CONGESTION CHARGING ZONE

- Zone applies Mon-Fri 7.00am to 6-30pm excluding public holidays.
- Daily charge allows unlimited travel within and multiple access to the zone.
- Payment must be made on the day of travel or in advance by telephone (0845 900 1234), via the website (www.cclondon.com) or by post.
- Exemptions include motorcycles, mopeds and bicycles. Registration for discount schemes, including disabled and residents, is available from Transport for London.
- There is a penalty charge for late or non-payment of the fee.

Geographers'
LONDON ATLAS

CONTENTS

REFERENCE

Motorway	M1	Built-up Area	BANK STREET
A Road	A2	Local Authority Boundary	
Under Construction		Posttown & London Postal District Boundary	
Proposed		Postcode Boundary (within Posttowns)	
B Road	B408	Map Continuation	56
Dual Carriageway			
One-way Street Traffic flow on A Roads is indicated by a heavy line on the drivers' left.		Church or Chapel	†
		Fire Station	■
Junction Name	MARBLE ARCH	Hospital	(H)
Restricted Access		House Numbers A & B Roads only	51 19 22 48
Pedestrianized Road		Information Centre	🛈
		National Grid Reference	530
Track & Footpath		Police Station	▲
Residential Walkway		Post Office	★
		Toilet with Facilities for the Disabled	♿
Railway	Tunnel / Level Crossing	Educational Establishment	
Stations:		Hospital or Hospice	
National Rail Network		Industrial Building	
Docklands Light Railway	DLR	Leisure or Recreational Facility	
Underground Station	⊖ is the registered trade mark of Transport for London	Place of Interest	
		Public Building	
Croydon Tramlink The boarding of Tramlink trams at stops may be limited to a single direction, indicated by the arrow.	Tunnel / Stop	Shopping Centre or Market	
		Other Selected Buildings	

SCALE
3.1 inches to 1 mile

0	¼	½	¾	1 Mile
0	250	500	750 Metres	1 Kilometre

1:20,438
7.87cm to 1 mile
4.89cm to 1 km

Geographers' A-Z Map Company Limited

Head Office:
Fairfield Road, Borough Green, Sevenoaks, Kent, TN15 8PP
Telephone: 01732 781000 (Enquiries & Trade Sales)
        01732 783422 (Retail Sales)
www.a-zmaps.co.uk

Ordnance Survey® This product includes mapping data licensed from Ordnance Survey® with the permission of the Controller of Her Majesty's Stationery Office.

© Crown Copyright 2003. All Rights Reserved.
Licence number 100017302

Edition 14 2001, Edition 14A* (Part Revision 2003)

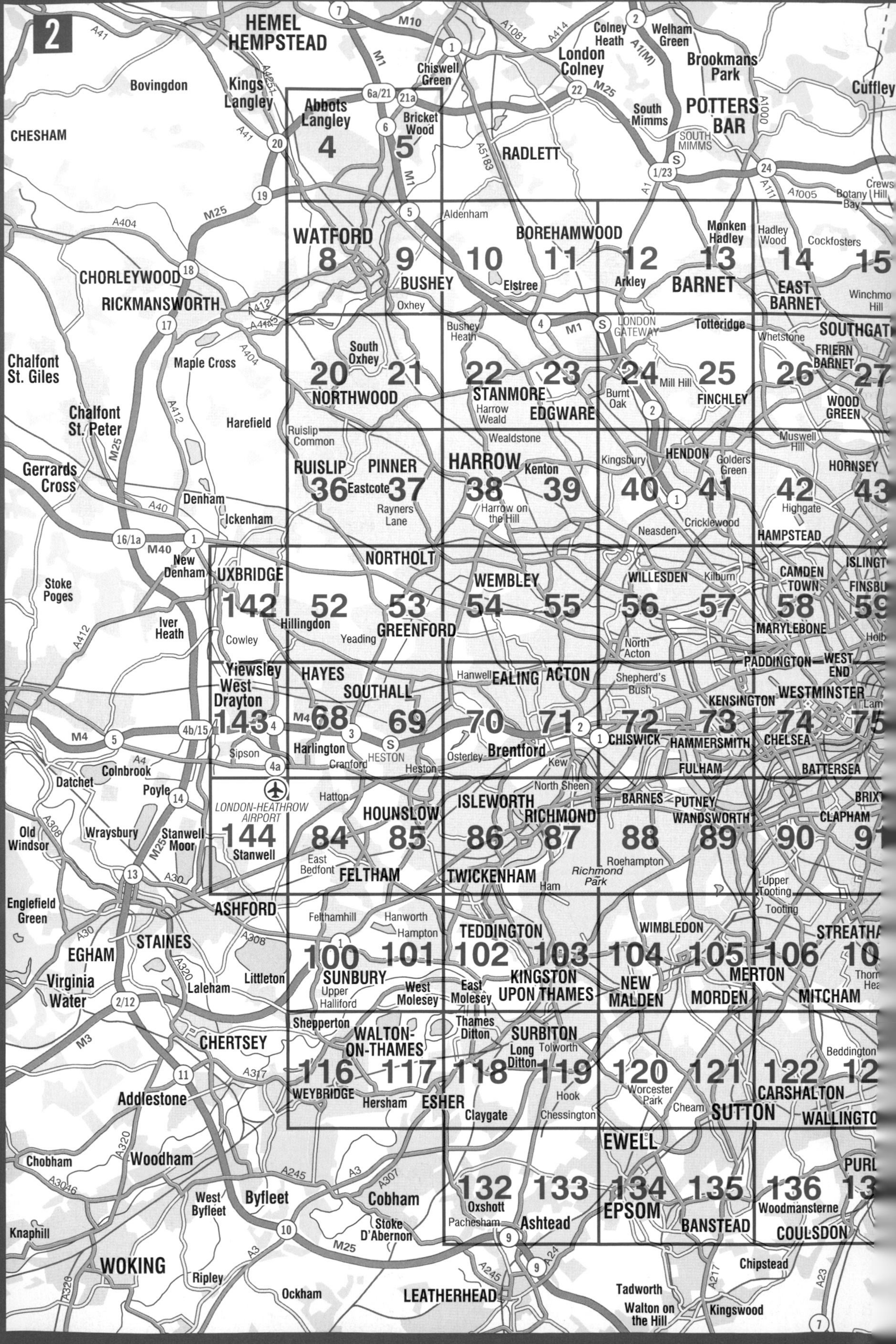

2
HEMEL HEMPSTEAD
M10
A1081
A414
Colney Heath
A1(M)
Welham Green
Brookmans Park
Cuffley
Chiswell Green
London Colney
M25
M1
A4251
Bovingdon
Kings Langley
Abbots Langley
4
Bricket Wood
5
South Mimms
POTTERS BAR
A1000
CHESHAM
A41
RADLETT
A5183
SOUTH MIMMS
A1
A111
A1005
Crews Hill
Botany Bay
A404
Aldenham
WATFORD
8
9
BUSHEY
10
Elstree
BOREHAMWOOD
11
12
Arkley
Monken Hadley
13
BARNET
Hadley Wood
Cockfosters
14
EAST BARNET
15
Winchmore Hill
CHORLEYWOOD
RICKMANSWORTH
A412
A4145
Oxhey
Bushey Heath
LONDON GATEWAY
Totteridge
Whetstone
SOUTHGATE
FRIERN BARNET
Chalfont St. Giles
Maple Cross
South Oxhey
20
21
NORTHWOOD
22
STANMORE
Harrow Weald
23
EDGWARE
24
Burnt Oak
Mill Hill
25
FINCHLEY
26
27
WOOD GREEN
Chalfont St. Peter
Harefield
Ruislip Common
Wealdstone
Muswell Hill
Gerrards Cross
RUISLIP
36
PINNER
Eastcote
37
Rayners Lane
HARROW
38
Harrow on the Hill
Kenton
39
Kingsbury
40
HENDON
41
Golders Green
Cricklewood
42
Highgate
HORNSEY
43
A40
Denham
Ickenham
Neasden
HAMPSTEAD
M40
New Denham
UXBRIDGE
142
NORTHOLT
52
Hillingdon
53
GREENFORD
Yeading
WEMBLEY
54
55
WILLESDEN
Kilburn
56
57
North Acton
CAMDEN TOWN
58
MARYLEBONE
ISLINGTON
FINSBURY
59
Holborn
Stoke Poges
Iver Heath
Cowley
PADDINGTON
WEST END
Yiewsley
West Drayton
143
HAYES
SOUTHALL
68
69
Hanwell
EALING
ACTON
70
71
Shepherd's Bush
72
CHISWICK
KENSINGTON
73
HAMMERSMITH
WESTMINSTER
74
CHELSEA
75
Lambeth
M4
Sipson
Harlington
Cranford
HESTON
Heston
Osterley
Brentford
Kew
FULHAM
BATTERSEA
A4
Colnbrook
Datchet
Poyle
LONDON-HEATHROW AIRPORT
144
Stanwell
Hatton
HOUNSLOW
84
85
East Bedfont
FELTHAM
North Sheen
ISLEWORTH
RICHMOND
86
87
TWICKENHAM
Ham
BARNES
PUTNEY
WANDSWORTH
88
Roehampton
Richmond Park
89
CLAPHAM
90
91
BRIXTON
Upper Tooting
Tooting
A308
Old Windsor
Wraysbury
Stanwell Moor
A30
Englefield Green
ASHFORD
Felthamhill
Hanworth
Hampton
TEDDINGTON
WIMBLEDON
STREATHAM
EGHAM
STAINES
A320
100
SUNBURY
Upper Halliford
101
West Molesey
102
East Molesey
103
KINGSTON UPON THAMES
104
NEW MALDEN
105
MORDEN
MERTON
106
MITCHAM
Thornton Heath
Virginia Water
Laleham
Littleton
Shepperton
WALTON-ON-THAMES
Thames Ditton
SURBITON
Long Ditton
Tolworth
M3
CHERTSEY
A317
116
WEYBRIDGE
117
Hersham
ESHER
118
Claygate
119
Hook
Chessington
120
Worcester Park
121
Cheam
SUTTON
Beddington
122
CARSHALTON
WALLINGTON
Addlestone
EWELL
Chobham
Woodham
A245
A3
A307
A3046
West Byfleet
Byfleet
Cobham
132
Oxshott
Pachesham
133
Ashtead
134
EPSOM
135
BANSTEAD
136
Woodmansterne
COULSDON
PURLEY
Knaphill
Stoke D'Abernon
WOKING
Ripley
Ockham
LEATHERHEAD
A24
Tadworth
Walton on the Hill
A217
Chipstead
Kingswood
A23

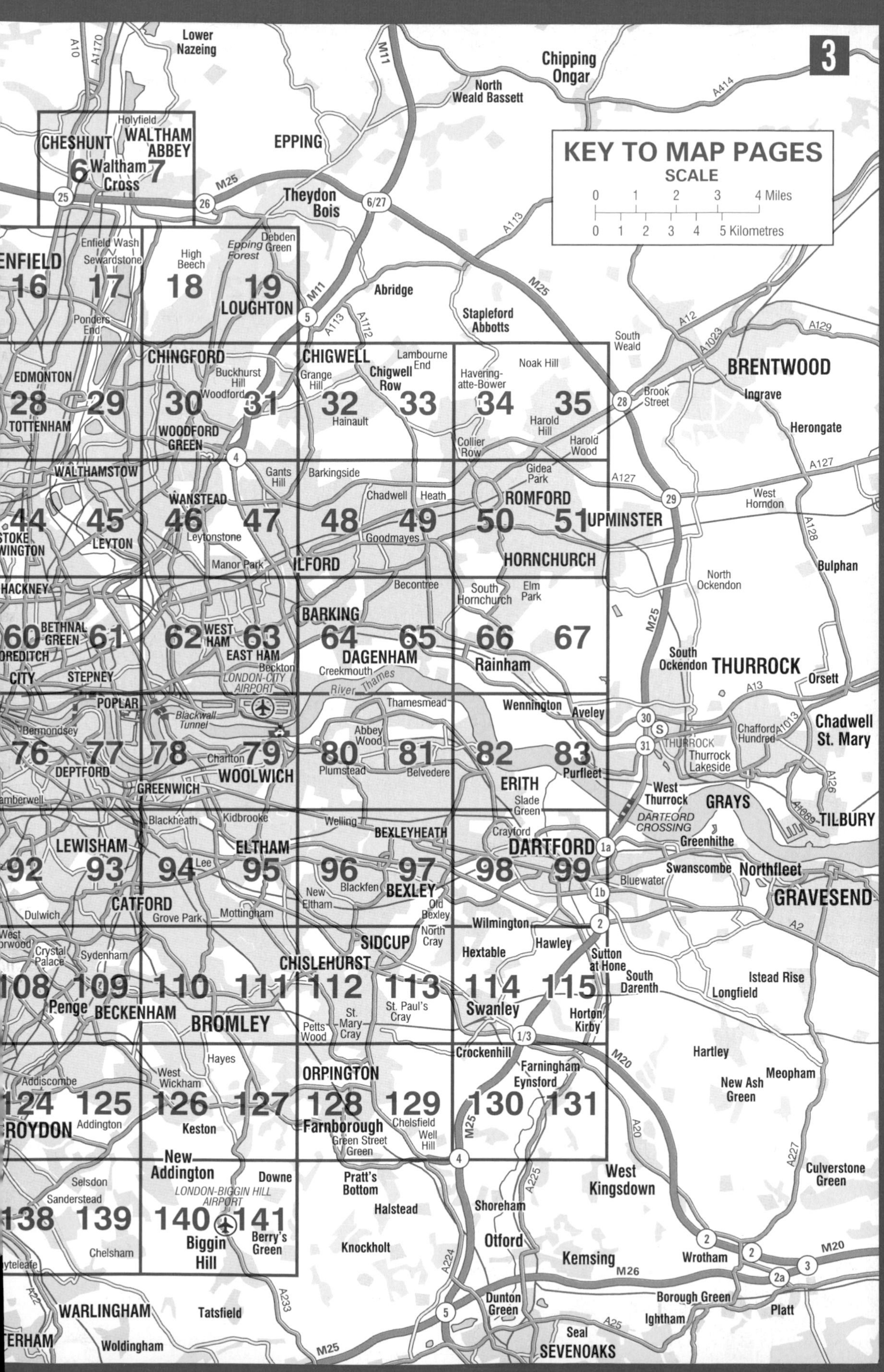

3

KEY TO MAP PAGES
SCALE

0	1	2	3	4 Miles

0	1	2	3	4	5 Kilometres

Lower Nazeing

Chipping Ongar

North Weald Bassett

Holyfield
CHESHUNT **WALTHAM ABBEY**
6 Waltham Cross **7**

EPPING

Theydon Bois

6/27

ENFIELD **16** Enfield Wash Sewardstone **17** High Beech **18** Epping Forest Debden Green **19** LOUGHTON

Ponders End

5

Abridge

Stapleford Abbotts

South Weald

BRENTWOOD

Brook Street
28

Ingrave

Herongate

EDMONTON **28** **29** **CHINGFORD** Buckhurst Hill Woodford **30** **31** **CHIGWELL** Grange Hill **32** Lambourne End Chigwell Row **33** Noak Hill Havering-atte-Bower **34** **35**

TOTTENHAM

WOODFORD GREEN

Hainault

Collier Row

Harold Hill

Harold Wood

West Horndon

WALTHAMSTOW **44** **45** LEYTON WANSTEAD **46** **47** Leytonstone Chadwell Heath **48** **49** Goodmayes Gidea Park **ROMFORD** **50** **51** UPMINSTER

STOKE NEWINGTON

Gants Hill

Barkingside

Manor Park

ILFORD

HORNCHURCH

North Ockendon

Bulphan

HACKNEY

Becontree

South Hornchurch

Elm Park

60 BETHNAL GREEN **61** **62** WEST HAM **63** EAST HAM **BARKING** **64** **65** **66** **67**

SHOREDITCH

CITY STEPNEY

Beckton LONDON CITY AIRPORT

DAGENHAM Creekmouth

Rainham

Wennington

Aveley

South Ockendon **THURROCK**

Orsett

30
31 S THURROCK Thurrock Lakeside

Chafford Hundred

Chadwell St. Mary

POPLAR Blackwall Tunnel

River Thames

Thamesmead

West Thurrock **GRAYS**

TILBURY

Bermondsey **76** **77** DEPTFORD **78** GREENWICH Charlton **79** **WOOLWICH** **80** Plumstead Abbey Wood **81** Belvedere **82** **83** Purfleet

ERITH Slade Green

DARTFORD CROSSING

Greenhithe

Camberwell

Blackheath

Kidbrooke

Welling

Crayford

Swanscombe Northfleet

Lewisham **92** **93** **94** Lee ELTHAM **95** **96** Blackfen **97** BEXLEY **98** **DARTFORD** **99**
1a

GRAVESEND

CATFORD Grove Park

New Eltham

Old Bexley

Bluewater
1b

West Norwood Crystal Palace Sydenham **108** **109** Penge BECKENHAM **110** **111** CHISLEHURST **112** SIDCUP North Cray **113** St. Paul's Cray **114** Swanley **115**

Dulwich

Mottingham

Wilmington

Hextable

Hawley

Sutton at Hone South Darenth

Istead Rise Longfield

2

BROMLEY Petts Wood St. Mary Cray

Crockenhill

Horton Kirby

1/3

Hartley

Meopham

Addiscombe **124** **125** Addington West Wickham Hayes **126** Keston **127** **ORPINGTON** **128** Farnborough **129** Chelsfield Well Hill **130** **131**

CROYDON

Green Street Green

Farningham Eynsford

West Kingsdown

New Ash Green

Culverstone Green

Selsdon Sanderstead **138** **139** New Addington LONDON-BIGGIN HILL AIRPORT **140** **141** Berry's Green

Downe

Pratt's Bottom

Halstead

Shoreham

Chelsham

Biggin Hill

Knockholt

Otford

Kemsing

Wrotham
2
2a
3

Borough Green

WARLINGHAM Tatsfield Woldingham

Dunton Green

Seal

SEVENOAKS

Ightham

Platt

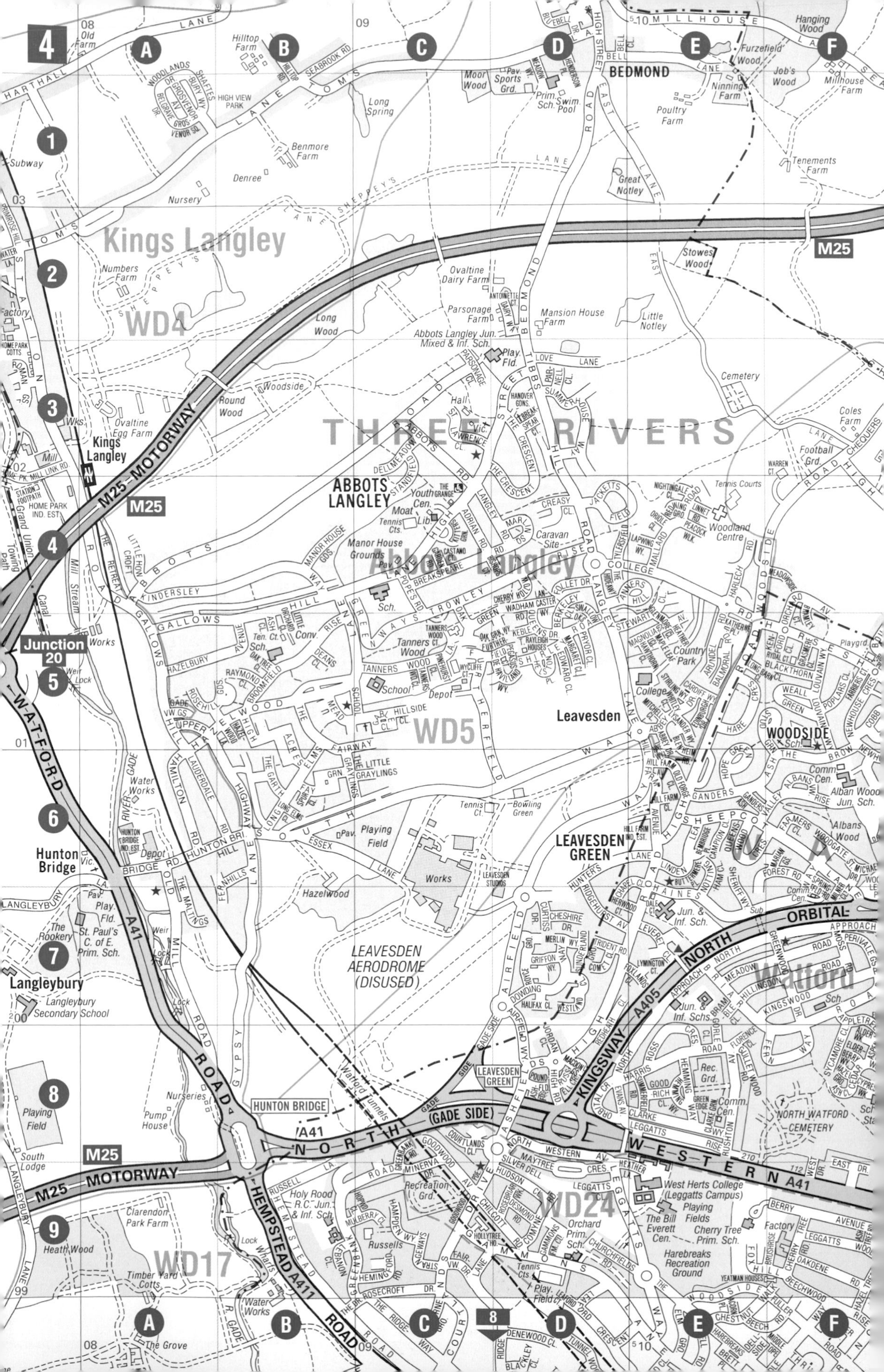
4
Kings Langley
WD4
THREE RIVERS
ABBOTS LANGLEY
Abbots Langley
WD5
Leavesden
LEAVESDEN GREEN
WOODSIDE
BEDMOND
M25 MOTORWAY
M25
Junction 20
Hunton Bridge
Langleybury
LEAVESDEN AERODROME (DISUSED)
NORTH ORBITAL
KINGSWAY A405
WATFORD ROAD
HEMPSTEAD A411 ROAD
NORTH WESTERN A41
WD24
WD17
Watford
West Herts College (Leggatts Campus)
NORTH WATFORD CEMETERY
8

5
G
H
J
K
L
M
1
2
3
4
5
6
7
8
9
12
13
14
Searches Farm
Searches Lane
Holt Wood
Holt Farm
Moat
Noke Lane
Burston Manor Farm
Burston Nurseries
How Wood
HOW WOOD
Birchwood Farm
Birch Wood
Junction 6a (M1)
Junction 21 (M25)
M25-MOTORWAY
Junction 21a
A405
NORTH ORBITAL ROAD
Tenterden House
Spielplatz
The Spinney
Hazel Rd.
Applecroft
Birchwood Way
Homewood Independent School
Cricket Grd.
Pav.
Blackgreen Wood
Winch Hill Wood
M1-MOTORWAY
M1
ST. ALBANS
Subway
Mobile Home Park
Black Green
Smug Oak Business Centre
Horseshoe Business Park
M25
Watford Road
Ashridge Drive
Jordan's Way
Hornbeams
North Riding
Oak Av.
Lye Lane
Smug Oak
Smug Oak Lane
St. Albans
Ash Dale
Russell Ct.
Black Boy Wood
Waterdell
Waterdale
Waterdell Lane
Bloom Wood
WATERDALE
Mount Pleasant Lane
Mount Pleasant Lane Mixed & Infant Sch.
Junction 6
BRICKET WOOD
AL2
Bricket Wood
Station Lane
Drop Lane
Rose Cotts.
Bricket Wood Sports Cen.
Running Track
Training Centre
Nottlers Wood
Nottlers House
Tennis Courts
Parmiter's Sch.
Playing Field
Elms Lane
St. Andrews Montessori Sch.
West Hertfordshire Crematorium
Brookdell Farm
Sports Ground
Building Research Station
Pumping Station
St. Michael's Catholic High Sch.
Francis Combe School & Community College
Tennis Courts
Sub.
Bucknalls Lane
Bucknalls Cl.
New Plantation
Jack William's Wood
Roman Villa (Site of)
Garston Manor Sch.
St. Catherine Siena R.C. Junior Mixed & Infant Sch.
Horseshoe Lodge
Woodside Arena
Watford Sports & Leisure Centre
Coates Way
Kytes Drive
KYTES ESTATE
Sch.
BRICKET WOOD COMMON
M1
Woodside Playing Fields
Bowling Alley & Cinema
Mutchetts Wood
Little Munden Farm
Woodbine Cottage
Coldharbour Plantation
Crab Wood
Four Acre Plantation
Munden
Commonmeadow Lane
Blackbirds
Garston Park
Pav.
Bus Depot
Peartree Wood
School Lane
Munden House
Munden Spring
Gaddesden Cres.
ROAD
Crown
A412
Garston Drive
Kingswood
Garston
Garston Lane
WD25
MERIDEN
Tibbles
Ravenscroft
GARSTON
HERTSMERE
River Colne
Open Air Theatre
UNIVERSITY OF HERTFORDSHIRE (Watford Campus)
Wall Hall Campus
Lea Farm Rec. Grd.
Lea Farm Jun. & Garston Inf. Schs.
Play. Fld.
THE DOME
Works
Superstore
Library
ST. ALBANS ROAD
A41 COLNE WY.
NORTH ORBITAL ROAD
Meriden Prim. Sch.
Meriden Pk.
M1-MOTORWAY
M1
Binghams
ALDENHAM GOLF COURSE & COUNTRY CLUB
Parkgate Sch.
Works
Comm. Cen.
9
Otterspool Farm
Cottage
Fish Pond

A
B
C
D
E
F
1
2
3
4
5
6
7
8
9
34
35
36
Rosedale
FLAMSTEAD END
Cheshunt Reservoir (North)
BROOKFIELD LA. WEST
BROOKFIELD
B156
Comm. Cen.
Rec. Grd.
Cheshunt Reservoir (South)
Playing Field
ANDREW'S LANE
ROSEDALE
CHURCHGATE
GOFF'S LANE
Goffs Sch.
St. Mary's High Sch.
Whit Hern Park
CHESHUNT
HIGH STREET
TURNER'S HILL
The Nightleys (Rec. Grnd.)
Turnford School
Brookland Inf. & Jun. Sch.
Turnford Brook
Youth Sail Training & Canoeing Base
COLLEGE RD.
B198
WINDMILL LANE
Cheshunt
Timber Yard
Grundy Park
Cheshunt School
Bonneygrove Prim. Sch.
Cemetery
LIEUTENANT ELLIS WY.
BURY GREEN
Waltham Cross
Albury Farm
Sports Ground
Rifle Range
Holy Trinity C. of E. Prim. Sch.
CROSSBROOK
Downfield Jun. & Inf. Sch.
Cheshunt Junction
Thistly Marsh Sand & Gravel Works
LEE VALL
Bowyer's Water
BROXBOURNE
Burygreen Plantation
Broom Hills
ELLIS WAY
A10
GREAT CAMBRIDGE ROAD
Hanging Plantation
EN7
EN8
Theobalds Grove
The Cedars Park
THEOBALDS LANE
Temple Bar
Temple House
Playground Tennis Courts Sports Ground
A121
WINSTON CHURCHILL WAY
OLDPARK RIDE
Caravan & Camping Site
Theobald's Park College
Theobald's Park Farm
Littlefield
Bullscross Farm
Theobalds Park Riding School
Theobalds Camp Site
Western Cemetery (Jewish)
Junction 25
Moat
Nursery
Playing Field
WALTHAM CROSS
ELEANOR CROSS RD.
MONARCHS WY.
Waltham Cross
Holdbrook
HOLMESDALE TUNNEL
M25 MOTORWAY
M25
Aqueduct
Meux Cottages
WHITE WEBBS LANE
Clydesdale Stud
Capel Manor Horticultural & Environmental Centre
Capel House
BULLSMOOR LANE
A1055
MOLLISON
Warehouse
Works
Lea Valley High Sch. & Bullsmoor Sports Cen.
Enfield
ENFIELD
EN2
EN3
EN1
BULLS CROSS
Sports Ground
Myddelton Farm
Myddelton House
New River (Old Course)
Turkey Brook
Capel Manor Prim. Sch.
Bullsmoor
A1010
HERTFORD ROAD
INNOVA BUSINESS PARK
FREEZY WATER
Business Innovation Centre
Aylands Sch.
Turkey St.
16
17
St. Ignatius College
ORDNANCE RD.
Maiden's Bri.
Aqueduct

7
G
H
J
K
L
M
38
39
40
Electricity Transformer Station
Breaker's Yard
Gate Cottages
Hayes Hill Farm
Hayes Hill
Hayes Hill Cottages
Greenview
Galley Hill
GALLEYHILL WOOD
CROOKED MILE
ROAD
MARSH HILL
B194
HOLYFIELD
Works
Seventy Acres
RIVER LEE NAVIGATION
Lock
Nursery
Stubbings Cottages
Woodside
North Lodge Farm
Grubb's Hill
Holy Field
PUCK LANE
Galley Wood House
Aimes Green
Broadgate Springs
CLAVERHAMBURY RD.
Aimesgreen Farm
Monkhams Cottage
Nightingales
Homefield Wood
FISHERS GREEN LA.
Sluice
Fishers Green
Holyfield Farm
Monkhams Hall
Stable Lodge
MONKHAMS
Kennel Wood
CLAYGATE LANE
Hooks Marsh
Hooksmarsh Ditch
E P P I N G
F O R E S T
Eagle Lodge
Poultry Farm
BREACH
BARNS
LANE
Dallance Farm
Powdermill Cut
Sluice
Hall Marsh
REGIONAL PARK
RIVER LEE NAVIGATION
LONG WALK
OLD RIVER LEA or LEE
Cornmill Stream
Arboretum
Tree Nursery
Nursery
Nurseries
Waltham Abbey
EN9
Royal Gunpowder Mills
Visitor Cen.
HORSEMILL STREAM
Waltham Marsh
Abbey Fish Ponds
Harold's Bridge
Subway
Cobbin's Brook
GALLEY HILL
Nurseries
PATERNOSTER HILL
UPSHIRE
PICK HILL
Jun. & Inf. Sch.
King Harold Sch.
Spts. Cen.
Tennis Courts
Playing Field
Sports Grds.
Infant Sch.
Junior Sch.
Play-ground
Comm. Cen.
Abbey Farm
Mkt.
Waltham Abbey Ch. (Rems. of)
Moat
Abbey Gdns.
Waltham Lock
Small Lea Bridge
A121
STATION RD.
HIGHBRIDGE ST.
ABBEY VIEW
WALTHAM ABBEY
Town Mead
Pit
Depot
Works
Rec. Grd.
Cemetery
Football Ground
Swimming Pool
King George's Field
Recreation Ground
Rec. Grd.
The Leverton Infant & Junior Sch.
Honeylands
Junction 26
M25
M25 MOTORWAY
Cobbins Brook
WALTHAM POINT
Quinton Hill Farm
A121
Meridian Park
RAMMEY MARSH
A1055
Lea Valley Walk
Rammey Marsh Flood Relief Channel
COUNTRY PARK
A112
SEWARDSTONE RD.
The Downing Nursery
Beechview Nursery
Round Hills
BEECH HILL PARK
Kennels
Portulaca
Normandy Nursery
17
18

8
A
B
C
D
E
F
4
20
1
2
3
4
5
6
7
8
9
Timber Yard Cotts.
The Grove
THE GROVE PARK
Grove Mill
Old Mill Ho.
Poultry Houses
Water Works
Deer Spring
WHIPPENDELL WOOD
JACOTTS HILL
WEST HERTS GOLF COURSE
Charlotte's Vale
Rough Wood
Sports Ground
Playing Field
Cassiobury Infant Sch.
Cassiobury Junior Sch.
Watercress Beds
Iron Bridge Lock
GRAND UNION CANAL
Boating Pond
CASSIOBURY PUBLIC PARK
WD17
WD18
WD3
WATFORD
Watford
NORTH WATFORD
WEST WATFORD
HEMPSTEAD ROAD
A411
A412
A4178
A4145
A4125
RICKMANSWORTH ROAD
CASSIO ROAD
VICARAGE ROAD
HAGDEN LANE
TOLPITS LANE
West Herts Sch. of Music
Nascot Wood Jun. & Inf. Schs.
West Herts Coll. (Cassio Campus)
Watford Tunnels
College
Swim. Pool
Watford Grammar Sch.
Swimming Pool
West Herts Golf Club
Fish Pond
Cassio Bridge Lock
Croxley Green
Croxley
Croxley Centre
HOLYWELL
Mail Centre
Westfield School
Watford West
Harwoods Rec. Grd.
WATFORD F.C. & SARACENS R.U.F.C. (Vicarage Rd. Stadium)
WATFORD GENERAL HOSP.
Laurance Haines Prim. Sch.
Watford Stadium
THE ROOKERY
Sewage Works
Electricity Transmission Station
King George V Playing Fields
Brightwells Farm Cotts.
Brightwells Farm
Oxhey Hall
Common Moor
Moor Park Crossing
Grand Union Canal Walk
Long Valley Wood
RIVER COLNE
RIVER GADE
Tolpits Ho.
Sports Ground
THREE RIVERS
Rickmansworth
Vicarage Road Cem.
Bowling Green
Sports Grd.
Pavilion

9
5
10
21
G
H
J
K
L
M
1
2
3
4
5
6
7
8
9
13
14
12
99
98
97
96
95
Watford North
WD24
Watford Junction
Watford High St.
Bushey
WD23
WD25
WD19
OXHEY
Oxhey Park
Watford Heath
Merry Hill
ALDENHAM
ALDENHAM GOLF COURSE & COUNTRY CLUB
HERTSMERE
Junction 5
BERRYGROVE
M1 MOTORWAY
M1
NORTH WESTERN AV.
A41 (NORTH WESTERN AV.)
ELTON WY.
OTTERSPOOL WAY
BUSHEY MILL LANE
COLNE WAY
STEPHENSON WAY
WATERFIELDS WAY
LONDON ROAD
HIGH STREET
CHALK HILL
PINNER ROAD
BUSHEY HALL ROAD
THE AVENUE
HARTSPRING LANE
LITTLE BUSHEY LANE
ALDENHAM ROAD
BUSHEY HALL GOLF COURSE
Scotts Wood
Bushey Hall Farm
Busheymill Bridge
Highwood Prim. Sch.
The Purcell School of Music
Metropolitan Police Sports Ground
Bushey Jewish Cemetery
Queens School
Queens Sch.
Bushey Leisure Cen.
Convent
Bushey Manor Jun. Mixed School
Bushey Hall School
Falconer Sch.
Swimming Pool
Bournehall Jun. Mixed & Inf. Sch.
Sacred Heart R.C. Jun. Mixed & Inf. Sch.
Haydon Dell Farm
Haydon Hill House
BUSHEY GOLF & COUNTRY CLUB
Bushey House
Club House
St. Margaret's School
Ashfield Jun. Sch.
Bromet Junior Mixed & Infant Sch.
Riding School
Nursery
Reservoir
Woodlands
Sherwoods
Front Lodge
Hartspring Sports Cen.
HARTSPRING INDUSTRIAL ESTATE
Hotel
Hartspring Cotts.
Gullimore Farm
WINFIELDS MOBILE HOME PARK
BUSHEY HALL MOBILE HOME PARK
Otterspool Farm
Otterspool
Binghams
Park Cottage
Berrygrove
Colne Bri.
Meriden Prim. Sch.
Meriden Pk.
Parkgate Sch.
Superstore
Library
Works
THE HARLEQUIN
COLONIAL BUSINESS PK.
Goods Shed
Depot
Sports Ground
Wiggenhall Bri.
Viaduct
COLNE VALLEY RETAIL PARK
WATFORD ARCHES RETAIL PK.
Watford Bri.
Meadow Wood Sch.
Moat Field
Tennis Courts
Playing Field
Red House
Club Ho.
Rec. Grd.
Play. Fld.
BUSHE

10
A
B
C
D
E
F
1
2
3
4
5
6
7
8
9
Kemprow
Fish Pond
Edge Grove Sch.
Playing Field
High Cross
High Cross Ho.
B462
ALDENHAM
Red House
Sounding Well
Play. Fld.
Red Lion Cl.
Round Bush
Four Want Ways
Radlett
Cobden Hill
Cobdenhill Dell
Wellhouse Dell
Rugby Football Ground
Battlers Green Farm
Battlers Green
Moses Dell
WD7
Little Kendals Farm
Little Kendals Wood
The Fruit Farm
COBDEN HILL A5183
WATLING ST
Roman Road
THE RIDGEWAY
LOOM LANE
LETCHMORE HEATH
Playing Field
Aldenham Grange
Aldenham Cottage
Holland Farm House
Patchetts Green
Watford
Bhaktivedanta Manor
Aldenham School
Boydens Hill
WARDS LANE
SAWYERS LANE
Delrow Ho.
Holland Farm
WD25
Electricity Transforming Station
H E R T S
Slades Farm
Letchmore Lodge
Kennels
Gullimore Farm
Caravan Site
Jewish Cemetery
Cemetery
Motel
ELTON WAY A41
TYLERS
BUTTERFLY LANE
Moats
Playing Field
ELSTREE AERODROME
Ham Farm
Flying School
Flying Club
HOG LANE
Page's Farm
Play. Fld.
Hilfield Farm
M1
Lodge
Hilfield Castle
Boat House
HILFIELD PARK RESERVOIR
Dam
Pumping Station
Sewage Works
Laboratories
ALDENHAM COU
Tyler's Farm
Kennels
Bushey Meads School
Meadow Wood Sch.
Works
Hart's Farm
Bushey
(NORTH WESTERN AV.) A41
M1 MOTORWAY
WD23
Prim. Sch.
Tennis Courts
BUSHEY
King George Rec. Grd.
Caldecote Farm
Berkeley Cottage
Rosary Priory
Immanuel College
Caldecote Hill
Stanmore
HA7
HARROW
LISMIRRANE INDUSTRIAL PARK
ELSTREE ROAD
WATFORD WAY
HEATHBOURNE ROAD A409
BUSHEY HOSP. (BUPA)
Sparrows Herne
Heath House
Inf. School
HERNE
HIGH RD.
A411
22
Works
Sch.
14
15
16
98
97
96
95
99

11
Borehamwood
WD6
BOREHAMWOOD
ELSTREE
ELSTREE GOLF COURSE
ALDENHAM PARK
BARNET
M1 MOTORWAY
Junction 4
Elstree & Borehamwood
Parkfields Open Space
Deacons Hill Open Space
Elstree Open Space
Lyndhurst School
Meryfield First Sch.
Cowley Hill First Sch.
Elstree Tunnel
Scratch Wood

12
Silver Hill Cotts.
High Canons
Holmshill Ho.
Buckettsland Farm
Wheatsheaf Farm
Well End Farm
Electricity Sub. Station
Well End
Strangeways Farm
Rowley Farm
DYRHAM PARK GOLF COURSE
DYRHAM PARK
Dyrham Park Country Club
Valentine's Farm
Hawksmoor School
Sports Cen.
Borehamwood
WD6
BOREHAMWOOD
The Venue (Swim. Pool)
Holmshill School
Hotel
Warehouse
Depot
BOREHAMWOOD IND. PARK
Sports Ground
A5135
ELSTREE WAY
YORK WAY
Subway
Works
Tennis Cts.
ELSTREE STUDIOS
Superstore
Hillside Sch.
Playing Field
MANOR PL. INDUSTRIAL ESTATE
HERTSMERE IND. PARK
King George's Field
Kenilworth First Sch.
ELSTREE DISTRIBUTION PARK
Playing Field
Laing's Sports Club
Club House
School
Comm. Cen.
Ripon Park
Laing Sports Club Golf Course
Tennis Courts.
Shooting Ground
Golf Driving Range
ARKLEY LANE OPEN SPACE
Arkley Lane Open Space
Woodlands Farm
Saffron Green
Fold Farm
Galley Lane Farm
Poor Clare Monastery
Playing Field
Rowley Green Farm
ARKLEY GOLF COURSE
Rowley Green
Arkley Manor
Arkley Rise Estate Open Space
Reservoir
Club House
Rowley Bank Nurseries
Sports Ground
Nursing Home
ARKLEY
B
BARNET A411 LANE
BARNET BY-PASS ROAD
A1
STIRLING CORNER
Memorial Sports Centre
Windmill
Tennis Courts
Sports Ground
BARNET GATE
ELSTREE PK. MOBILE HOMES
Froghall Wood
Scratchwood Open Space
Boys Hill Wood
Thistle Wood
Hyver Hall
Hyver Farm
Hyver Manor
Gravel Pit Wood
Moat Mount Open Space
Tanglewood
Barnet Gate Wood
NW7
MOAT MOUNT OPEN SPACE
B552
HENDON WOOD LANE
(Old Elizabethans) Playing Field
Pav.
Allendale
Brent Lodge Farm
Dollis
HENDON WOOD LANE OPEN SPACE
Sports Ground
Scratchwood Open Space
M1
Depot
Target Wood
Shrubbery
Clump of Trees Wood
Moat Mount Camp Site
24
11
A B C D E F
1 2 3 4 5 6 7 8 9
20 21 22

WROTHAM PARK
Wrotham Park
Three Oak Hill
Cockshot Hill
Ganwick Farm
Deadman's Bottom
WAGON ROAD
Lower Kitt's End Farm
Home Farm
Kitt's End
Kitt's End Farm
Knightsland Farm
Barnet
Bartram's Quash
Hadley Wood
EN4
OLD FOLD MANOR
GOLF COURSE
BRIDGEDOWN GOLF COURSE
ST. ALBANS ROAD
A1081
A1000 ROAD
GREAT NORTH ROAD (HADLEY HIGHSTONE)
Club House
Rectory Farm
Monken Hadley C. of E. Prim. Sch.
St. Martha's Convent R.C. School
CAMLET WAY
Bournwell Hill
Hadley Green
HADLEY ROAD
MONKEN HADLEY COMMON
MONKEN HADLEY
Electricity Transformer Sta.
Playing Field
HIGH BARNET
Christ Church C. of E. Prim. Sch.
Priddeon's Hill
COMMON
Tudor Park Golf Course
Tudor Sports Ground
Club House
HADLEY
King George's Field
EN5
Queen Elizabeth's School
BARNET
Cromer Road Prim. Sch.
WOOD STREET
A411
HIGH STREET
Queen Elizabeth Girls Sch.
High Barnet
Whalebone Park
BARNET HOSP.
Psychiatric Unit
CHIPPING BARNET
BARNET HILL
GREAT NORTH ROAD
STATION ROAD
A110
Barnet Vale
Lyonsdown
Whitings Hill Prim. Sch.
Barnet F.C. (Underhill Stadium)
Underhill
The Rainbow Cen.
Greenhill Gdns
Grasvenor Avenue Inf. Sch.
Ducks Island Recreation Ground
KING GEORGE PLAYING FIELDS
Cottage Farm
Grange Playing Fields
East Barnet Old Grammarians Playing Field
TOTTERIDGE PARK OPEN SPACE
GRANGE AVENUE OPEN SPACE
N20
Ravenscroft School
Playing Field
Tennis Courts
Wyatts Farm Open Space
Recreation Ground
Dollis Brook
SOUTH HERTS GOLF COURSE
Brook Farm Open Space
Pavilion
HIGH RD.
WHETSTONE
Fairlight Cottage
Hillsborough Cottage
Totteridge Park
Redings
TOTTERIDGE COMMON
Sports Ground
Club House
Warehouses
14
G H J K L M
1 2 3 4 5 6 7 8 9
24 25 26
99 98 97 96 95

Potters Bar
EN6
Hadley Wood
HADLEY WOOD
Barnet
E N F I E L D
BEECH HILL PARK
HADLEY WOOD GOLF COURSE
TRENT (Country)
EN4
Cockfosters
COCKFOSTERS
NEW BARNET
New Barnet
EAST BARNET
Lyonsdown
Barnet Vale
EN5
B A R N E T
OAK HILL PARK
Oakleigh Park
N20
WHETSTONE
South Barnet
HADLEY COMMON
TUDOR PARK GOLF COURSE
13
26

15
BOTANY BAY
Botany Bay Farm
East Lodge
Cricket Grd.
THE RIDGEWAY A1005
Salmon's Brook
CHASE
Cuckolds Hill
Parkside House
Park Farm
Park Farm Cottages
Reservoir
Parkside Farm
Pumping Station
Vicarage Farm
Wolverton
Enfield
EN2
ENFIELD
PARK
Ride Wood
Leeging Beech Gutter
Fish Pond
Icehouse Wood
Williams Wood
Tennis Courts
Middlesex University
Shaws Wood Cottages
Shaws Wood
Hog Hill
Miniature Rifle Range
Merryhills Brook
TRENT PARK
Merryhills GOLF COURSE
Eastpole Farm
Club House
Lodge
ENFIELD ROAD A110
SLADES HILL
WINDMILL HILL
Oakwood
World's End
Highlands School
Playing Fields
Playing Field
Grange Park Prim. Sch.
Club House
Moat
ENFIELD GOLF COURSE
GRANGE PARK
Grange Park
Highlands Village
Nursing Home
Superstore
Sports Ground
Boxer's Lake
N14
N21
OAKWOOD
Yacht Pond
OAKWOOD PARK
GROVELANDS PARK
Bowling Green
Tennis Courts
WINCHMORE HILL
Winchmore Hill
Rectory Farm
The Red House
KING'S OAK BMI HOSPITAL
CHASE FARM HOSP.
CEMETERY
Rendlesham Viaduct
Turkey Brook
Clovelly
Queenswood Farm
Kingswood
HILLY FIELDS
Gordon Hill
Sports Ground
Chase Side
Enfield Chase
The Golf Course
BUSH HILL GOLF COURSE
Southgate
Bournside Sports Centre
Boating
27
16

16
WHITEWEBBS GOLF COURSE
Turkey Brook
New River (Old Course)
Myddelton Ho.
Sports Ground
6
Brayside Farm
Club House
CLAY HILL
Kingswood
HILLY FIELDS PARK
Forty Hall Farm
Forty Hall & Museum
St. Ignatius College
Turkey Street
War Memorial
Maiden's Bri.
Aqueduct
Forty Hill C. of E. Prim. Sch.
Nursery
Worcesters Prim. Sch.
FORTY HILL
Enfield Crematorium
Cemy.
GREAT CAMBRIDGE ROAD
A10
Lavender Prim. Sch.
Play. Field
Rec. Ground
EN2
Gordon Hill
Chase Side
Sports Ground
Chase Community Sch.
Enfield
Cemetery
David Lloyd Raquet & Fitness Club
Running Track
Playing Field
Russet Ho. Sch.
Trinity Prim. Sch.
Prim. Sch.
Graeme Prim. Sch.
Suffolks Prim. Sch. & Bishop Stopford's Schs.
Martin Dale Industrial Estate
Factory
15
Enfield Grammar School (Lower)
Play. Field
Sports Ground
ENFIELD TOWN
Enfield Sch.
Civic Cen.
Playing Fields
ENFIELD
Nursery
WINDMILL HILL
Enfield Chase
CHURCH ST.
SOUTHBURY RD.
A110
Enfield Town
High Sch.
Kingsmead School
Cinema
Superstore
Enfield Retail Pk.
Warehouse
Northgate Business Park
Works
Southbury
EN1
Town Park
Tennis Courts
New River (old course)
Cricket Ground
Pav.
BUSH HILL PARK (Recreation Ground)
Club
Haslemere Business Centre
Martinbridge Trading Estate
Great Cambridge Ind. Est.
Grange Park
The Golf House
BUSH HILL PARK GOLF COURSE
Bush Hill
BUSH HILL PARK
Bush Hill Park
N21
LONDON ROAD
A105
VILLAGE RD.
Galliard Prim. Sch.
N9
Tennis Courts
Play. Field
Edmonton Sch.
King George's Field
Pavilion
Min. Golf Course
JUBILEE PARK
Prim. Sch.
Pav.
Recreation Ground
Tennis Courts
RIDGE AV.
Bury Lodge Park
28
Rec. Grd.
Salmon's Brook
Rec. Grd.
Churchfield
The Paulin Ground
GREEN LANES
HERTFORD

FREEZY WATER
Turkey St.
Turkey Brook
ORDNANCE
Enfield Lock
ENFIELD LOCK
Prince of Wales Prim. Sch.
ENFIELD WASH
ALBANY PARK
Albany Sch.
Enfield Island Village
COUNTRY PARK
Waltham Abbey
EN9
Sewardstone Hall
Kingsfield Nurseries
Barnfield Riding Stables
Hannah Nursery
Fouracres Nursery
Northfield Nursery
Northcroft Nursery
Marshfield Nursery
Luthers Farm
Amesbury Mead Farm
Caravan Park
Sewardstone Lodge
MILL LANE
SEWARDSTONE ROAD
A112
E4
Kennels
GILWELL
Yardley Hill
Valley Golf Course
Club Ho.
King George's Sailing Club
KING GEORGE'S RESERVOIR
WILLIAM GIRLING RESERVOIR
Overflow Channel
Pumping Station
River Lee Navigation
Small River Lee or Lea
Cattlegate Flood Relief Channel
River Lea (or Lee) Diversion
BRIMSDOWN
BRIMSDOWN INDUSTRIAL ESTATE
WATERMILL BUSINESS CENTRE
PLAZA BUSINESS CENTRE
LEASIDE BUSINESS CENTRE
SOVEREIGN BUSINESS CENTRE
CENTENARY TRADING ESTATE
MILL RIVER TRADING ESTATE
Brimsdown
Brimsdown Jun.& Inf. Schs.
ENFIELD HIGHWAY
Durants Park Athletic Ground
Enfield College
Cemetery
EN3
A1055
MOLLISON AVENUE
A1010
HERTFORD ROAD
A110
NAGS HEAD RD.
LEA VALLEY ROAD
PONDERS END
Ponders End
Rec. Grd.
Gas Works
PONDERS END INDUSTRIAL ESTATE
Warehouses
South Marsh
Weir
Locks
WHARF ROAD
MERIDIAN WAY
HIGH STREET
NIGHTINGALE RD.
Boundary Ditch
LEE VALLEY LEISURE GOLF COURSE
Cinema
KINGS HEAD HILL
MANSFIELD HILL
SEWARDSTONE ROAD
Playing Field
Superstore
G H J K L M
1 2 3 4 5 6 7 8 9
6 7 18 29

Waltham Abbey
EN9
EPPING
Loughton
E4
WALTHAM FOREST
EPPING FOREST
SEWARDSTONE
SEWARDSTONEBURY
HIGH BEECH
GILWELL PARK
The Downing
Beech Hill Nursery
BEECH HILL PARK
Tile Hill Farm
COUNTRY PARK
AVEY LANE
Avey Lane Nursery
Kennels
Portulaca
Providence Nursery
Normandy Nursery
Aveylane Farm
The Rookery
HIGH BEECH GOLF COURSE
Club House
BEECH HILL GS.
FOREST CL.
GREEN
WELLINGTON
Riding School
Bowling Green
Youth Hostel
RATS LA.
GRAVEL HILL
PYNEST GREEN LANE
Pynest Green
The Grange
High Beech Nurseries
Kennels
Piggery
Avey Cottages
Nursery
HAWES LA.
Sewardstone Hall
Sewardstone Nursery
Chandlers Farm
MOTT STREET
Mott Street Nursery
Thompson's Wood
BUTLERS DR.
Kingsfield Nurseries
Barnfield Riding Stables
Netherhouse Nursery
Beechside Nursery
Netherhouse Farm
Manor Farm
THOMPSON'S LANE
High Beech C. of E. Primary School
Manor House
Hall
MANOR
RESERVOIR RD.
GODWIN CL.
Hannah Nursery
Fouracres Nursery
Playing Field
Oak Farm
Cricket Ground
PEPPER ALLEY
Pav.
Wallsgrove House
Northfield Nursery
Northcroft Nursery
Aldergrove Wood
The Vicarage
Dairy Farm
Chapelfield Nursery
GREEN LANE
LIPPITTS HILL
Marshfield Nursery
Barn Hill
Camp Site
BLIND LANE
Day's Farm
Luthers
Amesbury Mead Farm
Woodlands Nursery
Fernhill Wood
THE ELMS
Field Study Centre
Hill Wood
Police Training Camp
Pipers Farm
Santa Maria Nursery
THE OWL CARAVAN SITE
DAWS HILL
Hall
Clock House Riding Stables
Gilwellbury
Springfield Farm
Lippittshill Lodge
CHURCH HILL
Picks Farm
Whitehouse Plain
Carrolls Farm
Round Thicket
GILWELL PARK
Club Ho.
North Long Hills
Sewardstone Green
BURY ROAD
WEST ESSEX GOLF COURSE
Ludgate Water
Caravan Site
Almshouse Plain
GILWELL LA.
Ludgate House
Reservoir (covered)
The White Cottage
Swimming Pool
Kennels
Bury Wood
Long Hills
GILWELL LANE
Ludgate Plain
Yardley Hill
Filter Beds
Bury Farm
Peartree Plain
Tennis Court
FARM END
Palmer's Bridge
Cuckoo Brook
Green Ride
Horse Ride
HORNBEAM LA.
WOODMAN LA.
Cuckoo Pits
Woodman's Glade
Bury Wood
Grimston's Oak
DEERLEAP GRO.
YARDLEY LANE
Hawkswood School & Centre
The Hawk Wood
Buttonseed Corner
Hawkwood Lodge Environmental Education Centre
HAWKWOOD CRESCENT
HAWKDENE
EPPING GLADE
Magpie Hill
Connaught Water
The Ching
WAY
MARK AV.
MARGARET AVENUE
ROYAL EPPING FOREST & CHINGFORD PUBLIC GOLF COURSE
Chingford Plain
Recreation Ground
NEW ROAD
A104
MANOR
SOUTH
Pole Hill
Obelisk
FOREST VIEW
WALSINGHAM HO.
ST. JOSEPH'S CT.
ST. THERESA CT.
CONNAUGHT
FARNLEY RD.
The Hawk Wood
Club Ho.
Queen Elizabeth's Hunting Lodge (Museum)
RANGER'S RD.
A1069
EPPING
Albany Ho.
Oak Hall
The Warren
Club
Tennis Courts
MORNINGTON
EGLINGTON
FREDERICA RD.
AVENUE
BUXTON RD.
Sch.
Chingford
FOREST AV.
GORDON ROAD
HADLEIGH CT.
CRESCENT RD.
WARREN POND RD.
Warren Pond
Barn Hoppet
POLE HILL RD.
A110
SUNNYSIDE DR.
WOODBERRY
PARKHILL RD.
MOUNT VIEW R
THE GREEN
STATION
HILL THE GN.
HEAD
DOUGLAS RD.
VICTORIA
Cricket Ground
BEECH GLADE
WARREN SIDE
Sch.
Nursy. Sch.
Play. Fld.
Council
ARDMORE
FERN-SIDE
Bowl. Grn.
St. John's C. Prim. Sch.
30
17
7
A
B
C
D
E
F
1
2
3
4
5
6
7
8
9
38
39
540
99
98
97
96
95

19
G
H
J
K
L
M
42
43
44
Honey Lane Quarters
Sunshine Plain
Dulsmead Hollow
Copley Plain
Birch Hall Farm
Epping CM16
Birch Wood
1
Wake Valley Pond
Wake Valley
Deershelter Plain
Furze Ground
Debden House Camp Site
DEBDEN GREEN
2
Rushey Plain
Epping Forest Nature Reserve
Epping Forest Conservation Centre
Great Monk Wood
Broadstrood Plain
Mount Pleasant
Court Hill
Bellringer's Hollow
Golding's Hill Ponds
LOUGHTON GOLF COURSE
Davenant Foundation School
Little Monk Wood
Blackweir Pond
Club House
3
Blackweir Hill
Baldwins Hill
Baldwins Pond
FOREST
Loughton Camp
Kate's Cellar
Shelleys Hill
Arewater Green
Ash Green
Dryad's Hall
4
Debden Slade
Woodbury Hollow
Hillyfields Open Space
NEW ROAD
A104
EPPING ROAD
EPPING FOREST
GOLDINGS HILL
A121
RECTORY HILL
A1168
CHURCH HILL
Strawberry Hill Ponds
5
Fairmead Bottom
IG10
Nursery
Cricket Grd.
Library
Swimming Pool
Epping Forest Coll.
East 15 Acting Sch.
Playing Fld.
Oakview Sch.
Loughton Hall
6
Tennis Courts
Oaklands Sch.
Roding Valley High Sch.
Council Offs.
Sports Hall
Playing Fields
OAKWOOD HILL IND. EST.
The Alderton Inf. & Jun. Schs.
7
Sports Grd.
Junction 5
LOUGHTON
Loughton
Warren Hill
Recreation Ground
River Roding
Foot Bridge
Chigwell IG7
8
M11
M11 MOTORWAY
Tennis Courts
Recreation Ground
RODING VALLEY MEADOWS NATURE RESERVE
Grange Farm Centre
9
Buckhurst Hill IG9
Hill Fm.
Swim. Pool
Recreation Ground
Playing Fields
RODING VALLEY NATURE RESERVE
Lake
David Lloyd Leisure
31

8
36
A
B
C
D
E
F
1
2
3
4
5
6
7
8
9
Moor Park Crossing
TOLPITS LANE
Tolpits Ho.
Tolpits Plantation
A4145
Brightwells Farm Cotts.
Brightwells Farm
Brightwells Spring
Oxhey Hall
Moat
RIVER COLNE
Hampermill Lake
Running Track
Merchant Taylors School
Playing Fields
Rifle Range
Pumping Works Station
HAMPERMILL LANE
A4125
The Withey Bed
Rickmansworth
Northwood Prep Sch.
Lodge
Manor of the Rose
EAST DRIVE
SANDY LODGE ROAD
SANDY LODGE LANE
Hampermill Wood
Ox Pasture Spring
South Oxhey Playing Fields
Big Wood
WD3
MOOR PARK
GOLF COURSE
Club House
Putting Green
Farm Cottage
Moor Park
Hampermill Spring
Round Spring
THREE RIVERS
SANDY LODGE GOLF COURSE
The Roughs
Old Furze Field
Little Furze Field
Young Hangings
Little Furze Jun. Mixed & Infant Sch.
Old Hangings
Beck Mason's Wood
THORNHILL ROAD
BATCHWORTH LANE
Bathend Clump
Batchworth Heath
EASTBURY
Sch.
The Plantation
Oxhey Wood Lodge
OXHEY WOODS
H.M.S. Warrior
Offices
Oxhey Woods House
B4542
Northwood
Bracken Hill Ho.
Wild Woods
Pretty Corner
Birchanger
Reservoir (covered)
HA6
Playing Field
St. Martin's Sch.
St. Helen's Sch.
Holy Trinity C.E. Sch.
MOUNT VERNON HOSPITAL
Ckt. Grd.
Park Farm
Esporta Riverside Northwood
London Bible Coll.
Frithwood Prim. Sch.
NORTHWOOD
St. John's School
GREEN LANE
B469
Northwood
Northwood College
Denville Hall
The Gravel Pits
A404
RICKMANSWORTH ROAD
WATFORD ROAD
HIGH ST.
Club House
A4180
NORTHWOOD GOLF COURSE
PINNER ROAD
HILLINGDON
Playing Field
NORTHWOOD HILLS
Rec. Grd.
Cemetery
Northwood Hills
Northwood School
Playing Fld.
Sports Cen.
Miniature Rifle Range
HASTE HILL GOLF COURSE
COPSE WOOD
Nature Reserve
B472
JOEL ST
Harlyn Primary Sch.
DUCK'S HILL RD.

21
G
H
J
K
L
M
9
Riding School
Nursery
Swimming Pool
Tennis Courts
Ashfield Jun. Sch.
Play. Fld.
Running Track
Tennis Court
St. Margaret's School
Inf. School
Police Sta.
Merry Hill Farm
Merry Hill House
Merry Hill
Hillside
Bushey
HERTSMERE
WD23
Hartsbourne Country C
HARTSBOURNE COUNTRY CLUB
GOLF COURSES
Watford Heath
Sherwoods Wood
Woodlands
Front Lodge
Oxhey Grange
Brick Works
Margeholes Wood
Driving Range
Club House
Tennis Courts
Oxhey Pav.
OXHEY PARK
GOLF COURSE
Watford
Warren Dell
Playground
OXHEY LANE
A4008
B4542
PRESTWICK ROAD
PENROSE AVENUE
CARPENDERS AVENUE
St. Meryl Sch.
Carpenders Park Farm
CARPENDERS PARK
Carpenders Park
Woodwalks
Cemetery
Mutton Wood
Valley View Farm
Levels Wood
Grim's Ditch
GRIM'S DYKE
GOLF COURSE
Weald Wood
Harrow
HA3
22
Stony Wood
Club House
Grimswood Lodge
Grimswood House
Highcroft
The Lodge
Oxheylane Farm
Social Cen.
Comm. Cen.
Pond Wood
School
Sandpit Wood
SOUTH OXHEY
Comm. Centre
WD19
Woodhall Jun. Mixed & Inf. Sch.
LITTLE OXHEY LANE
St. James Altham Pool
Play. Fld.
Nanscot Wood
Pinnerwood House
Pinnerwood Farm
Pinnerwood Cottage
Pinner Wood
PINNER HILL GOLF COURSE
First & Mid. Sch.
Shaftesbury Playing Fields
Cricket Club
Pav.
Saddlers Mead
HARROW
Hatch End
HATCH END
A410
UXBRIDGE ROAD
Superstore
Harrow Arts Cen.
Liby.
Playing Fields
The Cedars
High Sch.
Pinner
Pinnerwood Park
Pinner Wood First & Mid. Schs.
PINNER GREEN
Playing Field
A404
HA5
ST. THOMAS' DR.
GEORGE V AVENUE
Tennis Courts
Rugby Football Ground
Playing Field
PINNER PARK
Pinner Park Farm
Headstone Lane
River Pinn
Sports Ground
Model Railway
Tennis Courts
Pinner Park Schs.
HA2
Little Common
Superstore
37
Headstone Manor
12
13
14

22
A
B
C
D
E
F
1
2
3
4
5
6
7
8
9
10
21
38
94
93
92
91
90
14
15
16
SPARROWS HERNE
ELSTREE ROAD
HIGH ROAD
A4140
HEATHBOURNE RD.
A409
BUSHEY HEATH
Bushey
Heath House
BUSHEY HOSP. (BUPA)
Works
Belswood Cottage
STANMORE COMMON
HERTSMERE
Hartsbourne Country Club
Hartsbourne Jun. Mixed & Inf. Sch.
Kestrel Grove (Offices)
Tennis Courts
THE COMMON
WARREN LANE
Cricket Ground
Fish Pond
Grove Field
Pavilion
Husaini Shia Islamic Centre
Little Common
Stanmore
Stanmore Hall
Cloisters Wood
Sports Ground
SIR HENRY FLOYD CT.
ROYAL NATIONAL ORTHOPAEDIC HOSP.
Limes House
The Grove
Lodge
Swimming Pool
The Cedars
PRIORY DRIVE
Tanglewood
Peterborough & St. Margaret's School
Glenthorn (R.A.F.)
Bentley Priory (R.A.F.)
Priory Close
Heriots
Deer Park
Heriot's Wood
STANMORE HILL
St. John's First & Mid. Schs.
Levels Wood
HARROW WEALD COMMON
Grim's Ditch
Grim's Dyke
Grimsdyke Open Space
Harrow Weald Common
The City
Nurseries
The Old Barn
Weald Wood
REDDING LANE
COMMON ROAD
BROOKSHILL
OLD LODGE WAY
Scout Hall
Priory House
Harrow Weald Common
Hertfordshire & Middlesex Country Club
Copse Farm
Stony Wood
Lower Priory Farm
Nursery
Bentley Wood High Sch. for Girls
Hermitage Cottages
Hermitage Gate
Woodland Hall
Whyteways
Harrow Weald Cemetery
Boot Pond
CHURCH ROAD
STANMORE
HA3
HA7
Weald College
Brockhurst Cnr.
A410
Grave Yard
Play. Fld.
The Roger Bannister Sports Centre
UXBRIDGE ROAD
Playing Fields
Harrow
The Cedars
HIGH ROAD
KENTON LANE
GORDON AVENUE
Temple Pond
Club House
STANMORE GOLF COURSE
HARROW WEALD
Bus Depot
Recreation Ground
Weald Schs.
High Sch.
Cedars Schs.
First & Mid. Sch.
LONG ELMES
COLLEGE AVENUE
Salvatorian Coll.
Works
Sch.
Belmont First & Mid. Schs.
BELMONT
KENTON LANE
Kenton Lane Farm
HA2
PINNER PARK AVENUE
Sports Ground
Headstone Manor
WORKS
Library
ST. GEORGE
Cemetery
Byron
Play Field

23
Elstree Open Space
Norwegian Barn
Tennis Courts
The Dower House
Junction 4
M1 MOTORWAY
M1
EDGWARE
A5
A41
Brockleyhill Farm
Brockley Grange
Brockleyhill House
Pear Wood Cottages
Wood Farm
Pear Wood
Fish Pond
Bury Farm
Gate Cottages
Edgware Bury
Nursery Cottage
London Gateway Service Area
Depot
Edgwarebury Cemetery
Play. Fld.
Broadfields Inf. Sch.
Broadfields Jun. Sch.
Sports Grd.
Tennis Courts
NUTT GRO
(WATFORD BY-PASS)
(WATLING STREET)
ROMAN ROAD
Newlands
EDGWAREBURY PARK
Club Ho.
Edgwarebury Golf Course
Offices
Playing Field
BARNET
EDGWARE
A410
SPUR RD
STONEGROVE
Stonegrove
Edgware
St. Mary's Convent
A5100
Stanmore
LONDON ROAD
Aylward First & Mid. Sch.
Lake Grove Rec. Grd.
The Lake
Stonegrove Park
North London Collegiate School
King George V Memorial Gdns.
CANONS PARK
The Basin
Edgware Bus Sta.
BROADWALK SHOPPING CENTRE
Superstore
Works
Gas Works
Stanmore Marsh
Sports Ground
Whitchurch First & Mid. Schs.
Bowling Green
Stanburn Schs.
WHITCHURCH
Canons Park
Edgware Football Gd.
Chandos Recreation Ground
LITTLE STANMORE
DEANSBROOK
A5109
T.A. Cen.
BURNT OAK
EDGWARE COMM. HOSP.
HONEYPOT LANE
A4140
MARSH LANE
Little Stanmore First & Mid. School
Prince Edward Playing Field
Sports Ground
Canons High Sch.
School
Centenary Park
Park High Sch.
Pitch & Putt
Putting Green
Sports Ground
QUEENSBURY
Queensbury
BRENT
Wks.
BROADWAY
G
H
J
K
L
M
1
2
3
4
5
6
7
8
9
11
24
39

A
B
C
D
E
F
12
23
40
1
2
3
4
5
6
7
8
9
London Gateway Service Area
Scratchwood Open Space
Thistle Wood
Gravel Pit Wood
Moat Mount Open Space
Target Wood
The Shrubbery
MOAT MOUNT OPEN SPACE
Clump of Trees Wood
Moat Mount Camp Site
Leg of Mutton Pond
Mote End Farm
MILL HILL GOLF COURSE
M1 MOTORWAY
M1
Hemmings Wood
Stoney Wood Lake
Stoney Wood
Nut Wood
Mote Mount
White Lodge
Mill Hill High Sch.
Beech Wood
Highwood Park
Hendon Park
Highwood Ho.
Highwood Hill
Highwood Hill Cottage
Holcombe Dale
Holcombe Hill
HENDON WOOD LANE OPEN SPACE
Brent Lodge Farm
Allendale
Sports Ground
St. Edwards College
Farmleigh
Oak Lodge
Boundary House
The Lynch House
Fairlawn
HIGHWOOD HILL
TOTTERIDGE
BARNET WAY A1
MARSH LANE A5109
EDGWARE WAY A41
EDGWARE BY-PASS
WATFORD WAY A1
APEX CORNER
HALE LANE A5100
SELVAGE LANE A5109
DEANS LANE A5109
THE BROADWAY
DAWS LANE
HAMMERS LANE
BARNET BY-PASS A1
THE RIDGEWAY
MILL HILL CIRCUS
MILL HILL
NW7
St. Joseph's R.C. College
St. Mary's Abbey & Sch.
The Mill Field
Belmont Sch.
Belmont Farm
St. Paul's C. of E. Prim. Sch.
Mill Hill School
Riding School
Playing Field
Featherstone Hill
ARRANDENE OPEN SPACE
Garden Centre
Cricket Ground
MILL HILL PARK
Mill Hill Broadway
Lyndhurst Park
The Hale
Deansbrook School
Edgware
HA8
Watling
Burnt Oak
Grahame Park
NW9
Woodcroft Park
Sports Ground
Copthall School
Chase Lodge Playing Field
Powerleague Soccer Centre
Rugby Club
Copthall Swimming Pool
COPTHALL SPORTS CENTRE
Hasmonean High Sch.
Junction 2
FIVEWAYS CORNER
GREAT NORTH WAY
R.A.F. Museum Hendon
Battle of Britain Hall
Hendon Coll.
High Sch.
Montrose Recreation Ground
COLINDALE HOSPITAL
Colindale
COLINDALE
Peel Centre
SUNNY HILL PARK
EDGWARE RD A5
BROADWAY
Silk Stream
EUROPEAN BUSINESS CENTRE
Superstore
WATFORD WY. A41

G
H
J
K
L
M
13
26
41
1
2
3
4
5
6
7
8
9
SOUTH HERTS GOLF COURSE
Brook Farm Open Space
Warehouses
Sports Ground
Club House
Fairlight Cottage
Hillsborough Cottage
Totteridge Park
A5109 COMMON TOTTERIDGE
Redings
WYKEHAM RISE
TOTTERIDGE
Hillsdown
Montebello
Burnhams
Chestnut Cottages
The Warren
Ellern Mede Nursing Home
Ellern Mede Farm
Copped Hall
N20
VILLAGE
TOTTERIDGE LANE
A5109
Totteridge and Whetstone
Waverley
Prim. Sch.
Windyridge
Lyenells
The Croft
Cricket Ground
WHETSTONE
Swan Lane Open Space
Darland Lake Nature Reserve
Consolata Missionary College
Laurel Farm
Woodridge Prim. Sch.
Folly Farm
Sports Ground
Cricket Club
Burtonhole Lane Farm Estate
Nursery
Burtonhole Farm
North London Hospice
Medical Research Laboratory
St. Vincent's School
Works
Oakfields
Wentworth Hall
Drivers Hill
N12
Woodside Park Club
Woodside Park
Mill Hill Sub. Sta.
Riding School
Frith Manor Ho.
Frith Manor Prim. Sch.
Partingdale Manor
B552
RIDGEWAY
BITTACY
Watch Tower House
FINCHLEY GOLF COURSE
Inglis Barracks
Depot
MILL HILL CEMETERY
Bittacy Hill Park
Playgrd.
BITTACY BUSINESS CENTRE
Nether Court (Club House)
Mill Hill East
West Finchley
Jun. & Inf. Schs.
Dollis Inf. Schs.
Club House
Hendon Crematorium
HENDON CEMETERY
HENDON GOLF COURSE
NW4
DOLLIS
B1462
Playing Fields
CHURCH END
N3
FINCHLEY
Victoria Rec. Grd.
Finchley Central
Holders Hill
BARNET-BY-PASS
A1 - NORTH
HOLDERS HILL
HENDON LANE
A504
REGENTS PARK
A598
BALLARDS LA.
EAST END ROAD
Windsor Open Space
College
Avenue House Grounds
Sports Ground
Pentland Centre
Play. Fld. Club Ho.
NORTH CIRCULAR ROAD
St. Marylebone Crematorium
College Farm

A
B
C
D
E
F
1
2
3
4
5
6
7
8
9
14
25
42
Totteridge and Whetstone
WHETSTONE
OAKLEIGH PARK
South Barnet
OSIDGE
BRUNSWICK PARK
NEW SOUTHGATE CEMETERY
New Southgate Crematorium
NORTH MIDDLESEX GOLF COURSE
B A R N E T
N20
FRIERN BARNET
NORTH FINCHLEY
N11
New Southgate
NEW SOUTHGATE
COLNEY HATCH
N12
N3
N2
N10
ST. PANCRAS & ISLINGTON CEMETERY
Islington Crematorium
COLDFALL WOOD
Friary Park
Bethune Park
Recreation Ground
Owen's Centre Playing Field
North London Hospice
Finchley Mem. Hosp
Fallow Corner
Great North Leisure Park
Glebe Land Open Space
Coppetts Wood
Refuse Destructor
Swan Lane Open Space
Curtis Family Centre
Friern Bridge Retail Park
Hollickwood Park
HIGH ROAD A1000
WHETSTONE HIGH ROAD
A1000 FINCHLEY
HIGH ROAD
NORTH CIRCULAR ROAD A406
A406
PINKHAM WAY
WOODHOUSE RD. A1003
FRIERN BARNET LANE
FRIERN BARNET RD. A1003
COLNEY HATCH LANE B550
OAKLEIGH RD. NORTH
OAKLEIGH ROAD SOUTH A109
RUSSELL ROAD B1453
TOTTERIDGE LA. A5109
OAKLEIGH RD.
BALLARDS LANE A598
EAST FINCHLEY
ALEXANDRA
St. Marylebone Crematorium

27
G
H
J
K
L
M
1
2
3
4
5
6
7
8
9
15
28
43
WINCHMORE HILL
Winchmore Hill
GROVELANDS PARK
Bourneside Sports Centre
Boating Lake
GROVELANDS PRIORY HOSPITAL
Sports Grd.
Pitch & Putt Course
Club Ho.
Southgate
Southgate College
SOUTHGATE
Ashmole Sch.
Playing Fields
Morton Lodge
Southgate Cricket Club Ground
Cemetery
Superstore
SOUTHGATE INDUSTRIAL ESTATE
A111 BOURNE
BOURNE
THE BOURNE
HIGH STREET
A1004
A1003 ROAD
CANNON HILL
ALDERMANS HILL
A1004
N21
N13
N22
PALMERS GREEN
Palmers Green
ENFIELD
GREEN LANES
HEDGE LANE
A111
A105
Sports Ground
Highfield Schs.
Arnos Grove
ARNOS PARK
Putting Green
The Avenue
Broomfield Park
Bowling Greens
Tennis Courts
Sports Ground
POWYS LA.
WILMER WY. A1452
BROOMFIELD
Pymme's Brook
Broomfield Sch.
A1110
A406
NORTH CIRCULAR ROAD
CLOCKHOUSE JUNCTION
TELFORD RD.
BOUNDS GREEN RD.
Middlesex Univ.
Bounds Green
Scout Park
Bowes Park
Bowes & Tennis Club
B106
BROWNLOW RD.
GREEN LANES
HIGH RD.
A105
New River Sports and Recreation Centre
Tennis Courts
Playing Field
White Hart Lane Sch.
Football Ground
HARINGEY
DURNSFORD RD.
ALBERT RD.
Recreation Ground
A109
LORDSHIP LANE
NOEL PARK
Wood Green
WOOD GREEN
Civic Cen.
Alexandra Palace
Blandford Hall
Football Ground
Alexandra Pavilion
The Lake
ALEXANDRA
PARK
ALEXANDRA PALACE
Middlesex Univ. (Quicksilver Pl. Campus)
Reservoir
Filter Beds
Cricket Ground
Gas Works
Wood Gn. Common
STATION RD.
MAYES RD.
WESTBURY AV.
SHOPPING CITY
MUSWELL HILL

A
B
C
D
E
F
1
2
3
4
5
6
7
8
9
16
27
44
LOWER EDMONTON
EDMONTON
UPPER EDMONTON
TOTTENHAM
TOTTENHAM HALE
Edmonton Green
Silver Street
White Hart Lane
Bruce Grove
N9
N13
N18
N21
N17
N22
EDMONTON CEMETERY
TOTTENHAM CEMETERY
PYMMES PARK
JUBILEE PARK
LORDSHIP RECREATION GROUND
BRUCE CASTLE PARK
Craig Park
Tottenham Park Cemetery
Federation Cemetery Jewish
THE NORTH MIDDLESEX HOSP.
GREAT CAMBRIDGE JUNCTION
Tottenham Hotspur F.C. (White Hart Lane)
Middlesex University
Salmon's Brook
Pymmes Brook
Playing Fields
Recreation Ground
Sports Ground
Latymer School
Winchmore Sch.
Aylward School
West Lea Sch.
Haselbury Jun. & Inf. Schs.
Wilbury Prim. Sch.
Firs Farm Prim. Sch.
Churchfield Prim. Sch.
The Paulin Ground
Tatem Rec. Grd.
Hollywood Gardens
Open Air Theatre
The Moselle
WINGATE TRADING ESTATE
TRIUMPH TRADING EST.
BROADWATER FARM ESTATE
NORTH CIRCULAR A406 ROAD
STERLING WAY
ANGEL
GREAT CAMBRIDGE ROAD A10
CAMBRIDGE ROAD A10
A10 ROUNDWAY
LORDSHIP LANE A109
BRUCE GROVE
HIGH ROAD A1010
FORE ST. A1010
HERTFORD ROAD A1010
CHURCH STREET B154
SILVER STREET
LANSDOWNE ROAD B137
WILLOUGHBY LANE
MEYER A1055
WESTBURY AV.
DOWNHILLS WAY B155
A1080
A105
A111
HEDGE LANE

29
17
30
45
G
H
J
K
L
M
1
2
3
4
5
6
7
8
9
36
37
38
WILLIAM GIRLING RESERVOIR
LEE VALLEY LEISURE GOLF COURSE
Leisure Centre
Cinema
Golf Driving Range
Warehouse
Sewage Works
Pickett's Lock
Refuse Incineration Plant
Pumping Station
River Lee Diversion
River Lee Navigation
LEA VALLEY VIADUCT
MERIDIAN WAY
A1055
NIGHTINGALE ROAD
Salisbury Sch. (Lower) Playing Field
Playing Field
Montagu Rec. Grd.
Angel Rd.
Superstore
Works
BANBURY RESERVOIR
LEE VALLEY REGIONAL PARK
Valve Tower
Banbury Sailing Cen.
The Cottage
Chalk Bridge
Recreation Ground
LOCKWOOD RESERVOIR
HIGH MAYNARD RESR.
Low Maynard Resr.
BLACKHORSE LANE
HIGHAM HILL
CHINGFORD
SOUTH CHINGFORD
CHINGFORD MOUNT
Chingford Mount Cemetery
Ridgeway Park
Mansfield Park
Chingford Hall Park
Larkswood Playing Fields
Larkswood Park
Ainslie Wood Nature Reserve
Rolls Sports Grd
Highams Park
Walthamstow Stadium (Greyhound)
Peter May Sports Centre
Golf Driving Range
Sports Ground
LLOYD PARK
WALTHAMSTOW
Chapel End
E4
E17
WALTHAM WAY
A1037
OLD CHURCH ROAD
A112
HALL LANE
A1009
NEW ROAD
SOUTHEND ROAD
NORTH CIRCULAR ROAD
A406
CHINGFORD MOUNT RD.
CHINGFORD RD.
FOREST ROAD
THE BELL
CROOKED BILLET

A
B
C
D
E
F
1
2
3
4
5
6
7
8
9
RANGER'S ROAD
18
The Warren
Club
Tennis Courts
Warren Pond
Barn Hoppet
Albany Ho.
Oak Hall
KINGS HEAD HILL
A110
RIDGEWAY
STATION ROAD
A1069
Chingford
CHINGFORD
CHINGFORD GREEN
WHITEHALL RD.
Cricket Ground
Whitehall Plain
Pimp Hall Nurseries
Pimp Hall Park
Friday Hill
FRIDAY HILL
B146
Playing Field
Bluehouse Grove
Hatch Forest
Hatch Grove
Reed's Forest
EPPING NEW ROAD
A104
Bancroft's Sch.
WOODFORD GOLF COURSE
Football Ground
Knighton Wood
WOODFORD WELLS
HATCH LA.
NEW ROAD
A1009
Suffield Hatch
CHINGFORD HATCH
LARKSHALL RD.
B160
Larkswood Playing Fields
29
Larks Wood
Larkswood Park
Larkswood Club
WALTHAM FOREST
E4
CHINGFORD ROAD
The Lops
The Ching
Highams Park
Boating Lake
The Highams Park
Woodford Side
Woodford Green Prim. Sch.
WOODFORD GREEN
Cricket Ground
HIGHAMS PARK
Highams Park
HIGHAMS PARK INDUSTRIAL ESTATE
Rolls Sports Grd.
Naseberry Ct.
HALE END
Schools
River Ching
Rugby Football Grd.
Sports Grd. Woodford High Sch. for Girls
Cedar Lodge
BROADMEAD ROAD
G8
EPPING FOREST
WINCHESTER ROAD B160
Walthamstow Stadium
Sports Ground
The Peter May Sports Centre
WADHAM ROAD
SOUTHEND ROAD
A406
St. Aubyn's Sch.
HIGH ROAD WOODFORD GREEN
A1199
Churchfields Junior & Infant Schs.
Halls of Residence
Woodbridge High Sch.
WATERWORKS CORNER
WOODFORD NEW RD.
E17
Walthamstow Forest
Reservoir (Covered)
Gilbert's Slade
FOREST ROAD
A503
FULBOURNE RD.
Works
WALTHAMSTOW BUSINESS CEN.
Superstore
THE VIADUCT
GEORGE LA.
South Woodford
46
BROADWALK
38
39
40

G
H
J
K
L
M
19
47
32
1
2
3
4
5
6
7
8
9
Recreation Ground
Grange Farm Centre
Hill Fm.
Swim. Pool
RODING VALLEY NATURE RESERVE
David Lloyd Leisure
Lake
Playing Fields
Wakes Hall
Bramstons
Chigwell Hall
Chigwell Sch.
Sandon Lodge
Rodings
Buckhurst Hill
BUCKHURST HILL
LORD'S BUSHES
IG9
RODING LANE
B170
EPPING FOREST
River Roding
M11
Chigwell
CHIGWELL
IG7
New Barns Farm
Old Loughtonians Hockey Club
LUXBOROUGH LANE
Luxborough
Works
Chigwell Sewage Works
Roding Valley
Playing Fields
West Hatch High School
Hill House
CHIGWELL GOLF COURSE
Club House
HIGH ROAD
A113
A123
HAINAULT ROAD
Library
B173
MANOR ROAD
M11-MOTORWAY
TOMSWOOD ROAD
STRADBROKE DRIVE
Ray Park
Ray Lodge Prim. Sch.
Sports Ground
Football Grd.
WOODFORD BRIDGE
Roding Prim. Sch.
Orchard House
Claybury Hall
Eden Health Club
Claybury Hospital Woods Nature Reserve
Forest House
Hospital Hill Wood
Hospital Hill
Cocked Hat Plantation
Egg Clump
Ash Plantation
Sports Ground
Cemetery
Sewage Works
Winn Bridge
Junction 4
CHIGWELL ROAD
SOUTHEND RD.
A1400
WOODFORD AV.
CHARLIE BROWN'S ROUNDABOUT
NORTH CIRCULAR RD.
RAVENSBOURNE GDNS.
IG5
IG6
Caterham High Sch.
CLAYHALL AVENUE
CLAYHALL
Garden of Rest
Cemetery
FULLWELL CROSS

32
Chigwell
CHIGWELL
CHIGWELL ROW
GRANGE HILL
HAINAULT
FAIRLOP
FULLWELL CROSS
EPPING
REDBRIDGE
IG7
IG6
Ilford
High Wood
Patch Park
Grange Farm Camping & Sports Centre
The Grange
Broad Oaks
Old Farm
Chigwell Prim. Sch.
Rose Bridge
Oaks Farm
Hillside
Burnt House
Fulham's Farm
Water Works
Reservoir
Camping Site
Browning Farm
Taylors Farm
Thrift House
Sewage Works
Billingsbourne
The Chase
Miller's Fm.
Grove Cotts.
Res.
The Lodge
Cemetery
Wells Park School
Recreation Ground
Playing Fields
Tennis Courts
Coppice Prim. Sch.
Limes Farm Inf. & Jun. Schools
Depot
Grange Hill
Hainault
Forest Road Playing Field
Hainault Recreation Ground
Lloyds Sports Club
Fairlop Oak Recreation Ground
Powerleague Soccer Cen.
Playing Field
Oakfield Sch. Sports Centre
Redbridge Sports Centre
Forest Farm Cottages
Fairlop Lodge
Fairlop Lake
Slipways
FAIRLOP WATERS
Country Park
Activity Centre
King Solomon High Sch.
FAIRLOP WATERS GOLF COURSE
Nature Reserve
Lagoon
Works
Farm Cottages
Hainault Farm
Sports Ground
Club House
Hainault Forest High Sch.
Ilford High Sch.
Ilford Jewish Prim.Sch.
Fairlop Prim. Sch.
Cemetery
HIGH ROAD
A113
A123
A1112
B173
LAMBOURNE ROAD
GRAVEL LANE
ROMFORD ROAD
MANFORD WAY
MANOR ROAD
FENCEPIECE ROAD
HAINAULT ROAD
FOREST ROAD
NEW NORTH ROAD
VICARAGE LANE
PUDDING LANE
PAINTERS ROAD
31
48

G
H
J
K
L
M
48
49
50
Young's Farm
FEATHERBED LANE
Crabtree Hill
BOURNE BRIDGE
Bournebridge Farm
Crown Park Farm
Hop Pole Farm
HOE LANE
LAMBOURNE END
The Camelot
Bournebridge
Lambourne Well
FOREST
Harmes Farm
Three Cornered Plain
Cavill's Walk
Spurgate Plain
Spurgate Brook
LAMBOURNE SQ.
Banks Farm
Taylor's Plain
MANOR ROAD
RM4
94
WEDDRELL'S PLAIN
Lodge
Osier Bed
Cabin Plain
Cabin Hill
Mile Plantation
Sandhills
Sheep Water
Foreberry Wood North
Lower Sandhills
Park Farm
HAINAULT FOREST
(COUNTRY PARK)
93
WELLINGTON
Refreshment Room
Fox Burrows
FOX BURROW ROAD
The Lake
Foreberry Wood South
Lower Park Farm
River Rom
Churchpath Plantation
Old Hainault Oak
Dog Kennel Hill
HAINAULT FOREST GOLF COURSE
Nursery
FIVE OAKS LANE
Willoughby's Hill
THISTLEDENE AV.
Pinewood Prim. Sch.
34
Romford
Riding School
Havering Park
HAINAULT BUS. PK.
HAINAULT INDUSTRIAL ESTATE
Reservoirs (Covered)
Works
A1112
Hainault Lodge
Club Ho.
Golf Practice Ground
HAVERING
Clockhouse Jun. & Inf. Schools
Hog Hill
RIDGE
ROAD
RM5
Havering Lodge
COLLIER ROW
Forest Farm
Cold Blow Farm
WHALEBONE
ROMFORD B174 ROAD
HOG HILL RD.
Recreation Ground
COLLIER ROW 174 ROAD
RM6
Gobians Farm
Prim. Sch.
Works
Football Grd.
Marks Gate
LANE
NORTHGATE INDUSTRIAL PARK
RM7
Furze Cottage
Bowling Alley
Nursery
Whites Farm
Crownfield Jun. & Inf. Schs.
Furze House Farm
BARKING and DAGENHAM
NORTH
Mill Farm
Mawney
49
G
H
J
K
L
M
48
49
50

Bournebridge
EPPING FOREST
BRENTWOOD
Nuper's Hatch
Stapleford Common
Asheton Farm
Pygro Wood
Straights Plantation
Palace Plantation
Sandpits Plantation
Home Farm
Hilly Park
Witch Hill Plantation
Horseshoe Farm
Wilderness
Bower Farm
South Park Plantation
PYRGO PARK
Foxburrow Wood
RM4
Round House Farm
HAVERING-ATTE-BOWER
HAVERING COUNTRY PARK
Pine Wood
Bower Wood
Kiln Wood
Churchpath Plantation North
Upper Bedfords
Broxhill Common
Bedfords
Deer Park
Larch Wood
BEDFORDS PARK
St. Ursula's R.C. Jun. & Inf. Schs
Romford
Bower Park School
CHASE CROSS
RM5
COLLIER ROW
RM1
Sunnyside Farm
RISEBRIDGE GOLF COURSE
Club House
Rise Park Jun. & Inf. Schs.
RISE PARK
Sports Ground
ROMFORD GOLF COURSE
RM2
Marshalls Park Lower Sch.
RAPHAEL PARK
Fish Ponds
GIDEA PARK
EASTERN AVENUE
A12
B175
B174
B1459
33
50

Greyhound Training Track
Havering Plain
Sevenacre Plantation
Wabbing's Plantation
Frieze Hill Cottages
Lake
Lodge
St. Vincent's Hamlet
Rochetts Farm
Wright's Bridge
Old MacDonalds Educational Farm Park
Wrightsbridge Farm
Wealdside
Tennis Courts
M25
BRENTWOOD
Brentwood CM14
M25 MOTORWAY
Pentowan Farm
Spice Pits Wood
Spice Pits Farm
Hill Farm
Sports Ground
Widdrington Farm
Noakhill Common
NOAK HILL
Weald Brook
The Osiers
Lakeview Park
Kennels
Manor Farm
Burnt Wood
DAGNAM PARK
Fir Wood
Cock Wood
The Nursery
Havering College of Further & Higher Education
Hatters Wood
Dycorts Sch.
Harold Hill Community Sch.
Pyrgo Priory Prim. Sch.
MAYLANDS GOLF COURSE & COUNTRY CLUB
Duck Wood Community Nature Reserve
Central Park
Swim Pool
Golf Course
HAROLD HILL
The David Compton Lodge
Comm. Centre
Long Wood
Sage Wood
Club House
Maylands
Maylands Cottage
Sports Grd.
RM3
Mead Sch.
Football Ground
HAROLD PARK
Harold Court Prim. Sch.
Elms Industrial Estate
Bates Industrial Estate
Harold Hill Ind. Est.
Upminster
Bleasend Farm
The Chase
Harold Wood
HAROLD WOOD
HAROLD WOOD HOSPITAL
GALLOWS CORNER
Superstore
Cissbury Lodge Farm
Cockabourne Bridge
Miniature Golf Course
Pages Farm
Emanuel Cottage
Ivy Lodge Farm
HAROLD WOOD PARK
Pavilion
Ingrebourne River
COLCHESTER ROAD
A12
SOUTHEND ARTERIAL ROAD
A127
Stafford Ind. Est.
51
54
55
56

20
52
Northwood
HA6
HA4
UB9
UB10
Uxbridge
Ruislip
RUISLIP
RUISLIP COMMON
RUISLIP MANOR
Ruislip Manor
RUISLIP GARDENS
Ruislip Gardens
WEST RUISLIP
West Ruislip
ICKENHAM
Ickenham
EASTCOTE VILLAGE
HILLINGDON
COPSE WOOD
PARK WOOD
YOUNG WOOD
MAD BESS WOOD
Mad Bess Wood Cottage
HASTLE HILL GOLF COURSE
Haste Hill
Nature Reserve
Poor's Field
Cemetery
Eleanor's
Ruislip Lido Railway
Lakeside
RUISLIP LIDO
Ruislip Woodlands Centre
Landing Stage
Miniature Railway
Woody Bay
Breakspear Crematorium (Ruislip)
The Lodge
Football Ground
Cannons Bridge Farm
Hillingdon Athletic Club
Haydon School
Playing Field
St. Vincent's Farm
Nurseries
Joel Street Farm
White Cottage
Harlyn Primary Sch.
Grangewood School
Haydon Hall Park
Coteford Sch.
Playing Fields
Club
Offices
High Grove
Swimming Pool
Bishop Ramsey C.of E. Sch. (Upper)
Warrender Park
Warrender Prim. Sch.
Bishop Ramsey Sch.
Whiteheath Jun. & Inf. Schs.
Winston Churchill Hall
Youth Centre
Prim. Sch.
Church Field Gdns.
Playground
RUISLIP GOLF COURSE
Golf Driving Range
Club Ho.
Cricket Ground
Supermarket
Ruislip Rugby Club
Sacred Heart R.C. Primary School
Sports Ground
Community Cen.
Tennis Courts
Works
Playing Field
Recreation Ground
Ruislip Gardens Primary School
Glebe Primary School
Ickenham Manor
Moat
Weir
Brook
River Pinn
HILL ROAD A4180
BURY
HIGH STREET
EASTCOTE B466
WEST END ROAD A4180
KINGSEND
B466
B472
B466
HIGH ROAD
JOEL STREET
ICKENHAM ROAD
LONG LANE

37
G
H
J
K
L
M
21
53
12
13
14
1
2
3
4
5
6
7
8
9
38
Pinner
PINNER
NORTH HARROW
North Harrow
HARROW
Harrow
West Harrow
WEST HARROW
RAYNERS LANE
Rayners Lane
SOUTH RUISLIP
Eastcote
ROXETH
South Harrow
SOUTH HARROW
Northolt Pk.
HA5
HA2
HA1
Pinner Village Gardens (Rec. Grd.)
Pinner Memorial Park
Pinner New Cemetery
Nower Hill
Nower Hill High Sch.
Woodlands Open Space
Yeading Brook Open Space
Headstone Manor Recreation Ground
Harrow Museum & Heritage Cen.
Pinner Park Schs.
Sports Ground
Model Railway
Reddiford Sch.
West Lodge Schs.
Innellan Ho. Sch.
Cemetery
Superstore
Little Common
Cannon Lane First & Mid. Schs.
Heathfield Sch.
The Croft
Play. Fld.
Streamside Rec. Grd.
Longfield Schs.
Roxborough Rough
Roxbourne Park
Playground
Yeading Brook
Cavendish Recreation Ground
Miniature Railway
Roxbourne First & Mid. Schs.
Recreation Ground
Field End Jun. & Inf. Schs.
Newton Farm First & Mid. Sch.
Newton Park West
Newton Ecology Park
Alexandra Sch.
Alexandra Park
Grange Schs.
Whitmore High Sch.
High Sch.
Earlsmead Sch.
Harrow Borough F.C.
Depot
Deane Park
Deanesfield Prim. Sch.
Queensmead Sch.
Queensmead Sports Cen.
Playing Fields
Tennis Courts
Warehouses
GEORGE V AVENUE
A404
PINNER ROAD
A4090
IMPERIAL DRIVE
ALEXANDRA AVENUE
NORTHOLT ROAD
A312
B466
CUCKOO HILL
HIGH ST.
MARSH ROAD
RAYNERS LANE
CANNON LANE
EASTCOTE ROAD
VILLAGE WAY
VIEW EASTERN AVENUE
HEADSTONE DRIVE
SOMERVELL ROAD
WHITMORE ROAD

38
A
B
C
D
E
F
1
2
3
4
5
6
7
8
9
22
37
54
WEALDSTONE
Harrow & Wealdstone
HARROW
HEADSTONE
GREENHILL
KENTON
Kenton
Harrow-on-the-Hill
WEST HARROW
West Harrow
HARROW ON THE HILL
ROXETH
SOUTH HARROW
South Harrow
Northolt Pk.
Sudbury Hill
Sudbury Hill Harrow
SUDBURY
Wood End
HA1
HA2
HA3
UB5
Headstone Manor
Harrow Museum & Heritage Cen.
Headstone Manor Recreation Ground
Harrow Crown Court
Byron Recreation Ground
Harrow Driving, Cycling and Road Safety Centre
Swimming Pool
Leisure Cen.
Kenton Recreation Ground
Elmgrove First & Middle Schools
Priestmead Rec. Grd.
Harrow Recreation Ground
Harrow Cemetery
Civic Centre
St. Ann's Shopping Cen.
St. George's Shop. & Leis. Cen.
University of Westminster (Harrow Campus)
Northwick Park
NORTHWICK PARK HOSPITAL
ST. MARK'S HOSP.
NORTHWICK PARK
Harrow School
Harrow School Playing Fields
Harrow School Farm
School Lake
Miniature Rifle Range
Playing Fields
Parade Ground
Rugby Football Grounds
Whitmore High Sch.
Grange Schs.
Vaughan Schs.
Cricket Ground
St. Andrew's at Harrow
The Clementine Churchill Hospital
Burial Ground
Kennet End
Orley Farm Sch.
Harrow Ckt. Club
Toll Gate
David Lloyd Raquet & Fitness Club
Vale Farm Sports Centre
Wembley Football Club
Welldon Park First Sch.
Roxeth Rec. Grd.
PINNER ROAD
A404
A409
A312
A4005
A4006
A4127
B457
STATION ROAD
HIGH ST.
ST. GEORGE GANGE WAY
LOWLANDS RD.
KENTON RD.
WATFORD ROAD
SHEEPCOTE RD.
BESSBOROUGH RD.
LOWER RD.
ROXETH HILL
LONDON RD.
SUDBURY HILL
SUDBURY COURT DR.
HARROW ROAD
NORTHOLT ROAD
GREENFORD RD.

QUEENSBURY
23
Queensbury
Stanmore
HA7
HA3
HA8
NW9
HA0
HA9
Edgware
KINGSBURY
40
Kingsbury
HONEYPOT LANE
A4140
KENTON ROAD
A4006
KINGSBURY ROAD
FRYENT WAY
FRYENT COUNTRY PARK
Barn Hill
Barn Hill Open Space
Pond
SALMON
PRESTON
Preston Road
BRENT
Wembley
South Kenton
NORTH WEMBLEY
North Wembley
A4088
FORTY AVENUE
FORTY LANE
Wembley Park
WEMBLEY PARK
WEMBLEY ARENA
Conference Centre
WEMBLEY STADIUM
Wembley Stadium
EMPIRE WAY
B4565
PARK LANE
A4089
55
KING EDWARD VII PARK
WOODCOCK PARK
Preston Park
Kingsbury High Sch.
Roe Green Park
Recreation Ground
Sports Ground
Police Cadet Training Centre
Preston Manor High Sch.
Wembley Manor Jun. & Inf. Sch.
Chalkhill Prim. Sch.
Stanmore Junction
Wealdstone Brook
Palace of Industry
BOWMAN TRADING ESTATE
Superstore
Sherrins Farm
G
H
J
K
L
M
1
2
3
4
5
6
7
8
9

COLINDALE
Colindale
COLINDALE HOSPITAL
Recreation Ground
Peel Centre
(Metropolitan Police
Training Establishment)
Sports Ground
Library
Roe Green
Schools
Roe Green Park
Kingsbury Manor Studio
KINGSBURY ROAD
A4006
NW9
COLINDEEP
A5150
M1 MOTORWAY
M1
WATFORD WAY
A41
SUNNY HILL PARK
Middlesex University
Museum
HENDON
THE HYDE
Silk Stream
THE HYDE
WATLING STREET
A5
EDGWARE ROAD
STATION ROAD
A504
Hendon
Kingsbury Green
KINGSBURY
39
FRYENT
COUNTRY PARK
Recreation Ground
Kingsbury Grn. Prim. Sch.
St. Robert Sothwell Sch.
CHURCH LANE
B454
Silver Jubilee Park
WEST HENDON
PLAYING FIELDS
Cycle Track
Brent Reservoir
York Park
Youth Sailing Base
Cool Oak Bridge
WEST HENDON
WOODFIELD PARK
BRENT RESERVOIR
Field Study Centre
Woodfield Sch.
Welsh Harp Open Space
Sailing Club
Rifle Range
Nursery
Brent Bridge
Junc. 1
STAPLES CORNER
NORTH CIRCULAR ROAD
A406
Neasden Recreation Ground
Braintcroft Prim. Sch.
Technology Colleges
NEASDEN
SALMON STREET
A4140
BLACKBIRD HILL
NEASDEN LANE
Kingsbury Bridge
River Brent
NW10
St. Margaret Clitherow R.C. Prim. Sch.
Chalkhill Prim. Sch.
Play. Fld.
Railway Works
Neasden Depot
NEASDEN JUNCTION
A4088
DUDDEN HILL LANE
GLADSTONE PARK
Dollis Hill House
DOLLIS HILL
GREAT CENTRAL WAY
B4557
56
Neasden
Brent Park
Superstore
24
Battle of Britain Hall
Vernon Ho. Sch.

41
G
H
J
K
L
M
25
24
26
1
2
3
4
5
6
7
8
9
42
57
N3
NW4
NW11
NW3
NW6
CAMDEN
GREAT NORTH WAY
HENDON WAY
FINCHLEY ROAD
REGENTS PARK RD.
NORTH CIRCULAR ROAD
FALLODEN WAY
A1
A41
A406
A407
A502
A504
A598
A5
B551
B552
B510
HENLYS CORNER
HAMPSTEAD GARDEN SUBURB
Temple Fortune
GOLDERS GREEN
Golders Green
Brent Cross
BRENT CROSS INTERCHANGE
BRENT CROSS SHOPPING CENTRE
BRENT CROSS FLY OVER
HENDON PARK
CRICKLEWOOD
Cricklewood
CHILD'S HILL
Fortune Green
HAMPSTEAD
HEATH
GOLDERS HILL PARK
Golders Green Crematorium
Jewish Cemetery
St. Marylebone Crematorium
ST. MARYLEBONE CEMETERY
Clitterhouse Recreation Ground
Hendon Football Club
Hampstead School
Hampstead Cemetery
Sports Ground
Basing Hill Park
Princes Park
Big Wood
Little Wood
Leg of Mutton Pond
West Heath
Jack Straws Castle
Middlesex University
Brent Sidings
Depot
Bus Garage
Superstore
Superstores
Works
College Farm
Windsor Open Space
THE GARDEN HOSP
EAST END ROAD
NORTH END ROAD
FINCHLEY ROAD
GOLDERS GREEN ROAD
WEST HEATH ROAD
CRICKLEWOOD BROADWAY
CRICKLEWOOD LANE
HOLDERS HILL
BRENT STREET
QUEENS ROAD
HENDON WAY
ST. GOLDERS CIRCULAR
HOOP LANE
PLATTS LANE
REDINGTON ROAD
FROGNAL

42
A
B
C
D
E
F
1
2
3
4
5
6
7
8
9
26
27
28
41
58
EAST FINCHLEY
FORTIS GREEN
HAMPSTEAD GARDEN SUBURB
BARNET
N2
NW11
NW3
N6
CAMDEN
HIGHGATE
HAMPSTEAD
HAMPSTEAD HEATH
NORTH END
VALE OF HEALTH
DARTMOUTH PARK
GOSPEL OAK
Gospel Oak
Hampstead Heath
Hampstead
East Finchley
MARYLEBONE CEMETERY
HAMPSTEAD GOLF COURSE
HIGHGATE GOLF COURSE
Club House
HIGHGATE WOOD
QUEEN'S WOOD
Cranley Gardens
KEN WOOD
Kenwood House
Caen Wood Towers Farm
HIGHGATE CEMETERY
WATERLOW PARK
PARLIAMENT HILL
Highgate Ponds
Hampstead Ponds
Ladies' Bathing Pond
Bathing Pond
Sports Ground
Bunkers Hill
The Spaniards
Mount Tyndal
Jack Straws Castle
Whitestone Pond
West Heath
The Hill
Open Air Stage
Cherry Tree Wood
Parkland Walk
Stormont Lawn Tennis & Squash Club
Highgate Jun. Sch. Playing Field
HIGHGATE PRIVATE HOSP.
ATHLONE HOUSE
ST. LUKE'S WOODSIDE HOSP.
NATIONAL HOSP. FOR NEUROLOGY
William Ellis School
Parliament Hill School
Swimming Pool
Running Track
Fortismere Sch.
St. James C.E. Prim. Sch.
Oak Lodge Sch.
Highgate Wing
EAST END A504
A1000
FORTIS GREEN A504
LYTTELTON ROAD A1
AYLMER ROAD
GREAT NORTH RD
ARCHWAY RD A1
NORTH HILL B519
HAMPSTEAD LANE B519
SPANIARDS ROAD B519
NORTH END A502
MUSWELL HILL B550
SOUTHWOOD LANE B550
HIGHGATE HIGH ST.
HIGHGATE WEST HILL
MILLFIELD LA.
WINNINGTON ROAD
BISHOPS AVENUE
COURTENAY AV
COMPTON AV
SHELDON AV
STORMONT ROAD
DENEWOOD ROAD
WILDWOOD RD.
WEST HEATH RD
EAST HEATH RD
HEATH ST.
FITZJOHN'S AV.
ROSSLYN HILL
POND ST.
FLEET RD.
AGINCOURT RD.
MANSFIELD ROAD
GORDON HO. RD. B518
HIGHGATE RD.
SWAIN'S LANE
ROYAL FREE HOSPITAL

43
G
H
WOOD GREEN
J
K
L
M
27
ALEXANDRA PARK
ALEXANDRA PALACE
N22
MUSWELL HILL
Cricket Ground
Filter Beds
Playing Field
Gas Works
Reservoir
HORNSEY
Hornsey
PRIORY RD.
HIGH ST.
HORNSEY A504
TURNPIKE LA.
Turnpike La.
HIGH ROAD
WESTBURY A1080
GREEN LANES
A105
Priory Park
HORNSEY CENTRAL HOSPITAL
PARK ROAD
A1201
TOTTENHAM LA.
A103
HARRINGAY
Harringay
Harringay Grn. Lanes
GRAND PARADE
ST. ANN'S
HORNSEY VALE
Stationers Park
Town Hall
CROUCH END
CROUCH END HILL
CROUCH HILL
Crouch Hill
STROUD GREEN
Covered Reservoir
Parkland Walk
FINSBURY PARK
Finsbury Park
N4
Sports Arena
MANOR HOUSE
Manor House
SEVEN SISTERS
A503
STROUD GREEN RD.
HORNSEY RD.
HORNSEY RISE
A103
HORNSEY LANE
B540
ARCHWAY
Archway
HOLLOWAY RD.
A1
ISLINGTON
Upper Holloway
UPPER HOLLOWAY
ST. JOHN'S GR.
Whittington Park
JUNCTION RD.
A400
HOLLOWAY
NAG'S HEAD
N7
Isledon Village
Arsenal
BLACKSTOCK RD.
BROWNSWOOD PARK
HIGHBURY PARK
TUFNELL PARK
Tufnell Park
BRECKNOCK RD.
CAMDEN RD.
CALEDONIAN RD.
PARKHURST RD.
H.M.P. HOLLOWAY
Drayton Park
LOWER HOLLOWAY
HIGHBURY
59
44
1
2
3
4
5
6
7
8
9

A
B
C
D
E
F
1
2
3
4
5
6
7
8
9
28
43
60
The Moselle
Lordship Recreation Ground
Open Air Theatre
Bruce Grove
TOTTENHAM HALE
Tottenham Hale
MILLMEAD INDUSTRIAL CENTRE
Pymme's Brook
DOWNHILLS PARK
DOWNHILLS WY.
WEST GREEN
WEST GREEN ROAD
HARINGEY
PHILIP LANE
B153 LANE
MONUMENT WY
HALE RD.
FERRY A503 LANE
WATERMEAD
A1055
TOTTENHAM HALE GYRATORY
TOTTENHAM HALE RETAIL PARK
A504
BROAD LANE
Seven Sisters
SEVEN SISTERS ROAD
HIGH ROAD
A10
Town Hall
Leisure Cen.
Chestnuts Rec. Ground
ST. ANN'S ROAD
ST. ANN'S HOSPITAL
B152
South Tottenham
SOUTH TOTTENHAM
West Junction Mus.
Markfield Recreation Ground
WARWICK RESERVOIR (WEST)
WARWICK RESERVOIR (EAST)
RESERVOIR
Harringay Green Lanes
GREEN LANES
AMHURST PARK
A107
Stamford Hill
CLAPTON COMMON
EAST RESERVOIR
WEST RESERVOIR
Sir Thomas Abney Prim. Sch.
MANOR HOUSE
Manor House
A503
A105
STAMFORD HILL
SPRINGFIELD PARK
Springfield Marina
Coppermill Bridge
High Bri.
Cricket Ground
Sports Ground
UPPER CLAPTON
UPPER CLAPTON RD.
The Castle
The Castle (Indoor Climbing Cen.)
LORDSHIP PARK
B105
MANOR ROAD
ABNEY PARK CEMETERY
N16
STOKE NEWINGTON
Stoke Newington
STOKE NEWINGTON CHURCH
STOKE NEWINGTON HIGH ST
STAMFORD HILL A10
NORTHWOLD
B111
CLISSOLD PARK
Clissold Ho.
Lake
Council Offices
Paddling Pool
Leisure Cen.
BROWNSWOOD PARK
Rectory Road
RECTORY ROAD
EVERING RD.
AMHURST ROAD
SHACKLEWELL
Kingsland School
HACKNEY DOWNS
LOWER CLAPTON
Stormont House Sch.
DOWNS PARK
CRICKETFIELD R.
A104
HIGHBURY PARK
HIGHBURY GRANGE
HIGHBURY QUADRANT
N5
E8
N4
GUINNESS TRUST ESTATE
Superstore

45
G
H
J
K
L
M
1
2
3
4
5
6
7
8
9
WALTHAMSTOW
HIGHAM HILL
29
46
61
LOCKWOOD RESERVOIR
LOW MAYNARD RESERVOIR
HIGH MAYNARD RESERVOIR
RESERVOIR No. 4
RESERVOIR No. 5
FOREST ROAD
Blackhorse Rd.
BLACKHORSE ROAD
Walthamstow Central
Walthamstow Queens Rd.
St. James St. Walthamstow
E17
WALTHAMSTOW FOREST
WATER WORKS
Filter Beds
Low Hall Sports Ground
Leyton Marshes
MARKHOUSE ROAD
LEA BRIDGE ROAD
HIGH ST.
HOE ST.
CHINGFORD RD.
A503
A104
A112
A1006
A106
A12
B112
E10
LEYTON
Leyton Midland Rd.
ORIENT WAY
Recreation Ground
HACKNEY MARSH
RECREATION GROUND
LEA BRIDGE
CLAPTON PARK
E9
Temple Mills
EASTWAY
RUCKHOLT RD.
HOMERTON
LEA INTERCHANGE
HOMERTON HOSPITAL
NORTH MILLFIELDS Recreation Ground
SOUTH MILL FIELDS
Clapton Junction
MARSHES
Lee Valley Ice Centre
Middlesex Filter Beds Nature Reserve
Town Hall
THE BELL
NEW SPITALFIELDS MARKET

A
B
C
D
E
F
1
2
3
4
5
6
7
8
9
30
45
62
FOREST RD.
A503
WOOD ST.
THORPE COOMBE HOSP.
Wood St. Walthamstow
UPPER WALTHAMSTOW
E17
A104 NEW ROAD
WOODFORD NEW RD.
Gilbert's Slade
Reservoir (Covered)
Boating Pond
Community Hall
Sports Ground Forest Schs.
Round Pond
SNARESBROOK ROAD
Sports Ground
Horse Ride
E18
SOUTH WOODFORD
South Woodford
GEORGE LA.
HIGH RD.
WOODFORD RD.
HERMON HILL
SNARESBROOK
Snaresbrook
Eagle Pond
Snaresbrook Crown Court
Hollow Pond (Boating Lake)
WHIPPS CROSS HOSPITAL
WHIPPS CROSS ROAD
A114
Playing Field
LEA BRIDGE RD.
A104
HOLLYBUSH HILL
A1199
NEW WANSTEAD
A113
Recreation Grd.
CAMBRIDGE PARK
A106
EASTERN AV.
Wanstead
George Green
WANSTEAD
A12
GREEN MAN ROUNDABOUT
BUSH ROAD
A114
BLAKE HALL ROAD
A1008
E11
The Basin (Fish Pond)
WANSTEAD GOLF
Bush Wood
Reservoir Wood
Shoulder of Mutton Pond
WALTHAM FOREST
Leyton Midland Rd.
HIGH RD. LEYTON
FRANCIS RD.
B161
E10
Leytonstone
Leytonstone High Rd.
LEYTONSTONE
HIGH ROAD LEYTONSTONE
GAINSBOROUGH RD.
GROVE GREEN RD.
A106
CATHALL RD.
A12
Playing Field
Horse Ride
ALDERSBROOK
CENTRE ROAD
A114
WANSTEAD FLATS
St. Patrick's R.C. Cemetery
Leyton
Sidmouth Park
Leyton Orient F.C.
LEYTON
A112
Eastway Cycle Circuit
Mills
Eastway Spts. Cen.
Camp Site
Rec. Grd.
E15
Cann Hall
West Ham Cemetery
Cemetery
DAMES ROAD
HARROW RD.
E7
Wanstead Pk.
Forest Gate
WOODGRANGE RD.
CAPEL
SEBERT
CHANDOS
BUXTON
HAMPTON

47
31
63
48
G
H
J
K
L
M
1
2
3
4
5
6
7
8
9
CHARLIE BROWN'S ROUNDABOUT
NORTH CIRCULAR ROAD
SOUTHEND RD.
WOODFORD A1400
CLAYHALL
BARKINGSIDE
IG8
IG5
IG6
IG4
IG2
IG1
E12
M11
Hatton School
Sports Field
P.D.S.A. (Veterinary Centre)
RODING HOSPITAL (B.U.P.A.)
Beal High Sch.
CLAYHALL PARK
Garden of Rest
Cemetery
Nightingale Prim. Sch.
Recreation Ground
GANTS HILL
CRANBROOK
REDBRIDGE ROUNDABOUT
Redbridge
EASTERN AVENUE
A12
A406
A123
A116
A117
A118
B192
B165
SOUTH WOODFORD TO BARKING RELIEF ROAD
REDBRIDGE
Ilford
Gants Hill
P.L.A. Recreation Ground
Club House
Valentines High Sch.
The Ornamental Pond
VALENTINES PARK
Ilford Cricket Club
The Lake
Swim Pool
Wanstead High Sch.
Golf Course
Pumping Station
The Heronry
Lincoln Island
Rook Island
WANSTEAD PARK
The Temple
Keepers Lodge
Heronry Pond
Perch Pond
ILFORD GOLF COURSE
River Roding
Sewage Works
CITY OF LONDON CEMETERY
City of London Crematorium
Crematorium
Alders Brook
ALDERSBROOK
Aldersbrook Prim. Sch.
MANOR PARK
MANOR PARK CEMETERY
Manor Park Crem.
Manor Park
ROMFORD ROAD
FOREST DRIVE
ILFORD
THE EXCHANGE
Town Hall
Ilford
ILFORD HILL
WINSTON WAY
ILFORD LANE
CRANBROOK ROAD
Cranbrook Coll.
LITTLE ILFORD
Woodgrange
HIGH ST. N.

48
A
B
C
D
E
F
1
2
3
4
5
6
7
8
9
32
47
64
FAIRLOP WATERS
GOLF COURSE
Nature Reserve
Aldborough Hall
(School of Riding)
PAINTERS ROAD
BARKINGSIDE
Barkingside
Football Ground
Ilford Jewish Prim.Sch.
Barnardos
Fullwood Prim. Sch.
IG6
Aldborough Hall Farm
Aldborough Ho. Farm
ALDBOROUGH HATCH
Aldborough House
IG2
LITTLE HEATH
KING GEORGE HOSPITAL
GOODMAYES HOSPITAL
Oaks Park High Sch.
NEWBURY PARK
Newbury Park
Newbury Park Prim. Sch.
EASTERN AVENUE
A12
A123
HIGH ROAD
HORNS ROAD
CRANBROOK
Sports Ground
Playing Field
SEVEN KINGS PARK
Bandstand
REDBRIDGE
Ilford
SEVEN KINGS
Seven Kings
Railway Workshop
IG3
Goodmayes
GOODMAYES
GOODMAYES PARK
Superstore
A118
HIGH ROAD
GREEN LANE
A1083
GRIGGS APP.
WINSTON WY.
Cricklefield Rec. Grd.
Running Track
Cemetery
IG1
ILFORD
SOUTH PARK
The Lake
Mayespark Prim. Sch.
LONGBRIDGE RD.
A124
University of East London
LOXFORD PARK
LOXFORD
Woodlands Jun. & Inf. Schs.
Loxford Sch. of Science & Technology
Hyleford (Home for the Elderly)
Seven Kings Water
Cran Brook

G
H
J
K
L
M
33
Mawney
HAVERING
Romford
RM6
RM7
RM8
RM9
RM10
CHADWELL HEATH
Chadwell Heath
BARKING
and
DAGENHAM
BECONTREE
BEACONTREE HEATH
Crowlands
CENTRAL PARK
EASTERN AVENUE
A12
WEST AVENUE
WHALEBONE LANE NORTH
WHALEBONE LANE SOUTH
A1112
LONDON ROAD
A118
HIGH ROAD
RAINHAM ROAD
A124
WOOD LANE
A1083
A1240
HEATHWAY
BENNETT'S CASTLE LANE
B191
A1153
PORTERS AVENUE
RAINHAM ROAD NORTH
RAINHAM ROAD SOUTH
Chadwell Heath Cemetery
Jun. Sch.
Infant Sch.
Mill Farm
Warren Farm
MOBY DICK
Warren Park Golf Centre
Rec. Ground
Warren Jun. Sch.
ST. CHAD'S PARK
Crown Farm
Crown Cottages
St. Edward's C. of E. Comp. School
Westlands Playing Field
Sports Ground
Crowlands Sports Ground
CROWLANDS HEATH GOLF COURSE
Fords Sports Ground
Aqua Driving Range
Dagenham Civic Centre
CHADWELL HEATH INDUSTRIAL PARK
ELDENWALL INDUSTRIAL ESTATE
Playing Field
BECONTREE DAY HOSP.
VALENCE PARK
Valence Ho. Mus.
Bandstand
Youth Cen.
Swim. Pool
Trinity Sch.
Dagenham & Redbridge Grd.
Sydney Russell Comp. Sch.
King Georges Field
MAWNEY PARK
Red House Farm
Hainault House
Furze House Farm
Whites Farm
Miniature Golf Course
Pavilion
Nursery
50
65
1
2
3
4
5
6
7
8
9

50
A
B
C
D
E
F
1
2
3
4
5
6
7
8
9
34
49
66
RM1
RM2
RM7
RM10
ROMFORD
Romford
GIDEA PARK
HEATH PARK
RUSH GREEN
BARKING and DAGENHAM
Dagenham
Elm Park
ROMFORD GOLF COURSE
Marshalls Park Lower Sch.
Fish Ponds
Park Lake
Black's Bri.
LODGE FARM PARK
King Georges Field
MAWNEY PARK
Warehouse
Works
Bus Depot
Prim. Schs.
Lake
County Court
Town Hall
Mag. Court
Lib.
Superstore
ROGER REEDE'S ALMSHOUSES
Cottons Recreation Ground
Comm. Cen.
THE BREWERY
Romford Stadium (Greyhound)
OLDCHURCH HOSP.
Gas Works
Romford Ice Rink
OLDCHURCH PARK
Jutsums Rec. Grd.
Romford Cemetery
Crowlands Sports Ground
Pavilion
Recreation Ground
HYLANDS PARK
Depot
BROOKE TRAD. EST.
St. Mary's R.C. Jun. & Inf. Sch.
Playing Field
Grenfell Park
River Rom
Barking College
Miniature Golf Course
CENTRAL PARK
Nursing Home
Fels Farm
Eastbrookend House
Becontree Cemetery
Hook's Hall Farm
The Chase Nature Reserve
Lakes
Eastbrook Grove
Dagenham Playing Field
Eastbrook Comp. Sch.
Sports Ground
Dagenham & Redbridge F.C. Grd.
Driving Tuition Course
HARROW LODGE PARK
Boating Lake
Playground
The Albany School
Beam River
Gas Transmission Station
EASTERN AVENUE
A12 WEST
EASTERN AVENUE EAST
NORTH STREET
A125
A118
A124
A1112
MAIN ROAD
LONDON ROAD
WATERLOO RD.
ST. EDWARDS WAY
MERCURY GDNS.
THURLOE GDNS.
ROM VALLEY WAY
OLDCHURCH ROAD
RUSH GREEN ROAD
HORNCHURCH ROAD
UPPER RAINHAM ROAD
RAINHAM ROAD NORTH
RAINHAM RD. STH.
DAGENHAM ROAD
HAVERING RD.
SOUTH STREET
MAWNEY ROAD
CROW LANE
GORSEWAY
MARKS ROAD
HEATH PARK ROAD
BRENTWOOD ROAD
ELM PARK AVENUE

G
H
J
K
L
M
35
67
54
55
56
1
2
3
4
5
6
7
8
9
SOUTHEND
A127
ARTERIAL
ROAD
Romford
RM3
RM11
RM14
Squirrel's Heath
Gidea Park
ARDLEIGH GREEN
HAYNES PARK
EMERSON PARK
Hornchurch
HORNCHURCH
Upminster
UPMINSTER PARK
HAROLD WOOD PARK
Miniature Golf Course
Pages Farm
Tyes Cottage
Cornlands Farm
Prospect Farm
Ingrebourne Farm
Mount Pleasant Farm
Motel
Sunset
The Rosary
Grasslands
Lillyputts Farm
Harold Wood Prim. Sch.
Redden Ct. Sch.
The Campion School
College
Emerson Park School
Playing Field
UPMINSTER GOLF COURSE
Emerson Park
St. Andrew's Park
Council Offs.
Arts Centre
Sports Ground
Tower Inf. Sch.
Tower Jun. Sch.
Goodrington Sch.
Burnthouse Wood
Abbs Cross School
The Saunders Draper Sch.
Suttons Prim. Sch.
Hacton Junior Mixed & Inf. Sch.
Branfil Jun. & Inf. Schools
Sports Stadium
Cemetery
Mill Cott.
The Dell
Upminster Bridge
Upminster
Ingrebourne Centre
ST. GEORGES HOSPITAL
West Lodge
Hacton Parkway
River Ingrebourne
HIGH ROAD
HIGH STREET
UPMINSTER ROAD
ST. MARY'S LANE
A124
B187
B1421
CORBETS TEY RD
SUTTONS AVENUE
SYLVAN AVENUE
PARKSTONE AVENUE
HERBERT ROAD
WINGLETYE LANE
NELMES WAY
BILLET LANE
STATION LANE
HACTON LANE
Gaynes Parkway

A
B
C
D
E
F
36
1
2
3
4
5
6
7
8
9
142
68
08
09
10
185
84
83
82
81
Ickenham Manor
Glebe Primary School
Ickenham Marsh
Lane Farm
Freezeland Covert
WESTERN AVENUE
A40
Ruislip
R.A.F. NORTHOLT AERODROME
HA4
Yeading Brook
Cutthroat Wood
Gutteridge Wood
NORTH HILLINGDON
Uxbridge
Ryefield Primary Sch.
Recreation Ground
Ten Acres
The Gorse
UB10
Hare Plantation
Cycle Track
Westways Fm.
Lane Covert
West London Shooting Grounds
Home Covert
Swakeleys School
Charville Prim. Sch.
Hedgewood School
Grosvenor Playing Field
Corporation Yard
HILLINGDON
Hayes Shrub
Hayes Park
Mellow Lane Farm
Home Farm
HAYES END
The Paddocks Fm.
UB4
Hayes
Grange Park Jun. & Inf. Schs.
Belmore Primary School
Belmore Playing Fields
UXBRIDGE RD
A4020
UB8
WOOD END GREEN
Rosedale Park
The Hayes Manor Sch.
Hayes Manor Sports Cen.
UB3
The Beck Theatre
WOOD END
Barra Hall
Town Hall Park
Essoldo Theatre
Wood End Pk Prim. Sch.
HAYES
A437
HARLINGTON
WEST DRAYTON

53
G
H
J
K
L
M
1
2
3
4
5
6
7
8
9
37
54
69
South Ruislip
Deanesfield Prim. Sch.
Playing Fields
Queensmead Sports Cen.
Tennis Courts
Earlsmead Sch.
Harrow Borough F.C.
Harrow HA2
Northolt Pk.
Wood End
Warehouses
Victoria Retail Park
Waste Transfer Station
Depot
Play Centre
NORTHOLT PARK
Northolt High Sch.
Radio Station
Bourne Primary School
Sports Ground
Priors Fm.
Lord Halsbury Memorial Playing Flds.
Willow Tree Prim. Sch.
Com. Cen.
Northolt
Swim. Baths
THE FARMLANDS
NORTHOLT
Islips Manor Park
Playground
Youth & Comm. Cen.
Belvue Business Cen.
Works
Factory
Greenford Industrial Estate
Warehouse
Depot
Moat
Belvue Park
Mosque
LONDON GOLF COURSE
Walford First & Middle Sch.
Northolt Prim. Sch.
John Chilton Sch.
Walford High Sch.
TARGET ROUNDABOUT
Youth Cen.
Comm. Cen.
Golf Club
Golf Range
Superstore
Lime Tree Park
West End
Smith's Farm
Lorry Park
Playing Fields
NORTHOLT GOLF COURSE
Gifford Primary Sch.
RECTORY PARK
(Recreation Ground)
WHITE HART ROUNDABOUT
Greenford
UB6
GREENFORD
RAVENOR PARK
Ravenor Farm & London Motorcycle Museum
Greenford High Sch.
Greenford Sports Cen.
Playing Fields
Reservoir
Cricket Club
King George's Field
Sports & Social Club
Spts. Grd.
Public Open Space
Superstore
Southall
Rec. Grd.
GREENFORD PARK CEMETERY
Jubilee Park
UB1
Durdans Park Primary Sch.
Marina
Allenby Inf. Sch.
High Sch.
Mount Pleasant Leisure Cen.
Playing Field
Warren Park
Yeading Brook
Tennis Courts
Sports Grd.
Bowling Green
Athletic Grd.
GRAND UNION CANAL (PADDINGTON BRANCH)
Grand Union Canal Walk
A40 WESTERN AVENUE
A312 ROAD
MANDEVILLE ROAD
CHURCH ROAD
RUISLIP ROAD
B455
WEST END ROAD
A4180
THE PARKWAY
A312
A4090
PETT'S HILL
DORMER'S WELLS

A
B
C
D
E
F
1
2
3
4
5
6
7
8
9
38
53
70
Sudbury Hill
Harrow
Sudbury Hill Play. Flds.
HARROW
Wembley Football Club
David Lloyd Raquet & Fitness Club
Tennis Courts
Wood End
WHITTON
AVENUE
A4090
WEST
WHITTON
AVENUE
SUDBURY
Sudbury & Harrow Rd.
Maybank Open Space
Northolt
UB5
Factory
Greenford Green
Horsenden Primary Sch.
Horsenden Wood
Greenford
BERKELEY FIELDS
Horsenden Hill Rec. Grd.
HORSENDEN HILL GOLF COURSE
Horsenden Hill
Horsenden Farm
Nature Reserve
UB6
GRAND UNION CANAL
(PADDINGTON BRANCH)
Lyon's Dock
Warehouses
Greenford
GREENFORD INDUSTRIAL ESTATE
Works
Oldfield Rec. Grd.
Perivale Wood Local Nature Reserve
Comm. Centre
Library
PERIVALE
PERIVALE INDUSTRIAL PARK
Perivale
Sports Ground
Cayton Road Sports Ground
Selborne Prim. Sch.
A40
WESTERN
GREENFORD ROUNDABOUT
TEIGNMOUTH GDNS.
Superstore
South Greenford
Sports Arena
GREENFORD
RAVENOR PARK
Ravenor Farm & London Motorcycle Museum
Nature Reserve
PERIVALE PARK GOLF COURSE
PERIVALE PARK
Club House
EALING GOLF CO
Perivale Bri. Playing Fields
Swimming Pool
Playing Fields
EALING
THE BROADWAY
RUISLIP ROAD
B455
Stanhope Prim. Sch.
Greenford Bridge
Playing Field
High Sch.
R.C. Prim. Sch.
Cardinal Wiseman R.C. High Sch.
Elthorne Heights
GREENFORD PARK CEMETERY
Recreation Ground
Mayfield Prim. Sch.
W7
Hanwell Community Centre
Castle Bar Park
Castlebar Sch.
Pitshanger Park
SCOTCH COMMON
Cleveland Park
ARGYLE ROAD
B452
Ealing Coll.
Drayton Green
BRENT VALLEY GOLF COURSE
UB1
Hobbayne Prim. Sch.
DORMER'S WELLS
GREENFORD ROAD
A4127

G
H
J
K
L
M
39
WEMBLEY ARENA
Conference Centre
WEMBLEY STADIUM
KING EDWARD VII
Wembley Stadium
SOUTH WAY
B4557
ROAD
HARROW
Sherrins Farm Open Space
Oakington Manor Prim. Sch.
1
BARHAM PARK
Library
HARROW RD.
HIGH
A404
Wembley Central
WEMBLEY
Playing Field
Elsley Prim. Sch.
Wembley Brook
HA0
TOKYNGTON
2
Depot
Carriage Shed
Wembley
A4089
GOLF COURSE
Club House
Cemetery
One Tree Hill Rec. Grd.
Alperton Community Sch.
BRENT
Stonebridge Park
3
HARROW ROAD
BRENTFIELD
Brent Junction
Stone Bridge
Royal Mail Depot
A4005
Alperton
Bus Garage
Open Space
NORTHFIELD INDUSTRIAL ESTATE
4
ALPERTON
PARK ROYAL JUNCTION
A406
NORTH CIRCULAR
56
Metropolitan Police Traffic Unit
Alperton Sports Ground
Running Track
ALPERTON B456 LANE
HANGER
GRAND UNION CANAL
(Paddington Branch)
5
Twyford Abbey Prim. Sch.
NW10
PARK ROYAL
6
AVENUE
Subway
HANGER LANE
Hanger La.
Brentham Sports Club
WESTERN
Park Royal
7
A40
GOLF COURSE
Hanger Hill
St. Augustine Priory (Sch.)
A406
W5
Barclays Bank Sports Ground
Cricket Ground
West Acton
W3
NORTH ACTON PLAYING FIELDS
8
CASTLEBAR
B455
Nth. Ealing
Sports Ground
9
HAVEN
Ealing Broadway
EALING
71
Japanese Sch. London
G
H
J
K
L
M

56
40
55
72
A
B
C
D
E
F
1
2
3
4
5
6
7
8
9
GLADSTONE PARK
Railway Works
Neasden Depot
Neasden
Superstore
Dollis Hill
DUDDEN HILL
CHURCH END
WILLESDEN
WILLESDEN NEW CEMETERY
ROUNDWOOD PARK
NW10
HARLESDEN
Harlesden
Willesden Junction
STONEBRIDGE
Stonebridge Rec. Grd.
Royal Mail Depot
Lower Place
GRAND UNION CANAL (Paddington Branch)
CENTRAL MIDDLESEX HOSPITAL
Freightliner Depot
Canal Depot
NORTH ACTON
North Acton
OLD OAK COMMON
Old Oak Sidings
Carriage Shed
North Pole International Depot
HAMMERSMITH
WORMWOOD SCRUBS and PARK
FULHAM
H.M.P. Wormwood Scrubs
HAMMERSMITH & NEW QUEEN CHARLOTTE'S HOSP.
Linford Christie Stadium
EALING
GYPSY CORNER
Acton Main Line
East Acton
W12
NORTH CIRCULAR ROAD A406
HIGH ROAD A407
DUDDEN HILL LANE
CHURCH RD
BRENTFIELD
HILLSIDE
CRAVEN PK.
HIGH STREET
OLD OAK LANE
VICTORIA ROAD A4000
WESTERN AVENUE
SCRUBS LANE A219
HARROW ROAD
WEST WAY
DU CANE ROAD
ACTON LANE
ST MARY'S R.C. CEMETERY
WILLESDEN GREEN
WILLESDEN COMM. HOSP.
King Edward VII Recreation Ground

57
G
H
J
K
L
M
41
58
73
1
2
3
4
5
6
7
8
9
NW2
NW6
NW3
W10
W2
Fortune Green
WEST HAMPSTEAD
Finchley Rd. & Frognal
West Hampstead Thameslink
West Hampstead
SOUTH HAMPSTEAD
Willesden Green
Kilburn
Brondesbury
BRONDESBURY
Brondesbury Park
BRONDESBURY PARK
KENSAL RISE
Kensal Rise
KENSAL GREEN
Kensal Green
KENSAL GREEN CEMETERY
Kilburn High Road
KILBURN
Kilburn Park
Queens Park
WEST KILBURN
KENSAL TOWN
MAIDA HILL
MAIDA VALE
Maida Vale
NORTH KENSINGTON
WESTBOURNE GREEN
Westbourne Park
Royal Oak
BAYSWATER
Bayswater
Ladbroke Grove
Latimer Rd.
WHITE CITY
CAMDEN
WESTMINSTER
KENSINGTON and CHELSEA
QUEENS PARK
Willesden Lane Cemetery
Paddington Rec. Grd.
Kilburn Grange Park
Grand Union Canal
CRICKLEWOOD BROADWAY
SHOOT-UP-HILL
FINCHLEY ROAD
WEST END LANE
WILLESDEN LANE
KILBURN HIGH ROAD
MAIDA VALE
HARROW ROAD
WESTWAY
ABBEY ROAD
BELSIZE ROAD
KILBURN PARK ROAD
SHIRLAND ROAD
ELGIN AVENUE
CARLTON VALE
CHICHELE ROAD
WALM LANE
MORTIMER ROAD
HARVIST ROAD
LADBROKE GROVE
WESTBOURNE GROVE
CHEPSTOW RD.
ST. QUINTIN AV.
GREAT WESTERN RD.
KILBURN LANE
BRONDESBURY ROAD
SALUSBURY ROAD
Sports Ground
Superstore

58
A
B
C
D
E
F
1
2
3
4
5
6
7
8
9
42
57
74
Hampstead Heath
GOSPEL OAK
KENTISH TOWN
THE ROYAL FREE HOSPITAL
Finchley Rd. & Frognal
Finchley Rd.
Belsize Pk.
Kentish Town W.
Chalk Farm
SOUTH HAMPSTEAD
NW6
NW3
NW1
NW8
W9
W2
W1
Swiss Cottage
South Hampstead
Sigmund Freud Statue
PRIMROSE HILL
Reservoir (Covered)
Barrow Hill
St. John's Wood
ST. JOHN'S WOOD
Maida Vale
MAIDA VALE
Warwick Av
Little Venice
Royal Oak
BAYSWATER
Bayswater
Paddington
PADDINGTON
Paddington Basin
Edgware Rd.
MARYLEBONE
Baker St.
Regent's Park
Gt. Portland St.
Bond St.
Marble Arch
Lancaster Gate
Stanhope Place Gate
Speakers Corner
Albion Gate
Clarendon Gate
REGENT'S PARK
LONDON ZOO
Main Entrance
Gloucester Gate
Cumberland Gate
Golf & Tennis School
Winfield House
London Central Mosque
Macclesfield Bridge
Open-Air Theatre
QUEEN MARY'S GARDENS
St. John's Lodge
Boating Lake
The Holme
Regent's College
Clarence Gate
Hanover Gate
Parks Dept.
Refreshments
Middlesex C.C.Club
Lord's Cricket Ground
Lisson Green
Wallace Collection
Planetarium
Madame Tussaud's
Ryl. Academy of Music
WESTMINSTER
CAMDEN
FINCHLEY ROAD
WELLINGTON RD.
ST. JOHN'S WOOD RD.
PRINCE ALBERT ROAD
GROVE END RD.
PARK ROAD
BAKER STREET
GLOUCESTER PLACE
MARYLEBONE RD.
EDGWARE ROAD
WESTWAY
MARYLEBONE FLYOVER
HARROW ROAD
BISHOP'S BRIDGE ROAD
EASTBOURNE TER.
PRAED ST.
SUSSEX GS.
BAYSWATER RD.
OXFORD ST.
WIGMORE ST.
PORTLAND PL.
ALBANY ST.
PARKWAY
CHALK FARM RD.
HAVERSTOCK HILL
ADELAIDE ROAD
AVENUE ROAD
ABBEY ROAD
MAIDA VALE
FITZJOHN'S AVENUE
ROSSLYN HILL
MALDEN RD.
MANSFIELD RD.
FLEET RD.
POND ST.

59
43
60
75
G
H
J
K
L
M
1
2
3
4
5
6
7
8
9
Kentish Town
Holloway Rd.
LOWER HOLLOWAY
HIGHBURY
Highbury & Islington
Drayton Park
Canonbury
Caledonian Rd.
Caledonian Park
BARNSBURY
Caledonian Rd. and Barnsbury
CAMDEN TOWN
Camden Rd.
Channel Tunnel Rail Link (Under Construction)
ISLINGTON
Essex Rd.
Angel
PENTONVILLE
KING'S CROSS
King's Cross Thameslink
ST. PANCRAS
SOMERS TOWN
British Library
EUSTON
Euston
Euston Sq.
FINSBURY
CLERKENWELL
Farringdon
Barbican
ST. LUKE'S
Warren St.
Russell Sq.
BLOOMSBURY
British Museum
Goodge St.
Tottenham Court R.
SOHO
Covent Gdn.
HOLBORN
Holborn
Law Courts
City Thameslink
Leicester Sq.
Temple
BLACKFRIARS
THAMES

60
A
B
C
D
E
F
44
76
59
1
2
3
4
5
6
7
8
9
HIGHBURY
CANONBURY
Canonbury
Essex Rd.
N5
N1
E8
SHACKLEWELL
CLAPTON
HACKNEY DOWNS
Hackney Downs
Hackney Cen.
DALSTON
Dalston Kingsland
KINGSLAND
DE BEAUVOIR TOWN
HACKNEY
London Fields
HAGGERSTON
HOXTON
SHOREDITCH
Shoreditch
Old Street
BETHNAL GREEN
Bethnal Grn.
Cambridge Heath
SPITALFIELDS
LIVERPOOL ST.
Moorgate
Barbican
St. Paul's
Bank
Mansion Ho.
Monument
CITY
Aldgate
Aldgate East
WHITECHAPEL
Whitechapel
Tower Gateway
Tower Hill
BLACKFRIARS
BALLS POND RD.
GRAHAM RD.
KINGSLAND ROAD
QUEENSBRIDGE ROAD
HACKNEY ROAD
COLUMBIA RD.
BETHNAL GREEN RD.
NEW NORTH RD.
ESSEX RD.
CITY RD.
OLD ST.
GREAT EASTERN ST.
COMMERCIAL ST.
COMMERCIAL RD.
WHITECHAPEL RD.
BISHOPSGATE
HOUNDSDITCH
LONDON WALL
CHEAPSIDE
CANNON ST.
MOORGATE
ALDERSGATE ST.
CABLE ST.
A1199
A104
A1207
A10
A1208
A1209
A11
A1202
A1211
A501
A5201
A1
B100
B108
B118
B134
B135
B144
Regent's Canal
Kingsland Basin
Wenlock Basin
City Road Basin
Bunhill Fields Burial Grd.
H.A.C. Ground
Finsbury Circus
Old Spitalfields Mkt.
LONDON FIELDS
Mus. of London
Barbican Arts Centre

CLAPTON PARK
Changing Rooms
Dressing Rooms
Temple Mills
Play. Flds. Eastway Sports Cen.
45
LEA INTERCHANGE
Marshgate Bri.
Wick Field Recreation Ground
EASTWAY
EAST CROSS ROUTE
HOMERTON HOSPITAL
HOMERTON HIGH ST.
MARSH HILL
HOMERTON
Recreation Ground
Football Ground
Mabley Green
A12 EAST CROSS
Eastway Cycle Circuit
Container Terminal
Channelsea River
Kingsway International Christian Centre
Arena Field Rec. Grd.
Homerton
KENWORTHY RD.
URSWICK RD.
HACKNEY WICK
Cold Stores
CHANNEL TUNNEL RAIL LINK (UNDER CONSTRUCTION)
EAST CROSS CENTRE
Freight Terminal
Warehouses
Hackney Wick
CARPENTER'S RD.
WICK RD.
KENTON RD.
CASSLAND RD.
A106
WELL STREET COMMON
SOUTH HACKNEY
VICTORIA PARK
Tennis Courts
Playground
Bowling Green
Sports Ground
Bandstand
Victoria Fountain
Royal Gate East
Three Colt Bridge
OLD FORD
EAST CROSS ROUTE
Stratford Marsh
Works
Sun Wharf
E15
NEWHAM
Pudding Mill Lane
OLD FORD
BLACKWALL TUNNEL
BOW INTERCHANGE
62
St. Agnes Gate
Gore Gate
Bonner Hall Bri.
Crown Gate East
Crown Gate West
GROVE RD.
OLD FORD RD.
ROMAN RD.
PARNELL RD.
FAIRFIELD RD.
SEWARDSTONE RD.
THE LONDON CHEST HOSP.
Wennington Grn.
GLOBE TOWN
Suttons Wharf
MEATH GDNS.
BOW RD.
Bow Church
Bow Rd.
Bethnal Green
MILE END
ROYAL LONDON HOSP. MILE END
Queen Mary & Westfields College
Mile End
ROYAL LONDON HOSP. ST. CLEMENT'S
TOWER HAMLETS CEMETERY
BROMLEY
Bromley-by-Bow
ST. ANDREW'S HOSP.
DEVAS ST.
Devons Rd.
NORTHERN APPROACH
MILE END RD.
BURDETT RD.
A1205
Stepney Green
BOW COMMON
Shandy Park
Gas Works
Ragged Sch. Mus.
MILE END PARK
Stadium
Furze Grn.
Langdon Park
STEPNEY
BEN JONSON RD.
ST. PAULS WAY
RATCLIFF
Bartlett Park
LIMEHOUSE
COMMERCIAL RD.
Limehouse
EAST INDIA DOCK RD.
Limehouse Basin
77
Westferry
POPLAR
All Saints
CABLE ST.
HIGHWAY
NARROW ST.
COTTON ST.
TOWER HAMLETS
E14
E3
E9
E1
G H J K L M
1 2 3 4 5 6 7 8 9
36 37 38

62
A
B
C
D
E
F
46
61
78
1
2
3
4
5
6
7
8
9
STRATFORD NEW TOWN
STRATFORD
Stratford
Stratford (Low Level)
FOREST GATE
Forest Gate
Wanstead Park
Maryland
WEST HAM
WEST HAM PARK
West Ham
West Ham Cemetery
UPTON
PLASHET
PLAISTOW
Plaistow
CANNING TOWN
Canning Town
Mill Meads
Three Mills Green
Prescott Channel
Channelsea
East London Crematorium
EAST LONDON CEMETERY
Memorial Recreation Ground
Star Park
Container Terminal
Freight Terminal
Cold Stores
ROUTE OF CHANNEL TUNNEL (UNDER CONSTRUCTION)
Jubilee Line Depot
Bridge Rd. Depot
Gas Depot
Pumping Station
T.V. & Film Studios
The London Gas Museum
E15
E3
E14
E13
E7
E16
CHOBHAM RD.
LEYTON RD.
ANGEL LA.
GREAT EASTERN RD.
BROADWAY
ROMFORD RD.
WEST HAM LA.
PORTWAY
UPTON LA.
PLAISTOW RD.
NEW PLAISTOW R.
MANOR RD.
STEPHENSON ST.
HIGH ST.
BARKING RD.
NEWHAM WAY
SILVERTOWN WAY
LOWER LEA CROSSING
INDIA DOCK RD.
ABBOTT RD.
NORTHERN APPROACH
BLACKWALL TUNNEL
CARPENTER'S RD.
WOODGRANGE RD.
GREENGATE ST.
Bromley-by-Bow
All Saints
STH. BROMLEY
East India
LEAMOUTH
Royal Victoria
Custom House for ExCeL

Manor Park
Woodgrange Park
ROMFORD RD.
HIGH STREET NORTH
E12
PLASHET
Jewish Cemetery
PLASHET PARK
East Ham
LITTLE ILFORD
Little Ilford Park
STH.-WOODFORD-TO-BARKING-RELIEF RD.
NORTH CIRCULAR ROAD
BARKING
BARKING NORTHERN RELIEF RD.
WALLEND
Langdon School
UPTON PARK
West Ham Utd. F.C. (Upton Pk.)
BARKING ROAD
EAST HAM
CENTRAL PARK
E6
East Ham Jewish Cemetery
Gooseley's Playing Field
Refuse & Sewage Works
Hand Trough Creek
Cuckold's Haven
NEWHAM GENERAL HOSPITAL
Kingsford Community School
Terence McMillan Stadium
NEWHAM WAY A13
ALFREDS WAY A13
North Beckton
BECKTON
Winsor Park
Mid Beckton
CUSTOM HOUSE
West Beckton
Beckton Park
Gallions Reach
ROYAL DOCKS ROAD A1020
MANOR WAY A117
WOOLWICH MANOR WAY
VICTORIA DOCK RD.
ROYAL ALBERT WAY
Cyprus
Beckton Park
Prince Regent
Docklands Light Railway Depot
The Docklands Equestrian Centre
GATEWAY RETAIL PARK
Superstore
Nature Reserve

47
64
79

A
B
C
D
E
F
48
1
2
3
4
5
6
7
8
9
63
80
ILFORD LANE A123
LOXFORD
Loxford Sch. of Science & Technology
Hyleford (Home for the Elderly)
Woodlands Jun. & Inf. Schs.
LOXFORD PARK
University of East London
Play. Fld.
Playground
Football Ground
Running Track
Sports Ground
Tennis Courts
RM8
Playing Field
Tennis Courts
T.A. Centre
Bus Depot
Swimming Pool
FAIR CROSS
Putting Green
Tennis Courts
Pav.
BARKING PARK
Bowling Greens
Miniature Railway
FANSHAWE AV.
LONGBRIDGE ROAD
A124
Barking Abbey Comp. Sch.
Playing Field
Manor Jun. & Inf. Schs.
MAYESBROOK PARK
Boating Lake
Boat Ho.
Mayes Brook
AVENUE
PORTERS
BARKING NORTHERN RELIEF RD.
Barking
Playing Field
BARKING HOSP.
Upney
Upney Sidings
GREENSLADE RD.
VICARAGE FIELD SHOPPING CEN.
Courts
Lib.
T.H.
BARKING
Barking Abbey (Rem. of)
Prim. Sch.
ST. PAUL'S
RIPPLE
A123
RIPPLE ROAD JUNCTION
LODGE A1153
Cemetery
Schs.
Mus.
Offs.
Depot
BARKING INDUSTRIAL PARK
Rippleside
Depot
Warehouse
RENWICK INDUSTRIAL ESTATE
ALFREDS WAY INDUSTRIAL ESTATE
Ripple Lane Sidings
Greatfields Park
Playground
Barking
ABBEY PARK IND. EST.
Works
Adult Training Cen.
NEW ENGLAND INDUSTRIAL ESTATE
(EAST HAM AND BARKING BY-PASS)
A13
ALFREDS WAY
MOVERS LANE
LYON BUSINESS PARK
Hand Trough Creek
Cuckold's Haven
Subway
Library
Newlands Park
Thames View Jun. Sch.
Youth Centre
Jun. & Inf. Sch.
Hall
ENTERPRISE HO.
BARKING BUSINESS CEN.
RIVERSIDE INDUSTRIAL ESTATE
TRIUMPH HO.
THAMES ROAD
ABBEY WHARF INDUS. ESTATE
River Roding
Long Mark
Cinema
Bowling Alley
Lagoon
Powerleague Soccer Cen.
Refuse Transfer Station
CLARKE LANE
RIVER ROAD BUSINESS PARK
Works
Warehouses
Power Station (disused)
Thameside Community Nature Reserve
Beckton Sewage Treatment Works
Barking Creek
Long Reach
Wharf
TRAFALGAR BUSINESS CEN.
CREEKMOUTH
ANGLIAN INDUS. EST.
GATEWAY RETAIL PARK
NEWHAM
Warpool Reach
BALMORAL TRADING EST.
BUZZARD CREEK IND. EST.
Sewage Treatment Works
Tanks
Gas Works
E6
Barking Creek Flood Barrier
Jetty
Pier
Barking or False Point
Docklands Light Railway Depot
Engine Shed
Tanks
RIVER
BARKING REACH
Margaret or Tripcock Ness
Pumping Station
Library
Thamesmere Leisure Cen.
Gallions Reach
DLR
ROYAL DOCKS ROAD
ARMADA WAY
Works
Pier
Twin
44
45
46
81
82
83
84
85

65
PARSLOES PARK
DAGENHAM
Dagenham Heathway
Becontree
Dagenham East
OLD DAGENHAM PARK
Goresbrook Park
Goresbrook Leisure Centre
RIPPLE ROAD
THAMES AVENUE
A13
HEATHWAY
GORESBROOK INTERCHANGE
MOTOR WORKS
Dagenham Dock
ROUTE OF CHANNEL TUNNEL RAIL LINK (UNDER CONSTRUCTION)
Dagenham Breach
Power Station
Horse Shoe Corner
FORD INDUSTRIAL PARK
THAMES
Cross Ness
Thamesmead North
BEXLEY
RIVERSIDE GOLF COURSE
Hornchurch Shoot
49
81
66

A
B
C
D
E
F
1
2
3
4
5
6
7
8
9
50
82
65
BARKING and DAGENHAM
RM10
RM9
RM13
SOUTH HORNCHURCH
RAINHAM
Rainham
H A V
Elm Park
Dagenham East
Sports Ground
Gas Transmission Station
Playing Field
Bretons
Scargill Jun. & Inf. Schools
Brittons Sch.
Whybridge Inf. Sch.
Whybridge Jun. Sch.
Nason Walters Centre (Adult Training)
Dagenham Beam Bridge
Newtons Corner
Occupation Centre
THE LEYS
Mardyke Farm
Beam River
DOVERS CORNER
Rainham Steel Mills
SUTTONS BUSINESS PARK
MUDLANDS INDUSTRIAL ESTATE
Timber Yard
Sewage Works
ALBRIGHT INDUSTRIAL ESTATE
DENVER INDUSTRIAL ESTATE
HORNCHURCH MARSHES
Car Compound
Dagenham
Hornchurch Shoot
RIVER THAMES
Old Man's Head
Frog Island
FREIGHTMASTER ESTATE
STAR BUSINESS CENTRE
Silt Lagoons
RAINHAM MARSHES
ROUTE OF CHANNEL TUNNEL RAIL LINK (UNDER CONSTRUCTION)
RAINHAM ROAD
SOUTH DAGENHAM RD.
NEW ROAD A1306
THAMES GATE
MARSH WAY
WENNINGTON B1335
Ingrebourne River
Moat
Superstore
Rainham Hall
Jetty

51
83
G
H
J
K
L
M
1
2
3
4
5
6
7
8
9
54
55
56
Hornchurch
RM12
Upminster
RM14
South
Ockendon
RM15
THURROCK
HACTON
CORBETS
TEY
HORNCHURCH
COUNTRY PARK
Ingrebourne Centre
ST. GEORGES
HOSPITAL
Suttons Parkway
Suttons
Prim. Sch.
Park
Corner
Farm
West
Lodge
Play.
Fld.
Tennis
Cts.
Prim.
Sch.
Playing
Field
Runway
Wood
Airfield
Wood
Lightway Wood
Lake
Abbey
Wood
Berwick Pond
Watermeadow
Rainham Lodge
Farm
Lodge
Farm
Corbets Tey
School
Parklands
Weir Open Space
Harwood
Hall
The Lodge
West Lodge
Central
Cottages
Central
Farm
New
House
Llantrisant
Oaks
Greenacres
Refuse
Transfer Station
Gerpins
Farm
Damyn's
Hall
Damyn's
Hall Cotts.
Berwick
Cottages
Berwick Ponds
Farm
Berwick
Manor
Berwick Manor
Farm
Berwick Manor
Cottages
Landfill Site
White Post
Corner
Ayletts
Cottages
Sand & Gravel Pits
Warwick
Wood
White Post
Wood
Common
Watercourse
Jewish
Cemetery
Jun. & Inf.
School
Cem.
CHANDLERS
CORNER
Tennis Courts
Spring Farm
Park
Pavilion
IMPERIAL
TRAD. EST.
LAMBS LA.
IND. EST.
Playing
Field
The Chafford
School
Brady
Prim. Sch.
South Hall
Farm
East Hall
Farm
New
Cottages
Landthorpe
House
Halldare
Cottages
Wennington
Hall
The Willows
WENNINGTON
Bretts
Farm
Works
The
Orchard
Kennington's
Cottages
Moor
Hall
Kennington Park
(Belhus Woods Country Park)
NEW ROAD
A1306
B1335
B1421
HACTON LANE
PARK FARM ROAD
POND ROAD
BERWICK POND ROAD
GERPINS LANE
WARWICK LANE
NORTH ROAD
LAUNDERS LANE
AVELEY ROAD
HARWOOD HALL LANE
UPMINSTER ROAD
SOUTH ROAD
EAST HALL LANE
CHURCH LANE
WENNINGTON RD.
SUTTONS LANE
PATHWAY
EASTERN PATH
Ingrebourne River

68
52
84
143
HAYES
HAYES TOWN
Hayes
Stockley Park
STOCKLEY PARK GOLF COURSE
HILLINGDON
UB3
Hayes & Harlington
HARLINGTON
CRANFORD
CRANFORD PARK
AVENUE PARK
LONDON - HEATHROW AIRPORT
TW6
M4 MOTORWAY
Junction 4
Junction 3
DAWLEY ROAD
NORTH HYDE RD.
STATION RD.
HIGH STREET
UXBRIDGE RD.
THE PARKWAY
BATH ROAD
A4
A437
A312
Grand Union Canal
Frogs Ditch
River Crane

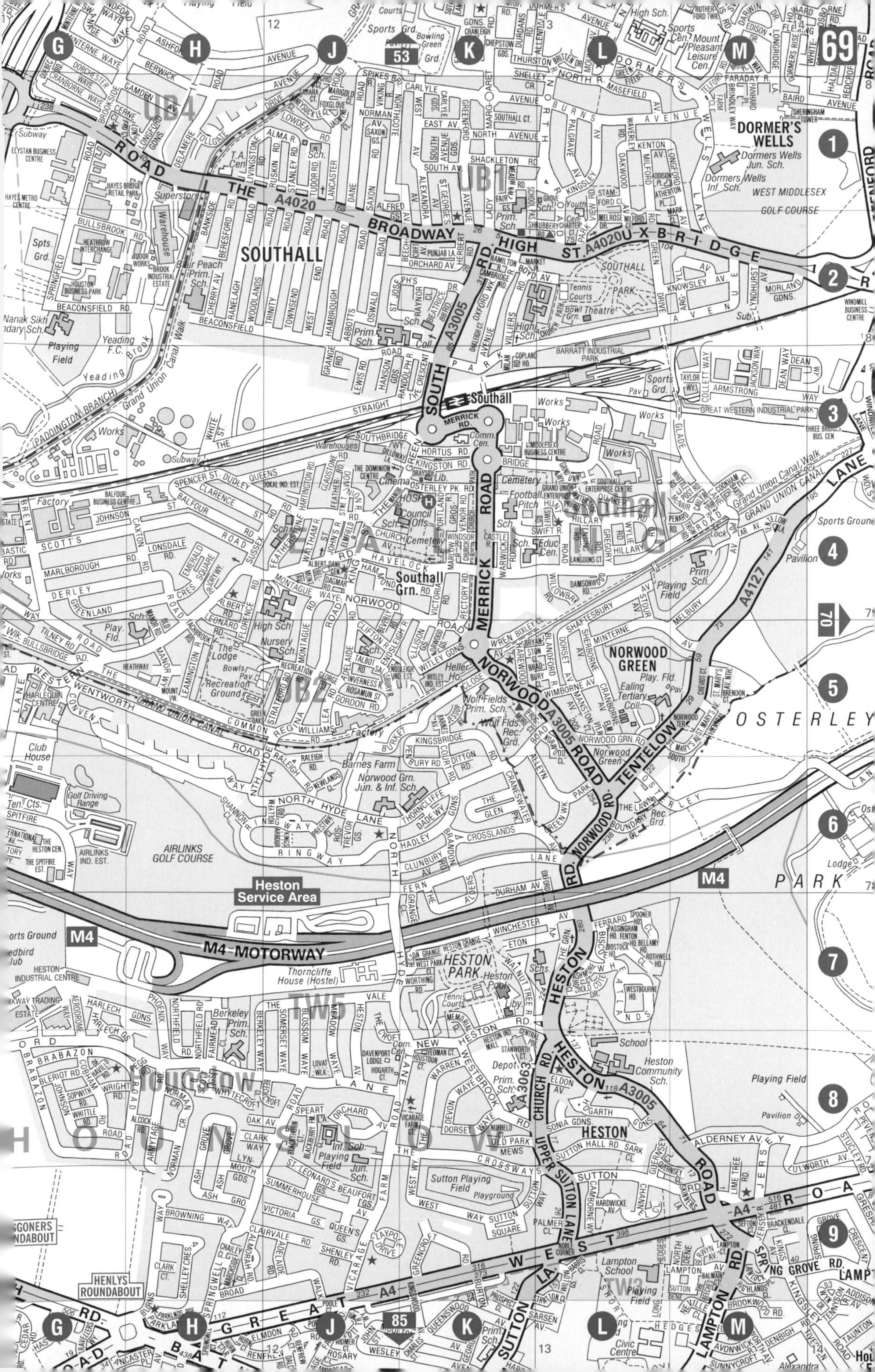
G
H
J
K
L
M
53
70
85
12
13
1
2
3
4
5
6
7
8
9
UB4
UB1
UB2
TW5
TW3
SOUTHALL
DORMER'S WELLS
Dormers Wells Jun. Sch.
Dormers Wells Inf. Sch.
WEST MIDDLESEX GOLF COURSE
THE BROADWAY
A4020
UXBRIDGE ROAD
HIGH ST.
SOUTHALL PARK
Southall
SOUTH RD.
A3005
MERRICK ROAD
Southall Grn.
NORWOOD
NORWOOD GREEN
NORWOOD ROAD
NORWOOD RD.
TENTELOW LANE
A4127
OSTERLEY PARK
Grand Union Canal Walk
GRAND UNION CANAL
Yeading Brook
Playing Field
Yeading F.C.
(PADDINGTON BRANCH)
Hayes Bridge Retail Park
Heathrow Interchange
Houston Business Park
Beaconsfield Rd.
Blair Peach Prim. Sch.
Superstore
Warehouse
Middlesex Business Centre
Great Western Industrial Park
Barratt Industrial Park
The Dominion Centre
Cemetery
Football Pitch
Southall Enterprise Centre
The Lodge
Recreation Ground
Nursery Sch.
High Sch.
Wolf Fields Prim. Sch.
Wolf Flds. Rec. Grd.
Barnes Farm
Norwood Grn. Jun. & Inf. Sch.
Ealing Tertiary Coll.
Club House
Golf Driving Range
AIRLINKS GOLF COURSE
Airlinks Ind. Est.
NORTH HYDE LANE
RINGWAY
Heston Service Area
M4
M4 MOTORWAY
Thorncliffe House (Hostel)
HESTON PARK
Heston Pool
Liby.
HESTON RD.
HESTON
A3063
CHURCH RD.
Heston Community Sch.
Berkeley Prim. Sch.
Sutton Playing Field
Playground
Playing Field
Hounslow
HOUNSLOW
Heston Industrial Centre
Henlys Roundabout
GREAT WEST ROAD
A4
Lampton School
Civic Centre
LAMPTON RD.
SPRING GROVE RD.
SUTTON LANE
UPPER SUTTON LANE
Windmill Business Centre
Three Bridges Bus. Cen.
Sports Ground
Pavilion
Lodge

54
69
86
A
B
C
D
E
F
1
2
3
4
5
6
7
8
9
BRENT VALLEY GOLF COURSE
Drayton Green
Ealing Coll.
West Ealing
DORMER'S WELLS
WEST MIDDLESEX GOLF COURSE
GREENFORD ROAD A4127
Brent Lodge Park
Churchfields Rec. Grd.
Hanwell
Kensington Cemetery
UB1
Iron Bridge
A4020
UXBRIDGE ROAD
BROADWAY
HANWELL
City of Westminster Cemetery
W7
WEST EALING
NORTHFIELD AV.
ST. BERNARD'S HOSPITAL
EALING HOSP.
Meadow Ho. Hospice
Hanwell Locks
Southall
Windmill Bridge
Grand Union Canal Walk
GRAND UNION CANAL
BOSTON RD.
A3002
Oaklands Primary Sch.
Elthorne Park
Elthorne Park High Sch.
Games Courts
Warren Farm School Sports Centre
UB2
WINDMILL LANE
B454
WATERSIDE TRADING CENTRE
BOSTON BUSINESS PARK
RIVER BRENT BUSINESS PARK
Playing Field
The Aviary Farm
The Aviary
Wincott Farm
Osterley Lock
Northfields
Northfields Depot
OSTERLEY
M4
MOTORWAY
Trumpers Wood
Boston Manor
Boston Manor Playing Field
Boston Manor House
Gallows Bridge
WYKE GREEN GOLF COURSE
Osterley Park Farm
Avenue Lodge
Lodge
Osterley Park House (N.T.)
PARK
HOUNSLOW
Lodges
Wyke Green
Sports Ground
Club House
Centaurs Rugby Club
CENTAURS BUSINESS CENTRE
WEST CROSS CENTRE
Isleworth
SYON LANE
West Cross Cen.
Factory
GILLETTE CNR.
BRENTFORD END
GREAT WEST TRAD. EST.
OSTERLEY
JERSEY ROAD
GREAT WEST RD.
A4
Osterley
Running Track
Brunel University
Indian Gymkhana Club
Campion Ho.
Crown Court
West Thames College
SPRING GROVE
Syon Lane
The Green Sch.
Busch Corner
TWICKENHAM RD.
A315
LONDON RD.
Syon Park Sch.
Cemetery
LAMPTON
GROVE B363
Hounslow East
TW3
TW7
Playing Field
Pavilion

71
55
87
72
G
H
J
K
L
M
1
2
3
4
5
6
7
8
9
18
19
EALING
Ealing Broadway
ACTON
W5
W3
W4
TW8
EALING COMMON
Ealing Common
WALPOLE PARK
Pitshanger Manor Mus.
Ealing Studios
Thames Valley University
South Ealing
Northfields
Little Ealing
GUNNERSBURY PARK
GUNNERSBURY
Gunnersbury
Museum
Boating Lake
Nurseries
Bowling Green
Miniature Golf Course
Refreshment Pavilion
Tennis Courts
Potomac (Fish Pond)
Kensington Cemetery
Acton Town
SOUTH ACTON
Acton
ACTON HOSP.
Reynolds Sports Cen.
Sports Ground
Depot
Works
CHISWICK PARK
CHISWICK HIGH ROAD
M4 MOTORWAY
M4
Junc. 2
Junc. 1
Kew Bridge
Steam Mus.
Musical Mus.
Brentford
BRENTFORD
Brentford F.C. Griffin Pk.
Old Brentford
Waterman's Arts Centre
Brentford Ait
Strand on the Green
Oliver's Island
Kew Pier
KEW
Kew Green
KEW GREEN
Kew Palace
Kew Gds.
Public Record Office
Warehouse
Refuse Depot
ROYAL BOTANIC GARDENS
KEW
RICHMOND
Richmond
THAMES
Orangery
Princess of Wales Conservatory
Palm House
Rose Garden
Azalea Garden
Bamboo Garden
Temple of Bellona
King William's Temple
Arboretum
Syon Vista
The Lake
Isleworth Ferry Gate (Closed)
Water Lily Pond
Evolution House
Temperate House
Marianne North Gallery
Queen Charlotte's
Syon Reach
Conservation Area
PARK
Syon Garden Centre
Syon House
THUMBERLAND
Mortlake
Westminster Boathouse
A4020 ROAD
UXBRIDGE ROAD
GUNNERSBURY LANE
GUNNERSBURY AVENUE
A406
A4000
B4491
POPES LANE
B455
SOUTH EALING ROAD
A315
KEW BRIDGE
KEW ROAD
A205
MORTLAKE RD.
A3000
GT. WEST RD.
A4
WELLESLEY
CEDARS
A3002
B452
WINDMILL

Acton Main Line
56
East Acton
WESTERN AVENUE
WESTWAY A40
SAVOY CIRCUS
EAST ACTON
W3
ACTON
EALING
Phoenix High Sch.
Acton Central
THE VALE A4020
UXBRIDGE ROAD
HAMMERSMITH
SOUTH ACTON
SOUTHFIELD
Southfields Rec. Grd.
BEDFORD PARK
ACTON GREEN
South Acton
71
GUNNERSBURY
Chiswick Pk.
Turnham Green
Stamford Brook
Ravenscourt Park
GOLDHAWK
CHISWICK HIGH ROAD A315
KING ST.
GREAT WEST ROAD A4
Gunnersbury
TURNHAM GREEN
W4
CEDARS RD.
ELLESMERE RD. A4 HOGARTH LA.
CHISWICK
HOUNSLOW
Chiswick House
Chiswick Eyot
St. Pauls School
SW13
RICHMOND upon THAMES
Castelnau
The Harrodian Sch.
Chiswick
GROVE PARK
University of Westminster Sports Ground
GREAT CHERTSEY ROAD A316
Riverside Lands
DUKE'S MEADOWS
RIVER THAMES
88
CHURCH RD. A3003
ROCKS LA. A306
Barn Elms Playing Fields
Mortlake Crematorium

G
H
J
K
L
M
57
1
2
3
4
5
6
7
8
9
74
89
White City
White City
Warehouse
Latimer Rd.
Proposed White City Development
SHEPHERD'S BUSH
Shepherd's Bush
Goldhawk Rd.
NOTTING HILL
Ladbroke Square Gardens
W11
Notting Hill Gate
Bayswater
Queensway
Holland Park
KENSINGTON
Holland Park
HOLLAND PARK
King George VI Memorial Youth Hostel
Holland Ho.
Commonwealth Inst.
W8
High St. Kensington
Kensington Palace
Round Pond
Kensington Olympia
Olympia
W14
Brook Green
Hammersmith
HAMMERSMITH
HAMMERSMITH FLYOVER
WEST KENSINGTON
West Kensington
Barons Court
Hammersmith Cemetery
Barons Court
The Queen's Club
EARLS COURT
Earls Court
Earls Court Exhibition Building
SW5
Gloucester Road
SOUTH KENSINGTON
West Brompton
SW10
Brompton Cemetery
WEST BROMPTON
Normand Park
Fulham Cross
Fulham Cemetery
Fulham Broadway
Chelsea F.C. (Stamford Bridge)
SW6
Eel Brook Common
WALHAM GREEN
Parsons Grn.
PARSONS GRN
FULHAM
Fulham F.C. (Craven Cottage)
Gas Works
SANDS END
Moat Garden
The Warren
Boat House
CROMWELL ROAD
TALGARTH ROAD
WEST CROMWELL ROAD
FULHAM PALACE ROAD
LILLIE ROAD
DAWES ROAD
FULHAM ROAD
KINGS ROAD
NEW KINGS ROAD
OLD BROMPTON ROAD
KENSINGTON HIGH STREET
HOLLAND PARK AVENUE
BAYSWATER ROAD
NORTH END ROAD
WEST CROSS ROUTE
WOOD LANE
SHEPHERD'S BUSH ROAD
UXBRIDGE R.
HOLLAND ROAD
ADDISON RD.
WARWICK GS.
EARLS COURT ROAD
REDCLIFFE GDNS.
FINBOROUGH RD.
WANDSWORTH BRI. RD.
HAR WOOD RD.
A219
A3220
A402
A315
A4
A3218
A3219
A308
B450
A4206
B405

74
A
B
C
D
E
F
58
73
90
1
2
3
4
5
6
7
8
9
Paddington
Bayswater
Queensway
BAYSWATER
Lancaster Gate
Marble Arch
OXFORD
Bond St
St. George's Field
W2
HYDE PARK
KENSINGTON
GARDENS
Round Pond
Kensington Palace
THE SERPENTINE
Serpentine Gallery
Albert Memorial
Rotten Row
Hyde Park Corner
MAYFAIR
W1
GREEN
KENSINGTON GORE
KNIGHTSBRIDGE
Knightsbridge
Harrods
Science Museum
Natural History Mus.
Victoria & Albert Museum
Brompton Oratory
BROMPTON
Gloucester Road
Sth. Kensington
SOUTH KENSINGTON
BELGRAVIA
VICTORIA
Sloane Square
CHELSEA
KENSINGTON
Royal Hospital Chelsea
EMBANKMENT
CHELSEA
BATTERSEA
WANDSWORTH
PARK
SW11
SW10
SW6
SANDS END
Battersea Park
Chelsea Harbour
Cremorne Gardens
Chelsea Wharf
Albert Bridge
Battersea Bridge
Chelsea Bridge
Grosvenor Bridge

G
H
J
K
L
M
SOHO
Covent Gdn
59
Piccadilly Circus
Leicester Sq.
SHAFTESBURY AV.
CHARING CROSS RD.
HAYMARKET
PICCADILLY
STRAND
ALDWYCH
EMBANKMENT
Temple
BLACKFRIARS
SOUTHWARK
Tate Modern
Embankment
CHARING CROSS
NORTHUMBERLAND AV.
WHITEHALL
VICTORIA EMBANKMENT
ST. JAMES'S PARK
Horse Guards Parade
Jubilee Gardens
London Eye
WATERLOO INTERNATIONAL
WATERLOO
Waterloo East
Southwark
Ryl. National Theatre
Westminster
WESTMINSTER BRI.
Houses of Parliament
Big Ben
St. James's Park
BUCKINGHAM GATE
VICTORIA ST.
ST. THOMAS' HOSPITAL
Lambeth Nth.
LAMBETH PALACE RD.
LAMBETH BRI.
MILLBANK
Lambeth Palace
Imperial War Mus.
Elephant & Castle
76
LAMBETH
KENNINGTON RD.
WESTMINSTER
Tate Britain
Pimlico
VAUXHALL BRIDGE RD.
ALBERT EMBANKMENT
VAUXHALL CROSS
Vauxhall
KENNINGTON
KENNINGTON LANE
Kennington
KENNINGTON PARK RD.
Oval
Surrey C.C.C. The Oval Cricket Grd.
VAUXHALL
Kennington Park
NINE ELMS
NEW COVENT GARDEN MARKET
SOUTH LAMBETH
CAMBERWELL NEW RD.
BRIXTON RD.
CLAPHAM RD.
Stockwell
91
Angell Town
MYATTS FIELDS
CAMBERWELL
Larkhall Park
WANDSWORTH RD.
RIVER THAMES
1
2
3
4
5
6
7
8
9

76
WHITECHAPEL
Mansion Ho.
Monument
FENCHURCH ST.
Tower Hill
Tower Gateway
Shadwell
CABLE ST.
CANNON STREET
THAMES ST.
TOWER HILL
THE TOWER
RIVER THAMES
SOUTHWARK
Bankside Jetty
Tate Modern
Golden Hinde
LONDON BRIDGE HOSP.
H.M.S. Belfast
City Hall
LONDON BRI.
THE BOROUGH
GUY'S HOSP.
TOOLEY ST.
TOWER BRI.
St. Katharine Docks
Tower Hotel
WAPPING
UPPER POOL
Pier Head
Wapping Old Stairs
Wapping New Stairs
BERMONDSEY
Cherry Garden Pier
Borough
JAMAICA RD.
LONG LANE
GREAT DOVER ST.
NEWINGTON
Elephant & Castle
NEW KENT RD.
BRICKLAYER'S ARMS
TOWER BRIDGE RD.
GRANGE RD.
ABBEY ST.
Bermondsey
SOUTHWARK PARK RD.
WALWORTH
WALWORTH RD.
OLD KENT RD.
ROTHERHITHE
BURGESS PARK
Burgess Park
ALBANY RD.
CAMBERWELL RD.
SOUTHAMPTON WAY
PECKHAM RD.
PECKHAM
PECKHAM HIGH ST.
QUEEN'S RD.
HANOVER PK.
CAMBERWELL GREEN
CAMBERWELL
DENMARK HILL
Peckham Rye
RYE LA.
60
75
92
A B C D E F
1 2 3 4 5 6 7 8 9

77
61
78
93
G
H
J
K
L
M
1
2
3
4
5
6
7
8
9
COMMERCIAL RD.
EAST INDIA DOCK RD.
HIGHWAY
CABLE ST.
LIMEHOUSE
Limehouse Basin
Westferry
POPLAR
ASPEN WAY
A1261
A1203
LINK
West India Quay
Canary Wharf
WEST INDIA DOCKS
Heron Quays
South Quay
ISLE OF DOGS
MILLWALL OUTER DOCK
MILLWALL
CUBITT TOWN
Crossharbour & London Arena
Mudchute
Island Gds.
MANCHESTER RD.
WESTFERRY RD.
A1206
RIVER THAMES
LIMEHOUSE REACH
GREENWICH REACH
Wapping
Shadwell Basin
King Edward Mem. Park
ROTHERHITHE TUNNEL
A101
BRUNEL RD.
Rotherhithe
Canada Water
ROTHERHITHE
SALTER RD.
B205
REDRIFF RD.
A2202
GREENLAND DOCK
SOUTH DOCK
Surrey Quays
LOWER RD.
A200
PLOUGH WAY
B206
EVELYN ST.
GROVE ST.
Pepys Park
CONVOY'S WHARF
DEPTFORD
Cutty Sark for Maritime Greenwich
CREEK RD.
DEPTFORD CHURCH ST.
A2209
Deptford
Greenwich
South Bermondsey
MILLWALL F.C. (The Den)
TRUNDLEYS RD.
B207
SANFORD ST.
LEWISHAM
NEW CROSS RD.
A2
New Cross
New Cross Gate
NEW CROSS GATE
NEW CROSS
Goldsmiths College
AMERSHAM RD.
LEWISHAM WAY
A20
Deptford Bri.
BROOKMILL RD.
BLACKHEATH RD.
GREENWICH HIGH RD.
A206
NORMAN RD.
B208
LEWISHAM RD.
St. Johns
ST. JOHNS
Elverson Road
QUEEN'S RD.
A2214
LAUSANNE RD.
POMEROY ST.
B2227
KENDER ST.
DLR
SE14
SE8

78
62
94
77
A
B
C
D
E
F
1
2
3
4
5
6
7
8
9
CANNING TOWN
Royal Victoria
Custom House for ExCeL
East India
LEAMOUTH
Blackwall
STH. BROMLEY
Poplar
All Saints
Billingsgate Fish Market
WEST INDIA
DOCKS
BLACKWALL BASIN
Virginia Quay
Blackwall Pier
Blackwall Point
MILLENNIUM DOME
North Greenwich
Ordnance Wharf
Delta Wharf
Victoria Deep Water Terminal
Primrose Wharf
Morden Wharf
Enderby's Wharf
Pipers Wharf
Badcock's Wharf
Granite Wharf
Lovell's Wharf
Cubitt Town Wharf
Newcastle Drawdock
Thames Wharf
London City Airport Pier
Tidal Basin Watersports Centre
Manhattan Wharf
Lyle Park
Plaistow Wharf
Deanston Wharf
KIERBECK BUSINESS COMPLEX
Millennium Village (under construction)
Greenwich Yacht Club
Christie's Wharf
RIVER THAMES
ROYAL VICTORIA
SILVERTOWN VIADUCT
SILVERTOWN WY.
NORTH WOOLWICH ROAD
LOWER LEA CROSSING
BLACKWALL TUNNEL
BLACKWALL TUNNEL SOUTHERN APPROACH
TUNNEL APPROACH
MILLENNIUM WAY
BUGSBY'S WAY
WOOLWICH RD.
TRAFALGAR RD.
ROMNEY RD.
PRESTON'S ROAD
MANCHESTER RD.
Crossharbour & London Arena
London Arena
CUBITT TOWN
TOWER HAMLETS
MUDCHUTE PARK
Mudchute
MILLWALL PARK
Island Gds.
Westcombe Park
Maze Hill
Cutty Sark for Maritime Greenwich
Greenwich
Old Royal Naval College
University of Greenwich
National Maritime Museum
GREENWICH
GREENWICH PARK
Royal Observatory Greenwich
The Wilderness (Deer Park)
Rangers Ho.
Reservoir (covered)
BLACK HEATH
SHOOTERS HILL
CHARLTON RD.
OLD DOVER RD.
VANBRUGH PARK
WESTCOMBE PARK
Christ's College for Boys
Morden College
KIDBROOKE PARK RD.
PRINCE OF WALES RD.
Blackheath Vale
A102
A2
A206
A2203
A2052
B209
B210
B212
A2213

79
West Beckton
Beckton Park
Gallions Reach
VICTORIA DOCK RD.
Prince Regent
ROYAL ALBERT WAY
Beckton Park
Cyprus
CYPRUS
Royal Albert
E16
London Regatta Centre
ROYAL ALBERT DOCK
LONDON CITY AIRPORT
NEWHAM
KING GEORGE V DOCK
CONNAUGHT BRIDGE
A1020
A112
A117
MANOR WAY
Gallions Point Marina
Terminal Building
Warehouse
Custom House
SILVERTOWN
Thames Barrier Park
Silvertown
THAMES ROAD INDUSTRIAL ESTATE
THAMESIDE INDUSTRIAL ESTATE
Sugar Refinery
STANDARD INDUSTRIAL ESTATE
North Woolwich
NORTH WOOLWICH
Royal Victoria Gardens
Hoba Wharf
GALLIONS REACH
WOOLWICH REACH
THAMES FLOOD BARRIER
RIVER THAMES
North Woolwich Pier
Woolwich Free Ferry
Waterfront Leisure Centre
THAMESMEAD WEST
Firepower (Royal Artillery Museum)
WOOLWICH HIGH ST.
BERESFORD ST.
A206
PLUMSTEAD RD
80
New Charlton
WOOLWICH CHURCH ST.
WOOLWICH ROAD
Woolwich Dockyard
Woolwich Arsenal
WOOLWICH
JOHN WILSON ST.
GRAND DEPOT RD.
A205
Maryon Park
Charlton Athletic F.C. (The Valley)
MARYON WILSON PARK
Museum of Artillery in the Rotunda
Repository Woods
Royal Artillery Barracks
Gun Park
SE18
SE7
Charlton Park Sch.
CHARLTON CEMETERY
CHARLTON
Charlton Ho.
CHARLTON PARK
Cricket Ground
QUEEN ELIZABETH HOSPITAL
WOOLWICH COMMON
Hornfair Park
Old Royal Military Academy
Eaglesfield School
SHOOTERS HILL
A207
Recreation Ground
Reservoir
Kidbrooke School
ELTHAM COMMON
MEMORIAL HOSPITAL
95
G
H
J
K
L
M
1
2
3
4
5
6
7
8
9
42
43
44

NEWHAM
THAMESMEAD CENTRAL
SE28
THAMESMEAD
THAMESMEAD WEST
GREENWICH
PLUMSTEAD
SE18
ABBEY WOOD
Welling
DA16
SHOOTERS HILL
Plumstead Common
SHREWSBURY PARK
BOSTALL WOODS
RIVER THAMES
Gallions Reach
Gallions Point
Thamesmead South West
H. M. P. BELMARSH
PLUMSTEAD MARSHES
WOOLWICH INDUSTRIAL ESTATE
PLUMSTEAD RD.
PLUMSTEAD HIGH STREET
BOSTALL HILL
WICKHAM LANE
SHOOTERS HILL
WESTERN WAY
EASTERN WAY
A206
A2016
A209
A2041
Woolwich Cemetery
Plumstead Cemetery
East Wickham Open Space
Shooters Hill Golf Course

64
79
96

G
H
J
K
L
M
65
97
Jetty
Tanks
RIVERSIDE GOLF COURSE
Playing Field
SEWAGE WORKS
Mill
Works
Belvedere Power Sta.
Tennis Courts
A2016
THAMESMEAD SOUTH
Lakeside Centre
Southmere Lake
THAMESMEAD EAST
ERITH
MARSHES
Erith
DA18
Thamesmead Community College
EASTERN INDUSTRIAL ESTATE
HARROW MANOR WAY
A2041
YARNTON WAY
CAPITAL INDUSTRIAL ESTATE
ELBOURNE TRADING ESTATE
Belvedere
Superstore
Belvedere Youth Cen.
Belvedere Jun. & Inf. Sch.
LOWER ROAD
B213
B253
B250
ABBEY ROAD
Abbey Wood
Lesnes Abbey Pk.
Remains of Lesnes Abbey
LESNES ABBEY WOODS
Belvedere
BELVEDERE
FRANK'S PARK
Trinity Sch. Belvedere
Abbey Wood Camping & Caravan Site
Cooperative Woods
Belvedere Private Clinic
Bostall Ho.
KNEE HILL
A206
ERITH ROAD
LESSNESS HEATH
Open Space
WOOLWICH HILL
WEST HEATH
Clam Field Recreation Ground
Bedonwell Prim. & Inf. Schs.
ERITH CEMETERY
Lime Wood
BEDONWELL ROAD
MANORWAY
Playing Field
Erith DA8
Bexleyheath
DA7
LONG LANE
BELMONT ROAD
Belmont Prim. Sch.
EAST WICKHAM
Stevens Park
Prim. Sch.
Comm. Cen.
Bursted Wood Sch.
Bursted Wood
Offices
St. Thomas More R.C. Prim. Sch.
Bram. Prim. Sch.
ERITH RD.
1
2
3
4
5
6
7
8
9
48
49
50
78
79
80
81

82
A
B
C
D
E
F
1
2
3
4
5
6
7
8
9
66
81
98
RIVER THAMES
ERITH REACH
ERITH RAN
RAINHAM MARSHES
HAVE
Rainham
RM13
Belvedere
Belvedere Power Sta.
Jenningtree Point
Lighthouse
Frog Island
FREIGHTMASTER ESTATE
Silt Lagoon
COLDHARBOUR LANE
Coldharbour Point
Depot
Jetty
Wharf
Pier
Works
Mill
Landing Stage
A17
BRONZE AGE WAY
A2016
MANORWAY
CAPITAL INDUSTRIAL ESTATE
RIVER WHARF BUSINESS PARK
CALLENDERS COTTS.
Sports Grd.
Tennis Courts
LOWER ROAD
B213
BELVEDERE
Belvedere Youth Cen.
Belvedere Jun. & Inf. Sch.
HILLSIDE
FRANK'S PARK
Bexley College
Trinity Sch. Belvedere
ERITH RD.
FRASER ROAD
A206 ROAD
EUROPA TRADING ESTATE
Sand and Gravel Pit
ERITH
Erith
Baths
Lib.
Chalk Farm Wharf
Garden Wharf
Superstore
Anchor Bay
Slipway
Concrete Works
MANFORD INDUSTRIAL ESTATE
A220 ROAD
QUEEN'S ROAD
BEXLEY ROAD
ERITH & DIST. HOSP.
Erith Stadium
Sports Centre Rec. Grd.
DA8
Monastery Prim. Sch.
Cemy.
Lime Wood
NORTHUMBERLAND HEATH
Erith Sch.
Pav. Playing Field
LESNEY FARM ESTATE
NORTHEND ROAD
A206
Playing Field
Slade Green Jun. & Inf. Schs.
CHURCH TRAD. EST.
ANCHOR BAY INDUS. EST.
NORTH END
Brick Works
School
Recreation Ground
Res. (covered)
Colyers Prim. Sch. Play. Fld.
Normandy Prim. Sch.
Bexleyheath
DA7
Slade Green
SLADE GREEN
Playing Field
Football Grd.
Howbury Farm
Moat
Rec. Grd.
Playgrd.
Bursted Wood Prim. Sch.
Bursted Wood
Barnehurst
Carriage

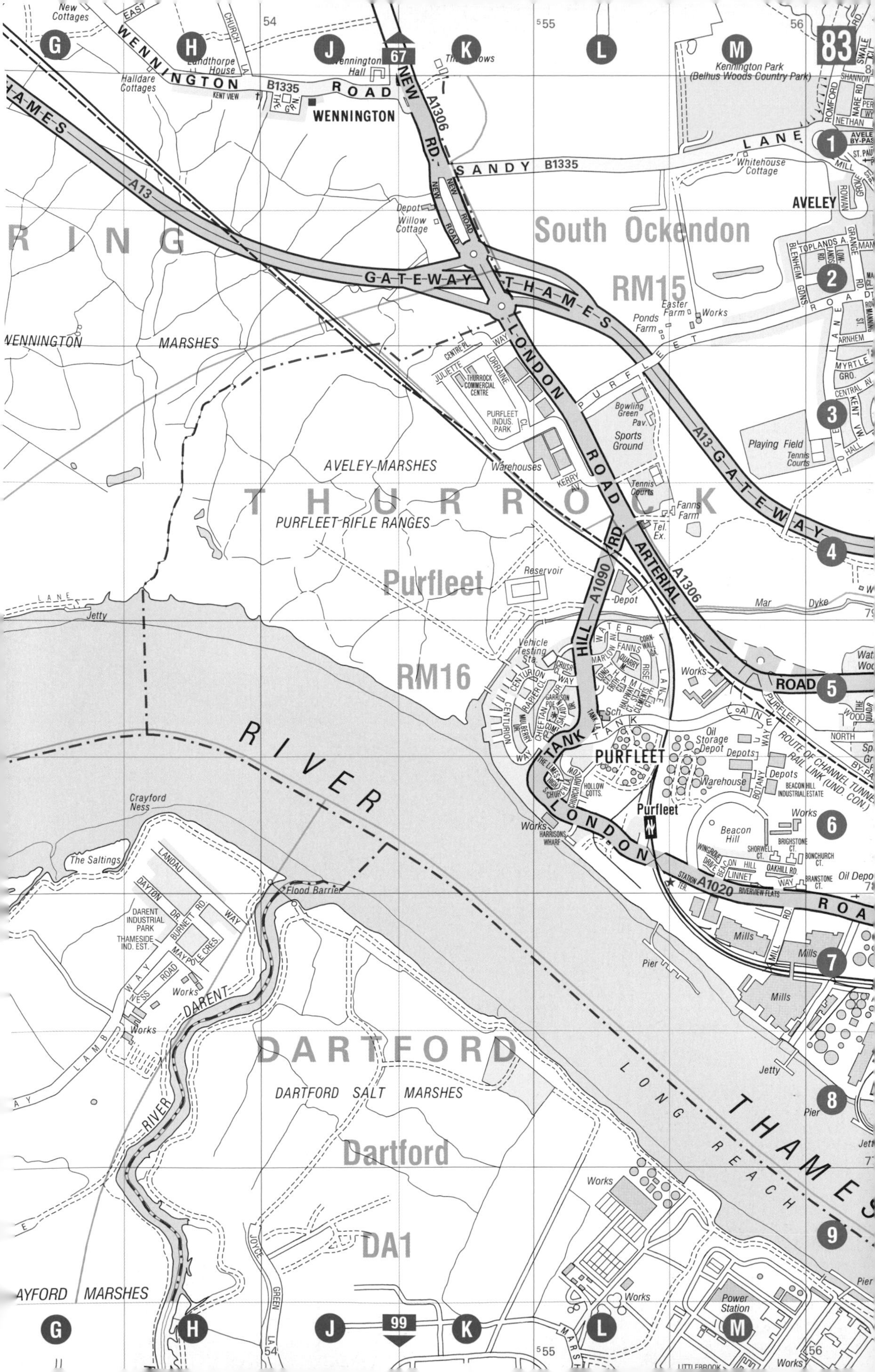

South Ockendon
RM15
THURROCK
Purfleet
RM16
PURFLEET
RIVER THAMES
LONG REACH
DARTFORD
Dartford
DA1
WENNINGTON
AVELEY
WENNINGTON MARSHES
AVELEY MARSHES
PURFLEET RIFLE RANGES
DARTFORD SALT MARSHES
Kennington Park (Belhus Woods Country Park)
A13
GATEWAY THAMES
LONDON ROAD
ARTERIAL RD. A1306
TANK HILL RD. A1090
A1020
WENNINGTON ROAD B1335
SANDY LANE B1335
NEW RD. A1306
THURROCK COMMERCIAL CENTRE
PURFLEET INDUS. PARK
DARENT INDUSTRIAL PARK
THAMESIDE IND. EST.
BEACON HILL INDUSTRIAL ESTATE
RIVER DARENT
Crayford Ness
The Saltings
Flood Barrier
Jetty
Pier
Mar Dyke
Power Station
Mills
Works
Depot
Warehouses
Reservoir
Sports Ground
Playing Field
Tennis Courts
Purfleet
Beacon Hill
Oil Storage Depot
Vehicle Testing Sta.
Fanns Farm
Ponds Farm
Easter Farm
Whitehouse Cottage
Willow Cottage
Landthorpe House
Halldare Cottages
New Cottages
Wennington Hall
ROUTE OF CHANNEL TUNNEL RAIL LINK (UND. CON.)
67
99

LONDON - HEATHROW
AIRPORT
HILLINGDON
TERMINAL 1
RMINAL 2
TERMINAL 4
Heathrow
Terminal 4
London Heathrow
Hilton Hotel
Compass
Base
Maintenance Area
Hatton Cross
HATTON
TW6
TW14
TW13
Airport
Car Park
Duds
Farm
Works
68
144
100
NORTHERN PERIMETER RD.
EASTERN PERIMETER ROAD
SOUTHERN PERIMETER ROAD
VANGUARD WAY
EASTCHURCH RD.
Boadicea
Ho.
Speedbird
Ho.
Comet
Ho.
ELMDON RD.
VISCOUNT WAY
LITHGOW'S RD.
GREAT SOUTH-WEST ROAD
A30
THE PARKWAY
THE CAUSEWAY
THE FAGG'S RD.
A312
HEATHROW
CAUSEWAY
CENTRE
Cranebank
Cranford
Inf. Sch.
Cranford
Jun. Sch.
Play.
Field
BERKELEY AV.
BYRON AV.
CHAUCER AV.
WESTWICK GS.
GREEN MAN LA.
Hatton
Farm
Warehouses
Hounslow
Urban Farm
Superstore
NORTH FELTHAM
TRADING ESTATE
Works
Rec. Grd.
Marjory
Kinnon Sch.
Bedfont Jun.
Inf. & Nursy.
Sch.
The Two
Bridges
Duke of Northumberland's River
Longford River
NORTHUMBERLAND CR.
KINGSTON
LONGFORD AV.
STAINES ROAD
A315
BEDFONT
RUSKIN
CASSIOBURY AV.
Playing
Field
School
Blenheim Park
Feltham
Arenas
Grandstand
FELTHAM
NORTH
FELTHAM
HARLINGTON ROAD WEST
HOUNSLOW
STATION
ESTATE
Feltham
Park
Hall
Warehouses
H.M. Customs
& Excise
Heathrow
Corporate
Cen.
Factory
Works
STANWELL
CLOCKHOUSE
ROUNDABOUT
CLOCKHOUSE
Bedfont
Green
Old People's
Home
HATCHETT RD.
DUDLEY
EAST
BEDFONT
Fairholme Jun.
Inf. & Nursy. Schs.
Playing
Field
NEW SQUARE
Bedfont
Cemetery
BEDFONT LAKES
COUNTRY PARK
Feltham
Edward Pauling
Prim. Sch.
Works
Playing
Field
Vineyard
Nurseries
H.M. Young Offenders
Institution Feltham
BEDFONT LAKES
COUNTRY PARK
BEDFONT
INDUSTRIAL PARK
BEDFONT PARK
INDUSTRIAL EST.
CHALLENGE
Grosvenor
Park
ROCHESTER AV.
VERNON
PERCIVAL
PRINCES
WESTBOURNE
Feltham Hill
Inf. Sch.
Feltham Hill
Jun. Sch.
LOWER
FELTHAM
ASHFORD RD.
HIGH ST.
A244
B377
B3377
Cemetery
Works
Croft
Farm
Rec.
Grd.
Pav.
ASHFORD ROAD
Piggeries
CHATTERN
SHIELD
Hall
GRANGE
MEWS
Ordnance
Depot
Feltham
Lib.
Schs.

HENLYS ROUNDABOUT
Hounslow
HOUNSLOW WEST
Hounslow West
Beaversfield Park
Cavalry Barracks
HEATHROW CORPORATE PARK
TW4
HOUNSLOW HEATH GOLF COURSE
HOUNSLOW HEATH
Heath Nurseries
The Heathland School
Lampton School
Civic Centre
LAMPTON PARK
Hounslow Central
TREATY CENTRE
HOUNSLOW
Maswell Park
Alexandra School
RICHMOND UPON THAMES
Twickenham
Twickenham Cemetery
TW2
Bridge Farm Nursery
Heathfield Jun. & Inf. Schs.
South West Middlesex Crematorium
Nature Reserve
Feltham Community College
Feltham Airparcs Leisure Centre
Hanworth Park House
HANWORTH PARK
Hounslow College
HANWORTH
APEX CORNER
HOSPITAL BRIDGE ROUNDABOUT
Fulwell Park
TWICKENHAM GOLF COURSE
FULWELL GOLF COURSE
GREAT WEST ROAD
A4
BATH ROAD
A3006
A3063
A3005
A315
A314
A312
A316
A305
B358
B361
UXBRIDGE ROAD
HANWORTH ROAD
HOUNSLOW ROAD
HAMPTON RD. WEST
CHERTSEY ROAD
STAINES ROAD
TWICKENHAM RD.
GREAT CHERTSEY ROAD
COUNTRY WAY
WHITTON ROAD
HOSPITAL BRIDGE ROAD
NELSON ROAD
69
86
101
G
H
J
K
L
M
1
2
3
4
5
6
7
8
9

86
70
85
102
A
B
C
D
E
F
1
2
3
4
5
6
7
8
9
76
75
74
73
72
14
15
16
LAMPTON
SPRING GROVE
Hounslow East
Bus Depot
WOODLANDS
Isleworth
ISLEWORTH
Playing Field
West Thames Coll.
Sports Ground
WEST MIDDLESEX UNIVERSITY HOSP.
Cemetery
Syon Park Sch.
Old Isleworth
Isleworth Ait
Nazareth Ho.
Brunel Univ.
Liby. & Isleworth Rec. Cen.
Clock Tower Ind. Est.
REDLEES PARK
Hounslow
HOUNSLOW
INWOOD PARK
Tennis Courts
Worton Hall Industrial Estate
Victory Business Centre
Waterside Business Centre
West Middlesex Drainage Works
TW3
TW7
TW1
TW2
Maswell Park
Queen's Bri.
Superstore
Heath Bus. Cen.
Murray Park
Royal Military Sch. of Music (Kneller Hall)
Sports Ground
The Museum of Rugby
Twickenham Trading Estate
Twickenham Rugby Union Football Grd.
Chase Bridge
Whitton Rd. R'bout
London Rd. Roundabout
Cole Park
Moor Mead Bridge
Moor Mead Gd.
Tennis Courts
St. Margarets
ST. MARGARETS
St. Margarets R'bout
St. Margarets Bus. Cen.
Pleasure Gdns.
Richmond upon Thames College
Harlequins R.U.F.C. (Stoop Meml. Grd.)
Play. Fld.
Twickenham
Whitton
WHITTON
Kneller Gdns.
Depot
Twickenham Green
Eel Pie Island
TWICKENHAM
Thames Eyot
Ham Riverside Lands
Nature Reserve
Wood
Miniature Rifle Range
Playing Field
Radnor Gardens
Swan Island
Strawberry Hill
STRAWBERRY HILL
St. Mary's Strawberry Hill
Thames Young Mariners Base
Ham Fields
Club House
St. James' R.C. Prim. Sch.
STRAWBERRY HILL GOLF COURSE
Waldegrave Sch. for Girls
Hospital Bri. Roundabout
Hosp. Bri.
FULWELL GOLF COURSE
Fulwell
Stanley Jun. & Inf. Schs.
Cemetery
Newland Ho. Sch.
LONDON ROAD A315
A310 TWICKENHAM ROAD
B363
A3004 ST. MARGARETS ROAD
A316 ROAD
CHERTSEY ROAD A316
WHITTON ROAD
KNELLER ROAD B361
HEATH ROAD A305
THE GREEN
A311 HAMPTON ROAD
STAINES ROAD A305
SIXTH CROSS ROAD B358
WALDEGRAVE ROAD A309
CROSS DEEP A310
STRAWBERRY VALE A310
RICHMOND ROAD
LONDON ROAD
MOGDEN LA.

87
Syon Garden Centre
Syon House
NORTHUMBERLAND ESTATE
RIVER THAMES
Isleworth Ferry Gate (Closed)
Syon Vista
The Lake
King William's Temple
Temple of Bellona
Arboretum
Berberis Dell
71
Water Lily Pond
KEW GARDENS
Evolution House
Temperate House
Pagoda
Marianne North Gallery
Conservation Area
Queen Charlotte's Cottage
Pavilion Restaurant
Japanese Gateway & Landscape
King's Steps Gate
OLD DEER PARK
ROYAL MID-SURREY GOLF COURSE
King's Observatory
Royal Mid-Surrey Golf Club
Richmond Athletic Ground
Rugby Club
Lion Gate
Cricket Grd.
Bowling Green
Grand Stand
Tennis Courts
Swimming Baths
Obelisk
Old Deer Park Recreation Ground
TWICKENHAM ROAD A316
RICHMOND CIRCUS
LOWER MORTLAKE RD.
KEW RD
A307
Richmond
RICHMOND
Richmond Green
Asgill Ho.
Corporation Island
PARADISE RD.
SHEEN RD
A305
PETERSHAM
RICHMOND HILL
QUEEN'S RD
KINGS RD
FRIARS STILE RD
B321
B322
B353
Terrace Gardens
Buccleugh Gdns.
Richmond Gate
Royal Star & Garter Home
Petersham Meadows
Petersham Farm
Petersham Common
STAR & GARTER HILL
Marble Hill Park
Marble Hill House
Glover's Island
Foot Ferry
RIVER THAMES
RICHMOND
Ham House
Polo Ground
The German Sch. London
The Russell Prim. Sch.
Strathmore Sch.
The Copse
PETERSHAM PARK
Sudbrook Park
Sudbrook Park (Club Ho.)
The Wilderness
RICHMOND GOLF COURSE
Grey Court School
Ham Green
HAM
Ham Common
B352
HAM GATE AV.
103
Pembroke Lodge (Cafeteria)
King Henry VIII Mound
SIDMOUTH WOOD
RICHMOND PARK
Kidney Wood
TW10
TW9
SAWYER'S HILL
(Open during daylight hours only)
Saw Pit Plantation
Jubilee Plantation
Queen's Ride
Queen Elizabeth's Plantation
Oak Lodge
Leg of Mutton Pond
Pen Ponds
Pond Plantation
Whiteash Lodge
Pond Slade
Ham Cross Plantation
Ham Bottom
Ham Gate
Ham Cross
Peg's Pond
Thomson's Pond
ISABELLA PLANTATION
HORNBEAM WALK
Horse Ride
Holly Lodge
Conduit Wood
Bishop's Pond
Cambrian Gate
Riding Ring
The Bog
Bog Gate
Barn Wood
Teck Plantation
Richmond Cemetery
East Sheen Cemetery
Pesthouse Common
Christ's Sch.
King's House Sch.
SHEEN COMMON
SW14
88
Football Ground
Playing Field
EAST SHEEN
UPPER RICHMOND ROAD
North Sheen
Holy Trinity C.E.Prim. Sch.
NORTH SHEEN
Recreation Ground
Playing Field
FULHAM (NORTH SHEEN) CEMETERY
Mortlake Crematorium
Hammersmith Cemetery
MORTLAKE RD.
A205
CLIFFORD AV.
LOWER RICHMOND RD.
SANDYCOMBE ROAD
MANOR ROAD
Refuse Depot
Westminster Boathouse
Chalker's Corner
Sheen Mt. Prim. Sch.
DEER PARK
King George Jubilee Plantation
Lawn

HOUNSLOW
W4
DUKE'S MEADOWS
Sports Ground
Driving Range
Playing Fields
Riverside Lands
Stadium
Yacht Basin
Sports Ground
Westminster Boathouse
Refuse Depot
Mortlake Crematorium
Hammersmith Cemetery
CHISWICK BRI.
GT. CHERTSEY RD.
CLIFFORD AV.
A316
RIVER THAMES
Barnes Bridge
THE TERRACE
MORTLAKE
A3003
MORTLAKE HIGH ST.
Brewery
Sports Ground
The Green
Mortlake
RICHMOND
CLIFFORD
UPPER RICHMOND RD. A205
WEST
UPPER (STH. CIRCULAR RD.)
A205
SHEEN LANE
B351
SW14
EAST SHEEN
Sheen Sch. & Sports Centre
E. Sheen Prim. Sch.
Beverley Brook
Sports Ground
Club House
Record Office
Clarence Farm
Palewell Common
Palewell Fields
Playing Fields
Pale Well
Pitch and Putt Course
ROEHAMPTON PRIORY HOSPITAL
ROEHAMPTON GOLF COURSE
Rosslyn Pk. R.U.F.C.
RED ROVER
Club House
Froebel College
Digby Stuart College
Roehampton Institute
QUEEN MARY'S UNIVERSITY HOSPITAL
SW15
ROEHAMPTON LANE
A306
BARNES
SW13
BARNES COMMON
Barnes
ROCKS LANE
A306
MILL HILL RD.
B349
Cricket Grounds
Cricket Ground
Football Ground
Barn Elms Playing Fields
Old Barnes Cemetery
Putney Cemetery
Running Track
Beverley Brook
BARNES HIGH ST.
CHURCH RD.
STATION RD.
QUEENS RIDE
B306
Cemy.
BARNES HOSP.
COMMON
Adam's Pond
Horse Ride
Playing Field
Roehampton Gate
East Sheen Gate
Sheen Wood
Teck Plantation
The Bog
RICHMOND
upon
THAMES
Richmond
TW10
Sheen Cross Wood
Polo Field
Barn Wood Pond
Deer Pen
White Lodge Plantation
Duchess' Wood
Queen's Ride
RICHMOND PARK
White Lodge (The Royal Ballet School)
Pen Ponds
Lawn Plantation
SPANKERS HILL WOOD
DEER PARK
King George V Jubilee Plantation
Plantation
Victory Plantation
Killcat Corner
RICHMOND PARK GOLF COURSE
Kingsfarm Plantation
Treebox Wood
(Open during daylight hours only)
College Halls
ROEHAMPTON
Maryfield Convent
Hyde Park Nursery
Chohole Gate
Silver Hill
STAG LANE
A3
KINGSTON VALE
ROEHAMPTON VALE
PUTNEY VALE
PUTNEY VALE CEMETERY
Putney Vale Crematorium
Superstore
Kingston University (Roehampton Vale Centre)
Playing Fields
Memorial Gardens
War Memorial
Hall School Wimbledon
WIMBLEDON COMMON
Silent Pools
Stag Bog
Jerry's Hill
Queen's Mere
Beverley Bridge
Robin Hood Gate
ROBIN HOOD
A308
KINGSTON BY-PASS
KINGSTON VALE
Tercentenary Plantation
Prince Charles's Spinney
Gibbet Wood
Thomson's Pond
Broomfield Hill Wood
Horse Ride
Gravelly Ride
PUTNEY
ROEHAMPTON LANE
72
87
104
A B C D E F
1 2 3 4 5 6 7 8 9

89
SANDS END
G
H
J
K
L
M
73
90
105
1
2
3
4
5
6
7
8
9
RIVER
THAMES
Barn Elms
Boat House
Barn Elms Schools Sports Centre
Stevenage Wharves
Fulham F.C. (Craven Cottage)
FULHAM PALACE RD.
Fulham Palace
Moat Garden
The Warren
Playground
Parsons Grn.
PARSONS GRN
KINGS RD.
NEW KINGS RD.
A308
A219
A3209
A205
A3
A217
A218
B306
SW6
SW15
SW18
SW19
HAMMERSMITH and FULHAM
HURLINGHAM PARK
Running Track
Hurlingham
The Hurlingham Club
Swim. Pool
Ckt. Grd.
SOUTH PARK
Putney Bri.
Putney Pier
Wharves
Trinidad Wharf
Hurlingham Wharf
Hurlingham Retail PK
Dock
Jetties
Jetty
River Wandle
Bell Lane Creek
Solid Waste Transfer Station
Works
WANDSWORTH BRIDGE
WANDSWORTH BRI. RD.
RICHMOND
PUTNEY
PUTNEY HIGH ST.
PUTNEY BRIDGE RD.
PUTNEY HILL
Putney
East Putney
WANDSWORTH
Wandsworth Town
WANDSWORTH HIGH ST.
WANDSWORTH GYRATORY
WANDSWORTH Leisure Cen.
WANDSWORTH PARK
Wandsworth Shop. Cen.
WANDSWORTH WORTH
WEST HILL
PUTNEY HEATH
HEATH
Cricket Ground
TIBBET'S CORNER
TIBBET'S RIDE
PUTNEY HEATH LA.
ROYAL HOSP. FOR NEURO-DISABILITY
Roehampton Institute Playing Fld.
Mosque
Play. Fld.
Elliott Sch.
Putney High Sch.
Water Scene
King George's Park
SOUTHFIELDS
Southfields
Southfields Comm. Coll.
T.A. Centre
Sports Grd.
Library
School
Depot
Superstore
Earlsfield
EARLSFIELD RD.
GARRATT LA.
BUCKHOLD RD.
MERTON RD.
DURNSFORD ROAD
KIMBER RD.
SOUTHFIELDS
WIMBLEDON PARK
WIMBLEDON PARK SIDE
PARKSIDE
WIMBLEDON PARK GOLF COURSE
Athletics Ground
Bowling Greens
Putting Green
Tennis Courts
Pavilion
Club House
Wimbledon Park
Aorangi Park
Cricket Ground
WIMBLEDON All England Lawn Tennis & Croquet Club
Sports Ground
PARKSIDE HOSP.
Clock House
King's Mere
Ladies Mile
Horse Ride
Subway
Recreation Ground
Carriage Cleaning Shed
Haslemere Ind. Est.
SUMMERSTOWN
Factory
Wimbledon Stadium (Greyhound)
Wimbledon Swan Stadium Bus. Cen.
MERTON

SANDS END
SW6
Chelsea Harbour Pier
Lensbury Wharf
Shell Wharf
London Westland Heliport
Fulham Wharf
BATTERSEA
CLAPHAM JUNCTION
CLAPHAM
Falcon Park
Wandsworth Town
Spencer Park
Emanuel School
BOLINGBROKE HOSPITAL
CLAPHAM COMMON
Clapham Sth.
Cricket Ground
H.M.P. Wandsworth
WANDSWORTH COMMON
Wandsworth Common
SW18
WANDSWORTH CEMETERY
EARLSFIELD
Earlsfield
Beatrix Potter Prim. Sch.
BALHAM
Balham
The Joan Bicknell Centre
THE CENTRAL LONDON GOLF CENTRE
SPRINGFIELD UNIVERSITY HOSPITAL
Burntwood School
Garratt Green
STREATHAM CEMETERY
UPPER TOOTING
Tooting Bec
Tooting Graveney Common
SW17
SUMMERSTOWN
River Wandle
LAVENDER HILL
NORTHCOTE ROAD
TRINITY ROAD
BURNTWOOD LANE
NIGHTINGALE LANE
BALHAM HIGH ROAD
TOOTING BEC ROAD
74
106
89

91
G
H
J
K
L
M
75
1
2
3
4
5
6
7
8
9
92
107
Larkhall Park
Stockwell
Angell Town
CAMBERWELL
SE5
Wandsworth Rd.
STOCKWELL
SW9
Loughborough Junc.
Clapham High St.
Clapham North
LAMBETH HOSPITAL
Clapham Comm.
CLAPHAM COMMON
Brixton
COLDHARBOUR LANE
A2217
BRIXTON
SW4
CLAPHAM PARK
Lambeth Coll.
HERNE HILL
SE24
Herne Hill
HALF MOON LA.
DULWICH ROAD
A2214
BROCKWELL PARK
Swimming Pool
Bowling Green
Tennis Courts
Open Air Theatre
The Mansion
New Lodge
Playground
H.M.P. Brixton
Windmill Gdns
Sports Ground
SW2
POYNDERS RD.
A205
ATKINS RD.
STREATHAM PL.
CHRISTCHURCH ROAD
A23
BRIXTON HILL
TULSE HILL
A204
STREATHAM HILL
Streatham Hill
SW16
STREATHAM HIGH ROAD
NORWOOD ROAD
A215
Tulse Hill
SE27
Knight's Hill
THURLOW PARK RD.
West Norwood
Football Pitch
BEC
COMMON
TOOTING
Swimming Pool
Hitherfield Prim. Sch.
Nature Gdns
Bus Depot
Res. (Covered)
Tonge Ho.
Library
CLAPHAM ROAD
A3
SOUTH SIDE
A24
A3036
OLD TOWN
BEDFORD RD.
ACRE LANE
EFFRA RD.
RAILTON RD.
MILKWOOD ROAD
CROXTED ROAD
LEIGHAM COURT
KINGS AV.
THORNTON AV.
B221
B222
B223

92
76
91
108
CAMBERWELL
PECKHAM
Peckham Rye
Denmark Hill
KINGS COLLEGE HOSPITAL
THE MAUDSLEY HOSP.
East Dulwich
EAST DULWICH
PECKHAM RYE COMMON
PECKHAM RYE PARK
North Dulwich
HERNE HILL
Herne Hill
DULWICH VILLAGE
DULWICH PARK
Dulwich Picture Gallery
DULWICH COLLEGE
DULWICH & SYDENHAM HILL GOLF COURSE
DULWICH
Dulwich Wood
West Dulwich
WEST DULWICH
TULSE HILL
Knight's Hill
West Norwood Cemetery and Crematorium
WEST NORWOOD
Sydenham Hill
UPPER SYDENHAM
Sydenham Wells Park
Horniman Gardens
Horniman Museum
Camberwell Old Cemetery
Herne Hill Stadium
Dulwich Hamlet F.C.
Superstore
SOUTHWARK
LAMBETH
SE5
SE15
SE22
SE24
SE21
SE26
SE27
COLDHARBOUR LA.
DENMARK HILL
CHAMPION PK.
GROVE LA.
DOG KENNEL HILL
GROVE VALE
EAST DULWICH ROAD
NUNHEAD
RYE LANE
PECKHAM RYE
EAST DULWICH GROVE
LORDSHIP LANE
BARRY ROAD
HALF MOON LA.
VILLAGE WAY
CROXTED ROAD
NORWOOD ROAD
THURLOW PARK ROAD
DULWICH COMMON
SOUTH CROXTED ROAD
LONDON ROAD
A215
A2216
A2214
A205
A2199
A2217
B219
B238

G
H
J
K
L
M
1
2
3
4
5
6
7
8
9
77
94
109
NEW CROSS
SE14
SE13
SE4
SE23
SE6
Nunhead
NUNHEAD
NUNHEAD CEMETERY
Telegraph Hill Park
DRAKEFELL ROAD
LEWISHAM
ST. JOHNS
St. Johns
Elverson Road
Lewisham
LOAMPIT VALE
LOAMPIT HILL
Lewisham College
Brockley
BROCKLEY
BROCKLEY ROAD
HILLY FIELDS
Prendergast School
ADELAIDE ROAD
LADYWELL
Ladywell
LEWISHAM UNIVERSITY HOSPITAL
Brockley Cemetery
Ladywell Cemetery
Crofton Park
Crofton Pk.
AQUARIUS GOLF COURSE
Newlands
Honor Oak Crematorium
Camberwell New Cemetery
ONE TREE HILL
HONOR OAK
Honor Oak Park
HONOR OAK PARK
STONDON PARK
Blythe Hill Fields
Blythe Hill
LEWISHAM
Catford Bridge
Catford
CATFORD
Catford Stadium (Greyhound)
Crofton School
Crofton Leisure & Youth Centre
Ladywell Fields
STANSTEAD ROAD
FOREST HILL
Forest Hill
PERRY VALE
PERRY RISE
PERRY HILL
CATFORD HILL
BROMLEY ROAD
RUSHEY GREEN
LEWISHAM HIGH STREET
Bellingham
BELLINGHAM
Powerleague Soccer Cen.
Catford Trading Estate
Sports Ground
Gasholder Station
Nature Reserve
Reservoirs (covered)
Playing Field

94
A
B
C
D
E
F
78
1
2
3
4
5
6
7
8
9
110
93
BLACKHEATH HILL
SHOOTERS HILL
BLACKHEATH
Blackheath Vale
Hollyhedge Ho.
PRINCE OF WALES RD.
Morden College
KIDBROOKE PARK A2213
LEWISHAM
A2211 ROAD
Lewisham
THURSTON RD.
LOAMPIT VALE
Superstore
College
Blackheath
Concert Halls
BELMONT HILL
LEE HIGH ROAD
A20
B220
B212
SE13
SE12
SE6
BLACKHEATH PARK
Sports Ground
Sports Grounds
Golf Driving Range
David Lloyd Leis.
Thomas Tallis Sch.
Manor House Gdns.
Manor Park
LEE
Lee
BURNT ASH RD.
A2212
ELTHAM RD.
Euro Cen.
Horn Park
Playing Field
Hither Green
HITHER GREEN
Depot
Lewisham Park
Ladywell
LADYWELL RD.
LEWISHAM HIGH ST.
A21
Baths
MOUNTSFIELD PARK
Playing Fields
Tennis Courts
Wks.
CHILTONIAN IND. EST.
WESTHORNE AVE.
A205
BROWNHILL ROAD
ST. MILDREDS ROAD
BARING ROAD
CATFORD
Catford Gyratory
RUSHEY GREEN
BROMLEY RD.
Prim. Sch.
Comm. Cen.
Hither Green Sidings
Northbrook Park
HITHER GREEN CEMETERY
Lewisham Crematorium
Lodge
Catford County School
FORSTER MEMORIAL PARK
Playground
Playing Field
Bellingham
SOUTHEND
Bromley BR1
GROVE PARK
Grove Park
CHINBROOK
Liby.
WHITEFOOT LANE
DOWNHAM WAY

G
H
J
K
L
M
1
2
3
4
5
6
7
8
9
42
43
44
79
96
111
KIDBROOKE
Kidbrooke School
Playing Fields
Sports Ground
Sam Montague Boys Club
Tennis Courts
CEMETERY
ELTHAM COMMON
MEMORIAL HOSPITAL
Severndroog Castle
CASTLE WOOD
Rose Cottage
JACK WOOD
SE18
Oxleas Meadows
Jackwood Ho.
SHOOTERS HILL
A207
ROYAL HERBERT PAVILIONS
WELL HALL ROAD
A205
WELL HALL ROUNDABOUT
ROCHESTER WAY
A2
ROCHESTER WAY RELIEF ROAD
KIDBROOKE ESTATE
Nature Res.
Tudor Barn
Eltham
ELTHAM PARK
ELTHAM PARK NORTH
ELTHAM PARK SOUTH
SHEPHERDLEAS WOOD
ELTHAM WARREN GOLF COURSE
GREENWICH
Greenwich Borough F.C.
Harrow Meadow
WESTHORNE AVENUE
ELTHAM ROAD
ELTHAM HILL
ELTHAM HIGH STREET
A210
BEXLEY ROAD
Eltham Hill Sch.
Eltham Green Sch.
ELTHAM
Supermarket
Moatbridge Sch.
Eltham Palace
SE9
Institute of Army Education
ROYAL BLACKHEATH GOLF COURSE
Club House
COURT ROAD
A208
FOOTSCRAY ROAD
A211
Bird Sanctuary
The Tarn
Mottingham
MOTTINGHAM
SIDCUP ROAD
A20
Carter's Hill
Mottingham Farm
Mottingham Hall
Eltham College Jun. Sch.
Eltham College
BROMLEY
Community Centre
Fairy Hill
Coldharbour Leisure Centre
Playing Fields
Netball Courts
New Eltham
NEW ELTHAM
St. Olave's Prep. School
FIVEWAYS
B263 GREEN LANE
B226
GROVE PARK
Lower Marvels Wood
AVERY
Sports Ground
Running Track
Rec. Grd.

A
B
C
D
E
F
1
2
3
4
5
6
7
8
9
80
95
112
SHOOTERS HILL
SHOOTERS HILL GOLF COURSE
Lowood Club Ho
Eaglesfield Rec. Grnd.
Woodlands Farm
Garden Centre
Abattoir
Council Offices
A207
SHOOTERS HILL
BELLEGROVE ROAD
Oxleas Meadows
OXLEAS WOOD
Eastcote Prim. Sch.
ROCHESTER WAY
WELLING WAY
Playing Field
SHEPHERDLEAS WOOD
Falconwood Field
Falconwood
FALCONWOOD
Inf. Sch.
Jun. Sch.
Coll.
Playing Field
Tennis Courts
Comm. Cen.
ELTHAM PARK NORTH
ELTHAM PARK SOUTH
ROCHESTER WAY RELIEF ROAD
Eltham Cemetery
Eltham Crematorium
ROCHESTER WAY
EAST
ELTHAM WARREN GOLF COURSE
Club House
Nature Study Centre
Crown Woods School
Playing Field
SE9
BEXLEY ROAD
A210
BLACKFEN ROAD
University of Greenwich (Avery Hill Campus)
AVERY HILL
AVERY HILL PARK
AVERY HILL RD.
B2214
(Halls of Residence)
Sports Ground
Alderwood Prim. Sch.
Parish Wood
Prim. Sch.
BLACKFEN
Days Lane Prim. Sch.
Hollyoak Wood Park
Lib.
DA15
DA16
Welling
Welling Corner
WELLING HIGH ST
A209
UPPER WICKHAM LANE
Hook La Prim. Sch.
Bexley Grammar Sch.
Playing Field
Prim. Sch.
ROCHESTER WAY
A2
Sherwood Prim. Sch.
Sparrow's Farm Leisure Cen.
Sports Ground
Playing Fields
Sidcup
HALFWAY STREET
Willersley Park
Marlborough Park
Marlborough Sch.
SIDCUP GOLF COURSE
Chatsworth Inf. Sch.
Lamorbey Adult Education Centre
Lamorbey
Lamorbey Park
The Barn Theatre
Chislehurst & Sidcup Grammar Sch.
The Glade
Comm. Cen.
Works
New Eltham
NEW ELTHAM
SIDCUP ROAD
A20
CRAY ROAD
A211
FOOTSCRAY ROAD
Dulverton Prim. Sch.
Wyncham Stream
Old Farm Park
FARM AVENUE
King George's Rec. Grd.
HURST ROAD
A222
Abbeyhill
Sidcup
STATION ROAD
Marlowe Ho.
Kings-Offs.
Baths
Club House
Birkbeck Prim. Sch.
WARING PARK
Rec. Grd.
LONGLANDS
World Of Golf At Sidcup
Pitch & Putt Course
Flamingo Park Sports Grd.
MAIN ROAD
SIDCUP BY-PASS
Ashen Grove
SIDCUP HIGH ST
44
45
46
72
73
74
75
76

97
G
H
J
K
L
M
1
2
3
4
5
6
7
8
9
81
98
113
48
49
50
DA7
DA6
DA5
DA14
BEXLEYHEATH
Bexleyheath
Bexley
BEXLEY
OLD BEXLEY
Bridgen
Blendon
Upton
A207 VIEW RD
CROOK LOG
BROADWAY
A207
WATLING
A220
GRAVEL HILL
BOURNE RD
ROCHESTER WAY
EAST
A2
ROCHESTER ROAD
A221 ROAD
DANSON ROAD
PENHILL RD.
A221
HURST ROAD
A222
BEXLEY ROAD
BLENDON B2210 RD
BRIDGEN RD.
PARKHILL B2210 ROAD
BOURNE A223
HIGH ST.
NORTH CRAY ROAD
A223
VICARAGE RD.
A2018
BUNKERS HILL
ALBION
MAYPLACE RD. W.
BROADWAY
DANSON PARK
The Boathouse
THE LAKE
The Mansion
DANSON INTERCHANGE
BLACK PRINCE INTERCHANGE
BEXLEYHEATH GOLF COURSE
Bexleyheath School
Playing Fields
Grammar Sch.
Upton Prim. Sch.
UPTON DAY HOSP.
Crook Log Jun. & Inf. Sch.
Westbrooke Sch.
Brampton Prim. Sch.
St. Thomas More R.C. Prim. Sch.
Bursted Wood Prim. Sch.
Bursted Wood
Russell Park
Civic Offices
Cinema
THE BROADWAY SHOP. CEN.
Gravel Hill Prim. Sch.
St. Catherine's Sch. for Girls
St. Columba's R.C. Boys Sch.
Martens Grove Park
Bexley Park Wood
Hurst Prim. Sch.
Old Bexley C.E. Prim. Sch.
Riverside Walk
River Shuttle
Cricket Ground
Upper College Farm
Albany Park
Royal Park Prim. Sch.
Playing Field
The Alders
Woollett Hall Farm
Sports Ground
Loring Hall
The Grove
Mount Mascal Farm
Home Close Farm
Keeper's Cottage
Pinewood Cottage
Sands Spinney
Little Mascal Farm
Bunkers Hill Pond Farm
Stable Meadow
Five Arch
North Cray Woods Nature Reserve
Cleeve Park Sch.
GATTONS PLANTATION
Rutland Shaw
Sidcup Cemy.
Welling United F.C.
Sports Grd.
Tennis Courts
Playground
Manor Ho.
Cemy.
Factory
Weir
Works
Nursery

98
A
B
C
D
E
F
1
2
3
4
5
6
7
8
9
82
97
114
50
51
52
76
75
74
73
72
Erith
DA8
DA7
DA6
DA5
DA2
Bexleyheath
Barnehurst
BARNEHURST
BARNEHURST GOLF COURSE
Mayplace (Club Ho.)
Recreation Ground
Slade Green
SLADE GREEN
Carriage Depot
The Grange
Crayford Creek Junction
Works
Refinery
Wharf
Crayford Creek
CENTURYAN PL.
CRAYSIDE INDUS. EST.
BEXLEY
Playing Field
BARNES CRAY
Dartford
Stanham
CRAYFORD
Crayford
Crayford Stadium (Greyhound)
Superstore
Sports Cen.
T.H.
Lib.
CRAYFORD IND. EST.
ACORN INDUSTRIAL ESTATE
TOWER RETAIL PK.
THE BOURNE INDUSTRIAL PARK
THE GREYHOUND COMMERCIAL CEN.
SHENSTONE PARK
Gas Works
Bigs Hill Wood
Martens Grove Park
Martens Grove
Mayplace Prim. Sch.
Youth Cen.
Manor House (Adult Ed. Cen.)
Rose Cott.
Spts. Grd.
Bowl. Grn.
Play. Fld.
Tennis Courts
Prim. Sch.
St. Catherine's Sch. for Girls
St. Columba's R.C. Boys Sch.
Bursted Wood Prim. Sch.
Bursted Wood
Hall Place & Visitor Cen.
Mus.
Weir
BLACK PRINCE INTERCHANGE
Hall Place Gardens
SPORTS FIELD
Pumping Station
The Old Orchard
Sports Ground
Rec. Grd.
Subway
Bexley
Churchfield Wood
OLD BEXLEY
Cemy.
COLDBLOW
MAYPOLE
BOWMANS
Playing Field
DARTFORD HEATH
Dartford Heath
Leyton Cross
Heath Side
THE BRACTON CENTRE
Bowling Green
Playing Fields
Cavey's Spring
Tennis Court
Nursery
Turnagain Farm
Turnagain Croft
Wilmington Hall Sch.
Wilmington Grammar Sch. for Boys
Grammar Sch. for Girls
Wilmington Common
Playing Field
Hook Green Farm
Hook Green
Joydens Wood Jun. Sch.
JOYDENS WOOD
JOYDENS WOOD (Nature Reserve)
Sands Spinney
Club Ho.
Howbury Farm
Football Grd.
Brick Works
WATLING ST.
A207
LONDON ROAD
(WATLING ST.)
CRAYFORD RD.
DARTFORD RD.
A226
BOURNE ROAD
A223
ROCHESTER WAY
A2
DARTFORD
A2018
OLD BEXLEY LA.
SHEPHERD'S LANE
PRINCES ROAD
B2174
THAMES ROAD
A206
NORTHEND ROAD
PERRY STREET
A2000
CRAYFORD HIGH ST.
CRAYFORD WAY
MAIDEN LANE
B2186
MAYPLACE ROAD EAST
MAYPLACE AVENUE
BARNEHURST ROAD
ERITH ROAD
VICARAGE RD.
DARTFORD RD.
TILE KILN LANE
OAKFIELD LANE
HEATH LANE
COMMON LANE
PARSONS LA.
HOOK GREEN LANE
BROAD LA.
BIRCHWOOD ROAD
LEYTON CROSS RD.
BALDWYNS PARK
DYKEWOOD CL.
CASTLETON AVENUE
EVERSLEY AVENUE
PARKSIDE AVENUE
NORTHUMBERLAND
STATION RD.
LOWER STATION RD.
IRON MILL LANE

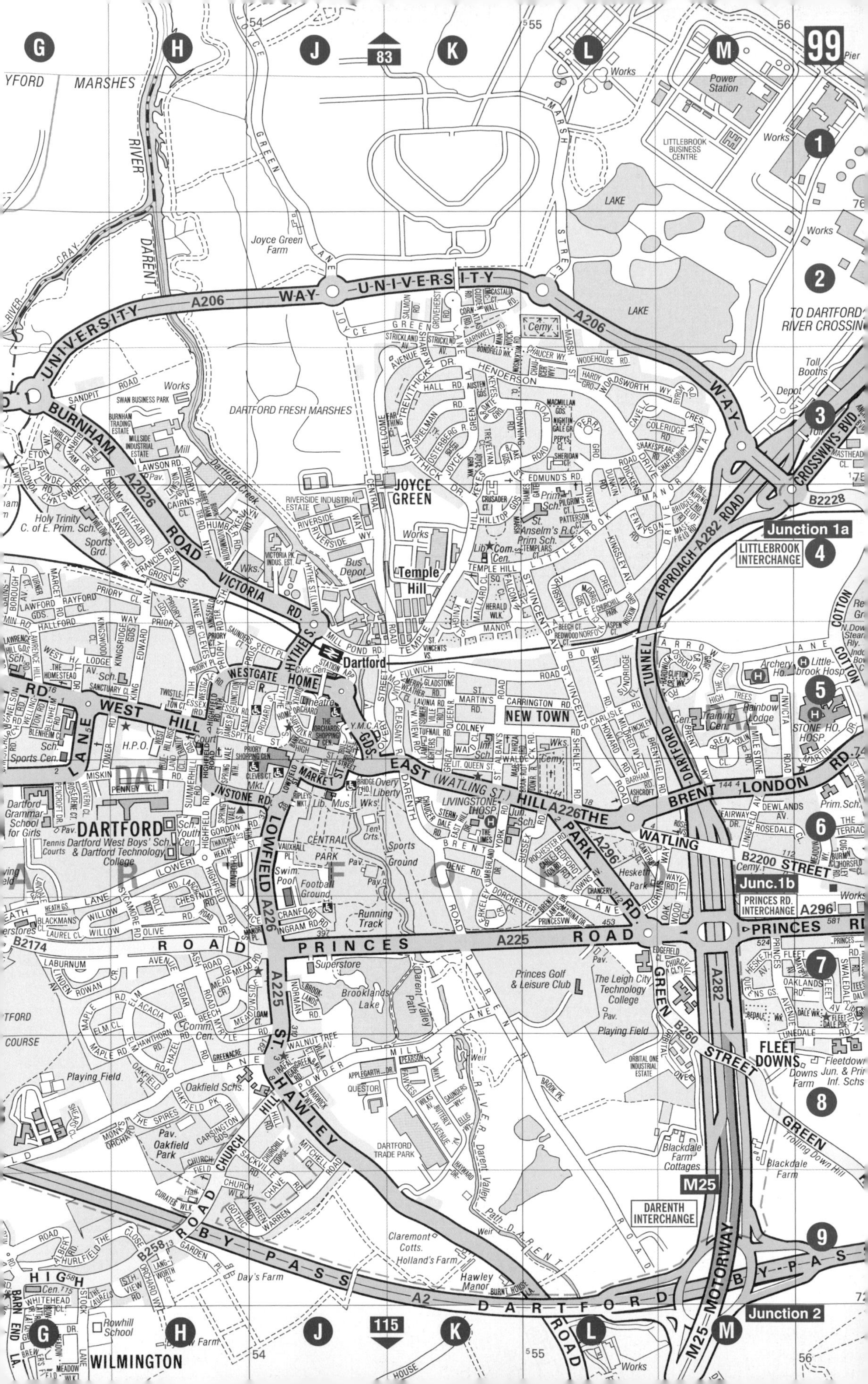
83
MARSHES
RIVER DARENT
JOYCE GREEN LANE
Joyce Green Farm
Power Station
LITTLEBROOK BUSINESS CENTRE
Works
LAKE
TO DARTFORD RIVER CROSSING
Toll Booths
Depot
UNIVERSITY WAY
A206
DARTFORD FRESH MARSHES
SWAN BUSINESS PARK
BURNHAM ROAD
A2026
Holy Trinity C. of E. Prim. Sch.
JOYCE GREEN
Temple Hill
RIVERSIDE INDUSTRIAL ESTATE
Bus Depot
VICTORIA RD.
St. Anselm's R.C. Prim Sch.
APPROACH A282 ROAD
B2228
Junction 1a
LITTLEBROOK INTERCHANGE
CROSSWAYS BVD.
Dartford
WEST HILL
HOME GDS.
THE ORCHARDS SHOPPING CEN.
PRIORY SHOPPING CEN.
EAST (WATLING ST.) HILL
A226
NEW TOWN
MARKET ST.
DA1
DARTFORD
Dartford Grammar School for Girls
Dartford West Boys' Sch. & Dartford Technology College
LOWFIELD A226
CENTRAL PARK
Sports Ground
Football Ground
Swim. Pool
Running Track
LIVINGSTONE HOSP.
THE BRENT
LONDON RD.
WATLING B2200 STREET
Junc. 1b
PRINCES RD. INTERCHANGE
A296
DARTFORD TUNNEL
Little-brook Hosp.
STONE HO. HOSP.
Hesketh Park
PRINCES ROAD
A225
B2174
Superstore
Brooklands Lake
Darent Valley Path
Princes Golf & Leisure Club
The Leigh City Technology College
Playing Field
GREEN B260 STREET
FLEET DOWNS
Fleetdown Jun. & Prim. Inf. Schs
A282
ORBITAL ONE INDUSTRIAL ESTATE
ST. HAWLEY ROAD
DARTFORD TRADE PARK
Oakfield Schs.
Oakfield Park
Playing Field
CHURCH ROAD
M25
DARENTH INTERCHANGE
Blackdale Farm Cottages
Blackdale Farm
Trolling Down Hill
Claremont Cotts.
Holland's Farm
Hawley Manor
Day's Farm
BY-PASS
A2
DARTFORD
Junction 2
M25 MOTORWAY
B258
HIGH ST.
Rowhill School
WILMINGTON
115

Bedfont Lakes Country Park
LOWER FELTHAM
CHATTERN HILL
FELTHAM
ASHFORD ROAD
CHERTSEY ROAD
A244
HOUNSLOW
Feltham
FELTHAMHILL
Ashford
ASHFORD COMMON
SUNBURY COMMON
Littleton Common
STAINES ROAD WEST
A308
TW15
SCHOOL ROAD JUNCTION
Junc.1
M3
SUNBURY CROSS
Sunbury
QUEEN MARY RESERVOIR
WINDMILL ROAD
Upper Halliford
M3 MOTORWAY
CHARLTON
Sunbury-on-Thames
TW16
SUNBURY
SPELTHORNE
Shepperton
HAZELWOOD GOLF CENTRE
SUNBURY GOLF COURSE
UPPER HALLIFORD
TW17
UPPER HALLIFORD BY-PASS
Shepperton
Elmbridge Leisure Centre

84
116

101
HANWORTH PARK
Fulwell Park
TWICKENHAM GOLF COURSE
FULWELL GOLF COURSE
HAMPTON HILL
Hounslow College
HANWORTH
Rectory Meadow
HOUNSLOW RD.
A316
A314
GREAT WEST
TWICKENHAM RD
APEX CORNER
HAMPTON RD. EAST
UXBRIDGE
A312
PARK RD
A313
Longford River
Superstore
Playing Field
Hampton Community College
Hampton School
Lady Eleanor Holles Sch.
TW13
The Linden Bennett Sch.
Reservoir
Sports Hall
Comm. Cen.
TW12
RICHMOND
UPON
THAMES
Clarendon Sch.
Reservoirs Aqueduct
Football Ground
Half Moon Covert
Hatherop Park
Carlisle Park
KEMPTON PARK RACECOURSE
Kempton Park
Football Ground
Oldfield Works
HAMPTON
Hampton
Hampton & Richmond Borough F.C.
KINGSWAY BUSINESS PARK
Hydes Field
Portlane Bridge
St. Mary's Lodge
102
EAST UPPER A308 SUNBURY ROAD
THAMES
Water Works
Grand Junction Reservoir
Filter Beds
Stain Hill West Reservoir
Stain Hill East Reservoir
Portlane Brook
Kenton Court Meadow
Sunbury Court
Hurst Park Open Space
Garrick's Ait
Platt's Eyot
Grand Junction Isle
RIVER THAMES
Sunnyside Reservoir
Sunbury Court Island
Rivermead Island
RESERVOIR
Reservoir
A3050
Recreation Ground
Cemetery
Church Farm
Mole Hall
WEST MOLESEY
West Molesey
Molesey F.C.
BESSBOROUGH RESERVOIR
KNIGHTS RESERVOIR
Walton-on-Thames
ELMBRIDGE
Apps Court Farm
The Cottage
KT12
KT8
Primary Sch.
Playing Field
MOLESEY HOSP.
WALTON B369
QUEEN ELIZABETH II RESERVOIR
Molesey Pony Farm
Pumping Station
Nielson Playing Field
117
G
H
J
K
L
M
1
2
3
4
5
6
7
8
9
12
13
14

FULWELL GOLF COURSE
Fulwell
HAMPTON HILL
TEDDINGTON
STRAWBERRY HILL
Hampton
TW12
TW11
BUSHY PARK
RICHMOND upon THAMES
Bushy House
National Physical Laboratory
Teddington Lock
Hampton Court Palace
HAMPTON COURT
HURST PARK
EAST MOLESEY
ELMBRIDGE
KT8
East Molesey
HAMPTON
The Long Water
HOME PARK GOLF COURSE
Thames Ditton
KT7
THAMES DITTON
Diana Fountain
Deer Pen
The Royal Paddocks
Stud House
86
101
118

G
H
J
K
L
M
87
104
119
1
2
3
4
5
6
7
8
9
HAM
Ham Bottom
Ham Cross Plantation
Peg's Pond
Thomson's Pond
Ham Cross
ISABELLA PLANTATION
HAM GATE B352 AVENUE
Ham Gate
Richmond
COMMON
Ham Dip
High Wood
Still Pond
Deer Fold
RICHMOND PARK
Coronation Plantation
The Flat
Dann's Pond
Coronation Plantation
Gallows Pond
King's Clump
(Open during daylight hours only)
Ladderstile Gate
THE CASSEL HOSP.
TW10
RICHMOND ROAD
A307
UPPER HAM RD.
Latchmere House
The Tiffin Girls' Sch.
Fernhill Prim. Sch.
Sports Grd.
Trowlock Island
Teddington Sch. & Sports Cen.
Recreation Ground
RIVER THAMES
Conifers
The Avenue Centre (Coll)
Steven's Eyot
Canbury Gardens
Kingston upon Thames
Sports Ground
R.C. Prim. Sch.
QUEENS B35 ROAD
Kingston Gate
KINGSTON ROAD
A308
COOMBE GOLF C
COOMBE WOOD GOLF COURSE
Holy Cross Preparatory R.C. Sch.
KINGSTON HOSPITAL
Park Hill Sch.
Hampton Wick
KT2
COOMBE ROAD
A238
Norbiton
NORBITON
Kingston
CROMWELL R.
LONDON A308 ROAD
CAMBRIDGE A2043 ROAD
KINGSTON ROAD
Tiffin Sch.
The Bentalls Centre
FAIRFIELD N.
The Fairfield Sch.
Recreation Ground
KINGSTON UPON THAMES
War Mem.
Kingston Cemetery
Kingston upon Thames Crematorium
Running Track
Kingstonian Football Club (Kingsmeadow)
New Malden
KT3
Sewage Works
Hogsmill River
Waste Disposal Centre
The Wilderness
Parkfield
County Hall
Kingston Univ.
KINGSTON upon THAMES
PENRHYN A240 RD.
SURBITON RD.
A307
PORTSMOUTH ROAD
KT5
Surbiton Cemetery
Berrylands
Recreation Ground
Surbiton
KT6
BERRYLANDS
CLAREMONT RD.
EWELL RD.
BRIGHTON RD.
Raven's Ait
Halls of Residence
Seething Wells

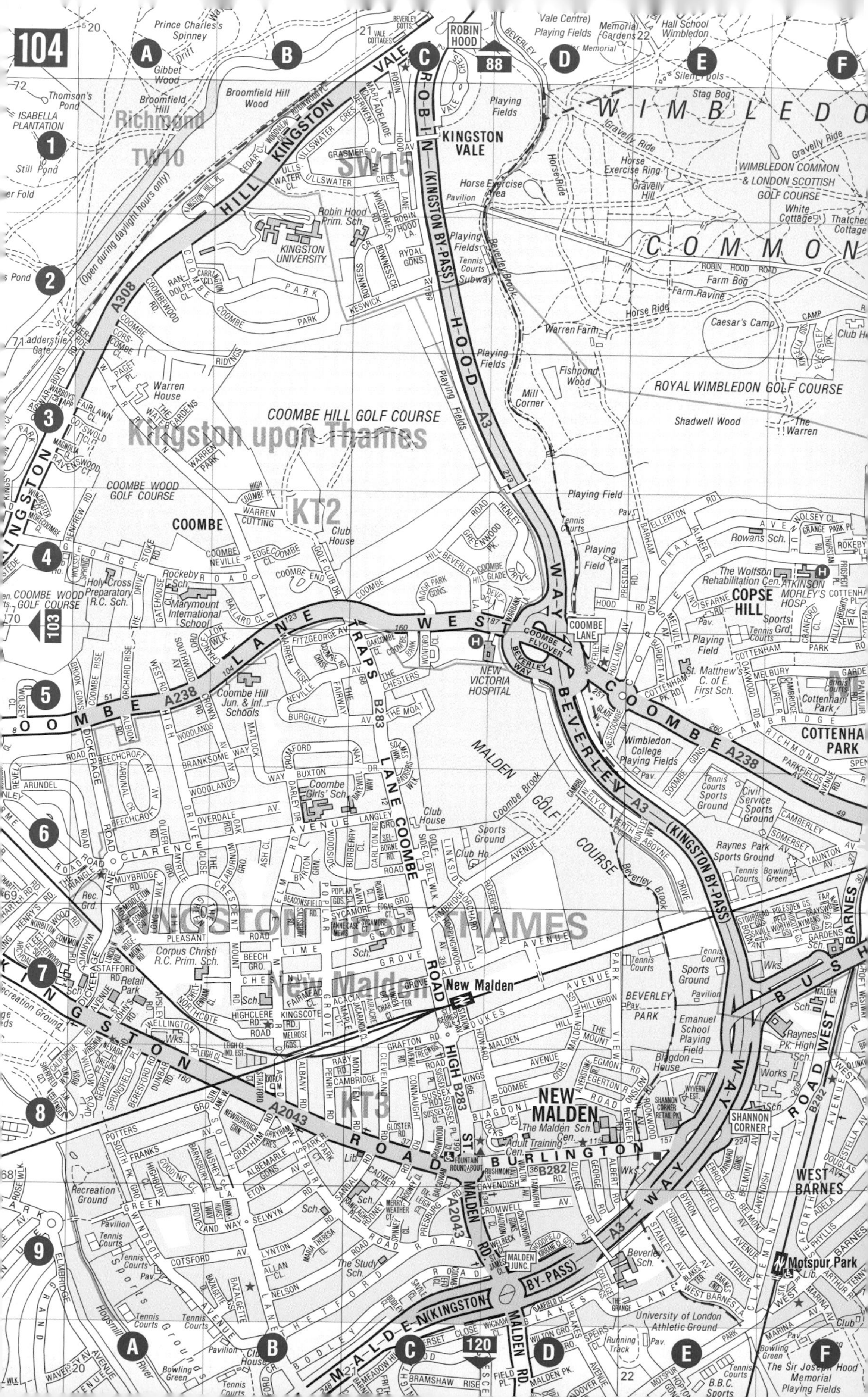

Prince Charles's Spinney
Gibbet Wood
Thomson's Pond
ISABELLA PLANTATION
Broomfield Hill
Broomfield Hill Wood
Richmond
TW10
Still Pond
ROBIN HOOD
88
Vale Centre
Playing Fields
Memorial Gardens
Hall School Wimbledon
Silent Pools
Stag Bog
WIMBLEDON
KINGSTON VALE
SW15
KINGSTON HILL
KINGSTON VALE
ROBIN HOOD WAY
(KINGSTON BY-PASS)
A3
(Open during daylight hours only)
Robin Hood Prim. Sch.
KINGSTON UNIVERSITY
COOMBE PARK
Horse Exercise Area
Pavilion
Playing Fields
Tennis Courts
Subway
Beverley Brook
Gravelly Ride
Horse Exercise Ring
Gravelly Hill
WIMBLEDON COMMON & LONDON SCOTTISH GOLF COURSE
White Cottage
Thatched Cottage
COMMON
ROBIN HOOD ROAD
Farm Bog
Farm Ravine
Horse Ride
Caesar's Camp
Warren Farm
Club Ho.
A308
Ladderstile Gate
Warren House
Fishpond Wood
Mill Corner
ROYAL WIMBLEDON GOLF COURSE
Shadwell Wood
The Warren
COOMBE HILL GOLF COURSE
Kingston upon Thames
COOMBE WOOD GOLF COURSE
COOMBE
KT2
Club House
Playing Field
Tennis Courts
Rowans Sch.
The Wolfson Rehabilitation Cen.
ATKINSON MORLEY'S HOSP.
COPSE HILL
Holy Cross Preparatory R.C. Sch.
Rockeby Sch.
Marymount International School
COOMBE WOOD GOLF COURSE
103
COOMBE LANE WEST
A238
TRAPS LANE
B283
NEW VICTORIA HOSPITAL
COOMBE LANE FLYOVER
COOMBE LANE
BEVERLEY WAY
Sports Grd.
St. Matthew's C. of E. First Sch.
Cottenham Park
COTTENHAM PARK
Coombe Hill Jun. & Inf. Schools
Wimbledon College Playing Fields
MALDEN GOLF COURSE
Coombe Brook
Coombe Girls' Sch.
Club House
Sports Ground
Club Ho.
Tennis Courts Sports Ground
Civil Service Sports Ground
Raynes Park Sports Ground
Tennis Courts
Bowling Green
COOMBE ROAD
KINGSTON upon THAMES
Rec. Grd.
Corpus Christi R.C. Prim. Sch.
Retail Park
New Malden
Tennis Courts
Sports Ground
Pavilion
BEVERLEY PARK
Emanuel School Playing Field
Blagdon House
Raynes Pk. High Sch.
Works
BUSHEY ROAD
WEST BARNES ROAD
KINGSTON ROAD
A2043
KT3
HIGH ST. B283
NEW MALDEN
The Malden Sch.
Adult Training Cen.
BURLINGTON RD.
B282
SHANNON CORNER RETAIL PK.
SHANNON CORNER
WEST BARNES
Recreation Ground
Pavilion
Tennis Courts
Sports Ground
The Study Sch.
MALDEN RD.
MALDEN JUNC.
Beverley Sch.
MALDEN WAY
(KINGSTON BY-PASS)
Motspur Park
University of London Athletic Ground
Running Track
120
Hogsmill River
Tennis Courts
Bowling Green
Club House
Tennis Courts
B.B.C. Sports
The Sir Joseph Hood Memorial Playing Fields

105
G
H
J
K
L
M
89
121
106
1
2
3
4
5
6
7
8
9
Wimbledon Park
Aorangi Park
WIMBLEDON All England Lawn Tennis & Croquet Club
WIMBLEDON PARK GOLF COURSE
SUMMERSTOWN
Wimbledon Cemetery
PARKSIDE
A219
HIGH ST
WIMBLEDON HILL RD.
ALEXANDRA RD.
THE BROADWAY
HARTFIELD RD.
DURNSFORD ROAD
A218
HAYDONS ROAD
PLOUGH ROAD
GAP ROAD
B235
WIMBLEDON
SW19
SOUTH WIMBLEDON
Wimbledon
South Wimbledon
MERTON HIGH ST.
MERTON
MORDEN ROAD
A24
KINGSTON ROAD
A238
WORPLE RD.
Wimbledon Chase
WOODHAYES RD.
CANNIZARO RD.
Cannizaro Park
Rushmere Pond
Wimbledon Coll.
Ursuline Convent Prep. Sch.
King's Coll. Sch.
Dundonald Rd.
Dundonald Recreation Ground
Merton Park
MERTON PARK
NELSON HOSP.
John Innes Park
Morden Rd.
Morden
Morden Hall
MARTIN WAY
South Merton
B286
CANNON HILL COMMON (Recreation Ground)
Cannon Hill
Joseph Hood Recreation Ground
Messines Playing Field
PRINCE GEORGE'S PLAYING FIELD
BUSHEY MEAD
David Lloyd Centre
A298
Raynes Park
Raynes Park Playing Fields
Morden
MORDEN
Morden South
SM4
LONDON RD.
CENTRAL ROAD
A239
MORDEN HALL RD.
Civic Cen.
Merton College
Morden Park School Sports Centre
School Playing Fields
MORDEN PARK
Swimming Baths
Recreation Grd.
Risley Sports Ground
Old Blues Rugby Football Grd.
Hatfield First Sch.
Croydon Tramlink
River Wandle

A
B
C
D
E
F
1
2
3
4
5
6
7
8
9
90
105
122
SUMMERSTOWN
Wimbledon Stadium (Greyhound)
STREATHAM CEMETERY
UPPER TOOTING
WANDSWORTH
Tooting Graveney Common
Tooting Broadway
ST. GEORGE'S HOSPITAL
TOOTING
LAMBETH CEMETERY
Haydons Road
Wandle Meadow Nature Park
TOOTING GRAVENEY
FURZEDOWN
SW17
Tooting
Colliers Wood
COLLIER'S WOOD
MERTON HIGH STREET
MERANTUN WAY
Superstore
TANDEM CENTRE RETAIL PARK
WESTERN ROAD
LONDON RD.
STREATHAM ROAD
Lonesome
MERTON
SW19
Eastfields High Sch.
Mitcham
MITCHAM
MORDEN HALL PARK
Phipps Bridge
Morden Hall
Morden Cottage
Morden Lodge
Ravensbury Park
Cricket Green
The Canons Leisure Cen. & Lib.
CR4
MITCHAM GOLF COURSE
Mitcham Junction
Morden
SM4
Bishopsford Comm.
Watermeads
Bennett's Hole
Bishopsford House
THE WILLOW BUSINESS CENTRE
River Wandle
Croydon Tramlink
CROYDON RD.
CARSHALTON RD.
CENTRAL ROAD
ST. HELIER AVENUE
BISHOPSFORD ROAD
LONDON ROAD
MORDEN ROAD
CRANMER RD.
COMMONSIDE WEST
A217
A24
A218
A236
A239
A297
A216
A237
B241
B235

G
H
J
K
L
M
91
108
123
1
2
3
4
5
6
7
8
9
STREATHAM
STREATHAM PARK
STREATHAM VALE
STREATHAM COMMON
Streatham
Streatham Common
LAMBETH
CROYDON
SW16
SE27
SE19
CR7
NORBURY
Norbury
NORBURY PARK
THORNTON HEATH
Thornton Heath
West Norwood
TOOTING BEC COMMON
Swimming Pool
STREATHAM HIGH RD.
STREATHAM COMMON NORTH
CROWN LA.
LONDON ROAD
MITCHAM ROAD
BRIGSTOCK
Norwood Grove Recreation Ground
Norbury Manor Girls High Sch.
Kensington Avenue Jun. & Inf. Schs.
Tamworth Manor High Sch.
William Morris Middle Sch.
Croydon Crematorium
CROYDON CEMETERY
MAYDAY UNIVERSITY HOSP.
Biggin Wood
Sports Ground
Powerleague Soccer Centre
Stanford Middle Sch.
Rowan High Sch.
Jewish Cemetery
Mill House
Playing Fields
THORNTON HEATH POND
A23
A214
A215
A216
A236
B242
B266
B272
B273

A
B
C
D
E
F
1
2
3
4
5
6
7
8
9
92
107
124
West Norwood Cemetery & Crematorium
West Norwood
WEST NORWOOD
SOUTHWARK
LAMBETH
UPPER SYDENHAM
Sydenham Wells Park
Sydenham Hill
Gipsy Hill
Kingswood Estate
DULWICH WD.
COLLEGE RD.
WESTWOOD HILL
CRYSTAL PALACE PARK
CRYSTAL PALACE PARADE
Crystal Palace Museum
NATIONAL SPORTS CENTRE
Sports Arena
Crystal Palace
T.V. Transmitter
Intermediate Lake
Lower Lake
Penge Entrance
Sydenham Entrance
Anerley Entrance
Rockhills Entrance Camping Site
CROWN DALE
CENTRAL HILL
NORWOOD PARK RD.
NORWOOD NEW TOWN
Convent Wood
Virgo Fidelis Convent Sch.
St. Joseph's R.C. Jun. & Inf. Schs.
Rockmount Prim. Sch.
WESTOW HILL
ANERLEY HILL
ANERLEY RD.
CHURCH RD.
SE19
NORWOOD
Westow Park
Recreation Ground
Westwood High Sch.
Downsview Prim. Sch.
UPPER NORWOOD
BEULAH HILL
SOUTH NORWOOD HILL
Harris City Technology Coll.
Beaulieu Heights
T.V. Station
Cypress Inf. Sch.
Cypress Jun. Sch.
South Norwood Lake
Athletic Grounds
Playing Field
Anerley Prim. Sch.
Orchard School Sports Centre
Nursing Home
ANERLEY
SE20
David Livingstone Prim. Sch.
CROYDON
Spurgeon's College
Grangewood Recreation Ground
Thornton Heath
CR7
THORNTON HEATH
BRIGSTOCK RD.
WHITEHORSE RD.
WHITEHORSE LANE
Crystal Palace F.C. & Wimbledon F.C. (Selhurst Park)
SE25
SOUTH NORWOOD
Norwood Junc.
Bromley Junction
PENGE RD.
CROYDON RD.
PORTLAND RD.
ST. GRANGE
Ecclesbourne Jun. & Inf. Schs.
Bensham Manor Sch.
St. Chad's R.C. Prim. Sch.
Heavers Farm Prim. Sch.
Adult Training Centre
Recreation Ground
Selhurst
SELHURST
SELHURST RD.
Depot
WOODSIDE
Croydon
Queen's Rd. Cemetery

BELL GREEN
BELLINGHAM
LWR. SYDENHAM
Sydenham
SYDENHAM
Mayow Park
SYDENHAM ROAD
A212
SOUTHEND LA.
A2218
Lower Sydenham
Southend Park
Beckenham Hill
BECKENHAM HILL ROAD
Stumpshill Wood
BECKENHAM PLACE PARK
GOLF COURSE
Beckenham Place Club House
Penge East
NEWLANDS PARK
A213
Alexandra Rec. Grd.
NEW BECKENHAM
New Beckenham
CATOR PARK
PENGE
A234
Kent House
Beckenham Road
Clock House
BECKENHAM
Beckenham Junc.
A2015
SOUTHEND ROAD
MANOR RD.
BROMLEY RD.
BECKENHAM HOSPITAL
Avenue Road
Birkbeck
Beckenham Crematorium
ELMERS END
Elmers End
A214
A222
Kelsey Park
Crease Park
Elgood Playing Field
PARK LANGLEY
Langley Court (Research Labs)
EDEN PARK
Eden Park
SOUTH EDEN PARK ROAD
B230
SOUTH NORWOOD COUNTRY PARK
Croydon Tramlink
Croydon Golf Driving Range
LONG LANE
A222
UPPER ELMERS END
Langley Park Schools
93
110
125
G H J K L M
1 2 3 4 5 6 7 8 9

SOUTHEND
LEWISHAM
DOWNHAM
Churchdown Christian Centre
Downham Fields
Beckenham Hill
Recreation Ground
Ash Plantation
Beckenham Place Club House
BECKENHAM PLACE PARK
GOLF COURSE
The Cottage
Summerhouse Hill Wood
Ravensbourne
BECKENHAM
Beckenham
BR3
Sports Ground
Playing Fields
Shaftesbury Park
Bromley Hill Cemy.
PLAISTOW
Sundridge Park
BR1
Bromley
Bromley Nth.
SHORTLANDS GOLF COURSE
BROMLEY PARK
THE SLOANE HOSP.
Bishop Challoner Sch.
Shortlands
Martin's Hill
Queen's Mead
BROMLEY
Leisure Cen.
Bromley Civic Centre
Bromley South
SHORTLANDS
PARK LANGLEY
BR2
BR4
South Hill Wood
Langley Court (Research Labs)
Langley Park Schools
Bromley F.C. Ground
Hayesford
Playing Field
Cricket Ground
Grove Park
CHINBROOK
King's Meadow Playing Grd.
Hall's Farm
BROMLEY ROAD
LONDON ROAD
BROMLEY HILL A2015
BECKENHAM LANE
WESTMORELAND ROAD
HAYES LANE
BURNT ASH LANE
COLLEGE RD. A2212
WIDMORE RD.
KENTISH WAY
MASONS HILL
A21
A222
B228
B251
B2212
B265
94
126
109
39
40
38

G
H
J
K
L
M
95
SE12
SE9
Lower Marvels Wood
Marvels Wood
Grove Park Cemetery
Castlecombe Prim. Sch.
ELMSTEAD WOOD
Sports Ground
New Farningham House
ELMSTEAD
Ravensbourne College
Garden Wood
SUNDRIDGE
Training Centre
High Grove
Sundridge Park Mansion
Botany Bay
Elmstead Woods
Rockpit Wood
SUNDRIDGE PARK
GOLF COURSE
Kyd Brook
Sira Institute
Chislehurst
CHISLEHURST WEST
Red Hill Prim. Sch.
Whyte's Woodland
Bird Sanctuary
Edgebury Prim. Sch.
CHISLEHURST
CAMDEN PARK
CHISLEHURST GOLF COURSE
Camden Place (Golf Club)
CHISLEHURST COMMON
BR7
112
Sundridge Park
Netball Courts
Bullers Wood Sch.
Widmore Green
Cricket Ground
Caves
Chalkpit Wood
Chislehurst
Bansome Wood
Rifle Range
Hawkwood Nursery
Birch Wood
Gosshill Wood
Avalon
Pond Wood
Hawkwood Farm
BICKLEY
Hadlow
Bickley Junc.
Bickley
WIDMORE
Playing Field
Gas Works
The Widmore Cen.
School
Chislehurst Junction
BR5
Great Thrift
Aquila (Ministry of Defence)
Blackbrook Wood
Bromley High School
JUBILEE COUNTRY PARK
Cycleway
Petts Wood Junction
Thornet Wood
Sydney Shaw
Recreation Ground
Sports Club
Whitehall Pleasure Ground
St. James' RC Prim. Sch.
Southborough Prim. Sch.
Southborough Open Space (Rec. Grd.)
127
A222
A208
A21
B264
B263
B265
BROMLEY COMMON
BICKLEY PARK ROAD
CHISLEHURST ROAD
WHITE HORSE HILL
SUMMER HILL
PRINCE IMPERIAL ROAD

112
A
B
C
D
E
F
1
2
3
4
5
6
7
8
9
96
111
128
44
45
46
72
71
70
69
68
LONGLANDS
World Of Golf) At Sidcup
Pitch & Putt Course
SIDCUP BY-PASS
A20
MAIN ROAD
A211
SIDCUP
Sports Ground
SIDCUP HIGH ST.
STATION RD.
ELM RD.
CHISLEHURST RD.
A222
A2001
Sidcup Green
Sidcup Place Park
QUEEN MARY'S HOSPITAL
FROGNAL
Frognal Ho.
Chestnut Ho.
Wall Ho.
FROGNAL CORNER
Spring Shaw
Ashen Grove
Kemnal Manor
Partridge Shaw
Esporta Health Club
Beavers Wood
Chislehurst Cemetery
Hoblands Wood
St. Mary & St. Joseph's Catholic Sch.
Playing Field
Garden Centre
Sports Ground
Old Elthamians Sports Club
Beaverwood Sch. for Girls
Athletic Ground
PERRY STREET
A222
Chislehurst
Edgebury Prim. Sch.
Foxbury
Lodge
Darul Uloom London Islamic Sch.
Westerland
Selwood
Mead Rd. Inf. Sch.
CHISLEHURST
CHISLEHURST COMMON
CENTRE COMN. RD.
A208
BROMLEY RD.
BROMLEY LANE
PERRY LANE
ROYAL PDE.
Farringtons & Stratford House
Icehouse Wood
Bank's Shaw
Square Clump
Bushy Clump
SCADBURY PARK WOOD NATURE RESERVE
Little Wood
Irish Plantation
Moat
Archway
PARK WOOD
Nature Reserve
Drive
Midfield Prim. Sch.
Youth Club
Playing Field
Kemnal Te College
Superstore
WATTS LA.
B264
MANOR PARK RD.
Coopers Sch.
Playing Field
Bansome Wood
Rifle Range
Hawkwood Nursery
Pond Wood
BR7
Hawkwood Estate
Hawkwood Farm
Tongs Farm
Walk Wood
ST. PAUL'S CRAY ROAD
A208
Hadresham
The Fantails
Holbrook Wood Lodge
Peasons
The Larches
The Gorse Children's Home
St. Peter & St. Paul RC Prim. Sch.
Playing Field
Mem.
St. Paul's Cray Common
Hoblingwell Wood
Brackenwood
ST. PAUL'S CRAY
Recreation Ground
Fairmile Ho.
Sports Cen.
Lib.
Leesons Prim. Sch.
Orpington
Factories
Warehouse
ORPINGTON RD.
PETTS WOOD
Edlmann Memorial Wood
Willett Memorial Wood
Meml.
Chislehurst Junction
Great Thrift
St. Mary Cray Junction
St. Mary Cray
JUBILEE COUNTRY PARK
Petts Wood Junction
Sydney Shaw
Cycleway
PETTS WOOD
Pav.
Rec. Grd.
Tennis Courts
Hall
Liby.
Petts Wood
POVEREST
Poverest Prim. Sch.
POVEREST RD.
CHISLEHURST RD.
A208
RAVENSQUAY BUSINESS CENTRE
Scout Halls
Covet Wood
Recreation

G
H
J
K
L
M
97
48
49
550
The Alders
Bunkers Hill
Little Mascal Farm
Cleeve Park Sch.
North Cray Woods Nature Reserve
Stable Meadow
Five Arch Bri.
Playing Field
Pond Farm
Home Wood
Hall
GATTONS PLANTATION
JOYDENS WOOD (Nature Reserve)
Dower House
Foots Cray Place
FOOTS CRAY MEADOWS
Gattons Wood
Nursy.
Nurseries
Bexley
DA5
NORTH CRAY
Manor Cotts.
Nature Trail (Starting Point)
Manor Farm
Picnic Site
North Cray Poultry Farm
Sidcup
David Lloyd Centre
Sports Ground
St. Peter Chanel R.C. Prim. Sch.
Bowling Green
Sidcup Technical Centre
Prim. Sch.
CHALK WOOD
DA14
FOOTS CRAY
Works
Factory
BIRCHWOOD PARK Club House GOLF COURSE
STONEHILL WOODS PARK
LEFA BUS. & IND EST.
RUXLEY CORNER IND. ESTATE
CRICHTON HO.
Superstore
RUXLEY
RUXLEY WOOD
CRITTALLS CORNER
Ruxley Manor Garden Centre
Upper Ruxley
Caravan Site
BY-PASS
A20
B2173
114
Grays Farm Cottages
Bromley Ski Centre
Sports Club
RUXLEY PARK GOLF COURSE
Driving Range
Club Ho.
Cookham Farm Cottage
CRAYFIELDS BUSINESS PARK
Home Farm Cotts.
Home Farm
Sports Ground
Playing Field
Club House
CRAY VALLEY GOLF COURSE
Burnt House Farm
CRAYFIELD INDUSTRIAL PARK
Garland Hill
The Lodge
Hockenden Lodge
Quoyne Cotts.
Pilgrim Manor
The Gardens
Barnfield Bank
Lower Hockenden Farm
Wycoombe
Vinsons Cotts.
Holly Cottage
Chestnut Cottage
HOCKENDEN
The Small House
Simon's Field Shaw
Hockenden House
PAULS CRAY HILL PARK
Swanley
SPRINGVALE RETAIL PARK
Hogspring Cotts.
Highlands Wood
HOCKENDEN WOOD
Milewood
BOURNE WOOD
Windmill Hill Wo
BR8
Cemetery
Hook Spring
Tile Kilns Wood
Sheepcote Farm
The Warren
Nature Reserve
Manor Oak Primary Sch.
Child's Wood
Kevington Hall
B258
129
DERRY DOWNS
KEVINGTOWN
Kevington Farm
Waldens Farm
Crouch Farm
1
2
3
4
5
6
7
8
9
72
71
170
69
68

Joydens Wood (Nature Reserve)
Bexley
Joydens Wood
DA5
Puddledock
Birchwood Park Golf Course
Stonehill Green
DA14
Hook Green
Hextable
Hextable Park
Swanley Village
Swanley
BR8
Swanley Park
Birchwood Corner
Crockenhill
Junction 3 (M25)
Swanley Interchange
Pedham Place Ind. Est.
The Olympic Golf & Leisure Centre
Wilmington Grammar Sch. for Boys
Rowhill Wood
Rowhill Grange
Hazelwood
Windmill Hill Wood
Tile Kilns Wood
Broom Hill

98
113
130

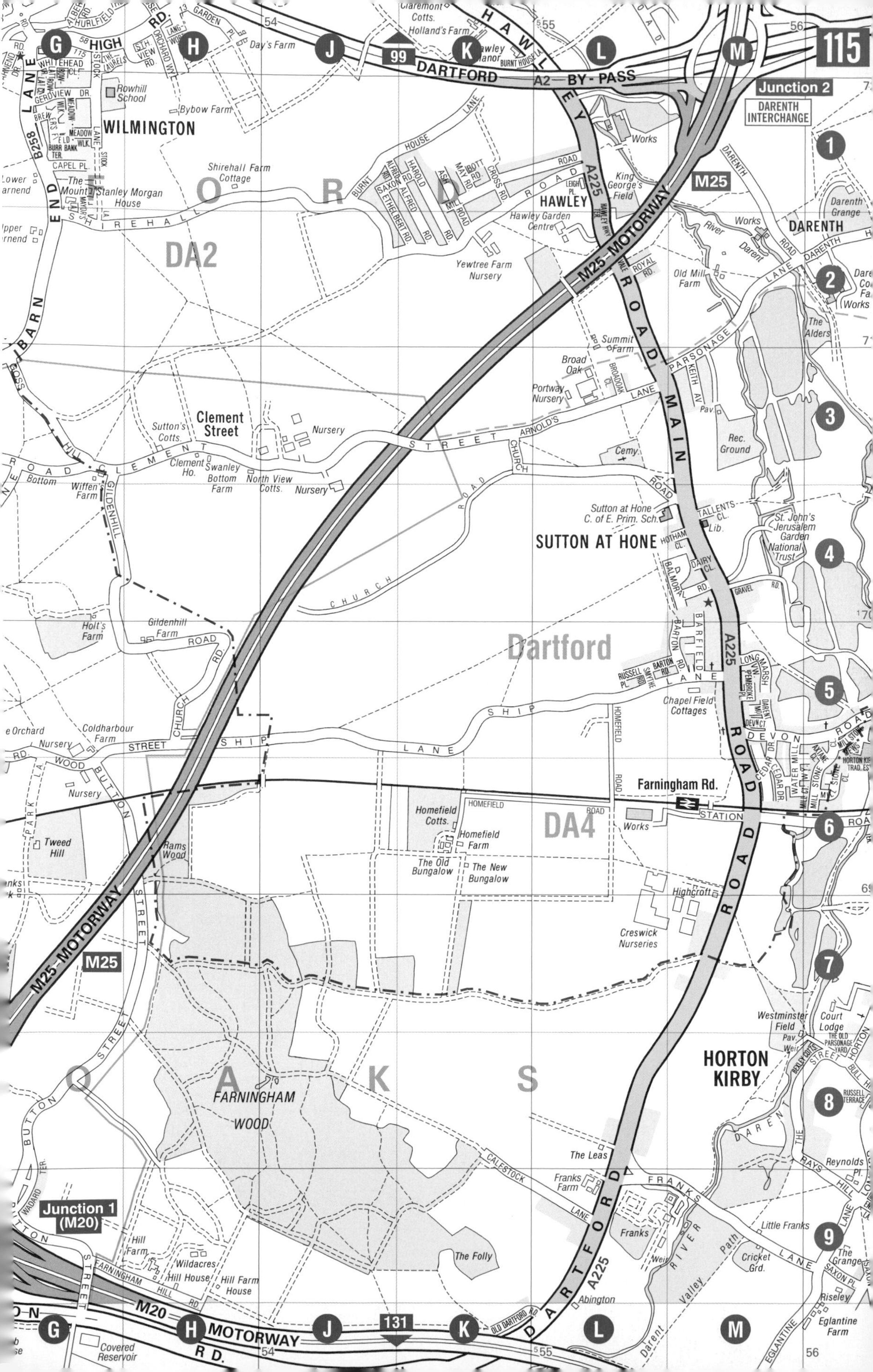
WILMINGTON
HAWLEY
DARENTH
SUTTON AT HONE
HORTON KIRBY
Clement Street
Dartford
DA2
DA4
Junction 2
DARENTH INTERCHANGE
Junction 1 (M20)
M25 MOTORWAY
DARTFORD A2 BY-PASS
M20 MOTORWAY
MAIN ROAD
DARTFORD ROAD
A225
99
131
Rowhill School
Day's Farm
Holland's Farm
Bybow Farm
Shirehall Farm Cottage
Stanley Morgan House
The Mount
Hawley Garden Centre
Yewtree Farm Nursery
King George's Field
Works
Darenth Grange
Old Mill Farm
The Alders
Summit Farm
Broad Oak
Portway Nursery
Nursery
Sutton's Cotts.
Clement Ho.
Swanley Bottom Farm
North View Cotts.
Wiffen's Farm
Rec. Ground
Cemy.
Sutton at Hone C. of E. Prim. Sch.
Lib.
St. John's Jerusalem Garden National Trust
Holt's Farm
Gildenhill Farm
Coldharbour Farm
Chapel Field Cottages
Farningham Rd.
Tweed Hill
Rams Wood
Homefield Cotts.
Homefield Farm
The Old Bungalow
The New Bungalow
Highcroft
Creswick Nurseries
Westminster Field
Court Lodge
FARNINGHAM WOOD
The Leas
Franks Farm
Franks
Little Franks
Cricket Grd.
The Folly
Hill Farm
Wildacres
Hill House
Hill Farm House
Abington
Riseley
Eglantine Farm
Covered Reservoir
Reynolds Pl.
The Grange
River Darent
Darent Valley Path
SHIREHALL ROAD
BURNT HOUSE LANE
CLEMENT STREET
ARNOLD'S LANE
CHURCH ROAD
GILDENHILL ROAD
SHIP LANE
STATION ROAD
PARSONAGE LANE
FRANKS LANE
CALFSTOCK LANE
BUTTON STREET
FARNINGHAM HILL RD.
HOMEFIELD ROAD
BARN END LANE
HIGH ST.
DEVON ROAD
O R D
O A K S
G H J K L M
1 2 3 4 5 6 7 8 9
54 55 56

A
B
C
D
E
F
1
2
3
4
5
6
7
8
9
100
SPELTHORNE
Shepperton
SHEPPERTON
Shepperton
Lower Halliford
TW17
River Ash Estate
Riverhouse Gds.
Shepperton Marina
Gravel Pit
RIVER
THAMES
Thames Meadow
Cowey Sale
DESBOROUGH ISLAND
Desborough Channel
Weybridge
Broad Water
Engine River
Greenlands Farm
Broadwater Farm
PORTMORE PARK
Golf Course
St. James C of E Prim. Sch.
WEYBRIDGE
OATLANDS PARK
KT13
WALTON-ON-THAMES
Ashley Park
ELM
Walton-on-Thames
Burwood Park
Burwood Park School
Upper Common
Rabbit Lane House
Burvale Cemetery
Burvale Farm
Kennels
BURHILL GOLF COURSE
Burhill
Practice Ground
Warren Pond
Recreation Ground
Thames Field Farm
Cricket Ground
Playing Field
Las Palmas Estate
Thamesmead School
Cleeves Jun.Sch.
Walton Leigh Sch.
Superstore
Swim. Pool
Walton & Hersham F.C.
GASTON BRIDGE RD.
WALTON BRIDGE RD.
HEPWORTH WY.
NEW ZEALAND AV.
CHURCH TERRACE
HERSHAM ROAD
OATLANDS DRIVE
QUEENS ROAD
ASHLEY ROAD
HILLS ROAD
BURWOOD ROAD
ST. GEORGE'S AVENUE
A3050
A244
A317
B365
B375
B376
A224
B373
B372
ST. GEORGE'S

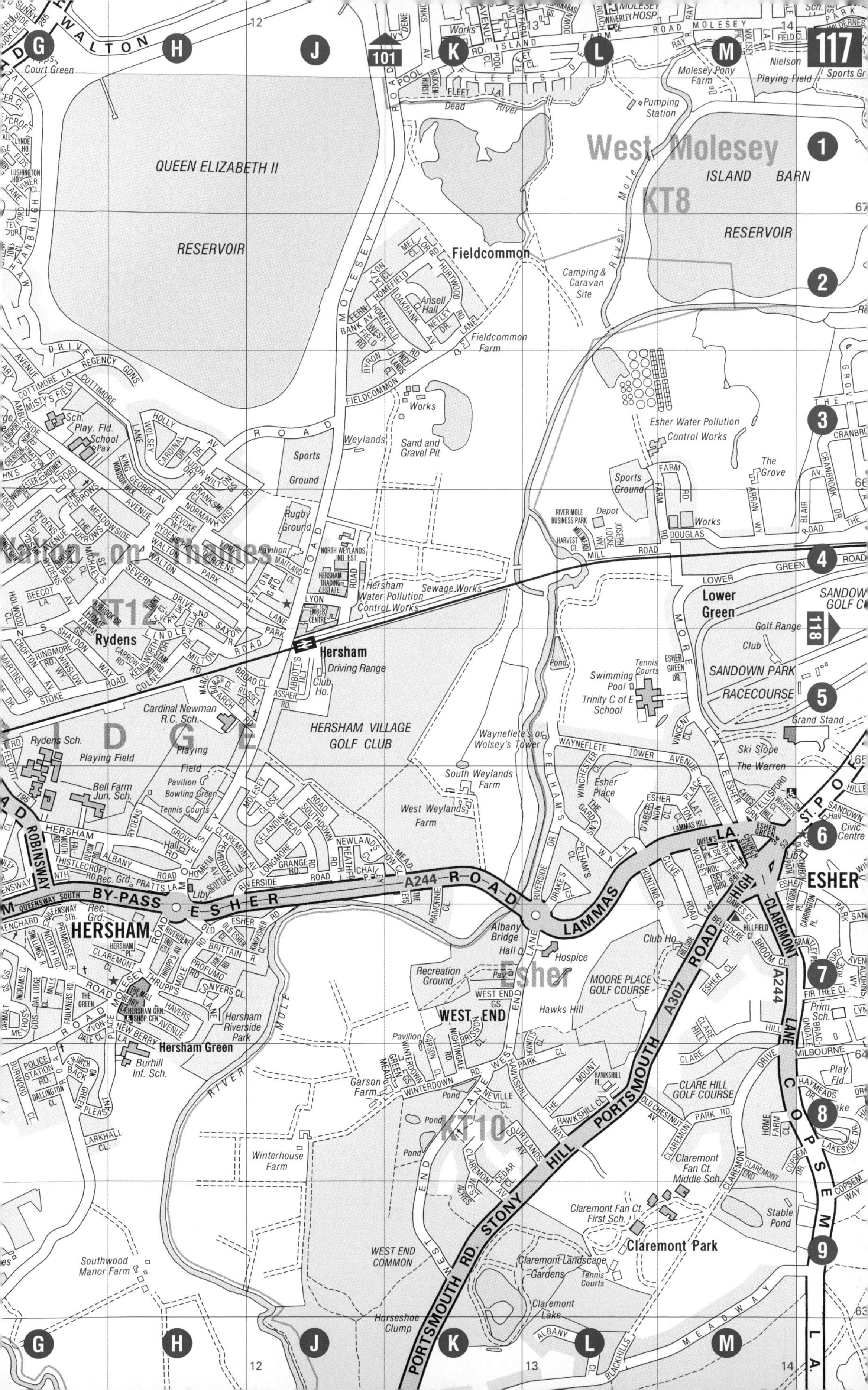
QUEEN ELIZABETH II
RESERVOIR
West Molesey
KT8
ISLAND BARN
RESERVOIR
Fieldcommon
Walton-on-Thames
KT12
Rydens
Hersham
HERSHAM VILLAGE
GOLF CLUB
HERSHAM
Hersham Green
Lower
Green
SANDOWN PARK
RACECOURSE
ESHER
Esher
KT10
WEST END
MOORE PLACE
GOLF COURSE
CLARE HILL
GOLF COURSE
Claremont Park
WEST END
COMMON
Esher Water Pollution
Control Works
Hersham
Water Pollution
Control Works

West Molesey
KT8
East Molesey
ISLAND BARN RESERVOIR
THAMES DITTON
Thames Ditton
HOME PARK GOLF COURSE
Weston Green
WESTON GREEN
KT7
Giggshill
Esher College
SANDOWN PARK GOLF COURSE
SANDOWN PARK RACECOURSE
Littleworth Common
HINCHLEY WOOD
Hinchley Wood
ELMBRIDGE
ESHER
Esher
SURBITON GOLF COURSE
KT10
Claygate
CLAYGATE
CLAYGATE COMMON
Loseberry
Arbrook Common
HAMPTON COURT WAY
PORTSMOUTH ROAD
KINGSTON BY-PASS
A309
A307
A244
B3379
B364
102
117
132

119
103
120
133
G
H
J
K
L
M
1
2
3
4
5
6
7
8
9
18
19
20
Surbiton
SURBITON
KT6
KT5
BERRYLANDS
LONG DITTON
Cockcrow Hill
SOUTHBOROUGH
TOLWORTH
Tolworth
TOLWORTH JUNCTION
HOOK
KINGSTON upon THAMES
Chessington
CHESSINGTON
KT9
Chessington North
Chessington South
Epsom
KT19
RUXLEY
EPSOM and EWELL
HORTON COUNTRY PARK
HORTON COUNTRY CLUB GOLF COURSE
CHESSINGTON GOLF CENTRE
Seething Wells
Halls of Residence
Surbiton Hosp.
Tolworth Hosp.
Government Offices
Tolworth Court Farm
Castle Hill
Butcher's Grove
Four Oaks Centre
KINGSTON BY-PASS
A3
A240
A243
A3210
B3364
B284
BRIGHTON ROAD
UPPER BRIGHTON ROAD
VICTORIA RD.
KINGSDOWNE RD.
EWELL ROAD
ALEXANDRA DRIVE
HOOK ROAD
LEATHERHEAD ROAD
CHESSINGTON RD.
MOOR LANE
HOOK RISE
KINGSTON ROAD

120
A
B
C
D
E
F
1
2
3
4
5
6
7
8
9
104
119
134
Motspur Park
MALDEN JUNC.
BY-PASS
University of London Athletic Ground
B.B.C. Sports Ground
MOTSPUR PARK
Gas Works
The Sir Joseph Hood Memorial Playing Fields
Playing Fields
Green Lane Prim. Sch.
Local Gov. Computer Centre
New Malden
KT3
MALDEN
A3 MALDEN WAY (KINGSTON BY-PASS)
Sports Grounds
Hogsmill River
Club House
Grand Avenue Prim. Sch.
MANOR PARK
A2043
Malden Manor
Malden Manor Prim. Sch.
Richard Challoner School
Sports Field
Surbiton
KT5
KINGSTON upon THAMES
OLD MALDEN
Malden Green
Worcester Park
Sports Ground
CENTRAL ROAD
CHEAM ROAD
Playing Field
Maori Sports Ground
Knollmead Prim. Sch.
Tolworth
Sports Ground
Riverhill
Cricket Ground
Linden Bridge Sch. & Spring Cen.
Wandgas Athletic Ground
Dancer Dick Wood
OLD MALDEN LANE
WORCESTER PARK RD. B284
Worcester Park
WORCESTER PARK
Shadbolt Park
KT4
Cuddington Recreation Ground
Tolworth Court Farm
Tolworth Court Bridge
Cuddington Prim. Sch.
King George's Field
Auriol Park
A240
KINGSTON ROAD
EPSOM and EWELL
Riverview C. of E. Prim. Sch.
Sports Ground
STONELEIGH
Stoneleigh
West Ewell Inf. Sch.
Epsom & Ewell High Sch.
KT19
Playing Field
KT17
Epsom
Pack Horse Bri.
King George's Field
Hogsmill River
Chamber Mead
BEGGAR'S HILL
EWELL A240 BY-PASS
A24
LONDON ROAD
WEST EWELL
HORTON COUNTRY PARK
HORTON COUNTRY PARK GOLF COURSE
Hook Arena
CHESSINGTON RD. B284
B2200
RUXLEY LANE
St. Ebba's Farm Cottage
Playing Field
Playing Fields
ORGAN CROSSROADS
Cherry Orchard Farm
Ewell West
Bourne Hall
Lower Mill
Playing Field

MORDEN PARK
MORDEN
Morden
NORTH EAST SURREY CREMATORIUM AND MORDEN CEMETERY
Merton & Sutton Joint Cemetery
SM4
Morden Farm Middle Sch.
King George's Field
Recreation Ground
Risley Sports Ground
St. Helier
ST. HELIER AVENUE
ROSE HILL ROUNDABOUT
ROSEHILL
Rosehill Recreation Ground
Sutton Cemetery
Glenthorne High Sch.
LONDON ROAD
STONECOT HILL
EPSOM ROAD
ST. ANTHONY'S HOSP.
Superstore
Sutton Common
BENHILTON
NORTH CHEAM
Sutton
SUTTON
SM1
SM3
SM2
Collingwood Road Recreation Ground
Sutton United F.C.
West Sutton
OLDFIELDS
ST. DUNSTAN'S HILL
Cheam High Sch.
Water Works
Cheam Recreation Ground
CHEAM
CHEAM PARK
Nonsuch Park
Nonsuch High Sch. for Girls
Cheam
EWELL RD.
A232
BELMONT RISE
BRIGHTON ROAD
Overton Grange High Sch.
Sports Ground
Glaisdale Sch.
105
122
135

A
B
C
D
E
F
1
2
3
4
5
6
7
8
9
106
121
136
GOLF COURSE
Club House
Mitcham Junction
MERTON
Mitcham
CR4
Sports Ground
Hundred Acre Bridge
Watermeads
Sports Ground
Tennis Courts
Bennett's Hole
Poulter Park
Bishopsford House
Bishopsford Comm. Sch.
Moreton Grn. First Sch.
Morden SM4
WORKS
THE WILLOW BUSINESS CENTRE
CAPITOL IND. EST.
EAGLE TRAD. EST.
Depot
Playing Fields
Open Space
Open Space
ST. HELIER
Hill Ho. Comm. Cen.
Carshalton Sports Arena
Running Track
Pavilion
St. Helier Open Space
ROSE HILL ROUNDABOUT
ROSEHILL
Rosehill Park East
Greenshaw Wood
ST. HELIER HOSPITAL
QUEEN MARY'S HOSPITAL FOR CHILDREN
Community Hall
Nature Reserves
BEDDINGTON CORNER
Irrigation Bridge
Mile Road Bridge
Hackbridge
HACKBRIDGE
Warehouses
Nature Reserve
Wandle Bri.
Carshalton
Muschamp Prim. Sch.
SM5
THE WRYTHE
Rushy Meadow Prim. Sch.
Playing Field
Royston Park
BENHILTON
SM1
Carshalton Coll.
Wrythe Rec. Grd.
Carshalton Athletic F.C.
Playing Field
Sutton
Benhill Rec. Grd.
Westcroft Leisure Cen.
The Grove
Council Offices
Heritage Cen.
Studio Thea.
WALLINGTON GRN.
St. Philomenas Convent
CARSHALTON
The Frying Pan
Hogpit Pond
CARSHALTON PARK
CARSHALTON WAR MEMORIAL HOSPL.
Manor Park
Superstore
Sutton
Wallington
Carshalton Beeches
Stanley Pk. Rec. Grd.
High Sch.
Little Holland Ho.
SM2
SUTTON HEIGHTS
Resrs (covered)
CARSHALTON ON THE HILL
CARSHALTON BEECHES
BISHOPSFORD ROAD
ST. HELIER AVENUE
WRYTHE LANE
CARSHALTON ROAD
LONDON ROAD
NIGHTINGALE RD.
HACKBRIDGE RD.
BRIGHTON ROAD
THROWLEY WAY
STANLEY PARK RD.
BOUNDARY RD.
MANOR RD.
A217
A237
A297
A232
B278
B271
B277
B2230

CROYDON ROAD
MITCHAM ROAD A236
THORNTON ROAD
LONDON ROAD A235
Thornton Heath
MAYDAY UNIVERSITY HOSP.
BROAD GREEN
ST. JAMES'S RD.
West Croydon
Croydon Crematorium
CROYDON CEMETERY
107
Beddington Lane
Croydon Tramlink
Therapia Lane
THE TRAMSHEDS INDUSTRIAL EST.
Transport Depot & Warehouse
Beddington Farm
Beddington Sewage Treatment Works
LOMBARD ROUNDABOUT
Ampere Way
PIONEERS INDUSTRIAL PARK
BEDDINGTON TRAD. EST.
Superstores
Cinema
Bingo Hall
Superstore
Warehouse
Electricity Switching Station
BEDDINGTON PARK
River Wandle
Carew Manor & Dovecot
BEDDINGTON
PURLEY WAY
Waddon Marsh
WANDLE PARK
Wandle Park
WADDON
Reeves Cnr.
124
CROYDON
DUPPAS HILL RD.
THE CROYDON FLYOVER
OLD TOWN
ROMAN WAY A236
Waddon
EPSOM RD.
A232
Duppas Hill
Recreation Ground
CR0
FIVEWAYS CORNER
Retail Park
Bandon Hill Cemetery
SM6
Bandonhill
WALLINGTON
Mellows Park
SOUTH BEDDINGTON
Roundshaw
Esporta Health & Raquets Club
Powerleague Soccer Cen.
PURLEY WAY PLAYING FIELDS
Haling Manor High Sch.
SOUTH CROYDON
Roundshaw Park (Playing Fields)
Amy Johnson Prim. Sch.
137
Nature Reserve
Russell Hill Resr. (covered)
CR2

108
138
123
A
B
C
D
E
F
1
2
3
4
5
6
7
8
9
SE25
CR0
CR2
CROYDON
Croydon
BROAD GREEN
SELHURST
Selhurst
WOODSIDE
Woodside
ADDISCOMBE
Addiscombe
West Croydon
East Croydon
South Croydon
SOUTH CROYDON
South Croydon
Sanderstead
LLOYD PARK
Lloyd Park
Queen's Road Cemetery
Croydon Coll.
Fairfield Halls
Law Courts
Park Hill
Coombe Cliff (Educ. Cen)
Trinity School Playing Field
Coombe Park
Coombe Farm
Coombe Lodge
Coombe Wood
Royal Russell Sch.
Royal Russell Preparatory Sch.
Ballards Plantation
Cottage in the Woods
Old Ballards Cottage
Croham Hurst Golf Club
CROHAM HURST GOLF COURSE
CROHAM HURST
Breakneck Hill
Thrift Wood
HALING PARK
Whitgift Sch.
Addiscombe Recreation Ground
Sandilands
Lebanon Rd.
Wellesley Rd.
George St.
Church St.
Blackhorse La.
Ashburton Park
WINDMILL RD
WHITEHORSE RD
ST. JAMES'S RD
LOWER ADDISCOMBE ROAD
MORLAND
ADDISCOMBE ROAD
WELLESLEY ROAD
PARK LANE
COOMBE ROAD
FLYOVER
BRIGHTON ROAD
SOUTH END
SELSDON RD.
CROHAM RD.
WARHAM B275 ROAD
UP. SELSDON RD.
WOODSIDE GREEN
SPRING LA.
SHIRLEY RD.
A212
A213
A222
A232
A235
B243
B274
B275
32
33
34
63
64
65
66
67

G
H
J
K
L
M
109
UPPER ELMERS END RD.
UPPER ELMERS END
Eden Park
Beckenham
BR3
BROMLEY
MONKS ORCHARD
THE BETHLEM ROYAL HOSPITAL
Langley Park Schools
SOUTH EDEN PARK RD.
BECKENHAM ROAD
A214
A232
A222
A212
A2022
B230
West Wickham
BR4
WEST WICKHAM
126
HIGH STREET
WICKHAM ROAD
SHIRLEY OAKS HOSPITAL
Shirley Oaks
Ashburton Playing Fields
SHIRLEY
UPPER SHIRLEY
SPRING PARK
Spring Park Wood
Parkfields Recreation Ground
Edenham High Sch.
Benson Prim. Sch.
Shirley High Sch.
Coloma Convent R.C. Sch.
Shirley Towermill (disused)
Foxes Wood
Kennel Wood
Wychwood
Threehalfpenny Wood
ADDINGTON GOLF COURSE
Addington Hills
ADDINGTON
ADDINGTON VILLAGE RD.
ADDINGTON PALACE GOLF COURSE
Addington Palace
ADDINGTON PARK
Addington Village
KENT GATE WAY
GRAVEL HILL
Gravel Hill
Croydon Tramlink
Heathfield
Applegarth Jun. & Inf. Schs.
Rowdown Fields
Fieldway
ADDINGTON COURT NEW GOLF COURSE
Gilbert Scott Jun. & Inf. Schs.
Monks Hill Sports Centre
John Ruskin College
SELSDON PARK ROAD
139
Y
D
O
N
1
2
3
4
5
6
7
8
9
35
36
37
38
64
65
66
67

110
125
140
A
B
C
D
E
F
1
2
3
4
5
6
7
8
9
38
39
40
63
64
65
66
67
Langley Park Schools
Play. Fld.
Tennis Courts
Beckenham
BR3
Sports Ground
Playing Field
LANGLEY PARK GOLF COURSE
Club House
The Rookery
LANGLEY PARK
West Wickham
West Wickham Pools
Blake Recreation Ground
Springfield
BR4
Cheyne Site
Sparrow's Den Playing Fields
SPRING PARK
FOX HILL
Foxhill Shaw
BIRCH WOOD
CROYDON
Croydon
CR0
Castlehill Ruffs
Electricity Sub Station
NEW ADDINGTON
Wolsey Jun. & Inf. Schs.
Pitch and Putt Course
ROWDOWN WOOD
Recreation Ground
Cupola Wood
Pickhurst Jun. & Inf. Schs.
Pickhurst Green
Sports Grounds
Hawes Down Jun. & Inf. Schs.
Glebe Sch.
WEST WICKHAM
Play Fld.
Hayes
Bromley
HAYES
Hayes Street Farm
Bromley F.C. Ground
Cricket Ground
Fishers Wood
Park & Ride
Athletic Track
Hayes Prim. Sch.
Playing Field
Baston Pre - Jun. School
Hayes Sch.
HAYES GROVE PRIORY HOSP.
Hayes Court
HAYES
West Wickham Common
The Warren
Nash Ho.
Sports Ground
CONEY HALL
Lodge Coney Hall Rec. Grd.
Bowling Green
Recreation Ground
Tower
Wickham Court
Emmaus Conference Centre
St. John Rigby R.C. College
Wickham Court Farm
The Cottages
The Bungalows
School
Playing Field
Hast Hill
Baston Manor
Keston Court Riding School
Rouse Farm
Arlington Orchard
Well Wood
Long Shaw
Cooper's Wood
Elm Farm
NASH
Fox Hill Nursery
Nash Farm
North Pole Farm
Waytes
Fuller's Wood
James's Wood
Baldwin Shaw
Bradmanshill Wood
Rushfield Shaw
Broomfieldbank Shaw
Pumping Sta.
A232
A2022
A214
B251
B265
CROYDON ROAD
GLEBE WAY
HIGH STREET
ADDINGTON ROAD
ADDINGTON VILLAGE RD.
BECKENHAM ROAD
STATION ROAD
HAYES LANE
HAYES ST.
BASTON ROAD
BASTON MANOR RD.
COMMON ROAD
PICKHURST LANE
WICKHAM ROAD
BUSHEY WAY
WICKHAM WAY
CORKSCREW HILL
LAYHAMS ROAD
NASH LANE
NORTH POLE LANE
WEST COMMON ROAD
BOURNE WAY
HAYES HILL
HARVEST BANK ROAD
GATES GREEN ROAD
KENT GATE WAY
RIDGEWAY
CHATHAM AVENUE
WEST WICKHAM HAWES LANE
HEATH RISE
MARDEN AVENUE
FAIR ACRES
HAYES GARDENS
HAYES CHASE
GOODHART WAY
WICKHAM CHASE
LANGLEY WAY
THE ALDERS
LODGE LANE

BROMLEY COMMON
SOUTHBOROUGH
BROMLEY GOLF COURSE
Bromley College of Further & Higher Education
Parkfield Recreation Ground
Princes Plain Prim. Sch.
Crofton Heath
Sparrow Wood
Sparrow Common
Roundabout Wood
BR5
BR2
Nobody's Wood
Pokeridden Wood
Knowlehill Wood
Hollydale Recreation Grounds
Ravens Wood Sch.
KESTON MARK
LOCKSBOTTOM
FARNBOROUGH HOSPITAL
Farnborough Recreation Ground
Darrick Wood Sec. Sch.
Darrick Wood Jun. & Inf. Schs.
KESTON
Keston
Orpington
FARNBOROUGH
SOUTH PARK
Caesars Camp
Holwood
Keston Common
Ninhams Wood
Lake Wood
Broom Bank
Woodlands Poultry Farm
The Larches
Sevenoaks Lodge
Lower Hook Farm
North End Farm
North End Farm Cotts
Blacklands
Wilberforce Oak
Keston Court Farm
The Temple (Roman Mausoleum)
War Bank
Westerham Lodge
Glebe Farm
Keston Postmill (dis.)
Heathfield House
Forest Lodge
Keston C.of E. Prim. Sch.
CROYDON ROAD
HASTINGS ROAD
FARNBOROUGH COMMON
CROFTON ROAD
OAKLEY ROAD
WESTERHAM ROAD
A21
A232
A233
B265
111
128
141

A
B
C
D
E
F
1
2
3
4
5
6
7
8
9
112
127
44
45
46
63
64
66
67
Petts Wood
Lakeswood Hall
Petts Wood Recreation Ground
Crofton Jun. Sch.
Crofton Inf. Sch.
BR5
Sparrow Common
Roundabout Wood
Gumping Common
CROFTON
CROFTON ROAD
A232
ORPINGTON
Orpington
Civic Halls
STATION ROAD
ROAD SPUR
BROOM HILL
BROMLEY
Scout Halls
Covet Wood
Recreation Ground
Playground
Bowling Green
Perry Hall Prim. Sch.
PERRY HALL RD.
A208
A224
HIGH ST.
Orpington Priory Gardens Mus.
Grave Yard
Leisure Cen.
Coll.
Orpington
Playing Field
Tennis Courts
St. Olave's Grammar Sch.
BR6
SEVENOAKS WAY
A223
Ontario Centre
Hospice
Orpington Hospital
Prim. Sch.
Play. Fld.
Swimming Pool
Darrick Wood Sec. Sch.
Darrick Wood
Darrick Wood Jun. & Inf. Schs.
Newstead Wood
Play. Fld
Newstead Wood Sch. For Girls
Playing Field
Tubbenden Jun. & Inf. Schools
Rec. Grd.
FARNBOROUGH HILL
FARNBOROUGH
HIGH B2158 STREET FARNBOROUGH
Farnborough Prim. Sch.
Club Pav.
Sports Ground
Scouts Hall
The Manse
The Green
SEVENOAKS RD.
A21
Ramus Wood
GREEN STREET GREEN
Cocksett Plantation
Cocksett Hill
Glentrammon Rec. Grd.
Pav.
High Beeches
Chelsfield Hall
WORLDS END LANE
Eleven Oaks
Chelsfield Hill Wood
Rounds Wood
Whitelands Wood
HIGH ELMS GOLF COURSE
High Elms
Club House
Tennis Ct.
Woodpiece
The Lodge
The Rookery
High Elms Clockhouse
Church Field Plantation
Blacklands
Rec. Grd.
SEVENOAKS ROAD
Sport Ground
RAVENSQUAY BUSINESS CENTRE

G
H
J
K
L
M
113
130
1
2
3
4
5
6
7
8
9
48
49
550
67
66
165
64
63
KEVINGTON
Kevington Hall
Kevington Farm
Kynaston Wood
Waldens Farm
Child's Wood
CROCKENHILL ROAD
B258
CRAY ROAD
Crouch Farm
Crouch Farm House
Crouch Farm Cottages
Felma House
Nursery
Middle Farm Nursery
Willow Farm
Walden Manor
Waldens Bungalow
Lark Rise
Heather's Holding
Bleak House Farm
East Hall Cottage
Green Cedar
Cock-mannings Farm
EAST HALL ROAD
DERRY DOWNS
Grigg's Cross
COCKMANNINGS ROAD
BR5
Swanley
BR8
Grassmeade Recreation Ground
Ramsden Jun. & Inf. Schs.
RAMSDEN
The Priory School
Playing Field
Play. Fld.
Piggery
Piggeries
Eastwood
Griff's Wood Cottage
Griff's Wood
Orchard View
The Oaks
Lone Barn Farm
GORSE ROAD
Brambles
Byways
Sage Wents
SKIBBS LANE
SKEET HILL LANE
Fairfield
Crown Wood Fm.
Crown Wood
Woodside
Cookham Hill Farm
Cookham Farm
Feathercot
Micklewood Farm
Pollard
Playing Field
Skeet Hill Farm
Davidson House
DALTONS ROAD
Blenheim Jun. & Inf. Schs.
Goddington Special Sch.
GODDINGTON
Goddington Park
CHELSFIELD ROAD
Rounds Smallams
Club
The Lodge
Pav.
Orpington Sports Club
Tennis Courts
Lilly's Wood
Black Bush Wood
Snow White Cottages
PARKGATE ROAD
Doctor's Wood
OWEN WOOD
COURT ROAD
A224
(ORPINGTON BY-PASS)
Chelsfield Village
CHELSFIELD PARK HOSPITAL
Cannock School
Woodlands Farm
CHELSFIELD
WARREN ROAD
BUCKS CROSS RD.
HAWSTEAD LANE
Bucks Cross Farm
Pav. Rec. Grd.
Court Lodge Farm
Court Lodge
MAYPOLE ROAD
WELL HILL
Maypole
Reservoir
Goat Hill
FIRMINGERS ROAD
HILL END
M25 MOTORWAY
SEVENOAKS
Pecks Cotts.
Chelsfield Riding School
Julian Brimstone
THE MEADOWS
BRIMSTONE CL.
Club House
CHELSFIELD LAKES GOLF CENTRE
Hewitts
HEWITTS ROUNDABOUT
Coneyearth Wood
Pascalls Wood
Westwood Farm
WEST WOOD
HOLLOWS WOOD
Junction 4
A21
Knockholt
M25
Sevenoaks TN14
CHELSFIELD HILL
LONDON RD.
Goss Bushes

114
129
Junction 3 (M25)
SWANLEY INTERCHANGE
Industrial Estate
PEDHAM PLACE IND. EST.
Nursery
Rec. Grd.
Pav.
Fleetfoot Fm.
Prim. Sch.
Peartrees
Crockenhill
Cemetery
Cemy.
Cherry Orchard
Gosenhill Farm
The Mount
Hall
CRAY B258 ROAD
EYNSFORD ROAD
Petham Court
Football Ground
Wested Farm Cotts.
Little Wested House
Wested Meadows
Wested Farm
Cacketshill Wood
WESTED ROAD
CROCKENHILL
Middle Farm Nursery
Willow Farm
GREEN RD.
Swanley
Highcroft Hall
Heathfield Shaw
BR8
Horncross Shaw
Pollard
M25 MOTORWAY
Hulberry
Baldwins Cottages
Hulberry Farm
Eagle Heights Birds of Prey Centre
SEVEN
Play. Fld.
Skeet Hill Farm
Lullingstone Roman Villa
Roughet
Lullingstone Park Farm
Snow White Cottages
PARKGATE ROAD
Orpington
Park Gate House
Tennis Court
Club House
LULLINGSTONE PARK GOLF COURSE
BR6
FIRMINGERS ROAD
UPPER BEECHEN WOOD
Nature Reserve
LOWER BEECHEN WOOD
River Darent
Lake
Lullingstone Park Visitors Centre
The Rookery
Picnic Area
HOME WOOD
REDMANS LANE
Great Cockerhurst
COCKERHURST
Ridge Farm
Homewood Farm
Sevenoaks
Castle Farm
Westwood Farm
Brent Farm
TN14
Darent Valley Path
Dalhanna
Junction 4
Longspring Wood
Coombe Hollow Cott.
CASTLE FARM ROAD
EYNSFORD A225
Preston Farm Cotts.
M25

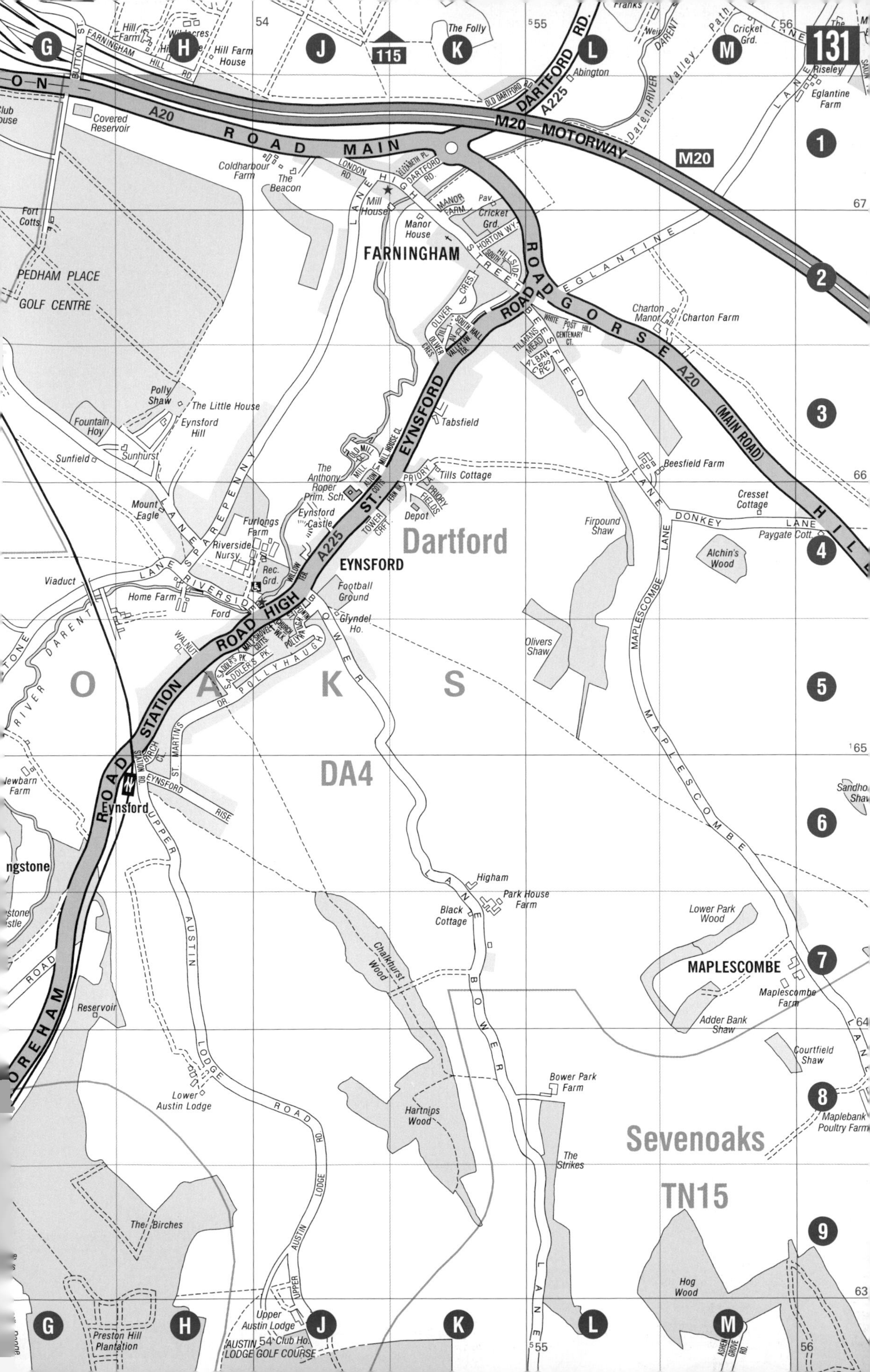

FARNINGHAM
EYNSFORD
MAPLESCOMBE
Dartford
Sevenoaks
DA4
TN15
O A K S
M20 MOTORWAY
A20 ROAD MAIN
DARTFORD RD.
A225
GORSE ROAD
HIGH STREET
EYNSFORD ROAD
HIGH ST.
STATION ROAD
RIVERSIDE
SPAREPENNY LANE
BOWER LANE
MAPLESCOMBE LANE
DONKEY LANE
EGLANTINE LANE
AUSTIN LODGE ROAD
UPPER AUSTIN LODGE RD.
BEESFIELD LANE
LANE
SHOREHAM ROAD
FARNINGHAM HILL RD.
BUTTON ST.
LONDON RD.
OLD DARTFORD RD.
POLLYHAUGH
EYNSFORD RISE
Hill Farm
Wildacres
Hill Farm House
The Folly
115
Abington
Cricket Grd.
Riseley
Eglantine Farm
Covered Reservoir
Coldharbour Farm
The Beacon
Mill House
Manor House
Cricket Grd.
Fort Cotts.
PEDHAM PLACE GOLF CENTRE
Charton Manor
Charton Farm
Polly Shaw
The Little House
Fountain Hoy
Eynsford Hill
Sunfield
Sunhurst
Tabsfield
The Anthony Roper Prim. Sch.
Tills Cottage
Beesfield Farm
Cresset Cottage
Paygate Cott.
Mount Eagle
Furlongs Farm
Eynsford Castle
Depot
Firpound Shaw
Alchin's Wood
Riverside Nursy.
Rec. Grd.
Football Ground
Viaduct
Home Farm
Ford
Glyndel Ho.
Olivers Shaw
Eynsford
Higham
Park House Farm
Black Cottage
Chalkhurst Wood
Lower Park Wood
Maplescombe Farm
Adder Bank Shaw
Courtfield Shaw
Reservoir
Lower Austin Lodge
Bower Park Farm
Hartnips Wood
Maplebank Poultry Farm
The Strikes
The Birches
Hog Wood
Upper Austin Lodge
Club Ho.
AUSTIN LODGE GOLF COURSE
Preston Hill Plantation
M20
RIVER DARENT
Darent Valley Path
54
55
56
67
66
65
64
63
G H J K L M
1 2 3 4 5 6 7 8 9

Esher
KT10
CLAYGATE
Claygate Common
Arbrook Common
Arbrook Farm
Vale Farm
Horridon Farm
Rowan Prep. Sch.
118
ESHER BY PASS
A3
COPSE LANE
A244
ESHER COMMON
Round Hill
Esher Common
Holroyd's Plantation
Birch Wood
Great Oaks
Sixty Acre Wood
Milbourneheld Plantation
Limekiln Wood
Jubilee Wood
B280
Old Carpenters Plantation
Stokesheath Farm Cottages
The Heckets
Brickyard Plantation
The Milbourneheld Wood
NEW WOOD
MALDEN RUSH
Byhurst Farm
OXSHOTT
OXSHOTT HEATH
Oxshott
WARREN LANE
OAK ROAD
ELMBRIDGE
Stoke Wood
Jessop's Well
PRINCE'S COVERTS
Bunkers Hill
Leatherhead
KT22
Adecroft Furze Field
Telegraph Hill
Reservoir (Covered)
D'Abernon Chase Cottage
Eleven Acres
Danes Hill School
Horns Hill
D'Abernon Ho.
LEATHERHEAD GOLF COURSE
Oxshott Flat
Fairways
Pachesham Lake
LEATHERHEAD COMMON
Club House
Pachesham Park
Clouds Hill Farm
Oxshott Mead
Little Brook Park
Crab Apple Court
OXSHOTT ROAD
KINGSTON ROAD
A243
Cobham
KT11
Woodland Court Farm
Woodlands Farm
Woodlands Park
WOODLANDS LA.
A245
Tyrwhitt House
Queen Elizabeth's Training Coll.
M25 MOTORWAY
A244
Junction 9
Old Parks Cottage
Little Park
East Lodge
WOODLANDS PARK
Dorincourt
Teazle Wood
Rowhurst Forge
B2430
Club House
PACHESHAM PARK GOLF CENTRE
Superstore
M25

133
119
134
G
H
J
K
L
M
1
2
3
4
5
6
7
8
9
18
19
20
KINGSTON
upon
THAMES
Chessington
KT9
KT19
KT18
KT21
EPSOM
and
EWELL
Epsom
MOLE
VALLEY
Ashtead
CHESSINGTON GOLF CENTRE
Recreation Ground
Sports Ground
Tennis Courts
Offices
BARWELL BUSINESS PARK
Chessington & Hook United F.C.
CHESSINGTON WORLD OF ADVENTURES
Main Entrance
South Entrance
Zoo
Burnt Stub
Park Farm
Acre Hill Farmhouse
Chessington Wood
SILVERGLADE BUSINESS PARK
Rushett Farm
Glanmire Farm
RUSHETT LANE B280
CHRIST CHURCH ROAD B280
CHALKY LA.
Bonesgate Stream
COUNTRY PARK
North Farm Cott.
Four Acre Wood
Pond Wood
HORTON
Aeronautical Radio Station
THE NEW EPSOM & EWELL COTTAGE HOSPITAL
Recreation Grd.
The Poplars
Riding Stables
Laundry Cott.
WEST PARK HOSPITAL, PARKLANDS DAY HOSPITAL
West Park Farm
Horton Park Children's Farm
Hollywood Lodge
Stew Pond
Gt. Wood
Cemetery
Horton Farm
Horton
Sports Grd.
Stamford Green Prim. Sch.
Stamford Green
Kingswood Ho. Sch.
St. Joseph's R.C. Prim. Sch.
Ebbisham Inf. Sch.
Rosebery Sch.
EPSOM COMMON
Newton Wood
THE FOREST
The Wells
ASHTEAD COMMON
Caen Wood
The Oaks
The Rye
Wood Field
Ashtead
WOODCOTE
Epsom Common
Woodcote Stud Farm
Woodcote Park
Ridgecourt
The Cottage in the Park
ASHTEAD PARK
Island Pond
Ashtead Ho.
Nursery
A24 ROAD DORKING
EPSOM
ASHTEAD
Rec. Grd.
Ckt. Grd.
Tennis Courts
Works

& COUNTRY CLUB
120
133
A
B
C
D
E
F
1
2
3
4
5
6
7
8
9
20
21
22
63
62
61
60
59
EWELL
Ewell West
Ewell East
EPSOM
Epsom
Epsom Downs
Horton
WOODCOTE
Woodcote Park
EPSOM Land EWELL
KT19
KT17
KT18
Cemetery
Horton Farm
St. Ebba's Farm Cottage
Playing Field
Cricket Gnd.
Hockey Gnd.
ST. EBBA'S
Sports Ground
Bowl. Green
Court Recreation Grd.
Gibraltar Rec. Grd.
Sewage Wks.
High Sch.
Longmead Business Cen.
Nonsuch Trad. Est.
Epsom Bus. Pk.
Shopping Centre
Peel Centre Industrial Estate
Glyn Tech. Sch.
Gypsy Site
Rainbow Leisure Centre
Water Works
Depot
Bourne Hall Museum
Glyn Ho.
Ewell Castle Sch.
Hatch Furlong
Priest Hill Cotts.
Reigate R.Br.
NESCOT Epsom's College of Further & Higher Education
Playing Field
Sports Cen
Wallace Fields Jun. Sch.
The Looe
The Downs Farm
Recreation Ground
Ashley Centre
Theatre
Epsom General Hospital
Epsom College
Rifle Range
Sports Grd.
Club House
Littlecourt
Littlecourt Cott.
Larkhall
Racing Stables
South Hatch
The Durdans
The Grove
Worlds End
Halfmoon Clump
Crockingham Wood
Fish Pond
Woodcote Park (Club House)
Tennis Courts
Tennis Court
Ridgecourt
R.A.C. COUNTRY CLUB GOLF COURSE
The Paddock
The Derby Day Experience
Grand Stand
Racecourse
Tattenham Corner
EPSOM DOWNS
EPSOM GOLF COURSE
Buckle's Gap
Cherry Orchard Farm
ORGAN CROSSROADS
Organ Crossroads
CHESSINGTON ROAD
HOOK ROAD
LONDON RD.
EWELL BY-PASS A24
CHEAM RD.
REIGATE ROAD
A240
EPSOM RD.
EAST ST.
HIGH ST.
UP. HIGH ST.
ALEXANDRA A2022 ROAD
COLLEGE ROAD
LONGDOWN LANE NORTH
LONGDOWN LANE SOUTH B288
WEST HILL B280
DORKING A24 ROAD
SOUTH STREET
ASHLEY AVENUE
ASHLEY RD.
CHURCH ST.
BURGH HEATH ROAD
DOWNS RD.
DOWNS ROAD
B290
B289
B284
B2200
B2221
B291
GRANDSTAND ROAD
TATTENHAM CORNER ROAD
YEW TREE
WOODCOTE RD.
WOODCOTE SIDE
WOODCOTE PARK RD.
WILMERHATCH LANE
HEADLEY RD.
LANGLEY VALE
MILL RD.
BRIDGE RD.
WINDMILL LA.
KINGSWAY
MEADOWVIEW
STATION AV.
FIRST AV.
LONGMEAD ROAD
MILES ROAD
TEMPLE ROAD
WATERLOO ROAD
HOOKFIELD
STAMFORD GRN. RD.
CHRIST CHURCH RD.
MANOR GREEN RD.
POUND LA.
HORTON LANE
GROVE ROAD
LOWER COURT RD.
CHASE RD.
HAWTHORNE PL.
THE PARADE
HEATHCOTE RD.
WORPLE RD.
CHALK LA.
HYLANDS RD.
CEDAR HILL
WARREN HILL
BARON'S HURST
TREADWELL RD.
BEECH WAY
CARTERS RD.
MOSPEY CRES.
LYNWOOD AV.
COLLEGE AV.
ASHDOWN RD.
KINGSDOWN RD.
LONGDOWN RD.
DOWNS HILL RD.
THE CHASE
RUDEN WAY
ST. MARGARET DR.

G
H
J
K
L
M
121
1
2
3
4
5
6
7
8
9
136
BELMONT
Belmont
SUTTON
Sutton
SM2
EAST EWELL
Overton Grange High Sch.
Sports Ground
The Avenue Prim. Sch.
SUTTON HOSP.
THE ROYAL HOSP.
Rugby Football Grd.
Sports Ground
CUDDINGTON GOLF COURSE
BANSTEAD DOWNS
BANSTEAD DOWNS GOLF COURSE
Gally Hills Tumuli
Club House
Resr. (Covered)
Priest Hill
Sports Ground
Sports Cen.
North Looe
North Looe Farm
Golf Course
Banstead
Rifle Range
Beecholme Recreation Gnd.
Depot
The Cutting
Littlecroft
H.M.P. HIGHDOWN
BANSTEAD
REIGATE and BANSTEAD
Banstead
SM7
NORK
NORK PARK
Round Wood
Warren Mead Inf. & Jun. Schs.
Park Wood
Nork Park Farm
Great Burgh
Tattenham Way Recreation Ground
Tumble Beacon
The Beacon Sch.
Tadworth
KT20
Aberdour School
Pages Acre
RUFFETT WOOD
Lady Neville Rec. Grd.
Cricket Grd.
Recreation Ground
Tech.Training Cen.
County Ambulance Cen.
The Larches
Lodge
Mint Farm
New Place
Apsley
A217
A232
A240
A2022
B2218
B2219
B2217
B2230
B2221
B2283
B284
BRIGHTON ROAD
BELMONT RISE
REIGATE RD.
WINKWORTH ROAD
FIR TREE ROAD
HIGH STREET
TATTENHAM WAY
NORTHEY AVENUE
CHEAM ROAD
SUTTON LANE
BURDON LA.
HIGHDOWN LANE
GARRATTS LANE
HOLLY LANE
CHIPSTEAD ROAD
WOOD LANE
24
25
26
59
60
61
62
63

136
A
B
C
D
E
F
1
2
3
4
5
6
7
8
9
26
27
28
63
62
61
60
59
122
135
CARSHALTON ON THE HILL
CARSHALTON BEECHES
Sutton
Carshalton
SM5
SM2
SM7
SUTTON
REIGATE
and
Banstead
BANSTEAD
WOODMANSTERNE
LITTLE WOODCOTE
WOODCOTE GREEN
Merton & Sutton Comm. N.H.S. Trust H.Q.
Banstead Mobility Cen.
ORCHARD HILL
Biological Research Labs.
Diamond Riding Centre
SUTTON GENERAL HOSPITAL
THE ROYAL MARSDEN HOSP. (SUTTON)
Seaton Ho. Prep. Sch.
White Lodge
OAKS SPORTS CENTRE GOLF COURSE
Club House
THE OAKS PARK
Woodland Craft Centre
South Lodge
Fairlawn Farm
Hunters Field Farm
April Cott.
The Oaks Farm
H.M.P. DOWNVIEW
H.M.P. HIGHDOWN
Little Woodcote Estate
Little Woodcote Farm
Little Woodcote Fm. Cotts.
Old Lodge Farm
Lower Pillory Downs
WOODCOTE PARK GOLF COURSE
Caravan Park
Rose Cott.
Hylands Nurseries
Hillside Cotts.
Sports Ground
Ruffet Wood
Big Wood
Woodmansterne Primary Sch.
Village Hall
Recreation Ground
Barn Grove
Weston Acres
Boundary Farm
Nicola Farm
Lodge
Hengest Farm
Littlecroft
Manor Cottage Farm
The Manor Ho.
The Old School
Woodcote Grove Farm
Orford House
Woodcote Grove House
Playground
Prospect Plantation
Apsley
The Shrubbery
Banstead Place
Place Fm.
Mint Farm
Courtlands Farm
Farmside
Piggery
Scratch Wood
Tall Trees
New Place
Haughdell House
Little Solom's Wood
Woodend
Great Solom's Wood
Soloms Court
Walwood
PARK DOWNS
Park Farm
HOW HILLS
White Hill
Page Hill
CHIPSTEAD GOLF COURSE
Chipstead
Chipstead Valley Prim. Sch.
Playing Fld.
Works
Recreation Ground
Tennis Courts
Portnalls
Woodmansterne
Playing Fields
High Sch. for G
ROYDON A2022
WOODMANSTERNE LANE
WOODMANSTERNE LA. LITTLE WOODCOTE
CARSHALTON ROAD B278
WOODMANSTERNE ROAD
RECTORY LANE
B278 LANE
CHIPSTEAD LANE
HOLLY LANE B2219
OUTWOOD B2032
FAIRLAWN ROAD
BANSTEAD ROAD SOUTH
SUTTON LANE
BRIGHTON ROAD
COTSWOLD RD.
CHILTERN ROAD
HIGHDOWN LANE
FREEDOWN LANE
SUTTON COUNTRYSIDE WALK
OAKS WALK
TELEGRAPH TRACK
PILLORY DOWN
UPPER PILLORY DOWN
LOWER PILLORY DOWN
GROVE LANE
MOUNT LANE
ST. ANDREWS
SOLOMS COURT ROAD
HIGHFIELD ROAD
PARK DOWNS ROAD
HIGH WOLD
RICKMAN HILL
PORTNALLS
MANOR WAY
PINES WALK
UPPER PINE WAY

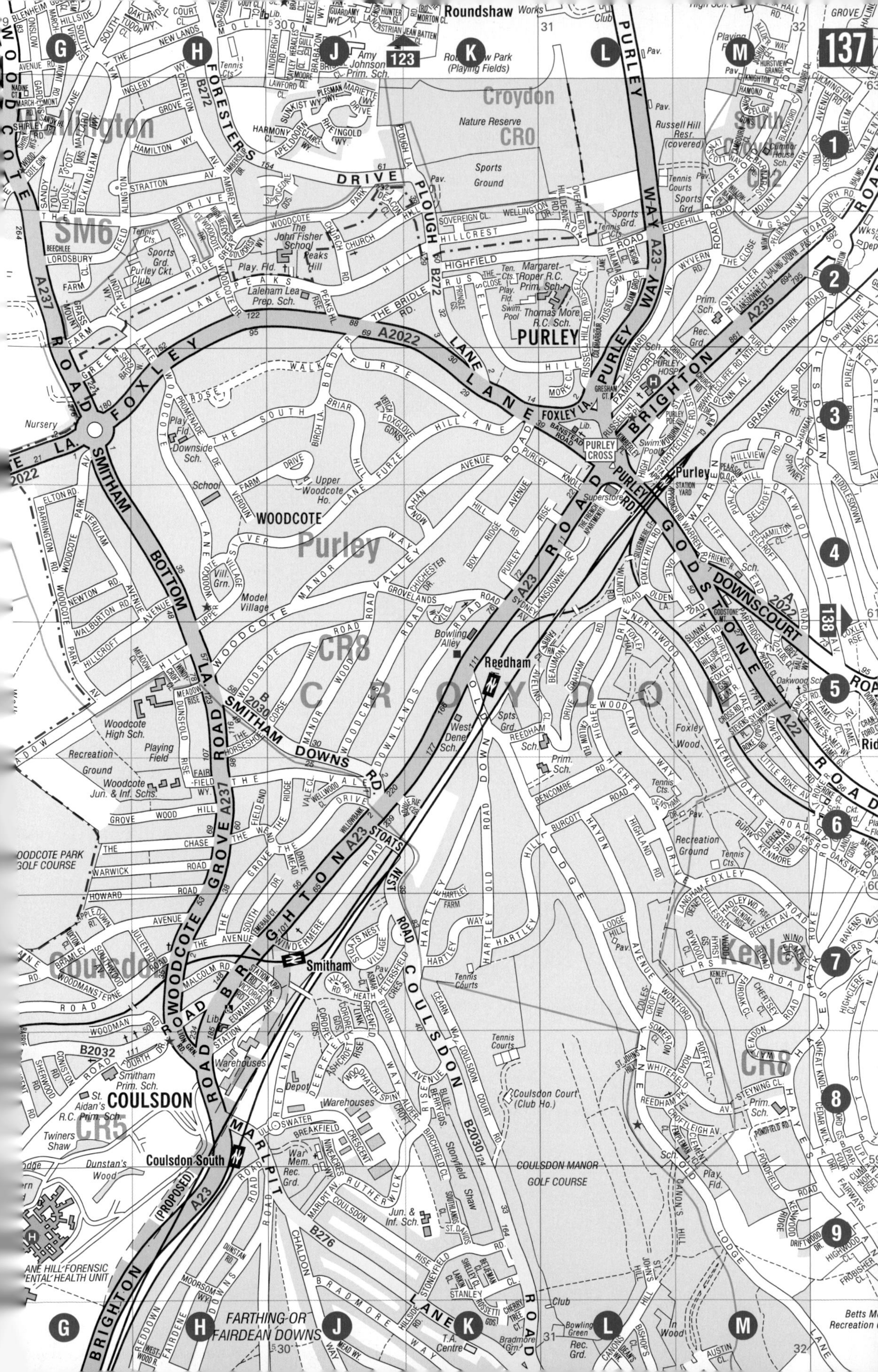
Roundshaw
Croydon
CR0
Nature Reserve
Sports Ground
Wallington
SM6
PURLEY
Purley
WOODCOTE
CR8
CROYDON
Reedham
Coulsdon
COULSDON
CR5
Coulsdon South
Smitham
Kenley
COULSDON MANOR GOLF COURSE
WOODCOTE PARK GOLF COURSE
FARTHING OR FAIRDEAN DOWNS
Foxley Wood
Purley Cross
BRIGHTON ROAD
GODSTONE ROAD
FOXLEY LANE
PURLEY WAY
WOODCOTE GROVE ROAD
SMITHAM BOTTOM LANE
123
138

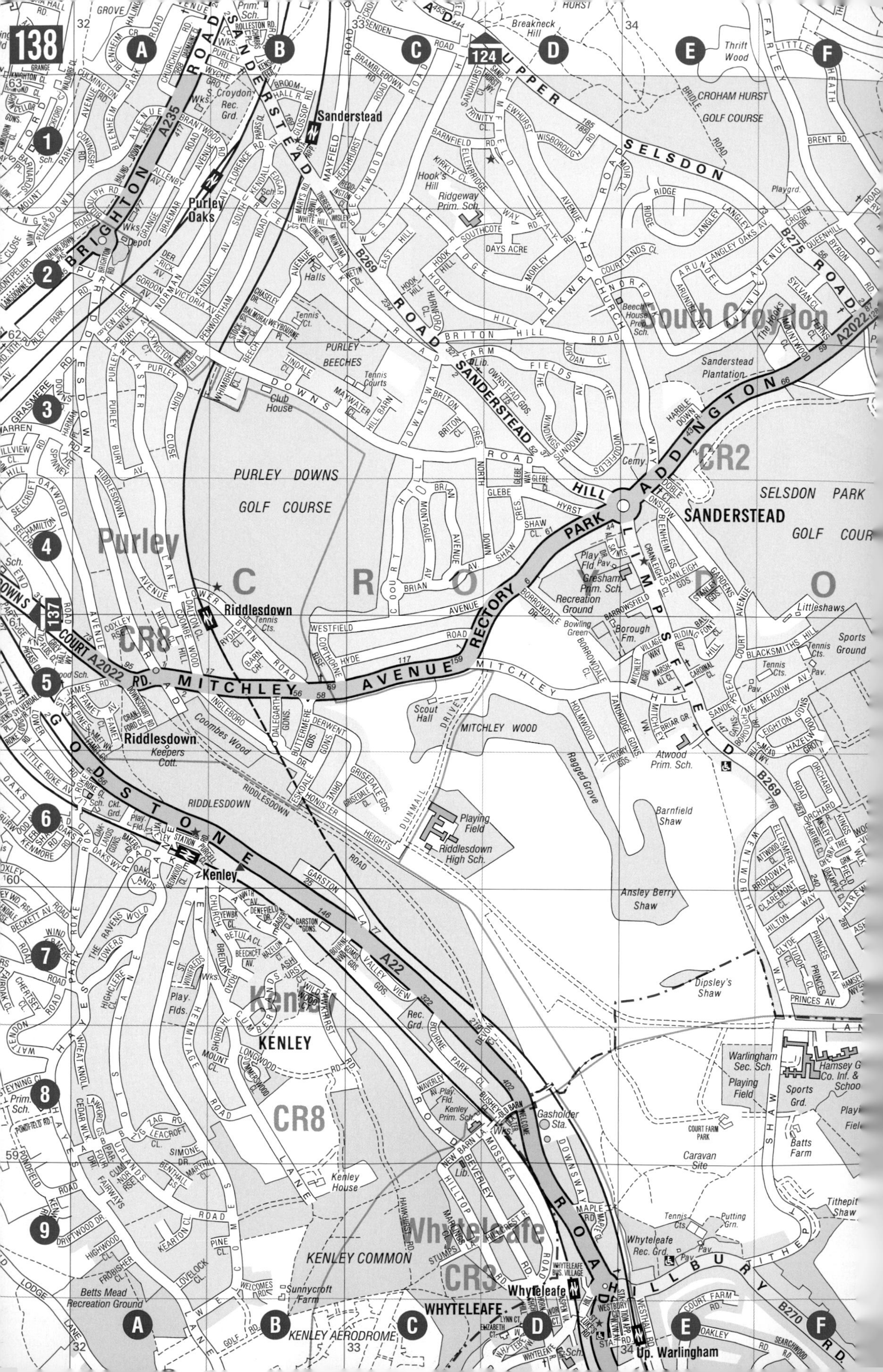

SELSDON
Croydon
CR0
FORESTDALE
SELSDON WOOD
(Nature Reserve)
ADDINGTON COURT
NEW GOLF COURSE
ADDINGTON COURT
OLD GOLF COURSE
FARLEIGH COURT
GOLF COURSE
FRITH WOOD
FRYLANDS WOOD
(Scout Camp)
PUPLET
WOOD
Farleigh
Common
FARLEIGH
GREATPARK WOOD
Cheverells
TANDRIDGE
Warlingham
CR6
WARLINGHAM
Chelsham
Common
CHELSHAM
Hamsey
Green
KINGS WOOD
Newlands
Wood
SELSDON PARK ROAD A2022
125
140
Crab Wood
Selsdon Park
Hotel
The Forestdale Centre
John Ruskin
College
Monks Hill
Sports Centre
North Down
New
Addington
Fieldway
Superstore
HOLT WOOD
Henley
Wood
Ledgers Park

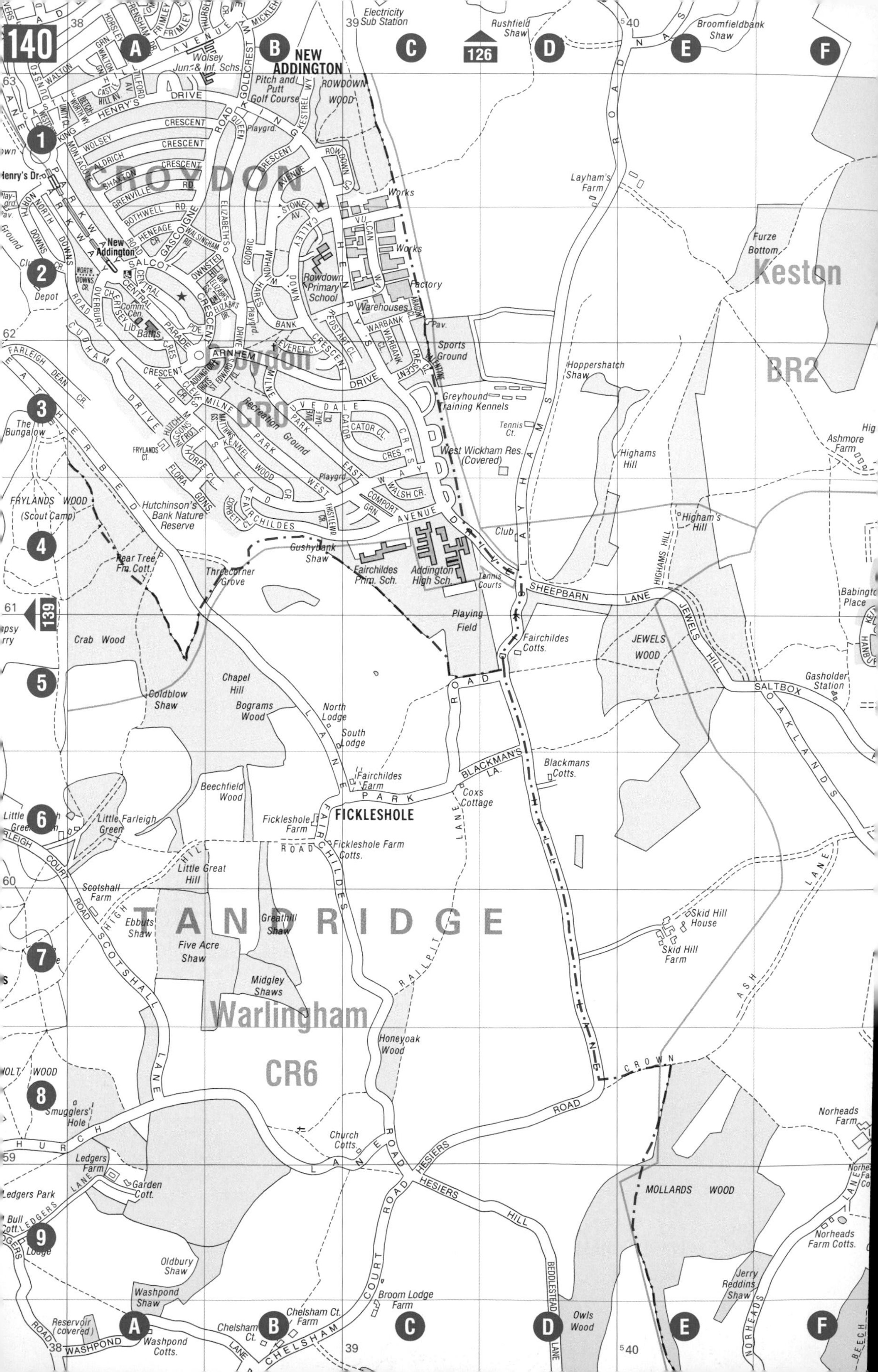

126
139
NEW ADDINGTON
CROYDON
Croydon
CR0
Keston
BR2
TANDRIDGE
Warlingham
CR6
FICKLESHOLE
Electricity Sub Station
Rushfield Shaw
Broomfieldbank Shaw
Wolsey Jun. & Inf. Schs.
Pitch and Putt Golf Course
ROWDOWN WOOD
Works
Factory
Warehouses
Rowdown Primary School
New Addington
Comm. Cen.
Lib.
Baths
Sports Ground
Pav.
Greyhound Training Kennels
Tennis Ct.
West Wickham Res. (Covered)
Recreation Ground
Playgrd.
Club
Fairchildes Prim. Sch.
Addington High Sch.
Tennis Courts
Playing Field
Gushybank Shaw
Threecorner Grove
Hutchinson's Bank Nature Reserve
FRYLANDS WOOD (Scout Camp)
The Bungalow
Pear Tree Fm. Cott.
Crab Wood
Coldblow Shaw
Chapel Hill
Bograms Wood
North Lodge
South Lodge
Fairchildes Farm
Fickleshole Farm
Fickleshole Farm Cotts.
Coxs Cottage
Blackmans Cotts.
Beechfield Wood
Little Farleigh Green
Little Great Hill
Scotshall Farm
Ebbuts Shaw
Five Acre Shaw
Greathill Shaw
Midgley Shaws
Honeyoak Wood
Smugglers' Hole
Church Cotts.
Ledgers Farm
Garden Cott.
Ledgers Park
Oldbury Shaw
Washpond Shaw
Reservoir (covered)
Washpond Cotts.
Chelsham Ct.
Chelsham Ct. Farm
Broom Lodge Farm
Owls Wood
MOLLARDS WOOD
Jerry Reddins Shaw
Norheads Farm
Norheads Farm Cotts.
Skid Hill House
Skid Hill Farm
Layham's Farm
Hoppershatch Shaw
Highams Hill
Higham's Hill
JEWELS WOOD
Fairchildes Cotts.
Furze Bottom
Ashmore Farm
Babington Place
Gasholder Station
KING HENRY'S DRIVE
PARKWAY
GASCOIGNE
SALCOT CRESCENT
CENTRAL PARADE
ARNHEM DRIVE
MILNE PARK
UVEDALE CRES.
EAST WAY
WEST WAY
FAIRCHILDES AVENUE
GOLDCREST WAY
KESTREL WY.
HENRY'S AVENUE
SHEEPBARN LANE
LAYHAMS ROAD
JEWELS HILL
SALTBOX
OAKLANDS
ASH LANE
BLACKMAN'S LA.
PARK LANE
FAIRCHILDES ROAD
RAILPIT LANE
CROWN ROAD
HESIERS ROAD
HESIERS HILL
BEDDLESTEAD LANE
CHELSHAM COURT ROAD
CHURCH LANE
SCOTSHALL LANE
FARLEIGH COURT ROAD
LEDGERS LANE
WASHPOND LANE
NORHEADS LANE
FARLEIGH DEAN CR.
CUDHAM DRIVE
FEATHERBED LANE
HIGH SCOTSHALL

127
Farthing Street
Westerham Lodge
Holwood Farm
Keston Court Farm
Glebe Farm
Longlands Nurseries
Kimberley Poultry Farm
Vale Farm
Farthing Street Farm
Farthings
Orange Court
Meadow Cott.
Green Acres
Hazels
Little Crowhill
The Rookery
Rookery Cotts.
Blacklands
North End Farm Cotts
HIGH ELMS GOLF COURSE
Cuckoo Lodge
Gorringes
Long Acre
Play. Fld.
Rec. Grd.
DOWNE
Orpington
Downe Hall
Petleys Farm
Petleys
Downe Hall Farm
WEST KENT GOLF COURSE
Club House
Downe Lodge
The Vicarage
Green Hill
Down House & Darwin Mus.
Buckston Browne Research Farm
Downe Court
Thompson Wood
BR6
Square Shaw
Downe Bank
Hang Grove
Beechwood
The Boundary
Shaws Cott.
Sevenoaks TN14
LEAVES GREEN
The Green
Greenacres Riding Sch.
Milking Lane Farm
Passenger Terminal
LONDON - BIGGIN HILL AIRPORT
B R O M L E Y
SOW WOOD
Snotsdale Wood
Cudham Lodge Woods
South London Aero Club
Ladies Wood
Cricket Grd.
Flora Nurseries
Spencers Grove
Luxted
Luxted Fm.
Greenacres
Brownsea Hut (Boy Scouts)
Twenty Acre Shaw
Downe Camp
Clock Tower
Leasons Wood
Bird House Wood
Great Southfield Shaw
Bromley Croft
Swim. Bath
Single Street
Bottom Barn
AIRPORT INDUSTRIAL ESTATE
BIGGIN HILL BUSINESS PARK
CONCORDE BUSINESS PK.
St. Julians Farm
Playing Fld.
Costains Farm
Strakes Shaw
Bertrey Cotts.
Charles Darwin School
Barn Farm
Primrose Farm
Parkfield Fm.
Cudham C.of E Prim.Sch.
Westerham
Cemetery
Biggin Hill Jun. & Inf. Schs.
Golden Acres
Littlewood Farm
Homeleigh Farm
BERRY'S GREEN
RESTAVON CARAVAN SITE
Blackbush Shaw
Recreation Ground
Grubb Grounds Farm
Brickyard Farm
Library
BIGGIN HILL
TN16
CHERRY LODGE GOLF COURSE
Club House
Oak Farm
Warren Farm
Foal Farm
Pimlico Wood
Laurel Farm
Valley View
APERFIELD
Oaklands Jun.Sch.
A233
WESTERHAM ROAD
LEAVES GREEN ROAD
MAIN ROAD
DOWNE ROAD
NEW ROAD HILL
HIGH ST.
NORTH END LANE
CUDHAM ROAD
HANGROVE HILL
LUXTED ROAD
CHURCHILL WAY
JAIL LANE
BERRY'S GREEN ROAD
SINGLE STREET
MILKING LANE
GREEN HILL WEST
SUNNINGVALE AVENUE
STOCK HILL
G H J K L M
1 2 3 4 5 6 7 8 9
42 43 44
59 60 61 62 63

142
WESTERN
A40
AVENUE
ICKENHAM
SWAKELEYS ROUNDABOUT
Vyners School
Sports Ground
WILLOWBANK
UB9
Hillingdon Ski Centre
Ski Slope
Uxbridge Common
Hillingdon House Farm Showground
Swimming Pool
Uxbridge College
Uxbridge
UXBRIDGE
UB10
HILLINGDON COURT PARK
(Recreation Ground)
American Community School
R.A.F. STATION
HILLINGDON
HILLINGDON GOLF COURSE
Abbotsfield School
UB8
BRUNEL UNIVERSITY
Uxbridge High Sch.
The Grove Nature Reserve
Hillingdon Cem.
Uxbridge Cem.
Bishopshalt School
COWLEY
COLHAM GREEN
HILLINGDON HEATH
HILLINGDON HOSPITAL
PIELD HEATH
COWLEY PEACHEY
Moorcroft School
West Drayton
Little Britain
Cowley Lake
Goulds Green
STOCKLEY PARK COUNTRY PARK
STILWELL ROUNDABOUT
143
52
A4020
A408
A437
A4007
B470
B483
B467
B466
B465
UXBRIDGE ROAD
HILLINGDON HILL
HARLINGTON ROAD
LONG LANE
COWLEY ROAD
HIGH STREET
PARK ROAD
FALLING LANE
WEST DRAYTON ROAD
GRAND UNION CANAL

YIEWSLEY
WEST DRAYTON
HARMONDSWORTH
SIPSON
Goulds Green
Uxbridge
UB8
Hayes
UB3
Iver
SL0
Hounslow
TW6
HILLINGDON
West Drayton
LONDON - HEATHROW AIRPORT
STOCKLEY PARK COUNTRY PARK
STOCKLEY PARK GOLF COURSE
HEATH PARK GOLF COURSE
Recreation Ground
R.A.F. Station
Crowne Plaza Hotel
Cherry Lane Roundabout
Junction 4b (M4)
Junction 4
Junction 4a
M4 MOTORWAY
A408
A3044
A4
COLNBROOK BY-PASS
BATH ROAD
FALLING LANE
STOCKLEY ROAD
HOLLOWAY LANE
HATCH LANE
SIPSON ROAD
SIPSON LANE
CHERRY LANE
NORTHERN PERIMETER ROAD
HIGH STREET
GRAND UNION CANAL
Grand Union Canal Walk
River Colne
Harmondsworth Immigration Detention Centre
The Crest Hotel
Excelsior Hotel
The Ramada Hotel
Heathrow Primary School
Longmead Prim. Sch.
West Drayton Prim. Sch.
Rabbsfarm Prim. Sch.
Harmondsworth Prim. Sch.
Cherry Lane Jun. & Inf. School
Little Harlington Field
Bourne Farm Playing Field
Burial Ground
Community Centre
Cricket Grd.
Playing Field
Cemetery
Government Offices
Stockley Bridge
Horton Bridge
Warehouses
Works
142
144
G H J K L M
1 2 3 4 5 6 7 8 9
06 07 08

LONDON-HEATHROW AIRPORT
HILLINGDON
Hounslow
TW6
PROPOSED TERMINAL 5 DEVELOPMENT AREA
Perry Oaks Sewage Works
West Drayton
UB7
TERMINAL 3
TERMINAL 2
TERMINAL 1
Heathrow Terminals 1,2&3
Heathrow Cen. Bus Sta.
Control Tower
D'Albiac House
Cargo Terminal
Cargo Tunnel
Vehicle Tunnel
Heathrow Express Rail Link
WESSEX ROAD
PERIMETER ROAD
NORTHERN PERIMETER ROAD
SOUTHERN PERIMETER ROAD
STANWELL
West Bedfont
WEST BEDFONT
Staines
TW19
STAINES RESERVOIRS
(BIRD SANCTUARY)
SPELTHORNE
HOUNSLOW
CLOCKHOUSE ROUNDABOUT
TW14
Feltham
Ashford
ASHFORD
TW15
Ashford Park
Ashford Park Prim. Sch.
Hengrove Farm
Cemetery
Shortwood Pond
Shortwood Common
LONDON ROAD (ROMAN ROAD) A30
STAINES ROAD A30
STANWELL MOOR ROAD A3044
B378
B3003
Recreation Ground
Ashford Football Ground
Westview Cotts.
Sports Ground
Playing Field
Piggeries
Factory
Depot
Mentone Farm
Longford River
Homers Farm
Nursery
Warehouses
Visitor Cen.
Bridge Farm
The Ashford High Sch.
St. David's School
Superstore
ASHFORD HOSP.
The Holloway Unit
Ashford Cemetery
Prim. Schs.
Prim. Sch.
Liby.
Play Fld.
Rec. Gd.
Cemetery
143
84

**CENTRAL LONDON
PLACES OF INTEREST**

Ⓤ Underground Station

⇄ Main Line Station

DLR Docklands Light Railway Station

ℹ Tourist Information Centre

■ Principal Shopping Areas

Scale: 1½ inches to 1 mile

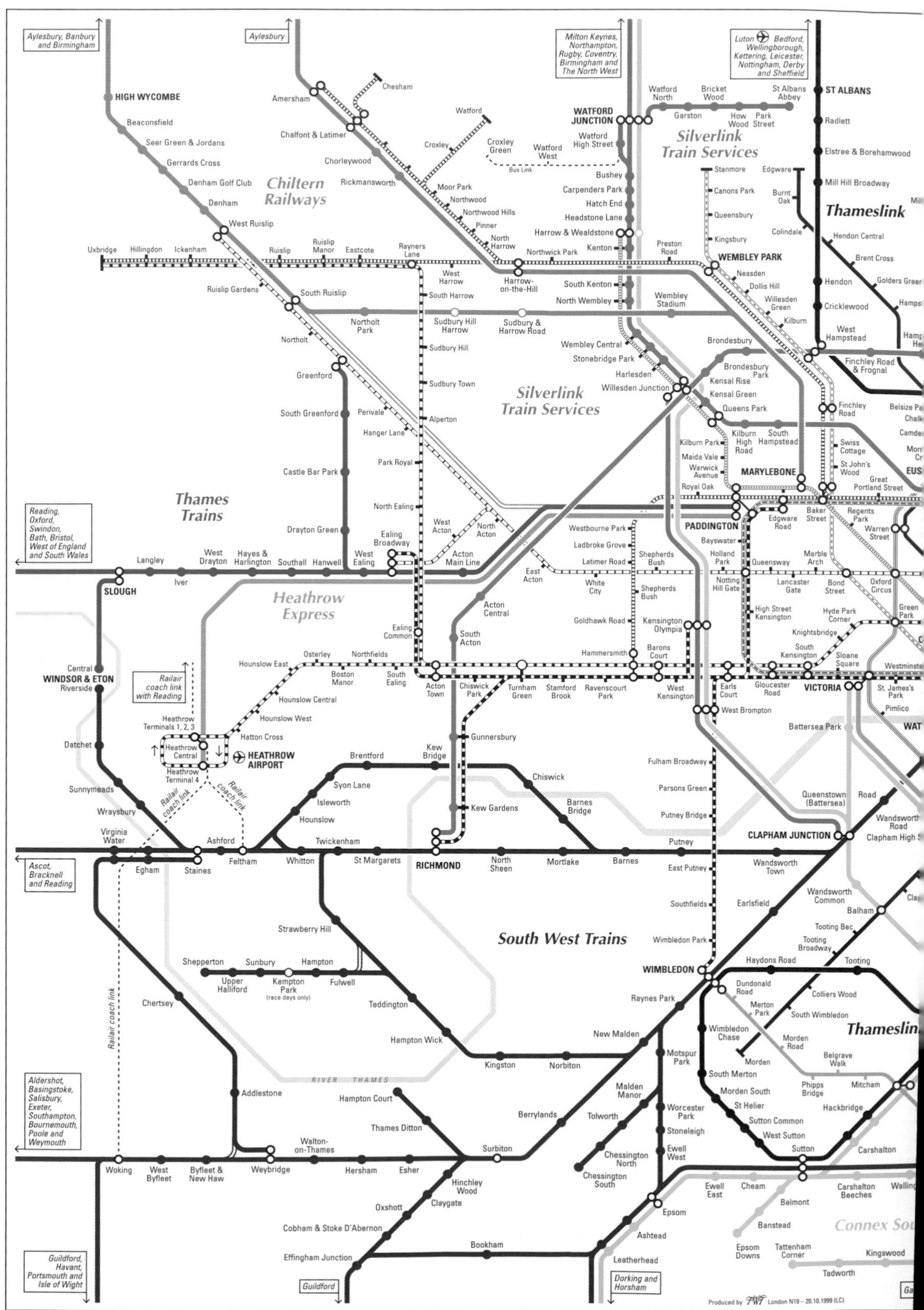

Aylesbury, Banbury and Birmingham
Aylesbury
Milton Keynes, Northampton, Rugby, Coventry, Birmingham and The North West
Luton Bedford, Wellingborough, Kettering, Leicester, Nottingham, Derby and Sheffield
HIGH WYCOMBE
Beaconsfield
Seer Green & Jordans
Gerrards Cross
Denham Golf Club
Denham
West Ruislip
Chiltern Railways
Amersham
Chesham
Chalfont & Latimer
Chorleywood
Rickmansworth
Watford
Croxley
Croxley Green
Watford West
Bus Link
Moor Park
Northwood
Northwood Hills
Pinner
North Harrow
WATFORD JUNCTION
Watford High Street
Bushey
Carpenders Park
Hatch End
Headstone Lane
Harrow & Wealdstone
Kenton
Watford North
Garston
Bricket Wood
How Wood
Park Street
St Albans Abbey
Silverlink Train Services
Stanmore
Canons Park
Queensbury
Kingsbury
Edgware
Burnt Oak
Colindale
ST ALBANS
Radlett
Elstree & Borehamwood
Mill Hill Broadway
Thameslink
Hendon Central
Brent Cross
Hendon
Golders Green
Cricklewood
West Hampstead
Uxbridge
Hillingdon
Ickenham
Ruislip
Ruislip Manor
Eastcote
Rayners Lane
West Harrow
Harrow-on-the-Hill
Northwick Park
Preston Road
WEMBLEY PARK
Neasden
Dollis Hill
Willesden Green
Kilburn
Ruislip Gardens
South Ruislip
South Harrow
South Kenton
North Wembley
Wembley Stadium
Northolt Park
Sudbury Hill Harrow
Sudbury & Harrow Road
Northolt
Sudbury Hill
Wembley Central
Stonebridge Park
Harlesden
Willesden Junction
Brondesbury
Brondesbury Park
Kensal Rise
Kensal Green
Queens Park
Finchley Road & Frognal
Greenford
Sudbury Town
Silverlink Train Services
South Greenford
Perivale
Hanger Lane
Alperton
Finchley Road
Kilburn Park
Kilburn High Road
South Hampstead
Maida Vale
Warwick Avenue
Swiss Cottage
St John's Wood
Castle Bar Park
Park Royal
MARYLEBONE
Royal Oak
Great Portland Street
Thames Trains
North Ealing
Edgware Road
Baker Street
Regents Park
Reading, Oxford, Swindon, Bath, Bristol, West of England and South Wales
Drayton Green
West Acton
North Acton
Westbourne Park
PADDINGTON
Warren Street
Ealing Broadway
Ladbroke Grove
Bayswater
Langley
West Drayton
Hayes & Harlington
Southall
Hanwell
West Ealing
Acton Main Line
Latimer Road
Shepherds Bush
Holland Park
Queensway
Marble Arch
Iver
SLOUGH
East Acton
White City
Shepherds Bush
Notting Hill Gate
Lancaster Gate
Bond Street
Oxford Circus
Heathrow Express
Acton Central
High Street Kensington
Hyde Park Corner
Green Park
Goldhawk Road
Kensington Olympia
Knightsbridge
Ealing Common
South Acton
Central
WINDSOR & ETON
Riverside
Osterley
Northfields
Hounslow East
Boston Manor
South Ealing
Hammersmith
Barons Court
South Kensington
Sloane Square
Westminster
Railair coach link with Reading
Acton Town
Chiswick Park
Turnham Green
Stamford Brook
Ravenscourt Park
West Kensington
Earls Court
Gloucester Road
VICTORIA
St. James's Park
Hounslow Central
Pimlico
Hounslow West
West Brompton
Heathrow Terminals 1, 2, 3
Hatton Cross
Battersea Park
Datchet
Heathrow Central
HEATHROW AIRPORT
Gunnersbury
Heathrow Terminal 4
Brentford
Kew Bridge
Chiswick
Fulham Broadway
Sunnymeads
Syon Lane
Railair coach link
Isleworth
Parsons Green
Barnes Bridge
Queenstown Road (Battersea)
Wraysbury
Hounslow
Kew Gardens
Putney Bridge
Wandsworth Road
Virginia Water
Ashford
Twickenham
CLAPHAM JUNCTION
Clapham High Street
Putney
Egham
Staines
Feltham
Whitton
St Margarets
RICHMOND
North Sheen
Mortlake
Barnes
East Putney
Wandsworth Town
Ascot, Bracknell and Reading
Southfields
Earlsfield
Wandsworth Common
Balham
Strawberry Hill
Tooting Bec
Tooting Broadway
South West Trains
Wimbledon Park
Shepperton
Sunbury
Hampton
Haydons Road
Tooting
Upper Halliford
Kempton Park (race days only)
Fulwell
WIMBLEDON
Dundonald Road
Railair coach link
Colliers Wood
Chertsey
Teddington
Raynes Park
Merton Park
South Wimbledon
Wimbledon Chase
Morden Road
Thameslink
New Malden
Hampton Wick
Motspur Park
Belgrave Walk
Kingston
Norbiton
Morden
South Merton
River Thames
Malden Manor
Phipps Bridge
Mitcham
Aldershot, Basingstoke, Salisbury, Exeter, Southampton, Bournemouth, Poole and Weymouth
Addlestone
Hampton Court
Morden South
St Helier
Berrylands
Tolworth
Worcester Park
Hackbridge
Thames Ditton
Sutton Common
Stoneleigh
West Sutton
Walton-on-Thames
Surbiton
Ewell West
Sutton
Carshalton
Chessington North
Woking
West Byfleet
Byfleet & New Haw
Weybridge
Hersham
Esher
Chessington South
Ewell East
Cheam
Carshalton Beeches
Hinchley Wood
Belmont
Claygate
Oxshott
Epsom
Banstead
Connex South
Cobham & Stoke D'Abernon
Ashtead
Epsom Downs
Tattenham Corner
Kingswood
Bookham
Effingham Junction
Leatherhead
Tadworth
Guildford, Havant, Portsmouth and Isle of Wight
Guildford
Dorking and Horsham
Produced by TWT London N19 – 20.10.1999 (LC)

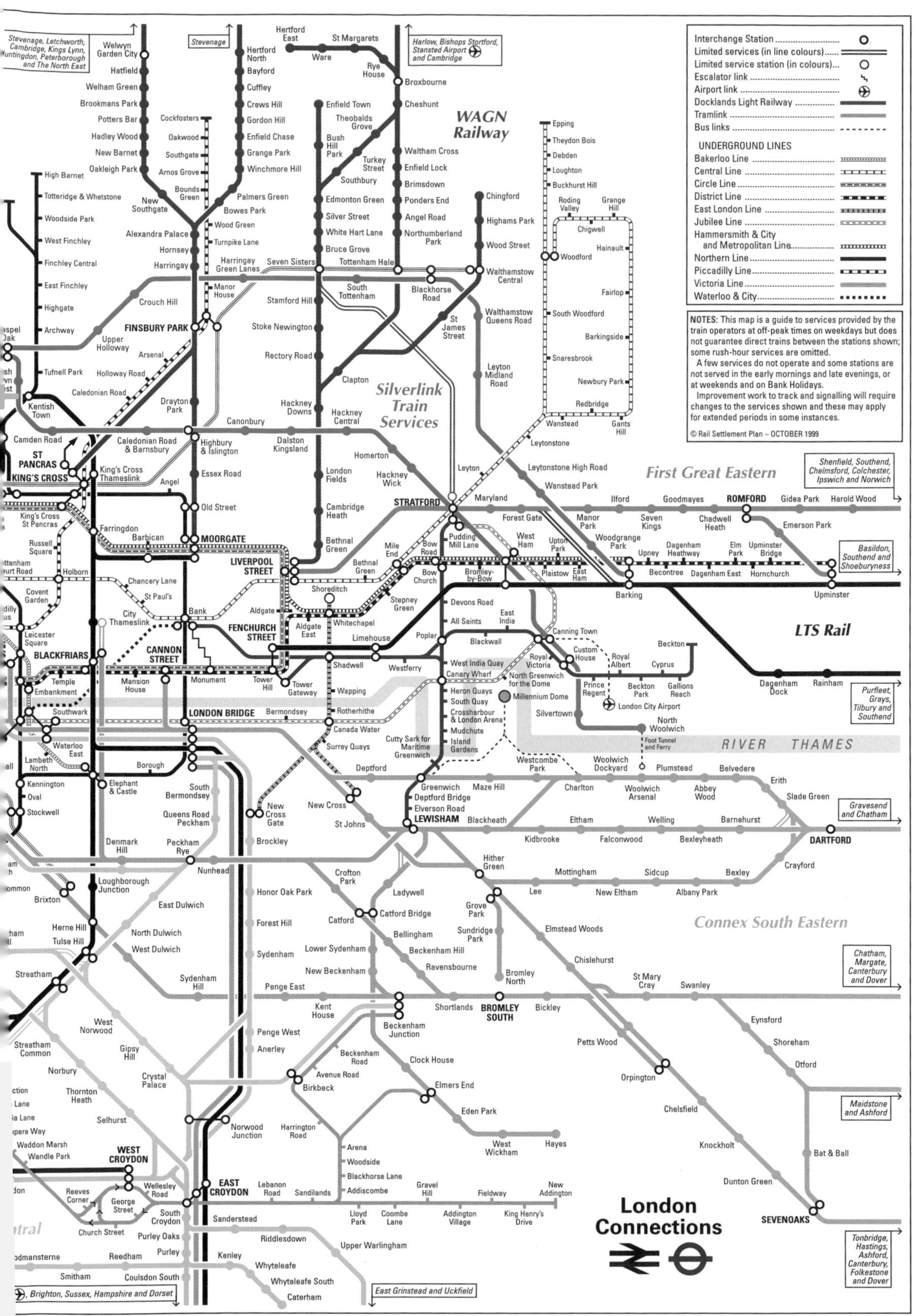
London Connections
WAGN Railway
Silverlink Train Services
First Great Eastern
LTS Rail
Connex South Eastern
RIVER THAMES
Interchange Station
Limited services (in line colours)
Limited service station (in colours)
Escalator link
Airport link
Docklands Light Railway
Tramlink
Bus links
UNDERGROUND LINES
Bakerloo Line
Central Line
Circle Line
District Line
East London Line
Jubilee Line
Hammersmith & City and Metropolitan Line
Northern Line
Piccadilly Line
Victoria Line
Waterloo & City
NOTES: This map is a guide to services provided by the train operators at off-peak times on weekdays but does not guarantee direct trains between the stations shown; some rush-hour services are omitted.
A few services do not operate and some stations are not served in the early mornings and late evenings, or at weekends and on Bank Holidays.
Improvement work to track and signalling will require changes to the services shown and these may apply for extended periods in some instances.
© Rail Settlement Plan – OCTOBER 1999
Stevenage, Letchworth, Cambridge, Kings Lynn, Huntingdon, Peterborough and The North East
Stevenage
Harlow, Bishops Stortford, Stansted Airport and Cambridge
Shenfield, Southend, Chelmsford, Colchester, Ipswich and Norwich
Basildon, Southend and Shoeburyness
Purfleet, Grays, Tilbury and Southend
Gravesend and Chatham
Chatham, Margate, Canterbury and Dover
Maidstone and Ashford
Tonbridge, Hastings, Ashford, Canterbury, Folkestone and Dover
East Grinstead and Uckfield
Brighton, Sussex, Hampshire and Dorset
Welwyn Garden City
Hatfield
Welham Green
Brookmans Park
Potters Bar
Hadley Wood
New Barnet
Oakleigh Park
High Barnet
Totteridge & Whetstone
Woodside Park
West Finchley
Finchley Central
East Finchley
Highgate
Archway
Tufnell Park
Kentish Town
Camden Road
ST PANCRAS
KING'S CROSS
Cockfosters
Oakwood
Southgate
Arnos Grove
Bounds Green
New Southgate
Alexandra Palace
Hornsey
Harringay
Crouch Hill
FINSBURY PARK
Upper Holloway
Arsenal
Holloway Road
Caledonian Road
Drayton Park
Caledonian Road & Barnsbury
King's Cross Thameslink
Angel
Highbury & Islington
Essex Road
Old Street
MOORGATE
Barbican
Farringdon
King's Cross St Pancras
Russell Square
Holborn
Chancery Lane
St Paul's
Covent Garden
City Thameslink
Leicester Square
BLACKFRIARS
Temple
Embankment
Mansion House
CANNON STREET
Monument
Bank
Hertford North
Bayford
Cuffley
Crews Hill
Gordon Hill
Enfield Chase
Grange Park
Winchmore Hill
Palmers Green
Bowes Park
Wood Green
Turnpike Lane
Harringay Green Lanes
Manor House
Hertford East
St Margarets
Ware
Rye House
Broxbourne
Cheshunt
Waltham Cross
Enfield Lock
Brimsdown
Ponders End
Angel Road
Northumberland Park
Tottenham Hale
Enfield Town
Theobalds Grove
Bush Hill Park
Turkey Street
Southbury
Edmonton Green
Silver Street
White Hart Lane
Bruce Grove
Seven Sisters
South Tottenham
Stamford Hill
Stoke Newington
Rectory Road
Hackney Downs
Clapton
Chingford
Highams Park
Wood Street
Walthamstow Central
Blackhorse Road
St James Street
Walthamstow Queens Road
Leyton Midland Road
Hackney Central
Canonbury
Dalston Kingsland
Homerton
Hackney Wick
London Fields
Cambridge Heath
Bethnal Green
LIVERPOOL STREET
Aldgate
Aldgate East
FENCHURCH STREET
Tower Hill
Tower Gateway
Shoreditch
Whitechapel
Mile End
Stepney Green
Bow Road
Bow Church
Limehouse
Shadwell
Wapping
Rotherhithe
Canada Water
Surrey Quays
Epping
Theydon Bois
Debden
Loughton
Buckhurst Hill
Roding Valley
Grange Hill
Chigwell
Hainault
Woodford
Fairlop
South Woodford
Barkingside
Snaresbrook
Newbury Park
Redbridge
Wanstead
Gants Hill
Leytonstone
Leyton
Leytonstone High Road
Wanstead Park
STRATFORD
Maryland
Forest Gate
Manor Park
Ilford
Seven Kings
Goodmayes
Chadwell Heath
ROMFORD
Gidea Park
Harold Wood
Emerson Park
Upminster
Woodgrange Park
Upney
Dagenham Heathway
Elm Park
Upminster Bridge
Becontree
Dagenham East
Hornchurch
Barking
Pudding Mill Lane
West Ham
Upton Park
Plaistow
East Ham
Bromley-by-Bow
Devons Road
All Saints
East India
Poplar
Blackwall
Canning Town
Custom House
Royal Victoria
Royal Albert
Beckton
Cyprus
Prince Regent
Beckton Park
Gallions Reach
London City Airport
Silvertown
North Woolwich
Foot Tunnel and Ferry
Dagenham Dock
Rainham
Westferry
West India Quay
Canary Wharf
North Greenwich for the Dome
Millennium Dome
Heron Quays
South Quay
Crossharbour & London Arena
Mudchute
Island Gardens
Cutty Sark for Maritime Greenwich
Deptford
Greenwich
Maze Hill
Westcombe Park
Woolwich Dockyard
Plumstead
Belvedere
Erith
Slade Green
Charlton
Woolwich Arsenal
Abbey Wood
Deptford Bridge
Elverson Road
LEWISHAM
Blackheath
Kidbrooke
Eltham
Falconwood
Welling
Bexleyheath
Barnehurst
DARTFORD
Crayford
Bexley
Sidcup
Albany Park
Mottingham
New Eltham
Hither Green
Lee
Grove Park
Sundridge Park
Bromley North
Elmstead Woods
Chislehurst
St Mary Cray
Swanley
Eynsford
Shoreham
Otford
Orpington
Petts Wood
Chelsfield
Knockholt
Dunton Green
SEVENOAKS
Bat & Ball
LONDON BRIDGE
Bermondsey
Borough
Waterloo East
Southwark
Lambeth North
Kennington
Oval
Stockwell
Elephant & Castle
South Bermondsey
Queens Road Peckham
Peckham Rye
Denmark Hill
Nunhead
Loughborough Junction
Brixton
Herne Hill
Tulse Hill
Streatham
East Dulwich
North Dulwich
West Dulwich
Sydenham Hill
New Cross
New Cross Gate
St Johns
Brockley
Honor Oak Park
Forest Hill
Sydenham
Crofton Park
Ladywell
Catford
Catford Bridge
Bellingham
Beckenham Hill
Ravensbourne
Lower Sydenham
New Beckenham
Penge East
Kent House
Shortlands
BROMLEY SOUTH
Bickley
Beckenham Junction
Penge West
Anerley
West Norwood
Gipsy Hill
Crystal Palace
Streatham Common
Norbury
Thornton Heath
Selhurst
Norwood Junction
Beckenham Road
Avenue Road
Birkbeck
Clock House
Elmers End
Eden Park
West Wickham
Hayes
Harrington Road
Arena
Woodside
Blackhorse Lane
Addiscombe
WEST CROYDON
EAST CROYDON
Waddon Marsh
Wandle Park
Reeves Corner
George Street
Church Street
Wellesley Road
South Croydon
Lebanon Road
Sandilands
Lloyd Park
Coombe Lane
Gravel Hill
Addington Village
Fieldway
King Henry's Drive
New Addington
Sanderstead
Riddlesdown
Upper Warlingham
Purley Oaks
Purley
Reedham
Kenley
Whyteleafe
Whyteleafe South
Caterham
Smitham
Coulsdon South

WEST END CINEMAS

ODEON TOTTENHAM COURT RD.
ABC SHAFTESBURY AVENUE
CURZON SOHO
PRINCE CHARLES
WARNER WEST END
UCI EMPIRE
METRO
UGC TROCADERO
ODEON WARDOUR ST.
ODEON LEICESTER SQUARE & MEZZANINE
ODEON WEST END
ABC PICCADILLY CIRCUS
ODEON HAYMARKET
ODEON PANTON STREET
UGC HAYMARKET
UCI PLAZA
ICA
NATIONAL FILM THEATRE
BFI IMAX

WEST END THEATRES

DOMINION
COCHRANE
ASTORIA
SHAFTESBURY
LONDON PALLADIUM
SOHO
PRINCE EDWARD
PHOENIX
NEW LONDON
DONMAR WAREHOUSE
PEACOCK
CAMBRIDGE
RAYMOND REVUEBAR
PALACE
ST. MARTINS
FORTUNE
NEW AMBASSADORS
DRURY LANE Theatre Royal
ARTS
ROYAL OPERA HOUSE
ALDWYCH
QUEENS
PICCADILLY
GIELGUD
STRAND
APOLLO
ALBERY
LYRIC
DUCHESS
LYCEUM
PRINCE OF WALES
Half Price Ticket Booth
WYNDHAMS
DUKE OF YORKS
SAVOY
CRITERION
COMEDY STORE
GARRICK
COLISEUM English National Opera
VAUDEVILLE
ADELPHI
COMEDY
JERMYN STREET
HAYMARKET Theatre Royal
ROYAL NATIONAL
PLAYERS
PURCELL ROOM
QUEEN ELIZABETH HALL
HER MAJESTY'S
ROYAL FESTIVAL HALL
PLAYHOUSE
ICA
WHITEHALL

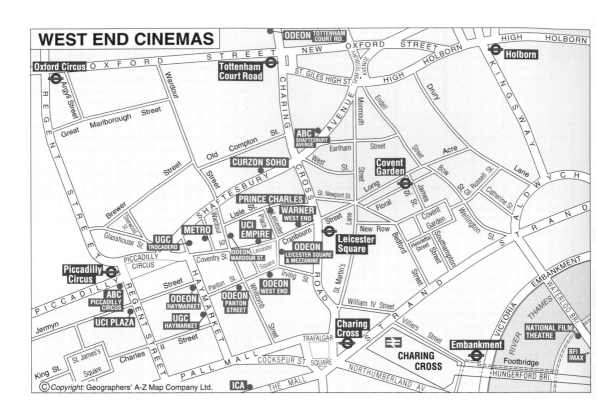

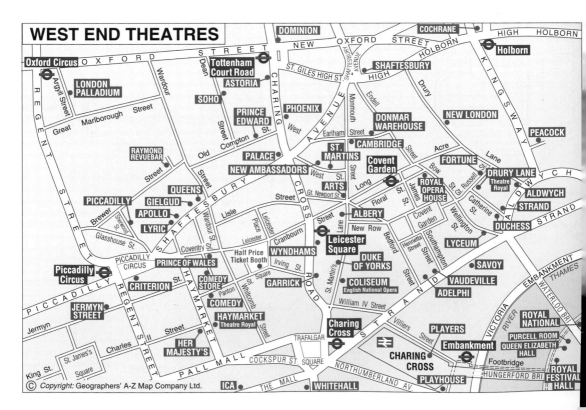

INDEX

Including Streets, Places & Areas, Industrial Estates, Selected Flats & Walkways,
Junction Names and Selected Places of Interest.

HOW TO USE THIS INDEX

1. Each street name is followed by its Postal District (or, if outside the London Postal District, by its Posttown or Postal Locality), and then by its map reference;
e.g. Aaron Hill Rd. *E6* . . . .*8L* **63** is in the East 6 Postal District and is to be found in square 8L on page **63**. The page number being shown in bold type.

2. A strict alphabetical order is followed in which Av., Rd., St., etc. (though abbreviated) are read in full and as part of the street name; e.g. Abbotstone Clo. appears after Abbots Ter. but before Abbot St.

3. Streets and a selection of flats and walkways too small to be shown on the maps, appear in the index in *Italics* with the thoroughfare to which it is connected shown in brackets;
e.g. *Abady Ho. SW1* . . . .*5H* **75** (off Page St.)

4. Places and areas are shown in the index in **blue type** and the map reference is to the actual map square in which the town centre or area is located and not to the place name shown on the map; e.g. **Abbey Wood** 5G 81

5. An example of a selected place of interest is Albert Memorial 3B 74

6. Junction names are shown in the index in **bold type**; e.g. **Aldgate (Junct.)** 9D 60

GENERAL ABBREVIATIONS

All : Alley	Cir : Circus	Gt : Great	M : Mews	Sq : Square
App : Approach	Clo : Close	Grn : Green	Mt : Mount	Sta : Station
Arc : Arcade	Comn : Common	Gro : Grove	Mus : Museum	St : Street
Av : Avenue	Cotts : Cottages	Ho : House	N : North	Ter : Terrace
Bk : Back	Ct : Court	Ind : Industrial	Pal : Palace	Trad : Trading
Boulevd : Boulevard	Cres : Crescent	Info : Information	Pde : Parade	Up : Upper
Bri : Bridge	Cft : Croft	Junct : Junction	Pk : Park	Va : Vale
B'way : Broadway	Dri : Drive	La : Lane	Pas : Passage	Vw : View
Bldgs : Buildings	E : East	Lit : Little	Pl : Place	Vs : Villas
Bus : Business	Embkmt : Embankment	Lwr : Lower	Quad : Quadrant	Vis : Visitors
Cvn : Caravan	Est : Estate	Mc : Mac	Res : Residential	Wlk : Walk
Cen : Centre	Fld : Field	Mnr : Manor	Ri : Rise	W : West
Chu : Church	Gdns : Gardens	Mans : Mansions	Rd : Road	Yd : Yard
Chyd : Churchyard	Gth : Garth	Mkt : Market	Shop : Shopping	
Circ : Circle	Ga : Gate	Mdw : Meadow	S : South	

POSTTOWN AND POSTAL LOCALITY ABBREVIATIONS

Ab L : Abbots Langley	*Chst* : Chislehurst	*Hack* : Hackbridge	*Mitc* : Mitcham	*Stan* : Stanmore
Abr : Abridge	*Clar P* : Claremont Park	*Hals* : Halstead	*Mit J* : Mitcham Junction	*Stanw* : Stanwell
A'ham : Aldenham	*Clay* : Claygate	*Ham* : Ham	*Mord* : Morden	*Stap A* : Stapleford Abbotts
Ark : Arkley	*Cob* : Cobham	*Hamp* : Hampton	*Nave* : Navestock	*Stoke D* : Stoke D'Abernon
Ashf : Ashford	*Cockf* : Cockfosters	*Hamp H* : Hampton Hill	*New Ad* : New Addington	*Stne* : Stone
Asht : Ashtead	*Col R* : Collier Row	*Hamp W* : Hampton Wick	*New Bar* : New Barnet	*S'leigh* : Stoneleigh
Ave : Aveley	*Coln* : Colnbrook	*Hanw* : Hanworth	*N Mald* : New Malden	*Sun* : Sunbury-on-Thames
Badg M : Badgers Mount	*Coul* : Coulsdon	*Hare* : Harefield	*Noak H* : Noak Hill	*Surb* : Surbiton
Bans : Banstead	*Cow* : Cowley	*Harm* : Harmondsworth	*N Har* : North Harrow	*Sutt* : Sutton
Bark : Barking	*Cran* : Cranford	*H Hill* : Harold Hill	*N Ock* : North Ockendon	*S at H* : Sutton at Hone
B'side : Barkingside	*Craw* : Crawley	*H Wood* : Harold Wood	*N'holt* : Northolt	*Swan* : Swanley
B'hurst : Barnehurst	*Cray* : Crayford	*Harr* : Harrow	*N Hth* : Northumberland Heath	*Tad* : Tadworth
Barn : Barnet	*Crock* : Crockenhill	*Har W* : Harrow Weald	*N'wd* : Northwood	*Tats* : Tatsfield
B Hth : Batchworth Heath	*Crox G* : Croxley Green	*H End* : Hatch End	*Orp* : Orpington	*Tedd* : Teddington
Bean : Bean	*Croy* : Croydon	*Hav* : Havering-atte-Bower	*Oxs* : Oxshott	*Th Dit* : Thames Ditton
Beck : Beckenham	*Cud* : Cudham	*Hawl* : Hawley	*Park* : Park Street	*T Hth* : Thornton Heath
Bedd : Beddington	*Dag* : Dagenham	*Hayes* : Hayes (Kent)	*Pet W* : Petts Wood	*Twic* : Twickenham
Bedf : Bedfont	*Dart* : Dartford	*Hay* : Hayes (Middlesex)	*Pil H* : Pilgrims Hatch	*Upm* : Upminster
Bedm : Bedmond	*Den* : Denham	*H'row* : Heathrow	*Pinn* : Pinner	*Uxb* : Uxbridge
Belm : Belmont	*Dit H* : Ditton Hill	*H'row A* : London Heathrow Airport	*Pot B* : Potters Bar	*Wall* : Wallington
Belv : Belvedere	*Dow* : Downe	*Hers* : Hersham	*Purf* : Purfleet	*Wal A* : Waltham Abbey
Berr G : Berrys Green	*E Barn* : East Barnet	*Hex* : Hextable	*Purl* : Purley	*Wal X* : Waltham Cross
Bex : Bexley	*Eastc* : Eastcote	*High Bar* : High Barnet	*Rad* : Radlett	*W on T* : Walton-on-Thames
Bexh : Bexleyheath	*E Mol* : East Molesey	*H Bee* : High Beech	*Rain* : Rainham	*Warl* : Warlingham
Big H : Biggin Hill	*Edgw* : Edgware	*Hil* : Hillingdon	*Rich* : Richmond	*Wat* : Watford
Borwd : Borehamwood	*Elm P* : Elm Park	*Hin W* : Hinchley Wood	*Rick* : Rickmansworth	*W'stone* : Wealdstone
Bren : Brentford	*Els* : Elstree	*Horn* : Hornchurch	*Ridg* : Ridgeway, The	*Well E* : West End
Brtwd : Brentwood	*Enf* : Enfield	*Hort K* : Horton Kirby	*Romf* : Romford	*Well* : Welling
Brick : Brickendon	*Epp* : Epping	*Houn* : Hounslow	*Ruis* : Ruislip	*Wemb* : Wembley
Brick W : Bricket Wood	*Eps* : Epsom	*Ick* : Ickenham	*Rush G* : Rush Green	*Wen* : Wennington
Brim : Brimsdown	*Eri* : Erith	*Ilf* : Ilford	*St Alb* : St Albans	*W Dray* : West Drayton
Brom : Bromley	*Esh* : Esher	*Iswth* : Isleworth	*St M* : St Mary Cray	*W End* : West End
Buck H : Buckhurst Hill	*Ewe* : Ewell	*Iver* : Iver	*St P* : St Pauls Cray	*W'ham* : Westerham
Bush : Bushey	*Eyns* : Eynsford	*Kenl* : Kenley	*Shenl* : Shenley	*W Ewe* : West Ewell
Bus H : Bushey Heath	*F'boro* : Farnborough	*Kent* : Kenton	*Shep* : Shepperton	*W Mol* : West Molesey
Cars : Carshalton	*F'ham* : Farningham	*Kes* : Keston	*Shor* : Shoreham	*W Wick* : West Wickham
Cat : Caterham	*Fawk* : Fawkham	*Kew* : Kew	*Short* : Shortlands	*Wey* : Weybridge
Chad H : Chadwell Heath	*Felt* : Feltham	*K Lan* : Kings Langley	*Sidc* : Sidcup	*W Vill* : Whiteley Village
Chan X : Chandlers Cross	*Frog* : Frogmore	*King T* : Kingston upon Thames	*S'hall* : Southall	*Whit* : Whitton
Cheam : Cheam	*Gid P* : Gidea Park	*Kgswd* : Kingswood	*S Croy* : South Croydon	*Whyt* : Whyteleafe
Chels : Chelsfield	*G Oak* : Goffs Oak	*Knat* : Knatts Valley	*S Dar* : South Darenth	*Wilm* : Wilmington
Chel : Chelsham	*Gnfd* : Greenford	*Lea* : Leatherhead	*S Harr* : South Harrow	*Wfd G* : Woodford Green
Chesh : Cheshunt	*Grnh* : Greenhithe	*Leav* : Leavesden	*S Ock* : South Ockendon	*Wor Pk* : Worcester Park
Chess : Chessington	*G Str* : Green Street Green (Dartford)	*Let H* : Letchmore Heath	*S Ruis* : South Ruislip	
Chig : Chigwell	*Grn St* : Green Street Green	*L Hth* : Little Heath	*S Wea* : South Weald	
Chips : Chipstead	(Orpington)	*Lou* : Loughton	*Stai* : Staines	

A	Abbess Clo. *E6* 8J **63**	Abbey Ct. *Hamp* 4L **101**	Abbey Gdns. *SE16* 5E **76**	Abbey Lodge. *NW8* 6C **58**
	Abbess Clo. *SW2* 7M **91**	Abbey Ct. *Wal A* 7H **7**	Abbey Gdns. *W6* 7J **73**	(off Park Rd.)
	Abbeville M. *SW4* 3H **91**	Abbey Cres. *Belv* 5L **81**	Abbey Gdns. *Chst* 5L **111**	Abbey Mead Ind. Est.
02 Centre. *NW3* 2A **58**	Abbeville Rd. *N8* 2H **43**	Abbeydale Ct. *E17* 1B **46**	Abbey Gro. *SE2* 5F **80**	*Wal A* 7J **7**
101 Bus. Units. *SW11* 2D **90**	Abbeville Rd. *SW4* 5G **91**	Abbeydale Ct. *S'hall* 9M **53**	Abbey Ho. *E15* 5C **62**	(in two parts)
198 Gallery. *5M* **91**	Abbey Av. *Wemb* 5J **55**	(off Dormers Ri.)	(off Baker's Row)	Abbey M. *E17* 3L **45**
(off Railton Rd.)	Abbey Bus. Cen.	Abbeydale Rd. *Wemb* 4K **55**	Abbey Ho. *NW8* 6A **58**	Abbey Mills. *Wal A* 6H **7**
	SW8 . . . . .9G **75**	Abbey Dri. *SW17* 2E **106**	(off Garden Rd.)	Abbey Mt. *Belv* 6K **81**
	Abbey Clo. *Hay* 2F **68**	Abbey Dri. *Ab L* 5E **4**	Abbey Ind. Est. *Mitc* 9D **106**	Abbey Orchard St. *SW1* 4H **75**
A	Abbey Clo. *N'holt* 6K **53**	Abbey Est. *NW8* 4M **57**	Abbey Ind. Est. *Wemb* 4K **55**	Abbey Orchard St. Est.
	Abbey Clo. *Pinn* 1F **36**	Abbeyfield Clo. *Mitc* 6C **106**	Abbey La. *E15* 5A **62**	*SW1* 4H **75**
Aaron Hill Rd. *E6* 8L **63**	Abbey Clo. *Romf* 4E **50**	Abbeyfield Rd. *SE16* 5G **77**	Abbey La. *Beck* 4L **109**	(in two parts)
Abady Ho. SW1 . . . .*5H* **75**	Abbey Ct. *NW8* 5A **58**	Abbeyfield Rd. *SE16* 5G **77**	Abbey La. Commercial Est.	Abbey Pde. *SW19* 4A **106**
(off Page St.)	(off Abbey Rd.)	(in two parts)	*E15* 5C **62**	(off Merton High St.)
Abberley M. *SW4* 2F **90**	Abbey Ct. *SE17* 6A **76**	Abbeyfields Clo. *NW10* 5L **55**	Abbey Life Ct. *E16* 8F **62**	Abbey Pde. *W5* 6K **55**
Abberton Wlk. *Rain* 4D **66**	(off Macleod St.)	Abbey Gdns. *NW8* 5A **58**		Abbey Pk. *Beck* 4L **109**

Adelphi Ct.—Aldebert Ter.

Adelphi Ct. SE16 3H 77
(off Garter Way)
Adelphi Ct. W4 7B 72
Adelphi Cres. Hay 6C 52
Adelphi Cres. Horn 7E 50
Adelphi Rd. Eps 5B 134
Adelphi Ter. WC2 1J 75
Adelphi Theatre. 1J 75
(off Strand)
Adelphi Way. Hay 6D 52
Adeney Clo. W6 7H 73
Aden Gro. N16 9B 44
Aden Ho. E1 8H 61
(off Duckett St.)
Adenmore Rd. SE6 6L 93
Aden Rd. Enf 6J 17
Aden Rd. Ilf 5A 48
Aden Ter. N16 9B 44
Adeyfield Ho. EC1 6B 60
(off Cranwood St.)
Adhara Rd. N'wd 5D 20
Adie Rd. W6 4G 73
Adine Rd. E13 7F 62
Adler Ind. Est. Hay 3B 68
Adler St. E1 9E 60
Adley St. E5 1J 61
Adlington Clo. N18 5C 28
Admark Ho. Eps 7M 133
Admaston Rd. SE18 8A 80
Admiral Clo. Orp 8H 113
Admiral Ct. SW10 9A 74
(off Admiral Sq.)
Admiral Ct. W1 8E 58
(off Blandford St.)
Admiral Ct. Bark 5F 64
Admiral Ct. Cars 3C 122
Admiral Ho. SW1 5G 75
(off Willow Pl.)
Admiral Ho. Tedd 1E 102
Admiral Hyson Ind. Est.
SE16 6F 76
Admiral M. W10 7H 57
Admiral Pl. SE16 2J 77
Admirals Clo. E18 2F 46
Admirals Ct. E6 9M 63
(off Trader Rd.)
Admirals Ct. SE1 2D 76
(off Horselydown La.)
Admiral Seymour Rd. SE9 3K 95
Admiral's Ga. SE10 9M 77
Admirals Lodge. Romf 2D 50
Admiral Sq. SW10 9A 74
Admiral St. SE8 1L 93
Admirals Wlk. NW3 8A 42
Admirals Way. E14 3L 77
Admiralty Arch. 2H 75
Admiralty Clo. SE8 8L 77
Admiralty Rd. Tedd 3D 102
Admiralty Way. Tedd 3D 102
Admiral Wlk. W9 8L 57
Adnams Wlk. Rain 2E 66
Adolf St. SE6 1M 109
Adolphus Rd. N4 7M 43
Adolphus St. SE8 8K 77
Adomar Rd. Dag 8H 49
Adpar St. W2 8B 58
Adrian Av. NW2 6F 40
Adrian Boult Ho. E2 6F 60
(off Mansford St.)
Adrian Clo. Barn 8H 13
Adrian Ho. N1 4K 59
(off Barnsbury Est.)
Adrian Ho. SW8 8J 75
(off Wyvil Rd.)
Adrian M. SW10 7M 73
Adrian Rd. Ab L 4C 4
Adriatic Building. E14 1J 77
(off Horseferry Rd.)
Adriatic Ho. E1 7H 61
(off Ernest St.)
Adrienne Av. S'hall 7K 53
Adron Ho. SE16 5G 77
(off Millender Wlk.)
Adstock Ho. N1 3M 59
(off Sutton Est., The)
Advance Rd. SE27 1A 108
Adventurers Ct. E14 1B 78
(off Newport Av.)
Advent Way. N18 5G 29
Adys Lawn. NW2 2F 56
Ady's Rd. SE15 2D 92
Aegon Ho. E14 4M 77
(off Lanark Sq.)
Aerodrome Rd.
NW9 & NW4 1D 40
Aerodrome Way. Houn 7G 69
Aeroville. NW9 9C 24
Affleck St. N1 5K 59
Afghan Rd. SW11 1C 90
Afsil Ho. EC1 8L 59
(off Viaduct Bldgs.)
Agamemnon Rd. NW6 9K 41
Agar Clo. Surb 4K 119
Agar Gro. NW1 3G 59
Agar Gro. Est. NW1 3H 59
Agar Ho. King T 7J 103
(off Denmark Rd.)
Agar Pl. NW1 3G 59
Agar St. WC2 1J 75
Agate Clo. E16 9H 63
Agate Rd. W6 4G 73
Agates La. Asht 9H 133
Agatha Clo. E1 2F 76
Agaton Rd. SE9 8A 96
Agave Rd. NW2 9G 41
Agdon St. EC1 7M 59
Agincourt Rd. NW3 9D 42
Agister Rd. Chig 5E 32
Agnes Av. Ilf 9L 47
Agnes Clo. E6 1L 79
Agnesfield Clo. N12 6C 26
Agnes Gdns. Dag 9H 49
Agnes Ho. W11 1H 73
(off St Ann's Rd.)
Agnes Rd. W3 2D 72
Agnes Scott Ct. Wey 5A 116
(off Palace Dri.)
Agnes St. E14 9K 61
Agnew Rd. SE23 6H 93
Agricola Pl. Enf 7D 16
Aidan Clo. Dag 8J 49
Aigburth Mans. SW9 8L 75
(off Mowll St.)
Aileen Wlk. E15 3D 62
Ailsa Av. Twic 4E 86
Ailsa Ho. E16 1L 79
(off University Way)
Ailsa Rd. Twic 4F 86
Ailsa St. E14 8A 62
Aimes Green. 2M 7
Ainger M. NW3 3D 58
(off Ainger Rd., in two parts)
Ainger Rd. NW3 3D 58
Ainsdale. NW1 5G 59
(off Harrington St.)
Ainsdale Clo. Orp 3B 128
Ainsdale Cres. Pinn 1L 37
Ainsdale Dri. SE1 6E 76
Ainsdale Rd. W5 7H 55
Ainsdale Rd. Wat 3G 21
Ainsley Av. Romf 4M 49
Ainsley Clo. N9 1C 28
Ainsley St. E2 6F 60
Ainslie Ct. Wemb 5J 55
Ainslie Wlk. SW12 6F 90
Ainslie Wood Cres. E4 5M 29
Ainslie Wood Gdns. E4 4M 29
Ainslie Wood Rd. E4 5L 29
Ainsty Est. SE16 3H 77
Ainsty St. SE16 3G 77
Ainsworth Clo. NW2 8E 40
Ainsworth Clo. SE15 1C 92
Ainsworth Ho. NW8 4M 57
(off Ainsworth Way)
Ainsworth Rd. E9 3G 61
Ainsworth Rd. Croy 3M 123
Ainsworth Way. NW8 4A 58
Aintree Av. E6 4J 63
Aintree Clo. Uxb 9F 142
Aintree Cres. Ilf 9A 32
Aintree Est. SW6 8J 73
(off Aintree St.)
Aintree Gro. Upm 8K 51
Aintree Rd. Gnfd 5F 54
Aintree St. SW6 8J 73
Airbourne Ho. Wall 6G 123
(off Maldon Rd.)
Air Call Bus. Cen. NW9 1B 40
Aird Ho. SE1 4A 76
(off Rockingham St.)
Airdrie Clo. N1 3K 59
Airdrie Clo. Hay 8J 53
Airedale Av. W4 5D 72
Airedale Av. S. W4 6D 72
Airedale Rd. SW12 6D 90
Airedale Rd. W5 4G 71
Airfield Pathway. Horn 3G 67
Airfield Way. Horn 2F 66
Airfield Way. Leav 7D 4
Airlie Gdns. W8 2L 73
Airlie Gdns. Ilf 6M 47
Airlinks Ind. Est. Houn 6G 69
Air Pk. Way. Felt 8F 84
Airport Ind. Est. Big H 7H 141
Air St. W1 1G 75
Airthrie Rd. Ilf 7F 48
Aisgill Av. W14 6K 73
(in two parts)
Aisher Rd. SE28 1G 81
Aislibie Rd. SE12 3C 94
Aiten Pl. W6 5E 72
Aithan Ho. E14 9K 61
(off Copenhagen Pl.)
Aitken Clo. E8 4E 60
Aitken Clo. Mitc 2D 122
Aitken Rd. SE6 8M 93
Aitken Rd. Barn 7G 13
Ajax Av. NW9 1C 40
Ajax Ho. E2 5F 60
(off Old Bethnal Grn. Rd.)
Ajax Rd. NW6 9K 41
Akabusi Clo. Croy 1E 124
Akbar Ho. E14 5M 77
(off Cahir St.)
Akehurst St. SW15 5E 88
Akenside Rd. NW3 1B 58
Akerman Rd. SW9 1M 91
Akerman Rd. Surb 1G 119
Akintaro Ho. SE8 7K 77
(off Alverton St.)
Alabama St. SE18 8B 80
Alacross Rd. W5 3G 71
Alan Clo. Dart 3G 99
Alandale Dri. Pinn 8F 20
Aland Ct. SE16 4J 77
Alander M. E17 2A 46
Alan Dri. Barn 8J 13
Alan Gdns. Romf 5L 49
Alan Hocken Way. E15 5C 62
Alan Preece Ct. NW6 3H 57
Alan Rd. SW19 2J 105
Alanthus Clo. SE12 5E 94
Alaska Bldgs. SE1 4C 76
Alaska St. SE1 2L 75
Alastor Ho. E14 4A 78
(off Strattondale Ho.)
Alba Clo. Hay 7H 53
Albacore Cres. SE13 5M 93
Alba Gdns. NW11 4J 41
Albain Cres. Ashf 8C 144
Alban Cres. Borwd 3M 11
Alban Cres. F'ham 3L 131
Alban Highwalk. EC2 8A 60
(off Addle St., in two parts)
Alban Ho. Borwd 3M 11
Albans Vw. Wat 6F 4
Albany. N12 6M 25
Albany. W1 1G 75
Albany Clo. N15 2M 43
Albany Clo. SW14 3M 87
Albany Clo. Bex 6G 97
Albany Clo. Bush 8B 10
Albany Clo. Esh 9L 117
Albany Clo. Uxb 1E 142
Albany Ct. E4 5K 29
Albany Ct. E10 5L 45
Albany Ct. EN3 8L 17
Albany Ct. NW8 5B 58
(off Abbey Rd.)
Albany Ct. NW10 6F 56
(off Trenmar Gdns.)
Albany Ct. Edgw 8B 24
Albany Courtyard. W1 1G 75
Albany Cres. Clay 8C 118
Albany Cres. Edgw 7L 23
Albany Mans. SW11 8C 74
Albany M. N1 3L 59
Albany M. SE5 7A 76
Albany M. Brom 3E 110
Albany M. King T 3H 103
Albany M. Sutt 7M 121
Albany Pde. Bren 7J 71
Albany Pk. 2J 17
Albany Pk. Av. Enf 3G 17
Albany Pk. Rd. King T 3H 103
Albany Pas. Rich 4J 87
Albany Pl. N7 9L 43
Albany Reach. Th Dit 9D 102
Albany Rd. E10 5L 45
Albany Rd. E12 9H 47
Albany Rd. E17 4J 45
Albany Rd. N4 4L 43
Albany Rd. N18 5G 29
Albany Rd. SE5 7B 76
Albany Rd. SW19 2M 105
Albany Rd. W13 1F 70
Albany Rd. Belv 7K 81
Albany Rd. Bex 6G 97
Albany Rd. Bren 7H 71
Albany Rd. Chst 2M 111
Albany Rd. Enf 1H 17
Albany Rd. Horn 6E 50
Albany Rd. N Mald 8B 104
Albany Rd. Rich 4K 87
Albany Rd. Romf 4K 49
Albany Rd. W on T 6H 117
Albany St. NW1 5F 58
Albany Ter. NW1 7F 58
(off Marylebone Rd.)
Albany Ter. Rich 4K 87
(off Albany Pas.)
Albany, The. Wfd G 4D 30
Albany Vw. Buck H 1E 30
Alba Pl. W11 9K 57
Albatross. NW9 9D 24
Albatross Gdns. S Croy 3H 139
Albatross St. SE18 8C 80
Albatross Way. SE16 3H 77
Albemarle. SW19 8H 89
Albemarle App. Ilf 4M 47
Albemarle Av. Chesh 1C 6
Albemarle Av. Twic 7K 85
Albemarle Gdns. Ilf 4M 47
Albemarle Gdns. N Mald 8B 104
Albemarle Ho. SE8 5K 77
(off Foreshore)
Albemarle Ho. SW9 2L 91
Albemarle Pk. Beck 5M 109
Albemarle Pk. Stan 5G 23
Albemarle Rd. Beck 5M 109
Albemarle Rd. E Barn 9C 14
Albemarle St. W1 1F 74
Albemarle Way. EC1 7M 59
Alberon Gdns. NW11 2K 41
Alberta Av. Sutt 6J 121
Alberta Est. SE17 6M 75
(off Alberta St.)
Alberta Ho. E14 2A 78
(off Gaselee St.)
Alberta Rd. Enf 8D 16
Alberta Rd. Eri 9A 82
Alberta St. SE17 6M 75
Albert Av. E4 4L 29
Albert Av. SW8 8K 75
Albert Barnes Ho. SE1 4A 76
(off New Kent Rd.)
Albert Bigg Point. E15 5A 62
(off Godfrey St.)
Albert Bri. SW3 & SW11 7C 74
Albert Bri. Rd. SW11 8C 74
Albert Carr Gdns. SW16 2J 107
Albert Clo. E9 4F 60
Albert Clo. N22 8H 27
Albert Cotts. E1 8E 60
(off Deal St.)
Albert Ct. E7 9E 46
Albert Ct. SW7 4B 74
Albert Ct. Ga. SW1 3D 74
(off Knightsbridge)
Albert Cres. E4 4L 29
Albert Dane Cen. S'hall 4J 69
Albert Dri. SW19 8J 89
Albert Embkmt. SE1 4K 75
(Lambeth Pal. Rd.)
Albert Embkmt. SE1 6J 75
(Vauxhall Cross)
Albert Gdns. E1 9H 61
Albert Ga. SW1 3D 74
Albert Gray Ho. SW10 8B 74
(off Worlds End Est.)
Albert Gro. SW20 5H 105
Albert Hall Mans. SW7 3B 74
(in two parts)
Albert Ho. E18 1F 46
(off Albert Rd.)
Albert Ho. SE28 3A 80
(off Erebus Dri.)
Albertine Clo. Eps 8F 134
Albert Mans. Croy 3B 124
(off Lansdowne Rd.)
Albert Memorial. 3B 74
Albert M. E14 1J 77
(off Northey St.)
Albert M. N4 6K 43
Albert M. SE4 3J 93
Albert M. W8 4A 74
Albert Pal. Mans.
SW11 9F 74
(off Lurline Gdns.)
Albert Pl. N3 8L 25
Albert Pl. N17 1D 44
Albert Pl. W8 4M 73
Albert Rd. E10 7A 46
Albert Rd. E16 2J 79
Albert Rd. E17 3L 45
Albert Rd. E18 1F 46
Albert Rd. N4 6K 43
Albert Rd. N15 4C 44
Albert Rd. N22 8G 27
Albert Rd. NW4 2H 41
Albert Rd. NW6 5K 57
Albert Rd. NW7 5D 24
Albert Rd. SE9 9J 95
Albert Rd. SE20 3H 109
Albert Rd. SE25 8E 108
Albert Rd. W5 7F 54
Albert Rd. Barn 6A 14
Albert Rd. Belv 6K 81
Albert Rd. Bex 5L 97
Albert Rd. Brom 9H 111
Albert Rd. Buck H 2H 31
Albert Rd. Chels 7E 128
Albert Rd. Dag 6L 49
Albert Rd. Dart 9G 99
Albert Rd. Eps 5D 134
Albert Rd. Hamp H 2A 102
Albert Rd. Harr 1A 38
Albert Rd. Hay 4C 68
Albert Rd. Houn 3L 85
Albert Rd. Ilf 8M 47
Albert Rd. King T 6K 103
Albert Rd. Mitc 7D 106
Albert Rd. N Mald 8D 104
Albert Rd. Rich 4J 87
Albert Rd. Romf 3D 50
Albert Rd. St M 1F 128
Albert Rd. S'hall 4H 69
Albert Rd. Sutt 7B 122
Albert Rd. Tedd 3D 102
Albert Rd. Twic 7D 86
Albert Rd. Warl 9K 139
Albert Rd. W Dray 2J 143
Albert Rd. Est. Belv 6K 81
Albert Rd. N. Wat 5F 8
Albert Rd. S. Wat 5F 8
Albert Sq. E15 1C 62
Albert Sq. SW8 8K 75
Albert Starr Ho. SE8 5H 77
(off Bush Rd.)
Albert St. N12 5A 26
Albert St. NW1 4F 58
Albert Studios. SW11 9D 74
Albert Ter. NW1 4E 58
Albert Ter. NW10 4A 56
Albert Ter. W5 7F 54
Albert Ter. Buck H 2J 31
Albert Ter. M. NW1 4E 58
Albert Victoria Ho. N22 8L 27
(off Pellatt Gro.)
Albert Wlk. E16 3L 79
Albert Way. SE15 8F 76
Albert Westcott Ho. SE17 6M 75
Albert Whicher Ho. E17 2A 46
Albert Yd. SE19 3C 108
Albery Ct. E8 3D 60
(off Middleton Rd.)
Albery Theatre. 1J 75
(off St Martin's La.)
Albion Av. N10 8E 26
Albion Av. SW8 1H 91
Albion Clo. W2 1C 74
Albion Clo. Romf 4B 50
Albion Ct. W6 5F 72
(off Albion Pl.)
Albion Dri. E8 3D 60
(in two parts)
Albion Est. SE16 3H 77
Albion Gdns. W6 5F 72
Albion Ga. W2 1C 74
(off Albion St., in two parts)
Albion Gro. N16 9C 44
Albion Hill. Lou 7G 19
Albion Ho. E16 2M 79
(off Church St.)
Albion Ho. SE8 8L 77
(off Watsons St.)
Albion M. N1 4L 59
Albion M. W2 1C 74
Albion M. W6 5F 72
Albion Pk. Lou 7H 19
Albion Pl. EC1 8M 59
Albion Pl. EC2 8B 60
Albion Pl. SE25 7E 108
Albion Pl. W6 5F 72
Albion Rd. E17 1A 46
Albion Rd. N16 9B 44
Albion Rd. N17 9E 28
Albion Rd. Bexh 3K 97
Albion Rd. Hay 9C 52
Albion Rd. Houn 3L 85
Albion Rd. King T 5A 104
Albion Rd. Sutt 8B 122
Albion Rd. Twic 7C 86
Albion Sq. E8 3D 60
Albion St. SE16 3G 77
Albion St. W2 9C 58
Albion St. Croy 3M 123
Albion Ter. E4 6M 17
Albion Ter. E8 3D 60
Albion Vs. Rd. SE26 9G 93
Albion Way. EC1 8A 60
Albion Way. SE13 3A 94
Albion Way. Wemb 8L 39
Albion Wharf. SW11 8C 74
Albion Yd. N1 5J 59
Albright Ind. Est. Rain 7D 66
Albrighton Rd. SE22 2C 92
Albuhera Clo. Enf 3L 15
Albury Av. Bexh 1J 97
Albury Av. Iswth 8D 70
Albury Av. Sutt 1G 135
Albury Clo. Eps 1M 133
Albury Clo. Hamp 3M 101
Albury Ct. Mitc 6B 106
Albury Ct. N'holt 6G 53
(off Canberra Dri.)
Albury Ct. S Croy 6A 124
(off Tanfield Rd.)
Albury Ct. Sutt 6A 122
Albury Dri. Pinn 8G 21
Albury Gro. Rd. Chesh 3D 6
Albury Ho. SE1 3M 75
(off Boyfield St.)
Albury M. E12 7G 47
Albury Ride. Chesh 4D 6
Albury Rd. Chess 7J 119
Albury Rd. W on T 8C 116
Albury St. SE8 7L 77
Albury Wlk. Chesh 3C 6
(in two parts)
Albyfield. Brom 8K 111
Albyn Rd. SE8 9L 77
Albyns Clo. Rain 3E 66
Alcester Cres. E5 7F 44
Alcester Ho. Romf 5H 35
(off Northallerton Way)
Alcester Rd. Wall 6F 122
Alcock Clo. Wall 9H 123
Alcock Rd. Houn 8H 69
Alconbury. Bexh 4M 97
Alconbury Rd. E5 7E 44
Alcorn Clo. Sutt 4L 121
Alcott Clo. W7 8D 54
Alcott Clo. Felt 7D 84
Alcuin Ct. Stan 7G 23
Aldam Pl. N16 7D 44
Aldborough Ct. Ilf 3D 48
(off Aldborough Rd. N.)
Aldborough Hatch. 2D 48
Aldborough Rd. Dag 2A 66
Aldborough Rd. Upm 7K 51
Aldborough Rd. N. Ilf 3D 48
Aldborough Rd. S. Ilf 6C 48
(in two parts)
Aldbourne Rd. W3 2D 72
(in two parts)
Aldbridge St. SE17 6C 76
Aldburgh M. W1 9E 58
(in two parts)
Aldbury Av. Wemb 3M 55
Aldbury Clo. Wat 9H 5
Aldbury Ho. SW3 5C 74
(off Ixworth Pl.)
Aldbury M. N9 9B 16
Aldebert Ter. SW8 8J 75

Aldeburgh Clo.—Alma St.

Aldeburgh Clo. E5 7F 44
Aldeburgh Pl. Wfd G 4E 30
Aldeburgh St. SE10 6E 78
Alden Av. E15 6D 62
Alden Ct. Croy 5C 124
Aldenham. 2M 9
Aldenham Av. Rad 1E 10
Aldenham Country Pk. 7F 10
Aldenham Dri. Uxb 7F 142
Aldenham Golf Course & Country Club. 1L 9
Aldenham Ho. NW1 5G 59
(off Aldenham St.)
Aldenham Pk. 6G 11
Aldenham Rd. Els 5E 10
Aldenham Rd. Let H & Els 3C 10
Aldenham Rd. Wat & Bush 8H 9
Aldenham St. NW1 5G 59
Aldenholme. Wey 8C 116
Alden Ho. E8 4F 60
(off Duncan Rd.)
Alden Mead. Pinn 6L 21
(off Avenue, The)
Aldensley Rd. W6 4F 72
Alder Av. Upm 9K 51
Alderbrook Rd. SW12 5F 90
Alderbury Rd. SW13 7E 72
Alder Clo. SE15 7D 76
Alder Clo. Park 1M 5
Aldercroft. Coul 8K 137
Alder Gro. NW2 7E 40
Aldergrove Gdns. Houn 1J 85
Aldergrove Wlk. Horn 2G 67
Alderholt Way. SE15 8C 76
Alder Ho. NW3 2D 58
Alder Ho. SE4 2L 93
Alder Ho. SE15 7D 76
(off Alder Clo.)
Alder Lodge. SW6 9G 73
Alderman Av. Bark 6E 64
Aldermanbury. EC2 9A 60
Aldermanbury Sq. EC2 8A 60
Alderman Clo. Dart 6C 98
Alderman Judge Mall. King T 6J 103
Aldermans Hill. N13 4J 27
Aldermans Wlk. EC2 8C 60
Aldermary Rd. Brom 5E 110
Alder M. N19 7G 43
Aldermoor Rd. SE6 9K 93
Alderney Av. Houn 8M 69
Alderney Gdns. N'holt 3K 53
Alderney Ho. N1 2A 60
(off Arran Wlk.)
Alderney Ho. Enf 2H 17
Alderney Rd. E1 7H 61
Alderney Rd. Eri 8E 82
Alderney St. SW1 5F 74
Alder Rd. SW14 2B 88
Alder Rd. Den 2A 142
Alder Rd. Sidc 9D 96
Alders Av. Wfd G 6C 30
Aldersbrook. 7F 46
Aldersbrook Av. Enf 4C 16
Aldersbrook Dri. King T 3K 103
Aldersbrook La. E12 8K 47
Aldersbrook Rd. E11 & E12 7F 46
Alders Clo. E11 7F 46
Alders Clo. W5 4H 71
Alders Clo. Edgw 5A 24
Aldersey Gdns. Bark 2B 64
Aldersford Clo. SE4 4H 93
Aldersgate St. EC1 8A 60
Alders Gro. E Mol 9B 102
Aldersgrove. Wal A 7L 7
Aldersgrove Av. SE9 9H 95
Aldershot Rd. NW6 4K 57
Aldershot Ter. SE18 8L 79
Aldersmead Av. Croy 1H 125
Aldersmead Rd. Beck 4J 109
Alderson Pl. S'hall 2A 70
Alderson St. W10 7J 57
Alders Rd. Edgw 5A 24
Alders, The. N21 8L 15
Alders, The. SW16 1G 107
Alders, The. Den 2A 142
Alders, The. Felt 1J 101
Alders, The. Houn 7K 69
Alders, The. W Wick 3M 125
Alderton Clo. NW10 8B 40
Alderton Clo. Lou 6L 19
Alderton Cres. NW4 3F 40
Alderton Hall La. Lou 6L 19
Alderton Hill. Lou 7J 19
Alderton M. Lou 6L 19
Alderton Ri. Lou 6L 19
Alderton Rd. SE24 2A 92
Alderton Rd. Croy 2D 124
Alderton Way. NW4 3F 40
Alderton Way. Lou 7K 19
Alderville Rd. SW6 1K 89
Alder Wlk. Ilf 1A 64
Alder Wlk. Wat 8F 4
Alder Way. Swan 6B 114
Alderwick Ct. N7 2K 59
(off Cornelia St.)
Alderwick Dri. Houn 2B 86
Alderwood M. Barn 2A 14
Alderwood Rd. SE9 5B 96
Aldford Ho. W1 2E 74
(off Park St.)
Aldford St. W1 2E 74
Aldgate (Junct.) 9D 60
Aldgate. E1 9D 60
(off Whitechapel High St.)
Aldgate. EC3 9C 60
Aldgate Av. E1 9D 60
Aldgate Barrs. E1 9D 60
(off Whitechapel High St.)
Aldgate High St. EC3 9D 60
Aldgate Triangle. E1 9E 60
(off Coke St.)
Aldham Ho. SE4 1K 93
(off Malpas Rd.)
Aldine Ct. W12 3G 73
(off Aldine St.)
Aldine Pl. W12 3G 73
Aldine St. W12 3G 73
Aldingham Ct. Horn 1F 66
(off Easedale Dri.)
Aldingham Gdns. Horn 1E 66
Aldington Clo. Dag 6G 49
Aldington Ct. E8 3E 60
(off London Field W. Side)
Aldington Rd. SE18 4H 79
Aldis M. SW17 2C 106
Aldis M. Enf 1L 17
Aldis St. SW17 2C 106
Aldred Rd. NW6 1L 57
Aldren Rd. SW17 9A 90
Aldrich Cres. New Ad 1A 140
Aldriche Way. E4 6A 30
Aldrich Gdns. Sutt 5K 121
Aldrich Ter. SW18 8A 90
Aldrick Ho. N1 4K 59
(off Barnsbury Est.)
Aldridge Av. Edgw 3M 23
Aldridge Av. Enf 2L 17
Aldridge Av. Ruis 7G 37
Aldridge Av. Stan 8J 23
Aldridge Ri. N Mald 2C 120
Aldridge Rd. Vs. W11 8K 57
Aldridge Wlk. N14 9J 15
Aldrington Rd. SW16 2G 107
Aldsworth Clo. W9 7M 57
Aldwick Clo. SE9 9B 96
Aldwick Rd. Croy 5K 123
Aldworth Gro. SE13 5A 94
Aldworth Rd. E15 3C 62
Aldwych. WC2 9K 59
Aldwych Av. Ilf 2A 48
Aldwych Clo. Horn 6E 50
Aldwych Ct. E8 3D 60
(off Middleton Rd.)
Aldwych Theatre. 9K 59
(off Aldwych)
Aldwyn Ho. SW8 8J 75
(off Davidson Gdns.)
Alers Rd. Bexh 4H 97
Alesia Clo. N22 7J 27
Alestan Beck Rd. E16 9H 63
Alexa Ct. W8 5L 73
Alexa Ct. Sutt 8L 121
Alexander Av. NW10 3F 56
Alexander Clo. Barn 6B 14
Alexander Clo. Brom 3E 126
Alexander Clo. Sidc 5C 96
Alexander Clo. S'hall 2A 70
Alexander Clo. Twic 8C 86
Alexander Ct. Beck 5B 110
Alexander Ct. Chesh 3D 6
Alexander Ct. Stan 1K 39
Alexander Evans M. SE23 8H 93
Alexander Fleming Mus. 9B 58
(off Praed St.)
Alexander Ho. E14 4L 77
(off Tiller Rd.)
Alexander M. W2 9M 57
Alexander Pl. SW7 5C 74
Alexander Rd. N19 8J 43
Alexander Rd. Bexh 1H 97
Alexander Rd. Chst 3M 111
Alexander Rd. Coul 7F 136
Alexander Sq. SW3 5C 74
Alexander St. W2 9L 57
Alexander Studios. SW11 3B 90
(off Haydon Way)
Alexandra Av. N22 8H 27
Alexandra Av. SW11 9E 74
Alexandra Av. W4 8B 72
Alexandra Av. Harr 6K 37
Alexandra Av. S'hall 1K 69
Alexandra Av. Sutt 5L 121
Alexandra Av. Warl 9K 139
Alexandra Clo. SE8 7K 77
Alexandra Clo. Ashf 4B 100
Alexandra Clo. Harr 8L 37
Alexandra Clo. Swan 6C 114
Alexandra Clo. W on T 4E 116
Alexandra Cotts. SE14 9K 77
Alexandra Ct. N14 7G 15
Alexandra Ct. SW7 4A 74
(off Queen's Ga.)
Alexandra Ct. W2 1M 73
(off Moscow Rd.)
Alexandra Ct. W9 7A 58
(off Maida Va.)
Alexandra Ct. Ashf 3B 100
Alexandra Ct. Gnfd 5M 53
Alexandra Ct. Houn 1M 85
Alexandra Ct. Wat 4G 9
Alexandra Cres. Brom 3D 110
Alexandra Dri. SE19 2C 108
Alexandra Dri. Surb 2L 119
Alexandra Gdns. N10 2F 42
Alexandra Gdns. W4 8C 72
Alexandra Gdns. Cars 9E 122
Alexandra Gdns. Houn 1M 85
Alexandra Gro. N4 6M 43
Alexandra Gro. N12 5M 25
Alexandra Ho. E16 2F 78
(off Wesley Av.)
Alexandra Ho. W6 6G 73
(off Queen Caroline St.)
Alexandra Mans. SW3 7B 74
(off Moravian Clo.)
Alexandra Mans. Eps 5D 134
(off Alexandra Rd.)
Alexandra M. N2 1D 42
Alexandra M. SW19 3K 105
Alexandra Palace. 1H 43
Alexandra Pal. Way. N22 2G 43
Alexandra Pde. Harr 9M 37
Alexandra Pk. Rd. N10 9F 26
Alexandra Pk. Rd. N22 8G 27
Alexandra Pl. NW8 4A 58
Alexandra Pl. SE25 9B 108
Alexandra Pl. Croy 3C 124
Alexandra Rd. E6 6L 63
Alexandra Rd. E10 8A 46
Alexandra Rd. E17 4K 45
Alexandra Rd. E18 1F 46
Alexandra Rd. N8 1L 43
Alexandra Rd. N9 9F 16
Alexandra Rd. N10 8F 26
Alexandra Rd. N15 3B 44
Alexandra Rd. NW4 2H 41
Alexandra Rd. NW8 4A 58
Alexandra Rd. SE26 3H 109
Alexandra Rd. SW14 2B 88
Alexandra Rd. SW19 3K 105
Alexandra Rd. W4 3B 72
Alexandra Rd. Ashf 4B 100
Alexandra Rd. Borwd 2B 12
Alexandra Rd. Bren 7H 71
Alexandra Rd. Chad H 4J 49
Alexandra Rd. Croy 3C 124
Alexandra Rd. Enf 6H 17
Alexandra Rd. Eps 5D 134
Alexandra Rd. Eri 7D 82
Alexandra Rd. Houn 1M 85
Alexandra Rd. King T 4L 103
Alexandra Rd. Mitc 4C 106
Alexandra Rd. Rain 4D 66
Alexandra Rd. Rich 1K 87
Alexandra Rd. Romf 4D 50
Alexandra Rd. Th Dit 9D 102
Alexandra Rd. Twic 5G 87
Alexandra Rd. Uxb 5B 142
Alexandra Rd. Warl 9K 139
Alexandra Rd. Wat 4E 8
Alexandra Rd. Ind. Est. Enf 6H 17
Alexandra Sq. Mord 9L 105
Alexandra St. E16 8E 62
Alexandra St. SE14 8J 77
Alexandra Ter. E14 6M 77
(off Westferry Rd.)
Alexandra Wlk. SE19 2C 108
Alexandra Way. Eps 3L 133
Alexandra Way. Wal X 7F 6
Alexandra Yd. E9 4H 61
Alexandria Rd. W13 1E 70
Alexis St. SE16 5E 76
Alfan La. Dart 2B 114
Alfearn Rd. E5 9G 45
Alford Ct. N1 5A 60
(off Shepherdess Wlk.)
Alford Grn. New Ad 8B 126
Alford Ho. N6 4G 43
Alford Pl. N1 5A 60
(in two parts)
Alford Rd. Eri 6A 82
Alfoxton Av. N8 2M 43
Alfreda St. SW11 9F 74
Alfred Clo. W4 5B 72
Alfred Finlay Ho. N22 9M 27
Alfred Gdns. S'hall 1J 69
Alfred Ho. E9 1J 61
(off Homerton Rd.)
Alfred Ho. E12 3J 63
(off Tennyson Av.)
Alfred M. W1 8H 59
Alfred Nunn Ho. NW10 4D 56
Alfred Pl. WC1 8H 59
Alfred Prior Ho. E12 9L 47
Alfred Rd. E15 1D 62
Alfred Rd. SE25 9E 108
Alfred Rd. W2 8L 57
Alfred Rd. W3 2A 72
Alfred Rd. Belv 6K 81
Alfred Rd. Buck H 2H 31
Alfred Rd. Dart 1J 115
(in two parts)
Alfred Rd. Felt 8G 85
Alfred Rd. King T 7J 103
Alfred Rd. Sutt 7A 122
Alfred's Gdns. Bark 5C 64
Alfred St. E3 6K 61
Alfreds Way. Bark 6M 63
Alfreds Way Ind. Est. Bark 4E 64
Alfreton Clo. SW19 9H 89
Alfriston. Surb 1K 119
Alfriston Av. Croy 2J 123
Alfriston Av. Harr 4L 37
Alfriston Clo. Dart 5C 98
Alfriston Clo. Surb 9K 103
Alfriston Rd. SW11 4D 90
Algar Clo. Iswth 2E 86
Algar Clo. Stan 5D 22
Algar Ho. SE1 3M 75
(off Webber Row)
Algar Rd. Iswth 2E 86
Algarve Rd. SW18 7M 89
Algernon Rd. NW4 4E 40
Algernon Rd. NW6 4L 57
Algernon Rd. SE13 3M 93
Algers Clo. Lou 7H 19
Algers Rd. Lou 7H 19
Alghers Mead. Lou 7H 19
Algiers Rd. SE13 3L 93
Alibon Gdns. Dag 1L 65
Alibon Rd. Dag 1K 65
Alice Clo. Barn 6A 14
(off Station App.)
Alice Gilliatt Ct. W14 7K 73
(off Star Rd.)
Alice La. E3 4K 61
Alice M. Tedd 2D 102
Alice Owen Technology Cen. EC1 6M 59
(off Goswell Rd.)
Alice Shepherd Ho. E14 3A 78
(off Manchester Rd.)
Alice St. SE1 4C 76
(in two parts)
Alice Thompson Clo. SE12 8G 95
Alice Walker Clo. SE24 3M 91
Alice Way. Houn 3M 85
Alicia Av. Harr 2F 38
Alicia Clo. Harr 3G 39
Alicia Gdns. Harr 2F 38
Alicia Ho. Well 9F 80
Alie St. E1 9D 60
Alington Cres. NW9 5A 40
Alington Gro. Wall 1G 137
Alison Clo. E6 9L 63
Alison Clo. Croy 3H 125
Alison Ct. SE1 6E 76
Aliwal Rd. SW11 3C 90
Alkerden Rd. W4 6C 72
Alkham Rd. N16 7D 44
Allan Barclay Clo. N15 4D 44
Allan Clo. N Mald 9B 104
Allandale Av. N3 1J 41
Allandale Pl. Orp 5H 129
Allandale Rd. Enf 9D 6
Allandale Rd. Horn 5D 50
Allanson Ct. E10 7L 45
(off Leyton Grange Est.)
Allan Way. W3 8A 56
Allard Clo. Orp 2G 129
Allard Cres. Bus H 1A 22
Allard Gdns. SW4 4H 91
Allardyce St. SW4 3K 91
Allbrook Clo. Tedd 2C 102
Allcott Ho. W12 9F 56
(off Du Cane Rd.)
Allcroft Rd. NW5 1E 58
Allder Way. S Croy 9M 123
Allenby Av. S Croy 1A 138
Allenby Clo. Gnfd 6L 53
Allenby Dri. Horn 6J 51
Allenby Rd. SE23 9J 93
Allenby Rd. Big H 9J 141
Allenby Rd. S'hall 6L 53
Allen Clo. Mitc 5F 106
Allen Clo. Sun 5F 100
Allen Ct. E17 4L 45
(off Yunus Khan Clo.)
Allen Ct. Gnfd 1D 54
Allendale Av. S'hall 9L 53
Allendale Clo. SE5 1B 92
Allendale Clo. SE26 2H 109
Allendale Rd. Gnfd 2F 54
Allen Edwards Dri. SW8 9J 75
Allenford Ho. SW15 5D 88
(off Tunworth Cres.)
Allen Rd. E3 5K 61
Allen Rd. N16 9C 44
Allen Rd. Beck 6H 109
Allen Rd. Croy 3L 123
Allen Rd. Rain 5G 67
Allen Rd. Sun 5F 100
Allensbury Pl. NW1 3H 59
Allens Rd. Enf 7G 17
Allen St. W8 4L 73
Allenswood Rd. SE9 2J 95
Allerford Ct. Harr 3A 38
Allerford Rd. SE6 9M 93
Allerton Clo. Borwd 2K 11
Allerton Ho. N1 6B 60
(off Provost Est.)
Allerton Rd. N16 7A 44
Allerton Rd. Borwd 2J 11
Allerton St. N1 6B 60
Allerton Wlk. N7 7K 43
Allestree Rd. SW6 8J 73
Alleyn Cres. SE21 8B 92
Alleyndale Rd. Dag 7G 49
Alleyn Ho. SE1 4B 76
(off Burbage Clo.)
Alleyn Pk. SE21 8B 92
Alleyn Pk. S'hall 6L 69
Alleyn Rd. SE21 9B 92
Allfarthing La. SW18 5M 89
Allgood Clo. Mord 1H 121
Allgood St. E2 5D 60
Allhallows La. EC4 1B 76
Allhallows Rd. E6 8J 63
All Hallows Rd. N17 8C 28
Alliance Clo. Wemb 9H 39
Alliance Ct. W3 8M 55
Alliance Rd. E13 8G 63
Alliance Rd. SE18 7E 80
Alliance Rd. W3 7M 55
Allied Ind. Est. W3 3C 72
Allied Way. W3 3C 72
Allingham Clo. W7 1D 70
Allingham St. N1 5A 60
Allington Av. N17 6C 28
Allington Av. Shep 7C 100
Allington Clo. SW19 2H 105
Allington Clo. Gnfd 3A 54
Allington Ct. SW1 4F 74
(off Allington St.)
Allington Ct. SW8 1G 91
Allington Ct. Enf 7H 17
(in two parts)
Allington Rd. NW4 3F 40
Allington Rd. W10 6J 57
Allington Rd. Harr 3A 38
Allington Rd. Orp 4B 128
Allington St. SW1 4F 74
Allison Clo. SE10 9A 78
Allison Clo. Wal A 5M 7
Allison Gro. SE21 7C 92
Allison Rd. N8 3L 43
Allison Rd. W3 9A 56
Alliston Ho. E2 6D 60
(off Gibraltar Wlk.)
Allitsen Rd. NW8 5C 58
(in two parts)
Allnutt Way. SW4 4H 91
Alloa Rd. SE8 6H 77
Alloa Rd. Ilf 7E 48
Allom Ho. W11 1J 73
(off Clarendon Rd.)
Allonby Dri. Ruis 5A 36
Allonby Gdns. Wemb 6G 39
Allonby Ho. E14 8J 61
(off Aston St.)
Allotment Way. NW2 8H 41
Alloway Rd. E3 6J 61
Allport Ho. SE5 2B 92
(off Denmark Hill)
All Saints Clo. N9 2E 28
All Saints Clo. Chig 3E 32
All Saints Ct. E1 1G 77
(off Johnson St.)
All Saints Ct. SW11 8F 74
(off Prince of Wales Dri.)
All Saints Ct. Houn 9H 69
(off Springwell Rd.)
All Saints Cres. Wat 6H 5
All Saints Dri. SE3 1C 94
(in two parts)
All Saints Dri. S Croy 4D 138
All Saints Ho. W11 8K 57
(off All Saints Rd.)
All Saints M. Harr 6C 22
All Saints Pas. SW18 4L 89
All Saints Rd. SW19 4A 106
(in two parts)
All Saints Rd. W3 4A 72
All Saints Rd. W11 8K 57
All Saints Rd. Sutt 5M 121
All Saints St. N1 5K 59
All Saints Tower. E10 5M 45
Allsop Pl. NW1 7D 58
All Souls Av. NW10 5F 56
All Souls' Pl. W1 8F 58
Allum La. Els 7J 11
Allum Way. N20 1A 26
Allwood Clo. SE26 1H 109
Alma Av. E4 7A 30
Alma Av. Horn 9J 51
Alma Birk Ho. NW6 3J 57
Almack Rd. E5 9G 45
Alma Clo. N10 8F 26
Alma Ct. Borwd 2K 11
Alma Ct. Harr 7B 38
Alma Cres. Sutt 7J 121
Alma Gro. SE1 5D 76
Alma Ho. Bren 7J 71
Alma Pl. NW10 6F 56
Alma Pl. SE19 4D 108
Alma Pl. T Hth 9L 107
Alma Rd. N10 7F 26
Alma Rd. SW18 3A 90
Alma Rd. Cars 7C 122
Alma Rd. Enf 7J 17
Alma Rd. Esh 3C 118
Alma Rd. Orp 4H 129
Alma Rd. Sidc 9E 96
Alma Rd. S'hall 1J 69
Alma Rd. Ind. Est. Enf 6H 17
Alma Row. Harr 8B 22
Alma Sq. NW8 5A 58
Alma St. E15 2B 62
Alma St. NW5 2F 58

Alma Ter.—Anglesea Rd.

Alma Ter. SW18 6B 90
Alma Ter. W8 4L 73
Almeida St. N1 4M 59
Almeida Theatre. 4M 59
(off Almeida St.)
Almeric Rd. SW11 3D 90
Almer Rd. SW20 4E 104
Almington St. N4 6K 43
Almond Av. W5 4H 71
Almond Av. Cars 4D 122
Almond Av. Uxb 8A 36
Almond Av. W Dray 4L 143
Almond Clo. SE15 1E 92
Almond Clo. Brom 2L 127
Almond Clo. Felt 7E 84
Almond Clo. Hay 1C 68
Almond Clo. Ruis 8D 36
Almond Clo. Shep 6A 100
Almond Dri. Swan 6B 114
Almond Gro. Bren 8F 70
Almond Rd. N17 7E 28
Almond Rd. SE16 5F 76
Almond Rd. Eps 3B 134
Almonds Av. Buck H 2E 30
Almond Way. Borwd 6M 11
Almond Way. Brom 2L 127
Almond Way. Harr 9M 21
Almond Way. Mitc 9H 107
Almorah Rd. N1 3B 60
Almorah Rd. Houn 9H 69
Almshouse La. Chess 1G 133
Almshouse La. Enf 1F 16
Almshouses. Lou 3K 19
Almshouses, The. Chesh 3D 6
(off Turner's Hill)
Alnmouth Ct. S'hall 9A 54
(off Fleming Rd.)
Alnwick. N17 7F 28
Alnwick Ct. Dart 5M 99
(off Osbourne Rd.)
Alnwick Gro. Mord 8M 105
Alnwick Rd. E16 9G 63
Alnwick Rd. SE12 5F 94
Alperton. 5J 55
Alperton La.
Gnfd & Wemb 6G 55
Alperton St. W10 7K 57
Alphabet Gdns. Cars 1B 122
Alphabet Sq. E3 8L 61
Alpha Bus. Cen. E17 3K 45
Alpha Clo. NW1 7C 58
Alpha Est. Hay 3C 68
Alpha Gro. E14 3L 77
Alpha Ho. NW6 5L 57
Alpha Ho. NW8 7C 58
(off Ashbridge St.)
Alpha Ho. SW9 3K 91
Alpha Pl. NW6 5L 57
Alpha Pl. SW3 7C 74
Alpha Pl. Mord 3H 121
Alpha Rd. E4 3L 29
Alpha Rd. N18 6E 28
Alpha Rd. SE14 9K 77
Alpha Rd. Croy 3C 124
Alpha Rd. Enf 6J 17
Alpha Rd. Surb 1K 119
Alpha Rd. Tedd 2B 102
Alpha Rd. Uxb 7F 142
Alpha St. SE15 1E 92
Alphea Clo. SW19 4C 106
Alpine Av. Surb 4A 120
Alpine Bus. Cen. E6 8L 63
Alpine Clo. Croy 5C 124
Alpine Copse. Brom 6L 111
Alpine Gro. E9 3G 61
Alpine Rd. E10 7M 45
Alpine Rd. SE16 5G 77
(in two parts)
Alpine Rd. W on T 2E 116
Alpine Vw. Cars 7C 122
Alpine Wlk. Stan 2C 22
Alpine Way. E6 8L 63
Alric Av. NW10 3B 56
Alric Av. N Mald 7C 104
Alroy Rd. N4 5L 43
Alsace Rd. SE17 6C 76
Alscot Rd. SE1 5D 76
(in two parts)
Alscot Rd. Ind. Est. SE1 4D 76
Alscot Way. SE1 5D 76
Alsike Rd. SE2 & Eri 4H 81
Alsom Av. Wor Pk 6E 120
Alston Clo. Surb 2F 118
Alston Rd. N18 5F 28
Alston Rd. SW17 1B 106
Alston Rd. Barn 5J 13
Altair Clo. N17 6D 28
Altair Way. N'wd 4D 20
Altash Way. SE9 8K 95
Altenburg Av. W13 4F 70
Altenburg Gdns. SW11 3D 90
Alt Gro. SW19 4K 105
Altham Ct. Harr 8M 21
Altham Rd. Pinn 7J 21
Althea St. SW6 1M 89
Althorne Gdns. E18 2D 46
Althorne Way. Dag 7L 49
Althorp Clo. Barn 9E 12
Althorpe M. SW11 9B 74
Althorpe Rd. Harr 3A 38
Althorp Rd. SW17 7D 90
Altior Ct. N6 4G 43
Altmore Av. E6 3K 63
Alton Av. Stan 7D 22
Alton Clo. Bex 7J 97
Alton Clo. Iswth 1D 86
Alton Cotts. F'ham 3J 131
Alton Gdns. Beck 4L 109
Alton Gdns. Twic 6B 86
Alton Rd. N17 1B 44
Alton Rd. SW15 7E 88
Alton Rd. Croy 5L 123
Alton Rd. Rich 3J 87
Alton St. E14 8M 61
Altyre Clo. Beck 9K 109
Altyre Rd. Croy 4B 124
Altyre Way. Beck 9K 109
Aluna Ct. SE15 2G 93
Alvanley Gdns. NW6 1M 57
Alva Way. Wat 2H 21
Alverstoke Rd. Romf 7J 35
Alverstone Av. SW19 8L 89
Alverstone Av. Barn 9C 14
Alverstone Gdns. SE9 7A 96
Alverstone Ho. SE11 7L 75
Alverstone Rd. E12 9L 47
Alverstone Rd. NW2 3G 57
Alverstone Rd. N Mald 8D 104
Alverstone Rd. Wemb 6K 39
Alverston Gdns. SE25 9C 108
Alverton St. SE8 6K 77
(in two parts)
Alveston Av. Harr 1F 38
Alvey St. SE17 6C 76
Alvia Gdns. Sutt 6A 122
Alvington Cres. E8 1D 60
Alway Av. Eps 7B 120
Alwin Pl. Wat 6C 8
Alwold Cres. SE12 5F 94
Alwyn Av. W4 6B 72
Alwyn Clo. Els 8K 11
Alwyn Clo. New Ad 9M 125
Alwyne Ho. N1 3M 59
(off Alwyne La.)
Alwyne La. N1 3M 59
Alwyne Pl. N1 2A 60
Alwyne Rd. N1 3A 60
Alwyne Rd. SW19 3K 105
Alwyne Rd. W7 1C 70
Alwyne Sq. N1 2A 60
Alwyne Vs. N1 3M 59
Alwyn Gdns. NW4 2E 40
Alwyn Gdns. W3 9M 55
Alyth Gdns. NW11 4L 41
Alzette Ho. E2 5H 61
(off Mace St.)
Amadeus Ho. Brom 7F 110
(off Elmfield Rd.)
Amalgamated Dri. Bren 7E 70
Amanda Clo. Chig 6B 32
Amanda M. Romf 3A 50
Amar Ct. SE18 5D 80
Amar Deep Ct. SE18 6D 80
Amazon St. E1 9E 60
Ambassador Clo. Houn 1J 85
Ambassador Gdns. E6 8K 63
Ambassadors Ct. E8 3D 60
(off Holly St.)
Ambassador's Ct. SW1 2G 75
(off St James' Pal.)
Ambassador Sq. E14 5M 77
Ambassadors Theatre. 1H 75
(off West St.)
Amber Av. E17 8J 29
Amberden Av. N3 1L 41
Ambergate St. SE17 6M 75
Amber Gro. NW2 6H 41
Amberley Clo. Orp 7D 128
Amberley Clo. Pinn 1K 37
Amberley Ct. Beck 4K 109
Amberley Ct. Sidc 2G 113
Amberley Gdns. Enf 9C 16
Amberley Gdns. Eps 6D 120
Amberley Gro. SE26 2F 108
Amberley Gro. Croy 2D 124
Amberley Rd. E10 5L 45
Amberley Rd. N13 2K 27
Amberley Rd. SE2 7H 81
Amberley Rd. W9 8L 57
Amberley Rd. Buck H 1G 31
Amberley Rd. Enf 9D 16
Amberley Ter. Wat 8J 9
(off Villiers Rd.)
Amberley Way. Houn 4G 85
Amberley Way. Mord 2K 121
Amberley Way. Romf 2M 49
Amberley Way. Uxb 5C 142
Amberside Clo. Iswth 5B 86
Amberwood Clo. Wall 7J 123
Amberwood Ri. N Mald 1C 120
Amblecote Clo. SE12 9F 94
Amblecote Meadows.
SE12 9F 94
Amblecote Rd. SE12 9F 94
Ambler Rd. N4 8M 43
Ambleside. NW1 5F 58
(off Augustus St.)
Ambleside. Brom 3B 110
Ambleside Av. SW16 1H 107
Ambleside Av. Beck 9J 109
Ambleside Av. Horn 1F 66
Ambleside Av. W on T 3G 117
Ambleside Clo. E9 1G 61
Ambleside Clo. E10 5M 45
Ambleside Cres. Enf 5H 17
Ambleside Dri. Felt 7D 84
Ambleside Gdns. SW16 2H 107
Ambleside Gdns. Ilf 2J 47
Ambleside Gdns. S Croy 1H 139
Ambleside Gdns. Sutt 8A 122
Ambleside Gdns. Wemb 6H 39
Ambleside Point. SE15 8G 77
(off Tustin Est.)
Ambleside Rd. NW10 3D 56
Ambleside Rd. Bexh 1L 97
Ambleside Wlk. Uxb 4B 142
(off Cumbrian Way)
Ambrey Way. Wall 1H 137
Ambrooke Rd. Belv 4L 81
Ambrosden Av. SW1 4G 75
Ambrose Av. NW11 5J 41
Ambrose Clo. E6 8K 63
Ambrose Clo. Cray 3D 98
Ambrose Clo. Orp 5D 128
Ambrose Ho. E14 8L 61
(off Selsey St.)
Ambrose M. SW11 1D 90
Ambrose St. SE16 5F 76
Ambrose Wlk. E3 5L 61
AMC Bus. Cen. NW10 6M 55
Amelia Clo. W3 2M 71
Amelia Ho. W6 6G 73
(off Queen Caroline St.)
Amelia St. SE17 6A 76
Amen Corner. EC4 9M 59
Amen Corner. SW17 3D 106
Amen Ct. EC4 9M 59
Amenity Way. Mord 2G 121
American International
University of London, The.
6J 87
(in Richmond University)
America Sq. EC3 1D 76
America St. SE1 2A 76
Amerland Rd. SW18 4K 89
Amersham Av. N18 6B 28
Amersham Clo. Romf 6K 35
Amersham Dri. Romf 6J 35
Amersham Gro. SE14 8K 77
Amersham Ho. Wat 9C 8
(off Chenies Way)
Amersham Rd. SE14 9K 77
Amersham Rd. Croy 1A 124
Amersham Rd. Romf 6J 35
Amersham Va. SE14 8K 77
Amersham Wlk. Romf 6K 35
Amery Gdns. NW10 4G 57
Amery Gdns. Romf 1H 51
Amery Ho. SE17 6C 76
(off Kinglake St.)
Amery Rd. Harr 7E 38
Amesbury. Wal A 5M 7
Amesbury Av. SW2 8J 91
Amesbury Clo. Wor Pk 3G 121
Amesbury Ct. Enf 4L 15
Amesbury Dri. E4 8M 17
Amesbury Rd. Brom 7H 111
Amesbury Rd. Dag 3H 65
Amesbury Rd. Felt 8H 85
Amesbury Tower. SW8 1G 91
Ames Cotts. E14 8J 61
(off Maroon St.)
Ames Ho. E2 5H 61
(off Mace St.)
Amethyst Clo. N11 7H 27
Amethyst Rd. E15 9B 46
Amherst Av. W13 9G 55
Amherst Clo. Orp 8E 112
Amherst Dri. Orp 8D 112
Amherst Gdns. W13 9G 55
(off Amherst Rd.)
Amherst Ho. SE16 3H 77
(off Wolfe Cres.)
Amherst Rd. W13 9G 55
Amhurst Gdns. Iswth 1E 86
Amhurst Pk. N16 5B 44
Amhurst Pas. E8 1E 60
Amhurst Rd. N16 & E8 9D 44
Amhurst Ter. E8 9E 44
Amhurst Wlk. SE28 2E 80
Amias Ho. EC1 7A 60
(off Central St.)
Amidas Gdns. Dag 9F 48
Amiel St. E1 7G 61
Amies St. SW11 2D 90
Amigo Ho. SE1 4L 75
(off Morley St.)
Amina Way. SE16 4E 76
Amis Av. Eps 8M 119
Amity Gro. SW20 5F 104
Amity Rd. E15 3D 62
Ammanford Grn. NW9 4C 40
Amner Rd. SW11 5E 90
Amor Rd. W6 4G 73
Amory Ho. N1 4K 59
(off Barnsbury Est.)
Amott Rd. SE15 2E 92
Amoy Pl. E14 9K 61
(in two parts)
Ampere Way. Croy 2J 123
(in two parts)
Ampleforth Clo. Orp 6G 129
Ampleforth Rd. SE2 3F 80
Ampthill Est. NW1 5G 59
Ampthill Ho. H Hill 5H 35
(off Montgomery Cres.)
Ampton Pl. WC1 6K 59
Ampton St. WC1 6K 59
Amroth Clo. SE23 7F 92
Amroth Grn. NW9 4C 40
Amstel Ct. SE15 8D 76
(off Garnies Clo.)
Amsterdam Rd. E14 4A 78
Amundsen Ct. E14 6L 77
(off Napier Av.)
Amunsden Ho. NW10 3B 56
(off Stonebridge Pk.)
Amwell Clo. Enf 7B 16
Amwell Clo. Wat 8J 5
Amwell Ct. Wal A 6M 7
Amwell Ct. Est. N16 7A 44
Amwell St. EC1 6L 59
Amwell Vw. Ilf 5F 32
Amyand Cotts. Twic 5F 86
Amyand La. Twic 6F 86
Amyand Pk. Gdns. Twic 6F 86
Amyand Pk. Rd. Twic 6E 86
Amy Clo. Wall 9J 123
Amy Johnson Ct. Edgw 9M 23
Amyruth Rd. SE4 4L 93
Amy's Clo. E16 2F 78
(off Pankhurst Av.)
Amy Warne Clo. E6 7J 63
Anatola Rd. N19 7F 42
Ancaster Cres. N Mald 1E 120
Ancaster M. Beck 7H 109
Ancaster Rd. Beck 7H 109
Ancaster St. SE18 8C 80
Anchor. SW18 3M 89
Anchorage Clo. SW19 2L 105
Anchorage Ho. E14 1B 78
(off Clove Cres.)
Anchorage Point. E14 3K 77
(off Cuba St.)
Anchorage Point Ind. Est.
SE7 4G 79
Anchor & Hope La. SE7 4F 78
Anchor Bay Ind. Est. Eri 7E 82
Anchor Boulevd. Dart 3M 99
Anchor Brewhouse. SE1 2D 76
Anchor Bus. Cen. Croy 5J 123
Anchor Clo. Bark 6F 64
Anchor Clo. Chesh 1D 6
Anchor Ct. SW1 5H 75
(off Vauxhall Bri. Rd.)
Anchor Ct. Enf 7C 16
Anchor Ct. Eri 8D 82
Anchor Dri. Rain 7F 66
Anchor Ho. E16 8D 62
(off Barking Rd.)
Anchor Ho. E16 9G 63
(off Prince Regent La.)
Anchor Ho. EC1 7A 60
(off Old St.)
Anchor M. SW12 5F 90
Anchor St. SE16 5F 76
Anchor Ter. E1 7G 61
(off Cephas Av.)
Anchor Wharf. E3 8M 61
(off Yeo St.)
Anchor Yd. EC1 7A 60
Ancient Almshouses. Wal X
3D 6
(off Turner's Hill)
Ancill Clo. W6 7J 73
Ancona Rd. NW10 5E 56
Ancona Rd. SE18 6B 80
Andace Pk. Gdns.
Brom 6G 111
Andalus Rd. SW9 2J 91
Andaman Ho. E1 8J 61
(off Duckett St.)
Ander Clo. Wemb 9H 39
Anderson Clo. N21 7K 15
Anderson Clo. W3 9B 56
Anderson Clo. Eps 4M 133
Anderson Clo. Sutt 3L 121
Anderson Ct. NW2 6G 41
Anderson Dri. Ashf 1A 100
Anderson Ho. E14 1A 78
(off Woolmore St.)
Anderson Ho. W12 9F 56
(off Du Cane Rd.)
Anderson Ho. Bark 4B 64
Anderson Pl. Houn 3M 85
Anderson Rd. E9 2H 61
Anderson Rd. Wey 5B 116
Anderson Rd. Wfd G 1H 47
Anderson Sq. N1 4M 59
(off Gaskin St.)
Anderson St. SW3 6D 74
Anderson Way. Belv 3A 82
Anderton Clo. SE5 2B 92
Anderton Ct. N22 9H 27
Andorra Ct. Brom 5G 111
Andover Av. E16 9H 63
Andover Clo. Eps 3B 134
Andover Clo. Felt 7D 84
Andover Clo. Gnfd 7M 53
Andover Clo. Uxb 5A 142
Andover Pl. NW6 5M 57
Andover Rd. N7 7K 43
Andover Rd. Orp 3B 128
Andover Rd. Twic 7B 86
Andoversford Ct. SE15 7C 76
(off Bibury Clo.)
Andreck Ct. Beck 6M 109
Andre St. E8 1E 60
Andrew Borde St. WC2 9H 59
Andrew Clo. Dart 4B 98
Andrew Clo. Ilf 6B 32
Andrew Ct. SE23 8H 93
Andrewes Gdns. E6 9J 63
Andrewes Highwalk. EC2 8A 60
(off Fore St.)
Andrewes Ho. EC2 8A 60
(off Fore St.)
Andrewes Ho. Sutt 6L 121
Andrew Pl. SW8 8H 75
Andrew Reed Ct. Wat 4G 9
(off Keele Clo.)
Andrews Clo. Buck H 2G 31
Andrew's Clo. Eps 6D 134
Andrews Clo. Harr 5B 38
Andrew's Clo. Orp 6H 113
Andrews Clo. Wor Pk 4H 121
Andrews Crosse. WC2 9L 59
(off Chancery La.)
Andrews Ho. NW3 3D 58
(off Fellows Rd.)
Andrew's Ho. S Croy 8A 124
Andrew's La. G Oak 1A 6
(in two parts)
Andrews Pl. SE9 5M 95
Andrews Pl. Bex 8C 98
Andrew's Rd. E8 4F 60
Andrew St. E14 9A 62
Andrews Wlk. SE17 7M 75
Andringham Lodge.
Brom 5F 110
(off Palace Gro.)
Andromeda Ct. H Hill 7G 35
Andwell Clo. SE2 3F 80
Anerley. 6F 108
Anerley Gro. SE19 4D 108
Anerley Hill. SE19 3D 108
Anerley Pk. SE20 4E 108
Anerley Pk. Rd. SE20 4F 108
Anerley Rd.
SE19 & SE20 4E 108
Anerley Sta. Rd. SE20 5F 108
Anerley Va. SE19 4D 108
Aneurin Bevan Ct. NW2 7F 40
Aneurin Bevan Ho. N11 7H 27
Anfield Clo. SW12 6G 91
Angas Ct. Wey 7A 116
Angel (Junct.) 5M 59
Angela Davies Ind. Est.
SE24 3M 91
Angel All. E1 9D 60
(off Whitechapel High St.)
Angel Cen., The. N1 5L 59
(off St John St.)
Angel Clo. N18 5D 28
Angel Corner Pde. N18 4E 28
Angel Ct. EC2 9B 60
Angel Ct. SW1 2G 75
Angel Edmonton (Junct.) 4E 28
Angelfield. Houn 3M 85
Angel Ga. EC1 6M 59
(in three parts)
Angel Hill. Sutt 5M 121
(in two parts)
Angel Hill Dri. Sutt 5M 121
Angelica Clo. W Dray 9C 142
Angelica Dri. E6 8L 63
Angelica Gdns. Croy 3H 125
Angelina Ho. SE15 9E 76
(off Goldsmith Rd.)
Angel La. E15 2B 62
Angel La. Hay 8B 52
Angell Pk. Gdns. SW9 2L 91
Angell Rd. SW9 2L 91
Angell Town. 9L 75
Angell Town Est. SW9 1L 91
Angel M. E1 1F 76
Angel M. N1 5L 59
Angel M. SW15 6E 88
Angel Pas. EC4 1B 76
Angel Pl. N18 4E 28
Angel Pl. SE1 3B 76
Angel Rd. N18 5E 28
Angel Rd. Harr 4C 38
Angel Rd. Th Dit 2E 118
Angel Rd. Works. N18 5G 29
Angel Sq. EC1 5L 59
Angel St. EC1 9A 60
Angel Wlk. W6 5G 73
Angel Way. Romf 3C 50
Angel Yd. N6 6E 42
Angerstein Bus. Pk. SE10 5E 78
Angerstein La. SE3 9D 78
Anglebury. W2 9L 57
(off Talbot Rd.)
Angle Clo. Uxb 4E 142
Angle Grn. Dag 6G 49
Anglers Clo. Rich 1G 103
Angler's La. NW5 2F 58
Anglers Reach. Surb 9H 103
Anglers, The. King T 7H 103
(off High St.)
Anglesea Av. SE18 5M 79
Anglesea Ho. King T 8H 103
(off Anglesea Rd.)
Anglesea Rd. SE18 5M 79

Anglesea Rd.—Argyle Rd.

Anglesea Rd. King T 8H 103
Anglesea Rd. Orp 1G 129
Anglesey Clo. Ashf 9E 144
Anglesey Ct. W7 7D 54
Anglesey Ct. Rd. Cars 8E 122
Anglesey Dri. Rain 7E 66
Anglesey Gdns. Cars 8E 122
Anglesey Ho. E14 9L 61
(off Lindfield St.)
Anglesey Rd. Enf 6F 16
Anglesey Rd. Wat 5G 21
Anglesmede Cres. Pinn 1L 37
Anglesmede Way. Pinn 1L 37
Angles Rd. SW16 1J 107
Anglia Clo. N17 7F 28
Anglia Ct. Dag 6H 49
(off Spring Clo.)
Anglia Ho. E14 9J 61
(off Salmon La.)
Anglian Clo. Wat 4G 9
Anglian Ind. Est. Bark 7D 64
Anglian Rd. E11 8B 46
Anglia Wlk. E6 4L 63
(off Napier Rd.)
Anglo Rd. E3 5K 61
Angrave Ct. E8 4D 60
(off Scriven St.)
Angrave Pas. E8 4D 60
Angus Clo. Chess 7L 119
Angus Dri. Ruis 9G 37
Angus Gdns. NW9 8B 24
Angus Ho. SW2 6H 91
Angus Rd. E13 6G 63
Angus St. SE14 8J 77
Anhalt Rd. SW11 8C 74
Ankerdine Cres. SE18 8M 79
Anlaby Rd. Tedd 2C 102
Anley Rd. W14 3H 73
Anmersh Gro. Stan 8H 23
Annabel Clo. E14 9M 61
Anna Clo. E8 4D 60
Annandale Gro. Uxb 8A 36
Annandale Rd. SE10 7D 78
Annandale Rd. W4 6C 72
Annandale Rd. Croy 4E 124
Annandale Rd. Sidc 6C 96
Annan Dri. Cars 1E 136
Anna Neagle Clo. E7 9E 46
Annan Way. Romf 8C 34
Anne Boleyn Ct. SE9 5A 96
Anne Boleyn's Wlk.
King T 2J 103
Anne Boleyn's Wlk. Sutt 9H 121
Anne Case M. N Mald 7B 104
Anne Compton M. SE12 6D 94
Anne Goodman Ho. E1 9G 61
(off Jubilee St.)
Anne Nastri Ct. Romf 3F 50
(off Heath Pk. Rd.)
Anne of Cleeves Ct. SE9 5B 96
Anne of Cleves Rd. Dart 4H 99
Annesley Av. NW9 1B 40
Annesley Clo. NW10 8C 40
Annesley Dri. Croy 5K 125
Annesley Ho. SW9 9L 75
Annesley Rd. SE3 9F 78
Annesley Wlk. N19 7G 43
Anne St. E13 7E 62
Anne Sutherland Ho.
Beck 4J 109
Annett Clo. Shep 8C 100
Annette Clo. Harr 9C 22
Annette Rd. N7 8K 43
(in two parts)
Annett Rd. W on T 2E 116
Annetts Cres. N1 3A 60
Anne Way. Ilf 6A 32
Anne Way. W Mol 8M 101
Annie Besant Clo. E3 4K 61
Annie Taylor Ho. E12 9L 47
(off Walton Rd.)
Anning St. EC2 7C 60
Annington Rd. N2 1D 42
Annis Rd. E9 2J 61
Ann La. SW10 7B 74
Ann Moss Way. SE16 4G 77
Ann's Clo. SW1 3D 74
(off Kinnerton St.)
Ann's Pl. E1 8D 60
(off Wentworth St.)
Ann St. SE18 6A 80
(in two parts)
Annsworthy Av. T Hth 7B 108
Annsworthy Cres. SE25 6B 108
Ansar Gdns. E17 3K 45
Ansdell Rd. SE15 1G 93
Ansdell St. W8 4M 73
Ansdell Ter. W8 4M 73
Ansell Gro. Cars 3E 122
Ansell Ho. E1 8G 61
(off Mile End Rd.)
Ansell Rd. SW17 9C 90
Anselm Clo. Croy 5D 124
Anselm Rd. SW6 7L 73
Anselm Rd. Pinn 7K 21
Ansford Rd. Brom 2A 110
Ansleigh Pl. W11 1H 73
Ansley Clo. S Croy 6F 138
Anson Clo. Romf 9M 33
Anson Ho. E1 7J 61
(off Shandy St.)
Anson Ho. SW1 7G 75
(off Churchill Gdns.)
Anson Pl. SE28 3B 80
Anson Rd. N7 9G 43
Anson Rd. NW2 9F 40
Anson Ter. N'holt 2M 53
Anson Wlk. N'wd 4A 20
Anstead Dri. Rain 5E 66
Anstey Ct. W3 3M 71
Anstey Ho. E9 4G 61
(off Templecombe Rd.)
Anstey Rd. SE15 2E 92
Anstey Wlk. N15 2M 43
Anstice Clo. W4 8C 72
Anstridge Path. SE9 5B 96
Anstridge Rd. SE9 5B 96
Antelope Rd. SE18 4K 79
Antenor Ho. E2 5F 60
(off Old Bethnal Grn. Rd.)
Anthony Clo. NW7 4C 24
Anthony Clo. Wat 1G 21
Anthony Cope Ct. N1 6B 60
(off Chart St.)
Anthony Ho. NW8 7C 58
(off Ashbridge St.)
Anthony La. Swan 5E 114
Anthony Rd. SE25 1E 124
Anthony Rd. Borwd 4K 11
Anthony Rd. Gnfd 6C 54
Anthony Rd. Well 9E 80
Anthony St. E1 9F 60
Anthony Way. N18 6H 29
Anthus M. N'wd 7C 20
Antigua Wlk. SE19 2B 108
Antilles Bay. E14 3A 78
Antill Rd. E3 6J 61
Antill Rd. N15 2E 44
Antill Ter. E1 9H 61
Antlers Hill. E4 7M 17
Antoinette Ct. Ab L 2D 4
Anton Cres. Sutt 5L 121
Antoneys Clo. Pinn 9H 21
Anton Pl. Wemb 8M 39
Anton St. E8 1E 60
Antony Ho. SE14 8H 77
(off Barlborough St.)
Antony Ho. SE16 5G 77
(off Raymouth Rd.)
Antrim Gro. NW3 2D 58
Antrim Rd. NW3 2D 58
Antrobus Clo. Sutt 7K 121
Antrobus Rd. W4 5A 72
Anvil Clo. SW16 4G 107
Anvil Rd. Sun 7E 100
Anworth Clo. Wfd G 6F 30
Apeldoorn Dri. Wall 1J 137
Aperfield. 9J 141
Aperfield Rd. Big H 9J 141
Aperfield Rd. Eri 7D 82
Aperfields. Big H 9J 141
Apex Clo. Beck 5M 109
Apex Clo. Wey 5B 116
Apex Corner (Junct.) 9K 85
(Feltham)
Apex Corner (Junct.) 4C 24
(Mill Hill)
Apex Ct. W13 1E 70
Apex Ind. Est. NW10 7D 56
Apex Pde. NW7 4B 24
(off Selvage La.)
Apex Retail Pk. Felt 9K 85
Aphrodite Ct. E14 5L 77
(off Homer Dri.)
Aplin Way. Iswth 9C 70
Apollo Av. Brom 5F 110
Apollo Av. N'wd 5E 20
Apollo Bus. Cen. SE8 6H 77
Apollo Clo. Horn 7F 50
Apollo Ct. E1 1E 76
(off Thomas More St.)
Apollo Ct. SW9 9L 75
(off Southey Rd.)
Apollo Ho. E2 5F 60
(off St Jude's Rd.)
Apollo Ho. N6 5D 42
Apollo Ho. SW10 8B 74
(off Riley St.)
Apollo Pl. E11 8C 46
Apollo Pl. SW10 8B 74
Apollo Theatre. 1H 75
(off Shaftesbury Av.)
Apollo Victoria Theatre. 4G 75
(off Wilton Rd.)
Apollo Way. SE28 4B 80
Apostle Way. T Hth 6M 107
Apothecary St. EC4 9M 59
Appach Rd. SW2 4L 91
Apple Blossom Ct. SW8 8H 75
(off Pascal St.)
Appleby Clo. E4 6A 30
Appleby Clo. N15 3B 44
Appleby Clo. Twic 8B 86
Appleby Dri. Romf 5G 35
Appleby Gdns. Felt 7D 84
Appleby Grn. Romf 5G 35
Appleby Ho. Eps 3B 134
Appleby Rd. E8 3E 60
Appleby Rd. E16 9E 62
Appleby St. E2 5D 60
Applecroft. Park 1M 5
Appledore Av. Bexh 9A 82
Appledore Av. Ruis 8F 36
Appledore Clo. SW17 8D 90
Appledore Clo. Brom 9D 110
Appledore Clo. Edgw 8L 23
Appledore Clo. Romf 8G 35
Appledore Cres. Sidc 9C 96
Appledown Ri. Coul 7G 137
Appleford Ho. W10 7J 57
(off Bosworth Rd.)
Appleford Rd. W10 7J 57
Apple Gth. Bren 5H 71
Applegarth. Clay 7D 118
Applegarth. New Ad 9M 125
(in two parts)
Applegarth Dri. Dart 8J 99
Applegarth Dri. Ilf 2D 48
Applegarth Ho. SE1 3M 75
(off Nelson Sq.)
Applegarth Ho. SE15 8E 76
(off Bird in Bush Rd.)
Applegarth Ho. Eri 1D 98
Applegarth Rd. SE28 2F 80
Applegarth Rd. W14 4H 73
Apple Gro. Chess 6J 119
Apple Gro. Enf 5C 16
Apple Mkt. King T 6H 103
Apple Orchard. Swan 8B 114
Apple Rd. E11 8C 46
Appleshaw Ho. SE5 2C 92
Appleton Clo. Bexh 1A 98
Appleton Dri. Dart 9F 98
Appleton Gdns. N Mald 1E 120
Appleton Rd. SE9 2J 95
Appleton Rd. Lou 5M 19
Appleton Sq. Mitc 5C 106
Appleton Way. Horn 6H 51
Apple Tree Av.
Uxb & W Dray 8D 142
Appletree Clo. SE20 5F 108
Appletree Gdns. Barn 6C 14
Appletree Wlk. Wat 7F 4
Apple Tree Yd. SW1 2G 75
Applewood Clo. N20 1C 26
(in two parts)
Applewood Clo. NW2 8F 40
Applewood Dri. E13 7F 62
Appleyard Ter. Enf 1G 17
Appold St. EC2 8C 60
Appold St. Eri 7D 82
Apprentice Way. E5 9F 44
Approach Clo. N16 9C 44
Approach Rd. E2 5G 61
Approach Rd. SW20 6G 105
Approach Rd. Ashf 3A 100
Approach Rd. Barn 6B 14
Approach Rd. Edgw 6L 23
Approach Rd. Purl 4L 137
Approach Rd. W Mol 9L 101
Approach, The. NW4 3H 41
Approach, The. W3 9B 56
Approach, The. Enf 4F 16
Approach, The. Orp 4D 128
Approach, The. Upm 8M 51
Aprey Gdns. NW4 2G 41
April Clo. W7 1C 70
April Clo. Asht 9K 133
April Clo. Felt 9E 84
April Clo. Orp 7D 128
April Ct. E2 5E 60
(off Teale St.)
April Glen. SE23 9H 93
April St. E8 9D 44
Apsley Clo. Harr 3A 38
Apsley House. 3E 74
Apsley Ho. E1 8G 61
(off Stepney Way)
Apsley Ho. NW8 5B 58
(off Finchley Rd.)
Apsley Ho. Houn 3K 85
Apsley Rd. SE25 8F 108
Apsley Rd. N Mald 7A 104
Apsley Way. NW2 7E 40
Apsley Way. W1 3E 74
(in two parts)
Aquarius. Twic 7F 86
Aquarius Bus. Pk. NW2 6E 40
(off Priestley Way)
Aquarius Way. N'wd 5E 20
Aquila Clo. N'wd 4E 20
Aquila St. NW8 5B 58
Aquinas St. SE1 2L 75
Arabella Dri. SW15 3C 88
Arabia Clo. E4 9B 18
Arabian Ho. E1 7J 61
(off Ernest St.)
Arabin Rd. SE4 3J 93
Aragon Av. Eps 2F 134
Aragon Av. Th Dit 9D 102
Aragon Clo. Brom 3K 127
Aragon Clo. Enf 2K 15
Aragon Clo. Lou 8J 19
Aragon Clo. New Ad 2C 140
Aragon Clo. Romf 6M 33
Aragon Clo. Sun 3D 100
Aragon Ct. E Mol 8A 102
Aragon Ct. Ilf 7A 32
Aragon Dri. Ilf 7A 32
Aragon Dri. Ruis 6H 37
Aragon Ho. E16 2E 78
(off Capulet M.)
Aragon Rd. King T 2J 103
Aragon Rd. Mord 1H 121
Aragon Tower. SE8 5K 77
Aral Ho. E1 7H 61
(off Ernest St.)
Aran Ct. Wey 4B 116
Arandora Cres. Romf 5F 48
Aran Dri. Stan 4G 23
Arapiles Ho. E14 9B 62
(off Blair St.)
Arbery Rd. E3 6J 61
Arbon Ct. N1 4A 60
(off Linton St.)
Arbor Clo. Beck 6M 109
Arbor Ct. N16 7B 44
Arboretum Ct. N1 2B 60
(off Dove Rd.)
Arborfield Clo. SW2 7K 91
Arborfield Ho. E14 1L 77
(off E. India Dock Rd.)
Arbor Rd. E4 3B 30
Arbour Ho. E1 9H 61
(off Arbour Sq.)
Arbour Rd. Enf 5H 17
Arbour Sq. E1 9H 61
Arbour Way. Horn 1F 66
Arbroath Grn. Wat 3E 20
Arbroath Rd. SE9 2J 95
Arbrook Chase. Esh 8A 118
Arbrook Clo. Orp 7E 112
Arbrook Hall. Clay 8D 118
Arbrook La. Esh 8A 118
Arbury Ct. SE20 5F 108
Arbury Ter. SE26 9E 92
Arbuthnot La. Bex 5J 97
Arbuthnot Rd. SE14 1H 93
Arbutus St. E8 4D 60
Arcade. Croy 4A 124
Arcade Pde. Chess 7H 119
Arcade Pl. Romf 3C 50
Arcade, The. E14 9M 61
Arcade, The. E17 2L 45
Arcade, The. EC2 8C 60
(off Liverpool St.)
Arcade, The. Bark 3A 64
Arcade, The. Croy 5A 124
(off High St.)
Arcade, The. Romf 5H 35
(off Farnham Rd.)
Arcadia Av. N3 9L 25
Arcadia Cen., The. W5 1H 71
Arcadia Clo. Cars 6E 122
Arcadia Ct. E1 9D 60
(off Old Castle St.)
Arcadian Av. Bex 5J 97
Arcadian Clo. Bex 5J 97
Arcadian Gdns. N22 7K 27
Arcadian Rd. Bex 5J 97
Arcadia St. E14 9L 61
Archangel St. SE16 3H 77
Archbishop's Pl. SW2 6K 91
Archdale Bus. Cen. Harr 7A 38
Archdale Ct. W12 2F 72
Archdale Ho. SE1 4C 76
(off Long La.)
Archdale Pl. King T 7M 103
Archdale Rd. SE22 4D 92
Archel Rd. W14 7K 73
Archer Clo. King T 4J 103
Archer Ho. SE14 9J 77
Archer Ho. SW11 9B 74
Archer Ho. W11 1K 73
(off Westbourne Gro.)
Archer Ho. W13 2F 70
(off Sherwood Clo.)
Archer M. Hamp H 3A 102
Archer Rd. SE25 8F 108
Archer Rd. Orp 9E 112
Archers Ct. Brom 8F 110
Archers Ct. S Croy 7A 124
(off Nottingham Rd.)
Archers Dri. Enf 4G 17
Archers Lodge. SE16 6E 76
(off Culloden Clo.)
Archer Sq. SE14 7J 77
Archer St. W1 1H 75
Archer Ter. W Dray 1J 143
Archer Way. Swan 6D 114
Archery Clo. W2 9C 58
Archery Clo. Harr 1D 38
Archery Rd. SE9 4K 95
Archery Steps. W2 1C 74
(off St George's Fields)
Arches Bus. Cen., The.
S'hall 3K 69
(off Merrick Rd.)
Arches, The. NW1 3F 58
Arches, The. SW8 8H 75
Arches, The. WC2 2J 75
(off Villiers St.)
Arches, The. Harr 7M 37
Archgate Bus. Cen. N12 5A 26
Archibald M. W1 1E 74
Archibald Rd. N7 9H 43
Archibald Rd. Romf 8L 35
Archibald St. E3 6L 61
Archie Clo. W Dray 3L 143
Arch Rd. W on T 5H 117
Arch St. SE1 4A 76
Archway (Junct.) 7G 43
Archway. Romf 6F 34
Archway Bus. Cen. N19 8H 43
Archway Clo. N19 7G 43
Archway Clo. SW19 9M 89
Archway Clo. W10 8H 57
Archway Clo. Wall 5H 123
Archway Mall. N19 7G 43
Archway M. SW15 3J 89
(off Putney Bri. Rd.)
Archway Rd. N6 & N19 4E 42
Archway St. SW13 2C 88
Arcola St. E8 1D 60
Arcon Ter. N9 9E 16
Arctic St. NW5 1F 58
Arcus Rd. Brom 3C 110
Ardbeg Rd. SE24 4B 92
Arden Clo. SE28 9H 65
Arden Clo. Bus H 9D 10
Arden Clo. Harr 8B 38
Arden Ct. Gdns. N2 4B 42
Arden Cres. E14 5L 77
Arden Cres. Dag 3G 65
Arden Est. N1 5C 60
Arden Grange. N12 4A 26
Arden Gro. Orp 6M 127
Arden Ho. N1 5C 60
(off Arden Est.)
Arden Ho. SE11 5K 75
(off Black Prince Rd.)
Arden Ho. SW9 1J 91
(off Grantham Rd.)
Arden M. E17 3M 45
Arden Mhor. Pinn 2F 36
Arden Rd. N3 1K 41
Arden Rd. W13 1G 71
Ardent Clo. SE25 7C 108
Ardent Ho. E3 5J 61
(off Roman Rd.)
Ardesley Wood. Wey 6C 116
Ardfern Av. SW16 7L 107
Ardfillan Rd. SE6 7B 94
Ardgowan Rd. SE6 6C 94
(in two parts)
Ardilaun Rd. N5 9A 44
Ardingly Clo. Croy 5H 125
Ardleigh Clo. Horn 1H 51
Ardleigh Gdns. Sutt 2L 121
Ardleigh Green. 2G 51
Ardleigh Grn. Rd. Horn 3H 51
Ardleigh Ho. Bark 4A 64
Ardleigh M. Ilf 8M 47
Ardleigh Rd. E17 8K 29
Ardleigh Rd. N1 2C 60
Ardleigh Ter. E17 8K 29
Ardley Clo. NW10 8C 40
Ardley Clo. SE6 9J 93
Ardley Clo. Ruis 5A 36
Ardlui Rd. SE27 8A 92
Ardmay Gdns. Surb 9J 103
Ardmere Rd. SE13 5B 94
Ardmore La. Buck H 9F 18
Ardmore Pl. Buck H 9F 18
Ardoch Rd. SE6 8B 94
Ardra Rd. N9 3H 29
Ardrossan Gdns. Wor Pk 5E 120
Ardross Av. N'wd 5C 20
Ardshiel Clo. SW15 2H 89
Ardwell Av. Ilf 3A 48
Ardwell Rd. SW2 8J 91
Ardwick Rd. NW2 9L 41
Arena Bus. Cen. N4 4A 44
Arena Est. N4 4M 43
Arena, The. Enf 2K 17
Ares Ct. E14 5L 77
(off Homer Dri.)
Arethusa Ho. E14 5L 77
(off Cahir St.)
Arewater Green. 4L 19
Argali Ho. Eri 4J 81
(off Kale Rd.)
Argall Av. E10 5H 45
Argall Way. E10 6H 45
Argenta Way.
Wemb & NW10 2L 55
Argent Cen., The. Hay 3E 68
Argent Ct. Chess 5L 119
Argon M. SW6 8L 73
Argon Rd. N18 5H 29
Argos Ct. SW9 9L 75
(off Caldwell St.)
Argos Ho. E2 5F 60
(off Old Bethnal Grn. Rd.)
Argosy Ho. SE8 5J 77
Argosy La. Stanw 6B 144
Argus Clo. Romf 8M 33
Argus Way. N'holt 6J 53
Argyle Av. Houn 5L 85
(in two parts)
Argyle Clo. W13 7E 54
Argyle Ct. Wat 6D 8
Argyle Ho. E14 4A 78
Argyle Pas. N17 8D 28
Argyle Pl. W6 5F 72
Argyle Rd. E1 7H 61
Argyle Rd. E15 9C 46
Argyle Rd. E16 9F 62
Argyle Rd. N12 5M 25
Argyle Rd. N17 8E 28
Argyle Rd. N18 4E 28
Argyle Rd. Barn 6G 13
Argyle Rd. Gnfd & W13 6D 54
Argyle Rd. Harr 4M 37
Argyle Rd. Houn 4M 85

Argyle Rd.—Ashenden Rd.

Argyle Rd. Ilf 7L 47
Argyle Sq. WC1 6J 59
Argyle St. WC1 6J 59
Argyle Wlk. WC1 6J 59
Argyle Way. SE16 6E 76
Argyll Av. S'hall 2M 69
Argyll Clo. SW9 2K 91
Argyll Gdns. Edgw 9M 23
Argyll Mans. SW3 7B 74
Argyll Mans. W14 5J 73
(off Hammersmith Rd.)
Argyll Rd. W8 3L 73
Argyll St. W1 9G 59
Arica Ho. SE16 4F 76
(off Slippers Pl.)
Arica Rd. SE4 3J 93
Ariel Ct. SE11 5M 75
Ariel Rd. NW6 2L 57
Ariel Way. W12 2G 73
Ariel Way. Houn 2F 84
Aristotle Rd. SW4 2H 91
Arkell Gro. SE19 4M 107
Arkindale Rd. SE6 9A 94
Arkley. 7E 12
Arkley Cres. E17 3K 45
Arkley Dri. Barn 6E 12
Arkley Golf Course. 6D 12
Arkley La. Barn 2D 12
(in two parts)
Arkley Pk. Ark 9B 12
Arkley Rd. E17 3K 45
Arkley Vw. Barn 6F 12
Arklow Ho. SE17 7B 76
(off Albany Rd.)
Arklow M. Surb 4J 119
Arklow Rd. SE14 7K 77
Arklow Rd. Trad. Est.
SE14 7J 77
Ark, The. W6 6H 73
(off Talgarth Rd.)
Arkwright Ho. SW2 6J 91
(off Streatham Pl.)
Arkwright Rd. NW3 1A 58
Arkwright Rd. S Croy 2D 138
Arlesey Clo. SW15 4J 89
Arlesford Rd. SW9 2J 91
Arlingford Rd. SW2 4L 91
Arlington. N12 3L 25
Arlington Av. N1 4A 60
(in two parts)
Arlington Clo. SE13 4B 94
Arlington Clo. Sidc 6C 96
Arlington Clo. Sutt 4L 121
Arlington Clo. Twic 5G 87
Arlington Ct. W3 3M 71
(off Mill Hill Rd.)
Arlington Ct. Hay 6C 68
Arlington Cres. Wal X 7E 6
Arlington Dri. Cars 4D 122
Arlington Dri. Ruis 4B 36
Arlington Gdns. W4 6A 72
Arlington Gdns. Ilf 6L 47
Arlington Gdns. Romf 8J 35
Arlington Ho. EC1 6L 59
(off Arlington Way)
Arlington Ho. SE8 7K 77
(off Evelyn St.)
Arlington Ho. SW1 2G 75
Arlington Ho. W12 2F 72
(off Tunis Rd.)
Arlington Lodge. SW2 3K 91
Arlington Lodge. Wey 6A 116
Arlington M. Twic 5F 86
Arlington M. Wal A 6J 7
(off Sun St.)
Arlington Pk. Mans. W4 6A 72
(off Sutton La. N.)
Arlington Pas. Tedd 1D 102
Arlington Pl. SE10 8A 78
Arlington Rd. N14 2F 26
Arlington Rd. NW1 4F 58
Arlington Rd. W13 9F 54
Arlington Rd. Rich 8H 87
Arlington Rd. Surb 1H 119
Arlington Rd. Tedd 1D 102
Arlington Rd. Twic 5G 87
Arlington Rd. Wfd G 8E 30
Arlington Sq. N1 4A 60
Arlington St. SW1 2G 75
Arlington Way. EC1 6L 59
Arliss Ho. Harr 3D 38
Arliss Way. N'holt 4G 53
Arlow Rd. N21 1L 27
Armada Ct. SE8 7L 77
Armadale Clo. N17 2F 44
Armadale Rd. SW6 8L 73
Armadale Rd. Felt 4E 84
Armada St. SE8 7L 77
(off McMillan St.)
Armada Way. E6 1M 79
Armagh Rd. E3 4K 61
Armand Clo. Wat 2D 8
Armfield Clo. W Mol 9K 101
Armfield Cres. Mitc 6D 106
Armfield Rd. Enf 3B 16
Arminger Rd. W12 2F 72
Armistice Gdns. SE25 7E 108
Armitage Rd. NW11 6J 41
Armitage Rd. SE10 6D 78
Armour Clo. N7 2K 59
Armoury Rd. SE8 1M 93
Armoury Way. SW18 4L 89
Armsby Ho. E1 8G 61
(off Stepney Way)
Armstead Wlk. Dag 3L 65
Armstrong Av. Wfd G 6C 30
Armstrong Clo. E6 9K 63
Armstrong Clo. Borwd 5A 12
Armstrong Clo. Brom 7J 111
Armstrong Clo. Dag 5H 49
Armstrong Clo. Pinn 4E 36
Armstrong Clo. W on T 1E 116
Armstrong Cres. Cockf 5B 14
Armstrong Rd. SW7 4B 74
Armstrong Rd. W3 2D 72
Armstrong Rd. Felt 2J 101
Armstrong Way. S'hall 3M 69
Armytage Rd. Houn 8H 69
Arnal Cres. SW18 6J 89
Arncliffe. NW6 5M 57
Arncliffe Clo. N11 6E 26
Arncroft Ct. Bark 6F 64
Arndale Wlk. SW18 4M 89
Arne Gro. Orp 5D 128
Arne Ho. SE11 6K 75
(off Worgan St.)
Arne St. WC2 9J 59
Arnett Sq. E4 6K 29
Arne Wlk. SE3 3D 94
Arneways Av. Romf 1H 49
Arneway St. SW1 4H 75
Arnewood Clo. SW15 7E 88
Arnewood Clo. Oxs 6A 132
Arneys La. Mitc 1E 122
Arngask Rd. SE6 6B 94
Arnhem Av. Ave 2M 83
Arnhem Dri. New Ad 3B 140
Arnhem Pl. E14 4L 77
Arnhem Way. SE22 4C 92
Arnhem Wharf. E14 4K 77
Arnison Rd. E Mol 8B 102
Arnold Av. E. Enf 2L 17
Arnold Av. W. Enf 2K 17
Arnold Cir. E2 6D 60
Arnold Clo. Harr 5K 39
Arnold Ct. N22 7J 27
Arnold Cres. Iswth 4B 86
Arnold Dri. Chess 8H 119
Arnold Est. SE1 3D 76
(in two parts)
Arnold Gdns. N13 5M 27
Arnold Ho. SE3 8G 79
(off Shooters Hill Rd.)
Arnold Ho. SE17 6M 75
(off Doddington Gro.)
Arnold Mans. W14 7K 73
(off Queen's Club Gdns.)
Arnold Rd. E3 6L 61
Arnold Rd. N15 1D 44
Arnold Rd. SW17 4D 106
Arnold Rd. Dag 3K 65
Arnold Rd. N'holt 2J 53
Arnold Rd. Wal A 8J 7
Arnold's La. S at H 3K 115
Arnold Ter. Stan 5D 22
Arnos Gro. N14 3H 27
Arnos Gro. Ct. N11 5G 27
(off Palmer's Rd.)
Arnos Rd. N11 4G 27
Arnot Ho. SE5 8A 76
(off Comber Gro.)
Arnott Clo. SE28 2G 81
Arnott Clo. W4 5B 72
Arnould Av. SE5 3B 92
Arnsberga Way. Bexh 3L 97
Arnside Gdns. Wemb 6H 39
Arnside Rd. Bexh 9L 81
Arnside St. SE17 7B 76
Arnulf St. SE6 1M 109
Arnulls Rd. SW16 3M 107
Arodene Rd. SW2 5K 91
Arosa Rd. Twic 5H 87
(in two parts)
Arpley Sq. SE20 4G 109
(off High St.)
Arragon Gdns. SW16 4J 107
Arragon Gdns. W Wick 5M 125
Arragon Rd. E6 4H 63
Arragon Rd. SW18 7L 89
Arragon Rd. Twic 6E 86
Arran Clo. Eri 7B 82
Arran Clo. Wall 6F 122
Arran Ct. NW9 9D 24
Arran Ct. NW10 8B 40
Arrandene Open Space. 6E 24
Arran Dri. E12 6H 47
Arran Grn. Wat 4H 21
Arran Ho. E14 2A 78
(off Raleana Rd.)
Arran M. W5 2K 71
Arranmore Ct. Bush 6J 9
Arran Rd. SE6 8M 93
Arran Wlk. N1 3A 60
Arran Way. Esh 4M 117
Arras Av. Mord 9A 106
Arrol Ho. SE1 4A 76
Arrol Rd. Beck 7G 109
Arrow Ct. SW5 5L 73
(off W. Cromwell Rd.)
Arrowhead Ct. E11 4B 46
Arrow Rd. E3 6M 61
Arrowscout Wlk. N'holt 6J 53
Arrowsmith Clo. Chig 5D 32
Arrowsmith Ho. SE11 6K 75
(off Wickham St.)
Arrowsmith Path. Chig 5D 32
Arrowsmith Rd. Chig 5C 32
Arsenal F.C. (Highbury) 8M 43
Arsenal Rd. SE9 1K 95
Artemis Ct. E14 5L 77
(off Homer Dri.)
Arterberry Rd. SW20 4G 105
Arterial Av. Rain 7F 66
Arterial Rd. Purf 4L 83
Artesian Clo. NW10 3B 56
Artesian Gro. Barn 6A 14
Artesian Rd. W2 9L 57
Artesian Wlk. E11 8C 46
Artespian Clo. Horn 4D 50
Arthingworth St. E15 4C 62
Arthur Ct. SW11 9E 74
Arthur Ct. W2 9M 57
(off Queensway)
Arthur Ct. W10 9H 57
(off Silchester Rd.)
Arthur Ct. Croy 5C 124
(off Fairfield Path)
Arthur Deakin Ho. E1 8E 60
(off Hunton St.)
Arthurdon Rd. SE4 4L 93
Arthur Gro. SE18 5A 80
Arthur Henderson Ho.
SW6 1K 89
(off Fulham Rd.)
Arthur Horsley Wlk. E7 1D 62
(off Tower Hamlets Rd.)
Arthur Rd. E6 5K 63
Arthur Rd. N7 9K 43
Arthur Rd. N9 2D 28
Arthur Rd. SW19 2K 105
Arthur Rd. Big H 7G 141
Arthur Rd. King T 4L 103
Arthur Rd. N Mald 9F 104
Arthur Rd. Romf 4G 49
Arthur St. EC4 1B 76
Arthur St. Bush 5H 9
Arthur St. Eri 8D 82
Artichoke Hill. E1 1F 76
Artichoke M. SE5 9B 76
(off Artichoke Pl.)
Artichoke Pl. SE5 9B 76
Artillery Clo. Ilf 4A 48
Artillery Ho. E15 2C 62
Artillery Ho. SE18 6L 79
(off Connaught M.)
Artillery La. E1 8C 60
Artillery La. W12 9E 56
Artillery Pas. E1 8D 60
(off Artillery La.)
Artillery Pl. SE18 6K 79
Artillery Pl. SW1 4H 75
Artillery Pl. Harr 7A 22
Artillery Row. SW1 4G 75
Artington Clo. Orp 6A 128
Artisan Clo. E6 9M 63
Artizan St. E1 9D 60
(off Harrow Pl.)
Arts Theatre. 1J 75
(off St Martin's St.)
Arun Ct. SE25 9E 108
Arundale. King T 8H 103
(off Anglesea Rd.)
Arundel Av. Eps 2F 134
Arundel Av. Mord 8K 105
Arundel Av. S Croy 2E 138
Arundel Bldgs. SE1 4C 76
(off Swan Mead)
Arundel Clo. E15 9C 46
Arundel Clo. SW11 4C 90
Arundel Clo. Bex 5K 97
Arundel Clo. Chesh 1C 6
Arundel Clo. Croy 5M 123
Arundel Clo. Hamp H 2M 101
Arundel Ct. N12 6C 26
Arundel Ct. N17 8E 28
Arundel Ct. SE16 6F 76
(off Varcoe Rd.)
Arundel Ct. SW3 6C 74
(off Jubilee Pl.)
Arundel Ct. SW13 7F 72
(off Arundel Ter.)
Arundel Ct. Brom 6C 110
Arundel Ct. S Harr 9L 37
Arundel Dri. Borwd 6A 12
Arundel Dri. Harr 9K 37
Arundel Dri. Orp 7F 128
Arundel Dri. Wfd G 7E 30
Arundel Gdns. N21 1L 27
Arundel Gdns. W11 1K 73
Arundel Gdns. Edgw 7B 24
Arundel Gdns. Ilf 7E 48
Arundel Gt. Ct. WC2 1K 75
Arundel Gro. N16 1C 60
Arundel Ho. W3 3M 71
(off Park Rd. N.)
Arundel Ho. Borwd 6A 12
(off Arundel Dri.)
Arundel Ho. Croy 7B 124
(off Heathfield Rd.)
Arundel Ho. Uxb 7A 142
Arundel Mans. SW6 9K 73
(off Kelvedon Rd.)
Arundel Pl. N1 2L 59
Arundel Rd. Ab L 5E 4
Arundel Rd. Cockf 5C 14
Arundel Rd. Croy 1B 124
Arundel Rd. Dart 3G 99
Arundel Rd. Houn 2G 85
Arundel Rd. King T 6M 103
Arundel Rd. Romf 7K 35
Arundel Rd. Sutt 9K 121
Arundel Rd. Uxb 5A 142
Arundel Sq. N7 2L 59
Arundel St. WC2 1K 75
Arundel Ter. SW13 7F 72
Arun Ho. King T 5H 103
Arvon Rd. N5 1L 59
(in two parts)
Asa Ct. Hay 4D 68
Asbridge Ct. W6 4F 72
(off Dalling Rd.)
Ascalon Ho. SW8 8G 75
(off Thessaly Rd.)
Ascalon St. SW8 8G 75
Ascension Rd. Romf 6A 34
Ascham Dri. E4 7M 29
Ascham End. E17 8J 29
Ascham St. NW5 1G 59
Aschurch Rd. Croy 2D 124
Ascot Clo. Els 7L 11
Ascot Clo. Ilf 6C 32
Ascot Clo. N'holt 1L 53
Ascot Ct. NW8 6B 58
(off Grove End Rd.)
Ascot Ct. Bex 6K 97
Ascot Ct. Brom 6J 111
Ascot Gdns. Enf 1G 17
Ascot Gdns. Horn 9J 51
Ascot Gdns. S'hall 7K 53
Ascot Ho. NW1 6F 58
(off Redhill St.)
Ascot Ho. W9 7L 57
(off Harrow Rd.)
Ascot Lodge. NW6 4M 57
Ascot M. Wall 1G 137
Ascot Pl. Stan 5G 23
Ascot Rd. E6 6K 63
Ascot Rd. N15 3B 44
Ascot Rd. N18 4E 28
Ascot Rd. SW17 3E 106
Ascot Rd. Felt 7E 144
Ascot Rd. Orp 8D 112
Ascot Rd. Wat 7C 8
(in two parts)
Ascott Av. W5 3J 71
Ascott Clo. Pinn 2E 36
Ashbee Ho. E2 6G 61
(off Portman Pl.)
Ashbourne Av. E18 2F 46
Ashbourne Av. N20 2D 26
Ashbourne Av. NW11 3K 41
Ashbourne Av. Bexh 8J 81
Ashbourne Av. Harr 7B 38
Ashbourne Clo. N12 4M 25
Ashbourne Clo. W5 8L 55
Ashbourne Ct. E5 9J 45
Ashbourne Ct. N12 4M 25
(off Ashbourne Clo.)
Ashbourne Gro. NW7 5B 24
Ashbourne Gro. SE22 3D 92
Ashbourne Gro. W4 6C 72
Ashbourne Pde. NW11 2K 41
Ashbourne Pde. W5 7K 55
Ashbourne Ri. Orp 6B 128
Ashbourne Rd. W5 7K 55
Ashbourne Rd. Mitc 4E 106
Ashbourne Rd. Romf 4G 35
Ashbourne Sq. N'wd 6C 20
Ashbourne Ter. SW19 4K 105
Ashbourne Way. NW11 2K 41
Ashbridge Rd. E11 5C 46
Ashbridge St. NW8 7C 58
Ashbrook. Edgw 6K 23
Ashbrook Rd. N19 6H 43
Ashbrook Rd. Dag 8M 49
Ashburn Gdns. SW7 5A 74
Ashburnham Av. Harr 4D 38
Ashburnham Clo. N2 1B 42
Ashburnham Clo. Wat 3E 20
Ashburnham Ct. Beck 6A 110
Ashburnham Ct. Pinn 1H 37
Ashburnham Dri. Wat 3E 20
Ashburnham Gdns. Harr 4D 38
Ashburnham Gdns. Upm 6M 51
Ashburnham Gro. SE10 8M 77
Ashburnham Mans.
SW10 8A 74
(off Ashburnham Rd.)
Ashburnham Pk. Esh 6A 118
Ashburnham Pl. SE10 8M 77
Ashburnham Retreat.
SE10 8M 77
Ashburnham Rd. NW10 6G 57
Ashburnham Rd. SW10 8A 74
Ashburnham Rd. Belv 5A 82
Ashburnham Rd. Rich 9F 86
Ashburnham Tower.
SW10 8B 74
(off Worlds End Est.)
Ashburn Pl. SW7 5A 74
Ashburton Av. Croy 3F 124
Ashburton Av. Ilf 1C 64
Ashburton Clo. Croy 3E 124
Ashburton Enterprise Cen.
SW15 5G 89
Ashburton Gdns. Croy 4E 124
Ashburton Gro. N7 9L 43
Ashburton Ho. W9 7K 57
(off Fernhead Rd.)
Ashburton Memorial Homes.
Croy 2F 124
Ashburton Rd. E16 9E 62
Ashburton Rd. Croy 4E 124
Ashburton Rd. Ruis 7E 36
Ashburton Ter. E13 5E 62
Ashbury Dri. Uxb 8A 36
Ashbury Gdns. Romf 3H 49
Ashbury Pl. SW19 3A 106
Ashbury Rd. SW11 2D 90
Ashby Av. Chess 8L 119
Ashby Clo. Horn 6L 51
Ashby Ct. NW8 7B 58
(off Pollitt Dri.)
Ashby Gro. N1 3A 60
Ashby Ho. N1 3A 60
(off Essex Rd.)
Ashby Ho. SW9 1M 91
Ashby M. SE4 1K 93
Ashby M. SW2 4J 91
(off Prague Pl.)
Ashby Rd. N15 3E 44
Ashby Rd. SE4 1K 93
Ashby Rd. Wat 2E 8
Ashby St. EC1 6M 59
Ashby Wlk. Croy 1A 124
Ashby Way. W Dray 8L 143
Aschurch Gro. W12 4E 72
Aschurch Pk. Vs. W12 4E 72
Aschurch Ter. W12 4E 72
Ash Clo. SE20 6G 109
Ash Clo. Ab L 5B 4
Ash Clo. Cars 4D 122
Ash Clo. Edgw 4A 24
Ash Clo. N Mald 6B 104
Ash Clo. Orp 9B 112
Ash Clo. Romf 7M 33
Ash Clo. Sidc 9F 96
Ash Clo. Stan 6E 22
Ash Clo. Swan 6A 114
Ash Clo. Wat 8F 4
Ashcombe Av. Surb 2H 119
Ashcombe Gdns. Edgw 4L 23
Ashcombe Pk. NW2 8C 40
Ashcombe Rd. SW19 2L 105
Ashcombe Rd. Cars 8E 122
Ashcombe Sq. N Mald 7A 104
Ashcombe St. SW6 1M 89
Ash Copse. Brick W 4K 5
Ash Ct. NW5 1G 59
Ash Ct. SW19 4J 105
Ash Ct. Eps 6A 120
Ashcroft. N14 2H 27
Ash Cft. Pinn 6L 21
Ashcroft Av. Sidc 5E 96
Ashcroft Ct. N20 2B 26
Ashcroft Ct. Dart 6L 99
Ashcroft Cres. Sidc 5E 96
Ashcroft Ho. SW8 9G 75
(off Wadhurst Rd.)
Ashcroft Ri. Coul 8J 137
Ashcroft Rd. E3 6J 61
Ashcroft Rd. Chess 5K 119
Ashcroft Sq. W6 5G 73
Ashcroft Theatre. 5B 124
(in Fairfield Halls)
Ashdale Clo. Stai 8C 144
Ashdale Clo. Twic 6A 86
Ashdale Gro. Stan 6D 22
Ashdale Ho. N4 5B 44
Ashdale Rd. SE12 7F 94
Ashdale Way. Twic 6M 85
Ashdene. SE15 8F 76
Ashdene. Pinn 1G 37
Ashdene Clo. Ashf 4A 100
Ashdon Clo. Wfd G 6F 30
Ashdon Rd. NW10 4D 56
Ashdon Rd. Bush 5H 9
Ashdown. W13 8F 54
(off Clivedon Ct.)
Ashdown Clo. Beck 6M 109
Ashdown Clo. Bex 6A 98
Ashdown Ct. Sutt 8A 122
Ashdown Cres. NW5 1E 58
Ashdown Cres. Chesh 1E 6
Ashdown Dri. Borwd 4K 11
Ashdowne Ct. N17 8E 28
Ashdown Est. E11 9B 46
Ashdown Gdns. S Croy 7F 138
Ashdown Ho. SW1 4G 75
(off Victoria St.)
Ashdown Pl. Th Dit 2E 118
Ashdown Rd. Enf 4G 17
Ashdown Rd. Eps 5D 134
Ashdown Rd. King T 6J 103
Ashdown Rd. Uxb 5E 142
Ashdown Wlk. E14 5L 77
(off Copeland Dri.)
Ashdown Wlk. Romf 8M 33
Ashdown Way. SW17 8E 90
Ashe Ho. Twic 5H 87
Ashen. E6 9L 63
Ashenden. SE17 5A 76
(off Deacon Way)
Ashenden Rd. E5 1J 61

Ashen Dri. Dart 6E 98
Ashen Gro. SW19 9L 89
Ashentree Ct. EC4 9L 59
(off Whitefriars St.)
Ashen Va. S Croy 1H 139
Asher Loftus Way. N11 6D 26
Asher Way. E1 1E 76
Ashfield Av. Bush 8M 9
Ashfield Av. Felt 7F 84
Ashfield Clo. Beck 4L 109
Ashfield Clo. Rich 7J 87
Ashfield Ho. W14 6K 73
(off W. Cromwell Rd.)
Ashfield La. Chst 3M 111
(in two parts)
Ashfield Pde. N14 1H 27
Ashfield Rd. N4 4A 44
Ashfield Rd. N14 3G 27
Ashfield Rd. W3 2D 72
Ashfields. Lou 4K 19
Ashfields. Wat 8D 4
(in two parts)
Ashfield St. E1 8F 60
Ashfield Yd. E1 8G 61
Ashford. 9D 144
Ashford Av. N8 2J 43
Ashford Av. Hay 9H 53
Ashford Bus. Complex. Ashf 2A 100
(Sandell's Av.)
Ashford Bus. Complex. Ashf 1A 100
(Shield Rd.)
Ashford Clo. E17 4K 45
Ashford Common. 4B 100
Ashford Ct. Edgw 3M 23
Ashford Cres. Ashf 9C 144
Ashford Cres. Enf 4G 17
Ashford Grn. Wat 5H 21
Ashford Ho. SE8 7K 77
Ashford Ho. SW9 3M 91
Ashford M. N17 8E 28
Ashford Park. 9B 144
Ashford Pas. NW2 9H 41
Ashford Rd. E6 3L 63
Ashford Rd. E18 9F 30
Ashford Rd. NW2 9H 41
Ashford Rd. Ashf 4A 100
Ashford Rd. Felt 1B 100
Ashford St. N1 6C 60
Ash Gro. E8 4F 60
(in two parts)
Ash Gro. N13 3A 28
Ash Gro. NW2 9H 41
Ash Gro. SE12 7E 94
Ash Gro. SE20 6G 109
Ash Gro. W5 3J 71
Ash Gro. Enf 9C 16
Ash Gro. Felt 7C 84
Ash Gro. Hay 1B 68
Ash Gro. Houn 9H 69
Ash Gro. S'hall 8L 53
Ash Gro. Wemb 9E 38
Ash Gro. W Dray 1K 143
Ash Gro. W Wick 4A 126
Ashgrove Ct. W9 8L 57
(off Elmfield Way)
Ashgrove Ho. SW1 6H 75
(off Lindsay Sq.)
Ashgrove Rd. Ashf 2A 100
Ashgrove Rd. Brom 3B 110
Ashgrove Rd. Ilf 6D 48
Ash Hill Clo. Bush 1M 21
Ash Hill Dri. Pinn 1G 37
Ash Ho. E14 3A 78
(off E. Ferry Rd.)
Ash Ho. SE1 5D 76
(off Longfield Est.)
Ash Ho. W10 7J 57
(off Heather Wlk.)
Ashingdon Clo. E4 3A 30
Ashington Ho. E1 7F 60
(off Barnsley St.)
Ashington Rd. SW6 1K 89
Ashlake Rd. SW16 1J 107
Ashland Pl. W1 8E 58
Ash La. Horn 2K 51
Ash La. Romf 6E 34
Ashlar Pl. SE18 5M 79
Ashleigh Commercial Est. SE7 4G 79
Ashleigh Ct. N14 9G 15
Ashleigh Ct. W5 5H 71
(off Murray Rd.)
Ashleigh Gdns. Sutt 4M 121
Ashleigh Point. SE23 9H 93
Ashleigh Rd. SE20 7F 108
Ashleigh Rd. SW14 2C 88
Ashley Av. Eps 5B 134
Ashley Av. Ilf 9M 31
Ashley Av. Mord 9L 105
Ashley Cen. Eps 5B 134
Ashley Clo. NW4 9G 25
Ashley Clo. Pinn 9F 20
Ashley Clo. W on T 3D 116
Ashley Ct. NW4 9G 25
Ashley Ct. NW9 9D 24
(off Guilfoyle)
Ashley Ct. SW1 4G 75
(off Morpeth Ter.)
Ashley Ct. Barn 7A 14
Ashley Ct. Eps 5B 134
Ashley Ct. N'holt 4J 53
Ashley Cres. N22 9L 27
Ashley Cres. SW11 2E 90
Ashley Dri. Bans 6L 135
Ashley Dri. Borwd 7A 12
Ashley Dri. Iswth 7C 70
Ashley Dri. Twic 6M 85
Ashley Dri. W on T 5E 116
Ashley Gdns. N13 4A 28
Ashley Gdns. SW1 4G 75
(in three parts)
Ashley Gdns. Orp 7C 128
Ashley Gdns. Rich 8H 87
Ashley Gdns. Wemb 7J 39
Ashley Gro. Lou 5J 19
Ashley La. NW4 7G 25
(in three parts)
Ashley La. Croy 6M 123
Ashley Park. 5E 116
Ashley Pk. Av. W on T 4D 116
Ashley Pk. Cres. W on T 3E 116
Ashley Pk. Rd. W on T 4E 116
Ashley Pl. SW1 4G 75
(in two parts)
Ashley Ri. W on T 6D 116
Ashley Rd. E4 6L 29
Ashley Rd. E7 3G 63
Ashley Rd. N17 1E 44
Ashley Rd. N19 6J 43
Ashley Rd. SW19 3M 105
Ashley Rd. Enf 4G 17
Ashley Rd. Eps 5B 134
Ashley Rd. Hamp 5L 101
Ashley Rd. Rich 2J 87
Ashley Rd. Th Dit 1D 118
Ashley Rd. T Hth 8K 107
Ashley Rd. Uxb 5A 142
Ashley Rd. W on T 6D 116
Ashley Sq. Eps 5B 134
(off Ashley Cen.)
Ashley Wlk. NW7 7H 25
Ashling Rd. Croy 3E 124
Ashlin Rd. E15 9B 46
Ashlone Rd. SW15 2G 89
Ashlyn Clo. Bush 6J 9
Ashlyn Ct. Wat 6J 9
Ashlyn Gro. Horn 1H 51
Ashlyns Way. Chess 8H 119
Ashmead. N14 7G 15
Ashmead Bus. Cen. E3 7B 62
Ashmead Ga. Brom 5G 111
Ashmead Ho. E9 1J 61
(off Homerton Rd.)
Ashmead M. SE8 1L 93
Ashmead Rd. SE8 1L 93
Ashmead Rd. Felt 7E 84
Ashmeads. Lou 5K 19
Ashmere Av. Beck 6B 110
Ashmere Clo. Sutt 7H 121
Ashmere Gro. SW2 3J 91
Ash M. Eps 5C 134
Ashmill St. NW1 8C 58
Ashmole Pl. SW8 7K 75
(in two parts)
Ashmole St. SW8 7K 75
Ashmore. NW1 3H 59
(off Agar Gro.)
Ashmore Clo. SE15 8D 76
Ashmore Ct. N11 6D 26
Ashmore Ct. Houn 7L 69
Ashmore Gro. Well 2B 96
Ashmore Ho. W14 4J 73
(off Russell Rd.)
Ashmore La. Kes 3G 141
Ashmore Rd. W9 5K 57
Ashmount Est. N19 5H 43
Ashmount Rd. N15 3D 44
Ashmount Rd. N19 5G 43
Ashmount Ter. W5 5H 71
Ashmour Gdns. Romf 9B 34
Ashneal Gdns. Harr 8B 38
Ashness Gdns. Gnfd 2F 54
Ashness Rd. SW11 4D 90
Ashpark Ho. E14 9K 61
(off Norbiton Rd.)
Ashridge Clo. Harr 4G 39
Ashridge Ct. N14 7G 15
Ashridge Ct. S'hall 9A 54
(off Redcroft Rd.)
Ashridge Cres. SE18 8A 80
Ashridge Dri. Brick W 3J 5
Ashridge Dri. Wat 5G 21
Ashridge Gdns. N13 5H 27
Ashridge Gdns. Pinn 2J 37
Ashridge Ho. Wat 9C 8
(off Chenies Way)
Ashridge Way. Mord 7K 105
Ashridge Way. Sun 3E 100
Ash Rd. E15 1C 62
Ash Rd. Croy 4L 125
Ash Rd. Dart 7H 99
Ash Rd. Hawl 1K 115
Ash Rd. Orp 9D 128
Ash Rd. Sutt 2J 121
Ash Row. Brom 2L 127
Ashtead. 9K 133
Ashtead Gap. Lea 8F 132
Ashtead Rd. E5 5E 44
Ashtead Woods Rd. Asht 9G 133
Ashton Clo. Sutt 6L 121
Ashton Clo. W on T 8F 116
Ashton Ct. Harr 8D 38
Ashton Gdns. Houn 3K 85
Ashton Gdns. Romf 4J 49
Ashton Ga. Romf 7H 35
Ashton Heights. SE23 7G 93
Ashton Ho. SW9 8L 75
Ashton Rd. E15 1B 62
Ashton Rd. Enf 9E 6
Ashton Rd. H Hill 7H 35
Ashton St. E14 1A 78
Ashtree Av. Mitc 6B 106
Ash Tree Clo. Croy 1J 125
Ashtree Clo. Orp 6M 127
Ash Tree Clo. Surb 4J 119
Ashtree Dell. NW9 3B 40
Ash Tree Rd. Wat 9F 4
Ash Tree Way. Croy 9H 109
Ashurst. Eps 6B 134
Ashurst Clo. SE20 5F 108
Ashurst Clo. Dart 2D 98
Ashurst Clo. Kenl 7B 138
Ashurst Clo. N'wd 7C 20
Ashurst Dri. Ilf 4M 47
Ashurst Gdns. SW2 7L 91
Ashurst Rd. N12 5C 26
Ashurst Rd. Barn 7D 14
Ashurst Wlk. Croy 4F 124
Ashvale Gdns. Romf 5B 34
Ashvale Rd. SW17 2D 106
Ashville Rd. E11 7B 46
Ash Wlk. Wemb 8G 39
Ashwater Rd. SE12 7E 94
Ashway Cen., The. King T 5J 103
Ashwell Clo. E6 9J 63
Ashwin St. E8 2D 60
Ashwood Av. Rain 7F 66
Ashwood Av. Uxb 9E 142
Ashwood Gdns. Hay 5D 68
Ashwood Gdns. New Ad 8M 125
Ashwood Ho. H End 6L 21
(off Avenue, The)
Ashwood Rd. E4 3B 30
Ashworth Clo. SE5 1B 92
Ashworth Est. Croy 3J 123
Ashworth Mans. W9 6M 57
(off Elgin Av.)
Ashworth Rd. W9 6M 57
Aske Ho. N1 6C 60
(off Fanshaw St., in two parts)
Asker Ho. N7 9J 43
Askern Clo. Bexh 3H 97
Aske St. N1 6C 60
Askew Cres. W12 3D 72
Askew Est. W12 2D 72
(off Uxbridge Rd.)
Askew Rd. W12 3D 72
Askew Rd. N'wd 2B 20
Askham Ct. W12 2E 72
Askham Rd. W12 2E 72
Askill Dri. SW15 4J 89
Askwith Rd. Rain 6B 66
Asland Rd. E15 4C 62
Aslett St. SW18 6M 89
Asmara Rd. NW2 1J 57
Asmar Clo. Coul 7J 137
Asmuns Hill. NW11 3L 41
Asmuns Pl. NW11 3K 41
Asolando Dri. SE17 5A 76
Aspen Clo. N19 7G 43
Aspen Clo. W5 3K 71
Aspen Clo. Brick W 3J 5
Aspen Clo. Orp 7E 128
Aspen Clo. Swan 5B 114
Aspen Clo. W Dray 2K 143
Aspen Copse. Brom 6K 111
Aspen Ct. Dart 5L 99
Aspen Dri. Wemb 8E 38
Aspen Gdns. W6 6F 72
Aspen Gdns. Ashf 2A 100
Aspen Gdns. Mitc 9E 106
Aspen Grn. Eri 4K 81
Aspen Gro. Upm 9L 51
Aspen Ho. SE15 7G 77
(off Sharratt St.)
Aspen Ho. Sidc 9E 96
Aspen La. N'holt 6J 53
Aspenlea Rd. W6 7H 73
Aspen Lodge. W8 4M 73
(off Abbots Wlk.)
Aspen Pk. Dri. Wat 8F 4
Aspen Sq. Wey 5B 116
Aspen Va. Whyt 9D 138
Aspen Way. E14 1M 77
Aspen Way. Bans 6H 135
Aspen Way. Enf 8D 6
Aspen Way. Felt 9F 84
Aspern Gro. NW3 1C 58
Aspinall Rd. SE4 2H 93
(in two parts)
Aspinden Rd. SE16 5F 76
Aspley Rd. SW18 4M 89
Asplins Rd. N17 8E 28
Asquith Clo. Dag 6G 49
Assam St. E1 9E 60
Assata M. N1 2M 59
Assembly Pas. E1 8G 61
Assembly Wlk. Cars 2C 122
Assher Rd. W on T 5J 117
Ass Ho. La. Harr 4M 21
Association Gallery, The. 7C 60
(off Leonard St.)
Astall Clo. Harr 8C 22
Astbury Bus. Pk. SE15 9G 77
Astbury Ho. SE11 4L 75
(off Lambeth Wlk.)
Astbury Rd. SE15 9G 77
Astede Pl. Asht 9K 133
Astell St. SW3 6C 74
Aste St. E14 3A 78
Astey's Row. N1 3A 60
Asthall Gdns. Ilf 2A 48
Astins Ho. E17 2M 45
Astle St. SW11 1E 90
Astley Av. NW2 1G 57
Astley Ho. SE1 6D 76
(off Rowcross St.)
Astley Ho. SW13 7F 72
(off Wyatt Dri.)
Aston Av. Harr 5G 39
Aston Clo. Bush 8A 10
Aston Clo. Sidc 9E 96
Aston Clo. Wat 4G 9
Aston Ct. Wfd G 6E 30
Aston Grn. Houn 1G 85
Aston Ho. SW8 9H 75
Aston Ho. W11 1K 73
(off Westbourne Gro.)
Aston M. Romf 5G 49
Aston Pl. SW16 3M 107
Aston Rd. SW20 6G 105
Aston Rd. W5 9H 55
Aston Rd. Clay 7C 118
Astons Rd. N'wd 3A 20
Aston St. E14 8J 61
Aston Ter. SW12 5F 90
Astonville St. SW18 7L 89
Aston Way. Eps 7D 134
Astor Av. Romf 4A 50
Astor Clo. King T 3M 103
Astor Ct. E16 9G 63
(off Ripley Rd.)
Astor Ct. SW6 8A 74
(off Maynard Clo.)
Astoria Mans. SW16 9J 91
Astoria Wlk. SW9 2L 91
Astra Clo. Horn 2F 66
Astra Ct. Wat 7D 8
Astra Ho. SE14 7K 77
(off Arklow Rd.)
Astrid Ho. Felt 8G 85
Astrop M. W6 4G 73
Astrop Ter. W6 3G 73
Astwood M. SW7 5A 74
Asylum Rd. SE15 8F 76
Atalanta Clo. Purl 2L 137
Atalanta St. SW6 8H 73
Atbara Rd. Tedd 3F 102
Atcham Rd. Houn 3A 86
Atcost Rd. Bark 8E 64
Atcraft Cen. Wemb 4J 55
Atheldene Rd. SW18 7M 89
Athelney St. SE6 9L 93
Athelstan Clo. Romf 9K 35
Athelstane Gro. E3 5K 61
Athelstane M. N4 6L 43
Athelstan Gdns. NW6 3J 57
Athelstan Ho. King T 8K 103
(off Athelstan Rd.)
Athelstan Rd. King T 8K 103
Athelstan Rd. Romf 8K 35
Athelstan Way. Orp 5E 112
Athelstone Rd. Harr 9B 22
Athena Clo. Harr 7B 38
Athena Clo. King T 7K 103
Athenaeum Ct. N5 9A 44
Athenaeum Pl. N10 1F 42
Athenaeum Rd. N20 1A 26
Athena Pl. N'wd 8D 20
Athenia Ho. E14 9B 62
(off Blair St.)
Athenlay Rd. SE15 4H 93
Athens Gdns. W9 7L 57
(off Harrow Rd.)
Atherden Rd. E5 9G 45
Atherfold Rd. SW9 2J 91
Atherley Way. Houn 6K 85
Atherstone Ct. W2 8M 57
(off Delamere Ter.)
Atherstone M. SW7 5A 74
Atherton Clo. Stanw 5B 144
Atherton Dri. SW19 1H 105
Atherton Heights. Wemb 2G 55
Atherton Ho. Romf 7J 35
(off Leyburn Cres.)
Atherton M. E7 2D 62
Atherton Pl. Harr 1B 38
Atherton Pl. S'hall 1L 69
Atherton Rd. E7 2D 62
Atherton Rd. SW13 8E 72
Atherton Rd. Ilf 9J 31
Atherton St. SW11 1C 90
Athlone. Clay 8C 118
Athlone Clo. E5 1F 60
Athlone Ct. E17 1B 46
Athlone Ho. E1 9G 61
(off Sidney St.)
Athlone Rd. SW2 6K 91
Athlone St. NW5 2E 58
Athlon Ind. Est. Wemb 4H 55
Athlon Rd. Wemb 5H 55
Athol Clo. Pinn 8F 20
Athole Gdns. Enf 7C 16
Athol Gdns. Pinn 8F 20
Atholl Ho. W9 6A 58
(off Maida Va.)
Atholl Rd. Ilf 5E 48
Athol Rd. Eri 6A 82
Athol Sq. E14 9A 62
Athol Way. Uxb 6E 142
Atkin Building. WC1 8K 59
(off Raymond Bldgs.)
Atkins Dri. W Wick 4B 126
Atkinson Clo. Orp 7E 128
Atkinson Ct. E10 5M 45
(off Kings Clo.)
Atkinson Ho. E2 5E 60
(off Pritchards Rd.)
Atkinson Ho. E13 7D 62
(off Sutton Rd.)
Atkinson Ho. SE17 5B 76
(off Catesby St.)
Atkinson Rd. E16 8G 63
Atkins Rd. E10 4M 45
Atkins Rd. SW12 6G 91
Atlanta Boulevd. Romf 4C 50
Atlanta Ho. SE16 4J 77
(off Brunswick Quay)
Atlantic Ct. E14 1B 78
(off Jamestown Way)
Atlantic Ho. E1 8J 61
(off Harford St.)
Atlantic Rd. SW9 3L 91
Atlantic Wharf. E1 1H 77
(off Jardine Rd.)
Atlantis Clo. Bark 6F 64
Atlas Bus. Cen. NW2 6F 40
Atlas Gdns. SE7 5G 79
Atlas M. E8 2D 60
Atlas M. N7 2K 59
Atlas Rd. E13 5E 62
Atlas Rd. N11 7E 26
Atlas Rd. NW10 6C 56
Atlas Rd. Dart 2K 99
Atlas Rd. Wemb 9A 40
Atlas Wharf. E9 2L 61
Atley Rd. E3 4L 61
Atlip Rd. Wemb 4J 55
Atney Rd. SW15 3J 89
Atria Rd. N'wd 5E 20
Attenborough Clo. Wat 3J 21
Atterbury Rd. N4 4L 43
Atterbury St. SW1 5J 75
Attewood Av. NW10 8C 40
Attewood Rd. N'holt 2J 53
Attfield Clo. N20 2B 26
Attfield Ct. King T 6K 103
(off Albert Rd.)
Attilburgh Ho. SE1 4D 76
(off Abbey St.)
Attleborough Ct. SE26 8E 92
Attle Clo. Uxb 5E 142
Attlee Clo. Hay 6F 52
Attlee Clo. T Hth 9A 108
Attlee Dri. Dart 4L 99
Attlee Rd. SE28 1F 80
Attlee Rd. Hay 6E 52
Attlee Ter. E17 2M 45
Attneave St. WC1 6L 59
Attwell's Yd. Uxb 3B 142
(off High St.)
Attwood Clo. S Croy 6F 138
Atwater Clo. SW2 7L 91
Atwell Clo. E10 4M 45
Atwell Pl. Th Dit 3D 118
Atwell Rd. SE15 1E 92
Atwood Av. Rich 1L 87
Atwood Ho. W14 5K 73
(off Beckford Clo.)
Atwood Rd. W6 5F 72
Atwoods All. Rich 9L 71
Aubert Ct. N5 9M 43
Aubert Pk. N5 9M 43
Aubert Rd. N5 9M 43
Aubretia Clo. H Wood 8J 35
Aubrey Beardsley Ho. SW1 5G 75
(off Vauxhall Bri. Rd.)
Aubrey Mans. NW1 8C 58
(off Lisson St.)
Aubrey Moore Point. E15 5A 62
(off Abbey La.)
Aubrey Pl. NW8 5A 58
Aubrey Rd. E17 1L 45
Aubrey Rd. N8 3J 43
Aubrey Rd. W8 2K 73
Aubrey Wlk. W8 2K 73
Auburn Clo. SE14 8J 77
Aubyn Hill. SE27 1A 108
Aubyn Sq. SW15 4E 88
Auckland Av. Rain 6D 66
Auckland Clo. SE19 5D 108
Auckland Clo. Enf 1F 16
Auckland Ct. Hay 7G 53
Auckland Gdns. SE19 5C 108
Auckland Hill. SE27 1A 108
Auckland Ho. W12 1F 72
(off White City Est.)
Auckland Ri. SE19 5C 108
Auckland Rd. E10 8M 45

Auckland Rd.—Badlow Clo.

Auckland Rd. SE19 ... 5D 108
Auckland Rd. SW11 ... 3C 90
Auckland Rd. Ilf ... 6M 47
Auckland Rd. King T ... 8K 103
Auckland St. SE11 ... 6K 75
Audax. NW9 ... 9D 24
Auden Pl. NW1 ... 4E 58
(in two parts)
Auden Pl. Cheam ... 6G 121
Audleigh Pl. Chig ... 6L 31
Audley Clo. N10 ... 7F 26
Audley Clo. SW11 ... 2E 90
Audley Clo. Borwd ... 5L 11
Audley Ct. E18 ... 2D 46
Audley Ct. N'holt ... 6G 53
Audley Ct. Pinn ... 9G 21
Audley Ct. Twic ... 9B 86
Audley Dri. E16 ... 2F 78
Audley Dri. Warl ... 7G 139
Audley Firs. W on T ... 6G 117
Audley Gdns. Ilf ... 7D 48
Audley Gdns. Wal A ... 7J 7
Audley Pl. Sutt ... 9M 121
Audley Rd. NW4 ... 3E 40
Audley Rd. W5 ... 8K 55
Audley Rd. Enf ... 4M 15
Audley Rd. Rich ... 4K 87
Audley Sq. W1 ... 2E 74
Audley Wlk. Orp ... 1G 129
Audrey Clo. Beck ... 1M 125
Audrey Gdns. Wemb ... 7F 38
Audrey Rd. Ilf ... 8M 47
Audrey St. E2 ... 5E 60
Audric Clo. King T ... 5L 103
Audwick Clo. Chesh ... 1E 6
Augurs La. E13 ... 6F 62
Augusta Clo. W Mol ... 8K 101
Augusta Rd. Twic ... 8A 86
Augusta St. E14 ... 9M 61
Augustine Rd. W14 ... 4H 73
Augustine Rd. Harr ... 8M 21
Augustine Rd. Orp ... 7H 113
Augustus Clo. W12 ... 3F 72
Augustus Clo. Bren ... 8G 71
Augustus Ct. SW16 ... 8H 91
Augustus Ct. Felt ... 1K 101
Augustus Ho. NW1 ... 5F 58
(off Augustus St.)
Augustus La. Orp ... 4E 128
Augustus Rd. SW19 ... 7H 89
Augustus St. NW1 ... 5F 58
Aultone Way. Cars ... 5D 122
Aultone Way. Sutt ... 4M 121
Aulton Pl. SE11 ... 6L 75
Aurelia Gdns. Croy ... 9K 107
Aurelia Rd. Croy ... 1J 123
Auriel Av. Dag ... 2B 66
Auriga M. N1 ... 1B 60
Auriol Clo. Wor Pk ... 5C 120
Auriol Dri. Gnfd ... 3B 54
Auriol Dri. Uxb ... 2E 142
Auriol Ho. W12 ... 2F 72
(off Ellerslie Rd.)
Auriol Pk. Rd. Wor Pk ... 5C 120
Auriol Rd. W14 ... 5J 73
Aurora Ho. E14 ... 9M 61
(off Kerbey St.)
Austell Gdns. NW7 ... 3C 24
Austell Heights. NW7 ... 3C 24
(off Austell Gdns.)
Austen Clo. SE28 ... 2F 80
Austen Gdns. Dart ... 3K 99
Austen Ho. NW6 ... 6L 57
(off Cambridge Rd.)
Austen Rd. Eri ... 8M 81
Austen Rd. Harr ... 7M 37
Austin Av. Brom ... 9J 111
Austin Clo. SE23 ... 6J 93
Austin Clo. Coul ... 9M 137
Austin Clo. Twic ... 4G 87
Austin Ct. E6 ... 4G 63
Austin Ct. SE15 ... 2E 92
(off Philip Wlk.)
Austin Ct. Enf ... 7C 16
Austin Friars. EC2 ... 9B 60
(in two parts)
Austin Friars Pas. EC2 ... 9B 60
(off Austin Friars)
Austin Friars Sq. EC2 ... 9B 60
(off Austin Friars)
Austin Ho. SE14 ... 8K 77
(off Achilles St.)
Austin Rd. SW11 ... 9E 74
Austin Rd. Hay ... 3D 68
Austin Rd. Orp ... 1E 128
Austin's La. Uxb ... 8A 36
(in two parts)
Austin St. E2 ... 6D 60
Austin Ter. SE1 ... 4L 75
(off Morley St.)
Austin Waye. Uxb ... 4A 142
Austral Clo. Sidc ... 9D 96
Austral Dri. Horn ... 5H 51
Australia Rd. W12 ... 1F 72
Austral St. SE11 ... 5M 75
Austyn Gdns. Surb ... 3M 119
Autumn Clo. SW19 ... 3A 106
Autumn Clo. Enf ... 3E 16
Autumn Dri. Sutt ... 1M 135
Autumn Lodge. S Croy ... 6C 124
(off S. Park Hill Rd.)
Autumn St. E3 ... 4L 61
Avalon Clo. SW20 ... 6J 105
Avalon Clo. W13 ... 8E 54
Avalon Clo. Enf ... 4L 15
Avalon Clo. Orp ... 5H 129
Avalon Clo. Wat ... 5J 5
Avalon Rd. SW6 ... 9M 73
Avalon Rd. W13 ... 7E 54
Avalon Rd. Orp ... 4F 128
Avard Gdns. Orp ... 6A 128
Avarn Rd. SW17 ... 3D 106
Avebury Ct. N1 ... 4B 60
(off Imber St.)
Avebury Pk. Surb ... 2H 119
Avebury Rd. E11 ... 6B 46
Avebury Rd. SW19 ... 5K 105
Avebury Rd. Orp ... 5B 128
Avebury St. N1 ... 4B 60
Aveley. ... 1M 83
Aveley By-Pass. S Ock ... 1M 83
Aveley Clo. Eri ... 7D 82
Aveley Mans. Bark ... 3M 63
(off Whiting Av.)
Aveley Rd. Romf ... 2B 50
Aveley Rd. Upm ... 2M 67
Aveline St. SE11 ... 6L 75
Aveling Clo. Purl ... 5K 137
Aveling Pk. Rd. E17 ... 9L 29
Avelon Rd. Rain ... 4E 66
Avelon Rd. Romf ... 6B 34
Ave Maria La. EC4 ... 9M 59
Avenell Rd. N5 ... 8M 43
Avenfield Ho. W1 ... 1D 74
(off Park La.)
Avening Rd. SW18 ... 6L 89
Avening Ter. SW18 ... 6L 89
Avenons Rd. E13 ... 7E 62
Avenue Clo. N14 ... 8G 15
Avenue Clo. NW8 ... 4C 58
Avenue Clo. Houn ... 9F 68
Avenue Clo. Romf ... 7K 35
Avenue Clo. W Dray ... 4H 143
Avenue Ct. N14 ... 8G 15
Avenue Ct. NW2 ... 8K 41
Avenue Ct. SW3 ... 5D 74
(off Draycott Av.)
Avenue Cres. W3 ... 3M 71
Avenue Cres. Houn ... 9F 68
Avenue Elmers. Surb ... 9J 103
Avenue Gdns. SE25 ... 6E 108
Avenue Gdns. SW14 ... 2C 88
Avenue Gdns. W3 ... 3M 71
Avenue Gdns. Houn ... 8F 68
Avenue Gdns. Tedd ... 4D 102
Avenue Ga. Lou ... 8G 19
Avenue Ho. NW8 ... 5C 58
(off Allitsen Rd.)
Avenue Ho. NW10 ... 5F 56
(off All Souls Av.)
Avenue Ind. Est. E4 ... 6K 29
Avenue Ind. Est. Romf ... 9H 35
Avenue Lodge. NW8 ... 3B 58
(off Avenue Rd.)
Avenue Mans. NW3 ... 1M 57
(off Finchley Rd.)
Avenue M. N10 ... 1F 42
Avenue Pde. N21 ... 9B 16
Avenue Pde. Sun ... 7F 100
Avenue Pk. Rd. SE27 ... 8M 91
Avenue Ri. Bush ... 7L 9
Avenue Rd. E7 ... 9F 46
Avenue Rd. N6 ... 5G 43
Avenue Rd. N12 ... 4A 26
Avenue Rd. N14 ... 9G 15
Avenue Rd. N15 ... 3B 44
Avenue Rd.
NW3 & NW8 ... 3B 58
Avenue Rd. NW10 ... 5D 56
Avenue Rd.
SE20 & Beck ... 5G 109
Avenue Rd. SE25 ... 6D 108
Avenue Rd. SW16 ... 6H 107
Avenue Rd. SW20 ... 6F 104
Avenue Rd. W3 ... 3M 71
Avenue Rd. Bans ... 7M 135
Avenue Rd. Belv ... 5A 82
Avenue Rd. Bexh ... 2J 97
Avenue Rd. Bren ... 6G 71
Avenue Rd. Chad H ... 6G 49
Avenue Rd. Eps ... 6B 134
Avenue Rd. Eri ... 8A 82
Avenue Rd. Felt ... 9D 84
Avenue Rd. Hamp ... 5M 101
Avenue Rd. H Wood ... 7K 35
Avenue Rd. Iswth ... 9D 70
Avenue Rd. King T ... 7J 103
Avenue Rd. N Mald ... 8C 104
Avenue Rd. Pinn ... 1J 37
Avenue Rd. S'hall ... 2K 69
Avenue Rd. Sutt ... 2L 135
Avenue Rd. Tedd ... 4E 102
Avenue Rd. Wall ... 9G 123
Avenue Rd. Wfd G ... 6G 31
Avenue S. Surb ... 2L 119
Avenue Ter. N Mald ... 7A 104
Avenue Ter. Wat ... 8J 9
Avenue, The. E4 ... 6B 30
Avenue, The. E11 ... 4F 46
Avenue, The. N3 ... 9L 25
Avenue, The. N8 ... 1L 43
Avenue, The. N10 ... 9G 27
Avenue, The. N11 ... 5F 26
Avenue, The. N17 ... 1B 44
Avenue, The. NW6 ... 4H 57
Avenue, The. SE9 ... 4K 95
Avenue, The. SE10 ... 8B 78
Avenue, The. SW4 ... 4E 90
Avenue, The. SW18 ... 6C 90
Avenue, The. W4 ... 4C 72
Avenue, The. W13 ... 9F 54
Avenue, The. Barn ... 5J 13
Avenue, The. Beck ... 5M 109
(in two parts)
Avenue, The. Bex ... 6H 97
Avenue, The. Brom ... 7H 111
Avenue, The. Buck H ... 2G 31
Avenue, The. Bush ... 6K 9
Avenue, The. Cars ... 9E 122
Avenue, The. Clay ... 8C 118
Avenue, The. Coul ... 7H 137
Avenue, The. Cow ... 7B 142
Avenue, The. Cran ... 9E 68
Avenue, The. Croy ... 5C 124
Avenue, The. Eps & Sutt ... 9F 120
Avenue, The. Hamp ... 3K 101
Avenue, The. Harr ... 8D 22
Avenue, The. H End ... 6K 21
Avenue, The. Horn ... 7G 51
Avenue, The. Houn ... 4M 85
Avenue, The. Kes ... 6H 127
Avenue, The. Lou ... 8H 19
Avenue, The. N'wd ... 6A 20
Avenue, The. Orp ... 4D 128
Avenue, The. Oxs ... 3D 132
Avenue, The. Pinn ... 5K 37
Avenue, The. Rich ... 1K 87
Avenue, The. Romf ... 2B 50
Avenue, The. St P ... 4F 112
Avenue, The. Sun ... 5F 100
Avenue, The. Surb ... 1K 119
Avenue, The. Sutt ... 2K 135
Avenue, The. Twic ... 4F 86
Avenue, The. Wat ... 4E 8
Avenue, The. Wemb ... 6J 39
Avenue, The. W Wick ... 2C 126
Avenue, The. Wor Pk ... 4D 120
Averil Gro. SW16 ... 3M 107
Averill St. W6 ... 7H 73
Avern Gdns. W Mol ... 8M 101
Avern Rd. W Mol ... 8M 101
Avery Farm Row. SW1 ... 5E 74
Avery Gdns. Ilf ... 3K 47
Avery Hill. ... 5B 96
Avery Hill Rd. SE9 ... 5B 96
Avery Row. W1 ... 1F 74
Avey La. Wal A & Lou ... 9K 7
Avia Pk. Felt ... 7F 144
Aviary Clo. E16 ... 8D 62
Aviemore Clo. Beck ... 9K 109
Aviemore Way. Beck ... 9J 109
Avignon Rd. SE4 ... 2H 93
Avington Ct. SE1 ... 5C 76
(off Old Kent Rd.)
Avington Gro. SE20 ... 4G 109
Avington Way. SE15 ... 8D 76
Avion Cres. NW9 ... 8E 24
Avior Dri. N'wd ... 4D 20
Avis Sq. E1 ... 9H 61
Avoca Rd. SW17 ... 1E 106
Avocet Clo. SE1 ... 6E 76
Avocet M. SE28 ... 4B 80
Avon Clo. Hay ... 7G 53
Avon Clo. Sutt ... 6A 122
Avon Clo. Wat ... 7G 5
Avon Clo. Wor Pk ... 4E 120
Avon Ct. E4 ... 1A 30
Avon Ct. N12 ... 5M 25
Avon Ct. W9 ... 8L 57
(off Elmfield Way)
Avon Ct. Buck H ... 1F 30
Avon Ct. Gnfd ... 7M 53
Avon Ct. Pinn ... 7L 21
(off Avenue, The)
Avondale Av. N12 ... 5M 25
Avondale Av. NW2 ... 8C 40
Avondale Av. Barn ... 1D 26
Avondale Av. Esh ... 5E 118
Avondale Av. Wor Pk ... 3D 120
Avondale Clo. Lou ... 9K 19
Avondale Clo. W on T ... 7G 117
Avondale Ct. E11 ... 6C 46
Avondale Ct. E16 ... 8C 62
Avondale Ct. E18 ... 8F 30
Avondale Cres. Enf ... 5J 17
Avondale Cres. Ilf ... 3H 47
Avondale Dri. Hay ... 2E 68
Avondale Dri. Lou ... 9K 19
Avondale Gdns. Houn ... 4K 85
Avondale Ho. SE1 ... 6E 76
(off Avondale Sq.)
Avondale Pk. Gdns. W11 ... 1J 73
Avondale Pk. Rd. W11 ... 1J 73
Avondale Ri. SE15 ... 2D 92
Avondale Rd. E16 ... 8C 62
Avondale Rd. E17 ... 5L 45
Avondale Rd. N3 ... 8A 26
Avondale Rd. N13 ... 2L 27
Avondale Rd. N15 ... 3M 43
Avondale Rd. SE9 ... 8J 95
Avondale Rd. SW14 ... 2C 88
Avondale Rd. SW19 ... 2M 105
Avondale Rd. Ashf ... 9B 144
Avondale Rd. Brom ... 3C 110
Avondale Rd. Harr ... 1D 38
Avondale Rd. S Croy ... 8A 124
Avondale Rd. Well ... 1G 97
Avondale Sq. SE1 ... 6E 76
Avonfield Ct. E17 ... 1B 46
Avon Ho. W8 ... 4L 73
(off Allen St.)
Avon Ho. W14 ... 5K 73
(off Kensington Village)
Avon Ho. King T ... 5H 103
Avonhurst Ho. NW2 ... 3J 57
Avonley Rd. SE14 ... 8G 77
Avon M. Pinn ... 7K 21
Avonmore Gdns. W14 ... 5K 73
Avonmore Pl. W14 ... 5J 73
Avonmore Rd. W14 ... 5J 73
Avonmouth Rd. Dart ... 4H 99
Avonmouth St. SE1 ... 4A 76
Avon Path. S Croy ... 8A 124
Avon Pl. SE1 ... 3A 76
Avon Rd. E17 ... 1B 46
Avon Rd. SE4 ... 2L 93
Avon Rd. Gnfd ... 7L 53
Avon Rd. Sun ... 4D 100
Avonstowe Clo. Orp ... 5A 128
Avon Way. E18 ... 1E 46
Avonwick Rd. Houn ... 1M 85
Avril Way. E4 ... 5A 30
Avro Ho. SW8 ... 8F 74
(off Havelock Ter.)
Avro Way. Wall ... 9J 123
Awberry Ct. Wat ... 8B 8
Awlfield Av. N17 ... 8B 28
Awliscombe Rd. Well ... 1D 96
Axe St. Bark ... 4A 64
(in two parts)
Axholme Av. Edgw ... 8L 23
Axminster Cres. Well ... 9G 81
Axminster Rd. N7 ... 8J 43
Axtaine Rd. Orp ... 2H 129
Axtane Clo. S at H ... 5M 115
Axwood. Eps ... 7A 134
Aybrook St. W1 ... 8E 58
Aycliffe Clo. Brom ... 8K 111
Aycliffe Rd. W12 ... 2E 72
Aycliffe Rd. Borwd ... 3J 11
Ayerst Ct. E10 ... 5A 46
Aylands Clo. Wemb ... 7J 39
Aylands Rd. Enf ... 9C 6
Aylesbury Clo. E7 ... 2D 62
Aylesbury Ct. Sutt ... 5A 122
Aylesbury Ho. SE15 ... 7E 76
(off Friary Est.)
Aylesbury Rd. SE17 ... 6B 76
Aylesbury Rd. Brom ... 7E 110
Aylesbury St. EC1 ... 7M 59
Aylesbury St. NW10 ... 8B 40
Aylesford Av. Beck ... 9J 109
Aylesford Ho. SE1 ... 3B 76
(off Long La.)
Aylesford St. SW1 ... 6H 75
Aylesham Cen., The. SE15 ... 9E 76
Aylesham Clo. NW7 ... 7E 24
Aylesham Rd. Orp ... 2D 128
Ayles Rd. Hay & N'holt ... 6F 52
Aylestone Av. NW6 ... 3H 57
Aylett Rd. SE25 ... 8F 108
Aylett Rd. Iswth ... 1C 86
Ayley Cft. Enf ... 7E 16
Ayliffe Clo. King T ... 6L 103
Aylmer Clo. Stan ... 4E 22
Aylmer Ct. N2 ... 3D 42
Aylmer Dri. Stan ... 4E 22
Aylmer Ho. SE10 ... 6B 78
Aylmer Pde. N2 ... 3D 42
Aylmer Rd. E11 ... 6D 46
Aylmer Rd. N2 ... 3C 42
Aylmer Rd. W12 ... 3D 72
Aylmer Rd. Dag ... 8J 49
Ayloffe Rd. Dag ... 2K 65
Ayloffs Clo. Horn ... 2H 51
Ayloffs Wlk. Horn ... 3H 51
Aylsham Dri. Uxb ... 7A 36
Aylsham La. Romf ... 4G 35
Aylton Est. SE16 ... 3G 77
Aylward Rd. SE23 ... 8H 93
Aylward Rd. SW20 ... 6K 105
Aylwards Ri. Stan ... 4E 22
Aylward St. E1 ... 9G 61
(Jamaica St.)
Aylward St. E1 ... 9G 61
(Jubilee St.)
Aylwin Est. SE1 ... 4C 76
Aynhoe Mans. W14 ... 5H 73
(off Aynhoe Rd.)
Aynhoe Rd. W14 ... 5H 73
Aynho St. Wat ... 7F 8
Aynscombe Angle. Orp ... 2E 128
Aynscombe Path.
SW14 ... 1A 88
Ayot Path. Borwd ... 1L 11
Ayr Ct. W3 ... 9L 55
Ayres Clo. E13 ... 6E 62
Ayres Cres. NW10 ... 3B 56
Ayres St. SE1 ... 3A 76
Ayr Grn. Romf ... 8C 34
Ayrsome Rd. N16 ... 8C 44
Ayrton Gould Ho. E2 ... 6H 61
(off Roman Rd.)
Ayrton Rd. SW7 ... 4B 74
Ayr Way. Romf ... 8C 34
Aysgarth Ct. Sutt ... 5M 121
Aysgarth Rd. SE21 ... 6C 92
Ayshford Ho. E2 ... 6F 60
(off Viaduct St.)
Ayston Ho. SE16 ... 5H 77
(off Plough Way)
Ayton Ho. SE5 ... 8B 76
(off Edmund St.)
Aytoun Pl. SW9 ... 1K 91
Aytoun Rd. SW9 ... 1K 91
Azalea Clo. W7 ... 2D 70
Azalea Clo. Ilf ... 1M 63
Azalea Ct. W7 ... 2D 70
Azalea Ct. Wfd G ... 6C 30
Azalea Dri. Swan ... 8B 114
Azalea Ho. SE14 ... 8K 77
(off Achilles St.)
Azalea Wlk. Pinn ... 3F 36
Azania M. NW5 ... 2F 58
Azenby Rd. SE15 ... 1D 92
Azof St. SE10 ... 5C 78
Azov Ho. E1 ... 7J 61
(off Commodore St.)
Aztec Ho. Ilf ... 8A 32

B

Baalbec Rd. N5 ... 1M 59
Babbacombe Clo. Chess ... 7H 119
Babbacombe Gdns. Ilf ... 2J 47
Babbacombe Rd. Brom ... 5E 110
Baber Bri. Cvn. Site. Felt ... 4G 85
Baber Dri. Felt ... 5G 85
Babington Ct. WC1 ... 8J 59
(off Orde Hall St.)
Babington Ho. SE1 ... 3A 76
(off Disney St.)
Babington Ri. Wemb ... 2L 55
Babington Rd. NW4 ... 2F 40
Babington Rd. SW16 ... 2H 107
Babington Rd. Dag ... 1G 65
Babington Rd. Horn ... 6F 50
Babmaes St. SW1 ... 1H 75
Bacchus Wlk. N1 ... 5C 60
(off Regan Way)
Bache's St. N1 ... 6B 60
Back All. EC3 ... 9C 60
(off Northumberland All.)
Bk. Church La. E1 ... 9E 60
Back Grn. W on T ... 8G 117
Back Hill. EC1 ... 7L 59
Backhouse Pl. SE17 ... 5C 76
Back La. N8 ... 3J 43
Back La. NW3 ... 9A 42
Back La. Bark ... 4A 64
Back La. Bex ... 6L 97
Back La. Bren ... 7H 71
Back La. Edgw ... 8A 24
Back La. Let H ... 3C 10
Back La. Romf ... 5H 49
Backley Gdns. SE25 ... 1E 124
Back Rd. Sidc ... 1E 112
Back Rd. Tedd ... 4C 102
Bacon Gro. SE1 ... 4D 76
Bacon La. NW9 ... 2M 39
(in two parts)
Bacon La. Edgw ... 8L 23
Bacon Link. Romf ... 6M 33
Bacons La. N6 ... 6E 42
Bacon St. E1 & E2 ... 7D 60
Bacon Ter. Dag ... 1F 64
Bacton St. E2 ... 6G 61
Badburgham Ct. Wal A ... 6M 7
Baddeley Clo. Enf ... 1L 17
Baddesley Ho. SE11 ... 6K 75
(off Jonathan St.)
Baddow Clo. Dag ... 4L 65
Baddow Clo. Wfd G ... 6G 31
Baddow Wlk. N1 ... 4A 60
(off New N. Rd.)
Baden Pl. SE1 ... 3B 76
Baden Powell Clo. Dag ... 4J 65
Baden Powell Clo. Surb ... 4K 119
Baden Powell Ho. SW7 ... 5A 74
(off Queens Ga.)
Baden Powell Ho. Belv ... 4L 81
(off Ambrooke Rd.)
Baden Rd. N8 ... 2H 43
Baden Rd. Ilf ... 1M 63
Bader Clo. Kenl ... 7B 138
Bader Way. Rain ... 2E 66
Badger Clo. Felt ... 9F 84
Badger Clo. Houn ... 2G 85
Badger Clo. Ilf ... 4A 48
Badger Ct. NW2 ... 8G 41
Badgers Clo. Borwd ... 4K 11
Badgers Clo. Enf ... 5M 15
Badgers Clo. Harr ... 4B 38
Badgers Clo. Hay ... 1C 68
Badgers Copse. Orp ... 4D 128
Badgers Copse. Wor Pk ... 4D 120
Badger's Ct. Eps ... 5C 134
Badgers Cft. N20 ... 9J 13
Badgers Cft. SE9 ... 9L 95
Badgers Hole. Croy ... 6H 125
Badgers Wlk. N Mald ... 6C 104
Badgers Wlk. Purl ... 3G 137
Badlis Rd. E17 ... 1L 45
Badlow Clo. Eri ... 8C 82

Badminton Clo.—Barkway Ct.

Badminton Clo. Borwd 4L 11
Badminton Clo. Harr 2C 38
Badminton Clo. N'holt 2L 53
Badminton Ho. Wat 4G 9
(off Anglian Clo.)
Badminton M. E16 2E 78
Badminton Rd. SW12 5E 90
Badsworth Rd. SE5 9A 76
Baffin Way. E14 2A 78
Bagley Clo. W Dray 3J 143
Bagley's La. SW6 9M 73
Bagleys Spring. Romf 2J 49
Bagnigge Ho. WC1 6L 59
(off Margery St.)
Bagot Clo. Asht 8K 133
Bagshot Ct. SE18 9L 79
Bagshot Ho. NW1 6F 58
(off Redhill St.)
Bagshot Rd. Enf 9D 16
Bagshot St. SE17 8K 77
Bahram Rd. Eps 2B 134
Baildon. E2 5G 61
(off Cyprus St.)
Baildon St. SE8 8K 77
Bailey Clo. E4 4A 30
Bailey Clo. N11 7H 27
Bailey Cres. Chess 9G 119
Bailey M. W4 7M 71
(off Hervert Gdns.)
Bailey Pl. SE26 3H 109
Baillie Clo. Rain 7F 66
Baillies Wlk. W5 3H 71
Bainbridge Clo. Ham 2J 103
Bainbridge Rd. Dag 9K 49
Bainbridge St. WC1 9H 59
Baines Clo. S Croy 7B 124
Baird Av. S'hall 1M 69
Baird Clo. E10 6L 45
Baird Clo. NW9 4A 40
Baird Clo. Bush 8M 9
Baird Gdns. SE19 1C 108
Baird Ho. W12 1F 72
(off White City Est.)
Baird Memorial Cotts. N14 2H 27
(off Balaams La.)
Baird Rd. Enf 5F 16
Baird St. EC1 7A 60
Bairstow Clo. Borwd 3J 11
Baisley Ho. Chesh 1A 6
Baizdon Rd. SE3 1C 94
Baker Beal Ct. Bexh 2M 97
Baker Boy La. Croy 5J 139
Baker Ct. Borwd 4M 11
Baker Ho. W7 2D 70
Baker Ho. WC1 7J 59
(off Colonnade)
Baker La. Mitc 6E 106
Baker Pas. NW10 4C 56
Baker Rd. NW10 4C 56
Baker Rd. SE18 8J 79
Bakers Av. E17 4M 45
Bakers Clo. Kenl 6A 138
Bakers Ct. SE25 7C 108
Bakers Ct. Uxb 3B 142
Bakerscroft. Chesh 1E 6
Bakers End. SW20 6J 105
Baker's Fld. N7 9J 43
Bakers Gdns. Cars 4C 122
Bakers Hall Ct. EC3 1C 76
(off Cross La.)
Bakers Hill. E5 6G 45
Bakers Hill. New Bar 4M 13
Bakers Ho. W5 2H 71
(off Grove, The)
Bakers La. N6 4D 42
Baker's M. W1 9E 58
Bakers M. Orp 8D 128
Bakers Pas. NW3 9A 42
(off Heath St.)
Baker's Rents. E2 6D 60
Bakers Rd. Chesh 3B 6
Bakers Rd. Uxb 3B 142
Baker's Row. E15 5C 62
Baker's Row. EC1 7L 59
Baker Street (Junct.) 7D 58
Baker St. NW1 & W1 7D 58
Baker St. Enf 5B 16
Baker St. Wey 6A 116
Baker's Yd. EC1 7L 59
(off Bakers Rd.)
Bakers Yd. Uxb 3B 142
Bakery Clo. SW9 8K 75
Bakery M. Surb 3L 119
Bakery Path. Edgw 6M 23
(off St Margaret's Rd.)
Bakery Pl. SW11 3D 90
Bakewell Way. N Mald 6C 104
Balaam Ho. Sutt 6L 121
Balaams La. N14 2H 27
Balaam St. E13 7E 62
Balaclava Rd. SE1 5D 76
Balaclava Rd. Surb 2G 119
Bala Grn. NW9 4C 40
(off Ruthin Clo.)
Balcaskie Rd. SE9 4K 95
Balchen Rd. SE3 1H 95
Balchier Rd. SE22 5F 92
Balcombe Clo. Bexh 3H 97
Balcombe Ho. NW1 7C 58
(off Taunton Pl.)
Balcombe St. NW1 7D 58
Balcon Ct. W5 9K 55
Balcon Way. Borwd 3A 12
Balcorne St. E9 3G 61
Balder Ri. SE12 8F 94
Balderton Flats. W1 9E 58
(off Balderton St.)
Balderton St. W1 9E 58
Baldewyne Ct. N17 8E 28
Baldock St. E3 5M 61
Baldock Way. Borwd 3K 11
Baldrey Ho. SE10 6D 78
(off Blackwall La.)
Baldry Gdns. SW16 3J 107
Baldwin Cres. SE5 9A 76
Baldwin Gdns. Houn 9A 70
Baldwin Ho. SW2 7L 91
Baldwins Gdns. EC1 8L 59
Baldwins Hill. Lou 4K 19
Baldwin's La. Crox G 6A 8
Baldwin St. EC1 6B 60
Baldwin Ter. N1 5A 60
Baldwyn Gdns. W3 1B 72
Baldwyn's Pk. Bex 8B 98
Baldwyn's Rd. Bex 8B 98
Bale Rd. E1 8J 61
Bales Ter. N9 3D 28
Balfern Gro. W4 6C 72
Balfern St. SW11 1C 90
Balfe St. N1 5J 59
Balfont Clo. S Croy 5E 138
Balfour Av. W7 2D 70
Balfour Bus. Cen. S'hall 4G 69
Balfour Gro. N20 3D 26
Balfour Ho. W10 8H 57
(off St Charles Sq.)
Balfour M. N9 3E 28
Balfour M. W1 2E 74
Balfour Pl. SW15 3F 88
Balfour Pl. W1 1E 74
Balfour Rd. N5 9A 44
Balfour Rd. SE25 9E 108
Balfour Rd. SW19 4M 105
Balfour Rd. W3 8A 56
Balfour Rd. W13 3E 70
Balfour Rd. Brom 9H 111
Balfour Rd. Cars 9D 122
Balfour Rd. Harr 3B 38
Balfour Rd. Houn 2M 85
Balfour Rd. Ilf 7M 47
Balfour Rd. S'hall 4H 69
Balfour St. SE17 5B 76
Balfour Ter. N3 9M 25
Balfron Tower. E14 9A 62
Balgonie Rd. E4 1B 30
Balgores Cres. Romf 1F 50
Balgores La. Romf 1F 50
Balgores Sq. Romf 2F 50
Balgowan Clo. N Mald 9C 104
Balgowan Rd. Beck 7J 109
Balgowan St. SE18 5D 80
Balham. 7F 90
Balham Continental Mkt. SW12 7F 90
(off Shipka Rd.)
Balham Gro. SW12 6E 90
Balham High Rd. SW17 & SW12 9E 90
Balham Hill. SW12 6F 90
Balham New Rd. SW12 6F 90
Balham Pk. Rd. SW12 7D 90
Balham Rd. N9 2E 28
Balham Sta. Rd. SW12 7F 90
Balin Ho. SE1 3B 76
(off Long La.)
Balkan Wlk. E1 1F 76
Balladier Wlk. E14 8M 61
Ballamore Rd. Brom 9E 94
Ballance Rd. E9 2H 61
Ballantine St. SW18 3A 90
Ballantrae Ho. NW2 9K 41
Ballard Clo. King T 4B 104
Ballard Ho. SE10 7M 77
(off Thames St.)
Ballards Clo. Dag 4M 65
Ballards Farm Rd. S Croy & Croy 8E 124
(in two parts)
Ballards La. N3 & N12 8L 25
Ballards M. Edgw 6L 23
Ballards Ri. S Croy 8E 124
Ballards Rd. NW2 7E 40
Ballards Rd. Dag 5M 65
Ballards Way. S Croy & Croy 8E 124
Ballast Quay. SE10 6B 78
Ballater Clo. Wat 4G 21
Ballater Rd. SW2 3J 91
Ballater Rd. S Croy 7D 124
Ball Ct. EC3 9B 60
(off Cornhill)
Ballina St. SE23 6H 93
Ballin Ct. E14 3A 78
(off Stewart St.)
Ballingdon Rd. SW11 5E 90
Ballinger Ct. Wat 5F 8
Balliol Av. E4 4C 30
Balliol Rd. N17 8C 28
Balliol Rd. W10 9G 57
Balliol Rd. Well 1F 96
Balloch Rd. SE6 7B 94
Ballogie Av. NW10 9C 40
Ballow Clo. SE5 8C 76
Ball's Pond Pl. N1 2B 60
Balls Pond Rd. N1 2B 60
Balmain Clo. W5 2H 71
Balmain Ct. Houn 9M 69
Balmain Lodge. Surb 8J 103
(off Cranes Pk. Av.)
Balman Ho. SE16 5H 77
(off Rotherhithe New Rd.)
Balmer Rd. E3 5K 61
Balmes Rd. N1 4B 60
Balmoral Av. N11 6E 26
Balmoral Av. Beck 8J 109
Balmoral Clo. SW15 5H 89
Balmoral Clo. Park 1M 5
Balmoral Ct. SE12 1F 110
Balmoral Ct. SE16 2H 77
(off King & Queen Wharf)
Balmoral Ct. SE27 1A 108
Balmoral Ct. Beck 5A 110
(off Avenue, The)
Balmoral Ct. Sutt 9L 121
Balmoral Ct. Wemb 8K 39
Balmoral Ct. Wor Pk 4F 120
Balmoral Cres. W Mol 7L 101
Balmoral Dri. Borwd 7B 12
Balmoral Dri. Hay 7C 52
Balmoral Dri. S'hall 7K 53
Balmoral Gdns. W13 4E 70
Balmoral Gdns. Bex 6K 97
Balmoral Gdns. Ilf 6D 48
Balmoral Gdns. S Croy 2B 138
Balmoral Gro. N7 2K 59
Balmoral Ho. E14 4M 77
(off Lanark Sq.)
Balmoral Ho. E16 2F 78
(off Keats Av.)
Balmoral Ho. W14 5J 73
(off Windsor Way)
Balmoral M. W12 4D 72
Balmoral Rd. E7 9G 47
Balmoral Rd. E10 7M 45
Balmoral Rd. NW2 2F 56
Balmoral Rd. Ab L 5E 4
Balmoral Rd. Enf 9D 6
Balmoral Rd. Harr 9L 37
Balmoral Rd. Horn 8H 51
Balmoral Rd. King T 8K 103
Balmoral Rd. Romf 3F 50
Balmoral Rd. S at H 4M 115
Balmoral Rd. Wat 2G 9
Balmoral Rd. Wor Pk 5F 120
Balmoral Trad. Est. Bark 8D 64
Balmoral Way. Sutt 2L 135
Balmore Cres. Barn 7E 14
Balmore St. N19 7F 42
Balmuir Gdns. SW15 3G 89
Balnacraig Av. NW10 9C 40
Balniel Ga. SW1 6H 75
Balquhain Clo. Asht 9H 133
Balsam Ho. E14 1M 77
(off E. India Dock Rd.)
Baltic Cen., The. Bren 6H 71
Baltic Clo. SW19 4B 106
Baltic Ct. SE16 3H 77
Baltic Ho. SE5 1A 92
Baltic Pl. N1 4C 60
Baltic St. E. EC1 7A 60
Baltic St. W. EC1 7A 60
Baltimore Ho. SE11 6L 75
(off Hotspur St.)
Baltimore Pl. Well 1D 96
Balvaird Pl. SW1 6H 75
Balvernie Gro. SW18 6K 89
Balvernie M. SW18 6L 89
Bamber Ho. Bark 4B 64
Bamborough Gdns. W12 3G 73
Bamburgh. N17 7F 28
Bamford Av. Wemb 4K 55
Bamford Ct. E15 1M 61
Bamford Rd. Bark 2A 64
Bamford Rd. Brom 2A 110
Bamford Way. Romf 5M 33
Bampfylde Clo. Wall 5G 123
Bampton Ct. W5 9H 55
Bampton Dri. NW7 7E 24
Bampton Rd. SE23 9H 93
Bampton Rd. Romf 7J 35
Banavie Gdns. Beck 5A 110
Banbury Clo. Enf 3M 15
Banbury Ct. WC2 1J 75
(off Long Acre)
Banbury Ct. Sutt 9L 121
Banbury Ho. E9 3H 61
Banbury Rd. E9 3H 61
Banbury Rd. E17 7H 29
Banbury St. SW11 1C 90
Banbury St. Wat 7E 8
Banbury Wlk. N'holt 5L 53
(off Brabazon Rd.)
Banchory Rd. SE3 8F 78
Bancroft Av. N2 3C 42
Bancroft Av. Buck H 2E 30
Bancroft Ct. SW8 8J 75
(off Allen Edwards Dri.)
Bancroft Ct. N'holt 4G 53
Bancroft Gdns. Harr 8A 22
Bancroft Gdns. Orp 3D 128
Bancroft Ho. E1 7G 61
(off Cephas St.)
Bancroft Rd. E1 6G 61
Bancroft Rd. Harr 9A 22
Bandon Clo. Uxb 5D 142
Bandonhill. 7H 123
Bandon Ri. Wall 7H 123
Banfield Rd. SE15 2F 92
Bangalore St. SW15 2G 89
Bangor Clo. N'holt 1M 53
Banim St. W6 5F 72
Banister Ho. E9 1H 61
Banister Ho. SW8 9G 75
(off Wadhurst Rd.)
Banister Ho. W10 6J 57
(off Bruckner St.)
Banister Rd. W10 6H 57
Bank Av. Mitc 6B 106
Bank Bldgs. E4 6B 30
(off Avenue, The)
Bank Ct. Dart 5J 99
Bank End. SE1 2A 76
Bankfoot Rd. Brom 1C 110
Bankhurst Rd. SE6 6K 93
Bank La. SW15 4C 88
Bank La. King T 4J 103
Bank M. Sutt 8A 122
Bank of England. 9B 60
Bank of England Mus. 9B 60
(off Bartholomew La.)
Bank of England Offices. EC4 9A 60
(off New Change)
Banks Ho. SE1 4A 76
(off Rockingham St.)
Banksian Wlk. Iswth 9C 70
Banksia Rd. N18 5H 29
Bankside. SE1 1A 76
(in two parts)
Bankside. Enf 3M 15
Bankside. S'hall 2H 69
Bankside. S Croy 8D 124
Bankside Art Gallery. 1M 75
Bankside Av. N'holt 5E 52
Bankside Clo. Bex 1B 114
Bankside Clo. Cars 8C 122
Bankside Clo. Iswth 3D 86
Bankside Dri. Th Dit 3F 118
Bankside Rd. Ilf 1A 64
Bankside Way. SE19 3C 108
Banks La. Bexh 3K 97
Banks Rd. Borwd 4A 12
Banks Way. E12 8L 47
Bank, The. N6 6F 42
Bankton Rd. SW2 3L 91
Bankwell Rd. SE13 3C 94
Bannerman Ho. SW8 7K 75
Banner St. EC1 7A 60
Banning St. SE10 6C 78
Bannister Clo. SW2 7L 91
Bannister Clo. Gnfd 1B 54
Bannister Gdns. Orp 7G 113
Bannister Ho. SE14 7H 77
(off John Williams Clo.)
Bannockburn Rd. SE18 5C 80
Banqueting House. 2J 75
Banstead. 7L 135
Banstead Gdns. N9 3C 28
Banstead Rd. Cars 1B 136
Banstead Rd. Eps & Bans 2F 134
Banstead Rd. Purl 3L 137
Banstead Rd. S. Sutt 3A 136
Banstead St. SE15 2G 93
Banstead Way. Wall 7J 123
Banstock Rd. Edgw 6M 23
Banting Dri. N21 7K 15
Banting Ho. NW2 8E 40
Bantock Ho. W10 6J 57
(off Third Av.)
Banton Clo. Enf 4F 16
Bantry Ho. E1 7H 61
(off Ernest St.)
Bantry St. SE5 8B 76
Banwell Rd. Bex 5H 97
Banyard Rd. SE16 4F 76
Banyards. Horn 2J 51
Bapchild Pl. Orp 8G 113
Baptist Gdns. NW5 2E 58
Barandon Rd. W11 1H 73
Barandon Wlk. W11 1H 73
Barbanel Ho. E1 7G 61
(off Cephas St.)
Barbara Brosnan Ct. NW8 5B 58
Barbara Clo. Shep 9A 100
Barbara Hucklesby Clo. N22 9M 27
Barbauld Rd. N16 8C 44
Barbel Clo. Wal X 7G 7
Barber Beaumont Ho. E1 6H 61
(off Bancroft Rd.)
Barber Clo. N21 9L 15
Barberry Clo. Romf 7G 35
Barbers All. E13 6F 62
Barbers Rd. E15 5M 61
Barbican Arts Cen. 8A 60
Barbican Cinema. 8A 60
(in Barbican)
Barbican Rd. Gnfd 9M 53
Barbican Theatre. 8A 60
(in Barbican)
Barb M. W6 4G 73
Barbon Clo. WC1 8K 59
Barbot Clo. N9 3E 28
Barchard St. SW18 4M 89
Barchester Clo. W7 2D 70
Barchester Clo. Uxb 7A 142
Barchester Rd. Harr 9B 22
Barchester St. E14 8M 61
Barclay Clo. SW6 8L 73
Barclay Clo. Wat 8E 8
Barclay Ho. E9 3G 61
(off Well St.)
Barclay Oval. Wfd G 4E 30
Barclay Path. E17 3A 46
Barclay Rd. E11 6D 46
(in two parts)
Barclay Rd. E13 7G 63
Barclay Rd. E17 3A 46
Barclay Rd. N18 6B 28
Barclay Rd. SW6 8L 73
Barclay Rd. Croy 5B 124
Barcombe Av. SW2 8J 91
Barcombe Clo. Orp 7D 112
Bardell Ho. SE1 3E 76
(off Dickens Est.)
Barden St. SE18 8C 80
Bardfield Av. Romf 1H 49
Bardney Rd. Mord 8M 105
Bardolph Av. Croy 1J 139
Bardolph Rd. N7 9J 43
Bardolph Rd. Rich 2K 87
Bard Rd. W10 1H 73
Bardsey Pl. E1 7G 61
(off Mile End Rd.)
Bardsey Wlk. N1 2A 60
(off Douglas Rd. N.)
Bardsley Clo. Croy 5D 124
Bardsley Ho. SE10 7A 78
(off Bardsley La.)
Bardsley La. SE10 7A 78
Barents Ho. E1 7H 61
(off White Horse La.)
Barfett St. W10 7K 57
Barfield. S at H 4M 115
Barfield Av. N20 2D 26
Barfield Rd. E11 6D 46
Barfield Rd. Brom 7L 111
Barfields. Lou 6L 19
Barfields Gdns. Lou 6L 19
Barfields Path. Lou 6L 19
Barfleur Ho. SE8 6K 77
Barford Clo. NW4 9E 24
Barford St. N1 4L 59
Barforth Rd. SE15 2F 92
Barfreston Way. SE20 5F 108
Bargate Clo. SE18 6D 80
Bargate Clo. N Mald 2E 120
Barge Ho. Rd. E16 3M 79
Barge Ho. St. SE1 2L 75
Bargery Rd. SE6 7M 93
Barge Wlk. E Mol 7B 102
Barge Wlk. Hamp W 5H 103
Barge Wlk. King T 7H 103
Bargrove Clo. SE20 4E 108
Bargrove Cres. SE6 8K 93
Barham Av. Els 5K 11
Barham Clo. Brom 3J 127
Barham Clo. Chst 2M 111
Barham Clo. Romf 9M 33
Barham Clo. Wemb 2F 54
Barham Clo. Wey 6A 116
Barham Ct. S Croy 6A 124
(off Barham Rd.)
Barham Ho. SE17 6C 76
(off Kinglake St.)
Barham Rd. SW20 4E 104
Barham Rd. Chst 2M 111
Barham Rd. Dart 6L 99
Barham Rd. S Croy 6A 124
Baring Clo. SE12 8E 94
Baring Ho. E14 9L 61
(off Canton St.)
Baring Rd. SE12 6E 94
Baring Rd. Cockf 6B 14
Baring Rd. Croy 3E 124
Baring St. N1 4B 60
Barker Clo. N Mald 8M 103
Barker Clo. N'wd 7D 20
Barker Dri. NW1 3G 59
Barker M. SW4 3F 90
Barkers Arc. W8 3M 73
Barker St. SW10 7A 74
Barker Wlk. SW16 9H 91
Barkham Rd. N17 7B 28
Barkham Ter. SE1 4L 75
(off Lambeth Rd.)
Bark Hart Rd. Orp 3F 128
Barking. 3A 64
Barking Bus. Cen. Bark 6E 64
Barking Ind. Pk. Bark 4D 64
Barking Northern Relief Rd. Bark 3M 63
Barking Railway (Miniature Railway) 2A 64
Barking Rd. E13 & E6 5G 63
Barking Rd. E16 & E13 8D 62
Barkingside. 1A 48
Bark Pl. W2 1M 73
Barkston Gdns. SW5 5M 73
Barkston Path. Borwd 2L 11
Barkway Ct. N4 7A 44

Barkwith Ho.—Bath Pl.

Barkwith Ho. SE14 . . . . .7H 77
(off Cold Blow La.)
Barkwood Clo. Romf 3A 50
Barkworth Rd. SE16 . . . . .6F 76
Barlborough St. SE14 . . . . . .8H 77
Barlby Gdns. W10 . . . . .7H 57
Barlby Rd. W10 . . . . .8G 57
Barlee Cres. Uxb 8A 142
Barley Brow. Wat 4F 4
Barley Clo. Bush 7M 9
Barleycorn Way. E14 . . . . . . .1K 77
Barleycorn Way. Horn 4K 51
Barleyfields Clo. Romf 4F 48
Barley La. Ilf & Romf 5E 48
Barley Mow Pas. EC1 . . . . . .8M 59
(off Long La.)
Barley Mow Pas. W4 . . . . . . .6B 72
Barley Shotts Bus. Pk.
W10 . . . . .8K 57
Barling. NW1 . . . . .2F 58
(off Castlehaven Rd.)
Barlings Ho. SE4 . . . . .3H 93
(off Frendsbury Rd.)
Barlow Clo. Wall 8J 123
Barlow Dri. SE18 . . . . .9J 79
Barlow Ho. N1 . . . . .6B 60
(off Provost Est.)
Barlow Ho. SE16 . . . . .5F 76
(off Rennie Est.)
Barlow Ho. W11 . . . . .1J 73
(off Walmer Rd.)
Barlow Pl. W1 . . . . .1F 74
Barlow Rd. NW6 . . . . .2K 57
Barlow Rd. W3 . . . . .2M 71
Barlow Rd. Hamp 4L 101
Barlow St. SE17 . . . . .5B 76
Barlow Way. Rain 8B 66
Barmeston Rd. SE6 . . . . .8M 93
Barmor Clo. Harr 9M 21
Barmouth Av. Gnfd 5D 54
Barmouth Rd. SW18 . . . . . . .5A 90
Barmouth Rd. Croy 4H 125
Barnabas Ct. N21 . . . . .6L 15
Barnabas Rd. E9 . . . . .1H 61
Barnaby Clo. Harr 7A 38
Barnaby Ct. NW9 . . . . .1C 40
Barnaby Ct. SE16 . . . . .3E 76
(off Scott Lidgett Cres.)
Barnaby Pl. SW7 . . . . .5B 74
(off Brompton Rd.)
Barnaby Way. Chig 3M 31
Barnacre Clo. Uxb 9B 142
Barnard Clo. SE18 . . . . .5L 79
Barnard Clo. Chst 5B 112
Barnard Clo. Sun 4F 100
Barnard Clo. Wall 9H 123
Barnard Ct. Dart 5M 99
(off Clifton Wlk.)
Barnard Gdns. Hay 7F 52
Barnard Gdns. N Mald 8E 104
Barnard Gro. E15 . . . . .3D 62
Barnard Hill. N10 . . . . .8F 26
Barnard Ho. E2 . . . . .6F 60
(off Ellsworth St.)
Barnard Lodge. W9 . . . . .8L 57
(off Admiral Wlk.)
Barnard Lodge. New Bar 6A 14
Barnard M. SW11 . . . . .3C 90
Barnardo Dri. Ilf 2A 48
Barnardo Gdns. E1 . . . . .1H 77
Barnardo St. E1 . . . . .9H 61
Barnardos Village. B'side 1A 48
Barnard Rd. SW11 . . . . .3C 90
Barnard Rd. Enf 4F 16
Barnard Rd. Mitc 7E 106
Barnards Ho. SE16 . . . . .3K 77
(off Wyatt Clo.)
Barnard's Inn. EC1 . . . . .9L 59
(off Fetter La., in two parts)
Barnards Pl. S Croy 1M 137
Barnbrough. NW1 . . . . .4G 59
(off Camden St.)
Barnby Sq. E15 . . . . .4C 62
Barnby St. E15 . . . . .4C 62
Barnby St. NW1 . . . . .5G 59
Barn Clo. NW5 . . . . .1H 59
(off Torriano Av.)
Barn Clo. Bans 7B 136
Barn Clo. Eps 7A 134
Barn Clo. N'holt 5G 53
Barn Cres. Purl 5B 138
Barn Cres. Stan 6G 23
Barncroft Clo. Lou 7L 19
Barncroft Clo. Uxb 8F 142
Barncroft Grn. Lou 7L 19
Barncroft Rd. Lou 7L 19
Barneby Clo. Twic 7C 86
Barnehurst. 2A 98
Barnehurst Av. Eri & Bexh . . .9A 82
Barnehurst Clo. Eri 9A 82
Barnehurst Rd. Bexh 1A 98
Barn Elms Pk. SW15 . . . . .2G 89
Barn End Dri. Dart 1G 115
Barn End La. Dart 2G 115
Barnes. 1D 88
Barnes All. Hamp 6A 102
Barnes Av. SW13 . . . . .8E 72
Barnes Av. S'hall 5K 69
Barnes Clo. E12 . . . . .9H 47
Barnes Ct. E16 . . . . .8G 63
Barnes Ct. N1 . . . . .3L 59
Barnes Ct. Wfd G 5H 31
Barnes Cray. 3E 98
Barnes Cray Rd. Dart 3E 98
Barnesdale Cres. Orp 1E 128
Barnes End. N Mald 9E 104
Barnes High St. SW13 . . . . . .1D 88
Barnes Ho. SE14 . . . . .7H 77
(off John Williams Clo.)
Barnes Ho. Bark 4B 64
Barnes Pikle. W5 . . . . .1H 71
Barnes Rd. N18 . . . . .4G 29
Barnes St. E14 . . . . .9J 61
Barnes Ter. SE8 . . . . .6K 77
Barnes Wallis Ct. Wemb 8A 40
Barnet. 5J 13
Barnet Bus. Cen. Barn 5J 13
Barnet By-Pass. NW7 . . . . . .6D 24
Barnet By-Pass Rd.
Borwd & Barn 8B 12
Barnet Dri. Brom 4J 127
Barnet F.C. (Underhill Stadium)
. . . . .7L 13
Barnet Gate. 7D 12
Barnet Ga. La. Barn 8D 12
Barnet Gro. E2 . . . . .6E 60
Barnet Hill. Barn 6K 13
Barnet Ho. N20 . . . . .2A 26
Barnet La. N20 & Barn 1K 25
Barnet La. Els & Borwd 8H 11
Barnet Rd. Ark 8C 12
Barnett Clo. Eri 1D 98
Barnet Trad. Est. High Bar . . .5K 13
Barnetts Ct. Harr 8M 37
Barnett St. E1 . . . . .9F 60
Barnett Wood La.
Lea & Asht 9H 133
Barnet Vale. 7M 13
Barnet Way.
NW7 & Borwd 3B 24
Barnet Wood Rd. Brom 4G 127
Barney Clo. SE7 . . . . .6G 79
Barn Fld. NW3 . . . . .1D 58
Barnfield. Bans 6M 135
Barnfield. N Mald 1C 120
Barnfield Av. Croy 4G 125
Barnfield Av. King T 1H 103
Barnfield Av. Mitc 8F 106
Barnfield Clo. N4 . . . . .5J 43
Barnfield Clo. SW17 . . . . .9B 90
Barnfield Clo. Swan 2A 130
Barnfield Gdns. SE18 . . . . . . .7M 79
Barnfield Gdns. King T 1J 103
Barnfield Pl. E14 . . . . .5L 77
Barnfield Rd. SE18 . . . . .7M 79
(in two parts)
Barnfield Rd. W5 . . . . .7G 55
Barnfield Rd. Belv 7K 81
Barnfield Rd. Edgw 8A 24
Barnfield Rd. Orp 7H 113
Barnfield Rd. S Croy 1C 138
Barnfield Wood Clo.
Beck 1B 126
Barnfield Wood Rd. Beck . . .1B 126
Barnham Dri. SE28 . . . . .2D 80
Barnham Rd. Gnfd 6A 54
Barnham St. SE1 . . . . .3C 76
Barnhill. Pinn 3G 37
Barn Hill. Wemb 6L 39
Barnhill Av. Brom 9D 110
Barnhill La. Hay 6F 52
Barnhill Rd. Hay 6F 52
Barnhill Rd. Wemb 8A 40
Barnhurst Path. Wat 5G 21
Barningham Way. NW9 . . . . .4B 40
Barnlea Clo. Felt 8J 85
Barnmead Gdns. Dag 1K 65
Barnmead Rd. Beck 5H 109
Barnmead Rd. Dag 1K 65
Barn M. S Harr 8L 37
Barnock Clo. Dart 5C 98
Barn Ri. Wemb 6L 39
Barnsbury. 3K 59
Barnsbury Clo. N Mald 8A 104
Barnsbury Cres. Surb 3A 120
Barnsbury Est. N1 . . . . .4K 59
(in two parts)
Barnsbury Gro. N7 . . . . .3K 59
Barnsbury Ho. SW4 . . . . .5H 91
Barnsbury La. Surb 4M 119
Barnsbury Pk. N1 . . . . .3L 59
Barnsbury Rd. N1 . . . . .5L 59
Barnsbury Sq. N1 . . . . .3L 59
Barnsbury St. N1 . . . . .3L 59
Barnsbury Ter. N1 . . . . .3K 59
Barnscroft. SW20 . . . . .7F 104
Barnsdale Av. E14 . . . . .5M 77
Barnsdale Clo. Borwd 3K 11
Barnsdale Rd. W9 . . . . .7K 57
Barnsfield Pl. Uxb 3A 142
Barnsley Rd. Romf 7K 35
Barnsley St. E1 . . . . .7F 60
Barnstable La. SE13 . . . . .3A 94
Barnstaple Ho. SE10 . . . . . . .8M 77
(off Devonshire Dri.)
Barnstaple Ho. SE12 . . . . . . .4D 94
(off Taunton Rd.)
Barnstaple Path. Romf 5G 35
Barnstaple Rd. Romf 5G 35
Barnstaple Rd. Ruis 8G 37
Barnston Wlk. N1 . . . . .4A 60
(off Popham St.)
Barn St. N16 . . . . .7C 44
Barn Way. Wemb 6L 39
Barnwell Ho. SE5 . . . . .9C 76
(off St Giles Rd.)
Barnwell Rd. SW2 . . . . .4L 91
Barnwell Rd. Dart 2K 99
Barnwood Clo. N20 . . . . .1K 25
Barnwood Clo. W9 . . . . .7M 57
Barnwood Clo. Ruis 7B 36
Baron Clo. N11 . . . . .5E 26
Baron Clo. Sutt 2M 135
Baroness Rd. E2 . . . . .6D 60
Baronet Gro. N17 . . . . .8E 28
Baronet Rd. N17 . . . . .8E 28
Baron Gdns. Ilf 1A 48
Baron Gro. Mitc 8C 106
Baron Rd. Dag 6H 49
Baronsclere Ct. N6 . . . . .5G 43
Barons Court. 6J 73
Barons Ct. Ilf 7B 48
Barons Ct. Wall 5H 123
Baron's Ct. Rd. W14 . . . . .6J 73
Barons Court Theatre. 6J 73
(off Comeragh Rd.)
Baronsfield Rd. Twic 5F 86
Barons Ga. W4 . . . . .4A 72
Barons Ga. Barn 8C 14
Baron's Hurst. Eps 8A 134
Barons Keep. W14 . . . . .6J 73
Barons Mead. Harr 2C 38
Baronsmead Rd. SW13 . . . . .9E 72
Baronsmede. W5 . . . . .3K 71
Baronsmere Ct. Barn 6J 13
Baronsmere Rd. N2 . . . . .2C 42
Baron's Pl. SE1 . . . . .3L 75
Barons, The. Twic 5F 86
Baron St. N1 . . . . .5L 59
Baron's Wlk. Croy 1J 125
Baron Wlk. E16 . . . . .8D 62
Baron Wlk. Mitc 8C 106
Barque M. SE8 . . . . .7L 77
Barrack Rd. Houn 3H 85
Barra Hall Cir. Hay 1C 68
Barra Hall Rd. Hay 1C 68
Barras Clo. Enf 1L 17
Barratt Av. N22 . . . . .9K 27
Barratt Ho. N1 . . . . .3M 59
(off Sable St.)
Barratt Ind. Pk. E3 . . . . .7A 62
Barratt Ind. Pk. S'hall 3L 69
Barratt Way. Harr 9B 22
Barrenger Rd. N10 . . . . .8D 26
Barret Ho. NW6 . . . . .4L 57
Barret Ho. SW9 . . . . .2K 91
(off Benedict Rd.)
Barrett Clo. Romf 7F 34
Barrett Ho. SE17 . . . . .6A 76
(off Browning St.)
Barrett Rd. E17 . . . . .2A 46
Barrett's Grn. Rd. NW10 . . . .6A 56
Barrett's Gro. N16 . . . . .1C 60
Barrett St. W1 . . . . .9E 58
Barrhill Rd. SW2 . . . . .8J 91
Barrie Clo. Coul 8G 137
Barrie Ct. New Bar 7A 14
(off Lyonsdown Rd.)
Barriedale. SE14 . . . . .1J 93
Barrie Est. W2 . . . . .1B 74
Barrie Ho. W2 . . . . .1A 74
(off Lancaster Ga.)
Barrier App. SE7 . . . . .4H 79
Barrier Point Rd. E16 . . . . . . .2G 79
Barringers Ct. Ruis 5B 36
Barringer Sq. SW17 . . . . . . .1E 106
Barrington Clo. NW5 . . . . . . .1E 58
Barrington Clo. Ilf 8K 31
Barrington Clo. Lou 5M 19
Barrington Ct. NW5 . . . . .1E 58
Barrington Ct. SW4 . . . . .1J 91
Barrington Ct. W3 . . . . .3M 71
(off Cheltenham Pl.)
Barrington Grn. Lou 5M 19
Barrington Lodge. Wey 7A 116
Barrington Rd. E12 . . . . .2L 63
Barrington Rd. N8 . . . . .3H 43
Barrington Rd. SW9 . . . . .2M 91
Barrington Rd. Bexh 1H 97
Barrington Rd. Lou 6M 19
Barrington Rd. Purl 4G 137
Barrington Rd. Sutt 4L 121
Barrington Vs. SE18 . . . . .9L 79
Barrington Wlk. SE19 . . . . . .3C 108
Barrosa Dri. Hamp 5L 101
Barrow Av. Cars 9D 122
Barrow Clo. N21 . . . . .3M 27
Barrow Ct. SE6 . . . . .7D 94
(off Cumberland Pl.)
Barrowdene Clo. Pinn 9J 21
Barrowell Grn. N21 . . . . .2M 27
Barrowfield Clo. N9 . . . . .3F 28
Barrowgate Rd. W4 . . . . .6A 72
Barrow Hedges Clo.
Cars 9C 122
Barrow Hedges Way.
Cars 9C 122
Barrowhill. Wor Pk 4C 120
Barrowhill Clo. Wor Pk 4C 120
Barrow Hill Est. NW8 . . . . . . .5C 58
(off Barrow Hill Rd.)
Barrow Hill Rd. NW8 . . . . . . .5C 58
Barrow La. Chesh 3A 6
Barrow Point Av. Pinn 9J 21
Barrow Point La. Pinn 9J 21
Barrow Rd. SW16 . . . . .3H 107
Barrow Rd. Croy 7L 123
Barrowsfield. S Croy 4D 138
Barrow Wlk. Bren 7G 71
Barrs Rd. NW10 . . . . .3B 56
Barry Av. N15 . . . . .4D 44
Barry Av. Bexh 8J 81
Barry Clo. Orp 5C 128
Barry Ct. Romf 5B 34
Barry Ct. Wat 7G 9
(off Cardiff Rd.)
Barrydene. N20 . . . . .1B 26
Barry Ho. SE16 . . . . .5F 76
(off Rennie Est.)
Barry Rd. E6 . . . . .9J 63
Barry Rd. NW10 . . . . .3A 56
Barry Rd. SE22 . . . . .5E 92
Barset Rd. SE15 . . . . .2G 93
(in three parts)
Barson Clo. SE20 . . . . .4G 109
Barston Rd. SE27 . . . . .9A 92
Barstow Cres. SW2 . . . . .7K 91
Barter St. WC1 . . . . .8J 59
Barters Wlk. Pinn 1J 37
Bartholomew Clo. EC1 . . . . . .8A 60
(in two parts)
Bartholomew Clo. SW18 . . . .3A 90
Bartholomew Ct. E14 . . . . . . .1B 78
(off Newport Av.)
Bartholomew Ct. EC1 . . . . . . .7A 60
(off Old St.)
Bartholomew Ct. Edgw 7H 23
Bartholomew Ct. Enf 1J 17
Bartholomew Dri.
H Wood 9H 35
Bartholomew La. EC2 . . . . . .9B 60
Bartholomew Pl. EC1 . . . . . . .8A 60
(off Kinghorn St.)
Bartholomew Rd. NW5 . . . . .2G 59
Bartholomew Sq. E1 . . . . .7F 60
Bartholomew Sq. EC1 . . . . . . .7A 60
Bartholomew St. SE1 . . . . . . .4B 76
Bartholomew Vs. NW5 . . . . .2G 59
Bartholomew Way. Swan . . .7C 114
Barth Rd. SE18 . . . . .5C 80
Bartle Av. E6 . . . . .5J 63
Bartle Rd. W11 . . . . .9J 57
Bartlett Clo. E14 . . . . .9L 61
Bartlett Ct. EC4 . . . . .9L 59
Bartlett Houses. Dag 3M 65
(off Vicarage Rd.)
Bartletts Pas. EC4 . . . . .9L 59
(off Fetter La.)
Bartlett St. S Croy 7B 124
Bartlow Gdns. Romf 8B 34
Barton Av. Romf 6M 49
Barton Clo. E6 . . . . .9K 63
Barton Clo. E9 . . . . .1G 61
Barton Clo. NW4 . . . . .3E 40
Barton Clo. SE15 . . . . .2F 92
Barton Clo. Bexh 4J 97
Barton Clo. Chig 2A 32
Barton Clo. Shep 1A 116
Barton Ct. W14 . . . . .6J 73
(off Baron's Ct. Rd.)
Barton Friars. Chig 2A 32
Barton Grn. N Mald 6B 104
Barton Ho. N1 . . . . .3M 59
(off Sable St.)
Barton Ho. SW6 . . . . .2M 89
(off Wandsworth Bri. Rd.)
Barton Meadows. Ilf 2M 47
Barton Rd. W14 . . . . .6J 73
Barton Rd. Horn 6E 50
Barton Rd. Sidc 3J 113
Barton Rd. S at H 5M 115
Bartons, The. Els 8H 11
Barton St. SW1 . . . . .4J 75
Bartonway. NW8 . . . . .4B 58
(off Queen's Ter.)
Barton Way. Borwd 4L 11
Bartram Clo. Uxb 7F 142
Bartram Rd. SE4 . . . . .4J 93
Bartrams La. Barn 2A 14
Bartrip St. E9 . . . . .2K 61
Barts Clo. Beck 9L 109
Barville Clo. SE4 . . . . .3J 93
Barwell Bus Pk. Chess 9H 119
Barwell Ho. E2 . . . . .7E 60
(off Menotti St.)
Barwick Dri. Uxb 8F 142
Barwick Ho. W3 . . . . .3A 72
(off Strafford Rd.)
Barwick Rd. E7 . . . . .9F 46
Barwood Av. W Wick 3M 125
Bascombe Gro. Dart 5C 98
Basden Gro. Felt 8L 85
Basden Ho. Felt 8L 85
Basedale Rd. Dag 3F 64
Baseing Clo. E6 . . . . .1L 79
Basevi Way. SE8 . . . . .7L 77
Bashley Rd. NW10 . . . . .7B 56
Basil Av. E6 . . . . .6J 63
Basildene Rd. Houn 2H 85
Basildon Av. Ilf 8L 31
Basildon Clo. Sutt 1M 135
Basildon Clo. Wat 8A 8
Basildon Ct. W1 . . . . .8E 58
(off Devonshire Rd.)
Basildon Rd. SE2 . . . . .6E 80
Basil Gdns. SE27 . . . . .2A 108
Basil Gdns. Croy 3H 125
Basil Ho. SW8 . . . . .8J 75
(off Wyvil Rd.)
Basilon Rd. Bexh 1J 97
Basil Spence Ho. N22 . . . . . . .8K 27
Basil St. SW3 . . . . .4D 74
Basin App. E14 . . . . .9J 61
Basing Clo. Th Dit 2D 118
Basing Ct. SE15 . . . . .9D 76
Basingdon Way. SE5 . . . . . . .3B 92
Basing Dri. Bex 5K 97
Basingfield Rd. Th Dit 2D 118
Basinghall Av. EC2 . . . . .9B 60
Basinghall Gdns. Sutt 1M 135
Basinghall St. EC2 . . . . .9B 60
Basing Hill. NW11 . . . . .6K 41
Basing Hill. Wemb 7K 39
Basing Ho. Bark 4B 64
(off St Margarets)
Basing Ho. Yd. E2 . . . . .6C 60
Basing Pl. E2 . . . . .6C 60
Basing Rd. Bans 6K 135
Basing St. W11 . . . . .9K 57
Basing Way. N3 . . . . .1L 41
Basing Way. Th Dit 2D 118
Basire St. N1 . . . . .4A 60
Baskerville Gdns. NW10 . . . .9C 40
Baskerville Rd. SW18 . . . . . .6C 90
Basket Gdns. SE9 . . . . .4J 95
Baslow Clo. Harr 8B 22
Baslow Wlk. E5 . . . . .9H 45
Basnett Rd. SW11 . . . . .2E 90
Basque Ct. SE16 . . . . .3H 77
(off Garter Way)
Bassano St. SE22 . . . . .4D 92
Bassant Rd. SE18 . . . . .7D 80
Bassein Pk. Rd. W12 . . . . . . .3D 72
Bassett Clo. Sutt 1M 135
Bassett Gdns. Iswth 8A 70
Bassett Rd. E7 . . . . .9H 47
Bassett Rd. W10 . . . . .9H 57
Bassett Rd. Uxb 3A 142
Bassett's Clo. Orp 6M 127
Bassett St. NW5 . . . . .2E 58
Bassett's Way. Orp 6M 127
Bassett Way. Gnfd 9M 53
Bassingbourn Ho. N1 . . . . . . .3L 59
(off Sutton Est., The)
Bassingham Rd. SW18 . . . . . .6A 90
Bassingham Rd. Wemb 3H 55
Bassishaw Highwalk. EC2 . . .8B 60
(off London Wall)
Basswood Clo. SE15 . . . . .2F 92
Bastable Av. Bark 5C 64
Basterfield Ho. EC1 . . . . .7A 60
(off Golden La. Est.)
Bastion Highwalk. EC2 . . . . . .8A 60
(off London Wall)
Bastion Ho. EC2 . . . . .8A 60
(off London Wall)
Bastion Rd. SE2 . . . . .6E 80
Baston Mnr. Rd. Brom 5F 126
Baston Rd. Brom 3F 126
Bastwick St. EC1 . . . . .7A 60
Basuto Rd. SW6 . . . . .9L 73
Batavia Clo. Sun 5F 100
Batavia Ho. SE14 . . . . .8J 77
(off Batavia Rd.)
Batavia M. SE14 . . . . .8J 77
Batavia Rd. SE14 . . . . .8J 77
Batavia Rd. Sun 5F 100
Batchelor St. N1 . . . . .4L 59
Batchwood Grn. Orp 7E 112
Batchworth La. N'wd 5A 20
Bateman Clo. Bark 2A 64
Bateman Ho. SE17 . . . . .7M 75
(off Otto St.)
Bateman Rd. E4 . . . . .6L 29
Bateman's Bldgs. W1 . . . . . . .9H 59
(off Bateman St.)
Bateman's Row. EC2 . . . . . . .7C 60
Bateman St. W1 . . . . .9H 59
Bates Bus. Cen. H Wood 7L 35
Bates Cres. SW16 . . . . .4G 107
Bates Cres. Croy 7L 123
Bates Ind. Est. H Wood 7L 35
Bateson St. SE18 . . . . .5C 80
Bates Point. E13 . . . . .4E 62
(off Pelly Rd.)
Bates Rd. Romf 7L 35
Bate St. E14 . . . . .1K 77
Bath Clo. SE15 . . . . .8F 76
Bath Ct. EC1 . . . . .7L 59
(off St Lukes Est.)
Bath Ct. SE26 . . . . .9E 92
(off Droitwich Clo.)
Bathgate Rd. SW19 . . . . .9H 89
Bath Gro. E2 . . . . .5E 60
(off Horatio St.)
Bath Ho. E2 . . . . .7E 60
(off Ramsey St.)
Bath Ho. SE1 . . . . .4A 76
(off Bath Ter.)
Bath Ho. Rd. Croy 3J 123
Bath Pas. King T 6H 103
Bath Pl. EC2 . . . . .6C 60
Bath Pl. W6 . . . . .6G 73
(off Fulham Pal. Rd.)
Bath Pl. Barn 5K 13

Beddington Farm Rd.—Belmont Av.

Beddington Farm Rd.
Croy 2J 123
Beddington Gdns.
Cars & Wall 8E 122
(in two parts)
Beddington Grn. Orp 5D 112
Beddington Gro. Wall 7H 123
Beddington La. Croy 9G 107
Beddington Pk. Cotts.
Wall 5H 123
Beddington Path. Orp 5D 112
Beddington Rd. Ilf 5D 48
Beddington Rd. Orp 5C 112
Beddington Ter. Croy 2K 123
Beddington Trad. Est.
Croy 3J 123
Beddlestead La. Warl 9D 140
Bede Clo. Pinn 8H 21
Bedefield. WC1 6J 59
Bede Ho. SE4 9K 77
(off Clare Rd.)
Bedens Rd. Sidc 3J 113
Bede Rd. Romf 4G 49
Bedfont Clo. Felt 5A 84
Bedfont Clo. Mitc 6E 106
Bedfont Ct. Stai 2A 144
Bedfont Grn. Clo. Felt 7A 84
Bedfont Ind. Pk. Ashf 9A 84
Bedfont Lakes Country Pk.
8A 84
Bedfont La. Felt 6D 84
Bedfont Pk. Ind. Est. Ashf 9A 84
Bedfont Rd. Felt 7A 84
Bedfont Rd. Stanw 5C 144
Bedford Av. WC1 8H 59
Bedford Av. Barn 7K 13
Bedford Av. Hay 9F 52
Bedfordbury. WC2 1J 75
Bedford Clo. N10 7E 26
Bedford Clo. W4 7C 72
Bedford Corner. W4 5C 72
(off South Pde.)
Bedford Ct. WC2 1J 75
(in two parts)
Bedford Ct. Croy 3A 124
(off Tavistock Rd.)
Bedford Ct. Mans. WC1 8H 59
(off Bedford Av.)
Bedford Cres. Enf 8E 6
Bedford Gdns. W8 2L 73
Bedford Gdns. Horn 7G 51
Bedford Hill.
SW12 & SW16 7F 90
Bedford Ho. SW4 3J 91
(off Solon New Rd. Est.)
Bedford M. N2 1C 42
Bedford Park. 4B 72
Bedford Pk. Croy 3A 124
Bedford Pk. Corner. W4 5C 72
Bedford Pk. Mans. W4 5B 72
Bedford Pas. SW6 8J 73
(off Dawes Rd.)
Bedford Pas. W1 8G 59
Bedford Pl. WC1 8J 59
Bedford Pl. Croy 3B 124
Bedford Rd. E6 4L 63
Bedford Rd. E17 9L 29
Bedford Rd. E18 9E 30
Bedford Rd. N2 1C 42
Bedford Rd. N8 4H 43
Bedford Rd. N9 9F 16
Bedford Rd. N15 2C 44
Bedford Rd. N22 8J 27
Bedford Rd. NW7 2C 24
Bedford Rd. SW4 3J 91
Bedford Rd. W4 4B 72
Bedford Rd. W13 1F 70
Bedford Rd. Dart 6L 99
Bedford Rd. Harr 4A 38
Bedford Rd. Ilf 8M 47
Bedford Rd. N'wd 3A 20
Bedford Rd. Orp 4F 128
Bedford Rd. Ruis 9D 36
Bedford Rd. Sidc 9C 96
Bedford Rd. Twic 9B 86
Bedford Rd. Wor Pk 4G 121
Bedford Row. WC1 8K 59
Bedford Sq. WC1 8H 59
Bedford St. WC2 1J 75
Bedford St. Wat 3F 8
Bedford Ter. SW4 4J 91
Bedford Way. WC1 7H 59
Bedgebury Gdns. SW19 8J 89
Bedgebury Rd. SE9 3H 95
Bedivere Rd. Brom 9E 94
Bedlam M. SE11 5L 75
(off Walnut Tree Wlk.)
Bedlow Way. Croy 6K 123
Bedmond. 1D 4
Bedmond Ho. SW3 6C 74
(off Ixworth Pl.)
Bedmond Rd. Ab L 2D 4
Bedonwell Rd.
SE2 & Belv 7J 81
Bedonwell Rd. Belv 7J 81
Bedonwell Rd. Bexh 9K 81
Bedser Clo. SE11 7K 75
Bedser Clo. T Hth 7A 108
Bedser Dri. Gnfd 1B 54
Bedster Gdns. W Mol 6M 101
Bedwardine Rd. SE19 4C 108
Bedwell Ct. Romf 5H 49
(off Broomfield Rd.)
Bedwell Gdns. Hay 6C 68
(in two parts)
Bedwell Ho. SW9 1L 91
Bedwell Rd. N17 8C 28
Bedwell Rd. Belv 6L 81
Beeby Rd. E16 8F 62
Beech Av. N20 1C 26
Beech Av. W3 2C 72
Beech Av. Bren 8F 70
Beech Av. Buck H 2F 30
Beech Av. Ruis 6F 36
Beech Av. Sidc 6E 96
Beech Av. S Croy 3B 138
Beech Av. Swan 8D 114
Beech Av. Upm 8M 51
Beech Clo. N9 8E 16
Beech Clo. SE8 7L 77
Beech Clo. SW15 6E 88
Beech Clo. SW19 3G 105
Beech Clo. Ashf 2B 100
Beech Clo. Cars 4D 122
Beech Clo. Horn 8F 50
Beech Clo. Lou 5M 19
Beech Clo. Stanw 6B 144
Beech Clo. Sun 6H 101
Beech Clo. W on T 6G 117
Beech Clo. W Dray 4L 143
Beech Copse. Brom 5K 111
Beech Copse. S Croy 7C 124
Beech Ct. W9 8L 57
(off Elmfield Way)
Beech Ct. Beck 4K 109
Beech Ct. Brom 5D 110
(off Blyth Rd.)
Beech Ct. Dart 5L 99
Beech Ct. N'holt 4J 53
Beech Ct. N'wd 7C 20
Beech Ct. Surb 2H 119
Beech Cres. Ct. N5 9M 43
Beechcroft. Chst 4L 111
Beechcroft Av. NW11 5K 41
Beechcroft Av. Bexh 9B 82
Beechcroft Av. Crox G 8A 8
Beechcroft Av. Harr 5L 37
Beechcroft Av. Kenl 7B 138
Beechcroft Av. N Mald 5A 104
Beechcroft Av. S'hall 2K 69
Beechcroft Clo. SW16 2K 107
Beechcroft Clo. Houn 8J 69
Beechcroft Clo. Orp 6B 128
Beechcroft Ct. NW11 5K 41
(off Beechcroft Av.)
Beechcroft Ct. Sutt 9A 122
Beechcroft Gdns. Wemb 8K 39
Beechcroft Ho. W5 8J 55
Beechcroft Mnr. Wey 5B 116
Beechcroft Rd. E18 9F 30
Beechcroft Rd. SW14 2A 88
Beechcroft Rd. SW17 8C 90
Beechcroft Rd. Bush 7J 9
Beechcroft Rd. Chess 5K 119
Beechcroft Rd. Orp 6B 128
Beechdale. N21 2K 27
Beechdale Rd. SW2 5K 91
Beech Dell. Kes 6K 127
Beechdene. SE15 9F 76
(off Carlton Gro.)
Beech Dri. N2 9D 26
Beech Dri. Borwd 4K 11
Beechen Cliff Way. Iswth 1D 86
Beechen Gro. Pinn 1K 37
Beechen Gro. Wat 5F 8
Beechenlea La. Swan 8E 114
Beechen Pl. SE23 8H 93
Beeches Av. Cars 9C 122
Beeches Clo. SE20 5G 109
Beeches Rd. SW17 9C 90
Beeches Rd. Sutt 3J 121
Beeches, The. E12 3J 63
Beeches, The. Bans 8M 135
Beeches, The. Houn 9M 69
Beeches, The. S Croy 7B 124
(off Blunt Rd.)
Beeches, The. Swan 4D 114
Beeches, The. Wat 5F 8
(off Halsey Rd.)
Beeches Wlk. Cars 1B 136
Beechey Ho. E1 2F 76
(off Watts St.)
Beechfield. Bans 5M 135
Beechfield Clo. Borwd 4J 11
Beechfield Cotts. Brom 5G 111
Beechfield Ct. S Croy 6A 124
(off Bramley Hill)
Beechfield Gdns. Romf 5A 50
Beechfield Rd. N4 4A 44
Beechfield Rd. SE6 7K 93
Beechfield Rd. Brom 6G 111
Beechfield Rd. Eri 8C 82
Beechfield Wlk. Wal A 8K 7
Beech Gdns. EC2 8A 60
(off Beech St.)
Beech Gdns. W5 3J 71
Beech Gdns. Dag 3A 66
Beech Gro. Eps 9F 134
Beech Gro. Ilf 6C 32
Beech Gro. Mitc 9H 107
(in two parts)
Beech Gro. N Mald 7B 104
Beech Hall Cres. E4 7B 30
Beech Hall Rd. E4 7A 30
Beech Haven Ct. Dart 4J 98
(off London Rd.)
Beech Hill. Barn 2B 14
Beech Hill Av. Barn 3A 14
Beech Hill Gdns. Wal A 1F 18
Beech Hill Pk. 3B 14
Beech Ho. E17 1B 46
Beech Ho. SE16 3G 77
(off Ainsty Est.)
Beech Ho. Rd. Croy 5B 124
Beechhill Rd. SE9 4L 95
Beech La. Buck H 2F 30
Beech Lawns. N12 5B 26
Beechlee. Wall 2G 137
Beechmont Clo. Brom 2C 110
Beechmore Gdns. Sutt 4H 121
Beechmore Rd. SW11 9D 74
Beechmount Av. W7 8B 54
Beecholme. N12 5M 25
Beecholme. Bans 6J 135
Beecholme Av. Mitc 5F 106
Beecholme Est. E5 8F 44
Beecholm M. Chesh 1E 6
(off Lawrence Gdns.)
Beechpark Way. Wat 1C 8
Beech Rd. N11 6J 27
Beech Rd. SW16 6J 107
Beech Rd. Big H 9F 140
Beech Rd. Dart 7H 99
Beech Rd. Eps 7D 134
Beech Rd. Felt 6C 84
Beech Rd. Orp 9E 128
Beech Rd. Wat 1E 8
Beech Rd. Wey 6B 116
Beechrow. Ham 1J 103
Beech St. EC2 8A 60
Beech St. Romf 2A 50
Beech Tree Clo. N1 3L 59
Beech Tree Clo. Stan 5G 23
Beech Tree Glade. E4 1D 30
Beech Tree Pl. Sutt 7M 121
Beechvale Clo. N12 5C 26
Beech Wlk. NW7 6C 24
Beech Wlk. Dart 3E 98
Beech Wlk. Eps 3E 134
Beech Way. NW10 3B 56
Beechway. Bex 5H 97
Beech Way. Eps 7D 134
Beech Way. S Croy 5H 139
Beech Way. Twic 9L 85
Beechwood Av. N3 1K 41
Beechwood Av. Coul 7F 136
Beechwood Av. Gnfd 6M 53
Beechwood Av. Harr 8M 37
Beechwood Av. Hay 1B 68
Beechwood Av. Orp 7C 128
Beechwood Av. Rich 9L 71
Beechwood Av. Ruis 7D 36
Beechwood Av. Sun 3E 100
Beechwood Av. T Hth 8M 107
Beechwood Av. Uxb 9E 142
Beechwood Av. Wey 6C 116
Beechwood Circ. Harr 8M 37
Beechwood Clo. N2 2D 42
(off Western Rd.)
Beechwood Clo. NW7 5C 24
Beechwood Clo. Surb 2G 119
Beechwood Clo. Wey 6C 116
Beechwood Ct. W4 7B 72
Beechwood Ct. Cars 6D 122
Beechwood Ct. Sun 3E 100
Beechwood Cres. Bexh 2H 97
Beechwood Dri. Kes 6H 127
Beechwood Dri. Wfd G 5D 30
Beechwood Gdns. NW10 6K 55
Beechwood Gdns. Harr 8M 37
Beechwood Gdns. Ilf 3K 47
Beechwood Gdns. Rain 8F 66
Beechwood Gro. W3 1C 72
Beechwood Gro. Surb 2G 119
Beechwood Hall. N3 1K 41
Beechwood Ho. E2 5E 60
(off Teale St.)
Beechwood Mnr. Wey 6C 116
Beechwood M. N9 2E 28
Beechwood Pk. E18 1E 46
Beechwood Ri. Chst 1M 111
Beechwood Ri. Wat 9F 4
Beechwood Rd. E8 2D 60
Beechwood Rd. N8 2H 43
Beechwood Rd. S Croy 2C 138
Beechwoods Ct. SE19 2D 108
Beechworth. NW6 3J 57
Beechworth Clo. NW3 7L 41
Beecot La. W on T 4G 117
Beecroft La. SE4 4J 93
Beecroft M. SE4 4J 93
Beecroft Rd. SE4 4J 93
Beehive Clo. E8 3D 60
Beehive Clo. Els 8H 11
Beehive Clo. Uxb 3D 142
Beehive Ct. Romf 7K 35
Beehive La. Ilf 3K 47
Beehive Pl. SW9 2L 91
Beeken Dene. Orp 6A 128
Beeleigh Rd. Mord 8M 105
Beemans Row. SW18 8A 90
Bee Pas. EC3 9C 60
(off Lime St.)
Beesfield La. F'ham 2L 131
Beeston Clo. E8 1E 60
Beeston Clo. Wat 4H 21
Beeston Ct. Dart 5M 99
(off Hardwick Cres.)
Beeston Dri. Chesh 1D 6
Beeston Ho. SE1 4B 76
(off Burbage Clo.)
Beeston Pl. SW1 4F 74
Beeston Rd. Barn 8B 14
Beeston Way. Felt 5G 85
Beethoven Rd. Els 8H 11
Beethoven St. W10 6J 57
Beeton Clo. Pinn 7L 21
Begbie Rd. SE3 9G 79
Beggars Bush La. Wat 7B 8
Beggar's Hill (Junct.) 8D 120
Beggar's Hill. Eps 9D 120
Beggars Hollow. Enf 1B 16
Beggars Roost La. Sutt 8L 121
Begonia Clo. E6 8K 63
Begonia Pl. Hamp 3L 101
Begonia Wlk. W12 9D 56
Beira St. SW12 6F 90
Beken Ct. Wat 8G 5
Bekesbourne St. E14 9J 61
Belcroft Clo. Brom 4D 110
Beldanes Lodge. NW10 3E 56
Beldham Gdns. W Mol 6M 101
Belfairs Dri. Romf 5G 49
Belfairs Grn. Wat 5H 21
Belfast Rd. N16 7D 44
Belfast Rd. SE25 8F 108
Belfield Rd. Eps 1B 134
Belfont Wlk. N7 9J 43
(in two parts)
Belford Gro. SE18 5L 79
Belford Ho. E8 4D 60
Belford Rd. Borwd 2K 11
Belfort Rd. SE15 1G 93
Belfry Clo. SE16 6F 76
Belgrade Rd. N16 9C 44
Belgrade Rd. Hamp 5M 101
Belgrave Av. Romf 1G 51
Belgrave Av. Wat 7D 8
Belgrave Clo. N14 7G 15
Belgrave Clo. NW7 5B 24
Belgrave Clo. W3 3M 71
Belgrave Clo. Orp 8G 113
Belgrave Clo. W on T 6F 116
Belgrave Ct. E13 7G 63
Belgrave Ct. E14 1K 77
(off Westferry Cir.)
Belgrave Ct. SW8 8G 75
(off Ascalon St.)
Belgrave Ct. W4 6A 72
Belgrave Cres. Sun 5F 100
Belgrave Dri. K Lan 1A 4
Belgrave Gdns. N14 6H 15
Belgrave Gdns. NW8 4M 57
Belgrave Gdns. Stan 5G 23
Belgrave Heights. E11 6E 46
Belgrave Ho. SW9 8L 75
Belgrave M. Uxb 7B 142
Belgrave M. N. SW1 3E 74
Belgrave M. S. SW1 4E 74
Belgrave M. W. SW1 4E 74
Belgrave Pl. SW1 4E 74
Belgrave Rd. E10 6A 46
Belgrave Rd. E11 7E 46
Belgrave Rd. E13 7G 63
Belgrave Rd. E17 3L 45
Belgrave Rd. SE25 8D 108
Belgrave Rd. SW1 5F 74
Belgrave Rd. SW13 8D 72
Belgrave Rd. Houn 2K 85
Belgrave Rd. Ilf 6K 47
Belgrave Rd. Mitc 7B 106
Belgrave Rd. Sun 5F 100
Belgrave Sq. SW1 4E 74
Belgrave St. E1 8H 61
Belgrave Ter. Wfd G 3E 30
Belgrave Wlk. Mitc 7B 106
Belgrave Yd. SW1 4F 74
(off Lwr. Belgrave St.)
Belgravia. 4E 74
Belgravia Clo. Barn 5K 13
Belgravia Ct. SW1 4F 74
(off Ebury St.)
Belgravia Gdns. Brom 3C 110
Belgravia Ho. SW1 4E 74
(off Halkin Pl.)
Belgravia Ho. SW4 5H 91
Belgravia M. King T 8H 103
Belgravia Workshops. N19 7J 43
(off Marlborough Rd.)
Belgrove St. WC1 6J 59
Belham Wlk. SE5 9B 76
Belhaven Ct. Borwd 3K 11
Belinda Rd. SW9 2M 91
Belitha Vs. N1 3K 59
Bellamine Clo. SE28 2D 80
Bellamy Clo. E14 3L 77
Bellamy Clo. W14 6K 73
Bellamy Clo. Edgw 2A 24
Bellamy Clo. Wat 3E 8
Bellamy Ct. Stan 8F 22
Bellamy Dri. Stan 8F 22
Bellamy Ho. Houn 7L 69
Bellamy Rd. E4 6M 29
Bellamy Rd. Chesh 2E 6
Bellamy Rd. Enf 4B 16
Bellamy's Ct. SE16 2H 77
(off Abbotshade Rd.)
Bellamy St. SW12 6F 90
Bellasis Av. SW2 8J 91
Bell Av. Romf 8F 34
Bell Av. W Dray 5K 143
Bell Clo. Bedm 1D 4
Bell Clo. Pinn 9G 21
Bell Clo. Ruis 8D 36
Bellclose Rd. W Dray 3J 143
Bell Corner. Upm 7M 51
Bell Ct. NW4 2G 41
Bell Dri. SW18 6J 89
Bellefield Rd. Orp 9F 112
Bellefields Rd. SW9 2K 91
Bellegrove Clo. Well 1D 96
Bellegrove Pde. Well 2D 96
Bellegrove Rd. Well 1B 96
Bellenden Rd. SE15 9D 76
Bellestaines Pleasaunce.
E4 2L 29
Belleville Rd. SW11 4C 90
Belle Vue. Gnfd 4B 54
Belle Vue Est. NW4 2H 41
Bellevue La. Bus H 1B 22
Bellevue M. N11 5E 26
Bellevue Pk. T Hth 7A 108
Bellevue Pl. E1 7G 61
Belle Vue Rd. E17 9B 30
Bellevue Rd. N11 4E 26
Belle Vue Rd. NW4 2H 41
Bellevue Rd. SW13 1E 88
Bellevue Rd. SW17 7C 90
Bellevue Rd. W13 7F 54
Bellevue Rd. Bexh 4K 97
Bellevue Rd. Horn 6K 51
Bellevue Rd. King T 7J 103
(in two parts)
Belle Vue Rd. Orp 2L 141
Belle Vue Rd. Romf 6A 34
Bellew St. SW17 9A 90
Bell Farm Av. Dag 8A 50
Bellfield. Croy 1J 139
Bellfield Av. Harr 6B 22
Bellflower Clo. E6 8J 63
Bellflower Path. Romf 7G 35
Bell Gdns. E10 6L 45
(off Church Rd.)
Bell Gdns. Orp 9G 113
Bellgate M. NW5 9F 42
Bell Green. 1J 109
Bell Grn. SE26 1K 109
Bell Grn. La. SE26 2K 109
Bell Hill. Croy 4A 124
Bell Ho. SE10 7A 78
(off Haddo St.)
Bellhouse Cotts. Hay 1C 68
Bell Ho. Rd. Romf 6A 50
Bellina M. NW5 9F 42
Bell Ind. Est. W4 5A 72
Bellingham. 9M 93
Bellingham. N17 7F 28
(off Park La.)
Bellingham Ct. Bark 6F 64
Bellingham Grn. SE6 9L 93
Bellingham Rd. SE6 9M 93
Bellingham Trad. Est.
SE6 9M 93
Bell Inn Yd. EC3 9B 60
Bell Junct. Houn 2M 85
Bell La. E1 8D 60
Bell La. E16 2D 78
Bell La. NW4 & NW11 2H 41
Bell La. Bedm 1D 4
Bell La. Enf 2H 17
Bell La. Twic 7E 86
Bell La. Wemb 8H 39
Bellmaker Ct. E3 8L 61
Bell Mdw. SE19 2C 108
Bell Moor. NW3 8A 42
(off E. Heath Rd.)
Bellmount Wood Av. Wat 3C 8
Bello Clo. SE24 6M 91
Bellot Gdns. SE10 6C 78
(off Bellot St.)
Bellot St. SE10 6C 78
Bellring Clo. Belv 7L 81
Bell Rd. E Mol 9B 102
Bell Rd. Enf 3B 16
Bell Rd. Houn 2M 85
Bells All. SW6 1L 89
Bells Hill. Barn 7H 13
Bell St. NW1 8C 58
Bell St. SE18 9J 79
Bell, The (Junct.) 1L 45
Belltrees Gro. SW16 2K 107
Bell Vw. Mnr. Ruis 5B 36
Bell Water Ga. SE18 4L 79
Bell Wharf La. EC4 1A 76
Bellwood Rd. SE15 3H 93
Bell Yd. WC2 9L 59
Belmarsh Rd. SE28 3C 80
Belmont. 9F 22
(Harrow)
Belmont. 2L 135
(Sutton)
Belmont. Wey 8A 116
Belmont Av. N9 1E 28
Belmont Av. N13 5K 27
Belmont Av. N17 1A 44

Belmont Av.—Berthon St.

Belmont Av. Barn 7D 14
Belmont Av. N Mald 9E 104
Belmont Av. S'hall 4J 69
Belmont Av. Upm 7K 51
Belmont Av. Well 1C 96
Belmont Av. Wemb 4K 55
Belmont Circ. Harr 8F 22
Belmont Clo. E4 5B 30
Belmont Clo. N20 1M 25
Belmont Clo. SW4 2G 91
Belmont Clo. Cockf 6D 14
Belmont Clo. Uxb 2B 142
Belmont Clo. Wfd G 4F 30
Belmont Ct. N5 9A 44
Belmont Ct. NW11 3K 41
Belmont Gro. SE13 2B 94
Belmont Gro. W4 5B 72
Belmont Hall Ct. SE13 2B 94
Belmont Hill. SE13 2A 94
Belmont La. Chst 2M 111
(in two parts)
Belmont La. Stan 8G 23
Belmont Lodge. Har W 7B 22
Belmont M. SW19 8H 89
Belmont Pde. NW11 3K 41
Belmont Pde. Chst 2A 112
Belmont Pk. SE13 3B 94
Belmont Pk. Clo. SE13 3C 94
Belmont Pk. Rd. E10 4M 45
Belmont Ri. Sutt 8K 121
Belmont Rd. N15 & N17 2A 44
Belmont Rd. SE25 9F 108
Belmont Rd. SW4 2G 91
Belmont Rd. W4 5B 72
Belmont Rd. Beck 6J 109
Belmont Rd. Bush 7J 9
Belmont Rd. Chst 2M 111
Belmont Rd. Eri 8L 81
Belmont Rd. Harr 1D 38
Belmont Rd. Horn 8H 51
Belmont Rd. Ilf 8A 48
Belmont Rd. Sutt 2L 135
Belmont Rd. Twic 8B 86
Belmont Rd. Uxb 3B 142
Belmont Rd. Wall 7F 122
Belmont St. NW1 3E 58
Belmont Ter. W4 5B 72
Belmor. Els 8L 11
Belmore Av. Hay 9E 52
Belmore La. N7 1H 59
Belmore St. SW8 9H 75
Beloe Clo. SW15 3E 88
Belsham St. E9 2G 61
Belsize Av. N13 6K 27
Belsize Av. NW3 2B 58
Belsize Av. W13 4F 70
Belsize Ct. NW3 1B 58
Belsize Ct. Garages. NW3 1B 58
(off Belsize La.)
Belsize Cres. NW3 1B 58
Belsize Gdns. Sutt 6M 121
Belsize Gro. NW3 2C 58
Belsize La. NW3 2B 58
Belsize M. NW3 2B 58
Belsize Pk. NW3 2B 58
Belsize Pk. Gdns. NW3 2B 58
Belsize Pk. M. NW3 2B 58
Belsize Pl. NW3 1B 58
Belsize Rd. NW6 4M 57
Belsize Rd. Harr 7B 22
Belsize Sq. NW3 2B 58
Belsize Ter. NW3 2B 58
Belson Rd. SE18 5K 79
Beltane Dri. SW19 9H 89
Belthorn Cres. SW12 6G 91
Beltinge Rd. Romf 9K 35
Beltona Gdns. Chesh 1D 6
Belton Rd. E7 3F 62
Belton Rd. E11 9C 46
Belton Rd. N17 1C 44
Belton Rd. NW2 2E 56
Belton Rd. Sidc 1E 112
Belton Way. E3 8L 61
Beltran Rd. SW6 1M 89
Beltwood Rd. Belv 5A 82
Belvedere. 4M 81
Belvedere Av. SW19 2J 105
Belvedere Av. Ilf 9M 31
Belvedere Bldgs. SE1 3M 75
Belvedere Clo. Esh 7M 117
Belvedere Clo. Tedd 2C 102
Belvedere Ct. NW2 2H 57
(off Willesden La.)
Belvedere Ct. SW15 3G 89
Belvedere Ct. Belv 4K 81
Belvedere Dri. SW19 2J 105
Belvedere Gdns. W Mol 9K 101
Belvedere Gro. SW19 2J 105
Belvedere M. SE3 8F 78
Belvedere M. SE15 2G 93
Belvedere Pl. SE1 3M 75
Belvedere Pl. SW2 3K 91
Belvedere Rd. E10 6J 45
Belvedere Rd. SE1 2K 75
Belvedere Rd. SE2 2G 81
Belvedere Rd. SE19 4D 108
Belvedere Rd. W7 4D 70
Belvedere Rd. Bexh 2K 97
Belvedere Rd. Big H 9K 141
Belvedere Sq. SW19 2J 105
Belvedere Strand. NW9 9D 24
Belvedere, The. SW10 9A 74
(off Chelsea Harbour)
Belvedere Way. Harr 4J 39
Belvoir Clo. SE9 9J 95
Belvoir Rd. SE22 6E 92
Belvue Bus. Cen. N'holt 3M 53
Belvue Clo. N'holt 3L 53
Belvue Rd. N'holt 3L 53
Bembridge Clo. NW6 3J 57
Bembridge Gdns. Ruis 7B 36
Bembridge Ho. SE8 5K 77
(off Longshore)
Bembridge Pl. Wat 6E 4
Bemersyde Point. E13 6F 62
(off Dongola Rd. W.)
Bemerton Est. N1 3J 59
Bemerton St. N1 4K 59
Bemish Rd. SW15 2H 89
Bempton Dri. Ruis 7F 36
Bemsted Rd. E17 1K 45
Benares Rd. SE18 5D 80
Benbow Ct. W6 4G 73
(off Benbow Rd.)
Benbow Ho. SE8 7L 77
(off Benbow St.)
Benbow Moorings. Uxb 8A 142
Benbow Rd. W6 4F 72
Benbow St. SE8 7L 77
Benbow Waye. Uxb 8A 142
Benbury Clo. Brom 2A 110
Bence Ho. SE8 6J 77
Bench Fld. S Croy 8D 124
Bench, The. Rich 9G 87
Bencombe Rd. Purl 6L 137
Bencroft Rd. SW16 4G 107
Bencurtis Pk. W Wick 5B 126
Bendall M. NW1 8C 58
(off Bell St.)
Bendemeer Rd. SW15 2H 89
Benden Ho. SE13 4A 94
(off Monument Gdns.)
Bendish Point. SE28 3A 80
(off Erebus Dri.)
Bendish Rd. E6 3J 63
Bendmore Av. SE2 6E 80
Bendon Valley. SW18 6M 89
Bendysh Rd. Bush 5J 9
Benedict Clo. Belv 4J 81
Benedict Clo. Orp 5C 128
Benedict Ct. Romf 4K 49
Benedict Dri. Felt 6B 84
Benedict Rd. SW9 2K 91
Benedict Rd. Mitc 7B 106
Benedict Way. N2 1A 42
Benedict Wharf. Mitc 7B 106
Benenden Grn. Brom 9E 110
Benets Rd. Horn 6L 51
Benett Gdns. SW16 6J 107
Ben Ezra Ct. SE17 5A 76
(off Asolando Dri.)
Benfleet Clo. Sutt 5A 122
Benfleet Ct. E8 4D 60
Benfleet Way. N11 2E 26
Bengal Ct. EC3 9B 60
(off Birchin La.)
Bengal Ho. E1 8H 61
(off Duckett St.)
Bengal Rd. Ilf 9M 47
Bengarth Dri. Harr 9B 22
Bengarth Rd. N'holt 4J 53
Bengeworth Rd. SE5 2A 92
Bengeworth Rd. Harr 7E 38
Ben Hale Clo. Stan 5F 22
Benham Clo. SW11 2B 90
Benham Clo. Chess 8G 119
Benham Gdns. Houn 4K 85
Benham Rd. W7 8C 54
Benham's Pl. NW3 9A 42
Benhill Av. Sutt 6M 121
Benhill Rd. SE5 8B 76
Benhill Rd. Sutt 5A 122
Benhill Wood Rd. Sutt 5A 122
Benhilton. 5A 122
Benhilton Gdns. Sutt 5M 121
Benhurst Av. Horn 9F 50
Benhurst Clo. S Croy 2H 139
Benhurst Ct. SW16 2L 107
Benhurst Gdns. S Croy 2G 139
Benhurst La. SW16 2L 107
Benin St. SE13 6B 94
Benjafield Clo. N18 4F 28
Benjamin Clo. E8 4E 60
Benjamin Clo. Horn 4E 50
Benjamin Ct. Belv 7K 81
Benjamin Franklin House. 2J 75
(off Craven St.)
Benjamin St. EC1 8M 59
Ben Jonson Ct. N1 5C 60
Ben Jonson Ho. EC2 8A 60
(off Beech St.)
Ben Jonson Pl. EC2 8A 60
(off Beech St.)
Ben Jonson Rd. E1 8H 61
Benledi St. E14 9B 62
Benneck Ho. Wat 8C 8
Bennelong Clo. W12 1F 72
Bennerley Rd. SW11 4C 90
Bennets Fld. Rd. Uxb 2M 143
Bennet's Hill. EC4 1A 76
Bennet St. SW1 2G 75
Bennett Clo. Hamp W 5G 103
Bennett Clo. N'wd 7D 20
Bennett Clo. Well 1E 96
Bennett Ct. N7 8K 43
Bennett Gro. SE13 9M 77
Bennett Ho. SW1 5H 75
(off Page St.)
Bennett Pk. SE3 2D 94
Bennett Rd. E13 7G 63
Bennett Rd. N16 9C 44
Bennett Rd. Romf 4J 49
Bennetts Av. Croy 4J 125
Bennetts Av. Gnfd 4C 54
Bennett's Castle La. Dag 7G 49
Bennetts Clo. N17 6D 28
Bennetts Clo. Mitc 5F 106
Bennetts Copse. Chst 3J 111
Bennett St. W4 7C 72
Bennetts Way. Croy 4J 125
Bennett's Yd. SW1 4H 75
Bennett's Yd. Uxb 3A 142
Benningholme Rd. Edgw 6C 24
Bennington Rd. N17 8C 28
Bennington Rd. Wfd G 7C 30
Bennions Clo. Horn 2H 67
Bennison Dri. H Wood 9H 35
Benn's All. Hamp 6M 101
Benn St. E9 2J 61
Benns Wlk. Rich 3J 87
(off Michelsdale Dri.)
Benrek Clo. Ilf 7A 32
Bensbury Clo. SW15 6F 88
Bensham Clo. T Hth 8A 108
Bensham Gro. T Hth 6A 108
Bensham La.
T Hth & Croy 9M 107
Bensham Mnr. Rd. T Hth 8A 108
Benskin Rd. Wat 7E 8
Benskins La. Noak H 1H 35
Bensley Clo. N11 5D 26
Ben Smith Way. SE16 4E 76
Benson Av. E6 5G 63
Benson Clo. Houn 3L 85
Benson Clo. Uxb 8C 142
Benson Ho. E2 7D 60
(off Ligonier St.)
Benson Ho. SE1 2M 75
(off Hatfields)
Benson Quay. E1 1G 77
Benson Rd. SE23 7G 93
Benson Rd. Croy 5L 123
Bentalls Cen., The.
King T 6H 103
Bentfield Gdns. SE9 9H 95
Benthall Gdns. Kenl 9A 138
Benthal Rd. N16 8E 44
Bentham Ct. N1 3A 60
(off Ecclesbourne Rd.)
Bentham Ct. SE1 4B 76
(off Falmouth Rd.)
Bentham Rd. E9 2H 61
Bentham Rd. SE28 1F 80
Bentham Wlk. NW10 1A 56
Ben Tillet Clo. E16 2K 79
Ben Tillet Clo. Bark 3E 64
Ben Tillet Ho. N15 1M 43
Bentinck Clo. NW8 5C 58
Bentinck Ho. W12 1F 72
(off White City Est.)
Bentinck M. W1 9E 58
Bentinck Rd. W Dray 2H 143
Bentinck St. W1 9E 58
Bentley Dri. NW2 8K 41
Bentley Dri. Ilf 4A 48
Bentley Ho. SE5 9C 76
(off Peckham Rd.)
Bentley Rd. N1 2C 60
Bentley Way. Stan 5E 22
Bentley Way. Wfd G 3E 30
Benton Rd. Ilf 6B 48
Benton Rd. Wat 5H 21
Bentons La. SE27 1A 108
Benton's Ri. SE27 2B 108
Bentry Clo. Dag 7J 49
Bentry Rd. Dag 7J 49
Bentworth Clo. W12 9F 56
(off Bentworth Rd.)
Bentworth Ct. E2 7E 60
(off Granby St.)
Bentworth Rd. W12 9F 56
Benville Ho. SW8 8K 75
(off Oval Pl.)
Benwell Ct. Sun 5E 100
Benwell Rd. N7 9L 43
Benwick Clo. SE16 5F 76
Benwood Ct. Sutt 5A 122
Benworth St. E3 6K 61
Benyon Ct. N1 4C 60
(off De Beauvoir Est.)
Benyon Ho. EC1 6L 59
(off Myddelton Pas.)
Benyon Rd. N1 4B 60
Berberis Ct. Ilf 2M 63
Berberis Ho. E3 8L 61
(off Gale St.)
Berberis Wlk. W Dray 5J 143
Berber Pl. E14 1L 77
Berber Rd. SW11 4D 90
Berberry Clo. Edgw 4A 24
Berceau Wlk. Wat 3C 8
Bercta Rd. SE9 8A 96
Berenger Tower. SW10 8B 74
(off Worlds End Est.)
Berenger Wlk. SW10 8B 74
(off Worlds End Est.)
Berens Ct. Sidc 1D 112
Berens Rd. NW10 6H 57
Berens Rd. Orp 9H 113
Berens Way. Chst 7D 112
Beresford Av. N20 2D 26
Beresford Av. W7 8B 54
Beresford Av. Surb 3M 119
Beresford Av. Twic 5G 87
Beresford Av. Wemb 4K 55
Beresford Dri. Brom 7J 111
Beresford Dri. Wfd G 4G 31
Beresford Gdns. Enf 6C 16
Beresford Gdns. Houn 4K 85
Beresford Gdns. Romf 3J 49
Beresford Rd. E4 1C 30
Beresford Rd. E17 8M 29
Beresford Rd. N2 1C 42
Beresford Rd. N5 1B 60
Beresford Rd. N8 3L 43
Beresford Rd. Harr 3B 38
Beresford Rd. King T 5K 103
Beresford Rd. N Mald 8A 104
Beresford Rd. S'hall 2H 69
Beresford Rd. Sutt 9K 121
Beresford Sq. SE18 5M 79
Beresford St. SE18 4M 79
Beresford Ter. N5 1A 60
Berestede Rd. W4 6D 72
Bere St. E1 1H 77
Bergen Ho. SE5 1A 92
(off Carew St.)
Bergen Sq. SE16 4J 77
Berger Clo. Orp 1B 128
Berger Rd. E9 2H 61
Berghem M. W14 4H 73
Bergholt Av. Ilf 3J 47
Bergholt Cres. N16 5C 44
Bergholt M. NW1 3G 59
Berglen Ct. E14 9J 61
Bering Sq. E14 6L 77
Bering Wlk. E16 9H 63
Berisford M. SW18 5A 90
Berkeley Av. Bexh 9H 81
Berkeley Av. Gnfd 2C 54
Berkeley Av. Houn 9E 68
Berkeley Av. Ilf 9L 31
Berkeley Av. Romf 7A 34
Berkeley Clo. Ab L 5D 4
Berkeley Clo. Bren 7E 70
Berkeley Clo. Els 7L 11
Berkeley Clo. Horn 7M 51
Berkeley Clo. King T 4J 103
Berkeley Clo. Orp 2C 128
Berkeley Clo. Ruis 8E 36
Berkeley Clo. Twic 9C 86
(off Wellesley Rd.)
Berkeley Ct. N3 8M 25
Berkeley Ct. N14 8G 15
Berkeley Ct. NW1 7D 58
(off Marylebone Rd.)
Berkeley Ct. NW10 9C 40
Berkeley Ct. NW11 5K 41
(off Ravenscroft Av.)
Berkeley Ct. W5 1G 71
(off Gordon Rd.)
Berkeley Ct. Crox G 7B 8
Berkeley Ct. Croy 6B 124
(off Coombe Rd.)
Berkeley Ct. Surb 2H 119
Berkeley Ct. Swan 7C 114
Berkeley Ct. Wall 5G 123
Berkeley Ct. Wey 4B 116
Berkeley Cres. Barn 7B 14
Berkeley Cres. Dart 7K 99
Berkeley Dri. Horn 6L 51
Berkeley Dri. W Mol 7K 101
Berkeley Gdns. N21 9B 16
Berkeley Gdns. W8 2L 73
Berkeley Gdns. Clay 8E 118
Berkeley Gdns. W on T 2D 116
Berkeley Ho. SE8 6K 77
(off Grove St.)
Berkeley Ho. Bren 7H 71
(off Albany Rd.)
Berkeley M. W1 9D 58
Berkeley Pl. SW19 3H 105
Berkeley Pl. Eps 8B 134
Berkeley Rd. E12 1J 63
Berkeley Rd. N8 3H 43
Berkeley Rd. N15 4B 44
Berkeley Rd. NW9 2L 39
Berkeley Rd. SW13 9E 72
Berkeley Rd. Uxb 3A 52
Berkeley Sq. W1 1F 74
Berkeley St. W1 1F 74
Berkeley Tower. E14 2K 77
(off Westferry Cir.)
Berkeley Wlk. N7 7K 43
(off Durham Rd.)
Berkeley Waye. Houn 7H 69
Berkely Clo. Sun 7G 101
Berkhampstead Rd. Belv 6L 81
Berkhamsted Av. Wemb 2K 55
Berkley Av. Wal X 7D 6
Berkley Gro. NW1 3E 58
Berkley Pl. Wal X 7D 6
Berkley Rd. NW1 3D 58
Berkshire Ct. W7 7D 54
(off Copley Clo.)
Berkshire Gdns. N13 6L 27
Berkshire Gdns. N18 5F 28
Berkshire Ho. SE6 1L 109
Berkshire Rd. E9 2K 61
Berkshire Sq. Mitc 8J 107
Berkshire Way. Horn 3L 51
Berkshire Way. Mitc 8J 107
Bermans Way. NW10 9C 40
Bermer Rd. Wat 3G 9
Bermondsey. 3E 76
Bermondsey Sq. SE1 4C 76
Bermondsey St. SE1 2C 76
Bermondsey Trad. Est.
SE16 6G 77
Bermondsey Wall E. SE16 3E 76
Bermondsey Wall W.
SE16 3E 76
Bernal Clo. SE28 1H 81
Bernard Angell Ho. SE10 7B 78
(off Trafalgar Rd.)
Bernard Ashley Dri. SE7 6F 78
Bernard Av. W13 4F 70
Bernard Cassidy St. E16 8D 62
Bernard Gdns. SW19 2K 105
Bernard Gro. Wal A 6H 7
Bernard Mans. WC1 7J 59
(off Bernard St.)
Bernard Rd. N15 3D 44
Bernard Rd. Romf 5A 50
Bernard Rd. Wall 6F 122
Bernards Clo. Ilf 7B 32
Bernard Shaw Ct. NW1 3G 59
(off St Pancras Way)
Bernard St. WC1 7J 59
Bernard Sunley Ho. SW9 8L 75
(off S. Island Pl.)
Bernays Clo. Stan 6G 23
Bernays Gro. SW9 3K 91
Bernel Dri. Croy 5K 125
Berne Rd. T Hth 9A 108
Berners Dri. W13 1E 70
Berners Ho. N1 5L 59
(off Barnsbury Est.)
Berners M. W1 8G 59
Berners Pl. W1 9G 59
Berners Rd. N1 4M 59
Berners Rd. N22 8L 27
Berners St. W1 8G 59
Berner Ter. E1 9E 60
(off Fairclough St.)
Berney Ho. Beck 9J 109
Berney Rd. Croy 2B 124
Bernhardt Cres. NW8 7C 58
Bernhart Clo. Edgw 7A 24
Bernice Clo. Rain 7G 67
Bernville Way. Harr 3K 39
Bernwell Rd. E4 3C 30
Berridge Grn. Edgw 7L 23
Berridge M. NW6 1L 57
Berridge Rd. SE19 2B 108
Berriman Rd. N7 8K 43
Berriton Rd. Harr 6K 37
Berry Av. Wat 9F 4
Berrybank Clo. E4 2A 30
Berry Clo. N21 1M 27
Berry Clo. NW10 3C 56
Berry Clo. Dag 1L 65
Berry Clo. Horn 1G 67
Berry Ct. Houn 4K 85
Berrydale Rd. Hay 7J 53
Berryfield Clo. E17 2M 45
Berryfield Clo. Brom 5J 111
Berryfield Rd. SE17 6M 75
Berrygrove (Junct.) 2L 9
Berry Gro. La. Wat 2J 9
(in two parts)
Berryhill. SE9 3M 95
Berry Hill. Stan 4H 23
Berryhill Gdns. SE9 3M 95
Berry Ho. E1 7F 60
(off Headlam St.)
Berrylands. 1L 119
Berrylands. SW20 7G 105
Berrylands. Orp 5G 129
Berrylands. Surb 1K 119
Berrylands Rd. Surb 1K 119
Berry La. SE21 1B 108
Berry La. W on T 7H 117
Berryman Clo. Dag 8G 49
Berryman's La. SE26 1H 109
Berry Meade. Asht 9K 133
Berrymead Gdns. W3 2A 72
Berrymede Rd. W4 4B 72
Berry Pl. EC1 6M 59
Berry's Green. 8M 141
Berry's Grn. Rd. Berr G 8M 141
Berry's Hill. Berr G 8M 141
Berry St. EC1 7M 59
Berry Way. W5 4J 71
Bertal Rd. SW17 1B 106
Bertha Hollamby Ct.
Sidc 2G 113
(off Sidcup Hill)
Bertha James Ct. Brom 8F 110
Berther Rd. Horn 5H 51
Berthold M. Wal A 6H 7
Berthons Gdns. E17 3B 46
(off Wood St.)
Berthon St. SE8 8L 77

Bertie Rd.—Birkbeck M.

Bertie Rd. NW10 .2E 56
Bertie Rd. SE26 .3H 109
Bertram Cotts. SW19 .4L 105
Bertram Rd. NW4 .4E 40
Bertram Rd. Enf .6E 16
Bertram Rd. King T .4L 103
Bertram St. N19 .7F 42
Bertrand Ho. SW16 .9J 91
(off Leigham Av.)
Bertrand St. SE13 .2M 93
Bertrand Way. SE28 .1F 80
Bert Rd. T Hth .9A 108
Bert Way. Enf .6D 16
Berwick Av. Hay .9H 53
Berwick Clo. Stan .6D 22
Berwick Clo. Wal X .7G 7
Berwick Cres. Sidc .6C 96
Berwick Ho. N2 .9B 26
Berwick Pond Clo. Rain .5H 67
Berwick Pond Rd.
Rain & Upm .5J 67
Berwick Rd. E16 .9F 62
Berwick Rd. N22 .8M 27
Berwick Rd. Borwd .2K 11
Berwick Rd. Rain .5H 67
Berwick Rd. Well .9F 80
Berwick St. W1 .9G 59
Berwick Way. Orp .3E 128
Berwyn Av. Houn .9M 69
Berwyn Rd. SE24 .7M 91
Berwyn Rd. Rich .3M 87
Beryl Av. E6 .8J 63
Beryl Rd. W6 .6H 73
Berystede. King T .4M 103
Besant Clo. NW2 .8J 41
Besant Ct. N1 .1B 60
Besant Ho. NW8 .4A 58
(off Boundary Rd.)
Besant Ho. Wat .4H 9
Besant Rd. NW2 .9J 41
Besant Wlk. N7 .7K 43
Besant Way. NW10 .1A 56
Besford Ho. E2 .5E 60
(off Pritchard's Rd.)
Besley St. SW16 .3G 107
Bessant Dri. Rich .9L 71
Bessborough Gdns. SW1 .6H 75
Bessborough Pl. SW1 .6H 75
Bessborough Rd. SW15 .7E 88
Bessborough Rd. Harr .6B 38
Bessborough St. SW1 .6H 75
Bessemer Ct. NW1 .3G 59
(off Rochester Sq.)
Bessemer Rd. SE5 .1A 92
Bessie Lansbury Clo. E6 .9L 63
Bessingby Rd. Ruis .7F 36
Bessingham Wlk. SE4 .3H 93
(off Aldersford Clo.)
Besson St. SE14 .9G 77
Bessy St. E2 .6G 61
Best Ter. Swan .1A 130
Bestwood St. SE8 .5H 77
Beswick M. NW6 .2M 57
Betam Rd. Hay .3B 68
Beta Pl. SW9 .3K 91
Betchworth Clo. Sutt .7B 122
Betchworth Rd. Ilf .7C 48
Betchworth Way.
New Ad .1A 140
Bethal Est. SE1 .2C 76
(off Tooley St.)
Betham Rd. Gnfd .6B 54
Bethany Waye. Felt .6C 84
Bethecar Rd. Harr .3C 38
Bethell Av. E16 .7D 62
Bethell Av. Ilf .5L 47
Bethel Rd. Well .2G 97
Bethersden Clo. Beck .4K 109
Bethersden Ho. SE17 .6C 76
(off Kinglake St.)
Bethlehem Ho. E14 .1K 77
(off Limehouse Causeway)
Bethnal Green. .6F 60
Bethnal Green Mus. of Childhood. .6G 61
Bethnal Grn. Rd. E1 & E2 .7D 60
Bethune Av. N11 .4D 26
Bethune Clo. N16 .6C 44
Bethune Rd. N16 .5B 44
Bethune Rd. NW10 .7B 56
Bethwin Rd. SE5 .8M 75
Betjeman Clo. Chesh .1A 6
Betjeman Clo. Coul .9K 137
Betjeman Clo. Pinn .2L 37
Betjeman Clo. W Dray .2H 143
Betley Ct. W on T .5F 116
Betony Clo. Croy .3H 125
Betony Rd. Romf .6G 35
Betoyne Av. E4 .4C 30
Betsham Ho. SE1 .3B 76
(off Newcomen St.)
Betsham Rd. Eri .8D 82
Betstyle Cir. N11 .4F 26
Betstyle Ho. N10 .7E 26
Betstyle Rd. N11 .4F 26
Betterton Dri. Sidc .8J 97
Betterton Ho. WC2 .9J 59
(off Betterton St.)
Betterton Rd. Rain .6C 66
Betterton St. WC2 .9J 59
Bettles Clo. Uxb .5A 142
Bettons Pk. E15 .4C 62
Bettridge Rd. SW6 .1K 89
Betts Clo. Beck .6J 109
Betts Ho. E1 .1F 76
(off Betts St.)
Betts M. E17 .4K 45
Betts Rd. E16 .1F 78
Betts St. E1 .1F 76
Betts Way. SE20 .5F 108
Betts Way. Surb .3F 118
Betty Brooks Ho. E11 .8B 46
Betty May Gray Ho. E14 .5A 78
(off Pier St.)
Betula Clo. Kenl .7B 138
Betula Wlk. Rain .6H 67
Beulah Av. T Hth .6A 108
Beulah Clo. Edgw .3M 23
Beulah Cres. T Hth .6A 108
Beulah Gro. Croy .1A 124
Beulah Hill. SE19 .3M 107
Beulah Path. E17 .3A 46
Beulah Rd. E17 .3M 45
Beulah Rd. SW19 .4K 105
Beulah Rd. Horn .8G 51
Beulah Rd. Sutt .6L 121
Beulah Rd. T Hth .7A 108
Beult Rd. Dart .3E 98
Bevan Av. Bark .3E 64
Bevan Ct. Croy .7L 123
Bevan Ho. WC1 .8J 59
(off Boswell St.)
Bevan Ho. Twic .5H 87
Bevan Ho. Wat .4H 9
Bevan Pk. Eps .2D 134
Bevan Pl. Swan .8D 114
Bevan Rd. SE2 .6F 80
Bevan Rd. Barn .6D 14
Bevan St. N1 .4A 60
Bevan Way. Horn .9K 51
Bev Callender Clo. SW8 .2F 90
Bevenden St. N1 .6B 60
Bevercote Wlk. Belv .7K 81
Beveridge Rd. NW10 .3C 56
Beverley Av. SW20 .5D 104
Beverley Av. Houn .3K 85
Beverley Av. Sidc .6D 96
Beverley Clo. N21 .1A 28
Beverley Clo. SW11 .3B 90
Beverley Clo. SW13 .1E 88
Beverley Clo. Chess .6G 119
Beverley Clo. Enf .6C 16
Beverley Clo. Eps .3G 135
Beverley Clo. Horn .5K 51
Beverley Clo. Wey .4C 116
Beverley Cotts. SW15 .9C 88
Beverley Ct. N2 .2D 42
(off Western Rd.)
Beverley Ct. N14 .9G 15
Beverley Ct. SE4 .2K 93
(in two parts)
Beverley Ct. W4 .6A 72
Beverley Ct. Harr .1B 38
Beverley Ct. Houn .3K 85
Beverley Ct. Kent .2G 39
Beverley Cres. Wfd G .8F 30
Beverley Dri. Edgw .1L 39
Beverley Gdns. NW11 .5J 41
Beverley Gdns. SW13 .2D 88
Beverley Gdns. Chesh .3A 6
Beverley Gdns. Horn .5K 51
Beverley Gdns. Stan .8E 22
Beverley Gdns. Wemb .6K 39
Beverley Gdns. Wor Pk .3E 120
Beverley Ho. Brom .2B 110
(off Brangbourne Rd.)
Beverley La. SW15 .9D 88
Beverley La. King T .4C 104
Beverley M. E4 .6B 30
Beverley Path. SW13 .1D 88
Beverley Rd. E4 .6B 30
Beverley Rd. E6 .6H 63
Beverley Rd. SE20 .6F 108
Beverley Rd. SW13 .2D 88
Beverley Rd. W4 .6D 72
Beverley Rd. Bexh .1A 98
Beverley Rd. Brom .4J 127
Beverley Rd. Dag .9J 49
Beverley Rd. King T .5G 103
Beverley Rd. Mitc .8H 107
Beverley Rd. N Mald .8E 104
Beverley Rd. Ruis .7E 36
Beverley Rd. S'hall .5J 69
Beverley Rd. Sun .5D 100
Beverley Rd. Whyt .8C 138
Beverley Rd. Wor Pk .4G 121
Beverley Trad. Est.
Mord .2H 121
Beverley Way.
SW20 & N Mald .5D 104
Beversbrook Rd. N19 .8H 43
Beverstone Rd. SW2 .4K 91
Beverstone Rd. T Hth .8L 107
Beverston M. W1 .8D 58
(off Up. Montagu St.)
Bevill Allen Clo. SW17 .2D 106
Bevill Clo. SE25 .7E 108
Bevin Clo. SE16 .2J 77
Bevin Ct. WC1 .6K 59
Bevington Path. SE1 .3D 76
(off Tanner St.)
Bevington Rd. W10 .8J 57
Bevington Rd. Beck .6M 109
Bevington St. SE16 .3E 76
Bevin Ho. E2 .6G 61
(off Butler St.)
Bevin Rd. Hay .6E 52
Bevin Sq. SW17 .9D 90
Bevin Way. WC1 .5L 59
Bevis Marks. EC3 .9C 60
Bewcastle Gdns.
Enf .6J 15
Bew Ct. SE22 .6E 92
Bewdley St. N1 .3L 59
Bewick M. SE15 .8F 76
Bewick St. SW8 .1F 90
Bewley Clo. Chesh .4D 6
Bewley Ho. E1 .1F 76
(off Bewley St.)
Bewley St. E1 .1G 77
Bewlys Rd. SE27 .2M 107
Bexhill Clo. Felt .8J 85
Bexhill Rd. N11 .5H 27
Bexhill Rd. SE4 .5K 93
Bexhill Rd. SW14 .2A 88
Bexhill Wlk. E15 .4C 62
Bexley. .6L 97
Bexley Clo. Dart .4C 98
Bexley Cotts. Hort K .8M 115
Bexley Gdns. N9 .3B 28
Bexley Gdns. Chad H .3F 48
Bexley Hall Place Vis. Cen.
(Hall Place) .5A 98
Bexleyheath. .3L 97
Bexley High St. Bex .6L 97
Bexley Ho. SE4 .3J 93
Bexley La. Dart .4C 98
Bexley La. Sidc .1G 113
Bexley Local Studies &
Archive Cen. .5A 98
(Hall Place)
Bexley Rd. SE9 .4M 95
Bexley Rd. Eri .9A 82
(in two parts)
Beynon Rd. Cars .7D 122
Bianca Rd. SE15 .7E 76
Bibsworth Rd. N3 .9K 25
Bibury Clo. SE15 .7C 76
(in two parts)
Bicester Rd. Rich .2L 87
Bickenhall Mans. W1 .8D 58
(off Bickenhall St., in two parts)
Bickenhall St. W1 .8D 58
Bickersteth Rd. SW17 .3D 106
Bickerton Rd. N19 .7G 43
Bickley. .7J 111
Bickley Cres. Brom .8J 111
Bickley Pk. Rd. Brom .7J 111
Bickley Rd. E10 .5M 45
Bickley Rd. Brom .6H 111
Bickley St. SW17 .2C 106
Bicknell Ho. E1 .9E 60
(off Ellen St.)
Bicknell Rd. SE5 .2A 92
Bicknoller Clo. Sutt .2M 135
Bicknoller Rd. Enf .3C 16
Bicknor Rd. Orp .2C 128
Bidborough Clo. Brom .9D 110
Bidborough St. WC1 .6J 59
Biddenden Way. SE9 .1L 111
Biddenham Ho. SE16 .5H 77
(off Plough Way)
Biddenham Turn. Wat .8G 5
Bidder St. E16 .8C 62
(in two parts)
Biddesden Ho. SW3 .5D 74
(off Cadogan St.)
Biddestone Rd. N7 .9K 43
Biddulph Ho. SE18 .5K 79
Biddulph Mans. W9 .6M 57
(off Elgin Av.)
Biddulph Rd. W9 .6M 57
Biddulph Rd. S Croy .2A 138
Bideford Av. Gnfd .5F 54
Bideford Clo. Edgw .8L 23
Bideford Clo. Felt .9K 85
Bideford Clo. Romf .8G 35
Bideford Gdns. Enf .9C 16
Bideford Rd. Brom .9D 94
Bideford Rd. Enf .2K 17
Bideford Rd. Ruis .8F 36
Bideford Rd. Well .8F 80
Bidwell Gdns. N11 .7G 27
Bidwell St. SE15 .9F 76
Big Ben. .3J 75
Bigbury Clo. N17 .7B 28
Biggerstaff Rd. E15 .4A 62
Biggerstaff St. N4 .7L 43
Biggin Av. Mitc .5D 106
Biggin Hill. .9H 141
Biggin Hill. SE19 .5M 107
Biggin Hill Airport. .4H 141
Biggin Hill Bus. Pk.
Big H .7H 141
Biggin Hill Clo. King T .2G 103
Biggin Way. SE19 .4M 107
Bigginwood Rd. SW16 .4M 107
Biggs Row. SW15 .2H 89
Big Hill. E5 .6F 44
Bigland St. E1 .9F 60
Bignell Rd. SE18 .6M 79
Bignold Rd. E7 .9E 46
Bigwood Ct. NW11 .3M 41
Bigwood Rd. NW11 .3M 41
Biko Clo. Uxb .9A 142
Bilberry Ho. E3 .8L 61
(off Watts Gro.)
Billet Clo. Romf .1H 49
Billet La. Horn .6H 51
Billet Rd. E17 .8H 29
Billet Rd. Romf .1F 48
Billets Hart Clo. W7 .3C 70
Bill Hamling Clo. SE9 .8K 95
Billing Clo. Dag .3G 65
Billingford Clo. SE4 .3H 93
Billing Ho. E1 .9H 61
(off Bower St.)
Billingley. NW1 .4G 59
(off Pratt St.)
Billing Pl. SW10 .8M 73
Billing Rd. SW10 .8M 73
Billingsgate Fish Market. .2M 77
Billing St. SW6 .8M 73
Billington Rd. SE14 .8H 77
Billinton Hill. Croy .4B 124
Billiter Sq. EC3 .9C 60
(off Fenchurch Av.)
Billiter St. EC3 .9C 60
Bill Nicholson Way. N17 .7D 28
(off High Rd.)
Billockby Clo. Chess .8K 119
Billson St. E14 .5A 78
Bilsby Gro. SE9 .1H 111
Bilsby Lodge. Wemb .8A 40
(off Chalklands)
Bilton Cen., The. Gnfd .4F 54
Bilton Rd. Eri .8E 82
Bilton Rd. Gnfd .4E 54
Bilton Towers. W1 .9D 58
(off Gt. Cumberland Pl.)
Bilton Way. Enf .3J 17
Bilton Way. Hay .3F 68
Bina Gdns. SW5 .5A 74
Binbrook Ho. W10 .8G 57
(off Sutton Way)
Bincote Rd. Enf .5K 15
Binden Rd. W12 .4D 72
Bindon Grn. Mord .8M 105
Binfield Rd. SW8 .9J 75
Binfield Rd. S Croy .7D 124
Bingfield St. N1 .4J 59
(in two parts)
Bingham Ct. N1 .3M 59
(off Halton Rd.)
Bingham Pl. W1 .8E 58
Bingham Rd. Croy .3E 124
Bingham St. N1 .2B 60
Bingley Rd. E16 .9G 63
Bingley Rd. Gnfd .7A 54
Bingley Rd. Sun .4E 100
Binley Ho. SW15 .5D 88
Binney St. W1 .9E 58
Binnie Ct. SE10 .8M 77
(off Greenwich High Rd.)
Binnie Ho. SE1 .4A 76
(off Bath Ter.)
Binns Rd. W4 .6C 72
Binns Ter. W4 .6C 72
Binsey Wlk. SE2 .3G 81
Binstead Clo. Hay .8J 53
Binyon Cres. Stan .5D 22
Birbetts Rd. SE9 .8K 95
Bircham Path. SE4 .3H 93
(off Aldersford Clo.)
Birchanger Rd. SE25 .9E 108
Birch Av. N13 .3A 28
Birch Av. W Dray .9D 142
Birch Clo. E16 .8C 62
Birch Clo. N19 .7G 43
Birch Clo. SE15 .1E 92
(off Bournemouth Clo.)
Birch Clo. Bren .8F 70
Birch Clo. Buck H .3H 31
Birch Clo. Eyns .5H 131
Birch Clo. Houn .1B 86
Birch Clo. Romf .1M 49
Birch Clo. Shep .6C 100
Birch Clo. Tedd .2E 102
Birch Copse. Brick W .3J 5
Birch Ct. N'wd .6A 20
Birch Ct. Wall .6F 122
Birch Cres. Horn .2J 51
Birch Cres. Uxb .4D 142
Birchdale Gdns. Romf .5H 49
Birchdale Rd. E7 .1G 63
Birchdene Dri. SE28 .2E 80
Birchen Clo. NW9 .7B 40
Birchend Clo. S Croy .8B 124
Birchen Gro. NW9 .7B 40
Birches Clo. Eps .7C 134
Birches Clo. Mitc .7D 106
Birches Clo. Pinn .3J 37
Birches, The. E12 .9J 47
Birches, The. N21 .8K 15
Birches, The. SE7 .7F 78
Birches, The. Brom .8D 110
(off Durham Av.)
Birches, The. Bush .7A 10
Birches, The. Houn .6K 85
Birches, The. Orp .6L 127
Birches, The. Swan .6C 114
Birches, The. Wal A .7M 7
Birchfield Clo. Coul .8K 137
Birchfield Gro. Eps .2G 135
Birchfield Ho. E14 .1L 77
(off Birchfield St.)
Birchfield Rd. Chesh .2B 6
Birchfield St. E14 .1L 77
Birch Gdns. Dag .8A 50
Birch Grn. NW9 .7C 24
Birch Gro. E11 .9C 46
Birch Gro. SE12 .6D 94
Birch Gro. W3 .2L 71
Birch Gro. Shep .6C 100
Birch Gro. Well .3E 96
Birch Hill. Croy .7H 125
Birch Ho. N22 .8L 27
(off Acacia Rd.)
Birch Ho. SE14 .9K 77
Birch Ho. SW2 .5L 91
(off Tulse Hill)
Birch Ho. W10 .7J 57
(off Droop St.)
Birchington Clo. Bexh .9M 81
Birchington Clo. Orp .3G 129
Birchington Ct. NW6 .4M 57
(off W. End La.)
Birchington Ho. E5 .1F 60
Birchington Rd. N8 .4H 43
Birchington Rd. NW6 .4L 57
Birchington Rd. Surb .2K 119
Birchin La. EC3 .9B 60
Birchlands Av. SW12 .6D 90
Birch La. Purl .3J 137
Birchmead. Orp .4L 127
Birchmead. Wat .2D 8
Birchmead Av. Pinn .2G 37
Birchmere Bus. Site. SE28 .3E 80
Birchmere Lodge. SE16 .6F 76
(off Sherwood Gdns.)
Birchmere Row. SE3 .1D 94
Birchmore Hall. N5 .8A 44
Birchmore Wlk. N5 .8A 44
Birch Pk. Harr .7A 22
Birch Rd. Felt .2H 101
Birch Rd. Romf .1M 49
Birch Row. Brom .2L 127
Birch Tree Av. W Wick .7D 126
Birch Tree Wlk. Wat .1D 8
Birch Tree Way. Croy .4F 124
Birch Va. Ct. NW8 .7B 58
(off Pollitt Dri.)
Birchville Ct. Bus H .1C 22
Birch Wlk. Borwd .3L 11
Birch Wlk. Eri .7A 82
Birch Wlk. Mitc .5F 106
Birchway. Hay .2E 68
Birch Way. Warl .9J 139
Birchwood. Wal A .7L 7
Birchwood Av. N10 .1E 42
Birchwood Av. Beck .8K 109
Birchwood Av. Sidc .8F 96
Birchwood Av. Wall .5E 122
Birchwood Clo. Mord .8M 105
Birchwood Ct. N13 .5M 27
Birchwood Ct. Edgw .9A 24
Birchwood Dri. NW3 .8M 41
Birchwood Dri. Dart .1C 114
Birchwood Gro. Hamp .3L 101
Birchwood La.
Esh & Oxs .1B 132
Birchwood Pde. Dart .1C 114
Birchwood Pk. Av. Swan .7C 114
Birchwood Rd. SW17 .2F 106
Birchwood Rd. Orp .8B 112
Birchwood Rd.
Swan & Dart .5A 114
Birchwood Way. Park .1M 5
Birdbrook Clo. Dag .3A 66
Birdbrook Ho. N1 .3A 60
(off Popham Rd.)
Birdbrook Rd. SE3 .3G 95
Birdcage Wlk. SW1 .3G 75
Birdham Clo. Brom .9J 111
Birdhouse La. Orp .7K 141
Birdhurst Av. S Croy .6B 124
Birdhurst Gdns. S Croy .6B 124
Birdhurst Ri. S Croy .7C 124
Birdhurst Rd. SW18 .4A 90
Birdhurst Rd. SW19 .3C 106
Birdhurst Rd. S Croy .7C 124
Bird in Bush Rd. SE15 .8E 76
Bird in Hand La. Brom .6H 111
Bird-in-Hand Pas. SE23 .8G 93
Bird in Hand Yd. NW3 .9A 42
Birdlip Clo. SE15 .7C 76
Birdsall Ho. SE5 .2C 92
Birds Farm Av. Romf .7M 33
Birdsfield La. E3 .4K 61
Birds Hill Dri. Oxs .5B 132
Birds Hill Ri. Oxs .5B 132
Birds Hill Rd. Oxs .4B 132
Bird St. W1 .9E 58
Bird Wlk. Twic .7K 85
Birdwood Clo. S Croy .3G 139
Birdwood Clo. Tedd .1C 102
Birkbeck Av. W3 .1A 72
Birkbeck Av. Gnfd .4A 54
Birkbeck College. .8H 59
Birkbeck Ct. W3 .2B 72
Birkbeck Gdns. Wfd G .2E 30
Birkbeck Gro. W3 .3B 72
Birkbeck Hill. SE21 .7M 91
Birkbeck M. E8 .1D 60

Birkbeck M. W3 . . . . .2B 72
Birkbeck Pl. SE21 . . . . .8A 92
Birkbeck Rd. E8 . . . . .1D 60
Birkbeck Rd. N8 . . . . .2J 43
Birkbeck Rd. N12 . . . . .5A 26
Birkbeck Rd. N17 . . . . .8D 28
Birkbeck Rd. NW7 . . . . .5D 24
Birkbeck Rd. SW19 . . . . . .2M 105
Birkbeck Rd. W3 . . . . .2B 72
Birkbeck Rd. W5 . . . . .5G 71
Birkbeck Rd. Beck 6G 109
Birkbeck Rd. Enf 3B 16
Birkbeck Rd. Ilf 3B 48
Birkbeck Rd. Romf 6B 50
Birkbeck Rd. Sidc 9E 96
Birkbeck St. E2 . . . . .6F 60
Birkbeck Way. Gnfd 4B 54
Birkdale Av. Pinn 1L 37
Birkdale Av. Romf 7K 35
Birkdale Clo. SE16 . . . . .6F 76
Birkdale Clo. SE28 . . . . .9H 65
Birkdale Clo. Orp 2B 128
Birkdale Ct. S'hall 9A 54
(off Redcroft Rd.)
Birkdale Gdns. Croy 6H 125
Birkdale Gdns. Wat 3H 21
Birkdale Rd. SE2 . . . . .5E 80
Birkdale Rd. W5 . . . . .7J 55
Birkenhead Av. King T 6K 103
Birkenhead St. WC1 . . . . . . .6J 59
Birken M. N'wd 5A 20
Birkhall Rd. SE6 . . . . .7B 94
Birkwood Clo. SW12 . . . . . . .6H 91
Birley Lodge. NW8 . . . . .5B 58
(off Acacia Rd.)
Birley Rd. N20 . . . . .2A 26
Birley St. SW11 . . . . .1E 90
Birling Rd. Eri 8B 82
Birnam Rd. N4 . . . . .7K 43
Birnbeck Ct. NW11 . . . . .3K 41
Birnbeck Ct. Barn 6H 13
Birrell Ho. SW9 . . . . .1K 91
(off Stockwell Rd.)
Birse Cres. NW10 . . . . .8C 40
Birstall Grn. Wat 4H 21
Birstall Rd. N15 . . . . .3C 44
Biscay Ho. E1 . . . . .7H 61
(off Mile End Rd.)
Biscay Rd. W6 . . . . .6H 73
Biscoe Clo. Houn 7L 69
Biscoe Way. SE13 . . . . .2B 94
Biscott Ho. E3 . . . . .7M 61
Bisenden Rd. Croy 4C 124
Bisham Clo. Cars 3D 122
Bisham Gdns. N6 . . . . .6E 42
Bishop Butt Clo. Orp 5D 128
Bishop Ct. N12 . . . . .4M 25
Bishop Ct. Rich 2J 87
Bishop Duppas Pk.
Shep 2C 116
Bishop Fox Way. W Mol 8K 101
Bishop Ken Rd. Harr 9D 22
Bishop King's Rd. W14 . . . . .5J 73
Bishop Rd. N14 . . . . .9F 14
Bishop's Av. E13 . . . . .4F 62
Bishop's Av. SW6 . . . . .1H 89
Bishops Av. Brom 6G 111
Bishops Av. Els 7K 11
Bishops Av. N'wd 4C 20
Bishops Av. Romf 4G 49
Bishops Av., The. N2 . . . . . . .4B 42
Bishop's Bri. Rd. W2 . . . . . . .9M 57
Bishops Clo. E17 . . . . .2M 45
Bishop's Clo. N19 . . . . .8G 43
Bishop's Clo. SE9 . . . . .8A 96
Bishops Clo. W4 . . . . .6A 72
Bishops Clo. Barn 8H 13
Bishop's Clo. Coul 9L 137
Bishops Clo. Enf 4F 16
Bishops Clo. Rich 9H 87
Bishop's Clo. Sutt 5L 121
Bishops Clo. Uxb 5E 142
Bishop's Ct. EC4 . . . . .9M 59
(off Old Bailey)
Bishops Ct. W2 . . . . .9M 57
(off Bishop's Bri. Rd.)
Bishop's Ct. WC2 . . . . .9L 59
(off Star Yd.)
Bishops Ct. Ab L 4D 4
Bishops Ct. Chesh 3B 6
Bishops Ct. Wemb 9F 38
Bishopsdale Ho. NW6 . . . . . .4L 57
(off Kilburn Va.)
Bishop's Dri. Felt 5B 84
Bishops Dri. N'holt 4J 53
Bishopsford Rd. Mord 2A 122
Bishopsgate. EC2 . . . . .9C 60
Bishopsgate Arc. EC2 . . . . . .8C 60
(off Bishopsgate)
Bishopsgate Chyd. EC2 . . . . .8C 60
Bishopsgate Institute & Libraries.
. . . . .8C 60
(off Bishopsgate)
Bishops Grn. Brom 5F 110
(off Up. Park Rd.)
Bishops Gro. N2 . . . . .4C 42
Bishop's Gro. Hamp 1K 101
Bishops Gro. Cvn. Site.
Hamp 1L 101
Bishop's Hall. King T 6H 103
Bishops Hill. W on T 2E 116
Bishops Ho. SW8 . . . . .8J 75
(off S. Lambeth Rd.)
Bishop's Mans. SW6 . . . . . . .1H 89
(in two parts)
Bishops Mead. SE5 . . . . .8A 76
(off Camberwell Rd.)
Bishopsmead Clo. Eps 2B 134
Bishop's Pk. Rd. SW6 . . . . . .1H 89
Bishops Pk. Rd. SW16 . . . . . .5J 107
Bishops Rd. N6 . . . . .4E 42
Bishops Rd. SW6 . . . . .9J 73
Bishop's Rd. SW11 . . . . .8C 74
Bishops Rd. W7 . . . . .3C 70
Bishop's Rd. Croy 2M 123
Bishop's Rd. Hay 9A 52
Bishop's Ter. SE11 . . . . .5L 75
Bishopsthorpe Rd. SE26 . . .1H 109
Bishop St. N1 . . . . .4A 60
Bishops Vw. Ct. N10 . . . . . . .2F 42
Bishops Wlk. Chst 5A 112
Bishops Wlk. Croy 7H 125
Bishops Wlk. Pinn 1J 37
Bishop's Way. E2 . . . . .5F 60
Bishopswood Rd. N6 . . . . . . .5D 42
Bishop Way. NW10 . . . . .3C 56
Bishop Wilfred Wood Clo.
SE15 . . . . .1E 92
Bishop Wilfred Wood Ct.
E13 . . . . .5G 63
(off Pragel St.)
Biskra. Wat 3E 8
Bisley Clo. Wal X 6D 6
Bisley Clo. Wor Pk 3G 121
Bison Ct. Felt 6F 84
Bispham Rd. NW10 . . . . .6K 55
Bissextile Ho. SE8 . . . . .1M 93
Bisson Rd. E15 . . . . .5A 62
Bisterne Av. E17 . . . . .1B 46
Bittacy Bus. Cen. NW7 . . . . . .6J 25
Bittacy Clo. NW7 . . . . .6H 25
Bittacy Ct. NW7 . . . . .7J 25
Bittacy Hill. NW7 . . . . .6H 25
Bittacy Pk. Av. NW7 . . . . . . .5H 25
Bittacy Ri. NW7 . . . . .6G 25
Bittacy Rd. NW7 . . . . .6H 25
Bittern Clo. Hay 8H 53
Bittern Ct. NW9 . . . . .9C 24
Bittern Ct. SE8 . . . . .7L 77
Bittern Ho. SE1 . . . . .3A 76
(off Gt. Suffolk St.)
Bittern Pl. N22 . . . . .9K 27
Bittern St. SE1 . . . . .3A 76
Bittoms Ct. King T 7H 103
Bittoms, The. King T 7H 103
(in two parts)
Bixley Clo. S'hall 5K 69
Blackall St. EC2 . . . . .7C 60
Blackberry Clo. Shep 8C 100
Blackberry Farm Clo.
Houn 8J 69
Blackberry Fld. Orp 5E 112
Blackbird Ct. NW9 . . . . .8B 40
Blackbird Hill. NW9 . . . . .7A 40
Blackbirds La. A'ham 7M 5
Blackbird Yd. E2 . . . . .6D 60
Blackborne Rd. Dag 2L 65
Black Boy La. N15 . . . . .3A 44
Black Boy Wood. Brick W 3L 5
Blackbrook La. Brom 9K 111
Blackburn. NW9 . . . . .9D 24
Blackburne's M. W1 . . . . .1E 74
Blackburn Rd. NW6 . . . . .2M 57
Blackbush Av. Romf 3H 49
Blackbush Clo. Sutt 9M 121
Blackdown Clo. N2 . . . . .9A 26
Blackett St. SW15 . . . . .2H 89
Black Fan Clo. Enf 3A 16
Blackfen. 5E 96
Blackfen Pde. Sidc 5E 96
Blackfen Rd. Sidc 4C 96
Blackford Clo. S Croy 1M 137
Blackford Rd. Wat 5H 21
Blackford's Path. SW15 . . . . .6E 88
Blackfriars Bri. EC4 . . . . . . .1M 75
Blackfriars Bri.
SE1 & EC4 . . . . .1M 75
Blackfriars Ct. EC4 . . . . .1M 75
(off New Bri. St.)
Black Friars La. EC4 . . . . . . .9M 59
(in two parts)
Blackfriars Pas. EC4 . . . . . . .1M 75
Blackfriars Rd. SE1 . . . . .3M 75
Blackfriars Underpass.
EC4 . . . . .1L 75
Black Gates. Pinn 1K 37
Blackheath. 1D 94
Blackheath Av. SE10 . . . . . . .8B 78
Blackheath Bus. Est. SE10 . . .9A 78
(off Blackheath Hill)
Blackheath Gro. SE3 . . . . . . .1D 94
Blackheath Hill. SE10 . . . . . .9A 78
Blackheath Park. 3E 94
Blackheath Pk. SE3 . . . . .2D 94
Blackheath Ri. SE13 . . . . .1A 94
Blackheath Rd. SE10 . . . . . . .9M 77
Blackheath Vale. 1D 94
Blackheath Va. SE3 . . . . .1C 94
Blackheath Village. SE3 . . . . .1D 94
Blackhills. Esh 9L 117
Black Horse Ct. SE1 . . . . .4B 76
(off Gt. Dover St.)
Blackhorse Lane (Junct.)
. . . . .2H 45
Blackhorse La. E17 . . . . .9H 29
Black Horse La. Croy 2E 124
Blackhorse M. E17 . . . . .1H 45
Black Horse Pde. Eastc 3F 36
Blackhorse Pl. Uxb 4A 142
Blackhorse Rd. E17 . . . . .2H 45
Blackhorse Rd. SE8 . . . . .7J 77
Blackhorse Rd. Sidc 1E 112
Black Horse Yd. Uxb 4A 142
Blacklands Dri. Hay 7A 52
Blacklands Rd. SE6 . . . . . . .1A 110
Blacklands Ter. SW3 . . . . . . .5D 74
Blackley Clo. Wat 1D 8
Black Lion La. W6 . . . . .5E 72
Black Lion M. W6 . . . . .5E 72
Blackmans Clo. Dart 7G 99
Blackman's La. Warl 6C 140
Blackmans Yd. E2 . . . . .7E 60
(off Grimsby St.)
Blackmoor La. Wat 7B 8
Blackmore Av. S'hall 2B 70
Blackmore Ho. N1 . . . . .4K 59
(off Barnsbury Est.)
Blackmore Rd. Buck H 9J 19
Blackmore's Gro. Tedd 3E 102
Blackmore Tower. W3 . . . . . .4A 72
(off Stanley Rd.)
Blackmore Way. Uxb 2B 142
Blackness La. Kes 1H 141
Black Path. E10 . . . . .5J 45
Blackpool Gdns. Hay 7C 52
Blackpool Rd. SE15 . . . . .1F 92
Black Prince Interchange (Junct.)
. . . . .5M 97
Black Prince Rd.
SE1 & SE11 . . . . .5K 75
Black Rod Clo. Hay 4D 68
Blackshaw Rd. SW17 . . . . . .1A 106
Blacksmiths Clo. Romf 4G 49
Blacksmiths Hill. S Croy 5E 138
Blacksmiths Ho. E17 . . . . . . .2L 45
(off Gillards M.)
Blacksmith's La. Orp 9G 113
Blacksmith's La. Rain 4D 66
Blacks Rd. W6 . . . . .6G 73
Blackstock M. N4 . . . . .7M 43
Blackstock Rd. N4 & N5 . . . .7M 43
Blackstone Est. E8 . . . . .3E 60
Blackstone Ho. SW1 . . . . . . .6G 75
(off Churchill Gdns.)
Blackstone Rd. NW2 . . . . . . .1G 57
Black Swan Yd. SE1 . . . . .3C 76
Blackthorn Av. W Dray 5L 143
Blackthorn Clo. Wat 5F 4
Blackthorn Ct. Houn 8J 69
Blackthorne Av. Croy 3G 125
Blackthorne Ct. SE15 . . . . . . .8D 76
(off Cator St.)
Blackthorne Ct. S'hall 2M 69
(off Dormer's Wells La.)
Blackthorne Dri. E4 . . . . .4B 30
Blackthorn Gro. Bexh 2J 97
Blackthorn Rd. Big H 8H 141
Blackthorn St. E3 . . . . .7L 61
Blacktree M. SW9 . . . . .2L 91
Blackwall. 1A 78
Blackwall La. SE10 . . . . .6C 78
(in two parts)
Blackwall Trad. Est.
E14 . . . . .8B 62
Blackwall Tunnel.
E14 & SE10 . . . . .2B 78
(in two parts)
Blackwall Tunnel App. E14 . . .9A 62
Blackwall Tunnel Northern App.
E3 & E14 . . . . .5L 61
Blackwall Tunnel Southern App.
SE10 . . . . .4C 78
Blackwall Way. E14 . . . . .2A 78
Blackwater Clo. E7 . . . . .9D 46
Blackwater Clo. Rain 8B 66
Blackwater Ho. NW8 . . . . . . .8B 58
(off Church St.)
Blackwater St. SE22 . . . . .4D 92
Blackwell Clo. E5 . . . . .9H 45
Blackwell Clo. Harr 7B 22
Blackwell Dri. Wat 8G 9
Blackwell Gdns. Edgw 4L 23
Blackwell Ho. SW4 . . . . .5H 91
Blackwood Av. N18 . . . . .5H 29
Blackwood Ho. E1 . . . . .7F 60
(off Collingwood St.)
Blackwood St. SE17 . . . . .6B 76
Blade M. SW15 . . . . .3K 89
Bladen Ho. E1 . . . . .9H 61
(off Dunelm St.)
Blades Ct. SW15 . . . . .3K 89
Blades Ct. W6 . . . . .6F 72
(off Lower Mall)
Blades Ho. SE11 . . . . .7L 75
(off Kennington Oval)
Bladindon Dri. Bex 6G 97
Bladon Clo. Wey 8B 116
Bladon Ct. SW16 . . . . .3J 107
Bladon Gdns. Harr 4M 37
Blagdens Clo. N14 . . . . .2H 27
Blagdens La. N14 . . . . .2H 27
Blagdon Ct. W7 . . . . .1C 70
Blagdon Rd. SE13 . . . . .5M 93
Blagdon Rd. N Mald 8D 104
(in two parts)
Blagdon Wlk. Tedd 3G 103
Blagrove Rd. W10 . . . . .8J 57
Blair Av. NW9 . . . . .5C 40
Blair Av. Esh 4A 118
Blair Clo. N1 . . . . .2A 60
Blair Clo. Hay 5E 68
Blair Clo. Sidc 4C 96
Blair Ct. NW8 . . . . .4B 58
Blair Ct. SE6 . . . . .7D 94
Blair Ct. Beck 5M 109
Blairderry Rd. SW2 . . . . .8J 91
Blairhead Dri. Wat 3F 20
Blair Ho. SW9 . . . . .1K 91
Blair St. E14 . . . . .9A 62
Blake Av. Bark 4C 64
Blakeborough Dri.
H Wood 9J 35
Blake Clo. Cars 3C 122
Blake Clo. Rain 4D 66
Blake Clo. Well 9C 80
Blake Ct. NW6 . . . . .6L 57
(off Stafford Clo.)
Blake Ct. SE16 . . . . .6F 76
(off Stubbs Dri.)
Blakeden Dri. Clay 8D 118
Blake Gdns. SW6 . . . . .9M 73
Blake Gdns. Dart 3K 99
Blake Hall Cres. E11 . . . . . . .6E 46
Blake Hall Rd. E11 . . . . .5E 46
Blakehall Rd. Cars 8D 122
Blake Ho. E14 . . . . .3L 77
(off Admirals Way)
Blake Ho. SE1 . . . . .4L 75
Blake Ho. SE8 . . . . .7L 77
(off New King St.)
Blakeley Cotts. SE10 . . . . . . .3B 78
Blakemore Rd. SW16 . . . . . . .9J 91
Blakemore Rd. T Hth 9K 107
Blakemore Way. Belv 4J 81
Blakeney Av. Beck 5K 109
Blakeney Clo. E8 . . . . .1E 60
Blakeney Clo. N20 . . . . .1A 26
Blakeney Clo. NW1 . . . . .3H 59
Blakeney Clo. Eps 3B 134
Blakeney Rd. Beck 4K 109
Blakenham Rd. SW17 . . . . . .1D 106
Blaker Ct. SE7 . . . . .8G 79
(in two parts)
Blake Rd. E16 . . . . .7D 62
Blake Rd. N11 . . . . .7G 27
Blake Rd. Croy 4C 124
Blake Rd. Mitc 7C 106
Blaker Rd. E15 . . . . .4A 62
Blakes Av. N Mald 9D 104
Blakes Clo. W10 . . . . .8G 57
Blake's Grn. W Wick 3A 126
Blakes La. N Mald 9D 104
Blakesley Av. W5 . . . . .9G 55
Blakesley Wlk. SW20 . . . . . .6K 105
Blake's Rd. SE15 . . . . .8C 76
Blakes Ter. N Mald 9E 104
Blakesware Gdns. N9 . . . . . . .9B 16
Blakewood Clo. Felt 1G 101
Blanchard Clo. SE9 . . . . .9J 95
Blanchard Gro. Enf 2M 17
Blanchard Ho. Twic 5H 87
(off Clevedon Rd.)
Blanchard M. Romf 7K 35
Blanchard Way. E8 . . . . .2E 60
Blanch Clo. SE15 . . . . .8G 77
Blanchedowne. SE5 . . . . .3B 92
Blanche St. E16 . . . . .7D 62
Blanchland Rd. Mord 9M 105
Blandfield Rd. SW12 . . . . . . .6E 90
Blandford Av. Beck 6J 109
Blandford Av. Twic 7M 85
Blandford Clo. N2 . . . . .2A 42
Blandford Clo. Croy 5J 123
Blandford Clo. Romf 2L 49
Blandford Ct. E8 . . . . .3C 60
(off St Peter's Way)
Blandford Ct. NW6 . . . . .3H 57
Blandford Cres. E4 . . . . .9A 18
Blandford Ho. SW8 . . . . .8K 75
(off Richborne Ter.)
Blandford Rd. W4 . . . . .4C 72
Blandford Rd. W5 . . . . .3H 71
Blandford Rd. Beck 7G 109
Blandford Rd. S'hall 5L 69
Blandford Rd. Tedd 2B 102
Blandford Sq. NW1 . . . . .7C 58
Blandford St. W1 . . . . .9D 58
Blandford Waye. Hay 9G 53
Bland Ho. SE11 . . . . .6K 75
(off Vauxhall St.)
Bland St. SE9 . . . . .3H 95
Blaney Cres. E6 . . . . .6M 63
Blanmerle Rd. SE9 . . . . .7M 95
Blann Clo. SE9 . . . . .5H 95
Blantyre St. SW10 . . . . .8B 74
Blantyre Tower. SW10 . . . . . .8B 74
(off Blantyre St.)
Blantyre Wlk. SW10 . . . . .8B 74
(off Worlds End Est.)
Blashford. NW3 . . . . .3D 58
(off Adelaide Rd.)
Blashford St. SE13 . . . . .6B 94
Blasker Wlk. E14 . . . . .6M 77
Blattner Clo. Els 6J 11
Blawith Rd. Harr 2C 38
Blaxland Ho. W12 . . . . .1F 72
(off White City Est.)
Blaxland Ter. Chesh 1D 6
(off Davison Dri.)
Blaydon Clo. N17 . . . . .7F 28
Blaydon Clo. Ruis 5C 36
Blaydon Ct. N'holt 2L 53
Blazer Ct. NW8 . . . . .6B 58
(off St John's Wood Rd.)
Bleak Hill La. SE18 . . . . .7D 80
Blean Gro. SE20 . . . . .4G 109
Blear Ho. Eps 3D 134
Bleasdale Av. Gnfd 5E 54
Blechynden Ho. W10 . . . . . . .9H 57
(off Kingsdown Clo.)
Blechynden St. W10 . . . . .1H 73
Bleddyn Clo. Sidc 5G 97
Bledlow Clo. SE28 . . . . .1G 81
Bledlow Ho. NW8 . . . . .7B 58
(off Capland St.)
Bledlow Ri. Gnfd 5A 54
Bleeding Heart Yd. EC1 . . . . .8L 59
(off Greville St.)
Blegborough Rd. SW16 . . . .3G 107
Blemundsbury. WC1 . . . . .8K 59
(off Dombey St.)
Blendon. 5H 97
Blendon Dri. Bex 5H 97
Blendon Path. Brom 4D 110
Blendon Rd. Bex 5H 97
Blendon Row. SE17 . . . . .5B 76
(off Townley St.)
Blendon Ter. SE18 . . . . .6A 80
Blendworth Way. SE15 . . . . .8C 76
(off Clanfield Way)
Blenheim Av. Ilf 4L 47
Blenheim Clo. N21 . . . . .1A 28
Blenheim Clo. SW20 . . . . . .7G 105
Blenheim Clo. Dart 5G 99
Blenheim Clo. Gnfd 5B 54
Blenheim Clo. Romf 2A 50
Blenheim Clo. Wall 9G 123
Blenheim Clo. Wat 9G 9
Blenheim Ct. N19 . . . . .7J 43
Blenheim Ct. SE16 . . . . .2H 77
(off King & Queen Wharf)
Blenheim Ct. Brom 8D 110
Blenheim Ct. Horn 1G 67
Blenheim Ct. Kent 4E 38
Blenheim Ct. Sidc 9B 96
Blenheim Ct. Sutt 8A 122
Blenheim Cres. W11 . . . . .1J 73
Blenheim Cres. Ruis 7B 36
Blenheim Cres. S Croy 9A 124
Blenheim Dri. Well 9D 80
Blenheim Gdns. NW2 . . . . . . .2G 57
Blenheim Gdns. SW2 . . . . . . .5K 91
Blenheim Gdns. Ave 2M 83
Blenheim Gdns. King T 4M 103
Blenheim Gdns. S Croy 4E 138
Blenheim Gdns. Wall 8G 123
Blenheim Gdns. Wemb 8J 39
Blenheim Gro. SE15 . . . . .1E 92
Blenheim Ho. E16 . . . . .2F 78
(off Constable Av.)
Blenheim Ho. Houn 2L 85
Blenheim Pde. Uxb 7F 142
Blenheim Pk. Rd. S Croy . . .1A 138
Blenheim Pas. NW8 . . . . .5A 58
(in two parts)
Blenheim Ri. N15 . . . . .2D 44
Blenheim Rd. E6 . . . . .6H 63
Blenheim Rd. E15 . . . . .9C 46
Blenheim Rd. E17 . . . . .1H 45
Blenheim Rd. NW8 . . . . .5A 58
Blenheim Rd. SE20 . . . . . . .4G 109
Blenheim Rd. SW20 . . . . . . .7G 105
Blenheim Rd. W4 . . . . .4C 72
Blenheim Rd. Ab L 5E 4
Blenheim Rd. Barn 5H 13
Blenheim Rd. Brom 8J 111
Blenheim Rd. Dart 5G 99
Blenheim Rd. Eps 3B 134
Blenheim Rd. Harr 4M 37
Blenheim Rd. N'holt 2M 53
Blenheim Rd. Orp 4G 129
Blenheim Rd. Sidc 7G 97
Blenheim Rd. Sutt 5L 121
Blenheim Shop. Cen.
SE20 . . . . .4G 109
Blenheim St. W1 . . . . .9F 58
Blenheim Ter. NW8 . . . . .5A 58
Blenheim Way. Iswth 9E 70
Blenkarne Rd. SW11 . . . . . . .5D 90
Bleriot. NW9 . . . . .9D 24
(off Belvedere Strand)
Bleriot Rd. Houn 8G 69
Blessbury Rd. Edgw 8A 24
Blessington Clo. SE13 . . . . . .2B 94
Blessington Rd. SE13 . . . . . . .2B 94
Blessing Way. Bark 6G 65
Bletchingley Clo. T Hth 8M 107
Bletchley Ct. N1 . . . . .5B 60
(off Bletchley St., in two parts)
Bletchley St. N1 . . . . .5B 60
Bletchmore Clo. Hay 6B 68
Bletsoe Wlk. N1 . . . . .5A 60
Blewbury Ho. SE2 . . . . .3H 81
Blewitts Cotts. Rain 6D 66
(off New Rd.)

Blick Ho.—Boundary Clo.

Blick Ho. SE16 4G **77** (off Neptune St.)
Blincoe Clo. *SW19* 8H **89**
Blind La. *Bans* 7C **136**
Blind La. *Lou* 4C **18**
Blindman's La. *Chesh* 3D **6**
Bliss Cres. *SE13* 1M **93**
Blissett St. *SE10* 9A **78**
Bliss M. *W10* 6J **57**
Blisworth Clo. *Hay* 7J **53**
Blisworth Ho. E2 4E **60** (off Whiston Rd.)
Blithbury Rd. *Dag* 2F **64**
Blithdale Rd. *SE2* 5E **80**
Blithfield St. *W8* 4M **73**
Blockley Rd. *Wemb* 7F **38**
Bloemfontein Av. *W12* 2F **72**
Bloemfontein Rd. *W12* 1F **72**
Bloemfontein Way. *W12* 2F **72**
Blomfield Ct. W9 7A **58** (off Maida Va.)
Blomfield Mans. W12 2G **73** (off Stanlake Rd.)
Blomfield Rd. *W9* 8M **57**
Blomfield St. *EC2* 8B **60**
Blomfield Vs. *W2* 8M **57**
Blomville Rd. *Dag* 8J **49**
Blondell Clo. *W Dray* 7H **143**
Blondel St. *SW11* 1E **90**
Blondin Av. *W5* 5G **71**
Blondin St. *E3* 5L **61**
Bloomburg St. *SW1* 5H **75**
Bloomfield Ct. *N6* 4E **42**
Bloomfield Cres. *Ilf* 4M **47**
Bloomfield Ho. E1 8E **60** (off Old Montague St.)
Bloomfield Pl. W1 1F **74** (off Grosvenor Hill)
Bloomfield Rd. *N6* 4E **42**
Bloomfield Rd. *SE18* 7M **79**
Bloomfield Rd. *Brom* 9H **111**
Bloomfield Rd. *King T* 8J **103**
Bloomfields, The. *Bark* 2A **64**
Bloomfield Ter. *SW1* 6E **74**
Bloom Gro. *SE27* 9M **91**
Bloomhall Rd. *SE19* 2B **108**
Bloom Pk. Rd. *SW6* 8K **73**
Bloomsbury. 8J **59**
Bloomsbury Clo. *NW7* 7E **24**
Bloomsbury Clo. *W5* 1K **71**
Bloomsbury Clo. *Eps* 2B **134**
Bloomsbury Ct. WC1 8J **59** (off Barter St.)
Bloomsbury Ct. *Houn* 9F **68**
Bloomsbury Ct. *Pinn* 1K **37**
Bloomsbury Ho. *SW4* 5H **91**
Bloomsbury Pl. *SW18* 4A **90**
Bloomsbury Pl. *WC1* 8J **59**
Bloomsbury Sq. *WC1* 8J **59**
Bloomsbury St. *WC1* 8H **59**
Bloomsbury Theatre. 7H **59** (off Gordon St.)
Bloomsbury Way. *WC1* 8J **59**
Blore Clo. *SW8* 9H **75**
Blore Ct. W1 9H **59** (off Berwick St.)
Blossom Clo. *W5* 3J **71**
Blossom Clo. *Dag* 4K **65**
Blossom Clo. *S Croy* 7D **124**
Blossom La. *Enf* 3A **16**
Blossom St. *E1* 7C **60**
Blossom Way. *Uxb* 3D **142**
Blossom Way. *W Dray* 5L **143**
Blossom Waye. *Houn* 7J **69**
Blount Ho. E14 8J **61** (off Maroon St.)
Blount St. *E14* 9J **61**
Bloxam Gdns. *SE9* 4J **95**
Bloxhall Rd. *E10* 6K **45**
Bloxham Cres. *Hamp* 4K **101**
Bloxworth Clo. *Wall* 5G **123**
Blucher Rd. *SE5* 8A **76**
Blue Anchor All. *Rich* 3J **87**
Blue Anchor La. *SE16* 5E **76**
Blue Anchor Yd. *E1* 1E **76**
Blue Ball Yd. *SW1* 2G **75**
Bluebell Av. *E12* 1H **63**
Bluebell Clo. *E9* 4G **61**
Bluebell Clo. *SE26* 1D **108**
Bluebell Clo. *Orp* 4A **128**
Bluebell Clo. *Rush G* 7C **50**
Bluebell Clo. *Wall* 3F **122**
Bluebell Dri. *Bedm* 1D **4**
Bluebell Way. *Ilf* 2M **63**
Blueberry Clo. *Wfd G* 6E **30**
Blueberry Gdns. *Coul* 8K **137**
Bluebird La. *Dag* 3L **65**
Bluebird Way. *SE28* 3B **80**
Bluebird Way. *Brick W* 3K **5**
Blue Cedars. *Bans* 6H **135**
Blue Elephant Theatre. 8A **76**
Bluefield Clo. *Hamp* 2L **101**
Bluegate M. *E1* 1F **76**
Bluegates. *Ewe* 9E **120**
Bluehouse Rd. *E4* 2C **30**
Blue Riband Ind. Est. *Croy* 4M **123**
Blue Water. *SW18* 3M **89**
Blundell Rd. *Edgw* 8B **24**
Blundell St. [illegible] 3J **59**
Blunden Clo. *Dag* 6G **49**
Blunt Rd. *S Croy* 7B **124**
Blunts Av. *W Dray* 8L **143**
Blunts Rd. *SE9* 4L **95**
Blurton Rd. *E5* 9G **45**
Blydon Ct. N21 7K **15** (off Chaseville Pk. Rd.)
Blyth Clo. *E14* 5B **78**
Blyth Clo. *Borwd* 3K **11**
Blyth Clo. *Twic* 5D **86**
Blyth Ct. Brom 5D **110** (off Blyth Rd.)
Blythe Clo. *SE6* 6K **93**
Blythe Hill. 6K **93**
Blythe Hill. *SE6* 6K **93**
Blythe Hill. *Orp* 5D **112**
Blythe Hill La. *SE6* 6K **93**
Blythe Ho. *SE11* 7L **75**
Blythe M. *W14* 4H **73**
Blythendale Ho. E2 5E **60** (off Mansford St.)
Blythe Rd. *W14* 4H **73** (in two parts)
Blythe St. *E2* 6F **60**
Blythe Va. *SE6* 7K **93**
Blyth Hill Pl. SE23 6J **93** (off Brockley Pk.)
Blyth Rd. *E17* 5K **45**
Blyth Rd. *SE28* 1G **81**
Blyth Rd. *Brom* 5D **110**
Blyth Rd. *Hay* 3C **68**
Blyth's Wharf. E14 1J **77** (off Narrow St.)
Blythswood Rd. *Ilf* 6E **48**
Blyth Wood Pk. *Brom* 5D **110**
Blythwood Rd. *N4* 5J **43**
Blythwood Rd. *Pinn* 8H **21**
Boades M. *NW3* 9B **42**
Boadicea St. *N1* 4K **59**
Boakes Clo. *NW9* 2A **40**
Boar Clo. *Chig* 5E **32**
Boardman Av. *E4* 7M **17**
Boardman Clo. *Barn* 7J **13**
Boardwalk Pl. *E14* 2A **78**
Boarhound. NW9 9D **24** (off Further Acre)
Boarley Ho. SE17 5C **76** (off Massinger St.)
Boars Head Yd. *Bren* 8H **71**
Boathouse Cen., The. W10 7H **57** (off Canal Clo.)
Boathouse Wlk. *SE15* 8D **76** (in two parts)
Boat Lifter Way. *SE16* 5J **77**
Bob Anker Clo. *E13* 6E **62**
Bobbin Clo. *SW4* 2G **91**
Bobby Moore Way. *N12* 7D **26**
Bob Marley Way. *SE24* 3L **91**
Bobs La. *Romf* 7E **34**
Bockhampton Rd. *King T* 4K **103**
Bocking St. *E8* 4F **60**
BOC Mus. 8H **59** (off Bedford Sq.,Association of Anaesthetists, The)
Boddicott Clo. *SW19* 8J **89**
Boddington Ho. SE14 9G **77** (off Pomeroy St.)
Boddington Ho. SW13 7F **72** (off Wyatt Dri.)
Bodeney Ho. SE5 9C **76** (off Peckham Rd.)
Boden Ho. E1 8E **60** (off Woodseer St.)
Bodiam Clo. *Enf* 4C **16**
Bodiam Rd. *SW16* 4H **107**
Bodicea M. *Houn* 5K **85**
Bodington Ct. *W12* 3H **73**
Bodley Clo. *N Mald* 9C **104**
Bodley Mnr. Way. *SW2* 6L **91**
Bodley Rd. *N Mald* 1B **120**
Bodmin. NW9 9D **24** (off Further Acre)
Bodmin Clo. *Harr* 8K **37**
Bodmin Clo. *Orp* 3G **129**
Bodmin Gro. *Mord* 9M **105**
Bodmin Pl. *SE27* 1M **107**
Bodmin St. *SW18* 7L **89**
Bodnant Gdns. *SW20* 7E **104**
Bodney Rd. *E8* 1F **60**
Boeing Way. *S'hall* 4F **68**
Boevey Path. *Belv* 6K **81**
Bogart Ct. E14 1L **77** (off Premiere Pl.)
Bogey La. *Orp* 9L **127**
Bognor Gdns. *Wat* 5G **21**
Bognor Rd. *Well* 9H **81**
Bohemia Pl. *E8* 2G **61**
Bohn Rd. *E1* 8J **61**
Bohun Gro. *Barn* 8C **14**
Boileau Pde. W5 9K **55** (off Boileau Rd.)
Boileau Rd. *SW13* 8E **72**
Boileau Rd. *W5* 9K **55**
Boisseau Ho. E1 8G **61** (off Stepney Way)
Bolden St. *SE8* 1M **93**
Boldero Pl. NW8 7C **58** (off Gateforth St.)
Bolderwood Way. *W Wick* 4M **125**
Boldmere Rd. *Pinn* 5G **37**
Boleyn Av. *Enf* 3F **16**
Boleyn Av. *Eps* 2F **134**
Boleyn Clo. *E17* 2L **45**
Boleyn Clo. *Lou* 8J **19**
Boleyn Ct. *Buck H* 1E **30**
Boleyn Dri. *Ruis* 7H **37**
Boleyn Dri. *W Mol* 7K **101**
Boleyn Gdns. *Dag* 3A **66**
Boleyn Gdns. *W Wick* 4M **125**
Boleyn Gro. *W Wick* 4A **126**
Boleyn Ho. E16 2E **78** (off Southey M.)
Boleyn Rd. *E6* 5H **63**
Boleyn Rd. *E7* 3E **62**
Boleyn Rd. *N16* 1C **60**
Boleyn Way. *Barn* 5A **14**
Boleyn Way. *Ilf* 6A **32**
Bolina Rd. *SE16* 6G **77**
Bolingbroke Gro. *SW11* 3C **90**
Bolingbroke Rd. *W14* 4H **73**
Bolingbroke Wlk. *SW11* 9B **74**
Bolingbroke Way. *Hay* 2B **68**
Bolliger Ct. *NW10* 7A **56**
Bollo Bri. Rd. *W3* 4M **71**
Bollo Ct. W3 4A **72** (off Bollo Bri. Rd.)
Bollo La. *W3 & W4* 3M **71**
Bolney Ga. *SW7* 3C **74**
Bolney St. *SW8* 8K **75**
Bolney Way. *Felt* 9J **85**
Bolsover St. *W1* 7F **58**
Bolstead Rd. *Mitc* 5F **106**
Bolster Gro. *N22* 7H **27**
Bolt Ct. *EC4* 9L **59**
Bolters La. *Bans* 6K **135**
Boltmore Clo. *NW4* 1H **41**
Bolton Clo. *SE20* 6E **108**
Bolton Clo. *Chess* 8H **119**
Bolton Cres. *SE5* 8M **75**
Bolton Gdns. *NW10* 5H **57**
Bolton Gdns. *SW5* 6M **73**
Bolton Gdns. *Brom* 3D **110**
Bolton Gdns. *Tedd* 3E **102**
Bolton Gdns. M. *SW10* 6A **74**
Bolton Ho. SE10 6C **78** (off Trafalgar Rd.)
Bolton Pl. NW8 4M **57** (off Bolton Rd.)
Bolton Rd. *E15* 2D **62**
Bolton Rd. *N18* 5D **28**
Bolton Rd. *NW8* 4M **57**
Bolton Rd. *NW10* 4C **56**
Bolton Rd. *W4* 8A **72**
Bolton Rd. *Chess* 8H **119**
Bolton Rd. *Harr* 2A **38**
Boltons Ct. SW5 6M **73** (off Old Brompton Rd.)
Bolton's La. *Hay* 8M **143**
Boltons Pl. *SW5* 6A **74**
Boltons, The. *SW10* 6A **74**
Boltons, The. *Wemb* 9D **38**
Bolton St. *W1* 2F **74**
Bolton Studios. *SW10* 6A **74**
Bolton Wlk. N7 7K **43** (off Durham Rd.)
Bombay St. *SE16* 5F **76**
Bomer Clo. *W Dray* 8L **143**
Bomore Rd. *W11* 1J **73**
Bonar Pl. *Chst* 4J **111**
Bonar Rd. *SE15* 8E **76**
Bonchester Clo. *Chst* 4L **111**
Bonchurch Clo. *Sutt* 9M **121**
Bonchurch Ct. *Purf* 6M **83**
Bonchurch Rd. *W10* 8J **57**
Bonchurch Rd. *W13* 2F **70**
Bond Clo. *W Dray* 9D **142**
Bond Ct. *EC4* 1B **76**
Bondfield Av. *Hay* 6E **52**
Bondfield Rd. *E6* 8K **63**
Bondfield Wlk. *Dart* 3K **99**
Bond Gdns. *Wall* 6G **123**
Bond Ho. NW6 5K **57** (off Rupert Rd.)
Bond Ho. SE14 8J **77** (off Goodwood Rd.)
Bonding Yd. Wlk. *SE16* 4J **77**
Bond Rd. *Mitc* 6C **106**
Bond Rd. *Surb* 4K **119**
Bond Rd. *Warl* 9H **139**
Bond St. *E15* 1C **62**
Bond St. *W4* 5B **72**
Bond St. *W5* 1H **71**
Bondway. *SW8* 7J **75**
Boneta Rd. *SE18* 4K **79**
Bonfield Rd. *SE13* 3A **94**
Bonham Gdns. *Dag* 7H **49**
Bonham Rd. *SW2* 4K **91**
Bonham Rd. *Dag* 7H **49**
Bonheur Rd. *W4* 3B **72**
Bonhill St. *EC2* 7B **60**
Boniface Gdns. *Harr* 7M **21**
Boniface Rd. *Uxb* 8A **36**
Boniface Wlk. *Harr* 7M **21**
Bonington Rd. *Horn* 1H **67**
Bonita M. *SE4* 2H **93**
Bon Marche Ter. M. *SE27* 1C **108**
Bonner Ct. Chesh 1D **6** (off Coopers Wlk.)
Bonner Hill Rd. *King T* 6K **103** (in two parts)
Bonner Rd. *E2* 5G **61**
Bonnersfield Clo. *Harr* 4D **38**
Bonnersfield La. *Harr* 4D **38**
Bonner St. *E2* 5G **61**
Bonnett M. *Horn* 6J **51**
Bonneville Gdns. *SW4* 5G **91**
Bonney Gro. *G Oak* 3A **6**
Bonney Way. *Swan* 6C **114**
Bonnington Ct. N'holt 5H **53** (off Gallery Gdns.)
Bonnington Ho. *N1* 5K **59**
Bonnington Sq. *SW8* 7K **75**
Bonny St. *NW1* 3G **59**
Bonser Rd. *Twic* 8D **86**
Bonsey's Yd. *Uxb* 3B **142**
Bonsor Ho. *SW8* 9G **75**
Bonsor St. *SE5* 8C **76**
Bonville Gdns. *NW4* 2F **40**
Bonville Rd. *Brom* 2D **110**
Bookbinders Cottage Homes. *N20* 3D **26**
Booker Clo. *E14* 8K **61**
Booker Rd. *N18* 5E **28**
Bookham Ct. *SW19* 7B **106**
Boomes Ind. Est. *Rain* 7D **66**
Boone Ct. *N9* 3G **29**
Boones Rd. *SE13* 3C **94**
Boone St. *SE13* 3C **94**
Boord St. *SE10* 4C **78**
Boothby Ct. *E4* 3A **30**
Boothby Rd. *N19* 7H **43**
Booth Clo. *E9* 4F **60**
Booth Clo. *SE28* 2F **80**
Booth La. EC4 1A **76** (off Baynard St.)
Boothman Ho. *Kent* 1H **39**
Booth Rd. *NW9* 9B **24**
Booth Rd. *Croy* 4M **123**
Booth's Pl. *W1* 8G **59**
Boot Pde. Edgw 6L **23** (off High St.)
Boot St. *N1* 6C **60**
Bordars Rd. *W7* 8C **54**
Bordars Wlk. *W7* 8C **54**
Borden Av. *Enf* 8B **16**
Border Cres. *SE26* 2F **108**
Border Gdns. *Croy* 6M **125**
Bordergate. *Mitc* 5C **106**
Border Rd. *SE26* 2F **108**
Border's La. *Lou* 6L **19**
Bordesley Rd. *Mord* 9M **105**
Bordeston Ct. Bren 8G **71** (off Augustus Clo.)
Bordon Wlk. *SW15* 6E **88**
Boreas Wlk. N1 5M **59** (off Nelson Pl.)
Boreham Av. *E16* 9E **62**
Boreham Clo. *E11* 6A **46**
Boreham Holt. *Els* 6K **11**
Boreham Rd. *N22* 9A **28**
Borehamwood. 5L **11**
Borehamwood Enterprise Cen. *Borwd* 5K **11**
Boreham Wood F.C. 4M **11**
Borehamwood Ind. Pk. *Borwd* 4B **12**
Boreman Ho. SE10 7A **78** (off Thames St.)
Borgard Rd. *SE18* 5K **79**
Borkwood Pk. *Orp* 6D **128**
Borkwood Way. *Orp* 6C **128**
Borland Rd. *SE15* 3G **93**
Borland Rd. *Tedd* 4F **102**
Borneo St. *SW15* 2G **89**
Borough High St. *SE1* 3A **76**
Borough Hill. *Croy* 5M **123**
Borough Rd. *SE1* 4M **75**
Borough Rd. *Iswth* 9C **70**
Borough Rd. *King T* 5L **103**
Borough Rd. *Mitc* 6C **106**
Borough Sq. SE1 3A **76** (off McCoid Way)
Borough, The. 3B **76**
Borrett Clo. *SE17* 6A **76**
Borrodaile Rd. *SW18* 5M **89**
Borrowdale. NW1 6G **59** (off Robert St.)
Borrowdale Av. *Harr* 9E **22**
Borrowdale Clo. *Ilf* 2J **47**
Borrowdale Clo. *S Croy* 5D **138**
Borrowdale Ct. *Enf* 3A **16**
Borrowdale Dri. *S Croy* 4D **138**
Borthwick M. *E15* 9C **46**
Borthwick Rd. *E15* 9C **46**
Borthwick Rd. *NW9* 4D **40**
Borthwick St. *SE8* 6L **77**
Borwick Av. *E17* 1K **45**
Bosanquet Clo. *Uxb* 7B **142**
Bosbury Rd. *SE6* 9A **94**
Boscastle Rd. *NW5* 8F **42**
Boscobel Ho. *E8* 2F **60**
Boscobel Pl. *SW1* 5E **74**
Boscobel St. *NW8* 7B **58**
Bosco Clo. *Orp* 6D **128**
Boscombe Av. *E10* 5B **46**
Boscombe Av. *Horn* 5H **51**
Boscombe Clo. *E5* 1J **61**
Boscombe Gdns. *SW16* 3J **107**
Boscombe Ho. Croy 3B **124** (off Sydenham Rd.)
Boscombe Rd. *SW17* 3E **106**
Boscombe Rd. *SW19* 5M **105**
Boscombe Rd. *W12* 2E **72**
Boscombe Rd. *Wor Pk* 3G **121**
Bose Clo. *N3* 8J **25**
Bosgrove. *E4* 2A **30**
Boss Ho. SE1 3D **76** (off Boss St.)
Boss St. *SE1* 3D **76**
Bostall Hill. *SE2* 6E **80**
Bostall La. *SE2* 5F **80**
Bostall Mnr. Way. *SE2* 5F **80**
Bostall Pk. Av. *Bexh* 8J **81**
Bostall Rd. *Orp* 4F **112**
Bostock Ho. *Houn* 7L **69**
Boston Bus. Pk. *W7* 4C **70**
Boston Gdns. *W4* 7C **72**
Boston Gdns. *W7* 5E **70**
Boston Gdns. *Bren* 5E **70**
Boston Gro. *Ruis* 4A **36**
Boston Manor. 5E **70**
Boston Manor House. 6F **70**
Boston Mnr. Rd. *Bren* 5F **70**
Boston Pde. *W7* 4E **70**
Boston Pk. Rd. *Bren* 6G **71**
Boston Pl. *NW1* 7D **58**
Boston Rd. *E6* 6J **63**
Boston Rd. *E17* 4L **45**
Boston Rd. *W7* 2C **70**
Boston Rd. *Croy* 1K **123**
Boston Rd. *Edgw* 7A **24**
Bostonthorpe Rd. *W7* 3C **70**
Boston Va. *W7* 5E **70**
Bosun Clo. *E14* 3L **77**
Boswell Clo. *Orp* 1G **129**
Boswell Ct. W14 4H **73** (off Blythe Rd.)
Boswell Ct. *WC1* 8J **59**
Boswell Ct. King T 5K **103** (off Clifton Rd.)
Boswell Ho. WC1 8J **59** (off Boswell St.)
Boswell Path. *Hay* 5D **68**
Boswell Rd. *T Hth* 8A **108**
Boswell St. *WC1* 8J **59**
Bosworth Clo. *E17* 8K **29**
Bosworth Cres. *Romf* 6G **35**
Bosworth Ho. W10 7J **57** (off Bosworth Rd.)
Bosworth Ho. Eri 6C **82** (off Saltford Clo.)
Bosworth Rd. *N11* 6H **27**
Bosworth Rd. *W10* 7J **57**
Bosworth Rd. *Barn* 5L **13**
Bosworth Rd. *Dag* 8L **49**
Botany Bay. 1H **15**
Botany Bay La. *Chst* 7A **112**
Botany Clo. *Barn* 6C **14**
Botany Way. *Purf* 6M **83**
Boteley Clo. *E4* 2B **30**
Botham Clo. *Edgw* 7A **24**
Botha Rd. *E13* 8F **62**
Bothwell Clo. *E16* 8D **62**
Bothwell Rd. *New Ad* 2A **140**
Bothwell St. *W6* 7H **73**
Botolph All. EC3 1C **76** (off Botolph La.)
Botolph La. *EC3* 1C **76**
Botsford Rd. *SW20* 6J **105**
Bott Rd. *Dart* 1K **115**
Botts M. *W2* 9L **57**
Botwell Comn. Rd. *Hay* 1B **68**
Botwell Cres. *Hay* 9C **52**
Botwell La. *Hay* 1C **68**
Boucher Clo. *Tedd* 2D **102**
Bouchier Ho. *N2* 9B **26**
Bouchier Wlk. *Rain* 2E **66**
Bough Beech Ct. *Enf* 1H **17**
Boughton Av. *Brom* 2D **126**
Boughton Ho. SE1 3B **76** (off Tennis St.)
Boughton Rd. *SE28* 4C **80**
Boulcott St. *E1* 9H **61**
Boulevard Cen., The. *Borwd* 5L **11**
Boulevard, The. *SW17* 8E **90**
Boulevard, The. *SW18* 3M **89**
Boulevard, The. *Pinn* 2L **37** (in two parts)
Boulevard, The. *Wat* 7B **8**
Boulevard, The. *Wfd G* 6L **31**
Boulevard 25. *Borwd* 5L **11**
Boulmer Rd. *Uxb* 6A **142**
Boulogne Ho. SE1 4D **76** (off Abbey St.)
Boulogne Rd. *Croy* 1A **124**
Boulter Gdns. *Rain* 2E **66**
Boulter Ho. SE14 9G **77** (off Kender St.)
Boulton Ho. *Bren* 6J **71**
Boulton Rd. *Dag* 7J **49**
Boultwood Rd. *E6* 9K **63**
Bounces La. *N9* 2F **28**
Bounces Rd. *N9* 2F **28**
Boundaries Rd. *SW12* 8D **90**
Boundaries Rd. *Felt* 7G **85**
Boundary Av. *E17* 5K **45**
Boundary Bus. Ct. *Mitc* 7B **106**
Boundary Clo. *SE25* 6E **108**

Boundary Clo.—Bramble Clo.

Boundary Clo. Barn 3K 13
Boundary Clo. Ilf 9C 48
Boundary Clo. King T 7M 103
Boundary Clo. S'hall 6L 69
Boundary Ct. N18 6D 28
(off Snells Pk.)
Boundary Ho. SE5 8A 76
Boundary La. E13 6H 63
(in two parts)
Boundary La. SE17 7A 76
Boundary M. NW8 4A 58
(off Boundary Rd.)
Boundary Pas. E1 7D 60
Boundary Rd. E13 5G 63
Boundary Rd. E17 5K 45
Boundary Rd. N2 8B 26
Boundary Rd. N9 8G 17
Boundary Rd. N22 1M 43
Boundary Rd. NW8 4M 57
Boundary Rd. SW19 3B 106
Boundary Rd. Bark 5A 64
(in two parts)
Boundary Rd. Cars & Wall 8F 122
Boundary Rd. Pinn 5H 37
Boundary Rd. Romf 4E 50
Boundary Rd. Sidc 4C 96
Boundary Rd. Upm 8L 51
Boundary Rd. Wemb 8J 39
Boundary Row. SE1 3M 75
Boundary St. E2 6D 60
(in two parts)
Boundary St. Eri 8D 82
Boundary Way. Croy 7L 125
Boundary Way. Wat 5F 4
Boundfield Rd. SE6 9C 94
Bounds Green. 6H 27
Bounds Grn. Ct. N11 6H 27
(off Bounds Grn. Rd.)
Bounds Grn. Ind. Est. N11 6G 27
Bounds Grn. Rd. N11 & N22 6G 27
Bourbon Ho. SE6 2A 110
Bourchier St. W1 1H 75
(in two parts)
Bourdon Pl. W1 1F 74
(off Bourdon St.)
Bourdon Rd. SE20 6G 109
Bourdon St. W1 1F 74
Bourke Clo. NW10 2C 56
Bourke Clo. SW4 5J 91
Bourlet Clo. W1 8G 59
Bourn Av. N15 2B 44
Bourn Av. Uxb 7E 142
Bournbrook Rd. SE3 2H 95
Bourne Av. N14 2J 27
Bourne Av. Barn 7B 14
Bourne Av. Hay 4A 68
Bourne Av. Ruis 1G 53
Bournebridge. 1M 33
Bournebridge La. Stap A 1M 33
Bourne Cir. Hay 4A 68
Bourne Clo. Th Dit 4D 118
Bourne Ct. W4 7A 72
Bourne Ct. S Ruis 1F 52
Bourne Ct. Wfd G 1H 47
Bourne Dri. Mitc 6B 106
Bourne End. Horn 5L 51
Bourne End Rd. N'wd 4C 20
Bourne Est. EC1 8L 59
Bourne Gdns. E4 4M 29
Bournehall. Bush 8L 9
Bournehall Av. Bush 7L 9
Bournehall La. Bush 8L 9
Bourne Hall Mus. 1D 134
Bournehall Rd. Bush 8L 9
Bourne Hill. N14 2J 27
Bourne Hill Clo. N13 2K 27
Bourne Ind. Pk., The. Dart 4C 98
Bourne Mead. Bex 4A 98
Bournemead Av. N'holt 5E 52
Bournemead Clo. N'holt 6E 52
Bournemead Way. N'holt 5F 52
Bourne M. W1 9E 58
Bournemouth Clo. SE15 1E 92
Bournemouth Rd. SE15 1E 92
Bournemouth Rd. SW19 5L 105
Bourne Pde. Bex 6M 97
Bourne Pk. Clo. Kenl 8C 138
Bourne Pl. W4 6B 72
Bourne Rd. E7 8D 46
Bourne Rd. N8 4J 43
Bourne Rd. Bex & Dart 6M 97
Bourne Rd. Brom 8H 111
Bourne Rd. Bush 7L 9
Bournes Ho. N15 4C 44
(off Chisley Rd.)
Bourneside Cres. N14 1H 27
Bourneside Gdns. SE6 2A 110
Bourne St. SW1 5E 74
Bourne St. Croy 4M 123
Bourne Ter. W2 8M 57
Bourne, The. N14 1H 27
Bourne Va. Brom 3D 126
Bournevale Rd. SW16 1J 107
Bourne Vw. Gnfd 2D 54
Bourne Vw. Kenl 7B 138
Bourne Way. Brom 4D 126
Bourne Way. Eps 6A 120
Bourne Way. Sutt 7K 121
Bourne Way. Swan 7A 114
Bournewood Rd. SE18 8E 80
Bournewood Rd. Orp 2F 128
Bournville Rd. SE6 6L 93
Bournwell Clo. Barn 5D 14
Bourton Clo. Hay 2E 68
Bousfield Rd. SE14 1H 93
Boutflower Rd. SW11 3C 90
Boutique Hall. SE13 3A 94
Bouverie Gdns. Harr 4H 39
Bouverie Gdns. Purl 6K 137
Bouverie M. N16 7C 44
Bouverie Pl. W2 9B 58
Bouverie Rd. N16 7C 44
Bouverie Rd. Harr 4A 38
Bouverie St. EC4 9L 59
Bouvier Rd. Enf 2G 17
Boveney Rd. SE23 6H 93
Bovill Rd. SE23 6H 93
Bovingdon Av. Wemb 2L 55
Bovingdon Clo. N19 7G 43
Bovingdon Cres. Wat 7H 5
Bovingdon La. NW9 8C 24
Bovingdon Rd. SW6 9M 73
Bovingdon Sq. Mitc 8J 107
Bow. 6L 61
Bow Arrow La. Dart 5L 99
(in two parts)
Bowater Clo. NW9 3B 40
Bowater Clo. SW2 5J 91
Bowater Gdns. Sun 6G 101
Bowater Ho. EC1 7A 60
(off Golden La. Est.)
Bowater Pl. SE3 8F 78
Bowater Rd. SE18 4H 79
Bow Bri. Est. E3 6M 61
Bow Brook, The. E2 5H 61
(off Mace St.)
Bow Chyd. EC4 9A 60
(off Cheapside)
Bow Common. 8L 61
Bow Comn. La. E3 7K 61
Bowden Clo. Felt 7C 84
Bowden Dri. Horn 6J 51
Bowden St. SE11 6L 75
Bowditch. SE8 5K 77
(in two parts)
Bowdon Rd. E17 5L 45
Bowen Dri. SE21 9C 92
Bowen Rd. Harr 5A 38
Bowen St. E14 9M 61
Bowens Wood. Croy 1K 139
Bower Av. SE10 9C 78
Bower Clo. N'holt 5G 53
Bower Clo. Romf 7B 34
Bower Ct. E4 1A 30
(off Ridgeway, The)
Bowerdean St. SW6 9M 73
Bower Farm Rd. Hav 3A 34
Bower Ho. SE14 9H 77
(off Besson St.)
Bower La. Eyns & Knat 4J 131
Bowerman Av. SE14 7J 77
Bowerman Ct. N19 7H 43
(off St John's Way)
Bower Rd. Swan 4E 114
Bower St. E1 9H 61
Bowers Wlk. E6 9K 63
Bowes Clo. Sidc 5F 96
Bowes Ct. Dart 5M 99
(off Osbourne Rd.)
Bowe's Ho. Bark 3M 63
Bowes-Lyon Hall. E16 2E 78
(off Wesley Av., in two parts)
Bowes Park. 7J 27
Bowes Rd. N11 & N13 5G 27
Bowes Rd. W3 1C 72
Bowes Rd. Dag 9G 49
Bowes Rd. W on T 4F 116
Bowfell Rd. W6 7G 73
Bowford Av. Bexh 9J 81
Bowhill Clo. SW9 8L 75
Bowie Clo. SW4 6H 91
Bow Ind. Pk. E15 3L 61
Bow Interchange (Junct.) 6A 62
Bowland Rd. SW4 3H 91
Bowland Rd. Wfd G 5G 31
Bowland Yd. SW1 3D 74
(off Kinnerton St.)
Bow La. EC4 9A 60
Bow La. N12 7A 26
Bow La. Mord 1J 121
Bowl Ct. EC2 7C 60
Bowles Grn. Enf 9B 6
Bowles Rd. SE1 7E 76
Bowley Clo. SE19 3D 108
Bowley Ho. SE16 4E 76
Bowley La. SE19 2D 108
Bowling Clo. Uxb 4D 142
Bowling Ct. Wat 6E 8
Bowling Grn. Clo. SW15 6F 88
Bowling Grn. Ct. Wemb 7K 39
Bowling Grn. La. EC1 7L 59
Bowling Grn. Pl. SE1 3B 76
Bowling Grn. Row. SE18 4K 79
Bowling Grn. St. SE11 7L 75
Bowling Grn. Wlk. N1 6C 60
Bowls Clo. Stan 5F 22
Bowls, The. Chig 3C 32
Bowman Av. E16 1D 78
Bowman M. SW18 7K 89
Bowmans. 6D 98
Bowman's Bldgs. NW1 8C 58
(off Penfold Pl.)
Bowmans Clo. W13 2F 70
Bowmans Grn. Wat 9J 5
Bowmans Lea. SE23 6G 93
Bowmans Mdw. Wall 5F 122
Bowman's M. E1 1E 76
Bowman's M. N7 8J 43
Bowman's Pl. N7 8J 43
Bowman's Rd. Dart 6D 98
Bowman Trad. Est. NW9 2L 39
Bowmead. SE9 8K 95
Bowmore Wlk. NW1 3H 59
Bowness Clo. E8 2D 60
(off Beechwood Rd.)
Bowness Cres. SW15 2C 104
Bowness Dri. Houn 3J 85
Bowness Ho. SE15 8G 77
(off Hillbeck Clo.)
Bowness Rd. SE6 6M 93
Bowness Rd. Bexh 1M 97
Bowness Way. Horn 1E 66
Bowood Rd. SW11 4E 90
Bowood Rd. Enf 4H 17
Bowring Grn. Wat 5G 21
Bow Rd. E3 6K 61
Bowrons Av. Wemb 3H 55
Bowry Ho. E14 8K 61
(off Wallwood St.)
Bowsley Ct. Felt 8E 84
Bowsprit Point. E14 4L 77
(off Westferry Rd.)
Bow St. E15 1C 62
Bow St. WC2 9J 59
Bow Triangle Bus. Cen. E3 7L 61
Bowyer Clo. E6 8K 63
Bowyer Ho. N1 4C 60
(off Whitmore Est.)
Bowyer Pl. SE5 8A 76
Bowyers Clo. Asht 9K 133
Bowyer St. SE5 8A 76
Boxall Rd. SE21 5C 92
Boxelder Clo. Edgw 5A 24
Boxford Clo. S Croy 4H 139
Boxgrove Rd. SE2 3F 80
Box La. Bark 5F 64
Boxley Rd. Mord 8A 106
Boxley St. E16 2F 78
Boxmoor Ho. W11 2H 73
(off Queensdale Cres.)
Boxmoor Rd. Harr 2F 38
Boxmoor Rd. Romf 5A 34
Boxoll Rd. Dag 9K 49
Box Ridge Av. Purl 4K 137
Boxted Clo. Buck H 1J 31
Box Tree Ho. SE8 7J 77
Boxtree La. Harr 8A 22
Boxtree Rd. Harr 7B 22
Box Tree Wlk. Orp 3H 129
Boxwood Clo. W Dray 3K 143
Boxwood Way. Warl 9H 139
Boxworth Clo. N12 5B 26
Boxworth Gro. N1 4K 59
Boyard Rd. SE18 6M 79
Boyce Clo. Borwd 3J 11
Boyce Ho. W10 6K 57
(off Bruckner St.)
Boyce Way. E13 7E 62
Boycroft Av. NW9 4A 40
Boyd Av. S'hall 2K 69
Boyd Clo. King T 4L 103
Boydell Ct. NW8 3B 58
(in two parts)
Boyden Ho. E17 1A 46
Boyd Rd. SW19 3B 106
Boyd St. E1 9E 60
Boyfield St. SE1 3M 75
Boyland Rd. Brom 2D 110
Boyle Av. Stan 6E 22
Boyle Clo. Uxb 5D 142
Boyle Farm Rd. Th Dit 1E 118
Boyle St. W1 1G 75
Boyne Av. NW4 2H 41
Boyne Rd. SE13 2A 94
Boyne Rd. Dag 8L 49
Boyne Ter. M. W11 2K 73
Boyseland Ct. Edgw 2A 24
Boyson Rd. SE17 7A 76
(in two parts)
Boyson Wlk. SE17 7B 76
Boyton Clo. E1 7G 61
Boyton Clo. N8 1J 43
Boyton Ho. NW8 5B 58
(off Wellington Rd.)
Boyton Rd. N8 1J 43
Brabant Ct. EC3 1C 76
(off Philpot La.)
Brabant Rd. N22 9K 27
Brabazon Av. Wall 9J 123
Brabazon Rd. Houn 8G 69
Brabazon Rd. N'holt 5L 53
Brabazon St. E14 9M 61
Brabner Ho. E2 6E 60
(off Wellington Row)
Brabourne Clo. SE19 2C 108
Brabourne Cres. Bexh 7K 81
Brabourne Heights. NW7 3C 24
Brabourne Ri. Beck 9A 110
Brabourn Gro. SE15 1G 93
Brabrook Ct. Wall 6F 122
Brabstone Ho. Gnfd 5D 54
Bracer Ho. N1 5C 60
(off Whitmore Est.)
Bracewell Av. Gnfd 1D 54
Bracewell Rd. W10 8G 57
Bracewood Gdns. Croy 5D 124
Bracey M. N4 7J 43
Bracey St. N4 7J 43
Bracken Av. SW12 5E 90
Bracken Av. Croy 5L 125
Brackenbridge Dri. Ruis 8H 37
Brackenbury. N4 6L 43
(off Osborne Rd.)
Brackenbury Gdns. W6 4F 72
Brackenbury Rd. N2 1A 42
Brackenbury Rd. W6 4F 72
Bracken Clo. E6 8K 63
Bracken Clo. Borwd 3M 11
Bracken Clo. Sun 3D 100
Bracken Clo. Twic 6L 85
Bracken Ct. Ilf 6D 32
Brackendale. N21 2K 27
Brackendale Clo. Houn 9M 69
Brackendale Gdns. Upm 9M 51
Brackendene. Brick W 3K 5
Brackendene. Dart 1C 114
Bracken Dri. Chig 6M 31
Bracken End. Iswth 4B 86
Brackenfield Clo. E5 8F 44
Bracken Gdns. SW13 1E 88
Brackenhill. Ruis 9J 37
Bracken Hill Clo. Brom 5D 110
Bracken Hill La. Brom 5D 110
Bracken Ho. E3 8L 61
(off Devons Rd.)
Bracken Ind. Est. Ilf 7C 32
Bracken M. E4 1A 30
Bracken M. Romf 4M 49
Bracken Path. Eps 5M 133
Brackens. Beck 4L 109
Brackens, The. Enf 9C 16
Brackens, The. Orp 7E 128
Bracken, The. E4 2A 30
Brackenwood. Sun 5E 100
Brackenwood Lodge. Barn 6L 13
(off Prospect Rd.)
Brackley. Wey 7B 116
Brackley Clo. Wall 9J 123
Brackley Ct. NW8 7B 58
(off Henderson Dri.)
Brackley Rd. W4 6C 72
Brackley Rd. Beck 4K 109
Brackley Sq. Wfd G 7H 31
Brackley St. EC1 7A 60
Brackley Ter. W4 6C 72
Bracklyn Ct. N1 5B 60
Bracklyn St. N1 5B 60
Bracknell Clo. N22 8L 27
Bracknell Gdns. NW3 9M 41
Bracknell Ga. NW3 1M 57
Bracknell Way. NW3 9M 41
Bracondale. Esh 7A 118
Bracondale Rd. SE2 5E 80
Bracton La. Bex 8D 98
Bradbeer Ho. E2 6G 61
(off Cornwall Av.)
Bradbourne Rd. Bex 6L 97
Bradbourne St. SW6 1L 89
Bradbury Clo. Borwd 3M 11
Bradbury Clo. S'hall 5K 69
Bradbury M. N16 1C 60
(off Bradbury St.)
Bradbury St. N16 1C 60
Braddock Clo. Iswth 1D 86
Braddon Ct. Barn 5J 13
Braddon Rd. Rich 2K 87
Braddyll St. SE10 6C 78
Bradenham. SE17 7B 76
(off Bradenham Clo.)
Bradenham Av. Well 3E 96
Bradenham Clo. SE17 7B 76
Bradenham Rd. Harr 2F 38
Bradenham Rd. Hay 6C 52
Braden St. W9 7M 57
Bradfield Ct. NW1 3F 58
(off Hawley Rd.)
Bradfield Dri. Bark 1E 64
Bradfield Rd. E16 3E 78
Bradfield Rd. Ruis 1J 53
Bradford Clo. N17 6D 28
Bradford Clo. SE26 1F 108
Bradford Clo. Brom 3K 127
Bradford Dri. Eps 8D 120
Bradford Ho. W14 4H 73
(off Spring Va. Ter.)
Bradford Rd. W3 3C 72
Bradford Rd. Ilf 6B 48
Bradgate Rd. SE6 5M 93
Brading Cres. E11 7F 46
Brading Rd. SW2 6K 91
Brading Rd. Croy 1K 123
Brading Ter. W12 4E 72
Bradiston Rd. W9 6K 57
Bradley Clo. N7 2J 59
Bradley Clo. Belm 2M 135
Bradley Ct. Enf 2J 17
(off Bradley Rd.)
Bradley Gdns. W13 9F 54
Bradley Ho. E2 5E 60
(off Claredale St.)
Bradley Ho. SE16 5G 77
(off Raymouth Rd.)
Bradley M. SW17 7D 90
Bradley Rd. N22 9K 27
Bradley Rd. SE19 3A 108
Bradley Rd. Enf 2J 17
Bradley Rd. Wal A 8J 7
Bradley's Clo. N1 5L 59
Bradley Stone Rd. E6 8K 63
Bradman Row. Edgw 7A 24
Bradmead. SW8 8F 74
Bradmore Pk. Rd. W6 5F 72
Bradmore Way. Coul 9J 137
Bradshaw Clo. SW19 3L 105
Bradshawe Waye. Uxb 8D 142
Bradshaw Rd. Wat 3G 9
Bradshaws Clo. SE25 7E 108
Bradstock Ho. E9 3H 61
Bradstock Rd. E9 2H 61
Bradstock Rd. Eps 7E 120
Brad St. SE1 2L 75
Bradwell Av. Dag 7L 49
Bradwell Clo. E18 2D 46
Bradwell Clo. Horn 2F 66
Bradwell Ho. NW6 4M 57
(off Mortimer Cres.)
Bradwell M. N18 4E 28
Bradwell Rd. Buck H 9J 19
Brady Av. Lou 4M 19
Brady Ct. Dag 6H 49
Brady Ho. SW8 9G 75
(off Corunna Rd.)
Bradymead. E6 9L 63
Brady St. E1 7F 60
Braeburn Ct. Barn 6B 14
Braemar Av. N22 8J 27
Braemar Av. NW10 8B 40
Braemar Av. SW19 8L 89
Braemar Av. Bexh 3A 98
Braemar Av. S Croy 2A 138
Braemar Av. T Hth 7L 107
Braemar Av. Wemb 3H 55
Braemar Clo. SE16 6F 76
(off Masters Dri.)
Braemar Ct. SE6 7D 94
Braemar Gdns. NW9 8B 24
Braemar Gdns. Horn 4L 51
Braemar Gdns. Sidc 9B 96
Braemar Gdns. W Wick 3A 126
Braemar Ho. W9 6A 58
(off Maida Va.)
Braemar Rd. E13 7D 62
Braemar Rd. N15 3C 44
Braemar Rd. Bren 7H 71
Braemar Rd. Wor Pk 5F 120
Braeside. Beck 2L 109
Braeside Av. SW19 5J 105
Braeside Clo. Pinn 7L 21
Braeside Cres. Bexh 3A 98
Braeside Rd. SW16 4G 107
Braes St. N1 3M 59
Braesyde Clo. Belv 5K 81
Brafferton Rd. Croy 6A 124
Braganza St. SE17 6M 75
Bragg Clo. Dag 2F 64
Bragg Rd. Tedd 3C 102
Braham Ho. SE11 6K 75
Braham St. E1 9D 60
Braid Av. W3 9C 56
Braid Clo. Felt 8K 85
Braid Ho. SE10 9A 78
(off Blackheath Hill)
Braidwood Pas. EC1 8A 60
(off Aldersgate St.)
Braidwood Rd. SE6 7B 94
Brailsford Clo. SW19 4C 106
Brailsford Rd. SW2 4L 91
Brainton Av. Felt 6F 84
Braintree Av. Ilf 2J 47
Braintree Ho. E1 7G 61
(off Malcolm Rd.)
Braintree Rd. Dag 8L 49
Braintree Rd. Ruis 9F 36
Braintree St. E2 6G 61
Braithwaite Av. Romf 5L 49
Braithwaite Gdns. Stan 8G 23
Braithwaite Ho. E14 9B 62
Braithwaite Ho. EC1 7B 60
(off Bunhill Row)
Braithwaite Rd. Enf 5K 17
Braithwaite Tower. W2 8B 58
(off Hall Pl.)
Bramah Grn. SW9 9L 75
Bramah Tea & Coffee Mus. 3D 76
(off Maguire St.)
Bramalea Clo. N6 4E 42
Bramall Clo. E15 1D 62
Bramall Ct. N7 1K 59
(off George's Rd.)
Bramber. WC1 6J 59
(off Cromer St.)
Bramber Ct. W5 5J 71
Bramber Ct. Dart 5M 99
(off Bow Arrow La.)
Bramber Rd. N12 5C 26
Bramber Rd. W14 7K 73
Brambleacres Clo. Sutt 9L 121
Bramble Banks. Cars 1E 136
Bramblebury Rd. SE18 6A 80
Bramble Clo. N15 2E 44

Bramble Clo.—Briar Way

Bramble Clo. Beck 9A 110
Bramble Clo. Croy 6L 125
Bramble Clo. Shep 7B 100
Bramble Clo. Stan 7H 23
Bramble Clo. Uxb 9D 142
Bramble Clo. Wat 7E 4
Bramble Ct. Ilf 6D 32
Bramble Cft. Eri 5A 82
Brambledown Clo. W Wick 9C 110
Brambledown Rd. Cars & Wall 9E 122
Brambledown Rd. S Croy 9C 124
Bramble Gdns. W12 1D 72
Bramble Ho. E3 8L 61 (off Devons Rd.)
Bramble La. Hamp 3K 101
Brambles Clo. Iswth 8F 70
Brambles Farm Dri. Uxb 6E 142
Brambles, The. SW19 2K 105 (off Woodside)
Brambles, The. Chesh 4D 6
Brambles, The. Chig 5A 32
Brambles, The. W Dray 5J 143
Bramble Wlk. Eps 6M 133
Bramblewood Clo. Cars 3C 122
Brambling Clo. Bush 6J 9
Brambling Ct. SE8 7K 77 (off Abinger Gro.)
Bramblings, The. E4 4B 30
Bramcote Av. Mitc 8D 106
Bramcote Gro. SE16 6G 77
Bramcote Rd. SW15 3F 88
Bramdean Cres. SE12 7E 94
Bramdean Gdns. SE12 7E 94
Bramerton. NW6 3H 57 (off Willesden La.)
Bramerton Rd. Beck 7K 109
Bramerton St. SW3 7C 74
Bramfield. Wat 7J 5
Bramfield Ct. N4 8A 44 (off Queens Dri.)
Bramfield Rd. SW11 5C 90
Bramford Ct. N14 2H 27
Bramford Rd. SW18 3A 90
Bramham Ct. N'wd 6C 20
Bramham Gdns. SW5 6M 73
Bramham Gdns. Chess 6H 119
Bramham Ho. SE15 2D 92
Bramhope La. SE7 7F 78
Bramlands Clo. SW11 2C 90
Bramleas. Wat 7D 8
Bramley Av. Coul 7G 137
Bramley Av. Shep 7C 100
Bramley Clo. E17 9J 29
Bramley Clo. N14 7F 14
Bramley Clo. Eastc 1D 36
Bramley Clo. Hay 1E 68
Bramley Clo. Orp 3M 127
Bramley Clo. S Croy 7A 124
Bramley Clo. Swan 8C 114
Bramley Clo. Twic 5A 86
Bramley Clo. Wfd G 7G 31
Bramley Ct. E4 1A 30 (off Ridgeway, The)
Bramley Ct. Barn 6C 14
Bramley Ct. Mitc 6B 106
Bramley Ct. S'hall 1A 70 (off Baird Av.)
Bramley Ct. Wat 5F 4
Bramley Ct. Well 9F 80
Bramley Cres. SW8 8H 75
Bramley Cres. Ilf 4L 47
Bramley Gdns. Wat 5G 21
Bramley Hill. S Croy 7M 123
Bramley Ho. SW15 5D 88 (off Tunworth Cres.)
Bramley Ho. W10 9H 57
Bramley Ho. Houn 3K 85
Bramley Ho. Ct. Enf 1B 16
Bramleyhyrst. S Croy 6A 124 (off Bramley Hill)
Bramley Pde. N14 6G 15
Bramley Pl. Dart 3E 98
Bramley Rd. N14 7F 14
Bramley Rd. W5 4G 71
Bramley Rd. W10 9H 57 (in two parts)
Bramley Rd. Cheam 1H 135
Bramley Rd. Sutt 7B 122
Bramley Shaw. Wal A 6M 7
Bramley Way. Asht 9K 133
Bramley Way. Houn 4K 85
Bramley Way. W Wick 4M 125
Brampton. WC1 8K 59 (off Red Lion Sq.)
Brampton Clo. E5 7F 44
Brampton Clo. Chesh 1A 6
Brampton Ct. NW4 2F 40
Brampton Gdns. N15 3A 44
Brampton Gdns. W on T 7G 117
Brampton Gro. NW4 2F 40
Brampton Gro. Harr 2E 38
Brampton Gro. Wemb 6L 39
Brampton La. NW4 2G 41
Brampton Pk. Rd. N8 1L 43
Brampton Rd. E6 6H 63
Brampton Rd. N15 3A 44
Brampton Rd. NW9 2L 39
Brampton Rd. SE2 & Bexh 7G 81
Brampton Rd. Croy 2D 124
Brampton Rd. Uxb 5F 142
Brampton Rd. Wat 3E 20
Brampton Ter. Borwd 2L 11 (off Stapleton Rd.)
Bramshaw Gdns. Wat 5H 21
Bramshaw Ri. N Mald 1C 120
Bramshaw Rd. E9 2H 61
Bramshill Clo. Chig 5C 32
Bramshill Gdns. NW5 8F 42
Bramshill Rd. NW10 5D 56
Bramshot Av. SE7 7E 78
Bramshot Way. Wat 2E 20
Bramshurst. NW8 4M 57 (off Abbey Rd.)
Bramston Clo. Ilf 6D 32
Bramston Rd. NW10 5E 56
Bramston Rd. SW17 9A 90
Bramwell Clo. Sun 6H 101
Bramwell Ho. SE1 4A 76
Bramwell Ho. SW1 6G 75 (off Churchill Gdns.)
Bramwell M. N1 4K 59
Brancaster Dri. NW7 7E 24
Brancaster Ho. E1 6H 61 (off Moody St.)
Brancaster La. Purl 2A 138
Brancaster Pl. Lou 5K 19
Brancaster Rd. E12 9K 47
Brancaster Rd. SW16 9J 91
Brancaster Rd. Ilf 4C 48
Brancepeth Gdns. Buck H 2E 30
Branch Hill. NW3 8A 42
Branch Hill Ho. NW3 8M 41
Branch Pl. N1 4B 60
Branch Rd. E14 1J 77
Branch Rd. Ilf 5F 32
Branch St. SE15 8C 76
Brancker Clo. Wall 9J 123
Brancker Rd. Harr 1H 39
Brancroft Way. Enf 3J 17
Brand Clo. N4 6M 43
Brandesbury Sq. Wfd G 7L 31
Brandlehow Rd. SW15 3K 89
Brandon. NW9 9D 24 (off Further Acre)
Brandon Est. SE17 7M 75
Brandon Ho. Beck 2M 109 (off Beckenham Hill Rd.)
Brandon Mans. W14 7J 73 (off Queen's Club Gdns.)
Brandon M. EC2 8B 60 (off Silk St.)
Brandon Rd. E17 2A 46
Brandon Rd. N7 3J 59
Brandon Rd. Dart 6L 99
Brandon Rd. S'hall 6K 69
Brandon Rd. Sutt 6M 121
Brandon St. SE17 5A 76 (in three parts)
Brandram M. SE13 3C 94 (off Brandram Rd.)
Brandram Rd. SE13 2C 94
Brandreth Ct. Harr 4D 38
Brandreth Rd. E6 9K 63
Brandreth Rd. SW17 8F 90
Brandries, The. Wall 5H 123
Brand St. SE10 8A 78
Brandt Ct. Borwd 4B 12 (off Elstree Way)
Brandville Gdns. Ilf 2M 47
Brandville Rd. W Dray 3J 143
Brandy Way. Sutt 9L 121
Branfill Rd. Upm 7M 51
Brangbourne Rd. Brom 2A 110
Brangton Rd. SE11 6K 75
Brangwyn Ct. W14 4J 73 (off Blythe Rd.)
Brangwyn Cres. SW19 5A 106
Branham Ho. SE18 6M 79
Branksea St. SW6 8J 73
Branksome Av. N18 6D 28
Branksome Clo. Tedd 1B 102
Branksome Clo. W on T 4H 117
Branksome Ho. SW8 8K 75 (off Meadow Rd.)
Branksome Rd. SW2 4J 91
Branksome Rd. SW19 5L 105
Branksome Way. Harr 4K 39
Branksome Way. N Mald 5A 104
Branksone Ct. N2 1A 42
Bransby Rd. Chess 8J 119
Branscombe. NW1 4G 59 (off Plender St.)
Branscombe Ct. Brom 9D 110
Branscombe Gdns. N21 9L 15
Branscombe St. SE13 2M 93
Bransdale Clo. NW6 4L 57
Bransell Clo. Swan 1A 130
Bransgrove Rd. Edgw 8K 23
Branston Cres. Orp 3B 128
Branstone Ct. Purf 6M 83
Branstone Rd. Rich 9K 71
Brants Wlk. W7 7C 54
Brantwood Av. Eri 8A 82
Brantwood Av. Iswth 3E 86
Brantwood Clo. E17 1M 45
Brantwood Gdns. Enf 6J 15
Brantwood Gdns. Ilf 2J 47
Brantwood Ho. SE5 8A 76 (off Wyndam Est.)
Brantwood Rd. N17 6E 28
Brantwood Rd. SE24 4A 92
Brantwood Rd. Bexh 1M 97
Brantwood Rd. S Croy 1A 138
Brantwood Way. Orp 7G 113
Branxholme Ct. Brom 5D 110 (off Highland Rd.)
Brasenose Dri. SW13 7G 73
Brasher Clo. Gnfd 1B 54
Brassett Point. E15 4C 62 (off Abbey Rd.)
Brassey Clo. Felt 7E 84
Brassey Ho. E14 5M 77 (off Cahir St.)
Brassey Rd. NW6 2K 57
Brassey Sq. SW11 2E 90
Brassie Av. W3 9C 56
Brass Talley All. SE16 3H 77
Brasted Clo. SE26 1G 109
Brasted Clo. Bexh 4H 97
Brasted Clo. Orp 4D 128
Brasted Clo. Sutt 2L 135
Brasted Lodge. Beck 4L 109
Brasted Rd. Eri 8C 82
Brathay. NW1 5G 59 (off Ampthill Est.)
Brathway Rd. SW18 6L 89
Bratley St. E1 7E 60
Bratten Ct. Croy 1B 124
Braund Av. Gnfd 7M 53
Braundton Av. Sidc 7D 96
Braunston Dri. Hay 7J 53
Bravington Pl. W9 7K 57
Bravington Rd. W9 5K 57
Brawne Ho. SE17 7M 75 (off Brandon Est.)
Braxfield Rd. SE4 3J 93
Braxted Pk. SW16 3K 107
Bray. NW3 3C 58
Brayards Rd. SE15 1F 92
Brayards Rd. Est. SE15 1G 93 (off Brayards Rd.)
Braybourne Clo. Uxb 2A 142
Braybourne Dri. Iswth 8D 70
Braybrooke Gdns. SE19 4C 108
Braybrook St. W12 8D 56
Brayburne Av. SW4 1G 91
Bray Clo. Borwd 3A 12
Bray Ct. SW16 2J 107
Braycourt Av. W on T 2F 116
Bray Cres. SE16 3H 77
Braydon Rd. N16 6E 44
Bray Dri. E16 1D 78
Brayfield Ter. N1 3L 59
Brayford Sq. E1 9G 61
Bray Lodge. Chesh 1E 6 (off High St.)
Bray Pas. E16 1E 78
Bray Pl. SW3 5D 74
Bray Rd. NW7 6H 25
Brays Springs. Wal A 7L 7
Brayton Gdns. Enf 6H 15
Braywood Rd. SE9 3B 96
Brazil Clo. Bedd 2J 123
Breach Barns La. Wal A 3M 7
Breach La. Dag 6L 65
Bread St. EC4 9A 60 (in two parts)
Breakfield. Coul 8J 137
Breakspear Ct. Ab L 3D 4
Breakspear Crematorium. Ruis 3A 36
Breakspeare Clo. Wat 2F 8
Breakspeare Rd. Ab L 4C 4
Breakspear Ho. Ruis 3B 36
Breakspear Rd. Ruis 5A 36
Breakspears Dri. Orp 5E 112
Breakspears M. SE4 1K 93
Breakspears Rd. SE4 3K 93
Bream Clo. N17 2F 44
Bream Gdns. E6 6L 63
Breamore Clo. SW15 7E 88
Breamore Ho. SE15 8E 76 (off Friary Est.)
Breamore Rd. Ilf 7D 48
Bream's Bldgs. EC4 9L 59
Bream St. E3 3L 61
Breamwater Gdns. Rich 9F 86
Brearley Clo. Edgw 7A 24
Brearley Clo. Uxb 2C 142
Breasley Clo. SW15 3F 88
Breasy Pl. NW4 2F 40 (off Burroughs Gdns.)
Brechin Pl. SW7 5A 74
Brecknock Rd. N19 & N7 9G 43
Brecknock Rd. Est. N19 9G 43
Breckonmead. Brom 6G 111
Brecon Clo. Mitc 7J 107
Brecon Clo. Wor Pk 4G 121
Brecon Grn. NW9 4C 40
Brecon Ho. W2 9A 58 (off Hallfield Est.)
Brecon M. NW5 1H 59
Brecon Rd. W6 7J 73
Brecon Rd. Enf 6G 17
Brecons, The. Wey 6B 116
Brede Clo. E6 6L 63
Bredel Ho. E14 8L 61 (off St Paul's Way)
Bredgar Rd. N19 7G 43
Bredhurst Clo. SE20 3G 109
Bredo Ho. Bark 6F 64
Bredon Rd. Croy 2D 124
Bredune. Kenl 7B 138
Breer St. SW6 2M 89
Breezers Ct. E1 1E 76 (off Highway, The)
Breezer's Hill. E1 1E 76
Breeze Ter. Chesh 1D 6
Brember Rd. Harr 7A 38
Bremer M. E17 2M 45
Bremner Clo. Swan 8E 114
Bremner Rd. SW7 4A 74
Brenchley Clo. Brom 1D 126
Brenchley Clo. Chst 5L 111
Brenchley Gdns. SE23 5G 93
Brenchley Rd. Orp 6D 112
Brendans Clo. Horn 6J 51
Brenda Rd. SW17 8D 90
Brende Gdns. W Mol 8M 101
Brendon Av. NW10 9C 40
Brendon Clo. Eri 9C 82
Brendon Clo. Esh 8A 118
Brendon Clo. Hay 8A 68
Brendon Ct. S'hall 5M 69
Brendon Dri. Esh 8A 118
Brendon Gdns. Harr 9M 37
Brendon Gdns. Ilf 3C 48
Brendon Gro. N2 9A 26
Brendon Rd. SE9 8B 96
Brendon Rd. Dag 6K 49
Brendon St. W1 9C 58
Brendon Vs. N21 1A 28
Brendon Way. Enf 9C 16
Brenley Clo. Mitc 7E 106
Brenley Gdns. SE9 3H 95
Brenley Ho. SE1 3B 76 (off Tennis St.)
Brennand Ct. N19 8G 43
Brent Clo. Bex 7J 97
Brent Clo. Dart 5M 99
Brentcot Clo. W13 7F 54
Brent Ct. NW11 5H 41
Brent Ct. W7 1B 70
Brent Cres. NW10 5K 55
Brent Cross. 5G 41
Brent Cross Fly-Over. NW4 5H 41
Brent Cross Gdns. NW4 4H 41
Brent Cross Interchange (Junct.) 4G 41
Brent Cross Shop. Cen. NW4 5G 41
Brentfield. NW10 3M 55
Brentfield Clo. NW10 2B 56
Brentfield Gdns. NW2 5H 41
Brentfield Ho. NW10 3B 56
Brentfield Rd. NW10 2B 56
Brentfield Rd. Dart 5L 99
Brentford. 7H 71
Brentford Bus. Cen. Bren 8J 71
Brentford Clo. Hay 7H 53
Brentford End. 8F 70
Brentford F.C. (Griffin Pk.) 7H 71
Brentford Ho. Twic 6F 86
Brentford Musical Mus. 7J 71
Brent Grn. NW4 3G 41
Brent Grn. Wlk. Wemb 8A 40
Brentham Way. W5 7H 55
Brent Ho. E9 2G 61 (off Frampton Pk. Rd.)
Brenthouse Rd. E9 3G 61
Brenthurst Rd. NW10 2D 56
Brentlands Dri. Dart 7L 99
Brent La. Dart 6K 99
Brent Lea. Bren 8G 71
Brentmead Clo. W7 1C 70
Brentmead Gdns. NW10 5K 55
Brentmead Pl. NW11 4H 41
Brent New Enterprise Cen. NW10 2D 56
Brenton St. E14 9J 61
Brent Pk. Ind. Est. S'hall 4F 68
Brent Pk. Rd. NW4 5F 40 (in two parts)
Brent Pl. Barn 7K 13
Brent Rd. E16 9E 62
Brent Rd. SE18 8M 79
Brent Rd. Bren 7G 71
Brent Rd. S'hall 4G 69
Brent Rd. S Croy 1F 138
Brent Side. Bren 7G 71
Brentside Clo. W13 7E 54
Brentside Executive Cen. Bren 7F 70
Brent St. NW4 2G 41
Brent Ter. NW2 6G 41 (in two parts)
Brent, The. Dart 6L 99
Brent Trad. Cen. NW10 1C 56
Brentvale Av. S'hall 2B 70
Brentvale Av. Wemb 4K 55
Brent Vw. Rd. NW9 4E 40
Brentwaters Bus. Pk. Bren 8G 71
Brent Way. N3 6L 25
Brent Way. Bren 8H 71
Brent Way. Dart 5M 99
Brent Way. Wemb 2M 55
Brentwick Gdns. Bren 5J 71
Brentwood Clo. SE9 7A 96
Brentwood Ho. SE18 8H 79 (off Portway Gdns.)
Brentwood Lodge. NW4 3H 41 (off Holmdale Gdns.)
Brentwood Rd. Romf 4D 50
Brereton Rd. N17 7D 28
Bressenden Pl. SW1 4F 74
Bressey Av. Enf 3E 16
Bressey Gro. E18 9D 30
Breton Highwalk. EC1 8A 60 (off Golden La.)
Breton Ho. EC1 8A 60 (off Beech St.)
Breton Ho. SE1 4D 76 (off Abbey St.)
Brett Clo. N16 7C 44
Brett Clo. N'holt 6H 53
Brett Ct. N9 2G 29
Brett Cres. NW10 4B 56
Brettell St. SE17 6B 76
Brettenham Av. E17 8L 29
Brettenham Rd. E17 9L 29
Brettenham Rd. N18 4E 28
Brett Gdns. Dag 3J 65
Brettgrave. Eps 2A 134
Brett Ho. Chesh 1D 6
Brett Ho. Clo. SW15 6H 89
Brettinghurst. SE1 6E 76 (off Avondale Sq.)
Brett Pas. E8 1F 60
Brett Pl. Wat 1E 8
Brett Rd. E8 1F 60
Brett Rd. Barn 7G 13
Brewer's Fld. Dart 1G 115
Brewer's Grn. SW1 4H 75 (off Buckingham Ga.)
Brewer's Hall Garden. EC2 8A 60 (off London Wall)
Brewers La. Rich 4H 87
Brewer St. W1 1G 75
Brewery Clo. Wemb 1E 54
Brewery Ind. Est., The. N1 5A 60 (off Wenlock Rd.)
Brewery La. Twic 6D 86
Brewery M. Cen. Iswth 2E 86
Brewery Rd. N7 3J 59
Brewery Rd. SE18 6B 80
Brewery Rd. Brom 3J 127
Brewery Sq. SE1 3D 76 (off Horselydown La.)
Brewery, The. Romf 3C 50
Brewhouse La. E1 2F 76
Brewhouse Rd. SE18 5K 79
Brewhouse St. SW15 2J 89
Brewhouse Wlk. SE16 2J 77
Brewhouse Yd. EC1 7M 59
Brewin Ter. Hay 8G 53
Brewood Rd. Dag 2F 64
Brewster Gdns. W10 8G 57
Brewster Ho. E14 1K 77 (off Three Colt St.)
Brewster Ho. SE1 5D 76 (off Dunton Rd.)
Brewster Rd. E10 6M 45
Brian Av. S Croy 4C 138
Brian Clo. Horn 9F 50
Briane Rd. Eps 2A 134
Brian Rd. Romf 3G 49
Briant Ho. SE1 4K 75 (off Hercules Rd.)
Briants Clo. Pinn 9K 21
Briant St. SE14 9H 77
Briar Av. SW16 4K 107
Briarbank Rd. W13 9E 54
Briar Banks. Cars 1E 136
Briar Clo. N2 1M 41
Briar Clo. N13 3A 28
Briar Clo. Buck H 2H 31
Briar Clo. Chesh 2C 6
Briar Clo. Hamp 2K 101
Briar Clo. Iswth 4D 86
Briar Ct. SW15 3F 88
Briar Ct. Sutt 6G 121
Briar Cres. N'holt 2M 53
Briardale Gdns. NW3 8L 41
Briarfield Av. N2 1M 41
Briarfield Av. N3 9M 25
Briar Gdns. Brom 3D 126
Briar Gro. S Croy 5E 138
Briar Hill. Purl 3J 137
Briaris Clo. N17 7F 28
Briar La. Cars 1E 136
Briar La. Croy 6M 125
Briar Rd. NW2 9G 41
Briar Rd. SW16 7J 107
Briar Rd. Bex 9B 98
Briar Rd. Harr 3G 39
Briar Rd. Romf 7G 35
Briar Rd. Twic 7C 86
Briar Rd. Wat 7E 4
Briars Ct. Oxs 6B 132
Briars, The. Bush 9C 10
Briars, The. Chesh 4E 6
Briars Wlk. Romf 9J 35
Briarswood Way. Orp 7D 128
Briar Wlk. SW15 3F 88
Briar Wlk. W10 7J 57
Briar Wlk. Edgw 7A 24
Briar Way. W Dray 3L 143

Briarwood Clo.—Broadmead Av.

Briarwood Clo. NW9 . . . . . . .4A 40
Briarwood Clo. Felt 1C 100
Briarwood Ct. Wor Pk 3E 120
(off Avenue, The)
Briarwood Dri. N'wd 9E 20
Briarwood Rd. SW4 . . . . .4H 91
Briarwood Rd. Eps 8E 120
Briary Clo. NW3 . . . . .3C 58
Briary Ct. Sidc 2F 112
Briary Gdns. Brom 2F 110
Briary Gro. Edgw 9M 23
Briary La. N9 . . . . .3D 28
Briary Lodge. Beck 5A 110
Briavels Ct. Eps 7C 134
Brickbarn Clo. SW10 . . . . . . .8A 74
(off King's Barn)
Brick Clo. Eri 7C 82
Brick Ct. EC4 . . . . .9L 59
Brickenden Ct. Wal A 6M 7
Brickett Clo. Ruis 3A 36
Bricket Wood. 3K 5
Bricket Wood Common. 5L 5
Brick Farm Clo. Rich 9M 71
Brickfield Clo. Bren 8G 71
Brickfield Cotts. SE18 . . . . . .8D 80
Brickfield Cotts. Chst 2L 111
Brickfield Farm Gdns.
Orp 6A 128
Brickfield La. Ark 8D 12
Brickfield La. Hay 7B 68
Brickfield Rd. SW19 . . . . . .1M 105
Brickfield Rd. T Hth 5M 107
Brickfields. Harr 7B 38
(in two parts)
Brickfields Cotts. Borwd 5K 11
Brickfields Way. W Dray . . .4K 143
Brick Kiln Clo. Wat 8J 9
Brick La. E2 & E1 . . . . .6D 60
Brick La. Enf 4F 16
Brick La. Stan 7H 23
Brick Lane Music Hall. 6C 60
(off Curtain Rd.)
Bricklayer's Arms (Junct.)
. . . . .5B 76
Bricklayers Arms Bus. Cen.
SE1 . . . . .5C 76
Brick St. W1 . . . . .2F 74
Brickwall La. Ruis 6C 36
Brickwood Clo. SE26 . . . . . . .9F 92
Brickwood Rd. Croy 4C 124
Brideale Clo. SE15 . . . . .7D 76
Bride Ct. EC4 . . . . .9M 59
(off Bride La.)
Bride La. EC4 . . . . .9M 59
Bridel M. N1 . . . . .4M 59
(off Colebrook Row)
Bride St. N7 . . . . .2K 59
Bridewain St. SE1 . . . . .4D 76
(in two parts)
Bridewell Pl. E1 . . . . .2F 76
Bridewell Pl. EC4 . . . . .9M 59
Bridewell, The (Theatre)
. . . . .9M 59
(off Bridewell Pl.)
Bridford M. W1 . . . . .8F 58
Bridge App. NW1 . . . . .3E 58
Bridge Av. W6 . . . . .5G 73
Bridge Av. W7 . . . . .8B 54
Bridge Av. Upm 8L 51
Bridge Av. Mans. W6 . . . . . . .6G 73
(off Bridge Av.)
Bridge Clo. W10 . . . . .9H 57
Bridge Clo. Enf 4F 16
Bridge Clo. Romf 4C 50
Bridge Clo. Tedd 1D 102
Bridge Clo. W on T 2D 116
Bridge Ct. E10 . . . . .6K 45
Bridgedown Golf Course.
. . . . .3G 13
Bridge Dri. N13 . . . . .4K 27
Bridge End. E17 . . . . .8A 30
Bridgefield Clo. Bans 7G 135
Bridgefield Rd. Sutt 8L 121
Bridgefoot. SE1 . . . . .6J 75
Bridgefoot. Sun 5D 100
Bridgeford Ho. Wat 5F 8
Bridge Gdns. Ashf 4A 100
Bridge Gdns. E Mol 8B 102
Bridge Ga. N21 . . . . .9A 16
Bridge Ho. E9 . . . . .2H 61
(off Shepherds La.)
Bridge Ho. NW3 . . . . .3E 58
(off Adelaide Rd.)
Bridge Ho. NW10 . . . . .5H 57
(off Chamberlayne Rd.)
Bridge Ho. SE4 . . . . .3K 93
Bridge Ho. SW1 . . . . .6F 74
(off Ebury Bri.)
Bridge Ho. Dart 6J 99
Bridge Ho. Sutt 8M 121
(off Bridge Rd.)
Bridgehouse Ct. SE1 . . . . . . .3M 75
(off Blackfriars Rd.)
Bridge Ho. Quay. E14 . . . . . . .2A 78
Bridgeland Rd. E16 . . . . .1E 78
Bridge La. NW11 . . . . .2J 41
Bridge La. SW11 . . . . .9C 74
Bridgeman Ho. E9 . . . . .3G 61
(off Frampton Pk. Rd.)
Bridgeman Rd. N1 . . . . .3K 59
Bridgeman Rd. Tedd 3E 102
Bridgeman St. NW8 . . . . .5C 58
Bridge Meadows. SE14 . . . . .7H 77
Bridgen. 6J 97
Bridgend Rd. SW18 . . . . .3A 90
Bridgend Rd. Enf 8C 6
Bridgenhall Rd. Enf 3D 16
Bridgen Ho. E1 . . . . .9F 60
(off Nelson St.)
Bridgen Rd. Bex 6J 97
Bridge Pde. N21 . . . . .9A 16
(off Ridge Av.)
Bridgepark. SW18 . . . . .4L 89
Bridge Pl. SW1 . . . . .5F 74
Bridge Pl. Croy 3B 124
Bridge Pl. Wat 7H 9
Bridgeport Pl. E1 . . . . .2E 76
Bridger Clo. Wat 6H 5
Bridge Rd. E6 . . . . .3K 63
Bridge Rd. E15 . . . . .3B 62
Bridge Rd. E17 . . . . .5K 45
Bridge Rd. N9 . . . . .3E 28
Bridge Rd. N22 . . . . .8J 27
Bridge Rd. NW10 . . . . .2C 56
Bridge Rd. Beck 4K 109
Bridge Rd. Bexh 1J 97
Bridge Rd. Chess 7J 119
Bridge Rd. E Mol 8B 102
Bridge Rd. Eps 4D 134
Bridge Rd. Eri 1D 98
Bridge Rd.
Houn & Iswth 2B 86
Bridge Rd. K Lan 6A 4
Bridge Rd. Orp 1F 128
Bridge Rd. Rain 7E 66
Bridge Rd. S'hall 3K 69
Bridge Rd. Sutt 8M 121
Bridge Rd. Twic 5F 86
Bridge Rd. Uxb 5A 142
Bridge Rd. Wall 7F 122
Bridge Rd. Wemb 8L 39
Bridge Row. Croy 3B 124
Bridges Ct. SW11 . . . . .2B 90
(in two parts)
Bridges Dri. Dart 4M 99
Bridges Ho. SE5 . . . . .8B 76
(off Elmington Est.)
Bridgeside Ho. N1 . . . . .5A 60
(off Wharf Rd.)
Bridges La. Croy 6J 123
Bridges Pl. SW6 . . . . .9K 73
Bridges Rd. SW19 . . . . .3M 105
Bridges Rd. Stan 5D 22
Bridges Rd. M. SW19 . . . . .3M 105
Bridge St. SW1 . . . . .3J 75
Bridge St. W4 . . . . .5B 72
Bridge St. Pinn 1J 37
Bridge St. Rich 4H 87
Bridge St. W on T 3C 116
Bridge Ter. E15 . . . . .3B 62
(in two parts)
Bridge, The. Harr 2D 38
Bridgetown Clo. SE19 . . . . .2C 108
Bridge Vw. W6 . . . . .6G 73
Bridgeview Ct. Ilf 6B 32
Bridgewalk Heights. SE1 . . . .3B 76
(off Weston St.)
Bridgewater Clo. Chst 7C 112
Bridgewater Gdns. Edgw 9K 23
Bridgewater Highwalk.
EC2 . . . . .8A 60
(off Beech St.)
Bridgewater Rd. E15 . . . . . . .4A 62
Bridgewater Rd. Ruis 9E 36
Bridgewater Rd. Wemb 2G 55
Bridgewater Rd. Wey 8B 116
Bridgewater Sq. EC2 . . . . . . .8A 60
Bridgewater St. EC2 . . . . .8A 60
Bridgewater Way. Bush 8M 9
Bridge Way. N11 . . . . .3G 27
Bridge Way. NW11 . . . . .3K 41
Bridgeway. Bark 3D 64
Bridge Way. Twic 6A 86
Bridge Way. Uxb 1F 142
Bridge Way. Wemb 3J 55
Bridgeway St. NW1 . . . . .5G 59
Bridge Wharf. E2 . . . . .5H 61
Bridge Wharf Rd. Isw th 2F 86
Bridgewood Clo. SE20 . . . . .4F 108
Bridgewood Rd. SW16 . . . .4H 107
Bridgewood Rd. Wor Pk . . .6E 120
Bridge Works. Uxb 7A 142
Bridge Yd. SE1 . . . . .2B 76
Bridgford St. SW18 . . . . .9A 90
Bridgman Rd. W4 . . . . .4A 72
Bridgnorth Ho. SE15 . . . . .7E 76
(off Friary Est.)
Bridgwater Clo. Romf 5H 35
Bridgwater Ho. W2 . . . . .9A 58
(off Hallfield Est.)
Bridgwater Rd. Romf 5G 35
Bridgwater Wlk. Romf 5H 35
Bridle Clo. Enf 1K 17
Bridle Clo. Eps 7B 120
Bridle Clo. King T 8H 103
Bridle Clo. Sun 7E 100
Bridle End. Eps 5D 134
Bridle La. W1 . . . . .1G 75
Bridle La. Stoke D & Oxs . . .7A 132
Bridle La. Twic 5F 86
Bridle Path. Croy 5J 123
(in two parts)
Bridle Path. Wat 4F 8
Bridle Path, The. Eps 2G 135
Bridle Path, The. Wfd G 7C 30
Bridlepath Way. Felt 7C 84
Bridle Rd. Clay 8F 118
Bridle Rd. Croy 5L 125
(in two parts)
Bridle Rd. Eps 5D 134
Bridle Rd. Pinn 4F 36
Bridle Rd. S Croy 1E 138
Bridle Rd., The. Purl 2J 137
Bridle Way. Croy 6L 125
Bridle Way. Orp 6A 128
Bridleway Clo. Eps 2G 135
Bridle Way, The. Croy 2J 139
Bridleway, The. Wall 7G 123
Bridlington Rd. N9 . . . . .9F 16
Bridlington Rd. Wat 3H 21
Bridport. SE17 . . . . .6B 76
(off Date St.)
Bridport Av. Romf 4M 49
Bridport Ho. N1 . . . . .4B 60
(off Bridport Pl.)
Bridport Pl. N1 . . . . .4B 60
(in two parts)
Bridport Rd. N18 . . . . .5C 28
Bridport Rd. Gnfd 4M 53
Bridport Rd. T Hth 7L 107
Bridstow Pl. W2 . . . . .9L 57
Brief St. SE5 . . . . .9M 75
Brierfield. NW1 . . . . .4G 59
(off Arlington Rd.)
Brierley. New Ad 8M 125
(in two parts)
Brierley Av. N9 . . . . .1G 29
Brierley Clo. SE25 . . . . .8E 108
Brierley Clo. Horn 4G 51
Brierley Ct. W7 . . . . .1C 70
Brierley Rd. E11 . . . . .9B 46
Brierley Rd. SW12 . . . . .8G 91
Brierly Gdns. E2 . . . . .5G 61
Brigade Clo. Harr 7B 38
Brigade St. SE3 . . . . .1D 94
(off Tranquil Va.)
Brigadier Av. Enf 2A 16
Brigadier Hill. Enf 2A 16
Briggeford Clo. E5 . . . . .7E 44
Briggs Clo. Mitc 5F 106
Briggs Ho. E2 . . . . .6D 60
(off Chambord St.)
Brighstone Ct. Purf 6M 83
Bright Clo. Belv 5H 81
Brightfield Rd. SE12 . . . . . . .4C 94
Brightling Rd. SE4 . . . . .5K 93
Brightlingsea Pl. E14 . . . . . . .1K 77
Brightman Rd. SW18 . . . . . . .7B 90
Brighton Av. E17 . . . . .3K 45
Brighton Bldgs. SE1 . . . . .4C 76
(off Tower Bri. Rd.)
Brighton Clo. Uxb 3F 142
Brighton Dri. N'holt 2L 53
Brighton Gro. SE14 . . . . .9J 77
Brighton Rd. E6 . . . . .6L 63
(in two parts)
Brighton Rd. N2 . . . . .9A 26
Brighton Rd. N16 . . . . .9C 44
Brighton Rd.
Coul & Purl 9G 137
Brighton Rd.
Purl & S Croy 3L 137
Brighton Rd. S Croy 7A 124
Brighton Rd. Surb 1G 119
Brighton Rd. Sutt 3L 135
Brighton Rd. Tad & Bans . . .9K 135
Brighton Rd. Wat 2E 8
Brighton Ter. SW9 . . . . .3K 91
Brights Av. Rain 7F 66
Brightside Rd. SE13 . . . . .5B 94
Brightside, The. Enf 3H 17
Bright St. E14 . . . . .9M 61
Brightview Clo. Brick W 2J 5
Brightwell Clo. Croy 3L 123
Brightwell Cres. SW17 . . . . .2D 106
Brightwell Rd. Wat 7E 8
Brig M. SE8 . . . . .7L 77
Brigstock Ho. SE5 . . . . .1A 92
Brigstock Rd. Belv 5M 81
Brigstock Rd. Coul 7F 136
Brigstock Rd. T Hth 9L 107
Brill Pl. NW1 . . . . .5H 59
Brim Hill. N2 . . . . .2A 42
Brimpsfield Clo. SE2 . . . . .4F 80
(in two parts)
Brimsdown. 4J 17
Brimsdown Av. Enf 4J 17
Brimsdown Ho. E3 . . . . .7M 61
Brimsdown Ind. Est. Enf 3K 17
(in two parts)
Brimstone Clo. Orp 9G 129
Brimstone Ho. E15 . . . . .3C 62
(off Victoria St.)
Brindle Ga. Sidc 7C 96
Brindles. Horn 2J 51
Brindles, The. Bans 9K 135
Brindley Clo. Bexh 2L 97
Brindley Clo. Gnfd 4H 55
Brindley St. SE14 . . . . .9K 77
Brindley Way. Brom 2E 110
Brindley Way. S'hall 1M 69
Brindwood Rd. E4 . . . . .3K 29
Brinkburn Clo. SE2 . . . . .5E 80
Brinkburn Clo. Edgw 1M 39
Brinkburn Gdns. Edgw 1L 39
Brinkley Rd. Wor Pk 4F 120
Brinklow Cres. SE18 . . . . . . .8M 79
Brinklow Ho. W2 . . . . .8M 57
(off Torquay St.)
Brinkworth Rd. Ilf 1J 47
Brinkworth Way. E9 . . . . .2K 61
Brinley Clo. Chesh 4D 6
Brinsdale Rd. NW4 . . . . .1H 41
Brinsley Ho. E1 . . . . .9G 61
(off Tarling St.)
Brinsley Rd. Harr 9B 22
Brinsley St. E1 . . . . .9F 60
Brinsmead Rd. Romf 9L 35
Brinsworth Clo. Twic 7B 86
Brinsworth Ho. Twic 8B 86
Brinton Wlk. SE1 . . . . .2M 75
(off Chancel St.)
Brion Pl. E14 . . . . .8A 62
Brisbane Av. SW19 . . . . . . .5M 105
Brisbane Ho. W12 . . . . .1F 72
(off White City Est.)
Brisbane Rd. E10 . . . . .7M 45
Brisbane Rd. W13 . . . . .3E 70
Brisbane Rd. Ilf 5M 47
Brisbane St. SE5 . . . . .8B 76
Briscoe Clo. E11 . . . . .7D 46
Briscoe Rd. SW19 . . . . .3B 106
Briscoe Rd. Rain 5G 67
Briset Rd. SE9 . . . . .2H 95
Briset St. EC1 . . . . .8M 59
Briset Way. N7 . . . . .7K 43
Brisson Clo. Esh 7K 117
Bristol Clo. Stanw 5C 144
Bristol Clo. Wall 9J 123
Bristol Ct. Stanw 5C 144
Bristol Gdns. SW15 . . . . .6G 89
Bristol Gdns. W9 . . . . .7M 57
Bristol Ho. SE11 . . . . .4L 75
(off Lambeth Wlk.)
Bristol Ho. Bark 3E 64
(off Margaret Bondfield Av.)
Bristol Ho. Borwd 4L 11
(off Eldon Av.)
Bristol M. W9 . . . . .7M 57
Bristol Pk. Rd. E17 . . . . .2J 45
Bristol Rd. E7 . . . . .2G 63
Bristol Rd. Gnfd 4M 53
Bristol Rd. Mord 9A 106
Briston Gro. N8 . . . . .4J 43
Briston M. NW7 . . . . .7E 24
Bristowe Clo. SW2 . . . . .5L 91
Bristow Rd. SE19 . . . . .2C 108
Bristow Rd. Bexh 9J 81
Bristow Rd. Croy 6J 123
Bristow Rd. Houn 2A 86
Britain Vis. Cen. 2H 75
(off Regent St.)
Britannia Bus. Cen. NW2 . . . .9H 41
Britannia Bus. Pk. Wal X 7F 6
Britannia Clo. SW4 . . . . .3H 91
Britannia Clo. N'holt 6H 53
Britannia Ct. W Dray 4H 143
Britannia Ga. E16 . . . . .2E 78
Britannia Junction (Junct.)
. . . . .3F 58
Britannia La. Twic 6A 86
Britannia Rd. E14 . . . . .5L 77
Britannia Rd. N12 . . . . .3A 26
Britannia Rd. SW6 . . . . .8M 73
(in two parts)
Britannia Rd. Ilf 8M 47
Britannia Rd. Surb 2K 119
Britannia Rd. Wal X 7F 6
Britannia Row. N1 . . . . .4M 59
Britannia St. WC1 . . . . .6K 59
Britannia Wlk. N1 . . . . .5B 60
(in two parts)
Britannia Way. NW10 . . . . . . .7M 55
Britannia Way. SW6 . . . . .8M 73
(off Britannia Rd.)
Britannia Way. Stanw 6B 144
Britannic Highwalk. EC2 . . . . .8B 60
(off Moor La.)
Britannic Tower. EC2 . . . . . . .8B 60
(off Ropemaker St.)
British Gro. W4 . . . . .6D 72
British Gro. Pas. W4 . . . . .6D 72
British Gro. S. W4 . . . . .6D 72
(off British Gro. Pas.)
British Legion Rd. E4 . . . . . . .2D 30
British Library. 6H 59
British Mus. 8J 59
British St. E3 . . . . .6K 61
British Telecom Cen. EC1 . . . .9A 60
(off Newgate St.)
British Wharf Ind. Est.
SE14 . . . . .6H 77
Britley Ho. E14 . . . . .9K 61
(off Copenhagen Pl.)
Briton Clo. S Croy 3C 138
Briton Cres. S Croy 3C 138
Briton Hill Rd. S Croy 2C 138
Brittain Ho. SE9 . . . . .7J 95
Brittain Rd. Dag 8J 49
Brittain Rd. W on T 7H 117
Brittania Clo. Eri 7D 82
Brittany Point. SE11 . . . . .5L 75
Britten Clo. NW11 . . . . .6M 41
Britten Clo. Els 8H 11
Britten Ct. E15 . . . . .5B 62
Brittenden Clo. Orp 8D 128
Brittenden Pde. G Str 8D 128
Britten Dri. S'hall 9L 53
Britten St. SW3 . . . . .6C 74
Britton Clo. SE6 . . . . .6B 94
Britton St. EC1 . . . . .7M 59
Brixham Cres. Ruis 6E 36
Brixham Gdns. Ilf 1C 64
Brixham Rd. Well 9H 81
Brixham St. E16 . . . . .2L 79
Brixton. 3K 91
Brixton Hill. SW2 . . . . .6J 91
Brixton Hill Ct. SW2 . . . . .4K 91
Brixton Hill Pl. SW2 . . . . .6J 91
Brixton Oval. SW9 . . . . .3L 91
Brixton Rd. SW9 & SE11 . . . .3L 91
Brixton Rd. Wat 3F 8
Brixton Sta. Rd. SW9 . . . . . . .2L 91
Brixton Water La. SW2 . . . . .4K 91
Broad Acre. Brick W 3J 5
Broadbent Clo. N6 . . . . .6F 42
Broadbent St. W1 . . . . .1F 74
Broadbridge Clo. SE3 . . . . . . .8E 78
Broadbury Ct. N18 . . . . .6F 28
Broad Clo. W on T 5H 117
Broad Comn. Est. N16 . . . . . .6E 44
(off Osbaldeston Rd.)
Broadcoombe. S Croy 9G 125
Broad Ct. WC2 . . . . .9J 59
Broadcroft Av. Stan 9H 23
Broadcroft Rd. Orp 2B 128
Broadeaves Clo. S Croy 7C 124
Broadfield. NW6 . . . . .2M 57
Broadfield Clo. NW2 . . . . . . .8G 41
Broadfield Clo. Croy 4K 123
Broadfield Clo. Romf 3D 50
Broadfield Ct. Bus H 2C 22
Broadfield Ct. N Har 8M 21
(off Broadfields)
Broadfield Heights. Edgw . . .4M 23
Broadfield La. NW1 . . . . .3J 59
Broadfield Pde. Edgw 3M 23
(off Glengall Rd.)
Broadfield Rd. SE6 . . . . .6C 94
Broadfields. E Mol 1C 118
Broadfields. Harr 9M 21
Broadfields Av. N21 . . . . .8L 15
Broadfields Av. Edgw 4M 23
Broadfields La. Wat 1F 20
Broadfield Sq. Enf 4F 16
Broadfields Way. NW10 . . . . .1D 56
Broadfield Way. Buck H 3G 31
Broadford Ho. E1 . . . . .7J 61
(off Commodore St.)
Broadgate. EC2 . . . . .8C 60
(off Broadgate Cir.)
Broadgate. Wal A 6M 7
Broadgate Circ. EC2 . . . . .8C 60
Broadgate Ice Rink. 8C 60
Broadgate Rd. E16 . . . . .9H 63
Broadgates Av. Barn 3M 13
Broadgates Ct. SE11 . . . . . . .6L 75
(off Cleaver St.)
Broadgates Rd. SW18 . . . . . .7B 90
Broad Green. 2M 123
Broad Grn. Av. Croy 2M 123
Broadhead Strand. NW9 . . . . .9D 24
Broadheath Dri. Chst 2K 111
Broadhinton Rd. SW4 . . . . . . .2F 90
Broadhurst. Asht 8J 133
Broadhurst Av. Edgw 4M 23
Broadhurst Av. Ilf 9D 48
Broadhurst Clo. NW6 . . . . . . .2A 58
Broadhurst Clo. Rich 4K 87
Broadhurst Gdns. NW6 . . . . .2M 57
Broadhurst Gdns. Chig 4A 32
(in two parts)
Broadhurst Gdns. Ruis 7G 37
Broadhurst Wlk. Rain 2E 66
Broadlands. E17 . . . . .1J 45
Broadlands. Hanw 9L 85
Broadlands Av. SW16 . . . . . . .8J 91
Broadlands Av. Enf 5F 16
Broadlands Av. Shep 1A 116
Broadlands Clo. N6 . . . . .5E 42
Broadlands Clo. SW16 . . . . . .8J 91
Broadlands Clo. Enf 5G 17
Broadlands Clo. Wal X 7C 6
Broadlands Ct. Rich 8L 71
(off Kew Gdns. Rd.)
Broadlands Lodge. N6 . . . . . .5D 42
Broadlands Rd. N6 . . . . .5D 42
Broadlands Rd. Brom 1F 110
Broadlands Way. N Mald . . .1D 120
Broad La. EC2 . . . . .8C 60
(in two parts)
Broad La. N8 . . . . .3K 43
Broad La. N15 . . . . .2D 44
Broad La. Dart 1E 114
Broad La. Hamp 4K 101
Broad Lawn. SE9 . . . . .8L 95
Broadlawns Ct. Harr 8D 22
Broadley St. NW8 . . . . .8B 58
Broadley Ter. NW1 . . . . .7C 58
Broadmayne. SE17 . . . . .6B 76
(off Portland St.)
Broadmead. SE6 . . . . .9L 93
Broadmead. W14 . . . . .5J 73
Broad Mead. Asht 9K 133
Broadmead Av. Wor Pk 2E 120

Broadmead Clo. Hamp 3L 101
Broadmead Clo. Pinn 7J 21
Broadmead Ct. Wfd G 6E 30
Broadmead Rd. Hay & N'holt 7J 53
Broadmead Rd. Wfd G 6E 30
Broadoak. Sun 3D 100
Broad Oak. Wfd G 5F 30
Broadoak Av. Enf 8D 6
Broad Oak Clo. E4 . . . . 5L 29
Broad Oak Clo. Orp 6E 112
Broadoak Clo. S at H 3L 115
Broadoak Ct. SW9 . . . . 2L 91
Broadoak Ho. NW6 . . . . 4M 57
(off Mortimer Cres.)
Broadoak Rd. Eri 8B 82
Broadoaks. Surb 4M 119
Broadoaks Way. Brom 9D 110
Broad Sanctuary. SW1 . . . . 3H 75
Broadstone Ho. SW8 . . . . 8K 75
(off Dorset Rd.)
Broadstone Pl. W1 . . . . 8E 58
Broadstone Rd. Horn 7E 50
Broad St. Dag 3L 65
Broad St. Tedd 3D 102
Broad St. Av. EC2 . . . . 8C 60
Broad St. Mkt. Dag 3L 65
Broad St. Pl. EC2 . . . . 8B 60
(off Blomfield St.)
Broadstrood. Lou 2L 19
Broad Vw. NW9 . . . . 4L 39
Broadview Rd. SW16 . . . . 4H 107
Broadwalk. E18 . . . . 1D 46
Broad Wlk. N21 . . . . 2K 27
Broad Wlk. NW1 . . . . 4E 58
Broad Wlk. SE3 . . . . 1G 95
Broad Wlk. W1 . . . . 1D 74
Broadwalk. Harr 3L 37
Broad Wlk. Houn 9H 69
Broad Wlk. Orp 5H 129
Broad Wlk. Rich 8K 71
Broadwalk Clo. E14 . . . . 2A 78
(off Broadwalk Pl.)
Broadwalk Ct. W8 . . . . 2L 73
(off Palace Gdns. Ter.)
Broadwalk Ho. EC2 . . . . 7C 60
Broadwalk Ho. SW7 . . . . 3A 74
(off Hyde Pk. Ga.)
Broad Wlk. La. NW11 . . . . 5K 41
Broadwalk Shop. Cen. Edgw 6M 23
Broad Wlk., The. W8 . . . . 2M 73
Broad Wlk., The. E Mol 8D 102
Broadwalk, The. N'wd 9A 20
Broadwall. SE1 . . . . 2L 75
Broadwater Clo. W on T 7E 116
Broadwater Farm Est. N17 . . . . 9B 28
Broadwater Gdns. Orp 6M 127
Broadwater Pl. Wey 4C 116
Broadwater Rd. N17 . . . . 8C 28
Broadwater Rd. SE28 . . . . 4B 80
Broadwater Rd. SW17 . . . . 1C 106
Broadwater Rd. N. W on T 7D 116
Broadwater Rd. S. W on T 7D 116
Broadway. E13 . . . . 5F 62
Broadway. E15 . . . . 3B 62
(in two parts)
Broadway. SW1 . . . . 4H 75
Broadway. W7 . . . . 2C 70
Broadway. W13 . . . . 2F 70
Broadway. Bark 4A 64
Broadway. Bexh 3J 97
(in three parts)
Broadway. Rain 7E 66
Broadway. Romf 9E 34
Broadway. Swan 1A 130
Broadway Arc. W6 . . . . 5G 73
(off Hammersmith B'way.)
Broadway Av. Croy 9B 108
Broadway Av. Twic 5F 86
Broadway Cen., The. W6 . . . . 5G 73
Broadway Chambers. W6 . . . . 5G 73
(off Hammersmith B'way.)
Broadway Clo. S Croy 6F 138
Broadway Clo. Wfd G 6F 30
Broadway Ct. SW19 . . . . 3L 105
Broadway Ct. Beck 7A 110
Broadway Gdns. Mitc 8C 106
Broadway Gdns. Wfd G 6F 30
Broadway Ho. E8 . . . . 4F 60
Broadway Ho. Brom 2B 110
(off Bromley Rd.)
Broadway Mkt. E8 . . . . 4F 60
Broadway Mkt. SW17 . . . . 1D 106
Broadway Mkt. Ilf 9B 32
(in two parts)
Broadway Mkt. M. E8 . . . . 4E 60
Broadway M. N13 . . . . 5K 27
Broadway M. N16 . . . . 5D 44
(in two parts)
Broadway M. N21 . . . . 1M 27
Broadway Pde. E4 . . . . 6A 30
Broadway Pde. N8 . . . . 4J 43
Broadway Pde. Harr 3M 37
Broadway Pde. Hay 2E 68
Broadway Pde. Horn 9F 50
(off Broadway, The)
Broadway Pl. SW19 . . . . 3K 105
Broadway Shop. Cen. Bexh 3L 97
Broadway Shop. Mall. SW1 . . . . 4H 75
Broadway Sq. Bexh 3L 97
Broadway, The. E4 . . . . 6B 30
Broadway, The. N8 . . . . 4J 43
Broadway, The. N9 . . . . 3E 28
Broadway, The. N11 . . . . 5E 26
(off Stanford Rd.)
Broadway, The. N14 . . . . 1H 27
(off Southgate Cir.)
Broadway, The. N22 . . . . 9L 27
Broadway, The. NW7 . . . . 7E 24
(off Colenso Dri.)
Broadway, The. NW7 . . . . 5C 24
(Watford Way)
Broadway, The. NW9 . . . . 4D 40
Broadway, The. SW14 . . . . 1C 88
Broadway, The. SW19 . . . . 3K 105
Broadway, The. W3 . . . . 3L 71
Broadway, The. W5 . . . . 1H 71
Broadway, The. Cheam 8J 121
Broadway, The. Croy 6J 123
Broadway, The. Dag 7K 49
Broadway, The. Gnfd 7A 54
Broadway, The. Horn 9F 50
Broadway, The. Lou 6M 19
Broadway, The. N'wd 9E 20
Broadway, The. S'hall 1H 69
Broadway, The. Stan 5G 23
Broadway, The. Sutt 7A 122
Broadway, The. Th Dit 3C 118
Broadway, The. Wat 5G 9
Broadway, The. W'stone 9C 22
Broadway, The. Wemb 8J 39
Broadway, The. Wfd G 6F 30
Broadway Theatre, The. . . . 6M 93
(off Catford B'way.)
Broadwell Ct. Houn 9H 69
(off Springwell Rd.)
Broadwick St. W1 . . . . 1G 75
Broadwood Av. Ruis 4C 36
Broadwood Ter. W14 . . . . 5K 73
(off Warwick Rd.)
Broad Yd. EC1 . . . . 7M 59
Brocas Clo. NW3 . . . . 3C 58
Brockbridge Ho. SW15 . . . . 5D 88
Brockdene Dri. Kes 6H 127
Brockdish Av. Bark 1D 64
Brockenhurst. W Mol 9K 101
Brockenhurst Av. Wor Pk 3C 120
Brockenhurst Gdns. NW7 . . . . 5C 24
Brockenhurst Gdns. Ilf 1A 64
Brockenhurst M. N18 . . . . 4E 28
Brockenhurst Rd. Croy 2F 124
Brockenhurst Way. SW16 . . . . 6H 107
Brocket Clo. Chig 4D 32
Brocket Ho. SW8 . . . . 1H 91
Brocket Way. Chig 5C 32
Brockham Clo. SW19 . . . . 2K 105
Brockham Cres. New Ad 9B 126
Brockham Dri. SW2 . . . . 6K 91
Brockham Dri. Ilf 4M 47
Brockham Ho. NW1 . . . . 4G 59
(off Bayham Pl.)
Brockham Ho. SW2 . . . . 6K 91
(off Brockham Dri.)
Brockham St. SE1 . . . . 4A 76
Brockhurst Clo. Stan 6D 22
Brockill Cres. SE4 . . . . 3J 93
Brocklebank Ho. E16 . . . . 2L 79
(off Glenister St.)
Brocklebank Ind. Est. SE7 . . . . 5E 78
Brocklebank Rd. SE7 . . . . 5F 78
Brocklebank Rd. SW18 . . . . 6A 90
Brocklehurst St. SE14 . . . . 8H 77
Brocklesbury Clo. Wat 5H 9
Brocklesby Rd. SE25 . . . . 8F 108
Brockley. . . . 3K 93
Brockley Av. Stan 3J 23
Brockley Clo. Stan 4J 23
Brockley Combe. Wey 6B 116
Brockley Cres. Romf 7A 34
Brockley Cross. SE4 . . . . 2J 93
Brockley Cross Bus. Cen. SE4 . . . . 2J 93
Brockley Footpath. SE4 . . . . 4J 93
(in two parts)
Brockley Footpath. SE15 . . . . 3G 93
Brockley Gdns. SE4 . . . . 1K 93
Brockley Gro. SE4 . . . . 4K 93
Brockley Hall Rd. SE4 . . . . 4J 93
Brockley Hill. Stan 1G 23
Brockley M. SE4 . . . . 4J 93
Brockley Pk. SE23 . . . . 6J 93
Brockley Ri. SE23 . . . . 7J 93
Brockley Rd. SE4 . . . . 2K 93
Brockley Side. Stan 4J 23
Brockley Vw. SE23 . . . . 6J 93
Brockley Way. SE4 . . . . 4H 93
Brockman Ri. Brom 1B 110
Brockmer Ho. E1 . . . . 1F 76
(off Crowder St.)
Brock Pl. E3 . . . . 7M 61
Brock Rd. E13 . . . . 8F 62
Brocks Dri. Sutt 5J 121
Brockshot Clo. Bren 6H 71
Brock St. SE15 . . . . 2G 93
Brockton Clo. Romf 2D 50
Brockway Clo. E11 . . . . 7C 46
Brockweir. E2 . . . . 5G 61
(off Cyprus St.)
Brockwell Clo. Orp 9D 112
Brockwell Ct. SW2 . . . . 4L 91
Brockwell Ho. SE11 . . . . 7K 75
(off Vauxhall St.)
Brockwell Pk. Gdns. SE24 . . . . 6L 91
Brockwell Pk. Row. SW2 . . . . 6L 91
Brodewater Rd. Borwd 4M 11
Brodia Rd. N16 . . . . 8C 44
Brodie Ho. SE1 . . . . 6D 76
(off Cooper's Rd.)
Brodie Rd. E4 . . . . 1A 30
Brodie Rd. Enf 2A 16
Brodie St. SE1 . . . . 6D 76
Brodlove La. E1 . . . . 1H 77
Brodrick Gro. SE2 . . . . 5F 80
Brodrick Rd. SW17 . . . . 8C 90
Brograve Gdns. Beck 6M 109
Broken Wharf. EC4 . . . . 1A 76
Brokesley St. E3 . . . . 6K 61
Broke Wlk. E8 . . . . 4D 60
Bromar Rd. SE5 . . . . 2C 92
Bromborough Grn. Wat 5G 21
Bromefield. Stan 8G 23
Bromefield Ct. Wal A 6M 7
Bromell's Rd. SW4 . . . . 3G 91
Brome Rd. SE9 . . . . 2K 95
Bromet Clo. Wat 2D 8
(in two parts)
Bromfelde Rd. SW4 . . . . 2H 91
Bromfelde Wlk. SW4 . . . . 1H 91
Bromfield St. N1 . . . . 4L 59
Bromhall Rd. Dag 2F 64
Bromhead Rd. E1 . . . . 9G 61
(off Jubilee St.)
Bromhead St. E1 . . . . 9G 61
Bromhedge. SE9 . . . . 9K 95
Bromholm Rd. SE2 . . . . 4F 80
Bromleigh Clo. Chesh 1E 6
Bromleigh Ct. SE23 . . . . 8E 92
Bromleigh Ho. SE1 . . . . 4D 76
(off Abbey St.)
Bromley. . . . 6M 61
(Bow)
Bromley. . . . 6E 110
(Chislehurst)
Bromley Av. Brom 4C 110
Bromley Common. . . . 3J 127
Bromley Comn. Brom 8G 111
Bromley Cres. Brom 7D 110
Bromley Cres. Ruis 9D 36
Bromley F.C. . . . 9F 110
Bromley Gdns. Brom 7D 110
Bromley Gro. Brom 6B 110
Bromley Hall Rd. E14 . . . . 8A 62
Bromley High St. E3 . . . . 6M 61
Bromley Hill. Brom 3C 110
Bromley Ind. Cen. Brom 7H 111
(off Waldo Rd.)
Bromley La. Chst 4A 112
Bromley Mus. . . . 2F 128
Bromley Park. . . . 5C 110
Bromley Pk. Brom 5D 110
Bromley Pl. W1 . . . . 8G 59
Bromley Rd. E10 . . . . 4M 45
Bromley Rd. E17 . . . . 1L 45
Bromley Rd. N17 . . . . 8D 28
Bromley Rd. N18 . . . . 3B 28
Bromley Rd. SE6 & Brom 7M 93
Bromley Rd. Beck & Short 5M 109
Bromley Rd. Chst 5M 111
Bromley St. E1 . . . . 8H 61
Brompton. . . . 4C 74
Brompton Arc. SW3 . . . . 3D 74
(off Brompton Rd.)
Brompton Clo. SE20 . . . . 6E 108
Brompton Clo. Houn 4K 85
Brompton Dri. Eri 8F 82
Brompton Gro. N2 . . . . 2C 42
Brompton Pk. Cres. SW6 . . . . 7M 73
Brompton Pl. SW3 . . . . 4C 74
Brompton Rd. SW3 & SW1 . . . . 5C 74
Brompton Sq. SW3 . . . . 4C 74
Brompton Ter. SE18 . . . . 9K 79
Bromwich Av. N6 . . . . 7E 42
Bromyard Av. W3 . . . . 1C 72
Bromyard Ho. SE15 . . . . 8F 76
(off Commercial Way)
Bron Ct. NW6 . . . . 4L 57
Brondesbury. . . . 3K 57
Brondesbury Ct. NW2 . . . . 2H 57
Brondesbury M. NW6 . . . . 3L 57
Brondesbury Park. . . . 4J 57
Brondesbury Pk. NW2 & NW6 . . . . 2F 56
Brondesbury Rd. NW6 . . . . 5K 57
Brondesbury Vs. NW6 . . . . 5K 57
Bronhill Ter. N17 . . . . 8E 28
Bronsart Rd. SW6 . . . . 8J 73
Bronson Rd. SW20 . . . . 6H 105
Bronte Clo. E7 . . . . 9E 46
Bronte Clo. Eri 8M 81
Bronte Clo. Ilf 2L 47
Bronte Ct. W14 . . . . 4H 73
(off Girdler's Rd.)
Bronte Gro. Dart 3K 99
Bronte Ho. N16 . . . . 1C 60
Bronte Ho. NW6 . . . . 6L 57
Bronte Ho. SW4 . . . . 6G 91
Bronti Clo. SE17 . . . . 6A 76
Bronwen Ct. NW8 . . . . 6B 58
(off Grove End Rd.)
Bronze Age Way. Belv & Eri 3M 81
Bronze St. SE8 . . . . 8L 77
Brook Av. Dag 3M 65
Brook Av. Edgw 6M 23
Brook Av. Wemb 8L 39
Brook Bank. Enf 1F 16
Brookbank Av. W7 . . . . 8B 54
Brookbank Rd. SE13 . . . . 2L 93
Brook Clo. NW7 . . . . 7J 25
Brook Clo. SW17 . . . . 8E 90
Brook Clo. SW20 . . . . 7F 104
Brook Clo. W5 . . . . 2L 71
Brook Clo. Borwd 4M 11
Brook Clo. Eps 1C 134
Brook Clo. Romf 8D 34
Brook Clo. Ruis 5C 36
Brook Clo. Stanw 6D 144
Brook Ct. E11 . . . . 8C 46
Brook Ct. E15 . . . . 1M 61
(off Clays La.)
Brook Ct. E17 . . . . 1J 45
Brook Ct. SE12 . . . . 9G 95
Brook Ct. Beck 5K 109
Brook Ct. Edgw 5M 23
Brook Cres. E4 . . . . 4L 29
Brook Cres. N18 . . . . 4F 28
Brookdale. N11 . . . . 4G 27
Brookdale Av. Upm 8L 51
Brookdale Clo. Upm 8M 51
Brookdale Rd. E17 . . . . 1L 45
Brookdale Rd. SE6 . . . . 6M 93
(in two parts)
Brookdale Rd. Bex 5J 97
Brookdales. NW4 . . . . 2J 41
Brookdene Av. Wat 9F 8
Brookdene Dri. N'wd 7D 20
Brookdene Rd. SE18 . . . . 5C 80
Brook Dri. SE11 . . . . 4L 75
Brook Dri. Harr 2A 38
Brook Dri. Ruis 5C 36
Brooke Av. Harr 8A 38
Brooke Clo. Bush 9A 10
Brooke Ho. SE14 . . . . 9J 77
Brookehowse Rd. SE6 . . . . 8L 93
Brookend Rd. Sidc 7C 96
Brooke Rd. E5 . . . . 8E 44
Brooke Rd. E17 . . . . 2A 46
Brooke Rd. N16 . . . . 8D 44
Brooker Rd. Wal A 7J 7
(in two parts)
Brookers Clo. Asht 9G 133
Brooke's Ct. EC1 . . . . 8L 59
Brooke's Mkt. EC1 . . . . 8L 59
(off Dorrington St.)
Brooke St. EC1 . . . . 8L 59
Brooke Trad. Est. Horn 5D 50
Brooke Way. Bush 9A 10
Brookfield. N6 . . . . 8E 42
Brookfield Av. E17 . . . . 2A 46
Brookfield Av. NW7 . . . . 6F 24
Brookfield Av. W5 . . . . 7H 55
Brookfield Av. Sutt 6C 122
Brookfield Clo. NW7 . . . . 6F 24
Brookfield Ct. Chesh 1D 6
Brookfield Ct. Gnfd 6A 54
Brookfield Cres. NW7 . . . . 6F 24
Brookfield Cres. Harr 3J 39
Brookfield Gdns. Chesh 1D 6
Brookfield Gdns. Clay 8D 118
Brookfield La. E. Chesh 1D 6
Brookfield La. W. Chesh 1B 6
(in two parts)
Brookfield Pk. NW5 . . . . 8F 42
Brookfield Path. Wfd G 6C 30
Brookfield Rd. E9 . . . . 2J 61
Brookfield Rd. N9 . . . . 3E 28
Brookfield Rd. W4 . . . . 3B 72
Brookfields. Enf 6H 17
Brookfields Av. Mitc 9C 106
Brook Gdns. E4 . . . . 4M 29
Brook Gdns. SW13 . . . . 2D 88
Brook Gdns. King T 5A 104
Brook Ga. W1 . . . . 1D 74
Brook Green. . . . 5H 73
Brook Grn. W6 . . . . 4H 73
Brook Grn. Flats. W14 . . . . 4H 73
(off Dunsany Rd.)
Brookhill Clo. SE18 . . . . 6M 79
Brookhill Clo. E Barn 7C 14
Brookhill Rd. SE18 . . . . 7M 79
Brookhill Rd. Barn 7C 14
Brook Ho. W6 . . . . 5G 73
(off Shepherd's Bush Rd.)
Brookhouse Gdns. E4 . . . . 4C 30
Brook Houses. NW1 . . . . 5G 59
(off Cranleigh St.)
Brook Ind. Est. Hay 2H 69
Brooking Rd. E7 . . . . 1E 62
Brookland Clo. NW11 . . . . 2L 41
Brookland Gth. NW11 . . . . 2L 41
Brookland Hill. NW11 . . . . 2M 41
Brookland Ri. NW11 . . . . 2L 41
Brooklands. Dart 7J 99
Brooklands App. Romf 2B 50
Brooklands Av. SW19 . . . . 8M 89
Brooklands Av. Sidc 8B 96
Brooklands Clo. Romf 2B 50
Brooklands Clo. Sun 5C 100
Brooklands Ct. N21 . . . . 7B 16
Brooklands Ct. NW6 . . . . 3K 57
Brooklands Ct. King T 8H 103
(off Surbiton Rd.)
Brooklands Ct. Mitc 6B 106
Brooklands Dri. Gnfd 4G 55
Brooklands Gdns. Horn 4G 51
Brooklands La. Romf 2B 50
(in two parts)
Brooklands Pk. SE3 . . . . 2E 94
Brooklands Pas. SW8 . . . . 9H 75
Brooklands Rd. Romf 2B 50
Brooklands Rd. Th Dit 3D 118
Brooklands, The. Iswth 9B 70
Brook La. SE3 . . . . 1F 94
Brook La. Bex 5H 97
Brook La. Brom 3E 110
Brook La. Bus. Cen. Bren 6H 71
Brook La. N. Bren 6H 71
(in three parts)
Brooklea Clo. NW9 . . . . 8C 24
Brook Lodge. Romf 2B 50
(off Medora Rd.)
Brooklyn Av. SE25 . . . . 8F 108
Brooklyn Av. Lou 6J 19
Brooklyn Clo. Cars 4C 122
Brooklyn Gro. SE25 . . . . 8F 108
Brooklyn Rd. SE25 . . . . 8F 108
Brooklyn Rd. Brom 9H 111
Brooklyn Way. W Dray 4H 143
Brookmarsh Ind. Est. SE8 . . . . 8M 77
Brook Mead. Eps 8C 120
Brookmead Av. Brom 9K 111
Brookmead Clo. Orp 2F 128
Brookmead Ind. Est. Croy 1G 123
Brook Mdw. N12 . . . . 3M 25
Brook Mdw. Clo. Wfd G 6C 30
Brookmead Rd. Croy 1G 123
Brookmead Way. Orp 1F 128
Brook M. WC2 . . . . 9H 59
Brook M. N. W2 . . . . 1A 74
Brookmill Clo. Wat 9F 8
Brookmill Rd. SE8 . . . . 9L 77
Brook Pde. Chig 3M 31
Brook Pk. Dart 8L 99
Brook Pk. Clo. N21 . . . . 7M 15
Brook Path. Lou 6J 19
Brook Pl. Barn 7L 13
Brook Ri. Chig 3L 31
Brook Rd. N2 . . . . 7C 26
Brook Rd. N8 . . . . 2J 43
Brook Rd. N22 . . . . 1K 43
Brook Rd. NW2 . . . . 7D 40
Brook Rd. Borwd 3L 11
Brook Rd. Buck H 2E 30
Brook Rd. Ilf 4C 48
Brook Rd. Lou 6J 19
Brook Rd. Romf 9D 34
Brook Rd. Surb 4J 119
Brook Rd. Swan 7B 114
Brook Rd. T Hth 8A 108
Brook Rd. Twic 5E 86
Brook Rd. Wal X 7F 6
Brook Rd. S. Bren 7H 71
Brooks Av. E6 . . . . 7K 63
Brooksbank St. E9 . . . . 2G 61
Brooksby M. N1 . . . . 3L 59
Brooksby St. N1 . . . . 3L 59
Brooksby's Wlk. E9 . . . . 1H 61
Brooks Clo. SE9 . . . . 8L 95
Brooks Ct. SW8 . . . . 8G 75
Brookscroft. E17 . . . . 1M 45
(off Forest Rd.)
Brookscroft. Croy 2K 139
Brookscroft Rd. E17 . . . . 8M 29
(in two parts)
Brookshill. Harr 5B 22
Brookshill Av. Harr 5B 22
Brookshill Dri. Harr 5B 22
Brookside. N21 . . . . 8K 15
Brookside. Cars 7E 122
Brookside. E Barn 8C 14
Brookside. Horn 3J 51
Brookside. Ilf 6A 32
Brookside. Orp 2D 128
Brookside. Uxb 3D 142
Brookside. Wal A 5L 7
Brookside. Wat 1H 9
Brookside Caravans. Wat 9F 8
Brookside Clo. Barn 8J 13
Brookside Clo. Felt 9E 84
Brookside Clo. Kent 3H 39
Brookside Clo. S Harr 9J 37
Brookside Cres. Wor Pk 3E 120
Brookside Gdns. Enf 1G 17
Brookside Rd. N9 . . . . 4F 28
(in two parts)
Brookside Rd. N19 . . . . 7G 43
Brookside Rd. NW11 . . . . 4J 41
Brookside Rd. Hay 1G 69
Brookside Rd. Wat 9F 8
Brookside S. E Barn 9E 14
Brookside Wlk. N12 . . . . 6L 25
Brookside Wlk. NW11 . . . . 2J 41

Brookside Way—Bugsby's Way Retail Est.

Brookside Way. Croy 1H 125
Brooks La. W4 7L 71
Brooks Lodge. N1 5C 60
(off Hoxton St.)
Brooks M. W1 1F 74
Brooks Rd. E13 4E 62
Brooks Rd. W4 6L 71
Brook St. N17 9D 28
Brook St. W1 1F 74
Brook St. W2 1B 74
Brook St. Belv & Eri 6M 81
Brook St. King T 6J 103
Brooksville Av. NW6 4J 57
Brooks Wlk. N3 1J 41
Brooks Way. Orp 6G 113
Brook Va. Eri 9M 81
Brookview Ct. Enf 7C 16
Brookview Rd. SW16 2G 107
Brookville Rd. SW6 8K 73
Brook Wlk. N2 8B 26
Brook Wlk. Edgw 6B 24
Brookway. SE3 2E 94
Brook Way. Chig 3L 31
Brook Way. Rain 8F 66
Brookwood Av. SW13 1D 88
Brookwood Clo. Brom 8D 110
Brookwood Ho. SE1 3M 75
(off Webber St.)
Brookwood Rd. SW18 7K 89
Brookwood Rd. Houn 1M 85
Broom Av. Orp 6F 112
Broom Clo. Brom 1J 127
Broom Clo. Esh 7M 117
Broom Clo. Tedd 4H 103
Broomcroft Av. N'holt 6G 53
Broome Rd. Hamp 4K 101
Broomer Pl. Chesh 2C 6
Broome Way. SE5 8B 76
Broomfield. E17 5K 45
Broomfield. NW1 3E 58
(off Ferdinand St.)
Broomfield. Sun 5E 100
Broomfield Av. N13 5K 27
Broomfield Av. Lou 8K 19
Broomfield Clo. Romf 7B 34
Broomfield Ct. SE16 4E 76
(off Ben Smith Way)
Broomfield Ho. SE17 5C 76
(off Massinger St.)
Broomfield Ho. Stan 3E 22
(off Stanmore Hill)
Broomfield La. N13 4J 27
Broomfield Pl. W13 2F 70
Broomfield Ride. Oxs 4B 132
Broomfield Ri. Ab L 5B 4
Broomfield Rd. N13 5J 27
Broomfield Rd. W13 2F 70
Broomfield Rd. Beck 7J 109
Broomfield Rd. Bexh 4L 97
Broomfield Rd. Rich 9K 71
Broomfield Rd. Romf 5H 49
Broomfield Rd. Surb 3K 119
Broomfield Rd. Tedd 3G 103
Broomfields. Esh 7A 118
Broomfield St. E14 8L 61
Broom Gdns. Croy 5L 125
Broom Gro. Wat 2E 8
Broomgrove Gdns. Edgw 8L 23
Broomgrove Rd. SW9 1K 91
Broom Hall. Oxs 6B 132
Broomhall Rd. S Croy 1B 138
Broom Hill. 2D 128
Broomhill Ct. Wfd G 6E 30
Broom Hill Ri. Bexh 4L 97
Broomhill Rd. SW18 4L 89
Broomhill Rd. Dart 5F 98
Broomhill Rd. Ilf 7E 48
Broomhill Rd. Orp 2E 128
Broomhill Rd. Wfd G 6E 30
(in two parts)
Broomhill Wlk. Wfd G 6D 30
Broomhouse La. SW6 1L 89
(in two parts)
Broomhouse Rd. SW6 1L 89
Broomleigh. Brom 5E 110
(off Tweedy Rd.)
Broomloan La. Sutt 4L 121
Broom Lock. Tedd 3G 103
Broom Mead. Bexh 5L 97
Broom Pk. Tedd 4H 103
Broom Rd. Croy 5L 125
Broom Rd. Tedd 2F 102
Broomsleigh Bus. Pk.
SE26 2K 109
Broomsleigh St. NW6 1K 57
Broomstick Hall Rd. Wal A 6L 7
Broom Water. Tedd 3G 103
Broom Water W. Tedd 2G 103
Broom Way. Wey 6C 116
Broomwood Clo. Bex 8B 98
Broomwood Clo. Croy 9H 109
Broomwood Rd. SW11 5D 90
Broomwood Rd. Orp 6F 112
Broseley Gdns. Romf 4J 35
Broseley Gro. SE26 2J 109
Broseley Rd. Romf 4J 35
Broster Gdns. SE25 7D 108
Brougham Ct. Dart 5M 99
(off Hardwick Cres.)
Brougham Rd. E8 4E 60
Brougham Rd. W3 9A 56
Brougham St. SW11 1D 90
Brough Clo. SW8 8J 75
Brough Clo. King T 2H 103
Broughinge Rd. Borwd 4M 11
Broughton Av. N3 1J 41
Broughton Av. Rich 9F 86
Broughton Ct. W13 1F 70
Broughton Dri. SW9 3L 91
Broughton Gdns. N6 4G 43
Broughton Rd. SW6 1M 89
Broughton Rd. W13 1F 70
Broughton Rd. Orp 4B 128
Broughton Rd. T Hth 1L 123
Broughton St. SW8 1E 90
Broughton St. Ind. Est.
SW11 1E 90
Brouncker Rd. W3 3A 72
Brow Clo. Orp 2H 129
Brow Cres. Orp 3G 129
Browells La. Felt 8F 84
(in two parts)
Brown Bear Ct. Felt 1H 101
Brown Clo. Wall 9J 123
Browne Clo. Romf 5M 33
Browne Ho. SE8 8L 77
(off Deptford Chu. St.)
Brownfield Area. E14 9M 61
Brownfield St. E14 9M 61
Browngraves Rd. Hay 8A 68
Brown Hart Gdns. W1 1E 74
Brownhill Rd. SE6 6M 93
Browning Av. W7 9D 54
Browning Av. Sutt 6C 122
Browning Av. Wor Pk 3F 120
Browning Clo. E17 2A 46
Browning Clo. W9 7A 58
Browning Clo. Col R 7K 33
Browning Clo. Hamp 1K 101
Browning Clo. Well 9C 80
Browning Ho. SE14 9J 77
(off Loring Rd.)
Browning Ho. W12 9G 57
(off Wood La.)
Browning M. W1 8F 58
Browning Rd. E11 5D 46
Browning Rd. E12 1K 63
Browning Rd. Dart 3K 99
Browning Rd. Enf 1B 16
Browning St. SE17 6A 76
Browning Way. Houn 9H 69
Brownlea Gdns. Ilf 7E 48
Brownlow Ct. N2 3A 42
Brownlow Ct. N11 6J 27
(off Brownlow Rd.)
Brownlow Ho. SE16 3E 76
(off George Row)
Brownlow M. WC1 7K 59
Brownlow Rd. E7 9E 46
Brownlow Rd. E8 4D 60
Brownlow Rd. N3 7M 25
Brownlow Rd. N11 6J 27
Brownlow Rd. NW10 3C 56
Brownlow Rd. W13 2E 70
Brownlow Rd. Borwd 6L 11
Brownlow Rd. Croy 6C 124
Brownlow St. WC1 8K 59
Browns Arc. W1 1G 75
(off Regent St.)
Brown's Bldgs. EC3 9C 60
Browns La. NW5 1F 58
Brownspring Dri. SE9 1M 111
Browns Rd. E17 1L 45
Brown's Rd. Surb 2K 119
Brown St. W1 9D 58
Brownswell Rd. N2 9B 26
Brownswood Park. 7M 43
Brownswood Rd. N4 8M 43
Brow, The. Wat 6F 4
Broxash Rd. SW11 5E 90
Broxbourne Av. E18 2F 46
Broxbourne Rd. E7 8E 46
Broxbourne Rd. Orp 3D 128
Broxhill Cen. Romf 4F 34
Broxhill Rd. Hav 3C 34
Broxholme Ho. SW6 9M 73
(off Harwood Rd.)
Broxholm Rd. SE27 9L 91
Broxted Rd. SE23 8K 93
Broxwood Way. NW8 4C 58
Bruce Av. Horn 7G 51
Bruce Av. Shep 1A 116
Bruce Castle Ct. N17 8D 28
(off Lordship La.)
Bruce Castle Mus. 8C 28
Bruce Castle Rd. N17 8D 28
Bruce Clo. W10 8H 57
Bruce Clo. Well 9F 80
Bruce Ct. Sidc 1D 112
Bruce Dri. S Croy 1H 139
Bruce Gdns. N20 3D 26
Bruce Gro. N17 8C 28
Bruce Gro. Orp 3E 128
Bruce Gro. Wat 2G 9
Bruce Hall M. SW17 1E 106
Bruce Ho. W10 8H 57
Bruce Rd. E3 6M 61
Bruce Rd. NW10 3B 56
Bruce Rd. SE25 8B 108
Bruce Rd. Barn 5J 13
Bruce Rd. Harr 9C 22
Bruce Rd. Mitc 4E 106
Bruce Way. Wal X 6D 6
Bruckner St. W10 6J 57
Brudenell Rd. SW17 9D 90
Bruffs Mdw. N'holt 2J 53
Bruges Pl. NW1 3G 59
(off Randolph St.)
Brumfield Rd. Eps 7A 120
Brummel Clo. Bexh 2A 98
Brune Ho. E1 8D 60
(off Bell La.)
Brunei Gallery. 8H 59
Brunel Clo. SE19 3D 108
Brunel Clo. Houn 8F 68
Brunel Clo. N'holt 6K 53
Brunel Clo. Romf 2C 50
Brunel Est. W2 8L 57
Brunel Ho. E14 6M 77
(off Ship Yd.)
Brunel Pl. S'hall 9M 53
Brunel Rd. E17 4J 45
Brunel Rd. SE16 3G 77
Brunel Rd. W3 8C 56
Brunel Rd. Wfd G 5K 31
Brunel Science Pk. Uxb 6C 142
Brunel St. E16 9D 62
Brunel University.
(Borough Rd., Isleworth) 8C 70
Brunel University.
(St Margaret's Rd., Isleworth) 3F 86
Brunel University (Uxbridge). 6C 142
Brunel Wlk. N15 2C 44
Brunel Wlk. Twic 6L 85
Brune St. E1 8D 60
Brunlees Ho. SE1 4A 76
(off Bath Ter.)
Brunner Clo. NW11 3M 41
Brunner Ho. SE6 1A 110
Brunner Rd. E17 3J 45
Brunner Rd. W5 7H 55
Bruno Pl. NW9 7A 40
Brunswick Av. N11 3E 26
(in two parts)
Brunswick Cen. WC1 7J 59
Brunswick Clo. Bexh 3H 97
Brunswick Clo. Pinn 4J 37
Brunswick Clo. Th Dit 3D 118
Brunswick Clo. Twic 9B 86
Brunswick Clo. W on T 4G 117
Brunswick Clo. Est. EC1 6M 59
Brunswick Ct. EC1 6M 59
(off Tompion St.)
Brunswick Ct. SE1 3C 76
Brunswick Ct. SW1 5H 75
(off Regency St.)
Brunswick Ct. Barn 7B 14
Brunswick Ct. Sutt 6M 121
Brunswick Cres. N11 3E 26
Brunswick Gdns. W5 7J 55
Brunswick Gdns. W8 2L 73
Brunswick Gdns. Ilf 7A 32
Brunswick Gro. N11 3E 26
Brunswick Ho. E2 5D 60
(off Thurtle Rd.)
Brunswick Ho. N3 8K 25
Brunswick Ho. SE16 4J 77
(off Brunswick Quay)
Brunswick Ind. Pk. N11 4F 26
Brunswick Mans. WC1 7J 59
(off Handel St.)
Brunswick M. SW16 3H 107
Brunswick M. W1 9D 58
Brunswick Park. 3E 26
Brunswick Pk. SE5 9C 76
Brunswick Pk. Gdns. N11 2E 26
Brunswick Pk. Rd. N11 2E 26
Brunswick Pl. N1 6B 60
Brunswick Pl. NW1 7E 58
(in two parts)
Brunswick Pl. SE19 4E 108
Brunswick Quay. SE16 4H 77
Brunswick Rd. E10 6A 46
Brunswick Rd. E14 9A 62
Brunswick Rd. N15 2C 44
(in two parts)
Brunswick Rd. W5 7H 55
Brunswick Rd. Bexh 3H 97
Brunswick Rd. Enf 2L 17
Brunswick Rd. King T 5L 103
Brunswick Rd. Sutt 6M 121
Brunswick Sq. N17 6D 28
Brunswick Sq. WC1 7J 59
Brunswick St. E17 3A 46
Brunswick Vs. SE5 9C 76
Brunswick Way. N11 4F 26
Brunton Pl. E14 9J 61
Brushfield St. E1 8C 60
(in two parts)
Brushrise. Wat 9F 4
Brussels Rd. SW11 3B 90
Bruton Clo. Chst 4K 111
Bruton La. W1 1F 74
Bruton Pl. W1 1F 74
Bruton Rd. Mord 8A 106
Bruton St. W1 1F 74
Bruton Way. W13 8E 54
Brutus Ct. SE11 5M 75
(off Kennington La.)
Bryan Av. NW10 3F 56
Bryan Clo. Sun 4E 100
Bryan Ho. NW10 3F 56
Bryan Ho. SE16 3K 77
Bryan Rd. SE16 3K 77
Bryan's All. SW6 1M 89
Bryanston Av. Twic 7M 85
Bryanston Clo. S'hall 5K 69
Bryanston Ct. W1 9D 58
(off Seymour Pl., in two parts)
Bryanstone Ct. Sutt 5A 122
Bryanstone Rd. N8 4H 43
Bryanstone Rd. Wal X 7F 6
Bryanston Mans. W1 8D 58
(off York St.)
Bryanston M. E. W1 8D 58
Bryanston M. W. W1 8D 58
Bryanston Pl. W1 8D 58
Bryanston Sq. W1 9D 58
Bryanston St. W1 9D 58
Bryant Av. Romf 8H 35
Bryant Clo. Barn 7K 13
Bryant Ct. E2 5D 60
(off Whiston Rd., in two parts)
Bryant Ct. W3 2B 72
Bryant Rd. N'holt 6G 53
Bryant Row. Noak H 2G 35
Bryant St. E15 3B 62
Bryantwood Rd. N7 1L 59
Brycedale Cres. N14 4G 27
Bryce Ho. SE14 7H 77
(off John Williams Clo.)
Bryce Rd. Dag 9G 49
Brydale Ho. SE16 5H 77
(off Rotherhithe New Rd.)
Bryden Clo. SE26 2J 109
Brydges Pl. WC2 1J 75
Brydges Rd. E15 1B 62
Brydon Wlk. N1 4J 59
Bryer Ct. EC2 8A 60
(off Beech St.)
Bryet Rd. N7 8J 43
Bryher Ct. SE11 6L 75
(off Sancroft St.)
Brymay Clo. E3 5L 61
Brynmaer Rd. SW11 9D 74
Brynmawr Rd. Enf 6D 16
Bryony Clo. Lou 6M 19
Bryony Clo. Uxb 8D 142
Bryony Rd. W12 1E 72
Bryony Way. Sun 3E 100
Buccleugh Ho. E5 5E 44
Buchanan Clo. N21 7K 15
Buchanan Clo. Ave 2M 83
Buchanan Clo. Borwd 4A 12
Buchanan Ct. SE16 5H 77
(off Worgan St.)
Buchanan Gdns. NW10 5F 56
Buchan Clo. Uxb 7A 142
Buchan Rd. SE15 2G 93
Bucharest Rd. SW18 6A 90
Buckbean Path. Romf 7G 35
Buckden Clo. N2 2D 42
Buckden Clo. SE12 5E 94
Buckettsland La. Borwd 2B 12
Buckfast Ct. W13 1E 70
Buckfast Rd. Mord 8M 105
Buckfast St. E2 6E 60
Buck Hill Wlk. W2 1B 74
Buckhold Rd. SW18 5L 89
Buckhurst Av. Cars 3C 122
Buckhurst Ct. Buck H 2H 31
(off Albert Rd.)
Buckhurst Hill. 2H 31
Buckhurst Hill Ho. Buck H 2F 30
Buckhurst Ho. N7 1H 59
Buckhurst St. E1 7F 60
Buckhurst Ter. Buck H 1H 31
Buckhurst Way. Buck H 4H 31
Buckingham Arc. WC2 1J 75
(off Strand)
Buckingham Av. N20 9A 14
Buckingham Av. Felt 5F 84
Buckingham Av. Gnfd 4E 54
Buckingham Av. T Hth 5L 107
Buckingham Av. Well 3C 96
Buckingham Av. W Mol 6M 101
Buckingham Chambers.
SW1 5G 75
(off Greencoat Pl.)
Buckingham Clo. W5 8G 55
Buckingham Clo. Enf 4C 16
Buckingham Clo. Hamp 2K 101
Buckingham Clo. Horn 4H 51
Buckingham Clo. Orp 2C 128
Buckingham Ct. NW4 1E 40
Buckingham Ct. W7 7D 54
(off Copley Clo.)
Buckingham Ct. N'holt 5J 53
Buckingham Ct. Sutt 1L 135
Buckingham Dri. Chst 1A 112
Buckingham Gdns. Edgw 7J 23
Buckingham Gdns. T Hth 6L 107
Buckingham Gdns. W Mol
6M 101
Buckingham Ga. SW1 4G 75
Buckingham Gro. Borwd 6B 12
Buckingham Gro. Uxb 5E 142
Buckingham La. SE23 6J 93
Buckingham Mans. NW6 1M 57
(off W. End La.)
Buckingham M. N1 2C 60
Buckingham M. NW10 5D 56
Buckingham M. SW1 4G 75
(off Stafford Pl.)
Buckingham Palace. 3F 74
Buckingham Pal. Rd. SW1 5F 74
Buckingham Pde. Stan 5G 23
Buckingham Pl. SW1 4G 75
Buckingham Rd. E10 8M 45
Buckingham Rd. E11 3G 47
Buckingham Rd. E15 1D 62
Buckingham Rd. E18 8D 30
Buckingham Rd. N1 2C 60
Buckingham Rd. N22 8J 27
Buckingham Rd. NW10 5D 56
Buckingham Rd. Borwd 6B 12
Buckingham Rd. Edgw 7K 23
Buckingham Rd. Hamp 1K 101
Buckingham Rd. Harr 3B 38
Buckingham Rd. Ilf 7B 48
Buckingham Rd. King T 8K 103
Buckingham Rd. Mitc 8J 107
Buckingham Rd. Rich 8H 87
Buckingham Rd. Wat 1G 9
Buckingham St. WC2 1J 75
Buckingham Way. Wall 1G 137
Buckland Ct. N1 5C 60
(off St Johns Est.)
Buckland Ct. Ick 7A 36
Buckland Cres. NW3 3B 58
Buckland Ri. Pinn 8G 21
Buckland Rd. E10 7A 46
Buckland Rd. Chess 7K 119
Buckland Rd. Orp 6C 128
Buckland Rd. Sutt 2G 135
Bucklands Rd. Tedd 3G 103
Buckland St. N1 5B 60
Buckland's Wharf.
King T 6H 103
Buckland Wlk. W3 3A 72
Buckland Wlk. Mord 8A 106
Buckland Way. Wor Pk 3G 121
Buck La. NW9 3B 40
Bucklebury. NW1 7G 59
(off Stanhope St.)
Buckleigh Av. SW20 7J 105
Buckleigh Rd. SW16 3H 107
Buckleigh Way. SE19 4D 108
Buckler Gdns. SE9 9K 95
Bucklers All. SW6 7K 73
(in two parts)
Bucklersbury. EC4 9B 60
(off Queen Victoria St.)
Bucklersbury Pas.
EC2 & EC4 9B 60
Buckler's Way. Cars 5D 122
Buckles Ct. Belv 5H 81
Buckle St. E1 9D 60
Buckles Way. Bans 8J 135
Buckley Clo. SE23 6F 92
Buckley Clo. Dart 1D 98
Buckley Ct. NW6 3K 57
Buckley Rd. NW6 3K 57
Buckmaster Clo. SW9 2L 91
(off Stockwell Pk. Rd.)
Buckmaster Ho. N7 9K 43
Buckmaster Rd. SW11 3C 90
Bucknalls Clo. Wat 5J 5
Bucknalls Dri. Brick W 4K 5
Bucknalls La. Wat 5H 5
Bucknall St. WC2 9J 59
Bucknall Way. Beck 8M 109
Bucknell Clo. SW9 3K 91
Buckner Rd. SW2 3K 91
Bucknill Ho. SW1 6F 74
(off Ebury Bri. Rd.)
Bucknills Clo. Eps 6A 134
Buckrell Rd. E4 2B 30
Buckridge Ho. EC1 8L 59
(off Portpool La.)
Buck's Av. Wat 9J 9
Bucks Cross Rd. Orp 7J 129
Buckstone Clo. SE23 5G 93
Buckstone Rd. N18 5E 28
Buck St. NW1 3F 58
Buckters Rents. SE16 2J 77
Buckthorne Rd. SE4 4J 93
Buckthorn Ho. Sidc 9D 96
(off Longlands Rd.)
Buckton Rd. Borwd 2K 11
Buck Wlk. E17 2B 46
Buckwheat Ct. Eri 4H 81
Budd Clo. N12 4M 25
Buddings Circ. Wemb 8A 40
Budd's All. Twic 4G 87
Bude Clo. E17 3K 45
Budge La. Mitc 2D 122
Budge Row. EC4 1B 76
Budge's Wlk. W2 2A 74
(off Broad Wlk., The)
Budleigh Cres. Well 9G 81
Budleigh Ho. SE15 8E 76
(off Bird in Bush Rd.)
Budoch Ct. Ilf 7E 48
Budoch Dri. Ilf 7E 48
Buer Rd. SW6 1J 89
Buff Av. Bans 6M 135
Bugsby's Way.
SE10 & SE7 5D 78
Bugsby's Way Retail Est.
SE7 5E 78
(off Bugsby's Way)

Bulbarrow—Bushey Hall Rd.

Bulbarrow. NW8 . . . . .4M 57
(off Abbey Rd.)
Bulganak Rd. T Hth 8A 108
Bulinga St. SW1 . . . . .5J 75
(off John Islip St.)
Bullace La. Dart 5J 99
Bullace Row. SE5 . . . . .9B 76
Bull All. Well 2F 96
Bullard Rd. Tedd 3C 102
Bullard's Pl. E2 . . . . .6H 61
Bullbanks Rd. Belv 5A 82
Bulleid Way. SW1 . . . . .5F 74
Bullen Ho. E1 . . . . .7F 60
(off Collingwood St.)
Bullen St. SW11 . . . . .1C 90
Buller Clo. SE15 . . . . .8E 76
Buller Rd. N17 . . . . .9E 28
Buller Rd. N22 . . . . .9L 27
Buller Rd. NW10 . . . . .6H 57
Buller Rd. Bark 3C 64
Buller Rd. T Hth 6B 108
Bullers Clo. Sidc 2J 113
Bullers Wood Dri. Chst 4K 111
Bullescroft Rd. Edgw 3L 23
Bullfinch Rd. S Croy 2H 139
Bullhead Rd. Borwd 5A 12
Bull Hill. Hort K 8M 115
Bullingham Mans. W8 . . . . . .3L 73
(off Pitt St. La.)
Bull Inn Ct. WC2 . . . . .1J 75
(off Strand)
Bullivant St. E14 . . . . .1A 78
Bull La. N18 . . . . .5C 28
Bull La. Chst 4B 112
Bull La. Dag 8M 49
Bull Rd. E15 . . . . .5D 62
Bullrush Clo. Cars 4C 122
Bullrush Clo. Croy 1C 124
Bullrush Gro. Uxb 7A 142
Bull's All. SW14 . . . . .1B 88
Bull's Bri. Cen. Hay 4F 68
Bull's Bri. Ind. Est. S'hall 5G 69
Bullsbridge Rd. S'hall 5G 69
Bullsbrook Rd. Hay 2G 69
Bulls Cross. 8B 6
Bull's Cross. Enf 8A 6
Bulls Cross Ride. Wal X 6A 6
Bulls Gdns. SW3 . . . . .5C 74
(in two parts)
Bulls Head Pas. EC3 . . . . . . .9C 60
(off Gracechurch St.)
Bulls Head Yd. Dart 5J 99
(off High St.)
Bullsmoor. 8C 6
Bullsmoor Clo. Wal X 8C 6
Bullsmoor Gdns. Wal X 8B 6
Bullsmoor La. Enf 8A 6
Bullsmoor Ride. Wal X 8C 6
Bullsmoor Way. Wal X 8C 6
Bullwell Cres. Chesh 2E 6
Bull Wharf La. EC4 . . . . .1A 76
Bull Yd. SE15 . . . . .9E 76
Bulmer Gdns. Harr 5H 39
Bulmer M. W11 . . . . .1L 73
Bulmer Pl. W11 . . . . .2L 73
Bulmer Wlk. Rain 5G 67
Bulow Est. SW6 . . . . .9M 73
(off Pearscroft Rd.)
Bulstrode Av. Houn 1K 85
Bulstrode Gdns. Houn 2L 85
Bulstrode Pl. W1 . . . . .8E 58
Bulstrode Rd. Houn 2L 85
Bulstrode St. W1 . . . . .9E 58
Bulwer Ct. E11 . . . . .6B 46
Bulwer Ct. Rd. E11 . . . . .6B 46
Bulwer Gdns. Barn 6A 14
Bulwer Rd. E11 . . . . .5B 46
Bulwer Rd. N18 . . . . .4C 28
Bulwer Rd. Barn 6M 13
Bulwer St. W12 . . . . .2G 73
Bunbury Ho. SE15 . . . . .8E 76
(off Fenham Rd.)
Bunbury Way. Eps 8F 134
Bunce's La. Wfd G 7D 30
Bungalow Rd. SE25 . . . . .8C 108
Bungalows, The. E10 . . . . . . .4A 46
Bungalows, The. SW16 . . . . .4F 106
Bungalows, The. Ilf 8C 32
Bungalows, The. Wall 7F 122
Bunhill Row. EC1 . . . . .7B 60
Bunhouse Pl. SW1 . . . . .6E 74
Bunkers Hill. NW11 . . . . .5A 42
Bunkers Hill. Belv 5L 81
Bunkers Hill. Sidc 9K 97
Bunning Way. N7 . . . . .3J 59
Bunns La. NW7 . . . . .6C 24
(in two parts)
Bunsen Ho. E3 . . . . .5J 61
(off Grove Rd.)
Bunsen St. E3 . . . . .5J 61
Buntingbridge Rd. Ilf 3B 48
Bunting Clo. N9 . . . . .1H 29
Bunting Clo. Mitc 9D 106
Bunting Ct. NW9 . . . . .9C 24
Bunton St. SE18 . . . . .4L 79
Bunyan Ct. EC2 . . . . .8A 60
(off Beech St.)
Bunyan Rd. E17 . . . . .1J 45
Buonaparte M. SW1 . . . . . . .6H 75
Burbage Clo. SE1 . . . . .4B 76
Burbage Clo. Chesh 4F 6
Burbage Clo. Hay 9B 52
Burbage Ho. N1 . . . . .4B 60
(off Poole St.)
Burbage Ho. SE14 . . . . .7H 77
(off Samuel Clo.)
Burbage Rd.
SE24 & SE21 . . . . .5A 92
Burberry Clo. N Mald 6C 104
Burbridge Way. N17 . . . . .9E 28
Burcham St. E14 . . . . .9M 61
Burcharbro Rd. SE2 . . . . .7H 81
Burchell Ct. Bush 9A 10
Burchell Ho. SE11 . . . . .6K 75
(off Jonathan St.)
Burchell Rd. E10 . . . . .6M 45
Burchell Rd. SE15 . . . . .9F 76
Burchetts Way. Shep 1A 116
Burchett Way. Romf 4K 49
Burchwall Clo. Romf 7A 34
Burcote. Wey 8B 116
Burcote Rd. SW18 . . . . .6B 90
Burcott Rd. Purl 6L 137
Burden Clo. Bren 6G 71
Burden Ho. SW8 . . . . .8J 75
(off Thorncroft St.)
Burdenshott Av. Rich 3M 87
Burden Way. E11 . . . . .7F 46
Burder Clo. N1 . . . . .2C 60
Burder Rd. N1 . . . . .2C 60
Burdett Av. SW20 . . . . .5E 104
Burdett Clo. W7 . . . . .2D 70
Burdett Clo. Sidc 2J 113
Burdett M. NW3 . . . . .2B 58
Burdett M. W2 . . . . .9M 57
Burdett Rd. E3 & E14 . . . . . . .7J 61
Burdett Rd. Croy 1B 124
Burdett Rd. Rich 1K 87
Burdetts Rd. Dag 4K 65
Burdock Clo. Croy 3H 125
Burdock Rd. N17 . . . . .1E 44
Burdon La. Sutt 9J 121
Burdon Pk. Sutt 1K 135
Bure Ct. New Bar 7M 13
Burfield Clo. SW17 . . . . . . .1B 106
Burford Clo. Dag 8G 49
Burford Clo. Ilf 2A 48
Burford Gdns. N13 . . . . .3K 27
Burford Ho. Bren 6H 71
Burford Ho. Eps 3G 135
Burford La. Eps 3G 135
Burford Rd. E6 . . . . .6J 63
Burford Rd. E15 . . . . .4B 62
Burford Rd. SE6 . . . . .8K 93
Burford Rd. Bren 6J 71
Burford Rd. Brom 8J 111
Burford Rd. Sutt 4L 121
Burford Rd. Wor Pk 2D 120
Burford Wlk. SW6 . . . . .8A 74
Burford Way. New Ad 8A 126
Burgate Clo. Dart 2D 98
Burge Rd. E7 . . . . .9H 47
Burges Clo. Horn 4K 51
Burges Gro. SW13 . . . . .8F 72
Burges Rd. E6 . . . . .3J 63
Burgess Av. NW9 . . . . .4B 40
Burgess Clo. Felt 1J 101
Burgess Ct. E6 . . . . .3L 63
Burgess Ct. Borwd 2K 11
(off Aycliffe Rd.)
Burgess Ct. S'hall 9M 53
(off Fleming Rd.)
Burgess Hill. NW2 . . . . .9L 41
Burgess Ind. Pk. SE5 . . . . . . .8B 76
Burgess M. SW19 . . . . .3M 105
Burgess Pk. 7C 76
Burgess Rd. E6 . . . . .3L 63
Burgess Rd. E15 . . . . .9C 46
Burgess Rd. Sutt 6M 121
Burgess St. E14 . . . . .8L 61
Burge St. SE1 . . . . .4B 76
Burgh Cft. Eps 7D 134
Burghfield. Eps 7D 134
Burgh Heath Rd. Eps 6D 134
Burghill Rd. SE26 . . . . .1J 109
Burghley Av. Borwd 7A 12
Burghley Av. N Mald 5B 104
Burghley Hall Clo. SW19 . . . .7J 89
Burghley Pl. Mitc 9D 106
Burghley Rd. E11 . . . . .6C 46
Burghley Rd. N8 . . . . .1L 43
Burghley Rd. NW5 . . . . .9F 42
Burghley Rd. SW19 . . . . . . .1H 105
Burghley Tower. W3 . . . . .1D 72
Burgh Mt. Bans 7K 135
Burgh St. N1 . . . . .5M 59
Burgh Wood. Bans 7J 135
Burgon St. EC4 . . . . .9M 59
Burgos Clo. Croy 8L 123
Burgos Gro. SE10 . . . . .9M 77
Burgoyne Rd. N4 . . . . .4M 43
Burgoyne Rd. SE25 . . . . . . .8D 108
Burgoyne Rd. SW9 . . . . .2K 91
Burgoyne Rd. Sun 3D 100
Burham Clo. SE20 . . . . .4G 109
Burhill. 9F 116
Burhill Gro. Pinn 9J 21
Burhill Rd. W on T 9F 116
Burke Clo. SW15 . . . . .3C 88
Burke Lodge. E13 . . . . .6F 62
Burke St. E16 . . . . .8D 62
(in two parts)
Burket Clo. S'hall 5J 69
Burland Rd. SW11 . . . . .4D 90
Burland Rd. Romf 6A 34
Burlea Clo. W on T 7F 116
Burleigh Av. Sidc 4D 96
Burleigh Av. Wall 5E 122
Burleigh Gdns. N14 . . . . .1G 27
Burleigh Gdns. Ashf 2A 100
Burleigh Ho. SW3 . . . . .7B 74
(off Beaufort St.)
Burleigh Ho. W10 . . . . .8J 57
(off St Charles Sq.)
Burleigh Pde. N14 . . . . .1H 27
Burleigh Pl. SW15 . . . . .4H 89
Burleigh Rd. Chesh 5E 6
Burleigh Rd. Enf 6C 16
Burleigh Rd. Sutt 3J 121
Burleigh Rd. Uxb 4F 142
Burleigh St. WC2 . . . . .1K 75
Burleigh Wlk. SE6 . . . . .7A 94
Burleigh Way. Enf 5B 16
Burley Clo. E4 . . . . .5L 29
Burley Clo. SW16 . . . . .6H 107
Burley Ho. E1 . . . . .9H 61
(off Chudleigh St.)
Burley Rd. E16 . . . . .9G 63
Burlington Arc. W1 . . . . .1G 75
Burlington Av. Rich 9L 71
Burlington Av. Romf 4M 49
Burlington Clo. E6 . . . . .9J 63
Burlington Clo. W9 . . . . .7L 57
Burlington Clo. Felt 6B 84
Burlington Clo. Orp 4M 127
Burlington Clo. Pinn 1F 36
Burlington Gdns. SW6 . . . . . .1J 89
Burlington Gdns. W1 . . . . . . .1G 75
Burlington Gdns. W3 . . . . . . .2A 72
Burlington Gdns. W4 . . . . . . .6A 72
Burlington Gdns. Romf 5J 49
Burlington La. W4 . . . . .8A 72
Burlington M. SW15 . . . . .4K 89
Burlington M. W3 . . . . .2A 72
Burlington Pl. SW6 . . . . .1J 89
Burlington Pl. Wfd G 3F 30
Burlington Ri. E Barn 1C 26
Burlington Rd. N10 . . . . .1E 42
Burlington Rd. N17 . . . . .8E 28
Burlington Rd. SW6 . . . . .1J 89
Burlington Rd. W4 . . . . .6A 72
Burlington Rd. Enf 3B 16
Burlington Rd. Iswth 9B 70
Burlington Rd. N Mald 8D 104
Burlington Rd. T Hth 6A 108
Burma M. N16 . . . . .9B 44
Burman Clo. Dart 6M 99
Burma Rd. N16 . . . . .9B 44
Burmarsh Ct. SE20 . . . . . . .5G 109
Burma Ter. SE19 . . . . .2C 108
Burmester Rd. SW17 . . . . . . .9A 90
Burnaby Cres. W4 . . . . .7A 72
Burnaby Gdns. W4 . . . . .7M 71
Burnaby St. SW10 . . . . .8A 74
Burnand Ho. W14 . . . . .4H 73
(off Redan St.)
Burnard Pl. N7 . . . . .1K 59
Burnaston Ho. E5 . . . . .8E 44
Burnbrae Clo. N12 . . . . .6M 25
Burnbury Rd. SW12 . . . . .7G 91
Burn Clo. Bush 5B 10
Burn Clo. Oxs 7B 132
Burncroft Av. Enf 4G 17
Burndell Way. Hay 8H 53
Burne Jones Ho. W14 . . . . . .5J 73
Burnell Av. Rich 2G 103
Burnell Av. Well 1E 96
Burnell Gdns. Stan 9H 23
Burnell Rd. Sutt 6M 121
Burnell Wlk. SE1 . . . . .6D 76
(off Abingdon Clo.)
Burnels Av. E6 . . . . .6L 63
Burness Clo. N7 . . . . .2K 59
Burness Clo. Uxb 5B 142
Burne St. NW1 . . . . .8C 58
Burnet Gro. Eps 5A 134
Burnett Clo. E9 . . . . .1G 61
Burnett Ho. SE13 . . . . .1A 94
(off Lewisham Hill)
Burnett Rd. Eri 7H 83
Burney Av. Surb 9K 103
Burney Dri. Lou 4M 19
(in two parts)
Burney St. SE10 . . . . .8A 78
Burnfoot Av. SW6 . . . . .9J 73
Burnham. NW3 . . . . .3C 58
Burnham Av. Uxb 9A 36
Burnham Clo. NW7 . . . . .7E 24
Burnham Clo. SE1 . . . . .5D 76
Burnham Clo. Enf 2C 16
Burnham Clo. W'stone 2E 38
Burnham Ct. W2 . . . . .1M 73
(off Moscow Rd.)
Burnham Cres. E11 . . . . .2G 47
Burnham Cres. Dart 3G 99
Burnham Dri. Wor Pk 4H 121
Burnham Est. E2 . . . . .6G 61
(off Burnham St.)
Burnham Gdns. Croy 2D 124
Burnham Gdns. Hay 4B 68
Burnham Gdns. Houn 9F 68
Burnham Rd. E4 . . . . .5K 29
Burnham Rd. Dag 3F 64
Burnham Rd. Dart 3G 99
Burnham Rd. Mord 8M 105
Burnham Rd. Romf 1B 50
Burnham Rd. Sidc 8J 97
Burnham St. E2 . . . . .6G 61
Burnham St. King T 5L 103
Burnham Ter. Dart 4H 99
Burnham Trad. Est. Dart 3H 99
Burnham Way. SE26 . . . . . .2K 109
Burnham Way. W13 . . . . .5F 70
Burnhill Rd. Beck 6L 109
Burnley Clo. Wat 5G 21
Burnley Rd. NW10 . . . . .1D 56
Burnley Rd. SW9 . . . . .1K 91
Burnsall St. SW3 . . . . .6C 74
Burns Av. Chad H 5G 49
Burns Av. Felt 5E 84
Burns Av. Sidc 5F 96
Burns Av. S'hall 1L 69
Burns Clo. E17 . . . . .2A 46
Burns Clo. SW19 . . . . .3B 106
Burns Clo. Cars 1E 136
Burns Clo. Eri 9D 82
Burns Clo. Hay 8D 52
Burns Clo. Well 9D 80
Burns Dri. Bans 6J 135
Burns Ho. E2 . . . . .6G 61
(off Cornwall Av.)
Burns Ho. SE17 . . . . .6M 75
(off Doddington Gro.)
Burn Side. N9 . . . . .3G 29
Burnside. Asht 9K 133
Burnside Av. E4 . . . . .6K 29
Burnside Clo. SE16 . . . . .2H 77
Burnside Clo. Barn 5L 13
Burnside Clo. Twic 5E 86
Burnside Cres. Wemb 4H 55
Burnside Ind. Est. Ilf 5F 32
Burnside Rd. Dag 7G 49
Burns Rd. NW10 . . . . .4D 56
Burns Rd. SW11 . . . . .1D 90
Burns Rd. W13 . . . . .3F 70
Burns Rd. Wemb 5J 55
Burns Way. Houn 1H 85
Burnt Ash Hill. SE12 . . . . . . .5D 94
(in two parts)
Burnt Ash La. Brom 4E 110
Burnt Ash Rd. SE12 . . . . .4D 94
Burnt Ho. La. Dart 1J 115
(in two parts)
Burnthwaite Rd. SW6 . . . . . .8K 73
Burnt Oak. 9A 24
Burnt Oak B'way. Edgw 7M 23
Burnt Oak Fields. Edgw 8A 24
Burnt Oak La. Sidc 5E 96
Burntwood Av. Horn 4H 51
Burntwood Clo. SW18 . . . . . .7C 90
Burntwood Grange Rd.
SW18 . . . . .7B 90
Burntwood La. SW17 . . . . . . .9A 90
Burntwood Vw. SE19 . . . . . .2D 108
Burnway. Horn 5J 51
Buross St. E1 . . . . .9F 60
Burpham Clo. Hay 8H 53
Burrage Ct. SE16 . . . . .5H 77
(off Worgan St.)
Burrage Gro. SE18 . . . . .5A 80
Burrage Pl. SE18 . . . . .6M 79
Burrage Rd. SE18 . . . . .7A 80
Burrard Rd. E16 . . . . .9F 62
Burrard Rd. NW6 . . . . .1L 57
Burr Bank Ter. Wilm 1G 115
Burr Clo. E1 . . . . .2E 76
Burr Clo. Bexh 2K 97
Burrell Clo. Croy 1J 125
Burrell Clo. Edgw 2M 23
Burrell Row. Beck 6L 109
Burrell St. SE1 . . . . .2M 75
Burrells Wharf Sq. E14 . . . . .6L 77
Burrell Towers. E10 . . . . .5L 45
Burrfield Dri. Orp 9H 113
Burrhill Ct. SE16 . . . . .4H 77
(off Worgan St.)
Burritt Rd. King T 6L 103
Burroughs Cotts. E14 . . . . . . .8J 61
(off Halley St.)
Burroughs Gdns. NW4 . . . . . .2F 40
Burroughs Pde. NW4 . . . . . . .2F 40
Burroughs, The. NW4 . . . . . . .2F 40
Burrow Clo. Chig 5D 32
Burrow Grn. Chig 5D 32
Burrow Ho. SW9 . . . . .1L 91
(off Stockwell Pk. Rd.)
Burrow Rd. SE22 . . . . .3C 92
Burrow Rd. Chig 5D 32
Burrows M. SE1 . . . . .3M 75
Burrows Rd. NW10 . . . . .6G 57
Burrow Wlk. SE21 . . . . .6A 92
Burr Rd. SW18 . . . . .7L 89
Bursar St. SE1 . . . . .2C 76
Bursdon Clo. Sidc 8D 96
Bursland Rd. Enf 6H 17
Burslem Av. Ilf 6E 32
Burslem St. E1 . . . . .9E 60
Burstock Rd. SW15 . . . . .3J 89
Burston Dri. Park 1M 5
Burston Rd. SW15 . . . . .4H 89
Burstow Rd. SW20 . . . . . . .5J 105
Burtenshaw Rd. Th Dit 2E 118
Burtley Clo. N4 . . . . .6A 44
Burton Av. Wat 6E 8
Burton Bank. N1 . . . . .3B 60
(off Yeate St.)
Burton Clo. Chess 9H 119
Burton Clo. T Hth 7B 108
Burton Ct. SE20 . . . . .6G 109
Burton Ct. SW3 . . . . .6D 74
(off Turks Row, in two parts)
Burton Dri. Enf 1L 17
Burton Gdns. Houn 9K 69
Burton Gro. SE17 . . . . .6B 76
Burtonhole Clo. NW7 . . . . . . .4H 25
Burtonhole La. NW7 . . . . . . .5G 25
(in two parts)
Burton Ho. SE16 . . . . .3F 76
(off Cherry Garden St.)
Burton La. SW9 . . . . .1L 91
(in two parts)
Burton M. SW1 . . . . .5E 74
Burton Pl. WC1 . . . . .7H 59
Burton Rd. E18 . . . . .1F 46
Burton Rd. NW6 . . . . .3K 57
Burton Rd. SW9 . . . . .1M 91
(Akerman Rd.)
Burton Rd. SW9 . . . . .1L 91
(Brixton Rd.)
Burton Rd. King T 4J 103
Burton Rd. Lou 6M 19
Burton's Rd. Hamp H 1M 101
Burton St. WC1 . . . . .6H 59
Burtonwood Ho. N4 . . . . .5B 44
Burt Rd. E16 . . . . .2G 79
Burtt Ho. N1 . . . . .6C 60
(off Aske St.)
Burtwell La. SE27 . . . . .1B 108
Burvale Ct. Wat 5F 8
Burwash Ct. St M 9G 113
Burwash Ho. SE1 . . . . .3B 76
(off Kipling Est.)
Burwash Rd. SE18 . . . . .6B 80
Burwell. King T 6L 103
(off Excelsior Rd.)
Burwell Av. Gnfd 2C 54
Burwell Clo. E1 . . . . .9F 60
Burwell Rd. E10 . . . . .6J 45
Burwell Rd. Ind. Est. E10 . . . .6J 45
Burwell Wlk. E3 . . . . .7L 61
Burwood Av. Brom 4F 126
Burwood Av. Kenl 6M 137
Burwood Av. Pinn 3F 36
Burwood Clo. Surb 3L 119
Burwood Clo. W on T 8G 117
Burwood Gdns. Rain 6D 66
Burwood Ho. SW9 . . . . .3M 91
Burwood Park. 7D 116
Burwood Pk. Rd.
W on T 6F 116
Burwood Pl. W2 . . . . .9C 58
Burwood Pl. Barn 3A 14
Burwood Rd. W on T 9C 116
Bury Av. Hay 5C 52
Bury Av. Ruis 4A 36
Bury Clo. SE16 . . . . .2H 77
Bury Ct. EC3 . . . . .9C 60
Bury Green. 4A 6
Bury Grn. Rd. Chesh 4A 6
(in two parts)
Bury Gro. Mord 9M 105
Bury Hall Vs. N9 . . . . .9D 16
Bury Pl. WC1 . . . . .8J 59
Bury Rd. E4 . . . . .5B 18
Bury Rd. N22 . . . . .9L 27
Bury Rd. Dag 1M 65
Buryside Clo. Ilf 2D 48
Bury St. EC3 . . . . .9C 60
Bury St. N9 . . . . .9D 16
Bury St. SW1 . . . . .2G 75
Bury St. Ruis 3A 36
Bury St. W. N9 . . . . .9B 16
Bury Wlk. SW3 . . . . .5C 74
Busbridge Ho. E14 . . . . .8L 61
(off Brabazon St.)
Busby M. NW5 . . . . .2H 59
Busby Pl. NW5 . . . . .2H 59
Busch Clo. Iswth 9F 70
Bushbaby Clo. SE1 . . . . .4C 76
Bushbarns. Chesh 2A 6
Bushberry Rd. E9 . . . . .2J 61
Bush Clo. Ilf 3B 48
Bush Cotts. SW18 . . . . .4L 89
Bush Ct. N14 . . . . .1H 27
Bush Ct. W12 . . . . .3H 73
Bushell Clo. SW2 . . . . .8K 91
Bushell Grn. Bus H 2B 22
Bushell St. E1 . . . . .2E 76
Bushell Way. Chst 2L 111
Bush Elms Rd. Horn 5E 50
Bushey. 8M 9
Bushey Av. E18 . . . . .1D 46
Bushey Av. Orp 2B 128
Bushey Clo. E4 . . . . .3A 30
Bushey Clo. Kenl 8D 138
Bushey Ct. SW20 . . . . .7F 104
Bushey Down. SW12 . . . . . . .8F 90
Bushey Golf & Country Club.
. . . . .9L 9
Bushey Grn. Rd. Bush 6H 9
Bushey Hall Dri. Bush 6J 9
Bushey Hall Golf Course. . . .5J 9
Bushey Hall Mobile Home Pk.
Bush 5J 9
Bushey Hall Rd. Bush 6H 9

Canterbury Ho.—Carshalton Pl.

Canterbury Ho. *Bark* 3E **64**
(off Margaret Bondfield Av.)
Canterbury Ho. *Borwd* 4L **11**
(off Stratfield Rd.)
Canterbury Ho. *Croy* 3B **124**
(off Sydenham Rd.)
Canterbury Ho. *Eri* 8D **82**
Canterbury Ho. *Wat* 4G **9**
(off Anglian Clo.)
Canterbury Ind. Pk. *SE15* 7G **77**
Canterbury M. *Oxs* 5A **132**
Canterbury Pl. *SE17* 6M **75**
Canterbury Rd. *E10* 5A **46**
Canterbury Rd. *NW6* 5K **57**
(in two parts)
Canterbury Rd. *Borwd* 4L **11**
Canterbury Rd. *Croy* 2K **123**
Canterbury Rd. *Felt* 8J **85**
Canterbury Rd. *Harr* 3M **37**
Canterbury Rd. *Mord* 2M **121**
Canterbury Rd. *Wat* 4F **8**
Canterbury Ter. *NW6* 5L **57**
Canterbury Way. *Crox G* 5A **8**
Cantium Retail Pk. *SE1* 7E **76**
Cantley Gdns. *SE19* 5D **108**
Cantley Gdns. *Ilf* 4A **48**
Cantley Rd. *W7* 4E **70**
Canton St. *E14* 9L **61**
Cantrel Lodge. *Enf* 9D **6**
Cantrell Rd. *E3* 7K **61**
Cantwell Rd. *SE18* 8M **79**
Canute Gdns. *SE16* 5H **77**
Canvey St. *SE1* 2A **76**
Cape Clo. *Bark* 3M **63**
Cape Henry Ct. *E14* 1B **78**
(off Jamestown Way)
Cape Ho. *E8* 2D **60**
(off Dalston La.)
Capel Av. *Wall* 7K **123**
Capel Clo. *N20* 3A **26**
Capel Clo. *Brom* 3J **127**
Capel Ct. *EC2* 9B **60**
(off Bartholomew La.)
Capel Ct. *SE20* 5G **109**
Capel Gdns. *Ilf* 9D **48**
Capel Gdns. *Pinn* 2K **37**
Capel Ho. *E9* 3G **61**
(off Loddiges Rd.)
Capella Rd. *N'wd* 4D **20**
Capel Pl. *Dart* 1G **115**
Capel Rd. *E7 & E12* 9F **46**
Capel Rd. *Barn* 8C **14**
Capel Rd. *Enf* 9B **6**
Capel Rd. *Wat* 8J **9**
Capelvere Wlk. *Wat* 3C **8**
Capener's Clo. *SW1* 3E **74**
(off Kinnerton St.)
Capern Rd. *SW18* 7A **90**
Cape Rd. *N17* 1E **44**
Cape Yd. *E1* 1E **76**
Capital Bus. Cen. *Wat* 9H **5**
Capital Bus. Cen. *Wemb* 5H **55**
Capital Ind. Est. *Belv* 4M **81**
Capital Ind. Est. *Mitc* 9D **106**
Capital Interchange Way.
Bren 6L **71**
Capital Pl. *Croy* 7K **123**
Capital Wharf. *E1* 2E **76**
Capitol Ind. Pk. *NW9* 1A **40**
Capitol Way. *NW9* 1A **40**
Capland Ho. *NW8* 7B **58**
(off Capland St.)
Capland St. *NW8* 7B **58**
Caple Ho. *SW10* 8A **74**
(off King's Rd.)
Caple Rd. *NW10* 5D **56**
Capper St. *W1* 7G **59**
Caprea Clo. *Hay* 8H **53**
Capricorn Cen. *Dag* 5K **49**
Capri Ho. *E17* 9K **29**
Capri Rd. *Croy* 3D **124**
Capstan Clo. *Romf* 4F **48**
Capstan Ct. *E1* 1G **77**
(off Wapping Wall)
Capstan Ct. *Dart* 3M **99**
Capstan Ho. *E14* 5A **78**
(off Stebondale St.)
Capstan Ho. *E14* 1B **78**
(off Clove Cres.)
Capstan Ride. *Enf* 4L **15**
Capstan Rd. *SE8* 5K **77**
Capstan Sq. *E14* 3A **78**
Capstan Way. *SE16* 2J **77**
Capstone Rd. *Brom* 1D **110**
Capthorne Av. *Harr* 6J **37**
Capuchin Clo. *Stan* 6F **22**
Capulet M. *E16* 2E **78**
Capworth St. *E10* 6L **45**
Caractacus Cottage Vw.
Wat 9E **8**
Caractacus Grn. *Wat* 8D **8**
Caradoc Clo. *W2* 9L **57**
Caradoc Evans Clo. *N11* 5F **26**
(off Springfield Rd.)
Caradoc St. *SE10* 6C **78**
Caradon Clo. *E11* 6C **46**
Caradon Way. *N15* 2B **44**
Caranday Villas. *W11* 2H **73**
(off Norland Rd.)
Caravel Clo. *E14* 4L **77**
Caravelle Gdns. *N'holt* 6H **53**
Caravel M. *SE8* 7L **77**
Caraway Clo. *E13* 8F **62**
Caraway Heights. *E14* 1A **78**
(off Poplar High St.)
Caraway Pl. *Wall* 5F **122**
Carberry Rd. *SE19* 3C **108**
Carbery Av. *W3* 3K **71**
Carbis Clo. *E4* 1B **30**
Carbis Rd. *E14* 9K **61**
Carbrooke Ho. *E9* 4G **61**
(off Templecombe Rd.)
Carbuncle Pas. Way. *N17* 9E **28**
Carburton St. *W1* 8F **58**
Carbury Clo. *Horn* 2G **67**
Cardale St. *E14* 3A **78**
Carden Rd. *SE15* 2F **92**
Cardiff Ho. *SE15* 7E **76**
(off Friary Est.)
Cardiff Rd. *W7* 4E **70**
Cardiff Rd. *Enf* 6F **16**
Cardiff Rd. *Wat* 8F **8**
(in two parts)
Cardiff Rd. Ind. Est. *Wat* 8F **8**
Cardiff St. *SE18* 8C **80**
Cardiff Way. *Ab L* 5E **4**
Cardigan Ct. *W7* 7D **54**
(off Copley Clo.)
Cardigan Gdns. *Ilf* 7E **48**
Cardigan Ho. *Romf* 5H **35**
(off Bridgwater Wlk.)
Cardigan Pl. *SE3* 1B **94**
Cardigan Rd. *E3* 5K **61**
Cardigan Rd. *SW13* 1E **88**
Cardigan Rd. *SW19* 3A **106**
Cardigan Rd. *Rich* 5J **87**
Cardigan St. *SE11* 6L **75**
Cardigan Wlk. *N1* 3A **60**
(off Ashby Gro.)
Cardinal Av. *Borwd* 5M **11**
Cardinal Av. *King T* 2J **103**
Cardinal Av. *Mord* 1J **121**
Cardinal Bourne St. *SE1* 4B **76**
Cardinal Cap All. *SE1* 2A **76**
Cardinal Clo. *Chst* 5B **112**
Cardinal Clo. *Edgw* 7A **24**
Cardinal Clo. *Mord* 1J **121**
Cardinal Clo. *S Croy* 5E **138**
Cardinal Clo. *Wor Pk* 6E **120**
Cardinal Ct. *E1* 1E **76**
(off Thomas More St.)
Cardinal Cres. *N Mald* 6A **104**
Cardinal Dri. *Ilf* 6A **32**
Cardinal Dri. *W on T* 3H **117**
Cardinal Hinsley Clo.
NW10 5E **56**
Cardinal Pl. *SW15* 3H **89**
Cardinal Rd. *Felt* 7F **84**
Cardinal Rd. *Ruis* 6H **37**
Cardinals Wlk. *Hamp* 4A **102**
Cardinals Wlk. *Sun* 3C **100**
Cardinals Way. *N19* 6H **43**
Cardinal Way. *Harr* 1C **38**
Cardinal Way. *Rain* 5H **67**
Cardine M. *SE15* 8F **76**
Cardington Rd. *H'row A* 2F **144**
Cardington Sq. *Houn* 3H **85**
Cardington St. *NW1* 6G **59**
Cardinham Rd. *Orp* 6D **128**
Cardozo Rd. *N7* 1J **59**
Cardrew Av. *N12* 5B **26**
Cardrew Clo. *N12* 5C **26**
Cardrew Ct. *N12* 5B **26**
Cardross Ho. *W6* 4F **72**
(off Cardross St.)
Cardross St. *W6* 4F **72**
Cardwell Rd. *N7* 9J **43**
Career Ct. *SE16* 3H **77**
(off Christopher Clo.)
Carew Clo. *N7* 7K **43**
Carew Ct. *SE14* 7H **77**
(off Samuel Clo.)
Carew Ct. *Sutt* 1M **135**
Carew Manor & Dovecote.
5G **123**
Carew Mnr. Cotts. *Wall* 5H **123**
Carew Rd. *N17* 9E **28**
Carew Rd. *W13* 3G **71**
Carew Rd. *Ashf* 3A **100**
Carew Rd. *Mitc* 6E **106**
Carew Rd. *N'wd* 6C **20**
Carew Rd. *T Hth* 8M **107**
Carew Rd. *Wall* 8G **123**
Carew St. *SE5* 1A **92**
Carew Way. *Wat* 3K **21**
Carey Ct. *SE5* 8A **76**
Carey Ct. *Bexh* 4M **97**
Carey Gdns. *SW8* 9G **75**
Carey La. *EC2* 9A **60**
Carey Mans. *SW1* 5H **75**
(off Rutherford St.)
Carey Pl. *SW1* 5H **75**
Carey Pl. *Wat* 6G **9**
Carey Rd. *Dag* 9J **49**
Carey St. *WC2* 9K **59**
Carey Way. *Wemb* 9M **39**
Carfax Pl. *SW4* 3H **91**
Carfax Rd. *Hay* 6D **68**
Carfax Rd. *Horn* 9D **50**
Carfree Clo. *N1* 3L **59**
Cargill Rd. *SW18* 7M **89**
Cargreen Pl. *SE25* 8D **108**
Cargreen Rd. *SE25* 8D **108**
Cargrey Ho. *Stan* 5G **23**
Carholme Rd. *SE23* 7K **93**
Carillon Ct. *W5* 1H **71**
Carina M. *SE27* 1A **108**
Carinthia Ct. *SE16* 5J **77**
(off Plough Way)
Carisbrooke Av. *Bex* 7H **97**
Carisbrooke Av. *Wat* 3H **9**
Carisbrooke Clo. *Enf* 3D **16**
Carisbrooke Clo. *Horn* 6L **51**
Carisbrooke Clo. *Stan* 9H **23**
Carisbrooke Ct. *W3* 3A **72**
(off Brouncker Rd.)
Carisbrooke Ct. *Cheam* 9K **121**
Carisbrooke Ct. *Dart* 5M **99**
(off Osbourne Rd.)
Carisbrooke Ct. *N'holt* 4K **53**
(off Eskdale Av.)
Carisbrooke Gdns. *SE15* 8D **76**
Carisbrooke Rd. *E17* 2J **45**
Carisbrooke Rd. *Brom* 8G **111**
Carisbrooke Rd. *Mitc* 8H **107**
Carker's La. *NW5* 1F **58**
Carleton Av. *Wall* 1H **137**
Carleton Clo. *Esh* 3B **118**
Carleton Gdns. *N19* 1G **59**
Carleton Rd. *N7* 1H **59**
Carleton Rd. *Chesh* 1D **6**
Carleton Rd. *Dart* 6L **99**
Carleton Vs. *NW5* 1G **59**
Carlile Clo. *E3* 5K **61**
Carlina Gdns. *Wfd G* 5F **30**
Carlingford Gdns. *Mitc* 4D **106**
Carlingford Rd. *N8* 1M **43**
Carlingford Rd. *NW3* 9B **42**
Carlingford Rd. *Mord* 1H **121**
Carlisle Av. *EC3* 9D **60**
Carlisle Av. *W3* 9C **56**
Carlisle Clo. *King T* 5L **103**
Carlisle Clo. *Pinn* 6J **37**
Carlisle Gdns. *Harr* 5H **39**
Carlisle Gdns. *Ilf* 4J **47**
Carlisle Ho. *Borwd* 4L **11**
Carlisle La. *SE1* 4K **75**
Carlisle Mans. *SW1* 5G **75**
(off Carlisle Pl.)
Carlisle M. *King T* 5L **103**
Carlisle Pl. *N11* 4F **26**
Carlisle Pl. *SW1* 4G **75**
Carlisle Rd. *E10* 6L **45**
Carlisle Rd. *N4* 5L **43**
Carlisle Rd. *NW6* 4J **57**
Carlisle Rd. *NW9* 1A **40**
Carlisle Rd. *Dart* 5L **99**
Carlisle Rd. *Hamp* 4M **101**
Carlisle Rd. *Romf* 3E **50**
Carlisle Rd. *Sutt* 8K **121**
Carlisle St. *W1* 9H **59**
Carlisle Wlk. *E8* 2D **60**
Carlisle Way. *SW17* 2E **106**
Carlos Pl. *W1* 1E **74**
Carlow St. *NW1* 5G **59**
Carlson Ct. *SW15* 3K **89**
Carlton Av. *N14* 7H **15**
Carlton Av. *Felt* 5G **85**
Carlton Av. *Harr* 3F **38**
Carlton Av. *Hay* 5C **68**
Carlton Av. *S Croy* 9C **124**
Carlton Av. E. *Wemb* 7H **39**
Carlton Av. W. *Wemb* 7F **38**
Carlton Clo. *NW3* 7L **41**
Carlton Clo. *Borwd* 6B **12**
Carlton Clo. *Chess* 8H **119**
Carlton Clo. *Edgw* 5L **23**
Carlton Clo. *N'holt* 1A **54**
Carlton Clo. *Upm* 7M **51**
Carlton Ct. *SE20* 5F **108**
Carlton Ct. *SW9* 9M **75**
Carlton Ct. *W9* 5M **57**
(off Maida Va.)
Carlton Ct. *Ilf* 1B **48**
Carlton Ct. *Uxb* 8B **142**
Carlton Ct. *Wat* 8H **9**
Carlton Cres. *Sutt* 6J **121**
Carlton Dri. *SW15* 4H **89**
Carlton Dri. *Ilf* 1B **48**
Carlton Gdns. *SW1* 2H **75**
Carlton Gdns. *W5* 9G **55**
Carlton Grn. *Sidc* 1D **112**
Carlton Gro. *SE15* 9F **76**
Carlton Hill. *NW8* 5M **57**
Carlton Ho. *NW6* 5L **57**
(off Canterbury Ter., in five parts)
Carlton Ho. *SE16* 3H **77**
(off Wolfe Cres.)
Carlton Ho. *Felt* 5D **84**
Carlton Ho. *Houn* 5L **85**
Carlton Ho. *Lou* 7H **19**
Carlton Ho. Ter. *SW1* 2H **75**
Carlton Lodge. *N4* 5L **43**
(off Carlton Rd.)
Carlton Mans. *NW6* 3L **57**
(off W. End La.)
Carlton Mans. *W9* 6M **57**
Carlton M. *NW6* 6L **57**
Carlton Pde. *Orp* 2F **128**
Carlton Pde. *Wemb* 7J **39**
Carlton Pk. Av. *SW20* 6H **105**
Carlton Pl. *N'wd* 5A **20**
Carlton Rd. *E11* 6D **46**
Carlton Rd. *E12* 9H **47**
Carlton Rd. *E17* 8J **29**
Carlton Rd. *N4* 5L **43**
Carlton Rd. *N11* 5E **26**
Carlton Rd. *SW14* 2A **88**
Carlton Rd. *W4* 3B **72**
Carlton Rd. *W5* 1G **71**
Carlton Rd. *Eri* 7M **81**
Carlton Rd. *N Mald* 6C **104**
Carlton Rd. *Romf* 3D **50**
Carlton Rd. *Sidc* 2D **112**
Carlton Rd. *S Croy* 8B **124**
Carlton Rd. *Sun* 4D **100**
Carlton Rd. *W on T* 2F **116**
Carlton Rd. *Well* 2F **96**
Carlton Sq. *E1* 7H **61**
(in two parts)
Carlton St. *SW1* 1H **75**
Carlton Ter. *E7* 3G **63**
Carlton Ter. *E11* 3F **46**
Carlton Ter. *N18* 3B **28**
Carlton Ter. *SE26* 9G **93**
Carlton Tower Pl.
SW1 4D **74**
Carlton Va. *NW6* 5K **57**
Carlwell St. *SW17* 2C **106**
Carlyle Av. *Brom* 7H **111**
Carlyle Av. *S'hall* 1K **69**
Carlyle Clo. *N2* 4A **42**
Carlyle Clo. *NW10* 4B **56**
Carlyle Clo. *W Mol* 6M **101**
Carlyle Ct. *SW6* 9M **73**
(off Imperial Rd.)
Carlyle Ct. *SW10* 9A **74**
(off Chelsea Harbour)
Carlyle Gdns. *S'hall* 1K **69**
Carlyle M. *E1* 7H **61**
Carlyle Pl. *SW15* 3H **89**
Carlyle Rd. *E12* 9J **47**
Carlyle Rd. *SE28* 1F **80**
Carlyle Rd. *W5* 5G **71**
Carlyle Rd. *Croy* 4E **124**
Carlyle's House. 7C **74**
(off Cheyne Row)
Carlyle Sq. *SW3* 6B **74**
Carlyon Av. *Harr* 9K **37**
Carlyon Clo. *Wemb* 4J **55**
Carlyon Rd. *Hay* 8G **53**
(in two parts)
Carlyon Rd. *Wemb* 5J **55**
Carlys Clo. *Beck* 6H **109**
Carmalt Gdns. *SW15* 3G **89**
Carmalt Gdns. *W on T* 7G **117**
Carmarthen Ct. *W7* 7D **54**
(off Copley Clo.)
Carmarthen Grn. *NW9* 3C **40**
Carmarthen Pl. *SE1* 3C **76**
Carmel Ct. *W8* 3M **73**
(off Holland St.)
Carmelite Clo. *Harr* 8A **22**
Carmelite Rd. *Harr* 8A **22**
Carmelite St. *EC4* 1L **75**
Carmelite Wlk. *Harr* 8A **22**
Carmelite Way. *Harr* 9A **22**
Carmen Ct. *Borwd* 3K **11**
(off Aycliffe Rd.)
Carmen St. *E14* 9M **61**
Carmichael Clo. *SW11* 2B **90**
Carmichael Ct. *SW13* 1D **88**
(off Grove Rd.)
Carmichael Ho. *E14* 1A **78**
(off Poplar High St.)
Carmichael M. *SW18* 6B **90**
Carmichael Rd. *SE25* 9D **108**
Carmine Ct. *Brom* 4D **110**
Carminia Rd. *SW17* 8F **90**
Carnaby St. *W1* 9G **59**
Carnac St. *SE27* 1B **108**
Carnanton Rd. *E17* 8B **30**
Carnarvon Av. *Enf* 5D **16**
Carnarvon Dri. *Hay* 4A **68**
Carnarvon Rd. *E10* 3A **46**
Carnarvon Rd. *E15* 2D **62**
Carnarvon Rd. *E18* 8D **30**
Carnarvon Rd. *Barn* 5J **13**
Carnation Clo. *Rush G* 7C **50**
Carnation St. *SE2* 6F **80**
Carnbrook Rd. *SE3* 2H **95**
Carnecke Gdns. *SE9* 4J **95**
Carnegie Clo. *Enf* 2M **17**
Carnegie Clo. *Surb* 4K **119**
Carnegie Pl. *SW19* 9H **89**
Carnegie Rd. *Harr* 5D **38**
Carnegie St. *N1* 4K **59**
Carnet Clo. *Dart* 6C **98**
Carnforth Clo. *Eps* 8M **119**
Carnforth Gdns. *Horn* 1D **66**
Carnforth Rd. *SW16* 4H **107**
Carnie Hall. *SW17* 9F **90**
Carnival Ho. *SE1* 3D **76**
(off Gainsford St.)
Carnoustie Clo. *SE28* 9H **65**
Carnoustie Dri. *N1* 3K **59**
(in two parts)
Carnwath Rd. *SW6* 2L **89**
Caroe Ct. *N9* 1F **28**
Carol Clo. *NW4* 2H **41**
Carolina Clo. *E15* 1C **62**
Carolina Rd. *T Hth* 6M **107**
Caroline Clo. *N10* 9F **26**
Caroline Clo. *SW16* 9K **91**
Caroline Clo. *W2* 1M **73**
(off Bayswater Rd.)
Caroline Clo. *Croy* 6C **124**
Caroline Clo. *Isw th* 8B **70**
Caroline Clo. *W Dray* 3H **143**
Caroline Ct. *SE6* 1B **110**
Caroline Ct. *Ashf* 3A **100**
Caroline Ct. *Stan* 6E **22**
Caroline Gdns. *E2* 6C **60**
Caroline Gdns. *SE15* 8F **76**
Caroline Ho. *W6* 6G **73**
(off Queen Caroline St.)
Caroline Pl. *SW11* 1E **90**
Caroline Pl. *W2* 1M **73**
Caroline Pl. *Hay* 8C **68**
Caroline Pl. *Wat* 8J **9**
Caroline Pl. M. *W2* 1M **73**
Caroline Rd. *SW19* 4K **105**
Caroline St. *E1* 9H **61**
Caroline Ter. *SW1* 5E **74**
Caroline Wlk. *W6* 7J **73**
(off Lillie Rd.)
Carol St. *NW1* 4G **59**
Carolyn Dri. *Orp* 5E **128**
Caronia Ct. *SE16* 5J **77**
(off Plough Way)
Carpenders Av. *Wat* 3J **21**
Carpenders Park. 3H **21**
Carpenter Clo. *Eps* 1D **134**
Carpenter Gdns. *N21* 2M **27**
Carpenter Ho. *E14* 8L **61**
(off Burgess St.)
Carpenter Ho. *NW11* 4A **42**
Carpenters Clo. *Barn* 8M **13**
Carpenters Ct. *NW1* 4G **59**
(off Pratt St.)
Carpenters Ct. *Twic* 8C **86**
Carpenters M. *N7* 1J **59**
Carpenters Pl. *SW4* 3H **91**
Carpenter's Rd. *E15* 2L **61**
Carpenters Rd. *Enf* 9C **6**
Carpenter St. *W1* 1F **74**
Carrack Ho. *Eri* 6C **82**
(off Saltford Clo.)
Carradale Ho. *E14* 9A **62**
(off St Leonard's Rd.)
Carrara M. *E8* 2E **60**
Carrara Wlk. *SE24* 3L **91**
Carrara Wharf. *SW6* 2J **89**
Carr Gro. *SE18* 5J **79**
Carr Ho. *Dart* 4C **98**
Carriage Dri. E. *SW11* 8E **74**
Carriage Dri. N. *SW11* 8D **74**
(in two parts)
Carriage Dri. S. *SW11* 9D **74**
Carriage Dri. W. *SW11* 8D **74**
Carriage M. *Ilf* 7A **48**
Carriage Pl. *N16* 8B **44**
Carriage Pl. *SW16* 2G **107**
Carrick Clo. *Isw th* 2E **86**
Carrick Dri. *Ilf* 8A **32**
Carrick Gdns. *N17* 7C **28**
Carrick Ga. *Esh* 5A **118**
Carrick Ho. *N7* 2K **59**
(off Caledonian Rd.)
Carrick Ho. *SE11* 6L **75**
Carrick M. *SE8* 7L **77**
Carrill Way. *Belv* 5H **81**
Carrington Av. *Borwd* 7M **11**
Carrington Av. *Houn* 4M **85**
Carrington Clo. *Ark* 7E **12**
Carrington Clo. *Borwd* 7A **12**
Carrington Clo. *Croy* 2J **125**
Carrington Clo. *King T* 2A **104**
Carrington Ct. *SW11* 3C **90**
(off Barnard Rd.)
Carrington Gdns. *E7* 9E **46**
Carrington Ho. *W1* 2F **74**
(off Carrington St.)
Carrington Pl. *Esh* 7A **118**
Carrington Rd. *Dart* 5K **99**
Carrington Rd. *Rich* 3L **87**
Carrington Sq. *Harr* 6A **22**
Carrington St. *W1* 2F **74**
Carrol Clo. *NW5* 9F **42**
Carroll Clo. *E15* 1D **62**
Carroll Ct. *W3* 4M **71**
(off Osborne Rd.)
Carroll Hill. *Lou* 5K **19**
Carroll Ho. *W2* 1B **74**
(off Craven Ter.)
Carronade Pl. *SE28* 4A **80**
Carron Clo. *E14* 9M **61**
Carroun Rd. *SW8* 8K **75**
Carroway La. *Gnfd* 6B **54**
Carrow Rd. *Dag* 3F **64**
Carrow Rd. *W on T* 5H **117**
Carr Rd. *E17* 9K **29**
Carr Rd. *N'holt* 2L **53**
Carrs La. *N21* 7A **16**
Carr St. *E14* 8J **61**
(in two parts)
Carshalton. 6E **122**
Carshalton Athletic F.C.
5C **122**
Carshalton Beeches. 1C **136**
Carshalton Gro. *Sutt* 6B **122**
Carshalton on the Hill. 9E **122**
Carshalton Pk. Rd.
Cars 7D **122**
Carshalton Pl. *Cars* 7E **122**

Cedar Ct.—Chantry Hurst

Cedar Ct. SE7 ... 7G 79
Cedar Ct. SW19 ... 9H 89
Cedar Ct. Bren ... 7G 71
Cedar Ct. Sutt ... 8A 122
Cedar Cres. Brom ... 5J 127
Cedarcroft Rd. Chess ... 6K 119
Cedar Dri. N2 ... 2C 42
Cedar Dri. Pinn ... 6L 21
Cedar Dri. S at H ... 6M 115
Cedar Gdns. Sutt ... 8A 122
Cedar Grange. Enf ... 7C 16
Cedar Gro. W5 ... 4J 71
Cedar Gro. Bex ... 5H 97
Cedar Gro. S'hall ... 8L 53
Cedar Gro. Wey ... 6A 116
Cedar Heights. NW2 ... 2K 57
Cedar Heights. Rich ... 7J 87
Cedar Hill. Eps ... 8A 134
Cedar Ho. E14 ... 3A 78
(off Manchester Rd.)
Cedar Ho. N22 ... 8L 27
(off Acacia Rd.)
Cedar Ho. SE14 ... 9H 77
Cedar Ho. SE16 ... 3H 77
(off Woodland Cres.)
Cedar Ho. W8 ... 4M 73
(off Marloes Rd.)
Cedar Ho. Hay ... 7G 53
Cedarhurst. Brom ... 4C 110
Cedarhurst Cotts. Bex ... 6L 97
Cedarhurst Dri. SE9 ... 4G 95
Cedarland Ter. SW20 ... 4F 104
Cedar Lawn Av. Barn ... 7J 13
Cedar Lodge. Chesh ... 1D 6
Cedar Mt. SE9 ... 7H 95
Cedarne Rd. SW6 ... 8M 73
Cedar Pk. Gdns. Romf ... 5H 49
Cedar Pk. Rd. Enf ... 2A 16
Cedar Pl. SE7 ... 6G 79
Cedar Pl. N'wd ... 6A 20
Cedar Ri. N14 ... 9E 14
Cedar Rd. N17 ... 8D 28
Cedar Rd. NW2 ... 9G 41
Cedar Rd. Brom ... 6G 111
Cedar Rd. Croy ... 4B 124
Cedar Rd. Dart ... 7H 99
Cedar Rd. E Mol ... 8C 102
Cedar Rd. Enf ... 2M 15
Cedar Rd. Eri ... 9E 82
Cedar Rd. Felt ... 7B 84
Cedar Rd. Horn ... 8G 51
Cedar Rd. Houn ... 1G 85
Cedar Rd. Romf ... 2A 50
Cedar Rd. Sutt ... 8A 122
Cedar Rd. Tedd ... 2E 102
Cedar Rd. Wat ... 8G 9
Cedars. Bans ... 6D 136
Cedars Av. E17 ... 3L 45
Cedars Av. Mitc ... 8E 106
Cedars Clo. NW4 ... 1H 41
Cedars Clo. SE13 ... 2B 94
Cedars Clo. Borwd ... 6M 11
Cedars Ct. N9 ... 2C 28
Cedars Dri. Uxb ... 5D 142
Cedars Ho. E17 ... 1M 45
Cedars M. SW4 ... 3F 90
(in two parts)
Cedars Rd. E15 ... 2C 62
Cedars Rd. N9 ... 2E 28
Cedars Rd. N21 ... 2M 27
Cedars Rd. SW4 ... 2F 90
Cedars Rd. SW13 ... 1E 88
Cedars Rd. W4 ... 6A 72
Cedars Rd. Beck ... 6J 109
Cedars Rd. Croy ... 5J 123
Cedars Rd. Hamp W ... 5G 103
Cedars Rd. Mord ... 8L 105
Cedars, The. E15 ... 3D 62
Cedars, The. W13 ... 9G 55
Cedars, The. Buck H ... 1E 30
Cedars, The. Tedd ... 3D 102
Cedars, The. Wall ... 6G 123
Cedar Ter. Rich ... 3J 87
Cedar Tree Gro. SE27 ... 2M 107
Cedar Vw. King T ... 7H 103
(off Milner Rd.)
Cedarville Gdns. SW16 ... 3K 107
Cedar Wlk. Clay ... 8D 118
Cedar Wlk. Kenl ... 8A 138
Cedar Wlk. Wal A ... 7K 7
Cedar Way. NW1 ... 3H 59
Cedar Way. Sun ... 4C 100
Cedar Way Ind. Est. NW1 ... 3H 59
Cedar Wood Dri. Wat ... 8F 4
Cedra Ct. N16 ... 6E 44
Cedric Av. Romf ... 1C 50
Cedric Rd. SE9 ... 9A 96
Celadon Clo. Enf ... 5J 17
Celandine Clo. E3 ... 8L 61
Celandine Ct. E4 ... 3M 29
Celandine Dri. E8 ... 3D 60
Celandine Dri. SE28 ... 2F 80
Celandine Rd. W on T ... 6J 117
Celandine Way. E15 ... 6C 62
Celbridge M. W2 ... 8M 57
Celestial Gdns. SE13 ... 3B 94
Celia Ho. N1 ... 5C 60
(off Arden Est.)
Celia Johnson Ct. Borwd ... 3A 12
Celia Rd. N19 ... 9G 43
Celtic Av. Brom ... 7C 110
Celtic St. E14 ... 8M 61
Cemetery La. SE7 ... 7J 79
Cemetery Rd. E7 ... 1D 62
Cemetery Rd. N17 ... 7C 28
Cemetery Rd. SE2 ... 8F 80
Cenacle Clo. NW3 ... 8L 41
Cenotaph. ... 3J 75
Centaur Ct. Bren ... 6J 71
Centaurs Bus. Cen. Iswth ... 7E 70
Centaur St. SE1 ... 4K 75
Centenary Ct. F'ham ... 2L 131
Centenary Rd. Enf ... 6K 17
Centenary Trad. Est. Enf ... 5K 17
Centennial Av. Els ... 9G 11
Centennial Pk. Els ... 9G 11
Central Av. E11 ... 7B 46
Central Av. N2 ... 9B 26
(East Finchley)
Central Av. N2 ... 2M 41
(St Marylebone Cemetery)
Central Av. N9 ... 3C 28
Central Av. SW11 ... 8D 74
Central Av. Ave ... 3M 83
Central Av. Enf ... 4F 16
Central Av. Hay ... 2D 68
Central Av. Houn ... 3A 86
Central Av. Pinn ... 4K 37
Central Av. Wall ... 7J 123
Central Av. Wal X ... 6E 6
Central Av. Well ... 1D 96
Central Av. W Mol ... 8K 101
Central Bus. Cen. NW10 ... 1C 56
Central Cir. NW4 ... 3F 40
Central Criminal Court
(Old Bailey). ... 9M 59
Central Dri. Horn ... 8J 51
Central Gdns. Mord ... 9M 105
Central Hill. SE19 ... 2A 108
Central Ho. E15 ... 5A 62
Central Mans. NW4 ... 3F 40
(off Watford Way)
Central Markets (Smithfield). ... 8M 59
(off Charterhouse St.)
Central Pde. E17 ... 2L 45
Central Pde. SE20 ... 4H 109
(off High St.)
Central Pde. W3 ... 3M 71
Central Pde. Enf ... 4G 17
Central Pde. Felt ... 6G 85
Central Pde. Gnfd ... 6E 54
Central Pde. Harr ... 3D 38
Central Pde. Houn ... 8K 69
Central Pde. Ilf ... 4B 48
Central Pde. New Ad ... 2A 140
Central Pde. Sidc ... 9E 96
Central Pde. Surb ... 1J 119
Central Pde. W Mol ... 8K 101
Central Pk. Av. Dag ... 8M 49
Central Pk. Est. Houn ... 4H 85
Central Pk. Rd. E6 ... 5H 63
Central Pl. SE25 ... 9E 108
Central Rd. Dart ... 3J 99
Central Rd. Mord ... 1L 121
Central Rd. Wemb ... 1F 54
Central Rd. Wor Pk ... 3E 120
Central School Path.
SW14 ... 2A 88
Central Sq. NW11 ... 4M 41
Central Sq. Wemb ... 1J 55
Central St. EC1 ... 6A 60
Central Ter. Beck ... 7H 109
Central Way. NW10 ... 6A 56
Central Way. SE28 ... 2E 80
Central Way. Cars ... 9C 122
Central Way. Felt ... 4E 84
Central Way. N'wd ... 7C 20
Centre Av. N2 ... 9C 26
Centre Av. NW10 ... 6G 57
Centre Av. W3 ... 2B 72
Centre Comn. Rd. Chst ... 3A 112
Centre Ct. Shop. Cen.
SW19 ... 3K 105
Centre Dri. E7 ... 9G 47
Cen. for the Magic Arts, The. ... 7G 59
(off Stephenson Way)
Centre Heights. NW3 ... 3B 58
(off Finchley Rd.)
Centre Pl. Ave ... 3K 83
Centre Point. SE1 ... 6E 76
Centrepoint. WC2 ... 9H 59
(off St Giles High St.)
Centre Point Ho. WC2 ... 9H 59
(off St Giles High St.)
Centre Rd. E11 & E7 ... 7E 46
Centre Rd. Dag ... 5M 65
Centre St. E2 ... 5F 60
Centre, The. Felt ... 8E 84
Centre, The. Houn ... 2M 85
Centre, The. W on T ... 3D 116
Centre Way. E17 ... 7A 30
Centre Way. N9 ... 2G 29
Centre Way. Ilf ... 7A 48
Centric Clo. NW1 ... 4E 58
Centro Ct. E6 ... 7K 63
Centurion Clo. N7 ... 3K 59
Centurion Ct. Hack ... 4F 122
Centurion La. E3 ... 4K 61
Centurion Way. Eri ... 4K 81
Centurion Way. Purf ... 5K 83
Centuryan Pl. Dart ... 3F 98
Century Clo. NW4 ... 3H 41
Century Ct. Wat ... 9A 8
Century Ho. SW15 ... 3H 89
Century M. E5 ... 9G 45
Century Pk. Ind. Est. Wat ... 7G 9
(off Local Board Rd.)
Century Pk. W. Wat ... 7G 9
Century Rd. E17 ... 1J 45
Century Yd. SE23 ... 8G 93
Cephas Av. E1 ... 7G 61
Cephas Ho. E1 ... 7G 61
(off Doveton St.)
Cephas St. E1 ... 7G 61
Ceres Rd. SE18 ... 5D 80
Cerise Rd. SE15 ... 9E 76
Cerne Clo. Hay ... 1G 69
Cerne Rd. Mord ... 1A 122
Cerney M. W2 ... 1B 74
Cervantes Ct. W2 ... 9M 57
Cervantes Ct. N'wd ... 7D 20
Cester St. E2 ... 4E 60
Ceylon Rd. W14 ... 4H 73
Chadacre Av. Ilf ... 1K 47
Chadacre Ct. E15 ... 4E 62
(off Vicars Clo.)
Chadacre Ho. SW9 ... 3M 91
(off Loughborough Pk.)
Chadacre Rd. Eps ... 8F 120
Chadbourn St. E14 ... 8M 61
Chadbury Ct. NW7 ... 7E 24
Chadd Dri. Brom ... 7J 111
Chadd Grn. E13 ... 4E 62
(in two parts)
Chadston Ho. N1 ... 3M 59
(off Halton Rd.)
Chadswell. WC1 ... 6J 59
(off Cromer St.)
Chadview Ct. Romf ... 5H 49
Chadville Gdns. Romf ... 3H 49
Chadway. Dag ... 6G 49
Chadwell Av. Chesh ... 1C 6
Chadwell Av. Romf ... 5F 48
Chadwell Heath. ... 5H 49
Chadwell Heath Ind. Pk.
Dag ... 6J 49
Chadwell Heath La.
Chad H & Romf ... 2F 48
Chadwell St. EC1 ... 6L 59
Chadwick Av. E4 ... 4B 30
Chadwick Av. N21 ... 7K 15
Chadwick Av. SW19 ... 3L 105
Chadwick Clo. SW15 ... 6D 88
Chadwick Clo. W7 ... 8D 54
Chadwick Clo. Tedd ... 3E 102
Chadwick Dri. H Wood ... 9H 35
Chadwick Pl. Surb ... 2G 119
Chadwick Rd. E11 ... 4C 46
Chadwick Rd. NW10 ... 4D 56
Chadwick Rd. SE15 ... 1D 92
Chadwick Rd. Ilf ... 8M 47
Chadwick St. SW1 ... 4H 75
Chadwick Way. SE28 ... 1H 81
Chadwin Rd. E13 ... 8F 62
Chadworth Ho. EC1 ... 6A 60
(off Lever St.)
Chadworth Ho. N4 ... 6A 44
Chadworth Way. Clay ... 7B 118
Chaffers Mead. Asht ... 8K 133
Chaffinch Av. Croy ... 1H 125
Chaffinch Bus. Pk. Beck ... 8H 109
Chaffinch Clo. N9 ... 1H 29
Chaffinch Clo. Croy ... 9H 109
Chaffinch Clo. Surb ... 5L 119
Chaffinch La. Wat ... 9D 8
Chaffinch Rd. Beck ... 5J 109
Chafford Wlk. Rain ... 5G 67
Chafford Way. Romf ... 2G 49
Chagford St. NW1 ... 7D 58
Chailey Av. Enf ... 4D 16
Chailey Clo. Houn ... 9H 69
Chailey Ind. Est. Hay ... 3E 68
Chailey Pl. W on T ... 6J 117
Chailey St. E5 ... 8G 45
Chalbury Wlk. N1 ... 5K 59
Chalcombe Rd. SE2 ... 4F 80
Chalcot Clo. Sutt ... 9L 121
Chalcot Cres. NW1 ... 4D 58
Chalcot Gdns. NW3 ... 2D 58
Chalcot M. SW16 ... 9J 91
Chalcot Rd. NW1 ... 3E 58
Chalcot Sq. NW1 ... 3E 58
(in two parts)
Chalcott Gdns. Surb ... 3G 119
Chalcroft Rd. SE13 ... 4C 94
Chaldon Ct. SE19 ... 5B 108
Chaldon Rd. SW6 ... 8J 73
Chaldon Way. Coul ... 9J 137
Chale Rd. SW2 ... 5J 91
Chalet Clo. Bex ... 1B 114
Chalet Est. NW7 ... 4E 24
Chale Wlk. Sutt ... 1M 135
Chalfont Av. Wemb ... 2M 55
Chalfont Ct. NW1 ... 7D 58
(off Baker St.)
Chalfont Ct. NW9 ... 1D 40
Chalfont Ct. Harr ... 4D 38
(off Northwick Pk. Rd.)
Chalfont Grn. N9 ... 3C 28
Chalfont Ho. SE16 ... 4F 76
(off Keetons Rd.)
Chalfont Ho. Wat ... 8C 8
Chalfont Rd. N9 ... 3C 28
Chalfont Rd. SE25 ... 7D 108
Chalfont Rd. Hay ... 3E 68
Chalfont Wlk. Pinn ... 9G 21
Chalfont Way. W13 ... 4F 70
Chalford. NW3 ... 2A 58
(off Finchley Rd.)
Chalford Clo. W Mol ... 8L 101
Chalforde Gdns. Romf ... 2F 50
Chalford Rd. SE21 ... 1B 108
Chalford Wlk. Wfd G ... 8H 31
Chalgrove Av. Mord ... 9L 105
Chalgrove Cres. Ilf ... 9J 31
Chalgrove Gdns. N3 ... 1J 41
Chalgrove Rd. N17 ... 8F 28
Chalgrove Rd. Sutt ... 9B 122
Chalice Clo. Wall ... 8H 123
Chalice Ct. N2 ... 2C 42
Chalkenden Clo. SE20 ... 4F 108
Chalker's Corner (Junct.) ... 2M 87
Chalk Farm. ... 3E 58
Chalk Farm Rd. NW1 ... 3E 58
Chalk Hill. Wat ... 8H 9
Chalk Hill Rd. W6 ... 5H 73
Chalkhill Rd. Wemb ... 8L 39
(in two parts)
Chalklands. Wemb ... 8A 40
Chalk La. Barn ... 5D 14
Chalk La. Eps ... 7B 134
(in two parts)
Chalkley Clo. Mitc ... 6D 106
Chalkmill Dri. Enf ... 5F 16
Chalk Paddock. Eps ... 7B 134
Chalk Pit Av. Orp ... 7G 113
Chalk Pit Rd. Bans ... 9L 135
Chalk Pit Way. Sutt ... 8A 122
Chalk Rd. E13 ... 8F 62
Chalkstone Clo. Well ... 9E 80
Chalkwell Ho. E1 ... 9H 61
(off Pitsea St.)
Chalkwell Pk. Av. Enf ... 6C 16
Chalky La. Chess ... 2H 133
Challenge Clo. NW10 ... 4C 56
Challenger Ho. E14 ... 1J 77
(off Victory Pl.)
Challenge Rd. Ashf ... 9B 84
Challice Way. SW2 ... 7K 91
Challin St. SE20 ... 5G 109
Challis Rd. Bren ... 6H 71
Challock Clo. Big H ... 8G 141
Challoner Clo. N2 ... 9B 26
Challoner Cres. W14 ... 6K 73
Challoners Clo. E Mol ... 8B 102
Challoner St. W14 ... 6K 73
Chalmers Ho. E17 ... 3M 45
Chalmers Rd. Ashf ... 2A 100
Chalmers Rd. Bans ... 7B 136
Chalmers Rd. E. Ashf ... 1A 100
Chalmers Wlk. SE17 ... 7M 75
(off Hillingdon St.)
Chalmers Way. Felt ... 4F 84
Chalsey Rd. SE4 ... 3K 93
Chalton Dri. N2 ... 4B 42
Chalton Ho. NW1 ... 6H 59
(off Chalton St.)
Chalton St. NW1 ... 5G 59
(in three parts)
Chamberlain Clo. SE28 ... 4B 80
Chamberlain Cotts.
SE5 ... 9B 76
Chamberlain Cres.
W Wick ... 3M 125
Chamberlain Gdns.
Houn ... 9A 70
Chamberlain Ho. E1 ... 1G 77
(off Cable St.)
Chamberlain Ho. NW1 ... 6H 59
(off Ossulston St.)
Chamberlain Ho. SE1 ... 3L 75
(off Westminster Bri. Rd.)
Chamberlain La. Pinn ... 2E 36
Chamberlain Pl. E17 ... 1J 45
Chamberlain Rd. N2 ... 9A 26
Chamberlain Rd. N9 ... 3E 28
Chamberlain Rd. W13 ... 3E 70
Chamberlain St. NW1 ... 3D 58
Chamberlain Wlk. Felt ... 1J 101
(off Swift Rd.)
Chamberlain Way. Pinn ... 1F 36
Chamberlain Way. Surb ... 2J 119
Chamberlayne Av. Wemb ... 8J 39
Chamberlayne Mans.
NW10 ... 6H 57
(off Chamberlayne Rd.)
Chamberlayne Rd. NW10 ... 4G 57
Chambers Gdns. N2 ... 8B 26
Chambers Ind. Pk.
W Dray ... 7L 143
Chambers La. NW10 ... 3F 56
Chambers Pl. S Croy ... 9B 124
Chambers Rd. N7 ... 9J 43
Chambers St. SE16 ... 3E 76
Chambers, The. SW10 ... 9A 74
(off Chelsea Harbour)
Chamber St. E1 ... 1D 76
Chambers Wlk. Stan ... 5F 22
Chambers Wharf. SE16 ... 3E 76
Chambon Pl. W6 ... 5E 72
Chambord St. E2 ... 6D 60
Chamomile Ct. E17 ... 4L 45
(off Yunus Khan Clo.)
Champion Cres. SE26 ... 1J 109
Champion Gro. SE5 ... 2B 92
Champion Hill. SE5 ... 2B 92
Champion Hill Est. SE5 ... 2C 92
Champion Pk. SE5 ... 1B 92
Champion Rd. SE26 ... 1J 109
Champion Rd. Upm ... 7M 51
Champlain Ho. W12 ... 1F 72
(off White City Est.)
Champness Clo. SE27 ... 1B 108
Champneys. Wat ... 2J 21
Champneys Clo. Sutt ... 9K 121
Chancel Ind. Est. NW10 ... 1D 56
Chancellor Gdns.
S Croy ... 1M 137
Chancellor Gro. SE21 ... 8A 92
Chancellor Ho. E1 ... 2F 76
(off Green Bank)
Chancellor Pas. E14 ... 2L 77
Chancellor Pl. NW9 ... 9D 24
Chancellors Ct. WC1 ... 8K 59
(off Olde Hall St.)
Chancellor's Rd. W6 ... 6G 73
Chancellor's St. W6 ... 6G 73
Chancellors Wharf. W6 ... 6G 73
Chancelot Rd. SE2 ... 5F 80
Chancel St. SE1 ... 2M 75
Chancery Bldgs. E1 ... 1F 76
(off Lowood St.)
Chancery Ct. Dart ... 6L 99
Chancery La. WC2 ... 9L 59
Chancery La. Beck ... 6M 109
Chancery M. SW17 ... 8C 90
Chance St. E2 & E1 ... 7D 60
Chanctonbury Clo. SE9 ... 9M 95
Chanctonbury Gdns.
Sutt ... 9M 121
Chanctonbury Way. N12 ... 4K 25
Chandler Av. E16 ... 8E 62
Chandler Clo. Hamp ... 5L 101
Chandler Ct. Felt ... 5E 84
Chandler Ho. NW6 ... 4K 57
(off Willesden La.)
Chandler Ho. WC1 ... 7J 59
(off Colonnade)
Chandler Rd. Lou ... 3M 19
Chandlers Clo. Felt ... 6D 84
Chandlers Corner (Junct.) ... 6G 67
Chandlers Corner. Rain ... 6G 67
Chandlers Ct. SE12 ... 7F 94
Chandlers Dri. Eri ... 5B 82
Chandlers M. E14 ... 3L 77
Chandler St. E1 ... 2F 76
Chandlers Way. SW2 ... 6L 91
Chandlers Way. Romf ... 3C 50
Chandler Way. SE15 ... 8D 76
(Diamond St.)
Chandler Way. SE15 ... 7C 76
(St George's Way)
Chandlery Ho. E1 ... 9E 60
(off Bk. Church La.)
Chandlery, The. SE1 ... 4L 75
(off Gerridge St.)
Chandon Lodge. Sutt ... 9A 122
Chandos Av. E17 ... 9L 29
Chandos Av. N14 ... 3G 27
Chandos Av. N20 ... 1A 26
Chandos Av. W5 ... 5G 71
Chandos Clo. Buck H ... 2F 30
Chandos Ct. N14 ... 2H 27
Chandos Ct. Edgw ... 7K 23
Chandos Cres. Edgw ... 7K 23
Chandos Pde. Edgw ... 7K 23
Chandos Pl. WC2 ... 1J 75
Chandos Rd. E15 ... 1B 62
Chandos Rd. N2 ... 9B 26
Chandos Rd. N17 ... 9C 28
Chandos Rd. NW2 ... 1G 57
Chandos Rd. NW10 ... 7C 56
Chandos Rd. Borwd ... 4K 11
Chandos Rd. Harr ... 3A 38
Chandos Rd. Pinn ... 5H 37
Chandos St. W1 ... 8F 58
Chandos Way. NW11 ... 6M 41
Change All. EC3 ... 9B 60
Channel Clo. Houn ... 9L 69
Channel Ga. Rd.
NW10 ... 6C 56
Channel Ho. E14 ... 8J 61
(off Aston St.)
Channel Islands Est. N1 ... 2A 60
(off Guernsey Rd.)
Channelsea Path. E15 ... 4B 62
Channelsea Rd. E15 ... 4B 62
Channing Clo. Horn ... 5K 51
Channon Ct. Surb ... 9J 103
(off Maple Rd)
Chanton Dri. Sutt ... 2G 135
Chantress Clo. Dag ... 4A 66
Chantrey Rd. SW9 ... 2K 91
Chantry Clo. NW7 ... 8D 12
Chantry Clo. W9 ... 7L 57
Chantry Clo. Enf ... 2A 16
Chantry Clo. Harr ... 3K 39
Chantry Clo. Sidc ... 2J 113
Chantry Clo. W Dray ... 1H 143
Chantry Ct. Cars ... 5C 122
Chantry Hurst. Eps ... 7B 134

Chaucer Mans.—Chesterton Rd.

Chaucer Mans. W14 7J 73 (off Queen's Club Gdns.)
Chaucer Pk. Dart 6K 99
Chaucer Rd. E7 2E 62
Chaucer Rd. E11 4H 46
Chaucer Rd. E17 9A 30
Chaucer Rd. SE24 4L 91
Chaucer Rd. W3 2A 72
Chaucer Rd. Romf 7F 34
Chaucer Rd. Sidc 7G 97
Chaucer Rd. Sutt 6L 121
Chaucer Rd. Well 9C 80
Chaucer Theatre 9D 60 (off Braham St.)
Chaucer Way. SW19 3A 106
Chaucer Way. Dart 3L 99 (in two parts)
Chaulden Ho. EC1 6B 60 (off Cranwood St.)
Chauncey Clo. N9 3E 28
Chauncey Ho. Wat 8C 8
Chaundrye Clo. SE9 5K 95
Chauntler Clo. E16 9F 62
Chave Rd. Dart 9J 99
Chaville Ho. N11 4E 26
Cheadle Ct. NW8 7B 58 (off Henderson Dri.)
Cheadle Ho. E14 9K 61 (off Copenhagen Pl.)
Cheam 8J 121
Cheam Comn. Rd. Wor Pk 4F 120
Cheam Mans. Sutt 9J 121
Cheam Pk. Way. Sutt 8J 121
Cheam Rd. Eps & Ewe 2E 134
Cheam Rd. Sutt 8K 121
Cheam St. SE15 2G 93
Cheam Village (Junct.) 8J 121
Cheapside. EC2 9A 60
Cheapside. N13 4B 28
Cheapside. N22 1L 43
Chearsley. SE17 5A 76 (off Deacon Way)
Cheddar Clo. N11 6D 26
Cheddar Waye. Hay 9F 52
Cheddington Ho. E2 4E 60 (off Whiston Rd.)
Cheddington Rd. N18 3C 28
Chedworth Clo. E16 9D 62
Cheeseman Clo. Hamp 3J 101
Cheesemans Ter. W14 6K 73 (in two parts)
Chelford Rd. Brom 2B 110
Chelmer Cres. Bark 5F 64
Chelmer Rd. E9 1H 61
Chelmsford Av. Romf 7B 34
Chelmsford Clo. E6 9K 63
Chelmsford Clo. W6 7H 73
Chelmsford Clo. Sutt 1L 135
Chelmsford Ct. N14 9H 15 (off Chelmsford Rd.)
Chelmsford Dri. Upm 8K 51
Chelmsford Gdns. Ilf 5J 47
Chelmsford Ho. N7 9K 43 (off Holloway Rd.)
Chelmsford Rd. E11 6B 46
Chelmsford Rd. E17 4L 45
Chelmsford Rd. E18 8D 30
Chelmsford Rd. N14 9G 15
Chelmsford Sq. NW10 4G 57
Chelmsine Ct. Ruis 3A 36
Chelsea 6C 74
Chelsea Bri. SW1 & SW8 7F 74
Chelsea Bri. Bus. Cen. SW8 8F 74
Chelsea Bri. Rd. SW1 6E 74
Chelsea Bri. Wharf. SW8 7F 74
Chelsea Cinema 6C 74 (off King's Rd.)
Chelsea Cloisters. SW3 5C 74
Chelsea Clo. NW10 4B 56
Chelsea Clo. Edgw 9L 23
Chelsea Clo. Hamp H 2A 102
Chelsea Clo. Wor Pk 2E 120
Chelsea College of Art & Design 6C 74
Chelsea Ct. Brom 7J 111
Chelsea Cres. NW2 2K 57
Chelsea Cres. SW10 9A 74
Chelsea Embkmt. SW3 7C 74
Chelsea Farm Ho. Studios. SW10 7B 74 (off Milman's St.)
Chelsea F.C. (Stamford Bridge) 8M 73
Chelsea Gdns. SW1 6E 74
Chelsea Gdns. W13 8D 54
Chelsea Gdns. Sutt 6J 121
Chelsea Ga. SW1 6E 74 (off Ebury Bri. Rd.)
Chelsea Harbour Design Cen. SW10 9A 74 (off Chelsea Harbour)
Chelsea Harbour Dri. SW10 9A 74
Chelsea Lodge. SW3 7D 74 (off Tite St.)
Chelsea Mnr. Ct. SW3 7C 74
Chelsea Mnr. Gdns. SW3 6C 74
Chelsea Mnr. St. SW3 6C 74
Chelsea M. Horn 6F 50
Chelsea Pk. Gdns. SW3 7B 74
Chelsea Physic Garden 7D 74
Chelsea Reach Tower. SW10 8B 74 (off Worlds End Est.)
Chelsea Sq. SW3 6B 74
Chelsea Studios. SW6 8M 73 (off Fulham Rd.)
Chelsea Towers. SW3 7C 74 (off Chelsea Mnr. Gdns.)
Chelsea Village. SW6 8M 73 (off Fulham Rd.)
Chelsea Wharf. SW10 8B 74 (off Lots Rd.)
Chelsfield 7F 128
Chelsfield Av. N9 9H 17
Chelsfield Gdns. SE26 9G 93
Chelsfield Grn. N9 9H 17
Chelsfield Hill. Orp 9G 129
Chelsfield Ho. SE17 5C 76 (off Massinger St.)
Chelsfield La. Orp (BR5) 2H 129
Chelsfield La. Orp (BR6) 9L 129
Chelsfield Rd. Orp 1G 129
Chelsfield Village 7J 129
Chelsham 9L 139
Chelsham Common 8L 139
Chelsham Comn. Rd. Warl 9L 139
Chelsham Ct. Rd. Warl 9B 140
Chelsham Rd. SW4 2H 91
Chelsham Rd. S Croy 9B 124
Chelsham Rd. Warl 9K 139
Chelsiter Ct. Sidc 1D 112
Chelston App. Ruis 7E 36
Chelston Rd. Ruis 6E 36
Chelsworth Clo. Romf 7K 35
Chelsworth Dri. SE18 7B 80
Chelsworth Dri. Romf 8J 35
Cheltenham Av. Twic 6E 86
Cheltenham Clo. N Mald 7A 104
Cheltenham Clo. N'holt 2M 53
Cheltenham Ct. Stan 5G 23 (off Marsh La.)
Cheltenham Gdns. E6 5J 63
Cheltenham Gdns. Lou 8J 19
Cheltenham Ho. Wat 4G 9 (off Exeter Clo.)
Cheltenham Pl. W3 2M 71
Cheltenham Pl. Harr 2J 39
Cheltenham Rd. E10 4A 46
Cheltenham Rd. SE15 3G 93
Cheltenham Rd. Orp 5E 128
Cheltenham Ter. SW3 6D 74
Chelverton Rd. SW15 3H 89
Chelwood. N20 2B 26
Chelwood Clo. E4 8M 17
Chelwood Clo. Eps 4D 134
Chelwood Clo. N'wd 7A 20
Chelwood Gdns. Rich 1L 87
Chelwood Gdns. Pas. Rich 1L 87
Chelwood Ho. W2 9B 58 (off Gloucester Sq.)
Chelwood Wlk. SE4 3J 93
Chenappa Clo. E13 6E 62
Chenduit Way. Stan 5D 22
Cheney Ct. SE23 7H 93
Cheney Rd. NW1 5J 59
Cheney Row. E17 8K 29
Cheneys Rd. E11 8C 46
Cheney St. Pinn 2G 37
Chenies Ho. W4 8D 72 (off Corney Reach Way)
Chenies M. WC1 7H 59
Chenies Pl. NW1 5H 59
Chenies St. WC1 8H 59
Chenies, The. NW1 5H 59 (off Pancras Rd.)
Chenies, The. Orp 1C 128
Chenies, The. Wilm 1C 114
Chenies Way. Wat 9C 8
Cheniston Gdns. W8 4M 73
Chepstow Av. Horn 8J 51
Chepstow Clo. SW15 5J 89
Chepstow Corner. W2 9L 57 (off Chepstow Pl.)
Chepstow Ct. W11 1L 73 (off Chepstow Vs.)
Chepstow Cres. W11 1L 73
Chepstow Cres. Ilf 4C 48
Chepstow Gdns. S'hall 9K 53
Chepstow Ho. Romf 5L 35 (off Leamington Rd.)
Chepstow Pl. W2 9L 57
Chepstow Ri. Croy 5C 124
Chepstow Rd. W2 9L 57
Chepstow Rd. W7 4E 70
Chepstow Rd. Croy 5C 124
Chepstow Vs. W11 1K 73
Chequers. Buck H 1F 30
Chequers Clo. NW9 1C 40
Chequers Clo. Orp 8D 112
Chequers Ct. EC1 7B 60 (off Chequer St.)
Chequers Ho. NW8 7C 58 (off Jerome Cres.)
Chequers La. Dag 8K 65
Chequers La. Wat 3F 4
Chequers Pde. N13 5A 28
Chequers Pde. SE9 5K 95 (off Eltham High St.)
Chequers Pde. Dag 4K 65
Chequers Rd. Lou 7L 19
Chequers Rd. Romf & S Wea 2J 35
Chequers Sq. Uxb 3A 142
Chequers, The. Pinn 1H 37
Chequer St. EC1 7A 60 (in two parts)
Chequers Wlk. Wal A 6M 7
Chequers Way. N13 5M 27
Cherbury Clo. SE28 9H 65
Cherbury Ct. N1 5B 60 (off St John's Est.)
Cherbury St. N1 5B 60
Cherchefelle M. Stan 5F 22
Cherimoya Gdns. W Mol 7M 101
Cherington Rd. W7 2C 70
Cheriton Av. Brom 9D 110
Cheriton Av. Ilf 9K 31
Cheriton Clo. W5 8G 55
Cheriton Clo. Barn 5D 14
Cheriton Ct. SE12 6E 94
Cheriton Ct. W on T 3G 117
Cheriton Dri. SE18 8B 80
Cheriton Sq. SW17 8E 90
Cherry Av. S'hall 2H 69
Cherry Av. Swan 8B 114
Cherry Blossom Clo. N13 5M 27
Cherry Clo. E17 3M 45
Cherry Clo. NW9 9C 24
Cherry Clo. SW2 6L 91
Cherry Clo. W5 4H 71
Cherry Clo. Bans 6H 135
Cherry Clo. Cars 4D 122
Cherry Clo. Mord 8J 105
Cherry Clo. Ruis 8D 36
Cherrycot Hill. Orp 6A 128
Cherrycot Ri. Orp 6A 128
Cherry Ct. W3 2C 72
Cherry Ct. Pinn 9H 21
Cherry Cres. Bren 8F 70
Cherrycroft Gdns. Pinn 7K 21
Cherrydale. Wat 6D 8
Cherrydown Av. E4 3K 29
Cherrydown Clo. E4 3L 29
Cherrydown Rd. Sidc 8H 97
Cherrydown Wlk. Romf 9M 33
Cherry Garden Ho. SE16 3F 76 (off Cherry Garden St.)
Cherry Gdns. Dag 1K 65
Cherry Gdns. N'holt 3M 53
Cherry Garden St. SE16 3F 76
Cherry Gth. Bren 6H 71
Cherry Gro. Hay 2F 68
Cherry Gro. Uxb 8F 142
Cherry Hill. Harr 6D 22
Cherry Hill. New Bar 8M 13
Cherry Hill Gdns. Croy 6K 123
Cherry Hills. Wat 5J 21
Cherry Hollow. Ab L 4D 4
Cherrylands Clo. NW9 7A 40
Cherry La. W Dray 5K 143
Cherry Laurel Wlk. SW2 5K 91
Cherry Orchard. SE7 7G 79
Cherry Orchard. W Dray 3J 143
Cherry Orchard Clo. Orp 9G 113
Cherry Orchard Gdns. Croy 3B 124
Cherry Orchard Gdns. W Mol 7K 101
Cherry Orchard Rd. Brom 4J 127
Cherry Orchard Rd. Croy 4B 124
Cherry Orchard Rd. W Mol 7L 101
Cherry Rd. Enf 2G 17
Cherry St. Romf 3B 50
Cherry Tree Av. W Dray 9D 142
Cherry Tree Clo. E9 4G 61
Cherry Tree Clo. Rain 5E 66
Cherry Tree Clo. Wemb 9E 38
Cherry Tree Ct. NW1 3G 59 (off Camden Rd.)
Cherry Tree Ct. NW9 2A 40
Cherry Tree Ct. SE7 7G 79
Cherry Tree Ct. Coul 9K 137
Cherrytree Dri. SW16 9J 91
Cherry Tree Grn. S Croy 6F 138
Cherry Tree Hill. N2 3C 42
Cherry Tree Ho. N22 7J 27
Cherry Tree La. Dart 9D 98
Cherry Tree La. Rain 6C 66
Cherry Tree Ri. Buck H 4G 31
Cherry Tree Rd. E15 1C 62
Cherry Tree Rd. N2 2D 42
Cherry Tree Rd. Wat 9F 4
Cherry Tree Wlk. EC1 7A 60
Cherry Tree Wlk. Beck 8K 109
Cherry Tree Wlk. Big H 9G 141
Cherry Tree Wlk. W Wick 6D 126
Cherrytree Way. Stan 6F 22
Cherry Wlk. Brom 3E 126
Cherry Wlk. Rain 5D 66
Cherry Way. Eps 8B 120
Cherry Way. Shep 8B 100
Cherrywood Clo. E3 6J 61
Cherry Wood Clo. King T 4L 103
Cherrywood Ct. Tedd 2E 102
Cherrywood Dri. SW15 4H 89
Cherrywood La. Mord 8J 105
Cherry Wood Way. W5 8L 55
Cherston Gdns. Lou 6L 19
Cherston Rd. Lou 6L 19
Chertsey Clo. Kenl 7M 137
Chertsey Ct. SW14 2M 87
Chertsey Cres. New Ad 2A 140
Chertsey Dri. Sutt 4J 121
Chertsey La. Eps 4L 133
Chertsey Rd. E11 7B 46
Chertsey Rd. Ashf 4B 100
Chertsey Rd. Felt 2C 100
Chertsey Rd. Ilf 9B 48
Chertsey Rd. Twic 8M 85
Chertsey St. SW17 2E 106
Chervil Clo. Felt 9E 84
Chervil M. SE28 2F 80
Cherwell Ct. Eps 6A 120
Cherwell Ho. NW8 7B 58 (off Church St. Est.)
Cherwell Way. Ruis 4A 36
Cheryls Clo. SW6 9M 73
Cheseman St. SE26 9F 92
Chesfield Rd. King T 4J 103
Chesham Av. Orp 1M 127
Chesham Clo. SW1 4E 74 (off Lyall St.)
Chesham Clo. Romf 2B 50
Chesham Clo. Sutt 2J 135
Chesham Ct. N'wd 6D 20
Chesham Cres. SE20 5G 109
Chesham Flats. W1 1E 74 (off Brown Hart Gdns.)
Chesham Ho. Romf 6J 35 (off Leyburn Cres.)
Chesham M. SW1 4E 74 (off Belgrave M. W.)
Chesham Pl. SW1 4E 74 (in two parts)
Chesham Rd. SE20 6G 109
Chesham Rd. SW19 2B 106
Chesham Rd. King T 6L 103
Chesham St. NW10 8B 40
Chesham St. SW1 4E 74
Chesham Ter. W13 3F 70
Chesham Way. Wat 8C 8
Cheshire Clo. E17 8M 29
Cheshire Clo. SE4 1K 93
Cheshire Clo. Horn 3L 51
Cheshire Clo. Mitc 7J 107
Cheshire Ct. EC4 9L 59 (off Fleet St.)
Cheshire Dri. Leav 7D 4
Cheshire Gdns. Chess 8H 119
Cheshire Ho. Mord 2M 121
Cheshire Rd. N22 7K 27
Cheshire St. E2 7D 60
Cheshir Ho. NW4 2G 41
Chesholm Rd. N16 8C 44
Cheshunt 1D 6
Cheshunt Ho. NW6 4M 57 (off Mortimer Cres.)
Cheshunt Rd. E7 2F 62
Cheshunt Rd. Belv 6L 81
Cheshunt Wash. Chesh 1E 6
Chesil Ct. E2 5G 61 (off Bishop's Way)
Chesil Ct. SW3 7C 74 (off St Loo Av.)
Chesilton Rd. SW6 9K 73
Chesil Way. Hay 6D 52
Chesley Gdns. E6 5H 63
Chesney Ct. W9 7L 57 (off Shirland Rd.)
Chesney Cres. New Ad 9A 126
Chesney Ho. SE13 3B 94 (off Mercator Rd.)
Chesney St. SW11 9E 74
Chesnut Gro. N17 1D 44
Chesnut Rd. N17 1D 44
Chesnut Row. N3 7L 25
Chessell Clo. T Hth 8M 107
Chessholme Rd. Ashf 3A 100
Chessing Ct. N2 1D 42 (off Fortis Grn.)
Chessington 7K 119
Chessington Av. N3 1J 41
Chessington Av. Bexh 8J 81
Chessington Clo. Eps 8A 120
Chessington Ct. N3 1K 41 (off Charter Way)
Chessington Ct. Pinn 2K 37
Chessington Hall Gdns. Chess 9H 119
Chessington Hill Pk. Chess 7L 119
Chessington Ho. SW8 1H 91
Chessington Ho. Eps 1D 134 (off Spring St.)
Chessington Lodge. N3 1K 41
Chessington Mans. E10 5L 45
Chessington Mans. E11 5C 46
Chessington Pde. Chess 8H 119
Chessington Rd. Eps & Ewe 8L 119
Chessington Way. W Wick 4M 125
Chessington World of Adventures 2G 133
Chesson Rd. W14 7K 73
Chesswood Way. Pinn 9H 21
Chestbrook Ct. Enf 7C 16 (off Forsyth Pl.)
Chester Av. Rich 5K 87
Chester Av. Twic 7K 85
Chester Clo. SW1 3F 74
Chester Clo. SW13 2F 88
Chester Clo. Ashf 2B 100
Chester Clo. Lou 3M 19
Chester Clo. Rich 5K 87
Chester Clo. Sutt 4L 121
Chester Clo. Uxb 9F 142
Chester Clo. N. NW1 6F 58
Chester Clo. S. NW1 6F 58
Chester Cotts. SW1 5E 74 (off Bourne St.)
Chester Ct. NW1 6F 58
Chester Ct. SE5 8B 76 (off Lomond Gro.)
Chester Ct. SE8 6H 77
Chester Ct. Brom 8E 110 (off Durham Rd.)
Chester Cres. E8 1D 60
Chester Dri. Harr 4K 37
Chesterfield Clo. SE13 1B 94
Chesterfield Clo. Orp 8J 113
Chesterfield Ct. Surb 9J 103 (off Cranes Pk.)
Chesterfield Dri. Dart 4F 98
Chesterfield Dri. Esh 4E 118
Chesterfield Flats. Barn 7H 13 (off Bells Hill)
Chesterfield Gdns. N4 3M 43
Chesterfield Gdns. SE10 9B 78
Chesterfield Gdns. W1 2F 74
Chesterfield Gro. SE22 4D 92
Chesterfield Hill. W1 2F 74
Chesterfield Ho. W1 2E 74 (off Chesterfield Gdns.)
Chesterfield Lodge. N21 9K 15 (off Church Hill)
Chesterfield Rd. E10 4A 46
Chesterfield Rd. N3 6L 25
Chesterfield Rd. W4 7A 72
Chesterfield Rd. Barn 7H 13
Chesterfield Rd. Enf 1J 17
Chesterfield Rd. Eps 9B 120
Chesterfield St. W1 2F 74
Chesterfield Wlk. SE10 9B 78
Chesterfield Way. SE15 8G 77
Chesterfield Way. Hay 3E 68
Chesterford Gdns. NW3 9M 41
Chesterford Ho. SE18 9H 79 (off Tellson Av.)
Chesterford Rd. E12 1K 63
Chester Gdns. W13 9F 54
Chester Gdns. Enf 8F 16
Chester Gdns. Mord 1A 122
Chester Ga. NW1 6F 58
Chester Grn. Lou 3M 19
Chester Ho. SE8 7K 77
Chester Ho. SW1 5F 74 (off Eccleston Pl.)
Chester Ho. SW9 8L 75 (off Brixton Rd.)
Chester Ho. Uxb 7A 142
Chesterman Ct. W4 8C 72 (off Corney Reach Way)
Chester M. E17 9L 29
Chester M. SW1 4F 74
Chester Path. Lou 3M 19
Chester Pl. NW1 6F 58
Chester Pl. N'wd 7C 20 (off Green La.)
Chester Rd. E7 3H 63
Chester Rd. E11 4F 46
Chester Rd. E16 7C 62
Chester Rd. E17 3H 45
Chester Rd. N9 1F 28
Chester Rd. N17 1B 44
Chester Rd. N19 7F 42
Chester Rd. NW1 6E 58
Chester Rd. SW19 3G 105
Chester Rd. Borwd 5A 12
Chester Rd. Chig 3L 31
Chester Rd. Houn 2F 84
Chester Rd. Ilf 6D 48
Chester Rd. H'row A 2E 144
Chester Rd. Lou 4M 19
Chester Rd. N'wd 7C 20
Chester Rd. Sidc 4C 96 (in two parts)
Chester Rd. Wat 7E 8
Chester Row. SW1 5E 74
Chester Sq. SW1 5E 74
Chester Sq. M. SW1 4F 74 (off Chester Sq.)
Chesters, The. N Mald 5C 104
Chester St. E2 7E 60
Chester St. SW1 4E 74
Chester Ter. NW1 6F 58 (in three parts)
Chester Ter. Bark 2B 64
Chesterton Clo. SW18 4L 89
Chesterton Clo. Gnfd 5M 53
Chesterton Ct. W3 4M 71 (off Bollo Bri. Rd.)
Chesterton Ct. W5 8H 55
Chesterton Dri. Stai 7D 144
Chesterton Ho. Croy 6B 124 (off Heathfield Rd.)
Chesterton Rd. E13 6E 62

Chesterton Rd.—Chudleigh Rd.

Chesterton Rd. W10 8H 57
Chesterton Sq. W8 5L 73
Chesterton Ter. E13 6E 62
Chesterton Ter. King T 6L 103
Chester Way. SE11 5L 75
Chesthunte Rd. N17 8A 28
Chestnut All. SW6 7K 73
Chestnut Av. E7 9F 46
Chestnut Av. N8 3J 43
Chestnut Av. SW14 2B 88
Chestnut Av. Bren 5H 71
Chestnut Av. Buck H 3H 31
Chestnut Av.
E Mol & Tedd 7D 102
Chestnut Av. Edgw 6J 23
Chestnut Av. Eps 6C 120
Chestnut Av. Esh 2B 118
Chestnut Av. Hamp 4L 101
Chestnut Av. Horn 7D 50
Chestnut Av. N'wd 9D 20
Chestnut Av. Wemb 1F 54
Chestnut Av. W Dray 1K 143
Chestnut Av. W Wick 7C 126
Chestnut Av. Wey 9A 116
Chestnut Av. W Vill 9C 116
Chestnut Av. N. E17 2B 46
Chestnut Av. S. E17 3A 46
Chestnut Clo. N14 7G 15
Chestnut Clo. N16 7B 44
Chestnut Clo. SE6 2A 110
Chestnut Clo. SE14 9K 77
Chestnut Clo. SW16 1L 107
Chestnut Clo. Buck H 2H 31
Chestnut Clo. Cars 3D 122
Chestnut Clo. Hay 1C 68
Chestnut Clo. Horn 9G 51
Chestnut Clo. Orp 7E 128
Chestnut Clo. Sidc 7E 96
Chestnut Clo. Sun 3D 100
Chestnut Clo. W Dray 8M 143
Chestnut Ct. N8 3J 43
Chestnut Ct. SW6 7K 73
Chestnut Ct. W8 4M 73
(off Abbots Wlk.)
Chestnut Ct. Felt 2H 101
Chestnut Ct. S Croy 6A 124
(off Bramley Hill)
Chestnut Dri. E11 4E 46
Chestnut Dri. Bexh 2H 97
Chestnut Dri. Harr 7D 22
Chestnut Dri. Pinn 4H 37
Chestnut Glen. Horn 7D 50
Chestnut Gro. SE20 4F 108
Chestnut Gro. SW12 6E 90
Chestnut Gro. W5 4H 71
Chestnut Gro. Barn 7D 14
Chestnut Gro. Dart 1B 114
Chestnut Gro. Ilf 6C 32
Chestnut Gro. Iswth 3E 86
Chestnut Gro. Mitc 9H 107
Chestnut Gro. N Mald 7B 104
Chestnut Gro. S Croy 9F 124
Chestnut Gro. Wemb 1F 54
Chestnut Ho. W4 5C 72
(off Orchard, The)
Chestnut La. N20 1J 25
Chestnut La. Wey 7A 116
Chestnut Pl. Eps 3E 134
Chestnut Ri. SE18 7B 80
Chestnut Ri. Bush 9M 9
Chestnut Rd. SE27 9M 91
Chestnut Rd. SW20 6H 105
Chestnut Rd. Dart 7H 99
Chestnut Rd. Enf 9E 6
Chestnut Rd. King T 4J 103
Chestnut Rd. Twic 8C 86
Chestnuts, The. N5 9A 44
(off Highbury Grange)
Chestnuts, The. Lou 7H 19
Chestnuts, The. Pinn 7K 21
Chestnuts, The. Uxb 3C 142
Chestnuts, The. W on T 4E 116
Chestnut Ter. Sutt 6M 121
Chestnut Wlk. Shep 8C 100
Chestnut Wlk. Wat 1E 8
Chestnut Wlk. Wfd G 5E 30
Chestnut Way. Felt 9F 84
Cheston Av. Croy 4J 125
Chestwood Gro. Uxb 3D 142
Cheswick Clo. Dart 3D 98
Chesworth Clo. Eri 1C 98
Chettle Clo. SE1 4B 76
(off Spurgeon St.)
Chettle Ct. N8 4L 43
Chetwode Ho. NW8 7C 58
(off Grendon St.)
Chetwode Rd. SW17 9D 90
Chetwood Wlk. E6 8J 63
(off Greenwich Cres.)
Chetwynd Av. E Barn 1D 26
Chetwynd Dri. Uxb 5D 142
Chetwynd Rd. NW5 9F 42
Chevalier Clo. Stan 4J 23
Cheval Pl. SW7 4C 74
Cheval St. E14 4L 77
Cheveley Clo. Romf 8J 35
Cheveney Wlk. Brom 7E 110
Chevening Rd. NW6 5H 57
Chevening Rd. SE10 6D 78
Chevening Rd. SE19 3B 108
Chevenings, The. Sidc 9G 97
Cheverell Ho. E2 5E 60
(off Pritchard's Rd.)
Cheverells. 7M 139
Cheverton Rd. N19 6H 43
Chevet St. E9 1J 61
Chevington. NW2 2K 57
Chevington Way. Horn 9H 51
Cheviot. N17 7F 28
(off Northumberland Gro.)
Cheviot Clo. Bans 7M 135
Cheviot Clo. Bexh 1C 98
Cheviot Clo. Bush 8A 10
Cheviot Clo. Enf 4B 16
Cheviot Clo. Hay 8B 68
Cheviot Clo. Sutt 1B 136
Cheviot Ct. SE14 7G 77
(off Avonley Rd.)
Cheviot Ct. S'hall 5M 69
Cheviot Gdns. NW2 7H 41
Cheviot Gdns. SE27 1M 107
Cheviot Ga. NW2 7J 41
Cheviot Ho. E1 9F 60
(off Commercial Rd.)
Cheviot Rd. SE27 2L 107
Cheviot Rd. Horn 5E 50
Cheviot Way. Ilf 2C 48
Chevron Clo. E16 9E 62
Chevy Rd. S'hall 3A 70
Chewton Rd. E17 2J 45
Cheyham Gdns. Sutt 2H 135
Cheyham Way. Sutt 2J 135
Cheylesmore Ho. SW1 6F 74
(off Ebury Bri. Rd.)
Cheyne Av. E18 1D 46
Cheyne Av. Twic 7K 85
Cheyne Clo. NW4 3G 41
Cheyne Clo. Brom 5J 127
Cheyne Ct. SW3 7D 74
Cheyne Ct. Bans 7M 135
Cheyne Ct. Bush 6J 9
Cheyne Gdns. SW3 7C 74
Cheyne Hill. Surb 8K 103
Cheyne M. SW3 7C 74
Cheyne Path. W7 8D 54
Cheyne Pl. SW3 7D 74
Cheyne Rd. Ashf 4B 100
Cheyne Row. SW3 7C 74
Cheyne Wlk. N21 7M 15
Cheyne Wlk. NW4 4G 41
Cheyne Wlk.
SW10 & SW3 8B 74
(in three parts)
Cheyne Wlk. Croy 4E 124
Cheyneys Av. Edgw 6H 23
Chichele Gdns. Croy 6C 124
Chichele Rd. NW2 1H 57
Chicheley Gdns. Harr 7A 22
(in two parts)
Chicheley Rd. Harr 7A 22
Chicheley St. SE1 3K 75
Chichester Av. Ruis 7B 36
Chichester Clo. E6 9J 63
Chichester Clo. SE3 8G 79
Chichester Clo. Hamp 3K 101
Chichester Ct. Edgw 6L 23
(off Whitchurch La.)
Chichester Ct. Eps 1D 134
Chichester Ct. N'holt 4J 53
Chichester Ct. Stan 1J 39
Chichester Dri. Purl 4K 137
Chichester Gdns. Ilf 5J 47
Chichester Ho. NW6 5L 57
Chichester Ho. SW9 8L 75
(off Brixton Rd.)
Chichester M. SE27 1L 107
Chichester Rents. WC2 9L 59
(off Chancery La.)
Chichester Rd. E11 8C 46
Chichester Rd. N9 1E 28
Chichester Rd. NW6 5L 57
Chichester Rd. W2 8M 57
Chichester Rd. Croy 5C 124
Chichester St. SW1 6G 75
Chichester Way. E14 5B 78
Chichester Way. Felt 6G 85
Chichester Way. Wat 6J 5
Chichester Wharf. Eri 6C 82
Chicken Shed Theatre. 7E 14
Chicksand Ho. E1 8E 60
(off Chicksand St.)
Chicksand St. E1 8D 60
(in two parts)
Chidbrook Ho. Wat 8C 8
Chiddingfold. N12 3L 25
Chiddingstone. SE13 4A 94
Chiddingstone Av. Bexh 8K 81
Chiddingstone Clo. Sutt 2L 135
Chiddingstone St. SW6 1L 89
Chieftan Dri. Purf 5L 83
Chieveley Pde. Bexh 3M 97
(off Chieveley Rd.)
Chieveley Pde. Bexh 2M 97
(Mayplace Rd. E.)
Chieveley Rd. Bexh 3M 97
Chignell Pl. W13 2E 70
Chigwell. 3M 31
Chigwell Hill. E1 1F 76
Chigwell Hurst Ct. Pinn 1H 37
Chigwell La. Lou & Chig 7M 19
Chigwell Pk. Chig 4M 31
Chigwell Pk. Dri. Chig 4L 31
Chigwell Ri. Chig 2L 31
Chigwell Rd. E18 & Wfd G 1F 46
Chigwell Row. 3F 32
Chigwell Vw. Romf 6L 33
Chilcot Clo. E14 9M 61
Chilcott Clo. Wemb 9G 39
Chilcott Rd. Wat 9C 4
Childebert Rd. SW17 8F 90
Childeric Rd. SE14 8J 77
Childerley St. SW6 9J 73
Childers St. SE8 7J 77
Childers, The. Wfd G 5K 31
Childs Clo. Horn 4G 51
Childs Ct. Hay 1E 68
Child's Hill. 8L 41
Childs Hill Wlk. NW2 8K 41
(off Cricklewood La.)
Child's La. SE19 3C 108
Child's Pl. SW5 5L 73
Child's St. SW5 5L 73
Child's Wlk. SW5 5L 73
(off Child's St.)
Childs Way. NW11 3K 41
Chilham Clo. Bex 6K 97
Chilham Clo. Gnfd 5E 54
Chilham Ho. SE1 4B 76
Chilham Ho. SE15 7G 77
Chilham Rd. SE9 1J 111
Chilham Way. Brom 2E 126
Chilianwalla Memorial. 7E 74
(in Royal Hospital Chelsea)
Chillerton Rd. SW17 2E 106
Chillingworth Gdns. Twic 9D 86
Chillingworth Rd. N7 1L 59
Chilmark Gdns. N Mald 1E 120
Chilmark Rd. SW16 6H 107
Chiltern Av. Bush 8A 10
Chiltern Av. Twic 7L 85
Chiltern Clo. Bexh 9C 82
Chiltern Clo. Borwd 4K 11
Chiltern Clo. Bush 8M 9
Chiltern Clo. Croy 5C 124
Chiltern Clo. Wor Pk 3G 121
Chiltern Ct. N10 9E 26
Chiltern Ct. NW1 7D 58
(off Baker St.)
Chiltern Ct. SE14 8G 77
(off Avonley Rd.)
Chiltern Ct. Harr 3B 38
Chiltern Ct. New Bar 7A 14
Chiltern Ct. Uxb 7F 142
Chiltern Dene. Enf 6K 15
Chiltern Dri. Surb 1L 119
Chiltern Gdns. NW2 8H 41
Chiltern Gdns. Brom 8D 110
Chiltern Gdns. Horn 8G 51
Chiltern Ho. SE17 7B 76
(off Portland St.)
Chiltern Ho. W5 8J 55
Chiltern Rd. E3 7L 61
Chiltern Rd. Ilf 3C 48
Chiltern Rd. Pinn 3G 37
Chiltern Rd. Sutt 1M 135
Chilterns, The. Brom 6F 110
(off Murray Av.)
Chilterns, The. Sutt 1M 135
Chiltern St. W1 8E 58
Chiltern Vw. Rd. Uxb 5A 142
Chiltern Way. Wfd G 3E 30
Chilthorne Clo. SE6 6K 93
Chilton Av. W5 5H 71
Chilton Ct. N22 7J 27
(off Truro Rd.)
Chilton Ct. W on T 6E 116
Chilton Gro. SE8 5H 77
Chiltonian Ind. Est. SE12 5D 94
Chilton Rd. Edgw 6L 23
Chilton Rd. Rich 2L 87
Chiltons Clo. Bans 7M 135
Chiltons, The. E18 9E 30
Chilton St. E2 7D 60
Chilvers Clo. Twic 8C 86
Chilver St. SE10 6D 78
Chilwell Gdns. Wat 4G 21
Chilworth Ct. SW19 7H 89
Chilworth Gdns. Sutt 5A 122
Chilworth M. W2 9B 58
Chilworth St. W2 9A 58
Chimes Av. N13 5L 27
Chimes Shop. Cen., The.
Uxb 3B 142
Chimney Ct. E1 2F 76
(off Brewhouse La.)
China Ct. E1 2F 76
(off Asher Way)
China M. SW2 6K 91
China Wharf. SE1 3E 76
Chinbrook Cres. SE12 9F 94
Chinbrook Rd. SE12 9F 94
Chinchilla Dri. Houn 1G 85
Chine, The. N10 2G 43
Chine, The. N21 8M 15
Chine, The. Wemb 1F 54
Ching Ct. WC2 9J 59
(off Monmouth St.)
Chingdale Rd. E4 3C 30
Chingford. 9C 18
Chingford Av. E4 3L 29
Chingford Green. 1B 30
Chingford Hall Est. E4 6K 29
Chingford Hatch. 4B 30
Chingford Ind. Est. E4 4J 29
Chingford La. Wfd G 4C 30
Chingford Mount. 4L 29
Chingford Mt. Rd. E4 4L 29
Chingford Rd. E4 6L 29
Chingford Rd. E17 8M 29
Chingley Clo. Brom 3C 110
Ching Way. E4 6K 29
(in two parts)
Chinnery Clo. Enf 3D 16
Chinnock's Wharf. E14 1J 77
(off Narrow St.)
Chinnor Cres. Gnfd 5M 53
Chipka St. E14 3A 78
(in two parts)
Chipley St. SE14 7J 77
Chipmunk Gro. N'holt 6J 53
Chippendale All. Uxb 3B 142
Chippendale Ho. SW1 6F 74
(off Churchill Gdns.)
Chippendale St. E5 8H 45
Chippendale Waye. Uxb 3B 142
Chippenham. King T 6K 103
(off Excelsior Clo.)
Chippenham Av. Wemb 1M 55
Chippenham Clo. Pinn 2D 36
Chippenham Clo. Romf 5H 35
Chippenham Gdns. NW6 6L 57
Chippenham Gdns. Romf 5H 35
Chippenham M. W9 7L 57
Chippenham Rd. W9 7L 57
Chippenham Rd. Romf 6H 35
Chippenham Wlk. Romf 6H 35
Chipperfield Ho. SW3 6C 74
(off Ixworth Pl.)
Chipperfield Rd.
Orp & St P 5E 112
Chipping Barnet. 6J 13
Chipping Clo. Barn 5J 13
Chipstead. 9D 136
Chipstead Av. T Hth 8M 107
Chipstead Clo. SE19 4D 108
Chipstead Clo. Coul 8E 136
Chipstead Clo. Sutt 1M 135
Chipstead Gdns. NW2 7F 40
Chipstead Rd. Bans 9K 135
(in two parts)
Chipstead Rd. Eri 8C 82
Chipstead Rd. H'row A 2E 144
Chipstead St. SW6 9L 73
Chipstead Valley Rd.
Coul 8E 136
Chipstead Way. Bans 8D 136
Chip St. SW4 2H 91
Chirdland Ho. Wat 8C 8
Chirk Clo. Hay 7J 53
Chisenhale Rd. E3 5J 61
Chisholm Ct. W6 6E 72
Chisholm Rd. Croy 4C 124
Chisholm Rd. Rich 5K 87
Chisledon Wlk. E9 2K 61
(off Osborne Rd.)
Chislehurst. 3M 111
Chislehurst Av. N12 7A 26
Chislehurst Caves. 5L 111
Chislehurst Rd.
Brom & Chst 6H 111
Chislehurst Rd. Orp 8C 112
Chislehurst Rd. Rich 4J 87
Chislehurst Rd. Sidc 2E 112
Chislehurst West. 2L 111
Chislet Clo. Beck 4L 109
Chisley Rd. N15 4C 44
Chiswell Ct. Wat 2G 9
Chiswell Sq. SE3 1F 94
Chiswell St. EC1 8A 60
Chiswick. 6B 72
Chiswick Bri. SW14 & W4 1A 88
Chiswick Clo. Croy 5K 123
Chiswick Comn. Rd. W4 5B 72
Chiswick Ct. W4 5M 71
Chiswick Ct. Pinn 1K 37
Chiswick High Rd.
Bren & W4 6L 71
(in two parts)
Chiswick House. 7C 72
Chiswick La. W4 6C 72
Chiswick La. S. W4 7D 72
Chiswick Mall. W4 & W6 7D 72
Chiswick Pk. W4 5M 71
Chiswick Plaza. W4 7A 72
Chiswick Quay. W4 9A 72
Chiswick Rd. N9 2E 28
Chiswick Rd. W4 5A 72
Chiswick Roundabout (Junct.)
6L 71
Chiswick Sq. W4 7C 72
Chiswick Staithe. W4 9A 72
Chiswick Ter. W4 5A 72
(off Chiswick Rd.)
Chiswick Village. W4 7L 71
Chiswick Wharf. W4 7D 72
Chitterfield Ga. W Dray 8L 143
Chitty's La. Dag 7H 49
Chitty St. W1 8G 59
Chivalry Rd. SW11 4C 90
Chive Clo. Croy 3H 125
Chivenor Gro. King T 2H 103
Chivers Rd. E4 3M 29
Choats Rd. Bark & Dag 5G 65
Chobham Gdns. SW19 8H 89
Chobham Rd. E15 1B 62
Cholmeley Cres. N6 5F 42
Cholmeley Lodge. N6 6F 42
Cholmeley Pk. N6 6F 42
Cholmley Gdns. NW6 1L 57
Cholmley Rd. Th Dit 1F 118
Cholmondeley Av. NW10 5E 56
Cholmondeley Wlk. Rich 4G 87
(in two parts)
Choppin's Ct. E1 2F 76
Chopwell Clo. E15 3B 62
Chorleywood Cres. Orp 6D 112
Choumert Gro. SE15 1E 92
Choumert Rd. SE15 2D 92
Choumert Sq. SE15 1E 92
Chow Sq. E8 1D 60
Chrislaine Clo. Stanw 5B 144
Chrisp Ho. SE10 7C 78
(off Maze Hill)
Chrisp St. E14 8M 61
(in two parts)
Christabel Clo. Iswth 2C 86
Christchurch Av. N12 6A 26
Christchurch Av. NW6 4H 57
Christchurch Av. Eri 7B 82
Christchurch Av. Harr 2D 38
Christchurch Av. Rain 5D 66
Christchurch Av. Tedd 2E 102
Christchurch Av. Wemb 2J 55
Christchurch Clo. N12 7B 26
Christchurch Clo. SW19 4B 106
Christchurch Clo. Enf 4A 16
Christchurch Ct. EC4 9M 59
(off Warwick La.)
Christ Church Ct. NW10 4C 56
Christchurch Ct. Hay 7G 53
(off Dunedin Way)
Christchurch Cres. Rad 1E 10
Christchurch Flats. Rich 2J 87
Christchurch Gdns. Eps 3M 133
Christchurch Gdns. Harr 2E 38
Christchurch Grn. Wemb 2J 55
Christchurch Hill. NW3 8B 42
Christchurch Ho. SW2 7K 91
(off Christchurch Rd.)
Christchurch La. Barn 4J 13
Christchurch Lodge. Barn 6D 14
Christ Chu. Mt. Eps 4M 133
(in two parts)
Christchurch Pk. Sutt 9A 122
Christchurch Pas. NW3 8A 42
Christchurch Pas.
High Bar 4J 13
Christchurch Path. Hay 4A 68
Christchurch Pl. SW8 1H 91
Christchurch Pl. Eps 3M 133
Christchurch Rd. N8 4J 43
Christchurch Rd. SW2 7K 91
Christ Chu. Rd. SW14 4M 87
Christchurch Rd. SW19 4B 106
Christ Chu. Rd. Beck 6L 109
Christchurch Rd. Dart 6G 99
Christ Chu. Rd. Eps 4J 133
Christchurch Rd. Ilf 6M 47
Christchurch Rd.
H'row A 2E 144
Christchurch Rd. Purl 3M 137
Christchurch Rd. Sidc 1D 112
Christchurch Rd. Surb 1K 119
Christchurch Sq. E9 4G 61
Christchurch St. SW3 7D 74
Christchurch Ter. SW3 7D 74
(off Christchurch St.)
Christchurch Way. SE10 6C 78
Christian Ct. SE16 2K 77
Christian Fields. SW16 4L 107
Christian Pl. E1 9E 60
(off Burslem St.)
Christian St. E1 9E 60
Christie Ct. N19 7J 43
Christie Dri. Croy 9E 108
Christie Gdns. Romf 4F 48
Christie Ho. SE10 6D 78
(off Blackwall La.)
Christie Rd. E9 2J 61
Christie Rd. Wal A 8H 7
Christina Sq. N4 6M 43
Christina St. EC2 7C 60
Christine Ct. Rain 8E 66
Christine Worsley Clo.
N21 1M 27
Christopher Av. W7 4E 70
Christopher Clo. SE16 3H 77
Christopher Clo. Horn 9H 51
Christopher Clo. Sidc 4D 96
Christopher Gdns. Dag 1H 65
Christopher Ho. Sidc 8E 96
(off Station Rd.)
Christopher Pl. NW1 6H 59
Christopher Rd. S'hall 5F 68
Christophers M. W11 2J 73
Christopher St. EC2 7B 60
Christy Rd. Big H 7G 141
Chryssell Rd. SW9 8L 75
Chubworthy St. SE14 7J 77
Chudleigh. Sidc 1F 112
Chudleigh Cres. Ilf 9C 48
Chudleigh Gdns. Sutt 5A 122
Chudleigh Rd. NW6 3H 57
Chudleigh Rd. SE4 4K 93
Chudleigh Rd. Romf 4J 35

Chudleigh Rd.—Clapton Sq.

Chudleigh Rd. Twic 5C 86 (in two parts)
Chudleigh St. E1 9H 61
Chudleigh Way. Ruis 6E 36
Chulsa Rd. SE26 2F 108
Chumleigh St. SE5 7C 76
Chumleigh Wlk. Surb 8K 103
Church All. A'ham 2A 10
Church All. Croy 3L 123
Church App. SE21 9B 92
Church App. Stanw 5B 144
Church Av. E4 6B 30
Church Av. N2 9B 26
Church Av. NW1 2F 58
Church Av. SW14 2B 88
Church Av. Beck 5L 109
Church Av. N'holt 3K 53
Church Av. Pinn 4J 37
Church Av. Ruis 6B 36
Church Av. Sidc 2E 112
Church Av. S'hall 4J 69
Churchbank. E17 2L 45 (off Teresa M.)
Churchbury Clo. Enf 4C 16
Churchbury La. Enf 5B 16
Churchbury Rd. SE9 6H 95
Churchbury Rd. Enf 4C 16
Church Cloisters. EC3 1C 76 (off Lovat La.)
Church Clo. N20 3C 26
Church Clo. W8 3M 73
Church Clo. Edgw 5A 24
Church Clo. Eps 5C 134
Church Clo. Hay 8B 52
Church Clo. Houn 1J 85
Church Clo. Lou 4K 19
Church Clo. N'wd 7D 20
Church Clo. Rad 1E 10
Church Clo. Uxb 5A 142
Church Clo. W Dray 4J 143
Church Ct. SE16 3K 77 (off Rotherhithe St.)
Church Ct. Rich 4H 87
Church Ct. Wfd G 6G 31
Church Cres. E9 3H 61
Church Cres. N3 8K 25
Church Cres. N10 2F 42
Church Cres. N20 3C 26
Churchcroft Clo. SW12 6E 90
Churchdown. Brom 1C 110
Church Dri. NW9 6B 40
Church Dri. Harr 4L 37
Church Dri. W Wick 5C 126
Church Elm La. Dag 2L 65
Church End. 8K 25 (Finchley)
Church End. 2C 56 (Willesden)
Church End. E17 2M 45
Church End. NW4 1F 40
Church Entry. EC4 9M 59 (off Carter La.)
Church Est. Almshouses. Rich 3K 87 (off Sheen Rd.)
Church Farm Clo. Swan 1A 130
Church Farm House Mus. 1F 40
Church Farm La. Sutt 8J 121
Church Farm Way. A'ham 2M 9
Church Fld. Dart 8H 99
Churchfield Av. N12 6B 26
Churchfield Clo. Harr 2A 38
Churchfield Clo. Hay 1D 68
Churchfield Mans. SW6 1K 89 (off New Kings Rd.)
Church Fld. Path. Chesh 2C 6 (in two parts)
Churchfield Rd. W3 2A 72
Churchfield Rd. W7 3C 70
Churchfield Rd. W13 2F 70
Churchfield Rd. W on T 3E 116
Churchfield Rd. Well 2E 96
Churchfields. E18 8E 30
Churchfields. SE10 7A 78
Churchfields. Lou 6J 19
Churchfields. W Mol 7L 101
Churchfields Av. Felt 9K 85
Churchfields Av. Wey 7A 116
Churchfields Rd. Beck 6H 109
Churchfields Rd. Wat 9D 4
Churchfield Way. N12 6A 26
Church Gdns. W5 3H 71
Church Gdns. Wemb 9E 38
Church Gth. N19 7H 43 (off St John's Gro.)
Churchgate. 3B 6
Church Ga. SW6 2J 89
Churchgate. Chesh 2B 6
Churchgate Rd. Chesh 2B 6
Church Grn. SW9 9L 75
Church Grn. Hay 9D 52
Church Grn. W on T 8G 117
Church Gro. SE13 4M 93
Church Gro. King T 5G 103
Church Hill. E17 2L 45
Church Hill. N21 9K 15
Church Hill. SE18 4K 79
Church Hill. SW19 2K 105
Church Hill. Cars 7D 122
Church Hill. Cray 3C 98
Church Hill. Cud 7M 141
Church Hill. Dart 8H 99
Church Hill. Harr 6C 38
Church Hill. Lou 5J 19
Church Hill. Orp 2E 128
Church Hill. Purl 2J 137
Church Hill Rd. E17 2M 45
Church Hill Rd. Barn & E Barn 8C 14
Church Hill Rd. Surb 9J 103
Church Hill Rd. Sutt 5H 121
Church Hill Wood. Orp 9D 112
Church Hollow. Purf 6L 83
Church Ho. SW1 4H 75 (off Gt. Smith St.)
Church Hyde. SE18 7C 80
Churchill Av. Harr 4F 38
Churchill Av. Uxb 6F 142
Churchill Clo. Dart 7M 99
Churchill Clo. Felt 7D 84
Churchill Clo. Uxb 6F 142
Churchill Clo. Warl 9G 139
Churchill Ct. N4 5L 43
Churchill Ct. W5 7K 55
Churchill Ct. N'holt 1L 53
Churchill Ct. N'wd 6B 20
Churchill Ct. Orp 7A 128
Churchill Ct. Pinn 8J 21
Churchill Ct. S Harr 3M 37
Churchill Dri. Wey 6A 116
Churchill Gdns. SW1 6G 75 (off Churchill Gdns., in three parts)
Churchill Gdns. W3 9L 55
Churchill Gdns. Rd. SW1 6F 74
Churchill Pk. Dart 4L 99
Churchill Pl. E14 2M 77
Churchill Pl. Harr 2C 38
Churchill Rd. E16 9G 63
Churchill Rd. NW2 2F 56
Churchill Rd. NW5 9F 42
Churchill Rd. Edgw 6K 23
Churchill Rd. Eps 3L 133
Churchill Rd. S Croy 1A 138
Churchill Ter. E4 4L 29
Churchill Theatre. 6E 110
Churchill Wlk. E9 1G 61
Churchill Way. Big H 5J 141
Churchill Way. Brom 6E 110
Churchill Way. Sun 2E 100
Church La. E11 6C 46
Church La. E17 2M 45
Church La. N2 1B 42
Church La. N8 2K 43
Church La. N9 2E 28
Church La. N17 8C 28
Church La. NW9 4A 40
Church La. SW17 2D 106
Church La. SW19 5K 105
Church La. W5 3G 71
Church La. A'ham 2M 9
Church La. Brom 3J 127
Church La. Chel 8M 139
Church La. Chesh 2B 6
Church La. Chess 8K 119
Church La. Chst 5A 112
Church La. Dag 3A 66
Church La. Enf 5B 16
Church La. Eps 9H 135
Church La. Harr 8D 22
Church La. Lou 5K 19
Church La. Pinn 1J 37
Church La. Purf 6L 83
Church La. Rich 7J 87
Church La. Romf 2C 50
Church La. Tedd 2D 102
Church La. Th Dit 1D 118
Church La. Twic 7E 86
Church La. Uxb 5A 142
Church La. Wall 5H 123
Church La. Warl 9H 139
Church La. Wen 9H 67
Churchley Rd. SE26 1F 108
Church Manorway. SE2 6E 80
Church Manorway. Eri 4B 82
Church Mead. SE5 8A 76 (off Camberwell Rd.)
Churchmead Clo. E Barn 8C 14
Church Mdw. Surb 4G 119
Churchmead Rd. NW10 2E 56
Churchmore Rd. SW16 5G 107
Church Mt. N2 3B 42
Chu. Paddock Ct. Wall 5H 123
Church Pas. EC2 9A 60 (off Guildhall Yd.)
Church Pas. Barn 5J 13
Church Pas. Surb 9J 103
Church Pas. Twic 7F 86
Church Path. E11 3E 46
Church Path. E17 2M 45
Church Path. N5 1M 59
Church Path. N12 4A 26
Church Path. N17 8C 28
Church Path. NW10 3C 56
Church Path. SW14 2B 88 (in two parts)
Church Path. SW19 6K 105 (in two parts)
Church Path. W3 & W4 3A 72 (in two parts)
Church Path. W7 2C 70
Church Path. Bark 4A 64
Church Path. Barn 6J 13
Church Path. Croy 4A 124
Church Path. Mitc 7C 106 (in two parts)
Church Path. Romf 3C 50
Church Path. S'hall (UB1) 2L 69
Church Path. S'hall (UB2) 4K 69 (in two parts)
Church Path. Swan 5F 114
Church Pl. SW1 1G 75
Church Pl. W5 3H 71
Church Pl. Ick 8A 36
Church Pl. Mitc 7C 106
Church Ri. SE23 8H 93
Church Ri. Chess 8K 119
Church Rd. E10 6L 45
Church Rd. E12 1J 63
Church Rd. E17 9J 29
Church Rd. N1 2A 60 (off Marquess Rd. S.)
Church Rd. N6 4E 42
Church Rd. N17 8C 28 (in two parts)
Church Rd. NW4 2F 40
Church Rd. NW10 3C 56
Church Rd. SE19 5C 108
Church Rd. SW13 1D 88
Church Rd. SW19 & Mitc 5B 106 (Christchurch Rd.)
Church Rd. SW19 9J 89 (Wimbledon Pk. Rd.)
Church Rd. W3 2A 72
Church Rd. W7 1B 70
Church Rd. Ashf 9D 144
Church Rd. Asht 9H 133
Church Rd. Bark 2A 64
Church Rd. Bexh 1K 97
Church Rd. Big H 9H 141
Church Rd. Brom 6E 110
Church Rd. Buck H 1F 30
Church Rd. Chels & Orp 9G 129
Church Rd. Clay 8D 118
Church Rd. Croy 5A 124 (in two parts)
Church Rd. E Mol 8B 102
Church Rd. Enf 8G 17
Church Rd. Eps 4C 134
Church Rd. Eri 6B 82
Church Rd. F'boro 7A 128
Church Rd. Felt 2H 101
Church Rd. Ham & Rich 1H 103
Church Rd. H Wood 8L 35
Church Rd. Hay 2D 68
Church Rd. H Bee 5E 18
Church Rd. Houn 6F 68 (High St.)
Church Rd. Houn 8L 69 (Up. Sutton La.)
Church Rd. Ilf 4C 48
Church Rd. Iswth 9B 70
Church Rd. Kenl 7B 138
Church Rd. Kes 9H 127
Church Rd. King T 6K 103
Church Rd. Noak H 1G 35
Church Rd. N'holt 5H 53
Church Rd. N'wd 7D 20
Church Rd. Purl 2J 137
Church Rd. Rich 3J 87
Church Rd. Shep 2A 116
Church Rd. Short 7C 110
Church Rd. Sidc 1E 112
Church Rd. S'hall 4K 69
Church Rd. Stan 5F 22
Church Rd. Surb 3G 119
Church Rd. Sutt 8J 121
Church Rd. S at H 3K 115 (in two parts)
Church Rd. Swan 2B 130 (Crockenhill)
Church Rd. Swan 5H 115 (Swanley Village)
Church Rd. Tedd 1C 102
Church Rd. Uxb 7B 142
Church Rd. Wall 5H 123
Church Rd. Warl 9H 139
Church Rd. Wat 3E 8
Church Rd. Well 1F 96
Church Rd. W Dray 4H 143
Church Rd. W Ewe 9B 120
Church Rd. Whyt 9D 138
Church Rd. Wor Pk 3C 120
Church Rd. Almshouses. E10 7M 45 (off Church Rd.)
Church Rd. Ind. Est. E10 6L 45
Church Rd. N. N2 9B 26
Church Rd. S. N2 9B 26
Church Row. NW3 9A 42
Church Row. Chst 5A 112
Church Row M. Chst 4A 112
Church Side. Eps 5M 133
Churchside Clo. Big H 9G 141
Church St. E15 4C 62
Church St. E16 2M 79
Church St. N9 9B 16
Church St. W2 & NW8 8B 58
Church St. W4 7D 72
Church St. Croy 5M 123
Church St. Dag 2M 65
Church St. Enf 5A 16
Church St. Eps 1E 134
Church St. Esh 6M 117
Church St. Ewe 5C 134
Church St. Hamp 5A 102
Church St. Iswth 2F 86
Church St. King T 6H 103
Church St. Sun 7F 100
Church St. Sutt 7M 121
Church St. Twic 7E 86
Church St. Wal A 6J 7
Church St. W on T 3E 116
Church St. Wat 6G 9
Church St. Est. NW8 7B 58 (in two parts)
Church St. N. E15 4C 62
Church St. Pas. E15 4C 62
Church Stretton Rd. Houn 4A 86
Church Ter. NW4 1F 40
Church Ter. SE13 2C 94
Church Ter. Rich 4H 87
Church Trad. Est. Eri 8D 82
Church Va. N2 1D 42
Church Va. SE23 8H 93
Church Vw. Rich 4J 87
Church Vw. Swan 7B 114
Church Vw. Upm 7M 51
Churchview Rd. Twic 7B 86
Church Wlk. N6 8E 42
Church Wlk. N16 8B 44 (in three parts)
Church Wlk. NW2 8K 41
Church Wlk. NW4 1G 41
Church Wlk. NW9 7B 40
Church Wlk. SW13 9E 72
Church Wlk. SW15 4F 88
Church Wlk. SW16 6G 107
Church Wlk. SW20 7G 105
Church Wlk. Bren 7G 71 (in two parts)
Church Wlk. Bush 8L 9
Church Wlk. Dart 9H 99
Church Wlk. Enf 5B 16
Church Wlk. Eyns 5J 131
Church Wlk. Hay 9C 52 (in three parts)
Church Wlk. Rich 4H 87
Church Wlk. Th Dit 1D 118
Church Wlk. W on T 3E 116
Churchward Ho. W14 6K 73 (off Ivatt Pl.)
Church Way. N20 3C 26
Churchway. NW1 6H 59 (in two parts)
Church Way. Barn 6D 14
Church Way. Edgw 6L 23
Church Way. S Croy 2D 138
Churchwell Path. E9 1G 61
Churchwood Gdns. Wfd G 4E 30
Churchyard Pas. SE5 1B 92
Churchyard Row. SE11 5M 75
Churnfield. N4 7L 43
Churston Av. E13 4F 62
Churston Clo. SW2 7L 91
Churston Dri. Mord 9H 105
Churston Gdns. N11 6G 27
Churton Pl. SW1 5G 75
Churton St. SW1 5G 75
Chusan Pl. E14 9K 61
Chute Ho. SW9 1L 91 (off Stockwell Pk. Rd.)
Chuters Gro. Eps 4D 134
Chyngton Clo. Sidc 9D 96
Cibber Rd. SE23 8H 93
Cicada Rd. SW18 5A 90
Cicely Ho. NW8 5B 58 (off Cochrane St.)
Cicely Rd. SE15 9E 76
Cinderella Path. NW11 6M 41
Cinderford Way. Brom 1C 110
Cine Lumiere. 5B 74 (off Queensberry Pl.)
Cinnabar Wharf Central. E1 2E 76 (off Wapping High St.)
Cinnabar Wharf E. E1 2E 76 (off Wapping High St.)
Cinnabar Wharf W. E1 2E 76 (off Wapping High St.)
Cinnamon Clo. Croy 2J 123
Cinnamon Row. SW11 2A 90
Cinnamon St. E1 2F 76
Cinnamon Wharf. SE1 3D 76 (off Shad Thames)
Cintra Pk. SE19 4D 108
Circle Gdns. SW19 6L 105
Circle, The. NW2 8C 40
Circle, The. NW7 6B 24
Circle, The. SE1 3D 76 (off Queen Elizabeth St.)
Circuits, The. Pinn 2G 37
Circular Rd. N2 9B 26
Circular Rd. N17 1D 44
Circular Way. SE18 7K 79
Circus Lodge. NW8 6B 58 (off Circus Rd.)
Circus M. W1 8D 58 (off Enford St.)
Circus Pl. EC2 8B 60
Circus Rd. NW8 6B 58
Circus St. SE10 8A 78
Cirencester St. W2 8M 57
Cirrus Clo. Wall 9J 123
Cissbury Ho. SE26 9E 92
Cissbury Ring N. N12 5K 25
Cissbury Ring S. N12 5K 25
Cissbury Rd. N15 3B 44
Citadel Pl. SE11 6K 75
Citizen Rd. N7 9L 43
Citrus Ho. SE8 6K 77 (off Alverton St.)
City Airport. 2J 79
City & Guilds of London Institute. 7L 59
City & Islington College. 7B 60
City Bus. Cen. SE16 4G 77
City Central Est. EC1 6A 60 (off Seward St.)
City Garden Row. N1 5M 59
City Harbour. E14 4M 77 (off Selsdon Way)
City Heights. SE1 2C 76 (off Weavers La.)
City Ho. Wall 3E 122 (off Corbet Clo.)
City of London. 9B 60
City of London Almshouses. SW9 3K 91
City of London College. 9D 60
City of London Crematorium. E12 8J 47
City of Westminster College. 1G 75
City Pavilion. EC1 8M 59 (off Britton St.)
City Rd. EC1 5M 59
City Tower. EC2 8B 60 (off Basinghall St.)
City University, The. 6M 59
City Vw. Ct. SE22 6E 92
Civic Way. Ilf 2A 48
Civic Way. Ruis 1H 53
Clabon M. SW1 4D 74
Clack La. Ruis 6A 36
Clack St. SE16 3G 77
Clacton Rd. E13 6H 63
Clacton Rd. E17 4J 45
Clacton Rd. N17 9D 28
Claigmar Gdns. N3 8M 25
Claire Ct. N12 4A 26
Claire Ct. NW2 2J 57
Claire Ct. Bush 1B 22
Claire Ct. Chesh 5E 6
Claire Ct. Pinn 7K 21
Claire Gdns. Stan 5G 23
Claire Ho. Edgw 9A 24 (off Burnt Oak B'way.)
Claire Pl. E14 4L 77
Clairvale. Horn 5J 51
Clairvale Rd. Houn 9H 69
Clairview Rd. SW16 2F 106
Clairville Gdns. W7 2C 70
Clairville Point. SE23 9H 93 (off Dacres Rd.)
Clammas Way. Uxb 8A 142
Clamp Hill. Stan 4B 22
Clancarty Rd. SW6 1L 89
Clandeboye Ho. E15 4D 62 (off John St.)
Clandon Clo. W3 3M 71
Clandon Clo. Eps 8D 120
Clandon Gdns. N3 1L 41
Clandon Ho. SE1 3M 75 (off Webber St.)
Clandon Rd. Ilf 7C 48
Clandon St. SE8 1L 93
Clandon Ter. SW20 6H 105
Clanfield Way. SE15 8C 76
Clanricarde Gdns. W2 1L 73
Clapgate Rd. Bush 8M 9
Clapham. 3G 91
Clapham Common (Junct.) 3H 91
Clapham Comn. N. Side. SW4 3D 90
Clapham Comn. S. Side. SW4 5F 90
Clapham Comn. W. Side. SW4 3D 90 (in five parts)
Clapham Cres. SW4 3H 91
Clapham High St. SW4 3H 91
Clapham Junction. 2C 90
Clapham Junct. App. SW11 2C 90
Clapham Mnr. Ct. SW4 2G 91
Clapham Mnr. St. SW4 2G 91
Clapham Park. 5H 91
Clapham Pk. Est. SW4 5H 91
Clapham Pk. Rd. SW4 3G 91
Clapham Pk. Ter. SW4 4J 91 (off Kings Av.)
Clapham Rd. SW4 & SW9 2J 91
Clapham Rd. Est. SW4 2J 91
Clap La. Dag 7M 49
Claps Ga. La. E6 7L 63
Clapton Comn. E5 5D 44 (in four parts)
Clapton Park. 9H 45
Clapton Pk. Est. E5 9H 45
Clapton Pas. E5 1G 61
Clapton Sq. E5 1G 61

Clapton Ter.—Clifford Av.

Clapton Ter. N16 . . . . .6E 44
Clapton Way. E5 . . . . .9E 44
Clara Grant Ho. E14 . . . . .4L 77
(off Mellish St.)
Clara Nehab Ho. NW11 . . . . .3K 41
(off Leeside Cres.)
Clara Pl. SE18 . . . . .5L 79
Clare Clo. N2 . . . . .1A 42
Clare Clo. Els 8K 11
Clare Corner. SE9 . . . . .6M 95
Clare Ct. WC1 . . . . .6J 59
(off Judd St.)
Clare Ct. Enf 8E 6
Claredale Ho. E2 . . . . .5F 60
(off Claredale St.)
Claredale St. E2 . . . . .5E 60
Clare Gdns. E7 . . . . .9E 46
Clare Gdns. W11 . . . . .9J 57
Clare Gdns. Bark 2D 64
Clare Hill. Esh 8M 117
Clare Ho. E16 . . . . .1L 79
(off University Way)
Clare La. N1 . . . . .3A 60
Clare Lawn Av. SW14 . . . . . .4A 88
Clare Mkt. WC2 . . . . .9K 59
Clare M. SW6 . . . . .8M 73
Claremont. Brick W 4L 5
Claremont. Chesh 2A 6
Claremont. Shep 1A 116
Claremont Av. Esh 8K 117
Claremont Av. Harr 3J 39
Claremont Av. N Mald 9E 104
Claremont Av. Sun 5F 100
Claremont Av. W on T 6H 117
Claremont Clo. E16 . . . . .2L 79
Claremont Clo. N1 . . . . .5L 59
Claremont Clo. SW2 . . . . .7J 91
Claremont Clo. Orp 6L 127
Claremont Clo. S Croy 7F 138
Claremont Clo. W on T 7G 117
Claremont Cres. Crox G 7A 8
Claremont Cres. Dart 3C 98
Claremont Dri. Esh 8M 117
Claremont End. Esh 8M 117
Claremont Gdns. Ilf 7C 48
Claremont Gdns. Surb 9J 103
Claremont Gro. W4 . . . . .8C 72
Claremont Gro. Wfd G 6G 31
Claremont Ho. Wat 8B 8
Claremont Landscape Garden.
. . . . .9L 117
Claremont La. Esh 7M 117
Claremont Park. 9L 117
Claremont Pk. N3 . . . . .8J 25
Claremont Pk. Rd. Esh 8M 117
Claremont Rd. E7 . . . . .1F 62
Claremont Rd. E11 . . . . .8B 46
Claremont Rd. E17 . . . . .9J 29
Claremont Rd. N6 . . . . .5G 43
Claremont Rd. NW2 . . . . .5H 41
Claremont Rd. W9 . . . . .5J 57
Claremont Rd. W13 . . . . .8E 54
Claremont Rd. Barn 2A 14
Claremont Rd. Brom 8J 111
Claremont Rd. Clay 9C 118
Claremont Rd. Croy 3E 124
Claremont Rd. Harr 9C 22
Claremont Rd. Horn 4E 50
Claremont Rd. Surb 9J 103
Claremont Rd. Swan 4C 114
Claremont Rd. Tedd 2D 102
Claremont Rd. Twic 6F 86
Claremont Sq. N1 . . . . .5L 59
Claremont St. E16 . . . . .3L 79
Claremont St. N18 . . . . .6E 28
Claremont St. SE10 . . . . .7M 77
Claremont Ter. Th Dit 2F 118
Claremont Way. NW2 . . . . . .6G 41
(in two parts)
Claremont Way Ind. Est.
NW2 . . . . .6G 41
Claremount Clo. Eps 9G 135
Claremount Gdns. Eps 9G 135
Clarence Av. SW4 . . . . .6H 91
Clarence Av. Brom 8J 111
Clarence Av. Ilf 4L 47
Clarence Av. N Mald 6A 104
Clarence Av. Upm 7L 51
Clarence Clo. Barn 7B 14
Clarence Clo. Bus H 9D 10
Clarence Clo. W on T 6F 116
Clarence Ct. NW7 . . . . .5C 24
Clarence Ct. W6 . . . . .5F 72
(off Cambridge Gro.)
Clarence Cres. SW4 . . . . .5H 91
Clarence Cres. Sidc 9F 96
Clarence Gdns. NW1 . . . . . . .6F 58
Clarence Ga. Wfd G 6K 31
(in four parts)
Clarence Ga. Gdns. NW1 . . . .7D 58
(off Glentworth St.)
Clarence House. 3G 75
(off St James's Pal.)
Clarence La. SW15 . . . . .5C 88
Clarence M. E5 . . . . .1F 60
Clarence M. SE16 . . . . .2H 77
Clarence M. SW12 . . . . .6F 90
Clarence Pas. NW1 . . . . .5J 59
Clarence Pl. E5 . . . . .1F 60
Clarence Rd. E5 . . . . .9F 44
Clarence Rd. E12 . . . . .9H 47
Clarence Rd. E16 . . . . .7C 62
Clarence Rd. E17 . . . . .9H 29
Clarence Rd. N15 . . . . .3A 44
Clarence Rd. N22 . . . . .7J 27
Clarence Rd. NW6 . . . . .3K 57
Clarence Rd. SE8 . . . . .7M 77
Clarence Rd. SE9 . . . . .8J 95
Clarence Rd. SW19 . . . . . . .3M 105
Clarence Rd. W4 . . . . .6L 71
Clarence Rd. Bexh 3J 97
Clarence Rd. Brom 7H 111
Clarence Rd. Croy 2B 124
Clarence Rd. Enf 7G 17
Clarence Rd. Rich 9K 71
Clarence Rd. Sidc 9F 96
Clarence Rd. Sutt 7M 121
Clarence Rd. Tedd 3D 102
Clarence Rd. Wall 7F 122
Clarence Rd. W on T 6F 116
Clarence St. King T 6H 103
(in three parts)
Clarence St. Rich 3J 87
Clarence St. S'hall 4H 69
Clarence Ter. NW1 . . . . .7D 58
Clarence Ter. Houn 3M 85
Clarence Wlk. SW4 . . . . .1J 91
Clarence Way. NW1 . . . . .3F 58
Clarenden Pl. Dart 2C 114
Clarendon Clo. E9 . . . . .3G 61
Clarendon Clo. W2 . . . . .1C 74
Clarendon Clo. Orp 7E 112
Clarendon Ct. NW2 . . . . .3G 57
Clarendon Ct. NW11 . . . . . . .2K 41
Clarendon Ct. Beck 5M 109
(off Albemarle Rd.)
Clarendon Ct. Houn 9E 68
Clarendon Ct. Rich 9K 71
Clarendon Cres. Twic 9B 86
Clarendon Cross. W11 . . . . . .1J 73
Clarendon Dri. SW15 . . . . . . .3G 89
Clarendon Flats. W1 . . . . .9E 58
(off Balderton St.)
Clarendon Gdns. NW4 . . . . . .1E 40
Clarendon Gdns. W9 . . . . . . .7A 58
Clarendon Gdns. Ilf 5K 47
Clarendon Gdns. Wemb 8H 39
Clarendon Grn. Orp 8E 112
Clarendon Gro. NW1 . . . . . . .6H 59
Clarendon Gro. Mitc 7D 106
Clarendon Gro. Orp 8E 112
Clarendon Ho. NW1 . . . . .5G 59
(off Werrington St.)
Clarendon M. W2 . . . . .1C 74
Clarendon M. Bex 7M 97
Clarendon M. Borwd 5L 11
Clarendon Pde. Chesh 2D 6
Clarendon Path. Orp 8E 112
(in two parts)
Clarendon Pl. W2 . . . . .1C 74
Clarendon Ri. SE13 . . . . .3A 94
Clarendon Rd. E11 . . . . .6B 46
Clarendon Rd. E17 . . . . .4M 45
Clarendon Rd. E18 . . . . .1E 46
Clarendon Rd. N8 . . . . .1K 43
Clarendon Rd. N15 . . . . .2A 44
Clarendon Rd. N18 . . . . .6E 28
Clarendon Rd. N22 . . . . .9K 27
Clarendon Rd. SW19 . . . . . .4C 106
Clarendon Rd. W5 . . . . .6J 55
Clarendon Rd. W11 . . . . .1J 73
Clarendon Rd. Ashf 9D 144
Clarendon Rd. Borwd 5L 11
Clarendon Rd. Chesh 2D 6
Clarendon Rd. Croy 4M 123
Clarendon Rd. Harr 4C 38
Clarendon Rd. Hay 3D 68
Clarendon Rd. Wall 8G 123
Clarendon Rd. Wat 4F 8
Clarendon St. SW1 . . . . .6F 74
Clarendon Ter. W9 . . . . .7A 58
Clarendon Wlk. W11 . . . . .9J 57
Clarendon Way. N21 . . . . .8A 16
Clarendon Way.
Chst & Orp 7D 112
Clarens St. SE6 . . . . .8K 93
Clare Pl. SW15 . . . . .6D 88
Clare Rd. E11 . . . . .4B 46
Clare Rd. NW10 . . . . .3E 56
Clare Rd. SE14 . . . . .9K 77
Clare Rd. Gnfd 2B 54
Clare Rd. Houn 2K 85
Clare Rd. Stanw 7B 144
Clare St. E2 . . . . .5F 60
Claret Gdns. SE25 . . . . . . .7C 108
Clareville Gro. SW7 . . . . .5A 74
Clareville Gro. M. SW7 . . . . .5A 74
(off Clareville St.)
Clareville Rd. Orp 4A 128
Clareville St. SW7 . . . . .5A 74
Clare Way. Bexh 9J 81
Clarewood Ct. W1 . . . . .8D 58
(off Seymour Pl.)
Clarewood Wlk. SW9 . . . . . . .3L 91
Clarges M. W1 . . . . .2F 74
Clarges St. W1 . . . . .2F 74
Claribel Rd. SW9 . . . . .1M 91
Clarice Way. Wall 1J 137
Claridge Ct. SW6 . . . . .1K 89
Claridge Rd. Dag 6H 49
Clarion Ho. E3 . . . . .5J 61
(off Roman Rd.)
Clarion Ho. SW1 . . . . .6G 75
(off Moreton Pl.)
Clarion Ho. W1 . . . . .9H 59
(off St Anne's Ct.)
Clarissa Ho. E14 . . . . .9M 61
(off Cordela St.)
Clarissa Rd. Romf 5H 49
Clarissa St. E8 . . . . .4D 60
Clark Clo. Eri 9E 82
Clark Ct. NW10 . . . . .3A 56
Clarke Grn. Wat 8E 4
Clarke Mans. Bark 3D 64
(off Upney La.)
Clarke M. N9 . . . . .3F 28
Clarke Path. N16 . . . . .6E 44
Clarkes Av. Wor Pk 3H 121
Clarkes Dri. Uxb 8C 142
Clarke's M. W1 . . . . .8E 58
Clarke Way. Wat 8E 4
Clarks Mead. Bush 9A 10
Clarkson Rd. E16 . . . . .9D 62
Clarkson Row. NW1 . . . . . . .5G 59
(off Mornington Ter.)
Clarksons, The. Bark 5A 64
Clarkson St. E2 . . . . .6F 60
Clark's Pl. EC2 . . . . .9C 60
Clarks Rd. Ilf 7B 48
Clark St. E1 . . . . .8F 60
Clark Way. Houn 8H 69
Classic Mans. E9 . . . . .3F 60
(off Wells St.)
Classon Clo. W Dray 3J 143
Claston Clo. Dart 3C 98
Claude Rd. E10 . . . . .7A 46
Claude Rd. E13 . . . . .4F 62
Claude Rd. SE15 . . . . .1F 92
Claude St. E14 . . . . .5L 77
Claudia Jones Ho. N17 . . . . .8A 28
Claudia Jones Way. SW2 . . . .5J 91
Claudia Pl. SW19 . . . . .7J 89
Claughton Rd. E13 . . . . .5G 63
Clauson Av. N'holt 1M 53
Clavell St. SE10 . . . . .7A 78
Claverdale Rd. SW2 . . . . .6K 91
Claverhambury Rd. Wal A 1M 7
(in two parts)
Clavering Av. SW13 . . . . .7F 72
Clavering Clo. Twic 1E 102
Clavering Ho. SE13 . . . . .3B 94
(off Blessington Rd.)
Clavering Ind. Est. N9 . . . . . .2G 29
(off Montagu Rd.)
Clavering Rd. E12 . . . . .6H 47
Claverley Gro. N3 . . . . .8M 25
Claverley Vs. N3 . . . . .7M 25
Claverton. Asht 9J 133
Claverton St. SW1 . . . . .6G 75
Clave St. E1 . . . . .2G 77
Claxton Gro. W6 . . . . .6H 73
Claxton Path. SE4 . . . . .3H 93
(off Coston Wlk.)
Clay Av. Mitc 6F 106
Claybank Gro. SE13 . . . . . . .2M 93
Claybourne M. SE19 . . . . . .4C 108
Claybridge Rd. SE12 . . . . . .1G 111
Claybrook Clo. N2 . . . . .1B 42
Claybrook Rd. W6 . . . . .7H 73
Claybury. Bush 9M 9
Claybury B'way. Ilf 1J 47
Claybury Rd. Wfd G 7J 31
Clay Ct. E17 . . . . .1B 46
Claydon. SE17 . . . . .5A 76
(off Deacon Way)
Claydon Dri. Croy 6J 123
Claydon Ho. NW4 . . . . .9H 25
(off Holders Hill Rd.)
Claydown M. SE18 . . . . .6L 79
Clay Farm Rd. SE9 . . . . .8A 96
Claygate. 8D 118
Claygate Clo. Horn 9E 50
Claygate Cres. New Ad 8A 126
Claygate La. Esh 4E 118
(in two parts)
Claygate La. Th Dit 3E 118
Claygate La. Wal A 3L 7
(in two parts)
Claygate Lodge Clo. Clay . . .9C 118
Claygate Rd. W13 . . . . .4F 70
Clayhall. 9K 31
Clayhall Av. Ilf 1J 47
Clay Hill. 1A 16
Clay Hill. Enf 1A 16
Clayhill. Surb 9L 103
Clayhill Cres. SE9 . . . . .1H 111
Claylands Pl. SW8 . . . . .8L 75
Claylands Rd. SW8 . . . . .7K 75
Clay La. Bus H 9C 10
Clay La. Edgw 2L 23
Clay La. Stanw 6D 144
Claymore Clo. Mord 2L 121
Claypit Hill. Wal A 1G 19
Claypole Ct. E17 . . . . .3L 45
(off Yunus Khan Clo.)
Claypole Dri. Houn 9J 69
Claypole Rd. E15 . . . . .5A 62
Clayponds Av.
W5 & Bren 5H 71
Claypons Gdns. W5 . . . . .5H 71
(in two parts)
Claypons La. Bren 6J 71
(in two parts)
Clay Ride. Lou 3H 19
(in two parts)
Clayside. Chig 5A 32
Clays La. E15 . . . . .1M 61
Clay's La. Lou 3L 19
Clays La. Clo. E15 . . . . .1M 61
Clay St. W1 . . . . .8D 58
Clayton Av. Upm 1M 67
Clayton Av. Wemb 3J 55
Clayton Clo. E6 . . . . .9K 63
Clayton Ct. E17 . . . . .9J 29
Clayton Cres. Bren 6H 71
Clayton Cft. Rd. Dart 8E 98
Clayton Fld. NW9 . . . . .7C 24
Clayton Ho. E9 . . . . .3G 61
(off Frampton Pk. Rd.)
Clayton Ho. SW13 . . . . .8G 73
(off Trinity Chu. Rd.)
Clayton M. SE10 . . . . .9B 78
Clayton Pde. Chesh 3D 6
Clayton Rd. SE15 . . . . .9E 76
Clayton Rd. Chess 6G 119
Clayton Rd. Eps 4C 134
Clayton Rd. Hay 3C 68
Clayton Rd. Iswth 2C 86
Clayton Rd. Romf 6A 50
Clayton St. SE11 . . . . .7L 75
Clayton Ter. Hay 8J 53
Clayton Way. Uxb 7B 142
Claywood Clo. Orp 2C 128
Clayworth Clo. Sidc 5F 96
Cleall Av. Wal A 7J 7
Cleanthus Clo. SE18 . . . . . . .9M 79
Cleanthus Rd. SE18 . . . . .1M 95
(in two parts)
Clearbrook Way. E1 . . . . .9G 61
Clearwater Pl. Surb 1G 119
Clearwater Ter. W11 . . . . .3J 73
(off Lorne Gdns.)
Clearwell Dri. W9 . . . . .7M 57
Cleave Av. Hay 5C 68
Cleave Av. Orp 8C 128
Cleaveland Rd. Surb 9H 103
Cleaverholme Clo. SE25 . . . .1F 124
Cleaver Ho. NW3 . . . . .3D 58
(off Adelaide Rd.)
Cleaver Sq. SE11 . . . . .6L 75
Cleaver St. SE11 . . . . .6L 75
Cleaves Almshouses.
King T 6J 103
(off London Rd.)
Cleeve Ct. Felt 7C 84
Cleeve Hill. SE23 . . . . .7F 92
Cleeve Pk. Gdns. Sidc 8F 96
Cleeves Vw. Dart 5H 99
(off Priory Pl.)
Cleeve Way. SW15 . . . . .6D 88
Cleeve Workshops. E2 . . . . . .6C 60
(off Boundary Rd.)
Clegg Ho. SE3 . . . . .3F 94
Clegg Ho. SE16 . . . . .4G 77
(off Moodkee St.)
Clegg St. E1 . . . . .2F 76
Clegg St. E13 . . . . .5E 62
Cleland Ho. E2 . . . . .5G 61
(off Sewardstone Rd.)
Cleland Path. Lou 3M 19
Clematis Clo. Romf 7G 35
Clematis Gdns. Wfd G 5E 30
Clematis St. W12 . . . . .1E 72
Clem Attlee Ct. SW6 . . . . . . .7K 73
Clem Attlee Pde. SW6 . . . . . .7K 73
(off N. End Rd.)
Clemence Rd. Dag 4A 66
Clemence St. E14 . . . . .8K 61
Clement Av. SW4 . . . . .3H 91
Clement Clo. NW6 . . . . .3G 57
Clement Clo. W4 . . . . .5B 72
Clement Clo. Purl 8M 137
Clement Gdns. Hay 5C 68
Clementhorpe Rd. Dag 2G 65
Clement Ho. SE8 . . . . .5J 77
Clement Ho. W10 . . . . .8G 57
(off Dalgarno Gdns.)
Clementina Rd. E10 . . . . .6K 45
Clementine Clo. W13 . . . . . . .3F 70
Clement Rd. SW19 . . . . .2J 105
Clement Rd. Beck 6H 109
Clement Rd. Chesh 1E 6
Clement's Av. E16 . . . . .1E 78
Clements Clo. Houn 3H 85
Clements Ct. Ilf 8M 47
Clement's Inn. WC2 . . . . .9K 59
Clement's Inn Pas. WC2 . . . . .9K 59
(off Grange Ct.)
Clements La. EC4 . . . . .1B 76
Clements La. Ilf 8M 47
Clements Pl. Bren 6H 71
Clements Rd. E6 . . . . .3J 63
Clement's Rd. SE16 . . . . .4E 76
Clements Rd. Ilf 8M 47
Clements Rd. W on T 4F 116
Clement Street. 3H 115
Clement St.
Swan & S at H 3H 115
Clement Way. Upm 8K 51
Clemson Ho. E8 . . . . .4D 60
Clendon Way. SE18 . . . . .5B 80
Clennam St. SE1 . . . . .3A 76
Clensham Ct. Sutt 4L 121
Clensham La. Sutt 4L 121
Clenston M. W1 . . . . .9D 58
Cleopatra's Needle. 1K 75
Clephane Rd. N1 . . . . .2A 60
(in two parts)
Clephane Rd. N. N1 . . . . .2A 60
Clere Pl. EC2 . . . . .7B 60
Clere St. EC2 . . . . .7B 60
Clerics Wlk. Shep 2B 116
Clerkenwell. 7L 59
Clerkenwell Clo. EC1 . . . . . . .7L 59
(in two parts)
Clerkenwell Grn. EC1 . . . . . . .7L 59
Clerkenwell Rd. EC1 . . . . .7L 59
Clerk's Piece. Lou 5K 19
Clermont Rd. E9 . . . . .4G 61
Clevedon. Wey 7B 116
Clevedon Clo. N16 . . . . .8D 44
Clevedon Ct. S Croy 7C 124
Clevedon Gdns. Hay 4B 68
Clevedon Gdns. Houn 9F 68
Clevedon Mans. NW5 . . . . . . .9E 42
Clevedon Pas. N16 . . . . .7D 44
Clevedon Rd. SE20 . . . . . . .5H 109
Clevedon Rd. King T 6L 103
Clevedon Rd. Twic 5H 87
(in two parts)
Cleve Ho. NW6 . . . . .3M 57
Cleveland Av. SW20 . . . . . . .6K 105
Cleveland Av. W4 . . . . .5D 72
Cleveland Av. Hamp 4K 101
Cleveland Clo. W on T 5F 116
Cleveland Ct. W13 . . . . .8F 54
Cleveland Cres. Borwd 7A 12
Cleveland Gdns. N4 . . . . .3A 44
Cleveland Gdns. NW2 . . . . . . .7H 41
Cleveland Gdns. SW13 . . . . . .1D 88
Cleveland Gdns. W2 . . . . .9A 58
Cleveland Gdns. Wor Pk . . .4C 120
Cleveland Gro. E1 . . . . .7G 61
Cleveland Ho. N2 . . . . .9B 26
(off Grange, The)
Cleveland La. N9 . . . . .9F 16
Cleveland Mans. SW9 . . . . . . .8L 75
(off Mowll St.)
Cleveland Mans. W9 . . . . .7L 57
Cleveland M. W1 . . . . .8G 59
Cleveland Pk. Stai 5C 144
Cleveland Pk. Av. E17 . . . . . .2L 45
Cleveland Pk. Cres. E17 . . . . .2L 45
Cleveland Pl. SW1 . . . . .2G 75
Cleveland Ri. Mord 2H 121
Cleveland Rd. E18 . . . . .1E 46
Cleveland Rd. N1 . . . . .3B 60
Cleveland Rd. SW13 . . . . .1D 88
Cleveland Rd. W4 . . . . .4A 72
Cleveland Rd. W13 . . . . .8E 54
Cleveland Rd. Ilf 8M 47
Cleveland Rd. Iswth 3E 86
Cleveland Rd. N Mald 8C 104
Cleveland Rd. Uxb 7B 142
Cleveland Rd. Well 1D 96
Cleveland Rd. Wor Pk 4C 120
Cleveland Row. SW1 . . . . .2G 75
Cleveland Sq. W2 . . . . .9A 58
Clevelands, The. Bark 2A 64
Cleveland St. W1 . . . . .7F 58
Cleveland Ter. W2 . . . . .9A 58
Cleveland Way. E1 . . . . .7G 61
Cleveley Clo. SE7 . . . . .5H 79
Cleveley Cres. W5 . . . . .5J 55
Cleveleys Rd. E5 . . . . .8F 44
Cleverly Est. W12 . . . . .2E 72
Cleve Rd. NW6 . . . . .3M 57
Cleve Rd. Sidc 9H 97
Cleves Av. Eps 1F 134
Cleves Clo. Lou 8J 19
Cleves Ct. Dart 6J 99
Cleves Ct. Eps 4D 134
Cleves Cres. New Ad 3A 140
Cleves Ho. E16 . . . . .2F 78
(off Southey M.)
Cleves Rd. E6 . . . . .4H 63
Cleves Rd. Rich 9G 87
Cleves Wlk. Ilf 7A 32
Cleves Way. Hamp 4K 101
Cleves Way. Ruis 6H 37
Cleves Way. Sun 3D 100
Cleves Wood. Wey 6C 116
Clewer Ct. E10 . . . . .6L 45
(off Leyton Grange Est.)
Clewer Cres. Harr 8B 22
Clewer Ho. SE2 . . . . .3H 81
(off Wolvercote Rd.)
Cley Ho. SE4 . . . . .3H 93
Clichy Est. E1 . . . . .8G 61
Clichy Ho. E1 . . . . .8G 61
(off Stepney Way)
Clifden Rd. E5 . . . . .1G 61
Clifden Rd. Bren 7H 71
Clifden Rd. Twic 7D 86
Cliffe Ho. SE10 . . . . .6D 78
(off Blackwall La.)
Cliff End. Purl 4M 137
Cliffe Rd. S Croy 7B 124
Cliffe Wlk. Sutt 7A 122
(off Greyhound Rd.)
Clifford Av. SW14 . . . . .2M 87
(in two parts)
Clifford Av. Chst 3K 111
Clifford Av. Ilf 8M 31
Clifford Av. Wall 6G 123

Clifford Clo.—Colchester Rd.

Clifford Clo. N'holt ... 4J 53
Clifford Ct. W2 ... 8M 57
(off Westbourne Pk. Vs.)
Clifford Dri. SW9 ... 3M 91
Clifford Gdns. NW10 ... 5G 57
Clifford Gdns. Hay ... 5C 68
Clifford Gro. Ashf ... 9E 144
Clifford Haigh Ho. SW6 ... 8H 73
Clifford Ho. W14 ... 5K 73
(off Edith Vs.)
Clifford Rd. E16 ... 7D 62
Clifford Rd. E17 ... 9A 30
Clifford Rd. N1 ... 4C 60
Clifford Rd. N9 ... 8G 17
Clifford Rd. SE25 ... 8E 108
Clifford Rd. Barn ... 5M 13
Clifford Rd. Houn ... 2H 85
Clifford Rd. Rich ... 8H 87
Clifford Rd. Wemb ... 3H 55
Clifford's Inn Pas. EC4 ... 9L 59
Clifford St. W1 ... 1G 75
Clifford Way. NW10 ... 9D 40
Cliff Rd. NW1 ... 2H 59
Cliffsend Ho. SW9 ... 9L 75
(off Cowley Rd.)
Cliff Ter. SE8 ... 1L 93
Cliffview Rd. SE13 ... 2L 93
Cliff Vs. NW1 ... 2H 59
Cliff Wlk. E16 ... 8D 62
(in two parts)
Clifton Av. E17 ... 1H 45
Clifton Av. N3 ... 8K 25
Clifton Av. W12 ... 2D 72
Clifton Av. Felt ... 9G 85
Clifton Av. Stan ... 9F 22
Clifton Av. Sutt ... 3M 135
Clifton Av. Wemb ... 2K 55
Clifton Clo. Chesh ... 2E 6
Clifton Clo. Orp ... 7A 128
Clifton Ct. N4 ... 7L 43
Clifton Ct. NW8 ... 7B 58
(off Maida Va.)
Clifton Ct. SE15 ... 8F 76
Clifton Ct. Beck ... 5M 109
Clifton Ct. Stanw ... 5C 144
Clifton Ct. Wfd G ... 6E 30
Clifton Cres. SE15 ... 8F 76
Clifton Est. SE15 ... 9F 76
Clifton Gdns. N15 ... 4D 44
Clifton Gdns. NW11 ... 4K 41
Clifton Gdns. W4 ... 5B 72
(in two parts)
Clifton Gdns. W9 ... 7A 58
Clifton Gdns. Enf ... 6J 15
Clifton Gdns. Uxb ... 5F 142
Clifton Gro. E8 ... 2E 60
Clifton Hill. NW6 ... 5M 57
Clifton Ho. E2 ... 7D 60
(off Club Row)
Clifton Ho. E11 ... 7C 46
Clifton Pde. Felt ... 1G 101
Clifton Pk. Av. SW20 ... 6G 105
Clifton Pl. SE16 ... 3G 77
Clifton Pl. W2 ... 9B 58
Clifton Pl. Bans ... 7L 135
Clifton Ri. SE14 ... 8J 77
(in two parts)
Clifton Rd. E7 ... 2H 63
Clifton Rd. E16 ... 8C 62
Clifton Rd. N3 ... 8A 26
Clifton Rd. N8 ... 4H 43
Clifton Rd. N22 ... 8G 27
Clifton Rd. NW10 ... 5E 56
Clifton Rd. SE25 ... 8C 108
Clifton Rd. SW19 ... 3H 105
Clifton Rd. W9 ... 7A 58
Clifton Rd. Coul ... 7F 136
Clifton Rd. Gnfd ... 7A 54
Clifton Rd. Harr ... 2K 39
Clifton Rd. Horn ... 4E 50
Clifton Rd. Ilf ... 4B 48
Clifton Rd. Iswth ... 1C 86
Clifton Rd. King T ... 4K 103
Clifton Rd. Lou ... 6J 19
Clifton Rd. Sidc ... 1C 112
Clifton Rd. S'hall ... 5J 69
Clifton Rd. Tedd ... 1C 102
Clifton Rd. Wall ... 7F 122
Clifton Rd. Wat ... 7F 8
Clifton Rd. Well ... 2G 97
Clifton St. EC2 ... 7C 60
(in two parts)
Clifton Ter. N4 ... 7L 43
Clifton Vs. W9 ... 8A 58
Cliftonville Ct. SE12 ... 7E 94
Clifton Wlk. W6 ... 5F 72
(off King St.)
Clifton Wlk. Dart ... 5M 99
Clifton Way. SE15 ... 8F 76
Clifton Way. Borwd ... 3L 11
Clifton Way. H'row A ... 2F 144
Clifton Way. Wemb ... 4J 55
Climsland Ho. SE1 ... 2L 75
Clinch Ct. E16 ... 8E 62
(off Plymouth Rd., in two parts)
Cline Rd. N11 ... 6G 27
Clinger Ct. N1 ... 4C 60
(off Hobbs Pl. Est.)
Clink Exhibition, The. ... 2B 76
(off Clink St.)
Clink St. SE1 ... 2B 76
Clink Wharf. SE1 ... 2B 76
(off Clink St.)
Clinton Av. E Mol ... 8A 102
Clinton Av. Well ... 3E 96
Clinton Clo. Wey ... 4A 116
Clinton Cres. Ilf ... 6C 32
Clinton Rd. E3 ... 6J 61
Clinton Rd. E7 ... 9E 46
Clinton Rd. N15 ... 2B 44
Clipper Clo. SE16 ... 3H 77
Clipper Ho. E14 ... 6A 78
(off Manchester Rd.)
Clipper Way. SE13 ... 3A 94
Clippesby Clo. Chess ... 8K 119
Clipstone M. W1 ... 8G 59
Clipstone Rd. Houn ... 2L 85
Clipstone St. W1 ... 8F 58
Clissold Clo. N2 ... 1D 42
Clissold Ct. N4 ... 7A 44
Clissold Cres. N16 ... 8B 44
Clissold Rd. N16 ... 8B 44
Clitheroe Av. Harr ... 6L 37
Clitheroe Gdns. Wat ... 3H 21
Clitheroe Rd. SW9 ... 1J 91
Clitheroe Rd. Romf ... 5A 34
Clitherow Av. W7 ... 4E 70
Clitherow Ct. Bren ... 6G 71
Clitherow Pas. Bren ... 6G 71
Clitherow Rd. Bren ... 6F 70
Clitterhouse Cres. NW2 ... 6G 41
Clitterhouse Rd. NW2 ... 6G 41
Clive Av. N18 ... 6E 28
Clive Av. Dart ... 5D 98
Clive Ct. W9 ... 7A 58
(off Maida Va.)
Cliveden Clo. N12 ... 4A 26
Cliveden Ho. E16 ... 2E 78
(off Fitzwilliam M.)
Cliveden Pl. SW1 ... 5E 74
Cliveden Pl. Shep ... 1A 116
Cliveden Rd. SW19 ... 5K 105
Clivedon Ct. W13 ... 8F 54
Clivedon Rd. E4 ... 5C 30
Clive Ho. SE10 ... 7A 78
(off Haddo St.)
Clive Lloyd Ho. N15 ... 3A 44
(off Woodlands Pk. Rd.)
Clive Lodge. NW4 ... 4H 41
Clive Pde. N'wd ... 7C 20
Clive Pas. SE21 ... 9B 92
Clive Rd. SE21 ... 9B 92
Clive Rd. SW19 ... 3C 106
Clive Rd. Belv ... 5L 81
Clive Rd. Enf ... 6E 16
Clive Rd. Esh ... 6M 117
Clive Rd. Felt ... 5E 84
Clive Rd. Romf ... 3F 50
Clive Rd. Twic ... 1D 102
Clivesdale Dri. Hay ... 2F 68
Clive Way. Enf ... 6E 16
Clive Way. Wat ... 3G 9
Cloak La. EC4 ... 1A 76
Clochar Ct. NW10 ... 4D 56
Clock House. ... 6F 136
Clock Ho. E3 ... 6A 62
Clock Ho. E17 ... 2B 46
(off Wood St.)
Clockhouse Av. Bark ... 4A 64
Clockhouse Clo. SW19 ... 8G 89
Clockhouse Ct. Beck ... 6J 109
Clockhouse Junction (Junct.)
... 5K 27
Clockhouse La.
Ashf & Felt ... 9E 144
Clockhouse La. Romf ... 7M 33
Clock Ho. Mead. Oxs ... 6A 132
Clock Ho. Pde. E11 ... 3F 46
Clockhouse Pde. N13 ... 5L 27
Clockhouse Pl. SW15 ... 5J 89
Clock Ho. Rd. Beck ... 7J 109
Clockhouse Roundabout (Junct.)
... 7A 84
Clock Mus., The. ... 9A 60
(off Aldermanbury)
Clock Pde. Enf ... 7B 16
Clock Pl. SE11 ... 5M 75
(off Newington Butts)
Clock Tower Ind. Est.
Iswth ... 2D 86
Clock Tower M. N1 ... 4A 60
Clock Tower M. SE28 ... 1F 80
Clock Tower Pl. N7 ... 2J 59
Clock Tower Rd. Iswth ... 2D 86
Cloister Clo. Rain ... 7F 66
Cloister Clo. Tedd ... 2F 102
Cloister Gdns. SE25 ... 1F 124
Cloister Gdns. Edgw ... 5A 24
Cloister Rd. NW2 ... 8K 41
Cloister Rd. W3 ... 8A 56
Cloisters Av. Brom ... 9K 111
Cloisters Bus. Cen.
SW8 ... 8F 74
(off Battersea Pk. Rd.)
Cloisters Ct. Bexh ... 2M 97
Cloisters Mall. King T ... 6J 103
Cloisters, The. ... 4J 75
(off Westminster Abbey)
Cloisters, The. E1 ... 8D 60
(off Commercial St.)
Cloisters, The. SW9 ... 9L 75
Cloisters, The. Bush ... 8M 9
Cloisters, The. Dart ... 5J 99
(off Orchard St.)
Cloisters, The. Wat ... 6G 9
Clonard Way. Pinn ... 6L 21
Clonbrock Rd. N16 ... 9C 44
Cloncurry St. SW6 ... 1H 89
Clonmel Clo. Harr ... 7B 38
Clonmell Rd. N17 ... 1B 44
Clonmel Rd. SW6 ... 8K 73
Clonmel Rd. Tedd ... 1B 102
Clonmore St. SW18 ... 7K 89
Cloonmore Av. Orp ... 6D 128
Clorane Gdns. NW3 ... 8L 41
Closemead Clo. N'wd ... 6A 20
Close, The. E4 ... 7A 30
Close, The. N10 ... 9F 26
Close, The. N14 ... 2H 27
Close, The. N20 ... 2K 25
Close, The. SE3 ... 1B 94
Close, The. SE25 ... 1E 124
Close, The. Beck ... 8J 109
Close, The. Berr G ... 8M 141
Close, The. Bex ... 5L 97
Close, The. Bush ... 8M 9
Close, The. Cars ... 1C 136
Close, The. E Barn ... 8D 14
Close, The. Eastc ... 5G 37
Close, The. Harr ... 9A 22
Close, The. Ilf ... 4C 48
Close, The. Iswth ... 1B 86
Close, The. Mitc ... 8D 106
Close, The. N Mald ... 6A 104
Close, The. Orp ... 1C 128
Close, The. Pinn ... 5K 37
Close, The. Purl ... 2M 137
(Pampisford Rd.)
Close, The. Purl ... 2K 137
(Russell Hill)
Close, The. Rich ... 2M 87
Close, The. Romf ... 4J 49
Close, The. Sidc ... 1F 112
Close, The. Surb ... 1J 119
Close, The. Sutt ... 2K 121
Close, The. Uxb ... 4E 142
Close, The. Wemb (HA0) ... 2J 55
Close, The. Wemb (HA9) ... 8A 40
Close, The. Wilm ... 9G 99
Cloth Ct. EC1 ... 8M 59
(off Cloth Fair)
Cloth Fair. EC1 ... 8M 59
Clothier St. E1 ... 9C 60
Cloth St. EC1 ... 8A 60
Clothworkers Rd. SE18 ... 8B 80
Cloudberry Rd. Romf ... 6H 35
Cloudesdale Rd. SW17 ... 8F 90
Cloudesley Pl. N1 ... 4L 59
Cloudesley Rd. N1 ... 4L 59
(in two parts)
Cloudesley Rd. Bexh ... 9K 81
Cloudesley Rd. Eri ... 9D 82
Cloudesley Sq. N1 ... 4L 59
Cloudesley St. N1 ... 4L 59
Clouston Clo. Wall ... 7J 123
Clova Rd. E7 ... 2D 62
Clove Cres. E14 ... 1A 78
Clove Hitch Quay.
SW11 ... 2A 90
Clovelly Av. NW9 ... 2D 40
Clovelly Av. Uxb ... 9A 36
Clovelly Clo. Pinn ... 1F 36
Clovelly Clo. Uxb ... 9A 36
Clovelly Ct. Horn ... 7L 51
Clovelly Gdns. SE19 ... 5D 108
Clovelly Gdns. Enf ... 9C 16
Clovelly Gdns. Romf ... 8M 33
Clovelly Ho. W2 ... 9A 58
(off Hallfield Est.)
Clovelly Rd. N8 ... 2H 43
Clovelly Rd. W4 ... 3B 72
Clovelly Rd. W5 ... 3G 71
Clovelly Rd. Bexh ... 7J 81
Clovelly Rd. Houn ... 1L 85
Clovelly Way. E1 ... 9G 61
Clovelly Way. Orp ... 1D 128
Clovelly Way. S Harr ... 7K 37
Clover Clo. E11 ... 7B 46
Cloverdale Gdns. Sidc ... 5D 96
Clover Fld., The. Bush ... 8K 9
Cloverleys. Lou ... 7H 19
Clover M. SW3 ... 7D 74
Clover Way. Wall ... 3E 122
Clove St. E13 ... 7E 62
Clowders Rd. SE6 ... 9K 93
Clowser Clo. Sutt ... 7A 122
Cloysters Grn. E1 ... 2E 76
Cloyster Wood. Edgw ... 7H 23
Club Gdns. Rd. Brom ... 2E 126
Club Row. E2 & E1 ... 7D 60
Clumps, The. Ashf ... 1B 100
Clunas Gdns. Romf ... 1H 51
Clunbury Av. S'hall ... 6K 69
Clunbury St. N1 ... 5B 60
Cluny Est. SE1 ... 4C 76
Cluny M. SW5 ... 5L 73
Cluny Pl. SE1 ... 4C 76
Cluse Ct. N1 ... 5A 60
(off St Peters St., in two parts)
Clutton St. E14 ... 8M 61
Clydach Rd. Enf ... 6D 16
Clyde Av. S Croy ... 7F 138
Clyde Cir. N15 ... 2C 44
Clyde Ct. NW1 ... 5H 59
(off Hampden Clo.)
Clyde Flats. SW6 ... 8K 73
(off Rhylston Rd.)
Clyde Ho. King T ... 5H 103
Clyde Pl. E10 ... 5M 45
Clyde Rd. N15 ... 2C 44
Clyde Rd. N22 ... 8H 27
Clyde Rd. Croy ... 4D 124
Clyde Rd. Stai ... 7B 144
Clyde Rd. Sutt ... 7L 121
Clyde Rd. Wall ... 8G 123
Clydesdale. Enf ... 6H 17
Clydesdale Av. Stan ... 1H 39
Clydesdale Clo. Borwd ... 7B 12
Clydesdale Clo. Iswth ... 2D 86
Clydesdale Ct. N20 ... 1B 26
Clydesdale Gdns. Rich ... 3M 87
Clydesdale Ho. W11 ... 9K 57
(off Clydesdale Rd.)
Clydesdale Ho. Eri ... 3J 81
(off Kale Rd.)
Clydesdale Path. Borwd ... 7B 12
(off Clydesdale Clo.)
Clydesdale Rd. W11 ... 9K 57
Clydesdale Rd. Horn ... 5D 50
Clyde St. SE8 ... 7K 77
Clyde Ter. SE23 ... 8G 93
Clyde Va. SE23 ... 8G 93
Clyde Way. Romf ... 7C 34
Clyde Wharf. E16 ... 2E 78
Clydon Clo. Eri ... 7C 82
Clyfford Rd. Ruis ... 9D 36
Clymping Dene. Felt ... 6F 84
Clynes Ho. E2 ... 6H 61
(off Knottisford St.)
Clynes Ho. Dag ... 8L 49
(off Uvedale Rd.)
Clyston Rd. Wat ... 8D 8
Clyston St. SW8 ... 1G 91
Coach & Horses Yd. W1 ... 1G 75
Coach Ho. La. N5 ... 9M 43
Coach Ho. La. SW19 ... 1H 105
Coach Ho. M. SE1 ... 3C 76
Coach Ho. M. SE20 ... 4F 108
Coach Ho. M. SE23 ... 5H 93
Coach Ho. Yd. NW3 ... 9A 42
(off Hampstead High St.)
Coach Ho. Yd. SW18 ... 3M 89
Coachmaker M. SW4 ... 2J 91
(off Fenwick Pl.)
Coach Yd. M. N19 ... 6J 43
Coaldale Wlk. SE21 ... 6A 92
Coalecroft Rd. SW15 ... 3G 89
Coalport Ho. SE11 ... 5L 75
(off Walnut Tree Wlk.)
Coates Av. SW18 ... 5C 90
Coates Dell. Wat ... 6J 5
Coates Hill Rd. Brom ... 6L 111
Coates Rd. Els ... 9H 11
Coate St. E2 ... 5E 60
Coates Wlk. Bren ... 7J 71
Coates Way. Wat ... 6H 5
Cobalt Sq. SW8 ... 7K 75
(off S. Lambeth Rd.)
Cobbett Clo. Enf ... 9C 6
Cobbett Rd. SE9 ... 2J 95
Cobbett Rd. Twic ... 7L 85
Cobbetts Av. Ilf ... 3H 47
Cobbetts Hill. Wey ... 9A 116
Cobbett St. SW8 ... 8K 75
Cobb Grn. Wat ... 5F 4
Cobbinsbank. Wal A ... 6K 7
Cobbins, The. Wal A ... 6L 7
Cobble La. N1 ... 3M 59
Cobble M. N4 ... 8A 44
Cobblers Wlk.
Hamp & Tedd ... 5A 102
(in two parts)
Cobblestone Pl. Croy ... 3A 124
Cobbold Ct. SW1 ... 5H 75
(off Elverton St.)
Cobbold Ind. Est. NW10 ... 2D 56
Cobbold M. W12 ... 3D 72
Cobbold Rd. E11 ... 8D 46
Cobbold Rd. NW10 ... 2D 56
Cobbold Rd. W12 ... 3C 72
Cobb's Ct. EC4 ... 9M 59
(off Carter La.)
Cobb's Hall. SW6 ... 7H 73
(off Fulham Pal. Rd.)
Cobb's Rd. Houn ... 3K 85
Cobbsthorpe Vs. SE26 ... 1H 109
Cobb St. E1 ... 8D 60
Cob Clo. Borwd ... 7B 12
Cobden Clo. Uxb ... 4A 142
Cobden Ct. Brom ... 8G 111
Cobden Hill. Rad ... 1F 10
Cobden Ho. E2 ... 6E 60
(off Nelson Gdns.)
Cobden Ho. NW1 ... 5G 59
(off Arlington Rd.)
Cobden M. SE26 ... 2F 108
Cobden Rd. E11 ... 8C 46
Cobden Rd. SE25 ... 9E 108
Cobden Rd. Orp ... 6B 128
Cobham Av. N Mald ... 9E 104
Cobham Clo. SW11 ... 5C 90
Cobham Clo. Brom ... 2J 127
Cobham Clo. Edgw ... 9M 23
Cobham Clo. Enf ... 5E 16
Cobham Clo. Sidc ... 5F 96
Cobham Clo. Wall ... 8J 123
Cobham Ct. Mitc ... 6B 106
Cobham Ho. Bark ... 4A 64
(in two parts)
Cobham Ho. Eri ... 8D 82
Cobham M. NW1 ... 3H 59
Cobham Pl. Bexh ... 4H 97
Cobham Rd. E17 ... 8A 30
Cobham Rd. N22 ... 1M 43
Cobham Rd. Houn ... 8G 69
Cobham Rd. Ilf ... 7C 48
Cobham Rd. King T ... 6L 103
Cobill Clo. Horn ... 2G 51
Cobland Rd. SE12 ... 1G 111
Coborn Rd. E3 ... 5K 61
Coborn St. E3 ... 6K 61
Cobourg Rd. SE5 ... 7D 76
Cobourg St. NW1 ... 6G 59
Coburg Clo. SW1 ... 5G 75
(off Windsor Pl.)
Coburg Cres. SW2 ... 7K 91
Coburg Dwellings. E1 ... 9G 61
(off Hardinge St.)
Coburg Gdns. Ilf ... 9H 31
Coburg Rd. N22 ... 1K 43
Cochrane Clo. NW8 ... 5B 58
(off Cochrane St.)
Cochrane Ct. E10 ... 6L 45
(off Leyton Grange Est.)
Cochrane Ho. E14 ... 3L 77
(off Admirals Way)
Cochrane Ho. Uxb ... 4A 142
Cochrane M. NW8 ... 5B 58
Cochrane Rd. SW19 ... 4J 105
Cochrane St. NW8 ... 5B 58
Cochrane Theatre, The. ... 8J 59
(off Theobald's Rd.)
Cockabourne Ct. H Wood ... 9L 35
(off Archibald Rd.)
Cockburn Ho. SW1 ... 6H 75
(off Aylesford St.)
Cockcrow Hill. ... 3H 119
Cockerell Rd. E17 ... 5J 45
Cockerhurst Rd. Shor ... 8B 130
Cocker Rd. Enf ... 9B 6
Cockfosters. ... 6E 14
Cockfosters Pde. Barn ... 6E 14
Cockfosters Rd.
Pot B & Barn ... 1C 14
Cock Hill. E1 ... 8C 60
Cock La. EC1 ... 8M 59
Cockmannings La. Orp ... 3H 129
Cockmannings Rd. Orp ... 2H 129
Cockpit Steps. SW1 ... 3H 75
(off Birdcage Wlk.)
Cockpit Theatre. ... 7C 58
(off Gateforth St.)
Cockpit Yd. WC1 ... 8K 59
Cocks Cres. N Mald ... 8D 104
Cocksett Av. Orp ... 8C 128
Cockspur Ct. SW1 ... 2H 75
Cockspur St. SW1 ... 2H 75
Cocksure La. Sidc ... 9L 97
Cock's Yd. Uxb ... 3B 142
(off Bakers Rd.)
Coda Cen., The. SW6 ... 8J 73
Code St. E1 ... 7D 60
Codicote Dri. Wat ... 7H 5
Codicote Ho. SE8 ... 5H 77
(off Chilton Gro.)
Codicote Ter. N4 ... 7A 44
Codling Clo. E1 ... 2E 76
Codling Way. Wemb ... 9H 39
Codrington Ct. E1 ... 7F 60
Codrington Ct. SE16 ... 1J 77
Codrington Hill. SE23 ... 6J 93
Codrington M. W11 ... 9J 57
Cody Clo. Harr ... 1H 39
Cody Clo. Wall ... 9H 123
Cody Rd. E16 ... 7B 62
Coe Av. SE25 ... 1E 124
Coe's All. Barn ... 6J 13
Cofers Circ. Wemb ... 7M 39
Coffey St. SE8 ... 8L 77
Cogan Av. E17 ... 8J 29
Cohen Clo. Chesh ... 4E 6
Coin St. SE1 ... 2L 75
(in two parts)
Coity Rd. NW5 ... 2E 58
Cokers La. SE21 ... 7B 92
Coke St. E1 ... 9E 60
Colas M. NW6 ... 4L 57
Colbeck M. SW7 ... 5M 73
Colbeck Rd. Harr ... 5A 38
Colberg Pl. N16 ... 5D 44
Colborne Ho. E14 ... 1L 77
(off E. India Dock Rd.)
Colborne Ho. Wat ... 8C 8
Colborne Way. Wor Pk ... 5G 121
Colbrook Av. Hay ... 4B 68
Colbrook Clo. Hay ... 4B 68
Colburn Av. Pinn ... 6J 21
Colburn Way. Sutt ... 5B 122
Colby M. SE19 ... 2C 108
Colby Rd. SE19 ... 2C 108
Colby Rd. W on T ... 3E 116
Colchester Av. E12 ... 9K 47
Colchester Dri. Pinn ... 3H 37
Colchester Rd. E10 ... 5A 46
Colchester Rd. E17 ... 4L 45

Comerell Pl.—Coopers Ct.

Comerell Pl. SE10 6D 78
Comerford Rd. SE4 3J 93
Comet Clo. E12 9H 47
Comet Clo. Purf 5L 83
Comet Clo. Wat 7D 4
Comet Pl. SE8 8L 77
(in two parts)
Comet Rd. Stanw 6B 144
Comet St. SE8 8L 77
Commerce Rd. N22 8K 27
Commerce Rd. Bren 7G 71
Commerce Way. Croy 4K 123
Commercial Dock Path. SE16 4K 77
(off Gulliver St.)
Commercial Rd. E1 & E14 9E 60
Commercial Rd. N18 5C 28
Commercial Rd. Ind. Est. N18 6D 28
Commercial St. E1 7D 60
Commercial Way. NW10 5M 55
Commercial Way. SE15 8D 76
Commerell St. SE10 6C 78
Commodity Quay. E1 1D 76
Commodore Ct. SE8 9L 77
(off Albyn Rd.)
Commodore Ho. E14 1A 78
(off Poplar High St.)
Commodore Sq. SW10 9A 74
Commodore St. E1 7J 61
Commondale. SW15 2G 89
Commonfield La. SW17 2C 106
Commonfield Rd. Bans 6L 135
Common La. Clay 9E 118
Common La. Dart 8E 98
Common La. Let H & Rad 3C 10
Commonmeadow La. Wat 7M 5
Common Rd. SW13 2F 88
Common Rd. Clay 8E 118
Common Rd. Stan 4B 22
Common Side. Eps 7L 133
Commonside. Kes 6G 127
Commonside Clo. Sutt 3M 135
Commonside E. Mitc 7E 106
(in two parts)
Commonside W. Mitc 7D 106
Common, The. E15 2C 62
(in two parts)
Common, The. W5 1J 71
(in two parts)
Common, The. Asht 8H 133
Common, The. S'hall 5G 69
Common, The. Stan 2C 22
Common, The. W Dray 5G 143
Commonwealth Av. W12 1F 72
(in three parts)
Commonwealth Av. Hay 9B 52
Commonwealth Institute. 4K 73
Commonwealth Rd. N17 7E 28
Commonwealth Way. SE2 6F 80
Community Clo. Houn 9F 68
Community Clo. Uxb 8A 36
Community La. N7 1H 59
Community Rd. E15 1B 62
Community Rd. Gnfd 4A 54
Community Way. Esh 6A 118
Como Rd. SE23 8J 93
Como St. Romf 3B 50
Compass Ct. SE1 2D 76
(off Shad Thames)
Compass Hill. Rich 5H 87
Compass Ho. SW18 3M 89
Compass Point. E14 1K 77
(off Grenade St.)
Compayne Gdns. NW6 3M 57
Comport Grn. New Ad 4C 140
Compton Av. E6 5H 63
Compton Av. N1 2M 59
Compton Av. N6 5C 42
Compton Av. Romf 1G 51
Compton Av. Wemb 9G 39
Compton Clo. E3 8L 61
Compton Clo. NW1 6F 58
(off Robert St.)
Compton Clo. NW11 8H 41
Compton Clo. SE15 8E 76
Compton Clo. W13 9E 54
Compton Clo. Edgw 7A 24
Compton Clo. Esh 8B 118
Compton Ct. SE19 3C 108
Compton Ct. Sutt 6A 122
Compton Cres. N17 7A 28
Compton Cres. W4 7A 72
Compton Cres. Chess 7J 119
Compton Cres. N'holt 4H 53
Compton Pas. EC1 7M 59
Compton Pl. WC1 7J 59
Compton Pl. Eri 7D 82
Compton Pl. Wat 3J 21
Compton Ri. Pinn 3J 37
Compton Rd. N1 2M 59
Compton Rd. N21 1L 27
Compton Rd. NW10 6H 57
Compton Rd. SW19 3K 105
Compton Rd. Croy 3F 124
Compton Rd. Hay 1C 68
Compton St. EC1 7M 59
Compton Ter. N1 2M 59
Compton Ter. N21 1L 27
Comreddy Clo. Enf 3M 15
Comus Ho. SE17 5C 76
(off Comus Pl.)
Comus Pl. SE17 5C 76
Comyne Rd. Wat 9D 4
Comyn Rd. SW11 3C 90
Comyns Clo. E16 8D 62
Comyns Rd. Dag 3L 65
Comyns, The. Bush 1A 22
Conant Ho. SE11 7M 75
(off St Agnes Pl.)
Conant M. E1 1E 76
Conaways Clo. Eps 2E 134
Concanon Rd. SW2 3K 91
Concert Hall App. SE1 2K 75
Concord Bus. Cen. W3 7M 55
Concord Clo. N'holt 6H 53
Concord Ct. King T 7K 103
(off Winery La.)
Concorde Bus. Pk. Big H 7H 141
Concorde Clo. Houn 1M 85
Concorde Clo. Uxb 5C 142
Concorde Dri. E6 8K 63
Concorde Ho. Horn 2F 66
(off Astra Clo.)
Concord Ho. N17 7D 28
(off Park La.)
Concordia Wharf. E14 2A 78
(off Coldharbour)
Concord Rd. W3 7M 55
Concord Rd. Enf 7G 17
Concourse, The. N9 2F 28
(off Plevna Rd.)
Concourse, The. NW9 8C 24
Condell Rd. SW8 9G 75
Conder St. E14 9J 61
Condor Path. N'holt 5L 53
(off Union Rd.)
Condor Wlk. Horn 3F 66
Condover Cres. SE18 8M 79
Condray Pl. SW11 8C 74
Conduit Av. SE10 9B 78
Conduit Ct. WC2 1J 75
(off Floral St.)
Conduit La. N18 5G 29
Conduit La. Enf 8J 17
Conduit La. S Croy 7E 124
(in two parts)
Conduit M. W2 9B 58
Conduit Pas. W2 9B 58
(off Conduit Pl.)
Conduit Pl. W2 9B 58
Conduit Rd. SE18 6M 79
Conduit St. W1 1F 74
Conduit Way. NW10 3A 56
Conewood St. N5 8M 43
Coney Acre. SE21 7A 92
Coney Burrows. E4 2C 30
Coney Gro. Uxb 6E 142
Coneygrove Path. N'holt 2J 53
(off Arnold Rd.)
Coney Hall. 6C 126
Coney Hall Pde. W Wick 5C 126
Coney Hill Rd. W Wick 4C 126
Coney Way. SW8 7K 75
Conference Clo. E4 2A 30
Conference Rd. SE2 5G 81
Congers Ho. SE8 8L 77
Congleton Gro. SE18 6A 80
Congo Rd. SE18 6B 80
Congress Rd. SE2 5G 81
Congreve Ho. N16 1C 60
Congreve Rd. SE9 2K 95
Congreve Rd. Wal A 6L 7
Congreve St. SE17 5C 76
Congreve Wlk. E16 8H 63
(off Fulmer Rd.)
Conical Corner. Enf 4A 16
Conifer Av. Romf 5M 33
Conifer Clo. Orp 6B 128
Conifer Clo. Wal X 2A 6
Conifer Gdns. SW16 9J 91
Conifer Gdns. Enf 8C 16
Conifer Gdns. Sutt 4M 121
Conifer Ho. SE4 3K 93
(off Brockley Rd.)
Conifer Pk. Eps 3C 134
Conifers. Wey 6C 116
Conifers Clo. Tedd 4F 102
Conifers, The. Wat 8G 5
Conifer Way. Hay 1E 68
Conifer Way. Swan 5A 114
Conifer Way. Wemb 8G 39
Coniffe Ct. SE9 4M 95
Coniger Rd. SW6 1L 89
Coningesby Dri. Wat 3C 8
Coningham Ct. SW10 8A 74
(off King's Rd.)
Coningham M. W12 2E 72
Coningham Rd. W12 3F 72
Coningsby Cotts. W5 3H 71
Coningsby Gdns. E4 6M 29
Coningsby Rd. N4 5M 43
Coningsby Rd. W5 3H 71
Coningsby Rd. S Croy 1A 138
Conington Rd. SE13 1M 93
Conisbee Ct. N14 7G 15
Conisborough Ct. Dart 5M 99
(off Osbourne Rd.)
Conisborough Cres. SE6 9A 94
Conisbrough. NW1 4G 59
(off Bayham St.)
Coniscliffe Clo. Chst 5L 111
Coniscliffe Rd. N13 3A 28
Coniston. NW1 6G 59
(off Harrington St.)
Coniston Av. Bark 3C 64
Coniston Av. Gnfd 6F 54
Coniston Av. Upm 9M 51
Coniston Av. Well 2C 96
Coniston Clo. N20 3A 26
Coniston Clo. SW13 8D 72
Coniston Clo. SW20 1H 121
Coniston Clo. W4 8A 72
Coniston Clo. Bark 3C 64
Coniston Clo. Bexh 9A 82
Coniston Clo. Dart 7F 98
Coniston Clo. Eri 8C 82
Coniston Ct. SE16 3H 77
(off Eleanor Clo.)
Coniston Ct. W2 9C 58
(off Kendal St.)
Conistone Way. N7 3J 59
Coniston Gdns. N9 1G 29
Coniston Gdns. NW9 3B 40
Coniston Gdns. Ilf 2J 47
Coniston Gdns. Pinn 2E 36
Coniston Gdns. Sutt 8B 122
Coniston Gdns. Wemb 6G 39
Coniston Ho. E3 7K 61
(off Southern Gro.)
Coniston Ho. SE5 8A 76
(off Wyndham Rd.)
Coniston Rd. N10 9F 26
Coniston Rd. N17 6E 28
Coniston Rd. Bexh 9A 82
Coniston Rd. Brom 3C 110
Coniston Rd. Coul 8G 137
Coniston Rd. Croy 2E 124
Coniston Rd. Twic 5M 85
Coniston Wlk. E9 1G 61
Coniston Way. Chess 5J 119
Coniston Way. Horn 1E 66
Conlan St. W10 7J 57
Conley Rd. NW10 2C 56
Conley St. SE10 6C 78
Connaught Av. E4 9B 18
Connaught Av. SW14 2A 88
Connaught Av. Ashf 9C 144
Connaught Av. E Barn 1D 26
Connaught Av. Enf 4C 16
Connaught Av. Houn 3J 85
Connaught Av. Lou 6H 19
Connaught Bri. E16 2H 79
Connaught Bus. Cen. NW9 3D 40
Connaught Bus. Cen. Mitc 9D 106
Connaught Clo. E10 7H 45
Connaught Clo. W2 9C 58
(off Connaught St.)
Connaught Clo. Enf 4C 16
Connaught Clo. Sutt 4B 122
Connaught Clo. Uxb 7A 52
Connaught Ct. E17 2M 45
(off Orford Rd.)
Connaught Dri. NW11 2L 41
Connaught Gdns. N10 3F 42
Connaught Gdns. N13 4M 27
Connaught Gdns. Mord 8A 106
Connaught Hall. 7H 59
(off Tavistock Sq., University of London)
Connaught Hill. Lou 6H 19
Connaught Ho. NW10 6F 56
(off Trenmar Gdns.)
Connaught Ho. W1 1F 74
(off Davies St.)
Connaught La. Ilf 7A 48
Connaught Lodge. N4 5L 43
(off Connaught Rd.)
Connaught M. NW3 9C 42
Connaught M. SE11 5L 75
(off Walcot Sq.)
Connaught M. SE18 6L 79
Connaught M. SW6 9J 73
Connaught Pl. W2 1D 74
Connaught Rd. E4 9C 18
Connaught Rd. E11 6B 46
Connaught Rd. E16 2H 79
(Albert Rd.)
Connaught Rd. E16 1H 79
(Connaught Bri.)
Connaught Rd. E17 3L 45
Connaught Rd. N4 5L 43
Connaught Rd. NW10 4C 56
Connaught Rd. SE18 6L 79
Connaught Rd. W13 1F 70
Connaught Rd. Barn 8H 13
Connaught Rd. Harr 8D 22
Connaught Rd. Horn 8H 51
Connaught Rd. Ilf 7B 48
Connaught Rd. N Mald 8C 104
Connaught Rd. Rich 4K 87
Connaught Rd. Sutt 4B 122
Connaught Rd. Tedd 2B 102
Connaught Roundabout (Junct.) 1H 79
Connaught Sq. W2 9D 58
Connaught St. W2 9C 58
Connaught Way. N13 4M 27
Connell Ct. SE14 7H 77
(off Myers La.)
Connell Cres. W5 7K 55
Connemara Clo. Borwd 8B 12
Connett Ho. E2 5E 60
(off Mansford St.)
Connington Cres. E4 3B 30
Connolly Pl. SW19 3A 106
Connop Rd. Enf 2H 17
Connor Clo. E11 5C 46
Connor Clo. Ilf 8A 32
Connor Ct. SW11 9F 74
Connor Rd. Dag 9K 49
Connor St. E9 4H 61
Conolly Rd. W7 2C 70
Conqueror Ct. H Hill 7H 35
Conrad Dri. Wor Pk 3G 121
Conrad Ho. E14 1J 77
(off Victory Pl.)
Conrad Ho. E16 2F 78
(off Wesley Av.)
Conrad Ho. N16 1C 60
(off Matthias Rd.)
Conrad Ho. SW8 8J 75
(off Wyvil Rd.)
Conrad Tower. W3 4M 71
(off Bollo La.)
Consec Farriers M. SE15 2G 93
Consfield Av. N Mald 8E 104
Consort Ho. E14 6M 77
(off St Davids Sq.)
Consort Ho. W2 1M 73
(off Queensway)
Consort Lodge. NW8 4D 58
(off Prince Albert Rd.)
Consort M. Iswth 4B 86
Consort Rd. SE15 9F 76
Cons St. SE1 3L 75
Constable Av. E16 2F 78
Constable Clo. NW11 4M 41
Constable Clo. Hay 5A 52
Constable Ct. SE16 6F 76
(off Stubbs Dri.)
Constable Ct. W4 6M 71
(off Chaseley Dri.)
Constable Cres. N15 3E 44
Constable Gdns. Edgw 8L 23
Constable Gdns. Iswth 4B 86
Constable Ho. NW3 3D 58
Constable Ho. N'holt 5H 53
(off Gallery Gdns.)
Constable M. Dag 9F 48
Constable Wlk. SE21 9C 92
Constance Allen Ho. W10 9H 57
(off Bridge Clo.)
Constance Cres. Brom 2D 126
Constance Rd. Croy 2M 123
Constance Rd. Enf 8C 16
Constance Rd. Sutt 6A 122
Constance Rd. Twic 6M 85
Constance St. E16 2J 79
Constant Ho. E14 1M 77
(off Harrow La.)
Constantine Pl. Hil 4D 142
Constantine Rd. NW3 9C 42
Constitution Hill. SW1 3F 74
Constitution Ri. SE18 9L 79
Consul Gdns. Swan 4E 114
Content St. SE17 5B 76
Contessa Clo. Orp 7C 128
Control Tower Rd. H'row A 2E 144
Convair Wlk. N'holt 6H 53
Convent Clo. Beck 4A 110
Convent Gdns. W5 5G 71
Convent Gdns. W11 9J 57
Convent Hill. SE19 3A 108
Convent Way. S'hall 5G 69
Conway Clo. Rain 3E 66
Conway Clo. Stan 6E 22
Conway Cres. Gnfd 5C 54
Conway Cres. Romf 4G 49
Conway Dri. Ashf 3A 100
Conway Dri. Hay 4A 68
Conway Dri. Sutt 8M 121
Conway Gdns. Enf 2C 16
Conway Gdns. Mitc 8J 107
Conway Gdns. Wemb 5G 39
Conway Gro. W3 8B 56
Conway Ho. E14 5L 77
(off Cahir St.)
Conway Ho. E17 3J 45
(off Mission Gro.)
Conway Ho. Borwd 6A 12
Conway M. W1 7G 59
(off Conway St.)
Conway Rd. N14 3J 27
Conway Rd. N15 3M 43
Conway Rd. NW2 7G 41
Conway Rd. SE18 5B 80
Conway Rd. SW20 5G 105
Conway Rd. Felt 2H 101
Conway Rd. Houn 6K 85
Conway Rd. H'row A 2F 144
Conway St. W1 7G 59
(in two parts)
Conway Wlk. Hamp 3K 101
Conybeare. NW3 3C 58
Conyers Clo. W on T 7H 117
Conyers Clo. Wfd G 6C 30
Conyer's Rd. SW16 2H 107
Conyer St. E3 5J 61
Conyers Way. Lou 5M 19
Cooden Clo. Brom 4F 110
Cook Ct. SE16 2G 77
(off Rotherhithe St.)
Cook Ct. Eri 8D 82
Cookes Clo. E11 7D 46
Cookes La. Sutt 8J 121
Cookham Clo. S'hall 4M 69
Cookham Cres. SE16 3H 77
Cookham Dene Clo. Chst 5B 112
Cookham Hill. Orp 5L 129
Cookham Ho. E2 7D 60
(off Montclare St.)
Cookham Rd. Swan 5L 113
Cookhill Rd. SE2 3F 80
Cook Rd. Dag 4J 65
Cook's Clo. Romf 8A 34
Cooks Hole Rd. Enf 2M 15
Cooks Mead. Bush 8M 9
Cookson Gro. Eri 8M 81
Cook Sq. Eri 8D 82
Cook's Rd. E15 5M 61
Cook's Rd. SE17 7M 75
Coolfin Rd. E16 9E 62
Coolgardie Av. E4 5B 30
Coolgardie Av. Chig 3L 31
Coolgardie Rd. Ashf 2A 100
Coolhurst Rd. N8 4H 43
Cool Oak La. NW9 6C 40
Coomassie Rd. W9 7K 57
Coombe. 4B 104
Coombe Av. Croy 6C 124
Coombe Bank. King T 5C 104
Coombe Clo. Edgw 9K 23
Coombe Clo. Houn 3L 85
Coombe Corner. N21 1M 27
Coombe Ct. Croy 6B 124
(off St Peter's Rd.)
Coombe Cres. Hamp 4K 101
Coombe Dri. Ruis 6F 36
Coombe End. King T 4B 104
Coombefield Clo. N Mald 9C 104
Coombe Gdns. SW20 6E 104
Coombe Gdns. N Mald 8D 104
Coombe Hill Glade. King T 4C 104
Coombe Hill Rd. King T 4C 104
Coombe Ho. E4 6K 29
Coombe Ho. N7 1H 59
Coombe Ho. Chase. N Mald 5B 104
Coombehurst Clo. Barn 4D 14
Coombe Lane (Junct.) 4D 104
Coombe La. SW20 5D 104
Coombe La. Croy 7F 124
Coombe La. W Vill 9D 116
Coombe La. Flyover. SW20 5D 104
Coombe La. W. King T 5M 103
Coombe Lea. Brom 7J 111
Coombe Lodge. SE7 7G 79
Coombe Neville. King T 4B 104
Coombe Pk. King T 2A 104
Coomber Ho. SW6 2M 89
(off Wandsworth Bri. Rd.)
Coombe Ridings. King T 2A 104
Coombe Ri. King T 5A 104
Coombe Rd. N22 9L 27
Coombe Rd. NW10 8B 40
Coombe Rd. SE26 1F 108
Coombe Rd. W4 6C 72
Coombe Rd. W13 4F 70
Coombe Rd. Bush 9B 10
Coombe Rd. Croy 6B 124
Coombe Rd. Hamp 3K 101
Coombe Rd. King T 5L 103
Coombe Rd. N Mald 6C 104
Coombe Rd. Romf 1K 51
Coomber Way. Croy 2H 123
Coombes Rd. Dag 4K 65
Coombe Wlk. Sutt 5M 121
Coombe Wood Dri. Romf 4K 49
Coombe Wood Hill. Purl 5A 138
Coombewood Rd. King T 2A 104
Coombs St. N1 5M 59
Coomer M. SW6 7K 73
Coomer Pl. SW6 7K 73
Coomer Rd. SW6 7K 73
Cooms Wlk. Edgw 8A 24
Cooperage Clo. N17 6D 28
Cooper Av. E17 8J 29
Cooper Clo. SE1 3L 75
Cooper Ct. E15 1M 61
Cooper Ct. SE18 7M 79
Cooper Cres. Cars 5D 122
Cooper Ho. NW8 7B 58
(off Lyons Pl.)
Cooper Ho. Houn 2K 85
Cooper Rd. NW4 4H 41
Cooper Rd. NW10 1D 56
Cooper Rd. Croy 6M 123
Coopersale Clo. Wfd G 7G 31
Coopersale Rd. E9 1H 61
Coopers Clo. E1 7G 61
Coopers Clo. Chig 2F 32
Coopers Clo. Dag 2M 65
Coopers Ct. W3 2A 72
(off Church Rd.)

Coopers Ct.—Cottesmore Av.

Coopers Ct. Iswth 1D 86
(off Woodlands Rd.)
Coopers Cres. Borwd 3A 12
Coopers La. E10 . . . . 6M 45
Coopers La. NW1 . . . . 5H 59
Cooper's La. SE12 . . . . 8F 94
Coopers Lodge. SE1 . . . . 3D 76
(off Tooley St.)
Coopers M. Wat 4G 5
Cooper's Rd. SE1 . . . . 6D 76
Coopers Row. EC3 . . . . 1D 76
Cooper St. E16 . . . . 8D 62
Coopers Wlk. E15 . . . . 1C 62
Coopers Wlk. Chesh 1D 6
Cooper's Yd. SE19 . . . . 3C 108
Coote Gdns. Dag 8K 49
Coote Rd. Bexh 9K 81
Coote Rd. Dag 8K 49
Cope Ho. EC1 . . . . 6A 60
(off Bath St.)
Copeland Dri. E14 . . . . 5L 77
Copeland Ho. SE11 . . . . 4L 75
(off Lambeth Wlk.)
Copeland Rd. E17 . . . . 4M 45
Copeland Rd. SE15 . . . . 1E 92
Copeman Clo. SE26 . . . . 2G 109
Copenhagen Gdns. W4 . . . . 3B 72
Copenhagen Ho. N1 . . . . 4K 59
(off Barnsbury Est.)
Copenhagen Pl. E14 . . . . 9K 61
(in two parts)
Copenhagen St. N1 . . . . 4J 59
Copenhagen Way.
W on T 5F 116
Cope Pl. W8 . . . . 4L 73
Copers Cope Rd. Beck 4K 109
Cope St. SE16 . . . . 5H 77
Copford Clo. Wfd G 6J 31
Copford Wlk. N1 . . . . 4A 60
(off Popham St.)
Copgate Path. SW16 . . . . 3K 107
Copinger Wlk. Edgw 8M 23
Copland Av. Wemb 1H 55
Copland Clo. Wemb 1G 55
Copland Ho. S'hall 3K 69
Copland M. Wemb 2J 55
Copland Rd. Wemb 2J 55
Copleston M. SE15 . . . . 1D 92
Copleston Pas. SE15 . . . . 1D 92
Copleston Rd. SE15 . . . . 2D 92
Copley Clo. SE17 . . . . 7A 76
Copley Clo. W7 . . . . 7D 54
Copley Dene. Brom 5H 111
Copley Pk. SW16 . . . . 3K 107
Copley Rd. Stan 5G 23
Copley St. E1 . . . . 8H 61
Copnor Way. SE15 . . . . 8C 76
Coppard Gdns. Chess 8G 119
Coppelia Rd. SE3 . . . . 3D 94
Coppen Rd. Dag 5K 49
Copperas St. SE8 . . . . 7M 77
Copperbeech Clo. NW3 . . . . 1B 58
Copper Beech Clo. Ilf 8K 31
Copper Beech Clo. Orp 9G 113
Copper Beech Ct. Lou 3L 19
Copper Beeches Ct.
Iswth 9B 70
Copper Clo. SE19 . . . . 4D 108
Copperdale Rd. Hay 3E 68
Copperfield. Chig 5B 32
Copperfield App. Chig 6B 32
Copperfield Av. Uxb 8E 142
Copperfield Clo. S Croy 3A 138
Copperfield Dri. N15 . . . . 2D 44
Copperfield Ho. SE1 . . . . 3E 76
(off Wolseley St.)
Copperfield Ho. W1 . . . . 8E 58
(off Marylebone High St.)
Copperfield Ho. W11 . . . . 2H 73
(off St Ann's Rd.)
Copperfield M. N18 . . . . 4C 28
Copperfield Rd. E3 . . . . 7J 61
Copperfield Rd. SE28 . . . . 9G 65
Copperfields. Beck 5A 110
Copperfields. Harr 5C 38
Copperfields Ct. W3 . . . . 3L 71
Copperfields Shop. Cen.
Dart 5J 99
Copperfield St. SE1 . . . . 3M 75
Copperfields Way. Romf 8H 35
Copperfield Way. Chst 3A 112
Copperfield Way. Pinn 2K 37
Coppergate Clo. Brom 5F 110
Copper Mead Clo. NW2 . . . . 8G 41
Copper Mill Dri. Iswth 1D 86
Coppermill La. E17 . . . . 4G 45
Copper Mill La. SW17 . . . . 1A 106
Copper Row. SE1 . . . . 2D 76
(off Horselydown La.)
Coppetts Cen. N11 . . . . 7D 26
Coppetts Clo. N12 . . . . 7C 26
Coppetts Rd. N10 . . . . 7D 26
Coppice Clo. SW20 . . . . 7G 105
Coppice Clo. Beck 8M 109
Coppice Clo. Ruis 4B 36
Coppice Clo. Stan 6D 22
Coppice Dri. SW15 . . . . 5F 88
Coppice Path. Chig 4F 32
Coppice, The. Ashf 3A 100
Coppice, The. Bex 9B 98
Coppice, The. Enf 6M 15
Coppice, The. New Bar 8M 13
(off Gt. North Rd.)
Coppice, The. Wat 8G 9
Coppice, The. W Dray 9C 142
Coppice Wlk. N20 . . . . 3L 25
Coppice Way. E18 . . . . 2D 46
Coppies Gro. N11 . . . . 4F 26
Copping Clo. Croy 6C 124
Coppins, The. Harr 6C 22
Coppins, The. New Ad 8M 125
Coppock Clo. SW11 . . . . 1C 90
Coppsfield. W Mol 7L 101
Copse Av. W Wick 5M 125
Copse Clo. SE7 . . . . 7F 78
Copse Clo. N'wd 9A 20
Copse Clo. W Dray 4H 143
Copse Edge Av. Eps 5D 134
Copse Glade. Surb 2H 119
Copse Hill. 4F 104
Copse Hill. SW20 . . . . 5E 104
Copse Hill. Purl 5J 137
Copse Hill. Sutt 9M 121
Copsem Dri. Esh 8M 117
Copsem La. Esh & Oxs 8M 117
Copsem Way. Esh 9A 118
Copsem Wood. Oxs 3A 132
Copse, The. E4 . . . . 1D 30
Copse, The. N2 . . . . 1D 42
Copse, The. Wat 5J 5
Copse Vw. S Croy 1H 139
Copsewood Clo. Sidc 5C 96
Copsewood Rd. Wat 3F 8
Copse Wood Way. N'wd 8A 20
Coptefield Dri. Belv 4H 81
Copthall Av. EC2 . . . . 9B 60
(in three parts)
Copthall Bldgs. EC2 . . . . 9B 60
(off Copthall Av.)
Copthall Clo. EC2 . . . . 9B 60
Copthall Dri. NW7 . . . . 7E 24
Copthall Gdns. NW7 . . . . 7E 24
Copthall Gdns. Twic 7D 86
Copthall Sports Cen. 8F 24
Copthorne Av. SW12 . . . . 6H 91
Copthorne Av. Brom 4K 127
Copthorne Av. Ilf 6M 31
Copthorne Clo. Shep 1A 116
Copthorne Gdns. Horn 3L 51
Copthorne M. Hay 5C 68
Copthorne Ri. S Croy 5B 138
Coptic St. WC1 . . . . 8J 59
Copwood Clo. N12 . . . . 4B 26
Coral Clo. Romf 2G 49
Coral Ho. E1 . . . . 7J 61
(off Harford St.)
Coraline Clo. S'hall 6K 53
Coralline Wlk. SE2 . . . . 3G 81
Coral Row. SW11 . . . . 2A 90
Coral St. SE1 . . . . 3L 75
Coram Ho. W4 . . . . 6C 72
(off Wood St.)
Coram Ho. WC1 . . . . 7J 59
(off Herbrand St.)
Coram St. WC1 . . . . 7J 59
Coran Clo. N9 . . . . 9H 17
Corban Rd. Houn 2L 85
Corbar Clo. Barn 3B 14
Corbden Clo. SE15 . . . . 9D 76
Corbet Clo. Wall 3E 122
Corbet Ct. EC3 . . . . 9B 60
Corbet Ho. N1 . . . . 5L 59
(off Barnsbury Est.)
Corbet Pl. E1 . . . . 8D 60
Corbet Rd. Eps 2C 134
Corbets Av. Upm 1M 67
Corbets Tey. 1M 67
Corbets Tey Rd. Upm 9M 51
Corbett Clo. Croy 4B 140
Corbett Ct. SE26 . . . . 1K 109
Corbett Gro. N22 . . . . 7J 27
Corbett Ho. SW10 . . . . 7A 74
(off Cathcart Rd.)
Corbett Rd. E11 . . . . 4G 47
Corbett Rd. E17 . . . . 1A 46
Corbetts La. SE16 . . . . 5G 77
(in two parts)
Corbetts Pas. SE16 . . . . 5G 77
(off Corbetts La.)
Corbetts Wharf. SE16 . . . . 3F 76
(off Bermondsey Wall E.)
Corbicum. E11 . . . . 5C 46
Corbidge Ct. SE8 . . . . 7M 77
(off Glaisher St.)
Corbiere Ct. SW19 . . . . 3H 105
Corbiere Ho. N1 . . . . 4C 60
(off De Beauvoir Est.)
Corbins La. Harr 8M 37
Corbridge. N17 . . . . 7F 28
Corbridge Cres. E2 . . . . 5F 60
Corbridge M. Romf 3D 50
Corby Cres. Enf 6J 15
Corbylands Rd. Sidc 6C 96
Corbyn St. N4 . . . . 6J 43
Corby Rd. NW10 . . . . 5B 56
Corby Way. E3 . . . . 7L 61
Cordelia Clo. SE24 . . . . 3M 91
Cordelia Gdns. Stai 6C 144
Cordelia Ho. N1 . . . . 5C 60
(off Arden Est.)
Cordelia Rd. Stai 6C 144
Cordelia St. E14 . . . . 9M 61
Cordell Clo. Chesh 1E 6
Cordell Ho. N15 . . . . 3E 44
(off Newton Rd.)
Cordingley Rd. Ruis 7B 36
Cording St. E14 . . . . 8M 61
Cordrey Gdns. Coul 7J 137
(in two parts)
Cordwainers Ct. E9 . . . . 3F 60
(off St Thomas's Sq.)
Cordwainers Wlk. E13 . . . . 5E 62
Cord Way. E14 . . . . 4L 77
Cordwell Rd. SE13 . . . . 4C 94
Corefield Clo. N11 . . . . 2E 26
Corelli Ct. SW5 . . . . 5L 73
(off W. Cromwell Rd.)
Corelli Rd. SE3 . . . . 1J 95
Corfe Av. Harr 9L 37
Corfe Clo. Asht 9G 133
Corfe Clo. Borwd 5B 12
Corfe Clo. Hay 9G 53
Corfe Ho. SW8 . . . . 8K 75
(off Dorset Rd.)
Corfe Tower. W3 . . . . 3M 71
Corfield Rd. N21 . . . . 7K 15
Corfield St. E2 . . . . 6F 60
Corfton Lodge. W5 . . . . 8J 55
Corfton Rd. W5 . . . . 9J 55
Corhaven Ho. Eri 8C 82
Coriander Av. E14 . . . . 9B 62
Cories Clo. Dag 7H 49
Corinium Clo. Wemb 9K 39
Corinne Rd. N19 . . . . 9G 43
Corinthian Manorway. Eri 5B 82
Corinthian Rd. Eri 5B 82
Corinthian Way. Stanw 6B 144
Corkers Path. Ilf 7A 48
Corker Wlk. N7 . . . . 7K 43
Corkran Rd. Surb 2H 119
Corkscrew Hill. W Wick 4A 126
Cork Sq. E1 . . . . 2F 76
Cork St. W1 . . . . 1G 75
Cork St. M. W1 . . . . 1G 75
(off Cork St.)
Cork Tree Est., The. E4 . . . . 5J 29
Cork Tree Ho. SE27 . . . . 2M 107
(off Lakeview Rd.)
Cork Tree Way. E4 . . . . 5J 29
Corlett St. NW1 . . . . 8C 58
Cormont Rd. SE5 . . . . 9M 75
Cormorant Clo. E17 . . . . 7J 29
Cormorant Ct. SE8 . . . . 7K 77
(off Pilot Clo.)
Cormorant Pl. Sutt 7K 121
Cormorant Rd. E7 . . . . 1D 62
Cormorant Wlk. Horn 2F 66
Cornbury Ho. SE8 . . . . 7K 77
(off Evelyn St.)
Cornbury Rd. Edgw 7H 23
Cornel Ho. Sidc 9E 96
Cornelia Dri. Hay 7G 53
Cornelia Ho. Twic 5H 87
(off Denton Rd.)
Cornelia Pl. Eri 7C 82
Cornelia St. N7 . . . . 2K 59
Cornell Building. E1 . . . . 9E 60
(off Coke St.)
Cornell Clo. Sidc 3J 113
Cornell Ho. S Harr 8K 37
Cornell Way. Romf 5L 33
Cornercroft. Sutt 7H 121
(off Wickham Av.)
Corner Fielde. SW2 . . . . 7K 91
Corner Grn. SE3 . . . . 1E 94
Corner Ho. St. WC2 . . . . 2J 75
(off Northumberland St.)
Corner Mead. NW9 . . . . 7D 24
Cornerside. Ashf 4A 100
Cornerstone Ho. Croy 2A 124
Corner, The. W5 . . . . 2J 71
Corney Reach Way. W4 . . . . 8C 72
Corney Rd. W4 . . . . 7C 72
Cornfield Clo. Uxb 5B 142
Cornfield Rd. Bush 6M 9
Cornflower La. Croy 3H 125
Cornflower Ter. SE22 . . . . 5F 92
Cornflower Way. Romf 8J 35
Cornford Clo. Brom 9E 110
Cornford Gro. SW12 . . . . 8F 90
Cornhill. EC3 . . . . 9B 60
Cornhill Dri. Enf 1J 17
(off Ordnance Rd.)
Cornick Ho. SE16 . . . . 4F 76
(off Slippers Pl.)
Cornish Ct. N9 . . . . 9F 16
Cornish Gro. SE20 . . . . 5F 108
Cornish Ho. SE17 . . . . 7M 75
(off Brandon Est.)
Cornish Ho. Bren 6K 71
Cornmill. Wal A 6H 7
Corn Mill Dri. Orp 2E 128
Cornmill La. SE13 . . . . 2A 94
Cornmow Dri. NW10 . . . . 1D 56
Cornshaw Rd. Dag 6H 49
Cornthwaite Rd. E5 . . . . 8G 45
Cornwall Av. E2 . . . . 6G 61
Cornwall Av. N3 . . . . 7L 25
Cornwall Av. N22 . . . . 8J 27
Cornwall Av. Clay 9D 118
Cornwall Av. S'hall 8K 53
Cornwall Av. Well 2C 96
Cornwall Clo. Bark 2D 64
Cornwall Clo. Horn 2L 51
Cornwall Clo. Wal X 6E 6
Cornwall Ct. W7 . . . . 7D 54
(off Copley Clo.)
Cornwall Ct. Pinn 7K 21
Cornwall Cres. W11 . . . . 9J 57
Cornwall Dri. Orp 4G 113
Cornwall Gdns. NW10 . . . . 2F 56
Cornwall Gdns. SE25 . . . . 8D 108
Cornwall Gdns. SW7 . . . . 4M 73
Cornwall Gdns. Wlk.
SW7 . . . . 4M 73
Cornwall Gro. W4 . . . . 6C 72
Cornwallis Av. N9 . . . . 2F 28
Cornwallis Av. SE9 . . . . 8B 96
Cornwallis Clo. Eri 7D 82
Cornwallis Ct. SW8 . . . . 9J 75
(off Lansdowne Grn.)
Cornwallis Gro. N9 . . . . 2F 28
Cornwallis Ho. SE16 . . . . 3F 76
(off Cherry Garden St.)
Cornwallis Ho. W12 . . . . 1F 72
(off India Way)
Cornwallis Rd. E17 . . . . 2H 45
Cornwallis Rd. N9 . . . . 2F 28
Cornwallis Rd. N19 . . . . 7J 43
Cornwallis Rd. Dag 9H 49
Cornwallis Sq. N19 . . . . 7J 43
Cornwallis Wlk. SE9 . . . . 2K 95
Cornwall Mans. SW10 . . . . 8A 74
(off Cremorne Rd.)
Cornwall Mans. W14 . . . . 4H 73
(off Blythe Rd.)
Cornwall M. S. SW7 . . . . 4A 74
Cornwall M. W. SW7 . . . . 4M 73
Cornwall Rd. N4 . . . . 5L 43
Cornwall Rd. N15 . . . . 3B 44
Cornwall Rd. N18 . . . . 5E 28
Cornwall Rd. SE1 . . . . 2L 75
Cornwall Rd. Croy 4M 123
Cornwall Rd. Dart 2K 99
Cornwall Rd. Harr 4A 38
Cornwall Rd. Pinn 7K 21
Cornwall Rd. Ruis 8D 36
Cornwall Rd. Sutt 9K 121
Cornwall Rd. Twic 6E 86
Cornwall Rd. Uxb 2B 142
Cornwall Sq. SE11 . . . . 6M 75
(off Seaton Clo.)
Cornwall St. E1 . . . . 1F 76
Cornwall Ter. NW1 . . . . 7D 58
Cornwall Ter. M. NW1 . . . . 7D 58
(off Allsop Pl.)
Corn Way. E11 . . . . 8B 46
Cornwell Cres. E7 . . . . 9G 47
Cornwood Clo. N2 . . . . 3B 42
Cornwood Dri. E1 . . . . 9G 61
Cornworthy Rd. Dag 1G 65
Corona Rd. SE12 . . . . 6E 94
Coronation Av. N16 . . . . 9D 44
Coronation Clo. Bex 5H 97
Coronation Clo. Ilf 2A 48
Coronation Ct. E15 . . . . 2D 62
Coronation Ct. W10 . . . . 8G 57
(off Brewster Gdns.)
Coronation Ct. Eri 8B 82
Coronation Dri. Horn 1F 66
Coronation Rd. E13 . . . . 6G 63
Coronation Rd. NW10 . . . . 6K 55
Coronation Rd. Hay 5D 68
Coronation Vs. NW10 . . . . 7M 55
Coronation Wlk. Twic 7L 85
Coronet Cinema. 2L 73
(off Notting Hill Ga.)
Coronet Pde. Wemb 2J 55
Coronet St. N1 . . . . 6C 60
Corporate Dri. Felt 9F 84
Corporate Ho. Har W 8B 22
Corporation Av. Houn 3J 85
Corporation Row. EC1 . . . . 7L 59
Corporation St. E15 . . . . 5C 62
Corporation St. N7 . . . . 1J 59
Corrance Rd. SW2 . . . . 3J 91
Corri Av. N14 . . . . 4H 27
Corrib Ct. N13 . . . . 3K 27
Corrib Dri. Sutt 7C 122
Corrigan Av. Coul 7E 136
Corrigan Clo. NW4 . . . . 1G 41
Corringham Ct. NW11 . . . . 5L 41
Corringham Ho. E1 . . . . 9H 61
(off Pitsea St.)
Corringham Rd. NW11 . . . . 5L 41
Corringham Rd. Wemb 7L 39
Corringway. NW11 . . . . 5M 41
Corringway. W5 . . . . 7L 55
Corris Grn. NW9 . . . . 3C 40
Corry Ho. E14 . . . . 1M 77
(off Wade's Pl.)
Corsair Clo. Stai 6B 144
Corsair Rd. Stai 6C 144
Corscombe Clo. King T 2A 104
Corsehill St. SW16 . . . . 3G 107
Corsham St. N1 . . . . 6B 60
Corsica St. N5 . . . . 2M 59
Corsley Way. E9 . . . . 2K 61
(off Osborne Rd.)
Cortayne Ct. Twic 8C 86
Cortayne Rd. SW6 . . . . 1K 89
Cortis Rd. SW15 . . . . 5F 88
Cortis Ter. SW15 . . . . 5F 88
Cortland Clo. Dart 5C 98
Corunna Rd. SW8 . . . . 9G 75
Corunna Ter. SW8 . . . . 9G 75
Corvette Sq. SE10 . . . . 7B 78
Corwell Gdns. Uxb 9A 52
Corwell La. Uxb 9A 52
(in two parts)
Coryton Path. W9 . . . . 7K 57
(off Ashmore Rd.)
Cosbycote Av. SE24 . . . . 4A 92
Cosdach Av. Wall 9H 123
Cosedge Cres. Croy 7L 123
Cosgrove Clo. N21 . . . . 2A 28
Cosgrove Clo. Hay 7J 53
Cosgrove Ho. E2 . . . . 4E 60
(off Whiston Rd.)
Cosmo Pl. WC1 . . . . 8J 59
Cosmur Clo. W12 . . . . 4D 72
Cossall Wlk. SE15 . . . . 1F 92
Cossar M. SW2 . . . . 4L 91
Cosser St. SE1 . . . . 4L 75
Costa St. SE15 . . . . 1E 92
Costons Av. Gnfd 6B 54
Costons La. Gnfd 6B 54
Coston Wlk. SE4 . . . . 3H 93
Cosway Mans. NW1 . . . . 8C 58
(off Shroton St.)
Cosway St. NW1 . . . . 8C 58
Cotall St. E14 . . . . 8L 61
Coteford Clo. Lou 4M 19
Coteford Clo. Pinn 3E 36
Coteford St. SW17 . . . . 1D 106
Cotelands. Croy 5C 124
Cotesbach Rd. E5 . . . . 8G 45
Cotes Ho. NW8 . . . . 7C 58
(off Broadley St.)
Cotesmore Gdns. Dag 9G 49
Cotford Rd. T Hth 8A 108
Cotham St. SE17 . . . . 5A 76
Cotherstone. Eps 2B 134
Cotherstone Rd. SW2 . . . . 7K 91
Cotleigh Av. Bex 8H 97
Cotleigh Rd. NW6 . . . . 3L 57
Cotleigh Rd. Romf 4B 50
Cotman Clo. NW11 . . . . 4A 42
Cotman Clo. SW15 . . . . 5H 89
Cotmandene Cres. Orp 6E 112
Cotman Gdns. Edgw 9L 23
Cotman Ho. NW8 . . . . 5C 58
(off Townshend Est.)
Cotman Ho. N'holt 5H 53
(off Academy Gdns.)
Cotman M. Dag 1G 65
(off Highgrove Rd.)
Cotmans Clo. Hay 2E 68
Coton Rd. Well 2E 96
Cotsford Av. N Mald 9A 104
Cotswold Av. Bush 8A 10
Cotswold Clo. N11 . . . . 4E 26
Cotswold Clo. Bexh 1C 98
Cotswold Clo. Hin W 4D 118
Cotswold Clo. King T 3A 104
Cotswold Clo. Uxb 4A 142
Cotswold Ct. EC1 . . . . 7A 60
(off Gee St.)
Cotswold Ct. Gnfd 5D 54
(off Hodder Dri.)
Cotswold Gdns. E6 . . . . 6H 63
Cotswold Gdns. NW2 . . . . 7H 41
Cotswold Gdns. Ilf 5B 48
Cotswold Ga. NW2 . . . . 6J 41
Cotswold Grn. Enf 6K 15
Cotswold M. SW11 . . . . 9B 74
Cotswold Ri. Orp 1D 128
Cotswold Rd. Hamp 2L 101
Cotswold Rd. Romf 9K 35
Cotswold Rd. Sutt 2M 135
Cotswold St. SE27 . . . . 1M 107
Cotswold Way. Enf 5K 15
Cotswold Way. Wor Pk 4G 121
Cottage Av. Brom 3J 127
Cottage Clo. E1 . . . . 7G 61
(off Hayfield Pas.)
Cottage Clo. Ruis 6B 36
Cottage Clo. Wat 4D 8
Cottage Fld. Clo. Sidc 7G 97
Cottage Gdns. Chesh 2D 6
Cottage Grn. SE5 . . . . 8B 76
Cottage Gro. SW9 . . . . 2J 91
Cottage Gro. Surb 1H 119
Cottage M. Horn 2G 51
Cottage Pl. SW3 . . . . 4C 74
Cottage Rd. Eps 9B 120
Cottage St. E14 . . . . 1M 77
Cottage Wlk. N16 . . . . 8D 44
Cottenham Dri. SW20 . . . . 4F 104
Cottenham Pde. SW20 . . . . 6F 104
Cottenham Park. 5F 104
Cottenham Pk. Rd.
SW20 . . . . 5E 104
(in two parts)
Cottenham Pl. SW20 . . . . 4F 104
Cottenham Rd. E17 . . . . 2K 45
Cotterill Rd. Surb 4J 119
Cottesbrook St. SE14 . . . . 8J 77
Cottesloe Ho. NW8 . . . . 7C 58
(off Jerome Cres.)
Cottesloe M. SE1 . . . . 4L 75
(off Emery St.)
Cottesloe Theatre. 2L 75
(in Royal National Theatre)
Cottesmore Av. Ilf 9L 31

Cranleigh Gdns. Ind. Est.—Cromer St.

Cranleigh Gdns. Ind. Est. S'hall .8K 53
Cranleigh Houses. NW1 .5G 59 (off Cranleigh St.)
Cranleigh M. SW11 .1C 90
Cranleigh Rd. N15 .3A 44
Cranleigh Rd. SW19 .7L 105
Cranleigh Rd. Esh .3A 118
Cranleigh Rd. Felt .1D 100
Cranleigh St. NW1 .5G 59
Cranley Dene Ct. N10 .2F 42
Cranley Dri. Ilf .5A 48
Cranley Dri. Ruis .7D 36
Cranley Gardens. .2F 42
Cranley Gdns. N10 .2F 42
Cranley Gdns. N13 .3K 27
Cranley Gdns. SW7 .6A 74
Cranley Gdns. Wall .9G 123
Cranley M. SW7 .6A 74
Cranley Pde. SE9 .1J 111 (off Beaconsfield Rd.)
Cranley Pl. SW7 .5B 74
Cranley Rd. E13 .8F 62
Cranley Rd. Ilf .4A 48
Cranley Rd. W on T .7D 116
Cranmer Av. W13 .4F 70
Cranmer Clo. Mord .1H 121
Cranmer Clo. Ruis .6H 37
Cranmer Clo. Stan .7G 23
Cranmer Clo. Warl .9J 139
Cranmer Ct. N3 .9J 25
Cranmer Ct. SW3 .5C 74
Cranmer Ct. SW4 .2H 91
Cranmere Ct. SE5 .9A 76
Cranmere Ct. Enf .4L 15
Cranmer Farm Clo. Mitc .8D 106
Cranmer Gdns. Dag .9A 50
Cranmer Gdns. Warl .9J 139
Cranmer Ho. SW9 .8L 75 (off Brixton Rd.)
Cranmer Rd. E7 .9F 46
Cranmer Rd. SW9 .8L 75
Cranmer Rd. Croy .5M 123
Cranmer Rd. Edgw .3M 23
Cranmer Rd. Hamp H .2M 101
Cranmer Rd. Hay .9B 52
Cranmer Rd. King T .2J 103
Cranmer Rd. Mitc .8D 106
Cranmer Ter. SW17 .2B 106
Cranmore Av. Iswth .8A 70
Cranmore Rd. Brom .9D 94
Cranmore Rd. Chst .2K 111
Cranmore Way. N10 .2G 43
Cranston Clo. Houn .1J 85
Cranston Clo. Uxb .7B 36
Cranston Est. N1 .5B 60
Cranston Gdns. E4 .6M 29
Cranston Pk. Av. Upm .9M 51
Cranston Rd. SE23 .7J 93
Cranswick Rd. SE16 .6F 76
Crantley Pl. Esh .7A 118
Crantock Rd. SE6 .8M 93
Cranwell Clo. E3 .7M 61
Cranwell Rd. H'row A .1F 144
Cranwich Av. N21 .9B 16
Cranwich Rd. N16 .5B 44
Cranwood Ct. EC1 .6B 60 (off Vince St.)
Cranwood St. EC1 .6B 60
Cranworth Cres. E4 .1B 30
Cranworth Gdns. SW9 .9L 75
Craster Rd. SW2 .6K 91
Crathie Rd. SE12 .5F 94
Cravan Av. Felt .8E 84
Craven Av. W5 .1G 71
Craven Av. S'hall .8K 53
Craven Clo. N16 .5E 44
Craven Clo. Hay .9E 52
Craven Ct. NW10 .4C 56
Craven Ct. Romf .4J 49
Craven Gdns. SW19 .2L 105
Craven Gdns. Bark .5C 64
Craven Gdns. Col R .5L 33
Craven Gdns. H Wood .6M 35
Craven Gdns. Ilf .9B 32
Craven Hill. W2 .1A 74
Craven Hill Gdns. W2 .1A 74 (in two parts)
Craven Hill M. W2 .1A 74
Craven Ho. N2 .9B 26 (off Central Av.)
Craven Lodge. W2 .1A 74 (off Craven Hill)
Craven M. SW11 .2E 90
Craven Pk. NW10 .4B 56
Craven Pk. M. NW10 .3C 56
Craven Pk. Rd. N15 .4D 44
Craven Pk. Rd. NW10 .4C 56
Craven Pas. WC2 .2J 75 (off Craven St.)
Craven Rd. NW10 .4B 56
Craven Rd. W2 .1A 74
Craven Rd. W5 .1G 71
Craven Rd. Croy .3F 124
Craven Rd. King T .5K 103
Craven Rd. Orp .5H 129
Craven St. WC2 .2J 75
Craven Ter. W2 .1A 74
Craven Wlk. N16 .5E 44
Crawford Av. Wemb .1H 55
Crawford Bldgs. W1 .8C 58 (off Homer St.)
Crawford Clo. Iswth .1C 86
Crawford Compton Clo. Horn .2G 67
Crawford Est. SE5 .1A 92
Crawford Gdns. N13 .3M 27
Crawford Gdns. N'holt .6K 53
Crawford Mans. W1 .8C 58 (off Crawford St.)
Crawford M. W1 .8D 58
Crawford Pas. EC1 .7L 59
Crawford Pl. W1 .9C 58
Crawford Point. E16 .9D 62 (off Wouldham Rd.)
Crawford Rd. SE5 .9A 76
Crawfords. Swan .4C 114
Crawford St. W1 .8C 58
Crawley Rd. E10 .6M 45
Crawley Rd. N22 .9A 28
Crawley Rd. Enf .9C 16
Crawshay Ct. SW9 .9L 75
Crawthew Gro. SE22 .3D 92
Cray Av. Asht .8J 133
Cray Av. Orp & St M .1F 128
Craybrooke Rd. Sidc .1F 112
Craybury End. SE9 .8A 96
Cray Clo. Dart .3E 98
Craydene Rd. Eri .9D 82
Crayfield Ind. Pk. Orp .6G 113
Crayfields Bus. Pk. Orp .5G 113 (off Rushet Rd.)
Crayford. .4C 98
Crayford Clo. E6 .9J 63
Crayford Greyhound Stadium. .5C 98
Crayford High St. Dart .3C 98
Crayford Ho. SE1 .3B 76 (off Long La.)
Crayford Ind. Est. Cray .4D 98
Crayford Rd. N7 .9H 43
Crayford Rd. Cray .4D 98
Crayford Way. Dart .4D 98
Crayke Hill. Chess .9J 119
Craylands. Orp .7G 113
Crayle Ho. EC1 .7M 59 (off Malta St.)
Craymill Sq. Dart .1D 98
Crayonne Clo. Sun .5C 100
Cray Rd. Belv .7L 81
Cray Rd. Dart .3E 98
Cray Rd. Sidc .3G 113
Cray Rd. Swan .1M 129
Crayside Ind. Est. Dart .3F 98
Crays Pde., The. Orp .6G 113
Cray Valley Rd. Orp .9E 112
Crealock Gro. Wfd G .5D 30
Crealock St. SW18 .5M 89
Creasey Clo. Horn .7F 50
Creasy Clo. Ab L .4D 4
Creasy Est. SE1 .4C 76
Crebor St. SE22 .5E 92
Credenhall Dri. Brom .3K 127
Credenhill Ho. SE15 .8F 76
Credenhill St. SW16 .3G 107
Crediton Hill. NW6 .1M 57
Crediton Rd. E16 .9E 62
Crediton Rd. NW10 .4H 57
Crediton Way. Clay .7E 118
Credon Rd. E13 .5G 63
Credon Rd. SE16 .6F 76
Creechurch La. EC3 .9C 60 (in two parts)
Creechurch Pl. EC3 .9C 60 (off Creechurch La.)
Creed Ct. EC4 .9M 59 (off Ludgate Hill)
Creed La. EC4 .9M 59
Creek Ho. W14 .4J 73 (off Russell Rd.)
Creekmouth. .7D 64
Creek Rd. SE8 & SE10 .7L 77
Creek Rd. Bark .6D 64
Creek Rd. E Mol .8C 102
Creekside. SE8 .8M 77
Creekside. Rain .7C 66
Creek, The. Sun .9E 100
Creek Way. Rain .8C 66
Creeland Gro. SE6 .7K 93
Cree Way. Romf .7C 34
Crefeld Clo. W6 .7J 73
Creffield Rd. W5 & W3 .1K 71
Creighton Av. E6 .5H 63
Creighton Av. N2 & N10 .1C 42
Creighton Clo. W12 .1E 72
Creighton Rd. N17 .7C 28
Creighton Rd. NW6 .5H 57
Creighton Rd. W5 .4H 71
Cremer Bus. Cen. E2 .5D 60 (off Cremer St.)
Cremer Ho. SE8 .8L 77 (off Deptford Chu. St.)
Cremer St. E2 .5D 60
Cremorne Est. SW10 .7B 74
Cremorne Gdns. Eps .2B 134
Cremorne Rd. SW10 .8A 74
Creon Ct. SW9 .8L 75 (off Caldwell St.)
Crescent. EC3 .1D 76
Crescent Av. Horn .7D 50
Crescent Ct. Surb .9H 103
Crescent Ct. Bus. Cen. E16 .7B 62
Crescent Dri. Orp .9M 111
Crescent E. Barn .2A 14
Crescent Gdns. SW19 .9L 89
Crescent Gdns. Ruis .5F 36
Crescent Gdns. Swan .6A 114
Crescent Gro. SW4 .3G 91
Crescent Gro. Mitc .8C 106
Crescent Ho. EC1 .7A 60 (off Golden La. Est.)
Crescent Ho. SE8 .1M 93
Crescent La. SW4 .3G 91
Crescent M. N22 .8J 27
Crescent Pde. Uxb .6E 142
Crescent Pl. SW3 .5C 74
Crescent Ri. N3 .8K 25
Crescent Ri. N22 .8H 27
Crescent Ri. Barn .7C 14
Crescent Rd. E4 .9C 18
Crescent Rd. E6 .4G 63
Crescent Rd. E10 .7M 45
Crescent Rd. E13 .4E 62
Crescent Rd. E18 .8G 31
Crescent Rd. N3 .8K 25
Crescent Rd. N8 .4H 43
Crescent Rd. N9 .1E 28
Crescent Rd. N11 .4D 26
Crescent Rd. N15 .1M 43
Crescent Rd. N22 .8H 27
Crescent Rd. SE18 .6M 79
Crescent Rd. SW20 .5H 105
Crescent Rd. Ave .3M 83
Crescent Rd. Barn .6B 14
Crescent Rd. Beck .6M 109
Crescent Rd. Brom .4E 110
Crescent Rd. Dag .8M 49
Crescent Rd. Enf .6M 15
Crescent Rd. Eri .7D 82
Crescent Rd. King T .4L 103
Crescent Rd. Shep .9A 100
Crescent Rd. Sidc .9D 96
Crescent Row. EC1 .7A 60
Crescent Stables. SW15 .4J 89
Crescent St. N1 .3K 59
Crescent, The. E17 .4J 45
Crescent, The. N9 .2F 28
Crescent, The. N11 .4D 26
Crescent, The. NW2 .8F 40
Crescent, The. SW13 .1D 88
Crescent, The. SW19 .9L 89
Crescent, The. W3 .9C 56
Crescent, The. Ab L .3D 4
Crescent, The. A'ham .2M 9
Crescent, The. Barn .4M 13
Crescent, The. Beck .5L 109
Crescent, The. Belm .3L 135
Crescent, The. Bex .6G 97
Crescent, The. Brick W .3L 5
Crescent, The. Croy .1B 124
Crescent, The. Eps .6L 133 (in two parts)
Crescent, The. Harr .6A 38
Crescent, The. Hay .8B 68
Crescent, The. Ilf .4L 47
Crescent, The. Lou .7H 19
Crescent, The. N Mald .7A 104
Crescent, The. Shep .2D 116
Crescent, The. Sidc .1D 112
Crescent, The. S'hall .3K 69
Crescent, The. Surb .9J 103
Crescent, The. Sutt .7B 122
Crescent, The. Wat .6G 9
Crescent, The. Wemb .7F 38
Crescent, The. W Mol .8L 101
Crescent, The. W Wick .1C 126
Crescent Vw. Lou .8H 19
Crescent Way. N12 .6C 26
Crescent Way. SE4 .2L 93
Crescent Way. SW16 .3K 107
Crescent Way. Orp .7C 128
Crescent W. Barn .3A 14
Crescent Wharf. E16 .2F 78 (off N. Woolwich Rd., in two parts)
Crescent Wood Rd. SE26 .9E 92
Cresford Rd. SW6 .9M 73
Crespigny Rd. NW4 .4F 40
Cressage Clo. S'hall .7L 53
Cressage Ho. Bren .7J 71 (off Ealing Rd.)
Cressal Ho. E14 .4L 77 (off Tiller Rd.)
Cresset Rd. E9 .2G 61
Cresset St. SW4 .2H 91
Cressfield Clo. NW5 .1E 58
Cressida Rd. N19 .6G 43
Cressingham Gdns. Est. SW2 .6L 91
Cressingham Gro. Sutt .6A 122
Cressingham Rd. SE13 .2A 94
Cressingham Rd. Edgw .6B 24
Cressington Clo. N16 .1C 60
Cress M. Brom .2B 110
Cresswell. NW9 .9D 24
Cresswell Gdns. SW5 .6A 74
Cresswell Pk. SE3 .2D 94
Cresswell Pl. SW10 .6A 74
Cresswell Rd. SE25 .8E 108
Cresswell Rd. Felt .9J 85
Cresswell Rd. Twic .5H 87
Cresswell Way. N21 .9L 15
Cressy Ct. E1 .8G 61
Cressy Ct. W6 .4F 72
Cressy Houses. E1 .8G 61 (off Hannibal Rd.)
Cressy Pl. E1 .8G 61
Cressy Rd. NW3 .1D 58
Cresta Ct. W5 .7K 55
Cresta Ho. NW3 .3B 58 (off Finchley Rd.)
Crestbrook Av. N13 .3M 27
Crestbrook Pl. N13 .3M 27 (off Green Lanes)
Crest Ct. NW4 .3G 41
Crest Dri. Enf .2G 17
Crestfield St. WC1 .6J 59
Crest Gdns. Ruis .8G 37
Creston Way. Wor Pk .3H 121
Crest Rd. NW2 .7E 40
Crest Rd. Brom .2D 126
Crest Rd. S Croy .9F 124
Crest, The. N13 .4L 27
Crest, The. NW4 .3G 41
Crest, The. Surb .9L 103
Crest Vw. Pinn .2H 37
Crest Vw. Dri. Orp .9M 111
Crestway. SW15 .5E 88
Crestwood Way. Houn .4J 85
Creswick Ct. W3 .1M 71
Creswick Rd. W3 .1M 71
Creswick Wlk. E3 .6L 61
Creswick Wlk. NW11 .2K 41
Creton St. SE18 .4L 79
Crewdson Rd. SW9 .8L 75
Crewe Pl. NW10 .6D 56
Crewe's Av. Warl .8G 139
Crewe's Clo. Warl .9G 139
Crewe's Farm La. Warl .8H 139
Crewe's La. Warl .8G 139 (in two parts)
Crewkerne Ct. SW11 .9B 74 (off Bolingbroke Wlk.)
Crews St. E14 .5L 77
Crewys Rd. NW2 .7K 41
Crewys Rd. SE15 .1F 92
Crichton Av. Wall .7H 123
Crichton Ho. Sidc .3H 113
Crichton Rd. Cars .8D 122
Crichton St. SW8 .1G 91
Cricketers Arms Rd. Enf .4A 16
Cricketers Clo. N14 .9G 15
Cricketers Clo. Chess .6H 119
Cricketers Clo. Eri .6C 82
Cricketers Ct. SE11 .5M 75 (off Kennington La.)
Cricketers M. SW18 .4M 89
Cricketers Ter. Cars .5C 122
Cricketers Wlk. SE26 .2G 109
Cricketfield Rd. E5 .9F 44
Cricket Fld. Rd. Uxb .4B 142
Cricketfield Rd. W Dray .5G 143
Cricket Grn. Mitc .7D 106
Cricket Ground Rd. Chst .5M 111 (in two parts)
Cricket La. Beck .3J 109
Cricket Way. Wey .4C 116
Cricklade Av. SW2 .8J 91
Cricklade Av. Romf .6H 35
Cricklewood. .8J 41
Cricklewood B'way. NW2 .8G 41
Cricklewood La. NW2 .9H 41
Cridland St. E15 .4D 62
Crieff Ct. Tedd .4G 103
Crieff Rd. SW18 .5A 90
Criffel Av. SW2 .8H 91
Crimscott St. SE1 .4C 76
Crimsworth Rd. SW8 .9H 75
Crinan St. N1 .5J 59
Cringle St. SW8 .8G 75
Cripplegate St. EC2 .8A 60
Cripps Grn. Hay .7F 52
Crispe Ho. N1 .4K 59 (off Barnsbury Est.)
Crispe Ho. Bark .5B 64
Crispen Rd. Felt .1J 101
Crispian Clo. NW10 .9C 40
Crispin Clo. Asht .9K 133
Crispin Clo. Croy .4J 123
Crispin Cres. Croy .5H 123
Crispin Lodge. N11 .5D 26
Crispin Rd. Edgw .6A 24
Crispin St. E1 .8D 60
Crispin Ter. Wfd G .6H 31
Crisp Rd. W6 .6G 73
Cristowe Rd. SW6 .1K 89
Criterion Ct. E8 .3D 60 (off Middleton Rd.)
Criterion M. N19 .7H 43
Criterion Theatre. .1G 75 (off Piccadilly)
Crittall's Corner (Junct.) .4F 112
Crockenhill. .1B 130
Crockenhill La. Eyns .2E 130
Crockenhill Rd. Orp & Swan .9H 113
Crockerton Rd. SW17 .8D 90
Crockham Way. SE9 .1L 111
Crocus Clo. Croy .3H 125
Crocus Fld. Barn .8K 13
Croft Av. W Wick .3A 126
Croft Clo. NW7 .3C 24
Croft Clo. Belv .6K 81
Croft Clo. Chst .2K 111
Croft Clo. Hay .8A 68
Croft Clo. Uxb .3E 142
Croft Ct. SE13 .5A 94
Croft Ct. Borwd .5B 12
Croft Ct. Ruis .6D 36
Croftdown Rd. NW5 .8E 42
Croft End Clo. Chess .5K 119 (off Ashcroft Rd.)
Crofters Clo. Iswth .4B 86
Crofters Clo. Stanw .5A 144
Crofters Ct. SE8 .5J 77 (off Croft St.)
Crofters Mead. Croy .1K 139
Crofters Rd. N'wd .4C 20
Crofters Way. NW1 .4H 59
Croft Gdns. W7 .3E 70
Croft Gdns. Ruis .6C 36
Croft Ho. E17 .2M 45
Croft Ho. W10 .6J 57 (off Third Av.)
Croftleigh Av. Purl .8L 137
Croft Lodge Clo. Wfd G .6F 30
Croft M. N12 .3A 26
Crofton. .4B 128
Crofton. Asht .9J 133
Crofton Av. W4 .8B 72
Crofton Av. Bex .6H 97
Crofton Av. Orp .4A 128
Crofton Av. W on T .5G 117
Croftongate Way. SE4 .4J 93
Crofton Gro. E4 .4B 30
Crofton La. Orp .4B 128
Crofton Park. .4K 93
Crofton Pk. Rd. SE4 .5K 93
Crofton Rd. E13 .7F 62
Crofton Rd. SE5 .9C 76
Crofton Rd. Orp .5L 127
Crofton Ter. E5 .1J 61
Crofton Ter. Rich .3K 87
Crofton Way. Barn .8M 13
Crofton Way. Enf .4L 15
Croft Rd. SW16 .5L 107
Croft Rd. SW19 .4A 106
Croft Rd. Brom .3E 110
Croft Rd. Enf .3J 17
Croft Rd. Sutt .7C 122
Crofts Ho. E2 .5E 60 (off Teale St.)
Croftside, The. SE25 .7E 108
Crofts La. N22 .7L 27
Crofts Rd. Harr .4E 38
Crofts St. E1 .1E 76
Crofts, The. Shep .8C 100
Croft St. SE8 .5J 77
Crofts Vs. Harr .4E 38
Croft, The. E4 .2C 30
Croft, The. NW10 .5D 56
Croft, The. W5 .8J 55
Croft, The. Barn .6J 13
Croft, The. Eps .6D 134
Croft, The. Houn .7J 69
Croft, The. Lou .4L 19
Croft, The. Pinn .5K 37
Croft, The. Ruis .9G 37
Croft, The. Swan .7A 114
Croft, The. Wemb .1G 55
Croftway. NW3 .9L 41
Croftway. Rich .9F 86
Croft Way. Sidc .9C 96
Crogsland Rd. NW1 .3E 58
Croham Clo. S Croy .9C 124
Croham Mnr. Rd. S Croy .9C 124
Croham Mt. S Croy .9C 124
Croham Pk. Av. S Croy .7C 124
Croham Rd. S Croy .7C 124
Croham Valley Rd. S Croy .8E 124
Croindene Rd. SW16 .5J 107
Crokesley Ho. Edgw .9A 24 (off Burnt Oak B'way.)
Cromartie Rd. N19 .5H 43
Cromarty Ct. SW2 .4K 91
Cromarty Ho. E1 .8J 61 (off Ben Jonson Rd.)
Cromarty Rd. Edgw .2M 23
Cromberdale Ct. N17 .8E 28 (off Spencer Rd.)
Crombie Clo. Ilf .3K 47
Crombie M. SW11 .1C 90
Crombie Rd. Sidc .7B 96
Crome Ho. N'holt .5J 53 (off Parkfield Dri.)
Cromer Clo. Uxb .9A 52
Cromerhyde. Mord .9M 105
Cromer Pl. Orp .3C 128
Cromer Rd. E10 .5B 46
Cromer Rd. N17 .9E 28
Cromer Rd. SE25 .7F 108
Cromer Rd. SW17 .3E 106
Cromer Rd. Chad H .4J 49
Cromer Rd. Horn .5H 51
Cromer Rd. H'row A .1E 144
Cromer Rd. New Bar .6A 14
Cromer Rd. Romf .4A 50
Cromer Rd. Wat .2G 9
Cromer Rd. Wfd G .4E 30
Cromer Rd. W. H'row A .2E 144
Cromer St. WC1 .6J 59

Cromer Ter.—Culverhouse

Cromer Ter. E8 1E 60
Cromer Vs. Rd. SW18 5K 89
Cromford Clo. Orp 5C 128
Cromford Path. E5 9H 45
Cromford Rd. SW18 4L 89
Cromford Way. N Mald 5B 104
Cromlix Clo. Chst 6M 111
Crompton Ho. SE1 4A 76 (off County St.)
Crompton Ho. W2 7B 58 (off Hall Pl.)
Crompton Pl. Enf 2L 17
Crompton St. W2 7B 58
Cromwell Av. N6 6F 42
Cromwell Av. W6 6F 72
Cromwell Av. Brom 8F 110
Cromwell Av. Chesh 3B 6
Cromwell Av. N Mald 9D 104
Cromwell Cen. NW10 6B 56
Cromwell Cen. Ilf 5F 32
Cromwell Cen., The. Dag 5K 49 (off Selinas La.)
Cromwell Clo. E1 2E 76
Cromwell Clo. N2 2B 42
Cromwell Clo. W3 2A 72 (in two parts)
Cromwell Clo. Brom 8F 110
Cromwell Clo. W on T 3F 116
Cromwell Ct. Enf 7H 17
Cromwell Cres. SW5 5L 73
Cromwell Gdns. SW7 4B 74
Cromwell Gro. W6 4G 73
Cromwell Highwalk. EC2 8A 60 (off Beech St.)
Cromwell Ho. Croy 5M 123
Cromwell Ind. Est. E10 6J 45
Cromwell Lodge. E1 7G 61 (off Cleveland Gro.)
Cromwell Lodge. Bexh 4J 97
Cromwell M. SW7 5B 74
Cromwell Pl. EC2 8A 60 (off Beech St.)
Cromwell Pl. N6 6F 42
Cromwell Pl. SW7 5B 74
Cromwell Pl. SW14 2A 88
Cromwell Rd. E7 3G 63
Cromwell Rd. E17 3A 46
Cromwell Rd. N3 8A 26
Cromwell Rd. N10 7E 26 (in two parts)
Cromwell Rd. SW5 & SW7 5L 73
Cromwell Rd. SW9 9M 75
Cromwell Rd. SW19 2L 105
Cromwell Rd. Beck 6J 109
Cromwell Rd. Borwd 3J 11
Cromwell Rd. Chesh 1B 6
Cromwell Rd. Croy 2B 124
Cromwell Rd. Felt 7F 84
Cromwell Rd. Hay 9B 52
Cromwell Rd. Houn 3L 85
Cromwell Rd. King T 5J 103
Cromwell Rd. Tedd 3E 102
Cromwell Rd. W on T 3F 116
Cromwell Rd. Wemb 5J 55
Cromwell Rd. Wor Pk 5B 120
Cromwells Mere. Romf 6B 34
Cromwell St. Houn 3L 85
Cromwell Tower. EC2 8A 60 (off Beech St.)
Crondace Rd. SW6 9L 73
Crondall Ct. N1 5C 60 (off St John's Est.)
Crondall St. N1 5B 60
Crone Ct. NW6 5K 57 (off Denmark Rd.)
Cronin St. SE15 8D 76
Crooked Billet (Junct.) 8L 29
Crooked Billet. SW19 3G 105
Crooked Billet Yd. E2 6C 60
Crooked Mile. Wal A 2J 7
Crooked Usage. N3 1J 41
Crooke Rd. SE8 6J 77
Crookham Rd. SW6 9K 73
Crook Log. Bexh 2H 97
Crookston Rd. SE9 2L 95
Croombs Rd. E16 8G 63
Croom's Hill. SE10 8A 78
Croom's Hill Gro. SE10 8A 78
Cropley Ct. N1 5B 60 (off Cropley St., in two parts)
Cropley St. N1 5B 60
Croppath Rd. Dag 9L 49
Cropthorne Ct. W9 6A 58
Crosbie. NW9 9D 24
Crosbie Ho. E17 1A 46 (off Prospect Hill)
Crosby Clo. Felt 9J 85
Crosby Ct. SE1 3B 76 (off Crosby Row)
Crosby Ct. Chig 3E 32
Crosby Ho. E7 2E 62
Crosby Ho. E14 4A 78 (off Manchester Rd.)
Crosby Rd. E7 2E 62
Crosby Rd. Dag 5M 65
Crosby Row. SE1 3B 76
Crosby Sq. EC3 9C 60
Crosby Wlk. E8 2D 60
Crosby Wlk. SW2 6L 91
Crosby Way. SW2 6L 91
Crosfield Ct. Wat 7G 9
Crosier Clo. SE3 9J 79
Crosier Rd. Ick 9A 36
Crosier Way. Ruis 8C 36
Crosland Pl. SW11 2E 90
Cross Av. SE10 7B 78
Crossbow Ho. W13 2F 70 (off Sherwood Clo.)
Crossbow Rd. Chig 5D 32
Crossbrook Rd. SE3 1J 95
Crossbrook St. Chesh 4D 6
Cross Clo. SE15 1F 92
Cross Deep. Twic 8D 86
Cross Deep Gdns. Twic 8D 86
Crossfield Ho. W11 1J 73 (off Mary Pl.)
Crossfield Rd. N17 1A 44
Crossfield Rd. NW3 2B 58
Crossfields. Lou 7M 19
Crossfield St. SE8 8L 77 (in two parts)
Crossford St. SW9 1K 91
Cross Ga. Edgw 3L 23
Crossgate. Gnfd 2F 54
Cross Keys Clo. N9 2E 28 (off Lacey Clo.)
Cross Keys Clo. W1 8E 58
Cross Keys Sq. EC1 8A 60 (off Little Britain)
Cross Lances Rd. Houn 3M 85
Crossland Rd. T Hth 1M 123
Crosslands Av. W5 2K 71
Crosslands Av. S'hall 6K 69
Crosslands Rd. Eps 8B 120
Cross La. EC3 1C 76
Cross La. N8 1K 43 (in two parts)
Cross La. Bex 6K 97
Crossleigh Ct. SE14 8K 77 (off New Cross Rd.)
Crosslet St. SE17 5B 76
Crosslet Va. SE10 9M 77
Crossley Clo. Big H 7H 141
Crossley St. N7 2L 59
Crossmead. SE9 7K 95
Crossmead. Wat 8F 8
Crossmead Av. Gnfd 6L 53
Crossmount Ho. SE5 8A 76 (off Bowyer St.)
Crossness Footpath. Eri 2K 81
Crossness La. SE28 1H 81
Crossness Rd. Bark 6D 64
Cross Rd. E4 1B 30
Cross Rd. N11 5F 26
Cross Rd. N22 7L 27
Cross Rd. SE5 1C 92
Cross Rd. SW19 4L 105
Cross Rd. Belm 2L 135
Cross Rd. Brom 4J 127
Cross Rd. Chad H 5G 49
Cross Rd. Croy 3B 124
Cross Rd. Dart 5G 99
Cross Rd. Enf 6C 16
Cross Rd. Felt 1J 101
Cross Rd. Harr 2B 38
Cross Rd. Hawl 1K 115
Cross Rd. King T 4K 103
Cross Rd. Orp 9F 112
Cross Rd. Purl 5M 137
Cross Rd. Romf 2L 49
Cross Rd. Sidc 1F 112
Cross Rd. S Harr 8M 37
Cross Rd. Sutt 7B 122
Cross Rd. Uxb 3A 142
Cross Rd. Wal X 6E 6
Cross Rd. Wat 8J 9
Cross Rd. W'stone 9E 22
Cross Rd. Wey 5B 116
Cross Rd. Wfd G 6K 31
Cross Roads. H Bee 4F 18
Cross St. N1 4M 59
Cross St. N18 5E 28
Cross St. SE5 2B 92
Cross St. SW13 1C 88
Cross St. Eri 7C 82
Cross St. Hamp H 2A 102
Cross St. Uxb 3A 142
Cross St. Wat 5G 9
Cross Ter. Wal A 7L 7 (off Stonyshotts)
Crossthwaite Av. SE5 3B 92
Crosswall. EC3 1D 76
Crossway. N12 6B 26
Crossway. N16 1C 60
Crossway. NW9 2D 40
Crossway. SE28 9F 64
Crossway. SW20 8G 105
Crossway. W13 7E 54
Crossway. Dag 8G 49
Crossway. Enf 9C 16
Crossway. Hay 2E 68
Crossway. Orp 8B 112
Cross Way. Pinn 9F 20
Crossway. Ruis 9G 37
Crossway. W on T 4F 116
Cross Way. Wfd G 4G 31
Crossway Ct. SE4 1J 93
Crossways. N21 8A 16
Crossways. Lou 7L 19
Crossways. Romf 1F 50
Crossways. S Croy 9J 125
Crossways. Sun 4D 100
Crossways. Sutt 1B 136
Crossways Boulevd. Dart 3M 99
Crossways Rd. Beck 8L 109
Crossways Rd. Mitc 7F 106
Crossways Ter. E5 9G 45
Crossways, The. Houn 8K 69
Crossways, The. Surb 3M 119
Crossways, The. Wemb 7L 39
Crossway, The. N22 7M 27
Crossway, The. SE9 8H 95
Cross Way, The. Harr 9C 22
Crossway, The. Uxb 5D 142
Crosswell Clo. Shep 6A 100
Croston St. E8 4E 60
Crothall Clo. N13 3K 27
Crouch Av. Bark 5F 64
Crouch Clo. Beck 3L 109
Crouch Cft. SE9 9L 95
Crouch End. 5H 43
Crouch End Hill. N8 5H 43
Crouch Hall Ct. N19 6J 43
Crouch Hall Rd. N8 4H 43
Crouch Hill. N8 & N4 4J 43
Crouchman's Clo. SE26 9D 92
Crouch Rd. NW10 3B 56
Crowborough Clo. Warl 9J 139
Crowborough Dri. Warl 9J 139
Crowborough Path. Wat 4H 21
Crowborough Rd. SW17 3E 106
Crowden Way. SE28 1G 81
Crowder St. E1 1F 76
Crowfield Ho. N5 9A 44
Crowfoot Clo. E9 1K 61
Crowhill. Orp 2L 141
Crowhurst Clo. SW9 1L 91
Crowhurst Ho. SW9 1K 91 (off Aytoun Rd.)
Crowhurst Way. Orp 9G 113
Crowland Av. Hay 5C 68
Crowland Gdns. N14 9J 15
Crowland Ho. NW8 4A 58 (off Springfield Rd.)
Crowland Rd. N15 3D 44
Crowland Rd. T Hth 8B 108
Crowlands Av. Romf 4M 49
Crowland Ter. N1 3B 60
Crowland Wlk. Mord 1M 121
Crow La. Romf 5K 49
Crowley Cres. Croy 7L 123
Crowline Wlk. N1 2A 60
Crowmarsh Gdns. SE23 6G 93
Crown Arc. King T 6H 103
Crown Ash Hill. Big H 6F 140
Crown Ash La. Warl & Big H 8E 140
Crownbourne Ct. Sutt 6M 121 (off St Nicholas Way)
Crown Bldgs. E4 1A 30
Crown Clo. E3 4L 61
Crown Clo. NW6 2M 57
Crown Clo. NW7 2D 24
Crown Clo. Hay 3D 68
Crown Clo. Orp 7E 128
Crown Clo. W on T 2G 117
Crown Clo. Bus. Cen. E3 4L 61 (off Crown Clo.)
Crown Cotts. Romf 8L 33
Crown Ct. EC4 9A 60 (off Cheapside)
Crown Ct. N10 7E 26
Crown Ct. SE12 5F 94
Crown Ct. WC2 9J 59
Crown Dale. SE19 3M 107
Crowndale Ct. NW1 5H 59 (off Crowndale Rd.)
Crowndale Rd. NW1 5G 59
Crownfield Av. Ilf 4C 48
Crownfield Rd. E15 9B 46
Crown Hill. Croy 4A 124
Crown Hill Rd. NW10 4D 56
Crownhill Rd. Wfd G 7J 31
Crown Ho. Ruis 6E 36
Crown La. N14 1G 27
Crown La. SW16 2L 107
Crown La. Brom 9H 111
Crown La. Chst 5A 112
Crown La. Mord 8L 105
Crown La. Gdns. SW16 2L 107
Crown La. Spur. Brom 1H 127
Crown Lodge. SW3 5C 74
Crownmead Way. Romf 2M 49
Crown M. E13 4G 63
Crown M. W6 5E 72
Crown Office Row. EC4 1L 75
Crown Pde. N14 1G 27
Crown Pde. SE19 3M 107
Crown Pde. Mord 7L 105
Crown Pas. SW1 2G 75
Crown Pas. King T 6H 103
Crown Pas. Wat 6G 9
Crown Pl. EC2 8C 60 (in two parts)
Crown Pl. NW5 2F 58
Crown Reach. SW1 6H 75
Crown Ri. Wat 7G 5
Crown Rd. N10 7E 26
Crown Rd. Borwd 3L 11
Crown Rd. Enf 6F 16
Crown Rd. Ilf 2B 48
Crown Rd. Mord 8M 105
Crown Rd. N Mald 5A 104
Crown Rd. Orp 7E 128
Crown Rd. Ruis 1H 53
Crown Rd. Sutt 6M 121
Crown Rd. Twic 5F 86
Crownstone Ct. SW2 4L 91
Crownstone Rd. SW2 4L 91
Crown St. SE5 8A 76
Crown St. W3 2M 71
Crown St. Dag 2A 66 (in two parts)
Crown St. Harr 6B 38
Crown Ter. N14 1H 27 (off Crown La.)
Crown Ter. Rich 3K 87
Crown Trad. Cen. Hay 3C 68
Crowntree Clo. Iswth 7D 70
Crown Wlk. Uxb 3A 142
Crown Wlk. Wemb 8K 39
Crown Way. W Dray 2K 143
Crown Wharf. E14 2A 78 (off Coldharbour)
Crown Wharf. SE8 6K 77 (off Grove St.)
Crown Woods. SE18 1M 95
Crown Woods Way. SE9 4B 96
Crown Yd. Houn 2A 86
Crowshott Av. Stan 9G 23
Crows Rd. E15 6B 62
Crows Rd. Bark 2M 63
Crowther Av. Bren 5J 71
Crowther Clo. SW6 7K 73 (off Buckers All.)
Crowther Rd. SE25 9E 108
Crowthorne Clo. SW18 6K 89
Crowthorne Rd. W10 9H 57
Croxall Ho. W on T 1G 117
Croxdale Rd. Borwd 4K 11
Croxden Clo. Edgw 1L 39
Croxden Wlk. Mord 1A 122
Croxford Gdns. N22 7M 27
Croxford Way. Romf 6B 50
Croxley Centre. 8B 8
Croxley Clo. Orp 6F 112
Croxley Grn. Orp 5F 112
Croxley Rd. W9 6K 57
Croxley Vw. Wat 8C 8
Croxted Clo. SE21 6A 92
Croxted M. SE24 5A 92
Croxted Rd. SE24 & SE21 5A 92
Croxteth Ho. SW8 1H 91
Croyde Av. Gnfd 6A 54
Croyde Av. Hay 5C 68
Croyde Clo. Sidc 6B 96
Croydon. 4A 124
Croydon. N17 9B 28 (off Gloucester Rd.)
Croydon Clock Tower. 5A 124 (off Katherine St.)
Croydon Crematorium. Croy 9K 107
Croydon Flyover, The. Croy 5A 124
Croydon Gro. Croy 3M 123
Croydon Ho. SE1 2L 75 (off Wootton St.)
Croydon La. Bans 6M 135
Croydon La. S. Bans 6A 136
Croydon Rd. E13 7D 62
Croydon Rd. SE20 6F 108
Croydon Rd. Beck 8H 109
Croydon Rd. Brom & Kes 5G 127
Croydon Rd. H'row A 1F 144
Croydon Rd. Mitc & Croy 8E 106
Croydon Rd. Wall & Croy 6F 122
Croydon Rd. W Wick & Brom 5C 126
Croydon Rd. Ind. Est. Beck 8H 109
Croyland Rd. N9 1E 28
Croylands Dri. Surb 2J 119
Croysdale Av. Sun 7E 100
Crozier Dri. S Croy 2F 138
Crozier Ho. SE3 2F 94
Crozier Ho. SW8 8K 75 (off Wilkinson St.)
Crozier Ter. E9 1H 61
Crucible Clo. Romf 4F 48
Crucifix La. SE1 3C 76
Cruden Ho. SE17 7M 75 (off Brandon Est.)
Cruden St. N1 4M 59
Cruikshank Ho. NW8 5C 58 (off Townshend Rd.)
Cruikshank Rd. E15 9C 46
Cruikshank St. WC1 6L 59
Crummock Gdns. NW9 3C 40
Crumpsall St. SE2 5G 81
Crundale Av. NW9 3L 39
Crunden Rd. S Croy 9B 124
Crusader Clo. Purf 5L 83
Crusader Ct. Dart 4K 99
Crusader Gdns. Croy 5C 124
Crusader Way. Wat 8D 8
Crusoe M. N16 7B 44
Crusoe Rd. Eri 6B 82
Crusoe Rd. Mitc 4D 106
Crutched Friars. EC3 1C 76
Crutchfield La. W on T 4F 116
Crutchley Rd. SE6 8C 94
Crystal Av. Horn 9J 51
Crystal Palace. 3D 108
Crystal Palace F.C. (Selhurst Pk.) 8C 108
Crystal Palace Mus. 3D 108
Crystal Palace National Sports Cen. 3E 108
Crystal Pal. Pde. SE19 3D 108
Crystal Pal. Pk. Rd. SE26 2E 108
Crystal Pal. Rd. SE22 5D 92
Crystal Pal. Sta. Rd. SE19 3E 108
Crystal Ter. SE19 3B 108
Crystal Vw. Ct. Brom 1B 110
Crystal Way. Dag 6G 49
Crystal Way. Harr 3D 38
Cuba Dri. Enf 4G 17
Cuba St. E14 3L 77
Cubitt Ho. SW4 5G 91
Cubitt Sq. S'hall 2A 70
Cubitt Steps. E14 2L 77
Cubitt St. WC1 6K 59
Cubitt St. Croy 7K 123
Cubitt's Yd. WC2 1J 75 (off James St.)
Cubitt Ter. SW4 2G 91
Cubitt Town. 5A 78
Cuckoo Av. W7 7C 54
Cuckoo Dene. W7 8B 54
Cuckoo Hall La. N9 9G 17
Cuckoo Hall Rd. N9 9G 17
Cuckoo Hill. Pinn 1G 37
Cuckoo Hill Dri. Pinn 1G 37
Cuckoo Hill Rd. Pinn 2G 37
Cuckoo La. W7 1C 70
Cuckoo Pound. Shep 9C 100
Cudas Clo. Eps 6D 120
Cuddington. SE17 5A 76 (off Deacon Way)
Cuddington Av. Wor Pk 5D 120
Cuddington Ct. Sutt 1H 135
Cuddington Glade. Eps 4L 133
Cuddington Pk. Clo. Bans 5K 135
Cuddington Way. Sutt 4H 135
Cudham Clo. Belm 2L 135
Cudham Dri. New Ad 2A 140
Cudham La. N. Cud & G Str 9C 128
Cudham Rd. Orp 3L 141
Cudham St. SE6 6A 94
Cudworth Ho. SW8 9G 75
Cudworth St. E1 7F 60
Cuff Cres. SE9 5H 95
Cuffley Av. Wat 7H 5
Cuffley Ho. W10 8G 57 (off Sutton Way)
Cuff Point. E2 6D 60 (off Columbia Rd.)
Cugley Rd. Dart 6M 99
Culford Gdns. SW3 5D 74
Culford Gro. N1 2C 60
Culford Mans. SW3 5D 74
Culford M. N1 2C 60
Culford Rd. N1 3C 60 (in two parts)
Culgaith Gdns. Enf 6J 15
Culham Ho. E2 6D 60 (off Palissy St.)
Cullen Way. NW10 7A 56
Cullera Clo. N'wd 6D 20
Cullerne Clo. Ewe 2D 134
Cullesden Rd. Kenl 7M 137
Cullinet Ho. Borwd 4B 12
Culling Rd. SE16 4G 77
Cullings Ct. Wal A 6M 7
Cullington Clo. Harr 2E 38
Cullingworth Rd. NW10 1E 56
Culloden Clo. SE16 6E 76
Culloden Rd. Enf 4M 15
Cullum St. EC3 1C 76
Cullum Welch Ct. N1 6B 60 (off Haberdasher St.)
Cullum Welch Ho. EC1 7A 60 (off Goswell Rd.)
Culmington Pde. W13 2G 71 (off Uxbridge Rd.)
Culmington Rd. W13 2G 71
Culmington Rd. S Croy 1A 138
Culmore Rd. SE15 8F 76
Culmstock Rd. SW11 4E 90
Culpeper Clo. Ilf 6M 31
Culpeper Ho. E14 9J 61
Culpepper Ct. SE11 5L 75 (off Kennington Rd.)
Culross Bldgs. NW1 5J 59 (off Battle Bri. Rd.)
Culross Clo. N15 2A 44
Culross Ho. W10 9H 57 (off Bridge Clo.)
Culross St. W1 1E 74
Culsac Rd. Surb 4J 119
Culverden Rd. SW12 8G 91
Culverden Rd. Wat 3F 20
Culver Gro. Stan 9G 23
Culverhay. Asht 8J 133
Culverhouse. WC1 8K 59 (off Red Lion Sq.)

Culverhouse Gdns.—Danby Ho.

Culverhouse Gdns. SW16 9K 91
Culverlands Clo. Stan 4F 22
Culverley Rd. SE6 7M 93
Culvers Av. Cars 4D 122
Culvers Retreat. Cars 3D 122
Culverstone Clo. Brom 1D 126
Culvers Way. Cars 4D 122
Culvert La. Uxb 5A 142
Culvert Pl. SW11 1E 90
Culvert Rd. N15 3C 44
Culvert Rd. SW11 1D 90
Culworth Ho. NW8 5C 58
(off Allitsen Rd.)
Culworth St. NW8 5C 58
Culzean Clo. SE27 9M 91
Cumberland Av. NW10 6M 55
Cumberland Av. Horn 8J 51
Cumberland Av. Well 2C 96
Cumberland Bus. Pk. NW10 6M 55
Cumberland Clo. E8 2D 60
Cumberland Clo. SW20 4H 105
Cumberland Clo. Eps 2C 134
Cumberland Clo. Horn 8J 51
Cumberland Clo. Ilf 8A 32
Cumberland Clo. Twic 5F 86
Cumberland Ct. SW1 6F 74
(off Cumberland St.)
Cumberland Ct. Croy 3B 124
Cumberland Ct. Harr 1C 38
(off Princes Dri.)
Cumberland Ct. Well 1C 96
Cumberland Cres. W14 5J 73
(in two parts)
Cumberland Dri. Bexh 8J 81
Cumberland Dri. Chess 5K 119
Cumberland Dri. Dart 6K 99
Cumberland Dri. Esh 4E 118
Cumberland Gdns. NW4 9J 25
Cumberland Gdns. WC1 6L 59
Cumberland Ga. W1 1D 74
Cumberland Ho. E16 2E 78
(off Wesley Av.)
Cumberland Ho. N9 1G 29
(off Cumberland Rd.)
Cumberland Ho. SE28 3A 80
(off Erebus Dri.)
Cumberland Ho. King T 4M 103
Cumberland Mans. W1 9D 58
(off George St.)
Cumberland Mkt. NW1 6F 58
Cumberland Mills Sq. E14 6B 78
Cumberland Pk. W3 1A 72
Cumberland Pk. Ind. Est. NW10 6E 56
Cumberland Pl. NW1 6F 58
Cumberland Pl. SE6 7D 94
Cumberland Pl. Sun 8E 100
Cumberland Rd. E12 9H 47
Cumberland Rd. E13 8F 62
Cumberland Rd. E17 9J 29
Cumberland Rd. N9 1G 29
Cumberland Rd. N22 9K 27
Cumberland Rd. SE25 1F 124
Cumberland Rd. SW13 9D 72
Cumberland Rd. W3 1A 72
Cumberland Rd. W7 3D 70
Cumberland Rd. Ashf 9B 144
Cumberland Rd. Brom 8C 110
Cumberland Rd. Harr 3M 37
Cumberland Rd. Rich 8L 71
Cumberland Rd. Stan 1K 39
Cumberlands. Kenl 7B 138
Cumberland St. SW1 6F 74
Cumberland Ter. NW1 5F 58
Cumberland Ter. M. NW1 5F 58
(off Cumberland Ter.)
Cumberland Vs. W3 1A 72
(off Cumberland Rd.)
Cumberlow Av. SE25 7D 108
Cumbernauld Gdns. Sun 2D 100
Cumberton Rd. N17 8B 28
Cumbrae Gdns. Surb 4H 119
Cumbrian Av. Bexh 1C 98
Cumbrian Gdns. NW2 7H 41
Cumbrian Way. Uxb 3B 142
Cuming Mus. 5A 76
(off Walworth Rd.)
Cummings Hall La. Noak H 3G 35
Cumming St. N1 5K 59
Cumnor Clo. SW9 1K 91
(off Robsart St.)
Cumnor Gdns. Eps 8E 120
Cumnor Ri. Kenl 9A 138
Cumnor Rd. Sutt 8A 122
Cunard Cres. N21 8B 16
Cunard Pl. EC3 9C 60
Cunard Rd. NW10 6B 56
Cunard Wlk. SE16 5H 77
Cundy Rd. E16 9G 63
Cundy St. SW1 5E 74
Cunliffe Pde. Eps 6D 120
Cunliffe Rd. Eps 6D 120
Cunliffe St. SW16 3G 107
Cunningham Av. Enf 9E 6
Cunningham Clo. Romf 3G 49
Cunningham Clo. W Wick 4M 125
Cunningham Ct. Chesh 1E 6
Cunningham Ho. SE5 8B 76
(off Elmington Est.)
Cunningham Pk. Harr 3A 38
Cunningham Pl. NW8 7B 58
Cunningham Rd. N15 2E 44
Cunningham Rd. Bans 7B 136
Cunningham Rd. Chesh 1E 6
Cunnington St. W4 4A 72
Cupar Rd. SW11 9E 74
Cupola Clo. Brom 2F 110
Curates Wlk. Dart 9H 99
Cureton St. SW1 5H 75
Curfew Ho. Bark 4A 64
Curie Ct. Harr 5F 38
Curie Gdns. NW9 9C 24
Curlew Clo. SE28 1H 81
Curlew Clo. Ilf 1L 47
Curlew Clo. S Croy 3H 139
Curlew Ct. W13 7D 54
Curlew Ct. Surb 5L 119
Curlew Ho. SE4 3J 93
(off St Norbert Rd.)
Curlew Ho. SE15 9D 76
Curlew St. SE1 3D 76
Curlew Way. Hay 8H 53
Curnick's La. SE27 1A 108
Curran Av. Sidc 4D 96
Curran Av. Wall 5E 122
Curran Clo. Uxb 7A 142
Curran Ho. SW3 5C 74
(off Lucan Pl.)
Currey Rd. Gnfd 2B 54
Curricle St. W3 2C 72
Currie Hill Clo. SW19 1K 105
Currie Ho. E14 9B 62
(off Abbott Rd.)
Curry Ri. NW7 6H 25
Cursitor St. EC4 9L 59
Curtain Pl. EC2 6C 60
(off Curtain Rd.)
Curtain Rd. EC2 7C 60
(in two parts)
Curthwaite Gdns. Enf 6H 15
Curtis Dri. W3 9B 56
Curtis Fld. Rd. SW16 1K 107
Curtis Ho. SE17 6B 76
(off Morecambe St.)
Curtis La. Wemb 1J 55
Curtismill Clo. Orp 7F 112
Curtismill Way. Orp 7F 112
Curtis Rd. Eps 6A 120
Curtis Rd. Horn 6K 51
Curtis Rd. Houn 6K 85
Curtiss Dri. Leav 7D 4
Curtis St. SE1 5D 76
Curtis Way. SE1 5D 76
Curtis Way. SE28 1F 80
Curtlington Ho. Edgw 9A 24
(off Burnt Oak B'way.)
Curvan Clo. Eps 2D 134
Curve, The. W12 1E 72
Curwen Av. E7 9F 46
Curwen Rd. W12 3E 72
Curzon Av. Enf 7H 17
Curzon Av. Stan 8E 22
Curzon Cinema. 2F 74
(off Curzon St.)
Curzon Cinema. 1H 75
(off Shaftesbury Av.)
Curzon Clo. Orp 6B 128
Curzon Ct. SW6 9A 74
(off Imperial Rd.)
Curzon Cres. NW10 3C 56
Curzon Cres. Bark 6D 64
Curzon Ga. W1 2E 74
Curzon Ga. Ct. Wat 3E 8
Curzon Pl. W1 2E 74
Curzon Pl. Pinn 3G 37
Curzon Rd. N10 9F 26
Curzon Rd. W5 7F 54
Curzon Rd. T Hth 1L 123
Curzon St. W1 2E 74
Cusack Clo. Twic 1D 102
Cussans Ho. Wat 8C 8
Cussons Clo. Chesh 2A 6
Custance Ho. N1 5B 60
(off Provost Est.)
Custance St. N1 6B 60
Custom House. 9G 63
Custom House. 1C 76
Custom Ho. Reach. SE16 3K 77
Custom Ho. Wlk. EC3 1C 76
Cutbush Ho. N7 1H 59
Cutcombe Rd. SE5 1A 92
Cuthberga Clo. Bark 3A 64
Cuthbert Gdns. SE25 7C 108
Cuthbert Harrowing Ho. EC1 7A 60
(off Golden La. Est.)
Cuthbert Ho. W2 8B 58
(off Hall Pl.)
Cuthbert Rd. E17 1A 46
Cuthbert Rd. N18 5E 28
Cuthbert Rd. Croy 4M 123
Cuthbert St. W2 8B 58
Cuthill Wlk. SE5 9B 76
Cutlers Gdns. E1 9C 60
(off Cutlers St.)
Cutlers Sq. E14 5L 77
Cutler St. E1 9C 60
Cut, The. SE1 3L 75
Cutthroat All. Rich 8G 87
Cutty Sark Clipper Ship. 7A 78
Cutty Sark Gdns. SE10 7A 78
(off King William Wlk.)
Cuxton. Orp 9A 112
Cuxton Clo. Bexh 4J 97
Cyclamen Clo. Hamp 3L 101
Cyclamen Rd. Swan 8B 114
Cyclamen Way. Eps 7A 120
Cyclops M. E14 5L 77
Cygnet Av. Felt 6G 85
Cygnet Clo. NW10 1B 56
Cygnet Clo. Borwd 3A 12
Cygnet Clo. N'wd 6A 20
Cygnets, The. Felt 1J 101
Cygnet St. E1 7D 60
Cygnet Way. Hay 8H 53
Cygnus Bus. Cen. NW10 1D 56
Cymbeline Ct. Harr 4D 38
(off Gayton Rd.)
Cynthia St. N1 5K 59
Cyntra Pl. E8 3F 60
Cypress Av. Twic 6A 86
Cypress Clo. Wal A 7K 7
Cypress Gdns. SE4 4J 93
Cypress Gro. Ilf 6C 32
Cypress Ho. SE14 9H 77
Cypress Ho. SE16 3H 77
(off Woodland Cres.)
Cypress Path. Romf 7H 35
Cypress Pl. W1 7G 59
Cypress Rd. SE25 6C 108
Cypress Rd. Harr 9B 22
Cypress Tree Clo. Sidc 7D 96
Cypress Wlk. Wat 8F 4
Cypress Way. Bans 6H 135
Cyprus. 1L 79
Cyprus Av. N3 9J 25
Cyprus Clo. N4 4M 43
Cyprus Gdns. N3 9J 25
Cyprus Pl. E2 5G 61
Cyprus Pl. E6 1L 79
Cyprus Rd. N3 9K 25
Cyprus Rd. N9 2D 28
Cyprus St. E2 5G 61
(in two parts)
Cyrena Rd. SE22 5D 92
Cyril Lodge. Sidc 1E 112
Cyril Mans. SW11 9D 74
Cyril Rd. Bexh 1J 97
Cyril Rd. Orp 2E 128
Cyrus Ho. EC1 7M 59
(off Cyrus St.)
Cyrus St. EC1 7M 59
(off Cyrus St.)
Czar St. SE8 7L 77

D

Dabbling Clo. Eri 7F 82
Dabbs Hill La. N'holt 2K 53
(in two parts)
Dabbs La. EC1 7L 59
(off Farringdon Rd.)
D'Abernon Chase. Lea 6E 132
D'Abernon Clo. Esh 6L 117
Dabin Cres. SE10 9A 78
Dacca St. SE8 7K 77
Dace Rd. E3 4L 61
Dacre Av. Ilf 9L 31
Dacre Clo. Chig 4A 32
Dacre Clo. Gnfd 5M 53
Dacre Gdns. SE13 3C 94
Dacre Gdns. Borwd 7B 12
Dacre Gdns. Chig 4A 32
Dacre Ho. SW3 7B 74
(off Beaufort St.)
Dacre Ind. Est. Chesh 2F 6
Dacre Pk. SE13 2C 94
Dacre Pl. SE13 2C 94
Dacre Rd. E11 6D 46
Dacre Rd. E13 4F 62
Dacre Rd. Croy 2J 123
Dacres Ho. SW4 2F 90
Dacres Rd. SE23 8H 93
Dacre St. SW1 4H 75
Dade Way. S'hall 6K 69
Daerwood Clo. Brom 3K 127
Daffodil Clo. Croy 3H 125
Daffodil Gdns. Ilf 1M 63
Daffodil Pl. Hamp 3L 101
Daffodil St. W12 1D 72
Dafforne Rd. SW17 9E 90
Da Gama Pl. E14 6L 77
Dagenham. 2L 65
Dagenham & Redbridge F.C. 1M 65
Dagenham Av. Dag 4J 65
(in two parts)
Dagenham Leisure Pk. Dag 4J 65
Dagenham Rd. E10 6K 45
Dagenham Rd. Dag 9A 50
Dagenham Rd. Rain 3B 66
Dagenham Rd. Romf 5B 50
Dagger La. Els 8E 10
Dagmar Av. Wemb 9K 39
Dagmar Ct. E14 4A 78
Dagmar Gdns. NW10 5H 57
Dagmar M. S'hall 4J 69
(off Dagmar Rd.)
Dagmar Pas. N1 4M 59
(off Cross St.)
Dagmar Rd. N4 5L 43
Dagmar Rd. N15 2B 44
Dagmar Rd. N22 8H 27
Dagmar Rd. SE5 9C 76
Dagmar Rd. SE25 9C 108
Dagmar Rd. Dag 3A 66
Dagmar Rd. King T 5K 103
Dagmar Rd. S'hall 4J 69
Dagmar Ter. N1 4M 59
Dagnall Cres. Uxb 8A 142
Dagnall Pk. SE25 1C 124
Dagnall Rd. SE25 9C 108
Dagnall St. SW11 1D 90
Dagnam Pk. Clo. Romf 5L 35
Dagnam Pk. Dri. Romf 5J 35
Dagnam Pk. Gdns. Romf 6L 35
(in two parts)
Dagnam Pk. Sq. Romf 6M 35
Dagnan Rd. SW12 6F 90
Dagobert Ho. E1 8G 61
(off Smithy St.)
Dagonet Gdns. Brom 9E 94
Dagonet Rd. Brom 9E 94
Dahlia Dri. Swan 6D 114
Dahlia Gdns. Ilf 2M 63
Dahlia Gdns. Mitc 8H 107
Dahlia Rd. SE2 5F 80
Dahomey Rd. SW16 3G 107
Daimler Way. Wall 9J 123
Dain Ct. W8 5L 73
(off Lexham Gdns.)
Daines Clo. E12 8K 47
Dainford Clo. Brom 2B 110
Dainton Clo. Brom 5F 110
Daintry Clo. Harr 2E 38
Daintry Lodge. N'wd 7D 20
Daintry Way. E9 2K 61
Dairsie Ct. Brom 5G 111
Dairsie Rd. SE9 2L 95
Dairy Clo. NW10 4E 56
Dairy Clo. Brom 4F 110
Dairy Clo. S at H 4M 115
Dairy Clo. T Hth 6A 108
Dairyglen Av. Chesh 4E 6
Dairy La. SE18 5K 79
Dairyman Clo. NW2 8H 41
Dairy M. SW9 2J 91
Dairy M. Wat 7E 8
Dairy Wlk. SW19 1J 105
Dairy Way. Ab L 2D 4
Daisy Clo. Croy 3H 125
Daisy Dobbings Wlk. N19 5J 43
(off Jessie Blythe La.)
Daisy La. SW6 2L 89
Daisy Rd. E16 7C 62
Daisy Rd. E18 9F 30
Dakota Clo. Wall 9K 123
Dakota Gdns. E6 7J 63
Dakota Gdns. N'holt 6J 53
Dalberg Rd. SW2 3L 91
(in two parts)
Dalberg Way. SE2 4H 81
Dalby Rd. SW18 3A 90
Dalbys Cres. N17 6C 28
Dalby St. NW5 2F 58
Dalcross Rd. Houn 1J 85
Dale Av. Edgw 8K 23
Dale Av. Houn 2J 85
Dalebury Rd. SW17 8D 90
Dale Clo. SE3 2E 94
Dale Clo. Dart 5D 98
Dale Clo. New Bar 8M 13
Dale Clo. Pinn 8F 20
Dale Ct. King T 4K 103
(off York Rd.)
Dale Ct. Wat 7E 4
Dale Dri. Hay 7D 52
Dale End. Dart 5D 98
Dale Gdns. Wfd G 4F 30
Dalegarth Gdns. Purl 5B 138
Dale Grn. Rd. N11 3F 26
Dale Gro. N12 5A 26
Daleham Dri. Uxb 9F 142
Daleham Gdns. NW3 1B 58
Daleham M. NW3 2B 58
Dalehead. NW1 5G 59
(off Harrington Sq.)
Dale Ho. NW8 4A 58
(off Boundary Rd.)
Dale Ho. SE4 3J 93
Dale Lodge. N6 4G 43
Dalemain M. E16 2E 78
Dale Pk. Av. Cars 4D 122
Dale Pk. Rd. SE19 5A 108
Dale Rd. NW5 1E 58
Dale Rd. SE17 7M 75
Dale Rd. Dart 5D 98
Dale Rd. Gnfd 8M 53
Dale Rd. Purl 4L 137
Dale Rd. Sun 4D 100
Dale Rd. Sutt 6K 121
Dale Rd. Swan 6A 114
Dale Rd. W on T 2D 116
Dale Row. W11 9J 57
Daleside. Orp 7E 128
Daleside Clo. Orp 8E 128
Daleside Gdns. Chig 3A 32
Daleside Rd. SW16 2F 106
Daleside Rd. Eps 8B 120
Dales Path. Borwd 7B 12
Dales Rd. Borwd 7B 12
Dalestone M. Romf 6F 34
Dale St. W4 6C 72
Dale, The. Kes 6H 127
Dale, The. Wal A 7L 7
Dale Vw. Eri 1D 98
Dale Vw. Av. E4 2A 30
Dale Vw. Cres. E4 2A 30
Dale Vw. Gdns. E4 3B 30
Daleview Rd. N15 4C 44
Dale Wlk. Dart 7M 99
Dalewood Clo. Horn 5K 51
Dalewood Gdns. Wor Pk 4F 120
Dale Wood Rd. Orp 2C 128
Daley Ho. W12 9F 56
Daley St. E9 2H 61
Daley Thompson Way. SW8 1F 90
Dalgarno Gdns. W10 8G 57
Dalgarno Way. W10 7G 57
Dalgleish St. E14 9J 61
Daling Way. E3 4J 61
Dali Universe. 3K 75
Dalkeith Ct. SW1 5H 75
(off Vincent St.)
Dalkeith Gro. Stan 5H 23
Dalkeith Ho. SW9 9M 75
(off Lothian Rd.)
Dalkeith Rd. SE21 7A 92
Dalkeith Rd. Ilf 8A 48
Dallas Rd. NW4 5E 40
Dallas Rd. SE26 9F 92
Dallas Rd. W5 8K 55
Dallas Rd. Sutt 8J 121
Dallas Ter. Hay 4D 68
Dallega Clo. Hay 1B 68
Dallinger Rd. SE12 5D 94
Dalling Rd. W6 5F 72
Dallington Clo. W on T 8G 117
Dallington St. EC1 7M 59
Dallin Rd. SE18 8M 79
Dallin Rd. Bexh 3H 97
Dalmain Rd. SE23 7H 93
Dalmally Rd. Croy 2D 124
Dalmeny Av. N7 9H 43
Dalmeny Av. SW16 6L 107
Dalmeny Clo. Wemb 2G 55
Dalmeny Cres. Houn 3B 86
Dalmeny Rd. N7 8H 43
(in three parts)
Dalmeny Rd. Cars 9E 122
Dalmeny Rd. Eri 9M 81
Dalmeny Rd. New Bar 8A 14
Dalmeny Rd. Wor Pk 5F 120
Dalmeyer Rd. NW10 2D 56
Dalmore Av. Clay 8D 118
Dalmore Rd. SE21 8A 92
Dalo Lodge. E3 8L 61
(off Gale St.)
Dalrymple Clo. N14 9H 15
Dalrymple Rd. SE4 3J 93
Dalston. 3D 60
Dalston Gdns. Stan 8J 23
Dalston La. E8 2D 60
Dalton Av. Mitc 6C 106
Dalton Clo. Hay 7B 52
Dalton Clo. Orp 5C 128
Dalton Clo. Purl 4A 138
Dalton Ho. SE14 7H 77
(off John Williams Clo.)
Dalton Ho. SW1 6F 74
(off Ebury Bri. Rd.)
Dalton Ho. Stan 5E 22
Dalton Rd. W'stone 9B 22
Daltons Rd. Orp & Swan 5M 129
Dalton St. SE27 8M 91
Dalton Way. Wat 7H 9
Dalwood St. SE5 9C 76
Daly Ct. E15 1M 61
Dalyell Rd. SW9 2K 91
Damascene Wlk. SE21 7A 92
Damask Cres. E16 7C 62
Damer Ter. SW10 8A 74
Dames Rd. E7 8E 46
Dame St. N1 5A 60
Damien Ct. E1 9F 60
(off Damien St.)
Damien St. E1 9F 60
Damon Clo. Sidc 9F 96
Damory Ho. SE16 5F 76
(off Abbeyfield Est.)
Damson Ct. Swan 8B 114
Damson Dri. Hay 1E 68
Damsonwood Rd. S'hall 4L 69
Danbrook Rd. SW16 5J 107
Danbury Clo. Romf 1H 49
Danbury Mans. Bark 3M 63
(off Whiting Av.)
Danbury M. Wall 6F 122
Danbury Rd. Lou 9J 19
Danbury Rd. Rain 4D 66
Danbury St. N1 5M 59
Danbury Way. Wfd G 6G 31
Danby Ct. Enf 5A 16
(off Horseshoe La.)
Danby Ho. E9 3G 61
(off Frampton Pk. Rd.)

Danby St.—Debden Ho.

Danby St. SE15 .... 2D 92
Dancer Rd. SW6 .... 9K 73
Dancer Rd. Rich 2L 87
Dancers Hill Rd. Barn 1G 13
Dandelion Clo. Rush G 7C 50
Dando Cres. SE3 .... 2F 94
Dandridge Clo. SE10 .... 6D 78
Dandridge Ho. E1 .... 8D 60
(off Lamb St.)
Danebury. New Ad 8A 126
Danebury Av. SW15 .... 5C 88
(in two parts)
Daneby Rd. SE6 .... 9M 93
Dane Clo. Bex 6L 97
Dane Clo. Orp 7B 128
Danecourt Gdns. Croy 5D 124
Danecroft Rd. SE24 .... 4A 92
Danehill Wlk. Sidc 9E 96
Danehurst Ct. Eps 5D 134
Danehurst Gdns. Ilf 3J 47
Danehurst St. SW6 .... 9J 73
Daneland. Barn 8D 14
Danemead Gro. N'holt 1M 53
Danemere St. SW15 .... 2G 89
Dane Pl. E3 .... 5J 61
Dane Rd. N18 .... 3G 29
Dane Rd. SW19 .... 5A 106
Dane Rd. W13 .... 2G 71
Dane Rd. Ashf 3A 100
Dane Rd. Ilf 1A 64
Dane Rd. S'hall 1J 69
Dane Rd. Warl 9H 139
Danesbury Rd. Felt 7F 84
Danes Clo. Oxs 6A 132
Danescombe. SE12 .... 7E 94
Danes Ct. NW8 .... 4D 58
(off St Edmund's Ter.)
Danes Ct. Wemb 8M 39
Danescourt Cres. Sutt 4A 122
Danescroft. NW4 .... 3H 41
Danescroft Av. NW4 .... 3H 41
Danescroft Gdns. NW4 .... 3H 41
Danesdale Rd. E9 .... 2J 61
Danesfield. SE5 .... 7C 76
(off Albany Rd.)
Danesfield Clo. W on T 5F 116
Danes Gate. Harr 1C 38
Daneshill Dri. Oxs 6B 132
Danes Ho. W10 .... 8G 57
(off Sutton Way)
Danes Rd. Romf 5A 50
Danes, The. Park 1M 5
Dane St. WC1 .... 8K 59
Danes Way. Oxs 6B 132
Daneswood Av. SE6 .... 9A 94
Daneswood Clo. Wey 7A 116
Danethorpe Rd. Wemb 2H 55
Danetree Clo. Eps 9A 120
Danetree Rd. Eps 9A 120
Danette Gdns. Dag 7L 49
Daneville Rd. SE5 .... 9B 76
Dangan Rd. E11 .... 4E 46
Daniel Bolt Clo. E14 .... 8M 61
Daniel Clo. N18 .... 4G 29
Daniel Clo. SW17 .... 3C 106
Daniel Clo. Houn 6K 85
Daniel Ct. NW9 .... 8C 24
Daniel Gdns. SE15 .... 8D 76
Daniel Ho. N1 .... 5B 60
(off Cranston Est.)
Daniell Way. Croy 3J 123
Daniel Pl. NW4 .... 5F 40
Daniel Rd. W5 .... 1K 71
Daniels La. Warl 8K 139
Daniels Rd. SE15 .... 2G 93
Daniel Way. Bans 6M 135
Danleigh Ct. N14 .... 9H 15
Dan Leno Wlk. SW6 .... 8M 73
Dansey Pl. W1 .... 1H 75
(off Wardour St.)
Dansington Rd. Well 3E 96
Danson Cres. Well 2E 96
Danson Interchange (Junct.)
.... 4G 97
Danson La. Well 3F 96
Danson Mead. Well 2G 97
Danson Rd. SE17 .... 6M 75
Danson Rd. Bex & Bexh 5G 97
(in two parts)
Danson Underpass. Sidc 5G 97
(in two parts)
Dante Pl. SE11 .... 5M 75
(off Dante Rd.)
Dante Rd. SE11 .... 5M 75
Danube Ct. SE15 .... 8D 76
(off Daniel Gdns.)
Danube St. SW3 .... 6C 74
Danvers Ho. E1 .... 9E 60
(off Christian St.)
Danvers Rd. N8 .... 2H 43
Danvers St. SW3 .... 7B 74
Danyon Clo. Rain 5G 67
Danziger Way. Borwd 3A 12
Da Palma Ct. SW6 .... 7L 73
(off Anselm Rd.)
Daphne Ct. Wor Pk 4C 120
Daphne Gdns. E4 .... 3A 30
Daphne Ho. N22 .... 8L 27
(off Acacia Rd.)
Daphne St. SW18 .... 5A 90
Daplyn St. E1 .... 8E 60
D'Arblay St. W1 .... 9G 59
Darby Cres. Sun 6G 101
Darby Dri. Wal A 6J 7
Darby Gdns. Sun 6G 101
Darcy Av. Wall 6G 123
Darcy Clo. N20 .... 2B 26
Darcy Clo. Chesh 4E 6
D'Arcy Dri. Harr 2H 39
Darcy Gdns. Dag 4K 65
D'Arcy Gdns. Harr 2J 39
Darcy Ho. E8 .... 4F 60
(off London Fields E. Side)
D'Arcy Pl. Asht 9K 133
D'Arcy Pl. Brom 8E 110
Darcy Rd. SW16 .... 6J 107
D'Arcy Rd. Asht 9K 133
Darcy Rd. Iswth 9E 70
D'Arcy Rd. Sutt 6H 121
Dare Ct. E10 .... 5A 46
Dare Gdns. Dag 8J 49
Darell Rd. Rich 2L 87
Darenth. 2M 115
Darenth Hill. Dart 2M 115
Darenth Interchange (Junct.)
.... 9L 99
Darent Ho. NW8 .... 8B 58
(off Church St. Est.)
Darent Ho. Brom 2B 110
Darenth Rd. N16 .... 5D 44
Darenth Rd. Dart 6K 99
Darenth Rd. Hawl 1M 115
Darenth Rd. Well 9E 80
Darent Ind. Pk. Eri 7H 83
Darent Mead. S at H 5M 115
Darfield. NW1 .... 4G 59
(off Bayham St.)
Darfield Rd. SE4 .... 4K 93
Darfield Way. W10 .... 9H 57
Darfur St. SW15 .... 2H 89
Dargate Clo. SE19 .... 4D 108
Darien Ho. E1 .... 8H 61
(off Shandy St.)
Darien Rd. SW11 .... 2B 90
Daring Ho. E3 .... 5J 61
(off Roman Rd.)
Dark Ho. Wlk. EC3 .... 1B 76
Dark La. Chesh 3A 6
Darland Lake Nature Reserve.
.... 3J 25
Darlands Dri. Barn 7H 13
Darlan Rd. SW6 .... 8K 73
Darlaston Rd. SW19 .... 4H 105
Darley Clo. Croy 1J 125
Darley Cft. Park 1M 5
Darley Dri. N Mald 6B 104
Darley Gdns. Mord 1A 122
Darley Ho. SE11 .... 6K 75
(off Laud St.)
Darley Rd. N9 .... 1D 28
Darley Rd. SW11 .... 5D 90
Darling Ho. Twic 5H 87
Darling Rd. SE4 .... 2L 93
Darling Row. E1 .... 7F 60
Darlington Ct. SE12 .... 7D 94
Darlington Gdns. Romf 5H 35
Darlington Ho. SW8 .... 8H 75
(off Hemans St.)
Darlington Path. Romf 5H 35
Darlington Rd. SE27 .... 2M 107
Darlton Clo. Dart 2D 98
Darmaine Clo. S Croy 9A 124
Darnall Ho. SE10 .... 9A 78
(off Royal Hill)
Darnay Ho. SE16 .... 4E 76
Darndale Clo. E17 .... 9K 29
Darnley Ho. E14 .... 9J 61
(off Camdenhurst St.)
Darnley Rd. E9 .... 2G 61
Darnley Rd. Wfd G 8E 30
Darnley Ter. W11 .... 2H 73
Darns Hill. Swan 2A 130
Darrell Charles Ct. Uxb 3C 142
Darrell Rd. SE22 .... 4E 92
Darren Clo. N4 .... 5K 43
Darrick Wood Rd. Orp 4B 128
Darrington Rd. Borwd 3J 11
Darris Clo. Hay 7J 53
Darsley Dri. SW8 .... 9H 75
Dartfields. Romf 6H 35
Dartford. 5J 99
Dartford Av. N9 .... 8G 17
Dartford Borough Mus. 6J 99
Dartford By-Pass.
Bex & Dart 6B 98
Dartford Gdns. Chad H 3F 48
Dartford Heath (Junct.) 7C 98
Dartford Ho. SE1 .... 5D 76
(off Longfield Est.)
Dartford Rd. Bex 7A 98
Dartford Rd. Dart 5E 98
Dartford Rd.
F'ham & Hort K 1K 131
(in two parts)
Dartford St. SE17 .... 7A 76
Dartford Trade Pk. Dart 8J 99
Dartford Tunnel App. Rd.
Dart 6M 99
Dartington. NW1 .... 4G 59
(off Plender St.)
Dartington Ho. SW8 .... 1H 91
(off Union Gro.)
Dartington Ho. W2 .... 8M 57
(off Senior St.)
Dartle Ct. SE16 .... 3E 76
(off Scott Lidgett Cres.)
Dartmoor Wlk. E14 .... 5L 77
(off Charnwood Gdns.)
Dartmouth Clo. W11 .... 9K 57
Dartmouth Ct. SE10 .... 9A 78
Dartmouth Gro. SE10 .... 9A 78
Dartmouth Hill. SE10 .... 9A 78
Dartmouth Park. 8F 42
Dartmouth Pk. Av. NW5 .... 8F 42
Dartmouth Pk. Hill.
N19 & NW5 .... 6F 42
Dartmouth Pk. Rd. NW5 .... 9F 42
Dartmouth Pl. SE23 .... 8G 93
Dartmouth Pl. W4 .... 7C 72
Dartmouth Rd. NW2 .... 2H 57
Dartmouth Rd. NW4 .... 4E 40
Dartmouth Rd.
SE26 & SE23 .... 9F 92
Dartmouth Rd. Brom 2E 126
Dartmouth Rd. Ruis 8E 36
Dartmouth Row. SE10 .... 1A 94
Dartmouth St. SW1 .... 3H 75
Dartmouth Ter. SE10 .... 9B 78
Dartnell Rd. Croy 2D 124
Darton Ct. W3 .... 2A 72
Dartrey Tower. SW10 .... 8A 74
(off Worlds End Est.)
Dartrey Wlk. SW10 .... 8A 74
Dart St. W10 .... 6J 57
Darville Rd. N16 .... 8D 44
Darwell Clo. E6 .... 5L 63
Darwin Clo. N11 .... 3F 26
Darwin Clo. Orp 7B 128
Darwin Ct. NW1 .... 4E 58
(in three parts)
Darwin Dri. S'hall 9M 53
Darwin Gdns. Wat 5G 21
Darwin Ho. SW1 .... 7G 75
(off Grosvenor Rd.)
Darwin Rd. N22 .... 8M 27
Darwin Rd. W5 .... 6G 71
Darwin Rd. Well 2D 96
Darwin St. SE17 .... 5B 76
(in two parts)
Darygnton Dri. Gnfd 5B 54
Darygnton Ho. SW8 .... 8J 75
(off Hartington Rd.)
Dashwood Clo. Bexh 4L 97
Dashwood Rd. N8 .... 4K 43
Dassett Rd. SE27 .... 2M 107
Data Point Bus. Cen. E16 .... 7B 62
Datchelor Pl. SE5 .... 9B 76
Datchet Ho. NW1 .... 6F 58
(off Augustus St.)
Datchet Rd. SE6 .... 8K 93
Datchworth Ct. Enf 7C 16
Datchworth Ho. N1 .... 3M 59
(off Sutton Est., The)
Date St. SE17 .... 6B 76
Daubeney Gdns. N17 .... 7A 28
Daubeney Rd. E5 .... 9J 45
Daubeney Rd. N17 .... 7A 28
Daubeney Tower. SE8 .... 6K 77
(off Bowditch)
Dault Rd. SW18 .... 5A 90
Dauncey Ho. SE1 .... 3M 75
(off Webber Row)
Davema Clo. Chst 5L 111
Davenant Rd. N19 .... 7H 43
Davenant Rd. Croy 6M 123
Davenant St. E1 .... 8E 60
Davenham Av. N'wd 5D 20
Davenport Clo. Tedd 3E 102
Davenport Ho. SE11 .... 5L 75
(off Walnut Tree Wlk.)
Davenport Lodge. Houn 8J 69
Davenport Rd. SE6 .... 5M 93
Davenport Rd. Sidc 8J 97
Daventer Dri. Stan 7D 22
Daventry Av. E17 .... 4L 45
Daventry Gdns. Romf 5G 35
Daventry Grn. Romf 5G 35
Daventry Rd. Romf 5G 35
Daventry St. NW1 .... 8C 58
Daver Ct. SW3 .... 6C 74
Daver Ct. W5 .... 7H 55
Davern Clo. SE10 .... 5D 78
Davey Clo. N7 .... 2K 59
Davey Clo. N13 .... 5K 27
Davey Rd. E9 .... 3L 61
Davey's Ct. WC2 .... 1J 75
(off Bedfordbury)
Davey St. SE15 .... 7D 76
David Av. Gnfd 6C 54
David Clo. Hay 8C 68
David Coffer Ct. Belv 5M 81
David Compton Lodge, The.
H Hill 5J 35
David Ct. N20 .... 3A 26
David Dri. Romf 6L 35
Davidge Ho. SE1 .... 3L 75
(off Coral St.)
Davidge St. SE1 .... 3M 75
David Ho. E14 .... 8M 61
(off Uamvar St.)
David Ho. SW8 .... 8J 75
(off Wyvil Rd.)
David Ho. Sidc 9E 96
David Lee Point. E15 .... 4C 62
(off Leather Gdns.)
David Lloyd Leisure. 4E 16
David M. W1 .... 8D 58
David Rd. Dag 7J 49
David's Ct. S'hall 9A 54
(off Whitecote Rd.)
Davidson Gdns. SW8 .... 8J 75
Davidson La. Harr 5D 38
Davidson Rd. Croy 3C 124
Davidson Terraces. E7 .... 1F 62
(off Claremont Rd., in two parts)
Davidson Tower. Brom 2F 110
Davidson Way. Romf 4C 50
David's Rd. SE23 .... 7G 93
David St. E15 .... 2B 62
David's Way. Ilf 7C 32
David Ter. Romf 7L 35
David Twigg Clo. King T 5J 103
Davies Clo. Croy 1D 124
Davies Clo. Rain 6G 67
Davies La. E11 .... 7C 46
Davies M. W1 .... 1F 74
Davies St. W1 .... 9F 58
Davies Wlk. Iswth 9B 70
Da Vinci Ct. SE16 .... 6F 76
(off Rossetti Rd.)
Davington Gdns. Dag 1F 64
Davington Rd. Dag 2F 64
Davinia Clo. Wfd G 6K 31
Davis Ho. W12 .... 1F 72
(off White City Est.)
Davison Clo. Chesh 1D 6
Davison Dri. Chesh 1D 6
Davis Rd. W3 .... 2D 72
Davis Rd. Chess 6L 119
Davis St. E13 .... 5F 62
Davisville Rd. W12 .... 3E 72
Davmor Ct. Bren 6G 71
Dawell Dri. Big H 9G 141
Dawes Av. Horn 8H 51
Dawes Av. Iswth 4E 86
Dawes Ct. Esh 6M 117
Dawes Ho. SE17 .... 5B 76
(off Orb St.)
Dawes Rd. SW6 .... 8J 73
Dawe's Rd. Uxb 5C 142
Dawes St. SE17 .... 6B 76
Dawley Av. Uxb 8A 52
Dawley Pde. Hay 1A 68
Dawley Pk. Hay 3B 68
Dawley Rd. Hay 1A 68
Dawlish Av. N13 .... 4J 27
Dawlish Av. SW18 .... 8M 89
Dawlish Av. Gnfd 5E 54
Dawlish Dri. Ilf 9C 48
Dawlish Dri. Pinn 3J 37
Dawlish Dri. Ruis 7E 36
Dawlish Rd. E10 .... 6A 46
Dawlish Rd. N17 .... 1E 44
Dawlish Rd. NW2 .... 2H 57
Dawlish Wlk. Romf 8G 35
Dawnay Gdns. SW18 .... 8B 90
Dawnay Rd. SW18 .... 8A 90
Dawn Clo. Houn 2J 85
Dawn Cres. E15 .... 4B 62
Dawpool Rd. NW2 .... 7D 40
Daws Hill. E4 .... 4A 18
Daws La. NW7 .... 5D 24
Dawson Av. Bark 3C 64
Dawson Av. Orp 6F 112
Dawson Clo. SE18 .... 5A 80
Dawson Clo. Hay 8B 52
Dawson Dri. Rain 3F 66
Dawson Dri. Swan 4C 114
Dawson Gdns. Bark 3D 64
Dawson Ho. E2 .... 6G 61
(off Sceptre Rd.)
Dawson Pl. W2 .... 1L 73
Dawson Rd. NW2 .... 1G 57
Dawson Rd. King T 7K 103
Dawson St. E2 .... 5D 60
Dawson Ter. N9 .... 9G 17
Daybrook Rd. SW19 .... 6M 105
Day Ho. SE5 .... 8A 76
(off Bethwin Rd.)
Daylesford Av. SW15 .... 3E 88
Daylop Dri. Chig 3F 32
Daymer Gdns. Pinn 2F 36
Days Acre. S Croy 2D 138
Daysbrook Rd. SW2 .... 7K 91
Days La. Sidc 6C 96
Dayton Dri. Eri 6H 83
Dayton Gro. SE15 .... 9G 77
Deacon Clo. Purl 1J 137
Deaconess Ct. N15 .... 2D 44
(off Tottenham Grn. E.)
Deacon Est., The. E4 .... 6K 29
Deacon Ho. SE11 .... 5K 75
(off Black Prince Rd.)
Deacon M. N1 .... 3B 60
Deacon Rd. NW2 .... 1E 56
Deacon Rd. King T 5K 103
Deacons Clo. Els 6L 11
Deacons Clo. Pinn 9F 20
Deacons Ct. Twic 8D 86
Deacons Heights. Els 8L 11
Deacons Hill. Borwd 8K 11
Deacons Hill. Wat 8G 9
Deacon's Hill Rd. Els 6K 11
Deacons Leas. Orp 6B 128
Deacon's Ri. N2 .... 3B 42
Deacons Wlk. Hamp 1L 101
Deacon Way. SE17 .... 5A 76
Deacon Way. Wfd G 7K 31
Deakin Clo. Wat 9C 8
Deakins Ter. Orp 2E 128
Deal Ct. NW9 .... 9D 24
(off Hazel Clo.)
Deal Ct. S'hall 9A 54
(off Haldane Rd.)
Deal Ho. SE15 .... 7H 77
(off Lovelinch La.)
Deal M. W5 .... 5H 71
Deal Porters Wlk. SE16 .... 3H 77
Deal Porters Way. SE16 .... 4G 77
Deal Rd. SW17 .... 3E 106
Deal's Gateway. SE10 .... 9L 77
Deal St. E1 .... 8E 60
Dealtry Rd. SW15 .... 3G 89
Deal Wlk. SW9 .... 8L 75
Dean Abbott Ho. SW1 .... 5H 75
(off Vincent St.)
Dean Bradley St. SW1 .... 4J 75
Dean Clo. E9 .... 1G 61
Dean Clo. SE16 .... 2H 77
Dean Clo. Uxb 3D 142
Dean Ct. SW8 .... 8J 75
(off Thorncroft St.)
Dean Ct. W3 .... 9B 56
Dean Ct. Edgw 6M 23
Dean Ct. Romf 3B 50
Dean Ct. Wat 6H 5
Dean Ct. Wemb 8F 38
Deancross St. E1 .... 9G 61
Dean Dri. Stan 9J 23
Deane Av. Ruis 1G 53
Deane Ct. N'wd 8C 20
Deane Cft. Rd. Pinn 4G 37
Deanery Clo. N2 .... 2C 42
Deanery M. W1 .... 2E 74
(off Deanery St.)
Deanery Rd. E15 .... 2C 62
Deanery St. W1 .... 2E 74
Deane Way. Ruis 4F 36
Dean Farrar St. SW1 .... 4H 75
Deanfield Gdns. Croy 6B 124
Dean Gdns. E17 .... 2B 46
Deanhill Ct. SW14 .... 3M 87
Deanhill Rd. SW14 .... 3M 87
Dean Ho. E1 .... 9G 61
(off Tarling St.)
Dean Ho. SE14 .... 8J 77
(off New Cross Rd.)
Dean Rd. NW2 .... 2G 57
Dean Rd. SE28 .... 2E 80
Dean Rd. Croy 6B 124
Dean Rd. Hamp 2L 101
Dean Rd. Houn 4M 85
Dean Ryle St. SW1 .... 5J 75
Deansbrook Clo. Edgw 7A 24
Deansbrook Rd. Edgw 7M 23
Dean's Bldgs. SE17 .... 5B 76
Deans Clo. W4 .... 7M 71
Deans Clo. Ab L 5B 4
Deans Clo. Croy 5D 124
Deans Clo. Edgw 6A 24
Dean's Ct. EC4 .... 9M 59
Deanscroft Av. NW9 .... 6A 40
Deans Dri. N13 .... 6M 27
Deans Dri. Edgw 5B 24
Deans Ga. Clo. SE23 .... 9H 93
Deanshanger Ho. SE8 .... 5H 77
(off Chilton Gro.)
Deans La. W4 .... 7M 71
(off Deans Clo.)
Deans La. Edgw 6A 24
Dean's M. W1 .... 9F 58
Deans Rd. W7 .... 2D 70
Deans Rd. Sutt 5M 121
Dean Stanley St. SW1 .... 4J 75
Deanston Wharf. E16 .... 3F 78
(in two parts)
Dean St. E7 .... 1E 62
Dean St. W1 .... 9H 59
Dean's Wlk. Coul 9L 137
Deansway. N2 .... 2B 42
Deansway. N9 .... 3C 28
Deans Way. Edgw 5A 24
Deanswood. N11 .... 6H 27
Dean's Yd. SW1 .... 4H 75
(off Sanctuary, The)
Dean Trench St. SW1 .... 4J 75
Dean Wlk. Edgw 6A 24
Dean Way. S'hall 3M 69
Dearne Clo. Stan 5E 22
Dearn Gdns. Mitc 7C 106
Dearsley Rd. Enf 5E 16
Deason St. E15 .... 4A 62
Deauville Ct. SE16 .... 3H 77
(off Eleanor Clo.)
Deauville Ct. SW4 .... 5G 91
De Barowe M. N5 .... 9M 43
Debdale Ho. E2 .... 4E 60
(off Whiston Rd.)
Debden. 6M 19
Debden. N17 .... 9B 28
(off Gloucester Rd.)
Debden Clo. King T 2H 103
Debden Clo. Wfd G 7H 31
Debden Green. 2M 19
Debden Ho. Lou 2M 19

Debden La.—Dersingham Rd.

Debden La. Lou 2M 19
Debden Rd. Lou 2M 19
Debden Wlk. Horn 2F 66
De Beauvoir Ct. N1 3B 60
(off Northchurch Rd.)
De Beauvoir Cres. N1 4C 60
De Beauvoir Est. N1 4C 60
De Beauvoir Pl. N1 2C 60
De Beauvoir Rd. N1 4C 60
De Beauvoir Sq. N1 3C 60
De Beauvoir Town. 4C 60
Debeham Ct. Barn 7G 13
Debenham Ct. E8 4E 60
(off Pownall Rd.)
Debenham Rd. Chesh 1B 6
Debham Ct. NW2 8G 41
Debnams Rd. SE16 5G 77
De Bohun Av. N14 8F 14
Deborah Clo. Iswth 9C 70
Deborah Ct. E18 1F 46
(off Victoria Rd.)
Deborah Cres. Ruis 5B 36
Deborah Lodge. Edgw 8M 23
Debrabant Clo. Eri 7B 82
De Brome Rd. Felt 7G 85
De Bruin Ct. E14 6A 78
(off Ferry St.)
De Burgh Pk. Bans 7M 135
De Burgh Rd. SW19 4A 106
Debussy. NW9 9D 24
Decima St. SE1 4C 76
Decimus Clo. T Hth 8B 108
Deck Clo. SE16 2H 77
Decoy Av. NW11 3J 41
De Crespigny Pk. SE5 1B 92
Dee Ct. W7 9B 54
(off Hobbayne Rd.)
Deeley Rd. SW8 9H 75
Deena Clo. W3 9K 55
Deepdale. SW19 1H 105
Deepdale Av. Brom 8D 110
Deepdale Clo. N11 6E 26
Deepdale Ct. S Croy 6B 124
(off Birdhurst Av.)
Deep Dene. W5 7K 55
Deepdene Av. Croy 5D 124
Deepdene Clo. E11 2E 46
Deepdene Ct. N21 8M 15
Deepdene Gdns. SW2 6K 91
Deepdene Path. Lou 6L 19
(in two parts)
Deepdene Point. SE23 9H 93
Deepdene Rd. SE5 3B 92
Deepdene Rd. Lou 6L 19
Deepdene Rd. Well 2E 96
Deepfield Way. Coul 8J 137
Deepway. SE8 6J 77
(off Evelyn St.)
Deepwell Clo. Iswth 9E 70
Deepwood La. Gnfd 6B 54
Deerbrook Rd. SE24 7M 91
Deerdale Rd. SE24 3A 92
Deere Av. Rain 2E 66
Deerfield Cotts. NW9 3D 40
Deerhurst Clo. Felt 1F 100
Deerhurst Cres. Hamp H 2A 102
Deerhurst Ho. SE15 7E 76
(off Haymerle Rd.)
Deerhurst Rd. NW2 2H 57
Deerhurst Rd. SW16 2K 107
Deerings Dri. Pinn 3E 36
Deerleap Gro. E4 7M 17
Dee Rd. Rich 3K 87
Deer Pk. Clo. King T 4M 103
Deer Pk. Gdns. Mitc 8B 106
Deer Pk. Rd. SW19 6M 105
Deerpark Way. Wal A 9H 7
Deer Pk. Way. W Wick 4D 126
Deeside Rd. SW17 9B 90
Dee St. E14 9A 62
Dee Way. Eps 2C 134
Dee Way. Romf 7C 34
Defiance Wlk. SE18 4K 79
Defiant. NW9 9D 24
(off Further Acre)
Defiant Way. Wall 9J 123
Defoe Av. Rich 8L 71
Defoe Clo. SE16 3K 77
Defoe Clo. SW17 3C 106
Defoe Clo. Eri 9C 82
Defoe Ho. EC2 8A 60
(off Beech St.)
Defoe Pl. EC2 8A 60
(off Beech St.)
Defoe Pl. SW17 1D 106
Defoe Rd. N16 8C 44
Defoe Way. Romf 6L 33
De Frene Rd. SE26 1H 109
Degema Rd. Chst 2M 111
Dehar Cres. NW9 5D 40
De Havilland Clo. N'holt 6H 53
De Havilland Rd. Edgw 9M 23
De Havilland Rd. Houn 8G 69
De Havilland Way. Ab L 5D 4
De Havilland Way. Stanw 5B 144
Dekker Ho. SE5 8B 76
(off Elmington Est.)
Dekker Rd. SE21 5C 92
Delacourt Rd. SE3 8F 78
Delafield Ho. E1 9E 60
(off Christian St.)
Delafield Rd. SE7 6F 78
Delaford Rd. SE16 6F 76
Delaford St. SW6 8J 73
Delamare Cres. Croy 1G 125
Delamare Rd. Chesh 3E 6
Delamere Gdns. NW7 6B 24
Delamere Rd. SW20 5H 105
Delamere Rd. W5 3J 71
Delamere Rd. Borwd 3M 11
Delamere Rd. Hay 1H 69
Delamere St. W2 8M 57
Delamere Ter. W2 8M 57
Delancey Pas. NW1 4F 58
(off Delancey St.)
Delancey St. NW1 4F 58
Delancey Studios.
NW1 4F 58
Delany Ho. SE10 7A 78
(off Thames St.)
Delaporte Clo. Eps 4C 134
De Lapre Clo. Orp 2H 129
Delarch Ho. SE1 3M 75
(off Webber Row)
De Laune St. SE17 6M 75
Delaware Mans. W9 7M 57
(off Delaware Rd.)
Delaware Rd. W9 7M 57
Delawyk Cres. SE24 5A 92
Delcombe Av. Wor Pk 3G 121
Delderfield Ho. Romf 9B 34
(off Portnoi Clo.)
Delft Ho. King T 4K 103
(off Acre Rd.)
Delft Way. SE22 4C 92
Delhi Rd. Enf 9D 16
Delhi St. N1 4J 59
(in two parts)
Delia St. SW18 6M 89
Delisle Rd. SE28 3C 80
(in two parts)
Delius Clo. Els 8G 11
Delius Gro. E15 5B 62
Della Path. E5 8E 44
Dellbow Rd. Felt 4F 84
Dell Clo. E15 4B 62
Dell Clo. Wall 6G 123
Dell Clo. Wfd G 3F 30
Dell Ct. Horn 7J 51
Dell Ct. N'wd 7B 20
Dell Farm Rd. Ruis 3B 36
Dellfield Clo. Beck 5A 110
Dellfield Clo. Wat 4E 8
Dellfield Cres. Uxb 7B 142
Dellfield Pde. Cow 7A 142
Dell La. Eps 7E 120
Dellmeadow. Ab L 3C 4
Dellors Clo. Barn 7H 13
Dellow Clo. Ilf 5B 48
Dellow Ho. E1 1F 76
(off Dellow St.)
Dellow St. E1 1F 76
Dell Rd. Enf 2G 17
Dell Rd. Eps 8E 120
Dell Rd. Wat 1E 8
Dell Rd. W Dray 5K 143
Dells Clo. E4 9M 17
Dells Clo. Tedd 3D 102
Dellside. Wat 1E 8
Dell's M. SW1 5G 75
(off Churton Pl.)
Dell, The. SE2 6E 80
Dell, The. SE19 5D 108
Dell, The. Bex 7C 98
Dell, The. Bren 7G 71
Dell, The. Felt 6F 84
Dell, The. N'wd 2C 20
Dell, The. Pinn 9H 21
Dell, The. Wemb 1F 54
Dell, The. Wfd G 3F 30
Dell Wlk. N Mald 6C 104
Dell Way. W13 9G 55
Dellwood Gdns. Ilf 1L 47
Delmaine Ho. E14 9J 61
(off Maroon St.)
Delmare Clo. SW9 3K 91
Delme Cres. SE3 1F 94
Delmer Ct. Borwd 2K 11
(off Aycliffe Rd.)
Delmerend Ho. SW3 6C 74
(off Ixworth Pl.)
Delmey Clo. Croy 5D 124
Deloraine Ho. SE8 9L 77
Delorme St. W6 7H 73
Delroy Ct. N20 9A 14
Delta Building. E14 9A 62
(off Ashton St.)
Delta Cen. Wemb 4K 55
Delta Clo. Wor Pk 5D 120
Delta Ct. NW2 7E 40
Delta Est. E2 6E 60
Delta Gain. Wat 2H 21
Delta Gro. N'holt 6H 53
Delta Pk. SW18 3M 89
Delta Point. Croy 3A 124
(off Wellesley Rd.)
Delta Rd. Wor Pk 5C 120
Delta St. E2 6E 60
De Luci Rd. Eri 6A 82
De Lucy St. SE2 5F 80
Delvan Clo. SE18 8L 79
Delvers Mead. Dag 9A 50
Delverton Ho. SE17 6M 75
(off Delverton Rd.)
Delverton Rd. SE17 6M 75
Delvino Rd. SW6 9L 73
De Mel Clo. Eps 4M 133
Demesne Rd. Wall 6H 123
Demeta Clo. Wemb 8A 40
De Montfort Pde. SW16 9J 91
De Montfort Rd. SW16 9J 91
De Morgan Rd. SW6 2M 89
Dempster Clo. Surb 3G 119
Dempster Rd. SW18 4A 90
Denbar Pde. Romf 2M 49
Denberry Dri. Sidc 9F 96
Denbigh Clo. NW10 3C 56
Denbigh Clo. W11 1K 73
Denbigh Clo. Chst 3K 111
Denbigh Clo. Horn 2L 51
Denbigh Clo. Ruis 7D 36
Denbigh Clo. S'hall 9K 53
Denbigh Clo. Sutt 7K 121
Denbigh Ct. E6 6H 63
Denbigh Ct. W7 8D 54
(off Copley Clo.)
Denbigh Dri. Hay 3A 68
Denbigh Gdns. Rich 4K 87
Denbigh Ho. SW1 4D 74
(off Hans Pl.)
Denbigh Ho. W11 1K 73
(off Westbourne Gro.)
Denbigh Ho. Romf 6J 35
(off Kingsbridge Cir.)
Denbigh M. SW1 5G 75
(off Denbigh St.)
Denbigh Pl. SW1 6G 75
Denbigh Rd. E6 6H 63
Denbigh Rd. W11 1K 73
Denbigh Rd. W13 1F 70
Denbigh Rd. Houn 1M 85
Denbigh Rd. S'hall 9K 53
Denbigh St. SW1 5G 75
(in two parts)
Denbigh Ter. W11 1K 73
Denbridge Rd. Brom 6K 111
Denby Ct. SE11 5K 75
(off Lambeth Wlk.)
Dence Ho. E2 6E 60
(off Turin St.)
Denchworth Ho. SW9 1L 91
Den Clo. Beck 7B 110
Dendridge Clo. Enf 1F 16
Dene Av. Houn 2K 85
Dene Av. Sidc 6F 96
Dene Clo. SE4 2J 93
Dene Clo. Brom 3D 126
Dene Clo. Dart 1C 114
Dene Clo. Wor Pk 4D 120
Dene Ct. W5 8G 55
Dene Ct. S Croy 7A 124
(off Warham Rd.)
Denecroft Cres. Uxb 4F 142
Dene Dri. Orp 5F 128
Denefield Dri. Kenl 7B 138
Dene Gdns. Stan 5G 23
Dene Gdns. Th Dit 4E 118
Dene Ho. N14 9H 15
Denehurst Gdns. NW4 4G 41
Denehurst Gdns. W3 2M 71
Denehurst Gdns. Rich 3L 87
Denehurst Gdns. Twic 6B 86
Denehurst Gdns. Wfd G 4F 30
Dene Rd. N11 1D 26
Dene Rd. Buck H 1H 31
Dene Rd. Dart 6K 99
Dene Rd. N'wd 6A 20
Denesmead. SE24 4A 92
Dene, The. W13 8F 54
Dene, The. Croy 6H 125
Dene, The. Sutt 3K 135
Dene, The. Wemb 9J 39
Dene, The. W Mol 9K 101
Denewood. Eps 5C 134
Denewood. New Bar 7A 14
Denewood Clo. Wat 1D 8
Denewood Rd. N6 4D 42
Denford St. SE10 6D 78
(off Glenforth St.)
Dengie Wlk. N1 4A 60
(off Basire St.)
Denham Clo. Well 2G 97
Denham Ct. SE26 9F 92
(off Kirkdale)
Denham Ct. S'hall 1A 70
(off Baird Av.)
Denham Cres. Mitc 8D 106
Denham Dri. Ilf 4A 48
Denham Ho. W12 1F 72
(off White City Est.)
Denham Lodge. Den 2A 142
Denham Rd. N20 3D 26
Denham Rd. Eps 4D 134
Denham Rd. Felt 6G 85
Denham St. SE10 6E 78
Denham Way. Bark 4D 64
Denham Way. Borwd 3A 12
Denholme Rd. W9 6K 57
Denholme Wlk. Rain 2D 66
Denison Clo. N2 1A 42
Denison Ho. E14 9L 61
(off Farrance St.)
Denison Rd. SW19 3B 106
Denison Rd. W5 7G 55
Denison Rd. Felt 1D 100
Deniston Av. Bex 7J 97
Denis Way. SW4 2H 91
Denland Ho. SW8 8K 75
(off Dorset Rd.)
Denleigh Gdns. N21 9L 15
Denleigh Gdns. Th Dit 1C 118
Denley Sq. Uxb 3B 142
Denman Dri. NW11 3L 41
Denman Dri. Ashf 3A 100
Denman Dri. Clay 7E 118
Denman Dri. N. NW11 3L 41
Denman Dri. S. NW11 3L 41
Denman Pl. W1 1H 75
(off Denman St.)
Denman Rd. SE15 9D 76
Denman St. W1 1H 75
Denmark Av. SW19 4J 105
Denmark Ct. Mord 1L 121
Denmark Gdns. Cars 5D 122
Denmark Gro. N1 5L 59
Denmark Hill. SE5 9B 76
Denmark Hill Dri. NW9 1E 40
Denmark Hill Est. SE5 3B 92
Denmark Mans. SE5 1A 92
(off Coldharbour La.)
Denmark Path. SE25 9F 108
Denmark Pl. WC2 9H 59
Denmark Rd. N8 2L 43
Denmark Rd. NW6 5K 57
(in two parts)
Denmark Rd. SE5 9A 76
Denmark Rd. SE25 9E 108
Denmark Rd. SW19 3H 105
Denmark Rd. W13 1F 70
Denmark Rd. Brom 5F 110
Denmark Rd. Cars 5D 122
Denmark Rd. King T 7J 103
Denmark Rd. Twic 9B 86
Denmark St. E11 8C 46
Denmark St. E13 8F 62
Denmark St. N17 8F 28
Denmark St. WC2 9H 59
Denmark St. Wat 4F 8
Denmark Ter. N2 1D 42
Denmark Wlk. SE27 1A 108
Denmead Ho. SW15 5D 88
(off Highcliffe Dri.)
Denmead Rd. Croy 3M 123
Denmead Way. SE15 8D 76
(off Pentridge St.)
Denmore Ct. Wall 7F 122
Dennan Rd. Surb 3K 119
Dennard Way. F'boro 6L 127
Denner Rd. E4 2L 29
Denne Ter. E8 4D 60
Dennett Rd. Croy 3L 123
Dennett's Gro. SE14 9G 77
Denning Av. Croy 6L 123
Denning Clo. NW8 6A 58
Denning Clo. Hamp 2K 101
Denning Point. E1 9D 60
(off Commercial St.)
Denning Rd. NW3 9B 42
Dennington Clo. E5 7G 45
Dennington Pk. Rd. NW6 2L 57
Denningtons, The.
Wor Pk 4C 120
Dennis Av. Wemb 1K 55
Dennis Clo. Ashf 4B 100
Dennis Gdns. Stan 5G 23
Dennis Ho. Sutt 6L 121
Dennis La. Stan 3F 22
Dennison Point. E15 3A 62
Dennis Pde. N14 1H 27
Dennis Pk. Cres. SW20 5J 105
Dennis Reeve Clo. Mitc 5D 106
Dennis Rd. E Mol 8A 102
Denny Av. Wal A 7K 7
Denny Clo. E6 8J 63
Denny Ct. Dart 5M 99
(off Bow Arrow La.)
Denny Cres. SE11 6L 75
Denny Gdns. Dag 3F 64
Denny Rd. N9 1F 28
Denny St. SE11 6L 75
Den Rd. Brom 7B 110
Densham Dri. Purl 6L 137
Densham Ho. NW8 5B 58
(off Cochrane St.)
Densham Rd. E15 4C 62
Densole Clo. Beck 5J 109
Denstone Ho. SE15 7E 76
(off Haymerle Rd.)
Densworth Gro. N9 2G 29
Dent Ho. SE17 5C 76
(off Tatum St.)
Denton. NW1 2E 58
Denton Clo. Barn 7G 13
Denton Gro. W on T 4J 117
Denton Ho. N1 3M 59
(off Halton Rd.)
Denton Rd. N8 3K 43
Denton Rd. N18 4C 28
Denton Rd. Bex 8C 98
Denton Rd. Dart 6C 98
Denton Rd. Twic 5H 87
Denton Rd. Well 8G 81
Denton St. SW18 5M 89
Denton Ter. Bex 8C 98
Denton Way. E5 8H 45
Dents Rd. SW11 5D 90
Denver Clo. Orp 1C 128
Denver Ind. Est. Rain 8D 66
Denver Rd. N16 5C 44
Denver Rd. Dart 6E 98
Denwood. SE23 9H 93
Denyer St. SW3 5C 74
Denys Ho. EC1 8L 59
(off Bourne Est.)
Denziloe Av. Uxb 6F 142
Denzil Rd. NW10 1D 56
Deodar Rd. SW15 3J 89
Deodora Clo. N20 3C 26
Depot App. NW2 9H 41
Depot Rd. W12 1G 73
Depot Rd. Eps 5C 134
Depot Rd. Houn 2B 86
Depot St. SE5 7B 76
Deptford. 7L 77
Deptford B'way. SE8 9L 77
Deptford Bus. Pk. SE15 7G 77
Deptford Chu. St. SE8 7L 77
(in two parts)
Deptford Creek Bri. SE8 7M 77
(off Creek Rd.)
Deptford Ferry Rd. E14 5L 77
Deptford Grn. SE8 7L 77
Deptford High St. SE8 7L 77
Deptford Pk. Bus. Cen.
SE8 6J 77
Deptford Strand. SE8 5K 77
Deptford Trad. Est. SE8 6J 77
Deptford Wharf. SE8 5K 77
(in two parts)
De Quincey Ho. SW1 6G 75
(off Lupus St.)
De Quincey M. E16 2E 78
De Quincey Rd. N17 8B 28
Derby Arms Rd. Eps 9D 134
Derby Av. N12 5A 26
Derby Av. Harr 8B 22
Derby Av. Romf 4A 50
Derby Av. Upm 8K 51
Derby Day Experience, The.
9D 134
Derby Ga. SW1 3J 75
(in two parts)
Derby Hill. SE23 8G 93
Derby Hill Cres. SE23 8G 93
Derby Ho. SE11 5L 75
(off Walnut Tree Wlk.)
Derby Ho. Pinn 9H 21
Derby Lodge. N3 9K 25
Derby Lodge. WC1 6K 59
(off Britannia St.)
Derby Rd. E7 3H 63
Derby Rd. E9 4H 61
Derby Rd. E18 8D 30
Derby Rd. N18 5G 29
Derby Rd. SW14 3M 87
Derby Rd. SW19 4L 105
Derby Rd. Croy 3M 123
Derby Rd. Enf 7F 16
Derby Rd. Gnfd 4M 53
Derby Rd. Houn 3M 85
Derby Rd. Surb 3L 119
Derby Rd. Sutt 8K 121
Derby Rd. Uxb 5A 142
Derby Rd. Wat 5G 9
(in two parts)
Derbyshire St. E2 6E 60
(in two parts)
Derby Sq., The. Eps 5B 134
(off High St.)
Derby Stables Rd. Eps 9D 134
Derby St. W1 2E 74
Dereham Clo. Romf 6M 33
Dereham Ho. SE4 3H 93
(off Frendsbury Rd.)
Dereham Pl. EC2 6C 60
Dereham Rd. Bark 1D 64
Derek Av. Eps 8L 119
Derek Av. Wall 6F 122
Derek Av. Wemb 3M 55
Derek Clo. Ewe 7M 119
Derek Walcott Clo. SE24 4M 91
Deri Av. Rain 7F 66
Dericote St. E8 4F 60
Deridene Clo. Stanw 5C 144
Derifall Clo. E6 8K 63
Dering Pl. S Croy 6A 124
Dering Rd. Croy 6A 124
Dering St. W1 9F 58
Dering Yd. W1 9F 58
Derinton Rd. SW17 1D 106
Derley Rd. S'hall 4G 69
Dermody Gdns. SE13 4B 94
Dermody Rd. SE13 4B 94
Deronda Est. SW2 7M 91
Deronda Rd. SE24 7M 91
Deroy Clo. Cars 8D 122
Derrick Av. S Croy 2A 138
Derrick Gdns. SE7 4G 79
Derrick Rd. Beck 7K 109
Derry Downs. 1G 129
Derry Downs. Orp 1G 129
Derry Rd. Croy 5J 123
Derry St. W8 3M 73
Dersingham Av. E12 9K 47
Dersingham Rd. NW2 8J 41

Derwent—Dolphin St.

Derwent. NW1 6G 59
(off Robert St.)
Derwent Av. N18 5B 28
Derwent Av. NW7 6B 24
Derwent Av. NW9 3C 40
Derwent Av. SW15 1C 104
Derwent Av. Barn 1D 26
Derwent Av. Pinn 6J 21
Derwent Clo. Clay 8C 118
Derwent Clo. Dart 7F 98
Derwent Clo. Felt 7D 84
Derwent Ct. SE16 3H 77
(off Eleanor Clo.)
Derwent Cres. N12 3A 26
Derwent Cres. Bexh 1L 97
Derwent Cres. Stan 9G 23
Derwent Dri. Hay 8C 52
Derwent Dri. Orp 2B 128
Derwent Dri. Purl 5B 138
Derwent Gdns. Ilf 2J 47
Derwent Gdns. Wemb 5G 39
Derwent Gro. SE22 3D 92
Derwent Ho. E3 7K 61
(off Southern Gro.)
Derwent Ho. SE20 6F 108
(off Derwent Rd.)
Derwent Ho. SW7 5A 74
(off Cromwell Rd.)
Derwent Lodge. Iswth 1B 86
Derwent Lodge. Wor Pk 4F 120
Derwent Ri. NW9 4C 40
Derwent Rd. N13 4K 27
Derwent Rd. SE20 6E 108
Derwent Rd. SW20 9H 105
Derwent Rd. W5 4G 71
Derwent Rd. S'hall 9K 53
Derwent Rd. Twic 5M 85
Derwent St. SE10 6C 78
Derwent Wlk. Wall 9F 122
Derwentwater Rd. W3 2A 72
Derwent Way. Horn 1F 66
Derwent Yd. W13 4G 71
(off Derwent Rd.)
De Salis Rd. Uxb 7A 52
Desborough Clo. W2 8M 57
Desborough Ho. W14 7K 73
(off N. End Rd.)
Desenfans Rd. SE21 5C 92
Desford Ct. Ashf 8E 144
Desford Rd. E16 7C 62
Desford Way. Ashf 8D 144
Design Mus. 3D 76
Desmond Ho. Barn 8C 14
Desmond Rd. Wat 9D 4
Desmond St. SE14 7J 77
Despard Rd. N19 6G 43
Dethick Ct. E3 4J 61
Detling Clo. Horn 1G 67
Detling Ho. SE17 5C 76
(off Congreve St.)
Detling Rd. Brom 2E 110
Detling Rd. Eri 8B 82
Detmold Rd. E5 7G 45
Devalls Clo. E6 1M 79
Devana End. Cars 5D 122
Devas Rd. SW20 5G 105
Devas St. E3 7M 61
Devenay Rd. E15 3D 62
Devenish Rd. SE2 3E 80
Deventer Cres. SE22 4C 92
De Vere Gdns. W8 3A 74
De Vere Gdns. Ilf 7K 47
Deverell St. SE1 4B 76
De Vere M. W8 4A 74
(off De Vere Gdns.)
Devereux Ct. WC2 9L 59
(off Essex St.)
Devereux Dri. Wat 2C 8
Devereux La. SW13 8F 72
Devereux Rd. SW11 5D 90
De Vere Wlk. Wat 4C 8
Deveron Way. Romf 8C 34
Devey Clo. King T 4D 104
Devitt Clo. Asht 8L 133
Devitt Ho. E14 1M 77
(off Wade's Pl.)
Devizes Ho. H Hill 5H 35
(off Montgomery Cres.)
Devizes St. N1 4B 60
Devoke Way. W on T 4H 117
Devon Av. Twic 7A 86
Devon Clo. N17 1D 44
Devon Clo. Buck H 2F 30
Devon Clo. Gnfd 4G 55
Devon Clo. Kenl 8D 138
Devon Ct. W7 8D 54
(off Copley Clo.)
Devon Ct. Hamp 4L 101
Devon Ct. S at H 5M 115
Devoncroft Gdns. Twic 6E 86
Devon Gdns. N4 4M 43
Devon Ho. E17 9K 29
Devonhurst Pl. W4 6B 72
Devonia Gdns. N18 6A 28
Devonia Rd. N1 5M 59
Devon Mans. SE1 3D 76
(off Tooley St.)
Devon Mans. Harr 3G 39
(off Woodcock Hill)
Devon Pde. Harr 3G 39
Devonport. W2 9C 58
Devonport Gdns. Ilf 4K 47
Devonport M. W12 3F 72
Devonport Rd. W12 2F 72
(in two parts)
Devonport St. E1 9H 61
Devon Ri. N2 2B 42
Devon Rd. Bark 4C 64
Devon Rd. S Dar 5M 115
Devon Rd. Sutt 1J 135
Devon Rd. W on T 6G 117
Devon Rd. Wat 3H 9
Devons Est. E3 6M 61
Devonshire Av. Dart 5F 98
Devonshire Av. Sutt 9A 122
Devonshire Clo. E15 9C 46
Devonshire Clo. N13 3L 27
Devonshire Clo. W1 8F 58
Devonshire Ct. E1 6G 61
(off Bancroft Rd.)
Devonshire Ct. WC1 8J 59
(off Boswell St.)
Devonshire Ct. Pinn 8K 21
(off Devonshire Rd.)
Devonshire Cres. NW7 7H 25
Devonshire Dri. SE10 8M 77
Devonshire Dri. Surb 3H 119
Devonshire Gdns. N17 6A 28
Devonshire Gdns. N21 9A 16
Devonshire Gdns. W4 8A 72
Devonshire Gro. SE15 7F 76
Devonshire Hall. E9 2G 61
(off Frampton Pk. Rd.)
Devonshire Hill La. N17 6M 27
(in two parts)
Devonshire Ho. NW6 2K 57
(off Kilburn High Rd.)
Devonshire Ho. SE1 4A 76
(off Bath Ter.)
Devonshire Ho. SW1 6H 75
(off Lindsay Sq.)
Devonshire Ho. Sutt 9A 122
Devonshire Ho. Bus. Cen.
Brom 8F 110
(off Devonshire Sq.)
Devonshire M. N13 4L 27
Devonshire M. SW10 7B 74
(off Camera Pl.)
Devonshire M. W4 6C 72
Devonshire M. N. W1 8F 58
Devonshire M. S. W1 8F 58
Devonshire M. W. W1 7E 58
Devonshire Pas. W4 6C 72
Devonshire Pl. NW2 8L 41
Devonshire Pl. W1 7E 58
Devonshire Pl. W8 4M 73
Devonshire Pl. M. W1 8E 58
Devonshire Rd. E16 9F 62
Devonshire Rd. E17 4L 45
Devonshire Rd. N9 1G 29
Devonshire Rd. N13 4K 27
Devonshire Rd. N17 6A 28
Devonshire Rd. NW7 7H 25
Devonshire Rd. SE9 8J 95
Devonshire Rd. SE23 7G 93
Devonshire Rd. SW19 4C 106
Devonshire Rd. W4 6C 72
Devonshire Rd. W5 4G 71
Devonshire Rd. Bexh 3J 97
Devonshire Rd. Cars 6E 122
Devonshire Rd. Croy 2B 124
Devonshire Rd. Eastc 4G 37
Devonshire Rd. Felt 9J 85
Devonshire Rd. Harr 4B 38
Devonshire Rd. Horn 7G 51
Devonshire Rd. Ilf 5C 48
Devonshire Rd. Orp 2E 128
Devonshire Rd. Pinn 8K 21
Devonshire Rd. S'hall 8L 53
Devonshire Rd. Sutt 9A 122
Devonshire Row. EC2 8C 60
Devonshire Row M. W1 7F 58
(off Devonshire St.)
Devonshire Sq.
EC2 & EC1 9C 60
Devonshire Sq. Brom 8F 110
Devonshire St. W1 8E 58
Devonshire St. W4 6C 72
Devonshire Ter. W2 9A 58
Devonshire Way. Croy 4J 125
Devonshire Way. Hay 9F 52
Devons Rd. E3 6M 61
Devon St. SE15 7F 76
Devon Way. Chess 7G 119
Devon Way. Eps 7M 119
Devon Way. Uxb 5D 142
Devon Waye. Houn 8K 69
Devon Wharf. E14 8A 62
(off Leven Rd.)
De Walden Ho. NW8 5C 58
(off Allitsen Rd.)
De Walden St. W1 8E 58
Dewar St. SE15 2E 92
Dewberry Gdns. E6 8J 63
Dewberry St. E14 8A 62
Dewey Path. Horn 2G 67
Dewey Rd. N1 5L 59
Dewey Rd. Dag 2M 65
Dewey St. SW17 2D 106
Dewgrass Gro. Wal X 8D 6
Dewhurst Rd. W14 4H 73
Dewhurst Rd. Chesh 2B 6
Dewlands Av. Dart 6M 99
Dewsbury Clo. Pinn 4J 37
Dewsbury Clo. Romf 6J 35
Dewsbury Ct. W4 5A 72
Dewsbury Gdns. Romf 6H 35
Dewsbury Gdns. Wor Pk 5E 120
Dewsbury Rd. NW10 1E 56
Dewsbury Rd. Romf 6H 35
Dewsbury Ter. NW1 4F 58
Dexter Ho. Eri 4J 81
(off Kale Rd.)
Dexter Rd. Barn 8H 13
Deyncourt Gdns. Upm 7M 51
Deyncourt Rd. N17 8A 28
Deynecourt Gdns. E11 2G 47
D'Eynsford Rd. SE5 9B 76
Dhonau Ho. SE1 5D 76
(off Longfield Est.)
Diadem Ct. W1 9H 59
(off Dean St.)
Dial Wlk., The. W8 3M 73
(off Broad Wlk., The)
Diamedes Av. Stanw 6B 144
Diameter Rd. Orp 2M 127
Diamond Clo. Dag 6G 49
Diamond Ct. Horn 6E 50
Diamond Est. SW17 9C 90
Diamond Ho. E3 5J 61
(off Roman Rd.)
Diamond Rd. Ruis 9H 37
Diamond Rd. Wat 2E 8
Diamond St. NW10 3B 56
Diamond St. SE15 8C 76
Diamond Ter. SE10 9A 78
Diamond Way. SE8 7L 77
Diana Clo. E18 8F 30
Diana Clo. SE8 7K 77
Diana Ct. Eri 7C 82
Diana Gdns. Surb 4K 119
Diana Ho. SW13 9D 72
Diana Rd. E17 1K 45
Dianne Way. Barn 6C 14
Dianthus Clo. SE2 6F 80
Diban Av. Horn 9F 50
Diban Ct. Horn 9F 50
(off Diban Av.)
Dibden Ho. SE5 8C 76
Dibden St. N1 4A 60
Dibdin Clo. Sutt 5L 121
Dibdin Ho. NW6 5M 57
Dibdin Rd. Sutt 5L 121
Diceland Rd. Bans 8K 135
Dicey Av. NW2 9G 41
Dickens Av. N3 8A 26
Dickens Av. Dart 3L 99
Dickens Av. Uxb 9F 142
Dickens Clo. Eri 8M 81
Dickens Clo. Hay 5C 68
Dickens Clo. Rich 8J 87
Dickens Ct. E11 2E 46
(off Makepeace Rd.)
Dickens Dri. Chst 3A 112
Dickens Est. SE1 & SE16 3E 76
Dickens Est. SE16 4E 76
Dickens House. 7K 59
Dickens Ho. NW6 6L 57
(off Malvern Rd.)
Dickens Ho. NW8 7B 58
(off Fisherton St.)
Dickens Ho. SE17 6M 75
(off Doddington Gro.)
Dickens Ho. WC1 7J 59
(off Herbrand St.)
Dickens La. N18 5C 28
Dickens M. EC1 8M 59
(off Turnmill St.)
Dickenson Clo. N9 1E 28
Dickenson Ho. N8 4K 43
Dickenson Rd. N8 5J 43
Dickenson Rd. Felt 2G 101
Dickensons La. SE25 9E 108
(in two parts)
Dickensons Pl. SE25 1E 124
Dickens Ri. Chig 3M 31
Dickens Rd. E6 5H 63
Dickens Sq. SE1 4A 76
Dickens St. SW8 1F 90
Dickens Way. Romf 2C 50
Dickenswood Clo. SE19 4M 107
Dickerage La. N Mald 7A 104
Dickerage Rd. King T 5A 104
Dicksee Ho. NW8 7B 58
(off Lyons Pl.)
Dickson. Chesh 1A 6
Dickson Fold. Pinn 2H 37
Dickson Ho. E1 9F 60
(off Philpot St.)
Dickson Rd. SE9 2J 95
Dick Turpin Way. Felt 3D 84
Didsbury Clo. E6 4K 63
Digby Bus. Cen. E9 2H 61
(off Digby Rd.)
Digby Cres. N4 7A 44
Digby Gdns. Dag 4L 65
Digby Mans. W6 6F 72
(off Hammersmith Bri. Rd.)
Digby Pl. Croy 5D 124
Digby Rd. E9 2H 61
Digby Rd. Bark 3D 64
Digby St. E2 6G 61
Digby Wlk. Horn 2G 67
Digdens Ri. Eps 7A 134
Diggens Ct. Lou 5J 19
Diggon St. E1 8H 61
Dighton Ct. SE5 7A 76
Dighton Rd. SW18 4A 90
Dignum St. N1 5L 59
Digswell Clo. Borwd 2L 11
Digswell St. N7 2L 59
Dilhorne Clo. SE12 9F 94
Dilke St. SW3 7D 74
Dilloway La. S'hall 3J 69
Dillwyn Clo. SE26 1J 109
Dilston Clo. N'holt 6G 53
Dilston Gro. SE16 5G 77
Dilton Gdns. SW15 7E 88
Dilwyn Ct. E17 9J 29
Dimes Pl. W6 5F 72
Dimmock Dri. Gnfd 1B 54
Dimond Clo. E7 9E 46
Dimsdale Dri. NW9 6A 40
Dimsdale Dri. Enf 9E 16
Dimsdale Wlk. E13 5E 62
Dimson Cres. E3 6L 61
Dingle Clo. Barn 8D 12
Dingle Gdns. E14 1L 77
Dingle Rd. Ashf 2A 100
Dingles Ct. Pinn 8H 21
Dingle, The. Uxb 6F 142
Dingley La. SW16 8H 91
Dingley Pl. EC1 6A 60
Dingley Rd. EC1 6A 60
Dingwall Av.
Croy & New Ad 4A 124
Dingwall Gdns. NW11 4L 41
Dingwall Rd. SW18 6A 90
Dingwall Rd. Cars 1D 136
Dingwall Rd. Croy 3B 124
Dinmont Est. E2 5E 60
Dinmont Ho. E2 5E 60
(off Pritchard's Rd.)
Dinmont St. E2 5F 60
Dinmore Ho. E9 4G 61
(off Templecombe Rd.)
Dinnington Ho. E1 7F 60
(off Coventry Rd.)
Dinsdale Gdns. SE25 9C 108
Dinsdale Gdns. New Bar 7M 13
Dinsdale Rd. SE3 7D 78
Dinsmore Rd. SW12 6F 90
Dinton Ho. NW8 7C 58
(off Lilestone St.)
Dinton Rd. SW19 3B 106
Dinton Rd. King T 4K 103
Diploma Av. N2 2C 42
Diploma Ct. N2 2C 42
Dirdene Clo. Eps 4D 134
Dirdene Gdns. Eps 4D 134
Dirdene Gro. Eps 4C 134
Dirleton Rd. E15 4D 62
Disbrowe Rd. W6 7J 73
Discovery Bus. Pk. SE16 4E 76
(off St James's Rd.)
Discovery Ho. E14 1A 78
(off Newby Pl.)
Discovery Wlk. E1 2F 76
Dishforth La. NW9 7C 24
Disley Ct. S'hall 9M 53
(off Howard Rd.)
Disney Pl. SE1 3A 76
Disney St. SE1 3A 76
Dison Clo. Enf 3H 17
Disraeli Clo. SE28 2G 81
Disraeli Clo. W4 4B 72
Disraeli Gdns. SW15 3K 89
Disraeli Rd. E7 2E 62
Disraeli Rd. NW10 5B 56
Disraeli Rd. SW15 3J 89
Disraeli Rd. W5 2H 71
Diss St. E2 6D 60
Distaff La. EC4 1A 76
Distillery La. W6 6G 73
Distillery Rd. W6 6G 73
Distillery Wlk. Bren 7J 71
Distin St. SE11 5L 75
District Rd. Wemb 1F 54
Ditch All. SE10 9M 77
Ditchburn St. E14 1A 78
Ditches Ride, The.
Lou & Epp 2L 19
Ditchfield Rd. Hay 7J 53
Ditchley Ct. W7 8D 54
(off Templeman Rd.)
Dittisham Rd. SE9 1J 111
Ditton Clo. Th Dit 2E 118
Dittoncroft Clo. Croy 6C 124
Ditton Grange Clo. Surb 3H 119
Ditton Grange Dri. Surb 3H 119
Ditton Hill. Surb 3G 119
Ditton Hill Rd. Surb 3G 119
Ditton Lawn. Th Dit 3E 118
Ditton Pl. SE20 5F 108
Ditton Reach. Th Dit 1F 118
Ditton Rd. Bexh 4H 97
Ditton Rd. S'hall 6K 69
Ditton Rd. Surb 4H 119
Divis Way. SW15 5F 88
(off Dover Pk. Dri.)
Dixon Clark Ct. N1 2M 59
Dixon Clo. E6 9K 63
Dixon Ho. W10 9H 57
(off Darfield Way)
Dixon Pl. W Wick 3M 125
Dixon Rd. SE14 9J 77
Dixon Rd. SE25 7C 108
Dixon's All. SE16 3F 76
Dobbin Clo. Harr 9E 22
Dobell Rd. SE9 4K 95
Doble Ct. S Croy 4E 138
Dobree Av. NW10 3F 56
Dobson Clo. NW6 3B 58
Dobson Ho. SE5 8B 76
(off Edmund St.)
Dobson Ho. SE14 7H 77
(off John Williams Clo.)
Doby Ct. EC4 1A 76
(off Skinners La.)
Dock Cotts. E1 1G 77
(off Highway, The)
Dockers Tanner Rd.
E14 4L 77
Dockhead. SE1 3D 76
Dockhead Wharf. SE1 3D 76
(off Shad Thames)
Dock Hill Av. SE16 2H 77
Docklands Mus. (Proposed)
1L 77
Dockland St. E16 2L 79
(in two parts)
Dockley Rd. SE16 4E 76
Dockley Rd. Ind. Est.
SE16 4E 76
(off Dockley Rd.)
Dock Offices. SE16 4G 77
(off Surrey Quays Rd.)
Dock Rd. E16 1D 78
Dock Rd. Bren 8H 71
Dockside Rd. E16 1H 79
Dock St. E1 1E 76
Dockwell Clo. Felt 3E 84
Doctor Johnson Av. SW17 9F 90
Doctors Clo. SE26 2G 109
Docwra's Bldgs. N1 2C 60
Dodbrooke Rd. SE27 9L 91
Dodd Ho. SE16 5F 76
(off Rennie Est.)
Doddington Gro. SE17 7M 75
Doddington Pl. SE17 7M 75
Dodsley Pl. N9 3G 29
Dodson St. SE1 3L 75
Dod St. E14 9K 61
Doebury Wlk. SE18 7E 80
(off Prestwood Clo.)
Doel Clo. SW19 4A 106
Dog & Duck Yd. WC1 8K 59
(off Princeton St.)
Doggett Rd. SE6 6L 93
Doggett's Corner. Horn 7K 51
Doggetts Courts. Barn 7C 14
Doghurst Av. Hay 8M 143
Doghurst Dri. W Dray 8M 143
Dog Kennel Hill. SE22 2C 92
Dog Kennel Hill Est. SE22 2C 92
(off Albrighton Rd.)
Dog La. NW10 9C 40
Doherty Rd. E13 7E 62
Dokal Ind. Est. S'hall 4J 69
Dolben Ct. SE8 5K 77
Dolben St. SE1 2M 75
(in two parts)
Dolby Rd. SW6 1K 89
Dolland Ho. SE11 6K 75
(off Newburn St.)
Dolland St. SE11 6K 75
Dollar Bay Ct. E14 3A 78
(off Lawn Ho. Clo.)
Dollary Pde. King T 7M 103
(off Kingston Rd.)
Dollis Av. N3 8K 25
Dollis Brook Wlk. Barn 8J 13
Dollis Cres. Ruis 6G 37
Dolliscroft. NW7 7J 25
Dollis Hill. 7F 40
Dollis Hill Av. NW2 8F 40
Dollis Hill Est. NW2 8E 40
Dollis Hill La. NW2 9D 40
Dollis M. N3 8L 25
Dollis Pk. N3 8K 25
Dollis Rd. NW7 & N3 7J 25
Dollis Valley Dri. Barn 8K 13
Dollis Valley Way. Barn 8K 13
Dolman Clo. N3 8A 26
Dolman Rd. W4 5B 72
Dolman St. SW4 3K 91
Dolphin App. Romf 2D 50
Dolphin Clo. SE16 3H 77
Dolphin Clo. SE28 9H 65
Dolphin Clo. Surb 9H 103
Dolphin Ct. NW11 4J 41
Dolphin Ct. SE8 7K 77
(off Wotton Rd.)
Dolphin Ct. Chig 3M 31
Dolphin Est. Sun 5C 100
Dolphin Ho. SW18 3M 89
Dolphin La. E14 1M 77
Dolphin Rd. N'holt 5K 53
Dolphin Rd. Sun 5C 100
Dolphin Rd. N. Sun 5C 100
Dolphin Rd. S. Sun 5C 100
Dolphin Rd. W. Sun 5C 100
Dolphin Sq. SW1 6G 75
Dolphin Sq. W4 8C 72
Dolphin St. King T 6J 103

Dolphin Tower—D'Oyley St.

Dolphin Tower. SE8 7K 77
(off Abinger Gro.)
Dombey Ho. SE1 3E 76
(off Wolseley St.)
Dombey Ho. W11 2H 73
(off St Ann's Rd.)
Dombey St. WC1 8K 59
(in two parts)
Dome Hill Pk. SE26 1D 108
Dome, The (Junct.) 9G 5
Domett Clo. SE5 3B 92
Domfe Pl. E5 9G 45
Domingo St. EC1 7A 60
Dominica Clo. E13 6G 63
Dominic Ct. Wal A 6H 7
Dominion Bus. Pk. N9 2H 29
Dominion Cen., The. S'hall 3J 69
Dominion Ct. E8 3D 60
(off Middleton Rd.)
Dominion Dri. Romf 6M 33
Dominion Ho. E14 6M 77
(off St Davids Sq.)
Dominion Pde. Harr 3D 38
Dominion Rd. Croy 2D 124
Dominion Rd. S'hall 3J 69
Dominion St. EC2 8B 60
Dominion Theatre. 9H 59
(off Tottenham Ct. Rd.)
Dominion Way. Rain 6E 66
Domitian Pl. Enf 7D 16
Domonic Dri. SE9 1M 111
Domville Clo. N20 2B 26
Donald Dri. Romf 3G 49
Donald Hunter Ho. E7 1F 62
(off Post Office App., in two parts)
Donald Rd. E13 4F 62
Donald Rd. Croy 2K 123
Donaldson Rd. NW6 4K 57
Donaldson Rd. SE18 9L 79
Donald Woods Gdns. Surb 4M 119
Doncaster Dri. N'holt 1K 53
Doncaster Gdns. N4 4A 44
Doncaster Gdns. N'holt 1K 53
Doncaster Grn. Wat 5G 21
Doncaster Rd. N9 9F 16
Doncaster Way. Upm 8K 51
Doncel Ct. E4 9B 18
Donegal Ho. E1 7F 60
(off Cambridge Heath Rd.)
Donegal St. N1 5K 59
Doneraile Ho. SW1 6F 74
(off Ebury Bri. Rd.)
Doneraile St. SW6 1H 89
Dongola Rd. E1 8J 61
Dongola Rd. E13 6F 62
Dongola Rd. N17 1C 44
Dongola Rd. W. E13 6F 62
Donington Av. Ilf 3A 48
Donkey All. SE22 6E 92
Donkey La. Enf 4E 16
Donkey La. F'ham 4M 131
Donkey La. W Dray 6G 143
Donkin Ho. SE16 5F 76
(off Rennie Est.)
Donmar Warehouse Theatre. 9J 59
(off Earlham St.)
Donnatt's Rd. SE14 9K 77
Donne Ct. SE24 5A 92
Donnefield Av. Edgw 7J 23
Donne Ho. E14 9L 61
(off Dod St.)
Donne Ho. SE14 7H 77
(off Samuel Clo.)
Donnelly Ct. SW6 8J 73
(off Dawes Rd.)
Donne Pl. SW3 5C 74
Donne Pl. Mitc 8F 106
Donne Rd. Dag 7G 49
Donnington Ct. NW1 3F 58
(off Castlehaven Rd.)
Donnington Ct. NW10 3F 56
Donnington Ct. Dart 5M 99
(off Bow Arrow La.)
Donnington Mans. NW10 4G 57
(off Donnington Rd.)
Donnington Rd. NW10 3F 56
Donnington Rd. Harr 3H 39
Donnington Rd. Wor Pk 4E 120
Donnybrook Rd. SW16 4G 107
Donoghue Cotts. E14 8J 61
(off Galsworthy Av.)
Donovan Av. N10 9F 26
Donovan Clo. Eps 2B 134
Donovan Ct. NW10 3A 56
Donovan Ct. SW10 6B 74
(off Drayton Gdns.)
Donovan Ho. E1 1G 77
(off Cable St.)
Donovan Pl. N21 7K 15
Don Phelan Clo. SE5 9B 76
Don Way. Romf 7C 34
Doone Clo. Tedd 3E 102
Doon St. SE1 2L 75
Dorado Gdns. Orp 5H 129
Dora Ho. E14 9K 61
(off Rhodeswell Rd.)
Dora Ho. W11 1H 73
(off St Ann's Rd.)
Doral Way. Cars 7D 122
Doran Ct. E6 5K 63
Dorando Clo. W12 1F 72
Doran Gro. SE18 8C 80
Doran Mnr. N2 3D 42
(off Gt. North Rd.)
Doran Wlk. E15 3A 62
Dora Rd. SW19 2L 105
Dora St. E14 9K 61
Dorchester Av. N13 4A 28
Dorchester Av. Bex 7H 97
Dorchester Av. Harr 4A 38
Dorchester Clo. Dart 6K 99
Dorchester Clo. N'holt 1M 53
Dorchester Clo. Orp 4F 112
Dorchester Ct. E18 8D 30
(off Buckingham Rd.)
Dorchester Ct. N1 3C 60
(off Englefield Rd.)
Dorchester Ct. N10 1F 42
Dorchester Ct. N14 9F 14
Dorchester Ct. NW2 8H 41
Dorchester Ct. SE24 4A 92
Dorchester Ct. Wat 8J 9
(off Chalk Hill)
Dorchester Dri. SE24 4A 92
Dorchester Dri. Felt 5C 84
Dorchester Gdns. E4 4L 29
Dorchester Gdns. NW11 2L 41
Dorchester Gro. W4 6C 72
Dorchester M. N Mald 8B 104
Dorchester M. Twic 5G 87
Dorchester Rd. Mord 2M 121
Dorchester Rd. N'holt 1M 53
Dorchester Rd. Wor Pk 3G 121
Dorchester Ter. NW2 8H 41
(off Gratton Ter.)
Dorchester Way. Harr 4K 39
Dorchester Waye. Hay 9F 52
(in two parts)
Dorcis Av. Bexh 1J 97
Dordrecht Rd. W3 2C 72
Dore Av. E12 1L 63
Doreen Av. NW9 6B 40
Doreen Capstan Ho. E11 8C 46
(off Apollo Pl.)
Dore Gdns. Mord 2M 121
Dorell Clo. S'hall 8K 53
Dorian Rd. Horn 6H 51
Doria Rd. SW6 1K 89
Doric Ho. E2 5H 61
(off Mace St.)
Doric Way. NW1 6H 59
Dorien Rd. SW20 6H 105
Doris Av. Eri 9A 82
Doris Emmerton Ct. SW11 3A 90
Doris Rd. E7 3E 62
Doris Rd. Ashf 3B 100
Doritt M. N18 5C 28
Dorking Clo. SE8 7K 77
Dorking Clo. Wor Pk 4H 121
Dorking Ct. N17 8E 28
(off Hampden La.)
Dorking Gdns. H Hill 5H 35
Dorking Glen. H Hill 4H 35
Dorking Ho. SE1 4B 76
Dorking Ri. H Hill 4H 35
Dorking Rd. Eps 8L 133
Dorking Rd. Romf 5H 35
Dorking Wlk. H Hill 4H 35
Dorlcote Rd. SW18 6C 90
Dorling Dri. Eps 4D 134
Dorly Clo. Shep 9C 100
Dorman Pl. N9 2E 28
Dormans Clo. N'wd 7B 20
Dorman Wlk. NW10 1B 56
Dorman Way. NW8 4B 58
Dorma Trad. Pk. E10 6H 45
Dormay St. SW18 4M 89
Dormer Clo. E15 2D 62
Dormer Clo. Barn 7H 13
Dormer's Av. S'hall 9L 53
Dormers Ct. E14 9L 61
Dormers Ri. S'hall 9M 53
Dormer's Wells. 1M 69
Dormer's Wells La. S'hall 9L 53
Dormstone Ho. SE17 5C 76
(off Beckway St.)
Dormywood. Ruis 3D 36
Dornberg Clo. SE3 8E 78
Dornberg Rd. SE3 8F 78
Dorncliffe Rd. SW6 1J 89
Dorney. NW3 3C 58
Dorney Ri. Orp 8D 112
Dorney Way. Houn 4J 85
Dornfell St. NW6 1K 57
Dornton Rd. SW12 8F 90
Dornton Rd. S Croy 8B 124
Dorothy Av. Wemb 3J 55
Dorothy Evans Clo. Bexh 3M 97
Dorothy Gdns. Dag 9F 48
Dorothy Pettingell Ho. Sutt 5M 121
(off Angel Hill)
Dorothy Rd. SW11 2D 90
Dorrell Pl. SW9 2L 91
Dorrien Wlk. SW16 8H 91
Dorrington Ct. SE25 5C 108
Dorrington Gdns. Horn 6H 51
Dorrington St. EC1 8L 59
Dorrit Ho. W11 2H 73
(off St Ann's Rd.)
Dorrit St. SE1 3A 76
Dorrit Way. Chst 3A 112
Dorrofield Clo. Crox G 7A 8
Dorryn Ct. SE26 2H 109
Dors Clo. NW9 6B 40
Dorset Av. Hay 6C 52
Dorset Av. Romf 2B 50
Dorset Av. S'hall 5L 69
Dorset Av. Well 3D 96
Dorset Bldgs. EC4 9M 59
Dorset Clo. NW1 8D 58
Dorset Clo. Hay 6C 52
Dorset Ct. N1 3C 60
(off Hertford Rd.)
Dorset Ct. W7 8D 54
(off Copley Clo.)
Dorset Ct. Eps 4D 134
Dorset Ct. N'wd 8D 20
Dorset Dri. Edgw 6K 23
Dorset Gdns. Mitc 8K 107
Dorset Ho. NW1 7D 58
(off Gloucester Pl.)
Dorset M. N3 8L 25
Dorset Pl. E15 2B 62
Dorset Ri. EC4 9M 59
Dorset Rd. E7 3G 63
Dorset Rd. N15 2B 44
Dorset Rd. N22 8J 27
Dorset Rd. SE9 8J 95
Dorset Rd. SW8 8J 75
Dorset Rd. SW19 5L 105
Dorset Rd. W5 4G 71
Dorset Rd. Ashf 9B 144
Dorset Rd. Beck 7H 109
Dorset Rd. Harr 4A 38
Dorset Rd. Mitc 6C 106
Dorset Rd. Sutt 2L 135
Dorset Sq. NW1 7D 58
Dorset Sq. Eps 2B 134
Dorset St. W1 8D 58
Dorset Way. Twic 7B 86
Dorset Way. Uxb 5D 142
Dorset Waye. Houn 8K 69
Dorton Clo. SE15 8C 76
Dorton Vs. W Dray 8L 143
Dorville Cres. W6 4F 72
Dorville Rd. SE12 4D 94
Dothill Rd. SE18 8A 80
Douai Gro. Hamp 5A 102
Doubleday Rd. Lou 5M 19
Doughty Ct. E1 2F 76
(off Prusom St.)
Doughty Ho. SW10 7A 74
(off Netherton Gro.)
Doughty M. WC1 7K 59
Doughty St. WC1 7K 59
Douglas Av. E17 8K 29
Douglas Av. N Mald 8F 104
Douglas Av. Romf 9J 35
Douglas Av. Wat 1H 9
Douglas Av. Wemb 3J 55
Douglas Clo. Stan 5E 22
Douglas Clo. Wall 8J 123
Douglas Ct. NW6 3L 57
(off Quex Rd.)
Douglas Ct. Big H 9J 141
Douglas Ct. King T 8J 103
(off Geneva Rd.)
Douglas Cres. Hay 7G 53
Douglas Dri. Croy 5L 125
Douglas Est. N1 2A 60
(off Marquess Rd.)
Douglas Ho. Surb 3K 119
Douglas Johnstone Ho. SW6 7K 73
(off Clem Attlee Ct.)
Douglas Mans. Houn 2M 85
Douglas M. NW2 8J 41
Douglas Pl. SW1 5H 75
(off Douglas St.)
Douglas Rd. E4 9C 18
Douglas Rd. E16 8E 62
Douglas Rd. N1 3A 60
Douglas Rd. N22 8L 27
Douglas Rd. NW6 4K 57
Douglas Rd. Esh 4M 117
Douglas Rd. Horn 4D 50
Douglas Rd. Houn 2M 85
Douglas Rd. Ilf 5E 48
Douglas Rd. King T 6M 103
Douglas Rd. Stanw 5B 144
Douglas Rd. Surb 4K 119
Douglas Rd. Well 9F 80
Douglas Rd. N. N1 2A 60
Douglas Rd. S. N1 2A 60
Douglas Robinson Ct. SW16 4J 107
(off Streatham High Rd.)
Douglas Sq. Mord 1L 121
Douglas St. SW1 5H 75
Douglas Ter. E17 8K 29
Douglas Waite Ho. NW6 3L 57
Douglas Way. SE8 8K 77
(Amersham Va., in two parts)
Douglas Way. SE8 8L 77
(Idonia St.)
Doulton Ho. SE11 4K 75
(off Lambeth Wlk.)
Doulton M. NW6 2M 57
Dounesforth Gdns. SW18 7M 89
Douro Pl. W8 4M 73
Douro St. E3 5L 61
Douthwaite Sq. E1 2E 76
Dove App. E6 8J 63
Dove Clo. NW7 7D 24
Dove Clo. N'holt 7H 53
Dove Clo. S Croy 3H 139
Dove Clo. Wall 9K 123
Dove Commercial Cen. NW5 1G 59
Dovecot Clo. Pinn 3G 37
Dovecote Av. N22 1L 43
Dove Cote Clo. Wey 5A 116
Dovecote Gdns. SW14 2B 88
Dove Ct. EC2 9B 60
(off Old Jewry)
Dovedale Av. Harr 4G 39
Dovedale Av. Ilf 9L 31
Dovedale Clo. Well 1E 96
Dovedale Ri. Mitc 4D 106
Dovedale Rd. SE22 4F 92
Dovedon Clo. N14 2J 27
Dovehouse Ct. N'holt 6H 53
(off Delta Gro.)
Dove Ho. Gdns. E4 2L 29
Dovehouse Grn. Wey 5B 116
Dovehouse Mead. Bark 5B 64
Dovehouse St. SW3 6B 74
Dove M. SW5 5A 74
Doveney Clo. Orp 7G 113
Dove Pk. Pinn 7L 21
Dover Clo. NW2 7H 41
Dover Clo. Romf 9A 34
Dovercourt Av. T Hth 9L 107
Dovercourt Est. N1 2B 60
Dovercourt Gdns. Stan 5J 23
Dovercourt La. Sutt 5A 122
Dovercourt Rd. SE22 5C 92
Doverfield Rd. SW2 6J 91
Dover Flats. SE1 5C 76
Dover Gdns. Cars 5D 122
Dover Ho. SE15 7G 77
Dover Ho. Rd. SW15 3E 88
Doveridge Gdns. N13 4M 27
Dove Rd. N1 2B 60
Dove Row. E2 4E 60
Dover Pk. Dri. SW15 5F 88
Dover Patrol. SE3 1F 94
Dover Rd. E12 7G 47
Dover Rd. N9 2G 29
Dover Rd. SE19 3B 108
Dover Rd. Romf 4J 49
Dovers Corner (Junct.) 6E 66
Dovers Corner. Rain 6E 66
Dovers Corner Ind. Est. Rain 6D 66
Dover St. W1 1F 74
Dover Ter. Rich 1K 87
(off Sandycombe Rd.)
Dover Way. Crox G 6A 8
Dover Yd. W1 2G 75
(off Berkeley St.)
Doves Clo. Brom 4J 127
Doves Cotts. Chig 3E 32
Doves Yd. N1 4L 59
Doveton Ho. E1 7G 61
(off Doveton St.)
Doveton Rd. S Croy 7B 124
Doveton St. E1 7G 61
Dovetree Ct. Romf 4H 35
(off N. Hill Dri.)
Dove Wlk. SW1 6E 74
Dove Wlk. Horn 2F 66
Dovey Lodge. N1 3L 59
(off Bewdley St.)
Dowanhill Rd. SE6 7B 94
Dowdeswell Clo. SW15 3C 88
Dowding Ho. N6 5E 42
(off Hillcrest)
Dowding Pl. Stan 6E 22
Dowding Rd. Big H 7H 141
Dowding Rd. Uxb 3D 142
Dowding Way. Horn 3F 66
Dowding Way. Leav 7D 4
Dowdney Clo. NW5 1G 59
Dowe Ho. SE3 2C 94
Dower Av. Wall 1F 136
Dowes Ho. SW16 9J 91
Dowgate Hill. EC4 1B 76
Dowland St. W10 6J 57
Dowlas St. SE5 8C 76
Dowler Ct. King T 5J 103
(off Burton Rd.)
Dowler Ho. E1 9E 60
(off Burslem St.)
Dowlerville Rd. Orp 8D 128
Dowling Ho. Belv 4K 81
Dowman Clo. SW19 5M 105
Downage. NW4 1G 41
Downalong. Bus H 1B 22
Downbank Av. Bexh 9B 82
Down Barns Rd. Ruis 8H 37
Downbury M. SW18 4L 89
Down Clo. N'holt 5F 52
Downderry Rd. Brom 9B 94
Downe. 3L 141
Downe Clo. Well 8G 81
Down End. SE18 8M 79
Downend Ct. SE15 7C 76
(off Longhope Clo.)
Downe Rd. Cud 5M 141
Downe Rd. Kes 1J 141
Downe Rd. Mitc 6D 106
Downer's Cottage. SW4 3G 91
Downes Clo. Twic 5F 86
Downes Ct. N21 1L 27
Downes Ho. Croy 6M 123
(off Violet La.)
Downe Ter. Rich 5J 87
Downey Ho. E1 7H 61
(off Globe Rd.)
Downfield. Wor Pk 3D 120
Downfield Clo. W9 7M 57
Downfield Rd. Chesh 4E 6
Down Hall Rd. King T 5H 103
Downham. 2B 110
Downham Clo. Romf 7L 33
Downham Enterprise Cen. SE6 8D 94
Downham La. Brom 2B 110
Downham Rd. N1 3B 60
Downham Way. Brom 2B 110
Downhills Av. N17 1B 44
Downhills Pk. Rd. N17 1A 44
Downhills Way. N17 1A 44
Down House Mus. 4L 141
Downhurst Av. NW7 5B 24
Downhurst Ct. NW4 1G 41
Downing Clo. Harr 1A 38
Downing Dri. Gnfd 4B 54
Downing Rd. Dag 4K 65
Downings. E6 9L 63
Downing St. SW1 3J 75
Downland Clo. N20 1A 26
Downland Gdns. Eps 9F 134
Downlands. Wal A 7L 7
Downlands Clo. Coul 6F 136
Downlands Rd. Purl 5J 137
Downland Way. Eps 9F 134
Downleys Clo. SE9 8J 95
Downman Rd. SE9 2J 95
Down Pl. W6 5F 72
Down Rd. Tedd 3F 102
Downs Av. Chst 2K 111
Downs Av. Dart 6L 99
Downs Av. Eps 6C 134
Downs Av. Pinn 4J 37
Downsbridge Rd. Beck 5B 110
Downscourt Rd. Purl 4M 137
Downsell Rd. E15 9A 46
Downsfield Rd. E17 4J 45
Downshall Av. Ilf 4C 48
Downs Hill. Beck 4B 110
Downs Hill Rd. Eps 6C 134
Downshire Hill. NW3 9B 42
Downside. Eps 6C 134
Downside. Sun 5E 100
Downside. Twic 9D 86
Downside Clo. SW19 3A 106
Downside Cres. NW3 1C 58
Downside Cres. W13 7E 54
Downside Rd. Sutt 8B 122
Downside Wlk. Bren 7H 71
(off Windmill Rd.)
Downside Wlk. N'holt 6K 53
Downs La. E5 9F 44
Downs Lodge Ct. Eps 6C 134
Downs Pk. Rd. E8 & E5 1D 60
Downs Rd. E5 9E 44
Downs Rd. Beck 6M 109
(in two parts)
Downs Rd. Coul 9H 137
Downs Rd. Enf 6C 16
Downs Rd. Eps 6C 134
Downs Rd. Purl 3M 137
Downs Rd. Sutt 2M 135
Downs Rd. T Hth 5A 108
Downs Side. Sutt 3K 135
Downs, The. SW20 4H 105
Down St. W1 2F 74
Down St. W Mol 9L 101
Down St. M. W1 2F 74
Downs Vw. Iswth 9D 70
Downsview Clo. Swan 7D 114
Downsview Gdns. SE19 4M 107
Downsview Rd. SE19 4A 108
Downs Way. Eps 8D 134
Downsway. Orp 7C 128
Downsway. S Croy 3C 138
Downsway. Whyt 8D 138
Downsway, The. Sutt 1A 136
Downs Wood. Eps 9F 134
Downton Av. SW2 8J 91
Downtown Rd. SE16 3J 77
Downway. N12 7C 26
Down Way. N'holt 5F 52
Dowrey St. N1 4L 59
Dowry Wlk. Wat 2D 8
Dowsett Rd. N17 9D 28
Dowson Clo. SE5 3B 92
Dowson Ho. E1 9H 61
(off Bower St.)
Doyce St. SE1 3A 76
Doyle Clo. Eri 9C 82
Doyle Gdns. NW10 4E 56
Doyle Ho. SW13 8G 73
(off Trinity Chu. Rd.)
Doyle Rd. SE25 8E 108
D'Oyley St. SW1 5E 74

D'Oyly Carte Island—Dunkeld Rd.

D'Oyly Carte Island. Wey ... 3A 116
Doynton St. N19 ... 7F 42
Draco Ga. SW15 ... 2G 89
Draco St. SE17 ... 7A 76
Dragonfly Clo. E13 ... 6F 62
Dragon Rd. SE15 ... 7C 76
Dragon Yd. WC1 ... 9J 59 (off High Holborn)
Dragoon Rd. SE8 ... 6K 77
Dragor Rd. NW10 ... 7A 56
Drake Clo. SE16 ... 3H 77
Drake Ct. W12 ... 3G 73 (off Scott's Rd.)
Drake Ct. Eri ... 8D 82 (off Frobisher Rd.)
Drake Ct. Surb ... 8J 103 (off Cranes Pk. Av.)
Drake Cres. SE28 ... 9G 65
Drakefell Rd. SE14 & SE4 ... 1H 93
Drakefield Rd. SW17 ... 9E 90
Drake Hall. E16 ... 2F 78 (off Wesley Av., in two parts)
Drake Ho. E1 ... 8G 61 (off Stepney Way)
Drake Ho. E14 ... 1J 77 (off Victory Pl.)
Drake Ho. SW1 ... 7H 75 (off Dolphin Sq.)
Drakeland Ho. W9 ... 7K 57 (off Fernhead Rd.)
Drakeley Ct. N5 ... 9M 43
Drake M. Horn ... 9F 50 (Calbourne Av.)
Drake M. Horn ... 2E 66 (Fulmar Rd.)
Drake Rd. SE4 ... 2L 93
Drake Rd. Chess ... 7L 119
Drake Rd. Croy ... 2K 123
Drake Rd. Harr ... 7K 37
Drake Rd. Mitc ... 1E 122
Drakes Clo. Chesh ... 1D 6
Drake's Clo. Esh ... 6L 117
Drakes Ct. SE23 ... 7G 93
Drakes Courtyard. NW6 ... 3K 57
Drake St. WC1 ... 8K 59
Drake St. Enf ... 3B 16
Drakes Wlk. E6 ... 4K 63 (in two parts)
Drakewood Rd. SW16 ... 4H 107
Draper Clo. Belv ... 5K 81
Draper Clo. Iswth ... 1B 86
Draper Ct. Brom ... 8J 111
Draper Ho. SE1 ... 5M 75 (off Elephant & Castle)
Draper Pl. N1 ... 4M 59 (off Dagmar Ter.)
Drapers' Cottage Homes. NW7 ... 4E 24 (in two parts)
Drapers Gdns. EC2 ... 9B 60
Drapers Rd. E15 ... 9B 46
Drapers Rd. N17 ... 1D 44
Drapers Rd. Enf ... 4M 15
Drappers Way. SE16 ... 5E 76
Draven Clo. Brom ... 2D 126
Drawdock Rd. SE10 ... 3B 78
Drawell Clo. SE18 ... 6C 80
Drax Av. SW20 ... 4E 104
Draxmont. SW19 ... 3J 105
Draycot Rd. E11 ... 4F 46
Draycot Rd. Surb ... 3L 119
Draycott Av. SW3 ... 5C 74
Draycott Av. Harr ... 4F 38
Draycott Clo. NW2 ... 8H 41
Draycott Clo. Harr ... 4F 38
Draycott Pl. SW3 ... 5D 74
Draycott Ter. SW3 ... 5D 74
Dray Ct. Wor Pk ... 3D 120
Drayford Clo. W9 ... 7K 57
Dray Gdns. SW2 ... 4K 91
Draymans Way. Iswth ... 2D 86
Drayside M. S'hall ... 3K 69
Drayson Clo. Wal A ... 5L 7
Drayson M. W8 ... 3L 73
Drayton Av. W13 ... 1E 70
Drayton Av. Lou ... 9K 19
Drayton Av. Orp ... 3M 127
Drayton Bri. Rd. W7 & W13 ... 1D 70
Drayton Clo. Houn ... 4K 85
Drayton Clo. Ilf ... 6B 48
Drayton Ct. W Dray ... 5K 143
Drayton Gdns. N21 ... 9M 15
Drayton Gdns. SW10 ... 6A 74
Drayton Gdns. W13 ... 1E 70
Drayton Gdns. W Dray ... 3J 143
Drayton Grn. W13 ... 1E 70
Drayton Grn. Rd. W13 ... 1F 70
Drayton Gro. W13 ... 1E 70
Drayton Ho. E11 ... 6B 46
Drayton Ho. SE5 ... 8B 76 (off Elmington Rd.)
Drayton Pk. N5 ... 9L 43
Drayton Pk. M. N5 ... 1L 59
Drayton Rd. E11 ... 6B 46
Drayton Rd. N17 ... 9C 28
Drayton Rd. NW10 ... 4D 56
Drayton Rd. W13 ... 1E 70
Drayton Rd. Borwd ... 6L 11
Drayton Rd. Croy ... 4M 123
Drayton Waye. Harr ... 4F 38
Dreadnought Wharf. SE10 ... 7M 77 (off Thames St.)
Drenon Sq. Hay ... 1D 68
Dresden Clo. NW6 ... 2M 57
Dresden Ho. SE11 ... 5K 75 (off Lambeth Wlk.)
Dresden Rd. N19 ... 6G 43
Dresden Way. Wey ... 7A 116
Dressington Av. SE4 ... 5L 93
Drew Av. NW7 ... 6J 25
Drewery Ct. SE3 ... 2C 94
Drewett Ho. E1 ... 9E 60 (off Christian St.)
Drew Gdns. Gnfd ... 2D 54
Drew Ho. SW16 ... 9J 91
Drewitts Ct. W on T ... 3D 116
Drew Rd. E16 ... 2H 79 (in three parts)
Drewstead Rd. SW16 ... 8H 91
Driffield Ct. NW9 ... 8C 24 (off Pageant Av.)
Driffield Rd. E3 ... 5J 61
Drift Bridge (Junct.) ... 6G 135
Drift, The. Brom ... 5H 127
Driftway, The. Bans ... 7G 135
Driftway, The. Mitc ... 5E 106
Driftwood Dri. Kenl ... 9M 137
Drill Hall Arts Cen. ... 8H 59 (off Chenies St.)
Drinkwater Ho. SE5 ... 8B 76 (off Picton St.)
Drinkwater Rd. Harr ... 7M 37
Drive Ct. Edgw ... 5L 23
Drive Mans. SW6 ... 1J 89 (off Fulham Rd.)
Drive Mead. Coul ... 6J 137
Drive, The. E4 ... 9B 18
Drive, The. E17 ... 1M 45
Drive, The. E18 ... 2E 46
Drive, The. N2 ... 3D 42
Drive, The. N3 ... 7L 25
Drive, The. N7 ... 2K 59 (in two parts)
Drive, The. N11 ... 6H 27
Drive, The. NW10 ... 4D 56
Drive, The. NW11 ... 5J 41
Drive, The. SW6 ... 1J 89
Drive, The. SW16 ... 7K 107
Drive, The. SW20 ... 4G 105
Drive, The. W3 ... 9A 56
Drive, The. Ashf ... 4B 100
Drive, The. Bans ... 9J 135
Drive, The. Bark ... 3D 64
Drive, The. Beck ... 6L 109
Drive, The. Bex ... 5G 97
Drive, The. Buck H ... 9G 19
Drive, The. Chesh ... 1B 6
Drive, The. Chst ... 7D 112
Drive, The. Col R ... 7B 34
Drive, The. Coul ... 6J 137
Drive, The. Edgw ... 5L 23
Drive, The. Enf ... 3B 16
Drive, The. Eps ... 8D 120
Drive, The. Eri ... 8M 81
Drive, The. Esh ... 3A 118
Drive, The. Felt ... 6G 85
Drive, The. H Wood ... 8J 35
Drive, The. Harr ... 5L 37
Drive, The. High Bar ... 5J 13
Drive, The. Houn & Iswth ... 1B 86
Drive, The. Ilf ... 4J 47
Drive, The. King T ... 4A 104
Drive, The. Lou ... 5J 19 (in two parts)
Drive, The. Mord ... 9A 106
Drive, The. New Bar ... 8A 14
Drive, The. N'wd ... 9C 20
Drive, The. Orp ... 4D 128
Drive, The. Sidc ... 9F 96
Drive, The. Surb ... 2J 119
Drive, The. Sutt ... 4K 135
Drive, The. T Hth ... 8B 108
Drive, The. Uxb ... 1C 142
Drive, The. Wall ... 2G 137
Drive, The. Wat ... 1B 8
Drive, The. Wemb ... 7A 40
Drive, The. W Wick ... 2B 126
Driveway, The. E17 ... 4M 45 (off Hoe St.)
Dr Johnson's House. ... 9L 59 (off Pemberton Row)
Droitwich Clo. SE26 ... 9E 92
Dromey Gdns. Harr ... 7D 22
Dromore Rd. SW15 ... 5J 89
Dronfield Gdns. Dag ... 1G 65
Dron Ho. E1 ... 8G 61 (off Adelina Gro.)
Droop St. W10 ... 6H 57
Drop La. Brick W ... 3M 5
Drovers Ct. King T ... 6J 103 (off Fairfield E.)
Drovers Pl. SE15 ... 8G 77
Drovers Rd. S Croy ... 7B 124
Droveway. Lou ... 4M 19
Druce Rd. SE21 ... 5C 92
Druid St. SE1 ... 3C 76
Druids Way. Brom ... 8B 110
Drumaline Ridge. Wor Pk ... 4C 120
Drummond Av. Romf ... 2B 50
Drummond Cen., The. Croy ... 4A 124
Drummond Clo. Eri ... 9C 82
Drummond Cres. NW1 ... 6H 59
Drummond Dri. Stan ... 7D 22
Drummond Gdns. Eps ... 3A 134
Drummond Ga. SW1 ... 6H 75
Drummond Ho. E2 ... 5E 60 (off Goldsmiths Row)
Drummond Pl. Twic ... 6F 86
Drummond Rd. E11 ... 4G 47
Drummond Rd. SE16 ... 4F 76
Drummond Rd. Croy ... 4A 124 (in two parts)
Drummond Rd. Romf ... 2B 50
Drummonds, The. Buck H ... 2F 30
Drummond St. NW1 ... 7G 59
Drum St. E1 ... 9D 60
Drury Cres. Croy ... 4L 123
Drury Ho. SW8 ... 9G 75
Drury La. WC2 ... 9J 59
Drury Lane Theatre. ... 1K 75 (off Catherine St.)
Drury Rd. Harr ... 5A 38
Drury Way. NW10 ... 1B 56
Drury Way Ind. Est. NW10 ... 1A 56
Dryad St. SW15 ... 2H 89
Dryburgh Gdns. NW9 ... 1L 39
Dryburgh Ho. SW1 ... 6F 74 (off Abbots Mnr.)
Dryburgh Rd. SW15 ... 2F 88
Dryden Av. W7 ... 9D 54
Dryden Clo. Ilf ... 6D 32
Dryden Ct. SE11 ... 5M 75
Dryden Mans. W14 ... 7J 73 (off Queen's Club Gdns.)
Dryden Rd. SW19 ... 3A 106
Dryden Rd. Enf ... 8C 16
Dryden Rd. Harr ... 8D 22
Dryden Rd. Well ... 9D 80
Dryden St. WC2 ... 9J 59
Dryden Way. Orp ... 3E 128
Dryfield Clo. NW10 ... 2A 56
Dryfield Rd. Edgw ... 6A 24
Dryfield Wlk. SE8 ... 7L 77
Dryhill Rd. Belv ... 7K 81
Dryland Av. Orp ... 6D 128
Drylands Rd. N8 ... 4J 43
Drynham Pk. Wey ... 5C 116
Drysdale Av. E4 ... 9M 17
Drysdale Clo. N'wd ... 7C 20
Drysdale Ho. N1 ... 6C 60 (off Drysdale St.)
Drysdale Pl. N1 ... 6C 60
Drysdale St. N1 ... 6C 60
Dublin Av. E8 ... 4E 60
Dublin Ct. S Harr ... 7B 38 (off Northolt Rd.)
Du Burstow Ter. W7 ... 3C 70
Ducal St. E2 ... 6D 60
Du Cane Clo. W12 ... 9G 57
Du Cane Ct. SW17 ... 7E 90
Du Cane Rd. W12 ... 9D 56
Ducavel Ho. SW2 ... 7K 91
Duchess Clo. N11 ... 5F 26
Duchess Clo. Sutt ... 6A 122
Duchess Gro. Buck H ... 2F 30
Duchess M. W1 ... 8F 58
Duchess of Bedford Ho. W8 ... 3L 73 (off Duchess of Bedford's Wlk.)
Duchess of Bedford's Wlk. W8 ... 3L 73
Duchess St. W1 ... 8F 58
Duchess Theatre. ... 1K 75 (off Catherine St.)
Duchy Rd. Barn ... 2B 14
Duchy St. SE1 ... 2L 75 (in two parts)
Ducie St. SW4 ... 3K 91
Duckett M. N4 ... 4M 43
Duckett Rd. N4 ... 4L 43
Ducketts Rd. Dart ... 4D 98
Duckett St. E1 ... 7H 61
Ducking Stool Ct. Romf ... 2C 50
Duck La. W1 ... 9H 59 (off Broadwick St.)
Duck Lees La. Enf ... 6J 17
Duck's Hill Rd. N'wd & Ruis ... 8A 20
Ducks Island. ... 8H 13
Ducks Wlk. Twic ... 4G 87
Du Cros Dri. Stan ... 6H 23
Du Cros Rd. W3 ... 2C 72
Dudden Hill. ... 1F 56
Dudden Hill La. NW10 ... 9D 40
Dudden Hill Pde. NW10 ... 9D 40
Duddington Clo. SE9 ... 1H 111
Dudley Av. Harr ... 9G 23
Dudley Av. Wal X ... 5D 6
Dudley Ct. NW11 ... 2K 41
Dudley Ct. W1 ... 9D 58 (off Up. Berkeley St.)
Dudley Ct. WC2 ... 9J 59
Dudley Dri. Mord ... 3J 121
Dudley Dri. Ruis ... 1F 52
Dudley Gdns. W13 ... 3F 70
Dudley Gdns. Harr ... 6B 38
Dudley Gdns. Romf ... 6H 35
Dudley Gro. Eps ... 6A 134
Dudley Ho. W2 ... 8B 58 (off N. Wharf Rd.)
Dudley Rd. E17 ... 9L 29
Dudley Rd. N3 ... 9M 25
Dudley Rd. NW6 ... 5J 57
Dudley Rd. SW19 ... 3L 105
Dudley Rd. Felt ... 7A 84
Dudley Rd. Harr ... 7A 38
Dudley Rd. Ilf ... 9M 47
Dudley Rd. King T ... 7K 103
Dudley Rd. Rich ... 1K 87
Dudley Rd. Romf ... 6H 35
Dudley Rd. S'hall ... 3H 69
Dudley Rd. W on T ... 1E 116
Dudley St. W2 ... 8B 58
Dudlington Rd. E5 ... 7G 45
Dudmaston M. SW3 ... 6B 74 (off Fulham Rd.)
Dudrich M. SE5 ... 8A 76 (off Pitman St.)
Dudrich M. Enf ... 3M 15
Dudsbury Rd. Dart ... 5F 98
Dudsbury Rd. Sidc ... 3F 112
Dudset La. Houn ... 9E 68
Duffell Ho. SE11 ... 6K 75 (off Loughborough St.)
Dufferin Av. EC1 ... 7B 60 (off Dufferin St.)
Dufferin Ct. EC1 ... 7B 60 (off Dufferin St.)
Dufferin St. EC1 ... 7A 60
Duffield Clo. Harr ... 3D 38
Duffield Dri. N15 ... 2D 44
Duff St. E14 ... 9M 61
Dufour's Pl. W1 ... 9G 59
Dugard Way. SE11 ... 5M 75
Duke Gdns. Ilf ... 2B 48
Duke Humphrey Rd. SE3 ... 9C 78 (in two parts)
Duke of Cambridge Clo. Twic ... 5B 86
Duke of Edinburgh Rd. Sutt ... 4B 122
Duke of Wellington Pl. SW1 ... 3E 74
Duke of York Column (Memorial) ... 2H 75 (off Carlton Ho. Ter.)
Duke of York's Theatre. ... 1J 75 (off St Martin's La.)
Duke of York St. SW1 ... 2G 75
Duke Rd. W4 ... 6B 72
Duke Rd. Ilf ... 2B 48
Dukes Av. N3 ... 8M 25
Duke's Av. N10 ... 1F 42
Duke's Av. W4 ... 6B 72
Duke's Av. Edgw ... 6K 23
Dukes Av. Harr ... 2C 38
Dukes Av. Houn ... 3J 85
Dukes Av. N Mald ... 7C 104
Dukes Av. N Har ... 4K 37
Dukes Av. N'holt ... 3J 53
Dukes Av. Rich ... 1G 103
Dukes Clo. Ashf ... 1A 100
Dukes Clo. Hamp ... 2K 101
Dukes Ct. E6 ... 4L 63
Dukes Ct. SE13 ... 1A 94
Dukes Ga. W4 ... 5A 72
Dukes Grn. Av. Felt ... 4E 84
Dukes Head Pas. Hamp ... 4A 102
Duke's Head Yd. N6 ... 6F 42
Duke Shore Wharf. E14 ... 1K 77
Duke's Ho. SW1 ... 5H 75 (off Vincent St.)
Dukes La. W8 ... 3M 73
Dukes M. N10 ... 1F 42
Duke's M. W1 ... 9E 58 (off Duke St.)
Dukes Orchard. Bex ... 7A 98
Duke's Pas. E17 ... 2A 46
Duke's Pl. EC3 ... 9C 60
Dukes Rd. E6 ... 4L 63
Dukes Rd. W3 ... 7L 55
Duke's Rd. WC1 ... 6H 59
Dukes Rd. W on T ... 7H 117
Dukesthorpe Rd. SE26 ... 1H 109
Duke St. SW1 ... 2G 75
Duke St. W1 ... 9E 58
Duke St. Rich ... 3H 87
Duke St. Sutt ... 6B 122
Duke St. Wat ... 5G 9
Duke St. Hill. SE1 ... 2B 76
Duke St. Mans. W1 ... 9E 58 (off Duke St.)
Dukes Way. Uxb ... 4A 142
Dukes Way. W Wick ... 5C 126
Duke's Yd. W1 ... 1E 74
Dulas St. N4 ... 6K 43
Dulford St. W11 ... 1J 73
Dulka Rd. SW11 ... 4D 90
Dulverton. NW1 ... 4G 59 (off Royal College St.)
Dulverton Mans. WC1 ... 7K 59 (off Gray's Inn Rd.)
Dulverton Rd. SE9 ... 8A 96
Dulverton Rd. Romf ... 6H 35
Dulverton Rd. Ruis ... 6E 36
Dulverton Rd. S Croy ... 2G 139
Dulwich. ... 8C 92
Dulwich Comn. SE21 ... 7C 92
Dulwich Hamlet F.C. ... 3C 92
Dulwich Lawn Clo. SE22 ... 4D 92
Dulwich Oaks Pl. SE21 ... 9C 92
Dulwich Picture Gallery. ... 6B 92
Dulwich Ri. Gdns. SE22 ... 4D 92
Dulwich Rd. SE24 ... 4L 91
Dulwich Village. ... 6C 92
Dulwich Village. SE21 ... 5B 92
Dulwich Wood Av. SE19 ... 1C 108
Dulwich Wood Pk. SE19 ... 1C 108
Dumain Ct. SE11 ... 5M 75 (off Opal St.)
Dumbarton Av. Wal X ... 7D 6
Dumbarton Ct. SW2 ... 5J 91
Dumbarton Rd. SW2 ... 5J 91
Dumbleton Clo. King T ... 5M 103
Dumbreck Rd. SE9 ... 3K 95
Dumfries Clo. Wat ... 3D 20
Dumont Rd. N16 ... 8C 44
Dumpton Pl. NW1 ... 3E 58
Dunally Pk. Shep ... 2B 116
Dunbar Av. SW16 ... 6L 107
Dunbar Av. Beck ... 8J 109
Dunbar Av. Dag ... 8L 49
Dunbar Clo. Hay ... 9F 52
Dunbar Ct. Brom ... 8E 110 (off Durham Rd.)
Dunbar Ct. Sutt ... 7B 122
Dunbar Ct. W on T ... 3G 117
Dunbar Gdns. Dag ... 1L 65
Dunbar Rd. E7 ... 2E 62
Dunbar Rd. N22 ... 8L 27
Dunbar Rd. N Mald ... 8A 104
Dunbar St. SE27 ... 9A 92
Dunbar Wharf. E14 ... 1K 77 (off Narrow St.)
Dunblane Clo. Edgw ... 2M 23
Dunblane Rd. SE9 ... 2J 95
Dunboe Pl. Shep ... 2A 116
Dunboyne Rd. NW3 ... 1D 58
Dunbridge Ho. SW15 ... 5D 88 (off Highcliffe Dri.)
Dunbridge St. E2 ... 7E 60
Duncan Clo. Barn ... 6A 14
Duncan Ct. N21 ... 1M 27
Duncan Gro. W3 ... 9C 56
Duncan Ho. NW3 ... 3D 58 (off Fellows Rd.)
Duncan Ho. SW1 ... 6G 75 (off Dolphin Sq.)
Duncannon Ho. SW1 ... 6H 75 (off Lindsay Sq.)
Duncannon St. WC2 ... 1J 75
Duncan Rd. E8 ... 4F 60
Duncan Rd. Rich ... 3J 87
Duncan St. N1 ... 5M 59
Duncan Ter. N1 ... 5M 59 (in two parts)
Duncan Way. Bush ... 4K 9
Dunch St. E1 ... 9F 60
Duncombe Hill. SE23 ... 6J 93
Duncombe Rd. N19 ... 6H 43
Duncrievie Rd. SE13 ... 5B 94
Duncroft. SE18 ... 8C 80
Dundalk Ho. E1 ... 9G 61 (off Clark St.)
Dundalk Rd. SE4 ... 2J 93
Dundas Gdns. W Mol ... 7M 101
Dundas M. Enf ... 1L 17
Dundas Rd. SE15 ... 1G 93
Dundee Ct. E1 ... 2F 76 (off Wapping High St.)
Dundee Ho. W9 ... 6A 58 (off Maida Va.)
Dundee Rd. E13 ... 5F 62
Dundee Rd. SE25 ... 9F 108
Dundee St. E1 ... 2F 76
Dundee Way. Enf ... 5J 17
Dundee Wharf. E14 ... 1K 77
Dundela Gdns. Wor Pk ... 6F 120
Dundonald Clo. E6 ... 9J 63
Dundonald Ho. E14 ... 3M 77 (off Admirals Way)
Dundonald Rd. NW10 ... 4H 57
Dundonald Rd. SW19 ... 4J 105 (in two parts)
Dundry Ho. SE26 ... 9E 92
Dunedin Ho. E16 ... 2K 79 (off Manwood St.)
Dunedin Rd. E10 ... 8M 45
Dunedin Rd. Ilf ... 6A 48
Dunedin Rd. Rain ... 6D 66
Dunedin Way. Hay ... 7G 53
Dunelm Gro. SE27 ... 9A 92
Dunelm St. E1 ... 9H 61
Dunfield Gdns. SE6 ... 2M 109
Dunfield Rd. SE6 ... 2M 109 (in two parts)
Dunford Ct. Pinn ... 7K 21
Dunford Rd. N7 ... 9K 43
Dungarvan Av. SW15 ... 3E 88
Dunheved Clo. T Hth ... 1L 123
Dunheved Rd. N. T Hth ... 1L 123
Dunheved Rd. S. T Hth ... 1L 123
Dunheved Rd. W. T Hth ... 1L 123
Dunholme Grn. N9 ... 3D 28
Dunholme La. N9 ... 3D 28
Dunholme Rd. N9 ... 3D 28
Dunkeld Ho. E14 ... 9B 62 (off Abbott Rd.)
Dunkeld Rd. SE25 ... 8B 108

Dunkeld Rd.—Eastholm

Dunkeld Rd. Dag 7F 48
Dunkery Rd. SE9 1H 111
Dunkin Rd. Dart 3L 99
Dunkirk St. SE27 1A 108
Dunlace Rd. E5 9G 45
Dunleary Clo. Houn 6K 85
Dunley Dri. New Ad 9M 125
Dunlin Ho. SE16 5H 77
(off Tawny Way)
Dunloe Av. N17 1B 44
Dunloe Ct. E2 5D 60
Dunloe St. E2 5D 60
Dunlop Pl. SE16 4D 76
Dunmall Dri. Purl 6C 138
Dunmore Point. E2 6D 60
(off Gascoigne Pl.)
Dunmore Rd. NW6 4J 57
Dunmore Rd. SW20 5G 105
Dunmow Clo. Felt 9J 85
Dunmow Clo. Lou 8J 19
Dunmow Clo. Romf 3G 49
Dunmow Dri. Rain 4D 66
Dunmow Ho. SE11 6K 75
(off Newburn St.)
Dunmow Rd. E15 9B 46
Dunmow Wlk. N1 4A 60
(off Popham St.)
Dunnage Cres. SE16 5J 77
(in two parts)
Dunnico Ho. SE17 6C 76
(off East St.)
Dunningford Clo. Horn 1D 66
Dunn Mead. NW9 7D 24
Dunnock Clo. E6 9J 63
Dunnock Clo. N9 1H 29
Dunnock Clo. Borwd 6L 11
Dunn's Pas. WC1 9J 59
(off High Holborn)
Dunn St. E8 1D 60
Dunnymans Rd. Bans 7K 135
Dunollie Pl. NW5 1G 59
Dunollie Rd. NW5 1G 59
Dunoon Gdns. SE23 6H 93
Dunoon Ho. N1 4K 59
(off Bemerton Est.)
Dunoon Rd. SE23 6G 93
Dunoran Home. Brom 5J 111
Dunraven Dri. Enf 4L 15
Dunraven Rd. W12 2E 72
Dunraven St. W1 1D 74
Dunsany Rd. W14 4H 73
Dunsbury Clo. Sutt 1M 135
Dunsfold Ri. Coul 5H 137
Dunsfold Way. New Ad 1M 139
Dunsford Way. SW15 5F 88
Dunsmore Clo. Bush 8B 10
Dunsmore Clo. Hay 7J 53
Dunsmore Rd. W on T 1F 116
Dunsmore Way. Bush 8B 10
Dunsmure Rd. N16 6C 44
Dunspring La. Ilf 9M 31
Dunstable Clo. Romf 6H 35
Dunstable M. W1 8E 58
Dunstable Rd. Rich 3J 87
Dunstable Rd. Romf 6H 35
Dunstable Rd. W Mol 8K 101
Dunstall Rd. SW20 3F 104
Dunstall Way. W Mol 7M 101
Dunstall Welling Est. Well 1F 96
Dunstan Clo. N2 1A 42
Dunstan Glade. Orp 1B 128
Dunstan Houses. E1 8G 61
(off Stepney Grn.)
Dunstan Rd. NW11 6K 41
Dunstan Rd. Coul 9H 137
Dunstan's Gro. SE22 5F 92
Dunstan's Rd. SE22 6E 92
Dunster Av. Mord 3H 121
Dunster Clo. Barn 6H 13
Dunster Clo. Romf 9A 34
Dunster Ct. EC3 1C 76
Dunster Ct. Borwd 5B 12
Dunster Cres. Horn 7L 51
Dunster Dri. NW9 6A 40
Dunster Gdns. NW6 3K 57
Dunster Ho. SE6 9A 94
Dunsterville Way. SE1 3B 76
Dunster Way. Harr 8J 37
Dunston Rd. E8 4D 60
Dunston Rd. SW11 1E 90
Dunston St. E8 4C 60
Dunton Clo. Surb 3J 119
Dunton Ct. SE23 8F 92
Dunton Rd. E10 5M 45
Dunton Rd. SE1 6D 76
Dunton Rd. Romf 2C 50
Duntshill Rd. SW18 7M 89
Dunvegan Clo. W Mol 8M 101
Dunvegan Rd. SE9 3K 95
Dunwich Rd. Bexh 9K 81
Dunworth M. W11 9K 57
Duplex Ride. SW1 3D 74
Dupont Rd. SW20 6H 105
Duppas Av. Croy 6M 123
Duppas Clo. Shep 9B 100
Duppas Ct. Croy 5M 123
(off Duppas Hill Ter.)
Duppas Hill La. Croy 6M 123
Duppas Hill Rd. Croy 6L 123
Duppas Hill Ter. Croy 5M 123
Duppas Rd. Croy 5L 123
Dupree Rd. SE7 6F 78
Duraden Clo. Beck 4M 109
Durand Clo. Cars 3D 122
Durand Gdns. SW9 9K 75
Durands Wlk. SE16 3K 77
Durand Way. NW10 3A 56
Durant Rd. Swan 3E 114
Durants Pk. Av. Enf 6H 17
Durants Rd. Enf 6G 17
Durant St. E2 5E 60
Durban Ct. E7 3H 63
Durban Gdns. Dag 3A 66
Durban Ho. W12 1F 72
(off White City Est.)
Durban Rd. E15 6C 62
Durban Rd. E17 8K 29
Durban Rd. N17 6C 28
Durban Rd. SE27 1A 108
Durban Rd. Beck 6K 109
Durban Rd. Ilf 6C 48
Durban Rd. E. Wat 6E 8
Durban Rd. W. Wat 6E 8
Durbin Rd. Chess 6J 119
Durdan Cotts. S'hall 9K 53
(off Denbigh Rd.)
Durdans Ho. NW1 3F 58
(off Farrier St.)
Durdans Rd. S'hall 9K 53
Durell Gdns. Dag 1H 65
Durell Ho. SE16 3H 77
(off Wolfe Cres.)
Durell Rd. Dag 1H 65
Durfey Ho. SE5 8B 76
(off Edmund St.)
Durford Cres. SW15 7F 88
Durham Av. Brom 8D 110
Durham Av. Houn 6K 69
Durham Av. Romf 2G 51
Durham Av. Wfd G 5H 31
Durham Clo. SW20 6F 104
Durham Ct. NW6 5L 57
(off Kilburn Pk. Rd., in five parts)
Durham Ct. Tedd 1C 102
Durham Hill. Brom 1D 110
Durham Ho. Bark 3E 64
(off Margaret Bondfield Av.)
Durham Ho. Borwd 4L 11
(off Canterbury Rd.)
Durham Ho. Brom 8C 110
Durham Ho. Dag 1A 66
Durham Ho. St. WC2 1J 75
(off John Adam St.)
Durham Pl. SW3 6D 74
Durham Pl. Ilf 9A 48
Durham Ri. SE18 6A 80
Durham Rd. E12 9H 47
Durham Rd. E16 7C 62
Durham Rd. N2 1C 42
Durham Rd. N7 7K 43
Durham Rd. N9 2E 28
Durham Rd. SW20 5F 104
Durham Rd. W5 4H 71
Durham Rd. Borwd 5A 12
Durham Rd. Brom 7D 110
Durham Rd. Dag 1A 66
Durham Rd. Felt 6G 85
Durham Rd. Harr 3M 37
Durham Rd. Sidc 2F 112
Durham Row. E1 8H 61
Durham St. SE11 7K 75
Durham Ter. W2 9M 57
Durham Wharf. Bren 8G 71
Durham Yd. E2 6F 60
Duriun Way. Eri 8F 82
Durley Av. Pinn 5J 37
Durley Gdns. Orp 5F 128
Durley Rd. N16 5C 44
Durlston Rd. E5 7E 44
Durlston Rd. King T 3J 103
Durnell Way. Lou 5L 19
Durnford Ho. SE6 9A 94
Durnford St. N15 3C 44
Durnford St. SE10 7A 78
Durning Rd. SE19 2B 108
Durnsford Av. SW19 8L 89
Durnsford Rd. N11 8H 27
Durnsford Rd. SW19 8L 89
Durrant Ct. Har W 9C 22
Durrants Clo. Rain 5G 67
Durrants Dri. Crox G 5A 8
Durrant Way. Orp 7B 128
Durrell Rd. SW6 9K 73
Durrell Way. Shep 1B 116
Durrels Ho. W14 5K 73
(off Warwick Gdns.)
Durrington Av. SW20 4G 105
Durrington Pk. Rd.
SW20 5G 105
Durrington Rd. E5 9J 45
Durrington Tower. SW8 1G 91
Durrisdeer Ho. NW2 9K 41
(off Lyndale)
Dursley Clo. SE3 1G 95
Dursley Ct. SE15 8C 76
(off Lydney Clo.)
Dursley Gdns. SE3 9H 79
Dursley Rd. SE3 1G 95
Durward St. E1 8F 60
Durweston M. W1 8D 58
(off Crawford St.)
Durweston St. W1 8D 58
Dury Falls Clo. Horn 6L 51
Dury Falls Ct. Romf 9A 34
Dury Rd. Barn 3K 13
Dutch Barn Clo. Stanw 5B 144
Dutch Gdns. King T 3M 103
Dutch Yd. SW18 4L 89
Dutton Bus. Pk. SE9 8L 95
Dutton St. SE10 9A 78
Duxberry Av. Felt 9G 85
Duxberry Clo. Brom 9J 111
Duxford Clo. Horn 2G 67
Duxford Ho. SE2 3H 81
(off Wolvercote Rd.)
Dwight Rd. Wat 9B 8
Dye Ho. La. E3 4L 61
Dyer Ho. Hamp 5M 101
Dyer's Bldgs. EC1 8L 59
Dyers Hall Rd. E11 6C 46
Dyers Hill Rd. E11 7B 46
Dyers La. SW15 3F 88
Dyers Way. Romf 7F 34
Dyke Dri. Orp 3G 129
Dykes Way. Brom 7D 110
Dykewood Clo. Bex 9B 98
Dylan Clo. Els 9H 11
Dylan Rd. SE24 3M 91
Dylan Rd. Belv 4L 81
Dylan Thomas Ho. N8 2K 43
Dylways. SE5 3B 92
Dymchurch Clo. Ilf 9L 31
Dymchurch Clo. Orp 6C 128
Dymes Path. SW19 8H 89
Dymock Ct. SE15 8C 76
(off Lydney Clo.)
Dymock St. SW6 2M 89
Dymoke Rd. Horn 5D 50
Dyneley Rd. SE12 9G 95
Dyne Rd. NW6 3J 57
Dynevor Rd. N16 8C 44
Dynevor Rd. Rich 4J 87
Dynham Rd. NW6 3L 57
Dyott St. WC1 9H 59
Dyrham La. Barn 1E 12
Dyrham Pk. 2F 12
Dyrham Pk. Golf Course. 1E 12
Dysart Av. King T 2G 103
Dysart St. EC2 7B 60
Dyson Ct. NW2 6G 41
Dyson Ct. Wat 7G 9
Dyson Ct. Wemb 9E 38
Dyson Ho. SE10 6D 78
(off Blackwall La.)
Dyson Rd. E11 4C 46
Dyson Rd. E15 2D 62
Dysons Clo. Wal X 6D 6
Dysons Rd. N18 5F 28

E

Eade Rd. N4 5A 44
Eagans Clo. N2 1B 42
Eagle Av. Romf 4J 49
Eagle Clo. SE16 6G 77
Eagle Clo. Enf 6G 17
Eagle Clo. Horn 2F 66
Eagle Clo. Wall 8J 123
Eagle Clo. Wal A 7M 7
Eagle Ct. E11 2E 46
Eagle Ct. EC1 8M 59
Eagle Dri. NW9 9C 24
Eagle Heights. 4F 130
Eagle Hill. SE19 3B 108
Eagle Ho. E1 7F 60
(off Headlam St.)
Eagle Ho. N1 5B 60
(off Eagle Wharf Rd.)
Eagle La. E11 2E 46
Eagle Lodge. NW11 5K 41
Eagle M. N1 2C 60
Eagle Pl. SW1 1G 75
(off Piccadilly)
Eagle Pl. SW7 6A 74
(off Rolandway)
Eagle Rd. Wemb 3H 55
Eagles Dri. Tats 9H 141
(in two parts)
Eaglesfield Rd. SE18 9M 79
Eagle St. WC1 8K 59
Eagle Ter. Wfd G 7F 30
Eagle Trad. Est. Mitc 1D 122
Eagle Wharf Ct. SE1 2D 76
(off Lafone St.)
Eagle Wharf E. E14 1J 77
(off Narrow St.)
Eagle Wharf Rd. N1 5A 60
Eagle Wharf W. E14 1J 77
(off Narrow St.)
Ealdham Sq. SE9 3G 95
Ealing. 1H 71
Ealing B'way. Cen. W5 1H 71
Ealing Clo. Borwd 3B 12
Ealing Common (Junct.) 2K 71
Ealing Downs Ct. Gnfd 6E 54
Ealing Grn. W5 2H 71
Ealing Pk. Gdns. W5 5G 71
Ealing Rd. Bren 5H 71
Ealing Rd. N'holt 4L 53
Ealing Rd. Wemb 2J 55
Ealing Rd. Trad. Est. Bren 6H 71
Ealing Village. W5 9J 55
Eamont Clo. Ruis 5A 36
Eamont Ct. NW8 5C 58
(off Eamont St.)
Eamont St. NW8 5C 58
Eardemont Clo. Dart 3D 98
Eardley Cres. SW5 6L 73
Eardley Rd. SW16 2G 107
Eardley Rd. Belv 6L 81
Earl Clo. N11 5F 26
Earldom Rd. SW15 3G 89
Earle Gdns. King T 4J 103
Earlham Gro. E7 1D 62
Earlham Gro. N22 7K 27
Earlham St. WC2 9J 59
Earl Ho. NW1 7C 58
(off Lisson Gro.)
Earlom Ho. WC1 6L 59
(off Margery St.)
Earl Ri. SE18 6B 80
Earl Rd. SW14 3A 88
Earl's Court. 6L 73
Earl's Court Exhibition Building.
6L 73
Earls Ct. Gdns. SW5 5M 73
Earls Ct. Rd. W8 & SW5 4L 73
Earl's Ct. Sq. SW5 6M 73
Earls Cres. Harr 2C 38
Earlsdown Ho. Bark 5B 64
Earlsferry Way. N1 3J 59
(in two parts)
Earlsfield. 7A 90
Earlsfield Rd. SW18 7A 90
Earlshall Rd. SE9 3K 95
Earlsmead. Harr 9K 37
Earlsmead Rd. N15 3D 44
Earlsmead Rd. NW10 6G 57
Earl's Path. Lou 4G 19
Earls Ter. W8 4K 73
Earlsthorpe M. SW12 5E 90
Earlsthorpe Rd. SE26 1H 109
Earlstoke St. EC1 6M 59
Earlston Gro. E9 4F 60
Earl St. EC2 8B 60
Earl St. Wat 5G 9
Earls Wlk. W8 4L 73
Earl's Wlk. Dag 9F 48
Earls Way. Orp 4E 128
Earlswood Av. T Hth 9L 107
Earlswood Clo. SE10 7C 78
Earlswood Gdns. Ilf 1L 47
Earlswood St. SE10 6C 78
Early M. NW1 4F 58
Earnshaw St. WC2 9H 59
Earsby St. W14 5J 73
(in three parts)
Easby Cres. Mord 1M 121
Easebourne Rd. Dag 1G 65
Easedale Dri. Horn 1E 66
Easleys M. W1 9E 58
East Acton. 1C 72
E. Acton Arc. W3 9C 56
E. Acton Ct. W3 1C 72
E. Acton La. W3 2C 72
E. Arbour St. E1 9H 61
East Av. E12 3J 63
East Av. E17 2M 45
East Av. N2 2M 41
East Av. Hay 2D 68
East Av. S'hall 1K 69
East Av. Wall 7K 123
East Bank. N16 5C 44
Eastbank Rd. Hamp H 2A 102
East Barnet. 8C 14
E. Barnet Rd. Barn 6B 14
E. Beckton District Cen.
E6 8K 63
East Bedfont. 6C 84
East Block. SE1 3K 75
(off York Rd.)
E. Boundary Rd. E12 8K 47
Eastbourne Av. W3 9B 56
Eastbourne Gdns. SW14 2A 88
Eastbourne M. W2 9A 58
Eastbourne Rd. E6 6L 63
(in two parts)
Eastbourne Rd. E15 4C 62
Eastbourne Rd. N15 4C 44
Eastbourne Rd. SW17 3E 106
Eastbourne Rd. W4 7A 72
Eastbourne Rd. Bren 6G 71
Eastbourne Rd. Felt 8H 85
Eastbourne Ter. W2 9A 58
Eastbournia Av. N9 3F 28
Eastbrook Av. N9 9G 17
Eastbrook Av. Dag 9A 50
Eastbrook Dri. Romf 8C 50
Eastbrook Rd. SE3 9F 78
Eastbrook Rd. Wal A 6L 7
Eastbury. 4D 20
Eastbury Av. Bark 4C 64
Eastbury Av. Enf 3D 16
Eastbury Av. N'wd 5C 20
Eastbury Ct. Bark 4C 64
Eastbury Ct. New Bar 7A 14
(off Lyonsdown Rd.)
Eastbury Ct. Wat 9G 9
Eastbury Gro. W4 6C 72
Eastbury Pl. N'wd 5D 20
Eastbury Rd. E6 7L 63
Eastbury Rd. King T 4J 103
Eastbury Rd. N'wd 6C 20
Eastbury Rd. Orp 1B 128
Eastbury Rd. Romf 4B 50
Eastbury Rd. Wat 9F 8
Eastbury Sq. Bark 4D 64
Eastbury Ter. E1 7H 61
Eastcastle St. W1 9G 59
Eastcheap. EC3 1C 76
E. Churchfield Rd. W3 2B 72
Eastchurch Rd. H'row A 1C 84
East Clo. W5 7L 55
East Clo. Barn 6E 14
East Clo. Gnfd 5A 54
East Clo. Rain 7F 66
Eastcombe Av. SE7 7F 78
Eastcote. 5F 36
Eastcote. Orp 3D 128
Eastcote Av. Gnfd 1E 54
Eastcote Av. Harr 7M 37
Eastcote Av. W Mol 9K 101
Eastcote Ho. Eps 4C 134
Eastcote Ind. Est. Ruis 5G 37
Eastcote La. Harr 9J 37
Eastcote La. N'holt 1K 53
(in three parts)
Eastcote La. N. N'holt 2K 53
Eastcote Pl. Pinn 4F 36
Eastcote Rd. Harr 8A 38
Eastcote Rd. Pinn 3H 37
Eastcote Rd. Ruis 5C 36
Eastcote Rd. Well 1B 96
Eastcote St. SW9 1K 91
Eastcote Vw. Pinn 2G 37
Eastcote Village. 3F 36
East Ct. Wemb 7G 39
East Cres. N11 4D 26
East Cres. Enf 7D 16
Eastcroft Rd. Eps 9C 120
E. Cross Cen. E15 2L 61
E. Cross Route. E9 & E3 3K 61
Eastdean Av. Eps 5M 133
E. Dene Dri. H Hill 5H 35
Eastdown Ct. SE13 3B 94
Eastdown Ho. E8 9E 44
Eastdown Pk. SE13 3B 94
East Dri. Cars 1C 136
East Dri. N'wd 2C 20
East Dri. Orp 1F 128
East Dri. Wat 9F 4
E. Duck Lees La. Enf 6J 17
East Dulwich. 3D 92
E. Dulwich Gro. SE22 4C 92
E. Dulwich Rd.
SE22 & SE15 3D 92
E. End Farm. Pinn 1K 37
E. End Rd. N3 & N2 9L 25
E. End Way. Pinn 1J 37
East Entrance. Dag 5M 65
Eastern Av. E11 & Ilf 4F 46
Eastern Av. Pinn 5H 37
Eastern Av. Wal X 6E 6
Eastern Av. E. Romf 1B 50
Eastern Av. W. Romf 2J 49
(in two parts)
Eastern Ind. Est. Eri 3L 81
Eastern Path. Horn 4G 67
Eastern Perimeter Rd.
H'row A 1D 84
Eastern Rd. E13 5F 62
Eastern Rd. E17 3A 46
Eastern Rd. N2 1D 42
Eastern Rd. N22 8J 27
Eastern Rd. SE4 3L 93
Eastern Rd. Romf 3C 50
Eastern Vw. Big H 9G 141
Easternville Gdns. Ilf 4A 48
Eastern Way. SE28 3E 80
East Ewell. 2G 135
E. Ferry Rd. E14 5M 77
Eastfield Av. Wat 3H 9
Eastfield Gdns. Dag 9L 49
Eastfield Rd. E17 2L 45
Eastfield Rd. N8 1J 43
Eastfield Rd. Dag 9K 49
Eastfield Rd. Enf 2H 17
Eastfield Rd. Wal X 4F 6
Eastfields. Pinn 3G 37
Eastfields Rd. W3 8A 56
Eastfields Rd. Mitc 6E 106
Eastfield St. E14 8J 61
East Finchley. 2C 42
East Gdns. SW17 3C 106
Eastgate. Bans 6K 135
Eastgate Clo. SE28 9H 65
Eastglade. N'wd 5D 20
Eastglade. Pinn 1K 37
E. Hall La. Wen 9H 67
E. Hall Rd. Orp 2J 129
East Ham. 4K 63
E. Ham and Barking By-Pass.
Bark 5C 64
Eastham Clo. Barn 7K 13
E. Ham Ind. Est. E6 7J 63
E. Ham Mnr. Way. E6 9L 63
E. Harding St. EC4 9L 59
E. Heath Rd. NW3 8A 42
East Hill. SW18 4M 89
East Hill. Dart 6K 99
East Hill. S Croy 2C 138
East Hill. Wemb 7L 39
E. Hill Dri. Dart 6K 99
Eastholm. NW11 2M 41

East Holme—Effie Pl.

East Holme. Eri 9B 82
East Holme. Hay 2E 68
E. India Bldgs. E14 1L 77 (off Saltwell St.)
E. India Dock Ho. E14 9A 62
E. India Dock Rd. E14 9L 61
Eastlake Ho. NW8 7B 58 (off Frampton St.)
Eastlake Rd. SE5 1A 92
Eastlands Cres. SE21 5D 92
East La. SE16 3E 76 (Chambers St.)
East La. SE16 3E 76 (Scott Lidgett Cres.)
East La. Bedm & Wat 1D 4 (in two parts)
East La. King T 7H 103
East La. Wemb 8F 38
East La. Bus. Pk. Wemb 7H 39
Eastlea Av. Wat 1J 9
Eastlea M. E16 7C 62
Eastleigh Av. Harr 7M 37
Eastleigh Clo. NW2 8C 40
Eastleigh Clo. Sutt 9M 121
Eastleigh Rd. E17 9K 29
Eastleigh Rd. Bexh 2A 98
Eastleigh Rd. H'row A 2D 84
Eastleigh Wlk. SW15 6E 88
Eastleigh Way. Felt 7E 84
East Lodge. E16 2E 78 (off Wesley Av.)
E. Lodge La. Enf 1H 15
East London Crematorium. E13 6D 62
Eastman Ho. SW4 5G 91
Eastman Rd. W3 3B 72
East Mascalls. SE7 7G 79
East Mead. Ruis 8H 37
Eastmead Av. Gnfd 6M 53
Eastmead Clo. Brom 6J 111
Eastmearn Rd. SE27 8A 92
East Molesey. 8B 102
Eastmont Rd. Esh 4C 118
Eastmoor Pl. SE7 4H 79
Eastmoor St. SE7 4H 79
E. Mount St. E1 8F 60 (in two parts)
Eastney Rd. Croy 3M 123
Eastney St. SE10 6B 78
Eastnor Rd. SE9 7A 96
Easton Gdns. Borwd 6C 12
Easton St. WC1 7L 59
E. Park Clo. Romf 3H 49
East Parkside. SE10 3C 78
East Pas. EC1 8A 60 (off Cloth St.)
East Pl. SE27 1A 108
East Point. SE1 6E 76
E. Pole Cotts. Barn 6H 15
E. Poultry Av. EC1 8M 59
East Ramp. H'row A 9M 143
East Rd. E15 4E 62
East Rd. N1 6B 60
East Rd. N2 8C 26
East Rd. SW19 3A 106
East Rd. Barn 1E 26
East Rd. Chad H 3J 49
East Rd. Edgw 8M 23
East Rd. Enf 2G 17
East Rd. Felt 6B 84
East Rd. Harr 5F 38
East Rd. King T 5J 103
East Rd. Rush G 5B 50
East Rd. Well 1F 96
East Rd. W Dray 5K 143
East Rd. Wey 9B 116
E. Rochester Way. Sidc & Bex 3C 96
East Row. E11 4E 46
East Row. W10 7J 57
Eastry Av. Brom 1D 126
Eastry Ho. SW8 8J 75 (off Hartington Rd.)
Eastry Rd. Eri 8L 81
East Sheen. 3A 88
E. Sheen Av. SW14 4B 88
Eastside Rd. NW11 2K 41
East Smithfield. E1 1D 76
East St. SE17 6A 76
East St. Bark 4A 64
East St. Bexh 3L 97
East St. Bren 8G 71
East St. Brom 6E 110
East St. Eps 5C 134
E. Surrey Gro. SE15 8D 76
E. Tenter St. E1 9D 60
East Ter. Sidc 7C 96
East Towers. Pinn 3H 37
East Va. W3 2D 72
East Vw. E4 5A 30
East Vw. Barn 4K 13
Eastview Av. SE18 8C 80
Eastville Av. NW11 4K 41
East Wlk. E Barn 9E 14
East Wlk. Hay 2E 68
Eastway. E9 2K 61 (in two parts)
East Way. E11 3F 46
East Way. Brom 2E 126
East Way. Croy 4J 125
Eastway. Eps 3B 134
East Way. Hay 2E 68
Eastway. Mord 9H 105
East Way. Ruis 6E 36
Eastway. Wall 6G 123
Eastwell Clo. Beck 4J 109
Eastwell Ho. SE1 4B 76 (off Weston St.)
E. W. Link Rd. King T 5H 103
East Wickham. 9G 81
Eastwick Rd. W on T 8F 116
Eastwood Clo. E18 9E 30
Eastwood Clo. N17 7F 28
Eastwood Dri. Rain 9F 66
Eastwood Rd. E18 9E 30
Eastwood Rd. N10 9E 26
Eastwood Rd. Ilf 5E 48
Eastwood Rd. W Dray 3L 143
East Woodside. Bex 7J 97
Eastwood St. SW16 3G 107
Eatington Rd. E10 3B 46
Eaton Clo. SW1 5E 74
Eaton Clo. Stan 4F 22
Eaton Dri. SW9 3M 91
Eaton Dri. King T 4L 103
Eaton Dri. Romf 7M 33
Eaton Gdns. Dag 3J 65
Eaton Ga. SW1 5E 74
Eaton Ga. N'wd 6A 20
Eaton Gro. N19 8H 43
Eaton Ho. E14 1K 77 (off Westferry Cir.)
Eaton Ho. SW11 9B 74
Eaton La. SW1 4F 74
Eaton Mans. SW1 5E 74 (off Bourne St.)
Eaton M. N. SW1 5E 74
Eaton M. S. SW1 5E 74
Eaton M. W. SW1 5E 74
Eaton Pk. Rd. N13 2L 27
Eaton Pl. SW1 5E 74
Eaton Ri. E11 3G 47
Eaton Ri. W5 8H 55
Eaton Rd. NW4 3G 41
Eaton Rd. Enf 5C 16
Eaton Rd. Houn 3B 86
Eaton Rd. Sidc 8H 97
Eaton Rd. Sutt 8A 122
Eaton Row. SW1 4F 74
Eatons Mead. E4 2L 29
Eaton Sq. SW1 5E 74
Eaton Ter. E3 6J 61
Eaton Ter. SW1 5E 74
Eaton Ter. M. SW1 5E 74 (off Eaton Ter.)
Eatonville Rd. SW17 8D 90
Eatonville Vs. SW17 8D 90
Ebbas Way. Eps 7M 133
Ebbisham Cen. Eps 5B 134
Ebbisham Dri. SW8 7K 75
Ebbisham Rd. Eps 6M 133
Ebbisham Rd. Wor Pk 4G 121
Ebbsfleet Rd. NW2 1J 57
Ebdon Way. SE3 2F 94
Ebenezer Ho. SE11 5M 75
Ebenezer Mussel Ho. E2 5G 61 (off Patriot Sq.)
Ebenezer St. N1 6B 60
Ebenezer Wlk. SW16 5G 107
Ebley Clo. SE15 7D 76
Ebner St. SW18 4M 89
Ebor Cotts. SW15 9C 88
Ebor St. E1 7D 60
Ebrington Rd. Harr 4H 39
Ebsworth St. SE23 6H 93
Eburne Rd. N7 8J 43
Ebury Bri. SW1 6F 74
Ebury Bri. Est. SW1 6F 74
Ebury Bri. Rd. SW1 6E 74
Ebury Clo. Kes 5J 127
Ebury Clo. N'wd 5A 20
Ebury M. SE27 9M 91
Ebury M. SW1 5F 74
Ebury M. E. SW1 4F 74
Ebury Rd. Wat 5G 9
Ebury Sq. SW1 5E 74
Ebury St. SW1 5E 74
Ecclesbourne Clo. N13 5L 27
Ecclesbourne Gdns. N13 5L 27
Ecclesbourne Rd. N1 3A 60
Ecclesbourne Rd. T Hth 9A 108
Eccleshill. Brom 8D 110 (off Durham Rd.)
Eccles Rd. SW11 3D 90
Eccleston Bri. SW1 5F 74
Eccleston Clo. Cockf 6D 14
Eccleston Clo. Orp 3B 128
Eccleston Cres. Romf 5F 48
Ecclestone Ct. Wemb 1J 55
Ecclestone M. Wemb 1J 55
Ecclestone Pl. Wemb 1K 55
Eccleston Ho. SW2 5L 91
Eccleston M. SW1 4E 74
Eccleston Pl. SW1 5F 74
Eccleston Rd. W13 1E 70
Eccleston Sq. SW1 5F 74
Eccleston Sq. M. SW1 5F 74
Eccleston St. SW1 4F 74
Echo Heights. E4 1M 29
Eckford St. N1 5L 59
Eckington Ho. N15 4B 44 (off Fladbury Rd.)
Eckstein Rd. SW11 3C 90
Eclipse Rd. E13 8F 62
Ector Rd. SE6 8C 94
Edam Ct. Sidc 9E 96
Edans Ct. W12 3D 72
Edbrooke Rd. W9 7L 57
Eddington St. N4 6L 43
Eddisbury Ho. SE26 9E 92
Eddiscombe Rd. SW6 1K 89
Eddy Clo. Romf 4M 49
Eddystone. Cars 3B 136
Eddystone Rd. SE4 4J 93
Eddystone Tower. SE8 6J 77
Eddystone Wlk. Stai 6C 144
Ede Clo. Houn 2K 85
Edenbridge Clo. SE16 6F 76 (off Masters Dri.)
Edenbridge Clo. Orp 8H 113
Edenbridge Rd. E9 3H 61
Edenbridge Rd. Enf 8C 16
Eden Clo. NW3 7L 41
Eden Clo. W8 4L 73
Eden Clo. Bex 1B 114
Eden Clo. Enf 1L 17
Eden Clo. Wemb 4H 55
Edencourt Rd. SW16 3F 106
Edendale. W3 1M 71
Edendale Rd. Bexh 9B 82
Edenfield Gdns. Wor Pk 5D 120
Eden Gro. E17 3M 45
Eden Gro. N7 1K 59
Edenhall Clo. Romf 5G 35
Edenhall Glen. Romf 5G 35
Edenhall Rd. Romf 5G 35
Edenham Way. W10 7K 57
Eden Ho. NW8 7C 58 (off Church St.)
Edenhurst Av. SW6 2K 89
Eden Lodge. NW6 3H 57
Eden M. SW17 9A 90
Eden Park. 9L 109
Eden Pk. Av. Beck 8J 109 (in two parts)
Eden Rd. E17 3M 45
Eden Rd. SE27 1M 107
Eden Rd. Beck 8J 109
Eden Rd. Bex 1A 114
Eden Rd. Croy 6B 124
Edensor Gdns. W4 8C 72
Edensor Rd. W4 8C 72
Eden St. King T 6H 103
Edenvale Clo. Mitc 4E 106
Edenvale Rd. Mitc 4E 106
Edenvale St. SW6 1A 90
Eden Wlk. King T 6J 103
Eden Way. Beck 9K 109
Ederline Av. SW16 7K 107
Edgar Clo. Swan 7D 114
Edgar Ct. N Mald 6C 104
Edgar Ho. E9 1J 61 (off Homerton Rd.)
Edgar Ho. E11 5E 46
Edgar Ho. SW8 8J 75 (off Wyvil Rd.)
Edgar Kail Way. SE22 3C 92
Edgarley Ter. SW6 9J 73
Edgar Rd. E3 6M 61
Edgar Rd. Houn 6K 85
Edgar Rd. Romf 5H 49
Edgar Rd. S Croy 1B 138
Edgar Rd. W Dray 1J 143
Edgbaston Rd. Wat 3F 20
Edgcott Ho. W10 8G 57 (off Sutton Way)
Edgeborough Way. Brom 4H 111
Edgebury. Chst 1M 111
Edgebury Wlk. Chst 1A 112
Edge Bus. Cen., The. NW2 7F 40
Edgecombe Ho. SE5 1C 92
Edgecoombe. S Croy 9G 125
Edgecoombe Clo. King T 4B 104
Edgecote Clo. W3 2A 72
Edgecot Gro. N15 3C 44
Edgefield Av. Bark 3D 64
Edgefield Clo. Dart 7M 99
Edgefield Ct. Bark 3D 64 (off Edgefield Av.)
Edge Hill. SE18 7M 79
Edge Hill. SW19 4H 105
Edge Hill Av. N3 2L 41
Edge Hill Ct. SW19 4H 105
Edge Hill Ct. Sidc 1D 112
Edgehill Ct. W on T 3G 117
Edgehill Gdns. Dag 9L 49
Edgehill Ho. SW9 1M 91
Edgehill Rd. W13 8G 55
Edgehill Rd. Chst 9A 96
Edgehill Rd. Mitc 5F 106
Edgehill Rd. Purl 2L 137
Edgeley La. SW4 2H 91
Edgeley Rd. SW4 2H 91
Edgel St. SW18 3M 89
Edgepoint Clo. SE27 2M 107
Edge St. W8 2L 73
Edgewood Dri. Orp 7D 128
Edgewood Grn. Croy 3H 125
Edgeworth Av. NW4 3E 40
Edgeworth Clo. NW4 3E 40
Edgeworth Ct. Barn 6C 14 (off Fordham Rd.)
Edgeworth Cres. NW4 3E 40
Edgeworth Ho. NW8 4A 58 (off Boundary Rd.)
Edgeworth Rd. SE9 3G 95
Edgeworth Rd. Cockf 6C 14
Edgington Rd. SW16 3H 107
Edgington Way. Sidc 4G 113
Edgson Ho. SW1 6F 74 (off Ebury Bri. Rd.)
Edgware. 6L 23
Edgware Bury. 3M 23
Edgwarebury Gdns. Edgw 5L 23
Edgwarebury Golf Course. 3J 23
Edgwarebury La. Edgw 1K 23 (in two parts)
Edgwarebury La. Els 9J 11 (in two parts)
Edgwarebury Pk. 3K 23
Edgware Ct. Edgw 6L 23
Edgware Rd. NW2 6F 40
Edgware Rd. NW9 9A 24
Edgware Rd. W2 7B 58
Edgware Way. Edgw & NW7 4K 23
Edgware Way. Els 1H 23
Edinburgh Clo. E2 5G 61
Edinburgh Clo. Pinn 5H 37
Edinburgh Clo. Uxb 9A 36
Edinburgh Ct. SE16 2H 77 (off Rotherhithe St.)
Edinburgh Ct. SW20 9H 105
Edinburgh Ct. Eri 8B 82
Edinburgh Ct. King T 7J 103 (off Watersplash Clo.)
Edinburgh Cres. Wal X 6E 6
Edinburgh Dri. Ab L 5E 4
Edinburgh Dri. Romf 2A 50
Edinburgh Dri. Uxb 9A 36 & 1F 142
Edinburgh Ga. SW1 3D 74
Edinburgh Ho. NW4 1G 41
Edinburgh Ho. W9 6M 57 (off Maida Va.)
Edinburgh Rd. E13 5F 62
Edinburgh Rd. E17 3L 45
Edinburgh Rd. N18 5E 28
Edinburgh Rd. W7 3D 70
Edinburgh Rd. Sutt 4A 122
Edington. NW5 2E 58
Edington Rd. SE2 4F 80
Edington Rd. Enf 4G 17
Edison Av. Horn 6D 50
Edison Building. E14 3L 77
Edison Clo. E17 3L 45
Edison Clo. Horn 6C 50
Edison Dri. S'hall 9M 53
Edison Dri. Wemb 8J 39
Edison Gro. SE18 8D 80
Edison Ho. Wemb 8A 40 (off Barnhill Rd.)
Edison Rd. N8 4H 43
Edison Rd. Brom 6E 110
Edison Rd. Enf 4K 17
Edison Rd. Well 9D 80
Edis St. NW1 4E 58
Edith Brinson Ho. E14 9B 62 (off Oban St.)
Edith Cavell Clo. N19 5J 43
Edith Gdns. Surb 2M 119
Edith Gro. SW10 7A 74
Edith Ho. W6 6G 73 (off Queen Caroline St.)
Edithna St. SW9 2J 91
Edith Neville Cotts. NW1 6H 59 (off Crace St.)
Edith Ramsay Ho. E1 8J 61 (off Duckett St.)
Edith Rd. E6 3H 63
Edith Rd. E15 1B 62
Edith Rd. N11 7H 27
Edith Rd. SE25 9B 108
Edith Rd. SW19 3M 105
Edith Rd. W14 5J 73
Edith Rd. Orp 7E 128
Edith Rd. Romf 5G 49
Edith Row. SW6 9M 73
Edith St. E2 5E 60
Edith Summerskill Ho. SW6 8K 73 (off Clem Attlee Est.)
Edith Ter. SW10 8A 74
Edith Vs. W14 5K 73
Edith Yd. SW10 8A 74
Edmansons Clo. N17 8D 28
Edmeston Clo. E9 2J 61
Edmond Ct. SE14 9G 77
Edmonscote. W13 8E 54
Edmonton. 4E 28
Edmonton Ct. SE16 4G 77 (off Canada Est.)
Edmonton Grn. Shop. Cen. N9 2E 28
Edmund Halley Way. SE10 3C 78
Edmund Ho. SE17 7M 75
Edmund Hurst Dri. E6 8M 63
Edmund Rd. Mitc 7C 106
Edmund Rd. Orp 1G 129
Edmund Rd. Rain 5C 66
Edmund Rd. Well 2E 96
Edmunds Av. Orp 7H 113
Edmundsbury Ct. Est. SW9 3K 91
Edmunds Clo. Hay 8G 53
Edmund St. SE5 8B 76
Edmunds Wlk. N2 2C 42
Ednam Ho. SE15 7E 76 (off Haymerle Rd.)
Edna Rd. SW20 6H 105
Edna St. SW11 9C 74
Edred Ho. E9 9J 45 (off Lindisfarne Way)
Edrich Ho. SW4 9J 75
Edric Ho. SW1 5H 75 (off Page St.)
Edrick Rd. Edgw 6A 24
Edrick Wlk. Edgw 6A 24
Edric Rd. SE14 8H 77
Edridge Clo. Bush 7A 10
Edridge Clo. Horn 1H 67
Edridge Rd. Croy 5A 124
Edulf Rd. Borwd 3M 11
Edward Amey Clo. Wat 9G 5
Edward Av. E4 6M 29
Edward Av. Mord 9B 106
Edward Bond Ho. WC1 6J 59 (off Cromer St.)
Edward Clo. N9 9D 16
Edward Clo. NW2 9H 41
Edward Clo. Ab L 5D 4
Edward Clo. Hamp H 2A 102
Edward Clo. N'holt 5G 53
Edward Clo. Romf 1G 51
Edward Ct. E16 8E 62
Edward Ct. Chesh 3E 6
Edward Ct. Wal A 6M 7
Edward Dodd Ct. N1 6B 60 (off Haberdasher St.)
Edward Edward's Ho. SE1 2M 75 (off Nicholson St.)
Edwardes Pl. W8 4K 73
Edwardes Sq. W8 4K 73
Edward Gro. Barn 7B 14
Edward Ho. SE11 6K 75 (off Newburn St.)
Edward Mann Clo. E1 9H 61 (off Caroline St.)
Edward Mans. Bark 3D 64 (off Upney La.)
Edward M. NW1 6F 58
Edward Pl. SE8 7K 77
Edward Rd. E17 2H 45
Edward Rd. SE20 4H 109
Edward Rd. Barn 7B 14
Edward Rd. Big H 9J 141
Edward Rd. Brom 4F 110
Edward Rd. Chst 2M 111
Edward Rd. Coul 7H 137
Edward Rd. Croy 2C 124
Edward Rd. Felt 4B 84
Edward Rd. Hamp H 2A 102
Edward Rd. Harr 1A 38
Edward Rd. N'holt 5G 53
Edward Rd. Romf 4J 49
Edward Robinson Ho. SE14 8H 77 (off Reaston St.)
Edward's Av. Ruis 2F 52
Edwards Clo. Wor Pk 4H 121
Edward's Cotts. N1 2M 59
Edwards Ct. S Croy 6B 124 (off S. Park Hill Rd.)
Edwards Dri. N11 7H 27
Edward VII Mans. NW10 6H 57 (off Chamberlayne Rd.)
Edwards Gdns. Swan 8B 114
Edward's La. N16 7B 44
Edwards M. N1 3L 59
Edwards M. W1 9E 58
Edward Sq. N1 4K 59
Edward Sq. SE16 2J 77
Edwards Rd. Belv 5L 81
Edward St. E16 7E 62 (in two parts)
Edward St. SE14 & SE8 8J 77
Edwards Yd. Wemb 4J 55
Edward Temme Av. E15 3D 62
Edward Tyler Rd. SE12 8G 95
Edward Way. Ashf 8D 144
Edwick Ct. Chesh 2D 6
Edwina Gdns. Ilf 3J 47
Edwin Arnold Ct. Sidc 1D 112
Edwin Av. E6 5L 63 (in two parts)
Edwin Clo. Bexh 7K 81
Edwin Clo. Rain 6D 66
Edwin Ho. SE15 8E 76
Edwin Pl. Croy 3C 124 (off Leslie Gro.)
Edwin Rd. Dart 9F 98
Edwin Rd. Edgw 6B 24
Edwin Rd. Twic 7C 86 (in two parts)
Edwin's Mead. E9 9J 45
Edwinstray Ho. Felt 8L 85
Edwin St. E1 7G 61
Edwin St. E16 8E 62
Edwin Ware Ct. Pinn 9G 21
Edwyn Clo. Barn 8G 13
Effie Pl. SW6 8L 73

Effie Rd.—Elmer Rd.

Effie Rd. SW6 . . . . 8L 73
Effingham Clo. Sutt 9M 121
Effingham Lodge. King T . . 8H 103
Effingham Rd. N8 . . . . 3L 43
Effingham Rd. SE12 . . . . 4C 94
Effingham Rd. Croy 2K 123
Effingham Rd. Surb 2F 118
Effort St. SW17 . . . . 2C 106
Effra Clo. SW19 . . . . 3M 105
Effra Ct. SW2 . . . . 4K 91
(off Brixton Hill)
Effra Pde. SW2 . . . . 4L 91
Effra Rd. SW2 . . . . 3L 91
Effra Rd. SW19 . . . . 3M 105
Effra Rd. Retail Pk. SW2 . . . 4L 91
Egan Way. Hay 1C 68
Egbert St. NW1 . . . . 4E 58
Egbury Ho. SW15 . . . . 5D 88
(off Tangley Gro.)
Egerton Av. Swan 4D 114
Egerton Clo. Dart 7F 98
Egerton Clo. Pinn 2E 36
Egerton Ct. E11 . . . . 5B 46
Egerton Cres. SW3 . . . . 5C 74
Egerton Dri. SE10 . . . . 9M 77
Egerton Gdns. NW4 . . . . 2F 40
Egerton Gdns. NW10 . . . . 4G 57
Egerton Gdns. SW3 . . . . 5C 74
Egerton Gdns. W13 . . . . 9F 54
Egerton Gdns. Ilf 8D 48
Egerton Gdns. M. SW3 . . . . 4C 74
Egerton Pl. SW3 . . . . 4C 74
Egerton Pl. Wey 8A 116
Egerton Rd. N16 . . . . 5D 44
Egerton Rd. SE25 . . . . 7C 108
Egerton Rd. N Mald 8D 104
Egerton Rd. Twic 6C 86
Egerton Rd. Wemb 3K 55
Egerton Rd. Wey 8A 116
Egerton Ter. SW3 . . . . 4C 74
Egerton Way. Hay 8M 143
Eggardon Ct. N'holt 2M 53
Egham Clo. SW19 . . . . 8J 89
Egham Clo. Sutt 4J 121
Egham Cres. Sutt 5J 121
Egham Rd. E13 . . . . 8F 62
Eglantine La.
F'ham & Hort K 2L 131
Eglantine Rd. SW18 . . . . 4A 90
Egleston Rd. Mord 1M 121
Eglington Ct. SE17 . . . . 7A 76
Eglington Rd. E4 . . . . 9B 18
Eglinton Hill. SE18 . . . . 7M 79
Eglinton Rd. SE18 . . . . 7L 79
Eglise Rd. Warl 9J 139
Egliston M. SW15 . . . . 2G 89
Egliston Rd. SW15 . . . . 2G 89
Eglon M. NW1 . . . . 3D 58
Egmont Av. Surb 3K 119
Egmont Rd. N Mald 8D 104
Egmont Rd. Surb 3K 119
Egmont Rd. Sutt 9A 122
Egmont Rd. W on T 2F 116
Egmont St. SE14 . . . . 8H 77
Egremont Ho. SE13 . . . . 1M 93
(off Russett Way)
Egremont Rd. SE27 . . . . 9L 91
Egret Ho. SE16 . . . . 5H 77
(off Tawny Way)
Egret Way. Hay 8H 53
Eider Clo. E7 . . . . 1D 62
Eider Clo. Hay 8H 53
Eider Ct. SE8 . . . . 7K 77
(off Pilot Clo.)
Eighteenth Rd. Mitc 8J 107
Eighth Av. E12 . . . . 9K 47
Eighth Av. Hay 2E 68
Eileen Rd. SE25 . . . . 9B 108
Eindhoven Clo. Cars 3E 122
Einstein Ho. Wemb 8A 40
Eisenhower Dri. E6 . . . . 8J 63
Elaine Gro. NW5 . . . . 1E 58
Elam Clo. SE5 . . . . 1M 91
Elam St. SE5 . . . . 1M 91
Elan Ct. E1 . . . . 8F 60
Eland Pl. Croy 5M 123
Eland Rd. SW11 . . . . 2D 90
Eland Rd. Croy 5M 123
Elba Pl. SE17 . . . . 5A 76
Elberon Av. Croy 1G 123
Elbe St. SW6 . . . . 1A 90
Elborough Rd. SE25 . . . . 9E 108
Elborough St. SW18 . . . . 7L 89
Elbourne Ct. SE16 . . . . 4H 77
(off Worgan St.)
Elbourne Trad. Est. Belv . . . 4M 81
Elbourn Ho. SW3 . . . . 6C 74
(off Cale St.)
Elbury Dri. E16 . . . . 9E 62
Elcho St. SW11 . . . . 8C 74
Elcot Av. SE15 . . . . 8F 76
Eldenwall Ind. Est. Dag . . . 6J 49
Elder Av. N8 . . . . 3J 43
Elderbek Clo. Chesh 1A 6
Elderberry Gro. SE27 . . . . 1A 108
Elderberry Rd. W5 . . . . 3J 71
Elderberry Way. Wat 8F 4
Elder Clo. N20 . . . . 2M 25
Elder Clo. Sidc 7D 96
Elder Clo. W Dray 1J 143
Elder Ct. Bush 2C 22
Elderfield Ho. E14 . . . . 1L 77
Elderfield Pl. SW17 . . . . 1F 106
Elderfield Rd. E5 . . . . 9H 45
Elderfield Wlk. E11 . . . . 3F 46
Elderflower Way. E15 . . . . 3C 62
Elder Gdns. SE27 . . . . 2A 108
Elder Oak Clo. SE20 . . . . 5F 108
Elder Oak Ct. SE20 . . . . 5F 108
(off Anerley Ct.)
Elder Rd. SE27 . . . . 1A 108
Elderslie Clo. Beck 9L 109
Elderslie Rd. SE9 . . . . 4L 95
Elder St. E1 . . . . 7D 60
(in two parts)
Elderton Rd. SE26 . . . . 1J 109
Eldertree Pl. Mitc 5G 107
Eldertree Way. Mitc 5G 107
Elder Wlk. N1 . . . . 4M 59
(off Popham St.)
Elder Way. Rain 6H 67
Elderwood Pl. SE27 . . . . 2A 108
Eldon Av. Borwd 4L 11
Eldon Av. Croy 4G 125
Eldon Av. Houn 8L 69
Eldon Ct. NW6 . . . . 4L 57
Eldon Gro. NW3 . . . . 1B 58
Eldon Pk. SE25 . . . . 8F 108
Eldon Rd. E17 . . . . 2K 45
Eldon Rd. N9 . . . . 1G 29
Eldon Rd. N22 . . . . 8M 27
Eldon Rd. W8 . . . . 4M 73
Eldon St. EC2 . . . . 8B 60
Eldon Way. NW10 . . . . 6M 55
Eldred Dri. Orp 3G 129
Eldred Rd. Bark 4C 64
Eldrick Ct. Felt 7B 84
Eldridge Clo. Felt 7E 84
Eldridge Ct. SE16 . . . . 4E 76
Eleanora Ter. Sutt 7A 122
(off Lind Rd.)
Eleanor Av. Eps 2B 134
Eleanor Clo. N15 . . . . 1D 44
Eleanor Clo. SE16 . . . . 3H 77
Eleanor Cres. NW7 . . . . 5H 25
Eleanor Cross Rd. Wal X 7E 6
(in two parts)
Eleanor Gdns. Barn 7H 13
Eleanor Gdns. Dag 7K 49
Eleanor Gro. SW13 . . . . 2C 88
Eleanor Gro. Ick 7A 36
Eleanor Ho. W6 . . . . 6G 73
(off Queen Caroline St.)
Eleanor Rd. E8 . . . . 2F 60
Eleanor Rd. E15 . . . . 2D 62
Eleanor Rd. N11 . . . . 6J 27
Eleanor Rd. Wal X 6E 6
Eleanor St. E3 . . . . 6L 61
Eleanor Wlk. SE18 . . . . 5J 79
Eleanor Way. Wal X 7F 6
Electric Av. SW9 . . . . 3L 91
Electric Av. Enf 9F 6
Electric La. SW9 & SW2 . . . 3L 91
(in two parts)
Electric Pde. E18 . . . . 9E 30
(off George La.)
Electric Pde. Ilf 7C 48
Electric Pde. Surb 1H 119
Elephant & Castle (Junct.)
. . . . 5M 75
Elephant & Castle. SE1 . . . . 5M 75
Elephant La. SE16 . . . . 3G 77
Elephant Rd. SE17 . . . . 5A 76
Elers Rd. W13 . . . . 3G 71
Elers Rd. Hay 5B 68
Eleven Acre Ri. Lou 5K 19
Eley Rd. N18 . . . . 4G 29
Eleys Est. N9 . . . . 3H 29
Eleys Est. N18 . . . . 4H 29
(in two parts)
Elfindale Rd. SE24 . . . . 4A 92
Elfin Gro. Tedd 2D 102
Elford Clo. SE3 . . . . 3F 94
Elford M. SW4 . . . . 4G 91
Elfort Rd. N5 . . . . 9L 43
Elfrida Cres. SE6 . . . . 1L 109
Elfrida Rd. Wat 7G 9
Elf Row. E1 . . . . 1G 77
Elfwine Rd. W7 . . . . 8C 54
Elgal Clo. Orp 7M 127
Elgar. N8 . . . . 1J 43
(off Boyton Clo.)
Elgar Av. NW10 . . . . 2B 56
(in two parts)
Elgar Av. SW16 . . . . 7J 107
Elgar Av. W5 . . . . 3J 71
Elgar Av. Surb 3L 119
Elgar Clo. E13 . . . . 5G 63
Elgar Clo. SE8 . . . . 8L 77
Elgar Clo. Buck H 2H 31
Elgar Clo. Els 9H 11
Elgar Ct. W14 . . . . 4J 73
(off Blythe Rd.)
Elgar Ho. NW6 . . . . 3A 58
(off Fairfax Rd.)
Elgar Ho. SW1 . . . . 6F 74
(off Churchill Gdns.)
Elgar St. SE16 . . . . 4J 77
Elgin Av. W9 . . . . 7K 57
Elgin Av. W12 . . . . 3F 72
Elgin Av. Ashf 3A 100
Elgin Av. Harr 9F 22
Elgin Av. Romf 7M 35
Elgin Ct. W9 . . . . 7M 57
Elgin Ct. S Croy 6A 124
(off Bramley Hill)
Elgin Cres. W11 . . . . 1J 73
Elgin Cres. H'row A 1C 84
Elgin Dri. N'wd 7C 20
Elgin Est. W9 . . . . 7L 57
(off Elgin Av.)
Elgin Ho. E14 . . . . 9M 61
(off Ricardo St.)
Elgin Mans. W9 . . . . 6M 57
Elgin M. W11 . . . . 9J 57
Elgin M. N. W9 . . . . 6M 57
Elgin M. S. W9 . . . . 6M 57
Elgin Pl. Wey 8A 116
Elgin Rd. N22 . . . . 9G 27
Elgin Rd. Chesh 3C 6
Elgin Rd. Croy 4D 124
Elgin Rd. Ilf 6C 48
Elgin Rd. Sutt 5A 122
Elgin Rd. Wall 8G 123
Elgood Av. N'wd 6D 20
Elgood Clo. W11 . . . . 1J 73
Elgood Ho. NW8 . . . . 5B 58
(off Wellington Rd.)
Elham Clo. Brom 4H 111
Elham Ho. E5 . . . . 1F 60
Elia M. N1 . . . . 5M 59
Elias Pl. SW8 . . . . 7L 75
Elia St. N1 . . . . 5M 59
Elibank Rd. SE9 . . . . 3K 95
Elim Est. SE1 . . . . 4C 76
Elim St. SE1 . . . . 4B 76
(off Weston St., in two parts)
Elim Way. E13 . . . . 6D 62
Eliot Bank. SE23 . . . . 8F 92
Eliot Cotts. SE3 . . . . 1C 94
Eliot Dri. Harr 7M 37
Eliot Gdns. SW15 . . . . 3E 88
Eliot Hill. SE13 . . . . 1A 94
Eliot M. NW8 . . . . 5A 58
Eliot Pk. SE13 . . . . 1A 94
Eliot Pl. SE3 . . . . 1C 94
Eliot Rd. Dag 9H 49
Eliot Rd. Dart 4M 99
Eliot Va. SE3 . . . . 1B 94
Elis David Almshouses.
Croy 5M 123
Elizabethan Clo. Stanw 6B 144
Elizabethan Way. Stanw . . . 6B 144
Elizabeth Av. N1 . . . . 4A 60
Elizabeth Av. Enf 5M 15
Elizabeth Av. Ilf 7B 48
Elizabeth Barnes Ct. SW6 . . . 1M 89
(off Marinefield Rd.)
Elizabeth Blackwell Ho.
N22 . . . . 8L 27
(off Progress Way)
Elizabeth Bri. SW1 . . . . 5F 74
Elizabeth Clo. E14 . . . . 9M 61
Elizabeth Clo. W9 . . . . 7A 58
Elizabeth Clo. Barn 5H 13
Elizabeth Clo. Romf 8M 33
Elizabeth Clo. Sutt 6K 121
Elizabeth Clyde Clo. N15 . . . 2C 44
Elizabeth Cotts. Kew 9K 71
Elizabeth Ct. E4 . . . . 5K 29
Elizabeth Ct. SW1 . . . . 4H 75
(off Milmans Ct.)
Elizabeth Ct. SW10 . . . . 7B 74
(off Milman's St.)
Elizabeth Ct. Brom 5D 110
(off Highland Rd.)
Elizabeth Ct. Tedd 2C 102
Elizabeth Ct. Wat 2D 8
Elizabeth Ct. Wey 6B 116
Elizabeth Ct. Whyt 9D 138
Elizabeth Ct. Wfd G 7G 31
Elizabeth Fry Ho. Hay 5D 68
Elizabeth Fry M. E8 . . . . 3F 60
Elizabeth Fry Pl. SE18 . . . . 9J 79
Elizabeth Gdns. W3 . . . . 2D 72
Elizabeth Gdns. Stan 6G 23
Elizabeth Gdns. Sun 7G 101
Elizabeth Garrett Anderson Ho.
Belv 4L 81
(off Ambrook Rd.)
Elizabeth Ho. SE11 . . . . 5L 75
(off Reedworth St.)
Elizabeth Ho. W6 . . . . 6G 73
(off Queen Caroline St.)
Elizabeth Ho. Wat 4G 9
Elizabeth Ind. Est. SE14 . . . . 7H 77
Elizabeth M. NW3 . . . . 2C 58
Elizabeth M. Harr 4C 38
Elizabeth Newcomen Ho.
SE1 . . . . 3B 76
(off Newcomen St.)
Elizabeth Pl. N15 . . . . 2B 44
Elizabeth Pl. F'ham 1K 131
Elizabeth Ride. N9 . . . . 9F 16
Elizabeth Rd. E6 . . . . 4H 63
Elizabeth Rd. N15 . . . . 3C 44
Elizabeth Rd. Rain 8F 66
Elizabeth Sq. SE16 . . . . 1J 77
(off Sovereign Cres.)
Elizabeth St. SW1 . . . . 5E 74
Elizabeth Ter. SE9 . . . . 5K 95
Elizabeth Way. SE19 . . . . 4B 108
Elizabeth Way. Felt 1G 101
Elizabeth Way. Orp 9G 113
Elkanet M. N20 . . . . 2A 26
Elkington Point. SE11 . . . . 5L 75
(off Lollard St.)
Elkington Rd. E13 . . . . 7F 62
Elkins, The. Romf 9C 34
Elkstone Ct. SE15 . . . . 7C 76
(off Birdlip Clo.)
Elkstone Rd. W10 . . . . 8K 57
Ellaline Rd. W6 . . . . 7H 73
Ella M. NW3 . . . . 9D 42
Ellanby Cres. N18 . . . . 4F 28
Elland Ho. E14 . . . . 9K 61
(off Copenhagen Pl.)
Elland Rd. SE15 . . . . 3G 93
Elland Rd. W on T 4H 117
Ella Rd. N8 . . . . 5J 43
Ellement Clo. Pinn 3H 37
Ellena Ct. N14 . . . . 3J 27
(off Conway Rd.)
Ellenborough Ho. W12 . . . . 1F 72
(off White City Est.)
Ellenborough Pl. SW15 . . . . 3E 88
Ellenborough Rd. N22 . . . . 8A 28
Ellenborough Rd. Sidc 2H 113
Ellenbridge Way. S Croy . . . 1C 138
Ellenbrook Clo. Wat 3G 9
Ellen Clo. Brom 7H 111
Ellen Ct. E4 . . . . 1A 30
(off Ridgeway, The)
Ellen Ct. N9 . . . . 2G 29
Ellen St. E1 . . . . 9E 60
Ellen Webb Dri. W'stone . . . 1C 38
Ellen Wilkinson Ho. E2 . . . . 6H 61
(off Usk St.)
Ellen Wilkinson Ho. SW6 . . . . 7K 73
(off Clem Attlee Ct.)
Ellen Wilkinson Ho. Dag 8L 49
Elleray Rd. Tedd 3D 102
Ellerby St. SW6 . . . . 9H 73
Ellerdale Clo. NW3 . . . . 9A 42
Ellerdale Rd. NW3 . . . . 1A 58
Ellerdale St. SE13 . . . . 3M 93
Ellerdine Rd. Houn 3A 86
Ellerker Gdns. Rich 5J 87
Ellerman Av. Twic 7K 85
Ellerslie Gdns. NW10 . . . . 4E 56
Ellerslie Rd. W12 . . . . 2F 72
Ellerslie Sq. Ind. Est. SW2 . . 4J 91
Ellerton Gdns. Dag 3G 65
Ellerton Lodge. N3 . . . . 9L 25
Ellerton Rd. SW13 . . . . 9E 72
Ellerton Rd. SW18 . . . . 7B 90
Ellerton Rd. SW20 . . . . 4E 104
Ellerton Rd. Dag 3G 65
Ellerton Rd. Surb 4K 119
Ellery Ho. SE17 . . . . 5B 76
Ellery Rd. SE19 . . . . 4B 108
Ellery St. SE15 . . . . 1F 92
Ellesborough Clo. Wat 5G 21
Ellesmere Av. NW7 . . . . 3B 24
Ellesmere Av. Beck 6M 109
Ellesmere Clo. E11 . . . . 3D 46
Ellesmere Clo. Ruis 5A 36
Ellesmere Ct. W4 . . . . 6B 72
Ellesmere Dri. S Croy 6F 138
Ellesmere Gdns. Ilf 3J 47
Ellesmere Gro. Barn 7K 13
Ellesmere Pl. W on T 7C 116
Ellesmere Rd. E3 . . . . 5J 61
Ellesmere Rd. NW10 . . . . 1E 56
Ellesmere Rd. W4 . . . . 7A 72
Ellesmere Rd. Gnfd 7A 54
Ellesmere Rd. Twic 5G 87
Ellesmere Rd. Wey 9C 116
Ellesmere St. E14 . . . . 9M 61
Elleswood Ct. Surb 2H 119
Ellie M. Ashf 8C 144
Ellingfort Rd. E8 . . . . 3F 60
Ellingham Rd. E15 . . . . 9B 46
Ellingham Rd. W12 . . . . 3E 72
Ellingham Rd. Chess 8H 119
Ellington Ct. N14 . . . . 2H 27
Ellington Ho. SE1 . . . . 4A 76
Ellington Rd. N10 . . . . 2F 42
Ellington Rd. Felt 1D 100
Ellington Rd. Houn 1M 85
Ellington St. N7 . . . . 2L 59
Ellington Way. Eps 9F 134
Elliot Clo. E15 . . . . 3C 62
Elliot Ho. W1 . . . . 8C 58
(off Cato St.)
Elliot Rd. NW4 . . . . 4F 40
Elliots Clo. Cow 8A 142
Elliott Av. Ruis 7F 36
Elliott Clo. Wemb 8L 39
Elliott Clo. Wfd G 6H 31
Elliott Gdns. Romf 8F 34
Elliott Rd. SW9 . . . . 9M 75
Elliott Rd. W4 . . . . 5C 72
Elliott Rd. Brom 8H 111
Elliott Rd. Stan 6E 22
Elliott Rd. T Hth 8M 107
Elliott's Pl. N1 . . . . 4M 59
Elliott Sq. NW3 . . . . 3C 58
Elliotts Row. SE11 . . . . 5M 75
Ellis Av. Rain 8E 66
Ellis Clo. NW10 . . . . 2F 56
Ellis Clo. SE9 . . . . 8A 96
Ellis Clo. Edgw 6C 24
Ellis Clo. Swan 8B 114
Elliscombe Mt. SE7 . . . . 7G 79
Elliscombe Rd. SE7 . . . . 6G 79
Ellis Ct. W7 . . . . 8D 54
Ellisfield Dri. SW15 . . . . 6E 88
Ellis Franklin Ct. NW8 . . . . 5A 58
(off Abbey Rd.)
Ellis Ho. SE17 . . . . 6B 76
(off Brandon St.)
Ellison Gdns. S'hall 5K 69
Ellison Ho. SE13 . . . . 1M 93
(off Lewisham Rd.)
Ellison Rd. SW13 . . . . 1D 88
Ellison Rd. SW16 . . . . 4H 107
Ellison Rd. Sidc 7B 96
Ellis Rd. Mitc 1D 122
Ellis Rd. S'hall 2A 70
Ellis St. SW1 . . . . 5E 74
Ellis Way. Dart 8K 99
Ellmore Clo. Romf 8F 34
Ellora Rd. SW16 . . . . 2H 107
Ellsworth St. E2 . . . . 6F 60
Ellwood Ct. W9 . . . . 7M 57
(off Clearwell Dri.)
Ellwood Ct. Wat 7F 4
Ellwood Gdns. Wat 7G 5
Elmar Rd. N15 . . . . 2B 44
Elm Av. W5 . . . . 2J 71
Elm Av. Ashf 8C 144
Elm Av. Ruis 6E 36
Elm Av. Upm 8M 51
Elm Av. Wat 9J 9
Elm Bank. N14 . . . . 9J 15
Elmbank Av. Barn 6G 13
Elm Bank Dri. Brom 6H 111
Elm Bank Gdns. SW13 . . . . 1C 88
Elmbank Way. W7 . . . . 8B 54
Elmbourne Dri. Belv 5M 81
Elmbourne Rd. SW17 . . . . 9E 90
Elmbridge Av. Surb 9M 103
Elmbridge Clo. Ruis 4E 36
Elmbridge Dri. Ruis 3D 36
Elmbridge Rd. Ilf 6E 32
Elmbridge Wlk. E8 . . . . 3E 60
Elmbrook Clo. Sun 5F 100
Elmbrook Gdns. SE9 . . . . 3J 95
Elmbrook Rd. Sutt 6K 121
Elm Clo. E11 . . . . 4F 46
Elm Clo. N19 . . . . 7G 43
Elm Clo. NW4 . . . . 3H 41
Elm Clo. SW20 . . . . 8G 105
Elm Clo. Buck H 2H 31
Elm Clo. Cars 3D 122
Elm Clo. Dart 7G 99
Elm Clo. Harr 4M 37
Elm Clo. Hay 9E 52
Elm Clo. Romf 8M 33
Elm Clo. S Croy 8C 124
Elm Clo. Stanw 7B 144
Elm Clo. Surb 2A 120
Elm Clo. Twic 8M 85
Elm Clo. Wal A 7K 7
Elm Clo. Warl 9H 139
Elmcote. Pinn 9H 21
Elm Cotts. Mitc 6D 106
Elm Ct. EC4 . . . . 9L 59
(off Terrace, The)
Elm Ct. SE13 . . . . 2B 94
Elm Ct. W9 . . . . 8L 57
(off Admiral Wlk.)
Elm Ct. Wat 5F 8
Elm Ct. W Mol 8M 101
Elmcourt Rd. SE27 . . . . 8M 91
Elm Cres. W5 . . . . 2J 71
Elm Cres. King T 5J 103
Elmcroft. N6 . . . . 5G 43
Elmcroft Av. E11 . . . . 3F 46
Elmcroft Av. N9 . . . . 8F 16
Elmcroft Av. NW11 . . . . 5K 41
Elmcroft Av. Sidc 6D 96
Elmcroft Clo. E11 . . . . 2F 46
Elmcroft Clo. N8 . . . . 3K 43
Elmcroft Clo. W5 . . . . 9H 55
Elmcroft Clo. Chess 5J 119
Elmcroft Clo. Felt 5D 84
Elmcroft Cres. NW11 . . . . 5J 41
Elmcroft Cres. Harr 1L 37
Elmcroft Dri. Chess 5J 119
Elmcroft Gdns. NW9 . . . . 2L 39
Elmcroft Rd. Orp 2E 128
Elmcroft St. E5 . . . . 9G 45
Elmcroft Ter. Uxb 9E 142
Elmdale Rd. N13 . . . . 5K 27
Elmdene. Surb 3A 120
Elmdene Av. Horn 3K 51
Elmdene Clo. Beck 1K 125
Elmdene Rd. SE18 . . . . 6M 79
Elmdon Rd. Houn 1H 85
Elmdon Rd. H'row A 2D 84
Elm Dri. Chesh 1E 6
Elm Dri. Harr 4M 37
Elm Dri. Sun 6G 101
Elm Dri. Swan 6B 114
Elmer Av. Hav 3C 34
Elmer Clo. Enf 5K 15
Elmer Clo. Rain 3E 66
Elmer Gdns. Edgw 7M 23
Elmer Gdns. Iswth 2B 86
Elmer Gdns. Rain 3E 66
Elmer Ho. NW8 . . . . 8C 58
(off Broadley St.)
Elmer Rd. SE6 . . . . 6A 94

End Way. Surb 2L 119
Endwell Rd. SE4 . . . . 1J 93
Endymion Rd. N4 . . . . 5L 43
Endymion Rd. SW2 . . . . 5K 91
Energen Clo. NW10 . . . . 2C 56
Enfield. 5B 16
Enfield Bus. Cen. Enf 4G 17
Enfield Cloisters. N1 . . . . 6C 60
(off Fanshaw St.)
Enfield Clo. Uxb 5B 142
Enfield Crematorium. Enf 1F 16
Enfield Golf Course. 6L 15
Enfield Highway. 4H 17
Enfield Ho. SW9 . . . . 1J 91
(off Stockwell Rd.)
Enfield Ho. Romf 7J 35
(off Leyburn Cres.)
Enfield Island Village. 2L 17
Enfield Lock. 1K 17
Enfield Retail Pk. Enf 5F 16
Enfield Rd. N1 . . . . 3C 60
Enfield Rd. W3 . . . . 3M 71
Enfield Rd. Bren 6H 71
Enfield Rd. Enf 6H 15
Enfield Rd. H'row A 1C 84
Enfield Town. 5B 16
Enfield Wlk. Bren 6H 71
Enfield Wash. 1H 17
Enford St. W1 . . . . 8D 58
Engadine Clo. Croy 5D 124
Engadine St. SW18 . . . . 7K 89
Engate St. SE13 . . . . 3A 94
Engayne Gdns. Upm 6M 51
Engel Pk. NW7 . . . . 6G 25
Engine Ct. SW1 . . . . 2G 75
(off Ambassadors' Ct.)
Engineer Clo. SE18 . . . . 7L 79
Engineers Way. Wemb 9L 39
England's La. NW3 . . . . 2D 58
Englands La. Lou 4L 19
England Way. N Mald 8M 103
Englefield. NW1 . . . . 6G 59
(off Clarence Gdns.)
Englefield Clo. Croy 1A 124
Englefield Clo. Enf 4L 15
Englefield Clo. Orp 9D 112
Englefield Cres. Orp 8D 112
Englefield Path. Orp 8E 112
Englefield Rd. N1 . . . . 3B 60
Engleheart Dri. Felt 5D 84
Engleheart Rd. SE6 . . . . 6M 93
Englemere Pk. Oxs 5A 132
Englewood Rd. SW12 . . . . 5F 90
English Grounds. SE1 . . . . . . 2C 76
English St. E3 . . . . 7K 61
Enid Clo. Brick W 4K 5
Enid St. SE16 . . . . 4D 76
Enmore Av. SE25 . . . . 9E 108
Enmore Gdns. SW14 . . . . 4B 88
Enmore Rd. SE25 . . . . 9E 108
Enmore Rd. SW15 . . . . 3G 89
Enmore Rd. S'hall 7L 53
Ennerdale. NW1 . . . . 6G 59
(off Varndell St.)
Ennerdale Av. Horn 1E 66
Ennerdale Av. Stan 1G 39
Ennerdale Clo. Felt 7D 84
Ennerdale Clo. Sutt 6K 121
Ennerdale Dri. NW9 . . . . 3C 40
Ennerdale Gdns. Wemb 6G 39
Ennerdale Ho. E3 . . . . 7K 61
Ennerdale Rd. Bexh 9L 81
Ennerdale Rd. Rich 1K 87
Ennersdale Rd. SE13 . . . . 4B 94
Ennis Ho. E14 . . . . 9M 61
(off Vesey Path)
Ennismore Av. W4 . . . . 5D 72
Ennismore Av. Gnfd 2C 54
Ennismore Gdns. SW7 . . . . . . 3C 74
Ennismore Gdns. Th Dit 1C 118
Ennismore Gdns. M. SW7 . . . 4C 74
Ennismore M. SW7 . . . . 4C 74
Ennismore St. SW7 . . . . 4C 74
Ennis Rd. N4 . . . . 6L 43
Ennis Rd. SE18 . . . . 7A 80
Ennor Ct. Sutt 6G 121
Ensbury Ho. SW8 . . . . 8K 75
(off Carroun Rd.)
Ensign Clo. Purl 2L 137
Ensign Clo. Stanw 7B 144
Ensign Dri. N13 . . . . 3A 28
Ensign Ho. E14 . . . . 3L 77
(off Admirals Way)
Ensign Ind. Cen. E1 . . . . 1E 76
(off Ensign St.)
Ensign St. E1 . . . . 1E 76
Ensign Way. Stanw 7B 144
Ensign Way. Wall 9J 123
Enslin Rd. SE9 . . . . 6L 95
Ensor M. SW7 . . . . 6B 74
Enstone Rd. Enf 5J 17
Enterprise Bus. Pk. E14 . . . . 3M 77
Enterprise Cen., The.
Beck 2J 109
(off Cricket La.)
Enterprise Clo. Croy 3L 123
Enterprise Ho. E9 . . . . 3G 61
(off Tudor Gro.)
Enterprise Ho. E14 . . . . 6M 77
(off St Davids Sq.)
Enterprise Ho. Bark 6D 64
Enterprise Ind. Est. SE16 . . . . 6G 77
Enterprise Way. NW10 . . . . . . 6D 56
Enterprise Way. SW18 . . . . . . 3L 89
Enterprise Way. Tedd 3D 102
Enterprize Way. SE8 . . . . 5K 77
Epcot M. NW10 . . . . 6H 57
Epirus M. SW6 . . . . 8L 73
Epirus Rd. SW6 . . . . 8K 73
Epping Clo. E14 . . . . 5L 77
Epping Clo. Romf 1M 49
Epping Forest. 1J 19
Epping Forest. 4H 19
Epping Glade. E4 . . . . 8A 18
Epping New Rd.
Buck H & Lou 2F 30
Epping Pl. N1 . . . . 2L 59
Epping Way. E4 . . . . 8M 17
Epple Rd. SW6 . . . . 9K 73
Epsom. 5B 134
Epsom Bus. Pk. Eps 3C 134
Epsom Clo. Bexh 2M 97
Epsom Clo. N'holt 1K 53
Epsom Gap. Lea 7F 132
Epsom Ho. Romf 5J 35
(off Dagnam Pk. Dri.)
Epsom Playhouse. 5B 134
(off Ashley Av.)
Epsom Rd. E10 . . . . 4A 46
Epsom Rd. Asht 9K 133
Epsom Rd. Croy 6L 123
Epsom Rd. Eps 3D 134
Epsom Rd. Ilf 4D 48
Epsom Rd. Sutt 2K 121
Epsom Sq. H'row A 1D 84
Epsom Way. Horn 9K 51
Epstein Rd. SE28 . . . . 2E 80
Epworth Rd. Iswth 8F 70
Epworth St. EC2 . . . . 7B 60
Equity Sq. E2 . . . . 6D 60
(off Shacklewell St.)
Erasmus St. SW1 . . . . 5H 75
Erconwald St. W12 . . . . 9D 56
Erebus Dri. SE28 . . . . 3A 80
Eresby Dri. Beck 3L 125
Eresby Ho. SW7 . . . . 3C 74
(off Rutland Ga.)
Eresby Pl. NW6 . . . . 3L 57
Erica Ct. Swan 8C 114
Erica Gdns. Croy 5M 125
Erica Ho. N22 . . . . 8L 27
(off Acacia Rd.)
Erica Ho. SE4 . . . . 2K 93
Erica St. W12 . . . . 1E 72
Eric Clarke La. Bark 7M 63
Eric Clo. E7 . . . . 9E 46
Ericcson Clo. SW18 . . . . 4L 89
Eric Fletcher Ct. N1 . . . . 3A 60
(off Essex Rd.)
Eric Rd. E7 . . . . 9E 46
Eric Rd. NW10 . . . . 2D 56
Eric Rd. Romf 5H 49
Ericson Ho. SE13 . . . . 3B 94
(off Blessington Rd.)
Eric St. E3 . . . . 7K 61
(in two parts)
Eric Wilkins Ho. SE1 . . . . . . 6E 76
(off Old Kent Rd.)
Eridge Grn. Clo. Orp 3G 129
Eridge Rd. W4 . . . . 4B 72
Erin Clo. Brom 4C 110
Erin Clo. Ilf 4E 48
Erindale. SE18 . . . . 7B 80
Erindale Ter. SE18 . . . . 7B 80
Eriswell Cres. W on T 8C 116
Eriswell Rd. W on T 6D 116
Erith. 6C 82
Erith Ct. Purf 5L 83
Erith Cres. Romf 8A 34
Erith High St. Eri 6C 82
Erith Mus. 6C 82
(in Library)
Erith Rd. Belv & Eri 6L 81
Erith Rd. Bexh & N Hth 3M 97
Erith Small Bus. Cen.
Eri 7D 82
(off Erith High St.)
Erlanger Rd. SE14 . . . . 9H 77
Erlesmere Gdns. W7 . . . . 4E 70
Erlich Cotts. E1 . . . . 8G 61
(off Sidney St.)
Ermine Clo. Chesh 4B 6
Ermine Clo. Houn 1G 85
Ermine Rd. N15 . . . . 4D 44
Ermine Rd. SE13 . . . . 3M 93
Ermine Side. Enf 7E 16
Ermington Rd. SE9 . . . . 8A 96
Ernald Av. E6 . . . . 5J 63
Erncroft Way. Twic 5D 86
Ernest Av. SE27 . . . . 1M 107
Ernest Clo. Beck 9L 109
Ernest Cotts. Eps 9D 120
Ernest Gdns. W4 . . . . 7M 71
Ernest Gro. Beck 9K 109
Ernest Harriss Ho. W9 . . . . . 7L 57
(off Elgin Av.)
Ernest Rd. Horn 4J 51
Ernest Rd. King T 6M 103
Ernest Sq. King T 6M 103
Ernest St. E1 . . . . 7H 61
Ernle Rd. SW20 . . . . 4F 104
Ernshaw Pl. SW15 . . . . 4J 89
Eros. 1H 75
Eros Ho. Shops. SE6 . . . . . . 6M 93
(off Brownhill Rd.)
Erpingham Rd. SW15 . . . . . . 2G 89
Erridge Rd. SW19 . . . . 6L 105
Errington Rd. W9 . . . . 7K 57
Errol Gdns. Hay 7F 52
Errol Gdns. N Mald 8E 104
Erroll Rd. Romf 2D 50
Errol St. EC1 . . . . 7A 60
Erskine Clo. Sutt 5C 122
Erskine Cres. N17 . . . . 2F 44
Erskine Hill. NW11 . . . . 2L 41
Erskine Ho. SW1 . . . . 6G 75
(off Churchill Gdns.)
Erskine M. NW3 . . . . 3D 58
(off Erskine Rd.)
Erskine Rd. E17 . . . . 2K 45
Erskine Rd. NW3 . . . . 3D 58
Erskine Rd. Sutt 6B 122
Erwood Rd. SE7 . . . . 6J 79
Esam Way. SW16 . . . . 2L 107
Escot Rd. Sun 4D 100
Escott Gdns. SE9 . . . . 1J 111
Escot Way. Barn 7G 13
Escreet Gro. SE18 . . . . 5L 79
Esher. 6M 117
Esher Av. Romf 4A 50
Esher Av. Sutt 5H 121
Esher Av. W on T 2E 116
Esher By-Pass.
Clay & Chess 1F 132
Esher By-Pass. Cob, Esh & Oxs
. . . . 2A 132
Esher Clo. Bex 7J 97
Esher Clo. Esh 7M 117
Esher Common (Junct.) . . . 1A 132
Esher Cres. H'row A 1D 84
Esher Gdns. SW19 . . . . 8H 89
Esher Grn. Esh 6M 117
Esher Green Dri. Esh 5M 117
Esher M. Mitc 7E 106
Esher Pk. Av. Esh 6M 117
Esher Pl. Av. Esh 6L 117
Esher Rd. E Mol 1B 118
Esher Rd. Ilf 8C 48
Esher Rd. W on T 7H 117
Eskdale. NW1 . . . . 5G 59
(off Stanhope St.)
Eskdale Av. N'holt 4K 53
Eskdale Clo. Wemb 7H 39
Eskdale Gdns. Purl 6B 138
Eskdale Rd. Bexh 1L 97
Eskmont Ridge. SE19 . . . . . 4B 108
Esk Rd. E13 . . . . 7E 62
Esk Way. Romf 7B 34
Esmar Cres. NW9 . . . . 5E 40
Esmeralda Rd. SE1 . . . . 5E 76
Esmond Clo. Rain 3F 66
Esmond Ct. W8 . . . . 4M 73
(off Thackeray St.)
Esmond Gdns. W4 . . . . 5B 72
Esmond Rd. NW6 . . . . 4K 57
Esmond Rd. W4 . . . . 5B 72
Esmond St. SW15 . . . . 3J 89
Esparto St. SW18 . . . . 6M 89
Esporta Riverside Northwood.
. . . . 6A 20
Essan Ho. W5 . . . . 8F 54
Essenden Rd. Belv 6L 81
Essenden Rd. S Croy 9C 124
Essendine Rd. W9 . . . . 6L 57
Essex Av. Iswth 2C 86
Essex Clo. E17 . . . . 2J 45
Essex Clo. Mord 2H 121
Essex Clo. Romf 2M 49
Essex Clo. Ruis 6H 37
Essex Ct. SW13 . . . . 1D 88
Essex Ct. WC2 . . . . 9L 59
(off Brick Ct.)
Essex Ct. Romf 7H 35
Essex Gdns. N4 . . . . 4M 43
Essex Gdns. Horn 3L 51
Essex Gro. SE19 . . . . 3B 108
Essex Hall. E17 . . . . 8H 29
Essex Ho. E14 . . . . 9M 61
(off Girauld St.)
Essex La. K Lan 6B 4
Essex Mans. E11 . . . . 5B 46
Essex Pk. N3 . . . . 6M 25
Essex Pk. M. W3 . . . . 2C 72
Essex Pl. W4 . . . . 5A 72
(in two parts)
Essex Pl. Sq. W4 . . . . 5B 72
Essex Rd. E4 . . . . 1C 30
Essex Rd. E10 . . . . 4A 46
Essex Rd. E12 . . . . 1J 63
Essex Rd. E17 . . . . 4J 45
Essex Rd. E18 . . . . 9F 30
Essex Rd. N1 . . . . 4M 59
Essex Rd. NW10 . . . . 3C 56
Essex Rd. W3 . . . . 1A 72
Essex Rd. W4 . . . . 5B 72
(in two parts)
Essex Rd. Bark 3B 64
Essex Rd. Borwd 5L 11
Essex Rd. Chad H 5G 49
Essex Rd. Dag 1A 66
Essex Rd. Dart 5H 99
(in two parts)
Essex Rd. Enf 6B 16
Essex Rd. Romf 2M 49
Essex Rd. Wat 4E 8
Essex Rd. S. E11 . . . . 5B 46
Essex St. E7 . . . . 1E 62
Essex St. SE18 . . . . 4A 80
Essex St. WC2 . . . . 9L 59
Essex Vs. W8 . . . . 3L 73
Essex Wharf. E5 . . . . 7H 45
Essian St. E1 . . . . 8J 61
Essoldo Way. Edgw 1K 39
Estate Way. E10 . . . . 6K 45
Estcourt Rd. SE25 . . . . 1F 124
Estcourt Rd. SW6 . . . . 8K 73
Estcourt Rd. Wat 5G 9
Estella Av. N Mald 8F 104
Estella Ho. W11 . . . . 1H 73
(off St Ann's Rd.)
Estelle Rd. NW3 . . . . 9D 42
Esterbrooke St. SW1 . . . . 5H 75
Este Rd. SW11 . . . . 2C 90
Esther Clo. N21 . . . . 9L 15
Esther Rd. E11 . . . . 5C 46
Estoria Clo. SW2 . . . . 6L 91
Estorick Collection of Modern
Italian Art. 2M 59
(off Canonbury Sq.)
Estreham Rd. SW16 . . . . . . 3H 107
Estridge Clo. Houn 3L 85
Estuary Clo. Bark 6F 64
Eswyn Rd. SW17 . . . . 1D 106
Etal Ho. N1 . . . . 3M 59
(off Sutton Est., The)
Etchingham Ct. N3 . . . . 7M 25
Etchingham Pk. Rd. N3 . . . . . 7M 25
Etchingham Rd. E15 . . . . 9A 46
Eternit Wlk. SW6 . . . . 9G 73
Etfield Gro. Sidc 2F 112
Ethel Bailey Clo. Eps 4L 133
Ethelbert Clo. Brom 6E 110
Ethelbert Ct. Brom 7E 110
(off Ethelbert Rd.)
Ethelbert Gdns. Ilf 3K 47
Ethelbert Rd. SW20 . . . . . . 5H 105
Ethelbert Rd. Brom 7E 110
Ethelbert Rd. Dart 1J 115
Ethelbert Rd. Eri 8A 82
Ethelbert Rd. Orp 7H 113
Ethelbert St. SW12 . . . . 7F 90
Ethel Brooks Ho. SE18 . . . . . 7M 79
Ethelburga Rd. Romf 8K 35
Ethelburga St. SW11 . . . . 9C 74
Ethelburga Tower. SW11 . . . 9C 74
(off Maskelyne Clo.)
Etheldene Av. N10 . . . . 2G 43
Ethelden Rd. W12 . . . . 2F 72
Ethel Rd. E16 . . . . 9F 62
Ethel St. SE17 . . . . 5A 76
Etheridge Grn. Lou 5M 19
Etheridge Rd. NW4 . . . . 5G 41
(in two parts)
Etheridge Rd. Lou 4M 19
Etherley Rd. N15 . . . . 3A 44
Etherow St. SE22 . . . . 6E 92
Etherstone Grn. SW16 . . . . 1L 107
Etherstone Rd. SW16 . . . . . 1L 107
Ethnard Rd. SE15 . . . . 7F 76
Ethronvi Rd. Bexh 2J 97
Etloe Rd. E10 . . . . 7L 45
Eton Av. N12 . . . . 7A 26
Eton Av. NW3 . . . . 3B 58
Eton Av. Barn 8C 14
Eton Av. Houn 7K 69
Eton Av. N Mald 9B 104
Eton Av. Wemb 9F 38
Eton Clo. SW18 . . . . 6M 89
Eton College Rd. NW3 . . . . . 2D 58
Eton Ct. NW3 . . . . 3B 58
(off Eton Av.)
Eton Ct. Wemb 9G 39
Eton Garages. NW3 . . . . 2C 58
Eton Gro. NW9 . . . . 1L 39
Eton Gro. SE13 . . . . 2C 94
Eton Hall. NW3 . . . . 2D 58
Eton Ho. N5 . . . . 9M 43
(off Leigh Rd.)
Eton Mnr. Ct. E10 . . . . 7L 45
(off Leyton Grange Est.)
Eton Pl. NW3 . . . . 3E 58
Eton Ri. NW3 . . . . 2D 58
Eton Rd. NW3 . . . . 3D 58
Eton Rd. Hay 8D 68
Eton Rd. Ilf 9A 48
Eton Rd. Orp 6F 128
Eton St. Rich 4J 87
Eton Vs. NW3 . . . . 2D 58
Eton Way. Dart 3G 99
Etta St. SE8 . . . . 7J 77
Etton Clo. Horn 7J 51
Ettrick St. E14 . . . . 9A 62
(in two parts)
Etwell Pl. Surb 1K 119
Eugene Clo. Romf 2G 51
Eugene Cotter Ho. SE17 . . . . 5B 76
(off Tatum St.)
Eugenia Rd. SE16 . . . . 5G 77
Eugenie M. Chst 5M 111
Eureka Rd. King T 6L 103
Euro Clo. NW10 . . . . 2E 56
Eurolink Bus. Cen. SW2 . . . . 4L 91
Europa Pl. EC1 . . . . 6A 60
Europa Trad. Est. Eri 6B 82
European Bus. Cen. NW9 . . . 1A 40
(Carlisle Rd.)
European Bus. Cen. NW9 . . . 1B 40
(Edgware Rd.)
Europe Rd. SE18 . . . . 4K 79
Eustace Ho. SE11 . . . . 5K 75
(off Old Paradise St.)
Eustace Pl. SE18 . . . . 5K 79
Eustace Rd. E6 . . . . 6J 63
Eustace Rd. SW6 . . . . 8L 73
Eustace Rd. Romf 5H 49
Euston Av. Wat 7D 8
Euston Cen. NW1 . . . . 7G 59
(in two parts)
Euston Gro. NW1 . . . . 6H 59
(off Euston Sq.)
Euston Rd. NW1 & N1 . . . . . 7F 58
Euston Rd. Croy 3L 123
Euston Sq. NW1 . . . . 6H 59
(in two parts)
Euston Sta. Colonnade.
NW1 . . . . 6H 59
Euston St. NW1 . . . . 6G 59
Euston Tower. NW1 . . . . 7G 59
Euston Underpass (Junct.)
. . . . 6F 58
Evandale Rd. SW9 . . . . 1L 91
Evangalist Ho. EC4 . . . . 9M 59
(off Black Friars La.)
Evangelist Rd. NW5 . . . . 9F 42
Evans Av. Wat 8D 4
Evans Clo. E8 . . . . 2D 60
Evansdale. Rain 6D 66
Evans Gro. Felt 8L 85
Evans Ho. SW8 . . . . 8H 75
(off Wandsworth Rd.)
Evans Ho. W12 . . . . 1F 72
(off White City Est.)
Evans Ho. Felt 8L 85
Evans Rd. SE6 . . . . 8C 94
Evanston Av. E4 . . . . 7A 30
Evanston Gdns. Ilf 4J 47
Eva Rd. Romf 5G 49
Evelina Mans. SE5 . . . . 8B 76
Evelina Rd. SE15 . . . . 2G 93
Evelina Rd. SE20 . . . . 4G 109
Eveline Rd. Mitc 5D 106
Evelyn Av. NW9 . . . . 2B 40
Evelyn Av. Ruis 5C 36
Evelyn Clo. Twic 6M 85
Evelyn Ct. E8 . . . . 9E 44
Evelyn Ct. N1 . . . . 5B 60
(off Evelyn Wlk., in two parts)
Evelyn Cres. Sun 5D 100
Evelyn Denington Ct. N1 . . . . 3M 59
(off Sutton Est., The)
Evelyn Denington Rd.
E6 . . . . 7J 63
Evelyn Dri. Pinn 7H 21
Evelyn Fox Ct. W10 . . . . 8G 57
Evelyn Gdns. SW7 . . . . 6A 74
Evelyn Gdns. Rich 3J 87
Evelyn Gro. W5 . . . . 2K 71
Evelyn Gro. S'hall 9K 53
Evelyn Ho. SE14 . . . . 9J 77
(off Loring Rd.)
Evelyn Ho. W12 . . . . 3D 72
(off Cobbold Rd.)
Evelyn Lowe Est. SE16 . . . . . 4E 76
Evelyn Mans. SW1 . . . . 4G 75
(off Carlisle Pl.)
Evelyn Mans. W14 . . . . 7J 73
(off Queen's Club Gdns.)
Evelyn Rd. E16 . . . . 2E 78
Evelyn Rd. E17 . . . . 2A 46
Evelyn Rd. SW19 . . . . 2M 105
Evelyn Rd. W4 . . . . 4B 72
Evelyn Rd. Cockf 6D 14
Evelyn Rd. Ham 9G 87
Evelyn Rd. Rich 2J 87
Evelyns Clo. Uxb 9E 142
Evelyn Sharp Clo. Romf 1H 51
Evelyn Sharp Ho. Romf 1H 51
Evelyn St. SE8 . . . . 5J 77
Evelyn Ter. Rich 2J 87
Evelyn Wlk. N1 . . . . 5B 60
Evelyn Way. Eps 3L 133
Evelyn Way. Sun 5D 100
Evelyn Way. Wall 6H 123
Evelyn Yd. W1 . . . . 9H 59
Evening Hill. Beck 4A 110
Evenlode Ho. SE2 . . . . 3G 81
(off Coralline Wlk.)
Evensyde. Wat 8A 8
Evenwood Clo. SW15 . . . . . . 4J 89
Everard Av. Brom 3E 126
Everard Ct. N13 . . . . 3K 27
Everard Ho. E1 . . . . 9E 60
(off Boyd St.)
Everard Way. Wemb 8J 39
Everatt Clo. SW18 . . . . 5K 89
Everdon Rd. SW13 . . . . 7E 72
Everest Pl. E14 . . . . 8A 62
Everest Pl. Swan 8B 114
Everest Rd. SE9 . . . . 4K 95
Everest Rd. Stanw 6B 144
Everett Clo. Bus H 1C 22
Everett Clo. Pinn 1D 36
Everett Ho. SE17 . . . . 6B 76
(off East St.)
Everett Wlk. Belv 6K 81

Fairway, The—Felton Clo.

Fairway, The. New Bar 8M 13
Fairway, The. N Mald 5B 104
Fairway, The. N'holt 2A 54
Fairway, The. N'wd 4C 20
Fairway, The. Ruis 9G 37
Fairway, The. Uxb 5D 142
Fairway, The. Wemb 8F 38
Fairway, The. W Mol 7M 101
Fairweather Clo. N15 . . . . . . .2C 44
Fairweather Ct. N13 . . . . .4K 27
Fairweather Rd. N16 . . . . . . .4E 44
Fairwyn Rd. SE26 . . . . .1J 109
Faithfield. Bush 7J 9
Fakenham Clo. NW7 . . . . . . .7E 24
Fakenham Clo. N'holt 2K 53
Fakruddin St. E1 . . . . .7E 60
Falcon. WC1 . . . . .8J 59
(off Old Gloucester St.)
Falcon Av. Brom 8J 111
Falconberg Ct. W1 . . . . .9H 59
Falconberg M. W1 . . . . .9H 59
Falcon Clo. SE1 . . . . .2M 75
Falcon Clo. W4 . . . . .7A 72
Falcon Clo. Dart 4K 99
Falcon Clo. N'wd 7C 20
Falcon Clo. Wal A 7M 7
Falcon Ct. E18 . . . . .1F 46
(off Albert Rd.)
Falcon Ct. EC4 . . . . .9L 59
Falcon Ct. N1 . . . . .5M 59
(off City Garden Row)
Falcon Ct. New Bar 6A 14
Falcon Ct. Ruis 7C 36
Falcon Cres. Enf 7H 17
Falcon Dri. Stanw 5B 144
Falconer Ct. N17 . . . . .7A 28
Falconer Rd. Bush 8K 9
Falconer Rd. Ilf 5F 32
Falconer Wlk. N7 . . . . .7K 43
Falconet Ct. E1 . . . . .2F 76
(off Wapping High St.)
Falcon Gro. SW11 . . . . .2C 90
Falcon Ho. E14 . . . . .6M 77
(off St Davids Sq.)
Falconhurst. Oxs 7B 132
Falcon La. SW11 . . . . .2C 90
Falcon Lodge. W9 . . . . .8L 57
(off Admiral Wlk.)
Falcon Pk. Ind. Est. NW10 . . .9C 40
Falcon Point. SE1 . . . . .1M 75
Falcon Rd. SW11 . . . . .1C 90
Falcon Rd. Enf 7H 17
Falcon Rd. Hamp 4K 101
Falconry Ct. King T 7J 103
(off Fairfield S.)
Falcons Clo. Big H 9H 141
Falcon St. E13 . . . . .7D 62
Falcon Ter. SW11 . . . . .2C 90
Falcon Way. E11 . . . . .2E 46
Falcon Way. E14 . . . . .5M 77
Falcon Way. NW9 . . . . .9C 24
Falcon Way. Felt 4F 84
Falcon Way. Harr 3J 39
Falcon Way. Horn 3E 66
Falcon Way. Sun 6C 100
Falcon Way. Wat 7J 5
Falconwood. 3D 96
Falconwood (Junct.) 3A 96
Falconwood Av. Well 1B 96
Falconwood Ct. SE3 . . . . .1D 94
(off Montpelier Row)
Falconwood Pde. Well 3C 96
Falconwood Rd. Croy 1K 139
Falcourt Clo. Sutt 7M 121
Falkirk Clo. Horn 6L 51
Falkirk Ct. SE16 . . . . .2H 77
(off Rotherhithe St.)
Falkirk Gdns. Wat 5H 21
Falkirk Ho. W9 . . . . .5M 57
(off Maida Va.)
Falkirk St. N1 . . . . .5C 60
Falkland Av. N3 . . . . .7L 25
Falkland Av. N11 . . . . .4F 26
Falkland Ho. SE6 . . . . .1A 110
Falkland Ho. W8 . . . . .4M 73
Falkland Ho. W14 . . . . .6K 73
(off Edith Vs.)
Falkland Pk. Av. SE25 . . . .7C 108
Falkland Pl. NW5 . . . . .1G 59
Falkland Rd. N8 . . . . .2L 43
Falkland Rd. NW5 . . . . .1G 59
Falkland Rd. Barn 4J 13
Fallaize Av. Ilf 9M 47
Falling La. W Dray 1J 143
Falloden Way. NW11 . . . . . . .2L 41
Fallodon Ho. W11 . . . . .8K 57
(off Tavistock Cres.)
Fallow Clo. Chig 5D 32
Fallow Corner. 7A 26
Fallow Ct. SE16 . . . . .6E 76
(off Argyle Way)
Fallow Ct. Av. N12 . . . . .7A 26
Fallowfield. Stan 4E 22
Fallowfield Ct. Stan 3E 22
Fallow Fields. Lou 8G 19
Fallowfields Dri. N12 . . . . . . .6C 26
Fallowhurst Path. N12 . . . . . .7A 26
Fallows Clo. N2 . . . . .9B 26
Fallsbrook Rd. SW16 . . . . . .3F 106
Falman Clo. N9 . . . . .1E 28
Falmer Rd. E17 . . . . .1M 45
Falmer Rd. N15 . . . . .3A 44
Falmer Rd. Enf 6C 16
Falmouth Av. E4 . . . . .5B 30
Falmouth Clo. N22 . . . . .7K 27
Falmouth Clo. SE12 . . . . .4D 94
Falmouth Gdns. Ilf 2H 47
Falmouth Ho. SE11 . . . . .6L 75
(off Seaton Clo.)
Falmouth Ho. W2 . . . . .1C 74
(off Clarendon Pl.)
Falmouth Ho. Pinn 7K 21
Falmouth Rd. SE1 . . . . .4A 76
Falmouth Rd. W on T 6G 117
Falmouth St. E15 . . . . .1B 62
Falstaff Clo. Dart 6C 98
Falstaff Ct. SE11 . . . . .5M 75
(off Opal St.)
Falstaff Ho. N1 . . . . .5C 60
(off Arden Est.)
Falstaff M. Hamp H 2B 102
(off Parkside)
Fambridge Clo. SE26 . . . . . .1K 109
Fambridge Ct. Romf 3B 50
(off Marks Rd.)
Fambridge Rd. Dag 6L 49
Famet Av. Purl 5A 138
Famet Clo. Purl 5A 138
Famet Gdns. Kenl 5A 138
Famet Wlk. Purl 5A 138
Fane Ho. E2 . . . . .4G 61
Fane St. W14 . . . . .7K 73
Fan Mus. 8A 78
(off Croom's Hill)
Fanns Ri. Purf 5L 83
Fann St. EC2 & EC1 . . . . .7A 60
(in two parts)
Fanshawe Av. Bark 2A 64
Fanshawe Cres. Dag 1J 65
Fanshawe Cres. Horn 4H 51
Fanshawe Rd. Rich 1G 103
Fanshaw St. N1 . . . . .6C 60
Fantail, The (Junct.) 6K 127
Fanthorpe St. SW15 . . . . .2G 89
Faraday Av. Sidc 8E 96
Faraday Clo. N7 . . . . .2K 59
Faraday Clo. Wat 8B 8
Faraday Ho. E14 . . . . .1K 77
(off Brightlingsea Pl.)
Faraday Ho. Wemb 8A 40
Faraday Mans. W14 . . . . .7J 73
(off Queen's Club Gdns.)
Faraday Mus. 1G 75
Faraday Rd. E15 . . . . .2D 62
Faraday Rd. SW19 . . . . .3L 105
Faraday Rd. W3 . . . . .1A 72
Faraday Rd. W10 . . . . .8J 57
Faraday Rd. S'hall 1M 69
Faraday Rd. Well 2E 96
Faraday Rd. W Mol 8L 101
Faraday Way. SE18 . . . . .4H 79
Faraday Way. Croy 3K 123
Faraday Way. Orp 8F 112
Fareham Rd. Felt 6G 85
Fareham St. W1 . . . . .9H 59
Farewell Pl. Mitc 5C 106
Faringdon Av. Brom 2L 127
Faringdon Av. Romf 8G 35
Faringford Rd. E15 . . . . .3C 62
Farington Acres. Wey 5B 116
Farjeon Ho. NW3 . . . . .3B 58
(off Hilgrove Rd.)
Farjeon Rd. SE3 . . . . .9H 79
Farleigh. 6K 139
Farleigh Av. Brom 2D 126
Farleigh Common. 6J 139
Farleigh Ct. S Croy 7A 124
Farleigh Ct. Rd. Warl 6K 139
Farleigh Dean Cres.
Croy 3M 139
Farleigh Pl. N16 . . . . .9D 44
Farleigh Rd. N16 . . . . .9D 44
Farleigh Rd. Warl 9H 139
Farleton Clo. Wey 8B 116
Farley Ct. NW1 . . . . .7D 58
(off Allsop Pl.)
Farley Dri. Ilf 6C 48
Farley Ho. SE26 . . . . .9F 92
Farley Pl. SE25 . . . . .8E 108
Farley Rd. SE6 . . . . .6M 93
Farley Rd. S Croy 9F 124
Farlington Pl. SW15 . . . . .6F 88
Farlow Rd. SW15 . . . . .2H 89
Farlton Rd. SW18 . . . . .7M 89
Farman Gro. N'holt 6H 53
Farm Av. NW2 . . . . .8J 41
Farm Av. SW16 . . . . .1J 107
Farm Av. Harr 5K 37
Farm Av. Swan 7A 114
Farm Av. Wemb 2G 55
Farmborough Clo. Harr 5B 38
Farm Clo. N14 . . . . .8F 14
Farm Clo. SW6 . . . . .8L 73
Farm Clo. Barn 7G 13
Farm Clo. Borwd 2H 11
Farm Clo. Buck H 3G 31
Farm Clo. Chesh 3C 6
Farm Clo. Dag 3A 66
Farm Clo. S'hall 1M 69
Farm Clo. Sutt 9B 122
Farm Clo. Wall 2G 137
Farm Clo. W Wick 5D 126
Farmcote Rd. SE12 . . . . .7E 94
Farm Ct. NW4 . . . . .1E 40
Farmdale Rd. SE10 . . . . .6E 78
Farmdale Rd. Cars 9C 122
Farm Dri. Croy 4K 125
Farm Dri. Purl 4H 137
Farm End. E4 . . . . .7C 18
Farmer Rd. E10 . . . . .6M 45
Farmers Clo. Wat 6F 4
Farmers Ct. Wal A 6M 7
Farmer's Rd. SE5 . . . . .8M 75
Farmer St. W11 & W8 . . . . . . .2L 73
Farmfield. Wat 2C 8
Farmfield Rd. Brom 2C 110
Farm Fields. S Croy 3C 138
Farm Hill Rd. Wal A 6K 7
Farm Ho. Ct. NW7 . . . . .7E 24
Farmhouse Rd. SW16 . . . . . .4G 107
Farmilo Rd. E17 . . . . .5K 45
Farmington Av. Sutt 5B 122
Farmlands. Enf 3L 15
Farmlands. Pinn 2E 36
Farmlands, The. N'holt 2K 53
Farmland Wlk. Chst 2M 111
Farm La. SW6 . . . . .7L 73
Farm La. Asht 9L 133
Farm La. Croy 4K 125
Farm La. Purl 2G 137
Farm La. Trad. Est. SW6 . . . .7L 73
Farmleigh. N14 . . . . .9G 15
Farmleigh Gro. W on T 7D 116
Farmleigh Ho. SW9 . . . . .4M 91
Farm M. Mitc 6F 106
Farm Pl. W8 . . . . .2L 73
Farm Pl. Dart 3E 98
Farm Rd. N21 . . . . .1A 28
Farm Rd. NW10 . . . . .4B 56
Farm Rd. Edgw 6M 23
Farm Rd. Esh 3M 117
Farm Rd. Houn 7J 85
Farm Rd. Mord 9M 105
Farm Rd. N'wd 5A 20
Farm Rd. Rain 6G 67
Farm Rd. Sutt 9B 122
Farmstead. Eps 1L 133
Farmstead Rd. SE6 . . . . . . .1M 109
Farmstead Rd. Harr 8B 22
Farm St. W1 . . . . .1F 74
Farm Va. Bex 5M 97
Farm Wlk. NW11 . . . . .3K 41
Farm Way. Buck H 4G 31
Farm Way. Bush 6M 9
Farmway. Dag 8G 49
Farm Way. Horn 9G 51
Farm Way. N'wd 4C 20
Farm Way. Wor Pk 5G 121
Farnaby Ho. W10 . . . . .6K 57
(off Bruckner St.)
Farnaby Rd. SE9 . . . . .3G 95
Farnaby Rd. Brom 4B 110
Farnan Av. E17 . . . . .9L 29
Farnan Rd. SW16 . . . . .2J 107
Farnborough. 7A 128
Farnborough Av. E17 . . . . . . .1J 45
Farnborough Av. S Croy . . .1H 139
Farnborough Clo. Wemb 7M 39
Farnborough Comn. Orp . . .5K 127
Farnborough Cres. Brom . . .3D 126
Farnborough Cres.
S Croy 1J 139
Farnborough Hill. Orp 7B 128
Farnborough Way. SE15 . . . .8C 76
Farnborough Way. Orp 7A 128
Farncombe St. SE16 . . . . . . .3E 76
Farndale Av. N13 . . . . .3M 27
Farndale Cres. Gnfd 6A 54
Farndale Ho. NW6 . . . . .4M 57
(off Kilburn Va.)
Farnell M. SW5 . . . . .6M 73
Farnell Rd. Iswth 2B 86
Farnes Dri. Romf 9G 35
Farnham Clo. N20 . . . . .9A 14
Farnham Ct. S'hall 1A 70
(off Redcroft Rd.)
Farnham Ct. Sutt 8J 121
Farnham Gdns. SW20 . . . . .6F 104
Farnham Ho. NW1 . . . . .7C 58
(off Harewood Av.)
Farnham Pl. SE1 . . . . .2M 75
Farnham Rd. Ilf 5D 48
Farnham Rd. Romf 5H 35
Farnham Rd. Well 1G 97
Farnham Royal. SE11 . . . . . .6K 75
Farningham. 2K 131
Farningham Ct. SW16 . . . . .4H 107
Farningham Hill Rd.
F'ham 9G 115
Farningham Ho. N4 . . . . .5B 44
Farningham Rd. N17 . . . . . . .7E 28
Farnley Ho. SW8 . . . . .1H 91
Farnley Rd. E4 . . . . .9C 18
Farnley Rd. SE25 . . . . .8B 108
Farnol Rd. Dart 4L 99
Farnworth Ho. E14 . . . . .5B 78
(off Manchester Rd.)
Faro Clo. Brom 6L 111
Faroe Rd. W14 . . . . .4H 73
Farorna Wlk. Enf 3L 15
Farquhar Rd. SE19 . . . . . . .2D 108
Farquhar Rd. SW19 . . . . .9L 89
Farquharson Rd. Croy 3A 124
Farraline Rd. Wat 6F 8
Farrance Rd. Romf 4J 49
Farrance St. E14 . . . . .9L 61
Farrans Ct. Harr 5F 38
Farrant Av. N22 . . . . .9L 27
Farrant Clo. Orp 9E 128
Farrant Way. Borwd 3J 11
Farr Av. Bark 5E 64
Farrell Ho. E1 . . . . .9G 61
(off Ronald St.)
Farren Rd. SE23 . . . . .8J 93
Farrer Ct. Twic 6H 87
Farrer Ho. SE8 . . . . .8L 77
Farrer M. N8 . . . . .2G 43
Farrer Rd. N8 . . . . .2G 43
Farrer Rd. Harr 3J 39
Farrer's Pl. Croy 6H 125
Farrier Clo. Brom 7H 111
Farrier Clo. Sun 7E 100
Farrier Clo. Uxb 9E 142
Farrier Rd. N'holt 5L 53
Farriers Clo. Eps 4C 134
Farriers Ct. Leav 5F 4
Farriers Ho. EC1 . . . . .7A 60
(off Errol St.)
Farriers Rd. Eps 4C 134
Farrier St. NW1 . . . . .3F 58
Farriers Way. Borwd 7B 12
Farrier Wlk. SW10 . . . . .7A 74
Farringdon La. EC1 . . . . .7L 59
Farringdon Rd. EC1 . . . . .7L 59
Farringdon St. EC4 . . . . .8M 59
Farrington Av. Orp 7F 112
Farrington Pl. Chst 4B 112
Farrington Pl. N'wd 4D 20
Farrins Rents. SE16 . . . . .2J 77
Farrow La. SE14 . . . . .8G 77
Farrow Pl. SE16 . . . . .4J 77
Farr Rd. Enf 3B 16
Farthingale Ct. Wal A 7M 7
Farthingale La. Wal A 7M 7
(in two parts)
Farthingale Wlk. E15 . . . . . . .3B 62
Farthing All. SE1 . . . . .3E 76
Farthing Barn La. Orp 1L 141
Farthing Clo. Dart 3K 99
Farthing Fields. E1 . . . . .2F 76
Farthings Clo. E4 . . . . .3C 30
Farthings Clo. Pinn 4F 36
Farthings, The. King T 5L 103
Farthing Street. 1K 141
Farthing St. Orp 9K 127
Farwell Rd. Sidc 1F 112
Farwig La. Brom 5D 110
Fashion St. E1 . . . . .8D 60
Fashoda Rd. Brom 8H 111
Fassett Rd. E8 . . . . .2E 60
Fassett Rd. King T 8J 103
Fassett Sq. E8 . . . . .2E 60
Fassnidge Vw. Uxb 3A 142
Fauconberg Ct. W4 . . . . .7A 72
(off Fauconberg Rd.)
Fauconberg Rd. W4 . . . . .7A 72
Faulkner Clo. Dag 5H 49
Faulkners All. EC1 . . . . .8M 59
Faulkners Rd. W on T 7G 117
Faulkner St. SE14 . . . . .9G 77
Fauna Clo. Romf 4G 49
Faunce Ho. SE17 . . . . .7M 75
(off Doddington Gro.)
Faunce St. SE17 . . . . .6M 75
Favart Rd. SW6 . . . . .9L 73
Faverolle Grn. Chesh 1C 6
Faversham Av. E4 . . . . .1C 30
Faversham Av. Enf 8B 16
Faversham Clo. Chig 2F 32
Faversham Ho. NW1 . . . . .4G 59
(off Bayham Pl.)
Faversham Ho. SE17 . . . . . . .6C 76
(off Kinglake St.)
Faversham Rd. SE6 . . . . .6K 93
Faversham Rd. Beck 6K 109
Faversham Rd. Mord 1M 121
Fawcett Clo. SW11 . . . . .1B 90
Fawcett Clo. SW16 . . . . . . .2L 107
Fawcett Est. E5 . . . . .6E 44
Fawcett Rd. NW10 . . . . .3D 56
Fawcett Rd. Croy 5A 124
Fawcett St. SW10 . . . . .7A 74
Fawcus Clo. Clay 8C 118
Fawe Pk. M. SW15 . . . . .3K 89
Fawe Pk. Rd. SW15 . . . . .3K 89
Fawe St. E14 . . . . .8M 61
Fawkes Av. Dart 8K 99
Fawkham Ho. SE1 . . . . .5D 76
(off Longfield Est.)
Fawley Lodge. E14 . . . . .5B 78
(off Millennium Dri.)
Fawley Rd. NW6 . . . . .1M 57
Fawnbrake Av. SE24 . . . . . . .4M 91
Fawn Rd. E13 . . . . .5G 63
Fawn Rd. Chig 5D 32
Fawns Mnr. Clo. Felt 7A 84
Fawns Mnr. Rd. Felt 7B 84
Fawood Av. NW10 . . . . .3A 56
Faygate Cres. Bexh 4L 97
Faygate Rd. SW2 . . . . .8K 91
Fay Grn. Ab L 6B 4
Fayland Av. SW16 . . . . .2G 107
Fazeley Ct. W9 . . . . .8L 57
(off Elmfield Way)
Fearnley Cres. Hamp 2J 101
Fearnley Ho. SE5 . . . . .1C 92
Fearnley St. Wat 6F 8
Fearon St. SE10 . . . . .6E 78
Featherbed La.
Croy & Warl 9K 125
Featherbed La. Romf 1J 33
Feathers Pl. SE10 . . . . .7B 78
Featherstone Av.
SE23 . . . . .8F 92
Featherstone Gdns.
Borwd 6B 12
Featherstone Ho. Hay 8G 53
Featherstone Ind. Est.
S'hall 3J 69
(off Straight, The)
Featherstone Rd. NW7 . . . . . .6F 24
Featherstone Rd. S'hall 4J 69
Featherstone St. EC1 . . . . . . .7B 60
Featherstone Ter. S'hall 4J 69
Featley Rd. SW9 . . . . .2M 91
Federal Rd. Gnfd 4G 55
Federal Way. Wat 3G 9
Federation Rd. SE2 . . . . .5F 80
Fee Farm Rd. Clay 9D 118
Felbridge Av. Stan 8E 22
Felbridge Clo. SW16 . . . . . .1L 107
Felbridge Clo. Sutt 1M 135
Felbridge Ct. Felt 7F 84
(off High St.)
Felbridge Ct. Hay 7B 68
Felbridge Ho. SE22 . . . . .2C 92
Felbrigge Rd. Ilf 7D 48
Felcott Clo. W on T 5G 117
Felcott Rd. W on T 5G 117
Felday Rd. SE13 . . . . .5M 93
Felden Clo. Pinn 7J 21
Felden Clo. Wat 7H 5
Felden St. SW6 . . . . .9K 73
Feldman Clo. N16 . . . . .6E 44
Felgate M. W6 . . . . .5F 72
Felhampton Rd. SE9 . . . . . . .8M 95
Felhurst Cres. Dag 9M 49
Feline Ct. Barn 8C 14
Felix Av. N8 . . . . .4J 43
Felix Ct. E17 . . . . .3M 45
Felix Ho. E16 . . . . .1L 79
(off University Way)
Felix La. Shep 1C 116
Felix Mnr. Chst 3C 112
Felix Rd. W13 . . . . .1E 70
Felix Rd. W on T 1E 116
Felixstowe Ct. E16 . . . . .2M 79
Felixstowe Rd. N9 . . . . .3E 28
Felixstowe Rd. N17 . . . . .1D 44
Felixstowe Rd. NW10 . . . . . . .6F 56
Felixstowe Rd. SE2 . . . . .4F 80
Felix St. E2 . . . . .5F 60
Fellbrigg Rd. SE22 . . . . .4D 92
Fellbrigg St. E1 . . . . .7F 60
Fellbrook. Rich 9F 86
Fellmongers Path. SE1 . . . . .3D 76
(off Tower Bri. Rd.)
Fellmongers Yd. Croy 5A 124
(off Surrey St.)
Fellowes Clo. Hay 7H 53
Fellowes Rd. Cars 5C 122
Fellows Ct. E2 . . . . .5D 60
(in two parts)
Fellows Rd. NW3 . . . . .3B 58
Fell Path. Borwd 7B 12
(off Clydesdale Clo.)
Fell Rd. Croy 5A 124
(in two parts)
Felltram Way. SE7 . . . . .6E 78
Fell Wlk. Edgw 8A 24
Felmersham Clo. SW4 . . . . . .3J 91
Felmingham Rd. SE20 . . . . .6G 109
Felnex Trad. Est. NW10 . . . . .5B 56
Felsberg Rd. SW2 . . . . .5J 91
Fels Clo. Dag 8M 49
Fels Farm Av. Dag 8A 50
Felsham M. SW15 . . . . .2H 89
(off Felsham Rd.)
Felsham Rd. SW15 . . . . .2G 89
Felspar Clo. SE18 . . . . .6D 80
Felstead Av. Ilf 8L 31
Felstead Gdns. E14 . . . . .6A 78
Felstead Rd. E9 . . . . .2K 61
Felstead Rd. E11 . . . . .5E 46
Felstead Rd. Eps 3B 134
Felstead Rd. Lou 9J 19
Felstead Rd. Orp 4E 128
Felstead Rd. Romf 7A 34
Felstead Rd. Wal X 5E 6
Felstead St. E9 . . . . .2K 61
Felstead Wharf. E14 . . . . .6A 78
Felsted Rd. E16 . . . . .9H 63
Feltham. 8E 84
Feltham Av. E Mol 8C 102
Felthambrook Ind. Est.
Felt 9F 84
Felthambrook Way. Felt 9F 84
Feltham Bus. Complex.
Felt 8F 84
Felthamhill. 2D 100
Feltham Hill Rd. Ashf 2A 100
Felthamhill Rd. Felt 1E 100
Feltham Rd. Ashf 1A 100
Feltham Rd. Mitc 6D 106
Felton Clo. Borwd 2J 11

First Way—Foresters Dri.

First Way. Wemb 9M 39
Firs Wlk. N'wd 6B 20
Firs Wlk. Wfd G 5E 30
Firswood Av. Eps 7C 120
Firth Gdns. SW6 9J 73
Firth Ho. E2 6E 60
(off Barnet Gro.)
Firtree Av. Mitc 6E 106
Fir Tree Av. W Dray 4L 143
Firtree Clo. SW16 2G 107
Fir Tree Clo. W5 9J 55
Fir Tree Clo. Eps 7G 135
Fir Tree Clo. Esh 7A 118
Firtree Clo. Ewe 6D 120
Fir Tree Clo. Orp 7D 128
Fir Tree Clo. Romf 1B 50
Firtree Ct. Borwd 6K 11
Firtree Gdns. Croy 6L 125
Fir Tree Gro. Cars 9D 122
Fir Tree Ho. SE14 8G 77
(off Avonley Rd.)
Fir Tree Rd. Bans 6G 135
Fir Tree Rd. Eps 8F 134
Fir Tree Rd. Houn 3J 85
Fir Trees Clo. SE16 2J 77
Fir Tree Wlk. Dag 8A 50
Fir Tree Wlk. Enf 5B 16
Fir Wlk. Sutt 8H 121
Fisher Athletic F.C.
(Surrey Docks Stadium)
2H 77
Fisher Clo. Croy 3D 124
Fisher Clo. Enf 1L 17
Fisher Clo. Gnfd 6L 53
Fisher Clo. W on T 6F 116
Fisher Ho. E1 1G 77
(off Cable St.)
Fisher Ho. N1 4L 59
(off Barnsbury Est.)
Fisherman Clo. Rich 1F 102
Fishermans Dri. SE16 3H 77
Fisherman's Pl. W4 7D 72
Fisherman's Wlk. E14 2L 77
Fishermans Wlk. SE28 3C 80
Fisher Rd. Harr 9D 22
Fisher's Clo. SW16 9H 91
Fishers Clo. Bush 5J 9
Fishers Clo. Wal X 7G 7
Fishers Ct. SE14 9H 77
Fishers Dene. Clay 9E 118
Fishers Green. 2H 7
Fishers Grn. La. Wal A 2H 7
Fisher's Ind. Est. Wat 7G 9
Fisher's La. W4 5B 72
Fisher St. E16 8E 62
Fisher St. WC1 8K 59
Fishers Way. Belv 2A 82
Fisherton St. NW8 7B 58
Fishguard Way. E16 2M 79
(in two parts)
Fishmongers Hall Wharf.
EC4 1B 76
(off Swan La.)
Fishponds Rd. SW17 1C 106
Fishponds Rd. Kes 7H 127
Fish St. Hill. EC3 1B 76
Fish Wharf. EC3 1B 76
(off Lwr. Thames St.)
Fiske Ct. N17 8E 28
Fiske Ct. Bark 5B 64
Fisons Rd. E16 2E 78
Fitzalan Ho. Ewe 2D 134
Fitzalan Rd. N3 1J 41
Fitzalan Rd. Clay 9C 118
Fitzalan St. SE11 5L 75
Fitzgeorge Av. W14 5J 73
Fitzgeorge Av. N Mald 5B 104
Fitzgerald Av. SW14 2C 88
Fitzgerald Ct. E10 6M 45
(off Leyton Grange Est.)
Fitzgerald Ho. E14 9M 61
(off E. India Dock Rd.)
Fitzgerald Ho. SW9 1L 91
Fitzgerald Rd. E11 3E 46
Fitzgerald Rd. SW14 2B 88
Fitzgerald Rd. Th Dit 1E 118
Fitzhardinge Ho. W1 9E 58
(off Portman Sq.)
Fitzhardinge St. W1 9E 58
Fitzhugh Gro. SW18 5B 90
Fitzilian Av. Romf 8K 35
Fitzjames Av. W14 5J 73
Fitzjames Av. Croy 4E 124
Fitzjohn Av. Barn 7J 13
Fitzjohn's Av. NW3 9A 42
Fitzmaurice Ho. SE16 5F 76
(off Rennie Est.)
Fitzmaurice Pl. W1 2F 74
Fitzneal St. W3 9D 56
Fitzrovia. 8F 58
Fitzroy Clo. N6 6D 42
Fitzroy Ct. N6 4G 43
Fitzroy Ct. W1 7G 59
(off Tottenham Ct. Rd.)
Fitzroy Ct. Croy 2B 124
Fitzroy Ct. Dart 7M 99
(off Churchill Clo.)
Fitzroy Cres. W4 8B 72
Fitzroy Gdns. SE19 4C 108
Fitzroy Ho. E14 8K 61
(off Wallwood St.)
Fitzroy Ho. SE1 6D 76
(off Coopers La.)
Fitzroy M. W1 7G 59
(off Cleveland St.)
Fitzroy Pk. N6 6D 42
Fitzroy Rd. NW1 4E 58
Fitzroy Sq. W1 7G 59
Fitzroy St. W1 7G 59
(in two parts)
Fitzroy Yd. NW1 4E 58
Fitzsimmons Ct. NW10 4B 56
Fitzstephen Rd. Dag 1F 64
Fitzwarren Gdns. N19 6G 43
Fitzwilliam Av. Rich 1K 87
Fitzwilliam Heights. SE23 8G 93
Fitzwilliam Ho. Rich 3H 87
Fitzwilliam M. E16 2E 78
Fitzwilliam Rd. SW4 2G 91
Fitzwygram Clo.
Hamp H 2A 102
Five Acre. NW9 9D 24
Fiveacre Clo. T Hth 1L 123
Five Acres Av. Brick W 2K 5
Five Bell All. E14 1K 61
(off Three Colt St.)
Five Elms Rd. Brom 4F 126
Five Elms Rd. Dag 8K 49
Five Fields Clo. Wat 2K 21
Five Oaks La. Chig 6J 33
Fives Ct. SE11 4M 75
Fiveways (Junct.) 8M 95
Fiveways. SE9 8M 95
Five Ways Bus. Cen. Felt 9F 84
Fiveways Corner (Junct.)
6K 123
(Croydon)
Fiveways Corner (Junct.)
8F 24
(Hendon)
Fiveways Rd. SW9 1L 91
Five Wents. Swan 6E 114
Flack Ct. E10 5M 45
Fladbury Rd. N15 4B 44
Fladgate Rd. E11 4C 46
Flag Clo. Croy 3H 125
Flagstaff Clo. Wal A 6H 7
Flagstaff Rd. Wal A 6H 7
Flag Wlk. Pinn 4E 36
Flambard Rd. Harr 4E 38
Flamborough Ho. SE15 9E 76
(off Clayton Rd.)
Flamborough Rd. Ruis 8E 36
Flamborough St. E14 9J 61
Flamborough Wlk. E14 9J 61
(off Flamborough St.)
Flamingo Ct. SE8 8L 77
(off Hamilton St.)
Flamingo Gdns. N'holt 6J 53
Flamingo Wlk. Horn 2E 66
Flamstead End. 1B 6
Flamstead End Rd. Chesh 1B 6
Flamstead Gdns. Dag 3G 65
Flamstead Ho. SW3 6C 74
(off Cale St.)
Flamstead Rd. Dag 3G 65
Flamsted Av. Wemb 2L 55
Flamsteed Rd. SE7 6J 79
Flanchford Rd. W12 4D 72
Flanders Ct. E17 5J 45
Flanders Cres. SW17 4D 106
Flanders Mans. W4 5D 72
Flanders Rd. E6 5K 63
Flanders Rd. W4 5C 72
Flanders Way. E9 2H 61
Flank St. E1 1E 76
Flansham Ho. E14 9K 61
(off Clemence St.)
Flash La. Enf 1M 15
Flask Wlk. NW3 9A 42
Flatford Ho. SE6 1A 110
Flatiron Yd. SE1 2A 76
(off Union St.)
Flaunden Ho. Wat 8C 8
Flavell M. SE10 6C 78
Flaxen Clo. E4 3M 29
Flaxen Rd. E4 3M 29
Flaxley Rd. Mord 2M 121
Flaxman Ct. W1 9H 59
(off Wardour St.)
Flaxman Ct. WC1 6H 59
(off Flaxman Ter.)
Flaxman Ct. Belv 6L 81
(off Hoddesdon Rd.)
Flaxman Ho. W4 6C 72
(off Devonshire St.)
Flaxman Rd. SE5 2M 91
Flaxman Ter. WC1 6H 59
Flaxton Rd. SE18 9B 80
Flecker Clo. Stan 5D 22
Flecker Ho. SE5 8B 76
(off Lomond Gro.)
Fleece Dri. N9 4E 28
Fleece Rd. Surb 3G 119
Fleece Wlk. N7 2J 59
Fleeming Clo. E17 9K 29
Fleeming Rd. E17 9K 29
Fleet Av. Dart 7M 99
Fleetbank Ho. EC4 9L 59
(off Salisbury Sq.)
Fleet Building. EC4 9M 59
(off Shoe La.)
Fleet Clo. Ruis 4A 36
Fleet Clo. W Mol 9K 101
Fleetdale Pde. Dart 7M 99
Fleet Downs. 7M 99
Fleetfield. WC1 6J 59
(off Birkenhead St.)
Fleet Ho. E14 1J 77
(off Victory Pl.)
Fleet La. W Mol 1K 117
Fleet Pl. EC4 9M 59
(off Limeburner La., in two parts)
Fleet Rd. NW3 1C 58
Fleet Rd. Dart 7M 99
Fleetside. W Mol 9K 101
Fleet Sq. WC1 6K 59
Fleet St. EC4 9L 59
Fleet St. Hill. E1 7E 60
Fleetway. WC1 6J 59
(off Birkenhead St.)
Fleetway Bus. Cen. NW2 6D 40
Fleetway W. Bus. Pk.
Gnfd 5F 54
Fleetwood Clo. E16 8H 63
Fleetwood Clo. Chess 9H 119
Fleetwood Clo. Croy 5D 124
Fleetwood Ct. E6 8K 63
(off Evelyn Dennington Rd.,
in three parts)
Fleetwood Ct. Stanw 5B 144
Fleetwood Rd. NW10 1E 56
Fleetwood Rd. King T 7M 103
Fleetwood Sq. King T 7M 103
Fleetwood St. N16 7C 44
Fleetwood Way. Wat 4G 21
Fleming. N8 1J 43
(off Boyton Clo.)
Fleming Clo. W9 7L 57
Fleming Ct. W2 8B 58
(off St Marys Sq.)
Fleming Ct. Croy 7L 123
Fleming Dri. N21 7K 15
Fleming Gdns. H Wood 9H 35
Fleming Ho. N4 6A 44
Fleming Ho. SE16 3E 76
(off George Row)
Fleming Ho. Wemb 8A 40
(off Barnhill Rd.)
Fleming Lodge. W9 8L 57
(off Admiral Wlk.)
Fleming Mead. Mitc 4C 106
Fleming Rd. SE17 7M 75
Fleming Rd. S'hall 9M 53
Fleming Wlk. NW9 1C 40
Fleming Way. SE28 1H 81
Fleming Way. Iswth 3D 86
Flemming Av. Ruis 6F 36
Flempton Rd. E10 6J 45
Fletcher Bldgs. WC2 9J 59
(off Martlett Ct.)
Fletcher Clo. E6 9M 63
Fletcher La. E10 5A 46
Fletcher Path. SE8 8L 77
Fletcher Rd. W4 4A 72
Fletcher Rd. Chig 5D 32
Fletchers Clo. Brom 8F 110
Fletcher St. E1 1E 76
Fletching Rd. E5 8G 45
Fletching Rd. SE7 7G 79
Flete Ho. Wat 8C 8
Fletton Rd. N11 7J 27
Fleur-de-Lis St. E1 7D 60
Fleur Gates. SW19 6H 89
Flexmere Gdns. N17 8B 28
Flexmere Rd. N17 8B 28
Flight App. NW9 9D 24
Flimwell Clo. Brom 2C 110
Flinders Ho. E1 2F 76
(off Green Bank)
Flint Clo. Bans 6M 135
Flint Clo. G Str 8D 128
Flint Down Clo. Orp 5E 112
Flintmill Cres. SE3 1J 95
(in three parts)
Flinton St. SE17 6C 76
Flint St. SE17 5B 76
Flitcroft St. WC2 9H 59
Flitton Ho. N1 3M 59
(off Sutton Est., The)
Flock Mill Pl. SW18 7M 89
Flockton St. SE16 3E 76
Flodden Rd. SE5 9A 76
Flood La. Twic 7E 86
Flood Pas. SE18 4J 79
Flood St. SW3 6C 74
Flood Wlk. SW3 7C 74
Flora Clo. E14 9M 61
Flora Gdns. W6 5F 72
(off Albion Gdns.)
Flora Gdns. Croy 3A 140
Flora Gdns. Romf 4G 49
Floral Ct. Asht 9G 133
Floral Pl. N1 1B 60
Floral St. WC2 1J 75
Flora St. Belv 6K 81
Florence Av. Enf 5A 16
Florence Av. Mord 9A 106
Florence Clo. Horn 7J 51
Florence Clo. W on T 2F 116
Florence Clo. Wat 8E 4
Florence Ct. E5 8E 44
Florence Ct. E11 2F 46
Florence Ct. N1 3M 59
(off Florence St.)
Florence Ct. SW19 3J 105
Florence Ct. W9 6A 58
(off Maida Va.)
Florence Dri. Enf 5A 16
Florence Elson Clo. E12 8L 47
(off Grantham Rd.)
Florence Gdns. W4 7A 72
Florence Ho. SE16 6F 76
(off Rotherhithe New Rd.)
Florence Ho. W11 1H 73
(off St Ann's Rd.)
Florence Ho. King T 4K 103
(off Florence Rd)
Florence Mans. NW4 3F 40
(off Vivian Av.)
Florence Nightingale Mus.
3K 75
Florence Rd. E6 4G 63
Florence Rd. E13 5D 62
Florence Rd. N4 5K 43
(in two parts)
Florence Rd. SE2 5G 81
Florence Rd. SE14 9K 77
Florence Rd. SW19 3M 105
Florence Rd. W4 4B 72
Florence Rd. W5 1J 71
Florence Rd. Beck 6J 109
Florence Rd. Brom 5E 110
Florence Rd. Felt 7F 84
Florence Rd. King T 4K 103
Florence Rd. S'hall 5H 69
Florence Rd. S Croy 1B 138
Florence Rd. W on T 2F 116
Florence St. E16 7D 62
Florence St. N1 3M 59
Florence St. NW4 2G 41
Florence Ter. SE14 9K 77
Florence Ter. SW15 9C 88
Florence Way. SW12 7D 90
Flores Ho. E1 8H 61
(off Shandy St.)
Florey Lodge. W9 8L 57
(off Admiral Wlk.)
Florfield Pas. E8 2F 60
(off Florfield Rd.)
Florfield Rd. E8 2F 60
Florian. SE5 9C 76
Florian Av. Sutt 6B 122
Florian Rd. SW15 3J 89
Florida Clo. Bus H 2B 22
Florida Ct. Brom 8D 110
(off Westmoreland Rd.)
Florida Rd. T Hth 5M 107
Florida St. E2 6E 60
Florin Ct. N18 4C 28
Florin Ct. SE1 3D 76
(off Tanner St.)
Floris Pl. SW4 2G 91
Floriston Av. Uxb 3A 52
Floriston Clo. Stan 8F 22
Floriston Ct. N'holt 1M 53
Floriston Gdns. Stan 8F 22
Floss St. SW15 1G 89
Flower & Dean Wlk.
E1 8D 60
Flower La. NW7 5D 24
Flowerpot Clo. N15 4D 44
Flowers Clo. NW2 8E 40
Flowersmead. SW17 8E 90
Flowers M. N19 7G 43
Flower Wlk., The. SW7 3A 74
Floyd Rd. SE7 6G 79
Fludyer St. SE13 3C 94
Flynn Ct. E14 1L 77
(off Garford St.)
Fogerty Clo. Enf 1M 17
Foley Ct. Dart 7M 99
(off Churchill Clo.)
Foley Ho. E1 9G 61
(off Tarling St.)
Foley M. Clay 8C 118
Foley Rd. Big H 9H 141
Foley Rd. Clay 9C 118
Foley St. W1 8G 59
Folgate St. E1 8C 60
(in two parts)
Foliot Ho. N1 5K 59
(off Priory Grn. Est.)
Foliot St. W3 9D 56
Folkestone Ct. N'holt 1M 53
(off Newmarket Av.)
Folkestone Rd. E6 5L 63
Folkestone Rd. E17 2M 45
Folkestone Rd. N18 4E 28
Folkingham La. NW9 8B 24
Folkington Corner. N12 5K 25
Folland. NW9 9D 24
(off Hundred Acre)
Follet Dri. Ab L 4D 4
Follett Ho. SW10 8B 74
(off Worlds End Est.)
Follett St. E14 9A 62
Follingham Ct. N1 6C 60
(off Drysdale Pl.)
Follyfield Rd. Bans 6L 135
Folly La. E17 8J 29
(in two parts)
Folly M. W11 9K 57
Folly Wall. E14 3A 78
Fonda Ct. E14 1L 77
(off Premiere Pl.)
Fontaine Rd. SW16 4K 107
Fontarabia Rd. SW11 3E 90
Fontayne Av. Chig 4A 32
Fontayne Av. Rain 3C 66
Fontayne Av. Romf 9C 34
Fontenelle Gdns. SE5 9C 76
Fontenoy Ho. SE11 5M 75
(off Kennington La.)
Fontenoy Rd. SW12 8F 90
Fonteyne Gdns. Wfd G 9H 31
Fonthill Clo. SE20 6E 108
Fonthill M. N4 7K 43
Fonthill Rd. N4 6K 43
Font Hills. N2 9A 26
Fontley Way. SW15 6E 88
Fontwell Clo. Harr 7C 22
Fontwell Clo. N'holt 2L 53
Fontwell Dri. Brom 9L 111
Fontwell Pk. Gdns. Horn 9J 51
Football La. Harr 6D 38
Footbury Hill Rd. Orp 1E 128
Footpath, The. SW15 5E 88
Foots Cray. 3G 113
Foots Cray High St. Sidc 3G 113
Foots Cray La. Sidc 7G 97
Footscray Rd. SE9 5L 95
Forber Ho. E2 6G 61
(off Cornwall Av.)
Forbes Clo. NW2 8E 40
Forbes Clo. Horn 6F 50
Forbes St. E1 9E 60
Forbes Way. Ruis 7F 36
Forburg Rd. N16 6E 44
Fordbridge Cvn. Pk. Sun 1D 116
Fordbridge Rd. Sun 1C 116
Ford Clo. E3 5J 61
Ford Clo. Bush 6A 10
Ford Clo. Harr 5B 38
Ford Clo. Rain 3D 66
Ford Clo. T Hth 9M 107
Fordcroft Rd. Orp 9F 112
Forde Av. Brom 7G 111
Fordel Rd. SE6 7A 94
Ford End. Wfd G 6F 30
Fordham. King T 6L 103
(off Excelsior Clo.)
Fordham Clo. Barn 5C 14
Fordham Clo. Horn 5L 51
Fordham Rd. Barn 5B 14
Fordham St. E1 9E 60
Fordhook Av. W5 2K 71
Ford Ho. Barn 7M 13
Ford Ind. Pk. Dag 7M 65
Fordingley Rd. W9 6K 57
Fordington Ho. SE26 9E 92
Fordington Rd. N6 3D 42
Ford La. Rain 3D 66
Fordmill Rd. SE6 8L 93
Ford Rd. E3 5K 61
Ford Rd. Dag 3K 65
Fords Gro. N21 1A 28
Fords Pk. Rd. E16 8E 62
Ford Sq. E1 8F 60
Ford St. E3 4J 61
Ford St. E16 9D 62
Fordwich Clo. Orp 2D 128
Fordwych Rd. NW2 9J 41
Fordyce Clo. Horn 5K 51
Fordyce Rd. SE13 5A 94
Fordyke Rd. Dag 7K 49
Foreign St. SE5 1M 91
Foreland Ct. NW4 8H 25
Foreland Ho. W11 1J 73
(off Walmer Rd.)
Foreland St. SE18 5B 80
Foreman Ct. Twic 7D 86
Foremark Clo. Ilf 5D 32
Foreshore. SE8 5K 77
Forest App. E4 9C 18
Forest App. Wfd G 7E 30
Forest Av. E4 9C 18
Forest Av. Chig 5L 31
Forest Bus. Pk. E10 5J 45
Forest Clo. E11 3E 46
Forest Clo. N10 8F 26
Forest Clo. Chst 5L 111
Forest Clo. Wal A 1F 18
Forest Clo. Wfd G 3F 30
Forest Ct. E4 1D 30
Forest Ct. E11 2C 46
Forest Ct. N12 5M 25
Forest Cres. Asht 8L 133
Forest Cft. SE23 8F 92
Forestdale. 1K 139
Forestdale. N14 4H 27
Forestdale Cen., The.
Croy 9K 125
Forest Dene Ct. Sutt 8A 122
Forest Dri. E12 8H 47
Forest Dri. Kes 6J 127
Forest Dri. Sun 4D 100
Forest Dri. Wfd G 7B 30
Forest Dri. E. E11 5B 46
Forest Dri. W. E11 5A 46
Forest Edge. Buck H 4G 31
Forester Rd. SE15 2F 92
Foresters Clo. Wall 9H 123
Foresters Dri. E17 2B 46
Foresters Dri. Wall 9H 123

Forest Gdns.—Fraser St.

Forest Gdns. N17 9D 28
Forest Gate. 1F 62
Forest Ga. NW9 2C 40
Forest Glade. E4 4C 30
Forest Glade. E11 4C 46
Forest Gro. E8 2D 60
Forest Hill. 8G 93
Forest Hill Bus. Cen. SE23 8G 93 (off Clyde Va.)
Forest Hill Ind. Est. SE23 8G 93
Forest Hill Rd. SE22 & SE23 4F 92
Forestholme Clo. SE23 8G 93
Forest Ind. Pk. Ilf 8C 32
Forest La. E15 & E7 1C 62
Forest La. Chig 5L 31
Forest Lodge. SE26 9G 93 (off Dartmouth Rd.)
Forest Mt. Rd. Wfd G 7B 30
Forest Point. E7 1F 62 (off Windsor Rd.)
Fore St. EC2 8A 60
Fore St. N18 & N9 6D 28
Fore St. Pinn 1D 36
Fore St. Av. EC2 8B 60
Forest Ridge. Beck 7L 109
Forest Ridge. Kes 6J 127
Forest Ri. E17 1B 46 (in three parts)
Forest Rd. E7 9E 46
Forest Rd. E8 2D 60
Forest Rd. E11 5B 46
Forest Rd. N9 1F 28
Forest Rd. N17 & E17 2G 45
Forest Rd. Chesh 2D 6
Forest Rd. Enf 9E 6
Forest Rd. Eri 9E 82
Forest Rd. Felt 8G 85
Forest Rd. Ilf 9B 32
Forest Rd. Lou 5H 19
Forest Rd. Rich 8L 71
Forest Rd. Romf 1M 49
Forest Rd. Sutt 3L 121
Forest Rd. Wat 6F 4
Forest Rd. Wfd G 3E 30
Forest Side. E4 9D 18
Forest Side. E7 9F 46
Forest Side. Buck H 1G 31
Forest Side. Wal A 1G 19
Forest Side. Wor Pk 3D 120
Forest St. E7 1E 62
Forest Ter. Chig 5L 31
Forest, The. E11 2C 46
Forest Trad. Est. E17 1H 45
Forest Vw. E4 9B 18
Forest Vw. E11 5D 46
Forest Vw. Av. E10 3B 46
Forest Vw. Rd. E12 9J 47
Forest Vw. Rd. E17 8A 30
Forest Vw. Rd. Lou 6H 19
Forest Wlk. Bush 3K 9
Forest Way. N19 7G 43
Forest Way. Asht 9K 133
Forest Way. Lou 5J 19
Forest Way. Orp 9D 112
Forest Way. Sidc 6B 96
Forest Way. Wfd G 4F 30
Forest Works Ind. Est. E17 1H 45
Forfar Rd. N22 8M 27
Forfar Rd. SW11 9E 74
Forge Clo. Brom 3E 126
Forge Clo. Hay 7B 68
Forge Cotts. W5 2H 71
Forge Dri. Clay 9E 118
Forge Fld. Big H 8H 141
Forge La. Felt 2J 101
Forge La. N'wd 7C 20
Forge La. Sun 7E 100
Forge La. Sutt 9J 121
Forge M. Croy 7L 125
Forge Pl. NW1 2E 58
Forge Steading. Bans 7M 135
Forman Pl. N16 9D 44
Formation, The. E16 3M 79 (off Woolwich Mnr. Way)
Formby Av. Stan 1G 39
Formby Ct. N7 1L 59 (off Morgan Rd.)
Formosa Ho. E1 7J 61 (off Ernest St.)
Formosa St. W9 7M 57
Formunt Clo. E16 8D 62
Forres Gdns. NW11 4L 41
Forrester Path. SE26 1G 109
Forresters Cres. Bexh 3M 97
Forrest Gdns. SW16 7K 107
Forris Av. Hay 2D 68
Forset Ct. W2 9C 58 (off Harrowby St.)
Forset St. W1 9C 58
Forstal Clo. Brom 7E 110
Forster Clo. E4 7B 30
Forster Ho. Brom 1B 110
Forster Rd. E17 4J 45
Forster Rd. N17 1D 44
Forster Rd. SW12 6J 91
Forster Rd. Beck 7J 109
Forsters Clo. Romf 4K 49
Forsters Way. Hay 9F 52
Forston St. N1 5A 60
Forsyte Cres. SE19 5C 108
Forsythe Shades Ct. Beck 5A 110
Forsyth Gdns. SE17 7M 75
Forsyth Ho. E9 3G 61 (off Frampton Pk. Rd.)
Forsyth Ho. SW1 6G 75 (off Tachbrook St.)
Forsythia Clo. Ilf 1M 63
Forsyth Pl. Enf 7C 16
Forterie Gdns. Ilf 8E 48
Fortescue Av. E8 3F 60
Fortescue Av. Twic 9A 86
Fortescue Rd. SW19 4B 106
Fortescue Rd. Edgw 8B 24
Fortess Gro. NW5 1G 59
Fortess Rd. NW5 1F 58
Fortess Wlk. NW5 1F 58
Fortess Yd. NW5 9F 42
Forthbridge Rd. SW11 3E 90
Fortis Clo. E16 9G 63
Fortis Ct. N10 1E 42
Fortis Green. 2D 42
Fortis Grn. N2 & N10 2C 42
Fortis Grn. Av. N2 1D 42
Fortis Grn. Rd. N10 1E 42
Fortismere Av. N10 1E 42
Fortnam Rd. N19 7H 43
Fortnum's Acre. Stan 6D 22
Fort Rd. SE1 5D 76
Fort Rd. N'holt 3L 53
Fortrose Gdns. SW2 7J 91
Fort St. E1 8C 60
Fort St. E16 2F 78
Fortuna Clo. N7 2K 59
Fortune Ct. Bark 5G 65
Fortunegate Rd. NW10 4C 56
Fortune Green. 9L 41
Fortune Grn. Rd. NW6 9L 41
Fortune Ho. EC1 7A 60 (off Fortune St.)
Fortune Ho. SE11 5L 75 (off Marylee Way)
Fortune La. Els 8H 11
Fortunes Mead. N'holt 2J 53
Fortune St. EC1 7A 60
***Fortune Theatre.* 9J 59 (off Russell St.)**
Fortune Wlk. SE28 4B 80 (off Broadwater Rd.)
Fortune Way. NW10 6E 56
Forty Acre La. E16 8E 62
Forty Av. Wemb 8K 39
Forty Clo. Wemb 8K 39
Forty Footpath. SW14 2A 88
Forty Foot Way. SE9 6A 96
Forty Hall & Mus. 1D 16
Forty Hill. 2C 16
Forty Hill. Enf 2C 16
Forty La. Wemb 7M 39
Forum Magnum Sq. SE1 3K 75 (off York Rd.)
Forumside. Edgw 6L 23
Forum, The. W Mol 8M 101
Forum Way. Edgw 6L 23
Forval Clo. Mitc 9D 106
Forward Bus. Cen. E16 7B 62
Forward Dri. Harr 2D 38
Fosbrooke Ho. SW8 8J 75 (off Davidson Gdns.)
Fosbury M. W2 1M 73
Foscote M. W9 7L 57
Foscote Rd. NW4 4F 40
Foskett Ho. N2 9B 26
Foskett Rd. SW6 1K 89
Foss Av. Croy 7L 123
Fossdene Rd. SE7 6F 78
Fossdyke Clo. Hay 8J 53
Fosset Lodge. Bexh 9A 82
Fosse Way. W13 8E 54
Fossil Rd. SE13 2L 93
Fossington Rd. Belv 5H 81
Foss Rd. SW17 1B 106
Fossway. Dag 7G 49
Foster Ct. E16 1D 78 (off Tarling Rd.)
Foster Ct. NW1 3G 59 (off Royal College St.)
Foster Ct. NW4 2G 41
Foster Ho. SE14 9K 77
Foster La. EC2 9A 60
Foster Rd. E13 7E 62
Foster Rd. W3 1C 72
Foster Rd. W4 6B 72
Fosters Clo. E18 8F 30
Fosters Clo. Chesh 3D 6
Fosters Clo. Chst 2K 111
Foster St. NW4 2G 41
Foster's Way. SW18 7M 89
Foster Wlk. NW4 2G 41
Fothergill Clo. E13 5E 62
Fothergill Dri. N21 7J 15
Fotheringham Rd. Enf 6D 16
Foubert's Pl. W1 9G 59
Foulden Rd. N16 9D 44
Foulden Ter. N16 9D 44
Foulis Ter. SW7 6B 74
Foulser Rd. SW17 9D 90
Foulsham Rd. T Hth 7A 108
Founder Clo. E6 9M 63
Founders Ct. EC2 9B 60 (off Lothbury)
Founders Gdns. SE19 4A 108
Founders Ho. SW1 6H 75 (off Aylesford St.)
Foundling Ct. WC1 7J 59 (off Brunswick Cen.)
Foundling Mus., The. 7J 59 **(Closed Until 2003)**
Foundry Clo. SE16 2J 77
Foundry Ho. E14 8M 61 (off Morris Rd.)
Foundry M. NW1 7G 59 (off Drummond St.)
Foundry Pl. SW18 6M 89
Fountain Clo. Uxb 8A 52
Fountain Ct. EC4 1L 75
Fountain Ct. SE23 8H 93
Fountain Ct. SW1 5F 74 (off Buckingham Pal. Rd.)
Fountain Ct. Eyns 4J 131
Fountain Ct. Sidc 5F 96
Fountain Dri. SE19 1D 108
Fountain Dri. Cars 9D 122
Fountain Grn. Sq. SE16 3E 76
Fountain Ho. NW6 3J 57
Fountain Ho. W1 2E 74 (off Park St.)
Fountain M. N5 9A 44 (off Highbury Grange)
Fountain M. NW3 2D 58
Fountain Pl. SW9 9L 75
Fountain Pl. Wal A 7J 7
Fountain Rd. SW17 2B 106
Fountain Rd. T Hth 7A 108
Fountain Roundabout. N Mald 8C 104
Fountains Av. Felt 9K 85
Fountains Clo. Felt 8K 85 (in two parts)
Fountains Cres. N14 9J 15
Fountain Sq. SW1 5F 74
Fountains, The. N3 7M 25 (off Ballards La.)
Fountains, The. Lou 9H 19
Fountayne Bus. Cen. N15 2E 44
Fountayne Rd. N15 2E 44
Fountayne Rd. N16 7E 44
Fount St. SW8 8H 75
Fouracres. NW1 6G 59 (off Stanhope St.)
Fouracres. Enf 3J 17
Fourland Wlk. Edgw 6A 24
Fournier St. E1 8D 60
Four Seasons Clo. E3 5L 61
Four Seasons Cres. Sutt 4K 121
Four Sq. Ct. Houn 5L 85
Fourth Av. E12 9K 47
Fourth Av. W10 7J 57
Fourth Av. Hay 2D 68
Fourth Av. Romf 6B 50
Fourth Av. Wat 8H 5
Fourth Cross Rd. Twic 8B 86
Fourth Dri. Coul 8G 137
Fourth Way. Wemb 9M 39
Four Tubs, The. Bush 9B 10
Four Wents, The. E4 2B 30
Fovant Ct. SW8 1G 91
Fowey Av. Ilf 3H 47
Fowey Clo. E1 2F 76
Fowey Ho. SE11 6L 75 (off Kennings Way)
Fowler Clo. SW11 2B 90
Fowler Ho. N15 3B 44 (off South Gro.)
Fowler Rd. E7 9E 46
Fowler Rd. N1 4M 59
Fowler Rd. Ilf 6F 32
Fowler Rd. Mitc 6E 106
Fowlers Clo. Sidc 2J 113
Fowler's Wlk. W5 7H 55
Fowley Clo. Wal X 7F 6
Fowley Mead Pk. Wal X 7G 7
Fownes St. SW11 2C 90
Fox All. Wat 7G 9
Fox & Knot St. EC1 8M 59 (off Charterhouse Sq.)
Foxberry Rd. SE4 2J 93
Foxborough Gdns. SE4 4L 93
Foxbourne Rd. SW17 8E 90
Fox Burrow Rd. Chig 4H 33
Foxbury Av. Chst 3B 112
Foxbury Clo. Brom 3F 110
Foxbury Clo. Orp 7E 128
Foxbury Dri. Orp 8E 128
Foxbury Rd. Brom 3E 110
Fox Clo. E1 7G 61
Fox Clo. E16 8E 62
Fox Clo. Bush 7M 9
Fox Clo. Els 8H 11
Fox Clo. Orp 7E 128
Fox Clo. Romf 5M 33
Fox Clo. Wey 7B 116
Foxcombe. New Ad 8M 125 (in two parts)
Foxcombe Clo. E6 5H 63
Foxcombe Rd. SW15 7E 88
Foxcote. SE5 6C 76
Foxcroft. WC1 5K 59 (off Penton Ri.)
Foxcroft Rd. SE18 9M 79
Foxdell. N'wd 6B 20
Foxearth Rd. S Croy 2G 139
Foxearth Spur. S Croy 1G 139
Foxes Dale. SE3 2E 94
Foxes Dale. Brom 7B 110
Foxes Dri. Wal X 2A 6
Foxes Pde. Wal A 7J 7 (off Rue de St Lawrence)
Foxfield. NW1 4F 58 (off Arlington Rd.)
Foxfield Clo. N'wd 6D 20
Foxfield Rd. Orp 4B 128
Foxglove Clo. S'hall 1J 69
Foxglove Clo. Stanw 7B 144
Foxglove Ct. Wemb 5J 55
Foxglove Gdns. E11 2G 47
Foxglove Gdns. Purl 3J 137
Foxglove La. Chess 6L 119
Foxglove Rd. Rush G 7C 50
Foxglove St. W12 1D 72
Foxglove Way. Wall 3F 122
Foxgrove. N14 3J 27
Fox Gro. W on T 2F 116
Foxgrove Av. Beck 4M 109
Foxgrove Path. Wat 5H 21
Foxgrove Rd. Beck 4M 109
Foxhall Rd. Upm 1M 67
Foxham Rd. N19 8H 43
Fox Hill. SE19 4D 108
Fox Hill. Kes 7G 127
Foxhill. Wat 9E 4
Fox Hill Gdns. SE19 4D 108
Foxhole Rd. SE9 4J 95
Foxholes. Wey 7B 116
Fox Hollow Clo. SE18 6C 80
Fox Hollow Dri. Bexh 2H 97
Foxholt Gdns. NW10 3A 56
Foxhome Clo. Chst 3L 111
Fox Ho. Rd. Belv 6M 81 (in two parts)
Foxlands Clo. Leav 7E 4
Foxlands Cres. Dag 1A 66
Foxlands La. Dag 1B 66
Foxlands Rd. Dag 1A 66
Fox La. N13 2K 27
Fox La. W5 7J 55 (in two parts)
Fox La. Kes 7F 126
Foxleas Ct. Brom 4C 110
Foxlees. Wemb 9E 38
Foxley Clo. E8 1E 60
Foxley Clo. Lou 4M 19
Foxley Ct. Sutt 9A 122
Foxley Gdns. Purl 5M 137
Foxley Hall. Purl 5L 137
Foxley Hill Rd. Purl 4L 137
Foxley La. Purl 3G 137
Foxley Rd. SW9 8L 75
Foxley Rd. Kenl 6M 137
Foxley Rd. T Hth 8M 107
Foxleys. Wat 3J 21
Foxley Sq. SW9 9M 75
Foxmead Clo. Enf 5K 15
Foxmore St. SW11 9D 74
Fox Rd. E16 8D 62
Fox's Path. Mitc 6C 106
Foxton Gro. Mitc 6B 106
Foxton Ho. E16 3L 79 (off Albert Rd.)
Foxtree Ho. Wat 9J 5
Foxwarren. Clay 1D 132
Foxwell M. SE4 2J 93
Foxwell St. SE4 2J 93
Foxwood Chase. Wal A 8J 7
Foxwood Clo. NW7 4C 24
Foxwood Clo. Felt 9F 84
Foxwood Grn. Clo. Enf 8C 16
Foxwood Rd. SE3 3D 94
Foyle Rd. N17 8E 28
Foyle Rd. SE3 7D 78
Framfield Clo. N12 3L 25
Framfield Ct. Enf 8C 16 (off Queen Annes Gdns.)
Framfield Rd. N5 1M 59
Framfield Rd. W7 9C 54
Framfield Rd. Mitc 4E 106
Framlingham Clo. E5 7G 45
Framlingham Cres. SE9 1J 111
Frampton. NW1 3H 59 (off Wrotham Rd.)
Frampton Clo. Sutt 9L 121
Frampton Ct. W3 3A 72 (off Avenue Rd.)
Frampton Ho. NW8 7B 58 (off Frampton St.)
Frampton Pk. Est. E9 3G 61
Frampton Pk. Rd. E9 2G 61
Frampton Rd. Houn 4J 85
Frampton St. NW8 7B 58
Francemary Rd. SE4 4L 93
Frances Ct. E17 4L 45
Frances Rd. E4 6L 29
Frances St. SE18 4K 79
Franche Ct. Rd. SW17 9A 90
Francis Av. Bexh 1L 97
Francis Av. Felt 9E 84
Francis Av. Ilf 7B 48
Francis Barber Clo. SW16 2K 107
Franciscan Rd. SW17 2D 106
Francis Chichester Way. SW11 9E 74
Francis Clo. E14 5B 78
Francis Clo. Eps 6B 120
Francis Ct. EC1 8M 59 (off Briset St.)
Francis Ct. NW7 5D 24 (off Watford Way)
Francis Ct. SE14 7H 77 (off Myers La.)
Francis Ct. Surb 8J 103 (off Cranes Pk. Av.)
Francis Greene Ho. Wal A 6H 7 (off Grove Ct.)
Francis Gro. SW19 3K 105 (in two parts)
Francis Ho. E17 4K 45
Francis Ho. N1 4C 60 (off Colville Est.)
Francis M. SE12 6E 94
Francis Rd. E10 6A 46
Francis Rd. N2 2D 42
Francis Rd. Croy 2M 123
Francis Rd. Dart 4H 99
Francis Rd. Gnfd 5F 54
Francis Rd. Harr 3E 38
Francis Rd. Houn 1H 85
Francis Rd. Ilf 7B 48
Francis Rd. Orp 7H 113
Francis Rd. Pinn 3G 37
Francis Rd. Wall 8G 123
Francis Rd. Wat 6F 8
Francis St. E15 1C 62
Francis St. SW1 5G 75
Francis St. Ilf 7B 48
Francis Ter. N19 8G 43
Francis Wlk. N1 4K 59
Francklyn Gdns. Edgw 3L 23
Francombe Gdns. Romf 3E 50
Franconia Rd. SW4 4H 91
Frank Bailey Wlk. E12 1L 63
Frank Beswick Ho. SW6 7K 73 (off Clem Attlee Ct.)
Frank Burton Clo. SE7 6F 78
Frank Dixon Clo. SE21 6C 92
Frank Dixon Way. SE21 7C 92
Frankfurt Rd. SE24 4A 92
Frankham Ho. SE8 8L 77 (off Frankham St.)
Frankham St. SE8 8L 77
Frank Ho. SW8 8J 75 (off Wyvil Rd.)
Frankland Clo. SE16 4F 76
Frankland Clo. Wfd G 5G 31
Frankland Rd. E4 5L 29
Frankland Rd. SW7 4B 74
Frankland Rd. Crox G 8A 8
Franklin Av. Chesh 3A 6
Franklin Building. E14 3L 77
Franklin Clo. N20 9A 14
Franklin Clo. SE13 9M 77
Franklin Clo. SE27 9M 91
Franklin Clo. King T 7L 103
Franklin Cotts. Stan 4F 22
Franklin Cres. Mitc 8G 107
Franklin Ho. E1 2F 76 (off Watts St.)
Franklin Pas. SE9 2J 95
Franklin Rd. SE20 4G 109
Franklin Rd. Bexh 9J 81
Franklin Rd. Horn 2G 67
Franklin Rd. Wat 4F 8
Franklins M. Harr 7A 38
Franklin Sq. W14 6K 73
Franklin's Row. SW3 6D 74
Franklin St. E3 6M 61
Franklin St. N15 4C 44
Franklin Way. Croy 2J 123
Franklyn Gdns. Ilf 6B 32
Franklyn Rd. NW10 2D 56
Franklyn Rd. W on T 1E 116
Frank Martin Ct. Chesh 3B 6
Franks Av. N Mald 8A 104
Franks La. Hort K 9M 115
Frank Soskice Ho. SW6 7K 73 (off Clem Attlee Ct.)
Frank St. E13 7E 62
Franks Wood Av. Orp 9M 111
Frankswood Av. W Dray 9D 142
Frank Towell Ct. Felt 6E 84
Frank Welsh Ct. Pinn 2G 37
Frank Whymark Ho. SE16 3G 77 (off Rupack St.)
Franlaw Cres. N13 4A 28
Franmil Rd. Horn 6E 50
Fransfield Gro. SE26 9F 92
Frans Hals Ct. E14 4B 78
Frant Clo. SE20 4G 109
Franthorne Way. SE6 8M 93
Frant Rd. T Hth 9M 107
Fraser Clo. E6 9J 63
Fraser Clo. Bex 7A 98
Fraser Ct. E14 6A 78 (off Ferry St.)
Fraser Ho. Bren 6K 71
Fraser Rd. E17 3M 45
Fraser Rd. N9 3F 28
Fraser Rd. Chesh 1E 6
Fraser Rd. Eri 6A 82
Fraser Rd. Gnfd 4F 54
Fraser St. W4 6C 72

Frating Cres.—Gainsborough Ct.

Frating Cres. Wfd G 6F 30
Frays Av. W Dray 3H 143
Frays Clo. W Dray 4H 143
Frayslea. Uxb 5A 142
Frays Waye. Uxb 4A 142
Frazer Av. Ruis 1G 53
Frazer Clo. Romf 5D 50
Frazier St. SE1 3L 75
Frean St. SE16 4E 76
Frearson Ho. WC1 6K 59
(off Penton Ri.)
Freda Corbett Clo. SE15 8E 76
Frederica Rd. E4 9B 18
Frederica St. N7 3K 59
Frederick Charrington Ho. E1 7G 61
(off Wickford St.)
Frederick Clo. W2 1D 74
Frederick Clo. Sutt 6K 121
Frederick Cres. SW9 8M 75
Frederick Cres. Enf 4G 17
Frederick Gdns. Croy 1M 123
Frederick Gdns. Sutt 6K 121
Frederick Pl. SE18 6M 79
Frederick Rd. SE17 7M 75
Frederick Rd. Rain 5B 66
Frederick Rd. Sutt 7K 121
Frederick's Pl. EC2 9B 60
Fredericks Pl. N12 4A 26
Frederick Sq. SE16 1J 77
(off Sovereign Cres.)
Frederick's Row. EC1 6M 59
Frederick St. WC1 6K 59
Frederick Ter. E8 3D 60
Frederic M. SW1 3D 74
(off Kinnerton St.)
Frederic St. E17 3J 45
Fredora Av. Hay 7D 52
Fred Styles Ho. SE7 7G 79
Fred White Wlk. N7 2J 59
Freeborne Gdns. Rain 2E 66
Freedom Clo. E17 2H 45
Freedom Rd. N17 9B 28
Freedom St. SW11 1D 90
Freedown La. Sutt 5M 135
Freegrove Rd. N7 1J 59
(in two parts)
Freehold Ind. Est. Houn 4G 85
Freeland Ct. Sidc 9E 96
Freeland Pk. NW4 9J 25
Freeland Rd. W5 1K 71
Freelands Av. S Croy 1H 139
Freelands Gro. Brom 5F 110
Freelands Rd. Brom 5F 110
Freeland Way. Eri 9E 82
Freeling Ho. NW8 4B 58
(off Dorman Way)
Freeling St. N1 3K 59
(Carnoustie Dri.)
Freeling St. N1 3J 59
(Pembroke St.)
Freeman Clo. N'holt 3J 53
Freeman Clo. Shep 8C 100
Freeman Dri. W Mol 8K 101
Freeman Rd. Mord 9B 106
Freemans La. Hay 1C 68
Freemantle Av. Enf 7H 17
Freemantle St. SE17 6C 76
Freeman Way. Horn 4K 51
Freemasons Rd. E16 8F 62
Freemasons Rd. Croy 3C 124
Freesia Clo. Orp 7D 128
Freethorpe Clo. SE19 4B 108
Free Trade Wharf. E1 1H 77
Freezeland Way. Hil 2F 142
Freezy Water. 9D 6
Freightmaster Est. Rain 9C 66
Freke Rd. SW11 2E 90
Fremantle Ho. E1 7F 60
(off Somerford St.)
Fremantle Rd. Belv 5L 81
Fremantle Rd. Ilf 9M 31
Fremont St. E9 4F 60
(in two parts)
French Apartments, The. Purl 4L 137
French Ordinary Ct. EC3 1C 76
(off Crutched Friars)
French Pl. E1 6C 60
French St. Sun 6G 101
Frendsbury Rd. SE4 3J 93
Frensham. Chesh 1A 6
Frensham Clo. S'hall 7K 53
Frensham Dri. SW15 9D 88
(in two parts)
Frensham Dri. New Ad 9A 126
Frensham Rd. SE9 8B 96
Frensham Rd. Kenl 6M 137
Frensham St. SE15 7E 76
Frensham Way. Eps 8G 135
Frere St. SW11 1C 90
Fresham Ho. Brom 7D 110
(off Durham Rd.)
Freshfield Av. E8 3D 60
Freshfield Clo. SE13 3B 94
Freshfield Dri. N14 9F 14
Freshfields. Croy 3K 125
Freshfields Av. Upm 1M 67
Freshford St. SW17 9A 90
Freshmount Gdns. Eps 3M 133
Freshwater Clo. SW17 3E 106
Freshwater Ct. W1 8C 58
(off Crawford St.)
Freshwater Ct. S'hall 6L 53
Freshwater Rd. SW17 3E 106
Freshwater Rd. Dag 6H 49
Freshwell Av. Romf 2G 49
Fresh Wharf Rd. Bark 4M 63
Freshwood Clo. Beck 5M 109
Freshwood Way. Wall 1F 136
Freston Gdns. Barn 7E 14
Freston Pk. N3 9K 25
Freston Rd. W10 & W11 1H 73
Freswick Ho. SE8 5H 77
(off Chilton Gro.)
Freta Rd. Bexh 4K 97
Freud Mus., The. 2A 58
Frewell Ho. EC1 8L 59
(off Bourne Est.)
Frewing Clo. Chst 3K 111
Frewin Rd. SW18 7B 90
Friar M. SE27 9M 91
Friar Rd. Hay 7H 53
Friar Rd. Orp 9E 112
Friars Av. N20 3C 26
Friars Av. SW15 9D 88
Friars Clo. E4 3A 30
Friars Clo. SE1 2M 75
(off Bear La.)
Friars Clo. Ilf 6B 48
Friars Clo. N'holt 6H 53
Friars Ct. E17 8K 29
Friars Gdns. W3 9B 56
Friars Ga. Clo. Wfd G 4E 30
Friars La. Rich 4H 87
Friars Mead. E14 4A 78
Friars M. SE9 4L 95
Friars Pl. La. W3 1B 72
Friars Rd. E6 4H 63
Friars Stile Pl. Rich 5J 87
Friars Stile Rd. Rich 5J 87
Friars, The. Chig 4C 32
Friar St. EC4 9M 59
Friars Wlk. N14 9F 14
Friars Wlk. SE2 6H 81
Friars Way. W3 9B 56
Friars Way. Bush 3K 9
Friarswood. Croy 1J 139
Friary Clo. N12 5C 26
Friary Ct. SW1 2G 75
(off Marlborough Rd.)
Friary Est. SE15 7E 76
(in two parts)
Friary La. Wfd G 4E 30
Friary Pk. Ct. W3 9A 56
Friary Rd. N12 4B 26
Friary Rd. SE15 8E 76
Friary Rd. W3 9A 56
Friary, The. Wal X 6F 6
Friary Way. N12 4C 26
Friday Hill. 2C 30
Friday Hill. E4 2C 30
Friday Hill E. E4 3C 30
Friday Hill W. E4 2C 30
Friday Rd. Eri 6B 82
Friday Rd. Mitc 4D 106
Friday St. EC4 1A 76
Frideswide Pl. NW5 1G 59
Friendly Pl. SE13 9M 77
Friendly St. SE8 1L 93
Friendly St. M. SE8 1L 93
Friends Av. Chesh 5D 6
Friendship Wlk. N'holt 6H 53
Friends Rd. Croy 5B 124
Friends Rd. Purl 4M 137
Friend St. EC1 6M 59
Friends Wlk. Uxb 3B 142
Friern Barnet. 5D 26
Friern Barnet La. N20 & N11 2B 26
Friern Barnet Rd. N11 5D 26
Friern Bri. Retail Pk. N11 6F 26
Friern Ct. N20 3B 26
Friern Mt. Dri. N20 9A 14
Friern Pk. N12 5A 26
Friern Rd. SE22 6E 92
Friern Watch Av. N12 4A 26
Frigate Ho. E14 5A 78
(off Stebondale St.)
Frigate M. SE8 7L 77
Frimley Av. Horn 6L 51
Frimley Av. Wall 7J 123
Frimley Clo. SW19 8J 89
Frimley Clo. New Ad 9A 126
Frimley Ct. Sidc 2G 113
Frimley Cres. New Ad 9A 126
Frimley Gdns. Mitc 7C 106
Frimley Rd. Chess 7H 119
Frimley Rd. Ilf 8C 48
Frimley St. E1 7H 61
(off Frimley Way)
Frimley Way. E1 7H 61
Fringewood Clo. N'wd 8A 20
Frinstead Ho. W10 1H 73
(off Freston Rd.)
Frinsted Gro. Orp 8H 113
Frinsted Rd. Eri 8B 82
Frinton Clo. Wat 2F 20
Frinton Ct. W13 8F 54
(off Hardwick Grn.)
Frinton Dri. Wfd G 7B 30
Frinton M. Ilf 4L 47
Frinton Rd. E6 6H 63
Frinton Rd. N15 4C 44
Frinton Rd. SW17 3E 106
Frinton Rd. Romf 7K 33
Frinton Rd. Sidc 8J 97
Friston Path. Chig 5C 32
Friston St. SW6 1M 89
Friswell Pl. Bexh 3L 97
Fritham Clo. N Mald 1C 120
Frith Ct. NW7 7J 25
Frith Ho. NW8 7B 58
(off Frampton St.)
Frith Knowle. W on T 8F 116
Frith La. NW7 7J 25
Frith Rd. E11 9A 46
Frith Rd. Croy 4A 124
Frith St. W1 9H 59
Frithville Ct. W12 2G 73
(off Frithville Gdns.)
Frithville Gdns. W12 2G 73
Frithwood Av. N'wd 6C 20
Frizlands La. Dag 7M 49
Frobisher Clo. Bush 8L 9
Frobisher Clo. Kenl 9A 138
Frobisher Clo. Pinn 5H 37
Frobisher Ct. NW9 9C 24
Frobisher Ct. SE10 7B 78
(off Old Woolwich Rd.)
Frobisher Ct. SE23 8F 92
Frobisher Ct. W12 3G 73
(off Lime Gro.)
Frobisher Ct. Sutt 9J 121
Frobisher Cres. EC2 8A 60
(off Beech St.)
Frobisher Cres. Stai 6C 144
Frobisher Gdns. E10 5M 45
Frobisher Gdns. Stai 6C 144
Frobisher Ho. E1 2F 76
(off Watts St.)
Frobisher Ho. SW1 7H 75
(off Dolphin Sq.)
Frobisher M. Enf 6B 16
Frobisher Pas. E14 2L 77
Frobisher Rd. E6 9K 63
Frobisher Rd. N8 2L 43
Frobisher Rd. Eri 8D 82
Frobisher St. SE10 7C 78
Froghall La. Chig 4B 32
Frog La. Frog 8B 66
Frogley Rd. SE22 3D 92
Frogmore. SW18 4L 89
Frogmore Av. Hay 7C 52
Frogmore Clo. Sutt 5H 121
Frogmore Cotts. Wat 7H 9
Frogmore Ct. S'hall 5K 69
Frogmore Gdns. Hay 7C 52
Frogmore Gdns. Sutt 6J 121
Frogmore Ind. Est. N5 1A 60
Frogmore Ind. Est. NW10 6A 56
Frogmore Ind. Est. Hay 3C 68
Frognal. NW3 9A 42
Frognal Av. Harr 2D 38
Frognal Av. Sidc 3E 112
Frognal Clo. NW3 1A 58
Frognal Corner (Junct.) 3D 112
Frognal Ct. NW3 2A 58
Frognal Gdns. NW3 9A 42
Frognal La. NW3 1M 57
Frognal Pde. NW3 2A 58
Frognal Pl. Sidc 3E 112
Frognal Ri. NW3 8A 42
Frognal Way. NW3 9A 42
Froissart Rd. SE9 4H 95
Frome Ho. SE15 3F 92
Frome Rd. N15 1M 43
Frome St. N1 5A 60
Fromondes Rd. Sutt 7J 121
Frontenac. NW10 3F 56
Frostic Wlk. E1 8E 60
Froude St. SW8 1F 90
Fruen Rd. Felt 6D 84
Fruiterers Pas. EC4 1A 76
(off Queen St. Pl.)
Fryatt Rd. N17 7B 28
(in two parts)
Fry Clo. Romf 5L 33
Fryent Clo. NW9 4L 39
Fryent Country Pk. 5L 39
Fryent Cres. NW9 4C 40
Fryent Fields. NW9 4C 40
Fryent Gro. NW9 4C 40
Fryent Way. NW9 3L 39
Fry Ho. E7 3G 63
Frying Pan All. E1 8D 60
(off Bell La.)
Frylands Ct. New Ad 3A 140
Fry Rd. E6 3H 63
Fry Rd. NW10 4D 56
Fryston Av. Coul 6F 136
Fryston Av. Croy 4E 124
Fuchsia Clo. Rush G 7C 50
Fuchsia St. SE2 6F 80
Fulbeck Dri. NW9 8C 24
Fulbeck Ho. N7 2K 59
(off Sutterton St.)
Fulbeck Rd. N19 9G 43
Fulbeck Wlk. Edgw 2M 23
Fulbeck Way. Harr 9A 22
Fulbourn. King T 6L 103
(off Eureka Rd.)
Fulbourne Rd. E17 8A 30
Fulbourne St. E1 8F 60
Fulbrook M. N19 9G 43
Fulcher Ho. N1 4C 60
(off Colville Ho.)
Fulcher Ho. SE8 6K 77
Fulford Gro. Wat 2F 20
Fulford Ho. Eps 9B 120
Fulford Rd. Eps 9B 120
Fulford St. SE16 3F 76
Fulham. 1J 89
Fulham Broadway (Junct.) 8L 73
Fulham B'way. SW6 8L 73
Fulham Clo. Uxb 7A 52
Fulham Ct. SW6 9L 73
Fulham F.C. (Craven Cottage) 9H 73
Fulham High St. SW6 1J 89
Fulham Pal. Rd. W6 & SW6 6G 73
Fulham Pk. Gdns. SW6 1K 89
Fulham Pk. Rd. SW6 1K 89
Fulham Rd. SW6, SW10 & SW3 1J 89
(in two parts)
Fullbrooks Av. Wor Pk 3D 120
Fuller Clo. E2 7E 60
(off Cheshire St.)
Fuller Clo. Orp 7D 128
Fuller Gdns. Wat 1F 8
Fuller Rd. Dag 8F 48
Fuller Rd. Wat 1F 8
Fullers Av. E18 7D 30
Fullers Av. Surb 4K 119
Fullers Clo. Romf 7A 34
Fullers Clo. Wal A 6M 7
Fuller's Griffin Brewery & Vis. Cen. 7D 72
Fullers La. Romf 7A 34
Fullers Rd. E18 7D 30
Fuller St. NW4 2G 41
Fullers Way N. Surb 5K 119
Fullers Way S. Chess 6J 119
Fuller's Wood. Croy 7L 125
Fullerton Ct. Tedd 3E 102
Fullerton Rd. SW18 4M 89
Fullerton Rd. Cars 1C 136
Fullerton Rd. Croy 2D 124
Fuller Way. Hay 6D 68
Fullwell Av. Ilf 8K 31
Fullwell Cross. Ilf 9B 32
Fullwell Pde. Ilf 8L 31
Fullwood's M. N1 6B 60
Fulmar Ct. Surb 1K 119
Fulmar Ho. SE16 5H 77
(off Tawny Way)
Fulmar Rd. Horn 3E 66
Fulmead St. SW6 9M 73
Fulmer Clo. Hamp 2J 101
Fulmer Ho. NW8 7C 58
(off Rossmore Rd.)
Fulmer Rd. E16 8H 63
Fulmer Way. W13 4F 70
Fulneck. E1 8G 61
(off Mile End Rd.)
Fulready Rd. E10 3B 46
Fulstone Clo. Houn 3K 85
Fulthorp Rd. SE3 1D 94
Fulton Ct. Borwd 2K 11
(off Aycliffe Rd.)
Fulton M. W2 1A 74
(off Porchester Ter.)
Fulton Rd. Wemb 8L 39
Fulwell. 1B 102
Fulwell Ct. S'hall 1A 70
(off Baird Av.)
Fulwell Cross. 9A 32
Fulwell Pk. Av. Twic 8M 85
Fulwell Rd. Tedd 1B 102
Fulwich Rd. Dart 5K 99
Fulwood Av. Wemb 5K 55
Fulwood Clo. Hay 9D 52
Fulwood Ct. Kent 4E 38
Fulwood Gdns. Twic 5D 86
Fulwood Pl. WC1 8K 59
Fulwood Wlk. SW19 7J 89
Furber St. W6 4F 72
Furham Fld. Pinn 7L 21
Furley Ho. SE15 8E 76
(off Peckham Pk. Rd.)
Furley Rd. SE15 8E 76
Furlong Clo. Wall 3F 122
Furlong Path. N'holt 2J 53
(off Cowings Mead)
Furlong Rd. N7 2L 59
Furmage St. SW18 6M 89
Furneaux Av. SE27 2M 107
Furner Clo. Dart 2D 98
Furness Ho. SW1 6F 74
(off Abbots Mnr.)
Furness Rd. NW10 5E 56
Furness Rd. SW6 1M 89
Furness Rd. Harr 5M 37
Furness Rd. Mord 1M 121
Furness Way. Horn 1E 66
Furnival Mans. W1 8G 59
(off Wells St.)
Furnival St. EC4 9L 59
Furrow La. E9 1G 61
Furrows, The. W on T 4G 117
Fursby Av. N3 6L 25
Fursecroft. W1 9D 58
(off George St.)
Further Acre. NW9 9D 24
Furtherfield. Ab L 5C 4
Furtherfield Clo. Croy 1L 123
Further Grn. Rd. SE6 6C 94
Furze Clo. Wat 5G 21
Furzedown. 2F 106
Furzedown Dri. SW17 2F 106
Furzedown Rd. SW17 2F 106
Furzedown Rd. Sutt 3A 136
Furze Farm Clo. Romf 9J 33
Furzefield. Chesh 1B 6
Furze Fld. Oxs 5B 132
Furzefield Clo. Chst 3M 111
Furzefield Rd. SE3 7F 78
Furzeground Way. Uxb 2A 68
Furzeham Rd. W Dray 3J 143
Furze Hill. Purl 3J 137
Furzehill Pde. Borwd 5L 11
Furzehill Rd. Borwd 6L 11
(in two parts)
Furzehill Sq. St M 8F 112
Furze La. Purl 3J 137
Furze Rd. T Hth 7A 108
Furze St. E3 8L 61
Furzewood. Sun 5E 100
Fye Foot La. EC4 1A 76
(off Queen Victoria St., in two parts)
Fyfe Way. Brom 6E 110
Fyfield. N4 7L 43
(off Six Acres Est.)
Fyfield Clo. Brom 8B 110
Fyfield Ct. E7 2E 62
Fyfield Ho. E6 4J 63
(off Ron Leighton Way)
Fyfield Rd. E17 1B 46
Fyfield Rd. SW9 2L 91
Fyfield Rd. Enf 5C 16
Fyfield Rd. Rain 4D 66
Fyfield Rd. Wfd G 7G 31
Fynes St. SW1 5H 75

G

Gable Clo. Ab L 5C 4
Gable Clo. Dart 4E 98
Gable Clo. Pinn 7L 21
Gable Ct. SE26 1F 108
Gables Av. Borwd 5K 11
Gables Clo. SE5 9C 76
Gables Clo. SE12 7E 94
Gables Lodge. Barn 2A 14
Gables, The. N10 1E 42
(off Fortis Grn.)
Gables, The. Bans 9K 135
Gables, The. Bark 2A 64
Gables, The. Brom 4F 110
Gables, The. Leav 6H 5
Gables, The. Oxs 4A 132
Gables, The. Wat 9G 9
Gables, The. Wemb 8L 39
Gables Way. Bans 9K 135
Gabriel Clo. Felt 1J 101
Gabriel Clo. Romf 7A 34
Gabriel Ho. SE11 5K 75
Gabrielle Clo. Wemb 8K 39
Gabrielle Ct. NW3 2B 58
Gabriel St. SE23 6H 93
Gabriels Wharf. SE1 2L 75
Gad Clo. E13 6F 62
Gaddesden Av. Wemb 2K 55
Gaddesden Cres. Wat 7H 5
Gaddesden Ho. EC1 6B 60
(off Cranwood St.)
Gade Av. Wat 6C 8
Gade Bank. Wat 6B 8
Gadebridge Ho. SW3 6C 74
(off Cale St.)
Gade Clo. Hay 2F 68
Gade Clo. Wat 6C 8
Gadesden Rd. Eps 8A 120
(in two parts)
Gade Side. Wat 8C 4
Gade Vw. Gdns. K Lan 5A 4
Gadsbury Clo. NW9 4D 40
Gadsden Ho. W10 7J 57
(off Hazlewood Cres.)
Gadswell Clo. Wat 9H 5
Gadwall Clo. E16 9F 62
Gadwall Way. SE28 3B 80
Gage Brown Ho. W10 9H 57
(off Bridge Clo.)
Gage Rd. E16 8C 62
Gage St. WC1 8J 59
Gainford Ho. E2 6F 60
(off Ellsworth St.)
Gainford St. N1 4L 59
Gainsboro Gdns. Gnfd 1C 54
Gainsborough Av. E12 1L 63
Gainsborough Av. Dart 4G 99
Gainsborough Clo. Beck 4L 109
Gainsborough Clo. Esh 3C 118
Gainsborough Ct. N12 5M 25
Gainsborough Ct. SE16 6F 76
(off Stubbs Dri.)
Gainsborough Ct. SE21 8C 92
Gainsborough Ct. W4 6M 71
(off Chaseley Dri.)

Gainsborough Ct.—Gay Clo.

Gainsborough Ct. W12 3G 73
Gainsborough Ct. W on T 6E 116
Gainsborough Dri. S Croy 5E 138
Gainsborough Gdns. NW3 8B 42
Gainsborough Gdns. NW11 5K 41
Gainsborough Gdns. Edgw 9K 23
Gainsborough Gdns. Iswth 4B 86
Gainsborough Ho. E14 1J 77 (off Victory Pl.)
Gainsborough Ho. SW1 5H 75 (off Erasmus St.)
Gainsborough Ho. Dag 9F 48 (off Gainsborough Rd.)
Gainsborough Lodge. Harr 3D 38 (off Hindes Rd.)
Gainsborough Mans. W14 7J 73 (off Queen's Club Gdns.)
Gainsborough M. SE26 9F 92
Gainsborough Pl. Chig 3D 32
Gainsborough Rd. E11 5C 46
Gainsborough Rd. E15 6C 62
Gainsborough Rd. N12 5M 25
Gainsborough Rd. W4 5D 72
Gainsborough Rd. Dag 9F 48
Gainsborough Rd. Eps 2A 134
Gainsborough Rd. Hay 5A 52
Gainsborough Rd. N Mald 1B 120
Gainsborough Rd. Rain 4E 66
Gainsborough Rd. Rich 1K 87
Gainsborough Rd. Wfd G 6J 31
Gainsborough Sq. Bexh 2H 97
Gainsborough Ter. Sutt 9K 121 (off Belmont Ri.)
Gainsborough Tower. N'holt 5H 53 (off Academy Gdns.)
Gainsfield Ct. E11 8C 46
Gainsford Rd. E17 2K 45
Gainsford St. SE1 3D 76
Gairloch Ho. NW1 3H 59 (off Stratford Vs.)
Gairloch Rd. SE5 1C 92
Gaisford St. NW5 2G 59
Gaitskell Ct. SW11 1C 90
Gaitskell Ho. E6 4H 63
Gaitskell Ho. E17 1M 45
Gaitskell Ho. SE17 7C 76 (off Villa St.)
Gaitskell Rd. SE9 7A 96
Galahad Rd. Brom 1E 110
Galata Rd. SW13 8E 72
Galatea Sq. SE15 2F 92
Galba Ct. Bren 8H 71
Galbraith St. E14 4A 78
Galdana Av. Barn 5A 14
Galeborough Av. Wfd G 7B 30
Gale Clo. Hamp 3J 101
Gale Clo. Mitc 7B 106
Gale Cres. Bans 9L 135
Galena Ho. W6 5F 72 (off Galena Rd.)
Galena Rd. W6 5F 72
Galen Clo. Eps 3L 133
Galen Pl. WC1 8J 59
Galesbury Rd. SW18 5A 90
Gales Gdns. E2 6F 60
Gale St. E3 8L 61
Gale St. Dag 1G 65
Gales Way. Wfd G 7J 31
Galgate Clo. SW19 7H 89
Gallants Farm Rd. E Barn 9C 14
Galleon Clo. SE16 3H 77
Galleon Clo. Eri 5B 82
Galleon Dri. Bark 6E 64
Galleon Ho. E14 5A 78 (off Glengarnock Av.)
Gallery Ct. SE1 3B 76 (off Pilgrimage St.)
Gallery Ct. SW10 7A 74 (off Gunter Gro.)
Gallery Gdns. N'holt 5H 53
Gallery Rd. SE21 7B 92
Galleyhill Rd. Wal A 6L 7 (in two parts)
Galley La. Barn 2E 12
Galleywall Rd. SE16 5F 76
Galleywall Rd. Trad. Est. SE16 5F 76 (off Galleywall Rd.)
Galleywood Cres. Romf 6B 34
Galleywood Ho. W10 8G 57 (off Sutton Way)
Galliard Clo. N9 8G 17
Galliard Ct. N9 8E 16
Galliard Rd. N9 9E 16
Gallia Rd. N5 1M 59
Gallions Clo. Bark 6E 64
Gallions Entrance. E16 2A 80
Gallions Rd. SE7 5F 78 (in two parts)
Gallions Vw. Rd. SE28 3C 80
Galliver Pl. E5 9F 44
Gallon Clo. SE7 5G 79
Gallop, The. S Croy 9F 124
Gallop, The. Sutt 1B 136
Gallosson Rd. SE18 5C 80
Galloway Dri. Rd. Dart 6C 98
Galloway Path. Croy 6B 124
Galloway Rd. W12 2E 72
Gallows Corner. 9G 35
Gallows Corner (Junct.) 8G 35
Gallows Hill. K Lan 5A 4
Gallows Hill La. Ab L 5A 4
Gallus Clo. N21 8K 15
Gallus Sq. SE3 2F 94
Galpin's Rd. T Hth 9J 107
Galsworthy Av. E14 8J 61
Galsworthy Av. Romf 5F 48
Galsworthy Clo. NW2 9J 41
Galsworthy Clo. SE28 2F 80
Galsworthy Ct. W3 4M 71 (off Bollo Bri. Rd.)
Galsworthy Cres. SE3 9G 79
Galsworthy Ho. W11 9J 57 (off Elgin Cres.)
Galsworthy Rd. NW2 9J 41
Galsworthy Rd. King T 4M 103
Galsworthy Ter. N16 8C 44
Galton St. W10 6J 57
Galva Clo. Barn 6E 14
Galvani Way. Croy 3K 123
Galveston Ho. E1 7J 61 (off Harford St.)
Galveston Rd. SW15 4K 89
Galway Clo. SE16 6F 76 (off Masters Dri.)
Galway Ho. E1 8H 61 (off White Horse La.)
Galway Ho. EC1 6A 60 (off Radnor St.)
Galway St. EC1 6A 60
Galy. NW9 9D 24
Gambetta St. SW8 1F 90
Gambia St. SE1 2M 75
Gambier Ho. EC1 6A 60 (off Mora St.)
Gambole Rd. SW17 1C 106
Games Rd. Barn 5D 14
Gamlen Rd. SW15 3H 89
Gammons Farm Clo. Wat 9D 4
Gammons La. Wat 9C 4 (in two parts)
Gamuel Clo. E17 4L 45
Gander Grn. Cres. Hamp 5L 101
Gander Grn. La. Sutt 4J 121
Ganders Ash. Wat 6E 4
Gandhi Clo. E17 4L 45
Gandhi Ct. Wat 4H 9
Gandolfi St. SE15 7C 76
Gant Ct. Wal A 7M 7
Ganton St. W1 1G 75
Ganton Wlk. Wat 4H 21
Gants Hill. 4L 47
Gants Hill (Junct.) 3L 47
Gantshill Cres. Ilf 3L 47
Gants Hill Cross. Ilf 4L 47
Gap Rd. SW19 2L 105
Garage Rd. W3 9L 55
Garbett Ho. SE17 7M 75 (off Doddington Gro.)
Garbrand Wlk. Eps 1D 134
Garbutt Pl. W1 8E 58
Garden Av. Bexh 2L 97
Garden Av. Mitc 4F 106
Garden City. Edgw 6L 23
Garden Clo. E4 5L 29
Garden Clo. SE12 9F 94
Garden Clo. SW15 6G 89
Garden Clo. Ark 6G 13
Garden Clo. Ashf 3A 100
Garden Clo. Bans 7L 135
Garden Clo. Hamp 2K 101
Garden Clo. N'holt 4J 53
Garden Clo. Ruis 7C 36
Garden Clo. Wall 7J 123
Garden Clo. Wat 4D 8
Garden Cotts. Orp 6G 113
Garden Ct. EC4 1L 75 (off Temple)
Garden Ct. W4 4A 72
Garden Ct. Croy 4D 124
Garden Ct. Hamp 2K 101
Garden Ct. Rich 9K 71
Garden Ct. Stan 5G 23
Gardener Gro. Felt 8K 85
Gardeners Clo. N11 2E 26
Gardeners Rd. Croy 3M 123
Garden Ho. N2 9B 26 (off Grange, The)
Gardenia Rd. Enf 8C 16
Gardenia Way. Wfd G 6E 30
Garden La. SW2 7K 91
Garden La. Brom 3F 110
Garden M. W2 1L 73
Garden Pl. E8 4D 60
Garden Pl. Dart 9H 99
Garden Rd. NW8 6A 58
Garden Rd. SE20 5G 109
Garden Rd. Ab L 4C 4
Garden Rd. Brom 4F 110
Garden Rd. Rich 2L 87
Garden Rd. W on T 1F 116
Garden Row. SE1 4M 75
Gardens, The. N8 2J 43 (in two parts)
Gardens, The. SE22 3E 92
Gardens, The. Beck 5A 110
Gardens, The. Esh 6L 117
Gardens, The. Felt 4B 84
Gardens, The. Harr 4A 38
Gardens, The. Pinn 4K 37
Gardens, The. Wat 4D 8
Garden St. E1 8H 61
Garden Ter. SW1 6H 75
Garden Ter. SW7 3C 74 (off Trevor Pl.)
Garden Vw. E7 9G 47
Garden Wlk. EC2 6C 60
Garden Wlk. Beck 5K 109
Garden Way. NW10 2A 56
Garden Way. Lou 2L 19
Gardiner Av. NW2 1G 57
Gardiner Clo. Enf 8H 17
Gardiner Clo. Orp 6G 113
Gardiner Ct. NW10 4B 56
Gardiner Ct. S Croy 8A 124
Gardiners Clo. Dag 9H 49
Gardner Clo. E11 4F 46
Gardner Ho. Felt 8K 85
Gardner Ho. S'hall 1H 69 (off Broadway, The)
Gardner Ind. Est. SE26 2K 109
Gardner Rd. E13 7F 62
Gardners La. EC4 1A 76
Gardnor Rd. NW3 9B 42
Gard St. EC1 6M 59
Garendon Gdns. Mord 2M 121
Garendon Rd. Mord 2M 121
Garenne Ct. E4 1A 30
Gareth Clo. Wor Pk 4H 121
Gareth Ct. SW16 9H 91
Gareth Ct. Borwd 2K 11 (off Aycliffe Rd.)
Gareth Gro. Brom 1E 110
Garfield. Enf 7B 16 (off Private Rd.)
Garfield Ct. NW6 3H 57 (off Willesden La.)
Garfield M. SW11 2E 90
Garfield Rd. E4 1B 30
Garfield Rd. E13 7D 62
Garfield Rd. SW11 2E 90
Garfield Rd. SW19 2A 106
Garfield Rd. Enf 6G 17
Garfield Rd. Twic 7E 86
Garfield St. Wat 2F 8
Garford St. E14 1L 77
Garganey Ct. NW10 2B 56 (off Elgar Av.)
Garganey Wlk. SE28 1G 81
Garibaldi St. SE18 5C 80
Garland Clo. Chesh 4E 6
Garland Ct. E14 1L 77 (off Premiere Pl.)
Garland Rd. SE18 8B 80
Garland Rd. Stan 8J 23
Garlands Ct. Croy 6B 124 (off Chatsworth Rd.)
Garland Way. Horn 2J 51
Garlichill Rd. Eps 9F 134
Garlick Hill. EC4 1A 76
Garlies Rd. SE23 9J 93
Garlinge Rd. NW2 2K 57
Garman Clo. N18 5B 28
Garman Rd. N17 7G 29
Garnault M. EC1 6L 59 (off Rosebery Av.)
Garnault Pl. EC1 6L 59
Garnault Rd. Enf 2D 16
Garner Clo. Dag 6H 49
Garner Rd. E17 8A 30
Garner St. E2 5E 60
Garnet Ho. E1 2G 77 (off Garnet St.)
Garnet Rd. NW10 2C 56
Garnet Rd. T Hth 8A 108
Garnet St. E1 1G 77
Garnett Clo. SE9 2K 95
Garnett Clo. Wat 1H 9
Garnett Dri. Brick W 2K 5
Garnett Rd. NW3 1D 58
Garnett Way. E17 8J 29 (off Swansland Gdns.)
Garnet Wlk. E6 8J 63
Garnham Clo. N16 7D 44
Garnham St. N16 7D 44
Garnies Clo. SE15 8D 76
Garrad's Rd. SW16 9H 91
Garrard Clo. Bexh 2L 97
Garrard Clo. Chst 2M 111
Garrard Rd. Bans 8L 135
Garrard Wlk. NW10 2C 56
Garratt Clo. Croy 6J 123
Garratt Ct. SW18 6M 89
Garratt La. SW18 & SW17 5M 89
Garratt Rd. Edgw 7L 23
Garratts La. Bans 8K 135
Garratts Rd. Bush 9A 10
Garratt Ter. SW17 1C 106
Garraway Ct. SW13 8G 73 (off Wyatt Dri.)
Garrett Clo. W3 8B 56
Garrett Ho. W12 9F 56 (off Du Cane Rd.)
Garrett St. EC1 7A 60
Garrick Av. NW11 4J 41
Garrick Clo. SW18 3A 90
Garrick Clo. W5 7J 55
Garrick Clo. Rich 4H 87
Garrick Clo. W on T 6F 116
Garrick Cres. Croy 4C 124
Garrick Dri. NW4 9G 25
Garrick Dri. SE28 4B 80
Garrick Gdns. W Mol 7L 101
Garrick Ho. W1 2F 74
Garrick Ho. W4 7C 72
Garrick Ho. King T 8J 103 (off Surbiton Rd.)
Garrick Ind. Est. NW9 3D 40
Garrick Pk. NW4 9H 25
Garrick Rd. NW9 4D 40
Garrick Rd. Gnfd 7M 53
Garrick Rd. Rich 1L 87
Garricks Ho. King T 6H 103 (off Wadbrook St.)
Garrick St. WC2 1J 75
Garrick Theatre. 1H 75 **(off Charing Cross Rd.)**
Garrick Way. NW4 2H 41
Garrick Yd. WC2 1J 75 (off St Martin's La.)
Garrison Clo. SE18 8L 79
Garrison Clo. Houn 4K 85
Garrison La. Chess 9H 119
Garrison Pde. Purf 5L 83
Garrolds Clo. Swan 6B 114
Garrowsfield. Barn 8K 13
Garry Clo. Romf 7C 34
Garry Way. Romf 7C 34
Garsdale Clo. N11 6E 26
Garsdale Ter. W14 6K 73 (off Aisgill Av.)
Garside Clo. SE28 4B 80
Garside Clo. Hamp 3M 101
Garsington M. SE4 2K 93
Garsmouth Way. Wat 9H 5
Garson Clo. Esh 8K 117
Garson Ho. W2 1B 74 (off Gloucester Ter.)
Garston. 8G 5
Garston Cres. Wat 7G 5
Garston Dri. Wat 7G 5
Garston Gdns. Kenl 7B 138
Garston Ho. N1 3M 59 (off Sutton Est., The)
Garston La. Kenl 6B 138
Garston La. Wat 7H 5
Garston Pk. Pde. Wat 7H 5
Garter Way. SE16 3H 77
Garth Clo. W4 6B 72
Garth Clo. King T 2K 103
Garth Clo. Mord 2H 121
Garth Clo. Ruis 6H 37
Garth Ct. W4 6B 72
Garth Ct. Harr 4D 38 (off Northwick Pk. Rd.)
Garthland Dri. Barn 7F 12
Garth M. W5 7J 55
Garthorne Rd. SE23 6H 93
Garth Rd. NW2 7K 41
Garth Rd. W4 6B 72
Garth Rd. King T 2K 103
Garth Rd. Mord 1G 121
Garth Rd. Ind. Est. Mord 3H 121
Garthside. Ham 2J 103
Garth, The. Ab L 6B 4
Garth, The. Hamp 3M 101
Garth, The. Harr 4K 39
Garthway. N12 6C 26
Gartlet Rd. Wat 5G 9
Gartmoor Gdns. SW19 7K 89
Gartmore Rd. Ilf 7D 48
Garton Pl. SW18 5A 90
Gartons Clo. Enf 6G 17
Gartons Way. SW11 2A 90
Garvary Rd. E16 9F 62
Garway Rd. W2 9M 57
Garwood Clo. N17 8F 28
Gascoigne Gdns. Wfd G 7C 30
Gascoigne Pl. E2 6D 60 (in two parts)
Gascoigne Rd. Bark 4A 64
Gascoigne Rd. New Ad 2A 140
Gascony Av. NW6 3L 57
Gascoyne Clo. Romf 7H 35
Gascoyne Dri. Dart 2D 98
Gascoyne Ho. E9 3J 61
Gascoyne Rd. E9 3H 61
Gaselee St. E14 2A 78 (off Baffin Way)
Gaskarth Rd. SW12 5F 90
Gaskarth Rd. Edgw 8A 24
Gaskell Rd. N6 4D 42
Gaskell St. SW4 1J 91
Gaskin St. N1 4M 59
Gaspar Clo. SW5 5M 73 (off Courtfield Gdns.)
Gaspar M. SW5 5M 73
Gassiot Rd. SW17 1D 106
Gassiot Way. Sutt 5B 122
Gasson Ho. SE14 7H 77 (off John Williams Clo.)
Gastein Rd. W6 7H 73
Gastigny Ho. EC1 6A 60 (off Pleydell Est.)
Gaston Bell Clo. Rich 2K 87
Gaston Bri. Rd. Shep 1B 116
Gaston Rd. Mitc 7E 106
Gaston Way. Shep 9B 100
Gataker Ho. SE16 4F 76 (off Slippers Pl.)
Gataker St. SE16 4F 76
Gatcombe Ct. Beck 4L 109
Gatcombe Ho. SE22 2C 92
Gatcombe M. W5 1K 71
Gatcombe Rd. E16 2E 78
Gatcombe Rd. N19 8H 43
Gatcombe Way. Barn 5D 14
Gateacre Ct. Sidc 1F 112
Gate Cen., The. Bren 8E 70
Gate Cinema. 1L 73 **(off Notting Hill Ga.)**
Gate Clo. Borwd 3A 12
Gate End. N'wd 7E 20
Gateforth St. NW8 7C 58
Gate Hill Ct. W11 2K 73 (off Ladbroke Ter.)
Gatehill Rd. N'wd 7D 20
Gatehouse Clo. King T 4A 104
Gatehouse Sq. SE1 2A 76 (off Porter St.)
Gateley Ho. SE4 3H 93 (off Coston Wlk.)
Gateley Rd. SW9 2K 91
Gate Lodge. W9 8L 57 (off Admiral Wlk.)
Gate M. SW7 3C 74 (off Rutland Ga.)
Gater Dri. Enf 3B 16
Gates. NW9 9D 24
Gatesborough St. EC2 7C 60
Gates Ct. SE17 6A 76
Gatesden. WC1 6J 59
Gates Grn. Rd. W Wick & Kes 5D 126
Gateshead Rd. Borwd 3K 11
Gateside Rd. SW17 9D 90
Gatestone Rd. SE19 3C 108
Gate St. WC2 9K 59
Gate Theatre, The. 2L 73 **(off Pembridge Rd.)**
Gateway. SE17 7A 76
Gateway. Wey 5A 116
Gateway Arc. N1 5M 59 (off Upper St.)
Gateway Clo. N'wd 6A 20
Gateway Ho. Bark 4A 64
Gateway Ind. Est. NW10 6D 56
Gateway M. E8 1D 60
Gateway Retail Pk. E6 7M 63
Gateway Rd. E10 8M 45
Gateways. Surb 9J 103 (off Surbiton Hill Rd.)
Gateways Ct. Wall 7F 122
Gateways, The. SW3 5C 74 (off Sprimont Pl.)
Gateways, The. Rich 3H 87 (off Park La.)
Gatfield Gro. Felt 8L 85
Gatfield Ho. Felt 8K 85
Gathorne Rd. N22 9L 27
Gathorne St. E2 5H 61
Gatley Av. Eps 7M 119
Gatliff Clo. SW1 6F 74 (off Ebury Bri. Rd.)
Gatliff Rd. SW1 6F 74 (in two parts)
Gatling Rd. SE2 6E 80
Gatonby St. SE15 9D 76
Gatting Clo. Edgw 7A 24
Gatting Way. Uxb 2C 142
Gattis Wharf. N1 5J 59 (off New Wharf Rd.)
Gatton Clo. Sutt 1M 135
Gatton Rd. SW17 1C 106
Gattons Way. Sidc 1K 113
Gatward Clo. N21 8M 15
Gatward Grn. N9 2D 28
Gatwick Ho. E14 9K 61 (off Clemence St.)
Gatwick Rd. SW18 6K 89
Gatwick Way. Horn 8K 51
Gauden Clo. SW4 2H 91
Gauden Rd. SW4 1H 91
Gaugin Ct. SE16 6F 76 (off Stubbs Dri.)
Gaumont App. Wat 5F 8
Gaumont Ter. W12 3G 73 (off Lime Gro.)
Gauntlet. NW9 9D 24 (off Five Acre)
Gauntlet Clo. N'holt 3J 53
Gauntlett Ct. Wemb 1F 54
Gauntlett Rd. Sutt 7B 122
Gaunt St. SE1 4A 76
Gautrey Rd. SE15 1G 93
Gautrey Sq. E6 9K 63
Gavel St. SE17 5B 76
Gavestone Cres. SE12 6F 94
Gavestone Rd. SE12 6F 94
Gaviller Pl. E5 9F 44
Gavina Clo. Mord 9C 106
Gawber St. E2 6G 61
Gawsworth Clo. E15 1D 62
Gawthorne Av. NW7 5J 25
Gay Clo. NW2 1F 56

Gaydon Ho. W2 . . . . .8M 57
(off Bourne Ter.)
Gaydon La. NW9 . . . . .8C 24
Gayfere Rd. Eps 7E 120
Gayfere Rd. Ilf 1K 47
Gayfere St. SW1 . . . . .4J 75
Gayford Rd. W12 . . . . .3D 72
Gay Gdns. Dag 9A 50
Gay Ho. N16 . . . . .1C 60
Gayhurst. SE17 . . . . .7B 76
(off Hopwood Rd.)
Gayhurst Ct. N'holt 6G 53
Gayhurst Ho. NW8 . . . . .7C 58
(off Mallory St.)
Gayhurst Rd. E8 . . . . .3E 60
Gaylor Rd. N'holt 1K 53
Gaymead. NW8 . . . . .4M 57
(off Abbey Rd.)
Gaynes Ct. Upm 9M 51
Gaynesford Rd. SE23 . . . . . .8H 93
Gaynesford Rd. Cars 9D 122
Gaynes Hill Rd. Wfd G 6J 31
Gaynes Pk. Rd. Upm 9L 51
Gaynes Rd. Upm 7M 51
Gay Rd. E15 . . . . .5B 62
Gaysham Av. Ilf 3L 47
Gaysham Hall. Ilf 1M 47
Gaysley Ho. SE11 . . . . .5L 75
(off Hotspur St.)
Gay St. SW15 . . . . .2H 89
Gayton Ct. Harr 4D 38
Gayton Cres. NW3 . . . . .9B 42
Gayton Rd. NW3 . . . . .9B 42
Gayton Rd. SE2 . . . . .4G 81
Gayton Rd. Harr 4D 38
Gayville Rd. SW11 . . . . .5D 90
Gaywood Av. Chesh 3D 6
Gaywood Clo. SW2 . . . . .7K 91
Gaywood Rd. E17 . . . . .1L 45
Gaywood St. SE1 . . . . .4M 75
Gaza St. SE17 . . . . .6M 75
Gaze Ho. E14 . . . . .9B 62
(off Blair St.)
Geariesville Gdns. Ilf 2M 47
Geary Rd. NW10 . . . . .1E 56
Geary St. N7 . . . . .1K 59
Geddes Pl. Bexh 3L 97
(off Arnsberga Way)
Geddes Rd. Bush 6A 10
Geddy Ct. Romf 1F 50
Gedeney Rd. N17 . . . . .8A 28
Gedling Pl. SE1 . . . . .4D 76
Geere Rd. E15 . . . . .4D 62
Gees Ct. W1 . . . . .9E 58
Gee St. EC1 . . . . .7A 60
Geffery's Ct. SE9 . . . . .9J 95
Geffrye Ct. N1 . . . . .5C 60
Geffrye Est. N1 . . . . .5C 60
Geffrye Mus. 5D 60
Geffrye St. E2 . . . . .5D 60
Geldart Rd. SE15 . . . . .8F 76
Geldeston Rd. E5 . . . . .7E 44
Gellatly Rd. SE14 . . . . .1G 93
Gelsthorpe Rd. Romf 7M 33
Gemini Bus. Cen. E16 . . . . . .7B 62
Gemini Bus. Est. SE14 . . . . . .6H 77
Gemini Ct. E1 . . . . .1E 76
(off Vaughan Way)
Gemini Gro. N'holt 6J 53
General Gordon Pl. SE18 . . . .5M 79
General's Wlk., The. Enf 1J 17
General Wolfe Rd. SE10 . . . .9B 78
Genesis Clo. Stanw 7D 144
Genesta Rd. SE18 . . . . .7M 79
Geneva Clo. Shep 6C 100
Geneva Ct. NW9 . . . . .3D 40
Geneva Dri. SW9 . . . . .3L 91
Geneva Gdns. Romf 3J 49
Geneva Rd. King T 8J 103
Geneva Rd. T Hth 9A 108
Genever Clo. E4 . . . . .5L 29
Genista Rd. N18 . . . . .5F 28
Genoa Av. SW15 . . . . .4G 89
Genoa Ho. E1 . . . . .7H 61
(off Ernest St.)
Genoa Rd. SE20 . . . . .5G 109
Genotin Rd. Enf 5B 16
Genotin Ter. Enf 6B 16
Gentlemans Row. Enf 5A 16
Gentry Gdns. E13 . . . . .7E 62
Geoffrey Av. Romf 6L 35
Geoffrey Clo. SE5 . . . . .1A 92
Geoffrey Ct. SE4 . . . . .1K 93
Geoffrey Gdns. E6 . . . . .5J 63
Geoffrey Ho. SE1 . . . . .4B 76
(off Pardoner St.)
Geoffrey Jones Ct. NW10 . . . .4E 56
Geoffrey Rd. SE4 . . . . .2K 93
Geographers' A-Z Shop. . . .8L 59
George Beard Rd. SE8 . . . . . .5K 77
George Belt Ho. E2 . . . . .6H 61
(off Smart St.)
George Comberton Wlk.
E12 . . . . .1L 63
George Ct. WC2 . . . . .1J 75
(off John Adam St.)
George Cres. N10 . . . . .7E 26
George Downing Est.
N16 . . . . .7D 44
George Eliot Ho. SW1 . . . . . .5G 75
(off Vauxhall Bri. Rd.)
George Elliston Ho. SE1 . . . . .6E 76
(off Old Kent Rd.)
George Eyre Ho. NW8 . . . . . .5B 58
(off Cochrane St.)
George V Av. Pinn 9K 21
George V Clo. Pinn 1L 37
George V Way. Gnfd 4F 54
George Gange Way. Harr 1C 38
George Gillett Ct. EC1 . . . . . .7A 60
(off Banner St.)
George Gro. Rd. SE20 . . . . .5E 108
George Inn Yd. SE1 . . . . .2B 76
George La. E18 . . . . .9E 30
(in two parts)
George La. SE13 . . . . .5M 93
George La. Brom 3F 126
George Lansbury Ho. N22 . . .8L 27
(off Progress Way)
George Lansbury Ho.
NW10 . . . . .3C 56
George Lindgren Ho.
SW6 . . . . .8K 73
(off Clem Attlee Ct.)
George Loveless Ho. E2 . . . . .6D 60
(off Diss St.)
George Lovell Dri. Enf 1L 17
George Lowe Ct. W2 . . . . . . .8M 57
(off Bourne Ter.)
George Mathers Rd.
SE11 . . . . .5M 75
George M. NW1 . . . . .6G 59
(off N. Gower St.)
George M. Enf 5B 16
(off Town, The)
George Peabody Ct. NW1 . . . .8C 58
(off Bell St.)
George Pl. N17 . . . . .1C 44
George Potter Ho. SW11 . . . .1B 90
(off George Potter Way)
George Potter Way. SW11 . . .1B 90
George Rd. E4 . . . . .6L 29
George Rd. King T 4M 103
(in two parts)
George Rd. N Mald 8D 104
George Row. SE16 . . . . .3E 76
Georges Clo. Orp 7G 113
Georges Mead. Els 8J 11
George Sq. SW19 . . . . .7L 105
George's Rd. N7 . . . . .1K 59
George's Sq. SW6 . . . . .7K 73
(off N. End Rd.)
George St. E16 . . . . .9D 62
George St. W1 . . . . .9D 58
George St. W7 . . . . .2C 70
George St. Bark 3A 64
George St. Croy 4A 124
George St. Houn 1K 85
George St. Rich 4H 87
George St. Romf 4D 50
George St. S'hall 5J 69
George St. Uxb 3B 142
George St. Wat 6G 9
George Tingle Ho. SE1 . . . . . .4D 76
(off Grange Wlk.)
Georgetown Clo. SE19 . . . . .2C 108
Georgette Pl. SE10 . . . . .8A 78
Georgeville Gdns. Ilf 2M 47
George Walter Ct. SE16 . . . . .5G 77
(off Millender Wlk.)
George Wyver Clo. SW19 . . . .6J 89
George Yd. EC3 . . . . .9B 60
George Yd. W1 . . . . .1E 74
Georgiana St. NW1 . . . . .4G 59
Georgian Clo. Brom 3F 126
Georgian Clo. Stan 7E 22
Georgian Ct. E9 . . . . .4G 61
Georgian Ct. N3 . . . . .8K 25
Georgian Ct. NW4 . . . . .3F 40
Georgian Ct. SW16 . . . . . . .1J 107
Georgian Ct. Croy 3B 124
(off Cross Rd.)
Georgian Ct. New Bar 6A 14
Georgian Ct. Wemb 2L 55
Georgian Ho. E16 . . . . .2E 78
(off Capulet M.)
Georgian Way. Harr 7B 38
Georgia Rd. N Mald 8A 104
Georgia Rd. T Hth 5M 107
Georgina Gdns. E2 . . . . .6D 60
Geraint Rd. Brom 1E 110
Geraldine Rd. SW18 . . . . . . .4A 90
Geraldine Rd. W4 . . . . .7L 71
Geraldine St. SE11 . . . . .4M 75
Gerald M. SW1 . . . . .5E 74
(off Gerald Rd.)
Gerald Rd. E16 . . . . .7D 62
Gerald Rd. SW1 . . . . .5E 74
Gerald Rd. Dag 7K 49
Gerald's Gro. Bans 6H 135
Gerard Av. Houn 6L 85
Gerard Gdns. Rain 5C 66
Gerard Rd. SW13 . . . . .9D 72
Gerard Rd. Harr 4E 38
Gerards Clo. SE16 . . . . .6G 77
Gerda Rd. SE9 . . . . .8A 96
Gerdview Dri. Dart 1G 115
Germander Way. E15 . . . . . . .6C 62
Gernon Clo. Rain 5H 67
Gernon Rd. E3 . . . . .5J 61
Geron Way. NW2 . . . . .7F 40
Gerpins La. Upm 5K 67
Gerrard Gdns. Pinn 3E 36
Gerrard Ho. SE14 . . . . .8G 77
(off Briant St.)
Gerrard Pl. W1 . . . . .1H 75
Gerrard Rd. N1 . . . . .5M 59
Gerrards Clo. N14 . . . . .7G 15
Gerrards Ct. W5 . . . . .4H 71
Gerrards Mead. Bans 8K 135
Gerrard St. W1 . . . . .1H 75
Gerridge Ct. SE1 . . . . .4L 75
(off Gerridge St.)
Gerridge St. SE1 . . . . .4L 75
Gerry Raffles Sq. E15 . . . . . .3B 62
Gertrude Rd. Belv 5L 81
Gertrude St. SW10 . . . . .7A 74
Gervase Clo. Wemb 8A 40
Gervase Rd. Edgw 8A 24
Gervase St. SE15 . . . . .8F 76
Gervis Ct. Houn 8A 70
Gews Corner. Chesh 2D 6
Ghent St. SE6 . . . . .8L 93
Ghent Way. E8 . . . . .2D 60
Giant Arches Rd. SE24 . . . . .6A 92
Giant Tree Hill. Bus H 1B 22
Gibbfield Clo. Romf 1J 49
Gibbings Ho. SE1 . . . . .3M 75
(off King James St.)
Gibbins Rd. E15 . . . . .3A 62
(in three parts)
Gibbon Ho. NW8 . . . . .7B 58
(off Fisherton St.)
Gibbon Rd. SE15 . . . . .1G 93
Gibbon Rd. W3 . . . . .1C 72
Gibbon Rd. King T 5J 103
Gibbons Clo. Borwd 3J 11
Gibbon's Rents. SE1 . . . . . . .2C 76
(off Magdalen St.)
Gibbons Rd. NW10 . . . . .2C 56
Gibbon Wlk. SW15 . . . . .3E 88
Gibbs Av. SE19 . . . . .2B 108
Gibbs Clo. SE19 . . . . .3B 108
Gibbs Clo. Chesh 2D 6
Gibbs Couch. Wat 3H 21
Gibbs Grn. W14 . . . . .6K 73
(in two parts)
Gibbs Grn. Edgw 4A 24
Gibbs Grn. Clo. W14 . . . . . . .6K 73
Gibbs Ho. Brom 5D 110
(off Longfield)
Gibb's Rd. N18 . . . . .4G 29
Gibbs Sq. SE19 . . . . .2B 108
Gibney Ter. Brom 1D 110
Gibraltar Cres. Eps 2C 134
Gibraltar Wlk. E2 . . . . .6D 60
(off Padbury Ct.)
Gibson Clo. E1 . . . . .7G 61
Gibson Clo. N21 . . . . .8L 15
Gibson Clo. Chess 7G 119
Gibson Clo. Iswth 2C 86
Gibson Ct. Esh 4D 118
Gibson Gdns. N16 . . . . .7D 44
Gibson Ho. Sutt 6L 121
Gibson M. Twic 5G 87
Gibson Pl. Stanw 5A 144
Gibson Rd. SE11 . . . . .5K 75
Gibson Rd. Dag 6G 49
Gibson Rd. Sutt 7M 121
Gibsons Hill. SW16 . . . . . . .4L 107
Gibson Sq. N1 . . . . .4L 59
Gibson St. SE10 . . . . .6C 78
Gidd Hill. Coul 8E 136
Gidea Av. Romf 1E 50
Gidea Clo. Romf 1E 50
Gidea Park. 1F 50
Gideon Clo. Belv 5M 81
Gideon M. W5 . . . . .3H 71
Gideon Rd. SW11 . . . . .2E 90
Gielgud Theatre. 1H 75
(off Shaftesbury Av.)
Giesbach Rd. N19 . . . . .7H 43
Giffard Rd. N18 . . . . .6C 28
Giffen Sq. Mkt. SE8 . . . . .8L 77
(off Giffen St.)
Giffin St. SE8 . . . . .8L 77
Gifford Gdns. W7 . . . . .8B 54
Gifford Ho. SE10 . . . . .6B 78
(off Eastney St.)
Gifford Ho. SW1 . . . . .6G 75
(off Churchill Gdns.)
Gifford St. N1 . . . . .3J 59
Gift La. E15 . . . . .4D 62
Giggshill. 2E 118
Giggs Hill. Orp 6E 112
Giggshill Gdns. Th Dit 3E 118
Giggshill Rd. Th Dit 2E 118
Gilbert Bri. EC2 . . . . .8A 60
(off Gilbert Ho.)
Gilbert Clo. SE18 . . . . .9K 79
Gilbert Clo. SW19 . . . . .4M 105
(off High Path)
Gilbert Collection. 1K 75
(off Lancaster Pl.)
Gilbert Ct. W5 . . . . .9K 55
(off Green Va.)
Gilbert Gro. Edgw 8B 24
Gilbert Ho. E2 . . . . .6H 61
(off Usk St.)
Gilbert Ho. E17 . . . . .1M 45
Gilbert Ho. EC2 . . . . .8A 60
(off Beech St.)
Gilbert Ho. SE8 . . . . .7L 77
Gilbert Ho. SW1 . . . . .6F 74
(off Churchill Gdns.)
Gilbert Ho. SW8 . . . . .8J 75
(off Wyvil Rd.)
Gilbert Ho. SW13 . . . . .8F 72
(off Trinity Chu. Rd.)
Gilbert Pl. WC1 . . . . .8J 59
Gilbert Rd. SE11 . . . . .5L 75
Gilbert Rd. SW19 . . . . .4A 106
Gilbert Rd. Belv 4L 81
Gilbert Rd. Brom 4E 110
Gilbert Rd. Pinn 2H 37
Gilbert Rd. Romf 2D 50
Gilbert Sheldon Ho. W2 . . . . .8B 58
(off Edgware Rd.)
Gilbertson Ho. E14 . . . . .4L 77
(off Mellish St.)
Gilbert St. E15 . . . . .9C 46
Gilbert St. W1 . . . . .9E 58
Gilbert St. Enf 1G 17
Gilbert St. Houn 2A 86
Gilbert Way. Croy 4K 123
Gilbey Clo. Uxb 9A 36
Gilbey Rd. SW17 . . . . .1C 106
Gilbeys Yd. NW1 . . . . .3E 58
Gilbourne Rd. SE18 . . . . .7D 80
Gilda Av. Enf 7J 17
Gilda Ct. NW7 . . . . .8E 24
Gilda Cres. N16 . . . . .6E 44
Gildea Clo. Pinn 7L 21
Gildea St. W1 . . . . .8F 58
Gilden Cres. NW5 . . . . .1E 58
Gildenhill Rd. Swan 4G 115
Gildersome St. SE18 . . . . . . .7L 79
Gilders Rd. Chess 9K 119
Giles Clo. Rain 5H 67
Giles Coppice. SE19 . . . . . .1D 108
Giles Ho. SE16 . . . . .4E 76
(off Old Jamaica Rd.)
Gilesmead. SE5 . . . . .9B 76
Gilesmead. Eps 6C 134
(off Downside)
Gilfrid Clo. Uxb 9F 142
Gilhams Av. Bans 4H 135
Gilkes Cres. SE21 . . . . .5C 92
Gilkes Pl. SE21 . . . . .5C 92
Gillam Ho. SE16 . . . . .5G 77
(off Silwood St.)
Gillam Way. Rain 2E 66
Gillan Ct. SE12 . . . . .9F 94
Gillan Grn. Bus H 2A 22
Gillards M. E17 . . . . .2L 45
Gillards Way. E17 . . . . .2L 45
Gill Av. E16 . . . . .9E 62
Gill Clo. Wat 8A 8
Gillender St. E3 & E14 . . . . . .7A 62
Gillespie Rd. N5 . . . . .8L 43
Gillett Av. E6 . . . . .5J 63
Gillette Corner (Junct.) 8E 70
Gillett Ho. N8 . . . . .1J 43
(off Campsfield Rd.)
Gillett Pl. N16 . . . . .1C 60
Gillett Rd. T Hth 8B 108
Gillett St. N16 . . . . .1C 60
Gillfoot. NW1 . . . . .5G 59
(off Hampstead Rd.)
Gillham Ter. N17 . . . . .6E 28
Gilliam Gro. Purl 2L 137
Gillian Cres. Romf 9G 35
Gillian Ho. Har W 6C 22
Gillian Pk. Rd. Sutt 3K 121
Gillian St. SE13 . . . . .4M 93
Gillies St. NW5 . . . . .1E 58
Gilling Ct. NW3 . . . . .2C 58
Gillingham Ho. Romf 5J 35
(off Lindfield Rd.)
Gillingham M. SW1 . . . . .5G 75
Gillingham Rd. NW2 . . . . .8J 41
Gillingham Row. SW1 . . . . . .5G 75
Gillingham St. SW1 . . . . .5G 75
Gillings Ct. Barn 6J 13
(off Wood St.)
Gillison Wlk. SE16 . . . . .4F 76
Gillman Dri. E15 . . . . .4D 62
Gillman Ho. E2 . . . . .5E 60
(off Pritchard's Rd.)
Gillmans Rd. Orp 3F 128
Gills Hill La. Rad 1D 10
Gill St. E14 . . . . .9K 61
Gillum Clo. E Barn 1D 26
Gilmore Ct. N11 . . . . .5D 26
Gilmore Rd. SE13 . . . . .3B 94
Gilmour Clo. Enf 8A 6
Gilpin Av. SW14 . . . . .3B 88
Gilpin Clo. Mitc 6C 106
Gilpin Cres. N18 . . . . .5D 28
Gilpin Cres. Twic 6M 85
Gilpin Rd. E5 . . . . .9J 45
Gilpin Way. Hay 8B 68
Gilray Ho. W2 . . . . .1B 74
(off Gloucester Ter.)
Gilroy Clo. Rain 2D 66
Gilroy Way. Orp 2F 128
Gilsland. Wal A 8L 7
Gilsland Rd. T Hth 8B 108
Gilstead Ho. Bark 5F 64
Gilstead Rd. SW6 . . . . .1M 89
Gilston Rd. SW10 . . . . .6A 74
Gilton Rd. SE6 . . . . .9C 94
Giltspur St. EC1 . . . . .9M 59
Gilwell Clo. E4 . . . . .6M 17
Gilwell La. E4 . . . . .6M 17
(in two parts)
Gilwell Park. 6B 18
Gilwell Pk. E4 . . . . .5B 18
Ginsburg Yd. NW3 . . . . .9A 42
Gippeswyck Clo. Pinn 8H 21
Gipsy Hill. SE19 . . . . .1C 108
Gipsy La. SW15 . . . . .2F 88
Gipsy La. Wey 4A 116
Gipsy Moth IV. 7A 78
Gipsy Rd. SE27 . . . . .1A 108
Gipsy Rd. Well 8H 81
Gipsy Rd. Gdns. SE27 . . . . .1A 108
Giralda Clo. E16 . . . . .8H 63
Giraud St. E14 . . . . .9M 61
Girdler's Rd. W14 . . . . .5H 73
Girdlestone Wlk. N19 . . . . . . .7G 43
Girdwood Rd. SW18 . . . . .6J 89
Girling Ho. N1 . . . . .4C 60
(off Colville Est.)
Girling Way. Felt 2E 84
Gironde Rd. SW6 . . . . .8K 73
Girtin Ho. N'holt 5H 53
(off Academy Gdns.)
Girtin Rd. Bush 7M 9
Girton Av. NW9 . . . . .1L 39
Girton Clo. N'holt 2A 54
Girton Ct. Chesh 3E 6
Girton Gdns. Croy 5L 125
Girton Rd. SE26 . . . . .2H 109
Girton Rd. N'holt 2A 54
Girton Vs. W10 . . . . .9H 57
Girton Way. Crox G 7A 8
Gisborne Gdns. Rain 6D 66
Gisbourne Clo. Wall 5H 123
Gisburne Way. Wat 1E 8
Gisburn Ho. SE15 . . . . .7E 76
(off Friary Est.)
Gisburn Rd. N8 . . . . .2K 43
Gissing Wlk. N1 . . . . .3L 59
Gittens Clo. Brom 1D 110
Given Wilson Wlk. E13 . . . . . .5D 62
Glacier Way. Wemb 5H 55
Gladbeck Way. Enf 6M 15
Gladding Rd. E12 . . . . .9H 47
Glade Clo. Surb 4H 119
Glade Ct. Ilf 8K 31
Glade Gdns. Croy 2J 125
Glade La. S'hall 3M 69
Glade Rd. E12 . . . . .8K 47
Gladeside. N21 . . . . .8K 15
Gladeside. Croy 1H 125
Gladeside Clo. Chess 9H 119
Gladesmere Ct. Wat 9F 4
Gladesmore Rd. N15 . . . . . . .4D 44
Glades Pl. Brom 6E 110
Glades Shop. Cen., The.
Brom 6E 110
Gladeswood Rd. Belv 5M 81
Glade, The. N20 . . . . .3B 26
Glade, The. N21 . . . . .8K 15
Glade, The. SE7 . . . . .8G 79
Glade, The. Brom 6H 111
Glade, The. Croy 1J 125
Glade, The. Enf 5L 15
Glade, The. Eps 8E 120
Glade, The. Ilf 8K 31
Glade, The. Sutt 1J 135
Glade, The. W Wick 5M 125
Glade, The. Wfd G 3F 30
Gladeway, The. Wal A 6K 7
Gladiator St. SE23 . . . . .6J 93
Glading Ter. N16 . . . . .8D 44
Gladioli Clo. Hamp 3L 101
Gladsdale Dri. Pinn 2E 36
Gladsmuir Clo. W on T 4G 117
Gladsmuir Rd. N19 . . . . .6G 43
Gladsmuir Rd. Barn 4J 13
Gladstone Av. E12 . . . . .3J 63
Gladstone Av. N22 . . . . .9L 27
Gladstone Av. Felt 5E 84
Gladstone Av. Twic 7B 86
Gladstone Ct. SW1 . . . . .5H 75
(off Regency St.)
Gladstone Ct. Bus. Cen.
SW8 . . . . .9F 74
(off Pagden St.)
Gladstone Gdns. Houn 9A 70
Gladstone Ho. E14 . . . . .9L 61
(off E. India Dock Rd.)
Gladstone M. N22 . . . . .9L 27
Gladstone M. NW6 . . . . .3K 57
(off Cavendish Rd.)
Gladstone M. SE20 . . . . . . .4G 109
Gladstone Pde. NW2 . . . . . . .7G 41
Gladstone Pk. Gdns.
NW2 . . . . .8F 40
Gladstone Pl. E3 . . . . .5K 61
Gladstone Pl. Barn 6H 13
Gladstone Pl. E Mol 9C 102
Gladstone Rd. SW19 . . . . . .4L 105
Gladstone Rd. W4 . . . . .4B 72
Gladstone Rd. Buck H 1G 31
Gladstone Rd. Croy 2B 124
Gladstone Rd. Dart 5K 99
Gladstone Rd. King T 7L 103
Gladstone Rd. Orp 7A 128
Gladstone Rd. S'hall 3J 69
Gladstone Rd. Surb 4H 119
Gladstone Rd. Wat 5G 9
Gladstone St. SE1 . . . . .4M 75

Godwin Clo.—Granada St.

Godwin Clo. N1 5A 60
Godwin Clo. Eps 8A 120
Godwin Ct. NW1 5G 59
(off Chalton St.)
Godwin Ho. NW6 5M 57
(off Tollgate Gdns., in three parts)
Godwin Rd. E7 9F 46
Godwin Rd. Brom 7G 111
Goffers Rd. SE3 9C 78
Goffs La. Craw 2A 6
(in two parts)
Goffs Rd. Ashf 3B 100
Goidel Clo. Wall 6H 123
Golborne Gdns. W10 7J 57
Golborne Ho. W10 7J 57
(off Adair Rd.)
Golborne M. W10 8J 57
Golborne Rd. W10 8J 57
Golda Clo. Barn 8H 13
Golda Ct. N3 9K 25
Goldbeaters Gro. Edgw 6C 24
Goldcliff Clo. Mord 2L 121
Goldcrest Clo. E16 8H 63
Goldcrest Clo. SE28 1G 81
Goldcrest M. W5 8H 55
Goldcrest Way. Bush 1A 22
Goldcrest Way. New Ad 1B 140
Goldcrest Way. Purl 2H 137
Golden Ct. Barn 6C 14
Golden Ct. Rich 4H 87
Golden Cres. Hay 2D 68
Golden Cross M. W11 9K 57
(off Portobello Rd.)
Golden Hinde Educational Mus. 2B 76
Golden Hind Pl. SE8 5K 77
(off Grove St.)
Golden La. EC1 7A 60
Golden La. Est. EC1 7A 60
Golden Mnr. W7 1C 70
Golden M. SE20 5G 109
Golden Pde. E17 1A 46
(off Wood St.)
Golden Plover Clo. E16 9E 62
Golden Sq. W1 1G 75
Golden Yd. NW3 9A 42
(off Holly Mt.)
Golders Clo. Edgw 5M 23
Golders Ct. NW11 5K 41
Golders Gdns. NW11 5J 41
Golders Green. 4J 41
Golders Green Crematorium. NW11 5L 41
Golders Grn. Cres. NW11 5K 41
Golders Grn. Rd. NW11 4J 41
Golderslea. NW11 6L 41
Golders Mnr. Dri. NW11 4H 41
Golders Pk. Clo. NW11 6L 41
Golders Ri. NW4 3H 41
Golders Way. NW11 5K 41
Golderton. NW4 2F 40
(off Prince of Wales Clo.)
Goldfinch Clo. Orp 7E 128
Goldfinch Rd. SE28 4B 80
Goldfinch Rd. S Croy 2J 139
Goldfinch Way. Borwd 6L 11
Goldhawk Ind. Est. W6 4F 72
Goldhawk M. W12 3F 72
Goldhawk Rd. W6 & W12 5D 72
Goldhaze Clo. Wfd G 7H 31
Gold Hill. Edgw 6B 24
Goldhurst Ter. NW6 3M 57
Goldie Ho. N19 5H 43
Golding Clo. Chess 8G 119
Golding Ct. Ilf 8L 47
Goldingham Av. Lou 4M 19
Goldings Hill. Lou 1K 19
Goldings Ri. Lou 3L 19
Goldings Rd. Lou 3L 19
Golding St. E1 9E 60
Golding Ter. E1 9E 60
Golding Ter. SW11 1E 90
Goldington Ct. NW1 4H 59
(off Royal College St.)
Goldington Cres. NW1 5H 59
Goldington St. NW1 5H 59
Gold La. Edgw 6B 24
Goldman Clo. E2 7E 60
Goldmark Ho. SE3 2F 94
Goldney Rd. W9 7L 57
Goldrill Dri. N11 2E 26
Goldrings Rd. Oxs 5A 132
Goldsboro' Rd. SW8 9H 75
Goldsborough Cres. E4 2M 29
Goldsborough Ho. E14 6M 77
(off St Davids Sq.)
Goldsdown Clo. Enf 4J 17
Goldsdown Rd. Enf 4H 17
Goldsel Rd. Swan 9B 114
Goldsmere Ct. Horn 6J 51
Goldsmid St. SE18 6C 80
Goldsmith Av. E12 2J 63
Goldsmith Av. NW9 3C 40
Goldsmith Av. W3 1B 72
Goldsmith Av. Romf 5L 49
Goldsmith Clo. Harr 6M 37
Goldsmith Ct. WC2 9J 59
(off Stukeley St.)
Goldsmith La. NW9 2M 39
Goldsmith Rd. E10 6L 45
Goldsmith Rd. E17 9H 29
Goldsmith Rd. N11 5D 26
Goldsmith Rd. SE15 9E 76
Goldsmith Rd. W3 2B 72
Goldsmith's Bldgs. W3 2B 72
Goldsmiths Clo. W3 2B 72
Goldsmith's Pl. NW6 4M 57
(off Springfield La.)
Goldsmith's Row. E2 5E 60
Goldsmith's Sq. E2 5E 60
Goldsmith St. EC2 9A 60
Goldsworthy Gdns. SE16 6G 77
Goldthorpe. NW1 4G 59
(off Camden St.)
Goldwell Ho. SE22 2C 92
Goldwell Rd. T Hth 8K 107
Goldwin Clo. SE14 9G 77
Goldwing Clo. E16 9E 62
Golf Clo. Bush 5H 9
Golf Clo. Stan 7G 23
Golf Clo. T Hth 5L 107
Golf Club Dri. King T 4B 104
Golfe Rd. Ilf 8B 48
Golf Rd. W5 9K 55
Golf Rd. Brom 7L 111
Golf Rd. Kenl 9B 138
Golf Side. Sutt 3J 135
Golf Side. Twic 9B 86
Golfside Clo. N20 3C 26
Golfside Clo. N Mald 6C 104
Goliath Clo. Wall 9J 123
Gollogly Ter. SE7 6G 79
Gomer Gdns. Tedd 3E 102
Gomer Pl. Tedd 3E 102
Gomm Rd. SE16 4G 77
Gomshall Av. Wall 7J 123
Gomshall Gdns. Kenl 7C 138
Gomshall Rd. Sutt 2G 135
Gondar Gdns. NW6 1K 57
Gonson St. SE8 7M 77
Gonston Clo. SW19 8J 89
Gonville Cres. N'holt 2M 53
Gonville Rd. T Hth 9K 107
Gonville St. SW6 2J 89
Gooch Ho. E5 8F 44
Gooch Ho. EC1 8L 59
(off Portpool La.)
Goodall Ho. SE4 3H 93
Goodall Rd. E11 8A 46
Gooden Ct. Harr 8C 38
Goodenough Rd. SW19 4K 105
Goodey Rd. Bark 3C 64
Goodfaith Ho. E14 1M 77
(off Simpson's Rd.)
Goodge Pl. W1 8G 59
Goodge St. W1 8G 59
Goodhall Clo. Stan 6F 22
Goodhall St. NW10 6D 56
(in two parts)
Goodhart Pl. E14 1J 77
Goodhart Way. W Wick 2C 126
Goodhew Rd. Croy 1E 124
Goodhope Ho. E14 1M 77
(off Poplar High St.)
Gooding Clo. N Mald 8A 104
Goodinge Clo. N7 2J 59
Gooding Ho. SE7 6G 79
Goodman Cres. SW2 8J 91
Goodman Rd. E10 5A 46
Goodman's Ct. E1 1D 76
(off Goodman's Yd.)
Goodmans Ct. Wemb 9H 39
Goodman's Stile. E1 9E 60
Goodmans Yd. E1 1D 76
Goodmayes. 6E 48
Goodmayes Av. Ilf 6E 48
Goodmayes La. Ilf 9E 48
Goodmayes Rd. Ilf 6E 48
Goodmead Rd. Orp 2E 128
Goodrich Clo. Wat 8E 4
Goodrich Ct. W10 9H 57
Goodrich Ho. E2 5G 61
(off Sewardstone Rd.)
Goodrich Rd. SE22 5D 92
Goodson Rd. NW10 3C 56
Goodson St. N1 5L 59
Goodspeed Ho. E14 1M 77
(off Simpson's Rd.)
Goods Way. NW1 5J 59
Goodway Gdns. E14 9B 62
Goodwill Ho. E14 1M 77
(off Simpson's Rd.)
Goodwin Clo. SE16 4D 76
Goodwin Clo. Mitc 7B 106
Goodwin Ct. N8 1J 43
(off Campsbourne Rd.)
Goodwin Ct. SW19 4C 106
Goodwin Ct. Barn 8C 14
Goodwin Ct. Chesh 1E 6
Goodwin Dri. Sidc 9H 97
Goodwin Gdns. Croy 8M 123
Goodwin Ho. N9 1G 29
Goodwin Ho. Wat 8C 8
Goodwin Rd. N9 1H 29
Goodwin Rd. W12 3E 72
Goodwin Rd. Croy 7M 123
Goodwins Ct. WC2 1J 75
Goodwin St. N4 7L 43
Goodwood Av. Enf 1G 17
Goodwood Av. Horn 9J 51
Goodwood Av. Wat 8C 4
Goodwood Clo. Mord 8L 105
Goodwood Clo. Stan 5G 23
Goodwood Ct. W1 8F 58
(off Devonshire St.)
Goodwood Dri. N'holt 2L 53
Goodwood Ho. SE14 9J 77
(off Goodwood St.)
Goodwood Pde. Beck 8J 109
Goodwood Pde. Wat 9C 4
Goodwood Path. Borwd 4L 11
Goodwood Rd. SE14 8J 77
Goodwyn Av. NW7 5C 24
Goodwyns Va. N10 8E 26
Goodyear Ho. N2 9B 26
(off Grange, The)
Goodyear Pl. SE5 7A 76
Goodyer Ho. SW1 6H 75
(off Tachbrook St.)
Goodyers Gdns. NW4 3H 41
Goosander Way. SE28 4B 80
Gooseacre La. Harr 3H 39
Goose Grn. Clo. Orp 6E 112
Goose Grn. Trad. Est. SE22 3D 92
Gooseley La. E6 6L 63
(in three parts)
Goosens Clo. Sutt 7A 122
Goose Sq. E6 9K 63
Gooshays Dri. Romf 5J 35
Gooshays Gdns. Romf 6J 35
Gophir La. EC4 1B 76
Gopsall St. N1 4B 60
Gordon Av. E4 6C 30
Gordon Av. SW14 3C 88
Gordon Av. Horn 7D 50
Gordon Av. S Croy 2A 138
Gordon Av. Stan 7D 22
Gordon Av. Twic 4E 86
Gordonbrock Rd. SE4 4L 93
Gordon Clo. E17 4L 45
Gordon Clo. N19 6G 43
Gordon Ct. W12 9G 57
Gordon Ct. Edgw 5J 23
Gordon Cres. Croy 3C 124
Gordon Cres. Hay 5E 68
Gordondale Rd. SW19 8L 89
Gordon Dri. Shep 2B 116
Gordon Gdns. Edgw 9M 23
Gordon Gro. SE5 1M 91
Gordon Hill. Enf 3A 16
Gordon Ho. E1 1G 77
(off Glamis Rd.)
Gordon Ho. SE10 8M 77
(off Tarves Way)
Gordon Ho. W5 6J 55
Gordon Ho. Rd. NW5 9E 42
Gordon Mans. W14 4H 73
(off Addison Gdns.)
Gordon Mans. WC1 7H 59
(off Torrington Pl.)
Gordon Pl. W8 3L 73
Gordon Rd. E4 9C 18
Gordon Rd. E11 4E 46
Gordon Rd. E15 9A 46
Gordon Rd. E18 8F 30
Gordon Rd. N3 7K 25
Gordon Rd. N9 2F 28
Gordon Rd. N11 7H 27
Gordon Rd. SE15 1F 92
Gordon Rd. W4 7M 71
Gordon Rd. W13 & W5 1F 70
Gordon Rd. Ashf 9C 144
Gordon Rd. Bark 4C 64
Gordon Rd. Beck 7K 109
Gordon Rd. Belv 5A 82
Gordon Rd. Cars 8D 122
Gordon Rd. Chad H 4K 49
Gordon Rd. Clay 9C 118
Gordon Rd. Dart 6H 99
Gordon Rd. Enf 3A 16
Gordon Rd. Harr 1C 38
Gordon Rd. Houn 3A 86
Gordon Rd. Ilf 8B 48
Gordon Rd. King T 5K 103
Gordon Rd. Rich 1K 87
Gordon Rd. Shep 1B 116
Gordon Rd. Sidc 4C 96
Gordon Rd. S'hall 5J 69
Gordon Rd. Surb 2K 119
Gordon Rd. Wal A 7G 7
Gordon Rd. W Dray 1J 143
Gordon Sq. WC1 7H 59
Gordon St. E13 6E 62
Gordon St. WC1 7H 59
Gordon Way. Barn 6K 13
Gordon Way. Brom 5E 110
Gore Ct. NW9 3L 39
Gorefield Ho. NW6 5L 57
(off Gorefield Pl., in three parts)
Gorefield Pl. NW6 5L 57
Gore Rd. E9 4G 61
Gore Rd. SW20 6G 105
Goresbrook Rd. Dag 4F 64
Gore St. SW7 4A 74
Gorham Ho. SE16 3H 77
(off Wolfe Cres.)
Gorham Pl. W11 1J 73
Goring Clo. Romf 8A 34
Goring Gdns. Dag 9G 49
Goring Rd. N11 6J 27
Goring Rd. Dag 2B 66
Goring St. EC3 9C 60
(off Houndsditch)
Goring Way. Gnfd 5A 54
Gorle Clo. Wat 8E 4
Gorleston Rd. N15 3B 44
Gorleston St. W14 5J 73
(in two parts)
Gorman Rd. SE18 5K 79
Gorringe Pk. Av. Mitc 4D 106
Gorse Clo. E16 9E 62
Gorsefield Ho. E14 1L 77
(off E. India Dock Rd.)
Gorse Hill. F'ham 2L 131
Gorse Ri. SW17 2E 106
Gorse Rd. Croy 6L 125
Gorse Rd. Orp 4L 129
Gorse Wlk. W Dray 9C 142
Gorseway. Romf 6C 50
Gorst Rd. NW10 7A 56
Gorst Rd. SW11 5D 90
Gorsuch Pl. E2 6D 60
Gorsuch St. E2 5D 60
Gosberton Rd. SW12 7D 90
Gosbury Hill. Chess 6J 119
Gosfield Rd. Dag 7L 49
Gosfield Rd. Eps 4B 134
Gosfield St. W1 8G 59
Gosford Gdns. Ilf 3K 47
Gosford Ho. Wat 8C 8
Gosforth La. Wat 3E 20
Gosforth Path. Wat 3E 20
Goshawk Gdns. Hay 6C 52
Goslett Yd. WC2 9H 59
Gosling Clo. Gnfd 6L 53
Gosling Ho. E1 1G 77
(off Sutton St.)
Gosling Way. SW9 9L 75
Gospatrick Rd. N17 7A 28
Gospel Oak. 9E 42
Gospel Oak Est. NW5 1D 58
Gosport Dri. Horn 2G 67
Gosport Rd. E17 3K 45
Gosport Wlk. N17 2F 44
Gosport Way. SE15 8D 76
Gossage Rd. SE18 6B 80
Gossage Rd. Uxb 3D 142
Gossamers, The. Wat 7J 5
Gosset St. E2 6D 60
Goss Hill. Swan 3G 115
Gosshill Rd. Chst 6L 111
Gossington Clo. Chst 1M 111
Gosterwood St. SE8 7J 77
Gostling Rd. Twic 7L 85
Goston Gdns. T Hth 7L 107
Goswell Pl. EC1 6M 59
(off Goswell Rd.)
Goswell Rd. EC1 5M 59
Gothic Clo. Dart 9H 99
Gothic Cotts. Enf 4A 16
(off Chase Grn. Av.)
Gothic Ct. SE5 8A 76
(off Wyndham Rd.)
Gothic Ct. Hay 7B 68
Gothic Rd. Twic 8B 86
Gottfried M. NW5 9G 43
Goudhurst Rd. Brom 2C 110
Gough Ho. N1 4M 59
(off Windsor St.)
Gough Ho. King T 6J 103
(off Eden St.)
Gough Rd. E15 9D 46
Gough Rd. Enf 4F 16
Gough Sq. EC4 9L 59
Gough St. WC1 7K 59
Gough Wlk. E14 9L 61
Goulden Ho. SW11 1C 90
Goulden Ho. App. SW11 1C 90
Goulding Gdns. T Hth 6A 108
Gouldman Ho. E1 7G 61
(off Wyllen Clo.)
Gould Rd. Felt 6C 84
Gould Rd. Twic 7C 86
Goulds Green. 9F 142
Gould's Grn. Uxb 1M 143
Gould Ter. E8 1F 60
Goulston St. E1 9D 60
Goulton Rd. E5 9F 44
Gourley Pl. N15 3C 44
Gourley St. N15 3C 44
Gourock Rd. SE9 4L 95
Govan St. E2 4E 60
Gover Ct. SW4 1J 91
Government Row. Enf 2L 17
Govett Av. Shep 9A 100
Govier Clo. E15 3C 62
Gowan Av. SW6 9J 73
Gowan Ho. E2 6D 60
(off Chambord St.)
Gowan Rd. NW10 2F 56
Gower Clo. SW4 5G 91
Gower Ct. WC1 7H 59
Gower Ho. E17 1M 45
Gower Ho. SE17 6A 76
(off Morecambe St.)
Gower M. WC1 8H 59
Gower M. Mans. WC1 8H 59
(off Gower M.)
Gower Pl. WC1 7H 59
Gower Rd. E7 2E 62
Gower Rd. Iswth 7D 70
Gower Rd. Wey 8B 116
Gower St. WC1 7G 59
Gower's Wlk. E1 9E 60
Gowland Pl. Beck 6K 109
Gowlett Rd. SE15 2E 92
Gowrie Rd. SW11 2E 90
Graburn Way. E Mol 7B 102
Grace Av. Bexh 1K 97
Gracechurch St. EC3 1B 76
Grace Clo. SE9 9H 95
Grace Clo. Borwd 3B 12
Grace Clo. Edgw 7A 24
Grace Clo. Ilf 6D 32
Grace Ct. Croy 5M 123
(off Waddon Rd.)
Gracedale Rd. SW16 2F 106
Gracefield Gdns. SW16 9J 91
Gracehill. E1 8G 61
(off Hannibal Rd.)
Grace Ho. SE11 7K 75
(off Vauxhall St.)
Grace Jones Clo. E8 2E 60
Grace M. SE20 6G 109
(off Marlow Rd.)
Grace Path. SE26 1G 109
Grace Pl. E3 6M 61
Grace Rd. Croy 1A 124
Graces All. E1 1E 76
Graces M. NW8 5A 58
Grace's M. SE5 1B 92
Grace's Rd. SE5 1C 92
Grace St. E3 6M 61
Gradient, The. SE26 1E 108
Graduate Pl. SE1 4C 76
(off Long La.)
Graeme Rd. Enf 4B 16
Graemesdyke Av. SW14 2M 87
Grafely Way. SE15 8D 76
Grafton Clo. W13 9E 54
Grafton Clo. Houn 7J 85
Grafton Clo. Wor Pk 5C 120
Grafton Ct. Felt 7B 84
Grafton Cres. NW1 2F 58
Grafton Gdns. N4 4A 44
Grafton Gdns. Dag 7J 49
Grafton Ho. SE8 6K 77
Grafton M. N1 5A 60
(off Frome St.)
Grafton M. W1 7G 59
Grafton Pk. Rd. Wor Pk 4C 120
Grafton Pl. NW1 6H 59
Grafton Rd. NW5 1E 58
Grafton Rd. W3 1A 72
Grafton Rd. Croy 3L 123
Grafton Rd. Dag 6J 49
Grafton Rd. Enf 5K 15
Grafton Rd. Harr 3A 38
Grafton Rd. N Mald 7C 104
Grafton Rd. Wor Pk 5B 120
Grafton Sq. SW4 2G 91
Graftons, The. NW2 8L 41
Grafton St. W1 1F 74
Grafton Ter. NW5 1D 58
Grafton Way. W1 & WC1 7G 59
Grafton Way. W Mol 8K 101
Grafton Yd. NW5 2F 58
Graham Av. W13 3F 70
Graham Av. Mitc 5E 106
Graham Clo. Croy 4L 125
Graham Ct. SE14 7H 77
(off Myers La.)
Graham Ct. N'holt 1K 53
Grahame Park. 8D 24
Grahame Pk. Est. NW9 8C 24
Grahame Pk. Way. NW7 & NW9 7D 24
Grahame White Ho. Kent 1H 39
Graham Gdns. Surb 3J 119
Graham Ho. N9 1G 29
(off Cumberland Rd.)
Graham Lodge. NW4 4F 40
Graham Mans. Bark 3E 64
(off Lansbury Av.)
Graham Rd. E8 2E 60
Graham Rd. E13 6E 62
Graham Rd. N15 1M 43
Graham Rd. NW4 4F 40
Graham Rd. SW19 4K 105
Graham Rd. W4 4B 72
Graham Rd. Bexh 3L 97
Graham Rd. Hamp 1L 101
Graham Rd. Harr 1C 38
Graham Rd. Mitc 5E 106
Graham Rd. Purl 5L 137
Graham St. N1 5M 59
Graham Ter. SW1 5E 74
Graham Ter. Sidc 5F 96
(off Westerham Dri.)
Grainger Clo. N'holt 1M 53
Grainger Ct. SE5 8A 76
Grainger Rd. N22 8A 28
Grainger Rd. Iswth 1D 86
Grainges Yd. Uxb 3A 142
Gramer Clo. E11 7B 46
Gramophone La. Hay 3C 68
Grampian Clo. Hay 8B 68
Grampian Clo. Orp 1D 128
Grampian Gdns. NW2 6J 41
Grampians, The. W6 3H 73
(off Shepherd's Bush Rd.)
Grampion Clo. Sutt 9A 122
Granada St. SW17 2C 106

Granard Av.—Greenacres

Granard Av. SW15 4F 88
Granard Bus. Cen. NW7 6C 24
Granard Ho. E9 2H 61
Granard Rd. SW12 6D 90
Granaries, The. Wal A 7L 7
Granary Clo. N9 9G 17
Granary Mans. SE28 3A 80
(off Erebus Dri.)
Granary Rd. E1 7F 60
Granary Sq. N1 2L 59
Granary St. NW1 4H 59
Granby Pk. Rd. Chesh 1A 6
Granby Pl. SE1 3L 75
(off Station App. Rd.)
Granby Rd. SE9 1K 95
Granby St. E2 7E 60
(in two parts)
Granby Ter. NW1 5G 59
Grand Arc. N12 5A 26
Grand Av. EC1 8M 59
(in three parts)
Grand Av. N10 2E 42
Grand Av. Surb 9M 103
Grand Av. Wemb 1L 55
Grand Av. E. Wemb 1M 55
Grand Depot Rd. SE18 6L 79
Grand Dri. SW20 6G 105
Grand Dri. S'hall 3A 70
Granden Rd. SW16 6J 107
Grandfield Av. Wat 3D 8
Grandfield Ct. W4 7B 72
Grandison Rd. SW11 4D 90
Grandison Rd. Wor Pk 4G 121
Grand Junct. Wharf. N1 5A 60
Grand Pde. N4 3M 43
Grand Pde. SW14 3A 88
(off Up. Richmond Rd. W.)
Grand Pde. Surb 3L 119
Grand Pde. Wemb 7L 39
Grand Pde. M. SW15 4J 89
Grandstand Rd. Eps 9D 134
Grand Union Cen. W10 7H 57
(off West Row)
Grand Union Clo. W9 8K 57
Grand Union Cres. E8 4E 60
Grand Union Enterprise Pk.
S'hall 4L 69
Grand Union Ind. Est.
NW10 5M 55
Grand Union Office Pk., The.
Uxb 9A 142
Grand Union Wlk. NW1 3F 58
(off Kentish Town Rd.)
Grand Union Way. S'hall 3L 69
Grand Vw. Av. Big H 9G 141
Grand Vitesse Ind. Cen.
SE1 2M 75
(off Dolben St.)
Grand Wlk. E1 7J 61
Granfield St. SW11 9B 74
Grange Av. N12 5A 26
Grange Av. N20 9J 13
Grange Av. SE25 6C 108
Grange Av. E Barn 1C 26
Grange Av. Stan 9F 22
Grange Av. Twic 8C 86
Grange Av. Wfd G 6E 30
Grangecliffe Gdns.
SE25 6C 108
Grange Clo. Edgw 5A 24
Grange Clo. Hay 8C 52
Grange Clo. Houn 7K 69
Grange Clo. Sidc 9E 96
Grange Clo. Wat 3E 8
Grange Clo. W Mol 8M 101
Grange Clo. Wfd G 7E 30
Grange Ct. NW10 8C 40
(off Neasden La.)
Grange Ct. WC2 9K 59
Grange Ct. Harr 8D 38
Grange Ct. Lou 7H 19
Grange Ct. N'holt 5G 53
Grange Ct. Pinn 1J 37
Grange Ct. Sutt 9M 121
Grange Ct. Wal A 7J 7
Grange Ct. W on T 4E 116
Grangecourt Rd. N16 6C 44
Grange Cres. SE28 9G 65
Grange Cres. Chig 5B 32
Grange Cres. Dart 5M 99
Grangedale Clo. N'wd 8C 20
Grange Dri. Chst 3J 111
Grange Farm Clo. Harr 7A 38
Grangefield. NW1 3H 59
(off Marquis Rd.)
Grange Gdns. N14 1H 27
Grange Gdns. NW3 8M 41
Grange Gdns. SE25 6C 108
Grange Gdns. Bans 5M 135
Grange Gdns. Pinn 1J 37
Grange Gro. N1 2A 60
Grange Hill. 5B 32
Grange Hill. SE25 6C 108
Grange Hill. Edgw 5A 24
Grangehill Pl. SE9 2K 95
Grangehill Rd. SE9 3K 95
Grange Ho. NW10 3F 56
Grange Ho. SE1 4D 76
Grange Ho. Eri 1E 98
Grange La. SE21 8D 92
Grange La. Let H 3B 10
Grange Lodge. SW19 3H 105
Grange Mans. Eps 9D 120
Grange Mdw. Bans 5M 135
Grange M. Felt 1E 100
Grangemill Rd. SE6 9L 93
Grangemill Way. SE6 8L 93
Grange Mus. of Community
History. 9C 40
Grange Park. 8M 15
Grange Pk. W5 2J 71
Grange Pk. Av. N21 8A 16
Grange Pk. Pl. SW20 4F 104
Grange Pk. Rd. E10 6M 45
Grange Pk. Rd. T Hth 8B 108
Grange Pl. NW6 3L 57
Grange Rd. E10 6L 45
Grange Rd. E13 6D 62
Grange Rd. E17 3J 45
(in two parts)
Grange Rd. N6 4E 42
Grange Rd. N17 & N18 6E 28
Grange Rd. NW10 2F 56
Grange Rd. SE1 4C 76
Grange Rd. SW13 9E 72
Grange Rd. W4 6M 71
Grange Rd. W5 2H 71
Grange Rd. Ave 2M 83
Grange Rd. Bush 7J 9
Grange Rd. Chess 6J 119
Grange Rd. Edgw 6B 24
Grange Rd. Els 7K 11
Grange Rd. Harr 3E 38
Grange Rd. Hay 9C 52
Grange Rd. Ilf 9M 47
Grange Rd. King T 7J 103
Grange Rd. Orp 4B 128
Grange Rd. Romf 6F 34
Grange Rd. S'hall 3J 69
Grange Rd. S Croy 2A 138
Grange Rd. S Harr 7B 38
Grange Rd. Sutt 9L 121
Grange Rd.
T Hth & SE25 8B 108
Grange Rd. W on T 6J 117
Grange Rd. W Mol 8M 101
Granger Way. Romf 4E 50
Grange St. N1 4B 60
Grange, The. E17 3J 45
(off Grange Rd.)
Grange, The. N2 9B 26
Grange, The. N20 1B 26
(Athenaeum Rd.)
Grange, The. N20 1A 26
(Chandos Av.)
Grange, The. SE1 4D 76
Grange, The. SW19 3H 105
Grange, The. W3 3M 71
Grange, The. W4 6M 71
Grange, The. W13 8G 55
Grange, The. W14 5K 73
Grange, The. Ab L 4C 4
Grange, The. Croy 4K 125
Grange, The. N Mald 9D 104
Grange, The. W on T 4F 116
Grange, The. Wemb 3L 55
Grange, The. Wor Pk 6B 120
Grange Va. Sutt 9M 121
Grangeview Rd. N20 1A 26
Grange Wlk. SE1 4C 76
Grange Wlk. M. SE1 4C 76
(off Grange Wlk.)
Grange Way. N12 4M 25
Grange Way. NW6 3L 57
Grange Way. Eri 8F 82
Grange Way. Wfd G 4G 31
Grangeway Gdns. Ilf 3J 47
Grangeway, The. N21 8M 15
Grangewood. Bex 7K 97
Grangewood Av. Rain 7G 67
Grangewood Clo. Pinn 3E 36
Grangewood Dri. Sun 4D 100
Grangewood La. Beck 3K 109
Grangewood St. E6 4H 63
Grangewood Ter. SE25 6B 108
Grange Yd. SE1 4D 76
Granham Gdns. N9 2D 28
Granite St. SE18 6D 80
Granleigh Rd. E11 7C 46
Gransden Av. E8 3F 60
Gransden Ho. SE8 6K 77
Gransden Rd. W12 3D 72
Grantbridge St. N1 5M 59
Grantchester. King T 6L 103
(off St Peters Rd.)
Grantchester Clo. Harr 8D 38
Grant Clo. N14 9G 15
Grant Clo. Shep 1A 116
Grant Ct. E4 1A 30
(off Ridgeway, The)
Grant Ct. NW9 9D 24
(off Hazel Clo.)
Grantham Clo. Edgw 3J 23
Grantham Ct. SE16 3H 77
(off Eleanor Clo.)
Grantham Ct. King T 2H 103
Grantham Ct. Romf 5K 49
Grantham Gdns. Romf 4K 49
Grantham Grn. Borwd 7A 12
Grantham Ho. SE15 7E 76
(off Friary Est.)
Grantham Pl. W1 2F 74
Grantham Rd. E12 9L 47
Grantham Rd. SW9 1J 91
Grantham Rd. W4 8C 72
Grantley Ho. SE14 7H 77
(off Myers La.)
Grantley Rd. Houn 1G 85
Grantley St. E1 6H 61
Grantock Rd. E17 8B 30
Granton Av. Upm 8K 51
Granton Rd. SW16 5G 107
Granton Rd. Ilf 6E 48
Granton Rd. Sidc 3G 113
Grant Pl. Croy 3D 124
Grant Rd. SW11 3B 90
Grant Rd. Croy 3D 124
Grant Rd. Harr 1D 38
Grants Clo. NW7 7G 25
Grants Quay Wharf. EC3 1B 76
Grant St. E13 6E 62
Grant St. N1 5L 59
Grantully Rd. W9 6M 57
Grant Way. Iswth 7E 70
Granville Arc. SW9 3L 91
Granville Av. N9 3G 29
Granville Av. Felt 8E 84
Granville Av. Houn 4L 85
Granville Clo. Croy 4C 124
Granville Clo. Wey 8A 116
Granville Ct. N1 4C 60
(off Colville Est.)
Granville Ct. SE14 8J 77
(off Nynehead St.)
Granville Gdns. SW16 5K 107
Granville Gdns. W5 2K 71
Granville Gro. SE13 2A 94
Granville Ho. E14 9L 61
(off E. India Dock Rd.)
Granville Mans. W12 3G 73
(off Shepherd's Bush Grn.)
Granville M. Sidc 1E 112
Granville M. Stan 5E 22
Granville Pk. SE13 2A 94
Granville Pl. N12 7A 26
Granville Pl. SW6 8M 73
Granville Pl. W1 9E 58
Granville Pl. Pinn 1H 37
Granville Point. NW2 7K 41
Granville Rd. E17 4M 45
Granville Rd. E18 9F 30
Granville Rd. N4 4K 43
Granville Rd. N12 7A 26
Granville Rd. N13 6K 27
Granville Rd. N22 8M 27
Granville Rd. NW2 7K 41
Granville Rd. NW6 5L 57
(in two parts)
Granville Rd. SW18 6K 89
Granville Rd. SW19 4L 105
Granville Rd. Barn 6G 13
Granville Rd. Hay 5D 68
Granville Rd. Ilf 6M 47
Granville Rd. Sidc 1E 112
Granville Rd. Uxb 2F 142
Granville Rd. Wat 6G 9
Granville Rd. Well 2G 97
Granville Rd. Wey 9A 116
Granville Sq. SE15 8C 76
Granville Sq. WC1 6K 59
Granville St. WC1 6K 59
Granwood Ct. Iswth 9C 70
Grape St. WC2 9J 59
Graphite Sq. SE11 6K 75
Grapsome Clo. Chess 9G 119
Grasdene Rd. SE18 8E 80
Grasgarth Clo. W3 1A 72
Grasmere. NW1 6F 58
(off Osnaburgh St.)
Grasmere Av. SW15 1B 104
Grasmere Av. SW19 7L 105
Grasmere Av. W3 1B 72
Grasmere Av. Houn 5M 85
Grasmere Av. Orp 5M 127
Grasmere Av. Ruis 5A 36
Grasmere Av. Wemb 5G 39
Grasmere Clo. Felt 7D 84
Grasmere Clo. Lou 4K 19
Grasmere Clo. Wat 5F 4
Grasmere Ct. N22 6K 27
Grasmere Ct. SE26 2E 108
Grasmere Ct. SW13 7E 72
(off Verdun Rd.)
Grasmere Ct. Sutt 8A 122
Grasmere Gdns. Harr 9E 22
Grasmere Gdns. Ilf 3K 47
Grasmere Gdns. Orp 5M 127
Grasmere Point. SE15 8G 77
(off Old Kent Rd.)
Grasmere Rd. E13 5E 62
Grasmere Rd. N10 8F 26
Grasmere Rd. N17 6E 28
Grasmere Rd. SE25 1F 124
Grasmere Rd. SW16 2K 107
Grasmere Rd. Bexh 1A 98
Grasmere Rd. Brom 5D 110
Grasmere Rd. Orp 5M 127
Grasmere Rd. Purl 3M 137
Grasshaven Way. SE28 2D 80
(in two parts)
Grassington Clo. N11 6E 26
Grassington Clo. Brick W 3L 5
Grassington Rd. Sidc 1E 112
Grassmere Rd. Horn 2K 51
Grassmount. SE23 8F 92
Grassmount. Purl 2G 137
Grass Pk. N3 8K 25
Grass Way. Wall 6G 123
Grasvenor Av. Barn 7L 13
Gratton Rd. W14 4J 73
Gratton Ter. NW2 8H 41
Gravel Clo. Chig 2E 32
Graveley Av. Borwd 7A 12
Gravel Hill. N3 9K 25
Gravel Hill. Bexh 4M 97
Gravel Hill. Croy 8H 125
Gravel Hill. Lou 2E 18
Gravel Hill. Uxb 1B 142
Gravel Hill Clo. Bexh 4M 97
Gravel La. E1 9D 60
Gravel La. Chig 1E 32
Gravel Pit La. SE9 4M 95
Gravel Pit Way. Orp 4E 128
Gravel Rd. Brom 5J 127
Gravel Rd. S at H 4M 115
Gravel Rd. Twic 7C 86
Gravelwood Clo. Chst 9A 96
Gravely Ho. SE8 5J 77
(off Chilton Gro.)
Gravenel Gdns. SW17 2C 106
(off Nutwell St.)
Graveney Gro. SE20 4G 109
Graveney Rd. SW17 1C 106
Gravesend Rd. W12 1E 72
Gray Av. Dag 6K 49
Gray Gdns. Rain 2E 66
Grayham Cres. N Mald 8A 104
Grayham Rd. N Mald 8B 104
Gray Ho. SE17 6A 76
(off King & Queen St.)
Grayland Clo. Brom 5H 111
Grayling Clo. E16 7C 62
Grayling Ct. W5 2H 71
(off Grange Rd.)
Grayling Rd. N16 7B 44
Grayling Sq. E2 6E 60
(off Nelson Gdns.)
Graylings, The. Ab L 6B 4
Grays Ct. Dag 3M 65
Grayscroft Rd. SW16 4H 107
Grays Farm Production Village.
Orp 5F 112
Grays Farm Rd. Orp 5F 112
Grayshott Rd. SW11 1E 90
Gray's Inn. 8K 59
Gray's Inn Bldgs. EC1 7L 59
(off Rosebery Av.)
Gray's Inn Pl. WC1 8K 59
Gray's Inn Rd. WC1 6J 59
Gray's Inn Sq. WC1 8K 59
Grays La. Ashf 9F 144 & 1A 100
Grayson Ho. EC1 6A 60
(off Pleydell Est.)
Grays Rd. Uxb 5C 142
Gray St. SE1 3L 75
Grayswood Gdns.
SW20 6F 104
Gray's Yd. W1 9E 58
(off James St.)
Graywood Ct. N12 7A 26
Grazebrook Rd. N16 7B 44
Grazeley Clo. Bexh 4A 98
Grazeley Ct. SE19 2C 108
Gt. Acre Ct. SW4 3H 91
Gt. Arthur Ho. EC1 7A 60
(off Golden La. Est.)
Gt. Bell All. EC2 9B 60
Great Benty. W Dray 5J 143
Great Brownings. SE21 1D 108
Great Burgh. 9G 135
Gt. Bushey Dri. N20 1M 25
Gt. Cambridge Ind. Est.
Enf 7F 16
Great Cambridge Junction
(Junct.) 5A 28
Gt. Cambridge Rd.
N18 & N9 4B 28
Gt. Cambridge Rd. Chesh 7C 6
Gt. Castle St. W1 9F 58
Gt. Central Av. Ruis 1G 53
Gt. Central St. NW1 8D 58
Gt. Central Way.
Wemb & NW10 9A 40
Gt. Chapel St. W1 9H 59
Gt. Chertsey Rd. W4 1A 88
Gt. Chertsey Rd.
Felt & Twic 9K 85
Gt. Church La. W6 5H 73
Gt. College St. SW1 4J 75
Great Cft. WC1 6J 59
(off Cromer St.)
Gt. Cross Av. SE10 8B 78
(in three parts)
Great Cullings. Romf 7C 50
Gt. Cumberland M. W1 9D 58
Gt. Cumberland Pl. W1 9D 58
Gt. Dover St. SE1 3A 76
Greatdown Rd. W7 7D 54
Gt. Eastern Bldgs. E1 8E 60
(off Fieldgate St.)
Gt. Eastern Enterprise Cen.
E14 3M 77
Gt. Eastern Rd. E15 3B 62
Gt. Eastern St. EC2 6C 60
Gt. Eastern Wlk. EC2 8C 60
(off Bishopsgate)
Gt. Eastern Wharf. SW11 8C 74
Great Ellshams. Bans 8L 135
Gt. Elms Rd. Brom 8G 111
Great Fld. NW9 8C 24
Greatfield Av. E6 7K 63
Greatfield Clo. N19 9G 43
Greatfield Clo. SE4 3L 93
Greatfields Dri. Uxb 8E 142
Greatfields Rd. Bark 4B 64
Gt. Fleete Way. Bark 5G 65
Gt. Galley Clo. Bark 6F 64
Gt. Gardens Rd. Horn 4F 50
Gt. Gatton Clo. Croy 2J 125
Gt. George St. SW1 3H 75
Great Gro. Bush 6M 9
Gt. Guildford Bus. Sq.
SE1 2A 76
(off Gt. Guildford St.)
Gt. Guildford St. SE1 2A 76
Great Hall. 6D 74
(Royal Hospital Chelsea)
Greatham Rd. Bush 5H 9
Greatham Wlk. SW15 7E 88
Gt. Harry Dri. SE9 9L 95
Gt. James St. WC1 8K 59
Gt. Marlborough St. W1 9G 59
Gt. Maze Pond. SE1 3B 76
(in two parts)
Gt. Nelmes Chase. Horn 3K 51
Gt. Newport St. WC2 1J 75
Gt. New St. EC4 9L 59
Gt. N. Leisure Pk. N12 7B 26
Gt. North Rd. N2 & N6 3C 42
Gt. North Rd. Barn 4K 13
Gt. North Rd. New Bar 7L 13
Gt. North Way. NW4 9F 24
Great Oaks. Chig 4A 32
Greatorex Ho. E1 8E 60
(off Greatorex St.)
Greatorex St. E1 8E 60
Gt. Ormond St. WC1 8J 59
Gt. Owl Rd. Chig 3L 31
Gt. Percy St. WC1 6K 59
Gt. Peter St. SW1 4H 75
Gt. Portland St. W1 7F 58
Gt. Pulteney St. W1 1G 75
Gt. Queen St. WC2 9J 59
Gt. Queen St. Dart 6K 99
Gt. Russell St. WC1 9H 59
Gt. St Helen's. EC3 9C 60
Gt. St Thomas Apostle.
EC4 1A 76
Gt. Scotland Yd. SW1 2J 75
Gt. Smith St. SW1 4H 75
Gt. South W. Rd.
Bedf & Felt 6A 84
Great Spilmans. SE22 4C 92
Great Strand. NW9 8D 24
Gt. Suffolk St. SE1 2M 75
Gt. Sutton St. EC1 7M 59
Gt. Swan All. EC2 9B 60
(in two parts)
Great Tattenhams. Eps 9H 135
Great Thrift. Orp 8A 112
Gt. Titchfield St. W1 7F 58
Gt. Tower St. EC3 1C 76
Gt. Trinity La. EC4 1A 76
Great Turnstile. WC1 8K 59
Gt. Western Ind. Pk.
S'hall 3M 69
Gt. Western Rd.
W9 & W11 8K 57
Gt. West Rd. W4 & W6 6D 72
Gt. West Rd. Houn 1H 85
Gt. West Rd.
Iswth & Bren 8C 70
Gt. West Trad. Est. Bren 7F 70
Gt. Winchester St. EC2 9B 60
Gt. Windmill St. W1 1H 75
Greatwood. Chst 4L 111
Gt. Woodcote Dri. Purl 2H 137
Gt. Woodcote Pk. Purl 2H 137
Great Yd. SE1 3C 76
(off Crucifix La.)
Greaves Clo. Bark 3B 64
Greaves Cotts. E14 8J 61
Greaves Pl. SW17 1C 106
Greaves Tower. SW10 8A 74
(off Worlds End Est.)
Grebe Av. Hay 9H 53
Grebe Clo. E7 1D 62
Grebe Clo. E17 7J 29
Grebe Ct. E14 3A 78
(off River Barge Clo.)
Grebe Ct. SE8 7K 77
(off Dorking Clo.)
Grebe Ct. Sutt 7K 121
Grebe Ter. King T 7J 103
Grecian Cres. SE19 3M 107
Greek Ct. W1 9H 59
Greek St. W1 9H 59
Greenacre. Dart 8H 99
Greenacre Clo. Barn 2K 13
Greenacre Clo. N'holt 1K 53
Greenacre Clo. Swan 8C 114
Greenacre Gdns. E17 2A 46
Greenacre Pl. Hack 4F 122
Greenacres. N3 9K 25
Greenacres. SE9 5L 95

Greenacres—Gresse St.

Greenacres. Bus H 2B 22
Green Acres. Croy 5D 124
Greenacres. Sidc 1E 112
Greenacres Clo. Orp 6A 128
Greenacres Clo. Rain 6J 67
Greenacres Dri. Stan 6F 22
Greenacre Sq. SE16 . . . . .3H 77
Greenacre Wlk. N14 . . . . .3H 27
Greenall Clo. Chesh 3E 6
Grn. Arbour Ct. EC4 . . . . . . .9M 59
(off Old Bailey)
Green Av. NW7 . . . . .4B 24
Green Av. W13 . . . . .4F 70
Greenaway Av. N18 . . . . .6H 29
Greenaway Gdns.
NW3 . . . . .9M 41
Greenaway Ho. NW8 . . . . . . .4A 58
(off Boundary Rd.)
Greenaway Ho. WC1 . . . . . . .6L 59
(off Fernsbury St.)
Green Bank. E1 . . . . .2F 76
Greenbank. N12 . . . . .4M 25
Greenbank. Chesh 1B 6
Greenbank Av. Wemb 1E 54
Grn. Bank Clo. E4 . . . . .2A 30
Greenbank Clo. Romf 3H 35
Greenbank Cres. NW4 . . . . . .2J 41
Greenbank Rd. Wat 9B 4
Greenbanks. Dart 8J 99
Greenbanks. Harr 9C 38
Greenbay Rd. SE7 . . . . .8H 79
Greenberry St. NW8 . . . . . . .5C 58
Greenbrook Av. Barn 3A 14
Green Clo. E15 . . . . .4C 62
Green Clo. NW9 . . . . .4A 40
Green Clo. NW11 . . . . .5A 42
Green Clo. Brom 7C 110
Green Clo. Cars 4D 122
Green Clo. Chesh 4E 6
Green Clo. Felt 2J 101
Greencoat Mans. SW1 . . . . . .4G 75
(off Greencoat Row)
Greencoat Pl. SW1 . . . . .5G 75
Greencoat Row. SW1 . . . . . .4G 75
Greencourt Av. Croy 4F 124
Greencourt Av. Edgw 8M 23
Greencourt Gdns. Croy 3F 124
Greencourt Ho. E1 . . . . .7H 61
(off Mile End Rd.)
Greencourt Rd. Orp 9B 112
Green Ct. Rd. Swan 1B 130
Greencrest Pl. NW2 . . . . .8E 40
Greencroft. Edgw 5A 24
Greencroft Av. Ruis 7G 37
Greencroft Clo. E6 . . . . .8H 63
Greencroft Gdns. NW6 . . . . .3M 57
Greencroft Gdns. Enf 5C 16
Greencroft Rd. Houn 9K 69
Green Curve. Bans 6K 135
Greendale. NW7 . . . . .4C 24
Green Dale. SE5 . . . . .3B 92
Green Dale. SE22 . . . . .4C 92
Grn. Dale Clo. SE22 . . . . . . .4C 92
Grn. Dragon Ct. SE1 . . . . . . .2B 76
(off Bedale St.)
Grn. Dragon La. N21 . . . . . . .8L 15
Grn. Dragon La. Bren 6J 71
Grn. Dragon Yd. E1 . . . . .8E 60
Green Dri. S'hall 2L 69
Greene Ct. SE14 . . . . .7H 77
(off Samuel Clo.)
Green Edge. Wat 8E 4
Greene Ho. SE1 . . . . .4B 76
(off Burbage Clo.)
Green End. N21 . . . . .2M 27
Green End. Chess 6J 119
Greenend Rd. W4 . . . . .3C 72
Greener Ho. SW4 . . . . .2H 91
Grn. Farm Clo. Orp 8D 128
Greenfell Mans. SE8 . . . . . . .7M 77
Greenfield Av. Surb 2M 119
Greenfield Av. Wat 2H 21
Greenfield Dri. N2 . . . . .2D 42
Greenfield Dri. Brom 6G 111
Greenfield Gdns. NW2 . . . . . .7J 41
Greenfield Gdns. Dag 4H 65
Greenfield Gdns. Orp 2B 128
Greenfield Link. Coul 7J 137
Greenfield Rd. E1 . . . . .8E 60
Greenfield Rd. N15 . . . . .3C 44
Greenfield Rd. Dag 3G 65
Greenfield Rd. Dart 2B 114
Greenfields. Lou 6L 19
Greenfields. S'hall 9L 53
Greenfields Clo. Lou 6L 19
Greenfield St. Wal A 7J 7
Greenfield Way. Harr 1M 37
Greenford. 6A 54
Greenford Av. W7 . . . . .7C 54
Greenford Av. S'hall 1K 69
Greenford Bus. Cen. Gnfd . . .3B 54
Greenford Gdns. Gnfd 6M 53
Greenford Green. 2C 54
Greenford Ind. Est. N'holt . . .3M 53
Greenford Rd. S'hall 2A 70
Greenford Rd. Sutt 6M 121
(in two parts)
Greenford Roundabout (Junct.)
. . . . .5B 54
Green Gdns. Orp 7A 128
Greengate. Gnfd 2F 54
Greengate Lodge. E13 . . . . . .5F 62
(off Hollybush St.)
Greengate St. E13 . . . . .5F 62
Green Glades. Horn 4K 51
Greenhalgh Wlk. N2 . . . . .2A 42
Greenham Clo. SE1 . . . . .3L 75
Greenham Cres. E4 . . . . .6K 29
Greenham Ho. E9 . . . . .4G 61
(off Templecombe Rd.)
Greenham Ho. Houn 2B 86
Greenham Rd. N10 . . . . .9E 26
Greenhaven Dri. SE28 . . . . . .9F 64
Greenhayes Av. Bans 6L 135
Greenhayes Gdns. Bans 7L 135
Greenheath Bus. Cen. E2 . . . .7F 60
(off Three Colts La.)
Green Hedge. Twic 4G 87
Greenheys Clo. N'wd 8C 20
Greenheys Dri. E18 . . . . .1D 46
Greenhill. 3C 38
Greenhill. NW3 . . . . .9B 42
Green Hill. SE18 . . . . .6K 79
Greenhill. Buck H 1G 31
Green Hill. Orp 4K 141
Greenhill. Sutt 4A 122
Greenhill. Wemb 7M 39
Greenhill Ct. SE18 . . . . .6K 79
Greenhill Ct. New Bar 7M 13
Greenhill Cres. Wat 8B 8
Greenhill Gdns. N'holt 5K 53
Greenhill Gro. E12 . . . . .9J 47
Grn. Hill La. Warl 9J 139
Greenhill Pde. New Bar 7M 13
Greenhill Pk. NW10 . . . . .4C 56
Greenhill Pk. New Bar 7M 13
Greenhill Rd. NW10 . . . . .4C 56
Greenhill Rd. Harr 4C 38
Greenhill Rd. Wat 8C 8
Greenhill's Rents. EC1 . . . . . .8M 59
Greenhills Ter. N1 . . . . .2B 60
Greenhill Ter. SE18 . . . . .6K 79
Greenhill Ter. N'holt 5K 53
Greenhill Way. Harr 4C 38
Greenhill Way. Wemb 7M 39
Greenhithe Clo. Sidc 6C 96
Greenholm Rd. SE9 . . . . .4M 95
Grn. Hundred Rd. SE15 . . . . . .7E 76
Greenhurst Rd. SE27 . . . . . .2L 107
Greening St. SE2 . . . . .5G 81
Greenland Cres. S'hall 4G 69
Greenland Ho. E1 . . . . .7J 61
(off Ernest St.)
Greenland M. SE8 . . . . .6H 77
Greenland Pl. NW1 . . . . .4F 58
Greenland Quay. SE16 . . . . . .5H 77
Greenland Rd. NW1 . . . . .4G 59
Greenland Rd. Barn 8G 13
Greenlands Rd. Wey 5A 116
Greenland St. NW1 . . . . .4F 58
Green La. E4 . . . . .3C 18
Green La. NW4 . . . . .2H 41
Green La. SE9 & Chst 7M 95
Green La. SE20 . . . . .4H 109
Green La. SW16 & T Hth 4K 107
Green La. W7 . . . . .3C 70
Green La. Asht 9G 133
Green La. Chess 1H 133
(in two parts)
Green La. Chig 1A 32
Green La. Edgw 4K 23
Green La. Felt 2J 101
Green La. Harr 8C 38
Green La. Houn 2F 84
Green La. Ilf 7B 48
Green La. Mord 2G 121
(Battersea Cemetery)
Green La. Mord 1L 121
(Morden)
Green La. N Mald 9A 104
Green La. N'wd 6B 20
Green La. Purl 3G 137
Green La. Shep 1A 116
Green La. Stan 4F 22
Green La. Sun 4D 100
Green La. Uxb 8A 52
Green La. W on T 8F 116
Green La. Warl 8J 139
Green La. Wat 9G 9
Green La. W Mol 9M 101
Green La. Wor Pk 3E 120
Green La. Av. W on T 7G 117
Green La. Cotts. Stan 4F 22
Green La. Gdns. T Hth 6A 108
Green Lanes. N8 & N4 . . . . . .1M 43
Green Lanes. N13 & N21 . . . . .3L 27
Green Lanes. Eps 1C 134
(in two parts)
Greenlaw Ct. W5 . . . . .9H 55
(off Mt. Park Rd.)
Greenlaw Gdns. N Mald 2D 120
Greenlawns. N12 . . . . .6M 25
Green Lawns. Ruis 6G 37
Greenlaw St. SE18 . . . . .4L 79
Grn. Leaf Av. Wall 6H 123
Greenleaf Clo. SW2 . . . . .6L 91
Greenleafe Dri. Ilf 1M 47
Greenleaf Rd. E6 . . . . .4G 63
Greenleaf Rd. E17 . . . . .1K 45
Green Leas. King T 7J 103
(off Mill St.)
Green Leas. Sun 3D 100
Greenleas. Wal A 7L 7
Grn. Leas Clo. Sun 3D 100
Greenleaves Ct. Ashf 3A 100
Greenleigh Av. St P 8F 112
Grn. Man Gdns. W13 . . . . . . .1E 70
Grn. Man La. W13 . . . . .1E 70
Grn. Man La. Felt 3E 84
(Faggs Rd.)
Grn. Man La. Felt 3F 84
(Heron Way)
Green Man Pas. W13 . . . . . . .1F 70
(in two parts)
Green Man Roundabout (Junct.)
. . . . .4D 46
Greenman St. N1 . . . . .3A 60
Greenmead. Eri 4J 81
Green Mead. Esh 8K 117
Greenmead Clo. SE25 . . . . .9E 108
Green Moor Link. N21 . . . . . .9M 15
Greenmoor Rd. Enf 4G 17
Greenoak Pl. Cockf 4D 14
Green Oaks. S'hall 5H 69
Greenoak Way. SW19 . . . . . .1H 105
Greenock Rd. SW16 . . . . . . .5H 107
Greenock Rd. W3 . . . . .4M 71
Greenock Way. Romf 7C 34
Green Pde. Houn 4M 85
Green Pk. 3F 74
Greenpark Ct. Wemb 3G 55
Grn. Park Way. Gnfd 3C 54
(in two parts)
Green Pl. Dart 4C 98
Green Point. E15 . . . . .2C 62
Grn. Pond Clo. E17 . . . . .1J 45
Grn. Pond Rd. E17 . . . . .1J 45
Green Ride. Lou 6G 19
(in two parts)
Green Rd. N14 . . . . .8F 14
Green Rd. N20 . . . . .3A 26
Greens Clo., The. Lou 4L 19
Green's Ct. W1 . . . . .1H 75
(off Brewer St.)
Green's End. SE18 . . . . .5M 79
Greenshank Clo. E17 . . . . . . .7J 29
Greenshields Ind. Est. E16 . . .3E 78
Greenside. Bex 7J 97
Greenside. Borwd 2L 11
Green Side. Dag 6G 49
Greenside. Swan 6B 114
Greenside Clo. N20 . . . . .2B 26
Greenside Clo. SE6 . . . . .8B 94
Greenside Rd. W12 . . . . .4E 72
Greenside Rd. Croy 2L 123
Greenslade Rd. Bark 3B 64
Grn. Slip Rd. Barn 4K 13
Greenstead Av. Wfd G 7G 31
Greenstead Clo. Wfd G 6G 31
Greenstead Gdns. SW15 . . . .4F 88
Greenstead Gdns. Wfd G 6G 31
Greensted Rd. Lou 9J 19
Greenstone M. E11 . . . . .4E 46
Green St. E7 & E13 . . . . .2F 62
Green St. W1 . . . . .1E 74
Green St. Enf 4G 17
Green St. Shenl & Borwd 1L 11
Green St. Sun 5E 100
Green Street Green. 8D 128
Green St. Grn. Rd. Dart 7M 99
(in three parts)
Greenstreet Hill. SE14 . . . . . .1H 93
Greensward. Bush 8M 9
Green Ter. EC1 . . . . .6L 59
Green, The. E4 . . . . .1A 30
Green, The. E11 . . . . .4F 46
Green, The. E15 . . . . .2C 62
Green, The. N9 . . . . .2E 28
Green, The. N14 . . . . .2H 27
Green, The. N17 . . . . .6A 28
Green, The. N21 . . . . .9L 15
Green, The. SW19 . . . . .2H 105
Green, The. W3 . . . . .9C 56
Green, The. W5 . . . . .2H 71
Green, The. Bexh 9L 81
Green, The. Brom 9E 94
(in two parts)
Green, The. Buck H 1F 30
Green, The. Cars 6E 122
Green, The. Chesh 1C 6
Green, The. Clay 8D 118
Green, The. Croy 1K 139
Green, The. Eps 3E 134
Green, The. Felt 8F 84
Green, The. Hav 3C 34
Green, The. Hayes 2E 126
Green, The. Hers 7G 117
Green, The. Houn 7L 69
Green, The. Ick 7A 36
Green, The. Let H 3C 10
Green, The. Mord 8J 105
Green, The. N Mald 7B 104
Green, The. Noak H 2G 35
Green, The. Orp (BR5) 4F 112
Green, The. Orp (BR6) 6M 127
Green, The. Rich 4H 87
Green, The. Shep 8C 100
Green, The. Sidc 1E 112
Green, The. S'hall 4J 69
Green, The. Sutt 5M 121
Green, The. Twic 7C 86
Green, The. Wal A 7J 7
Green, The. Warl 9H 139
Green, The. Well 3C 96
Green, The. Wemb 7E 38
Green, The. Wen 1J 83
Green, The. W Dray 4H 143
Green, The. Wfd G 5E 30
Green Va. W5 . . . . .9K 55
Green Va. Bexh 4H 97
Greenvale Rd. SE9 . . . . .3K 95
Green Verges. Stan 7H 23
Green Vw. Chess 9K 119
Greenview Av. Beck 1J 125
Greenview Av. Croy 1J 125
Greenview Clo. W3 . . . . .2C 72
Greenview Ct. Ashf 9D 144
Green Wlk. NW4 . . . . .3H 41
Green Wlk. SE1 . . . . .4C 76
Green Wlk. Dart 4D 98
Green Wlk. Hamp 3K 101
Green Wlk. Lou 9J 19
Green Wlk. Ruis 6D 36
Green Wlk. S'hall 6L 69
Green Wlk. Wfd G 6J 31
Green Wlk., The. E4 . . . . .1B 30
Greenway. N14 . . . . .2J 27
Greenway. N20 . . . . .2L 25
Green Way. SE9 . . . . .4H 95
Greenway. SW20 . . . . .8G 105
Green Way. Brom 1J 127
Greenway. Chst 2L 111
Greenway. Dag 7G 49
Greenway. Hay 6E 52
Greenway. Kent 3J 39
Greenway. Pinn 9F 20
Greenway. Romf 6M 35
Green Way. Sun 8E 100
Greenway. Wall 6G 123
Green Way. Wfd G 5G 31
Greenway Av. E17 . . . . .2B 46
Greenway Clo. N4 . . . . .7A 44
Greenway Clo. N11 . . . . .6E 26
Greenway Clo. N15 . . . . .2D 44
Greenway Clo. N20 . . . . .2L 25
Greenway Clo. NW9 . . . . .9B 24
Greenway Gdns. NW9 . . . . . . .9B 24
Greenway Gdns. Croy 5K 125
Greenway Gdns. Gnfd 6L 53
Greenway Gdns. Harr 9C 22
Greenways. Ab L 5C 4
Greenways. Beck 7L 109
Greenways. Esh 6C 118
Greenways Ct. Horn 4H 51
Greenways, The. Twic 5E 86
Greenway, The. NW9 . . . . . . .9B 24
Greenway, The. Enf 8D 6
Greenway, The. Eps 6L 133
Greenway, The. Houn 3K 85
Greenway, The. Ick 7A 36
Greenway, The. Orp 1F 128
Green Way, The. Pinn 4K 37
Greenway, The. Uxb 5B 142
Green Way, The. W'stone 8C 22
Greenwell St. W1 . . . . .7F 58
Greenwich. 8A 78
Greenwich Bus. Pk. SE10 . . .8M 77
Greenwich Chu. St. SE10 . . . .7A 78
Greenwich Cinema. 8A 78
Greenwich Commercial Cen.
SE10 . . . . .8M 77
Greenwich Ct. E1 . . . . .9F 60
(off Cavell St.)
Greenwich Ct. Wal X 7E 6
Greenwich Cres. E6 . . . . .8J 63
Greenwich Gateway Vis. Cen.
. . . . .7A 78
Greenwich High Rd.
SE10 . . . . .9M 77
Greenwich Ind. Est. SE7 . . . . .5F 78
Greenwich Ind. Est. SE10 . . .8M 77
Greenwich Mkt. SE10 . . . . . . .7A 78
Greenwich Pk. 8B 78
Greenwich Pk. St. SE10 . . . . .7B 78
Greenwich Quay. SE8 . . . . . .7M 77
Greenwich S. St. SE10 . . . . .9M 77
Greenwich University. 4L 79
(Beresford St.)
Greenwich University. 5A 96
(Besley Rd., Avery Hill Campus)
Greenwich University. 5L 79
(Wellington St.)
Greenwich Vw. Pl. E14 . . . . .4M 77
Greenwich Way. Wal A 9J 7
Greenwood Av. Chesh 4B 6
Greenwood Av. Dag 9M 49
Greenwood Av. Enf 4J 17
Greenwood Bus. Cen.
Croy 2D 124
Greenwood Clo. Bus H 9C 10
Greenwood Clo. Chesh 4B 6
Greenwood Clo. Mord 8J 105
Greenwood Clo. Orp 1C 128
Greenwood Clo. Sidc 8E 96
Greenwood Clo. Th Dit 3E 118
Greenwood Dri. E4 . . . . .5B 30
Greenwood Dri. Wat 7F 4
Greenwood Gdns. N13 . . . . .3M 27
Greenwood Gdns. Ilf 7A 32
Greenwood Ho. N22 . . . . .8L 27
Greenwood Ho. SE4 . . . . .3H 93
Greenwood La. Hamp H . . .2M 101
Greenwood Mans. Bark 3E 64
(off Lansbury Av.)
Greenwood Pk. King T 4C 104
Greenwood Pl. NW5 . . . . .1F 58
Greenwood Rd. E8 . . . . .2E 60
Greenwood Rd. E13 . . . . .5D 62
Greenwood Rd. Bex 1B 114
Greenwood Rd. Chig 4F 32
Greenwood Rd. Croy 2M 123
Greenwood Rd. Isw th 2D 86
Greenwood Rd. Mitc 7H 107
Greenwood Rd. Th Dit 3E 118
Greenwoods, The. S Harr 8A 38
Greenwood Ter. NW10 . . . . . .4B 56
Grn. Wrythe Cres. Cars 3C 122
Grn. Wrythe La. Cars 1B 122
Green Yd. WC1 . . . . .7K 59
(off Gough St.)
Greenyard. Wal A 6J 7
Green Yd., The. EC3 . . . . .9C 60
(off Leadenhall St.)
Greer Rd. Harr 8A 22
Greet Ho. SE1 . . . . .3L 75
(off Frazier St.)
Greet St. SE1 . . . . .2L 75
Greg Clo. E10 . . . . .4A 46
Gregory Clo. Brom 8C 110
Gregory Cres. SE9 . . . . .6H 95
Gregory M. Wal A 5H 7
Gregory Pl. W8 . . . . .3M 73
Gregory Rd. Romf 2H 49
Gregory Rd. S'hall 4L 69
Gregson Clo. Borwd 3A 12
Gregson's Ride. Lou 2L 19
Greig Clo. N8 . . . . .3J 43
Greig Ter. SE17 . . . . .7M 75
Grenaby Av. Croy 2B 124
Grenaby Rd. Croy 2B 124
Grenada Ho. E14 . . . . .1K 77
(off Limehouse Causeway)
Grenada Rd. SE7 . . . . .8G 79
Grenade St. E14 . . . . .1K 77
Grenadier St. E16 . . . . .2L 79
Grena Gdns. Rich 3K 87
Grenard Clo. SE15 . . . . .8E 76
Grena Rd. Rich 3K 87
Grendon Gdns. Wemb 7L 39
Grendon Ho. E9 . . . . .3G 61
(off Shore Pl.)
Grendon Ho. N1 . . . . .5K 59
(off Calshot St.)
Grendon Lodge. Edgw 2A 24
Grendon St. NW8 . . . . .7C 58
Grenfell Av. Horn 6D 50
Grenfell Clo. Borwd 3A 12
Grenfell Ct. NW7 . . . . .6F 24
Grenfell Gdns. Harr 5J 39
Grenfell Gdns. Ilf 3D 48
Grenfell Ho. SE5 . . . . .8A 76
Grenfell Rd. SW17 . . . . . . .3D 106
Grenfell Rd. W11 . . . . .1H 73
Grenfell Tower. W11 . . . . .1H 73
Grenfell Wlk. W11 . . . . .1H 73
Grenier Apartments. SE15 . . .8F 76
Grennell Clo. Sutt 4B 122
Grennell Rd. Sutt 4A 122
Grenoble Gdns. N13 . . . . . . .6L 27
Grenside Rd. Wey 5A 116
Grenville Clo. N3 . . . . .8J 25
Grenville Clo. Surb 3A 120
Grenville Clo. Wal X 5D 6
Grenville Ct. W13 . . . . .8F 54
Grenville Gdns. Wfd G 8G 31
Grenville Ho. E3 . . . . .5J 61
(off Arbery Rd.)
Grenville Ho. SE8 . . . . .7L 77
(off New King St.)
Grenville Ho. SW1 . . . . .7H 75
(off Dolphin Sq.)
Grenville M. SW7 . . . . .5A 74
(off Harrington Gdns.)
Grenville M. Hamp 2M 101
Grenville Pl. NW7 . . . . .5B 24
Grenville Pl. SW7 . . . . .4A 74
Grenville Rd. N19 . . . . .6J 43
Grenville Rd. New Ad 1A 140
Grenville St. WC1 . . . . .7J 59
Gresham Av. N20 . . . . .4D 26
Gresham Clo. Bex 5J 97
Gresham Clo. Enf 5A 16
Gresham Ct. Purl 3L 137
Gresham Dri. Romf 3F 48
Gresham Gdns. NW11 . . . . . . .6J 41
Gresham Lodge. E17 . . . . . . .3M 45
Gresham M. W4 . . . . .4A 72
Gresham Rd. E6 . . . . .5K 63
Gresham Rd. E16 . . . . .9F 62
Gresham Rd. NW10 . . . . .1B 56
Gresham Rd. SE25 . . . . .8E 108
Gresham Rd. SW9 . . . . .2L 91
Gresham Rd. Beck 6J 109
Gresham Rd. Edgw 6K 23
Gresham Rd. Hamp 3L 101
Gresham Rd. Houn 9A 70
Gresham Rd. Uxb 5E 142
Gresham St. EC2 . . . . .9A 60
Gresham Way. SW19 . . . . . . .9M 89
Gresley Clo. E17 . . . . .4J 45
Gresley Clo. N15 . . . . .2B 44
Gresley Ct. Enf 8C 6
Gresley Rd. N19 . . . . .6G 43
Gressenhall Rd. SW18 . . . . . .5K 89
Gresse St. W1 . . . . .9H 59

Gresswell Clo.—Guinness Trust Bldgs.

Gresswell Clo. Sidc 9E 96
Greswell St. SW6 9H 73
Gretton Ho. E2 6G 61
(off Globe Rd.)
Gretton Rd. N17 7D 28
Greville Av. S Croy 2H 139
Greville Clo. Twic 6F 86
Greville Ct. E5 9F 44
(off Napoleon Rd.)
Greville Ct. Harr 9C 38
Greville Hall. NW6 5M 57
Greville Lodge. E13 4F 62
Greville Lodge. N12 5M 25
Greville Lodge. Edgw 4M 23
(off Broadhurst Av.)
Greville M. NW6 4M 57
(off Greville Rd.)
Greville Pk. Av. Asht 9J 133
Greville Pk. Rd. Asht 9J 133
Greville Pl. NW6 5M 57
Greville Rd. E17 2A 46
Greville Rd. NW6 5M 57
Greville Rd. Rich 5K 87
Greville St. EC1 8L 59
(in two parts)
Grey Alders. Bans 6G 135
Greycaine Rd. Wat 1H 9
Greycaine Trad. Est. Wat 1H 9
Grey Clo. NW11 4A 42
Greycoat Gdns. SW1 4H 75
(off Greycoat St.)
Greycoat Pl. SW1 4H 75
Greycoat St. SW1 4H 75
Greycot Rd. Beck 2L 109
Grey Eagle St. E1 7D 60
Greyfell Clo. Stan 5G 23
Greyfields Clo. Purl 5M 137
Greyfriars. SE26 9E 92
(off Wells Pk. Rd.)
Greyfriars Pas. EC1 9M 59
Greyhound Commercial Cen., The. Dart 4C 98
Greyhound Ct. WC2 1K 75
Greyhound Hill. NW4 1E 40
Greyhound La. SW16 3H 107
Greyhound Mans. W6 7J 73
(off Greyhound Rd.)
Greyhound Rd. N15 1C 44
Greyhound Rd. NW10 6F 56
Greyhound Rd. W6 & W14 7H 73
Greyhound Rd. Sutt 7A 122
Greyhound Ter. SW16 5G 107
Greyhound Way. Dart 4C 98
Grey Ho. W12 1F 72
(off White City Est.)
Grey Ho., The. Wat 4E 8
Greyladies Gdns. SE10 1A 94
Greys Pk. Clo. Kes 7H 127
Greystead Rd. SE23 6G 93
Greystoke Av. Pinn 1L 37
Greystoke Ct. W5 7J 55
Greystoke Dri. Ruis 5A 36
Greystoke Gdns. W5 7J 55
Greystoke Gdns. Enf 6H 15
Greystoke Ho. SE15 7E 76
(off Peckham Pk. Rd.)
Greystoke Ho. W5 7J 55
Greystoke Lodge. W5 7K 55
(off Hanger La.)
Greystoke Pk. Ter. W5 6H 55
Greystoke Pl. EC4 9L 59
Greystone Clo. S Croy 3G 139
Greystone Gdns. Harr 4G 39
Greystone Gdns. Ilf 9A 32
Greystone Path. E11 5D 46
(off Mornington Rd.)
Greyswood Av. N18 6H 29
Greyswood St. SW16 3F 106
Grey Towers Av. Horn 5H 51
Grey Towers Gdns. Horn 5G 51
Grey Turner Ho. W12 9E 56
Grice Av. Big H 5F 140
Gridiron Pl. Upm 8M 51
Grierson Rd. SE23 6H 93
Griffin Cen. Felt 4F 84
Griffin Cen., The. King T 6H 103
(off Market Pl.)
Griffin Clo. NW10 1F 56
Griffin Ct. W4 6D 72
Griffin Ct. Bren 7J 71
Griffin Ho. E14 9M 61
(off Ricardo St.)
Griffin Ho. W6 5H 73
(off Hammersmith Rd.)
Griffin Mnr. Way. SE28 4B 80
Griffin Rd. N17 9C 28
Griffin Rd. SE18 6B 80
Griffins Clo. N21 9B 16
Griffin Way. Sun 6E 100
Griffith Clo. Dag 5G 49
Griffiths Clo. Wor Pk 4F 120
Griffiths Rd. SW19 4L 105
Griffon Way. Leav 7D 4
Griggs App. Ilf 7A 48
Griggs Gdns. Horn 1G 67
Grigg's Pl. SE1 4C 76
Griggs Rd. E10 4A 46
Grilse Clo. N9 4F 28
Grimaldi Ho. N1 5K 59
(off Calshot St.)
Grimsby Gro. E16 3M 79
Grimsby St. E2 7D 60
Grimsdyke Cres. Barn 5G 13
Grim's Dyke Golf Course. 4L 21
Grimsdyke Rd. Pinn 7J 21
Grimsel Path. SE5 8M 75
Grimshaw Clo. N6 5E 42
Grimshaw Way. Romf 3D 50
Grimstone Clo. Romf 6M 33
Grimston Rd. SW6 1K 89
Grimthorpe Ho. EC1 7M 59
(off Agdon St.)
Grimwade Av. Croy 5E 124
Grimwade Clo. SE15 2G 93
Grimwood Rd. Twic 6D 86
Grindall Clo. Croy 6M 123
Grindall Ho. E1 7F 60
(off Darling Row)
Grindal St. SE1 3L 75
Grindleford Av. N11 2E 26
Grindley Gdns. Croy 1D 124
Grindley Ho. E3 8K 61
(off Leopold St.)
Grinling Pl. SE8 7L 77
Grinstead Rd. SE8 6J 77
Grisedale. NW1 6G 59
(off Cumberland Mkt.)
Grisedale Clo. Purl 6C 138
Grisedale Gdns. Purl 6C 138
Grittleton Av. Wemb 2M 55
Grittleton Rd. W9 7L 57
Grizedale Ter. SE23 8F 92
Grocer's Hall Ct. EC2 9B 60
Grocer's Hall Gdns. EC2 9B 60
(off Prince's St.)
Grogan Clo. Hamp 3K 101
Groombridge Clo. W on T 7F 116
Groombridge Clo. Well 4E 96
Groombridge Rd. E9 3H 61
Groom Clo. Brom 8F 110
Groom Cres. SW18 6B 90
Groome Ho. SE11 5K 75
Groomfield Clo. SW17 1E 106
Groom Pl. SW1 4E 74
Grooms Dri. Pinn 3E 36
Grosmont Rd. SE18 7D 80
Grosse Way. SW15 5F 88
Grosvenor Av. N5 1A 60
Grosvenor Av. SW14 2C 88
Grosvenor Av. Cars 8D 122
Grosvenor Av. Harr 4M 37
Grosvenor Av. Hay 5D 52
Grosvenor Av. K Lan 1A 4
Grosvenor Av. Rich 4J 87
Grosvenor Clo. Lou 3M 19
Grosvenor Cotts. SW1 5E 74
Grosvenor Ct. E10 6M 45
Grosvenor Ct. N14 9G 15
Grosvenor Ct. NW6 4H 57
Grosvenor Ct. NW7 5B 24
(off Hale La.)
Grosvenor Ct. SE5 7A 76
Grosvenor Ct. W3 2L 71
Grosvenor Ct. W5 1J 71
(off Grove, The)
Grosvenor Ct. Crox G 7B 8
Grosvenor Ct. Mans. W2 9D 58
(off Edgware Rd.)
Grosvenor Cres. NW9 2L 39
Grosvenor Cres. SW1 3E 74
Grosvenor Cres. Dart 4H 99
Grosvenor Cres. Uxb 3F 142
Grosvenor Cres. M. SW1 3E 74
Grosvenor Dri. Horn 6G 51
Grosvenor Dri. Lou 4M 19
Grosvenor Est. SW1 5H 75
Grosvenor Gdns. E6 6H 63
Grosvenor Gdns. N10 1G 43
Grosvenor Gdns. N14 7H 15
Grosvenor Gdns. NW2 1G 57
Grosvenor Gdns. NW11 4K 41
Grosvenor Gdns. SW1 4F 74
Grosvenor Gdns. SW14 2C 88
Grosvenor Gdns. King T 3H 103
Grosvenor Gdns. Wall 9G 123
Grosvenor Gdns. Wfd G 6E 30
Grosvenor Gdns. M. E. SW1 4F 74
(off Beeston Pl.)
Grosvenor Gdns. M. N. SW1 4F 74
(off Ebury St.)
Grosvenor Gdns. M. S. SW1 4F 74
(off Ebury St.)
Grosvenor Ga. W1 1E 74
Grosvenor Hill. SW19 3J 105
Grosvenor Hill. W1 1F 74
Grosvenor Hill Ct. W1 1F 74
(off Bourdon St.)
Grosvenor Pde. W5 2L 71
(off Uxbridge Rd.)
Grosvenor Pk. SE5 8A 76
Grosvenor Pk. Rd. E17 3L 45
Grosvenor Path. Lou 3M 19
Grosvenor Pl. SW1 3E 74
Grosvenor Pl. Wey 5B 116
Grosvenor Ri. E. E17 3M 45
Grosvenor Rd. E6 4H 63
Grosvenor Rd. E7 2F 62
Grosvenor Rd. E10 6A 46
Grosvenor Rd. E11 3F 46
Grosvenor Rd. N3 7K 25
Grosvenor Rd. N9 1F 28
Grosvenor Rd. N10 8F 26
Grosvenor Rd. SE25 8D 108
Grosvenor Rd. SW1 7F 74
Grosvenor Rd. W4 6M 71
Grosvenor Rd. W7 2E 70
Grosvenor Rd. Belv 7L 81
Grosvenor Rd. Bexh 4H 97
Grosvenor Rd. Borwd 5L 11
Grosvenor Rd. Bren 7H 71
Grosvenor Rd. Dag 6K 49
Grosvenor Rd. Houn 2K 85
Grosvenor Rd. Ilf 8A 48
Grosvenor Rd. N'wd 5D 20
Grosvenor Rd. Orp 1C 128
Grosvenor Rd. Rich 4J 87
Grosvenor Rd. Romf 5B 50
Grosvenor Rd. S'hall 4K 69
Grosvenor Rd. Twic 7E 86
Grosvenor Rd. Wall 8F 122
Grosvenor Rd. Wat 6G 9
Grosvenor Rd. W Wick 3M 125
Grosvenor Sq. W1 1E 74
Grosvenor Sq. K Lan 1A 4
Grosvenor St. W1 1F 74
Grosvenor Ter. SE5 8A 76
Grosvenor Va. Ruis 7D 36
Grosvenor Way. E5 7G 45
Grosvenor Wharf Rd. E14 5B 78
Grotes Bldgs. SE3 1C 94
Grote's Pl. SE3 1C 94
Groton Rd. SW18 8M 89
Grotto Ct. SE1 3M 75
Grotto Pas. W1 8E 58
Grotto Rd. Twic 8D 86
Grotto Rd. Wey 5A 116
Grove Av. N3 7L 25
Grove Av. N10 9G 27
Grove Av. W7 9C 54
Grove Av. Eps 5C 134
Grove Av. Pinn 2J 37
Grove Av. Sutt 8L 121
Grove Av. Twic 7D 86
Grove Bank. Wat 1H 21
Grovebury Clo. Eri 7B 82
Grovebury Ct. N14 9H 15
Grovebury Ct. Bexh 4M 97
Grovebury Rd. SE2 3F 80
Grove Clo. N14 9G 15
Grove Clo. SE23 7J 93
Grove Clo. Brom 4E 126
Grove Clo. Eps 2L 133
Grove Clo. Felt 1J 101
Grove Clo. King T 8K 103
Grove Clo. Uxb 1E 142
Grove Cotts. W4 7C 72
Grove Ct. NW8 6B 58
(off Grove End Rd.)
Grove Ct. SW10 6A 74
(off Drayton Gdns.)
Grove Ct. W5 2J 71
Grove Ct. E Mol 8B 102
Grove Ct. Houn 3L 85
Grove Ct. King T 7J 103
(off Grove Cres.)
Grove Ct. Upm 9L 51
Grove Ct. Wal A 6H 7
Grove Cres. E18 9D 30
Grove Cres. NW9 2A 40
Grove Cres. Felt 1J 101
Grove Cres. King T 7J 103
Grove Cres. W on T 2F 116
Grove Cres. Rd. E15 2B 62
Grovedale Clo. Chesh 3A 6
Grovedale Rd. N19 7H 43
Grove Dwellings. E1 8G 61
Grove End. E18 9D 30
Grove End. NW5 9F 42
Grove End Gdns. NW8 5B 58
Grove End Ho. NW8 6B 58
(off Grove End Rd.)
Grove End La. Esh 3B 118
Grove End Rd. NW8 5B 58
Grove Farm Pk. N'wd 5B 20
Grovefield. N11 4F 26
(off Coppies Gro.)
Grove Footpath. Surb 8J 103
Grove Gdns. NW4 3E 40
Grove Gdns. NW8 6C 58
Grove Gdns. Dag 8A 50
Grove Gdns. Enf 2H 17
Grove Gdns. Rich 5K 87
Grove Gdns. Tedd 1E 102
Grove Grn. N'wd 5B 20
Grove Grn. Rd. E10 8A 46
Grove Hall Ct. NW8 6A 58
Grove Hall Rd. Bush 6J 9
Groveherst Rd. Dart 2K 99
Grove Hill. E18 9D 30
Grove Hill. Harr 5C 38
Grovehill Ct. Brom 3D 110
Grove Hill Rd. SE5 2C 92
Grove Hill Rd. Harr 5D 38
Grove Ho. SW3 7C 74
(off Chelsea Mnr. St.)
Grove Ho. Bush 8K 9
Grove Ho. Chesh 3B 6
Grove Ho. Rd. N8 2J 43
Groveland Av. SW16 4K 107
Groveland Ct. EC4 9A 60
(off Bow La.)
Groveland Rd. Beck 7K 109
Grovelands. King T 8H 103
(off Palace Rd.)
Grovelands. W Mol 8L 101
Grovelands Clo. SE5 1C 92
Grovelands Clo. Harr 8M 37
Grovelands Ct. N14 9H 15
Grovelands Pk. 1K 27
Grovelands Rd. N13 4K 27
Grovelands Rd. N15 4E 44
Grovelands Rd. Orp 4E 112
Grovelands Rd. Purl 4J 137
Groveland Way. N Mald 9A 104
Grove La. SE5 9B 76
Grove La. Chig 3D 32
Grove La. Coul 4D 136
(in two parts)
Grove La. King T 8J 103
Grove La. Uxb 7D 142
Grove La. Ter. SE5 1B 92
Groveley Rd. Sun 2D 100
Grove Mans. W6 3G 73
(off Hammersmith Gro.)
Grove Mkt. Pl. SE9 5K 95
Grove M. W6 4G 73
Grove Mill La. Wat 2A 8
Grove Mill Pl. Cars 5E 122
Grove Nature Reserve, The. 7D 142
Grove Park. 9F 94
(Bromley)
Grove Park. 9A 72
(Chiswick)
Grove Pk. E11 4F 46
Grove Pk. NW9 2A 40
Grove Pk. SE5 1C 92
Gro. Park Av. E4 7M 29
Gro. Park Bri. W4 8A 72
Gro. Park Gdns. W4 8M 71
Gro. Park Ind. Est. NW9 2B 40
Gro. Park M. W4 8A 72
Gro. Park Rd. N15 2C 44
Gro. Park Rd. SE9 9G 95
Gro. Park Rd. W4 8M 71
Gro. Park Rd. Rain 4E 66
Gro. Park Ter. W4 8M 71
(in two parts)
Grove Pas. E2 5F 60
Grove Path. Chesh 4A 6
Grove Pl. NW3 8B 42
Grove Pl. SW12 6F 90
Grove Pl. W3 2A 72
Grove Pl. Bark 3A 64
Grove Pl. Wey 7A 116
Grover Ct. SE13 1M 93
Grover Ho. SE11 6K 75
Grove Rd. E3 4H 61
Grove Rd. E4 4A 30
Grove Rd. E11 5D 46
Grove Rd. E17 4M 45
Grove Rd. E18 9D 30
Grove Rd. N11 5F 26
Grove Rd. N12 5B 26
Grove Rd. N15 3C 44
Grove Rd. NW2 2G 57
Grove Rd. SW13 1D 88
Grove Rd. SW19 4A 106
Grove Rd. W3 2A 72
Grove Rd. W5 1H 71
Grove Rd. Belv 7K 81
Grove Rd. Bexh 3A 98
Grove Rd. Borwd 3L 11
Grove Rd. Bren 6G 71
Grove Rd. Chad H 5F 48
Grove Rd. Cockf 5C 14
Grove Rd. E Mol 8B 102
Grove Rd. Edgw 6L 23
Grove Rd. Eps 5C 134
Grove Rd. Houn 3L 85
Grove Rd. Iswth 9C 70
Grove Rd. Mitc 7E 106
(in two parts)
Grove Rd. N'wd 5B 20
Grove Rd. Pinn 3K 37
Grove Rd. Rich 5K 87
Grove Rd. Shep 1A 116
Grove Rd. Surb 9H 103
Grove Rd. Sutt 8L 121
Grove Rd. T Hth 8L 107
Grove Rd. Twic 9B 86
Grove Rd. Uxb 3B 142
Grove Rd. W. Enf 1G 17
Grover Rd. Wat 9H 9
Groveside Clo. W3 8L 55
Groveside Clo. Cars 4C 122
Groveside Rd. E4 2C 30
Grovestile Waye. Felt 6B 84
Grove St. N18 5D 28
Grove St. SE8 5K 77
Grove Ter. NW5 8F 42
Grove Ter. S'hall 1L 69
Grove Ter. Tedd 1E 102
Grove Ter. M. NW5 8F 42
Grove, The (Junct.) 7E 92
Grove, The. E15 2C 62
Grove, The. N3 8L 25
Grove, The. N4 5K 43
Grove, The. N6 6E 42
Grove, The. N8 3H 43
Grove, The. N13 4L 27
(in two parts)
Grove, The. N14 7G 15
Grove, The. NW9 3B 40
Grove, The. NW11 5J 41
Grove, The. W5 2H 71
Grove, The. Bexh 3H 97
Grove, The. Big H 9H 141
Grove, The. Coul 7H 137
Grove, The. Edgw 4M 23
Grove, The. Enf 4L 15
Grove, The. Eps 5C 134
(Epsom)
Grove, The. Eps 2D 134
(Ewell)
Grove, The. Gnfd 9A 54
Grove, The. Iswth 9C 70
Grove, The. Sidc 1J 113
Grove, The. Stan 2E 22
Grove, The. Swan 7D 114
Grove, The. Tedd 1E 102
Grove, The. Twic 5F 86
Grove, The. Upm 9M 51
Grove, The. Uxb (UB8) 7D 142
Grove, The. Uxb (UB10) 1E 142
Grove, The. W on T 2F 116
Grove, The. W Wick 5M 125
Grove Va. SE22 3D 92
Grove Va. Chst 3L 111
Grove Vs. E14 1M 77
Groveway. SW9 9K 75
Groveway. Dag 8H 49
Grove Way. Esh 2A 118
Grove Way. Uxb 3B 142
Grove Way. Wemb 1M 55
Grovewood. Rich 9L 71
Grove Wood Hill. Coul 6G 137
Grovewood Pl. Wfd G 6K 31
Grummant Rd. SE15 9D 76
Grundy St. E14 9M 61
Gruneisen Rd. N3 7M 25
Guardian Bus. Cen. H Hill 7H 35
Guardian Clo. Horn 6F 50
Guardian Ct. SE12 4C 94
Guards Memorial. 2H 75
Guards' Mus. 3G 75
Gubbins La. H Wood 7K 35
Gubyon Av. SE24 4M 91
Guerin Sq. E3 6K 61
Guernsey Clo. Houn 8L 69
Guernsey Gro. SE24 6A 92
Guernsey Ho. N1 2A 60
(off Douglas Rd. N.)
Guernsey Ho. Enf 2H 17
(off Eastfield Rd.)
Guernsey Rd. E11 6B 46
Guernsey Rd. N1 2A 60
Guibal Rd. SE12 6F 94
Guildersfield Rd. SW16 4J 107
Guildford Av. Felt 8D 84
Guildford Ct. SW8 8J 75
(off Guildford Rd.)
Guildford Gdns. Romf 6J 35
Guildford Gro. SE10 9M 77
Guildford Rd. E6 9K 63
Guildford Rd. E17 8A 30
Guildford Rd. SW8 9J 75
Guildford Rd. Croy 1B 124
Guildford Rd. Ilf 7C 48
Guildford Rd. Romf 6J 35
Guildford Way. Wall 7J 123
Guildhall. 9A 60
Guildhall Art Gallery. 9B 60
Guildhall Bldgs. EC2 9B 60
(off Basinghall St.)
Guildhall Library. 9A 60
Guildhall Offices. EC2 9A 60
(off Basinghall St.)
Guildhall School of Music & Drama. 8A 60
(off Silk St.)
Guildhall Yd. EC2 9A 60
Guildhouse St. SW1 5G 75
Guildown Av. N12 4M 25
Guild Rd. SE7 7H 79
Guild Rd. Eri 8D 82
Guildsway. E17 8K 29
Guilford Av. Surb 9K 103
Guilford Pl. WC1 7K 59
Guilford St. WC1 7J 59
Guilfoyle. NW9 9D 24
Guillemot Pl. N22 9K 27
Guilsborough Clo. NW10 3C 56
Guinevere Gdns. Wal X 4E 6
Guinness Clo. E9 3J 61
Guinness Clo. Hay 4B 68
Guinness Ct. E1 9D 60
(off Mansell St.)
Guinness Ct. EC1 6A 60
(off Lever St.)
Guinness Ct. NW8 4C 58
Guinness Ct. SE1 3C 76
(off Snowsfields)
Guinness Ct. SW3 5D 74
Guinness Ct. Croy 4D 124
Guinness Sq. SE1 5C 76
Guinness Trust Bldgs. SE11 6M 75

Guinness Trust Bldgs.—Hambro Av.

Guinness Trust Bldgs. W6 .6H 73
(off Fulham Pal. Rd.)
Guinness Trust Est. E15 .4D 62
Guinness Trust Est. N16 .6C 44
Guion Rd. SW6 .1K 89
Gulland Clo. Bush .7A 10
Gulland Wlk. N1 .3A 60
(off Oronsay Wlk.)
Gull Clo. Wall .9J 123
Gullet Wood Rd. Wat .8E 4
Gulliver Clo. N'holt .4K 53
Gulliver Rd. Sidc .8B 96
Gulliver's Ho. EC1 .7A 60
(off Goswell Rd.)
Gulliver St. SE16 .4J 77
Gull Wlk. Horn .3F 66
Gulston Wlk. SW3 .5D 74
(off Blackland Ter.)
Gumleigh Rd. W5 .5G 71
Gumley Gdns. Iswth .2E 86
Gumping Rd. Orp .4A 128
Gundulph Rd. Brom .7G 111
Gun Ho. E1 .2F 76
(off Wapping High St.)
Gunmaker's La. E3 .4J 61
Gunnell Clo. SE26 .1E 108
Gunnell Clo. Croy .1D 124
Gunner Dri. Enf .1L 17
Gunner La. SE18 .6L 79
Gunnersbury. .6M 71
Gunnersbury Av.
W5, W3 & W4 .2K 71
Gunnersbury Clo. W4 .6M 71
Gunnersbury Ct. W3 .3M 71
Gunnersbury Cres. W3 .3L 71
Gunnersbury Dri. W5 .3K 71
Gunnersbury Gdns. W3 .3L 71
Gunnersbury La. W3 .4L 71
Gunnersbury Mnr. W5 .2K 71
Gunnersbury M. W4 .6M 71
Gunnersbury Park (Junct.)
.4L 71
Gunnersbury Pk. Mus. .4L 71
Gunners Gro. E4 .3A 30
Gunners Rd. SW18 .8B 90
Gunning St. SE18 .5C 80
Gunpowder Sq. EC4 .9L 59
(off Gough Sq., in two parts)
Gunstor Rd. N16 .9C 44
Gun St. E1 .8D 60
Gunter Gro. SW10 .7A 74
Gunter Gro. Edgw .8B 24
Gunters Mead. Oxs .3A 132
Gunterstone Rd. W14 .5J 73
Gunthorpe St. E1 .8D 60
Gunton Rd. E5 .8F 44
Gunton Rd. SW17 .3E 106
Gunwhale Clo. SE16 .2H 77
Gun Wharf. E1 .2G 77
(off Wapping High St.)
Gun Wharf Bus. Cen. E3 .4J 61
(off Old Ford Rd.)
Gurdon Ho. E14 .9L 61
(off Dod St.)
Gurdon Rd. SE7 .6E 78
Gurnard Clo. W Dray .1H 143
Gurnell Gro. W13 .7D 54
Gurney Clo. E15 .1C 62
Gurney Clo. E17 .8H 29
Gurney Clo. Bark .2M 63
Gurney Cres. Croy .3K 123
Gurney Dri. N2 .2A 42
Gurney Ho. E2 .5E 60
(off Goldsmith Row)
Gurney Ho. Hay .6C 68
Gurney Rd. E15 .1C 62
Gurney Rd. SW6 .2A 90
Gurney Rd. Cars .6E 122
Gurney Rd. N'holt .6F 52
Guthrie Ct. SE1 .4L 75
(off Morley St.)
Guthrie St. SW3 .6B 74
Gutter La. EC2 .9A 60
Guyatt Gdns. Mitc .6E 106
Guy Barnett Gro. SE3 .2E 94
Guy Rd. Wall .5H 123
Guyscliff Rd. SE13 .4A 94
Guysfield Clo. Rain .4E 66
Guysfield Dri. Rain .4E 66
Guys Retreat. Buck H .9G 19
Guy St. SE1 .3B 76
Gwalior Rd. SW15 .3H 89
Gwendolen Av. SW15 .3H 89
Gwendolen Clo. SW15 .4H 89
Gwendoline Av. E13 .4F 62
Gwendwr Rd. W14 .6J 73
Gweneth Cotts. Edgw .6L 23
Gwent Clo. Wat .7H 5
Gwent Ct. SE16 .2H 77
(off Rotherhithe St.)
Gwillim Clo. Sidc .4E 96
Gwilym Maries Ho.
E2 .6F 60
(off Blythe St.)
Gwydor Rd. Beck .7H 109
Gwydyr Rd. Brom .7D 110
Gwyn Clo. SW6 .8A 74
Gwynne Av. Croy .2H 125
Gwynne Clo. W4 .7D 72
Gwynne Ho. E1 .8F 60
(off Turner St.)
Gwynne Ho. WC1 .6L 59
(off Lloyd Baker St.)
Gwynne Pk. Av. Wfd G .6K 31
Gwynne Pl. WC1 .6K 59
Gwynne Rd. SW11 .1B 90
Gyfford Wlk. Chesh .4B 6
Gylcote Clo. SE5 .3B 92
Gyles Pk. Stan .8G 23
Gyllyngdune Gdns. Ilf .7D 48
Gypsy Corner (Junct.) .8A 56
Gypsy La. K Lan .8B 4

H

Haarlem Rd. W14 .4H 73
Haberdasher Est. N1 .6B 60
Haberdasher Pl. N1 .6B 60
(off Haberdasher St.)
Haberdashers Ct. SE14 .2H 93
Haberdasher St. N1 .6B 60
Habgood Rd. Lou .5J 19
Habington Ho. SE5 .8B 76
(off Notley St.)
Haccombe Rd. SW19 .3A 106
Hackbridge. .4E 122
Hackbridge Grn. Wall .4E 122
Hackbridge Pk. Gdns.
Cars .4D 122
Hackbridge Rd. Wall .4E 122
Hackford Rd. SW9 .9K 75
Hackford Wlk. SW9 .9K 75
Hackforth Clo. Barn .7F 12
Hackington Cres. Beck .3L 109
Hackney. .4F 60
Hackney Clo. Borwd .7B 12
Hackney Gro. E8 .2F 60
Hackney Rd. E2 .6D 60
Hackney Wick. .2L 61
Hackney Wick (Junct.) .2J 61
Hacton. .1K 67
Hacton Dri. Horn .9H 51
Hacton La. Horn & Upm .7K 51
Hacton Pde. Horn .8K 51
Hadar Clo. N20 .1L 25
Haddenham Ct. Wat .3H 21
Hadden Rd. SE28 .4C 80
Hadden Way. Gnfd .2B 54
Haddington Ct. SE10 .8M 77
(off Tarves Way)
Haddington Rd. Brom .9B 94
Haddo Ho. SE10 .7M 77
(off Haddo St.)
Haddon Clo. Borwd .4L 11
Haddon Clo. Enf .8E 16
Haddon Clo. N Mald .9D 104
Haddon Clo. Wey .5C 116
Haddon Ct. NW4 .1G 41
Haddon Ct. W3 .1D 72
Haddonfield. SE8 .5H 77
Haddon Gro. Sidc .6D 96
Haddon Rd. Orp .9G 113
Haddon Rd. Sutt .6M 121
Haddo St. SE10 .7M 77
Haden Ct. N4 .7L 43
Haden La. N11 .4G 27
Hadfield Clo. S'hall .6K 53
Hadfield Ho. E1 .9E 60
(off Ellen St.)
Hadfield Rd. Stanw .5B 144
Hadleigh Clo. E1 .7G 61
Hadleigh Clo. SW20 .6K 105
Hadleigh Ct. E4 .9C 18
Hadleigh Dri. Sutt .1L 135
Hadleigh Ho. E1 .7G 61
(off Hadleigh Clo.)
Hadleigh Rd. N9 .9F 16
Hadleigh St. E2 .6G 61
Hadleigh Wlk. E6 .9J 63
Hadley. .5K 13
Hadley Clo. N21 .8L 15
Hadley Clo. Els .8K 11
Hadley Comn. Barn .4L 13
Hadley Ct. N16 .6E 44
Hadley Ct. New Bar .5M 13
Hadley Gdns. W4 .6B 72
Hadley Gdns. S'hall .6K 69
Hadley Grn. Rd. Barn .4K 13
Hadley Grn. W. Barn .4K 13
Hadley Gro. Barn .4J 13
Hadley Highstone.
Barn .3K 13
Hadley Mnr. Trad. Est.
Barn .5K 13
Hadley M. Barn .5K 13
Hadley Pde. Barn .5J 13
(off High St.)
Hadley Ridge. Barn .5K 13
Hadley Rd. Barn & Enf (EN4,EN2)
.2E 14
Hadley Rd. Barn (EN5) .4M 13
Hadley Rd. Belv .5K 81
Hadley Rd. Mitc .8H 107
Hadley St. NW1 .2F 58
(in two parts)
Hadley Way. N21 .8L 15
Hadley Wood. .2A 14
Hadley Wood Golf Course.
.3B 14
Hadley Wood Ri. Kenl .7M 137
Hadley Wood Rd. Barn .4A 14
Hadlow Ho. SE17 .6C 76
(off Kinglake Est.)
Hadlow Pl. SE19 .4E 108
Hadlow Rd. Sidc .1E 112
Hadlow Rd. Well .8G 81
Hadrian Clo. Stai .6C 144
Hadrian Ct. Sutt .9M 121
Hadrian Est. E2 .5E 60
Hadrians Ride. Enf .7D 16
Hadrian St. SE10 .6C 78
Hadrian Way. Stanw .6B 144
(in two parts)
Hadstock Ho. NW1 .6H 59
(off Ossulston St.)
Hadyn Pk. Ct. W12 .3E 72
(off Curwen Rd.)
Hadyn Pk. Rd. W12 .3E 72
Hafer Rd. SW11 .3D 90
Hafton Rd. SE6 .7C 94
Hagden La. Wat .6D 8
Haggard Rd. Twic .6F 86
Hagger Ct. E17 .1B 46
Haggerston. .5D 60
Haggerston Rd. E8 & E2 .3D 60
Haggerston Rd. Borwd .2J 11
Hague St. E2 .6E 60
Ha Ha Rd. SE18 .7K 79
Haig Ho. E2 .5E 60
(off Shipton St.)
Haig Pl. Mord .1L 121
Haig Rd. Big H .9J 141
Haig Rd. Stan .5G 23
Haig Rd. Uxb .8F 142
Haig Rd. E. E13 .6G 63
Haig Rd. W. E13 .6G 63
Haigville Gdns. Ilf .2M 47
Hailes Clo. SW19 .3A 106
Haileybury Av. Enf .8D 16
Haileybury Rd. Orp .6E 128
Hailey Rd. Eri .3L 81
Hailsham Av. SW2 .8K 91
Hailsham Clo. Romf .5G 35
Hailsham Clo. Surb .2H 119
Hailsham Cres. Bark .2D 64
Hailsham Dri. Harr .1B 38
Hailsham Gdns. Romf .5G 35
Hailsham Rd. SW17 .3E 106
Hailsham Rd. Romf .5G 35
Hailsham Ter. N18 .5B 28
Haimo Rd. SE9 .4H 95
Hainault. .5E 32
Hainault Bus. Pk. Ilf .5G 33
Hainault Ct. E17 .2B 46
Hainault Forest Country Pk.
.3H 33
Hainault Gore. Romf .3J 49
Hainault Gro. Chig .4A 32
Hainault Ind. Est. Ilf .5G 33
Hainault Rd. E11 .6A 46
Hainault Rd. Chad H .4K 49
Hainault Rd. Chig .3M 31
Hainault Rd. Col R .9A 34
Hainault Rd. Romf .7F 32
Hainault St. SE9 .7M 95
Hainault St. Ilf .7A 48
Haines Ct. Wey .7B 116
Haines St. SW8 .8G 75
Haines Wlk. Mord .2M 121
Haines Way. Wat .7E 4
Hainford Clo. SE4 .3H 93
Haining Clo. W4 .6L 71
Hainthorpe Rd. SE27 .9M 91
Hainton Clo. E1 .9F 60
Halberd M. E5 .7F 44
Halbutt Gdns. Dag .8K 49
Halbutt St. Dag .9K 49
Halcomb St. N1 .4C 60
Halcot Av. Bexh .4M 97
Halcrow St. E1 .8F 60
Halcyon. Enf .7C 16
(off Private Rd.)
Halcyon Way. Horn .6K 51
Halcyon Wharf. E1 .2E 76
(off Hermitage Wall)
Haldane Clo. N10 .7F 26
Haldane Clo. Enf .2M 17
Haldane Pl. SW18 .7M 89
Haldane Rd. E6 .6H 63
Haldane Rd. SE28 .1H 81
Haldane Rd. SW6 .8K 73
Haldane Rd. S'hall .1A 70
Haldan Rd. E4 .6A 30
Haldon Clo. Chig .5C 32
Haldon Rd. SW18 .5K 89
Hale Clo. E4 .3A 30
Hale Clo. Edgw .5A 24
Hale Clo. Orp .6A 128
Hale Ct. Edgw .5A 24
Hale Dri. NW7 .6A 24
Hale End. .6B 30
Hale End. Romf .6F 34
Hale End Clo. Ruis .4E 36
Hale End Rd. E4 & Wfd G .6B 30
Halefield Rd. N17 .8F 28
Hale Gdns. N17 .2E 44
Hale Gdns. W3 .2L 71
Hale Gro. Gdns. NW7 .5C 24
Hale Ho. SW1 .6H 75
(off Lindsay Sq.)
Hale Ho. Horn .4E 50
(off Benjamin Clo.)
Hale La. NW7 .5B 24
Hale La. Edgw .5M 23
Hale Path. SE27 .1M 107
Hale Rd. E6 .7J 63
Hale Rd. N17 .1E 44
Halesowen Rd. Mord .2M 121
Hales Prior. N1 .5K 59
(off Calshot St.)
Hales St. SE8 .8L 77
Hale St. E14 .1M 77
Halesworth Clo. E5 .7G 45
Halesworth Clo. Romf .7J 35
Halesworth Rd. SE13 .2M 93
Halesworth Rd. Romf .6J 35
Hale, The. .5A 24
Hale, The. E4 .7B 30
Hale, The. N17 .1E 44
Hale Wlk. W7 .8C 54
Haley Rd. NW4 .4G 41
Half Acre. Bren .7H 71
Half Acre. Stan .6G 23
Half Acre Rd. W7 .2C 70
Halfhides. Wal A .6K 7
Half Moon Ct. EC1 .8A 60
(off Bartholomew Clo.)
Half Moon Cres. N1 .5K 59
(in two parts)
Half Moon La. SE24 .5A 92
Half Moon Pas. E1 .9D 60
(in two parts)
Half Moon St. W1 .2F 74
Halford Clo. Edgw .9M 23
Halford Rd. E10 .3B 46
Halford Rd. SW6 .7L 73
Halford Rd. Rich .4J 87
Halford Rd. Uxb .1E 142
Halfway Ct. Purf .5L 83
Halfway Grn. W on T .5F 116
Halfway St. Sidc .6B 96
Haliburton Rd. Twic .4E 86
Haliday Ho. N1 .2B 60
(off Mildmay St.)
Haliday Wlk. N1 .2B 60
Halidon Clo. E9 .1G 61
Halidon Ri. Romf .6M 35
Halifax. NW9 .9D 24
Halifax Clo. Leav .7D 4
Halifax Clo. Tedd .3C 102
Halifax Ho. Romf .5J 35
(off Lindfield Rd.)
Halifax Rd. Enf .4A 16
Halifax Rd. Gnfd .4M 53
Halifax St. SE26 .9F 92
Halifield Dri. Belv .4J 81
Haling Down Pas. Purl .2M 137
(in two parts)
Haling Gro. S Croy .9A 124
Haling Pk. Gdns. Croy .8M 123
Haling Pk. Rd. S Croy .7M 123
Haling Rd. S Croy .8B 124
Haliwell Ho. NW6 .4M 57
(off Mortimer Cres.)
Halkin Arc. SW1 .4D 74
(in two parts)
Halkin M. SW1 .4E 74
Halkin Pl. SW1 .4E 74
Halkin St. SW1 .3E 74
Hallam Clo. Chst .2K 111
Hallam Clo. Wat .4G 9
Hallam Ct. W1 .8F 58
(off Hallam St.)
Hallam Gdns. Pinn .7J 21
Hallam Ho. SW1 .6G 75
(off Churchill Gdns.)
Hallam M. W1 .8F 58
Hallam Rd. N15 .2M 43
Hallam Rd. SW13 .2F 88
Hallam St. W1 .7F 58
Halland Way. N'wd .6B 20
Hallane Ho. SE27 .2A 108
Hall Clo. W5 .8J 55
Hall Ct. Tedd .2D 102
Hall Cres. Ave .3M 83
Hall Dri. SE26 .2G 109
Hall Dri. W7 .9C 54
Halley Gdns. SE13 .3B 94
Halley Ho. E2 .5E 60
(off Pritchards Rd.)
Halley Ho. SE10 .6D 78
(off Armitage Rd.)
Halley Rd. E7 & E12 .2G 63
Halley Rd. Wal A .9H 7
Halley St. E14 .8J 61
Hall Farm Clo. Stan .4F 22
Hall Farm Dri. Twic .6B 86
Hallfield Est. W2 .9A 58
(in two parts)
Hallford Way. Dart .5G 99
Hall Gdns. E4 .4K 29
Hall Ga. NW8 .6B 58
Halliards, The. W on T .1E 116
Halliday Sq. S'hall .2B 70
Halliford Clo. Shep .8B 100
Halliford Rd.
Shep & Sun .9C 100
Halliford St. N1 .3A 60
Hallingbury Ct. E17 .1M 45
Halliwell Ct. SE22 .4E 92
Halliwell Rd. SW2 .5K 91
Halliwick Ct. Pde. N12 .6D 26
(off Woodhouse Rd.)
Halliwick Rd. N10 .8E 26
Hall Lane (Junct.) .4H 29
Hall La. E4 .5J 29
Hall La. NW4 .8E 24
Hall La. Hay .8B 68
Hall La. Upm .9M 35 & 6M 51
Hallmark Trad. Cen.
Wemb .9A 40
Hallmead Rd. Sutt .5M 121
Hall Oak Wlk. NW6 .2K 57
Hallowell Av. Croy .6J 123
Hallowell Clo. Mitc .7E 106
Hallowell Rd. N'wd .7C 20
Hallowes Cres. Wat .3E 20
Hallowfield Way. Mitc .7C 106
Hall Pk. Rd. Upm .1M 67
Hall Place. .5A 98
Hall Pl. W2 .7B 58
(in two parts)
Hall Pl. Cres. Bex .4A 98
Hall Pl. Dri. Wey .7C 116
Hall Place Mus. .5A 98
Hall Rd. E6 .4K 63
Hall Rd. E15 .9B 46
Hall Rd. NW8 .6A 58
Hall Rd. Ave .3M 83
Hall Rd. Chad H .4G 49
Hall Rd. Dart .3K 99
Hall Rd. Gid P .1F 50
Hall Rd. Iswth .4B 86
Hall Rd. Wall .1F 136
Hallside Rd. Enf .2D 16
Hall St. EC1 .6M 59
Hall St. N12 .5A 26
Hallsville Rd. E16 .9D 62
Hallswelle Pde. NW11 .3K 41
Hallswelle Rd. NW11 .3K 41
Hall Ter. Romf .7L 35
Hall, The. SE3 .2E 94
Hall Tower. W2 .8B 58
(off Hall Pl.)
Hall Vw. SE9 .8H 95
Hall Way. Purl .5M 137
Hallywell Cres. E6 .8K 63
Halons Rd. SE9 .6L 95
Halpin Pl. SE17 .5B 76
Halsbrook Rd. SE3 .2G 95
Halsbury Clo. Stan .4F 22
Halsbury Ct. Stan .5F 22
Halsbury Rd. W12 .2F 72
Halsbury Rd. E. N'holt .9A 38
Halsbury Rd. W. N'holt .1M 53
Halsend. Hay .2F 68
Halsey M. SW3 .5D 74
Halsey Pl. Wat .2F 8
Halsey Rd. Wat .5F 8
Halsey St. SW3 .5D 74
Halsmere Rd. SE5 .9M 75
Halstead Clo. Croy .5A 124
Halstead Ct. E17 .5K 45
Halstead Ct. N1 .5B 60
(off Fairbank Est.)
Halstead Gdns. N21 .1B 28
Halstead Ho. Romf .6H 35
(off Dartfields)
Halstead Rd. E11 .3E 46
Halstead Rd. N21 .1B 28
Halstead Rd. Enf .6C 16
Halstead Rd. Eri .9C 82
Halston Clo. SW11 .5D 90
Halstow Rd. NW10 .6H 57
Halstow Rd. SE10 .6E 78
Halsway. Hay .2E 68
Halter Clo. Borwd .7B 12
Halton Clo. N11 .6D 26
Halton Clo. Park .1M 5
Halton Cross St. N1 .4M 59
Halton Mans. N1 .3M 59
Halton Pl. N1 .4A 60
Halton Rd. N1 .3M 59
Halt Robin La. Belv .5M 81
Halt Robin Rd. Belv .5L 81
(in two parts)
Halyard Ho. E14 .4A 78
Ham. .9G 87
Hamara Ghar. E13 .4G 63
Hamblat Rd. SW4 .4G 91
Hamble Clo. Ruis .7C 36
Hamble Ct. Wat .6E 8
Hambleden Pl. SE21 .7C 92
Hambledon. SE17 .7B 76
(off Villa St.)
Hambledon Clo. Uxb .7F 142
Hambledon Ct. SE22 .3C 92
Hambledon Ct. W5 .1J 71
Hambledon Gdns. SE25 .7D 108
Hambledon Hill. Eps .8A 134
Hambledon Rd. SW18 .6K 89
Hambledon Va. Eps .8A 134
Hambledown Rd. Sidc .6B 96
Hamblehyrst. Beck .6M 109
Hamble St. SW6 .2M 89
Hambleton Clo. Wor Pk .4G 121
Hamble Wlk. N'holt .5L 53
(off Brabazon Rd.)
Hambley Ho. SE16 .5F 76
(off Camilla Rd.)
Hamblin Ho. S'hall .1J 69
(off Broadway, The)
Hambridge Way. SW2 .6L 91
Hambro Av. Brom .3E 126

Hambrook Rd.—Hardwicke Rd.

Hambrook Rd. SE25 7F 108
Hambro Rd. SW16 3H 107
Hambrough Ho. Hay 8G 53
Hambrough Rd. S'hall 2J 69
Hamburgh Ct. Chesh 1D 6
Ham Clo. Rich 9G 87
(in two parts)
Ham Comn. Rich 9H 87
Ham Ct. NW9 9C 24
Hamden Cres. Dag 8M 49
Hamel Clo. Harr 2H 39
Hame Way. E6 7L 63
Ham Farm Rd. Rich 1H 103
Hamfrith Rd. E15 2D 62
Ham Ga. Av. Rich 9H 87
Ham House. 7G 87
Hamilton Av. N9 9E 16
Hamilton Av. Ilf 2M 47
Hamilton Av. Romf 9B 34
Hamilton Av. Surb 4L 119
Hamilton Av. Sutt 4J 121
Hamilton Bldgs. EC2 7C 60
(off Gt. Eastern St.)
Hamilton Clo. N17 1D 44
Hamilton Clo. NW8 6B 58
Hamilton Clo. SE16 3J 77
Hamilton Clo. Brick W 4L 5
Hamilton Clo. Cockf 6C 14
Hamilton Clo. Eps 4A 134
Hamilton Clo. Felt 2D 100
Hamilton Clo. Purl 4M 137
Hamilton Clo. Stan 2C 22
Hamilton Ct. SE6 7D 94
Hamilton Ct. SW15 2J 89
Hamilton Ct. W5 1J 71
Hamilton Ct. W9 6A 58
(off Maida Va.)
Hamilton Ct. Croy 3E 124
Hamilton Ct. Eri 8D 82
(off Frobisher Rd.)
Hamilton Cres. N13 4L 27
Hamilton Cres. Harr 8K 37
Hamilton Cres. Houn 4M 85
Hamilton Dri. Romf 9J 35
Hamilton Gdns. NW8 6A 58
Hamilton Ho. E14 1K 77
(off Victory Pl.)
Hamilton Ho. E14 6M 77
(off St Davids Sq.)
Hamilton Ho. NW8 6B 58
(off Hall Rd.)
Hamilton Ho. W4 7C 72
Hamilton La. N5 9M 43
Hamilton Lodge. E1 7G 61
(off Cleveland Gro.)
Hamilton M. SW18 7L 89
Hamilton M. SW19 4L 105
Hamilton M. W1 3F 74
Hamilton Pde. Felt 1D 100
Hamilton Pk. N5 9M 43
Hamilton Pk. W. N5 9M 43
Hamilton Pl. W1 2E 74
Hamilton Pl. Sun 4F 100
Hamilton Rd. E15 6C 62
Hamilton Rd. E17 9J 29
Hamilton Rd. N2 1A 42
Hamilton Rd. N9 9E 16
Hamilton Rd. NW10 1E 56
Hamilton Rd. NW11 5H 41
Hamilton Rd. SE27 1B 108
Hamilton Rd. SW19 4M 105
Hamilton Rd. W4 3C 72
Hamilton Rd. W5 1J 71
Hamilton Rd. Bexh 1J 97
Hamilton Rd. Bren 7H 71
Hamilton Rd. Cockf 6C 14
Hamilton Rd. Felt 1D 100
Hamilton Rd. Harr 3C 38
Hamilton Rd. Hay 1F 68
Hamilton Rd. Ilf 9M 47
Hamilton Rd. K Lan 6A 4
Hamilton Rd. Romf 3F 50
Hamilton Rd. Sidc 1E 112
Hamilton Rd. S'hall 2K 69
Hamilton Rd. T Hth 7B 108
Hamilton Rd. Twic 7C 86
Hamilton Rd. Uxb 7B 142
Hamilton Rd. Wat 3F 20
Hamilton Rd. Ind. Est.
SE27 1B 108
(off Hamilton Rd.)
Hamilton Rd. M. SW19 4M 105
Hamilton Sq. N12 6B 26
Hamilton Sq. SE1 3B 76
(off Kipling St.)
Hamilton St. SE8 7L 77
Hamilton St. Wat 7G 9
Hamilton Ter. NW8 5M 57
Hamilton Wlk. Eri 8D 82
Hamilton Way. N3 6L 25
Hamilton Way. N13 4M 27
Hamilton Way. Wall 1H 137
Hamlea Clo. SE12 4E 94
Hamlet Clo. SE13 3C 94
Hamlet Clo. Brick W 3K 5
Hamlet Clo. Romf 7L 33
Hamlet Ct. SE11 6M 75
(off Opal St.)
Hamlet Ct. W6 5E 72
Hamlet Ct. Enf 7C 16
Hamlet Gdns. W6 5E 72
Hamlet Ho. Eri 8C 82
Hamlet Ind. Est. E9 3L 61
Hamlet Rd. SE19 4D 108
Hamlet Rd. Romf 7L 33
Hamlet Sq. NW2 8J 41
Hamlets Way. E3 7K 61
(in two parts)
Hamlet, The. SE5 2B 92
Hamlet Way. SE1 3B 76
Hamlin Cres. Pinn 3G 37
Hamlyn Clo. Edgw 3J 23
Hamlyn Gdns. SE19 4C 108
Hammelton Ct. Brom 5D 110
(off London Rd.)
Hammelton Grn. SW9 9M 75
Hammelton Rd. Brom 5D 110
Hammerfield Ho. SW3 6C 74
(off Marlborough St.)
Hammers La. NW7 5E 24
Hammersley Ho. SE14 8G 77
(off Pomeroy St.)
Hammersmith. 5G 73
Hammersmith Bri.
SW13 & W6 7F 72
Hammersmith Bri. Rd. W6 6G 73
Hammersmith Broadway (Junct.)
4G 73
Hammersmith B'way. W6 5G 73
Hammersmith Flyover (Junct.)
6G 73
Hammersmith Flyover. W6 6G 73
Hammersmith Gro. W6 3G 73
Hammersmith Ind. Est.
W6 7G 73
Hammersmith Rd.
W6 & W14 5H 73
Hammersmith Ter. W6 6E 72
Hammet Clo. Hay 8H 53
Hammett St. EC3 1D 76
Hammond Av. Mitc 6F 106
Hammond Clo. Barn 7J 13
Hammond Clo. Gnfd 1B 54
Hammond Clo. Hamp 5L 101
Hammond Ct. E10 7M 45
(off Crescent Rd.)
Hammond Ct. E17 3J 45
(off Maude Rd.)
Hammond Ho. E14 4L 77
(off Tiller Rd.)
Hammond Ho. SE14 8G 77
(off Lubbock St.)
Hammond Lodge. W9 8L 57
(off Admiral Wlk.)
Hammond Rd. Enf 4F 16
Hammond Rd. S'hall 4J 69
Hammonds Clo. Dag 8G 49
Hammond St. NW5 2G 59
Hammond Way. SE28 1F 80
Hamond Clo. S Croy 1M 137
Hamonde Clo. Edgw 2M 23
Hamond Sq. N1 5C 60
(off Hoxton St.)
Ham Pk. Rd. E15 & E7 3D 62
Hampden Av. Beck 6J 109
Hampden Clo. NW1 5H 59
Hampden Ct. N10 7E 26
Hampden Cres. Chesh 4B 6
Hampden Gurney St. W1 9D 58
Hampden Ho. SW9 1L 91
Hampden La. N17 8D 28
Hampden Rd. N8 2L 43
Hampden Rd. N10 7E 26
Hampden Rd. N17 8E 28
Hampden Rd. N19 7H 43
Hampden Rd. Beck 6J 109
Hampden Rd. Harr 8A 22
Hampden Rd. King T 7L 103
Hampden Rd. Romf 7M 33
Hampden Sq. N14 1F 26
Hampden Way. N14 1F 26
Hampden Way. Wat 9C 4
Hampermill La. Wat 2D 20
Hampshire Clo. N18 5F 28
Hampshire Hog La. W6 6F 72
Hampshire Rd. N22 7K 27
Hampshire Rd. Horn 2L 51
Hampshire St. NW5 2H 59
Hampson Way. SW8 9K 75
Hampstead. 9B 42
Hampstead Clo. SE28 2F 80
Hampstead Gdns. NW11 4L 41
Hampstead Gdns. Chad H 3F 48
Hampstead Garden Suburb.
3A 42
Hampstead Grn. NW3 1C 58
Hampstead Gro. NW3 8A 42
Hampstead Heath. 7B 42
Hampstead Heights. N2 1A 42
Hampstead High St.
NW3 9B 42
Hampstead Hill Gdns.
NW3 9B 42
Hampstead La.
NW3 & N6 6B 42
Hampstead Mus. 9B 42
(off New End Sq.)
Hampstead Rd. NW1 5G 59
Hampstead Sq. NW3 8A 42
Hampstead Theatre Club.
3B 58
(off Avenue Rd.)
Hampstead Wlk. E3 4K 61
Hampstead Way. NW11 3K 41
Hampstead W. NW6 2L 57
Hampton. 5M 101
Hampton & Richmond
Borough F.C. 5M 101
Hampton Clo. N11 5F 26
Hampton Clo. NW6 6L 57
Hampton Clo. SW20 4G 105
Hampton Court. 8C 102
Hampton Court (Junct.) 7C 102
Hampton Ct. N1 2M 59
Hampton Ct. N22 8G 27
Hampton Ct. SE16 1H 77
(off King & Queen Wharf)
Hampton Ct. Av. E Mol 1B 118
Hampton Ct. Bri. E Mol 8C 102
Hampton Ct. Cres. E Mol 7B 102
Hampton Court Palace. 8D 102
Hampton Ct. Pde. E Mol 8C 102
Hampton Ct. Rd.
E Mol & King T 7D 102
Hampton Ct. Rd.
Hamp & E Mol 6A 102
Hampton Ct. Way.
Th Dit & E Mol 4C 118
Hampton Farm Ind. Est.
Felt 9J 85
Hampton Gro. Eps 3D 134
Hampton Hill. 2A 102
Hampton Ho. Bexh 1M 97
(off Erith Rd.)
Hampton La. Felt 1J 101
Hampton Mead. Lou 5M 19
Hampton M. NW10 6B 56
Hampton Ri. Harr 4J 39
Hampton Rd. E4 5K 29
Hampton Rd. E7 1F 62
Hampton Rd. E11 6B 46
Hampton Rd. Croy 1A 124
Hampton Rd. Ilf 9A 48
Hampton Rd. Tedd 2B 102
Hampton Rd. Twic 9B 86
Hampton Rd. Wor Pk 4E 120
Hampton Rd. E. Felt 1K 101
Hampton Rd. W. Felt 9J 85
Hampton St. SE17 & SE1 5M 75
Hampton Wick. 5G 103
Ham Ridings. Rich 2K 103
Hamsey Green. 8F 138
Hamsey Grn. Gdns. Warl 8F 138
Hamsey Way. S Croy 7F 138
Hamshades Clo. Sidc 9D 96
Ham St. Rich 7F 86
Ham, The. Bren 8G 71
Ham Vw. Croy 1J 125
Ham Yd. W1 1H 75
Hanah Ct. SW19 4H 105
Hanameel St. E16 2E 78
Hanbury Clo. NW4 1G 41
Hanbury Clo. Chesh 2E 6
Hanbury Ct. Harr 4D 38
Hanbury Dri. N21 7K 15
Hanbury Dri. Big H 5F 140
Hanbury Ho. E1 8E 60
(off Hanbury St.)
Hanbury Ho. SW8 8J 75
(off Regent's Bri. Gdns.)
Hanbury M. N1 4A 60
Hanbury Rd. N17 9F 28
Hanbury Rd. W3 3M 71
Hanbury St. E1 8D 60
Hanbury Wlk. Bex 9C 98
Hancock Ct. Borwd 3A 12
Hancock Nunn Ho. NW3 2D 58
(off Fellows Rd.)
Hancock Rd. E3 6A 62
Hancock Rd. SE19 3B 108
Handa Wlk. N1 2B 60
Hand Ct. WC1 8K 59
Handcroft Rd. Croy 2M 123
Handel Clo. Edgw 6K 23
Handel House Mus. 8F 58
(off Brook St.)
Handel Mans. SW13 8G 73
Handel Mans. WC1 7J 59
(off Handel St.)
Handel Pde. Edgw 7L 23
(off Whitchurch La.)
Handel Pl. NW10 2B 56
Handel St. WC1 7J 59
Handel Way. Edgw 7L 23
Handen Rd. SE12 4C 94
Handforth Rd. SW9 8L 75
Handforth Rd. Ilf 8M 47
Handley Ga. Brick W 2K 5
Handley Gro. NW2 8H 41
Handley Page Rd. Wall 9K 123
Handley Rd. E9 3G 61
Handowe Clo. NW4 2E 40
Handside Clo. Wor Pk 3H 121
Hands Wlk. E16 9E 62
Handsworth Av. E4 6B 30
Handsworth Clo. Wat 3E 20
Handsworth Rd. N17 1B 44
Handtrough Way. Bark 5M 63
Hanford Clo. SW18 7L 89
Hanford Row. SW19 3G 105
Hangar Ruding. Wat 3K 21
Hangboy Slade. Lou 1L 19
Hanger Ct. W5 7K 55
Hanger Grn. W5 7L 55
Hanger Hill. 7K 55
Hanger Hill. Wey 7A 116
Hanger Lane (Junct.) 7K 55
Hanger La. W5 5J 55
Hanger Va. La. W5 9K 55
(in two parts)
Hanger Vw. Way. W3 9L 55
Hanging Sword All. EC4 9L 59
(off Whitefriars St.)
Hangrove Hill. Orp 5M 141
Hankey Pl. SE1 3B 76
Hankins La. NW7 2C 24
Hanley Gdns. N4 6K 43
Hanley Pl. Beck 4L 109
Hanley Rd. N4 6J 43
Hanmer Wlk. N7 7K 43
Hannah Barlow Ho. SW8 9K 75
Hannah Clo. NW10 9A 40
Hannah Clo. Beck 7A 110
Hannah Mary Way. SE1 5E 76
Hannah M. Wall 9G 123
Hannards Way. Ilf 5F 32
Hannay La. N8 5H 43
Hannay Wlk. SW16 8H 91
Hannell Rd. SW6 8J 73
Hannen Rd. SE27 9M 91
Hannibal Rd. E1 8G 61
Hannibal Rd. Stanw 6B 144
Hannibal Way. Croy 7K 123
Hannington Point. E9 2K 61
(off Eastway)
Hannington Rd. SW4 2F 90
Hanover Av. E16 2E 78
Hanover Av. Felt 7E 84
Hanover Circ. Hay 9A 52
Hanover Clo. Rich 8L 71
Hanover Clo. Sutt 6J 121
Hanover Ct. NW9 1C 40
Hanover Ct. SW15 3D 88
Hanover Ct. W12 2E 72
(off Uxbridge Rd.)
Hanover Ct. Ruis 8E 36
Hanover Ct. Wal A 6J 7
(off Quakers La.)
Hanover Dri. Chst 1A 112
Hanover Flats. W1 1E 74
(off Binney St., in two parts)
Hanover Gdns. SE11 7L 75
Hanover Gdns. Ab L 3D 4
Hanover Gdns. Ilf 7A 32
Hanover Ga. NW8 & NW1 6C 58
Hanover Ga. Mans. NW1 7C 58
Hanover Ho. E14 2K 77
(off Westferry Cir.)
Hanover Ho. NW8 5C 58
(off St John's Wood High St.)
Hanover Ho. SW9 2L 91
Hanover Mans. SW2 4L 91
Hanover Mead. NW11 3J 41
Hanover Pk. SE15 9E 76
Hanover Pl. E3 6K 61
Hanover Pl. WC2 9J 59
Hanover Rd. N15 2D 44
Hanover Rd. NW10 3G 57
Hanover Rd. SW19 4A 106
Hanover Sq. W1 9F 58
Hanover Steps. W2 9C 58
(off St George's Fields)
Hanover St. W1 9F 58
Hanover St. Croy 5M 123
Hanover Ter. NW1 6C 58
Hanover Ter. Iswth 9E 70
Hanover Ter. M. NW1 6C 58
Hanover Trad. Est. N7 1J 59
Hanover Wlk. Wey 5B 116
Hanover Way. Bexh 2H 97
Hanover W. Ind. Est.
NW10 6B 56
Hanover Yd. N1 5A 60
(off Noel Rd.)
Hansard M. W14 3H 73
(in two parts)
Hansart Way. Enf 3L 15
Hanscomb M. SW4 3G 91
Hans Cres. SW1 4D 74
Hanselin Clo. Stan 5D 22
Hansen Dri. N21 7K 15
Hanshaw Dri. Edgw 8B 24
Hansler Gro. E Mol 8B 102
Hansler Rd. SE22 4D 92
Hansol Rd. Bexh 4J 97
Hansom Ter. Brom 5F 110
(off Freelands Gro.)
Hanson Clo. SW12 6F 90
Hanson Clo. SW14 2A 88
Hanson Clo. Beck 3M 109
Hanson Clo. Lou 4M 19
Hanson Clo. W Dray 4K 143
Hanson Ct. E17 4M 45
Hanson Dri. Lou 4M 19
Hanson Gdns. S'hall 3J 69
Hanson Grn. Lou 4M 19
Hanson St. W1 8G 59
Hans Pl. SW1 4D 74
Hans Rd. SW3 4D 74
Hans St. SW1 4D 74
Hanway Pl. W1 9H 59
Hanway Rd. W7 9B 54
Hanway St. W1 9H 59
Hanwell. 2D 70
Hanworth. 2J 101
Hanworth Ho. SE5 8M 75
(in two parts)
Hanworth Rd. Felt 7F 84
Hanworth Rd. Hamp 1K 101
Hanworth Rd. Houn 7J 85
Hanworth Rd. Sun 4E 100
(in two parts)
Hanworth Ter. Houn 3M 85
Hanworth Trad. Est. Felt 9J 85
Hapgood Clo. Gnfd 1B 54
Harad's Pl. E1 1E 76
Harben Pde. NW3 3A 58
(off Finchley Rd.)
Harben Rd. NW6 3A 58
Harberson Rd. E15 4D 62
Harberson Rd. SW12 7F 90
Harbert Gdns. Park 2M 5
Harberton Rd. N19 6G 43
Harbet Rd. N18 & E4 5J 29
Harbet Rd. W2 8B 58
Harbex Clo. Bex 6M 97
Harbinger Rd. E14 5M 77
Harbledown Ho. SE1 3B 76
(off Manciple St.)
Harbledown Pl. Orp 8G 113
Harbledown Rd. SW6 9L 73
Harbledown Rd. S Croy 3E 138
Harbord Clo. SE5 1B 92
Harbord Ho. SE16 5H 77
(off Cope St.)
Harbord St. SW6 9H 73
Harborne Clo. Wat 5G 21
Harborough Av. Sidc 6C 96
Harborough Rd. SW16 1K 107
Harbour Av. SW10 9A 74
Harbourer Clo. Ilf 5F 32
Harbourer Rd. Ilf 5F 32
Harbour Exchange Sq.
E14 3M 77
Harbourfield Rd. Bans 7M 135
Harbour Quay. E14 2A 78
Harbour Rd. SE5 2A 92
Harbour Yd. SW10 9A 74
Harbridge Av. SW15 6D 88
Harbury Rd. Cars 1C 136
Harbut Rd. SW11 3B 90
(in two parts)
Harcombe Rd. N16 8C 44
Harcourt Av. E12 9K 47
Harcourt Av. Edgw 3A 24
Harcourt Av. Sidc 5G 97
Harcourt Av. Wall 6F 122
Harcourt Bldgs. EC4 1L 75
(off Middle Temple La.)
Harcourt Clo. Iswth 2E 86
Harcourt Fld. Wall 6F 122
Harcourt Lodge. Wall 6F 122
Harcourt M. Romf 3D 50
Harcourt Rd. E15 5D 62
Harcourt Rd. N22 8H 27
Harcourt Rd. SE4 2K 93
Harcourt Rd. SW19 4L 105
Harcourt Rd. Bexh 3J 97
Harcourt Rd. Bush 7M 9
Harcourt Rd. T Hth 1K 123
Harcourt Rd. Wall 6F 122
Harcourt St. W1 8C 58
Harcourt Ter. SW10 6M 73
Hardcastle Clo. Croy 1E 124
Hardcastle Ho. SE14 9J 77
(off Loring Rd.)
Hardcourts Clo. W Wick 5M 125
Hardel Ri. SW2 7M 91
Hardel Wlk. SW2 6L 91
Harden Ct. SE7 5J 79
Harden Ho. SE5 1C 92
Harden's Manorway. SE7 4H 79
(in three parts)
Harders Rd. SE15 1F 92
Hardess St. SE24 2A 92
Hardie Clo. NW10 1B 56
Hardie Rd. Dag 8A 50
Harding Clo. SE17 7A 76
Harding Clo. Croy 5D 124
Harding Clo. Wat 6G 5
Hardinge Clo. Uxb 8F 142
Hardinge La. E1 9G 61
(in two parts)
Hardinge Rd. N18 6C 28
Hardinge Rd. NW10 4F 56
Harding Ho. SW13 7F 72
(off Wyatt Dri.)
Harding Ho. Hay 9F 52
Harding Rd. Bexh 1K 97
Harding's Clo. King T 5K 103
Hardings La. SE20 3H 109
Hardingstone Ct. Wal X 7F 6
Hardington. NW1 3E 58
(off Belmont St.
Hardley Cres. Horn 2H 51
Hardman Rd. SE7 6F 78
Hardman Rd. King T 6J 10
Hardwick Clo. Oxs 7A 13
Hardwick Clo. Stan 5G 2
Hardwick Ct. Eri 7B 8
Hardwick Cres. Dart 5M 9
Hardwicke Av. Houn 9L 6
Hardwicke M. WC1 6K 5
(off Lloyd Baker M
Hardwicke Rd. N13 6J 2

Hardwicke Rd.—Harvel Cres.

Hardwicke Rd. W4 5B 72
Hardwicke Rd. Rich 1G 103
Hardwicke St. Bark 4A 64
Hardwick Grn. W13 8F 54
Hardwick Ho. NW8 7C 58 (off Lilestone St.)
Hardwick St. EC1 6L 59
Hardwicks Way. SW18 4L 89
Hardwidge St. SE1 3C 76
Hardy Av. E16 2E 78
Hardy Av. Ruis 1F 52
Hardy Clo. SE16 3H 77
Hardy Clo. Barn 8J 13
Hardy Clo. Pinn 5H 37
Hardy Cotts. SE10 7B 78
Hardy Ct. Eri 8D 82
Hardy Gro. Dart 3L 99
Hardy Ho. SW4 6G 91
Hardying Ho. E17 2J 45
Hardy Rd. E4 6K 29
Hardy Rd. SE3 8D 78
Hardy Rd. SW19 4M 105
Hardys Clo. E Mol 8C 102
Hardy Way. Enf 3L 15
Hare & Billet Rd. SE3 9B 78
Harebell Dri. E6 8L 63
Harebell Way. Romf 7H 35
Harebreaks, The. Wat 1E 8
Harecastle Clo. Hay 7J 53
Hare Ct. EC4 9L 59
Harecourt Rd. N1 2A 60
Hare Cres. Wat 5E 4
Haredale Rd. SE24 3A 92
Haredon Clo. SE23 6H 93
Harefield. Esh 5C 118
Harefield Av. Sutt 1J 135
Harefield Clo. Enf 3L 15
Harefield Grn. NW7 6G 25
Harefield M. SE4 2K 93
Harefield Rd. N8 3H 43
Harefield Rd. SE4 2K 93
Harefield Rd. SW16 4K 107
Harefield Rd. Sidc 9H 97
Harefield Rd. Uxb 3A 142
Harehall La. Romf 2F 50
Hare La. Clay 7B 118
Hare Marsh. E2 7E 60
Hare Pl. EC4 9L 59 (off Pleydell St.)
Hare Row. E2 5F 60
Hares Bank. New Ad 2B 140
Haresfield Rd. Dag 2L 65
Hare St. SE18 4L 79
Hare Wlk. N1 5C 60 (in two parts)
Harewood Av. NW1 7C 58
Harewood Av. N'holt 3K 53
Harewood Clo. N'holt 3K 53
Harewood Dri. Ilf 9K 31
Harewood Gdns. S Croy 7F 138
Harewood Pl. W1 9F 58
Harewood Rd. SW19 3C 106
Harewood Rd. Iswth 8D 70
Harewood Rd. S Croy 8C 124
Harewood Rd. Wat 3F 20
Harewood Row. NW1 8C 58
Harewood Ter. S'hall 5K 69
Harfield Gdns. SE5 2C 92
Harfield Rd. Sun 6H 101
Harfleur Ct. SE11 5M 75 (off Opal St.)
Harford Clo. E4 9M 17
Harford Dri. Wat 2C 8
Harford Ho. SE5 7A 76 (off Bethwin Rd.)
Harford Ho. W11 8K 57
Harford M. N19 8H 43
Harford Rd. E4 9M 17
Harford St. E1 7J 61
Harford Wlk. N2 2B 42
Harfst Way. Swan 5A 114
Hargood Clo. Harr 4J 39
Hargood Rd. SE3 9G 79
Hargrave Mans. N19 7H 43
Hargrave Pk. N19 7G 43
Hargrave Pl. NW5 1H 59
Hargrave Rd. N19 7G 43
Hargraves Ho. W12 1F 72 (off White City Est.)
Hargreaves Av. Chesh 4B 6
Hargreaves Clo. Chesh 4B 6
Hargwyne St. SW9 2K 91
Haringey Pk. N8 4J 43
Haringey Pas. N8 2L 43
Haringey Rd. N8 2J 43
Harington Ter. N13 3B 28
Harkett Clo. Harr 9D 22
Harkett Ct. W'stone 9D 22
Harkness. Chesh 2B 6
Harkness Clo. Eps 8G 135
Harkness Clo. Romf 5K 35
Harkness Ho. E1 9E 60 (off Christian St.)
Harkness Ind. Est. Borwd 7L 11
Harland Av. Croy 5D 124
Harland Av. Sidc 9B 96
Harland Clo. SW19 7M 105
Harland Rd. SE12 7E 94
Harlands Gro. Orp 6M 127
Harlech Gdns. Houn 7G 69
Harlech Gdns. Pinn 6H 37
Harlech Rd. N14 3J 27
Harlech Rd. Ab L 4E 4
Harlech Tower. W3 3A 72
Harlequin Av. Bren 7E 70
Harlequin Cen. S'hall 5G 69
Harlequin Clo. Hay 8H 53
Harlequin Clo. Iswth 4C 86
Harlequin Ct. NW10 2B 56 (off Mitchellbrook Way)
Harlequin Ct. W5 1G 71
Harlequin Ho. Eri 4J 81 (off Kale Rd.)
Harlequin Rd. Tedd 4F 102
Harlequins R.U.F.C. (Stoop Memorial Ground) 6C 86
Harlequin, The. Wat 6G 9
Harlescott Rd. SE15 3H 93
Harlesden. 5D 56
Harlesden Clo. Romf 6K 35
Harlesden Gdns. NW10 4D 56
Harlesden La. NW10 4E 56
Harlesden Plaza. NW10 5D 56
Harlesden Rd. NW10 4E 56
Harlesden Rd. Romf 6K 35
Harlesden Wlk. Romf 7K 35
Harleston Clo. E5 7G 45
Harley Clo. Wemb 2H 55
Harley Ct. E11 5E 46
Harley Ct. N20 3A 26
Harley Ct. Harr 2B 38
Harley Cres. Harr 2B 38
Harleyford. Brom 5F 110
Harleyford Ct. SE11 7K 75 (off Harleyford Rd.)
Harleyford Mnr. W3 2A 72 (off Edgecote Clo.)
Harleyford Rd. SE11 7K 75
Harleyford St. SE11 7L 75
Harley Gdns. SW10 6A 74
Harley Gdns. Orp 6C 128
Harley Gro. E3 6K 61
Harley Ho. E11 5B 46
Harley Ho. NW1 7E 58 (off Marylebone Rd.)
Harley Ho. Borwd 4M 11 (off Brook Clo.)
Harley Pl. W1 8F 58
Harley Rd. NW3 3B 58
Harley Rd. NW10 5C 56
Harley Rd. Harr 2B 38
Harley St. W1 7F 58
Harley Vs. NW10 5C 56
Harling Ct. SW11 1D 90
Harlinger St. SE18 4J 79
Harlington. 7B 68
Harlington Clo. Hay 8A 68
Harlington Corner (Junct.) 9B 68
Harlington Rd. Bexh 2J 97
Harlington Rd. Uxb 6E 142
Harlington Rd. E. Felt 6F 84
Harlington Rd. W. Felt 5F 84
Harlowe Clo. E8 4E 60
Harlowe Ho. E8 4D 60 (off Clarissa St.)
Harlow Gdns. Romf 6A 34
Harlow Mans. Bark 3M 63 (off Whiting Av.)
Harlow Rd. N13 3B 28
Harlow Rd. Rain 4D 66
Harlton Ct. Wal A 7M 7
Harlyn Dri. Pinn 1F 36
Harlynwood. SE5 8A 76 (off Wyndham Rd.)
Harman Av. Wfd G 6D 30
Harman Clo. E4 4B 30
Harman Clo. NW2 8J 41
Harman Clo. SE1 6E 76
Harman Dri. NW2 8J 41
Harman Dri. Sidc 5D 96
Harman Pl. Purl 3M 137
Harman Rd. Enf 7D 16
Harmondsworth. 7H 143
Harmondsworth La. W Dray 7J 143
Harmondsworth Rd. W Dray 6J 143
Harmon Ho. SE8 5K 77
Harmont Ho. W1 8F 58 (off Harley St.)
Harmony Clo. NW11 3J 41
Harmony Clo. Wall 1H 137
Harmony Way. NW4 2G 41
Harmony Way. Brom 6E 110
Harmood Gro. NW1 3F 58
Harmood Ho. NW1 3F 58 (off Harmood St.)
Harmood Pl. NW1 3F 58
Harmood St. NW1 2F 58
Harmsworth M. SE11 4L 75
Harmsworth St. SE17 6M 75
Harmsworth Way. N20 1K 25
Harness Rd. SE28 3E 80
Harnetts Clo. Swan 2B 130
Harold Av. Belv 6K 81
Harold Av. Hay 4D 68
Harold Ct. SE16 3H 77 (off Christopher Clo.)
Harold Ct. H Wood 7M 35
Harold Ct. Rd. Romf 6M 35
Harold Cres. Wal A 5J 7
Harold Est. SE1 4C 76
Harold Gibbons Ct. SE7 7G 79
Harold Hill. 6K 35
Harold Hill Ind. Est. H Hill 7H 35
Harold Ho. E2 5H 61 (off Mace St.)
Harold Laski Ho. EC1 6M 59 (off Percival St.)
Harold Maddison Ho. SE17 6M 75 (off Penton Pl.)
Harold Park. 6M 35
Harold Pl. SE11 6L 75
Harold Rd. E4 4A 30
Harold Rd. E11 6C 46
Harold Rd. E13 4F 62
Harold Rd. N8 3K 43
Harold Rd. N15 3D 44
Harold Rd. NW10 6B 56
Harold Rd. SE19 4B 108
Harold Rd. Dart 1K 115
Harold Rd. Sutt 6B 122
Harold Rd. Wfd G 8E 30
Haroldstone Rd. E17 3H 45
Harold Vw. Romf 9K 35
Harold Wilson Ho. SE28 2F 80
Harold Wilson Ho. SW6 7K 73 (off Clem Attlee Ct.)
Harold Wood. 8K 35
Harold Wood Hall. H Hill 8H 35 (off Widecombe Clo.)
Harp All. EC4 9M 59
Harp Bus. Cen. NW2 6E 40 (off Apsley Way)
Harpenden Rd. E12 7G 47
Harpenden Rd. SE27 9M 91
Harpenmead Point. NW2 7K 41
Harper Clo. N14 7G 15
Harper Ho. SW9 2M 91
Harper M. SW17 9A 90
Harper Rd. E6 9K 63
Harper Rd. SE1 4A 76
Harper's Yd. N17 8D 28
Harp Island Clo. NW10 7B 40
Harp La. EC3 1C 76
Harpley Sq. E1 7G 61
Harpour Rd. Bark 2A 64
Harp Rd. W7 7D 54
Harpsden St. SW11 9E 74
Harpur M. WC1 8K 59
Harpur St. WC1 8K 59
Harraden Rd. SE3 9G 79
Harrier Av. E11 4F 46
Harrier Clo. Horn 2F 66
Harrier Ct. Houn 2J 85
Harrier M. SE28 3B 80
Harrier Rd. NW9 9C 24
Harriers Clo. W5 1J 71
Harrier Way. E6 8K 63
Harrier Way. Wal A 7M 7
Harriescourt. Wal A 5M 7
Harries Rd. Hay 7G 53
Harriet Clo. E8 4E 60
Harriet Gdns. Croy 4E 124
Harriet Ho. SW6 8M 73 (off Wandon Rd.)
Harriet St. SW1 3D 74
Harriet Tubman Clo. SW2 6K 91
Harriet Wlk. SW1 3D 74
Harriet Way. Bush 9B 10
Harringay. 3M 43
Harringay Gdns. N8 2M 43
Harringay Rd. N15 3M 43 (in two parts)
Harrington Clo. NW10 8B 40
Harrington Clo. Croy 4J 123
Harrington Ct. W10 6K 57
Harrington Ct. Croy 4B 124
Harrington Gdns. SW7 5M 73
Harrington Hill. E5 6F 44
Harrington Ho. NW1 6G 59 (off Harrington St.)
Harrington Rd. E11 6C 46
Harrington Rd. SE25 8E 108
Harrington Rd. SW7 5B 74
Harrington Sq. NW1 5G 59
Harrington St. NW1 5G 59 (in two parts)
Harrington Way. SE18 4H 79
Harriott Clo. SE10 5D 78
Harriott Ho. E1 8G 61 (off Jamaica St.)
Harris Bldgs. E1 9E 60 (off Burslem St.)
Harris Clo. Enf 3M 15
Harris Clo. Houn 9L 69
Harris Ct. Wemb 8K 39
Harris Ho. SW9 2L 91 (off St James's Cres.)
Harris Lodge. SE6 7A 94
Harrison Clo. N20 1C 26
Harrison Clo. N'wd 6A 20
Harrison Ho. SE17 6B 76 (off Brandon St.)
Harrison Rd. Dag 2M 65
Harrisons Ct. SE14 7H 77 (off Myers La.)
Harrison's Ri. Croy 5M 123
Harrison St. WC1 6J 59
Harrisons Wharf. Purf 6L 83
Harrison Wlk. Chesh 3D 6
Harris Rd. Bexh 9J 81
Harris Rd. Dag 1K 65
Harris Rd. Wat 8E 4
Harris St. E17 5K 45
Harris St. SE5 8B 76
Harris Way. Sun 5C 100
Harrods. 4D 74
Harrogate Ct. N11 6E 26
Harrogate Ct. SE12 6E 94
Harrogate Ct. SE26 9E 92 (off Droitwich Clo.)
Harrogate Rd. Wat 3G 21
Harrold Ho. NW6 3B 58
Harrold Rd. Dag 1F 64
Harrovian Bus. Village. Harr 5C 38
Harrow. 4C 38
Harrow Av. Enf 8D 16
Harroway Rd. SW11 1B 90
Harrow Borough F.C. 9L 37
Harrowby St. W1 9C 58
Harrow Clo. Chess 9H 119
Harrow Clo. Horn 6F 50
Harrow Cres. Romf 7F 34
Harrowdene Clo. Wemb 9H 39
Harrowdene Gdns. Tedd 3E 102
Harrowdene Rd. Wemb 8H 39
Harrow Dri. N9 1D 28
Harrow Dri. Horn 4F 50
Harrowes Meade. Edgw 3L 23
Harrow Fields Gdns. Harr 8C 38
Harrow Gdns. Orp 6F 128
Harrow Gdns. Warl 8K 139
Harrowgate Ho. E9 2H 61
Harrowgate Rd. E9 2J 61
Harrow Grn. E11 8C 46
Harrow La. E14 1M 77
Harrow Lodge. NW8 7B 58 (off Northwick Ter.)
Harrow Mnr. Way. SE2 2G 81
Harrow Mus. & Heritage Cen. 1A 38
Harrow on the Hill. 6C 38
Harrow Pk. Harr 7C 38
Harrow Pl. E1 9C 60
Harrow Road (Junct.) 2M 55
Harrow Rd. E6 4J 63
Harrow Rd. E11 8C 46
Harrow Rd. NW10 6E 56
Harrow Rd. W2 & NW1 8A 58 (in two parts)
Harrow Rd. W10 & W9 7J 57
Harrow Rd. Bark 4C 64
Harrow Rd. Cars 8C 122
Harrow Rd. Felt 8E 144
Harrow Rd. Ilf 9A 48
Harrow Rd. Warl 7K 139
Harrow Rd. Wemb (HA0) 9D 38 (in two parts)
Harrow Rd. Wemb (HA9) 1L 55
Harrow Rd. Bri. W2 8A 58
Harrow School Old Speech Room Gallery. 6C 38 (off High St., in Harrow School)
Harrow St. NW1 8C 58 (off Daventry St.)
Harrow Vw. Harr 9A 22
Harrow Vw. Hay 9E 52
Harrow Vw. Uxb 6A 52
Harrow Vw. Rd. W5 7F 54
Harrow Way. Shep 6A 100
Harrow Way. Wat 3J 21
Harrow Weald. 8C 22
Harrow Weald Pk. Harr 6B 22
Harry Hinkins Ho. SE17 6A 76 (off Bronti Clo.)
Harry Lambourn Ho. SE15 8F 76 (off Gervase St.)
Harston Dri. Enf 2L 17
Hartcliff Ct. W7 3D 70
Hart Ct. E6 3L 63
Hart Cres. Chig 5D 32
Hart Dyke Cres. Swan 7B 114
Hart Dyke Rd. Orp 4H 129
Hart Dyke Rd. Swan 6B 114
Harte Rd. Houn 1K 85
Hartfield Av. Els 6L 11
Hartfield Av. N'holt 5F 52
Hartfield Clo. Els 7L 11
Hartfield Cres. SW19 4K 105
Hartfield Cres. W Wick 5E 126
Hartfield Gro. SE20 5G 109
Hartfield Ho. N'holt 5F 52 (off Hartfield Av.)
Hartfield Rd. SW19 4K 105
Hartfield Rd. Chess 7H 119
Hartfield Rd. W Wick 6E 126
Hartfield Ter. E3 5L 61
Hartford Av. Harr 1E 38
Hartforde Rd. Borwd 4L 11
Hartford Rd. Bex 5L 97
Hartford Rd. Eps 8M 119
Hart Gro. W5 2L 71
Hart Gro. S'hall 8L 53
Hart Gro. Ct. W5 2L 71
Harthall La. K Lan 1A 4
Hartham Clo. N7 1J 59
Hartham Clo. Iswth 9E 70
Hartham Rd. N7 1J 59
Hartham Rd. N17 9D 28
Hartham Rd. Iswth 9D 70
Harting Rd. SE9 9J 95
Hartington Clo. F'boro 7A 128
Hartington Clo. Harr 9C 38
Hartington Ct. SW8 9J 75
Hartington Ct. W4 8M 71
Hartington Ho. SW1 6H 75 (off Drummond Ga.)
Hartington Rd. E16 9F 62
Hartington Rd. E17 4J 45
Hartington Rd. SW8 9J 75
Hartington Rd. W4 8M 71
Hartington Rd. W13 1F 70
Hartington Rd. S'hall 4J 69
Hartington Rd. Twic 6F 86
Hartismere Rd. SW6 8K 73
Hartlake Rd. E9 2H 61
Hartland. NW1 4G 59 (off Royal College St.)
Hartland Clo. N21 8A 16
Hartland Clo. Edgw 2L 23
Hartland Ct. N11 5D 26 (off Hartland Rd.)
Hartland Dri. Edgw 2L 23
Hartland Dri. Ruis 8F 36
Hartland Rd. E15 3D 62
Hartland Rd. N11 5D 26
Hartland Rd. NW1 3F 58
Hartland Rd. NW6 5K 57
Hartland Rd. Chesh 3D 6
Hartland Rd. Hamp H 1M 101
Hartland Rd. Horn 7E 50
Hartland Rd. Iswth 2E 86
Hartland Rd. Mord 2L 121
Hartlands Clo. Bex 5K 97
Hartlands, The. Houn 7F 68
Hartland Way. Croy 5J 125
Hartland Way. Mord 2K 121
Hartlepool Ct. E16 2M 79
Hartley Av. E6 4J 63
Hartley Av. NW7 5D 24
Hartley Clo. NW7 5D 24
Hartley Clo. Brom 6K 111
Hartley Down. Purl 7K 137
Hartley Farm. Purl 7K 137
Hartley Hill. Purl 7K 137
Hartley Ho. SE1 5D 76 (off Longfield Est.)
Hartley Old Rd. Purl 7K 137
Hartley Rd. E11 6D 46
Hartley Rd. Croy 2A 124
Hartley Rd. Well 8G 81
Hartley St. E2 6G 61 (in two parts)
Hartley Way. Purl 7K 137
Hart Lodge. High Bar 5J 13
Hartmann Rd. E16 2H 79
Hartmoor M. Enf 1H 17
Hartnoll St. N7 1K 59
Harton Clo. Brom 5H 111
Harton Rd. N9 2F 28
Harton St. SE8 9L 77
Hartop Point. SW6 8J 73 (off Pellant Rd.)
Hartsbourne Av. Bus H 2A 22
Hartsbourne Clo. Bus H 2B 22
Hartsbourne Country Club Golf Courses. 2L 21
Hartsbourne Ct. S'hall 9A 54 (off Fleming Rd.)
Hartsbourne Pk. Bush 2C 22
Hartsbourne Rd. Bus H 2B 22
Harts Clo. Bush 4L 9
Harts Cft. Croy 1J 139
Harts Gro. Wfd G 5E 30
Hartshill Clo. Uxb 3F 142
Hartshorn All. EC3 9C 60 (off Leadenhall St.)
Hartshorn Gdns. E6 7L 63
Hart's La. SE14 9J 77
Harts La. Bark 2M 63
Hartslock Dri. SE2 3H 81
Hartsmead Rd. SE9 8K 95
Hartspring Ind. Est. Wat 4L 9
Hartspring La. Bush & Wat 4L 9
Hart St. EC3 1C 76
Hartsway. Enf 6G 17
Hartswood Gdns. W12 4D 72
Hartswood Rd. W12 3D 72
Hartsworth Clo. E13 5D 62
Hartville Rd. SE18 5C 80
Hartwell Dri. E4 6A 30
Hartwell Ho. SE7 6F 78 (off Troughton Rd.)
Hartwell St. E8 2D 60
Hartwood Grn. Bush 2B 22
Harvard Ct. NW6 1M 57
Harvard Hill. W4 7M 71
Harvard Ho. SE17 7M 75 (off Doddington Gro.)
Harvard La. W4 6A 72
Harvard Rd. SE13 4A 94
Harvard Rd. W4 6M 71
Harvard Rd. Iswth 9C 70
Harvard Wlk. Horn 9E 50
Harvel Clo. Orp 7E 112
Harvel Cres. SE2 6H 81

Harvest Bank Rd.—Hayes Ct.

Harvest Bank Rd.
W Wick 5D 126
Harvest Ct. Esh 4L 117
Harvest End. Wat 9H 5
Harvester Rd. Eps 2B 134
Harvesters Clo. Iswth 4B 86
Harvest La. Lou 9H 19
Harvest La. Th Dit 1E 118
Harvest Rd. Bush 6M 9
Harvest Rd. Felt 1E 100
Harvest Way. Swan 2B 130
Harvey Ct. E17 . . . . .3L 45
Harvey Ct. Eps 1M 133
Harvey Dri. Hamp 5M 101
Harveyfields. Wal A 7J 7
Harvey Gdns. E11 . . . . .6D 46
Harvey Gdns. SE7 . . . . .6G 79
Harvey Gdns. Lou 5M 19
Harvey Ho. E1 . . . . .7F 60
(off Brady St.)
Harvey Ho. N1 . . . . .4B 60
(off Colville Est.)
Harvey Ho. SW1 . . . . .6H 75
(off Aylesford St.)
Harvey Ho. Bren 6J 71
Harvey Ho. Romf 2H 49
Harvey Lodge. W9 . . . . .8L 57
(off Admiral Wlk.)
Harvey Point. E16 . . . . .8E 62
(off Fife Rd.)
Harvey Rd. E11 . . . . .6C 46
Harvey Rd. N8 . . . . .3K 43
Harvey Rd. SE5 . . . . .9B 76
(in two parts)
Harvey Rd. Houn 6K 85
Harvey Rd. Ilf 1M 63
Harvey Rd. N'holt 3G 53
Harvey Rd. Uxb 5E 142
Harvey Rd. W on T 2D 116
Harvey's Bldgs. WC2 . . . . . . .1J 75
Harveys La. Romf 7B 50
Harvey St. N1 . . . . .4B 60
Harvill Rd. Sidc 2J 113
Harvington Wlk. E8 . . . . .3E 60
Harvist Est. N7 . . . . .9L 43
Harvist Rd. NW6 . . . . .5H 57
Harwater Dri. Lou 4K 19
Harwell Clo. Ruis 6B 36
Harwell Pas. N2 . . . . .2D 42
Harwood Av. Brom 6F 110
Harwood Av. Horn 1J 51
Harwood Av. Mitc 7C 106
Harwood Clo. N12 . . . . .6C 26
Harwood Clo. Wemb 9H 39
Harwood Ct. N1 . . . . .4B 60
(off Colville Est.)
Harwood Ct. SW15 . . . . .3G 89
Harwood Dri. Uxb 4D 142
Harwood Hall La. Upm 2M 67
Harwood M. SW6 . . . . .8L 73
Harwood Point. SE16 . . . . . .3K 77
Harwood Rd. SW6 . . . . .8L 73
Harwoods Rd. Wat 6E 8
Harwoods Yd. N21 . . . . .9L 15
Harwood Ter. SW6 . . . . .9M 73
Haselbury Rd. N18 & N9 . . . .4C 28
Haseley End. SE23 . . . . .6G 93
Haselrigge Rd. SW4 . . . . . . .3H 91
Haseltine Rd. SE26 . . . . . . .1K 109
Haselwood Dri. Enf 6M 15
Haskard Rd. Dag 9H 49
Hasker St. SW3 . . . . .5C 74
Haslam Av. Sutt 3J 121
Haslam Clo. N1 . . . . .3L 59
Haslam Clo. Uxb 7A 36
Haslam Ct. N11 . . . . .4F 26
Haslam St. SE15 . . . . .8D 76
Haslemere and Heathrow Est., The.
Houn 1F 84
Haslemere Av. NW4 . . . . .4H 41
Haslemere Av. SW18 . . . . . .8M 89
Haslemere Av. W7 & W13 . . .4E 70
Haslemere Av. Barn 1D 26
Haslemere Av. Houn 1G 85
Haslemere Av. Mitc 6B 106
Haslemere Bus. Cen.
Enf 6F 16
Haslemere Clo. Hamp 2K 101
Haslemere Clo. Wall 7J 123
Haslemere Gdns. N3 . . . . . . .1K 41
Haslemere Ind. Est.
SW18 . . . . .8M 89
Haslemere Rd. N8 . . . . .5H 43
Haslemere Rd. N21 . . . . .2M 27
Haslemere Rd. Bexh 1K 97
Haslemere Rd. Ilf 7D 48
Haslemere Rd. T Hth 9M 107
Hasler Clo. SE28 . . . . .1F 80
Haslers Wharf. E3 . . . . .4J 61
(off Old Ford Rd.)
Haslett Rd. Shep 6C 100
Haslingden Ho. Romf 5J 35
(off Dagnam Pk. Dri.)
Hasluck Gdns. New Bar 8M 13
Hassard St. E2 . . . . .5D 60
Hassendean Rd. SE3 . . . . . . .7F 78
Hassett Rd. E9 . . . . .2H 61
Hassocks Clo. SE26 . . . . .9F 92
Hassocks Rd. SW16 . . . . . . .5H 107
Hassock Wood. Kes 6H 127
Hassop Rd. NW2 . . . . .9H 41
Hassop Wlk. SE9 . . . . .1J 111
Hasted Rd. SE7 . . . . .6H 79
Haste Hill Golf Course. 9C 20
Hastings Av. Ilf 2A 48
Hastings Clo. SE15 . . . . .8E 76
Hastings Clo. Barn 6A 14
Hastings Clo. Wemb 9G 39
Hastings Ct. Tedd 2B 102
Hastings Dri. Surb 1G 119
Hastings Ho. SE18 . . . . .5K 79
(off Mulgrave Rd.)
Hastings Ho. W12 . . . . .1F 72
(off White City Est.)
Hastings Ho. W13 . . . . .1F 70
Hastings Ho. WC1 . . . . .6J 59
(off Hastings St.)
Hastings Rd. N11 . . . . .5G 27
Hastings Rd. N17 . . . . .1B 44
Hastings Rd. W13 . . . . .1F 70
Hastings Rd. Brom 3J 127
Hastings Rd. Croy 3D 124
Hastings Rd. Romf 3F 50
Hastings St. WC1 . . . . .6J 59
Hastings Way. Bush 6J 9
Hastings Way. Crox G 6A 8
Hastingwood Ct. E17 . . . . . .3M 45
Hastingwood Trad. Est.
N18 . . . . .5H 29
Hastoe Clo. Hay 7J 53
Hat & Mitre Ct. EC1 . . . . . . .7M 59
(off St John St.)
Hatcham M. Bus. Cen.
SE14 . . . . .9H 77
Hatcham Pk. M. SE14 . . . . . .9H 77
Hatcham Pk. Rd. SE14 . . . . .9H 77
Hatcham Rd. SE15 . . . . .7G 77
Hatchard Rd. N19 . . . . .7H 43
Hatchcroft. NW4 . . . . .1F 40
Hatch End. 7K 21
Hatchers M. SE1 . . . . .3C 76
(off Bermondsey St.)
Hatchett Rd. Felt 7A 84
Hatchfield Ho. N15 . . . . .4C 44
(off Albert Rd.)
Hatch Gro. Romf 2J 49
Hatch La. E4 . . . . .4B 30
(in two parts)
Hatch La. Coul 7D 136
Hatch La. W Dray 8H 143
Hatch Pl. King T 2K 103
Hatch Rd. SW16 . . . . .6J 107
Hatch Side. Chig 5L 31
Hatch, The. Enf 3H 17
Hatchwood Clo. Wfd G 4D 30
Hatcliffe Almshouses.
SE10 . . . . .6C 78
(off Tuskar St.)
Hatcliffe Clo. SE3 . . . . .2D 94
Hatcliffe St. SE10 . . . . .6D 78
Hatfield Clo. SE14 . . . . .8H 77
Hatfield Clo. Horn 1H 67
Hatfield Clo. Ilf 1M 47
Hatfield Clo. Mitc 8B 106
Hatfield Clo. Sutt 1M 135
Hatfield Ct. SE3 . . . . .8E 78
Hatfield Ct. N'holt 6G 53
(off Canberra Dri.)
Hatfield Ho. EC1 . . . . .7A 60
(off Golden La. Est.)
Hatfield Mead. Mord 9L 105
Hatfield Rd. E15 . . . . .1C 62
Hatfield Rd. W4 . . . . .3B 72
Hatfield Rd. W13 . . . . .2E 70
Hatfield Rd. Dag 2J 65
Hatfield Rd. Wat 3F 8
Hatfields. SE1 . . . . .2L 75
Hatfields. Lou 5M 19
Hathaway Clo. Brom 3K 127
Hathaway Clo. Ruis 9D 36
Hathaway Clo. Stan 5E 22
Hathaway Cres. E12 . . . . . . .2K 63
Hathaway Gdns. W13 . . . . . . .8E 54
Hathaway Gdns. Romf 3H 49
Hathaway Ho. N1 . . . . .5C 60
Hathaway Rd. Croy 2M 123
Hatherleigh Clo. Chess 7H 119
Hatherleigh Clo. Mord 8L 105
Hatherleigh Rd. Ruis 7E 36
Hatherleigh Way. Romf 8H 35
Hatherley Ct. W2 . . . . .9M 57
(off Hatherley Gro.)
Hatherley Cres. Sidc 8E 96
Hatherley Gdns. E6 . . . . .6H 63
Hatherley Gdns. N8 . . . . .4J 43
Hatherley Gro. W2 . . . . .9M 57
Hatherley Ho. E17 . . . . .2L 45
Hatherley M. E17 . . . . .2L 45
Hatherley Rd. E17 . . . . .2K 45
Hatherley Rd. Rich 9K 71
Hatherley Rd. Sidc 1E 112
Hatherley St. SW1 . . . . .5G 75
Hathern Gdns. SE9 . . . . .1L 111
Hatherop Rd. Hamp 4K 101
Hathersage Ct. N1 . . . . .1B 60
Hathorne Clo. SE15 . . . . .1F 92
Hathway St. SE15 . . . . .1H 93
Hathway Ter. SE15 . . . . .1H 93
(off Hathway St.)
Hatley Av. Ilf 2A 48
Hatley Clo. N11 . . . . .5D 26
Hatley Rd. N4 . . . . .7K 43
Hatteraick St. SE16 . . . . .3G 77
Hattersfield Clo. Belv 5K 81
Hatters La. Wat 8B 8
Hatton. 3D 84
Hatton Clo. SE18 . . . . .8B 80
Hatton Cross (Junct.) 2D 84
Hatton Garden. EC1 . . . . .8L 59
Hatton Gdns. Mitc 9D 106
Hatton Grn. Felt 3E 84
Hatton Gro. W Dray 3H 143
Hatton Ho. King T 6K 103
(off Victoria Rd.)
Hatton Pl. EC1 . . . . .8L 59
Hatton Rd. Chesh 2D 6
Hatton Rd. Croy 3L 123
Hatton Rd. Felt 6A 84
Hatton Rd. S. Felt 3D 84
Hatton Row. NW8 . . . . .7B 58
(off Hatton St.)
Hatton St. NW8 . . . . .7B 58
Hatton Wall. EC1 . . . . .8L 59
Haughmond. N12 . . . . .4M 25
Haunch of Venison Yd.
W1 . . . . .9F 58
Hauteville Ct. Gdns. W6 . . . . .4D 72
(off South Side)
Havana Clo. Romf 3C 50
Havana Rd. SW19 . . . . .8L 89
Havannah St. E14 . . . . .3L 77
Havant Rd. E17 . . . . .1A 46
Havelock Clo. W12 . . . . .1F 72
Havelock Ct. S'hall 4K 69
(off Havelock Rd.)
Havelock Ho. SE23 . . . . .7G 93
Havelock Pl. Harr 4C 38
Havelock Rd. N17 . . . . .9E 28
Havelock Rd. SW19 . . . . . . .2A 106
Havelock Rd. Belv 5K 81
Havelock Rd. Brom 8G 111
Havelock Rd. Croy 4D 124
Havelock Rd. Dart 6F 98
Havelock Rd. Harr 1C 38
Havelock Rd. S'hall 4J 69
Havelock St. N1 . . . . .4J 59
Havelock St. Ilf 7M 47
Havelock Ter. SW8 . . . . .9F 74
Havelock Wlk. SE23 . . . . .7G 93
Haven Clo. SE9 . . . . .9K 95
Haven Clo. SW19 . . . . .9H 89
Haven Clo. Hay 7C 52
Haven Clo. Sidc 3G 113
Haven Clo. Swan 6D 114
Haven Ct. Beck 6A 110
Haven Ct. Surb 1K 119
Haven Grn. W5 . . . . .9H 55
Haven Grn. Ct. W5 . . . . .9H 55
Havenhurst Ri. Enf 4L 15
Haven La. W5 . . . . .9J 55
Haven Lodge. Enf 8C 16
(off Village Rd.)
Haven M. E3 . . . . .8K 61
Haven Pl. W5 . . . . .1H 71
Havenpool. NW8 . . . . .4M 57
(off Abbey Rd.)
Haven Rd. Ashf 9F 144
Haven St. NW1 . . . . .3F 58
Haven, The. N14 . . . . .8F 14
Haven, The. Rich 2L 87
Haven, The. Sun 4E 100
Havent Ho. Romf 7J 35
(off Kingsbridge Cir.)
Haven Wood. Wemb 8M 39
Haverfield Gdns. Rich 8L 71
Haverfield Rd. E3 . . . . .6J 61
Haverford Way. Edgw 8K 23
Haverhill Rd. E4 . . . . .1A 30
Haverhill Rd. SW12 . . . . .7G 91
Havering. NW1 . . . . .3F 58
(off Castlehaven Rd.)
Havering-atte-Bower. 3C 34
Havering Country Pk. 4A 34
Havering Dri. Romf 2C 50
Havering Gdns. Romf 3G 49
Havering Park. 5M 33
Havering Rd. Romf 5B 34
Havering St. E1 . . . . .9H 61
Havering Way. Bark 6F 64
Havers Av. W on T 7H 117
Haversham Clo. Twic 5H 87
Haversham Ct. Gnfd 2D 54
Haversham Pl. N6 . . . . .7D 42
Haverstock Ct. Orp 6F 112
(off Cotmandene Cres.)
Haverstock Hill. NW3 . . . . . . .1C 58
Haverstock Pl. N1 . . . . .6M 59
(off Haverstock St.)
Haverstock Rd. NW5 . . . . . . .1E 58
Haverstock St. N1 . . . . .5M 59
Haverthwaite Rd. Orp 4B 128
Havil St. SE5 . . . . .8C 76
Havisham Ho. SE16 . . . . .3E 76
Havisham Pl. SE19 . . . . .4M 107
Hawarden Gro. SE24 . . . . . . .6A 92
Hawarden Hill. NW2 . . . . .8E 40
Hawarden Rd. E17 . . . . .2H 45
Hawbridge Rd. E11 . . . . .6B 46
Hawes Clo. N'wd 7D 20
Hawes Ho. E17 . . . . .2H 45
Hawes La. E4 . . . . .2A 18
Hawes La. W Wick 3A 126
Hawes Rd. N18 . . . . .6F 28
Hawes Rd. Brom 5F 110
(in two parts)
Hawes St. N1 . . . . .3M 59
Haweswater Dri. Wat 6G 5
Hawfield Bank. Orp 5H 129
Hawgood St. E3 . . . . .8L 61
Hawk Clo. Wal A 7M 7
Hawkdene. E4 . . . . .8M 17
Hawke Ct. Hay 7G 53
(off Perth Av.)
Hawke Ho. E1 . . . . .7H 61
(off Ernest St.)
Hawke Pk. Rd. N22 . . . . .1M 43
Hawke Pl. SE16 . . . . .3H 77
Hawker Ct. King T 6K 103
(off Church Rd.)
Hawke Rd. SE19 . . . . .3B 108
Hawkesbury Rd. SW15 . . . . . .4F 88
Hawkesfield Rd. SE23 . . . . . .8J 93
Hawkesley Clo. Twic 1E 102
Hawkes Rd. Felt 6E 84
Hawkes Rd. Mitc 5D 106
Hawkesworth Clo. N'wd 7C 20
Hawke Tower. SE14 . . . . .7J 77
Hawkewood Rd. Sun 7E 100
Hawkfield Ct. Iswth 1C 86
Hawkhirst Rd. Kenl 7B 138
Hawkhurst Gdns. Chess 6J 119
Hawkhurst Gdns. Romf 6B 34
Hawkhurst Rd. SW16 . . . . . .5H 107
Hawkhurst Rd. Kenl 9C 138
Hawkhurst Way. N Mald . . .9B 104
Hawkhurst Way.
W Wick 4M 125
Hawkinge. N17 . . . . .9B 28
(off Gloucester Rd.)
Hawkinge Wlk. Orp 7F 112
Hawkinge Way. Horn 2G 67
Hawkins Clo. NW7 . . . . .5B 24
Hawkins Clo. Borwd 4A 12
Hawkins Clo. Harr 5B 38
Hawkins Ct. SE18 . . . . .5J 79
Hawkins Ho. SE8 . . . . .7L 77
(off New King St.)
Hawkins Ho. SW1 . . . . .7G 75
(off Dolphin Sq.)
Hawkins Rd. Tedd 3F 102
Hawkins Way. SE6 . . . . .2L 109
Hawkley Gdns. SE27 . . . . . . .8M 91
Hawkridge Clo. Romf 4G 49
Hawksbrook La. Beck 1M 125
(in two parts)
Hawkshaw Clo. SW2 . . . . . . .6J 91
Hawkshead. NW1 . . . . .6G 59
(off Stanhope St.)
Hawkshead Clo. Brom 4C 110
Hawkshead Rd. NW10 . . . . . .3D 56
Hawkshead Rd. W4 . . . . .3C 72
Hawkshill Clo. Esh 8L 117
Hawkshill Pl. Esh 8L 117
Hawkshill Way. Esh 8K 117
Hawkslade Rd. SE15 . . . . . . .4H 93
Hawksley Rd. N16 . . . . .8C 44
Hawksmead Clo. Enf 9D 6
Hawks M. SE10 . . . . .8A 78
Hawksmoor Clo. E6 . . . . .9J 63
Hawksmoor Clo. SE18 . . . . . .6C 80
Hawksmoor Ho. E14 . . . . .8J 61
(off Aston St.)
Hawksmoor M. E1 . . . . .1F 76
Hawksmoor Pl. E2 . . . . .7E 60
(off Cheshire St.)
Hawksmoor St. W6 . . . . .7H 73
Hawksmouth. E4 . . . . .9A 18
Hawks Pas. King T 6K 103
(off Minerva Rd.)
Hawks Rd. King T 6K 103
Hawkstone Rd. SE16 . . . . . . .5G 77
Hawkwell Ct. E4 . . . . .3A 30
Hawkwell Wlk. N1 . . . . .4A 60
(off Maldon Rd.)
Hawkwood Cres. E4 . . . . . . .8M 17
Hawkwood La. Chst 5A 112
Hawkwood Mt. E5 . . . . .6F 44
Hawlands Dri. Pinn 5J 37
Hawley. 1K 115
Hawley Clo. Hamp 3K 101
Hawley Cres. NW1 . . . . .3F 58
Hawley M. NW1 . . . . .3F 58
Hawley Rd. N18 . . . . .5H 29
Hawley Rd. NW1 . . . . .3F 58
(in two parts)
Hawley Rd. Dart & S at H . . .8J 99
Hawley St. NW1 . . . . .3F 58
Hawley Ter. Dart 1L 115
Hawley Va. Dart 2L 115
(in two parts)
Hawstead La. Orp 7K 129
Hawstead Rd. SE6 . . . . .5M 93
Hawsted. Buck H 9F 18
Hawter. NW9 . . . . .8D 24
Hawthorn Av. E3 . . . . .4K 61
Hawthorn Av. N13 . . . . .5J 27
Hawthorn Av. Rain 7F 66
Hawthorn Cen. Harr 3D 38
Hawthorn Clo. Ab L 5E 4
Hawthorn Clo. Bans 6J 135
Hawthorn Clo. Hamp 2L 101
Hawthorn Clo. Houn 8F 68
Hawthorn Clo. Orp 1B 128
Hawthorn Clo. Wat 2D 8
Hawthorn Cotts. Well 2E 96
(off Hook La.)
Hawthorn Ct. Pinn 9G 21
(off Rickmansworth Rd.)
Hawthorn Ct. Rich 9M 71
Hawthorn Cres. SW17 . . . . .2E 106
Hawthorn Cres. S Croy 3G 139
Hawthornden Clo. N12 . . . . . .6C 26
Hawthorndene Clo.
Brom 4D 126
Hawthorndene Rd. Brom . . .4D 126
Hawthorn Dri. Den 2A 142
Hawthorn Dri. Harr 4L 37
Hawthorn Dri. W Wick 6C 126
Hawthorne Av. Big H 7H 141
Hawthorne Av. Cars 9E 122
Hawthorne Av. Chesh 4B 6
Hawthorne Av. Harr 4E 38
Hawthorne Av. Mitc 6B 106
Hawthorne Av. Ruis 4F 36
Hawthorne Av. T Hth 5M 107
Hawthorne Clo. N1 . . . . .2C 60
Hawthorne Clo. Brom 7K 111
Hawthorne Clo. Chesh 4B 6
Hawthorne Clo. Sutt 4A 122
Hawthorne Ct. W5 . . . . .2J 71
Hawthorne Ct. N'wd 9E 20
Hawthorne Ct. Stanw 6B 144
(off Hawthorne Way)
Hawthorne Cres. W Dray . . .3K 143
Hawthorne Farm Av.
N'holt 4J 53
Hawthorne Gro. NW9 . . . . . . .5A 40
Hawthorne Ho. SW1 . . . . .6G 75
(off Churchill Gdns.)
Hawthorne M. Gnfd 9A 54
Hawthorne Pl. Eps 4C 134
Hawthorne Pl. Hay 1D 68
Hawthorne Rd. E17 . . . . .1L 45
Hawthorne Rd. Brom 7J 111
Hawthorne Way. Stanw 6B 144
Hawthorn Gdns. W5 . . . . .4H 71
Hawthorn Gro. SE20 . . . . . . .4F 108
Hawthorn Gro. Barn 8D 12
Hawthorn Gro. Enf 2B 16
Hawthorn Hatch. Bren 8F 70
Hawthorn M. NW7 . . . . .8J 25
Hawthorn Pl. Eri 6A 82
Hawthorn Rd. N8 . . . . .1H 43
Hawthorn Rd. N18 . . . . .6D 28
Hawthorn Rd. NW10 . . . . .3E 56
Hawthorn Rd. Bexh 3K 97
Hawthorn Rd. Bren 8F 70
Hawthorn Rd. Buck H 4H 31
Hawthorn Rd. Dart 8H 99
Hawthorn Rd. Sutt 8C 122
Hawthorn Rd. Wall 9F 122
Hawthorns. S Croy 6M 123
(off Bramley Hill)
Hawthorns. Wfd G 3E 30
Hawthorns, The. Eps 9D 120
Hawthorns, The. Lou 6L 19
Hawthorn Ter. Sidc 4D 96
Hawthorn Wlk. W10 . . . . .7J 57
Hawthorn Way. N9 . . . . .2C 28
Hawthorn Way. Shep 8B 100
Hawtrey Av. N'holt 5H 53
Hawtrey Dri. Ruis 5E 36
Hawtrey Rd. NW3 . . . . .3C 58
Haxted Rd. Brom 5F 110
Hayburn Way. Horn 6D 50
Hay Clo. E15 . . . . .3C 62
Hay Clo. Borwd 4A 12
Haycroft Gdns. NW10 . . . . . .4E 56
Haycroft Rd. SW2 . . . . .4J 91
Haycroft Rd. Surb 4H 119
Hay Currie St. E14 . . . . .9M 61
Hayday Rd. E16 . . . . .8E 62
(in three parts)
Hayden Rd. Wal A 8J 7
Haydens Clo. Orp 1G 129
Haydens M. W3 . . . . .9A 56
Hayden's Pl. W11 . . . . .9K 57
Hayden Way. Romf 9A 34
Haydn Av. Purl 6L 137
Haydock Av. N'holt 2L 53
Haydock Clo. Horn 9K 51
Haydock Grn. N'holt 2L 53
Haydock Grn. Flats. N'holt . . .2L 53
(off Haydock Grn.)
Haydon Clo. NW9 . . . . .2A 40
Haydon Clo. Enf 8C 16
Haydon Dell. Bush 8K 9
Haydon Dri. Pinn 2E 36
Haydon Pk. Rd. SW19 . . . . . .2L 105
Haydon Rd. Dag 7G 49
Haydon Rd. Wat 8J 9
Haydons Rd. SW19 . . . . . . .2M 105
Haydon St. EC3 . . . . .1D 76
Haydon Wlk. E1 . . . . .9D 60
Haydon Way. SW11 . . . . .3B 90
Hayes. 3E 126
(Bromley)
Hayes. 9C 52
(Hillingdon)
Hayes Bri. Retail Pk. Hay 1G 69
Hayes Chase. W Wick 1B 126
Hayes Clo. Brom 4E 126
Hayes Ct. SE5 . . . . .8A 76
(off Camberwell New Rd.)
Hayes Ct. SW2 . . . . .7J 91

Hayes Cres.—Hedingham Clo.

Hayes Cres. NW11 ....3K 41
Hayes Cres. Sutt 6H 121
Hayes Dri. Rain 3F 66
Hayes End. 8B 52
Hayes End Clo. Hay 8B 52
Hayes End Dri. Hay 7B 52
Hayes End Rd. Hay 7B 52
Hayes F.C. 1D 68
Hayesford Pk. Dri. Brom ...9D 110
Hayes Garden. Brom 4E 126
Hayes Hill. Brom 3C 126
Hayes Hill Rd. Brom 3D 126
Hayes La. Beck 7A 110
Hayes La. Brom 9E 110
Hayes La. Kenl 8M 137
Hayes Mead Rd. Brom 3C 126
Hayes Metro Cen. Hay 1G 69
Hayes Pl. NW1 ....7C 58
Hayes Rd. Brom 8E 110
Hayes Rd. S'hall 5F 68
Hayes St. Brom 3F 126
Hayes Town. 3D 68
Hayes Way. Beck 8A 110
Hayes Wood Av. Brom 3F 126
Hayfield Clo. Bush 6M 9
Hayfield Pas. E1 ....7G 61
Hayfield Rd. Orp 9E 112
Hayfield Yd. E1 ....7G 61
Haygarth Pl. SW19 ....2H 105
Haygreen Clo. King T 3M 103
Hay Hill. W1 ....1F 74
Hayland Clo. NW9 ....2B 40
Hay La. NW9 ....2A 40
Hayles Bldgs. SE11 ....5M 75
(off Elliotts Row)
Hayles St. SE11 ....5M 75
Haylett Gdns. King T 8H 103
Hayling Av. Felt 9E 84
Hayling Clo. N16 ....1C 60
Hayling Ct. Sutt 6G 121
Hayling Rd. Wat 3E 20
Haymaker Clo. Uxb 3D 142
Hayman Cres. Hay 5B 52
Haymans Point. SE11 ......5K 75
Hayman St. N1 ....3M 59
Haymarket. SW1 ....1H 75
Haymarket Arc. SW1 ....1H 75
(off Haymarket)
Haymarket Theatre Royal. *1H 75*
(off Haymarket)
Haymeads Dri. Esh 8A 118
Haymer Gdns. Wor Pk 5E 120
Haymerle Ho. SE15 ....7E 76
(off Haymerle Rd.)
Haymerle Rd. SE15 ....7E 76
Haymill Clo. Gnfd 6D 54
Hayne Ho. W11 ....2J 73
(off Penzance Pl.)
Hayne Rd. Beck 6K 109
Haynes Clo. N11 ....3E 26
Haynes Clo. N17 ....7F 28
Haynes Clo. SE3 ....2C 94
Haynes Dri. N9 ....3F 28
Haynes La. SE19 ....3C 108
Haynes Rd. Horn 2H 51
Haynes Rd. Wemb 3J 55
Hayne St. EC1 ....8M 59
Haynt Wlk. SW20 ....7J 105
Hay's Galleria. SE1 ....2C 76
Hays La. SE1 ....2C 76
Haysleigh Gdns. SE20 .....6E 108
Hay's M. W1 ....2F 74
Haysoms Clo. Romf 2C 50
Haystall Clo. Hay 5C 52
Hay St. E2 ....4E 60
Hays Wlk. Sutt 2H 135
Hayter Ct. E11 ....7F 46
Hayter Rd. SW2 ....4J 91
Hayton Clo. E8 ....2D 60
Hayward Clo. SW19 ......4M 105
Hayward Clo. Dart 4B 98
Hayward Ct. SW9 ....1J 91
(off Clapham Rd.)
Hayward Dri. Dart 8K 99
Hayward Gallery. *2K 75*
(off Belvedere Rd.)
Hayward Gdns. SW15 ....5G 89
Hayward Rd. N20 ....2A 26
Hayward Rd. Th Dit 3D 118
Haywards Clo. Chad H 3F 48
Hayward's Pl. EC1 ....7M 59
Haywards Yd. SE4 ....4K 93
(off Lindal Rd.)
Haywood Clo. Pinn 9H 21
Haywood Ct. Wal A 7M 7
Haywood Lodge. N11 ....6J 27
(off Oak La.)
Haywood Ri. Orp 7C 128
Haywood Rd. Brom 8H 111
Hayworth Clo. Enf 4J 17
Hazel Av. W Dray 4L 143
Hazel Bank. SE25 ....6C 108
Hazel Bank. Surb 3A 120
Hazelbank Rd. SE6 ....8B 94
Hazelbourne Rd. SW12 .....5F 90
Hazelbrouck Gdns. Ilf 7B 32
Hazelbury Av. Ab L 5A 4
Hazelbury Clo. SW19 ....6L 105
Hazelbury Grn. N9 ....3C 28
Hazelbury La. N9 ....3C 28
Hazel Clo. N13 ....3B 28
Hazel Clo. N19 ....7G 43
Hazel Clo. NW9 ....9C 24
Hazel Clo. SE15 ....1E 92
Hazel Clo. Bren 8F 70
Hazel Clo. Croy 2H 125
Hazel Clo. Horn 8F 50
Hazel Clo. Mitc 8H 107
Hazel Clo. Twic 6A 86
Hazel Ct. W5 ....1J 71
Hazel Ct. Lou 5K 19
Hazel Cres. Romf 8M 33
Hazel Cft. Pinn 6M 21
Hazelcroft Clo. Uxb 3D 142
Hazeldean Rd. NW10 ....3B 56
Hazeldene. Wal X 5E 6
Hazeldene Ct. Kenl 7B 138
Hazeldene Dri. Pinn 1G 37
Hazeldene Gdns. Uxb 4A 52
Hazeldene Rd. Ilf 7F 48
Hazeldene Rd. Well 1G 97
Hazeldon Rd. SE4 ....4J 93
Hazel Dri. Eri 9E 82
Hazeleigh Gdns. Wfd G 5J 31
Hazel End. Swan 9C 114
Hazel Gdns. Edgw 4M 23
Hazelgreen Clo. N21 ....1M 27
Hazel Gro. SE26 ....1H 109
Hazel Gro. Felt 7E 84
Hazel Gro. Orp 4M 127
Hazel Gro. Romf 1J 49
Hazel Gro. Wat 8F 4
Hazel Gro. Wemb 4J 55
Hazelhurst. Beck 5B 110
Hazelhurst Ct. SE6 ....2A 110
(off Beckenham Hill Rd.)
Hazelhurst Rd. SW17 ......1A 106
Hazel La. Rich 8J 87
Hazellville Rd. N19 ....5H 43
Hazel Mead. Barn 7F 12
Hazel Mead. Eps 2E 134
Hazelmere Clo. Felt 5C 84
Hazelmere Clo. N'holt 5K 53
Hazelmere Ct. SW2 ....7K 91
Hazelmere Dri. N'holt 5K 53
Hazelmere Gdns. Horn 3G 51
Hazelmere Rd. NW6 ....4K 57
Hazelmere Rd. N'holt 5K 53
Hazelmere Rd. Orp 8A 112
Hazelmere Wlk. N'holt 5K 53
(in two parts)
Hazelmere Way. Brom 1E 126
Hazel Ri. Horn 4G 51
Hazel Rd. E15 ....1C 62
Hazel Rd. NW10 ....6F 56
(in two parts)
Hazel Rd. Dart 8H 99
Hazel Rd. Eri 9E 82
Hazel Rd. Park 1M 5
Hazeltree La. N'holt 6J 53
Hazel Tree Rd. Wat 1F 8
Hazel Wlk. Brom 1L 127
Hazel Way. E4 ....6K 29
Hazel Way. SE1 ....5D 76
Hazelwood. Lou 7H 19
Hazelwood Av. Mord 8M 105
Hazelwood Clo. W5 ....3J 71
Hazelwood Clo. Harr 2M 37
Hazelwood Ct. N13 ....4L 27
(off Hazelwood La.)
Hazelwood Ct. NW10 ....8C 40
Hazelwood Ct. Surb 1J 119
Hazelwood Cres. N13 ....4L 27
Hazelwood Dri. Pinn 9F 20
Hazelwood Gro. S Croy 5F 138
Hazelwood Ho. SE8 ....5J 77
Hazelwood Houses. Short 7C 110
Hazelwood La. N13 ....4L 27
Hazelwood La. Ab L 5A 4
Hazelwood Pk. Clo. Chig 5C 32
Hazelwood Rd. E17 ....3J 45
Hazelwood Rd. Crox G 8A 8
Hazelwood Rd. Enf 8D 16
Hazlebury Rd. SW6 ....1M 89
Hazledean Rd. Croy 4B 124
Hazledene Rd. W4 ....7A 72
Hazlemere Gdns. Wor Pk 3E 120
Hazlewell Rd. SW15 ....4G 89
Hazlewood Clo. E5 ....8J 45
Hazlewood Cres. W10 ....7J 57
Hazlewood Tower. W10 .....7J 57
(off Golborne Gdns.)
Hazlitt Clo. Felt 1J 101
Hazlitt M. W14 ....4J 73
Hazlitt Rd. W14 ....4J 73
Hazon Way. Eps 4A 134
Heacham Av. Uxb 8A 36
Headbourne Ho. SE1 ....4B 76
Headcorn Pl. T Hth 8K 107
Headcorn Rd. N17 ....7D 28
Headcorn Rd. Brom 2D 110
Headcorn Rd. T Hth 8K 107
Headfort Pl. SW1 ....3E 74
Headingley Clo. Ilf 6D 32
Headington Ct. Croy 6A 124
(off Tanfield Rd.)
Headington Rd. SW18 ....8A 90
Headlam Rd. SW4 ....5H 91
(in two parts)
Headlam St. E1 ....7F 60
Headley App. Ilf 3M 47
Headley Av. Wall 7K 123
Headley Clo. Eps 8L 119
Headley Ct. SE26 ....2G 109
Headley Dri. Ilf 4M 47
Headley Dri. New Ad 9M 125
Headley Rd. Eps 9M 133
(in two parts)
Head's M. W11 ....9L 57
Headstone. 2A 38
Headstone Dri. Harr 1B 38
Headstone Gdns. Harr 2A 38
Headstone La. Harr 7M 21
Headstone Pde. Harr 2B 38
Headstone Rd. Harr 3C 38
Head St. E1 ....9H 61
(in two parts)
Headway Clo. Rich 1G 103
Headway, The. Eps 1D 134
Heald St. SE14 ....9L 77
Healey Ho. SW9 ....8L 75
Healey Rd. Wat 8D 8
Healey St. NW1 ....2F 58
Healy Dri. Orp 6D 128
Hearne Rd. W4 ....7L 71
Hearn Ri. N'holt 4H 53
Hearn Rd. Romf 4D 50
Hearn's Bldgs. SE17 ....5B 76
Hearnshaw Ho. E14 ....8J 61
(off Halley St.)
Hearn's Rd. Orp 8G 113
Hearn St. EC2 ....7C 60
Hearnville Rd. SW12 ....7E 90
Heatham Pk. Twic 6D 86
Heath Av. Bexh 7H 81
Heathbourne Rd. Bus H 1C 22
Heath Brow. NW3 ....8A 42
Heath Bus. Cen. Houn 3A 86
Heath Clo. NW11 ....5M 41
Heath Clo. W5 ....7K 55
Heath Clo. Bans 6M 135
Heath Clo. Hay 8B 68
Heath Clo. Orp 2G 129
Heath Clo. Romf 1E 50
Heath Clo. Stanw 5A 144
Heathclose. Swan 6C 114
Heathclose Av. Dart 6F 98
Heathclose Rd. Dart 7E 98
Heathcock Ct. WC2 ....1J 75
(off Exchange Ct.)
Heathcote Av. Ilf 9K 31
Heathcote Ct. Ilf 8K 31
(in two parts)
Heathcote Gro. E4 ....3A 30
Heathcote Rd. Eps 6B 134
Heathcote Rd. Twic 5F 86
Heathcote St. WC1 ....7K 59
Heathcote Way. W Dray ...2H 143
Heath Ct. Croy 6B 124
(off Heathfield Rd.)
Heath Ct. Houn 3K 85
Heath Ct. Uxb 3B 142
Heathcroft. NW11 ....6M 41
Heathcroft. W5 ....7K 55
Heathcroft Av. Sun 4D 100
Heathcroft Gdns. E17 ....8B 30
Heathdale Av. Houn 2J 85
Heathdene Dri. Belv 5M 81
Heathdene Mnr. Wat 3D 8
Heathdene Rd. SW16 ......4K 107
Heathdene Rd. Wall 9F 122
Heath Dri. NW3 ....9M 41
Heath Dri. SW20 ....8G 105
Heath Dri. Romf 8E 34
Heath Dri. Sutt 1A 136
Heathedge. SE26 ....8F 92
Heath End Rd. Bex 7C 98
Heather Av. Romf 9B 34
Heatherbank. SE9 ....1K 95
Heatherbank. Chst 6L 111
Heatherbank Clo. Dart 5C 98
Heather Clo. E6 ....9L 63
Heather Clo. N7 ....8K 43
Heather Clo. SE13 ....6B 94
Heather Clo. SW8 ....2F 90
Heather Clo. Ab L 5E 4
Heather Clo. Hamp 5K 101
Heather Clo. Iswth 4B 86
Heather Clo. Romf 8B 34
Heather Clo. Uxb 8D 142
Heather Ct. Sidc 3H 113
Heatherdale Clo. King T 3L 103
Heatherdene Clo. N12 ......7A 26
Heatherdene Clo. Mitc 8B 106
Heather Dri. Dart 6E 98
Heather Dri. Enf 4M 15
Heather Dri. Romf 9B 34
Heather End. Swan 8B 114
Heatherfold Way. Pinn 1D 36
Heather Gdns. NW11 ....4J 41
Heather Gdns. Romf 9B 34
Heather Gdns. Sutt 8L 121
Heather Glen. Romf 9B 34
Heather Ho. E14 ....9A 62
(off Dee St.)
Heatherlands. Sun 3E 100
Heather La. Wat 9D 4
Heather La. W Dray 9C 142
Heatherley Ct. E5 ....8E 44
Heatherley Dri. Ilf 1J 47
Heather Pk. Dri. Wemb 3L 55
Heather Pk. Pde. Wemb 3K 55
(off Heather Pk. Dri.)
Heather Pl. Esh 6M 117
Heather Ri. Bush 4K 9
Heather Rd. E4 ....6K 29
Heather Rd. NW2 ....7D 40
Heather Rd. SE12 ....8E 94
Heatherset Clo. Esh 7A 118
Heatherset Gdns. SW16 ...4K 107
Heatherside Rd. Eps 9B 120
Heatherside Rd. Sidc 9G 97
Heathers, The. Stai 6D 144
Heatherton Ter. N3 ....9M 25
Heather Wlk. W10 ....7J 57
Heather Wlk. Edgw 5M 23
Heather Wlk. Twic 6L 85
(off Stephenson Rd.)
Heather Way. Romf 9B 34
Heather Way. S Croy 1H 139
Heather Way. Stan 6D 22
Heatherwood Clo. E12 ......7G 47
Heatherwood Dri. Hay 5B 52
Heath Farm Ct. Wat 1B 8
Heathfield. E4 ....3A 30
Heathfield. Chst 3A 112
Heathfield. Harr 5D 38
Heathfield Av. SW18 ....6B 90
Heathfield Clo. E16 ....8H 63
Heathfield Clo. Kes 7G 127
Heathfield Ct. SE20 ....4G 109
Heathfield Ct. W4 ....6B 72
Heathfield Dri. Mitc 5C 106
Heathfield Gdns. NW11 .....4H 41
Heathfield Gdns. SE3 ....1C 94
(off Baizdon Rd.)
Heathfield Gdns. SW18 .....5B 90
Heathfield Gdns. W4 ....6A 72
Heathfield Gdns. Croy 6B 124
Heathfield Ho. SE3 ....1C 94
Heathfield La. Chst 3M 111
Heathfield N. Twic 6C 86
Heathfield Pde. Swan 6A 114
Heathfield Pk. NW2 ....2G 57
Heathfield Pk. Dri. Romf 3F 48
Heathfield Ri. Ruis 5A 36
Heathfield Rd. SW18 ....5A 90
Heathfield Rd. W3 ....3M 71
Heathfield Rd. Bexh 3K 97
Heathfield Rd. Brom 4D 110
Heathfield Rd. Bush 6J 9
Heathfield Rd. Croy 6B 124
Heathfield Rd. Kes 7G 127
Heathfield Rd. W on T 6J 117
Heathfields Ct. Houn 4J 85
Heathfield S. Twic 6D 86
Heathfield Sq. SW18 ....6B 90
Heathfield St. W11 ....1J 73
(off Portland Rd.)
Heathfield Ter. SE18 ....7C 80
Heathfield Ter. W4 ....6A 72
Heathfield Va. S Croy 1H 139
Heath Gdns. Dart 7G 99
Heath Gdns. Twic 7D 86
Heathgate. NW11 ....4M 41
Heathgate Pl. NW3 ....1D 58
Heath Gro. SE20 ....4G 109
Heath Gro. Sun 4D 100
Heath Ho. Sidc 1D 112
Heath Hurst Rd. NW3 ....9C 42
Heathhurst Rd. S Croy 1B 138
Heathland Rd. N16 ....6C 44
Heathlands Clo. Sun 6E 100
Heathlands Clo. Twic 8D 86
Heathlands Ri. Dart 5F 98
Heathlands Way. Houn 4J 85
Heath La. SE3 ....1B 94
(in two parts)
Heath La. (Lower) Dart 7G 99
Heath La. (Upper) Dart 8E 98
Heathlee Rd. SE3 ....3D 94
Heathlee Rd. Dart 5C 98
Heathley End. Chst 3A 112
Heath Lodge. Bush 1C 22
Heathmans Rd. SW6 ....9K 73
Heath Mead. SW19 ....9H 89
Heath Park. 4E 50
Heath Pk. Ct. Romf 3E 50
Heath Pk. Dri. Brom 7J 111
Heath Pk. Rd. Romf 3E 50
Heath Pas. NW3 ....7M 41
Heathpool Ct. E1 ....7F 60
Heath Ri. SW15 ....5H 89
Heath Ri. Brom 1D 126
Heath Rd. SW8 ....1F 90
Heath Rd. Bex 7A 98
Heath Rd. Dart 5D 98
Heath Rd. Harr 5A 38
Heath Rd. Houn 3M 85
Heath Rd. Oxs 4A 132
Heath Rd. Romf 5H 49
Heath Rd. T Hth 7A 108
Heath Rd. Twic 7D 86
Heath Rd. Uxb 7A 52
Heath Rd. Wat 9H 9
Heathrow Airport. 2F 144
Heathrow Boulevd. W Dray 8K 143
(in two parts)
Heathrow Causeway Cen. Houn 2E 84
Heathrow Clo. W Dray 9G 143
Heathrow Corporate Pk. Houn 2G 85
Heathrow Interchange. Hay 2G 69
Heathrow International Trad. Est. Houn 2F 84
Heaths Clo. Enf 4C 16
Heath Side. 8D 98
Heath Side. NW3 ....9B 42
Heathside. NW11 ....6L 41
Heathside. SE13 ....1A 94
Heathside. Esh 5C 118
Heathside. Houn 6K 85
Heathside. Orp 3A 128
Heathside. Wey 7A 116
Heathside Av. Bexh 9J 81
Heathside Clo. Esh 5C 118
Heathside Clo. N'wd 5B 20
Heathside Rd. N'wd 4B 20
Heathstan Rd. W12 ....9E 56
Heath St. NW3 ....8A 42
Heath St. Dart 6H 99
Heath, The. 8A 116
Heath, The. W7 ....2C 70
Heath Vw. N2 ....2A 42
Heathview. NW5 ....9E 42
Heathview Av. Dart 5C 98
Heath Vw. Clo. N2 ....2A 42
Heathview Cres. Dart 7E 98
Heathview Dri. SE2 ....7H 81
Heathview Gdns. SW15 .....6G 89
Heathview Rd. T Hth 8L 107
Heath Vs. NW3 ....8B 42
Heath Vs. SE18 ....6D 80
Heathville Rd. N19 ....5J 43
Heathwall St. SW11 ....2D 90
Heathway (Junct.) **5L 65**
Heathway. SE3 ....8E 78
Heathway. Croy 5K 125
Heathway. Dag 8K 49
Heath Way. Eri 9A 82
Heathway. S'hall 5H 69
Heath Way. Wfd G 5G 31
Heathway Ct. NW11 ....7L 41
Heathway Ind. Est. Dag 9M 49
Heathwood Gdns. SE7 ....5J 79
Heathwood Gdns. Swan 6A 114
Heathwood Point. SE23 .....9H 93
Heathwood Wlk. Bex 7C 98
Heaton Av. Romf 7F 34
Heaton Clo. E4 ....3A 30
Heaton Clo. Romf 7G 35
Heaton Ct. Chesh 2D 6
Heaton Grange Rd. Romf 9D 34
Heaton Rd. SE15 ....1F 92
Heaton Rd. Mitc 4E 106
Heaton Way. Romf 7G 35
Heaven Tree Clo. N1 ....2A 60
Heaver Rd. SW11 ....2B 90
Heavitree Clo. SE18 ....6B 80
Heavitree Rd. SE18 ....6B 80
(in two parts)
Hebden Ct. E2 ....4D 60
Hebden Ter. N17 ....6C 28
Hebdon Rd. SW17 ....9C 90
Heber Mans. W14 ....7J 73
(off Queen's Club Gdns.)
Heber Rd. NW2 ....1H 57
Heber Rd. SE22 ....5D 92
Hebron Rd. W6 ....4G 73
Hecham Clo. E17 ....9J 29
Heckets Ct. Esh 2A 132
Heckfield Pl. SW6 ....8L 73
Heckford Clo. Wat 8A 8
Heckford Ho. E14 ....9M 61
(off Grundy St.)
Heckford St. E1 ....1H 77
Hector. NW9 ....8D 24
(off Five Acre)
Hector Ct. SW9 ....8L 75
(off Caldwell St.)
Hector Ho. E2 ....5F 60
(off Old Bethnal Grn. Rd.)
Hector St. SE18 ....5C 80
Heddington Gro. N7 ....1K 59
Heddon Clo. Iswth 3E 86
Heddon Ct. Av. Barn 7D 14
Heddon Ct. Pde. Barn 7E 14
Heddon Rd. Cockf 7D 14
Heddon St. W1 ....1G 75
(in two parts)
Hedgegate Ct. W11 ....9K 57
Hedge Hill. Enf 3M 15
Hedge La. N13 ....3M 27
Hedgemans Rd. Dag 3H 65
Hedgemans Way. Dag 2J 65
Hedgerley Gdns. Gnfd 5A 54
Hedgerow La. Ark 7F 12
Hedgerow Wlk. Chesh 3D 6
Hedgers Clo. Lou 6L 19
Hedgers Gro. E9 ....2J 61
Hedger St. SE11 ....5M 75
Hedgeside Rd. N'wd 5A 20
Hedge Wlk. SE6 ....2M 109
Hedgewood Gdns. Ilf 3L 47
Hedgley. Ilf 2K 47
Hedgley M. SE12 ....4D 94
Hedgley St. SE12 ....4D 94
Hedingham Clo. N1 ....3A 60

Hedingham Rd.—Hertsmere Ind. Pk.

Hedingham Rd. *Dag* 1F **64**
Hedingham Rd. *Horn* 6L **51**
Hedley Ho. E14 . . . . *4A* **78**
(off Stewart St.)
Hedley Rd. *Twic* 6L **85**
Hedley Row. *N5* 1B **60**
Hedley St. *Romf* 3C **50**
Hedsor Ho. E2 . . . . *7D* **60**
(off Ligonier St.)
Hedworth Av. *Wal X* 6D **6**
Heenan Clo. *Bark* 2A **64**
Heene Rd. *Enf* 3B **16**
Hega Ho. E14 . . . . *8A* **62**
(off Ullin St.)
Heidegger Cres. *SW13* 8F **72**
Heigham Rd. *E6* 4H **63**
Heighton Gdns. *Croy* 7M **123**
Heights Clo. *SW20* 4F **104**
Heights Clo. *Bans* 8J **135**
Heights, The. *SE7* 6G **79**
Heights, The. *Beck* 4A **110**
(in two parts)
Heights, The. *Lou* 4K **19**
Heights, The. *N'holt* 1K **53**
Heiron St. *SE17* 7M **75**
Helby Rd. *SW4* 5H **91**
Heldar Ct. *SE1* 3B **76**
Helder Gro. *SE12* 6D **94**
Helder St. *S Croy* 8B **124**
Heldmann Clo. *Houn* 3B **86**
Helegan Clo. *Orp* 6D **128**
Helena Clo. *Barn* 2B **14**
Helena Ct. *W5* 8H **55**
Helena Pl. *E9* 4F **60**
Helena Rd. *E13* 5D **62**
Helena Rd. *E17* 3L **45**
Helena Rd. *NW10* 1F **56**
Helena Rd. *W5* 8H **55**
Helena Sq. SE16 . . . . *1J* **77**
(off Sovereign Cres.)
Helen Av. *Felt* 6F **84**
Helen Clo. *N2* 1A **42**
Helen Clo. *Dart* 6F **98**
Helen Clo. *W Mol* 8M **101**
Helen Gladstone Ho. SE1 . . . *3M* **75**
(off Surrey Row)
Helen Ho. E2 . . . . *5F* **60**
(off Old Bethnal Grn. Rd.)
Helen Mackay Ho. E14 . . . . . *9B* **62**
(off Blair St.)
Helen Peele Cotts. SE16 . . . . *4G* **77**
(off Lower Rd.)
Helen Rd. *Horn* 1H **51**
Helenslea Av. *NW11* 6L **41**
Helen's Pl. *E2* 6G **61**
Helen St. *SE18* 5M **79**
Helen Taylor Ho. SE16 . . . . . *4E* **76**
(off Evelyn Lowe Est.)
Helford Clo. *Ruis* 7C **36**
Helgiford Gdns. *Sun* 4C **100**
Heliport Ind. Est. *SW11* 1B **90**
Helix Gdns. *SW2* 5K **91**
Helix Rd. *SW2* 5K **91**
Hellings St. *E1* 2E **76**
Helm Clo. *Eps* 4L **133**
Helme Clo. *SW19* 2K **105**
Helmet Row. *EC1* 7A **60**
(in two parts)
Helmore Rd. *Bark* 3D **64**
Helmsdale Clo. *Hay* 7J **53**
Helmsdale Clo. *Romf* 7C **34**
Helmsdale Ho. NW6 . . . . *5M* **57**
(off Carlton Va.)
Helmsdale Rd. *SW16* 5H **107**
Helmsdale Rd. *Romf* 7C **34**
Helmsley Ho. Romf *7J* **35**
(off Leyburn Cres.)
Helmsley Pl. *E8* 3F **60**
Helmsley St. *E8* 3F **60**
Helperby Rd. *NW10* 3C **56**
Helsby Ct. NW8 . . . . *7B* **58**
(off Pollitt Dri.)
Helsinki Sq. *SE16* 4J **77**
Helston. NW1 . . . . *4G* **59**
(off Camden St.)
Helston Clo. *Pinn* 7K **21**
Helston Ct. N15 . . . . *3C* **44**
(off Culvert Rd.)
Helston Ho. SE11 . . . . *6L* **75**
(off Kennings Way)
Helston Pl. *Ab L* 5D **4**
Helvetia St. *SE6* 8K **93**
Helwys Ct. *E4* 6M **29**
Hemans St. *SW8* 8H **75**
Hemans St. Est. *SW8* 8H **75**
Hemberton Rd. *SW9* 2J **91**
Hemery Rd. *Gnfd* 1B **54**
Hemingford Clo. *N12* 5B **26**
Hemingford Rd. *N1* 4K **59**
Hemingford Rd. *Sutt* 6G **121**
Hemingford Rd. *Wat* 9C **4**
Heming Rd. *Edgw* 7M **23**
Hemington Av. *N11* 5D **26**
Hemingway Clo. *NW5* 9E **42**
Hemlington Ho. E14 . . . . *8J* **61**
(off Aston St.)
Hemlock Rd. *W12* 1D **72**
(in two parts)
Hemmen La. *Hay* 9D **52**
Hemming Clo. *Hamp* 5L **101**
Hemmings Clo. *Sidc* 8F **96**
Hemming St. *E1* 7E **60**
Hemming Way. *Wat* 8E **4**
Hempshaw Av. *Bans* 8D **136**
Hempstead Clo. *Buck H* 2E **30**
Hempstead Rd. *E17* 1B **46**
Hempstead Rd. *Wat* 9B **4**
Hemp Wlk. *SE17* 5B **76**
Hemsby Rd. *Chess* 8K **119**
Hemstal Rd. *NW6* 3L **57**
Hemsted Rd. *Eri* 8C **82**
Hemswell Dri. *NW9* 8C **24**
Hemsworth Ct. *N1* 5C **60**
Hemsworth St. *N1* 5C **60**
Hemus Pl. *SW3* 6C **74**
Hen & Chicken Ct. EC4 . . . . . *9L* **59**
(off Fleet St.)
Henbane Path. *Romf* 7H **35**
Henbury Way. *Wat* 3H **21**
Henchman St. *W12* 9D **56**
Hendale Av. *NW4* 1F **40**
Henderson Clo. *NW10* 2A **56**
Henderson Clo. *Horn* 7F **50**
Henderson Ct. SE14 . . . . *7H* **77**
(off Myers La.)
Henderson Dri. *NW8* 7B **58**
Henderson Dri. *Dart* 3K **99**
Henderson Ho. Dag *8L* **49**
(off Kershaw Rd.)
Henderson Pl. *Bedm* 1D **4**
Henderson Rd. *E7* 2G **63**
Henderson Rd. *N9* 1F **28**
Henderson Rd. *SW18* 6C **90**
Henderson Rd. *Big H* 4G **141**
Henderson Rd. *Croy* 1B **124**
Henderson Rd. *Hay* 6E **52**
Hendham Rd. *SW17* 8C **90**
Hendon. 3F **40**
Hendon Av. *N3* 8J **25**
Hendon Crematorium.
NW4 . . . . 8H **25**
Hendon F.C. 6H **41**
Hendon Gdns. *Romf* 6A **34**
Hendon Golf Course. 8G **25**
Hendon Gro. *Eps* 1L **133**
Hendon Hall Ct. *NW4* 1H **41**
Hendon Ho. *NW4* 3H **41**
Hendon La. *N3* 1J **41**
Hendon Lodge. *NW4* 1F **40**
Hendon Pk. Mans. *NW4* 3G **41**
Hendon Pk. Row. *NW11* 4K **41**
Hendon Rd. *N9* 2E **28**
Hendon Way. *NW4 & NW2* . . 4F **40**
Hendon Way. *Stanw* 5B **144**
Hendon Wood La. *NW7* 8D **12**
Hendren Clo. *Gnfd* 1B **54**
Hendre Rd. *SE1* 5C **76**
Hendrick Av. *SW12* 6D **90**
Heneage Cres. *New Ad* 2A **140**
Heneage La. *EC3* 9C **60**
Heneage Pl. *EC3* 9C **60**
Heneage St. *E1* 8D **60**
Henfield Clo. *N19* 6G **43**
Henfield Clo. *Bex* 5L **97**
Henfield Rd. *SW19* 5K **105**
Hengelo Gdns. *Mitc* 8B **106**
Hengist Rd. *SE12* 6F **94**
Hengist Rd. *Eri* 8M **81**
Hengist Way. *Brom* 8C **110**
Hengrave Rd. *SE23* 5G **93**
Hengrove Ct. *Bex* 7J **97**
Hengrove Cres. *Ashf* 9B **144**
Henham Ct. *Romf* 8A **34**
Henley Av. *Sutt* 5J **121**
Henley Clo. SE16 . . . . *3G* **77**
(off St Marychurch St.)
Henley Clo. *Gnfd* 5A **54**
Henley Clo. *Iswth* 9D **70**
Henley Ct. *N14* 9G **15**
Henley Ct. *NW2* 2H **57**
Henley Dri. *SE1* 5D **76**
Henley Dri. *King T* 4D **104**
Henley Gdns. *Pinn* 1F **36**
Henley Gdns. *Romf* 3J **49**
Henley Ho. E2 . . . . *7D* **60**
(off Swanfield St.)
Henley Prior. N1 . . . . *5K* **59**
(off Collier St.)
Henley Rd. *E16* 3K **79**
Henley Rd. *N18* 4C **28**
Henley Rd. *NW10* 4G **57**
Henley Rd. *Ilf* 9A **48**
Henley St. *SW11* 1E **90**
Henley Way. *Felt* 2H **101**
Henlow Pl. *Rich* 8H **87**
Henlys Corner (Junct.) **2K 41**
Henlys Roundabout (Junct.)
. . . . **1G 85**
Hennel Clo. *SE23* 9G **93**
Hennessey Rd. *N9* 2G **29**
Henniker Gdns. *E6* 6H **63**
Henniker M. *SW3* 7B **74**
Henniker Point. E15 . . . . *1C* **62**
(off Leytonstone Rd.)
Henniker Rd. *E15* 1B **62**
Henningham Rd. *N17* 8B **28**
Henning St. *SW11* 9C **74**
Henrietta Clo. *SE8* 7L **77**
Henrietta Ct. Twic *6G* **87**
(off Richmond Rd.)
Henrietta Ho. N15 . . . . *4C* **44**
(off St Ann's Rd.)
Henrietta Ho. W6 . . . . *6G* **73**
(off Queen Caroline St.)
Henrietta M. *WC1* 7J **59**
Henrietta Pl. *W1* 9F **58**
Henrietta St. *E15* 1A **62**
Henrietta St. *WC2* 1J **75**
Henriques St. *E1* 9E **60**
Henry Addlington Clo. *E6* . . . 8M **63**
Henry Clo. *Enf* 2C **16**
Henry Cooper Way. *SE9* 9H **95**
Henry Darlot Dri. *NW7* 5H **25**
Henry Dickens Ct. *W11* 1H **73**
Henry Doulton Dri.
SW17 . . . . 1E **106**
Henry Hatch Wlk. *Sutt* 9A **122**
Henry Ho. *SE1* 2L **75**
Henry Ho. SW8 . . . . *8J* **75**
(off Wyvil Rd.)
Henry Jackson Rd. *SW15* . . . 2H **89**
Henry Macaulay Av.
King T 5H **103**
Henry Peters Dri. Tedd *2C* **102**
(off Somerset Gdns.)
Henry Purcell Ho. E16 . . . . . . *2F* **78**
(off Evelyn Rd.)
Henry Rd. *E6* 5J **63**
Henry Rd. *N4* 6A **44**
Henry Rd. *Barn* 7B **14**
Henrys Av. *Wfd G* 5D **30**
Henryson Rd. *SE4* 4L **93**
Henry St. *Brom* 5F **110**
Henry's Wlk. *Ilf* 7B **32**
Henry Tate M. *SW16* 2L **107**
Henry Wise Ho. SW1 . . . . *5G* **75**
(off Vauxhall Bri. Rd.)
Hensford Gdns. *SE26* 1F **108**
Henshall St. *N1* 2B **60**
Henshawe Rd. *Dag* 8H **49**
Henshaw St. *SE17* 5B **76**
Henslowe Rd. *SE22* 4E **92**
Henslow Ho. SE15 . . . . *8E* **76**
(off Peckham Pk. Rd.)
Henson Av. *NW2* 1G **57**
Henson Clo. *Orp* 4M **127**
Henson Path. *Harr* 1H **39**
Henson Pl. *N'holt* 4G **53**
Henstridge Pl. *NW8* 4C **58**
Henty Clo. *SW11* 8C **74**
Henty Wlk. *SW15* 4F **88**
Henville Rd. *Brom* 5F **110**
Henwick Rd. *SE9* 2H **95**
Henwood Side. *Wfd G* 6K **31**
Hepburn Gdns. *Brom* 3C **126**
Hepburn M. *SW11* 4D **90**
Hepple Clo. *Iswth* 1F **86**
Hepplestone Clo. *SW15* 5F **88**
Hepscott Rd. *E9* 2L **61**
Hepworth Ct. N1 . . . . *4M* **59**
(off Gaskin St.)
Hepworth Ct. *NW3* 1C **58**
Hepworth Ct. *Sutt* 3L **121**
Hepworth Gdns. *Bark* 1E **64**
Hepworth Rd. *SW16* 4J **107**
Hepworth Way. *W on T* 3D **116**
Heracles. NW9 . . . . *8D* **24**
(off Five Acre)
Heracles Clo. *Wall* 9J **123**
Hera Ct. E14 . . . . *5L* **77**
(off Homer Dri.)
Herald Gdns. *Wall* 4F **122**
Herald's Pl. *SE11* 5M **75**
Herald St. *E2* 7F **61**
Herald Wlk. *Dart* 4K **99**
Herbal Hill. *EC1* 7L **59**
Herbal Hill Gdns. *EC1* 7L **59**
Herbal Pl. EC1 . . . . *7L* **59**
(off Herbal Hill)
Herbert Cres. *SW1* 4D **74**
Herbert Gdns. *NW10* 5F **56**
Herbert Gdns. *W4* 7M **71**
Herbert Gdns. *Romf* 5H **49**
Herbert Ho. E1 . . . . *9D* **60**
(off Old Castle St.)
Herbert Morrison Ho.
SW6 . . . . *7K* **73**
(off Clem Attlee Ct.)
Herbert Pl. *SE18* 7M **79**
Herbert Rd. *E12* 9J **47**
Herbert Rd. *E17* 5K **45**
Herbert Rd. *N11* 7J **27**
Herbert Rd. *N15* 3D **44**
Herbert Rd. *NW9* 4E **40**
Herbert Rd. *SE18* 8L **79**
(in two parts)
Herbert Rd. *SW19* 4K **105**
(in two parts)
Herbert Rd. *Bexh* 1J **97**
Herbert Rd. *Brom* 9H **111**
Herbert Rd. *Horn* 5J **51**
Herbert Rd. *Ilf* 7C **48**
Herbert Rd. *King T* 7K **103**
Herbert Rd. *S'hall* 2K **69**
Herbert Rd. *Swan* 3F **114**
Herbert St. *E13* 5E **62**
Herbert St. *NW5* 2E **58**
Herbrand Est. *WC1* 7J **59**
Herbrand St. *WC1* 7J **59**
Hercies Rd. *Uxb* 3D **142**
Hercules Pl. *N7* 8J **43**
(in two parts)
Hercules Rd. *SE1* 4K **75**
Hercules St. *N7* 8J **43**
Hercules Tower. *SE14* 7J **77**
Hercules Wharf. E14 . . . . *1C* **78**
(off Orchard Pl.)
Hercules Yd. *N7* 8J **43**
Hereford Av. *Barn* 1D **26**
Hereford Bldgs. SW3 . . . . *7B* **74**
(off Old Church St.)
Hereford Clo. *Eps* 5B **134**
Hereford Ct. W7 . . . . *8D* **54**
(off Copley Clo.)
Hereford Ct. *Harr* 2C **38**
Hereford Ct. *Sutt* 9L **121**
Hereford Gdns. *SE13* 4C **94**
Hereford Gdns. *Ilf* 5J **47**
Hereford Gdns. *Pinn* 3J **37**
Hereford Gdns. *Twic* 7A **86**
Hereford Ho. NW6 . . . . *5L* **57**
(off Carlton Va.)
Hereford Ho. SW3 . . . . *4C* **74**
(off Old Brompton Rd.)
Hereford Ho. SW10 . . . . *8M* **73**
(off Fulham Rd.)
Hereford M. *W2* 9L **57**
Hereford Pl. *SE14* 8K **77**
Hereford Retreat. *SE15* 8E **76**
Hereford Rd. *E11* 3F **46**
Hereford Rd. *W2* 9L **57**
Hereford Rd. *W3* 1M **71**
Hereford Rd. *W5* 4G **71**
Hereford Rd. *Felt* 7G **85**
Hereford Sq. *SW7* 5A **74**
Hereford St. *E2* 7E **60**
Hereford Way. *Chess* 7G **119**
Herent Dri. *Ilf* 2J **47**
Hereward Av. *Purl* 3L **137**
Hereward Clo. *Wal A* 5K **7**
Hereward Gdns. *N13* 5L **27**
Hereward Grn. *Lou* 3M **19**
Hereward Rd. *SW17* 1D **106**
Herga Ct. *Harr* 8C **38**
Herga Ct. *Wat* 4E **8**
Herga Rd. *Harr* 2D **38**
Heriot Av. *E4* 2L **29**
Heriot Rd. *NW4* 3G **41**
Heriots Clo. *Stan* 4E **22**
Heritage Clo. *SW9* 2M **91**
Heritage Clo. *Uxb* 7A **142**
Heritage Ct. SE8 . . . . *6H* **77**
(off Trundley's Rd.)
Heritage Hill. *Kes* 7G **127**
Heritage Vw. *Harr* 8D **38**
Herkomer Clo. *Bush* 8M **9**
Herkomer Rd. *Bush* 7L **9**
Herlwyn Av. *Ruis* 7C **36**
Herlwyn Gdns. *SW17* 1D **106**
Her Majesty's Theatre. ***2H 75***
(off Haymarket)
Herm Clo. *Iswth* 8A **70**
Hermes Clo. *W9* 7L **57**
Hermes Ct. SW9 . . . . *9L* **75**
(off Southey Rd.)
Hermes St. *N1* 5L **59**
Hermes Wlk. *N'holt* 5L **53**
Hermes Way. *Wall* 9H **123**
Herm Ho. *N1* 2A **60**
Herm Ho. *Enf* 2H **17**
Hermiston Av. *N8* 3J **43**
Hermitage Clo. *E18* 2D **46**
Hermitage Clo. *Clay* 8E **118**
Hermitage Clo. *Enf* 4M **15**
Hermitage Ct. E1 . . . . *2E* **76**
(off Knighten St.)
Hermitage Ct. *E18* 2E **46**
Hermitage Ct. *NW2* 8L **41**
Hermitage Gdns. *NW2* 8L **41**
Hermitage Gdns. *SE19* 4A **108**
Hermitage Grn. *SW16* 5J **107**
Hermitage La. *N18* 5B **28**
Hermitage La. *NW2* 8L **41**
Hermitage La. *SE25* 1E **124**
(in two parts)
Hermitage La. *SW16* 4K **107**
Hermitage Path. *SW16* 5J **107**
Hermitage Rd. *N4 & N15* . . . 5M **43**
Hermitage Rd. *SE19* 4A **108**
Hermitage Rd. *Kenl* 7A **138**
Hermitage Rooms. ***1K 75***
(off Embankment)
Hermitage Row. *E8* 1E **60**
Hermitage St. *W2* 8B **58**
Hermitage, The. *SE13* 1A **94**
Hermitage, The. *SE23* 7G **93**
Hermitage, The. *SW13* 9D **72**
Hermitage, The. *Felt* 9D **84**
Hermitage, The. *King T* 8H **103**
Hermitage, The. *Rich* 4J **87**
Hermitage, The. *Uxb* 2B **142**
Hermitage Wlk. *E18* 2D **46**
Hermitage Wall. *E1* 2E **76**
Hermitage Waterside. E1 . . . . *2E* **76**
(off Thomas More St.)
Hermitage Way. *Stan* 8E **22**
Hermit Pl. *NW6* 4M **57**
Hermit Rd. *E16* 8D **62**
Hermit St. *EC1* 6M **59**
Hermon Gro. *Hay* 2E **68**
Hermon Hill. *E11 & E18* 3E **46**
Herndon Rd. *SW18* 4A **90**
Herne Clo. *NW10* 1B **56**
Herne Ct. *Bush* 9A **10**
Herne Hill. 4A **92**
Herne Hill. *SE24* 5A **92**
Herne Hill Ho. SE24 . . . . *5M* **91**
(off Railton Rd.)
Herne Hill Rd. *SE24* 2A **92**
Herne Hill Stadium. 3B **92**
Herne M. *N18* 4E **28**
Herne Pl. *SE24* 4M **91**
Herne Rd. *Bush* 8M **9**
Herne Rd. *Surb* 4H **119**
Heron Clo. *E17* 9K **29**
Heron Clo. *NW10* 2C **56**
Heron Clo. *Buck H* 1E **30**
Heron Clo. *Sutt* 7K **121**
Heron Clo. *Uxb* 2B **142**
Heron Ct. E14 . . . . *4A* **78**
(off New Union Clo.)
Heron Ct. *Brom* 8G **111**
Heron Ct. *Eps* 6E **134**
Heron Ct. *Ilf* 7M **47**
Heron Ct. *King T* 7J **103**
Heron Ct. *Ruis* 7B **36**
Heron Cres. *Sidc* 9C **96**
Herondale. *S Croy* 1H **139**
Herondale Av. *SW18* 7B **90**
Heron Dri. *N4* 7A **44**
Heron Flight Av. *Horn* 3E **66**
Herongate Clo. *Enf* 4D **16**
Herongate Rd. *E12* 7G **47**
Herongate Rd. *Swan* 3C **114**
Heron Hill. *Belv* 6K **81**
Heron Ho. *E6* 3J **63**
Heron Ho. NW8 . . . . *5C* **58**
(off Barrow Hill Est.)
Heron Ho. SW11 . . . . *8C* **74**
(off Searles Clo.)
Heron Ho. *W13* 7E **54**
Heron Ho. *Sidc* 9F **96**
Heron Ind. Est. *E15* 5M **61**
Heron Mead. *Enf* 2L **17**
Heron M. *Ilf* 7M **47**
Heron Pl. *SE16* 2J **77**
Heron Pl. W1 . . . . *9E* **58**
(off Thayer St.)
Heron Quay. *E14* 2L **77**
Heron Rd. *SE24* 3A **92**
Heron Rd. *Croy* 4C **124**
Heron Rd. *Twic* 3E **86**
Heronry, The. *W on T* 8E **116**
Herons Cft. *Wey* 8A **116**
Heronsforde. *W13* 9G **55**
Herons Ga. *Edgw* 5L **23**
Heron's Lea. *N6* 4D **42**
Herons Lea. *Wat* 9G **5**
Heronslea Dri. *Stan* 5J **23**
Heron's Pl. *Iswth* 2F **86**
Heron Sq. *Rich* 4H **87**
Herons Ri. *New Bar* 6C **14**
Herons, The. *E11* 4D **46**
Herons, The. *Horn* 6H **51**
Heronswood. *Wal A* 7L **7**
Heron Trad. Est. *W3* 8M **55**
Heron Wlk. *N'wd* 4C **20**
Heron Way. *Felt* 3E **84**
Heron Way. *Wfd G* 4G **31**
Herrick Ho. SE5 . . . . *8B* **76**
(off Elmington Est.)
Herrick Rd. *N5* 8A **44**
Herrick St. *SW1* 5H **75**
Herries St. *W10* 5J **57**
Herringham Rd. *SE7* 4G **79**
Herron Ct. *Brom* 8D **110**
Hersant Clo. *NW10* 4E **56**
Herschell M. *SE5* 2A **92**
Herschell Rd. *SE23* 6J **93**
Hersham. 7H **117**
Hersham By-Pass.
W on T 7F **116**
Hersham Clo. *SW15* 6E **88**
Hersham Gdns. *W on T* 6F **116**
Hersham Green. 7H **117**
Hersham Grn. Shop. Cen.
W on T 7H **117**
Hersham Pl. *W on T* 7H **117**
Hersham Rd. *W on T* 3E **116**
Hersham Trad. Est.
W on T 4J **117**
Hershell Ct. *SW14* 3M **87**
Hertford Av. *SW14* 4B **88**
Hertford Clo. *Barn* 5B **14**
Hertford Ct. E6 . . . . *6K* **63**
(off Vicarage La.)
Hertford Ct. *N13* 3L **27**
Hertford Pl. *W1* 7G **59**
Hertford Rd. *N1* 4C **60**
(in two parts)
Hertford Rd. *N2* 1C **42**
Hertford Rd. *N9* 2F **28**
Hertford Rd. *Bark* 3L **63**
Hertford Rd. *Barn* 5A **14**
Hertford Rd. *Ilf* 4C **48**
Hertfordshire & Middlesex
Country Club. **5A 22**
Hertford Sq. *Mitc* 8J **107**
Hertford St. *W1* 2F **74**
Hertford Wlk. *Belv* 6L **81**
Hertford Way. *Mitc* 8J **107**
Hertslet Rd. *N7* 8K **43**
Hertsmere Ho. E14 . . . . *1L* **77**
(off Hertsmere Rd.)
Hertsmere Ind. Pk. *Borwd* . . 5B **12**

Hertsmere Rd.—High Trees

Hertsmere Rd. E14 . . . 2L 77
Hertswood Ct. Barn . . . 6J 13
Hervey Clo. N3 . . . 8L 25
Hervey Pk. Rd. E17 . . . 2J 45
Hervey Rd. SE3 . . . 9F 78
Hervey Way. N3 . . . 8L 25
Hesa Rd. Hay . . . 9E 52
Hesewall Clo. SW4 . . . 1G 91
Hesiers Hill. Warl . . . 9C 140
Hesiers Rd. Warl . . . 8C 140
Hesketh Av. Dart . . . 7M 99
Hesketh Pl. W11 . . . 1J 73
Hesketh Rd. E7 . . . 8E 46
Heslop Rd. SW12 . . . 7D 90
Hesper M. SW5 . . . 5M 73
Hesperus Clo. E14 . . . 5M 77
Hesperus Cres. E14 . . . 5M 77
Hessel Rd. W13 . . . 3E 70
Hessel St. E1 . . . 9F 60
Hesselyn Dri. Rain . . . 3F 66
Hessle Gro. Eps . . . 3D 134
Hestercombe Av. SW6 . . . 1J 89
Hesterman Way. Croy . . . 3K 123
Hester Rd. N18 . . . 5E 28
Hester Rd. SW11 . . . 8C 74
Hester Ter. Rich . . . 2L 87
Heston. . . . 8L 69
Heston Av. Houn . . . 7J 69
Heston Cen., The. Houn . . . 6G 69
Heston Grange. Houn . . . 7K 69
Heston Grange La. Houn . . . 7K 69
Heston Ho. SE8 . . . 9L 77
Heston Ind. Cen. Houn . . . 7G 69
Heston Ind. Mall. Houn . . . 8K 69
Heston Rd. Houn . . . 8L 69
Heston St. SE14 . . . 9L 77
Heswell Grn. Wat . . . 3E 20
Hetherington Rd. SW4 . . . 3J 91
Hetherington Rd. Shep . . . 6A 100
Hethpool Ho. W2 . . . 7B 58
(off Hall Pl.)
Hetley Gdns. SE19 . . . 4D 108
Hetley Rd. W12 . . . 2F 72
Heton Gdns. NW4 . . . 2F 40
Hevelius Clo. SE10 . . . 6D 78
Hever Cft. SE9 . . . 1L 111
Hever Gdns. Brom . . . 6L 111
Heverham Rd. SE18 . . . 5C 80
Hever Ho. SE15 . . . 7H 77
(off Lovelinch Clo.)
Heversham Ho. SE15 . . . 7G 77
Heversham Rd. Bexh . . . 1L 97
Hewens Rd. Uxb . . . 7A 52
Hewer St. W10 . . . 8H 57
Hewett Clo. Stan . . . 4F 22
Hewett Pl. Swan . . . 8B 114
Hewett Rd. Dag . . . 1H 65
Hewett St. EC2 . . . 7C 60
Hewins Clo. Wal A . . . 5L 7
Hewish Rd. N18 . . . 4C 28
Hewison St. E3 . . . 5K 61
Hewitt Av. N22 . . . 9M 27
Hewitt Clo. Croy . . . 5L 125
Hewitt Rd. N8 . . . 3L 43
Hewitts Rd. Orp . . . 9K 129
Hewitts Roundabout (Junct.) . . . 9K 129
Hewlett Ho. SW8 . . . 8F 74
(off Havelock Ter.)
Hewlett Rd. E3 . . . 5J 61
Hexagon Ho. Romf . . . 3D 50
(off Mercury Gdns.)
Hexagon, The. N6 . . . 6D 42
Hexal Rd. SE6 . . . 9C 94
Hexham Gdns. Iswth . . . 8E 70
Hexham Rd. SE27 . . . 8A 92
Hexham Rd. Barn . . . 6M 13
Hexham Rd. Mord . . . 3M 121
Hextable. . . . 4D 114
Heybourne Rd. N17 . . . 7F 28
Heybridge. NW1 . . . 2F 58
(off Lewis St.)
Heybridge Av. SW16 . . . 4J 107
Heybridge Dri. Ilf . . . 9B 32
Heybridge Way. E10 . . . 5J 45
Heydon Ho. SE14 . . . 9G 77
(off Kender St.)
Heyford Av. SW8 . . . 8J 75
Heyford Av. SW20 . . . 7K 105
Heyford Rd. Mitc . . . 6C 106
Heyford Rd. Rad . . . 1D 10
Heyford Ter. SW8 . . . 8J 75
Heygate St. SE17 . . . 5A 76
Heylyn Sq. E3 . . . 6K 61
Heynes Rd. Dag . . . 9G 49
Heysham Dri. Wat . . . 5G 21
Heysham La. NW3 . . . 8M 41
Heysham Rd. N15 . . . 4B 44
Heythorp St. SW18 . . . 7K 89
Heythrop College. . . . 4M 73
(off Kensington Sq., University of London)
Heywood Av. NW9 . . . 8C 24
Heywood Ct. Stan . . . 5G 23
Heywood Ho. SE14 . . . 7H 77
(off Myers La.)
Heyworth Rd. E5 . . . 9F 44
Heyworth Rd. E15 . . . 1D 62
Hibbert Av. Wat . . . 2H 9
Hibbert Ho. E14 . . . 4L 77
(off Tiller Rd.)
Hibbert Rd. E17 . . . 5K 45
Hibbert Rd. Harr . . . 9D 22
Hibbert St. SW11 . . . 2B 90
Hibbs Clo. Swan . . . 6B 114
Hibernia Gdns. Houn . . . 3L 85
Hibernia Point. SE2 . . . 3H 81
(off Wolvercote Rd.)
Hibernia Rd. Houn . . . 3L 85
Hibiscus Clo. Edgw . . . 4A 24
Hichisson Rd. SE15 . . . 4G 93
Hickes Ho. NW6 . . . 3B 58
Hickey's Almshouses. Rich . . . 3K 87
Hickin Clo. SE7 . . . 5H 79
Hickin St. E14 . . . 4A 78
Hickleton. NW1 . . . 4G 59
(off Camden St.)
Hickling Ho. SE16 . . . 4F 76
(off Slippers Pl.)
Hickling Rd. Ilf . . . 1M 63
Hickman Av. E4 . . . 6A 30
Hickman Clo. E16 . . . 8H 63
Hickman Rd. Romf . . . 5G 49
Hickmore Wlk. SW4 . . . 2H 91
Hickory Clo. N9 . . . 9E 16
Hicks Av. Gnfd . . . 6B 54
Hicks Clo. SW11 . . . 2C 90
Hicks Ct. Dag . . . 8M 49
Hicks St. SE8 . . . 6J 77
Hidcote Gdns. SW20 . . . 7F 104
Hide. E6 . . . 9L 63
Hideaway, The. Ab L . . . 4D 4
Hide Pl. SW1 . . . 5H 75
Hider Ct. SE3 . . . 8G 79
Hide Rd. Harr . . . 2A 38
Hides St. N7 . . . 2K 59
Hide Tower. SW1 . . . 5H 75
(off Regency St.)
Higgins Ho. N1 . . . 4C 60
(off Colville Est.)
Higginson Ho. NW3 . . . 3D 58
(off Fellows Rd.)
Higgins Wlk. Hamp . . . 3J 101
(off Abbott Clo.)
Higgs Ind. Est. SE24 . . . 2M 91
High Acres. Ab L . . . 5B 4
High Acres. Enf . . . 5M 15
Higham Hill. . . . 9J 29
Higham Hill Rd. E17 . . . 8J 29
Higham Path. E17 . . . 1J 45
Higham Pl. E17 . . . 1J 45
Higham Rd. N17 . . . 1B 44
Higham Rd. Wfd G . . . 6E 30
Highams Ct. E4 . . . 3B 30
Highams Hill. Warl . . . 4E 140
Highams Lodge Bus. Cen. E17 . . . 1H 45
Highams Park. . . . 6B 30
Highams Pk. Ind. Est. E4 . . . 6A 30
Highams Sta. Av. E4 . . . 6L 29
Highams, The. E17 . . . 8A 30
Higham St. E17 . . . 1J 45
Highbanks Clo. Well . . . 8F 80
Highbanks Rd. Pinn . . . 6M 21
Highbank Way. N8 . . . 4L 43
High Barnet. . . . 4H 13
Highbarrow Rd. Croy . . . 3E 124
High Beech. . . . 2F 18
High Beech. N21 . . . 8K 15
High Beech. S Croy . . . 9C 124
High Beeches. Bans . . . 6G 135
High Beeches. Orp . . . 8E 128
High Beeches. Sidc . . . 2J 113
High Beeches Clo. Purl . . . 2H 137
High Beech Rd. Lou . . . 6H 19
High Birch Ct. New Bar . . . 6C 14
(off Park Rd.)
High Bri. SE10 . . . 6B 78
Highbridge Ct. SE14 . . . 8G 77
(off Farrow La.)
Highbridge Ind. Est. Uxb . . . 3A 142
Highbridge Retail Pk. Wal A . . . 7H 7
Highbridge Rd. Bark . . . 4M 63
Highbridge St. Wal A . . . 6H 7
(in two parts)
High Bri. Wharf. SE10 . . . 6B 78
(off High Bri.)
Highbrook Rd. SE3 . . . 2H 95
High Broom Cres. W Wick . . . 2M 125
Highbury. . . . 9M 43
Highbury Av. T Hth . . . 6L 107
Highbury Barn. N5 . . . 9A 44
Highbury Clo. N Mald . . . 8A 104
Highbury Clo. W Wick . . . 4M 125
Highbury Corner (Junct.) . . . 2L 59
Highbury Cres. N5 . . . 1M 59
Highbury Est. N5 . . . 1A 60
Highbury Gdns. Ilf . . . 7C 48
Highbury Grange. N5 . . . 9A 44
Highbury Gro. N5 . . . 1M 59
Highbury Gro. Ct. N5 . . . 2A 60
Highbury Hill. N5 . . . 8L 43
Highbury New Pk. N5 . . . 1A 60
Highbury Pk. N5 . . . 8M 43
Highbury Pk. M. N5 . . . 9A 44
Highbury Pl. N5 . . . 2M 59
Highbury Quad. N5 . . . 8A 44
Highbury Rd. SW19 . . . 2J 105
Highbury Sta. Rd. N1 . . . 2L 59
Highbury Ter. N5 . . . 1M 59
Highbury Ter. M. N5 . . . 1M 59
High Canons. Borwd . . . 1A 12
High Cedar Dri. SW20 . . . 4G 105
Highclere Clo. Kenl . . . 7A 138
Highclere Rd. N Mald . . . 7B 104
Highclere St. SE26 . . . 1J 109
Highcliffe. W13 . . . 8F 54
(off Clivedon Ct.)
Highcliffe Dri. SW15 . . . 5D 88
(in two parts)
Highcliffe Gdns. Ilf . . . 3J 47
Highcombe. SE7 . . . 7F 78
Highcombe Clo. SE9 . . . 7H 95
High Coombe Pl. King T . . . 3B 104
Highcroft. NW9 . . . 3C 40
Highcroft Av. Wemb . . . 3L 55
High Cft. Cotts. Swan . . . 8E 114
Highcroft Est. N19 . . . 5J 43
Highcroft Gdns. NW11 . . . 4K 41
Highcroft Rd. N19 . . . 5J 43
High Cross. . . . 1B 10
High Cross. A'ham . . . 1B 10
High Cross Cen., The. N15 . . . 2E 44
High Cross Rd. N17 . . . 1E 44
Highcross Way. SW15 . . . 7E 88
Highdaun Dri. SW16 . . . 8K 107
Highdown. Wor Pk . . . 4C 120
Highdown La. Sutt . . . 3M 135
Highdown Rd. SW15 . . . 5F 88
High Dri. N Mald . . . 5A 104
High Dri. Oxs . . . 6B 132
High Elms. Chig . . . 4C 32
High Elms. Wfd G . . . 5E 30
High Elms Clo. N'wd . . . 6A 20
High Elms La. Wat . . . 4F 4
High Elms Rd. Dow & Orp . . . 3L 141 & 9A 128
Higher Dri. Bans . . . 4H 135
Higher Dri. Purl . . . 5L 137
Higher Grn. Eps . . . 5E 134
Highfield. Bans . . . 9C 136
Highfield. Bus H . . . 2C 22
Highfield. Wat . . . 3K 21
Highfield Av. NW9 . . . 3A 40
Highfield Av. NW11 . . . 5H 41
Highfield Av. Eri . . . 7M 81
Highfield Av. Gnfd . . . 1C 54
Highfield Av. Orp . . . 8D 128
Highfield Av. Pinn . . . 3K 37
Highfield Av. Wemb . . . 8K 39
Highfield Clo. N22 . . . 8L 27
Highfield Clo. NW9 . . . 3A 40
Highfield Clo. SE13 . . . 5B 94
Highfield Clo. N'wd . . . 8C 20
Highfield Clo. Oxs . . . 3B 132
Highfield Clo. Romf . . . 6A 34
Highfield Clo. Surb . . . 3G 119
Highfield Cotts. Dart . . . 3F 114
Highfield Ct. N14 . . . 8G 15
Highfield Ct. NW11 . . . 4J 41
Highfield Cres. Horn . . . 7K 51
Highfield Cres. N'wd . . . 8C 20
Highfield Dri. Brom . . . 8C 110
Highfield Dri. Eps . . . 8D 120
Highfield Dri. W Wick . . . 4M 125
Highfield Gdns. NW11 . . . 4J 41
Highfield Hill. SE19 . . . 4B 108
Highfield Link. Romf . . . 6A 34
Highfield Rd. N21 . . . 2M 27
Highfield Rd. NW11 . . . 4J 41
Highfield Rd. W3 . . . 8M 55
Highfield Rd. Bexh . . . 4K 97
Highfield Rd. Big H . . . 9G 141
Highfield Rd. Brom . . . 8K 111
Highfield Rd. Bush . . . 7J 9
Highfield Rd. Chst . . . 7D 112
Highfield Rd. Dart . . . 6H 99
Highfield Rd. Felt . . . 8E 84
(in two parts)
Highfield Rd. Horn . . . 7K 51
Highfield Rd. Iswth . . . 9D 70
Highfield Rd. N'wd . . . 8C 20
Highfield Rd. Purl . . . 2K 137
Highfield Rd. Romf . . . 7A 34
Highfield Rd. Sun . . . 9D 100
Highfield Rd. Surb . . . 2A 120
Highfield Rd. Sutt . . . 7C 122
Highfield Rd. W on T . . . 3E 116
Highfield Rd. Wfd G . . . 7J 31
Highfield Rd. N. Dart . . . 5H 99
Highfield Rd. S. Dart . . . 6H 99
Highfields. Sutt . . . 4L 121
Highfields Gro. N6 . . . 6D 42
Highfield Towers. Romf . . . 5B 34
Highfield Way. Horn . . . 7K 51
High Firs. Swan . . . 8C 114
High Foleys. Clay . . . 9F 118
High Gables. Brom . . . 6C 110
High Gables. Lou . . . 7H 19
High Garth. Esh . . . 8A 118
Highgate. . . . 6F 42
Highgate Av. N6 . . . 5F 42
Highgate Cemetery. . . . 7F 42
Highgate Clo. N6 . . . 5E 42
Highgate Edge. N2 . . . 3C 42
Highgate Heights. N6 . . . 4G 43
Highgate High St. N6 . . . 6E 42
Highgate Hill. N6 & N19 . . . 6F 42
Highgate Ho. SE26 . . . 9E 92
Highgate Rd. NW5 . . . 8E 42
Highgate Spinney. N8 . . . 4H 43
Highgate Wlk. SE23 . . . 8G 93
Highgate W. Hill. N6 . . . 7E 42
High Gro. SE18 . . . 8B 80
High Gro. Brom . . . 5H 111
Highgrove Clo. N11 . . . 5E 26
Highgrove Clo. Chst . . . 5J 111
Highgrove Ct. Beck . . . 4L 109
Highgrove Ct. Sutt . . . 8L 121
Highgrove Ct. Wal X . . . 7C 6
Highgrove M. Cars . . . 5D 122
Highgrove Rd. Dag . . . 1G 65
Highgrove Way. Ruis . . . 4E 36
High Hill Est. E5 . . . 6F 44
High Hill Ferry. E5 . . . 6F 44
High Hill Rd. Warl . . . 7A 140
(in two parts)
High Holborn. WC1 . . . 9J 59
Highland Av. W7 . . . 9C 54
Highland Av. Dag . . . 8A 50
Highland Av. Lou . . . 8J 19
Highland Cotts. Wall . . . 6G 123
Highland Ct. E18 . . . 8F 30
Highland Cft. Beck . . . 2M 109
Highland Dri. Bush . . . 9M 9
Highland Pk. Felt . . . 1D 100
Highland Rd. SE19 . . . 3C 108
Highland Rd. Bexh . . . 4L 97
Highland Rd. Brom . . . 5D 110
Highland Rd. N'wd . . . 9D 20
Highland Rd. Purl . . . 6L 137
Highlands. N20 . . . 2B 26
Highlands. Wat . . . 1G 21
Highlands Av. N21 . . . 7K 15
Highlands Av. W3 . . . 1A 72
Highlands Clo. N4 . . . 5J 43
Highlands Clo. Houn . . . 9M 69
Highlands Ct. SE19 . . . 3C 108
Highlands Farm Bus. Pk. Swan . . . 5E 114
Highlands Gdns. Ilf . . . 6K 47
Highlands Heath. SW15 . . . 6G 89
Highlands Hill. Swan . . . 5E 114
Highlands Rd. Barn . . . 7L 13
Highlands Rd. Orp . . . 2F 128
Highlands, The. Barn . . . 6L 13
Highlands, The. Edgw . . . 9M 23
Highlands Village. . . . 7K 15
Highland Ter. SE13 . . . 2M 93
(off Algernon Rd.)
High La. W7 . . . 8B 54
(in two parts)
Highlawn Hall. Harr . . . 8C 38
Highlea Clo. NW9 . . . 7C 24
High Level Dri. SE26 . . . 1E 108
Highlever Rd. W10 . . . 8G 57
Highmead. N18 . . . 5E 28
(off Alpha Rd.)
Highmead. SE18 . . . 8D 80
High Mead. Cars . . . 3B 136
(off Pine Cres.)
High Mead. Chig . . . 2A 32
High Mead. Harr . . . 3C 38
High Mead. W Wick . . . 4B 126
Highmead Cres. Wemb . . . 3K 55
High Mdw. Clo. Pinn . . . 2G 37
High Mdw. Cres. NW9 . . . 3B 40
High Meadows. Chig . . . 5B 32
High Meads Rd. E16 . . . 9H 63
Highmore Rd. SE3 . . . 8C 78
High Mt. NW4 . . . 4E 40
High Oaks. Enf . . . 2K 15
High Oaks. N'wd . . . 5D 20
High Pde., The. SW16 . . . 9J 91
High Pk. Av. Rich . . . 9L 71
High Pk. Rd. Rich . . . 9L 71
High Path. SW19 . . . 5M 105
High Pine Clo. Wey . . . 7A 116
Highpoint. N6 . . . 5E 42
High Point. SE9 . . . 9M 95
High Ridge. N10 . . . 8F 26
Highridge Clo. Eps . . . 6C 134
High Ridge Pl. Enf . . . 2K 15
(off Oak Av.)
High Rd. E18 . . . 8E 30
High Rd. N11 . . . 5F 26
High Rd. N15 & N17 . . . 3D 44
High Rd. N22 . . . 8K 27
High Rd. NW10 . . . 2C 56
High Rd. Buck H . . . 2F 30
High Rd. Bus H . . . 1B 22
High Rd. Chig . . . 5L 31
High Rd. Cow . . . 8A 142
High Rd. Dart . . . 9G 99
High Rd. Eastc . . . 4E 36
High Rd. Harr . . . 7C 22
High Rd. Hay . . . 8C 52
High Rd. Ick . . . 8A 36
High Rd. Ilf & Romf . . . 8M 47
(in five parts)
High Rd. Leav . . . 8D 4
High Rd. Romf . . . 5H 49
High Rd. Wemb . . . 1H 55
High Rd. E. Finchley. N2 . . . 8B 26
High Rd. Leyton. E10 & E15 . . . 4M 45
High Rd. Leytonstone. E11 & E15 . . . 9C 46
High Rd. N. Finchley. N12 . . . 3A 26
High Rd. Whetstone. N20 . . . 9A 14
High Rd. Woodford Grn. Wfd G . . . 6D 30
High Sheldon. N6 . . . 4D 42
Highshore Rd. SE15 . . . 1D 92
(in two parts)
High Silver. Lou . . . 6H 19
Highstead Cres. Eri . . . 9C 82
Highstone Av. E11 . . . 4E 46
Highstone Ct. E11 . . . 4D 46
(off New Wanstead)
Highstone Mans. NW1 . . . 3G 59
(off Camden Rd.)
High St. E11 . . . 3E 46
High St. E13 . . . 5E 62
High St. E15 . . . 5A 62
High St. E17 . . . 3J 45
High St. N14 . . . 1H 27
High St. NW7 . . . 5F 24
High St. SE20 . . . 3G 109
High St. SE25 . . . 8D 108
High St. SW19 . . . 2H 105
High St. W3 . . . 2M 71
High St. W5 . . . 2H 71
High St. Ab L . . . 4C 4
High St. Bans . . . 7L 135
High St. B'side . . . 1A 48
High St. Barn . . . 5J 13
High St. Beck . . . 6L 109
High St. Bedm . . . 1D 4
High St. Bren . . . 8G 71
High St. Brom . . . 6E 110
(in two parts)
High St. Bush . . . 8L 9
High St. Cars . . . 7E 122
High St. Cheam . . . 8J 121
High St. Chesh . . . 2D 6
High St. Chst . . . 3M 111
High St. Clay . . . 8D 118
High St. Cow . . . 7A 142
High St. Cran . . . 9E 68
High St. Croy . . . 4A 124
(in two parts)
High St. Dart . . . 5J 99
High St. Dow . . . 3L 141
High St. Edgw . . . 6L 23
High St. Els . . . 8H 11
High St. Enf . . . 8G 17
High St. Eps . . . 5B 134
High St. Esh . . . 6M 117
High St. Ewe . . . 1D 134
High St. Eyns . . . 4J 131
High St. F'boro . . . 7M 127
High St. F'ham . . . 1J 131
High St. Felt . . . 9D 84
High St. G Str . . . 9D 128
High St. Hamp . . . 5A 102
High St. Hamp H . . . 3A 102
High St. Hamp W . . . 5G 103
High St. Harm . . . 7H 143
High St. Harr (HA1) . . . 6C 38
High St. Harr (HA3) . . . 9C 22
High St. Hay . . . 7B 68
High St. Horn . . . 6H 51
High St. Houn . . . 2M 85
(in three parts)
High St. King T . . . 7H 103
High St. N Mald . . . 8C 104
High St. N'wd . . . 8D 20
High St. Orp . . . 4E 128
High St. Oxs . . . 5B 132
High St. Pinn . . . 1J 37
High St. Purf . . . 6L 83
High St. Purl . . . 3L 137
High St. Romf . . . 3C 50
High St. Ruis . . . 5C 36
High St. St M . . . 1G 129
High St. Shep . . . 1A 116
High St. S'hall . . . 2K 69
High St. Stanw . . . 5B 144
High St. Sutt . . . 6M 121
High St. Swan . . . 7D 114
High St. Tedd . . . 2D 102
High St. Th Dit . . . 1E 118
High St. T Hth . . . 8A 108
High St. Uxb . . . 3A 142
(in two parts)
High St. Wal X . . . 6E 6
(in two parts)
High St. W on T . . . 3E 116
High St. Wat . . . 5F 8
(in four parts)
High St. Wemb . . . 9K 39
High St. W Dray . . . 1H 143
High St. W Mol . . . 8L 101
High St. W Wick . . . 3M 125
High St. Whit . . . 6A 86
High St. Colliers Wood. SW19 . . . 4B 106
High St. Harlesden. NW10 . . . 5D 56
High St. Hornsey. N8 . . . 2J 43
High St. M. SW19 . . . 2J 105
High St. N. E12 & E6 . . . 1J 63
High St. S. E6 . . . 5K 63
High Timber St. EC4 . . . 1A 76
High Tor Clo. Brom . . . 4F 110
High Trees. N20 . . . 3A 26
High Trees. SW2 . . . 7L 91
High Trees. Barn . . . 7C 14
High Trees. Croy . . . 3J 125

High Trees—Hockington Ct.

High Trees. Dart 5M 99
Hightrees Ct. W7 1C 70
Highview. N6 4G 43
Highview. NW7 3B 24
Highview. N'holt 6J 53
High Vw. Pinn 2G 37
High Vw. Sutt 3K 135
High Vw. Wat 8D 8
Highview Av. Edgw 4A 24
Highview Av. Wall 7K 123
High Vw. Clo. SE19 6D 108
High Vw. Clo. Lou 7G 19
High Vw. Ct. Har W 7C 22
Highview Ct. Lou 7H 19
Highview Gdns. N3 1J 41
Highview Gdns. N11 5G 27
Highview Gdns. Edgw 4A 24
Highview Gdns. Upm 7M 51
Highview Ho. Romf 2J 49
Highview Lodge. Enf 5M 15
(off Ridgeway, The)
High Vw. Pde. Ilf 3K 47
High Vw. Pk. K Lan 1B 4
Highview Path. Bans 7L 135
High Vw. Rd. E18 9D 30
High Vw. Rd. N2 8D 26
Highview Rd. SE19 3B 108
Highview Rd. W13 8E 54
High Vw. Rd. Dow 2L 141
High Vw. Rd. Sidc 1F 112
Highway Bus. Pk., The. E1 1H 77
(off Heckford St.)
Highway, The. E1 & E14 1E 76
Highway, The. Orp 7F 128
Highway, The. Stan 8D 22
Highway, The. Sutt 1A 136
Highway Trad. Cen., The. E1 1H 77
(off Heckford St.)
Highwold. Coul 9E 136
Highwood. Brom 7C 110
Highwood Av. N12 4A 26
Highwood Av. Bush 3K 9
Highwood Clo. Kenl 9A 138
Highwood Clo. Orp 4A 128
Highwood Ct. N12 3A 26
Highwood Ct. Barn 7L 13
Highwood Dri. Orp 4A 128
Highwood Gdns. Ilf 3K 47
Highwood Gro. NW7 5B 24
Highwood Hill. 3D 24
Highwood Hill. NW7 2D 24
Highwood La. Lou 7L 19
Highwood Rd. N19 8J 43
High Worple. Harr 5K 37
Highworth Rd. N11 6H 27
Highworth St. NW1 8C 58
(off Daventry St.)
Hi-Gloss Cen. SE8 6J 77
Hilary Av. Mitc 7E 106
Hilary Clo. E11 3E 46
Hilary Clo. SW6 8M 73
Hilary Clo. Eri 9M 81
Hilary Clo. Horn 1H 67
Hilary Dennis Ct. E11 2E 46
Hilary Rd. W12 9D 56
(in two parts)
Hilbert Rd. Sutt 5H 121
Hilborough Ct. E8 3D 60
Hilborough Way. Orp 7B 128
Hilda Ct. Surb 2H 119
Hilda May Av. Swan 7C 114
Hilda Rd. E6 3H 63
Hilda Rd. E16 7C 62
Hilda Ter. SW9 1L 91
Hilda Va. Clo. Orp 6M 127
Hilda Va. Rd. Orp 6L 127
Hildenborough Gdns. Brom 3C 110
Hildenborough Ho. Beck 4K 109
(off Bethersden Clo.)
Hilden Dri. Eri 8F 82
Hildenlea Pl. Brom 6B 110
Hilderley Ho. King T 7K 103
(off Winery La.)
Hilders, The. Asht 9M 133
Hildreth St. SW12 7F 90
Hildyard Rd. SW6 7L 73
Hiley Rd. NW10 6G 57
Hilfield La. A'ham 3M 9
Hilfield La. S. Bush 8D 10
Hilgrove Rd. NW6 3A 58
Hiliary Gdns. Stan 9G 23
Hillars Heath Rd. Coul 7J 137
Hillary. N8 1J 43
(off Boyton Clo.)
Hillary Ct. W12 3G 73
(off Titmuss St.)
Hillary Cres. W on T 3G 117
Hillary Dri. Iswth 4D 86
Hillary Ho. Borwd 5M 11
(off Eldon Av.)
Hillary Ri. Barn 6L 13
Hillary Rd. S'hall 4L 69
Hill Barn. S Croy 3C 138
Hillbeck Clo. SE15 8G 77
Hillbeck Ho. SE15 7G 77
(off Hillbeck Clo.)
Hillbeck Way. Gnfd 4B 54
Hillborne Clo. Hay 6E 68
Hillboro Ct. E11 5B 46
Hillborough Clo. SW19 4A 106
Hillbrook Rd. SW17 9D 90
Hill Brow. Brom 5H 111
Hill Brow. Dart 5D 98
Hillbrow. N Mald 7D 104
Hill Brow Clo. Bex 1B 114
Hillbrow Rd. Brom 4C 110
Hillbrow Rd. Esh 6A 118
Hillbury Av. Harr 3F 38
Hillbury Rd. SW17 9F 90
Hillbury Rd. Whyt & Warl 9E 138
Hill Clo. NW2 8F 40
Hill Clo. NW11 4L 41
Hill Clo. Barn 7G 13
Hill Clo. Chst 2M 111
Hill Clo. Harr 8C 38
Hill Clo. Purl 5A 138
Hill Clo. Stan 4F 22
Hillcote Av. SW16 4L 107
Hill Ct. W5 7K 55
Hill Ct. Barn 6C 14
Hill Ct. N'holt 1L 53
Hill Ct. Romf 2D 50
Hillcourt Av. N12 6M 25
Hillcourt Est. N16 6B 44
Hillcourt Rd. SE22 5F 92
Hill Cres. N20 2M 25
Hill Cres. Bex 7A 98
Hill Cres. Harr 3E 38
Hill Cres. Horn 4G 51
Hill Cres. Surb 9K 103
Hill Cres. Wor Pk 4G 121
Hillcrest. N6 5E 42
Hillcrest. N21 9L 15
Hillcrest. SE5 3B 92
Hillcrest. Sidc 6E 96
Hill Crest. Surb 2J 119
Hillcrest. Wey 6A 116
Hillcrest Av. NW11 3K 41
Hillcrest Av. Edgw 4M 23
Hillcrest Av. Pinn 2H 37
Hillcrest Clo. SE26 1E 108
Hillcrest Clo. Beck 1K 125
Hillcrest Clo. Eps 7D 134
Hillcrest Ct. Romf 8B 34
Hillcrest Ct. Sutt 8B 122
Hillcrest Gdns. N3 2J 41
Hill Crest Gdns. NW2 8E 40
Hillcrest Gdns. Esh 5D 118
Hillcrest Pde. Coul 6F 136
Hillcrest Rd. E17 9B 30
Hillcrest Rd. E18 9E 30
Hillcrest Rd. W3 2M 71
Hillcrest Rd. W5 8J 55
Hillcrest Rd. Big H 8H 141
Hillcrest Rd. Brom 2E 110
Hillcrest Rd. Dart 6C 98
Hillcrest Rd. Horn 5E 50
Hillcrest Rd. Lou 8H 19
Hillcrest Rd. Orp 4E 128
Hillcrest Rd. Purl 2K 137
Hillcrest Rd. Whyt 9D 138
Hillcrest Vw. Beck 1K 125
Hillcroft. Lou 4L 19
Hillcroft Av. Pinn 4K 37
Hillcroft Av. Purl 5G 137
Hillcroft Cres. W5 9J 55
Hillcroft Cres. Ruis 8H 37
Hillcroft Cres. Wat 1F 20
Hillcroft Cres. Wemb 9K 39
Hillcroft Rd. E6 8M 63
Hillcroome Rd. Sutt 8B 122
Hillcross Av. Mord 1H 121
Hilldale Rd. Sutt 6K 121
Hilldeane Rd. Purl 1L 137
Hilldene Av. Romf 6G 35
Hilldene Clo. H Hill 5H 35
Hilldown Ct. SW16 4J 107
Hilldown Rd. SW16 4J 107
Hilldown Rd. Brom 3C 126
Hill Dri. NW9 6A 40
Hill Dri. SW16 7K 107
Hilldrop Cres. N7 1H 59
Hilldrop Est. N7 9H 43
Hilldrop La. N7 1H 59
Hilldrop Rd. N7 1H 59
Hilldrop Rd. Brom 3F 110
Hille Bus. Cen. Wat 3F 8
Hillend. SE18 9L 79
Hill End. Orp 4D 128
Hillersden Ho. SW1 6F 74
(off Ebury Bri. Rd.)
Hillersdon Av. SW13 1E 88
Hillersdon Av. Edgw 5K 23
Hillery Clo. SE17 5B 76
Hill Farm Av. Wat 5E 4
Hill Farm Clo. Wat 6E 4
Hill Farm Cotts. Ruis 5A 36
Hill Farm Ind. Est. Wat 6E 4
Hill Farm Rd. W10 8G 57
Hill Farm Rd. Uxb 9B 36
Hillfield Av. N8 3J 43
Hillfield Av. NW9 3C 40
Hillfield Av. Mord 1C 122
Hillfield Av. Wemb 3J 55
Hillfield Clo. Harr 2A 38
Hillfield Ct. NW3 1C 58
Hillfield Ct. Esh 7M 117
Hillfield Ho. N5 1A 60
Hillfield Pk. N10 2F 42
Hillfield Pk. N21 2L 27
Hillfield Pk. M. N10 2F 42
Hillfield Rd. NW6 1K 57
Hill Fld. Rd. Hamp 4K 101
Hillfoot Av. Romf 8A 34
Hillfoot Rd. Romf 8A 34
Hillgate Pl. SW12 6F 90
Hillgate Pl. W8 2L 73
Hillgate St. W8 2L 73
Hill Gro. Felt 8K 85
Hill Gro. Romf 1C 50
Hill Ho. E5 6F 44
(off Harrington Hill)
Hill Ho. Brom 6D 110
Hillhouse. Wal A 6M 7
Hillhouse Av. Stan 7D 22
Hill Ho. Clo. N21 9L 15
Hill Ho. Dri. Hamp 5L 101
Hill Ho. Rd. SW16 2K 107
Hilliard Ho. E1 2F 76
(off Prusom St.)
Hilliard Rd. N'wd 8D 20
Hilliards Ct. E1 2G 77
Hilliards Rd. Uxb 9B 142
Hillier Clo. New Bar 8M 13
Hillier Gdns. Croy 7L 123
Hillier Ho. NW1 3H 59
(off Camden Sq.)
Hillier Lodge. Tedd 2B 102
Hillier Pl. Chess 8H 119
Hillier Rd. SW11 5D 90
Hilliers Av. Uxb 6E 142
Hilliers La. Croy 5J 123
Hillingdale. Big H 9F 140
Hillingdon. 6E 142
Hillingdon Av. Stai 7C 144
Hillingdon Cir. Hil 2F 142
Hillingdon Ct. Harr 2H 39
Hillingdon Heath. 7F 142
Hillingdon Hill. Uxb 5C 142
Hillingdon Rd. Bexh 1A 98
Hillingdon Rd. Uxb 4B 142
Hillingdon Rd. Wat 7E 4
Hillingdon St. SE5 & SE17 7M 75
(in two parts)
Hillington Gdns. Wfd G 9H 31
Hill La. Ruis 6A 36
Hillman Clo. Horn 1H 51
Hillman Clo. Uxb 1C 142
Hillman Dri. W10 7G 57
Hillman St. E8 2F 60
Hillmarton Rd. N7 1J 59
Hillmead Dri. SW9 3M 91
Hillmont Rd. Esh 5C 118
Hillmore Ct. SE13 2B 94
(off Belmont Hill)
Hillmore Gro. SE26 2J 109
Hill Path. SW16 2K 107
Hillreach. SE18 6K 79
Hill Ri. N9 8F 16
Hill Ri. NW11 2M 41
Hill Ri. SE23 7F 92
Hill Ri. Esh 4F 118
Hill Ri. Gnfd 3A 54
Hill Ri. Rich 4H 87
Hill Ri. Ruis 6A 36
Hill Ri. Upm 7L 51
Hill Ri. W on T 2D 116
Hillrise Av. Wat 2H 9
Hillrise Mans. N19 5J 43
(off Warltersville Rd.)
Hillrise Rd. N19 5J 43
Hillrise Rd. Romf 6A 34
Hill Rd. N10 8D 26
Hill Rd. NW8 6A 58
Hill Rd. Cars 8C 122
Hill Rd. Dart 8J 99
Hill Rd. Harr 3E 38
Hill Rd. Mitc 5F 106
Hill Rd. N'wd 6B 20
Hill Rd. Pinn 3J 37
Hill Rd. Purl 4K 137
Hill Rd. Sutt 7M 121
Hill Rd. Wemb 8F 38
Hillsboro' Rd. SE22 4C 92
Hillsborough Ct. NW6 4M 57
(off Mortimer Cres.)
Hillsborough Grn. Wat 3E 20
Hillsgrove Clo. Well 8G 81
Hillside. 5A 82
Hillside. N8 4H 43
Hillside. NW5 8E 42
Hillside. NW9 2B 40
Hillside. NW10 3A 56
Hillside. SE10 8B 78
(off Crooms Hill)
Hillside. SW19 3H 105
Hillside. Bans 7J 135
Hillside. Eri 5A 82
Hillside. Esh 7M 117
Hillside. F'ham 2K 131
Hillside. H Hill 4H 35
Hillside. New Bar 7A 14
Hillside Av. N11 6D 26
Hillside Av. Borwd 6M 11
Hillside Av. Chesh 4D 6
Hillside Av. Purl 5M 137
Hillside Av. Wemb 9K 39
Hillside Av. Wfd G 6G 31
Hillside Clo. NW8 5M 57
Hillside Clo. Ab L 5C 4
Hillside Clo. Bans 8J 135
Hillside Clo. Mord 8J 105
Hillside Clo. Wfd G 5G 31
Hillside Ct. Chesh 4D 6
Hillside Ct. Swan 8E 114
Hillside Cres. Chesh 4D 6
Hillside Cres. Enf 2B 16
Hillside Cres. Harr 6A 38
Hillside Cres. N'wd 8E 20
Hillside Cres. Wat 8J 9
Hillside Dri. Edgw 6L 23
Hillside Est. N15 4D 44
Hillside Gdns. E17 1B 46
Hillside Gdns. N6 4F 42
Hillside Gdns. N11 6G 27
Hillside Gdns. SW2 8L 91
Hillside Gdns. Barn 6J 13
Hillside Gdns. Edgw 4K 23
Hillside Gdns. Harr 5J 39
Hillside Gdns. N'wd 7E 20
Hillside Gdns. Wall 9G 123
Hillside Gro. N14 9H 15
Hillside Gro. NW7 7E 24
Hillside Ho. Croy 6M 123
(off Violet La.)
Hillside La. Brom 4D 126
(in two parts)
Hillside Mans. Barn 6K 13
Hillside Pas. SW16 8K 91
Hillside Ri. N'wd 7E 20
Hillside Rd. N16 5C 44
Hillside Rd. SW2 8K 91
Hillside Rd. W5 8J 55
Hillside Rd. Asht 9K 133
Hillside Rd. Brom 7D 110
Hillside Rd. Bush 7J 9
Hillside Rd. Coul 9J 137
Hillside Rd. Croy 7M 123
Hillside Rd. Dart 5E 98
Hillside Rd. Eps 2G 135
Hillside Rd. N'wd 7E 20
Hillside Rd. Pinn 7F 20
Hillside Rd. S'hall 7L 53
Hillside Rd. Surb 8K 103
Hillside Rd. Sutt 9K 121
Hillside, The. Orp 9F 128
Hills La. N'wd 8C 20
Hillsleigh Rd. W8 2K 73
Hillsmead Way. S Croy 5E 138
Hills M. W5 1J 71
Hills Pl. W1 9G 59
Hills Rd. Buck H 1F 30
Hillstowe St. E5 8G 45
Hill St. W1 2E 74
Hill St. Rich 4H 87
Hilltop. E17 1M 45
Hilltop. NW11 2M 41
Hill Top. Lou 4L 19
Hill Top. Mord 1L 121
Hill Top. Sutt 2K 121
Hill Top Clo. Lou 5L 19
Hilltop Ct. NW8 3A 58
(off Alexandra Rd.)
Hill Top Ct. Wfd G 6K 31
Hilltop Gdns. NW4 9F 24
Hilltop Gdns. Dart 4K 99
Hilltop Gdns. Orp 4C 128
Hill Top Pl. Lou 5L 19
Hilltop Rd. NW6 3L 57
Hilltop Rd. K Lan 1B 4
Hilltop Rd. Whyt 9C 138
Hill Top Vw. Wfd G 6K 31
Hilltop Way. Stan 3E 22
Hillview. SW20 4F 104
Hillview Av. Harr 3J 39
Hillview Av. Horn 4G 51
Hillview Clo. Pinn 6K 21
Hillview Clo. Purl 3M 137
Hillview Clo. Wemb 7K 39
Hill Vw. Cres. Ilf 4K 47
Hill Vw. Cres. Orp 3C 128
Hill Vw. Dri. SE28 2C 80
Hill Vw. Dri. Well 1C 96
Hillview Gdns. NW4 2H 41
Hill Vw. Gdns. NW9 3B 40
Hillview Gdns. Harr 1L 37
Hillview Rd. NW7 4H 25
Hillview Rd. Chst 2L 111
Hill Vw. Rd. Clay 9E 118
Hill Vw. Rd. Orp 3D 128
Hillview Rd. Pinn 7K 21
Hillview Rd. Sutt 5A 122
Hill Vw. Rd. Twic 5E 86
Hillway. N6 7E 42
Hillway. NW9 6C 40
Hillwood Ho. NW1 5G 59
(off Polygon Rd.)
Hillworth. Beck 6M 109
Hillworth Rd. SW2 6L 91
Hillyard Ho. SW9 9L 75
Hillyard Rd. W7 8C 54
Hillyard St. SW9 9L 75
Hillyfield. E17 9J 29
Hillyfields. Lou 4L 19
Hilly Fields Cres. SE4 2L 93
Hilly Fields Pk. 2A 16
Hilsea St. E5 9G 45
Hilton Av. N12 5B 26
Hilton Clo. Uxb 5A 142
Hilton Ho. SE4 3H 93
Hilton Way. S Croy 7F 138
Hilton Wharf. SE10 7M 77
(off Norman Rd.)
Hilversum Cres. SE22 4C 92
Himalayan Way. Wat 8D 8
Himley Rd. SW17 2C 106
Hinchinbrook Ho. NW6 4M 57
(off Mortimer Cres.)
Hinchley Clo. Esh 6D 118
Hinchley Dri. Esh 5D 118
Hinchley Way. Esh 5E 118
Hinchley Wood. 5D 118
Hinckley Rd. SE15 3E 92
Hind Clo. Chig 5D 32
Hind Ct. EC4 9L 59
Hind Cres. Eri 7B 82
Hinde Ho. W1 9E 58
(off Hinde St.)
Hinde M. W1 9E 58
(off Marlebone La.)
Hindes Rd. Harr 3B 38
Hinde St. W1 9E 58
Hind Gro. E14 9L 61
Hindhead Clo. N16 6C 44
Hindhead Clo. Uxb 8F 142
Hindhead Gdns. N'holt 4J 53
Hindhead Grn. Wat 5G 21
Hindhead Way. Wall 7J 123
Hind Ho. SE14 7H 77
(off Myers La.)
Hindlip Ho. SW8 9H 75
Hindmans Rd. SE22 4E 92
Hindmans Way. Dag 7K 65
Hindmarsh Clo. E1 1E 76
Hindrey Rd. E5 1F 60
Hindsley's Pl. SE23 8G 93
Hinkler Rd. Harr 1H 39
Hinksey Path. SE2 3H 81
Hinstock. NW6 4M 57
(off Belsize Rd.)
Hinstock Rd. SE18 7A 80
Hinton Av. Houn 3H 85
Hinton Clo. SE9 7J 95
Hinton Ct. E10 7M 45
(off Leyton Grange Est.)
Hinton Ho. W5 9G 55
Hinton Rd. N18 4C 28
Hinton Rd. SW9 2M 91
Hinton Rd. Uxb 4A 142
Hinton Rd. Wall 8G 123
Hippodrome M. W11 1J 73
Hippodrome Pl. W11 1J 73
Hiroshima Promenade. SE7 4G 79
Hissocks Ho. NW10 3A 56
(off Stilton Cres.)
Hitcham Rd. E17 5K 45
Hitchin Clo. Romf 4G 35
Hitchin Sq. E3 5J 61
Hitherbroom Rd. Hay 2E 68
Hither Farm Rd. SE3 2G 95
Hitherfield Rd. SW16 8K 91
Hitherfield Rd. Dag 7J 49
Hither Green. 5C 94
Hither Grn. La. SE13 4A 94
Hitherwell Dri. Harr 8B 22
Hitherwood Clo. Horn 9H 51
Hitherwood Dri. SE19 1D 108
Hive Clo. Bus H 2B 22
Hive Rd. Bus H 2B 22
(in two parts)
HMS Belfast. 2C 76
Hoadly Rd. SW16 9H 91
Hobart Clo. N20 2C 26
Hobart Clo. Hay 7H 53
Hobart Ct. S Croy 7B 124
(off S. Park Hill Rd.)
Hobart Dri. Hay 7H 53
Hobart Gdns. T Hth 7B 108
Hobart La. Hay 7H 53
Hobart Pl. SW1 4F 74
Hobart Pl. Rich 6K 87
Hobart Rd. Dag 9H 49
Hobart Rd. Hay 7H 53
Hobart Rd. Ilf 9A 32
Hobart Rd. Wor Pk 5F 120
Hobbayne Rd. W7 9B 54
Hobbes Wlk. SW15 4F 88
Hobbs Clo. Chesh 2D 6
Hobbs Ct. SE1 3D 76
(off Mill St.)
Hobbs Grn. N2 1A 42
Hobbs M. Ilf 7D 48
Hobbs Pl. N1 4C 60
Hobbs Pl. Est. N1 4C 6
(off Hobbs Pl.
Hobbs Rd. SE27 1A 10
Hobday St. E14 9M 6
Hobill Wlk. Surb 1K 11
Hoblands End. Chst 3C 11
Hobson's Pl. E1 8E 6
Hobury St. SW10 7A 7
Hockenden. 7L 11
Hockenden La. Swan 7L 11
Hocker St. E2 6D 6
Hockett Clo. SE8 5J 7
Hockington Ct. New Bar 6M 1

Hockley Av.—Holyport Rd.

Hockley Av. E6 . . . . .5J 63
Hockley Ct. E18 . . . . .8E 30
Hockley Dri. Romf 9F 34
Hockley M. Bark 6C 64
Hockliffe Ho. W10 . . . . .8G 57
(off Sutton Way)
Hockney Ct. SE16 . . . . .6F 76
(off Rossetti Rd.)
Hocroft Av. NW2 . . . . .8K 41
Hocroft Ct. NW2 . . . . .8K 41
Hocroft Rd. NW2 . . . . .8K 41
Hocroft Wlk. NW2 . . . . .8K 41
Hodder Dri. Gnfd 5D 54
Hoddesdon Rd. Belv 6L 81
Hodes Row. NW3 . . . . .9E 42
Hodford Rd. NW11 . . . . .6K 41
Hodges Way. Wat 8E 8
Hodgkin Clo. SE28 . . . . .1H 81
Hodister Clo. SE5 . . . . .8A 76
Hodnet Gro. SE16 . . . . .5H 77
Hodsoll Ct. Orp 9H 113
Hodson Clo. Harr 8K 37
Hodson Cres. Orp 9H 113
Hodson Pl. Enf 2L 17
Hoecroft Ct. Enf 2G 17
(off Hoe La.)
Hoe La. Abr 1H 33
Hoe La. Enf 2E 16
Hoe St. E17 . . . . .2L 45
Hoe, The. Wat 2H 21
Hoever Ho. SE6 . . . . .1A 110
Hofland Rd. W14 . . . . .4J 73
Hogan M. W2 . . . . .8A 58
Hogan Way. E5 . . . . .7E 44
Hogarth Av. Ashf 3A 100
Hogarth Bus. Cen. W4 . . . . . .7C 72
Hogarth Clo. E16 . . . . .8H 63
Hogarth Clo. W5 . . . . .8J 55
Hogarth Ct. E1 . . . . .9E 60
(off Batty St.)
Hogarth Ct. EC3 . . . . .9C 60
Hogarth Ct. NW1 . . . . .3G 59
(off St Pancras Way)
Hogarth Ct. SE19 . . . . .1D 108
Hogarth Ct. Bush 9M 9
Hogarth Ct. Houn 8J 69
Hogarth Cres. SW19 . . . . . .5B 106
Hogarth Cres. Croy 2A 124
Hogarth Gdns. Houn 8L 69
Hogarth Hill. NW11 . . . . .2K 41
Hogarth Ho. SW1 . . . . .5H 75
(off Erasmus St.)
Hogarth Ho. N'holt 5H 53
(off Gallery Gdns.)
Hogarth Ind. Est. NW10 . . . . .7E 56
Hogarth La. W4 . . . . .7C 72
Hogarth Pl. SW5 . . . . .5M 73
(off Hogarth Rd.)
Hogarth Reach. Lou 7K 19
Hogarth Rd. SW5 . . . . .5M 73
Hogarth Rd. Dag 1F 64
Hogarth Rd. Edgw 9L 23
Hogarth Roundabout (Junct.)
. . . . .7D 72
Hogarth's House. 7C 72
(off Hogarth La.)
Hogarth Ter. W4 . . . . .7C 72
Hogarth Way. Hamp 5A 102
Hog Hill Rd. Romf 7K 33
Hog La. Els 6E 10
Hogshead Pas. E1 . . . . .1F 76
(off Reunion Row)
Hogsmill Ho. King T 7K 103
(off Vineyard Clo.)
Hogsmill Wlk. King T 7J 103
(off Penrhyn Rd.)
Hogsmill Way. Eps 7A 120
Hogs Orchard. Swan 5F 114
Holbeach Gdns. Sidc 5C 96
Holbeach M. SW12 . . . . .7F 90
Holbeach Rd. SE6 . . . . .6L 93
Holbeck Row. SE15 . . . . .8E 76
Holbein Ga. N'wd 5C 20
Holbein Ho. SW1 . . . . .6E 74
(off Holbein M.)
Holbein M. SW1 . . . . .6E 74
Holbein Pl. SW1 . . . . .5E 74
Holbein Ter. Dag 9G 49
(off Marlborough Rd.)
Holberton Gdns. NW10 . . . . .6F 56
Holborn. 8L 59
Holborn. EC1 . . . . .8L 59
Holborn Cir. EC1 . . . . .8L 59
Holborn Pl. WC2 . . . . .8K 59
(off High Holborn)
Holborn Rd. E13 . . . . .8F 62
Holborn Viaduct.
EC4 & EC1 . . . . .8L 59
Holborn Way. Mitc 6D 106
Holbrook Clo. N19 . . . . .6F 42
Holbrook Clo. Enf 3D 16
Holbrooke Ct. N7 . . . . .8J 43
Holbrooke Pl. Rich 4H 87
Holbrook Ho. Chst 5B 112
Holbrook La. Chst 4B 112
Holbrook Rd. E15 . . . . .5D 62
Holbrook Way. Brom 1K 127
Holburne Clo. SE3 . . . . .9G 79
Holburne Gdns. SE3 . . . . . . .9H 79
Holburne Rd. SE3 . . . . .9G 79
Holcombe Hill. NW7 . . . . . . .3E 24
Holcombe Ho. SW9 . . . . .2J 91
(off Landor Rd.)
Holcombe Pl. SE4 . . . . .2J 93
(off St Asaph Rd.)
Holcombe Rd. N17 . . . . .1D 44
(in two parts)
Holcombe Rd. Ilf 5L 47
Holcombe St. W6 . . . . .5F 72
Holcote Clo. Belv 4J 81
Holcroft Ct. W1 . . . . .8G 59
(off Clipstone St.)
Holcroft Ho. SW11 . . . . .2B 90
Holcroft Rd. E9 . . . . .3G 61
Holdbrook. 7F 6
Holdbrook N. Wal X 6F 6
Holdbrook S. Wal X 7F 6
Holdbrook Way. Romf 9K 35
Holden Av. N12 . . . . .5M 25
Holden Av. NW9 . . . . .6A 40
Holdenby Rd. SE4 . . . . .4J 93
Holden Clo. Dag 8F 48
Holden Ho. N1 . . . . .4A 60
(off Prebend St.)
Holden Ho. SE8 . . . . .8L 77
Holdenhurst Av. N12 . . . . . . .7A 26
Holden Rd. N12 . . . . .5M 25
Holden St. SW11 . . . . .1E 90
Holder Clo. N3 . . . . .7M 25
Holdernesse Clo. Iswth 9E 70
Holdernesse Rd. SW17 . . . . .9D 90
Holderness Ho. SE5 . . . . .2C 92
Holderness Way. SE27 . . . .2M 107
Holders Hill. 9H 25
Holder's Hill Av. NW4 . . . . . .9H 25
Holders Hill Cir. NW7 . . . . . .7J 25
Holders Hill Cres. NW4 . . . . .9H 25
Holders Hill Dri. NW4 . . . . . .1H 41
Holder's Hill Gdns. NW4 . . . .9J 25
Holders Hill Pde. NW4 . . . . . .8J 25
Holders Hill Rd.
NW4 & NW7 . . . . .9H 25
Holecroft. Wal A 7L 7
Holford Ho. SE16 . . . . .5F 76
(off Camilla Rd.)
Holford M. WC1 . . . . .6L 59
(off Cruikshank St.)
Holford Pl. WC1 . . . . .6K 59
Holford Rd. NW3 . . . . .8A 42
Holford St. WC1 . . . . .6K 59
Holford Yd. WC1 . . . . .5L 59
(off Cruikshank St.)
Holgate Av. SW11 . . . . .2B 90
Holgate Ct. Romf 3C 50
(off Western Rd.)
Holgate Gdns. Dag 2L 65
Holgate Rd. Dag 1L 65
Holgate St. SE7 . . . . .4H 79
Hollam Ho. N8 . . . . .2K 43
Holland Av. SW20 . . . . .5D 104
Holland Av. Sutt 1L 135
Holland Clo. Brom 4D 126
Holland Clo. New Bar 9B 14
Holland Clo. Romf 3A 50
Holland Clo. Stan 5F 22
Holland Ct. E17 . . . . .2A 46
(off Evelyn Rd.)
Holland Ct. NW7 . . . . .6E 24
Holland Ct. Surb 2H 119
Holland Dri. SE23 . . . . .9J 93
Holland Gdns. W14 . . . . .4J 73
Holland Gdns. Wat 8G 5
Holland Gro. SW9 . . . . .8L 75
Holland Ho. E4 . . . . .4B 30
Holland Ho. NW10 . . . . .5F 56
(off Holland Rd.)
Holland Park. 2K 73
Holland Pk. 3K 73
Holland Pk. W11 . . . . .2J 73
Holland Pk. Av. W11 . . . . . . .3J 73
Holland Pk. Av. Ilf 4C 48
Holland Pk. Gdns. W14 . . . . .3J 73
Holland Pk. M. W11 . . . . .2J 73
Holland Pk. Rd. W14 . . . . . . .4K 73
Holland Park Roundabout (Junct.)
. . . . .3J 73
Holland Pk. Theatre. 3K 73
(in Holland Pk., Open Air)
Holland Pas. N1 . . . . .4A 60
(off Basire St.)
Holland Pl. W8 . . . . .3M 73
(off Kensington Chu. St.)
Holland Pl. Chambers.
W8 . . . . .3M 73
(off Holland Pl.)
Holland Ri. Ho. SW9 . . . . . . .8K 75
(off Clapham Rd.)
Holland Rd. E6 . . . . .4K 63
Holland Rd. E15 . . . . .6C 62
Holland Rd. NW10 . . . . .4E 56
Holland Rd. SE25 . . . . .9E 108
Holland Rd. W14 . . . . .3H 73
Holland Rd. Wemb 2H 55
Hollands, The. Felt 1H 101
Hollands, The. Wor Pk 3D 120
Holland St. SE1 . . . . .2M 75
Holland St. W8 . . . . .3L 73
Holland Vs. Rd. W14 . . . . . . .3J 73
Holland Wlk. N19 . . . . .6H 43
Holland Wlk. W8 . . . . .2K 73
(off Holland Pk. Av.)
Holland Wlk. Stan 5E 22
Holland Way. Brom 4D 126
Hollar Rd. N16 . . . . .8D 44
Hollen St. W1 . . . . .9H 59
Holles Clo. Hamp 3L 101
Holles Ho. SW9 . . . . .1L 91
Holles St. W1 . . . . .9F 58
Holley Rd. W3 . . . . .3C 72
Hollick Wood Av. N12 . . . . . .6D 26
Holliday Sq. SW11 . . . . .2B 90
(off Fowler Clo.)
Hollidge Way. Dag 3M 65
Hollies Av. Sidc 8D 96
Hollies Clo. SW16 . . . . . . .3L 107
Hollies Clo. Twic 8D 86
Hollies End. NW7 . . . . .5F 24
Hollies Rd. W5 . . . . .5G 71
Hollies, The. E11 . . . . .3E 46
(off New Wanstead)
Hollies, The. N20 . . . . .1B 26
Hollies, The. Harr 2E 38
Hollies Way. SW12 . . . . .6E 90
Holligrave Rd. Brom 5E 110
Hollingbourne Av. Bexh 9K 81
Hollingbourne Gdns. W13 . . .8F 54
Hollingbourne Rd. SE24 . . . .4A 92
Hollingsworth Ct. Surb 2H 119
Hollingsworth Rd. Croy . . .8F 124
Hollington Ct. Chst 3M 111
Hollington Cres. N Mald . . .1D 120
Hollington Rd. E6 . . . . .6K 63
Hollington Rd. N17 . . . . .9E 28
Hollingworth Clo. W Mol . . .8K 101
Hollingworth Rd. Orp 1M 127
Hollins Ho. N7 . . . . .9J 43
Hollisfield. WC1 . . . . .6J 59
(off Cromer St.)
Hollman Gdns. SW16 . . . . .3M 107
Holloway. 8J 43
Holloway Clo. W Dray 6J 143
Holloway Ho. NW2 . . . . .8G 41
(off Stoll Clo.)
Holloway La. W Dray 7H 143
Holloway Rd. E6 . . . . .6K 63
Holloway Rd. E11 . . . . .8B 46
Holloway Rd. N19 & N7 . . . . .7H 43
Holloway St. Houn 2M 85
Hollow Cotts. Purf 6L 83
Hollowfield Wlk. N'holt 3J 53
Hollows, The. Bren 7K 71
Hollows Wood. 9M 129
Hollow, The. Wfd G 4D 30
Holly Av. Stan 9J 23
Holly Av. W on T 3H 117
Hollybank Clo. Hamp 2L 101
Hollyberry La. NW3 . . . . .9A 42
Hollybrake Clo. Chst 4B 112
Hollybush Clo. E11 . . . . .3E 46
Hollybush Clo. Harr 8C 22
Hollybush Clo. Wat 9G 9
Hollybush Gdns. E2 . . . . .6F 60
Hollybush Hill. E11 . . . . .4D 46
Hollybush Hill. NW3 . . . . .9A 42
Hollybush Ho. E2 . . . . .6F 60
Holly Bush La. Hamp 4K 101
Holly Bush La. Orp 8L 129
Hollybush Pl. E2 . . . . .6F 60
Hollybush Rd. King T 2J 103
Hollybush Steps. NW3 . . . . . .9A 42
(off Holly Mt.)
Hollybush St. E13 . . . . .6F 62
Holly Bush Va. NW3 . . . . .9A 42
Hollybush Wlk. SW9 . . . . . . .3M 91
Hollybush Way. Chesh 1A 6
Holly Clo. NW10 . . . . .3C 56
Holly Clo. Beck 8A 110
Holly Clo. Buck H 3H 31
Holly Clo. Felt 2J 101
Holly Clo. Wall 9F 122
Holly Cottage M. Uxb 8E 142
Holly Ct. N15 . . . . .2C 44
Holly Ct. Sidc 1F 112
(off Sidcup Hill)
Holly Ct. Sutt 9L 121
Holly Cres. Beck 9K 109
Holly Cres. Wfd G 7B 30
Hollycroft Av. NW3 . . . . .8L 41
Hollycroft Av. Wemb 7K 39
Hollycroft Clo. S Croy 7C 124
Hollycroft Clo. W Dray 7L 143
Hollycroft Gdns. W Dray . . .7L 143
Hollydale Clo. N'holt 9M 37
Hollydale Dri. Brom 5K 127
Hollydale Rd. SE15 . . . . .9G 77
Hollydene. SE15 . . . . .9F 76
Hollydene. Brom 5D 110
(off Beckenham Rd.)
Hollydown Way. E11 . . . . . . .8B 46
Holly Dri. E4 . . . . .9M 17
Holly Farm Rd. S'hall 6J 69
Hollyfield Av. N11 . . . . .5D 26
Hollyfield Rd. Surb 2K 119
Holly Gdns. Bexh 3A 98
Holly Gdns. W Dray 3K 143
Holly Grn. Wey 6B 116
Holly Gro. NW9 . . . . .5A 40
Holly Gro. SE15 . . . . .1D 92
Hollygrove. Bush 9B 10
Holly Gro. Pinn 8J 21
Hollygrove Clo. Houn 3K 85
Holly Hedge Ter. SE13 . . . . .4B 94
Holly Hill. N21 . . . . .8K 15
Holly Hill. NW3 . . . . .9A 42
Holly Hill Dri. Bans 9L 135
Holly Hill Rd. Belv 6M 81
Holly Ho. W10 . . . . .7J 57
(off Hawthorn Wlk.)
Holly Ho. Iswth 7G 71
Holly Ind. Pk. Wat 3G 9
Holly La. Bans 8L 135
Holly La. E. Bans 8M 135
Holly La. W. Bans 9L 135
Holly Lodge. Harr 3B 38
Holly Lodge Gdns. N6 . . . . . .7E 42
Holly Lodge Mans. N6 . . . . . .7E 42
Hollymead. Cars 5D 122
Holly M. SW10 . . . . .6A 74
(off Drayton Gdns.)
Hollymoor La. Eps 2B 134
Holly Mt. NW3 . . . . .9A 42
Hollymount Clo. SE10 . . . . . .9A 78
Holly Pk. N3 . . . . .1K 41
Holly Pk. N4 . . . . .5J 43
(in two parts)
Holly Pk. Est. N4 . . . . .5K 43
Holly Pk. Gdns. N3 . . . . .1L 41
Holly Pk. Rd. N11 . . . . .5E 26
Holly Pk. Rd. W7 . . . . .2D 70
Holly Pl. NW3 . . . . .9A 42
(off Holly Berry La.)
Holly Rd. E11 . . . . .5D 46
Holly Rd. W4 . . . . .5B 72
Holly Rd. Dart 7H 99
Holly Rd. Enf 9D 6
Holly Rd. Hamp 3A 102
Holly Rd. Houn 3M 85
Holly Rd. Orp 9E 128
Holly Rd. Twic 7D 86
Holly St. E8 . . . . .3D 60
Holly Ter. N6 . . . . .6E 42
Holly Ter. N20 . . . . .2A 26
Hollytree Av. Swan 6C 114
Holly Tree Clo. SW19 . . . . . . .7H 89
Holly Tree Ho. SE4 . . . . .2K 93
(off Brockley Rd.)
Hollytree Ho. Wat 9C 4
Hollytree Pde. Sidc 3G 113
(off Sidcup Hill)
Holly Vw. Clo. NW4 . . . . .4E 40
Holly Village. N6 . . . . .7F 42
Holly Wlk. NW3 . . . . .9A 42
Holly Wlk. Enf 5A 16
Holly Way. Mitc 8H 107
Hollywood Ct. W5 . . . . .1K 71
Hollywood Ct. Borwd 6L 11
Hollywood Gdns. Hay 9F 52
Hollywood M. SW10 . . . . .7A 74
Hollywood Rd. E4 . . . . .5J 29
Hollywood Rd. SW10 . . . . . . .7A 74
Hollywoods. Croy 1K 139
Hollywood Way. Eri 8F 82
Hollywood Way. Wfd G 7B 30
Holman Ct. Eps 1E 134
Holman Ho. E2 . . . . .6H 61
(off Roman Rd.)
Holman Hunt Ho. W6 . . . . . . .6J 73
(off Field Rd.)
Holman Rd. SW11 . . . . .1B 90
Holman Rd. Eps 7A 120
Holmbank Dri. Shep 8C 100
Holmbridge Gdns. Enf 6H 17
Holmbrook. NW1 . . . . .5G 59
(off Eversholt St.)
Holmbrook Dri. NW4 . . . . . . .3H 41
Holmbury Ct. SW17 . . . . .9D 90
Holmbury Ct. S Croy 7C 124
Holmbury Gdns. Hay 2D 68
Holmbury Gro. Croy 9K 125
Holmbury Ho. SE24 . . . . .4M 91
Holmbury Mnr. Sidc 1E 112
Holmbury Pk. Brom 4J 111
Holmbury Vw. E5 . . . . .6F 44
Holmbush Rd. SW15 . . . . . . .5J 89
Holmcote Gdns. N5 . . . . .1A 60
Holm Ct. SE12 . . . . .9F 94
Holmcroft Ho. E17 . . . . .2M 45
Holmcroft Way. Brom 9K 111
Holmdale Clo. Borwd 4K 11
Holmdale Gdns. NW4 . . . . . . .3H 41
Holmdale Rd. NW6 . . . . .1L 57
Holmdale Rd. Chst 2A 112
Holmdale Ter. N15 . . . . .5C 44
Holmdene. N12 . . . . .5M 25
Holmdene Av. NW7 . . . . .6E 24
Holmdene Av. SE24 . . . . .4A 92
Holmdene Av. Harr 1M 37
Holmdene Clo. Beck 6A 110
Holmead Rd. SW6 . . . . .8M 73
Holmebury Clo. Bush 2C 22
Holme Chase. Wey 8A 116
Holme Clo. Chesh 4E 6
Holme Lacey Rd. SE12 . . . . . .5D 94
Holme Lea. Wat 7G 5
Holme Pk. Borwd 4K 11
Holme Rd. E6 . . . . .4J 63
Holme Rd. Horn 6L 51
Holmes Av. E17 . . . . .1K 45
Holmes Av. NW7 . . . . .5J 25
Holmesdale. Wal X 8C 6
Holmesdale Av. SW14 . . . . . .2M 87
Holmesdale Clo. SE25 . . . . .7D 108
Holmesdale Ho. NW6 . . . . . . .4L 57
(off Kilburn Va.)
Holmesdale Rd. N6 . . . . .5F 42
Holmesdale Rd. Bexh 1H 97
Holmesdale Rd.
Croy & SE25 . . . . .9B 108
Holmesdale Rd. Rich 9K 71
Holmesdale Rd. Tedd 4G 103
Holmesdale Tunnel. Wal X 7D 6
Holmesley Rd. SE23 . . . . .5J 93
Holmes Pl. SW10 . . . . .7A 74
Holmes Rd. NW5 . . . . .1F 58
Holmes Rd. SW19 . . . . .4A 106
Holmes Rd. Twic 8D 86
Holmes Ter. SE1 . . . . .3L 75
(off Waterloo Rd.)
Holmeswood Ct. N22 . . . . . . .9L 27
Holme Way. Stan 6D 22
Holmewood Gdns. SW2 . . . . .6K 91
Holmewood Rd. SE25 . . . . .7C 108
Holmewood Rd. SW2 . . . . . . .6J 91
Holmfield Av. NW4 . . . . .3H 41
Holmfield Ct. NW3 . . . . .1C 58
Holm Gro. Uxb 3E 142
Holmhurst Rd. Belv 6M 81
Holmlea Ct. Croy 6B 124
(off Chatsworth Rd.)
Holmleigh Av. Dart 4G 99
Holmleigh Ct. Enf 6G 17
Holmleigh Rd. N16 . . . . .6C 44
Holmleigh Rd. Est. N16 . . . . .6C 44
Holmoak Clo. SW15 . . . . .5K 89
Holm Oak M. SW4 . . . . .4J 91
Holm Oak Pk. Wat 7D 8
Holmoaks Ho. Beck 6A 110
Holmsdale Gro. Bexh 1C 98
Holmsdale Ho. E14 . . . . .1M 77
(off Poplar High St.)
Holmsdale Ho. N11 . . . . .4F 26
(off Coppies Gro.)
Holmshaw Clo. SE26 . . . . . .1J 109
Holmshill La. Borwd 1C 12
Holmside Ri. Wat 3F 20
Holmside Rd. SW12 . . . . .5E 90
Holmsley Clo. N Mald 1D 120
Holmsley Ho. SW15 . . . . .6D 88
(off Tangley Gro.)
Holmstall Av. Edgw 1A 40
Holmstall Pde. Edgw 9A 24
Holm Wlk. SE3 . . . . .1E 94
Holmwood Av. S Croy 5D 138
Holmwood Clo. Harr 1A 38
Holmwood Clo. N'holt 2M 53
Holmwood Clo. Sutt 1H 135
Holmwood Gdns. N3 . . . . . . .9L 25
Holmwood Gdns. Wall 8F 122
Holmwood Gro. NW7 . . . . . . .5B 24
Holmwood Rd. Chess 7H 119
Holmwood Rd. Enf 9D 6
Holmwood Rd. Ilf 7C 48
Holmwood Rd. Sutt 1G 135
Holmwood Vs. SE7 . . . . .6E 78
Holne Chase. N2 . . . . .4A 42
Holne Chase. Mord 1K 121
Holness Rd. E15 . . . . .2D 62
Holroyd Clo. Clay 1D 132
Holroyd Rd. SW15 . . . . .3G 89
Holroyd Rd. Clay 1D 132
Holst Ct. SE1 . . . . .4L 75
(off Westminster Bri. Rd.)
Holstein Way. Eri 4H 81
Holst Mans. SW13 . . . . .7G 73
Holstock Rd. Ilf 7A 48
Holsworth Clo. Harr 3A 38
Holsworthy Ho. H Hill 8H 35
Holsworthy Sq. WC1 . . . . . . .7K 59
(off Elm St.)
Holsworthy Way. Chess 7G 119
Holt Clo. N10 . . . . .2E 42
Holt Clo. SE28 . . . . .1F 80
Holt Clo. Chig 5D 32
Holt Clo. Els 6K 11
Holt Ct. E15 . . . . .1A 62
Holt Ho. SW2 . . . . .5L 91
Holton St. E1 . . . . .7H 61
Holt Rd. E16 . . . . .2J 79
Holt Rd. Wemb 8F 38
Holtsmere Clo. Wat 8G 5
Holt, The. Ilf 6A 32
Holt, The. Mord 8L 105
Holt, The. Wall 6G 123
Holt Way. Chig 5D 32
Holtwhites Av. Enf 4A 16
Holtwhite's Hill. Enf 3M 15
Holtwood Rd. Oxs 5A 132
Holwell Pl. Pinn 2J 37
Holwood Clo. W on T 4G 117
Holwood Pk. Av. Orp 6K 127
Holwood Pl. SW4 . . . . .3H 91
Holybourne Av. SW15 . . . . . .6E 88
Holybush. Chesh 1B 6
Holyfield. 2K 7
Holyfield Rd. Wal A 2J 7
Holyhead Clo. E3 . . . . .6L 61
Holyhead Clo. E6 . . . . .8K 63
Holyhead Ct. King T 8H 103
(off Anglesea Rd.)
Holyoake Ct. SE16 . . . . .3K 77
Holyoake Ho. W5 . . . . .7G 55
Holyoake Wlk. N2 . . . . .1A 42
Holyoake Wlk. W5 . . . . .7G 55
Holyoak Rd. SE11 . . . . .5M 75
Holyport Rd. SW6 . . . . .8H 73

Holyrood Av.—Houston Pl.

Holyrood Av. Harr ... 9J 37
Holyrood Ct. Wat ... 6F 8
Holyrood Gdns. Edgw ... 1M 39
Holyrood M. E16 ... 2E 78
(off Badminton M.)
Holyrood Rd. New Bar ... 8A 14
Holyrood St. SE1 ... 2C 76
Holywell. ... 8D 8
Holywell Clo. SE3 ... 7E 78
Holywell Clo. SE16 ... 6F 76
Holywell Clo. Orp ... 6E 128
Holywell Clo. Stai ... 7C 144
Holywell La. EC2 ... 7C 60
Holywell Rd. Wat ... 7E 8
Holywell Row. EC2 ... 7C 60
Holywell Way. Stai ... 7C 144
Homan Ct. N12 ... 4B 26
Homebush Ho. E4 ... 9M 17
Home Clo. Cars ... 4D 122
Home Clo. N'holt ... 6K 53
Home Ct. Surb ... 9H 103
Homecroft Gdns. Lou ... 6M 19
Homecroft Rd. N22 ... 8A 28
Homecroft Rd. SE26 ... 2G 109
Home Farm Clo. Eps ... 9H 135
Home Farm Clo. Esh ... 8M 117
Home Farm Clo. Shep ... 8C 100
Home Farm Clo. Th Dit ... 2D 118
Home Farm Gdns.
W on T ... 4G 117
Homefarm Rd. W7 ... 9C 54
Home Fld. Barn ... 7K 13
Homefield. Mord ... 8L 105
Homefield. Wal A ... 5M 7
Homefield Av. Ilf ... 3C 48
Homefield Av. W on T ... 6H 117
Homefield Clo. NW10 ... 2A 56
Homefield Clo. Hay ... 7H 53
Homefield Clo. St P ... 8F 112
Homefield Clo. Swan ... 7D 114
Homefield Ct. SW16 ... 9J 91
Homefield Gdns. N2 ... 1B 42
Homefield Gdns. Mitc ... 6A 106
Homefield Ho. SE23 ... 9H 93
Homefield M. Beck ... 5L 109
Homefield Pk. Sutt ... 8M 121
Homefield Ri. Orp ... 3E 128
Homefield Rd. SW19 ... 3H 105
Homefield Rd. W4 ... 5D 72
Homefield Rd. Brom ... 5G 111
Homefield Rd. Bush ... 6L 9
Homefield Rd. Edgw ... 6B 24
Homefield Rd. Rad ... 1D 10
Homefield Rd. S at H ... 5L 115
Homefield Rd. W on T ... 2J 117
Homefield Rd. Wemb ... 9E 38
Homefield St. N1 ... 5C 60
Homefirs Ho. Wemb ... 8K 39
Home Gdns. Dag ... 8A 50
Home Gdns. Dart ... 5J 99
Home Hill. Swan ... 4D 114
Homeland Dri. Sutt ... 1M 135
Homelands Dri. SE19 ... 4C 108
Home Lea. Orp ... 7D 128
Homeleigh Ct. Chesh ... 2B 6
Homeleigh Rd. SE15 ... 4H 93
Homeleigh St. Chesh ... 3B 6
Homemanor Ho. Wat ... 5F 8
(off Cassio Rd.)
Home Mead. Stan ... 8G 23
Home Mdw. Bans ... 8L 135
Homemead Rd. Brom ... 9K 111
Homemead Rd. Croy ... 1G 123
Home Orchard. Dart ... 5J 99
(in two parts)
Home Pk. Cotts. K Lan ... 3A 4
Home Pk. Ct. King T ... 8H 103
(off Palace Rd.)
Home Pk. Ind. Est. K Lan ... 4A 4
Home Pk. Mill Link Rd.
K Lan ... 3A 4
Home Pk. Pde. King T ... 6H 103
(off High St.)
Home Pk. Rd. SW19 ... 1K 105
Home Pk. Ter. King T ... 6H 103
(off Hampton Ct. Rd.)
Home Pk. Wlk. King T ... 8H 103
Homer Clo. Bexh ... 9A 82
Homer Dri. E14 ... 5L 77
Home Rd. SW11 ... 1C 90
Homer Rd. E9 ... 2J 61
Homer Rd. Croy ... 1H 125
Homer Row. W1 ... 8C 58
Homersham Rd. King T ... 6L 103
Homer St. W1 ... 8C 58
Homerton. ... 1H 61
Homerton Gro. E9 ... 1H 61
Homerton High St. E9 ... 1H 61
Homerton Rd. E9 ... 1J 61
Homerton Row. E9 ... 1G 61
Homerton Ter. E9 ... 2G 61
(in two parts)
Homesdale Clo. E11 ... 3E 46
Homesdale Rd. Brom ... 8G 111
Homesdale Rd. Orp ... 2C 128
Homesfield. NW11 ... 3L 41
Homestall Rd. SE22 ... 4G 93
Homestead Ct. Barn ... 7L 13
Homestead Gdns. Clay ... 7C 118
Homestead Paddock. N14 ... 7F 14
Homestead Pk. NW2 ... 8D 40
Homestead Rd. SW6 ... 8K 73
Homestead Rd. Dag ... 7K 49
Homestead Rd. Orp ... 9F 128
Homesteads, The. N11 ... 4F 26
Homestead, The. Dart ... 4C 98
(off Crayford High St.)
Homestead, The. Dart ... 5G 99
(W. Hill Dri.)
Homestead Way.
New Ad ... 3A 140
Homewater Ho. Eps ... 5C 134
Homewaters Av. Sun ... 5D 100
Homeway. Romf ... 6M 35
Homewillow Clo. N21 ... 8M 15
Homewood Clo. Hamp ... 3K 101
Homewood Cres. Chst ... 3C 112
Homewoods. SW12 ... 6G 91
Homildon Ho. SE26 ... 9E 92
Honduras St. EC1 ... 7A 60
Honeybourne Rd. NW6 ... 1M 57
Honeybourne Way. Orp ... 3B 128
Honey Brook. Wal A ... 6L 7
Honeybrook Rd. SW12 ... 6G 91
Honey Clo. Dag ... 2M 65
Honeycroft. Lou ... 6M 19
Honeycroft Hill. Uxb ... 3C 142
Honeyden Rd. Sidc ... 3J 113
Honeyfield. Swan ... 3D 114
Honey Hill. Uxb ... 3D 142
Honey La. EC2 ... 9A 60
(off Trump St.)
Honey La. Wal A ... 6L 7
Honey La. Ho. Wal A ... 7M 7
Honeyman Clo. NW6 ... 3H 57
(in two parts)
Honeymead. N8 ... 1J 43
(off Campsfield Rd.)
Honeypot Bus. Cen. Stan ... 8J 23
Honeypot Clo. NW9 ... 2K 39
Honeypot La.
Stan & NW9 ... 7H 23
Honeysett Rd. N17 ... 9D 28
Honeysuckle Clo. Romf ... 6G 35
Honeysuckle Clo. S'hall ... 1J 69
Honeysuckle Ct. E12 ... 2M 63
Honeysuckle Gdns. Croy ... 2H 125
Honeysuckle La. N22 ... 9A 28
Honeytree Ct. Lou ... 4M 19
Honeywell Rd. SW11 ... 5D 90
Honeywood Heritage Cen.
... 6D 122
Honeywood Rd. NW10 ... 5D 56
Honeywood Rd. Iswth ... 3E 86
Honeywood Wlk. Cars ... 6D 122
Honister Clo. Stan ... 8F 22
Honister Gdns. Stan ... 7F 22
Honister Heights. Purl ... 6B 138
Honister Pl. Stan ... 8F 22
Honiton Gdns. SE15 ... 1G 93
(off Gibbon Rd.)
Honiton Rd. NW6 ... 5K 57
Honiton Rd. Romf ... 4B 50
Honiton Rd. Well ... 1D 96
Honley Rd. SE6 ... 6M 93
Honnor Gdns. Iswth ... 1B 86
Honor Oak. ... 5G 93
Honor Oak Crematorium.
SE23 ... 4J 93
Honor Oak Park. ... 6J 93
Honor Oak Pk. SE23 ... 5G 93
Honor Oak Ri. SE23 ... 5G 93
Honor Oak Rd. SE23 ... 7G 93
Hood Av. N14 ... 8F 14
Hood Av. SW14 ... 4A 88
Hood Av. Orp ... 9F 112
Hood Clo. Croy ... 3M 123
Hoodcote Gdns. N21 ... 9M 15
Hood Ct. EC4 ... 9L 59
(off Fleet St.)
Hood Ho. SE5 ... 8B 76
(off Elmington Est.)
Hood Ho. SW1 ... 6H 75
(off Dolphin Sq.)
Hood Rd. SW20 ... 4D 104
Hood Rd. Rain ... 5C 66
Hood Wlk. Romf ... 8M 33
Hook. ... 7H 119
Hooke Ho. E3 ... 5J 61
(off Gernon Rd.)
Hookers Rd. E17 ... 1H 45
Hook Farm Rd. Brom ... 9H 111
Hookfield. Eps ... 5A 134
Hookfield M. Eps ... 5A 134
Hook Ga. Enf ... 9B 6
Hook Green. ... 1E 114
Hook Grn. La. Dart ... 9D 98
Hookham Ct. SW8 ... 9H 75
Hook Hill. S Croy ... 2C 138
(in two parts)
Hooking Grn. Harr ... 3M 37
Hook Junction (Junct.) ... 5H 119
Hook La. Well ... 4D 96
Hook Ri. Bus. Cen.
Chess ... 5L 119
Hook Ri. N. Surb ... 5J 119
Hook Ri. S. Surb ... 5J 119
Hook Ri. S. Ind. Pk.
Chess ... 5K 119
Hook Rd. Chess & Surb ... 7H 119
Hook Rd. Eps ... 9A 120
Hooks Clo. SE15 ... 9F 76
Hookshall Dri. Dag ... 8A 50
Hookstone Way. Wfd G ... 7H 31
Hook, The. New Bar ... 8B 14
Hook Wlk. Edgw ... 6A 24
Hooper Rd. E16 ... 9E 62
Hooper's Ct. SW3 ... 3D 74
Hooper's M. W3 ... 2A 72
Hooper Sq. E1 ... 9E 60
(off Hooper St.)
Hooper St. E1 ... 9E 60
Hoop La. NW11 ... 5K 41
(in two parts)
Hope Clo. N1 ... 2A 60
Hope Clo. SE12 ... 9F 94
Hope Clo. Bren ... 6J 71
Hope Clo. Chad H ... 2H 49
Hope Clo. Sutt ... 7A 122
Hope Clo. Wfd G ... 6G 31
Hope Ct. NW10 ... 6H 57
(off Chamberlayne Rd.)
Hopedale Rd. SE7 ... 7F 78
Hopefield Av. NW6 ... 5J 57
Hope Grn. Wat ... 6E 4
Hope Ho. Croy ... 6C 124
(off Steep Hill)
Hope Pk. Brom ... 4D 110
Hopes Clo. Houn ... 7L 69
Hope St. SW11 ... 2B 90
Hopetown St. E1 ... 8D 60
Hopewell St. SE5 ... 8B 76
Hopewell Yd. SE5 ... 8B 76
(off Hopewell St.)
Hope Wharf. SE16 ... 3G 77
Hop Gdns. WC2 ... 1J 75
Hop Garden Way. Wat ... 4G 5
Hopgood St. W12 ... 2G 73
Hopkins Clo. N10 ... 7E 26
Hopkins Clo. Romf ... 1G 51
Hopkins Ho. E14 ... 9L 61
(off Canton St.)
Hopkins M. E15 ... 4D 62
Hopkinsons Pl. NW1 ... 4E 58
Hopkins St. W1 ... 9G 59
Hoppers Rd. N21 ... 2L 27
Hoppett Rd. E4 ... 2C 30
Hopping La. N1 ... 2M 59
Hoppingwood Av.
N Mald ... 7C 104
Hoppner Rd. Hay ... 5B 52
Hopton Ct. Brom ... 3F 126
Hopton Gdns. N Mald ... 1E 120
Hopton Rd. SW16 ... 2J 107
Hopton's Gdns. SE1 ... 2M 75
(off Hopton St.)
Hopton St. SE1 ... 2M 75
Hoptree Clo. N12 ... 5M 25
Hopwood Clo. SW17 ... 9A 90
Hopwood Clo. Wat ... 9C 4
Hopwood Rd. SE17 ... 7B 76
Hopwood Wlk. E8 ... 3E 60
Horace Av. Romf ... 6A 50
Horace Rd. E7 ... 9F 46
Horace Rd. Ilf ... 1A 48
Horace Rd. King T ... 7K 103
Horatio Ct. SE16 ... 2G 77
(off Rotherhithe St.)
Horatio Ho. E2 ... 5D 60
(off Horatio St.)
Horatio Ho. W6 ... 6H 73
(off Fulham Pal. Rd.)
Horatio Pl. E14 ... 2A 78
(off Preston's Rd.)
Horatio Pl. SW19 ... 5L 105
Horatio St. E2 ... 5D 60
(in two parts)
Horatius Way. Croy ... 7K 123
Horbury Cres. W11 ... 1L 73
Horbury M. W11 ... 1K 73
Horder Rd. SW6 ... 9J 73
Hordle Promenade E.
SE15 ... 8D 76
Hordle Promenade N.
SE15 ... 8D 76
Hordle Promenade S.
SE15 ... 8D 76
(off Quarley Way)
Hordle Promenade W.
SE15 ... 8C 76
(off Clanfield Way)
Horizon Building. E14 ... 1L 77
(off Hertsmere Rd.)
Horizon Ho. Eps ... 5C 134
Horizon Ho. Swan ... 8C 114
Horizon Way. SE7 ... 5F 78
Horle Wlk. SW9 ... 1M 91
Horley Clo. Bexh ... 4L 97
Horley Rd. SE9 ... 1J 111
Hormead Rd. W9 ... 7K 57
Hornbeam Av. Upm ... 9L 51
Hornbeam Clo. NW7 ... 3D 24
Hornbeam Clo. SE11 ... 5L 75
Hornbeam Clo. Borwd ... 3L 11
Hornbeam Clo. Buck H ... 3H 31
Hornbeam Clo. Ilf ... 1B 64
Hornbeam Clo. N'holt ... 1K 53
Hornbeam Cres. Bren ... 8F 70
Hornbeam Gro. E4 ... 3C 30
Hornbeam Ho. Buck H ... 3H 31
Hornbeam La. E4 ... 7C 18
Hornbeam La. Bexh ... 1A 98
Hornbeam Rd. Buck H ... 3H 31
Hornbeam Rd. Hay ... 8G 53
Hornbeams. Brick W ... 3K 5
Hornbeams Av. Enf ... 8C 6
Hornbeams Ri. N11 ... 6E 26
Hornbeam Ter. Cars ... 3C 122
Hornbeam Wlk. Rich ... 8K 87
Hornbeam Way. Brom ... 1L 127
Hornbeam Way. Wal X ... 2A 6
Hornbill Clo. Uxb ... 9B 142
Hornblower Clo. SE16 ... 4J 77
Hornbuckle Clo. Harr ... 7B 38
Hornby Clo. NW3 ... 3B 58
Hornby Ho. SE11 ... 7L 75
(off Clayton St.)
Horncastle Clo. SE12 ... 6E 94
Horncastle Rd. SE12 ... 6E 94
Hornchurch. ... 6J 51
Hornchurch. N17 ... 9B 28
(off Gloucester Rd.)
Hornchurch Clo. King T ... 1H 103
Hornchurch Country Pk. ... 3G 67
Hornchurch Hill. Whyt ... 9D 138
Hornchurch Rd. Horn ... 6E 50
Horndean Clo. SW15 ... 7E 88
Horndon Clo. Romf ... 8A 34
Horndon Grn. Romf ... 8A 34
Horndon Rd. Romf ... 8A 34
Horner Ho. N1 ... 4C 60
(off Whitmore Est.)
Horner La. Mitc ... 6B 106
Hornets, The. Wat ... 6F 8
Horne Way. SW15 ... 1G 89
Hornfair Rd. SE7 ... 7G 79
Hornford Way. Romf ... 5C 50
Horniman Dri. SE23 ... 7F 92
Horniman Mus. ... 7F 92
Horning Clo. SE9 ... 1J 111
Horn La. SE10 ... 6E 78
(in two parts)
Horn La. W3 ... 1A 72
(in two parts)
Horn La. Wfd G ... 6E 30
Horn Link Way. SE10 ... 5E 78
Hornminster Glen. Horn ... 7L 51
Horn Park. ... 4F 94
Horn Pk. Clo. SE12 ... 4F 94
Hornpark La. SE12 ... 4F 94
Horns End Pl. Pinn ... 2G 37
Hornsey. ... 2J 43
Hornsey La. N6 ... 6F 42
Hornsey La. Est. N19 ... 5H 43
Hornsey La. Gdns. N6 ... 5G 43
Hornsey Pk. Rd. N8 ... 1K 43
Hornsey Ri. N19 ... 5H 43
Hornsey Ri. Gdns. N19 ... 5H 43
Hornsey Rd. N19 & N7 ... 6J 43
Hornsey St. N7 ... 1K 59
Hornsey Vale. ... 3K 43
Hornshay St. SE15 ... 7G 77
Horns Rd. Ilf ... 2B 48
Hornton Ct. W8 ... 3L 73
(off Kensington High St.)
Hornton Pl. W8 ... 3M 73
Hornton St. W8 ... 3L 73
Horsa Rd. SE12 ... 6G 95
Horsa Rd. Eri ... 8M 81
Horse & Dolphin Yd. W1 ... 1H 75
(off Macclesfield St.)
Horsebridge Clo. Dag ... 4J 65
Horsecroft. Bans ... 9K 135
Horsecroft Clo. Orp ... 3F 128
Horsecroft Rd. Edgw ... 7B 24
Horse Fair. King T ... 6H 103
Horseferry Pl. SE10 ... 7A 78
Horseferry Rd. E14 ... 1J 77
Horseferry Rd. SW1 ... 4H 75
Horseferry Rd. Est. SW1 ... 4H 75
(off Horseferry Rd.)
Horseguards Av. SW1 ... 2J 75
Horse Guards Rd. SW1 ... 2H 75
Horse Leaze. E6 ... 9L 63
Horsell Rd. N5 ... 1L 59
(in two parts)
Horsell Rd. Orp ... 5F 112
Horselydown La. SE1 ... 3D 76
Horselydown Mans. SE1 ... 3D 76
(off Lafone St.)
Horsemongers M. SE1 ... 3A 76
(off Cole St.)
Horsenden Av. Gnfd ... 1D 54
Horsenden Cres. Gnfd ... 1D 54
Horsenden La. N. Gnfd ... 2C 54
Horsenden La. S. Gnfd ... 4E 54
Horse Ride. SW1 ... 2G 75
Horse Ride. Cars ... 2C 136
Horseshoe Bus. Pk.
Brick W ... 3M 5
Horseshoe Clo. E14 ... 6A 78
Horseshoe Clo. NW2 ... 7F 40
Horse Shoe Cres. N'holt ... 5L 53
Horseshoe Dri. Uxb ... 9E 142
Horse Shoe Grn. Sutt ... 4M 121
Horseshoe La. N20 ... 1H 25
Horseshoe La. Enf ... 5A 16
Horseshoe La. Wat ... 5F 4
Horseshoe, The. Bans ... 7K 135
Horseshoe, The. Coul ... 5H 137
Horseshoe Wharf. SE1 ... 2B 76
(off Clink St.)
Horse Yd. N1 ... 4M 59
(off Essex Rd.)
Horsfeld Gdns. SE9 ... 4J 95
Horsfeld Rd. SE9 ... 4H 95
Horsfield Clo. Dart ... 6M 99
Horsfield Ho. N1 ... 3A 60
(off Northampton St.)
Horsford Rd. SW2 ... 4K 91
Horsham Av. N12 ... 5C 26
Horsham Ct. N17 ... 8E 28
(off Lansdowne Rd.)
Horsham Rd. Bexh ... 4L 97
Horsham Rd. Felt ... 5A 84
Horsley Clo. Eps ... 5B 134
Horsley Dri. King T ... 2H 103
Horsley Dri. New Ad ... 9A 126
Horsley Rd. E4 ... 2A 30
Horsley Rd. Brom ... 5F 110
Horsley St. SE17 ... 7B 76
Horsman Ho. SE5 ... 7A 76
(off Bethwin Rd.)
Horsman St. SE5 ... 7A 76
Horsmonden Clo. Orp ... 2D 128
Horsmonden Rd. SE4 ... 4K 93
Hortensia Ho. SW10 ... 8A 74
(off Hortensia Rd.)
Hortensia Rd. SW10 ... 8A 74
Horticultural Pl. W4 ... 6B 72
Horton. ... 3A 134
Horton Av. NW2 ... 9J 41
Horton Bri. Rd. W Dray ... 2K 143
Horton Clo. W Dray ... 2L 143
Horton Country Pk. ... 2K 133
Horton Footpath. Eps ... 3A 134
Horton Gdns. Eps ... 3A 134
Horton Hill. Eps ... 3A 134
Horton Ho. SE15 ... 7G 77
Horton Ho. SW8 ... 8K 75
Horton Ho. W6 ... 6J 73
(off Field Rd.)
Horton Ind. Pk. W Dray ... 2K 143
Horton Kirby. ... 8M 115
Horton Kirby Trad. Est.
S Dar ... 6M 115
Horton La. Eps ... 3L 133
Horton Pde. W Dray ... 2J 143
Horton Pk. Children's Farm.
... 2L 133
Horton Rd. E8 ... 2F 60
Horton Rd.
Hort K & S Dar ... 8M 115
Horton Rd. W Dray ... 2J 143
Horton Rd. Ind. Est.
W Dray ... 2K 143
Horton St. SE13 ... 2M 93
Horton Way. Croy ... 9H 109
Horton Way. F'ham ... 2K 131
Hortus Rd. E4 ... 2A 30
Hortus Rd. S'hall ... 3K 69
Horvath Clo. Wey ... 6B 116
Horwood Ct. Wat ... 1H 9
Horwood Ho. E2 ... 6F 60
(off Pott St.)
Horwood Ho. NW8 ... 7C 58
(off Paveley St.)
Hosack Rd. SW17 ... 8E 90
Hoser Av. SE12 ... 8E 94
Hosier La. EC1 ... 8M 59
Hoskins Clo. E16 ... 9G 63
Hoskins Clo. Hay ... 6D 68
Hoskins St. SE10 ... 6B 78
Hospital Bri. Rd. Twic ... 6M 85
Hospital Bridge Roundabout
(Junct.) ... 8M 85
Hospital Cres. Romf ... 8K 35
Hospital Rd. E9 ... 1H 61
Hospital Rd. Houn ... 2L 85
Hospital Way. SE13 ... 5B 94
Hotham Clo. S at H ... 4M 115
Hotham Clo. Swan ... 5F 114
Hotham Clo. W Mol ... 7L 101
Hotham Rd. SW15 ... 2G 89
Hotham Rd. SW19 ... 4A 106
Hotham Rd. M. SW19 ... 4A 106
Hotham St. E15 ... 4C 62
Hothfield Pl. SE16 ... 4G 77
Hotspur Ind. Est. N17 ... 6F 28
Hotspur Rd. N'holt ... 5L 53
Hotspur St. SE11 ... 5L 75
Houblon Rd. Rich ... 4J 87
Houghton Clo. E8 ... 2D 60
Houghton Clo. Hamp ... 3J 101
Houghton Rd. N15 ... 2D 44
Houghton St. WC2 ... 9K 59
(in two parts)
Houlder Cres. Croy ... 8M 123
Houndsden Rd. N21 ... 8K 15
Houndsditch. EC3 ... 9C 60
Houndsfield Rd. N9 ... 9F 16
Hounslow. ... 2M 85
Hounslow Av. Houn ... 4M 85
Hounslow Bus. Pk. Houn ... 3L 85
Hounslow Cen. Houn ... 2M 85
Hounslow Gdns. Houn ... 4M 85
Hounslow Rd. Felt ... 7F 84
Hounslow Rd. Hanw ... 1H 10
Hounslow Rd. Twic ... 5M 85
Hounslow Urban Farm. ... 4E 8
Hounslow West. ... 1J 85
Houseman Way. SE5 ... 8B 76
Houses of Parliament. ... 4J 7
Houston Bus. Pk. Hay ... 2G 6
Houston Pl. Esh ... 3B 11

Hylton St.—Ivere Dri.

Hylton St. SE18 . . . 5D 80
Hyndewood. SE23 . . . 9H 93
Hyndman Ho. Dag . . . 8L 49
(off Kershaw Rd.)
Hyndman St. SE15 . . . 7F 76
Hynton Rd. Dag . . . 7G 49
Hyperion Ho. E3 . . . 5J 61
(off Arbery Rd.)
Hyperion Ho. SW2 . . . 5K 91
Hyperion Pl. Eps . . . 1B 134
Hyrstdene. S Croy . . . 6M 123
Hyson Rd. SE16 . . . 6F 76
Hythe Av. Bexh . . . 8J 81
Hythe Clo. N18 . . . 4E 28
Hythe Clo. Orp . . . 8G 113
Hythe Ho. SE16 . . . 3G 77
(off Swan Rd.)
Hythe Ho. W6 . . . 5G 73
(off Shepherd's Bush Rd.)
Hythe Rd. NW10 . . . 6D 56
Hythe Rd. T Hth . . . 6B 108
Hythe Rd. Ind. Est. NW10 . . . 6E 56
Hythe St. Dart . . . 5J 99
(in two parts)
Hythe St. (Lwr.). Dart . . . 4J 99
Hyver Hill. NW7 . . . 8B 12

I

Ian Bowater Ct. N1 . . . 6B 60
(off East Rd.)
Ian Ct. SE23 . . . 8G 93
Ian Sq. Enf . . . 3H 17
Ibberton Ho. SW8 . . . 8K 75
(off Meadow Rd.)
Ibberton Ho. W14 . . . 4J 73
(off Russell Rd.)
Ibbetson Path. Lou . . . 5M 19
Ibbotson Av. E16 . . . 9D 62
Ibbott St. E1 . . . 7G 61
Iberia Ho. N19 . . . 5H 43
Iberian Av. Wall . . . 6H 123
Ibis Ct. SE8 . . . 7K 77
(off Edward Pl.)
Ibis La. W4 . . . 9A 72
Ibis Way. Hay . . . 9H 53
Ibrox Ct. Buck H . . . 2G 31
Ibscott Clo. Dag . . . 2A 66
Ibsley Gdns. SW15 . . . 7E 88
Ibsley Way. Cockf . . . 7C 14
ICA Cinema. . . . 2H 75
(off Mall, The)
ICA Theatre. . . . 2H 75
(off Mall, The)
Iceland Rd. E3 . . . 4L 61
Ice Wharf Marina. N1 . . . 5J 59
(off New Wharf Rd.)
Ickburgh Est. E5 . . . 7F 44
Ickburgh Rd. E5 . . . 8F 44
Ickenham. . . . 8A 36 & 1C 142
Ickenham Clo. Ruis . . . 7B 36
Ickenham Grn. Uxb . . . 6A 36
Ickenham Rd. Ruis . . . 7A 36
Ickleton Rd. SE9 . . . 1J 111
Icknield Dri. Ilf . . . 3M 47
Icknield Ho. SW3 . . . 6C 74
(off Marlborough St.)
Ickworth Pk. Rd. E17 . . . 2J 45
Ida Rd. N15 . . . 2B 44
Ida St. E14 . . . 9A 62
(in three parts)
Iden Clo. Brom . . . 7C 110
Idlecombe Rd. SW17 . . . 3E 106
Idmiston Rd. E15 . . . 9D 46
Idmiston Rd. SE27 . . . 9A 92
Idmiston Rd. Wor Pk . . . 2D 120
Idmiston Sq. Wor Pk . . . 2D 120
Idol La. EC3 . . . 1C 76
Idonia St. SE8 . . . 8L 77
Iffley Clo. Uxb . . . 3B 142
Iffley Rd. W6 . . . 4F 72
Ifield Rd. SW10 . . . 7M 73
Ifor Evans Pl. E1 . . . 7H 61
Ightham Ho. SE17 . . . 5C 76
(off Comus Pl.)
Ightham Ho. Beck . . . 4K 109
(off Bethersden Clo.)
Ightham Rd. Eri . . . 8L 81
Ikona Ct. Wey . . . 7A 116
Ilbert St. W10 . . . 6H 57
Ilchester Gdns. W2 . . . 1M 73
Ilchester Pl. W14 . . . 4K 73
Ilchester Rd. Dag . . . 1F 64
Ildersly Gro. SE21 . . . 8B 92
Ilderton Rd. SE16 & SE15 . . . 6G 77
Ilderton Wharf. SE15 . . . 7G 77
(off Rollins St.)
Ilex Clo. Sun . . . 6G 101
Ilex Rd. NW10 . . . 2D 56
Ilex Way. SW16 . . . 2L 107
Ilford. . . . 8M 47
Ilford Hill. Ilf . . . 8L 47
Ilford Ho. N1 . . . 2B 60
(off Dove Rd.)
Ilford La. Ilf . . . 8M 47
Ilfracombe Cres. Horn . . . 9G 51
Ilfracombe Flats. SE1 . . . 3A 76
(off Marshalsea Rd.)
Ilfracombe Gdns. Romf . . . 5F 48
Ilfracombe Rd. Brom . . . 9D 94
Iliffe St. SE17 . . . 6M 75
Iliffe Yd. SE17 . . . 6M 75
(off Crampton St.)
Ilkeston Ct. E5 . . . 9H 45
(off Clapton Pk. Est.)
Ilkley Clo. SE19 . . . 3B 108
Ilkley Rd. E16 . . . 8G 63
Ilkley Rd. Wat . . . 5H 21
Illingworth Clo. Mitc . . . 7B 106
Illingworth Way. Enf . . . 7C 16
Ilmington Rd. Harr . . . 4H 39
Ilminster Gdns. SW11 . . . 3C 90
Imani Mans. SW11 . . . 1B 90
IMAX Cinema. . . . 2L 75
Imber Clo. N14 . . . 9G 15
Imber Clo. Esh . . . 3B 118
Imber Ct. Trad. Est.
E Mol . . . 1B 118
Imber Cross. Th Dit . . . 1D 118
Imber Gro. Esh . . . 2B 118
Imber Pk. Rd. Esh . . . 3B 118
Imber St. N1 . . . 4B 60
Impact Bus. Pk. Gnfd . . . 5F 54
Impact Ct. SE20 . . . 6F 108
Imperial Av. N16 . . . 9C 44
Imperial Clo. Harr . . . 4L 37
Imperial College. . . . 4B 74
Imperial College Rd. SW7 . . . 4B 74
Imperial Ct. N6 . . . 4G 43
Imperial Ct. N20 . . . 3A 26
Imperial Ct. NW8 . . . 5C 58
(off Prince Albert Rd.)
Imperial Ct. SE11 . . . 6L 75
Imperial Ct. S Harr . . . 5L 37
Imperial Dri. Harr . . . 5L 37
Imperial Gdns. Mitc . . . 7F 106
Imperial Ho. E3 . . . 6J 61
(off Grove Rd.)
Imperial Ho. E14 . . . 1K 77
(off Victory Pl.)
Imperial M. E6 . . . 5H 63
Imperial Pde. EC4 . . . 9M 59
(off New Bri. St.)
Imperial Pk. Way. Wat . . . 3G 9
Imperial Pl. Borwd . . . 5M 11
Imperial Pl. Chst . . . 5L 111
Imperial Rd. N22 . . . 7J 27
(in two parts)
Imperial Rd. SW6 . . . 9M 73
Imperial Rd. Felt . . . 6C 84
Imperial Sq. SW6 . . . 9M 73
Imperial St. E3 . . . 6A 62
Imperial Trad. Est. Rain . . . 7H 67
Imperial War Mus. . . . 4L 75
Imperial Way. Chst . . . 9A 96
Imperial Way. Croy . . . 8K 123
Imperial Way. Harr . . . 4J 39
Imperial Way. Wat . . . 3G 9
Imre Clo. W12 . . . 2F 72
Inca Dri. SE9 . . . 6M 95
Ince Rd. W on T . . . 8C 116
Inchmery Rd. SE6 . . . 8M 93
Inchwood. Croy . . . 6M 125
Independent Ind. Est.
W Dray . . . 2J 143
Independent Pl. E8 . . . 1D 60
Independents Rd. SE3 . . . 2D 94
Inderwick Rd. N8 . . . 3K 43
Indescon Ct. E14 . . . 3L 77
India Pl. WC2 . . . 1K 75
(off Montreal Pl.)
India St. EC3 . . . 9D 60
India Way. W12 . . . 1F 72
Indigo M. E14 . . . 1A 78
Indigo M. N16 . . . 8B 44
Indus Rd. SE7 . . . 8G 79
Infirmary Ct. SW3 . . . 7D 74
(off West Rd.)
Ingal Rd. E13 . . . 7E 62
Ingate Pl. SW8 . . . 9F 74
Ingatestone Rd. E12 . . . 6G 47
Ingatestone Rd. SE25 . . . 8F 108
Ingatestone Rd. Wfd G . . . 7F 30
Ingelow Ho. W8 . . . 3M 73
(off Holland St.)
Ingelow Rd. SW8 . . . 1F 90
Ingersoll Rd. W12 . . . 2F 72
Ingersoll Rd. Enf . . . 2G 17
Ingestre Pl. W1 . . . 9G 59
Ingestre Rd. E7 . . . 9E 46
Ingestre Rd. NW5 . . . 9F 42
Ingham Clo. S Croy . . . 1H 139
Ingham Rd. NW6 . . . 9L 41
Ingham Rd. S Croy . . . 1G 139
Inglebert St. EC1 . . . 6L 59
Ingleboro Dri. Purl . . . 5B 138
Ingleborough Ct. N17 . . . 1D 44
Ingleborough St. SW9 . . . 1L 91
Ingleby Dri. Harr . . . 8B 38
Ingleby Gdns. Chig . . . 3F 32
Ingleby Rd. N7 . . . 8J 43
Ingleby Rd. Dag . . . 2M 65
Ingleby Rd. Ilf . . . 6M 47
Ingleby Way. Chst . . . 2L 111
Ingleby Way. Wall . . . 1H 137
Ingle Clo. Pinn . . . 1J 37
Ingledew Rd. SE18 . . . 6B 80
Inglefield Sq. E1 . . . 2F 76
(off Prusom St.)
Ingleglen. Horn . . . 5L 51
Inglehurst Gdns. Ilf . . . 3K 47
Inglemere Rd. SE23 . . . 9H 93
Inglemere Rd. Mitc . . . 4D 106
Inglenorth Ct. Swan . . . 1A 130
Inglesham Wlk. E9 . . . 2K 61
Ingleside Clo. Beck . . . 4L 109
Ingleside Gro. SE3 . . . 7D 78
Inglethorpe St. SW6 . . . 9H 73
Ingleton Av. Well . . . 4E 96
Ingleton Rd. N18 . . . 6E 28
Ingleton Rd. Cars . . . 1C 136
Ingleton St. SW9 . . . 1L 91
Ingleway. N12 . . . 6B 26
Inglewood. Croy . . . 1J 139
Inglewood. Swan . . . 6C 114
Inglewood Clo. E14 . . . 5L 77
Inglewood Clo. Horn . . . 9H 51
Inglewood Clo. Ilf . . . 6D 32
Inglewood Copse. Brom . . . 6J 111
Inglewood Rd. NW6 . . . 1L 57
Inglewood Rd. Bexh . . . 3B 98
Inglis Rd. W5 . . . 1K 71
Inglis Rd. Croy . . . 3D 124
Inglis St. SE5 . . . 9M 75
Ingoldisthorpe Gro. SE15 . . . 7D 76
Ingram Av. NW11 . . . 5A 42
Ingram Clo. SE11 . . . 5K 75
Ingram Clo. Stan . . . 5G 23
Ingram Ho. E3 . . . 4J 61
Ingram Rd. N2 . . . 2C 42
Ingram Rd. Dart . . . 7J 99
Ingram Rd. T Hth . . . 5A 108
Ingrams Clo. W on T . . . 7G 117
Ingram Way. Gnfd . . . 4B 54
Ingrave Rd. Romf . . . 2C 50
Ingrave St. SW11 . . . 2B 90
Ingrebourne Ct. E4 . . . 3M 29
Ingrebourne Gdns. Upm . . . 6M 51
Ingrebourne Ho. NW8 . . . 8B 58
(off Broadley St.)
Ingrebourne Ho. Brom . . . 2B 110
(off Brangbourne Rd.)
Ingrebourne Rd. Rain . . . 7F 66
Ingress St. W4 . . . 6C 72
Ingreway. Romf . . . 6M 35
Inigo Jones Rd. SE7 . . . 8J 79
Inigo Pl. WC2 . . . 1J 75
(off Bedford St.)
Inkerman Rd. NW5 . . . 2F 58
Inkerman Ter. W8 . . . 4L 73
(off Allen St.)
Inks Grn. E4 . . . 5A 30
Inkwell Clo. N12 . . . 3A 26
Inman Rd. NW10 . . . 4C 56
Inman Rd. SW18 . . . 6A 90
Inmans Row. Wfd G . . . 4E 30
Inner Circ. NW1 . . . 6E 58
Inner Pk. Rd. SW19 . . . 7H 89
Inner Ring E. H'row A . . . 2F 144
Inner Ring W. H'row A . . . 2E 144
Inner Temple Hall. . . . 9L 59
(off Inner Temple La.)
Inner Temple La. EC4 . . . 9L 59
Innes Clo. SW20 . . . 6J 105
Innes Gdns. SW15 . . . 5F 88
Innes Yd. Croy . . . 5A 124
Innis Ho. SE17 . . . 6C 76
(off East St.)
Inniskilling Rd. E13 . . . 5G 63
Inn of Court & City Yeomanry Mus. . . . 8K 59
Innova Bus. Pk. Enf . . . 9F 6
Innovation Cen., The. E14 . . . 3A 78
(off Marsh Wall)
Innovation Clo. Wemb . . . 4J 55
Innova Way. Enf . . . 9F 6
Inskip Clo. E10 . . . 7M 45
Inskip Dri. Horn . . . 6J 51
Inskip Rd. Dag . . . 6H 49
Inspirations Way. Orp . . . 2E 128
Institute for English Studies. . . . 8H 59
(in University of London, Senate House)
Institute of Advanced Legal Studies. . . . 7J 59
(off Russell Sq.)
Institute of Classical Studies. . . . 8H 59
(in University of London, Senate House)
Institute of Commonwealth Studies. . . . 8J 59
(off Russell Sq.)
Institute of Contemporary Arts. . . . 2H 75
(off Carlton Ho. Ter.)
Institute of Education. . . . 7H 59
(off Bedford Way)
Institute of Germanic Studies. . . . 8J 59
(off Russell Sq.)
Institute of Historical Research. . . . 8H 59
(in University of London, Senate House)
Institute of Latin American Studies. . . . 7H 59
Institute of Romance Studies. . . . 8H 59
(in University of London, Senate House)
Institute of United States Studies. . . . 8H 59
(in University of London, Senate House)
Institute Pl. E8 . . . 1F 60
Instone Rd. Dart . . . 6H 99
Integer Gdns. E11 . . . 5B 46
Interface Ho. Houn . . . 2L 85
(off Staines Rd.)
International Av. Houn . . . 6G 69
International Ho. E1 . . . 1D 76
(off St Katharine's Way)
International Trad. Est.
S'hall . . . 4F 68
Inverary Pl. SE18 . . . 7B 80
Inver Clo. E5 . . . 7G 45
Inverclyde Gdns. Romf . . . 2G 49
(in two parts)
Inver Ct. W2 . . . 9M 57
Inveresk Gdns. Wor Pk . . . 5E 120
Inverforth Clo. NW3 . . . 7A 42
Inverforth Rd. N11 . . . 5F 26
Invergarry Ho. NW6 . . . 5M 57
(off Carlton Va.)
Inverine Rd. SE7 . . . 6F 78
Invermore Pl. SE18 . . . 5A 80
Inverness Av. Enf . . . 3C 16
Inverness Ct. SE6 . . . 7D 94
Inverness Dri. Ilf . . . 6C 32
Inverness Gdns. W8 . . . 2M 73
Inverness M. E16 . . . 2A 80
Inverness M. W2 . . . 1M 73
Inverness Pl. W2 . . . 1M 73
Inverness Rd. N18 . . . 5F 28
Inverness Rd. Houn . . . 3K 85
Inverness Rd. S'hall . . . 5J 69
Inverness Rd. Wor Pk . . . 3H 121
Inverness St. NW1 . . . 4F 58
Inverness Ter. W2 . . . 9M 57
Inverton Rd. SE15 . . . 3H 93
Invicta Clo. Chst . . . 2L 111
Invicta Clo. Felt . . . 7D 84
Invicta Gro. N'holt . . . 6K 53
Invicta Pde. Sidc . . . 1F 112
Invicta Plaza. SE1 . . . 2M 75
Invicta Rd. SE3 . . . 8E 78
Invicta Rd. Dart . . . 5M 99
Inville Rd. SE17 . . . 6B 76
Inville Wlk. SE17 . . . 6B 76
Inwen Ct. SE8 . . . 6J 77
(in three parts)
Inwood Av. Houn . . . 2A 86
Inwood Clo. Croy . . . 4J 125
Inwood Ct. NW1 . . . 3G 59
(off Rochester Sq.)
Inwood Ct. W on T . . . 4G 117
Inwood Rd. Houn . . . 3M 85
Inworth St. SW11 . . . 1C 90
Inworth Wlk. N1 . . . 4A 60
(off Popham St.)
Iona Clo. SE6 . . . 6L 93
Iona Clo. Mord . . . 2M 121
Ion Ct. E2 . . . 5E 60
Ionian Building. E14 . . . 1J 77
Ionian Ho. E1 . . . 7H 61
(off Duckett St.)
Ion Sq. E2 . . . 5E 60
Ipsden Bldgs. SE1 . . . 3L 75
(off Great St.)
Ipswich Ho. SE4 . . . 4H 93
Ipswich Rd. SW17 . . . 3E 106
Ireland Clo. E6 . . . 8K 63
Ireland Pl. N22 . . . 7J 27
Ireland Yd. EC4 . . . 9M 59
Irene M. W7 . . . 2D 70
(off Uxbridge Rd.)
Irene Rd. SW6 . . . 9L 73
Irene Rd. Orp . . . 2D 128
Ireton Av. W on T . . . 4C 116
Ireton Clo. N10 . . . 7E 26
Ireton St. E3 . . . 6L 61
Iris Av. Bex . . . 5J 97
Iris Clo. E6 . . . 8J 63
Iris Clo. Croy . . . 3H 125
Iris Clo. Surb . . . 2K 119
Iris Ct. SE14 . . . 9G 77
(off Briant St.)
Iris Cres. Bexh . . . 7K 81
Iris Path. Romf . . . 7G 35
Iris Rd. W Ewe . . . 7M 119
Iris Wlk. Edgw . . . 4A 24
Iris Way. E4 . . . 6K 29
Irkdale Av. Enf . . . 3D 16
Iron Bri. Clo. NW10 . . . 1C 56
Ironbridge Clo. S'hall . . . 2A 70
Iron Bri. Ho. NW1 . . . 3D 58
Iron Bri. Rd. W Dray . . . 2L 143
Iron Mill La. Dart . . . 3C 98
Iron Mill Pl. SW18 . . . 5M 89
Iron Mill Pl. Dart . . . 3D 98
Iron Mill Rd. SW18 . . . 5M 89
Ironmonger La. EC2 . . . 9A 60
Ironmonger Pas. EC1 . . . 6A 60
(off Ironmonger Row)
Ironmonger Row. EC1 . . . 6A 60
Ironmongers Pl. E14 . . . 5L 77
Ironside Clo. SE16 . . . 3H 77
Ironside Ho. E9 . . . 9J 45
Irons Way. Romf . . . 7A 34
Irvine Av. Harr . . . 1E 38
Irvine Clo. N20 . . . 2C 26
Irvine Ho. E14 . . . 8M 61
(off Uamvar St.)
Irvine Ho. N7 . . . 2K 59
(off Caledonian Rd.)
Irvine Way. Orp . . . 2D 128
Irving Av. N'holt . . . 4H 53
Irving Gro. SW9 . . . 1K 91
Irving Ho. SE17 . . . 6M 75
(off Doddington Gro.)
Irving Mans. W14 . . . 7J 73
(off Queen's Club Gdns.)
Irving M. N1 . . . 2A 60
Irving Rd. W14 . . . 4H 73
Irving St. WC2 . . . 1H 75
Irving Way. NW9 . . . 3E 40
Irving Way. Swan . . . 6B 114
Irwell Ct. W7 . . . 9B 54
(off Hobbayne Rd.)
Irwell Est. SE16 . . . 4G 77
Irwin Av. SE18 . . . 8C 80
Irwin Gdns. NW10 . . . 4F 56
Isabel Hill Clo. Hamp . . . 6M 101
Isabella Clo. N14 . . . 9G 15
Isabella Ct. Rich . . . 5K 87
(off Kings Mead)
Isabella Dri. Orp . . . 6A 128
Isabella Ho. SE11 . . . 6M 75
(off Othello Clo.)
Isabella Ho. W6 . . . 6G 73
(off Queen Caroline St.)
Isabella Plantation. . . . 1M 103
Isabella Rd. E9 . . . 1G 61
Isabella St. SE1 . . . 2M 75
Isabel St. SW9 . . . 9K 75
Isambard Clo. Uxb . . . 7B 142
Isambard M. E14 . . . 4A 78
Isambard Pl. SE16 . . . 2G 77
Isard Ho. Brom . . . 3F 126
Isbell Gdns. Romf . . . 7C 34
Isel Way. SE22 . . . 4C 92
Isham Rd. SW16 . . . 6J 107
Isis Clo. SW15 . . . 3G 89
Isis Clo. Ruis . . . 4A 36
Isis Ct. W4 . . . 8M 71
Isis Ho. N18 . . . 6D 28
Isis Ho. NW8 . . . 7B 58
(off Church St. Est.)
Isis St. SW18 . . . 8A 90
Island Cen. Way. Enf . . . 1L 17
Island Farm Av. W Mol . . . 9K 101
Island Farm Rd. W Mol . . . 9K 101
Island Rd. Mitc . . . 4D 106
Island Row. E14 . . . 9K 61
Island, The. Th Dit . . . 1E 118
Island, The. W Dray . . . 8G 143
Isla Rd. SE18 . . . 7A 80
Islay Gdns. Houn . . . 4H 85
Isleden Ho. N1 . . . 4A 60
(off Prebend St.)
Isledon Rd. N7 . . . 8L 43
Isledon Village. . . . 8L 43
Islehurst Clo. Chst . . . 5L 111
Isleworth. . . . 2E 86
Isleworth Bus. Complex.
Iswth . . . 1D 86
Isleworth Promenade.
Twic . . . 3F 86
Isley Ct. SW8 . . . 1G 91
Islington. . . . 3M 59
Islington Crematorium.
N2 . . . 8D 26
Islington Grn. N1 . . . 4M 59
Islington High St. N1 . . . 5L 59
(in two parts)
Islington Pk. M. N1 . . . 3M 59
Islington Pk. St. N1 . . . 3L 59
Islip Gdns. Edgw . . . 7B 24
Islip Gdns. N'holt . . . 3J 53
Islip Mnr. Rd. N'holt . . . 3J 53
Islip St. NW5 . . . 1G 59
Ismailia Rd. E7 . . . 3F 62
Isobel Ho. Harr . . . 3D 38
Isom Clo. E13 . . . 6F 62
Isopad Ho. Borwd . . . 5M 11
(off Shenley Rd.)
Itaska Cotts. Bush . . . 1C 22
Ivanhoe Clo. Uxb . . . 8B 142
Ivanhoe Dri. Harr . . . 1E 38
Ivanhoe Ho. E3 . . . 5J 61
(off Grove Rd.)
Ivanhoe Rd. SE5 . . . 2D 92
Ivanhoe Rd. Houn . . . 2H 85
Ivatt Pl. W14 . . . 6K 73
Ivatt Way. N17 . . . 1M 43
Iveagh Av. NW10 . . . 5L 55
Iveagh Clo. E9 . . . 4H 61
Iveagh Clo. NW10 . . . 5L 55
Iveagh Clo. N'wd . . . 8A 20
Iveagh Ct. E1 . . . 9D 60
(off Haydon Wlk.)
Iveagh Ct. Beck . . . 7A 110
Iveagh Ho. SW9 . . . 1M 91
Iveagh Ho. SW10 . . . 8A 74
(off King's Rd.)
Iveagh Ter. NW10 . . . 5L 55
(off Iveagh Av.)
Ivedon Rd. Well . . . 1G 97
Ive Farm Clo. E10 . . . 7L 45
Ive Farm La. E10 . . . 7L 45
Iveley Rd. SW4 . . . 1G 91
Ivere Dri. New Bar . . . 8M 13

Iverhurst Clo.—John's Ct.

Iverhurst Clo. Bexh ... 4H 97
Iver La. Iver & Uxb ... 7A 142
Iverna Ct. W8 ... 4L 73
Iverna Gdns. W8 ... 4L 73
Iverna Gdns. Felt ... 4B 84
Iverson Rd. NW6 ... 2K 57
Ivers Way. New Ad ... 9M 125
Ives Gdns. Romf ... 2D 50
Ives Rd. E16 ... 8C 62
Ives St. SW3 ... 5C 74
Ivestor Ter. SE23 ... 6G 93
Ivimey St. E2 ... 6E 60
Ivinghoe Clo. Enf ... 3C 16
Ivinghoe Clo. Wat ... 8H 5
Ivinghoe Ho. N7 ... 1H 59
Ivinghoe Rd. Bush ... 9B 10
Ivinghoe Rd. Dag ... 1F 64
Ivor Ct. N8 ... 4J 43
Ivor Ct. NW1 ... 7D 58
(off Gloucester Pl.)
Ivor Gro. SE9 ... 7M 95
Ivories, The. N1 ... 3A 60
(off Northampton St.)
Ivor Pl. NW1 ... 7D 58
Ivor St. NW1 ... 3G 59
Ivory Ct. Felt ... 8E 84
Ivorydown. Brom ... 1E 110
Ivory Ho. E1 ... 2D 76
Ivory Sq. SW11 ... 2A 90
Ivybridge Clo. Twic ... 6E 86
Ivybridge Clo. Uxb ... 6C 142
Ivybridge Ct. NW1 ... 3F 58
(off Lewis St.)
Ivybridge Ct. Chst ... 5L 111
(off Old Hill)
Ivybridge La. WC2 ... 1J 75
Ivy Bri. Retail Pk. Iswth ... 4D 86
Ivychurch Clo. SE20 ... 4G 109
Ivychurch La. SE17 ... 6D 76
Ivy Clo. Dart ... 5L 99
Ivy Clo. Harr ... 9K 37
Ivy Clo. Pinn ... 5G 37
Ivy Clo. Sun ... 6G 101
Ivy Cotts. E14 ... 1A 78
Ivy Cotts. Uxb ... 6E 142
Ivy Ct. SE16 ... 6E 76
(off Argyle Way)
Ivy Cres. W4 ... 5A 72
Ivydale Rd. SE15 ... 2H 93
Ivydale Rd. Cars ... 4D 122
Ivyday Gro. SW16 ... 9K 91
Ivydene. W Mol ... 9K 101
Ivydene Clo. Sutt ... 6A 122
Ivy Gdns. N8 ... 4J 43
Ivy Gdns. Mitc ... 7H 107
Ivy Ho. Flats. Wat ... 8H 9
Ivyhouse Rd. Dag ... 2H 65
Ivyhouse Rd. Uxb ... 8A 36
Ivy La. Houn ... 3K 85
Ivy Lodge La. H Wood ... 8M 35
Ivymount Rd. SE27 ... 9L 91
Ivy Rd. E16 ... 9E 62
Ivy Rd. E17 ... 4L 45
Ivy Rd. N14 ... 9G 15
Ivy Rd. NW2 ... 9G 41
Ivy Rd. SE4 ... 3K 93
Ivy Rd. SW17 ... 2C 106
Ivy Rd. Houn ... 3M 85
Ivy Rd. Surb ... 3L 119
Ivy St. N1 ... 5C 60
Ivy Wlk. Dag ... 2J 65
Ivy Wlk. N'wd ... 8C 20
Ixworth Pl. SW3 ... 6C 74
Izane Rd. Bexh ... 3K 97

J

Jacaranda Clo. N Mald ... 7C 104
Jacaranda Gro. E8 ... 3D 60
Jackass La. Kes ... 7F 126
Jack Barnett Way. N22 ... 9K 27
Jack Clow Rd. E15 ... 5C 62
Jack Cook Ho. Bark ... 3M 63
Jack Cornwell St. E12 ... 9L 47
Jack Dash Ho. E14 ... 3A 78
(off Lawn Ho. Clo.)
Jack Dash Way. E6 ... 7J 63
Jackets La. Hare & N'wd ... 8A 20
(in two parts)
Jacketts Fld. Ab L ... 4D 4
Jack Goodchild Way.
King T ... 7M 103
Jacklin Grn. Wfd G ... 4E 30
Jackman Ho. E1 ... 2F 76
(off Watts St.)
Jackman M. NW10 ... 8C 40
Jackman St. E8 ... 4F 60
Jackson Clo. E9 ... 3G 61
Jackson Clo. Eps ... 6B 134
Jackson Clo. Horn ... 2K 51
Jackson Clo. Uxb ... 3C 142
Jackson Ct. E7 ... 2F 62
Jackson Rd. N7 ... 9K 43
Jackson Rd. Bark ... 4B 64
Jackson Rd. Barn ... 8C 14
Jackson Rd. Brom ... 4K 127
Jackson Rd. Uxb ... 3C 142
Jacksons Dri. Chesh ... 1A 6
Jacksons La. N6 ... 5E 42
Jacksons Pl. Croy ... 3B 124
Jackson St. SE18 ... 7L 79
Jackson's Way. Croy ... 5L 125
Jackson Way. Eps ... 1L 133
Jackson Way. S'hall ... 3M 69
Jack Walker Ct. N5 ... 9M 43
Jacob Ho. Eri ... 3H 81
Jacobin Lodge. N7 ... 1J 59
Jacobs Av. H Wood ... 9J 35
Jacobs Clo. Dag ... 9M 49
Jacobs Ho. E13 ... 6G 63
(off New City Rd.)
Jacob St. SE1 ... 3E 76
Jacob's Well M. W1 ... 8E 58
Jacotts Ho. W10 ... 7G 57
(off Sutton Way)
Jacqueline Clo. N'holt ... 4J 53
Jacqueline Creft Ter. N6 ... 4E 42
(off Grange Rd.)
Jacqueline Vs. E17 ... 3A 46
(off Shernhall St.)
Jade Clo. E16 ... 9H 63
Jade Clo. NW2 ... 5H 41
Jade Clo. Dag ... 6G 49
Jade Ho. Rain ... 7E 66
Jade Ter. NW6 ... 3A 58
Jaffe Rd. Ilf ... 6B 48
Jaffray Pl. SE27 ... 1M 107
Jaffray Rd. Brom ... 8H 111
Jaggard Way. SW12 ... 6D 90
Jagger Ho. SW11 ... 9D 74
(off Rosenau Rd.)
Jago Clo. SE18 ... 7A 80
Jago Wlk. SE5 ... 8B 76
Jail La. Big H ... 8H 141
Jamaica Rd. SE1 & SE16 ... 3D 76
Jamaica Rd. T Hth ... 1M 123
Jamaica St. E1 ... 9G 61
James Anderson Ct. N1 ... 5C 60
(off Kingsland Rd.)
James Av. NW2 ... 1G 57
James Av. Dag ... 6K 49
James Bedford Clo. Pinn ... 9G 21
James Boswell Clo.
SW16 ... 1K 107
James Brine Ho. E2 ... 6D 60
(off Ravenscroft St.)
James Campbell Ho. E2 ... 5G 61
(off Old Ford Rd.)
James Clo. E13 ... 5E 62
James Clo. NW11 ... 4J 41
James Clo. Bush ... 7J 9
James Clo. Romf ... 3E 50
James Collins Clo. W9 ... 7K 57
James Ct. N1 ... 4A 60
(off Raynor Pl.)
James Ct. NW9 ... 9C 24
James Ct. N'holt ... 5J 53
(off Church Rd.)
James Ct. N'wd ... 8D 20
James Docherty Ho. E2 ... 5F 60
(off Patriot Sq.)
James Dudson Ct. NW10 ... 3A 56
James Est. Mitc ... 6D 106
James Gdns. N22 ... 7M 27
James Hammett Ho. E2 ... 6D 60
(off Ravenscroft St.)
James Ho. E1 ... 7J 61
(off Solebay St.)
James Ho. SE16 ... 3H 77
(off Wolfe Cres.)
James Joyce Wlk. SE24 ... 3M 91
James La. E10 & E11 ... 5A 46
James Lee Sq. Enf ... 2L 17
James Lind Ho. SE8 ... 5K 77
(off Grove St.)
James Middleton Ho. E2 ... 6F 60
(off Middleton St.)
James Newham Ct. SE9 ... 9L 95
Jameson Clo. W3 ... 3A 72
Jameson Ct. E2 ... 5G 61
(off Russia La.)
Jameson Ho. SE11 ... 6K 75
(off Glasshouse Wlk.)
Jameson Lodge. N6 ... 4G 43
Jameson St. W8 ... 2L 73
James Pl. N17 ... 8D 28
James Rd. Dart ... 6E 98
James's Cotts. Rich ... 8L 71
James Stewart Ho.
NW6 ... 3K 57
James St. W1 ... 9E 58
James St. WC2 ... 1J 75
James St. Bark ... 3A 64
James St. Enf ... 7D 16
James St. Houn ... 2B 86
James Stroud Ho. SE17 ... 6A 76
(off Bronti Clo.)
James Ter. SW14 ... 2B 88
(off Church Path)
James Terry Ct. S Croy ... 7A 124
(off Warham Rd.)
Jamestown Rd. NW1 ... 4F 58
Jamestown Way. E14 ... 1B 78
James Watt Way. Eri ... 7D 82
James Yd. E4 ... 6B 30
Jamieson Ho. Houn ... 5K 85
Jamilah Ho. E16 ... 1M 79
(off University Way)
Jamuna Clo. E14 ... 8J 61
Jane Austen Hall. E16 ... 2F 78
(off Wesley Av., in two parts)
Jane Austen Ho. SW1 ... 6G 75
(off Churchill Gdns.)
Jane Seymour Ct. SE9 ... 6A 96
Jane St. E1 ... 9F 60
Janet St. E14 ... 4L 77
Janeway Pl. SE16 ... 3F 76
Janeway St. SE16 ... 3E 76
Janice M. Ilf ... 7M 47
Jansen Wlk. SW11 ... 2B 90
Janson Clo. E15 ... 1C 62
Janson Clo. NW10 ... 8C 40
Janson Rd. E15 ... 1C 62
Jansons Rd. N15 ... 1C 44
Japan Cres. N4 ... 6K 43
Japan Rd. Chad H ... 4H 49
Jardine Rd. E1 ... 1H 77
Jarman Ho. E1 ... 8G 61
(off Jubilee St.)
Jarman Ho. SE16 ... 5H 77
(off Hawkstone Rd.)
Jarrett Clo. SW2 ... 7M 91
Jarrow Clo. Mord ... 9M 105
Jarrow Rd. N17 ... 2F 44
Jarrow Rd. SE16 ... 5G 77
Jarrow Rd. Romf ... 4G 49
Jarrow Way. E9 ... 9K 45
Jarvis Clo. Bark ... 4B 64
Jarvis Clo. Barn ... 7H 13
Jarvis Rd. SE22 ... 3C 92
Jarvis Rd. S Croy ... 8B 124
Jarvis Way. H Wood ... 9J 35
Jashoda Ho. SE18 ... 6L 79
(off Connaught M.)
Jasmin Clo. N'wd ... 8D 20
Jasmin Ct. SE12 ... 5D 94
Jasmine Clo. Ilf ... 1M 63
Jasmine Clo. Orp ... 4M 127
Jasmine Clo. S'hall ... 1J 69
Jasmine Ct. SW19 ... 2L 105
Jasmine Gdns. Croy ... 5M 125
Jasmine Gdns. Harr ... 7L 37
Jasmine Gro. SE20 ... 5F 108
Jasmine Rd. Rush G ... 7C 50
Jasmine Ter. W Dray ... 3L 143
Jasmine Way. E Mol ... 8C 102
Jasmin Lodge. SE16 ... 6F 76
(off Sherwood Gdns.)
Jasmin Rd. Eps ... 7M 119
Jason Clo. Wey ... 7A 116
Jason Ct. SW9 ... 9L 75
(off Southey Rd.)
Jason Ct. W1 ... 9E 58
(off Wigmore St.)
Jason Wlk. SE9 ... 1L 111
Jasper Clo. Enf ... 2G 17
Jasper Pas. SE19 ... 3D 108
Jasper Rd. E16 ... 9H 63
Jasper Rd. SE19 ... 2D 108
Jasper Wlk. N1 ... 6B 60
Java Wharf. SE1 ... 3D 76
(off Shad Thames)
Javelin Way. N'holt ... 6H 53
Jaycroft. Enf ... 3L 15
Jay Gdns. Chst ... 1K 111
Jay M. SW7 ... 3A 74
Jazzfern Ter. Wemb ... 1E 54
Jeal Oakwood Ct. Eps ... 6C 134
Jean Batten Clo. Wall ... 9K 123
Jean Darling Ho. SW10 ... 7B 74
(off Milman's St.)
Jean Pardies Ho. E1 ... 8G 61
(off Jubilee St.)
Jebb Av. SW2 ... 5J 91
(in two parts)
Jebb St. E3 ... 5L 61
Jedburgh Rd. E13 ... 6G 63
Jedburgh St. SW11 ... 3E 90
Jeddo M. W3 ... 3D 72
Jeddo Rd. W12 ... 3D 72
Jefferson Building. E14 ... 3L 77
Jefferson Clo. W13 ... 4F 70
Jefferson Clo. Ilf ... 3M 47
Jefferson Wlk. SE18 ... 7L 79
Jeffrey Row. SE12 ... 4F 94
Jeffrey's Pl. NW1 ... 3G 59
Jeffreys Rd. SW4 ... 1J 91
Jeffreys Rd. Enf ... 6J 17
Jeffrey's St. NW1 ... 3G 59
Jeffries Ho. NW10 ... 3B 56
Jeffs Clo. Hamp ... 3M 101
Jeffs Rd. Sutt ... 6K 121
Jeger Av. E2 ... 4D 60
Jeken Rd. SE9 ... 3G 95
Jelf Rd. SW2 ... 4L 91
Jellicoe Gdns. Stan ... 6D 22
Jellicoe Ho. E2 ... 5E 60
(off Ropley St.)
Jellicoe Ho. NW1 ... 7F 58
Jellicoe Rd. E13 ... 7E 62
Jellicoe Rd. N17 ... 7B 28
Jellicoe Rd. Wat ... 8E 8
Jemmett Clo. King T ... 5M 103
Jemotts Ct. SE14 ... 7H 77
(off Myers La.)
Jem Paterson Ct. Harr ... 9C 38
Jengar Clo. Sutt ... 6M 121
Jenkins Av. Brick W ... 3J 5
Jenkins La. Bark ... 5A 64
Jenkinson Ho. E2 ... 6H 61
(off Usk St.)
Jenkins Rd. E13 ... 7F 62
Jenner Av. W3 ... 8B 56
Jenner Ho. SE3 ... 7C 78
(off Restell Clo.)
Jenner Ho. WC1 ... 7J 59
(off Hunter St.)
Jenner Pl. SW13 ... 7F 72
Jenner Rd. N16 ... 8D 44
Jenner Way. Eps ... 1L 133
Jennett Rd. Croy ... 5L 123
Jennifer Ho. SE11 ... 5L 75
(off Reedworth St.)
Jennifer Rd. Brom ... 9D 94
Jenningsbury Ho. SW3 ... 6C 74
(off Marlborough St.)
Jennings Clo. Surb ... 2G 119
Jennings Ho. SE10 ... 6B 78
(off Old Woolwich Rd.)
Jennings Rd. SE22 ... 5D 92
Jennings Way. Barn ... 5G 13
Jenningtree Rd. Eri ... 8F 82
Jenningtree Way. Belv ... 3A 82
Jenny Hammond Clo. E11 ... 8D 46
Jenny Path. Romf ... 7H 35
Jenson Way. SE19 ... 4D 108
Jenton Av. Bexh ... 9J 81
Jephson Ct. SW4 ... 1J 91
Jephson Ho. SE17 ... 7M 75
(off Doddington Gro.)
Jephson Rd. E7 ... 3G 63
Jephson St. SE5 ... 9B 76
Jephtha Rd. SW18 ... 5L 89
Jeppos La. Mitc ... 8D 106
Jepson Ho. SW6 ... 9M 73
(off Pearscroft Rd.)
Jerdan Pl. SW6 ... 8L 73
Jeremiah St. E14 ... 9M 61
Jeremy Bentham Ho. E2 ... 6E 60
(off Mansford St.)
Jeremy's Grn. N18 ... 4F 28
Jermyn St. SW1 ... 2G 75
Jermyn Street Theatre. ... 1H 75
(off Jermyn St.)
Jerningham Av. Ilf ... 9M 31
Jerningham Ct. SE14 ... 9J 77
Jerningham Rd. SE14 ... 1J 93
Jerome Cres. NW8 ... 7C 58
Jerome Ho. NW1 ... 8C 58
(off Lisson Gro.)
Jerome Ho. SW7 ... 5B 74
(off Glendower Pl.)
Jerome Ho. Hamp W ... 6H 103
(off Old Bri. St.)
Jerome St. E1 ... 7D 60
Jerome Tower. W3 ... 3M 71
Jerrard St. SE13 ... 2M 93
Jerrold St. N1 ... 5C 60
Jersey Av. Stan ... 9F 22
Jersey Dri. Orp ... 1B 128
Jersey Ho. N1 ... 2A 60
Jersey Ho. Enf ... 2H 17
(off Eastfield Rd.)
Jersey Rd. E11 ... 6B 46
Jersey Rd. E16 ... 9G 63
Jersey Rd. N1 ... 2A 60
Jersey Rd. SW17 ... 3F 106
Jersey Rd. W7 ... 3E 70
Jersey Rd. Houn & Iswth ... 9M 69
Jersey Rd. Ilf ... 9M 47
Jersey Rd. Rain ... 3E 66
Jersey St. E2 ... 6F 60
Jerusalem Pas. EC1 ... 7M 59
Jervis Av. Enf ... 8E 6
Jervis Bay Ho. E14 ... 9B 62
(off Blair St.)
Jervis Ct. SE10 ... 9A 78
(off Blissett St.)
Jervis Ct. W1 ... 9F 58
(off Princes St.)
Jervis Ct. Dag ... 2M 65
Jerviston Gdns. SW16 ... 3L 107
Jerwood Space Art Gallery.
... 3M 75
(off Union St.)
Jesmond Av. Wemb ... 2K 55
Jesmond Clo. Mitc ... 7F 106
Jesmond Rd. Croy ... 2D 124
Jesmond Way. Stan ... 5J 23
Jessam Av. E5 ... 6F 44
Jessamine Rd. W7 ... 2D 70
Jessel Dri. Lou ... 3M 19
Jessel Ho. SW1 ... 5H 75
(off Page St.)
Jessel Ho. WC1 ... 6J 59
(off Judd St.)
Jessel Mans. W14 ... 7J 73
(off Queen's Club Gdns.)
Jesse Rd. E10 ... 6A 46
Jessett Clo. Eri ... 5B 82
Jessica Rd. SW18 ... 5A 90
Jessie Blythe La. N19 ... 5J 43
Jessie Wood Ct. SW9 ... 8L 75
(off Caldwell St.)
Jesson Ho. SE17 ... 5B 76
(off Orb St.)
Jessop Av. S'hall ... 5K 69
Jessop Ct. N1 ... 5M 59
Jessop Ct. Wal A ... 7M 7
Jessop Rd. SE24 ... 3M 91
Jessop Sq. E14 ... 2L 77
(off Heron Quay)
Jessops Way. Croy ... 1G 123
Jessup Clo. SE18 ... 5A 80
Jetstar Way. N'holt ... 6J 53
Jevington Way. SE12 ... 7F 94
Jewel House. ... 1D 76
(in Tower of London, The)
Jewel Rd. E17 ... 1L 45
Jewels Hill. Big H ... 4E 140
Jewel Tower. ... 4J 75
(off College M.)
Jewish Mus. ... 4F 58
(Camden Town)
Jewish Mus., The. ... 9M 25
(off E. End Rd., Finchley)
Jewry St. EC3 ... 9D 60
Jew's Row. SW18 ... 3M 89
Jews' Wlk. SE26 ... 1F 108
Jeymer Av. NW2 ... 1F 56
Jeymer Dri. Gnfd ... 4M 53
(in two parts)
Jeypore Pas. SW18 ... 5A 90
Jeypore Rd. SW18 ... 6A 90
Jillian Clo. Hamp ... 4L 101
Jim Bradley Clo. SE18 ... 5L 79
Jim Griffiths Ho. SW6 ... 7K 73
(off Clem Attlee Ct.)
Joan Cres. SE9 ... 6H 95
Joan Gdns. Dag ... 7J 49
Joanna Ho. W6 ... 6G 73
(off Queen Caroline St.)
Joan Rd. Dag ... 7J 49
Joan St. SE1 ... 2M 75
Jocelin Ho. N1 ... 4K 59
(off Barnsbury Est.)
Jocelyn Rd. Rich ... 2J 87
Jocelyn St. SE15 ... 9E 76
Jockey's Fields. WC1 ... 8K 59
Jodane St. SE8 ... 5K 77
Jodrell Clo. Iswth ... 9E 70
Jodrell Rd. E3 ... 4K 61
Joe Hunte Ct. SE27 ... 2M 107
Joel St. N'wd & Pinn ... 9E 20
Johanna St. SE1 ... 3L 75
John Adams Ct. N9 ... 2D 28
John Adam St. WC2 ... 1J 75
John Aird Ct. W2 ... 8A 58
(off Howley Pl., in two parts)
John Archer Way. SW18 ... 5B 90
John Ashby Clo. SW2 ... 5J 91
John Austin Clo. King T ... 5K 103
John Baird Ct. SE26 ... 1G 109
John Barker Ct. NW6 ... 3J 57
(off Brondesbury Pk.)
John Barnes Wlk. E15 ... 2D 62
John Betts' Ho. W12 ... 4D 72
John Bradshaw Rd. N14 ... 1H 27
John Brent Ho. SE8 ... 5H 77
(off Bush Rd.)
John Buck Ho. NW10 ... 4D 56
John Burns Dri. Bark ... 3C 64
Johnby Clo. Enf ... 1J 17
John Campbell Rd. N16 ... 1C 60
John Carpenter St. EC4 ... 1M 75
John Cartwright Ho. E2 ... 6F 60
(off Old Bethnal Grn. Rd.)
John Drinkwater Clo. E11 ... 5D 46
John Felton Rd. SE16 ... 3E 76
John Fielden Ho. E2 ... 6F 60
(off Canrobert St.)
John Fisher St. E1 ... 1E 76
John Gale Ct. Eps ... 1D 134
(off West St.)
John Goddard Way. Felt ... 8F 84
John Gooch Dri. Enf ... 3M 15
John Harrison Way. SE10 ... 4D 78
John Islip St. SW1 ... 5H 75
John Kennedy Ct. N1 ... 2B 60
(off Newington Grn. Rd.)
John Kennedy Ho. SE16 ... 5H 77
(off Rotherhithe Old Rd.)
John Kirk Ho. E6 ... 9L 63
(off Pearl Clo.)
John Knight Lodge. SW6 ... 8L 73
John Lamb Ct. Harr ... 8C 22
John Masefield Ho. N15 ... 4B 44
(off Fladbury Rd.)
John Maurice Clo. SE17 ... 5B 76
John McDonald Ho. E14 ... 4A 78
(off Glengall Gro.)
John McKenna Wlk.
SE16 ... 4E 76
John Newton Ct. Well ... 2F 96
John Parker Clo. Dag ... 3M 65
John Parker Sq. SW11 ... 2B 90
John Parry Ct. N1 ... 5C 60
(off Hare Wlk.)
John Penn Ho. SE14 ... 8K 77
(off Amersham Va.)
John Penn St. SE13 ... 9M 77
John Perrin Pl. Harr ... 5J 39
John Pound Ho. SW18 ... 6M 89
John Prince's St. W1 ... 9F 58
John Pritchard Ho. E1 ... 7E 60
(off Buxton St.)
John Ratcliffe Ho. NW6 ... 6L 57
(off Chippenham Gdns.)
John Rennie Wlk. E1 ... 1F 76
John Roll Way. SE16 ... 4E 76
John Ruskin St. SE5 ... 8M 75
John's Av. NW4 ... 2G 41
John's Clo. Ashf ... 1A 100
John's Ct. Sutt ... 8M 121

John Scurr Ho.—Kemerton Rd.

John Scurr Ho. E14 9J 61
(off Ratcliffe La.)
John Silkin La. SE8 6H 77
John's La. Mord 9A 106
John's M. WC1 7K 59
John Smith Av. SW6 8K 73
Johnson Clo. E8 4E 60
Johnson Ho. E2 6E 60
(off Roberta St.)
Johnson Ho. NW1 5G 59
(off Cranleigh St.)
Johnson Ho. NW3 3D 58
(off Adelaide Rd.)
Johnson Ho. SW1 5E 74
(off Cundy St.)
Johnson Ho. SW8 8H 75
(off Wandsworth Rd.)
Johnson Lodge. W9 8L 57
(off Admiral Wlk.)
Johnson Mans. W14 7J 73
(off Queen's Club Gdns.)
Johnson Rd. NW10 4B 56
Johnson Rd. Brom 9H 111
Johnson Rd. Croy 2B 124
Johnson Rd. Houn 8G 69
Johnsons Clo. Cars 4D 122
Johnson's Ct. EC4 9L 59
Johnsons Dri. Hamp 5A 102
Johnsons Ind. Est. Hay 3D 68
Johnson's Pl. SW1 6G 75
Johnson St. E1 1G 77
Johnson St. S'hall 4G 69
Johnsons Way. NW10 7M 55
Johnson's Yd. Uxb 3A 142
John Spencer Sq. N1 2M 59
John's Pl. E1 9F 60
John's Ter. Croy 3C 124
John's Ter. Romf 6M 35
Johnston Clo. SW9 9K 75
Johnstone Ho. SE13 2B 94
(off Belmont Hill)
Johnstone Rd. E6 6K 63
Johnston Rd. Wfd G 6E 30
Johnston Ter. NW2 8H 41
John Strachey Ho. SW6 7K 73
(off Clem Attlee Ct.)
John St. E15 4D 62
John St. SE25 8E 108
John St. WC1 7K 59
John St. Enf 7D 16
John St. Houn 1J 85
John Strype Ct. E10 6M 45
John Trundle Ct. EC2 8A 60
(off Beech St.)
John Trundle Highwalk.
EC2 8A 60
(off Beech St.)
John Tucker Ho. E14 4L 77
(off Mellish St.)
John Watkin Clo. Eps 1M 133
John Wesley Ct. Twic 7E 86
John Wesley Highwalk.
EC1 8A 60
(off Barbican)
John Wheatley Ho. SW6 7K 73
(off Clem Attlee Ct.)
John Williams Clo. SE14 7H 77
John Williams Clo.
King T 5H 103
John Wilson St. SE18 4L 79
John Woolley Clo. SE13 3C 94
Joiners Arms Yd. SE5 9B 76
Joiners Pl. N5 9B 44
Joiner St. SE1 2B 76
Joint Rd. N2 8C 26
Jollys La. Harr 6B 38
Jollys La. Hay 8H 53
Jonathans. Horn 6J 51
(off High St.)
Jonathan St. SE11 6K 75
Jones Cotts. Barn 7E 12
Jones Ho. E14 9B 62
(off Blair St.)
Jones M. SW15 3J 89
Jones Rd. E13 8F 62
Jones St. W1 1F 74
Jones Wlk. Rich 5K 87
Jonquil Gdns. Hamp 3L 101
Jonson Clo. Hay 8E 52
Jonson Clo. Mitc 8F 106
Jonson Ho. SE1 4B 76
(off Burbage Clo.)
Jordan Clo. Dag 9M 49
Jordan Clo. Harr 8K 37
Jordan Clo. Leav 8D 4
Jordan Clo. S Croy 3D 138
Jordan Ho. N1 4B 60
(off Colville Est.)
Jordan Ho. SE4 3H 93
(off St Norbert Rd.)
Jordan Rd. Gnfd 4F 54
Jordans Clo. Iswth 9C 70
Jordans Clo. Stanw 6A 144
Jordans Ho. NW8 7B 58
(off Capland St.)
Jordans M. Twic 8C 86
Jordan's Way. Brick W 3J 5
Jordans Way. Rain 5H 67
Joscoyne Ho. E1 9F 60
(off Philpot St.)
Joseph Av. W3 9B 56
Joseph Conrad Ho. SW1 5G 75
(off Tachbrook St.)
Joseph Ct. N15 4C 44
(off Amhurst Pk.)
Joseph Gdns. SE18 4J 79
Joseph Hardcastle Clo.
SE14 8H 77
Josephine Av. SW2 4K 91
Joseph Irwin Ho. E14 1K 77
(off Gill St.)
Joseph Lister Ct. E7 3E 62
Joseph Locke Way. Esh 4L 117
Joseph Powell Clo. SW12 5F 90
Joseph Priestley Ho. E2 6F 60
(off Canrobert St.)
Joseph Ray Rd. E11 7C 46
Joseph St. E3 7K 61
Joseph Trotter Clo. EC1 6L 59
(off Finsbury Est.)
Joshua Clo. S Croy 9M 123
Joshua St. E14 9A 62
Joshua Wlk. Wal X 7G 7
Joslings Clo. W12 1E 72
Joslyn Clo. Enf 2L 17
Josseline Ct. E3 5J 61
(off Ford St.)
Joubert St. SW11 1D 90
Jowett St. SE15 8D 76
Jowitt Ho. E2 6H 61
(off Morpeth St.)
Joyce Av. N18 5D 28
Joyce Butler Ho. N22 8K 27
Joyce Ct. Wal A 7K 7
Joyce Dawson Way. SE28 1E 80
Joyce Green. 3K 99
Joyce Grn. La. Dart 3K 99
Joyce Grn. Wlk. Dart 3K 99
Joyce Page Clo. SE7 7H 79
Joyce Wlk. SW2 5L 91
Joydens Wood. 1B 114
Joydens Wood Rd. Bex 1B 114
Joydon Dri. Romf 4F 48
Joyes Clo. Romf 4H 35
Joyners Clo. Dag 9K 49
Joystone Ct. New Bar 6C 14
(off Park Rd.)
Jubb Powell Ho. N15 4C 44
Jubilee Av. E4 6A 30
Jubilee Av. Romf 3M 49
Jubilee Av. Twic 7A 86
Jubilee Bldgs. NW8 4B 58
Jubilee Clo. NW9 4B 40
Jubilee Clo. King T 5G 103
Jubilee Clo. Pinn 9G 21
Jubilee Clo. Romf 3M 49
Jubilee Clo. Stanw 6A 144
Jubilee Ct. N10 1E 42
Jubilee Ct. Dart 6H 99
(off Spring Va. S.)
Jubilee Ct. Harr 5J 39
Jubilee Ct. Houn 2A 86
(off Bristow Rd.)
Jubilee Ct. Wal A 6M 7
Jubilee Cres. E14 4A 78
Jubilee Cres. N9 1E 28
Jubilee Dri. Ruis 9H 37
Jubilee Gdns. S'hall 8L 53
Jubilee Ho. SE11 5L 75
(off Reedworth St.)
Jubilee Ho. WC1 7K 59
(off Gray's Inn Rd.)
Jubilee Ho. Stan 5H 23
Jubilee Mans. E1 9G 61
(off Jubilee St.)
Jubilee Mkt. Wfd G 6G 31
Jubilee Pde. Wfd G 6G 31
Jubilee Pl. SW3 6C 74
Jubilee Rd. Gnfd 4F 54
Jubilee Rd. Orp 8L 129
Jubilee Rd. Sutt 9H 121
Jubilee Rd. Wat 2E 8
Jubilee St. E1 9G 61
Jubilee, The. SE10 8M 77
Jubilee Vs. Esh 3B 118
Jubilee Wlk. Wat 4F 20
Jubilee Walkway. SE1 1M 75
Jubilee Way. SW19 5M 105
Jubilee Way. Chess 6L 119
Jubilee Way. Felt 7E 84
Jubilee Way. Sidc 8E 96
Jubilee Yd. SE1 3D 76
(off Lafone St.)
Judd St. WC1 6J 59
Jude St. E16 9D 62
Judge Heath La. Hay 9A 52
Judge St. Wat 2F 8
Judges Wlk. NW3 8A 42
Judge Wlk. Clay 8C 118
Judith Av. Romf 6M 33
Juer Ho. SW11 8C 74
(off Juer St.)
Juer St. SW11 8C 74
Jug Hill. Big H 8H 141
Juglans Rd. Orp 3E 128
Jules Thorn Av. Enf 6E 16
Julia Ct. E17 3M 45
Julia Gdns. Bark 5H 65
Julia Garfield M. E16 2F 78
Juliana Clo. N2 9A 26
Julian Av. W3 1M 71
Julian Clo. New Bar 5M 13
Julian Hill. Harr 7C 38
Julian Pl. E14 6M 77
Julian Rd. Orp 8E 128
Julian Taylor Path.
SE23 8F 92
Julia St. NW5 9E 42
Julien Rd. W5 4G 71
Julien Rd. Coul 7H 137
Juliet Ho. N1 5C 60
(off Arden Est.)
Juliette Rd. E13 5E 62
Juliette Way. S Ock 3K 83
Julius Nyerere Clo. N1 4K 59
(off Copenhagen St.)
Junction App. SE13 2A 94
Junction App. SW11 2C 90
Junction Av. NW10 7G 57
Junction M. W2 9C 58
Junction Pl. W2 9B 58
(off Praed St.)
Junction Rd. E13 5F 62
Junction Rd. N9 1E 28
Junction Rd. N17 1E 44
Junction Rd. N19 9G 43
Junction Rd. W5 5G 71
Junction Rd. Ashf 2A 100
Junction Rd. Dart 5H 99
Junction Rd. Harr 4C 38
Junction Rd. Romf 2D 50
Junction Rd. S Croy 7B 124
Junction Rd. E. Romf 5J 49
Junction Rd. W. Romf 5J 49
June Clo. Coul 6F 136
Juniper Av. Brick W 4L 5
Juniper Clo. Barn 7H 13
Juniper Clo. Big H 9J 141
Juniper Clo. Chess 7K 119
Juniper Clo. Wemb 1L 55
Juniper Ct. W8 4M 73
(off St Mary's Pl.)
Juniper Ct. Harr 8D 22
Juniper Ct. Houn 3M 85
(off Grove Rd.)
Juniper Ct. N'wd 8E 20
Juniper Ct. Romf 4F 48
Juniper Cres. NW1 3E 58
Juniper Gdns. SW16 5G 107
Juniper Gdns. Sun 3D 100
Juniper Gro. Wat 2E 8
Juniper Ho. SE15 8G 77
Juniper Ho. W10 7J 57
(off Fourth Av.)
Juniper La. E6 8J 63
Juniper Rd. Ilf 8L 47
Juniper St. E1 1G 77
Juniper Wlk. Swan 6B 114
Juniper Way. Hay 1B 68
Juniper Way. Romf 8J 35
Juno Ct. SW9 8L 75
(off Caldwell St.)
Juno Way. SE14 7H 77
Juno Way Ind. Est. SE14 7H 77
Jupiter Ct. SW9 8L 75
(off Caldwell St.)
Jupiter Ct. N'holt 6H 53
(off Seasprite Clo.)
Jupiter Heights. Uxb 4D 142
Jupiter Ho. E14 6M 77
(off St Davids Sq.)
Jupiter Way. N7 2K 59
Jupp Rd. E15 3B 62
Jupp Rd. W. E15 4B 62
Jura Ho. SE16 5H 77
(off Plough Way)
Jurston Ct. SE1 3L 75
(off Gerridge St.)
Justice Wlk. SW3 7C 74
(off Lawrence St.)
Justin Clo. Bren 8H 71
Justin Rd. E4 6K 29
Jute La. Brim 4J 17
(in two parts)
Jutland Clo. N19 6J 43
Jutland Ho. SE5 1A 92
Jutland Rd. E13 7E 62
Jutland Rd. SE6 6A 94
Jutsums Av. Romf 4M 49
Jutsums Ct. Romf 4M 49
Jutsums La. Romf 4M 49
Juxon Clo. Harr 8M 21
Juxon St. SE11 5K 75
JVC Bus. Pk. NW2 6E 40

K

Kaduna Clo. Pinn 3E 36
Kale Rd. Eri 3J 81
Kambala Rd. SW11 2B 90
Kangley Bri. Rd. SE26 3K 109
Kangley Bus. Cen. SE26 2K 109
Kaplan Dri. N21 7K 15
Kara Way. NW2 9H 41
Karen Clo. Rain 5C 66
Karen Ct. Brom 5D 110
Karen Ter. E11 7D 46
Karina Clo. Chig 5C 32
Karoline Gdns. Gnfd 5B 54
Kashgar Rd. SE18 5D 80
Kashmir Rd. SE7 8H 79
Kassala Rd. SW11 9D 74
Kates Clo. Barn 7E 12
Katharine Ho. Croy 5A 124
(off Katharine St.)
Katharine St. Croy 5A 124
Katherine Clo. SE16 2H 77
Katherine Ct. SE23 7F 92
Katherine Gdns. SE9 3H 95
Katherine Gdns. Ilf 7A 32
Katherine Pl. Ab L 5E 4
Katherine Rd. E7 & E6 1G 63
Katherine Rd. Twic 7E 86
Katherine Sq. W11 2J 73
Kathleen Av. W3 8A 56
Kathleen Av. Wemb 3J 55
Kathleen Godfree Ct.
SW19 3L 105
Kathleen Rd. SW11 2D 90
Kayemoor Rd. Sutt 8B 122
Kay Rd. SW9 1J 91
Kay St. E2 5E 60
Kay St. E15 3B 62
Kay St. Well 9F 80
Kay Ter. E18 8D 30
Kay Way. SE10 8A 78
(off Greenwich High Rd.)
Kean Ho. SE17 7M 75
Kean Ho. Twic 5H 87
(off Arosa Rd.)
Kean St. WC2 9K 59
Kearton Clo. Kenl 9A 138
Keatley Grn. E4 6K 29
Keats Av. E16 2F 78
Keats Av. Romf 7F 34
Keats Clo. E11 3F 46
Keat's Clo. NW3 9C 42
Keats Clo. SE1 5D 76
Keats Clo. SW19 3B 106
Keats Clo. Chig 6A 32
Keats Clo. Enf 7H 17
Keats Clo. Hay 8E 52
Keat's Gro. NW3 9C 42
Keats House. 9C 42
Keats Ho. E2 6G 61
(off Roman Rd.)
Keats Ho. SE5 8A 76
(off Elmington Est.)
Keats Ho. SW1 7G 75
(off Churchill Gdns.)
Keats Ho. Cray 4C 98
Keats Pde. N9 2E 28
(off Church St.)
Keats Pl. EC2 8B 60
(off Moorfields)
Keats Rd. Belv 4A 82
Keats Rd. Well 9C 80
Keats Way. Croy 1G 125
Keats Way. Gnfd 8M 53
Keats Way. W Dray 5K 143
Kebbell Ter. E7 1F 62
(off Claremont Rd.)
Keble Clo. N'holt 1A 54
Keble Clo. Wor Pk 3D 120
Keble Pl. SW13 7F 72
Keble St. SW17 1A 106
Keble Ter. Ab L 5D 4
Kechill Gdns. Brom 2E 126
Kedeston Ct. Sutt 3M 121
Kedge Ho. E14 4L 77
(off Tiller Rd.)
Kedleston Dri. Orp 1D 128
Kedleston Wlk. E2 6F 60
Kedyngton Ho. Edgw 9A 24
(off Burnt Oak B'way.)
Keeble Clo. SE18 7M 79
Keedonwood Rd. Brom 2C 110
Keel Clo. SE16 2H 77
Keel Clo. Bark 5G 65
Keele Clo. Wat 4G 9
Keeley Rd. Croy 4A 124
Keeley St. WC2 9K 59
Keeling Ho. E2 5F 60
(off Claredale St.)
Keeling Rd. SE9 4H 95
Keely Clo. Barn 7C 14
Keemor Clo. SE18 8L 79
Keens Clo. SW16 2H 107
Keens Rd. Croy 6A 124
Keen's Yd. N1 2M 59
Keepers Ct. S Croy 7A 124
(off Warham Rd.)
Keepers M. Tedd 3G 103
Keepier Wharf. E14 1H 77
(off Narrow St.)
Keep, The. SE3 1E 94
Keep, The. King T 3K 103
Keeton's Rd. SE16 4F 76
(in two parts)
Keevil Dri. SW19 6H 89
Keighley Clo. N7 1J 59
Keighley Rd. Romf 7J 35
Keightley Dri. SE9 7A 96
Keilder Clo. Uxb 5E 142
Keildon Rd. SW11 3D 90
Keir Hardie Ct. NW10 3D 56
Keir Hardie Est. E5 6F 44
Keir Hardie Ho. N19 5H 43
Keir Hardie Ho. W6 7H 73
(off Fulham Pal. Rd.)
Keir Hardie Way. Bark 3E 64
Keir Hardie Way. Hay 6E 52
Keir, The. SW19 2G 105
Keith Av. S at H 3M 115
Keith Connor Clo. SW8 2F 90
Keith Gro. W12 3E 72
Keith Ho. NW6 6M 57
(off Carlton Va.)
Keith Pk. Cres. Big H 4F 140
Keith Pk. Rd. Uxb 3D 142
Keith Rd. E17 8K 29
Keith Rd. Bark 5B 64
Keith Rd. Hay 4C 68
Keith Way. Horn 5J 51
Kelbrook Rd. SE3 1J 95
Kelburn Way. Rain 6E 66
Kelby Ho. N7 2K 59
(off Sutterton St.)
Kelby Path. SE9 9M 95
Kelceda Clo. NW2 7E 40
Kelf Gro. Hay 9D 52
Kelfield Ct. W10 9H 57
Kelfield Gdns. W10 9G 57
Kelfield M. W10 9H 57
Kelland Clo. N8 3H 43
Kelland Rd. E13 7E 62
Kellaway Rd. SE3 1H 95
Keller Cres. E12 9H 47
Kellerton Rd. SE13 4C 94
Kellet Houses. WC1 6J 59
(off Tankerton St.)
Kellett Ho. N1 4C 60
(off Colville Est.)
Kellett Rd. SW2 3L 91
Kelling Gdns. Croy 2M 123
Kellino St. SW17 1D 106
Kellner Rd. SE28 4D 80
Kellogg Tower. Gnfd 1C 54
Kellow Ho. SE1 3B 76
(off Tennis St.)
Kell St. SE1 4M 75
Kelly Av. SE15 8D 76
Kelly Clo. NW10 8B 40
Kelly Clo. Shep 6C 100
Kelly Ct. E14 1L 77
(off Garford St.)
Kelly Ct. Borwd 4B 12
Kelly M. W9 7K 57
Kelly Rd. NW7 6J 25
Kelly St. NW1 2F 58
Kelly Way. Romf 3J 49
Kelman Clo. SW4 1H 91
Kelman Clo. Wal X 4D 6
Kelmore Gro. SE22 3E 92
Kelmscott Clo. E17 8K 29
Kelmscott Clo. Wat 7E 8
Kelmscott Cres. Wat 7E 8
Kelmscott Gdns. W12 4E 72
Kelmscott Rd. SW11 4C 90
Kelross Pas. N5 9A 44
Kelross Rd. N5 9A 44
Kelsall Clo. SE3 1F 94
Kelsey Ga. Beck 6M 109
Kelsey La. Beck 6L 109
(in two parts)
Kelsey Pk. Av. Beck 6M 109
Kelsey Pk. Rd. Beck 6L 109
Kelsey Rd. Orp 6F 112
Kelsey Sq. Beck 6L 109
Kelsey St. E2 7E 60
Kelsey Way. Beck 7L 109
Kelshall. Wat 9J 5
Kelsie Way. Ilf 6C 32
Kelson Ho. E14 4A 78
Kelso Pl. W8 4M 73
Kelso Rd. Cars 2A 122
Kelston Rd. Ilf 9M 31
Kelvedon Av. W on T 9C 116
Kelvedon Clo. King T 3L 103
Kelvedon Ho. SW8 9J 75
Kelvedon Rd. SW6 8K 73
Kelvedon Wlk. Rain 4D 66
Kelvedon Way. Wfd G 6K 31
Kelvin Av. N13 6K 27
Kelvin Av. Tedd 3C 102
Kelvinbrook. W Mol 7M 101
Kelvin Clo. Eps 8L 119
Kelvin Ct. SE20 5F 108
Kelvin Ct. W11 1L 73
Kelvin Ct. Iswth 1C 86
Kelvin Cres. Harr 7C 22
Kelvin Dri. Twic 5F 86
Kelvin Gdns. Croy 2J 123
Kelvin Gdns. S'hall 9L 53
Kelvin Gro. SE26 9F 92
Kelvin Gro. Chess 5H 119
Kelvington Clo. Croy 2J 125
Kelvington Rd. SE15 4H 93
Kelvin Pde. Orp 3C 128
Kelvin Rd. N5 9A 44
Kelvin Rd. Well 2E 96
Kember St. N1 3K 59
Kemble Clo. Wey 6B 116
Kemble Ct. SE15 8C 76
(off Lydney Clo.)
Kemble Dri. Brom 5J 127
Kemble Ho. SW9 2M 91
(off Barrington Rd.)
Kemble Rd. N17 8E 28
Kemble Rd. SE23 7H 93
Kemble Rd. Croy 5M 123
Kembleside Rd. Big H 9G 141
Kemble St. WC2 9K 59
Kemerton Rd. SE5 2A 92

Kemerton Rd.—Keswick Av.

Kemerton Rd. Beck 6M 109
Kemerton Rd. Croy 2D 124
Kemeys St. E9 1J 61
Kemnal Rd. Chst 1B 112
(in two parts)
Kemp. NW9 8D 24
(off Concourse, The)
Kemp Ct. SW8 8J 75
(off Hartington Rd.)
Kempe Ho. SE1 4B 76
(off Burge St.)
Kempe Rd. NW6 5H 57
Kempe Rd. Enf 9B 6
(in two parts)
Kemp Gdns. Croy 1A 124
Kemp Ho. E2 5H 61
(off Sewardstone Rd.)
Kemp Ho. E6 2L 63
Kemp Ho. W1 1H 75
(off Berwick St.)
Kempis Way. SE22 4C 92
Kemplay Rd. NW3 9B 42
Kemp Pl. Bush 8L 9
Kemp Rd. Dag 6H 49
Kemprow. 1B 10
Kemprow. A'ham 1B 10
Kemps Ct. W1 9H 59
(off Hopkins St.)
Kemps Dri. E14 1L 77
Kemps Dri. N'wd 7D 20
Kempsford Gdns. SW5 6L 73
Kempsford Rd. SE11 5L 75
(Reedworth St.)
Kempsford Rd. SE11 5M 75
(Renfrew Rd.)
Kemps Gdns. SE13 4A 94
Kempshott Rd. SW16 4H 107
Kempson Rd. SW6 9L 73
Kempthorne Rd. SE8 5K 77
Kempton Av. Horn 9K 51
Kempton Av. N'holt 2L 53
Kempton Av. Sun 5F 100
Kempton Clo. Eri 7A 82
Kempton Clo. Uxb 9A 36
Kempton Ct. E1 8F 60
Kempton Ct. Sun 5F 100
Kempton Pk. Racecourse. 4G 101
Kempton Rd. E6 4K 63
Kempton Rd. Hamp 6K 101
(in three parts)
Kempton Wlk. Croy 1J 125
Kempt St. SE18 7L 79
Kemsing Clo. Bex 6J 97
Kemsing Clo. Brom 4D 126
Kemsing Clo. T Hth 8A 108
Kemsing Ho. SE1 3B 76
(off Long La.)
Kemsing Rd. SE10 6E 78
Kemsley Ct. W13 2G 71
Kenbrook Ho. W14 4K 73
Kenbury Gdns. SE5 1A 92
Kenbury Mans. SE5 1A 92
(off Kenbury St.)
Kenbury St. SE5 1A 92
Kenchester Clo. SW8 8J 75
Kencot Way. Eri 3K 81
Kendal. NW1 6F 58
(off Augustus St.)
Kendal Av. N18 4B 28
Kendal Av. W3 7L 55
(in two parts)
Kendal Av. Bark 4C 64
Kendal Clo. SW9 8M 75
Kendal Clo. Felt 7D 84
Kendal Clo. Hay 5C 52
Kendal Clo. Wfd G 2D 30
Kendal Ct. W3 8L 55
Kendal Ct. Borwd 4A 12
Kendal Cft. Horn 1E 66
Kendale Rd. Brom 2C 110
Kendal Gdns. N18 4B 28
Kendal Gdns. Sutt 4A 122
Kendal Ho. E9 4G 61
Kendal Ho. N1 5K 59
(off Priory Grn. Est.)
Kendal Ho. SE20 6E 108
(off Derwent Rd.)
Kendall Av. Beck 6J 109
Kendall Av. S Croy 1B 138
Kendall Av. S. S Croy 2A 138
Kendall Ct. SW19 3B 106
Kendall Ct. Sidc 9E 96
Kendall Lodge. Brom 5F 110
(off Willow Tree Wlk.)
Kendall Pl. W1 8E 58
Kendall Rd. SE18 9J 79
Kendall Rd. Beck 6J 109
Kendall Rd. Iswth 1E 86
Kendalmere Clo. N10 8F 26
Kendal Pde. N18 4B 28
Kendal Pl. SW9 8M 75
(off Kendal Clo.)
Kendal Pl. SW15 4K 89
Kendal Rd. NW10 9E 40
Kendal Rd. Wal A 8J 7
Kendals Clo. Rad 1C 10
Kendal Steps. W2 9C 58
(off St George's Fields)
Kendal St. W2 9C 58
Kender St. SE14 8G 77
Kendoa Rd. SW4 3H 91
Kendon Clo. E11 3F 46
Kendor Av. Eps 3A 134
Kendra Hall Rd. S Croy 9M 123
Kendrey Gdns. Twic 6C 86
Kendrick Ct. SE15 9F 76
(off Woods Rd.)
Kendrick M. SW7 5B 74
Kendrick Pl. SW7 5B 74
Kenelm Clo. Harr 8E 38
Kenerne Dri. Barn 7J 13
Kenford Clo. Wat 5F 4
Kenilford Rd. SW12 6F 90
Kenilworth Av. E17 9L 29
Kenilworth Av. SW19 2L 105
Kenilworth Av. Harr 9K 37
Kenilworth Av. Romf 6M 35
Kenilworth Av. Stoke D 6A 132
Kenilworth Clo. Bans 8M 135
Kenilworth Clo. Borwd 5A 12
Kenilworth Ct. Dart 5M 99
(off Bow Arrow La.)
Kenilworth Ct. Wat 3E 8
Kenilworth Cres. Enf 3C 16
Kenilworth Dri. Borwd 5A 12
Kenilworth Dri. Crox G 6A 8
Kenilworth Dri. W on T 5H 117
Kenilworth Gdns. SE18 1M 95
Kenilworth Gdns. Hay 8D 52
Kenilworth Gdns. Horn 8G 51
Kenilworth Gdns. Ilf 7D 48
Kenilworth Gdns. Lou 8K 19
Kenilworth Gdns. S'hall 6K 53
Kenilworth Gdns. Wat 5G 21
Kenilworth Rd. E3 5J 61
Kenilworth Rd. NW6 4K 57
Kenilworth Rd. SE20 5H 109
Kenilworth Rd. W5 2J 71
Kenilworth Rd. Ashf 9B 144
Kenilworth Rd. Edgw 3A 24
Kenilworth Rd. Eps 7E 120
Kenilworth Rd. Orp 1A 128
Kenley. 6A 138
Kenley Av. NW9 8C 24
Kenley Clo. Barn 6C 14
Kenley Clo. Bex 6L 97
Kenley Clo. Chst 7C 112
Kenley Ct. Kenl 7M 137
Kenley Gdns. Horn 7K 51
Kenley Gdns. T Hth 8M 107
Kenley La. Kenl 6A 138
Kenley Rd. SW19 6L 105
Kenley Rd. King T 6M 103
Kenley Rd. Twic 5F 86
Kenley Wlk. W11 1J 73
Kenley Wlk. Sutt 6H 121
Kenlor Rd. SW17 2B 106
Kenmare Dri. Mitc 4D 106
Kenmare Gdns. N13 4A 28
Kenmare Rd. T Hth 1L 123
Kenmere Gdns. Wemb 4L 55
Kenmere Rd. Well 1G 97
Kenmont Gdns. NW10 6F 56
Kenmore Av. Harr 2E 38
Kenmore Clo. Rich 8L 71
Kenmore Cres. Hay 6D 52
Kenmore Gdns. Edgw 9M 23
Kenmore Rd. Harr 1H 39
Kenmore Rd. Kenl 6M 137
Kenmure Rd. E8 1F 60
Kenmure Yd. E8 1F 60
Kennacraig Clo. E16 2E 78
Kennard Ho. SW11 1E 90
Kennard Rd. E15 3B 62
Kennard Rd. N11 5D 26
Kennard St. E16 2K 79
Kennard St. SW11 9E 74
Kennedy Av. Enf 8G 17
Kennedy Clo. E13 5E 62
Kennedy Clo. Chesh 1E 6
Kennedy Clo. Mitc 5E 106
Kennedy Clo. Orp 3B 128
Kennedy Clo. Pinn 6K 21
Kennedy Ct. Beck 1K 125
Kennedy Ct. Bush 2B 22
Kennedy Cox Ho. E16 8D 62
(off Burke St.)
Kennedy Ho. SE11 6K 75
(off Vauxhall Wlk.)
Kennedy Path. W7 7D 54
Kennedy Rd. W7 8C 54
Kennedy Rd. Bark 4C 64
Kennedy Wlk. SE17 5B 76
(off Elsted St.)
Kennel Wood Cres.
New Ad 3B 140
Kennet Clo. SW11 3B 90
Kennet Ct. W9 8L 57
(off Elmfield Way)
Kenneth Av. Ilf 9M 47
Kenneth Campbell Ho.
NW8 7B 58
(off Orchardson St.)
Kenneth Ct. SE11 5L 75
Kenneth Cres. NW2 1F 56
Kenneth Gdns. Stan 6E 22
Kenneth More Rd. Ilf 8M 47
Kenneth More Theatre. 8M 47
Kennet Ho. NW8 7B 58
(off Church St. Est.)
Kenneth Rd. Bans 7B 136
Kenneth Rd. Romf 5H 49
Kenneth Robbins Ho. N17 7F 28
Kenneth Younger Ho.
SW6 7K 73
(off Clem Attlee Ct.)
Kennet Rd. W9 7K 57
Kennet Rd. Dart 2E 98
Kennet Rd. Iswth 2D 86
Kennet Sq. SW19 5B 106
Kennet St. E1 2E 76
Kennett Ct. W4 8M 71
Kennett Ct. Swan 7C 114
(off Oakleigh Clo.)
Kennett Ct. Wat 6F 8
(off Whippendell Rd.)
Kennett Dri. Hay 8J 53
Kennett Wharf La. EC4 1A 76
Kenninghall (Junct.) 5G 29
Kenninghall Rd. E5 8E 44
Kenninghall Rd. N18 5G 29
Kenning Ho. N1 4C 60
(off Colville Est.)
Kenning St. SE16 3G 77
Kennings Way. SE11 6L 75
Kennington. 7L 75
Kennington Grn. SE11 6L 75
Kennington Gro. SE11 7K 75
Kennington La. SE11 6K 75
Kennington Oval (Junct.) 7L 75
Kennington Oval. SE11 7K 75
Kennington Pal. Ct. SE11 6L 75
(off Sancroft St.)
Kennington Pk. Gdns.
SE11 7M 75
Kennington Pk. Ho. SE11 6L 75
(off Kennington Pk. Pl.)
Kennington Pk. Pl. SE11 7L 75
Kennington Pk. Rd. SE11 7L 75
Kennington Rd.
SE1 & SE11 4L 75
Kennistoun Ho. NW5 1G 59
Kenny Dri. Cars 1E 136
Kennyland Ct. NW4 4F 40
(off Hendon Way)
Kennylands Rd. Ilf 7E 32
Kenny Rd. NW7 6J 25
Kenrick Pl. W1 8E 58
Kensal Green. 6G 57
Kensal Ho. W10 7H 57
(off Ladbroke Gro.)
Kensal Rise. 5H 57
Kensal Rd. W10 7J 57
Kensal Town. 7J 57
Kensington. 3M 73
Kensington Arc. W8 3M 73
(off Kensington High St.)
Kensington Av. E12 2J 63
Kensington Av. T Hth 5L 107
Kensington Av. Wat 6D 8
Kensington Cen. W14 5J 73
(in two parts)
Kensington Chu. Ct. W8 3M 73
Kensington Chu. St. W8 2L 73
Kensington Chu. Wlk. W8 3M 73
(in two parts)
Kensington Clo. N11 6E 26
Kensington Ct. SE16 2H 77
(off King & Queen Wharf)
Kensington Ct. W8 3M 73
Kensington Ct. Gdns. W8 4M 73
(off Kensington Ct. Pl.)
Kensington Ct. M. W8 4M 73
(off Kensington Ct. Pl.)
Kensington Ct. Pl. W8 4M 73
Kensington Dri. Wfd G 9H 31
Kensington Gardens. 2A 74
Kensington Gdns. Ilf 6K 47
Kensington Gdns.
King T 7H 103
(in two parts)
Kensington Gdns. Sq.
W2 9M 57
(in two parts)
Kensington Ga. W8 4A 74
Kensington Gore. SW7 3A 74
Kensington Hall Gdns.
W14 6K 73
Kensington Heights. W8 2L 73
Kensington Heights. Harr 4D 38
(off Sheepcote Rd.)
Kensington High St.
W14 & W8 4K 73
Kensington Ho. W14 3H 73
Kensington Mall. W8 2L 73
Kensington Mans. SW5 6L 73
(off Trebovir Rd., in two parts)
Kensington Palace. 3M 73
Kensington Pal. Gdns.
W8 2M 73
Kensington Pk. Gdns.
W11 1K 73
Kensington Pk. M. W11 9K 57
Kensington Pk. Rd. W11 9K 57
Kensington Pl. W8 2L 73
Kensington Rd.
W8 & SW7 3A 74
Kensington Rd. N'holt 6L 53
Kensington Rd. Romf 4A 50
Kensington Sq. W8 4M 73
Kensington Ter. S Croy 9B 124
Kensington Village. W14 5K 73
Kensington Way. Borwd 5B 12
Kensington W. W14 5J 73
Kenswick Ct. SE13 4M 93
Kensworth Ho. EC1 6B 60
(off Cranwood St.)
Kent Av. W13 8F 54
Kent Av. Dag 7L 65
Kent Av. Well 4D 96
Kent Clo. Borwd 2B 12
Kent Clo. Mitc 8J 107
Kent Clo. Orp 8C 128
Kent Clo. Uxb 2A 142
Kent Ct. E2 5D 60
Kent Ct. NW9 9C 24
Kent Dri. Cockf 6E 14
Kent Dri. Horn 9H 51
Kent Dri. Tedd 2C 102
Kentford Way. N'holt 4J 53
Kent Gdns. W13 8F 54
Kent Gdns. Ruis 4E 36
Kent Ga. Way. Croy 8K 125
Kent Ho. SE1 6D 76
Kent Ho. SW1 6H 75
(off Aylesford St.)
Kent Ho. W4 6C 72
(off Devonshire St.)
Kent Ho. La. Beck 3J 109
Kent Ho. Rd.
SE26 & Beck 2J 109
Kentish Bldgs. SE1 3B 76
Kentish Rd. Belv 5L 81
Kentish Town. 1F 58
Kentish Town Ind. Est.
NW5 1F 58
Kentish Town Rd.
NW1 & NW5 3F 58
Kentish Way. Brom 6E 110
Kentlea Rd. SE28 3C 80
Kentmere Ho. SE15 7G 77
Kentmere Mans. W5 7F 54
Kentmere Rd. SE18 5C 80
Kenton. 3G 39
Kenton Av. Harr 5D 38
Kenton Av. S'hall 1L 69
Kenton Av. Sun 6H 101
Kenton Ct. SE26 1J 109
(off Adamsrill Rd.)
Kenton Ct. W14 4K 73
Kenton Ct. Kent 4F 38
Kenton Ct. Twic 5H 87
Kentone Ct. SE25 8F 108
Kenton Gdns. Harr 3G 39
Kenton Ho. E1 7G 61
(off Mantus Clo.)
Kenton La. Harr 6D 22
Kenton Pk. Av. Harr 2H 39
Kenton Pk. Clo. Harr 2G 39
Kenton Pk. Cres. Harr 2H 39
Kenton Pk. Mans. Kent 3G 39
(off Kenton Rd.)
Kenton Pk. Pde. Harr 3G 39
Kenton Pk. Rd. Harr 2G 39
Kenton Rd. E9 2H 61
Kenton Rd. Harr 5D 38
Kenton St. WC1 7J 59
Kenton Way. Hay 6C 52
Kent Pk. Ind. Est. SE15 7F 76
Kent Pas. NW1 7D 58
Kent Rd. N21 1B 28
Kent Rd. W4 4A 72
Kent Rd. Dag 1M 65
Kent Rd. Dart 5H 99
Kent Rd. E Mol 8A 102
Kent Rd. King T 7H 103
Kent Rd. Orp 1F 128
Kent Rd. Rich 8L 71
Kent Rd. W Wick 3M 125
Kent's Pas. Hamp 5K 101
Kent St. E2 5D 60
Kent St. E13 6F 62
Kent Ter. NW1 6C 58
Kent Vw. Ave 3M 83
Kent Vw. Wen 1H 83
Kent Vw. Gdns. Ilf 7C 48
Kent Wlk. SW9 3M 91
Kent Way. Surb 5J 119
Kentwell Clo. SE4 3J 93
Kent Wharf. SE8 8M 77
(off Creekside)
Kentwode Grn. SW13 8E 72
Kent Yd. SW7 3C 74
Kenver Av. N12 6B 26
Kenward Rd. SE9 4G 95
Kenward Way. SW11 1E 90
Kenway. Rain 6H 67
Kenway. Romf 9A 34
Ken Way. Wemb 8A 40
Kenway Clo. Rain 6G 67
Kenway Rd. SW5 5M 73
Kenway Wlk. Rain 6H 67
Ken Wilson Ho. E2 5E 60
(off Pritchards Rd.)
Kenwood Av. N14 7H 15
Kenwood Clo. NW3 6B 42
Kenwood Clo. W Dray 7L 143
Kenwood Dri. Beck 7A 110
Kenwood Dri. W on T 8F 116
Kenwood Gdns. E18 1F 46
Kenwood Gdns. Ilf 2L 47
Kenwood House. 6C 42
Kenwood Ho. SW9 3M 91
Kenwood Ho. Wat 9B 8
Kenwood Pk. Wey 8B 116
Kenwood Ridge. Kenl 9M 137
Kenwood Rd. N6 4D 42
Kenwood Rd. N9 1E 28
Kenworth Clo. Wal X 6D 6
Kenworthy Rd. E9 1J 61
Kenwrick Ho. N1 4K 59
(off Barnsbury Est.)
Kenwyn Dri. NW2 7C 40
Kenwyn Lodge. N2 2D 42
Kenwyn Rd. SW4 3H 91
Kenwyn Rd. SW20 5G 105
Kenwyn Rd. Dart 4H 99
Kenya Rd. SE7 8H 79
Kenyngton Ct. Sun 2E 100
Kenyngton Dri. Sun 2E 100
Kenyngton Pl. Harr 3G 39
Kenyon Mans. W14 7J 73
(off Queen's Club Gdns.)
Kenyon St. SW6 9H 73
Keogh Rd. E15 2C 62
Kepler Ho. SE10 6D 78
(off Armitage Rd.)
Kepler Rd. SW4 3J 91
Keppel Ho. SE8 6K 77
Keppel Rd. E6 3K 63
Keppel Rd. Dag 9J 49
Keppel Row. SE1 2A 76
Keppel St. WC1 8H 59
Kerbela St. E2 7E 60
Kerbey St. E14 9M 61
Kerfield Cres. SE5 9B 76
Kerfield Pl. SE5 9B 76
Kernow Clo. Horn 7J 51
Kerri Clo. Barn 6G 13
Kerridge Ct. N1 2C 60
(off Balls Pond Rd.)
Kerrington Ct. W12 3G 73
(off Uxbridge Rd.)
Kerrison Pl. W5 2H 71
Kerrison Rd. E15 4B 62
Kerrison Rd. SW11 2C 90
Kerrison Rd. W5 2H 71
Kerrison Vs. W5 2H 71
Kerry. N7 2J 59
Kerry Av. Ave 4L 83
Kerry Av. Stan 4G 23
Kerry Clo. E16 9F 62
Kerry Clo. N13 2K 27
Kerry Ct. Stan 4H 23
Kerry Ho. E1 9G 61
(off Sidney St.)
Kerry Path. SE14 7K 77
Kerry Rd. SE14 7K 77
Kersey Dri. S Croy 4G 139
Kersey Gdns. SE9 1J 111
Kersey Gdns. Romf 7J 35
Kersfield Rd. SW15 5H 89
Kershaw Clo. SW18 5B 90
Kershaw Clo. Horn 5J 51
Kershaw Rd. Dag 8L 49
Kersley M. SW11 9D 74
Kersley Rd. N16 7C 44
Kersley St. SW11 1D 90
Kerstin Clo. Hay 1D 68
Kerswell Clo. N15 3C 44
Kerwick Clo. N7 3J 59
Keslake Mans. NW10 5H 57
(off Station Ter.)
Keslake Rd. NW6 5H 57
Kessock Clo. N17 3F 44
Kesteven Clo. Ilf 6D 32
Kestlake Rd. Bex 5G 97
Keston. 7G 127
Keston Av. Kes 7G 127
Keston Clo. N18 3B 28
Keston Clo. Well 8G 81
Keston Ct. Bex 6K 97
Keston Ct. Surb 9K 103
(off Cranes Pk.)
Keston Gdns. Kes 6G 127
Keston Ho. SE17 6C 76
(off Kinglake St.)
Keston Mark. 6J 127
Keston Mark (Junct.) 6H 127
Keston M. Wat 4F 8
Keston Pk. Clo. Kes 5K 127
Keston Rd. N17 1B 44
Keston Rd. SE15 2E 92
Keston Rd. T Hth 1L 123
Kestral Clo. Wat 7J 5
Kestrel Av. E6 8J 63
Kestrel Av. SE24 4M 91
Kestrel Clo. NW9 9C 24
Kestrel Clo. NW10 1B 56
Kestrel Clo. Eps 3M 133
Kestrel Clo. Horn 3F 66
Kestrel Clo. Ilf 4F 32
Kestrel Clo. King T 1H 103
Kestrel Ct. E17 9H 29
Kestrel Ct. Ruis 7B 36
Kestrel Ct. S Croy 8A 124
Kestrel Ho. EC1 6A 60
(off Pickard St.)
Kestrel Pl. SE14 7J 77
Kestrel Rd. Wal A 7M 7
Kestrels, The. Brick W 4K 5
Kestrel Way. Hay 3B 68
Kestrel Way. New Ad 1B 140
Keswick Av. SW15 2C 104

Keswick Av.—Kingsgate Pl.

Keswick Av. SW19 . . . . 6L 105
Keswick Av. Horn 6H 51
Keswick Av. Shep 7C 100
Keswick Clo. Sutt 6A 122
Keswick Ct. SE6 . . . . 7D 94
Keswick Ct. Brom 8D 110
Keswick Dri. Enf 9C 6
Keswick Gdns. Ilf 2J 47
Keswick Gdns. Ruis 4B 36
Keswick Gdns. Wemb 9J 39
Keswick Ho. SE5 . . . . 1A 92
Keswick Ho. Romf 6H 35
(off Dartfields)
Keswick M. W5 . . . . 2J 71
Keswick Rd. SW15 . . . . 4J 89
Keswick Rd. Bexh 9L 81
Keswick Rd. Orp 3D 128
Keswick Rd. Twic 5A 86
Keswick Rd. W Wick 4C 126
Kettering Rd. Enf 1H 17
Kettering Rd. Romf 7J 35
Kettering St. SW16 . . . . . . 3G 107
Kett Gdns. SW2 . . . . 4K 91
Kettlebaston Rd. E10 . . . . . . 6K 45
Kettleby Ho. SW9 . . . . 2M 91
(off Barrington Rd.)
Kettlewell Clo. N11 . . . . 6E 26
Kettlewell Ct. Swan 6D 114
Ketton Ho. W10 . . . . 7G 57
(off Sutton Way)
Kevan Ct. E17 . . . . 2L 45
Kevan Ho. SE5 . . . . 8A 76
Kevelioc Rd. N17 . . . . 8A 28
Kevere Ct. N'wd 5A 20
Kevin Clo. Houn 1H 85
Kevington. 1J 129
Kevington Clo. Orp 8D 112
Kevington Dri.
Chst & Orp 8C 112
Kew. 8L 71
Kew Bridge (Junct.) 7L 71
Kew Bri. Bren 7K 71
Kew Bri. Arches. Rich 7L 71
Kew Bri. Ct. W4 . . . . 6L 71
Kew Bri. Distribution Cen.
Bren 6K 71
Kew Bri. Rd. Bren 7K 71
Kew Bridge Steam Mus. . . . 6K 71
Kew Cres. Sutt 5J 121
Kewferry Dri. N'wd 5A 20
Kewferry Rd. N'wd 6A 20
Kew Foot Rd. Rich 3J 87
Kew Gardens Plants & People Exhibition. 8K 71
Kew Gdns. Rd. Rich 8K 71
Kew Green (Junct.) 8K 71
Kew Grn. Rich 7K 71
Kew Mdw. Path. Rich 1A 88
(Thames Bank)
Kew Mdw. Path. Rich 9M 71
(W. Park Av.)
Kew Palace. 8J 71
Kew Retail Pk. Rich 9M 71
Kew Rd. Rich 7L 71
Keybridge Ho. SW8 . . . . 7J 75
(off Miles St.)
Key Clo. E1 . . . . 7G 61
Keyes Ho. SW1 . . . . 6H 75
(off Dolphin Sq.)
Keyes Rd. NW2 . . . . 1H 57
Keyes Rd. Dart 3K 99
Key Ho. SE11 . . . . 7L 75
Keymer Clo. Big H 8G 141
Keymer Rd. SW2 . . . . 8K 91
Keynes Clo. N2 . . . . 2D 42
Keynsham Av. Wfd G 4C 30
Keynsham Gdns. SE9 . . . . . . 4J 95
Keynsham Rd. SE9 . . . . 4H 95
Keynsham Rd. Mord 3M 121
Keynsham Wlk. Mord 3M 121
Keys Ct. Croy 5B 124
(off Beech Ho. Rd.)
Keyse Rd. SE1 . . . . 4D 76
Keysham Av. Houn 9E 68
Keystone Cres. N1 . . . . 5J 59
Keywood Dri. Sun 3E 100
Keyworth Clo. E5 . . . . 9J 45
Keyworth Pl. SE1 . . . . 4M 75
(off Keyworth St.)
Keyworth St. SE1 . . . . 4M 75
Kezia St. SE8 . . . . 6J 77
Khama Rd. SW17 . . . . 1C 106
Khartoum Rd. E13 . . . . 6F 62
Khartoum Rd. SW17 . . . . . . 1B 106
Khartoum Rd. Ilf 1M 63
Khyber Rd. SW11 . . . . 1C 90
Kibworth St. SW8 . . . . 8K 75
Kidbrooke. 1F 94
Kidbrooke Est. SE3 . . . . 2G 95
Kidbrooke Gdns. SE3 . . . . . . 1E 94
Kidbrooke Gro. SE3 . . . . 9E 78
Kidbrooke La. SE9 . . . . 3J 95
Kidbrooke Pk. Clo. SE3 . . . . 9F 78
Kidbrooke Pk. Rd. SE3 . . . . . 9F 78
Kidbrooke Way. SE3 . . . . 1F 94
Kidderminster Pl. Croy . . . 3M 123
Kidderminster Rd. Croy . . . 3M 123
Kidderpore Av. NW3 . . . . 9L 41
Kidderpore Gdns. NW3 . . . . 9L 41
Kidd Pl. SE7 . . . . 6J 79
Kidlington Way. NW9 . . . . . . 9B 24
Kidman Clo. Romf 1G 51
Kielder Clo. Ilf 6D 32
Kierbeck Bus. Complex.
E16 . . . . 3F 78
Kiffen St. EC2 . . . . 7B 60
Kilberry Clo. Iswth 9B 70
Kilbrennan Ho. E14 . . . . 9A 62
(off Findhorn St.)
Kilburn. 5K 57
Kilburn Bri. NW6 . . . . 4L 57
Kilburn Ga. NW6 . . . . 5M 57
Kilburn High Rd. NW6 . . . . . 3K 57
Kilburn Ho. NW6 . . . . 5K 57
(off Malvern Pl.)
Kilburn La. W10 & W9 . . . . . 6H 57
Kilburn Pk. Rd. NW6 . . . . . . 6L 57
Kilburn Pl. NW6 . . . . 4L 57
Kilburn Priory. NW6 . . . . 4M 57
Kilburns Mill Clo. Wall 4F 122
Kilburn Sq. NW6 . . . . 4L 57
Kilburn Va. NW6 . . . . 4M 57
Kilburn Va. Est. NW6 . . . . . . 4M 57
(off Kilburn Va.)
Kilby Clo. Wat 8H 5
Kilcorral Clo. Eps 6E 134
Kildare Clo. Ruis 6G 37
Kildare Gdns. W2 . . . . 9L 57
Kildare Rd. E16 . . . . 8E 62
Kildare Ter. W2 . . . . 9L 57
Kildare Wlk. E14 . . . . 9L 61
Kildonan Clo. Wat 3D 8
Kildoran Rd. SW2 . . . . 4J 91
Kildowan Rd. Ilf 6E 48
Kilgour Rd. SE23 . . . . 5J 93
Kilkie St. SW6 . . . . 1A 90
Killarney Rd. SW18 . . . . 5A 90
Killearn Rd. SE6 . . . . 7B 94
Killester Gdns. Wor Pk 6F 120
Killewarren Way. Orp 1G 129
Killick Ho. Sutt 6M 121
Killick St. N1 . . . . 5K 59
Killieser Av. SW2 . . . . 8J 91
Killigarth Ct. Sidc 1E 112
Killip Clo. E16 . . . . 9D 62
Killoran Ho. E14 . . . . 4A 78
(off Galbraith St.)
(in two parts)
Killowen Av. N'holt 1A 54
Killowen Rd. E9 . . . . 2H 61
Killyon Rd. SW8 . . . . 1G 91
Killyon Ter. SW8 . . . . 1G 91
Kilmaine Rd. SW6 . . . . 8J 73
Kilmarnock Gdns. Dag 8G 49
Kilmarnock Rd. Wat 4H 21
Kilmarsh Rd. W6 . . . . 5G 73
Kilmartin Av. SW16 . . . . . . 7L 107
Kilmartin Rd. Ilf 7E 48
Kilmartin Way. Horn 1F 66
Kilmington Rd. SW13 . . . . . . 7E 72
Kilmiston Av. Shep 1A 116
Kilmore Ho. E14 . . . . 9M 61
(off Vesey Path)
Kilmorey Gdns. Twic 4F 86
Kilmorey Rd. Twic 3F 86
Kilmorie Rd. SE23 . . . . 7J 93
Kilmuir Ho. SW1 . . . . 5E 74
(off Bury St.)
Kiln Clo. Hay 7B 68
Kiln Ct. E14 . . . . 1K 77
(off Newell St.)
Kilner Ho. E16 . . . . 8F 62
(off Freemasons Rd.)
Kilner Ho. SE11 . . . . 7L 75
(off Clayton St.)
Kilner St. E14 . . . . 8L 61
Kilnfields. Orp 8L 129
Kiln La. Eps 3C 134
Kiln M. SW17 . . . . 2B 106
Kiln Pl. NW5 . . . . 1E 58
Kilnside. Clay 9E 118
Kiln Way. N'wd 6C 20
Kiln Wood La. Romf 5B 34
Kilpatrick Way. Hay 8J 53
Kilravock St. W10 . . . . 6J 57
Kilronan. W3 . . . . 9B 56
Kilross Rd. Felt 7B 84
Kilrue La. W on T 6D 116
Kilsby Wlk. Dag 2F 64
Kilsha Rd. W on T 1G 117
Kilsmore La. Chesh 1D 6
Kilvinton Dri. Enf 2B 16
Kimbell Gdns. SW6 . . . . 9J 73
Kimbell Pl. SE3 . . . . 3G 95
Kimberley Av. E6 . . . . 5J 63
Kimberley Av. SE15 . . . . 1F 92
Kimberley Av. Ilf 5B 48
Kimberley Av. Romf 4A 50
Kimberley Dri. Sidc 8H 97
Kimberley Gdns. N4 . . . . 3M 43
Kimberley Gdns. Enf 5D 16
Kimberley Ga. Brom 4C 110
Kimberley Ho. E14 . . . . 4A 78
(off Galbraith St.)
Kimberley Ind. Est. E17 . . . . 8K 29
Kimberley Pl. Purl 3L 137
Kimberley Rd. E4 . . . . 1C 30
Kimberley Rd. E11 . . . . 7B 46
Kimberley Rd. E16 . . . . 7D 62
Kimberley Rd. E17 . . . . 8J 29
Kimberley Rd. N17 . . . . 9E 28
Kimberley Rd. N18 . . . . 6F 28
Kimberley Rd. NW6 . . . . 4J 57
Kimberley Rd. SW9 . . . . 1J 91
Kimberley Rd. Beck 6H 109
Kimberley Rd. Croy 1M 123
Kimberley Wlk. W on T 2F 116
Kimberley Way. E4 . . . . 1C 30
Kimber Rd. SW18 . . . . 6L 89
Kimble Clo. Wat 9C 8
Kimble Cres. Bush 9A 10
Kimble Ho. NW8 . . . . 7C 58
(off Lilestone St.)
Kimble Rd. SW19 . . . . 3B 106
Kimbolton Clo. SE12 . . . . . . 5D 94
Kimbolton Ct. SW3 . . . . 5C 74
(off Fulham Rd.)
Kimbolton Grn. Borwd 6A 12
Kimbolton Row. SW3 . . . . . . 5C 74
(off Fulham Rd.)
Kimmeridge Gdns. SE9 . . . 1J 111
Kimmeridge Rd. SE9 . . . . . 1J 111
Kimpton Ind. Est. Sutt 4K 121
Kimpton Pl. Wat 7H 5
Kimpton Rd. SE5 . . . . 9B 76
Kimpton Rd. Sutt 4K 121
Kinburn St. SE16 . . . . 3H 77
Kincaid Rd. SE15 . . . . 8F 76
Kincardine Gdns. W9 . . . . . . 7L 57
(off Harrow Rd.)
Kincha Lodge. King T 5K 103
(off Elm Rd.)
Kinch Gro. Wemb 5K 39
Kinder Clo. SE28 . . . . 1H 81
Kinder Ho. N1 . . . . 5B 60
(off Cranston Est.)
Kindersley Ho. E1 . . . . 9E 60
(off Pinchin St.)
Kindersley Way. Ab L 4A 4
Kinder St. E1 . . . . 9F 60
Kinefold Ho. N7 . . . . 2J 59
Kinetic Bus. Cen. Borwd 5L 11
Kinetic Cres. Enf 9F 6
Kinfauns Av. Horn 4G 51
Kinfauns Rd. SW2 . . . . 8L 91
Kinfauns Rd. Ilf 6E 48
Kingaby Gdns. Rain 3E 66
King Alfred Av. SE6 . . . . . . 1L 109
King Alfred Rd. Romf 9K 35
King & Queen Clo. SE9 . . . . 1J 111
King & Queen St. SE17 . . . . . 6A 76
King & Queen Wharf.
SE16 . . . . 1H 77
King Arthur Clo. SE15 . . . . . 8G 77
King Arthur Ct. Chesh 4E 6
King Charles Ct. SE17 . . . . . 7M 75
(off Royal Rd.)
King Charles Cres. Surb . . . 2K 119
King Charles Ho. SW6 . . . . . 8M 73
(off Wandon Rd.)
King Charles Rd. Surb 9K 103
King Charles's Ct. SE10 . . . . 7A 78
(off Park Row)
King Charles St. SW1 . . . . . 3H 75
King Charles Ter. E1 . . . . 1F 76
(off Sovereign Clo.)
King Charles Wlk. SW19 . . . . 7J 89
King Ct. E10 . . . . 5M 45
Kingcup Clo. Croy 2H 125
King David La. E1 . . . . 1G 77
Kingdom Way. Uxb 8B 142
Kingdon Ho. E14 . . . . 4A 78
(off Galbraith St.)
Kingdon Rd. NW6 . . . . 2L 57
King Edward Av. Dart 5H 99
King Edward Av. Rain 5H 67
King Edward Building.
EC1 . . . . 9M 59
King Edward Dri. Chess 5J 119
King Edward Mans. E8 . . . . . 4F 60
(off Mare St.)
King Edward M. SW13 . . . . . 9E 72
King Edward Rd. E10 . . . . . . 6A 46
King Edward Rd. E17 . . . . . . 1J 45
King Edward Rd. Barn 6L 13
King Edward Rd. Romf 4D 50
King Edward Rd. Wal X 6E 6
King Edward Rd. Wat 8J 9
King Edward's Gdns. W3 . . . . 2L 71
King Edwards Gro. Tedd . . . 3F 102
King Edwards Mans. SW6 . . . 8L 73
(off Fulham Rd.)
King Edward's Pl. W3 . . . . . . 2L 71
King Edward's Rd.
E8 & E9 . . . . 4F 60
King Edward's Rd. N9 . . . . . . 9F 16
King Edwards Rd. Bark 4B 64
King Edward's Rd. Enf 6H 17
King Edward's Rd. Ruis 6B 36
King Edward St. EC1 . . . . . . 9A 60
King Edward III M. SE16 . . . . 3F 76
King Edward Wlk. SE1 . . . . . 4L 75
Kingfield Rd. W5 . . . . 7H 55
Kingfield St. E14 . . . . 5A 78
Kingfisher Av. E11 . . . . 4F 46
Kingfisher Clo. SE28 . . . . . . 1G 81
Kingfisher Clo. Har W 7D 22
Kingfisher Clo. Orp 8H 113
Kingfisher Clo. W on T 7J 117
Kingfisher Ct. E14 . . . . 3A 78
(off River Barge Clo.)
Kingfisher Ct. SW19 . . . . 8H 89
Kingfisher Ct. Enf 2K 15
Kingfisher Ct. Houn 4M 85
Kingfisher Dri. Rich 1F 102
Kingfisher Gdns. S Croy . . . 3H 139
Kingfisher M. SE13 . . . . 3L 93
Kingfisher Pl. N22 . . . . 9K 27
Kingfisher Pl. S Dar 6M 115
Kingfisher Sq. SE8 . . . . 7K 77
(off Clyde St.)
Kingfisher St. E6 . . . . 8J 63
Kingfisher Wlk. NW9 . . . . 9C 24
Kingfisher Way. NW10 . . . . . 2B 56
Kingfisher Way. Beck 9H 109
King Frederick IX Tower.
SE16 . . . . 4K 77
King Gdns. Croy 7M 123
King George Av. E16 . . . . . . 9G 63
King George Av. Bush 8M 9
King George Av. Ilf 3B 48
King George Av. W on T . . . 3H 117
King George Clo. Romf 1A 50
King George Clo. Sun 2C 100
King George Rd. Wal A 7J 7
King George's Av. Wat 7C 8
King George's Dri. S'hall . . . 8K 53
King George VI Av.
Big H 8H 141
King George VI Av. Mitc . . 8D 106
King George VI Memorial. 2H 75
King George Sq. Rich 5K 87
King George's Trad. Est.
Chess 6L 119
King George St. SE10 . . . . . . 8A 78
Kingham Clo. SW18 . . . . 6A 90
Kingham Clo. W11 . . . . 3J 73
(off Holland Pk. Av.)
King Harold Ct. Wal A 6J 7
(off Sun St.)
King Harolds Way.
Bexh & Belv 8H 81
King Henry M. Orp 7D 128
King Henry's Dri.
New Ad 1M 139
King Henry's M. Enf 1L 17
(off Mollison Av.)
King Henry's Reach. W6 . . . . 7G 73
King Henry's Rd. NW3 . . . . . 3C 58
King Henry's Rd. King T . . . 7M 103
King Henry St. N16 . . . . 1C 60
King Henry's Wlk. N1 . . . . . . 2C 60
King Henry Ter. E1 . . . . 1F 76
(off Sovereign Clo.)
Kinghorn St. EC1 . . . . 8A 60
King Ho. W12 . . . . 9F 56
King James Ct. SE1 . . . . 3M 75
(off King James St.)
King James St. SE1 . . . . 3M 75
King John Ct. EC2 . . . . 7C 60
King John St. E1 . . . . 8H 61
King John's Wlk. SE9 . . . . . . 6J 95
(Middle Pk. Av., in two parts)
King John's Wlk. SE9 . . . . . . 7H 95
(Mottingham La.)
Kinglake Est. SE17 . . . . 6C 76
Kinglake St. SE17 . . . . 6C 76
(in two parts)
Kingly Ct. W1 . . . . 1G 75
(off Beak St.)
Kingly St. W1 . . . . 9G 59
Kingsand Rd. SE12 . . . . 8E 94
Kings Arbour. S'hall 6J 69
King's Arms All. Bren 7H 71
Kings Arms Ct. E1 . . . . 8E 60
Kings Arms Yd. EC2 . . . . 9B 60
Kings Arms Yd. Romf 3C 50
Kingsash Dri. Hay 7J 53
King's Av. N10 . . . . 1E 42
Kings Av. N21 . . . . 1M 27
Kings Av. SW12 & SW4 . . . . . 7H 91
Kings Av. W5 . . . . 9H 55
Kings Av. Brom 3D 110
King's Av. Buck H 2H 31
King's Av. Cars 9C 122
King's Av. Gnfd 8M 53
King's Av. Houn 9M 69
Kings Av. N Mald 8C 104
Kings Av. Romf 4K 49
King's Av. Sun 2D 100
King's Av. Wat 6D 8
King's Av. Wfd G 6F 30
King's Bench St. SE1 . . . . . . 3M 75
King's Bench Wlk. EC4 . . . . . 9L 59
Kingsbridge Av. W5 . . . . 3K 71
Kingsbridge Cir. Romf 6J 35
Kingsbridge Clo. Romf 6J 35
Kingsbridge Ct. E14 . . . . 4L 77
(off Dockers Tanner Rd.)
Kingsbridge Ct. NW1 . . . . 3F 58
(off Castlehaven Rd.)
Kingsbridge Cres. S'hall 8K 53
Kingsbridge Rd. W10 . . . . . . 9G 57
Kingsbridge Rd. Bark 5B 64
Kingsbridge Rd. Mord 1H 121
Kingsbridge Rd. Romf 6J 35
Kingsbridge Rd. S'hall 5K 69
Kingsbridge Rd. W on T . . . 2F 116
Kingsbridge Way. Hay 6C 52
Kingsbrook. Lea 9E 132
Kingsbury. 5B 40
Kingsbury Circ. NW9 . . . . . . 3L 39
Kingsbury Green. 3A 40
Kingsbury Rd. N1 . . . . 2C 60
Kingsbury Rd. NW9 . . . . 3L 39
Kingsbury Ter. N1 . . . . 2C 60
Kingsbury Trad. Est. NW9 . . . 4B 40
Kings Chase. E Mol 7A 102
Kings Chase Vw. Ridg 4L 15
Kingsclere Clo. SW15 . . . . . . 6E 88
Kingsclere Ct. N12 . . . . 5C 26
Kingsclere Pl. Enf 4A 16
Kingscliffe Gdns. SW19 . . . . 7K 89
Kings Clo. E10 . . . . 5M 45
King's Clo. NW4 . . . . 2H 41
King's Clo. Dart 3C 98
Kings Clo. N'wd 6D 20
Kings Clo. Th Dit 1E 118
Kings Clo. W on T 3F 116
King's Clo. Wat 6F 8
Kings College Ct. NW3 . . . . . 3C 58
King's College London. 2L 75
(Waterloo Campus)
King's College London. 1K 75
(Strand Campus)
King's College London. 6B 74
(Chelsea Campus)
King's College London Dental Institute. 1B 92
King's College Rd. NW3 . . . . 3C 58
Kings College Rd. Ruis 4D 36
King's College School of Medicine & Dentistry. 1A 92
Kingscote Rd. W4 . . . . 4B 72
Kingscote Rd. Croy 2F 124
Kingscote Rd. N Mald 7B 104
Kingscote St. EC4 . . . . 1M 75
King's Ct. E13 . . . . 4F 62
Kings Ct. N7 . . . . 3K 59
(off Caledonian Rd.)
Kings Ct. NW8 . . . . 4D 58
(off Prince Albert Rd.)
King's Ct. SE1 . . . . 3M 75
Kings Ct. W6 . . . . 5E 72
Kings Ct. Buck H 2H 31
Kings Ct. N. SW3 . . . . 6C 74
Kingscourt Rd. SW16 . . . . . . 9H 91
Kings Ct. S. SW3 . . . . 6C 74
(off King's Rd.)
King's Cres. N4 . . . . 8A 44
Kings Cres. Est. N4 . . . . 7A 44
Kingscroft. SW4 . . . . 5J 91
Kingscroft Rd. NW2 . . . . 2K 57
Kingscroft Rd. Bans 7B 136
Kings Cross. 5J 59
King's Cross (Junct.) 5J 59
King's Cross Bri. N1 . . . . 6J 59
(off Gray's Inn Rd.)
King's Cross Rd. WC1 . . . . . . 6K 59
Kingsdale Gdns. W11 . . . . . . 2H 73
Kingsdale Rd. SE18 . . . . 8D 80
Kingsdale Rd. SE20 . . . . . . 4H 109
Kingsdown Av. W3 . . . . 1C 72
Kingsdown Av. W13 . . . . 3F 70
Kingsdown Av. S Croy 2M 137
Kingsdown Clo. SE16 . . . . . . 6F 76
(off Masters Dri.)
Kingsdown Clo. W10 . . . . 9H 57
Kingsdowne Rd. Surb 2J 119
Kingsdown Ho. E8 . . . . 1E 60
Kingsdown Rd. E11 . . . . 8C 46
Kingsdown Rd. N19 . . . . 7J 43
Kingsdown Rd. Eps 5E 134
Kingsdown Rd. Sutt 7J 121
Kingsdown Way. Brom 2E 126
King's Dri. Edgw 4K 23
Kings Dri. Surb 2L 119
Kings Dri. Tedd 2B 102
Kings Dri. Th Dit 2F 118
Kings Dri. W on T 9D 116
Kings Dri. Wemb 7M 39
Kingsend. Ruis 6B 36
Kingsend Ct. Ruis 6C 36
Kings Farm. E17 . . . . 8M 29
Kings Farm Av. Rich 3L 87
Kingsfield Av. Harr 2M 37
Kingsfield Ct. Wat 9H 9
Kingsfield Dri. Enf 8D 6
Kingsfield Ho. SE9 . . . . 9H 95
Kingsfield Rd. Harr 5B 38
Kingsfield Rd. Wat 9H 9
Kingsfield Ter. Dart 4H 99
Kingsfield Ter. Harr 6B 38
Kingsfield Way. Enf 8D 6
Kingsford St. NW5 . . . . 1D 58
Kingsford Way. E6 . . . . 8K 63
King's Gdns. NW6 . . . . 3L 57
Kings Gdns. Ilf 6B 48
Kings Gth. M. SE23 . . . . 8G 93
Kingsgate. Wemb 8A 40
Kingsgate Av. N3 . . . . 1L 41
Kingsgate Bus. Cen.
King T 5J 103
(off Kingsgate Rd.)
Kingsgate Clo. Bexh 9J 81
Kingsgate Clo. Orp 6G 113
Kingsgate Est. N1 . . . . 2C 60
Kingsgate Ho. SW9 . . . . 9L 75
Kingsgate Mans. WC1 . . . . . . 8K 59
(off Red Lion Sq.)
Kingsgate Pde. SW1 . . . . 4G 75
(off Victoria St.)
Kingsgate Pl. NW6 . . . . 3L 57

Kingsgate Rd.—Knaresborough Dri.

Kingsgate Rd. NW6 . . . . .3L 57
Kingsgate Rd. King T 5J 103
Kings Grange. Ruis 6D 36
Kings Grn. Lou 5J 19
Kingsground. SE9 . . . . .6H 95
King's Gro. SE15 . . . . .8F 76
(in two parts)
Kings Gro. Romf 3E 50
Kingshall M. SE13 . . . . .2A 94
Kings Hall Rd. Beck 4J 109
Kings Head Hill. E4 . . . . .9M 17
Kings Head Pas. SW4 . . . . . .3H 91
(off Clapham Pk. Rd.)
Kings Head Theatre. 4M 59
(off Upper St.)
King's Head Yd. SE1 . . . . . . .2B 76
King's Highway. SE18 . . . . . .7C 80
Kingshill. SE17 . . . . .5A 76
King's Hill. Lou 4J 19
Kingshill Av. Harr 2F 38
Kingshill Av. Hay & N'holt . . .6C 52
Kingshill Av. Romf 6A 34
Kingshill Av. Wor Pk 2E 120
Kingshill Ct. Barn 6J 13
Kingshill Dri. Harr 9F 22
Kingshold Rd. E9 . . . . .3G 61
Kingsholm Gdns. SE9 . . . . . .3H 95
Kings Ho. SW8 . . . . .8J 75
(off S. Lambeth Rd.)
Kingshurst Rd. SE12 . . . . . . .6E 94
Kings Keep. SW15 . . . . .4H 89
Kings Keep. Brom 7C 110
Kings Keep. King T 8J 103
Kingsland. 3C 60
Kingsland. NW8 . . . . .4C 58
Kingsland Grn. E8 . . . . .2C 60
Kingsland High St. E8 . . . . . .2D 60
Kingsland Pas. E8 . . . . .2C 60
Kingsland Rd. E2 & E8 . . . . .6C 60
Kingsland Rd. E13 . . . . .6G 63
Kingsland Shop. Cen. E8 . . . .2D 60
Kings La. Sutt 8B 122
Kingslawn Clo. SW15 . . . . . . .4F 88
Kingsleigh Pl. Mitc 7D 106
Kingsleigh Wlk. Brom 8D 110
(off Stamford Dri.)
Kingsley Av. W13 . . . . .8E 54
Kingsley Av. Bans 7L 135
Kingsley Av. Borwd 4K 11
Kingsley Av. Chesh 2B 6
Kingsley Av. Dart 4L 99
Kingsley Av. Houn 1A 86
Kingsley Av. S'hall 1L 69
Kingsley Av. Sutt 6B 122
Kingsley Clo. N2 . . . . .3A 42
Kingsley Clo. Dag 9M 49
Kingsley Ct. NW2 . . . . .2F 56
Kingsley Ct. Bexh 4L 97
Kingsley Ct. Edgw 3M 23
Kingsley Ct. Romf 4F 50
Kingsley Ct. Sutt 9M 121
Kingsley Ct. Wor Pk 4D 120
(off Avenue, The)
Kingsley Dri. Wor Pk 4D 120
Kingsley Flats. SE1 . . . . .5C 76
(off Old Kent Rd.)
Kingsley Gdns. E4 . . . . .5L 29
Kingsley Gdns. Horn 2H 51
Kingsley Ho. SW3 . . . . .7B 74
(off Beaufort St.)
Kingsley Mans. W14 . . . . . . .7J 73
(off Greyhound Rd.)
Kingsley M. E1 . . . . .1F 76
Kingsley M. W8 . . . . .4M 73
Kingsley M. Chst 3M 111
Kingsley Pl. N6 . . . . .5E 42
Kingsley Rd. E7 . . . . .3E 62
Kingsley Rd. E17 . . . . .9A 30
Kingsley Rd. N13 . . . . .4L 27
Kingsley Rd. NW6 . . . . .4K 57
Kingsley Rd. SW19 . . . . . . .2M 105
Kingsley Rd. Croy 3L 123
Kingsley Rd. Harr 9A 38
Kingsley Rd. Houn 9M 69
Kingsley Rd. Ilf 8A 32
Kingsley Rd. Orp 9D 128
Kingsley Rd. Pinn 2K 37
Kingsley St. SW11 . . . . .2D 90
Kingsley Way. N2 . . . . .4A 42
Kingsley Wood Dri. SE9 . . . . .9K 95
Kingslyn Cres. SE19 . . . . . .5C 108
Kings Lynn Clo. H Hill 6H 35
Kings Lynn Dri. Romf 6H 35
Kings Lynn Path. H Hill 6H 35
Kings Mall. W6 . . . . .5G 73
Kingsman Pde. SE18 . . . . . . .4K 79
Kingsman St. SE18 . . . . .4K 79
Kingsmead. Barn 6L 13
Kingsmead. Big H 8H 141
Kings Mead. Rich 5K 87
Kingsmead. Wal X 1D 6
Kingsmead Av. N9 . . . . .1F 28
Kingsmead Av. NW9 . . . . . . .5B 40
Kingsmead Av. Mitc 7G 107
Kingsmead Av. Romf 4C 50
Kingsmead Av. Sun 6G 101
Kingsmead Av. Surb 4L 119
Kingsmead Av. Wor Pk 4F 120
Kingsmead Clo. Eps 9B 120
Kingsmead Clo. Sidc 8E 96
Kingsmead Clo. Tedd 3F 102
Kingsmead Cotts. Brom 3J 127
Kingsmead Ct. N6 . . . . .5H 43
Kingsmead Dri. N'holt 3K 53
Kingsmead Ho. E9 . . . . .9J 45
Kingsmead Mans. Romf 4D 50
(off Kingsmead Av.)
Kings Mead Pk. Clay 9C 118
Kingsmead Rd. SW2 . . . . . . .8L 91
King's Mead Way. E9 . . . . . . .9J 45
Kingsmere Clo. SW15 . . . . . .2H 89
Kingsmere Pk. NW9 . . . . . . .6M 39
Kingsmere Pl. N16 . . . . .6B 44
Kingsmere Rd. SW19 . . . . . .8H 89
King's M. SW4 . . . . .4J 91
King's M. WC1 . . . . .7K 59
Kings M. Chig 2A 32
Kingsmill. NW8 . . . . .5B 58
(off Kingsmill Ter.)
Kingsmill Bus. Pk.
King T 7K 103
Kingsmill Gdns. Dag 1K 65
Kingsmill Ho. SW3 . . . . .6C 74
(off Marlborough St.)
Kingsmill Rd. Dag 1K 65
Kingsmill Ter. NW8 . . . . .5B 58
Kingsnorth Ho. W10 . . . . . . .9H 57
Kingsnympton Pk.
King T 4M 103
King's Orchard. SE9 . . . . .5J 95
King's Paddock. Hamp 5A 102
Kings Pde. N17 . . . . .1D 44
Kings Pde. NW10 . . . . .4G 57
Kings Pde. W12 . . . . .4E 72
King's Pde. Cars 5D 122
(off Wrythe La.)
King's Pde. Edgw 5L 23
(off Edgwarebury La.)
Kingspark Ct. E18 . . . . .1E 46
Kings Pas. E11 . . . . .5C 46
King's Pas. King T (KT1) . . .6H 103
King's Pas. King T (KT2) . . .5H 103
King's Pl. SE1 . . . . .3A 76
King's Pl. W4 . . . . .6A 72
Kings Pl. Buck H 2G 31
Kings Pl. Lou 9H 19
King Sq. EC1 . . . . .6A 60
King's Quay. SW10 . . . . .9A 74
(off Chelsea Harbour)
Kings Reach Tower. SE1 . . . . .2L 75
(off Hatfields)
Kings Ride Ga. Rich 3L 87
Kingsridge. SW19 . . . . .8J 89
Kingsridge Gdns. Dart 5H 99
Kings Rd. E4 . . . . .1B 30
King's Rd. E6 . . . . .4G 63
Kings Rd. E11 . . . . .5C 46
King's Rd. N17 . . . . .8D 28
King's Rd. N18 . . . . .5E 28
King's Rd. N22 . . . . .8K 27
King's Rd. NW10 . . . . .3F 56
King's Rd. SE25 . . . . .7E 108
King's Rd.
SW6, SW10 & SW3 . . .8M 73
Kings Rd. SW14 . . . . .2B 88
Kings Rd. SW19 . . . . .3L 105
Kings Rd. W5 . . . . .8H 55
Kings Rd. Bark 3A 64
Kings Rd. Barn 5G 13
Kings Rd. Big H 8G 141
Kings Rd. Felt 7G 85
Kings Rd. Harr 7K 37
King's Rd. King T 5J 103
Kings Rd. Mitc 7E 106
King's Rd. Orp 6D 128
Kings Rd. Rich 5K 87
King's Rd. Romf 3E 50
King's Rd. Surb 3G 119
Kings Rd. Sutt 2L 135
King's Rd. Tedd 2B 102
Kings Rd. Twic 5F 86
King's Rd. Uxb 5B 142
Kings Rd. Wal X 6E 6
Kings Rd. W on T 4F 116
Kings Rd. W Dray 3K 143
Kings Rd. Bungalows.
S Harr 9K 37
King's Scholars' Pas.
SW1 . . . . .4G 75
(off Carlisle Pl.)
King's Shade Wlk. Eps 5B 134
King Stairs Clo. SE16 . . . . . . .3F 76
King's Ter. NW1 . . . . .4G 59
King's Ter. Iswth 3E 86
Kingsthorpe Rd. SE26 . . . . .1H 109
Kingston Av. Felt 5C 84
Kingston Av. Sutt 5J 121
Kingston Av. W Dray 1K 143
(in three parts)
Kingston Bri. King T 6H 103
Kingston Bus. Cen.
Chess 5J 119
Kingston By-Pass.
SW15 & SW20 . . . . . .1C 104
Kingston By-Pass.
N Mald 9C 104
Kingston By-Pass. Surb 5H 119
Kingston By-Pass Rd.
Esh & Surb 4C 118
Kingston Clo. N'holt 4K 53
Kingston Clo. Romf 1J 49
(in two parts)
Kingston Clo. Tedd 3F 102
Kingston Cres. Beck 5K 109
Kingston Gdns. Croy 5J 123
Kingston Hall Rd. King T . . .7H 103
Kingston Hill. King T 5L 103
Kingston Hill Av. Romf 1J 49
Kingston Hill Pl. King T 1A 104
Kingston Ho. NW6 . . . . .3J 57
Kingston Ho. King T 8H 103
(off Surbiton Rd.)
Kingston Ho. E. SW7 . . . . . . .3C 74
(off Prince's Ga.)
Kingston Ho. Est. Surb 1F 118
Kingston Ho. N. SW7 . . . . . . .3C 74
(off Prince's Ga.)
Kingston Ho. S. SW7 . . . . . . .3C 74
(off Ennismore Gdns.)
Kingstonian F.C. 7M 103
Kingston La. Tedd 2E 102
Kingston La. Uxb 6C 142
Kingston La. W Dray 3K 143
Kingston Pl. Harr 7D 22
Kingston Rd. N9 . . . . .2E 28
Kingston Rd.
SW15 & SW19 . . . . . . .8E 88
Kingston Rd.
SW20 & SW19 . . . . . .6H 105
Kingston Rd. Barn 7B 14
Kingston Rd. Eps 1D 134
Kingston Rd. Ilf 9M 47
Kingston Rd.
King T & N Mald 7M 103
Kingston Rd. Lea 9E 132
(in two parts)
Kingston Rd. Romf 2D 50
Kingston Rd. S'hall 3K 69
Kingston Rd. Surb & Eps . .4M 119
Kingston Rd. Tedd 2F 102
Kingston Sq. SE19 . . . . .2B 108
Kingston University. 7J 103
(Grange Rd.)
Kingston University. 2B 104
(Kingston Hill)
Kingston University. 8J 103
(Penrhyn Rd.)
Kingston upon Thames.
. . . . .6H 103
Kingston upon Thames
Crematorium. King T
. . . . .7L 103
Kingston upon Thames Library,
Art Gallery & Mus. . . .6J 103
Kingston Vale. 1C 104
Kingston Va. SW15 . . . . . . .1B 104
Kingstown St. NW1 . . . . .4E 58
(in two parts)
King St. E13 . . . . .7E 62
King St. EC2 . . . . .9A 60
King St. N2 . . . . .1B 42
King St. N17 . . . . .8D 28
King St. SW1 . . . . .2G 75
King St. W3 . . . . .2A 72
King St. W6 . . . . .5E 72
King St. WC2 . . . . .1J 75
King St. Rich 4H 87
King St. S'hall 4J 69
King St. Twic 7E 86
King St. Wat 6G 9
King St. Cloisters. W6 . . . . . .5F 72
(off King St.)
King St. Pde. Twic 7E 86
(off King St.)
Kingsville Ct. W Dray 1H 143
Kings Wlk. S Croy 6F 138
Kings Wlk. Shop. Cen.
SW3 . . . . .6D 74
Kings Warren. Oxs 3A 132
Kingswater Pl. SW11 . . . . . . .8C 74
Kingsway. N12 . . . . .6A 26
Kingsway. SW14 . . . . .2M 87
Kingsway. WC2 . . . . .9K 59
King's Way. Croy 7K 123
Kingsway. Enf 7F 16
Kings Way. Harr 2C 38
Kingsway. Hay 8A 52
Kingsway. N Mald 8G 105
Kingsway. Orp 9B 112
Kingsway. Stai 7B 144
Kingsway. Wemb 9J 39
Kingsway. W Wick 5C 126
Kings Way. Wfd G 5J 31
Kingsway Av. S Croy 1G 139
Kingsway Bus. Pk.
Hamp 5K 101
Kingsway Cres. Harr 2A 38
Kingsway Est. N18 . . . . .6H 29
Kingsway Mans. WC1 . . . . . .8K 59
(off Red Lion Sq.)
Kingsway N. Orbital Rd.
Wat 8D 4
Kingsway Pl. EC1 . . . . .7L 59
(off Corporation Row)
Kingsway Rd. Sutt 9J 121
Kingsway, The. Eps 3C 134
Kingswear Rd. NW5 . . . . .8F 42
Kingswear Rd. Ruis 7E 36
Kingswood. 7F 4
Kingswood. E2 . . . . .5G 61
(off Cyprus St.)
Kingswood Av. NW6 . . . . .4J 57
Kingswood Av. Belv 5K 81
Kingswood Av. Brom 7C 110
Kingswood Av. Hamp 3M 101
Kingswood Av. Houn 9K 69
Kingswood Av. S Croy 7F 138
Kingswood Av. Swan 8D 114
Kingswood Av. T Hth 9L 107
Kingswood Clo. N20 . . . . .9A 14
Kingswood Clo. SW8 . . . . . . .8J 75
Kingswood Clo. Dart 5G 99
Kingswood Clo. Enf 7C 16
Kingswood Clo. N Mald 1D 120
Kingswood Clo. Orp 2C 128
Kingswood Clo. Surb 2J 119
Kingswood Ct. E4 . . . . .5L 29
Kingswood Ct. NW6 . . . . .3L 57
(off W. End La.)
Kingswood Dri. SE19 . . . . . .1C 108
Kingswood Dri. Cars 3D 122
Kingswood Dri. Sutt 1M 135
Kingswood Est. SE21 . . . . . .1C 108
Kingswood La. Warl 7G 139
(in two parts)
Kingswood Pk. N3 . . . . .8K 25
Kingswood Pl. SE13 . . . . .3C 94
Kingswood Rd. E11 . . . . .5C 46
Kingswood Rd. SE20 . . . . . .3G 109
Kingswood Rd. SW2 . . . . .5J 91
Kingswood Rd. SW19 . . . . . .4K 105
Kingswood Rd. W4 . . . . .4A 72
Kingswood Rd. Brom 8B 110
Kingswood Rd. Ilf 6E 48
Kingswood Rd. Wat 7F 4
Kingswood Rd. Wemb 8L 39
Kingswood Ter. W4 . . . . .4A 72
Kingswood Way. S Croy . . .5G 139
(in two parts)
Kingswood Way. Wall 7J 123
Kingsworth Clo. Beck 9J 109
Kingsworthy Clo.
King T 7K 103
Kings Yd. E9 . . . . .2L 61
Kings Yd. SW15 . . . . .2G 89
(off Lwr. Richmond Rd.)
Kingthorpe Rd. NW10 . . . . . .3B 56
Kingthorpe Ter. NW10 . . . . . .2B 56
Kington Ho. NW6 . . . . .4M 57
(off Mortimer Cres.)
Kingward Ho. E1 . . . . .8E 60
(off Hanbury St.)
Kingwell Rd. Barn 2B 14
Kingweston Clo. NW2 . . . . . .8J 41
King William IV Gdns.
SE20 . . . . .3G 109
King William La. SE10 . . . . . .6C 78
King William's Ct. SE10 . . . . .7B 78
(off Park Row)
King William St. EC4 . . . . . . .9B 60
King William Wlk. SE10 . . . . .7A 78
(in two parts)
Kingwood Rd. SW6 . . . . .9J 73
Kinlet Rd. SE18 . . . . .9A 80
Kinloch Dri. NW9 . . . . .5B 40
Kinloch St. N7 . . . . .8K 43
Kinloss Ct. N3 . . . . .2K 41
Kinloss Gdns. N3 . . . . .1K 41
Kinloss Rd. Cars 2A 122
Kinnaird Av. W4 . . . . .8A 72
Kinnaird Av. Brom 3D 110
Kinnaird Clo. Brom 3D 110
Kinnaird Way. Wfd G 6K 31
Kinnear Rd. W12 . . . . .3D 72
Kinnerton Pl. N. SW1 . . . . . . .3D 74
(off Kinnerton St.)
Kinnerton Pl. S. SW1 . . . . . . .3D 74
(off Kinnerton St.)
Kinnerton St. SW1 . . . . .3E 74
Kinnerton Yd. SW1 . . . . .3E 74
(off Kinnerton St.)
Kinnoul Rd. W6 . . . . .7J 73
Kinross Av. Wor Pk 4E 120
Kinross Clo. Edgw 2M 23
Kinross Clo. Harr 3K 39
Kinross Clo. Sun 2D 100
Kinross Ct. SE6 . . . . .7D 94
Kinross Ct. Brom 5D 110
(off Highland Rd.)
Kinross Dri. Sun 2D 100
Kinross Ter. E17 . . . . .9K 29
Kinsale Rd. SE15 . . . . .2E 92
Kinsella Gdns. SW19 . . . . . .2F 104
Kinsham Ho. E2 . . . . .7E 60
(off Ramsey St.)
Kintore Way. SE1 . . . . .5D 76
Kintyre Clo. SW16 . . . . .6K 107
Kintyre Ct. SW2 . . . . .6J 91
Kintyre Ho. E14 . . . . .2A 78
(off Coldharbour)
Kinveachy Gdns. SE7 . . . . . . .6J 79
Kinver Rd. SE26 . . . . .1G 109
Kipling Ct. W7 . . . . .1D 70
Kipling Dri. SW19 . . . . .3B 106
Kipling Est. SE1 . . . . .3B 76
Kipling Ho. E16 . . . . .2F 78
(off Southampton M.)
Kipling Ho. SE5 . . . . .8B 76
(off Elmington Est.)
Kipling Pl. Stan 6D 22
Kipling Rd. Bexh 9J 81
Kipling Rd. Dart 4M 99
Kipling St. SE1 . . . . .3B 76
Kipling Ter. N13 . . . . .3B 28
Kipling Tower. W3 . . . . .4A 72
(off Palmerston Rd.)
Kippington Dri. SE9 . . . . .7H 95
Kirby Clo. Eps 7D 120
Kirby Clo. Ilf 6C 32
Kirby Clo. Lou 9J 19
Kirby Clo. N'wd 6D 20
Kirby Clo. Romf 5L 35
Kirby Est. SE16 . . . . .4F 76
Kirby Est. W Dray 1H 143
Kirby Gro. SE1 . . . . .3C 76
Kirby St. EC1 . . . . .8L 59
Kirby Way. Uxb 7D 142
Kirby Way. W on T 1G 117
Kirchen Rd. W13 . . . . .1F 70
Kirkby Clo. N11 . . . . .6E 26
Kirkcaldy Grn. Wat 3G 21
Kirkdale. SE26 . . . . .8F 92
Kirkdale Corner. SE26 . . . . .1G 109
Kirkdale Rd. E11 . . . . .6C 46
Kirkeby Ho. EC1 . . . . .8L 59
(off Leather La.)
Kirkfield Clo. W13 . . . . .2F 70
Kirkgate, The. Eps 5C 134
Kirkham Ho. Romf 5H 35
(off Montgomery Cres.)
Kirkham Rd. E6 . . . . .9J 63
Kirkham St. SE18 . . . . .7C 80
Kirkland Av. Ilf 9L 31
Kirkland Clo. Sidc 5C 96
Kirkland Dri. Enf 3A 16
Kirkland Ho. E14 . . . . .6M 77
(off Westferry Rd.)
Kirkland Ho. E14 . . . . .6M 77
(off St Davids Sq.)
Kirkland Wlk. E8 . . . . .2D 60
Kirk La. SE18 . . . . .7A 80
Kirkleas Rd. Surb 3J 119
Kirklees Rd. Dag 1G 65
Kirklees Rd. T Hth 9L 107
Kirkley Rd. SW19 . . . . .5L 105
Kirkly Clo. S Croy 1C 138
Kirkman Pl. W1 . . . . .8H 59
(off Tottenham Ct. Rd.)
Kirkmichael Rd. E14 . . . . . . .9A 62
Kirk Ri. Sutt 5M 121
Kirk Rd. E17 . . . . .4K 45
Kirkside Rd. SE3 . . . . .7E 78
Kirkstall Av. N17 . . . . .2B 44
Kirkstall Gdns. SW2 . . . . .7J 91
Kirkstall Rd. SW2 . . . . .7H 91
Kirksted Rd. Mord 3M 121
Kirkstone. NW1 . . . . .6G 59
(off Harrington St.)
Kirkstone Way. Brom 4C 110
Kirk St. WC1 . . . . .7K 59
(off Northington St.)
Kirkton Rd. N15 . . . . .2C 44
Kirkwall Pl. E2 . . . . .6G 61
Kirkwood Pl. NW1 . . . . .3E 58
Kirkwood Rd. SE15 . . . . .1F 92
Kirn Rd. W13 . . . . .1F 70
Kirrane Clo. N Mald 9D 104
Kirtley Ho. SW8 . . . . .9G 75
Kirtley Rd. SE26 . . . . .1J 109
Kirtling St. SW8 . . . . .8G 75
Kirton Clo. W4 . . . . .5B 72
Kirton Clo. Horn 2G 67
Kirton Gdns. E2 . . . . .6D 60
(in two parts)
Kirton Lodge. SW18 . . . . . . .5M 89
Kirton Rd. E13 . . . . .5G 63
Kirton Wlk. Edgw 7A 24
Kirwyn Way. SE5 . . . . .8M 75
Kitcat Ter. E3 . . . . .6L 61
Kitchener Rd. E7 . . . . .2F 62
Kitchener Rd. E17 . . . . .8M 29
Kitchener Rd. N2 . . . . .1C 42
Kitchener Rd. N17 . . . . .1C 44
Kitchener Rd. Dag 2M 65
Kitchener Rd. T Hth 7B 108
Kite Pl. E2 . . . . .6E 60
(off Lampern Sq.)
Kite Yd. SW11 . . . . .9D 74
(off Cambridge Rd.)
Kitley Gdns. SE19 . . . . .5D 108
Kitson Rd. SE5 . . . . .8B 76
Kitson Rd. SW13 . . . . .9E 72
Kitters Grn. Ab L 4C 4
Kittiwake Clo. S Croy 2J 139
Kittiwake Ct. SE8 . . . . .7K 77
(off Abinger Gro.)
Kittiwake Pl. Sutt 7K 121
Kittiwake Rd. N'holt 6H 53
Kittiwake Way. Hay 8H 53
Kitto Rd. SE14 . . . . .1H 93
Kitt's End. 1J 13
Kitts End Rd. Barn 1J 13
Kiver Rd. N19 . . . . .7H 43
Klea Av. SW4 . . . . .5G 91
Klein's Wharf. E14 . . . . .4L 77
(off Westferry Rd.)
Knapdale Clo. SE23 . . . . .8F 92
Knapmill Rd. SE6 . . . . .8L 93
Knapmill Way. SE6 . . . . .8M 93
Knapp Clo. NW10 . . . . .2C 56
Knapp Rd. E3 . . . . .7L 61
Knapp Rd. Ashf 9D 144
Knapton M. SW17 . . . . .3E 106
Knaresborough Dri.
SW18 . . . . .7M 89

Knaresborough Pl.—Lampton Ct.

Knaresborough Pl. SW5 5M 73
Knatchbull Rd. NW10 4B 56
Knatchbull Rd. SE5 1M 91
Knebworth Av. E17 8L 29
Knebworth Ho. SW8 1H 91
Knebworth Path. Borwd 6B 12
Knebworth Rd. N16 9C 44
Knee Hill. SE2 5G 81
Kneehill Cres. SE2 5G 81
Kneller Gdns. Iswth 5B 86
Kneller Ho. N'holt 5H 53
(off Academy Gdns.)
Kneller Rd. SE4 3J 93
Kneller Rd. N Mald 2C 120
Kneller Rd. Twic 5A 86
Knight Clo. Dag 7G 49
Knight Ct. E4 1A 30
(off Ridgeway, The)
Knight Ct. N15 3C 44
Knighten St. E1 2F 76
Knighthead Point. E14 3L 77
Knight Ho. SE17 5C 76
(off Tatum St.)
Knightland Rd. E5 7F 44
Knightleas Ct. NW2 2G 57
Knighton Clo. Romf 4B 50
Knighton Clo. S Croy 1M 137
Knighton Clo. Wfd G 4F 30
Knighton Dri. Wfd G 4F 30
Knighton Grn. Buck H 2F 30
Knighton La. Buck H 2F 30
Knighton Pk. Rd. SE26 2H 109
Knighton Rd. E7 8E 46
Knighton Rd. Romf 4A 50
Knightrider Ct. EC4 1A 76
(off Knightrider St.)
Knightrider St. EC4 9M 59
Knights Arc. SW1 3D 74
(off Knightsbridge)
Knights Av. W5 3J 71
Knightsbridge. 3C 74
Knightsbridge. SW7 & SW1 3D 74
Knightsbridge Ct. SW7 & SW1 3D 74
(off Sloane St.)
Knightsbridge Gdns. Romf 3B 50
Knightsbridge Grn. SW1 3D 74
(in two parts)
Knights Clo. E9 1G 61
Knights Ct. Brom 9D 94
Knights Ct. King T 7J 103
Knights Hill. SE27 2M 107
Knight's Hill Sq. SE27 1M 107
Knights Ho. SW8 8J 75
(off S. Lambeth Rd.)
Knights La. N9 3E 28
Knights Mnr. Way. Dart 4K 99
Knight's Pk. King T 7J 103
Knight's Pl. Twic 7C 86
Knights Ridge. Orp 7F 128
Knight's Rd. E16 3E 78
Knights Rd. Stan 4G 23
Knight's Wlk. SE11 5M 75
(in two parts)
Knights Way. Ilf 6A 32
Knightswood Clo. Edgw 2A 24
Knightswood Ct. N6 5H 43
Knightswood Ho. N12 6A 26
Knightswood Rd. Rain 5E 66
Knightwood Cres. N Mald 1C 120
Knivet Rd. SW6 7L 73
Knobs Hill Rd. E15 4M 61
Knockholt Clo. Sutt 2M 135
Knockholt Rd. SE9 4H 95
Knole Clo. Croy 1G 125
Knole Ct. N'holt 6G 53
(off Broomcroft Av.)
Knole Ga. Sidc 9C 96
Knole Rd. Dart 6E 98
Knole, The. SE9 1L 111
Knoll Cres. N'wd 8C 20
(in two parts)
Knoll Dri. N14 9E 14
Knoll Ho. NW8 5A 58
(off Carlton Hill)
Knollmead. Surb 3A 120
Knoll Ri. Orp 3D 128
Knoll Rd. SW18 4A 90
Knoll Rd. Bex 6L 97
Knoll Rd. Sidc 2F 112
Knolls Clo. Wor Pk 5F 120
Knolls, The. Eps 8G 135
Knoll, The. W13 8G 55
Knoll, The. Beck 5M 109
Knoll, The. Brom 4E 126
Knollys Clo. SW16 9L 91
Knolly's Ho. WC1 7J 59
(off Tavistock Pl.)
Knollys Rd. SW16 9K 91
Knottisford St. E2 6G 61
Knotts Grn. M. E10 4M 45
Knotts Grn. Rd. E10 4M 45
Knowlden Ho. E1 1G 77
(off Cable St.)
Knowle Av. Bexh 8J 81
Knowle Clo. SW9 2L 91
Knowle Rd. Brom 4K 127
Knowle Rd. Twic 7C 86
Knowles Clo. W Dray 2J 143
Knowles Ct. Harr 4D 38
(off Gayton Rd.)
Knowles Hill Cres. SE13 4B 94
Knowles Wlk. SW4 2G 91
Knowl Pk. Els 7J 11
Knowlton Grn. Brom 9D 110
Knowlton Ho. SW9 9L 75
(off Cowley Rd.)
Knowl Way. Els 7K 11
Knowsley Av. S'hall 2M 69
Knowsley Rd. SW11 1D 90
Knox Ct. SW4 1J 91
Knox Rd. E7 2D 62
Knox St. NW1 8D 58
Knoyle St. SE14 7J 77
Knutsford Av. Wat 2H 9
Koblenz Ho. N8 1J 43
(off Newland Rd.)
Kohat Rd. SW19 2M 105
Koh-I-Nor Av. Bush 8L 9
Komeheather Ho. Ilf 3K 47
Koonowla Clo. Big H 7H 141
Kossuth St. SE10 6C 78
Kotree Way. SE1 5E 76
Kramer M. SW5 6L 73
Kreedman Wlk. E8 1E 60
Kreisel Wlk. Rich 7K 71
Kristina Ct. Sutt 8L 121
(off Overton Rd.)
Krupnik Pl. EC2 7C 60
(off Bateman's Row)
Kuala Gdns. SW16 5K 107
Kubrick Bus. Est. E7 9F 46
(off Station App.)
Kuhn Way. E7 1E 62
Kwame Ho. E16 1M 79
(off University Way)
Kydbrook Clo. Orp 2A 128
Kylemore Clo. E6 5H 63
Kylemore Rd. NW6 3L 57
Kylestrome Ho. SW1 5E 74
(off Cundy St.)
Kymberley Rd. Harr 4C 38
Kyme Rd. Horn 4D 50
Kymes Ct. S Harr 7B 38
Kynance Clo. Romf 3G 35
Kynance Gdns. Stan 8G 23
Kynance Mp. SW7 4M 73
Kynance Pl. SW7 4A 74
Kynaston Av. N16 8D 44
Kynaston Av. T Hth 9A 108
Kynaston Clo. Harr 7B 22
Kynaston Cres. T Hth 9A 108
Kynaston Rd. N16 8C 44
Kynaston Rd. Brom 2E 110
Kynaston Rd. Enf 3B 16
Kynaston Rd. Orp 2F 128
Kynaston Rd. T Hth 9A 108
Kynaston Wood. Harr 7B 22
Kynnersley Clo. Cars 5D 122
Kynoch Rd. N18 4G 29
Kyrle Rd. SW11 5E 90
Kytes Dri. Wat 6H 5
Kytes Est. Wat 6H 5
Kyverdale Rd. N16 6D 44

L

Laburnum Av. N9 2D 28
Laburnum Av. N17 7B 28
Laburnum Av. Dart 7G 99
Laburnum Av. Horn 7E 50
Laburnum Av. Sutt 5C 122
Laburnum Av. Swan 7B 114
Laburnum Av. W Dray 1K 143
Laburnum Clo. E4 6K 29
Laburnum Clo. N11 6E 26
Laburnum Clo. SE15 8G 77
Laburnum Clo. Chesh 4D 6
Laburnum Clo. Wemb 4L 55
Laburnum Ct. E2 4D 60
Laburnum Ct. SE16 3G 77
(off Albion St.)
Laburnum Ct. SE19 5D 108
Laburnum Ct. Harr 4M 37
Laburnum Ct. Stan 4G 23
Laburnum Cres. Sun 5F 100
Laburnum Gdns. N21 2A 28
Laburnum Gdns. Croy 2H 125
Laburnum Gro. N21 2A 28
Laburnum Gro. NW9 5A 40
Laburnum Gro. Houn 3K 85
Laburnum Gro. N Mald 6B 104
Laburnum Gro. Ruis 4B 36
Laburnum Gro. S'hall 7K 53
Laburnum Ho. Short 5B 110
Laburnum Lodge. N3 9K 25
Laburnum Pl. SE9 4L 95
Laburnum Rd. SW19 4A 106
Laburnum Rd. Eps 5C 134
Laburnum Rd. Hay 5D 68
Laburnum Rd. Mitc 6E 106
Laburnums, The. E6 7J 63
Laburnum St. E2 4D 60
Laburnum Wlk. Horn 1G 67
Laburnum Way. Brom 2L 127
Laburnum Way. Stai 7D 144
La Caye Apartments. E14 5B 78
(off Glenaffric Av.)
Lacebark Clo. Sidc 6D 96
Lacey Clo. N9 2E 28
Lacey Dri. Edgw 4K 23
Lacey Dri. Hamp 5K 101
Lacey Wlk. E3 5L 61
Lacine Ct. SE16 3H 77
(off Christopher Clo.)
Lackford Rd. Coul 9D 136
Lackington St. EC2 8B 60
Lackland Ho. SE1 6D 76
(off Rowcross St.)
Lackmore Rd. Enf 8C 6
Lacland Ho. SW10 8B 74
(off Worlds End Est.)
Lacock Clo. SW19 3A 106
Lacock Ct. W13 2E 70
(off Tewkesbury Rd.)
Lacon Ho. WC1 8K 59
(off Theobalds Rd.)
Lacon Rd. SE22 3E 92
Lacrosse Way. SW16 5H 107
Lacy Dri. Dag 8G 49
Lacy Rd. SW15 3H 89
(in two parts)
Ladas Rd. SE27 1A 108
Ladbroke Cres. W11 9J 57
Ladbroke Gdns. W11 1K 73
Ladbroke Gro. W10 & W11 7H 57
Ladbroke Gro. Ho. W11 1K 73
(off Ladbroke Gro.)
Ladbroke M. W11 2J 73
Ladbroke Rd. W11 2K 73
Ladbroke Rd. Enf 8D 16
Ladbroke Rd. Eps 6B 134
Ladbroke Sq. W11 1K 73
Ladbroke Ter. W11 1K 73
Ladbroke Wlk. W11 2K 73
Ladbrook Clo. Pinn 3K 37
Ladbrooke Cres. Sidc 9H 97
Ladbrook Rd. SE25 8B 108
Ladderstile Ride. King T 2M 103
Ladderswood Way. N11 5G 27
Ladds Way. Swan 8B 114
Ladlands. SE22 6E 92
Lady Aylesford Av. Stan 5E 22
Lady Booth Rd. King T 6J 103
Ladycroft Gdns. Orp 7A 128
Ladycroft Rd. SE13 2M 93
Ladycroft Wlk. Stan 8H 23
Ladycroft Way. Orp 7A 128
Lady Dock Wlk. SE16 3J 77
Lady Elizabeth Ho. SW14 2A 88
Ladyfields. Lou 6M 19
Ladyfields Clo. Lou 6M 19
Lady Forsdyke Way. Eps 1L 133
Ladygate La. Ruis 4A 36
Ladygrove. Croy 1J 139
Lady Harewood Way. Eps 1L 133
Lady Hay. Wor Pk 4D 120
Lady Margaret Rd. NW5 & N19 1G 59
Lady Margaret Rd. S'hall 1K 69
Lady Micos Almshouses. E1 9G 61
(off Aylward St.)
Lady Sarah Ho. N11 6D 26
(off Asher Loftus Way)
Lady's Clo. Wat 6G 9
Lady Shaw Ct. N13 2K 27
Ladyship Ter. SE22 6E 92
Ladysmith Av. E6 5J 63
Ladysmith Av. Ilf 5C 48
Ladysmith Clo. NW7 7E 24
Ladysmith Rd. E16 6D 62
Ladysmith Rd. N17 9E 28
Ladysmith Rd. N18 5F 28
Ladysmith Rd. SE9 5L 95
Ladysmith Rd. Enf 5C 16
(in two parts)
Ladysmith Rd. Harr 9C 22
Lady Somerset Rd. NW5 9F 42
Ladywell. 4M 93
Ladywell Clo. SE4 4L 93
Ladywell Heights. SE4 5K 93
Ladywell Rd. SE13 4L 93
Ladywell St. E15 4D 62
Ladywood Av. Orp 9C 112
Ladywood Rd. Surb 4L 119
Lafone Av. Felt 8G 85
Lafone St. SE1 3D 76
Lagado M. SE16 2H 77
Lagonda Av. Ilf 6D 32
Lagonda Way. Dart 3G 99
Lagoon Rd. Orp 9G 113
Laidlaw Dri. N21 7K 15
Laing Clo. Ilf 6B 32
Laing Dean. N'holt 4G 53
Laing Ho. SE5 8A 76
Laings Av. Mitc 6D 106
Laing Sports Club Golf Course. 7C 12
Lainlock Pl. Houn 9M 69
Lainson St. SW18 6L 89
Lairdale Clo. SE21 7A 92
Laird Ho. SE5 8A 76
(off Redcar St.)
Lairs Clo. N7 1J 59
Laitwood Rd. SW12 7F 90
Lakanal. SE5 9C 76
(off Dalwood St.)
Lake Av. Brom 3E 110
Lake Av. Rain 5H 67
Lake Bus. Cen. N17 7E 28
Lake Clo. SW19 2K 105
Lakedale Rd. SE18 7C 80
Lake Dri. Bush 2B 22
Lakefield Clo. SE20 4F 108
Lakefield Rd. N22 9M 27
Lakefields Clo. Rain 5H 67
Lake Footpath. SE2 3H 81
Lake Gdns. Dag 1L 65
Lake Gdns. Rich 8F 86
Lake Gdns. Wall 5F 122
Lakehall Gdns. T Hth 9M 107
Lakehall Rd. T Hth 9M 107
Lake Ho. SE1 3A 76
(off Southwark Bri. Rd.)
Lake Ho. Rd. E11 8E 46
Lakehurst Rd. Eps 7C 120
Lakeland Clo. Chig 4F 32
Lakeland Clo. Harr 6B 22
Lakenheath. N14 7H 15
Laker Ct. SW4 9J 75
Laker Ind. Est. SE26 2J 109
(off Kent Ho. La.)
Lake Ri. Romf 9D 34
Lake Rd. SW19 2K 105
Lake Rd. Croy 4K 125
Lake Rd. Romf 2H 49
Laker Pl. SW15 5J 89
Lakers Ri. Bans 8C 136
Lakeside. N3 9M 25
Lakeside. W13 9G 55
Lakeside. Beck 7M 109
Lakeside. Enf 6H 15
Lakeside. Eps 8C 120
Lakeside. Rain 5J 67
Lakeside. Wall 6F 122
Lakeside. Wey 4C 116
Lakeside Av. SE28 3E 80
Lakeside Av. Ilf 2H 47
Lakeside Clo. SE25 6E 108
Lakeside Clo. Ruis 2A 36
Lakeside Clo. Sidc 4G 97
Lakeside Ct. N4 7A 44
Lakeside Ct. Els 7L 11
Lakeside Cres. Barn 7D 14
Lakeside Dri. Brom 5J 127
Lakeside Dri. Esh 8A 118
Lakeside Grange. Wey 5A 116
Lakeside Rd. N13 4K 27
Lakeside Rd. W14 4H 73
Lakeside Rd. Chesh 1C 6
Lakeside Ter. EC2 8A 60
(off Beech St.)
Lakeside Way. SE2 4H 81
Lakeside Way. Wemb 9L 39
Lakes Rd. Kes 7G 127
Lakeswood Rd. Orp 1M 127
Lake, The. Bush 1B 22
Lake Vw. Edgw 5K 23
Lake Vw. Ct. SW1 4F 74
(off Bressenden Pl.)
Lake Vw. Est. E3 5J 61
Lakeview Pk. Noak H 3G 35
Lakeview Rd. SE27 2L 107
Lakeview Rd. Well 3F 96
Lake Vw. Ter. N18 4D 28
(off Sweet Briar Wlk.)
Lakis Clo. NW3 9A 42
Laleham Av. NW7 3B 24
Laleham Ho. E2 7D 60
(off Camlet St.)
Laleham Rd. SE6 6A 94
Laleham Rd. Shep 9A 100
Lalor St. SW6 1J 89
Lambarde Av. SE9 1L 111
Lambard Ho. SE10 8A 78
(off Langdale Rd.)
Lamb Clo. Wat 7G 5
Lamb Ct. E14 1J 77
(off Narrow St.)
Lamberhurst Clo. Orp 3H 129
Lamberhurst Ho. SE15 7G 77
Lamberhurst Rd. SE27 1L 107
Lamberhurst Rd. Dag 6K 49
Lambert Av. Rich 2L 87
Lambert Clo. Big H 8H 141
Lambert Ct. Eri 7A 82
(off Park Cres.)
Lambert Ct. Wat 6H 9
Lambert Jones M. EC2 8A 60
(off Beech St.)
Lambert Lodge. Bren 6H 71
(off Layton Rd.)
Lamberton Ct. Borwd 3L 11
(off Gateshead Rd.)
Lambert Rd. E16 9F 62
Lambert Rd. N12 5B 26
Lambert Rd. SW2 4J 91
Lambert Rd. Bans 6L 135
Lambert's Pl. Croy 3B 124
Lamberts Rd. Surb 9J 103
Lambert St. N1 3L 59
Lambert Wlk. Wemb 8H 39
Lambert Way. N12 5A 26
Lambeth. 4K 75
Lambeth Bri. SW1 & SE1 5J 75
Lambeth Crematorium. SW17 1A 106
Lambeth High St. SE1 5K 75
Lambeth Hill. EC4 1A 76
Lambeth Pal. Rd. SE1 4K 75
Lambeth Rd. SE1 & SE11 5K 75
Lambeth Rd. Croy 2L 123
Lambeth Towers. SE11 4L 75
(off Kennington Rd.)
Lambeth Wlk. SE1 & SE11 5K 75
(in two parts)
Lambfold Ho. N7 2J 59
Lamb Ho. SE5 8A 76
(off Elmington Est.)
Lamb Ho. SE10 7A 78
(off Haddo St.)
Lamb La. E8 3F 60
Lamble St. NW5 1E 58
Lambley Rd. Dag 2F 64
Lambolle Pl. NW3 2C 58
Lambolle Rd. NW3 2C 58
Lambourn Chase. Rad 1D 10
Lambourn Clo. NW5 9G 43
Lambourn Clo. W7 3D 70
Lambourn Clo. S Croy 1M 137
Lambourne Av. SW19 1K 105
Lambourne Clo. Chig 3F 32
Lambourne Ct. Uxb 4A 142
Lambourne Ct. Wfd G 7G 31
Lambourne Cres. Chig 2F 32
Lambourne End. 1J 33
Lambourne Gdns. E4 2L 29
Lambourne Gdns. Bark 3D 64
Lambourne Gdns. Enf 4D 16
Lambourne Gdns. Horn 7H 51
Lambourne Ho. NW8 8B 58
(off Broadley St.)
Lambourne Ho. SE16 5H 77
Lambourne Pl. SE3 9F 78
Lambourne Rd. E11 5A 46
Lambourne Rd. Bark 3C 64
Lambourne Rd. Chig 4D 32
Lambourne Rd. Ilf 7C 48
Lambourne Sq. Abr 1G 33
Lambourn Gro. King T 6M 103
Lambourn Rd. SW4 2F 90
Lambrook Ho. SE15 9E 76
Lambrook Ter. SW6 9J 73
Lamb's Bldgs. EC1 7B 60
Lamb's Clo. N9 2E 28
Lamb's Conduit Pas. WC1 8K 59
Lamb's Conduit St. WC1 7K 59
(in three parts)
Lambscroft Av. SE9 9G 95
Lambs La. Ind. Est. Rain 7G 67
Lamb's La. N. Rain 7H 67
Lamb's La. S. Rain 8F 66
Lambs Mdw. Wfd G 9H 31
Lamb's M. N1 4M 59
Lamb's Pas. EC1 7B 60
Lambs Ter. N9 2B 28
Lamb St. E1 8C 60
Lamb's Wlk. Enf 4A 16
Lambton Av. Wal X 5D 6
Lambton Pl. W11 1K 73
Lambton Rd. N19 6J 43
Lambton Rd. SW20 5G 105
Lamb Wlk. SE1 3C 76
***LAMDA Theatre.** 5L 73*
(off Logan Pl.)
Lamerock Rd. Brom 1D 110
Lamerton Rd. Ilf 9M 31
Lamerton St. SE8 7L 77
Lamford Clo. N17 7B 28
Lamington St. W6 5F 72
Lamlash St. SE11 5M 75
Lamley Ho. SE10 8M 77
(off Ashburnham Pl.)
Lammas Av. Mitc 6E 106
Lammas Grn. SE26 9F 92
Lammas Hill. Esh 6M 117
Lammas La. Esh 7L 117
Lammas Pk. Gdns. W5 2G 71
Lammas Pk. Rd. W5 3H 71
Lammas Rd. E9 3H 61
Lammas Rd. E10 7J 45
Lammas Rd. Rich 1G 103
Lammas Rd. Wat 7G 9
Lammermoor Rd. SW12 6F 90
Lamont Rd. SW10 7B 74
Lamont Rd. Pas. SW10 7B 74
(off Lamont Rd.)
Lamorbey. 7D 96
Lamorbey Clo. Sidc 7D 96
Lamorna Clo. E17 9A 30
Lamorna Clo. Orp 2E 128
Lamorna Gro. Stan 8H 23
Lampard Gro. N16 6D 44
Lampern Sq. E2 6E 60
Lampeter Clo. NW9 4C 40
Lampeter Ho. Romf 7J 35
(off Kingsbridge Cir.)
Lampeter Sq. W6 7J 73
Lamplighter Clo. E1 7G 61
Lamplighters Clo. Dart 5K 99
Lampmead Rd. SE12 4D 94
Lamp Office Ct. WC1 7K 59
(off Conduit St.)
Lamport Clo. SE18 5K 79
Lamps Ct. SE5 8A 76
Lampton. 9M 69
Lampton Av. Houn 9M 69
Lampton Ct. Houn 9M 69

Lampton Ho. Clo.—Larcombe Ct.

Lampton Ho. Clo. SW19 ... 1H 105
Lampton Pk. Rd. Houn ... 1M 85
Lampton Rd. Houn ... 1M 85
Lamson Rd. Rain ... 7D 66
Lanacre Av. HA8 ... 8B 24
Lanain Ct. SE12 ... 6D 94
Lanark Clo. W5 ... 8G 55
Lanark Ct. N'holt ... 1L 53
(off Newmarket Av.)
Lanark Ho. SE1 ... 6E 76
(off Old Kent Rd.)
Lanark Mans. W9 ... 7A 58
(off Lanark Rd.)
Lanark Mans. W12 ... 3G 73
(off Pennard Rd.)
Lanark M. W9 ... 6A 58
Lanark Pl. W9 ... 7A 58
Lanark Rd. W9 ... 5M 57
Lanark Sq. E14 ... 4M 77
Lanata Wlk. Hay ... 7H 53
(off Alba Clo.)
Lanbury Rd. SE15 ... 3H 93
Lancashire Ct. W1 ... 1F 74
(off New Bond St.)
Lancaster Av. E18 ... 2F 46
Lancaster Av. SE27 ... 8M 91
Lancaster Av. SW19 ... 2H 105
Lancaster Av. Bark ... 3C 64
Lancaster Av. Barn ... 2A 14
Lancaster Av. Mitc ... 9J 107
Lancaster Clo. N1 ... 3C 60
Lancaster Clo. N17 ... 7E 28
Lancaster Clo. NW9 ... 7D 24
Lancaster Clo. SE27 ... 8M 91
Lancaster Clo. W2 ... 1M 73
(off St Petersburgh Pl.)
Lancaster Clo. Ashf ... 9C 144
Lancaster Clo. Brom ... 8D 110
Lancaster Clo. King T ... 2H 103
Lancaster Clo. Stanw ... 5C 144
Lancaster Cotts. Rich ... 5J 87
Lancaster Ct. SE27 ... 8M 91
Lancaster Ct. SW6 ... 8K 73
Lancaster Ct. W2 ... 1A 74
(off Lancaster Ga.)
Lancaster Ct. Bans ... 6K 135
Lancaster Ct. Eps ... 2B 134
Lancaster Ct. Sutt ... 9L 121
(off Mulgrave Rd.)
Lancaster Ct. W on T ... 2E 116
Lancaster Dri. E14 ... 2A 78
Lancaster Dri. NW3 ... 2C 58
Lancaster Dri. Horn ... 1F 66
Lancaster Dri. Lou ... 8J 19
Lancaster Gdns. SW19 ... 2J 105
Lancaster Gdns. W13 ... 3F 70
Lancaster Gdns. King T ... 2H 103
Lancaster Ga. W2 ... 1A 74
Lancaster Gro. NW3 ... 2B 58
Lancaster Hall. E16 ... 2E 78
(off Wesley Av., in two parts)
Lancaster Ho. Enf ... 3B 16
Lancaster Lodge. W11 ... 9J 57
(off Lancaster Rd.)
Lancaster M. SW18 ... 4M 89
Lancaster M. W2 ... 1A 74
Lancaster M. Rich ... 5J 87
Lancaster Pk. Rich ... 4J 87
Lancaster Pl. SW19 ... 2H 105
Lancaster Pl. WC2 ... 1K 75
Lancaster Pl. Houn ... 1G 85
Lancaster Pl. Ilf ... 1A 64
Lancaster Pl. Twic ... 5E 86
Lancaster Rd. E7 ... 3E 62
Lancaster Rd. E11 ... 7C 46
Lancaster Rd. E17 ... 9H 29
Lancaster Rd. N4 ... 5K 43
Lancaster Rd. N11 ... 6H 27
Lancaster Rd. N18 ... 5D 28
Lancaster Rd. NW10 ... 1E 56
Lancaster Rd. SE25 ... 6D 108
Lancaster Rd. SW19 ... 2H 105
Lancaster Rd. W11 ... 9J 57
Lancaster Rd. Barn ... 6B 14
(in two parts)
Lancaster Rd. Enf ... 3B 16
Lancaster Rd. Harr ... 3L 37
Lancaster Rd. N'holt ... 2A 54
Lancaster Rd. S'hall ... 1J 69
Lancaster Rd. Uxb ... 2B 142
Lancaster Stables. NW3 ... 2C 58
Lancaster St. SE1 ... 3M 75
Lancaster Ter. W2 ... 1B 74
Lancaster Wlk. W2 ... 2A 74
Lancaster Wlk. Hay ... 9A 52
Lancaster Way. Ab L ... 4D 4
Lancastrian Rd. Wall ... 9J 123
Lancefield Ct. W10 ... 5J 57
Lancefield Ho. SE15 ... 3F 92
Lancefield St. W10 ... 6K 57
Lancell St. N16 ... 7C 44
Lancelot Av. Wemb ... 9H 39
Lancelot Ct. Orp ... 4F 128
Lancelot Cres. Wemb ... 9H 39
Lancelot Gdns. E Barn ... 9E 14
Lancelot Pl. SW7 ... 3D 74
Lancelot Rd. Ilf ... 6C 32
Lancelot Rd. Well ... 3E 96
Lancelot Rd. Wemb ... 9H 39
Lance Rd. Harr ... 5A 38
Lancer Sq. W8 ... 3M 73
Lancey Clo. SE7 ... 5J 79
Lanchester Ct. W2 ... 9D 58
(off Seymour St.)
Lanchester Rd. N6 ... 3D 42
Lancing Gdns. N9 ... 1D 28
Lancing Ho. Croy ... 6B 124
(off Coombe Rd.)
Lancing Ho. Wat ... 4G 9
(off Hallam Clo.)
Lancing Rd. W13 ... 1F 70
Lancing Rd. Croy ... 2K 123
Lancing Rd. Felt ... 8D 84
Lancing Rd. Ilf ... 4B 48
Lancing Rd. Orp ... 4E 128
Lancing Rd. Romf ... 7J 35
Lancing St. NW1 ... 6H 59
Lancing Way. Crox G ... 7A 8
Lancresse Clo. Uxb ... 2B 142
Lancresse Ct. N1 ... 4C 60
(off De Beauvoir Est.)
Landale Gdns. Dart ... 6G 99
Landale Ho. SE16 ... 4G 77
(off Lower Rd.)
Landau Ct. S Croy ... 7A 124
(off Warham Rd.)
Landau Way. Eri ... 6H 83
Land Clo. Asht ... 9J 133
Landcroft Rd. SE22 ... 4D 92
Landells Rd. SE22 ... 5D 92
Landford Rd. SW15 ... 2G 89
Landgrove Rd. SW19 ... 2L 105
Landin Ho. E14 ... 9L 61
(off Thomas Rd.)
Landleys Fld. NW5 ... 1H 59
(off Long Mdw.)
Landmann Ho. SE16 ... 5F 76
(off Rennie Est.)
Landmann Way. SE14 ... 6H 77
Landmark Commercial Cen.
N18 ... 6C 28
Landmark Ho. W6 ... 6G 73
(off Hammersmith Bri. Rd.)
Landmead Rd. Chesh ... 2E 6
Landon Pl. SW1 ... 4D 74
Landon's Clo. E14 ... 2A 78
Landon Wlk. E14 ... 1M 77
Landon Way. Ashf ... 3A 100
Landor Ho. SE5 ... 8B 76
(off Elmington Est.)
Landor Rd. SW4 ... 2J 91
Landor Wlk. W12 ... 3E 72
Landra Gdns. N21 ... 8M 15
Landrake. NW1 ... 4G 59
(off Plender St.)
Landridge Dri. Enf ... 2F 16
Landridge Rd. SW6 ... 1K 89
Landrock Rd. N8 ... 4J 43
Landscape Rd. Wfd G ... 7F 30
Landseer Av. E12 ... 1L 63
Landseer Clo. SW19 ... 5A 106
Landseer Clo. Edgw ... 9L 23
Landseer Clo. Horn ... 6F 50
Landseer Ct. Hay ... 5B 52
Landseer Ho. NW8 ... 7B 58
(off Frampton St.)
Landseer Ho. SW1 ... 5H 75
(off Herrick St.)
Landseer Ho. SW11 ... 9E 74
Landseer Ho. N'holt ... 5H 53
(off Parkfield Dri.)
Landseer Rd. N19 ... 8J 43
(in two parts)
Landseer Rd. Enf ... 7E 16
Landseer Rd. N Mald ... 2B 120
Landseer Rd. Sutt ... 8L 121
Lands End. Els ... 8H 11
Landstead Rd. SE18 ... 8B 80
Landulph Ho. SE11 ... 6L 75
(off Kennings Way)
Landward Ct. W1 ... 9C 58
(off Harrowby St.)
Landway, The. Orp ... 7G 113
Lane App. NW7 ... 5J 25
Lane Clo. NW2 ... 8F 40
Lane End. SW15 ... 5H 89
Lane End. Bexh ... 2M 97
Lane End. Eps ... 6M 133
Lane Gdns. Bus H ... 9C 10
Lane Jane Ct. King T ... 6K 103
(off London Rd.)
Lane M. E12 ... 8K 47
Lanercost Clo. SW2 ... 8L 91
Lanercost Gdns. N14 ... 9J 15
Lanercost Rd. SW2 ... 8L 91
Lanesborough Pl. SW1 ... 3E 74
(off Grosvenor Pl.)
Laneside. Chst ... 2M 111
Laneside. Edgw ... 5A 24
Laneside Av. Dag ... 5K 49
Lane, The. NW8 ... 5A 58
Lane, The. SE3 ... 2E 94
Laneway. SW15 ... 4F 88
Laney Ho. EC1 ... 8L 59
(off Leather La.)
Lanfranc Ct. Harr ... 8D 38
Lanfranc Rd. E3 ... 5J 61
Lanfrey Pl. W14 ... 6K 73
Langbourne Av. N6 ... 7E 42
Langbourne Ct. E17 ... 4J 45
Langbourne Mans. N6 ... 7E 42
Langbourne Pl. E14 ... 6M 77
Langbourne Way. Clay ... 8E 118
Langbrook Rd. SE3 ... 2H 95
Langcroft Clo. Cars ... 5D 122
Langdale. NW1 ... 6G 59
(off Stanhope St.)
Langdale Av. Mitc ... 7D 106
Langdale Clo. SE17 ... 7A 76
Langdale Clo. SW14 ... 3M 87
Langdale Clo. Dag ... 6G 49
Langdale Clo. Orp ... 5M 127
Langdale Cres. Bexh ... 8L 81
Langdale Dri. Hay ... 5C 52
Langdale Gdns. Gnfd ... 6F 54
Langdale Gdns. Horn ... 1E 66
Langdale Gdns. Wal X ... 8D 6
Langdale Ho. SW1 ... 6G 75
(off Churchill Gdns.)
Langdale Pde. Mitc ... 7D 106
Langdale Rd. SE10 ... 8A 78
Langdale Rd. T Hth ... 8L 107
Langdale St. E1 ... 9F 60
Langdale Ter. Borwd ... 5A 12
Langdon Ct. EC1 ... 5M 59
(off City Rd.)
Langdon Ct. NW10 ... 4C 56
Langdon Cres. E6 ... 5L 63
Langdon Dri. NW9 ... 6A 40
Langdon Ho. E14 ... 9A 62
Langdon Pk. Rd. N6 ... 5G 43
Langdon Pl. SW14 ... 2A 88
Langdon Rd. E6 ... 4L 63
Langdon Rd. Brom ... 7F 110
Langdon Rd. Mord ... 9A 106
Langdons Ct. S'hall ... 4L 69
Langdon Shaw. Sidc ... 2D 112
Langdon Wlk. Mord ... 9A 106
Langdon Way. SE1 ... 5E 76
Langford Clo. E8 ... 1E 60
Langford Clo. NW8 ... 5A 58
Langford Clo. W3 ... 3M 71
Langford Ct. NW8 ... 5A 58
(off Abbey Rd.)
Langford Cres. Cockf ... 6D 14
Langford Grn. SE5 ... 2C 92
Langford Ho. SE8 ... 7L 77
Langford Pl. NW8 ... 5A 58
Langford Pl. Sidc ... 9E 96
Langford Rd. SW6 ... 1M 89
Langford Rd. Cockf ... 6D 14
Langford Rd. Wfd G ... 6G 31
Langfords. Buck H ... 2H 31
Langham Clo. N15 ... 1M 43
(off Langham Rd.)
Langham Ct. NW4 ... 3H 41
Langham Ct. Horn ... 5H 51
Langham Ct. Ruis ... 1F 52
Langham Dene. Kenl ... 7M 137
Langham Dri. Romf ... 4F 48
Langham Gdns. N21 ... 7L 15
Langham Gdns. W13 ... 1F 70
Langham Gdns. Edgw ... 7A 24
Langham Gdns. Rich ... 1G 103
Langham Gdns. Wemb ... 7G 39
Langham Ho. Clo. Rich ... 1H 103
Langham Mans. SW5 ... 6M 73
(off Earl's Ct. Sq.)
Langham Pl. N15 ... 1M 43
Langham Pl. W1 ... 8F 58
Langham Pl. W4 ... 7C 72
Langham Rd. N15 ... 1M 43
Langham Rd. SW20 ... 5G 105
Langham Rd. Edgw ... 6A 24
Langham Rd. Tedd ... 2F 102
Langham St. W1 ... 8F 58
Langhedge Clo. N18 ... 6D 28
Langhedge La. N18 ... 6D 28
Langhedge La. Ind. Est.
N18 ... 6D 28
Langholm Clo. SW12 ... 6H 91
Langholme. Bush ... 1A 22
Langhorn Dri. Twic ... 6C 86
Langhorne Ct. NW8 ... 3B 58
(off Dorman Way)
Langhorne Rd. Dag ... 3L 65
Lang Ho. SW8 ... 8J 75
(off Hartington Rd.)
Langland Ct. N'wd ... 7A 20
Langland Cres. Stan ... 9H 23
Langland Dri. Pinn ... 7J 21
Langland Gdns. NW3 ... 1M 57
Langland Gdns. Croy ... 4K 125
Langland Ho. SE5 ... 8B 76
(off Edmund St.)
Langlands Ri. Eps ... 5A 134
Langler Rd. NW10 ... 5G 57
Langley Av. Ruis ... 7F 36
Langley Av. Surb ... 3H 119
Langley Av. Wor Pk ... 3H 121
Langleybury. ... 7A 4
Langleybury La. Wat ... 7A 4
Langley Clo. Romf ... 7H 35
Langley Ct. WC2 ... 1J 75
Langley Cres. E11 ... 5G 47
Langley Cres. Dag ... 3G 65
Langley Cres. Edgw ... 3A 24
Langley Cres. Hay ... 8D 68
Langley Dri. E11 ... 5F 46
Langley Dri. W3 ... 3M 71
Langley Gdns. Brom ... 8G 111
Langley Gdns. Dag ... 3H 65
Langley Gdns. Orp ... 1M 127
Langley Gro. N Mald ... 6C 104
Langley La. SW8 ... 7J 75
Langley La. Ab L ... 4D 4
Langley Mans. SW8 ... 7K 75
(off Langley La.)
Langley Oaks Av. S Croy ... 2E 138
Langley Pk. NW7 ... 6C 24
Langley Pk. Rd. Sutt ... 7A 122
Langley Rd. SW19 ... 5K 105
Langley Rd. Ab L ... 4C 4
Langley Rd. Beck ... 8J 109
Langley Rd. Iswth ... 1D 86
Langley Rd. S Croy ... 1H 139
Langley Rd. Surb ... 2J 119
Langley Rd. Wat ... 3D 8
Langley Rd. Well ... 7G 81
Langley Row. Barn ... 3K 13
Langley St. WC2 ... 9J 59
Langley Va. Rd. Eps ... 9C 134
Langley Way. Wat ... 4C 8
Langley Way. W Wick ... 3B 126
Langmead Dri. Bus H ... 1C 22
Langmead St. SE27 ... 1M 107
Langmore Ct. Bexh ... 2H 97
Langmore Ho. E1 ... 9E 60
(off Stutfield St.)
Langport Ct. W on T ... 3G 117
Langport Ho. SW9 ... 1M 91
Langport Ho. Romf ... 7J 35
(off Leyburn Rd.)
Langridge M. Hamp ... 3K 101
Langroyd Rd. SW17 ... 8D 90
Langside Av. SW15 ... 3E 88
Langside Cres. N14 ... 3H 27
Langston Hughes Clo.
SE24 ... 3M 91
Lang St. E1 ... 7G 61
Langthorn Ct. EC2 ... 9B 60
Langthorne Ct. SE6 ... 1A 110
Langthorne Ho. Hay ... 5C 68
Langthorne Rd. E11 ... 8A 46
Langthorne St. SW6 ... 8H 73
Langton Av. E6 ... 6L 63
Langton Av. N20 ... 9A 14
Langton Av. Eps ... 3D 134
Langton Clo. WC1 ... 7K 59
Langton Gro. N'wd ... 5A 20
Langton Ho. SE11 ... 5K 75
(off Lambeth Wlk.)
Langton Pl. SW18 ... 7L 89
Langton Ri. SE23 ... 6F 92
Langton Rd. NW2 ... 8G 41
Langton Rd. SW9 ... 8M 75
Langton Rd. Harr ... 7A 22
Langton Rd. W Mol ... 8A 102
Langton St. SW10 ... 7A 74
Langton Way. SE3 ... 9D 78
Langton Way. Croy ... 5C 124
Langtry Pl. SW6 ... 7L 73
Langtry Rd. NW8 ... 4M 57
Langtry Rd. N'holt ... 5H 53
Langtry Wlk. NW8 ... 4M 57
Langwood Chase. Tedd ... 3G 103
Langwood Clo. Asht ... 9L 133
Langwood Gdns. Wat ... 3E 8
Langworth Clo. Dart ... 9H 99
Langworth Dri. Hay ... 9E 52
Langworthy. Pinn ... 6L 21
Lanhill Rd. W9 ... 7L 57
Lanier Rd. SE13 ... 5B 94
Lanigan Dri. Houn ... 4M 85
Lankaster Gdns. N2 ... 8B 26
Lankers Dri. Harr ... 4K 37
Lankton Clo. Beck ... 5A 110
Lannock Rd. Hay ... 2D 68
Lannoy Point. SW6 ... 8J 73
(off Pellant Rd.)
Lannoy Rd. SE9 ... 7A 96
Lanrick Ho. E14 ... 9B 62
(off Lanrick Rd.)
Lanrick Rd. E14 ... 9B 62
Lanridge Rd. SE2 ... 4H 81
Lansbury Av. N18 ... 5B 28
Lansbury Av. Bark ... 3E 64
Lansbury Av. Felt ... 5F 84
Lansbury Av. Romf ... 3J 49
Lansbury Clo. NW10 ... 1A 56
Lansbury Cres. Dart ... 4L 99
Lansbury Dri. Hay ... 5C 52
Lansbury Est. E14 ... 9M 61
Lansbury Gdns. E14 ... 9B 62
Lansbury Rd. Enf ... 3H 17
Lansbury Way. N18 ... 5C 28
Lanscombe Wlk. SW8 ... 9J 75
Lansdell Ho. SW2 ... 5L 91
(off Tulse Hill)
Lansdell Rd. Mitc ... 6E 106
Lansdown Clo. W on T ... 3G 117
Lansdowne Av. Bexh ... 8H 81
Lansdowne Av. Orp ... 3M 127
Lansdowne Clo. SW20 ... 4H 105
Lansdowne Clo. Surb ... 4M 119
Lansdowne Clo. Twic ... 7D 86
Lansdowne Clo. Wat ... 8H 5
Lansdowne Ct. W11 ... 1J 73
(off Lansdowne Ri.)
Lansdowne Ct. Ilf ... 1J 47
Lansdowne Ct. Purl ... 2M 137
Lansdowne Ct. Wor Pk ... 4E 120
Lansdowne Cres. W11 ... 1J 73
Lansdowne Dri. E8 ... 2E 60
Lansdowne Gdns. SW8 ... 9J 75
Lansdowne Grn. Est. SW8 ... 9J 75
Lansdowne Gro. NW10 ... 9C 40
Lansdowne Hill. SE27 ... 9M 91
Lansdowne La. SE7 ... 7H 79
Lansdowne M. SE7 ... 6H 79
Lansdowne M. W11 ... 2K 73
Lansdowne Pl. SE1 ... 4B 76
Lansdowne Pl. SE19 ... 4D 108
Lansdowne Ri. W11 ... 1J 73
Lansdowne Rd. E4 ... 2L 29
Lansdowne Rd. E11 ... 7D 46
Lansdowne Rd. E17 ... 4L 45
Lansdowne Rd. E18 ... 1E 46
Lansdowne Rd. N3 ... 7L 25
Lansdowne Rd. N10 ... 9G 27
Lansdowne Rd. N17 ... 8D 28
Lansdowne Rd. SW20 ... 4G 105
Lansdowne Rd. W11 ... 1J 73
Lansdowne Rd. Brom ... 4E 110
Lansdowne Rd. Croy ... 4B 124
Lansdowne Rd. Eps ... 9A 120
Lansdowne Rd. Harr ... 5C 38
Lansdowne Rd. Houn ... 2M 85
Lansdowne Rd. Ilf ... 6D 48
Lansdowne Rd. Purl ... 4L 137
Lansdowne Rd. Stan ... 6G 23
Lansdowne Rd. Uxb ... 9A 52
Lansdowne Row. W1 ... 2F 74
Lansdowne Ter. WC1 ... 7J 59
Lansdowne Wlk. W11 ... 2K 73
Lansdowne Way. SW8 ... 9H 75
Lansdowne Wood Clo.
SE27 ... 9M 91
Lansdowne Workshops.
SE7 ... 6G 79
Lansdown Rd. E7 ... 3G 63
Lansdown Rd. Sidc ... 9F 96
Lansfield Av. N18 ... 4E 28
Lantern Clo. SW15 ... 3E 88
Lantern Clo. Wemb ... 1H 55
Lanterns Ct. E14 ... 4L 77
Lantern Way. W Dray ... 3J 143
Lant Ho. SE1 ... 3A 76
(off Toulmin St.)
Lantry Ct. W3 ... 2M 71
Lant St. SE1 ... 3A 76
Lanvanor Rd. SE15 ... 1G 93
Lanyard Ho. SE8 ... 5K 77
Lapford Clo. W9 ... 7K 57
Lapponum Wlk. Hay ... 7H 53
Lapse Wood Wlk. SE23 ... 7F 92
Lapstone Gdns. Harr ... 4G 39
Lapwing Clo. Eri ... 8F 82
Lapwing Clo. S Croy ... 2J 139
Lapwing Ct. Surb ... 5L 119
Lapwing Pl. Wat ... 5G 5
Lapwing Tower. SE8 ... 7K 77
(off Taylor Clo.)
Lapwing Way. Ab L ... 4E 4
Lapwing Way. Hay ... 9H 53
Lapworth. N11 ... 4F 26
(off Coppies Gro.)
Lapworth Clo. Orp ... 4G 129
Lapworth Ct. W2 ... 8M 57
(off Chichester Rd.)
Lara Clo. SE13 ... 5A 94
Lara Clo. Chess ... 9J 119
Larbert Rd. SW16 ... 4G 107
Larby Pl. Eps ... 2C 134
Larch Av. W3 ... 2C 72
Larch Av. Brick W ... 3J 5
Larch Clo. E13 ... 7F 62
Larch Clo. N11 ... 7E 26
Larch Clo. N19 ... 7G 43
Larch Clo. SE8 ... 7K 77
Larch Clo. SW12 ... 8F 90
Larch Ct. W9 ... 8L 57
(off Admiral Wlk.)
Larch Cres. Eps ... 8M 119
Larch Cres. Hay ... 8G 53
Larch Dene. Orp ... 4L 127
Larch Dri. W4 ... 6L 71
Larches Av. SW14 ... 3B 88
Larches Av. Enf ... 8C 6
Larches, The. N13 ... 3A 28
Larches, The. Bush ... 7H 9
Larches, The. N'wd ... 6A 20
Larches, The. Uxb ... 6F 142
Larch Grn. NW9 ... 8C 24
Larch Gro. Sidc ... 7D 96
Larch Ho. SE16 ... 3G 77
(off Ainsty Est.)
Larch Ho. W10 ... 7J 57
(off Rowan Wlk.)
Larch Ho. Hay ... 8G 53
Larch Ho. Short ... 5C 110
Larch Rd. E10 ... 7L 45
Larch Rd. NW2 ... 9G 41
Larch Rd. Dart ... 6H 99
Larch Tree Way. Croy ... 5L 125
Larchvale Ct. Sutt ... 9M 121
Larch Wlk. Swan ... 6B 114
Larch Way. Brom ... 2L 127
Larchwood Av. Romf ... 6M 33
Larchwood Clo. Bans ... 7J 135
Larchwood Clo. Romf ... 6A 34
Larchwood Rd. SE9 ... 8M 95
Larcombe Clo. Croy ... 6D 124
Larcombe Ct. Sutt ... 9M 121
(off Worcester Rd.)

Leather Clo.—Leybourne Rd.

Leather Clo. *Mitc* . . . 6E **106**
Leatherdale St. *E1* . . . 7G **61**
(in two parts)
Leather Gdns. *E15* . . . 4C **62**
Leatherhead Clo. *N16* . . . 6D **44**
Leatherhead Rd. *Chess* . . . 6F **132**
Leatherhead Rd. *Oxs* . . . 6B **132**
Leather La. *EC1* . . . 8L **59**
(in two parts)
Leather La. *Horn* . . . 6H **51**
Leathermarket Ct. *SE1* . . . 3C **76**
Leathermarket St. *SE1* . . . 3C **76**
Leathersellers Clo. *Barn* . . . 5J **13**
Leathsail Rd. *Harr* . . . 8M **37**
Leathwaite Rd. *SW11* . . . 3D **90**
Leathwell Rd. *SE8* . . . 1M **93**
Lea Va. *Dart* . . . 3B **98**
Lea Valley Rd. *Enf & E4* . . . 7J **17**
Lea Valley Trad. Est. *N18* . . . 6H **29**
Lea Valley Viaduct. *N18 & E4* . . . 5H **29**
Leaveland Clo. *Beck* . . . 8L **109**
Leaver Gdns. *Gnfd* . . . 5B **54**
Leavesden. . . . 5D 4
Leavesden Green. . . . 6E 4
Leavesden Green (Junct.) . . . 8C 4
Leavesden Rd. *Stan* . . . 6E **22**
Leavesden Rd. *Wat* . . . 2F **8**
Leavesden Rd. *Wey* . . . 7A **116**
Leavesden Studios. *Leav* . . . 6D **4**
Leaves Green. . . . 3H 141
Leaves Grn. Cres. *Kes* . . . 3G **141**
Leaves Grn. Rd. *Kes* . . . 3H **141**
Lea Vw. *Wal A* . . . 6H **7**
Lea Vw. Ho. *E5* . . . 6F **44**
Leaway. *E10* . . . 6H **45**
Lebanon Av. *Felt* . . . 2H **101**
Lebanon Clo. *Wat* . . . 9B **4**
Lebanon Gdns. *SW18* . . . 5L **89**
Lebanon Gdns. *Big H* . . . 9H **141**
Lebanon Pk. *Twic* . . . 6F **86**
Lebanon Rd. *SW18* . . . 4L **89**
Lebanon Rd. *Croy* . . . 3C **124**
Lebrun Sq. *SE3* . . . 3F **94**
Lebus Ho. NW8 . . . 5C **58**
(off Cochrane St.)
Le Chateau. Croy . . . 5B **124**
(off Chatsworth Rd.)
Lechmere App. *Wfd G* . . . 9G **31**
Lechmere Av. *Chig* . . . 4A **32**
Lechmere Av. *Wfd G* . . . 9H **31**
Lechmere Rd. *NW2* . . . 2F **56**
Leckford Rd. *SW18* . . . 8A **90**
Leckhampton Pl. *SW2* . . . 6L **91**
Leckwith Av. *Bexh* . . . 7J **81**
Lecky St. *SW7* . . . 6B **74**
Leclair Ho. *SE3* . . . 2F **94**
Leconfield Av. *SW13* . . . 2D **88**
Leconfield Ho. *SE5* . . . 3C **92**
Leconfield Rd. *N5* . . . 9B **44**
Leconfield Wlk. *Horn* . . . 2G **67**
Leda Av. *Enf* . . . 2H **17**
Leda Ct. SW9 . . . 8L **75**
(off Caldwell St.)
Ledam Ho. EC1 . . . 8L **59**
(off Bourne Est.)
Leda Rd. *SE18* . . . 4K **79**
Ledbury Ho. *SE22* . . . 2C **92**
Ledbury Ho. W11 . . . 9K **57**
(off Colville Rd.)
Ledbury M. N. *W11* . . . 1L **73**
Ledbury M. W. *W11* . . . 1L **73**
Ledbury Pl. *Croy* . . . 6A **124**
Ledbury Rd. *W11* . . . 9K **57**
Ledbury Rd. *Croy* . . . 6B **124**
Ledbury St. *SE15* . . . 8E **76**
Ledgers La. *Warl* . . . 9M **139**
Ledgers Rd. *Warl* . . . 8L **139**
Ledrington Rd. *SE19* . . . 3E **108**
Ledway Dri. *Wemb* . . . 5K **39**
Lee. . . . 4D 94
Lee Av. *Romf* . . . 4J **49**
Lee Bri. *SE13* . . . 2A **94**
Leechcroft Av. *Sidc* . . . 4D **96**
Leechcroft Av. *Swan* . . . 7D **114**
Leechcroft Rd. *Wall* . . . 5E **122**
Lee Chu. St. *SE13* . . . 3C **94**
Lee Clo. *E17* . . . 8H **29**
Lee Clo. *Barn* . . . 6A **14**
Lee Conservancy Rd. *E9* . . . 1K **61**
Lee Ct. SE13 . . . 3B **94**
(off Lee High Rd.)
Leecroft Rd. *Barn* . . . 7J **13**
Leeds Clo. *Orp* . . . 4H **129**
Leeds Pl. *N4* . . . 6K **43**
Leeds Rd. *Ilf* . . . 6B **48**
Leeds St. *N18* . . . 5E **28**
Leefern Rd. *W12* . . . 3E **72**
Lee Gdns. Av. *Horn* . . . 6L **51**
Leegate. *SE12* . . . 4D **94**
Lee Green (Junct.) . . . 4D 94
Lee Grn. *Orp* . . . 9E **112**
Lee Gro. *Chig* . . . 2M **31**
Lee High Rd. *SE13 & SE12* . . . 2A **94**
Lee Ho. EC2 . . . 8A **60**
(off Monkwell Sq.)
Leeke St. *WC1* . . . 6K **59**
Leeland Rd. *W13* . . . 2E **70**
Leeland Ter. *W13* . . . 2E **70**
Leeland Way. *NW10* . . . 9D **40**
Leeming Rd. *Borwd* . . . 3K **11**
Leemount Clo. *NW4* . . . 2H **41**
Leemount Ho. *NW4* . . . 2H **41**
Lee Pk. *SE3* . . . 3D **94**
Lee Pk. Way. *N18 & N9* . . . 4H **29**
Leerdam Dri. *E14* . . . 4A **78**
Lee Rd. *NW7* . . . 7H **25**
Lee Rd. *SE3* . . . 2D **94**
Lee Rd. *SW19* . . . 5M **105**
Lee Rd. *Enf* . . . 8E **16**
Lee Rd. *Gnfd* . . . 4G **55**
Lees Av. *N'wd* . . . 8D **20**
Lees Ct. W1 . . . 1E **74**
(off Lees Pl.)
Leeside. *Barn* . . . 7J **13**
Leeside Ct. SE16 . . . 2H **77**
(off Rotherhithe St.)
Leeside Cres. *NW11* . . . 4J **41**
Leeside Ind. Est. *N17* . . . 7G **29**
Leeside Rd. *N17* . . . 6F **28**
Leeside Works. *N17* . . . 7G **29**
Leeson Ho. *Twic* . . . 6F **86**
Leeson Rd. *SE24* . . . 3L **91**
Leesons Hill. *Chst & Orp* . . . 7C **112**
Leeson's Way. *Orp* . . . 6D **112**
Lees Pde. *Uxb* . . . 7F **142**
Lees Pl. *W1* . . . 1E **74**
Lees Rd. *Uxb* . . . 7F **142**
Lees, The. *Croy* . . . 4K **125**
Lee St. *E8* . . . 4D **60**
Lee Ter. *SE3* . . . 2C **94**
Lee, The. *N'wd* . . . 5D **20**
Lee Valley Ice Cen. . . . 7H 45
Lee Valley Leisure Golf Course. . . . 9J 17
Lee Valley Technopark. *N17* . . . 1E **44**
Lee Vw. *Enf* . . . 3M **15**
Leeward Ct. *E1* . . . 1E **76**
Leeward Gdns. *SW19* . . . 2J **105**
Leeway. *SE8* . . . 6K **77**
Leeway Clo. *H End* . . . 7K **21**
Leeways, The. *Sutt* . . . 8J **121**
Leewood Clo. *SE12* . . . 5D **94**
Leewood Pl. *Swan* . . . 8B **114**
Lefa Bus. & Ind. Est. *Sidc* . . . 3H **113**
Lefevre Wlk. *E3* . . . 4K **61**
Leff Ho. *NW6* . . . 4J **57**
Lefroy Ho. SE1 . . . 3A **76**
(off Southwark Bri. Rd.)
Lefroy Rd. *W12* . . . 3D **72**
Legard Rd. *N5* . . . 8M **43**
Legatt Rd. *SE9* . . . 4H **95**
Leggatt Rd. *E15* . . . 5A **62**
Leggatts Clo. *Wat* . . . 9D **4**
Leggatts Ri. *Wat* . . . 8E **4**
Leggatts Way. *Wat* . . . 9D **4**
Leggatts Wood Av. *Wat* . . . 9F **4**
Legge St. *SE13* . . . 4A **94**
Leghorn Rd. *NW10* . . . 5D **56**
Leghorn Rd. *SE18* . . . 6B **80**
Legion Clo. *N1* . . . 3L **59**
Legion Ct. *Mord* . . . 1L **121**
Legion Rd. *Gnfd* . . . 4A **54**
Legion Ter. *E3* . . . 4K **61**
Legion Way. *N12* . . . 7C **26**
Legon Av. *Romf* . . . 6A **50**
Legrace Av. *Houn* . . . 1H **85**
Leicester Av. *Mitc* . . . 8J **107**
Leicester Clo. *Wor Pk* . . . 6G **121**
Leicester Ct. W9 . . . 8L **57**
(off Elmfield Way)
Leicester Ct. WC2 . . . 1H **75**
(off Lisle St.)
Leicester Ct. Twic . . . 5H **87**
(off Clevedon Rd.)
Leicester Fields. WC2 . . . 1H **75**
(off Leicester Sq.)
Leicester Gdns. *Ilf* . . . 5C **48**
Leicester Ho. SW9 . . . 2M **91**
(off Loughborough Rd.)
Leicester M. *N2* . . . 1C **42**
Leicester Pl. *WC2* . . . 1H **75**
Leicester Rd. *E11* . . . 3F **46**
Leicester Rd. *N2* . . . 1C **42**
Leicester Rd. *NW10* . . . 3B **56**
Leicester Rd. *Barn* . . . 7M **13**
Leicester Rd. *Croy* . . . 2C **124**
Leicester Sq. *WC2* . . . 1H **75**
Leicester St. *WC2* . . . 1H **75**
Leigham Av. *SW16* . . . 9J **91**
Leigham Clo. *SW16* . . . 9K **91**
Leigham Ct. Rd. *SW16* . . . 8J **91**
Leigham Dri. *Iswth* . . . 8C **70**
Leigham Hall Pde. SW16 . . . 9J **91**
(off Streatham High Rd.)
Leigham Va. *SW16 & SW2* . . . 9K **91**
Leigh Av. *Ilf* . . . 2H **47**
Leigh Clo. *N Mald* . . . 8A **104**
Leigh Clo. Ind. Est. *N Mald* . . . 8B **104**
Leigh Ct. *Borwd* . . . 4B **12**
Leigh Ct. *Harr* . . . 6C **38**
Leigh Cres. *New Ad* . . . 9M **125**
Leigh Dri. *Romf* . . . 4H **35**
Leigh Gdns. *NW10* . . . 5G **57**
Leigh Hunt Dri. *N14* . . . 1H **27**
Leigh Orchard Clo. *SW16* . . . 9K **91**
Leigh Pl. *EC1* . . . 8L **59**
Leigh Pl. *Dart* . . . 1L **115**
Leigh Pl. *Well* . . . 1E **96**
Leigh Rd. *E6* . . . 2L **63**
Leigh Rd. *E10* . . . 5A **46**
Leigh Rd. *N5* . . . 9M **43**
Leigh Rd. *Houn* . . . 3B **86**
Leigh Rodd. *Wat* . . . 3K **21**
Leigh St. *WC1* . . . 6J **59**
Leigh Ter. *Orp* . . . 7F **112**
Leighton Av. *E12* . . . 1L **63**
Leighton Av. *Pinn* . . . 1J **37**
Leighton Clo. *Edgw* . . . 9L **23**
Leighton Ct. *Chesh* . . . 2D **6**
Leighton Cres. *NW5* . . . 1G **59**
Leighton Gdns. *NW10* . . . 5F **56**
Leighton Gdns. *Croy* . . . 3M **123**
Leighton Gdns. *S Croy* . . . 5F **138**
Leighton Gro. *NW5* . . . 1G **59**
Leighton Ho. SW1 . . . 5H **75**
(off Herrick St.)
Leighton House Mus. & Art Galley. . . . 4K 73
Leighton Mans. W14 . . . 7J **73**
(off Greyhound Rd.)
Leighton Pl. *NW5* . . . 1G **59**
Leighton Rd. *NW5* . . . 1G **59**
Leighton Rd. *W13* . . . 3E **70**
Leighton Rd. *Enf* . . . 7D **16**
Leighton Rd. *Har W* . . . 9B **22**
Leighton St. *Croy* . . . 3M **123**
Leighton Way. *Eps* . . . 6B **134**
Leila Parnell Pl. *SE7* . . . 7G **79**
Leinster Av. *SW14* . . . 2A **88**
Leinster Gdns. *W2* . . . 9A **58**
Leinster M. *W2* . . . 1A **74**
Leinster Pl. *W2* . . . 9A **58**
Leinster Rd. *N10* . . . 2F **42**
Leinster Sq. *W2* . . . 9L **57**
(in two parts)
Leinster Ter. *W2* . . . 1A **74**
Leisure Way. *N12* . . . 7B **26**
Leisure West. *Felt* . . . 8F **84**
Leith Clo. *NW9* . . . 6B **40**
Leithcote Gdns. *SW16* . . . 1K **107**
Leithcote Path. *SW16* . . . 9K **91**
Leith Hill. *Orp* . . . 5E **112**
Leith Hill Grn. *Orp* . . . 5E **112**
Leith Mans. W9 . . . 6M **57**
(off Grantully Rd.)
Leith Rd. *N22* . . . 8M **27**
Leith Rd. *Eps* . . . 4C **134**
Leith Towers. *Sutt* . . . 9M **121**
Lela Av. *Houn* . . . 1G **85**
Lelita Clo. *E8* . . . 4E **60**
Lely Ho. N'holt . . . 5H **53**
(off Academy Gdns.)
Leman Pas. E1 . . . 9E **60**
(off Leman St.)
Leman St. *E1* . . . 9D **60**
Lemark Clo. *Stan* . . . 6G **23**
Le May Av. *SE12* . . . 9F **94**
Lemmon Rd. *SE10* . . . 7C **78**
Lemna Rd. *E11* . . . 5D **46**
Le Moal Ho. E1 . . . 8G **61**
(off Stepney Way)
Lemon Fld. Dri. *Wat* . . . 5J **5**
Lemon Gro. *Felt* . . . 7E **84**
Lemonwell Dri. *SE9* . . . 5A **96**
Lemsford Clo. *N15* . . . 4E **44**
Lemsford Ct. *N4* . . . 7A **44**
Lemsford Ct. *Borwd* . . . 6A **12**
Lemuel St. *SW18* . . . 5A **90**
Lena Cres. *N9* . . . 2G **29**
Lena Gdns. *W6* . . . 4G **73**
Lena Kennedy Clo. *E4* . . . 6A **30**
Lenanton Steps. E14 . . . 3L **77**
(off Manilla St.)
Len Clifton Ho. SE18 . . . 5K **79**
(off Cambridge Barracks Rd.)
Lendal Ter. *SW4* . . . 2H **91**
Lenderyou Ct. Dart . . . 6H **99**
(off Phoenix Pl.)
Lenelby Rd. *Surb* . . . 3L **119**
Len Freeman Pl. *SW6* . . . 7K **73**
Lenham Ho. SE1 . . . 4B **76**
(off Long La.)
Lenham Rd. *SE12* . . . 3D **94**
Lenham Rd. *Bexh* . . . 7K **81**
Lenham Rd. *Sutt* . . . 6M **121**
Lenham Rd. *T Hth* . . . 6B **108**
Lennard Av. *W Wick* . . . 4C **126**
Lennard Clo. *W Wick* . . . 4C **126**
Lennard Rd. *SE20 & Beck* . . . 3H **109**
Lennard Rd. *Brom* . . . 3K **127**
Lennard Rd. *Croy* . . . 3A **124**
Lennon Rd. *NW2* . . . 1G **57**
Lennox Clo. *Romf* . . . 4D **50**
Lennox Gdns. *NW10* . . . 9D **40**
Lennox Gdns. *SW1* . . . 4D **74**
Lennox Gdns. *Croy* . . . 6M **123**
Lennox Gdns. *Ilf* . . . 6K **47**
Lennox Gdns. M. *SW1* . . . 4D **74**
Lennox Ho. Belv . . . 4L **81**
(off Picardy St.)
Lennox Ho. Twic . . . 5H **87**
(off Clevedon Rd.)
Lennox Lewis Cen. *E5* . . . 7G **45**
Lennox Rd. *E17* . . . 4K **45**
Lennox Rd. *N4* . . . 7K **43**
Lenor Clo. *Bexh* . . . 3J **97**
Lensbury Clo. *Chesh* . . . 1E **6**
Lensbury Way. *SE2* . . . 4G **81**
Lens Rd. *E7* . . . 3G **63**
Lenthall Ho. SW1 . . . 6G **75**
(off Churchill Gdns.)
Lenthall Rd. *E8* . . . 3E **60**
Lenthorp Rd. *SE10* . . . 5D **78**
Lentmead Rd. *Brom* . . . 9D **94**
Lenton Path. *SE18* . . . 7B **80**
Lenton Ri. *Rich* . . . 2J **87**
Lenton Rd. *SE18* . . . 5B **80**
Len Williams Ct. *NW6* . . . 5L **57**
Leo Ct. *Bren* . . . 8H **71**
Leof Cres. *SE6* . . . 2M **109**
Leominster Rd. *Mord* . . . 1A **122**
Leominster Wlk. *Mord* . . . 1A **122**
Leonard Av. *Mord* . . . 9A **106**
Leonard Av. *Romf* . . . 6B **50**
Leonard Ct. *WC1* . . . 7H **59**
Leonard Ct. *Har W* . . . 8C **22**
Leonard Rd. *E4* . . . 6L **29**
Leonard Rd. *E7* . . . 9E **46**
Leonard Rd. *N9* . . . 3D **28**
Leonard Rd. *SW16* . . . 5G **107**
Leonard Rd. *S'hall* . . . 4H **69**
Leonard Robbins Path. SE28 . . . 1F **80**
(off Tawney Rd.)
Leonard St. *E16* . . . 2J **79**
Leonard St. *EC2* . . . 7B **60**
Leonora Ho. W9 . . . 7A **58**
(off Lanark Rd.)
Leontine Clo. *SE15* . . . 8E **76**
Leopards Ct. EC1 . . . 8L **59**
(off Baldwins Gdns.)
Leopold Av. *SW19* . . . 2K **105**
Leopold Bldgs. E2 . . . 6D **60**
(off Columbia Rd.)
Leopold Rd. *E17* . . . 3L **45**
Leopold Rd. *N2* . . . 1B **42**
Leopold Rd. *N18* . . . 5F **28**
Leopold Rd. *NW10* . . . 3C **56**
Leopold Rd. *SW19* . . . 1K **105**
Leopold Rd. *W5* . . . 2K **71**
Leopold St. *E3* . . . 8K **61**
Leopold Ter. *SW19* . . . 2K **105**
Leo St. *SE15* . . . 8F **76**
Leo Yd. EC1 . . . 7M **59**
(off St John St.)
Leppoc Rd. *SW4* . . . 4H **91**
Leroy St. *SE1* . . . 5C **76**
Lerry Clo. *W14* . . . 7K **73**
Lerwick Ct. *Enf* . . . 7C **16**
Lescombe Clo. *SE23* . . . 9J **93**
Lescombe Rd. *SE23* . . . 9J **93**
Lesley Clo. *Bex* . . . 6M **97**
Lesley Clo. *Swan* . . . 7B **114**
Leslie Gdns. *Sutt* . . . 8L **121**
Leslie Gro. *Croy* . . . 3C **124**
Leslie Gro. Pl. *Croy* . . . 3C **124**
Leslie Pk. Rd. *Croy* . . . 3C **124**
Leslie Prince Ct. *SE5* . . . 8B **76**
Leslie Rd. *E11* . . . 9A **46**
Leslie Rd. *E16* . . . 9F **62**
Leslie Rd. *N2* . . . 1B **42**
Leslie Smith Sq. *SE18* . . . 7L **79**
Lesnes Abbey (Remains of) . . . 5H 81
Lesney Farm Est. *Eri* . . . 8B **82**
Lesney Pk. *Eri* . . . 7B **82**
Lesney Pk. Rd. *Eri* . . . 7B **82**
Lessar Av. *SW4* . . . 5G **91**
Lessingham Av. *SW17* . . . 1D **106**
Lessingham Av. *Ilf* . . . 1L **47**
Lessing St. *SE23* . . . 6J **93**
Lessington Av. *Romf* . . . 4A **50**
Lessness Av. *Bexh* . . . 8H **81**
Lessness Heath. . . . 6L 81
Lessness Pk. *Belv* . . . 6K **81**
Lessness Rd. *Belv* . . . 7L **81**
Lessness Rd. *Mord* . . . 1A **122**
Lester Av. *E15* . . . 7C **62**
Lester Ct. *Wat* . . . 1G **9**
Leston Clo. *Rain* . . . 6F **66**
Leswin Pl. *N16* . . . 8D **44**
Leswin Rd. *N16* . . . 8D **44**
Letchford Gdns. *NW10* . . . 6E **56**
Letchford M. *NW10* . . . 6E **56**
Letchford Ter. *Harr* . . . 8M **21**
Letchmore Heath. . . . 3C 10
Letchmore Ho. W10 . . . 7G **57**
(off Sutton Way)
Letchworth Av. *Felt* . . . 6D **84**
Letchworth Clo. *Brom* . . . 9E **110**
Letchworth Clo. *Wat* . . . 5H **21**
Letchworth Dri. *Brom* . . . 9E **110**
Letchworth St. *SW17* . . . 1D **106**
Lethbridge Clo. *SE13* . . . 9A **78**
Letterstone Rd. *SW6* . . . 8K **73**
Lettice St. *SW6* . . . 9K **73**
Lett Rd. *E15* . . . 3B **62**
Lettsom St. *SE5* . . . 1C **92**
Lettsom Wlk. *E13* . . . 5E **62**
Leucha Rd. *E17* . . . 3J **45**
Levana Clo. *SW19* . . . 7J **89**
Levant Ho. E1 . . . 7H **61**
(off Ernest St.)
Levehurst Ho. *SE27* . . . 2A **108**
Leven Clo. *Wal X* . . . 6D **6**
Leven Clo. *Wat* . . . 5H **21**
Levendale Rd. *SE23* . . . 8J **93**
Leven Dri. *Wal X* . . . 6D **6**
Levenhurst Way. *SW4* . . . 1J **91**
Leven Rd. *E14* . . . 8A **62**
Leven Way. *Hay* . . . 9C **52**
Leveret Clo. *New Ad* . . . 3B **140**
Leveret Clo. *Wat* . . . 7E **4**
Leverett St. *SW3* . . . 5C **74**
Leverholme Gdns. *SE9* . . . 9L **95**
Leverington Pl. N1 . . . 6B **60**
(off Charles Sq.)
Leverson St. *SW16* . . . 3G **107**
Leverstock Ho. SW3 . . . 6C **74**
(off Cale St.)
Lever St. *EC1* . . . 6M **59**
Leverton Pl. *NW5* . . . 1G **59**
Leverton St. *NW5* . . . 1G **59**
Leverton Way. *Wal A* . . . 6J **7**
Levett Gdns. *Ilf* . . . 9D **48**
Levett Rd. *Bark* . . . 2C **64**
Levine Gdns. *Bark* . . . 5H **65**
Levison Way. *N19* . . . 6H **43**
Levita Ho. NW1 . . . 6H **59**
(off Ossulston St., in two parts)
Lewes Clo. *N'holt* . . . 2L **53**
Lewesdon Clo. *SW19* . . . 7H **89**
Lewes Ho. SE1 . . . 3C **76**
(off Druid St.)
Lewes Ho. SE15 . . . 7E **76**
(off Friary Est.)
Lewes Rd. *N12* . . . 5C **26**
Lewes Rd. *Brom* . . . 6H **111**
Lewes Rd. *Romf* . . . 4H **35**
Leweston Pl. *N16* . . . 5D **44**
Lewes Way. *Crox G* . . . 6A **8**
Lewey Ho. E3 . . . 7K **61**
(off Joseph St.)
Lewgars Av. *NW9* . . . 4A **40**
Lewing Clo. *Orp* . . . 3C **128**
Lewin Rd. *SW14* . . . 2B **88**
Lewin Rd. *SW16* . . . 3H **107**
Lewin Rd. *Bexh* . . . 4J **97**
Lewins Rd. *Eps* . . . 6M **133**
Lewis Av. *E17* . . . 8L **29**
Lewis Clo. *N14* . . . 9G **15**
Lewis Ct. SE16 . . . 6F **76**
(off Stubbs Dri.)
Lewis Cres. *NW10* . . . 1B **56**
Lewis Gdns. *N2* . . . 9B **26**
Lewis Gro. *SE13* . . . 3A **94**
Lewisham. . . . 2A 94
Lewisham Bus. Cen. *SE14* . . . 7H **77**
Lewisham Cen. *SE13* . . . 3A **94**
Lewisham Crematorium. *SE6* . . . 8D **94**
Lewisham Heights. *SE23* . . . 7G **93**
Lewisham High St. *SE13* . . . 2A **94**
(Lewisham Rd.)
Lewisham High St. *SE13* . . . 5M **93**
(Rushey Grn.)
Lewisham Hill. *SE13* . . . 1A **94**
Lewisham Model Mkt. SE13 . . . 3A **94**
(off Lewisham High St.)
Lewisham Pk. *SE13* . . . 4A **94**
Lewisham Rd. *SE13* . . . 9M **77**
Lewisham St. *SW1* . . . 3H **75**
(in two parts)
Lewisham Way. *SE14 & SE4* . . . 9K **77**
Lewis Ho. E14 . . . 2A **78**
(off Coldharbour)
Lewis Pl. *E8* . . . 1E **60**
Lewis Rd. *Horn* . . . 4G **51**
Lewis Rd. *Mitc* . . . 6B **106**
(in two parts)
Lewis Rd. *Rich* . . . 4H **87**
Lewis Rd. *Sidc* . . . 9G **97**
Lewis Rd. *S'hall* . . . 3J **69**
Lewis Rd. *Sutt* . . . 6M **121**
Lewis Rd. *Well* . . . 2G **97**
Lewis Silkin Ho. SE15 . . . 7G **77**
(off Lovelinch Clo.)
Lewis St. *NW1* . . . 2F **58**
(in two parts)
Lewis Way. *Dag* . . . 2M **65**
Lexden Dri. *Romf* . . . 4F **48**
Lexden Rd. *W3* . . . 1M **71**
Lexden Rd. *Mitc* . . . 8H **107**
Lexden Ter. Wal A . . . 7J **7**
(off Sewardstone Rd.)
Lexham Gdns. *W8* . . . 5L **73**
Lexham Gdns. M. *W8* . . . 4M **73**
Lexham Ho. Bark . . . 4B **64**
(off St Margarets)
Lexham M. *W8* . . . 5L **73**
Lexham Wlk. *W8* . . . 4M **73**
Lexington Apartments. *EC1* . . . 7B **60**
Lexington Clo. *Borwd* . . . 5K **11**
Lexington Ct. *Purl* . . . 2A **138**
Lexington St. *W1* . . . 1G **75**
Lexington Way. *Barn* . . . 6H **13**
Lexton Gdns. *SW12* . . . 7H **91**
Leybourne Av. *W13* . . . 3F **70**
Leyborne Pk. *Rich* . . . 9L **71**
Leybourne Clo. *Brom* . . . 1E **126**
Leybourne Ho. *E14* . . . 9K **61**
Leybourne Ho. *SE15* . . . 7G **77**
Leybourne Rd. *E11* . . . 6D **46**
Leybourne Rd. *NW1* . . . 3F **58**

Leybourne Rd.—Linkside

Leybourne Rd. NW9 3L 39
Leybourne Rd. Uxb 4A 52
Leybourne St. NW1 3F 58
Leybridge Ct. SE12 4E 94
Leyburn Clo. E17 2M 45
Leyburn Cres. Romf 7J 35
Leyburn Gdns. Croy 4C 124
Leyburn Gro. N18 6E 28
Leyburn Rd. N18 6E 28
Leyburn Rd. Romf 7J 35
Leycroft Clo. Lou 7L 19
Leycroft Gdns. Eri 9F 82
Leydenhatch La. Swan 5A 114
Leyden Mans. N19 5J 43
Leyden St. E1 8D 60
Leydon Clo. SE16 2H 77
Leyes Rd. E16 1H 79
Leyfield. Wor Pk 3C 120
Leyhill Clo. Swan 9C 114
Leyland Av. Enf 4J 17
Leyland Clo. Chesh 1C 6
Leyland Gdns. Wfd G 5G 31
Leyland Ho. E14 1M 77 (off Hale St.)
Leyland Rd. SE12 4E 94
Leylang Rd. SE14 8H 77
Leys Av. Dag 4A 66
Leys Clo. Dag 3B 66 (in two parts)
Leys Clo. Harr 3B 38
Leys Ct. SW9 1L 91
Leysdown Av. Bexh 3A 98
Leysdown Ho. SE17 6C 76 (off Madron St.)
Leysdown Rd. SE9 8J 95
Leysfield Rd. W12 4E 72
Leys Gdns. Barn 7E 14
Leyspring Rd. E11 6D 46
Leys Rd. Oxs 4B 132
Leys Rd. E. Enf 3J 17
Leys Rd. W. Enf 3J 17
Leys Sq. N3 8M 25
Leys, The. N2 2A 42
Leys, The. Harr 4K 39
Leys, The. W on T 6K 117
Ley St. Ilf 7M 47
Leyswood Dri. Ilf 3C 48
Leythe Rd. W3 3A 72
Leyton. 8A 46
Leyton Bus. Cen. E10 7L 45
Leyton Ct. SE23 7G 93
Leyton Cross. 9E 98
Leyton Cross Rd. Dart 9D 98
Leyton Grange Est. E10 7L 45
Leyton Grn. Rd. E10 4A 46
Leyton Ind. Village. E17 5H 45
Leyton Orient F.C. (Brisbane Rd.) 8M 45
Leyton Pk. Rd. E10 8A 46
Leyton Rd. E15 1A 62
Leyton Rd. SW19 4A 106
Leytonstone. 6C 46
Leytonstone Rd. E15 9C 46
Leyton Way. E11 5C 46
Leywick St. E15 5C 62
Lezayre Rd. Orp 8D 128
Liardet St. SE14 7J 77
Liberia Rd. N5 2M 59
Liberty Av. SW19 5A 106
Liberty Ct. Bark 5F 64
Liberty M. N22 8M 27
Liberty M. SW12 5F 90
Liberty St. SW9 9K 75
Liberty, The. Romf 3C 50
Liberty 2 Cen. (Shop. Cen.) Romf 2D 50
Libra Ct. E4 4L 29
Libra Rd. E3 5K 61
Libra Rd. E13 5E 62
Library Ct. N17 1D 44
Library Mans. W12 3G 73 (off Pennard Rd.)
Library Pde. NW10 4C 56 (off Craven Pk. Rd.)
Library Pl. E1 1F 76
Library St. SE1 3M 75
Library Way. Twic 6A 86
Lichfield Clo. Barn 5D 14
Lichfield Ct. Rich 3J 87
Lichfield Ct. Surb 9J 103 (off Claremont Rd.)
Lichfield Gdns. Rich 3J 87
Lichfield Gro. N3 8L 25
Lichfield Rd. E3 6J 61
Lichfield Rd. E6 6H 63
Lichfield Rd. N9 2E 28
Lichfield Rd. NW2 9J 41
Lichfield Rd. Dag 9F 48
Lichfield Rd. Houn 2G 85
Lichfield Rd. N'wd 1E 36
Lichfield Rd. Rich 9K 71
Lichfield Rd. Wfd G 4C 30
Lichfield Ter. Rich 4J 87
Lichfield Way. S Croy 2H 139
Lichlade Clo. Orp 6D 128
Lickey Ho. W14 7K 73 (off N. End Rd.)
Lidbury Rd. NW7 6J 25
Lidcote Gdns. SW9 1K 91
Liddall Way. W Dray 2K 143
Liddell Clo. Harr 1H 39
Liddell Gdns. NW10 5G 57
Liddell Rd. NW6 2L 57
Lidding Rd. Harr 3H 39
Liddington Rd. E15 4D 62
Liddon Rd. E13 6F 62
Liddon Rd. Brom 7G 111
Liden Clo. E17 5K 45
Lidfield Rd. N16 9B 44
Lidgate Rd. SE15 8D 76
Lidiard Rd. SW18 8A 90
Lidlington Pl. NW1 5G 59
Lido Sq. N17 9B 28
Lidyard Rd. N19 6G 43
Lieutenant Ellis Way. Chesh & Wal X 3A 6
Lifetimes Mus. 5A 124 (off High St., Croydon)
Liffler Rd. SE18 6C 80
Liffords Pl. SW13 1D 88
Lifford St. SW15 3H 89
Lightcliffe Rd. N13 4L 27
Lighter Clo. SE16 5J 77
Lighterman Ho. E14 1A 78
Lighterman M. E1 9H 61
Lightermans Rd. E14 3L 77
Lightermans Wlk. SW18 3L 89
Lightfoot Rd. N8 3J 43
Light Horse Ct. SW3 6E 74 (off Royal Hospital Rd.)
Lightley Clo. Wemb 4J 55
Ligonier St. E2 7D 60
Lilac Clo. E4 6K 29
Lilac Clo. Chesh 4B 6
Lilac Ct. E13 4G 63
Lilac Ct. Tedd 1D 102
Lilac Gdns. W5 4H 71
Lilac Gdns. Croy 5L 125
Lilac Gdns. Hay 9C 52
Lilac Gdns. Romf 6C 50
Lilac Gdns. Swan 7B 114
Lilac Ho. SE4 2L 93
Lilac Pl. SE11 5K 75
Lilac Pl. W Dray 1K 143
Lilacs Av. Enf 9C 6
Lilac St. W12 1E 72
Lila Pl. Swan 8C 114
Lilburne Gdns. SE9 4J 95
Lilburne Rd. SE9 4J 95
Lilburne Wlk. NW10 2A 56
Lile Cres. W7 8C 54
Lilestone Ho. NW8 7B 58 (off Frampton St.)
Lilestone St. NW8 7C 58
Lilford Ho. SE5 1A 92
Lilford Rd. SE5 1M 91
Lilian Barker Clo. SE12 4E 94
Lilian Board Way. Gnfd 1B 54
Lilian Clo. N16 8C 44
Lilian Gdns. Wfd G 8F 30
Lilian Rd. SW16 5G 107
Lillechurch Rd. Dag 2F 64
Lilleshall Rd. Mord 1B 122
Lilley Clo. E1 2E 76
Lilley La. NW7 5B 24
Lillian Av. W3 3L 71
Lillian Rd. SW13 7E 72
Lillie Mans. SW6 7J 73 (off Lillie Rd.)
Lillie Rd. SW6 7J 73
Lillie Rd. Big H 9H 141
Lillieshall Rd. SW4 2F 90
Lillie Yd. SW6 7L 73
Lillington Gdns. Est. SW1 5G 75 (off Vauxhall Bri. Rd.)
Lilliput Av. N'holt 4J 53
Lilliput Ct. SE12 4F 94
Lilliput Rd. Romf 5B 50
Lily Clo. W14 5H 73 (in two parts)
Lily Dri. W Dray 5G 143
Lily Gdns. Wemb 5G 55
Lily Nichols Ho. E16 2H 79 (off Connaught Rd.)
Lily Pl. EC1 8L 59
Lily Rd. E17 4L 45
Lilyville Rd. SW6 9K 73
Limberg Ho. SE8 5K 77
Limborough Ho. E14 8L 61 (off Thomas Rd.)
Limbourne Av. Dag 5K 49
Limburg Rd. SW11 3C 90
Lime Av. Upm 9L 51
Lime Av. W Dray 1K 143
Limeburner La. EC4 9M 59
Lime Clo. E1 2E 76
Lime Clo. Brom 8J 111
Lime Clo. Buck H 2H 31
Lime Clo. Cars 4D 122
Lime Clo. Harr 9E 22
Lime Clo. Pinn 1D 36
Lime Clo. Romf 2A 50
Lime Clo. Wat 9H 9
Lime Ct. E11 7C 46 (off Trinity Clo.)
Lime Ct. E17 3A 46
Lime Ct. SE9 8M 95
Lime Ct. Harr 4D 38
Lime Ct. Mitc 6B 106
Lime Cres. Sun 6G 101
Limecroft Clo. Eps 9B 120
Limedene Clo. Pinn 8H 21
Lime Gro. E4 6K 29
Lime Gro. N20 1K 25
Lime Gro. W12 3G 73
Lime Gro. Hay 1B 68
Lime Gro. Ilf 6D 32
Lime Gro. N Mald 7B 104
Lime Gro. Orp 4M 127
Lime Gro. Ruis 4F 36
Lime Gro. Sidc 5D 96
Lime Gro. Twic 5D 86
Limeharbour. E14 4M 77
Limehouse. 9K 61
Limehouse Causeway. E14 1K 77
Limehouse Ct. E14 9L 61 (off Dod St.)
Limehouse Cut. E14 8M 61 (off Morris Rd.)
Limehouse Fields Est. E1 8J 61
Limehouse Link. E14 9J 61
Lime Kiln Dri. SE7 7F 78
Limekiln Pl. SE19 4D 108
Lime Mdw. Av. S Croy 5E 138
Limerick Clo. SW12 6G 91
Lime Rd. Eri 4K 81
Lime Rd. Rich 3K 87
Lime Rd. Swan 7B 114
Lime Row. Eri 4K 81
Limerston St. SW10 7A 74
Limes Av. E11 2F 46
Limes Av. E12 8J 47
Limes Av. N12 4A 26
Limes Av. NW7 6C 24
Limes Av. NW11 5J 41
Limes Av. SE20 4F 108
Limes Av. SW13 1D 88
Limes Av. Cars 3D 122
Limes Av. Chig 5A 32
Limes Av. Croy 5L 123
Limes Av., The. N11 5F 26
Limes Clo. N11 5G 27
Limes Ct. NW6 3J 57 (off Brondesbury Pk.)
Limesdale Gdns. Edgw 9A 24
Limes Fld. Rd. SW14 2C 88
Limesford Rd. SE15 3H 93
Limes Gdns. SW18 5L 89
Limes Gro. SE13 3A 94
Limes Pl. Croy 2B 124
Limes Rd. Beck 6M 109
Limes Rd. Chesh 5E 6
Limes Rd. Croy 1B 124
Limes Row. F'boro 7M 127
Limes, The. SW18 5L 89
Limes, The. W2 1L 73
Limes, The. Brom 4J 127
Limes, The. Dart 6K 99
Limes, The. E Mol 8M 101
Limes, The. Horn 1H 51
Limes, The. Purf 6L 83
Limestone Wlk. Eri 3H 81
Lime St. E17 2J 45
Lime St. EC3 1C 76
Lime St. Pas. EC3 9C 60
Limes Wlk. SE15 3G 93
Limes Wlk. W5 3H 71
Lime Ter. W7 1C 70
Lime Tree Av. Esh 3B 118
Limetree Clo. SW2 7K 91
Limetree Ct. Pinn 7L 21 (off Avenue, The)
Lime Tree Ct. S Croy 8A 124
Lime Tree Gro. Croy 5K 125
Lime Tree Pl. Mitc 5F 106
Lime Tree Rd. Houn 9M 69
Limetree Ter. SE6 7K 93
Limetree Ter. Well 2E 96
Limetree Wlk. SW17 2E 106
Lime Tree Wlk. Bush 1C 22
Lime Tree Wlk. Enf 2A 16
Lime Tree Wlk. W Wick 6D 126
Lime Wlk. E15 4C 62
Lime Wlk. Den 1A 142
Limewood Clo. E17 2K 45
Limewood Clo. W13 9F 54
Limewood Clo. Beck 9A 110
Limewood Ct. Ilf 3K 47
Limewood Rd. Eri 8A 82
Limpsfield Av. SW19 8H 89
Limpsfield Av. T Hth 9K 107
Limpsfield Rd. S Croy 4E 138
Linacre Clo. SE15 2F 92
Linacre Ct. W6 6H 73
Linacre Rd. NW2 2F 56
Linale Ho. N1 5B 60 (off Murray Gro.)
Linberry Wlk. SE8 5K 77
Linchmere Rd. SE12 6D 94
Lincoln Av. N14 3G 27
Lincoln Av. SW19 9H 89
Lincoln Av. Romf 7B 50
Lincoln Av. Twic 8A 86
Lincoln Clo. SE25 1E 124
Lincoln Clo. Eri 1D 98
Lincoln Clo. Gnfd 4A 54
Lincoln Clo. Harr 3K 37
Lincoln Clo. Horn 3L 51
Lincoln Ct. N16 5B 44
Lincoln Ct. SE12 9G 95
Lincoln Ct. Borwd 7B 12
Lincoln Ct. S Croy 7A 124 (off Warham Rd.)
Lincoln Cres. Enf 7C 16
Lincoln Dri. Wat 3G 21
Lincoln Gdns. Ilf 5J 47
Lincoln Grn. Rd. Orp 9D 112
Lincoln Ho. SW3 3D 74
Lincoln Ho. SW9 & SE5 8L 75
Lincoln M. NW6 4K 57
Lincoln M. SE21 8B 92
Lincoln Pde. N2 1C 42
Lincoln Rd. E7 2H 63
Lincoln Rd. E13 7F 62
Lincoln Rd. E18 8D 30
Lincoln Rd. N2 1C 42
Lincoln Rd. SE25 7F 108
Lincoln Rd. Enf 6C 16
Lincoln Rd. Eri 1D 98 (in two parts)
Lincoln Rd. Felt 9K 85
Lincoln Rd. Harr 3K 37
Lincoln Rd. Mitc 9J 107
Lincoln Rd. N Mald 7A 104
Lincoln Rd. N'wd 1D 36
Lincoln Rd. Sidc 2F 112
Lincoln Rd. Wemb 2H 55
Lincoln Rd. Wor Pk 3F 120
Lincolnsfield Cen., The. Bush 6K 9
Lincolns Inn Fields. WC2 9K 59
Lincoln's Inn Hall. 9K 59
Lincolns, The. NW7 3D 24
Lincoln St. E11 7C 46
Lincoln St. SW3 5D 74
Lincoln Wlk. Eps 2B 134 (in two parts)
Lincoln Way. Enf 7F 16
Lincoln Way. Sun 5C 100
Lincombe Rd. Brom 9D 94
Lindal Cres. Enf 6J 15
Lindal Rd. SE4 4K 93
Lindbergh Rd. Wall 9J 123
Linden Av. NW10 5H 57
Linden Av. Coul 8F 136
Linden Av. Dart 7G 99
Linden Av. Enf 3E 16
Linden Av. Houn 4M 85
Linden Av. Ruis 6E 36
Linden Av. T Hth 8M 107
Linden Av. Wemb 1K 55
Linden Clo. N14 8G 15
Linden Clo. Orp 7E 128
Linden Clo. Ruis 6E 36
Linden Clo. Stan 5F 22
Linden Clo. Th Dit 2D 118
Linden Clo. Wal X 3B 6
Linden Ct. W12 2G 73
Linden Ct. Sidc 1C 112
Linden Cres. Gnfd 2D 54
Linden Cres. King T 6K 103
Linden Cres. Wfd G 6F 30
Lindenfield. Chst 6M 111
Linden Gdns. W2 1L 73
Linden Gdns. W4 6C 72
Linden Gdns. Enf 3E 16
Linden Gro. SE15 2F 92
Linden Gro. SE26 3G 109
Linden Gro. N Mald 7C 104
Linden Gro. Tedd 2D 102
Linden Gro. W on T 4D 116
Linden Gro. Warl 9J 139
Linden Ho. SE8 7K 77 (off Abinger Gro.)
Linden Ho. SE15 2F 92
Linden Ho. Hamp 3L 101
Linden Lawns. Wemb 9K 39
Linden Lea. N2 3A 42
Linden Lea. Pinn 7K 21
Linden Lea. Wat 6E 4
Linden Leas. W Wick 4B 126
Linden M. N1 1B 60
Linden M. W2 1L 73
Linden Pl. Eps 4C 134
Linden Pl. Mitc 8C 106
Linden Rd. N10 2F 42
Linden Rd. N11 2D 26
Linden Rd. N15 2A 44
Linden Rd. Hamp 4L 101
Lindens, The. E17 2M 45 (off Prospect Hill)
Lindens, The. N12 5B 26
Lindens, The. W4 9A 72
Lindens, The. Lou 7K 19
Lindens, The. New Ad 8A 126
Linden St. Romf 2B 50
Linden Wlk. N19 7G 43
Linden Way. N14 8G 15
Linden Way. Purl 2G 137
Linden Way. Shep 9A 100
Lindeth Clo. Stan 6F 22
Lindfield Gdns. NW3 1M 57
Lindfield Rd. W5 7G 55
Lindfield Rd. Croy 1D 124
Lindfield Rd. Romf 5J 35
Lindfield St. E14 9L 61
Lindhill Clo. Enf 4H 17
Lindholme Ct. NW9 8C 24 (off Pageant Av.)
Lindisfarne Rd. SW20 4E 104
Lindisfarne Rd. Dag 8G 49
Lindisfarne Way. E9 9J 45
Lindley Ct. King T 5G 103
Lindley Est. SE15 8E 76
Lindley Ho. E1 8G 61 (off Lindley St.)
Lindley Ho. SE15 8E 76 (off Peckham Pk. Rd.)
Lindley Pl. Kew 9L 71
Lindley Rd. E10 7A 46
Lindley Rd. W on T 5H 117
Lindley St. E1 8G 61
Lindop Ho. E1 7J 61 (off Mile End Rd.)
Lindore Rd. SW11 3D 90
Lindores Rd. Cars 2A 122
Lindo St. SE15 1G 93
Lind Rd. Sutt 7A 122
Lindrop St. SW6 1A 90
Lindsay Clo. Chess 9J 119
Lindsay Clo. Eps 5A 134
Lindsay Clo. Stanw 4B 144
Lindsay Ct. Croy 6B 124 (off Eden Rd.)
Lindsay Dri. Harr 4J 39
Lindsay Dri. Shep 1B 116
Lindsay Pl. Chesh 3B 6
Lindsay Rd. Hamp H 1M 101
Lindsay Rd. Wor Pk 4F 120
Lindsay Sq. SW1 6H 75
Lindsell St. SE10 9A 78
Lindsey Clo. Brom 7H 111
Lindsey Clo. Mitc 8J 107
Lindsey Ct. N13 3L 27 (off Green Lanes)
Lindsey Gdns. Felt 6B 84
Lindsey Ho. W5 5H 71
Lindsey M. N1 3A 60
Lindsey Rd. Dag 9G 49
Lindsey St. EC1 8M 59
Lindsey Way. Horn 3G 51
Lind St. SE8 1L 93
Lindum Rd. Tedd 4G 103
Lindway. SE27 2M 107
Lindwood Clo. E6 9K 63
Linfield. WC1 6K 59 (off Sidmouth St.)
Linfield Clo. NW4 2G 41
Linfield Clo. W on T 7F 116
Linford Christie Stadium. 8E 56
Linford Rd. E17 1A 46
Linford St. SW8 9G 75
Lingard Ho. E14 4A 78 (off Marshfield St.)
Lingards Rd. SE13 3A 94
Lingey Clo. Sidc 8D 96
Lingfield Av. Dart 6M 99
Lingfield Av. King T 8J 103
Lingfield Av. Upm 8K 51
Lingfield Clo. Enf 8C 16
Lingfield Clo. N'wd 7C 20
Lingfield Ct. N'holt 5L 53
Lingfield Cres. SE9 3B 96
Lingfield Gdns. N9 9F 16
Lingfield Ho. SE1 3M 75 (off Lancaster St.)
Lingfield Rd. SW19 2H 105
Lingfield Rd. Wor Pk 5G 121
Lingfield Way. Wat 2D 8
Lingham St. SW9 1J 91
Lingholm Way. Barn 7H 13
Lingmere Clo. Chig 2A 32
Lingmoor Dri. Wat 6G 5
Ling Rd. E16 8E 62
Ling Rd. Eri 7A 82
Lingrove Gdns. Buck H 2F 30
Lings Coppice. SE21 8B 92
Lingwell Rd. SW17 9C 90
Lingwood. Bexh 1M 97
Lingwood Gdns. Iswth 8C 70
Lingwood Rd. E5 5E 44
Linhope St. NW1 7D 58
Linkenholt Mans. W6 5D 72 (off Stamford Brook Av.)
Linkfield. Brom 1E 126
Linkfield. W Mol 7M 101
Linkfield Rd. Iswth 1D 86
Link Ho. E3 5M 61
Link Ho. W10 9H 57 (off Kingsdown Clo.)
Link La. Wall 8H 123
Linklea Clo. NW9 7C 24
Link Pl. Ilf 6D 32
Link Rd. E1 1E 76
Link Rd. N8 1L 43 (in two parts)
Link Rd. N11 4E 26
Link Rd. Dag 5M 65
Link Rd. Felt 6D 84
Link Rd. Wall 3E 122
Link Rd. Wat & Bush 4H 9
Links Av. Mord 8L 105 (in two parts)
Links Av. Romf 9F 34
Links Clo. Asht 9G 133
Links Dri. N20 1L 25
Links Dri. Els 5K 11
Links Gdns. SW16 4L 107
Linkside. N12 6L 25
Linkside. Chig 5A 32
Linkside. N Mald 6C 104

Linkside Clo. *Enf* 5K 15
Linkside Gdns. *Enf* 5K 15
Links Pl. *Asht* 9H 133
Links Rd. *NW2* 7D 40
Links Rd. *SW17* 3E 106
Links Rd. *W3* 9L 55
Links Rd. *Asht* 9G 133
Links Rd. *Eps* 5E 134
Links Rd. *W Wick* 3A 126
Links Rd. *Wfd G* 5E 30
Links Side. *Enf* 5K 15
Links, The. *E17* 2J 45
Links, The. *W on T* 4E 116
Link St. *E9* 2G 61
Linksview. N2 3D 42
(off Gt. North Rd.)
Links Vw. *N3* 7K 25
Links Vw. *Dart* 7F 98
Links Vw. Clo. *Stan* 7E 22
Links Vw. Ct. *Hamp* 1B 102
Links Vw. Rd. *Croy* 5L 125
Links Vw. Rd. *Hamp H* 2A 102
Linksway. *NW4* 9H 25
Links Way. *Beck* 1L 125
Links Way. *Crox G* 5A 8
Links Way. *N'wd* 7A 20
Links Yd. E1 8E 60
(off Spelman St.)
Link, The. SE9 9L 95
(off William Barefoot Dri.)
Link, The. *W3* 9M 55
Link, The. *Enf* 3J 17
Link, The. *N'holt* 1K 53
Link, The. *Pinn* 5G 37
Link, The. *Tedd* 3D 102
Link, The. *Wemb* 6G 39
Linkway. *N4* 5A 44
Linkway. *SW20* 8F 104
Link Way. *Brom* 2J 127
Linkway. *Dag* 9G 49
Link Way. *Horn* 6J 51
Link Way. *Pinn* 8H 21
Linkway. *Rich* 8F 86
Linkway, The. *Barn* 8M 13
Linkway, The. *Sutt* 1A 136
Linkwood Wlk. *NW1* 3H 59
Linley Ct. *Sutt* 6A 122
Linley Cres. *Romf* 1M 49
Linley Rd. *N17* 9C 28
Linley Sambourne House. *4L 73*
(off Stafford Ter.)
Linnell Clo. *NW11* 4M 41
Linnell Dri. *NW11* 4M 41
Linnell Ho. E1 8D 60
(off Folgate St.)
Linnell Rd. *N18* 5E 28
Linnell Rd. *SE5* 1C 92
Linnet Clo. *N9* 1H 29
Linnet Clo. *SE28* 1G 81
Linnet Clo. *Bush* 9A 10
Linnet Clo. *S Croy* 2H 139
Linnet M. *SW12* 6E 90
Linnet Rd. *Ab L* 4E 4
Linnett Clo. *E4* 4A 30
Linnet Way. *Purf* 6M 83
Linom Rd. *SW4* 3J 91
Linscott Rd. *E5* 9G 45
Linsdell Rd. *Bark* 4A 64
Linsey Ct. E10 6L 45
(off Grange Rd.)
Linsey St. *SE16* 5E 76
(in two parts)
Linslade Clo. *Houn* 4J 85
Linslade Clo. *Pinn* 1F 36
Linslade Ho. *E2* 4E 60
Linslade Ho. NW8 7C 58
(off Paveley St.)
Linslade Rd. *Orp* 8E 128
Linstead St. *NW6* 3L 57
Linstead Way. *SW18* 6J 89
Linster Gro. *Borwd* 7A 12
Lintaine Clo. *W6* 7J 73
Linthorpe Av. *Wemb* 2G 55
Linthorpe Rd. *N16* 5C 44
Linthorpe Rd. *Cockf* 5C 14
Linton Av. *Borwd* 3K 11
Linton Clo. *SE7* 6G 79
Linton Clo. *Mitc* 2D 122
Linton Clo. *Well* 9F 80
Linton Ct. *Romf* 9C 34
Linton Gdns. *E6* 9J 63
Linton Glade. *Croy* 1J 139
(in two parts)
Linton Gro. *SE27* 2M 107
Linton Ho. E3 8L 61
(off St Paul's Way)
Linton Rd. *Bark* 3A 64
Lintons La. *Eps* 4C 134
Lintons, The. *Bark* 3A 64
Linton St. *N1* 4A 60
(in two parts)
Lintott Ct. *Stanw* 5B 144
Linver Rd. *SW6* 1L 89
Linwood Clo. *SE5* 1D 92
Linwood Cres. *Enf* 3E 16
Linzee Rd. *N8* 2J 43
Lion Av. *Twic* 7D 86
Lion Clo. *SE4* 5L 93
Lion Ct. E1 1H 77
(off Highway, The)
Lion Ct. N1 4K 59
(off Copenhagen St.)
Lion Ct. SE1 2C 76
(off Magdalen St.)
Lion Ct. *Borwd* 3A 12
Lionel Gdns. *SE9* 4H 95
Lionel Mans. W14 4H 73
(off Haarlem Rd.)
Lionel M. *W10* 8J 57
Lionel Rd. *SE9* 4H 95
Lionel Rd. N. *Bren* 4J 71
Lionel Rd. S. *Bren* 6K 71
Lion Ga. Gdns. *Rich* 2K 87
Lion Ga. M. *SW18* 6L 89
Liongate M. *E Mol* 7D 102
Lion Grn. Rd. *Coul* 8H 137
Lion Mills. *E2* 5E 60
Lion Pk. Av. *Chess* 6L 119
Lion Rd. *E6* 8K 63
Lion Rd. *N9* 2E 28
Lion Rd. *Bexh* 3J 97
Lion Rd. *Croy* 9A 108
Lion Rd. *Twic* 7D 86
Lions Clo. *SE9* 9H 95
Lion Way. *Bren* 8H 71
Lion Wharf Rd. *Iswth* 2F 86
Lion Yd. *SW4* 3H 91
Liphook Clo. *Horn* 9D 50
Liphook Cres. *SE23* 6G 93
Liphook Rd. *Wat* 4H 21
Lippitts Hill. *Lou* 3C 18
Lipsham Clo. *Bans* 5B 136
Lipton Clo. *SE28* 1G 81
Lipton Rd. *E1* 9H 61
Lisbon Av. *Twic* 8A 86
Lisbon Clo. *E17* 9K 29
Lisburne Rd. *NW3* 9D 42
Lisford St. *SE15* 9D 76
Lisgar Ter. *W14* 5K 73
Liskeard Clo. *Chst* 3A 112
Liskeard Gdns. *SE3* 9E 78
Liskeard Ho. SE11 6L 75
(off Kennings Way)
Lisle Clo. *SW17* 1F 106
Lisle Ct. *NW2* 8J 41
Lisle St. *WC2* 1H 75
Lismirrane Ind. Pk. *Els* 8F 10
Lismore. SW19 2K 105
(off Woodside)
Lismore Cir. *NW5* 1E 58
Lismore Clo. *Iswth* 1E 86
Lismore Ho. *SE15* 2F 92
Lismore Rd. *N17* 1B 44
Lismore Rd. *S Croy* 8C 124
Lismore Wlk. N1 2A 60
(off Clephane Rd.)
Lisselton Ho. NW4 2H 41
(off Belle Vue Est.)
Lissenden Gdns. *NW5* 9E 42
(in two parts)
Lissenden Mans. *NW5* 9E 42
Lisson Grn. Est. NW8 7C 58
(off Tresham Cres.)
Lisson Grove. 8C 58
Lisson Gro. *NW8 & NW1* 7B 58
Lisson Ho. NW1 8C 58
(off Lisson St.)
Lisson St. *NW1* 8C 58
Lister Av. *H Wood* 9H 35
Lister Clo. *W3* 8B 56
Lister Clo. *Mitc* 5C 106
Lister Cotts. *Els* 7E 10
Lister Ct. *Harr* 5F 38
Lister Gdns. *N18* 5A 28
Listergate Ct. *SW15* 3G 89
Lister Ho. *E1* 8E 60
Lister Ho. SE3 7C 78
(off Restell Clo.)
Lister Ho. *Hay* 5C 68
Lister Ho. Wemb 8A 40
(off Barnhill Rd.)
Lister Lodge. W2 8L 57
(off Admiral Wlk.)
Lister M. *N7* 9K 43
Lister Rd. *E11* 6C 46
Lister Wlk. *SE28* 1H 81
Liston Rd. *N17* 8E 28
Liston Rd. *SW4* 2G 91
Liston Way. *Wfd G* 7G 31
Listowel Clo. *SW9* 8L 75
Listowel Rd. *Dag* 8L 49
Listria Pk. *N16* 7C 44
Litcham Ho. E1 6H 61
(off Longnor Rd.)
Litchfield Av. *E15* 2C 62
Litchfield Av. *Mord* 2K 121
Litchfield Ct. *E17* 4L 45
Litchfield Gdns. *NW10* 2E 56
Litchfield Rd. *Sutt* 6A 122
Litchfield St. *WC2* 1H 75
Litchfield Way. *NW11* 3M 41
Lithgow's Rd. *H'row A* 3C 84
Lithos Rd. *NW3* 2M 57
Little Acre. *Beck* 7L 109
Lit. Albany St. NW1 6F 58
(off Longford St., in two parts)
Little Angel Theatre. *4M 59*
(off Dagmar Pas.)
Lit. Argyll St. *W1* 9G 59
Lit. Aston Rd. *Romf* 7L 35
Little Benty. *W Dray* 6H 143
Little Birches. *Sidc* 8C 96
Lit. Boltons, The.
SW5 & SW10 6M 73
Little Bornes. *SE21* 1C 108
Littlebourne. *SE13* 6C 94
Little Britain. 9A 142
Little Britain. *EC1* 8M 59
Littlebrook Bus. Cen.
Dart 1M 99
Littlebrook Clo. *Croy* 1H 125
Littlebrook Gdns. *Chesh* 3D 6
Littlebrook Interchange (Junct.)
3M 99
Littlebrook Mnr. Way. *Dart* 4L 99
Little Brownings. *SE23* 8F 92
Littlebury Ct. *Wat* 6E 8
Littlebury Rd. *SW4* 2H 91
Lit. Bury St. *N9* 1B 28
Lit. Bushey La. *Bush* 4L 9
Little Cedars. *N12* 4A 26
Lit. Chester St. *SW1* 4F 74
Little Cloisters. *SW1* 4J 75
Lit. College La. EC4 1B 76
(off College St.)
Lit. College St. *SW1* 4J 75
Littlecombe. *SE7* 7F 78
Littlecombe Clo. *SW15* 5H 89
Little Common. *Stan* 3E 22
Littlecote Clo. *SW19* 6J 89
Littlecote Pl. *Pinn* 8J 21
Little Ct. *W Wick* 4C 126
Little Cft. *SE9* 2L 95
Littledale. *SE2* 7E 80
Lit. Dean's Yd. SW1 4J 75
(off Dean's Yd.)
Little Dimocks. *SW12* 8F 90
Lit. Dorrit Ct. *SE1* 3A 76
Little Dragons. *Lou* 6H 19
Little Ealing. 4H 71
Lit. Ealing La. *W5* 5G 71
Lit. Edward St. *NW1* 6F 58
Little Elms. *Hay* 8B 68
Lit. Essex St. WC2 1L 75
(off Essex St.)
Lit. Ferry Rd. *Twic* 7F 86
Littlefield Clo. *N19* 9G 43
Littlefield Clo. *King T* 6J 103
Littlefield Ho. King T 6J 103
(off Littlefield Clo)
Littlefield Rd. *Edgw* 7A 24
Lit. Friday Rd. *E4* 2C 30
Lit. Gaynes Gdns. *Upm* 9M 51
Lit. Gaynes La. *Upm* 9K 51
Little Gearies. *Ilf* 2M 47
Lit. George St. *SW1* 3J 75
Lit. Gerpins La. *Upm* 4K 67
Lit. Goldings Est. *Lou* 3L 19
Little Grange. *Gnfd* 6E 54
Little Graylings. *Ab L* 6C 4
Little Grn. *Rich* 3H 87
Lit. Green La. *Crox G* 5A 8
Lit. Green St. *NW5* 9F 42
Little Gro. *Bush* 6M 9
Littlegrove. *E Barn* 8C 14
Little Halliards. *W on T* 1E 116
Little Heath. 2F 48
Little Heath. *SE7* 7J 79
Little Heath. *Chad H* 2F 48
Lit. Heath Rd. *Bexh* 9K 81
Littleheath Rd. *S Croy* 9F 124
Little Holt. *E11* 3E 46
Lit. How Cft. *Ab L* 4A 4
Little Ilford. 9L 47
Lit. Ilford La. *E12* 9K 47
Lit. John Rd. *W7* 9D 54
Littlejohn Rd. *Orp* 1E 128
Little Larkins. *Barn* 8J 13
Lit. London Clo. *Uxb* 8F 142
Lit. London Ct. SE1 3D 76
(off Wolseley St.)
Lit. Marlborough St. W1 9G 59
(off Kingly St.)
Little Martins. *Bush* 7M 9
Littlemead. *Esh* 6B 118
Littlemede. *SE9* 9K 95
Littlemoor Rd. *Ilf* 8B 48
Littlemore Rd. *SE2* 3E 80
Lit. Moss La. *Pinn* 9J 21
Lit. Newport St. *WC2* 1H 75
Lit. New St. *EC4* 9L 59
Lit. Orchard Clo. *Ab L* 5B 4
Lit. Orchard Clo. *Pinn* 9J 21
Little Orchards. Eps 6C 134
(off Worple Rd.)
Lit. Oxhey La. *Wat* 5H 21
Lit. Park Dri. *Felt* 8J 85
Lit. Park Gdns. *Enf* 5A 16
Lit. Pluckett's Way.
Buck H 1H 31
Lit. Portland St. *W1* 9G 59
Little Potters. *Bush* 9B 10
Lit. Queen's Rd. *Tedd* 3D 102
Lit. Queen St. *Dart* 6K 99
Little Redlands. *Brom* 6J 111
Little Rd. *Hay* 3D 68
Lit. Roke Av. *Kenl* 6M 137
Lit. Roke Rd. *Kenl* 6A 138
Littlers Clo. *SW19* 5A 106
Lit. Russell St. *WC1* 8J 59
Lit. St James's St. *SW1* 2G 75
Lit. St Leonard's. *SW14* 2A 88
Little Sanctuary. *SW1* 3H 75
Lit. Smith St. *SW1* 4H 75
Lit. Somerset St. *E1* 9D 60
Little Stanmore. 7K 23
Littlestone Clo. *Beck* 3L 109
Little Strand. *NW9* 9D 24
Lit. Stream Clo. *N'wd* 5C 20
Little St. *Wal A* 9J 7
Little Theatre, The. 5E 110
Little Thrift. *Orp* 8A 112
Lit. Titchfield St. *W1* 8G 59
Littleton Av. *E4* 1D 30
Littleton Common. 4A 100
Littleton Cres. *Harr* 7D 38
Littleton Ho. SW1 6G 75
(off Lupus St.)
Littleton Rd. *Ashf* 4A 100
Littleton Rd. *Harr* 7D 38
Littleton St. *SW18* 8A 90
Lit. Trinity La. *EC4* 1A 76
Little Turnstile. *WC1* 8K 59
Lit. Warkworth Ho. *Iswth* 1F 86
Littlewood. *SE13* 5A 94
Littlewood Clo. *W13* 4F 70
Lit. Wood Clo. *Orp* 5E 112
Little Woodcote. 3E 136
Lit. Woodcote Est. *Cars* 3E 136
Lit. Woodcote La. *Cars* 4F 136
Lit. Wood St. *King T* 6H 103
Littleworth Av. *Esh* 7B 118
Littleworth Comn. Rd.
Esh 5B 118
Littleworth La. *Esh* 6B 118
Littleworth Pl. *Esh* 6B 118
Littleworth Rd. *Esh* 7B 118
Livermere Ct. E8 4D 60
(off Queensbridge Rd.)
Livermere Rd. *E8* 4D 60
Liverpool Gro. *SE17* 6A 76
Liverpool Rd. *E10* 4A 46
Liverpool Rd. *E16* 8C 62
Liverpool Rd. *N7 & N1* 1L 59
Liverpool Rd. *W5* 3H 71
Liverpool Rd. *King T* 4L 103
Liverpool Rd. *T Hth* 7A 108
Liverpool Rd. *Wat* 7F 8
Liverpool St. *EC2* 8C 60
Livesey Clo. *King T* 7K 103
Livesey Mus. 7F 76
Livesey Pl. *SE15* 7E 76
Livesley Clo. *SE28* 3A 80
Livingstone College Towers.
E10 4A 46
Livingstone Ct. *E10* 4A 46
Livingstone Ct. *W'stone* 1D 38
Livingstone Ho. *NW10* 3B 56
Livingstone Ho. SE5 8A 76
(off Wyndham Rd.)
Livingstone Lodge. W9 8L 57
(off Admiral Wlk.)
Livingstone Mans. W14 7J 73
(off Queen's Club Gdns.)
Livingstone Pl. *E14* 6A 78
Livingstone Rd. *E15* 4A 62
Livingstone Rd. *E17* 4M 45
Livingstone Rd. *N13* 6J 27
Livingstone Rd. *SW11* 2B 90
Livingstone Rd. *Houn* 3A 86
Livingstone Rd. *S'hall* 1H 69
Livingstone Rd. *T Hth* 6A 108
Livingstone Ter. *Rain* 4C 66
Livonia St. *W1* 9G 59
Lizard St. *EC1* 6A 60
Lizban St. *SE3* 8F 78
Llandovery Ho. E14 3A 78
(off Chipka St.)
Llanelly Rd. *NW2* 7K 41
Llanover Rd. *SE18* 7L 79
Llanover Rd. *Wemb* 8H 39
Llanthony Rd. *Mord* 9B 106
Llanvanor Rd. *NW2* 7K 41
Llewellyn Ct. *SE20* 5G 109
Llewellyn St. *SE16* 3E 76
Lloyd Av. *SW16* 5J 107
Lloyd Av. *Coul* 6E 136
Lloyd Baker St. *WC1* 6K 59
(in two parts)
Lloyd Ct. *Pinn* 3H 37
Lloyd M. *Enf* 2L 17
Lloyd Pk. Av. *Croy* 6D 124
Lloyd Pk. Ho. *E17* 1L 45
Lloyd Rd. *E6* 4K 63
Lloyd Rd. *E17* 2H 45
Lloyd Rd. *Dag* 2K 65
Lloyd Rd. *Wor Pk* 5G 121
Lloyd's Av. *EC3* 9C 60
Lloyds Building. 9C 60
Lloyd's Pl. *SE3* 1C 94
Lloyd Sq. *WC1* 6L 59
Lloyd's Row. *EC1* 6L 59
Lloyd St. *WC1* 6L 59
Lloyds Way. *Beck* 9J 109
Lloyds Wharf. SE1 3D 76
(off Mill St.)
Lloyd Thomas Ct. *N22* 7K 27
Lloyd Vs. SE4 1L 93
(off Lewisham Way)
Loam Ct. *Dart* 7J 99
Loampit Hill. *SE13* 1L 93
Loampit Vale (Junct.) 2A 94
Loampit Va. *SE13* 2M 93
Loanda Clo. *E8* 4D 60
Loates La. *Wat* 5G 9
Loats Rd. *SW2* 5J 91
Lobelia Clo. *E6* 8J 63
Local Board Rd. *Wat* 7G 9
Locarno Ct. *SW16* 2G 107
Locarno Rd. *W3* 2A 72
Locarno Rd. *Gnfd* 7B 54
Lochaber Rd. *SE13* 3C 94
Lochaline St. *W6* 7G 73
Lochan Clo. *Hay* 7J 53
Lochinvar St. *SW12* 6F 90
Lochleven Ho. N2 9B 26
(off Grange, The)
Lochmere Clo. *Eri* 7M 81
Lochmore Ho. SW1 5E 74
(off Cundy St.)
Lochnagar St. *E14* 8A 62
Lockbridge Ct. W9 8L 57
(off Elmfield Way)
Lock Chase. *SE3* 2C 94
Lock Clo. *S'hall* 3A 70
Locke Clo. *Rain* 2D 66
Locke Ho. SW8 9G 75
(off Wadhurst Rd.)
Lockesley Dri. *Orp* 1D 128
Lockesley Sq. *Surb* 1H 119
Locket Rd. *Harr* 1C 38
Lockfield Av. *Brim* 4J 17
Lockgate Clo. *E9* 1K 61
Lockhart Clo. *N7* 2K 59
Lockhart Clo. *Enf* 7C 16
Lockhart Ho. SE10 8M 77
(off Tarves Way)
Lockhart St. *E3* 7K 61
Lockhurst St. *E5* 9H 45
Lockie Pl. *SE25* 7E 108
Lockier Wlk. *Wemb* 8H 39
Lockington Rd. *SW8* 9F 74
Lock Keepers Quay. SE16 4H 77
(off Brunswick Quay)
Lockmead Rd. *N15* 4E 44
Lockmead Rd. *SE13* 2A 94
Lock Rd. *Rich* 1G 103
Locksbottom. 5L 127
Locksfield Pl. *E14* 6M 77
Locksfields. SE17 5B 76
(off Catesby St.)
Lockside. E14 1J 77
(off Narrow St.)
Locks La. *Mitc* 5E 106
Locksley Est. *E14* 9K 61
Locksley St. *E14* 8K 61
Locksmeade Rd. *Rich* 1G 103
Lockswood Clo. *Barn* 6D 14
Lock Vw. Ct. E14 1J 77
(off Narrow St.)
Lockwood Clo. *SE26* 1H 109
Lockwood Ho. *SE11* 7L 75
Lockwood Ind. Pk. *N17* 1F 44
Lockwood Sq. *SE16* 4F 76
Lockwood Wlk. *Romf* 3C 50
Lockwood Way. *E17* 9H 29
Lockwood Way. *Chess* 7L 119
Lockyer Est. SE1 3B 76
(off Kipling St., in two parts)
Lockyer Ho. SE10 6D 78
(off Armitage Rd.)
Lockyer Ho. SW8 8H 75
(off Wandsworth Rd.)
Lockyer Ho. *SW15* 2H 89
Lockyer St. *SE1* 3B 76
Locomotive Dri. *Felt* 7E 84
Locton Grn. *E3* 4K 61
Loddiges Ho. *E9* 3G 61
Loddiges Rd. *E9* 3G 61
Loder St. *SE15* 8G 77
Lodge Av. *SW14* 2C 88
Lodge Av. *Croy* 5L 123
Lodge Av. *Dag* 4E 64
Lodge Av. *Dart* 5G 99
Lodge Av. *Els* 7K 11
Lodge Av. *Harr* 2J 39
Lodge Av. *Romf* 2E 50
Lodge Clo. *N18* 5A 28
Lodge Clo. *Chig* 3E 32
Lodge Clo. *Edgw* 6K 23
Lodge Clo. *Eps* 2G 135
Lodge Clo. *Iswth* 9F 70
Lodge Clo. *Orp* 3F 128
Lodge Clo. *Uxb* 7A 142
Lodge Clo. *Wall* 3E 122
Lodge Ct. *Horn* 7J 51
Lodge Ct. *Wemb* 2J 55
Lodge Cres. *Orp* 3F 128
Lodge Cres. *Wal X* 7D 6
Lodge Dri. *N13* 4L 27
Lodge End. *Crox G* 6B 8
Lodge Gdns. *Beck* 9K 109
Lodge Hill. *Ilf* 2J 47
Lodge Hill. *Purl* 7L 137
Lodge Hill. *Well* 8F 80
Lodgehill Pk. Clo. *Harr* 7M 37
Lodge La. *N12* 5A 26
Lodge La. *Bex* 5H 97
Lodge La. *New Ad* 8L 125
Lodge La. *Romf* 7L 33
Lodge La. *Wal A* 8K 7
Lodge Pl. *Sutt* 7M 121
Lodge Rd. *NW4* 2G 41
Lodge Rd. *NW8* 6B 58

Lodge Rd.—Lothrop St.

Lodge Rd. Brom 4F 110
Lodge Rd. Croy 1M 123
Lodge Rd. Wall 7F 122
Lodge, The. Wat 4G 9
(off Orphanage Rd.)
Lodge Vs. Wfd G 6D 30
Lodge Way. Ashf 8C 144
Lodge Way. Shep 6A 100
Lodore Gdns. NW9 3C 40
Lodore St. E14 9A 62
Loft Ho. Pl. Chess 8G 119
Loftie St. SE16 3E 76
Lofting Rd. N1 3K 59
Loftus Rd. W12 2F 72
Loftus Road (Queen's Pk. Rangers F.C.) 2F 72
Logan Clo. Enf 3H 17
Logan Clo. Houn 2K 85
Logan M. W8 5L 73
Logan Pl. W8 5L 73
Logan Rd. N9 2F 28
Logan Rd. Wemb 7H 39
Loggetts. SE21 8C 92
Logs Hill. Chst 4J 111
Logs Hill Clo. Chst 5J 111
Lohmann Ho. SE11 7L 75
(off Kennington Oval)
Lois Dri. Shep 9A 100
Lolesworth Clo. E1 8D 60
Lollard St. SE11 5K 75
(in two parts)
Loman St. SE1 3M 75
Lomas Clo. Croy 9A 126
Lomas St. E1 8E 60
Lombard Av. Enf 3G 17
Lombard Av. Ilf 6C 48
Lombard Bus. Cen., The. SW11 1B 90
Lombard Bus. Pk. Croy 2K 123
Lombard Ct. EC3 1B 76
Lombard Ct. W3 2M 71
Lombard Ct. Romf 2A 50
(off Poplar St.)
Lombard La. EC4 9L 59
Lombard Rd. N11 5F 26
Lombard Rd. SW11 1B 90
Lombard Rd. SW19 6M 105
Lombard Roundabout (Junct.) 2K 123
Lombards, The. Horn 5K 51
Lombard St. EC3 9B 60
Lombard St. Hort K 9M 115
Lombard Trad. Est. SE7 5F 78
Lombard Wall. SE7 4F 78
(in two parts)
Lombardy Pl. W2 1M 73
Lombardy Retail Pk. Hay 1F 68
Lombardy Way. Borwd 3J 11
Lomond Clo. N15 3C 44
Lomond Clo. Wemb 3K 55
Lomond Gdns. S Croy 9J 125
Lomond Gro. SE5 8B 76
Lomond Ho. SE5 8B 76
Loncroft Rd. SE5 7C 76
Londesborough Rd. N16 9C 44
Londinium Tower. E1 1D 76
(off W. Tenter St.)
London Academy of Music & Dramatic Art. 5L 73
(off Cromwell Rd.)
London Aquarium. 3K 75
London Arena. 4M 77
London Biggin Hill Airport. 4H 141
London Bri. SE1 & EC4 2B 76
London Bri. St. SE1 2B 76
London Bri. Wlk. SE1 2B 76
(off Duke St. Hill)
London Broncos Rugby League Football Club (Brentford F.C.) 7H 71
London Business School. 7D 58
London Butterfly House. 9F 70
London Canal Mus. 5J 59
London City Airport. 2J 79
London City College. 2L 75
(in Schiller University)
London Coliseum. 1J 75
(off St Martin's La.)
London College of Fashion. 7A 60
(Baltic St. E.)
London College of Fashion. 7C 60
(Curtain Rd.)
Londonderry Pde. Eri 8B 82
London Dungeon. 2B 76
(off Tooley St.)
London Eye. 3K 75
London Fields E. Side. E8 3F 60
(in two parts)
London Fields W. Side. E8 3E 60
London Fruit Exchange. E1 8D 60
(off Brushfield St.)
London Guidhall University. 9E 60
(Commercial Rd.)
London Guidhall University. 9E 60
(Manningtree St.)
London Guidhall University. 1D 76
(Minories)
London Guildhall University. 9E 60
(Commercial Rd.)
London Guildhall University. 9D 60
(off Jewry St.)
London Guildhall University. 8B 60
(Moorgate)
London Guildhall University. 9E 60
(Whitechapel High St., Central Ho.)
London Heathrow Airport. 2F 144
London Ho. NW8 5C 58
(off Avenue Rd.)
London Ho. WC1 7K 59
London Ind. Pk., The. E6 8M 63
London Knights Ice Hockey (London Arena). 4M 77
London La. E8 3F 60
London La. Brom 4D 110
London Leopards Basketball (London Arena). 4M 77
London Master Bakers Almshouses. E10 4M 45
London M. W2 9B 58
London Motorcycle Mus. 6A 54
London Palladium. 9G 59
(off Argyll St.)
London Planetarium. 7E 58
London Rd. E13 5E 62
London Rd. SE1 4M 75
London Rd. SE23 7F 92
London Rd. SW16 5K 107
London Rd. SW17 & Mitc 4D 106
London Rd. Ave 2K 83
London Rd. Badg M 9K 129
London Rd. Bark 3M 63
London Rd. Brom 4D 110
London Rd. Bush 8J 9
London Rd. Cray 4B 98
London Rd. Enf 5B 16
London Rd. Ewe & Sutt 1D 134
London Rd. Harr 7C 38
London Rd. Houn & Iswth 2A 86
London Rd. Iswth & Twic 4E 86
(Linkfield Rd.)
London Rd. Iswth & Bren 1D 86
(Twickenham Rd.)
London Rd. King T 6K 103
(in two parts)
London Rd. Mitc & Wall 2E 122
London Rd. Mord 9L 105
London Rd. Purf 6L 83
London Rd. Romf 4L 49
London Rd. Shenl & Borwd 1A 12
London Rd. Stai & Ashf 9A 144
London Rd. Stan 5G 23
London Rd. Stne & Grnh 6M 99
London Rd. Swan & F'ham 5A 114
(in four parts)
London Rd. T Hth & Croy 9L 107
London Rd. Wemb 1J 55
London Road Roundabout (Junct.) 5E 86
London School of Economics & Politics, The. 9K 59
Londons Clo. Upm 1M 67
London Scottish R.U.F.C. 2H 87
London Stile. W4 6L 71
London St. EC3 1C 76
London St. W2 9B 58
London Ter. E2 5E 60
London Towers Basketball (Crystal Palace National Sports Cen.) 3E 108
London Transport Mus. 1J 75
London Underwriting Cen. EC3 1C 76
London Wall. EC2 8A 60
London Wall Bldgs. EC2 8B 60
(off London Wall)
London Westland Heliport. 1B 90
London Wharf. E2 4F 60
(off Wharf Pl.)
London Zoo. 5E 58
Lonesome. 5G 107
Lonesome Way. SW16 5F 106
Long Acre. WC2 1J 75
Long Acre. Orp 4H 129
Longacre Clo. Enf 5A 16
Long Acre Ct. W13 8E 54
Longacre Pl. Cars 8E 122
Longacre Rd. E17 8B 30
Long Barn Clo. Wat 5E 4
Longbeach Rd. SW11 2D 90
Longberrys. NW2 8K 41
Longboat Row. S'hall 9K 53
Longbridge Ho. Dag 9F 48
(off Gainsborough Rd.)
Longbridge Rd. Bark 2B 64
Longbridge Way. SE13 4A 94
Longbury Clo. Orp 7F 112
Longbury Dri. Orp 7F 112
Long Cliffe Path. Wat 3E 20
Long Ct. Purf 5L 83
Longcroft. SE9 9K 95
Longcroft. Wat 9F 8
Longcroft Av. Bans 6A 136
Long Cft. Dri. Wal X 7F 6
Longcrofte Rd. Edgw 7H 23
Longcroft Ri. Lou 7L 19
Longcrofts. Wal A 7L 7
Long Deacon Rd. E4 1C 30
Long Ditton. 3G 119
Longdon Ct. Romf 3D 50
Longdon Wood. Kes 5J 127
Longdown La. N. Eps 6E 134
Longdown La. S. Eps 6E 134
Longdown Rd. SE6 1L 109
Longdown Rd. Eps 6E 134
Long Dri. W3 9C 56
Long Dri. Gnfd 4M 53
Long Dri. Ruis 1G 53
Long Dri. W Dray 3J 143
Long Elmes. Harr 8M 21
Long Elms. Ab L 6B 4
Long Elms Clo. Ab L 6B 4
Longfellow Rd. E17 4K 45
Longfellow Rd. Wor Pk 4E 120
Longfellow Way. SE1 5D 76
Long Fld. NW9 7C 24
Longfield. Brom 5D 110
Longfield. Lou 7H 19
Longfield Av. E17 2J 45
Longfield Av. NW7 7E 24
Longfield Av. W5 1G 71
Longfield Av. Enf 1G 17
Longfield Av. Horn 5D 50
Longfield Av. Wall 3E 122
Longfield Av. Wemb 6J 39
Longfield Cres. SE26 9G 93
Longfield Dri. SW14 4M 87
Longfield Dri. Mitc 4C 106
Longfield Est. SE1 5D 76
Longfield La. Chesh 1A 6
Longfield Rd. W5 9G 55
Longfield St. SW18 6L 89
Longfield Wlk. W5 9G 55
Longford. 9G 143
Longford Av. Felt 5C 84
Longford Av. S'hall 1M 69
Longford Av. Stai 7C 144
Longford Clo. Hamp H 1L 101
Longford Clo. Hanw 9J 85
Longford Clo. Hay 1H 69
Longford Ct. NW4 2H 41
Longford Ct. Eps 6A 120
Longford Ct. S'hall 2L 69
(off Uxbridge Rd.)
Longford Gdns. Hay 1H 69
Longford Gdns. Sutt 5A 122
Longford Ho. E1 9G 61
(off Jubilee St.)
Longford Ho. Brom 2B 110
(off Brangbourne Rd.)
Longford Ho. Hamp 1L 101
Longford Rd. Twic 7L 85
Longford St. NW1 7F 58
Longford Wlk. SW2 6L 91
Longford Way. Stai 7C 144
Long Grn. Chig 4C 32
Long Gro. H Wood 9J 35
Long Gro. Rd. Eps 2M 133
Longhayes Av. Romf 2H 49
Longhayes Ct. Romf 2H 49
Longheath Gdns. Croy 9G 109
Longhedge Ho. SE26 1E 108
(off High Level Dri.)
Long Hedges. Houn 1L 85
Longhedge St. SW11 1E 90
Longhill Rd. SE6 8B 94
Longhook Gdns. N'holt 5E 52
Longhope Clo. SE15 7C 76
Longhurst Rd. SE13 4B 94
Longhurst Rd. Croy 1F 124
Longland Ct. SE1 6E 76
Longland Dri. N20 3M 25
Longlands. 9B 96
Longlands Av. Coul 6E 136
Longlands Clo. Chesh 5D 6
Longlands Ct. W11 1K 73
(off Westbourne Gro.)
Longlands Ct. Sidc 9D 96
Longlands Pk. Cres. Sidc 9C 96
Longlands Rd. Sidc 9C 96
Long La. EC1 8M 59
Long La. N3 & N2 8M 25
(in two parts)
Long La. SE1 3B 76
Long La. Bexh 8H 81
Long La. Croy 1F 124
Long La. Hil 2F 142
Long La. Stai & Stanw 8D 144
Long La. Uxb 6E 142
Longleat Ho. SW1 6H 75
(off Rampayne St.)
Longleat M. Orp 8G 113
Longleat Rd. Enf 7C 16
Longleat Way. Felt 6B 84
Longleigh Ho. SE5 9C 76
(off Peckham Rd.)
Longleigh La. SE2 7G 81
Long Lents Ho. NW10 4B 56
Longley Av. Wemb 4K 55
Longley Ct. SW8 9J 75
Longley Rd. SW17 3C 106
Longley Rd. Croy 2M 123
Longley Rd. Harr 3A 38
Long Leys. E4 6M 29
Longley St. SE1 5E 76
Longley Way. NW2 8G 41
Long Lodge Dri. W on T 5G 117
Longman Ho. E2 5H 61
(off Mace St.)
Longman Ho. E8 4D 60
(off Haggerston Rd.)
Longmans Clo. Wat 8A 8
Long Mark Rd. E16 8H 63
Longmarsh Vw. S at H 5M 115
Long Mead. NW9 8D 24
Longmead. Chst 6L 111
Longmead Bus. Cen. Eps 3B 134
Longmead Dri. Sidc 8H 97
Longmead Ho. SE27 2A 108
Long Mdw. NW5 1H 59
Long Mdw. Noak H 2G 35
Long Mdw. Clo. W Wick 2A 126
Longmeadow Rd. Sidc 7C 96
Longmead Rd. SW17 2D 106
Longmead Rd. Eps 3B 134
Longmead Rd. Hay 1D 68
Longmead Rd. Th Dit 2C 118
Long Moor. Chesh 2E 6
Longmoore St. SW1 5G 75
Longmore Av. Barn & E Barn 8A 14
Longmore Rd. W on T 6J 117
Longnor Est. E1 6H 61
Longnor Rd. E1 6H 61
Long Pond Rd. SE3 9C 78
Longport Clo. Ilf 6E 32
Longreach Ct. Bark 5B 64
Long Reach Rd. Bark 7D 64
Longreach Rd. Eri 8F 82
Longridge Ho. SE1 4A 76
Longridge La. S'hall 9M 53
Longridge Rd. SW5 5L 73
Longridge Rd. Bark 3A 64
Long Ridges. N10 1E 42
(off Fortis Grn.)
Long Rd. SW4 3F 90
Long's Ct. WC2 1H 75
(off Orange St.)
Longs Ct. Rich 3K 87
Longshaw Rd. E4 3B 30
Longshore. SE8 5K 77
Longshott Ct. SW5 5L 73
(off W. Cromwell Rd.)
Longspring. Wat 2F 8
Longstaff Cres. SW18 5L 89
Longstaff Rd. SW18 5L 89
Longstone Av. NW10 3D 56
Longstone Rd. SW17 2F 106
Long St. E2 6D 60
Longthornton Rd. SW16 6G 107
Longton Av. SE26 1E 108
Longton Gro. SE26 1F 108
Longtown Clo. Romf 5G 35
Longtown Ct. Dart 5M 99
(off Osbourne Rd.)
Longtown Rd. Romf 5G 35
Longview Vs. Romf 8K 33
Longview Way. Romf 8B 34
Longville Rd. SE11 5M 75
Long Wlk. SE1 4C 76
Long Wlk. SE18 7M 79
Long Wlk. SW13 1C 88
Long Wlk. N Mald 7A 104
Long Wlk. Wal A 3G 7
Longwalk Rd. Uxb 2M 143
Long Wall. E15 6B 62
Longwater Ho. King T 7H 103
(off Portsmouth Rd.)
Longwood Clo. Upm 1M 67
Longwood Ct. Upm 1M 67
(off Corbets Tey Rd.)
Longwood Dri. SW15 5E 88
Longwood Gdns. Ilf 2K 47
Longwood Rd. Kenl 8B 138
(in two parts)
Longworth Clo. SE28 9H 65
Long Yd. WC1 7K 59
Loning, The. NW9 2D 40
Loning, The. Enf 2G 17
Lonsdale Av. E6 7H 63
Lonsdale Av. Romf 4A 50
Lonsdale Av. Wemb 1J 55
Lonsdale Clo. E6 7J 63
Lonsdale Clo. SE9 9H 95
Lonsdale Clo. Edgw 5K 23
Lonsdale Clo. Pinn 7J 21
Lonsdale Clo. Uxb 8A 52
Lonsdale Ct. Surb 2H 119
Lonsdale Cres. Ilf 4M 47
Lonsdale Dri. Enf 6H 15
Lonsdale Gdns. SW16 8K 107
Lonsdale Ho. W11 9K 57
(off Lonsdale Rd.)
Lonsdale M. W11 9K 57
(off Lonsdale Rd.)
Lonsdale M. Rich 9L 71
Lonsdale Pl. N1 3L 59
Lonsdale Rd. E11 4D 46
Lonsdale Rd. NW6 4K 57
Lonsdale Rd. SE25 8F 108
Lonsdale Rd. SW13 9D 72
Lonsdale Rd. W4 5D 72
Lonsdale Rd. W11 9K 57
Lonsdale Rd. Bexh 1K 97
Lonsdale Rd. S'hall 4H 69
Lonsdale Sq. N1 3L 59
Lonsdale Yd. W11 1L 73
Loobert Rd. N15 1C 44
Looe Gdns. Ilf 1M 47
Loom La. Rad 1D 10
Loom Pl. Rad 1E 10
Loop Rd. Chst 3A 112
Loop Rd. Eps 8A 134
Lopen Rd. N18 4C 28
Lopez Ho. SW9 2J 91
Lorac Ct. Sutt 9L 121
Loraine Clo. Enf 7G 17
Loraine Ct. Chst 2M 111
Loraine Gdns. Asht 9J 133
Loraine Ho. Wall 6F 122
Loraine Rd. N7 9K 43
Loraine Rd. W4 7M 71
Lorane Ct. Wat 4E 8
Lord Amory Way. E14 3A 78
Lord Av. Ilf 2K 47
Lord Chancellor Wlk. King T 5A 104
Lordell Pl. SW19 3G 105
Lorden Wlk. E2 6E 60
Lord Gdns. Ilf 2J 47
Lord Hills Bri. W2 8M 57
Lord Hills Rd. W2 8M 57
Lord Holland La. SW9 1L 91
Lord Knyvett Clo. Stanw 5B 144
Lord Knyvetts Ct. Stanw 5B 144
Lord Napier Pl. W6 6E 72
Lord N. St. SW1 4J 75
Lord Roberts M. SW6 8M 73
Lord Robert's Ter. SE18 6L 79
Lordsbury Fld. Wall 2G 137
Lords Clo. SE21 8A 92
Lords Clo. Felt 8J 85
Lord's Cricket Ground. 6B 58
(Marylebone & Middlesex County Cricket Clubs)
Lordship Gro. N16 7B 44
Lordship La. N22 & N17 9L 27
Lordship La. SE22 3D 92
Lordship La. Est. SE21 6E 92
Lordship Pk. N16 7A 44
Lordship Pk. M. N16 7A 44
Lordship Pl. SW3 7C 74
Lordship Rd. N16 6B 44
Lordship Rd. Chesh 3B 6
Lordship Rd. N'holt 3J 53
Lordship Ter. N16 7B 44
Lordsmead Rd. N17 8C 28
Lord St. E16 2J 79
Lord St. Wat 5G 9
Lords Vw. NW8 6B 58
Lord Warwick St. SE18 4K 79
Loreburn Ho. N7 9K 43
Lorenzo St. WC1 6K 59
Loretto Gdns. Harr 2J 39
Lorian Clo. N12 4M 25
Loring Rd. N20 2C 26
Loring Rd. SE14 9J 77
Loring Rd. Iswth 1D 86
Loris Rd. W6 4G 73
Lorn Ct. SW9 1L 91
Lorne Av. Croy 2H 125
Lorne Clo. NW8 6C 58
Lorne Gdns. E11 2G 47
Lorne Gdns. W11 3H 73
Lorne Gdns. Croy 2H 125
Lorne Ho. E1 8J 61
(off Ben Jonson Rd.)
Lorne Rd. E7 9F 46
Lorne Rd. E17 3L 45
Lorne Rd. N4 6K 43
Lorne Rd. Harr 9D 22
Lorne Rd. Rich 4K 87
Lorne Ter. N3 9K 25
Lorn Rd. SW9 1K 91
Lorraine Clo. S Ock 3K 83
Lorraine Ct. NW1 3F 58
Lorraine Pk. Harr 7C 22
Lorrimore Rd. SE17 7M 75
Lorrimore Sq. SE17 7M 75
Lorton Ho. NW6 4L 57
(off Kilburn Va.)
Loseberry Rd. Clay 7B 118
Lothair Rd. W5 3H 71
Lothair Rd. N. N4 4M 43
Lothair Rd. S. N4 5L 43
Lothbury. EC2 9B 60
Lothian Av. Hay 8F 52
Lothian Clo. Wemb 9E 38
Lothian Rd. SW9 9M 75
Lothrop St. W10 6J 57

Lymington Lodge. E14 . . . . .4B 78
(off Schooner Clo.)
Lymington Rd. NW6 . . . . .2M 57
Lymington Rd. Dag 6H 49
Lyminster Clo. Hay 8J 53
Lympne. N17 . . . . .9B 28
(off Gloucester Rd.)
Lympstone Gdns. SE15 . . . .8E 76
Lynbridge Gdns. N13 . . . .4M 27
Lynbrook Clo. Rain 5B 66
Lynbury Ct. Wat 5E 8
Lynch Clo. SE3 . . . . .1D 94
Lynch Clo. Uxb 3A 142
Lynchen Clo. Houn 9F 68
Lynch, The. Uxb 3A 142
Lynch Wlk. SE8 . . . . .7K 77
(off Dacca St.)
Lyncott Cres. SW4 . . . . . .3F 90
Lyncourt. SE3 . . . . .1B 94
Lyncroft Av. Pinn 3J 37
Lyncroft Gdns. NW6 . . . . .1L 57
Lyncroft Gdns. W13 . . . . .3G 71
Lyncroft Gdns. Eps 1D 134
Lyncroft Gdns. Hous 4A 86
Lyncroft Gdns. NW6 . . . . .1L 57
Lyndale. NW2 . . . . .9K 41
Lyndale. Th Dit 2C 118
Lyndale Av. NW2 . . . . . . .8K 41
Lyndale Clo. SE3 . . . . . . .7D 78
Lynde Ho. SW4 . . . . .2H 91
Lynde Ho. W on T 1G 117
Lynden Hyrst. Croy 4D 124
Lynden Way. Swan 7A 114
Lyndhurst Av. N12 . . . . . .6D 26
Lyndhurst Av. NW7 . . . . . .6C 24
Lyndhurst Av. SW16 . . . . .6H 107
Lyndhurst Av. Pinn 8F 20
Lyndhurst Av. S'hall 2M 69
Lyndhurst Av. Sun 7E 100
Lyndhurst Av. Surb 3M 119
Lyndhurst Av. Twic 7K 85
Lyndhurst Clo. NW10 . . . . .8B 40
Lyndhurst Clo. Bexh 2M 97
Lyndhurst Clo. Croy 5D 124
Lyndhurst Clo. Orp 6M 127
Lyndhurst Ct. E18 . . . . . . .8E 30
Lyndhurst Ct. NW8 . . . . . .4B 58
(off Finchley Rd.)
Lyndhurst Ct. Sutt 9L 121
(off Grange Rd.)
Lyndhurst Dri. E10 . . . . . .5A 46
Lyndhurst Dri. Horn 6G 51
Lyndhurst Dri. N Mald 2C 120
Lyndhurst Gdns. N3 . . . . .8J 25
Lyndhurst Gdns. NW3 . . . .1B 58
Lyndhurst Gdns. Bark 2C 64
Lyndhurst Gdns. Enf 6C 16
Lyndhurst Gdns. Ilf 4B 48
Lyndhurst Gdns. Pinn 8F 20
Lyndhurst Gro. SE15 . . . . .1C 92
Lyndhurst Lodge. E14 . . . .5B 78
(off Millennium Dri.)
Lyndhurst Ri. Chig 4L 31
Lyndhurst Rd. E4 . . . . . . .7A 30
Lyndhurst Rd. N18 . . . . . .4E 28
Lyndhurst Rd. N22 . . . . . .6L 27
Lyndhurst Rd. NW3 . . . . . .1B 58
Lyndhurst Rd. Bexh 2M 97
Lyndhurst Rd. Coul 8E 136
Lyndhurst Rd. Gnfd 7M 53
Lyndhurst Rd. T Hth 8L 107
Lyndhurst Sq. SE15 . . . . . .9D 76
Lyndhurst Ter. NW3 . . . . . .1B 58
Lyndhurst Way. SE15 . . . . .9D 76
Lyndhurst Way. Sutt 1L 135
Lyndon Av. Pinn 6J 21
Lyndon Av. Sidc 4D 96
Lyndon Av. Wall 5E 122
Lyndon Rd. Belv 5L 81
Lyne Cres. E17 . . . . .8K 29
Lynegrove Av. Ashf 2A 100
Lyneham Wlk. E5 . . . . . . .1J 61
Lyneham Wlk. Pinn 1D 36
Lynette Av. SW4 . . . . .5F 90
Lyn M. E3 . . . . .6K 61
Lyn M. N16 . . . . .9C 44
Lynmouth Av. Enf 8D 16
Lynmouth Av. Mord 1H 121
Lynmouth Av. Ruis 7F 36
Lynmouth Gdns. Gnfd 4F 54
Lynmouth Gdns. Hous 8H 69
Lynmouth Rd. Romf 5J 35
(off Dagnam Pk. Dri.)
Lynmouth Ri. Orp 8F 112
Lynmouth Rd. E17 . . . . . .4J 45
Lynmouth Rd. N2 . . . . . . .1D 42
Lynmouth Rd. N16 . . . . . .6D 44
Lynmouth Rd. Gnfd 4F 54
Lynn Clo. Ashf 2B 100
Lynn Clo. Harr 9B 22
Lynn Ct. Whyt 9D 138

Lynne Clo. SE23 . . . . .6K 93
Lynne Clo. Orp 8D 128
Lynne Clo. S Croy 3G 139
Lynne Ct. S Croy 6C 124
(off Birdhurst Rd.)
Lynnett Rd. Dag 7H 49
Lynne Wlk. Esh 7A 118
Lynne Way. N'holt 5H 53
Lynn Ho. SE15 . . . . .7F 76
(off Friary Est.)
Lynn M. E11 . . . . .7C 46
Lynn Rd. E11 . . . . .7C 46
Lynn Rd. SW12 . . . . .6F 90
Lynn Rd. Ilf 5B 48
Lynn St. Enf 3B 16
Lynross Clo. Romf 9K 35
Lynscott Way. S Croy 1M 137
Lynstead Ct. Beck 6J 109
Lynstead Clo. Bexh 4M 97
Lynsted Clo. Brom 6G 111
Lynsted Gdns. SE9 . . . . . .2H 95
Lynton Av. N12 . . . . .4B 26
Lynton Av. NW9 . . . . .2D 40
Lynton Av. W13 . . . . .9E 54
Lynton Av. Orp 8F 112
Lynton Av. Romf 8L 33
Lynton Clo. NW10 . . . . . . .1C 56
Lynton Clo. Chess 6J 119
Lynton Clo. Iswth 3D 86
Lynton Cres. Ilf 4M 47
Lynton Est. SE1 . . . . .5E 76
Lynton Gdns. N11 . . . . . . .6H 27
Lynton Gdns. Enf 9C 16
Lynton Grange. N2 . . . . . .1D 42
Lynton Ho. W2 . . . . .9A 58
(off Hallfield Est.)
Lynton Ho. Ilf 7A 48
Lynton Mans. SE1 . . . . . . .4L 75
(off Kennington Rd.)
Lynton Mead. N20 . . . . . . .3L 25
Lynton Pde. Chesh 3E 6
Lynton Rd. E4 . . . . .5M 29
Lynton Rd. N8 . . . . .3J 43
(in two parts)
Lynton Rd. NW6 . . . . .5K 57
Lynton Rd. SE1 . . . . .5D 76
Lynton Rd. W3 . . . . .1L 71
Lynton Rd. Croy 1L 123
Lynton Rd. Harr 7J 37
Lynton Rd. N Mald 9B 104
Lynton Ter. W3 . . . . .9A 56
Lynton Wlk. Hay 6C 52
Lynwood Av. Coul 7F 136
Lynwood Av. Eps 6D 134
Lynwood Clo. E18 . . . . . . .8G 31
Lynwood Clo. Harr 8J 37
Lynwood Clo. Romf 6M 33
Lynwood Ct. Eps 5D 134
Lynwood Ct. King T 6M 103
Lynwood Dri. N'wd 8D 20
Lynwood Dri. Romf 6M 33
Lynwood Dri. Wor Pk 4E 120
Lynwood Gdns. Croy 6K 123
Lynwood Gdns. S'hall 9K 53
Lynwood Gro. N21 . . . . . .1L 27
Lynwood Gro. Orp 2C 128
Lynwood Rd. SW17 . . . . . .9D 90
Lynwood Rd. W5 . . . . . . .6H 55
Lynwood Rd. Eps 6D 134
Lynwood Rd. Th Dit 4D 118
Lyon Bus. Pk. Bark 5C 64
Lyon Ct. Ruis 6D 36
Lyon Ho. NW8 . . . . .7C 58
(off Broadley St.)
Lyon Ind. Est. NW2 . . . . . .7F 40
Lyon Meade. Stan 8G 23
Lyon Pk. Av. Wemb 2J 55
(in two parts)
Lyon Rd. SW19 . . . . .5A 106
Lyon Rd. Harr 4D 38
Lyon Rd. Romf 5D 50
Lyon Rd. W on T 4J 117
Lyonsdown Av. New Bar . . .8A 14
Lyonsdown Rd. Barn 8A 14
Lyons Ind. Est. Uxb 1H 143
Lyons Pl. NW8 . . . . .7B 58
Lyon St. N1 . . . . .3K 59
Lyons Wlk. W14 . . . . .5J 73
Lyoth Way. Gnfd 4C 54
Lyoth Rd. Orp 4A 128
Lyric Dri. Gnfd 7M 53
Lyric M. SE26 . . . . .1G 109
Lyric Rd. SW13 . . . . .9D 72
Lyric Theatre. 5G 73
(Hammersmith)
Lyric Theatre. 1H 75
(off Shaftesbury Av.,
Westminster)
Lysander. NW9 . . . . .8D 24
Lysander Gdns. Surb 1K 119
Lysander Gro. N19 . . . . . .6H 43
Lysander Ho. E2 . . . . .5F 60
(off Temple St.)
Lysander M. N19 . . . . .6G 43
Lysander Rd. Croy 8K 123
Lysander Rd. Ruis 7B 36
Lysander Way. Ab L 5H 5
Lysander Way. Orp 5A 128
Lysia Ct. SW6 . . . . .8H 73
(off Lysia St.)

Lysias Rd. SW12 . . . . .5F 90
Lysia St. SW6 . . . . .8H 73
Lysons Wlk. SW15 . . . . . . .3E 88
Lytchet Rd. Brom 4E 110
Lytchet Way. Enf 3G 17
Lytchgate Clo. S Croy 9C 124
Lytcott Dri. W Mol 7K 101
Lytcott Gro. SE22 . . . . . . .4C 92
Lytham Av. Wat 5H 21
Lytham Clo. SE28 . . . . . . .9J 65
Lytham Ct. S'hall 9M 53
(off Whitecote Rd.)
Lytham Gro. W5 . . . . .6K 55
Lytham St. SE17 . . . . .6B 76
Lyttelton Clo. NW3 . . . . . .3C 58
Lyttelton Ct. N2 . . . . .3A 42
Lyttelton Ho. E9 . . . . .3G 61
(off Well St.)
Lyttelton Rd. E10 . . . . . . .8M 45
Lyttelton Rd. N2 . . . . .3A 42
Lyttelton Theatre. 2L 75
(in Royal National Theatre)
Lyttleton Ct. Hay 7G 53
(off Dunedin Way)
Lyttleton Rd. N8 . . . . .1L 43
Lytton Av. N13 . . . . .2L 27
Lytton Av. Enf 2J 17
Lytton Clo. N2 . . . . .4B 42
Lytton Clo. N'holt 3K 53
Lytton Gdns. Wall 6H 123
Lytton Gro. SW15 . . . . . . .4H 89
Lytton Rd. E11 . . . . .5C 46
Lytton Rd. Barn 6A 14
Lytton Rd. Pinn 7J 21
Lytton Rd. Romf 3F 50
Lytton Strachey Path.
  SE28 . . . . .1F 80
Lyveden Rd. SE3 . . . . .8F 78
Lyveden Rd. SW17 . . . . . .3D 106

M

Mabbett Ho. SE18 . . . . . . .7L 79
(off Nightingale Pl.)
Mabbutt Clo. Brick W 3J 5
Mabel Evetts Ct. Hay 1F 68
Mabel Rd. Swan 3E 114
Maberley Cres. SE19 . . . . .4E 108
Maberley Rd. SE19 . . . . . .5D 108
Maberley Rd. Beck 7H 109
Mabledon Pl. WC1 . . . . . . .6G 59
(off Mabledon Pl.)
Mablethorpe Rd. SW6 . . . .8J 73
Mabley St. E9 . . . . .1J 61
Mablin Lodge. Buck H 1G 31
McAdam Dri. Enf 4M 15
Macaret Clo. N20 . . . . . . .9M 13
Macarthur Clo. E7 . . . . . . .2E 62
MacArthur Clo. Eri 6C 82
Macarthur Ter. SE7 . . . . . .7H 79
Macartney Ho. SE10 . . . . .8B 78
(off Chesterfield Wlk.)
Macartney Ho. SW9 . . . . . .9L 75
(off Gosling Way)
Macaulay Av. Esh 4D 118
Macaulay Ct. SW4 . . . . . . .2F 90
Macaulay Rd. E6 . . . . .5H 63
Macaulay Rd. SW4 . . . . . .2F 90
Macaulay Sq. SW4 . . . . . .3F 90
Macaulay Way. SE28 . . . . .2F 80
McAuley Clo. SE1 . . . . . . .4L 75
McAuley Clo. SE9 . . . . . . .4M 95
Macauley M. SE13 . . . . . . .9A 78
Macbean St. SE18 . . . . . . .4M 79
Macbeth Ho. N1 . . . . .5C 60
Macbeth St. W6 . . . . .6F 72
McCall Clo. SW4 . . . . .1J 91
McCall Cres. SE7 . . . . . . .6J 79
McCall Ho. N7 . . . . .9J 43
McCarthy Rd. Felt 2H 101
Macclesfield Ho. EC1 . . . . .6A 60
(off Central St.)
Macclesfield Ho. Romf 5J 35
(off Dagnam Pk. Dri.)
Macclesfield Rd. EC1 . . . . .6A 60
Macclesfield Rd. SE25 . . . .9G 109
Macclesfield St. W1 . . . . . .1H 75
McClintock Pl. Enf 1M 17
McCoid Way. SE1 . . . . . . .3A 76
McCrone M. NW3 . . . . .2B 58
McCudden Rd. Dart 2K 99
McCullum Rd. E3 . . . . .4K 61
McDermott Clo. SW11 . . . .2C 90
McDermott Rd. SE15 . . . . .2E 92
Macdonald Av. Dag 8M 49
Macdonald Av. Horn 1J 51
Macdonald Rd. E7 . . . . . . .9E 46
Macdonald Rd. E17 . . . . . .9A 30
Macdonald Rd. N11 . . . . . .5D 26
Macdonald Rd. N19 . . . . . .7G 43
Macdonald Way. Horn 2J 51
Macdonnell Gdns. Wat 3G 8
McDonough Clo. Chess . . .6J 119
McDowall Clo. E16 . . . . . . .8D 62
McDowall Rd. SE5 . . . . . . .9A 76
Macduff Rd. SW11 . . . . . . .9E 74
Mace Clo. E1 . . . . .2F 76
Mace Gateway. E16 . . . . . .1E 78
McEntee Av. E17 . . . . .8J 29

Mace St. E2 . . . . .5H 61
McEwen Way. E15 . . . . . . .4B 62
Macey St. SE10 . . . . .7A 78
(off Thames St.)
Macfarlane La. Iswth 7D 70
Macfarlane Rd. W12 . . . . .2G 73
Macfarren Pl. NW1 . . . . . . .7E 58
McGlashon Ho. E1 . . . . . . .7E 60
(off Hunton St.)
McGrath Rd. E15 . . . . .1D 62
McGredy. Chesh 2B 6
McGregor Ct. N1 . . . . .6C 60
(off Hoxton St.)
MacGregor Rd. E16 . . . . . .8G 63
McGregor Rd. W11 . . . . . . .9J 57
Machell Rd. SE15 . . . . . . .2G 93
McIndoe Ct. N1 . . . . .4B 60
(off Sherborne St.)
McIntosh Clo. Romf 1C 50
McIntosh Clo. Wall 9J 123
McIntosh Ho. SE16 . . . . . .5G 77
(off Millender Wlk.)
Macintosh Ho. W1 . . . . . . .8E 58
(off Beaumont St.)
McIntyre Ct. SE18 . . . . . . .5J 79
(off Prospect Va.)
Mackay Ho. W12 . . . . .1F 72
(off White City Est.)
Mackay Rd. SW8 . . . . .2F 90
McKay Rd. SW20 . . . . . . .4F 104
McKay Trad. Est. W10 . . . .7J 57
McKellar Clo. Bus H 2A 22
Mackennal St. NW8 . . . . . .5C 58
Mackenzie Clo. W12 . . . . .1F 72
Mackenzie Ho. NW2 . . . . . .8E 40
Mackenzie Rd. N7 . . . . . . .2K 59
Mackenzie Rd. Beck 6G 109
Mackenzie Wlk. E14 . . . . . .2L 77
McKenzie Way. Eps 1L 133
McKerrell Rd. SE15 . . . . . .9E 76
Mackeson Rd. NW3 . . . . . .9D 42
Mackie Rd. SW2 . . . . .6L 91
McKillop Way. Sidc 4G 113
Mackintosh La. E9 . . . . . . .1H 61
Macklin St. WC2 . . . . .9J 59
Mackonochie Ho. EC1 . . . .8L 59
(off Baldwins Gdns.)
Mackrow Wlk. E14 . . . . . . .1A 78
Mack's Rd. SE16 . . . . .5E 76
Mackworth Ho. NW1 . . . . . .6G 59
(off Augustus St.)
Mackworth St. NW1 . . . . . .6G 59
Maclaren M. SW15 . . . . . . .3G 89
Maclean Rd. SE23 . . . . . . .5J 93
Maclennan Av. Rain 6H 67
McLeod Ct. SE22 . . . . .7E 92
McLeod Rd. N21 . . . . .7J 15
McLeod Rd. SE2 . . . . .5F 80
McLeod's M. SW7 . . . . . . .5M 73
(in two parts)
Macleod St. SE17 . . . . .6A 76
Maclise Ho. SW1 . . . . .5J 75
(off Marsham St.)
Maclise Rd. W14 . . . . .4J 73
Macmillan Ct. S Harr 6L 37
Macmillan Gdns. Dart 3L 99
McMillan Ho. SE4 . . . . . . .2J 93
(off Arica Rd.)
McMillan Ho. SE14 . . . . . .9J 77
McMillan St. SE8 . . . . .7L 77
Macmillan Way. SW17 . . . .1F 106
McNair Rd. S'hall 4M 69
Macnamara Ho. SW10 . . . .8B 74
(off Worlds End Est.)
McNeil Rd. SE5 . . . . .1C 92
McNicol Dri. NW10 . . . . . .5A 56
Macoma Rd. SE18 . . . . . . .7B 80
Macoma Ter. SE18 . . . . . . .7B 80
Maconochies Rd.
  E14 . . . . .6M 77
Macquarie Way. E14 . . . . .5M 77
McRae La. Mitc 2D 122
Macready Ho. W1 . . . . .8C 58
(off Crawford St.)
Macready Pl. N7 . . . . .9J 43
Macroom Rd. W9 . . . . .6K 57
Macs Ho. E17 . . . . .1M 45
Mac's Pl. EC4 . . . . .9L 59
Madame Tussaud's. 7E 58
Madans Wlk. Eps 7B 134
(in two parts)
Mada Rd. Orp 5M 127
Maddams St. E3 . . . . .7M 61
Maddison Clo. Tedd 3D 102
Maddocks Clo. Sidc 2J 113
Maddocks Ho. E1 . . . . .1F 76
(off Cornwall St.)
Maddox St. W1 . . . . .1F 74
Madeira Av. Brom 4C 110
Madeira Gro. Wfd G 6G 31
Madeira Rd. E11 . . . . .6B 46
Madeira Rd. N13 . . . . .4M 27
Madeira Rd. SW16 . . . . . . .2J 107
Madeira Rd. Mitc 8D 106
Madeline Clo. Romf 4G 49
Madeley Rd. W5 . . . . .9H 55
Madeline Gro. Ilf 1B 64
Madeline Rd. SE20 . . . . . .4E 108

Madge Gill Way. E6 . . . . . .4J 63
(off High St. N.)
Madge Hill. W7 . . . . .1B 70
Madinah Rd. E8 . . . . .2E 60
Madison Cres. Bexh 8G 81
Madison Gdns. Bexh 8G 81
Madison Gdns. Brom 7D 110
Madison Ho. E1 . . . . .1K 77
(off Victory Pl.)
Madison, The. SE1 . . . . . . .3B 76
(off Long La.)
Madras Pl. N7 . . . . .2L 59
Madras Rd. Ilf 9M 47
Madrid Rd. SW13 . . . . .9E 72
Madrigal La. SE5 . . . . .8M 75
Madron St. SE17 . . . . .6C 76
Mafeking Av. E6 . . . . .5J 63
Mafeking Av. Bren 7J 71
Mafeking Av. Ilf 5B 48
Mafeking Rd. E16 . . . . .7D 62
Mafeking Rd. N17 . . . . . . .9E 28
Mafeking Rd. Enf 5D 16
Magdala Av. N19 . . . . .7G 43
Magdala Rd. Iswth 2E 86
Magdala Rd. S Croy 9B 124
Magdalen Clo. SE15 . . . . . .1F 92
Magdalene Gdns. E6 . . . . . .7L 63
Magdalen Gro. Orp 6F 128
Magdalen Ho. E16 . . . . . . .2F 78
(off Keats Av.)
Magdalen Pas. E1 . . . . . . .1D 76
Magdalen Rd. SW18 . . . . . .7A 90
Magdalen St. SE1 . . . . . . .2C 76
Magee St. SE11 . . . . .7L 75
Magellan Ct. NW10 . . . . . . .3B 56
(off Stonebridge Pk.)
Magellan Ho. E1 . . . . .7H 61
(off Ernest St.)
Magellan Pl. E14 . . . . .5L 77
Magnaville Rd. Bus H 9C 10
Magnet Rd. Wemb 7H 39
Magnin Clo. E8 . . . . .4E 60
Magnolia Av. Ab L 5E 4
Magnolia Clo. E10 . . . . . . .7L 45
Magnolia Clo. King T 3M 103
Magnolia Ct. Felt 7E 84
Magnolia Ct. Harr 5K 39
Magnolia Ct. N'holt 7J 53
Magnolia Ct. Rich 9M 71
Magnolia Ct. Sutt 9L 121
(off Grange Rd.)
Magnolia Ct. Uxb 2F 142
Magnolia Ct. Wall 7F 122
Magnolia Dri. Big H 8H 141
Magnolia Gdns. E10 . . . . . .7L 45
Magnolia Gdns. Edgw 4A 24
Magnolia Ho. SE8 . . . . . . .7K 77
(off Evelyn St.)
Magnolia Lodge. E4 . . . . . .3M 29
Magnolia Pl. SW4 . . . . .4J 91
Magnolia Pl. W5 . . . . .8H 55
Magnolia Rd. W4 . . . . .7M 71
Magnolia St. W Dray 6H 143
Magnolia Way. Eps 7A 120
Magnum Clo. Rain 7F 66
Magpie All. EC4 . . . . .9L 59
Magpie Clo. E7 . . . . .1D 62
Magpie Clo. NW9 . . . . .9C 24
Magpie Clo. Enf 3E 16
Magpie Hall Clo. Brom 1J 127
Magpie Hall La. Brom 2J 127
Magpie Hall Rd. Bus H 2C 22
Magpie Pl. SE14 . . . . .7J 77
Magpie Pl. Wat 5G 5
Magri Wlk. E1 . . . . .8G 61
Maguire Dri. Rich 1G 103
Maguire St. SE1 . . . . .3D 76
Mahatma Gandhi Ind. Est.
  SE24 . . . . .3M 91
Mahlon Av. Ruis 1F 52
Mahogany Clo. SE16 . . . . .2J 77
Mahon Clo. Enf 3D 16
Maida Av. E4 . . . . .9M 17
Maida Av. W2 . . . . .8A 58
Maida Hill. 7K 57
Maida Rd. Belv 4L 81
Maida Vale. 6M 57
Maida Va. W9 . . . . .5L 57
Maida Va. Rd. Dart 4E 98
Maida Way. E4 . . . . .9M 17
Maiden Erlegh Av. Bex 7J 97
Maiden La. NW1 . . . . .3H 59
Maiden La. SE1 . . . . .2A 76
Maiden La. WC2 . . . . .1J 75
Maiden La. Dart 2E 98
Maiden Pl. NW5 . . . . .8G 43
Maiden Rd. E15 . . . . .3C 62
Maidenshaw Rd. Eps 4B 134
Maidenstone Hill. SE10 . . . .9A 78
Maids of Honour Row.
  Rich 4H 87
Maidstone Av. Romf 9A 34
Maidstone Bldgs. SE1 . . . . .2A 76
Maidstone Ho. E14 . . . . . . .9M 61
(off Carmen St.)
Maidstone Rd. N11 . . . . . . .6G 27
Maidstone Rd. Sidc 3H 113
Main Av. Enf 7D 16

Main Av.—Manor Rd.

Main Av. N'wd 3A 20
Main Dri. Wemb 8H 39
Mainridge Rd. Chst 1L 111
Main Rd. Big H & Kes 5G 141
Main Rd. Crock 1B 130
Main Rd. Eyns 1J 131
Main Rd. F'ham 3M 141
Main Rd. Hex 4D 114
Main Rd. Orp 7G 113
Main Rd. Romf 2D 50
Main Rd. Sidc 9B 96
Main Rd. S at H 3M 115
Main St. Felt 2H 101
Mais Ho. SE26 8F 92
Maisie Webster Clo.
Stanw 6A 144
Maismore St. SE15 7E 76
Maisonettes, The. Sutt 7K 121
Maitland Clo. SE10 8M 77
Maitland Clo. Houn 2K 85
Maitland Clo. W on T 4J 117
Maitland Ct. W2 1B 74
(off Lancaster Ter.)
Maitland Ho. SW1 7G 75
(off Churchill Gdns.)
Maitland Pk. Est. NW3 2D 58
Maitland Pk. Rd. NW3 2D 58
Maitland Pk. Vs. NW3 2D 58
Maitland Pl. E5 9F 44
Maitland Rd. E15 2D 62
Maitland Rd. SE26 3H 109
Maitlands. Lou 5K 19
Maitland Yd. W13 2E 70
Maize Row. E14 1K 77
Majendie Rd. SE18 6B 80
Majestic Way. Mitc 6D 106
Major Rd. E15 1B 62
Major Rd. SE16 4E 76
Makepeace Av. N6 7E 42
Makepeace Mans. N6 7E 42
Makepeace Rd. E11 2E 46
Makepeace Rd. N'holt 5J 53
Makinen Ho. Buck H 1G 31
Makins St. SW3 5C 74
Malabar Ct. W12 1F 72
(off India Way)
Malabar St. E14 3L 77
Malam Ct. SE11 5L 75
Malam Gdns. E14 1M 77
Malan Clo. Big H 9J 141
Malan Sq. Rain 2F 66
Malbrook Rd. SW15 3F 88
Malcolm Ct. E7 2D 62
Malcolm Ct. NW4 4E 40
Malcolm Ct. Stan 5G 23
Malcolm Cres. NW4 4E 40
Malcolm Dri. Surb 3H 119
Malcolm Ho. N1 5C 60
(off Arden Est.)
Malcolm Pl. E2 7G 61
Malcolm Rd. E1 7G 61
Malcolm Rd. SE20 4G 109
Malcolm Rd. SE25 1E 124
Malcolm Rd. SW19 3J 105
Malcolm Rd. Coul 7H 137
Malcolm Sargent Ho. E16 2F 78
(off Evelyn Rd.)
Malcolmson Ho. SW1 6H 75
(off Aylesford St.)
Malcolm Way. E11 3E 46
Malcombs Way. N14 7G 15
Malden Av. SE25 8F 108
Malden Av. Gnfd 1C 54
Malden Ct. N4 4A 44
Malden Ct. N Mald 7F 104
Malden Cres. NW5 2E 58
Malden Fields. Bush 7H 9
Malden Green. 3E 120
Malden Grn. Av. Wor Pk 3D 120
Malden Hill. N Mald 7D 104
Malden Hill Gdns.
N Mald 7D 104
Malden Junction (Junct.)
9C 104
Malden Pk. N Mald 1D 120
Malden Pl. NW5 1E 58
Malden Rd. NW5 1D 58
Malden Rd. Borwd 5L 11
Malden Rd. N Mald 9C 104
Malden Rd. Sutt 6G 121
Malden Rd. Wat 4F 8
Malden Rushett. 3G 133
Malden Way. N Mald 1B 120
Maldon Clo. E15 1C 62
Maldon Clo. N1 4A 60
Maldon Clo. SE5 2C 92
Maldon Ct. E6 4L 63
Maldon Ct. Wall 7G 123
Maldon Rd. N9 3D 28
Maldon Rd. W3 1A 72
Maldon Rd. Romf 5A 50
Maldon Rd. Wall 7F 122
Maldon Wlk. Wfd G 6G 31
Malet Pl. WC1 7H 59
Malet St. WC1 7H 59
Maley Av. SE27 8M 91
Malford Ct. E18 9E 30
Malford Gro. E18 2D 46
Malfort Rd. SE5 2C 92
Malham Clo. N11 6E 26
Malham Rd. SE23 7H 93
Malham Ter. N18 6F 28
(off Dysons Rd.)
Malibu Ct. SE26 9F 92
Malins Clo. Barn 7F 12
Mallams M. SW9 2M 91
Mallard Clo. E9 2K 61
Mallard Clo. NW6 5L 57
Mallard Clo. W7 3C 70
Mallard Clo. Dart 4K 99
Mallard Clo. New Bar 8B 14
Mallard Clo. Twic 6L 85
Mallard Ct. E17 1B 46
Mallard Ho. NW8 5C 58
(off Barrow Hill Est.)
Mallard Path. SE28 4B 80
(off Goosander Way)
Mallard Pl. N22 9K 27
Mallard Pl. Twic 9E 86
Mallard Rd. Ab L 4E 4
Mallard Rd. S Croy 2H 139
Mallards. E11 5E 46
(off Blake Hall Rd.)
Mallards Ct. Wat 3K 21
(off Hangar Ruding)
Mallards Reach. Wey 4B 116
Mallards Rd. Wfd G 7F 30
Mallard Wlk. Beck 9H 109
Mallard Wlk. Sidc 3G 113
Mallard Way. NW9 5A 40
Mallard Way. N'wd 7A 20
Mallard Way. Wall 1G 137
Mallard Way. Wat 1J 9
Mall Chambers. W8 2L 73
(off Kensington Mall)
Mallet Dri. N'holt 1K 53
Mallet Rd. SE13 5B 94
Mall Galleries. 2H 75
(off Carlton Ho. Ter.)
Mall Gallery. WC2 9J 59
(off Thomas Neals Shop. Mall)
Malling Clo. Croy 1G 125
Malling Gdns. Mord 1A 122
Malling Way. Brom 2D 126
Mallinson Clo. Horn 1G 67
Mallinson Rd. SW11 4C 90
Mallinson Rd. Croy 5H 123
Mallion Ct. Wal A 6M 7
Mallon Gdns. E1 9D 60
(off Commercial St.)
Mallord St. SW3 7B 74
Mallory Clo. SE4 3J 93
Mallory Gdns. E Barn 9E 14
Mallory Ho. E14 8M 61
(off Teviot St.)
Mallory St. NW8 7C 58
Mallow Clo. Croy 3H 125
Mallow Mead. NW7 7J 25
Mallows, The. Uxb 8A 36
Mallow St. EC1 7B 60
Mall Rd. W6 6F 72
Mall, The. E15 3B 62
Mall, The. N14 3J 27
Mall, The. SW1 3G 75
Mall, The. SW14 4A 88
Mall, The. W5 1J 71
Mall, The. Bexh 3L 97
Mall, The. Bren 7H 71
Mall, The. Brom 7E 110
Mall, The. Croy 4A 124
Mall, The. Dag 2L 65
Mall, The. Harr 4K 39
Mall, The. Horn 6F 50
Mall, The. Park 1M 5
Mall, The. Surb 9H 103
Mall, The. Swan 7C 114
Mall, The. W on T 7H 117
Mallys Pl. S Dar 5M 115
Malmains Clo. Beck 8B 110
Malmains Way. Beck 8A 110
Malmesbury. E2 5G 61
(off Cyprus St.)
Malmesbury Clo. Pinn 2D 36
Malmesbury Rd. E3 6K 61
Malmesbury Rd. E16 8C 62
Malmesbury Rd. E18 8D 30
Malmesbury Rd. Mord 2A 122
Malmesbury Ter. E16 8D 62
Malmsey Ho. SE11 6K 75
Malpas Dri. Pinn 3H 37
Malpas Rd. E8 1F 60
Malpas Rd. SE4 1K 93
Malpas Rd. Dag 2H 65
Malsmead Ho. E9 1K 61
(off Homerton Rd.)
Malta Rd. E10 6L 45
Malta St. EC1 7M 59
Maltby Clo. Orp 3E 128
Maltby Dri. Enf 2F 16
Maltby Rd. Chess 8L 119
Maltby St. SE1 3D 76
Malthouse Dri. W4 7D 72
Malthouse Dri. Felt 2H 101
Malthouse Pas. SW13 1D 88
(off Maltings Clo.)
Malthus Path. SE28 2G 81
Malting Ho. E14 1K 77
(off Oak La.)
Maltings. W4 6L 71
Maltings Clo. SW13 1D 88
Maltings Lodge. W4 7C 72
(off Corney Reach Way)
Maltings M. Sidc 9E 96
Maltings Pl. SE1 3C 76
(off Tower Bri. Rd.)
Maltings Pl. SW6 9M 73
Maltings, The. K Lan 7A 4
Maltings, The. Orp 3D 128
Maltings, The. Romf 5D 50
Malting Way. Iswth 2D 86
Malton M. SE18 7C 80
Malton M. W10 9J 57
Malton Rd. W10 9J 57
Malton St. SE18 7C 80
Maltravers St. WC2 1K 75
Malt Shovel Cotts. Eyns 5H 131
Malt St. SE1 7E 76
Malva Clo. SW18 4M 89
Malvern Av. E4 7B 30
Malvern Av. Bexh 8J 81
Malvern Av. Harr 8J 37
Malvern Clo. SE20 6E 108
Malvern Clo. W10 8K 57
Malvern Clo. Bush 8A 10
Malvern Clo. Mitc 7G 107
Malvern Clo. Surb 3J 119
Malvern Ct. SW7 5B 74
(off Onslow Sq.)
Malvern Ct. W12 3E 72
(off Hadyn Pk. Rd.)
Malvern Ct. Eps 6B 134
Malvern Ct. Sutt 9L 121
Malvern Dri. Felt 2H 101
Malvern Dri. Ilf 9D 48
Malvern Dri. Wfd G 5G 31
Malvern Gdns. NW2 7J 41
Malvern Gdns. Harr 2J 39
Malvern Gdns. Lou 8K 19
Malvern Ho. N16 6D 44
Malvern Ho. Wat 8B 8
Malvern M. NW6 6L 57
Malvern Pl. NW6 6K 57
Malvern Rd. E6 4J 63
Malvern Rd. E8 3E 60
Malvern Rd. E11 7C 46
Malvern Rd. N8 1L 43
Malvern Rd. N17 1E 44
Malvern Rd. NW6 6L 57
(in two parts)
Malvern Rd. Enf 1J 17
Malvern Rd. Hamp 4L 101
Malvern Rd. Hay 8C 68
Malvern Rd. Horn 4E 50
Malvern Rd. Orp 6F 128
Malvern Rd. Surb 4J 119
Malvern Rd. T Hth 8L 107
Malvern Ter. N1 4L 59
Malvern Ter. N9 1D 28
Malvern Way. W13 8F 54
Malvern Way. Crox G 7A 8
Malwood Rd. SW12 5F 90
Malyons Rd. SE13 5M 93
Malyons Rd. Swan 4D 114
Malyons Ter. SE13 4M 93
Malyons, The. Shep 1B 116
Managers St. E14 2A 78
Manatee Pl. Wall 5H 123
Manaton Clo. SE15 2F 92
Manaton Cres. S'hall 9L 53
Manbey Gro. E15 2C 62
Manbey Pk. Rd. E15 2C 62
Manbey Rd. E15 2C 62
Manbey St. E15 2C 62
Manbre Rd. W6 7G 73
Manbrough Av. E6 6L 63
Manchester Ct. E16 9F 62
(off Garvary Rd.)
Manchester Dri. W10 7J 57
Manchester Gro. E14 6A 78
Manchester Ho. SE17 6A 76
Manchester M. W1 8E 58
(off Manchester St.)
Manchester Rd. E14 6A 78
Manchester Rd. N15 4B 44
Manchester Rd. T Hth 7A 108
Manchester Sq. W1 9E 58
Manchester St. W1 8E 58
Manchester Way. Dag 9M 49
Manchuria Rd. SW11 5E 90
Manciple St. SE1 3B 76
Mandalay Rd. SW4 4G 91
Mandarin Ct. NW10 2B 56
(off Mitchellbrook Way)
Mandarin Ct. SE8 7K 77
Mandarin St. E14 1L 77
Mandarin Way. Hay 9J 53
Mandela Clo. NW10 3A 56
Mandela Clo. W12 1F 72
Mandela Ct. Uxb 8A 142
Mandela Ho. E2 6D 60
(off Virginia Rd.)
Mandela Ho. SE5 1M 91
Mandela Pl. Wat 4H 9
Mandela Rd. E16 9E 62
Mandela St. NW1 4G 59
Mandela St. SW9 8L 75
(in two parts)
Mandela Way. SE1 5C 76
Mandeville Clo. SE3 8D 78
Mandeville Clo. SW20 4J 105
Mandeville Clo. Wat 2D 8
Mandeville Ct. E4 5J 29
Mandeville Dri. Surb 3H 119
Mandeville Ho. SE1 6D 76
(off Rolls Rd.)
Mandeville Ho. SW4 4G 91
Mandeville M. SW4 3H 91
Mandeville Pl. W1 9E 58
Mandeville Rd. N14 2F 26
Mandeville Rd. Enf 9D 6
Mandeville Rd. Iswth 1E 86
Mandeville Rd. N'holt 3L 53
Mandeville St. E5 8J 45
Mandrake Rd. SW17 9D 90
Mandrake Way. E15 3C 62
Mandrell Rd. SW2 4J 91
Manesty Ct. N14 9H 15
(off Ivy Rd.)
Manette St. W1 9H 59
Manford Clo. Chig 4E 32
Manford Cross. Chig 5E 32
Manford Ind. Est. Eri 7F 82
Manford Way. Chig 5C 32
Manfred Rd. SW15 4K 89
Manger Rd. N7 2J 59
Mangold Way. Eri 4H 81
Manilla St. E14 3L 77
Man in the Moon Theatre.
7B 74
(off King's Rd.)
Manister Rd. SE2 4E 80
Manitoba Ct. SE16 3G 77
(off Canada Est.)
Manitoba Gdns. G Str 8D 128
Manley Ct. N16 8D 44
Manley Ho. SE11 5L 75
Manley St. NW1 4E 58
Manly Dixon Dri. Enf 1J 17
Mann Clo. Croy 5A 124
Manneby Prior. N1 5K 59
(off Cumming St.)
Manning Ct. Wat 8H 9
Manningford Clo. EC1 6M 59
Manning Gdns. Harr 5H 39
Manning Pl. Rich 5K 87
Manning Rd. E17 3J 45
Manning Rd. Dag 2L 65
Manning Rd. Orp 9H 113
Manning St. Ave 2M 83
Manningtree Clo. SW19 7J 89
Manningtree Rd. Ruis 9F 36
Manningtree St. E1 9E 60
Mannin Rd. Romf 5F 48
Mannock Dri. Lou 4M 19
Mannock M. E18 8G 31
Mannock Rd. N22 1M 43
Mannock Rd. Dart 2K 99
Mann's Clo. Iswth 4D 86
Manns Rd. Edgw 6L 23
Manny Shinwell Ho. SW6 7K 73
(off Clem Attlee Ct.)
Manoel Rd. Twic 9A 86
Manor Av. E7 9G 47
Manor Av. SE4 1K 93
Manor Av. Horn 3G 51
Manor Av. Houn 2H 85
Manor Av. N'holt 3K 53
Manor Brook. SE3 3E 94
Manor Chase. Wey 7A 116
Manor Circus (Junct.) 2K 87
Manor Clo. E17 8J 29
Manor Clo. NW7 5B 24
Manor Clo. NW9 3M 39
Manor Clo. SE28 1G 81
Manor Clo. Ave 2M 83
Manor Clo. Barn 6J 13
Manor Clo. Cray 3B 98
Manor Clo. Dag 2B 66
Manor Clo. Romf 3E 50
Manor Clo. Ruis 6D 36
Manor Clo. Warl 9J 139
Manor Clo. Wilm 9E 98
Manor Clo. Wor Pk 3C 120
Manor Clo. S. Ave 2M 83
Manor Cotts. N2 9A 26
(off Manor Cotts. App.)
Manor Cotts. N'wd 8D 20
Manor Cotts. App. N2 9A 26
Manor Ct. E4 1C 30
Manor Ct. E10 6M 45
Manor Ct. N2 3D 42
(off Aylmer Rd.)
Manor Ct. N14 2H 27
Manor Ct. N20 3D 26
(off York Way)
Manor Ct. SW2 4K 91
Manor Ct. SW6 9M 73
Manor Ct. SW16 9J 91
Manor Ct. W3 5L 71
Manor Ct. Bark 3D 64
Manor Ct. Bexh 3M 97
Manor Ct. Chesh 4D 6
Manor Ct. Enf 9B 6
Manor Ct. Harr 4D 38
Manor Ct. King T 5L 103
Manor Ct. Twic 8A 86
Manor Ct. Wemb 1J 55
Manor Ct. W Mol 8L 101
Manor Ct. W Wick 3M 125
Manor Ct. Wey 6A 116
Manor Ct. Rd. W7 1C 70
Manor Cres. Eps 4L 133
Manor Cres. Horn 3G 51
Manor Cres. Surb 1L 119
Manorcroft Pde. Chesh 3D 6
Manor Dene. SE28 9G 65
Manordene Clo. Th Dit 3E 118
Manordene Rd. SE28 9H 65
Manor Dri. N14 1F 26
Manor Dri. N20 4D 26
Manor Dri. NW7 5B 24
Manor Dri. Eps 8C 120
Manor Dri. Esh 4D 118
Manor Dri. Felt 2H 101
Manor Dri. Sun 6E 100
Manor Dri. Surb 1K 119
Manor Dri. Wemb 9K 39
Manor Dri. N.
N Mald & Wor Pk 2B 120
Manor Dri., The. Wor Pk 3C 120
Manor Est. SE16 5F 76
Manor Farm. F'ham 1K 131
Mnr. Farm Av. Shep 1A 116
Mnr. Farm Clo. Wor Pk 3C 120
Mnr. Farm Ct. E6 6K 63
(off Holloway Rd.)
Mnr. Farm Dri. E4 3C 30
Mnr. Farm Rd. SW16 6L 107
Mnr. Farm Rd. Enf 8B 6
Mnr. Farm Rd. Wemb 5H 55
Manorfield Clo. N19 9G 43
(off Fulbrook M.)
Manor Fields. SW15 5H 89
Manorfields Clo. Chst 7D 112
Manor Gdns. N7 8J 43
Manor Gdns. SW4 1G 91
(off Larkhall Ri.)
Manor Gdns. SW20 6K 105
Manor Gdns. W3 5L 71
Manor Gdns. W4 6C 72
Manor Gdns. Hamp 4M 101
Manor Gdns. Rich 3K 87
Manor Gdns. Ruis 1G 53
Manor Gdns. S Croy 8D 124
Manor Gdns. Sun 5E 100
Manor Ga. N'holt 3J 53
Manorgate Rd. King T 5L 103
Mnr. Green Rd. Eps 5M 133
Manor Gro. SE15 7G 77
Manor Gro. Beck 6M 109
Manor Gro. Rich 3L 87
Mnr. Hall Av. NW4 9H 25
Mnr. Hall Dri. NW4 9H 25
Manorhall Gdns. E10 6L 45
Manor Hill. Bans 7D 136
Manor House (Junct.) 6A 44
Manor Ho. NW1 8C 58
(off Marylebone Rd.)
Manor Ho. S'hall 4J 69
Manor Ho. Ct. W9 7A 58
(off Warrington Gdns.)
Manor Ho. Ct. Eps 5A 134
Manor Ho. Ct. Shep 2A 116
Manor Ho. Dri. NW6 3H 57
Manor Ho. Dri. N'wd 7A 20
Manor Ho. Est. Stan 6F 22
Manor Ho. Garden. E11 4F 46
Manor Ho. Gdns. Ab L 4B 4
Manor Ho. Way. Iswth 2F 86
Manor La. SE13 & SE12 4C 94
Manor La. Felt 8E 84
Manor La. Hay 7B 68
Manor La. Sun 6E 100
Manor La. Sutt 7A 122
Manor La. Ter. SE13 3C 94
Manor M. NW6 5L 57
(off Cambridge Av., in two parts)
Manor M. SE4 1K 93
Manor Mt. SE23 7G 93
Manor Pde. N16 7D 44
Manor Pde. NW10 5D 56
(off High St.)
Manor Pde. Harr 4D 38
Manor Park. 9J 47
Manor Pk. SE13 3B 94
Manor Pk. Chst 6B 112
Manor Pk. Eri 7E 82
Manor Pk. Rich 3K 87
Mnr. Park Clo. W Wick 3M 125
Manor Park Crematorium.
E7 9G 47
Mnr. Park Cres. Edgw 6L 23
Mnr. Park Dri. Harr 1M 37
Mnr. Park Gdns. Edgw 5L 23
Mnr. Park Pde. SE13 3B 94
(off Lee High Rd.)
Mnr. Park Rd. E12 9H 47
Mnr. Park Rd. N2 1A 42
Mnr. Park Rd. NW10 4D 56
Mnr. Park Rd. Chst 5A 112
Mnr. Park Rd. Sutt 7A 122
Mnr. Park Rd. W Wick 3M 125
Manor Pl. SE17 6M 75
Manor Pl. Chst 6B 112
Manor Pl. Dart 7J 99
Manor Pl. Felt 7E 84
Manor Pl. Mitc 7G 107
Manor Pl. Sutt 6M 121
Manor Pl. W on T 2E 116
(off Thames St., in two parts)
Manor Pl. Ind. Est. Borwd 5A 12
Manor Rd. E10 5L 45
Manor Rd. E15 & E16 5C 62
Manor Rd. E17 9J 29
Manor Rd. N16 7B 44

Manor Rd.—Mark St.

Manor Rd. N17 8E 28
Manor Rd. N22 6J 27
Manor Rd. SE25 8E 108
Manor Rd. SW20 6K 105
Manor Rd. W13 1E 70
Manor Rd. Abr 2G 33
Manor Rd. Bark 2D 64
Manor Rd. Barn 6J 13
Manor Rd. Beck 6M 109
Manor Rd. Bex 7M 97
Manor Rd. Chad H 4H 49
Manor Rd. Dag 2A 66
Manor Rd. Dart 3C 98
Manor Rd. E Mol 8B 102
Manor Rd. Enf 4A 16
Manor Rd. Eri 7D 82
Manor Rd. Harr 4E 38
Manor Rd. Hay 9E 52
Manor Rd. H Bee 3F 18
Manor Rd. Lou 8F 18
Manor Rd. Mitc 8G 107
Manor Rd. Rich 3L 87
Manor Rd. Romf 3E 50
Manor Rd. Ruis 6B 36
Manor Rd. Sidc 9D 96
Manor Rd. Sutt 9K 121
Manor Rd. Tedd 2E 102
(in two parts)
Manor Rd. Twic 8A 86
Manor Rd. Wall 6F 122
Manor Rd. Wal A 6K 7
Manor Rd. W on T 2D 116
Manor Rd. Wat 3F 8
Manor Rd. W Wick 4M 125
Manor Rd. Wfd G & Chig 6K 31
Manor Rd. Ho. Harr 4E 38
Manor Rd. N. Esh 5D 118
Manor Rd. N. Wall 6F 122
Manor Rd. S. Esh 6C 118
Manorside. Barn 6J 13
Manorside Clo. SE2 5G 81
Manor Sq. Dag 7G 49
Manor Va. Bren 6G 71
Manor Vw. N3 9M 25
Manor Way. E4 4B 30
Manor Way. NW9 2C 40
Manor Way. SE3 3D 94
Manor Way. Bans 8D 136
Manor Way. Beck 6L 109
Manor Way. Bex 7L 97
Manor Way. Bexh 2B 98
Manor Way. Borwd 5A 12
Manor Way. Brom 1J 127
Manor Way. Chesh 3E 6
Manorway. Enf 9C 16
Manor Way. Harr 2M 37
Manor Way. Mitc 7G 107
Manor Way. Orp 8A 112
Manor Way. Oxs 7A 132
Manor Way. Purl 4J 137
Manor Way. Rain 7C 66
Manor Way. Ruis 5C 36
Manor Way. S'hall 5H 69
Manor Way. S Croy 8C 124
Manor Way. Wfd G 5G 31
Manor Way. Wor Pk 3C 120
Manor Way Bus. Cen.
Rain 8B 66
Manor Waye. Uxb 4B 142
Manor Way, The. Wall 6F 122
Mnr. Wood Rd. Purl 5J 137
Manpreet Ct. E12 1K 63
Manresa Rd. SW3 6C 74
Mansard Beeches. SW17 2E 106
Mansard Clo. Horn 7E 50
Mansard Clo. Pinn 1H 37
Manse Clo. Hay 7B 68
Mansel Gro. E17 8L 29
Mansell Rd. W3 3B 72
Mansell Rd. Gnfd 8M 53
Mansell St. E1 9D 60
Mansel Rd. SW19 3J 105
Manse Pde. Swan 8E 114
Mansergh Clo. SE18 8J 79
Manse Rd. N16 8D 44
Manser Rd. Rain 6C 66
Manse Way. Swan 8E 114
Mansfield Av. N15 2B 44
Mansfield Av. Barn 8D 14
Mansfield Av. Ruis 6F 36
Mansfield Clo. N9 8E 16
Mansfield Clo. Orp 2H 129
Mansfield Ct. E2 4D 60
(off Whiston Rd.)
Mansfield Dri. Hay 7C 52
Mansfield Gdns. Horn 7H 51
Mansfield Heights. N2 3C 42
Mansfield Hill. E4 9M 17
Mansfield M. W1 8F 58
Mansfield Pl. NW3 9A 42
Mansfield Pl. S Croy 8B 124
Mansfield Rd. E11 4F 46
Mansfield Rd. E17 2K 45
Mansfield Rd. NW3 1D 58
Mansfield Rd. W3 7M 55
Mansfield Rd. Chess 7G 119
Mansfield Rd. Ilf 7L 47
Mansfield Rd. S Croy 8B 124
Mansfield Rd. Swan 3C 114
Mansfield St. W1 8F 58
Mansford St. E2 5E 60
Manship Rd. Mitc 4E 106
Mansion Clo. SW9 9L 75
(in two parts)
Mansion Gdns. NW3 8M 41
Mansion House. 9B 60
Mansion Ho. Pl. EC4 9B 60
Mansion Ho. St. EC4 9B 60
(off Victoria St.)
Mansions, The. SW5 6M 73
Manson M. SW7 5B 74
Manson Pl. SW7 5B 74
Manstead Gdns. Rain 9F 66
Mansted Gdns. Romf 5G 49
Manston. N17 9B 28
(off Adams Rd.)
Manston. NW1 3G 59
(off Agar Gro.)
Manston Av. S'hall 5L 69
Manston Clo. SE20 5G 109
Manston Clo. Chesh 3C 6
Manstone Rd. NW2 1J 57
Manston Gro. King T 2H 103
Manston Ho. W14 4J 73
(off Russell Rd.)
Manston Way. Horn 2F 66
Manthorp Rd. SE18 6A 80
Mantilla Rd. SW17 1E 106
Mantle Rd. SE4 2J 93
Mantlet Clo. SW16 4G 107
Mantle Way. E15 3C 62
Manton Av. W7 3D 70
Manton Clo. Hay 1C 68
Manton Rd. SE2 5E 80
Manton Rd. Enf 1L 17
Mantua St. SW11 2B 90
Mantus Clo. E1 7G 61
Mantus Rd. E1 7G 61
Manus Way. N20 2A 26
Manville Gdns. SW17 9F 90
Manville Rd. SW17 8E 90
Manwood Rd. SE4 4K 93
Manwood St. E16 2K 79
Manygate La. Shep 2A 116
Manygate Mobile Home Est.
Shep 1B 116
(off Mitre Clo.)
Manygates. SW12 8F 90
Mapesbury Rd. NW2 3J 57
Mapeshill Pl. NW2 2G 57
Mapes Ho. NW6 3J 57
Mape St. E2 7F 60
Maple Av. E4 5K 29
Maple Av. W3 2C 72
Maple Av. Harr 7M 37
Maple Av. Upm 8M 51
Maple Av. W Dray 1J 143
Maple Clo. N3 6L 25
Maple Clo. N16 4E 44
Maple Clo. SW4 5H 91
Maple Clo. Buck H 3H 31
Maple Clo. Bush 4J 9
Maple Clo. Hamp 3J 101
Maple Clo. Hay 6H 53
Maple Clo. Horn 8F 50
Maple Clo. Ilf 5C 32
Maple Clo. Mitc 5F 106
Maple Clo. Orp 9B 112
Maple Clo. Ruis 4F 36
Maple Clo. Swan 6C 114
Maple Clo. Whyt 9D 138
Maple Ct. E6 8L 63
Maple Ct. SE6 7M 93
Maple Ct. Borwd 6L 11
(off Drayton Rd.)
Maple Ct. Croy 6A 124
(off Lwr. Coombe St.)
Maple Ct. Croy 6A 124
(off Waldrons, The)
Maple Ct. N Mald 7B 104
Maple Ct. Wat 9H 5
Maple Cres. Sidc 5E 96
Maplecroft Clo. E6 9H 63
Mapledale Av. Croy 4E 124
Mapledene. Chst 2A 112
Mapledene Est. E8 3E 60
Mapledene Rd. E8 3D 60
Maplefield. Park 2M 5
Maple Gdns. Edgw 7C 24
Maple Gdns. Stai 8C 144
Maple Ga. Lou 4L 19
Maple Gro. NW9 5A 40
Maple Gro. W5 4H 71
Maple Gro. Bren 8F 70
Maple Gro. S'hall 8K 53
Maple Gro. Wat 3E 8
Maple Gro. Bus. Cen.
Houn 3G 85
Maple Ho. E17 1M 45
Maple Ho. SE8 8K 77
(off Idonia St.)
Maple Ho. King T 9J 103
(off Maple Rd.)
Maplehurst. Brom 6C 110
Maplehurst Clo. King T 8J 103
Maple Ind. Est. Felt 9E 84
Maple Leaf Clo. Ab L 5E 4
Maple Leaf Clo. Big H 8H 141
Mapleleaf Clo. S Croy 3G 139
Maple Leaf Dri. Sidc 7D 96
Mapleleafe Gdns. Ilf 1M 47
Maple Leaf Sq. SE16 3H 77
Maple Lodge. W8 4M 73
(off Abbots Wlk.)
Maple M. NW6 5M 57
Maple M. SW16 2K 107
Maple Pl. N17 7E 28
Maple Pl. W1 7G 59
Maple Pl. Bans 6H 135
Maple Pl. W Dray 2J 143
Maple Rd. E11 4C 46
Maple Rd. SE20 5F 108
Maple Rd. Dart 7G 99
Maple Rd. Hay 6G 53
Maple Rd. Surb 1H 119
Maple Rd. Whyt 9D 138
Maplescombe. 7M 131
Maplescombe La. F'ham 5L 131
Maples Pl. E1 8F 60
Maple Springs. Wal A 6M 7
Maplestead Rd. SW2 6K 91
Maplestead Rd. Dag 4F 64
Maples, The. Bans 6M 135
Maples, The. Borwd 3L 11
Maples, The. Clay 9E 118
Maples, The. King T 4G 103
Maple St. W1 8G 59
Maple St. Romf 2A 50
Maplethorpe Rd. T Hth 8L 107
Mapleton Clo. Brom 1E 126
Mapleton Cres. SW18 5M 89
Mapleton Cres. Enf 2G 17
Mapleton Rd. E4 3A 30
Mapleton Rd. SW18 5L 89
(in two parts)
Mapleton Rd. Enf 4F 16
Maple Wlk. W10 6H 57
Maple Wlk. Sutt 2M 135
Maple Way. Felt 9E 84
Maplin Clo. N21 8K 15
Maplin Ho. SE2 3H 81
(off Wolvercote Rd.)
Maplin Rd. E16 9E 62
Maplin St. E3 6K 61
Mapperley Clo. E11 4D 46
Mapperley Dri. Wfd G 7C 30
Maran Way. Eri 4H 81
Marathon Ho. NW1 8D 58
(off Marylebone Rd.)
Marathon Way. SE28 3D 80
Marban Rd. W9 6K 57
Marble Arch (Junct.) 1C 74
Marble Arch. 1D 74
(off Marble Arch)
Marble Arch. W1 1D 74
Marble Arch Apartments.
W1 9D 58
(off Harrowby St.)
Marble Clo. W3 2M 71
Marble Dri. NW2 6H 41
Marble Hill Clo. Twic 6F 86
Marble Hill Gdns. Twic 6F 86
Marble Hill House. 6G 87
Marble Ho. W9 7K 57
Marble Quay. E1 2E 76
Marbrook Ct. SE12 9G 95
Marcella Rd. SW9 1L 91
Marcellina Way. Orp 5C 128
Marcet Rd. Dart 4G 99
March. NW9 8D 24
(off Concourse, The)
Marchant Ct. SE1 6D 76
Marchant Rd. E11 7B 46
Marchant St. SE14 7J 77
Marchbank Rd. W14 7K 73
March Ct. SW15 3F 88
Marchmant Clo. Horn 8G 51
Marchmont Rd. Rich 4K 87
Marchmont Rd. Wall 9G 123
Marchmont St. WC1 7J 59
March Rd. Twic 6E 86
Marchside Clo. Houn 9H 69
Marchwood Clo. SE5 8C 76
Marchwood Cres. W5 9G 55
Marcia Rd. SE1 5C 76
Marcilly Rd. SW18 4B 90
Marcon Ct. E8 1F 60
(off Amhurst Rd.)
Marconi Pl. N11 4F 26
Marconi Rd. E10 6L 45
Marconi Way. S'hall 9M 53
Marcon Pl. E8 1F 60
Marco Polo Ho. SW8 8F 74
Marco Rd. W6 4G 73
Marcourt Lawns. W5 7J 55
Marcus Ct. E15 4C 62
Marcus Garvey M. SE22 5F 92
Marcus Garvey Way. SE24 3L 91
Marcus Rd. Dart 6E 98
Marcus St. E15 4C 62
Marcus St. SW18 5M 89
Marcus Ter. SW18 5M 89
Mardale Ct. NW7 7E 24
Mardale Dri. NW9 3B 40
Mardell Rd. Croy 9H 109
Marden Av. Brom 1D 126
Marden Clo. Chig 2F 32
Marden Cres. Bex 4A 98
Marden Cres. Croy 1K 123
Marden Ho. E5 1F 60
Marden Rd. N17 9C 28
Marden Rd. Croy 1K 123
Marden Rd. Romf 4C 50
Marden Sq. SE16 4F 76
Marder Rd. W13 3E 70
Mardon. Pinn 7K 21
Mardyke Ho. SE17 5B 76
(off Mason St.)
Marechal Niel Av. Sidc 9B 96
Marechal Niel Pde. Sidc 9B 96
(off Main Rd.)
Maresby Ho. E4 2M 29
Mares Fld. Croy 5C 124
Maresfield Gdns. NW3 1A 58
Mare St. E8 & E2 1F 60
Marfleet Clo. Cars 4C 122
Margaret Av. E4 8M 17
Margaret Bondfield Av.
Bark 3E 64
Margaret Bldgs. N16 6D 44
Margaret Clo. Ab L 5D 4
Margaret Clo. Romf 3F 50
Margaret Clo. Wal A 6K 7
Margaret Ct. W1 9G 59
(off Margaret St.)
Margaret Ct. Barn 6B 14
Margaret Dri. Horn 6K 51
Margaret Gardner Dri.
SE9 8K 95
Margaret Herbison Ho.
SW6 7K 73
(off Clem Attlee Ct.)
Margaret Ho. W6 6G 73
(off Queen Caroline St.)
Margaret Ingram Clo.
SW6 7K 73
(off Rylston Rd.)
Margaret Lockwood Clo.
King T 8K 103
Margaret Rd. N16 6D 44
Margaret Rd. Barn 6B 14
Margaret Rd. Bex 5H 97
Margaret Rd. Romf 3F 50
Margaret Sq. Uxb 4A 142
Margaret St. W1 9F 58
Margaretta Ter. SW3 7C 74
Margaretting Rd. E12 6G 47
Margaret Way. Ilf 4J 47
Margaret White Ho. NW1 6H 59
(off Chalton St.)
Margate Rd. SW2 4J 91
Margeholes. Wat 2J 21
Margery Fry Ct. N7 8J 43
Margery Pk. Rd. E7 2E 62
Margery Rd. Dag 8H 49
Margery St. WC1 6L 59
Margherita Pl. Wal A 7M 7
Margherita Rd. Wal A 7M 7
Margin Dri. SW19 2H 105
Margravine Gdns. W6 6H 73
Margravine Rd. W6 6H 73
Marham Gdns. SW18 7C 90
Marham Gdns. Mord 1A 122
Maria Clo. SE1 5F 76
Mariam Gdns. Horn 7K 51
Marian Clo. Hay 7H 53
Marian Ct. E9 1G 61
Marian Ct. Sutt 7M 121
Marian Gdns. Leav 6F 4
Marian Pl. E2 5F 60
Marian Rd. SW16 5G 107
Marian Sq. E2 5F 60
Marian St. E2 5F 60
Marian Way. NW10 3D 56
Maria Ter. E1 8H 61
Maria Theresa Clo.
N Mald 9B 104
Maribor. SE10 8A 78
(off Burney St.)
Maricas Av. Harr 8B 22
Marie Curie. SE5 9C 76
Marie Lloyd Gdns. N19 5J 43
Marie Lloyd Ho. N1 5B 60
(off Murray Gro.)
Marie Lloyd Wlk. E8 2D 60
Mariette Way. Wall 1J 137
Marigold All. SE1 1M 75
(off Upper Ground)
Marigold Clo. S'hall 1J 69
Marigold Rd. N17 7G 29
Marigold St. SE16 3F 76
Marigold Way. Croy 3H 125
Marina App. Hay 8J 53
Marina Av. N Mald 9F 104
Marina Clo. Brom 7E 110
Marina Dri. Dart 7L 99
Marina Dri. Well 1C 96
Marina Gdns. Chesh 3C 6
Marina Gdns. Romf 3M 49
Marina Way. Tedd 4H 103
Marine Ct. Eri 8D 82
Marine Dri. SE18 5K 79
Marine Dri. Bark 6F 64
Marinefield Rd. SW6 1M 89
Marinel Ho. SE5 8A 76
Mariner Gdns. Rich 9G 87
Mariner Rd. E12 9L 47
Mariners M. E14 5B 78
Mariners Wlk. Eri 7D 82
Marine St. SE16 4E 76
Marine Tower. SE8 7K 77
(off Abinger Gro.)
Marion Av. Shep 9A 100
Marion Clo. Bush 3K 9
Marion Clo. Ilf 7B 32
Marion Cres. Orp 9E 112
Marion Gro. Wfd G 5C 30
Marion Rd. NW7 5E 24
Marion Rd. T Hth 9A 108
Marischal Rd. SE13 2B 94
Maritime Ind. Est. SE7 5F 78
Maritime Quay. E14 6L 77
Maritime St. E3 7K 61
Marius Pas. SW17 8E 90
Marius Rd. SW17 8E 90
Marjorams Av. Lou 4L 19
Marjorie Gro. SW11 3D 90
Marjorie M. E1 9H 61
Markab Rd. N'wd 5D 20
Mark Av. E4 8M 17
Mark Clo. Bexh 9J 81
Mark Clo. S'hall 1M 69
Marke Clo. Kes 6J 127
Markeston Grn. Wat 4H 21
Market Cen., The. S'hall 5F 68
Market Chambers. Enf 5B 16
(off Church St.)
Market Ct. W1 9G 59
(off Market Pl.)
Market Entrance. SW8 8G 75
Market Est. N7 2J 59
Market Hill. SE18 4L 79
Market La. Edgw 8A 24
Market Link. Romf 2C 50
Market Mdw. Orp 8G 113
Market M. W1 2F 74
Market Pde. E10 4A 46
(off High Rd. Leyton)
Market Pde. E17 1K 45
(off Forest Rd.)
Market Pde. N9 2E 28
(off Winchester Rd.)
Market Pde. Brom 5E 110
(off East St.)
Market Pde. Felt 9J 85
Market Pde. Sidc 1F 112
Market Pavilion. E10 8L 45
Market Pl. N2 1C 42
Market Pl. NW11 2M 41
Market Pl. SE16 5E 76
(in two parts)
Market Pl. W1 9G 59
Market Pl. W3 2A 72
Market Pl. Bexh 3L 97
Market Pl. Bren 8G 71
Market Pl. Dart 6J 99
Market Pl. Enf 5B 16
Market Pl. King T 6H 103
Market Pl. Romf 3C 50
Market Pl. S'hall 2K 69
Market Rd. N7 2J 59
Market Rd. Rich 2L 87
Market Row. SW9 3L 91
Market Sq. E14 9M 61
Market Sq. Brom 6E 110
(in two parts)
Market Sq. Uxb 3A 142
Market Sq. Wal A 6J 7
Market Sq., The. N9 2F 28
(off Plevna Rd.)
Market St. E6 5K 63
Market St. SE18 5L 79
Market St. Dart 6J 99
Market St. Wat 6F 8
Market Ter. Bren 7J 71
(off Albany Rd.)
Market, The. Sutt 3A 122
Market Way. E14 9M 61
Market Way. Wemb 1J 55
Market Yd. M. SE1 3C 76
Markfield. Croy 2K 139
(in three parts)
Markfield Gdns. E4 9M 17
Markfield Rd. N15 2E 44
Markham Clo. Borwd 4K 11
Markham Ho. Dag 8L 49
(off Uvedale Rd.)
Markham Pl. SW3 6D 74
Markham Sq. SW3 6D 74
Markham St. SW3 6C 74
Markhole Clo. Hamp 4K 101
Mark Ho. E2 5H 61
(off Sewardstone Rd.)
Markhouse Av. E17 4J 45
Markhouse Pas. E17 4K 45
(off Markhouse Rd.)
Markhouse Rd. E17 4K 45
Markland Ho. W10 1H 73
(off Darfield Way)
Mark La. EC3 1C 76
Mark Lodge. Cockf 6C 14
(off Edgeworth Rd.)
Markmanor Av. E17 5J 45
Mark Rd. N22 8M 27
Marksbury Av. Rich 2L 87
Marks Gate. 8J 33
Marks Lodge. Romf 3B 50
Mark Sq. EC2 7C 60
Marks Rd. Romf 3A 50
(in two parts)
Marks Rd. Warl 9J 139
Markstone Ho. SE1 3M 75
(off Lancaster St.)
Mark St. E15 3C 62
Mark St. EC2 7C 60

Mast Ct.—Meadow Way

Mast Ct. SE16 5J 77
(off Boat Lifter Way)
Master Brewer (Junct.) 1F 142
Master Gunners Pl. SE18 8J 79
Masterman Ho. SE5 8B 76
(off Elmington Est.)
Masterman Rd. E6 6J 63
Masters Clo. SW16 3G 107
Masters Dri. SE16 6F 76
Masters Lodge. E1 9G 61
(off Johnson St.)
Masters St. E1 8H 61
Masthead Clo. Dart 3M 99
Mast Ho. Ter. E14 5L 77
(in two parts)
Mastmaker Ct. E14 3L 77
Mastmaker Rd. E14 3L 77
Maswell Park. 4A 86
Maswell Pk. Cres. Houn 4A 86
Maswell Pk. Rd. Houn 4M 85
Matcham Ct. Twic 5H 87
(off Clevedon Rd.)
Matcham Rd. E11 8C 46
Matchless Dri. SE18 8L 79
Matfield Clo. Brom 9E 110
Matfield Rd. Belv 7L 81
Matham Gro. SE22 3D 92
Matham Rd. E Mol 9B 102
Matheson Lang Ho. SE1 3L 75
(off Baylis Rd.)
Matheson Rd. W14 5K 73
Mathews Av. E6 5L 63
Mathews Pk. Av. E15 2D 62
Mathews Yd. WC2 9J 59
Mathias Clo. Eps 5A 134
Mathieson Ct. SE1 3M 75
(off King James St.)
Matilda Clo. SE19 4B 108
Matilda Ho. E1 2E 76
(off St Katherine's Way)
Matilda St. N1 4K 59
Matlock Clo. SE24 3A 92
Matlock Clo. Barn 7H 13
Matlock Ct. SE5 3B 92
Matlock Cres. Sutt 6J 121
Matlock Cres. Wat 3G 21
Matlock Gdns. Horn 8J 51
Matlock Gdns. Sutt 6J 121
Matlock Pl. Sutt 6J 121
Matlock Rd. E10 4A 46
Matlock St. E14 9J 61
Matlock Way. N Mald 5B 104
Maton Ho. SW6 8K 73
(off Estcourt Rd.)
Matrimony Pl. SW8 1G 91
Matson Ct. Wfd G 7C 30
Matson Ho. SE16 4F 76
Matthew Clo. W10 7H 57
Matthew Ct. E17 1A 46
Matthew Ct. Mitc 9H 107
Matthew Parker St. SW1 3H 75
Matthews Clo. Romf 8K 35
Matthews Ct. E17 8L 29
(off Chingford Rd.)
Matthews Gdns. New Ad 3B 140
Matthews Ho. E14 8L 61
(off Burgess St.)
Matthews Rd. Gnfd 1B 54
Matthews St. SW11 1D 90
Matthias Rd. N16 1C 60
Mattingley Way. SE15 8D 76
Mattison Rd. N4 4L 43
Mattock La. W13 & W5 2F 70
Maud Cashmore Way. SE18 4K 79
Maude Cres. Wat 2F 8
Maude Ho. E2 5E 60
(off Ropley St.)
Maude Rd. E17 3J 45
Maude Rd. SE5 9C 76
Maude Rd. Swan 3E 114
Maude Ter. E17 3J 45
Maud Gdns. E13 4D 62
Maud Gdns. Bark 5D 64
Maudlins Grn. E1 2E 76
Maud Rd. E10 8A 46
Maud Rd. E13 5D 62
Maudslay Rd. SE9 2K 95
Maudsley Ho. Bren 6J 71
Maud St. E16 8D 62
Maudsville Cotts. W7 2C 70
Maud Wilkes Clo. NW5 1G 59
Maugham Ct. W3 4A 72
(off Palmerston Rd.)
Mauleverer Rd. SW2 4J 91
Maundeby Wlk. NW10 2C 56
Maunder Rd. W7 2D 70
Maunsel St. SW1 5H 75
Maureen Ct. Beck 6G 109
Mauretania Building. E1 1H 77
(off Jardine Rd.)
Maurice Av. N22 9M 27
Maurice Bishop Ter. N6 4E 42
(off View Rd.)
Maurice Brown Clo. NW7 5H 25
Maurice Ct. Bren 8H 71
Maurice Drummond Ho. SE10 9M 77
(off Catherine Gro.)
Maurice St. W12 9F 56
Maurice Wlk. NW11 2A 42
Maurier Clo. N'holt 4G 53
Mauritius Rd. SE10 5C 78
Maury Rd. N16 7E 44
Mauveine Gdns. Houn 3L 85
Mavelstone Clo. Brom 5J 111
Mavelstone Rd. Brom 5H 111
Maverton Rd. E3 4L 61
Mavis Av. Eps 7C 120
Mavis Clo. Eps 7C 120
Mavis Gro. Horn 7J 51
Mavis Wlk. E6 8J 63
(off Greenwich Cres.)
Mavor Ho. N1 4K 59
(off Barnsbury Est.)
Mawbey Ho. SE1 6D 76
Mawbey Pl. SE1 6D 76
Mawbey Rd. SE1 6D 76
Mawbey St. SW8 8J 75
Mawdley Ho. SE1 3L 75
(off Webber Row)
Mawney. 2A 50
Mawney Clo. Romf 9M 33
Mawney Rd. Romf 9M 33
Mawson Clo. SW20 6J 105
Mawson Ho. EC1 8L 59
(off Baldwins Gdns.)
Mawson La. W4 7D 72
Maxden Ct. SE15 2D 92
Maxey Gdns. Dag 9J 49
Maxey Rd. SE18 5A 80
Maxey Rd. Dag 1J 65
Maxfield Clo. N20 9A 14
Maxilla Wlk. W10 9H 57
(off Westway)
Maximfeldt Rd. Eri 6C 82
Maxim Rd. N21 8L 15
Maxim Rd. Dart 4C 98
Maxim Rd. Eri 5C 82
Maxted Pk. Harr 5C 38
Maxted Rd. SE15 2D 92
Maxwell Clo. Croy 3J 123
Maxwell Clo. Hay 1E 68
Maxwell Ct. SE22 7E 92
Maxwell Ct. SW4 4H 91
Maxwell Gdns. Orp 5D 128
Maxwell Ri. Wat 9J 9
Maxwell Rd. SW6 8M 73
Maxwell Rd. Ashf 3A 100
Maxwell Rd. Borwd 5M 11
Maxwell Rd. N'wd 7B 20
Maxwell Rd. Well 2D 96
Maxwell Rd. W Dray 5K 143
Maxwelton Av. NW7 5B 24
Maxwelton Clo. NW7 5B 24
Maya Angelou Ct. E4 4A 30
Maya Clo. SE15 1F 92
Mayall Rd. SE24 4M 91
Maya Rd. N2 2A 42
May Av. Orp 9F 112
Maybank Av. E18 9F 30
Maybank Av. Horn 1F 66
Maybank Av. Wemb 1D 54
Maybank Gdns. Pinn 3E 36
Maybank Lodge. Horn 1G 67
Maybank Rd. E18 8F 30
May Bate Av. King T 5H 103
Maybells Commercial Est. Bark 5H 65
Mayberry Ct. Beck 4K 109
(off Copers Cope Rd.)
Mayberry Pl. Surb 2K 119
Maybourne Clo. SE26 3F 108
Maybrick Rd. Horn 4G 51
Maybury Av. Chesh 1B 6
Maybury Av. Dart 7M 99
Maybury Clo. Enf 2F 16
Maybury Clo. Lou 6M 19
Maybury Clo. Orp 9M 111
Maybury Ct. W1 8E 58
(off Marylebone St.)
Maybury Ct. Harr 4B 38
Maybury Ct. S Croy 7M 123
(off Haling Pk. Rd.)
Maybury Gdns. NW10 2F 56
Maybury M. N6 5G 43
Maybury Rd. E13 7G 63
Maybury Rd. Bark 5D 64
Maybury St. SW17 2C 106
Maybush Rd. Horn 5J 51
Maychurch Clo. Stan 7H 23
May Clo. Chess 8K 119
Maycock Gro. N'wd 6D 20
May Cotts. Wat 7G 9
(off Lammas Rd.)
Maycroft. Pinn 9F 20
Maycross Av. Mord 8K 105
Mayday Gdns. SE3 1J 95
Mayday Rd. T Hth 1M 123
Maydew Ho. SE16 5G 77
(off Abbeyfield Est.)
Maydwell Ho. E14 8L 61
(off Thomas Rd.)
Maydwell Lodge. Borwd 4K 11
Mayerne Rd. SE9 4H 95
Mayer Rd. Wal A 9H 7
Mayesbrook Rd. Bark 4D 64
Mayesbrook Rd. Ilf 8E 48
Mayes Clo. Swan 8E 114
Mayes Clo. Warl 9H 139
Mayesford Rd. Romf 5G 49
Mayes Rd. N22 9K 27
Mayeswood Rd. SE12 1G 111
Mayfair. 1F 74
Mayfair Av. Bexh 9H 81
Mayfair Av. Ilf 7K 47
Mayfair Av. Romf 4H 49
Mayfair Av. Twic 6A 86
Mayfair Av. Wor Pk 3E 120
Mayfair Clo. Beck 5M 109
Mayfair Clo. Surb 3J 119
Mayfair Gdns. N17 6A 28
Mayfair Gdns. Wfd G 7E 30
Mayfair M. NW1 3D 58
(off Regents Pk. Rd.)
Mayfair Pl. W1 2F 74
Mayfair Rd. Dart 4H 99
Mayfair Ter. N14 9H 15
Mayfare. Crox G 7B 8
Mayfield. Bexh 2K 97
Mayfield. Wal A 7K 7
Mayfield Av. N12 4A 26
Mayfield Av. N14 2H 27
Mayfield Av. W4 5C 72
Mayfield Av. W13 4F 70
Mayfield Av. Harr 3F 38
Mayfield Av. Orp 3D 128
Mayfield Av. Wfd G 6E 30
Mayfield Cvn. Pk. W Dray 4G 143
Mayfield Clo. E8 2D 60
Mayfield Clo. SE20 5F 108
Mayfield Clo. SW4 4H 91
Mayfield Clo. Th Dit 3F 118
Mayfield Clo. Uxb 6F 142
Mayfield Clo. W on T 6E 116
Mayfield Cres. N9 8F 16
Mayfield Cres. T Hth 8K 107
Mayfield Dri. Pinn 2K 37
Mayfield Gdns. NW4 4H 41
Mayfield Gdns. W7 9B 54
Mayfield Gdns. W on T 6E 116
Mayfield Ho. E2 5F 60
(off Cambridge Heath Rd.)
Mayfield Rd. E4 2A 30
Mayfield Rd. E8 3D 60
Mayfield Rd. E13 7D 62
Mayfield Rd. E17 9J 29
Mayfield Rd. N8 3K 43
Mayfield Rd. SW19 5K 105
Mayfield Rd. W3 1M 71
Mayfield Rd. W12 3C 72
Mayfield Rd. Belv 5A 82
Mayfield Rd. Brom 9J 111
Mayfield Rd. Dag 6G 49
Mayfield Rd. Enf 4H 17
Mayfield Rd. S Croy 1B 138
Mayfield Rd. Sutt 8B 122
Mayfield Rd. T Hth 8K 107
Mayfield Rd. W on T 6E 116
Mayfield Rd. Flats. N8 4K 43
Mayfields. Wemb 7L 39
Mayfields Clo. Wemb 7L 39
Mayflower Clo. SE16 5H 77
Mayflower Clo. Ruis 4A 36
Mayflower Ho. Bark 4B 64
(off Westbury Rd.)
Mayflower Rd. SW9 2J 91
Mayflower St. SE16 3G 77
Mayfly Clo. Eastc 5G 37
Mayfly Clo. Orp 8H 113
Mayfly Gdns. N'holt 6H 53
Mayford. NW1 5G 59
(in three parts)
Mayford Clo. SW12 6D 90
Mayford Clo. Beck 7H 109
Mayford Rd. SW12 6D 90
May Gdns. Els 8H 11
May Gdns. Wemb 6G 55
Maygoods Clo. Uxb 8B 142
Maygoods Grn. Uxb 8B 142
Maygoods La. Uxb 8B 142
Maygood St. N1 5L 59
Maygoods Vw. Cow 8A 142
Maygreen Cres. Horn 5E 50
Maygrove Rd. NW6 2K 57
Mayhew Clo. E4 3L 29
Mayhew Ct. SE5 3B 92
Mayhill Rd. SE7 7F 78
Mayhill Rd. Barn 8J 13
Mayland Mans. Bark 3M 63
(off Whiting Av.)
Maylands Av. Horn 9F 50
Maylands Dri. Sidc 9H 97
Maylands Dri. Uxb 2B 142
Maylands Ho. SW3 5C 74
(off Elystan St.)
Maylands Rd. Wat 4G 21
Maylands Way. Romf 6M 35
Maynard Clo. N15 3C 44
Maynard Clo. SW6 8M 73
Maynard Clo. Eri 8D 82
Maynard Ct. Wal A 7M 7
Maynard Path. E17 3A 46
Maynard Rd. E17 3A 46
Maynards. Horn 5J 51
Maynards Quay. E1 1G 77
Mayne Ct. SE26 2F 108
Maynooth Gdns. Cars 2D 122
Mayo Clo. Chesh 1C 6
Mayo Ct. W13 4F 70
Mayo Ho. E1 8G 61
(off Lindley St.)
Mayola Rd. E5 9G 45
Mayo Rd. NW10 2C 56
Mayo Rd. Croy 9B 108
Mayo Rd. W on T 2E 116
Mayor's La. Dart 1G 115
Mayow Rd. SE26 & SE23 1H 109
Mayplace Av. Dart 3E 98
Mayplace Clo. Bexh 2M 97
Mayplace La. SE18 7M 79
(in two parts)
Mayplace Rd. E. Bexh 2M 97
Mayplace Rd. W. Bexh 3L 97
Maypole. 7C 98
(Bexley)
Maypole. 8L 129
(Orpington)
Maypole Ct. S'hall 3K 69
(off Merrick Rd.)
Maypole Cres. Eri 7H 83
Maypole Cres. Ilf 7B 32
Maypole Dri. Chig 3E 32
Maypole Rd. Orp 7K 129
May Rd. E4 6L 29
May Rd. E13 5E 62
May Rd. Dart 1K 115
May Rd. Twic 7C 86
Mayroyd Av. Surb 4L 119
May's Bldgs. M. SE10 8A 78
May's Ct. SE10 8B 78
Mays Ct. WC2 1J 75
Mays Hill Rd. Brom 6C 110
Mays La. Barn 9F 12
Maysoule Rd. SW11 3B 90
Mays Rd. Tedd 2B 102
Mayston M. SE10 6E 78
(off Ormiston Rd.)
May St. W14 6K 73
Mayswood Gdns. Dag 2A 66
Maythorne Clo. Wat 6C 8
Mayton St. N7 8K 43
Maytree Clo. Edgw 3A 24
Maytree Clo. Rain 5C 66
Maytree Ct. N'holt 6J 53
Maytree Cres. Wat 8D 4
Maytree Gdns. W5 3H 71
May Tree Ho. SE4 2K 93
(off Wickham Rd.)
Maytree La. Stan 7E 22
Maytrees. Rad 1E 10
Maytree Wlk. SW2 8L 91
Mayville Est. N16 1C 60
Mayville Rd. E11 7C 46
Mayville Rd. Ilf 1M 63
May Wlk. E13 5F 62
Mayward Ho. SE5 9C 76
(off Peckham Rd.)
Maywater Clo. S Croy 3B 138
Maywin Dri. Horn 6K 51
Maywood Clo. Beck 4M 109
May Wynne Ho. E16 1F 78
(off Murray Sq.)
Maze Hill. SE10 & SE3 7C 78
Maze Hill Lodge. SE10 7B 78
(off Park Vista)
Mazenod Av. NW6 3L 57
Maze Rd. Rich 8L 71
M.C.C. Cricket Mus. & Tours. 6B 58
Mead Clo. NW1 2E 58
Mead Clo. Harr 8B 22
Mead Clo. Lou 4M 19
Mead Clo. Romf 9E 34
Mead Clo. Swan 9E 114
Mead Ct. NW9 3A 40
Mead Ct. Wal A 7H 7
Mead Cres. E4 4A 30
Mead Cres. Dart 7H 99
Mead Cres. Sutt 5C 122
Meadcroft Rd. SE11 7M 75
(in two parts)
Meade Clo. W4 7L 71
Mead End. Asht 9K 133
Meader Ct. SE14 8H 77
Meades, The. Wey 8A 116
Meadfield. Edgw 2M 23
(in two parts)
Mead Fld. Harr 8K 37
Meadfield Grn. Edgw 2M 23
Meadfoot Rd. SW16 4G 107
Meadgate Av. Wfd G 5J 31
Mead Gro. Romf 1H 49
Mead Ho. W11 2K 73
(off Ladbroke Rd.)
Mead Ho. La. Hay 7B 52
Meadhurst Pk. Sun 3C 100
Meadlands Dri. Rich 8H 87
Mead Lodge. W4 3B 72
Meadow Av. Croy 1H 125
Meadow Bank. N21 8K 15
Meadowbank. NW3 3D 58
Meadowbank. Surb 1K 119
Meadowbank. Wat 9G 9
Meadowbank Clo. SW6 8G 73
Meadowbank Clo. Barn 7E 12
Meadowbank Gdns. Houn 9E 68
Meadowbank Rd. NW9 5B 40
Meadowbanks. Barn 7E 12
Meadowbrook Ct. Iswth 2C 86
Meadow Clo. E4 1M 29
Meadow Clo. E9 1K 61
Meadow Clo. SE6 2L 109
Meadow Clo. SW20 8G 105
Meadow Clo. Barn 8K 13
Meadow Clo. Bexh 4K 97
Meadow Clo. Brick W 2L 5
Meadow Clo. Chst 2M 111
Meadow Clo. Enf 2J 17
Meadow Clo. Esh 5D 118
Meadow Clo. Houn 5L 85
Meadow Clo. Noak H 3G 35
Meadow Clo. N'holt 5L 53
Meadow Clo. Purl 5H 137
Meadow Clo. Rich 7J 87
Meadow Clo. Ruis 4D 36
Meadow Clo. Sutt 4A 122
Meadow Clo. W on T 6K 117
Meadow Ct. N1 5C 60
Meadow Ct. Eps 5A 134
Meadow Ct. Houn 5M 85
Meadowcourt Rd. SE3 3D 94
Meadowcroft. W4 6L 71
(off Brooks Rd.)
Meadowcroft. Brom 7K 111
Meadowcroft. Bush 8M 9
(off High St.)
Meadowcroft Clo. N13 2L 27
Meadowcroft Rd. N13 2L 27
Meadowcross. Wal A 7L 7
Meadow Dri. N10 1F 42
Meadow Dri. NW4 9G 25
Meadowford Clo. SE28 1E 80
Meadow Gdns. Edgw 6M 23
Meadow Gth. NW10 2A 56
(in two parts)
Meadow Ga. Asht 9J 133
(off Meadow Rd.)
Meadow Hill. Coul 6G 137
Meadow Hill. N Mald 1C 120
Meadowlands. Horn 5J 51
Meadow La. SE12 9F 94
Meadowlea Clo. Harm 7H 143
Meadow M. SW8 7K 75
Meadow Pl. SW8 8J 75
Meadow Pl. W4 8C 72
Meadow Ri. Coul 5H 137
Meadow Rd. SW8 8K 75
Meadow Rd. SW19 4A 106
Meadow Rd. Ashf 2B 100
Meadow Rd. Asht 9J 133
Meadow Rd. Bark 3D 64
Meadow Rd. Borwd 4M 11
Meadow Rd. Brom 6C 110
Meadow Rd. Bush 7M 9
Meadow Rd. Clay 8C 118
Meadow Rd. Dag 2K 65
Meadow Rd. Felt 8J 85
Meadow Rd. Lou 7J 19
Meadow Rd. Pinn 2H 37
Meadow Rd. Romf 6A 50
Meadow Rd. S'hall 1K 69
Meadow Rd. Sutt 6C 122
Meadow Rd. Wat 7E 4
Meadow Row. SE1 4A 76
Meadows Clo. E10 7L 45
Meadows Ct. Sidc 3F 112
Meadows End. Sun 5E 100
Meadowside. SE9 3G 95
Meadowside. Dart 7H 99
Meadowside. Twic 6H 87
Meadowside. W on T 4G 117
Meadowside. Wat 4F 4
Meadowside Rd. Sutt 1J 135
Meadowside Rd. Upm 1M 67
Meadows Leigh Clo. Wey 5A 116
Meadows, The. Orp 8G 129
Meadows, The. Warl 9H 139
Meadow Stile. Croy 5A 124
Meadowsweet Clo. E16 8H 63
Meadowsweet Clo. SW20 8G 105
Meadow, The. N10 1E 42
Meadow, The. Chst 3A 112
Meadow Vw. Cow 8A 142
(in three parts)
Meadow Vw. Harr 6C 38
Meadow Vw. Orp 7G 113
Meadow Vw. Sidc 6F 96
Meadowview Rd. SE6 2K 109
Meadowview Rd. Bex 5J 97
Meadowview Rd. Eps 1C 134
Meadow Vw. Rd. Hay 7B 52
Meadow Vw. Rd. T Hth 9M 107
Meadow Wlk. E18 2E 46
Meadow Wlk. Dag 2K 65
Meadow Wlk. Dart 1G 115
(in two parts)
Meadow Wlk. Eps 8C 120
(in two parts)
Meadow Wlk. Wall 5F 122
Meadow Way. NW9 3B 40
Meadow Way. Bedm 1D 4
Meadow Way. Chess 7J 119
Meadow Way. Chig 3A 32
Meadow Way. Dart 6M 99
Meadow Way. Orp 5L 127
Meadow Way. Ruis 4F 36
Meadow Way. Tad 9J 135
Meadow Way. Upm 8M 51

Meadow Way—Merryweather Ct.

Meadow Way. Wemb 9H 39
Meadow Waye. Houn 7J 69
Meadow Way, The. Harr 8C 22
Mead Path. SW17 1A 106
Mead Pl. E9 2G 61
Mead Pl. Croy 3A 124
Mead Plat. NW10 2A 56
Mead Rd. Chst 3A 112
Mead Rd. Dart 7H 99
Mead Rd. Edgw 6L 23
Mead Rd. Rich 9G 87
Mead Rd. Uxb 3B 142
Mead Rd. W on T 6J 117
Mead Row. SE1 4L 75
Meads Ct. E15 2D 62
Meadside Clo. Beck 5J 109
Meads La. Ilf 5C 48
Meads Rd. N22 9M 27
Meads Rd. Enf 3J 17
Meads, The. Brick W 2K 5
Meads, The. Edgw 6B 24
Meads, The. Mord 9C 106
Meads, The. Sutt 5J 121
Meads, The. Uxb 7C 142
Mead Ter. Wemb 9H 39
Mead, The. N2 9A 26
Mead, The. W13 8F 54
Mead, The. Beck 5A 110
Mead, The. Chesh 2C 6
Mead, The. Wall 8H 123
Mead, The. Wat 3J 21
Mead, The. W Wick 3B 126
Meadvale Rd. W5 7F 54
Meadvale Rd. Croy 2D 124
Meadway. N14 2H 27
Meadway. NW11 4L 41
Mead Way. SW20 8G 105
Meadway. Ashf 9E 144
Meadway. Barn 6L 13
Meadway. Beck 5A 110
Mead Way. Brom 1D 126
Mead Way. Bush 4J 9
Mead Way. Coul 9J 137
Mead Way. Croy 4J 125
Meadway. Enf 9C 6
Meadway. Eps 4A 134
Meadway. Esh
9M 117 & 1A 132
Meadway. Ilf 9C 48
Meadway. Oxs 6C 132
Meadway. Romf 9E 34
Mead Way. Ruis 4B 36
Meadway. Surb 3A 120
Meadway. Twic 7B 86
Meadway. Warl 8G 139
Mead Way. Wfd G 5G 31
Meadway Clo. NW11 4M 41
Meadway Clo. Barn 6L 13
Meadway Clo. Pinn 6M 21
Meadway Ct. NW11 4M 41
Meadway Ct. W5 7K 55
Meadway Ct. Dag 7K 49
Meadway Ct. Tedd 2G 103
Meadway Gdns. Ruis 4B 36
Meadway Ga. NW11 4L 41
Meadway, The. SE3 1B 94
Meadway, The. Buck H 1H 31
Meadway, The. Lou 8K 19
Meadway, The. Orp 8F 128
Meaford Way. SE20 4F 108
Meakin Est. SE1 4C 76
Meanley Rd. E12 9J 47
Meard St. W1 9H 59
(in two parts)
Meath Clo. Orp 9F 112
Meath Rd. E15 5D 62
Meath Rd. Ilf 8A 48
Meath St. SW11 9F 74
Mechanic's Path. SE8 8L 77
(off Deptford High St.)
Mecklenburgh Pl. WC1 7K 59
Mecklenburgh Sq. WC1 7K 59
Mecklenburgh St. WC1 7K 59
Medburn St. NW1 5H 59
Medcalf Rd. Enf 1K 17
Medcroft Gdns. SW14 3A 88
Medebourne Clo. SE3 2E 94
Mede Ho. Brom 2F 110
(off Pike Clo.)
Medesenge Way. N13 6M 27
Medfield St. SW15 6E 88
Medhurst Clo. E3 5J 61
(in two parts)
Median Rd. E5 1G 61
Medina Av. Esh 5C 118
Medina Gro. N7 8L 43
Medina Ho. Eri 8C 82
Medina Rd. N7 8L 43
Medina Sq. Eps 1L 133
Medland Clo. Wall 3E 122
Medland Ho. E14 1J 77
Medlar Clo. N'holt 5H 53
Medlar Ho. Sidc 9E 96
Medlar St. SE5 9A 76
Medley Rd. NW6 2L 57
Medman Clo. Uxb 5A 142
Medmenham. Cars 3B 136
(off Pine Cres.)
Medora Rd. SW2 6K 91
Medora Rd. Romf 2B 50
Medusa Rd. SE6 5M 93
Medway Bldgs. E3 5J 61
(off Medway Rd.)
Medway Clo. Croy 1G 125
Medway Clo. Ilf 1A 64
Medway Clo. Wat 7G 5
Medway Ct. WC1 6J 59
(off Judd St.)
Medway Dri. Gnfd 5D 54
Medway Gdns. Wemb 9E 38
Medway Ho. NW8 7C 58
(off Penfold St.)
Medway Ho. SE1 3B 76
(off Hankey Pl.)
Medway Ho. King T 5H 103
Medway M. E3 5J 61
Medway Pde. Gnfd 5D 54
Medway Rd. E3 5J 61
Medway Rd. Dart 2E 98
Medway St. SW1 4H 75
Medwin St. SW4 3K 91
Meerbrook Rd. SE3 2G 95
Meeson Rd. E15 3D 62
Meeson St. E5 9J 45
Meeting All. Wat 5F 8
Meeting Fld. Path. E9 2G 61
Meeting Ho. All. E1 2F 76
Meeting Ho. La. SE15 9F 76
Mehetabel Rd. E9 1G 61
Meister Clo. Ilf 6B 48
Melancholy Wlk. Rich 8G 87
Melanda Clo. Chst 2K 111
Melanie Clo. Bexh 9J 81
Melba Way. SE13 9M 77
Melbourne Av. N13 6K 27
Melbourne Av. W13 2E 70
Melbourne Av. Pinn 1M 37
Melbourne Clo. SE20 4E 108
Melbourne Clo. Orp 2C 128
Melbourne Clo. Wall 7G 123
Melbourne Ct. N10 7F 26
Melbourne Ct. W9 7A 58
(off Randolph Av.)
Melbourne Gdns. Romf 3J 49
Melbourne Gro. SE22 3C 92
Melbourne Ho. W8 2L 73
(off Kensington Pl.)
Melbourne Ho. Hay 7G 53
Melbourne Mans. W14 7J 73
(off Musard Rd.)
Melbourne M. SE6 6A 94
Melbourne M. SW9 9L 75
Melbourne Pl. WC2 9K 59
Melbourne Rd. E6 5K 63
Melbourne Rd. E10 5M 45
Melbourne Rd. E17 2J 45
Melbourne Rd. SW19 5L 105
Melbourne Rd. Bush 7M 9
Melbourne Rd. Ilf 6M 47
Melbourne Rd. Tedd 3G 103
Melbourne Rd. Wall 7F 122
Melbourne Sq. SW9 9L 75
Melbourne Ter. SW6 8M 73
(off Moore Pk. Rd.)
Melbourne Way. Enf 8D 16
Melbray M. SW6 1K 89
Melbreak Ho. SE22 2C 92
Melbury Av. S'hall 4M 69
Melbury Clo. Chst 3J 111
Melbury Clo. Clay 8F 118
Melbury Ct. W8 4K 73
Melbury Dri. SE5 8C 76
Melbury Gdns. SW20 5F 104
Melbury Ho. SW8 8K 75
(off Richborne Ter.)
Melbury Rd. W14 4K 73
Melbury Rd. Harr 3K 39
Melbury Ter. NW1 7C 58
Melchester. W11 9K 57
(off Ledbury Rd.)
Melchester Ho. N19 8H 43
(off Wedmore St.)
Melcombe Ct. NW1 8D 58
(off Melcombe Pl.)
Melcombe Gdns. Harr 4K 39
Melcombe Ho. SW8 8K 75
(off Dorset Rd.)
Melcombe Pl. NW1 8D 58
Melcombe Regis Ct. W1 8E 58
(off Weymouth St.)
Melcombe St. NW1 7D 58
Meldex Clo. NW7 6G 25
(off Prince of Wales Clo.)
Meldon Clo. SW6 9M 73
Meldone Clo. Surb 2M 119
Meldrum Clo. Orp 1G 129
Meldrum Rd. Ilf 7E 48
Melfield Gdns. SE6 1A 110
Melford Av. Bark 2C 64
Melford Clo. Chess 7K 119
Melford Ct. SE1 4C 76
(off Fendall St.)
Melford Ct. SE22 7E 92
Melford Pas. SE22 6E 92
Melford Rd. E6 7K 63
Melford Rd. E11 7C 46
Melford Rd. E17 2J 45
Melford Rd. SE22 6E 92
Melford Rd. Ilf 7B 48
Melfort Av. T Hth 7M 107
Melfort Rd. T Hth 7M 107
Melgund Rd. N5 1L 59
Melina Clo. Hay 8B 52
Melina Ct. SW15 2E 88
Melina Pl. NW8 6B 58
Melina Rd. W12 3F 72
Melior Ct. N6 4G 43
Melior Pl. SE1 3C 76
Melior St. SE1 3C 76
Meliot Rd. SE6 8B 94
Melksham Clo. Romf 7K 35
Melksham Dri. Romf 7K 35
Melksham Gdns. Romf 7J 35
Melksham Grn. Romf 7K 35
Meller Clo. Croy 5J 123
Melling Dri. Enf 3E 16
Melling St. SE18 7C 80
Mellish Clo. Bark 4D 64
Mellish Flats. E10 5L 45
Mellish Gdns. Wfd G 5E 30
Mellish Ho. E1 9F 60
(off Varden St.)
Mellish Ind. Est. SE18 4H 79
Mellish St. E14 4L 77
Mellish Way. Horn 3G 51
Mellison Rd. SW17 2C 106
Mellitus St. W12 8D 56
Mellor Clo. W on T 2K 117
Mellow Clo. Bans 6A 136
Mellow La. E. Hay 6A 52
Mellow La. W. Uxb 6A 52
Mellows Rd. Ilf 1K 47
Mellows Rd. Wall 7H 123
Mells Cres. SE9 1K 111
Mell St. SE10 6C 78
Melody La. N5 1A 60
Melody Rd. SW18 4A 90
Melody Rd. Big H 9G 141
Melon Pl. W8 3L 73
Melon Rd. E11 8C 46
Melon Rd. SE15 9E 76
Melrose Av. N22 8M 27
Melrose Av. NW2 1F 56
Melrose Av. SW16 7K 107
Melrose Av. SW19 8K 89
Melrose Av. Borwd 7M 11
Melrose Av. Dart 5C 98
Melrose Av. Gnfd 5M 53
Melrose Av. Mitc 4F 106
Melrose Av. Twic 6M 85
Melrose Clo. SE12 7E 94
Melrose Clo. Gnfd 5M 53
Melrose Clo. Hay 8E 52
Melrose Ct. Chesh 2D 6
Melrose Cres. Orp 6B 128
Melrose Dri. S'hall 2L 69
Melrose Gdns. W6 4G 73
Melrose Gdns. Edgw 1M 39
Melrose Gdns. N Mald 7B 104
Melrose Gdns. W on T 7G 117
Melrose Ho. E14 4M 77
(off Lanark Sq.)
Melrose Ho. NW6 6L 57
(off Carlton Va.)
Melrose Pl. Wat 2D 8
Melrose Rd. SW13 1D 88
Melrose Rd. SW18 5K 89
Melrose Rd. SW19 6L 105
Melrose Rd. W3 4A 72
Melrose Rd. Big H 8G 141
Melrose Rd. Coul 7F 136
Melrose Rd. Pinn 2K 37
Melrose Ter. W6 4G 73
Melrose Tudor. Wall 7J 123
(off Plough La.)
Melsa Rd. Mord 1A 122
Melstock Av. Upm 9M 51
Melthorne Dri. Ruis 8G 37
Melthorpe Gdns. SE3 9J 79
Melton Clo. Ruis 6G 37
Melton Ct. SW7 5B 74
(in two parts)
Melton Ct. Sutt 9A 122
Melton Fields. Eps 1B 134
Melton Gdns. Romf 5D 50
Melton Pl. Eps 1B 134
Melton St. NW1 6G 59
Melville Av. SW20 4E 104
Melville Av. Gnfd 1D 54
Melville Av. S Croy 7D 124
Melville Clo. Uxb 7B 36
Melville Ct. SE8 5J 77
Melville Ct. W12 4F 72
(off Goldhawk Rd.)
Melville Ct. H Hill 7J 35
Melville Ct. N'wd 6B 20
Melville Gdns. N13 5M 27
Melville Ho. SE10 9A 78
Melville Ho. New Bar 7B 14
Melville Pl. N1 3A 60
Melville Rd. E17 1K 45
Melville Rd. NW10 3B 56
Melville Rd. SW13 9E 72
Melville Rd. Rain 7E 66
Melville Rd. Romf 7M 33
Melville Rd. Sidc 8G 97
Melville Vs. Rd. W3 2A 72
Melvin Rd. SE20 5G 109
Melwood Ho. E1 9F 60
(off Watney Mkt.)
Melyn Clo. N7 9G 43
Memel Ct. EC1 7A 60
(off Memel St.)
Memel St. EC1 7A 60
Memess Path. SE18 7L 79
Memorial Av. E15 6C 62
Memorial Clo. Houn 7K 69
Mendham Ho. SE1 4C 76
(off Cluny Pl.)
Mendip Clo. SE26 1G 109
Mendip Clo. SW19 8J 89
Mendip Clo. Hay 8B 68
Mendip Clo. Wor Pk 3G 121
Mendip Ct. SE14 7G 77
(off Avonley Rd.)
Mendip Ct. SW18 2A 90
Mendip Dri. NW2 7J 41
Mendip Houses. E2 6G 61
(off Welwyn St.)
Mendip Rd. SW11 2A 90
Mendip Rd. Bexh 9C 82
Mendip Rd. Bush 8A 10
Mendip Rd. Horn 5E 50
Mendip Rd. Ilf 3C 48
Mendora Rd. SW6 8J 73
Mendoza Clo. Horn 3J 51
Menelik Rd. NW2 9J 41
Menlo Gdns. SE19 4B 108
Menlo Lodge. N13 3K 27
(off Crothall Clo.)
Menon Dri. N9 3F 28
Menotti St. E2 7E 60
Menteath Ho. E14 9L 61
(off Dod St.)
Menthone Pl. Horn 5H 51
Mentmore Clo. Harr 4G 39
Mentmore Ter. E8 3F 60
Meon Ct. Iswth 1C 86
Meon Rd. W3 3A 72
Meopham Rd. Mitc 5G 107
Mepham Cres. Harr 7A 22
Mepham Gdns. Harr 7A 22
Mepham St. SE1 2L 75
Mera Dri. Bexh 3L 97
Merantun Way. SW19 5M 105
Merbury Clo. SE13 4B 94
Merbury Rd. SE28 3C 80
Mercator Pl. E14 6L 77
Mercator Rd. SE13 3B 94
Mercer Clo. Th Dit 2E 118
Mercer Ho. SW1 6F 74
(off Ebury Bri. Rd.)
Merceron Houses. E2 6G 61
(off Globe Rd.)
Merceron St. E1 7F 60
Mercer Pl. Pinn 9G 21
Mercers Clo. SE10 5D 78
Mercer's Cotts. E1 9J 61
(off White Horse Rd.)
Mercers Pl. W6 5H 73
Mercers Rd. N19 8H 43
(in two parts)
Mercer St. WC2 9J 59
Mercer Wlk. Uxb 3A 142
Merchant Ct. E1 2G 77
(off Wapping Wall)
Merchant Ind. Ter. NW10 7A 56
Merchants Lodge. E17 2L 45
(off Westbury Rd.)
Merchant St. E3 6K 61
Merchiston Rd. SE6 8B 94
Merchland Rd. SE9 7A 96
Mercia Gro. SE13 3A 94
Mercia Ho. SE5 1A 92
(off Denmark Rd.)
Mercier Rd. SW15 4J 89
Mercury. NW9 8D 24
(off Concourse, The)
Mercury Cen. Felt 4E 84
Mercury Ct. E14 5L 77
(off Homer Dri.)
Mercury Gdns. Romf 2C 50
Mercury Ho. Bren 7G 71
(off Glenhurst Rd.)
Mercury Rd. Bren 7G 71
Mercury Way. SE14 7H 77
Mercy Ter. SE13 4M 93
Merebank La. Croy 7K 123
Mere Clo. SW15 6H 89
Mere Clo. Orp 4L 127
Meredith Av. NW2 1G 57
Meredith Clo. Pinn 7H 21
Meredith Ho. N16 1C 60
Meredith M. SE4 3K 93
Meredith St. E13 6E 62
Meredith St. EC1 6M 59
Meredyth Rd. SW13 1E 88
Mere End. Croy 2H 125
Mere Rd. Shep 1A 116
Mere Rd. Wey 5B 116
Mere Side. Orp 4L 127
Meretone Clo. SE4 3J 93
Merevale Cres. Mord 1A 122
Mereway Rd. Twic 7B 86
Merewood Clo. Brom 6L 111
Merewood Rd. Bexh 1A 98
Mereworth Clo. Brom 9D 110
Mereworth Dri. SE18 8M 79
Mereworth Ho. SE15 7G 77
Merganser Ct. SE8 7K 77
(off Edward St.)
Merganser Gdns. SE28 4B 80
Meriden. 9J 5
Meriden Clo. Brom 4H 111
Meriden Clo. Ilf 8A 32
Meriden Ct. SW3 6C 74
(off Chelsea Mnr. St.)
Meriden Way. Wat 9J 5
Meridian Ga. E14 3A 78
Meridian Ho. SE10 5C 78
(off Azof St.)
Meridian Ho. SE10 8A 78
(off Royal Hill)
Meridian Park. 9J 7
Meridian Pl. E14 3M 77
Meridian Rd. SE7 8H 79
Meridian Sq. E15 3B 62
Meridian Trad. Est. SE7 5F 78
Meridian Wlk. N17 6C 28
Meridian Way. N18 & N9 5G 29
Merifield Rd. SE9 3G 95
Merino Clo. E11 2G 47
Merino Pl. Sidc 5E 96
Merioneth Ct. W7 8D 54
(off Copley Clo.)
Merivale Rd. SW15 3J 89
Merivale Rd. Harr 5A 38
Merlewood Dri. Chst 5K 111
Merlewood Pl. SE9 4K 95
Merley Ct. NW9 6A 40
Merlin. NW9 8D 24
(off Concourse, The)
Merlin Clo. Croy 6C 124
Merlin Clo. Ilf 5G 33
Merlin Clo. Mitc 7C 106
Merlin Clo. N'holt 6G 53
Merlin Clo. Romf 6B 34
Merlin Clo. Wall 8K 123
Merlin Clo. Wal A 7M 7
Merlin Ct. Brom 7D 110
Merlin Ct. Ruis 7B 36
Merlin Cres. Edgw 8K 23
Merlin Gdns. Brom 9E 94
Merlin Gdns. Romf 6B 34
Merling Clo. Chess 7G 119
Merlin Gro. Beck 8K 109
Merlin Gro. Ilf 7M 31
Merlin Rd. E12 7H 47
Merlin Rd. Romf 6B 34
Merlin Rd. Well 3E 96
Merlin Rd. N. Well 3E 96
Merlins Av. Harr 8K 37
Merlins Ct. WC1 6L 59
(off Margery St.)
Merlin St. WC1 6L 59
Merlin Way. Leav 7D 4
Mermagen Dri. Rain 3F 66
Mermaid Ct. E8 3D 60
(off Celandine Dri.)
Mermaid Ct. SE1 3B 76
Mermaid Ct. SE16 2K 77
Mermaid Ho. E14 1A 78
(off Bazely St.)
Mermaid Tower. SE8 7K 77
(off Abinger Gro.)
Meroe Ct. N16 7C 44
Merredene St. SW2 5K 91
Merriam Clo. E4 5A 30
Merrick Rd. S'hall 3K 69
Merrick Sq. SE1 4B 76
Merridene. N21 8M 15
Merrielands Cres. Dag 5K 65
Merrielands Retail Pk.
Dag 4K 65
Merrilands Rd. Wor Pk 3G 121
Merrilees Rd. Sidc 7C 96
Merrilyn Clo. Clay 8E 118
Merriman Rd. SE3 9G 79
Merrington Rd. SW6 7L 73
Merrion Av. Stan 5H 23
Merritt Gdns. Chess 8G 119
Merritt Ho. Romf 5D 50
(off Frazer Clo.)
Merritt Rd. SE4 4K 93
Merritt's Bldgs. EC2 7C 60
(off Worship St.)
Merrivale. N14 8H 15
Merrivale. NW1 4G 59
(off Camden St.)
Merrivale Av. Ilf 2H 47
Merrivale M. W Dray 2H 143
Merrow Ct. Mitc 6B 106
Merrow Rd. Sutt 1H 135
Merrows Clo. N'wd 6A 20
Merrow St. SE17 6B 76
Merrow Wlk. SE17 6B 76
Merrow Way. New Ad 8A 126
Merrydown Way. Chst 5J 111
Merryfield. SE3 1D 94
Merryfield Gdns. Stan 5G 23
Merryfield Ho. SE9 9G 95
(off Grove Pk. Rd.)
Merryfields. Uxb 5B 142
(in two parts)
Merryfields Way. SE6 6M 93
Merry Hill. 1L 21
Merryhill Clo. E4 9M 17
Merry Hill Mt. Bush 1M 21
Merry Hill Rd. Bush 8K 9
Merryhills Clo. Big H 8H 141
Merryhills Ct. N14 7G 15
Merryhills Dri. Enf 6H 15
Merrymeet. Bans 6D 136
Merryweather Clo. Dart 5K 99
Merryweather Ct. N19 8G 43

Merryweather Ct.—Mill Plat Av.

Merryweather Ct. N Mald ... 9C 104
Mersea Ho. Bark ... 2M 63
Mersey Ct. King T ... 5H 103
Mersey Rd. E17 ... 1K 45
Mersey Wlk. N'holt ... 5L 53
Mersham Dri. NW9 ... 3L 39
Mersham Pl. SE20 ... 5F 108
Mersham Rd. T Hth ... 7B 108
Merten Rd. Romf ... 5J 49
Merthyr Ter. SW13 ... 7F 72
Merton. ... 4A 106
Merton Av. W4 ... 5D 72
Merton Av. N'holt ... 1A 54
Merton Av. Uxb ... 3F 142
Merton Ct. Ilf ... 4J 47
Merton Ct. Well ... 1F 96
Merton Gdns. Orp ... 9M 111
Merton Hall Gdns. SW20 ... 5J 105
Merton Hall Rd. SW19 ... 4J 105
Merton High St. SW19 ... 4M 105
Merton Ind. Pk. SW19 ... 5M 105
Merton La. N6 ... 7D 42
Merton Lodge. New Bar ... 7A 14
Merton Mans. SE8 ... 9L 77 (off Brookmill Rd.)
Merton Mans. SW20 ... 6H 105
Merton Park. ... 6L 105
Merton Pk. Pde. SW19 ... 5K 105
Merton Pl. SW19 ... 5A 106 (off Nelson Gro. Rd.)
Merton Ri. NW3 ... 3C 58 (in two parts)
Merton Rd. E17 ... 3A 46
Merton Rd. SE25 ... 9E 108
Merton Rd. SW18 ... 5L 89
Merton Rd. SW19 ... 4M 105
Merton Rd. Bark ... 3D 64
Merton Rd. Enf ... 2B 16
Merton Rd. Harr ... 6A 38
Merton Rd. Ilf ... 5D 48
Merton Rd. Wat ... 6F 8
Merton Way. Uxb ... 3F 142
Merton Way. W Mol ... 8M 101
Mertoun Ter. W1 ... 8D 58 (off Seymour Pl.)
Merttins Rd. SE15 & SE4 ... 4H 93
Meru Clo. NW5 ... 9E 42
Mervan Rd. SW2 ... 3L 91
Mervyn Av. SE9 ... 9A 96
Mervyn Rd. W13 ... 4E 70
Mervyn Rd. Shep ... 2A 116
Meryfield Clo. Borwd ... 4K 11
Messaline Av. W3 ... 9A 56
Messant Clo. H Wood ... 9J 35
Messent Rd. SE9 ... 4G 95
Messeter Pl. SE9 ... 5L 95
Messina Av. NW6 ... 3L 57
Messiter Ho. N1 ... 4K 59 (off Barnsbury Est.)
Metcalf Rd. Ashf ... 2A 100
Metcalf Wlk. Felt ... 1J 101
Meteor St. SW11 ... 3E 90
Meteor Way. Wall ... 9J 123
Metford Cres. Enf ... 2L 17
Metheringham Way. NW9 ... 8C 24
Methley St. SE11 ... 6L 75
Methuen Clo. Edgw ... 7L 23
Methuen Pk. N10 ... 1F 42
Methuen Rd. Belv ... 5M 81
Methuen Rd. Bexh ... 3K 97
Methuen Rd. Edgw ... 7L 23
Methwold Rd. W10 ... 8H 57
Metro Bus. Cen., The. SE26 ... 3K 109
Metro Central Heights. SE1 ... 4A 76 (off Newington Causeway)
Metro Cen. Orp ... 1F 128
Metro Cinema. ... 1H 75 (off Rupert St.)
Metro Ind. Cen. Iswth ... 1C 86
Metropolis. SE11 ... 4M 75 (off Oswin St.)
Metropolitan Bus. Cen. N1 ... 3C 60 (off Enfield Rd.)
Metropolitan Clo. E14 ... 8L 61
Metropolitan Sta. App. Wat ... 5D 8
Metropolitan Wharf. E1 ... 2G 77
Metro Trad. Est. Wemb ... 9M 39
Meux Clo. Chesh ... 4A 6
Mews End. Big H ... 9H 141
Mews Pl. Wfd G ... 4E 30
Mews St. E1 ... 2E 76
Mews, The. N1 ... 4A 60
Mews, The. N8 ... 1L 43
Mews, The. Ilf ... 3H 47
Mews, The. Romf ... 2C 50
Mews, The. Sidc ... 1E 112
Mews, The. Twic ... 5F 86
Mews, The. Wat ... 6G 9 (off Smith St.)
Mexborough. NW1 ... 4G 59
Mexfield Rd. SW15 ... 4K 89
Meyer Grn. Enf ... 2E 16
Meyer Rd. Eri ... 7B 82
Meymott St. SE1 ... 2M 75
Meynell Cres. E9 ... 3H 61
Meynell Gdns. E9 ... 3H 61
Meynell Rd. E9 ... 3H 61
Meynell Rd. Romf ... 7F 34
Meyrick Ho. E14 ... 8L 61 (off Burgess St.)
Meyrick Rd. NW10 ... 2E 56
Meyrick Rd. SW11 ... 2B 90
Mezen Clo. N'wd ... 5B 20
Miah Ter. E1 ... 2E 76
Miall Wlk. SE26 ... 1J 109
Micawber Av. Uxb ... 7E 142
Micawber Ct. N1 ... 6A 60 (off Windsor Ter.)
Micawber Ho. SE16 ... 3E 76 (off Llewellyn St.)
Micawber St. N1 ... 6A 60
Michael Cliffe Ho. EC1 ... 6M 59 (off Finsbury Est.)
Michael Faraday Ho. SE17 ... 6C 76 (off Beaconsfield Rd.)
Michael Gdns. Horn ... 2H 51
Michael Gaynor Clo. W7 ... 2D 70
Michael Manley Ind. Est. SW8 ... 1G 91 (off Clyston St.)
Michaelmas Clo. SW20 ... 7G 105
Michael Rd. E11 ... 6D 46
Michael Rd. SE25 ... 7C 108
Michael Rd. SW6 ... 9M 73
Michaels Clo. SE13 ... 3C 94
Michael Stewart Ho. SW6 ... 7K 73 (off Clem Attlee Ct.)
Michelangelo Ct. SE16 ... 6F 76 (off Stubbs Dri.)
Micheldever Rd. SE12 ... 5C 94
Michelham Gdns. Twic ... 9D 86
Michelle Ct. N12 ... 5A 26
Michelle Ct. W3 ... 1B 72
Michelle Ct. Brom ... 5D 110 (off Blyth Rd.)
Michelsdale Dri. Rich ... 3J 87
Michelson Ho. SE11 ... 5K 75 (off Black Prince Rd.)
Michel's Row. Rich ... 3J 87 (off Michelsdale Dri.)
Michigan Av. E12 ... 9K 47
Michigan Ho. E14 ... 5L 77
Michleham Down. N12 ... 4K 25
Mickledore. NW1 ... 5G 59 (off Ampthill Est.)
Micklefield Way. Borwd ... 2J 11
Mickleham Clo. Orp ... 6D 112
Mickleham Gdns. Sutt ... 8J 121
Mickleham Rd. Orp ... 5D 112
Mickleham Way. New Ad ... 9B 126
Micklethwaite Rd. SW6 ... 7L 73
Midas Metropolitan Ind. Est. Mord ... 2G 121
Mid Beckton. ... 9K 63
Midcroft. Ruis ... 6C 36
Middleborough Ho. Romf ... 7J 35 (off Kingsbridge Cir.)
Middle Clo. Eps ... 4C 134
Middle Dene. NW7 ... 3B 24
Middlefield. NW8 ... 4B 58
Middlefielde. W13 ... 8F 54
Middlefield Gdns. Ilf ... 4M 47
Middlefields. Croy ... 1J 139
Middle Furlong. Bush ... 6M 9
Middle Grn. Clo. Surb ... 1K 119
Middleham Ct. Dart ... 5M 99 (off Osbourne Rd.)
Middleham Gdns. N18 ... 6E 28
Middleham Rd. N18 ... 6E 28
Middle La. N8 ... 3J 43
Middle La. Eps ... 4C 134
Middle La. Tedd ... 3D 102
Middle La. M. N8 ... 3J 43
Middle Mill Hall. King T ... 7K 103
Middle Ope. Wat ... 1F 8
Middle Pk. Av. SE9 ... 5H 95
Middle Path. Harr ... 6B 38
Middle Rd. E13 ... 5E 62
Middle Rd. SW16 ... 6H 107
Middle Rd. E Barn ... 8C 14
Middle Rd. Harr ... 7B 38
Middle Row. W10 ... 7J 57
Middlesborough Rd. N18 ... 6E 28
Middlesex Bus. Cen. S'hall ... 3K 69
Middlesex County Cricket Club. (Lord's Cricket Ground) ... 6B 58
Middlesex Ct. W4 ... 6D 72
Middlesex Ct. Harr ... 3D 38
Middlesex Pas. EC1 ... 8M 59 (off Bartholomew Clo.)
Middlesex Pl. E9 ... 2G 61 (off Elsdale St.)
Middlesex Rd. Mitc ... 9J 107
Middlesex St. E1 ... 8C 60
Middlesex University (Bounds Grn. Campus) ... 6G 27
Middlesex University (Enfield Campus) ... 7F 16
Middlesex University (Hendon Campus) ... 2F 40
Middlesex University (Tottenham Campus) ... 6C 28
Middlesex Wharf. E5 ... 7G 45
Middle St. EC1 ... 8A 60
Middle St. Croy ... 4A 124 (in two parts)
Middle Temple Hall. ... 1L 75 (off Middle Temple La.)
Middle Temple La. EC4 ... 9L 59
Middleton Av. E4 ... 4K 29
Middleton Av. Gnfd ... 5B 54
Middleton Av. Sidc ... 3F 112
Middleton Bldgs. W1 ... 8G 59 (off Langham St.)
Middleton Clo. E4 ... 3K 29
Middleton Dri. SE16 ... 3H 77
Middleton Dri. Pinn ... 1E 36
Middleton Gdns. Ilf ... 4M 47
Middleton Gro. N7 ... 1J 59
Middleton Ho. E8 ... 3D 60
Middleton Ho. SE1 ... 4B 76 (off Burbage Clo.)
Middleton Ho. SW1 ... 5H 75 (off Causton St.)
Middleton M. N7 ... 1J 59
Middleton Rd. E8 ... 3D 60
Middleton Rd. NW11 ... 5L 41
Middleton Rd. Eps ... 2B 134
Middleton Rd. Hay ... 8B 52
Middleton Rd. Mord ... 1M 121
Middleton Rd. N Mald ... 7A 104
Middleton St. E2 ... 6F 60
Middleton Way. SE13 ... 3B 94
Middleway. NW11 ... 3M 41
Middle Way. SW16 ... 6H 107
Middle Way. Eri ... 4J 81
Middle Way. Hay ... 7G 53
Middle Way. Wat ... 1E 8
Middle Way, The. Harr ... 9D 22
Middle Yd. SE1 ... 2C 76
Midfield Av. Bexh ... 2A 98
Midfield Av. Swan ... 3E 114
Midfield Pde. Bexh ... 2A 98
Midfield Way. Orp ... 5F 112
Midford Ho. NW4 ... 2H 41 (off Belle Vue Est.)
Midford Pl. W1 ... 7G 59
Midgarth Clo. Oxs ... 6A 132
Midholm. Wemb ... 6L 39
Midholm Clo. NW11 ... 2M 41
Midholm Rd. Croy ... 5J 125
Midhope Ho. WC1 ... 6J 59 (off Midhope St.)
Midhope St. WC1 ... 6J 59
Midhurst. SE26 ... 3G 109
Midhurst Av. N10 ... 1E 42
Midhurst Av. Croy ... 2L 123
Midhurst Clo. Horn ... 9E 50
Midhurst Gdns. Uxb ... 4A 52
Midhurst Hill. Bexh ... 5L 97
Midhurst Ho. E14 ... 9K 61 (off Salmon La.)
Midhurst Pde. N10 ... 1E 42 (off Fortis Grn.)
Midhurst Rd. W13 ... 3E 70
Midhurst Way. E5 ... 9E 44
Midland Cres. NW3 ... 2A 58
Midland Pde. NW6 ... 2M 57
Midland Pl. E14 ... 6A 78
Midland Rd. E10 ... 5A 46
Midland Rd. NW1 ... 5H 59
Midland Ter. NW2 ... 8H 41
Midland Ter. NW10 ... 7C 56 (in two parts)
Midmoor Rd. SW12 ... 7G 91
Midmoor Rd. SW19 ... 5H 105
Midship Clo. SE16 ... 2H 77
Midship Point. E14 ... 3L 77 (off Quarterdeck, The)
Midstrath Rd. NW10 ... 9C 40
Midsummer Av. Houn ... 3K 85
Midway. Sutt ... 2K 121
Midway. W on T ... 4F 116
Midway Ho. EC1 ... 6M 59 (off Manningford Clo.)
Midwinter Clo. Well ... 2E 96
Midwood Clo. NW2 ... 8F 40
Miena Way. Asht ... 9H 133
Miers Clo. E6 ... 4L 63
Mighell Av. Ilf ... 3H 47
Milan Rd. S'hall ... 3K 69
Milborne Gro. SW10 ... 6A 74
Milborne St. E9 ... 2G 61
Milborough Cres. SE12 ... 5C 94
Milbourne Ct. Wat ... 4E 8
Milbourne La. Esh ... 8A 118
Milbrook. Esh ... 8A 118
Milburn Dri. W Dray ... 1J 143
Milburn Wlk. Eps ... 7C 134
Milby Ct. Borwd ... 3K 11
Milcote St. SE1 ... 3M 75
Mildenhall Ho. Romf ... 5L 35 (off Redcar Rd.)
Mildenhall Rd. E5 ... 9G 45
Mildmay Av. N1 ... 2B 60
Mildmay Gro. N. N1 ... 1B 60
Mildmay Gro. S. N1 ... 1B 60
Mildmay Pk. N1 ... 1B 60
Mildmay Pl. N16 ... 1C 60
Mildmay Rd. N1 ... 1B 60
Mildmay Rd. Ilf ... 8M 47
Mildmay Rd. Romf ... 3A 50
Mildmay St. N1 ... 2B 60
Mildred Av. Borwd ... 6L 11 (in two parts)
Mildred Av. Hay ... 5B 68
Mildred Av. N'holt ... 1M 53
Mildred Av. Wat ... 6D 8
Mildred Clo. Dart ... 5L 99
Mildred Rd. Eri ... 6C 82
Mildura Ct. N8 ... 2K 43
Mile Clo. Wal A ... 6J 7
Mile End. ... 6J 61
Mile End Pk. ... 6J 61
Mile End Pl. E1 ... 7H 61
Mile End Rd. E1 & E3 ... 8G 61
Mile End, The. E17 ... 8H 29
Mile Rd. Wall ... 3F 122
Miles Bldgs. NW1 ... 8C 58 (off Penfold Pl.)
Miles Ct. E1 ... 9F 60 (off Tillman St.)
Miles Ct. Croy ... 4M 123 (off Cuthbert Rd.)
Miles Dri. SE28 ... 2C 80
Miles Ho. SE10 ... 6C 78 (off Tuskar St.)
Miles Lodge. Harr ... 3B 38
Milespit Hill. NW7 ... 5F 24
Miles Pl. NW1 ... 8B 58 (off Broadley St.)
Miles Pl. Surb ... 8K 103
Miles Rd. N8 ... 1J 43
Miles Rd. Eps ... 4B 134
Miles Rd. Mitc ... 7C 106
Miles St. SW8 ... 7J 75 (in two parts)
Miles St. Bus. Est. SW8 ... 7J 75
Milestone Clo. N9 ... 2E 28
Milestone Clo. Sutt ... 9B 122
Milestone Green (Junct.) ... 3B 88
Milestone Ho. King T ... 7H 103 (off Surbiton Rd.)
Milestone Rd. SE19 ... 3D 108
Milestone Rd. Dart ... 5M 99
Miles Way. N20 ... 2C 26
Milfoil St. W12 ... 1E 72
Milford Clo. SE2 ... 7J 81
Milford Ct. S'hall ... 2L 69
Milford Gdns. Croy ... 9G 109
Milford Gdns. Edgw ... 7L 23
Milford Gdns. Wemb ... 9H 39
Milford Gro. Sutt ... 6A 122
Milford La. WC2 ... 1L 75
Milford M. SW16 ... 9K 91
Milford Rd. W13 ... 2F 70
Milford Rd. S'hall ... 1L 69
Milford Towers. SE6 ... 6M 93
Milking La. Kes ... 3H 141 (in two parts)
Milk St. E16 ... 2M 79
Milk St. EC2 ... 9A 60
Milk St. Brom ... 3F 110
Milkwell Gdns. Wfd G ... 7F 30
Milkwell Yd. SE5 ... 9A 76
Milkwood Rd. SE24 ... 4M 91
Milk Yd. E1 ... 1G 77
Millais Av. E12 ... 1L 63
Millais Ct. N'holt ... 5H 53 (off Academy Gdns.)
Millais Gdns. Edgw ... 9L 23
Millais Ho. SW1 ... 5J 75 (off Marsham St.)
Millais Rd. E11 ... 9A 46
Millais Rd. Enf ... 7D 16
Millais Rd. N Mald ... 2C 120
Millais Way. Eps ... 6A 120
Milland Ct. Borwd ... 3B 12
Millard Clo. N16 ... 1C 60
Millard Ho. SE8 ... 6K 77 (off Leeway)
Millard Ter. Dag ... 2L 65
Mill Av. Uxb ... 5A 142
Millbank. SW1 ... 4J 75
Millbank Ct. SW1 ... 5J 75 (off John Islip St.)
Millbank Tower. SW1 ... 5J 75
Millbank Way. SE12 ... 4E 94
Millbourne Rd. Felt ... 1J 101
Mill Bri. Barn ... 8K 13
Mill Bri. Pl. Uxb ... 5A 142
Millbro. Swan ... 5E 114
Millbrook. Wey ... 6C 116
Millbrook Av. Well ... 3B 96
Millbrook Gdns. Chad H ... 4K 49
Millbrook Gdns. Gid P ... 9C 34
Millbrook Ho. SE15 ... 7E 76 (off Peckham Pk. Rd.)
Millbrook Pas. SW9 ... 2M 91
Millbrook Pl. NW1 ... 5G 59 (off Hampstead Rd.)
Millbrook Rd. N9 ... 1F 28
Millbrook Rd. SW9 ... 2M 91
Millbrook Rd. Bush ... 3K 9
Mill Brook Rd. St M ... 8G 113
Mill Clo. Cars ... 4E 122
Mill Clo. W Dray ... 4H 143
Mill Corner. Barn ... 3K 13
Mill Ct. E10 ... 8A 46
Mill Ct. Hort K ... 6M 115
Millcroft Ho. SE6 ... 1A 110 (off Melfield Gdns.)
Millender Wlk. SE16 ... 5G 77
Millennium Bridge. ... 1M 75
Millennium Bus. Cen. NW2 ... 7F 40
Millennium Clo. E16 ... 9F 62
Millennium Clo. Uxb ... 5A 142
Millennium Dome. ... 2C 78
Millennium Dri. E14 ... 5B 78
Millennium Ho. E17 ... 3H 45
Millennium Pl. E2 ... 5F 60
Millennium Sq. SE1 ... 3D 76
Millennium Way. SE10 ... 3C 78
Miller Av. Enf ... 2L 17
Miller Clo. Mitc ... 2D 122
Miller Clo. Pinn ... 9G 21
Miller Ct. Bexh ... 2A 98
Miller Rd. SW19 ... 3B 106
Miller Rd. Croy ... 3K 123
Miller's Av. E8 ... 1D 60
Millers Clo. NW7 ... 4E 24
Millers Clo. Chig ... 2F 32
Miller's Ct. W4 ... 6D 72
Millers Ct. Wemb ... 5J 55 (off Vicars Bri. Clo.)
Millers Grn. Clo. Enf ... 5M 15
Miller's La. Chig ... 1F 32
Millers Mdw. Clo. SE3 ... 4D 94
Miller's Ter. E8 ... 1D 60
Miller St. NW1 ... 5G 59 (in two parts)
Millers Way. W6 ... 3G 73
Millers Wharf Ho. E1 ... 2E 76 (off St Katherine's Way)
Miller Wlk. SE1 ... 2L 75
Millet Rd. Gnfd ... 5M 53
Mill Farm Av. Sun ... 4C 100
Mill Farm Bus. Pk. Houn ... 6J 85
Mill Farm Clo. Pinn ... 9G 21
Mill Farm Cres. Houn ... 7J 85
Millfield. N4 ... 7L 43
Millfield. King T ... 7K 103
Millfield. Sun ... 5B 100
Millfield Av. E17 ... 8J 29
Millfield Cotts. Orp ... 7F 112
Millfield Ho. Wat ... 8B 8
Millfield La. N6 ... 6C 42 (in two parts)
Millfield Pl. N6 ... 7E 42
Millfield Rd. Edgw ... 9A 24
Millfield Rd. Houn ... 7J 85
Millfields Clo. Orp ... 8F 112
Millfields Rd. E5 ... 9G 45
Mill Gdns. SE26 ... 9F 92
Mill Grn. Mitc ... 2E 122
Mill Grn. Bus. Pk. Mitc ... 2E 122
Mill Grn. Rd. Mitc ... 2E 122
Millgrove St. SW11 ... 9E 74
Millharbour. E14 ... 3M 77
Millhaven Clo. Romf ... 4F 48
Mill Hill. ... 5C 24
Mill Hill. SW13 ... 1E 88
Mill Hill Circus (Junct.) ... 5D 24
Mill Hill Golf Course. ... 1B 24
Mill Hill Gro. W3 ... 2A 72
Mill Hill Ind. Est. NW7 ... 6D 24
Mill Hill Pk. ... 6D 24
Mill Hill Rd. SW13 ... 1E 88
Mill Hill Rd. W3 ... 3M 71
Mill Hill Ter. W3 ... 2M 71
Mill Hill Yd. W3 ... 3M 71
Millhoo Ct. Wal A ... 7M 7
Mill Ho. Wfd G ... 5D 30
Mill Ho. Clo. Eyns ... 3J 131
Millhouse La. Bedm ... 1E 4
Millhouse Pl. SE27 ... 1M 107
Millicent Fawcett Ct. N17 ... 8D 28
Millicent Rd. E10 ... 6K 45
Milligan St. E14 ... 1K 77
Milliners Ct. Lou ... 4L 19
Milling Rd. Edgw ... 7B 24
Millington Ho. N16 ... 8B 44
Millington Rd. Hay ... 4C 68
Mill La. E4 ... 5M 17
Mill La. NW6 ... 1K 57
Mill La. SE18 ... 6L 79
Mill La. Cars ... 6D 122
Mill La. Chesh ... 1E 6
Mill La. Crox G ... 8A 8
Mill La. Croy ... 5K 123
Mill La. Eps ... 1D 134
Mill La. Eyns ... 3J 131
Mill La. Orp ... 2L 141
Mill La. Romf ... 4J 49
Mill La. Wfd G ... 5D 30
Millman M. WC1 ... 7K 59
Millman Pl. WC1 ... 7K 59 (off Millman St.)
Millman St. WC1 ... 7K 59
Millmark Gro. SE14 ... 1J 93
Millmarsh La. Brim ... 4J 17
Millmead. Esh ... 4L 117
Millmead Ind. Cen. N17 ... 9F 28
Mill Mead Rd. N17 ... 1F 44
Mill Meads. ... 5B 62
Mill Pk. Av. Horn ... 7J 51
Mill Pl. E14 ... 9J 61
Mill Pl. Chst ... 5M 111
Mill Pl. Dart ... 3E 98
Mill Pl. King T ... 7K 103
Mill Plat. Iswth ... 1E 86 (in two parts)
Mill Plat Av. Iswth ... 1E 86

Mill Pond Clo.—Monmouth St.

Mill Pond Clo. SW8 8H 75
Millpond Est. SE16 3F 76
Mill Pond Rd. Dart 5J 99
Mill Ridge. Edgw 5K 23
Mill River Trad. Est. Enf 5J 17
Mill Rd. E16 2F 78
Mill Rd. SW19 4A 106
Mill Rd. Ave 1M 83
Mill Rd. Dart 1K 115
Mill Rd. Eps 4D 134
Mill Rd. Eri 8A 82
Mill Rd. Esh 4L 117
Mill Rd. Ilf 8L 47
Mill Rd. Purf 7M 83
Mill Rd. Twic 8A 86
Mill Rd. W Dray 4G 143
Mill Row. N1 4C 60
Mill Row. Bex 7M 97
Mills Clo. Uxb 5E 142
Mills Ct. EC2 7C 60 (off Curtain Rd.)
Mills Gro. E14 9A 62
Mills Gro. NW4 1H 41
Millshot Clo. SW6 9G 73
Mills Ho. E17 1B 46
Mills Ho. SW8 9G 75 (off Thessaly Rd.)
Millside. Cars 4D 122
Millside Ind. Est. Dart 3H 99
Millside Pl. Iswth 1F 86
Millsmead Way. Lou 4K 19
Millson Clo. N20 2B 26
Mills Rd. W on T 7G 117
Mills Row. W4 5B 72
Mill Stone Clo. S Dar 6M 115
Mill Stone M. S Dar 5M 115
Millstream Clo. N13 5L 27
Millstream Ho. SE16 3F 76 (off Jamaica Rd.)
Millstream Rd. SE1 3D 76
Mill St. SE1 3D 76
Mill St. W1 1F 74
Mill St. King T 7J 103
Mill Trad. Est., The. NW10 6A 56
Mill Va. Brom 6D 110
Mill Vw. Clo. Ewe 9D 120
Mill Vw. Gdns. Croy 5H 125
Millwall. 5L 77
Millwall Dock Rd. E14 4L 77
Millwall F.C. (New Den, The) 6G 77
Millway. NW7 4C 24
Mill Way. Bush 4J 9
Mill Way. Felt 4F 84
Millway Gdns. N'holt 2K 53
Millwell Cres. Chig 5B 32
Millwood Rd. Houn 4A 86
Millwood Rd. Orp 7G 113
Millwood St. W10 8J 57
Mill Yd. E1 1E 76
Milman Clo. Pinn 1H 37
Milman Rd. NW6 5H 57
Milman's St. SW10 7B 74
Milne Fld. Pinn 7L 21
Milne Gdns. SE9 4J 95
Milne Ho. SE18 5K 79 (off Ogilby St.)
Milne Pk. E. New Ad 3B 140
Milne Pk. W. New Ad 3B 140
Milner Clo. Wat 7F 4
Milner Ct. Bush 8M 9
Milner Dri. Twic 6B 86
Milner Pl. N1 4L 59
Milner Pl. Cars 6E 122
Milner Rd. E15 6C 62
Milner Rd. SW19 5M 105
Milner Rd. Dag 7G 49
Milner Rd. King T 7H 103
Milner Rd. Mord 9B 106
Milner Rd. T Hth 7B 108
Milner Sq. N1 3M 59
Milner St. SW3 5D 74
Milner Wlk. Sidc 8B 96
Milnthorpe Rd. W4 7B 72
Milo Gdns. SE22 5D 92
Milo Rd. SE22 5D 92
Milrood Ho. E1 8H 61 (off Stepney Grn.)
Milroy Wlk. SE1 2M 75
Milson Rd. W14 4H 73
Milstead Ho. E5 1F 60
Milton Av. E6 3H 63
Milton Av. N6 5G 43
Milton Av. NW9 1A 40
Milton Av. NW10 4A 56
Milton Av. Barn 7K 13
Milton Av. Croy 2B 124
Milton Av. Horn 7D 50
Milton Av. Sutt 5B 122
Milton Clo. N2 3A 42
Milton Clo. SE1 5D 76
Milton Clo. Hay 9E 52
Milton Clo. Sutt 5B 122
Milton Ct. E17 2L 45
Milton Ct. EC2 8B 60
Milton Ct. SE14 7K 77
Milton Ct. SW18 4L 89
Milton Ct. Chad H 5G 49
Milton Ct. Twic 9C 86
Milton Ct. Uxb 8A 36
Milton Ct. Wal A 7J 7
Milton Ct. Rd. SE14 7J 77
Milton Ct. Wlk. EC2 8B 60 (off Silk St.)
Milton Cres. Ilf 5M 47
Milton Dri. Borwd 7M 11
Milton Garden Est. N16 9B 44
Milton Gdns. Eps 6C 134
Milton Gdns. Stai 7D 144
Milton Gro. N11 5G 27
Milton Gro. N16 9B 44
Milton Ho. E2 6G 61 (off Roman Rd.)
Milton Ho. E17 2L 45
Milton Ho. SE5 8B 76 (off Elmington Est.)
Milton Ho. Sutt 5L 121
Milton Lodge. Sidc 1E 112
Milton Lodge. Twic 6D 86
Milton Mans. W14 7J 73 (off Queen's Club Gdns.)
Milton Pk. N6 5G 43
Milton Pl. N7 1L 59
Milton Rd. E17 2L 45
Milton Rd. N6 5G 43
Milton Rd. N15 2M 43
Milton Rd. NW7 5E 24
Milton Rd. NW9 5E 40
Milton Rd. SE24 4M 91
Milton Rd. SW14 2B 88
Milton Rd. SW19 3A 106
Milton Rd. W3 2B 72
Milton Rd. W7 1D 70
Milton Rd. Belv 5L 81
Milton Rd. Croy 3B 124
Milton Rd. Hamp 4L 101
Milton Rd. Harr 2C 38
Milton Rd. Mitc 4E 106
Milton Rd. Romf 4E 50
Milton Rd. Sutt 5L 121
Milton Rd. Uxb 9A 36
Milton Rd. Wall 8G 123
Milton Rd. W on T 5H 117
Milton Rd. Well 9D 80
Milton St. EC2 8B 60
Milton St. Wal A 7J 7
Milton St. Wat 2F 8
Milton Way. W Dray 5K 143
Milverton Dri. Uxb 9A 36
Milverton Gdns. Ilf 7D 48
Milverton Ho. SE23 9J 93
Milverton Rd. NW6 3G 57
Milverton St. SE11 6L 75
Milverton Way. SE9 1L 111
Milward Wlk. E1 8F 60
Milward Wlk. SE18 7L 79
Mimosa Clo. Orp 4G 129
Mimosa Clo. Romf 7G 35
Mimosa Ho. Hay 8G 53
Mimosa Lodge. NW10 1D 56
Mimosa Rd. Hay 8G 53
Mimosa St. SW6 9K 73
Minard Rd. SE6 6C 94 (in two parts)
Mina Rd. SE17 6C 76
Mina Rd. SW19 5L 105
Minchenden Ct. N14 2H 27
Minchenden Cres. N14 3G 27
Minchin Ho. E14 9L 61 (off Dod St.)
Mincing La. EC3 1C 76
Minden Rd. SE20 5F 108
Minden Rd. Sutt 4K 121
Minehead Ho. Romf 5J 35 (off Dagnam Pk. Dri.)
Minehead Rd. SW16 2K 107
Minehead Rd. Harr 8L 37
Mineral St. SE18 5C 80
Minera M. SW1 5E 74
Minerva Clo. SW9 8L 75 (in two parts)
Minerva Clo. Sidc 1C 112
Minerva Dri. Wat 9C 4
Minerva Rd. E4 7M 29
Minerva Rd. NW10 7A 56
Minerva Rd. King T 6K 103
Minerva St. E2 5F 60
Minerva Wlk. EC1 9M 59
Minet Av. NW10 5C 56
Minet Dri. Hay 2E 68
Minet Gdns. NW10 5C 56
Minet Gdns. Hay 2F 68
Minet Rd. SW9 1M 91
Minford Gdns. W14 3H 73
Minford Ho. W14 3H 73 (off Minford Gdns.)
Mingard Wlk. N7 7K 43
Ming St. E14 1L 77
Minimax Clo. Felt 5E 84
Ministry Way. SE9 8K 95
Miniver Pl. EC4 1A 76 (off Garlick Hill)
Mink Ct. Houn 1G 85
Minniedale. Surb 9K 103
Minnow St. SE17 5C 76
Minnow Wlk. SE17 5C 76
Minories. EC3 9D 60
Minshaw Ct. Sidc 1D 112
Minshill St. SW8 9H 75
Minshull Pl. Beck 4L 109
Minson Rd. E9 4H 61
Minstead Gdns. SW15 6D 88
Minstead Way. N Mald 1C 120
Minster Av. Sutt 4L 121
Minster Ct. EC3 1C 76 (off Mincing La.)
Minster Ct. W5 7J 55
Minster Ct. Horn 7L 51
Minster Dri. Croy 6C 124
Minster Gdns. W Mol 8K 101
Minsterley Av. Shep 8C 100
Minster Pavement. EC3 1C 76 (off Mincing La.)
Minster Rd. NW2 1J 57
Minster Rd. Brom 4F 110
Minster Wlk. N8 2J 43
Minster Way. Horn 6K 51
Minstrel Gdns. Surb 8K 103
Mint Bus. Pk. E16 8F 62
Mint Clo. Hil 6F 142
Mintern Clo. N13 3M 27
Minterne Av. S'hall 5L 69
Minterne Rd. Harr 3K 39
Minterne Waye. Hay 9G 53
Mintern St. N1 5B 60
Minton Ho. SE11 5L 75 (off Walnut Tree Wlk.)
Minton M. NW6 2M 57
Mint Rd. Bans 8A 136
Mint Rd. Wall 6F 122
Mint St. SE1 3A 76
Mint Wlk. Croy 5A 124
Mint Wlk. Warl 9H 139
Mirabel Rd. SW6 8K 73
Miramar Way. Horn 1H 67
Miranda Clo. E1 8G 61
Miranda Ct. W3 9K 55
Miranda Rd. N19 6G 43
Mirfield St. SE7 5H 79
Miriam Rd. SE18 6C 80
Mirravale Trad. Est. Dag 5J 49
Mirren Clo. Harr 9K 37
Mirror Path. SE9 9G 95
Misbourne Rd. Uxb 4E 142
Miskin Rd. Dart 6G 99
Missenden. SE17 6B 76 (off Roland Way)
Missenden Clo. Felt 7D 84
Missenden Gdns. Mord 1A 122
Missenden Ho. NW8 7C 58 (off Jerome Cres.)
Missenden Ho. Wat 9C 8 (off Chenies Way)
Mission Gro. E17 3J 45
Mission Pl. SE15 9E 76
Mission Sq. Bren 7J 71
Mission, The. E14 9K 61 (off Commercial Rd.)
Mistletoe Clo. Croy 3H 125
Mistral. SE5 9C 76
Misty's Fld. W on T 3G 117
Mitali Pas. E1 9E 60 (in two parts)
Mitcham. 7D 106
Mitcham Garden Village. Mitc 9E 106
Mitcham Ho. SE5 9A 76
Mitcham Ind. Est. Mitc 5F 106
Mitcham La. SW16 3G 107
Mitcham Pk. Mitc 8C 106
Mitcham Rd. E6 6J 63
Mitcham Rd. SW17 2D 106
Mitcham Rd. Croy 1J 123
Mitcham Rd. Ilf 5D 48
Mitchell. NW9 8D 24 (off Concourse, The)
Mitchellbrook Way. NW10 2B 56
Mitchell Clo. SE2 5G 81
Mitchell Clo. Ab L 5E 4
Mitchell Clo. Belv 4A 82
Mitchell Clo. Dart 8J 99
Mitchell Clo. Rain 5G 67
Mitchell Ho. W12 1F 72 (off White City Est.)
Mitchell Rd. N13 5A 28
Mitchell Rd. Orp 6D 128
Mitchell's Pl. SE21 5C 92 (off Aysgarth Rd.)
Mitchell St. EC1 7A 60 (in two parts)
Mitchell Wlk. E6 8J 63 (off Neats Ct. Rd.)
Mitchell Wlk. E6 8K 63 (Elmley Clo.)
Mitchell Way. NW10 2A 56
Mitchell Way. Brom 5E 110
Mitchison Rd. N1 2B 60
Mitchley Av. Purl & S Croy 5A 138
Mitchley Gro. S Croy 5E 138
Mitchley Hill. S Croy 5D 138
Mitchley Rd. N17 1E 44
Mitchley Vw. S Croy 5E 138
Mitford Clo. Chess 8G 119
Mitford Rd. N19 7J 43
Mitre Av. E17 1L 45
Mitre Bri. Ind. Pk. W10 7F 56
Mitre Clo. Brom 6D 110
Mitre Clo. Shep 1B 116
Mitre Clo. Sutt 9A 122
Mitre Ct. EC2 9A 60 (off Wood St.)
Mitre Rd. E15 5C 62
Mitre Rd. SE1 3L 75
Mitre Sq. EC3 9C 60
Mitre St. EC3 9C 60
Mitre, The. E14 1K 77
Mitre Way. NW10 & W10 7F 56
Mitre Yd. SW3 5C 74
Mixbury Gro. Wey 8B 116
Moat Clo. Bush 7M 9
Moat Clo. Orp 8D 128
Moat Ct. SE9 5K 95
Moat Ct. Asht 9J 133
Moat Ct. Sidc 9D 96
Moat Cres. N3 1M 41
Moat Cft. Well 2G 97
Moat Dri. E13 5G 63
Moat Dri. Harr 2A 38
Moat Dri. Ruis 5C 36
Moat Farm Rd. N'holt 2K 53
Moatfield. NW6 3J 57
Moatfield Rd. Bush 7M 9
Moat Gdns. SE28 1G 81
Moatlands Ho. WC1 6J 59 (off Cromer St.)
Moat La. Eri 9E 82
Moat Mount Open Space. 1C 24
Moat Pl. SW9 2K 91
Moat Pl. W3 9M 55
Moat Side. Enf 6H 17
Moat Side. Felt 1G 101
Moat, The. N Mald 5C 104
Moat Vw. Ct. Bush 7M 9
Moberley Rd. SW4 6H 91
Mobil Ct. WC2 9K 59 (off Clement's Inn)
Mobile Way. W3 8B 56
Moby Dick (Junct.) 2J 49
Mocatta Ho. E1 7F 60 (off Brady St.)
Modbury Gdns. NW5 2E 58
Modder Pl. SW15 3H 89
Model Bldgs. WC1 6K 59 (off Cubitt St.)
Model Cotts. SW14 3A 88
Model Cotts. W13 3F 70
Model Farm Clo. SE9 9J 95
Modern Ct. EC4 9M 59 (off Farringdon St.)
Modling Ho. E2 5H 61 (off Mace St.)
Moelwyn. N7 1H 59
Moelyn M. Harr 3E 38
Moffat Ct. SW19 2L 105
Moffat Ho. SE5 8A 76
Moffat Rd. N13 6J 27
Moffat Rd. SW17 1D 106
Moffat Rd. T Hth 6A 108
Mogden La. Iswth 4D 86
Mohammedi Pk. N'holt 4L 53
Mohawk Ho. E3 5J 61 (off Gernon Rd.)
Mohmmad Khan Rd. E11 6D 46
Moineau. NW9 8D 24 (off Concourse, The)
Moira Clo. N17 9C 28
Moira Rd. SE9 3K 95
Moir Clo. S Croy 1E 138
Mokswell Ct. N10 8E 26
Moland Mead. SE16 6H 77 (in two parts)
Molash Rd. Orp 8H 113
Molasses Ho. SW11 2A 90 (off Clove Hitch Quay)
Molasses Row. SW11 2A 90
Mole Abbey Gdns. W Mol 7M 101
Mole Ct. Eps 6A 120
Molember Ct. E Mol 8C 102
Molember Rd. E Mol 9C 102
Mole Rd. W on T 7H 117
Molescroft. SE9 9A 96
Molesey Av. W Mol 9K 101
Molesey Clo. W on T 6J 117
Molesey Dri. Sutt 4J 121
Molesey Pk. Av. W Mol 9M 101
Molesey Pk. Clo. E Mol 9A 102
Molesey Pk. Rd. W Mol 9M 101
Molesey Rd. W on T & W Mol 7H 117
Molesford Rd. SW6 9L 73
Molesham Clo. W Mol 7M 101
Molesham Way. W Mol 7M 101
Moles Hill. Oxs 3B 132
Molesworth Ho. SE17 7M 75 (off Brandon Est.)
Molesworth St. SE13 3A 94
Moliner Ct. Beck 4L 109
Mollis Ho. E3 8L 61 (off Gale St.)
Mollison Av. Enf 8E 6
Mollison Dri. Wall 9H 123
Mollison Way. Edgw 9K 23
Molly Huggins Clo. SW12 6G 91
Molteno Rd. Wat 2E 8
Molton Ho. N1 4K 59 (off Barnsbury Est.)
Molyneux Dri. SW17 1F 106
Molyneux St. W1 8C 58
Monach Clo. Rain 5E 66
Monahan Av. Purl 4K 137
Monarch Clo. Felt 6C 84
Monarch Clo. W Wick 6D 126
Monarch Ct. N2 3B 42
Monarch Dri. E16 8H 63
Monarch M. E17 4M 45
Monarch M. SW16 2L 107
Monarch Pde. Mitc 6D 106
Monarch Pl. Buck H 2G 31
Monarch Rd. Belv 4L 81
Monarchs Way. Ruis 6B 36
Monarchs Way. Wal X 7E 6
Mona Rd. SE15 1G 93
Monastery Gdns. Enf 4B 16
Mona St. E16 8D 62
Monaveen Gdns. W Mol 7M 101
Moncks Row. SW18 5K 89
Monck St. SW1 4H 75
Monclar Rd. SE5 3B 92
Moncorvo Clo. SW7 3C 74 (off Ennismore Gdns.)
Moncrieff Clo. E6 9J 63
Moncrieff Pl. SE15 1E 92
Moncrieff St. SE15 1E 92
Mondial Way. Hay 8A 68
Monega Rd. E7 & E12 2G 63
Monet Ct. SE16 6F 76 (off Stubbs Dri.)
Moneyer Ho. N1 5B 60 (off Provost Est.)
Money La. W Dray 4H 143
Mongers Almshouses. E9 3H 61 (off Church Cres.)
Mongers La. Eps 2D 134 (in two parts)
Mongomery Ct. W4 8A 72
Monica Clo. Wat 4G 9
Monica Ct. Enf 7C 16
Monica James Ho. Sidc 9E 96
Monica Shaw Ct. NW1 5H 59 (off Purchese St., in two parts)
Monier Rd. E3 3L 61
Monivea Rd. Beck 4K 109
Monkchester Clo. Lou 3K 19
Monk Ct. W12 2E 72
Monk Dri. E16 1E 78
Monken Hadley. 4K 13
Monken Hadley Common. 4M 13
Monkfrith Av. N14 8F 14
Monkfrith Clo. N14 9F 14
Monkfrith Way. N14 9E 14
Monkhams. Wal A 3J 7
Monkham's Av. Wfd G 5F 30
Monkham's Dri. Wfd G 5F 30
Monkham's La. Buck H 3F 30
Monkham's La. Wfd G 5E 30 (in two parts)
Monkleigh Rd. Mord 7J 105
Monk Pas. E16 1E 78 (off Monk Dri.)
Monks Av. Barn 8A 14
Monks Av. W Mol 9K 101
Monks Clo. SE2 5H 81
Monks Clo. Enf 4A 16
Monks Clo. Harr 7L 37
Monks Clo. Ruis 9H 37
Monks Cres. W on T 3F 116
Monksdene Gdns. Sutt 5M 121
Monks Dri. W3 8L 55
Monksgrove. Lou 7L 19
Monksmead. Borwd 6A 12
Monks Orchard. 2J 125
Monks Orchard. Dart 8G 99
Monks Orchard Rd. Beck 3L 125
Monks Pk. Wemb 2M 55
Monks Pk. Gdns. Wemb 3M 55
Monks Rd. Bans 9L 135
Monks Rd. Enf 4M 15
Monk St. SE18 5L 79
Monks Way. NW11 2K 41
Monks Way. Beck 1L 125
Monks Way. Orp 3A 128
Monks Way. W Dray 7J 143
Monkswood Av. Wal A 6K 7
Monkswood Gdns. Borwd 7B 12
Monkswood Gdns. Ilf 1L 47
Monkton Ho. E5 1F 60
Monkton Ho. SE16 3H 77 (off Wolfe Cres.)
Monkton Rd. Well 1D 96
Monkton St. SE11 5L 75
Monkville Av. NW11 2K 41
Monkville Pde. NW11 2K 41
Monkwell Sq. EC2 8A 60
Monkwood Clo. Romf 3E 50
Monmouth Av. E18 1F 46
Monmouth Av. King T 4G 103
Monmouth Clo. W4 4A 72
Monmouth Clo. Mitc 8J 107
Monmouth Clo. Well 3E 96
Monmouth Ct. W7 8D 54 (off Copley Clo.)
Monmouth Gro. W5 5J 71
Monmouth Pl. W2 9M 57 (off Monmouth Rd.)
Monmouth Rd. E6 6K 63
Monmouth Rd. N9 2F 28
Monmouth Rd. W2 9L 57
Monmouth Rd. Dag 1K 65
Monmouth Rd. Hay 5C 68
Monmouth Rd. Wat 5F 8
Monmouth St. WC2 9J 59

Monnery Rd.—Mortimer Ho.

Monnery Rd. N19 8G 43
Monnow Rd. SE1 6E 76
Mono La. Felt 8F 84
Monoux Almshouses. E17 2M 45
Monoux Gro. E17 8L 29
Monroe Cres. Enf 3F 16
Monroe Dri. SW14 4M 87
Monro Gdns. Harr 7C 22
Monro Ind. Est. Wal X 7E 6
Monro Pl. Eps 1L 133
Monsell Ct. N4 8M 43
Monsell Rd. N4 8L 43
Monson Rd. NW10 5E 56
Monson Rd. SE14 8H 77
Mons Way. Brom 1J 127
Montacute Rd. SE6 6K 93
Montacute Rd. Bus H 9C 10
Montacute Rd. Mord 1B 122
Montacute Rd. New Ad 1A 140
Montagu Cres. N18 4F 28
Montague Av. SE4 3K 93
Montague Av. W7 2D 70
Montague Av. S Croy 4C 138
Montague Clo. SE1 2B 76
Montague Clo. W on T 2F 116
Montague Ct. Sidc 9E 96
Montague Gdns. W3 1L 71
Montague Hall Pl. Bush 8L 9
Montague Ho. E16 2F 78
(off Wesley Av.)
Montague Pas. Uxb 3B 142
Montague Pl. WC1 8H 59
Montague Pl. Swan 8D 114
Montague Rd. E8 1E 60
Montague Rd. E11 7D 46
Montague Rd. N8 3K 43
Montague Rd. N15 2E 44
Montague Rd. SW19 4M 105
Montague Rd. W7 2D 70
Montague Rd. W13 9F 54
Montague Rd. Croy 3M 123
Montague Rd. Houn 2M 85
Montague Rd. Rich 5J 87
Montague Rd. S'hall 5J 69
Montague Rd. Uxb 3B 142
Montague Sq. SE15 8G 77
Montague St. EC1 8A 60
Montague St. WC1 8J 59
Montague Ter. Brom 8D 110
Montague Waye. S'hall 4J 69
Montagu Gdns. N18 4F 28
Montagu Gdns. Wall 6G 123
Montagu Mans. W1 8D 58
Montagu M. N. W1 8D 58
Montagu M. S. W1 9D 58
Montagu M. W. W1 9D 58
Montagu Pl. W1 8D 58
Montagu Rd. N18 & N9 5F 28
Montagu Rd. NW4 4E 40
Montagu Rd. Ind. Est. N18 4G 29
Montagu Row. W1 8D 58
Montagu Sq. W1 8D 58
Montagu St. W1 9D 58
Montalt Rd. Wfd G 4D 30
Montana Clo. S Croy 2B 138
Montana Gdns. SE26 2K 109
Montana Gdns. Sutt 7A 122
Montana Rd. SW17 9E 90
Montana Rd. SW20 5G 105
Montayne Rd. Chesh 5D 6
Montbelle Rd. SE9 9M 95
Montbretia Clo. Orp 8G 113
Montcalm Clo. Brom 1E 126
Montcalm Clo. Hay 6F 52
Montcalm Ho. E14 5K 77
Montcalm Rd. SE7 8H 79
Montclare St. E2 7D 60
Monteagle Av. Bark 2A 64
Monteagle Ct. N1 5C 60
Monteagle Way. E5 8E 44
Monteagle Way. SE15 2F 92
Montefiore St. SW8 1F 90
Montego Clo. SE24 3L 91
Montem Rd. SE23 6K 93
Montem Rd. N Mald 8C 104
Montem St. N4 6K 43
Montenotte Rd. N8 3G 43
Monterey Clo. Bex 8A 98
Monterey Pl. Shop. Cen. NW7 5C 24
Montesole Ct. Pinn 9G 21
Montesquieu Ter. E16 9D 62
(off Clarkson Rd.)
Montevetro. SW11 9B 74
Montford Pl. SE11 6L 75
Montford Rd. Sun 8E 100
Montfort Gdns. Ilf 6A 32
Montfort Ho. E2 6G 61
(off Victoria Pk. Sq.)
Montfort Ho. E14 4A 78
(off Galbraith St.)
Montfort Pl. SW19 7H 89
Montgolfier Wlk. N'holt 6J 53
Montgomery Av. Esh 4C 118
Montgomery Clo. Mitc 8J 107
Montgomery Clo. Sidc 5D 96
Montgomery Ct. S Croy 7C 124
(off Birdhurst Rd.)
Montgomery Cres. Romf 5G 35
Montgomery Dri. Chesh 1E 6
Montgomery Lodge. E1 7G 61
(off Cleveland Gro.)
Montgomery Rd. W4 5A 72
Montgomery Rd. Edgw 6K 23
Montholme Rd. SW11 5D 90
Monthope Rd. E1 8E 60
Montolieu Gdns. SW15 4F 88
Montpelier Av. W5 8G 55
Montpelier Av. Bex 6H 97
Montpelier Clo. Uxb 4E 142
Montpelier Ct. W5 8H 55
Montpelier Ct. Brom 8D 110
(off Westmoreland Rd.)
Montpelier Gdns. E6 6H 63
Montpelier Gdns. Romf 5G 49
Montpelier Gro. NW5 1G 59
Montpelier M. SW7 4C 74
Montpelier Pl. E1 9G 61
Montpelier Pl. SW7 4C 74
Montpelier Ri. NW11 5J 41
Montpelier Ri. Wemb 6H 39
Montpelier Rd. N3 8A 26
Montpelier Rd. SE15 9F 76
Montpelier Rd. W5 8H 55
Montpelier Rd. Purl 2M 137
Montpelier Rd. Sutt 6A 122
Montpelier Row. SE3 1D 94
Montpelier Row. Twic 6G 87
Montpelier Sq. SW7 3C 74
Montpelier St. SW7 4C 74
Montpelier Ter. SW7 3C 74
Montpelier Va. SE3 1D 94
Montpelier Wlk. SW7 4C 74
Montpelier Way. NW11 5J 41
Montpellier Ho. Chig 5A 32
Montrave Rd. SE20 3G 109
Montreal Pl. WC2 1K 75
Montreal Rd. Ilf 5A 48
Montrell Rd. SW2 7J 91
Montrose Av. NW6 5J 57
Montrose Av. Edgw 9A 24
Montrose Av. Romf 9G 35
Montrose Av. Sidc 6E 96
Montrose Av. Twic 6M 85
Montrose Av. Well 2B 96
Montrose Clo. Ashf 3A 100
Montrose Clo. Well 2D 96
Montrose Clo. Wfd G 4E 30
Montrose Ct. NW9 9A 24
Montrose Ct. NW11 2K 41
Montrose Ct. SE6 7D 94
Montrose Ct. SW7 3B 74
Montrose Ct. Harr 3M 37
Montrose Cres. N12 6A 26
Montrose Cres. Wemb 2J 55
Montrose Gdns. Mitc 6D 106
Montrose Gdns. Oxs 4B 132
Montrose Gdns. Sutt 4M 121
Montrose Ho. E14 4L 77
Montrose Pl. SW1 3E 74
Montrose Rd. Felt 5B 84
Montrose Rd. Harr 9C 22
Montrose Ter. W Dray 1H 143
(off Trout Rd.)
Montrose Wlk. Stan 6F 22
Montrose Way. SE23 7H 93
Montrouge Cres. Eps 8G 135
Montserrat Av. Wfd G 7B 30
Montserrat Clo. SE19 2B 108
Montserrat Rd. SW15 3J 89
Monument Gdns. SE13 4A 94
Monument Hill. Wey 6A 116
Monument Rd. Wey 6A 116
Monument St. EC3 1B 76
Monument, The. 1B 76
(off Monument St.)
Monument Way. N17 1D 44
Monza St. E1 1G 77
Moodkee St. SE16 4G 77
Moody Rd. SE15 9D 76
Moody St. E1 6H 61
Moon Ct. SE12 3E 94
Moon La. Barn 5K 13
Moon St. N1 4M 59
Moorcroft. Edgw 8M 23
Moorcroft Gdns. Brom 9J 111
Moorcroft La. Uxb 8E 142
Moorcroft Rd. SW16 9J 91
Moorcroft Way. Pinn 3J 37
Moordown. SE18 8M 79
Moore Clo. SW14 2A 88
Moore Clo. Mitc 6F 106
Moore Clo. Wall 9J 123
Moore Ct. N1 4M 59
(off Gaskin St.)
Moore Cres. Dag 4F 64
Moorehead Way. SE3 2E 94
Moore Ho. E1 1G 77
(off Cable St.)
Moore Ho. E2 6G 61
(off Roman Rd.)
Moore Ho. N8 2J 43
(off Pembroke Rd.)
Moore Ho. SE10 6D 78
(off Armitage Rd.)
Moore Ho. Horn 4E 50
(off Globe Rd.)
Mooreland Rd. Brom 4D 110
Moore Pk. Ct. SW6 8M 73
(off Fulham Rd.)
Moore Pk. Rd. SW6 8L 73
Moore Rd. SE19 3A 108
Moore St. SW3 5D 74
Moore Wlk. E7 9E 46
Moore Way. Sutt 1L 135
Moorey Clo. E15 4D 62
Moorfield Av. W5 7H 55
Moorfield Rd. N17 9D 28
Moorfield Rd. Chess 7J 119
Moorfield Rd. Enf 3G 17
Moorfield Rd. Orp 2E 128
Moorfield Rd. Uxb 9B 142
Moorfields. EC2 8B 60
Moorfields Highwalk. EC2 8B 60
(off Moor La., in two parts)
Moorgate. EC2 9B 60
Moorgate Pl. EC2 9B 60
(off Swan All.)
Moorgreen Ho. EC1 6M 59
(off Spencer St.)
Moorhen Clo. Eri 8F 82
Moorhouse. NW9 8D 24
Moorhouse Rd. W2 9L 57
Moorhouse Rd. Harr 1H 39
Moorings, The. E16 8G 63
(off Prince Regent La.)
Moor Junction (Junct.) 8G 143
Moorland Clo. Romf 7M 33
Moorland Clo. Twic 6L 85
Moorland M. N1 3L 59
Moorland Rd. SW9 3M 91
Moorland Rd. W Dray 7G 143
Moorlands. N'holt 4J 53
Moorlands Av. NW7 6F 24
Moor La. EC2 8B 60
(in two parts)
Moor La. Chess 6J 119
Moor La. Rick 1A 20
Moor La. W Dray 7G 143
Moor La. Crossing. Wat 9A 8
Moormead Dri. Eps 7C 120
Moor Mead Rd. Twic 5E 86
Moor Park. 3A 20
Moor Pk. Gdns. King T 4C 104
Moor Pk. Golf Course. 2A 20
Moor Pk. Ind. Cen. Wat 9A 8
Moor Pk. Rd. N'wd 5B 20
Moor Pl. EC2 8B 60
Moorside Rd. Brom 9C 94
Moorsom Way. Coul 9H 137
Moor St. W1 9H 59
Moortown Rd. Wat 4G 21
Moor Vw. Wat 9E 8
Moot Ct. NW9 3L 39
Moran Clo. Brick W 4K 5
Moran Ho. E1 2F 76
(off Wapping La.)
Morant Gdns. Romf 5M 33
Morant Pl. N22 8K 27
Morant St. E14 1L 77
Mora Rd. NW2 9G 41
Mora St. EC1 6A 60
Morat St. SW9 9K 75
Moravian Clo. SW10 7B 74
Moravian Pl. SW10 7B 74
Moravian St. E2 5G 61
Moray Av. Hay 2D 68
Moray Clo. Edgw 2M 23
Moray Clo. Romf 7C 34
Moray Ct. S Croy 7A 124
(off Warham Rd.)
Moray Ho. E1 7J 61
(off Harford St.)
Moray M. N7 7K 43
Moray Rd. N4 7K 43
Moray Way. Romf 7B 34
Mordaunt Gdns. Dag 3J 65
Mordaunt Ho. NW10 4B 56
Mordaunt Rd. NW10 4B 56
Mordaunt St. SW9 2K 91
Morden. 7M 105
Morden Ct. Mord 8M 105
Morden Ct. Pde. Mord 8M 105
Morden Gdns. Gnfd 1D 54
Morden Gdns. Mitc 8B 106
Morden Hall Rd. Mord 7M 105
Morden Hill. SE13 1A 94
(in two parts)
Morden La. SE13 9A 78
Morden Park. 1J 121
Morden Rd. SE3 1E 94
Morden Rd. SW19 5M 105
Morden Rd. Mord & Mitc 8A 106
Morden Rd. Romf 5J 49
Morden Rd. M. SE3 1E 94
Morden St. SE13 9M 77
Morden Way. Sutt 2L 121
Morden Wharf. SE10 4C 78
(off Morden Wharf Rd.)
Morden Wharf Rd. SE10 4C 78
Mordern Ho. NW1 7C 58
(off Harewood Av.)
Mordon Rd. Ilf 5D 48
Mordred Rd. SE6 8C 94
Morecambe Clo. E1 8H 61
Morecambe Clo. Horn 1F 66
Morecambe Gdns. Stan 4H 23
Morecambe Ho. Romf 5J 35
(off Chudleigh Rd.)
Morecambe St. SE17 5A 76
Morecambe Ter. N18 4B 28
(off Gt. Cambridge Rd.)
More Clo. E16 9D 62
More Clo. W14 5H 73
More Clo. Purl 3L 137
Morecoombe Clo. King T 4M 103
Moree Way. N18 4E 28
Moreland Ct. NW2 8L 41
Moreland St. EC1 6M 59
Moreland Way. E4 3M 29
More La. Esh 5M 117
Morella Rd. SW12 6D 90
Morello Av. Uxb 8F 142
Morello Clo. Swan 8B 114
Moremead. Wal A 6K 7
Moremead Rd. SE6 1K 109
Morena St. SE6 6M 93
Moresby Av. Surb 2M 119
Moresby Rd. E5 6F 44
Moresby Wlk. SW8 1G 91
More's Garden. SW3 7B 74
(off Cheyne Wlk.)
Moretaine Rd. Ashf 9B 144
Moreton Av. Iswth 9C 70
Moreton Clo. E5 7F 44
Moreton Clo. N15 4B 44
Moreton Clo. NW7 6G 25
Moreton Clo. SW1 6G 75
(off Moreton Ter.)
Moreton Clo. Chesh 1B 6
Moreton Clo. Swan 6C 114
Moreton Ct. Dart 2D 98
Moreton Gdns. Wfd G 5J 31
Moreton Ho. SE16 4F 76
Moreton Ind. Est. Swan 8F 114
Moreton Pl. SW1 6G 75
Moreton Rd. N15 4B 44
Moreton Rd. S Croy 7B 124
Moreton Rd. Wor Pk 4E 120
Moreton St. SW1 6G 75
Moreton Ter. SW1 6G 75
Moreton Ter. M. N. SW1 6G 75
Moreton Ter. M. S. SW1 6G 75
Moreton Tower. W3 2M 71
Morford Clo. Ruis 5F 36
Morford Way. Ruis 5F 36
Morgan Av. E17 2B 46
Morgan Clo. Dag 3L 65
Morgan Clo. N'wd 6D 20
Morgan Ct. Cars 6D 122
Morgan Gdns. A'ham 2M 9
Morgan Ho. SW1 5G 75
(off Vauxhall Bri. Rd.)
Morgan Ho. SW8 9G 75
(off Wadhurst Rd.)
Morgan Mans. N7 1L 59
(off Morgan Rd.)
Morgan Rd. N7 1L 59
Morgan Rd. W10 8K 57
Morgan Rd. Brom 4E 110
Morgan Rd. Tedd 3C 102
Morgan's La. SE1 2C 76
Morgan's La. Hay 8B 52
Morgan St. E3 6J 61
Morgan St. E16 8D 62
Morgan Wlk. Beck 8M 109
Morgan Way. Rain 6G 67
Morgan Way. Wfd G 6J 31
Moriatry Clo. N7 9J 43
Morie St. SW18 4M 89
Morieux Rd. E10 6K 45
Moring Rd. SW17 1E 106
Morkyns Wlk. SE21 9C 92
Morland Av. Croy 3C 124
Morland Av. Dart 4F 98
Morland Clo. NW11 6M 41
Morland Clo. Hamp 2K 101
Morland Clo. Mitc 7C 106
Morland Ct. W12 3F 72
(off Coningham Rd.)
Morland Est. E8 3E 60
Morland Gdns. NW10 3B 56
Morland Gdns. S'hall 2M 69
Morland Ho. NW1 5G 59
(off Cranleigh St.)
Morland Ho. NW6 4L 57
Morland Ho. SW1 5J 75
(off Marsham St.)
Morland Ho. W11 9J 57
(off Lancaster Rd.)
Morland Rd. E17 3H 45
Morland Rd. SE20 3H 109
Morland Rd. Croy 3C 124
Morland Rd. Dag 3L 65
Morland Rd. Harr 3J 39
Morland Rd. Ilf 7M 47
Morland Rd. Sutt 7A 122
Morland Way. Chesh 1E 6
Morley Av. E4 7B 30
Morley Av. N18 4E 28
Morley Av. N22 9L 27
Morley Clo. Orp 4M 127
Morley Ct. E4 5K 29
Morley Ct. Brom 8D 110
Morley Cres. Edgw 2A 24
Morley Cres. Ruis 7G 37
Morley Cres. E. Stan 9G 23
Morley Cres. W. Stan 1G 39
Morley Hill. Enf 2B 16
Morley Ho. N16 7E 44
Morley Rd. E10 6A 46
Morley Rd. E15 5D 62
Morley Rd. SE13 3A 94
Morley Rd. Bark 4B 64
Morley Rd. Chst 5A 112
Morley Rd. Romf 3J 49
Morley Rd. S Croy 2D 138
Morley Rd. Sutt 3K 121
Morley Rd. Twic 5H 87
Morley St. SE1 4L 75
Morna Rd. SE5 1A 92
Morning La. E9 2G 61
Morningside Rd. Wor Pk 4F 120
Mornington Av. W14 5K 73
Mornington Av. Brom 7G 111
Mornington Av. Ilf 5L 47
Mornington Clo. Big H 9H 141
Mornington Clo. Wfd G 4E 30
Mornington Ct. NW1 5G 59
(off Mornington Cres.)
Mornington Ct. Bex 7B 98
Mornington Cres. NW1 5G 59
Mornington Cres. Houn 9F 68
Mornington Gro. E3 6L 61
Mornington M. SE5 9A 76
Mornington Pl. NW1 5G 59
Mornington Pl. SE8 8K 77
(off Mornington Rd.)
Mornington Rd. E4 9B 18
Mornington Rd. E11 5D 46
(in two parts)
Mornington Rd. SE8 8K 77
Mornington Rd. Ashf 2A 100
Mornington Rd. Gnfd 8M 53
Mornington Rd. Lou 5M 19
Mornington Rd. Wfd G 4D 30
Mornington St. NW1 5F 58
Mornington Ter. NW1 4F 58
Mornington Wlk. Rich 1G 103
Morocco St. SE1 3C 76
Morpeth Av. Borwd 2K 11
Morpeth Gro. E9 4H 61
Morpeth Mans. SW1 5G 75
(off Morpeth Ter.)
Morpeth Rd. E9 4H 61
Morpeth St. E2 6G 61
Morpeth Ter. SW1 4G 75
Morpeth Wlk. N17 7F 28
Morrab Gdns. Ilf 8D 48
Morrel Ct. E2 5E 60
(off Goldsmiths Row)
Morrell Clo. New Bar 5A 14
Morris Av. E12 1K 63
Morris Blitz Ct. N16 9D 44
Morris Clo. Croy 9J 109
Morris Clo. Orp 5C 128
Morris Ct. E4 3M 29
Morris Ct. Wal A 7M 7
Morris Gdns. SW18 6L 89
Morris Gdns. Dart 4L 99
Morris Ho. E2 6G 61
(off Roman Rd.)
Morris Ho. NW8 7C 58
(off Salisbury St.)
Morrish Rd. SW2 6J 91
Morrison Av. E4 6L 29
Morrison Av. N17 1C 44
Morrison Bldgs. N. E1 9E 60
(off Commercial Rd.)
Morrison Bldgs. S. E1 9E 60
(off Commercial Rd.)
Morrison Ct. Barn 6J 13
(off Manor Way)
Morrison Rd. Bark 5J 65
Morrison Rd. Hay 6F 52
Morrison St. SW11 2E 90
Morris Pl. N4 7L 43
Morris Rd. E14 8M 61
Morris Rd. E15 9C 46
Morris Rd. Dag 7K 49
Morris Rd. Iswth 2D 86
Morris Rd. Romf 7F 34
Morriss Ho. SE16 3F 76
(off Cherry Garden St.)
Morris St. E1 9F 60
Morriston Clo. Wat 5G 21
Morritt Ho. Wemb 1H 55
(off Talbot Rd.)
Morse Clo. E13 6E 62
Morshead Mans. W9 6L 57
(off Morshead Rd.)
Morshead Rd. W9 6L 57
Morson Rd. Enf 8J 17
Morston Gdns. SE9 1K 111
Mortain Ho. SE16 5F 76
(off Roseberry St.)
Morten Clo. SW4 5H 91
Morteyne Rd. N17 8B 28
Mortgramit Sq. SE18 4L 7
Mortham St. E15 4C 62
Mortimer Clo. NW2 7K 4
Mortimer Clo. SW16 8H 9
Mortimer Clo. Bush 8M
Mortimer Ct. NW8 5A 5
(off Abbey Rd
Mortimer Cres. NW6 4M 5
Mortimer Cres. Wor Pk 5B 12
Mortimer Dri. Enf 8B 1
Mortimer Est. NW6 4M 5
(off Mortimer P
Mortimer Ho. W11 2H 7

Mortimer Ho.—Mutrix Rd.

Mortimer Ho. W14 . . . . *5J* ***73***
(off N. End Rd.)
Mortimer Mkt. *WC1* 7G **59**
Mortimer Mkt. Cen. WC1 . . . . *7G* ***59***
(off Mortimer Mkt.)
Mortimer Pl. *NW6* 4M **57**
Mortimer Rd. *E6* 6K **63**
Mortimer Rd. *N1* 3C **60**
(in two parts)
Mortimer Rd. *NW10* 6G **57**
Mortimer Rd. *W13* 9G **55**
Mortimer Rd. *Big H* 4G **141**
Mortimer Rd. *Eri* 7B **82**
Mortimer Rd. *Mitc* 5D **106**
Mortimer Rd. *Orp* 3E **128**
Mortimer Sq. *W11* 1H **73**
Mortimer St. *W1* 9G **59**
Mortimer Ter. *NW5* 9F **42**
Mortlake. 2B 88
Mortlake Clo. *Croy* 5J **123**
Mortlake Crematorium.
Rich 1A **88**
Mortlake Dri. *Mitc* 5C **106**
Mortlake High St. *SW14* . . . 2B **88**
Mortlake Rd. *E16* 9F **62**
Mortlake Rd. *Ilf* 9A **48**
Mortlake Rd. *Rich* 8L **71**
Mortlake Ter. Rich *8L* ***71***
(off Mortlake Rd.)
Mortlock Clo. *SE15* 9F **76**
Mortlock Ct. *E7* 9H **47**
Morton Clo. *Wall* 9K **123**
Morton Ct. *N'holt* 1A **54**
Morton Cres. *N14* 4H **27**
Morton Gdns. *Wall* 7G **123**
Morton M. *SW5* 5M **73**
Morton Pl. *SE1* 4L **75**
Morton Rd. *E15* 3D **62**
Morton Rd. *N1* 3A **60**
Morton Rd. *Mord* 9B **106**
Morton Way. *N14* 3G **27**
Morvale Clo. *Belv* 5K **81**
Morval Rd. *SW2* 4L **91**
Morven Rd. *SW17* 9D **90**
Morville St. *E3* 5L **61**
Morwell St. *WC1* 8H **59**
Moscow Pl. *W2* 1M **73**
Moscow Rd. *W2* 1L **73**
Mosedale. NW1 . . . . *6G* ***59***
(off Cumberland Mkt.)
Moselle Av. *N22* 9L **27**
Moselle Clo. *N8* 1K **43**
Moselle Ho. N17 . . . . *7D* ***28***
(off William St.)
Moselle Pl. *N17* 7D **28**
Moselle Rd. *Big H* 9J **141**
Moselle St. *N17* 7D **28**
Mospey Cres. *Eps* 7D **134**
Mossborough Clo. *N12* 6M **25**
Mossbury Rd. *SW11* 2C **90**
Moss Clo. *E1* 8E **60**
Moss Clo. *Pinn* 9K **21**
Mossdown Clo. *Belv* 5L **81**
Mossford Ct. *Ilf* 9M **31**
Mossford Grn. *Ilf* 1M **47**
Mossford La. *Ilf* 9M **31**
Mossford St. *E3* 7K **61**
Moss Gdns. *Felt* 8E **84**
Moss Gdns. *S Croy* 9H **125**
Moss Hall Ct. *N12* 6M **25**
Moss Hall Cres. *N12* 6M **25**
Moss Hall Gro. *N12* 6M **25**
Mossington Gdns. *SE16* 5G **77**
Moss La. *Pinn* 8J **21**
Moss La. *Romf* 4D **50**
Mosslea Rd. *SE20* 3G **109**
(in two parts)
Mosslea Rd. *Brom* 9H **111**
Mosslea Rd. *Orp* 5A **128**
Mosslea Rd. *Whyt* 8D **138**
Mossop St. *SW3* 5C **74**
Moss Rd. *Dag* 3L **65**
Moss Rd. *Wat* 7F **4**
Moss Side. *Brick W* 3K **5**
Mossville Gdns. *Mord* 7K **105**
Mosswell Ho. *N10* 8E **26**
Moston Clo. *Hay* 6D **68**
Mostyn Av. *Wemb* 1K **55**
Mostyn Gdns. *NW10* 6H **57**
Mostyn Gro. *E3* 5L **61**
Mostyn Rd. *SW9* 9L **75**
Mostyn Rd. *SW19* 5K **105**
Mostyn Rd. *Bush* 7A **10**
Mostyn Rd. *Edgw* 7C **24**
Mosul Way. *Brom* 1J **127**
Mosyer Dri. *Orp* 4H **129**
Mota M. *N3* 8L **25**
Motcomb St. *SW1* 4E **74**
Moth Clo. *Wall* 9J **123**
Mothers Sq. *E5* 9F **44**
Motley Av. EC2 . . . . *7C* ***60***
(off Christina St.)
Motley St. *SW8* 1G **91**
Motspur Park. 1E 120
Motspur Pk. *N Mald* 1D **120**
Mottingham. 8J 95
Mottingham Gdns. *SE9* 7H **95**
Mottingham La. *SE9* 7G **95**
Mottingham Rd. *N9* 8H **17**
Mottingham Rd. *SE9* 8J **95**
Mottisfont Rd. *SE2* 4E **80**
Mott St. *E4* 2B **18**
Mouchotte Clo. *Big H* 4F **140**
Moules Ct. *SE5* 8A **76**
Moulins Rd. *E9* 3G **61**
Moulsford Ho. *N7* 1H **59**
Moultain Hill. *Swan* 8E **114**
Moulton Av. *Houn* 1J **85**
Moundfield Rd. *N16* 4E **44**
Mound, The. *SE9* 9L **95**
Mounsey Ho. W10 . . . . *6J* ***57***
(off Third Av.)
Mountacre Clo. *SE26* 1D **108**
Mt. Adon Pk. *SE22* 6E **92**
Montague Pl. *E14* 1A **78**
Mountain Ho. *SE11* 5K **75**
Mt. Angelus Rd. *SW15* 6D **88**
Mt. Ararat Rd. *Rich* 4J **87**
Mount Arlington. Brom *6C* ***110***
(off Pk. Hill Rd.)
Mt. Ash Rd. *SE26* 9F **92**
Mount Av. *E4* 3L **29**
Mount Av. *W5* 8G **55**
Mount Av. *Romf* 6M **35**
Mount Av. *S'hall* 9L **53**
Mountbatten Clo. *SE18* 7C **80**
Mountbatten Clo. *SE19* 2C **108**
Mountbatten Ct. SE16 . . . . . *2G* ***77***
(off Rotherhithe St.)
Mountbatten Ct. *Buck H* 2H **31**
Mountbatten Gdns. *Beck* . . . 8J **109**
Mountbatten Ho. N6 . . . . *5E* ***42***
(off Hillcrest)
Mountbatten Ho. *N'wd* 6C **20**
Mountbatten M. *SW18* 6A **90**
Mountbel Rd. *Stan* 8E **22**
Mt. Carmel Chambers.
W8 . . . . *3L* ***73***
(off Dukes La.)
Mount Clo. *W5* 8G **55**
Mount Clo. *Brom* 5J **111**
Mount Clo. *Cars* 1E **136**
Mount Clo. *Cockf* 6E **14**
Mount Clo. *Kenl* 8B **138**
Mountcombe Clo. *Surb* 2J **119**
Mount Ct. *SW15* 2J **89**
Mount Ct. *W Wick* 4C **126**
Mt. Culver Av. *Sidc* 3H **113**
Mount Dri. *Bexh* 4J **97**
Mount Dri. *Harr* 3K **37**
Mount Dri. *Wemb* 7A **40**
Mountearl Gdns. *SW16* 9K **91**
Mt. Eaton Ct. W5 . . . . *8G* ***55***
(off Mount Av.)
Mt. Echo Av. *E4* 2M **29**
Mt. Echo Dri. *E4* 1M **29**
Mt. Ephraim La. *SW16* 9H **91**
Mt. Ephraim Rd. *SW16* 9H **91**
Mount Felix. *W on T* 3D **116**
Mountfield Clo. *SE6* 6B **94**
Mountfield Rd. *E6* 5L **63**
Mountfield Rd. *N3* 1K **41**
Mountfield Rd. *W5* 9H **55**
Mountfield Way. *Orp* 8G **113**
Mountford Rd. *E8* 1E **60**
Mountford St. *E1* 9E **60**
Mountfort Cres. *N1* 3L **59**
Mountfort Ter. *N1* 3L **59**
Mount Gdns. *SE26* 9F **92**
Mount Gro. *Edgw* 3A **24**
Mountgrove Rd. *N5* 8M **43**
Mounthurst Rd. *Brom* 2D **126**
Mountington Pk. Clo.
Harr 4H **39**
Mountjoy Clo. EC2 . . . . *8A* ***60***
(off Thomas More Highwalk)
Mountjoy Clo. *SE2* 3F **80**
Mountjoy Ho. EC2 . . . . *8A* ***60***
(off Beech St.)
Mount Lodge. *N6* 4G **43**
Mount M. *Hamp* 5M **101**
Mount Mills. *EC1* 6M **59**
Mt. Nod Rd. *SW16* 9K **91**
Mt. Olive Ct. *W7* 3C **70**
Mount Pde. *Barn* 6C **14**
Mount Pk. *Cars* 9E **122**
Mt. Park Av. *Harr* 7B **38**
Mt. Park Av. *S Croy* 1M **137**
Mt. Park Cres. *W5* 9H **55**
Mt. Park Rd. *W5* 8H **55**
Mount Pk. Rd. *Harr* 8B **38**
Mount Pk. Rd. *Pinn* 3E **36**
Mount Pl. *W3* 2M **71**
Mount Pleasant. N14 . . . . . . *9H* ***15***
(off Wells, The)
Mount Pleasant. *SE27* 1A **108**
Mount Pleasant. *WC1* 7L **59**
Mount Pleasant. *Barn* 6C **14**
Mount Pleasant. *Big H* 9H **141**
Mount Pleasant. *Eps* 2D **134**
Mount Pleasant. *Ilf* 1A **64**
Mount Pleasant. *Ruis* 7G **37**
Mount Pleasant. *Wemb* 4J **55**
Mt. Pleasant Cres. *N4* 6K **43**
Mt. Pleasant Hill. *E5* 7F **44**
Mt. Pleasant La. *E5* 6F **44**
Mt. Pleasant La. *Brick W* 3J **5**
Mt. Pleasant Pl. *SE18* 5B **80**
Mt. Pleasant Rd. *E17* 9J **29**
Mt. Pleasant Rd. *N17* 9C **28**
Mt. Pleasant Rd. *NW10* 3G **57**
Mt. Pleasant Rd. *SE13* 5M **93**
Mt. Pleasant Rd. *W5* 7G **55**
Mt. Pleasant Rd. *Chig* 4B **32**
Mt. Pleasant Rd. *Dart* 5K **99**
Mt. Pleasant Rd. *N Mald* . . . 7A **104**
Mt. Pleasant Rd. *Romf* 6B **34**
Mt. Pleasant Vs. *N4* 5K **43**
Mt. Pleasant Wlk. *Bex* 4A **98**
Mount Rd. *NW2* 8F **40**
Mount Rd. *NW4* 4E **40**
Mount Rd. *SW19* 8L **89**
Mount Rd. *Barn* 7C **14**
Mount Rd. *Chess* 7K **119**
Mount Rd. *Dag* 6K **49**
Mount Rd. *Dart* 5D **98**
Mount Rd. *Felt* 9J **85**
Mount Rd. *Hay* 3E **68**
Mount Rd. *Mitc* 6B **106**
Mount Rd. *N Mald* 7B **104**
Mount Row. *W1* 1F **74**
Mountsfield Ct. *SE13* 5B **94**
Mountside. *Stan* 8D **22**
Mounts Pond Rd. *SE3* 1B **94**
(in two parts)
Mount Sq., The. *NW3* 8A **42**
Mounts Rd. *Bexh* 4H **97**
Mt. Stewart Av. *Harr* 5H **39**
Mount St. *W1* 1E **74**
Mount St. M. *W1* 1F **74**
Mount Ter. *E1* 8F **60**
Mount, The. *E5* 7F **44**
(in two parts)
Mount, The. *N20* 2A **26**
Mount, The. *NW3* 8A **42**
Mount, The. *W3* 2A **72**
Mount, The. *Bexh* 4M **97**
Mount, The. *Coul* 7E **136**
Mount, The. *Eps* 2D **134**
Mount, The. *Esh* 8L **117**
Mount, The. *N Mald* 7D **104**
Mount, The. *N'holt* 1M **53**
Mount, The. *Romf* 3G **35**
Mount, The. S Croy *7A* ***124***
(off Warham Rd.)
Mount, The. *Wemb* 7M **39**
Mount, The. *Wey* 4C **116**
Mount, The. *Wor Pk* 6F **120**
Mount Vernon. *NW3* 9A **42**
Mount Vw. *NW7* 3B **24**
Mount Vw. *W5* 7H **55**
Mount Vw. *Enf* 2K **15**
Mount Vw. *N'wd* 6D **20**
Mount Vw. *S'hall* 5H **69**
Mountview Clo. *NW11* 6M **41**
Mountview Ct. *N8* 2M **43**
Mount Vw. Rd. *E4* 9B **18**
Mount Vw. Rd. *N4* 5J **43**
Mount Vw. Rd. *NW9* 3B **40**
Mount Vw. Rd. *Clay* 9F **118**
Mountview Rd. *Orp* 2E **128**
(in two parts)
Mount Vs. *SE27* 9M **91**
Mount Way. *Cars* 1E **136**
Mount Wood. *W Mol* 7M **101**
Mountwood Clo. *S Croy* . . . 2F **138**
Movers Lane (Junct.) **5C 64**
Movers La. *Bark* 4B **64**
Mowat Ct. Wor Pk *4D* ***120***
(off Avenue, The)
Mowat Ind. Est. Wat *1G* ***9***
(off Sandown Rd.)
Mowatt Clo. *N19* 7H **43**
Mowbray Ct. *N22* 8L **27**
Mowbray Ct. *SE19* 4D **108**
Mowbray Gdns. *N'holt* 4L **53**
Mowbray Ho. N2 . . . . *9B* ***26***
(off Grange, The)
Mowbray Pde. *Edgw* 4L **23**
Mowbray Pde. *N'holt* 4L **53**
Mowbray Rd. *NW6* 3J **57**
Mowbray Rd. *SE19* 5D **108**
Mowbray Rd. *Edgw* 4L **23**
Mowbray Rd. *New Bar* 7A **14**
Mowbray Rd. *Rich* 9G **87**
Mowbrays Clo. *Romf* 8A **34**
Mowbrays Rd. *Romf* 9A **34**
Mowlem St. *E2* 5F **60**
Mowlem Trad. Est. *N17* 7G **29**
Mowll St. *SW9* 8L **75**
Moxom Av. *Chesh* 3E **6**
Moxon Clo. *E13* 5D **62**
Moxon St. *W1* 8E **58**
Moxon St. *Barn* 5K **13**
Moye Clo. *E2* 5E **60**
Moyers Rd. *E10* 5A **46**
Moylan Rd. *W6* 7J **73**
Moyle Ho. SW1 . . . . *6G* ***75***
(off Churchill Gdns.)
Moyne Ho. *SW9* 4M **91**
Moyne Pl. *NW10* 5L **55**
Moynihan Dri. *N21* 7J **15**
Moys Clo. *Croy* 1J **123**
Moyser Rd. *SW16* 2F **106**
Mozart St. *W10* 6K **57**
Mozart Ter. *SW1* 5E **74**
Muchelney Rd. *Mord* 1A **122**
Mudlands Ind. Est. *Rain* 6C **66**
Mudlarks Way.
SE10 & SE7 . . . . 4D **78**
(in two parts)
Muggeridge Clo. *S Croy* . . . 7B **124**
Muggeridge Rd. *Dag* 9M **49**
Muirdown Av. *SW14* 3B **88**
Muir Dri. *SW18* 5C **90**
Muirfield. *W3* 9C **56**
Muirfield Clo. *SE16* 6F **76**
Muirfield Clo. *Wat* 5G **21**
Muirfield Cres. *E14* 4M **77**
Muirfield Grn. *Wat* 4F **20**
Muirfield Rd. *Wat* 4F **20**
Muirkirk Rd. *SE6* 7A **94**
Muir Rd. *E5* 9E **44**
Muir St. *E16* 2J **79**
(in two parts)
Mulberry Av. *Stai* 7C **144**
Mulberry Bus. Cen. *SE16* . . . 3H **77**
Mulberry Clo. *E4* 2L **29**
Mulberry Clo. *N8* 3J **43**
Mulberry Clo. *NW3* 9B **42**
Mulberry Clo. *NW4* 1G **41**
Mulberry Clo. *SE7* 7H **79**
Mulberry Clo. *SE22* 4E **92**
Mulberry Clo. *SW3* 7B **74**
Mulberry Clo. *SW16* 1G **107**
Mulberry Clo. *Barn* 6B **14**
Mulberry Clo. *N'holt* 5J **53**
Mulberry Clo. *Park* 1M **5**
Mulberry Clo. *Romf* 2G **51**
Mulberry Clo. *Wat* 9B **4**
Mulberry Clo. *Wey* 5A **116**
Mulberry Ct. EC1 . . . . *6M* ***59***
(off Tompion St.)
Mulberry Ct. *Bark* 3D **64**
Mulberry Ct. *Surb* 2H **119**
Mulberry Ct. *Twic* 9D **86**
Mulberry Cres. *Bren* 8F **70**
Mulberry Cres. *W Dray* 3L **143**
Mulberry Dri. *Purf* 5K **83**
Mulberry Ho. E2 . . . . *6G* ***61***
(off Victoria Pk. Sq.)
Mulberry Ho. *SE8* 7K **77**
Mulberry Ho. *Short* 5C **110**
Mulberry Housing Co-operative.
SE1 . . . . *2L* ***75***
(off Upper Rd.)
Mulberry La. *Croy* 3D **124**
Mulberry Lodge. Wat *8H* ***9***
(off Eastbury Rd.)
Mulberry M. *SE14* 9K **77**
Mulberry M. *Wall* 8G **123**
Mulberry Pde. *W Dray* 4L **143**
Mulberry Pl. E14 . . . . *1A* ***78***
(off Clove Cres.)
Mulberry Pl. *W6* 6E **72**
Mulberry Rd. *E8* 3D **60**
Mulberry St. *E1* 9E **60**
Mulberry Trees. *Shep* 2B **116**
Mulberry Wlk. *SW3* 7B **74**
Mulberry Way. *E18* 9F **30**
Mulberry Way. *Belv* 3A **82**
Mulberry Way. *Ilf* 2A **48**
Mulgrave Ct. Sutt *8M* ***121***
(off Mulgrave Rd.)
Mulgrave Rd. *NW10* 9D **40**
Mulgrave Rd. *SE18* 5K **79**
Mulgrave Rd. *SW6* 7K **73**
Mulgrave Rd. *W5* 6H **55**
Mulgrave Rd. *Croy* 5B **124**
Mulgrave Rd. *Harr* 7E **38**
Mulgrave Rd. *Sutt* 9K **121**
Mulholland Clo. *Mitc* 6F **106**
Mulkern Rd. *N19* 6H **43**
Mullards Clo. *Mitc* 3D **122**
Mullen Tower. EC1 . . . . *7L* ***59***
(off Mount Pleasant)
Muller Ho. *SE18* 6L **79**
Muller Rd. *SW4* 5H **91**
Mullet Gdns. *E2* 6E **60**
Mulletsfield. WC1 . . . . *6J* ***59***
(off Cromer St.)
Mullins Path. *SW14* 2B **88**
Mullion Clo. *Harr* 8M **21**
Mullion Wlk. *Wat* 4H **21**
Mull Wlk. N1 . . . . *2A* ***60***
(off Clephane Rd.)
Mulready Ho. SW1 . . . . *5J* ***75***
(off Marsham St.)
Mulready St. *NW8* 7C **58**
Multimedia Ho. *NW10* 7A **56**
Multi Way. *W3* 3C **72**
Multon Ho. *E9* 3G **61**
Multon Rd. *SW18* 6B **90**
Mulvaney Way. *SE1* 3B **76**
(in two parts)
Mumford Ct. *EC2* 9A **60**
Mumford Rd. *SE24* 4M **91**
Muncaster Rd. *SW11* 4D **90**
Muncies M. *SE6* 8A **94**
Mundania Rd. *SE22* 5F **92**
Munday Ho. SE1 . . . . *4B* ***76***
(off Deverell St.)
Munday Rd. *E16* 1E **78**
Munden. 7M 5
Munden Dri. *Wat* 1J **9**
Munden Gro. *Wat* 2G **9**
Munden St. *W14* 5J **73**
Mundesley Clo. *Wat* 4G **21**
Mundford Rd. *E5* 7G **45**
Mundon Gdns. *Ilf* 6B **48**
Mund St. *W14* 6K **73**
Mundy Ho. *W10* 6J **57**
Mundy St. *N1* 6C **60**
Mungo Pk. Clo. *Bus H* 2A **22**
Mungo Pk. Rd. *Rain* 2E **66**
Mungo Pk. Way. *Orp* 2G **129**
Munnery Way. *Orp* 5L **127**
Munnings Gdns. *Iswth* 4B **86**
Munnings Ho. E16 . . . . *2F* ***78***
(off Portsmouth M.)
Munro Dri. *N11* 6G **27**
Munro Ho. *SE1* 3L **75**
Munro M. *W10* 8J **57**
(in two parts)
Munro Rd. *Bush* 7M **9**
Munro Ter. *SW10* 8B **74**
Munslow Gdns. *Sutt* 6B **122**
Munster Av. *Houn* 4J **85**
Munster Ct. *SW6* 1K **89**
Munster Ct. *Tedd* 3G **103**
Munster Gdns. *N13* 4M **27**
Munster M. *SW6* 8J **73**
Munster Rd. *SW6* 8J **73**
Munster Rd. *Tedd* 3F **102**
Munster Sq. *NW1* 6F **58**
Munton Rd. *SE17* 5A **76**
Murchison Av. *Bex* 7H **97**
Murchison Rd. *E10* 7A **46**
Murdoch Ho. SE16 . . . . *4G* ***77***
(off Moodkee St.)
Murdock Clo. *E16* 9D **62**
Murdock St. *SE15* 7F **76**
Murfett Clo. *SW19* 8J **89**
Murfitt Way. *Upm* 9L **51**
Muriel Av. *Wat* 7G **9**
Muriel Ct. *E10* 5M **45**
Muriel St. *N1* 5K **59**
(in two parts)
Murillo Rd. *SE13* 3B **94**
Murphy Ho. SE1 . . . . *4M* ***75***
(off Borough Rd.)
Murphy St. *SE1* 3L **75**
Murray Av. *Brom* 7F **110**
Murray Av. *Houn* 4M **85**
Murray Bus. Cen. *Orp* 7F **112**
Murray Ct. *Harr* 4D **38**
Murray Ct. *Twic* 8B **86**
Murray Cres. *Pinn* 8H **21**
Murray Gro. *N1* 5A **60**
Murray Ho. SE18 . . . . *5K* ***79***
(off Rideout St.)
Murray M. *NW1* 3H **59**
Murray Rd. *SW19* 3H **105**
Murray Rd. *W5* 5G **71**
Murray Rd. *N'wd* 8C **20**
Murray Rd. *Orp* 7F **112**
Murray Rd. *Rich* 8F **86**
Murray Sq. *E16* 9E **62**
Murray St. *NW1* 3G **59**
Murray Ter. *NW3* 9A **42**
Murray Ter. *W5* 5H **71**
Mursell Est. *SW8* 9K **75**
Murtwell Dri. *Chig* 6A **32**
Musard Rd. *W6* 7J **73**
Musbury St. *E1* 9G **61**
Muscal. W6 . . . . *7J* ***73***
(off Field Rd.)
Muscatel Pl. *SE5* 9C **76**
Muschamp Rd. *SE15* 2D **92**
Muschamp Rd. *Cars* 4C **122**
Muscovy Ho. Eri *4J* ***81***
(off Kale Rd.)
Muscovy St. *EC3* 1C **76**
Museum Chambers. WC1 . . . *8J* ***59***
(off Bury Pl.)
Mus. in Docklands. 1L 77
Museum La. SW7 . . . . *4B* ***74***
(off Exhibition Rd.)
Mus. of Artillery in the Rotunda.
. . . . 6K 79
Mus. of Classical Art. *7H 59*
(off Gower Pl.)
Mus. of Fulham Palace. . . . 1J 89
Mus. of Garden History. . . . 4K 75
Mus. of London. 8A 60
Mus. of Richmond. *4H 87*
(off Whittaker Av.)
Mus. of Rugby, The. 5C 86
Mus. of the Order of St John, The.
. . . . *7M 59*
(off St John's La.)
Museum Pas. *E2* 6G **61**
Museum St. *WC1* 8J **59**
Musgrave Clo. *Barn* 3A **14**
Musgrave Ct. *SW11* 9C **74**
Musgrave Cres. *SW6* 8L **73**
Musgrave Rd. *Iswth* 9D **70**
Musgrove Rd. *SE14* 9H **77**
Musjid Rd. *SW11* 1B **90**
Musket Clo. *E Barn* 8B **14**
Musquash Way. *Houn* 1G **85**
Mussenden La.
Hort K & Fawk 9M **115**
Muston Rd. *E5* 7F **44**
Mustow Pl. *SW6* 1K **89**
Muswell Av. *N10* 8F **26**
Muswell Hill. 1F 42
Muswell Hill. *N10* 1F **42**
Muswell Hill B'way. *N10* 1F **42**
Muswell Hill Pl. *N10* 2F **42**
Muswell Hill Rd. *N6* 4E **42**
Muswell M. *N10* 1F **42**
Muswell Rd. *N10* 1F **42**
Mutchetts Clo. *Wat* 6J **5**
Mutrix Rd. *NW6* 4L **57**

Mutton Pl.—Newbarn La.

Mutton Pl. NW1 2E 58
Muybridge Rd. N Mald 6A 104
Myatt Rd. SW9 9M 75
Myatts Fields S. SW9 1L 91
(off St Lawrence Way)
Mycenae Rd. SE3 8E 78
Myddelton Av. Enf 2C 16
Myddelton Clo. Enf 3D 16
Myddelton Gdns. N21 9A 16
Myddelton Pk. N20 3B 26
Myddelton Pas. EC1 6L 59
Myddelton Rd. N8 1J 43
Myddelton Sq. EC1 6L 59
Myddelton St. EC1 6L 59
Myddleton Av. N4 7A 44
Myddleton Ho. N1 5L 59
(off Pentonville Rd.)
Myddleton M. N22 7J 27
Myddleton Path. Chesh 4B 6
Myddleton Rd. N22 7J 27
Myddleton Rd. Uxb 4A 142
Myers La. SE14 7H 77
Mygrove Clo. Rain 5H 67
Mygrove Gdns. Rain 5H 67
Mygrove Rd. Rain 5H 67
Mylis Clo. SE26 1F 108
Mylius Clo. SE14 8G 77
Myline Clo. W6 6E 72
Mylne Clo. Chesh 1C 6
Mylne St. EC1 6L 59
Mynn's Clo. Eps 6M 133
Myra St. SE2 6E 80
Myrdle St. E1 8E 60
Myrna Clo. SW19 4C 106
Myron Pl. SE13 2A 94
Myrtle Av. Felt 4C 84
Myrtle Av. Ruis 5E 36
Myrtleberry Clo. E8 2D 60
(off Beechwood Rd.)
Myrtle Clo. E Barn 1D 26
Myrtle Clo. Eri 9C 82
Myrtle Clo. Uxb 8D 142
Myrtle Clo. W Dray 4K 143
Myrtledene Rd. SE2 6E 80
Myrtle Gdns. W7 2C 70
Myrtle Gro. Ave 3M 83
Myrtle Gro. Enf 2B 16
Myrtle Gro. N Mald 6A 104
Myrtle Rd. E6 4K 63
Myrtle Rd. E17 4J 45
Myrtle Rd. N13 3A 28
Myrtle Rd. W3 2A 72
Myrtle Rd. Croy 5L 125
Myrtle Rd. Dart 7H 99
Myrtle Rd. Hamp H 3A 102
Myrtle Rd. Houn 1A 86
Myrtle Rd. Ilf 7M 47
Myrtle Rd. Romf 6G 35
Myrtle Rd. Sutt 7A 122
Myrtleside Clo. N'wd 7B 20
Myrtle Wlk. N1 5C 60
Mysore Rd. SW11 2D 90
Myton Rd. SE21 9B 92
Mytton Ho. SW8 8K 75
(off St Stephens Ter.)

N

Nadine Ct. Wall 1G 137
Nadine St. SE7 6G 79
Nafferton Ri. Lou 7H 19
Nagasaki Wlk. SE7 4F 78
Nagle Clo. E17 9B 30
Nag's Head (Junct.) 8J 43
Nags Head Ct. EC1 7A 60
(off Golden La.)
Nags Head La. Upm 8M 35
Nags Head La. Well 2F 96
Nags Head Rd. Enf 6G 17
Nags Head Shop. Cen. N7 9K 43
Nailsworth Ct. SE15 7C 76
(off Birdlip Clo.)
Nainby Ho. SE11 5L 75
(off Hotspur St.)
Nairne Gro. SE24 4B 92
Nairn Grn. Wat 3E 20
Nairn Rd. Ruis 2G 53
Nairn St. E14 8A 62
Naish Ct. N1 4J 59
(in three parts)
Naldera Gdns. SE3 7E 78
Nallhead Rd. Felt 2G 101
Namba Roy Clo. SW16 1K 107
Namton Dri. T Hth 8K 107
Nan Clark's La. NW7 2C 24
Nancy Downs. Wat 9G 9
Nankin St. E14 9L 61
Nansen Ho. NW10 3B 56
(off Stonebridge Pk.)
Nansen Rd. SW11 2E 90
Nansen Village. N12 4M 25
Nant Ct. NW2 7K 41
Nantes Clo. SW18 3A 90
Nantes Pas. E1 8D 60
Nant Rd. NW2 7K 41
Nant St. E2 6F 60
Nantwich Ho. Romf 5J 35
(off Lindfield Rd.)
Naoroji St. WC1 6L 59
Napier. NW9 8D 24
Napier Av. E14 6L 77
Napier Av. SW6 2K 89
Napier Clo. SE8 8K 77
Napier Clo. W14 4J 73
Napier Clo. Horn 6F 50
Napier Clo. W Dray 4K 143
Napier Ct. N1 5B 60
(off Cropley St.)
Napier Ct. SW6 2K 89
(off Ranelagh Gdns.)
Napier Ct. Chesh 1B 6
Napier Ct. Hay 7G 53
(off Dunedin Way)
Napier Gro. N1 5A 60
Napier Ho. Rain 6D 66
(off Dunedin Rd.)
Napier Pl. W14 4K 73
Napier Rd. E6 4L 63
Napier Rd. E11 9C 46
Napier Rd. E15 5C 62
(in two parts)
Napier Rd. N17 1C 44
Napier Rd. NW10 6F 56
Napier Rd. SE25 8F 108
Napier Rd. W14 4J 73
Napier Rd. Ashf 4B 100
Napier Rd. Belv 5K 81
Napier Rd. Brom 8F 110
Napier Rd. Enf 7H 17
Napier Rd. Iswth 3E 86
Napier Rd. H'row A 9H 143
Napier Rd. S Croy 9B 124
Napier Rd. Wat 6J 9
Napier Rd. Wemb 2H 55
Napier St. SE8 8K 77
(off Napier Clo.)
Napier Ter. N1 3M 59
Napier Wlk. Ashf 4B 100
Napoleon Rd. E5 8F 44
Napoleon Rd. Twic 6F 86
Napton Clo. Hay 7J 53
Narbonne Av. SW4 4G 91
Narboro Ct. Romf 3E 50
Narborough Clo. Uxb 7A 36
Narborough St. SW6 1M 89
Narcissus Rd. NW6 1L 57
Nardini. NW9 8D 24
(off Concourse, The)
Nare Rd. Ave 1M 83
Naresby Fold. Stan 6G 23
Narford Rd. E5 8E 44
Narrow Boat Clo. SE28 3B 80
Narrow St. E14 1H 77
(off Highway, The)
Narrow St. W3 2M 71
Narrow Way. Brom 1J 127
Narvic Ho. SE5 1A 92
Nascot Pl. Wat 4F 8
Nascot Rd. Wat 4F 8
Nascot St. W12 9G 57
Nascot St. Wat 4F 8
Nascot Wood Rd. Wat 1D 8
Naseby Clo. NW6 3A 58
Naseby Clo. Iswth 9C 70
Naseby Ct. Sidc 1D 112
Naseby Ct. W on T 4G 117
Naseby Rd. SE19 3B 108
Naseby Rd. Dag 8L 49
Naseby Rd. Ilf 8K 31
Nash. 8E 126
Nash Clo. Els 6K 11
Nash Clo. Sutt 5B 122
Nash Ct. E14 2M 77
(off Nash Pl.)
Nash Ct. Kent 4F 38
Nashe Ho. SE1 4B 76
(off Burbage Clo.)
Nash Grn. Brom 3E 110
Nash Ho. E17 1M 45
Nash Ho. SW1 6F 74
(off Lupus St.)
Nash La. Kes 9E 126
Nash Pl. E14 2M 77
Nash Rd. N9 2G 29
Nash Rd. SE4 3J 93
Nash Rd. Chad H 2H 49
Nash St. NW1 6F 58
Nash's Yd. Uxb 3B 142
Nash Way. Kent 4F 38
Nasmyth St. W6 4F 72
Nassau Path. SE28 2G 81
Nassau Rd. SW13 9D 72
Nassau St. W1 8G 59
Nassington Rd. NW3 9D 42
Natalie Clo. Felt 6B 84
Natalie M. Twic 9B 86
Natal Rd. N11 6J 27
Natal Rd. SW16 3H 107
Natal Rd. Ilf 9M 47
Natal Rd. T Hth 7B 108
Natasha Ct. Romf 7G 35
Nathan Ct. N9 9G 17
(off Causeyware Rd.)
Nathan Ho. SE11 5L 75
(off Reedworth St.)
Nathaniel Clo. E1 8D 60
Nathaniel Ct. E17 5J 45
Nathans Rd. Wemb 6G 39
Nathan Way. SE28 5B 80
National Army Mus. 7D 74
National Film Theatre, The. 2K 75
(off Waterloo Rd.)
National Gallery. 1H 75
National Gallery (Sainsbury Wing) 1H 75
(off National Gallery)
National Maritime Mus. 7B 78
National Portrait Gallery. 1H 75
(off St Martin's Pl.)
Nation Way. E4 1A 30
Natural History Mus. 4B 74
Naunton Way. Horn 8H 51
Nautilus Building, The. EC1 6L 59
(off Myddelton Pas.)
Naval Ho. E14 1B 78
(off Quixley St.)
Naval Row. E14 1A 78
Naval Wlk. Brom 6E 110
(off Mitre Clo.)
Navarino Gro. E8 2E 60
Navarino Mans. E8 2E 60
Navarino Rd. E8 2E 60
Navarre Gdns. Romf 5M 33
Navarre Rd. E6 5J 63
Navarre St. E2 7D 60
Navenby Wlk. E3 7L 61
Navestock Clo. E4 3A 30
Navestock Cres. Wfd G 7G 31
Navestock Ho. Bark 5F 64
Navigation Dri. Enf 2L 17
Navigator Dri. S'hall 3A 70
Navy St. SW4 2H 91
Nayland Ho. SE6 1A 110
Naylor Gro. Enf 7H 17
Naylor Ho. W10 6J 57
Naylor Rd. N20 2A 26
Naylor Rd. SE15 8F 76
Nazareth Gdns. SE15 1F 92
Nazeing Wlk. Rain 3D 66
Nazrul St. E2 6D 60
Neagle Clo. Borwd 3A 12
Neagle Ho. NW2 8G 41
(off Stoll Clo.)
Neal Av. S'hall 7K 53
Neal Clo. N'wd 8E 20
Neal Ct. Wal A 6M 7
Nealden St. SW9 2K 91
Neale Clo. N2 1A 42
Neal St. WC2 9J 59
Neal St. Wat 7G 9
Neal's Yd. WC2 9J 59
Near Acre. NW9 8D 24
Neasden. 8C 40
Neasden Clo. NW10 1C 56
Neasden Junction (Junct.) 9B 40
Neasden La. NW10 8C 40
(in two parts)
Neasden La. N. NW10 8B 40
Neasham Rd. Dag 1F 64
Neatby Ct. Chesh 1D 6
Neate St. SE5 7C 76
(in two parts)
Neath Gdns. Mord 1A 122
Neath Ho. SE24 5M 91
(off Dulwich Rd.)
Neathouse Pl. SW1 5G 75
Neats Acre. Ruis 5B 36
Neatscourt Rd. E6 8H 63
Neave Cres. Romf 8G 35
Nebraska St. SE1 3B 76
Neckinger. SE16 4D 76
Neckinger Est. SE16 4D 76
Neckinger St. SE1 3D 76
Nectarine Way. SE13 1M 93
Needham Ho. SE11 6L 75
(off Hotspur St.)
Needham Rd. W11 9L 57
Needham Ter. NW2 8H 41
Needleman St. SE16 3H 77
Needwood Ho. N4 6A 44
Neela Clo. Uxb 9A 36
Neeld Cres. NW4 3F 40
Neeld Cres. Wemb 1L 55
Neeld Pde. Wemb 1K 55
Neil Clo. Ashf 2A 100
Neil Wates Cres. SW2 7L 91
Nelgarde Rd. SE6 6L 93
Nella Rd. W6 7H 73
Nelldale Rd. SE16 5G 77
Nellgrove Rd. Uxb 7F 142
Nell Gwynne Av. Shep 1B 116
Nell Gwynne Clo. Eps 3L 133
Nello James Gdns. SE27 1B 108
Nelmes Clo. Horn 3K 51
Nelmes Cres. Horn 3J 51
Nelmes Rd. Horn 5J 51
Nelmes Way. Horn 2H 51
Nelson Clo. NW6 6L 57
(off Cambridge Rd.)
Nelson Clo. Big H 9J 141
Nelson Clo. Croy 3M 123
Nelson Clo. Felt 7D 84
Nelson Clo. Romf 8M 33
Nelson Clo. Uxb 6F 142
Nelson Clo. W on T 3F 116
Nelson Ct. SE1 3M 75
Nelson Ct. SE16 2G 77
(off Brunel Rd.)
Nelson Ct. Eri 8D 82
(off Frobisher Rd.)
Nelson Gdns. E2 6E 60
Nelson Gdns. Houn 5L 85
Nelson Gro. Rd. SW19 5A 106
Nelson Ho. SW1 7G 75
(off Dolphin Sq.)
Nelson Ho. Romf 5J 35
(off Lindfield Rd.)
Nelson Ind. Est. SW19 5M 105
Nelson La. Uxb 6F 142
Nelson Mandela Clo. N10 9E 26
Nelson Mandela Rd. SE3 2G 95
Nelson Pas. EC1 6A 60
Nelson Pl. N1 5M 59
Nelson Pl. Sidc 1E 112
Nelson Rd. E4 6M 29
Nelson Rd. E11 2E 46
Nelson Rd. N8 3K 43
Nelson Rd. N9 2F 28
Nelson Rd. N15 2C 44
Nelson Rd. SE10 7A 78
Nelson Rd. SW19 4M 105
Nelson Rd. Belv 6K 81
Nelson Rd. Brom 8G 111
Nelson Rd. Dart 5G 99
Nelson Rd. Enf 8H 17
Nelson Rd. Harr 6B 38
Nelson Rd. Houn & Twic 5L 85
Nelson Rd. H'row A 9K 143
Nelson Rd. N Mald 9B 104
Nelson Rd. Rain 5D 66
Nelson Rd. Sidc 1E 112
Nelson Rd. Stan 6G 23
Nelson Rd. Uxb 6F 142
Nelson Rd. M. SW19 4M 105
Nelson's Column. 2J 75
Nelson Sq. SE1 3M 75
Nelson's Row. SW4 3H 91
Nelson St. E1 9F 60
Nelson St. E6 5K 63
(in two parts)
Nelson St. E16 1D 78
(in two parts)
Nelsons Yd. NW1 5G 59
(off Mornington Cres.)
Nelson Ter. N1 5M 59
Nelson Wlk. SE16 2J 77
Nelson Wlk. Eps 1L 133
Nelwyn Av. Horn 3K 51
Nemoure Rd. W3 1A 72
Nene Gdns. Felt 8K 85
Nene Rd. H'row A 9M 143
Nene Rd. Roundabout (Junct.) 9M 143
Nene Rd. Roundabout. H'row A 9M 143
Nepaul Rd. SW11 1C 90
Nepean St. SW15 5E 88
Neptune Clo. Rain 5D 66
Neptune Ct. E14 5L 77
(off Homer Dri.)
Neptune Ct. Borwd 5L 11
Neptune Ct. Eri 8D 82
(off Frobisher Rd.)
Neptune Ho. SE16 4G 77
(off Moodkee St.)
Neptune Rd. Harr 4B 38
Neptune Rd. H'row A 9A 68
Neptune St. SE16 4G 77
Neptune Wlk. Eri 5B 82
Nero Ct. Bren 8H 71
Nesbit Rd. SE9 3H 95
Nesbitt Clo. SE3 2C 94
Nesbitts All. Barn 5K 13
Nesbitt Sq. SE19 4C 108
Nesham St. E1 1E 76
Ness Rd. Eri 7H 83
Ness St. SE16 4E 76
Nesta Rd. Wfd G 6C 30
Nestles Av. Hay 4D 68
Neston Rd. Wat 1G 9
Nestor Av. N21 8M 15
Nestor Ho. E2 5F 60
(off Old Bethnal Grn. Rd.)
Nethan Dri. Ave 1M 83
Netheravon Rd. W4 5D 72
Netheravon Rd. W7 2D 70
Netheravon Rd. S. W4 6D 72
Netherbury Rd. W5 4H 71
Netherby Gdns. Enf 6J 15
Netherby Pk. Wey 7C 116
Netherby Rd. SE23 6G 93
Nether Clo. N3 7L 25
Nethercourt Av. N3 6L 25
Netherfield Gdns. Bark 2B 64
Netherfield Rd. N12 5M 25
Netherfield Rd. SW17 9E 90
Netherford Rd. SW4 1G 91
Netherhall Gdns. NW3 2A 58
Netherhall Way. NW3 1A 58
Netherlands Rd. Barn 8B 14
Netherleigh Clo. N6 6F 42
Netherpark Dri. Romf 9D 34
Nether St. N3 & N12 8L 25
Netherton Gro. SW10 7A 74
Netherton Rd. N15 4B 44
Netherton Rd. Twic 4E 86
Netherwood. N2 9B 26
Netherwood Pl. W14 4H 73
(off Netherwood Rd.)
Netherwood Rd. W14 4H 73
Netherwood St. NW6 3K 57
Nethewode Ct. Belv 4M 81
(off Lwr. Park Rd.)
Netley. SE5 9C 76
(off Redbridge Gdns.)
Netley Clo. Cheam 7H 121
Netley Clo. New Ad 9A 126
Netley Dri. W on T 2K 117
Netley Gdns. Mord 2A 122
Netley Rd. E17 3K 45
Netley Rd. Bren 7J 71
Netley Rd. Ilf 3B 48
Netley Rd. Mord 2A 122
Netley St. NW1 6G 59
Nettlecombe. NW1 3H 59
(off Agar Gro.)
Nettlecombe Clo. Sutt 1M 135
Nettleden Av. Wemb 2L 55
Nettleden Ho. SW3 5C 74
(off Marlborough St.)
Nettlefold Pl. SE27 9M 91
Nettlestead Clo. Beck 4K 109
Nettleton Ct. EC2 8A 60
(off London Wall)
Nettleton Rd. SE14 9H 77
Nettleton Rd. H'row A 9M 143
Nettlewood Rd. SW16 4H 107
Neuchatel Rd. SE6 8K 93
Nevada Clo. N Mald 8A 104
Nevada St. SE10 7A 78
Nevern Mans. SW5 6L 73
(off Warwick Rd.)
Nevern Pl. SW5 5L 73
Nevern Rd. SW5 5L 73
Nevern Sq. SW5 5L 73
Nevil Clo. N'wd 5B 20
Nevil Ho. SW9 1M 91
(off Loughborough Est.)
Nevill Ct. EC4 9L 59
(off E. Harding St.)
Neville Av. N Mald 5B 104
Neville Clo. E11 8D 46
Neville Clo. NW1 5H 59
Neville Clo. NW6 5K 57
Neville Clo. SE15 9E 76
Neville Clo. W3 3A 72
Neville Clo. Bans 6M 135
Neville Clo. Esh 8K 117
Neville Clo. Houn 1M 85
Neville Clo. Sidc 1D 112
Neville Ct. NW8 5B 58
(off Abbey Rd.)
Neville Dri. N2 4A 42
Neville Gdns. Dag 8H 49
Neville Gill Clo. SW18 5L 89
Neville Ho. N11 4E 26
Neville Ho. N22 8K 27
(off Neville Pl.)
Neville Ho. Yd. King T 6J 103
Neville Pl. N22 8K 27
Neville Rd. E7 3E 62
Neville Rd. NW6 5K 57
Neville Rd. W5 7H 55
Neville Rd. Croy 2B 124
Neville Rd. Dag 7H 49
Neville Rd. Ilf 8A 32
Neville Rd. King T 6L 103
Neville Rd. Rich 9G 87
Nevilles Ct. NW2 8E 40
Neville St. SW7 6B 74
Neville Ter. SW7 6B 74
Neville Wlk. Cars 2C 122
Nevill Gro. Wat 3F 8
Nevill Rd. N16 9C 44
Nevill Way. Lou 8J 19
Nevin Dri. E4 1M 29
Nevin Ho. Hay 4A 68
Nevinson Clo. SW18 5B 90
Nevis Clo. Romf 6C 34
Nevis Rd. SW17 8E 90
Nevitt Ho. N1 5B 60
(off Cranston Est.)
New Acres Rd. SE28 3C 80
(in three parts)
New Addington. 2A 140
Newall Ho. SE1 4A 76
(off Bath Ter.)
Newall Rd. H'row A 9A 68
New Arcade. Uxb 4B 142
Newark Ct. W on T 3G 117
Newark Cres. NW10 6B 56
Newarke Ho. SW9 1M 91
Newark Grn. Borwd 5B 12
Newark Knok. E6 9L 63
Newark Pde. NW4 1E 40
Newark Rd. S Croy 8B 124
Newark St. E1 8F 60
(in two parts)
Newark Way. NW4 2E 40
New Ash Clo. N2 1B 42
New Atlas Wharf. E14 4L 77
(off Arnhem Pl.)
New Baltic Wharf. SE8 6J 77
(off Evelyn St.)
New Barn Clo. Wall 8K 12
New Barnet. 6B 1
Newbarn La. W'ham & Cud 9M 14

248 Geographers' London Atlas

New Barn La.—Nicosia Rd.

New Barn La. Whyt 8C 138
New Barn Rd. Swan 5C 114
New Barns Av. Mitc 8H 107
(in two parts)
New Barn St. E13 7E 62
New Barns Way. Chig 3M 31
New Beckenham 3K 109
New Bentham Ct. N1 3A 60
(off Ecclesbourne Rd.)
New Berry La. W on T 7H 117
Newbery Ho. N1 3A 60
(off Northampton St.)
Newbery Rd. Eri 9D 82
Newbiggin Path. Wat 4G 21
Newbold Cotts. E1 9G 61
Newbolt Av. Sutt 7G 121
Newbolt Ho. SE17 6B 76
(off Brandon St.)
Newbolt Rd. Stan 5D 22
New Bond St. W1 9F 58
Newborough Grn. N Mald 8B 104
New Brent St. NW4 3G 41
Newbridge Point. SE23 9H 93
(off Windrush La.)
New Bri. St. EC4 9M 59
New Broad St. EC2 8C 60
New B'way. W5 1H 71
New B'way. Hamp H 2B 102
New B'way. Uxb 6F 142
New B'way. Bldgs. W5 1H 71
Newburgh Rd. W3 2A 72
Newburgh St. W1 9G 59
New Burlington M. W1 1G 75
New Burlington Pl. W1 1G 75
New Burlington St. W1 1G 75
Newburn Ho. SE11 6K 75
(off Newburn St.)
Newburn St. SE11 6K 75
Newbury Av. Enf 2K 17
Newbury Clo. N'holt 2K 53
Newbury Clo. Romf 6G 35
Newbury Ct. Sidc 1D 112
Newbury Gdns. Eps 6D 120
Newbury Gdns. Romf 6H 35
Newbury Gdns. Upm 8K 51
Newbury Ho. N22 8J 27
Newbury Ho. SW9 1M 91
Newbury Ho. W2 9M 57
(off Hallfield Est.)
Newbury M. NW5 2E 58
Newbury Park 3A 48
Newbury Rd. E4 6A 30
Newbury Rd. Brom 7E 110
Newbury Rd. Ilf 4C 48
Newbury Rd. H'row A 9K 143
Newbury Rd. Romf 5H 35
Newbury St. EC1 8A 60
Newbury Wlk. Romf 5H 35
Newbury Way. N'holt 2J 53
New Bus. Cen., The. NW10 6D 56
New Butt La. SE8 8L 77
New Butt La. N. SE8 8L 77
(off Hales St.)
Newby. NW1 6G 59
(off Robert St.)
Newby Clo. Enf 4C 16
Newby Ho. E14 1A 78
(off Newby Pl.)
Newby Pl. E14 1A 78
Newby St. SW8 2F 90
New Caledonian Wharf. SE16 4K 77
Newcastle Av. Ilf 6E 32
Newcastle Clo. EC4 9M 59
Newcastle Ct. EC4 1A 76
(off College Hill)
Newcastle Ho. W1 8E 58
(off Luxborough St.)
Newcastle Pl. W2 8B 58
Newcastle Row. EC1 7L 59
New Cavendish St. W1 8E 58
New Change. EC4 9A 60
New Chapel Sq. Felt 7F 84
New Charles St. EC1 6M 59
New Charlton 5G 79
New Chu. Rd. SE5 8A 76
(in three parts)
New City Rd. E13 6G 63
New Clo. SW19 7A 106
New Clo. Felt 2J 101
New Colebrooke Ct. Cars 9E 122
(off Stanley Rd.)
New College Ct. NW3 2A 58
(off Finchley Rd.)
New College M. N1 3L 59
New College Pde. NW3 2B 58
(off College Cres.)
Newcombe Gdns. SW16 1J 107
Newcombe Gdns. Houn 3K 85
Newcombe Pk. NW7 5C 24
Newcombe Pk. Wemb 4K 55
Newcombe Ri. W Dray 9C 142
Newcombe St. W8 2L 73
Newcomen Rd. E11 8D 46
Newcomen Rd. SW11 2B 90
Newcomen St. SE1 3B 76
New Compton St. WC2 9H 59
New Concordia Wharf. SE1 3E 76
New Cotts. Wal X 7C 6
New Ct. EC4 1L 75
(off Fountain Ct.)
New Ct. N'holt 1M 53
Newcourt. Uxb 8A 142
Newcourt Ho. E2 6F 60
(off Pott St.)
Newcourt St. NW8 5C 58
New Covent Garden Market. 8H 75
New Coventry St. W1 1H 75
New Crane Pl. E1 2G 77
New Crane Wharf. E1 2G 77
(off New Crane Pl.)
New Cres. Yd. NW10 5D 56
Newcroft Clo. Uxb 8D 142
New Cross 8K 77
New Cross (Junct.) 9J 77
New Cross Gate 9H 77
New Cross Gate (Junct.) 9H 77
New Cross Rd. SE15 & SE14 8G 77
Newdales Clo. N9 2E 28
Newdene Av. N'holt 5H 53
New Den, The (Millwall F.C.) 6G 77
Newdigate Ho. E14 9K 61
(off Norbiton Rd.)
Newell St. E14 9K 61
New Eltham 8A 96
New End. NW3 9A 42
New End Sq. NW3 9B 42
New England Ind. Est. Bark 5A 64
Newent Clo. SE15 8C 76
New Era Est. N1 4C 60
(off Phillipp St.)
New Farm Av. Brom 8E 110
New Farm La. N'wd 8C 20
New Fetter La. EC4 9L 59
Newfield Clo. Hamp 5L 101
Newfield Ri. NW2 8F 40
New Ford Rd. Wal X 7F 6
New Forest La. Chig 6L 31
Newgale Gdns. Edgw 8K 23
New Garden Dri. W Dray 3J 143
Newgate. Croy 3A 124
Newgate Clo. Felt 8J 85
Newgate St. E4 3C 30
(in two parts)
Newgate St. EC1 9M 59
New Globe Wlk. SE1 2A 76
New Goulston St. E1 9D 60
New Grn. Pl. SE19 3C 108
Newhall Ct. Wal A 6M 7
New Hall Dri. Romf 8J 35
Newhall Gdns. W on T 4G 117
Newham Grn. N22 8L 27
Newham's Row. SE1 3C 76
Newham Way. E16 & E6 8D 62
Newhaven Clo. Hay 5D 68
Newhaven Cres. Ashf 2B 100
Newhaven Gdns. SE9 3H 95
Newhaven La. E16 7D 62
Newhaven Rd. SE25 9B 108
New Heston Rd. Houn 8K 69
New Horizons Ct. Bren 7G 71
Newhouse Av. Romf 1H 49
Newhouse Clo. N Mald 2C 120
Newhouse Cres. Wat 5F 4
Newhouse Wlk. Mord 2A 122
Newick Clo. Bex 5M 97
Newick Rd. E5 9F 44
Newing Grn. Brom 4H 111
Newington 4A 76
Newington Barrow Way. N7 8K 43
Newington Butts. SE11 & SE1 5M 75
Newington Causeway. SE1 4M 75
Newington Ct. Bus. Cen. SE1 4A 76
(off Newington Causeway)
Newington Grn. N1 & N16 1B 60
Newington Grn. Mans. N16 1B 60
Newington Grn. Rd. N1 2B 60
Newington Ind. Est. SE17 5A 76
(off Crampton St.)
New Inn B'way. EC2 7C 60
New Inn Pas. WC2 9K 59
(off Houghton St.)
New Inn Sq. EC2 7C 60
(off Bateman's Row)
New Inn St. EC2 7C 60
New Inn Yd. EC2 7C 60
New Jubilee Ct. Wfd G 7E 30
New Jubilee Wharf. E1 2G 77
(off Wapping Wall)
New Kelvin Av. Tedd 3C 102
New Kent Rd. SE1 4A 76
New Kings Rd. SW6 1K 89
New King St. SE8 7L 77
Newland Clo. Pinn 6J 21
Newland Ct. EC1 7B 60
(off St Luke's Est.)
Newland Dri. Enf 3F 16
Newland Gdns. W13 3E 70
Newland Ho. N8 1J 43
(off Newland Rd.)
Newland Ho. SE14 7H 77
(off John Williams Clo.)
Newland Rd. N8 1J 43
Newlands 4H 93
(Brockley)
Newlands 3J 23
(Edgware)
Newlands. NW1 6G 59
(off Harrington St.)
Newlands Av. Th Dit 3C 118
Newlands Clo. Edgw 3J 23
Newlands Clo. S'hall 6J 69
Newlands Clo. W on T 6J 117
Newlands Clo. Wemb 2G 55
Newlands Ct. SE9 5L 95
Newlands Pk. SE26 3G 109
Newlands Pl. Barn 7H 13
Newlands Quay. E1 1G 77
Newlands Rd. SW16 6J 107
Newlands Rd. Wfd G 2D 30
Newlands, The. Wall 9G 123
Newland St. E16 2J 79
Newlands Wlk. Wat 6H 5
Newlands Way. Chess 7G 119
Newlands Wood. Croy 1K 139
Newling Clo. E6 9K 63
New London St. EC3 1C 76
(off Hart St.)
New London Theatre. 9J 59
(off Drury La.)
New Lydenburg Commercial Est. SE7 4G 79
New Lydenburg St. SE7 4G 79
Newlyn. NW1 4G 59
(off Plender St.)
Newlyn Clo. Brick W 3J 5
Newlyn Clo. Orp 6E 128
Newlyn Clo. Uxb 8E 142
Newlyn Gdns. Harr 5K 37
Newlyn Ho. Pinn 7K 21
Newlyn Rd. N17 8D 28
Newlyn Rd. Barn 6K 13
Newlyn Rd. Well 1D 96
New Malden 8C 104
Newman Clo. Horn 3J 51
Newman Pas. W1 8G 59
Newman Rd. E13 6F 62
Newman Rd. E17 3H 45
Newman Rd. Brom 5E 110
Newman Rd. Croy 3K 123
Newman Rd. Hay 1F 68
Newman Rd. Ind. Est. Croy 2K 123
Newmans Clo. Lou 5L 19
Newman's Ct. EC3 9B 60
(off Cornhill)
Newmans La. Lou 5L 19
Newmans La. Surb 1H 119
Newman's Row. WC2 8K 59
Newman St. W1 8G 59
Newman's Way. Barn 3A 14
Newman Yd. W1 9G 59
Newmarket Av. N'holt 1L 53
Newmarket Grn. SE9 6H 95
Newmarket Ho. Romf 5J 35
(off Lindfield Rd.)
Newmarket Way. Horn 9J 51
Newmarsh Rd. SE28 2D 80
Newmill Ho. E3 7A 62
New Mill Rd. Orp 5G 113
Newminster Rd. Mord 1A 122
New Mt. St. E15 3B 62
Newnes Path. SW15 3F 88
Newnet Clo. Cars 3D 122
Newnham Av. Ruis 6G 37
Newnham Clo. Lou 8H 19
Newnham Clo. N'holt 2A 54
Newnham Clo. T Hth 6A 108
Newnham Gdns. N'holt 2A 54
Newnham Ho. Lou 8H 19
Newnham Lodge. Belv 6L 81
(off Erith Rd.)
Newnham M. N22 7K 27
Newnham Pde. Chesh 3D 6
Newnham Rd. N22 8K 27
Newnhams Clo. Brom 7K 111
Newnham Ter. SE1 4L 75
Newnham Way. Harr 3J 39
New N. Pl. EC2 7C 60
New N. Rd. N1 3A 60
New N. Rd. Ilf 7B 32
New N. St. WC1 8K 59
Newnton Clo. N4 5B 44
(in two parts)
New Oak Rd. N2 9A 26
New Orleans Wlk. N19 5H 43
New Oxford St. WC1 9H 59
New Pde. W Dray 2J 143
New Pk. Av. N13 3A 28
New Pk. Clo. N'holt 2J 53
New Pk. Est. N18 5G 29
New Pk. Ho. N13 4K 27
New Pk. Pde. SW2 6J 91
(off New Pk. Rd.)
New Pk. Rd. SW2 7H 91
New Pk. Rd. Ashf 2A 100
New Peachey La. Uxb 9B 142
Newpiece. Lou 5M 19
New Pl. Croy 8L 125
New Pl. Sq. SE16 4F 76
New Plaistow Rd. E15 4C 62
New Plymouth Ho. Rain 6D 66
(off Dunedin Rd.)
New Pond Pde. Ruis 8E 36
Newport Av. E13 7F 62
Newport Av. E14 1B 78
Newport Clo. Enf 1J 17
Newport Ct. WC2 1H 75
Newport Ho. E3 6J 61
(off Strahan Rd.)
Newport Lodge. Enf 7C 16
(off Village Rd.)
Newport Mead. Wat 4H 21
Newport Pl. WC2 1H 75
Newport Rd. E10 7A 46
Newport Rd. E17 2J 45
Newport Rd. SW13 9E 72
Newport Rd. Hay 8B 52
Newport Rd. H'row A 9L 143
Newports. Swan 2B 130
Newport St. SE11 5K 75
New Priory Ct. NW6 3L 57
(off Mazenod Av.)
Newquay Cres. Harr 7J 37
Newquay Gdns. Wat 2F 20
Newquay Ho. SE11 6L 75
Newquay Rd. SE6 8M 93
New Quebec St. W1 9D 58
New Ride. SW7 & SW1 3C 74
New River Ct. N5 9A 44
New River Ct. Chesh 4B 6
New River Cres. N13 4M 27
New River Head. EC1 6L 59
New River Wlk. N1 2A 60
New River Way. N4 5B 44
New Rd. E1 8F 60
New Rd. E4 4M 29
New Rd. N8 3J 43
New Rd. N9 3E 28
New Rd. N17 8D 28
New Rd. N22 8A 28
New Rd. NW7 9D 12
(Highwood Hill)
New Rd. NW7 7J 25
(Mill Hill)
New Rd. SE2 5H 81
New Rd. Bedf 7F 84
New Rd. Bren 7H 71
New Rd. Crox G 8A 8
New Rd. Dag 5L 65
New Rd. Els 8H 11
New Rd. Esh 5A 118
New Rd. Felt 5B 84
New Rd. Hanw 2J 101
New Rd. Harr 9D 38
New Rd. Hay 8A 68
New Rd. Hex 4D 114
New Rd. Houn 3M 85
New Rd. Ilf 7C 48
New Rd. King T 4L 103
New Rd. Let H 3C 10
New Rd. Mitc 3D 122
New Rd. Orp 2E 128
New Rd. Oxs 3D 132
New Rd. Rad 1C 10
New Rd. Rich 1G 103
New Rd. Shep 7A 100
New Rd. Swan 7D 114
New Rd. Uxb 7A 52
New Rd. Wat 6G 9
New Rd. Well 1F 96
New Rd. W Mol 8L 101
New Rd. Wey 7A 116
New Rd. Hill. Kes & Orp 1J 141
New Rochford St. NW5 1D 58
New Row. WC2 1J 75
Newry Rd. Twic 4E 86
Newsam Av. N15 3B 44
Newsholme Av. N21 7K 15
New Southgate 5F 26
New Southgate Crematorium. N11 3F 26
New Southgate Ind. Est. N11 5G 27
New Spitalfields Market. 8M 45
New Spring Gdns. Wlk. SE1 & SE11 6J 75
New Sq. WC2 9L 59
New Sq. Felt 7A 84
New Sq. Pas. WC2 9L 59
(off Star Yd.)
Newstead Av. Orp 5B 128
Newstead Clo. N12 6C 26
Newstead Ct. N'holt 6J 53
Newstead Ho. Romf 4H 35
(off Troopers Dri.)
Newstead Rd. SE12 6D 94
Newstead Wlk. Cars 2A 122
Newstead Way. SW19 1H 105
New St. EC2 8C 60
New St. Wat 6G 9
New St. Hill. Brom 2F 110
New St. Sq. EC4 9L 59
Newteswell Dri. Wal A 5K 7
Newton Av. N10 8E 26
Newton Av. W3 3A 72
Newton Clo. E17 4J 45
Newton Clo. Harr 7L 37
Newton Cres. Borwd 6A 12
Newton Gro. W4 5C 72
Newton Ho. E1 1F 76
(off Cornwall St.)
Newton Ho. E17 1M 45
(off Prospect Hill)
Newton Ho. NW8 4M 57
(off Abbey Rd.)
Newton Ho. SE20 4H 109
Newton Ho. Borwd 5B 12
(off Chester Rd.)
Newton Ind. Est. Romf 2H 49
Newton Mans. W14 7J 73
(off Queen's Club Gdns.)
Newton Pl. E14 5L 77
Newton Point. E16 9D 62
(off Clarkson Rd.)
Newton Rd. E15 1B 62
Newton Rd. N15 3E 44
Newton Rd. NW2 9G 41
Newton Rd. SW19 4J 105
Newton Rd. W2 9M 57
Newton Rd. Chig 5F 32
Newton Rd. Harr 9C 22
Newton Rd. Iswth 1D 86
Newton Rd. H'row A 9J 143
Newton Rd. Purl 4G 137
Newton Rd. Well 2E 96
Newton Rd. Wemb 3K 55
Newtons Clo. Rain 3D 66
Newton St. WC2 9J 59
Newton's Yd. SW18 4L 89
Newton Ter. Brom 1H 127
Newton Wlk. Edgw 8M 23
Newton Way. N18 5A 28
Newton Wood Rd. Asht 8K 133
New Tower Bldgs. E1 2F 76
New Town 5L 99
Newtown Rd. Den 2A 142
Newtown St. SW11 9F 74
New Trinity Rd. N2 1B 42
New Turnstile. WC1 8K 59
(off High Holborn)
New Union Clo. E14 4A 78
New Union St. EC2 8B 60
New Wanstead. E11 4D 46
New Way Rd. NW9 2C 40
New Wharf Rd. N1 5J 59
New Windsor St. Uxb 4A 142
New Zealand Av. W on T 3D 116
New Zealand Way. W12 1F 72
New Zealand Way. Rain 6D 66
Niagara Av. W5 5G 71
Niagara Clo. Chesh 2D 6
Niagra Clo. N1 5A 60
Niagra Ct. SE16 4G 77
(off Canada Est.)
Nibthwaite Rd. Harr 3C 38
Nicholas Clo. Gnfd 5M 53
Nicholas Clo. Wat 1F 8
Nicholas Ct. W4 7C 72
(off Corney Reach Way)
Nicholas Gdns. W5 3H 71
Nicholas La. EC4 1B 76
(in two parts)
Nicholas M. W4 7C 72
Nicholas Pas. EC4 1B 76
(off Nicholas La.)
Nicholas Rd. E1 7G 61
Nicholas Rd. Croy 6J 123
Nicholas Rd. Dag 7K 49
Nicholas Rd. Els 8K 11
Nicholas Stacey Ho. SE7 6F 78
(off Frank Burton Clo.)
Nicholas Way. N'wd 8A 20
Nichola Ter. Bexh 9J 81
Nicholay Rd. N19 6H 43
Nichol Clo. N14 1H 27
Nicholes Rd. Houn 3L 85
Nichol La. Brom 4E 110
Nicholl Ho. N4 6A 44
Nicholls Av. Uxb 7E 142
Nichollsfield Wlk. N7 1K 59
Nicholls Point. E13 4E 62
(off Park Gro.)
Nicholl St. E2 4E 60
Nichols Clo. N4 6L 43
(off Osborne Rd.)
Nichols Clo. Chess 8G 119
Nichols Grn. W5 8J 55
Nicholson Ct. E17 2J 45
Nicholson Dri. Bush 1A 22
Nicholson Ho. SE17 6B 76
Nicholson M. King T 8J 103
Nicholson Rd. Croy 3D 124
Nicholson St. SE1 2M 75
Nickelby Clo. SE28 9G 65
Nickleby Clo. Uxb 9F 142
Nickleby Ho. SE16 3E 76
(off George Row)
Nicola Clo. Harr 9B 22
Nicola Clo. S Croy 8A 124
Nicola M. Ilf 7M 31
Nicol Clo. Twic 5F 86
Nicoll Ct. N10 7F 26
Nicoll Ct. NW10 4C 56
Nicoll Pl. NW4 4F 40
Nicoll Rd. NW10 4C 56
Nicoll Way. Borwd 7B 12
Nicolson. NW9 8C 24
Nicolson Rd. Orp 2H 129
Nicosia Rd. SW18 6C 90

Niederwald Rd.—Northfields

Niederwald Rd. *SE26* 1J 109
Nield Rd. *Hay* 3D 68
Nigel Clo. *N'holt* 4J 53
Nigel Ct. *N3* 7M 25
Nigel Fisher Way. *Chess* 9G 119
Nigel Ho. EC1 8L 59
(off Portpool La.)
Nigel M. *Ilf* 9M 47
Nigel Playfair Av. *W6* 5F 72
Nigel Rd. *E7* 1G 63
Nigel Rd. *SE15* 2E 92
Nigeria Rd. *SE7* 8G 79
Nighthawk. *NW9* 8D 24
Nightingale Av. *E4* 5C 30
Nightingale Av. *Harr* 6F 38
Nightingale Clo. *E4* 4B 30
Nightingale Clo. *W4* 7A 72
Nightingale Clo. *Ab L* 4E 4
Nightingale Clo. *Big H* 7G 141
Nightingale Clo. *Cars* 4E 122
Nightingale Clo. *Eps* 4L 133
Nightingale Clo. *Pinn* 3G 37
Nightingale Clo. *Rad* 1D 10
Nightingale Corner. *Orp* 8H 113
Nightingale Ct. E14 3A 78
(off Ovex Clo.)
Nightingale Ct. N4 7K 43
(off Tollington Pk.)
Nightingale Ct. SW6 9M 73
(off Maltings Pl.)
Nightingale Ct. *Short* 6C 110
Nightingale Dri. *Eps* 8M 119
Nightingale Gro. *SE13* 4B 94
Nightingale Gro. *Dart* 3L 99
Nightingale Heights.
SE18 7M 79
Nightingale Ho. E1 2E 76
(off Thomas More St.)
Nightingale Ho. N1 4C 60
(off Wilmer Gdns.)
Nightingale Ho. SE18 6L 79
(off Connaught M.)
Nightingale Ho. W12 9G 57
(off Du Cane Rd.)
Nightingale Ho. Eps 4C 134
(off East St.)
Nightingale La. *E11* 2F 46
Nightingale La. *N8* 2J 43
Nightingale La.
SW12 & SW4 6D 90
Nightingale La. *Brom* 6G 111
Nightingale La. *Rich* 6J 87
Nightingale Lodge. W9 8L 57
(off Admiral Wlk.)
Nightingale M. *E3* 5H 61
Nightingale M. *SE11* 5M 75
Nightingale M. King T 7H 103
(off South La.)
Nightingale Pl. *SE18* 7L 79
Nightingale Pl. *SW10* 7A 74
Nightingale Rd. *E5* 8F 44
Nightingale Rd. *N9* 8G 17
Nightingale Rd. *N22* 7J 27
Nightingale Rd. *NW10* 5D 56
Nightingale Rd. *W7* 2D 70
Nightingale Rd. *Bush* 7L 9
Nightingale Rd. *Cars* 5D 122
Nightingale Rd. *Esh* 7K 117
Nightingale Rd. *Hamp* 2L 101
Nightingale Rd. *Orp* 1A 128
Nightingale Rd. *S Croy* 3H 139
Nightingale Rd. *W on T* 2G 117
Nightingale Rd. *W Mol* 9M 101
Nightingales. *Wal A* 7L 7
Nightingale Sq. *SW12* 6E 90
Nightingales, The. *Stai* 6D 144
Nightingale Va. *SE18* 7L 79
Nightingale Wlk. *SW4* 5F 90
Nightingale Way. *E6* 8J 63
Nightingale Way. *Swan* 7C 114
Nikols Wlk. *SW18* 3M 89
Nile Clo. *N16* 8D 44
Nile Dri. *N9* 2G 29
Nile Path. *SE18* 7L 79
Nile Rd. *E13* 5G 63
Nile St. *N1* 6A 60
Nile Ter. *SE15* 6D 76
Nimbus Rd. *Eps* 2B 134
Nimegen Way. *SE22* 4C 92
Nimmo Dri. *Bus H* 9B 10
Nimrod. *NW9* 8C 24
Nimrod Clo. *N'holt* 6H 53
Nimrod Ho. E16 8F 62
(off Vanguard Clo.)
Nimrod Pas. *N1* 2C 60
Nimrod Rd. *SW16* 3F 106
Nina Mackay Clo. *E15* 4C 62
Nine Acres Clo. *E12* 1J 63
Nineacres Way. *Coul* 8J 137
Nine Elms. 8G 75
Nine Elms Av. *Uxb* 8B 142
Nine Elms Clo. *Felt* 7D 84
Nine Elms Clo. *Uxb* 8B 142
Nine Elms La. *SW8* 8G 75
Ninefields. *Wal A* 6M 7
Nineteenth Rd. *Mitc* 8J 107
Ninhams Wood. *Orp* 6L 127
Ninth Av. *Hay* 1E 68
Nita Ct. *SE12* 7E 94
Nithdale Rd. *SE18* 8M 79
Nithsdale Gro. *Uxb* 8A 36
Niton Clo. *Barn* 8H 13
Niton Rd. *Rich* 2L 87
Niton St. *SW6* 8H 73
Niven Clo. *Borwd* 3A 12
Noak Hill. 2J 35
Noak Hill Rd. *Noak H* 5F 34
Nobel Dri. *Hay* 9B 68
Nobel Ho. *SE5* 1A 92
Nobel Rd. *N18* 4G 29
Noble Corner. *Houn* 9L 69
Noble Ct. *E1* 1F 76
Noble Ct. *Mitc* 6B 106
Noblefield Heights. *N2* 3C 42
Noble St. *EC2* 9A 60
Noel. *NW9* 8C 24
Noel Ct. *Houn* 2K 85
Noel Coward Ho. SW1 5G 75
(off Vauxhall Bri. Rd.)
Noel Ho. NW3 3B 58
(off Harben Rd.)
Noel Park. 9M 27
Noel Pk. Rd. *N22* 9L 27
Noel Rd. *E6* 7J 63
Noel Rd. *N1* 5M 59
Noel Rd. *W3* 1L 71
Noel Sq. *Dag* 9G 49
Noel St. *W1* 9G 59
Noel Ter. *SE23* 8G 93
Noel Ter. *Sidc* 1F 112
Noke La. *St Alb* 1K 5
Nolan Way. *E5* 9E 44
Nolton Pl. *Edgw* 8K 23
Nonsuch Clo. *Ilf* 6M 31
Nonsuch Ct. Av. *Eps* 2F 134
Nonsuch Pl. *Sutt* 9H 121
Nonsuch Trad. Est. *Eps* 3C 134
Nonsuch Wlk. *Sutt* 2G 135
(in two parts)
Nora Gdns. *NW4* 2H 41
Norbiton. 6L 103
Norbiton Av. *King T* 5L 103
Norbiton Comn. Rd.
King T 7M 103
Norbiton Hall. *King T* 6K 103
Norbiton Rd. *E14* 9K 61
Norbreck Gdns. *NW10* 6K 55
Norbreck Pde. *NW10* 6J 55
Norbroke St. *W12* 1D 72
Norburn St. *W10* 8J 57
Norbury. 6K 107
Norbury Av. *SW16* 5K 107
Norbury Av. *Houn* 3B 86
Norbury Av. *Wat* 3G 9
Norbury Clo. *SW16* 5L 107
Norbury Ct. Rd. *SW16* 7J 107
Norbury Cres. *SW16* 5K 107
Norbury Cross. *SW16* 7J 107
Norbury Gdns. *Romf* 3H 49
Norbury Gro. *NW7* 3C 24
Norbury Hill. *SW16* 4L 107
Norbury Ri. *SW16* 7J 107
Norbury Rd. *E4* 5L 29
Norbury Rd. *T Hth* 6A 108
Norbury Trad. Est. *SW16* 6K 107
Norcombe Gdns. *Harr* 4G 39
Norcombe Ho. N19 8H 43
(off Wedmore St.)
Norcott Clo. *Hay* 7G 53
Norcott Rd. *N16* 7E 44
Norcroft Gdns. *SE22* 6E 92
Norcutt Rd. *Twic* 7C 86
Nordenfeldt Rd. *Eri* 6B 82
Norden Ho. E2 6F 60
(off Pott St.)
Norfield Rd. *Dart* 1A 114
Norfolk Av. *N13* 6M 27
Norfolk Av. *N15* 4D 44
Norfolk Av. *S Croy* 2D 138
Norfolk Av. *Wat* 2G 9
Norfolk Clo. *N2* 1C 42
Norfolk Clo. *N13* 6M 27
Norfolk Clo. *Barn* 6E 14
Norfolk Clo. *Dart* 5L 99
Norfolk Clo. *Twic* 5F 86
Norfolk Ct. *Barn* 6J 13
Norfolk Cres. *W2* 9C 58
Norfolk Cres. *Sidc* 6C 96
Norfolk Gdns. *Bexh* 9K 81
Norfolk Gdns. *Borwd* 6B 12
Norfolk Gdns. *Houn* 4K 85
Norfolk Ho. SE3 7C 78
(off Restell Clo.)
Norfolk Ho. *SE8* 9L 77
Norfolk Ho. *SE20* 5G 109
Norfolk Ho. SW1 5H 75
(off Page St.)
Norfolk Ho. Rd. *SW16* 9H 91
Norfolk Mans. SW11 9D 74
(off Prince of Wales Dri.)
Norfolk M. W10 8K 57
(off Blagrove Rd.)
Norfolk Pl. *W2* 9B 58
(in two parts)
Norfolk Pl. *Well* 1E 96
Norfolk Rd. *E6* 4K 63
Norfolk Rd. *E17* 9H 29
Norfolk Rd. *NW8* 4B 58
Norfolk Rd. *NW10* 3C 56
Norfolk Rd. *SW19* 4C 106
Norfolk Rd. *Bark* 3C 64
Norfolk Rd. *Barn* 5L 13
Norfolk Rd. *Clay* 7C 118
Norfolk Rd. *Dag* 1M 65
Norfolk Rd. *Enf* 8F 16
Norfolk Rd. *Felt* 7G 85
Norfolk Rd. *Harr* 3M 37
Norfolk Rd. *Ilf* 6C 48
Norfolk Rd. *Romf* 4A 50
Norfolk Rd. *T Hth* 7A 108
Norfolk Rd. *Upm* 8L 51
Norfolk Rd. *Uxb* 2B 142
Norfolk Row. *SE1* 5K 75
(in two parts)
Norfolk Sq. *W2* 9B 58
Norfolk Sq. M. W2 9B 58
(off London St.)
Norfolk St. *E7* 1E 62
Norfolk Ter. *W6* 6J 73
Norgrove St. *SW12* 6E 90
Norham Ct. Dart 5M 99
(off Osbourne Rd.)
Norheads La.
Warl & Big H 9E 140
(in two parts)
Norhyrst Av. *SE25* 7D 108
Nork. 7H 135
Nork Gdns. *Bans* 6J 135
Nork Ri. *Bans* 8H 135
Nork Way. *Bans* 8G 135
Norland Ho. W11 2H 73
(off Queensdale Cres.)
Norland Pl. *W11* 2J 73
Norland Rd. W11 2H 73
(off Queensdale Cres.)
Norlands Cres. *Chst* 5M 111
Norland Sq. *W11* 2J 73
Norland Sq. Mans. W11 2J 73
(off Norland Sq.)
Norley Va. *SW15* 7E 88
Norlington Rd. *E10* 6A 46
Norman Av. *N22* 8M 27
Norman Av. *Eps* 4D 134
Norman Av. *Felt* 8J 85
Norman Av. *S'hall* 1J 69
Norman Av. *S Croy* 2A 138
Norman Av. *Twic* 6G 87
Normanby Clo. *SW15* 4K 89
Normanby Rd. *NW10* 9D 40
Norman Clo. *N22* 8A 28
Norman Clo. *Orp* 5A 128
Norman Clo. *Romf* 8M 33
Norman Clo. *Wal A* 6K 7
Norman Colyer Ct. *Eps* 2B 134
Norman Ct. *N4* 5L 43
Norman Ct. *NW10* 3E 56
Norman Ct. W13 2F 70
(off Kirkfield Clo.)
Norman Ct. Brom 5E 110
(off Tweedy Rd.)
Norman Ct. *Ilf* 5B 48
Norman Cres. *Houn* 8H 69
Norman Cres. *Pinn* 8G 21
Normand Gdns. W14 7J 73
(off Greyhound Rd.)
Normand M. *W14* 7J 73
Normand Rd. *W14* 7K 73
Normandy Av. *Barn* 7K 13
Normandy Clo. *SE26* 9J 93
Normandy Dri. *Hay* 9A 52
Normandy Ho. E14 3A 78
(off Plevna St.)
Normandy Rd. *SW9* 9L 75
Normandy Ter. *E16* 9F 62
Normandy Way. *Eri* 9C 82
Norman Gro. *E3* 5J 61
Norman Hay Ind. Est.
W Dray 8K 143
Norman Ho. SW8 8J 75
(off Wyvil Rd.)
Norman Ho. Felt 8K 85
(off Watermill Way)
Normanhurst Av. *Bexh* 9H 81
Normanhurst Dri. *Twic* 4E 86
Normanhurst Rd. *SW2* 8K 91
Normanhurst Rd. *Orp* 6F 112
Normanhurst Rd.
W on T 4H 117
Norman Pde. *Sidc* 8H 97
Norman Rd. *E6* 7K 63
Norman Rd. *E11* 7B 46
Norman Rd. *N15* 3D 44
Norman Rd. *SE10* 8M 77
Norman Rd. *SW19* 4A 106
Norman Rd. *Ashf* 3B 100
Norman Rd. *Belv* 4M 81
(in two parts)
Norman Rd. *Dart* 7J 99
Norman Rd. *Horn* 5E 50
Norman Rd. *Ilf* 1M 63
Norman Rd. *Sutt* 7L 121
Norman Rd. *T Hth* 9M 107
Norman's Clo. *NW10* 2B 56
Normans Clo. *Uxb* 7D 142
Normansfield Av. *Tedd* 4G 103
Normans Fld. Clo. *Bush* 9M 9
Normanshire Dri. *E4* 4L 29
Norman's Mead. *NW10* 2B 56
Norman St. *EC1* 6A 60
Normanton Av. *SW19* 8L 89
Normanton Pk. *E4* 2C 30
Normanton Rd. *S Croy* 7C 124
Normanton St. *SE23* 8H 93
Norman Way. *N14* 2J 27
Norman Way. *W3* 8M 55
Normington Clo. *SW16* 2L 107
Norrice Lea. *N2* 3B 42
Norris. NW9 8D 24
(off Concourse, The)
Norris Ho. E9 4G 61
(off Handley Rd.)
Norris Ho. N1 4C 60
(off Colville Est.)
Norris Ho. SE8 6K 77
(off Grove St.)
Norris St. *SW1* 1H 75
Norris Way. *Dart* 2D 98
Norroy Rd. *SW15* 3H 89
Norry's Clo. *Cockf* 6D 14
Norry's Rd. *Cockf* 6D 14
Norseman Clo. *Ilf* 6F 48
Norseman Way. *Gnfd* 4M 53
Norstead Pl. *SW15* 8E 88
N. Access Rd. *E17* 4H 45
North Acre. *NW9* 8C 24
North Acre. *Bans* 8K 135
North Acton. 7B 56
N. Acton Rd. *NW10* 5B 56
Northallerton Way. *Romf* 5H 35
Northall Rd. *Bexh* 1A 98
Northampton Gro. *N1* 1A 60
Northampton Hall City University (Halls) 7B 60
Northampton Ho. Romf 4J 35
(off Broseley Rd.)
Northampton Pk. *N1* 2A 60
Northampton Rd. *EC1* 7L 59
Northampton Rd. *Croy* 4E 124
Northampton Rd. *Enf* 6J 17
Northampton Row. EC1 7L 59
(off Rosoman Pl.)
Northampton Sq. *EC1* 6M 59
Northampton St. *N1* 3A 60
Northanger Rd. *SW16* 3J 107
North App. *N'wd* 2A 20
North App. *Wat* 8D 4
N. Audley St. *W1* 9E 58
North Av. *N18* 4E 28
North Av. *NW10* 6G 57
North Av. *W13* 8F 54
North Av. *Cars* 9E 122
North Av. *Harr* 4M 37
North Av. *Hay* 1E 68
North Av. *Rich* 9L 71
North Av. *S'hall* 1K 69
North Av. *W Vill* 9C 116
North Bank. *NW8* 6C 58
Northbank Rd. *E17* 9A 30
North Beckton. 8J 63
N. Birkbeck Rd. *E11* 8B 46
North Block. SE1 3K 75
(off York Rd.)
Northborough Rd.
SW16 7H 107
Northbourne. *Brom* 2E 126
Northbourne Rd. *SW4* 4H 91
N. Branch Av. *NW10* 6G 57
Northbrook Dri. *N'wd* 8C 20
Northbrook Rd. *N22* 7J 27
Northbrook Rd. *SE13* 4C 94
Northbrook Rd. *Barn* 8J 13
Northbrook Rd. *Croy* 9B 108
Northbrook Rd. *Ilf* 7L 47
Northburgh St. *EC1* 7M 59
N. Carriage Dri. W2 1C 74
(off Bayswater Rd.)
North Cheam. 5H 121
Northchurch. *SE17* 6B 76
(in three parts)
Northchurch Rd. *N1* 3B 60
(in two parts)
Northchurch Rd. *Wemb* 2L 55
Northchurch Ter. *N1* 3C 60
(in two parts)
N. Circular Rd. *E4* 6K 29
N. Circular Rd. *N3 & N12* 1L 41
N. Circular Rd. *N13* 5L 27
N. Circular Rd. *NW2* 8C 40
N. Circular Rd. *NW4* 5G 41
N. Circular Rd. *NW10* 5K 55
Northcliffe Clo. *Wor Pk* 5C 120
Northcliffe Dri. *N20* 1K 25
North Clo. *Barn* 7G 13
North Clo. *Bexh* 3H 97
North Clo. *Chig* 5E 32
North Clo. *Dag* 4L 65
North Clo. *Felt* 5B 84
North Clo. *Mord* 8J 105
N. Colonnade, The. *E14* 2L 77
North Comn. *Wey* 6A 116
N. Common Rd. *W5* 1J 71
N. Common Rd. *Uxb* 1B 142
Northcote. *Oxs* 6A 132
Northcote. *Pinn* 9G 21
Northcote Av. *W5* 1J 71
Northcote Av. *Iswth* 4E 86
Northcote Av. *S'hall* 1J 69
Northcote Av. *Surb* 2M 119
Northcote M. *SW11* 3C 90
Northcote Rd. *E17* 2J 45
Northcote Rd. *NW10* 3C 56
Northcote Rd. *SW11* 4C 90
Northcote Rd. *Croy* 1B 124
Northcote Rd. *N Mald* 7A 104
Northcote Rd. *Sidc* 1C 112
Northcote Rd. *Twic* 4E 86
Northcott Av. *N22* 8J 27
Northcotts. Ab L 6B 4
(off Long Elms Clo.)
N. Countess Rd. *E17* 9K 29
North Ct. *SE24* 2M 91
North Ct. SW1 4J 75
(off Gt. Peter St.)
North Ct. *W1* 8G 59
North Ct. Brom 5E 110
(off Palace Gro.)
North Cray. 2J 113
N. Cray Rd. *Sidc & Bex* 3J 113
North Cres. *E16* 7B 62
North Cres. *N3* 9K 25
North Cres. *WC1* 8H 59
Northcroft Ct. *W12* 3E 72
Northcroft Rd. *W13* 3F 70
Northcroft Rd. *Eps* 9C 120
North Crofts. *SE23* 7F 92
Northcroft Ter. *W13* 3F 70
N. Cross Rd. *SE22* 4D 92
N. Cross Rd. *Ilf* 2A 48
Northdale Ct. *SE25* 7D 108
North Dene. *NW7* 3B 24
Northdene. *Chig* 5B 32
North Dene. *Houn* 9M 69
Northdene Gdns. *N15* 4D 44
North Down. *S Croy* 3C 138
Northdown Clo. *Ruis* 8D 36
Northdown Gdns. *Ilf* 3C 48
Northdown Rd. *Horn* 5F 50
Northdown Rd. *Sutt* 2L 135
Northdown Rd. *Well* 1F 96
N. Downs Cres. *New Ad* 1M 139
(in two parts)
N. Downs Rd. *New Ad* 2M 139
Northdown St. *N1* 5J 59
North Dri. *SW16* 1G 107
North Dri. *Beck* 8M 109
North Dri. *Houn* 1A 86
North Dri. *Orp* 6C 128
North Dri. *Romf* 1G 51
North Dri. *Ruis* 5C 36
North East Surrey Crematorium.
Mord 1G 121
North End. 9D 82
(Erith)
North End. 7A 42
(Hampstead)
North End. *NW3* 7A 42
North End. *Buck H* 9G 19
North End. *Croy* 4A 124
North End. *Noak H* 2G 35
N. End Av. *NW3* 7A 42
(in two parts)
N. End Cres. *W14* 5K 73
N. End Ho. *W14* 5J 73
N. End La. *Orp* 3L 141
N. End Pde. W14 5J 73
(off N. End Rd.)
N. End Rd. *NW11* 6L 41
N. End Rd. *W14 & SW6* 5J 73
Northend Rd. *Eri* 8D 82
N. End Rd. *Wemb* 8L 39
Northend Trad. Est. *Eri* 9C 82
N. End Way. *NW3* 7A 42
Northern Av. *N9* 2C 28
Northernhay Wlk. *Mord* 8J 105
Northern Perimeter Rd.
H'row A 9M 143
Northern Perimeter Rd. W.
H'row A 9J 143
Northern Rd. *E13* 5F 62
Northesk Ho. E1 7F 60
(off Tent St.)
Northey Av. *Sutt* 2H 135
N. Eyot Gdns. *W6* 6D 72
Northey St. *E14* 1J 77
North Feltham. 5F 84
N. Feltham Trad. Est.
Felt 4F 84
Northfield. *Lou* 6H 19
Northfield Av. *W13 & W5* 2F 70
Northfield Av. *Orp* 1G 129
Northfield Av. *Pinn* 2H 37
Northfield Clo. *Brom* 5J 111
Northfield Clo. *Hay* 4D 68
Northfield Cres. *Sutt* 6J 121
Northfield Gdns. *Dag* 9K 49
Northfield Gdns. *Wat* 1G 9
Northfield Ho. *SE15* 7E 76
Northfield Ind. Est. *NW10* 6L 55
Northfield Ind. Est. *Wemb* 4L 55
Northfield Pde. *Hay* 4C 68
Northfield Pk. *Hay* 4D 68
Northfield Path. *Dag* 9K 49
Northfield Pl. *Wey* 9A 116
Northfield Rd. *E6* 3K 63
Northfield Rd. *N16* 5C 44
Northfield Rd. *W13* 3F 70
Northfield Rd. *Barn* 5C 14
Northfield Rd. *Borwd* 3M 11
Northfield Rd. *Dag* 9K 49
Northfield Rd. *Enf* 7F 1
Northfield Rd. *Houn* 7H 6
Northfield Rd. *Wal X* 5E
Northfields. 4F 7
Northfields. *SW18* 3L 8
Northfields. *Eps* 3C 13

Northfields Prospect Bus. Cen.—Oakdene Clo.

Northfields Prospect Bus. Cen.
SW18 .... 3L 89
Northfields Rd. W3 .... 8M 55
North Finchley. 5A 26
Northfleet Ho. SE1 .... 3B 76
(off Tennis St.)
N. Flock St. SE16 .... 3E 76
N. Flower Wlk. W2 .... 1A 74
(off Lancaster Wlk.)
North Garden. E14 .... 2K 77
North Gdns. SW19 .... 4B 106
North Ga. NW8 .... 5C 58
(off Prince Albert Rd.)
Northgate. N'wd 7A 20
Northgate Bus. Pk. Enf 5F 16
Northgate Dri. NW9 .... 4C 40
Northgate Ho. E14 .... 1L 77
(off E. India Dock Rd.)
Northgate Ind. Pk. Romf 8K 33
Northgate Path. Borwd 2K 11
N. Glade, The. Bex 6K 97
N. Gower St. NW1 .... 6G 59
North Grn. NW9 .... 7C 24
North Gro. N6 .... 5E 42
North Gro. N15 .... 3B 44
North Harrow. 3M 37
N. Hatton Rd. H'row A 9B 68
North Hill. N6 .... 4D 42
N. Hill Av. N6 .... 4E 42
N. Hill Dri. Romf 3H 35
N. Hill Grn. Romf 4H 35
North Hillingdon. 3A 52
North Ho. SE8 .... 6K 77
N. Hyde Gdns. Hay 5E 68
N. Hyde La. S'hall 6H 69
N. Hyde Rd. Hay 4C 68
Northiam. N12 .... 4L 25
(in two parts)
Northiam. WC1 .... 6J 59
(off Cromer St.)
Northiam St. E9 .... 4F 60
Northington St. WC1 .... 7K 59
North Kensington. 8H 57
Northlands Av. Orp 6C 128
Northlands St. SE5 .... 1A 92
North La. Tedd 3D 102
Northleach Ct. SE15 .... 7C 76
(off Birdlip Clo.)
North Lodge. E16 .... 2F 78
(off Wesley Av.)
North Lodge. New Bar 7A 14
N. Lodge Clo. SW15 .... 4H 89
North Looe. 5G 135
North Mall. N9 .... 2F 28
(off Plevna Rd.)
North M. WC1 .... 7K 59
North Mt. N20 .... 2A 26
(off High Rd.)
Northolm. Edgw 4B 24
Northolme Gdns. Edgw 8L 23
Northolme Ri. Orp 4C 128
Northolme Rd. N5 .... 9A 44
Northolt. 3L 53
Northolt. N17 .... 9C 28
(off Griffin Rd.)
Northolt Av. Ruis 1F 52
Northolt Gdns. Gnfd 1D 54
Northolt Rd. Harr 9M 37
Northolt Rd. H'row A 9H 143
Northolt Way. Horn 2G 67
N. Orbital Rd.
Wat & Brick W 6H 5
Northover. Brom 9D 94
North Pde. Chess 7K 119
North Pde. Edgw 9L 23
North Pde. S'hall 9L 53
(off North Rd.)
North Pk. SE9 .... 5K 95
North Pl. SW18 .... 4L 89
North Pl. Mitc 4D 106
North Pl. Tedd 3D 102
North Pl. Wal A 6H 7
N. Pole La. Kes 8D 126
N. Pole Rd. W10 .... 8G 57
Northport St. N1 .... 4B 60
North Ride. W2 .... 1C 74
North Riding. Brick W 3L 5
North Ri. W2 .... 9C 58
North Rd. N2 .... 9C 26
North Rd. N6 .... 5E 42
North Rd. N7 .... 2J 59
North Rd. N9 .... 1F 28
North Rd. SE18 .... 5C 80
North Rd. SW19 .... 3A 106
North Rd. W5 .... 4H 71
North Rd. Belv 4M 81
North Rd. Bren 7J 71
North Rd. Brom 5F 110
North Rd. Chad H 3J 49
North Rd. Dart 5D 98
North Rd. Edgw 8M 23
North Rd. Felt 5B 84
North Rd. Harr 5E 38
North Rd. Hav 3C 34
North Rd. Hay 8B 52
North Rd. Ilf 7C 48
North Rd. Purf 5M 83
(in two parts)
North Rd. Rich 2L 87
North Rd. S'hall 9L 53
North Rd. Surb 1H 119
North Rd. Wal X 6E 6
North Rd. W on T 7G 117
North Rd. W Dray 4K 143
North Rd. W Wick 3M 125
Northrop Rd. H'row A 9C 68
North Row. W1 .... 1D 74
N. Row Bldgs. W1 .... 1E 74
(off North Row)
North Several. SE3 .... 1B 94
North Sheen. 2L 87
Northside Rd. Brom 5E 110
N. Side Wandsworth Comn.
SW18 .... 4B 90
Northspur Rd. Sutt 5L 121
North Sq. N9 .... 2F 28
(off Hertford Rd.)
North Sq. NW11 .... 3L 41
Northstead Rd. SW2 .... 8L 91
North St. E13 .... 5F 62
North St. NW4 .... 3G 41
North St. SW4 .... 2G 91
North St. Bark 2M 63
(Barking Northern Relief Rd.)
North St. Bark 3A 64
(London Rd.)
North St. Bexh 3L 97
North St. Brom 5E 110
North St. Cars 5D 122
North St. Dart 6H 99
North St. Horn 5H 51
North St. Iswth 2E 86
North St. Romf 1B 50
(in two parts)
N. Street Pas. E13 .... 5F 62
N. Tenter St. E1 .... 9D 60
North Ter. SW3 .... 4C 74
Northumberland All. EC3 .... 9C 60
(in two parts)
Northumberland Av. E12 .... 6G 47
Northumberland Av. WC2 .... 2J 75
Northumberland Av. Enf 3F 16
Northumberland Av. Horn 3G 51
Northumberland Av. Iswth 9D 70
Northumberland Av. Well 3B 96
Northumberland Clo. Eri 8A 82
Northumberland Clo.
Stanw 5C 144
Northumberland Cres.
Felt 5C 84
Northumberland Gdns.
N9 .... 3D 28
Northumberland Gdns.
Brom 8L 111
Northumberland Gdns.
Iswth 8E 70
Northumberland Gdns.
Mitc 9H 107
Northumberland Gro. N17 .... 7F 28
Northumberland Heath. 8A 82
Northumberland Ho. WC2 .... 2J 75
(off Northumberland Av.)
Northumberland Pk. N17 .... 7D 28
Northumberland Pk. Eri 8A 82
Northumberland Pk. Ind. Est.
N17 .... 7F 28
Northumberland Pl. W2 .... 9L 57
Northumberland Pl. Rich 4H 87
Northumberland Rd. E6 .... 9J 63
Northumberland Rd. E17 .... 5L 45
Northumberland Rd. Harr 3K 37
Northumberland Rd.
New Bar 8A 14
Northumberland Row.
Twic 7C 86
Northumberland St. WC2 .... 2J 75
Northumberland Way. Eri 9A 82
Northumbria St. E14 .... 9L 61
N. Verbena Gdns. W6 .... 6E 72
Northview. N7 .... 8J 43
North Vw. SW19 .... 2G 105
North Vw. W5 .... 7G 55
North Vw. Pinn 5G 37
Northview. Swan 6C 114
N. View Cres. NW10 .... 9D 40
N. View Cres. Eps 9F 134
Northview Dri. Wfd G 9H 31
N. View Rd. N8 .... 2H 43
North Vs. NW1 .... 2H 59
North Wlk. W8 & W2 .... 1M 73
(off Bayswater Rd.)
North Wlk. New Ad 8M 125
(in two parts)
North Watford. 1F 8
North Way. N9 .... 2H 29
North Way. N11 .... 6G 27
North Way. NW9 .... 1M 39
Northway. NW11 .... 3M 41
Northway. Mord 7J 105
North Way. Pinn 2H 37
North Way. Uxb 3C 142
Northway. Wall 6G 123
Northway Cir. NW7 .... 4B 24
Northway Cres. NW7 .... 4B 24
Northway Gdns. NW11 .... 3M 41
Northway Rd. SE5 .... 2A 92
Northway Rd. Croy 1D 124
Northways Pde. NW3 .... 3B 58
(off College Cres., in two parts)
Northweald La. King T 2H 103
North Wembley. 8H 39
N. Western Av. A'ham 4M 9
N. Western Av. Wat 8B 4
(in two parts)
N. Western Commercial Cen.
NW1 .... 3J 59
Northwest Pl. N1 .... 5L 59
N. Weylands Ind. Est.
W on T 4J 117
North Wharf. E14 .... 2A 78
(off Coldharbour)
N. Wharf Rd. W2 .... 8B 58
Northwick Av. Harr 4E 38
Northwick Circ. Harr 4G 39
Northwick Clo. NW8 .... 7B 58
Northwick Clo. Harr 6F 38
Northwick Ho. NW8 .... 7A 58
(off St John's Wood Rd.)
Northwick Pk. Rd. Harr 4D 38
Northwick Rd. Wat 4G 21
Northwick Rd. Wemb 4H 55
Northwick Ter. NW8 .... 7B 58
Northwick Wlk. Harr 5D 38
Northwold Dri. Pinn 9G 21
Northwold Est. E5 .... 7E 44
Northwold Rd. N16 & E5 .... 7D 44
Northwood. 6C 20
Northwood Av. Horn 9E 50
Northwood Av. Purl 4L 137
N. Wood Ct. SE25 .... 7E 108
Northwood Gdns. N12 .... 5B 26
Northwood Gdns. Gnfd 1D 54
Northwood Gdns. Ilf 2L 47
Northwood Golf Course. 8B 20
Northwood Hills. 9E 20
Northwood Hills Cir. N'wd 8E 20
Northwood Ho. SE27 .... 1B 108
Northwood Pl. Eri 4K 81
Northwood Rd. N6 .... 5F 42
Northwood Rd. SE23 .... 7K 93
Northwood Rd. Cars 8E 122
Northwood Rd. H'row A 9H 143
Northwood Rd. T Hth 6M 107
Northwood Way. SE19 .... 3B 108
Northwood Way. N'wd 7D 20
North Woolwich. 2L 79
North Woolwich Old Station Mus.
.... 3L 79
N. Woolwich Rd. E16 .... 2D 78
N. Worple Way. SW14 .... 2B 88
Norton Almshouses. Chesh 3D 6
(off Turner's Hill)
Norton Av. Surb 2M 119
Norton Clo. E4 .... 5L 29
Norton Clo. Borwd 3L 11
Norton Clo. Enf 4F 16
Norton Folgate. E1 .... 8C 60
Norton Folgate Houses.
E1 .... 8D 60
(off Puma Ct.)
Norton Gdns. SW16 .... 6J 107
Norton Ho. E1 .... 9F 60
(off Bigland St.)
Norton Ho. E2 .... 5H 61
(off Mace St.)
Norton Ho. SW1 .... 4H 75
(off Arneway St.)
Norton Ho. SW9 .... 1K 91
(off Aytoun Rd.)
Norton Rd. E10 .... 6K 45
Norton Rd. Dag 2B 66
Norton Rd. Uxb 6B 142
Norton Rd. Wemb 2H 55
Norval Rd. Wemb 7F 38
Norvic Ho. Eri 8D 82
Norway Ga. SE16 .... 4J 77
Norway Pl. E14 .... 9K 61
Norway St. SE10 .... 7M 77
Norway Wlk. Rain 7G 67
Norway Wharf. E14 .... 9K 61
(off Norway Pl.)
Norwich Ho. E14 .... 9M 61
(off Cordelia St.)
Norwich Ho. Borwd 4L 11
(off Stratfield Rd.)
Norwich M. Ilf 6E 48
Norwich Pl. Bexh 3L 97
Norwich Rd. E7 .... 1E 62
Norwich Rd. Dag 5L 65
Norwich Rd. Gnfd 4M 53
Norwich Rd. N'wd 1D 36
Norwich Rd. T Hth 7A 108
Norwich St. EC4 .... 9L 59
Norwich Wlk. Edgw 7A 24
Norwich Way. Crox G 5A 8
Norwood. 3C 108
Norwood Av. Romf 5C 50
Norwood Av. Wemb 4K 55
Norwood Clo. NW2 .... 8J 41
Norwood Clo. S'hall 5L 69
Norwood Clo. Twic 8B 86
Norwood Ct. Dart 4L 99
(off Farnol Rd.)
Norwood Dri. Harr 4K 37
Norwood Gdns. Hay 7G 53
Norwood Gdns. S'hall 5K 69
Norwood Green. 5L 69
Norwood Grn. Rd. S'hall 5L 69
Norwood High St. SE27 .... 9M 91
Norwood Ho. E14 .... 1M 77
(off Poplar High St.)
Norwood New Town. 3A 108
Norwood Pk. Rd. SE27 .... 2A 108
Norwood Rd. SE24 .... 7M 91
Norwood Rd. SE27 .... 8M 91
Norwood Rd. Chesh 3E 6
Norwood Rd. S'hall 4J 69
Norwood Ter. S'hall 5M 69
Notley St. SE5 .... 8B 76
Notson Rd. SE25 .... 8F 108
Notting Barn Rd. W10 .... 7H 57
Nottingdale Sq. W11 .... 2J 73
Nottingham Av. E16 .... 8G 63
Nottingham Clo. Wat 6E 4
Nottingham Ct. WC2 .... 9J 59
Nottingham Ho. WC2 .... 9J 59
(off Shorts Gdns.)
Nottingham Pl. W1 .... 8E 58
Nottingham Rd. E10 .... 4A 46
Nottingham Rd. SW17 .... 7D 90
Nottingham Rd. Iswth 1D 86
Nottingham Rd. S Croy 6A 124
Nottingham St. W1 .... 8E 58
Nottingham Ter. NW1 .... 7E 58
(off York Ter. W.)
Notting Hill. 1K 73
Notting Hill Ga. W11 .... 2L 73
Nottingwood Ho. W11 .... 1J 73
(off Clarendon Rd.)
Nova M. Sutt 3J 121
Novar Clo. Orp 2D 128
Nova Rd. Croy 3M 123
Novar Rd. SE9 .... 7A 96
Novello St. SW6 .... 9L 73
Novello Way. Borwd 3B 12
Nowell Rd. SW13 .... 7E 72
Nower Ct. Pinn 2K 37
Nower Hill. Pinn 2K 37
Noyna Rd. SW17 .... 9D 90
Nubia Way. Brom 9C 94
Nuding Clo. SE13 .... 2L 93
Nuffield Ct. Houn 8K 69
Nuffield Lodge. N6 .... 4G 43
Nuffield Lodge. W9 .... 8L 57
(off Admiral Wlk.)
Nuffield Rd. Swan 3E 114
Nugent Ind. Pk. Orp 8G 113
Nugent Rd. N19 .... 6J 43
Nugent Rd. SE25 .... 7D 108
Nugents Ct. Pinn 8J 21
Nugent's Pk. Pinn 8J 21
Nugent Ter. NW8 .... 5A 58
Numa Ct. Bren 8H 71
Nun Ct. EC2 .... 9B 60
(off Coleman St.)
Nuneaton Rd. Dag 3J 65
Nunhead. 2F 92
Nunhead Cres. SE15 .... 2F 92
Nunhead Est. SE15 .... 3F 92
Nunhead Grn. SE15 .... 2F 92
Nunhead Gro. SE15 .... 2F 92
Nunhead La. SE15 .... 2F 92
Nunhead Pas. SE15 .... 2E 92
Nunnington Clo. SE9 .... 9J 95
Nunns Rd. Enf 4A 16
Nuper's Hatch. 1C 34
Nupton Dri. Barn 8G 13
Nurse Clo. Edgw 8A 24
Nursery App. N12 .... 6C 26
Nursery Av. N3 .... 9A 26
Nursery Av. Bexh 2K 97
Nursery Av. Croy 4H 125
Nursery Clo. SE4 .... 1K 93
Nursery Clo. SW15 .... 3H 89
Nursery Clo. Croy 4H 125
Nursery Clo. Enf 3H 17
Nursery Clo. Eps 2C 134
Nursery Clo. Felt 6F 84
(in two parts)
Nursery Clo. Orp 2D 128
Nursery Clo. Romf 4H 49
Nursery Clo. Swan 6A 114
Nursery Clo. Wfd G 5F 30
Nursery Ct. N17 .... 7D 28
Nursery Ct. W13 .... 8E 54
Nursery Gdns. Chst 3M 111
Nursery Gdns. Enf 3H 17
Nursery Gdns. Hamp 1K 101
Nursery Gdns. Houn 4K 85
Nursery Gdns. Sun 6D 100
Nursery La. E2 .... 4D 60
Nursery La. E7 .... 2E 62
Nursery La. W10 .... 8G 57
Nursery La. Uxb 7B 142
Nurserymans Rd. N11 .... 2E 26
Nursery Rd. E9 .... 2G 61
Nursery Rd. N2 .... 8B 26
Nursery Rd. N14 .... 9G 15
Nursery Rd. SW9 .... 3K 91
Nursery Rd. SW19 .... 6M 105
(Merton)
Nursery Rd. SW19 .... 4J 105
(Wimbledon)
Nursery Rd. H Bee 3G 19
Nursery Rd. Lou 7G 19
Nursery Rd. Pinn 1G 37
Nursery Rd. Sun 6C 100
Nursery Rd. Sutt 6A 122
Nursery Rd. T Hth 8B 108
Nursery Row. Barn 5J 13
Nursery St. N17 .... 7D 28
Nursery, The. Eri 8D 82
Nursery Wlk. NW4 .... 1G 41
Nursery Wlk. Romf 5B 50
Nursery Waye. Uxb 4B 142
Nurstead Rd. Eri 8L 81
Nutbourne St. W10 .... 6J 57
Nutbrook St. SE15 .... 2E 92
Nutbrowne Rd. Dag 4K 65
Nutcroft Rd. SE15 .... 8F 76
Nutfield Clo. N18 .... 6D 28
Nutfield Clo. Cars 5C 122
Nutfield Gdns. Ilf 7D 48
Nutfield Gdns. N'holt 5G 53
Nutfield Rd. E15 .... 9A 46
Nutfield Rd. NW2 .... 8E 40
Nutfield Rd. SE22 .... 3D 92
Nutfield Rd. Coul 8E 136
Nutfield Rd. T Hth 8M 107
Nutfield Way. Orp 4M 127
Nutford Pl. W1 .... 9D 58
Nuthatch Clo. Stai 7D 144
Nuthatch Gdns. SE28 .... 3B 80
(in two parts)
Nuthurst Av. SW2 .... 8K 91
Nutkin Wlk. Uxb 3C 142
Nutley Clo. Swan 5D 114
Nutley Ter. NW3 .... 2A 58
Nutmead Clo. Bex 7A 98
Nutmeg Clo. E16 .... 7C 62
Nutmeg La. E14 .... 9B 62
Nuttall St. N1 .... 5C 60
Nutter La. E11 .... 4G 47
Nuttfield Clo. Crox G 8A 8
Nutt Gro. Edgw 2H 23
Nut Tree Clo. Orp 5H 129
Nutt St. SE15 .... 8D 76
Nutty La. Shep 7A 100
Nutwell St. SW17 .... 2C 106
Nuxley Rd. Belv 7K 81
Nyanza St. SE18 .... 7B 80
Nye Bevan Est. E5 .... 8H 45
Nye Bevan Ho. SW6 .... 8K 73
(off St Thomas's Way)
Nylands Av. Rich 9L 71
Nymans Gdns. SW20 .... 7F 104
Nynehead St. SE14 .... 8J 77
Nyon Gro. SE6 .... 8K 93
Nyssa Clo. Wfd G 6K 31
Nyssa Ct. E15 .... 6C 62
(off Teasel Way)
Nyton Clo. N19 .... 6J 43

O

Oakapple Clo. S Croy 6F 138
Oak Apple Ct. SE12 .... 7E 94
Oak Av. N8 .... 2J 43
Oak Av. N10 .... 7F 26
Oak Av. N17 .... 7B 28
Oak Av. Brick W 3L 5
Oak Av. Croy 3L 125
Oak Av. Enf 2K 15
Oak Av. Hamp 2J 101
Oak Av. Houn 8H 69
Oak Av. Upm 8M 51
Oak Av. Uxb 7A 36
Oak Av. W Dray 4L 143
Oak Bank. New Ad 8A 126
Oakbank Av. W on T 2K 117
Oakbank Gro. SE24 .... 3A 92
Oakbrook Clo. Brom 1F 110
Oakbury Rd. SW6 .... 1M 89
Oak Clo. N14 .... 9F 14
Oak Clo. Dart 3C 98
Oak Clo. Sutt 4A 122
Oak Clo. Wal A 7K 7
Oakcombe Clo. N Mald 5C 104
Oak Cottage Clo. SE6 .... 7D 94
Oak Cotts. W7 .... 3C 70
Oak Ct. SE15 .... 8D 76
(off Sumner Rd.)
Oak Ct. N'wd 6B 20
Oak Cres. E16 .... 8C 62
Oakcroft Bus. Cen.
Chess 6K 119
Oakcroft Clo. Pinn 9F 20
Oakcroft Rd. SE13 .... 1B 94
Oakcroft Rd. Chess 6K 119
Oakcroft Vs. Chess 6K 119
Oakdale. N14 .... 1F 26
Oakdale Av. Harr 3J 39
Oakdale Av. N'wd 9E 20
Oakdale Clo. Wat 4G 21
Oakdale Ct. E4 .... 5A 30
Oakdale Gdns. E4 .... 5A 30
Oakdale Rd. E7 .... 3F 62
Oakdale Rd. E11 .... 7B 46
Oakdale Rd. E18 .... 9F 30
Oakdale Rd. N4 .... 4A 44
Oakdale Rd. SE15 & SE4 .... 2G 93
Oakdale Rd. SW16 .... 2J 107
Oakdale Rd. Eps 1B 134
Oakdale Rd. Wat 3G 21
Oakdale Way. Mitc 2E 122
Oakdene. SE15 .... 9F 76
Oakdene. W13 .... 8F 54
Oakdene. Chesh 3E 6
Oakdene. Romf 9K 35
Oakdene Av. Chst 2L 111
Oakdene Av. Eri 7A 82
Oakdene Av. Th Dit 3E 118
Oakdene Clo. Horn 4F 50
Oakdene Clo. Pinn 7K 21

Oakdene Ct.—Offley Pl.

Oakdene Ct. *W on T* 5F 116
Oakdene Dri. *Surb* 2A 120
Oakdene M. *Sutt* 3K 121
Oakdene Pk. *N3* 7K 25
Oakdene Rd. *Orp* 9D 112
Oakdene Rd. *Uxb* 5F 142
Oakdene Rd. *Wat* 9F 4
Oakden St. *SE11* 5L 75
Oake Ct. *SW15* 4J 89
Oakeford Ho. W14 *4J 73*
(off Russell Rd.)
Oakend Ho. *N4* 5B 44
Oaken Dri. *Clay* 8D 118
Oakenholt Ho. *SE2* 2H 81
Oaken La. *Clay* 6C 118
Oakenshaw Clo. *Surb* 2J 119
Oakes Clo. *E6* 9K 63
Oakeshott Av. *N6* 7E 42
Oakey La. *SE1* 4L 75
Oak Farm. *Borwd* 7A 12
Oakfield. *E4* 5M 29
Oakfield Av. *Harr* 1F 38
Oakfield Cen. *SE20* 4F 108
Oakfield Clo. *N Mald* 9D 104
Oakfield Clo. *Ruis* 4D 36
Oakfield Clo. *Wey* 6A 116
Oakfield Ct. *N8* 5J 43
Oakfield Ct. *NW11* 5H 41
Oakfield Ct. *Borwd* 5M 11
Oakfield Gdns. *N18* 4C 28
Oakfield Gdns. *SE19* 2C 108
(in two parts)
Oakfield Gdns. *Beck* 9M 109
Oakfield Gdns. *Cars* 3C 122
Oakfield Gdns. *Gnfd* 7B 54
Oakfield Glade. *Wey* 6A 116
Oakfield Ho. E3 *8L 61*
(off Gale St.)
Oakfield La. *Dart* 8C 98
Oakfield La. *Kes* 6G 127
Oakfield Lodge. Ilf *8M 47*
(off Albert Rd.)
Oakfield Pk. Rd. *Dart* 8H 99
Oakfield Pl. *Dart* 8H 99
Oakfield Rd. *E6* 4J 63
Oakfield Rd. *E17* 9J 29
Oakfield Rd. *N3* 8M 25
Oakfield Rd. *N8* 4L 43
Oakfield Rd. *N14* 2J 27
Oakfield Rd. *SE20* 4F 108
Oakfield Rd. *SW19* 9H 89
Oakfield Rd. *Asht* 9H 133
Oakfield Rd. *Croy* 3A 124
Oakfield Rd. *Ilf* 8M 47
Oakfield Rd. *Orp* 2E 128
Oakfield Rd. Ind. Est.
SE20 4F 108
Oakfields. *Lou* 7L 19
Oakfields. *W on T* 3E 116
Oakfields Rd. *NW11* 4J 41
Oakfield St. *SW10* 7A 74
Oakford Rd. *NW5* 9G 43
Oak Gdns. *Croy* 4L 125
Oak Gdns. *Edgw* 9M 23
Oak Glade. *Eps* 4L 133
Oak Glade. *N'wd* 8A 20
Oak Glen. *Horn* 1J 51
Oak Grn. *Ab L* 5C 4
Oak Grn. Way. *Ab L* 5C 4
Oak Gro. *NW2* 9J 41
Oak Gro. *Ruis* 5F 36
Oak Gro. *Sun* 4E 100
Oak Gro. *W Wick* 3A 126
Oak Gro. Rd. *SE20* 5G 109
Oakhall Ct. *E11* 4F 46
Oakhall Dri. *Sun* 2D 100
Oak Hall Rd. *E11* 4F 46
Oakham Clo. *SE6* 8K 93
Oakham Clo. *Barn* 5D 14
Oakham Dri. *Brom* 8D 110
Oakham Ho. W10 *7G 57*
(off Sutton Way)
Oakhampton Rd. *NW7* 7H 25
Oakhill. *Clay* 8E 118
Oak Hill. *Eps* 8B 134
Oakhill. *Surb* 2J 119
Oak Hill. *Wfd G* 7B 30
Oakhill Av. *NW3* 9M 41
Oakhill Av. *Pinn* 9J 21
Oakhill Clo. *Asht* 9G 133
Oak Hill Clo. *Wfd G* 7B 30
Oakhill Ct. *SE23* 5G 93
Oakhill Ct. *SW19* 4H 105
Oak Hill Ct. *Wfd G* 7B 30
Oakhill Cres. *Surb* 2J 119
Oak Hill Cres. *Wfd G* 7B 30
Oakhill Dri. *Surb* 2J 119
Oakhill Gdns. *Wey* 4C 116
Oak Hill Gdns. *Wfd G* 8C 30
Oakhill Gro. *Surb* 1J 119
Oak Hill Pk. *NW3* 9M 41
Oak Hill Pk. M. *NW3* 9A 42
Oakhill Path. *Surb* 1J 119
Oakhill Pl. *SW15* 4L 89
Oakhill Rd. *SW15* 4K 89
Oakhill Rd. *SW16* 5J 107
Oakhill Rd. *Asht* 9G 133
Oakhill Rd. *Beck* 6A 110
Oakhill Rd. *Orp* 3D 128
Oakhill Rd. *Purf* 6M 83
Oak Hill Rd. *Stap A* 1B 34
Oakhill Rd. *Surb* 1J 119
Oakhill Rd. *Sutt* 5M 121
Oak Hill Way. *NW3* 9A 42
Oak Ho. *N2* 9B 26
Oak Ho. W10 *7J 57*
(off Sycamore Wlk.)
Oakhouse Rd. *Bexh* 4L 97
Oakhurst Av. *Barn* 9C 14
Oakhurst Av. *Bexh* 8J 81
Oakhurst Clo. *E17* 2C 46
Oakhurst Clo. *Chst* 5K 111
Oakhurst Clo. *Ilf* 8M 31
Oakhurst Clo. *Tedd* 2C 102
Oakhurst Ct. E17 *2C 46*
(off Woodford New Rd.)
Oakhurst Gdns. *E4* 1D 30
Oakhurst Gdns. *E17* 2C 46
Oakhurst Gdns. *Bexh* 8J 81
Oakhurst Gro. *SE22* 3E 92
Oakhurst Pl. *Wat* 6D 8
Oakhurst Ri. *Cars* 2C 136
Oakhurst Rd. *Enf* 9D 6
Oakhurst Rd. *Eps* 8A 120
Oakington Av. *Harr* 5L 37
Oakington Av. *Hay* 5B 68
Oakington Av. *Wemb* 8K 39
Oakington Ct. Enf *4M 15*
(off Ridgeway, The)
Oakington Dri. *Sun* 6G 101
Oakington Mnr. Dri.
Wemb 1L 55
Oakington Rd. *W9* 7L 57
Oakington Way. *N8* 5J 43
Oakland Pl. *Buck H* 2E 30
Oakland Rd. *E15* 9B 46
Oaklands. *N13* 2K 27
Oaklands. *W13* 8E 54
Oaklands. *Beck* 5M 109
Oaklands. *Kenl* 6A 138
Oaklands Av. *N9* 8F 16
Oaklands Av. *Esh* 3B 118
Oaklands Av. *Iswth* 7D 70
Oaklands Av. *Romf* 1C 50
Oaklands Av. *Sidc* 6D 96
Oaklands Av. *T Hth* 8L 107
Oaklands Av. *Wat* 1F 20
Oaklands Av. *W Wick* 5M 125
Oaklands Clo. *Bexh* 4K 97
Oaklands Clo. *Chess* 6G 119
Oaklands Clo. *Orp* 1C 128
Oaklands Clo. *Wemb* 1H 55
Oaklands Ct. NW10 *4C 56*
(off Nicoll Rd.)
Oaklands Ct. SE20 *4G 109*
(off Chestnut Gro.)
Oaklands Ct. *Wat* 3E 8
Oaklands Ct. *Wemb* 1H 55
Oaklands Dri. *Twic* 6A 86
Oaklands Est. *SW4* 5G 91
Oaklands Gdns. *Kenl* 6A 138
Oaklands Ga. *N'wd* 6C 20
Oaklands Gro. *W12* 2E 72
Oaklands La. *Barn* 6F 12
(in two parts)
Oaklands La. *Big H* 5F 140
Oaklands M. NW2 *9H 41*
(off Oaklands Rd.)
Oaklands Pk. Av. *Ilf* 7A 48
Oaklands Pas. NW2 *9H 41*
(off Oaklands Rd.)
Oaklands Pl. *SW4* 3G 91
Oaklands Rd. *N20* 9K 13
Oaklands Rd. *NW2* 9H 41
Oaklands Rd. *SW14* 2B 88
Oaklands Rd. *W7* 3D 70
(in two parts)
Oaklands Rd. *Bexh* 3K 97
Oaklands Rd. *Brom* 4C 110
Oaklands Rd. *Dart* 7M 99
Oaklands Way. *Wall* 9H 123
Oakland Way. *Eps* 8C 120
Oak La. *E14* 1K 77
Oak La. *N2* 9B 26
Oak La. *N11* 6H 27
Oak La. *Iswth* 3C 86
Oak La. *Twic* 6E 86
Oak La. *Wfd G* 4D 30
Oaklawn Rd. *Lea* 9C 132
Oak Leaf Clo. *Eps* 4A 134
Oakleafe Gdns. *Ilf* 1M 47
Oaklea Lodge. *Ilf* 8E 48
Oaklea Pas. *King T* 7H 103
Oakleigh Av. *N20* 2B 26
Oakleigh Av. *Edgw* 9M 23
Oakleigh Av. *Surb* 3L 119
Oakleigh Clo. *N20* 3D 26
Oakleigh Clo. *Swan* 7C 114
Oakleigh Ct. *Barn* 8C 14
Oakleigh Ct. *Edgw* 9A 24
Oakleigh Ct. *S'hall* 2K 69
Oakleigh Cres. *N20* 2C 26
Oakleigh Dri. *Crox G* 8A 8
Oakleigh Flats. *Eps* 6C 134
Oakleigh Gdns. *N20* 1A 26
Oakleigh Gdns. *Edgw* 5K 23
Oakleigh Gdns. *Orp* 6C 128
Oakleigh M. *N20* 1A 26
Oakleigh Park. 1B 26
Oakleigh Pk. Av. *Chst* 5L 111
Oakleigh Pk. N. *N20* 1B 26
Oakleigh Pk. S. *N20* 9C 14
Oakleigh Rd. *Pinn* 6K 21
Oakleigh Rd. *Uxb* 3A 52
Oakleigh Rd. N. *N20* 2B 26
Oakleigh Rd. S. *N11* 3E 26
Oakleigh Way. *Mitc* 5F 106
Oakleigh Way. *Surb* 3L 119
Oakley Av. *W5* 1L 71
Oakley Av. *Bark* 3D 64
Oakley Av. *Croy* 6K 123
Oakley Clo. *E4* 3A 30
Oakley Clo. *E6* 9J 63
Oakley Clo. *W7* 1C 70
Oakley Clo. *Iswth* 9B 70
Oakley Ct. *Lou* 4L 19
Oakley Cres. *EC1* 5M 59
Oakley Dri. *SE9* 7B 96
Oakley Dri. *SE13* 5B 94
Oakley Dri. *Brom* 5J 127
Oakley Dri. *Romf* 5L 35
Oakley Gdns. *N8* 3K 43
Oakley Gdns. *SW3* 7C 74
Oakley Gdns. *Bans* 7M 135
Oakley Grange. *Harr* 8A 38
Oakley Ho. *SW1* 5D 74
Oakley Ho. *W3* 1L 71
Oakley Pk. *Bex* 6G 97
Oakley Pl. *SE1* 6D 76
Oakley Rd. *N1* 3B 60
Oakley Rd. *SE25* 9F 108
Oakley Rd. *Brom* 5J 127
Oakley Rd. *Harr* 4C 38
Oakley Rd. *Warl* 9E 138
Oakley Sq. *NW1* 5G 59
Oakley St. *SW3* 7C 74
Oakley Wlk. *W6* 7H 73
Oakley Yd. E2 *7D 60*
(off Bacon St.)
Oak Lodge. *E11* 4E 46
Oak Lodge. W8 *4M 73*
(off Chantry Sq.)
Oak Lodge Av. *Chig* 5B 32
Oak Lodge Clo. *Stan* 5G 23
Oak Lodge Clo. *W on T* 7G 117
Oak Lodge Dri.
W Wick 2M 125
Oaklodge Way. *NW7* 5D 24
Oakmead Av. *Brom* 1E 126
Oakmead Ct. *Stan* 4G 23
Oak Meade. *Pinn* 6L 21
Oakmead Gdns. *Edgw* 4B 24
Oakmead Grn. *Eps* 7A 134
Oakmead Pl. *Mitc* 5C 106
Oakmead Rd. *SW12* 7E 90
Oakmead Rd. *Croy* 1H 123
Oakmede. *Barn* 6H 13
Oakmere Rd. *SE2* 7E 80
Oakmont Pl. *Orp* 3B 128
Oakmoor Way. *Chig* 5C 32
Oak Pk. Gdns. *SW19* 7H 89
Oak Pk. M. *N16* 8D 44
Oak Path. Bush *8M 9*
(off Mortimer Clo.)
Oak Pl. *SW18* 4M 89
Oakridge. *Brick W* 2K 5
Oakridge Dri. *N2* 1B 42
Oakridge La. *Brom* 2B 110
Oakridge Rd. *Brom* 1B 110
Oak Ri. *Buck H* 3H 31
Oak Rd. *W5* 1H 71
Oak Rd. *Eri* 8A 82
(Mill Rd.)
Oak Rd. *Eri* 1E 98
(Moat La.)
Oak Rd. *N Mald* 6B 104
Oak Rd. *Orp* 9E 128
Oak Rd. *Romf* 8K 35
Oak Row. *SW16* 6G 107
Oaks Av. *SE19* 2C 108
Oaks Av. *Felt* 8J 85
Oaks Av. *Romf* 9A 34
Oaks Av. *Wor Pk* 5F 120
Oaks Cvn. Pk., The.
Chess 5G 119
Oaksford Av. *SE26* 9F 92
Oaks Gro. *E4* 2C 30
Oakshade Rd. *Brom* 1B 110
Oakshade Rd. *Oxs* 6A 132
Oakshaw Rd. *SW18* 6M 89
Oakshott Ct. *NW1* 5H 59
(in two parts)
Oakside. *Den* 2A 142
Oaks La. *Croy* 5G 125
(in two parts)
Oaks La. *Ilf* 3C 48
Oaks Rd. *Croy* 7F 124
Oaks Rd. *Kenl* 6M 137
Oaks Rd. *Stanw* 5B 144
Oaks Shop. Cen., The.
W3 2A 72
Oaks Sq., The. Eps *5B 134*
(off High St.)
Oaks, The. *N12* 4M 25
Oaks, The. NW6 *3H 57*
(off Brondesbury Pk.)
Oaks, The. *NW10* 3F 56
Oaks, The. *SE18* 6A 80
Oaks, The. *Borwd* 3L 11
Oaks, The. *Brom* 1L 127
Oaks, The. *Dart* 5M 99
Oaks, The. Enf *5M 15*
(off Byculluh Rd.)
Oaks, The. *Eps* 6C 134
Oaks, The. *Hay* 5A 52
Oaks, The. *Mord* 8J 105
Oaks, The. *Ruis* 5C 36
Oaks, The. *Swan* 6C 114
Oaks, The. *Wat* 1G 21
Oaks, The. *Wfd G* 7C 30
Oaks Track. *Cars* 3D 136
Oak St. E14 *3A 78*
(off Stewart St.)
Oak St. *Romf* 3A 50
Oaks Way. *Cars* 9D 122
Oaks Way. *Kenl* 6A 138
Oaksway. *Surb* 3H 119
Oakthorpe Ct. *N13* 5A 28
Oakthorpe Pk. Est. *N13* 5A 28
Oakthorpe Rd. *N13* 5L 27
Oaktree Av. *N13* 3M 27
Oak Tree Clo. *W5* 9G 55
Oak Tree Clo. *Ab L* 5B 4
Oak Tree Clo. *Lou* 3M 19
Oak Tree Clo. *Stan* 7G 23
Oak Tree Ct. *W3* 1M 71
Oaktree Ct. *Els* 8J 11
Oak Tree Ct. *N'holt* 5G 53
Oak Tree Dell. *NW9* 3B 40
Oak Tree Dri. *N20* 1M 25
Oak Tree Gdns. *Brom* 2F 110
Oaktree Gro. *Ilf* 1B 64
Oak Tree Ho. W9 *7L 57*
(off Shirland Rd.)
Oak Tree Rd. *NW8* 6C 58
Oakview Clo. *Chesh* 1B 6
Oakview Gdns. *N2* 2B 42
Oakview Gro. *Croy* 3J 125
Oakview Lodge. NW11 *5K 41*
(off Beechcroft Av.)
Oakview Rd. *SE6* 2M 109
Oak Village. *NW5* 9E 42
Oak Vs. NW11 *4K 41*
(off Hendon Pk. Row)
Oak Way. *N14* 9F 14
Oak Way. *SW20* 8G 105
Oak Way. *W3* 2C 72
Oak Way. *Asht* 8L 133
Oakway. *Brom* 6B 110
Oak Way. *Croy* 1H 125
Oak Way. *Felt* 7C 84
Oakway Clo. *Bex* 5J 97
Oakways. *SE9* 5M 95
Oakwood. 7G 15
Oakwood. *Wall* 1F 136
Oakwood. *Wal A* 8L 7
Oakwood Av. *N14* 9H 15
Oakwood Av. *Beck* 6A 110
Oakwood Av. *Borwd* 6M 11
Oakwood Av. *Brom* 7F 110
Oakwood Av. *Eps* 1L 133
Oakwood Av. *Mitc* 6B 106
Oakwood Av. *Purl* 4M 137
Oakwood Av. *S'hall* 1L 69
Oakwood Bus. Pk.
NW10 7B 56
Oakwood Chase. *Horn* 4K 51
Oakwood Clo. *N14* 8G 15
Oakwood Clo. *Chst* 3K 111
Oakwood Clo. *Dart* 7M 99
Oakwood Clo. *Wfd G* 6J 31
Oakwood Ct. *E6* 3J 63
Oakwood Ct. *W14* 4K 73
Oakwood Ct. *Harr* 4B 38
Oakwood Ct. Swan *6A 114*
(off Lawn Clo.)
Oakwood Cres. *N21* 8J 15
Oakwood Cres. *Gnfd* 2E 54
Oakwood Dri. *SE19* 3B 108
Oakwood Dri. *Bexh* 3A 98
Oakwood Dri. *Edgw* 6A 24
Oakwood Gdns. *Ilf* 7D 48
Oakwood Gdns. *Orp* 4A 128
Oakwood Gdns. *Sutt* 4L 121
Oakwood Hill. *Lou* 8K 19
Oakwood Hill Ind. Est.
Lou 7M 19
Oakwood La. *W14* 4K 73
Oakwood Lodge. N14 *8G 15*
(off Avenue Rd.)
Oakwood Pk. 8J 15
Oakwood Pk. Rd. *N14* 9H 15
Oakwood Pl. *Croy* 1L 123
Oakwood Rd. *NW11* 2L 41
Oakwood Rd. *SW20* 5E 104
Oakwood Rd. *Brick W* 2K 5
Oakwood Rd. *Croy* 1L 123
Oakwood Rd. *Orp* 4A 128
Oakwood Rd. *Pinn* 9F 20
Oakwood Vw. *N14* 8H 15
Oakworth Rd. *W10* 8G 57
Oarsman Pl. *E Mol* 8C 102
Oasis, The. *Brom* 6G 111
Oast Ct. E14 *1K 77*
(off Newell St.)
Oasthouse Way. *Orp* 8F 112
Oast Lodge. W4 *8C 72*
(off Corney Reach Way)
Oates Clo. *Brom* 7B 110
Oates Rd. *Romf* 5M 33
Oatfield Ho. N15 *4C 44*
(off Perry Ct.)
Oatfield Rd. *Orp* 3D 128
Oatland Ri. *E17* 9J 29
Oatlands Av. *Wey* 7B 116
Oatlands Chase. *Wey* 5C 116
Oatlands Clo. *Wey* 6A 116
Oatlands Dri. *Wey* 6A 116
Oatlands Grn. *Wey* 5B 116
Oatlands Mere. *Wey* 5B 116
Oatlands Park. 5C 116
Oatlands Rd. *Enf* 3G 17
Oat La. *EC2* 9A 60
Oatwell Ho. SW3 *6C 74*
(off Marlborough St.)
Oban Clo. *E13* 7G 63
Oban Ho. E14 *9B 62*
(off Oban St.)
Oban Ho. *Bark* 5B 64
Oban Rd. *E13* 6G 63
Oban Rd. *SE25* 8B 108
Oban St. *E14* 9B 62
Oberon Clo. *Borwd* 3A 12
Oberon Ho. N1 *5C 60*
(off Arden Est.)
Oberstein Rd. *SW11* 3B 90
Oborne Clo. *SE24* 4M 91
O'Brien Ho. E2 *6H 61*
(off Roman Rd.)
Observatory Gdns.
W8 3L 73
Observatory M. *E14* 5B 78
Observatory Rd. *SW14* 3A 88
Occupation La. *SE18* 9M 79
Occupation La. *W5* 5H 71
Occupation Rd. *SE17* 6A 76
Occupation Rd. *W13* 3F 70
Occupation Rd. *Eps* 9B 120
Occupation Rd. *Wat* 7F 8
Ocean Est. *E1* 8J 61
(Ben Jonson Rd.)
Ocean Est. *E1* 7H 61
(Ernest St.)
Ocean St. *E1* 8H 61
Ocean Wharf. *E14* 3K 77
Ockbrook. E1 *8G 61*
(off Hannibal Rd.)
Ockendon M. *N1* 2B 60
Ockendon Rd. *N1* 2B 60
Ockendon Rd. *N Ock* 1M 67
Ockham Dri. *Orp* 4E 112
Ockley Ct. *Sidc* 9C 96
Ockley Ct. *Sutt* 6A 122
Ockley Rd. *SW16* 1J 107
Ockley Rd. *Croy* 2K 123
Octagon Arc. *EC2* 8C 60
Octagon Ct. SE16 *2H 77*
(off Rotherhithe St.)
Octavia Clo. *Mitc* 9C 106
Octavia Ct. *Wat* 4G 9
Octavia Ho. SW1 *4H 75*
(off Medway St.)
Octavia Ho. *W10* 7J 57
Octavia Rd. *Iswth* 2C 86
Octavia St. *SW11* 9C 74
Octavia Way. *SE28* 1F 80
Octavius St. *SE8* 8L 77
October Pl. *NW4* 1H 41
Odard Rd. *W Mol* 8L 101
Oddesey Rd. *Borwd* 3M 11
Oddmark Rd. *Bark* 5B 64
Odeon Cinema. ***4F 58***
(off Camden Town)
Odeon Cinema. ***9D 58***
(off Edgware Rd.)
Odeon Cinema. ***1H 75***
(off Leicester Sq.)
Odeon Cinema. ***1H 75***
(off Panton St.)
Odeon Cinema. ***9H 59***
(off Shaftesbury Av.)
Odeon Cinema. ***1H 75***
(off Swiss Cen.)
Odeon Cinema. ***8H 59***
(off Tottenham Ct. Rd.)
Odeon Ct. *E16* 8E 62
Odeon Ct. *NW10* 4C 56
Odeon Pde. Gnfd *2F 54*
(off Allendale Rd.)
Odessa Rd. *E7* 8D 46
Odessa Rd. *NW10* 5E 56
Odessa St. *SE16* 3M 77
Odette Duval Ho. E1 *8G 61*
(off Stepney Way)
Odger St. *SW11* 1D 90
Odhams Trad. Est. *Wat* 1G 9
Odhams Wlk. *WC2* 9J 59
Odin Ho. *SE5* 1A 92
O'Donnell Ct. *WC1* 7J 59
Odontological Mus., The.
9K 59
(off Lincoln's Inn Fields,
Royal College of Surgeons)
O'Driscoll Ho. *W12* 9F 56
Odyssey Bus. Pk. *Ruis* 1F 52
Offa's Mead. *E9* 9K 45
Offenbach Ho. E2 *5H 61*
(off Mace St.)
Offenham Rd. *SE9* 1K 111
Offers Ct. *King T* 7K 103
Offerton Rd. *SW4* 2G 91
Offham Ho. SE17 *5C 76*
(off Beckway St.)
Offham Slope. *N12* 5K 25
Offley Pl. *Iswth* 1B 86

Offley Rd.—Orchard Dri.

Offley Rd. SW9 .... 8L 75
Offord Clo. N17 .... 6E 28
Offord Rd. N1 .... 3K 59
Offord St. N1 .... 3K 59
Ogden Ho. Felt 9J 85
Ogilby St. SE18 .... 5K 79
Ogilvie Ho. E1 .... 9H 61
(off Stepney Causeway)
Oglander Rd. SE15 .... 3D 92
Ogle St. W1 .... 8G 59
Oglethorpe Rd. Dag 8K 49
O'Gorman Ho. SW10 .... 8A 74
(off King's Rd.)
O'Grady Ho. E17 .... 1M 45
Ohio Cotts. Pinn 9G 21
Ohio Rd. E13 .... 7D 62
Oil Mill La. W6 .... 6E 72
Okeburn Rd. SW17 .... 2E 106
Okehampton Clo. N12 .... 5B 26
Okehampton Cres. Well 9F 80
Okehampton Rd. NW10 .... 4G 57
Okehampton Rd. H Hill 6G 35
Okehampton Sq. Romf 6G 35
Okemore Gdns. Orp 8G 113
Olaf St. W11 .... 1H 73
Oldacre M. SW12 .... 6E 90
Old Av. Wey 9A 116
Old Bailey. EC4 .... 9M 59
Old Bailey
(Central Criminal Court)
.... 9M 59
Old Barge Ho. All. SE1 .... 1L 75
(off Barge Ho. St.)
Old Barn Clo. Sutt 9J 121
Old Barn La. Kenl 8D 138
Old Barn Rd. Eps 9A 134
Old Barn Way. Bexh 2B 98
Old Barrack Yd. SW1 .... 3E 74
(in two parts)
Old Barrowfield. E15 .... 4C 62
Old Bellgate Wharf. E14 .... 4K 77
Oldberry Rd. Edgw 6B 24
Old Bethnal Grn. Rd. E2 .... 6E 60
Old Bexley. 6M 97
Old Bexley Bus. Pk. Bex 6M 97
Old Bexley La. Bex & Dart 8B 98
(in two parts)
Old Billingsgate Mkt. EC3 .... 1C 76
(off Lwr. Thames St.)
Old Billingsgate Wlk. EC3 .... 1C 76
Old Bond St. W1 .... 1G 75
Oldborough Rd. Wemb 8G 39
Old Brentford. 8H 71
Old Brewer's Yd. WC2 .... 9J 59
Old Brewery M. NW3 .... 9B 42
Old Bri. Clo. N'holt 5L 53
Old Bri. St. Hamp W 6H 103
Old Broad St. EC2 .... 9B 60
Old Bromley Rd. Brom 2B 110
Old Brompton Rd.
SW5 & SW7 .... 6L 73
Old Bldgs. WC2 .... 9L 59
(off Chancery La.)
Old Burlington St. W1 .... 1G 75
Oldbury Clo. Orp 8G 113
Oldbury Pl. W1 .... 8E 58
Oldbury Rd. Enf 4E 16
Old Canal M. SE15 .... 6D 76
(off Trafalgar Av.)
Old Castle St. E1 .... 9D 60
Old Cavendish St. W1 .... 9F 58
Old Change Ct. EC4 .... 9A 60
(off Carter La.)
Old Chapel Pl. SW9 .... 1L 91
Old Chapel Rd. Swan 2A 130
Old Charlton Rd. Shep 9A 100
Old Chelsea M. SW3 .... 7C 74
Old Chestnut Av. Clar P 8L 117
Old Chiswick Yd. W4 .... 7C 72
(off Pumping Sta. Rd.)
Old Church Ct. N11 .... 5F 26
Oldchurch Gdns. Romf 5B 50
Old Church La. NW9 .... 7B 40
Old Church La. Gnfd 6E 54
Old Church La. Stan 5F 22
Old Church Path. Esh 6A 118
Oldchurch Ri. Romf 5C 50
Old Church Rd. E1 .... 9H 61
Old Church Rd. E4 .... 4L 29
Oldchurch Rd. Romf 5B 50
Old Church St. SW3 .... 6B 74
Old Claygate La. Clay 8E 118
Old Compton St. W1 .... 1H 75
Old Cote Dri. Houn 7L 69
Old Ct. Ho. W8 .... 3M 73
(off Old Ct. Pl.)
Old Ct. Pl. W8 .... 3M 73
Old Courtyard, The.
Brom 5F 110
Old Curiosity Shop. 8K 59
(off Portsmouth St.)
Old Dairy M. NW5 .... 2F 58
Old Dairy M. SW12 .... 7E 90
Old Dartford Rd. F'ham 1K 131
Old Deer Pk. Gdns. Rich 2J 87
Old Devonshire Rd. SW12 .... 6F 90
Old Dock Clo. Rich 7L 71
Old Dover Rd. SE3 .... 8E 78
Oldegate Ho. E6 .... 3H 63
Olden La. Purl 4L 137
Old Esher Clo. W on T 7H 117
Old Esher Rd. W on T 7H 117
Old Farleigh Rd.
S Croy & Warl 2G 139
Old Farm Av. N14 .... 9G 15
Old Farm Av. Sidc 7B 96
Old Farm Clo. SW17 .... 8C 90
Old Farm Clo. Houn 3K 85
Old Farm Gdns. Swan 7D 114
Old Farm Ho. Dri. Oxs 7B 132
Old Farm Pas. Hamp 5A 102
Old Farm Rd. N2 .... 8B 26
Old Farm Rd. Hamp 3K 101
(in two parts)
Old Farm Rd. W Dray 3H 143
Old Farm Rd. E. Sidc 8E 96
Old Farm Rd. W. Sidc 8D 96
Oldfield Clo. Brom 8K 111
Oldfield Clo. Chesh 1E 6
Oldfield Clo. Gnfd 1C 54
Oldfield Clo. Stan 5E 22
Oldfield Ct. Surb 8K 103
(off Cranes Pk. Cres.)
Oldfield Dri. Chesh 1E 6
Oldfield Farm Gdns. Gnfd 4B 54
Oldfield Gro. SE16 .... 5H 77
Oldfield Ho. W4 .... 6C 72
(off Devonshire Rd.)
Oldfield La. N. Gnfd 5B 54
Oldfield La. S. Gnfd 7A 54
Oldfield M. N6 .... 5G 43
Oldfield Rd. N16 .... 8C 44
Oldfield Rd. NW10 .... 3D 56
Oldfield Rd. SW19 .... 3J 105
Oldfield Rd. W3 .... 3D 72
Oldfield Rd. Bexh 1J 97
Oldfield Rd. Brom 8K 111
Oldfield Rd. Hamp 5K 101
Oldfields Cir. N'holt 2A 54
Oldfields Rd. Sutt 5K 121
Oldfields Trad. Est. Sutt 5L 121
Old Fish St. Hill. EC4 .... 1A 76
(off Victoria St.)
Old Fleet La. EC4 .... 9M 59
Old Fold Clo. Barn 3K 13
Old Fold La. Barn 3K 13
Old Fold Manor Golf Course.
.... 2H 13
Old Fold Vw. Barn 5G 13
Old Ford. 4K 61
Old Ford (Junct.) 4L 61
Old Ford Rd. E2 & E3 .... 6G 61
Old Forge Clo. Stan 4E 22
Old Forge Clo. Wat 6E 4
Old Forge Cres. Shep 1A 116
Old Forge M. W12 .... 3F 72
Old Forge Rd. Enf 2D 16
Old Forge Way. Sidc 1F 112
Old Gannon Clo. N'wd 4A 20
Old Gloucester St. WC1 .... 8J 59
Old Hall Clo. Pinn 8J 21
Old Hall Dri. Pinn 8J 21
Oldham Ter. W3 .... 2A 72
(in two parts)
Old Hatch Mnr. Ruis 5D 36
Old Hill. Chst 5L 111
Old Hill. Orp 8B 128
Oldhill St. N16 .... 6E 44
Old Homesdale Rd.
Brom 8G 111
Old Hospital Clo. SW17 .... 7D 90
Old Ho. Clo. SW19 .... 2J 105
Old Ho. Clo. Eps 2D 134
Old Ho. Gdns. Twic 5G 87
Old Howlett's La. Ruis 4B 36
Old Isleworth. 2F 86
Old Jamaica Rd. SE16 .... 4E 76
Old James St. SE15 .... 2F 92
Old Jewry. EC2 .... 9B 60
Old Kenton La. NW9 .... 3M 39
Old Kent Rd. SE1 & SE15 .... 5C 76
Old Kingston Rd.
Wor Pk 4A 120
Old Laundry, The. Chst 5A 112
Old Lodge La. Purl 5K 137
Old Lodge Pl. Twic 5F 86
Old Lodge Way. Stan 5E 22
Old London Rd. Eps 9E 134
(in two parts)
Old London Rd. King T 6J 103
Old London Rd. Sidc 4L 113
Old Macdonalds Educational
Farm Pk. 1K 35
Old Maidstone Rd. Sidc 4K 113
Old Malden. 3C 120
Old Malden La. Wor Pk 4B 120
Old Mnr. Ct. NW8 .... 5A 58
Old Mnr. Dri. Iswth 5A 86
Old Mnr. Rd. S'hall 5H 69
Old Mnr. Way. Bexh 1B 98
Old Mnr. Way. Chst 2K 111
Old Mnr. Yd. SW5 .... 5M 73
Old Mkt. Sq. E2 .... 6D 60
Old Marylebone Rd. NW1 .... 8C 58
Oldmead Ho. Dag 2M 65
Old M. Harr 3C 38
Old Mill Clo. E18 .... 1G 47
Old Mill Clo. Eyns 3J 131
Old Mill La. Uxb 9A 142
Old Mill Pde. Romf 3D 50
Old Mill Pl. Romf 4B 50
Old Mill Rd. SE18 .... 7B 80
Old Mill Rd. K Lan 6A 4
Old Mitre Ct. EC4 .... 9L 59
Old Montague St. E1 .... 8E 60
Old Nichol St. E2 .... 7D 60
Old N. St. WC1 .... 8K 59
(off Theobald's Rd.)
Old Nursery Pl. Ashf 2A 100
Old Oak Clo. Chess 6K 119
Old Oak Common. 7C 56
Old Oak Comn. La.
W3 & NW10 .... 8C 56
Old Oak La. NW10 .... 6C 56
Old Oak Rd. W3 .... 1D 72
Old Oaks. Wal A 5L 7
Old Orchard. Sun 6G 101
Old Orchard Clo. Barn 2B 14
Old Orchard Clo. Uxb 9E 142
Old Orchard, The. NW3 .... 9D 42
Old Pal. La. Rich 4G 87
Old Pal. Rd. Croy 5M 123
Old Pal. Rd. Wey 5A 116
Old Pal. Ter. Rich 4H 87
Old Pal. Yd. SW1 .... 4J 75
Old Pal. Yd. Rich 4G 87
Old Paradise St. SE11 .... 5K 75
Old Pk. Av. SW12 .... 5E 90
Old Pk. Av. Enf 7A 16
Old Pk. Gro. Enf 6A 16
Old Pk. La. W1 .... 2F 74
Old Pk. M. Houn 8K 69
Oldpark Ride. Wal X 6A 6
(in three parts)
Old Pk. Ridings. N21 .... 8M 15
Old Pk. Rd. N13 .... 4K 27
Old Pk. Rd. SE2 .... 6E 80
Old Pk. Rd. Enf 5M 15
Old Pk. Rd. S. Enf 6M 15
Old Pk. Vw. Enf 5L 15
Old Parsonage Yd., The.
Hort K 8M 115
Old Perry St. Chst 3C 112
Old Pound Clo. Iswth 1E 86
Old Pye St. SW1 .... 4H 75
Old Pye St. Est. SW1 .... 4H 75
(off Old Pye St.)
Old Quebec St. W1 .... 9D 58
Old Queen St. SW1 .... 3H 75
Old Rectory Gdns. Edgw 6L 23
Old Redding. Harr 5M 21
Old Red Lion Theatre. 5L 59
(off St John St.)
Oldridge Rd. SW12 .... 6E 90
Old River Works. N17 .... 6A 28
Old Rd. SE13 .... 3C 94
Old Rd. Dart 4B 98
Old Rd. Enf 3G 17
Old Royal Free Pl. N1 .... 4L 59
Old Royal Free Sq. N1 .... 4L 59
Old Royal Naval College.
.... 6B 78
Old Ruislip Rd. N'holt 5G 53
Old's App. Wat 1A 20
Old School Clo. SE10 .... 4C 78
Old School Clo. SW19 .... 6L 105
Old School Clo. Beck 6H 109
Old School Ct. N17 .... 1D 44
Old School Cres. E7 .... 2E 62
Old School M. Wey 6B 116
Old School Rd. Uxb 7D 142
Old Schools La. Eps 1D 134
Old School Sq. E14 .... 9L 61
(off Pelling St.)
Old School Sq. Th Dit 1D 118
Old's Clo. Wat 9A 8
Old Seacoal La. EC4 .... 9M 59
Old S. Clo. H End 8H 21
Old S. Lambeth Rd. SW8 .... 8J 75
Old Spitalfields Market. 8D 60
Old Sq. WC2 .... 9K 59
Old Stable M. N5 .... 8A 44
Old Sta. Gdns. Tedd 3E 102
(off Victoria Rd.)
Old Sta. Rd. Hay 4D 68
Old Sta. Rd. Lou 7J 19
Oldstead Rd. Brom 1A 110
Old Stockley Rd.
W Dray 3M 143
Old Street (Junct.) 7A 60
Old St. E13 .... 5F 62
Old St. EC1 .... 7A 60
Old Sungate Cotts. Romf 8K 33
Old Sun Wharf. E14 .... 1J 77
(off Narrow St.)
Old Swan Wharf. SW11 .... 9B 74
Old Swan Yd. Cars 6D 122
Old Thackeray School.
SW8 .... 1F 90
Old Theatre Ct. SE1 .... 2A 76
(off Porter St.)
Old Town. SW4 .... 2G 91
Old Town. Croy 5M 123
Old Tramyard. SE18 .... 5C 80
Old Tye Av. Big H 8J 141
Old Vic Theatre, The. 3L 75
(off Cut, The)
Old Watford Rd. Brick W 3J 5
Old Woolwich Rd. SE10 .... 7B 78
Old York Rd. SW18 .... 4M 89
Oleander Clo. Orp 7B 128
O'Leary Sq. E1 .... 8G 61
Olga St. E3 .... 5J 61
Olinda Rd. N16 .... 4D 44
Oliphant St. W10 .... 6H 57
Oliver Av. SE25 .... 7D 108
Oliver Bus. Pk. NW10 .... 5A 56
Oliver Clo. W4 .... 7M 71
Oliver Ct. SE18 .... 5A 80
Oliver Cres. F'ham 2K 131
Oliver Gdns. E6 .... 8J 63
Oliver Goldsmith Est.
SE15 .... 9E 76
Oliver Gro. SE25 .... 8D 108
Oliver Ho. SE16 .... 3E 76
(off George Row)
Oliver Ho. SW8 .... 8J 75
(off Wyvil Rd.)
Oliver M. SE15 .... 1E 92
Olive Rd. E13 .... 6G 63
Olive Rd. NW2 .... 9G 41
Olive Rd. SW19 .... 4A 106
Olive Rd. W5 .... 4H 71
Olive Rd. Dart 7H 99
Oliver Rd. E10 .... 7M 45
Oliver Rd. E17 .... 3A 46
Oliver Rd. NW10 .... 5A 56
Oliver Rd. N Mald 6A 104
Oliver Rd. Rain 4D 66
Oliver Rd. Sutt 6B 122
Oliver Rd. Swan 7B 114
Olivers Wharf. E1 .... 2F 76
(off Wapping High St.)
Olivers Yd. EC1 .... 7B 60
Olive St. Romf 3B 50
Olive Tree Ho. SE15 .... 7G 77
(off Sharratt St.)
Olivette St. SW15 .... 2H 89
Olive Waite Ho. NW6 .... 3L 57
Olivia Ct. Enf 3A 16
(off Chase Side)
Olivier Theatre. 2L 75
(in Royal National Theatre)
Ollard's Ct. Lou 7H 19
Ollard's Gro. Lou 6H 19
Ollerton Grn. E3 .... 4K 61
Ollerton Rd. N11 .... 5H 27
Olley Clo. Wall 9J 123
Ollgar Clo. W12 .... 2D 72
Olliffe St. E14 .... 4A 78
Olmar St. SE1 .... 7E 76
Olney Ho. NW8 .... 7C 58
(off Tresham Cres.)
Olney Rd. SE17 .... 7M 75
(in two parts)
Olron Cres. Bexh 4H 97
Olven Rd. SE18 .... 7A 80
Olveston Wlk. Cars 1B 122
Olwen M. Pinn 9H 21
Olyffe Av. Well 9E 80
Olympia. 4J 73
Olympia Ind. Est. N22 .... 1K 43
Olympia M. W2 .... 1M 73
Olympian Ct. E14 .... 5L 77
(off Homer Dri.)
Olympia Way. W14 .... 4J 73
Olympic Way. Gnfd 4A 54
Olympic Way. Wemb 8L 39
(in three parts)
Olympus Sq. E5 .... 8E 44
O'Mahoney Ct. SW17 .... 9A 90
Oman Av. NW2 .... 9G 41
O'Meara St. SE1 .... 2A 76
Omega Clo. E14 .... 4M 77
Omega Pl. N1 .... 5J 59
(off Caledonian Rd.)
Omega St. SE14 .... 9L 77
Ommaney Rd. SE14 .... 9H 77
Omnibus Way. E17 .... 9L 29
Ondine Rd. SE15 .... 3D 92
Onega Ga. SE16 .... 4J 77
O'Neill Ho. NW8 .... 5C 58
(off Cochrane St.)
O'Neill Path. SE18 .... 7L 79
One Owen St. EC1 .... 5M 59
(off Goswell St.)
One Tree Clo. SE23 .... 5G 93
Ongar Clo. Romf 3G 49
Ongar Rd. SW6 .... 7L 73
Ongar Way. Rain 4C 66
Onra Rd. E17 .... 5L 45
Onslow Av. Rich 4J 87
Onslow Av. Sutt 2K 135
Onslow Clo. E4 .... 2A 30
Onslow Clo. Th Dit 3C 118
Onslow Cres. Chst 5M 111
Onslow Dri. Sidc 8H 97
Onslow Gdns. E18 .... 1F 46
Onslow Gdns. N10 .... 3F 42
Onslow Gdns. N21 .... 7L 15
Onslow Gdns. SW7 .... 5B 74
Onslow Gdns. S Croy 4E 138
Onslow Gdns. Th Dit 3C 118
Onslow Gdns. Wall 8G 123
Onslow Ho. King T 5K 103
(off Acre Rd.)
Onslow M. E. SW7 .... 5B 74
Onslow M. W. SW7 .... 5B 74
Onslow Mills Trad. Est.
W Dray 1H 143
Onslow Pde. N14 .... 1F 26
Onslow Rd. Croy 2K 123
Onslow Rd. N Mald 8E 104
Onslow Rd. Rich 4J 87
Onslow Rd. W on T 6D 116
Onslow Sq. SW7 .... 5B 74
Onslow St. EC1 .... 7L 59
Onslow Way. Th Dit 3C 118
Ontario St. SE1 .... 4M 75
Ontario Way. E14 .... 1L 77
(in two parts)
On the Hill. Wat 2J 21
Opal Clo. E16 .... 9H 63
Opal M. NW6 .... 4K 57
Opal M. Ilf 7M 47
Opal St. SE11 .... 6M 75
Openshaw Rd. SE2 .... 5F 80
Open University, The
(Parsifal College). 9L 41
Openview. SW18 .... 7A 90
Opera Ct. N19 .... 8H 43
(off Wedmore St.)
Operating Theatre Mus. 2B 76
(off St Thomas St.)
Ophelia Gdns. NW2 .... 8J 41
Ophelia Ho. W6 .... 6H 73
(off Fulham Pal. Rd.)
Ophir Ter. SE15 .... 9E 76
Opie Ho. NW8 .... 5C 58
(off Townshend Est.)
Opossum Way. Houn 2G 85
Oppenheim Rd. SE13 .... 1A 94
Oppidans Rd. NW3 .... 3D 58
Orange Ct. La. Orp 1L 141
Orange Gro. E11 .... 8C 46
(in two parts)
Orange Gro. Chig 6A 32
Orange Hill Rd. Edgw 7A 24
Orange Pl. SE16 .... 4G 77
Orangery La. SE9 .... 4K 95
Orangery, The. 2M 73
(in Kensington Gardens)
Orangery, The. Rich 8G 87
Orange St. WC2 .... 1H 75
Orange Tree Ct. SE5 .... 8C 76
(off Havil St.)
Orange Tree Hill. Hav 5B 34
Orange Yd. W1 .... 9H 59
(off Manette St.)
Oransay Rd. N1 .... 2A 60
Oratory La. SW3 .... 6B 74
(off Stewart's Gro.)
Oratory, The. 4C 74
Orbain Rd. SW6 .... 8J 73
Orbel St. SW11 .... 9C 74
Orbital Cen., The. Wfd G 9H 31
Orbital Cres. Wat 8D 4
Orbital One. Dart 8M 99
Orbital One Ind. Est. Dart 8L 99
Orb St. SE17 .... 5B 76
Orchard Av. N3 .... 1L 41
Orchard Av. N14 .... 8G 15
Orchard Av. N20 .... 2B 26
Orchard Av. Ashf 3A 100
Orchard Av. Belv 7J 81
Orchard Av. Croy 4J 125
Orchard Av. Dart 6F 98
Orchard Av. Felt 4B 84
Orchard Av. Houn 8J 69
Orchard Av. Mitc 3E 122
Orchard Av. N Mald 6C 104
Orchard Av. Rain 7G 67
Orchard Av. S'hall 2K 69
Orchard Av. Th Dit 3E 118
Orchard Av. Wat 5F 4
Orchard Bus. Cen. SE26 .... 2K 109
Orchard Clo. E4 .... 4L 29
Orchard Clo. E11 .... 2F 46
Orchard Clo. N1 .... 3A 60
Orchard Clo. NW2 .... 8E 40
Orchard Clo. SE23 .... 5G 93
Orchard Clo. SW20 .... 8G 105
Orchard Clo. W10 .... 8K 57
Orchard Clo. Ashf 3A 100
Orchard Clo. Bans 6M 135
Orchard Clo. Bexh 9J 81
Orchard Clo. Bus H 1B 22
Orchard Clo. Den 2A 142
Orchard Clo. Edgw 6J 23
Orchard Clo. Els 6K 11
Orchard Clo. N'holt 2A 54
Orchard Clo. Rad 1C 10
Orchard Clo. Ruis 5A 36
Orchard Clo. Surb 3F 118
Orchard Clo. W on T 2F 116
Orchard Clo. Wat 4D 8
Orchard Clo. Wemb 4J 55
Orchard Clo. W Ewe 8M 119
Orchard Cotts. Hay 3C 68
Orchard Cotts. King T 5K 103
Orchard Ct. E10 .... 6M 45
Orchard Ct. N14 .... 8G 15
Orchard Ct. Edgw 5K 23
Orchard Ct. Iswth 8B 70
Orchard Ct. New Bar 5M 13
Orchard Ct. Twic 8B 86
Orchard Ct. Wall 7F 122
Orchard Ct. W Dray 8G 143
Orchard Ct. Wor Pk 3E 120
Orchard Cres. Edgw 5A 24
Orchard Cres. Enf 3D 16
Orchard Dri. SE3 .... 1B 94
Orchard Dri. Edgw 5K 23
Orchard Dri. Shep 7C 100
Orchard Dri. Uxb 7B 142

Orchard Dri.—Overton Dri.

Orchard Dri. Wat 3D 8
Orchard End. Wey 4C 116
Orchard Gdns. Chess 6J 119
Orchard Gdns. Eps 6A 134
Orchard Gdns. Sutt 7L 121
Orchard Gdns. Wal A 7J 7
Orchard Ga. NW9 2C 40
Orchard Ga. Esh 3B 118
Orchard Ga. Gnfd 2F 54
Orchard Grn. Orp 4C 128
Orchard Gro. SE20 4E 108
Orchard Gro. Croy 2J 125
Orchard Gro. Edgw 8L 23
Orchard Gro. Harr 3K 39
Orchard Gro. Orp 4D 128
Orchard Hill. SE13 1M 93
Orchard Hill. Cars 7D 122
Orchard Hill. Dart 4C 98
Orchard Ho. SE5 9A 76
(off County Gro.)
Orchard Ho. SE16 4G 77
Orchard Ho. SW6 8K 73
(off Varna Rd.)
Orchard Ho. W1 9E 58
(off Fitzhardinge St.)
Orchard Ho. W12 2E 72
Orchard Ho. Eri 9D 82
Orchard La. SW20 5F 104
Orchard La. E Mol 1B 118
Orchard La. Wfd G 4G 31
Orchardleigh Av. Enf 4G 17
Orchard Mead Ho.
NW2 7L 41
Orchardmede. N21 8B 16
Orchard M. N1 3B 60
Orchard Pl. E14 1C 78
(in two parts)
Orchard Pl. N17 7D 28
Orchard Pl. Chesh 3D 6
Orchard Pl. Cow 3B 142
Orchard Pl. Kes 1G 141
Orchard Pl. Orp 7G 113
Orchard Ri. Croy 3J 125
Orchard Ri. King T 5A 104
Orchard Ri. Pinn 1D 36
Orchard Ri. Rich 3M 87
Orchard Ri. E. Sidc 4C 96
Orchard Ri. W. Sidc 4C 96
Orchard Rd. N6 5F 42
Orchard Rd. SE3 1C 94
Orchard Rd. SE18 5B 80
Orchard Rd. Barn 6K 13
Orchard Rd. Belv 5L 81
Orchard Rd. Bren 7G 71
Orchard Rd. Brom 5G 111
Orchard Rd. Chess 6J 119
Orchard Rd. Dag 4L 65
Orchard Rd. Enf 7G 17
Orchard Rd. F'boro 7M 127
Orchard Rd. Felt 7E 84
Orchard Rd. Hamp 4K 101
Orchard Rd. Hay 1E 68
Orchard Rd. Houn 4K 85
Orchard Rd. King T 6J 103
Orchard Rd. Mitc 3E 122
Orchard Rd. Rich 2L 87
Orchard Rd. Romf 8M 33
Orchard Rd. Sidc 1C 112
Orchard Rd. S Croy 6F 138
Orchard Rd. Sun 4F 100
Orchard Rd. Sutt 7L 121
Orchard Rd. Twic 4E 86
Orchard Rd. Well 2F 96
Orchardson Ho. NW8 7B 58
(off Orchardson St.)
Orchardson St. NW8 7B 58
Orchard Sq. W14 6K 73
Orchards Shop. Cen., The.
Dart 5J 99
Orchards, The. Dart 5J 99
Orchard St. E17 2J 45
Orchard St. W1 9E 58
Orchard St. Dart 5J 99
Orchard Studios. W6 5H 73
(off Brook Grn.)
Orchard Ter. Enf 8E 16
Orchard, The. N14 7F 14
Orchard, The. N21 8B 16
Orchard, The. NW11 3L 41
Orchard, The. SE3 1B 94
Orchard, The. W4 5B 72
Orchard, The. W5 8H 55
(off Montpelier Rd.)
Orchard, The. Bans 7L 135
Orchard, The. Eps 9D 120
(Meadow Wlk.)
Orchard, The. Eps 2D 134
(Tayles Hill)
Orchard, The. Houn 1A 86
Orchard, The. Swan 6B 114
Orchard, The. Wey 6A 116
Orchard Theatre. 5J 99
Orchard Vw. Uxb 7B 142
Orchard Way. Ashf 8D 144
Orchard Way. Chig 3E 32
Orchard Way. Croy 3J 125
Orchard Way. Dart 9H 99
Orchard Way. Enf 5C 16
Orchard Way. Esh 8A 118
Orchard Way. Sutt 6B 122
Orchard Waye. Uxb 5B 142
Orchard Wharf. E14 1C 78
(off Orchard Pl.)
Orchid Clo. E6 8J 63
Orchid Clo. Chess 9G 119
Orchid Clo. S'hall 1J 69
Orchid Ct. Rush G 7C 50
Orchid Ct. Wemb 7J 39
Orchid Grange. N14 9G 15
Orchid Mead. Bans 6M 135
Orchid Rd. N14 9G 15
Orchid St. W12 1E 72
Orchis Way. Romf 6K 35
Orde. NW9 8D 24
Orde Hall St. WC1 7K 59
Ordell Rd. E3 5K 61
Ordnance Clo. Felt 8E 84
Ordnance Cres. SE10 3B 78
Ordnance Hill. NW8 4B 58
Ordnance M. NW8 5B 58
Ordnance Rd. E16 8D 62
Ordnance Rd. SE18 7L 79
Ordnance Rd. Enf 1H 17
Oregano Clo. W Dray 9C 142
Oregano Dri. E14 9B 62
Oregon Av. E12 9K 47
Oregon Clo. N Mald 8A 104
Oregon Sq. Orp 3B 128
Orestes M. NW6 1L 57
Oreston Rd. Rain 6H 67
Orford Ct. SE27 8M 91
Orford Ct. Dart 5M 99
(off Osbourne Rd.)
Orford Ct. Stan 6G 23
Orford Gdns. Twic 8D 86
Orford Rd. E17 3L 45
Orford Rd. E18 1F 46
Orford Rd. SE6 9M 93
Organ Crossroads (Junct.)
9E 120
Organ Hall Rd. Borwd 3J 11
Organ La. E4 2A 30
(in two parts)
Oriana Ho. E14 1K 77
(off Victory Pl.)
Oriel Clo. Mitc 8H 107
Oriel Ct. NW3 9A 42
Oriel Ct. Croy 3B 124
Oriel Dri. SW13 7G 73
Oriel Gdns. Ilf 1K 47
Oriel Pl. NW3 9A 42
(off Heath St.)
Oriel Rd. E9 2H 61
Oriel Way. N'holt 3M 53
Oriental Rd. E16 2H 79
Oriental St. E14 1L 77
(off Pennyfields)
Orient Ind. Pk. E10 7L 45
Orient St. SE11 5M 75
Orient Way. E5 8H 45
Orient Way. E10 6J 45
Orient Wharf. E1 2F 76
(off Wapping High St.)
Oriole Clo. Ab L 4E 4
Oriole Way. SE28 1F 80
Orion Bus. Cen. SE14 6H 77
Orion Cen., The. Croy 4J 123
Orion Ho. E1 7F 60
(off Coventry Rd.)
Orion Rd. N11 7E 26
Orion Way. N'wd 4D 20
Orissa Rd. SE18 6C 80
Orkney Ho. N1 4K 59
(off Bemerton Est.)
Orkney St. SW11 1E 90
Orlando Gdns. Eps 2B 134
Orlando Rd. SW4 2G 91
Orleans Clo. Esh 4B 118
Orleans Ct. Twic 6F 86
Orleans House Gallery.
7F 86
Orleans Rd. SE19 3B 108
Orleans Rd. Twic 6F 86
Orlestone Gdns. Orp 7J 129
Orleston M. N7 2L 59
Orleston Rd. N7 2L 59
Orley Ct. Harr 9D 38
Orley Farm Rd. Harr 8C 38
Orlop St. SE10 6C 78
Ormanton Rd. SE26 1E 108
Orme Ct. W2 1M 73
Orme Ct. M. W2 1M 73
(off Orme La.)
Orme Ho. E8 4D 60
Orme La. W2 1M 73
Ormeley Rd. SW12 7F 90
Orme Rd. King T 6M 103
Ormerod Gdns. Mitc 6E 106
Ormesby Clo. SE28 1H 81
Ormesby Way. Harr 4K 39
Orme Sq. W2 1M 73
Ormiston Gro. W12 2F 72
Ormiston Rd. SE10 6E 78
Ormond Av. Hamp 5M 101
Ormond Av. Rich 4H 87
Ormond Clo. WC1 8J 59
Ormond Clo. H Wood 9H 35
Ormond Cres. Hamp 5M 101
Ormond Dri. Hamp 4M 101
Ormonde Av. Eps 2B 134
Ormonde Av. Orp 4A 128
Ormonde Ct. SW15 3G 89
Ormonde Ct. Horn 5D 50
(off Clydesdale Rd.)
Ormonde Ga. SW3 6D 74
Ormonde Pl. SW1 5E 74
Ormonde Ri. Buck H 1G 31
Ormonde Rd. SW14 2A 88
Ormonde Rd. N'wd 4B 20
Ormonde Ter. NW8 4D 58
Ormond M. WC1 7J 59
Ormond Rd. N19 6J 43
Ormond Rd. Rich 4H 87
Ormond Yd. SW1 2G 75
Ormsby. Sutt 9M 121
Ormsby Gdns. Gnfd 5A 54
Ormsby Lodge. W4 4C 72
Ormsby Pl. N16 8D 44
Ormsby St. E2 5D 60
Ormside St. SE15 7G 77
Ormskirk Rd. Wat 4H 21
Ornan Rd. NW3 1C 58
Orpen Wlk. N16 8C 44
Orphanage Rd. Wat 4G 9
Orpheus St. SE5 9B 76
Orpington. 3E 128
Orpington By-Pass. Orp 4F 128
Orpington By-Pass Rd.
Orp & Badg M 9K 129
Orpington Gdns. N18 3C 28
Orpington Mans. N21 1M 27
Orpington Priory Gardens.
2F 128
Orpington Retail Pk.
Orp 8G 113
Orpington Rd. N21 1M 27
Orpington Rd. Chst 7C 112
Orpwood Clo. Hamp 3K 101
Orsett M. W2 9M 57
(in two parts)
Orsett St. SE11 6K 75
Orsett Ter. W2 9M 57
Orsett Ter. Wfd G 7G 31
Orsman Rd. N1 4C 60
Orton Ho. Romf 7J 35
(off Leyburn Rd.)
Orton St. E1 2E 76
Orville Rd. SW11 1B 90
Orwell Clo. Hay 1C 68
Orwell Clo. Rain 8B 66
Orwell Ct. E8 4E 60
(off Pownall Rd.)
Orwell Ct. N5 9A 44
Orwell Ct. Wat 5H 9
Orwell Rd. E13 5G 63
Osbaldeston Rd. N16 7E 44
Osberton Rd. SE12 4E 94
Osbert St. SW1 5H 75
Osborn Clo. E8 4E 60
Osborne Av. Stai 7D 144
Osborne Clo. Barn 5D 14
Osborne Clo. Beck 8J 109
Osborne Clo. Felt 2H 101
Osborne Clo. Horn 4F 50
Osborne Ct. E10 5M 45
Osborne Ct. W5 8J 55
Osborne Gdns. T Hth 6A 108
Osborne Gro. E17 2K 45
Osborne Gro. N4 6L 43
Osborne Ho. E16 2E 78
(off Wesley Av.)
Osborne M. E17 2K 45
Osborne Pl. Sutt 7B 122
Osborne Rd. E7 1F 62
Osborne Rd. E9 2K 61
Osborne Rd. E10 7M 45
Osborne Rd. N4 6L 43
Osborne Rd. N13 3L 27
Osborne Rd. NW2 2F 56
Osborne Rd. W3 4M 71
Osborne Rd. Belv 6K 81
Osborne Rd. Buck H 1F 30
Osborne Rd. Dag 1K 65
Osborne Rd. Enf 4J 17
Osborne Rd. Horn 4F 50
Osborne Rd. Houn 2K 85
Osborne Rd. King T 4J 103
Osborne Rd. S'hall 9A 54
Osborne Rd. T Hth 6A 108
Osborne Rd. Uxb 3A 142
Osborne Rd. W on T 3E 116
Osborne Rd. Wat 2G 9
Osborne Sq. Dag 9K 49
Osborne Ter. SW17 2D 106
(off Church La.)
Osborne Way. Chess 7K 119
(off Bridge Rd.)
Osborn Gdns. NW7 7H 25
Osborn La. SE23 6J 93
Osborn St. E1 8D 60
Osborn Ter. SE3 3D 94
Osbourne Ct. Harr 2M 37
Osbourne Ho. Twic 8A 86
Osbourne Rd. Dart 5M 99
Oscar Faber Pl. N1 3C 60
Oscar St. SE4 1L 93
(in two parts)
Oseney Cres. NW5 1G 59
Osgood Av. Orp 7D 128
Osgood Gdns. Orp 7D 128
O'Shea Gro. E3 4K 61
Osidge. 1F 26
Osidge La. N14 1E 26
Osier Ct. E1 7H 61
(off Osier St.)
Osier Ct. Bren 7J 71
(off Ealing Rd.)
Osier Ct. Romf 4B 50
Osier Cres. N10 8D 26
Osier M. W4 7C 72
Osiers Ct. King T 5H 103
(off Steadfast Rd.)
Osiers Rd. SW18 3L 89
Osier St. E1 7G 61
Osier Way. E10 8M 45
Osier Way. Bans 6J 135
Osier Way. Mitc 9D 106
Oslac Rd. SE6 2M 109
Oslo Ct. NW8 5C 58
(off Prince Albert Rd.)
Oslo Ho. SE5 1A 92
(off Carew St.)
Oslo Sq. SE16 4J 77
Osman Clo. N15 4B 44
Osman Rd. N9 3E 28
Osman Rd. W6 4G 73
Osmington Ho. SW8 8K 75
(off Dorset Rd.)
Osmond Clo. Harr 7A 38
Osmond Gdns. Wall 7G 123
Osmund St. W12 8D 56
Osnaburgh St. NW1 6F 58
(off Robert St.)
Osnaburgh St. NW1 7F 58
(Longford St.)
Osnaburgh Ter. NW1 7F 58
Osney Ho. SE2 3H 81
Osney Wlk. Cars 1B 122
Osprey. NW9 8D 24
Osprey Clo. E6 8J 63
Osprey Clo. E11 2E 46
Osprey Clo. E17 7J 29
Osprey Clo. Sutt 7K 121
Osprey Clo. Wat 7J 5
Osprey Clo. W Dray 3H 143
Osprey Ct. Beck 4L 109
Osprey Ct. Wal A 7M 7
Osprey Gdns. S Croy 2J 139
Osprey Ho. E14 1J 77
(off Victory Pl.)
Osprey M. Enf 7G 17
Osprey Rd. Wal A 7M 7
Ospringe Clo. SE20 4G 109
Ospringe Ho. SE1 3L 75
(off Wootton St.)
Ospringe Rd. NW5 9G 43
Osram Ct. W6 4G 73
Osram Rd. Wemb 8H 39
Osric Path. N1 5C 60
Ossian M. N4 5K 43
Ossian Rd. N4 5K 43
Ossington Bldgs. W1 8E 58
Ossington Clo. W2 1L 73
Ossington St. W2 1L 73
Ossory Rd. SE1 7E 76
Ossulston St. NW1 5H 59
Ossulton Pl. N2 1A 42
Ossulton Way. N2 2A 42
Ostade Rd. SW2 6K 91
Ostell Cres. Enf 2L 17
Ostend Pl. SE1 5A 76
Osten M. SW7 4M 73
Osterberg Rd. Dart 3K 99
Osterley. 8B 70
Osterley Av. Iswth 8B 70
Osterley Clo. Orp 5E 112
Osterley Ct. Iswth 9B 70
Osterley Ct. N'holt 6G 53
(off Canberra Dri.)
Osterley Cres. Iswth 9C 70
Osterley Gdns. S'hall 3A 70
Osterley Gdns. T Hth 6A 108
Osterley Ho. E14 9M 61
(off Giraud St.)
Osterley La.
S'hall & Iswth 6L 69
(in two parts)
Osterley Lodge. Iswth 8C 70
(off Church Rd.)
Osterley Pk. House. 7A 70
Osterley Pk. Rd. S'hall 4K 69
Osterley Pk. Vw. Rd.
W7 3C 70
Osterley Rd. N16 9C 44
Osterley Rd. Iswth 8C 70
Osterley Views. S'hall 2A 70
Oster Ter. E17 3H 45
Ostliffe Rd. N13 5A 28
Oswald Rd. S'hall 2J 69
Oswald's Mead. E9 9J 45
Oswald St. E5 8H 45
Oswald Ter. NW2 8G 41
Osward. Croy 1K 139
(in four parts)
Osward Pl. N9 2F 28
Osward Rd. SW17 8D 90
Oswell Ho. E1 2F 76
(off Farthing Fields)
Oswin St. SE11 5M 75
Oswyth Rd. SE5 1C 92
Otford Clo. SE20 5G 109
Otford Clo. Bex 5M 97
Otford Clo. Brom 7L 111
Otford Cres. SE4 5K 93
Otford Ho. SE1 3B 76
(off Staple St.)
Otford Ho. SE15 7G 77
(off Lovelinch Clo.)
Othello Clo. SE11 6M 75
Otho Ct. Bren 8H 71
Otis St. E3 6A 62
Otley App. Ilf 4M 47
Otley Dri. Ilf 3M 47
Otley Ho. N4 8L 43
Otley Rd. E16 9G 63
Otley Ter. E5 8H 45
Otley Way. Wat 3G 21
Otlinge Rd. Orp 8H 113
Ottawa Gdns. Dag 3B 66
Ottaway Ct. E5 8E 44
Ottaway St. E5 8E 44
Otterbourne Rd. E4 3B 30
Otterbourne Rd. Croy 4A 124
Otterburn Gdns. Iswth 8E 70
Otterburn Ho. SE5 8A 76
(off Sultan St.)
Otterburn St. SW17 3D 106
Otter Clo. E15 4A 62
Otterden Clo. Orp 5C 128
Otterden St. SE6 1L 109
Otterfield Rd. W Dray 1J 143
Otter Rd. Gnfd 7A 54
Otters Clo. Orp 8H 113
Otterspool La. Wat 2J 9
Otterspool Way. Wat 2K 9
Otto Clo. SE26 9F 92
Ottoman Ter. Wat 5G 9
Otto St. SE17 7M 75
Otway Gdns. Bush 9C 10
Oulton Clo. E5 7G 45
Oulton Clo. SE28 9G 65
Oulton Cres. Bark 1D 64
Oulton Rd. N15 3B 44
Oulton Way. Wat 4K 21
Oundle Av. Bush 8A 10
Oundle Ho. H Hill 5H 35
(off Montgomery Cres.)
Ousden Clo. Chesh 3E 6
Ousden Dri. Chesh 3E 6
Ouseley Rd. SW12 7D 90
Outer Circ. NW1 5C 58
Outgate Rd. NW10 3D 56
Outram Pl. N1 4J 59
Outram Pl. Wey 7A 116
Outram Rd. E6 4J 63
Outram Rd. N22 8H 27
Outram Rd. Croy 4D 124
Outwich St. EC3 9C 60
(off Houndsditch)
Outwood Ho. SW2 6K 91
(off Deepdene Gdns.)
Outwood La.
Kgswd & Coul 9C 136
Oval Ct. Edgw 7A 24
Oval Cricket Ground
(Surrey County Cricket Club)
7K 75
Oval Ho. Croy 3C 124
(off Oval Rd.)
Oval House Theatre. 7L 75
(off Kennington Oval)
Oval Mans. SE11 7K 75
Oval Pl. SW8 8K 75
Oval Rd. NW1 4F 58
Oval Rd. Croy 4B 124
Oval Rd. N. Dag 4M 65
Oval Rd. S. Dag 5M 65
Oval, The. E2 5F 60
Oval, The. Bans 6L 135
Oval, The. Sidc 6E 96
Oval Way. SE11 6K 75
Overbrae. Beck 3L 109
Overbrook Wlk. Edgw 7L 23
(in two parts)
Overbury Av. Beck 7M 109
Overbury Cres. New Ad 2A 140
Overbury Rd. N15 4B 44
Overbury St. E5 9H 45
Overcliff Rd. SE13 2L 93
Overcourt Clo. Sidc 5F 96
Overdale. Asht 7J 133
Overdale Av. N Mald 6A 104
Overdale Rd. W5 4G 71
Overdown Rd. SE6 1L 109
Overhill Rd. SE22 6E 92
Overhill Rd. Purl 1L 137
Overhill Way. Beck 9B 110
Overlea Rd. E5 5E 44
Overmead. SE9 6B 96
Overmead. Swan 9C 114
Oversley Ho. W2 8L 57
(off Alfred Rd.)
Overstand Clo. Beck 9L 109
Overstone Gdns. Croy 2K 125
Overstone Ho. E14 9L 61
(off E. India Dock Rd.)
Overstone Rd. W6 4G 73
Overstrand Mans.
SW11 9D 74
Overton Clo. NW10 2A 56
Overton Clo. Iswth 9D 70
Overton Ct. E11 5E 46
Overton Ct. Sutt 9L 121
Overton Dri. E11 5E 46
Overton Dri. Romf 5G 49

Overton Ho.—Paradise Wlk.

Overton Ho. SW15 6D 88
(off Tangley Gro.)
Overton Rd. E10 6J 45
Overton Rd. N14 7J 15
Overton Rd. SE2 4G 81
Overton Rd. SW9 1L 91
Overton Rd. Sutt 8L 121
Overton Rd. E. SE2 4H 81
Overton's Yd. Croy 5A 124
Overy Ho. SE1 3M 75
Overy St. Dart 5J 99
Ovesdon Av. Harr 6K 37
Ovett Clo. SE19 3C 108
Ovex Clo. E14 3A 78
Ovington Gdns. SW3 4C 74
Ovington M. SW3 4C 74
(off Ovington M.)
Ovington Sq. SW3 4C 74
Ovington St. SW3 5C 74
Owen Clo. SE28 2G 81
Owen Clo. Croy 1B 124
Owen Clo. Hay 6F 52
Owen Clo. Romf 6M 33
Owen Gdns. Wfd G 6J 31
Owen Ho. Twic 6F 86
Owenite St. SE2 5F 80
Owen Mans. W14 7J 73
(off Queen's Club Gdns.)
Owen Rd. N13 5A 28
Owen Rd. Hay 6F 52
Owen's Ct. EC1 6M 59
Owen's Row. EC1 6M 59
Owen St. EC1 5M 59
(in two parts)
Owens Way. SE23 6J 93
Owen Wlk. SE20 5E 108
Owen Way. NW10 2A 56
Owgan Clo. SE5 8B 76
Owl Cvn. Site, The. Lou 5D 18
Owl Clo. S Croy 2H 139
Owlets Hall Clo. Horn 1K 51
Ownstead Gdns. S Croy 3D 138
Ownsted Hill. New Ad 2A 140
Oxberry Av. SW6 1J 89
Oxenden Wood Rd. Orp 8F 128
Oxendon St. SW1 1H 75
Oxenford St. SE15 2D 92
Oxenham Ho. SE8 7L 77
(off Benbow St.)
Oxenholme. NW1 5G 59
(off Harrington Sq.)
Oxenpark Av. Wemb 5J 39
Oxestall's Rd. SE8 6J 77
Oxford & Cambridge Mans.
NW1 8C 58
(off Old Marylebone Rd.)
Oxford Av. NW10 6F 56
Oxford Av. SW20 6J 105
Oxford Av. Hay 8D 68
Oxford Av. Horn 2L 51
Oxford Av. Houn 6L 69
Oxford Cir. W1 9G 59
(off Oxford St.)
Oxford Cir. Av. W1 9G 59
Oxford Clo. N9 2F 28
Oxford Clo. Ashf 4A 100
Oxford Clo. Chesh 2D 6
Oxford Clo. Mitc 7G 107
Oxford Clo. N'wd 4B 20
Oxford Ct. EC4 1B 76
(off Cannon St.)
Oxford Ct. W3 9L 55
Oxford Ct. W4 6M 71
Oxford Ct. W7 8D 54
(off Copley Clo.)
Oxford Ct. W9 8L 57
(off Elmfield Way)
Oxford Ct. Felt 1H 101
Oxford Cres. N Mald 1B 120
Oxford Dri. SE1 2C 76
Oxford Dri. Ruis 7G 37
Oxford Gdns. N20 1B 26
Oxford Gdns. N21 9A 16
Oxford Gdns. W4 6L 71
Oxford Gdns. W10 9G 57
Oxford Ga. W6 5H 73
Oxford Ho. Borwd 4L 11
(off Stratfield Rd.)
Oxford M. Bex 6L 97
Oxford Pl. NW10 8B 40
(off Press Rd.)
Oxford Rd. E15 2B 62
(in two parts)
Oxford Rd. N4 6L 43
Oxford Rd. N9 2F 28
Oxford Rd. NW6 5L 57
Oxford Rd. SE19 3B 108
Oxford Rd. SW15 3J 89
Oxford Rd. W5 1H 71
Oxford Rd. Cars 8C 122
Oxford Rd. Den & Uxb 1A 142
Oxford Rd. Enf 7F 16
Oxford Rd. Harr 4A 38
Oxford Rd. Ilf 1A 64
Oxford Rd. Romf 6K 35
Oxford Rd. Sidc 2F 112
Oxford Rd. Tedd 2B 102
Oxford Rd. Wall 7G 123
Oxford Rd. W'stone 1D 38
Oxford Rd. Wfd G 5H 31
Oxford Rd. N. W4 6M 71
Oxford Rd. S. W4 6L 71
Oxford Sq. W2 9C 58
Oxford St. W1 9E 58
Oxford St. Wat 7F 8
Oxford Wlk. S'hall 2K 69
Oxford Way. Felt 1H 101
Oxgate Cen. NW2 7F 40
Oxgate Ct. NW2 7E 40
Oxgate Gdns. NW2 8F 40
Oxgate La. NW2 7F 40
Oxgate Pde. NW2 7E 40
Oxhawth Cres. Brom 9L 111
Oxhey. 8H 9
Oxhey Av. Wat 9H 9
Oxhey Dri. N'wd & Wat 5F 20
Oxhey La. Wat & Pinn 1J 21
Oxhey Pk. 8G 9
Oxhey Pk. Golf Course. 2G 21
Oxhey Ridge Clo. N'wd 4F 20
Oxhey Rd. Wat 9G 9
Ox La. Eps 1E 134
Oxleas. E6 9M 63
Oxleas Clo. Well 1B 96
Oxleay Rd. Harr 6L 37
Oxleigh Clo. N Mald 9C 104
Oxley Clo. SE1 6D 76
Oxley Clo. Romf 9G 35
Oxleys Rd. NW2 8F 40
Oxlip Clo. Croy 3H 125
Oxlow La. Dag 9K 49
Oxonian St. SE22 3D 92
Oxo Tower Wharf. 1L 75
Oxshott. 5B 132
Oxshott Rd. Lea 8C 132
Oxted Clo. Mitc 7B 106
Oxted Ho. Romf 5K 35
(off Redcar Rd.)
Oxtoby Way. SW16 5H 107
Oystercatchers Clo. E16 9F 62
Oystergate Wlk. EC4 1B 76
(off Swan La.)
Oyster Row. E1 9G 61
Ozolins Way. E16 9E 62

P

Pablo Neruda Clo. SE24 3M 91
Pace Heath Clo. Romf 6B 34
Pace Pl. E1 9F 60
Pachesham Dri. Lea 8D 132
Pachesham Park. 8E 132
Pachesham Pk. Lea 8E 132
Pacific Clo. Felt 7D 84
Pacific Ho. E1 7H 61
(off Ernest St.)
Pacific Rd. E16 9E 62
Pacific Wharf. SE16 2H 77
Packenham Ho. E2 6D 60
(off Wellington Row)
Packet Boat La. Uxb 9A 142
Packham Clo. Orp 4G 129
Packhorse La. Borwd 1C 12
Packington Rd. W3 4A 72
Packington Sq. N1 4A 60
(in three parts)
Packington St. N1 4M 59
Packmores Rd. SE9 4B 96
Padbury. SE17 6C 76
(off Bagshot St.)
Padbury Clo. Felt 7B 84
Padbury Ct. E2 6D 60
Padbury Ho. NW8 7C 58
(off Tresham Cres.)
Padcroft Rd. W Dray 2H 143
Paddenswick Rd. W6 4E 72
Paddington. 9B 58
Paddington Clo. Hay 7H 53
Paddington Ct. W7 8D 54
(off Copley Clo.)
Paddington Grn. W2 8B 58
Paddington St. W1 8E 58
Paddock Clo. SE3 1E 94
Paddock Clo. SE26 1H 109
Paddock Clo. F'boro 6M 127
Paddock Clo. N'holt 5L 53
Paddock Clo. Wat 8J 9
Paddock Clo. Wor Pk 3C 120
Paddock Gdns. SE19 3C 108
Paddock Lodge. Enf 7C 16
(off Village Rd.)
Paddock Pas. SE19 3C 108
(off Paddock Gdns.)
Paddock Rd. NW2 8E 40
Paddock Rd. Bexh 3J 97
Paddock Rd. Ruis 8H 37
Paddocks Clo. Harr 9M 37
Paddocks Clo. Orp 4H 129
Paddocks Grn. NW9 6M 39
Paddocks, The. W5 4H 71
(off Popes La.)
Paddocks, The. Cockf 5D 14
Paddocks, The. Croy 8L 125
Paddocks, The. Wemb 7M 39
Paddocks, The. Wey 5C 116
Paddock, The. NW9 3L 39
Paddock, The. Uxb 9A 36
Paddock Way. Chst 4B 112
Paddock Way. Eps 3G 135
Padfield Ct. Wemb 8K 39
Padfield Rd. SE5 2A 92
Padgets, The. Wal A 7L 7
Padley Clo. Chess 7K 119
Padnall Ct. Romf 1H 49
Padnall Rd. Chad H 1H 49
Padstow Clo. Orp 6D 128
Padstow Ho. E14 1K 77
(off Three Colt St.)
Padstow Rd. Enf 3M 15
Padstow Wlk. Felt 7D 84
Padua Rd. SE20 5G 109
Pagden St. SW8 9F 74
Pageant Av. NW9 8B 24
Pageant Cres. SE16 2J 77
Pageantmaster Ct. EC4 9M 59
(off Ludgate Hill)
Pageant Wlk. Croy 5C 124
Page Av. Wemb 8A 40
Page Clo. Dag 1J 65
Page Clo. Hamp 3J 101
Page Clo. Harr 4K 39
Page Cres. Croy 7M 123
Page Cres. Eri 8D 82
Page Grn. Rd. N15 3E 44
Page Grn. Ter. N15 3D 44
Page Heath La. Brom 7H 111
Page Heath Vs. Brom 7H 111
Page Ho. SE10 7A 78
(off Welland St.)
Pagehurst Rd. Croy 2F 124
Page Mdw. NW7 7F 24
Page Rd. Felt 5B 84
Pages Hill. N10 9E 26
Pages La. N10 9E 26
Pages La. Romf 9M 35
Pages La. Uxb 2A 142
Page St. NW7 8E 24
Page St. SW1 5H 75
Page's Wlk. SE1 5C 76
Pages Yd. W4 7D 72
Paget Av. Sutt 5B 122
Paget Clo. Hamp 1B 102
Paget Gdns. Chst 5M 111
Paget La. Iswth 2B 86
Paget Pl. King T 3A 104
Paget Pl. Th Dit 3D 118
Paget Ri. SE18 7L 79
Paget Rd. N16 6B 44
Paget Rd. Ilf 9M 47
Paget Rd. Uxb 7A 52
Paget St. EC1 6M 59
Paget Ter. SE18 7M 79
Pagham Ho. W10 7G 57
(off Sutton Way)
Pagin Ho. N15 3C 44
(off Braemar Rd.)
Pagitts Gro. Barn 3M 13
Pagnell St. SE14 8K 77
Pagoda Av. Rich 2K 87
Pagoda Gdns. SE3 1B 94
Paignton Rd. N15 4C 44
Paignton Rd. Ruis 8E 36
Paines Brook Rd. Romf 6K 35
Paines Brook Way. Romf 6K 35
Paines Clo. Pinn 1J 37
Paines La. Pinn 8J 21
Pain's Clo. Mitc 6F 106
Painsthorpe Rd. N16 8C 44
Painswick Ct. SE15 8D 76
(off Daniel Gdns.)
Painters La. Enf 8E 6
Painters Rd. Ilf 1D 48
Paisley Rd. N22 8M 27
Paisley Rd. Cars 3B 122
Pakeman Ho. SE1 3M 75
(off Surrey Row)
Pakeman St. N7 8K 43
Pakenham Clo. SW12 7E 90
Pakenham St. WC1 6K 59
Pakington Ho. SW9 1J 91
(off Stockwell Gdns. Est.)
Palace Av. W8 3M 73
Palace Ct. NW3 1M 57
Palace Ct. W2 1M 73
(off Moscow Rd., in two parts)
Palace Ct. Brom 5F 110
(off Palace Gro.)
Palace Ct. Harr 4J 39
Palace Ct. Gdns. N10 1G 43
Palace Dri. Wey 5A 116
Palace Gdns. Buck H 1H 31
Palace Gdns. Enf 6B 16
Palace Gdns. M. W8 2M 73
Palace Gdns. Shop. Cen.
Enf 6B 16
(off Palace Gdns.)
Palace Gdns. Ter. W8 2L 73
Palace Ga. W8 3A 74
Palace Gates Rd. N22 8H 27
Palace Grn. W8 2M 73
Palace Grn. Croy 9K 125
Palace Gro. SE19 4D 108
Palace Gro. Brom 5F 110
Palace Mans. W14 5J 73
(off Hammersmith Rd.)
Palace Mans. King T 8H 103
(off Palace Rd.)
Palace M. E17 2K 45
Palace M. SW1 5E 74
(off Eaton Ter.)
Palace M. SW6 8L 73
Palace M. Enf 5B 16
Palace Pde. E17 2K 45
Palace Pl. SW1 4G 75
Palace Pl. Mans. W8 3M 73
(off Kensington Ct.)
Palace Rd. N8 3H 43
(in two parts)
Palace Rd. N11 7J 27
Palace Rd. SE19 4D 108
Palace Rd. SW2 7K 91
Palace Rd. Brom 5F 110
Palace Rd. E Mol 7B 102
Palace Rd. King T 8H 103
Palace Rd. Ruis 9J 37
Palace Sq. SE19 4D 108
Palace St. SW1 4G 75
Palace Theatre. 9H 59
(off Shaftesbury Av.)
Palace Vw. SE12 8E 94
Palace Vw. Brom 7F 110
(in two parts)
Palace Vw. Croy 6K 125
Palace Vw. Rd. E4 5M 29
Palace Way. Wey 5A 116
Palace Wharf. W6 8G 73
(off Rainville Rd.)
Palamon Ct. SE1 6D 76
(off Cooper's Rd.)
Palamos Rd. E10 6L 45
Palatine Av. N16 9C 44
Palatine Rd. N16 9C 44
Palermo Rd. NW10 5E 56
Palestine Gro. SW19 5B 106
Palewell Clo. Orp 6F 112
Palewell Comn. Dri.
SW14 4B 88
Palewell Pk. SW14 4B 88
Paley Gdns. Lou 5M 19
Palfrey Pl. SW8 8K 75
Palgrave Av. S'hall 1L 69
Palgrave Gdns. NW1 7C 58
Palgrave Ho. SE5 8A 76
(off Wyndham Est.)
Palgrave Ho. Twic 6A 86
Palgrave Rd. W12 4D 72
Palissy St. E2 6D 60
(in two parts)
Pallant Ho. SE1 4B 76
(off Tabard St.)
Pallant Way. Orp 5L 127
Pallett Way. SE18 9J 79
Palliser Ct. W14 6J 73
(off Palliser Rd.)
Palliser Dri. Rain 8E 66
Palliser Ho. E1 7H 61
(off Ernest St.)
Palliser Ho. SE10 7B 78
(off Trafalgar Rd.)
Palliser Rd. W14 6J 73
Pall Mall. SW1 2G 75
Pall Mall E. SW1 2H 75
Pall Mall Pl. SW1 2G 75
(off Pall Mall)
Palmar Cres. Bexh 2L 97
Palmar Rd. Bexh 1L 97
Palmarsh Rd. Orp 8H 113
Palm Av. Sidc 3H 113
Palm Clo. E10 8M 45
Palm Ct. SE15 8D 76
(off Garnies Clo.)
Palmeira Rd. Bexh 2H 97
Palmer Av. Bush 7M 9
Palmer Av. Sutt 6G 121
Palmer Clo. Houn 9L 69
Palmer Clo. W Wick 5B 126
Palmer Ct. NW10 4B 56
(in two parts)
Palmer Cres. King T 7J 103
Palmer Gdns. Barn 7H 13
Palmer Pl. N7 1L 59
Palmer Rd. E13 7F 62
Palmer Rd. Dag 6H 49
Palmer's Ct. N11 5G 27
(off Palmer's Rd.)
Palmersfield Rd. Bans 6L 135
Palmers Green. 4L 27
Palmers Gro. W Mol 8L 101
Palmers La. Enf 3F 16
(in two parts)
Palmers Pas. SW14 2A 88
(off Palmers Rd.)
Palmer's Rd. E2 5H 61
Palmer's Rd. N11 5G 27
Palmers Rd. SW14 2A 88
Palmers Rd. SW16 6K 107
Palmers Rd. Borwd 3M 11
Palmerston Cen. W'stone 1D 38
Palmerston Ct. E3 5H 61
(off Old Ford Rd.)
Palmerston Ct. Buck H 1G 31
Palmerston Ct. Surb 2H 119
Palmerston Cres. N13 5K 27
Palmerston Cres. SE18 7A 80
Palmerston Gro. SW19 4L 105
Palmerston Ho. SE1 3L 75
(off Westminster Bri. Rd.)
Palmerston Ho. W8 2L 73
(off Kensington Pl.)
Palmerston Mans. W14 7J 73
(off Queen's Club Gdns.)
Palmerston Rd. E7 2F 62
Palmerston Rd. E17 1K 45
Palmerston Rd. N22 7K 27
Palmerston Rd. NW6 3K 57
(in two parts)
Palmerston Rd. SW14 3A 88
Palmerston Rd. SW19 4L 105
Palmerston Rd. W3 4A 72
Palmerston Rd. Buck H 2F 30
Palmerston Rd. Cars 6D 122
Palmerston Rd. Croy 9B 108
Palmerston Rd. Harr 1C 38
Palmerston Rd. Houn 9A 70
Palmerston Rd. Orp 6A 128
Palmerston Rd. Rain 5G 67
Palmerston Rd. Sutt 7A 122
Palmerston Rd. Twic 5C 86
Palmerston Way. SW8 8F 74
Palmer St. SW1 4H 75
(in two parts)
Palmers Way. Chesh 2E 6
Palm Gro. W5 4J 71
Palm Rd. Romf 3A 50
Palm Tree Ho. SE14 8H 77
(off Barlborough St.)
Pamela Ct. N3 6M 25
Pamela Gdns. Pinn 3F 36
Pamela Ho. E8 4D 60
(off Haggerston Rd.)
Pampisford Rd. Purl 3L 137
Pams Way. Eps 7B 120
Panama Ho. E1 8H 61
(off Beaumont Sq.)
Pancras La. EC4 9A 60
Pancras Rd. NW1 5H 59
Pandora Rd. NW6 2L 57
Panfield M. Ilf 4L 47
Panfield Rd. SE2 4E 80
Pangbourne. NW1 6G 59
(off Stanhope St.)
Pangbourne Av. W10 8G 57
Pangbourne Dri. Stan 5H 23
Panhard Pl. S'hall 1M 69
Pank Av. Barn 7A 14
Pankhurst Av. E16 2F 78
Pankhurst Clo. SE14 8H 77
Pankhurst Clo. Iswth 2D 86
Pankhurst Pl. Wat 5G 9
Pankhurst Rd. W on T 2G 117
Panmuir Rd. SW20 5F 104
Panmure Clo. N5 9M 43
Panmure Ct. S'hall 9A 54
(off Osborne Rd.)
Panmure Rd. SE26 9F 92
Panorama Ct. N6 4G 43
Pansy Gdns. W12 1E 72
Panter's. Swan 4D 114
Panther Dri. NW10 1B 56
Pantile Rd. Wey 6B 116
Pantiles Clo. N13 5M 27
Pantiles, The. NW11 3K 41
Pantiles, The. Bexh 8K 81
Pantiles, The. Brom 7J 111
Pantiles, The. Bush 1B 22
Pantile Wlk. Uxb 3A 142
Panton Clo. Croy 3M 123
Panton St. SW1 1H 75
Paper Bldgs. EC4 1L 75
(off Crown Office Row)
Papermill Clo. Cars 6E 122
Paper Mill Wharf. E14 1J 77
Papillons Wlk. SE3 1E 94
Papworth Gdns. N7 1K 59
Papworth Way. SW2 6L 91
Parade Mans. NW4 3F 40
Parade M. SE27 8M 91
Parade, The. N4 6L 43
Parade, The. SE4 1K 93
(off Up. Brockley Rd.)
Parade, The. SE26 9F 92
(off Wells Pk. Rd.)
Parade, The. SW11 8D 74
Parade, The. Cars 7D 122
(off Beynon Rd.)
Parade, The. Clay 8C 118
Parade, The. Croy 1J 123
Parade, The. Dart 4D 98
Parade, The. Eps 5B 134
(in two parts)
Parade, The. Gnfd 1F 54
Parade, The. Hamp 2B 102
Parade, The. King T 6J 103
(off London Rd.)
Parade, The. Romf 6M 35
Parade, The. Sun 4D 100
Parade, The. Sutt 5K 121
Parade, The. Wat 3H 21
(Fairfield Av.)
Parade, The. Wat 5F 8
(High St.)
Parade, The. Wat 3J 21
(Parade, The)
Parade, The. Wor Pk 6D 120
Paradise Clo. Chesh 1B 6
Paradise Pas. N7 1L 59
Paradise Pl. SE18 5J 79
Paradise Rd. SW4 1J 91
Paradise Rd. Rich 4H 87
Paradise Rd. Wal A 7J 7
Paradise Row. E2 6F 60
Paradise St. SE16 3F 76
Paradise Wlk. SW3 7D 74

Paragon Clo.—Parkview Ho.

Paragon Clo. E16 9E 62
Paragon Gro. Surb 1K 119
Paragon M. SE1 5B 76
Paragon Pl. SE3 1D 94
Paragon Pl. W13 7D 54
Paragon Pl. Surb 1K 119
Paragon Rd. E9 2G 61
Paragon, The. SE3 1D 94
Paramount Building. EC1 7M 59
(off St John St.)
Paramount Ct. WC1 7G 59
(off University St.)
Paramount Ind. Est. Wat 1G 9
(off Sandown Rd.)
Parbury Ri. Chess 8J 119
Parbury Rd. SE23 5J 93
Parchmore Rd. T Hth 6M 107
Parchmore Way. T Hth 6M 107
Pardoner Ho. SE1 4B 76
(off Pardoner St.)
Pardoner St. SE1 4B 76
(in two parts)
Pardon St. EC1 7M 59
Parfett St. E1 8E 60
(in two parts)
Parfitt Clo. NW3 6A 42
Parfour Dri. Kenl 8A 138
Parfrey St. W6 7G 73
Pargreaves Ct. Wemb 7L 39
Parham Dri. Ilf 4M 47
Parham Way. N10 9G 27
Paris Garden. SE1 2M 75
Parish Clo. Horn 7F 50
Parish Clo. Wat 7G 5
Parish Cotts. Dag 7L 49
Parish Ct. Surb 9J 103
Parish Ga. Dri. Sidc 5C 96
Parish La. SE20 3H 109
Parish M. SE20 4H 109
Paris Ho. E2 5F 60
(off Old Bethnal Grn. Rd.)
Parish Wharf Pl. SE18 5J 79
Park App. SE16 4F 76
Park App. Well 3F 96
Park Av. E6 4L 63
Park Av. E15 2C 62
Park Av. N3 8M 25
Park Av. N13 3L 27
Park Av. N18 4E 28
Park Av. N22 9J 27
Park Av. NW2 2G 57
Park Av. NW10 5K 55
(in two parts)
Park Av. NW11 6M 41
Park Av. SW14 3B 88
Park Av. Bark 2A 64
Park Av. Brom 4D 110
Park Av. Bush 4E 9
Park Av. Cars 8E 122
Park Av. Enf 7B 16
Park Av. Houn 5M 85
Park Av. Ilf 6L 47
Park Av. Mitc 4F 106
Park Av. Orp 5K 127
(Farnborough Rd.)
Park Av. Orp 4E 128
(Sevenoaks Rd.)
Park Av. Ruis 4B 36
Park Av. Shep 7C 100
Park Av. S'hall 3K 69
Park Av. Wat 6E 8
Park Av. W Wick 4A 126
Park Av. Wfd G 5F 30
Park Av. E. Eps 8E 120
Park Av. Maisonettes.
Bush 4K 9
Park Av. M. Mitc 4F 106
Park Av. N. N8 1H 43
Park Av. N. NW10 1F 56
Park Av. Rd. N17 7F 28
Park Av. S. N8 2H 43
Park Av. W. Eps 8E 120
Park Boulevd. Romf 8D 34
Park Bus. Cen. NW6 6L 57
Park Chase. Wemb 9K 39
Park Clo. E9 4G 61
Park Clo. N20 3B 26
Park Clo. NW2 8F 40
Park Clo. NW10 6K 55
Park Clo. SW1 3D 74
Park Clo. W4 7B 72
Park Clo. W14 4K 73
Park Clo. Bush 5H 9
Park Clo. Cars 8D 122
Park Clo. Esh 8L 117
Park Clo. Hamp 5A 102
Park Clo. Harr 8C 22
Park Clo. Houn 4A 86
Park Clo. King T 5L 103
Park Clo. Rick 4A 20
Park Clo. W on T 4D 116
Park Ct. E4 2A 30
Park Ct. E17 3M 45
Park Ct. N11 7H 27
Park Ct. N17 7E 28
Park Ct. SE26 3F 108
Park Ct. SW11 9F 74
Park Ct. W6 5E 72
Park Ct. Hamp W 5G 103
Park Ct. Harr 5J 39
Park Ct. N Mald 8B 104
Park Ct. S Croy 7A 124
(off Warham Rd.)
Park Ct. Uxb 4B 142
Park Ct. Wemb 1J 55
Park Cres. N3 7A 26
Park Cres. W1 7F 58
Park Cres. Els 5K 11
Park Cres. Enf 6B 16
Park Cres. Eri 7A 82
Park Cres. Harr 8C 22
Park Cres. Horn 5E 50
Park Cres. Twic 7B 86
Park Cres. M. E. W1 7F 58
Park Cres. M. W. W1 7F 58
Park Cres. Rd. Eri 7B 82
Park Cft. Edgw 8A 24
Parkcroft Rd. SE12 6D 94
Parkdale. N11 6H 27
Parkdale Cres. Wor Pk 5B 120
Parkdale Rd. SE18 6C 80
Park Dri. N21 8A 16
Park Dri. NW11 6M 41
Park Dri. SE7 7J 79
Park Dri. SW14 4B 88
Park Dri. W3 4L 71
Park Dri. Asht 9L 133
Park Dri. Dag 8A 50
Park Dri. Har W 6B 22
Park Dri. N Har 5L 37
Park Dri. Romf 2B 50
Park Dri. Upm 9M 51
Park Dwellings. NW3 1D 58
Park End. NW3 9C 42
Park End. Brom 5D 110
Pk. End Rd. Romf 2C 50
Parker Clo. E16 2J 79
Parker Clo. Cars 8D 122
Parker Ho. E14 3L 77
(off Admirals Way)
Parker M. WC2 9J 59
Parke Rd. SW13 9E 72
Parke Rd. Sun 8E 100
Parker Rd. Croy 6A 124
Parkers Row. SE1 3E 76
Parker St. E16 2J 79
Parker St. WC2 9J 59
Parker St. Wat 3F 8
Parkes Rd. Chig 5C 32
Pk. Farm Clo. N2 1A 42
Pk. Farm Clo. Pinn 3F 36
Pk. Farm Ct. Hay 1C 68
Pk. Farm Rd. Brom 5H 111
Pk. Farm Rd. King T 4J 103
Pk. Farm Rd. Upm 1K 67
Parkfield. Iswth 9C 70
Parkfield Av. SW14 3C 88
Parkfield Av. Felt 9E 84
Parkfield Av. Harr 9A 22
Parkfield Av. Hil 6F 142
Parkfield Av. N'holt 5H 53
Parkfield Clo. Edgw 6M 23
Parkfield Clo. N'holt 5J 53
Parkfield Ct. SE14 9K 77
(off Parkfield Rd.)
Parkfield Cres. Felt 9E 84
Parkfield Cres. Harr 9A 22
Parkfield Cres. Ruis 7J 37
Parkfield Dri. N'holt 5H 53
Parkfield Gdns. Harr 1M 37
Parkfield Ho. N Har 8M 21
Parkfield Ind. Est. SW11 1E 90
Parkfield Pde. Felt 9E 84
Parkfield Rd. NW10 3F 56
Parkfield Rd. SE14 9K 77
Parkfield Rd. Felt 9E 84
Parkfield Rd. Harr 8A 38
Parkfield Rd. N'holt 5J 53
Parkfield Rd. Uxb & Ick 7A 36
Parkfields. SW15 3G 89
Parkfields. Croy 3K 125
Parkfields. Oxs 3B 132
Parkfields Av. NW9 6B 40
Parkfields Av. SW20 5F 104
Parkfields Clo. Cars 6E 122
Parkfields Rd. King T 2K 103
Parkfield St. N1 5L 59
Parkfield Way. Brom 1K 127
Park Gdns. E10 6L 45
Park Gdns. NW9 1M 39
Park Gdns. Eri 5B 82
Park Gdns. King T 2K 103
Park Ga. N2 1B 42
Park Ga. N21 9K 15
Park Ga. SE3 2D 94
Park Ga. W5 8H 55
Parkgate Av. Barn 3A 14
Pk. Gate Clo. King T 3M 103
Pk. Gate Ct. Hamp H 3A 102
Parkgate Cres. Barn 3A 14
Parkgate Gdns. SW14 4B 88
Parkgate M. N6 5G 43
Parkgate Rd. SW11 8C 74
Parkgate Rd. Orp 6M 129
Parkgate Rd. Wall 7E 122
Parkgate Rd. Wat 1G 9
Park Gates. Harr 9L 37
Park Gro. E15 4E 62
Park Gro. N11 7H 27
Park Gro. Bexh 3A 98
Park Gro. Brom 5F 110
Park Gro. Edgw 5K 23
Park Gro. Rd. E11 7C 46
Park Hall. SE10 8B 78
(off Crooms Hill)
Parkhall Rd. N2 2C 42
Pk. Hall Rd. SE21 9A 92
Pk. Hall Trad. Est. SE21 9A 92
Parkham Ct. Brom 6C 110
Parkham St. SW11 9C 74
Park Hill. SE23 8F 92
Park Hill. SW4 4H 91
Park Hill. W5 8H 55
Park Hill. Brom 8J 111
Park Hill. Cars 8C 122
Park Hill. Lou 7H 19
Park Hill. Rich 5K 87
Pk. Hill Clo. Cars 7C 122
Parkhill Clo. Horn 7G 51
Pk. Hill Ct. SW17 9D 90
Pk. Hill M. S Croy 7B 124
Pk. Hill Ri. Croy 4C 124
Parkhill Rd. E4 1A 30
Parkhill Rd. NW3 1D 58
Parkhill Rd. Bex 6K 97
Pk. Hill Rd. Brom 6C 110
Pk. Hill Rd. Croy 4C 124
Parkhill Rd. Eps 3D 134
Pk. Hill Rd. Sidc 9B 96
Pk. Hill Rd. Wall 9F 122
Parkhill Wlk. NW3 1D 58
Parkholme Rd. E8 2E 60
Park Ho. E9 3G 61
(off Shore Rd.)
Park Ho. N21 9K 15
Park Ho. Gdns. Twic 4G 87
Park Ho. Pas. N6 5E 42
Parkhouse St. SE5 8B 76
Parkhurst. Eps 2A 134
Parkhurst Ct. N7 9J 43
Parkhurst Gdns. Bex 6L 97
Parkhurst Rd. E12 9L 47
Parkhurst Rd. E17 2J 45
Parkhurst Rd. N7 9J 43
Parkhurst Rd. N11 5E 26
Parkhurst Rd. N17 9E 28
Parkhurst Rd. N22 6K 27
Parkhurst Rd. Bex 6L 97
Parkhurst Rd. Sutt 6B 122
Parkinson Ho. E9 3G 61
(off Frampton Pk. Rd.)
Parkinson Ho. SW1 5G 75
(off Tachbrook St.)
Parkland Av. Romf 1C 50
Parkland Av. Upm 1M 67
Parkland Ct. E15 1C 62
(off Maryland Pk.)
Parkland Gdns. SW19 7H 89
Parkland Gro. Ashf 9E 144
Parkland Rd. N22 9K 27
Parkland Rd. Ashf 9E 144
Parkland Rd. Wfd G 7F 30
Parklands. N6 6F 42
Parklands. Chig 2A 32
Parklands. Surb 9K 103
Parklands. Wal A 6J 7
Parklands Clo. SW14 4A 88
Parklands Clo. Barn 2B 14
Parklands Clo. Chig 3A 32
Parklands Clo. Ilf 5A 48
Parklands Ct. Houn 1H 85
Parklands Dri. N3 1J 41
Parklands Gro. Iswth 9D 70
Parklands Pde. Houn 1H 85
Parklands Rd. SW16 2F 106
Parklands Way. Wor Pk 4C 120
Park La. E15 4B 62
Park La. N9 3C 28
Park La. N17 7D 28
(in two parts)
Park La. W1 1D 74
Park La. Cars 6E 122
Park La. Chad H 4H 49
Park La. Chesh 1B 6
Park La. Cran 8E 68
Park La. Croy 5B 124
Park La. Elm P 2F 66
Park La. Harr 8M 37
Park La. Hay 8C 52
Park La. Horn 4D 50
Park La. Rich 3H 87
Park La. Stan 3E 22
Park La. Sutt 8J 121
Park La. Swan 6G 115
Park La. Tedd 3D 102
Park La. Wal X 6C 6
Park La. Wemb 1J 55
Park La. Clo. N17 7E 28
Park La. Mans.
Croy 5B 124
(off Edridge Rd.)
Park Langley 8A 110
Parklawn Av. Eps 5M 133
Pk. Lawn Rd. Wey 6A 116
Park Lawns. Wemb 9K 39
Parklea Clo. NW9 8C 24
Pk. Lee Ct. N16 5C 44
Parkleigh Rd. SW19 6M 105
Parkleys. Rich 1H 103
Parkleys Pde. Rich 1H 103
Park Lodge. NW8 3B 58
Park Lofts. SW2 4J 91
(off Mandrell Rd.)
Park Lorne. NW8 6C 58
(off Park Rd.)
Park Mnr. Sutt 9A 122
(off Christchurch Pk.)
Park Mans. NW4 3F 40
Park Mans. NW8 5C 58
(off Allitsen Rd.)
Park Mans. SW1 3D 74
(off Knightsbridge)
Park Mans. SW8 7J 75
Park Mans. SW11 9D 74
(off Prince of Wales Dri.)
Parkmead. SW15 5F 88
Park Mead. Harr 8M 37
Parkmead. Lou 7L 19
Park Mead. Sidc 4F 96
Parkmead Gdns. NW7 6D 24
Park M. SE24 6A 92
Park M. W10 5J 57
Park M. Chst 3M 111
Park M. Rain 2E 66
Park M. Stanw 6D 144
Parkmore Clo. Wfd G 4E 30
Pk. Nook Gdns. Enf 1B 16
Park Pde. NW10 5D 56
Park Pde. W5 4L 71
Park Pde. Hay 9C 52
Park Pl. E14 2L 77
Park Pl. SW1 2G 75
Park Pl. W3 5L 71
Park Pl. W5 2H 71
Park Pl. Brom 5F 110
(off Park Rd.)
Park Pl. Hamp H 3A 102
Park Pl. Wemb 9K 39
Park Pl. Vs. W2 8A 58
Park Ridings. N8 1L 43
Park Ri. SE23 7J 93
Park Ri. Harr 8C 22
Park Ri. Rd. SE23 7J 93
Park Rd. E6 4G 63
Park Rd. E10 6L 45
Park Rd. E12 6F 46
Park Rd. E15 4E 62
Park Rd. E17 3K 45
Park Rd. N2 1B 42
Park Rd. N8 2G 43
Park Rd. N11 7H 27
Park Rd. N14 1H 27
Park Rd. N15 2M 43
Park Rd. N18 4E 28
Park Rd. NW4 5E 40
Park Rd. NW8 & NW1 6C 58
Park Rd. NW9 5B 40
Park Rd. NW10 4C 56
Park Rd. SE25 8C 108
Park Rd. SW19 3B 106
Park Rd. W4 8A 72
Park Rd. W7 1D 70
Park Rd. Ashf 2A 100
Park Rd. Bans 7M 135
Park Rd. Barn 6B 14
Park Rd. Beck 4K 109
Park Rd. Brom 5F 110
Park Rd. Bush 8L 9
Park Rd. Cheam 8J 121
Park Rd. Chst 3M 111
Park Rd. Dart 6L 99
Park Rd. E Mol 8A 102
Park Rd. Enf 9E 6
Park Rd. Esh 6M 117
Park Rd. Felt 1H 101
Park Rd. Hack 4F 122
Park Rd. Hamp H 1M 101
Park Rd. Hamp W 5G 103
Park Rd. Hay 8C 52
Park Rd. High Bar 6K 13
Park Rd. Houn 4M 85
Park Rd. Ilf 8B 48
Park Rd. Iswth 9F 70
Park Rd. Kenl 7A 138
Park Rd. King T 2K 103
Park Rd. N Mald 8B 104
Park Rd. Orp 9G 113
Park Rd. Rich 5K 87
Park Rd. Stanw 5A 144
Park Rd. Sun 4F 100
Park Rd. Surb 1K 119
Park Rd. Swan 8D 114
Park Rd. Tedd 3D 102
Park Rd. Twic 5G 87
Park Rd. Uxb 3C 142
Park Rd. Wall 7F 122
Park Rd. Wal X 6D 6
Park Rd. Warl 6C 140
Park Rd. Wat 3E 8
Park Rd. Wemb 2J 55
Park Rd. E. W3 3M 71
Park Rd. E. Uxb 5B 142
Park Rd. Ho. King T 4L 103
Park Rd. Ind. Est. Swan 7D 114
Park Rd. N. W3 3M 71
Park Rd. N. W4 6B 72
Park Row. SE10 6B 78
Park Royal 6M 55
Park Royal Junction (Junct.)
4M 55
Pk. Royal Metro Cen.
NW10 7M 55
Pk. Royal Rd.
NW10 & W3 6A 56
Pk. Royal S. Leisure Complex.
W3 7L 55
Parkshot. Rich 3H 87
Parkside. N3 8M 25
Parkside. NW2 8E 40
Parkside. NW7 6E 24
Parkside. SE3 8D 78
Parkside. SW1 3D 74
(off Knightsbridge)
Parkside. SW19 9H 89
Parkside. W3 2C 72
Parkside. W5 1J 71
Parkside. Buck H 2F 30
Parkside. Hamp H 2B 102
Parkside. Hay 1C 68
Parkside. Sidc 8F 96
Parkside. Sutt 8J 121
Parkside. Wal X 7E 6
Parkside. Wat 8G 9
Parkside Av. SW19 2H 105
Parkside Av. Bexh 1B 98
Parkside Av. Brom 8J 111
Parkside Av. Romf 1B 50
Parkside Bus. Est. SE8 7J 77
(Blackhorse Rd.)
Parkside Bus. Est. SE8 7J 77
(Rolt St.)
Parkside Clo. SE20 4G 109
Parkside Ct. E11 4E 46
(off Wanstead Pl.)
Parkside Ct. N22 6K 27
Parkside Cres. N7 8L 43
Parkside Cres. Surb 1A 120
Parkside Cross. Bexh 1C 98
Parkside Dri. Edgw 3L 23
Parkside Dri. Wat 4C 8
Parkside Est. E9 4G 61
Parkside Gdns. SW19 1H 105
Parkside Gdns. Coul 9F 136
Parkside Gdns. E Barn 1D 26
Parkside Ho. Dag 8A 50
Parkside Lodge. Belv 6A 82
Parkside Pde. Dart 1D 98
(off Northend Rd.)
Parkside Rd. SW11 9E 74
Parkside Rd. Belv 5M 81
Parkside Rd. Houn 4M 85
Parkside Rd. N'wd 5D 20
Parkside Ter. N18 4B 28
Parkside Ter. Orp 5M 127
(off Willow Wlk.)
Parkside Way. Harr 2M 37
Park Sq. Esh 6M 117
Park Sq. E. NW1 7F 58
Park Sq. M. NW1 7E 58
(off Up. Harley St.)
Park Sq. W. NW1 7F 58
Parkstead Rd. SW15 4E 88
Park Steps. W2 1C 74
(off St George's Fields)
Parkstone Av. N18 6D 28
Parkstone Av. Horn 4J 51
Parkstone Rd. E17 1A 46
Parkstone Rd. SE15 1E 92
Park St. SE1 2A 76
Park St. W1 1E 74
Park St. Croy 5A 124
Park St. Tedd 3C 102
Park St. La. Brick W 3M 5
Park Ter. Cars 5C 122
Park Ter. Enf 2J 17
Park Ter. Wor Pk 3E 120
Park, The. N6 4E 42
Park, The. NW11 6M 41
Park, The. SE19 4C 108
Park, The. SE23 7G 93
Park, The. W5 2H 71
Park, The. Cars 7D 122
Park, The. Sidc 2E 112
Parkthorne Clo. Harr 4M 37
Parkthorne Dri. Harr 4L 37
Parkthorne Rd. SW12 6H 91
Park Towers. W1 2F 74
(off Brick St.)
Park Vw. N5 9A 44
Park Vw. N21 9K 15
Park Vw. W3 8A 56
Park Vw. Chad H 4H 49
Parkview. Eri 4H 81
Parkview. Gnfd 6E 54
(off Perivale La.)
Park Vw. N Mald 7D 104
Park Vw. Pinn 8K 21
Park Vw. Wemb 1M 55
Park Vw. W Dray 1J 143
Pk. View Ct. N12 4C 26
Pk. View Ct. SE20 5F 108
Parkview Ct. SW6 1J 89
Parkview Ct. SW18 4L 89
Parkview Ct. Har W 7C 22
Pk. View Cres. N11 4F 26
Pk. View Est. E2 5H 61
Pk. View Gdns. N22 8L 27
Pk. View Gdns. NW4 3G 41
Pk. View Gdns. Bark 5C 64
Pk. View Gdns. Ilf 2K 47
Pk. View Ho. E4 5L 29
Parkview Ho. N9 9F 16
Pk. View Ho. SE24 5M 9
(off Hurst St.)
Parkview Ho. Wat 8H 9

Pk. View Mans.—Peel Clo.

Pk. View Mans. N4 5M 43
Pk. View Rd. N3 8M 25
Pk. View Rd. N17 1E 44
Pk. View Rd. NW10 9D 40
Parkview Rd. SE9 7M 95
Pk. View Rd. W5 8J 55
Pk. View Rd. Croy 3E 124
Pk. View Rd. Pinn 7F 20
Pk. View Rd. S'hall 2L 69
Pk. View Rd. Uxb 9D 142
Pk. View Rd. Well 2G 97
Pk. Village E. NW1 5F 58
Pk. Village W. NW1 5F 58
Park Vs. Romf 4H 49
Parkville Rd. SW6 8K 73
Park Vista. SE10 7B 78
Park Wlk. N6 5E 42
Park Wlk. SE10 8B 78
Park Wlk. SW10 7A 74
Park Wlk. Barn 5B 14
Parkway. N14 2J 27
Park Way. N20 4D 26
Parkway. NW1 4F 58
Park Way. NW11 3J 41
Parkway. SW20 8H 105
Park Way. Bex 9C 98
Park Way. Edgw 8M 23
Park Way. Enf 4L 15
Parkway. Eri 4J 81
Park Way. Felt 6F 84
Parkway. Ilf 8D 48
Parkway. New Ad 1M 139
Parkway. Rain 7E 66
Parkway. Romf 9D 34
Park Way. Ruis 6E 36
Parkway. Uxb 3E 142
Park Way. W Mol 7M 101
Park Way. Wey 5B 116
Park Way. Wfd G 5G 31
Pk. Way Ct. Ruis 6D 36
Parkway, The. Hay (UB3) 4F 68
Parkway, The.
Hay & N'holt (UB4,UB5)
9G 53
Parkway, The. Houn 7E 68
(Church Rd.)
Parkway, The.
Houn & S'hall 6E 68
(Watersplash La.)
Parkway Trad. Est. Houn 7G 69
Park West. W2 9C 58
(off Edgware Rd.)
Park W. Pl. W2 9C 58
Park Wharf. SE8 6J 77
(off Evelyn St.)
Parkwood. N20 3D 26
Parkwood. NW8 4D 58
(off St Edmund's Ter.)
Parkwood. Beck 4L 109
Parkwood Av. Esh 3A 118
Pk. Wood Clo. Bans 7H 135
Parkwood Flats. N20 3D 26
Parkwood Gro. Sun 7E 100
Parkwood M. N6 4F 42
Parkwood Rd. SW19 2K 105
Pk. Wood Rd. Bans 7H 135
Pk. Wood Rd. Bex 6K 97
Parkwood Rd. Iswth 9D 70
Pk. Wood Vw. Bans 8G 135
Parliament Ct. E1 8C 60
(off Artillery La.)
Parliament Hill. 8D 42
Parliament Hill. NW3 9C 42
Parliament Hill Mans.
NW5 9E 42
Parliament M. SW14 1A 88
Parliament Sq. SW1 3J 75
Parliament St. SW1 3J 75
Parliament Vw. SE1 5K 75
Parma Cres. SW11 3D 90
Parmiter Ind. Est. E2 5F 60
(off Parmiter St.)
Parmiter St. E2 5F 60
Parmoor Ct. EC1 7A 60
(off Gee St.)
Parndon Ho. Lou 9J 19
Parnell Clo. W12 4F 72
Parnell Clo. Ab L 3D 4
Parnell Clo. Edgw 4M 23
Parnell Ho. WC1 8H 59
Parnell Rd. E3 4K 61
(in two parts)
Parnham St. E14 9J 61
(in two parts)
Parolles Rd. N19 6G 43
Paroma Rd. Belv 4L 81
Parr Av. Eps 1F 134
Parr Clo. N9 & N18 4F 28
Parr Ct. N1 5B 60
(off New N. Rd.)
Parr Ct. Felt 1G 101
Parr Ho. E16 2F 78
(off Beaulieu Av.)
Parrington Ho. SW4 5H 91
Parr Rd. E6 4H 63
Parr Rd. Stan 8H 23
Parrs Clo. S Croy 1B 138
Parrs Pl. Hamp 4L 101
Parr St. N1 5B 60
Parry Av. E6 9K 63
Parry Clo. Eps 9F 120
Parry Ho. E1 2F 76
(off Green Bank)
Parry Pl. SE18 5M 79
Parry Rd. SE25 7C 108
Parry Rd. W10 6J 57
(in two parts)
Parry St. SW8 7J 75
Parsifal Rd. NW6 1L 57
Parsley Gdns. Croy 3H 125
Parsloes Av. Dag 9H 49
Parsonage Clo. Ab L 3C 4
Parsonage Clo. Hay 9D 52
Parsonage Clo. Warl 8K 139
Parsonage Ct. Lou 6M 19
(off Rectory La.)
Parsonage Gdns. Enf 4A 16
Parsonage La. Enf 4A 16
Parsonage La. Sidc 1K 113
Parsonage La. S at H 3M 115
Parsonage Manorway.
Belv 7L 81
Parsonage Rd. Rain 5G 67
Parsonage St. E14 5A 78
Parson's Cres. Edgw 3L 23
Parsonsfield Clo. Bans 7H 135
Parsonsfield Rd. Bans 8H 135
Parsons Green. 9L 73
Parson's Grn. SW6 9L 73
Parson's Grn. La. SW6 9L 73
Parson's Gro. Edgw 3L 23
Parsons Hill. SE18 4L 79
(off Powis St.)
Parsons Ho. W2 7B 58
(off Hall Pl.)
Parsons La. Dart 9F 98
Parsons Lodge. NW6 3M 57
(off Priory Rd.)
Parson's Mead. Croy 3M 123
Parsons Mead. E Mol 7A 102
Parson's Rd. E13 5G 63
Parson St. NW4 2G 41
Parthenia Rd. SW6 9L 73
Partingdale La. NW7 5H 25
Partington Clo. N19 6H 43
Partridge Clo. E16 8H 63
Partridge Clo. Barn 8G 13
Partridge Clo. Bush 1A 22
Partridge Clo. Stan 4J 23
Partridge Ct. EC1 7M 59
(off Cyprus St.)
Partridge Dri. Orp 5A 128
Partridge Grn. SE9 9L 95
Partridge Knoll. Purl 4M 137
Partridge Mead. Bans 7G 135
Partridge Rd. Hamp 3K 101
Partridge Rd. Sidc 9C 96
Partridge Sq. E6 8J 63
Partridge Way. N22 8J 27
Parvills. Wal A 5K 7
Pasadena Clo. Hay 3E 68
Pasadena Clo. Trad. Est.
Hay 3F 68
Pascall Ho. SE17 7A 76
(off Draco St.)
Pascal St. SW8 8H 75
Pascoe Rd. SE13 4B 94
Pasfield. Wal A 6K 7
Pasley Clo. SE17 6M 75
Pasquier Rd. E17 1J 45
Passage, The. Rich 4J 87
Passey Pl. SE9 5K 95
Passfield Dri. E14 8M 61
Passfield Path. SE28 1F 80
Passfields. SE6 9M 93
Passfields. W14 6K 73
(off Star St.)
Passing All. EC1 8M 59
(off St John St.)
Passingham Ho. Houn 7L 69
Passmore Gdns. N11 6H 27
Passmore St. SW1 6E 74
Pasteur Clo. NW9 9C 24
Pasteur Ct. Harr 6F 38
Pasteur Dri. H Wood 9H 35
Pasteur Gdns. N18 5M 27
Paston Clo. E5 8H 45
Paston Clo. Wall 5G 123
Paston Cres. SE12 6F 94
Pastor Ct. N6 4G 43
Pastor St. SE11 5M 75
(in two parts)
Pasture Clo. Bush 9A 10
Pasture Clo. Wemb 8F 38
Pasture Rd. SE6 7D 94
Pasture Rd. Dag 9K 49
Pasture Rd. Wemb 7F 38
Pastures Mead. Uxb 2E 142
Pastures, The. N20 1K 25
Pastures, The. Wat 9G 9
Patcham Ter. SW8 9F 74
Patch Clo. Uxb 4D 142
Patchetts Green. 3A 10
Patching Way. Hay 8J 53
Patchway Ct. SE15 7C 76
(off Newent Clo.)
Patent Ho. E14 8M 61
(off Morris Rd.)
Paternoster Clo. Wal A 6M 7
Paternoster Hill. Wal A 5M 7
Paternoster La. EC4 9M 59
Paternoster Row. EC4 9A 60
Paternoster Row. Noak H 1G 35
Paternoster Sq. EC4 9M 59
Paterson Ct. EC1 6B 60
(off St Lukes Est.)
Pater St. W8 4L 73
Pates Mnr. Dri. Felt 6B 84
Pathfield Rd. SW16 3H 107
Path, The. SW19 5M 105
Pathway, The. Rad 1D 10
(in two parts)
Pathway, The. Wat 1H 21
Patience Rd. SW11 1C 90
Patio Clo. SW4 5H 91
Patmore Est. SW8 9G 75
Patmore Ho. N16 1C 60
Patmore La. W on T 8D 116
Patmore Lodge. N6 2D 42
Patmore Rd. Wal A 7L 7
Patmore St. SW8 9G 75
Patmore Way. Romf 5M 33
Patmos Lodge. SW9 9M 75
(off Elliott Rd.)
Patmos Rd. SW9 8M 75
Paton Clo. E3 6L 61
Paton Ho. SW9 1K 91
(off Stockwell Rd.)
Paton St. EC1 6A 60
Patricia Ct. Chst 5B 112
Patricia Ct. Well 8F 80
Patricia Dri. Horn 6J 51
Patricia Gdns. Sutt 3L 135
Patrick Coman Ho. EC1 6M 59
(off Finsbury Est.)
Patrick Connolly Gdns.
E3 6M 61
Patrick Gro. Wal A 6H 7
Patrick Pas. SW11 1C 90
Patrick Rd. E13 6G 63
Patrington Clo. Uxb 6A 142
Patriot Sq. E2 5F 60
Patrol Pl. SE6 5M 93
Pat Shaw Ho. E1 7H 61
(off Globe Rd.)
Patshull Pl. NW5 2G 59
Patshull Rd. NW5 2G 59
Patten All. Rich 4H 87
Pattenden Rd. SE6 7K 93
Patten Ho. N16 6A 44
Patten Rd. SW18 6C 90
Patterdale. NW1 6F 58
(off Osnaburgh St.)
Patterdale Clo. Brom 3D 110
Patterdale Rd. SE15 8G 77
Pattern Ho. EC1 7M 59
Patterson Ct. SE19 4D 108
Patterson Ct. Dart 4L 99
Patterson Rd. SE19 3D 108
Pattina Wlk. SE16 2J 77
(off Capstan Way)
Pattinson Point. E16 8E 62
(off Fife Rd.)
Pattison Ho. E1 9H 61
(off Wellesley St.)
Pattison Ho. SE1 3A 76
(off Redcross Way)
Pattison Rd. NW2 8L 41
Pattison Wlk. SE18 6A 80
Paul Byrne Ho. N2 1A 42
Paul Clo. E15 3C 62
Paul Ct. N18 4E 28
(off Fairfield Rd.)
Paul Ct. Romf 3A 50
Paulet Rd. SE5 1M 91
Paul Gdns. Croy 4D 124
Paul Gdns. Hay 7B 68
Paulhan Rd. Harr 2H 39
Paulin Dri. N21 9L 15
Pauline Cres. Twic 7A 86
Pauline Ho. E1 8E 60
(off Old Montague St.)
Paulinus Clo. Orp 6G 113
Paul Julius Clo. E14 1B 78
Paul Robeson Clo. E6 6L 63
Pauls Grn. Wal X 6E 6
Pauls Ho. E3 8K 61
(off Timothy Rd.)
Paul St. E15 4C 62
Paul St. EC2 7B 60
Paul's Wlk. EC4 1A 76
Paultons Sq. SW3 7B 74
Paultons St. SW3 7B 74
Pauntley St. N19 6G 43
Pavan Ct. E2 6G 61
(off Sceptre Rd.)
Paved Ct. Rich 4H 87
Paveley Dri. SW11 8C 74
Paveley Ho. N1 5K 59
(off Priory Grn. Est.)
Paveley St. NW8 6C 58
Pavement M. Romf 5H 49
Pavement Sq. Croy 3E 124
Pavement, The. E11 6A 46
(off Hainault Rd.)
Pavement, The. SW4 3G 91
Pavement, The. W5 4J 71
Pavement, The. Iswth 2E 86
(off South St.)
Pavet Clo. Dag 2M 65
Pavilion. NW8 6B 58
Pavilion Ct. NW6 6L 57
(off Stafford Rd.)
Pavilion Lodge. Harr 6B 38
Pavilion M. N3 1L 41
Pavilion Rd. SW1 4D 74
Pavilion Rd. Ilf 5K 47
Pavilion Shop. Cen., The.
Wal X 6E 6
Pavilions, The. Uxb 3A 142
Pavilion St. SW1 4D 74
Pavilion Ter. W12 9G 57
(off Wood La.)
Pavilion Ter. Ilf 3C 48
Pavilion, The. SW8 8H 75
Pavilion Way. Edgw 7M 23
Pavilion Way. Ruis 7G 37
Pawleyne Clo. SE20 4G 109
Pawsey Clo. E13 4F 62
Pawsons Rd. Croy 1A 124
Paxfold. Stan 5H 23
Paxford Rd. Wemb 7F 38
Paxton Clo. Rich 1K 87
Paxton Clo. W on T 2G 117
Paxton Ct. SE12 9G 95
Paxton Ct. SE26 1J 109
(off Adamsrill Rd.)
Paxton Ct. Borwd 6A 12
Paxton Pl. SE27 1C 108
Paxton Rd. N17 7D 28
Paxton Rd. SE23 9J 93
Paxton Rd. W4 7C 72
Paxton Rd. Brom 4E 110
Paxton Ter. SW1 7F 74
Paymal Ho. E1 8G 61
(off Stepney Way)
Payne Clo. Bark 3D 64
Payne Ho. N1 4K 59
(off Barnsbury Est.)
Paynell Ct. SE3 2C 94
Payne Rd. E3 5M 61
Paynesfield Av. SW14 2B 88
Paynesfield Rd. Bus H 9D 10
Payne St. SE8 8K 77
Paynes Wlk. W6 7J 73
Payzes Gdns. Wfd G 6D 30
Peabody Av. SW1 6F 74
Peabody Bldgs. E1 1E 76
(off John Fisher St.)
Peabody Bldgs. EC1 7A 60
(off Roscoe St.)
Peabody Bldgs. SW3 7C 74
(off Lawrence St.)
Peabody Clo. SE10 9M 77
Peabody Clo. SW1 6F 74
Peabody Clo. Croy 3G 125
Peabody Cotts. N17 8C 28
Peabody Ct. EC1 7A 60
(off Roscoe St.)
Peabody Ct. SE5 9B 76
(off Kimpton Rd.)
Peabody Est. E1 1H 77
(off Glasmis Pl.)
Peabody Est. E2 5F 60
(off Minerva St.)
Peabody Est. EC1 7A 60
(off Whitecross St., in two parts)
Peabody Est. EC1 7L 59
(off Farringdon La.)
Peabody Est. N1 4A 60
Peabody Est. SE1 2L 75
(Hatfield St.)
Peabody Est. SE1 3A 76
(off Mint St., Mint St.)
Peabody Est. SE1 2A 76
(Southwark St.)
Peabody Est. SE24 6M 91
Peabody Est. SW1 5G 75
(off Vauxhall Bri. Rd.)
Peabody Est. SW3 7C 74
Peabody Est. SW6 7L 73
(off Lillie Rd.)
Peabody Est. SW11 3C 90
Peabody Est. W6 6G 73
Peabody Est. W10 8G 57
Peabody Hill. SE21 7M 91
Peabody Sq. SE1 3M 75
(in two parts)
Peabody Tower. EC1 7A 60
(off Golden La.)
Peabody Trust. SE17 5B 76
Peabody Yd. N1 4A 60
Peace Clo. N14 7F 14
Peace Clo. SE25 8C 108
Peace Clo. Chesh 2B 6
Peace Clo. Gnfd 4B 54
Peace Dri. Wat 5E 8
Peace Gro. Wemb 8M 39
Peace Pagoda. 8D 74
Peace Prospect. Wat 5E 8
Peace St. SE18 7L 79
Peaches Clo. Sutt 9J 121
Peachey Clo. Uxb 8B 142
Peachey Edwards Ho. E2 6F 60
(off Teesdale St.)
Peachey La. Uxb 8B 142
Peach Rd. W10 6H 57
Peach Rd. Felt 7E 84
Peach Tree Av. W Dray 9D 142
Peachum Rd. SE3 7D 78
(in two parts)
Peachwalk M. E3 5H 61
Peacock Av. Felt 7B 84
Peacock Clo. Dag 6G 49
Peacock Clo. Horn 2J 51
Peacock Gdns. S Croy 2J 139
Peacock Ind. Est. N17 7D 28
Peacock St. SE17 5M 75
Peacock Theatre. 9K 59
(off Portugal St.)
Peacock Wlk. E16 9F 62
(off Mortlake Rd.)
Peacock Wlk. N6 5F 42
Peacock Wlk. Ab L 4E 4
Peacock Yd. SE17 6M 75
(off Iliffe St.)
Peakes Way. Chesh 1A 6
Peaketon Av. Ilf 2H 47
Peak Hill. SE26 1G 109
Peak Hill Av. SE26 1G 109
Peak Hill Gdns. SE26 1G 109
Peak Ho. N4 6A 44
(off Woodberry Down Est.)
Peaks Hill. Purl 2H 137
Peaks Hill Ri. Purl 2J 137
Peak, The. SE26 9G 93
Peal Gdns. W13 6E 54
Peall Rd. Croy 1K 123
Peall Rd. Ind. Est. Croy 1K 123
Pearce Clo. Mitc 6E 106
Pearcefield Av. SE23 7G 93
Pearce Rd. W Mol 7M 101
Pear Clo. NW9 2B 40
Pear Clo. SE14 8J 77
Pear Ct. SE15 8D 76
(off Thruxton Way)
Pearcroft Rd. E11 7B 46
Peardon St. SW8 1F 90
Peareswood Gdns. Stan 8H 23
Peareswood Rd. Eri 9D 82
Pearfield Rd. SE23 9J 93
Pearl Clo. E6 9L 63
Pearl Clo. NW2 5H 41
Pearl Rd. E17 1L 45
Pearl St. E1 2F 76
Pearmain Clo. Shep 9A 100
Pearman St. SE1 4L 75
Pear Pl. SE1 3L 75
Pear Rd. E11 8B 46
Pears Av. Shep 7C 100
Pearscroft Ct. SW6 9M 73
Pearscroft Rd. SW6 9M 73
Pearse St. SE15 7C 76
Pearson Clo. Purl 3M 137
Pearson's Av. SE14 9L 77
Pearson St. E2 5D 60
Pearson Way. Dart 8K 99
Pears Rd. Houn 2A 86
Peartree. SE26 2J 109
Peartree Av. SW17 9A 90
Pear Tree Av. W Dray 9D 142
Pear Tree Clo. E2 4D 60
Pear Tree Clo. Chess 7L 119
Peartree Clo. Eri 9B 82
Peartree Clo. Mitc 6C 106
Peartree Clo. S Croy 6F 138
Pear Tree Clo. Swan 6B 114
Pear Tree Ct. E18 8F 30
Pear Tree Ct. EC1 7L 59
Peartree Ct. Wat 9H 5
Peartree Gdns. Dag 9F 48
Peartree Gdns. Romf 9M 33
Pear Tree Ho. SE4 2K 93
Peartree La. E1 1G 77
Pear Tree Rd. Ashf 2A 100
Peartree Rd. Enf 5C 16
Peartrees. W Dray 1H 143
Pear Tree St. EC1 7A 60
Pear Tree Way. SE10 5E 78
Peary Ho. NW10 3B 56
Peary Pl. E2 6G 61
Pease Clo. Horn 3F 66
Peas Mead Ter. E4 4A 30
Peatfield Clo. Sidc 9C 96
Pebble Way. W3 2M 71
(off Steyne Rd.)
Pebworth Rd. Harr 7E 38
Peckarmans Wood. SE26 9E 92
Peckett Sq. N5 9A 44
Peckford Pl. SW9 1L 91
Peckham. 9E 76
Peckham Gro. SE15 8C 76
Peckham High St. SE15 9E 76
Peckham Hill St. SE15 8E 76
Peckham Pk. Rd. SE15 8E 76
Peckham Rd. SE5 & SE15 9C 76
Peckham Rye.
SE15 & SE22 2E 92
Peckham Sq. SE15 9E 76
Pecks Yd. E1 8D 60
(off Hanbury St.)
Peckwater St. NW5 1G 59
Pedham Pl. Ind. Est.
Swan 9E 114
Pedhoulas. N14 3J 27
Pedlar's Wlk. N7 1K 59
Pedley Rd. Dag 6G 49
Pedley St. E1 7D 60
Pedro St. E5 8H 45
Pedworth Gdns. SE16 5G 77
Peebles Ct. S'hall 9A 54
(off Haldane Rd.)
Peek Cres. SW19 2H 105
Peel Cen. Ind. Est. Eps 3C 134
Peel Clo. E4 2M 29

Peel Clo.—Perkins Ho.

Peel Clo. N9 3E 28
Peel Dri. Ilf 1J 47
Peel Gro. E2 5G 61
(in two parts)
Peel La. NW9 1E 40
Peel Pas. W8 2L 73
(off Peel St.)
Peel Pl. Ilf 9J 31
Peel Precinct. NW6 5L 57
Peel Rd. E18 8D 30
Peel Rd. Harr 1D 38
(in two parts)
Peel Rd. Orp 7A 128
Peel Rd. Wemb 8H 39
Peel St. W8 2L 73
Peel Way. Romf 9K 35
Peel Way. Uxb 8C 142
Peerage Way. Horn 5K 51
Peerglow Est. Enf 7G 17
Peerglow Ind. Est. Wat 1A 20
Peerless St. EC1 6B 60
Pegamoid Rd. N18 3G 29
Pegasus Clo. N5 9B 44
Pegasus Ct. NW10 6F 56
(off Trenmar Gdns.)
Pegasus Ct. Ab L 5D 4
Pegasus Ct. Bren 6K 71
Pegasus Ct. King T 7H 103
Pegasus Ho. E1 7H 61
(off Beaumont Sq.)
Pegasus Pl. SE11 7L 75
Pegasus Pl. SW6 9L 73
Pegasus Way. N11 6F 26
Pegelm Gdns. Horn 5K 51
Peggotty Way. Uxb 9F 142
Pegg Rd. Houn 8H 69
Pegley Gdns. SE12 8E 94
Pegmire La. A'ham 3A 10
Pegwell St. SE18 8C 80
Pekin Clo. E14 9L 61
(off Pekin St.)
Pekin St. E14 9L 61
Pelabon Ho. Twic 5H 87
(off Clevedon Rd.)
Peldon Ct. Rich 3K 87
Peldon Pas. Rich 3K 87
Peldon Wlk. N1 4M 59
(off Popham St.)
Pelham Av. Bark 4D 64
Pelham Clo. SE5 2C 92
Pelham Cotts. Bex 7M 97
Pelham Ct. SW3 5C 74
(off Fulham Rd.)
Pelham Ct. Sidc 9E 96
Pelham Cres. SW7 5C 74
Pelham Ho. W14 5K 73
(off Mornington Av.)
Pelham Pl. SW7 5C 74
Pelham Pl. W13 7D 54
Pelham Rd. E18 1F 46
Pelham Rd. N15 2D 44
Pelham Rd. N22 9L 27
Pelham Rd. SW19 4L 105
Pelham Rd. Beck 6G 109
Pelham Rd. Bexh 2L 97
Pelham Rd. Ilf 7B 48
Pelham's Clo. Esh 6L 117
Pelhams, The. Wat 8H 5
Pelham St. SW7 5B 74
Pelham's Wlk. Esh 6L 117
Pelican Est. SE15 9D 76
Pelican Ho. SE8 5K 77
Pelican Pas. E1 7G 61
Pelican Wlk. SW9 3M 91
Pelican Wharf. E1 2G 77
(off Wapping Wall)
Pelier St. SE17 7A 76
Pelinore Rd. SE6 8C 94
Pella Ho. SE11 6K 75
Pellant Rd. SW6 8J 73
Pellatt Gro. N22 8L 27
Pellatt Rd. SE22 4D 92
Pellatt Rd. Wemb 7H 39
(in two parts)
Pellerin Rd. N16 1C 60
Pellew Ho. E1 7F 60
(off Somerford St.)
Pelling St. E14 9L 61
Pellipar Clo. N13 3L 27
Pellipar Gdns. SE18 6K 79
Pellipar Rd. SE18 6K 79
Pelly Rd. E13 4E 62
(in two parts)
Pelter St. E2 6D 60
(in two parts)
Pelton Av. Sutt 2M 135
Pelton Rd. SE10 6C 78
Pembar Av. E17 1J 45
Pemberley Chase.
W Ewe 7M 119
Pemberley Clo. W Ewe 7M 119
Pember Rd. NW10 6H 57
Pemberton Av. Romf 1F 50
Pemberton Ct. E1 6H 61
(off Portelet Rd.)
Pemberton Gdns. N19 8G 43
Pemberton Gdns. Romf 3J 49
Pemberton Gdns. Swan 7C 114
Pemberton Ho. SE26 1E 108
(off High Level Dri.)
Pemberton Pl. E8 3F 60
Pemberton Pl. Esh 5A 118
Pemberton Rd. N4 3L 43
Pemberton Rd. E Mol 8A 102
Pemberton Row. EC4 9L 59
Pemberton Ter. N19 8G 43
Pembrey Way. Horn 2G 67
Pembridge Av. Twic 7K 85
Pembridge Cres. W11 1L 73
Pembridge Gdns. W2 1L 73
Pembridge M. W11 1L 73
Pembridge Pl. SW15 4L 89
Pembridge Pl. W2 1L 73
Pembridge Rd. W11 1L 73
Pembridge Sq. W2 1L 73
Pembridge Vs. W11 & W2 1L 73
Pembroke Av. Enf 2F 16
Pembroke Av. Harr 1E 38
Pembroke Av. Pinn 6H 37
Pembroke Av. Surb 9M 103
Pembroke Av. W on T 6H 117
Pembroke Bldgs. NW10 6E 56
Pembroke Cen., The. Ruis 6D 36
Pembroke Clo. SW1 3E 74
Pembroke Clo. Bans 9M 135
Pembroke Clo. Horn 2K 51
Pembroke Cotts. W8 4L 73
(off Pembroke Sq.)
Pembroke Ct. W7 9D 54
(off Copley Clo.)
Pembroke Gdns. W8 5K 73
Pembroke Gdns. Dag 8M 49
Pembroke Gdns. Clo. W8 4L 73
Pembroke Hall. NW4 1G 41
(off Mulberry Clo.)
Pembroke Ho. W2 9M 57
(off Hallfield Est.)
Pembroke Ho. W3 3A 72
(off Park Rd. E.)
Pembroke Ho. Borwd 6L 11
(off Station Rd.)
Pembroke Lodge. Stan 6G 23
Pembroke M. E3 6J 61
Pembroke M. N10 8F 26
Pembroke M. W8 4L 73
Pembroke Pde. Eri 6A 82
Pembroke Pl. W8 4L 73
Pembroke Pl. Edgw 7L 23
Pembroke Pl. Iswth 1C 86
Pembroke Pl. S at H 5M 115
Pembroke Rd. E6 8K 63
Pembroke Rd. E17 3M 45
Pembroke Rd. N8 2J 43
Pembroke Rd. N10 8E 26
Pembroke Rd. N13 3A 28
Pembroke Rd. N15 3D 44
Pembroke Rd. SE25 8C 108
Pembroke Rd. W8 5K 73
Pembroke Rd. Brom 6G 111
Pembroke Rd. Eri 6A 82
Pembroke Rd. Gnfd 7M 53
Pembroke Rd. Ilf 6D 48
Pembroke Rd. Mitc 6E 106
Pembroke Rd. N'wd 3A 20
Pembroke Rd. Ruis 6C 36
Pembroke Rd. Wemb 8H 39
Pembroke Sq. W8 4L 73
Pembroke St. N1 3J 59
(in two parts)
Pembroke Vs. W8 5L 73
Pembroke Vs. Rich 3H 87
Pembroke Wlk. W8 5L 73
Pembroke Way. Hay 4A 68
Pembrook M. SW11 3B 90
Pembry Clo. SW9 9L 75
Pembury Av. Wor Pk 3E 120
Pembury Clo. E5 1F 60
Pembury Clo. Brom 2D 126
Pembury Clo. Coul 6E 136
Pembury Ct. Hay 7B 68
Pembury Cres. Sidc 8J 97
Pembury Pl. E5 1F 60
Pembury Rd. E5 1F 60
Pembury Rd. N17 8D 28
Pembury Rd. SE25 8E 108
Pembury Rd. Bexh 8J 81
Pemdevon Rd. Croy 2L 123
Pemell Clo. E1 7G 61
Pemell Ho. E1 7G 61
(off Pemell Clo.)
Pemerich Clo. Hay 6D 68
Pempath Pl. Wemb 7H 39
Penally Pl. N1 4B 60
Penang Ho. E1 2F 76
(off Prusom St.)
Penang St. E1 2F 76
Penard Rd. S'hall 4M 69
Penarth Cen. SE15 7G 77
Penarth St. SE15 7G 77
Penates. Esh 6B 118
Penberth Rd. SE6 8A 94
Penbury Rd. S'hall 5K 69
Pencombe M. W11 1K 73
Pencraig Way. SE15 7F 76
Pencroft Dri. Dart 6G 99
Pendall Clo. Barn 6C 14
Penda Rd. Eri 8M 81
Pendarves Rd. SW20 5G 105
Penda's Mead. E9 9J 45
Pendell Av. Hay 8D 68
Pendennis Ho. SE8 5J 77
Pendennis Rd. N17 1B 44
Pendennis Rd. SW16 1J 107
Pendennis Rd. Orp 4G 129
Penderel Rd. Houn 4L 85
Penderry Ri. SE6 8B 94
Penderyn Way. N7 9H 43
Pendlebury Ct. Surb 8J 103
(off Cranes Pk.)
Pendle Ct. Uxb 4F 142
Pendle Ho. SE26 9E 92
Pendle Rd. SW16 3F 106
Pendlestone Rd. E17 3M 45
Pendragon Rd. Brom 9D 94
Pendragon Wlk. NW9 4C 40
Pendrell Ho. WC2 9H 59
(off New Compton St.)
Pendrell Rd. SE4 1J 93
Pendrell St. SE18 7B 80
Pendula Dri. Hay 7H 53
Pendulum M. E8 1D 60
Penerley Rd. SE6 7M 93
Penerley Rd. Rain 8F 66
Penfield Lodge. W9 8L 57
(off Admiral Wlk.)
Penfields Ho. N7 2J 59
Penfold Clo. Croy 5L 123
Penfold La. Bex 8H 97
(in two parts)
Penfold Pl. NW1 8C 58
Penfold Rd. N9 1H 29
Penfold St. NW8 & NW1 7B 58
Penfold Trad. Est. Wat 3G 9
Penford Gdns. SE9 2H 95
Penford St. SE5 1M 91
Pengarth Rd. Bex 4H 97
Penge. 4G 109
Penge Ho. SW11 2B 90
Penge La. SE20 4G 109
Pengelly Clo. Chesh 3B 6
Penge Rd. E13 4G 63
Penge Rd. SE25 & SE20 7E 108
Penhale Clo. Orp 6E 128
Penhall Rd. SE7 5H 79
Penhill Rd. Bex 5G 97
Penhurst Pl. SE1 4K 75
(off Carlisle La.)
Penhurst Rd. Ilf 7M 31
Penifather La. Gnfd 6B 54
Peninsula Ct. E14 4M 77
(off E. Ferry Rd.)
Peninsula Heights. SE1 6J 75
Peninsula Pk. SE7 5E 78
(off Peninsula Pk. Rd.,
in two parts)
Peninsula Pk. Rd. SE7 5E 78
Peninsular Clo. Felt 5B 84
Penistone Rd. SW16 4J 107
Penistone Wlk. Romf 6G 35
Penketh Dri. Harr 8B 38
Penley Ct. WC2 1K 75
Penmayne Ho. SE11 6L 75
(off Kennings Way)
Penmon Rd. SE2 4E 80
Pennack Rd. SE15 7D 76
Penn Almshouses. SE10 9A 78
(off Greenwich S. St.)
Pennant M. W8 5M 73
Pennant Ter. E17 9K 29
Pennard Mans. W12 3G 73
(off Goldhawk Rd.)
Pennard Rd. W12 3G 73
Pennards, The. Sun 7G 101
Penn Clo. Gnfd 5M 53
Penn Clo. Harr 2G 39
Penn Clo. Uxb 7B 142
Penn Ct. NW9 1B 40
Penner Clo. SW19 8J 89
Penners Gdns. Surb 2J 119
Pennethorne Clo. E9 4G 61
Pennethorne Ho. SW11 2B 90
Pennethorne Rd. SE15 8F 76
Penney Clo. Dart 6H 99
Penn Gdns. Chst 6M 111
Penn Gdns. Romf 7L 33
Penn Ho. NW8 7C 58
(off Mallory St.)
Pennine Dri. NW2 7H 41
Pennine La. NW2 7J 41
Pennine Pde. NW2 7J 41
Pennine Way. Bexh 9C 82
Pennine Way. Hay 8B 68
Pennington Clo. SE27 1B 108
Pennington Clo. Romf 5L 33
Pennington Ct. SE16 2J 77
Pennington Dri. N21 7J 15
Pennington Dri. Wey 5C 116
Pennington Lodge. Surb 9J 103
(off Cranes Dri.)
Pennington St. E1 1F 76
Pennington Way. SE12 8F 94
Penniston Clo. N17 9A 28
Penn La. Bex 4H 97
(in two parts)
Penn Rd. N7 1J 59
Penn Rd. Park 1M 5
Penn Rd. Wat 3F 8
Penn St. N1 4B 60
Penny Clo. Rain 6F 66
Penny Ct. Wat 4F 8
(off Westland Rd.)
Pennycroft. Croy 1J 139
Pennyfather La. Enf 5A 16
Pennyfields. E14 1L 77
(in two parts)
Pennyford Ct. NW8 7B 58
(off St John's Wood Rd.)
Penny La. Shep 2C 116
Penny M. SW12 6F 90
Pennymoor Wlk. W9 7K 57
(off Ashmore Rd.)
Penny Rd. NW10 6M 55
Penny Royal. Wall 8H 123
Pennyroyal Av. E6 9L 63
Penpoll Rd. E8 2F 60
Penpool La. Well 2F 96
Penrhyn Av. E17 8K 29
Penrhyn Cres. E17 8L 29
Penrhyn Cres. SW14 3A 88
Penrhyn Gdns. King T 8H 103
Penrhyn Gro. E17 8L 29
Penrhyn Rd. King T 8J 103
Penrith Clo. SW15 4J 89
Penrith Clo. Beck 5M 109
Penrith Clo. Uxb 3B 142
Penrith Cres. Rain 1E 66
Penrith Pl. SE27 8M 91
Penrith Rd. N15 3B 44
Penrith Rd. Ilf 6D 32
Penrith Rd. N Mald 8B 104
Penrith Rd. Romf 6L 35
Penrith Rd. T Hth 6A 108
Penrith St. SW16 3G 107
Penrose Av. Wat 2J 21
Penrose Dri. Eps 3L 133
Penrose Gro. SE17 6A 76
Penrose Ho. SE17 6A 76
(in two parts)
Penrose St. SE17 6A 76
Penryn Ho. SE11 6L 75
(off Seaton Clo.)
Penryn St. NW1 5H 59
Penry St. SE1 5C 76
Pensbury Pl. SW8 1G 91
Pensbury St. SW8 1G 91
Penscroft Gdns. Borwd 6B 12
Pensford Av. Rich 1L 87
Penshurst. NW5 2E 58
Penshurst Av. Sidc 5E 96
Penshurst Gdns. Edgw 5M 23
Penshurst Grn. Brom 9D 110
Penshurst Ho. SE15 7G 77
(off Lovelinch Clo.)
Penshurst Rd. E9 3H 61
Penshurst Rd. N17 7D 28
Penshurst Rd. Bexh 9K 81
Penshurst Rd. T Hth 9M 107
Penshurst Wlk. Brom 9D 110
Penshurst Way. Orp 8G 113
Penshurst Way. Sutt 9L 121
Pensilver Clo. Barn 6C 14
Penstemon Clo. N3 6L 25
Penta Ct. Borwd 6L 11
(off Station Rd.)
Pentagon, The. W13 1E 70
Pentavia Retail Pk. NW7 7D 24
Pentelow Gdns. Felt 5E 84
Pentire Rd. E17 8B 30
Pentland Av. Edgw 2M 23
Pentland Clo. N9 2G 29
Pentland Clo. NW11 7J 41
Pentland Gdns. SW18 5A 90
Pentland Pl. N'holt 4J 53
Pentland Rd. Bush 8A 10
Pentlands Clo. Mitc 7F 106
Pentland St. SW18 5A 90
Pentland Way. Uxb 8A 36
Pentlow St. SW15 2G 89
Pentlow Way. Buck H 9J 19
Pentney Rd. E4 1B 30
Pentney Rd. SW12 7G 91
Pentney Rd. SW19 5J 105
Penton Dri. Chesh 2D 6
Penton Gro. N1 5L 59
Penton Ho. N1 5L 59
(off Donegal St.)
Penton Ho. SE2 2H 81
Penton Pl. SE17 6M 75
Penton Ri. WC1 6K 59
Penton St. N1 5L 59
Pentonville. 5K 59
Pentonville Rd. N1 5K 59
Pentrich Av. Enf 2E 16
Pentridge St. SE15 8D 76
Pentyre Av. N18 5B 28
Penwerris Av. Iswth 8A 70
Penwerris Ct. Houn 8A 70
Penwith Rd. SW18 8L 89
Penwood Ct. Pinn 2K 37
Penwood Ho. SW15 5D 88
Penwortham Ct. N22 9K 27
Penwortham Rd. SW16 3F 106
Penwortham Rd. S Croy 2A 138
Penylan Pl. Edgw 7L 23
Penywern Rd. SW5 6L 73
Penzance Gdns. Romf 6L 35
(in two parts)
Penzance Ho. SE11 6L 75
(off Seaton Clo.)
Penzance Pl. W11 2J 73
Penzance Rd. Romf 6L 35
Penzance St. W11 2J 73
Peony Ct. Wfd G 6C 30
Peony Gdns. W12 1E 72
Peperfield. WC1 6K 59
(off Cromer St.)
Pepler Ho. W10 7J 57
(off Wornington Rd.)
Pepler M. SE5 6D 76
Peploe Rd. NW6 5H 57
(in two parts)
Peplow Clo. W Dray 2H 143
Pepper All. Lou 4D 18
Pepper Clo. E6 8K 63
Peppercorn Clo. T Hth 6B 108
Peppermead Sq. SE4 4L 93
Peppermint Clo. Croy 2J 123
Peppermint Pl. E11 8C 46
Pepper St. E14 4M 77
Pepper St. SE1 3A 76
Peppie Clo. N16 7C 44
(in two parts)
Pepys Clo. Asht 9L 133
Pepys Clo. Dart 3L 99
Pepys Cres. E16 2E 78
Pepys Cres. Barn 7G 13
Pepys Ho. E2 6G 61
(off Kirkwall Pl.)
Pepys Ri. Orp 3D 128
Pepys Rd. SE14 9H 77
Pepys Rd. SW20 5G 105
Pepys St. EC3 1C 76
Perceval Av. NW3 1C 58
Perceval Ct. N'holt 1L 53
Perceval Ho. W5 1G 71
Percheron Clo. Iswth 2D 86
Percheron Rd. Borwd 8B 12
Perch St. E8 9D 44
Percival Clo. Oxs 3A 132
Percival Ct. N17 7D 28
Percival Ct. Chesh 3E 6
Percival David Foundation of Chinese Art. 7H 59
(off Gordon Sq.)
Percival Gdns. Romf 4G 49
Percival Rd. SW14 3A 88
Percival Rd. Enf 6D 16
Percival Rd. Felt 8D 84
Percival Rd. Horn 4G 51
Percival Rd. Orp 4M 127
Percival St. EC1 7M 59
Percival Way. Eps 6B 120
Percy Bryant Rd. Sun 4C 100
Percy Bush Rd. W Dray 4K 143
Percy Cir. WC1 6K 59
Percy Gdns. Enf 7H 17
Percy Gdns. Hay 6C 52
Percy Gdns. Iswth 2E 86
Percy Gdns. Wor Pk 3C 120
Percy M. W1 8H 59
(off Rathbone Pl.)
Percy Pas. W1 8G 59
(off Rathbone St.)
Percy Rd. E11 5C 46
Percy Rd. E16 8C 62
Percy Rd. N12 5A 26
Percy Rd. N21 9A 16
Percy Rd. SE20 5H 109
Percy Rd. SE25 9E 108
Percy Rd. W12 3E 72
(in two parts)
Percy Rd. Bexh 1J 97
Percy Rd. Hamp 4L 101
Percy Rd. Ilf 5E 48
Percy Rd. Iswth 3E 86
Percy Rd. Mitc 2E 122
Percy Rd. Romf 1M 49
Percy Rd. Twic 7M 85
Percy Rd. Wat 6F 8
Percy St. W1 8H 59
Percy Way. Twic 7A 86
Percy Yd. WC1 6K 59
Peregrine Clo. NW10 1B 56
Peregrine Clo. Wat 7J 5
Peregrine Ct. SE8 7L 77
(off Edward St.)
Peregrine Ct. SW16 1K 107
Peregrine Ct. Well 9D 80
Peregrine Gdns. Croy 4J 125
Peregrine Ho. EC1 6M 59
(off Hall St.)
Peregrine Rd. Ilf 5F 32
Peregrine Rd. Sun 6D 100
Peregrine Wlk. Horn 2F 66
Peregrine Way. SW19 4G 105
Peregrin Rd. Wal A 7M 7
Perham Rd. W14 6J 73
Peridot St. E6 8J 63
Perifield. SE21 7A 92
Perimeade Rd. Gnfd 5G 55
Periton Rd. SE9 3H 95
Perivale. 4G 55
Perivale Gdns. W13 7F 54
Perivale Gdns. Wat 7F 4
Perivale Grange. Gnfd 6E 54
Perivale Ind. Pk. Gnfd 5F 54
Perivale La. Gnfd 6E 54
Perivale Lodge. Gnfd 6E 54
(off Perivale La.)
Perivale New Bus. Cen.
Gnfd 5G 55
Perkin Clo. Houn 3L 85
Perkin Clo. Wemb 1F 54
Perkins Ho. E14 8K 61
(off Wallwood St.)

Perkin's Rents. SW1 4H 75
Perkins Rd. Ilf 3B 48
Perkins Sq. SE1 2A 76
Perks Clo. SE3 2C 94
Perley Ho. E3 8K 61
(off Weatherley Clo.)
Perpins Rd. SE9 5B 96
Perran Rd. SW2 7M 91
Perran Wlk. Bren 6J 71
Perren St. NW5 2F 58
Perrers Rd. W6 5F 72
Perring Est. E3 8L 61
(off Gale St.)
Perrin Ho. NW6 6L 57
Perrin Rd. Wemb 9F 38
Perrin's Ct. NW3 9A 42
Perrin's La. NW3 9A 42
Perrin's Wlk. NW3 9A 42
Perronet Ho. SE1 4M 75
(off Princess St.)
Perrott St. SE18 5A 80
Perry Av. W3 9B 56
Perry Clo. Rain 5B 66
Perry Clo. Uxb 9F 142
Perry Ct. E14 6L 77
(off Maritime Quay)
Perry Ct. N15 4C 44
Perryfield Way. NW9 4D 40
Perryfield Way. Rich 9F 86
Perry Gdns. N9 3B 28
Perry Gth. N'holt 4G 53
Perry Gro. Dart 3L 99
Perry Hall Clo. Orp 2E 128
Perry Hall Rd. Orp 1D 128
Perry Hill. SE6 9K 93
Perry How. Wor Pk 3D 120
Perrymans Farm Rd. Ilf 4B 48
Perry Mead. Bush 8A 10
Perry Mead. Enf 4M 15
Perrymead St. SW6 9L 73
Perryn Ct. Twic 5E 86
Perryn Ho. W3 1C 72
Perryn Rd. SE16 4F 76
Perryn Rd. W3 2B 72
Perry Oaks Dri.
W Dray & H'row A 1A 144
Perry Ri. SE23 9J 93
Perry Rd. Dag 8K 65
Perry's Pl. W1 9H 59
Perry St. Chst 3B 112
Perry St. Dart 3C 98
Perry St. Gdns. Chst 3C 112
Perry St. Shaw. Chst 4C 112
Perry Va. SE23 8G 93
Perry Way. Ave 1M 83
Persant Rd. SE6 8C 94
Perseverance Pl. SW9 8L 75
Perseverance Pl. Rich 3J 87
Perseverance Works. E2 6C 60
(off Kingsland Rd.)
Persfield Clo. Eps 2D 134
Persfield M. Eps 2D 134
Pershore Clo. Ilf 3M 47
Pershore Gro. Cars 1B 122
Pert Clo. N10 7F 26
Perth Av. NW9 5B 40
Perth Av. Hay 7G 53
Perth Clo. SE5 3B 92
Perth Clo. SW20 6D 104
Perth Ho. N1 3K 59
(off Bemerton Est.)
Perth Rd. E10 6J 45
Perth Rd. E13 5F 62
Perth Rd. N4 6L 43
Perth Rd. N22 8M 27
Perth Rd. Bark 5B 64
Perth Rd. Beck 6A 110
Perth Rd. Ilf 4L 47
Perth Ter. Ilf 5A 48
Perwell Av. Harr 6K 37
Perystreete. SE23 8G 93
Petands Ct. Horn 8H 51
(off Randall Dri.)
Petavel Rd. Tedd 3C 102
Peter Av. NW10 3F 56
Peter Best Ho. E1 9F 60
(off Nelson St.)
Peterboat Clo. SE10 5C 78
Peterborough Ct. EC4 9L 59
Peterborough Gdns. Ilf 5J 47
Peterborough Ho. Borwd 4L 11
(off Stratfield Rd.)
Peterborough M. SW6 1L 89
Peterborough Rd. E10 3A 46
Peterborough Rd. SW6 1L 89
Peterborough Rd. Cars 1C 122
Peterborough Rd. Harr 6C 38
Peterborough Vs. SW6 9M 73
Peter Butler Ho. SE1 3E 76
(off Wolseley St.)
Peterchurch Ho. SE15 7F 76
(off Commercial Way)
Petergate. SW11 3A 90
Peterhead Ct. S'hall 9A 54
(off Osborne Rd.)
Peter Heathfield Ho. E15 4B 62
(off Wise Rd.)
Peter Ho. SW8 8J 75
(off Luscombe Way)
Peter James Bus. Cen.
Hay 3E 68
Peter James Enterprise Cen.
NW10 6A 56
Peterley Bus. Cen. E2 5F 60
Peter Pan Statue. 2B 74
Peters Clo. Dag 6H 49
Peters Clo. Stan 6H 23
Peters Clo. Well 1C 96
Peter Scott Vis. Cen., The.
9F 72
Peters Ct. W2 9M 57
(off Porchester Rd.)
Petersfield Av. Romf 6J 35
Petersfield Clo. N18 5A 28
Petersfield Clo. Romf 6L 35
Petersfield Cres. Coul 7J 137
Petersfield Ri. SW15 7F 88
Petersfield Rd. W3 3A 72
Petersham. 7J 87
Petersham Clo. Rich 8H 87
Petersham Clo. Sutt 7K 121
Petersham Dri. Orp 6D 112
Petersham Gdns. Orp 6D 112
Petersham Ho. SW7 5B 74
(off Kendrick M.)
Petersham La. SW7 4A 74
Petersham M. SW7 4A 74
Petersham Pl. SW7 4A 74
Petersham Rd. Rich 5H 87
Petersham Ter. Croy 5J 123
(off Richmond Grn.)
Peter's Hill. EC4 1A 76
Peter Shore Ct. E1 8H 61
(off Beaumont Sq.)
Peter's La. EC1 8M 59
Peterson Ct. Lou 4L 19
Peter's Path. SE26 1F 108
Peterstone Rd. SE2 3F 80
Peterstow Clo. SW19 8J 89
Peter St. W1 1H 75
Peterwood Pk. Croy 4K 123
Peterwood Way. Croy 4K 123
Petherton Ct. NW10 4H 57
(off Tiverton Rd.)
Petherton Ct. Harr 4D 38
(off Gayton Rd.)
Petherton Ho. N4 6A 44
(off Woodberry Down Est.)
Petherton Rd. N5 1A 60
Petiver Clo. E9 3G 61
Petley Rd. W6 7H 73
Peto Pl. NW1 7F 58
Peto St. N. E16 9D 62
Petrie Clo. NW2 2J 57
Petrie Ho. SE18 7L 79
(off Woolwich Comn.)
Petrie Mus. of Egyptian
Archaeology. 7H 59
Petros Gdns. NW3 2A 58
Pett Clo. Horn 7F 50
Petten Clo. Orp 3H 129
Petten Gro. Orp 3G 129
Petters Rd. Asht 8K 133
Petticoat La. E1 8C 60
Petticoat Lane Market. 9D 60
(in Middlesex St.)
Petticoat Sq. E1 9D 60
Petticoat Tower. E1 9D 60
(off Petticoat Sq.)
Pettits Boulevd. Romf 8C 34
Pettits Clo. Romf 9C 34
Pettits La. Romf 9C 34
Pettits La. N. Romf 8B 34
Pettits Pl. Dag 1L 65
Pettits Rd. Dag 1L 65
Pettiward Clo. SW15 3G 89
Pettley Gdns. Romf 3B 50
Pettman Cres. SE28 4B 80
Pettsgrove Av. Wemb 1G 55
Pett's Hill. N'holt 1M 53
Pett St. SE18 5J 79
Petts Wood. 9A 112
Petts Wood Rd. Orp 9A 112
Petty France. SW1 4G 75
Pettys Clo. Chesh 1D 6
Petworth Clo. N'holt 3K 53
Petworth Gdns. SW20 7F 104
Petworth Gdns. Uxb 4A 52
Petworth Rd. N12 5C 26
Petworth Rd. Bexh 4L 97
Petworth St. SW11 9C 74
Petworth Way. Horn 9D 50
Petyt Pl. SW3 7C 74
Petyward. SW3 5C 74
Pevensey Av. N11 5H 27
Pevensey Av. Enf 4C 16
Pevensey Clo. Iswth 8A 70
Pevensey Ct. W3 3M 71
Pevensey Ho. E1 8H 61
(off Ben Jonson Rd.)
Pevensey Rd. E7 9D 46
Pevensey Rd. SW17 1B 106
Pevensey Rd. Felt 7J 85
Peverel. E6 9L 63
Peverel Ho. Dag 7L 49
Peveret Clo. N11 5F 26
Peveril Ct. Dart 5M 99
(off Clifton Wlk.)
Peveril Dri. Tedd 2B 102
Peveril Ho. SE1 4B 76
(off Rephidim St.)
Pewsey Clo. E4 5L 29
Peyton Pl. SE10 8A 78
Pharamond. NW2 2H 57
Pharaoh Clo. Mitc 2D 122
Pheasant Clo. E16 9F 62
Pheasant Clo. Purl 5M 137
Phelp St. SE17 7B 76
Phelps Way. Hay 5D 68
Phene St. SW3 7C 74
Philadelphia Ct. SW10 8A 74
(off Uverdale Rd.)
Philan Way. Romf 6B 34
Philbeach Gdns. SW5 6K 73
Phil Brown Pl. SW8 2F 90
(off Wandsworth Rd.)
Philchurch Pl. E1 9E 60
Philimore Clo. SE18 6C 80
Philip Av. Romf 6B 50
Philip Av. Swan 8B 114
Philip Clo. Romf 6B 50
Philip Ct. W2 8B 58
(off Hall Pl.)
Philip Gdns. Croy 4K 125
Philip Ho. NW6 4M 57
(off Mortimer Pl.)
Philip La. N15 2B 44
Philipot Path. SE9 5K 95
Philippa Gdns. SE9 4H 95
Philip Rd. Rain 6C 66
Philips Clo. Cars 3E 122
Philip St. E13 7E 62
Philip Wlk. SE15 2E 92
(in two parts)
Phillida Rd. Romf 9L 35
Phillimore Ct. Rad 1C 10
Phillimore Gdns. NW10 4G 57
Phillimore Gdns. W8 3L 73
Phillimore Gdns. Clo. W8 4L 73
Phillimore Pl. W8 3L 73
Phillimore Pl. Rad 1C 10
Phillimore Ter. W8 4L 73
(off Allen St.)
Phillimore Wlk. W8 4L 73
Phillipers. Wat 9H 5
Phillipp St. N1 4C 60
(in two parts)
Phillips Clo. Dart 5F 98
Phillips Ct. Edgw 6L 23
Philosophy Programme. 8H 59
(in University of London,
Senate House)
Philpot La. EC3 1C 76
Philpot Path. Ilf 8A 48
Philpots Clo. W Dray 1H 143
Philpot Sq. SW6 2M 89
Philpot St. E1 9F 60
Phineas Pett Rd. SE9 2J 95
Phipps Bri. Rd. SW19 6A 106
Phipps Hatch La. Enf 2A 16
Phipps Ho. SE7 6F 78
(off Woolwich Rd.)
Phipps Ho. W12 1F 72
(off White City Est.)
Phipp St. EC2 7C 60
Phoebeth Rd. SE13 4L 93
Phoenix Bus. Cen. E3 8L 61
Phoenix Cen. Brom 8F 110
Phoenix Clo. E8 4D 60
Phoenix Clo. Eps 4L 133
Phoenix Clo. N'wd 4D 20
Phoenix Clo. W Wick 4B 126
Phoenix Ct. E4 3M 29
Phoenix Ct. E14 5L 77
Phoenix Ct. NW1 5H 59
(off Purchese St.)
Phoenix Ct. SE14 7J 77
(off Chipley St.)
Phoenix Ct. Houn 4H 85
Phoenix Ct. S Croy 7D 124
Phoenix Dri. Kes 6H 127
Phoenix Ho. Sutt 6M 121
Phoenix Ind. Est. Harr 2D 38
Phoenix Lodge Mans. W6 5H 73
(off Brook Grn.)
Phoenix Pl. WC1 7K 59
Phoenix Pl. Dart 6H 99
Phoenix Rd. NW1 6H 59
Phoenix Rd. SE20 3G 109
Phoenix St. WC2 9H 59
Phoenix Theatre. 9H 59
(off Charing Cross Rd.)
Phoenix Trad. Est. Gnfd 4G 55
Phoenix Trad. Pk. Bren 6H 71
Phoenix Way. Houn 7H 69
Phoenix Wharf. E1 2F 76
(off Wapping High St.)
Phoenix Wharf Rd. SE1 3D 76
(off Tanner St.)
Phoenix Yd. WC1 6K 59
(off Kings Cross Rd.)
Photographers' Gallery. 1J 75
(off Gt. Newport St.)
Phyllis Av. N Mald 9F 104
Phyllis Ho. Croy 6M 123
(off Ashley La.)
Physic Pl. SW3 7D 74
Piazza, The. WC2 1J 75
(off Covent Garden, in two parts)
Piazza, The. Uxb 3B 142
Picardy Manorway. Belv 4M 81
Picardy Rd. Belv 6L 81
Picardy St. Belv 4L 81
Piccadilly. W1 2F 74
Piccadilly Arc. SW1 2G 75
(off Piccadilly)
Piccadilly Circus. 1H 75
Piccadilly Cir. W1 1H 75
Piccadilly Pl. W1 1G 75
(off Piccadilly)
Piccadilly Theatre. 1G 75
(off Denman St.)
Pickard St. EC1 6M 59
Pickering Av. E6 5L 63
Pickering Clo. E9 3H 61
Pickering Ct. Dart 5M 99
(off Osbourne Rd.)
Pickering Gdns. N11 6E 26
Pickering Gdns. Croy 1D 124
Pickering Ho. W2 9A 58
(off Hallfield Est.)
Pickering Ho. W5 5G 71
(off Windmill Rd.)
Pickering M. W2 9M 57
Pickering Pl. SW1 2G 75
(off St James's St.)
Pickering St. N1 4M 59
Pickets Clo. Bus H 1B 22
Pickets St. SW12 6F 90
Pickett Cft. Stan 8H 23
Picketts Lock La. N9 2G 29
Picketts Lock La. Ind. Est.
N9 2J 29
Picketts Ter. SE22 4E 92
Pickford Clo. Bexh 1J 97
Pickford La. Bexh 1J 97
Pickford Rd. Bexh 2J 97
Pickfords Wharf. N1 5A 60
Pickfords Wharf. SE1 2B 76
Pickfords Yd. N17 6D 28
Pick Hill. Wal A 5M 7
Pickhurst Grn. Brom 2D 126
Pickhurst La.
W Wick & Brom 9C 110
Pickhurst Mead. Brom 2D 126
Pickhurst Pk. Brom 9C 110
Pickhurst Ri. W Wick 2A 126
Pickwick Clo. Houn 4J 85
Pickwick Ho. SE16 3E 76
(off George Row)
Pickwick Ho. W11 2H 73
(off St Ann's Rd.)
Pickwick M. N18 4C 28
Pickwick Pl. Harr 5C 38
Pickwick Rd. SE21 6B 92
Pickwick St. SE1 3A 76
Pickwick Way. Chst 3A 112
Pickworth Clo. SW8 8J 75
Picquets Way. Bans 8J 135
Picton Pl. W1 9E 58
Picton St. SE5 8B 76
Pied Bull Yd. WC1 8J 59
(off Bury Pl.)
Piedmont Rd. SE18 6B 80
(in two parts)
Pield Heath. 8C 142
Pield Heath Av. Uxb 7E 142
Pield Heath Rd. Uxb 7C 142
Pier Head. E1 2F 76
(in two parts)
Pierhead Wharf. E1 2F 76
(off Wapping High St.)
Pier Ho. SW3 7C 74
Piermont Pl. Brom 6J 111
Piermont Rd. SE22 4F 92
Pier Pde. E16 2L 79
(off Pier Rd.)
Pierpoint Building. E14 3K 77
Pierrepoint Rd. W3 1M 71
Pierrepont Arc. N1 5M 59
(off Pierrepont Row)
Pierrepont Row. N1 5M 59
(off Camden Pas.)
Pier Rd. E16 3K 79
Pier Rd. Eri 7C 82
(in two parts)
Pier Rd. Felt 4F 84
Pier St. E14 5A 78
(in two parts)
Pier Ter. SW18 3M 89
Pier Way. SE28 3A 80
Pigeon La. Hamp 1L 101
Piggott Ho. E2 5H 61
(off Sewardstone Rd.)
Pigott St. E14 9L 61
Pike Clo. Brom 2F 110
Pike Clo. Uxb 4D 142
Pikemans Ct. SW5 5L 73
(off W. Cromwell Rd.)
Pike Rd. NW7 4B 24
Pikes Cotts. Barn 6G 13
Pike's End. Pinn 2F 36
Pikes Hill. Eps 5C 134
Pikestone Clo. Hay 7J 53
Pikethorne. SE23 8H 93
Pilgrimage St. SE1 3B 76
Pilgrim Clo. Mord 2M 121
Pilgrim Hill. SE27 1A 108
Pilgrim Ho. SE1 4B 76
(off Lansdowne Pl.)
Pilgrims Cloisters. SE5 8C 76
(off Sedgmoor Pl.)
Pilgrims Clo. N13 4K 27
Pilgrims Clo. N'holt 1A 54
Pilgrims Clo. Wat 6H 5
Pilgrim's Ct. Dart 4L 99
Pilgrim's La. NW3 9B 42
Pilgrims M. E14 1C 78
Pilgrim's Pl. NW3 9B 42
Pilgrims Ri. Barn 7C 14
Pilgrim St. EC4 9M 59
Pilgrims Way. E6 4J 63
Pilgrims Way. N19 6H 43
Pilgrims Way. Dart 7L 99
Pilgrims Way. S Croy 7D 124
Pilgrim's Way. Wemb 6M 39
Pilkington Rd. SE15 1F 92
Pilkington Rd. Orp 5A 128
Pillions La. Hay 7B 52
Pilot Clo. SE8 7K 77
Pilot Ind. Cen. NW10 7B 56
Pilsden Clo. SW19 7H 89
Piltdown Rd. Wat 4H 21
Pilton Est., The. Croy 4M 123
Pilton Pl. SE17 6A 76
(off Pingle St.)
Pilton Pl. Est. SE17 6A 76
Pimento Ct. W5 4H 71
Pimlico. 6G 75
Pimlico Ho. SW1 6F 74
(off Ebury Bri. Rd.)
Pimlico Rd. SW1 6E 74
Pimlico Wlk. N1 6C 60
(off Aske St.)
Pimpernel Way. Romf 6H 35
Pinchbeck Rd. Orp 8D 128
Pinchin St. E1 1E 76
Pincombe Ho. SE17 6B 76
Pincott Pl. SE4 2H 93
Pincott Rd. SW19 4A 106
Pincott Rd. Bexh 4L 97
Pindar St. EC2 8C 60
Pindock M. W9 7M 57
Pineapple Ct. SW1 4G 75
(off Wilfred St.)
Pine Av. E15 1B 62
Pine Av. W Wick 3M 125
Pine Clo. E10 7M 45
Pine Clo. N14 9G 15
Pine Clo. N19 7G 43
Pine Clo. SE20 5G 109
Pine Clo. Chesh 1D 6
Pine Clo. Kenl 9B 138
Pine Clo. Stan 4F 22
Pine Clo. Swan 8D 114
Pine Coombe. Croy 6H 125
Pine Ct. N21 7K 15
Pine Ct. N'holt 7J 53
Pinecourt. Upm 9M 51
Pine Cres. Cars 3B 136
Pinecrest Gdns. Orp 6M 127
Pinecroft. Gid P 2G 51
Pinecroft Ct. Well 8E 80
Pinecroft Cres. Barn 6J 13
Pinedene. SE15 9F 76
Pinefield Clo. E14 1L 77
Pine Gdns. Ruis 6F 36
Pine Gdns. Surb 1L 119
Pine Glade. Orp 6K 127
Pine Gro. N4 7J 43
Pine Gro. N20 1K 25
Pine Gro. SW19 2K 105
Pine Gro. Brick W 3K 5
Pine Gro. Bush 4K 9
Pine Gro. Wey 7A 116
Pine Gro. M. Wey 7A 116
Pine Hill. Eps 7B 134
Pine Ho. SE16 3G 77
(off Ainsty Est.)
Pine Ho. W10 7J 57
(off Droop St.)
Pinehurst Clo. Ab L 5C 4
Pinehurst Ct. W11 9K 57
(off Colville Gdns.)
Pinehurst Wlk. Orp 3B 128
Pinemartin Clo. NW2 8G 41
Pine M. NW10 5H 57
Pine Pl. Bans 6H 135
Pine Pl. Hay 7D 52
Pine Ridge. Cars 9E 122
Pineridge Ct. Barn 6H 13
Pine Rd. N11 2E 26
Pine Rd. NW2 9G 41
Pines Av. Enf 9C 6
Pines Clo. N'wd 6C 20
Pines Rd. Brom 6J 111
Pines, The. N14 7G 15
Pines, The. SE19 4M 107
Pines, The. Borwd 4K 11
Pines, The. Coul 9F 136
Pines, The. Purl 5A 138
Pines, The. Sun 7E 100
Pines, The. Wfd G 3E 30
Pine St. EC1 7L 59
Pine Tree Clo. Houn 9F 68
Pine Tree Ho. SE14 8H 77
(off Reaston St.)
Pinetree Ho. Wat 9J 5
Pine Tree Lodge. Brom 8D 110
Pineview Ct. E4 1A 30
Pine Wlk. Bans 9D 136
Pine Wlk. Cars 2B 136
Pine Wlk. Surb 1L 119
Pine Wlk. E. Cars 3B 136
Pine Wlk. W. Cars 2B 136

Pine Wood—Poppleton Rd.

Pine Wood. Sun 5E 100
Pinewood Av. Pinn 6M 21
Pinewood Av. Rain 7F 66
Pinewood Av. Sidc 7C 96
Pinewood Av. Uxb 9D 142
Pinewood Clo. Borwd 3B 12
Pinewood Clo. Croy 5J 125
Pinewood Clo. N'wd 5E 20
Pinewood Clo. Orp 3B 128
Pinewood Clo. Pinn 6M 21
Pinewood Clo. Wat 3E 8
Pinewood Ct. SW4 5H 91
Pinewood Ct. Enf 5M 15
Pinewood Dri. Orp 7C 128
Pinewood Gro. W5 9G 55
Pinewood Lodge. Bush 1B 22
Pinewood M. Stai 5B 144
Pinewood Pl. Eps 6B 120
Pinewood Rd. SE2 7H 81
Pinewood Rd. Brom 8E 110
Pinewood Rd. Felt 9F 84
Pinewood Rd. Hav 4A 34
Pinfold Rd. SW16 1J 107
Pinfold Rd. Bush 4K 9
Pinglestone Clo. W Dray 8J 143
Pinkcoat Clo. Felt 9F 84
Pinkerton Pl. SW16 1H 107
Pinkham Mans. W4 6L 71
Pinkham Way. N11 7E 26
Pink's Hill. Swan 9C 114
Pinkwell Av. Hay 5B 68
Pinkwell La. Hay 5A 68
Pinley Gdns. Dag 4F 64
Pinnace Ho. E14 4A 78
(off Manchester Rd.)
Pinnacle Hill. Bexh 3M 97
Pinnacle Hill N. Bexh 2M 97
Pinnacle Pl. Stan 4F 22
Pinnacles. Wal A 7L 7
Pinn Clo. Uxb 9B 142
Pinnell Rd. SE9 3H 95
Pinner. 2J 37
Pinner Ct. NW8 7B 58
(off St John's Wood Rd.)
Pinner Ct. Pinn 2L 37
Pinner Green. 9G 21
Pinner Grn. Pinn 9G 21
Pinner Gro. Pinn 2J 37
Pinner Hill. Pinn 7F 20
(in two parts)
Pinner Hill Farm. Pinn 8F 20
Pinner Hill Golf Course. 7G 21
Pinner Hill Rd. Pinn 7F 20
Pinner Pk. 8L 21
Pinner Pk. Pinn 9L 21
Pinner Pk. Av. Harr 1M 37
Pinner Pk. Gdns. Harr 9A 22
Pinner Rd. Harr 2L 37
Pinner Rd. N'wd & Pinn 8D 20
Pinner Rd. Pinn 2K 37
Pinner Rd. Wat 8H 9
Pinner Vw. Harr 2A 38
Pinnerwood Park. 8G 21
Pinn Way. Ruis 5B 36
Pintail Clo. E6 8J 63
Pintail Ct. SE8 7K 77
(off Pilot Clo.)
Pintail Rd. Wfd G 7F 30
Pintail Way. Hay 8H 53
Pinter Ho. SW9 1J 91
(off Grantham Rd.)
Pinto Clo. Borwd 8B 12
Pinto Way. SE3 3F 94
Pioneer Mkt. Ilf 8M 47
(off Winston Way)
Pioneer Pl. Croy 1L 139
Pioneers Ind. Pk. Croy 3J 123
Pioneer St. SE15 9E 76
Pioneer Way. W12 9F 56
Pioneer Way. Swan 7C 114
Pioneer Way. Wat 8D 8
Piper Clo. N7 1K 59
Piper Rd. King T 7L 103
Piper's Gdns. Croy 2J 125
Pipers Grn. NW9 3A 40
Pipers Grn. La. Edgw 3J 23
(in two parts)
Pipewell Rd. Cars 1C 122
Pippin Clo. NW2 8E 40
Pippin Clo. Croy 3K 125
Pippins Clo. W Dray 4H 143
Pippins, The. Wat 7G 5
Piquet Rd. SE20 6G 109
Pirbright Cres. New Ad 8A 126
Pirbright Rd. SW18 7K 89
Pirie Clo. SE5 2B 92
Pirie St. E16 2F 78
Pitcairn Clo. Romf 2L 49
Pitcairn Ho. E8 3G 61
Pitcairn Rd. Mitc 4D 106
Pitcairn's Path. Harr 8A 38
Pitchford St. E15 3B 62
Pitfield Cres. SE28 2E 80
Pitfield Est. N1 6C 60
Pitfield St. N1 6C 60
Pitfield Way. NW10 2A 56
Pitfield Way. Enf 3G 17
Pitfold Clo. SE12 5E 94
Pitfold Rd. SE12 5E 94
Pitlake. Croy 4M 123
Pitman Ho. SE8 9L 77
Pitman St. SE5 8A 76
(in two parts)
Pitmaston Ho. SE13 1A 94
(off Lewisham Rd.)
Pitsea Pl. E1 9H 61
Pitsea St. E1 9H 61
Pitshanger La. W5 7F 54
Pitshanger Manor. 2H 71
Pitt Cres. SW19 1M 105
Pittman Gdns. Ilf 1A 64
Pitt Pl. Eps 6C 134
Pitt Rd. Eps 6C 134
Pitt Rd. Orp 6A 128
Pitt Rd. T Hth & Croy 9A 108
Pitt's Head M. W1 2E 74
Pittsmead Av. Brom 2E 126
Pitt St. W8 3L 73
Pittville Gdns. SE25 7E 108
Pixfield Ct. Brom 6D 110
(off Beckenham La.)
Pixley St. E14 9K 61
Pixton Way. Croy 1J 139
Place Farm Av. Orp 3B 128
Place, The. 6H 59
(off Flaxman Ter.)
Plaisterers Highwalk. EC2 8A 60
(off Noble St.)
Plaistow. 4E 110
(Bromley)
Plaistow. 6F 62
(West Ham)
Plaistow Gro. E15 4D 62
Plaistow Gro. Brom 4F 110
Plaistow La. Brom 4E 110
(in two parts)
Plaistow Pk. Rd. E13 5F 62
Plaistow Rd. E15 & E13 4D 62
Plaistow Wharf. E16 2E 78
Plane Ho. Short 6C 110
Plane St. SE26 9F 92
Planetree Ct. W6 5M 73
(off Brook Grn.)
Plane Tree Cres. Felt 9F 84
Plane Tree Ho. SE8 7J 77
(off Etta St.)
Plane Tree Wlk. N2 1C 42
Plane Tree Wlk. SE19 3C 108
Plantaganet Pl. Wal A 6H 7
Plantagenet Clo. Wor Pk 6B 120
Plantagenet Gdns. Romf 5H 49
Plantagenet Ho. SE18 4K 79
(off Leda Rd.)
Plantagenet Pl. Romf 5H 49
Plantagenet Rd. Barn 6A 14
Plantain Gdns. E11 8B 46
(off Hollydown Way, in two parts)
Plantain Pl. SE1 3B 76
Plantation Dri. Orp 3H 129
Plantation Rd. Eri 9E 82
Plantation Rd. Swan 4E 114
Plantation, The. SE3 1E 94
Plantation Wharf. SW11 2A 90
Plasel Ct. E13 4F 62
(off Pawsey Clo.)
Plashet. 2J 63
Plashet Gro. E6 4G 63
Plashet Rd. E13 4E 62
Plassy Rd. SE6 6M 93
Plate Ho. E14 6M 77
(off Burrells Wharf Sq.)
Platford Grn. Horn 2J 51
Platina St. EC2 7B 60
(off Tabernacle St.)
Plato Rd. SW2 3J 91
Platt Halls. NW9 9D 24
Platt's La. NW3 9L 41
Platts Rd. Enf 3G 17
Platt St. NW1 5H 59
Platt, The. SW15 2H 89
Plawsfield Rd. Beck 5H 109
Plaxtol Clo. Brom 5G 111
Plaxtol Rd. Eri 8L 81
Plaxton Ct. E11 8D 46
Players Theatre. 2J 75
(off Villiers St.)
Playfair Ho. E14 9L 61
(off Saracen St.)
Playfair Mans. W14 7J 73
(off Queen's Club Gdns.)
Playfair St. W6 6G 73
Playfield Av. Romf 8A 34
Playfield Cres. SE22 4D 92
Playfield Rd. Edgw 9A 24
Playford Rd. N4 7K 43
(in two parts)
Playgreen Way. SE6 9L 93
Playground Clo. Beck 6H 109
Playhouse Theatre. 2J 75
(off Northumberland Av.)
Playhouse Yd. EC4 9M 59
Plaza Bus. Cen. Enf 4J 17
Plaza Cinema. 1H 75
(off Regent St.)
Plaza Pde. NW6 5M 57
Plaza Shop. Cen., The.
W1 9G 59
Pleasance Rd. SW15 4F 88
Pleasance Rd. Orp 6F 112
Pleasance, The. SW15 3F 88
Pleasant Gro. Croy 5K 125
Pleasant Pl. N1 3M 59
Pleasant Pl. S Harr 6B 38
Pleasant Pl. W on T 8G 117
Pleasant Row. NW1 4F 58
Pleasant Vw. Eri 6C 82
Pleasant Vw. Pl. Orp 7M 127
Pleasant Way. Wemb 5G 55
Pleasure Pit Rd. Asht 9M 133
Plender Pl. NW1 4G 59
(off Plender St.)
Plender St. NW1 4G 59
Pleshey Rd. N7 9H 43
Plesman Way. Wall 1J 137
Plevna Cres. N15 4C 44
Plevna Rd. N9 3E 28
Plevna Rd. Hamp 5M 101
Plevna St. E14 4A 78
Pleydell Av. SE19 4D 108
Pleydell Av. W6 5D 72
Pleydell Ct. EC4 9L 59
(off Lombard La.)
Pleydell Est. EC1 6A 60
(off Radnor St.)
Pleydell St. EC4 9L 59
(off Bouverie St.)
Plimsoll Clo. E14 9M 61
Plimsoll Rd. N4 8L 43
Plough Ct. EC3 1B 76
Plough Farm Clo. Ruis 4B 36
Plough La. SE22 5D 92
Plough La. SW19 & SW17
2M 105
Plough La. Purl 1J 137
Plough La. Tedd 2E 102
Plough La. Wall 6J 123
Plough La. Clo. Wall 7J 123
Ploughmans Clo. NW1 4H 59
Ploughmans End. Iswth 4B 86
Ploughmans Wlk. N2 9A 26
(off Long La.)
Plough Pl. EC4 9L 59
Plough Rd. SW11 2B 90
Plough Rd. Eps 1B 134
Plough St. E1 9D 60
Plough Ter. SW11 3B 90
Plough Way. SE16 5H 77
Plough Yd. EC2 7C 60
Plover Ho. SW9 8L 75
(off Brixton Rd.)
Plover Way. SE16 4J 77
Plover Way. Hay 9H 53
Plowden Bldgs. EC4 1L 75
(off Middle Temple La.)
Plowman Clo. N18 5B 28
Plowman Way. Dag 6G 49
Plumber's Row. E1 8E 60
Plumbridge St. SE10 9M 77
Plum Clo. Felt 7E 84
Plume Ho. SE10 7M 77
(off Creek Rd.)
Plum Gth. Bren 5H 71
Plum La. SE18 8M 79
Plummer La. Mitc 6D 106
Plummer Rd. SW4 6H 91
Plumpton Av. Horn 9J 51
Plumpton Clo. N'holt 2L 53
Plumpton Way. Cars 5C 122
Plumstead. 5C 80
Plumstead Common. 7B 80
Plumstead Comn. Rd.
SE18 7M 79
Plumstead High St. SE18 5B 80
Plumstead Rd. SE18 5M 79
Plumtree Clo. Dag 2M 65
Plumtree Clo. Wall 9H 123
Plumtree Ct. EC4 9M 59
Plumtree Mead. Lou 5L 19
Plymouth Ct. Surb 8J 103
(off Cranes Pk. Av.)
Plymouth Ho. SE10 8M 77
(off Devonshire Dri.)
Plymouth Ho. Bark 3E 64
(off Keir Hardie Way)
Plymouth Rd. E16 8E 62
Plymouth Rd. Brom 5F 110
Plymouth Wharf. E14 5B 78
Plympton Av. NW6 3K 57
Plympton Clo. Belv 4J 81
Plympton Pl. NW8 7C 58
Plympton Rd. NW6 3K 57
Plympton St. NW8 7C 58
Plymstock Rd. Well 8G 81
Pocklington Clo. NW9 9C 24
Pocklington Clo. W12 4E 72
(off Ashchurch Pk. Vs.)
Pocklington Lodge. W12 4E 72
Pocock Av. W Dray 4K 143
Pocock St. SE1 3M 75
Podmore Rd. SW18 3A 90
Poet's Rd. N5 1B 60
Poets Way. Harr 2C 38
Pointalls Clo. N3 9A 26
Point Clo. SE10 9A 78
Pointer Clo. SE28 9H 65
Pointers Clo. E14 6M 77
Pointers Cotts. Rich 8G 87
Point Hill. SE10 8A 78
Point Pl. Wemb 3M 55
Point Pleasant. SW18 3L 89
Point Ter. E7 1F 62
(off Claremont Rd.)
Point, The. Ruis 9E 36
Point West. SW7 5M 73
Poland St. W1 9G 59
Polebrook Rd. SE3 2G 95
Pole Cat All. Brom 4D 126
Polecroft La. SE6 8K 93
Polehamptons, The.
Hamp 4A 102
Pole Hill Rd. E4 9A 18
Pole Hill Rd. Uxb & Hil 7F 142
Polesden Gdns. SW20 6F 104
Polesteeple Hill. Big H 9H 141
Polesworth Ho. W2 8L 57
(off Alfred Rd.)
Polesworth Rd. Dag 3H 65
Police Sta. La. Bush 9M 9
Police Sta. Rd. W on T 8G 117
Polish War Memorial (Junct.)
2G 53
Pollard Clo. E16 1E 78
Pollard Clo. N7 9K 43
Pollard Clo. Chig 5E 32
Pollard Ho. N1 5K 59
(off Northdown St.)
Pollard Rd. N20 2C 26
Pollard Rd. Mord 9B 106
Pollard Row. E2 6E 60
Pollards Clo. Lou 7G 19
Pollards Cres. SW16 7J 107
Pollards Hill E. SW16 7K 107
Pollards Hill N. SW16 7J 107
Pollards Hill S. SW16 7J 107
Pollards Hill W. SW16 7K 107
Pollard St. E2 6E 60
Pollards Wood Rd.
SW16 7J 107
Pollard Wlk. Sidc 3G 113
Pollen St. W1 9G 59
Pollitt Dri. NW8 7B 58
Pollock Ho. W10 7J 57
(off Kensal Rd.)
Pollock's Toy Mus. 8G 59
Pollyhaugh. Eyns 5H 131
Polperro Clo. Orp 1D 128
Polperro M. SE11 5M 75
Polsted Rd. SE6 6K 93
Polsten M. Enf 1L 17
Polthorne Gro. SE18 5A 80
Polworth Rd. SW16 2J 107
Polygon Rd. NW1 5H 59
Polygon, The. NW8 4B 58
(off Avenue Rd.)
Polygon, The. SW4 3G 91
Polytechnic St. SE18 5L 79
Pomell Way. E1 9D 60
Pomeroy Cres. Wat 9F 4
Pomeroy Ho. E2 5H 61
(off St James's Av.)
Pomeroy Ho. W11 9J 57
(off Lancaster Rd.)
Pomeroy St. SE14 8G 77
Pomfret Rd. SE5 2M 91
Pomoja La. N19 7J 43
Pomona Ho. SE8 5J 77
(off Evelyn St.)
Pond Clo. N12 6C 26
Pond Clo. SE3 1E 94
Pond Clo. W on T 8D 116
(in two parts)
Pond Cottage La. Beck 3L 125
Pond Cotts. SE21 7C 92
Ponders End. 7G 17
Ponders End Ind. Est. Enf 7J 17
Ponder St. N7 3K 59
(in two parts)
Pond Farm Est. E5 8G 45
Pond Fld. End. Lou 9H 19
Pondfield Ho. SE27 2A 108
Pondfield Rd. Brom 3C 126
Pondfield Rd. Dag 1M 65
Pondfield Rd. Kenl 8M 137
(in two parts)
Pondfield Rd. Orp 5M 127
Pond Grn. Ruis 7C 36
Pond Hill Gdns. Sutt 8J 121
Pond Ho. SW3 5C 74
Pond Ho. Stan 6F 22
Pond Lees Clo. Dag 3B 66
Pond Mead. SE21 5B 92
Pond Path. Chst 3M 111
Pond Piece. Oxs 5A 132
Pond Pl. SW3 5C 74
Pond Pl. Asht 9J 133
Pond Rd. E15 5C 62
Pond Rd. SE3 1D 94
Pondside Clo. Hay 7B 68
Pond Sq. N6 6E 42
Ponds, The. Wey 8B 116
Pond St. NW3 1C 58
Pond Way. Tedd 3G 103
Pondwood Ri. Orp 2C 128
Ponler St. E1 9F 60
Ponsard Rd. NW10 6F 56
Ponsford St. E9 2G 61
Ponsonby Pl. SW1 6H 75
Ponsonby Rd. SW15 6F 88
Ponsonby Ter. SW1 6H 75
Pontefract Ct. N'holt 1M 53
(off Newmarket Av.)
Pontefract Rd. Brom 2D 110
Ponton Rd. SW8 8H 75
Pont St. SW1 4D 74
Pont St. M. SW1 4D 74
Pontypool Pl. SE1 3M 75
Pontypool Wlk. Romf 6G 35
Pool Clo. Beck 2L 109
Pool Clo. W Mol 9K 101
Pool Ct. SE6 8L 93
Poole Clo. Ruis 7C 36
Poole Ct. N1 3C 60
(off St Peter's Way)
Poole Ct. Houn 1J 85
Poole Ct. Rd. Houn 1J 85
Poole Ho. SE11 4L 75
(off Lambeth Wlk.)
Poole Rd. E9 2H 61
Poole Rd. Eps 8B 120
Poole Rd. Horn 5K 51
Pooles Bldgs. WC1 7L 59
(off Mount Pleasant)
Pooles Cotts. Rich 8H 87
Pooles La. SW10 8A 74
Pooles La. Dag 5J 65
Pooles Pk. N4 7L 43
Poole St. N1 4B 60
Poole Way. Hay 6C 52
Pool Ho. NW8 8B 58
(off Penfold St.)
Poolmans St. SE16 3H 77
Pool Rd. Harr 5B 38
Pool Rd. W Mol 9K 101
Poolsford Rd. NW9 2C 40
Poonah St. E1 9G 61
Pope Clo. SW19 3B 106
Pope Clo. Felt 7D 84
Pope Ho. SE5 8B 76
(off Elmington Est.)
Pope Ho. SE16 5F 76
(off Manor Est.)
Pope Rd. Brom 9H 111
Popes Av. Twic 8C 86
Popes Ct. Twic 8C 86
Popes Dri. N3 8L 25
Popes Gro. Croy 5K 125
Popes Gro. Twic 8C 86
Pope's Head All. EC3 9B 60
Popes La. W5 4H 71
Popes La. Wat 1F 8
Pope's Rd. SW9 2L 91
Pope's Rd. Ab L 4C 4
Pope St. SE1 3C 76
Popham Clo. Hanw 9K 85
Popham Gdns. Rich 2L 87
Popham Rd. N1 4A 60
Popham St. N1 4M 59
(in two parts)
Pop-In Commercial Cen.
Wemb 1M 55
Popinjays Row. Cheam 7H 121
(off Netley Clo.)
Poplar. 1M 77
Poplar Av. Mitc 5D 106
Poplar Av. Orp 4M 127
Poplar Av. S'hall 4M 69
Poplar Av. W Dray 1K 143
Poplar Bath St. E14 9M 61
Poplar Bus. Pk. E14 1A 78
Poplar Clo. E9 1K 61
Poplar Clo. Pinn 8H 21
Poplar Ct. SW19 2L 105
Poplar Ct. N'holt 5G 53
Poplar Ct. Twic 5G 87
Poplar Cres. Eps 8A 120
Poplar Dri. Bans 6H 135
Poplar Farm Clo. Eps 8A 120
Poplar Gdns. SE28 1G 81
Poplar Gdns. N Mald 6B 104
Poplar Gro. N11 6E 26
Poplar Gro. W6 3G 73
Poplar Gro. N Mald 6B 104
Poplar Gro. Wemb 8A 40
Poplar High St. E14 1M 77
Poplar Ho. SE4 3K 93
(off Wickham Rd.)
Poplar Ho. SE16 3H 77
(off Woodland Cres.)
Poplar M. W12 2G 73
Poplar Mt. Belv 5M 81
Poplar Pl. SE28 1G 81
Poplar Pl. W2 1M 73
Poplar Pl. Hay 1E 68
Poplar Rd. SE24 3A 92
Poplar Rd. SW19 6L 105
Poplar Rd. Ashf 2A 100
Poplar Rd. Den 1A 142
Poplar Rd. Sutt 3K 121
Poplar Rd. S. SW19 7L 105
Poplars Av. NW2 2G 57
Poplars Clo. Ruis 6C 36
Poplars Clo. Wat 5F 4
Poplar Shaw. Wal A 6M 7
Poplars Rd. E17 4M 45
Poplars, The. N14 7F 14
Poplars, The. Borwd 3L 11
Poplar St. Romf 2A 50
Poplar Vw. Wemb 7H 39
Poplar Wlk. SE24 2A 92
(in two parts)
Poplar Wlk. Croy 4A 124
Poplar Way. Felt 9E 84
Poplar Way. Ilf 2A 48
Poppins Ct. EC4 9M 59
Poppleton Rd. E11 4C 46

Poppy Clo.—Prince of Wales Clo.

Poppy Clo. Belv 4M 81
Poppy Clo. Wall 3E 122
Poppy La. Croy 2G 125
Porchester Clo. SE5 . . . . 3A 92
Porchester Clo. Horn 4J 51
Porchester Ct. W2 . . . . 1M 73
(off Porchester Gdns.)
Porchester Gdns. W2 . . . . . . 1M 73
Porchester Gdns. M. W2 . . . . 9M 57
Porchester Ga. W2 . . . . 1M 73
(off Bayswater Rd., in two parts)
Porchester Ho. E1 . . . . 9F 60
(off Philpot St.)
Porchester Mead. Beck 3L 109
Porchester M. W2 . . . . 9M 57
Porchester Pl. W2 . . . . 9C 58
Porchester Rd. W2 . . . . 9M 57
Porchester Rd. King T 6M 103
Porchester Sq. W2 . . . . 9M 57
Porchester Ter. W2 . . . . 1A 74
Porchester Ter. N. W2 . . . . . . 9M 57
Porchfield Clo. Sutt 2M 135
Porch Way. N20 . . . . 3D 26
Porcupine Clo. SE9 . . . . 8J 95
Porden Rd. SW2 . . . . 3K 91
Porlock Av. Harr 6A 38
Porlock Ho. SE26 . . . . 9E 92
Porlock Rd. W10 . . . . 7H 57
Porlock Rd. Enf 9D 16
Porlock St. SE1 . . . . 3B 76
Porrington Clo. Chst 5K 111
Porson Ct. SE13 . . . . 2M 93
Portal Clo. SE27 . . . . 9L 91
Portal Clo. Ruis 9E 36
(in two parts)
Portal Clo. Uxb 3C 142
(in two parts)
Portbury Clo. SE15 . . . . 9E 76
Port Cres. E13 . . . . 7F 62
Portcullis Ho. SW1 . . . . 3J 75
(off Bridge St.)
Portcullis Lodge Rd. Enf 5B 16
Portelet Ct. N1 . . . . 4C 60
(off De Beauvoir Est.)
Portelet Rd. E1 . . . . 6H 61
Porten Houses. W14 . . . . 4J 73
(off Porten Rd.)
Porten Rd. W14 . . . . 4J 73
Porter Rd. E6 . . . . 9K 63
Porters & Walters Almshouses.
N22 . . . . 7K 27
(off Nightingale Rd.)
Porters Av. Dag 2F 64
Porter Sq. N19 . . . . 6J 43
Porter St. SE1 . . . . 2A 76
Porter St. W1 . . . . 8D 58
Porters Wlk. E1 . . . . 1F 76
(off Balkan Wlk.)
Porters Way. W Dray 4K 143
Porteus Rd. W2 . . . . 8A 58
Portgate Clo. W9 . . . . 7K 57
Porthallow Clo. Orp 6D 128
Porthcawe Rd. SE26 . . . . . . 1J 109
Porthkerry Av. Well 3E 96
Port Ho. E14 . . . . 6M 77
(off Burrells Wharf Sq.)
Portia Ct. SE11 . . . . 6M 75
(off Opal St.)
Portia Ct. Bark 3E 64
Portia Way. E3 . . . . 7K 61
Porticos, The. SW3 . . . . 7B 74
(off Kings Rd.)
Portinscale Rd. SW15 . . . . . . 4J 89
Portland Av. N16 . . . . 5D 44
Portland Av. N Mald 2D 120
Portland Av. Sidc 5E 96
Portland Clo. Romf 3J 49
Portland Commercial Est.
Bark 5G 65
Portland Ct. N1 . . . . 3C 60
(off St Peter's Way)
Portland Ct. SE1 . . . . 4B 76
(off Gt. Dover St.)
Portland Ct. SE14 . . . . 7J 77
(off Whitcher Clo.)
Portland Cres. SE9 . . . . 8J 95
Portland Cres. Felt 1B 100
Portland Cres. Gnfd 7M 53
Portland Cres. Stan 9H 23
Portland Dri. Chesh 4A 6
Portland Dri. Enf 2C 16
Portland Gdns. N4 . . . . 4M 43
Portland Gdns. Romf 3H 49
Portland Gro. SW8 . . . . 9K 75
Portland Heights. N'wd 4D 20
Portland Ho. SW1 . . . . 4G 75
(off Stag Pl.)
Portland M. W1 . . . . 9G 59
Portland Pl. SE25 . . . . 8E 108
(off Portland Rd.)
Portland Pl. W1 . . . . 7F 58
Portland Pl. Eps 4C 134
Portland Ri. N4 . . . . 6M 43
Portland Ri. Est. N4 . . . . 6A 44
Portland Rd. N15 . . . . 2D 44
Portland Rd. SE9 . . . . 8J 95
Portland Rd. SE25 . . . . 8E 108
Portland Rd. W11 . . . . 1J 73
Portland Rd. Ashf 9C 144
Portland Rd. Brom 1G 111
Portland Rd. Hay 6C 52
Portland Rd. King T 7J 103
Portland Rd. Mitc 6C 106
Portland Rd. S'hall 4K 69
Portland Sq. E1 . . . . 2F 76
Portland St. SE17 . . . . 6B 76
Portland Ter. Rich 3H 87
Portland Wlk. SE17 . . . . 7B 76
Portmadoc Ho. Romf 4J 35
(off Broseley Rd.)
Portman Av. SW14 . . . . 2B 88
Portman Clo. W1 . . . . 9D 58
Portman Clo. Bex 7C 98
Portman Clo. Bexh 2J 97
Portman Dri. Wfd G 9H 31
Portman Gdns. NW9 . . . . 9B 24
Portman Gdns. Uxb 3E 142
Portman Ga. NW1 . . . . 7C 58
(off Broadley Ter.)
Portman Mans. W1 . . . . 8D 58
(off Chiltern St.)
Portman M. S. W1 . . . . 9E 58
Portman Pl. E2 . . . . 6G 61
Portman Rd. King T 6K 103
Portman Sq. W1 . . . . 9E 58
Portman St. W1 . . . . 9E 58
Portman Towers. W1 . . . . 9D 58
Portmeadow Wlk. SE2 . . . . . . 3H 81
Port Meers Clo. E17 . . . . 4K 45
Portmore Gdns. Romf 5L 33
Portnall Rd. W9 . . . . 5K 57
Portnalls Clo. Coul 8F 136
Portnalls Ri. Coul 8G 137
Portnalls Rd. Coul 9F 136
Portnoi Clo. Romf 9B 34
Portobello Ct. Est. W11 . . . . . 9K 57
Portobello M. W11 . . . . 1L 73
Portobello Rd. W10 . . . . 8J 57
Portobello Rd. W11 . . . . 9K 57
Portobello Road Market. . . . 8J 57
Portpool La. EC1 . . . . 8L 59
Portree Clo. N22 . . . . 7K 27
Portree St. E14 . . . . 9B 62
Portrush Ct. S'hall 9A 54
(off Whitecote Rd.)
Portsdown. Edgw 5L 23
Portsdown Av. NW11 . . . . 4K 41
Portsdown M. NW11 . . . . 4K 41
Portsea Hall. W2 . . . . 9D 58
(off Portsea Pl.)
Portsea M. W2 . . . . 9C 58
(off Portsea Pl.)
Portsea Pl. W2 . . . . 9C 58
Portslade Rd. SW8 . . . . 1G 91
Portsmouth Av. Th Dit 2E 118
Portsmouth M. E16 . . . . 2F 78
Portsmouth Rd. SW15 . . . . . . 6F 88
Portsmouth Rd.
Cob & Esh 9K 117
Portsmouth Rd. Esh 8L 117
(Stony Hill)
Portsmouth Rd. Esh & Th Dit
. . . . 6A 118
(High St.)
Portsmouth Rd.
Th Dit, Surb & Kin 2E 118
Portsmouth St. WC2 . . . . 9K 59
Portsoken St. E1 . . . . 1D 76
Portswood Pl. SW15 . . . . 5D 88
Portugal Gdns. Twic 8A 86
Portugal St. WC2 . . . . 9K 59
Portway. E15 . . . . 4D 62
Portway. Eps 1E 134
Portway Cres. Eps 1E 134
Portway Gdns. SE18 . . . . 8H 79
Pory Ho. SE11 . . . . 5K 75
Poseidon Ct. E14 . . . . 5L 77
(off Homer Dri.)
Postern Grn. Enf 4L 15
Postern, The. EC2 . . . . 8A 60
(off Wood St.)
Post La. Twic 7B 86
Postmill Clo. Croy 5G 125
Post Office All. Hamp 6M 101
Post Office App. E7 . . . . 1F 62
Post Office Ct. EC4 . . . . 9B 60
(off Barbican)
Post Office Way. SW8 . . . . . . 8H 75
Post Rd. S'hall 4M 69
Postway M. Ilf 8M 47
(in two parts)
Potier St. SE1 . . . . 4B 76
Potter Clo. Mitc 6F 106
Potteries, The. Barn 7L 13
Potterne Clo. SW19 . . . . 6H 89
Potters Clo. Croy 3J 125
Potters Clo. Lou 4J 19
Potters End. Pinn 6F 20
Potters Fld. Enf 6C 16
(off Lincoln Rd.)
Potters Fields. SE1 . . . . 2C 76
Potters Gro. N Mald 8A 104
Potters Heights Clo. Pinn 7F 20
Potter's La. SW16 . . . . 3H 107
Potters La. Barn 6L 13
(in two parts)
Potters La. Borwd 3A 12
Potters Lodge. E14 . . . . 6A 78
(off Manchester Rd.)
Potters M. Els 8H 11
Potters Rd. SW6 . . . . 1A 90
Potter's Rd. Barn 6M 13
Potter St. N'wd 8E 20
Potter St. Pinn 8F 20
Potter St. Hill. Pinn 6F 20
Pottery La. W11 . . . . 2J 73
Pottery Rd. Bex 8A 98
Pottery Rd. Bren 7J 71
Pottery St. SE16 . . . . 3F 76
Pott St. E2 . . . . 6F 60
Poulett Gdns. Twic 7E 86
Poulett Rd. E6 . . . . 5K 63
Poulters Wood. Kes 7H 127
Poulton Av. Sutt 5B 122
Poulton Clo. E8 . . . . 2F 60
Poultry. EC2 . . . . 9B 60
Pound Clo. Orp 4B 128
Pound Clo. Surb 3G 119
Pound Ct. Dri. Orp 4B 128
Poundfield. Wat 8D 4
Poundfield Rd. Lou 7L 19
Pound Grn. Bex 6L 97
Pound La. NW10 . . . . 2E 56
Pound La. Eps 4A 134
Pound Pk. Rd. SE7 . . . . 5H 79
Pound Pl. SE9 . . . . 5L 95
Pound Rd. Bans 9K 135
Pound St. Cars 7D 122
Pound Way. Chst 4A 112
Pountney Rd. SW11 . . . . 2E 90
Poverest. 9E 112
Poverest Rd. Orp 9D 112
Povey Ho. SE17 . . . . 5C 76
(off Tatum St.)
Powder Mill La. Dart 8J 99
Powder Mill La. Twic 6K 85
Powdermill La. Wal A 6H 7
Powdermill M. Wal A 6H 7
(off Powdermill La.)
Powell Clo. Chess 7H 119
Powell Clo. Edgw 6K 23
Powell Clo. Wall 9J 123
Powell Ct. E17 . . . . 1M 45
Powell Ct. S Croy 6M 123
(off Bramley Hill)
Powell Gdns. Dag 9L 49
Powell Rd. E5 . . . . 8F 44
Powell Rd. Buck H 9G 19
Powell's Wlk. W4 . . . . 7C 72
Power Dri. Enf 9F 6
Powergate Bus. Pk.
NW10 . . . . 6B 56
Power Rd. W4 . . . . 5L 71
Powers Ct. Twic 6H 87
Powerscroft Rd. E5 . . . . 9G 45
Powerscroft Rd. Sidc 3G 113
Power Works. Eri 9E 82
Powis Ct. W11 . . . . 9K 57
(off Powis Gdns.)
Powis Ct. Bus H 1B 22
(off Rutherford Way)
Powis Gdns. NW11 . . . . 5K 41
Powis Gdns. W11 . . . . 9K 57
Powis M. W11 . . . . 9K 57
Powis Pl. WC1 . . . . 7J 59
Powis Rd. E3 . . . . 6M 61
Powis Sq. W11 . . . . 9K 57
(in two parts)
Powis St. SE18 . . . . 4L 79
Powis Ter. W11 . . . . 9K 57
Powlett Ho. NW1 . . . . 2F 58
(off Powlett Pl.)
Powlett Pl. NW1 . . . . 3E 58
(in two parts)
Pownall Gdns. Houn 3M 85
Pownall Rd. E8 . . . . 4E 60
Pownall Rd. Houn 3M 85
Pownsett Ter. Ilf 1A 64
Powster Rd. Brom 2E 110
Powys Clo. Bexh 7H 81
Powys Ct. N11 . . . . 5J 27
Powys Ct. Borwd 5B 12
Powys La. N14 & N13 . . . . . . 4J 27
Poynders Ct. SW4 . . . . 5G 91
Poynders Gdns. SW4 . . . . 6G 91
Poynders Rd. SW4 . . . . 5G 91
Poynings Clo. Orp 4G 129
Poynings Rd. N19 . . . . 8G 43
Poynings Way. N12 . . . . 5L 25
Poynings Way. H Wood 8J 35
Poyntell Cres. Chst 5B 112
Poynter Ct. N'holt 5H 53
(off Gallery Gdns.)
Poynter Ho. NW8 . . . . 7B 58
(off Fisherton St.)
Poynter Ho. W11 . . . . 2H 73
(off Queensdale Cres.)
Poynter Rd. Enf 7D 16
Poynton Rd. N17 . . . . 9E 28
Poyntz Rd. SW11 . . . . 1D 90
Poyser St. E2 . . . . 5F 60
Praed M. W2 . . . . 9B 58
Praed St. W2 . . . . 9B 58
Pragel St. E13 . . . . 5G 63
Pragnell Rd. SE12 . . . . 8F 94
Prague Pl. SW2 . . . . 4J 91
Prah Rd. N4 . . . . 7L 43
Prairie St. SW8 . . . . 1E 90
Pratt M. NW1 . . . . 4G 59
Pratts La. W on T 6H 117
Pratts Pas. King T 6J 103
Pratt St. NW1 . . . . 4G 59
Pratt Wlk. SE11 . . . . 5K 75
Prayle Gro. NW2 . . . . 6H 41
Preachers Ct. EC1 . . . . 7M 59
(off Charterhouse Sq.)
Prebend Gdns. W6 & W4 . . . 5D 72
(in two parts)
Prebend Mans. W4 . . . . 5D 72
(off Chiswick High Rd.)
Prebend St. N1 . . . . 4A 60
Precinct Rd. Hay 1E 68
Precincts, The. Mord 1L 121
Precinct, The. N1 . . . . 4A 60
(in two parts)
Precinct, The. W Mol 7M 101
Premier Corner. W9 . . . . 5K 57
Premier Ct. Enf 2H 17
Premiere Pl. E14 . . . . 1L 77
Premier Ho. N1 . . . . 3M 59
(off Waterloo Ter.)
Premier Pk. NW10 . . . . 4M 55
Premier Pk. Rd. NW10 . . . . . 5M 55
Premier Pl. SW15 . . . . 3J 89
Prendergast Rd. SE3 . . . . 2C 94
Prentice Ct. SW19 . . . . 2K 105
Prentis Rd. SW16 . . . . 1H 107
Prentiss Ct. SE7 . . . . 5H 79
Presburg Rd. N Mald 9C 104
Presburg St. E5 . . . . 8H 45
Prescelly Pl. Edgw 8K 23
Prescot St. E1 . . . . 1D 76
Prescott Av. Orp 1M 127
Prescott Clo. SW16 . . . . 4J 107
Prescott Grn. Lou 5M 19
Prescott Ho. SE17 . . . . 7M 75
(off Hillingdon St.)
Prescott Pl. SW4 . . . . 2H 91
Prescott Rd. Chesh 1E 6
Presentation M. SW2 . . . . 8K 91
Preshaw Cres. Mitc 7C 106
President Dri. E1 . . . . 2F 76
President Ho. EC1 . . . . 6M 59
President Quay. E1 . . . . 2D 76
(off St Katherine's Way)
President St. EC1 . . . . 6A 60
(off Central St.)
Prespa Clo. N9 . . . . 2G 29
Press Ho. NW10 . . . . 8B 40
Press Rd. NW10 . . . . 8B 40
Press Rd. Uxb 2B 142
Prestage Way. E14 . . . . 1A 78
Prestbury Cres. Bans 8D 136
Prestbury Rd. E7 . . . . 3G 63
Prestbury Sq. SE9 . . . . 1K 111
Prested Rd. SW11 . . . . 3C 90
Prestige Way. NW4 . . . . 3G 41
Preston. 6J 39
Preston Av. E4 . . . . 6B 30
Preston Clo. SE1 . . . . 5C 76
Preston Clo. Twic 9C 86
Preston Ct. New Bar 6A 14
Preston Ct. Sidc 1D 112
(off Crescent, The)
Preston Ct. W on T 3G 117
Preston Dri. E11 . . . . 3G 47
Preston Dri. Bexh 9H 81
Preston Dri. Eps 8C 120
Preston Gdns. NW10 . . . . 2D 56
Preston Gdns. Enf 1J 17
Preston Gdns. Ilf 4J 47
Preston Gro. Asht 9G 133
Preston Hill. Harr 5J 39
Preston Ho. SE1 . . . . 5C 76
(off Preston Clo.)
Preston Ho. SE1 . . . . 4D 76
(off Stanworth St.)
Preston Ho. Dag 8L 49
(off Uvedale Rd.)
Preston Pl. NW2 . . . . 2E 56
Preston Pl. Rich 4J 87
Preston Rd. E11 . . . . 4C 46
Preston Rd. SE19 . . . . 3M 107
Preston Rd. SW20 . . . . 4D 104
Preston Rd. Romf 4H 35
Preston Rd. Wemb 6J 39
Preston's Rd. E14 . . . . 1A 78
Prestons Rd. Brom 5E 126
Preston St. E2 . . . . 5H 61
Preston Waye. Harr 6J 39
Prestwich Ter. SW4 . . . . 4G 91
Prestwick Clo. S'hall 6J 69
Prestwick Ct. S'hall 1A 70
(off Baird Av.)
Prestwick Rd. Wat 1G 21
Prestwood. Wat 2J 21
Prestwood Av. Harr 2F 38
Prestwood Clo. SE18 . . . . 7E 80
Prestwood Clo. Harr 2F 38
Prestwood Dri. Romf 5A 34
Prestwood Gdns. Croy 2A 124
Prestwood Ho. SE16 . . . . 4F 76
(off Drummond Rd.)
Prestwood St. N1 . . . . 5A 60
Pretoria Av. E17 . . . . 2J 45
Pretoria Clo. N17 . . . . 7D 28
Pretoria Cres. E4 . . . . 1A 30
Pretoria Ho. Eri 8C 82
Pretoria Rd. E4 . . . . 1A 30
Pretoria Rd. E11 . . . . 6B 46
Pretoria Rd. E16 . . . . 7D 62
Pretoria Rd. N17 . . . . 7D 28
Pretoria Rd. SW16 . . . . 3F 106
Pretoria Rd. Ilf 1M 63
Pretoria Rd. Romf 2A 50
Pretoria Rd. Wat 6E 8
Pretoria Rd. N. N18 . . . . 6D 28
Prevost Rd. N11 . . . . 2E 26
Priam Ho. E2 . . . . 5F 60
(off Old Bethnal Grn. Rd.)
Price Clo. NW7 . . . . 6J 25
Price Clo. SW17 . . . . 9D 90
Price' Ct. SW11 . . . . 2B 90
Price Ho. N1 . . . . 4A 60
(off Britannia Row)
Price Rd. Croy 7M 123
Price's St. SE1 . . . . 2M 75
Price's Yd. N1 . . . . 4K 59
Price Way. Hamp 3J 101
Prichard Ct. N7 . . . . 2K 59
Pricklers Hill. Barn 8M 13
Prickley Wood. Brom 3D 126
Priddy's Yd. Croy 4A 124
Prideaux Pl. W3 . . . . 1B 72
Prideaux Pl. WC1 . . . . 6K 59
Prideaux Rd. SW9 . . . . 2J 91
Pridham Rd. T Hth 8B 108
Priestfield Rd. SE23 . . . . 9J 93
Priestlands Pk. Rd. Sidc 9D 96
Priestley Clo. N16 . . . . 5D 44
Priestley Gdns. Romf 4F 48
Priestley Ho. EC1 . . . . 7A 60
(off Old St.)
Priestley Ho. Wemb 8A 40
(off Barnhill Rd.)
Priestley Rd. Mitc 6E 106
Priestley Way. E17 . . . . 1H 45
Priestley Way. NW2 . . . . 6E 40
Priest Pk. Av. Harr 7L 37
Priests Av. Romf 9B 34
Priest's Bri.
SW14 & SW15 . . . . 2C 88
Priest's Ct. EC2 . . . . 9A 60
(off Foster La.)
Prima Rd. SW9 . . . . 8L 75
Prime Meridian Line, The.
. . . . 8B 78
(Greenwich Royal Observatory)
Primrose Av. Enf 3B 16
Primrose Av. Romf 5F 48
Primrose Clo. N3 . . . . 9M 25
Primrose Clo. SE6 . . . . 2A 110
Primrose Clo. Harr 8K 37
Primrose Clo. Wall 2F 122
Primrose Ct. SW12 . . . . 6H 91
Primrose Dri. W Dray 4H 143
Primrose Gdns. NW3 . . . . 2C 58
Primrose Gdns. Bush 9M 9
Primrose Gdns. Ruis 1G 53
Primrose Glen. Horn 2J 51
Primrose Hill. 4E 58
Primrose Hill. EC4 . . . . 9L 59
Primrose Hill. K Lan 2A 4
Primrose Hill Ct. NW3 . . . . . . 3D 58
Primrose Hill Rd. NW3 . . . . . 3D 58
Primrose Hill Studios.
NW1 . . . . 4E 58
Primrose La. Croy 3G 125
Primrose Mans. SW11 . . . . . . 9E 74
Primrose M. NW1 . . . . 3D 58
(off Sharpleshall St.)
Primrose M. SE3 . . . . 8E 78
Primrose Path. Chesh 4A 6
Primrose Rd. E10 . . . . 6M 45
Primrose Rd. E18 . . . . 9F 30
Primrose Rd. W on T 7G 117
Primrose Sq. E9 . . . . 3G 61
Primrose St. EC2 . . . . 8C 60
Primrose Wlk. SE14 . . . . 8J 77
Primrose Wlk. Eps 9D 120
Primrose Way. Wemb 5H 55
Primula St. W12 . . . . 9E 56
Prince Albert Ct. NW8 . . . . . . 4D 58
(off Prince Albert Rd.)
Prince Albert Rd.
NW1 & NW8 . . . . 6C 58
Prince Arthur M. NW3 . . . . . . 9A 42
Prince Arthur Rd. NW3 . . . . . 1A 58
Prince Charles Cinema. . . . 1H 75
(off Leicester Pl.)
Prince Charles Dri. NW4 . . . . 5G 41
Prince Charles Rd. SE3 . . . . . 1D 94
Prince Charles Way. Wall . . . 5F 122
Prince Consort Dri. Chst . . . 5B 112
Prince Consort Rd. SW7 . . . . . 4A 74
Princedale Rd. W11 . . . . 2J 73
Prince Edward Mans. W2 . . . . 1L 73
(off Hereford Rd.)
Prince Edward Rd. E9 . . . . . . 2K 61
Prince Edward Theatre. . . . 9H 59
(off Old Compton St.)
Prince George Av. N14 . . . . . 7G 15
Prince George Rd. N16 . . . . . 9C 44
Prince George's Av.
SW20 . . . . 6G 105
Prince George's Rd.
SW19 . . . . 5B 106
Prince Henry Rd. SE7 . . . . . . 8H 79
Prince Imperial Rd. SE18 . . . 9K 79
Prince Imperial Rd.
Chst 5M 111
Prince John Rd. SE9 . . . . 4J 95
Princelet St. E1 . . . . 8D 60
Prince of Wales Clo.
NW4 . . . . 2F 40

Prince of Wales Dri.—Purves Rd.

Prince of Wales Dri. SW11 & SW8 ...9C **74**
Prince of Wales Footpath. Enf ...2H **17**
Prince of Wales Mans. SW11 ...9E **74**
Prince of Wales Pas. NW1 ...6G **59**
(off Hampstead Rd.)
Prince of Wales Rd. E16 ...9G **63**
Prince of Wales Rd. NW5 ...2E **58**
Prince of Wales Rd. SE3 ...1D **94**
Prince of Wales Rd. Sutt ...4B **122**
Prince of Wales Ter. W4 ...6C **72**
Prince of Wales Ter. W8 ...3M **73**
Prince of Wales Theatre. ...1H 75
(off Coventry St.)
Prince Regent Ct. NW8 ...5C **58**
(off Avenue Rd.)
Prince Regent Ct. SE16 ...1J **77**
(off Edward Sq.)
Prince Regent La. E13 & E16 ...6F **62**
Prince Regent M. NW1 ...6G **59**
(off Hampstead Rd.)
Prince Regent Rd. Houn ...2A **86**
Prince Regents Ga. NW8 ...7C **58**
Prince Rd. SE25 ...9C **108**
Prince Rupert Rd. SE9 ...3K **95**
Princes Arc. SW1 ...2G **75**
(off Piccadilly)
Princes Av. N3 ...8L **25**
Princes Av. N10 ...1F **42**
Princes Av. N13 ...5L **27**
Princes Av. N22 ...8H **27**
Princes Av. NW9 ...2L **39**
Princes Av. W3 ...4L **71**
Princes Av. Cars ...9D **122**
Princes Av. Dart ...7M **99**
Princes Av. Enf ...9E **6**
Prince's Av. Gnfd ...9M **53**
Princes Av. Orp ...9C **112**
Princes Av. S Croy ...7F **138**
Princes Av. Surb ...3L **119**
Prince's Av. Wat ...7D **8**
Princes Av. Wfd G ...4F **30**
Princes Cir. WC2 ...9J **59**
Princes Clo. N4 ...6M **43**
Princes Clo. NW9 ...2L **39**
Princes Clo. SW4 ...2G **91**
Princes Clo. Edgw ...5L **23**
Princes Clo. Sidc ...9H **97**
Princes Clo. S Croy ...7F **138**
Prince's Clo. Tedd ...1B **102**
Prince's Ct. SE16 ...4K **77**
Prince's Ct. SW3 ...4D **74**
(off Brompton Rd.)
Princes Ct. Wemb ...1J **55**
Princes Ct. Bus. Cen. E1 ...1F **76**
Princes Dri. Harr ...1C **38**
Prince's Dri. Oxs ...4C **138**
Prince's Gdns. SW7 ...4B **74**
Princes Gdns. W3 ...8L **55**
Princes Gdns. W5 ...7G **55**
Prince's Ga. SW7 ...3B **74**
(in six parts)
Prince's Ga. Ct. SW7 ...3B **74**
Prince's Ga. M. SW7 ...4B **74**
Princes La. N10 ...1F **42**
Prince's M. W2 ...1M **73**
Princes M. W6 ...6F **72**
(off Down Pl.)
Princes M. Houn ...3L **85**
Princes Pde. NW11 ...4J **41**
(off Golders Grn. Rd.)
Princes Pk. Rain ...3E **66**
Princes Pk. Av. NW11 ...4J **41**
Princes Pk. Av. Hay ...1B **68**
Princes Pk. Circ. Hay ...1B **68**
Princes Pk. Clo. Hay ...1B **68**
Princes Pk. La. Hay ...1B **68**
Princes Pk. Pde. Hay ...1B **68**
Princes Pl. SW1 ...2G **75**
(off Duke St.)
Princes Pl. W11 ...2J **73**
Prince's Plain. Brom ...2J **127**
Prince's Ri. SE13 ...1A **94**
Princes Riverside Rd. SE16 ...2H **77**
Princes Rd. N18 ...4G **29**
Princes Rd. SE20 ...3H **109**
Princes Rd. SW14 ...2B **88**
Prince's Rd. SW19 ...3L **105**
Princes Rd. W13 ...2F **70**
Princes Rd. Buck H ...2G **31**
Princes Rd. Dart (DA1) ...5E **98**
Princes Rd. Dart (DA2) ...7M **99**
Princes Rd. Felt ...8D **84**
Princes Rd. Ilf ...2B **48**
Princes Rd. Kew ...9K **71**
Princes Rd. King T ...4L **103**
Princes Rd. Rich ...4K **87**
Prince's Rd. Romf ...3E **50**
Princes Rd. Swan ...3E **114**
Prince's Rd. Tedd ...1B **102**
Princes Rd. Wey ...7A **116**
Princes Road Interchange (Junct.) ...7L 99
Princessa Ct. Enf ...7B **16**
Princess Alice Ho. W10 ...7G **57**
Princess Alice Way. SE28 ...3B **80**
Princess Av. Wemb ...7J **39**
Princess Clo. SE28 ...9H **65**
Princess Ct. N6 ...5G **43**
Princess Ct. W1 ...8D **58**
(off Bryanston Pl.)
Princess Ct. W2 ...1M **73**
(off Queensway)
Princess Ct. King T ...7K **103**
(off Horace Rd.)
Princess Cres. N4 ...7M **43**
Princesses Pde. Dart ...4C **98**
(off Waterside)
Princess La. Ruis ...6C **36**
Princess Louise Clo. W2 ...8B **58**
Princess Mary Ho. SW1 ...5H **75**
(off Vincent St.)
Princess May Rd. N16 ...9C **44**
Princess M. NW3 ...1B **58**
Princess M. King T ...7K **103**
Princess Pde. Dag ...5L **65**
Princess Pde. Orp ...5L **127**
Princess Pk. Mnr. N11 ...5E **26**
Prince's Sq. W2 ...1M **73**
(in two parts)
Princess Rd. NW1 ...4E **58**
Princess Rd. NW6 ...5L **57**
Princess Rd. Croy ...1A **124**
Princess St. SE1 ...4M **75**
Prince's St. EC2 ...9B **60**
Princes St. N17 ...6C **28**
Princes St. W1 ...9F **58**
Princes St. Bexh ...2K **97**
Princes St. Rich ...3J **87**
Princes St. Sutt ...6B **122**
Princes Ter. E13 ...4F **62**
Prince's Tower. SE16 ...3G **77**
(off Elephant La.)
Prince St. SE8 ...7K **77**
Prince St. Wat ...5G **9**
Princes Vw. Dart ...7L **99**
Princes Way. SW19 ...6H **89**
Princes Way. Buck H ...2G **31**
Princes Way. Croy ...7K **123**
Princes Way. Ruis ...9J **37**
Princes Way. W Wick ...6D **126**
Prince's Yd. W11 ...2J **73**
(off Princedale Rd.)
Princethorpe Ho. W2 ...8M **57**
(off Woodchester Sq.)
Princethorpe Rd. SE26 ...1H **109**
Princeton Ct. SW15 ...2H **89**
Princeton M. King T ...5L **103**
Princeton St. WC1 ...8K **59**
Principal Sq. E9 ...1H **61**
Pringle Gdns. SW16 ...1G **107**
(in two parts)
Pringle Gdns. Purl ...2K **137**
Printers Inn Ct. EC4 ...9L **59**
Printers M. E3 ...4J **61**
Printer St. EC4 ...9L **59**
Printinghouse La. Hay ...3C **68**
Printing Ho. Yd. E2 ...6C **60**
Printon Ho. E14 ...8K **61**
(off Wallwood St.)
Print Village. SE15 ...1D **92**
Printwork Apartments. SE1 ...4C **76**
(off Long La.)
Priolo Rd. SE7 ...6G **79**
Prior Av. Sutt ...9C **122**
Prior Bolton St. N1 ...2M **59**
Prioress Rd. SE27 ...9M **91**
Prioress St. SE1 ...4C **76**
Prior Rd. Ilf ...8L **47**
Priors Cft. E17 ...9J **29**
Priors Fld. N'holt ...2J **53**
Priorsford Av. Orp ...8E **112**
Priors Gdns. Ruis ...1G **53**
Priors Mead. Enf ...3C **16**
Priors Pk. Horn ...8G **51**
Prior St. SE10 ...8A **78**
Priory Apartments, The. SE6 ...7M **93**
Priory Av. E4 ...3K **29**
Priory Av. E17 ...3L **45**
Priory Av. N8 ...2H **43**
Priory Av. W4 ...5C **72**
Priory Av. Orp ...1B **128**
Priory Av. Sutt ...6H **121**
Priory Av. Wemb ...9D **38**
Priory Clo. E4 ...3K **29**
Priory Clo. E18 ...8E **30**
Priory Clo. N3 ...8K **25**
Priory Clo. N14 ...7F **14**
Priory Clo. N20 ...9K **13**
Priory Clo. SW19 ...5M **105**
Priory Clo. Beck ...7J **109**
Priory Clo. Chst ...5K **111**
Priory Clo. Dart ...4G **99**
Priory Clo. Hamp ...5K **101**
Priory Clo. Hay ...1F **68**
Priory Clo. Ruis ...6D **36**
Priory Clo. Stan ...3D **22**
Priory Clo. Sun ...4E **100**
Priory Clo. W on T ...5E **116**
Priory Clo. Wemb ...9D **38**
Priory Ct. E6 ...4G **63**
Priory Ct. E9 ...1H **61**
Priory Ct. E17 ...9K **29**
Priory Ct. EC4 ...9M **59**
(off Pilgrim St.)
Priory Ct. SW8 ...9H **75**
Priory Ct. Bush ...1A **22**
Priory Ct. Dart ...5H **99**
Priory Ct. Eps ...1D **134**
Priory Ct. Houn ...2M **85**
Priory Ct. King T ...7J **103**
(off Denmark Rd.)
Priory Ct. Sutt ...6J **121**
Priory Ct. Wemb ...5J **55**
Priory Ct. Est. E17 ...9K **29**
Priory Cres. SE19 ...4A **108**
Priory Cres. Sutt ...6H **121**
Priory Cres. Wemb ...8E **38**
Priory Dri. SE2 ...6H **81**
Priory Dri. Stan ...3D **22**
Priory Field Dri. Edgw ...4M **23**
Priory Fields. Eyns ...4K **131**
Priory Gdns. N6 ...4F **42**
Priory Gdns. SE25 ...8D **108**
Priory Gdns. SW13 ...2D **88**
Priory Gdns. W4 ...5C **72**
Priory Gdns. W5 ...6J **55**
Priory Gdns. Ashf ...2B **100**
Priory Gdns. Dart ...4H **99**
Priory Gdns. Hamp ...4K **101**
Priory Gdns. Wemb ...9E **38**
Priory Grange. N2 ...1D **42**
(off Fortis Grn.)
Priory Grn. Est. N1 ...5K **59**
Priory Gro. SW8 ...9J **75**
Priory Gro. Barn ...7L **13**
Priory Gro. Romf ...3J **35**
Priory Hill. Dart ...4H **99**
Priory Hill. Wemb ...9E **38**
Priory Ho. E1 ...8D **60**
(off Folgate St.)
Priory Ho. EC1 ...7M **59**
(off Sans Wlk.)
Priory Ho. SW1 ...6H **75**
(off Rampayne St.)
Priory La. SW15 ...5C **88**
Priory La. Eyns ...3K **131**
Priory La. Rich ...8L **71**
Priory La. W Mol ...8M **101**
Priory Leas. SE9 ...7J **95**
Priory M. SW8 ...9J **75**
Priory M. Horn ...6F **50**
Priory Pk. SE3 ...2D **94**
Priory Pk. Rd. NW6 ...4K **57**
(in two parts)
Priory Pk. Rd. Wemb ...9E **38**
Priory Path. Romf ...3J **35**
Priory Pl. Dart ...5H **99**
Priory Pl. W on T ...5E **116**
Priory Rd. E6 ...4H **63**
Priory Rd. N8 ...2G **43**
Priory Rd. NW6 ...4M **57**
Priory Rd. SW19 ...4B **106**
Priory Rd. W4 ...4B **72**
Priory Rd. Bark ...3B **64**
Priory Rd. Chess ...5J **119**
Priory Rd. Croy ...2L **123**
Priory Rd. Hamp ...4K **101**
Priory Rd. Houn ...4A **86**
Priory Rd. Lou ...6J **19**
Priory Rd. Rich ...7L **71**
Priory Rd. Romf ...3J **35**
Priory Rd. Sutt ...6H **121**
Priory Rd. N. Dart ...3H **99**
Priory Rd. S. Dart ...5H **99**
Priory Shop. Cen. Dart ...5H **99**
Priory St. E3 ...6M **61**
Priory Ter. NW6 ...4M **57**
Priory Ter. Sun ...4E **100**
Priory, The. SE3 ...3D **94**
(in two parts)
Priory, The. Croy ...6L **123**
Priory Vw. Bus H ...9C **10**
Priory Vs. N11 ...6D **26**
(off Colney Hatch La.)
Priory Wlk. SW10 ...6A **74**
Priory Way. Harr ...2M **37**
Priory Way. S'hall ...4H **69**
Priory Way. W Dray ...7J **143**
Pritchard Ho. E2 ...5F **60**
(off Ada Pl.)
Pritchard's Rd. E2 ...4E **60**
Pritchett Clo. Enf ...1L **17**
Priter Rd. SE16 ...4E **76**
Priter Way. SE16 ...4E **76**
Private Rd. Enf ...7B **16**
Probert Rd. SW2 ...4L **91**
Probyn Ho. SW1 ...5H **75**
(off Page St.)
Probyn Rd. SW2 ...8M **91**
Procter Ho. SE1 ...6E **76**
(off Avondale Sq.)
Procter Ho. SE5 ...8B **76**
(off Picton St.)
Procter St. WC1 ...8K **59**
Proctor Clo. Mitc ...5E **106**
Proctors Clo. Felt ...7E **84**
Profumo Rd. W on T ...7H **117**
Progress Bus. Pk., The. Croy ...4K **123**
Progress Cen., The. N9 ...3C **28**
Progress Cen., The. Enf ...5H **17**
Progress Way. N22 ...8L **27**
Progress Way. Croy ...4K **123**
Progress Way. Enf ...7E **16**
Project Pk. E3 ...7B **62**
Promenade App. Rd. W4 ...8C **72**
Promenade de Verdun. Purl ...3H **137**
Promenade, The. W4 ...1C **88**
Promenade, The. Edgw ...5L **23**
Prospect Clo. SE26 ...1F **108**
Prospect Clo. Belv ...5L **81**
Prospect Clo. Houn ...9K **69**
Prospect Clo. Ruis ...5H **37**
Prospect Cotts. SW18 ...3L **89**
Prospect Cres. Twic ...5A **86**
Prospect Hill. E17 ...2M **45**
Prospect Ho. E17 ...1A **46**
(off Prospect Hill)
Prospect Ho. N1 ...5L **59**
(off Donegal St.)
Prospect Ho. SE1 ...4M **75**
(off Gaywood St.)
Prospect Ho. W10 ...9H **57**
(off Bridge Clo.)
Prospect Ho. Eps ...1M **133**
Prospect Pl. E1 ...2G **77**
(in two parts)
Prospect Pl. N2 ...2B **42**
Prospect Pl. N7 ...9J **43**
Prospect Pl. N17 ...7C **28**
Prospect Pl. NW2 ...8K **41**
Prospect Pl. NW3 ...9A **42**
Prospect Pl. SE8 ...7K **77**
(off Evelyn St.)
Prospect Pl. SW20 ...4F **104**
Prospect Pl. W4 ...6B **72**
Prospect Pl. Brom ...7F **110**
Prospect Pl. Dart ...5J **99**
Prospect Pl. Eps ...4C **134**
Prospect Pl. Romf ...9A **34**
Prospect Quay. SW18 ...3L **89**
(off Lightermans Wlk.)
Prospect Ring. N2 ...1B **42**
Prospect Rd. NW2 ...8K **41**
Prospect Rd. Barn ...6L **13**
Prospect Rd. Chesh ...2C **6**
Prospect Rd. Horn ...1K **51**
Prospect Rd. Surb ...1G **119**
Prospect Rd. Wfd G ...6G **31**
Prospect St. SE16 ...4F **76**
Prospect Va. SE18 ...5J **79**
Prospect Wharf. E1 ...1G **77**
Prospero Rd. N19 ...6H **43**
Protea Clo. E16 ...7D **62**
Protheroe Ho. N17 ...1D **44**
Prothero Gdns. NW4 ...3F **40**
Prothero Ho. NW10 ...3B **56**
Prothero Rd. SW6 ...8J **73**
Prout Gro. NW10 ...9C **40**
Prout Rd. E5 ...8F **44**
Provence St. N1 ...5A **60**
Providence Clo. E9 ...4H **61**
Providence Ct. W1 ...1E **74**
Providence La. Hay ...8B **68**
Providence Pl. N1 ...4M **59**
Providence Pl. Eps ...4C **134**
Providence Pl. Romf ...8K **33**
Providence Rd. W Dray ...2J **143**
Providence Row. N1 ...5K **59**
(off Pentonville Rd.)
Providence Row Clo. E2 ...6F **60**
Providence Sq. SE1 ...3E **76**
Providence Tower. SE16 ...3E **76**
(off Bermondsey Wall W.)
Providence Yd. E2 ...6E **60**
(off Ezra St.)
Provost Ct. NW3 ...2D **58**
(off Eton Rd.)
Provost Est. N1 ...5B **60**
(off Provost St.)
Provost Rd. NW3 ...3D **58**
Provost St. N1 ...5B **60**
Prowse Av. Bus H ...1A **22**
Prowse Pl. NW1 ...3G **59**
Proyers Path. Harr ...5F **38**
Pruden Clo. N14 ...2G **27**
Prudent Pas. EC2 ...9A **60**
(off King St.)
Prudhoe Ct. Dart ...5M **99**
(off Osbourne Rd.)
Prusom's Island. E1 ...2G **77**
(off Cinnamon St.)
Prusom St. E1 ...2F **76**
Pryor Clo. Ab L ...5D **4**
Pryors, The. NW3 ...8B **42**
Public Record Office. ...8M 71
Puck La. Wal A ...2L **7**
Pudding La. EC3 ...1B **76**
Pudding La. Chig ...1D **32**
Pudding Mill La. E15 ...4M **61**
Puddledock. ...2C 114
Puddle Dock. EC4 ...1M **75**
(in two parts)
Puddledock La. Dart ...2C **114**
Puffin Clo. Bark ...6F **64**
Puffin Clo. Beck ...9H **109**
Pugin Ct. N1 ...3L **59**
(off Liverpool Rd.)
Pulborough Ho. Romf ...7J **35**
(off Kingsbridge Cir.)
Pulborough Rd. SW18 ...6K **89**
Pulborough Way. Houn ...3G **85**
Pulford Rd. N15 ...4B **44**
Pulham Av. N2 ...2A **42**
Pulham Ho. SW8 ...8K **75**
(off Dorset Rd.)
Pullen's Bldgs. SE17 ...6M **75**
(off Iliffe St.)
Puller Rd. Barn ...4J **13**
Pulleyns Av. E6 ...6J **63**
Pullman Ct. SW2 ...7J **91**
Pullman Gdns. SW15 ...5G **89**
Pullman M. SE12 ...9F **94**
Pullman Pl. SE9 ...4J **95**
Pulross Rd. SW9 ...2K **91**
Pulteney Clo. E3 ...4K **61**
Pulteney Gdns. E18 ...1F **46**
Pulteney Rd. E18 ...1F **46**
Pulteney Ter. N1 ...4K **59**
(in two parts)
Pulton Ho. SE4 ...3J **93**
(off Turnham Rd.)
Pulton Pl. SW6 ...8L **73**
Puma Ct. E1 ...8D **60**
Pump All. Bren ...8H **71**
Pump Clo. N'holt ...5L **53**
Pump Ct. EC4 ...9L **59**
Pumphandle Path. N2 ...9B **26**
(off Oak La.)
Pump Hill. Lou ...4K **19**
Pump Ho. Clo. SE16 ...3G **77**
Pump Ho. Clo. Brom ...6C **110**
Pumping Sta. Rd. W4 ...8C **72**
Pump La. SE14 ...8G **77**
Pump La. Hay ...3E **68**
Pump La. Orp ...7M **129**
Pump La. Ind. Est. Hay ...3E **68**
Pump Pail N. Croy ...5A **124**
Pump Pail S. Croy ...5A **124**
Punderson's Gdns. E2 ...6F **60**
Punjab La. S'hall ...2K **69**
Purbeck Av. N Mald ...1D **120**
Purbeck Dri. NW2 ...7H **41**
Purbeck Ho. SW8 ...8K **75**
(off Bolney St.)
Purbeck Rd. Horn ...5E **50**
Purberry Gro. Eps ...2D **134**
Purbrock Av. Wat ...9G **5**
Purbrook Est. SE1 ...3C **76**
Purbrook St. SE1 ...4C **76**
Purcell Clo. Borwd ...3H **11**
Purcell Clo. Kenl ...6A **138**
Purcell Cres. SW6 ...8H **73**
Purcell Ho. SW10 ...7B **74**
(off Milman's St.)
Purcell Mans. W14 ...7J **73**
(off Queen's Club Gdns.)
Purcell M. NW10 ...3C **56**
Purcell Rd. Gnfd ...8M **53**
Purcell Room. ...2K 75
(off Waterloo Rd.)
Purcells Av. Edgw ...5L **23**
Purcell St. N1 ...5C **60**
Purchese St. NW1 ...5H **59**
Purdon Ho. SE15 ...9E **76**
(off Peckham High St.)
Purdy Ct. Wor Pk ...4E **120**
Purdy St. E3 ...7M **61**
Purelake M. SE13 ...2B **94**
(off Marischal Rd.)
Purfleet. ...6L 83
Purfleet By-Pass. Purf ...5M **83**
Purfleet Ind. Pk. Ave ...3K **83**
Purfleet Rd. Ave ...3L **83**
Purland Clo. Dag ...6K **49**
Purland Rd. SE28 ...3D **80**
Purleigh Av. Wfd G ...6J **31**
Purley. ...3L 137
Purley Av. NW2 ...7J **41**
Purley Bury Av. Purl ...3A **138**
Purley Bury Clo. Purl ...3A **138**
Purley Clo. Ilf ...9L **31**
Purley Cross (Junct.) ...4L 137
Purley Downs Rd. Purl ...2A **138**
Purley Hill. Purl ...4M **137**
Purley Knoll. Purl ...3K **137**
Purley Oaks Rd. S Croy ...1B **138**
Purley Pde. Purl ...3L **137**
Purley Pk. Rd. Purl ...2M **137**
Purley Pl. N1 ...3M **59**
Purley Ri. Purl ...4K **137**
Purley Rd. N9 ...3C **28**
Purley Rd. Purl ...3L **137**
Purley Rd. S Croy ...9B **124**
Purley Va. Purl ...5M **137**
Purley Vw. Ter. S Croy ...9B **124**
(off Sanderstead Rd.)
Purley Way. Croy ...2K **123**
Purley Way Cen., The. Croy ...4L **123**
Purley Way Corner. Croy ...2K **123**
Purley Way Cres. Croy ...2K **123**
Purlings Rd. Bush ...7M **9**
Purneys Rd. SE9 ...3H **95**
Purrett Rd. SE18 ...6D **80**
Purser Ho. SW2 ...5L **91**
(off Tulse Hill)
Pursers Cross Rd. SW6 ...9K **73**
(in two parts)
Purse Wardens Clo. W13 ...2G **71**
Pursley Gdns. Borwd ...2L **11**
Pursley Rd. NW7 ...7F **24**
Purves Rd. NW10 ...6F **56**

Pusey Ho.—Questor

Pusey Ho. E14 . . . 9L 61
(off Saracen St.)
Puteaux Ho. E2 . . . 5H 61
(off Mace St.)
Putney. . . . 3J 89
Putney Bri. SW15 & SW6 . . . 2J 89
Putney Bri. App. SW6 . . . 2J 89
Putney Bri. Rd.
SW15 & SW18 . . . 3J 89
Putney Comn. SW15 . . . 2G 89
Putney Exchange Shop. Cen.
SW15 . . . 3H 89
Putney Gdns. Chad H . . . 3F 48
Putney Heath. . . . 5G 89
Putney Heath. SW15 . . . 6F 88
Putney Heath La. SW15 . . . 5H 89
Putney High St. SW15 . . . 3H 89
Putney Hill. SW15 . . . 6H 89
(in two parts)
Putney Pk. Av. SW15 . . . 3E 88
Putney Pk. La. SW15 . . . 3F 88
(in two parts)
Putney Rd. Enf . . . 9D 6
Putney Vale. . . . 9E 88
Putney Vale Crematorium.
SW15 . . . 8E 88
Puttenham Clo. Wat . . . 2G 21
Pycroft Way. N9 . . . 4D 28
Pyecombe Corner. N12 . . . 4K 25
Pylbrook Rd. Sutt . . . 5L 121
Pylon Trad. Est. E16 . . . 7C 62
Pylon Way. Croy . . . 3J 123
Pym Clo. E Barn . . . 7B 14
Pymers Mead. SE21 . . . 7A 92
Pymmes Brook Ho. N10 . . . 7E 26
Pymmes Clo. N13 . . . 5K 27
Pymmes Clo. N17 . . . 8F 28
Pymmes Gdns. N. N9 . . . 3D 28
Pymmes Gdns. S. N9 . . . 3D 28
Pymmes Grn. Rd. N11 . . . 4F 26
Pymmes Rd. N13 . . . 6J 27
Pymms Brook Dri. Barn . . . 6C 14
Pyne Rd. Surb . . . 3L 119
Pynest Grn. La. Wal A . . . 2E 18
Pynfolds. SE16 . . . 3F 76
Pynham Clo. SE2 . . . 4F 80
Pynnacles Clo. Stan . . . 5F 22
Pynnersmead. SE24 . . . 4A 92
Pyramid Ho. Houn . . . 1J 85
Pyrcroft La. Wey . . . 7A 116
Pyrford Ho. SW9 . . . 3M 91
Pyrland Rd. N5 . . . 1B 60
Pyrland Rd. Rich . . . 5K 87
Pyrles Grn. Lou . . . 3M 19
Pyrles La. Lou . . . 4M 19
Pyrmont Gro. SE27 . . . 9M 91
Pyrmont Rd. W4 . . . 7L 71
Pytchley Cres. SE19 . . . 3A 108
Pytchley Rd. SE22 . . . 2C 92

Q

Quadrangle Clo. SE1 . . . 5C 76
Quadrangle, The. SE24 . . . 4A 92
Quadrangle, The. SW6 . . . 8J 73
Quadrangle, The. SW10 . . . 9A 74
Quadrangle, The. W2 . . . 9C 58
Quadrangle, The. W12 . . . 9F 56
(off Du Cane Rd.)
Quadrangle, The. Stan . . . 7G 23
Quadrant Arc. W1 . . . 1G 75
(off Regent St.)
Quadrant Arc. Romf . . . 3C 50
Quadrant Clo. NW4 . . . 3F 40
Quadrant Gro. NW5 . . . 1D 58
Quadrant Ho. SE1 . . . 2M 75
(off Burrell St.)
Quadrant Rd. Rich . . . 3H 87
Quadrant Rd. T Hth . . . 8M 107
Quadrant, The. NW4 . . . 2G 41
Quadrant, The. SW20 . . . 5J 105
Quadrant, The. W10 . . . 6H 57
Quadrant, The. Bexh . . . 8H 81
Quadrant, The. Edgw . . . 6L 23
Quadrant, The. Eps . . . 5C 134
Quadrant, The. Harr . . . 1B 38
Quadrant, The. Purf . . . 5M 83
Quadrant, The. Rich . . . 3H 87
Quadrant, The. Sutt . . . 8A 122
Quad Rd. Wemb . . . 8H 39
Quaggy Wlk. SE3 . . . 3E 94
Quail Gdns. S Croy . . . 2J 139
Quain Mans. W14 . . . 7J 73
(off Queen's Club Gdns.)
Quainton St. NW10 . . . 8B 40
Quaker Ct. E1 . . . 7D 60
(off Quaker St.)
Quaker Ct. EC1 . . . 7A 60
(off Banner St.)
Quaker La. S'hall . . . 4L 69
Quaker La. Wal A . . . 7J 7
Quakers Course. NW9 . . . 8D 24
Quakers La. Iswth . . . 8E 70
(in three parts)
Quakers Pl. E7 . . . 1H 63
Quaker St. E1 . . . 7D 60
Quakers Wlk. N21 . . . 8B 16
Quality Ct. WC2 . . . 9L 59
(off Chancery La.)
Quantock Clo. Hay . . . 8B 68
Quantock Dri. Wor Pk . . . 4G 121
Quantock Gdns. NW2 . . . 7H 41
Quantock Ho. N16 . . . 6D 44
Quantock Rd. Bexh . . . 1C 98
Quarles Clo. Romf . . . 7L 33
Quarley Way. SE15 . . . 8D 76
Quarrendon St. SW6 . . . 1L 89
Quarr Rd. Cars . . . 1B 122
Quarry M. Purf . . . 5L 83
Quarry Pk. Rd. Sutt . . . 8K 121
Quarry Ri. Sutt . . . 8K 121
Quarry Rd. SW18 . . . 5A 90
Quarterdeck, The. E14 . . . 3L 77
Quarter Mile La. E10 . . . 9M 45
Quastel Ho. SE1 . . . 3B 76
(off Long La.)
Quatre Ports. E4 . . . 5B 30
Quay Ho. E14 . . . 3L 77
(off Admirals Way)
Quayside Cotts. E1 . . . 2E 76
(off Mew St.)
Quayside Ct. SE16 . . . 2H 77
(off Abbotshade Rd.)
Quayside Ho. E14 . . . 2K 77
Quay Vw. Apartments.
E14 . . . 4L 77
(off Arden Cres.)
Quebec M. W1 . . . 9D 58
Quebec Rd. Hay . . . 9G 53
Quebec Rd. Ilf . . . 5M 47
Quebec Way. SE16 . . . 3H 77
Quebec Way Ind. Est.
SE16 . . . 3J 77
Quedgeley Ct. SE15 . . . 7D 76
(off Ebley Clo.)
Queen Adelaide Ct. SE20 . . . 3G 109
Queen Adelaide Rd.
SE20 . . . 3G 109
Queen Alexandra Mans.
WC1 . . . 6J 59
(off Bidborough St.)
Queen Alexandra's Ct.
SW19 . . . 2K 105
Queen Alexandra's Way.
Eps . . . 3L 133
Queen Anne Av. Brom . . . 7D 110
Queen Anne Dri. Clay . . . 9C 118
Queen Anne Ho. E16 . . . 2E 78
(off Hardy Av.)
Queen Anne M. W1 . . . 8F 58
Queen Anne Rd. E9 . . . 2H 61
Queen Anne's Clo. Twic . . . 9B 86
Queen Anne's Ct. SE10 . . . 6B 78
(off Park Row)
Queen Anne's Gdns. W4 . . . 4C 72
Queen Anne's Gdns. W5 . . . 3J 71
Queen Anne's Gdns. Enf . . . 8C 16
Queen Anne's Gdns.
Mitc . . . 7D 106
Queen Anne's Ga. SW1 . . . 3H 75
Queen Anne's Ga. Bexh . . . 2H 97
Queen Anne's Gro. W4 . . . 4C 72
Queen Anne's Gro. W5 . . . 3J 71
Queen Anne's Gro. Enf . . . 9B 16
Queen Anne's Pl. Enf . . . 8C 16
Queen Anne St. W1 . . . 9F 58
Queen Anne's Wlk. WC1 . . . 7J 59
(off Queen Sq.)
Queen Anne Ter. E1 . . . 1F 76
(off Sovereign Clo.)
Queenborough Gdns.
Chst . . . 3B 112
Queenborough Gdns. Ilf . . . 2L 47
Queen Caroline St. W6 . . . 6G 73
(in two parts)
Queen Catherine Ho.
SW6 . . . 8M 73
(off Wandon Rd.)
Queen Charlotte's Cottage.
. . . 1H 87
Queen Elizabeth Bldgs.
EC4 . . . 1L 75
(off Middle Temple La.)
Queen Elizabeth Ct.
High Bar . . . 5K 13
Queen Elizabeth Gdns.
Mord . . . 8L 105
Queen Elizabeth Hall. . . . 2K 75
Queen Elizabeth Ho.
SW12 . . . 6E 90
Queen Elizabeth II
Conference Cen. . . . 3H 75
Queen Elizabeth Rd.
E17 . . . 1J 45
Queen Elizabeth Rd.
King T . . . 6K 103
Queen Elizabeth's Clo.
N16 . . . 7B 44
Queen Elizabeth's College.
SE10 . . . 8A 78
Queen Elizabeth's Dri.
N14 . . . 1J 27
Queen Elizabeth's Dri.
New Ad . . . 1B 140
Queen Elizabeth's Gdns.
New Ad . . . 2B 140
Queen Elizabeth St. SE1 . . . 3C 76
Queen Elizabeth's Wlk.
N16 . . . 6B 44
Queen Elizabeth's Wlk.
Wall . . . 6H 123
Queen Elizabeth Wlk.
SW13 . . . 9E 72
(in two parts)
Queengate Ct. N12 . . . 5M 25
Queenhill Rd. S Croy . . . 2F 138
Queenhithe. EC4 . . . 1A 76
Queen Isabella Way. EC1 . . . 9M 59
(off King Edward St.)
Queen Margaret Flats. E2 . . . 6F 60
(off St Jude's Rd.)
Queen Margaret's Gro. N1 . . . 1C 60
Queen Mary Av. Mord . . . 9H 105
Queen Mary Clo. Romf . . . 4D 50
Queen Mary Clo. Surb . . . 5M 119
Queen Mary Ho. E16 . . . 2F 78
(off Wesley Av.)
Queen Mary Rd. SE19 . . . 3M 107
Queen Mary Rd. Shep . . . 6A 100
Queen Mary's Av. Cars . . . 9D 122
Queen Mary's Av. Wat . . . 6C 8
Queen Marys Bldgs. SW1 . . . 5G 75
(off Stillington St.)
Queen Mary's Ct. SE10 . . . 7B 78
(off Park Row)
Queen Marys Ct. Wal A . . . 9J 7
Queen Mary Works. Wat . . . 6C 8
Queen of Denmark Ct.
SE16 . . . 4K 77
Queens Acre. Sutt . . . 9H 121
Queens Av. N3 . . . 7A 26
Queens Av. N10 . . . 1E 42
Queens Av. N20 . . . 2B 26
Queens Av. N21 . . . 1M 27
Queens Av. Felt . . . 1G 101
Queen's Av. Gnfd . . . 9M 53
Queens Av. Stan . . . 1G 39
Queen's Av. Wat . . . 6D 8
Queen's Av. Wfd G . . . 5F 30
Queensberry M. W. SW7 . . . 5B 74
Queensberry Pl. E12 . . . 1H 63
Queensberry Pl. SW7 . . . 5B 74
Queensberry Way. SW7 . . . 5B 74
Queensborough Ct. NW11 . . . 2K 41
(off N. Circular Rd.)
Queensborough M. W2 . . . 1A 74
Queensborough Pas. W2 . . . 1A 74
(off Queensborough M.)
Queensborough Studios.
W2 . . . 1A 74
(off Queensborough M.)
Queensborough Ter. W2 . . . 1M 73
Queensbridge Ct. E2 . . . 4D 60
(off Queensbridge Rd.)
Queensbridge Pk. Iswth . . . 4C 86
Queensbridge Rd.
E8 & E2 . . . 2D 60
Queensbury. . . . 1J 39
Queensbury Circ. Pde.
Harr . . . 1J 39
Queensbury Ho. Rich . . . 4G 87
Queensbury Rd. NW9 . . . 5B 40
Queensbury Rd. Wemb . . . 5K 55
Queensbury Sta. Pde.
Edgw . . . 1K 39
Queensbury St. N1 . . . 3A 60
Queen's Cir. SW8 . . . 8F 74
Queens Clo. Edgw . . . 5L 23
Queen's Clo. Esh . . . 6M 117
Queens Clo. Wall . . . 7F 122
Queen's Club Gdns. W14 . . . 7J 73
Queen's Club (Tennis) . . . 6J 73
Queens Ct. NW6 . . . 1M 57
Queen's Ct. NW8 . . . 5B 58
(off Queen's Ter.)
Queens Ct. NW11 . . . 3K 41
Queens Ct. SE23 . . . 8F 92
Queens Ct. W2 . . . 1M 73
(off Queensway)
Queen's Ct. Belm . . . 3L 135
Queens Ct. Rich . . . 5K 87
Queens Ct. S Croy . . . 7A 124
(off Warham Rd.)
Queen's Ct. Wat . . . 5G 9
(off Queen's Rd.)
Queens Ct. W'stone . . . 9F 22
Queenscourt. Wemb . . . 9J 39
Queens Ct. Wey . . . 7B 116
Queen's Cres. NW5 . . . 2E 58
Queen's Cres. Rich . . . 4K 87
Queenscroft Rd. SE9 . . . 4H 95
Queensdale Cres. W11 . . . 2H 73
Queensdale Pl. W11 . . . 2J 73
Queensdale Rd. W11 . . . 2H 73
Queensdale Wlk. W11 . . . 2J 73
Queensdown Rd. E5 . . . 9F 44
Queens Dri. E10 . . . 5L 45
Queen's Dri. N4 . . . 7M 43
Queens Dri. W5 & W3 . . . 9K 55
Queens Dri. Ab L . . . 5D 4
Queen's Dri. Oxs . . . 3A 132
Queen's Dri. Surb . . . 2L 119
Queen's Dri. Th Dit . . . 1E 118
Queen's Dri. Wal X . . . 7G 7
Queen's Elm Pde. SW3 . . . 6B 74
(off Old Church St.)
Queen's Elm Sq. SW3 . . . 6B 74
Queens Ferry Wlk. N17 . . . 2F 44
Queensfield Ct. Sutt . . . 6G 121
Queens Gallery. . . . 3F 74
Queen's Gdns. NW4 . . . 3G 41
Queen's Gdns. W2 . . . 1A 74
Queen's Gdns. W5 . . . 7G 55
Queens Gdns. Dart . . . 7M 99
Queen's Gdns. Houn . . . 9J 69
Queen's Gdns. Rain . . . 5B 66
Queen's Ga. SW7 . . . 3A 74
Queensgate. Wal X . . . 7F 6
Queen's Ga. Gdns. SW7 . . . 4A 74
Queens Ga. Gdns. SW15 . . . 3F 88
Queensgate Gdns. Chst . . . 5B 112
Queen's Ga. M. SW7 . . . 4A 74
Queensgate Pl. NW6 . . . 3L 57
Queen's Ga. Pl. SW7 . . . 4A 74
Queen's Ga. Pl. M. SW7 . . . 4A 74
Queen's Ga. Ter. SW7 . . . 4A 74
Queens Ga. Vs. E9 . . . 3J 61
Queen's Gro. NW8 . . . 4B 58
Queens Gro. Rd. E4 . . . 1B 30
Queen's Gro. Studios.
NW8 . . . 4B 58
Queen's Head Pas. EC4 . . . 9A 60
Queen's Head St. N1 . . . 4M 59
Queen's Head Yd. SE1 . . . 2B 76
(off Borough High St.)
Queens Ho. SW8 . . . 8J 75
(off S. Lambeth Rd.)
Queens Ho. Tedd . . . 3D 102
Queen's House, The. . . . 7B 78
(off National Maritime Mus.)
Queen's Ice Club. . . . 1M 73
(off Queensway)
Queen's Keep. Twic . . . 5G 87
Queensland Av. N18 . . . 6A 28
Queensland Av. SW19 . . . 5M 105
Queensland Ho. E16 . . . 2L 79
(off Rymill St.)
Queensland Pl. N7 . . . 9L 43
Queensland Rd. N7 . . . 9L 43
Queens La. N10 . . . 1F 42
Queens La. Ashf . . . 9D 144
Queen's Mans. W6 . . . 5H 73
(off Brook Grn.)
Queen's Mkt. E13 . . . 4G 63
Queensmead. NW8 . . . 4B 58
Queensmead. Oxs . . . 3A 132
Queensmead Av. Eps . . . 2F 134
Queen's Mead Rd. Brom . . . 6D 110
Queensmere Clo. SW19 . . . 8H 89
Queensmere Ct. SW13 . . . 8D 72
Queensmere Rd. SW19 . . . 8H 89
Queen's M. W2 . . . 1M 73
(in two parts)
Queensmill Rd. SW6 . . . 8H 73
Queens Pde. N8 . . . 2M 43
Queen's Pde. N11 . . . 5D 26
(off Friern Barnet Rd.)
Queen's Pde. NW2 . . . 2G 57
(off Walm La.)
Queens Pde. NW4 . . . 3G 41
(off Queens Rd.)
Queens Pde. W5 . . . 9K 55
Queens Pde. Clo. N11 . . . 5D 26
Queen's Pk. Ct. W10 . . . 6H 57
Queen's Pk. Gdns. Felt . . . 9D 84
Queen's Pk. Rangers F.C.
(Loftus Rd.). . . . 2F 72
Queen's Pk. Rd. Romf . . . 8L 35
Queens Pas. Chst . . . 3M 111
Queens Pl. Mord . . . 8L 105
Queens Pl. Wat . . . 5G 9
Queen's Promenade.
King T . . . 8H 103
Queen Sq. WC1 . . . 7J 59
Queen Sq. Pl. WC1 . . . 7J 59
(off Queen Sq.)
Queen's Quay. EC4 . . . 1A 76
(off Up. Thames St.)
Queens Reach. E Mol . . . 8C 102
Queens Reach. King T . . . 6H 103
Queens Ride.
SW13 & SW15 . . . 2E 88
Queens Ri. Rich . . . 5K 87
Queens Rd. E11 . . . 5B 46
Queens Rd. E13 . . . 4F 62
Queens Rd. E17 . . . 4K 45
Queens Rd. N3 . . . 8A 26
Queens Rd. N9 . . . 3F 28
Queens Rd. N11 . . . 7J 27
Queens Rd. NW4 . . . 3G 41
Queen's Rd. SE15 & SE14 . . . 9F 76
Queen's Rd. SW14 . . . 2B 88
Queens Rd. SW19 . . . 3K 105
Queens Rd. W5 . . . 9J 55
Queens Rd. Bark . . . 2A 64
Queens Rd. Barn . . . 5H 13
Queens Rd. Beck . . . 6J 109
Queens Rd. Brom . . . 6E 110
Queens Rd. Buck H . . . 2F 30
Queens Rd. Chst . . . 3M 111
Queens Rd. Croy . . . 1M 123
Queen's Rd. Enf . . . 6C 16
Queen's Rd. Eri . . . 7C 82
Queen's Rd. Felt . . . 7F 84
Queen's Rd. Hamp H . . . 1M 101
Queen's Rd. Hay . . . 9C 52
Queen's Rd. Houn . . . 2M 85
Queen's Rd. King T . . . 4L 103
Queen's Rd. Lou . . . 5J 19
Queens Rd. Mord . . . 8L 105
Queens Rd. N Mald . . . 8D 104
Queen's Rd. Rich . . . 6K 87
Queens Rd. S'hall . . . 3H 69
Queen's Rd. Sutt . . . 2L 135
Queen's Rd. Tedd . . . 3D 102
Queen's Rd. Th Dit . . . 9D 102
Queens Rd. Twic . . . 7E 86
Queen's Rd. Uxb . . . 6A 142
Queens Rd. Wall . . . 7F 122
Queen's Rd. Wal X . . . 6E 6
Queen's Rd. Wat . . . 5G 9
(in three parts)
Queen's Rd. Well . . . 1E 96
Queens Rd. W Dray . . . 3K 143
Queen's Rd.
Wey & W on T . . . 6A 116
Queens Rd. W. E13 . . . 5E 62
Queen's Row. SE17 . . . 7B 76
Queens Ter. E1 . . . 7G 61
Queen's Ter. E13 . . . 4F 62
Queen's Ter. NW8 . . . 4B 58
Queens Ter. Iswth . . . 3E 86
Queen's Ter. Cotts. W7 . . . 3C 70
Queens Theatre. . . . 6H 51
(Hornchurch)
Queen's Theatre. . . . 1H 75
(off Shaftesbury Av.,
Westminster)
Queensthorpe Rd. SE26 . . . 1H 109
Queenstown Gdns. Rain . . . 6D 66
Queenstown M. SW11 . . . 1F 90
Queenstown Rd. SW8 . . . 7F 74
Queen St. EC4 . . . 1A 76
(in two parts)
Queen St. N17 . . . 6C 28
Queen St. W1 . . . 2F 74
Queen St. Bexh . . . 2K 97
Queen St. Croy . . . 6A 124
Queen St. Eri . . . 7C 82
Queen St. Romf . . . 4B 50
Queen St. Pl. EC4 . . . 1A 76
Queensville Rd. SW12 . . . 6H 91
Queens Wlk. E4 . . . 1B 30
Queens Wlk. NW9 . . . 7A 40
Queen's Wlk. SW1 . . . 2G 75
Queen's Wlk. W5 . . . 7G 55
Queen's Wlk. Ashf . . . 9B 144
Queens Wlk. Harr . . . 2C 38
Queens Wlk. Ruis . . . 7G 37
Queens Wlk. Ter. Ruis . . . 8G 37
Queen's Wlk., The. SE1 . . . 1L 75
(Barge Ho. St.)
Queen's Wlk., The. SE1 . . . 2C 76
(Morgan's La.)
Queen's Wlk., The. SE1 . . . 2K 75
(Waterloo Rd.)
Queen's Way. NW4 . . . 3G 41
Queensway. W2 . . . 9M 57
Queensway. Croy . . . 8K 123
Queensway. Enf . . . 6F 16
Queens Way. Felt . . . 1G 101
Queensway. Orp . . . 9A 112
Queensway. Sun . . . 6F 100
Queens Way. Wal X . . . 7F 6
Queensway. W Wick . . . 5C 126
Queensway Bus. Cen. Enf . . . 6G 16
Queensway Ind. Est. Enf . . . 6G 17
Queensway N. W on T . . . 6G 117
(in two parts)
Queensway S. W on T . . . 7G 117
(in two parts)
Queenswell Av. N20 . . . 3C 26
Queens Wharf. W6 . . . 6G 73
Queenswood Av. E17 . . . 8A 30
Queenswood Av. Hamp . . . 3M 101
Queenswood Av. Houn . . . 1K 85
Queenswood Av. T Hth . . . 9L 107
Queenswood Av. Wall . . . 6H 123
Queenswood Ct. SE27 . . . 1B 108
Queenswood Ct. SW4 . . . 4J 91
Queenswood Cres. Wat . . . 6E 4
Queenswood Gdns. E11 . . . 6F 46
Queenswood Pk. N3 . . . 9J 25
Queens Wood Rd. N10 . . . 4F 42
Queenswood Rd. SE23 . . . 9H 93
Queenswood Rd. Sidc . . . 4D 96
Queen's Yd. W1 . . . 8G 59
Queen Victoria (Junct.) . . . 5G 121
Queen Victoria Av. Wemb . . . 3H 55
Queen Victoria Memorial.
. . . 3G 75
Queen Victoria Seaman's Rest. E14
9M 61
(off E. India Dock Rd.)
Queen Victoria St. EC4 . . . 1M 75
Queen Victoria Ter. E1 . . . 1F 76
(off Sovereign Clo.)
Quemerford Rd. N7 . . . 1K 59
Quendon Dri. Wal A . . . 6K 7
Quendon Ho. W10 . . . 7G 57
(off Sutton Way)
Quenington Ct. SE15 . . . 7D 76
Quentin Ho. SE1 . . . 3L 75
(off Gray St., in two parts)
Quentin Pl. SE13 . . . 2C 94
Quentin Rd. SE3 . . . 2C 94
Quentins Dri. Berr G . . . 8M 141
Quernmore Clo. Brom . . . 3E 110
Quernmore Rd. N4 . . . 4L 43
Quernmore Rd. Brom . . . 3E 110
Querrin St. SW6 . . . 1A 90
Quested Ct. E8 . . . 1F 60
(off Brett Rd.)
Questor. Dart . . . 8J 99

Quex M.—Ravensbourne Rd.

Quex M. NW6 4L 57
Quex Rd. NW6 4L 57
Quick Rd. W4 6C 72
Quicks Rd. SW19 4M 105
Quick St. N1 5M 59
Quick St. M. N1 5M 59
Quickswood. NW3 3C 58
Quiet Nook. Brom 5H 127
Quill La. SW15 3H 89
Quillot, The. W on T 7D 116
Quill St. N4 8L 43
Quill St. W5 5J 55
Quilp St. SE1 3A 76
(in two parts)
Quilter Gdns. Orp 3G 129
Quilter Ho. W10 6K 57
(off Dart St.)
Quilter Rd. Orp 3G 129
Quilter St. E2 6E 60
Quilter St. SE18 6D 80
Quilting Ct. SE16 3H 77
(off Garter Way)
Quinta Dri. Barn 7F 12
Quintin Av. SW20 5K 105
Quintin Clo. Pinn 2F 36
Quinton Clo. Beck 7A 110
Quinton Clo. Houn 8F 68
Quinton Clo. Wall 6F 122
Quinton Ho. SW8 8J 75
(off Wyvil Rd.)
Quinton Rd. Th Dit 3E 118
Quinton St. SW18 8A 90
Quixley St. E14 1B 78
Quorn Rd. SE22 3C 92

R

Rabbit La. W on T 9E 116
Rabbit Row. W8 2L 73
Rabbits Rd. E12 9J 47
Rabbs Mill Ho. Uxb 5A 142
Rabournmead Dri. N'holt 1J 53
Raby Rd. N Mald 8B 104
Raby St. E14 9J 61
Raccoon Way. Houn 1G 85
Rachel Clo. Ilf 1B 48
Rachel Point. E5 9E 44
Racine. SE5 9C 76
(off Peckham Rd.)
Rackham M. SW16 3G 107
Rackman Clo. Well 1F 96
Rackstraw Ho. NW3 3D 58
Racton Rd. SW6 7L 73
R.A.D.A. 8H 59
(off Chenies St.)
R.A.D.A. 8H 59
(off Gower St.)
Radbourne Av. W5 5G 71
Radbourne Clo. E5 9H 45
Radbourne Ct. Harr 4F 38
Radbourne Cres. E17 9B 30
Radbourne Rd. SW12 6G 91
Radcliffe Av. NW10 5E 56
Radcliffe Av. Enf 3A 16
Radcliffe Gdns. Cars 1C 136
Radcliffe Ho. SE16 5F 76
(off Anchor St.)
Radcliffe M. Hamp H 2A 102
Radcliffe Path. SW8 1F 90
Radcliffe Rd. N21 1M 27
Radcliffe Rd. SE1 4C 76
Radcliffe Rd. Croy 4D 124
Radcliffe Rd. Harr 9E 22
Radcliffe Sq. SW15 5H 89
Radcliffe Way. N'holt 6H 53
Radcot Point. SE23 9H 93
Radcot St. SE11 6L 75
Raddington Rd. W10 8J 57
Radfield Way. Sidc 6B 96
(in two parts)
Radford Ho. E14 8M 61
(off St Leonard's Rd.)
Radford Ho. N7 1K 59
Radford Rd. SE13 5A 94
Radford Way. Bark 6D 64
Radipole Rd. SW6 9K 73
Radius Pk. Felt 3D 84
Radland Rd. E16 9D 62
Radlet Av. SE26 9F 92
Radlett Clo. E7 2D 62
Radlett Pl. NW8 4C 58
Radlett Rd. A'ham 2M 9
Radlett Rd. Wat 5G 9
Radley Av. Ilf 9E 48
Radley Clo. Felt 7D 84
Radley Ct. SE16 3H 77
Radley Gdns. Harr 2J 39
Radley Ho. NW1 7D 58
(off Gloucester Pl.)
Radley Ho. SE2 3H 81
(off Wolvercote Rd.)
Radley M. W8 4L 73
Radley Rd. N17 9C 28
Radley's La. E18 9E 30
Radleys Mead. Dag 2M 65
Radley Sq. E5 7G 45
Radley Ter. E16 8D 62
(off Hermit Rd.)
Radlix Rd. E10 6L 45
Radnor Av. Harr 3C 38
Radnor Av. Well 4F 96
Radnor Clo. Chst 3C 112
Radnor Clo. Mitc 8J 107
Radnor Ct. W7 9D 54
(off Copley Clo.)
Radnor Ct. Har W 8D 22
Radnor Cres. SE18 8E 80
Radnor Cres. Ilf 3K 47
Radnor Gdns. Enf 3C 16
Radnor Gdns. Twic 8D 86
Radnor Gro. Uxb 5E 142
Radnor Hall Mobile Homes. Borwd 7J 11
Radnor M. W2 9B 58
Radnor Pl. W2 9C 58
Radnor Rd. NW6 4J 57
Radnor Rd. SE15 8E 76
Radnor Rd. Harr 3B 38
Radnor Rd. Twic 7D 86
Radnor St. EC1 6A 60
Radnor Ter. W14 5K 73
Radnor Ter. Sutt 9L 121
Radnor Wlk. E14 5L 77
(off Barnsdale Av.)
Radnor Wlk. SW3 6C 74
Radnor Wlk. Croy 1J 125
Radnor Way. NW10 7M 55
Radstock Av. Harr 1E 38
Radstock Clo. N11 6E 26
Radstock Ho. H Hill 5H 35
(off Darlington Gdns.)
Radstock St. SW11 8C 74
(in two parts)
Raebarn Gdns. Barn 7F 12
Raeburn Av. Dart 4F 98
Raeburn Av. Surb 3M 119
Raeburn Clo. NW11 4A 42
Raeburn Clo. King T 4H 103
Raeburn Ho. N'holt 5H 53
(off Academy Gdns.)
Raeburn Rd. Edgw 8L 23
Raeburn Rd. Hay 5B 52
Raeburn Rd. Sidc 5C 96
Raeburn St. SW2 3J 91
Raffles Ct. NW4 2F 40
Raffles St. E15 3B 62
Rafford Way. Brom 6F 110
R.A.F. Mus. Hendon. 9E 24
R.A.F. Northolt. 2D 52
Ragged School Mus. 8J 61
Raggleswood. Chst 5L 111
Raglan Av. Wal X 7D 6
Raglan Clo. Houn 4K 85
Raglan Ct. SE12 4E 94
Raglan Ct. S Croy 7M 123
Raglan Ct. Wemb 9K 39
Raglan Gdns. Wat 1F 20
Raglan Rd. E17 3A 46
Raglan Rd. SE18 6M 79
Raglan Rd. Belv 5K 81
Raglan Rd. Brom 8G 111
Raglan Rd. Enf 9D 16
Raglan St. NW5 2F 58
Raglan Ter. Harr 9M 37
Raglan Way. N'holt 2A 54
Ragley Clo. W3 3A 72
Raider Clo. Romf 8L 33
Railey M. NW5 1G 59
Railpit La. Warl 7C 140
Railshead Rd. Iswth 3F 86
Railton Rd. SE24 3L 91
Railway App. N4 4L 43
Railway App. SE1 2B 76
Railway App. Harr 2D 38
Railway App. Twic 6E 86
Railway App. Wall 7F 122
Railway Arches. E7 9E 46
(off Winchelsea Rd.)
Railway Arches. E10 5M 45
(off Capworth St.)
Railway Arches. E11 7C 46
(off Leytonstone High Rd.)
Railway Arches. E11 6B 46
(off Sidings, The)
Railway Arches. E17 3L 45
(off Yunus Khan Clo.)
Railway Arches. W12 3G 73
(off Shepherd's Bush Mkt.)
Railway Av. SE16 3G 77
(in two parts)
Railway Children Wlk. Brom 8E 94
Railway Cotts. SW19 1M 105
Railway Cotts. W6 3G 73
(off Sulgrave Rd.)
Railway Cotts. Borwd 6L 11
(off Station Rd.)
Railway Cotts. Twic 5L 85
Railway Cotts. Wat 3F 8
Railway Gro. SE14 8K 77
Railway M. E3 6L 61
(off Wellington Way)
Railway M. W11 9J 57
Railway Mus. 3L 79
Railway Pas. Tedd 3E 102
Railway Pl. SW19 3K 105
Railway Pl. Belv 4L 81
Railway Ri. SE22 3C 92
Railway Rd. Tedd 1C 102
Railway Rd. Wal X 6F 6
Railway Side. SW13 2C 88
(in two parts)
Railway St. N1 5J 59
Railway St. Romf 5G 49
Railway Ter. E17 8A 30
Railway Ter. SE13 4M 93
Railway Ter. Coul 7H 137
(off Station App.)
Railway Ter. Felt 7E 84
Rainborough Clo. NW10 2A 56
Rainbow Av. E14 6M 77
Rainbow Ct. SE14 7J 77
(off Chipley St.)
Rainbow Ct. Wat 8G 9
Rainbow Ind. Est. W Dray 1H 143
Rainbow Quay. SE16 4J 77
(in two parts)
Rainbow St. SE5 8C 76
Rainer Clo. Chesh 2D 6
Raine St. E1 2F 76
Rainham. 7E 66
Rainham Clo. SE9 5C 96
Rainham Clo. SW11 5C 90
Rainham Hall. 7E 66
Rainham Ho. NW1 4G 59
(off Bayham Pl.)
Rainham Rd. NW10 6G 57
Rainham Rd. Horn 1D 66
Rainham Rd. N. Dag 7L 49
Rainham Rd. S. Dag 9M 49
Rainham Trad. Est. Rain 7D 66
Rainhill Way. E3 6L 61
(in two parts)
Rainsborough Av. SE8 5J 77
Rainsford Clo. Stan 4G 23
Rainsford Rd. NW10 5M 55
(in two parts)
Rainsford St. W2 9C 58
Rainsford Way. Horn 6E 50
Rainton Rd. SE7 6E 78
Rainville Rd. W6 7G 73
Raisins Hill. Pinn 1G 37
Raith Av. N14 3H 27
Raleana Rd. E14 2A 78
Raleigh Av. Hay 8F 52
Raleigh Av. Wall 6H 123
Raleigh Clo. NW4 3G 41
Raleigh Clo. Eri 7D 82
Raleigh Clo. Pinn 5H 37
Raleigh Clo. Ruis 7D 36
Raleigh Ct. SE16 2H 77
(off Clarence M.)
Raleigh Ct. W12 3G 73
(off Scott's Rd.)
Raleigh Ct. W13 8F 54
Raleigh Ct. Beck 5M 109
Raleigh Ct. Eri 8D 82
Raleigh Ct. Wall 8F 122
Raleigh Dri. N20 3C 26
Raleigh Dri. Clay 7B 118
Raleigh Dri. Surb 3A 120
Raleigh Gdns. SW2 5K 91
Raleigh Gdns. Mitc 7D 106
(in two parts)
Raleigh Ho. E14 3M 77
(off Admirals Way)
Raleigh Ho. SW1 7H 75
(off Dolphin Sq.)
Raleigh M. N1 4M 59
(off Packington St.)
Raleigh M. Orp 7D 128
Raleigh Rd. N2 9C 26
Raleigh Rd. N8 2L 43
Raleigh Rd. SE20 4H 109
Raleigh Rd. Enf 6B 16
Raleigh Rd. Felt 9D 84
Raleigh Rd. Rich 2K 87
Raleigh Rd. S'hall 6J 69
Raleigh St. N1 4M 59
Raleigh Way. N14 1H 27
Raleigh Way. Felt 2G 101
Ralph Brook Ct. N1 6B 60
(off Chart St.)
Ralph Ct. W2 9M 57
(off Queensway)
Ralph Perring Ct. Beck 8L 109
Ralston St. SW3 6D 74
Ralston Way. Wat 2H 21
Ramac Ind. Est. SE7 5F 78
Rama Clo. SW16 4J 107
Rama Ct. Harr 7C 38
Ramac Way. SE7 5F 78
Rama La. SE19 4D 108
Ramar Ho. E1 8E 60
(off Hanbury St.)
Rambler Clo. SW16 1G 107
Rame Clo. SW17 2E 106
Ramilles Clo. SW2 5J 91
Ramillies Pl. W1 9G 59
Ramillies Rd. NW7 2C 24
Ramillies Rd. W4 5B 72
Ramillies Rd. Sidc 5F 96
Ramillies St. W1 9G 59
Ramney Dri. Enf 9E 6
Ramones Ter. Mitc 8J 107
Ramornie Clo. W on T 7K 117
Rampart St. E1 9F 60
Ram Pas. King T 6H 103
Rampayne St. SW1 6H 75
Ram Pl. E9 2G 61
Rampton Clo. E4 3L 29
Ramsay Gdns. Romf 8G 35
Ramsay Ho. NW8 5C 58
(off Townshend Est.)
Ramsay M. SW3 7C 74
Ramsay Pl. Harr 6C 38
Ramsay Rd. E7 9C 46
Ramsay Rd. W3 4A 72
Ramscroft Clo. N9 9C 16
Ramsdale Rd. SW17 2E 106
Ramsden. 3G 129
Ramsden Clo. Orp 3G 129
Ramsden Dri. Romf 7L 33
Ramsden Rd. N11 5D 26
Ramsden Rd. SW12 5E 90
Ramsden Rd. Eri 8B 82
Ramsden Rd. Orp 2F 128
Ramsey Clo. NW9 4D 40
Ramsey Clo. Gnfd 1B 54
Ramsey Ct. Croy 4M 123
(off Church St.)
Ramsey Ho. SW9 8L 75
Ramsey Rd. T Hth 1K 123
Ramsey St. E2 7E 60
Ramsey Wlk. N1 2B 60
(off Handa Wlk.)
Ramsey Way. N14 9G 15
Ramsfort Ho. SE16 5F 76
(off Camilla Rd.)
Ramsgate Clo. E16 2F 78
Ramsgate St. E8 2D 60
Ramsgill App. Ilf 2D 48
Ramsgill Dri. Ilf 3D 48
Rams Gro. Romf 2J 49
Ram St. SW18 4M 89
Ramulis Dri. Hay 7H 53
Ramuswood Av. Orp 7C 128
Rancliffe Gdns. SE9 3J 95
Rancliffe Rd. E6 5J 63
Randall Av. NW2 7C 40
Randall Clo. SW11 9C 74
Randall Clo. Eri 7A 82
Randall Ct. NW7 7E 24
Randall Dri. Horn 9G 51
Randall Pl. SE10 8A 78
Randall Rd. SE11 6K 75
Randall Row. SE11 5K 75
Randalls Rents. SE16 4K 77
(off Gulliver St.)
Randalls Wlk. Brick W 3K 5
Randell's Rd. N1 4J 59
(in two parts)
Randisbourne Gdns. SE6 9M 93
Randle Rd. Rich 1G 103
Randlesdown Rd. SE6 1L 109
(in two parts)
Randolph App. E16 9G 63
Randolph Av. W9 5M 57
Randolph Clo. Bexh 2A 98
Randolph Clo. King T 2A 104
Randolph Ct. H End 7L 21
(off Avenue, The)
Randolph Cres. W9 7A 58
Randolph Gdns. NW6 5M 57
Randolph Gro. Romf 3G 49
Randolph M. W9 7A 58
Randolph Rd. E17 3M 45
Randolph Rd. W9 7A 58
Randolph Rd. Brom 3K 127
Randolph Rd. Eps 6D 134
Randolph Rd. S'hall 3K 69
Randolph St. NW1 3G 59
Randon Clo. Harr 9M 21
Ranelagh Av. SW6 2K 89
Ranelagh Av. SW13 1E 88
Ranelagh Bri. W2 8M 57
Ranelagh Clo. Edgw 4L 23
Ranelagh Dri. Edgw 4L 23
Ranelagh Dri. Twic 3F 86
Ranelagh Gdns. E11 3G 47
Ranelagh Gdns. SW6 2J 89
(in two parts)
Ranelagh Gdns. W4 8A 72
Ranelagh Gdns. W6 5D 72
Ranelagh Gdns. Ilf 6K 47
Ranelagh Gdns. Mans. SW6 2J 89
(off Ranelagh Gdns.)
Ranelagh Gro. SW1 6E 74
Ranelagh Ho. SW3 6D 74
(off Elystan Pl.)
Ranelagh M. W5 3H 71
Ranelagh Pl. N Mald 9C 104
Ranelagh Rd. E6 4L 63
Ranelagh Rd. E11 9C 46
Ranelagh Rd. E15 5C 62
Ranelagh Rd. N17 1C 44
Ranelagh Rd. N22 8K 27
Ranelagh Rd. NW10 5D 56
Ranelagh Rd. SW1 6G 75
Ranelagh Rd. W5 3H 71
Ranelagh Rd. S'hall 2H 69
Ranelagh Rd. Wemb 2H 55
Ranfurly Rd. Sutt 4L 121
Rangbourne Ho. N7 1J 59
Rangefield Rd. Brom 2C 110
Rangemoor Rd. N15 3D 44
Ranger's House. 9B 78
Ranger's Rd. E4 9C 18
Rangers Sq. SE10 9B 78
Rangeworth Pl. Sidc 9D 96
Rangoon St. EC3 9D 60
(off Crutched Friars)
Rankin Clo. NW9 1C 40
Rankine Ho. SE1 4A 76
(off Bath Ter.)
Ranleigh Gdns. Bexh 8K 81
Ranmere St. SW12 7F 90
Ranmoor Clo. Harr 2B 38
Ranmoor Gdns. Harr 2B 38
Ranmore Av. Croy 5D 124
Ranmore Path. Orp 8E 112
Ranmore Pl. Wey 7A 116
(off Princes Rd.)
Ranmore Rd. Sutt 1H 135
Rannoch Clo. Edgw 2M 23
Rannoch Rd. W6 7G 73
Rannock Av. NW9 5B 40
Ranskill Ct. Borwd 3L 11
Ranskill Rd. Borwd 3L 11
Ransom Clo. Wat 9G 9
Ransome's Dock Bus. Cen. SW11 8C 74
Ransom Rd. SE7 5G 79
Ranston St. NW1 8C 58
Ranulf Rd. NW2 9K 41
Ranwell Clo. E3 4K 61
Ranworth Clo. Eri 1C 98
Ranworth Rd. N9 2G 29
Ranyard Clo. Chess 5K 119
Raphael Av. Romf 1D 50
Raphael Ct. SE16 6F 76
(off Stubbs Dri.)
Raphael Dri. Th Dit 2D 118
Raphael Dri. Wat 4H 9
Raphael St. SW7 3D 74
Rapier Clo. Purf 5K 83
Rapley Ho. E2 6E 60
(off Turin St.)
Rashleigh Ct. SW8 1F 90
Rashleigh Ho. WC1 6J 59
(off Thanet St.)
Rasper Rd. N20 2A 26
Rastell Av. SW2 8H 91
Ratcliff. 9J 61
Ratcliffe Clo. SE12 6E 94
Ratcliffe Clo. Uxb 6B 142
Ratcliffe Cross St. E1 9H 61
Ratcliffe Ho. E14 9J 61
Ratcliffe La. E14 9J 61
Ratcliffe Orchard. E1 1H 77
Ratcliff Rd. E7 1G 63
Rathbone Ho. E16 9D 62
(off Rathbone St.)
Rathbone Ho. NW6 4L 57
Rathbone Mkt. E16 8D 62
Rathbone Pl. W1 8H 59
Rathbone Point. E5 9E 44
Rathbone Sq. Croy 6A 124
Rathbone St. E16 8D 62
Rathbone St. W1 8G 59
Rathcoole Av. N8 3K 43
Rathcoole Gdns. N8 3K 43
Rathfern Rd. SE6 7K 93
Rathgar Av. W13 2F 70
Rathgar Clo. N3 9K 25
Rathgar Rd. SW9 2M 91
Rathmell Dri. SW4 5H 91
Rathmore Rd. SE7 6F 78
Rats La. Lou 2F 18
(in two parts)
Rattray Ct. SE6 8D 94
Rattray Rd. SW2 3L 91
Raul Rd. SE15 1E 92
Raveley St. NW5 9G 43
(in two parts)
Raven Clo. NW9 9C 24
Ravendale Rd. Sun 6D 100
Ravenet St. SW11 9F 74
(in two parts)
Ravenfield Rd. SW17 9D 90
Ravenhill Rd. E13 5G 63
Raven Ho. SE16 5H 77
(off Tawny Way)
Ravenings Pde. Ilf 6E 48
Ravenna Rd. SW15 4H 89
Ravenoak Way. Chig 5C 32
Ravenor Ct. Gnfd 7M 53
Ravenor Pk. Rd. Gnfd 6M 53
Raven Rd. E18 9G 31
Raven Row. E1 8F 60
(in two parts)
Ravensbourne Av. Brom 4B 110
Ravensbourne Av. Stai 7C 144
Ravensbourne Ct. SE6 6L 93
Ravensbourne Cres. Romf 1K 51
Ravensbourne Gdns. W13 8F 54
Ravensbourne Gdns. Ilf 8L 31
Ravensbourne Ho. NW8 8C 58
(off Broadley St.)
Ravensbourne Ho. Brom 2B 110
Ravensbourne Mans. SE8 7L 77
(off Berthon St.)
Ravensbourne Pk. SE6 6L 93
Ravensbourne Pk. Cres. SE6 6K 93
Ravensbourne Pl. SE13 1M 93
Ravensbourne Rd. SE6 6K 93
Ravensbourne Rd. Brom 7E 110
Ravensbourne Rd. Dart 2E 98
Ravensbourne Rd. Twic 5G 87

Ravensbury Av.—Reedsfield Clo.

Ravensbury Av. Mord 9A 106
Ravensbury Ct. Mitc 8B 106
(off Ravensbury Gro.)
Ravensbury Gro. Mitc 8B 106
Ravensbury La. Mitc 8B 106
Ravensbury Path. Mitc 8B 106
Ravensbury Rd. SW18 . . . . .8L 89
Ravensbury Rd. Orp 7D 112
Ravensbury Ter. SW18 . . . . .8M 89
Ravenscar. NW1 . . . . .4G 59
(off Bayham St.)
Ravenscar Rd. Brom 1C 110
Ravenscar Rd. Surb 4K 119
Ravens Clo. Brom 6D 110
Ravens Clo. Enf 4C 16
Ravens Clo. Surb 1H 119
Ravens Ct. King T 9H 103
(off Uxbridge Rd.)
Ravenscourt. Sun 5D 100
Ravenscourt Av. W6 . . . . .5E 72
Ravenscourt Clo. Horn 8J 51
Ravenscourt Clo. Ruis 5A 36
Ravenscourt Dri. Horn 8J 51
Ravenscourt Gdns. W6 . . . . .5E 72
Ravenscourt Gro. Horn 7J 51
Ravenscourt Pk. W6 . . . . . . .4E 72
Ravenscourt Pk. Barn 6H 13
Ravenscourt Pk. Mans.
W6 . . . . .4F 72
(off Paddenswick Rd.)
Ravenscourt Pl. W6 . . . . .5F 72
Ravenscourt Rd. W6 . . . . . . .5F 72
(in two parts)
Ravenscourt Rd. Orp 7E 112
Ravenscourt Sq. W6 . . . . . . .4E 72
Ravenscraig Rd. N11 . . . . . . .4G 27
Ravenscroft. Wat 8J 5
Ravenscroft Av. NW11 . . . . . .5K 41
Ravenscroft Av. Wemb 6J 39
Ravenscroft Clo. E16 . . . . . . .8E 62
Ravenscroft Cotts. Barn 6L 13
Ravenscroft Cres. SE9 . . . . . .9K 95
Ravenscroft Pk. Barn 5H 13
Ravenscroft Rd. E16 . . . . . . .8E 62
Ravenscroft Rd. W4 . . . . .5A 72
Ravenscroft Rd. Beck 6G 109
Ravenscroft St. E2 . . . . .5D 60
Ravensdale Av. N12 . . . . .4A 26
Ravensdale Gdns. SE19 . . . . .4B 108
Ravensdale Rd. N16 . . . . . . .5D 44
Ravensdale Rd. Houn 2J 85
Ravensdon St. SE11 . . . . . . .6L 75
Ravensfield Clo. Dag 9H 49
Ravensfield Gdns. Eps 7C 120
Ravenshaw St. NW6 . . . . . . .1K 57
Ravenshead Clo. S Croy . . .3G 139
Ravenshill. Chst 5M 111
Ravenshurst Av. NW4 . . . . . . .2G 41
Ravenside. King T 9H 103
(off Portsmouth Rd.)
Ravenside Clo. N18 . . . . .5H 29
Ravenside Retail Pk. N18 . . .5H 29
Ravenslea Rd. SW12 . . . . . . .6D 90
Ravensleigh Gdns. Brom . . .2F 110
Ravensmead Rd. Brom 4B 110
Ravensmede Way. W4 . . . . . .5D 72
Ravens M. SE12 . . . . .4E 94
Ravensquay Bus. Cen.
Orp 9F 112
Ravenstone. SE17 . . . . .6C 76
Ravenstone Rd. N8 . . . . .1L 43
Ravenstone Rd. NW9 . . . . . . .4D 40
Ravenstone St. SW12 . . . . . .7E 90
Ravens Way. SE12 . . . . .4E 94
Ravens Wold. Kenl 7A 138
Ravenswood. Bex 7J 97
Ravenswood Av. Surb 4K 119
Ravenswood Av. W Wick . . .3A 126
Ravenswood Clo. Romf 5M 33
Ravenswood Ct. King T 3M 103
Ravenswood Cres. Harr 7K 37
Ravenswood Cres.
W Wick 3A 126
Ravenswood Gdns. Iswth . . .9C 70
Ravenswood Ind. Est. E17 . . .2A 46
Ravenswood Pk. N'wd 6E 20
Ravenswood Rd. E17 . . . . . . .2A 46
Ravenswood Rd. SW12 . . . . .6F 90
Ravenswood Rd. Croy 5M 123
Ravensworth Ct. SW6 . . . . . .8L 73
(off Fulham Rd.)
Ravensworth Rd. NW10 . . . . .6F 56
Ravensworth Rd. SE9 . . . . . .9K 95
Ravent Rd. SE11 . . . . .5K 75
Ravey St. EC2 . . . . .7C 60
Ravine Gro. SE18 . . . . .7C 80
Rav Pinter Clo. N16 . . . . . . .5C 44
Rawalpindi Ho. E16 . . . . .7D 62
Rawchester Clo. SW18 . . . . .7K 89
Rawlings Clo. Orp 7D 128
Rawlings Cres. Wemb 8M 39
Rawlings St. SW3 . . . . .5D 74
Rawlins Clo. N3 . . . . .1J 41
Rawlins Clo. S Croy 9J 125
Rawlinson Ct. NW2 . . . . .5G 41
Rawlinson Ho. SE13 . . . . .3B 94
(off Mercator Rd.)
Rawlinson Point. E16 . . . . . .8D 62
(off Fox Rd.)
Rawlinson Ter. N17 . . . . .1D 44
Rawnsley Av. Mitc 9B 106
Rawreth Wlk. N1 . . . . .4A 60
(off Basire St.)
Rawson St. SW11 . . . . .9E 74
(in two parts)
Rawsthorne Clo. E16 . . . . . . .2K 79
Rawsthorne Ct. Houn 3K 85
Rawstone Wlk. E13 . . . . .5E 62
Rawstorne Pl. EC1 . . . . .6M 59
Rawstorne St. EC1 . . . . .6M 59
Raybell Ct. Iswth 1D 86
Rayburne Ct. W14 . . . . .4J 73
Rayburne Ct. Buck H 1G 31
Rayburn Rd. Horn 5L 51
Ray Clo. Chess 8G 119
Raydean Rd. New Bar 7M 13
Raydon Rd. Chesh 5D 6
Raydons Gdns. Dag 9J 49
Raydons Rd. Dag 1J 65
Raydon St. N19 . . . . .7F 42
Rayfield Clo. Brom 1J 127
Rayford Av. SE12 . . . . .6D 94
Rayford Clo. Dart 4G 99
Ray Gdns. Bark 5E 64
Ray Gdns. Stan 5F 22
Ray Gunter Ho. SE17 . . . . . . .6M 75
(off Marsland Clo.)
Ray Ho. N1 . . . . .4B 60
(off Colville Est.)
Ray Lamb Way. Eri 7F 82
Rayleas Clo. SE18 . . . . .9M 79
Rayleigh Av. Tedd 3C 102
Rayleigh Clo. N13 . . . . .3B 28
Rayleigh Ct. N22 . . . . .8A 28
Rayleigh Ct. King T 6L 103
Rayleigh Ho. Brom 5E 110
(off Hammelton Rd.)
Rayleigh Houses. Ab L 5D 4
Rayleigh Ri. S Croy 8C 124
Rayleigh Rd. E16 . . . . .2F 78
Rayleigh Rd. N13 . . . . .3A 28
Rayleigh Rd. SW19 . . . . . . .5K 105
Rayleigh Rd. Wfd G 6G 31
Ray Lodge Rd. Wfd G 6G 31
Ray Massey Way. E6 . . . . . . .4J 63
(off High St. N.)
Raymead Av. T Hth 9L 107
Raymede Towers. W10 . . . . . .8H 57
(off Treverton St.)
Raymere Gdns. SE18 . . . . . . .8B 80
Raymond Av. E18 . . . . .1D 46
Raymond Av. W13 . . . . .4E 70
Raymond Bldgs. WC1 . . . . . .8K 59
Raymond Clo. SE26 . . . . . . .2G 109
Raymond Clo. Ab L 5B 4
Raymond Ct. N10 . . . . .7F 26
Raymond Ct. Sutt 8M 121
Raymond Gdns. Chig 3F 32
Raymond Postage Ct.
SE28 . . . . .1F 80
Raymond Revuebar. 1H 75
(off Walkers Ct.)
Raymond Rd. E13 . . . . .4G 63
Raymond Rd. SW19 . . . . . . .3J 105
Raymond Rd. Beck 8J 109
Raymond Rd. Ilf 5B 48
Raymond Way. Clay 8E 118
Raymouth Rd. SE16 . . . . .5F 76
Raynald Ho. SW16 . . . . .9J 91
Rayne Ct. E18 . . . . .2D 46
Rayne Ho. W9 . . . . .7M 57
(off Delaware Rd.)
Rayner Ct. W12 . . . . .3G 73
(off Bamborough Gdns.)
Rayners Clo. Wemb 1H 55
Rayners Cres. N'holt 6F 52
Rayners Gdns. N'holt 5F 52
Rayners Lane. 6K 37
Rayners La. Pinn & Harr 3K 37
Rayners Rd. SW15 . . . . .4J 89
Rayner Towers. E10 . . . . .5L 45
(off Albany Rd.)
Raynes Av. E11 . . . . .5G 47
Raynes Park. 8G 105
Raynes Pk. Bri. SW20 . . . . .6G 105
Raynham. W2 . . . . .9C 58
(off Norfolk Cres.)
Raynham Av. N18 . . . . .6E 28
Raynham Ho. E1 . . . . .7H 61
(off Harpley Sq.)
Raynham Rd. N18 . . . . .5E 28
Raynham Rd. W6 . . . . .5F 72
Raynham Ter. N18 . . . . .5E 28
Raynor Clo. S'hall 2K 69
Raynor Pl. N1 . . . . .3A 60
Raynton Clo. Harr 6J 37
Raynton Clo. Hay 7D 52
Raynton Dri. Hay 7D 52
Raynton Rd. Enf 1H 17
Ray Rd. Romf 5M 33
Ray Rd. W Mol 9M 101
Rays Av. N18 . . . . .4G 29
Rays Hill. Hort K 8M 115
Rays Rd. N18 . . . . .4G 29
Rays Rd. W Wick 2A 126
Ray St. EC1 . . . . .7L 59
Ray St. Bri. EC1 . . . . .7L 59
(off Farringdon Rd.)
Ray Wlk. N7 . . . . .7K 43
Raywood Clo. Hay 8A 68
Reachview Clo. NW1 . . . . . . .3G 59
Read Clo. Th Dit 2E 118
Read Ct. E17 . . . . .4L 45
Read Ct. Wal A 6M 7
Reade Ct. W3 . . . . .4A 72
(off Stanley Rd.)
Reade Ho. SE10 . . . . .7B 78
(off Trafalgar Gro.)
Readens, The. Bans 8C 136
Reade Wlk. NW10 . . . . .3C 56
Read Ho. SE11 . . . . .7L 75
(off Clayton St.)
Reading Ho. SE15 . . . . .7E 76
(off Friary Est.)
Reading Ho. W2 . . . . .9A 58
(off Hallfield Est.)
Reading La. E8 . . . . .2F 60
Reading Rd. N'holt 1M 53
Reading Rd. Sutt 7A 122
Reading Way. NW7 . . . . .5H 25
Read Rd. Asht 9H 133
Reads Clo. Ilf 8M 47
Reapers Clo. NW1 . . . . .4H 59
Reapers Way. Iswth 4B 86
Reardon Ct. N21 . . . . .2M 27
Reardon Ho. E1 . . . . .2F 76
(off Reardon St.)
Reardon Path. E1 . . . . .2F 76
(in two parts)
Reardon St. E1 . . . . .2F 76
Reaston St. SE14 . . . . .8H 77
Rebecca Ct. Sidc 1F 112
Reckitt Rd. W4 . . . . .6C 72
Record St. SE15 . . . . .7G 77
Recovery St. SW17 . . . . . . .2C 106
Recreation Av. H Wood 9K 35
Recreation Av. Romf 3A 50
Recreation Rd. SE26 . . . . . .1H 109
Recreation Rd. Brom 6D 110
Recreation Rd. Sidc 9C 96
Recreation Rd. S'hall 5J 69
Recreation Way. Mitc 7H 107
Rector St. N1 . . . . .4A 60
Rectory Bus. Cen. Sidc 1F 112
Rectory Clo. E4 . . . . .3L 29
Rectory Clo. N3 . . . . .8K 25
Rectory Clo. SW20 . . . . . . .7G 105
Rectory Clo. Dart 3C 98
Rectory Clo. Sidc 1F 112
Rectory Clo. Stan 5F 22
Rectory Clo. Surb 3G 119
Rectory Ct. E18 . . . . .8D 30
Rectory Ct. Felt 1G 101
Rectory Ct. Wall 6G 123
Rectory Cres. E11 . . . . .4G 47
(in two parts)
Rectory Farm Rd. Enf 2K 15
Rectory Fld. Cres. SE7 . . . . . .8G 79
Rectory Gdns. N8 . . . . .2J 43
Rectory Gdns. SW4 . . . . .2G 91
Rectory Gdns. Beck 5L 109
(off Rectory Rd.)
Rectory Gdns. N'holt 4K 53
Rectory Grn. Beck 5K 109
Rectory Gro. SW4 . . . . .2G 91
Rectory Gro. Croy 4M 123
Rectory Gro. Hamp 1K 101
Rectory La. SW17 . . . . .3E 106
Rectory La. Bans 6D 136
Rectory La. Edgw 6L 23
Rectory La. Lou 4L 19
Rectory La. Sidc 1F 112
Rectory La. Stan 5F 22
Rectory La. Surb 3F 118
Rectory La. Wall 6G 123
Rectory Orchard. SW19 . . . . .1J 105
Rectory Pk. S Croy 5C 138
Rectory Pk. Av. N'holt 6K 53
Rectory Pl. SE18 . . . . .5L 79
Rectory Rd. E12 . . . . .1K 63
Rectory Rd. E17 . . . . .2M 45
Rectory Rd. N16 . . . . .7D 44
Rectory Rd. SW13 . . . . .1E 88
Rectory Rd. W3 . . . . .2M 71
Rectory Rd. Beck 6L 109
Rectory Rd. Dag 2M 65
Rectory Rd. Hay 9E 52
Rectory Rd. Houn 1G 85
Rectory Rd. Kes 9H 127
Rectory Rd. S'hall 4K 69
Rectory Rd. Sutt 5L 121
Rectory Sq. E1 . . . . .8H 61
Rectory Way. Uxb 7A 36
Reculver Ho. SE15 . . . . .7G 77
(off Lovelinch Clo.)
Reculver M. N18 . . . . .4E 28
Reculver Rd. SE16 . . . . .6H 77
Red Anchor Clo. SW3 . . . . . . .7B 74
Redan Pl. W2 . . . . .9M 57
Redan St. W14 . . . . .4H 73
Redan Ter. SE5 . . . . .1M 91
Redbarn Clo. Purl 3M 137
Red Barracks Rd. SE18 . . . . .5K 79
Redberry Gro. SE26 . . . . .9G 93
Redbourne Av. N3 . . . . .8L 25
Redbourne Dri. SE28 . . . . . . .9H 65
Redbourne Ho. E14 . . . . .9K 61
(off Norbiton Rd.)
Redbourn Ho. W10 . . . . .7G 57
(off Sutton Way)
Redbridge. 4H 47
Redbridge Enterprise Cen.
Ilf 7A 48
Redbridge Foyer. Ilf 7A 48
(off Sylvan Rd.)
Redbridge Gdns. SE5 . . . . . . .8C 76
Redbridge La. E. Ilf 4H 47
Redbridge La. W. E11 . . . . . . .4F 46
Redbridge Roundabout (Junct.)
. . . . 4G 47
Redburn St. SW3 . . . . .7D 74
Redburn Trad. Est. Enf 8H 17
Redbury Clo. Rain 7G 67
Redcar Clo. N'holt 1M 53
Redcar Rd. Romf 5K 35
Redcar St. SE5 . . . . .8A 76
Redcastle Clo. E1 . . . . .1G 77
Red Cedars Rd. Orp 2C 128
Redchurch St. E2 . . . . .7D 60
Redcliffe Clo. SW5 . . . . .6M 73
(off Old Brompton Rd.)
Redcliffe Ct. E5 . . . . .8F 44
(off Napoleon Rd.)
Redcliffe Gdns.
SW5 & SW10 . . . . .6M 73
Redcliffe Gdns. W4 . . . . .8M 71
Redcliffe Gdns. Ilf 6L 47
Redcliffe M. SW10 . . . . .6M 73
Redcliffe Pl. SW10 . . . . .7A 74
Redcliffe Rd. SW10 . . . . .6A 74
Redcliffe Sq. SW10 . . . . .6M 73
Redcliffe St. SW10 . . . . .7M 73
Redclose Av. Mord 9L 105
Redclyffe Rd. E6 . . . . .4G 63
Redclyf Ho. E1 . . . . .7G 61
(off Cephas St.)
Redcourt. Croy 5C 124
Redcroft Rd. S'hall 1A 70
Redcross Way. SE1 . . . . .3A 76
Redden Ct. Romf 9K 35
Redden Ct. Rd. Romf 1J 51
Redding Ho. SE18 . . . . .4J 79
Redding Ho. Wat 8C 8
Reddings Av. Bush 7M 9
Reddings Clo. NW7 . . . . .4D 24
Reddings, The. NW7 . . . . . . .3D 24
Reddings, The. Borwd 5K 11
Reddington Clo. S Croy 1B 138
Reddins Rd. SE15 . . . . .7E 76
Reddons Rd. Beck 4J 109
Reddown Rd. Coul 9H 137
Reddy Rd. Eri 7D 82
Rede Ct. Wey 5A 116
(off Old Pal. Rd.)
Redenham Ho. SW15 . . . . . . .6E 88
(off Ellisfield Dri.)
Rede Pl. W2 . . . . .9L 57
Redesdale Gdns. Iswth 8E 70
Redesdale St. SW3 . . . . .7C 74
Redfern Av. Houn 6L 85
Redfern Clo. Uxb 4A 142
Redfern Ct. Wat 7C 8
Redfern Gdns. Romf 9H 35
Redfern Ho. E15 . . . . .4D 62
(off Redriffe Rd.)
Redfern Rd. NW10 . . . . .3C 56
Redfern Rd. SE6 . . . . .6A 94
Redfield La. SW5 . . . . .5L 73
Redfield M. SW5 . . . . .5M 73
Redford Av. Coul 6F 136
Redford Av. T Hth 8K 107
Redford Av. Wall 8J 123
Redford Clo. Felt 8D 84
Redford Ho. W10 . . . . .6K 57
(off Dowland St.)
Redford Wlk. N1 . . . . .4A 60
(off Popham St.)
Redford Way. Uxb 3B 142
Redgate Dri. Brom 4F 126
Redgate Ter. SW15 . . . . .5H 89
Redgrave Clo. Croy 1D 124
Redgrave Rd. SW15 . . . . .2H 89
Redgrave Ter. E2 . . . . .6E 60
(off Derbyshire St.)
Redheath Clo. Wat 8D 4
Red Hill. Chst 2M 111
Redhill Ct. SW2 . . . . .8L 91
Redhill Dri. Edgw 9M 23
Redhill St. NW1 . . . . .5F 58
Red Ho. La. Bexh 3H 97
Red Ho. La. W on T 4E 116
Redhouse Rd. Croy 1H 123
Red Ho. Sq. N1 . . . . .2A 60
Redington Gdns. NW3 . . . . .9M 41
Redington Ho. N1 . . . . .5K 59
(off Priory Grn. Est.)
Redington Rd. NW3 . . . . .8M 41
Redland Gdns. W Mol 8K 101
Redlands. N15 . . . . .2B 44
Redlands. Coul 8J 137
Redlands. Tedd 3E 102
Redlands Ct. Brom 4D 110
Redlands Rd. Enf 3J 17
Redlands, The. Beck 6M 109
Redlands Way. SW2 . . . . .6K 91
Red La. Clay 8E 118
Redleaf Clo. Belv 7L 81
Redleaves Av. Ashf 3A 100
Redlees Clo. Iswth 3E 86
Red Leys. Uxb 3C 142
Red Lion Bus. Pk. Surb 5K 119
Red Lion Clo. SE17 . . . . .7B 76
(off Red Lion Row)
Red Lion Clo. A'ham 1A 10
Red Lion Clo. Orp 1G 129
Red Lion Ct. EC4 . . . . .9L 59
Red Lion Ct. SE1 . . . . .2A 76
Red Lion Hill. N2 . . . . .9B 26
Red Lion La. SE18 . . . . .8L 79
Red Lion Pde. Pinn 1J 37
Red Lion Pl. SE18 . . . . .9L 79
Red Lion Rd. Surb 4K 119
Red Lion Row. SE17 . . . . .7A 76
Red Lion Sq. SW18 . . . . .4L 89
Red Lion Sq. WC1 . . . . .8K 59
Red Lion St. WC1 . . . . .8K 59
Red Lion St. Rich 4H 87
Red Lion Yd. W1 . . . . .2F 74
(off Waverton St.)
Red Lion Yd. Wat 6G 9
Red Lodge. W Wick 3A 126
Red Lodge Cres. Bex 9B 98
Red Lodge Rd. Bex 9B 98
Red Lodge Rd. W Wick 3A 126
Redman Clo. N'holt 5G 53
Redman Ho. EC1 . . . . .8L 59
(off Bourne Est.)
Redman Ho. SE1 . . . . .3A 76
(off Borough High St.)
Redmans La. Shor 8A 130
Redman's Rd. E1 . . . . .8G 61
Redmead La. E1 . . . . .2E 76
Redmead Rd. Hay 5C 68
Redmill Ho. E1 . . . . .7F 60
(off Headlam St.)
Redmond Ho. N1 . . . . .4K 59
(off Barnsbury Est.)
Redmore Rd. W6 . . . . .5F 72
Red Oak Clo. Orp 5M 127
Redo Ho. E12 . . . . .1L 63
(off Dore Av.)
Red Path. E9 . . . . .2J 61
Red Pl. W1 . . . . .1E 74
Redpoll Way. Eri 4H 81
Red Post Hill.
SE24 & SE21 . . . . .3B 92
Red Post Ho. E6 . . . . .3H 63
Redriffe Rd. E13 . . . . .4D 62
Redriff Est. SE16 . . . . .4K 77
Redriff Rd. SE16 . . . . .5H 77
Redriff Rd. Romf 9M 33
Red Rd. Borwd 5K 11
Redroofs Clo. Beck 5M 109
Redrose Trad. Cen. Barn 7B 14
Red Rover (Junct.) 3D 88
Redrup Ho. SE14 . . . . .7H 77
(off John Williams Clo.)
Redruth Clo. N22 . . . . .7K 27
Redruth Gdns. Romf 5K 35
Redruth Ho. Sutt 9M 121
Redruth Rd. E9 . . . . .4G 61
Redruth Rd. Romf 5K 35
Redruth Wlk. Romf 5K 35
Redstart Clo. E6 . . . . .8J 63
Redstart Clo. SE14 . . . . .8J 77
Redstart Clo. New Ad 2B 140
Redston Rd. N8 . . . . .2H 43
Redvers Rd. N22 . . . . .9L 27
Redvers St. N1 . . . . .6C 60
Redwald Rd. E5 . . . . .9H 45
Redway Dri. Twic 6A 86
Redwing Clo. S Croy 3H 139
Redwing Ct. H Hill 7H 35
Redwing Gro. Ab L 4E 4
Redwing Path. SE28 . . . . .3B 80
Redwing Rd. Wall 8J 123
Redwood Clo. N14 . . . . .9H 15
Redwood Clo. SE16 . . . . .2J 77
Redwood Clo. Buck H 2F 30
Redwood Clo. Kenl 6A 138
Redwood Clo. Sidc 6E 96
Redwood Clo. Uxb 5F 142
Redwood Clo. Wat 4H 21
Redwood Ct. N19 . . . . .5H 43
Redwood Ct. NW6 . . . . .3J 57
Redwood Ct. Dart 5L 99
Redwood Ct. N'holt 6J 53
Redwood Ct. Surb 2H 119
Redwood Est. Houn 7F 68
Redwood Gdns. E4 . . . . .8M 17
Redwood Gdns. Chig 5E 32
Redwood Mans. W8 . . . . .4M 73
(off Chantry Sq.)
Redwood M. SW4 . . . . .2F 90
Redwood Ri. Borwd 1L 11
Redwoods. SW15 . . . . .7E 88
Redwood Wlk. Surb 3H 119
Redwood Way. Barn 7H 13
Reece M. SW7 . . . . .5B 74
Reed Av. Orp 5C 128
Reed Clo. E16 . . . . .8E 62
Reed Clo. SE12 . . . . .4E 94
Reede Gdns. Dag 1M 65
Reede Rd. Dag 2L 65
Reede Way. Dag 2M 65
Reedham Clo. N17 . . . . .2F 44
Reedham Clo. Brick W 2L 5
Reedham Dri. Purl 5K 137
Reedham Pk. Av. Purl 8L 137
Reedham St. SE15 . . . . .1E 92
Reedholm Vs. N16 . . . . .9B 44
Reed Pond Wlk. Romf 9D 34
Reed Rd. N17 . . . . .9D 28
Reeds Cres. Wat 4G 9
Reedsfield Clo. Ashf 9F 144

Reedsfield Rd.—Rickman Hill

Reedsfield Rd. Ashf 9F 144 & 1A 100
Reed's Pl. NW1 3G 59
Reeds Wlk. Wat 4G 9 (in two parts)
Reedworth St. SE11 5L 75
Reef Ho. E14 4A 78 (off Manchester St.)
Reenglass Rd. Stan 4H 23
Rees Dri. Stan 4J 23
Rees Gdns. Croy 1D 124
Reesland Clo. E12 2L 63
Rees St. N1 4A 60
Reets Farm Clo. NW9 4C 40
Reeves Av. NW9 5B 40
Reeves Corner. Croy 4M 123
Reeves Cres. Swan 7B 114
Reeves Ho. SE1 3L 75 (off Baylis Rd.)
Reeves M. W1 1E 74
Reeves Path. Hay 5D 68
Reeves Rd. E3 7M 61
Reeves Rd. SE18 7M 79
Reflection, The. E16 3M 79 (off Woolwich Mnr. Way)
Reform Row. N17 9D 28
Reform St. SW11 1D 90
Regal Clo. E1 8E 60
Regal Clo. W5 8H 55
Regal Ct. N18 5D 28
Regal Cres. Wall 5F 122
Regal Dri. N11 5F 26
Regal La. NW1 4E 58
Regal Pl. E3 6K 61
Regal Pl. SW6 8M 73
Regal Row. SE15 9G 77
Regal Way. Harr 4J 39
Regal Way. Wat 2G 9
Regan Ho. N18 6D 28
Regan Way. N1 5C 60
Regarder Rd. Chig 5E 32
Regarth Av. Romf 4C 50
Regatta Ho. Tedd 1E 102
Regatta Point. Bren 7K 71
Regency Clo. W5 9J 55
Regency Clo. Chig 5A 32
Regency Clo. Hamp 2K 101
Regency Ct. Enf 7B 16
Regency Ct. Sutt 6M 121
Regency Ct. Tedd 3F 102
Regency Ct. Wat 3E 8 (off Langley Rd.)
Regency Cres. NW4 9H 25
Regency Dri. Ruis 6C 36
Regency Gdns. Horn 5G 51
Regency Gdns. W on T 3G 117
Regency Ho. E16 2E 78 (off Pepys Cres.)
Regency Ho. NW1 7F 58 (off Osnaburgh St.)
Regency Lawn. NW5 8F 42
Regency Lodge. NW3 3B 58 (off Adelaide Rd.)
Regency Lodge. Buck H 2H 31
Regency M. NW10 2E 56
Regency M. SW9 8M 75
Regency M. Beck 4A 110
Regency M. Iswth 4C 86
Regency Pl. SW1 5H 75
Regency St. SW1 5H 75
Regency Ter. SW7 6B 74 (off Fulham Rd.)
Regency Wlk. Croy 1K 125
Regency Wlk. Rich 4J 87 (off Grosvenor Av.)
Regency Way. Bexh 2H 97
Regent Av. Uxb 3F 142
Regent Bus. Cen. Hay 3F 68
Regent Clo. N12 5A 26
Regent Clo. Harr 4J 39
Regent Clo. Houn 9F 68
Regent Ct. N3 7M 25
Regent Ct. N20 2A 26
Regent Ct. NW8 6C 58 (off North Bank)
Regent Gdns. Ilf 5E 48
Regent Ga. Wal X 7D 6
Regent Ho. W14 5J 73 (off Windsor Way)
Regent Ho. Eps 3C 134
Regent Pl. SW19 2A 106
Regent Pl. W1 1G 75
Regent Pl. Croy 3D 124
Regent Rd. SE24 5M 91
Regent Rd. Surb 9K 103
Regents Av. N13 5L 27
Regent's Bri. Gdns. SW8 8J 75
Regents Canal Ho. E14 9J 61 (off Commercial Rd.)
Regents Clo. Hay 8D 52
Regents Clo. S Croy 8C 124
Regents Clo. Stan 4J 23
Regent's College. 7D 58
Regents Ct. E8 4D 60 (off Pownall Rd.)
Regents Ct. Brom 4D 110
Regents Ct. King T 5J 103 (off Sopwith Way)
Regents Ct. Pinn 9H 21
Regents Dri. Kes 7H 127
Regents Ga. Ho. E14 1J 77 (off Horseferry Rd.)
Regents M. NW8 5A 58
Regent's Park. 5F 58
Regent's Pk. 6D 58
Regents Pk. Est. NW1 6G 59 (off Robert St.)
Regent's Pk. Gdns. M. NW1 4D 58
Regent's Pk. Ho. NW8 6C 58 (off Park Rd.)
Regent's Pk. Open Air Theatre. 6E 58
Regents Pk. Rd. N3 1K 41
Regent's Pk. Rd. NW1 3D 58 (in two parts)
Regent's Pk. Ter. NW1 4F 58
Regent's Pl. SE3 1E 94
Regents Pl. Lou 9H 19
Regents Plaza. NW6 5M 57 (off Kilburn High Rd.)
Regent Sq. E3 6M 61
Regent Sq. WC1 6J 59
Regent Sq. Belv 5M 81
Regent's Row. E8 4E 60
Regent St. NW10 6H 57
Regent St. SW1 1H 75
Regent St. W1 9F 58
Regent St. W4 6L 71
Regent St. Wat 2F 8
Regents Wharf. E8 4F 60 (off Wharf Pl.)
Regents Wharf. N1 5K 59
Regina Clo. Barn 5H 13
Regina Ho. SE20 5H 109
Reginald Pl. SE8 8L 77 (off Deptford High St.)
Reginald Rd. E7 3E 62
Reginald Rd. SE8 8L 77
Reginald Rd. N'wd 8D 20
Reginald Rd. Romf 8L 35
Reginald Sq. SE8 8L 77
Regina Point. SE16 3G 77
Regina Rd. N4 6K 43
Regina Rd. SE25 7E 108
Regina Rd. W13 2E 70
Regina Rd. S'hall 5J 69
Regina Ter. W13 2F 70
Regis Ct. N8 2K 43
Regis Ct. NW1 8D 58 (off Melcombe Pl.)
Regis Ho. W1 8E 58 (off Beaumont St.)
Regis Pl. SW2 3K 91
Regis Rd. NW5 1F 58
Regnart Bldgs. NW1 6G 59 (off Euston St.)
Reid Clo. Coul 8F 136
Reid Clo. Pinn 2E 36
Reidhaven Rd. SE18 5C 80
Reigate Av. Sutt 3L 121
Reigate Rd. Brom 9D 94
Reigate Rd. Eps & Tad (KT8,KT20) 9H 135
Reigate Rd. Eps (KT17) 2D 134
Reigate Rd. Ilf 7D 48
Reigate Way. Wall 7J 123
Reighton Rd. E5 8E 44
Reinickendorf Av. SE9 5A 96
Relay Rd. W12 2G 73
Relf Rd. SE15 2E 92
Reliance Arc. SW9 3L 91
Reliance Sq. EC2 7C 60 (off Anning St.)
Relko Ct. Eps 3B 134
Relko Gdns. Sutt 7B 122
Relton M. SW7 4C 74
Rembold Ho. SE10 9A 78 (off Blissett St.)
Rembrandt Clo. E14 4B 78
Rembrandt Clo. SW1 6E 74 (off Graham Ter.)
Rembrandt Ct. SE16 6F 76 (off Stubbs Dri.)
Rembrandt Ct. Eps 8D 120
Rembrandt Rd. SE13 3C 94
Rembrandt Rd. Edgw 9L 23
Rembrandt Way. W on T 4F 116
Remembrance Rd. E7 9H 47
Remington Rd. E6 9J 63
Remington Rd. N15 4B 44
Remington St. N1 5M 59
Remnant St. WC2 9K 59
Remsted Ho. NW6 4M 57 (off Mortimer Cres.)
Remus Building, The. EC1 6L 59 (off Hardwick St.)
Remus Rd. E3 3L 61
Renaissance Ho. Eps 5C 134 (off Up. High St.)
Rendle Clo. Croy 9D 108
Rendlesham Av. Rad 1D 10
Rendlesham Rd. E5 9E 44
Rendlesham Rd. Enf 3M 15
Renforth St. SE16 4G 77
Renfree Way. Shep 1A 116
Renfrew Clo. E6 1L 79
Renfrew Ct. Houn 1J 85
Renfrew Ho. E17 9K 29
Renfrew Rd. SE11 5M 75
Renfrew Rd. Houn 1H 85
Renfrew Rd. King T 4M 103
Renmans, The. Asht 8K 133
Renmuir St. SW17 3D 106
Rennell St. SE13 2A 94
Rennels Way. Iswth 1C 86
Renness Rd. E17 1J 45
Rennets Clo. SE9 4C 96
Rennets Wood Rd. SE9 4B 96
Rennie Clo. Ashf 9B 144
Rennie Cotts. E1 7G 61 (off Pemell Clo.)
Rennie Ct. SE1 2M 75 (off Stamford St.)
Rennie Est. SE16 5F 76
Rennie Ho. SE1 4A 76 (off Bath Ter.)
Rennie St. SE1 2M 75 (in two parts)
Renoir Cinema. 7J 59 (off Brunswick Sq.)
Renoir Ct. SE16 6F 76 (off Stubbs Dri.)
Renovation, The. E16 3M 79 (off Woolwich Mnr. Way)
Renown Clo. Croy 3M 123
Renown Clo. Romf 8L 33
Rensburg Rd. E17 3H 45
Renshaw Clo. Belv 7K 81
Renters Av. NW4 4G 41
Renton Clo. SW2 5K 91
Renton Dri. Orp 2H 129
Renwick Ind. Est. Bark 5F 64
Renwick Rd. Bark 7F 64
Repens Way. Hay 7H 53
Rephidim St. SE1 4C 76
Replingham Rd. SW18 7K 89
Reporton Rd. SW6 8J 73
Repository Rd. SE18 7K 79
Repton Av. Hay 5B 68
Repton Av. Romf 1E 50
Repton Av. Wemb 9G 39
Repton Clo. Cars 7C 122
Repton Ct. Beck 5M 109
Repton Ct. Ilf 8K 31
Repton Dri. Romf 2E 50
Repton Gdns. Romf 1E 50
Repton Gro. Ilf 8K 31
Repton Ho. E14 9J 61 (off Repton St.)
Repton Ho. SW1 5G 75 (off Charlwood St.)
Repton Rd. Harr 2K 39
Repton Rd. Orp 5E 128
Repton St. E14 9J 61
Repulse Clo. Romf 8L 33
Reservoir Clo. T Hth 8B 108
Reservoir Rd. N14 7G 15
Reservoir Rd. SE4 1J 93
Reservoir Rd. Lou 3F 18
Reservoir Rd. Ruis 2B 36
Reservoir Studios. E1 9H 61 (off Cable St.)
Resolution Wlk. SE18 4K 79
Restavon Cvn. Site. Berr G 8M 141
Restell Clo. SE3 7C 78
Restmor Way. Wall 4E 122
Reston Clo. Borwd 2L 11
Reston Path. Borwd 2L 11
Reston Pl. SW7 3A 74
Restons Cres. SE9 5B 96
Restoration Sq. SW11 9B 74
Restormel Clo. Houn 4L 85
Restormel Ho. SE11 5L 75 (off Chester Way)
Retcar Clo. N19 7F 42
Retcar Pl. N19 7F 42 (off Retcar Clo.)
Retford Clo. Borwd 2L 11
Retford Clo. Romf 6L 35
Retford Path. Romf 6L 35
Retford Rd. Romf 6K 35
Retford St. N1 5C 60
Retingham Way. E4 2M 29
Retles Ct. Harr 5C 38
Retreat Clo. Harr 3G 39
Retreat Ho. E9 2G 61
Retreat Pl. E9 2G 61
Retreat Rd. Rich 4H 87
Retreat, The. NW9 3B 40
Retreat, The. SW14 2C 88
Retreat, The. Harr 5L 37
Retreat, The. K Lan 4A 4
Retreat, The. Orp 8F 128
Retreat, The. Surb 1K 119
Retreat, The. T Hth 8B 108
Retreat, The. Wor Pk 4F 120
Retreat Way. Chig 3F 32
Reubens Ct. W4 6M 71 (off Chaseley Dri.)
Reunion Row. E1 1F 76
Reveley Sq. SE16 3J 77
Revell Ri. SE18 7D 80
Revell Rd. King T 6M 103
Revell Rd. Sutt 8K 121
Revelon Rd. SE4 3J 93
Revelstoke Rd. SW18 8K 89
Reventlow Rd. SE9 7A 96
Reverdy Rd. SE1 5E 76
Reverend Clo. Harr 8M 37
Revesby Rd. Cars 1B 122
Review Rd. NW2 7D 40
Review Rd. Dag 4M 65
Rewell St. SW6 8A 74
Rewley Rd. Cars 1B 122
Rex Clo. Romf 7M 33
Rex Pl. W1 1E 74
Reydon Av. E11 3G 47
Reynard Clo. SE4 2J 93
Reynard Clo. Brom 7L 111
Reynard Dri. SE19 4D 108
Reynard Mills Trad. Est. Bren 6G 71
Reynard Pl. SE14 7J 77
Reynardson Rd. N17 7A 28
Reynards Way. Brick W 2K 5
Reynolds Av. E12 1L 63
Reynolds Av. Chad H 5G 49
Reynolds Av. Chess 9J 119
Reynolds Clo. NW11 5M 41
Reynolds Clo. SW19 5B 106
Reynolds Clo. Cars 3D 122
Reynolds Ct. Romf 1H 49
Reynolds Dri. Edgw 1K 39
Reynolds Ho. E2 5G 61 (off Approach Rd.)
Reynolds Ho. NW8 5B 58 (off Wellington Rd.)
Reynolds Ho. SW1 5H 75 (off Erasmus St.)
Reynolds Pl. SE3 8F 78
Reynolds Pl. Rich 5K 87
Reynolds Rd. SE15 3G 93
Reynolds Rd. W4 4A 72
Reynolds Rd. Hay 7G 53
Reynolds Rd. N Mald 2B 120
Reynolds Way. Croy 6C 124
Rheidol M. N1 5A 60
Rheidol Ter. N1 4A 60
Rheingold Way. Wall 1J 137
Rhein Ho. N8 1J 43 (off Campsfield Rd.)
Rheola Clo. N17 8D 28
Rhoda St. E2 7D 60
Rhodes Av. N22 8G 27
Rhodes Ho. N1 6B 60 (off Provost Est.)
Rhodes Ho. W12 2F 72
Rhodesia Rd. E11 7B 46
Rhodesia Rd. SW9 1J 91
Rhodesmoor Ho. Ct. Mord 1L 121
Rhodes St. N7 1K 59
Rhodes Way. Wat 4H 9
Rhodeswell Rd. E14 8J 61
Rhodrons Av. Chess 7J 119
Rhondda Gro. E3 6J 61
Rhyl Rd. Gnfd 5D 54
Rhyl St. NW5 2E 58
Rhys Av. N11 7H 27
Rialto Rd. Mitc 6E 106
Ribble Clo. Wfd G 6G 31
Ribblesdale Av. N11 6E 26
Ribblesdale Av. N'holt 2M 53
Ribblesdale Ho. NW6 4L 57 (off Kilburn Va.)
Ribblesdale Rd. N8 2K 43
Ribblesdale Rd. SW16 3F 106
Ribblesdale Rd. Dart 7M 99
Ribbon Ct. N11 6E 26 (off Ribblesdale Av.)
Ribbon Dance M. SE5 9B 76
Ribchester Av. Gnfd 6D 54
Ribston Clo. Brom 3K 127
Ricardo Path. SE28 2G 81
Ricardo St. E14 9M 61
Ricards Rd. SW19 2K 105
Riccall Ct. NW9 8C 24 (off Pageant Av.)
Rice Pde. Orp 9B 112
Riceyman Ho. WC1 6L 59 (off Lloyd Baker St.)
Richard Anderson Ct. SE14 8H 77 (off Monson Rd.)
Richard Burbidge Mans. SW13 7G 73 (off Brasenose Dri.)
Richard Clo. SE18 5J 79
Richard Fell Ho. E12 9L 47 (off Walton Rd.)
Richard Ho. SE16 5G 77 (off Silwood St.)
Richard Ho. Dri. E16 9H 63
Richard Neale Ho. E1 1F 76 (off Cornwall St.)
Richards Av. Romf 4A 50
Richards Clo. Bush 9B 10
Richards Clo. Harr 3E 38
Richards Clo. Hay 7B 68
Richards Clo. Uxb 4E 142
Richards Fld. Eps 1B 134
Richard Sharples Ct. Sutt 9A 122
Richardson Clo. E8 4D 60
Richardson Ct. SW4 1J 91 (off Studley Rd.)
Richardson Rd. E15 5C 62
Richardson's M. W1 7G 59 (off Warren St.)
Richards Pl. E17 1L 45
Richard's Pl. SW3 5C 74
Richard St. E1 9F 60
Richbell Clo. Asht 9H 133
Richbell Pl. WC1 8K 59
Richborne Ter. SW8 8K 75
Richborough Clo. Orp 8H 113
Richborough Ho. SE15 7G 77 (off Sharratt St.)
Richborough Rd. NW2 9J 41
Richens Clo. Houn 1B 86
Riches Rd. Ilf 7A 48
Richfield Rd. Bush 9A 10
Richford Ga. W6 4G 73
Richford Rd. E15 4D 62
Richford St. W6 3G 73
Rich Ind. Est. SE15 7F 76
Richland Av. Coul 6E 136
Richlands Av. Eps 6E 120
Rich La. SW5 6M 73
Richman Ho. SE8 6K 77 (off Grove St.)
Richmer Rd. Eri 8E 82
Richmond. 4H 87
Richmond Av. E4 5B 30
Richmond Av. N1 4K 59
Richmond Av. NW10 2G 57
Richmond Av. SW20 5J 105
Richmond Av. Felt 5C 84
Richmond Av. Uxb 2F 142
Richmond Bri. Twic & Rich 5H 87
Richmond Bldgs. W1 9H 59
Richmond Circus (Junct.) 3J 87
Richmond Clo. E17 4K 45
Richmond Clo. Borwd 7B 12
Richmond Clo. Chesh 2C 6
Richmond Clo. Eps 6C 134
Richmond Cotts. W14 5J 73 (off Hammersmith Rd.)
Richmond Ct. E8 3F 60 (off Mare St.)
Richmond Ct. NW6 3H 57 (off Willesden La.)
Richmond Ct. SW1 3D 74 (off Sloane St.)
Richmond Ct. Lou 7H 19
Richmond Ct. Mitc 7B 106
Richmond Ct. Wemb 8K 39
Richmond Cres. E4 5B 30
Richmond Cres. N1 4K 59
Richmond Cres. N9 1E 28
Richmond Dri. Shep 1B 116
Richmond Dri. Wat 4C 8
Richmond Gdns. NW4 3E 40
Richmond Gdns. Harr 7D 22
Richmond Grn. Croy 5J 123
Richmond Gro. N1 3M 59 (in two parts)
Richmond Gro. Surb 1K 119
Richmond Hill. Rich 5J 87
Richmond Hill Ct. Rich 5J 87
Richmond Ho. NW1 5F 58 (off Park Village E.)
Richmond Ho. SE17 6B 76 (off Portland St.)
Richmond Mans. Twic 5H 87
Richmond M. W1 9H 59
Richmond M. Tedd 2D 102
Richmond Pde. Twic 5G 87 (off Richmond Rd.)
Richmond Pk. 7L 87
Richmond Pk. Lou 9H 19
Richmond Pk. Rd. SW14 4A 88
Richmond Pk. Rd. King T 5J 103
Richmond Pl. SE18 5A 80
Richmond Rd. E4 1B 30
Richmond Rd. E7 1F 62
Richmond Rd. E8 3D 60
Richmond Rd. E11 7B 46
Richmond Rd. N2 9A 26
Richmond Rd. N11 6J 27
Richmond Rd. N15 4C 44
Richmond Rd. SW20 5F 104
Richmond Rd. W5 3J 71
Richmond Rd. Coul 7F 136
Richmond Rd. Croy 5J 123
Richmond Rd. Ilf 8A 48
Richmond Rd. Iswth 2E 86
Richmond Rd. King T 1H 103
Richmond Rd. New Bar 7M 13
Richmond Rd. Romf 4D 50
Richmond Rd. T Hth 7M 107
Richmond Rd. Twic 6F 86
Richmond R.U.F.C. 2H 87
Richmond St. E13 5E 62
Richmond Ter. SW1 3J 75
Richmond Way. E11 7E 46
Richmond Way. W12 & W14 3H 73
Richmond Way. Crox G 6A 8
Richmount Gdns. SE3 2E 94
Rich St. E14 1K 77
Rickard Clo. NW4 2F 40
Rickard Clo. SW2 7L 91
Rickard Clo. W Dray 4H 143
Rickards Clo. Surb 4J 119
Ricketts Hill Rd. Tats 9H 141
Rickett St. SW6 7L 73
Rickman Hill. Coul 9F 136

Roberts Ct.—Rosalind Ct.

Roberts Ct. SE20 . . . . .5G 109
(off Maple Rd.)
Roberts M. SW1 . . . . .4E 74
Roberts M. Orp 3E 128
Robertson Rd. E15 . . . . .4A 62
Robertson St. SW8 . . . . .2F 90
Roberts Pl. EC1 . . . . .7L 59
Roberts Rd. E17 . . . . .8M 29
Roberts Rd. NW7 . . . . .6J 25
Roberts Rd. Belv 6L 81
Roberts Rd. Wat 7G 9
Robert St. E16 . . . . .2M 79
Robert St. NW1 . . . . .6F 58
Robert St. SE18 . . . . .6B 80
(in two parts)
Robert St. WC2 . . . . .1J 75
Robert St. Croy 5A 124
Robert Sutton Ho. E1 . . . . . .9G 61
(off Tarling St.)
Robeson St. E3 . . . . .8K 61
Robeson Way. Borwd 3A 12
Robina Clo. Bexh 3H 97
Robina Clo. N'wd 8D 20
Robina Ct. Swan 8E 114
Robin Clo. NW7 . . . . .3C 24
Robin Clo. Hamp 2J 101
Robin Clo. Romf 7B 34
Robin Ct. E14 . . . . .3A 78
Robin Ct. SE16 . . . . .5E 76
Robin Cres. E6 . . . . .8H 63
Robin Gro. N6 . . . . .7E 42
Robin Gro. Bren 7G 71
Robin Gro. Harr 4K 39
Robin Hill Dri. Chst 3J 111
Robin Hood (Junct.) 9C 88
Robinhood Clo. Mitc 7G 107
Robin Hood Dri. Bush 3K 9
Robin Hood Dri. Harr 7D 22
Robin Hood Gdns. E14 . . . . .1A 78
(off Woolmore St., in two parts)
Robin Hood Grn. Orp 9E 112
Robin Hood La. E14 . . . . .1A 78
Robin Hood La. SW15 . . . . . .9C 88
Robin Hood La. Bexh 4J 97
Robinhood La. Mitc 7G 107
Robin Hood La. Sutt 7L 121
Robin Hood Rd.
SW19 & SW15 . . . . . .2E 104
Robin Hood Way.
SW15 & SW20 . . . . . . .9C 88
Robin Hood Way. Gnfd 2D 54
Robin Ho. NW8 . . . . .5C 58
(off Barrow Hill Est.)
Robinia Clo. Ilf 6C 32
Robinia Cres. E10 . . . . .7M 45
Robin Pl. Wat 5F 4
Robins Clo. Uxb 8A 142
Robins Ct. SE12 . . . . .9G 95
Robin's Ct. Beck 6B 110
Robins Ct. S Croy 6C 124
(off Birdhurst Rd.)
Robinscroft M. SE10 . . . . . . .9A 78
Robins Gro. W Wick 5E 126
Robinson Clo. E11 . . . . .8C 46
Robinson Clo. Horn 3F 66
Robinson Ct. N1 . . . . .4M 59
(off St Mary's Path)
Robinson Cres. Bus H 1A 22
Robinson Ho. E14 . . . . .8L 61
(off Selsey St.)
Robinson Ho. W10 . . . . .9H 57
(off Bramley Rd.)
Robinson Rd. E2 . . . . .5G 61
Robinson Rd.
SW17 & SW19 . . . . .3C 106
Robinson Rd. Dag 9L 49
Robinson's Clo. W13 . . . . . . .8E 54
Robinson St. SW3 . . . . .7D 74
Robins Way. Wal A 7L 7
Robinsway. W on T 6G 117
Robin Way. Orp 7F 112
Robinwood Pl. SW15 . . . . . .1B 104
Roborough Wlk. Horn 2G 67
Robsart St. SW9 . . . . .1K 91
Robson Av. NW10 . . . . .3E 56
Robson Clo. E6 . . . . .9J 63
Robson Clo. Enf 4M 15
Robson Rd. SE27 . . . . .9M 91
Robsons Clo. Chesh 2C 6
Roby Ho. EC1 . . . . .7A 60
(off Mitchell St.)
Roch Av. Edgw 9K 23
Rochdale Rd. E17 . . . . .5L 45
Rochdale Rd. SE2 . . . . .6F 80
Rochdale Way. SE8 . . . . .8L 77
Roche Ho. E14 . . . . .1K 77
(off Beccles St.)
Rochelle Clo. SW11 . . . . .3B 90
Rochelle St. E2 . . . . .6D 60
(in two parts)
Rochemont Wlk. E8 . . . . .4E 60
(off Pownell Rd.)
Roche Rd. SW16 . . . . .5K 107
Rochester Av. E13 . . . . .4G 63
Rochester Av. Brom 6F 110
Rochester Av. Felt 8D 84
Rochester Clo. SW16 . . . . . .4J 107
Rochester Clo. Enf 3C 16
Rochester Clo. Sidc 5F 96
Rochester Ct. E2 . . . . .7F 60
(off Wilmot St.)
Rochester Ct. NW1 . . . . .3G 59
(off Rochester Sq.)
Rochester Dri. Bex 5K 97
Rochester Dri. Pinn 3H 37
Rochester Dri. Wat 8G 5
Rochester Gdns. Croy 5C 124
Rochester Gdns. Ilf 5K 47
Rochester Ho. SE1 . . . . .3B 76
(off Manciple St.)
Rochester Ho. SE15 . . . . . . .7G 77
(off Sharratt St.)
Rochester M. NW1 . . . . .3G 59
Rochester M. W5 . . . . .5G 71
Rochester Pde. Felt 8E 84
Rochester Pl. NW1 . . . . .2G 59
Rochester Rd. NW1 . . . . .2G 59
Rochester Rd. Cars 6D 122
Rochester Rd. Dart 6L 99
Rochester Rd. N'wd 1D 36
Rochester Row. SW1 . . . . . . .5G 75
Rochester Sq. NW1 . . . . .3G 59
Rochester St. SW1 . . . . .4H 75
Rochester Ter. NW1 . . . . .2G 59
Rochester Wlk. SE1 . . . . .2B 76
Rochester Way.
SE3 & SE9 . . . . .9F 78
Rochester Way. Dart 6B 98
Rochester Way Relief Rd.
SE3 & SE9 . . . . .9F 78
Roche Wlk. Cars 1B 122
Rochford. N17 . . . . .9C 28
(off Griffin Rd.)
Rochford Av. Lou 5M 19
Rochford Av. Romf 3G 49
Rochford Av. Wal A 7K 7
Rochford Clo. E6 . . . . .5H 63
Rochford Clo. Horn 2F 66
Rochford Grn. Lou 5M 19
Rochford Wlk. E8 . . . . .3E 60
Rochford Way. Croy 1J 123
Rochfort Ho. SE8 . . . . .6K 77
Rock Av. SW14 . . . . .2B 88
Rockbourne M. SE23 . . . . . . .7H 93
Rockbourne Rd. SE23 . . . . . .7H 93
Rockchase Gdns. Horn 4J 51
Rock Clo. Mitc 6B 106
Rockell's Pl. SE22 . . . . .5F 92
Rockfield Ho. NW4 . . . . .2H 41
(off Belle Vue Est.)
Rockfield Ho. SE10 . . . . .7A 78
(off Welland St.)
Rockford Av. Gnfd 5E 54
Rock Gdns. Dag 1M 65
Rock Gro. Way. SE16 . . . . . . .5E 76
(in two parts)
Rockhall Rd. NW2 . . . . .9H 41
Rockhall Way. NW2 . . . . .8H 41
Rockhampton Clo. SE27 . . . .1L 107
Rockhampton Rd. SE27 . . . .1L 107
Rockhampton Rd.
S Croy 8C 124
Rock Hill. SE26 . . . . .1D 108
(in two parts)
Rock Hill. Orp 8M 129
Rockingham Av. Horn 4F 50
Rockingham Clo. SW15 . . . . .3D 88
Rockingham Clo. Uxb 4A 142
Rockingham Ga. Bush 8A 10
Rockingham Pde. Uxb 3A 142
Rockingham Rd. Uxb 4A 142
Rockingham St. SE1 . . . . . . .4A 76
Rockland Rd. SW15 . . . . .3J 89
Rocklands Dri. Stan 9F 22
Rockley Ct. W14 . . . . .3H 73
(off Rockley Rd.)
Rockley Rd. W14 . . . . .3H 73
Rockmount Rd. SE18 . . . . . . .6D 80
Rockmount Rd. SE19 . . . . . .3B 108
Rocks La. SW13 . . . . .9E 72
Rock St. N4 . . . . .7L 43
Rockware Av. Gnfd 4B 54
Rockware Av. Bus. Cen.
Gnfd 4B 54
Rockways. Barn 8D 12
Rockwell Gdns. SE19 . . . . . .2C 108
Rockwell Rd. Dag 1M 65
Rockwood Pl. W12 . . . . .3G 73
Rocliffe St. N1 . . . . .5M 59
Rocombe Cres. SE23 . . . . . . .6G 93
Rocque Ho. SW6 . . . . .8K 73
(off Estcourt Rd.)
Rocque La. SE3 . . . . .2D 94
Rodale Mans. SW18 . . . . .5M 89
Rodborough Ct. W9 . . . . .7L 57
(off Hermes Clo.)
Rodborough Rd. NW11 . . . . . .6L 41
Roden Gdns. Croy 1C 124
Rodenhurst Rd. SW4 . . . . . . .5G 91
Roden St. N7 . . . . .8K 43
Roden St. Ilf 8L 47
Roden Way. Ilf 8L 47
(off Roden St.)
Rodeo Clo. Eri 9F 82
Roderick Ho. SE16 . . . . .5G 77
(off Raymouth Rd.)
Roderick Rd. NW3 . . . . .9D 42
Rodgers Clo. Els 8H 11
Rodgers Ho. SW4 . . . . .6H 91
(off Clapham Pk. Est.)
Rodin Ct. N1 . . . . .4M 59
(off Essex Rd.)
Roding Av. Wfd G 6J 31
Roding Gdns. Lou 8J 19
Roding Ho. N1 . . . . .4L 59
(off Barnsbury Est.)
Roding La. Buck H 1J 31
Roding La. N. Wfd G 6J 31
Roding La. S. Ilf 2H 47
Roding M. E1 . . . . .2E 76
Roding Rd. E5 . . . . .9H 45
Roding Rd. E6 . . . . .8M 63
Roding Rd. Lou 7J 19
Rodings Row. Barn 6J 13
(off Leecroft Rd.)
Rodings, The. Wfd G 6G 31
Roding Trad. Est. Bark 3M 63
Roding Vw. Buck H 1H 31
Roding Way. Rain 5H 67
Rodmarton St. W1 . . . . .8D 58
Rodmell. WC1 . . . . .6J 59
(off Regent Sq.)
Rodmell Clo. Hay 7J 53
Rodmell Slope. N12 . . . . .5K 25
Rodmere St. SE10 . . . . .6C 78
Rodmill La. SW2 . . . . .6J 91
Rodney Clo. Croy 3M 123
Rodney Clo. N Mald 9C 104
Rodney Clo. Pinn 5J 37
Rodney Clo. W on T 3G 117
Rodney Ct. W9 . . . . .7A 58
Rodney Ct. Barn 5K 13
Rodney Gdns. Pinn 3F 36
Rodney Gdns. W Wick 6E 126
Rodney Grn. W on T 4G 117
Rodney Ho. E14 . . . . .5M 77
(off Cahir St.)
Rodney Ho. N1 . . . . .5K 59
(off Donegal St.)
Rodney Ho. SW1 . . . . .6G 75
(off Dolphin Sq.)
Rodney Ho. W11 . . . . .1L 73
(off Pembridge Cres.)
Rodney Pl. E17 . . . . .9J 29
Rodney Pl. SE17 . . . . .5A 76
Rodney Pl. SW19 . . . . .5A 106
Rodney Rd. E11 . . . . .2F 46
Rodney Rd. SE17 . . . . .5A 76
(in two parts)
Rodney Rd. Mitc 7C 106
Rodney Rd. N Mald 9C 104
Rodney Rd. Twic 5L 85
Rodney Rd. W on T 4G 117
Rodney St. N1 . . . . .5K 59
Rodney Way. Romf 8M 33
Rodway Rd. SW15 . . . . .6E 88
Rodway Rd. Brom 5F 110
Rodwell Clo. Ruis 6G 37
Rodwell Pl. Edgw 6L 23
Rodwell Rd. SE22 . . . . .5D 92
Roe. NW9 . . . . .7D 24
Roebourne Way. E16 . . . . . . .2L 79
Roebuck Clo. Felt 1F 100
Roebuck Ho. SW1 . . . . .4G 75
(off Palace Ho.)
Roebuck La. N17 . . . . .6D 28
Roebuck La. Buck H 9G 19
Roebuck Rd. Chess 7L 119
Roebuck Rd. Ilf 5F 32
Roebuck Rd. Trad. Est. Ilf . . .6F 32
Roedean Av. Enf 3G 17
Roedean Clo. Enf 3G 17
Roedean Clo. Orp 6F 128
Roedean Cres. SW15 . . . . . . .5C 88
Roedean Dri. Romf 2C 50
Roe End. NW9 . . . . .2A 40
Roe Green. 2A 40
Roe Grn. NW9 . . . . .3A 40
Roehampton. 6E 88
Roehampton Clo. SW15 . . . . .3E 88
Roehampton Dri. Chst 3A 112
Roehampton Ga. SW15 . . . . .5C 88
Roehampton High St.
SW15 . . . . .6E 88
Roehampton Lane (Junct.)
. . . . .7F 88
Roehampton La. SW15 . . . . .3E 88
Roehampton Va. SW15 . . . . .9D 88
Roe La. NW9 . . . . .2M 39
Rofant Rd. N'wd 6C 20
Roffey Clo. Purl 8M 137
Roffey St. E14 . . . . .3A 78
Rogate Ho. E5 . . . . .8E 44
Roger Bannister Sports Cen., The.
. . . . .6A 22
Roger Dowley Ct. E2 . . . . . . .5G 61
Roger Harriss Almshouses.
E15 . . . . .4D 62
(off Gift La.)
Roger Reede's Almshouses.
Romf 2C 50
Rogers Ct. E14 . . . . .1L 77
(off Premiere Pl.)
Rogers Ct. Swan 8E 114
Rogers Est. E2 . . . . .6G 61
Rogers Gdns. Dag 1L 65
Rogers Ho. SW1 . . . . .5H 75
(off Page St.)
Roger's Ho. Dag 8L 49
Rogers La. Warl 9K 139
Rogers Rd. E16 . . . . .9D 62
Rogers Rd. SW17 . . . . .1B 106
Rogers Rd. Dag 1L 65
Rogers Ruff. N'wd 8A 20
Roger St. WC1 . . . . .7K 59
Rogers Wlk. N12 . . . . .3M 25
Rohere Ho. EC1 . . . . .6A 60
Rojack Rd. SE23 . . . . .7H 93
Rokeby Gdns. Wfd G 8E 30
Rokeby Pl. SW20 . . . . .4F 104
Rokeby Rd. SE4 . . . . .1K 93
Rokeby Rd. Harr 1B 38
Rokeby St. E15 . . . . .4B 62
Roke Clo. Kenl 6A 138
Rokell Ho. Beck 2M 109
(off Beckenham Hill Rd.)
Roke Lodge Rd. Kenl 5M 137
Roke Rd. Kenl 7A 138
Rokesby Clo. Well 1B 96
Rokesby Pl. Wemb 1H 55
Rokesly Av. N8 . . . . .3J 43
Roland Gdns. SW7 . . . . .6A 74
Roland Ho. SW7 . . . . .6A 74
(off Cranley M.)
Roland M. E1 . . . . .8H 61
Roland Rd. E17 . . . . .2B 46
Roland Way. SE17 . . . . .6B 76
Roland Way. SW7 . . . . .6A 74
Roland Way. Wor Pk 4D 120
Roles Gro. Romf 2H 49
Rolfe Clo. Barn 6C 14
Rolinsden Way. Kes 7H 127
Rolland Ho. W7 . . . . .8C 54
Rollesby Rd. Chess 8L 119
Rollesby Way. SE28 . . . . . . .9G 65
Rolleston Av. Orp 1M 127
Rolleston Clo. Orp 2M 127
Rolleston Rd. S Croy 9B 124
Roll Gdns. Ilf 3L 47
Rollins St. SE15 . . . . .7G 77
Rollit Cres. Houn 4L 85
Rollit St. N7 . . . . .1L 59
Rollo Rd. Swan 4D 114
Rolls Bldgs. EC4 . . . . .9L 59
Rollscourt Av. SE24 . . . . .4A 92
Rolls Pk. Av. E4 . . . . .5L 29
Rolls Pk. Rd. E4 . . . . .5M 29
Rolls Pas. EC4 . . . . .9L 59
(off Chancery La.)
Rolls Rd. SE1 . . . . .6D 76
Rolt St. SE8 . . . . .7J 77
(in two parts)
Rolvenden Gdns. Brom 4H 111
Rolvenden Pl. N17 . . . . .8E 28
Roman Clo. W3 . . . . .3M 71
Roman Clo. Felt 4G 85
Roman Clo. Rain 5B 66
Roman Ct. N7 . . . . .2K 59
Romanfield Rd. SW2 . . . . . . .6K 91
Roman Gdns. K Lan 3A 4
Roman Ho. EC2 . . . . .8A 60
(off Wood St.)
Romanhurst Av. Brom 8C 110
Romanhurst Gdns.
Brom 8C 110
Roman Ind. Est. Croy 2C 124
Roman Ri. SE19 . . . . .3B 108
Roman Rd. E2 & E3 . . . . .6G 61
Roman Rd. E3 . . . . .4K 61
Roman Rd. E6 . . . . .7H 63
Roman Rd. N10 . . . . .7F 26
Roman Rd. NW2 . . . . .8G 41
Roman Rd. W4 . . . . .5C 72
Roman Rd. Ilf 2M 63
Roman Sq. SE28 . . . . .2E 80
Roman Wlk. Rad 1D 10
Roman Way. N7 . . . . .2K 59
Roman Way. SE15 . . . . .8G 77
Roman Way. Cars 1D 136
Roman Way. Croy 4M 123
Roman Way. Dart 4C 98
Roman Way. Enf 7D 16
Roman Way Ind. Est. N7 . . . .3K 59
(off Roman Way)
Romany Gdns. E17 . . . . .8J 29
Romany Gdns. Sutt 2L 121
Romany Ri. Orp 3A 128
Roma Read Clo. SW15 . . . . . .6F 88
Roma Rd. E17 . . . . .1J 45
Romayne Ho. SW4 . . . . .2H 91
Romberg Rd. SW17 . . . . .9E 90
Romborough Gdns. SE13 . . .4A 94
Romborough Way. SE13 . . . .4A 94
Rom Cres. Romf 5D 50
Romeland. Els 8H 11
Romeland. Wal A 6J 7
Romer Ho. W10 . . . . .6K 57
(off Dowland St.)
Romero Clo. SW9 . . . . .2K 91
Romero Sq. SE3 . . . . .3G 95
Romeyn Rd. SW16 . . . . .9K 91
Romford. 3C 50
Romford Greyhound Stadium.
. . . . .4A 50
Romford Ice Rink. 5C 50
Romford Rd. E15 & E7 . . . . .2C 62
Romford Rd. Ave 1M 83
Romford Rd. Chig 3F 32
Romford Rd. Romf 7J 33
Romford St. E1 . . . . .8E 60
Romilly Dri. Wat 4J 21
Romilly Rd. N4 . . . . .7M 43
Romilly St. W1 . . . . .1H 75
Romily Ct. SW6 . . . . .1K 89
Rommany Rd. SE27 . . . . . .1B 108
(in two parts)
Romney Chase. Horn 4L 51
Romney Clo. N17 . . . . .8F 28
Romney Clo. NW11 . . . . .6A 42
Romney Clo. SE14 . . . . .8G 77
Romney Clo. Ashf 2A 100
Romney Clo. Chess 6J 119
Romney Clo. Harr 5L 37
Romney Ct. NW3 . . . . .2C 58
Romney Ct. W12 . . . . .3H 73
(off Shepherd's Bush Grn.)
Romney Dri. Brom 4H 111
Romney Dri. Harr 5L 37
Romney Gdns. Bexh 9K 81
Romney M. W1 . . . . .8E 58
Romney Pde. Hay 5B 52
Romney Rd. SE10 . . . . .7B 78
Romney Rd. Hay 5B 52
Romney Rd. N Mald 1B 120
Romney Row. NW2 . . . . .7H 41
(off Brent Ter.)
Romney St. SW1 . . . . .4J 75
Romola Rd. SE24 . . . . .7M 91
Romsey Clo. Orp 6M 127
Romsey Gdns. Dag 4H 65
Romsey Rd. W13 . . . . .1E 70
Romsey Rd. Dag 4H 65
Romulus Ct. Bren 8H 71
Rom Valley Way. Romf 5C 50
Ronald Av. E15 . . . . .6C 62
Ronald Buckingham Ct.
SE16 . . . . .3G 77
(off Kenning St.)
Ronald Clo. Beck 8K 109
Ronald Ct. Brick W 2K 5
Ronald Ct. New Bar 5M 13
Ronald Ho. SE3 . . . . .3G 95
Ronald Rd. Romf 8L 35
Ronaldshay. N4 . . . . .6L 43
Ronalds Rd. N5 . . . . .1L 59
(in three parts)
Ronalds Rd. Brom 5E 110
Ronaldstone Rd. Sidc 5C 96
Ronald St. E1 . . . . .9G 61
Rona Rd. NW3 . . . . .9E 42
Ronart St. W'stone 1D 38
Rona Wlk. N1 . . . . .2B 60
(off Ramsey Wlk.)
Rondel Ct. Bex 5J 97
Rondu Rd. NW2 . . . . .1J 57
Ronelean Rd. Surb 4K 119
Roneo Corner. Horn 6D 50
Roneo Link. Horn 6D 50
Ronfearn Av. Orp 9H 113
Ron Leighton Way. E6 . . . . . .4J 63
Ronneby Clo. Wey 5C 116
Ronver Rd. SE12 . . . . .7D 94
Rood La. EC3 . . . . .1C 76
Rookby Ct. N21 . . . . .2M 27
Rook Clo. Horn 3E 66
Rook Clo. Wemb 8M 39
Rookeries Clo. Felt 9F 84
Rookery Clo. NW9 . . . . .3D 40
Rookery Cres. Dag 3M 65
Rookery Dri. Chst 5L 111
Rookery Gdns. Orp 9G 113
Rookery La. Brom 1H 127
Rookery Rd. SW4 . . . . .3G 91
Rookery Rd. Orp 2K 141
Rookery, The. 9F 8
Rookery Way. NW9 . . . . .3D 40
Rookesley Rd. Orp 2H 129
Rooke Way. SE10 . . . . .6D 78
Rookfield Av. N10 . . . . .2G 43
Rookfield Clo. N10 . . . . .2G 43
Rookley Clo. Sutt 1M 135
Rooksmead Rd. Sun 6D 100
Rooks Ter. W Dray 3J 143
Rookstone Rd. SW17 . . . . . .2D 106
Rook Wlk. E6 . . . . .9H 63
Rookwood Av. N Mald 8E 104
Rookwood Av. Wall 6H 123
Rookwood Gdns. E4 . . . . . . .2D 30
Rookwood Ho. Bark 5B 64
Rookwood Rd. N16 . . . . .5D 44
Roosevelt Memorial. 1E 74
Roosevelt Way. Dag 2B 66
Rootes Dri. W10 . . . . .8H 57
Ropemaker Rd. SE16 . . . . . . .3J 77
Ropemaker's Fields. E14 . . . .1K 77
Ropemaker St. EC2 . . . . .8B 60
Roper La. SE1 . . . . .3C 76
Ropers Av. E4 . . . . .5M 29
Ropers Orchard. SW3 . . . . . .7C 74
(off Danvers St.)
Roper St. SE9 . . . . .4K 95
Ropers Wlk. SW2 . . . . .6L 91
Roper Way. Mitc 6E 106
Ropery Bus. Pk. SE7 . . . . . . .5G 79
Ropery St. E3 . . . . .7K 61
Rope St. SE16 . . . . .5J 77
Rope Wlk. Sun 7G 101
Rope Wlk. Gdns. E1 . . . . .9E 60
Ropewalk M. E8 . . . . .3E 60
(off Middleton Rd.)
Rope Yd. Rails. SE18 . . . . . . .4M 79
Ropley St. E2 . . . . .5E 60
Rosa Alba M. N5 . . . . .9A 44
Rosalind Ct. Bark 3E 64
(off Meadow Rd.)

Rosalind Ho.—Rowantree Rd.

Rosalind Ho. N1 5C 60
(off Arden Ho.)
Rosaline Rd. SW6 8J 73
Rosaline Ter. SW6 8J 73
(off Rosaline Rd.)
Rosamond St. SE26 9F 92
Rosamund Clo. S Croy 6B 124
Rosamun St. S'hall 5J 69
Rosary Clo. Houn 1J 85
Rosary Gdns. SW7 5A 74
Rosary Gdns. Ashf 1A 100
Rosary Gdns. Bush 9C 10
Rosaville Rd. SW6 8K 73
Roscoe St. EC1 7A 60
(in two parts)
Roscoe St. Est. EC1 7A 60
Roscoff Clo. Edgw 8A 24
Roseacre Clo. W13 8F 54
Roseacre Clo. Horn 5K 51
Roseacre Rd. Well 2F 96
Rose All. EC2 8C 60
(off Bishopsgate)
Rose All. SE1 2A 76
Rose & Crown Ct. EC2 9A 60
(off Foster La.)
Rose & Crown Pas. Iswth 9E 70
Rose & Crown Yd. SW1 2G 75
Roseary Clo. W Dray 5H 143
Rose Av. E18 9F 30
Rose Av. Mitc 5D 106
Rose Av. Mord 9A 106
Rosebank. SE20 4F 108
Rosebank. SW6 8G 73
Rosebank. W3 9B 56
Rosebank. Eps 6A 134
Rosebank. Wal A 6L 7
Rosebank Av. Horn 1G 67
Rosebank Av. Wemb 9D 38
Rose Bank Clo. N12 5C 26
Rosebank Clo. Tedd 3E 102
Rosebank Gdns. E3 5K 61
Rosebank Gdns. W3 9B 56
Rosebank Gro. E17 1K 45
Rosebank Rd. E17 4M 45
Rosebank Rd. W7 3C 70
Rosebank Vs. E17 2L 45
Rosebank Wlk. NW1 3H 59
Rosebank Wlk. SE18 5J 79
Rosebank Way. W3 9B 56
Rose Bates Dri. NW9 2L 39
Roseberry Av. T Hth 6A 108
Roseberry Ct. Wat 3E 8
(in two parts)
Roseberry Gdns. N4 4M 43
Roseberry Gdns. Dart 6G 99
Roseberry Gdns. Orp 5C 128
Roseberry Pl. E8 2D 60
Roseberry St. SE1 5F 76
Rosebery Av. E12 2J 63
Rosebery Av. EC1 7L 59
Rosebery Av. N17 9E 28
Rosebery Av. Eps 6C 134
Rosebery Av. Harr 9J 37
Rosebery Av. N Mald 6D 104
Rosebery Av. Sidc 6C 96
Rosebery Clo. Mord 1H 121
Rosebery Ct. EC1 7L 59
(off Rosebery Av.)
Rosebery Gdns. N8 3J 43
Rosebery Gdns. W13 9E 54
Rosebery Gdns. Sutt 6M 121
Rosebery Ho. E2 5H 61
(off Sewardstone Rd.)
Rosebery Ind. Est. N17 9F 28
Rosebery Ind. Pk. N17 9F 28
Rosebery M. N10 9G 27
Rosebery Rd. N9 3E 28
Rosebery Rd. N10 9G 27
Rosebery Rd. SW2 5J 91
Rosebery Rd. Bush 9M 9
Rosebery Rd. Houn 4A 86
Rosebery Rd. King T 6M 103
Rosebery Rd. Sutt 8K 121
Rosebery Sq. EC1 7L 59
(off Rosebery Av.)
Rosebery Sq. King T 6M 103
Rosebine Av. Twic 6B 86
Rosebriars. Esh 7A 118
(in two parts)
Rosebriar Wlk. Wat 9D 4
Rosebury Rd. SW6 1M 89
Rosebury Sq. Wfd G 7L 31
Rosebury Va. Ruis 7E 36
Rose Bush Ct. NW3 1D 58
Rosebushes. Eps 8F 134
Rose Cotts. Brick 3M 5
Rose Cotts. Kes 3G 141
Rose Ct. E1 8D 60
(off Wentworth St.)
Rose Ct. E8 3D 60
(off Richmond Rd.)
Rose Ct. SE16 5H 77
Rose Ct. Chesh 1A 6
Rose Ct. S Harr 7A 38
Rose Ct. Wemb 5J 55
(off Vicars Bri. Clo.)
Rosecourt Rd. Croy 1K 123
Rosecroft. N14 2J 27
Rosecroft Av. NW3 8L 41
Rosecroft Clo. Big H 9K 141
Rosecroft Clo. Orp 1G 129
Rosecroft Ct. N'wd 6A 20
Rosecroft Dri. Wat 9C 4
Rosecroft Gdns. NW2 8E 40
Rosecroft Gdns. Twic 7B 86
Rosecroft Rd. S'hall 7L 53
Rosecroft Wlk. Pinn 3H 37
Rosecroft Wlk. Wemb 1H 55
Rosedale. 1A 6
Rosedale. Asht 9G 133
Rose Dale. Orp 4M 127
Rosedale Av. Chesh 2A 6
Rosedale Av. Hay 8B 52
Rosedale Clo. SE2 4F 80
Rosedale Clo. W7 3D 70
Rosedale Clo. Brick W 3J 5
Rosedale Clo. Dart 6M 99
Rosedale Clo. Stan 6F 22
Rosedale Ct. N5 9M 43
Rosedale Ct. Harr 9D 38
Rosedale Gdns. Dag 3F 64
Rosedale Ho. N16 6B 44
Rosedale Pl. Croy 2H 125
Rosedale Rd. E7 1G 63
Rosedale Rd. Dag 3F 64
Rosedale Rd. Eps 7E 120
Rosedale Rd. Rich 2J 87
Rosedale Rd. Romf 9A 34
Rosedale Ter. W6 4F 72
(off Dalling Rd.)
Rosedale Way. Chesh 1A 6
Rosedene. NW6 4H 57
(in three parts)
Rosedene Av. SW16 9K 91
Rosedene Av. Croy 2J 123
Rosedene Av. Gnfd 6L 53
Rosedene Av. Mord 9L 105
Rosedene Ct. Dart 6G 99
Rosedene Ct. Ruis 6C 36
Rosedene Gdns. Ilf 2L 47
Rosedene Ter. E10 7M 45
Rosedew Rd. W6 7H 73
Rose End. Wor Pk 3H 121
Rosefield Clo. Cars 7C 122
Rosefield Gdns. E14 1L 77
Roseford Ct. W12 3H 73
(off Shepherd's Bush Grn.)
Rose Garden Clo. Edgw 6J 23
Rose Gdns. W5 4H 71
Rose Gdns. Felt 8E 84
Rose Gdns. S'hall 7L 53
Rose Gdns. Stanw 6B 144
Rose Gdns. Wat 7E 8
Rose Glen. NW9 2B 40
Rose Glen. Romf 6C 50
Rosehart M. W11 9L 57
Rosehatch Av. Romf 1H 49
Roseheath Rd. Houn 4K 85
Rosehill. 3A 122
Rosehill. Clay 8E 118
Rosehill. Hamp 5L 101
Rosehill. Sutt 4M 121
Rosehill Av. Sutt 3A 122
Rosehill Ct. Mord 2A 122
(off St Helier Av.)
Rosehill Ct. Pde. Mord 2A 122
(off St Helier Av.)
Rosehill Farm Mdw.
Bans 7M 135
Rosehill Gdns. Ab L 5A 4
Rosehill Gdns. Gnfd 1D 54
Rosehill Gdns. Sutt 4M 121
Rosehill Pk. W. Sutt 3A 122
Rosehill Rd. SW18 5A 90
Rosehill Rd. Big H 9G 141
Rose Hill Roundabout (Junct.)
2A 122
Roseland Clo. N17 7B 28
Rose La. Romf 1H 49
Rose Lawn. Bus H 1A 22
Roseleigh Av. N5 9M 43
Roseleigh Clo. Twic 5H 87
Rosemary Av. N2 2M 41
Rosemary Av. N3 9M 25
Rosemary Av. N9 1F 28
Rosemary Av. Enf 3C 16
Rosemary Av. Houn 1H 85
Rosemary Av. Romf 1D 50
Rosemary Av. W Mol 7L 101
Rosemary Clo. Croy 1J 123
Rosemary Clo. Uxb 8E 142
Rosemary Ct. SE8 7K 77
(off Dorking Clo.)
Rosemary Ct. H End 7L 21
(off Avenue, The)
Rosemary Dri. E14 9B 62
Rosemary Dri. Ilf 3H 47
Rosemary Gdns. SW14 2A 88
Rosemary Gdns. Chess 6J 119
Rosemary Gdns. Dag 6K 49
Rosemary Ho. N1 4B 60
(off Colville Est.)
Rosemary La. SW14 2A 88
Rosemary Rd. SE15 8D 76
Rosemary Rd. SW17 9A 90
Rosemary Rd. Well 9D 80
Rosemary St. N1 4B 60
Rosemead. NW9 5D 40
Rosemead Av. Felt 8D 84
Rosemead Av. Mitc 7G 107
Rosemead Av. Wemb 1J 55
Rose M. N18 4F 28
Rosemont Av. N12 6A 26
Rosemont Rd. NW3 2A 58
Rosemont Rd. W3 1M 71
Rosemont Rd. N Mald 7A 104
Rosemont Rd. Rich 5J 87
Rosemoor St. SW3 5D 74
Rosemount Clo. Wfd G 6K 31
Rosemount Dri. Brom 8K 111
Rosemount Point. SE23 9H 93
Rosemount Rd. W13 9E 54
Rosenau Cres. SW11 9D 74
Rosenau Rd. SW11 9C 74
Rosendale Rd.
SE24 & SE21 6A 92
Roseneath Av. N21 1M 27
Roseneath Clo. Orp 9G 129
Roseneath Rd. SW11 5E 90
Roseneath Wlk. Enf 6C 16
Rosen's Wlk. Edgw 3M 23
Rosenthal Rd. SE6 5M 93
Rosenthorpe Rd. SE15 4H 93
Rose Pk. Clo. Hay 8G 53
Rosepark Ct. Ilf 9K 31
Roserton St. E14 3A 78
Rosery, The. Croy 1H 125
Rose Sq. SW3 6B 74
Roses, The. Wfd G 7D 30
Rose St. EC4 9M 59
Rose St. WC2 1J 75
(in two parts)
Rosethorn Clo. SW12 6H 91
Rosetta Clo. SW8 8J 75
(off Kenchester Clo.)
Rosetti Ter. Dag 9F 48
(off Marlborough Rd.)
Roseveare Rd. SE12 1G 111
Rose Vs. Dart 6M 99
Roseville Av. Houn 4L 85
Roseville Rd. Hay 6E 68
Rosevine Rd. SW20 5G 105
Rose Wlk. Purl 3H 137
Rose Wlk. Surb 9M 103
Rose Wlk. W Wick 4A 126
Rose Wlk., The. Rad 1F 10
Rose Way. SE12 4E 94
Roseway. SE21 5B 92
Rose Way. Edgw 4A 24
Rosewell Clo. SE20 4F 108
Rosewood. Dart 1C 114
Rosewood. Sutt 2A 136
Rosewood. Th Dit 4E 118
Rosewood Av. Gnfd 1E 54
Rosewood Av. Horn 1E 66
Rosewood Clo. Sidc 9G 97
Rosewood Ct. E11 9B 46
Rosewood Ct. Brom 5G 111
Rosewood Gdns. SE13 1A 94
Rosewood Gro. Sutt 4A 122
Rosewood Ho. SW8 7K 75
Rosewood Sq. W12 9E 56
Rosher Clo. E15 3B 62
Roshni Ho. SW17 3C 106
Rosina St. E9 2H 61
Roskell Rd. SW15 2H 89
Roslin Ho. E1 1H 77
(off Brodlove La.)
Roslin Rd. W3 4M 71
Roslin Way. Brom 2E 110
Roslyn Clo. Mitc 6B 106
Roslyn Gdns. Romf 9D 34
Roslyn Rd. N15 3B 44
Rosmead Rd. W11 1J 73
Rosoman Pl. EC1 7L 59
Rosoman St. EC1 6L 59
Rossall Clo. Horn 4E 50
Rossall Cres. NW10 6K 55
Ross Av. NW7 5J 25
Ross Av. Dag 7K 49
Ross Clo. Harr 7A 22
Ross Clo. Hay 5B 68
Ross Clo. N'holt 9B 38
Ross Ct. E5 9F 44
(off Napoleon Rd.)
Ross Ct. NW9 1C 40
Ross Ct. W13 8F 54
(off Cleveland Rd.)
Rosscourt Mans. SW1 4F 74
(off Buckingham Pal. Rd.)
Ross Cres. Wat 8E 4
Rossdale. Sutt 7C 122
Rossdale Dri. N9 8G 17
Rossdale Dri. NW9 6A 40
Rossdale Rd. SW15 3G 89
Rosse M. SE3 9F 78
Rossendale Clo. Enf 1M 15
Rossendale St. E5 7F 44
Rossendale Way. NW1 4G 59
Rossetti Ct. WC1 8H 59
(off Ridgmount Pl.)
Rossetti Gdns. Coul 9K 137
Rossetti Ho. SW1 5H 75
(off Erasmus St.)
Rossetti M. NW8 4B 58
Rossetti Rd. SE16 6F 76
Rosshaven Pl. N'wd 8D 20
Ross Ho. E1 2F 76
(off Prusom St.)
Rossignol Gdns. Cars 4E 122
Rossindel Rd. Houn 4L 85
Rossington Av. Borwd 2J 11
Rossington Clo. Enf 2F 16
Rossington St. E5 7E 44
Rossiter Fields. Barn 8K 13
Rossiter Rd. SW12 7F 90
Rossland Clo. Bexh 4M 97
Rosslyn Av. E4 2D 30
Rosslyn Av. SW13 2C 88
Rosslyn Av. Dag 5K 49
Rosslyn Av. E Barn 8C 14
Rosslyn Av. Felt 5E 84
Rosslyn Av. Romf 9J 35
Rosslyn Clo. Hay 8B 52
Rosslyn Clo. Sun 3C 100
Rosslyn Clo. W Wick 5D 126
Rosslyn Cres. Harr 2D 38
Rosslyn Cres. Wemb 9J 39
Rosslyn Gdns. Wemb 8J 39
(off Rosslyn Cres.)
Rosslyn Hill. NW3 9B 42
Rosslyn Mans. NW6 3A 58
(off Goldhurst Ter.)
Rosslyn M. NW3 9B 42
Rosslyn Pk. Wey 6B 116
Rosslyn Pk. M. NW3 1B 58
Rosslyn Pk. R.U.F.C. 3D 88
Rosslyn Rd. E17 2A 46
Rosslyn Rd. Bark 3B 64
Rosslyn Rd. Twic 5G 87
Rosslyn Rd. Wat 5F 8
Rossmore Clo. NW1 7C 58
(off Rossmore Rd.)
Rossmore Ct. NW1 7D 58
Rossmore Rd. NW1 7C 58
Ross Pde. Wall 8F 122
Ross Rd. SE25 7B 108
Ross Rd. Dart 5E 98
Ross Rd. Twic 7M 85
Ross Rd. Wall 7G 123
Ross Way. SE9 2J 95
Ross Way. N'wd 4D 20
Rossway Dri. Bush 7A 10
Rosswood Gdns. Wall 8G 123
Ross Wyld Lodge. E17 1L 45
(off Forest Rd.)
Rostella Rd. SW17 1B 106
Rostrevor Av. N15 4D 44
Rostrevor Gdns. Hay 2C 68
Rostrevor Gdns. S'hall 6J 69
Rostrevor M. SW6 9K 73
Rostrevor Rd. SW6 9K 73
Rostrevor Rd. SW19 2L 105
Roswell Clo. Chesh 3E 6
Rotary St. SE1 4M 75
Rothay. NW1 6F 58
(off Albany St.)
Rothbury Av. Rain 8F 66
Rothbury Gdns. Iswth 8E 70
Rothbury Hall. SE10 5C 78
(off Azof St.)
Rothbury Rd. E9 3K 61
Rothbury Wlk. N17 7E 28
Rotheley Ho. E9 3G 61
(off Balcorne St.)
Rother Clo. Wat 7G 5
Rotherfield Ct. N1 3B 60
(off Rotherfield St., in two parts)
Rotherfield Rd. Cars 6E 122
Rotherfield Rd. Enf 1H 17
Rotherfield St. N1 3A 60
Rotherham Wlk. SE1 2M 75
(off Nicholson St.)
Rotherhill Av. SW16 3H 107
Rotherhithe. 3G 77
Rotherhithe New Rd.
SE16 6F 76
Rotherhithe Old Rd. SE16 5H 77
Rotherhithe St. SE16 3G 77
Rotherhithe Tunnel.
SE16 & E1 2H 77
Rother Ho. SE15 3F 92
Rothermere Rd. Croy 7K 123
Rotherwick Hill. W5 7K 55
Rotherwick Ho. E1 1E 76
(off Thomas More St.)
Rotherwick Rd. NW11 5L 41
Rotherwood Clo. SW20 5J 105
Rotherwood Rd. SW15 2H 89
Rothery St. N1 4M 59
(off St Marys Path)
Rothesay Av. SW20 6J 105
Rothesay Av. Gnfd 2A 54
(in two parts)
Rothesay Av. Rich 3M 87
Rothesay Ct. SE6 8D 94
(off Cumberland Pl.)
Rothesay Ct. SE11 7L 75
(off Harleyford St.)
Rothesay Ct. SE12 9F 94
Rothesay Rd. SE25 8B 108
Rothley Ct. NW8 7B 58
(off St John's Wood Rd.)
Rothsay Rd. E7 3G 63
Rothsay St. SE1 4C 76
Rothsay Wlk. E14 5L 77
(off Charnwood Gdns.)
Rothschild Rd. W4 5A 72
Rothschild St. SE27 1M 107
Roth Wlk. N7 7K 43
Rothwell Ct. Harr 3D 38
Rothwell Gdns. Dag 3G 65
Rothwell Ho. Houn 7L 69
Rothwell Rd. Dag 4G 65
Rothwell St. NW1 4D 58
Rotten Row. NW3 6A 42
Rotten Row. SW7 & SW1 3C 74
Rotterdam Dri. E14 4A 78
Rotunda, The. Romf 3B 50
(off Yew Tree Gdns.)
Rouel Rd. SE16 4E 76
(Old Jamaica Rd.)
Rouel Rd. SE16 5E 76
(Yalding Rd.)
Rougemont Av. Mord 1L 121
Roughs, The. N'wd 3C 20
Roughwood Clo. Wat 2C 8
Roundabout Ho. N'wd 8E 20
Roundacre. SW19 8H 89
Roundaway Rd. Ilf 8K 31
Round Bush. 2B 10
Roundel Clo. SE4 3K 93
Round Gro. Croy 2H 125
Roundhay Clo. SE23 8H 93
Roundhedge Way. Enf 2K 15
Round Hill. SE26 8G 93
(in two parts)
Roundhill Dri. Enf 6K 15
Roundhills. Wal A 7L 7
Roundhouse Theatre, The.
3E 58
Roundlyn Gdns. St M 8F 112
Roundmead Av. Lou 4L 19
Roundmead Clo. Lou 5L 19
Roundmoor Dri. Chesh 2E 6
Roundshaw. 9J 123
Roundshaw Cen. Wall 9J 123
(off Mollison Dri.)
Roundtable Rd. Brom 9D 94
Roundtree Rd. Wemb 1F 54
Roundway. Big H 8G 141
Roundways. Ruis 8D 36
Roundway, The. N17 8A 28
Roundway, The. Clay 8D 118
Roundway, The. Wat 8D 8
Roundwood. Chst 6M 111
Roundwood Av. Uxb 2A 68
Roundwood Clo. Ruis 5B 36
Roundwood Rd. NW10 2D 56
Roundwood Vw. Bans 7H 135
Roundwood Way. Bans 7H 135
Rounton Dri. Wat 2D 8
Rounton Rd. E3 7L 61
Rounton Rd. Wal A 6L 7
Roupell Ho. King T 4K 103
(off Florence Rd.)
Roupell Rd. SW2 7K 91
Roupell St. SE1 2L 75
Rousden St. NW1 3G 59
Rousebarn La.
Chan X & Crox G 4A 8
(in two parts)
Rouse Gdns. SE21 1C 108
Rous Rd. Buck H 1J 31
Routemaster Clo. E13 6F 62
Routh Ct. Felt 7B 84
Routh Rd. SW18 6C 90
Routh St. E6 8K 63
Rover Av. Ilf 6D 32
Rover Ho. N1 4C 60
(off Whitmore Est.)
Rowallan Rd. SW6 8J 73
Rowallen Pde. Dag 6G 49
Rowan. N10 9F 26
Rowan Av. E4 6K 29
Rowan Clo. SW16 5G 107
Rowan Clo. W5 3J 71
Rowan Clo. Brick W 4L 5
Rowan Clo. Ilf 1B 64
Rowan Clo. N Mald 6C 104
Rowan Clo. Stan 6D 22
Rowan Clo. Wemb 8E 38
Rowan Ct. E13 5F 62
(off High St.)
Rowan Ct. SE15 8D 76
(off Garnies Clo.)
Rowan Ct. SW11 5D 90
Rowan Cres. SW16 5G 107
Rowan Cres. Dart 7G 99
Rowan Dri. NW9 1E 40
Rowan Gdns. Croy 5D 124
Rowan Grn. Wey 6B 116
Rowan Gro. Ave 1M 83
Rowan Ho. SE16 3H 77
(off Woodland Cres.)
Rowan Ho. Short 6C 110
Rowan Ho. Sidc 9D 96
Rowan Lodge. W8 4M 73
(off Chantry Sq.)
Rowan Pl. Hay 1D 68
Rowan Rd. SW16 6G 107
Rowan Rd. W6 5H 73
Rowan Rd. Bexh 2J 97
Rowan Rd. Bren 8F 70
Rowan Rd. Swan 7B 114
Rowan Rd. W Dray 5H 143
Rowans Bowl. N4 7L 43
Rowans, The. N13 3M 27
Rowans, The. Ave 2M 83
Rowans, The. Sun 2D 100
Rowans Way. Lou 6K 19
Rowan Ter. W6 5H 73
(off Rowan Rd.)
Rowantree Clo. N21 1B 28
Rowantree Rd. N21 1B 28

Rowantree Rd.—Russell Av.

Rowantree Rd. Enf 4M 15
Rowan Wlk. N2 3A 42
Rowan Wlk. N19 7G 43
Rowan Wlk. W10 7J 57
Rowan Wlk. Barn 7M 13
Rowan Wlk. Brom 5K 127
Rowan Wlk. Horn 2H 51
Rowan Way. Romf 1G 49
Rowanwood Av. Sidc 7E 96
Rowanwood M. Enf 4M 15
Rowben Clo. N20 1M 25
Rowberry Clo. SW6 8G 73
Rowcross St. SE1 6D 76
Rowdell Rd. N'holt 4L 53
Rowden Pk. Gdns. E4 7L 29
(off Chingford Rd.)
Rowden Rd. E4 6M 29
Rowden Rd. Beck 5J 109
Rowden Rd. Eps 6M 119
Rowditch La. SW11 1E 90
Rowdon Av. NW10 3F 56
Rowdown Cres. New Ad 1B 140
Rowdowns Rd. Dag 4K 65
Rowe Gdns. Bark 5D 64
Rowe La. E9 1G 61
Rowena Cres. SW11 1C 90
Rowe Wlk. Harr 8L 37
Rowfant Rd. SW17 7E 90
Rowhill Rd. E5 9F 44
Rowhill Rd.
Swan & Dart 3D 114
Rowhurst Av. Lea 9D 132
Rowington Clo. W2 8M 57
Rowland Av. Harr 1G 39
Rowland Ct. E16 7D 62
Rowland Cres. Chig 4C 32
Rowland Gro. SE26 9F 92
Rowland Hill Av. N17 7A 28
Rowland Hill Ho. SE1 3M 75
Rowland Hill St. NW3 1C 58
Rowland Pl. N'wd 7C 20
Rowlands Av. Pinn 5L 21
Rowlands Clo. N6 4E 42
Rowlands Clo. NW7 7E 24
Rowlands Clo. Chesh 3D 6
Rowlands Rd. Dag 7K 49
Rowland Wlk. Hav 3C 34
Rowland Way. SW19 5M 105
Rowland Way. Ashf 4B 100
Rowlatt Clo. Dart 1G 115
Rowlatt Rd. Dart 1G 115
Rowley Av. Sidc 6F 96
Rowley Clo. Wat 8J 9
Rowley Clo. Wemb 3K 55
Rowley Ct. Enf 7C 16
(off Wellington Rd.)
Rowley Gdns. N4 5A 44
Rowley Gdns. Chesh 1D 6
Rowley Green. 6D 12
Rowley Grn. Rd. Barn 7D 12
Rowley Ho. SE8 6L 77
(off Watergate St.)
Rowley Ind. Pk. W3 4M 71
Rowley La. Barn 6C 12
Rowley La. Borwd 3B 12
Rowley Rd. N15 3A 44
Rowley Way. NW8 4M 57
Rowlheys Pl. W Dray 4J 143
Rowlls Rd. King T 7K 103
Rowney Gdns. Dag 2G 65
Rowney Rd. Dag 2F 64
Rowntree Clifford Clo.
E13 7E 62
Rowntree Clo. NW6 2L 57
Rowntree Path. SE28 2F 80
Rowntree Rd. Twic 7C 86
Rowse Clo. E15 4A 62
Rowsley Av. NW4 1G 41
Rowstock Gdns. N7 1H 59
Rowton Rd. SE18 8A 80
Rowzill Rd. Swan 3D 114
Roxborough Av. Harr 5B 38
Roxborough Av. Iswth 8D 70
Roxborough Heights.
Harr 4C 38
(off College Rd.)
Roxborough Pk. Harr 5C 38
Roxborough Rd. Harr 3B 38
Roxbourne Clo. N'holt 2J 53
Roxbourne Pk. Miniature Railway.
7H 37
Roxburgh Rd. SE27 2M 107
Roxburn Way. Ruis 8D 36
Roxby Pl. SW6 7L 73
Roxeth. 7B 38
Roxeth Grn. Av. Harr 8M 37
Roxeth Gro. Harr 9M 37
Roxeth Hill. Harr 7B 38
Roxford Clo. Shep 9C 100
Roxley Rd. SE13 5M 93
Roxton Gdns. Croy 7L 125
Roxwell. NW1 2F 58
(off Hartland Rd.)
Roxwell Ho. Lou 9J 19
Roxwell Rd. W12 3E 72
Roxwell Rd. Bark 5E 64
Roxwell Trad. Pk. E17 5J 45
Roxwell Way. Wfd G 7G 31
Roxy Av. Romf 5G 49
Royal Academy of Arts
(Burlington House) 1G 75
Royal Academy of Music.
7E 58
Royal Academy of Music Mus.
7E 58
(in Royal Academy of Music)
Royal Air Force Memorial.
2J 75
Royal Albert Hall. 3B 74
Royal Albert Roundabout (Junct.)
1J 79
Royal Albert Way. E16 1H 79
Royal Arc. W1 1G 75
(off Old Bond St.)
Royal Arsenal West.
SE18 4M 79
Royal Artillery Mus. of
Fire Power, The. 4M 79
Royal Av. SW3 6D 74
Royal Av. Wal X 6E 6
Royal Av. Wor Pk 4C 120
Royal Av. Ho. SW3 6D 74
(off Royal Av.)
Royal Belgrave Ho. SW1 5F 74
(off Hugh St.)
Royal Botanic Gardens Kew, The.
9J 71
Royal Ceremonial Dress
Collection, The 2M 73
(in Kensington Palace)
Royal Cir. SE27 9L 91
Royal Clo. N16 6C 44
Royal Clo. SE8 7K 77
Royal Clo. SW19 8H 89
Royal Clo. Ilf 5E 48
Royal Clo. Orp 6M 127
Royal Clo. Uxb 9D 142
Royal Clo. Wor Pk 4C 120
Royal College of Art. 8C 74
(Howie St.)
Royal College of Art. 3B 74
(Kensington Gore)
Royal College of Music. 4B 74
Royal College of Obstetricians &
Gynaecologists. 7D 58
Royal College of Physicians.
7F 58
Royal College of Surgeons.
9K 59
Royal College St. NW1 3G 59
Royal Connaught Apartments.
E16 2H 79
(off Connaught Rd.)
Royal Ct. EC3 9B 60
(off Finch La.)
Royal Ct. SE16 4K 77
Royal Ct. Enf 8C 16
Royal Courts of Justice. 9L 59
Royal Court Theatre. 5E 74
(off Sloane Sq.)
Royal Cres. W11 2H 73
Royal Cres. Ruis 9J 37
Royal Cres. M. W11 2H 73
Royal Docks Rd. E6 9M 63
Royal Dri. N11 5E 26
Royal Duchess M. SW12 6F 90
Royal Epping Forest &
Chingford (Public) Golf Course.
8B 18
Royal Exchange. 9B 60
Royal Exchange Av. EC3 9B 60
(off Finch La.)
Royal Exchange Bldgs.
EC3 9B 60
(off Threadneedle St.)
Royal Festival Hall. 2K 75
Royal Fusiliers Mus. 1D 76
(in Tower of London, The)
Royal Gdns. W7 4E 70
Royal Gunpowder Mills Vis. Cen.
5H 7
Royal Herbert Pavilions.
SE18 9K 79
Royal Hill. SE10 8A 78
Royal Hill Ct. SE10 8A 78
(off Greenwich High St.)
Royal Hospital Chelsea Mus.
6E 74
Royal Hospital Rd. SW3 7D 74
Royal La. Uxb & W Dray 8D 142
Royal London Ind. Est.
NW10 5B 56
Royal M. SW1 4F 74
Royal Mews, The. 4F 74
Royal Mint Ct. EC3 & E1 1D 76
Royal Mint Pl. E1 1E 76
Royal Mint St. E1 1D 76
Royal National Theatre. 2K 75
Royal Naval Pl. SE14 8K 77
Royal Oak Ct. N1 6C 60
(off Pitfield St.)
Royal Oak Pl. SE22 5F 92
Royal Oak Rd. E8 2F 60
Royal Oak Rd. Bexh 4K 97
(in two parts)
Royal Oak Yd. SE1 3C 76
Royal Observatory Greenwich.
8B 78
Royal Opera Arc. SW1 2H 75
Royal Opera House. 9J 59
Royal Orchard Clo. SW18 6J 89
Royal Pde. SE3 1D 94
Royal Pde. SW6 8J 73
Royal Pde. W5 6J 55
Royal Pde. Chst 4A 112
Royal Pde. Dag 2M 65
(off Church St.)
Royal Pde. Rich 9L 71
(off Layton Pl.)
Royal Pde. M. SE3 1D 94
(off Royal Pde.)
Royal Pde. M. Chst 4A 112
(off Royal Pde.)
Royal Pl. SE10 8A 78
Royal Rd. E16 9H 63
Royal Rd. SE17 7M 75
Royal Rd. Dart 2L 115
Royal Rd. Sidc 9H 97
Royal Rd. Tedd 2B 102
Royal Route. Wemb 9K 39
Royal St. SE1 4K 75
Royal Tower Lodge. E1 1E 76
(off Cartwright St.)
Royalty M. W1 9H 59
Royalty Studios. W11 9J 57
(off Lancaster Rd.)
Royal Victoria Patriotic Building.
SW18 5B 90
Royal Victoria Pl. E16 2F 78
Royal Victor Pl. E3 5H 61
Royal Wlk. Wall 4F 122
Royal Westminster Lodge.
SW1 5H 75
(off Elverton St.)
Royce Gro. Leav 7D 4
Roycraft Av. Bark 5D 64
Roycroft Clo. E18 8F 30
Roycroft Clo. SW2 7L 91
Roydene Rd. SE18 7C 80
Roydon Clo. SW11 1D 90
(off Battersea Pk. Rd.)
Roydon Clo. Lou 9J 19
Roydon Ct. W on T 6F 116
Roy Gdns. Ilf 2C 48
Roy Gro. Hamp 3M 101
Royle Building. N1 5A 60
(off Wenlock Rd.)
Royle Clo. Romf 3F 50
Royle Cres. W13 7E 54
Roymount Ct. Twic 9C 86
Roy Rd. N'wd 7D 20
Roy Sq. E14 1J 77
Royston Av. E4 5L 29
Royston Av. Sutt 5B 122
Royston Av. Wall 6H 123
Royston Clo. Houn 9F 68
Royston Clo. W on T 3E 116
Royston Ct. E13 4E 62
(off Stopford Rd.)
Royston Ct. SE24 5A 92
Royston Ct. Hin W 4D 118
Royston Ct. Rich 9K 71
Royston Gdns. Ilf 4H 47
Royston Gro. Pinn 6L 21
Royston Ho. N11 4D 26
Royston Ho. SE15 7F 76
(off Friary Est.)
Royston Pde. Ilf 4H 47
Royston Pk. Rd. Pinn 6K 21
Royston Rd. SE20 5H 109
Royston Rd. Dart 5D 98
Royston Rd. Rich 4J 87
Royston Rd. Romf 7L 35
Roystons, The. Surb 9M 103
Royston St. E2 5G 61
Rozel Ct. N1 4C 60
Rozel Rd. SW4 2G 91
Rozel Ter. Croy 4A 124
(off Church Rd.)
Rubastic Rd. S'hall 4G 69
Rubens Pl. SW4 3J 91
Rubens Rd. N'holt 5G 53
Rubens St. SE6 8K 93
Rubin Pl. Enf 1L 17
Ruby M. E17 1L 45
Ruby Rd. E17 1L 45
Ruby St. NW10 3B 56
Ruby St. SE15 7F 76
Ruby Triangle. SE15 7F 76
Ruckholt Clo. E10 8M 45
Ruckholt Rd. E10 9M 45
Rucklidge Av. NW10 5D 56
Rucklidge Pas. NW10 5D 56
(off Rucklidge Av.)
Rudall Cres. NW3 9B 42
Rudbeck Ho. SE15 8E 76
(off Peckham Pk. Rd.)
Ruddington Clo. E5 9J 45
Ruddock Clo. Edgw 7A 24
Ruddstreet Clo. SE18 5M 79
Ruddy Way. NW7 6D 24
Ruden Way. Eps 8F 134
Rudge Ho. SE16 4E 76
(off Jamaica Rd.)
Rudgwick Ct. SE18 5J 79
(off Woodville St., in two parts)
Rudgwick Ter. NW8 4C 58
Rudland Rd. Bexh 2M 97
Rudloe Rd. SW12 6G 91
Rudolf Pl. SW8 7J 75
Rudolph Rd. E13 5D 62
Rudolph Rd. NW6 5L 57
Rudolph Rd. Bush 8L 9
Rudyard Gro. NW7 6A 24
Rue de St Lawrence.
Wal A 7J 7
Ruegg Ho. SE18 7L 79
(off Woolwich Comn.)
Ruffetts Clo. S Croy 9F 124
Ruffetts, The. S Croy 9F 124
Ruffle Clo. W Dray 3J 143
Rufford Clo. Harr 4E 38
Rufford Clo. Wat 1D 8
Rufford St. N1 4J 59
Rufford Tower. W3 2M 71
Rufforth Ct. NW9 8C 24
(off Pageant Av.)
Rufus Clo. Ruis 8J 37
Rufus Ho. SE1 4D 76
(off Abbey St.)
Rufus St. N1 6C 60
Rugby Av. N9 1D 28
Rugby Av. Gnfd 2B 54
Rugby Av. Wemb 1F 54
Rugby Clo. Harr 2C 38
Rugby Gdns. Dag 2G 65
Rugby La. Sutt 1H 135
Rugby Mans. W14 5J 73
(off Bishop King's Rd.)
Rugby Rd. NW9 2M 39
Rugby Rd. W4 3C 72
Rugby Rd. Dag 2F 64
Rugby Rd. Twic 4C 86
Rugby St. WC1 7K 59
Rugg St. E14 1L 77
Rugless Ho. E14 3A 78
(off E. Ferry Rd.)
Rugmere. NW1 3E 58
(off Ferdinand St.)
Ruislip. 6C 36
Ruislip Clo. Gnfd 7M 53
Ruislip Common. 2A 36
Ruislip Ct. Ruis 7D 36
Ruislip Gardens. 8E 36
Ruislip Lido Railway. 2B 36
Ruislip Manor. 6E 36
Ruislip Rd. Gnfd 6L 53
Ruislip Rd.
N'holt & S'hall 4G 53
Ruislip Rd. E.
Gnfd & W7 7B 54
Ruislip St. SW17 1D 106
Rumball Ho. SE5 8C 76
(off Harris St.)
Rumbold Rd. SW6 8M 73
Rum Clo. E1 1G 77
Rumford Ho. SE1 4A 76
(off Tiverton St.)
Rumford Shopping Hall.
Romf 2C 50
(off Market Pl.)
Rumney Ct. N'holt 5H 53
(off Parkfield Dri.)
Rumsey Clo. Hamp 3K 101
Rumsey M. N4 8M 43
Rumsey Rd. SW9 2K 91
Runacres Ct. SE17 6A 76
Runbury Circ. NW9 7B 40
Runcorn Clo. N17 2F 44
Runcorn Ho. Romf 6J 35
(off Kingsbridge Cir.)
Runcorn Pl. W11 1J 73
Rundell Cres. NW4 3F 40
Rundell Tower. SW8 9K 75
Runes Clo. Mitc 8B 106
Runnel Fld. Harr 8C 38
Running Horse Yd. Bren 7J 71
Runnymede. SW19 5A 106
Runnymede Clo. Twic 5M 85
Runnymede Ct. SW15 7E 88
Runnymede Ct. Dart 7M 99
Runnymede Cres. SW16 5H 107
Runnymede Gdns. Gnfd 5C 54
Runnymede Gdns. Twic 5M 85
Runnymede Ho. E9 9J 45
Runnymede Rd. Twic 5M 85
Runway, The. Ruis 1F 52
Rupack St. SE16 3G 77
Rupert Av. Wemb 1J 55
Rupert Ct. W1 1H 75
Rupert Ct. W Mol 8L 101
(off St Peters Rd.)
Rupert Gdns. SW9 1M 91
Rupert Ho. SE11 5L 75
Rupert Rd. N19 8H 43
(in two parts)
Rupert Rd. NW6 5K 57
Rupert Rd. W4 4C 72
Rupert St. W1 1H 75
Rural Clo. Horn 6F 50
Rural Way. SW16 4F 106
Rusbridge Clo. E8 1E 60
Ruscoe Rd. E16 9D 62
Ruscombe Way. Felt 6D 84
Rusham Rd. SW12 5D 90
Rushbrook Cres. E17 8K 29
Rushbrook Rd. SE9 8A 96
Rushbury Ct. Hamp 5L 101
Rush Common M. SW2 6K 91
Rushcroft Rd. E4 7M 29
Rushcroft Rd. SW2 3L 91
Rushcutters Ct. SE16 5J 77
(off Boat Lifter Way)
Rushden Clo. SE19 4B 108
Rushdene. SE2 4G 81
(in two parts)
Rushdene Av. Barn 9C 14
Rushdene Clo. N'holt 5G 53
Rushdene Cres. N'holt 5F 52
Rushdene Rd. Pinn 4H 37
Rushdene Wlk. Big H 9H 141
Rushden Gdns. NW7 6G 25
Rushden Gdns. Ilf 9L 31
Rushdon Clo. Romf 3E 50
Rush Dri. Wal A 9J 7
Rushen Wlk. Cars 3B 122
Rushes Mead. Uxb 4A 142
Rushet Rd. Orp 6E 112
Rushett Clo. Th Dit 3F 118
Rushett La. Chess 3G 133
Rushett Rd. Th Dit 2F 118
Rushey Clo. N Mald 8B 104
Rushey Grn. SE6 6M 93
Rushey Hill. Enf 6K 15
Rushey Mead. SE4 4L 93
Rushford Rd. SE4 5K 93
Rush Green. 6B 50
Rush Grn. Gdns. Romf 6A 50
Rush Grn. Rd. Romf 6M 49
Rushgrove Av. NW9 3C 40
Rushgrove Pde. NW9 3C 40
Rushgrove St. SE18 5K 79
Rush Hill M. SW11 2E 90
(off Rush Hill Rd.)
Rush Hill Rd. SW11 2E 90
Rushleigh Av. Chesh 4D 6
Rushley Clo. Kes 6H 127
Rushmead. E2 6F 60
Rushmead. Rich 9F 86
Rushmead Clo. Croy 6D 124
Rushmead Clo. Edgw 2M 23
Rushmere Ct. Wor Pk 4E 120
Rushmere Pl. SW19 2H 105
Rushmon Gdns. W on T 5F 116
Rushmon Pl. Cheam 8J 121
Rushmon Vs. N Mald 8D 104
Rushmoor Clo. Pinn 2F 36
Rushmoor Ct. Wat 8A 8
Rushmore Clo. Brom 7J 111
Rushmore Cres. E5 9H 45
Rushmore Ho. W14 4J 73
(off Russell Rd.)
Rushmore Rd. E5 9G 45
(in three parts)
Rusholme Av. Dag 8L 49
Rusholme Gro. SE19 2C 108
Rusholme Rd. SW15 5H 89
Rushout Av. Harr 4F 38
Rush, The. SW19 5K 105
(off Kingston Rd.)
Rushton Av. Wat 8E 4
Rushton Ct. Chesh 2D 6
Rushton Ho. SW8 1H 91
Rushton St. N1 5B 60
Rushworth Av. NW4 1E 40
Rushworth Gdns. NW4 1E 40
Rushworth St. SE1 3M 75
Rushy Mdw. La. Cars 5C 122
Ruskin Av. E12 2J 63
Ruskin Av. Felt 5D 84
Ruskin Av. Rich 8L 71
(in two parts)
Ruskin Av. Wal A 7L 7
Ruskin Av. Well 1E 96
Ruskin Clo. NW11 4M 41
Ruskin Ct. N21 9K 15
Ruskin Ct. SE5 2B 92
(off Champion Hill)
Ruskin Dri. Orp 5C 128
Ruskin Dri. Well 2E 96
Ruskin Dri. Wor Pk 4F 120
Ruskin Gdns. W5 7H 55
Ruskin Gdns. Harr 3K 39
Ruskin Gdns. Romf 7F 34
Ruskin Gro. Dart 4L 99
Ruskin Gro. Well 1E 96
Ruskin Ho. SW1 5H 75
(off Herrick St.)
Ruskin Ho. S Croy 7B 124
(off Selsdon Rd.)
Ruskin Mans. W14 7J 73
(off Queen's Club Gdns.)
Ruskin Pde. S Croy 7B 124
(off Selsdon Rd.)
Ruskin Pk. Ho. SE5 2B 92
Ruskin Rd. N17 8D 28
Ruskin Rd. Belv 5L 81
Ruskin Rd. Cars 7D 122
Ruskin Rd. Croy 4M 123
Ruskin Rd. Iswth 2D 86
Ruskin Rd. S'hall 1J 69
Ruskin Wlk. N9 2E 28
Ruskin Wlk. SE24 4A 92
Ruskin Wlk. Brom 1K 127
Ruskin Way. SW19 5B 106
Rusland Av. Orp 5B 128
Rusland Heights. Harr 2C 38
Rusland Pk. Rd. Harr 2C 38
Rusper Clo. NW2 8G 41
Rusper Clo. Stan 4G 23
Rusper Ct. SW9 1J 91
(off Clapham Rd.)
Rusper Rd. N22 & N17 9M 27
Rusper Rd. Dag 2G 65
Russell Av. N22 9L 27

Russell Clo.—St Anthony's Clo.

Russell Clo. NW10 . . . . .3A 56
Russell Clo. SE7 . . . . .8G 79
Russell Clo. W4 . . . . .7D 72
Russell Clo. Beck 7M 109
Russell Clo. Bexh 3L 97
Russell Clo. Dart 3E 98
Russell Clo. N'wd 5A 20
Russell Clo. Ruis 7G 37
Russell Ct. E10 . . . . .5M 45
Russell Ct. N14 . . . . .8H 15
Russell Ct. SE15 . . . . .1F 92
(off Heaton Rd.)
Russell Ct. SW1 . . . . .2G 75
(off Cleveland Row)
Russell Ct. SW16 . . . . .2K 107
Russell Ct. WC1 . . . . .7J 59
(off Woburn Pl.)
Russell Ct. Brick W 3L 5
Russell Ct. New Bar 6A 14
Russell Ct. Purl 2L 137
Russell Ct. Wall 7G 123
(off Ross Rd.)
Russell Cres. Wat 8D 4
Russell Dri. Stanw 5B 144
Russell Flint Ho. E16 . . . . .2F 78
(off Pankhurst Av.)
Russell Gdns. N20 . . . . .2C 26
Russell Gdns. NW11 . . . . . . .4J 41
Russell Gdns. W14 . . . . .4J 73
Russell Gdns. Ilf 5B 48
Russell Gdns. Rich 8G 87
Russell Gdns. W Dray 6L 143
Russell Gdns. M. W14 . . . . . . .3J 73
Russell Grn. Clo. Purl 2L 137
Russell Gro. NW7 . . . . .5C 24
Russell Gro. SW9 . . . . .8L 75
Russell Hill. Purl 2K 137
Russell Hill Pl. Purl 3L 137
Russell Hill Rd. Purl 3L 137
Russell Ho. E14 . . . . .9L 61
(off Saracen St.)
Russell Ho. SW1 . . . . .6G 75
(off Cambridge St.)
Russell Kerr Clo. W4 . . . . . . .8A 72
Russell La. N20 . . . . .2C 26
Russell La. Wat 9B 4
Russell Lodge. E4 . . . . .2A 30
Russell Lodge. SE1 . . . . .4B 76
(off Spurgeon St.)
Russell Mead. Har W 8D 22
Russell Pde. NW11 . . . . .4J 41
(off Golders Grn. Rd.)
Russell Pl. NW3 . . . . .1C 58
Russell Pl. SE16 . . . . .4J 77
Russell Pl. Sutt 9M 121
Russell Pl. S at H 5L 115
Russell Rd. E4 . . . . .4K 29
Russell Rd. E10 . . . . .4M 45
Russell Rd. E16 . . . . .9E 62
Russell Rd. E17 . . . . .1K 45
Russell Rd. N8 . . . . .4H 43
Russell Rd. N13 . . . . .6K 27
Russell Rd. N15 . . . . .3C 44
Russell Rd. N20 . . . . .2C 26
Russell Rd. NW9 . . . . .4D 40
Russell Rd. SW19 . . . . .4L 105
Russell Rd. W14 . . . . .4J 73
Russell Rd. Buck H 1F 30
Russell Rd. Enf 2D 16
Russell Rd. Mitc 7C 106
Russell Rd. N'holt 1A 54
Russell Rd. N'wd 5A 20
Russell Rd. Shep 2A 116
Russell Rd. Twic 5D 86
Russell Rd. W on T 1E 116
Russell's Footpath.
SW16 . . . . .2J 107
Russell Sq. WC1 . . . . .8J 59
Russell's Ride. Chesh 4E 6
Russell St. WC2 . . . . .1J 75
Russell Ter. Hort K 8M 115
Russell Wlk. Rich 5K 87
Russell Way. Sutt 7M 121
Russell Way. Wat 9F 8
Russell Yd. SW15 . . . . .3J 89
Russet Av. Shep 7C 100
Russet Clo. Uxb 7A 52
Russet Clo. W on T 5H 117
Russet Cres. N7 . . . . .1K 59
Russet Dri. Croy 3J 125
Russets Clo. E4 . . . . .4B 30
Russett Clo. Orp 7F 128
Russettings. Pinn 7K 21
(off Westfield Pk.)
Russetts. Horn 2J 51
Russett Way. SE13 . . . . .1M 93
Russett Way. Swan 6B 114
Russia Ct. EC2 . . . . .9A 60
(off Russia Row)
Russia Dock Rd. SE16 . . . . . .2J 77
Russia La. E2 . . . . .5G 61
Russia Row. EC2 . . . . .9A 60
Russia Wlk. SE16 . . . . .3J 77
Russington Rd. Shep 1B 116
Rusthall Av. W4 . . . . .5B 72
Rusthall Clo. Croy 1G 125
Rustic Av. SW16 . . . . .4F 106
Rustic Pl. Wemb 9H 39
Rustic Wlk. E16 . . . . .9F 62
(off Lambert Rd.)
Rustington Wlk. Mord 2K 121
Ruston Av. Surb 2M 119
Ruston Gdns. N14 . . . . .8E 14
Ruston M. W11 . . . . .9J 57
Ruston Rd. SE18 . . . . .4J 79
Ruston St. E3 . . . . .4K 61
Rust Sq. SE5 . . . . .8B 76
Rutford Rd. SW16 . . . . .2J 107
Ruth Clo. Stan 2K 39
Ruth Ct. E3 . . . . .5J 61
Ruthen Clo. Eps 6M 133
Rutherford Clo. Borwd 4A 12
Rutherford Clo. Sutt 8B 122
Rutherford Clo. Uxb 7D 142
Rutherford Ho. E1 . . . . .7F 60
(off Brady St.)
Rutherford Ho. Wemb 8A 40
(off Barnhill Rd.)
Rutherford St. SW1 . . . . .5H 75
Rutherford Tower. S'hall 9M 53
Rutherford Way. Bus H 1B 22
Rutherford Way. Wemb 9L 39
Rutherglen Rd. SE2 . . . . .7E 80
Rutherwick Ri. Coul 9J 137
Rutherwyke Clo. Eps 8E 120
Ruth Ho. W10 . . . . .7J 57
(off Kensal Rd.)
Ruthin Clo. NW9 . . . . .4C 40
Ruthin Rd. SE3 . . . . .7E 78
Ruthven Av. Wal X 6D 6
Ruthven St. E9 . . . . .4H 61
Rutland App. Horn 3L 51
Rutland Av. Sidc 6E 96
Rutland Clo. SW14 . . . . .2M 87
Rutland Clo. SW19 . . . . . . .4C 106
Rutland Clo. Asht 9J 133
Rutland Clo. Bex 8H 97
Rutland Clo. Chess 8K 119
Rutland Clo. Dart 6H 99
Rutland Clo. Eps 2B 134
Rutland Ct. SE5 . . . . .3B 92
Rutland Ct. SE9 . . . . .8A 96
Rutland Ct. SW7 . . . . .3C 74
(off Rutland Gdns.)
Rutland Ct. W3 . . . . .9L 55
Rutland Ct. Chst 5L 111
Rutland Ct. Enf 7F 16
Rutland Ct. King T 8H 103
(off Palace Rd.)
Rutland Dri. Horn 3L 51
Rutland Dri. Mord 1K 121
Rutland Dri. Rich 7H 87
Rutland Gdns. N4 . . . . .4M 43
Rutland Gdns. SW7 . . . . .3C 74
Rutland Gdns. W13 . . . . .8E 54
Rutland Gdns. Croy 6C 124
Rutland Gdns. Dag 1G 65
Rutland Gdns. M. SW7 . . . . .3C 74
Rutland Ga. SW7 . . . . .3C 74
Rutland Ga. Belv 6M 81
Rutland Ga. Brom 8D 110
Rutland Ga. M. SW7 . . . . . . .3C 74
(off Rutland Ga.)
Rutland Gro. W6 . . . . .6F 72
Rutland Ho. W8 . . . . .4M 73
(off Marloes Rd.)
Rutland Ho. N'holt 2L 53
(off Farmlands, The)
Rutland M. NW8 . . . . .4M 57
Rutland M. E. SW7 . . . . .4C 74
(off Ennismore St.)
Rutland M. S. SW7 . . . . .4C 74
(off Ennismore St.)
Rutland M. W. SW7 . . . . .4C 74
(off Rutland Ga.)
Rutland Pk. NW2 . . . . .2G 57
Rutland Pk. SE6 . . . . .8K 93
Rutland Pk. Gdns. NW2 . . . . .2G 57
(off Rutland Pk.)
Rutland Pk. Mans. NW2 . . . .2G 57
Rutland Pl. EC1 . . . . .7M 59
Rutland Pl. Bush 1B 22
Rutland Rd. E7 . . . . .3H 63
Rutland Rd. E9 . . . . .4H 61
Rutland Rd. E11 . . . . .3F 46
Rutland Rd. E17 . . . . .4L 45
Rutland Rd. SW19 . . . . .4C 106
Rutland Rd. Harr 4A 38
Rutland Rd. Hay 5B 68
Rutland Rd. Ilf 8M 47
Rutland Rd. S'hall 8L 53
Rutland Rd. Twic 8B 86
Rutland St. SW7 . . . . .4C 74
Rutland Wlk. SE6 . . . . .8K 93
Rutland Way. Orp 1G 129
Rutley Clo. SE17 . . . . .7M 75
Rutley Clo. H Wood 9H 35
Rutlish Rd. SW19 . . . . .5L 105
Rutter Gdns. Mitc 8A 106
Rutters Clo. W Dray 3L 143
Rutt's Ter. SE14 . . . . .9H 77
Rutts, The. Bush 1B 22
Ruvigny Gdns. SW15 . . . . . . .2H 89
Ruxley. 3H 113
Ruxley Clo. Eps 7M 119
Ruxley Clo. Sidc 3H 113
Ruxley Corner Ind. Est.
Sidc 3H 113
Ruxley Ct. Eps 7A 120
Ruxley Cres. Clay 8F 118
Ruxley La. Eps 8M 119
Ruxley M. Eps 7M 119
Ruxley Ridge. Clay 9E 118
Ruxley Towers. Clay 9E 118
Ruxton Clo. Coul 7G 137
Ruxton Clo. Swan 7C 114
Ruxton Ct. Swan 7C 114
Ryall Clo. Brick W 2J 5
Ryalls Ct. N20 . . . . .3D 26
Ryan Clo. SE3 . . . . .3F 94
Ryan Clo. Ruis 6F 36
Ryan Ct. SW16 . . . . .4J 107
Ryan Dri. Bren 7E 70
Ryan Way. Wat 3G 9
Ryarsh Cres. Orp 6C 128
Rybrook Dri. W on T 4G 117
Rycott Path. SE22 . . . . .6E 92
Rycroft Way. N17 . . . . .1D 44
Ryculff Sq. SE3 . . . . .1D 94
Rydal Clo. NW4 . . . . .8J 25
Rydal Clo. Purl 5B 138
Rydal Ct. Edgw 5K 23
Rydal Ct. Leav 5F 4
Rydal Ct. Wemb 5K 39
Rydal Cres. Gnfd 6F 54
Rydal Dri. Bexh 9L 81
Rydal Dri. W Wick 4C 126
Rydal Gdns. NW9 . . . . .3C 40
Rydal Gdns. SW15 . . . . .2C 104
Rydal Gdns. Houn 5M 85
Rydal Gdns. Wemb 6G 39
Rydal Mt. Brom 8D 110
Rydal Rd. SW16 . . . . .1H 107
Rydal Water. NW1 . . . . .6G 59
Rydal Way. Enf 8G 17
Rydal Way. Ruis 9G 37
Rydens. 5G 117
Rydens Av. W on T 4F 116
Rydens Clo. W on T 4G 117
Rydens Gro. W on T 6H 117
Rydens Ho. SE9 . . . . .9G 95
Rydens Pk. W on T 4H 117
Rydens Rd. W on T 5F 116
Ryde Pl. Twic 5H 87
Ryder Clo. Brom 2F 110
Ryder Clo. Bush 8M 9
Ryder Ct. E10 . . . . .7M 45
Ryder Ct. SW1 . . . . .2G 75
(off Ryder St.)
Ryder Dri. SE16 . . . . .6F 76
Ryder Gdns. Rain 2D 66
Ryder Ho. E1 . . . . .7G 61
(off Colebert Av.)
Ryder M. E9 . . . . .1G 61
Ryder's Ter. NW8 . . . . .5A 58
Ryder St. SW1 . . . . .2G 75
Ryder Yd. SW1 . . . . .2G 75
Ryde Va. Rd. SW12 . . . . .8G 91
Rydon M. SW19 . . . . .4G 105
Rydons Clo. SE9 . . . . .2J 95
Rydon St. N1 . . . . .4A 60
Rydston Clo. N7 . . . . .3J 59
Ryebridge Clo. Lea 9E 132
Ryebrook Rd. Lea 9E 132
Rye Clo. Bex 5M 97
Rye Clo. Horn 1G 67
Ryecotes Mead. SE21 . . . . . .7C 92
Rye Cres. Orp 3G 129
Ryecroft Av. Ilf 9M 31
Ryecroft Av. Twic 6M 85
Ryecroft Cres. Barn 7F 12
Ryecroft Lodge. SW16 . . . .3M 107
Ryecroft Rd. SE13 . . . . .4A 94
Ryecroft Rd. SW16 . . . . .3L 107
Ryecroft Rd. Orp 1B 128
Ryecroft St. SW6 . . . . .9M 73
Ryedale. SE22 . . . . .5F 92
Rye Fld. Asht 8H 133
Rye Fld. Orp 3H 129
Ryefield Av. Uxb 3F 142
Ryefield Ct. N'wd 9E 20
Ryefield Cres. N'wd 9E 20
Ryefield Path. SW15 . . . . . . .7E 88
Ryefield Pde. N'wd 9E 20
(off Joel St.)
Ryefield Rd. SE19 . . . . .3A 108
Rye Hill Pk. SE15 . . . . .3G 93
Rye Ho. SE16 . . . . .3G 77
(off Swan Rd.)
Rye Ho. SW1 . . . . .6F 74
(off Ebury Bri. Rd.)
Ryeland Clo. W Dray 9C 142
Ryelands Cres. SE12 . . . . . . .5G 95
Ryelands Pl. Wey 5C 116
Rye La. SE15 . . . . .9E 76
Rye Pas. SE15 . . . . .2E 92
Rye Rd. SE15 . . . . .3H 93
Rye, The. N14 . . . . .9H 15
Rye Wlk. SW15 . . . . .4H 89
Rye Way. Edgw 6K 23
Ryfold Rd. SW19 . . . . .9L 89
Ryhope Rd. N11 . . . . .4F 26
Ryland Clo. Felt 1D 100
Rylandes Rd. NW2 . . . . .8E 40
Rylandes Rd. S Croy 1F 138
Ryland Rd. NW5 . . . . .2F 58
Rylett Cres. W12 . . . . .3D 72
Rylett Rd. W12 . . . . .3D 72
Rylston Rd. N13 . . . . .3B 28
Rylston Rd. SW6 . . . . .7K 73
Rymer Rd. Croy 2C 124
Rymer St. SE24 . . . . .5M 91
Rymill St. E16 . . . . .2L 79
Rysbrack St. SW3 . . . . .4D 74
Rythe Ct. Th Dit 2E 118
Rythe Rd. Clay 7B 118
Rythe, The. Esh 2A 132

S

Sabbarton St. E16 . . . . .9D 62
Sabella Ct. E3 . . . . .5K 61
Sabine Rd. SW11 . . . . .2D 90
Sable Clo. Houn 2G 85
Sable St. N1 . . . . .3M 59
Sach Rd. E5 . . . . .7F 44
Sackville Av. Brom 3E 126
Sackville Clo. Harr 8B 38
Sackville Cres. Romf 8J 35
Sackville Gdns. Ilf 6K 47
Sackville Ho. SW16 . . . . .9J 91
Sackville Rd. Dart 8H 99
Sackville Rd. Sutt 9L 121
Sackville St. W1 . . . . .1G 75
Saddlebrook Pk. Sun 4C 100
Saddlers Clo. Ark 7F 12
Saddlers Clo. Borwd 7B 12
Saddlers Clo. Pinn 6L 21
Saddlers M. SW8 . . . . .9J 75
Saddlers M. King T 5G 103
Saddlers M. Wemb 9D 38
Saddler's Pk. Eyns 5H 131
Saddlers Path. Borwd 7B 12
(off Farriers Way)
Saddlescombe Way. N12 . . . . .5L 25
Saddleworth Rd. H Hill 6G 35
Saddleworth Sq. Romf 6G 35
Saddle Yd. W1 . . . . .2F 74
Sadler Clo. Mitc 6D 106
Sadler Ho. EC1 . . . . .6M 59
(off Spa Grn. Est.)
Sadlers Ride. W Mol 6A 102
Sadler's Wells Theatre. 6L 59
Saffron Av. E14 . . . . .1B 78
Saffron Clo. NW11 . . . . .4K 41
Saffron Clo. Croy 1J 123
Saffron Ct. E15 . . . . .1C 62
(off Maryland Pk.)
Saffron Ct. Felt 6A 84
Saffron Green. 3E 12
Saffron Hill. EC1 . . . . .8L 59
Saffron Rd. Romf 9B 34
Saffron St. EC1 . . . . .8L 59
Saffron Way. Surb 3H 119
Saffron Wharf. SE1 . . . . .3D 76
(off Shad Thames)
Sage Clo. E6 . . . . .8K 63
Sage St. E1 . . . . .1G 77
Sage Way. WC1 . . . . .6K 59
(off Cubitt St.)
Sahara Ct. S'hall 1J 69
Saigasso Clo. E16 . . . . .9H 63
Sailmakers Ct. SW6 . . . . .1A 90
Sail St. SE11 . . . . .5K 75
Saimel. NW9 . . . . .7D 24
(off Satchell Mead)
Sainfoin Rd. SW17 . . . . .8E 90
Sainsbury Rd. SE19 . . . . . . .2C 108
St Agatha's Dri. King T 3K 103
St Agatha's Gro. Cars 3D 122
St Agnes Clo. E9 . . . . .4G 61
St Agnes Pl. SE11 . . . . .7L 75
St Agnes Well. EC1 . . . . .7B 60
(off City Rd.)
St Aidans Ct. Bark 5F 64
St Aidan's Rd. SE22 . . . . .5F 92
St Aidan's Rd. W13 . . . . .3F 70
St Alban's Av. E6 . . . . .6K 63
St Alban's Av. W4 . . . . .5B 72
St Albans Av. Felt 2H 101
St Alban's Clo. NW11 . . . . . . .6L 41
St Albans Ct. EC2 . . . . .9A 60
(off Wood St.)
St Alban's Cres. N22 . . . . .8L 27
St Alban's Cres. Wfd G 7E 30
St Alban's Gdns. Tedd 2E 102
St Alban's Gro. W8 . . . . .4M 73
St Alban's Gro. Cars 2C 122
St Alban's La. NW11 . . . . .6L 41
St Albans Mans. W8 . . . . . . .4M 73
(off Kensington Ct. Pl.)
St Alban's Pl. N1 . . . . .4M 59
St Albans Rd. NW5 . . . . .8E 42
St Albans Rd. NW10 . . . . .4C 56
St Albans Rd. Barn 1G 13
St Alban's Rd. Dart 6K 99
St Albans Rd. Ilf 6D 48
St Alban's Rd. King T 3J 103
St Alban's Rd. Sutt 6K 121
St Albans Rd. Wat (WD17,WD24)
. . . . .4F 8
St Albans Rd. Wat (WD25)
. . . . .9G 5
St Alban's Rd. Wfd G 7E 30
St Alban's St. SW1 . . . . .1H 75
(in two parts)
St Albans Ter. W6 . . . . .7J 73
St Albans Tower. E4 . . . . .6K 29
St Albans Vs. NW5 . . . . .8E 42
St Alfege Pas. SE10 . . . . .7A 78
St Alfege Rd. SE7 . . . . .7H 79
St Alphage Garden. EC2 . . . . .8A 60
(in two parts)
St Alphage Highwalk. EC2 . . .8A 60
(off London Wall)
St Alphage Ho. EC2 . . . . .8B 60
(off Fore St.)
St Alphage Wlk. Edgw 9A 24
St Alphege Rd. N9 . . . . .9G 17
St Alphonsus Rd. SW4 . . . . . .3G 91
St Amunds Clo. SE6 . . . . . . .1L 109
St Andrew's Av. Horn 1D 66
St Andrew's Av. Wemb 9E 38
St Andrews Chambers.
W1 . . . . .8G 59
(off Wells St.)
St Andrew's Clo. N12 . . . . . . .4A 26
St Andrew's Clo. NW2 . . . . . . .8F 40
St Andrews Clo. SE16 . . . . . . .6F 76
St Andrews Clo. SE28 . . . . . . .9H 65
St Andrew's Clo. Iswth 9C 70
St Andrew's Clo. Ruis 7H 37
St Andrew's Clo. Shep 8B 100
St Andrews Clo. Stan 9G 23
St Andrew's Ct. SW18 . . . . . . .8A 90
St Andrews Ct. Sutt 5C 122
St Andrews Ct. Swan 7C 114
St Andrews Ct. Wat 3F 8
St Andrew's Dri. Orp 1F 128
St Andrews Dri. Stan 8G 23
St Andrew's Gro. N16 . . . . . . .6B 44
St Andrew's Hill. EC4 . . . . . .1M 75
(in two parts)
St Andrews Mans. W1 . . . . . .8E 58
(off Dorset St.)
St Andrews Mans. W14 . . . . . .7J 73
(off St Andrews Rd.)
St Andrew's M. N16 . . . . .6C 44
St Andrew's M. SE3 . . . . .8E 78
St Andrews M. SW12 . . . . . . .7H 91
St Andrew's Pl. NW1 . . . . . . .7F 58
St Andrew's Rd. E11 . . . . .4C 46
St Andrew's Rd. E13 . . . . .6F 62
St Andrew's Rd. E17 . . . . . . .9H 29
St Andrew's Rd. N9 . . . . .9G 17
St Andrew's Rd. NW9 . . . . . . .6B 40
St Andrew's Rd. NW10 . . . . . .2F 56
St Andrew's Rd. NW11 . . . . . .4K 41
St Andrew's Rd. W3 . . . . .1C 72
St Andrews Rd. W7 . . . . .3C 70
St Andrew's Rd. W14 . . . . . . .7J 73
St Andrew's Rd. Cars 5C 122
St Andrew's Rd. Coul 8E 136
St Andrew's Rd. Croy 6A 124
St Andrew's Rd. Enf 5B 16
St Andrew's Rd. Ilf 5K 47
St Andrew's Rd. Romf 4B 50
St Andrew's Rd. Sidc 9H 97
St Andrew's Rd. Surb 1H 119
St Andrew's Rd. Uxb 4C 142
St Andrews Rd. Wat 3H 21
St Andrews Sq. W11 . . . . .9J 57
St Andrew's Sq. Surb 1H 119
St Andrews Ter. Wat 5G 21
St Andrew's Tower. S'hall . . .1A 70
(off Baird Av.)
St Andrew St. EC1 & EC4 . . .8L 59
St Andrews Way. E3 . . . . . . .7M 61
St Andrew's Wharf. SE1 . . . .3D 76
St Anna Rd. Barn 7H 13
St Anne's Av. Stanw 6B 144
St Anne's Clo. N6 . . . . .8E 42
St Anne's Clo. Chesh 1A 6
St Anne's Clo. Wat 4G 21
St Anne's Ct. NW6 . . . . .4J 57
St Anne's Ct. W1 . . . . .9H 59
St Anne's Ct. W Wick 6C 126
St Anne's Flats. NW1 . . . . . . .6H 59
(off Doric Way)
St Anne's Gdns. NW10 . . . . . .6K 55
St Anne's Pas. E14 . . . . .9K 61
St Anne's Rd. E11 . . . . .7B 46
St Anne's Rd. Wemb 1H 55
St Anne's Row. E14 . . . . .9K 61
St Annes Ter. Ilf 5C 32
St Anne's Trad. Est. E14 . . . . .9K 61
(off St Anne's Row)
St Anne St. E14 . . . . .9K 61
St Ann's. Bark 4A 64
St Ann's Ct. NW4 . . . . .1F 40
St Ann's Cres. SW18 . . . . . . .5M 89
St Ann's Gdns. NW5 . . . . .2E 58
St Ann's Hill. SW18 . . . . .4M 89
St Ann's Ho. WC1 . . . . .6L 59
(off Margery St.)
St Ann's La. SW1 . . . . .4H 75
St Ann's Pk. Rd. SW18 . . . . . .5A 90
St Ann's Pas. SW13 . . . . .2C 88
St Ann's Rd. N9 . . . . .2D 28
St Ann's Rd. N15 . . . . .3M 43
St Ann's Rd. SW13 . . . . .1D 88
St Ann's Rd. W11 . . . . .1H 73
St Ann's Rd. Bark 4A 64
St Ann's Rd. Harr 4C 38
St Ann's Shop. Cen. Harr 4C 38
St Ann's St. SW1 . . . . .4H 75
St Ann's Ter. NW8 . . . . .5B 58
St Ann's Vs. W11 . . . . .2H 73
St Anns Way. Berr G 8M 141
St Ann's Way. S Croy 8M 123
St Anselm's Pl. W1 . . . . .1F 74
St Anselm's Rd. Hay 3D 68
St Anthony's Av. Wfd G 6G 31
St Anthony's Clo. E1 . . . . .2E 76

St Anthony's Clo. SW17 . . . . .8C 90
St Anthony's Flats. NW1 . . . .5H 59
(off Aldenham St.)
St Anthony's Way. Felt 3D 84
St Antony's Rd. E7 . . . . .3F 62
St Arvan's Clo. Croy 5C 124
St Asaph Rd. SE4 . . . . .2H 93
St Aubins Ct. N1 . . . . .4B 60
St Aubyn's Av. SW19 . . . . . .2K 105
St Aubyn's Av. Houn 4L 85
St Aubyn's Clo. Orp 5D 128
St Aubyn's Gdns. Orp 4D 128
St Aubyn's Rd. SE19 . . . . . .3D 108
St Audrey Av. Bexh 1L 97
St Augustine's Av. W5 . . . . . .5J 55
St Augustine's Av. Brom 9J 111
St Augustine's Av.
S Croy 8A 124
St Augustine's Av. Wemb 8J 39
St Augustine's Ho. NW1 . . . .6H 59
(off Werrington St.)
St Augustine's Mans.
SW1 . . . . .5G 75
(off Bloomburg St.)
St Augustine's Path. N5 . . . . .9A 44
St Augustine's Rd. NW1 . . . . .3H 59
St Augustine's Rd. Beck 5K 81
St Austell Clo. Edgw 9K 23
St Austell Rd. SE13 . . . . .1A 94
St Awdry's Rd. Bark 3B 64
St Awdry's Wlk. Bark 3A 64
St Barnabas Clo. SE22 . . . . . .4C 92
St Barnabas Clo. Beck 6A 110
St Barnabas Ct. Har W 8A 22
St Barnabas Gdns.
W Mol 9L 101
St Barnabas Rd. E17 . . . . . . .4L 45
St Barnabas Rd. Mitc 4E 106
St Barnabas Rd. Sutt 7B 122
St Barnabas Rd. Wfd G 8F 30
St Barnabas St. SW1 . . . . . . .6E 74
St Barnabas Ter. E9 . . . . .1H 61
St Barnabas Vs. SW8 . . . . . . .9J 75
St Bartholomew's Clo.
SE26 . . . . .1F 108
St Bartholomew's Ct. E6 . . . .5J 63
(off St Bartholomew's Rd.)
St Bartholomew's Hospital Mus.
. . . . .8M 59
(off St Bartholomew's Hospital)
St Bartholomew's Rd. E6 . . . .5K 63
St Benedict's Clo. SW17 . . . .1E 106
St Benet's Clo. SW17 . . . . . . .8C 90
St Benet's Gro. Cars 2A 122
St Benet's Pl. EC3 . . . . .1B 76
St Bernards. Croy 5C 124
St Bernard's Clo. SE27 . . . . .1B 108
St Bernards Ho. E14 . . . . . . .4A 78
(off Galbraith St.)
St Bernard's Rd. E6 . . . . .4H 63
St Blaise Av. Brom 6F 110
St Botolph Row. EC3 . . . . . . .9D 60
St Botolph St. EC3 . . . . .9D 60
St Brelades Ct. N1 . . . . .4C 60
St Bride's Av. EC4 . . . . .9M 59
(off Bride La.)
St Bride's Av. Edgw 8K 23
St Bride's Church. 9M 59
St Brides Clo. Eri 3H 81
St Bride's Crypt Mus. 9M 59
(in St Bride's Church)
St Bride's Pas. EC4 . . . . .9M 59
(off Dorset Ri.)
St Bride St. EC4 . . . . .9M 59
St Catherines Clo. Chess . . .8H 119
St Catherine's Clo. SW17 . . . .8C 90
St Catherine's Ct. W4 . . . . . . .4C 72
St Catherines Ct. Felt 7E 84
St Catherine's Dri. SE14 . . . . .1H 93
St Catherine's Farm Ct.
Ruis 4A 36
St Catherines M. SW3 . . . . . .5D 74
St Catherine's Rd. E4 . . . . . . .2L 29
St Catherine's Rd. Ruis 4B 36
St Catherines Tower. E10 . . . .5M 45
St Cecilia's Clo. Sutt 3J 121
St Chads Clo. Surb 2G 119
St Chad's Gdns. Romf 5J 49
St Chad's Pl. WC1 . . . . .6J 59
St Chad's Rd. Romf 5J 49
St Chad's St. WC1 . . . . .6J 59
(in two parts)
St Charles Pl. W10 . . . . .8J 57
St Charles Sq. W10 . . . . .8H 57
St Christopher Rd. Uxb 9B 142
St Christopher's Clo.
Iswth 9C 70
St Christophers Dri. Hay 1F 68
St Christopher's Gdns.
T Hth 7L 107
St Christopher's Ho. NW1 . . .5G 59
(off Bridgeway St.)
St Christopher's M. Wall 7G 123
St Christopher's Pl. W1 . . . . . .9E 58
St Clair Clo. Ilf 9K 31
St Clair Dri. Wor Pk 5F 120
St Clair Rd. E13 . . . . .5F 62
St Clair's Rd. Croy 4C 124
St Clare Bus. Pk. Hamp 3A 102
St Clare St. EC3 . . . . .9D 60
St Clement Clo. Uxb 9B 142

St Clement's Ct. EC4 . . . . . . .1B 76
(off Clements La.)
St Clement's Ct. N7 . . . . .2K 59
St Clement's Ct. SE14 . . . . . .7H 77
(off Myers La.)
St Clements Ct. W11 . . . . . . .1H 73
(off Stoneleigh St.)
St Clements Ct. Purf 5L 83
St Clement's Heights.
SE26 . . . . .9E 92
St Clement's La. WC2 . . . . . . .9K 59
St Clements Mans. SW6 . . . . .7H 73
(off Lillie Rd.)
St Clements St. N7 . . . . .2L 59
St Clements Yd. SE22 . . . . . .3D 92
St Cloud Rd. SE27 . . . . .1A 108
St Columbas Ho. E17 . . . . . . .2M 45
St Crispin's Clo. NW3 . . . . . . .9C 42
St Crispin's Clo. S'hall 9K 53
St Cross St. EC1 . . . . .8L 59
St Cuthberts Gdns. Pinn 7K 21
St Cuthbert's Rd. NW2 . . . . . .2K 57
St Cyprian's St. SW17 . . . . . .1D 106
St Daniel Ct. Beck 4L 109
(off Brackley Rd.)
St David Clo. Uxb 8B 142
St David's. Coul 9K 137
St Davids Clo. SE16 . . . . .6F 76
(off Masters Dri.)
St David's Clo. Wemb 8A 40
St David's Clo. W Wick 2M 125
St David's Dri. Edgw 8K 23
St Davids M. E3 . . . . .6J 61
(off Morgan St.)
St David's Pl. NW4 . . . . .5F 40
St Davids Rd. Swan 3D 114
St Davids Sq. E14 . . . . .6M 77
St Denis Rd. SE27 . . . . .1B 108
St Dionis Rd. SW6 . . . . .1K 89
St Domingo Ho. SE18 . . . . . . .4K 79
(off Leda Rd.)
St Donatt's Rd. SE14 . . . . . . .9K 77
St Dunstan's (Junct.) 8K 121
St Dunstan's All. EC3 . . . . . . .1C 76
(off St Dunstans Hill)
St Dunstans Av. W3 . . . . .1B 72
St Dunstan's Clo. Hay 6D 68
St Dunstan's Ct. EC4 . . . . . . .9L 59
St Dunstans Gdns. W3 . . . . . .1B 72
St Dunstan's Hill. EC3 . . . . . . .1C 76
St Dunstan's Hill. Sutt 6J 121
St Dunstan's La. EC3 . . . . . . .1C 76
St Dunstan's La. Beck 1A 126
St Dunstan's Rd. E7 . . . . .2F 62
St Dunstan's Rd. SE25 . . . . . .8D 108
St Dunstan's Rd. W6 . . . . .6H 73
St Dunstan's Rd. W7 . . . . .3C 70
St Dunstan's Rd. Felt 9D 84
St Dunstan's Rd. Houn 1F 84
(in two parts)
St Edith Clo. Eps 6A 134
St Edmund's Av. Ruis 4B 36
St Edmund's Clo. NW8 . . . . . .4D 58
St Edmund's Clo. SW17 . . . . .8C 90
St Edmunds Clo. Eri 3H 81
St Edmund's Ct. NW8 . . . . . . .4D 58
(off St Edmund's Ter.)
St Edmund's Dri. Stan 8E 22
St Edmund's La. Twic 6M 85
St Edmund's Rd. N9 . . . . .9E 16
St Edmund's Rd. Dart 3K 99
St Edmund's Rd. Ilf 6M 47
St Edmunds Sq. SW13 . . . . . .7G 73
St Edmund's Ter. NW8 . . . . . .4C 58
St Edward's Clo. NW11 . . . . . .4L 41
St Edward's Clo. New Ad . . .3B 140
St Edwards Ct. E10 . . . . .5M 45
St Edwards Ct. NW11 . . . . . . .4L 41
St Edwards Way. Romf 3B 50
St Egberts Way. E4 . . . . .1A 30
St Elizabeth Ct. E10 . . . . .5M 45
St Elizabeth Dri. Eps 6A 134
St Elmo Rd. W12 . . . . .2D 72
(in two parts)
St Elmos Rd. SE16 . . . . .3J 77
St Erkenwald M. Bark 4B 64
St Erkenwald Rd. Bark 4B 64
St Ermin's Hill. SW1 . . . . .4H 75
(off Broadway)
St Ervan's Rd. W10 . . . . .8K 57
St Ethelburga St. Romf 9L 35
St Eugene Ct. NW6 . . . . .4J 57
(off Salusbury Rd.)
St Fabian Tower. E4 . . . . .6K 29
St Faith's Clo. Enf 3A 16
St Faith's Rd. SE21 . . . . .7M 91
St Fidelis Rd. Eri 5B 82
St Fillans Rd. SE6 . . . . .7A 94
St Frances Way. Ilf 9B 48
St Francis Clo. Orp 1C 128
St Francis Clo. Wat 1F 20
St Francis' Ho. NW1 . . . . .5H 59
(off Bridgeway St.)
St Francis Rd. SE22 . . . . .3C 92
St Francis Rd. Eri 5B 82
St Francis Tower. E4 . . . . .6K 29
(off Burnside Av.)
St Frideswides M. E14 . . . . . . .9A 62
St Gabriel's Clo. E11 . . . . .6F 46
St Gabriels Mnr. SE5 . . . . . . .9M 75
(off Cormont Rd.)

St Gabriels Rd. NW2 . . . . . . .1H 57
St George's Av. E7 . . . . .3F 62
St George's Av. N7 . . . . .9H 43
St George's Av. NW9 . . . . . . .2B 40
St George's Av. W5 . . . . .3H 71
St George's Av. Horn 5K 51
St George's Av. S'hall 1K 69
St George's Av. Wey 8A 116
St George's Bldgs. SE1 . . . . .4M 75
(off St George's Rd.)
St George's Cir. SE1 . . . . .4M 75
St George's Clo. NW11 . . . . . .4K 41
St George's Clo. SE28 . . . . . . .9H 65
St George's Clo. SW8 . . . . . . .9G 75
St George's Clo. Wemb 8E 38
St George's Clo. Wey 7A 116
St Georges Ct. E6 . . . . .7K 63
St Georges Ct. E17 . . . . .3B 46
St Georges Ct. EC4 . . . . .9M 59
St Georges Ct. SW15 . . . . . . .3K 89
St Georges Ct. Harr 4E 38
(off Kenton Rd.)
St George's Dri. SW1 . . . . . . .5F 74
St George's Dri. Wat 3J 21
St George's Fields. W2 . . . . . .9C 58
St George's Gdns. Eps 6D 134
St George's Gdns. Surb 4M 119
St George's Gro. SW17 . . . . . .9B 90
St George's Ho. NW1 . . . . . . .5H 59
(off Bridgeway St.)
St Georges Ind. Est. N17 . . . .7M 27
St George's Ind. Est.
King T 2H 103
St George's La. EC3 . . . . .1B 76
(off Pudding La.)
St George's Mans. SW1 . . . . .6H 75
(off Causton St.)
St George's M. NW1 . . . . .3D 58
St George's M. SE1 . . . . .4L 75
(off Westminster Bri. Rd.)
St Georges Pde. SE6 . . . . . . .8K 93
St George's Path. SE4 . . . . . . .3L 93
(off Adelaide Av.)
St George's Pl. Twic 7E 86
St George's Rd. E7 . . . . .3F 62
St George's Rd. E10 . . . . .8A 46
St George's Rd. N9 . . . . .3E 28
St George's Rd. N13 . . . . .3K 27
St George's Rd. NW11 . . . . . . .4K 41
St George's Rd. SE1 . . . . .4L 75
St George's Rd. SW19 . . . . . .4K 105
(in two parts)
St George's Rd. W4 . . . . .3B 72
St George's Rd. W7 . . . . .2D 70
St George's Rd. Beck 5M 109
St George's Rd. Brom 6K 111
(in two parts)
St George's Rd. Dag 1J 65
St George's Rd. Enf 2D 16
St George's Rd. Felt 1H 101
St George's Rd. King T 4L 103
St George's Rd. Mitc 7F 106
St George's Rd. Orp 1B 128
St Georges Rd. Rich 2K 87
St Georges Rd. Sidc 3H 113
St George's Rd. Swan 8D 114
St George's Rd. Twic 4F 86
St George's Rd. Wall 7F 122
St George's Rd. Wat 2F 8
St George's Rd. Wey 8B 116
St George's Rd. W. Brom 6J 111
St George's Shop. & Leisure Cen.
Harr 4C 38
St Georges Sq. E7 . . . . .3F 62
St George's Sq. E14 . . . . .1J 77
St George's Sq. SE8 . . . . .5K 77
St George's Sq. SW1 . . . . . . .6H 75
St George's Sq. N Mald 7C 104
St George's Sq. M. SW1 . . . . .6H 75
St George Ter. NW1 . . . . .3D 58
St George's Wlk. Croy 5A 124
St George's Way. SE15 . . . . . .7C 76
St George's Wharf. SE1 . . . . .3D 76
(off Shad Thames)
St George Wharf. SW8 . . . . . .7J 75
St Gerards Clo. SW4 . . . . .4G 91
St German's Pl. SE3 . . . . .9E 78
St German's Rd. SE23 . . . . . . .7J 93
St Giles Av. Dag 3M 65
St Giles Av. Uxb 9A 36
St Giles Cir. W1 . . . . .9H 59
St Giles Clo. Dag 3M 65
St Giles Clo. Orp 7B 128
St Giles Ct. WC2 . . . . .9J 59
(off St Giles High St.)
St Giles Ct. Enf 8C 6
St Giles High St. WC2 . . . . . . .9H 59
St Giles Pas. WC2 . . . . .9J 59
(off New Compton St.)
St Giles Rd. SE5 . . . . .8C 76
St Giles Ter. EC2 . . . . .8A 60
(off Beech St.)
St Giles Tower. SE5 . . . . .9C 76
(off Gables Clo.)
St Gilles Ho. E2 . . . . .5H 61
(off Mace St.)
St Gothard Rd. SE27 . . . . . . .1B 108
(in two parts)

St Gregory Clo. Ruis 9G 37
St Helena Ho. WC1 . . . . .6L 59
(off Margery St.)
St Helena Rd. SE16 . . . . .5H 77
St Helena St. WC1 . . . . .6L 59
St Helen Clo. Uxb 8B 142
St Helens. Th Dit 2D 118
St Helen's Ct. Rain 7E 66
St Helen's Cres. SW16 . . . . . .5K 107
St Helen's Gdns. W10 . . . . . . .8H 57
St Helen's Pl. EC3 . . . . .9C 60
St Helen's Rd. SW16 . . . . . . .5K 107
St Helen's Rd. W13 . . . . .2F 70
St Helen's Rd. Eri 3H 81
St Helen's Rd. Ilf 4K 47
St Helier. 2C 122
St Helier Av. Mord 2A 122
St Helier Ct. N1 . . . . .4C 60
(off De Beauvoir Est.)
St Helier Ct. SE16 . . . . .3H 77
(off Poolmans St.)
St Helier's Av. Houn 4L 85
St Helier's Rd. E10 . . . . .4A 46
St Hilda's Clo. NW6 . . . . .3H 57
St Hilda's Clo. SW17 . . . . . . .8C 90
St Hilda's Rd. SW13 . . . . .7F 72
St Hilda's Wharf. E1 . . . . .2G 77
(off Wapping High St.)
St Hubert's Ho. E14 . . . . .4L 77
(off Janet St.)
St Hughes Clo. SW17 . . . . . . .8C 90
St Hugh's Rd. SE20 . . . . .5F 108
St Ives Clo. Romf 7K 35
St Ivian's Dri. Romf 1E 50
St James Apartments.
E17 . . . . .3J 45
(off High St.)
St James Av. N20 . . . . .3C 26
St James Av. W13 . . . . .2E 70
St James Av. Eps 3D 134
St James Av. Sutt 7L 121
St James Clo. N20 . . . . .3C 26
St James Clo. SE18 . . . . .6A 80
St James Clo. Barn 6B 14
St James Clo. Eps 6C 134
St James Clo. N Mald 9D 104
St James Clo. Ruis 7G 37
St James Ct. E2 . . . . .6E 60
(off Bethnal Grn. Rd.)
St James Ct. E12 . . . . .7G 47
St James Ct. SE3 . . . . .9F 78
St James' Ct. SW1 . . . . .4G 75
St James Ct. Asht 9H 133
St James Ct. Romf 2D 50
St James Gdns. Ilf 2F 48
St James Gdns. Wemb 3H 55
St James Ga. Buck H 1F 30
St James Gro. SW11 . . . . . . .1D 90
St James Ho. Romf 3D 50
(off Eastern Rd.)
St James' Mans. NW6 . . . . . . .3L 57
(off W. End La.)
St James' M. E14 . . . . .4A 78
St James M. E17 . . . . .3J 45
(off St James's St.)
St James Pl. Dart 5H 99
St James Pl. S Croy 8C 124
St James Residences. W1 . . . .1H 75
(off Brewer St.)
St James' Rd. E15 . . . . .1D 62
St James' Rd. N9 . . . . .2F 28
St James Rd. Cars 5C 122
St James' Rd. Mitc 4E 106
St James' Rd. Purl 5M 137
St James' Rd. Surb 1H 119
St James' Rd. Sutt 7L 121
St James Rd. Wat 7F 8
St James's. 2H 75
St James's. SE14 . . . . .9J 77
St James's. SW1 . . . . .2G 75
St James's App. EC2 . . . . .7C 60
St James's Av. E2 . . . . .5G 61
St James's Av. Beck 7J 109
St James's Av. Hamp H 2A 102
St James's Chambers.
SW1 . . . . .2G 75
(off Jermyn St.)
St James's Clo. NW8 . . . . .4D 58
(off St James's Ter M.)
St James's Clo. SW17 . . . . . .8D 90
St James's Cotts. Rich 4H 87
St James's Ct. N18 . . . . .6D 28
(off Fore St.)
St James's Ct. Harr 2A 38
St James's Ct. King T 7J 103
St James's Cres. SW9 . . . . . . .2L 91
St James's Dri.
SW17 & SW12 . . . . . . .7D 90
St James's Gdns. W11 . . . . . .2J 73
(in two parts)
St James's La. N10 . . . . .2F 42
St James's Mkt. SW1 . . . . . . .1H 75
St James's Palace. 3G 75
St James's Pk. 3H 75
St James's Pk. Croy 2A 124
St James's Pas. EC3 . . . . .9C 60
(off Duke's Pl.)
St James's Pl. SW1 . . . . .2G 75
St James's Rd.
SE1 & SE16 . . . . .7E 76
St James's Rd. SE16 . . . . . . .4E 76

St James's Rd. Croy 2M 123
St James's Rd. Hamp H 2M 101
St James's Rd. King T 6H 103
St James's Sq. SW1 . . . . .2G 75
St James's St. E17 . . . . .3J 45
St James's St. SW1 . . . . .2G 75
St James's Ter. NW8 . . . . .4D 58
(off Prince Albert Rd.)
St James's Ter. M. NW8 . . . . .4D 58
St James's Wlk. EC1 . . . . .7M 59
St James's Wlk. W6 . . . . .6G 73
St James Ter. SW12 . . . . .7E 90
St James Way. Sidc 2J 113
St Jeromes Gro. Hay 9A 52
St Joan's Rd. N9 . . . . .2D 28
St John Fisher Rd. Eri 4H 81
St John's. 1L 93
St John's Av. N11 . . . . .5D 26
St John's Av. NW10 . . . . .4D 56
St John's Av. SW15 . . . . .4H 89
St John's Av. Eps 4E 134
St Johns Cvn. Pk. Enf 1M 15
St Johns Chu. Rd. E9 . . . . . . .1G 61
St Johns Clo. N14 . . . . .8G 15
St John's Clo. N20 . . . . .3A 26
(off Rasper Rd.)
St John's Clo. SW6 . . . . .8L 73
St John's Clo. Rain 3E 66
St John's Clo. Uxb 4A 142
St John's Clo. Wemb 1J 55
St John's Cotts. SE20 . . . . . . .4G 109
St John's Ct. E1 . . . . .2F 76
(off Scandrett St.)
St John's Ct. N4 . . . . .7M 43
St John's Ct. N5 . . . . .9M 43
St John's Ct. SE13 . . . . .1A 94
St John's Ct. W6 . . . . .5F 72
(off Glenthorne Rd.)
St John's Ct. Buck H 1F 30
St John's Ct. Eri 5B 82
St John's Ct. Harr 4D 38
St John's Ct. Iswth 1D 86
St John's Ct. King T 8J 103
(off Beaufort Rd.)
St John's Ct. N'wd 8E 20
(off Murray Rd.)
St Johns Cres. SW9 . . . . .2L 91
St Johns Dri. SW18 . . . . .7M 89
St John's Dri. W on T 3G 117
St John's Est. N1 . . . . .5B 60
St John's Est. SE1 . . . . .3D 76
(off Fair St.)
St John's Gdns. W11 . . . . . . .1J 73
St John's Gate. 7M 59
(off St John's La.)
St John's Gro. N19 . . . . .7G 43
St John's Gro. SW13 . . . . .1D 88
St John's Gro. Rich 3J 87
St John's Hill. SW11 . . . . .4B 90
St John's Hill. Coul 9L 137
(in two parts)
St John's Hill. Purl 8L 137
St John's Hill Gro. SW11 . . . . .3B 90
St John's Ho. E14 . . . . .5A 78
(off Pier St.)
St Johns Ho. SE17 . . . . .7B 76
(off Lytham St.)
St John's Jerusalem Garden.
. . . . .4M 115
St John's La. EC1 . . . . .7M 59
St John's M. W11 . . . . .9L 57
St Johns Pde. Sidc 1E 112
(off Sidcup High St.)
St John's Pk. SE3 . . . . .8D 78
St John's Pk. Mans. N19 . . . . .8G 43
St John's Pas. SW19 . . . . .3J 105
St John's Path. EC1 . . . . .7M 59
(off Britton St.)
St Johns Pathway. SE23 . . . . .7G 93
St John's Pl. EC1 . . . . .7M 59
St Johns Ri. Berr G 8M 141
St John's Rd. E4 . . . . .4M 29
St John's Rd. E6 . . . . .4J 63
St John's Rd. E16 . . . . .9E 62
St John's Rd. E17 . . . . .9M 29
St John's Rd. N15 . . . . .4C 44
St John's Rd. NW11 . . . . .4K 41
St John's Rd. SE20 . . . . .3G 109
St John's Rd. SW11 . . . . .3C 90
St John's Rd. SW19 . . . . .4J 105
St John's Rd. Bark 4C 64
St John's Rd. Cars 5C 122
St John's Rd. Croy 5M 123
St John's Rd. Dart 6M 99
St John's Rd. E Mol 8B 102
St John's Rd. Eri 6B 82
St John's Rd. Felt 1J 101
St John's Rd. Hamp W 6G 103
St John's Rd. Harr 4D 38
St John's Rd. Ilf 5C 48
St John's Rd. Iswth 1D 86
St John's Rd. Lou 4K 19
St John's Rd. N Mald 7A 104
St John's Rd. Orp 1B 128
St John's Rd. Rich 3J 87
St Johns Rd. Romf 5A 34
St John's Rd. Sidc 1F 112
St John's Rd. S'hall 4J 69
St John's Rd. Sutt 4M 121
St John's Rd. Uxb 4A 142

St John's Rd.—St Peter's Rd.

St John's Rd. Wat 4F 8
St John's Rd. Well 2F 96
St John's Rd. Wemb 9H 39
St John's Sq. EC1 7M 59
St John's Ter. E7 2F 62
St John's Ter. SE18 7A 80
St John's Ter. SW15 9C 88
(off Kingston Va.)
St John's Ter. W10 7H 57
St John's Ter. Enf 1B 16
St John St. EC1 5L 59
St John's Va. SE8 1L 93
St John's Vs. N11 5D 26
(off Friern Barnet Rd.)
St John's Vs. N19 7H 43
St John's Vs. W8 4M 73
St John's Way. N19 7G 43
St John's Wood. 5B 58
St John's Wood Ct. NW8 6B 58
(off St John's Wood Rd.)
St John's Wood High St. NW8 5B 58
St John's Wood Pk. NW8 4B 58
St John's Wood Rd. NW8 7B 58
St John's Wood Ter. NW8 5B 58
St John's Yd. N17 7D 28
St Joseph's Clo. W10 8J 57
St Joseph's Clo. Orp 5D 128
St Joseph's Ct. E4 9B 18
St Josephs Ct. SE7 7F 78
St Joseph's Dri. S'hall 2J 69
St Joseph's Flats. NW1 6H 59
(off Drummond Cres.)
St Joseph's Gro. NW4 2F 40
St Joseph's Ho. W6 5H 73
(off Brook Grn.)
St Joseph's Rd. N9 9F 16
St Joseph's Rd. Wal X 6E 6
St Joseph's St. SW8 9F 74
St Joseph's Va. SE3 2B 94
St Jude's Rd. E2 5F 60
St Jude St. N16 1C 60
St Julian's Clo. SW16 1L 107
St Julian's Farm Rd. SE27 1L 107
St Julian's Rd. NW6 4L 57
St Justin Clo. St P 7H 113
St Katharine Docks. 2E 76
St Katharine's Pier. E1 2D 76
(off Tower Bri. App.)
St Katharine's Precinct. NW1 5F 58
St Katharine's Way. E1 2D 76
(in two parts)
St Katherine's Rd. Eri 3H 81
St Katherine's Row. EC3 1C 76
(off Fenchurch St.)
St Katherines Wlk. W11 2H 73
(off St Ann's Rd.)
St Kathryn's Pl. Upm 7M 51
St Keverne Rd. SE9 1J 111
St Kilda Rd. W13 2E 70
St Kilda Rd. Orp 3D 128
St Kilda's Rd. N16 6B 44
St Kilda's Rd. Harr 4C 38
St Kitts Ter. SE19 2C 108
St Laurence Clo. NW6 4H 57
St Laurence Clo. Orp 7H 113
St Laurence Clo. Uxb 8A 142
St Lawrence Bus. Cen. Twic 8F 84
St Lawrence Clo. Ab L 3C 4
St Lawrence Clo. Edgw 7K 23
St Lawrence Cotts. E14 2A 78
(off St Lawrence St.)
St Lawrence Ct. N1 3B 60
(off De Beauvoir Est.)
St Lawrence Dri. Pinn 3F 36
St Lawrence Ho. SE1 4C 76
(off Purbrook St.)
St Lawrence Rd. Upm 7M 51
St Lawrence St. E14 2A 78
St Lawrence Ter. W10 8J 57
St Lawrence Way. SW9 1L 91
St Lawrence Way. Brick W 3K 5
St Leonard M. N1 5C 60
St Leonard's Av. E4 6B 30
St Leonard's Av. Harr 3G 39
St Leonard's Clo. Bush 6J 9
St Leonard's Clo. Well 2E 96
St Leonard's Ct. N1 6B 60
(off New N. Rd.)
St Leonards Ct. SW14 2A 88
St Leonard's Gdns. Houn 9J 69
St Leonard's Gdns. Ilf 1A 64
St Leonards Hamlet. 6F 50
St Leonard's Ri. Orp 6C 128
St Leonard's Rd. E14 8M 61
(in two parts)
St Leonard's Rd. NW10 7B 56
St Leonard's Rd. SW14 2M 87
St Leonard's Rd. W13 1G 71
St Leonard's Rd. Clay 8D 118
St Leonard's Rd. Croy 5M 123
St Leonard's Rd. Surb 9H 103
St Leonard's Rd. Th Dit 1E 118
St Leonards Sq. NW5 2E 58
St Leonards Sq. Surb 9H 103
St Leonard's St. E3 6M 61
St Leonard's Ter. SW3 6D 74
St Leonard's Wlk. SW16 4K 107
St Leonards Way. Horn 7F 50
St Loo Av. SW3 7C 74
St Louis Rd. SE27 1B 108
St Loy's Rd. N17 9C 28
St Lucia Dri. E15 4D 62
St Luke Clo. Uxb 9B 142
St Luke's. 7A 60
St Luke's Av. SW4 3H 91
St Luke's Av. Enf 2B 16
St Luke's Av. Ilf 1M 63
St Luke's Clo. EC1 7A 60
St Luke's Clo. SE25 1F 124
St Luke's Clo. Swan 6B 114
St Lukes Ct. E10 5M 45
(off Capworth St.)
St Luke's Est. EC1 6B 60
St Luke's M. W11 9K 57
St Luke's Pas. King T 5K 103
St Luke's Path. Ilf 1M 63
St Luke's Rd. W11 8K 57
St Luke's Rd. Uxb 3C 142
St Luke's Rd. Whyt 9D 138
St Luke's Sq. E16 9D 62
St Luke's St. SW3 6C 74
St Luke's Yd. W9 5K 57
(in two parts)
St Malo Av. N9 3G 29
St Margaret Dri. Eps 6A 134
St Margarets. 5F 86
St Margaret's. Bark 4A 64
St Margaret's Av. N15 2M 43
St Margaret's Av. N20 1A 26
St Margaret's Av. Ashf 2A 100
St Margarets Av. Berr G 8M 141
St Margaret's Av. Harr 8A 38
St Margaret's Av. Sidc 9B 96
St Margaret's Av. Sutt 5J 121
St Margarets Av. Uxb 7E 142
St Margarets Bus. Cen. Twic 5F 86
St Margarets Clo. EC2 9B 60
(off Lothbury)
St Margaret's Clo. Orp 6F 128
St Margaret's Ct. N11 4E 26
St Margarets Ct. SE1 2A 76
St Margarets Ct. SW15 3F 88
St Margarets Ct. Edgw 5M 23
St Margaret's Cres. SW15 4F 88
St Margaret's Dri. Twic 4F 86
St Margaret's Gro. E11 8D 46
St Margaret's Gro. SE18 7A 80
St Margaret's Gro. Twic 5E 86
St Margaret's La. W8 4M 73
St Margaret's Pas. SE13 2C 94
(in two parts)
St Margarets Path. SE18 6A 80
St Margaret's Rd. E12 7G 47
St Margaret's Rd. N17 1C 44
St Margaret's Rd. NW10 6G 57
St Margarets Rd. SE4 3K 93
(in two parts)
St Margaret's Rd. W7 3C 70
St Margaret's Rd. Edgw 5M 23
St Margarets Rd. Iswth & Twic 3F 86
St Margaret's Rd. Ruis 4B 36
St Margarets Roundabout (Junct.) 5F 86
St Margaret's Ter. SE18 6A 80
St Margaret St. SW1 3J 75
St Mark's Clo. SE10 8A 78
St Marks Clo. SW6 9L 73
St Marks Clo. Harr 5F 38
St Mark's Clo. New Bar 5M 13
St Marks Ct. E10 5M 45
(off Capworth St.)
St Marks Ct. NW8 5A 58
(off Abercorn Pl.)
St Marks Ct. W7 3C 70
(off Lwr. Boston Rd.)
St Mark's Cres. NW1 4E 58
St Mark's Ga. E9 3K 61
St Mark's Gro. SW10 8M 73
St Mark's Hill. Surb 1J 119
St Marks Ho. SE17 7B 76
(off Lytham St.)
St Marks Ind. Est. E16 2H 79
St Mark's Pl. SW19 3K 105
St Mark's Pl. W11 9J 57
St Mark's Ri. E8 1D 60
St Mark's Rd. SE25 8E 108
St Mark's Rd. W5 2J 71
St Mark's Rd. W7 3C 70
St Mark's Rd. W10 & W11 8H 57
St Mark's Rd. Brom 7E 110
St Marks Rd. Enf 8D 16
St Marks Rd. Mitc 6D 106
St Mark's Rd. Tedd 4F 102
St Mark's Sq. NW1 4E 58
St Mark St. E1 9D 60
St Martin Clo. Uxb 9B 142
St Martin-in-the-Fields Church. 1J 75
(off St Martin's Pl.)
St Martins. N'wd 5B 20
St Martin's Almshouses. NW1 4G 59
St Martin's App. Ruis 5C 36
St Martin's Av. E6 5H 63
St Martin's Av. Eps 6C 134
St Martin's Clo. NW1 4G 59
St Martin's Clo. Enf 3F 16
St Martins Clo. Eps 5C 134
St Martin's Clo. Eri 3H 81
St Martins Clo. Wat 4G 21
St Martin's Clo. W Dray 4H 143
St Martins Ct. N1 4C 60
(off De Beauvoir Est.)
St Martin's Ct. WC2 1J 75
St Martin's Dri. Eyns 6H 131
St Martins Dri. W on T 5G 117
St Martins Est. SW2 7L 91
St Martin's La. WC2 1J 75
St Martins La. Beck 9M 109
St Martin's le-Grand. EC1 9A 60
St Martin's Pl. WC2 1J 75
St Martin's Rd. N9 2F 28
St Martin's Rd. SW9 1K 91
St Martin's Rd. Dart 5K 99
St Martin's Rd. W Dray 4H 143
St Martin's St. WC2 1H 75
(in two parts)
St Martins Ter. N10 1E 42
St Martin's Theatre. 1J 75
(off West St.)
St Martins Way. SW17 9A 90
St Mary Abbot's Ct. W14 4K 73
(off Warwick Gdns.)
St Mary Abbot's Pl. W8 4K 73
St Mary Abbot's Ter. W14 4K 73
St Mary at Hill. EC3 1C 76
St Mary Av. Wall 5E 122
St Mary Axe. EC3 9C 60
St Marychurch St. SE16 3G 77
St Mary Cray. 8G 113
St Mary Graces Ct. E1 1D 76
St Marylebone Crematorium. N2 1M 41
St Mary le-Park Ct. SW11 8C 74
(off Parkgate Rd.)
St Mary Newington Clo. SE17 6C 76
(off Surrey Sq.)
St Mary Rd. E17 2L 45
St Mary's. Bark 4B 64
St Marys. Wey 5B 116
St Mary's App. E12 1K 63
St Mary's Av. E11 5F 46
St Mary's Av. N3 9J 25
St Mary's Av. Brom 7C 110
St Mary's Av. N'wd 5C 20
St Mary's Av. Stanw 6B 144
St Mary's Av. Tedd 3D 102
St Mary's Av. Central. S'hall 5M 69
St Mary's Av. N. S'hall 5M 69
St Mary's Av. S. S'hall 5M 69
St Mary's Clo. N17 8D 28
St Mary's Clo. Chess 9K 119
St Mary's Clo. Eps 9D 120
St Mary's Clo. Orp 6F 112
St Mary's Clo. Stanw 6B 144
St Mary's Clo. Sun 8E 100
St Mary's Clo. Wat 6F 8
(off Church St.)
St Mary's Ct. E6 7K 63
St Mary's Ct. SE7 8H 79
St Mary's Ct. W5 3H 71
St Mary's Ct. W12 4D 72
St Mary's Ct. Wall 6G 123
St Mary's Cres. NW4 1F 40
St Mary's Cres. Hay 1D 68
St Mary's Cres. Iswth 8B 70
St Mary's Cres. Stanw 6B 144
St Mary's Dri. Felt 6A 84
St Mary's Est. SE16 3G 77
(off St Marychurch St.)
St Mary's Flats. NW1 6H 59
(off Drummond Cres.)
St Mary's Gdns. SE11 5L 75
St Mary's Ga. W8 4M 73
St Mary's Grn. N2 9A 26
St Mary's Grn. Big H 9G 141
St Mary's Gro. N1 2M 59
St Mary's Gro. SW13 2F 88
St Mary's Gro. W4 7M 71
St Mary's Gro. Big H 9G 141
St Mary's Gro. Rich 3K 87
St Mary's Ho. N1 4M 59
(off St Mary's Path)
St Mary's La. N Ock 7L 51
St Mary's Mans. W2 8B 58
St Mary's M. NW6 3M 57
(in two parts)
St Marys M. Rich 8G 87
St Mary's Path. N1 4M 59
St Mary's Pl. SE9 5K 95
St Mary's Pl. W5 3H 71
St Mary's Pl. W8 4M 73
St Mary's Rd. E10 8A 46
St Mary's Rd. E13 5F 62
St Mary's Rd. N8 2J 43
St Mary's Rd. N9 1F 28
St Mary's Rd. NW10 4C 56
St Mary's Rd. NW11 5J 41
St Mary's Rd. SE15 9G 77
St Mary's Rd. SE25 7C 108
St Mary's Rd. SW19 2J 105
St Marys Rd. W5 3H 71
St Mary's Rd. Barn 9D 14
St Mary's Rd. Bex 7A 98
St Mary's Rd. Chesh 2C 6
St Mary's Rd. Dit H 2G 119
St Mary's Rd. E Mol 9B 102
St Mary's Rd. Hay 1D 68
St Mary's Rd. Ilf 7B 48
St Mary's Rd. S Croy 2B 138
St Mary's Rd. Surb 1H 119
St Mary's Rd. Swan 8B 114
St Mary's Rd. Wat 6F 8
St Mary's Rd. Wey 6B 116
St Mary's Rd. Wor Pk 4C 120
St Mary's Sq. W2 8B 58
St Mary's Sq. W5 3H 71
St Mary's Ter. W2 8B 58
St Mary's Tower. EC1 7A 60
(off Fortune St.)
St Mary St. SE18 5K 79
St Mary's Vw. Harr 3G 39
St Mary's Vw. Wat 6G 9
(off King St.)
St Mary's Wlk. SE11 5L 75
St Mary's Wlk. Hay 1D 68
St Mary's Way. Chig 5L 31
St Matthew Clo. Uxb 9B 142
St Matthew's Av. Surb 3J 119
St Matthew's Clo. Rain 3E 66
St Matthews Clo. Wat 8H 9
St Matthews Ct. E10 5M 45
St Matthews Ct. N10 9E 26
St Matthews Ct. SE1 4A 76
(off Meadow Row)
St Matthew's Dri. Brom 7K 111
St Matthews Ho. SE17 7B 76
(off Phelp St.)
St Matthew's Lodge. NW1 5G 59
(off Oakley Sq.)
St Matthew's Rd. SW2 3K 91
St Matthew's Rd. W5 2J 71
St Matthew's Row. E2 6E 60
St Matthew St. SW1 4H 75
St Matthias Clo. NW9 3D 40
St Maur Rd. SW6 9K 73
St Mellion Clo. SE28 9H 65
St Merryn Clo. SE18 8B 80
St Merryn Ct. Beck 4L 109
St Michael's All. EC3 9B 60
St Michael's Av. N9 9G 17
St Michael's Av. Wemb 2L 55
St Michaels Clo. E16 8H 63
St Michael's Clo. N3 9K 25
St Michael's Clo. N12 5C 26
St Michael's Clo. Brom 7J 111
St Michael's Clo. Eri 3H 81
St Michael's Clo. W on T 4G 117
St Michael's Clo. Wor Pk 4D 120
St Michaels Ct. E14 8A 62
(off St Leonards Rd.)
St Michael's Ct. SE1 3A 76
(off Trinity St.)
St Michael's Ct. Wey 7A 116
(off Princes Rd.)
St Michael's Cres. Pinn 4J 37
St Michaels Dri. Wat 6F 4
St Michael's Flats. NW1 5H 59
(off Aldenham St.)
St Michael's Gdns. W10 8J 57
St Michael's Pde. Wat 2F 8
St Michael's Ri. Well 9F 80
St Michael's Rd. NW2 9G 41
St Michael's Rd. SW9 1K 91
St Michael's Rd. Croy 3A 124
St Michael's Rd. Wall 8G 123
St Michael's Rd. Well 2F 96
St Michael's St. W2 9B 58
St Michaels Ter. N6 6E 42
(off South Gro.)
St Michael's Ter. N22 8J 27
St Mildred's Ct. EC2 9B 60
St Mildreds Rd. SE12 6C 94
St Mirren Ct. New Bar 7A 14
St Neots Clo. Borwd 2L 11
St Neot's Rd. Romf 7K 35
St Nicholas Av. Horn 8E 50
St Nicholas Cen. Sutt 7M 121
St Nicholas Clo. Els 8H 11
St Nicholas Clo. Uxb 9B 142
St Nicholas Ct. King T 8J 103
(off Surbiton Rd.)
St Nicholas' Flats. NW1 5H 59
(off Werrington St.)
St Nicholas Glebe. SW17 2E 106
St Nicholas Ho. SE8 7L 77
(off Deptford Grn.)
St Nicholas Ho. SE18 8J 79
(off Shrapnel Clo.)
St Nicholas Rd. SE18 6D 80
St Nicholas Rd. Sutt 7M 121
St Nicholas Rd. Th Dit 1D 118
St Nicholas St. SE8 9K 77
St Nicholas Way. Sutt 6M 121
St Nicolas La. Chst 5J 111
St Ninian's Ct. N20 3D 26
St Norbert Grn. SE4 3J 93
St Norbert Rd. SE4 4H 93
St Normans Way. Eps 2E 134
St Olaf Ho. SE1 2B 76
(off Tooley St.)
St Olaf's Rd. SW6 8J 73
St Olaf Stairs. SE1 2B 76
(off Tooley St.)
St Olave's Ct. EC2 9B 60
St Olave's Est. SE1 3C 76
St Olave's Gdns. SE11 5L 75
St Olave's Mans. SE11 5L 75
(off Walnut Tree Wlk.)
St Olave's Rd. E6 4L 63
St Olave's Ter. SE1 3C 76
(off Fair St.)
St Olaves Wlk. SW16 6G 107
St Olav's Sq. SE16 3G 77
St Onge Pde. Enf 5B 16
(off Southbury Rd.)
St Oswald's Pl. SE11 6K 75
St Oswald's Rd. SW16 5M 107
St Oswulf St. SW1 5H 75
St Owen Ho. SE1 4C 76
(off Fendall St.)
St Pancras. 6J 59
St Pancras Commercial Cen. NW1 4G 59
(off Pratt St.)
St Pancras Ct. N2 9B 26
St Pancras Way. NW1 3G 59
St Patrick's Ct. Wfd G 7C 30
St Paul Clo. Uxb 8B 142
St Paul's Av. NW2 2F 56
St Paul's Av. SE16 2H 77
St Paul's Av. Harr 2K 39
St Paul's Cathedral. 9A 60
St Paul's Chyd. EC4 9M 59
(in two parts)
St Pauls Clo. SE7 6H 79
St Paul's Clo. W5 3K 71
St Paul's Clo. Ashf 2A 100
St Paul's Clo. Ave 1M 83
St Paul's Clo. Cars 3C 122
St Paul's Clo. Chess 6H 119
St Paul's Clo. Hay 6B 68
St Paul's Clo. Houn 1J 85
St Pauls Ct. SW4 4H 91
St Paul's Ct. Houn 2J 85
St Pauls Courtyard. SE8 8L 77
(off Crossfield St.)
St Paul's Cray. 6F 112
St Paul's Cray Rd. Chst 5B 112
St Paul's Cres. NW1 3H 59
(in two parts)
St Paul's Dri. E15 1B 62
St Paul's M. NW1 3H 59
St Paul's Pl. N1 2B 60
St Pauls Pl. Ave 1M 83
St Paul's Ri. N13 6M 27
St Paul's Rd. N1 2M 59
St Paul's Rd. N17 7E 28
St Paul's Rd. Bark 4A 64
St Paul's Rd. Bren 7H 71
St Paul's Rd. Eri 8A 82
St Paul's Rd. Rich 2K 87
St Paul's Rd. T Hth 7A 108
St Paul's Shrubbery. N1 2B 60
St Paul's Sq. Brom 6D 110
St Paul's Studios. W6 6J 73
(off Talgarth Rd.)
St Pauls Ter. SE17 7M 75
St Pauls Tower. E10 5M 45
(off Beaumont Rd.)
St Paul St. N1 4A 60
(in two parts)
St Pauls Vw. Apartments. EC1 6L 59
(off Amwell St.)
St Paul's Wlk. King T 4L 103
St Pauls Way. E3 8K 61
St Paul's Way. N3 7M 25
St Pauls Way. Wal A 6K 7
St Pauls Way. Wat 4G 9
St Paul's Wood Hill. Orp 6C 112
St Peter's All. EC3 9B 60
(off Cornhill)
St Peter's Av. E2 5E 60
St Peter's Av. E17 2C 46
St Peters Av. N2 7C 26
St Peter's Av. N18 4E 28
St Peters Av. Berr G 8M 141
St Petersburgh M. W2 1M 73
St Petersburgh Pl. W2 1M 73
St Peter's Cen. E1 2F 76
(off Reardon St.)
St Peter's Chu. Ct. N1 4M 59
(off Devonia Rd.)
St Peter's Clo. E2 5E 60
St Peter's Clo. SW17 8C 90
St Peter's Clo. Barn 7F 12
St Peters Clo. Bus H 1B 22
St Peter's Clo. Chst 4B 112
St Peter's Clo. Ilf 2C 48
St Peter's Clo. Ruis 7H 37
St Peter's Ct. NW4 3G 41
St Peters Ct. W Mol 8L 101
St Peter's Gdns. SE27 9L 91
St Peter's Gro. W6 5E 72
St Peters Ho. SE17 7B 76
St Peter's Ho. WC1 6J 59
(off Regent Sq.)
St Peter's La. St P 6E 112
St Peters Pl. W9 7M 57
St Peter's Rd. N9 1F 28
St Peter's Rd. W6 6E 72
St Peter's Rd. Croy 6B 124
St Peter's Rd. King T 6L 103
St Peter's Rd. S'hall 8L 53
St Peter's Rd. Twic 4F 86

St Peters Rd.—Sandringham Ho.

St Peters Rd. Uxb 8B 142
St Peter's Rd. W Mol 8L 101
St Peter's Sq. E2 ....5E 60
St Peter's Sq. W6 ....5D 72
St Peter's St. N1 ....4M 59
St Peter's St. S Croy 7B 124
St Peter's St. M. N1 ....5M 59
(off St Peters St.)
St Peter's Ter. SW6 ....8K 73
St Peter's Vs. W6 ....5E 72
St Peter's Way. N1 ....3C 60
St Peter's Way. W5 ....8H 55
St Peters Way. Hay 6B 68
St Peter's Wharf. W4 ....6E 72
St Philip Ho. WC1 ....6L 59
(off Lloyd Baker St.)
St Philips Av. N2 ....7C 26
St Philip's Av. Wor Pk 4F 120
St Philip's Ga. Wor Pk 4F 120
St Philip Sq. SW8 ....1F 90
St Philip's Rd. E8 ....2E 60
St Philips Rd. Surb 1H 119
St Philip St. SW8 ....1F 90
St Philip's Way. N1 ....4A 60
St Quentin Rd. Well 2D 96
St Quintin Av. W10 ....8G 57
St Quintin Gdns. W10 ....8G 57
St Quintin Rd. E13 ....6F 62
St Raphael's Way. NW10 ....1A 56
St Regis Clo. N10 ....9F 26
St Regis Heights. NW3 ....8M 41
St Richard's Ho. NW1 ....6H 59
(off Eversholt St.)
St Ronan's Clo. Barn 2B 14
St Ronan's Cres. Wfd G 7E 30
St Rule St. SW8 ....1G 91
St Saviour's College.
SE27 ....1B 108
St Saviour's Ct. N10 ....9F 26
(off Alexandra Pk. Rd.)
St Saviours Ct. Harr 3C 38
St Saviour's Est. SE1 ....3D 76
St Saviour's Rd. SW2 ....4K 91
St Saviour's Rd. Croy 1M 123
St Saviours Wlk. Dart 5J 99
(off Bullace La.)
St Saviour's Wharf. SE1 ....3D 76
(Mill St.)
St Saviour's Wharf. SE1 ....3D 76
(off Shad Thames)
Saints Clo. SE27 ....1M 107
Saints Dri. E7 ....1H 63
St Silas Pl. NW5 ....2E 58
St Simon's Av. SW15 ....4G 89
Saints M. Mitc 7C 106
St Stephen's Av. E17 ....3A 46
St Stephen's Av. W12 ....2F 72
(in two parts)
St Stephen's Av. W13 ....9F 54
St Stephen's Av. Asht 8J 133
St Stephen's Clo. E17 ....3M 45
St Stephen's Clo. NW8 ....4C 58
St Stephen's Clo. S'hall 8L 53
St Stephens Ct. N8 ....4K 43
St Stephens Ct. W13 ....9F 54
St Stephen's Ct. Enf 8C 16
(off Park Av.)
St Stephen's Cres. W2 ....9L 57
St Stephen's Cres. T Hth 7L 107
St Stephen's Gdns. SW15 ....4K 89
St Stephen's Gdns. W2 ....9L 57
(in two parts)
St Stephen's Gdns. Twic 5G 87
St Stephens Gro. SE13 ....2A 94
St Stephens Ho. SE17 ....7B 76
(off Lytham St.)
St Stephens M. W2 ....8L 57
St Stephens Pde. E7 ....3G 63
St Stephen's Pas. Twic 5G 87
St Stephen's Rd. E3 ....4J 61
St Stephen's Rd. E6 ....3G 63
St Stephen's Rd. E17 ....3M 45
St Stephen's Rd. W13 ....9F 54
St Stephen's Rd. Barn 7H 13
St Stephens Rd. Enf 1H 17
St Stephen's Rd. Houn 5L 85
St Stephen's Rd. W Dray 2H 143
St Stephen's Row. EC4 ....9B 60
(off Walbrook)
St Stephen's Ter. SW8 ....8K 75
St Stephen's Wlk. SW7 ....5A 74
(off Southwell Gdns.)
St Swithins La. EC4 ....1B 76
St Swithun's Rd. SE13 ....5B 94
St Theresa Clo. Eps 6A 134
St Theresa Ct. E4 ....9B 18
St Theresa's Rd. Felt 3D 84
St Thomas Clo. Surb 3K 119
St Thomas Ct. E10 ....5M 45
(off Beaumont Rd.)
St Thomas Ct. Bex 6L 97
St Thomas Ct. Pinn 8J 21
St Thomas Dri. Orp 3A 128
St Thomas' Dri. Pinn 8J 21
St Thomas Gdns. Ilf 2A 64
St Thomas Ho. E1 ....9H 61
(off W. Arbour St.)
St Thomas Rd. E16 ....9E 62
St Thomas Rd. N14 ....9H 15
St Thomas Rd. W4 ....7A 72
St Thomas Rd. Belv 3A 82
St Thomas's Gdns. NW5 ....2E 58
St Thomas's Pl. E9 ....3G 61
St Thomas's Rd. N4 ....7L 43
St Thomas's Rd. NW10 ....4C 56
St Thomas's Sq. E9 ....3G 61
St Thomas St. SE1 ....2B 76
St Thomas's Way. SW6 ....8K 73
St Timothys M. Brom 5F 110
St Ursula Gro. Pinn 3H 37
St Ursula Rd. S'hall 9L 53
St Vincent Clo. SE27 ....2M 107
St Vincent De Paul Ho. E1 ....8G 61
(off Jubilee St.)
St Vincent Ho. SE1 ....4D 76
(off Fendall St.)
St Vincent Rd. Twic 5A 86
St Vincent Rd. W on T 5F 116
St Vincents Av. Dart 4L 99
St Vincent's Cotts. Wat 6F 8
(off Marlborough Rd.)
St Vincent's Hamlet. 1M 35
St Vincents Rd. Dart 5L 99
St Vincent St. W1 ....8E 58
St Vincents Vs. Dart 5K 99
St Wilfrid's Clo. Barn 7C 14
St Wilfrid's Rd. New Bar 7C 14
St Winefride's Av. E12 ....1K 63
St Winifreds. Kenl 7A 138
St Winifred's Clo. Chig 5A 32
St Winifred's Rd. Big H 9K 141
St Winifred's Rd. Tedd 3F 102
Saladin Dri. Purf 5L 83
Sala Ho. SE3 ....3F 94
Salamanca Pl. SE1 ....5K 75
Salamanca St.
SE1 & SE11 ....5K 75
Salamander Clo. King T 2G 103
Salamander Quay.
King T 5H 103
Salamons Way. Rain 9C 66
Salcombe Dri. Mord 3H 121
Salcombe Dri. Romf 4K 49
Salcombe Gdns. NW7 ....6G 25
Salcombe Pk. Lou 7H 19
Salcombe Rd. E17 ....5K 45
Salcombe Rd. N16 ....1C 60
Salcombe Rd. Ashf 9C 144
Salcombe Way. Hay 6C 52
Salcombe Way. Ruis 7E 36
Salcot Cres. New Ad 2A 140
Salcott Rd. SW11 ....4C 90
Salcott Rd. Croy 5J 123
Salehurst Clo. Harr 3J 39
Salehurst Rd. SE4 ....5K 93
Salem Pl. Croy 5A 124
Salem Rd. W2 ....1M 73
Sale Pl. W2 ....8C 58
Sale St. E2 ....7E 60
Salford Ho. E14 ....5A 78
(off Seyssel St.)
Salford Rd. SW2 ....7H 91
Salhouse Clo. SE28 ....9G 65
Salisbury Av. N3 ....1K 41
Salisbury Av. Bark 3B 64
Salisbury Av. Sutt 8K 121
Salisbury Av. Swan 8E 114
Salisbury Clo. SE17 ....5B 76
Salisbury Clo. Wor Pk 5D 120
Salisbury Ct. EC4 ....9M 59
Salisbury Ct. Cars 7D 122
Salisbury Ct. Edgw 6L 23
Salisbury Ct. Enf 6B 16
(off London Rd.)
Salisbury Ct. N'holt 1M 53
(off Newmarket Av.)
Salisbury Cres. Chesh 5D 6
Salisbury Gdns. SW19 ....4J 105
Salisbury Gdns. Buck H 2H 31
Salisbury Hall Gdns. E4 ....6L 29
Salisbury Ho. E14 ....9M 61
(off Hobday St.)
Salisbury Ho. EC2 ....8B 60
(off London Wall)
Salisbury Ho. N1 ....4M 59
(off St Mary's Path)
Salisbury Ho. SW1 ....6H 75
(off Drummond Ga.)
Salisbury Ho. SW9 ....8L 75
(off Cranmer Rd.)
Salisbury Ho. Stan 6E 22
Salisbury Mans. N4 ....3M 43
Salisbury M. SW6 ....8K 73
Salisbury Pas. SW6 ....8K 73
(off Dawes Rd.)
Salisbury Pavement. SW6 ....8K 73
(off Dawes Rd.)
Salisbury Pl. SW9 ....8M 75
Salisbury Pl. W1 ....8D 58
Salisbury Rd. E4 ....3L 29
Salisbury Rd. E7 ....2E 62
Salisbury Rd. E10 ....7A 46
Salisbury Rd. E12 ....1H 63
Salisbury Rd. E17 ....3A 46
Salisbury Rd. N4 ....3M 43
Salisbury Rd. N9 ....3E 28
Salisbury Rd. N22 ....8M 27
Salisbury Rd. SE25 ....1E 124
Salisbury Rd. SW19 ....4J 105
Salisbury Rd. W13 ....3F 70
Salisbury Rd. Bans 6M 135
Salisbury Rd. Barn 5J 13
Salisbury Rd. Bex 7L 97
Salisbury Rd. Brom 9J 111
Salisbury Rd. Cars 8D 122
Salisbury Rd. Dag 2M 65
Salisbury Rd. Enf 1K 17
Salisbury Rd. Felt 7G 85
Salisbury Rd. Harr 3B 38
Salisbury Rd. Houn 2G 85
Salisbury Rd. Ilf 7C 48
Salisbury Rd. H'row A 4A 84
Salisbury Rd. N Mald 7B 104
Salisbury Rd. Pinn 2E 36
Salisbury Rd. Rich 3J 87
Salisbury Rd. Romf 3F 50
Salisbury Rd. S'hall 5J 69
Salisbury Rd. Uxb 5A 142
Salisbury Rd. Wat 2F 8
Salisbury Rd. Wor Pk 6B 120
Salisbury Sq. EC4 ....9L 59
Salisbury St. NW8 ....7C 58
Salisbury St. W3 ....3A 72
Salisbury Ter. SE15 ....2G 93
Salisbury Wlk. N19 ....7G 43
Salix Clo. Sun 4F 100
Salix Ct. N3 ....6L 25
Salliesfield. Twic 5B 86
Sally Murray Clo. E12 ....9L 47
(off Grantham Rd.)
Salmen Rd. E13 ....5D 62
Salmond Clo. Stan 6E 22
Salmon La. E14 ....9J 61
Salmon M. NW6 ....1L 57
Salmon Rd. Belv 6M 81
Salmon Rd. Dart 2K 99
Salmons Rd. N9 ....1E 28
Salmons Rd. Chess 8J 119
Salmon St. E14 ....9K 61
Salmon St. NW9 ....6M 39
Salomons Rd. E13 ....8G 63
Salop Rd. E17 ....4H 45
Saltash Clo. Sutt 6K 121
Saltash Rd. Ilf 7B 32
Saltash Rd. Well 9G 81
Saltbox Hill. Big H 5F 140
Saltcoats Rd. W4 ....3C 72
Saltcote Clo. Dart 5C 98
Saltcroft Clo. Wemb 6M 39
Saltdene. N4 ....6K 43
Salter Clo. Harr 9K 37
Salterford Rd. SW17 ....3E 106
Salter Rd. SE16 ....2H 77
Salters Ct. EC4 ....9A 60
(off Bow La.)
Salters Gdns. Wat 3E 8
Salter's Hall Ct. EC4 ....1B 76
(off Cannon St.)
Salter's Hill. SE19 ....2B 108
Salters Rd. E17 ....2B 46
Salters Rd. W10 ....7H 57
Salter St. E14 ....1K 77
Salter St. NW10 ....6E 56
Salterton Rd. N7 ....8K 43
Saltford Clo. Eri 6C 82
Salt Hill Clo. Uxb 1C 142
Saltley Clo. E6 ....9J 63
Saltoun Rd. SW2 ....3L 91
Saltram Clo. N15 ....2D 44
Saltram Cres. W9 ....6K 57
Saltwell St. E14 ....1L 77
Saltwood Clo. Orp 6G 129
Saltwood Gro. SE17 ....6B 76
Saltwood Ho. SE15 ....7G 77
(off Lovelinch Clo.)
Salusbury Rd. NW6 ....4J 57
Salutation Rd. SE10 ....5C 78
Salvador. SW17 ....2D 106
Salvia Gdns. Gnfd 5E 54
Salvin Rd. SW15 ....2H 89
Salway Clo. Wfd G 7E 30
Salway Pl. E15 ....2B 62
Salway Rd. E15 ....2B 62
Samantha Clo. E17 ....5K 45
Samantha M. Hav 3C 34
Sam Bartram Clo. SE7 ....6G 79
Sambrook Ho. E1 ....8G 61
(off Jubilee St.)
Sambrook Ho. SE11 ....5L 75
(off Hotspur St.)
Sambruck M. SE6 ....7M 93
Samels Ct. W6 ....6E 72
Samford Ho. N1 ....4L 59
(off Barnsbury Est.)
Samford St. NW8 ....7B 58
Samira Clo. E17 ....4L 45
Sam Manners Ho.
SE10 ....6C 78
(off Tuskar St.)
Sam March Ho. E14 ....9B 62
(off Blair St.)
Samos Rd. SE20 ....6F 108
Sampson Av. Barn 7H 13
Sampson Clo. Belv 4H 81
Sampson Ho. SE1 ....2M 75
Sampsons Ct. Shep 9A 100
Sampson St. E1 ....2E 76
Samsbrooke Ct. Enf 8C 16
Samson St. E13 ....5G 63
Samuda Est. E14 ....4A 78
Samuel Clo. E8 ....4D 60
Samuel Clo. SE14 ....7H 77
Samuel Clo. SE18 ....5J 79
Samuel Gray Gdns.
King T 5H 103
Samuel Ho. E8 ....4D 60
(off Clarissa St.)
Samuel Johnson Clo.
SW16 ....1K 107
Samuel Jones Ind. Est.
SE15 ....8C 76
(off Peckham Gro.)
Samuel Lewis Bldgs. N1 ....2L 59
Samuel Lewis Trust Dwellings.
N15 ....4C 44
Samuel Lewis Trust Dwellings.
SE5 ....9A 76
(off Warner Rd.)
Samuel Lewis Trust Dwellings.
SW3 ....5C 74
(off Ixworth Pl., in two parts)
Samuel Lewis Trust Dwellings.
SW6 ....8L 73
(off Vanston Pl.)
Samuel Lewis Trust Dwellings.
W14 ....5K 73
(off Lisgar Ter.)
Samuel Palmer Ct. Orp 2E 128
(off Chislehurst Rd.)
Samuel Richardson Ho.
W14 ....5K 73
(off N. End Cres.)
Samuel's Clo. W6 ....5G 73
Samuel St. SE15 ....8D 76
Samuel St. SE18 ....5K 79
Sancroft Clo. NW2 ....8F 40
Sancroft Ho. SE11 ....6K 75
(off Sancroft St.)
Sancroft Rd. Harr 9D 22
Sancroft St. SE11 ....6K 75
Sanctuary Clo. Dart 5G 99
Sanctuary Rd. H'row A 5E 144
Sanctuary St. SE1 ....3A 76
Sanctuary, The. SW1 ....4H 75
(off Broad Sanctuary)
Sanctuary, The. Bex 5H 97
Sanctuary, The. Mord 1L 121
Sandale Clo. N16 ....8B 44
Sandall Clo. W5 ....7J 55
Sandall Ho. E3 ....5J 61
Sandall Rd. NW5 ....2G 59
Sandall Rd. W5 ....7J 55
Sandal Rd. N18 ....5E 28
Sandal Rd. N Mald 9B 104
Sandal St. E15 ....4C 62
Sandalwood Clo. E1 ....7J 61
Sandal Wood Dri. Ruis 5A 36
Sandalwood Ho. Sidc 9D 96
Sandalwood Mans. W8 ....4M 73
(off Stone Hall Gdns.)
Sandalwood Rd. Felt 9F 84
Sandbach Pl. SE18 ....5A 80
Sandbanks. Felt 7C 84
Sandbourne. NW8 ....4M 57
(off Abbey Rd.)
Sandbourne. W11 ....9L 57
(off Dartmouth Clo.)
Sandbourne Av. SW19 ....6M 105
Sandbourne Rd. SE4 ....1J 93
Sandbrook Clo. NW7 ....6B 24
Sandbrook Rd. N16 ....8C 44
Sandby Grn. SE9 ....2J 95
Sandby Ho. NW6 ....4L 57
Sandcliff Rd. Eri 5B 82
Sandcroft Clo. N13 ....6M 27
Sandell's Av. Ashf 1A 100
Sandell St. SE1 ....3L 75
Sanderling Ct. SE8 ....7K 77
(off Abinger Gro.)
Sanderling Ct. SE28 ....1G 81
Sanders Clo. Hamp H 2A 102
Sandersfield Gdns. Bans 7L 135
Sandersfield Rd. Bans 7M 135
Sanders Ho. WC1 ....6L 59
(off Gt. Percy St.)
Sanders La. NW7 ....7G 25
(in three parts)
Sanderson Clo. NW5 ....9F 42
Sanderson Ho. SE8 ....6K 77
(off Grove St.)
Sanderson Rd. Uxb 2A 142
Sanderstead. 4E 138
Sanderstead Av. NW2 ....7J 41
Sanderstead Clo. SW12 ....6G 91
Sanderstead Ct. Av.
S Croy 5E 138
Sanderstead Hill. S Croy 3C 138
Sanderstead Rd. E10 ....6J 45
Sanderstead Rd. Orp 1F 128
Sanderstead Rd. S Croy 9B 124
Sanders Way. N19 ....6H 43
Sandfield. WC1 ....6J 59
(off Cromer St.)
Sandfield Gdns. T Hth 7M 107
Sandfield Rd. T Hth 7M 107
Sandford Av. N22 ....8A 28
Sandford Av. Lou 5M 19
Sandford Clo. E6 ....7K 63
Sandford Ct. N16 ....6C 44
Sandford Ct. New Bar 5M 13
Sandford Rd. E6 ....6J 63
Sandford Rd. Bexh 3J 97
Sandford Rd. Brom 7E 110
Sandford Row. SE17 ....6B 76
Sandford St. SW6 ....8M 73
Sandgate Clo. Romf 5A 50
Sandgate Ho. E5 ....1F 60
Sandgate Ho. W5 ....8G 55
Sandgate La. SW18 ....7C 90
Sandgate Rd. Well 8G 81
Sandgate St. SE15 ....7F 76
Sandgate Trad. Est. SE15 ....7F 76
(off Sandgate St.)
Sandham Ct. SW4 ....9J 75
Sandhills. Wall 6H 123
Sandhills Mdw. Shep 2A 116
Sandhills, The. SW10 ....7A 74
(off Limerston St.)
Sandhurst Av. Harr 4M 37
Sandhurst Av. Surb 2M 119
Sandhurst Cen. Wat 3G 9
Sandhurst Clo. NW9 ....1L 39
Sandhurst Clo. S Croy 1C 138
Sandhurst Ct. SW2 ....3J 91
Sandhurst Dri. Ilf 9D 48
Sandhurst Ho. E1 ....8G 61
(off Wolsy St.)
Sandhurst Mkt. SE6 ....7A 94
(off Sandhurst Rd.)
Sandhurst Rd. N9 ....8G 17
Sandhurst Rd. NW9 ....1L 39
Sandhurst Rd. SE6 ....7B 94
Sandhurst Rd. Bex 4H 97
Sandhurst Rd. Orp 5E 128
Sandhurst Rd. Sidc 9D 96
Sandhurst Way. S Croy 9C 124
Sandifer Dri. NW2 ....8H 41
Sandiford Rd. Sutt 4K 121
Sandiland Cres. Brom 4D 126
Sandilands. Croy 4E 124
Sandilands Rd. SW6 ....9M 73
Sandison St. SE15 ....2E 92
Sandland St. WC1 ....8K 59
Sandling Ri. SE9 ....9L 95
Sandlings Clo. SE15 ....1F 92
Sandlings, The. N22 ....1M 43
Sandmere Rd. SW4 ....3J 91
Sandon Clo. Esh 2B 118
Sandon Rd. Chesh 3C 6
Sandow Cres. Hay 4D 68
Sandown Av. Dag 2A 66
Sandown Av. Esh 7A 118
Sandown Av. Horn 7H 51
Sandown Clo. Houn 9E 68
Sandown Ct. SE26 ....9F 92
Sandown Ct. Stan 5G 23
Sandown Ct. Sutt 9M 121
Sandown Dri. Cars 1E 136
Sandown Ga. Esh 5B 118
Sandown Lodge. Eps 6B 134
Sandown Pk. Racecourse.
....5A 118
Sandown Rd. SE25 ....9F 108
Sandown Rd. Coul 8E 136
Sandown Rd. Esh 6A 118
Sandown Rd. Wat 2G 9
Sandown Rd. Ind. Est. Wat 1G 9
Sandown Way. N'holt 2J 53
Sandpiper Clo. E17 ....7H 29
Sandpiper Clo. SE16 ....3K 77
Sandpiper Ct. E14 ....4A 78
(off New Union Clo.)
Sandpiper Ct. SE8 ....7L 77
(off Edward Pl.)
Sandpiper Dri. Eri 8F 82
Sandpiper Rd. S Croy 3H 139
Sandpiper Rd. Sutt 7K 121
Sandpiper Way. Orp 8H 113
Sandpit Pl. SE7 ....6J 79
Sandpit Rd. Brom 2C 110
Sandpit Rd. Dart 3G 99
Sandpits Rd. Croy 6H 125
Sandpits Rd. Rich 8H 87
Sandra Clo. N22 ....8A 28
Sandra Clo. Houn 4M 85
Sandridge Clo. Harr 2C 38
Sandridge Ct. N4 ....7A 44
Sandridge St. N19 ....7G 43
Sandringham Av. SW20 ....5J 105
Sandringham Clo. SW19 ....7H 89
Sandringham Clo. Enf 4C 16
Sandringham Clo. Ilf 1A 48
Sandringham Ct. SE16 ....2H 77
(off King & Queen Wharf)
Sandringham Ct. W1 ....9G 59
(off Dufour's Pl.)
Sandringham Ct. W9 ....6A 58
(off Maida Va.)
Sandringham Ct. Sidc 5D 96
Sandringham Ct. Sutt 1L 135
Sandringham Ct. Uxb 7A 52
Sandringham Cres. Harr 7L 37
Sandringham Dri. Ashf 9B 144
Sandringham Dri. Bex 8C 98
Sandringham Dri. Well 1C 96
Sandringham Flats. WC2 ....1H 75
(off Charing Cross Rd.)
Sandringham Gdns. N8 ....4J 43
Sandringham Gdns. N12 ....6B 26
Sandringham Gdns. Houn 9E 68
Sandringham Gdns. Ilf 1A 48
Sandringham Gdns.
W Mol 8L 101
Sandringham Ho. W14 ....5J 73
(off Windsor Way)

Sandringham M.—Seaforth Cres.

Sandringham M. W5 . . . . . . .1H 71
Sandringham Rd. E7 . . . . . . .1G 63
Sandringham Rd. E8 . . . . . . .1D 60
Sandringham Rd. E10 . . . . . .4B 46
Sandringham Rd. N22 . . . . . .1A 44
Sandringham Rd. NW2 . . . . . .2F 56
Sandringham Rd. NW11 . . . .5J 41
Sandringham Rd. Bark 1D 64
Sandringham Rd. Brom 2E 110
Sandringham Rd.
H'row A 4C 144
Sandringham Rd. N'holt 3L 53
Sandringham Rd. T Hth 9A 108
Sandringham Rd. Wat 1G 9
Sandringham Rd.
Wor Pk 5E 120
Sandringham Way. Wal X 7C 6
Sandrock Pl. Croy 6H 125
Sandrock Rd. SE13 . . . . .2L 93
Sands End. 9A 74
Sand's End La. SW6 . . . . . . .9M 73
Sandstone Pl. N19 . . . . .7F 42
Sandstone Rd. SE12 . . . . . . .8F 94
Sands Way. Wfd G 6K 31
Sandtoft Rd. SE7 . . . . .7F 78
Sandway Path. St M 8G 113
(off Okemore Gdns.)
Sandway Rd. Orp 8G 113
Sandwell Cres. NW6 . . . . . . .2L 57
Sandwich Ho. SE16 . . . . .3G 77
(off Swan Rd.)
Sandwich Ho. WC1 . . . . .6J 59
(off Sandwich St.)
Sandwich St. WC1 . . . . .6J 59
Sandwick Clo. NW7 . . . . .7E 24
Sandy Bury. Orp 5B 128
Sandycombe Rd. Felt 7E 84
Sandycombe Rd. Rich 2K 87
Sandycoombe Rd. Twic 5G 87
Sandycroft. SE2 . . . . .7E 80
Sandy Cft. Eps 2G 135
Sandy Dri. Felt 7C 84
Sandy Hill Av. SE18 . . . . . . .6M 79
Sandy Hill Rd. SE18 . . . . . . .5M 79
Sandyhill Rd. Ilf 9M 47
Sandy Hill Rd. Wall 1G 137
Sandy La. Ave 1K 83
Sandy La. Bush 5A 10
Sandy La. Cob & Oxs 3A 132
Sandy La. Harr 4K 39
Sandy La. Mitc 5E 106
(in two parts)
Sandy La. N'wd 2D 20
Sandy La. Orp 2E 128
Sandy La. Rich 8G 87
Sandy La. St P & Sidc 6H 113
Sandy La. Sutt 9J 121
Sandy La.
Tedd & Hamp W 4E 102
Sandy La. W on T 1F 116
Sandy La. N. Wall 7H 123
Sandy La. S. Wall 1G 137
Sandy Lodge. N'wd 2C 20
Sandy Lodge. Pinn 6L 21
Sandy Lodge Ct. N'wd 5C 20
Sandy Lodge Golf Course.
. . . . .3B 20
Sandy Lodge La. N'wd 2B 20
Sandy Lodge Rd. Rick 2A 20
Sandy Lodge Way. N'wd 5B 20
Sandy Mead. Eps 2L 133
Sandymount Av. Stan 5G 23
Sandy Ridge. Chst 3L 111
Sandy Rd. NW3 . . . . .7M 41
(in two parts)
Sandys Row. E1 . . . . .8C 60
Sandy Way. Croy 5K 125
Sandy Way. W on T 3D 116
Sanford La. N16 . . . . .8D 44
(in two parts)
Sanford St. SE14 . . . . .7J 77
Sanford Ter. N16 . . . . .8D 44
Sanford Wlk. N16 . . . . .7D 44
Sanford Wlk. SE14 . . . . .7J 77
Sanger Av. Chess 7J 119
Sangley Rd. SE6 . . . . .6M 93
Sangley Rd. SE25 . . . . .8C 108
Sangora Rd. SW11 . . . . .3B 90
Sankey Ho. E2 . . . . .5G 61
(off St James's Av.)
Sansom Rd. E11 . . . . .7D 46
Sansom St. SE5 . . . . .9B 76
Sans Wlk. EC1 . . . . .7L 59
Santley Ho. SE1 . . . . .3L 75
Santley St. SW4 . . . . .3K 91
Santos Rd. SW18 . . . . .4L 89
Santway, The. Stan 5C 22
Sapcote Trad. Cen. NW10 . . .2D 56
Saperton Wlk. SE11 . . . . .5K 75
(off Juxon St.)
Saphora Clo. Orp 7B 128
Sapperton Ct. EC1 . . . . .7A 60
(off Gee St.)
Sapphire Clo. E6 . . . . .9L 63
Sapphire Clo. Dag 6G 49
Sapphire Ct. E1 . . . . .1E 76
(off Cable St.)
Sapphire Rd. SE8 . . . . .5J 77
Saracen Clo. Croy 1B 124
Saracens Head Yd. EC3 . . . . .9D 60
(off Jewry St.)
Saracens R.U.F.C. (Watford F.C.)
. . . . .7F 8
Saracens Rugby Football Club.
. . . . .8F 14
Saracen St. E14 . . . . .9L 61
Sarah Ct. N'holt 4K 53
Sarah Ho. E1 . . . . .9F 60
(off Commercial Rd.)
Sara Ho. Eri 8C 82
Sarah St. N1 . . . . .6C 60
Sarah Swift Ho. SE1 . . . . . . .3B 76
(off Kipling St.)
Sara La. Ct. N1 . . . . .5C 60
(off Stanway St.)
Saratoga Rd. E5 . . . . .9G 45
Sara Turnbull Ho. SE18 . . . . .5K 79
Sardinia St. WC2 . . . . .9K 59
Sargeant Clo. Uxb 6B 142
Sarita Clo. Harr 9B 22
Sarjant Path. SW19 . . . . .8H 89
(off Blincoe Clo.)
Sark Clo. Houn 8L 69
Sark Ho. Enf 2H 17
Sark Tower. SE28 . . . . .3A 80
(off Erebus Dri.)
Sark Wlk. E16 . . . . .9F 62
Sarnes Ct. N11 . . . . .4F 26
(off Oakleigh Rd. S.)
Sarnesfield Ho. SE15 . . . . . . .7F 76
(off Pencraig Way)
Sarnesfield Rd. Enf 6B 16
Sarratt Ho. W10 . . . . .8G 57
(off Sutton Way)
Sarre Av. Horn 2G 67
Sarre Rd. NW2 . . . . .1K 57
Sarre Rd. Orp 9G 113
Sarsen Av. Houn 1L 85
Sarsfeld Rd. SW12 . . . . .8D 90
Sarsfield Rd. Gnfd 5F 54
Sartor Rd. SE15 . . . . .3H 93
Sarum Complex. Uxb 6A 142
Sarum Grn. Wey 5C 116
Sarum Ter. E3 . . . . .7K 61
Sassoon. NW9 . . . . .8D 24
Satanita Clo. E16 . . . . .9H 63
Satchell Mead. NW9 . . . . . . .8D 24
Satchwell Rd. E2 . . . . .6E 60
Satchwell St. E2 . . . . .6E 60
Satis Ct. Eps 3D 134
Sattar M. N16 . . . . .8B 44
(off Clissold Rd.)
Saul Ct. SE15 . . . . .7D 76
Sauls Grn. E11 . . . . .8C 46
Saunders Clo. E14 . . . . .1K 77
(off Limehouse Causeway)
Saunders Clo. Chesh 1D 6
Saunders Ho. SE16 . . . . .3H 77
(off Quebec Way)
Saunders Ho. W11 . . . . .2H 73
Saunders Ness Rd. E14 . . . . .6A 78
Saunders Rd. SE18 . . . . .6D 80
Saunders Rd. Uxb 3D 142
Saunders St. SE11 . . . . .5L 75
Saunders Way. SE28 . . . . .1F 80
Saunders Way. Dart 8K 99
Saunderton Rd. Wemb 1F 54
Saunton Av. Hay 8D 68
Saunton Ct. S'hall 1A 70
(off Haldane Rd.)
Saunton Rd. Horn 7E 50
Savage Gdns. E6 . . . . .9K 63
Savage Gdns. EC3 . . . . .1C 76
(in two parts)
Savernake Ct. Stan 6G 23
Savernake Ho. N4 . . . . .5A 44
Savernake Rd. N9 . . . . .8E 16
Savernake Rd. NW3 . . . . .9D 42
Savery Dri. Surb 2G 119
Savile Clo. N Mald 9C 104
Savile Clo. Th Dit 3D 118
Savile Gdns. Croy 4D 124
Savile Row. W1 . . . . .1G 75
Saville Cres. Ashf 3B 100
Saville Rd. E16 . . . . .2J 79
Saville Rd. W4 . . . . .4B 72
Saville Rd. Romf 4K 49
Saville Rd. Twic 7D 86
Saville Row. Brom 3D 126
Saville Row. Enf 4H 17
Savill Gdns. SW20 . . . . .7E 104
Savill Ho. E16 . . . . .2M 79
(off Robert St.)
Savill Ho. SW4 . . . . .5H 91
Savill Row. Wfd G 6D 30
Savin Lodge. Sutt 9A 122
(off Walnut M.)
Savona Clo. SW19 . . . . .4H 105
Savona Ho. SW8 . . . . .8G 75
(off Savona St.)
Savona St. SW8 . . . . .8G 75
Savoy Av. Hay 6C 68
Savoy Bldgs. WC2 . . . . .1K 75
(off Strand)
Savoy Circus (Junct.) 1D 72
Savoy Clo. E15 . . . . .4C 62
Savoy Clo. Edgw 5L 23
Savoy Ct. NW3 . . . . .8A 42
Savoy Ct. WC2 . . . . .1K 75
Savoy Hill. WC2 . . . . .1K 75
Savoy Pde. Enf 5C 16
Savoy Pl. WC2 . . . . .1J 75
Savoy Rd. Dart 4H 99
Savoy Row. WC2 . . . . .1K 75
(off Savoy St.)
Savoy Steps. WC2 . . . . .1K 75
(off Savoy St.)
Savoy St. WC2 . . . . .1K 75
Savoy Theatre. 1J 75
(off Strand)
Savoy Way. WC2 . . . . .1K 75
(off Savoy Hill)
Sawbill Clo. Hay 8H 53
Sawkins Clo. SW19 . . . . .8J 89
Sawley Rd. W12 . . . . .2D 72
Sawmill Yd. E3 . . . . .4J 61
Sawtry Clo. Cars 2C 122
Sawtry Way. Borwd 2L 11
Sawyer Clo. N9 . . . . .2E 28
Sawyer Ct. NW10 . . . . .3B 56
Sawyers Clo. Dag 2A 66
Sawyer's Hill. Rich 6K 87
Sawyers La. Els 3F 10
Sawyers Lawn. W13 . . . . .9E 54
Sawyer St. SE1 . . . . .3A 76
Saxby Rd. SW2 . . . . .6J 91
Saxham Rd. Bark 4C 64
Saxlingham Rd. E4 . . . . .3B 30
Saxon Av. Felt 8J 85
Saxonbury Av. Sun 7F 100
Saxonbury Clo. Mitc 7B 106
Saxonbury Ct. N7 . . . . .1J 59
Saxonbury Gdns. Surb 3G 119
Saxon Bus. Cen. SW19 . . . .6A 106
Saxon Clo. E17 . . . . .5L 45
Saxon Clo. Romf 9K 35
Saxon Clo. Surb 1H 119
Saxon Clo. Uxb 8D 142
Saxon Ct. Borwd 3J 11
Saxon Dri. W3 . . . . .9L 55
Saxonfield Clo. SW2 . . . . . . .7K 91
Saxon Gdns. S'hall 1J 69
Saxon Ho. Felt 8K 85
Saxon Lodge. Croy 3A 124
(off Tavistock Rd.)
Saxon Pl. Hort K 9M 115
Saxon Rd. E3 . . . . .5K 61
Saxon Rd. E6 . . . . .7K 63
Saxon Rd. N22 . . . . .8M 27
Saxon Rd. SE25 . . . . .9B 108
Saxon Rd. Ashf 3B 100
Saxon Rd. Brom 4D 110
Saxon Rd. Dart 1J 115
Saxon Rd. Ilf 2M 63
Saxon Rd. King T 5J 103
Saxon Rd. S'hall 1J 69
Saxon Rd. W on T 5H 117
Saxon Rd. Wemb 8A 40
Saxon Wlk. Sidc 3G 113
Saxon Way. N14 . . . . .8H 15
Saxon Way. Wal A 6J 7
Saxon Way. W Dray 7G 143
Saxon Way Ind. Est.
W Dray 7G 143
Saxony Pde. Hay 8A 52
Saxton Clo. SE13 . . . . .2B 94
Saxton M. Wat 4E 8
Saxville Rd. Orp 7F 112
Sayers Ho. N2 . . . . .9B 26
(off Grange, The)
Sayer's Wlk. Rich 6K 87
Sayesbury La. N18 . . . . .5E 28
Sayes Ct. SE8 . . . . .7K 77
Sayes Ct. Rd. Orp 8E 112
Sayes Ct. St. SE8 . . . . .7K 77
Scadbury Gdns. Orp 6E 112
Scads Hill Clo. Orp 1D 128
Scafell. NW1 . . . . .6G 59
(off Stanhope St.)
Scala St. W1 . . . . .8G 59
Scales Rd. N17 . . . . .1D 44
Scammell Way. Wat 8D 8
Scampston M. W10 . . . . .9H 57
Scampton Rd. H'row A 5D 144
Scandrett St. E1 . . . . .2F 76
Scarba Wlk. N1 . . . . .2B 60
(off Marquess Rd.)
Scarborough Clo. Sutt 3K 135
Scarborough Rd. E11 . . . . . . .6B 46
Scarborough Rd. N4 . . . . .6L 43
Scarborough Rd. N9 . . . . .9G 17
Scarborough Rd. H'row A . . .5A 84
Scarborough St. E1 . . . . .9D 60
Scarbrook Rd. Croy 5A 124
Scarle Rd. Wemb 2H 55
Scarlet Clo. St P 8F 112
Scarlet Rd. SE6 . . . . .9C 94
Scarlette Mnr. Way.
SW2 . . . . .6L 91
Scarsbrook Rd. SE3 . . . . .2H 95
Scarsdale Pl. W8 . . . . .4M 73
Scarsdale Rd. Harr 8A 38
Scarsdale Vs. W8 . . . . .4L 73
Scarth Rd. SW13 . . . . .2D 88
Scawen Clo. Cars 6E 122
Scawen Rd. SE8 . . . . .6J 77
Scawfell St. E2 . . . . .5D 60
S.C.C. Smallholdings Rd.
Eps 6G 135
(in two parts)
Sceaux Gdns. SE5 . . . . .9C 76
Sceptre Ct. EC3 . . . . .1D 76
(off Tower Hill)
Sceptre Ho. E1 . . . . .7G 61
(off Malcolm Rd.)
Sceptre Rd. E2 . . . . .6G 61
Sceynes Link. N12 . . . . .4L 25
Schafer Ho. NW1 . . . . .6G 59
Schiller International University.
. . . . .2L 75
Schofield Wlk. SE3 . . . . .8F 78
Scholars Rd. E4 . . . . .1B 30
Scholars Rd. SW12 . . . . .7G 91
Scholars, The. Wat 6G 9
(off Lady's Clo.)
Scholefield Rd. N19 . . . . .6H 43
Scholey Ho. SW11 . . . . .2C 90
Schomberg Ho. SW1 . . . . .5H 75
(off Page St.)
Schonfeld Sq. N16 . . . . .7B 44
School All. Twic 7E 86
School App. E2 . . . . .6C 60
Schoolbank Rd. SE10 . . . . . . .4D 78
Schoolbell M. E3 . . . . .5J 61
School Cres. Cray 3D 98
School Ho. SE1 . . . . .5C 76
(off Quadrangle Clo.)
Schoolhouse Gdns. Lou 6M 19
School Ho. La. E1 . . . . .1H 77
School Ho. La. Tedd 4F 102
School La. Brick W 7K 5
School La. Bush 9M 9
School La. Chig 4D 32
School La. King T 5G 103
School La. Pinn 2J 37
School La. Shep 1A 116
School La. Surb 3L 119
School La. Swan 5F 114
School La. Well 2F 96
School Mead. Ab L 5C 4
School of Advanced Study.
. . . . .8H 59
(in University of London,
Senate House)
**School of Hygiene &
Tropical Medicine.** . . .8H 59
(off Keppel St.)
**School of Oriental &
African Studies.** 7H 59
(off Thornhaugh St.)
School of Pharmacy, The.
. . . . .7J 59
(off Brunswick Sq.)
**School of Slavonic &
East European Studies.**
. . . . .8H 59
(in University of London,
Senate House)
School Pas. King T 6K 103
School Pas. S'hall 1K 69
School Rd. E12 . . . . .9K 47
School Rd. NW10 . . . . .7B 56
School Rd. Ashf 3A 100
School Rd. Chst 5A 112
School Rd. Dag 4L 65
School Rd. E Mol 8B 102
School Rd. Hamp H 3A 102
School Rd. Houn 2A 86
School Rd. King T 5G 103
School Rd. W on T 7D 116
School Rd. W Dray 7H 143
School Rd. Av. Hamp H 3A 102
School Road Junction (Junct.)
. . . . .3A 100
School Wlk. Sun 8D 100
School Way. N12 . . . . .6B 26
School Way. Dag 8G 49
Schooner Clo. E14 . . . . .4B 78
Schooner Clo. SE16 . . . . .3H 77
Schooner Clo. Bark 6F 64
Schopwick Pl. Els 8H 11
(off St Nicholas Clo.)
Schubert Rd. SW15 . . . . .4K 89
Schubert Rd. Els 8H 11
Science Mus. 4B 74
Scilly Isles (Junct.) 4C 118
Sclater St. E1 . . . . .7D 60
Scoble Pl. N16 . . . . .9D 44
Scoles Cres. SW2 . . . . .7L 91
Scope Way. King T 8J 103
Scoresby St. SE1 . . . . .2M 75
Scorton Av. Gnfd 5E 54
Scorton Ho. N1 . . . . .5C 60
(off Whitmore Est.)
Scotch Comn. W13 . . . . .8E 54
Scotch House (Junct.) 3D 74
Scoter Clo. Wfd G 7F 30
Scoter Ct. SE8 . . . . .7K 77
(off Abinger Gro.)
Scot Gro. Pinn 7H 21
Scotia Building. E1 . . . . .1H 77
(off Jardine Rd.)
Scotia Ct. SE16 . . . . .3G 77
(off Canada Est.)
Scotia Rd. SW2 . . . . .6L 91
Scotland Grn. N17 . . . . .9D 28
Scotland Grn. Rd. Enf 7H 17
Scotland Grn. Rd. N. Enf 6H 17
Scotland Pl. SW1 . . . . .2J 75
Scotland Rd. Buck H 1G 31
Scotney Clo. Orp 6L 127
Scotney Ho. E9 . . . . .2G 61
Scotney Wlk. Horn 1G 67
Scots Clo. Stanw 7B 144
Scotsdale Clo. Orp 8C 112
Scotsdale Clo. Sutt 9J 121
Scotsdale Rd. SE12 . . . . .4F 94
Scotshall La. Warl 7A 140
Scotson Ho. SE11 . . . . .5L 75
(off Marylee Way)
Scotswood St. EC1 . . . . .7L 59
Scotswood Wlk. N17 . . . . .7E 28
Scott Clo. SW16 . . . . .5K 107
Scott Clo. Eps 7A 120
Scott Clo. W Dray 5K 143
Scott Ct. W3 . . . . .3B 72
Scott Cres. Eri 9D 82
Scott Cres. Harr 6M 37
Scott Ellis Gdns. NW8 . . . . . .6B 58
Scottes La. Dag 6H 49
Scott Farm Clo. Th Dit 3F 118
Scott Gdns. Houn 8H 69
Scott Ho. E13 . . . . .5E 62
(off Queens Rd. W.)
Scott Ho. E14 . . . . .3L 77
(off Admirals Way)
Scott Ho. N1 . . . . .4B 60
(off Sherborne St.)
Scott Ho. N7 . . . . .2K 59
(off Caledonian Rd.)
Scott Ho. NW8 . . . . .7C 58
(off Ashmill St.)
Scott Ho. NW10 . . . . .3B 56
(off Stonebridge Pk.)
Scott Ho. Belv 6K 81
Scott Ho. Horn 4E 50
(off Benjamin Clo.)
Scott Lidgett Cres. SE16 . . . .3E 76
Scott Russell Pl. E14 . . . . . . .6M 77
Scotts Av. Brom 6B 110
Scotts Av. Sun 4C 100
Scotts Clo. Horn 1G 67
Scotts Ct. W12 . . . . .3G 73
(off Scott's Rd.)
Scotts Dri. Hamp 4M 101
Scotts Farm Rd. Eps 8A 120
Scott's La. Brom 7B 110
Scotts La. W on T 6H 117
Scotts Pas. SE18 . . . . .5M 79
Scott's Rd. E10 . . . . .6A 46
Scott's Rd. W12 . . . . .3F 72
Scotts Rd. Brom 4E 110
Scott's Rd. S'hall 4G 69
Scott's Sufferance Wharf.
SE1 . . . . .3D 76
(off Mill St.)
Scott St. E1 . . . . .7F 60
Scotts Way. Sun 4C 100
Scottswood Clo. Bush 4J 9
Scottswood Rd. Bush 4J 9
Scott's Yd. EC4 . . . . .1B 76
Scott Trimmer Way. Houn . . .1J 85
Scottwell Dri. NW9 . . . . .3D 40
Scoulding Ho. E14 . . . . .4L 77
(off Mellish St.)
Scoulding Rd. E16 . . . . .9E 62
Scouler St. E14 . . . . .1A 78
Scout App. NW10 . . . . .9C 40
Scout La. SW4 . . . . .2G 91
Scout Way. NW7 . . . . .4B 24
Scovell Cres. SE1 . . . . .3A 76
(off McCoid Way)
Scovell Rd. SE1 . . . . .3A 76
Scrattons Ter. Bark 5H 65
Screen on Baker St. (Cinema)
. . . . .8D 58
(off Baker St.)
Screen on the Green (Cinema)
. . . . .4M 59
Scriven Ct. E8 . . . . .4D 60
Scriven St. E8 . . . . .4D 60
Scrooby St. SE6 . . . . .5M 93
Scrope Ho. EC1 . . . . .8L 59
(off Bourne Est.)
Scrubs La. NW10 & W10 . . . .6E 56
Scrutton Clo. SW12 . . . . .6H 91
Scrutton St. EC2 . . . . .7C 60
Scudamore La. NW9 . . . . .2A 40
Scutari Rd. SE22 . . . . .4G 93
Scylla Cres. H'row A 5F 144
Scylla Rd. SE15 . . . . .2E 92
(in two parts)
Scylla Rd. H'row A 5F 144
Seabright St. E2 . . . . .6F 60
Seabrook Dri. W Wick 4C 126
Seabrook Gdns. Romf 5L 49
Seabrook Rd. Dag 8H 49
Seabrook Rd. K Lan 1B 4
Seaburn Clo. Rain 5C 66
Seacole Clo. W3 . . . . .9B 56
Seacourt Rd. SE2 . . . . .3H 81
Seacroft Gdns. Wat 3H 21
Seafield Rd. N11 . . . . .4H 27
Seaford Clo. Ruis 6B 36
Seaford Ho. SE16 . . . . .3G 77
(off Swan Rd.)
Seaford Rd. E17 . . . . .1M 45
Seaford Rd. N15 . . . . .3B 44
Seaford Rd. W13 . . . . .2F 70
Seaford Rd. Enf 6C 16
Seaford Rd. H'row A 4B 144
Seaford St. WC1 . . . . .6K 59
Seaforth Av. N Mald 9F 104
Seaforth Clo. Romf 7C 34
Seaforth Cres. N5 . . . . .1A 60

Seaforth Dri.—Shakspeare M.

Seaforth Dri. Wal X 7D 6
Seaforth Gdns. N21 9K 15
Seaforth Gdns. Eps 6D 120
Seaforth Gdns. Wfd G 5G 31
Seaforth Pl. SW1 4G 75
(off Buckingham Ga.)
Seagar Bldgs. SE8 9L 77
Seagar Pl. E3 8K 61
Seagrave Clo. E1 8H 61
Seagrave Lodge. SW6 7L 73
(off Seagrave Rd.)
Seagrave Rd. SW6 7L 73
Seagry Rd. E11 5E 46
Sealand Rd. H'row A 5E 144
Sealand Wlk. N'holt 6H 53
Seal Ho. SE1 4B 76
(off Pardoner St.)
Seal St. E8 9D 44
Searches La. Bedm 1F 4
Searchwood Rd. Warl 9F 138
Searle Pl. N4 6K 43
Searles Clo. SW11 8C 74
Searles Dri. E6 8M 63
Searles Rd. SE1 5B 76
Searson Ho. SE17 5M 75
(off Canterbury Pl.)
Sears St. SE5 8B 76
Seasprite Clo. N'holt 6H 53
Seaton Av. Ilf 1D 64
Seaton Clo. E13 7E 62
Seaton Clo. SE11 6L 75
Seaton Clo. SW15 7F 88
Seaton Clo. Twic 5B 86
Seaton Dri. Ashf 8C 144
Seaton Gdns. Ruis 8D 36
Seaton Point. E5 9E 44
Seaton Rd. Dart 6E 98
Seaton Rd. Hay 5B 68
Seaton Rd. Mitc 6C 106
Seaton Rd. Twic 5A 86
Seaton Rd. Well 8G 81
Seaton Rd. Wemb 5J 55
Seaton St. N18 5E 28
Sebastian Ho. N1 5C 60
(off Hoxton St.)
Sebastian St. EC1 6M 59
Sebastopol Rd. N9 4E 28
Sebbon St. N1 3M 59
Sebergham Gro. NW7 7E 24
Sebert Rd. E7 1F 62
Sebright Ho. E2 5E 60
(off Coate St.)
Sebright Pas. E2 5E 60
Sebright Rd. Barn 4H 13
Secker Cres. Harr 8A 22
Secker Ho. SW9 1M 91
(off Loughborough Est.)
Secker St. SE1 2L 75
Secombe Theatre. 7M 121
Second Av. E12 9J 47
Second Av. E13 6E 62
Second Av. E17 3L 45
Second Av. N18 4G 29
Second Av. NW4 2H 41
Second Av. SW14 2C 88
Second Av. W3 2D 72
Second Av. W10 7J 57
Second Av. Dag 4M 65
Second Av. Enf 7D 16
Second Av. Hay 2D 68
Second Av. Romf 3G 49
Second Av. W on T 1F 116
Second Av. Wat 8H 5
Second Av. Wemb 7H 39
Second Clo. W Mol 8A 102
Second Cross Rd. Twic 8C 86
Second Way. Wemb 9M 39
Sedan Way. SE17 6C 76
Sedcombe Clo. Sidc 1F 112
Sedcote Rd. Enf 7G 17
Sedding St. SW1 5E 74
Sedding Studios. SW1 5E 74
(off Sedding St.)
Seddon Highwalk. EC2 8A 60
(off Seddon Ho.)
Seddon Ho. EC2 8A 60
(off Beech St.)
Seddon Rd. Mord 9B 106
Seddon St. WC1 6K 59
Sedgebrook Rd. SE3 1H 95
Sedgecombe Av. Harr 3G 39
Sedgefield Clo. Romf 4K 35
Sedgefield Ct. N'holt 1M 53
(off Newmarket Av.)
Sedgefield Cres. Romf 5K 35
Sedgeford Rd. W12 2D 72
Sedgehill Rd. SE6 1L 109
Sedgemere Av. N2 1A 42
Sedgemere Rd. SE2 4G 81
Sedgemoor Dri. Dag 9L 49
Sedge Rd. N17 7G 29
Sedgeway. SE6 7D 94
Sedgewick Av. Uxb 3F 142
Sedgewood Clo. Brom 2D 126
Sedgmoor Pl. SE5 8C 76
Sedgwick Ho. E3 8L 61
(off Gale St.)
Sedgwick Rd. E10 7A 46
Sedgwick St. E9 1H 61
Sedleigh Rd. SW18 5K 89
Sedlescombe Rd. SW6 7L 73
Sedley Clo. Enf 2F 16
Sedley Ct. SE26 8F 92
Sedley Ho. SE11 6K 75
(off Newburn St.)
Sedley Pl. W1 9F 58
Sedley Ri. Lou 4K 19
Sedum Clo. NW9 3M 39
Seeley Dri. SE21 1C 108
Seelig Av. NW9 5E 40
Seely Rd. SW17 3E 106
Seething La. EC3 1C 76
Seething Wells. 1G 119
Seething Wells La. Surb 1G 119
Sefton Av. NW7 5B 24
Sefton Av. Harr 9B 22
Sefton Clo. Orp 8D 112
Sefton Ct. Enf 4M 15
(in two parts)
Sefton Ct. Houn 9M 69
Sefton Rd. Croy 3E 124
Sefton Rd. Eps 2B 134
Sefton Rd. Orp 8D 112
Sefton St. SW15 2G 89
Sefton Way. Uxb 9A 142
Segal Clo. SE23 6J 93
Sekforde St. EC1 7M 59
Sekhon Ter. Felt 9L 85
Selah Dri. Swan 5A 114
Selan Gdns. Hay 8F 52
Selbie Av. NW10 1D 56
Selborne Av. E12 9L 47
Selborne Av. Bex 7J 97
Selborne Gdns. NW4 2E 40
Selborne Gdns. Gnfd 4E 54
Selborne Rd. E17 3K 45
Selborne Rd. N14 3J 27
Selborne Rd. SE5 1B 92
Selborne Rd. Croy 5C 124
Selborne Rd. Ilf 7L 47
Selborne Rd. N Mald 6C 104
Selborne Rd. Sidc 1F 112
Selborne Wlk. E17 3K 45
Selborne Wlk. Shop. Cen.
E17 2K 45
Selbourne Av. Surb 4K 119
Selbourne Ho. SE1 3B 76
(off Gt. Dover St.)
Selbourne Rd. N22 8K 27
Selby Chase. Ruis 7F 36
Selby Clo. E6 8J 63
Selby Clo. Chess 9J 119
Selby Clo. Chst 3L 111
Selby Gdns. S'hall 7L 53
Selby Grn. Cars 2C 122
Selby Ho. W10 6J 57
(off Beethoven St.)
Selby Rd. E11 8C 46
Selby Rd. E13 8F 62
Selby Rd. N17 7C 28
Selby Rd. SE20 6E 108
Selby Rd. W5 7F 54
Selby Rd. Ashf 3A 100
Selby Rd. Cars 2C 122
Selby St. E1 7E 60
Selcroft Ho. SE10 6D 78
(off Glenister Rd.)
Selcroft Rd. Purl 4M 137
Selden Ho. SE15 1G 93
(off Selden Rd.)
Selden Rd. SE15 1G 93
Selden Wlk. N7 7K 43
Seldon Ho. SW1 6G 75
(off Churchill Gdns.)
Seldon Ho. SW8 8G 75
(off Stewart's Rd.)
Selfridges. 9E 58
(off Oxford St.)
Selhurst. 1B 124
Selhurst Clo. SW19 7H 89
Selhurst New Rd. SE25 1C 124
Selhurst Pk.
(Crystal Palace F.C. &
Wimbledon F.C.)
8C 108
Selhurst Pl. SE25 1C 124
Selhurst Rd. N9 3B 28
Selhurst Rd. SE25 1C 124
Selina Ho. NW8 7B 58
(off Frampton St.)
Selinas La. Dag 5J 49
Selkirk Dri. Eri 9C 82
Selkirk Rd. SW17 1C 106
Selkirk Rd. Twic 8A 86
Sellers Clo. Borwd 3A 12
Sellers Hall Clo. N3 7L 25
Sellincourt Rd. SW17 2C 106
Sellindge Clo. Beck 4K 109
Sellons Av. NW10 4D 56
Selma Ho. W12 9F 56
(off Du Cane Rd.)
Selsdon. 2G 139
Selsdon Av. S Croy 8B 124
Selsdon Clo. Romf 8A 34
Selsdon Clo. Surb 9J 103
Selsdon Ct. S'hall 9M 53
(off Dormers Ri.)
Selsdon Cres. S Croy 2G 139
Selsdon Pk. Rd.
S Croy & Croy 1H 139
Selsdon Rd. E11 5E 46
Selsdon Rd. E13 4G 63
Selsdon Rd. NW2 7D 40
Selsdon Rd. SE27 9L 91
Selsdon Rd. S Croy 7B 124
Selsdon Way. E14 4M 77
Selsea Pl. N16 1C 60
Selsey Cres. Well 9H 81
Selsey St. E14 8L 61
Selvage La. NW7 5B 24
Selway Clo. Pinn 2F 36
Selway Ho. SW8 9J 75
(off S. Lambeth Rd.)
Selwood Clo. Stanw 5A 144
Selwood Dri. Barn 7H 13
Selwood Gdns. Stanw 5A 144
Selwood Pl. SW7 6B 74
Selwood Rd. Chess 6H 119
Selwood Rd. Croy 4F 124
Selwood Rd. Sutt 3K 121
Selwoods. SW2 6L 91
Selwood Ter. SW7 6B 74
Selworthy Clo. E11 3E 46
Selworthy Rd. SE6 9K 93
Selwyn Av. E4 6A 30
Selwyn Av. Ilf 4D 48
Selwyn Av. Rich 2J 87
Selwyn Clo. Houn 3J 85
Selwyn Ct. E17 3L 45
(off Yunus Khan Clo.)
Selwyn Ct. SE3 2D 94
Selwyn Ct. Edgw 7M 23
Selwyn Ct. Wemb 8A 40
Selwyn Cres. Well 2F 96
Selwyn Pl. Orp 7F 112
Selwyn Rd. E3 5K 61
Selwyn Rd. E13 4F 62
Selwyn Rd. NW10 3B 56
Selwyn Rd. N Mald 9B 104
Semley Ga. E9 2K 61
Semley Ho. SW1 5F 74
(off Semley Pl.)
Semley Pl. SW1 5E 74
Semley Rd. SW16 6J 107
Senate St. SE15 1G 93
Senators Lodge. E3 5J 61
(off Roman Rd.)
Senator Wlk. SE28 4B 80
Seneca Rd. T Hth 8A 108
Senga Rd. Wall 3E 122
Senhouse Rd. Sutt 5H 121
Senior St. W2 8M 57
Senlac Rd. SE12 7F 94
Sennen Rd. Enf 9D 16
Sennen Wlk. SE9 9J 95
Senrab St. E1 9H 61
Sentinel Clo. N'holt 7J 53
Sentinel Sq. NW4 2G 41
Sentis Ct. N'wd 6C 20
September Ct. S'hall 2M 69
(off Dormer's Wells La.)
September Ct. Uxb 5B 142
September Way. Stan 6F 22
Septimus Pl. Enf 7E 16
Sequoia Clo. Bus H 1B 22
Sequoia Gdns. Orp 2D 128
Sequoia Pk. Pinn 6M 21
Seraph Ct. EC1 6A 60
(off Moreland St.)
Serbin Clo. E10 5A 46
Serenaders Rd. SW9 1L 91
Sergeant Ind. Est. SW18 5M 89
Serica Ct. SE10 8A 78
Serjeants Inn. EC4 9L 59
Serle St. WC2 9K 59
Sermon Dri. Swan 7A 114
Sermon La. EC4 9A 60
(off Carter La.)
Serpentine Gallery. 3B 74
Serpentine Rd. W2 2C 74
Serviden Dri. Brom 5H 111
Servite Ho. Wor Pk 4D 120
(off Avenue, The)
Servius Ct. Bren 8H 71
Setchell Rd. SE1 5D 76
Setchell Way. SE1 5D 76
Seth St. SE16 3G 77
Seton Gdns. Dag 3G 65
Settle Rd. E13 5E 62
Settle Rd. Romf 4L 35
Settles St. E1 8E 60
Settrington Rd. SW6 1M 89
Seven Acres. Cars 4C 122
Seven Acres. N'wd 6F 20
Seven Acres. Swan 1B 130
Seven Dials. WC2 9J 59
Seven Dials Ct. WC2 9J 59
(off Shorts Gdns.)
Sevenex Pde. Wemb 1J 55
Seven Hills Clo. W on T 9C 116
Seven Hills Rd. W on T 9C 116
Seven Kings. 6C 48
Seven Kings Rd. Ilf 6C 48
Seven Kings Way.
King T 5J 103
Sevenoaks Clo. Bexh 3M 97
Sevenoaks Clo. Romf 4G 35
Sevenoaks Clo. Sutt 2L 135
Sevenoaks Ct. N'wd 7A 20
Sevenoaks Rd. SE4 5J 93
Sevenoaks Rd.
Grn St & Hals 9D 128
Sevenoaks Rd. Orp 7D 128
Sevenoaks Way.
Sidc & Orp 4G 113
Seven Sisters (Junct.) 3D 44
Seven Sisters Rd.
N7 & N4 8K 43
Seven Sisters Rd. N15 4B 44
Seven Stars Corner. W6 4E 72
Seventh Av. E12 9K 47
Seventh Av. Hay 2E 68
Severnake Clo. E14 5L 77
Severn Av. Romf 1F 50
Severn Ct. King T 5H 103
Severn Dri. Enf 2E 16
Severn Dri. Esh 4E 118
Severn Dri. W on T 4H 117
Severn Way. NW10 1D 56
Severn Way. Wat 7G 5
Severus Rd. SW11 3C 90
Seville M. N1 3C 60
Seville St. SW1 3D 74
Sevington Rd. NW4 4F 40
Sevington St. W9 7M 57
Seward Rd. W7 3E 70
Seward Rd. Beck 6H 109
Sewardstone. 3A 18
Sewardstonebury. 7C 18
Sewardstone Gdns. E4 7M 17
Sewardstone Rd. E2 5G 61
Sewardstone Rd.
E4 & Wal A 9M 17
Sewardstone Rd.
Wal A & E4 7J 7
Sewardstone St. Wal A 7J 7
Seward St. EC1 6M 59
Sewdley St. E5 8H 45
Sewell Rd. SE2 4E 80
Sewell St. E13 6E 62
Sextant Av. E14 5B 78
Sexton Clo. Rain 4D 66
Sextons Ho. SE10 7A 78
(off Bardsley La.)
Seymer Rd. Romf 1B 50
Seymour Av. N17 9E 28
Seymour Av. Eps 1F 134
Seymour Av. Mord 2H 121
Seymour Clo. E Mol 9A 102
Seymour Clo. Lou 8J 19
Seymour Clo. Pinn 8K 21
Seymour Ct. E4 2D 30
Seymour Ct. N10 9E 26
Seymour Ct. N21 8K 15
Seymour Ct. NW2 7F 40
Seymour Dri. Brom 3K 127
Seymour Gdns. SE4 2J 93
Seymour Gdns. Felt 1G 101
Seymour Gdns. Ilf 6K 47
Seymour Gdns. Ruis 6H 37
Seymour Gdns. Surb 9K 103
Seymour Gdns. Twic 6F 86
Seymour Ho. E16 2E 78
(off De Quincey M.)
Seymour Ho. NW1 6H 59
(off Churchway)
Seymour Ho. WC1 7J 59
(off Tavistock Pl.)
Seymour Ho. Sutt 8M 121
(off Mulgrave Rd.)
Seymour M. W1 9E 58
Seymour M. Ewe 2E 134
Seymour Pl. SE25 8F 108
Seymour Pl. W1 8D 58
Seymour Rd. E4 1M 29
Seymour Rd. E6 5H 63
Seymour Rd. E10 6K 45
Seymour Rd. N3 7M 25
Seymour Rd. N8 3L 43
Seymour Rd. N9 2F 28
Seymour Rd. SW18 6K 89
Seymour Rd. SW19 9H 89
Seymour Rd. W4 5A 72
Seymour Rd. Cars 7E 122
Seymour Rd. E Mol 9A 102
Seymour Rd. Hamp H 2A 102
Seymour Rd. King T 5H 103
Seymour Rd. Mitc 2E 122
Seymours, The. Lou 3L 19
Seymour St. W2 & W1 9D 58
Seymour Ter. SE20 5F 108
Seymour Vs. SE20 5F 108
Seymour Wlk. SW10 7A 74
Seymour Way. Sun 4D 100
Seyssel St. E14 5A 78
Shaa Rd. W3 1B 72
Shacklegate La. Tedd 1C 102
Shackleton Clo. SE23 8F 92
Shackleton Ct. E14 6L 77
(off Maritime Quay)
Shackleton Ct. W12 3F 72
Shackleton Ho. E1 2G 77
(off Prusom St.)
Shackleton Ho. NW10 3B 56
Shackleton Rd. S'hall 1K 69
Shackleton Way. Ab L 5E 4
(off Lysander Way)
Shacklewell. 9D 44
Shacklewell Grn. E8 9D 44
Shacklewell Ho. E8 9D 44
Shacklewell La. N16 1D 60
Shacklewell Rd. N16 9D 44
Shacklewell Row. E8 9D 44
Shacklewell St. E2 6D 60
Shadbolt Clo. Wor Pk 4D 120
Shad Thames. SE1 2D 76
Shadwell. 1F 76
Shadwell Ct. N'holt 5K 53
Shadwell Dri. N'holt 6K 53
Shadwell Gdns. E1 1G 77
(off Sutton St.)
Shadwell Pierhead. E1 1G 77
Shadwell Pl. E1 1G 77
(off Shadwell Gdns.)
Shadybush Clo. Bush 9A 10
Shady La. Wat 4F 8
Shaef Way. Tedd 4E 102
Shafter Rd. Dag 2A 66
Shaftesbury. Lou 5H 19
Shaftesbury Av.
W1 & WC2 9J 59
Shaftesbury Av. Enf 4H 17
Shaftesbury Av. Felt 5E 84
Shaftesbury Av. Harr 6M 37
Shaftesbury Av. Kent 3H 39
Shaftesbury Av. New Bar 6A 14
Shaftesbury Av. S'hall 5L 69
Shaftesbury Cen. W10 7H 57
(off Barlby Rd.)
Shaftesbury Circ. S Harr 6A 38
Shaftesbury Ct. E6 9L 63
(off Sapphire Clo.)
Shaftesbury Ct. N1 5B 60
(off Shaftesbury St.)
Shaftesbury Ct. SW6 9M 73
(off Maltings Pl.)
Shaftesbury Ct. SW16 9H 91
Shaftesbury Ct. Crox G 7A 8
Shaftesbury Gdns. NW10 7C 56
Shaftesbury La. Dart 3M 99
Shaftesbury Lodge. E14 9M 61
(off Up. North St.)
Shaftesbury M. SE1 4B 76
(off Falmouth Rd.)
Shaftesbury M. SW4 4G 91
Shaftesbury M. W8 4L 73
(off Stratford Rd.)
Shaftesbury Pde. S Harr 6A 38
Shaftesbury Pl. EC2 8A 60
(off London Wall)
Shaftesbury Pl. W14 5K 73
(off Warwick Rd.)
Shaftesbury Point. E13 5E 62
(off High St.)
Shaftesbury Rd. E4 1B 30
Shaftesbury Rd. E7 3G 63
Shaftesbury Rd. E10 6L 45
Shaftesbury Rd. E17 4M 45
Shaftesbury Rd. N18 6C 28
Shaftesbury Rd. N19 6J 43
Shaftesbury Rd. Beck 6K 109
Shaftesbury Rd. Cars 2B 122
Shaftesbury Rd. Rich 2J 87
Shaftesbury Rd. Romf 4D 50
Shaftesbury Rd. Wat 5G 9
Shaftesburys, The. Bark 5A 64
Shaftesbury St. N1 5A 60
(in two parts)
Shaftesbury Theatre. 9J 59
(off Shaftesbury Av.)
Shaftesbury Way. K Lan 1A 4
Shaftesbury Way. Twic 9B 86
Shaftesbury Waye. Hay 8G 53
Shafto M. SW1 4D 74
Shafton M. E9 4H 61
Shafton Rd. E9 4H 61
Shaftsbury Ct. SE5 3B 92
Shaftsbury Ct. Eri 9D 82
(off Selkirk Dri.)
Shafts Ct. EC3 9C 60
Shahjalal Ho. E2 5E 60
(off Pritchards Rd.)
Shakespeare Av. N11 5G 27
Shakespeare Av. NW10 4B 56
Shakespeare Av. Felt 5E 84
Shakespeare Av. Hay 9E 52
(in two parts)
Shakespeare Clo. Harr 4L 39
Shakespeare Ct. Harr 5L 39
Shakespeare Ct. New Bar 5M 13
Shakespeare Cres. E12 2K 63
Shakespeare Cres. NW10 4B 56
Shakespeare Dri. Harr 4K 39
Shakespeare Gdns. N2 2D 42
Shakespeare Ho. E9 3G 61
(off Lyme Gro.)
Shakespeare Ho. N14 2H 27
Shakespeare Ind. Est. Wat 2E 8
Shakespeare Rd. E17 9H 29
Shakespeare Rd. N3 8L 25
Shakespeare Rd. NW7 4D 24
Shakespeare Rd. SE24 4M 91
Shakespeare Rd. W3 2A 72
Shakespeare Rd. W7 1D 70
Shakespeare Rd. Bexh 9J 81
Shakespeare Rd. Dart 3L 99
Shakespeare Rd. Romf 4D 50
Shakespeare's Globe Theatre &
Exhibition. 2A 76
Shakespeare Sq. Ilf 6A 32
Shakespeare St. Wat 2F 8
Shakespeare Tower. EC2 8A 60
(off Beech St.)
Shakespeare Way. Felt 1G 101
Shakspeare M. N16 9C 44

Shakspeare Wlk.—Shirebrook Rd.

akspeare Wlk. N16 .... 9C 44
albourne Sq. E9 .... 2K 61
alcomb St. SW10 .... 7A 74
alcross Dri. Chesh 3F 6
alden Ho. SW15 .... 5D 88
aldon Dri. Mord 9J 105
aldon Dri. Ruis 8G 37
aldon Rd. Edgw 9K 23
aldon Way. W on T 5G 117
alfleet Dri. W10 .... 1H 73
alford Clo. Orp 6A 128
alford Ct. N1 .... 5M 59
(off Charlton Pl.)
alford Ho. SE1 .... 4B 76
alimar Gdns. W3 .... 1A 72
alimar Rd. W3 .... 1A 72
allons Rd. SE9 .... 1M 111
alstone Rd. SW14 .... 2M 87
alston Vs. Surb 1K 119
amrock Rd. Croy 1K 123
amrock St. SW4 .... 2H 91
amrock Way. N14 .... 1F 26
andon Rd. SW4 .... 5G 91
and St. SE1 .... 3C 76
andy St. E1 .... 8H 61
anklin Clo. Chesh 2A 6
anklin Gdns. Wat 4G 21
anklin Ho. E17 .... 9K 29
anklin Rd. N8 .... 3H 43
annon Clo. NW2 .... 8H 41
annon Clo. S'hall 6H 69
annon Corner (Junct.) 8E 104
annon Corner Retail Pk. N Mald 8E 104
annon Ct. N16 .... 8C 44
annon Ct. Croy 3A 124
(off Tavistock Rd.)
annon Gro. SW9 .... 3K 91
annon Pl. NW8 .... 5C 58
annon Way. Ave 1M 83
annon Way. Beck 3M 109
anti Ct. SW18 .... 7L 89
ap Cres. Cars 3D 122
apland Way. N13 .... 5K 27
ap St. E2 .... 5D 60
apwick Clo. N11 .... 5D 26
ardcroft Av. SE24 .... 4M 91
ardeloes Rd. SE14 .... 1K 93
ard's Sq. SE15 .... 7E 76
arland Clo. T Hth 1L 123
arman Ct. Sidc 1E 112
(off Carlton Rd.)
arnbrooke Clo. Well 2G 97
arnbrook Ho. W14 .... 7L 73
aron Clo. Eps 5A 134
aron Clo. Surb 3G 119
haron Ct. S Croy 7A 124
(off Warham Rd.)
haron Gdns. E9 .... 4G 61
haron Rd. W4 .... 6B 72
haron Rd. Enf 4J 17
harpe Clo. W7 .... 8D 54
harp Ho. SW8 .... 2F 90
harp Ho. Twic 5H 87
harpleshall St. NW1 .... 3D 58
harpness Clo. Hay 8J 53
harpness Ct. SE15 .... 8D 76
(off Daniel Gdns.)
harp's La. Ruis 5B 36
harp Way. Dart 2K 99
harratt St. SE15 .... 7G 77
harsted St. SE17 .... 6M 75
harvel La. N'holt 4F 52
harwood. WC1 .... 5K 59
(off Penton Ri.)
haver's Pl. SW1 .... 1H 75
(off Coventry St.)
haw Av. Bark 5J 65
hawbrooke Rd. SE9 .... 4G 95
hawbury Rd. SE22 .... 4D 92
haw Clo. SE28 .... 2F 80
haw Clo. Bus H 2C 22
haw Clo. Chesh 1C 6
haw Clo. Eps 3D 134
haw Clo. Horn 6F 50
haw Clo. S Croy 4D 138
Shaw Ct. W3 .... 4A 72
(off All Saints Rd.)
Shaw Cres. S Croy 4D 138
Shaw Dri. W on T 2G 117
Shawfield Ct. W Dray 4J 143
Shawfield Pk. Brom 6H 111
Shawfield St. SW3 .... 6C 74
Shawford Ct. SW15 .... 6E 88
Shawford Rd. Eps 8B 120
Shaw Gdns. Bark 5J 65
Shaw Ho. E16 .... 2L 79
(off Claremont St.)
Shaw Ho. Belv 6K 81
Shawley Cres. Eps 9G 135
Shawley Way. Eps 9F 134
Shaw Path. Brom 9D 94
Shaw Rd. SE22 .... 3C 92
Shaw Rd. Brom 9D 94
Shaw Rd. Enf 3H 17
Shaws Cotts. SE23 .... 9J 93
Shaws Path. Hamp W 5G 103
(off Bennett Clo.)
Shaw Sq. E17 .... 8J 29
Shaw Way. Wall 9J 123

Shaxton Cres. New Ad 1A 140
Shearing Dri. Cars 2A 122
Shearling Way. N7 .... 2J 59
Shearman Rd. SE3 .... 3D 94
Shears Clo. Dart 8G 99
Shears Ct. Sun 4C 100
Shears, The (Junct.) 4C 100
Shearwater Ct. SE8 .... 7K 77
(off Abinger Gro.)
Shearwater Rd. Sutt 7K 121
Shearwater Way. Hay 9H 53
Shearwood Cres. Dart 2D 98
Sheath's La. Oxs 5A 132
Sheaveshill Av. NW9 .... 2C 40
Sheaveshill Ct. NW9 .... 2B 40
Sheaveshill Pde. NW9 .... 2C 40
(off Sheaveshill Av.)
Sheba Ct. N17 .... 6E 28
(off Altair Clo.)
Sheen Comn. Dri. Rich 3L 87
Sheen Ct. Rich 3L 87
Sheen Ct. Rd. Rich 3L 87
Sheendale Rd. Rich 3K 87
Sheenewood. SE26 .... 1F 108
Sheen Ga. Gdns. SW14 .... 3A 88
Sheengate Mans. SW14 .... 3B 88
Sheen Gro. N1 .... 4L 59
Sheen La. SW14 .... 4A 88
Sheen Pk. Rich 3K 87
Sheen Rd. Orp 8D 112
Sheen Rd. Rich 4J 87
Sheen Way. Wall 7K 123
Sheen Wood. SW14 .... 4A 88
Sheepbarn La. Warl 4D 140
Sheepcot Dri. Wat 7G 5
Sheepcote Clo. Houn 8E 68
Sheepcote La. SW11 .... 1D 90
Sheepcote La. Orp & Swan 9K 113
Sheepcote Rd. Harr 4D 38
Sheepcotes Rd. Romf 2J 49
Sheepcot La. Wat 6E 4
(in two parts)
Sheephouse Way. N Mald 3B 120
Sheep La. E8 .... 4F 60
Sheep Wlk. M. SW19 .... 3H 105
Sheerness M. E16 .... 3M 79
Sheerwater Rd. E16 .... 8H 63
Sheffield Dri. Romf 5L 35
Sheffield Gdns. Romf 5L 35
Sheffield Rd. H'row A 5A 84
Sheffield Sq. E3 .... 6K 61
Sheffield St. WC2 .... 9K 59
Sheffield Ter. W8 .... 2L 73
Sheffield Way. H'row A 4B 84
Shefton Ri. N'wd 7E 20
Sheila Clo. Romf 7M 33
Sheila Rd. Romf 7M 33
Sheilings, The. Horn 3K 51
Shelbourne Clo. Pinn 1K 37
Shelbourne Pl. Beck 4K 109
Shelbourne Rd. N17 .... 9F 28
Shelburne Dri. Houn 5L 85
Shelburne Rd. N7 .... 9K 43
Shelbury Clo. Sidc 9E 96
Shelbury Rd. SE22 .... 4F 92
Sheldon Av. N6 .... 5C 42
Sheldon Av. Ilf 9M 31
Sheldon Clo. SE12 .... 4F 94
Sheldon Clo. SE20 .... 5F 108
Sheldon Ct. SW8 .... 9J 75
(off Lansdowne Grn.)
Sheldon Ct. Barn 6M 13
Sheldon Rd. N18 .... 4C 28
Sheldon Rd. NW2 .... 9H 41
Sheldon Rd. Bexh 9K 81
Sheldon Rd. Dag 3J 65
Sheldon St. Croy 5A 124
Sheldrake Clo. E16 .... 2K 79
Sheldrake Ct. E6 .... 5J 63
(off St Bartholomew's Rd.)
Sheldrake Ho. SE16 .... 5H 77
(off Tawny Way)
Sheldrake Pl. W8 .... 3L 73
Sheldrick Clo. SW19 .... 6B 106
Shelduck Clo. E15 .... 1D 62
Shelduck Ct. SE8 .... 7K 77
(off Pilot Clo.)
Sheldwich Ter. Brom 1J 127
Shelford Pl. N16 .... 8B 44
Shelford Ri. SE19 .... 4D 108
Shelford Rd. Barn 8G 13
Shelgate Rd. SW11 .... 4C 90
Shell Clo. Brom 1J 127
Shellduck Clo. NW9 .... 9C 24
Shelley. N8 .... 1J 43
(off Boyton Rd.)
Shelley Av. E12 .... 2J 63
Shelley Av. Gnfd 6B 54
Shelley Av. Horn 7D 50
Shelley Clo. SE15 .... 1F 92
Shelley Clo. Bans 7H 135
Shelley Clo. Coul 9K 137
Shelley Clo. Edgw 4L 23
Shelley Clo. Gnfd 6B 54
Shelley Clo. Hay 8E 52
Shelley Clo. N'wd 5D 20
Shelley Clo. Orp 5C 128
Shelley Ct. E10 .... 5M 45
(off Skelton's La.)

Shelley Ct. E11 .... 2F 46
(off Makepeace Rd.)
Shelley Ct. N4 .... 6K 43
Shelley Ct. SW3 .... 7D 74
(off Tite St.)
Shelley Ct. Wal A 6M 7
(off Ninefields)
Shelley Cres. Houn 9H 69
Shelley Cres. S'hall 9K 53
Shelley Dri. Well 9C 80
Shelley Gdns. Wemb 7G 39
Shelley Gro. Lou 6K 19
Shelley Ho. E2 .... 6G 61
(off Cornwall Av.)
Shelley Ho. SE17 .... 6A 76
(off Browning St.)
Shelley Ho. SW1 .... 7G 75
(off Churchill Gdns.)
Shelley Rd. NW10 .... 4B 56
Shelley Way. SW19 .... 3B 106
Shellness Rd. E5 .... 1F 60
Shell Rd. SE13 .... 2M 93
Shellwood Rd. SW11 .... 1D 90
Shelmerdine Clo. E3 .... 8L 61
Shelson Av. Felt 9D 84
Shelton Av. Warl 9G 139
Shelton Clo. Warl 9G 139
Shelton Rd. SW19 .... 5L 105
Shelton St. WC2 .... 9J 59
(in two parts)
Shene Ho. EC1 .... 8L 59
(off Bourne Est.)
Shenfield Ho. SE18 .... 9H 79
(off Portway Gdns.)
Shenfield Rd. Wfd G 7F 30
Shenfield St. N1 .... 5C 60
(in two parts)
Shenley Av. Ruis 7D 36
Shenley Rd. SE5 .... 9C 76
Shenley Rd. Borwd 6L 11
Shenley Rd. Dart 5L 99
Shenley Rd. Houn 9J 69
Shenstone. W5 .... 2G 71
Shenstone Clo. Dart 3B 98
Shenstone Gdns. Romf 8G 35
Shenwood Ct. Borwd 1L 11
Shepherd Clo. W1 .... 1E 74
(off Lees Pl.)
Shepherd Clo. Felt 1J 101
Shepherdess Pl. N1 .... 6A 60
Shepherdess Wlk. N1 .... 5A 60
Shepherd Ho. E14 .... 9M 61
(off Annabel Clo.)
Shepherd Mkt. W1 .... 2F 74
Shepherd's Bush. 3G 73
Shepherd's Bush Grn. W12 .... 3G 73
Shepherd's Bush Mkt. W12 .... 3G 73
(in two parts)
Shepherd's Bush Pl. W12 .... 3H 73
Shepherd's Bush Rd. W6 .... 5G 73
Shepherd's Clo. N6 .... 4F 42
Shepherd's Clo. Orp 5D 128
Shepherds Clo. Romf 3H 49
Shepherds Clo. Uxb 7A 142
Shepherds Ct. W12 .... 3H 73
(off Shepherd's Bush Grn.)
Shepherds Grn. Chst 4B 112
Shepherd's Hill. N6 .... 4F 42
Shepherds Hill. Romf 9L 35
Shepherds La. E9 .... 2H 61
Shepherd's La. Dart 7E 98
Shepherds Leas. SE9 .... 3A 96
Shepherd's Path. NW3 .... 1B 58
(off Lyndhurst Rd.)
Shepherds Path. N'holt 2J 53
(off Arnold Rd.)
Shepherds Pl. W1 .... 1E 74
Shepherd's Rd. Wat 5D 8
Shepherd St. W1 .... 2F 74
Shepherds Wlk. NW2 .... 7E 40
Shepherd's Wlk. NW3 .... 1B 58
(in two parts)
Shepherds Wlk. Bus H 2B 22
Shepherds Way. S Croy 9H 125
Shepiston La. Hay 5M 143
Shepley Clo. Cars 5E 122
Shepley Clo. Horn 1H 67
Shepley M. Enf 1L 17
Sheppard Clo. Enf 3F 16
Sheppard Clo. King T 8J 103
Sheppard Dri. SE16 .... 6F 76
Sheppard Ho. E2 .... 5E 60
(off Warner Pl.)
Sheppard Ho. SW2 .... 7L 91
Sheppards College. Brom 5E 110
(off London Rd.)
Sheppard St. E16 .... 7D 62
Shepperton. 1A 116
Shepperton Bus. Pk. Shep 9A 100
Shepperton Clo. Borwd 3B 12
Shepperton Ct. Dri. Shep 9A 100
Shepperton Rd. N1 .... 4A 60
Shepperton Rd. Orp 1A 128
Sheppey Clo. Eri 8F 82
Sheppey Gdns. Dag 3G 65
Sheppey Rd. Dag 3F 64

Sheppey's La. K Lan & Ab L 2A 4
Sheppey Wlk. N1 .... 3A 60
(off Oronsay Wlk.)
Shepton Houses. E2 .... 6G 61
(off Welwyn St.)
Sherard Ct. N7 .... 8J 43
Sherard Ho. E9 .... 3G 61
(off Frampton Pk. Rd.)
Sherard Rd. SE9 .... 4J 95
Sheraton Bus. Cen. Gnfd 5G 55
Sheraton Clo. Els 7K 11
Sheraton Dri. Eps 5A 134
Sheraton Ho. SW1 .... 7F 74
(off Churchill Gdns.)
Sheraton M. Wat 6C 8
Sheraton St. W1 .... 9H 59
Sherborne Av. Enf 4G 17
Sherborne Av. S'hall 5L 69
Sherborne Clo. Eps 9G 135
Sherborne Clo. Hay 9G 53
Sherborne Cotts. Wat 7G 9
(off Muriel Av.)
Sherborne Cres. Cars 2C 122
Sherborne Gdns. NW9 .... 1L 39
Sherborne Gdns. W13 .... 8F 54
Sherborne Gdns. Romf 5L 33
Sherborne Gdns. Shep 2C 116
Sherborne Ho. SW1 .... 6F 74
Sherborne Ho. SW8 .... 8K 75
(off Bolney St.)
Sherborne La. EC4 .... 1B 76
Sherborne Pl. N'wd 6B 20
Sherborne Rd. Chess 7J 119
Sherborne Rd. Felt 7B 84
(in two parts)
Sherborne Rd. Orp 8D 112
Sherborne Rd. Sutt 4L 121
Sherborne St. N1 .... 4B 60
Sherborne Way. Crox G 7A 8
Sherboro Rd. N15 .... 4D 44
Sherbourne Ct. Sutt 8A 122
Sherbourne Ho. Wat 8B 8
Sherbourne Pl. Stan 6E 22
Sherbrooke Clo. Bexh 3L 97
Sherbrooke Ho. E2 .... 5G 61
(off Bonner Rd.)
Sherbrooke Rd. SW6 .... 8J 73
Sherbrook Gdns. N21 .... 9M 15
Shere Av. Sutt 2G 135
Shere Clo. Chess 7H 119
Sheredan Rd. E4 .... 5B 30
Shere Ho. SE1 .... 4B 76
(off Gt. Dover St.)
Shere Rd. Ilf 3L 47
Sherfield Clo. N Mald 8M 103
Sherfield Gdns. SW15 .... 5D 88
Sheridan Bldgs. WC2 .... 9J 59
(off Martlett Ct.)
Sheridan Clo. Romf 7G 35
Sheridan Clo. Swan 8D 114
Sheridan Clo. Uxb 7A 52
Sheridan Ct. NW6 .... 3A 58
(off Belsize Rd.)
Sheridan Ct. W7 .... 1D 70
(off Milton Rd.)
Sheridan Ct. Croy 6C 124
(off Coombe Rd.)
Sheridan Ct. Dart 3L 99
Sheridan Ct. Harr 4B 38
Sheridan Ct. Houn 4J 85
Sheridan Ct. N'holt 1M 53
Sheridan Cres. Chst 6M 111
Sheridan Gdns. Harr 4H 39
Sheridan Ho. E1 .... 9G 61
(off Tarling St.)
Sheridan Ho. SE11 .... 5L 75
(off Wincott St.)
Sheridan Lodge. Brom 8G 111
(off Homesdale Rd.)
Sheridan M. E11 .... 4F 46
(off High St.)
Sheridan Pl. SW13 .... 2D 88
Sheridan Pl. Hamp 5M 101
Sheridan Rd. E7 .... 8D 46
Sheridan Rd. E12 .... 1J 63
Sheridan Rd. SW19 .... 5K 105
Sheridan Rd. Belv 5L 81
Sheridan Rd. Bexh 2J 97
Sheridan Rd. Rich 9G 87
Sheridan Rd. Wat 9H 9
Sheridan St. E1 .... 9F 60
Sheridan Ter. N'holt 1M 53
Sheridan Wlk. NW11 .... 4L 41
Sheridan Wlk. Cars 7D 122
Sheridan Way. Beck 5K 109
Sheriden Pl. Harr 5C 38
Sheriff Way. Wat 6E 4
Sheringham. NW8 .... 4B 58
Sheringham Av. E12 .... 9K 47
Sheringham Av. N14 .... 7H 15
Sheringham Av. Felt 9E 84
Sheringham Av. Romf 4A 50
Sheringham Av. Twic 7K 85
Sheringham Ct. Enf 5M 15
Sheringham Ct. Felt 9E 84
(off Sheringham Av.)
Sheringham Dri. Bark 1D 64
Sheringham Ho. NW1 .... 8C 58
(off Lisson St.)
Sheringham Rd. N7 .... 2K 59

Sheringham Rd. SE20 .... 7G 109
Sheringham Tower. S'hall 1M 69
Sherington Av. Pinn 7L 21
Sherington Rd. SE7 .... 7F 78
Sherland Rd. Twic 7D 86
Sherlies Av. Orp 4C 128
Sherlock Ct. NW8 .... 4B 58
(off Dorman Way)
Sherlock Holmes Mus. 7D 58
(off Baker St.)
Sherlock M. W1 .... 8E 58
Shermanbury Pl. Eri 8D 82
Sherman Gdns. Romf 4G 49
Sherman Rd. Brom 5E 110
Shernbroke Rd. Wal A 7M 7
Shernhall St. E17 .... 1A 46
Sherrard Rd. E7 & E12 .... 2G 63
Sherrards Way. Barn 7L 13
Sherren Ho. E1 .... 7G 61
(off Nicholas Rd.)
Sherrick Grn. Rd. NW10 .... 1F 56
Sherriff Rd. NW6 .... 2L 57
Sherringham Av. N17 .... 9E 28
Sherrin Rd. E10 .... 9M 45
Sherrock Gdns. NW4 .... 2E 40
Sherry M. Bark 3B 64
Sherston Ct. SE1 .... 5M 75
(off Newington Butts)
Sherston Ct. WC1 .... 6L 59
(off Attneave St.)
Sherwin Ho. SE11 .... 7L 75
(off Kennington Rd.)
Sherwin Rd. SE14 .... 9H 77
Sherwood. NW6 .... 3J 57
Sherwood Av. E18 .... 1F 46
Sherwood Av. SW16 .... 4H 107
Sherwood Av. Gnfd 2C 54
Sherwood Av. Hay 7F 52
Sherwood Av. Ruis 4C 36
Sherwood Clo. E17 .... 9K 29
Sherwood Clo. SW13 .... 2F 88
Sherwood Clo. W13 .... 2F 70
Sherwood Clo. Bex 5G 97
Sherwood Ct. SW11 .... 2A 90
Sherwood Ct. W1 .... 8D 58
(off Bryanston Pl.)
Sherwood Ct. S Croy 7A 124
(off Nottingham Rd.)
Sherwood Ct. S Harr 7M 37
Sherwood Ct. Wat 7D 4
Sherwood Gdns. E14 .... 5L 77
Sherwood Gdns. SE16 .... 6E 76
Sherwood Gdns. Bark 3B 64
Sherwood Pk. Av. Sidc 6E 96
Sherwood Pk. Rd. Mitc 8G 107
Sherwood Pk. Rd. Sutt 7L 121
Sherwood Rd. NW4 .... 1G 41
Sherwood Rd. SW19 .... 4K 105
Sherwood Rd. Coul 8G 137
Sherwood Rd. Croy 2F 124
Sherwood Rd. Hamp H 2A 102
Sherwood Rd. Harr 7A 38
Sherwood Rd. Ilf 2B 48
Sherwood Rd. Well 1C 96
Sherwoods Rd. Wat 9J 9
Sherwood St. N20 .... 3B 26
Sherwood St. W1 .... 1G 75
Sherwood Ter. N20 .... 3B 26
Sherwood Way. W Wick 4A 126
Shetland Clo. Borwd 8B 12
Shetland Rd. E3 .... 5K 61
Shewens Rd. Wey 6B 116
Shield Dri. Bren 7E 70
Shieldhall St. SE2 .... 5G 81
Shield Rd. Ashf 1A 100
Shifford Path. SE23 .... 9H 93
Shillaker Ct. W3 .... 2D 72
Shillibeer Pl. W1 .... 8C 58
(off York St.)
Shillibeer Wlk. Chig 3D 32
Shillingford St. N1 .... 3M 59
Shilling Pl. W7 .... 3E 70
Shillingstone Ho. W14 .... 4J 73
(off Russell Rd.)
Shinfield St. W12 .... 9G 57
Shingle Ct. Wal A 6M 7
Shingle End. Bren 8G 71
Shinglewell Rd. Eri 8L 81
Shinners Clo. SE25 .... 9E 108
Ship All. W4 .... 7L 71
Ship & Mermaid Row. SE1 .... 3B 76
Shipka Rd. SW12 .... 7F 90
Shiplake Ho. E2 .... 6D 60
(off Arnold Cir.)
Ship La. SW14 .... 2A 88
Ship La. S at H 5H 115
Shipman Rd. E16 .... 9F 62
Shipman Rd. SE23 .... 8H 93
Ship St. SE8 .... 9L 77
Ship Tavern Pas. EC3 .... 1C 76
Shipton Clo. Dag 8H 49
Shipton Ho. E2 .... 5D 60
(off Shipton St.)
Shipton St. E2 .... 5D 60
Shipway Ter. N16 .... 8D 44
Shipwright Rd. SE16 .... 3J 77
Shipwright Yd. SE1 .... 2C 76
Ship Yd. E14 .... 6M 77
Shirburn Clo. SE23 .... 6G 93
Shirebrook Rd. SE3 .... 2H 95

Shire Ct.—Sistova Rd.

Shire Ct. Eps 9D 120
Shire Ct. Eri 4H 81
Shirehall Clo. NW4 4H 41
Shirehall Gdns. NW4 4H 41
Shirehall La. NW4 4H 41
Shirehall Pk. NW4 3H 41
Shirehall Rd. Dart 2G 115
Shire Horse Way. Iswth 2D 86
Shire La. Kes 1J 141
(in two parts)
Shire La. Orp 7C 128
Shiremeade. Borwd 7K 11
Shire M. Whit 5A 86
Shire Pl. SW18 6A 90
Shire Pl. Bren 8G 71
Shires, The. Ham 1J 103
Shires, The. Wat 4F 4
Shirland M. W9 6K 57
Shirland Rd. W9 6K 57
Shirlbutt St. E14 1M 77
Shirley. 4G 125
Shirley Av. Bex 6H 97
Shirley Av. Cheam 1K 135
Shirley Av. Croy 3G 125
Shirley Av. Sutt 6B 122
Shirley Chu. Rd. Croy 5G 125
Shirley Clo. Chesh 2C 6
Shirley Clo. Dart 3G 99
Shirley Clo. Houn 4A 86
Shirley Ct. SW16 4J 107
Shirley Ct. Lou 4K 19
Shirley Cres. Beck 8J 109
Shirley Dri. Houn 4A 86
Shirley Gdns. W7 2D 70
Shirley Gdns. Bark 2C 64
Shirley Gdns. Horn 7G 51
Shirley Gro. N9 9G 17
Shirley Gro. SW11 2E 90
Shirley Heights. Wall 1G 137
Shirley Hills Rd. Croy 7G 125
Shirley Ho. SE5 8B 76
(off Picton St.)
Shirley Ho. Dri. SE7 8G 79
Shirley Oaks. 3H 125
Shirley Oaks Rd. Croy 3H 125
Shirley Pk. Croy 4G 125
Shirley Pk. Rd. Croy 3F 124
Shirley Rd. E15 3C 62
Shirley Rd. W4 3B 72
Shirley Rd. Ab L 5D 4
Shirley Rd. Croy 2F 124
Shirley Rd. Enf 5A 16
Shirley Rd. Sidc 9C 96
Shirley Rd. Wall 1G 137
Shirleys Clo. E17 3M 45
Shirley St. E16 9D 62
Shirley Way. Croy 5J 125
Shirlock Rd. NW3 9D 42
Shobden Rd. N17 8B 28
Shobroke Clo. NW2 8G 41
Shoebury Rd. E6 3K 63
Shoelands Ct. NW9 1B 40
Shoe La. EC4 9L 59
Sholden Gdns. Orp 9G 113
Shooters Av. Harr 2G 39
Shooters Hill. 9L 79
Shooters Hill.
SE18 & Well 9K 79
Shooters Hill Rd.
SE3 & SE18 8G 79
Shooters Hill Rd.
SE10 & SE3 9B 78
Shooters Rd. Enf 3M 15
Shoot Up Hill. NW2 1J 57
Shop. Hall, The. E6 4J 63
Shord Hill. Kenl 8B 138
Shore Bus. Cen. E9 3G 61
Shore Clo. Felt 6E 84
Shore Clo. Hamp 3J 101
Shoreditch. 6C 60
Shoreditch Ct. E8 3D 60
(off Queensbridge Rd.)
Shoreditch High St. E1 7C 60
Shore Gro. Felt 8K 85
Shoreham Clo. SW18 4M 89
Shoreham Clo. Bex 7H 97
Shoreham Clo. Croy 1G 125
Shoreham La. Orp 8L 129
Shoreham Rd. Eyns 8G 131
Shoreham Rd. Orp 5F 112
Shoreham Rd. Shor 9F 130
Shoreham Rd. E.
H'row A 4C 144
Shoreham Rd. W.
H'row A 4C 144
Shoreham Way. Brom 1E 126
Shore Ho. SW8 2F 90
Shore M. E9 3G 61
(off Shore Rd.)
Shore Pl. E9 3G 61
Shore Rd. E9 3G 61
Shorncliffe Rd. SE1 6D 76
Shorndean St. SE6 7A 94
Shorne Clo. Orp 8H 113
Shorne Clo. Sidc 5F 96
Shornefield Clo. Brom 7L 111
Shornells Way. SE2 5G 81
Shorrold's Rd. SW6 8K 73
Shortcroft Mead Ct.
NW10 1E 56
(off Cooper Rd.)
Shortcroft Rd. Eps 9D 120
Shortcrofts Rd. Dag 2K 65
Shorter St. EC3 & E1 1D 76
Short Ga. N12 4K 25
Short Hedges. Houn 9L 69
Short Hill. Harr 6C 38
Shortlands. 6C 110
Shortlands. W6 5H 73
Shortlands. Hay 7B 68
Shortlands Clo. N18 3B 28
Shortlands Clo. Belv 4K 81
Shortlands Gdns. Brom 6C 110
Shortlands Gro. Brom 7B 110
Shortlands Ho. E17 3K 45
Shortlands Rd. E10 5M 45
Shortlands Rd. Brom 7B 110
Shortlands Rd. King T 4K 103
Short La. Brick W 2J 5
Short La. Stai 6D 144
Shortmead Dri. Chesh 4E 6
Short Path. SE18 7M 79
Short Rd. E11 7C 46
Short Rd. W4 7C 72
Short Rd. H'row A 5C 144
Shorts Cft. NW9 2M 39
Shorts Gdns. WC2 9J 59
Shorts Rd. Cars 6C 122
Short St. NW4 2G 41
Short St. SE1 3L 75
Short Wall. E15 6A 62
Short Way. N12 6C 26
Short Way. SE9 2J 95
Short Way. Twic 6A 86
Shortwood Av. Stai 9A 144
Shorwell Ct. Purf 6M 83
Shotfield. Wall 8F 122
Shott Clo. Sutt 7A 122
Shottendane Rd. SW6 9L 73
Shottery Clo. SE9 9J 95
Shottfield Av. SW14 3C 88
Shottsford. W2 9L 57
(off Ledbury Rd.)
Shoulder of Mutton All.
E14 1J 77
Shouldham St. W1 8C 58
Showers Way. Hay 2E 68
Shrapnel Clo. SE18 8J 79
Shrapnel Rd. SE9 2K 95
Shrewsbury Av. SW14 3A 88
Shrewsbury Av. Harr 2J 39
Shrewsbury Clo. Surb 4J 119
Shrewsbury Ct. EC1 7A 60
(off Whitecross St.)
Shrewsbury Cres. NW10 4B 56
Shrewsbury Ho. SW8 7K 75
(off Meadow Rd.)
Shrewsbury La. SE18 9M 79
Shrewsbury M. W2 8L 57
(off Chepstow Rd.)
Shrewsbury Rd. E7 1H 63
Shrewsbury Rd. N11 6G 27
Shrewsbury Rd. W2 9L 57
Shrewsbury Rd. Beck 7J 109
Shrewsbury Rd. Cars 2C 122
Shrewsbury Rd. H'row A 5A 84
Shrewsbury St. W10 7G 57
Shrewsbury Wlk. Iswth 2E 86
Shrewton Rd. SW17 4D 106
Shroffold Rd. Brom 1C 110
Shropshire Clo. Mitc 8J 107
Shropshire Ct. W7 9D 54
(off Copley Clo.)
Shropshire Pl. WC1 7G 59
Shropshire Rd. N22 7K 27
Shroton St. NW1 8C 58
Shrubberies, The. E18 9E 30
Shrubberies, The. Chig 5A 32
Shrubbery Clo. N1 4A 60
Shrubbery Gdns. N21 9M 15
Shrubbery Rd. N9 3E 28
Shrubbery Rd. SW16 1J 107
Shrubbery Rd. S'hall 2K 69
Shrubbery, The. E11 3F 46
Shrubbery, The. Surb 3J 119
Shrubbery, The. Upm 8M 51
Shrubland Clo. N20 1B 26
Shrubland Gro. Wor Pk 5G 121
Shrubland Rd. E8 4E 60
Shrubland Rd. E10 5L 45
Shrubland Rd. E17 3L 45
Shrubland Rd. Bans 8K 135
Shrublands Av. Croy 5L 125
Shrublands Clo. SE26 9G 93
Shrublands Clo. Chig 6A 32
Shrubsall Clo. SE9 7J 95
Shuna Wlk. N1 2B 60
Shurland Av. Barn 8B 14
Shurland Gdns. SE15 8D 76
Shurlock Av. Swan 6B 114
Shurlock Dri. Orp 6A 128
Shuters Sq. W14 6K 73
Shuttle Clo. Sidc 6D 96
Shuttlemead. Bex 6K 97
Shuttle Rd. Dart 2E 98
Shuttle St. E1 7E 60
Shuttleworth Rd. SW11 1C 90
Sibella Rd. SW4 1H 91
Sibley Clo. Bexh 4J 97
Sibley Ct. Uxb 8A 52
Sibley Gro. E12 3J 63
Sibthorpe Rd. SE12 5F 94
Sibthorp Rd. Mitc 6D 106
Sibton Rd. Cars 2C 122
Sicilian Av. WC1 8J 59
(off Vernon Pl.)
Sickle Corner. Dag 7M 65
Sidbury St. SW6 9J 73
Sidcup. 1E 112
Sidcup By-Pass.
Chst & Sidc 9B 96
Sidcup High St. Sidc 1E 112
Sidcup Hill. Sidc 1F 112
Sidcup Hill Gdns. Sidc 2G 113
Sidcup Pl. Sidc 2E 112
Sidcup Rd. SE12 & SE9 5G 95
Sidcup Technical Cen.
Sidc 3H 113
Siddeley Dri. Houn 2J 85
Siddons Ho. W2 8B 58
(off Harbet Rd.)
Siddons La. NW1 7D 58
Siddons Rd. N17 8E 28
Siddons Rd. SE23 8J 93
Siddons Rd. Croy 5L 123
Side Rd. E17 3K 45
Sidewood Rd. SE9 7B 96
Sidford Ho. SE1 4L 75
(off Cosser St.)
Sidford Pl. SE1 4L 75
Sidgwick Ho. SW9 1K 91
(off Lingham St.)
Sidings M. N7 8L 43
Sidings, The. E11 6A 46
Sidings, The. Lou 8J 19
Sidlaw Ho. N16 6D 44
Sidmouth Av. Iswth 1C 86
Sidmouth Clo. Wat 2F 20
Sidmouth Ct. Dart 7M 99
(off Churchill Clo.)
Sidmouth Dri. Ruis 8E 36
Sidmouth Ho. SE15 8E 76
(off Lympstone Gdns.)
Sidmouth Ho. W1 9C 58
(off Cato St.)
Sidmouth Pde. NW2 3G 57
Sidmouth Rd. E10 8A 46
Sidmouth Rd. NW2 3G 57
Sidmouth Rd. Orp 9F 112
(in two parts)
Sidmouth Rd. Well 8G 81
Sidmouth St. WC1 6K 59
Sidney Av. N22 5K 27
Sidney Boyd Ct. NW6 3L 57
Sidney Clo. Uxb 3A 142
Sidney Elson Way. E6 5L 63
Sidney Est. E1 9G 61
(Bromhead St.)
Sidney Est. E1 8G 61
(Jubilee St.)
Sidney Gdns. Bren 7H 71
Sidney Godley (VC) Ho.
E2 6G 61
(off Digby St.)
Sidney Gro. EC1 5M 59
Sidney Ho. E2 5H 61
(off Old Ford Rd.)
Sidney Miller Ct. W3 2M 71
(off Crown St.)
Sidney Rd. E7 8E 46
Sidney Rd. N22 7K 27
Sidney Rd. SE25 9E 108
Sidney Rd. SW9 1K 91
Sidney Rd. Beck 6J 109
Sidney Rd. Harr 1A 38
Sidney Rd. Twic 5E 86
Sidney Rd. W on T 2E 116
Sidney Sq. E1 8G 61
Sidney St. E1 8F 60
Sidworth St. E8 3F 60
Siebert Rd. SE3 7E 78
Siege Ho. E1 9F 60
(off Sidney St.)
Siemens Rd. SE18 4H 79
Sienna Ter. NW2 7E 40
Sigdon Pas. E8 1E 60
Sigdon Rd. E8 1E 60
Sigers, The. Pinn 4F 36
Sigmund Freud Statue. 2B 58
Signmakers Yd. NW1 4F 58
(off Delancey St.)
Sigrist Sq. King T 5J 103
Silbury Av. Mitc 5C 106
Silbury Ho. SE26 9E 92
Silbury St. N1 6B 60
Silchester Rd. W10 9H 57
Silecroft Rd. Bexh 9L 81
Silesia Bldgs. E8 3F 60
Silex St. SE1 3M 75
Silicone Bus. Cen. Gnfd 5G 55
Silk Clo. SE12 4E 94
Silk Ct. E2 6E 60
(off Squirries St.)
Silkfield Rd. NW9 3C 40
Silk Ho. NW9 1B 40
Silk Mill Ct. Wat 8F 8
Silk Mill Rd. Wat 9F 8
Silk Mills Pas. SE13 1M 93
Silk Mills Path. SE13 1M 93
Silk Mills Sq. E9 2K 61
Silks Ct. E11 6D 46
Silkstream Pde. Edgw 8A 24
Silkstream Rd. Edgw 8A 24
Silk St. EC2 8A 60
Sillitoe Ho. N1 4B 60
(off Colville Est.)
Silsoe Ho. NW1 5F 58
Silsoe Rd. N22 9K 27
Silver Birch Av. E4 5K 29
Silverbirch Clo. N11 6E 26
Silverbirch Clo. SE6 9K 93
Silver Birch Clo. SE28 2E 80
Silver Birch Clo. Dart 1C 114
Silver Birch Clo. Uxb 1C 142
Silverbirch Ct. Chesh 4D 6
Silver Birch Gdns. E6 7K 63
Silver Birch M. Ilf 6A 32
Silverbirch Wlk. NW5 2E 58
Silverburn Ho. SW9 9M 75
(off Lothian Rd.)
Silver Chase Ct. Enf 2M 15
Silvercliffe Gdns. Barn 6C 14
Silver Clo. SE14 8J 77
Silver Clo. Harr 7B 22
Silver Cres. W4 5M 71
Silverdale. NW1 6G 59
(off Hampstead Rd.)
Silverdale. SE26 1G 109
Silverdale. Enf 6J 15
Silverdale Av. Ilf 3C 48
Silverdale Av. Oxs 6A 132
Silverdale Av. W on T 4D 116
Silverdale Cen., The.
Wemb 4K 55
Silverdale Clo. W7 2C 70
Silverdale Clo. N'holt 1K 53
Silverdale Clo. Sutt 6K 121
Silverdale Ct. EC1 7M 59
(off Goswell Rd.)
Silverdale Dri. SE9 8J 95
Silverdale Dri. Horn 1F 66
Silverdale Dri. Sun 6F 100
Silverdale Factory Cen.
Hay 4E 68
Silverdale Gdns. Hay 3E 68
Silverdale Ind. Est. Hay 4E 68
Silverdale Rd. E4 6B 30
Silverdale Rd. Bexh 1M 97
Silverdale Rd. Bush 7J 9
Silverdale Rd. Hay 3D 68
Silverdale Rd. Pet W 8A 112
Silverdale Rd. St P 7E 112
Silver Dell. Wat 9D 4
Silverdene. N12 6M 25
(off Thyra Gro.)
Silverglade Bus. Pk.
Chess 4G 133
Silverhall St. Iswth 2E 86
Silver Hill. Well E 1A 12
Silverholme Clo. Harr 5J 39
Silver Jubilee Way. Houn 1F 84
Silverland St. E16 2K 79
Silver La. Purl 4H 137
Silver La. W Wick 4B 126
Silverleigh Rd. T Hth 8K 107
Silvermead. E18 8E 30
Silvermere Av. Romf 6M 33
Silvermere Ct. Purl 4L 137
Silvermere Dri. N18 6H 29
Silvermere Rd. SE6 6M 93
Silver Pl. W1 9G 59
Silver Rd. SE13 2M 93
(in two parts)
Silver Rd. W12 1H 73
Silver Spring Clo. Eri 7M 81
Silverston Way. Stan 6G 23
Silver St. N18 4B 28
Silver St. Enf 5B 16
Silver St. Wal A 7J 7
Silverthorn. NW8 4M 57
(off Abbey Rd.)
Silverthorne Rd. SW8 1F 90
Silverthorn Gdns. E4 2L 29
Silverton Rd. W6 7H 73
Silvertown. 2H 79
Silvertown Way. E16 9C 62
Silver Tree Clo. W on T 5E 116
Silvertree La. Gnfd 6B 54
Silver Trees. Brick W 3K 5
Silver Wlk. SE16 2J 77
Silver Way. Hil 5F 142
Silver Way. Romf 1M 49
Silver Wing Ind. Est.
Croy 8K 123
Silverwood Clo. Beck 4L 109
Silverwood Clo. Croy 1K 139
Silverwood Clo. N'wd 8A 20
Silvester Ho. E1 9F 60
(off Varden St.)
Silvester Ho. E2 6G 61
(off Sceptre Rd.)
Silvester Ho. W11 9K 57
(off Basing St.)
Silvester Rd. SE22 4D 92
Silvester St. SE1 3B 76
Silvocea Way. E14 9B 62
Silwood Est. SE16 5G 77
Silwood St. SE16 5G 77
Simla Ho. SE1 3B 76
(off Kipling Est.)
Simmil Rd. Clay 7C 118
Simmons Clo. N20 2C 26
Simmons Clo. Chess 8G 119
Simmons La. E4 2B 30
Simmons Rd. SE18 6M
Simmons Way. N20 2C
Simms Clo. Cars 4C 1
Simms Gdns. N2 9A
Simms Rd. SE1 5E
Simnel Rd. SE12 6F
Simon Clo. W11 1K
Simon Ct. W9 6L
(off Saltram Cre
Simon Ct. Bush 8L
Simonds Rd. E10 7L
Simone Clo. Brom 5H 1
Simone Ct. SE26 9G
Simone Dri. Kenl 8A 1
Simon Peter Ct. Enf 4M
Simons Ct. N16 7D
Simons Wlk. E15 1B
Simpson Clo. N21 7J
Simpson Dri. W3 9B
Simpson Ho. NW8 6C
Simpson Ho. SE11 6K
Simpson Rd. Houn 5K
Simpson Rd. Rain 2D
Simpson Rd. Rich 1G 1
Simpson's Rd. E14 1M
Simpsons Rd. Brom 7E 1
Simpson St. SW11 1C
Simpson Way. Surb 1G 1
Simrose Ct. SW18 4L
Sims Clo. Romf 2D
Sims Wlk. SE3 3D
Sinclair Ct. Croy 4C 1
Sinclair Dri. Sutt 1M 1
Sinclair Gdns. W14 3H
Sinclair Gro. NW11 4H
Sinclair Ho. WC1 6J
(off Sandwich S
Sinclair Mans. W12 3H
(off Richmond Wa
Sinclair Pl. SE4 5L
Sinclair Rd. E4 5K
Sinclair Rd. W14 3H
Sinclare Clo. Enf 3D
Sinderby Clo. Borwd 3K
Singapore Rd. W13 2E
Singer St. EC2 6B
Single Street. 7M 1
Single St. Berr G 7M 1
Singleton Clo. SW17 4D 1
Singleton Clo. Croy 2A 1
Singleton Clo. Horn 9D
Singleton Rd. Dag 1K
Singleton Scarp. N12 5L 2
Singret Pl. Cow 7A 14
Sinnott Rd. E17 8H 2
Sion Ct. Twic 7F 8
Sion Rd. Twic 7F 8
Sippets Ct. Ilf 6B
Sipson. 7L 14
Sipson Clo. W Dray 7L 14
Sipson La.
W Dray & Hay 7L 14
Sipson Rd. W Dray 4K 14
(in two part
Sipson Way. W Dray 8L 14
Sir Abraham Dawes Cotts.
SW15 3J 8
Sir Alexander Clo. W3 2D 7
Sir Alexander Rd. W3 2D 7
Sir Cyril Black Way.
SW19 4L 10
Sirdar Rd. N22 1M 4
Sirdar Rd. W11 1H 7
Sirdar Rd. Mitc 3E 10
Sir Henry Floyd Ct. Stan 2F 2
Sirinham Point. SW8 7K 7
(off Meadow Rd
Sirius Building. E1 1H 7
(off Jardine Rd
Sirius Rd. N'wd 5E 2
Sir John Soane's Mus. 9K 5
Sir Nicholas Garrow Ho.
W10 7J 5
(off Kensal Rd
Sir Oswald Stoll Foundation, The.
SW6 8M 7
(off Fulham Rd
Sir Oswald Stoll Mans.
SW6 8M 7
(off Fulham Rd
Sir William Atkins Ho.
Eps 6B 13
Sir William Powell's Almshouses.
SW6 1J 8
Sise La. EC4 9B 6
(off Queen Victoria St
Siskin Clo. Borwd 6L 1
Siskin Clo. Bush 6J
Siskin Ho. SE16 5H 7
(off Tawny Way
Siskin Ho. Wat 8B
Sisley Rd. Bark 4C 6
Sispara Gdns. SW18 5K 8
Sissinghurst Clo. Brom 2C 11
Sissinghurst Ho. SE15 7G 7
(off Sharratt St.
Sissinghurst Rd. Croy 2E 12
Sissulu Ct. E6 4G 6
Sister Mabel's Way. SE15 8E 7
Sisters Av. SW11 2D 9
Sistova Rd. SW12 7F 9

Sisulu Pl.—S. Eaton Pl.

ulu Pl. SW9 ... 2L 91
ingbourne Av. N21 ... 8B 16
well Gro. Stan ... 5D 22
erst Clo. N'holt ... 2M 53
ill Ho. E2 ... 6D 60
(off Columbia Rd.)
iter Way. Dag ... 3M 65
vard Rd. N17 ... 8B 28
vard Rd. SW17 ... 9A 90
vard Rd. Brom ... 7F 110
Acres Est. N4 ... 7K 43
Bridges Ind. Est. SE1 ... 6E 76
th Av. E12 ... 9K 47
th Av. W10 ... 6J 57
th Av. Hay ... 2D 68
th Av. Wat ... 8H 5
th Cross Rd. Twic ... 9A 86
ardu Rd. NW2 ... 1J 57
arnings Ct. Wal A ... 6M 7
eena Hill. SW18 ... 6J 89
eet Hill La. Orp ... 3J 129
effington Rd. E6 ... 4K 63
eggs Ho. E14 ... 4A 78
(off Glengall St.)
egness Ho. N7 ... 3K 59
(off Sutterton St.)
elbrook St. SW18 ... 8A 90
elgill Rd. SW15 ... 3K 89
elley Rd. E15 ... 3D 62
elton Clo. E8 ... 2D 60
elton Rd. E7 ... 2E 62
elton's La. E10 ... 5M 45
elwith Rd. W6 ... 7G 73
enfrith Ho. SE15 ... 7F 76
(off Commercial Way)
erne Rd. King T ... 5H 103
erne Wlk. King T ... 5H 103
(off Skerne Rd.)
etchley Gdns. SE16 ... 6H 77
etty Rd. Enf ... 5D 16
ibbs La. Orp ... 7J 129
id Hill La. Warl ... 4D 140
iers St. E15 ... 4C 62
iffington Clo. SW2 ... 7L 91
illen Lodge. Pinn ... 8H 21
kinner Pl. SW1 ... 5E 74
(off Bourne St.)
kinners La. EC4 ... 1A 76
kinners La. Asht ... 9H 133
kinners La. Houn ... 9M 69
kinner's Row. SE10 ... 9M 77
kinner St. EC1 ... 6L 59
kipper Ct. Bark ... 4A 64
kipsey Av. E6 ... 6K 63
kipton Clo. N11 ... 6E 26
kipton Dri. Hay ... 4A 68
kipton Ho. SE4 ... 3J 93
kipwith Ho. EC1 ... 8L 59
(off Bourne Est.)
kipworth Rd. E9 ... 4G 61
kua Ct. SE8 ... 7K 77
(off Dorking Clo.)
kyline Ct. S Croy ... 5B 124
(off Park La.)
kyline Plaza Building. E1 ... 9E 60
(off Commercial Rd.)
kylines. E14 ... 3A 78
ky Peals Rd. Wfd G ... 7B 30
kyport Dri. W Dray ... 8H 143
Skyview Apartments.
S Croy ... 4A 124
(off Park St.)
Sladebrook Rd. SE3 ... 2H 95
Slade Ct. New Bar ... 5M 13
Sladedale Rd. SE18 ... 6C 80
Slade Gdns. Eri ... 9D 82
Slade Green. ... 9E 82
Slade Grn. Rd. Eri ... 8F 82
Slade Ho. Houn ... 5K 85
Sladen Pl. E5 ... 9F 44
Slades Clo. Enf ... 5L 15
Slades Dri. Chst ... 1A 112
Slades Gdns. Enf ... 4L 15
Slades Hill. Enf ... 5L 15
Slades Ri. Enf ... 5L 15
Slade, The. SE18 ... 7C 80
Slade Tower. E10 ... 7L 45
(off Leyton Grange Est.)
Slade Wlk. SE17 ... 7M 75
Slagrove Pl. SE4 ... 4L 93
Slaidburn St. SW10 ... 7A 74
Slaithwaite Rd. SE13 ... 3A 94
Slaney Ct. NW10 ... 3G 57
Slaney Pl. N7 ... 1L 59
Slaney Rd. Romf ... 3C 50
Slater Clo. SE18 ... 6L 79
Slatter. NW9 ... 7D 24
Slattery Rd. Felt ... 7H 85
Sleaford Grn. Wat ... 3H 21
Sleaford Ind. Est. SW8 ... 8G 75
Sleaford St. SW8 ... 8G 75
Sledmere Ct. Felt ... 7C 84
Sleigh Ho. E2 ... 6G 61
(off Bacton St.)
Slewins Clo. Horn ... 3G 51
Slewins La. Horn ... 3G 51
Slievemore Clo. SW4 ... 2H 91
Sligo Ho. E1 ... 7H 61
(off Beaumont Gro.)
Slindon Ct. N16 ... 8D 44
Slingsby Pl. WC2 ... 1J 75
Slippers Pl. SE16 ... 4F 76
Slipway Ho. E14 ... 6M 77
(off Burrells Wharf Sq.)
Sloane Av. SW3 ... 5C 74
Sloane Ct. E. SW3 ... 6E 74
Sloane Ct. W. SW3 ... 6E 74
Sloane Gdns. SW1 ... 5E 74
Sloane Gdns. Orp ... 5A 128
Sloane Ho. E9 ... 3G 61
(off Loddiges Rd.)
Sloane Sq. SW1 ... 5D 74
Sloane St. SW1 ... 3D 74
Sloane Ter. SW1 ... 5E 74
Sloane Ter. Mans. SW1 ... 5E 74
Sloane Wlk. Croy ... 1K 125
Slocum Clo. SE28 ... 1G 81
Sloman Ho. W10 ... 6J 57
(off Beethoven St.)
Slough La. NW9 ... 3A 40
Sly St. E1 ... 9F 60
Smaldon Clo. W Dray ... 4L 143
Smallberry Av. Iswth ... 1D 86
Smallbrook M. W2 ... 9B 58
Smalley Clo. N16 ... 8D 44
Smalley Rd. Est. N16 ... 8D 44
(off Smalley Clo.)
Smallwood Rd. SW17 ... 1B 106
Smarden Clo. Belv ... 6L 81
Smarden Gro. SE9 ... 1K 111
Smart Clo. Romf ... 8F 34
Smart's La. Lou ... 6H 19
Smart's Pl. N18 ... 5E 28
Smart's Pl. WC2 ... 9J 59
Smart St. E2 ... 6H 61
Smeaton Clo. Chess ... 8H 119
Smeaton Clo. Wal A ... 5L 7
Smeaton Ct. SE1 ... 4A 76
Smeaton Rd. SW18 ... 6L 89
Smeaton Rd. Enf ... 1L 17
Smeaton Rd. Wfd G ... 5K 31
Smeaton St. E1 ... 2F 76
Smedley St. SW8 & SW4 ... 1H 91
Smeed Rd. E3 ... 3L 61
Smiles Pl. SE13 ... 1A 94
Smitham Bottom La.
Purl ... 3G 137
Smitham Downs Rd.
Purl ... 5H 137
Smith Clo. SE16 ... 2H 77
Smithfield St. EC1 ... 8M 59
Smith Hill. Bren ... 7J 71
Smithies Ct. E15 ... 1A 62
Smithies Rd. SE2 ... 5F 80
Smith's Ct. W1 ... 1H 75
(off Gt. Windmill St.)
Smithson Rd. N17 ... 8B 28
Smiths Point. E13 ... 4E 62
(off Brooks Rd.)
Smith Sq. SW1 ... 4J 75
Smith St. SW3 ... 6D 74
Smith St. Surb ... 1K 119
Smith St. Wat ... 6G 9
Smith's Yd. SW18 ... 8A 90
Smiths Yd. Croy ... 5A 124
(off St George's Wlk.)
Smith Ter. SW3 ... 6D 74
Smithwood Clo. SW19 ... 7J 89
Smithy St. E1 ... 8G 61
Smock Wlk. Croy ... 1A 124
Smokehouse Yd. EC1 ... 8M 59
(off St John St.)
Smoothfield. Houn ... 3L 85
Smugglers Way. SW18 ... 3M 89
Smug Oak. ... 3M 5
Smug Oak Bus. Cen.
Brick W ... 2M 5
Smug Oak La. Brick W ... 3M 5
Smyrk's Rd. SE17 ... 6C 76
Smyrna Rd. NW6 ... 3L 57
Smythe Rd. S at H ... 5L 115
Smythe St. E14 ... 1M 77
Snag La. Cud ... 9D 128
(in two parts)
Snakes La. Barn ... 5F 14
Snakes La. E. Wfd G ... 6G 31
Snakes La. W. Wfd G ... 5E 30
Snaresbrook. ... 3E 46
Snaresbrook Dri. Stan ... 4H 23
Snaresbrook Hall. E18 ... 2E 46
Snaresbrook Rd. E11 ... 2C 46
Snarsgate St. W10 ... 8G 57
Sneath Av. NW11 ... 5K 41
Snellings Rd. W on T ... 7G 117
Snells Pk. N18 ... 6D 28
Sneyd Rd. NW2 ... 1G 57
Snipe Clo. Eri ... 8F 82
Snodland Clo. Orp ... 2L 141
Snowberry Clo. E15 ... 9B 46
Snowbury Rd. SW6 ... 1M 89
Snowden Av. Uxb ... 5F 142
Snowden Dri. NW9 ... 4C 40
Snowden St. EC2 ... 7C 60
Snow Dome (Proposed). ... 8L 63
Snowdon Cres. Hay ... 4A 68
Snowdon Rd. H'row A ... 5A 84
Snowdown Clo. SE20 ... 5G 109
Snowdrop Clo. Hamp ... 3L 101
Snowdrop Pl. Romf ... 7H 35
Snow Hill. EC1 ... 8M 59
Snow Hill Ct. EC1 ... 9M 59
(in two parts)
Snowman Ho. NW6 ... 4M 57
Snowsfields. SE1 ... 3B 76
Snowshill Rd. E12 ... 1J 63
Snowy Fielder Waye.
Iswth ... 1F 86
Soames St. SE15 ... 2D 92
Soames Wlk. N Mald ... 5C 104
Soane Clo. W5 ... 3H 71
Soane Ct. NW1 ... 3G 59
(off St Pancras Way)
Sobraon Ho. King T ... 4K 103
(off Elm Rd.)
Socket La. Brom ... 1F 126
Soham Rd. Enf ... 1K 17
Soho. ... 9G 59
Soho Sq. W1 ... 9H 59
Soho St. W1 ... 9H 59
Soho Theatre & Writers Cen.
... 9H 59
(off Dean St.)
Sojourner Truth Clo. E8 ... 2F 60
Solander Gdns. E1 ... 1G 77
Solar Ct. N3 ... 7M 25
Solar Ct. Wat ... 7D 8
Solar Ho. E6 ... 8L 63
Solarium Ct. SE1 ... 5D 76
(off Alscot Rd.)
Solar Way. Enf ... 9F 6
Soldene Ct. N7 ... 1K 59
(off George's Rd.)
Solebay St. E1 ... 7J 61
Solent Ho. E1 ... 8J 61
(off Ben Jonson Rd.)
Solent Ri. E13 ... 6E 62
Solent Rd. NW6 ... 1L 57
Solent Rd. H'row A ... 5D 144
Soley M. WC1 ... 6L 59
Solna Av. SW15 ... 4G 89
Solna Rd. N21 ... 1B 28
Solomon Av. N18 ... 4E 28
Solomon's Pas. SE15 ... 3F 92
Soloms Ct. Rd. Bans ... 9B 136
(in two parts)
Solon New Rd. SW4 ... 3J 91
Solon New Rd. Est. SW4 ... 3J 91
Solon Rd. SW2 ... 3J 91
Solway Clo. E8 ... 2D 60
(off Queensbridge Rd.)
Solway Clo. Houn ... 2J 85
Solway Ho. E1 ... 7H 61
(off Ernest St.)
Solway Rd. N22 ... 8M 27
Solway Rd. SE22 ... 3E 92
Somaford Gro. Barn ... 8B 14
Somali Rd. NW2 ... 1K 57
Somerby Rd. Bark ... 3B 64
Somercoates Clo. Barn ... 5C 14
Somer Ct. SW6 ... 7L 73
(off Anselm Rd.)
Somerden Rd. Orp ... 2H 129
Somerfield Ho. SE16 ... 6H 77
Somerfield Rd. N4 ... 7M 43
Somerford Clo. Pinn ... 2E 36
Somerford Gro. N16 ... 9D 44
Somerford Gro. N17 ... 7E 28
(in two parts)
Somerford Gro. Est. N16 ... 9D 44
Somerford St. E1 ... 7F 60
Somerford Way. SE16 ... 3J 77
Somerhill Av. Sidc ... 6F 96
Somerhill Rd. Well ... 1F 96
Somerleyton Pas. SW9 ... 3M 91
Somerleyton Rd. SW9 ... 3L 91
Somersby Gdns. Ilf ... 3K 47
Somers Clo. NW1 ... 5H 59
Somers Cres. W2 ... 9C 58
Somerset Av. SW20 ... 6F 104
Somerset Av. Chess ... 6H 119
Somerset Av. Well ... 4D 96
Somerset Clo. N17 ... 9B 28
Somerset Clo. Eps ... 1B 134
Somerset Clo. N Mald ... 1C 120
Somerset Clo. W on T ... 7F 116
Somerset Clo. Wfd G ... 8E 30
Somerset Ct. W7 ... 9D 54
(off Copley Clo.)
Somerset Ct. Buck H ... 2G 31
Somerset Est. SW11 ... 9B 74
Somerset Gdns. N6 ... 5E 42
Somerset Gdns. N17 ... 7C 28
Somerset Gdns. SE13 ... 1M 93
Somerset Gdns. SW16 ... 7K 107
Somerset Gdns. Horn ... 6L 51
Somerset Gdns. Tedd ... 2C 102
Somerset Hall. N17 ... 7C 28
Somerset House. ... 1K 75
Somerset Lodge. Bren ... 7H 71
Somerset Rd. E17 ... 4L 45
Somerset Rd. N17 ... 1D 44
Somerset Rd. N18 ... 5D 28
Somerset Rd. NW4 ... 2G 41
Somerset Rd. SW19 ... 9H 89
Somerset Rd. W4 ... 4B 72
Somerset Rd. W13 ... 2F 70
Somerset Rd. Bren ... 7G 71
Somerset Rd. Dart ... 5F 98
Somerset Rd. Enf ... 2L 17
Somerset Rd. Harr ... 3A 38
Somerset Rd. King T ... 6K 103
Somerset Rd. New Bar ... 7M 13
Somerset Rd. Orp ... 2E 128
Somerset Rd. S'hall ... 8K 53
Somerset Rd. Tedd ... 2C 102
Somerset Sq. W14 ... 3J 73
Somerset Waye. Houn ... 7J 69
Somersham Rd. Bexh ... 1J 97
Somers Pl. SW2 ... 6K 91
Somers Rd. E17 ... 2K 45
Somers Rd. SW2 ... 5K 91
Somers Town. ... 6H 59
Somers Way. Bush ... 9A 10
Somerton Av. Rich ... 2M 87
Somerton Clo. Purl ... 7L 137
Somerton Rd. NW2 ... 8J 41
Somerton Rd. SE15 ... 3F 92
Somertrees Av. SE12 ... 8F 94
Somervell Rd. Harr ... 1K 53
Somerville Av. SW13 ... 7F 72
Somerville Point. SE16 ... 3K 77
Somerville Rd. SE20 ... 4H 109
Somerville Rd. Dart ... 5K 99
Somerville Rd. Romf ... 4G 49
Sonderburg Rd. N7 ... 7K 43
Sondes St. SE17 ... 7B 76
Sonia Clo. Wat ... 9G 9
Sonia Ct. Edgw ... 7K 23
Sonia Ct. Harr ... 4D 38
Sonia Gdns. N12 ... 4A 26
Sonia Gdns. NW10 ... 9D 40
Sonia Gdns. Houn ... 8L 69
Sonning Gdns. Hamp ... 3J 101
Sonning Ho. E2 ... 6D 60
(off Swanfield St.)
Sonning Rd. SE25 ... 1E 124
Sontan Ct. Twic ... 7B 86
Soper Clo. E4 ... 5K 29
Soper Clo. SE23 ... 7H 93
Soper M. Enf ... 2L 17
Sophia Clo. N7 ... 2K 59
Sophia Ho. W6 ... 6G 73
(off Queen Caroline St.)
Sophia Rd. E10 ... 6M 45
Sophia Rd. E16 ... 9F 62
Sophia Sq. SE16 ... 1J 77
(off Sovereign Cres.)
Sopwith. NW9 ... 7D 24
Sopwith Av. Chess ... 7J 119
Sopwith Clo. Big H ... 8H 141
Sopwith Clo. King T ... 2K 103
Sopwith Rd. Houn ... 8G 69
Sopwith Way. SW8 ... 8F 74
Sopwith Way. King T ... 5J 103
Sorbie Clo. Wey ... 8B 116
Sorensen Ct. E10 ... 7M 45
(off Leyton Grange Est.)
Sorrel Bank. Croy ... 2J 139
Sorrel Clo. SE28 ... 2E 80
Sorrel Gdns. E6 ... 8J 63
Sorrel La. E14 ... 9B 62
Sorrell Clo. SE14 ... 8J 77
Sorrell Clo. SW9 ... 1L 91
Sorrel Wlk. Romf ... 1D 50
Sorrento Rd. Sutt ... 5L 121
Sotheby Rd. N5 ... 8M 43
Sotheran Clo. E8 ... 4E 60
Sotherby Lodge. E2 ... 5G 61
(off Sewardstone Rd.)
Sotheron Rd. SW6 ... 8M 73
Sotheron Rd. Wat ... 5G 9
Soudan Rd. SW11 ... 9D 74
Souldern Rd. W14 ... 4H 73
Souldern St. Wat ... 7F 8
Sounds Lodge. Swan ... 1A 130
S. Access Rd. E17 ... 5J 45
Southacre. W2 ... 9C 58
(off Hyde Pk. Cres.)
Southacre Way. Pinn ... 8G 21
South Acton. ... 3M 71
S. Africa Rd. W12 ... 2F 72
Southall. ... 2K 69
Southall Ct. S'hall ... 1K 69
Southall Enterprise Cen.
S'hall ... 3L 69
Southall Green. ... 4J 69
Southall Ho. Romf ... 6J 35
(off Kingsbridge Cir.)
Southall La. Houn & S'hall ... 7F 68
Southall Pl. SE1 ... 3B 76
Southampton Bldgs. WC2 ... 8L 59
Southampton Gdns. Mitc ... 9J 107
Southampton M. E16 ... 2F 78
Southampton Pl. WC1 ... 8J 59
Southampton Rd. NW5 ... 1D 58
Southampton Rd.
H'row A ... 5C 144
Southampton Row. WC1 ... 8J 59
Southampton St. WC2 ... 1J 75
Southampton Way. SE5 ... 8B 76
Southampton Way.
Stanw ... 5C 144
Southam St. W10 ... 7J 57
South App. N'wd ... 3B 20
S. Audley St. W1 ... 1E 74
South Av. E4 ... 9M 17
South Av. N2 ... 2M 41
South Av. NW10 ... 7G 57
South Av. Cars ... 9E 122
South Av. Rich ... 1L 87
South Av. S'hall ... 1K 69
South Av. Gdns. S'hall ... 1K 69
South Bank. Surb ... 1J 119
Southbank. Th Dit ... 2F 118
S. Bank Bus. Cen. SW8 ... 7H 75
South Bank Cen. ... 2K 75
S. Bank Ter. Surb ... 1J 119
South Bank University
(New Kent Rd. Hall)
... 4A 76
(off New Kent Rd.)
South Barnet. ... 1E 26
South Beddington. ... 8H 123
South Bermondsey. ... 6G 77
S. Birkbeck Rd. E11 ... 8B 46
S. Black Lion La. W6 ... 6E 72
South Block. SE1 ... 3K 75
(off Westminster Bri. Rd.)
S. Bolton Gdns. SW5 ... 6A 74
S. Border, The. Purl ... 3H 137
Southborough. ... 9K 111
(Bromley)
Southborough. ... 3J 119
(Surbiton)
Southborough Clo. Surb ... 3H 119
Southborough Ho. SE17 ... 6C 76
(off Surrey Gro.)
Southborough La. Brom ... 9J 111
Southborough Rd. E9 ... 4H 61
Southborough Rd. Brom ... 7J 111
Southborough Rd. Surb ... 3J 119
S. Boundary Rd. E12 ... 8K 47
Southbourne. Brom ... 2E 126
Southbourne Av. NW9 ... 9A 24
Southbourne Clo. Pinn ... 5J 37
Southbourne Ct. NW9 ... 9A 24
Southbourne Cres. NW4 ... 2J 41
Southbourne Gdns. SE12 ... 4F 94
Southbourne Gdns. Ilf ... 1A 64
Southbourne Gdns. Ruis ... 6F 36
S. Branch Av. NW10 ... 7G 57
Southbridge Pl. Croy ... 6A 124
Southbridge Rd. Croy ... 6A 124
Southbridge Way. S'hall ... 3J 69
South Bromley. ... 9B 62
Southbrook Dri. Chesh ... 1D 6
Southbrook M. SE12 ... 5D 94
Southbrook Rd. SE12 ... 5D 94
Southbrook Rd. SW16 ... 5J 107
Southbury. NW8 ... 4A 58
(off Loudoun Rd.)
Southbury Av. Enf ... 6E 16
Southbury Clo. Horn ... 1H 67
Southbury Rd. Enf ... 5C 16
S. Carriage Dri.
SW7 & SW1 ... 3B 74
South Chingford. ... 5K 29
Southchurch Ct. E6 ... 5K 63
(off High St. S.)
Southchurch Rd. E6 ... 5K 63
S. Circular Rd. SW15 ... 3E 88
South Clo. N6 ... 4F 42
South Clo. Barn ... 5K 13
South Clo. Bexh ... 3H 97
South Clo. Dag ... 4L 65
South Clo. Mord ... 1L 121
South Clo. Pinn ... 5K 37
South Clo. Twic ... 9L 85
South Clo. W Dray ... 4K 143
S. Colonnade, The. E14 ... 2L 77
Southcombe St. W14 ... 5J 73
S. Common Rd. Uxb ... 2C 142
Southcote Av. Felt ... 8D 84
Southcote Av. Surb ... 2M 119
Southcote Ri. Ruis ... 5B 36
Southcote Rd. E17 ... 3H 45
Southcote Rd. N19 ... 9G 43
Southcote Rd. SE25 ... 9F 108
Southcote Rd. S Croy ... 2C 138
S. Countess Rd. E17 ... 1K 45
South Cres. E16 ... 7B 62
South Cres. WC1 ... 8H 59
Southcroft Av. Well ... 2C 96
Southcroft Av. W Wick ... 4A 126
Southcroft Rd.
SW17 & SW16 ... 3E 106
Southcroft Rd. Orp ... 5C 128
S. Cross Rd. Ilf ... 3A 48
S. Croxted Rd. SE21 ... 9B 92
South Croydon. ... 7B 124
Southdale. Chig ... 6B 32
Southdean Gdns. SW19 ... 8K 89
South Dene. NW7 ... 3B 24
Southdene Ct. N11 ... 3F 26
Southdown. N7 ... 2J 59
Southdown Av. W7 ... 4E 70
Southdown Cres. Harr ... 6A 38
Southdown Cres. Ilf ... 3C 48
Southdown Dri. SW20 ... 4H 105
Southdown Rd. SW20 ... 5H 105
Southdown Rd. Cars ... 1E 136
Southdown Rd. Horn ... 5F 50
Southdown Rd. W on T ... 6J 117
South Dri. E12 ... 8J 47
South Dri. Bans ... 5C 136
South Dri. Coul ... 7H 137
South Dri. Orp ... 7C 128
South Dri. Romf ... 1G 51
South Dri. Ruis ... 6C 36
South Dri. Sutt ... 2J 135
S. Ealing Rd. W5 ... 3H 71
S. Eastern Av. N9 ... 3D 28
South Eastern University.
... 8K 43
S. Eaton Pl. SW1 ... 5E 74

S. Eden Pk. Rd.—Spikes Bri. Rd.

S. Eden Pk. Rd. Beck 1M 125
S. Edwardes Sq. W8 4K 73
Southend. 1B 110
South End. W8 4M 73
South End. Croy 6A 124
Southend Arterial Rd.
Gid P 9H 35
S. End Clo. NW3 9C 42
Southend Clo. SE9 5M 95
Southend Cres. SE9 5M 95
S. End Grn. NW3 9C 42
Southend La.
SE26 & SE6 1K 109
Southend Rd. E4 & E17 5J 29
Southend Rd. E6 3K 63
Southend Rd.
E18 & Wfd G 8E 30
S. End Rd. NW3 9C 42
Southend Rd. Beck 5L 109
S. End Rd. Rain 4E 66
S. End Row. W8 4M 73
Southerland Clo. Wey 6A 116
Southern Av. SE25 7D 108
Southern Av. Felt 7E 84
Southern Dri. Lou 8K 19
Southerngate Way. SE14 8J 77
Southern Gro. E3 6K 61
Southernhay. Lou 7H 19
Southern Perimeter Rd.
H'row A 4A 144
Southern Pl. Swan 8B 114
Southern Rd. E13 5F 62
Southern Rd. N2 2D 42
Southern Row. W10 7J 57
Southern St. N1 5K 59
Southern Way. Romf 4L 49
Southernwood Retail Pk.
SE1 6D 76
Southerton Rd. W6 5G 73
S. Esk Rd. E7 2G 63
Southey Ho. SE17 6A 76
(off Browning St.)
Southey M. E16 2E 78
Southey Rd. N15 3C 44
Southey Rd. SW9 9L 75
Southey Rd. SW19 4L 105
Southey St. SE20 4H 109
Southfield. Barn 8H 13
Southfield Av. Wat 2G 9
Southfield Clo. Uxb 7E 142
Southfield Cotts. W7 3D 70
(in two parts)
Southfield Ct. E11 8D 46
Southfield Gdns. Twic 1D 102
Southfield Pk. Harr 2M 37
Southfield Pl. Wey 9A 116
Southfield Rd. N17 9C 28
Southfield Rd. W4 3B 72
Southfield Rd. Chst 7E 112
Southfield Rd. Enf 8F 16
Southfield Rd. Wal X 5E 6
Southfields. 6L 89
Southfields. NW4 1F 40
Southfields. E Mol 1C 118
Southfields. Swan 4C 114
Southfields Av. Ashf 3A 100
Southfields Ct. Sutt 4L 121
Southfields M. SW18 5L 89
Southfields Pas. SW18 5L 89
Southfields Rd. SW18 5L 89
Southfleet Rd. Orp 5C 128
South Gdns. SW19 4B 106
South Gdns. Wemb 7L 39
Southgate. 1H 27
Southgate Av. Felt 1B 100
Southgate Cir. N14 1H 27
Southgate Gro. N1 3B 60
Southgate Ho. Chesh 3E 6
Southgate Ind. Est.
N14 9H 15
Southgate Rd. N1 4B 60
S. Gipsy Rd. Well 2H 97
S. Glade, The. Bex 7K 97
South Grn. NW9 8C 24
South Gro. E17 3K 45
South Gro. N6 6E 42
South Gro. N15 3B 44
South Gro. Ho. N6 6E 42
South Hackney. 3H 61
S. Hall Clo. F'ham 2K 131
S. Hall Dri. Rain 8F 66
South Hampstead. 3A 58
South Harrow. 8A 38
S. Harrow Ind. Est. S Harr 7A 38
South Herts Golf Course.
9L 13
South Hill. Chst 3K 111
South Hill. N'wd 8C 20
S. Hill Av. Harr 8A 38
S. Hill Gro. Harr 9C 38
S. Hill Pk. NW3 9C 42
S. Hill Pk. Gdns. NW3 8C 42
S. Hill Rd. Brom 7C 110
Southholme Clo. SE19 5C 108
South Hornchurch. 4D 66
Southill Ct. Brom 9D 110
Southill La. Pinn 2E 36
Southill Rd. Chst 4J 111
Southill St. E14 9M 61
S. Island Pl. SW9 8K 75
South Kensington. 5B 74
S. Kensington Sta. Arc.
SW7 5B 74
(off Pelham St.)
South Lambeth. 8J 75
S. Lambeth Pl. SW8 6J 75
S. Lambeth Rd. SW8 7J 75
Southland Rd. SE18 8D 80
Southlands Av. Orp 6B 128
Southlands Clo. Coul 9K 137
Southlands Dri. SW19 8H 89
Southlands Gro. Brom 7J 111
Southlands Rd. Brom 9G 111
Southland Way. Houn 4B 86
South La. King T 7H 103
(in two parts)
South La. N Mald 8B 104
South La. W. N Mald 8B 104
South Lodge. E16 2F 78
(off Audley Dri.)
South Lodge. NW8 5B 58
South Lodge. SW7 3C 74
(off Knightsbridge)
South Lodge. Twic 5A 86
S. Lodge Av. Mitc 8J 107
S. Lodge Cres. Enf 6H 15
(in two parts)
S. Lodge Dri. N14 6H 15
S. Lodge Rd. W on T 9E 116
South London Crematorium.
Mitc 6G 107
***South London Gallery.* 9C 76**
(off Peckham Rd.)
Southly Clo. Sutt 5L 121
South Mall. N9 3E 28
(off Plevna Rd.)
South Mead. NW9 8D 24
South Mead. Eps 9D 120
Southmead Cres. Chesh 3E 6
South Meadows. Wemb 1K 55
Southmead Rd. SW19 7J 89
S. Molton La. W1 9F 58
S. Molton Rd. E16 9E 62
S. Molton St. W1 9F 58
Southmont Rd. Esh 4C 118
Southmoor Way. E9 2K 61
South Mt. N20 2A 26
(off High Rd.)
South Norwood. 8D 108
South Norwood Country Pk.
8G 109
S. Norwood Hill. SE25 5C 108
S. Oak Rd. SW16 1K 107
Southold Ri. SE9 9K 95
Southolm St. SW11 9F 74
S. Ordnance Rd. Enf 2L 17
Southover. N12 3L 25
Southover. Brom 2E 110
South Oxhey. 4H 21
South Pde. SW3 6B 74
South Pde. W4 5B 72
South Pde. Edgw 9L 23
South Pde. Wall 8G 123
S. Park Ct. Beck 4L 109
S. Park Cres. SE6 7C 94
S. Park Cres. Ilf 8B 48
S. Park Dri. Ilf 7C 48
S. Park Gro. N Mald 8A 104
S. Park Hill Rd. S Croy 7B 124
S. Park M. SW6 2M 89
S. Park Rd. SW19 3L 105
S. Park Rd. Ilf 8B 48
S. Park Ter. Ilf 8C 48
S. Park Vs. Ilf 9C 48
S. Park Way. Ruis 2G 53
South Pl. EC2 8B 60
South Pl. Enf 7G 17
South Pl. Surb 2K 119
South Pl. Wal A 6J 7
South Pl. M. EC2 8B 60
Southport Rd. SE18 5B 80
S. Quay Plaza. E14 3M 77
Southridge Pl. SW20 4H 105
South Riding. Brick W 3K 5
South Ri. W2 1C 74
(off St George's Fields)
South Ri. Cars 1C 136
South Ri. Way. SE18 6B 80
South Rd. N9 1E 28
South Rd. SE23 8H 93
South Rd. SW19 3A 106
South Rd. W5 5H 71
South Rd. Chad H 4J 49
South Rd. Edgw 8M 23
South Rd. Eri 8D 82
South Rd. Felt 2H 101
South Rd. Hamp 3J 101
South Rd. Harr 6E 38
South Rd. L Hth 3G 49
South Rd. S'hall 3K 69
South Rd. Twic 9B 86
South Rd. W Dray 4L 143
South Rd. Wey 7A 116
South Row. SE3 1D 94
South Ruislip. 9G 37
Southsea Av. Wat 6E 8
Southsea Ho. H Hill 5H 35
(off Darlington Gdns.)
Southsea Rd. King T 8J 103
S. Sea St. SE16 4K 77
South Side. N15 2D 44
South Side. W6 4D 72
Southside Comn. SW19 3G 105
Southside House. 3G 105
Southside Ind. Est. SW8 9G 75
(off Havelock Ter.)
Southspring. Sidc 6B 96
South Sq. NW11 4M 41
South Sq. WC1 8L 59
South St. W1 2E 74
South St. Brom 6E 110
South St. Enf 7G 17
South St. Eps 5B 134
South St. Iswth 2E 86
South St. Rain 5A 66
South St. Romf 3C 50
(in two parts)
S. Tenter St. E1 1D 76
South Ter. SW7 5C 74
South Ter. F'ham 2K 131
South Ter. Surb 1J 119
South Tottenham. 3D 44
Southvale. SE19 3C 108
South Va. Harr 9C 38
Southvale Rd. SE3 1C 94
South Vw. Brom 6G 111
South Vw. Eps 2L 133
Southview Av. NW10 1D 56
Southview Clo. SW17 2E 106
S. View Clo. Bex 5K 97
S. View Clo. Swan 8E 114
S. View Ct. SE19 4A 108
Southview Cres. Ilf 4M 47
S. View Dri. E18 1F 46
S. View Dri. Upm 8L 51
Southview Gdns. Wall 9G 123
Southview Pde. Rain 6B 66
S. View Rd. N8 1H 43
Southview Rd. Brom 1B 110
S. View Rd. Dart 9H 99
S. View Rd. Lou 8K 19
S. View Rd. Pinn 6F 20
Southviews. S Croy 2H 139
South Vs. NW1 2H 59
Southville. SW8 9H 75
Southville Clo. Eps 1B 134
Southville Clo. Felt 7C 84
Southville Cres. Felt 7C 84
Southville Rd. Felt 7C 84
Southville Rd. Th Dit 2E 118
South Wlk. Hay 8B 52
South Wlk. W Wick 5C 126
Southwark. 2A 76
Southwark Bri.
SE1 & EC4 1A 76
Southwark Bri. Bus. Cen.
SE1 2A 76
(off Southwark Bri. Rd.)
Southwark Bri. Office Village.
SE1 2A 76
(off Southwark Bri. Rd.)
Southwark Bri. Rd. SE1 4M 75
Southwark Cathedral. 2B 76
Southwark Ho. Borwd 4L 11
(off Stratfield Rd.)
Southwark Pk. Est. SE16 4F 76
Southwark Pk. Rd. SE16 5D 76
Southwark Pl. Brom 7K 111
Southwark St. SE1 2M 75
Southwater Clo. E14 9K 61
Southwater Clo. Beck 4M 109
South Way. N9 2G 29
South Way. N11 6G 27
Southway. N20 2L 25
Southway. NW11 4M 41
Southway. SW20 9G 105
South Way. Ab L 6B 4
South Way. Cars 2B 136
South Way. Croy 5J 125
South Way. Harr 2L 37
South Way. Hayes 2E 126
Southway. Wall 6G 123
South Way. Wemb 1L 55
Southway Clo. W12 3F 72
(off Scott's Rd.)
Southways Pde. Ilf 3L 47
S. Weald Dri. Wal A 6K 7
Southwell Av. N'holt 2L 53
Southwell Gdns. SW7 5A 74
Southwell Gro. Rd. E11 7C 46
Southwell Ho. SE16 5F 76
(off Anchor St.)
Southwell Rd. SE5 2A 92
Southwell Rd. Croy 1L 123
Southwell Rd. Kent 4H 39
S. Western Rd. Twic 5E 86
S. W. India Dock Entrance.
E14 3A 78
South West Middlesex
Crematorium. Felt 7J 85
Southwest Rd. E11 6B 46
S. Wharf Rd. W2 9B 58
Southwick M. W2 9B 58
Southwick Pl. W2 9C 58
Southwick St. W2 9C 58
Southwick Yd. W2 9C 58
(off Titchborne Row)
South Wimbledon. 3M 105
Southwold Dri. Bark 1E 64
Southwold Mans. W9 6L 57
(off Widley Rd.)
Southwold Rd. E5 7F 44
Southwold Rd. Bex 5M 97
Southwold Rd. Wat 1G 9
Southwood Av. N6 5F 42
Southwood Av. Coul 7G 137
Southwood Av. King T 5A 104
Southwood Clo. Brom 8K 111
Southwood Clo. Wor Pk 3H 121
Southwood Ct. EC1 6M 59
(off Wynyatt St.)
Southwood Ct. NW11 3M 41
Southwood Dri. Surb 2A 120
South Woodford. 9E 30
S. Woodford to Barking Relief Rd.
E11 3H 47
Southwood Gdns. Esh 5E 118
Southwood Gdns. Ilf 2M 47
Southwood Hall. N6 4F 42
Southwood Heights. N6 5F 42
Southwood Ho. W11 1J 73
(off Avondale Pk. Rd.)
Southwood La. N6 6E 42
Southwood Lawn Rd. N6 5E 42
Southwood Mans. N6 4E 42
(off Southwood La.)
Southwood Pk. N6 5E 42
Southwood Rd. SE9 8M 95
Southwood Rd. SE28 2F 80
Southwood Smith Ho. E2 6F 60
(off Florida St.)
Southwood Smith St. N1 4M 59
S. Worple Av. SW14 2C 88
S. Worple Way. SW14 2B 88
Southwyck Ho. SW9 3M 91
Sovereign Bus. Cen. Enf 5K 17
Sovereign Clo. E1 1F 76
Sovereign Clo. W5 8G 55
Sovereign Clo. Purl 2K 137
Sovereign Clo. Ruis 6C 36
Sovereign Ct. Houn 2L 85
Sovereign Ct. N'wd 8E 20
Sovereign Ct. S Croy 7A 124
(off Warham Rd.)
Sovereign Ct. S at H 5M 115
(off Ship La.)
Sovereign Ct. Wat 6E 8
Sovereign Ct. W Mol 8K 101
Sovereign Cres. SE16 1J 77
Sovereign Gro. Wemb 8H 39
Sovereign Ho. E1 7F 60
(off Cambridge Heath Rd.)
Sovereign Ho. SE18 4K 79
(off Leda Rd.)
Sovereign M. E2 5D 60
Sovereign M. Barn 5D 14
Sovereign Pk. NW10 7M 55
Sovereign Pk. Trad. Est.
NW10 7M 55
Sovereign Pl. Harr 3D 38
Sovereign Rd. Bark 6G 65
Sowerby Clo. SE9 4J 95
Sowrey Av. Rain 2D 66
Space Waye. Felt 4E 84
Spa Clo. SE25 5C 108
Spa Ct. SW16 1K 107
Spa Dri. Eps 6L 133
Spafield St. EC1 7L 59
Spa Grn. Est. EC1 6M 59
Spa Hill. SE19 5B 108
Spalding Ho. SE4 3J 93
Spalding Rd. NW4 5G 41
Spalding Rd. SW17 2F 106
Spanbrook. Chig 3M 31
Spanby Rd. E3 7L 61
Spaniards Clo. NW3 6B 42
Spaniards End. NW3 6A 42
Spaniards Rd. NW3 7A 42
Spanish Pl. W1 9E 58
Spanish Rd. SW18 4A 90
Spanswick Lodge. N15 2M 43
Spareleaze Hill. Lou 6K 19
Sparepenny La.
Eyns & F'ham 4H 131
Sparkbridge Rd. Harr 2C 38
Sparke Ter. E16 9D 62
(off Clarkson Rd.)
Sparkford Gdns. N11 5E 26
Sparks Clo. W3 9B 56
Sparks Clo. Dag 7H 49
Sparks Clo. Hamp 3J 101
Spa Rd. SE16 4D 76
Sparrick's Row. SE1 3B 76
Sparrow Clo. Hamp 3J 101
Sparrow Dri. Orp 3A 128
Sparrow Farm Dri. Felt 6G 85
Sparrow Farm Rd. Eps 6E 120
Sparrow Grn. Dag 8M 49
Sparrow Ho. E1 7G 61
(off Cephas Av.)
Sparrows Herne. Bush 9M 9
Sparrows La. SE9 6A 96
Sparrows Way. Bush 9A 10
Sparsholt Clo. Bark 4C 64
(off Sparsholt Rd.)
Sparsholt Rd. N19 6K 43
Sparsholt Rd. Bark 4C 64
Sparta St. SE10 9A 78
Speaker's Corner. 1D 74
Speakers Ct. Croy 3B 124
Speakman Ho. SE4 2J 93
(off Arica Rd.)
Spearman Ho. E14 9L 61
(off Up. North St.)
Spearman St. SE18 7L
Spear M. SW5 5L
Spearpoint Gdns. Ilf 3D
Spears Rd. N19 6J
Speart La. Houn 8J
Spectacle Works. E13 6G
Spedan Clo. NW3 8A
Speedbird Way. Harm 8G 1
Speed Highwalk. EC2 8A
(off Silk
Speed Ho. EC2 8B
(off Silk
Speedway Ind. Est. Hay 3B
Speedwell Ho. N12 4M
Speedwell St. SE8 8L
Speedy Pl. WC1 6J
(off Cromer
Speer Rd. Th Dit 1D 1
Speirs Clo. N Mald 1D 1
Speke Hill. SE9 9K
Speke Rd. T Hth 6B 1
Speke's Monument. 2A
Speldhurst Clo. Brom 9D 1
Speldhurst Rd. E9 3H
Speldhurst Rd. W4 4B
Spellbrook Wlk. N1 4A
Spelman Ho. E1 8E
(off Spelman S
Spelman St. E1 8E
(in two par
Spelthorne Gro. Sun 4D 1
Spelthorne La. Ashf 5A 1
Spence Clo. SE16 3K
Spencer Av. N13 6K
Spencer Av. Hay 8E
Spencer Clo. N3 9L
Spencer Clo. NW10 6K
Spencer Clo. Orp 4C 1
Spencer Clo. Uxb 6A 1
Spencer Clo. Wfd G 5G
Spencer Ct. Orp 7A 1
Spencer Dri. N2 4A
Spencer Gdns. SE9 4K
Spencer Gdns. SW14 4A
Spencer Hill Rd. SW19 4J 1
***Spencer House.* 2G**
(off St James's P
Spencer Ho. NW4 3F
Spencer Mans. W14 7J
(off Queen's Club Gdn
Spencer M. SW9 9K
(off S. Lambeth R
Spencer M. W6 7J 7
Spencer Park. 4B
Spencer Pk. SW18 4B 9
Spencer Pk. E Mol 9A 10
Spencer Pl. N1 3M 5
Spencer Pl. Croy 2B 12
Spencer Ri. NW5 9F 4
Spencer Rd. E6 4H 6
Spencer Rd. E17 9A 3
Spencer Rd. N8 3K 4
(in two parts
Spencer Rd. N11 4F 2
Spencer Rd. N17 8E 2
Spencer Rd. SW11 3B 9
Spencer Rd. SW19 3J 10
Spencer Rd. SW20 5F 10
Spencer Rd. W3 2A 7
Spencer Rd. W4 8A 7
Spencer Rd. Brom 4D 11
Spencer Rd. E Mol 8A 10
Spencer Rd. Harr 9C 2
Spencer Rd. Ilf 6D 4
Spencer Rd. Iswth 9A 7
Spencer Rd. Mitc 7E 10
Spencer Rd. Mit J 2E 12
Spencer Rd. Rain 6B 6
Spencer Rd. S Croy 7C 12
Spencer Rd. Twic 9C 8
Spencer Rd. Wemb 7G 3
Spencer St. EC1 6M 5
Spencer St. S'hall 3H 6
Spencer Wlk. NW3 9B 4
Spencer Wlk. SW15 3H 8
Spenlow Ho. SE16 4E 7
(off Jamaica Rd
Spenser Cres. Upm 5M 5
Spenser Gro. N16 1C 6
(in two parts
Spenser M. SE21 8B 9
Spenser Rd. SE24 4M 9
Spenser St. SW1 4G 7
Spensley Wlk. N16 8B 4
Speranza Rd. SE18 6D 8
Sperling Rd. N17 9C 2
Spert St. E14 1J 7
Speyside. N14 8G 1
Spey St. E14 8A 6
Spey Way. Romf 7C 3
Spezia Rd. NW10 5E 5
Spice Ct. E1 1E 7
Spice Quay Heights. SE1 2D 7
Spicer Clo. SW9 1M 9
Spicer Clo. W on T 1G 117
Spicer Ct. Enf 5C 1
Spicers Fld. Oxs 5B 132
Spice's Yd. Croy 6A 124
Spielman Rd. Dart 3K 9
Spigurnell Rd. N17 8B 2
Spikes Bri. Rd. S'hall 9J 53

Spilsby Clo.—Stanhope Gdns.

Spilsby Clo. NW9 8C 24
Spilsby Rd. H Hill 7H 35
Spindle Clo. SE18 4J 79
Spindlewood Gdns. Croy 6C 124
Spindrift Av. E14 5L 77
Spinel Clo. SE18 6D 80
Spingate Clo. Horn 1H 67
Spinnaker Clo. Bark 6F 64
Spinnaker Ct. Hamp W 5H 103 (off Beckets Pl.)
Spinnaker Ho. E14 3L 77 (off Byng St.)
Spinnells Rd. Harr 6K 37
Spinney Clo. Beck 8M 109
Spinney Clo. N Mald 9C 104
Spinney Clo. Rain 5C 66
Spinney Clo. W Dray 1J 143
Spinney Clo. Wor Pk 4D 120
Spinney Cft. Oxs 7B 132
Spinney Dri. Felt 6A 84
Spinney Gdns. SE19 2D 108
Spinney Gdns. Dag 1J 65
Spinney Oak. Brom 6J 111
Spinneys, The. Brom 6K 111
Spinney, The. N21 9L 15
Spinney, The. SW13 8F 72
Spinney, The. SW16 9G 91
Spinney, The. Barn 4M 13
Spinney, The. Chesh 3B 6
Spinney, The. Eps 5C 134
Spinney, The. Lou 6M 19
Spinney, The. Oxs 4A 132
Spinney, The. Purl 3M 137
Spinney, The. Sidc 2J 113
Spinney, The. Stan 4J 23
Spinney, The. Sun 5E 100
Spinney, The. Sutt 6G 121
Spinney, The. Swan 6C 114
Spinney, The. Wat 3E 8
Spinney, The. Wemb 8E 38
Spire Ho. W2 1A 74 (off Lancaster Ga.)
Spires Shop. Cen., The. Barn 5J 13
Spires, The. Dart 8H 99
Spirit Quay. E1 2E 76
Spitalfields. 8D 60
Spital Sq. E1 8C 60
Spital St. E1 8E 60
Spital St. Dart 5H 99
Spital Yd. E1 8C 60
Spitfire Est., The. Houn 6G 69
Spitfire Rd. H'row A 5A 84
Spitfire Rd. Wall 9J 123
Spitfire Way. Houn 6G 69
Splendour Wlk. SE16 6G 77 (off Verney Rd.)
Spode Ho. SE11 4L 75 (off Lambeth Wlk.)
Spode Wlk. NW6 1M 57
Spondon Rd. N15 2E 44
Spoonbill Way. Hay 8H 53
Spooner Ho. Houn 7L 69
Spooners Dri. Park 1M 5
Spooners M. W3 2B 72
Spooner Wlk. Wall 7J 123
Sportsbank St. SE6 6A 94
Spottons Gro. N17 8A 28
Spout Hill. Croy 7L 125
Spout La. N. Stai 3A 144
Spratt Hall Rd. E11 4E 46
Spray La. Twic 5C 86
Spray St. SE18 5M 79
Spread Eagle Wlk. Eps 5B 134
Spreighton Rd. W Mol 8M 101
Spriggs Ho. N1 3M 59 (off Canonbury Rd.)
Sprimont Pl. SW3 6D 74
Springall St. SE15 8F 76
Springalls Wharf. SE16 3E 76 (off Bermondsey Wall W.)
Spring Bank. N21 8K 15
Springbank Av. Horn 1G 67
Springbank Rd. SE13 5B 94
Springbank Wlk. NW1 3H 59
Springbourne Ct. Beck 5A 110 (in two parts)
Spring Bri. M. W5 1H 71
Springbridge Rd. W5 1H 71
Spring Clo. Barn 7H 13
Spring Clo. Borwd 3L 11
Spring Clo. Dag 6H 49
Spring Clo. La. Sutt 8J 121
Spring Corner. Felt 9E 84
Spring Cotts. Surb 9H 103
Spring Ct. NW6 2K 57
Spring Ct. W7 1B 70
Spring Ct. Eps 1D 134
Spring Ct. Rd. Enf 2L 15
Springcroft Av. N2 2D 42
Spring Crofts. Bush 7L 9
Springdale M. N16 9B 44
Springdale Rd. N16 9B 44
Spring Dri. Pinn 4E 36
Springfarm Clo. Rain 6H 67
Springfield. E5 6F 44
Springfield. Bus H 1B 22
Springfield Av. N10 1G 43
Springfield Av. SW20 7K 105
Springfield Av. Hamp 3M 101
Springfield Av. Swan 8D 114
Springfield Clo. N12 5M 25
Springfield Clo. Crox G 7A 8
Springfield Clo. Stan 3E 22
Springfield Ct. NW3 3C 58 (off Eton Av.)
Springfield Ct. Ilf 1M 63
Springfield Ct. King T 7J 103 (off Springfield Rd.)
Springfield Ct. Wall 7F 122
Springfield Dri. Ilf 3A 48
Springfield Gdns. E5 6F 44
Springfield Gdns. NW9 3B 40
Springfield Gdns. Brom 8K 111
Springfield Gdns. Ruis 6F 36
Springfield Gdns. Upm 8M 51
Springfield Gdns. W Wick 4M 125
Springfield Gdns. Wfd G 7G 31
Springfield Gro. SE7 7G 79
Springfield Gro. Sun 5D 100
Springfield La. NW6 4M 57
Springfield Mt. NW9 3C 40
Springfield Pde. M. N13 4L 27
Springfield Pl. N Mald 8A 104
Springfield Ri. SE26 9F 92 (in two parts)
Springfield Rd. E4 1C 30
Springfield Rd. E6 3K 63
Springfield Rd. E15 6C 62
Springfield Rd. E17 4K 45
Springfield Rd. N11 5F 26
Springfield Rd. N15 2E 44
Springfield Rd. NW8 4A 58
Springfield Rd. SE26 2F 108
Springfield Rd. SW19 2K 105
Springfield Rd. W7 2C 70
Springfield Rd. Bexh 2M 97
Springfield Rd. Brom 8K 111
Springfield Rd. Chesh 5E 6
Springfield Rd. Eps 2G 135
Springfield Rd. Harr 4C 38
Springfield Rd. Hay 2G 69
Springfield Rd. King T 7J 103
Springfield Rd. Tedd 2E 102
Springfield Rd. T Hth 5A 108
Springfield Rd. Twic 7L 85
Springfield Rd. Wall 7F 122
Springfield Rd. Wat 6F 4
Springfield Rd. Well 2F 96
Springfields. New Bar 7M 13 (off Somerset Rd.)
Springfields. Wal A 7L 7
Springfield Wlk. NW6 4M 57
Spring Gdns. N5 1A 60
Spring Gdns. SW1 2H 75 (in two parts)
Spring Gdns. Big H 9G 141
Spring Gdns. Horn 9F 50
Spring Gdns. Orp 8F 128
Spring Gdns. Romf 3A 50
Spring Gdns. Wall 7G 123
Spring Gdns. Wat 8G 5
Spring Gdns. W Mol 9M 101
Spring Gdns. Wfd G 7G 31
Spring Grove. 9C 70
Spring Gro. SE19 4D 108
Spring Gro. W4 6L 71
Spring Gro. Hamp 5M 101
Spring Gro. Lou 8H 19
Spring Gro. Mitc 5E 106
Spring Gro. Cres. Houn 9A 70
Spring Gro. Rd. Houn & Iswth 9M 69
Spring Gro. Rd. Rich 4K 87
Springhead Rd. Eri 7D 82
Spring Hill. E5 5E 44
Spring Hill. SE26 1G 109
Springhill Clo. SE5 2B 92
Springholm Clo. Big H 9G 141
Spring Ho. WC1 6L 59 (off Margery St.)
Springhurst Clo. Croy 6K 125
Spring Lake. Stan 4F 22
Spring La. E5 5F 44
Spring La. N10 1E 42
Spring La. SE25 1F 124
Spring M. W1 8D 58
Spring M. Eps 1D 134
Spring Park. 5L 125
Spring Pk. Av. Croy 4H 125
Spring Pk. Dri. N4 6A 44
Springpark Dri. Beck 7A 110
Spring Pk. Rd. Croy 4H 125
Spring Pas. SW15 2H 89
Spring Path. NW3 1B 58
Spring Pl. N3 1L 41
Spring Pl. NW5 1F 58
Springpond Rd. Dag 1J 65
Springrice Rd. SE13 5B 94
Spring Rd. Felt 9D 84
Spring Shaw Rd. Orp 5E 112
Spring St. W2 9B 58
Spring St. Eps 1D 134
Spring Ter. Rich 4J 87
Spring Tide Clo. SE15 9E 76
Spring Va. Bexh 3M 97
Springvale Av. Bren 6H 71
Spring Va. Clo. Swan 5D 114
Spring Va. N. Dart 6H 99
Springvale Retail Pk. Orp 7G 113
Spring Va. S. Dart 6H 99
Spring Va. Ter. W14 4H 73
Springvale Way. Orp 7G 113
Spring Villa Rd. Edgw 7L 23
Spring Wlk. E1 8E 60
Springwater. WC1 8K 59 (off New N. St.)
Springwater Clo. SE18 9L 79
Springway. Harr 5B 38
Springwell Av. NW10 4D 56
Springwell Clo. SW16 1K 107
Springwell Ct. Houn 1H 85
Springwell Rd. SW16 1L 107
Springwell Rd. Houn 1H 85
Springwood Ct. S Croy 6C 124 (off Birdhurst Rd.)
Springwood Cres. Edgw 2M 23
Springwood Way. Romf 3E 50
Sprowston M. E7 2E 62
Sprowston Rd. E7 1E 62
Spruce Ct. W5 4J 71
Sprucedale Clo. Swan 6C 114
Sprucedale Gdns. Croy 6H 125
Sprucedale Gdns. Wall 1J 137
Spruce Hills Rd. E17 9A 30
Spruce Ho. SE16 3H 77 (off Woodland Cres.)
Spruce Pk. Brom 8D 110
Spruce Rd. Big H 8H 141
Sprules Rd. SE4 1J 93
Spur Clo. Ab L 6B 4
Spurfield. W Mol 7M 101
Spurgeon Av. SE19 5B 108
Spurgeon Rd. SE19 5B 108
Spurgeon St. SE1 4B 76
Spurling Rd. SE22 3D 92
Spurling Rd. Dag 2K 65
Spurrell Av. Bex 1B 114
Spur Rd. N15 2B 44
Spur Rd. SE1 3L 75
Spur Rd. SW1 3G 75
Spur Rd. Edgw 4J 23
Spur Rd. Felt 3F 84
Spur Rd. Iswth 8E 70
Spur Rd. Orp 4E 128
Spurstowe Rd. E8 2F 60
Spurstowe Ter. E8 2F 60
Spur, The. Chesh 1D 6
Spurway Pde. Ilf 3K 47 (off Woodford Av.)
Squadrons App. Horn 2G 67
Square Rigger Row. SW11 2A 90
Square, The. W6 6G 73
Square, The. Cars 7E 122
Square, The. Ilf 5L 47
Square, The. Rich 4H 87
Square, The. Swan 7B 114
Square, The. Uxb 2B 68
Square, The. Wat 1F 8
Square, The. W Dray 9G 143
Square, The. Wey 6A 116
Square, The. Wfd G 5E 30
Squarey St. SW17 9A 90
Squire Gdns. NW8 6B 58 (off Grove End Rd.)
Squires Ct. SW4 9J 75
Squires Ct. SW19 1L 105
Squires Fld. Hex 5E 114
Squires La. N3 9M 25
Squires Mt. NW3 8B 42
Squires, The. Romf 4A 50
Squires Wlk. Ashf 4B 100
Squires Way. Dart 1B 114
Squires Wood Dri. Chst 4J 111
Squirrel Clo. Houn 2G 85
Squirrel Clo. Orp 3C 128
Squirrel M. W13 1D 70
Squirrels Clo. N12 4A 26
Squirrels Clo. Uxb 3E 142
Squirrels Ct. Wor Pk 4E 120 (off Avenue, The)
Squirrels Drey. Brom 6C 110 (off Park Hill Rd.)
Squirrels Grn. Wor Pk 4D 120
Squirrel's Heath. 1H 51
Squirrels Heath Av. Romf 1F 50
Squirrels Heath La. Romf 2G 51
Squirrels Heath Rd. Romf 1J 51
Squirrel's La. Buck H 3H 31
Squirrels, The. SE13 2B 94
Squirrels, The. Bush 8B 10
Squirrels, The. Pinn 1K 37
Squirrels Trad. Est., The. Hay 4D 68
Squirrels Way. Eps 6B 134
Squirries St. E2 6E 60
Stable Clo. N'holt 5L 53
Stables End. Orp 5A 128
Stables Market, The. 3F 58
Stables Mkt., The. NW1 3F 58
Stables M. SE27 2A 108
Stables, The. Buck H 9G 19
Stables Way. SE11 6L 75
Stable Wlk. N2 8B 26
Stable Way. W10 9G 57
Stable Yd. SW1 3G 75 (off Stable Yd. Rd.)
Stable Yd. SW15 2G 89
Stable Yd. Rd. SW1 3G 75 (in two parts)
Stableyard, The. SW9 1K 91
Stacey Av. N18 4G 29
Stacey Clo. E10 3B 46
Stacey St. N7 8L 43
Stacey St. WC2 9H 59
Stack Ho. SW1 5E 74 (off Cundy St.)
Stackhouse St. SW3 4D 74 (off Pavilion Rd.)
Stacy Path. SE5 8C 76
Stadium Bus. Cen. Wemb 8M 39
Stadium Retail Pk. Wemb 8L 39
Stadium Rd. SE18 8K 79
Stadium Rd. E. NW4 5F 40
Stadium St. SW10 8A 74
Stadium Way. Dart 4C 98
Stadium Way. Wemb 9K 39
Staffa Rd. E10 6J 45
Stafford Av. Horn 1H 51
Stafford Clo. E17 4K 45 (in two parts)
Stafford Clo. N14 7G 15
Stafford Clo. NW6 6L 57 (in two parts)
Stafford Clo. Chesh 2B 6
Stafford Clo. Sutt 8J 121
Stafford Ct. SW8 8J 75
Stafford Ct. W7 9D 54 (off Copley Clo.)
Stafford Cripps Ho. E2 6G 61 (off Globe Rd.)
Stafford Cripps Ho. SW6 7K 73 (off Clem Attlee Ct.)
Stafford Cross Bus. Pk. Croy 7K 123
Stafford Gdns. Croy 7K 123
Stafford Ind. Est. Horn 1H 51
Stafford Mans. SW1 4G 75 (off Stafford Pl.)
Stafford Mans. SW4 3J 91
Stafford Mans. SW11 8D 74 (off Albert Bri. Rd.)
Stafford Mans. W14 4H 73 (off Haarlem Rd.)
Stafford Pl. SW1 4G 75
Stafford Pl. Rich 6K 87
Stafford Rd. E3 5K 61
Stafford Rd. E7 3G 63
Stafford Rd. NW6 6L 57
Stafford Rd. Harr 7A 22
Stafford Rd. N Mald 7A 104
Stafford Rd. Ruis 9D 36
Stafford Rd. Sidc 1C 112
Stafford Rd. Wall & Croy 8G 123
Staffordshire St. SE15 9E 76
Stafford Sq. Wey 6B 116
Stafford St. W1 2G 75
Stafford Ter. W8 4L 73
Staff St. EC1 6B 60
Stag Clo. Edgw 9M 23
Stag Ct. King T 5L 103 (off Coombe Rd.)
Staggart Grn. Chig 5D 32
Stagg Hill. Barn 1C 14
Stag Lane (Junct.) 8D 88
Stag La. SW15 9D 88
Stag La. Buck H 2F 30
Stag La. Edgw & NW9 9M 23
Stag Leys Clo. Bans 7B 136
Stag Pl. SW1 4G 75
Stags Way. Iswth 8D 70
Stainbank Rd. Mitc 7F 106
Stainby Clo. W Dray 4J 143
Stainby Rd. N15 2D 44
Stainer Ho. SE3 3G 95
Stainer Rd. Borwd 3H 11
Stainer St. SE1 2B 76
Staines Av. Sutt 4H 121
Staines Reservoir Bird Sanctuary. 7A 144
Staines Rd. Felt & Houn 7E 144 (in two parts)
Staines Rd. Ilf 1A 64
Staines Rd. Twic 9L 85
Staines Rd. E. Sun 4E 100
Staines Rd. W. Ashf & Sun 4A 100
Staines Wlk. Sidc 3G 113
Stainford Clo. Ashf 2B 100
Stainforth Rd. E17 2L 45
Stainforth Rd. Ilf 5B 48
Staining La. EC2 9A 60
Stainmore Clo. Chst 5B 112
Stainsbury St. E2 5G 61
Stainsby Pl. E14 9L 61
Stainsby Rd. E14 9L 61
Stains Clo. Chesh 1E 6
Stainton Rd. SE6 5B 94
Stainton Rd. Enf 3G 17
Stalbridge Flats. W1 9E 58 (off Lumley St.)
Stalbridge St. NW1 8C 58
Stalham St. SE16 4F 76
Stalham Way. Ilf 8M 31
Stalisfield Pl. Dow 2L 141
Stambourne Way. SE19 4C 108
Stambourne Way. W Wick 4A 126
Stamford Bridge (Chelsea F.C.) 8M 73
Stamford Brook Arches. W6 5E 72
Stamford Brook Av. W6 4D 72
Stamford Brook Gdns. W6 4D 72
Stamford Brook Mans. W6 5D 72 (off Goldhawk Rd.)
Stamford Brook Rd. W6 4D 72
Stamford Clo. N15 3E 44
Stamford Clo. NW3 8A 42 (off Heath St.)
Stamford Clo. Harr 7C 22
Stamford Clo. S'hall 1L 69
Stamford Ct. W6 5E 72
Stamford Dri. Brom 8D 110
Stamford Gdns. Dag 3G 65
Stamford Ga. SW6 8M 73
Stamford Green. 5M 133
Stamford Grn. Rd. Eps 5M 133
Stamford Gro. E. N16 6E 44
Stamford Gro. W. N16 6E 44
Stamford Hill. 6D 44
Stamford Hill. N16 7D 44
Stamford Lodge. N16 5D 44
Stamford Rd. E6 4J 63
Stamford Rd. N1 3C 60
Stamford Rd. N15 3E 44
Stamford Rd. Dag 4F 64
Stamford Rd. W on T 5H 117
Stamford Rd. Wat 4F 8
Stamford St. SE1 2L 75
Stamp Pl. E2 5D 60
Stanard Clo. N16 5C 44
Stanborough Av. Borwd 1L 11
Stanborough Clo. Borwd 2L 11
Stanborough Clo. Hamp 3K 101
Stanborough Pk. Wat 8F 4
Stanborough Pas. E8 2D 60
Stanborough Rd. Houn 2B 86
Stanbridge Pl. N21 2M 27
Stanbridge Rd. SW15 2G 89
Stanbrook Rd. SE2 3F 80
Stanbury Av. Wat 1C 8
Stanbury Ct. NW3 2D 58
Stanbury Rd. SE15 1F 92 (in two parts)
Stancroft. NW9 3C 40
Standale Gro. Ruis 3A 36
Standard Ind. Est. E16 3K 79
Standard Pl. EC2 6C 60 (off Rivington St.)
Standard Rd. NW10 7A 56
Standard Rd. Belv 6L 81
Standard Rd. Bexh 3J 97
Standard Rd. Dow 2L 141
Standard Rd. Enf 2J 17
Standard Rd. Houn 2J 85
Standen Av. Horn 8J 51
Standen Rd. SW18 6K 89
Standfield. Ab L 4C 4
Standfield Gdns. Dag 2L 65
Standfield Rd. Dag 1L 65
Standish Ho. SE3 3F 94 (off Elford Clo.)
Standish Ho. W6 5E 72 (off St Peter's Gro.)
Standish Rd. W6 5E 72
Standlake Point. SE23 9H 93
Stane Clo. SW19 4M 105
Stane Pas. SW16 2J 107
Stanesgate Ho. SE15 8E 76 (off Friary Est.)
Stane Way. SE18 8H 79
Stane Way. Eps 2E 134
Stanfield Ho. NW8 7B 58 (off Frampton St.)
Stanfield Ho. N'holt 5H 53 (off Academy Gdns.)
Stanfield Rd. E3 5J 61
Stanford Clo. Hamp 3K 101
Stanford Clo. Romf 4M 49
Stanford Clo. Ruis 4A 36
Stanford Clo. Wfd G 5J 31
Stanford Ct. SW6 9M 73
Stanford Ct. Wal A 6M 7
Stanford Ho. Bark 5F 64
Stanford Pl. SE17 5C 76
Stanford Rd. N11 5D 26
Stanford Rd. SW16 6H 107
Stanford Rd. W8 4M 73
Stanfords, The. Eps 4D 134 (off East St.)
Stanford St. SW1 5H 75
Stanford Way. SW16 6H 107
Stangate. SE1 4K 75 (off Royal St.)
Stangate Cres. Borwd 7B 12
Stangate Gdns. Stan 4F 22
Stangate Lodge. N21 8K 15
Stanger Rd. SE25 8E 108
Stanham Pl. Dart 3E 98
Stanham Rd. Dart 4G 99
Stanhill Cotts. Dart 4B 114
Stanhope Av. N3 1K 41
Stanhope Av. Brom 3D 126
Stanhope Av. Harr 8B 22
Stanhope Clo. SE16 3H 77
Stanhope Gdns. N4 4M 43
Stanhope Gdns. N6 4F 42
Stanhope Gdns. NW7 5D 24
Stanhope Gdns. SW7 5A 74
Stanhope Gdns. Dag 8K 49

Stanhope Gdns.—Steed Clo.

Stanhope Gdns. Ilf 6K 47
Stanhope Ga. W1 ....2E 74
Stanhope Gro. Beck 9K 109
Stanhope Heath. Stanw 5A 144
Stanhope Ho. N11 ....4F 26
(off Coppies Gro.)
Stanhope Ho. SE8 ....8K 77
(off Adolphus St.)
Stanhope M. E. SW7 ....5A 74
Stanhope M. S. SW7 ....5A 74
Stanhope M. W. SW7 ....5A 74
Stanhope Pde. NW1 ....6G 59
Stanhope Pk. Rd. Gnfd 7A 54
Stanhope Pl. W2 ....1D 74
Stanhope Rd. E17 ....3M 45
Stanhope Rd. N6 ....4G 43
Stanhope Rd. N12 ....5A 26
Stanhope Rd. Barn 8G 13
Stanhope Rd. Bexh 1J 97
Stanhope Rd. Cars 9E 122
Stanhope Rd. Croy 5C 124
Stanhope Rd. Dag 7K 49
Stanhope Rd. Gnfd 8A 54
Stanhope Rd. Rain 5E 66
Stanhope Rd. Sidc 1E 112
Stanhope Rd. Wal X 6E 6
Stanhope Row. W1 ....2F 74
Stanhope St. NW1 ....5G 59
Stanhope Ter. W2 ....1B 74
Stanhope Ter. Twic 6D 86
Stanhope Way. Stanw 5A 144
Stanier Clo. W14 ....6K 73
Stanlake M. W12 ....2G 73
Stanlake Rd. W12 ....2G 73
Stanlake Vs. W12 ....2G 73
Stanley Av. Bark 6D 64
Stanley Av. Beck 6A 110
Stanley Av. Dag 6K 49
Stanley Av. Gnfd 4A 54
Stanley Av. N Mald 9E 104
Stanley Av. Romf 2E 50
Stanley Av. Wemb 3J 55
Stanley Bldgs. NW1 ....5J 59
(off Stanley Pas.)
Stanley Clo. SW8 ....7K 75
Stanley Clo. Coul 9K 137
Stanley Clo. Horn 7G 51
Stanley Clo. Romf 2E 50
Stanley Clo. Uxb 5B 142
Stanley Clo. Wemb 3J 55
Stanley Cohen Ho. EC1 ....7A 60
(off Golden La. Est.)
Stanley Ct. W5 ....8G 55
Stanley Ct. Cars 9E 122
Stanley Ct. Sutt 9M 121
Stanley Cres. W11 ....1K 73
Stanleycroft Clo. Iswth 9C 70
Stanley Gdns. NW2 ....1G 57
Stanley Gdns. W3 ....3C 72
Stanley Gdns. W11 ....1K 73
Stanley Gdns. Borwd 3J 11
Stanley Gdns. Mitc 3E 106
Stanley Gdns. S Croy 4E 138
Stanley Gdns. Wall 8G 123
Stanley Gdns. W on T 8G 117
Stanley Gdns. M. W11 ....1K 73
(off Kensington Pk. Rd.)
Stanley Gdns. Rd. Tedd 2C 102
Stanley Gro. N17 ....7D 28
Stanley Gro. SW8 ....1E 90
Stanley Gro. Croy 1L 123
Stanley Holloway Ct. E16 ....9E 62
(off Coolfin Rd.)
Stanley Ho. E14 ....9L 61
(off Saracen St.)
Stanley Pk. Dri. Wemb 4K 55
Stanley Pk. Rd. Cars 9D 122
Stanley Pas. NW1 ....5J 59
Stanley Rd. E4 ....1B 30
Stanley Rd. E10 ....4M 45
Stanley Rd. E12 ....1J 63
Stanley Rd. E15 ....4B 62
Stanley Rd. E18 ....8D 30
Stanley Rd. N2 ....1B 42
Stanley Rd. N9 ....1D 28
Stanley Rd. N10 ....7F 26
Stanley Rd. N11 ....6H 27
Stanley Rd. N15 ....2M 43
Stanley Rd. NW9 ....5E 40
Stanley Rd. SW14 ....3M 87
Stanley Rd. SW19 ....3L 105
Stanley Rd. W3 ....4A 72
Stanley Rd. Brom 8F 110
Stanley Rd. Cars 9E 122
Stanley Rd. Croy 2L 123
Stanley Rd. Enf 5C 16
Stanley Rd. Harr 7A 38
Stanley Rd. Horn 7G 51
Stanley Rd. Houn 3A 86
Stanley Rd. Ilf 7B 48
Stanley Rd. Mitc 4E 106
Stanley Rd. Mord 8L 105
Stanley Rd. N'wd 8E 20
Stanley Rd. Orp 3E 128
Stanley Rd. Sidc 9E 96
Stanley Rd. S'hall 1J 69
Stanley Rd. Sutt 8M 121
Stanley Rd. Twic 9B 86
Stanley Rd. Wat 6G 9
Stanley Rd. Wemb 2K 55
Stanley Rd. N. Rain 4C 66
Stanley Rd. S. Rain 5D 66
Stanley Sq. Cars 1D 136
Stanley St. SE8 ....8K 77
Stanley Ter. N19 ....7J 43
Stanley Way. Orp 9F 112
Stanmer St. SW11 ....9C 74
Stanmore. 5F 22
Stanmore Gdns. Rich 2K 87
Stanmore Gdns. Sutt 5A 122
Stanmore Golf Course. 7E 22
Stanmore Hill. Stan 3E 22
Stanmore Lodge. Stan 4F 22
Stanmore Pl. NW1 ....4F 58
Stanmore Rd. E11 ....6D 46
Stanmore Rd. N15 ....2M 43
Stanmore Rd. Belv 5A 82
Stanmore Rd. Rich 2K 87
Stanmore Rd. Wat 3F 8
Stanmore St. N1 ....4K 59
Stanmore Ter. Beck 6L 109
Stanmore Way. Lou 3L 19
Stannard Cotts. E1 ....7G 61
(off Fox Clo.)
Stannard M. E8 ....2E 60
(off Stannard Rd.)
Stannard Rd. E8 ....2E 60
Stannary Pl. SE11 ....6L 75
Stannary St. SE11 ....7L 75
Stannet Way. Wall 6G 123
Stannington Path. Borwd 3L 11
Stansbury Ho. W10 ....6J 57
(off Beethoven St.)
Stansfeld Rd. E6 & E16 ....8H 63
Stansfield Ho. SE1 ....5D 76
(off Balaclava Rd.)
Stansfield Rd. SW9 ....2K 91
Stansfield Rd. Houn 1F 84
Stansgate Rd. Dag 7L 49
Stanstead Clo. Brom 9D 110
Stanstead Gro. SE6 ....7K 93
Stanstead Mnr. Sutt 8L 121
Stanstead Rd. E11 ....3F 46
Stanstead Rd.
SE23 & SE6 ....7H 93
Stanstead Rd. H'row A 5D 144
Stansted Clo. Horn 2F 66
Stansted Cres. Bex 7H 97
Stanswood Gdns. SE5 ....8C 76
Stanthorpe Clo. SW16 ....2J 107
Stanthorpe Rd. SW16 ....2J 107
Stanton Av. Tedd 3C 102
Stanton Clo. Eps 7M 119
Stanton Clo. Orp 2G 129
Stanton Clo. Wor Pk 3H 121
Stanton Ct. S Croy 7C 124
(off Birdhurst Ri.)
Stanton Ho. SE10 ....7A 78
(off Thames St.)
Stanton Ho. SE16 ....3K 77
(off Rotherhithe St.)
Stanton Rd. SE26 ....1K 109
Stanton Rd. SW13 ....1D 88
Stanton Rd. SW20 ....5H 105
Stanton Rd. Croy 2A 124
Stanton Sq. SE26 ....1K 109
Stanton Way. SE26 ....1K 109
Stanway Clo. Chig 5C 32
Stanway Ct. N1 ....5C 60
Stanway Gdns. W3 ....2L 71
Stanway Gdns. Edgw 5A 24
Stanway St. N1 ....5C 60
Stanwell. 5B 144
Stanwell Clo. Stanw 5B 144
Stanwell Gdns. Stanw 5B 144
Stanwell Moor Rd.
Stai & Stanw (TW18)
....5A 144
Stanwell Moor Rd.
Stai & W Dray (TW19)
....3A 144
Stanwell Rd. Ashf 8C 144
Stanwell Rd. Felt 6F 144
Stanwick Rd. W14 ....5K 73
Stanworth Ct. Houn 8K 69
Stanworth St. SE1 ....4D 76
Stanwyck Dri. Chig 5A 32
Stanwyck Gdns. H Hill 5F 34
Stanyhurst. SE23 ....7J 93
Stapenhill Rd. Wemb 8F 38
Staple Clo. Bex 9B 98
Staplefield Clo. SW2 ....7J 91
Staplefield Clo. Pinn 7J 21
Stapleford. N17 ....9C 28
(off Willan Rd.)
Stapleford Av. Ilf 3C 48
Stapleford Clo. E4 ....3A 30
Stapleford Clo. SW19 ....6J 89
Stapleford Clo. King T 6L 103
Stapleford Gdns. Romf 6L 33
Stapleford Rd. Wemb 3H 55
Stapleford Way. Bark 6F 64
Staplehurst Rd. SE13 ....4B 94
Staplehurst Rd. Cars 9C 122
Staple Inn. WC1 ....8L 59
(off Staple Inn Bldgs.)
Staple Inn Bldgs. WC1 ....8L 59
Staples Clo. SE16 ....2J 77
Staples Corner (Junct.) 6F 40
Staples Corner Bus. Pk. NW2 6F 40
Staples Ho. E6 ....9L 63
(off Savage Gdns.)
Staple's Rd. Lou 5J 19
Staples, The. Swan 5F 114
Staple St. SE1 ....3B 76
Stapleton Cres. Rain 2E 66
Stapleton Gdns. Croy 7L 123
Stapleton Hall Rd. N4 ....6K 43
Stapleton Ho. E2 ....6F 60
(off Ellsworth St.)
Stapleton Rd. SW17 ....9E 90
Stapleton Rd. Bexh 8K 81
Stapleton Rd. Borwd 2L 11
Stapleton Rd. Orp 5D 128
Stapley Rd. Belv 6L 81
Stapylton Rd. Barn 5J 13
Star All. EC3 ....1C 76
(off Fenchurch St.)
Star & Garter Hill.
Rich 7J 87
Starboard Way. E14 ....4L 77
Star Bus. Cen. Rain 8B 66
Starch Ho. La. Ilf 9B 32
Star Clo. Enf 8G 17
Starcross St. NW1 ....6G 59
Starfield Rd. W12 ....3E 72
Star Hill. Dart 4C 98
Star La. E16 ....7C 62
Star La. Orp 8G 113
Starling Clo. Buck H 1E 30
Starling Clo. Pinn 1G 37
Starling Ho. NW8 ....5C 58
(off Barrow Hill Est.)
Starling Pl. Wat 5G 5
Starlings, The. Oxs 5A 132
Starling Wlk. Hamp 2J 101
Starmans Clo. Dag 4J 65
Star Path. N'holt 5L 53
(off Brabazon Rd.)
Star Pl. E1 ....1E 76
Star Rd. W14 ....7K 73
Star Rd. Iswth 1B 86
Star Rd. Uxb 7A 52
Star St. W2 ....9C 58
Starts Clo. Orp 5L 127
Starts Hill Av. F'boro 6M 127
Starts Hill Rd. Orp 5L 127
Starveall Clo. W Dray 4K 143
Star Yd. WC2 ....9L 59
State Farm Av. Orp 6M 127
Staten Gdns. Twic 7D 86
Statham Gro. N16 ....9B 44
Statham Gro. N18 ....5C 28
Statham Ho. SW8 ....9G 75
(off Wadhurst Rd.)
Station App. E4 ....6B 30
Station App. E7 ....9F 46
Station App. E11 ....3E 46
Station App. E17 ....3L 45
(in two parts)
Station App. E18 ....9F 30
Station App. N11 ....5F 26
Station App. N12 ....4M 25
Station App. NW10 ....6D 56
Station App. SE3 ....2F 94
Station App. SE12 ....5E 94
(off Burnt Ash Hill)
Station App. SE26 ....1G 109
(Sydenham Rd.)
Station App. SE26 ....2K 109
(Westerley Cres.)
Station App. SW6 ....2J 89
Station App. SW14 ....2A 88
Station App. SW16 ....3H 107
(Estreham Rd.)
Station App. SW16 ....2H 107
(Streatham High Rd.)
Station App. W7 ....2C 70
Station App. Ashf 9D 144
Station App. B'hurst 1A 98
Station App. Beck 5L 109
Station App. Belm 2M 135
Station App. Bex 7L 97
Station App. Bexh 1J 97
Station App. Bren 7G 71
(off Sidney Gdns.)
Station App. Brom 7E 110
(off High St.)
Station App. Buck H 4H 31
Station App. Cars 6D 122
Station App. Cheam 9J 121
Station App. Chels 7F 128
Station App. Chips 9D 136
Station App. Chst 3J 111
(Elmstead La.)
Station App. Chst 5L 111
(Lower Camden)
Station App. Coul 8H 137
Station App. Cray 5D 98
Station App. Dart 5J 99
Station App. Eps 5B 134
Station App. Ewe 2F 134
(Ewell East)
Station App. Ewe 1D 134
(Ewell West)
Station App. Gnfd 3A 54
Station App. Hamp 5L 101
Station App. Harr 5C 38
Station App. Hayes 3E 126
Station App. Hay 4D 68
Station App. High Bar 6A 14
Station App. Hin W 5D 118
Station App. King T 5L 103
Station App. Lou 6M 19
(Debden)
Station App. Lou 7J 19
(Loughton)
Station App. N'wd 7C 20
Station App. Orp 4D 128
Station App. Oxs 4A 132
Station App. Pinn 1J 37
Station App. Purl 3L 137
Station App. Rich 9L 71
Station App. Ruis 6C 36
(Pembroke Rd.)
Station App. Ruis 1F 52
(W. End Rd.)
Station App. St M 8F 112
Station App. Shep 9A 100
Station App. S Croy 1B 138
Station App. S'leigh 7E 120
Station App. Sun 5E 100
Station App. Swan 8C 114
Station App. Upm 7M 51
Station App. Wal X 7E 6
Station App. Wat 3H 21
Station App. Well 1E 96
(in three parts)
Station App. Wemb 2F 54
Station App. W Dray 2J 143
Station App. W Wick 2A 126
Station App. Whyt 9E 138
Station App. Wor Pk 3E 120
Station App. N. Sidc 8E 96
Station App. Rd. SE1 ....3L 75
Station App. Rd. W4 ....8A 72
Station App. Rd. Coul 7H 137
Station Av. SW9 ....2M 91
Station Av. Eps 1C 134
Station Av. Kew 9L 71
Station Av. N Mald 7C 104
Station Av. W on T 6E 116
Station Bldgs. King T 6J 103
(off Fife Rd.)
Station Clo. N3 ....8L 25
Station Clo. N12 ....4M 25
Station Clo. Hamp 5M 101
Station Cotts. Chels 4D 128
Station Ct. E10 ....5M 45
(off Kings Clo.)
Station Cres. N15 ....2B 44
Station Cres. SE3 ....6E 78
Station Cres. Ashf 9B 144
Station Cres. Wemb 2F 54
Stationer's Hall Ct. EC4 ....9M 59
Station Est. Beck 7H 109
Station Est. Rd. Felt 7F 84
Station Footpath. K Lan 4A 4
(in two parts)
Station Garage M. SW16 ....3H 107
Station Gdns. W4 ....8A 72
Station Gro. Wemb 2J 55
Station Hill. Brom 4E 126
Station Ho. M. N9 ....4E 28
Station La. Horn 8H 51
Station Pde. E11 ....3E 46
Station Pde. N14 ....1H 27
Station Pde. NW2 ....2G 57
Station Pde. SW12 ....7E 90
Station Pde. W3 ....9L 55
Station Pde. W4 ....8A 72
Station Pde. W5 ....2K 71
Station Pde. Ashf 9D 144
Station Pde. Bark 3A 64
Station Pde. Barn 6E 14
Station Pde. Bexh 1J 97
(off Pickford La.)
Station Pde. Buck H 4H 31
Station Pde. Chips 9D 136
Station Pde. Dag 2L 65
Station Pde. Edgw 7J 23
Station Pde. Elm P 9F 50
Station Pde. Eri 6C 82
Station Pde. Felt 7F 84
Station Pde. Harr (HA2) 9M 37
Station Pde. Harr (HA3) 9E 22
Station Pde. N Har 9M 37
Station Pde. N'holt 3L 53
Station Pde. N'wd 7C 20
Station Pde. Rich 9L 71
Station Pde. Romf 4C 50
Station Pde. Sidc 8E 96
Station Pde. Sutt 8A 122
(off High St.)
Station Pas. E18 ....9F 30
Station Pas. SE15 ....9G 77
Station Path. E8 ....2F 60
(off Graham Rd.)
Station Path. SW6 ....2K 89
Station Pl. N4 ....7L 43
Station Ri. SE27 ....8M 91
Station Rd. E4 ....1B 30
Station Rd. E7 ....9E 46
Station Rd. E10 ....8A 46
Station Rd. E12 ....9J 47
Station Rd. E17 ....4J 45
Station Rd. N3 ....8L 25
Station Rd. N11 ....5F 26
Station Rd. N17 ....1E 44
Station Rd. N19 ....8G 43
Station Rd. N21 ....1M 27
Station Rd. N22 ....9J 27
Station Rd. NW4 ....4E 40
Station Rd. NW7 ....6C 24
Station Rd. NW10 ....5D 5
Station Rd. SE13 ....2A 9
Station Rd. SE20 ....3G 10
Station Rd. SE25 ....8D 10
Station Rd. SW13 ....1D 8
Station Rd. SW19 ....5A 10
Station Rd. W5 ....9K 5
Station Rd. W7 ....2C 7
Station Rd. Ashf 9D 14
Station Rd. B'side 1B 4
Station Rd. Barn 7M 1
Station Rd. Belv 4L 8
Station Rd. Bexh 2J 9
Station Rd. Borwd 6L 1
Station Rd. Brick W 4L
Station Rd. Brom 5E 11
Station Rd. Cars 6D 12
Station Rd. Chad H 5H 4
Station Rd. Chess 7J 11
Station Rd. Chig 3M 3
Station Rd. Clay 8C 11
Station Rd. Cray 6D 9
Station Rd. Croy 3A 12
Station Rd. Edgw 6L 2
Station Rd. Esh 4B 11
Station Rd. Eyns 6H 13
Station Rd. Gid P 2F 5
Station Rd. Hamp 5L 10
Station Rd. Hamp W 5G 10
Station Rd. H Wood 8K 3
Station Rd. Harr 2D 3
Station Rd. Hay 5C 6
(in three parts)
Station Rd. Houn 3M 8
Station Rd. Ilf 8M 4
Station Rd. Kenl 6A 13
Station Rd. K Lan 2A 4
Station Rd. King T 5L 10
Station Rd. Lou 6J 1
Station Rd. N Mald 9F 10
Station Rd. N Har 3M 3
Station Rd. Orp 4D 12
Station Rd. St P 8G 11
Station Rd. Shep 9A 10
Station Rd. Short 6C 11
Station Rd. Sidc 8E 9
Station Rd. S Dar 6M 11
Station Rd. Sun 4E 10
Station Rd. Sutt 2L 13
Station Rd. Swan 8C 114
Station Rd. Tedd 3E 102
Station Rd. Th Dit 2D 118
Station Rd. Twic 7D 86
Station Rd. Upm 7M 51
Station Rd. Uxb 7A 142
Station Rd. Wal A 7G 7
Station Rd. Wat 4F 8
Station Rd. W Dray 3J 143
Station Rd. W Wick 3A 126
Station Rd. Whyt 9D 138
Station Rd. N. Belv 4M 81
Station Sq. Gid P 2F 50
Station Sq. Orp 9A 112
Station St. E16 ....2M 79
Station Ter. NW10 ....5H 57
Station Ter. SE5 ....9A 76
Station Ter. Purf 6M 83
Station Ter. M. SE3 ....6E 78
Station Vw. Gnfd 4B 54
Station Way. SE15 ....1E 92
Station Way. Buck H 4G 31
Station Way. Clay 8C 118
Station Way. Eps 5B 134
Station Way. Sutt 8J 121
Station Yd. Purl 4M 137
Station Yd. Twic 6E 86
Staunton Ho. SE17 ....5C 76
(off Tatum St.)
Staunton Rd. King T 3J 103
Staunton St. SE8 ....7K 77
Staveley. NW1 ....6G 59
(off Varndell St.)
Staveley Clo. E9 ....1G 61
Staveley Clo. N7 ....9J 43
Staveley Clo. SE15 ....9F 76
Staveley Gdns. W4 ....9B 72
Staveley Rd. W4 ....7A 72
Staveley Rd. Ashf 3B 100
Staverton Rd. NW2 ....3G 57
Staverton Rd. Horn 4H 51
Stave Yd. Rd. SE16 ....2J 77
Stavordale Rd. N5 ....9M 43
Stavordale Rd. Cars 2A 122
Stayner's Rd. E1 ....7H 61
Stayton Rd. Sutt 5L 121
Steadfast Rd. King T 5H 103
Steadman Ct. EC1 ....7A 60
(off Old St.)
Steadman Ho. Dag 8L 49
(off Uvedale Rd.)
Stead St. SE17 ....5B 76
Steam Farm La. Felt 3D 84
Stean St. E8 ....4D 60
Stebbing Ho. W11 ....2H 7
(off Queensdale Cres
Stebbing Way. Bark 5E 6
Stebondale St. E14 ....5A 7
Stedham Pl. WC1 ....9J 5
(off New Oxford St
Stedman Clo. Bex 9C 9
Steed Clo. Horn 7F 5

Stratford Shop. Cen.—Sunna Gdns.

Stratford Shop. Cen. E15 . . . .3B 62
(off Stratford Cen., The)
Stratford Studios. W8 . . . . . .4L 73
Stratford Vs. NW1 . . . . .3G 59
Stratford Way. Brick W 2K 5
Stratford Way. Wat 4D 8
Stratham Ct. N19 . . . . .8J 43
(off Alexander Rd.)
Strathan Clo. SW18 . . . . .5J 89
Strathaven Rd. SE12 . . . . . . .5F 94
Strathblaine Rd. SW11 . . . . .4B 90
Strathbrook Rd. SW16 . . . . .4K 107
Strathcona Rd. Wemb 7H 39
Strathdale. SW16 . . . . .2K 107
Strathdon Dri. SW17 . . . . . . .9B 90
Strathearn Av. Hay 8D 68
Strathearn Av. Twic 7M 85
Strathearn Pl. W2 . . . . .9C 58
Strathearn Rd. SW19 . . . . . .2L 105
Strathearn Rd. Sutt 7L 121
Stratheden Pde. SE3 . . . . . . .8E 78
Stratheden Rd. SE3 . . . . .9E 78
Strathfield Gdns. Bark 2B 64
Strathleven Rd. SW2 . . . . . . .4J 91
Strathmore Ct. NW8 . . . . . . .6C 58
(off Park Rd.)
Strathmore Gdns. N3 . . . . . .8M 25
Strathmore Gdns. W8 . . . . . .2L 73
Strathmore Gdns. Edgw 9M 23
Strathmore Gdns. Horn 6D 50
Strathmore Rd. SW19 . . . . . . .9L 89
Strathmore Rd. Croy 2B 124
Strathmore Rd. Tedd 1C 102
Strathnairn St. SE1 . . . . .5E 76
Strathray Gdns. NW3 . . . . . . .2C 58
Strath Ter. SW11 . . . . .3C 90
Strathville Rd. SW18 . . . . . . .8L 89
Strathyre Av. SW16 . . . . . . .7L 107
Stratton Av. Enf 1B 16
Stratton Av. Wall 1H 137
Stratton Clo. SW19 . . . . . . .6L 105
Stratton Clo. Bexh 2J 97
Stratton Clo. Edgw 6K 23
Stratton Clo. Houn 9L 69
Stratton Clo. W on T 3G 117
Stratton Ct. N1 . . . . .3C 60
(off Hertford Rd.)
Stratton Ct. Pinn 7K 21
(off Devonshire Rd.)
Strattondale St. E14 . . . . .4A 78
Stratton Dri. Bark 1C 64
Stratton Gdns. S'hall 9K 53
Stratton Rd. SW19 . . . . .6L 105
Stratton Rd. Bexh 2J 97
Stratton Rd. Romf 5L 35
Stratton Rd. Sun 6D 100
Stratton St. W1 . . . . .2F 74
Stratton Wlk. Romf 5L 35
Strauss Rd. W4 . . . . .3B 72
Strawberry Fields. Swan . . .5C 114
Strawberry Hill. 9D 86
Strawberry Hill. Twic 9D 86
Strawberry Hill Clo. Twic 9D 86
Strawberry Hill House. 9D 86
(off Strawberry Va.)
Strawberry Hill Rd. Twic 9D 86
Strawberry La. Cars 5E 122
Strawberry Ter. N10 . . . . .8D 26
Strawberry Va. N2 . . . . .8B 26
Strawberry Va. Twic 9E 86
(in two parts)
Strayfield Rd. Enf 1L 15
Streakes Fld. Rd. NW2 . . . . . .7E 40
Streamdale. SE2 . . . . .7F 80
Stream La. Edgw 5M 23
Streamline Ct. SE22 . . . . .7E 92
(off Streamline M.)
Streamline M. SE22 . . . . .7E 92
Streamside Clo. N9 . . . . .1D 28
Streamside Clo. Brom 8E 110
Stream Way. Belv 7K 81
Streatfield Av. E6 . . . . .4K 63
Streatfield Rd. Harr 1G 39
Streatham. 2J 107
Streatham Clo. SW16 . . . . . . .8J 91
Streatham Common. 3J 107
Streatham Comn. N.
SW16 . . . . .2J 107
Streatham Comn. S.
SW16 . . . . .3J 107
Streatham Ct. SW16 . . . . .9J 91
Streatham High Rd.
SW16 . . . . .1J 107
Streatham Hill. 8J 91
Streatham Hill. SW2 . . . . .8J 91
Streatham Ice Rink. 2H 107
Streatham Park. 2G 107
Streatham Pl. SW2 . . . . .6J 91
Streatham Rd.
Mitc & SW16 . . . . .5E 106
Streatham St. WC1 . . . . .9J 59
Streatham Vale. 4G 107
Streatham Va. SW16 . . . . . .5G 107
Streathbourne Rd. SW17 . . . .8E 90
Streatley Pl. NW3 . . . . .9A 42
Streatley Rd. NW6 . . . . .3K 57
Streeters La. Wall 5H 123
Streetfield M. SE3 . . . . .2E 94
Street, The. Hort K 8M 115
Streimer Rd. E15 . . . . .5A 62
Strelley Way. W3 . . . . .1C 72
Stretton Mans. SE8 . . . . .6L 77
Stretton Rd. Croy 2C 124
Stretton Rd. Rich 8G 87
Stretton Way. Borwd 2J 11
Strickland Av. Dart 2K 99
(in two parts)
Strickland Ct. SE15 . . . . .2E 92
Strickland Ho. E2 . . . . .6D 60
(off Chambord St.)
Strickland Row. SW18 . . . . . .6B 90
Strickland St. SE8 . . . . .1L 93
Strickland Way. Orp 6D 128
Stride Rd. E13 . . . . .5D 62
Strimon Clo. N9 . . . . .2G 29
Stringer Ho. N1 . . . . .4C 60
(off Whitmore Est.)
Stripling Way. Wat 8E 8
Strode Clo. N10 . . . . .7E 26
Strode Rd. E7 . . . . .9E 46
Strode Rd. N17 . . . . .9C 28
Strode Rd. NW10 . . . . .2E 56
Strode Rd. SW6 . . . . .8J 73
Strome Ho. NW6 . . . . .5M 57
(off Carlton Va.)
Strone Rd. E7 & E12 . . . . . . .2G 63
Strone Way. Hay 7J 53
Strongbow Cres. SE9 . . . . . . .4K 95
Strongbow Rd. SE9 . . . . .4K 95
Strongbridge Clo. Harr 6L 37
Stronsa Rd. W12 . . . . .3D 72
Strood Av. Romf 6B 50
Strood Ho. SE1 . . . . .3B 76
(off Staple St.)
Stroud Cres. SW15 . . . . .9E 88
Stroudes Clo. Wor Pk 2C 120
Stroud Fld. N'holt 2J 53
Stroud Ga. Harr 9M 37
Stroud Green. 5K 43
Stroud Grn. Gdns. Croy 2G 125
Stroud Grn. Rd. N4 . . . . .6K 43
Stroud Grn. Way. Croy 2F 124
Stroud Ho. Romf 5H 35
(off Montgomery Cres.)
Stroudley Ho. SW8 . . . . .9G 75
Stroudley Wlk. E3 . . . . .6M 61
Stroud Rd. SE25 . . . . .1E 124
Stroud Rd. SW19 . . . . .9L 89
Stroud's Clo. Chad H 3F 48
Stroudwater Pk. Wey 8A 116
Stroud Way. Ashf 3A 100
Strouts Pl. E2 . . . . .6D 60
Strudwick Ct. SW4 . . . . .9J 75
(off Binfield Rd.)
Strutton Ground. SW1 . . . . . .4H 75
Strype St. E1 . . . . .8D 60
Stuart Av. NW9 . . . . .5E 40
Stuart Av. W5 . . . . .3K 71
Stuart Av. Brom 3E 126
Stuart Av. Harr 8K 37
Stuart Av. W on T 3F 116
Stuart Clo. Swan 4D 114
Stuart Clo. Uxb 2E 142
Stuart Ct. Croy 5M 123
(off St John's Rd.)
Stuart Ct. Els 8H 11
Stuart Cres. N22 . . . . .8K 27
Stuart Cres. Croy 5K 125
Stuart Cres. Hay 9A 52
Stuart Evans Clo. Well 2G 97
Stuart Gro. Tedd 2C 102
Stuart Ho. E16 . . . . .2F 78
(off Beaulieu Av.)
Stuart Ho. W14 . . . . .5J 73
(off Windsor Way)
Stuart Mantle Way. Eri 8C 82
Stuart Mill Ho. N1 . . . . .5K 59
(off Killick St.)
Stuart Pl. Mitc 5D 106
Stuart Rd. NW6 . . . . .6L 57
(in two parts)
Stuart Rd. SE15 . . . . .3G 93
Stuart Rd. SW19 . . . . .9L 89
Stuart Rd. W3 . . . . .2A 72
Stuart Rd. Bark 3D 64
Stuart Rd. E Barn 9C 14
Stuart Rd. Harr 1D 38
Stuart Rd. Rich 8F 86
Stuart Rd. T Hth 8A 108
Stuart Rd. Well 9F 80
Stuarts. Horn 6K 51
(off High St.)
Stuart Tower. W9 . . . . .6A 58
(off Maida Va.)
Stuart Way. Chesh 4B 6
Stubbings Hall La. Wal A 1J 7
Stubbs Ct. W4 . . . . .6M 71
(off Chaseley Dri.)
Stubbs Dri. SE16 . . . . .6F 76
Stubbs Ho. E2 . . . . .6H 61
(off Bonner St.)
Stubbs Ho. SW1 . . . . .5H 75
(off Erasmus St.)
Stubbs M. Dag 9F 48
(off Marlborough Rd.)
Stubbs Point. E13 . . . . .7E 62
Stubbs Way. SW19 . . . . .5B 106
Stucley Pl. NW1 . . . . .3F 58
Stucley Rd. Houn 8A 70
Studdridge St. SW6 . . . . .1L 89
(in two parts)
Studd St. N1 . . . . .4M 59
Stud Grn. Wat 5E 4
Studholme Ct. NW3 . . . . .9L 41
Studholme St. SE15 . . . . .8F 76
Studio La. W5 . . . . .2H 71
Studio Pl. SW1 . . . . .3D 74
(off Kinnerton St.)
Studios, The. Bush 8L 9
Studio Way. Borwd 4A 12
Studland. SE17 . . . . .6B 76
(off Portland St.)
Studland Clo. Sidc 9D 96
Studland Ho. E14 . . . . .9J 61
(off Aston St.)
Studland Rd. SE26 . . . . . . .2H 109
Studland Rd. W7 . . . . .9B 54
Studland Rd. King T 3J 103
Studland St. W6 . . . . .5F 72
Studley Av. E4 . . . . .7B 30
Studley Clo. E5 . . . . .1J 61
Studley Ct. E14 . . . . .1B 78
(off Jamestown Way)
Studley Ct. Sidc 2F 112
Studley Dri. Ilf 4H 47
Studley Est. SW4 . . . . .9J 75
Studley Grange Rd. W7 . . . . .3C 70
Studley Rd. E7 . . . . .2F 62
Studley Rd. SW4 . . . . .9J 75
Studley Rd. Dag 3H 65
Stukeley Rd. E7 . . . . .3F 62
Stukeley St. WC2 . . . . .9J 59
Stumps Hill La. Beck 3L 109
Stumps La. Whyt 9C 138
Stunell Ho. SE14 . . . . .7H 77
(off John Williams Clo.)
Sturdee Ho. E2 . . . . .5E 60
(off Horatio St.)
Sturdy Ho. E3 . . . . .5J 61
(off Gernon Rd.)
Sturdy Rd. SE15 . . . . .1F 92
Sturge Av. E17 . . . . .9M 29
Sturgeon Rd. SE17 . . . . .6A 76
Sturges Fld. Chst 3B 112
Sturgess Av. NW4 . . . . .5F 40
Sturge St. SE1 . . . . .3A 76
Sturlas Way. Wal X 6D 6
Sturmer Way. N7 . . . . .1K 59
Sturminster Clo. Hay 9G 53
Sturminster Ho. SW8 . . . . . . .8K 75
(off Dorset Rd.)
Sturrock Clo. N15 . . . . .2B 44
Sturry St. E14 . . . . .9M 61
Sturt St. N1 . . . . .5A 60
(off Wenlock Rd.)
Stutfield St. E1 . . . . .9E 60
Styles Gdns. SW9 . . . . .2M 91
Styles Ho. SE1 . . . . .2M 75
(off Hatfields)
Styles Way. Beck 8A 110
Sudbourne Rd. SW2 . . . . .4J 91
Sudbrooke Rd. SW12 . . . . . . .5D 90
Sudbrook Gdns. Rich 9H 87
Sudbrook La. Rich 7J 87
Sudbury. 1F 54
Sudbury. E6 . . . . .8L 63
Sudbury Av. Wemb 8G 39
Sudbury Ct. E5 . . . . .9J 45
Sudbury Ct. SW8 . . . . .9H 75
Sudbury Ct. Dri. Harr 8D 38
Sudbury Ct. Rd. Harr 8D 38
Sudbury Cres. Brom 3E 110
Sudbury Cres. Wemb 1F 54
Sudbury Cft. Wemb 9D 38
Sudbury Gdns. Croy 6C 124
Sudbury Heights Av. Gnfd . . .1D 54
Sudbury Hill. Harr 7C 38
Sudbury Hill Clo. Wemb 9D 38
Sudbury Ho. SW18 . . . . .4M 89
Sudbury Rd. Bark 1D 64
Sudeley St. N1 . . . . .5M 59
Sudicamps Ct. Wal A 6M 7
Sudlow Rd. SW18 . . . . .4L 89
Sudrey St. SE1 . . . . .3A 76
Suez Av. Gnfd 5D 54
Suez Rd. Enf 6J 17
Suffield Clo. S Croy 4H 139
Suffield Hatch. 4A 30
Suffield Ho. SE17 . . . . .6M 75
(off Berryfield Rd.)
Suffield Rd. E4 . . . . .3M 29
Suffield Rd. N15 . . . . .3D 44
Suffield Rd. SE20 . . . . .6G 109
Suffolk Clo. Borwd 7B 12
Suffolk Ct. E10 . . . . .5L 45
Suffolk Ct. Ilf 4C 48
Suffolk Ho. SE20 . . . . .5H 109
(off Croydon Rd.)
Suffolk Ho. Croy 4B 124
(off George St.)
Suffolk La. EC4 . . . . .1B 76
Suffolk Pk. Rd. E17 . . . . .2J 45
Suffolk Pl. SW1 . . . . .2H 75
Suffolk Rd. E13 . . . . .6E 62
Suffolk Rd. N15 . . . . .3B 44
Suffolk Rd. NW10 . . . . .3C 56
Suffolk Rd. SE25 . . . . .8D 108
Suffolk Rd. SW13 . . . . .8D 72
Suffolk Rd. Bark 3B 64
Suffolk Rd. Dag 1A 66
Suffolk Rd. Dart 5J 99
(in two parts)
Suffolk Rd. Enf 7F 16
Suffolk Rd. Harr 4K 37
Suffolk Rd. Ilf 4C 48
Suffolk Rd. Sidc 3G 113
Suffolk Rd. Wor Pk 4D 120
Suffolk St. E7 . . . . .9E 46
Suffolk St. SW1 . . . . .1H 75
Suffolk Way. Horn 2L 51
Sugar Bakers Ct. EC3 . . . . . . .9C 60
(off Creechurch La.)
Sugar Ho. La. E15 . . . . .5A 62
Sugar Loaf Wlk. E2 . . . . .6G 61
Sugar Quay. EC3 . . . . .1C 76
(off Lwr. Thames St.)
Sugar Quay Wlk. EC3 . . . . . . .1C 76
Sugden Rd. SW11 . . . . .2E 90
Sugden Rd. Th Dit 3F 118
Sugden St. SE5 . . . . .7B 76
(off Depot St.)
Sugden Way. Bark 5D 64
Sulby Ho. SE4 . . . . .3J 93
(off Turnham Rd.)
Sulgrave Gdns. W6 . . . . .3G 73
Sulgrave Rd. W6 . . . . .4G 73
Sulina Rd. SW2 . . . . .6J 91
Sulivan Ct. SW6 . . . . .1L 89
Sulivan Enterprise Cen.
SW6 . . . . .2M 89
Sulivan Rd. SW6 . . . . .2L 89
Sulkin Ho. E2 . . . . .6H 61
(off Knottisford St.)
Sullivan Av. E16 . . . . .8H 63
Sullivan Clo. SW11 . . . . .2C 90
Sullivan Clo. Dart 5F 98
Sullivan Clo. Hay 8G 53
Sullivan Clo. W Mol 7M 101
Sullivan Ct. N16 . . . . .5D 44
Sullivan Ho. SE11 . . . . .5K 75
(off Vauxhall St.)
Sullivan Ho. SW1 . . . . .7F 74
(off Churchill Gdns.)
Sullivan Rd. SE11 . . . . .5L 75
Sullivans Reach. W on T . . .2D 116
Sullivan Way. Els 8G 11
Sultan Rd. E11 . . . . .2F 46
Sultan St. SE5 . . . . .8A 76
Sultan St. Beck 6H 109
Sultan Ter. N22 . . . . .9L 27
Sumatra Rd. NW6 . . . . .1L 57
Sumburgh Rd. SW12 . . . . .5E 90
Summer Av. E Mol 9C 102
Summercourt Rd. E1 . . . . . . .9G 61
Summerene Clo. SW16 . . . .4G 107
Summerfield Av. NW6 . . . . . .5J 57
Summerfield La. Surb 4H 119
Summerfield Rd. W5 . . . . . . .7F 54
Summerfield Rd. Lou 8H 19
Summerfield Rd. Wat 8E 4
Summerfields. Brom 5F 110
(off Freelands Rd.)
Summerfields Av. N12 . . . . . .6C 26
Summerfield St. SE12 . . . . . .6D 94
Summer Gdns. E Mol 9C 102
Summer Gro. Els 8H 11
Summer Hill. Chst 6L 111
Summer Hill. Els 7L 11
Summerhill Clo. Orp 5C 128
Summerhill Gro. Enf 8C 16
Summerhill Rd. N15 . . . . .2B 44
Summerhill Rd. Dart 6H 99
Summerhill Vs. Chst 5L 111
(off Susan Wood)
Summerhill Way. Mitc 5E 106
Summerhouse Av. Houn 9J 69
Summerhouse Dri.
Bex & Dart 1B 114
Summerhouse La. A'ham 4A 10
Summerhouse La.
W Dray 7H 143
Summerhouse Rd. N16 . . . . . .7C 44
Summerhouse Way. Ab L 3D 4
Summerland Gdns. N10 . . . . .1F 42
Summerland Grange. N10 . . .1F 42
Summerlands Av. W3 . . . . . .1A 72
Summerlands Lodge.
Orp 6L 127
Summerlee Av. N2 . . . . .2D 42
Summerlee Gdns. N2 . . . . . . .2D 42
Summerleigh. Wey 8B 116
(off Gower Rd.)
Summerley St. SW18 . . . . . .8M 89
Summer Pl. Wat 8D 8
Summer Rd.
E Mol & Th Dit 9C 102
Summersby Rd. N6 . . . . .4F 42
Summers Clo. Sutt 9L 121
Summers Clo. Wemb 6M 39
Summerskille Clo. N9 . . . . . . .3F 28
Summers La. N12 . . . . .7B 26
Summers Row. N12 . . . . .6C 26
Summers St. EC1 . . . . .7L 59
Summerstown. 9A 90
Summerstown. SW17 . . . . . . .9A 90
Summerswood Clo. Kenl 8B 138
Summerswood La. Borwd . . .1C 12
Summerton Way. SE28 . . . . . .9H 65
Summer Trees. Sun 5F 100
Summerville Gdns. Sutt 8K 121
Summerwood Rd. Iswth 4D 86
Summit Av. NW9 . . . . .3B 40
Summit Bus. Pk. Sun 4E 100
Summit Clo. N14 . . . . .2G 27
Summit Clo. NW2 . . . . .1J 5
Summit Clo. NW9 . . . . .2B 4
Summit Clo. Edgw 7L 2
Summit Dri. Wfd G 9H 3
Summit Est. N16 . . . . .5E 4
Summit Rd. E17 . . . . .2M 4
Summit Rd. N'holt 3L 5
Summit, The. Lou 3K 1
Summit Way. N14 . . . . .2F 2
Summit Way. SE19 . . . . .4C 10
Sumner Av. SE15 . . . . .9D 7
Sumner Bldgs. SE1 . . . . .2A 7
(off Sumner S
Sumner Clo. Orp 6A 12
Sumner Ct. SW8 . . . . .8J 7
Sumner Est. SE15 . . . . .8D 7
Sumner Gdns. Croy 3L 12
Sumner Ho. E3 . . . . .8M 6
(off Watts Gro
Sumner Pl. SW7 . . . . .5B 7
Sumner Pl. M. SW7 . . . . .5B 7
Sumner Rd. SE15 . . . . .7D 7
(in two part
Sumner Rd. Croy 3L 12
Sumner Rd. Harr 5A 3
Sumner Rd. S. Croy 3L 12
Sumner St. SE1 . . . . .2M 7
Sumpter Clo. NW3 . . . . .2A 5
Sun All. Rich 3J 8
Sunbeam Cres. W10 . . . . . . .7G 5
Sunbeam Rd. NW10 . . . . .7A 5
Sunbury. 7G 10
Sunbury Av. NW7 . . . . .5B 2
Sunbury Av. SW14 . . . . .3B 8
Sunbury Av. Pas. SW14 . . . . .3C 8
Sunbury Clo. W on T 1E 11
Sunbury Common. 4D 10
Sunbury Ct. Barn 6J 1
Sunbury Ct. Island. Sun . . .7H 10
Sunbury Ct. M. Sun 6H 10
Sunbury Ct. Rd. Sun 6G 10
Sunbury Cres. Felt 1D 10
Sunbury Cross (Junct.)
. . . . .4E 10
Sunbury Cross Shop. Cen.
Sun 4D 10
Sunbury Gdns. NW7 . . . . .5B 2
Sunbury Ho. E2 . . . . .6D 6
(off Swanfield S
Sunbury Ho. SE14 . . . . .7H 7
(off Myers La
Sunbury La. SW11 . . . . .9B 7
(in two part
Sunbury La. W on T 1E 11
Sunburylock Ait. W on T . . .8F 10
Sunbury Pk. Walled Garden.
. . . . .7F 10
Sunbury Rd. Felt 9D 8
Sunbury Rd. Sutt 5H 12
Sunbury St. SE18 . . . . .4K 7
Sunbury Way. Hanw 2G 10
Sunbury Workshops. E2 . . . .6D 6
(off Swanfield S
Sun Ct. EC3 . . . . .9B 6
(off Cornh
Sun Ct. Eri 1D 9
Suncroft Pl. SE26 . . . . .9G 9
Sundale Av. S Croy 2G 13
Sunderland Ct. SE22 . . . . . . .6E 9
Sunderland Ct. Stanw 5C 14
Sunderland Gro. Leav 7D
Sunderland Mt. SE23 . . . . . . .8H 9
Sunderland Rd. SE23 . . . . . . .7H 9
Sunderland Rd. W5 . . . . .4H 7
Sunderland Rd. H'row A . . .5C 14
Sunderland Ter. W2 . . . . .9M 5
Sunderland Way. E12 . . . . . . .7H 4
Sundew Av. W12 . . . . .1E 7
Sundew Clo. W12 . . . . .1E 7
Sundew Ct. Wemb 5J 3
(off Elmore Cl
Sundial Av. SE25 . . . . .7D 10
Sundorne Rd. SE7 . . . . .6G 7
Sundown Av. S Croy 3D 13
Sundown Rd. Ashf 2A 10
Sundra Wlk. E1 . . . . .7H 6
Sundridge. 3G 11
Sundridge Av. Brom 5H 11
Sundridge Av. Well 1B 9
Sundridge Clo. Dart 5L 9
Sundridge Ho. E9 . . . . .3H
(off Church Cres
Sundridge Pde. Brom 4F 11
Sundridge Park. 4F 11
Sundridge Pl. Croy 3E 12
Sundridge Rd. Croy 2D 12
Sunfields Pl. SE3 . . . . .8F 7
Sunflower Way. Romf 8H 3
Sungate Cotts. Romf 8K 3
Sun-in-the-Sands (Junct.)
. . . . .8F 7
Sunken Rd. Croy 7G 12
Sunkist Way. Wall 1J 13
Sunland Av. Bexh 3J 9
Sun La. SE3 . . . . .8F 7
Sunleigh Rd. Wemb 4J 5
Sunley Gdns. Gnfd 4E 5
Sunlight Clo. SW19 . . . . .3A 10
Sunlight Sq. E2 . . . . .6F 6
Sunmead Rd. Sun 7E 10
Sunna Gdns. Sun 6F 10

Sybil Thorndike Casson Ho.—Tavistock Rd.

Sybil Thorndike Casson Ho.
SW5 . . . . 6L 73
(off Old Brompton Rd.)
Sybourn St. E17 . . . . . 5K 45
Sycamore App. Crox G 7A 8
Sycamore Av. E3 . . . . . 4K 61
Sycamore Av. W5 . . . . . 4H 71
Sycamore Av. Hay 1C 68
Sycamore Av. Sidc 5D 96
Sycamore Av. Upm 8L 51
Sycamore Clo. E16 . . . . . 7C 62
Sycamore Clo. N9 . . . . . 4E 28
Sycamore Clo. SE9 . . . . . 8J 95
Sycamore Clo. W3 . . . . . 2C 72
Sycamore Clo. Barn 8B 14
Sycamore Clo. Bush 4J 9
Sycamore Clo. Cars 6D 122
Sycamore Clo. Edgw 4A 24
Sycamore Clo. Felt 9E 84
Sycamore Clo. Lou 4M 19
Sycamore Clo. N'holt 4J 53
Sycamore Clo. S Croy 7C 124
Sycamore Clo. Wat 8F 4
Sycamore Clo. W Dray 1K 143
Sycamore Ct. E7 . . . . . 2E 62
Sycamore Ct. NW6 . . . . . 4L 57
(off Bransdale Clo.)
Sycamore Ct. Eri 6B 82
(off Sandcliff Rd.)
Sycamore Ct. Houn 3J 85
Sycamore Ct. N Mald 7C 104
Sycamore Dri. Swan 7C 114
Sycamore Gdns. N15 . . . . . 2D 44
Sycamore Gdns. W6 . . . . . 3F 72
Sycamore Gdns. Mitc 6B 106
Sycamore Gro. NW9 . . . . . 5A 40
Sycamore Gro. SE6 . . . . . 5A 94
Sycamore Gro. SE20 . . . . . 5E 108
Sycamore Gro. N Mald 7B 104
Sycamore Hill. N11 . . . . . 6E 26
Sycamore Ho. N2 . . . . . 9B 26
(off Grange, The)
Sycamore Ho. SE16 . . . . . 3H 77
(off Woodland Cres.)
Sycamore Ho. W6 . . . . . 3F 72
Sycamore Ho. Buck H 2H 31
Sycamore Ho. Short 6C 110
Sycamore Lodge. W8 . . . . . 4M 73
(off Stone Hall Pl.)
Sycamore Lodge. Orp 4D 128
Sycamore M. SW4 . . . . . 2G 91
Sycamore M. Eri 6B 82
(off St John's Rd.)
Sycamore Ri. Bans 6H 135
Sycamore Rd. SW19 . . . . . 3G 105
Sycamore Rd. Crox G 7A 8
Sycamore Rd. Dart 7H 99
Sycamore St. EC1 . . . . . 7A 60
Sycamore Wlk. W10 . . . . . 7J 57
Sycamore Wlk. Ilf 2A 48
Sycamore Way. Tedd 3G 103
Sycamore Way. T Hth 9L 107
Sydcote. SE21 . . . . . 7A 92
Sydenham. 1G 109
Sydenham Av. N21 . . . . . 7K 15
Sydenham Av. SE26 . . . . . 2F 108
Sydenham Clo. Romf 1D 50
Sydenham Cotts. SE12 . . . . . 8G 95
Sydenham Ct. Croy 3B 124
(off Sydenham Rd.)
Sydenham Hill.
SE23 & SE26 . . . . . 7F 92
Sydenham Pk. SE26 . . . . . 9G 93
Sydenham Pk. Mans.
SE26 . . . . . 9G 93
(off Sydenham Pk.)
Sydenham Pk. Rd. SE26 . . . . 9G 93
Sydenham Pl. SE27 . . . . . 9M 91
Sydenham Ri. SE23 . . . . . 8F 92
Sydenham Rd. SE26 . . . . . 1G 109
Sydenham Rd. Croy 3A 124
Sydmons Ct. SE23 . . . . . 6G 93
Sydner M. N16 . . . . . 9D 44
Sydner Rd. N16 . . . . . 9D 44
Sydney Av. Purl 4K 137
Sydney Clo. SW3 . . . . . 5B 74
Sydney Ct. Hay 7G 53
Sydney Gro. NW4 . . . . . 3G 41
Sydney M. SW3 . . . . . 5B 74
Sydney Pl. SW7 . . . . . 5B 74
Sydney Rd. E11 . . . . . 4F 46
Sydney Rd. N8 . . . . . 2L 43
Sydney Rd. N10 . . . . . 8E 26
Sydney Rd. SE2 . . . . . 4G 81
Sydney Rd. SW20 . . . . . 6H 105
Sydney Rd. W13 . . . . . 2E 70
Sydney Rd. Bexh 3H 97
Sydney Rd. Enf 5B 16
(in two parts)
Sydney Rd. Felt 7E 84
Sydney Rd. Ilf 9A 32
Sydney Rd. Rich 3J 87
Sydney Rd. Sidc 1C 112
Sydney Rd. Sutt 6L 121
Sydney Rd. Tedd 2D 102
Sydney Rd. Wat 7C 8
Sydney Rd. Wfd G 4E 30
Sydney St. SW3 . . . . . 6C 74
Sylvana Clo. Uxb 4D 142
Sylvan Av. N3 . . . . . 9L 25
Sylvan Av. N22 . . . . . 7K 27
Sylvan Av. NW7 . . . . . 6C 24
Sylvan Av. Horn 4J 51
Sylvan Av. Romf 4K 49
Sylvan Clo. S Croy 2F 138
Sylvan Ct. N12 . . . . . 3M 25
Sylvan Est. SE19 . . . . . 5D 108
Sylvan Gdns. Surb 2H 119
Sylvan Gro. NW2 . . . . . 9H 41
Sylvan Gro. SE15 . . . . . 7F 76
Sylvan Hill. SE19 . . . . . 5C 108
Sylvan Rd. E7 . . . . . 2E 62
Sylvan Rd. E11 . . . . . 3E 46
Sylvan Rd. E17 . . . . . 3L 45
Sylvan Rd. SE19 . . . . . 5D 108
Sylvan Wlk. Brom 7K 111
Sylvan Way. Chig 3F 32
Sylvan Way. Dag 9F 48
Sylvan Way. W Wick 6C 126
Sylverdale Rd. Croy 5M 123
Sylverdale Rd. Purl 5M 137
Sylvester Av. Chst 3K 111
Sylvester Gdns. Ilf 5F 32
Sylvester Path. E8 . . . . . 2F 60
Sylvester Rd. E8 . . . . . 2F 60
Sylvester Rd. E17 . . . . . 5K 45
Sylvester Rd. N2 . . . . . 9A 26
Sylvester Rd. Wemb 1G 55
Sylvestrus Clo. King T 5L 103
Sylvia Av. Pinn 6J 21
Sylvia Ct. N1 . . . . . 5B 60
Sylvia Ct. Wemb 3M 55
Sylvia Gdns. Wemb 3M 55
Sylvia Pankhurst Ho. Dag 8L 49
(off Wythenshawe Rd.)
Symes M. NW1 . . . . . 5G 59
Symington Ho. SE1 . . . . . 4B 76
(off Deverell St.)
Symington M. E9 . . . . . 1H 61
Symister M. N1 . . . . . 6C 60
(off Coronet St.)
Symonds Ct. Chesh 1D 6
Symons St. SW3 . . . . . 5D 74
Symphony M. W10 . . . . . 6J 57
Syon Ga. Way. Bren 8E 70
Syon House & Pk. 9G 71
Syon La. Iswth 7C 70
Syon Lodge. SE12 . . . . . 6E 94
Syon Pk. Gdns. Iswth 8D 70
Syracuse Av. Rain 6J 67
Syringa Ho. SE4 . . . . . 2K 93

T

Tabard Ct. E14 . . . . . 9A 62
(off Lodore St.)
Tabard Garden Est. SE1 . . . . 4B 76
Tabard Ho. SE1 . . . . . 4B 76
(off Manciple St.)
Tabard St. SE1 . . . . . 3A 76
Tabarin Way. Eps 8G 135
Tabernacle Av. E13 . . . . . 7E 62
Tabernacle St. EC2 . . . . . 7B 60
Tableer Av. SW4 . . . . . 4G 91
Tabley Rd. N7 . . . . . 9J 43
Tabor Ct. Sutt 8J 121
Tabor Gdns. Sutt 8K 121
Tabor Gro. SW19 . . . . . 4K 105
Tabor Rd. W6 . . . . . 4F 72
Tachbrook Est. SW1 . . . . . 6H 75
Tachbrook M. SW1 . . . . . 5G 75
Tachbrook Rd. Felt 6D 84
Tachbrook Rd. S'hall 5H 69
Tachbrook Rd. Uxb 5A 142
Tachbrook Rd. W Dray 2J 143
Tachbrook St. SW1 . . . . . 5G 75
(in two parts)
Tack M. SE4 . . . . . 2L 93
Tadema Ho. NW8 . . . . . 7B 58
(off Penfold St.)
Tadema Rd. SW10 . . . . . 8A 74
Tadlow. King T 7L 103
(off Washington Rd.)
Tadlows Clo. Upm 1M 67
Tadmor Clo. Sun 8D 100
Tadmor St. W12 . . . . . 2H 73
Tadworth Av. N Mald 8D 104
Tadworth Ho. SE1 . . . . . 3M 75
(off Webber St.)
Tadworth Pde. Horn 9F 50
Tadworth Rd. NW2 . . . . . 7E 40
Taeping St. E14 . . . . . 5M 77
Taffrail Ho. E14 . . . . . 6M 77
(off Burrells Wharf Sq.)
Taffy's Row. Mitc 7C 106
Taft Way. E3 . . . . . 6M 61
Tailor Ho. WC1 . . . . . 7J 59
(off Colonnade)
Tailworth St. E1 . . . . . 8E 60
(off Chicksand St.)
Tailworth St. Houn 1A 86
Tait Ct. E3 . . . . . 4K 61
(off St Stephen's Rd.)
Tait Ct. SW8 . . . . . 9J 75
(off Lansdowne Grn.)
Tait Ho. SE1 . . . . . 2L 75
(off Greet St.)
Tait Rd. Croy 2C 124
Takeley Clo. Romf 9B 34
Takeley Clo. Wal A 6K 7
Takhar M. SW11 . . . . . 1C 90
Talacre Rd. NW5 . . . . . 2E 58
Talbot Av. N2 . . . . . 1B 42
Talbot Av. Wat 9J 9
Talbot Clo. N15 . . . . . 2D 44
Talbot Ct. EC3 . . . . . 1B 76
(off Gracechurch St.)
Talbot Ct. NW9 . . . . . 8B 40
Talbot Cres. NW4 . . . . . 3E 40
Talbot Gdns. Ilf 7E 48
Talbot Gro. Ho. W11 . . . . . 9J 57
(off Lancaster Rd.)
Talbot Ho. E14 . . . . . 9M 61
(off Girauld St.)
Talbot Pl. SE3 . . . . . 1C 94
Talbot Rd. E6 . . . . . 5L 63
Talbot Rd. E7 . . . . . 9E 46
Talbot Rd. N6 . . . . . 4E 42
Talbot Rd. N15 . . . . . 2D 44
Talbot Rd. N22 . . . . . 9G 27
Talbot Rd. SE22 . . . . . 3C 92
Talbot Rd. W11 & W2 . . . . . 9K 57
(in two parts)
Talbot Rd. W13 . . . . . 2E 70
Talbot Rd. Cars 7E 122
Talbot Rd. Dag 2K 65
Talbot Rd. Harr 9D 22
Talbot Rd. Iswth 3E 86
Talbot Rd. S'hall 5J 69
Talbot Rd. T Hth 8B 108
Talbot Rd. Twic 7C 86
Talbot Rd. Wemb 2H 55
Talbot Sq. W2 . . . . . 9B 58
Talbot Wlk. NW10 . . . . . 2C 56
Talbot Wlk. W11 . . . . . 9J 57
Talbot Yd. SE1 . . . . . 2B 76
Talcott Path. SW2 . . . . . 7L 91
Talfourd Pl. SE15 . . . . . 9D 76
Talfourd Rd. SE5 . . . . . 9D 76
Talgarth Ho. Romf 6J 35
(off Kingsbridge Cir.)
Talgarth Mans. W14 . . . . . 6J 73
(off Talgarth Rd.)
Talgarth Rd. W6 & W14 . . . . 6H 73
Talgarth Wlk. NW9 . . . . . 3C 40
Talia Ho. E14 . . . . . 4A 78
(off Manchester Rd.)
Talina Cen. SW6 . . . . . 9A 74
Talisman Clo. Ilf 6F 48
Talisman Sq. SE26 . . . . . 1E 108
Talisman Way. Eps 8G 135
Talisman Way. Wemb 8K 39
Tallack Clo. Harr 7C 22
Tallack Rd. E10 . . . . . 6K 45
Tall Elms Clo. Brom 9D 110
Tallents Clo. S at H 4M 115
Talleyrand Ho. SE5 . . . . . 1A 92
(off Lilford Rd.)
Tallis Clo. E16 . . . . . 9F 62
Tallis Gro. SE7 . . . . . 7F 78
Tallis St. EC4 . . . . . 1L 75
Tallis Vw. NW10 . . . . . 2B 56
Tallis Way. Borwd 3H 11
Tall Pines. Eps 3D 134
Tall Trees. SW16 . . . . . 7K 107
Tall Trees Clo. Horn 3J 51
Talma Gdns. Twic 5C 86
Talmage Clo. SE23 . . . . . 6G 93
Talman Gro. Stan 6H 23
Talma Rd. SW2 . . . . . 3L 91
Talwin St. E3 . . . . . 6M 61
Tamar Clo. E3 . . . . . 4K 61
Tamar Dri. Ave 9M 67
Tamar Ho. E14 . . . . . 3A 78
(off Plevna St.)
Tamar Ho. SE11 . . . . . 6L 75
(off Kennington La.)
Tamarind Ct. W8 . . . . . 4M 73
(off Stone Hall Gdns.)
Tamarind Yd. E1 . . . . . 2E 76
(off Kennet St.)
Tamarisk Sq. W12 . . . . . 1D 72
Tamar Sq. Wfd G 6F 30
Tamar St. SE7 . . . . . 4J 79
Tamar Way. N17 . . . . . 1E 44
Tamesis Gdns. Wor Pk 4C 120
Tamian Ind. Est. Houn 3G 85
Tamian Way. Houn 3G 85
Tamplin Ho. W10 . . . . . 6K 57
(off Dowland St.)
Tamworth. N7 . . . . . 2J 59
Tamworth Av. Wfd G 6C 30
Tamworth La. Mitc 6F 106
Tamworth Pk. Mitc 8F 106
Tamworth Pl. Croy 4A 124
Tamworth Rd. Croy 4M 123
Tamworth St. SW6 . . . . . 7L 73
Tamworth Vs. Mitc 8F 106
Tancred Rd. N4 . . . . . 5M 43
Tandem Cen. Retail Pk.
SW19 . . . . . 5B 106
Tandem Way. SW19 . . . . . 5B 106
Tandridge Dri. Orp 3B 128
Tandridge Gdns. S Croy 5D 138
Tandridge Pl. Orp 3B 128
Tanfield Av. NW2 . . . . . 9D 40
Tanfield Rd. Croy 6A 124
Tangent Link. H Hill 8H 35
Tangier Rd. Rich 3L 87
Tangier Way. Tad 9J 135
Tangier Wood. Tad 9J 135
Tangleberry Clo. Brom 8K 111
Tangle Tree Clo. N3 . . . . . 9M 25
Tanglewood Clo. Croy 5G 125
Tanglewood Clo. Stan 2C 22
Tanglewood Clo. Uxb 7E 142
Tanglewood Ct. Orp 7G 113
Tanglewood Way. Felt 9F 84
Tangley Gro. SW15 . . . . . 5D 88
Tangley Pk. Rd. Hamp 2K 101
Tangmere. N17 . . . . . 9B 28
(off Willan Rd.)
Tangmere. WC1 . . . . . 6K 59
(off Sidmouth St.)
Tangmere Cres. Horn 2F 66
Tangmere Gdns. N'holt 5G 53
(in two parts)
Tangmere Gro. King T 2H 103
Tangmere Way. NW9 . . . . . 9C 24
Tanhurst Ho. SW2 . . . . . 6K 91
(off Redlands Way)
Tanhurst Wlk. SE2 . . . . . 4H 81
Tankerton Houses. WC1 . . . . 6J 59
(off Tankerton St.)
Tankerton Rd. Surb 4K 119
Tankerton St. WC1 . . . . . 6J 59
Tankerton Ter. Croy 1K 123
Tankerville Rd. SW16 . . . . . 4H 107
Tank Hill Rd. Purf 5L 83
Tank La. Purf 5L 83
Tankridge Rd. NW2 . . . . . 7F 40
Tanner Ho. SE1 . . . . . 3C 76
(off Tanner St.)
Tanneries, The. E1 . . . . . 7G 61
(off Cephas Av.)
Tanner Point. E13 . . . . . 4E 62
(off Pelly Rd.)
Tanners Clo. W on T 1F 116
Tanners End La. N18 . . . . . 4C 28
Tanner's Hill. SE8 . . . . . 9K 77
Tanners Hill. Ab L 4D 4
Tanners La. B'side 1A 48
Tanner St. SE1 . . . . . 3C 76
(in two parts)
Tanner St. Bark 2A 64
Tanners Wood Clo. Ab L 5C 4
Tanners Wood Ct. Ab L 5C 4
Tanners Wood La. Ab L 5C 4
Tannery Clo. Beck 9H 109
Tannery Clo. Dag 8M 49
Tannington Ter. N5 . . . . . 8M 43
Tannsfeld Rd. SE26 . . . . . 2H 109
Tansley Clo. N7 . . . . . 1H 59
Tanswell St. SE1 . . . . . 3L 75
Tansy Clo. E6 . . . . . 9L 63
Tansy Clo. Romf 6J 35
Tantallon Rd. SW12 . . . . . 7E 90
Tant Av. E16 . . . . . 9D 62
Tantony Gro. Romf 1H 49
Tanworth Clo. N'wd 6A 20
Tanworth Gdns. Pinn 9F 20
Tanyard La. Bex 6L 97
Tanza Rd. NW3 . . . . . 9D 42
Tapestry Clo. Sutt 9M 121
Tapley Ho. SE1 . . . . . 3E 76
(off Wolseley St.)
Taplins Trad. Est.
W Dray 1H 143
Taplow. SE17 . . . . . 6B 76
(off Thurlow St.)
Taplow Ct. Mitc 8C 106
Taplow Ho. E2 . . . . . 6D 60
(off Palissy St.)
Taplow Rd. N13 . . . . . 4A 28
Taplow St. N1 . . . . . 5A 60
Tappesfield Rd. SE15 . . . . . 2G 93
Tapp St. E1 . . . . . 7F 60
Tapster St. Barn 5K 13
Tara Ct. Beck 6M 109
Tara M. N8 . . . . . 4J 43
Taranto Ho. E1 . . . . . 8H 61
(off Master's St.)
Tarbert M. N15 . . . . . 3C 44
Tarbert Rd. SE22 . . . . . 4C 92
Tarbert Wlk. E1 . . . . . 1G 77
Target Clo. Felt 5C 84
Target Ho. W13 . . . . . 2F 70
(off Sherwood Clo.)
Target Roundabout (Junct.)
. . . . . 4K 53
Tariff Cres. SE8 . . . . . 5K 77
Tariff Rd. N17 . . . . . 6E 28
Tarleton Ct. N22 . . . . . 9L 27
Tarleton Gdns. SE23 . . . . . 8F 92
Tarling Clo. Sidc 9F 96
Tarling Ho. E1 . . . . . 9F 60
(off Tarling St.)
Tarling Rd. E16 . . . . . 9D 62
Tarling Rd. N2 . . . . . 9A 26
Tarling St. E1 . . . . . 9F 60
Tarling St. Est. E1 . . . . . 9G 61
Tarmac Way. W Dray 8G 143
Tarn Bank. Enf 7J 15
Tarns, The. NW1 . . . . . 6G 59
(off Varndell St.)
Tarn St. SE1 . . . . . 4A 76
Tarnwood Pk. SE9 . . . . . 6K 95
Tarnworth Rd. Romf 5L 35
Tarplett Ho. SE14 . . . . . 7G 77
(off John Williams Clo.)
Tarquin Ho. SE26 . . . . . 1E 108
(off High Level Dri.)
Tarragon Clo. SE14 . . . . . 8J 77
Tarragon Gro. SE26 . . . . . 3H 1
Tarranbrae. NW6 . . . . . 3J
Tarrant Ho. E2 . . . . . 6G
(off Roman R
Tarrant Pl. W1 . . . . . 8D
Tarrington Clo. SW16 . . . . . 9H
Tartan Ho. E14 . . . . . 9A
(off Dee S
Tarver Rd. SE17 . . . . . 6M
Tarves Way. SE10 . . . . . 8M
Tash Pl. N11 . . . . . 5F 2
Tasker Clo. Hay 8A
Tasker Ho. E14 . . . . . 8K
(off Wallwood S
Tasker Ho. Bark 5B
Tasker Rd. NW3 . . . . . 1D
Tasman Ct. E14 . . . . . 5M
(off Westferry R
Tasman Ct. Sun 4C 1
Tasman Ho. E1 . . . . . 2F
(off Clegg S
Tasmania Ter. N18 . . . . . 6A 2
Tasman Rd. SW9 . . . . . 2J
Tasman Wlk. E16 . . . . . 9H 6
Tasso Rd. W6 . . . . . 7J 7
Tasso Yd. W6 . . . . . 7J 7
(off Tasso R
Tatam Rd. NW10 . . . . . 3B 5
Tatchbury Ho. SW15 . . . . . 5D 8
(off Tunworth Cres
Tate Britain. 5J 7
Tate Gdns. Bush 9C 1
Tate Ho. E2 . . . . . 5H 6
(off Mace S
Tate Modern. 2M 7
Tate Rd. E16 . . . . . 2K 7
(in two parts
Tate Rd. Sutt 7L 12
Tatnell Rd. SE23 . . . . . 5J 9
Tatsfield Ho. SE1 . . . . . 4B 7
(off Pardoner S
Tattenham Corner Rd.
Eps 9D 13
Tattenham Cres. Eps 9E 13
Tattenham Way. Tad 9H 13
Tattersall Clo. SE9 . . . . . 4J 9
Tatton Cres. N16 . . . . . 5D 4
Tatum St. SE17 . . . . . 5B 7
Tauber Clo. Els 6K 1
Tauheed Clo. N4 . . . . . 7A 4
Taunton Av. SW20 . . . . . 6F 10
Taunton Av. Houn 1A 8
Taunton Clo. Bexh 1B 9
Taunton Clo. Ilf 6D 3
Taunton Clo. Sutt 3L 12
Taunton Dri. N2 . . . . . 9A 2
Taunton Dri. Enf 5L 1
Taunton Ho. W2 . . . . . 9A 5
(off Hallfield Est
Taunton Ho. Romf 5K 3
(off Redcar Rd
Taunton M. NW1 . . . . . 7D 5
Taunton Pl. NW1 . . . . . 7D 5
Taunton Rd. SE12 . . . . . 4C 9
Taunton Rd. Gnfd 4M 5
Taunton Rd. Romf 4G 3
Taunton Way. Stan 9J 2
Tavern Clo. Cars 2C 12
Taverners Clo. W11 . . . . . 2J 7
Taverners Ct. E3 . . . . . 6J 6
(off Grove Rd.
Taverner Sq. N5 . . . . . 9A 4
Taverners Way. E4 . . . . . 1C 3
Tavern La. SW9 . . . . . 1L 9
Tavern Quay. SE16 . . . . . 5J 7
Tavistock Av. E17 . . . . . 1H 4
Tavistock Av. NW7 . . . . . 7H 2
Tavistock Av. Gnfd 5E 54
Tavistock Clo. N16 . . . . . 1C 60
Tavistock Clo. Romf 8H 35
Tavistock Ct. WC1 . . . . . 7H 59
(off Tavistock Sq.
Tavistock Ct. Croy 3B 124
(off Tavistock Rd.
Tavistock Cres. W11 . . . . . 8K 57
(in three parts)
Tavistock Cres. Mitc 8J 107
Tavistock Gdns. Ilf 9C 48
Tavistock Ga. Croy 3B 124
Tavistock Gro. Croy 2B 124
Tavistock Ho. WC1 . . . . . 7H 59
Tavistock M. E18 . . . . . 2E 46
Tavistock M. W11 . . . . . 9K 57
Tavistock Pl. E18 . . . . . 2E 46
Tavistock Pl. N14 . . . . . 9F 14
Tavistock Pl. WC1 . . . . . 7J 59
Tavistock Rd. E7 . . . . . 9D 46
Tavistock Rd. E15 . . . . . 2D 62
Tavistock Rd. E18 . . . . . 1E 46
Tavistock Rd. N4 . . . . . 4B 44
Tavistock Rd. NW10 . . . . . 5D 56
Tavistock Rd. W11 . . . . . 9K 57
(in two parts)
Tavistock Rd. Brom 8D 110
Tavistock Rd. Cars 3B 122
Tavistock Rd. Croy 3B 124
Tavistock Rd. Edgw 8L 23
Tavistock Rd. Uxb 1B 52
Tavistock Rd. Wat 3H 9
Tavistock Rd. Well 9G 81
Tavistock Rd. W Dray 2H 143

Thanet Lodge. NW2 2J 57
(off Mapesbury Rd.)
Thanet Pl. Croy 6A 124
Thanet Rd. Bex 6L 97
Thanet Rd. Eri 8C 82
Thanet St. WC1 6J 59
Thanet Wharf. SE8 7M 77
(off Copperas St.)
Thane Vs. N7 8K 43
Thane Works. N7 8K 43
Thant Clo. E10 8M 45
Tharp Rd. Wall 7H 123
Thatcham Ct. N20 9A 14
Thatcham Gdns. N20 9A 14
Thatcher Clo. W Dray 3J 143
Thatcher Ct. Dart 6H 99
Thatchers Clo. Lou 4M 19
Thatchers Way. Iswth 4B 86
Thatches Gro. Romf 2J 49
Thavie's Inn. EC1 9L 59
Thaxted Ct. N1 5B 60
(off Fairbank Est.)
Thaxted Ho. SE16 5G 77
(off Abbeyfield Est.)
Thaxted Ho. Dag 3M 65
Thaxted Pl. SW20 4H 105
Thaxted Rd. SE9 9A 96
Thaxted Rd. Buck H 9J 19
Thaxted Wlk. Rain 3C 66
Thaxted Way. Wal A 6K 7
Thaxton Rd. W14 7K 73
Thayers Farm Rd. Beck 5J 109
Thayer St. W1 9E 58
Theatre Ct. Eps 5B 134
Theatre Mus. 1J 75
(off Russell St.)
Theatre Royal (Stratford)
2B 62
Theatre Sq. E15 2B 62
Theatre St. SW11 2D 90
Theatro Technis. 4G 59
Theberton St. N1 4L 59
Theed St. SE1 2L 75
Thelma Gdns. SE3 9H 79
Thelma Gro. Tedd 3E 102
Theobald Cres. Harr 8A 22
Theobald Rd. E17 5K 45
Theobald Rd. Croy 4M 123
Theobalds Av. N12 4A 26
Theobalds Ct. N4 8A 44
Theobalds La. Wal X 5A 6
(in three parts)
Theobalds Pk. Rd. Enf 1M 15
Theobald's Rd. WC1 8K 59
Theobald St. SE1 4B 76
Theobald St.
Rad & Borwd 1G 11
Theodora Way. Pinn 1D 36
Theodore Ct. SE13 5B 94
Theodore Rd. SE13 5B 94
Therapia La. Croy 2H 123
(in two parts)
Therapia Rd. SE22 5G 93
Theresa Rd. W6 5E 72
Theresa's Wlk. S Croy 1B 138
Therfield Ct. N4 7A 44
Thermopylae Ga. E14 5M 77
Theseus Wlk. N1 5M 59
(off City Garden Row)
Thesiger Rd. SE20 4H 109
Thessaly Ho. SW8 8G 75
(off Thessaly Rd.)
Thessaly Rd. SW8 8G 75
(in two parts)
Thesus Ho. E14 9A 62
(off Blair St.)
Thetford Clo. N13 6M 27
Thetford Gdns. Dag 4J 65
Thetford Ho. SE1 4D 76
(off Maltby St.)
Thetford Rd. Ashf 9C 144
Thetford Rd. Dag 3H 65
Thetford Rd. N Mald 1B 120
Thetis Ter. Rich 7L 71
Theydon Gdns. Rain 3C 66
Theydon Gro. Wfd G 6G 31
Theydon Rd. E5 7G 45
Theydon St. E17 5K 45
Thicket Cres. Sutt 6A 122
Thicket Gro. SE19 4E 108
Thicket Gro. Dag 2G 65
Thicket Rd. SE20 4E 108
Thicket Rd. Sutt 6A 122
Thicket, The. W Dray 9C 142
Third Av. E12 9J 47
Third Av. E13 6E 62
Third Av. E17 3L 45
Third Av. W3 2D 72
Third Av. W10 6J 57
Third Av. Dag 4M 65
Third Av. Enf 7D 16
Third Av. Hay 2D 68
Third Av. Romf 4G 49
Third Av. Wat 8H 5
Third Av. Wemb 7H 39
Third Clo. W Mol 8A 102
Third Cross Rd. Twic 8B 86
Third Way. Wemb 9M 39
Thirleby Rd. SW1 4G 75
Thirleby Rd. Edgw 8B 24
Thirlestane Ct. N10 9E 26
Thirlmere. NW1 6F 58
(off Cumberland Mkt.)
Thirlmere Av. Gnfd 6G 55
Thirlmere Gdns. N'wd 5A 20
Thirlmere Gdns. Wemb 6G 39
Thirlmere Ri. Brom 3D 110
Thirlmere Rd. N10 8F 26
Thirlmere Rd. SW16 1H 107
Thirlmere Rd. Bexh 1A 98
Thirsk Clo. N'holt 2L 53
Thirsk Rd. SE25 8B 108
Thirsk Rd. SW11 2E 90
Thirsk Rd. Borwd 1L 11
Thirsk Rd. Mitc 4E 106
Thirston Path. Borwd 4L 11
Thirza Rd. Dart 5K 99
Thistlebrook. SE2 3G 81
Thistle Ct. Dart 7M 99
(off Churchill Clo.)
Thistlecroft Gdns. Stan 8H 23
Thistlecroft Rd. W on T 6G 117
Thistledene. Th Dit 1C 118
Thistledene Av. Harr 8J 37
Thistledene Av. Romf 5M 33
Thistlefield Clo. Bex 7H 97
Thistle Gro. SW10 6A 74
Thistle Ho. E14 9A 62
(off Dee St.)
Thistlemead. Chst 6M 111
Thistle Mead. Lou 5L 19
Thistlewaite Rd. E5 8F 44
Thistlewood Clo. N7 7K 43
Thistlewood Cres.
New Ad 4B 140
Thistleworth Clo. Iswth 8B 70
Thistleworth Marina.
Iswth 3F 86
(off Railshead Rd.)
Thistley Clo. N12 6C 26
Thistley Ct. SE8 7M 77
Thomas A'Beckett Clo.
Wemb 9D 38
Thomas Baines Rd. SW11 2B 90
Thomas Burt Ho. E2 6F 60
(off Canrobert St.)
Thomas Cribb M. E6 9L 63
Thomas Darby Ct. W11 9J 57
(off Lancaster Rd.)
Thomas Dean Rd. SE26 1K 109
Thomas Dinwiddy Rd.
SE12 8F 94
Thomas Doyle St. SE1 4M 75
Thomas England Ho.
Romf 4B 50
(off Waterloo Gdns.)
Thomas Hewlett Ho. Harr 9C 38
Thomas Hollywood Ho.
E2 5G 61
(off Approach Rd.)
Thomas Ho. Sutt 9M 121
Thomas La. SE6 6L 93
Thomas Lodge. E17 3M 45
Thomas More Highwalk.
EC2 8A 60
(off Beech St.)
Thomas More Ho. EC2 8A 60
(off Beech St.)
Thomas More Ho. Ruis 6C 36
Thomas More Sq. E1 1E 76
(off Thomas More St.)
Thomas More St. E1 1E 76
Thomas More Way. N2 1A 42
Thomas Neal's Shop. Mall.
WC2 9J 59
Thomas N. Ter. E16 8D 62
(off Barking Rd.)
Thomas Pl. W8 4M 73
Thomas Rd. E14 9K 61
Thomas Rd. Ind. Est. E14 8L 61
Thomas Sims Ct. Horn 2F 66
Thomas St. SE18 5M 79
Thomas Turner Path.
Croy 4A 124
(off George St.)
Thomas Wall Clo. Sutt 7M 121
Thomas Watson Cottage Homes.
Barn 6J 13
(off Leecroft Rd.)
Thompson Av. Rich 2L 87
Thompson Clo. Ilf 7A 48
Thompson Clo. Sutt 3L 121
Thompson Ho. SE14 7G 77
(off John Williams Clo.)
Thompson Rd. SE22 5D 92
Thompson Rd. Dag 8K 49
Thompson Rd. Houn 3M 85
Thompson Rd. Uxb 4C 142
Thompson's Av. SE5 8A 76
Thompson's La. Lou 2E 18
Thomson Cres. Croy 3L 123
Thomson Ho. E14 9L 61
(off Saracen St.)
Thomson Ho. SE17 5C 76
(off Tatum St.)
Thomson Ho. SW1 6H 75
(off Bessborough Pl.)
Thomson Ho. S'hall 1J 69
(off Broadway, The)
Thomson Rd. Harr 1C 38
Thorburn Sq. SE1 5E 76
Thorburn Way. SW19 5B 106
Thoresby St. N1 6A 60
Thorkhill Gdns. Th Dit 3E 118
Thorkhill Rd. Th Dit 3E 118
Thornaby Gdns. N18 6E 28
Thornaby Ho. E2 6F 60
(off Canrobert St.)
Thorn Av. Bus H 1A 22
Thorn Bank. Edgw 6L 23
Thornbury. NW4 2F 40
(off Prince of Wales Clo.)
Thornbury Av. Iswth 8B 70
Thornbury Clo. N16 1C 60
Thornbury Ct. W11 1L 73
(off Chepstow Vs.)
Thornbury Ct. Iswth 8C 70
Thornbury Ct. S Croy 7B 124
(off Blunt Rd.)
Thornbury Gdns. Borwd 6A 12
Thornbury Ho. Romf 5H 35
(off Bridgwater Wlk.)
Thornbury Rd. SW2 5J 91
Thornbury Rd. Iswth 8B 70
Thornbury Sq. N6 6G 43
Thornby Rd. E5 8G 45
Thorncliffe Rd. SW4 5J 91
Thorncliffe Rd. S'hall 6K 69
Thorn Clo. Brom 1L 127
Thorn Clo. N'holt 6K 53
Thorncombe Rd. SE22 4C 92
Thorncroft. Horn 4F 50
Thorncroft Rd. Sutt 7M 121
Thorncroft St. SW8 8J 75
Thorndean St. SW18 8A 90
Thorndene. SE28 1F 80
Thorndene Av. N11 1E 26
Thorndike Av. N'holt 4H 53
Thorndike Clo. SW10 8A 74
Thorndike Ho. SW1 6H 75
(off Vauxhall Bri. Rd.)
Thorndike St. SW1 5H 75
Thorndon Clo. Orp 6D 112
Thorndon Gdns. Eps 7C 120
Thorndon Rd. Orp 6D 112
Thorndyke Ct. Pinn 6K 21
Thorne Clo. E11 9C 46
Thorne Clo. E16 9E 62
Thorne Clo. Ashf 4A 100
Thorne Clo. Eri 7M 81
Thorne Ho. E2 6G 61
(off Roman Rd.)
Thorne Ho. E14 4A 78
(off Launch St.)
Thorne Ho. Clay 9F 118
Thorneloe Gdns. Croy 7L 123
Thorne Pas. SW13 1C 88
Thorne Rd. SW8 8J 75
Thornes Clo. Beck 7A 110
Thorne St. SW13 2C 88
Thornet Wood Rd. Brom 7L 111
Thornewill Ho. E1 1G 77
(off Cable St.)
Thorney. 4G 143
Thorney Ct. W8 3A 74
(off Palace Ga.)
Thorney Cres. SW11 8B 74
Thorneycroft Clo.
W on T 1G 117
Thorneycroft Dri. Enf 1L 17
Thorney Hedge Rd. W4 5M 71
Thorney Mill Rd.
Iver & W Dray 4G 143
Thorney St. SW1 5J 75
Thornfield Av. NW7 8J 25
Thornfield Ct. NW7 8J 25
Thornfield Ho. E14 1L 77
(off Rosefield Gdns.)
Thornfield Pde. NW7 7J 25
(off Holders Hill Rd.)
Thornfield Rd. W12 3F 72
(in four parts)
Thornfield Rd. Bans 9L 135
Thornford Rd. SE13 4A 94
Thorngate Rd. W9 7L 57
Thorngrove Rd. E13 4F 62
Thornham Gro. E15 1B 62
Thornham St. SE10 7M 77
Thornhaugh M. WC1 7H 59
Thornhaugh St. WC1 7H 59
Thornhill Av. SE18 8C 80
Thornhill Av. Surb 4J 119
Thornhill Bri. Wharf. N1 4K 59
Thornhill Cres. N1 3K 59
Thornhill Gdns. E10 7M 45
Thornhill Gdns. Bark 3C 64
Thornhill Gro. N1 3K 59
Thornhill Ho. W4 6C 72
(off Wood St.)
Thornhill Houses. N1 3L 59
Thornhill Rd. E10 7M 45
Thornhill Rd. N1 3L 59
Thornhill Rd. Croy 2A 124
Thornhill Rd. N'wd 4A 20
Thornhill Rd. Surb 4J 119
Thornhill Sq. N1 3K 59
Thorn Ho. Borwd 4A 12
(off Elstree Way)
Thornicroft Ho. SW9 1K 91
(off Stockwell Rd.)
Thorn La. Rain 5H 67
Thornlaw Rd. SE27 1L 107
Thornley Clo. N17 7E 28
Thornley Dri. Harr 7M 37
Thornley Pl. SE10 6C 78
Thornsbeach Rd. SE6 7A 94
Thornsett Pl. SE20 6F 108
Thornsett Rd. SE20 6F 108
Thornsett Rd. SW18 7M 89
Thornsett Ter. SE20 6F 108
(off Croydon Rd.)
Thorn Ter. SE15 2G 93
Thornton Av. SW2 7H 91
Thornton Av. W4 5C 72
Thornton Av. Croy 1K 123
Thornton Av. W Dray 4K 143
Thornton Clo. W Dray 4K 143
Thornton Dene. Beck 6L 109
Thornton Gdns. SW12 7H 91
Thornton Gro. Pinn 6L 21
Thornton Heath. 8A 108
Thornton Heath Pond (Junct.)
9L 107
Thornton Hill. SW19 4J 105
Thornton Ho. SE17 5C 76
(off Townsend St.)
Thornton Pl. W1 8D 58
Thornton Rd. E11 7B 46
Thornton Rd. N18 3G 29
Thornton Rd. SW12 6H 91
Thornton Rd. SW14 3B 88
Thornton Rd. SW19 3H 105
Thornton Rd. Barn 5J 13
Thornton Rd. Belv 5M 81
Thornton Rd. Brom 2E 110
Thornton Rd. Cars 3B 122
Thornton Rd.
Croy & T Hth 2K 123
Thornton Rd. Ilf 9M 47
Thornton Rd. E. SW19 3H 105
Thornton Row. T Hth 9L 107
Thornton's Farm Av. Romf 6A 50
Thornton St. SW9 1L 91
Thornton Way. NW11 3M 41
Thorntree Ct. W5 8J 55
Thorntree Rd. SE7 6H 79
Thornville Gro. Mitc 6B 106
Thornville St. SE8 9L 77
Thornwell Ct. W7 3C 70
(off Du Burstow Ter.)
Thornwood Clo. E18 9F 30
Thornwood Ho. Buck H 9J 19
Thornwood Rd. SE13 4C 94
Thornycroft Ho. W4 6C 72
(off Fraser St.)
Thorogood Gdns. E15 1C 62
Thorogood Way. Rain 4C 66
Thorold Clo. S Croy 2H 139
Thorold Ho. SE1 3A 76
(off Pepper St.)
Thorold Rd. N22 7J 27
Thorold Rd. Ilf 7M 47
Thorparch Rd. SW8 9H 75
Thorpebank Rd. W12 2E 72
Thorpe Clo. SE26 1H 109
Thorpe Clo. W10 9J 57
Thorpe Clo. New Ad 3A 140
Thorpe Clo. Orp 4C 128
Thorpe Ct. Enf 5M 15
Thorpe Cres. E17 9K 29
Thorpe Cres. Wat 9G 9
Thorpedale Gdns. Ilf 2L 47
Thorpedale Rd. N4 7J 43
Thorpe Hall Rd. E17 8A 30
Thorpe Ho. N1 4K 59
(off Barnsbury Est.)
Thorpe Lodge. Horn 4J 51
Thorpe Rd. E6 4K 63
Thorpe Rd. E7 9D 46
Thorpe Rd. E17 9A 30
Thorpe Rd. N15 4C 44
Thorpe Rd. Bark 3B 64
Thorpe Rd. King T 4J 103
Thorpewood Av. SE26 8F 92
Thorpland Av. Uxb 8A 36
Thorsden Way. SE19 2C 108
Thorverton Rd. NW2 8J 41
Thoydon Rd. E3 5J 61
Thrale Rd. SW16 1G 107
Thrale St. SE1 2A 76
Thrapston Ho. Romf 5J 35
(off Dagnam Pk. Dri.)
Thrasher Clo. E8 4D 60
Thrawl St. E1 8D 60
Thrayle Ho. SW9 2K 91
(off Benedict Rd.)
Threadgold Ho. N1 2B 60
(off Dovercourt Est.)
Threadneedle St. EC2 9B 60
Three Barrels Wlk. EC4 1A 76
(off Queen St. Pl.)
Three Bridges Bus. Cen.
S'hall 3A 70
Three Colt Corner.
E2 & E1 7E 60
(off Cheshire St.)
Three Colts La. E2 7F 60
Three Colt St. E14 9K 61
Three Corners. Bexh 1M 97
Three Cranes Wlk. EC4 1A 76
(off Bell Wharf La.)
Three Cups Yd. WC1 8K 59
(off Sandland St.)
Three Kings Yd. W1 1F 74
Three Meadows M. Harr 8D 22
Three Mill La. E3 6A 62
(in two parts)
Three Oak La. SE1 3D 76
Three Quays. EC3 1C 76
(off Tower Hill)
Three Quays Wlk. EC3 1C 76
Three Valleys Way. Bush 7H 9
Threshers Pl. W11 1J 73
Thriffwood. SE26 9G 93
Thrift Farm La. Borwd 4A 12
Thrigby Rd. Chess 8K 119
Thring Ho. SW9 1K 91
(off Stockwell Rd.)
Throckmorten Rd. E16 9F 62
Throgmorton Av. EC2 9B 60
(in two parts)
Throgmorton St. EC2 9B 60
Throstle Pl. Wat 5G 5
Throwley Clo. SE2 4G 81
(in two parts)
Throwley Rd. Sutt 7M 121
Throwley Way. Sutt 6M 121
Thrums. Wat 1F 8
Thrupp Clo. Mitc 6F 106
Thrupp's Av. W on T 7H 117
Thrupp's La. W on T 7H 117
Thrush Grn. Harr 2L 37
Thrush St. SE17 6A 76
Thurbarn Rd. SE6 2M 109
Thurland Ho. SE16 5F 76
(off Camilla Rd.)
Thurland Rd. SE16 4E 76
Thurlby Clo. Harr 4E 38
Thurlby Clo. Wfd G 5K 31
Thurlby Cft. NW4 1G 41
(off Mulberry Clo.)
Thurlby Rd. SE27 1L 107
Thurlby Rd. Wemb 2H 55
Thurleigh Av. SW12 5E 90
Thurleigh Rd. SW12 6D 90
Thurleston Av. Mord 9J 105
Thurlestone Av. N12 6D 26
Thurlestone Av. Ilf 9D 48
Thurlestone Clo. Shep 1A 116
Thurlestone Ct. S'hall 9M 53
(off Howard Rd.)
Thurlestone Pde. Shep 1A 116
(off High St.)
Thurlestone Rd. SE27 9L 91
Thurloe Clo. SW7 5C 74
Thurloe Ct. SW3 5C 74
(off Fulham Ct.)
Thurloe Gdns. Romf 4D 50
Thurloe Pl. SW7 5B 74
Thurloe Pl. M. SW7 5B 74
(off Thurloe Pl.)
Thurloe Sq. SW7 5C 74
Thurloe St. SW7 5B 74
Thurlow Clo. E4 6A 30
Thurlow Gdns. Ilf 6B 32
Thurlow Gdns. Wemb 1H 55
Thurlow Hill. SE21 7A 92
Thurlow Ho. SW16 9J 91
Thurlow Pk. Rd. SE21 8M 91
Thurlow Rd. NW3 1B 58
Thurlow Rd. W7 3E 70
Thurlow St. SE17 6B 76
(in two parts)
Thurlow Ter. NW5 1E 58
Thurlow Wlk. SE17 6C 76
(in two parts)
Thurlstone Rd. Ruis 8E 36
Thurnby Ct. Twic 9C 86
Thurnscoe. NW1 4G 59
(off Pratt St.)
Thurrock Commercial Cen.
Ave 3K 83
Thursland Rd. Sidc 2J 113
Thursley Cres. New Ad 9A 126
Thursley Gdns. SW19 8H 89
Thursley Ho. SW2 6K 91
(off Holmewood Gdns.)
Thursley Rd. SE9 9K 95
Thurso Clo. Romf 6M 35
Thurso Ho. NW6 5M 57
Thurso St. SW17 1B 106
Thurstan Dwellings. WC2 9J 59
(off Newton St.)
Thurstan Rd. SW20 4F 104
Thurston Ind. Est. SE13 2M 93
Thurston Rd. SE13 1M 93
Thurston Rd. S'hall 9K 53
Thurtle Rd. E2 5D 60
Thwaite Clo. Eri 7A 82
Thyer Clo. Orp 6A 128
Thyra Gro. N12 6M 25
Tibbatt's Rd. E3 7M 61
Tibbenham Pl. SE6 8L 93
Tibbenham Wlk. E13 5D 62
Tibberton Sq. N1 4A 60
Tibbet's Clo. SW19 7H 89
Tibbet's Corner (Junct.)
6H 89
Tibbet's Ride. SW15 6H 89
Tibbles Clo. Wat 8J 5
Tibbs Hill Rd. Ab L 3D 4
Tiber Gdns. N1 4J 59
Ticehurst Clo. Orp 4E 112
Ticehurst Rd. SE23 8J 93
Tichmarsh. Eps 2A 134

Tickford Clo.—Tower Bldgs.

Tickford Clo. SE2 . . . . 3G 81
Tickford Ho. NW8 . . . . 6C 58
Tidal Basin Rd. E16 . . . . 1D 78
Tidbury Ct. SW8 . . . . 8G 75
(off Stewart's Rd.)
Tidelea Tower. SE28 . . . . 3A 80
(off Erebus Dri.)
Tidenham Gdns. Croy 5C 124
Tideside Ct. SE18 . . . . 4J 79
Tideswell Rd. SW15 . . . . . . 3G 89
Tideswell Rd. Croy 5L 125
Tideway Clo. Rich 1F 102
Tideway Ct. SE16 . . . . 2H 77
Tideway Ho. E14 . . . . 3L 77
(off Strafford St.)
Tideway Ind. Est. SW8 . . . . . . 7G 75
Tideway Wlk. SW8 . . . . 7G 75
Tidey St. E3 . . . . 8L 61
Tidford Rd. Well 1D 96
Tidlock Ho. SE28 . . . . 3B 80
(off Erebus Dri.)
Tidworth Rd. E3 . . . . 7L 61
Tiepigs La. W Wick 4C 126
Tierney Ct. Croy 4C 124
Tierney Rd. SW2 . . . . 7J 91
Tiffany Heights. SW18 . . . . . . 6L 89
Tiger La. Brom 8F 110
Tiger Way. E5 . . . . 9F 44
Tigris Clo. N9 . . . . 2G 29
Tilbrook Rd. SE3 . . . . 2G 95
Tilbury Clo. SE15 . . . . 8D 76
Tilbury Clo. Orp 6F 112
Tilbury Ho. SE14 . . . . 7H 77
(off Myers La.)
Tilbury Rd. E6 . . . . 5K 63
Tilbury Rd. E10 . . . . 5A 46
Tildesley Rd. SW15 . . . . 5G 89
Tile Farm Rd. Orp 5B 128
Tilehouse Clo. Borwd 5K 11
Tilehurst Point. SE2 . . . . 3H 81
Tilehurst Rd. SW18 . . . . 7B 90
Tilehurst Rd. Sutt 7J 121
Tile Kiln La. N6 . . . . 6F 42
Tile Kiln La. N13 . . . . 5A 28
(in two parts)
Tile Kiln La. Bex 8A 98
(in three parts)
Tile Kiln La. Hare 5A 36
Tile Kiln Studios. N6 . . . . 5G 43
Tile Yd. E14 . . . . 9K 61
Tileyard Rd. N7 . . . . 3J 59
Tilford Av. New Ad 1A 140
Tilford Gdns. SW19 . . . . 7H 89
Tilford Ho. SW2 . . . . 6K 91
(off Holmewood Gdns.)
Tilia Clo. Sutt 7K 121
Tilia Rd. E5 . . . . 9F 44
Tilia Wlk. SW9 . . . . 3M 91
Till Av. F'ham 2K 131
Tilleard Ho. W10 . . . . 6J 57
(off Herries St.)
Tiller Rd. E14 . . . . 4L 77
Tillett Clo. NW10 . . . . 2A 56
Tillett Sq. SE16 . . . . 3J 77
Tillet Way. E2 . . . . 6E 60
Tillingbourne Gdns. N3 . . . . . 1K 41
Tillingbourne Grn. Orp 8D 112
Tillingbourne Way. N3 . . . . . . 2K 41
Tillingham Ct. Wal A 6M 7
Tillingham Way. N12 . . . . 4L 25
Tilling Rd. NW2 . . . . 6G 41
Tilling Way. Wemb 8H 39
Tillman St. E1 . . . . 9F 60
Tilloch St. N1 . . . . 3K 59
Tillotson Ct. SW8 . . . . 8H 75
(off Wandsworth Rd.)
Tillotson Rd. N9 . . . . 2D 28
Tillotson Rd. Harr 7M 21
Tillotson Rd. Ilf 5L 47
Tilmans Mead. F'ham 3K 131
Tilney Ct. EC1 . . . . 7A 60
Tilney Ct. Buck H 2E 30
Tilney Dri. Buck H 2E 30
Tilney Gdns. N1 . . . . 2B 60
Tilney Rd. Dag 2K 65
(in two parts)
Tilney Rd. S'hall 5G 69
Tilney St. W1 . . . . 2E 74
Tilson Clo. SE5 . . . . 8C 76
Tilson Gdns. SW12 . . . . 6J 91
Tilson Ho. SW2 . . . . 6J 91
Tilson Rd. N17 . . . . 8E 28
Tilston Clo. E11 . . . . 8D 46
Tilton St. SW6 . . . . 7J 73
Tiltwood, The. W3 . . . . 1A 72
Tilt Yd. App. SE9 . . . . 5K 95
Timber Clo. Chst 6L 111
Timbercroft. Eps 6C 120
Timbercroft La. SE18 . . . . 7C 80
Timberdene. NW4 . . . . 9H 25
Timberdene Av. Ilf 8M 31
Timberland Clo. SE15 . . . . . . 8E 76
Timberland Rd. E1 . . . . 9F 60
Timberling Gdns. S Croy . . . 1B 138
Timber Mill Way. SW4 . . . . . . 2H 91
Timber Pond Rd. SE16 . . . . . . 2H 77
Timberslip Dri. Wall 1H 137
Timbers, The. Sutt 8J 121
Timber St. EC1 . . . . 7A 60
Timbertop Rd. Big H 9G 141
Timberwharf Rd. N16 . . . . . . 4E 44
Timber Wharves Est. E14 . . . . 5L 77
(off Copeland Dri.)
Timbrell Pl. SE16 . . . . 2K 77
Time Sq. E8 . . . . 1D 60
Times Sq. Sutt 7M 121
Timor Ho. E1 . . . . 7J 61
(off Duckett St.)
Timothy Clo. SW4 . . . . 4G 91
Timothy Clo. Bexh 4J 97
Timothy Ho. Eri 3J 81
(off Kale Rd.)
Timothy Rd. E3 . . . . 8K 61
Timsbury Wlk. SW15 . . . . 7E 88
Tindale Clo. S Croy 3B 138
Tindall Clo. Romf 9K 35
Tindal St. SW9 . . . . 9M 75
Tinderbox All. SW14 . . . . 2B 88
Tine Rd. Chig 5C 32
(in two parts)
Tinniswood Clo. N5 . . . . 1L 59
Tinsley Rd. E1 . . . . 8G 61
Tintagel Clo. Eps 6D 134
Tintagel Ct. Horn 6L 51
Tintagel Cres. SE22 . . . . 3D 92
Tintagel Dri. Stan 4H 23
Tintagel Gdns. SE22 . . . . 3D 92
Tintagel Rd. Orp 4G 129
Tintern Av. NW9 . . . . 1M 39
Tintern Clo. SW15 . . . . 4J 89
Tintern Clo. SW19 . . . . 3A 106
Tintern Ct. W13 . . . . 1E 70
Tintern Gdns. N14 . . . . 9J 15
Tintern Ho. NW1 . . . . 5F 58
(off Augustus St.)
Tintern Ho. SW1 . . . . 5F 74
(off Abbots Mnr.)
Tintern Path. NW9 . . . . 4C 40
(off Fryent Gro.)
Tintern Rd. N22 . . . . 8A 28
Tintern Rd. Cars 3B 122
Tintern St. SW4 . . . . 3J 91
Tintern Way. Harr 6M 37
Tinto Rd. E16 . . . . 7E 62
Tinwell M. Borwd 7B 12
Tinworth St. SE11 . . . . 6J 75
Tippett Ct. E6 . . . . 5K 63
Tippetts Clo. Enf 3A 16
Tipthorpe Rd. SW11 . . . . 2E 90
Tipton Dri. Croy 6C 124
Tiptree. NW1 . . . . 3F 58
(off Castlehaven Rd.)
Tiptree Clo. E4 . . . . 3A 30
Tiptree Clo. Horn 6L 51
Tiptree Cres. Ilf 9L 31
Tiptree Dri. Enf 6B 16
Tiptree Rd. Ruis 9F 36
Tirlemont Rd. S Croy 9A 124
Tirrell Rd. Croy 1A 124
Tisbury Ct. W1 . . . . 1H 75
(off Wardour St.)
Tisbury Rd. SW16 . . . . 6J 107
Tisdall Pl. SE17 . . . . 5B 76
Tissington Ct. SE16 . . . . 5G 77
Titan Bus. Est. SE8 . . . . 8L 77
(off Ffinch St.)
Titan Ct. Bren 6K 71
Titchborne Row. W2 . . . . 9C 58
Titchfield Rd. NW8 . . . . 4C 58
Titchfield Rd. Cars 3B 122
Titchfield Rd. Enf 1J 17
Titchfield Wlk. Cars 2B 122
Titchwell Rd. SW18 . . . . 7B 90
Tite St. SW3 . . . . 6D 74
Tithe Barn Clo. King T 5K 103
Tithe Barn Way. N'holt 5F 52
Tithe Clo. NW7 . . . . 8E 24
Tithe Clo. Hay 8D 52
Tithe Clo. W on T 1F 116
Tithe Farm Av. Harr 8L 37
Tithe Farm Clo. Harr 8L 37
Tithe Meadow. Wat 9B 8
Tithepit Shaw La. Warl 9F 138
Tithe Wlk. NW7 . . . . 8E 24
Titian Av. Bus H 9C 10
Titley Clo. E4 . . . . 5L 29
Titmus Clo. Uxb 9A 52
Titmuss Av. SE28 . . . . 1F 80
Titmuss St. W12 . . . . 3G 73
Tivendale. N8 . . . . 1J 43
Tiverton Av. Ilf 1L 47
Tiverton Clo. Croy 2D 124
Tiverton Dri. SE9 . . . . 7A 96
Tiverton Gro. Romf 5L 35
Tiverton M. Houn 1A 86
Tiverton Rd. N15 . . . . 4B 44
Tiverton Rd. N18 . . . . 5C 28
Tiverton Rd. NW10 . . . . 4H 57
Tiverton Rd. Edgw 9K 23
Tiverton Rd. Houn 1A 86
Tiverton Rd. Ruis 8E 36
Tiverton Rd. T Hth 9L 107
Tiverton Rd. Wemb 5J 55
Tiverton St. SE1 . . . . 4A 76
Tiverton Way. Chess 7H 119
Tivoli Ct. SE16 . . . . 2K 77
Tivoli Gdns. SE18 . . . . 5J 79
(in two parts)
Tivoli Rd. N8 . . . . 3H 43
Tivoli Rd. SE27 . . . . 2A 108
Tivoli Rd. Houn 3J 85
Toad La. Houn 3K 85
Tobacco Dock. E1 . . . . 1F 76
Tobacco Quay. E1 . . . . 1F 76
Tobago St. E14 . . . . 3L 77
Tobin Clo. NW3 . . . . 3C 58
Toby Ct. N9 . . . . 9G 17
(off Tramway Av.)
Toby La. E1 . . . . 7J 61
Toby Way. Surb 4M 119
Todd Clo. Rain 7H 67
Todd Ho. N2 . . . . 9B 26
(off Grange, The)
Todds Wlk. N7 . . . . 7K 43
Todhunter Ter. Barn 6L 13
Tokenhouse Yd. EC2 . . . . 9B 60
Token Yd. SW15 . . . . 3J 89
Tokyngton. 2M 55
Tokyngton Av. Wemb 2L 55
Toland Sq. SW15 . . . . 4E 88
Tolbut Ct. Romf 4D 50
Tolcairn Ct. Belv 6L 81
Tolcarne Dri. Pinn 9E 20
Tolchurch. W11 . . . . 9K 57
(off Dartmouth Clo.)
Toley Av. Wemb 5J 39
Toll Bar Ct. Sutt 1M 135
Tollbridge Clo. W10 . . . . 7J 57
Tollesbury Gdns. Ilf 1B 48
Tollet St. E1 . . . . 7H 61
Tollgate Dri. SE21 . . . . 8C 92
Tollgate Dri. Hay 1H 69
Tollgate Gdns. NW6 . . . . 5M 57
Tollgate Ho. NW6 . . . . 5M 57
(off Tollgate Gdns.)
Tollgate Rd. E16 & E6 . . . . . 8G 63
Tollgate Rd. Wal X 8D 6
Tollgate Sq. E6 . . . . 8K 63
Tollhouse La. Wall 1G 137
Tollhouse Way. N19 . . . . 7G 43
Tollington Pk. N4 . . . . 7K 43
Tollington Pl. N4 . . . . 7K 43
Tollington Rd. N7 . . . . 9K 43
Tollington Way. N7 . . . . 8J 43
Tolmers Sq. NW1 . . . . 7G 59
(in two parts)
Tolpaide Ho. SE11 . . . . 5L 75
(off Hotspur St.)
Tolpits Clo. Wat 7D 8
Tolpits La. Wat 1A 20
Tolpits La. Cvn. Site. Wat 9C 8
Tolpuddle Av. E13 . . . . 4G 63
(off Queens Rd.)
Tolpuddle St. N1 . . . . 5L 59
Tolsford Rd. E5 . . . . 1F 60
Tolson Rd. Iswth 2E 86
Tolverne Rd. SW20 . . . . 5G 105
Tolworth. 4M 119
Tolworth B'way. Surb 3M 119
Tolworth Clo. Surb 3M 119
Tolworth Gdns. Romf 3H 49
Tolworth Junction (Toby Jug) (Junct.) 4M 119
Tolworth Pde. Chad H 3J 49
Tolworth Pk. Rd. Surb 4K 119
Tolworth Ri. N. Surb 3M 119
Tolworth Ri. S. Surb 4M 119
Tolworth Rd. Surb 4J 119
Tolworth Tower. Surb 4M 119
Tomahawk Gdns. N'holt 6H 53
Tom Coombs Clo. SE9 . . . . . . 3J 95
Tom Cribb Rd. SE28 . . . . 4A 80
Tom Groves Clo. E15 . . . . 1B 62
Tom Hood Clo. E15 . . . . 1B 62
Tom Jenkinson Rd. E16 . . . . . 2E 78
Tomkins Clo. Borwd 3J 11
Tomkyns Ho. SE11 . . . . 5L 75
(off Distin St.)
Tomlin Clo. Eps 3B 134
Tomlin Ct. Eps 3B 134
Tomlins All. Twic 7E 86
Tomlin's Gro. E3 . . . . 6L 61
Tomlinson Clo. E2 . . . . 6D 60
Tomlinson Clo. W4 . . . . 6M 71
Tomlins Orchard. Bark 4A 64
Tomlins Ter. E14 . . . . 9J 61
Tomlins Wlk. N7 . . . . 7K 43
Tom Mann Clo. Bark 4C 64
Tom Nolan Clo. E15 . . . . 5C 62
Tom Oakman Cen. E4 . . . . 2B 30
Tomo Ind. Est. Uxb 9A 142
Tompion Ho. EC1 . . . . 7M 59
(off Percival St.)
Tompion St. EC1 . . . . 6M 59
(in two parts)
Tom's La. K Lan 2A 4
Tom Smith Clo. SE10 . . . . 7C 78
Tomson Ho. SE1 . . . . 4D 76
(off Riley Rd.)
Tomswood Ct. Ilf 8A 32
Tomswood Hill. Ilf 6M 31
Tomswood Rd. Chig 6L 31
Tom Williams Ho. SW6 . . . . . 7K 73
(off Clem Attlee Ct.)
Tonbridge Clo. Bans 6D 136
Tonbridge Cres. Harr 2J 39
Tonbridge Houses. WC1 . . . . 6J 59
(off Tonbridge St.)
Tonbridge Rd. H Hill 7H 35
Tonbridge Rd. W Mol 8K 101
Tonbridge St. WC1 . . . . 6J 59
Tonbridge Wlk. WC1 . . . . 6J 59
(off Tonbridge St.)
Toneborough. NW8 . . . . 4M 57
(off Abbey Rd.)
Tonfield Rd. Sutt 3K 121
Tonge Clo. Beck 9L 109
Tonsley Hill. SW18 . . . . 4M 89
Tonsley Pl. SW18 . . . . 4M 89
Tonsley Rd. SW18 . . . . 4M 89
Tonsley St. SW18 . . . . 4M 89
Tonstall Rd. Eps 2B 134
Tonstall Rd. Mitc 6E 106
Tony Cannell M. E3 . . . . 6K 61
Tony Law Ho. SE20 . . . . 5F 108
Tooke Clo. Pinn 8J 21
Tookey Clo. Harr 5K 39
Took's Ct. EC4 . . . . 9L 59
Tooley St. SE1 . . . . 2B 76
Toomy Cen. E16 . . . . 2F 78
(off Evelyn Rd.)
Toorack Rd. Harr 9B 22
Tooting. 2C 106
Tooting Bec. 9E 90
Tooting Bec Gdns. SW16 . . . . 1H 107
(in two parts)
Tooting Bec Rd. SW17 & SW16 . . . . 9E 90
Tooting B'way. SW17 . . . . . 2C 106
Tooting Graveney. 3D 106
Tooting Gro. SW17 . . . . 2C 106
Tooting High St. SW17 . . . . 3C 106
Tooting Mkt. SW17 . . . . 1D 106
Tootswood Rd. Brom 9C 110
Topaz Wlk. NW2 . . . . 5H 41
Topcliffe Dri. Orp 6B 128
Top Dartford Rd. Swan & Dart 4D 114
Topham Ho. SE10 . . . . 8A 78
(off Prior St.)
Topham Sq. N17 . . . . 8A 28
Topham St. EC1 . . . . 7L 59
Top Ho. Ri. E4 . . . . 9A 18
Topiary Sq. Rich 2K 87
Toplands Av. Ave 2M 83
Topley St. SE9 . . . . 3G 95
Topmast Point. E14 . . . . 3L 77
Top Pk. Beck 9C 110
Topping La. Uxb 6B 142
Topp Wlk. NW2 . . . . 7G 41
Topsfield Clo. N8 . . . . 3H 43
Topsfield Pde. N8 . . . . 3J 43
(off Tottenham La.)
Topsfield Rd. N8 . . . . 3J 43
Topsham Rd. SW17 . . . . 9D 90
Torbay Ct. NW1 . . . . 3F 58
Torbay Mans. NW6 . . . . 4K 57
(off Willesden La.)
Torbay Rd. NW6 . . . . 3K 57
Torbay Rd. Harr 7J 37
Torbay St. NW1 . . . . 3F 58
Torbitt Way. Ilf 3D 48
Torbridge Clo. Edgw 7J 23
Torbrook Clo. Bex 5J 97
Tor Ct. W8 . . . . 3L 73
Torcross Dri. SE23 . . . . 8G 93
Torcross Rd. Ruis 8F 36
Tor Gdns. W8 . . . . 3L 73
Tor Ho. N6 . . . . 4F 42
Torland Dri. Oxs 5B 132
Tormead Clo. Sutt 8L 121
Tormount Rd. SE18 . . . . 7C 80
Tornay Ho. N1 . . . . 5K 59
(off Priory Grn. Est.)
Torney Ho. E9 . . . . 3G 61
Toronto Av. E12 . . . . 9K 47
Toronto Rd. E11 . . . . 9B 46
Toronto Rd. Ilf 6M 47
Torquay Gdns. Ilf 2H 47
Torquay St. W2 . . . . 8M 57
Torrance Clo. SE7 . . . . 7H 79
Torrance Clo. Horn 6F 50
Torrens Ct. SE5 . . . . 2B 92
Torrens Rd. E15 . . . . 2D 62
Torrens Rd. SW2 . . . . 4K 91
Torrens Sq. E15 . . . . 2D 62
Torrens St. EC1 . . . . 5L 59
Torres Sq. E14 . . . . 6L 77
Torre Wlk. Cars 3C 122
Torriano Av. NW5 . . . . 1H 59
Torriano Cotts. NW5 . . . . 1G 59
Torriano M. NW5 . . . . 1G 59
Torridge Gdns. SE15 . . . . 3G 93
Torridge Rd. T Hth 9M 107
Torridon Ho. NW6 . . . . 5M 57
(off Randolph Gdns.)
Torridon Rd. SE6 . . . . 6B 94
Torrington Av. N12 . . . . 5B 26
Torrington Clo. N12 . . . . 4B 26
Torrington Clo. Clay 8C 118
Torrington Ct. SE26 . . . . 2E 108
(off Crystal Pal. Pk. Rd.)
Torrington Dri. Harr 9M 37
Torrington Dri. Lou 6M 19
Torrington Gdns. N11 . . . . . . 6G 27
Torrington Gdns. Gnfd 4G 55
Torrington Gro. N12 . . . . 5C 26
Torrington Pk. N12 . . . . 5A 26
Torrington Pl. E1 . . . . 2E 76
Torrington Pl. WC1 . . . . 8H 59
Torrington Rd. E18 . . . . 1E 46
Torrington Rd. Clay 8C 118
Torrington Rd. Dag 6K 49
Torrington Rd. Gnfd 4G 55
Torrington Rd. Ruis 8E 36
Torrington Sq. WC1 . . . . 7H 59
Torrington Sq. Croy 2B 124
Torrington Way. Mord 1L 121
Tor Rd. Well 9G 81
Torr Rd. SE20 . . . . 4H 109
Tortington Ho. SE15 . . . . 8E 76
(off Friary Est.)
Torver Rd. Harr 2C 38
Torver Way. Orp 5B 128
Torwood Rd. SW15 . . . . 4E 88
Torworth Rd. Borwd 3K 11
Tothill Ho. SW1 . . . . 5H 75
(off Page St.)
Tothill St. SW1 . . . . 3H 75
Totnes Rd. Well 8F 80
Totnes Vs. N11 . . . . 5G 27
(off Telford Rd.)
Totnes Wlk. N2 . . . . 2B 42
Tottan Ter. E1 . . . . 9H 61
Tottenhall. NW1 . . . . 3E 58
(off Ferdinand St.)
Tottenhall Rd. N13 . . . . 6L 27
Tottenham. 9D 28
Tottenham Ct. Rd. W1 . . . . . 7G 59
Tottenham Grn. E. N15 . . . . . 2D 44
Tottenham Hale. 9E 28
Tottenham Hale Gyratory (Junct.) 1D 44
Tottenham Hale Gyratory. N15 . . . . 2E 44
Tottenham Hale Retail Pk. N15 . . . . 2E 44
Tottenham Hotspur F.C. (White Hart Lane) 7E 28
Tottenham La. N8 . . . . 4J 43
Tottenham M. W1 . . . . 8G 59
Tottenham Rd. N1 . . . . 2C 60
Tottenham St. W1 . . . . 8G 59
Totterdown St. SW17 . . . . . 1D 106
Totteridge. 1K 25
Totteridge Comn. N20 . . . . . . 2E 24
Totteridge Grn. N20 . . . . 2L 25
Totteridge La. N20 . . . . 2L 25
Totteridge Rd. Enf 1H 17
Totteridge Village. N20 . . . . . 1J 25
Totternhoe Clo. Harr 3G 39
Totton Rd. T Hth 7L 107
Toulmin St. SE1 . . . . 3A 76
Toulon St. SE5 . . . . 8A 76
Toulouse Ct. SE16 . . . . 6F 76
(off Rossetti Rd.)
Tourist Info. Cen. 5A 98
(Bexley)
Tourist Info. Cen. 3L 97
(Bexleyheath)
Tourist Info. Cen. 9A 60
(City of London)
Tourist Info. Cen. 5A 124
(Croydon)
Tourist Info. Cen. 7A 78
(Greenwich)
Tourist Info. Cen. 2C 38
(Harrow)
Tourist Info. Cen. 2F 144
(Heathrow Airport)
Tourist Info. Cen. 3B 142
(Hillingdon)
Tourist Info. Cen. 2M 85
(Hounslow)
Tourist Info. Cen. 6H 103
(Kingston)
Tourist Info. Cen. 6H 103
(Kingston upon Thames)
Tourist Info. Cen. 3A 94
(Lewisham)
Tourist Info. Cen. 8M 47
(Redbridge)
Tourist Info. Cen. 4H 87
(Richmond upon Thames)
Tourist Info. Cen. 2B 76
(off Tooley St., Southwark)
Tourist Info. Cen. 7C 114
(Swanley)
Tourist Info. Cen. 7F 86
(Twickenham)
Tourist Info. Cen. 3K 75
(Waterloo International Terminal)
Tournay Rd. SW6 . . . . 8K 73
Tours Pas. SW11 . . . . 3A 90
Toussaint Wlk. SE16 . . . . 4E 76
Tovil Clo. SE20 . . . . 6F 108
Tovy Ho. SE1 . . . . 6E 76
(off Avondale Sq.)
Towcester Rd. E3 . . . . 7M 61
Tower Bri. SE1 & E1 . . . . 2D 76
Tower Bri. App. E1 . . . . 2D 76
Tower Bri. Bus. Complex. SE16 . . . . 4E 76
Tower Bri. Bus. Sq. SE16 . . . . 5F 76
Tower Bridge Experience. 2D 76
(off Tower Bri.)
Tower Bri. Plaza. SE1 . . . . . . 2D 76
Tower Bri. Rd. SE1 . . . . 4C 76
Tower Bri. Sq. SE1 . . . . 3D 76
(off Queen Elizabeth St.)
Tower Bri. Wharf. E1 . . . . 2E 76
Tower Bldgs. E1 . . . . 2F 76
(off Brewhouse La.)

Tower Clo.—Troon Clo.

Tower Clo. NW3 1B 58
Tower Clo. SE20 4F 108
Tower Clo. Ilf 6M 31
Tower Clo. Orp 4D 128
Tower Ct. E5 5D 44
Tower Ct. N1 3A 60
(off Canonbury St.)
Tower Ct. NW8 5C 58
(off Mackennal St.)
Tower Ct. WC2 9J 59
(off Tower St.)
Tower Cft. Eyns 4J 131
Tower 42. 9C 60
Tower Gdns. Clay 9F 118
Tower Gdns. Rd. N17 8A 28
Towergate Clo. Uxb 1C 142
Tower Gro. Wey 4C 116
Tower Hamlets Rd. E7 9D 46
Tower Hamlets Rd. E17 1L 45
Tower Hill (Junct.) 2D 76
Tower Hill. EC3 1C 76
Tower Hill Ter. EC3 1C 76
(off Byward St.)
Tower Ho. E1 8E 60
(off Fieldgate St.)
Tower La. Wemb 8H 39
Tower M. E17 2L 45
Tower of London, The. 1D 76
Tower Pk. Rd. Cray 4D 98
Tower Pl. EC3 1C 76
(off Lwr. Thames St.)
Tower Retail Pk. Dart 4D 98
Tower Ri. Rich 2J 87
Tower Rd. NW10 3E 56
Tower Rd. Belv 5A 82
Tower Rd. Bexh 3L 97
Tower Rd. Dart 5G 99
Tower Rd. Orp 4D 128
Tower Rd. Twic 9D 86
Tower Royal. EC4 1B 76
Towers Av. Hil 6A 52
Towers Bus. Pk. Wemb 9A 40
(off Carey Way)
Towers Ct. Uxb 6A 52
Towers Pl. Rich 4J 87
Towers Rd. Pinn 8J 21
Towers Rd. S'hall 7L 53
Towers, The. Kenl 7A 138
Tower St. WC2 9J 59
Towers Wlk. Wey 8A 116
Tower Ter. N22 9K 27
Tower Vw. Croy 3J 125
Tower Yd. Rich 4K 87
Towfield Ct. Felt 8K 85
Towfield Rd. Felt 8K 85
Towgar Ct. N20 9A 14
Towncourt Cres. Orp 9A 112
Towncourt La. Orp 1B 128
Towncourt Path. N4 6A 44
Towneley Cotts. Stap A 1C 34
Town End Pde. King T 7H 103
(off High St.)
Towney Mead. N'holt 5K 53
Towney Mead Ct. N'holt 5K 53
Town Farm Way. Stanw 6B 144
Townfield Rd. Hay 2D 68
Townfield Sq. Hay 1D 68
Town Fld. Way. Iswth 1E 86
Town Hall App. Rd. N15 2D 44
Town Hall Av. W4 6B 72
Town Hall Rd. SW11 2D 90
Town Hall Wlk. N16 9C 44
(off Church Wlk.)
Townholm Cres. W7 4D 70
Town La. Stanw 5B 144
(in two parts)
Townley Ct. E15 2D 62
Townley Rd. SE22 4C 92
Townley Rd. Bexh 4K 97
Townley St. SE17 6B 76
(in two parts)
Townmead Bus. Cen.
SW6 2A 90
Town Mdw. Bren 7H 71
Town Mdw. Rd. Bren 8H 71
Townmead Rd. SW6 2M 89
Townmead Rd. Rich 1M 87
Townmead Rd. Wal A 7J 7
Town Quay. Bark 4M 63
Town Quay Wharf. Bark 4M 63
Town Rd. N9 2F 28
Townsend Av. N14 4H 27
Townsend Ho. SE1 5E 76
(off Strathnairn St.)
Townsend Ind. Est. NW10 5A 56
Townsend La. NW9 5B 40
Townsend Rd. N15 3D 44
Townsend Rd. S'hall 2J 69
Townsend St. SE17 5C 76
Townsend Way. N'wd 7D 20
Townsend Yd. N6 6F 42
Townshend Clo. Sidc 3F 112
Townshend Ct. NW8 5C 58
(off Townshend Rd.)
Townshend Est. NW8 5C 58
Townshend Rd. NW8 4C 58
(in two parts)
Townshend Rd. Chst 2M 111
Townshend Rd. Rich 3K 87
Townshend Ter. Rich 3K 87
Towns Ho. SW4 2H 91
Townson Av. N'holt 5E 52
Townson Way. N'holt 5E 52
Town Sq. Eri 7C 82
Town Sq. Iswth 2F 86
(off Swan St.)
Town, The. Enf 5B 16
Town Wharf. Iswth 2F 86
Towpath. W on T 9E 100
Towpath Rd. N18 6H 29
Towpath, The. SW10 9B 74
Towpath Wlk. E9 1K 61
Towpath Way. SE25 1D 124
Towton Rd. SE27 8A 92
Toynbec Clo. Chst 1M 111
Toynbee Rd. SW20 5J 105
Toynbee St. E1 8D 60
Toynbee Studios
(College & Theatre) 9D 60
Toyne Way. N6 4D 42
Tracery, The. Bans 7M 135
Tracey Av. NW2 1G 57
Tracy Ct. Stan 7G 23
Trade Clo. N13 4L 27
Trader Rd. E6 9M 63
Tradescant Ho. E9 3G 61
(off Frampton Pk. Rd.)
Tradescant Rd. SW8 8J 75
Tradewinds Ct. E1 1E 76
Trading Est. Rd. NW10 7A 56
Trafalgar Av. N17 6C 28
Trafalgar Av. SE15 6D 76
Trafalgar Av. Wor Pk 3H 121
Trafalgar Bus. Cen. Bark 7D 64
Trafalgar Clo. SE16 4J 77
Trafalgar Ct. E1 2G 77
(off Wapping Wall)
Trafalgar Ct. Eri 8D 82
(off Frobisher Rd.)
Trafalgar Dri. W on T 5F 116
Trafalgar Gdns. E1 8H 61
Trafalgar Gdns. W8 4M 73
(off South End)
Trafalgar Gro. SE10 7B 78
Trafalgar Ho. SE17 6A 76
(off Bronti Clo.)
Trafalgar Pl. E11 2E 46
Trafalgar Pl. N18 5E 28
Trafalgar Rd. SE10 7B 78
Trafalgar Rd. SW19 4M 105
Trafalgar Rd. Dart 8J 99
Trafalgar Rd. Rain 5D 66
Trafalgar Rd. Twic 8B 86
Trafalgar Square. 2J 75
Trafalgar Sq. WC2 2H 75
Trafalgar St. SE17 6B 76
Trafalgar Ter. Harr 6C 38
Trafalgar Trad. Est. Enf 6J 17
Trafalgar Way. E14 2A 78
Trafalgar Way. Croy 4L 123
Trafford Clo. E15 1M 61
Trafford Clo. Ilf 6D 32
Trafford Ho. N1 5B 60
(off Cranston Est.)
Trafford Rd. T Hth 9K 107
Traitors' Gate. 2D 76
(in Tower of London, The)
Tralee Ct. SE16 6F 76
(off Masters Dri.)
Tramsheds Ind. Est.
Croy 2H 123
Tramway Av. E15 3C 62
Tramway Av. N9 9F 16
Tramway Path. Mitc 8C 106
(in three parts)
Tranley M. NW3 9C 42
Tranmere Ct. Sutt 9A 122
Tranmere Rd. N9 9D 16
Tranmere Rd. SW18 8A 90
Tranmere Rd. Twic 6M 85
Tranquil Pas. SE3 1D 94
(off Montpelier Va.)
Tranquil Ri. Eri 6C 82
Tranquil Va. SE3 1C 94
Transay Wlk. N1 2B 60
Transept St. NW1 8C 58
Transmere Clo. Orp 1A 128
Transmere Rd. Orp 1A 128
Transom Clo. SE16 5J 77
Transom Sq. E14 6M 77
Transport Av. Bren 6E 70
Tranton Rd. SE16 4E 76
Trappes Ho. SE16 5F 76
(off Camilla Rd.)
Trap's Hill. Lou 5K 19
Traps La. N Mald 5C 104
Travellers Site. E17 6K 29
Travellers Way. Houn 1G 85
Travers Clo. E17 8H 29
Travers Ho. SE10 7B 78
(off Trafalgar Gro.)
Travers Rd. N7 8L 43
Travis Ho. SE10 9A 78
Treacy Clo. Bus H 2A 22
Treadgold Ho. W11 1H 73
(off Bomore Rd.)
Treadgold St. W11 1H 73
Treadway St. E2 5F 60
Treadwell Rd. Eps 8C 134
Treasury Pas. SW1 3J 75
(off Downing St.)
Treaty Cen. Houn 2M 85
Treaty St. N1 4K 59
Trebeck St. W1 2F 74
Trebovir Rd. SW5 6L 73
Treby St. E3 7K 61
Trecastle Way. N7 9H 43
Tredegar M. E3 6K 61
Tredegar Rd. E3 5K 61
Tredegar Rd. N11 7H 27
Tredegar Rd. Dart 8E 98
Tredegar Sq. E3 6K 61
Tredegar Ter. E3 6K 61
Trederwen Rd. E8 4E 60
Tredown Rd. SE26 2G 109
Tredwell Clo. SW2 8K 91
Tredwell Clo. Brom 8J 111
Tredwell Rd. SE27 1M 107
Treebourne Rd. Big H 9G 141
Tree Clo. Rich 7H 87
Treemount Ct. Eps 5C 134
Treen Av. SW13 2D 88
Tree Rd. E16 9G 63
Treeside Clo. W Dray 5H 143
Tree Top M. Dag 2B 66
Treetops Clo. SE2 6J 81
Treetops Clo. N'wd 5B 20
Treeview Clo. SE19 5C 108
Treewall Gdns. Brom 1F 110
Trefgarne Rd. Dag 7L 49
Trefil Wlk. N7 9J 43
Trefoil Ho. Eri 3J 81
(off Kale Rd.)
Trefoil Rd. SW18 4A 90
Trefusis Ct. Houn 9F 68
Trefusis Wlk. Wat 3C 8
Tregaron Av. N8 4J 43
Tregaron Gdns. N Mald 8C 104
Tregarvon Rd. SW11 3E 90
Tregenna Av. Harr 9L 37
Tregenna Clo. N14 7G 15
Tregenna Ct. S Harr 9L 37
Tregony Rd. Orp 6D 128
Trego Rd. E9 3L 61
Tregothnan Rd. SW9 2J 91
Tregunter Rd. SW10 7M 73
Trehearn Rd. Ilf 7B 32
Treherne Ct. SW9 9M 75
Treherne Ct. SW17 1E 106
Trehern Rd. SW14 2B 88
Trehurst St. E5 1J 61
Trelawney Est. E9 2G 61
Trelawney Ho. SE1 3A 76
(off Pepper St.)
Trelawney Rd. Ilf 7B 32
Trelawn Rd. E10 8A 46
Trelawn Rd. SW2 4L 91
Trelawny Clo. E17 2M 45
Trellick Tower. W10 7K 57
(off Golborne Rd.)
Trellis Sq. E3 6K 61
Treloar Gdns. SE19 3B 108
Tremadoc Rd. SW4 3H 91
Tremaine Clo. SE4 1L 93
Tremaine Rd. SE20 6F 108
Trematon Ho. SE11 6L 75
(off Kennings Way)
Trematon Pl. Tedd 4G 103
Tremlett Gro. N19 8G 43
Tremlett M. N19 8G 43
Trenance Gdns. Ilf 8E 48
Trenchard Av. Ruis 9F 36
Trenchard Clo. NW9 8C 24
Trenchard Clo. Stan 6E 22
Trenchard Clo. W on T 7G 117
Trenchard Ct. NW4 3E 40
Trenchard Ct. Mord 1L 121
Trenchard St. SE10 6B 78
Trenchold St. SW8 7J 75
Trendell Ho. E14 9L 61
(off Dod St.)
Trenear Clo. Orp 6E 128
Trenham Dri. Warl 8G 139
Trenholme Clo. SE20 4F 108
Trenholme Rd. SE20 4F 108
Trenholme Ter. SE20 4F 108
Trenmar Gdns. NW10 6F 56
Trent Av. W5 4G 71
Trentbridge Clo. Ilf 6D 32
Trent Ct. S Croy 7A 124
(off Nottingham Rd.)
Trent Gdns. N14 8F 14
Trentham Dri. Orp 8E 112
Trentham St. SW18 7L 89
Trent Ho. SE15 3G 93
Trent Ho. King T 5H 103
Trent Pk. (Country Pk.) 3F 14
Trent Pk. Golf Course. 5G 15
Trent Rd. SW2 4K 91
Trent Rd. Buck H 1F 30
Trent Way. Hay 5C 52
Trent Way. Wor Pk 5G 121
Trentwood Side. Enf 5K 15
Treport St. SW18 6M 89
Tresco Clo. Brom 3C 110
Trescoe Gdns. Harr 5J 37
Trescoe Gdns. Romf 5A 34
Tresco Gdns. Ilf 7E 48
Tresco Ho. SE11 6L 75
(off Sancroft St.)
Tresco Rd. SE15 3F 92
Tresham Cres. NW8 7C 58
Tresham Rd. Bark 3D 64
Tresham Wlk. E9 1G 61
Tresidder Ho. SW4 6H 91
Tresilian Av. N21 7K 15
Tressell Clo. N1 3M 59
Tressillian Cres. SE4 2L 93
Tressillian Rd. SE4 3K 93
Tress Pl. SE1 2M 75
(off Blackfriars Rd.)
Trestis Clo. Hay 7H 53
Treswell Rd. Dag 4J 65
Tretawn Gdns. NW7 4C 24
Tretawn Pk. NW7 4C 24
Trevanion Rd. W14 5J 73
Treve Av. Harr 5B 38
Trevellance Way. Wat 6H 5
Trevelyan Av. E12 9K 47
Trevelyan Clo. Dart 3K 99
Trevelyan Cres. Harr 5H 39
Trevelyan Gdns. NW10 4G 57
Trevelyan Ho. E2 6H 61
(off Morpeth St.)
Trevelyan Ho. SE5 8M 75
(off John Ruskin St.)
Trevelyan Rd. E15 9D 46
Trevelyan Rd. SW17 2C 106
Trevenna Ho. SE23 9H 93
(off Dacres Rd.)
Trevera Ct. Enf 7J 17
Trevera Ct. Wal X 6E 6
(off Eleanor Rd.)
Treveris St. SE1 2M 75
Treverton St. W10 7J 57
Treverton Towers. W10 8H 57
(off Treverton St.)
Treves Clo. N21 7K 15
Treves Ho. E1 7E 60
(off Vallance Rd.)
Treville St. SW15 6F 88
Treviso Rd. SE23 8H 93
Trevithick Clo. Felt 7D 84
Trevithick Dri. Dart 3K 99
Trevithick Ho. SE16 5F 76
(off Rennie Est.)
Trevithick St. SE8 7L 77
Trevone Ct. SW2 6J 91
(off Doverfield Rd.)
Trevone Gdns. Pinn 4J 37
Trevor Clo. Brom 2D 126
Trevor Clo. E Barn 8B 14
Trevor Clo. Harr 7D 22
Trevor Clo. Iswth 4D 86
Trevor Clo. N'holt 5G 53
Trevor Cres. Ruis 9D 36
Trevor Gdns. Edgw 8B 24
Trevor Gdns. N'holt 5G 53
Trevor Gdns. Ruis 9E 36
Trevor Pl. SW7 3C 74
Trevor Rd. SW19 4J 105
Trevor Rd. Edgw 8B 24
Trevor Rd. Hay 3C 68
Trevor Rd. Wfd G 7E 30
Trevor Sq. SW7 3D 74
Trevor St. SW7 3C 74
Trevor Wlk. SW7 3C 74
(off Trevor Pl.)
Trevose Ho. SE11 6K 75
(off Orsett St.)
Trevose Rd. E17 8B 30
Trevose Way. Wat 3G 21
Trewenna Dri. Chess 7H 119
Trewince Rd. SW20 5G 105
Trewint St. SW18 8A 90
Trewsbury Ho. SE2 2H 81
Trewsbury Rd. SE26 2H 109
Triandra Way. Hay 8H 53
Triangle Bus. Cen., The.
NW10 6D 56
Triangle Cen. S'hall 2B 70
Triangle Ct. E16 8H 63
Triangle Pas. Barn 6A 14
Triangle Pl. SW4 3H 91
Triangle Rd. E8 4F 60
Triangle, The. E8 4F 60
Triangle, The. N13 4K 27
Triangle, The. Bark 2A 64
Triangle, The. King T 6M 103
Triangle, The. Sidc 6E 96
(off Burnt Oak La.)
Trickett Ho. Sutt 1M 135
Tricycle Cinema. 3K 57
Tricycle Theatre. 3K 57
(off Kilburn High Rd.)
Trident Bus. Cen. SW17 2D 106
Trident Gdns. N'holt 6H 53
Trident Ho. E14 9A 62
(off Blair St.)
Trident Rd. Wat 7D 4
Trident St. SE16 5H 77
Trident Way. S'hall 4F 68
Trig La. EC4 1A 76
Trigo Ct. Eps 3B 134
Trigon Rd. SW8 8K 75
Trilby Rd. SE23 8H 93
Trillo Ct. Ilf 5C 48
Trimdon. NW1 4G 59
Trimmer Wlk. Bren 7J 71
Trim St. SE14 7K 77
Trinder Gdns. N19 6J 43
Trinder Rd. N19 6J 43
Trinder Rd. Barn 7G 13
Tring Av. W5 2K 71
Tring Av. S'hall 9K 53
Tring Av. Wemb 2L 55
Tring Clo. Ilf 3B 48
Tring Clo. Romf 4K 35
Tring Ct. Twic 1E 102
Tring Gdns. Romf 4J 35
Tring Grn. Romf 4J 35
Tring Ho. Wat 9C 8
Tring Wlk. Romf 4J 35
Trinidad Gdns. Dag 3B 66
Trinidad Ho. E14 1K 77
(off Gill St.)
Trinidad St. E14 1K 77
Trinity Av. N2 1B 42
Trinity Av. Enf 8D 16
Trinity Buoy Wharf. E14 1C 78
(off Orchard Pl.)
Trinity Bus. Pk. E4 6K 29
Trinity Chu. Pas. SW13 7F 72
Trinity Chu. Rd. SW13 7F 72
Trinity Chu. Sq. SE1 4A 76
Trinity Clo. E8 2D 60
Trinity Clo. E11 7C 46
Trinity Clo. NW3 9B 42
Trinity Clo. SE13 3B 94
Trinity Clo. SW4 3G 91
Trinity Clo. Brom 3J 127
Trinity Clo. Houn 3J 85
Trinity Clo. N'wd 6C 20
Trinity Clo. S Croy 1C 138
Trinity Clo. Stanw 5A 144
Trinity Cotts. Rich 2K 87
Trinity Ct. N1 4C 60
(off Downham Rd.
Trinity Ct. NW2 1G 57
Trinity Ct. SE1 4A 76
(off Brockham St.
Trinity Ct. SE7 5H 79
Trinity Ct. SE25 1C 124
Trinity Ct. SE26 9G 93
Trinity Ct. W2 9A 58
(off Gloucester Ter.
Trinity Ct. WC1 7K 59
(off Gray's Inn Rd.
Trinity Ct. Croy 4A 124
Trinity Ct. Dart 7M 99
(off Churchill Clo.
Trinity Ct. Enf 4A 16
Trinity Cres. SW17 8D 90
Trinity Gdns. E16 8D 62
Trinity Gdns. SW9 3K 91
Trinity Gdns. Dart 5H 99
Trinity Grn. E1 7G 61
Trinity Gro. SE10 9A 78
Trinity Hall Clo. Wat 5G
Trinity Hospital (Almshouses)
SE10 6B 78
Trinity Ho. SE1 4A 76
(off Bath Ter.
Trinity Ho. Wal X 5E
Trinity La. Wal X 5E
Trinity M. E1 8G 6
(off Redman's Rd
Trinity M. SE20 5F 10
Trinity M. W10 9H 5
Trinity Path. SE23 9G 9
Trinity Pl. EC3 1D 7
Trinity Pl. Bexh 3K 9
Trinity Ri. SW2 7L 9
Trinity Rd. N2 1B 4
Trinity Rd. N22 7J 2
(in two parts
Trinity Rd. SW18 & SW17 3A 9
Trinity Rd. SW19 3L 10
Trinity Rd. Ilf 1A 4
Trinity Rd. Rich 2K 8
Trinity Rd. S'hall 2J 6
Trinity Sq. EC3 1C 7
Trinity St. E16 8D 6
Trinity St. SE1 3A 7
(in two parts
Trinity St. Enf 4A 1
Trinity Tower. E1 1E 7
(off Vaughan Wa
Trinity Wlk. NW3 2A 5
Trinity Way. E4 6K 2
Trinity Way. W3 1C 7
Trio Pl. SE1 3A 7
Tristan Ct. SE8 7K 7
(off Dorking Cl
Tristan Sq. SE3 2C 9
Tristram Clo. E17 1B 4
Tristram Rd. Brom 1D 11
Triton Ho. E14 5M 7
(off Cahir S
Triton Sq. NW1 7G 5
Tritton Av. Croy 6J 12
Tritton Rd. SE21 9B 9
Triumph Clo. Hay 9A 6
Triumph Ho. Bark 6E 6
Triumph Rd. E6 9K 6
Triumph Trad. Est. N17 6E 2
Trocadero Cen. 1H 7
Trocette Mans. SE1 4C 7
(off Bermondsey St
Trojan Ct. NW6 3J 5
Trojan Ind. Est. NW10 2D 5
Trojan Way. Croy 5K 12
Troon Clo. SE16 6F 7
Troon Clo. SE28 9H 6

Troon Ho.—Udimore Ho.

Troon Ho. E1 9J 61
(off White Horse Rd.)
Troon St. E1 9J 61
Troopers Dri. Romf 4H 35
Tropical Ct. W10 6H 57
(off Kilburn La.)
Trosley Rd. Belv 7L 81
Trossachs Rd. SE22 4C 92
Trothy Rd. SE1 5E 76
Trotman Ho. SE14 9G 77
(off Pomeroy St.)
Trotters Bottom. Barn 1E 12
Trotter Way. Eps 4M 133
Trott Rd. N10 7D 26
Trott St. SW11 9C 74
Trot Wood. Chig 5B 32
Troughton Rd. SE7 6F 78
Troutbeck. NW1 6F 58
(off Albany St.)
Troutbeck Rd. SE14 9J 77
Trout La. W Dray 1G 143
Trout Rd. W Dray 2H 143
Trouville Rd. SW4 5G 91
Trowbridge Rd. E9 2K 61
Trowbridge Rd. Romf 6H 35
Trowley Ri. Ab L 4C 4
Trowlock Av. Tedd 3G 103
Trowlock Way. Tedd 3H 103
Troy Ct. SE18 5M 79
Troy Ct. W8 4L 73
(off Kensington High St.)
Troy Ind. Est. Harr 3D 38
Troy Rd. SE19 3B 108
Troy Town. SE15 2E 92
Trubshaw Rd. S'hall 4M 69
Truesdale Rd. E6 9K 63
Trulock Ct. N17 7E 28
Trulock Rd. N17 7E 28
Truman Clo. Edgw 7M 23
Trumans Rd. N16 1D 60
Trumble Gdns. T Hth 8M 107
Trumpers Way. W7 4C 70
Trumper Way. Uxb 3A 142
Trumpington Rd. E7 9D 46
Trump St. EC2 9A 60
Trundlers Way. Bush 1C 22
Trundle St. SE1 3A 76
Trundleys Rd. SE8 6H 77
Trundley's Ter. SE8 5H 77
Trunks All. Swan 6M 113
Truro Gdns. Ilf 5J 47
Truro Ho. Pinn 7K 21
Truro Rd. E17 2K 45
Truro Rd. N22 7J 27
Truro St. NW5 2E 58
Truro Wlk. Romf 6G 35
Truro Way. N'holt 6C 52
Truslove Rd. SE27 2L 107
Trussley Rd. W6 4G 73
Truston's Gdns. Horn 5E 50
Trust Rd. Wal X 7E 6
Trust Wlk. SE21 7M 91
Tryfan Clo. Ilf 3H 47
Tryon Cres. E9 4G 61
Tryon St. SW3 6D 74
Trystings Clo. Clay 8E 118
Tuam Rd. SE18 7B 80
Tubbenden Clo. Orp 5C 128
Tubbenden Dri. Orp 6B 128
Tubbenden La. Orp 6B 128
Tubbenden La. S. Orp 7B 128
Tubbs Rd. NW10 5D 56
Tucker St. Wat 7G 9
Tucklow Wlk. SW15 6D 88
Tuck Rd. Rain 2E 66
Tudor Av. Chesh 4A 6
Tudor Av. Hamp 3L 101
Tudor Av. Romf 1E 50
Tudor Av. Wat 2H 9
Tudor Av. Wor Pk 5F 120
Tudor Clo. N6 5G 43
Tudor Clo. NW3 1C 58
Tudor Clo. NW7 6E 24
Tudor Clo. NW9 7A 40
Tudor Clo. SW2 5K 91
Tudor Clo. Ashf 9C 144
Tudor Clo. Bans 7J 135
Tudor Clo. Chesh 4B 6
Tudor Clo. Chess 7J 119
Tudor Clo. Chig 4L 31
Tudor Clo. Chst 5K 111
Tudor Clo. Dart 5F 98
Tudor Clo. Eps 2D 134
Tudor Clo. Hamp 2A 102
Tudor Clo. Pinn 3E 36
Tudor Clo. S Croy 7F 138
Tudor Clo. Sutt 7H 121
Tudor Clo. Wall 9G 123
Tudor Clo. Wfd G 5F 30
Tudor Ct. E17 5K 45
Tudor Ct. N1 2C 60
Tudor Ct. N22 7J 27
Tudor Ct. SE9 3J 95
Tudor Ct. SE16 2H 77
(off Princes Riverside Rd.)
Tudor Ct. W3 3L 71
Tudor Ct. Big H 9J 141
Tudor Ct. Borwd 4J 11
Tudor Ct. Crock 2A 130
Tudor Ct. Felt 1G 101
Tudor Ct. Romf 6M 35
Tudor Ct. Sidc 9E 96
Tudor Ct. Stanw 5C 144
Tudor Ct. Tedd 3D 102
Tudor Ct. N. Wemb 1L 55
Tudor Ct. S. Wemb 1L 55
Tudor Cres. Enf 3A 16
Tudor Cres. Ilf 6M 31
Tudor Dri. King T 2H 103
Tudor Dri. Mord 1H 121
Tudor Dri. Romf 2E 50
Tudor Dri. W on T 3H 117
Tudor Dri. Wat 2H 9
Tudor Enterprise Pk. Harr (HA1) 8D 38
Tudor Enterprise Pk. Harr (HA3) 1B 38
Tudor Est. NW10 5M 55
Tudor Gdns. NW9 7A 40
Tudor Gdns. SW13 2C 88
Tudor Gdns. W3 8L 55
Tudor Gdns. Harr 9B 22
Tudor Gdns. Romf 2E 50
Tudor Gdns. Twic 7D 86
Tudor Gdns. Upm 7M 51
Tudor Gdns. W Wick 5A 126
Tudor Gro. E9 3G 61
Tudor Ho. E9 3G 61
Tudor Ho. E16 2F 78
(off Wesley Av.)
Tudor Ho. W14 5H 73
(off Windsor Way)
Tudor Ho. Pinn 9G 21
(off Pinner Hill Rd.)
Tudor Mnr. Gdns. Wat 5H 5
Tudor M. Romf 3D 50
Tudor Pde. SE9 3J 95
Tudor Pde. Romf 5H 49
Tudor Pk. Golf Course. 4A 14
Tudor Pl. SE19 4D 108
Tudor Pl. Mitc 4C 106
Tudor Rd. E4 6M 29
Tudor Rd. E6 4G 63
Tudor Rd. E9 4F 60
Tudor Rd. N9 9F 16
Tudor Rd. SE19 4D 108
Tudor Rd. SE25 9F 108
Tudor Rd. Ashf 3B 100
Tudor Rd. Bark 4D 64
Tudor Rd. Barn 5L 13
Tudor Rd. Beck 7A 110
Tudor Rd. Hamp 4L 101
Tudor Rd. Harr 9B 22
Tudor Rd. Hay 9B 52
Tudor Rd. Houn 3B 86
Tudor Rd. King T 4L 103
Tudor Rd. Pinn 9G 21
Tudor Rd. S'hall 1J 69
Tudor Sq. Hay 8B 52
Tudor Stacks. SE24 3A 92
Tudor St. EC4 1L 75
Tudor Wlk. Bex 5J 97
Tudor Wlk. Wat 1H 9
Tudor Wlk. Wey 5A 116
Tudor Way. N14 1H 27
Tudor Way. W3 3L 71
Tudor Way. Orp 1B 128
Tudor Way. Uxb 2E 142
Tudor Way. Wal A 6K 7
Tudor Well Clo. Stan 5F 22
Tudor Works. Hay 2H 69
Tudway Rd. SE3 2F 94
Tuffnell Ct. Chesh 1D 6
(off Coopers Wlk.)
Tufnail Rd. Dart 5K 99
Tufnell Park. 9G 43
Tufnell Pk. Rd.
N19 & N7 9G 43
Tufter Rd. Chig 5D 32
Tufton Ct. SW1 4J 75
(off Tufton St.)
Tufton Gdns. W Mol 6M 101
Tufton Rd. E4 4L 29
Tufton St. SW1 4J 75
Tugboat St. SE28 3C 80
Tugela Rd. Croy 1B 124
Tugela St. SE6 8K 93
Tugmutton Clo. Orp 6M 127
Tulip Clo. E6 8K 63
Tulip Clo. Croy 3H 125
Tulip Clo. Hamp 3K 101
Tulip Clo. Romf 6G 35
Tulip Clo. S'hall 3A 70
Tulip Gdns. E4 3B 30
Tulip Gdns. Ilf 2M 63
Tulip Tree Ct. Belm 3L 135
Tulip Way. W Dray 5H 143
Tullis Ho. E9 3G 61
(off Frampton Pk. Rd.)
Tull St. Mitc 2D 122
Tulse Clo. Beck 7A 110
Tulse Hill. 7M 91
Tulse Hill. SW2 5L 91
Tulse Hill Est. SW2 5L 91
Tulse Ho. SW2 5L 91
Tulsemere Rd. SE27 8A 92
Tumblewood Rd. Bans 8J 135
Tumbling Bay. W on T 1E 116
Tummons Gdns. SE25 6C 108
Tunbridge Ho. EC1 6M 59
(off Spa Grn. Est.)
Tuncombe Rd. N18 4C 28
Tunis Rd. W12 2G 73
Tunley Grn. E14 8K 61
Tunley Rd. NW10 4C 56
Tunley Rd. SW17 7E 90
Tunmarsh La. E13 6F 62
Tunnanleys. E6 9L 63
Tunnel App. E14 1J 77
Tunnel App. SE10 3C 78
Tunnel App. SE16 3G 77
Tunnel Av. SE10 3B 78
(in three parts)
Tunnel Av. Trad. Est. SE10 3B 78
Tunnel Gdns. N11 7G 27
Tunnel Link Rd. H'row A 4E 144
Tunnel Rd. SE16 3G 77
Tunnel Rd. E. H'row A 9M 143
Tunnel Rd. W. H'row A 9L 143
Tunnel Wood Clo. Wat 1D 8
Tunnel Wood Rd. Wat 1D 8
Tunstall Av. Ilf 6E 32
Tunstall Clo. Orp 6C 128
Tunstall Rd. SW9 3K 91
Tunstall Rd. Croy 3C 124
Tunstall Wlk. Bren 7J 71
Tunstock Way. Belv 4J 81
Tunworth Clo. NW9 4A 40
Tunworth Cres. SW15 5D 88
Tun Yd. SW8 1F 90
(off Silverthorne Rd.)
Tupelo Rd. E10 7M 45
Tupman Ho. SE16 3E 76
(off Scott Lidgett Cres.)
Tuppy St. SE28 3A 80
Turenne Clo. SW18 3A 90
Turin Rd. N9 9G 17
Turin St. E2 6E 60
Turkey Oak Clo. SE19 4C 108
Turkey Street. 1G 17
Turkey St. Enf 9A 6
(in two parts)
Turks Clo. Uxb 6E 142
Turk's Head Yd. EC1 8M 59
Turk's Row. SW3 6D 74
Turle Rd. N4 7K 43
Turle Rd. SW16 6J 107
Turlewray Clo. N4 6K 43
Turley Clo. E15 4C 62
Turnagain La. EC4 9M 59
(off Farringdon St.)
Turnage Rd. Dag 6J 49
Turnberry Clo. NW4 9H 25
Turnberry Clo. SE16 6F 76
Turnberry Ct. Wat 3G 21
Turnberry Dri. Brick W 3J 5
Turnberry Quay. E14 4M 77
Turnberry Way. Orp 3B 128
Turnbull Ho. N1 4M 59
Turnbury Clo. SE28 9H 65
Turnchapel M. SW4 2F 90
Turner Av. N15 2C 44
Turner Av. Mitc 5D 106
Turner Av. Twic 9A 86
Turner Clo. NW11 4M 41
Turner Clo. SW9 8M 75
Turner Clo. Hay 5A 52
Turner Clo. Wemb 2H 55
Turner Ct. SE16 3G 77
(off Albion St.)
Turner Ct. Dart 4G 99
Turner Dri. NW11 4M 41
Turner Ho. NW8 5C 58
(off Townshend Est.)
Turner Ho. SW1 5H 75
(off Herrick St.)
Turner Ho. Twic 5H 87
(off Clevedon Rd.)
Turner Pl. SW11 4C 90
Turner Rd. E17 1A 46
Turner Rd. Big H 4G 141
Turner Rd. Bush 6A 10
Turner Rd. Edgw 9J 23
Turner Rd. N Mald 2B 120
Turner's All. EC3 1C 76
Turner's Hill. Chesh 2D 6
Turners La. W on T 8F 116
Turners Mdw. Way. Beck 5K 109
Turners Rd. E14 & E3 8K 61
Turner St. E1 8F 60
Turner St. E16 9D 62
Turner's Way. Croy 4L 123
Turners Wood. NW11 5A 42
Turneville Rd. W14 7K 73
Turney Rd. SE21 6A 92
Turnham Green. 5C 72
Turnham Grn. Ter. W4 5C 72
Turnham Grn. Ter. M. W4 5C 72
Turnham Rd. SE4 4J 93
Turnmill St. EC1 7M 59
Turnour Ho. E1 9F 60
(off Walburgh St.)
Turnpike Clo. SE8 8K 77
Turnpike Ct. Bexh 3H 97
Turnpike Ho. EC1 6M 59
Turnpike La. N8 2K 43
Turnpike La. Sutt 7A 122
Turnpike La. Uxb 6C 142
Turnpike Link. Croy 4C 124
Turnpike Pde. N8 1M 43
(off Green Lanes)
Turnpike Way. Iswth 9E 70
Turnpin La. SE10 7A 78
Turnstone Clo. E13 6E 62
Turnstone Clo. NW9 9C 24
Turnstone Clo. Ick 1F 142
Turnstone Clo. S Croy 2J 139
Turnstones, The. Wat 9J 5
Turpentine La. SW1 6F 74
Turpin Av. Romf 6L 33
Turpin Clo. Enf 1L 17
Turpington Clo. Brom 1J 127
Turpington La. Brom 2J 127
Turpin Ho. SW11 9F 74
Turpin La. Eri 8E 82
Turpin Rd. Felt 5D 84
Turpin's La. Wfd G 5K 31
Turpin Way. N19 7H 43
(in two parts)
Turpin Way. Wall 9F 122
Turquand St. SE17 5A 76
Turret Gro. SW4 2G 91
Turton Rd. Wemb 1J 55
Turville Ho. NW8 7C 58
(off Grendon St.)
Turville St. E2 7D 60
Tuscan Ho. E2 6G 61
(off Knottisford St.)
Tuscan Rd. SE18 6B 80
Tuscany Ho. E17 9K 29
Tuskar St. SE10 7C 78
Tustin Est. SE15 7G 77
Tuttlebee La. Buck H 2E 30
Tuttle Ho. SW1 6H 75
(off Aylesford St.)
Tuxford Clo. Borwd 2J 11
Tweedale Ct. E15 1A 62
Tweed Ct. W7 9C 54
(off Hanway Rd.)
Tweeddale Gro. Uxb 8A 36
Tweeddale Rd. Cars 3B 122
Tweed Glen. Romf 7B 34
Tweed Grn. Romf 7B 34
Tweed Ho. E14 7A 62
(off Teviot St.)
Tweedmouth Rd. E13 5F 62
Tweed Way. Romf 7B 34
Tweedy Clo. Enf 7D 16
Tweedy Rd. Brom 5E 110
Tweezer's All. WC2 1L 75
(off Milford La.)
Twelvetrees Cres.
E3 & E16 7A 62
(in three parts)
Twentyman Clo. Wfd G 5E 30
Twickenham. 7E 86
Twickenham Bri.
Twic & Rich 4G 87
Twickenham Clo. Croy 5K 123
Twickenham Gdns. Gnfd 1E 54
Twickenham Gdns. Harr 7C 22
Twickenham Rd. E11 7A 46
Twickenham Rd. Felt 9K 85
Twickenham Rd. Iswth 4E 86
Twickenham Rd. Rich 3G 87
Twickenham Rd. Tedd 1E 102
(in two parts)
Twickenham Rugby Union Football Ground. 5C 86
Twickenham Stadium Tours. 5C 86
(in Museeum of Rugby, The, Twickenham Rugby Union Football Ground)
Twickenham Trad. Est.
Twic 5D 86
Twig Folly Clo. E2 5H 61
Twigg Clo. Eri 8C 82
Twilley St. SW18 6M 89
Twin Bridges Bus. Pk.
S Croy 8B 124
Twine Clo. Bark 6F 64
Twine Ct. E1 1G 77
Twineham Grn. N12 4L 25
Twine Ter. E3 7K 61
(off Ropery St.)
Twining Av. Twic 9A 86
Twinn Rd. NW7 6J 25
Twin Tumps Way. SE28 1E 80
Twisden Rd. NW5 9F 42
Twistleton Ct. Dart 5H 99
Twybridge Way. NW10 3A 56
Twycross M. SE10 6C 78
Twyford Abbey Rd. NW10 6K 55
Twyford Av. N2 1D 42
Twyford Av. W3 1L 71
Twyford Ct. N10 1E 42
Twyford Ct. Wemb 5J 55
(off Vicars Bri. Clo.)
Twyford Cres. W3 2L 71
Twyford Ho. N5 8M 43
Twyford Ho. N15 4C 44
(off Chisley Rd.)
Twyford Pl. WC2 9K 59
Twyford Rd. Cars 3B 122
Twyford Rd. Harr 6M 37
Twyford Rd. Ilf 1A 64
Twyford St. N1 4K 59
Tyas Rd. E16 7D 62
Tybenham Rd. SW19 7L 105
Tyberry Rd. Enf 5F 16
Tyburn La. Harr 5D 38
Tyburn Way. W1 1D 74
Tycehurst Hill. Lou 6K 19
Tye La. Orp 7A 128
Tyers Est. SE1 3C 76
(off Bermondsey St.)
Tyers Ga. SE1 3C 76
Tyers St. SE11 6K 75
Tyers Ter. SE11 6K 75
Tyeshurst Clo. SE2 6J 81
Tyfield Clo. Chesh 3C 6
Tykeswater La. Els 4G 11
Tylecroft Rd. SW16 6J 107
Tyle Grn. Horn 2J 51
Tylehurst Gdns. Ilf 1A 64
Tyler Clo. E2 5D 60
Tyler Gro. Dart 3K 99
(in two parts)
Tyler Rd. S'hall 4M 69
Tylers Clo. Lou 9J 19
Tylers Ct. E17 2L 45
(off Westbury Rd.)
Tyler's Ct. W1 9H 59
(off Wardour St.)
Tylers Ct. Wemb 5J 55
Tylers Cres. Horn 1G 67
Tylersfield. Ab L 4D 4
Tylers Ga. Harr 4J 39
Tylers Grn. Rd. Swan 1A 130
Tylers Path. Cars 6D 122
Tyler St. SE10 6C 78
(in two parts)
Tylers Way. Wat 5A 10
Tylney Av. SE19 2D 108
(in two parts)
Tylney Ho. E1 9F 60
(off Nelson St.)
Tylney Rd. E7 9G 47
Tylney Rd. Brom 6H 111
Tynamara. King T 8H 103
(off Portsmouth Rd.)
Tynan Clo. Felt 7E 84
Tyndale Ct. E14 6M 77
(off Transom Sq.)
Tyndale La. N1 3M 59
Tyndale Mans. N1 3M 59
(off Upper St.)
Tyndale Ter. N1 3M 59
Tyndall Gdns. E10 7A 46
Tyndall Rd. E10 7A 46
Tyndall Rd. Well 2D 96
Tyne Ct. W7 9C 54
(off Hanway Rd.)
Tyneham Clo. SW11 2E 90
Tyneham Rd. SW11 1E 90
Tyne Ho. King T 5H 103
Tynemouth Clo. E6 9M 63
Tynemouth Dri. Enf 2E 16
Tynemouth Rd. N15 2D 44
Tynemouth Rd. SE18 6C 80
Tynemouth Rd. Mitc 4E 106
Tynemouth St. SW6 1A 90
Tyne St. E1 9D 60
Tynsdale Clo. NW10 2C 56
Tynwald Ho. SE26 9E 92
Type St. E2 5H 61
Tyrawley Rd. SW6 9M 73
Tyre La. NW9 2C 40
Tyrell Clo. Harr 9C 38
Tyrell Ct. Cars 6D 122
Tyrell Ho. Beck 2M 109
(off Beckenham Hill Rd.)
Tyrells Clo. Upm 7M 51
Tyrols Rd. SE23 7H 93
Tyrone Rd. E6 5K 63
Tyron Way. Sidc 1C 112
Tyrrell Av. Well 4E 96
Tyrrell Ho. SW1 7G 75
(off Churchill Gdns.)
Tyrrell Rd. SE22 3E 92
Tyrrell Sq. Mitc 5C 106
Tyrrel Way. NW9 5D 40
Tyrwhitt Rd. SE4 2L 93
Tysea Hill. Stap A 1D 34
Tysoe Av. Enf 9F 6
Tysoe St. EC1 6L 59
Tyson Gdns. SE23 6G 93
Tyson Rd. SE23 6G 93
Tyssen Pas. E8 2D 60
Tyssen Rd. N16 8D 44
Tyssen St. E8 2D 60
Tyssen St. N1 5C 60
Tytherton. E2 5G 61
(off Cyprus St.)
Tytherton Rd. N19 8H 43

U

Uamvar St. E14 8M 61
UCI Cinema. 4H 77
(Teredo St.)
UCI Cinema. 9M 57
(in Whiteleys Cen.)
UCI Empire Cinema. 1H 75
(off Leicester Sq.)
UCI Filmworks. 3D 78
Uckfield Gro. Mitc 4E 106
Uckfield Rd. Enf 1H 17
Udall Gdns. Romf 6L 33
Udall St. SW1 5G 75
Udimore Ho. W10 8G 57
(off Sutton Way)

Udney Pk. Rd.—Valetta Gro.

Udney Pk. Rd. Tedd 3E 102
Uffington Rd. NW10 4E 56
Uffington Rd. SE27 1L 107
Ufford Clo. Harr 7M 21
Ufford Rd. Harr 7M 21
Ufford St. SE1 3L 75
Ufton Ct. N'holt 6H 53
Ufton Gro. N1 3B 60
Ufton Rd. N1 3B 60
(in two parts)
UGC Cinema. 6A 74
(off Fulham Rd.)
UGC Cinema (Haymarket) 1H 75
(off Haymarket)
UGC Cinema (Trocadero) 1H 75
(off Windmill St.)
Uhura Sq. N16 8C 44
Ujima Ct. SW16 1J 107
Ullathorne Rd. SW16 1G 107
Ulleswater Rd. N14 3J 27
Ullin St. E14 8A 62
Ullswater Clo. SW15 1B 104
Ullswater Clo. Brom 4C 110
Ullswater Clo. Hay 5C 52
Ullswater Ct. Harr 5L 37
Ullswater Cres. SW15 1B 104
Ullswater Cres. Coul 8H 137
Ullswater Ho. SE15 7G 77
(off Hillbeck Clo.)
Ullswater Rd. SE27 8M 91
Ullswater Rd. SW13 8E 72
Ullswater Way. Horn 1E 66
Ulster Gdns. N13 4A 28
Ulster Pl. NW1 7F 58
Ulster Ter. NW1 7E 58
(off Outer Circ.)
Ulundi Rd. SE3 7C 78
Ulva Rd. SW15 4H 89
Ulverscroft Rd. SE22 4D 92
Ulverstone Rd. SE27 8M 91
Ulverston Ho. Romf 6J 35
(off Kingsbridge Cir.)
Ulverston Rd. E17 9B 30
Ulysses Rd. NW6 1K 57
Umberston St. E1 9E 60
Umbria St. SW15 5E 88
Umfreville Rd. N4 4M 43
Undercliff Rd. SE13 2L 93
Underhill. 7L 13
Underhill. Barn 7L 13
Underhill Ct. Barn 7L 13
Underhill Ho. E14 8L 61
(off Burgess St.)
Underhill Pas. NW1 4F 58
(off Camden High St.)
Underhill Rd. SE22 4E 92
Underhill St. NW1 4F 58
Underne Av. N14 2F 26
Undershaft. EC3 9C 60
Undershaw Rd. Brom 9D 94
Underwood. New Ad 7A 126
Underwood Ct. E10 6M 45
(off Leyton Grange Est.)
Underwood Ho. W6 4F 72
(off Sycamore Gdns.)
Underwood Rd. E1 7E 60
Underwood Rd. E4 5M 29
Underwood Rd. Wfd G 7G 31
Underwood Row. N1 6A 60
Underwood St. N1 6A 60
Underwood, The. SE9 8K 95
Undine Rd. E14 5M 77
Undine St. SW17 2D 106
Uneeda Dri. Gnfd 4B 54
Unicorn Building. E1 1H 77
(off Jardine Rd.)
Union Clo. E11 9B 46
Union Cotts. E15 3C 62
Union Ct. EC2 9C 60
(off Old Broad St.)
Union Ct. SW4 1J 91
Union Ct. W9 8L 57
(off Elmfield Way)
Union Ct. Rich 4J 87
Union Dri. E1 7J 61
Union Gro. SW8 1H 91
Union M. SW4 1J 91
Union Rd. N11 6H 27
Union Rd. SW8 & SW4 1H 91
Union Rd. Brom 9H 111
Union Rd. Croy 2A 124
Union Rd. N'holt 5L 53
Union Rd. Wemb 2J 55
Union Sq. N1 4A 60
Union St. E15 4B 62
Union St. SE1 2M 75
Union St. Barn 5J 13
Union St. King T 6H 103
Union Theatre. 2M 75
(off Union St.)
Union Wlk. E2 6C 60
Union Wharf. N1 4A 60
Union Yd. W1 9F 58
Unitair Cen. Felt 5A 84
Unit Workshops. E1 9E 60
(off Adler St.)
Unity Clo. NW10 2E 56
Unity Clo. SE19 2A 108
Unity Clo. New Ad 1M 139
Unity M. NW1 5H 59
Unity Rd. Enf 1G 17
Unity Trad. Est. Wfd G 9H 31
Unity Way. SE7 4H 79
Unity Wharf. SE1 3D 76
(off Mill St.)
University Clo. NW7 7D 24
University Clo. Bush 6L 9
University College. 7H 59
University Gdns. Bex 6K 97
University of Central London. 7G 59
(Gordon St., Chemistry Building)
University of Central London. 7G 59
(Taviton St., Campbell Ho.)
University of East London (Docklands Campus) 1L 79
University of Greenwich. 7B 78
(Romney Rd.)
University of Greenwich (Dartford Campus). 8F 98
University of London Observatory. 6D 24
University of London (Senate House). 8H 59
University of London Union. 7H 59
University of North London. 1A 60
(Highbury Grove)
University of North London. 1L 59
(Holloway Rd.)
University of Westminster. 7G 59
(Euston Cen.)
University of Westminster. (Cavendish Campus) 8F 58
(Bolsover St.)
University of Westminster. (Cavendish Campus) 8G 59
(Hanson St.)
University of Westminster. (Harrow Campus). 5E 38
University of Westminster Library. 8G 59
University of Westminster. (Marylebone Campus) 8E 58
University of Westminster (Regent Campus) 8G 59
(off Lit. Titchfield St.)
University of Westminster. (Regent Campus) 9F 58
(Regent St.)
University of Westminster. (Regent Campus) 8G 59
(off Wells St.)
University Pl. Eri 8A 82
University Rd. SW19 3B 106
University St. WC1 7G 59
University Way. E16 1L 79
University Way. Dart 3G 99
(in two parts)
Unwin Av. Felt 4B 84
Unwin Clo. SE15 7E 76
Unwin Mans. W14 7K 73
(off Queen's Club Gdns.)
Unwin Rd. SW7 4B 74
Unwin Rd. Iswth 2C 86
Upbrook M. W2 9A 58
Upcerne Rd. SW10 8A 74
Upchurch Clo. SE20 4F 108
Upcott Ho. E9 3G 61
(off Frampton Pk. Rd.)
Upcroft Av. Edgw 5A 24
Updale Rd. Sidc 1D 112
Upfield. Croy 5F 124
Upfield Rd. W7 8D 54
Upgrove Mnr. Way. SE24 6L 91
Uphall Rd. Ilf 1M 63
Upham Pk. Rd. W4 5C 72
Uphill Dri. NW7 5C 24
Uphill Dri. NW9 3A 40
Uphill Gro. NW7 4C 24
Uphill Rd. NW7 4C 24
Upland Ct. Rd. Romf 9K 35
Upland M. SE22 4E 92
Upland Rd. E13 7E 62
Upland Rd. SE22 4E 92
Upland Rd. Bexh 2K 97
Upland Rd. S Croy 7B 124
Upland Rd. Sutt 9B 122
Uplands. Beck 6L 109
Uplands Av. E17 9H 29
Uplands Bus. Pk. E17 1H 45
Uplands Clo. SW14 4M 87
Uplands Ct. N21 9L 15
(off Green, The)
Uplands Dri. Oxs 6B 132
Uplands End. Wfd G 7J 31
Uplands Pk. Rd. Enf 4L 15
Uplands Rd. N8 3K 43
Uplands Rd. E Barn 1E 26
Uplands Rd. Kenl 8A 138
Uplands Rd. Orp 3F 128
Uplands Rd. Romf 1H 49
Uplands Rd. Wfd G 7J 31
Uplands, The. Brick W 3J 5
Uplands, The. Lou 5K 19
Uplands, The. Ruis 6E 36
Uplands Way. N21 7L 15
Upland Way. Eps 9G 135
Upminster Rd. Horn & Upm 7K 51
Upminster Rd. N. Rain 6G 67
Upminster Rd. S. Rain 7E 66
Upminster Smockmill. 7M 51
Upnall Ho. SE15 7G 77
Upney Clo. Horn 1H 67
Upney La. Bark 1C 64
Upnor Way. SE17 6C 76
Uppark Dri. Ilf 4A 48
Up. Abbey Rd. Belv 5K 81
Up. Addison Gdns. W14 3J 73
Up. Austin Lodge Rd. Eyns 6H 131
Up. Bardsey Wlk. N1 2A 60
(off Douglas Rd. N.)
Up. Belgrave St. SW1 4E 74
Up. Berenger Wlk. SW10 8B 74
(off Berenger Wlk.)
Up. Berkeley St. W1 9D 58
Up. Beulah Hill. SE19 5C 108
Up. Blantyre Wlk. SW10 8B 74
(off Blantyre Wlk.)
Up. Brentwood Rd. Romf 2G 51
Up. Brighton Rd. Surb 1H 119
Up. Brockley Rd. SE4 2K 93
Up. Brook St. W1 1E 74
Up. Butts. Bren 7G 71
Up. Caldy Wlk. N1 3A 60
(off Caldy Wlk.)
Up. Camelford Wlk. W11 9J 57
(off St Mark's Rd.)
Up. Cavendish Av. N3 1L 41
Up. Cheyne Row. SW3 7C 74
(off Up. Cheyne Row)
Upper Clapton. 7F 44
Up. Clapton Rd. E5 7F 44
Up. Clarendon Wlk. W11 9J 57
(off Clarendon Rd.)
Up. Court Rd. Eps 3A 134
Up. Dartrey Wlk. SW10 8A 74
(off Whistler Wlk.)
Up. Dengie Wlk. N1 4A 60
(off Baddow Wlk.)
Upper Dri. Big H 9G 141
Upper Dunnymans. Bans 6K 135
Upper Edmonton. 5F 28
Upper Elmers End. 9K 109
Up. Elmers End Rd. Beck 8J 109
Up. Farm Rd. W Mol 8K 101
Upper Feilde. W1 1E 74
(off Park St.)
Upper Fosters. NW4 2G 41
(off New Brent St.)
Up. Green E. Mitc 7D 106
Up. Green W. Mitc 6D 106
(in two parts)
Up. Grosvenor St. W1 1E 74
Up. Grotto Rd. Twic 8D 86
Upper Ground. SE1 2L 75
Upper Gro. SE25 8C 108
Up. Grove Rd. Belv 7K 81
Up. Gulland Wlk. N1 2A 60
(off Oronsay Wlk.)
Upper Halliford. 8C 100
Up. Halliford By-Pass. Shep 9C 100
Up. Halliford Grn. Shep 8C 100
Up. Halliford Rd. Shep 7C 100
Up. Hampstead Wlk. NW3 9A 42
Up. Ham Rd. Rich 1H 103
Up. Handa Wlk. N1 2B 60
(off Handa Wlk.)
Up. Hawkwell Wlk. N1 4A 60
(off Baddow Wlk.)
Up. High St. Eps 5C 134
Up. Highway. Ab L 5A 4
Up. Hilldrop Est. N7 1H 59
Upper Hitch. Wat 1J 21
Upper Holloway. 7G 43
Up. Holly Hill Rd. Belv 6M 81
Up. James St. W1 1G 75
Up. John St. W1 1G 75
Up. Lismore Wlk. N1 2B 60
(off Clephane St.)
Upper Mall. W6 6E 72
(in two parts)
Upper Marsh. SE1 4K 75
Up. Montagu St. W1 8D 58
Up. Mulgrave Rd. Sutt 9J 121
Up. North St. E14 8L 61
Upper Norwood. 5C 108
Up. Paddock Rd. Wat 8J 9
Up. Palace Rd. E Mol 7A 102
Upper Pk. Lou 6H 19
Up. Park Rd. N11 5F 26
Up. Park Rd. NW3 1D 58
Up. Park Rd. Belv 5M 81
Up. Park Rd. Brom 5F 110
Up. Park Rd. King T 3L 103
Up. Phillimore Gdns. W8 3L 73
Up. Pillory Down. Cars 5E 136
Upper Pines. Bans 9D 136
Up. Rainham Rd. Horn 6D 50
Up. Ramsey Wlk. N1 2B 60
(off Ramsey Wlk.)
Up. Rawreth Wlk. N1 4A 60
(off Basire St.)
Up. Richmond Rd. SW15 3D 88
Up. Richmond Rd. W. Rich & SW14 3L 87
Upper Rd. E13 6E 62
Upper Rd. Wall 7H 123
Upper Ruxley. 4L 113
Up. St Martin's La. WC2 1J 75
Up. Sawley Wood. Bans 6K 135
Up. Selsdon Rd. S Croy 9D 124
Up. Sheridan Rd. Belv 5L 81
Upper Shirley. 6H 125
Up. Shirley Rd. Croy 4G 125
Upper Sq. Iswth 2E 86
Upper St. N1 5L 59
Up. Sunbury Rd. Hamp 5J 101
Up. Sutton La. Houn 8L 69
Upper Sydenham. 9F 92
Up. Tachbrook St. SW1 5G 75
Upper Tail. Wat 3J 21
Up. Talbot Wlk. W11 9J 57
(off Talbot Wlk.)
Up. Teddington Rd. King T 4G 103
Upper Ter. NW3 8A 42
Up. Thames St. EC4 1M 75
Up. Tollington Pk. N4 6L 43
(in two parts)
Upperton Rd. Sidc 2D 112
Upperton Rd. E. E13 6G 63
Upperton Rd. W. E13 6G 63
Upper Tooting. 9D 90
Up. Tooting Pk. SW17 8D 90
Up. Tooting Rd. SW17 1D 106
Up. Town Rd. Gnfd 7M 53
Up. Tulse Hill. SW2 6K 91
Up. Vernon Rd. Sutt 7B 122
Upper Walthamstow. 2B 46
Up. Walthamstow Rd. E17 2A 46
Up. Whistler Wlk. SW10 8A 74
(off Worlds End Est.)
Up. Wickham La. Well 8F 80
Up. Wimpole St. W1 8E 58
Up. Woburn Pl. WC1 6H 59
Up. Woodcote Village. Purl 4H 137
Uppingham Av. Stan 8F 22
Upsdell Av. N13 6L 27
Upshire Ho. E17 9K 29
Upshire Rd. Wal A 5M 7
Upstall St. SE5 9M 75
Upton. 4H 97
(Bexleyheath)
Upton. 3E 62
(Plaistow)
Upton Av. E7 3E 62
Upton Clo. NW2 8J 41
Upton Clo. Bex 5K 97
Upton Ct. SE20 4G 109
Upton Dene. Sutt 9M 121
Upton Gdns. Harr 3F 38
Upton Ho. H Hill 5H 35
(off Barnstaple Rd.)
Upton La. E7 3E 62
Upton Lodge. E7 2E 62
Upton Lodge Clo. Bush 9A 10
Upton Park. 5H 63
Upton Pk. Rd. E7 3F 62
Upton Rd. N18 5E 28
Upton Rd. SE18 7A 80
Upton Rd. Bexh 3J 97
Upton Rd. Houn 2L 85
Upton Rd. T Hth 6B 108
Upton Rd. Wat 5F 8
Upton Rd. S. Bex 5K 97
Upton Vs. Bexh 3J 97
Upward Ct. Romf 2D 50
Upway. N12 6C 26
Upwey Ho. N1 4C 60
Upwood Rd. SE12 5E 94
Upwood Rd. SW16 5J 107
Urban Av. Horn 8G 51
Urlwin St. SE5 7A 76
Urlwin Wlk. SW9 9L 75
Urmston Dri. SW19 7J 89
Urmston Ho. E14 5A 78
(off Seyssel St.)
Urquhart Ct. Beck 4K 109
Ursula Lodges. Sidc 2F 112
(off Eynswood Dri.)
Ursula M. N4 6A 44
Ursula St. SW11 9C 74
Urswick Gdns. Dag 3J 65
Urswick Rd. E9 1G 61
Urswick Rd. Dag 3H 65
Usborne M. SW8 8K 75
Usher Rd. E3 4K 61
Usk Rd. SW11 3A 90
Usk Rd. Ave 9M 67
Usk St. E2 6H 61
Utopia Village. NW1 3E 58
Uvedale Clo. New Ad 3B 140
Uvedale Cres. New Ad 3B 140
Uvedale Rd. Dag 8L 49
Uvedale Rd. Enf 7B 16
Uverdale Rd. SW10 8A 74
Uxbridge. 3A 142
Uxbridge Ct. King T 9H 103
(off Uxbridge Rd.)
Uxbridge Ind. Est. Uxb 5A 142
Uxbridge Moor. 5A 142
Uxbridge Rd. W5 & W3 1J 71
Uxbridge Rd. W7 2D 70
Uxbridge Rd. W12 2D 72
Uxbridge Rd. W13 & W5 2F 70
Uxbridge Rd. Felt 8G 85
Uxbridge Rd. Hamp H 1L 101
Uxbridge Rd. Harr & Stan 7A 22
Uxbridge Rd. Hil & Hay 6E 142
Uxbridge Rd. King T 8H 103
Uxbridge Rd. Pinn 9G 21
Uxbridge Rd. S'hall 2L 69
Uxbridge St. W8 2L 73
Uxendon Cres. Wemb 6J 39
Uxendon Hill. Wemb 6K 39

V

Vaillant Rd. Wey 6A 116
Vaizeys Wharf. SE7 4F 78
(off Riverside)
Valan Leas. Brom 7C 110
Vale Av. Borwd 7M 11
Vale Border. S Croy 3H 139
Vale Clo. N2 1D 42
Vale Clo. W9 6A 58
Vale Clo. Coul 6J 137
Vale Clo. Orp 6L 127
Vale Clo. Twic 9E 86
Vale Clo. Wey 5B 116
Vale Cotts. SW15 9C 88
Vale Ct. W3 2D 72
Vale Ct. W9 6A 58
Vale Ct. New Bar 6M 13
Vale Ct. Wey 5B 116
Vale Cres. SW15 1C 104
Vale Cft. Clay 1D 132
Vale Cft. Pinn 3J 37
Vale Dri. Barn 6K 13
Vale End. SE22 3D 92
Vale Est., The. W3 2C 72
Vale Gro. N4 5A 44
Vale Gro. W3 3B 72
Vale Ind. Est. Wat 9A 8
Vale La. W3 8L 55
Vale Lodge. SE23 8G 93
Valence Av. E4 1C 30
Valence Av. Dag 6H 49
Valence Cir. Dag 8H 49
Valence Dri. Chesh 1A 6
Valence House Mus. 8J 49
Valence Rd. Eri 8B 82
Valence Wood Rd. Dag 8H 49
Valencia Rd. Stan 4G 23
Valency Clo. N'wd 4D 20
Valentia Pl. SW9 3L 91
Valentine Av. Bex 8J 97
Valentine Ct. SE23 8H 93
(in two parts)
Valentine Pl. SE1 3M 75
Valentine Rd. E9 2H 61
Valentine Rd. Harr 8M 37
Valentine Row. SE1 3M 75
Valentines Rd. Ilf 6M 47
Valentine's Way. Romf 7C 50
Valentyne Clo. New Ad 3C 140
Vale of Health. 8A 42
Vale of Health. NW3 8B 42
Vale Pde. SW15 9C 88
Valerian Way. E15 6C 62
Valerie Ct. Sutt 9M 121
Vale Ri. NW11 6K 41
Vale Rd. E7 2F 62
Vale Rd. N4 5A 44
Vale Rd. Brom 5L 111
Vale Rd. Bush 7J 9
Vale Rd. Clay 1C 132
Vale Rd. Dart 7F 98
Vale Rd. Eps 6D 120
Vale Rd. Mitc 7H 107
Vale Rd. Sutt 6M 121
Vale Rd. Wey 5B 116
Vale Rd. Wor Pk 5D 120
Vale Rd. N. Surb 4J 119
Vale Rd. S. Surb 4J 119
Vale Row. N5 8M 43
Vale Royal. N7 3J 59
Vale Royal Ho. WC2 1H 75
(off Charing Cross Rd.)
Valery Pl. Hamp 4L 101
Valeside Ct. Barn 6M 13
Vale St. SE27 9B 92
Valeswood Rd. Brom 2D 110
Vale Ter. N4 4A 44
Vale, The. N10 8E 26
Vale, The. N14 9H 15
Vale, The. NW11 8H 41
Vale, The. SW3 7B 74
Vale, The. W3 2B 72
Vale, The. Coul 6H 137
Vale, The. Croy 4H 125
Vale, The. Felt 5F 84
Vale, The. Houn 7J 69
Vale, The. Ruis 9G 37
Vale, The. Sun 3E 100
Vale, The. Wfd G 7E 30
Valetta Gro. E13 5E 62

Valetta Rd.—Victoria Point

aletta Rd. W3 3C 72
alette Ct. N10 2F 42
(off St James's La.)
alette Ho. E9 2G 61
alette St. E9 2G 61
aliant Clo. N'holt 6H 53
aliant Clo. Romf 9M 33
aliant Ho. E14 3A 78
(off Plevna St.)
aliant Ho. SE7 6G 79
aliant Way. E6 8K 63
allance Rd. E2 & E1 6E 60
allance Rd. N10 9G 27
allentin Rd. E17 2A 46
alley Av. N12 4B 26
alley Clo. Dart 5D 98
alley Clo. Lou 8K 19
alley Clo. Pinn 9F 20
alley Clo. Wal A 5J 7
alley Dri. NW9 4L 39
alleyfield Rd. SW16 2K 107
alley Fields Cres. Enf 4L 15
alley Gdns. SW19 4B 106
alley Gdns. Wemb 3K 55
alley Gro. SE7 6G 79
alley Hill. Lou 9J 19
alleylink Est. Enf 8J 17
alley M. Twic 8D 86
alley Pk. Wat 9A 8
alley Ri. Wat 6F 4
alley Rd. SW16 2K 107
Valley Rd. Belv 5M 81
Valley Rd. Brom 6C 110
Valley Rd. Dart 5D 98
Valley Rd. Eri 5A 82
Valley Rd. Kenl 7B 138
Valley Rd. Orp 5F 112
Valley Rd. Uxb 5C 142
Valley Side. E4 2L 29
Valley Side. SE7 6H 79
Valley Side Pde. E4 2L 29
Valley Vw. Barn 8J 13
Valley Vw. Big H 9G 141
Valley Vw. Gdns. Kenl 7C 138
Valley Vw. Ter. F'ham 3K 131
Valley Wlk. Crox G 7A 8
Valley Wlk. Croy 4G 125
Valliere Rd. NW10 6E 56
Valliers Wood Rd. Sidc 7C 96
Vallis Way. W13 8E 54
Vallis Way. Chess 6H 119
Valmar Rd. SE5 9A 76
Valmar Trad. Est. SE5 9A 76
Val McKenzie Av. N7 8L 43
Valnay St. SW17 2D 106
Valognes Av. E17 8J 29
Valois Ho. SE1 4D 76
(off Grange, The)
Valonia Gdns. SW18 5K 89
Vambery Rd. SE18 7A 80
Vanbrough Cres. N'holt 4G 53
Vanbrugh Castle. SE3 7C 78
(off Maze Hill)
Vanbrugh Clo. E16 8H 63
Vanbrugh Ct. SE11 5L 75
(off Wincott St.)
Vanbrugh Dri. W on T 2G 117
Vanbrugh Fields. SE3 7D 78
Vanbrugh Hill. SE10 & SE3 6D 78
Vanbrugh Ho. E9 3G 61
(off Loddiges Rd.)
Vanbrugh Pk. SE3 8D 78
Vanbrugh Pk. Rd. SE3 8D 78
Vanbrugh Pk. Rd. W. SE3 8D 78
Vanbrugh Rd. W4 4B 72
Vanbrugh Ter. SE3 9D 78
Vanburgh Clo. Orp 3C 128
Vanburgh Ho. E1 8D 60
(off Folgate St.)
Vancouver Clo. Eps 3A 134
Vancouver Clo. Orp 6E 128
Vancouver Ho. E1 2F 76
(off Reardon Path)
Vancouver Mans. Edgw 8M 23
Vancouver Rd. SE23 8J 93
Vancouver Rd. Edgw 8M 23
Vancouver Rd. Hay 7F 52
Vancouver Rd. Rich 1G 103
Vanderbilt Rd. SW18 7M 89
Vanderville Gdns. N2 9A 26
Vandome Clo. E16 9F 62
Vandon Ct. SW1 4G 75
(off Petty France)
Vandon Pas. SW1 4G 75
Vandon St. SW1 4G 75
Van Dyck Av. N Mald 2B 120
Vandyke Clo. SW15 6H 89
Vandyke Cross. SE9 4J 95
Vandy St. EC2 7C 60
Vane Clo. NW3 1B 58
Vane Clo. Harr 4K 39
Vanessa Clo. Belv 6L 81
Vanessa Way. Bex 9B 98
Vane St. SW1 5G 75
Vangaurd. NW9 7C 24
Vange Ho. W10 8G 57
(off Sutton Way)
Van Gogh Clo. Iswth 2E 86
Van Gogh Ct. E14 4B 78
Vanguard Building. E14 3K 77
Vanguard Clo. E16 8E 62
Vanguard Clo. Croy 3M 123
Vanguard Clo. Romf 9L 33
Vanguard St. SE8 9L 77
Vanguard Trad. Est. E15 4A 62
Vanguard Way. H'row A 1C 84
Vanguard Way. Wall 9J 123
Vanneck Sq. SW15 4E 88
Vanoc Gdns. Brom 1E 110
Vanryne Ho. Lou 6J 19
Vansittart Rd. E7 9D 46
Vansittart St. SE14 8J 77
Vanston Pl. SW6 8L 73
Vantage M. E14 2A 78
(off Preston's Rd.)
Vantage Pl. W8 4L 73
Vantage W. W3 5K 71
Vantrey Ho. SE11 5L 75
(off Marylee Way)
Vant Rd. SW17 2D 106
Varcoe Rd. SE16 6F 76
Vardens Rd. SW11 3B 90
Varden St. E1 9F 60
Vardon Clo. W3 9B 56
Vardon Ho. SE10 9A 78
Varley Ho. NW6 4L 57
Varley Pde. NW9 2C 40
Varley Rd. E16 9F 62
Varley Way. Mitc 6B 106
Varna Rd. SW6 8J 73
Varna Rd. Hamp 5M 101
Varndell St. NW1 6G 59
Varney Clo. Chesh 1A 6
Varsity Dri. Twic 4C 86
Varsity Row. SW14 1A 88
Vartry Rd. N15 4B 44
Vassall Ho. E3 6J 61
(off Antill Rd.)
Vassall Rd. SW9 8L 75
Vat Ho. SW8 8J 75
(off Rita Rd.)
Vauban Est. SE16 4D 76
Vauban St. SE16 4D 76
Vaudeville Ct. N4 7L 43
Vaudeville Theatre. 1J 75
(off Strand)
Vaughan Av. NW4 3E 40
Vaughan Av. W6 5D 72
Vaughan Av. Horn 9H 51
Vaughan Clo. Hamp 3J 101
Vaughan Est. E2 6D 60
(off Diss St.)
Vaughan Gdns. Ilf 5K 47
Vaughan Ho. SE1 3M 75
(off Blackfriars Rd.)
Vaughan Ho. SW4 6G 91
Vaughan Rd. E15 2D 62
Vaughan Rd. SE5 1A 92
Vaughan Rd. Harr 5A 38
Vaughan Rd. Th Dit 2F 118
Vaughan Rd. Well 1D 96
Vaughan St. SE16 3K 77
Vaughan Way. E1 1E 76
Vaughan Williams Clo. SE8 8L 77
Vaux Cres. W on T 8F 116
Vauxhall. 6J 75
Vauxhall Bri. SW1 & SE1 6J 75
Vauxhall Bri. Rd. SW1 4G 75
Vauxhall Cross (Junct.) 6J 75
Vauxhall Cross. SE1 6J 75
Vauxhall Distribution Pk. SW8 7H 75
(off Post Office Way)
Vauxhall Gdns. S Croy 8A 124
Vauxhall Gro. SW8 7K 75
Vauxhall Pl. Dart 6J 99
Vauxhall St. SE11 6K 75
Vauxhall Wlk. SE11 6K 75
Vawdrey Clo. E1 7G 61
Veals Mead. Mitc 5C 106
Vectis Gdns. SW17 3F 106
Vectis Rd. SW17 3F 106
Veda Rd. SE13 3L 93
Vega Cres. N'wd 5D 20
Vega Rd. Bush 9A 10
Veitch Clo. Felt 6D 84
Veitch Rd. Wal A 7J 7
Veldene Way. Harr 8K 37
Velde Way. SE22 4C 92
Velletri Ho. E2 5H 61
(off Mace St.)
Vellum Dri. Cars 5E 122
Venables Clo. Dag 9M 49
Venables St. NW8 7B 58
Vencourt Pl. W6 5E 72
Venetian Rd. SE5 1A 92
Venetia Rd. N4 4M 43
Venetia Rd. W5 3H 71
Venette Clo. Rain 8F 66
Venice Ct. SE5 8A 76
(off Bowyer St.)
Venner Rd. SE26 3G 109
Venners Clo. Bexh 1C 98
Venn Ho. N1 4K 59
(off Barnsbury Est.)
Venn St. SW4 3G 91
Ventnor Av. Stan 8F 22
Ventnor Dri. N20 3M 25
Ventnor Gdns. Bark 2C 64
Ventnor Rd. SE14 8H 77
Ventnor Rd. Sutt 9M 121
Venture Clo. Bex 6J 97
Venture Ct. SE12 6E 94
Venture Ho. W10 9H 57
(off Bridge Clo.)
Venue St. E14 8A 62
Venue, The. 4A 12
(Swimming Pool)
Venus Rd. SE18 4K 79
Veny Cres. Horn 1H 67
Vera Av. N21 7L 15
Vera Ct. Wat 9H 9
Vera Lynn Clo. E7 9E 46
Vera Rd. SW6 9J 73
Verbena Clo. E16 7D 62
Verbena Clo. W Dray 6H 143
Verbena Gdns. W6 6E 72
Verdant Ct. SE6 6C 94
(off Verdant La.)
Verdant La. SE6 6C 94
Verdayne Av. Croy 3H 125
Verdayne Gdns. Warl 8G 139
Verderers Rd. Chig 5E 32
Verdi Ho. W10 5J 57
(off Herries St.)
Verdun Rd. SE18 7E 80
Verdun Rd. SW13 7E 72
Verdure Clo. Wat 5J 5
Vereker Dri. Sun 7E 100
Vereker Rd. W14 6J 73
Vere Rd. Lou 6M 19
Vere St. W1 9F 58
Veritas Ho. Sidc 8E 96
(off Station Rd.)
Verity Clo. W11 1J 73
Vermeer Ct. E14 4B 78
Vermeer Gdns. SE15 3G 93
Vermont Clo. Enf 6M 15
Vermont Ho. E17 9K 29
Vermont Rd. SE19 3B 108
Vermont Rd. SW18 5M 89
Vermont Rd. Sutt 5M 121
Verne Ct. W3 4A 72
(off Vincent Rd.)
Verney Gdns. Dag 9J 49
Verney Ho. NW8 7C 58
(off Jerome Cres.)
Verney Rd. SE16 7E 76
Verney Rd. Dag 9J 49
(in two parts)
Verney St. NW10 8B 40
Verney Way. SE16 6F 76
Vernham Rd. SE18 7A 80
Vernon Av. E12 9K 47
Vernon Av. SW20 6H 105
Vernon Av. Enf 9E 6
Vernon Av. Wfd G 7F 30
Vernon Clo. Eps 8A 120
Vernon Clo. Orp 7F 112
Vernon Ct. NW2 8K 41
Vernon Ct. W5 1G 71
Vernon Ct. Stan 8F 22
Vernon Cres. Barn 8E 14
Vernon Dri. Stan 8E 22
Vernon Ho. SE11 6K 75
(off Vauxhall St.)
Vernon Ho. WC1 8J 59
(off Vernon Pl.)
Vernon M. E17 3K 45
Vernon M. W14 5J 73
Vernon Pl. WC1 8J 59
Vernon Ri. WC1 6K 59
Vernon Ri. Gnfd 1B 54
Vernon Rd. E3 5K 61
Vernon Rd. E11 6C 46
Vernon Rd. E15 3C 62
Vernon Rd. E17 3K 45
Vernon Rd. N8 1L 43
Vernon Rd. SW14 2B 88
Vernon Rd. Bush 7J 9
Vernon Rd. Felt 8D 84
Vernon Rd. Ilf 6D 48
Vernon Rd. Romf 5A 34
Vernon Rd. Sutt 7A 122
Vernon Sq. WC1 6K 59
Vernon St. W14 5J 73
Vernon Yd. W11 1K 73
Veroan Rd. Bexh 1J 97
Verona Clo. Uxb 9A 142
Verona Ct. SE14 7H 77
(off Myers La.)
Verona Dri. Surb 4J 119
Verona Ho. Eri 8D 82
Verona Rd. E7 3E 62
Veronica Clo. Romf 7G 35
Veronica Gdns. SW16 5G 107
Veronica Ho. SE4 2K 93
Veronica Rd. SW17 8F 90
Veronique Gdns. Ilf 3A 48
Verran Rd. SW12 6F 90
Versailles Rd. SE20 4E 108
Verulam Av. E17 4K 45
Verulam Av. Purl 4G 137
Verulam Bldgs. WC1 8K 59
(off Grays Inn)
Verulam Ct. NW9 5E 40
Verulam Ct. S'hall 9A 54
(off Haldane Rd.)
Verulam Ho. W6 3F 72
(off Hammersmith Gro.)
Verulam Pas. Wat 4F 8
Verulam Rd. Gnfd 7L 53
Verulam St. WC1 8L 59
Verwood Dri. Barn 5D 14
Verwood Ho. SW8 8K 75
(off Cobbett St.)
Verwood Lodge. E14 4B 78
(off Manchester Rd.)
Verwood Rd. Harr 9A 22
Veryan Clo. Orp 8G 113
Veryan Ct. N8 3H 43
Vesage Ct. EC1 8L 59
(off Leather La.)
Vesey Path. E14 9M 61
Vespan Rd. W12 3E 72
Vesta Rd. SE4 1J 93
Vestris Rd. SE23 8H 93
Vestry Ct. SW1 4H 75
(off Monck St.)
Vestry House Mus. 2M 45
Vestry M. SE5 9C 76
Vestry Rd. E17 2M 45
Vestry Rd. SE5 9C 76
Vestry St. N1 6B 60
Vevey St. SE6 8K 93
Veysey Gdns. Dag 8L 49
Viaduct Bldgs. EC1 8L 59
Viaduct Pl. E2 6F 60
Viaduct Rd. N2 9B 26
Viaduct St. E2 6F 60
Viaduct Ter. S Dar 6M 115
Viaduct, The. E18 9E 30
Viaduct, The. Wemb 4J 55
Vian Av. Enf 8E 6
Vian St. SE13 2M 93
Viant Ho. NW10 3B 56
Vibart Gdns. SW2 6K 91
Vibart Wlk. N1 4J 59
(off Outram Pl.)
Vibia Clo. Stanw 6B 144
Vicarage Clo. Eri 7A 82
Vicarage Clo. N'holt 3K 53
Vicarage Clo. Ruis 5B 36
Vicarage Clo. Wor Pk 3C 120
Vicarage Ct. W8 3M 73
Vicarage Ct. Beck 7J 109
Vicarage Ct. Felt 6A 84
Vicarage Ct. Ilf 1M 63
Vicarage Cres. SW11 9B 74
Vicarage Dri. SW14 4B 88
Vicarage Dri. Bark 3A 64
Vicarage Dri. Beck 5L 109
Vicarage Farm Ct. Houn 8K 69
Vicarage Farm Rd. Houn 1J 85
Vicarage Fields. W on T 1G 117
Vicarage Fld. Shop. Cen. Bark 3A 64
Vicarage Gdns. SW14 4A 88
Vicarage Gdns. W8 2L 73
Vicarage Gdns. Mitc 7C 106
Vicarage Ga. W8 2M 73
Vicarage Gro. SE5 9B 76
Vicarage Ho. King T 6K 103
(off Cambridge Rd.)
Vicarage La. E6 6K 63
Vicarage La. E15 3C 62
Vicarage La. Chig 2A 32
Vicarage La. Eps 1E 134
(in two parts)
Vicarage La. Ilf 6B 48
Vicarage M. NW9 7B 40
Vicarage Pde. N15 2A 44
Vicarage Pk. SE18 6A 80
Vicarage Path. N8 5J 43
Vicarage Rd. E10 5L 45
Vicarage Rd. E15 3D 62
Vicarage Rd. N17 8E 28
Vicarage Rd. NW4 4E 40
Vicarage Rd. SE18 6A 80
(in two parts)
Vicarage Rd. SW14 4A 88
Vicarage Rd. Bex 7M 97
Vicarage Rd. Croy 5L 123
Vicarage Rd. Dag 3M 65
Vicarage Rd. Hamp W 5G 103
Vicarage Rd. Horn 6E 50
Vicarage Rd. King T 6H 103
Vicarage Rd. Sun 2D 100
Vicarage Rd. Sutt 6M 121
Vicarage Rd. Tedd 2E 102
Vicarage Rd. Twic 8C 86
(Green, The)
Vicarage Rd. Twic 5A 86
(Kneller Rd.)
Vicarage Rd. Wat 8E 8
Vicarage Rd. Wfd G 7J 31
Vicarage Rd. Precinct. Wat 6F 8
(off Vicarage Rd.)
Vicarage Wlk. SW11 9B 74
Vicarage Wlk. W on T 2E 116
Vicarage Way. NW10 8B 40
Vicarage Way. Harr 5L 37
Vicars Bri. Clo. Wemb 5J 55
Vicar's Clo. E9 4G 61
Vicars Clo. E15 4E 62
Vicars Clo. Enf 4C 16
Vicar's Hill. SE13 3M 93
Vicars Moor La. N21 9L 15
Vicars Oak Rd. SE19 3C 108
Vicar's Rd. NW5 1E 58
Vicars Wlk. Dag 8F 48
Viceroy Clo. N2 2C 42
Viceroy Ct. NW8 5C 58
(off Prince Albert Rd.)
Viceroy Ct. Croy 3B 124
Viceroy Pde. N2 2C 42
(off High Rd.)
Viceroy Rd. SW8 9J 75
Vickers Clo. Wall 9K 123
Vickers Rd. Eri 6B 82
Vickers Way. Houn 4J 85
Vickery Ct. EC1 7A 60
(off Mitchell St.)
Victor App. Horn 6H 51
Victor Cazalet Ho. N1 4M 59
(off Gaskin St.)
Victor Clo. Horn 6H 51
Victor Ct. Horn 6H 51
(off Victor Wlk.)
Victor Gdns. Horn 6H 51
Victor Gro. Wemb 3J 55
Victoria & Albert Mus. 4B 74
Victoria Arc. SW1 4F 74
(off Victoria St.)
Victoria Av. E6 4H 63
Victoria Av. EC2 8C 60
Victoria Av. N3 8K 25
Victoria Av. Barn 6B 14
Victoria Av. Houn 4L 85
Victoria Av. Romf 6M 33
Victoria Av. S Croy 2A 138
Victoria Av. Surb 1H 119
Victoria Av. Uxb 2F 142
Victoria Av. Wall 5E 122
Victoria Av. Wemb 2M 55
Victoria Av. W Mol 7M 101
Victoria Bldgs. E8 4F 60
(off Mare St.)
Victoria Clo. Barn 6B 14
Victoria Clo. Harr 4D 38
Victoria Clo. Hay 9B 52
Victoria Clo. W Mol 7L 101
Victoria Clo. Wey 5B 116
Victoria Colonnade. WC1 8J 59
(off Southampton Row)
Victoria Cotts. E1 8E 60
(off Deal St.)
Victoria Cotts. N10 9E 26
Victoria Cotts. Rich 9K 71
Victoria Ct. E18 1F 46
Victoria Ct. SE26 3G 109
Victoria Ct. W3 3L 71
Victoria Ct. Romf 3E 50
Victoria Ct. Wat 5G 9
Victoria Ct. Wemb 2L 55
Victoria Cres. N15 3C 44
Victoria Cres. SE19 3C 108
Victoria Cres. SW19 4K 105
Victoria Dock Rd. E16 9D 62
Victoria Dri. SW19 6H 89
Victoria Embkmt. SW1 & WC2 3J 75
Victoria Gdns. W11 2L 73
Victoria Gdns. Big H 7G 141
Victoria Gdns. Houn 9J 69
Victoria Gro. N12 5B 26
Victoria Gro. W8 4A 74
Victoria Gro. M. W2 1L 73
Victoria Hall. E16 2E 78
(off Wesley Av., in two parts)
Victoria Hill Rd. Swan 5D 114
Victoria Ho. E6 9L 63
Victoria Ho. SW1 5G 75
(off Francis St.)
Victoria Ho. SW1 6F 74
(off Ebury Bri. Rd.)
Victoria Ho. SW8 8J 75
(off S. Lambeth Rd.)
Victoria Ho. Edgw 6M 23
Victoria Ind. Est. W3 8C 56
Victoria La. Barn 6K 13
Victoria La. Hay 6A 68
Victoria Mans. NW10 3F 56
Victoria Mans. SW8 8J 75
(off S. Lambeth Rd.)
Victoria M. NW6 4L 57
Victoria M. SW4 3F 90
Victoria M. SW18 7A 90
Victorian Gro. N16 9C 44
Victorian Rd. N16 8C 44
Victoria Palace Theatre. 4G 75
(off Victoria St.)
Victoria Pde. Rich 9L 71
(off Sandycombe Rd.)
Victoria Pk. 4J 61
Victoria Pk. Ct. E9 3G 61
(off Well St.)
Victoria Pk. Ind. Cen. E9 3L 61
(off Rothbury Rd.)
Victoria Pk. Ind. Est. Dart 4J 99
Victoria Pk. Rd. E9 4G 61
Victoria Pk. Sq. E2 6G 61
Victoria Pas. NW8 7B 58
(off Fisherton St.)
Victoria Pas. Wat 6F 8
Victoria Pl. Eps 4C 134
Victoria Pl. Esh 6M 117
Victoria Pl. Rich 4H 87
Victoria Pl. Shop. Cen. SW1 5F 74
(off Buckingham Palace Rd.)
Victoria Point. E13 5E 62
(off Victoria Rd.)

Victoria Retail Pk.—Walden Way

Victoria Retail Pk. Ruis 1H 53
Victoria Ri. SW4 2F 90
Victoria Rd. E4 1C 30
Victoria Rd. E11 9C 46
Victoria Rd. E13 5E 62
Victoria Rd. E17 9A 30
Victoria Rd. E18 9F 30
Victoria Rd. N4 5K 43
Victoria Rd. N15 2E 44
Victoria Rd. N18 & N9 4D 28
Victoria Rd. N22 8G 27
Victoria Rd. NW4 2G 41
Victoria Rd. NW6 5K 57
Victoria Rd. NW7 5D 24
Victoria Rd. NW10 8B 56
Victoria Rd. SW14 2B 88
Victoria Rd. W3 8B 56
Victoria Rd. W5 8F 54
Victoria Rd. W8 4A 74
Victoria Rd. Bark 2M 63
Victoria Rd. Barn 6B 14
Victoria Rd. Bexh 3L 97
Victoria Rd. Brom 9H 111
Victoria Rd. Buck H 2H 31
Victoria Rd. Bush 1M 21
Victoria Rd. Chst 2L 111
Victoria Rd. Coul 7H 137
Victoria Rd. Dag 1M 65
Victoria Rd. Dart 4H 99
Victoria Rd. Eri 7C 82
(in two parts)
Victoria Rd. Felt 7F 84
Victoria Rd. King T 6K 103
Victoria Rd. Mitc 4C 106
Victoria Rd. Romf 4D 50
Victoria Rd. Ruis 6E 36
Victoria Rd. Sidc 9D 96
Victoria Rd. S'hall 4K 69
Victoria Rd. Surb 1H 119
Victoria Rd. Sutt 7B 122
Victoria Rd. Tedd 3E 102
Victoria Rd. Twic 6F 86
Victoria Rd. Uxb 3A 142
Victoria Rd. Wal A 7J 7
Victoria Rd. Wat 2F 8
Victoria Rd. Wey 5B 116
Victoria Scott Ct. Dart 2D 98
Victoria Sq. SW1 4F 74
Victoria St. E15 3C 62
Victoria St. SW1 4G 75
Victoria St. Belv 6K 81
Victoria Ter. N4 6L 43
Victoria Ter. NW10 7D 56
Victoria Ter. SW8 1F 90
Victoria Ter. W5 2H 71
Victoria Ter. Harr 6C 38
Victoria Vs. Rich 2K 87
Victoria Way. SE7 6F 78
Victoria Way. Ruis 1H 53
Victoria Way. Wey 5B 116
Victoria Wharf. E2 5H 61
(off Palmers Rd.)
Victoria Wharf. E14 1J 77
Victoria Wharf. SE8 6K 77
(off Dragoon Rd.)
Victoria Works. NW2 7F 40
Victoria Yd. E1 9E 60
Victor Rd. NW10 6F 56
Victor Rd. SE20 4H 109
Victor Rd. Harr 1A 38
Victor Rd. Tedd 1C 102
Victors Dri. Hamp 3J 101
Victor Smith Ct. Brick W 4L 5
Victors Way. Barn 5K 13
Victor Vs. N9 3B 28
Victor Wlk. Horn 6H 51
Victory Av. Mord 9A 106
Victory Bus. Cen. Iswth 3D 86
Victory Ct. W9 7L 57
(off Hermes Clo.)
Victory Ct. Eri 8D 82
(off Frobisher Rd.)
Victory Pk. Wemb 8H 39
Victory Pl. E14 1J 77
Victory Pl. SE17 5B 76
Victory Pl. SE19 4C 108
Victory Rd. E11 2F 46
Victory Rd. SW19 4A 106
Victory Rd. Rain 5E 66
Victory Rd. M. SW19 4A 106
Victory Wlk. SE8 9L 77
Victory Way. SE16 3J 77
Victory Way. Houn 6G 69
Victory Way. Romf 9M 33
Vidler Clo. Chess 8G 119
Vienna Clo. Ilf 9H 31
View Clo. N6 5D 42
View Clo. Big H 8G 141
View Clo. Chig 5B 32
View Clo. Harr 2B 38
View Ct. SE12 9G 95
View Cres. N8 3H 43
Viewfield Clo. Harr 5J 39
Viewfield Rd. SW18 5K 89
Viewfield Rd. Bex 7G 97
Viewland Rd. SE18 6D 80
View Rd. N6 5D 42
View, The. SE2 6J 81
Viga Rd. N21 8L 15
Vigilant Clo. SE26 1E 108
Vignoles Rd. Romf 5L 49
Vigo St. W1 1G 75
Viking Clo. E3 5J 61
Viking Ct. SW6 7L 73
Viking Gdns. E6 7J 63
Viking Ho. SE5 1A 92
(off Denmark Rd.)
Viking Pl. E10 6K 45
Viking Rd. S'hall 1J 69
Viking Way. Eri 4A 82
Viking Way. Rain 7E 66
Villa Ct. Dart 8J 99
Villacourt Rd. SE18 8E 80
Village Arc. E4 1B 30
Village Clo. E4 5A 30
Village Clo. NW3 1B 58
(off Belsize La.)
Village Clo. Wey 5B 116
Village Ct. SE3 2C 94
(off Hurren Clo.)
Village Gdns. Eps 2D 134
Village Grn. Av. Big H 9J 141
Village Grn. Rd. Dart 3E 98
Village Grn. Way. Big H 9J 141
Village Heights. Wfd G 5D 30
Village M. NW9 7B 40
Village Pk. Clo. Enf 8C 16
Village Rd. N3 9J 25
Village Rd. Enf 7C 16
Village Row. Sutt 9L 121
Village, The. NW3 7A 42
Village, The. SE7 7G 79
Village Way. NW10 9B 40
Village Way. SE24 5B 92
Village Way. Ashf 9D 144
Village Way. Beck 6L 109
Village Way. Pinn 5J 37
Village Way. S Croy 5E 138
Village Way E. Harr 5L 37
Villa Rd. SW9 2L 91
Villas on the Heath. NW3 8A 42
Villas Rd. SE18 6A 80
(in three parts)
Villa St. SE17 6B 76
Villa Wlk. SE17 6B 76
(off Inville Rd.)
Villiers Av. Surb 9K 103
Villiers Av. Twic 7K 85
Villiers Clo. E10 7L 45
Villiers Clo. Surb 8K 103
Villiers Gro. Sutt 1H 135
Villiers M. NW2 2E 56
Villiers Path. Surb 9J 103
Villiers Rd. NW2 2E 56
Villiers Rd. Beck 6H 109
Villiers Rd. Iswth 1C 86
Villiers Rd. King T 8K 103
Villiers Rd. S'hall 2K 69
Villiers Rd. Wat 8J 9
Villiers St. WC2 2J 75
Villiers, The. Wey 8B 116
Villier St. Uxb 6B 142
Vincam Clo. Twic 6L 85
Vincennes Est. SE27 1B 108
Vincent Av. Cars 3B 136
Vincent Av. Surb 4A 120
Vincent Clo. SE16 3J 77
Vincent Clo. Barn 5M 13
Vincent Clo. Brom 8F 110
Vincent Clo. Chesh 1E 6
Vincent Clo. Esh 5M 117
Vincent Clo. Ilf 6A 32
Vincent Clo. Sidc 7C 96
Vincent Clo. W Dray 7L 143
Vincent Ct. N4 6J 43
Vincent Ct. NW4 2H 41
Vincent Ct. SW9 9K 75
Vincent Ct. W1 9D 58
(off Seymour Pl.)
Vincent Ct. N'wd 8D 20
Vincent Dri. Shep 7C 100
Vincent Dri. Uxb 4D 142
Vincent Gdns. NW2 8D 40
Vincent Ho. SW1 5H 75
(off Vincent Sq.)
Vincent M. E3 5L 61
Vincent Rd. E4 6B 30
Vincent Rd. N15 2A 44
Vincent Rd. N22 9L 27
Vincent Rd. SE18 5M 79
Vincent Rd. W3 4A 72
Vincent Rd. Coul 8G 137
Vincent Rd. Croy 2C 124
Vincent Rd. Dag 3J 65
Vincent Rd. Houn 1H 85
Vincent Rd. Iswth 9B 70
Vincent Rd. King T 7L 103
Vincent Rd. Rain 7G 67
Vincent Rd. Wemb 3K 55
Vincent Row. Hamp H 3A 102
Vincents Path. N'holt 2J 53
(off Arnold Rd.)
Vincent Sq. N22 9L 27
Vincent Sq. SW1 5H 75
Vincent Sq. Big H 5G 141
Vincent Sq. Mans. SW1 5G 75
(off Walcott St.)
Vincent St. E16 8D 62
Vincent St. SW1 5H 75
Vincent Ter. N1 5M 59
Vince St. EC1 6B 60
Vine Clo. Surb 1K 119
Vine Clo. Sutt 5A 122
Vine Clo. W Dray 5L 143
Vine Cotts. E1 9G 61
(off Sidney Sq.)
Vine Ct. E1 8E 60
Vine Ct. Harr 4J 39
Vinegar All. E17 2M 45
Vine Gdns. Ilf 1A 64
Vinegar St. E1 2F 76
Vinegar Yd. SE1 3C 76
Vine Gro. Uxb 3E 142
Vine Hill. EC1 7L 59
Vine La. SE1 2C 76
Vine La. Uxb 4D 142
Vine Pl. W5 2J 71
(off St Mark's Rd.)
Vine Pl. Houn 3M 85
Viner Clo. W on T 1G 117
Vineries Bank. NW7 5F 24
Vineries Clo. Dag 2K 65
Vineries Clo. W Dray 7L 143
Vineries, The. N14 8G 15
Vineries, The. SE6 7L 93
Vineries, The. Enf 5C 16
Vine Rd. E15 3D 62
Vine Rd. SW13 2D 88
Vine Rd. E Mol 8A 102
Vine Rd. Orp 8D 128
Vinery Way. W6 4F 72
Vines Av. N3 8M 25
Vine Sq. W14 6K 73
(off Star Rd.)
Vine St. EC3 9D 60
Vine St. W1 1G 75
Vine St. Romf 2A 50
Vine St. Uxb 4B 142
Vine St. Bri. EC1 7L 59
Vine Yd. SE1 3A 76
(off Sanctuary St.)
Vineyard Av. NW7 7J 25
Vineyard Clo. SE6 7L 93
Vineyard Clo. King T 7K 103
Vineyard Gro. N3 8M 25
Vineyard Hill Rd. SW19 1K 105
Vineyard M. EC1 7L 59
(off Vineyard Wlk.)
Vineyard Pas. Rich 4J 87
Vineyard Path. SW14 2B 88
Vineyard Rd. Felt 9E 84
Vineyard Row. Hamp W 5G 103
Vineyards, The. Felt 9E 84
(off High St.)
Vineyards, The. Sun 7E 100
Vineyard, The. Rich 4J 87
Vineyard Wlk. EC1 7L 59
Viney Bank. Croy 1K 139
Viney Rd. SE13 2M 93
Vining St. SW9 3L 91
Vinopolis, City of Wine. 2B 76
Vinson Clo. Orp 3E 128
Vintners Ct. EC4 1A 76
Vintner's Pl. EC4 1A 76
Vintry M. E17 2L 45
Viola Av. SE2 5F 80
Viola Av. Felt 5G 85
Viola Av. Stai 7B 144
Viola Sq. W12 1D 72
Violet Av. Enf 2B 16
Violet Av. Uxb 8D 142
Violet Clo. E16 7C 62
Violet Clo. SE8 7K 77
Violet Clo. Wall 3E 122
Violet Gdns. Croy 7M 123
Violet Hill. NW8 5A 58
Violet Hill Ho. NW8 5A 58
(off Violet Hill, in two parts)
Violet La. Croy 8M 123
Violet Rd. E3 7M 61
Violet Rd. E17 4L 45
Violet Rd. E18 9F 30
Violet St. E2 7F 60
V.I.P. Trading Est. SE7 5G 79
Virgil Pl. W1 8D 58
Virgil St. SE1 4K 75
Virginia Clo. N Mald 8A 104
Virginia Clo. Romf 7A 34
Virginia Clo. Wey 8A 116
Virginia Ct. SE16 3H 77
(off Eleanor Clo.)
Virginia Ct. WC1 7H 59
(off Burton St.)
Virginia Gdns. Ilf 9A 32
Virginia Ho. E14 1A 78
(off Newby Pl.)
Virginia Rd. E2 6D 60
Virginia Rd. T Hth 5M 107
Virginia St. E1 1E 76
Virginia Wlk. SW2 5K 91
Viscount Clo. N11 6F 26
Viscount Ct. W2 9L 57
(off Pembridge Vs.)
Viscount Dri. E6 8K 63
Viscount Gro. N'holt 6H 53
Viscount Rd. Stanw 7C 144
Viscount St. EC1 7A 60
Viscount Way. H'row A 3C 84
(in two parts)
Vista Av. Enf 4H 17
Vista Dri. Ilf 3H 47
Vista, The. SE9 5H 95
Vista, The. Sidc 2D 112
Vista Way. Harr 4J 39
Vittoria Ho. N1 4K 59
(off High Rd.)
Viveash Clo. Hay 4D 68
Vivian Av. NW4 3F 40
Vivian Av. Wemb 1L 55
Vivian Clo. Wat 1E 20
Vivian Comma Clo. N4 8M 43
Vivian Ct. N12 5M 25
Vivian Gdns. Wat 1E 20
Vivian Gdns. Wemb 1L 55
Vivian Mans. NW4 3F 40
(off Vivian Av.)
Vivian Rd. E3 5J 61
Vivian Sq. SE15 2F 92
Vivian Way. N2 3B 42
Vivien Clo. Chess 9J 119
Vivienne Clo. Twic 5H 87
Vixen M. E8 3D 60
(off Haggerston Rd.)
Voce Rd. SE18 8B 80
Voewood Clo. N Mald 1D 120
Vogans Mill. SE1 3D 76
Vogler Ho. E1 1G 77
(off Cable St.)
Vogue Ct. Brom 5F 110
Vollasky Ho. E1 8E 60
(off Daplyn St.)
Volta Clo. N9 3G 29
Voltaire Rd. SW4 2H 91
Voltaire Way. Hay 1C 68
Volt Av. NW10 6C 56
Volta Way. Croy 3K 123
Voluntary Pl. E11 4E 46
Vorley Rd. N19 7G 43
Voss Ct. SW16 3J 107
Voss St. E2 6E 60
Voyager Bus. Est. SE16 4E 76
(off Spa Rd.)
Voyagers Clo. SE28 9G 65
Vulcan Clo. E6 9L 63
Vulcan Ga. Enf 4L 15
Vulcan Rd. SE4 1K 93
Vulcan Sq. E14 5M 77
Vulcan Ter. SE4 1K 93
Vulcan Way. N7 2K 59
Vulcan Way. New Ad 2C 140
Vyner Rd. W3 1B 72
Vyner St. E2 4F 60
Vyner's Way. Uxb 1E 142
Vyne, The. Bexh 2M 97
Vyse Clo. Barn 6G 13

W

W12 Shop. Cen. W12 3H 73
Wadard Ter. Swan 9G 115
Wadbrook St. King T 6H 103
Wadding St. SE17 5B 76
Waddington Clo. Enf 6C 16
Waddington Rd. E15 1B 62
Waddington St. E15 2B 62
Waddington Way. SE19 4A 108
Waddon. 5L 123
Waddon Clo. Croy 5L 123
Waddon Ct. Rd. Croy 5L 123
Waddon Marsh Way.
Croy 3K 123
Waddon New Rd. Croy 5M 123
Waddon Pk. Av. Croy 6L 123
Waddon Rd. Croy 5L 123
Waddon Way. Croy 8L 123
Wade Av. Orp 2H 129
Wade Ct. N10 7F 26
Wade Ho. SE1 3E 76
(off Parkers Row)
Wade Ho. Enf 7B 16
Wades Gro. N21 9L 15
Wades Hill. N21 8L 15
Wades La. Tedd 2E 102
Wadeson St. E2 5F 60
Wade's Pl. E14 1M 77
Wadeville Av. Romf 4J 49
Wadeville Clo. Belv 7L 81
Wadham Av. E17 7M 29
Wadham Clo. Shep 2A 116
Wadham Gdns. NW3 4C 58
Wadham Gdns. Gnfd 2B 54
Wadham Rd. E17 7M 29
Wadham Rd. SW15 3J 89
Wadham Rd. Ab L 4D 4
Wadhurst Clo. SE20 6F 108
Wadhurst Rd. SW8 9G 75
Wadhurst Rd. W4 4B 72
Wadley Rd. E11 5C 46
Wadsworth Bus. Cen.
Gnfd 5G 55
Wadsworth Clo. Enf 7H 17
Wadsworth Clo. Gnfd 5G 55
Wadsworth Rd. Gnfd 5F 54
Wager St. E3 7K 61
Waggoners Roundabout (Junct.) 9F 68
Waggon La. N17 6E 28
Waggon M. N14 1G 27
Waghorn Rd. E13 4G 63
Waghorn Rd. Harr 1H 39
Waghorn St. SE15 2E 92
Wagner St. SE15 8G 77
Wagon Rd. Barn 1M 13
Wagstaff Gdns. Dag 3G
Wagtail Clo. NW9 9C
Wagtail Gdns. S Croy 2J 1
Wagtail Wlk. Beck 9A 1
Wagtail Way. Orp 8H 1
Waid Clo. Dart 5K
Waight's Ct. King T 5J 1
Wainfleet Av. Romf 9A
Wainford Clo. SW19 6H
Wainwright Gro. Iswth 3B
Wainwright Ho. E1 2G
(off Garnet S
Waite Davies Rd. SE12 6D
Waite St. SE15 7D
Waithman St. EC4 9M
(off Apothecary S
Wakefield Ct. SE26 3G 1
Wakefield Gdns. SE19 4C 1
Wakefield Gdns. Ilf 4J
Wakefield Ho. SE15 9E
Wakefield M. WC1 6J
Wakefield Rd. N11 5H
Wakefield Rd. N15 3D
Wakefield Rd. Rich 4H
Wakefield St. E6 4H
Wakefield St. N18 5E
Wakefield St. WC1 7J
Wakefields Wlk. Chesh 4E
Wakeford Clo. SW4 4G
Wakehams Hill. Pinn 1K
Wakeham St. N1 2B
Wakehurst Rd. SW11 4C
Wakeling Rd. W7 8D
Wakeling St. E14 9J
Wakelin Ho. N1 3M
(off Sebbon S
Wakelin Ho. SE23 6J 9
Wakelin Rd. E15 5C
Wakeman Ho. NW10 6H 5
(off Wakeman Rd
Wakeman Rd. NW10 6G 5
Wakemans Hill Av. NW9 3B 4
Wakerfield Clo. Horn 3K 5
Wakering Rd. Bark 2A 6
(in two parts
Wakerings, The. Bark 2A 6
Wakerley Clo. E6 9K 6
Wake Rd. Lou 2G 1
Wakley St. EC1 6M 5
Walberswick St. SW8 8J 7
Walbrook. EC4 1B 7
(in three parts
Walbrook Ho. N9 2G 2
(off Huntingdon Ro
Walbrook Wharf. EC4 1A 7
(off Bell Wharf La
Walburgh St. E1 9F 6
Walburton Rd. Purl 5G 13
Walcorde Av. SE17 5A 7
Walcot Gdns. SE11 5L 7
(off Kennington Rd.
Walcot Rd. Enf 4K 1
Walcot Sq. SE11 5L 7
Walcott St. SW1 5G 7
Waldair Ct. E16 3M 7
Waldeck Gro. SE27 9M 9
Waldeck Rd. N15 2M 4
Waldeck Rd. SW14 2A 8
Waldeck Rd. W4 7L 7
Waldeck Rd. W13 9F 5
Waldeck Rd. Dart 6K 9
Waldeck Ter. SW14 2A 8
(off Waldeck Rd.
Waldegrave Av. Tedd 2D 102
Waldegrave Ct. Bark 4B 64
Waldegrave Ct. Upm 6M 51
Waldegrave Gdns. Twic 8D 86
Waldegrave Gdns. Upm 6M 51
Waldegrave Pk. Twic 1D 102
Waldegrave Rd. N8 1L 43
Waldegrave Rd. SE19 4D 108
Waldegrave Rd. W5 1K 71
Waldegrave Rd. Brom 8J 111
Waldegrave Rd. Dag 7G 49
Waldegrave Rd.
Tedd & Twic 1D 102
Waldegrove. Croy 5D 124
Waldemar Av. SW6 9J 73
Waldemar Av. W13 2G 71
Waldemar Rd. SW19 2L 105
Walden Av. N13 4A 28
Walden Av. Chst 1K 11
Walden Av. Rain 5B 66
Walden Clo. Belv 6K 81
Walden Ct. SW8 9H 75
Walden Gdns. T Hth 7K 107
Walden Ho. SW1 5E 74
(off Pimlico Rd.
Waldenhurst Rd. Orp 2H 12
Walden Pde. Chst 3K 11
(in two parts
Walden Rd. N17 8B 28
Walden Rd. Chst 3K 11
Walden Rd. Horn 4H 5
Waldens Clo. Orp 2H 12
Waldenshaw Rd. SE23 7G 9
Waldens Rd. Orp 2J 12
Walden St. E1 9F 6
Walden Way. NW7 6H 2
Walden Way. Horn 4H 5
Walden Way. Ilf 7C 3

Waldo Clo.—Warner Pl.

Waldo Clo. *SW4* 4G **91**
Waldo Ho. NW10 6F **56**
(off Waldo Rd.)
Waldo Ind. Est. *Brom* 7H **111**
Waldo Pl. *Mitc* 4C **106**
Waldorf Clo. *S Croy* 1M **137**
Waldo Rd. *NW10* 6E **56**
(in two parts)
Waldo Rd. *Brom* 7H **111**
Waldram Cres. *SE23* 7G **93**
Waldram Pk. Rd. *SE23* 7H **93**
Waldram Pl. *SE23* 7G **93**
Waldrist Way. *Eri* 3K **81**
Waldron Gdns. *Brom* 7B **110**
Waldronhyrst. *S Croy* 6M **123**
Waldron M. *SW3* 7B **74**
Waldron Rd. *SW18* 9A **90**
Waldron Rd. *Harr* 6C **38**
Waldron's Path. *S Croy* 6A **124**
Waldrons, The. *Croy* 6M **123**
Waldrons Yd. *S Harr* 7B **38**
Waldstock Rd. *SE28* 1E **80**
Waleran Clo. *Stan* 5D **22**
Walerand Rd. *SE13* 1A **94**
Waleran Flats. *SE1* 5C **76**
Wales Av. *Cars* 7C **122**
Wales Clo. *SE15* 8F **76**
Wales Farm Rd. *W3* 8B **56**
Waleton Acres. *Wall* 8G **123**
Waley St. *E1* 8J **61**
Walfield Av. *N20* 9M **13**
Walford Ho. *E1* 9E **60**
Walford Rd. *N16* 9C **44**
Walford Rd. *Uxb* 5A **142**
Walfrey Gdns. *Dag* 3J **65**
Walham Green. 9M 73
Walham Grn. Ct. SW6 8M **73**
(off Waterford Rd.)
Walham Gro. *SW6* 8L **73**
Walham Ri. *SW19* 3J **105**
Walham Yd. *SW6* 8L **73**
Walkato Lodge. *Buck H* 1G **31**
Walkden Rd. *Chst* 2L **111**
Walker Clo. *N11* 4G **27**
Walker Clo. *SE18* 5A **80**
Walker Clo. *W7* 2C **70**
Walker Clo. *Dart* 2D **98**
Walker Clo. *Felt* 6D **84**
Walker Clo. *Hamp* 3K **101**
Walker Ho. *NW1* 5H **59**
Walker's Ct. W1 1H **75**
(off Brewer St.)
Walkerscroft Mead. *SE21* 7A **92**
Walkers Pl. *SW15* 3J **89**
Walkfield Dri. *Eps* 9F **134**
Walkinshaw Ct. N1 3A **60**
(off Rotherfield St.)
Walkley Rd. *Dart* 4F **98**
Walks, The. *N2* 1B **42**
Walk, The. N13 3L **27**
(off Fox La.)
Walk, The. *Horn* 7K **51**
Walk, The. *Sun* 4D **100**
Wallace Clo. *SE28* 1H **81**
Wallace Clo. *Shep* 8B **100**
Wallace Clo. *Uxb* 5C **142**
Wallace Collection. 9E 58
Wallace Ct. NW1 8C **58**
(off Old Marylebone Rd.)
Wallace Cres. *Cars* 7D **122**
Wallace Fields. *Eps* 5E **134**
Wallace Ho. N7 2K **59**
(off Caledonian Rd.)
Wallace Rd. *N1* 2A **60**
Wallace Way. N19 7H **43**
(off St John's Way)
Wallbrook Bus. Cen. *Houn* 2F **84**
Wallbutton Rd. *SE4* 1J **93**
Wallcote Av. *NW2* 6H **41**
Wall Ct. N4 6K **43**
(off Stroud Grn. Rd.)
Wallend. 4L 63
Wall End Ct. E6 4L **63**
(off Wall End Rd.)
Wall End Rd. *E6* 3K **63**
Wallenger Av. *Romf* 1F **50**
Waller Dri. *N'wd* 9E **20**
Waller Rd. *SE14* 9H **77**
Wallers Clo. *Dag* 4J **65**
Wallers Clo. *Wfd G* 6K **31**
Waller's Hoppet. *Lou* 4K **19**
Waller Way. *SE10* 8M **77**
Wallflower St. *W12* 1D **72**
Wallgrave Rd. *SW5* 5M **73**
Wallhouse Rd. *Eri* 8F **82**
Wallingford Av. *W10* 8H **57**
Wallingford Ho. Romf 6J **35**
(off Kingsbridge Rd.)
Wallingford Rd. *Uxb* 5A **142**
Wallington. 8G 123
Wallington Clo. *Ruis* 4A **36**
Wallington Corner. Wall 6F **122**
(off Manor Rd. N.)
Wallington Ct. Wall 8F **122**
(off Stanley Pk. Rd.)
Wallington Green (Junct.) **6F 122**
Wallington Rd. *Ilf* 5D **48**
Wallington Sq. *Wall* 8F **122**
Wallis All. SE1 3A **76**
(off Marshalsea Rd.)
Wallis Clo. *SW11* 2B **90**
Wallis Clo. *Dart* 9D **98**
Wallis Clo. *Horn* 6F **50**
Wallis Ho. *SE14* 9J **77**
Wallis M. N8 1L **43**
(off Courcy Rd.)
Wallis Rd. *E9* 2K **61**
Wallis Rd. *S'hall* 9M **53**
Wallis's Cotts. *SW2* 6J **91**
Wallman Pl. *N22* 8K **27**
Wallorton Gdns. *SW14* 3B **88**
Wallside. EC2 8A **60**
(off Beech St.)
Wall St. *N1* 2B **60**
Wallwood Rd. *E11* 5B **46**
Wallwood St. *E14* 8K **61**
Walmar Clo. *Barn* 3B **14**
Walmer Clo. *E4* 2M **29**
Walmer Clo. *F'boro* 6B **128**
Walmer Clo. *Romf* 9M **33**
Walmer Ct. Surb 9J **103**
(off Cranes Pk.)
Walmer Gdns. *W13* 3E **70**
Walmer Ho. W10 9H **57**
(off Bramley Rd.)
Walmer Pl. W1 8D **58**
(off Walmer St.)
Walmer Rd. *W10* 9G **57**
Walmer Rd. *W11* 1J **73**
Walmer St. *W1* 8D **58**
Walmer Ter. *SE18* 5A **80**
Walmgate Rd. *Gnfd* 4F **54**
Walmington Fold. *N12* 6L **25**
Walm La. *NW2* 2G **57**
Walney Wlk. *N1* 2A **60**
Walnut Av. *W Dray* 4L **143**
Walnut Clo. *SE8* 7K **77**
Walnut Clo. *Cars* 7D **122**
Walnut Clo. *Eps* 7D **134**
Walnut Clo. *Eyns* 5H **131**
Walnut Clo. *Hay* 1C **68**
Walnut Clo. *Ilf* 2A **48**
Walnut Ct. *E17* 2A **46**
Walnut Ct. *W5* 3J **71**
Walnut Ct. W8 4M **73**
(off St Mary's Ga.)
Walnut Fields. *Eps* 1D **134**
Walnut Gdns. *E15* 1C **62**
Walnut Grn. *Bush* 4K **9**
Walnut Gro. *Bans* 6H **135**
Walnut Gro. *Enf* 7B **16**
Walnut M. *Sutt* 9A **122**
Walnut Rd. *E10* 7L **45**
Walnuts Rd. *Orp* 3F **128**
Walnuts, The. *Orp* 3E **128**
Walnut Tree Av. *Dart* 8J **99**
Walnut Tree Av. *Mitc* 7C **106**
Walnut Tree Clo. *SW13* 9D **72**
Walnut Tree Clo. *Bans* 4J **135**
Walnut Tree Clo. *Chesh* 4D **6**
Walnut Tree Clo. *Chst* 5B **112**
Walnut Tree Clo. *Shep* 7A **100**
Walnut Tree Cotts. *SW19* 2J **105**
Walnut Tree Ho. SW10 7M **73**
(off Tregunter Rd.)
Walnut Tree Rd. *SE10* 6C **78**
(in two parts)
Walnut Tree Rd. *Bren* 7J **71**
Walnut Tree Rd. *Dag* 7J **49**
Walnut Tree Rd. *Eri* 6C **82**
Walnut Tree Rd. *Houn* 7K **69**
Walnut Tree Rd. *Shep* 6A **100**
Walnut Tree Wlk. *SE11* 5L **75**
Walnut Way. *Buck H* 3H **31**
Walnut Way. *Ruis* 2G **53**
Walnut Way. *Swan* 6B **114**
Walpole Av. *Rich* 1K **87**
Walpole Clo. *W13* 3G **71**
Walpole Clo. *Pinn* 6L **21**
Walpole Ct. W14 4H **73**
(off Blythe Rd.)
Walpole Ct. *Twic* 8C **86**
Walpole Cres. *Tedd* 2D **102**
Walpole Gdns. *W4* 6A **72**
Walpole Gdns. *Twic* 8C **86**
Walpole Ho. SE1 3L **75**
(off Westminster Bri. Rd.)
Walpole Lodge. *W5* 2G **71**
Walpole M. *NW8* 4B **58**
Walpole M. *SW19* 3B **106**
Walpole Pl. *SE18* 5M **79**
Walpole Pl. *Tedd* 2D **102**
Walpole Rd. *E6* 3G **63**
Walpole Rd. *E17* 2J **45**
Walpole Rd. *E18* 8D **30**
Walpole Rd. *N17* 9A **28**
(in two parts)
Walpole Rd. *SW19* 3B **106**
Walpole Rd. *Brom* 9H **111**
Walpole Rd. *Croy* 4B **124**
Walpole Rd. *Surb* 2J **119**
Walpole Rd. *Tedd* 2D **102**
Walpole Rd. *Twic* 8C **86**
Walpole St. *SW3* 6D **74**
Walpole Way. *Barn* 7G **13**
Walrond Av. *Wemb* 1J **55**
Walsham Clo. *N16* 6E **44**
Walsham Clo. *SE28* 1H **81**
Walsham Ho. *SE14* 1H **93**
Walsham Ho. SE17 6B **76**
(off Blackwood St.)
Walsham Rd. *SE14* 1H **93**
Walsham Rd. *Felt* 6F **84**
Walsh Cres. *New Ad* 4C **140**
Walshford Way. *Borwd* 2L **11**
Walsingham. *NW8* 4B **58**
Walsingham Gdns. *Eps* 6C **120**
Walsingham Ho. *E4* 9B **18**
Walsingham Lodge. *SW13* 9E **72**
Walsingham Mans. SW6 8M **73**
(off Fulham Rd.)
Walsingham Pk. *Chst* 6B **112**
Walsingham Pl. *SW11* 5E **90**
Walsingham Rd. *E5* 8E **44**
Walsingham Rd. *W13* 2E **70**
Walsingham Rd. *Enf* 6B **16**
Walsingham Rd. *Mitc* 9D **106**
Walsingham Rd. *New Ad* 2A **140**
Walsingham Rd. *Orp* 5F **112**
Walsingham Wlk. *Belv* 7L **81**
Walston Ho. SW1 6H **75**
(off Aylesford St.)
Walter Besant Ho. E1 6H **61**
(off Bancroft Rd.)
Walter Ct. W3 9A **56**
(off Lynton Ter.)
Walter Grn. Ho. SE15 9G **77**
(off Lausanne Rd.)
Walter Hurford Pde. *E12* 9L **47**
Walter Langley Ct. SE16 3G **77**
(off Brunel Rd.)
Walter Rodney Clo. *E6* 2K **63**
Walters Clo. SE17 5B **76**
(off Brandon St.)
Walters Clo. *Hay* 3D **68**
Walters Ho. SE17 7M **75**
(off Otto St.)
Walters Mead. *Asht* 9J **133**
Walters Rd. *SE25* 8C **108**
Walters Rd. *Enf* 6G **17**
Walter St. *E2* 6H **61**
Walter St. *King T* 5J **103**
Walters Way. *SE23* 5H **93**
Walters Yd. *Brom* 6E **110**
Walter Ter. *E1* 9H **61**
Walterton Rd. *W9* 7K **57**
Walter Wlk. *Edgw* 6A **24**
Waltham Abbey. 6J 7
Waltham Abbey Church. 6J 7
(Remains of)
Waltham Av. *NW9* 4L **39**
Waltham Av. *Hay* 4A **68**
Waltham Clo. *Dart* 5E **98**
Waltham Clo. *Orp* 3H **129**
Waltham Cross. 7E 6
Waltham Dri. *Edgw* 9L **23**
Waltham Gdns. *Enf* 9C **6**
Waltham Ho. *NW8* 4A **58**
Waltham Pk. Way. *E17* 8L **29**
Waltham Point. *Wal A* 8J **7**
Waltham Rd. *Cars* 2B **122**
Waltham Rd. *S'hall* 4J **69**
Waltham Rd. *Wfd G* 6J **31**
Walthamstow. 2L 45
Walthamstow Av. *E4* 6K **29**
Walthamstow Bus. Cen. *E17* 9A **30**
Walthamstow Greyhound Stadium. 7M 29
Waltham Way. *E4* 3K **29**
Waltheof Av. *N17* 8B **28**
Waltheof Gdns. *N17* 8B **28**
Walton & Hersham F.C. **4E 116**
Walton Av. *Harr* 1K **53**
Walton Av. *N Mald* 8D **104**
Walton Av. *Sutt* 5K **121**
Walton Av. *Wemb* 8M **39**
Walton Bri. *Shep & W on T* 2C **116**
Walton Bri. Rd. *Shep* 2C **116**
Walton Clo. *E5* 8H **45**
Walton Clo. *NW2* 7F **40**
Walton Clo. *SW8* 8J **75**
Walton Clo. *Harr* 2B **38**
Walton Ct. *New Bar* 7A **14**
Walton Ct. S Croy 7A **124**
(off Warham Rd.)
Walton Cft. *Harr* 9C **38**
Walton Dri. *NW10* 2B **56**
Walton Dri. *Harr* 2B **38**
Walton Gdns. *W3* 8M **55**
Walton Gdns. *Felt* 1D **100**
Walton Gdns. *Wal A* 6H **7**
Walton Gdns. *Wemb* 7J **39**
Walton Grn. *New Ad* 1M **139**
Walton Ho. *E2* 7D **60**
Walton Ho. E4 5L **29**
(off Chingford Mt. Rd.)
Walton Ho. E17 1M **45**
(off Drive, The)
Walton La. *Shep* 2B **116**
Walton La. *Wey* 4A **116**
Walton-on-Thames. 3E 116
Walton Pk. *W on T* 4H **117**
Walton Pk. La. *W on T* 4H **117**
Walton Pl. *SW3* 4D **74**
Walton Rd. *E12* 9L **47**
(in three parts)
Walton Rd. *E13* 5G **63**
Walton Rd. *N15* 2D **44**
Walton Rd. *Bush* 6H **9**
Walton Rd. *Eps* 9D **134**
(in two parts)
Walton Rd. *Harr* 2B **38**
Walton Rd. *Romf* 7K **33**
Walton Rd. *Sidc* 8G **97**
Walton Rd. *W on T & W Mol* 9G **101**
Walton Rd. *W Mol* 8K **101**
Walton St. *SW3* 5C **74**
Walton St. *Enf* 3B **16**
Walton Way. *W3* 8M **55**
Walton Way. *Mitc* 8G **107**
Walt Whitman Clo. *SE24* 3M **91**
Walverns Clo. *Wat* 8G **9**
Walworth. 6A 76
Walworth Pl. *SE17* 6A **76**
Walworth Rd. *SE1 & SE17* 5A **76**
Walwyn Av. *Brom* 7H **111**
Wanborough Dri. *SW15* 7F **88**
Wanderer Dri. *Bark* 6G **65**
Wandle Bank. *SW19* 4B **106**
Wandle Bank. *Croy* 5J **123**
Wandle Ct. *Croy* 5J **123**
Wandle Ct. *Eps* 6A **120**
Wandle Ct. Gdns. *Croy* 5J **123**
Wandle Ho. NW8 8C **58**
(off Penfold St.)
Wandle Ho. *Brom* 2B **110**
Wandle Pk. Trad. Est., The. *Croy* 3M **123**
Wandle Rd. *SW17* 8C **90**
Wandle Rd. *Bedd* 5J **123**
Wandle Rd. *Croy* 5A **124**
Wandle Rd. *Mord* 8A **106**
Wandle Rd. *Wall* 5F **122**
Wandle Side. *Croy* 5K **123**
Wandle Side. *Wall* 5F **122**
Wandle Way. *SW18* 7M **89**
Wandle Way. *Mitc* 9D **106**
Wandon Rd. *SW6* 8M **73**
(in two parts)
Wandsworth. 4K 89
Wandsworth Bri. *SW6 & SW18* 2M **89**
Wandsworth Bri. Rd. *SW6* 9M **73**
Wandsworth Common. 7D 90
Wandsworth Comn. W. Side. *SW18* 4A **90**
Wandsworth Gyratory (Junct.) **4M 89**
Wandsworth High St. *SW18* 4L **89**
Wandsworth Plain. *SW18* 4M **89**
Wandsworth Rd. *SW8* 2F **90**
Wandsworth Shop. Cen. *SW18* 5M **89**
Wangey Rd. *Chad H* 5H **49**
Wangford Ho. SW9 3M **91**
(off Loughborough Pk.)
Wanless Rd. *SE24* 2A **92**
Wanley Rd. *SE5* 3B **92**
Wanlip Rd. *E13* 7F **62**
Wannock Gdns. *Ilf* 7M **31**
Wansbeck Ct. Enf 5M **15**
(off Waverley Rd.)
Wansbeck Rd. *E9 & E3* 3K **61**
Wansbury Way. *Swan* 9E **114**
Wansey St. *SE17* 5A **76**
Wansford Pk. *Borwd* 6B **12**
Wansford Rd. *Wfd G* 8G **31**
Wanstead. 3F 46
Wanstead Clo. *Brom* 6G **111**
Wanstead Gdns. *Ilf* 4H **47**
Wanstead La. *Ilf* 4H **47**
Wanstead Pk. Av. *E12* 6H **47**
Wanstead Pk. Rd. *Ilf* 4H **47**
Wanstead Pl. *E11* 4E **46**
Wanstead Rd. *Brom* 6G **111**
Wansunt Rd. *Bex* 7A **98**
Wantage Rd. *SE12* 4D **94**
Wantz La. *Rain* 7F **66**
(in two parts)
Wantz Rd. *Dag* 9M **49**
Wapping. 2F 76
Wapping Dock St. *E1* 2F **76**
Wapping High St. *E1* 2E **76**
Wapping La. *E1* 1F **76**
Wapping Wall. *E1* 2G **77**
Warbank Clo. *New Ad* 2C **140**
Warbank Cres. *New Ad* 2C **140**
Warbank La. *King T* 4D **104**
Warberry Rd. *N22* 9K **27**
Warboys App. *King T* 3M **103**
Warboys Cres. *E4* 5A **30**
Warboys Rd. *King T* 3M **103**
Warbreck Rd. *W12* 2F **72**
Warburg Institute. 7H 59
Warburton Clo. N1 2C **60**
(off Culford Rd.)
Warburton Clo. *Harr* 6B **22**
Warburton Ct. *Ruis* 7E **36**
Warburton Ho. E8 4F **60**
(off Warburton St.)
Warburton Rd. *E8* 4F **60**
Warburton Rd. *Twic* 7M **85**
Warburton St. *E8* 4F **60**
Warburton Ter. *E17* 9M **29**
Wardalls Gro. *SE14* 8G **77**
Wardalls Ho. SE8 7K **77**
(off Staunton St.)
Ward Clo. *Eri* 7B **82**
Ward Clo. *S Croy* 8C **124**
Wardell Clo. *NW7* 7C **24**
Wardell Fld. *NW9* 8C **24**
Wardell Ho. SE10 7A **78**
(off Welland St.)
Warden Av. *Harr* 6K **37**
Warden Av. *Romf* 5A **34**
Warden Rd. *NW5* 2E **58**
Wardens Fld. Clo. *G Str* 8C **128**
Wardens Gro. *SE1* 2A **76**
Ward Gdns. *H Wood* 9J **35**
Ward La. *Warl* 8G **139**
Wardle St. *E9* 1H **61**
Wardley St. *SW18* 6M **89**
Wardo Av. *SW6* 9J **73**
Wardour Ct. Dart 5M **99**
(off Bow Arrow La.)
Wardour M. W1 9G **59**
(off D'Arblay St.)
Wardour St. *W1* 9G **59**
Ward Point. *SE11* 5L **75**
Ward Rd. *E15* 4B **62**
Ward Rd. *N19* 8G **43**
Ward Rd. *SW19* 5A **106**
Wardrobe Pl. EC4 9M **59**
(off Carter La.)
Wardrobe Ter. EC4 1M **75**
(off Addle Hill)
Wardrobe, The. Rich 4H **87**
(off Old Pal. Yd.)
Wards La. *Els* 4D **10**
Wards Rd. *Ilf* 5B **48**
Ware Ct. *Sutt* 6K **121**
Wareham Clo. *Houn* 3M **85**
Wareham Ct. N1 3C **60**
(off Hertford Rd.)
Wareham Ho. *SW8* 8K **75**
Warehouse Theatre. **4B 124**
Waremead Rd. *Ilf* 3M **47**
Warenford Way. *Borwd* 3L **11**
Warepoint Dri. *SE28* 3B **80**
Warfield Rd. *NW10* 6H **57**
Warfield Rd. *Felt* 6C **84**
Warfield Rd. *Hamp* 5M **101**
Warfield Yd. NW10 6H **57**
(off Warfield Rd.)
Wargrave Av. *N15* 4D **44**
Wargrave Ho. E2 6D **60**
(off Navarre St.)
Wargrave Rd. *Harr* 8A **38**
Warham Rd. *N4* 3L **43**
Warham Rd. *Harr* 9D **22**
Warham Rd. *S Croy* 7M **123**
Warham St. *SE5* 8M **75**
Waring & Gillow Est. *W3* 7L **55**
Waring Clo. *Orp* 8D **128**
Waring Dri. *Orp* 8D **128**
Waring Rd. *Sidc* 3G **113**
Waring St. *SE27* 1A **108**
Warkworth Gdns. *Iswth* 8E **70**
Warkworth Rd. *N17* 7B **28**
Warland Rd. *SE18* 8B **80**
Warley Av. *Dag* 5K **49**
Warley Av. *Hay* 9E **52**
Warley Clo. *E10* 6K **45**
Warley Rd. *N9* 2G **29**
Warley Rd. *Hay* 9E **52**
Warley Rd. *Ilf* 8L **31**
Warley Rd. *Wfd G* 7F **30**
Warley St. *E2* 6H **61**
Warlingham. 9H 139
Warlingham Rd. *T Hth* 8M **107**
Warlock Rd. *W9* 7K **57**
Warlow Clo. *Enf* 1L **17**
Warlters Clo. *N7* 9J **43**
Warlters Rd. *N7* 9J **43**
Warltersville Mans. *N19* 5J **43**
Warltersville Rd. *N19* 5J **43**
Warmington Clo. *E5* 8H **45**
Warmington Rd. *SE24* 5A **92**
Warmington St. *E13* 7E **62**
Warmington Tower. *SE14* 9J **77**
Warminster Gdns. *SE25* 6E **108**
Warminster Ho. Romf 5K **35**
(off Redcar Rd.)
Warminster Rd. *SE25* 6D **108**
Warminster Sq. *SE25* 6E **108**
Warminster Way. *Mitc* 5F **106**
Warmley Ct. SE15 7C **76**
(off Newent Ct.)
Warmsworth. NW1 4G **59**
(off Pratt St.)
Warndon St. *SE16* 5H **77**
Warneford Pl. *Wat* 8J **9**
Warneford Rd. *Harr* 1H **39**
Warneford St. *E9* 4F **60**
Warne Pl. *Sidc* 5F **96**
Warner Av. *Sutt* 4J **121**
Warner Clo. *E15* 1C **62**
Warner Clo. *NW9* 5D **40**
Warner Clo. *Hamp* 2K **101**
Warner Clo. *Hay* 8B **68**
Warner Ho. *NW8* 6A **58**
Warner Ho. SE13 1M **93**
(off Russett Way)
Warner Pde. *Hay* 8B **68**
Warner Pl. *E2* 5E **60**

Warner Rd.—Waverley Rd.

Warner Rd. E17 2J 45
Warner Rd. N8 2H 43
Warner Rd. SE5 9A 76
Warner Rd. Brom 4D 110
Warners Clo. Wfd G 5E 30
Warners La. King T 1H 103
Warners Path. Wfd G 5E 30
Warner St. EC1 7L 59
Warner Ter. E14 8L 61
(off Broomfield St.)
Warner Village West End Cinema. 1H 75
(off Leicester Ct.)
Warner Yd. EC1 7L 59
(off Warner St.)
Warnford Ho. SW15 5C 88
(off Tunworth Cres.)
Warnford Ind. Est. Hay 3C 68
Warnford Rd. Orp 7D 128
Warnham. WC1 6K 59
(off Sidmouth St.)
Warnham Ct. Rd. Cars 9D 122
Warnham Ho. SW2 6K 91
(off Up. Tulse Hill)
Warnham Rd. N12 5C 26
Warpiner Dri. N9 3E 28
Warple M. W3 3C 72
Warple Way. W3 2C 72
(in two parts)
Warren Av. E10 8A 46
Warren Av. Brom 4C 110
Warren Av. Orp 7D 128
Warren Av. Rich 3M 87
Warren Av. S Croy 9H 125
Warren Av. Sutt 2K 135
Warren Clo. N9 9H 17
Warren Clo. SE21 6A 92
Warren Clo. Bexh 4L 97
Warren Clo. Esh 6M 117
Warren Clo. Hay 8G 53
Warren Clo. Wemb 7H 39
Warren Ct. N17 1E 44
(off High Cross Rd.)
Warren Ct. NW1 7G 59
(off Warren St.)
Warren Ct. W5 8G 55
Warren Ct. Beck 4L 109
Warren Ct. Chig 4B 32
Warren Ct. Croy 3C 124
Warren Ct. Wat 3F 4
Warren Cres. N9 9D 16
Warren Cutting. King T 4B 104
Warrender Rd. N19 8G 43
Warrender Way. Ruis 5E 36
Warren Dri. Gnfd 7M 53
Warren Dri. Horn 9E 50
Warren Dri. Orp 7F 128
Warren Dri. Ruis 5H 37
Warren Dri. N. Surb 3M 119
Warren Dri. S. Surb 3A 120
Warren Dri., The. E11 5G 47
Warreners La. Wey 9B 116
Warren Farm Cotts. Romf 2K 49
Warrenfield Clo. Chesh 4A 6
Warren Fields. Stan 4G 23
Warren Footpath. Twic 7G 87
Warren Gdns. E15 1B 62
Warren Gdns. Orp 7E 128
Warren Gro. Borwd 6B 12
Warren Hill. Eps 8B 134
Warren Hill. Lou 7G 19
Warren Ho. W14 5K 73
(off Beckford Clo.)
Warren La. SE18 4M 79
Warren La. Oxs 3A 132
Warren La. Stan 2E 22
Warren Mead. Bans 7G 135
Warren M. W1 7G 59
Warren Pk. King T 3A 104
Warren Pk. Warl 9H 139
Warren Pk. Rd. Sutt 8B 122
Warren Pl. E1 9H 61
(off Caroline St.)
Warren Pond Rd. E4 1D 30
(in two parts)
Warren Ri. N Mald 5B 104
Warren Rd. E4 2A 30
Warren Rd. E10 8A 46
Warren Rd. E11 4G 47
(in two parts)
Warren Rd. NW2 7D 40
Warren Rd. SW19 3C 106
Warren Rd. Ashf 4C 100
Warren Rd. Bans 6G 135
Warren Rd. Bexh 4L 97
Warren Rd. Brom 4E 126
Warren Rd. Bus H 1A 22
Warren Rd. Croy 3C 124
Warren Rd. Dart 9J 99
Warren Rd. Ilf 3B 48
Warren Rd. King T 3A 104
Warren Rd. Orp & Chels 7D 128
Warren Rd. Purl 4M 137
Warren Rd. Sidc 9G 97
Warren Rd. Twic 5A 86
Warren Rd. Uxb 1C 142
Warrens Shawe La. Edgw 2M 23
Warren St. W1 7G 59
Warren Ter. Romf 2H 49
(in two parts)
Warren, The. E12 9J 47
Warren, The. Cars 1B 136
Warren, The. Hay 9E 52
Warren, The. Houn 8K 69
Warren, The. Oxs 4A 132
Warren, The. Wor Pk 6B 120
Warren Wlk. SE7 7G 79
Warren Way. NW7 6J 25
Warren Way. Wey 7A 116
Warren Wood Clo. Brom 4D 126
Warriner Av. Horn 7H 51
Warriner Gdns. SW11 9D 74
Warrington Ct. Croy 5M 123
(off Warrington Rd.)
Warrington Cres. W9 7A 58
Warrington Gdns. W9 7A 58
Warrington Gdns. Horn 4G 51
Warrington Pl. E14 2A 78
(off Yabsley St.)
Warrington Rd. Croy 5M 123
Warrington Rd. Dag 7H 49
Warrington Rd. Harr 3C 38
Warrington Rd. Rich 4H 87
Warrington Sq. Dag 7H 49
Warrior Sq. E12 9L 47
Warsaw Clo. Ruis 2F 52
Warspite Ho. E14 5M 77
(off Cahir St.)
Warspite Rd. SE18 4J 79
Warton Rd. E15 3A 62
Warwall. E6 9M 63
Warwick. W14 5K 73
(off Kensington Village)
Warwick Av. W9 & W2 7M 57
Warwick Av. Edgw 3M 23
Warwick Av. Harr 9K 37
Warwick Chambers. W8 4L 73
(off Pater St.)
Warwick Clo. Barn 7B 14
Warwick Clo. Bex 6K 97
Warwick Clo. Bus H 9C 10
Warwick Clo. Hamp 4A 102
Warwick Clo. Orp 5E 128
Warwick Ct. W7 9D 54
(off Copley Clo.)
Warwick Ct. WC1 8K 59
Warwick Ct. Brom 6C 110
Warwick Ct. Eri 8D 82
Warwick Ct. Harr 1C 38
Warwick Ct. New Bar 7M 13
(off Station Rd.)
Warwick Ct. N'holt 1L 53
(off Newmarket Av.)
Warwick Cres. W2 8A 58
Warwick Cres. Hay 7D 52
Warwick Dene. W5 2J 71
Warwick Dri. SW15 2F 88
Warwick Dri. Chesh 1D 6
Warwick Est. W2 8M 57
Warwick Gdns. N4 3A 44
Warwick Gdns. W14 4K 73
Warwick Gdns. Asht 9G 133
Warwick Gdns. Barn 2K 13
Warwick Gdns. Ilf 6M 47
Warwick Gdns. Romf 1G 51
Warwick Gdns. Th Dit 9D 102
Warwick Gdns. T Hth 7L 107
Warwick Gro. E5 7F 44
Warwick Gro. Surb 2K 119
Warwick Ho. E16 2E 78
(off Wesley Av.)
Warwick Ho. SW9 1L 91
Warwick Ho. King T 5J 103
(off Acre Rd.)
Warwick Ho. Swan 8C 114
Warwick Ho. St. SW1 2H 75
Warwick La. EC4 9M 59
Warwick La. Rain 6K 67
Warwick Lodge. Twic 9M 85
Warwick Pde. Harr 9F 22
Warwick Pas. EC4 9M 59
(off Old Bailey)
Warwick Pl. W5 3H 71
Warwick Pl. W9 8A 58
Warwick Pl. Borwd 5B 12
Warwick Pl. Th Dit 1E 118
Warwick Pl. Uxb 3A 142
Warwick Pl. N. SW1 5G 75
Warwick Rd. E4 5L 29
Warwick Rd. E11 3F 46
Warwick Rd. E12 1J 63
Warwick Rd. E15 2D 62
Warwick Rd. E17 8K 29
Warwick Rd. N11 6H 27
Warwick Rd. N18 4C 28
Warwick Rd. SE20 7F 108
Warwick Rd. W5 3H 71
Warwick Rd. W14 & SW5 5K 73
Warwick Rd. Barn 6M 13
Warwick Rd. Borwd 5B 12
Warwick Rd. Coul 6G 137
Warwick Rd. Enf 1K 17
Warwick Rd. Houn 2F 84
Warwick Rd. King T 5G 103
Warwick Rd. N Mald 7A 104
Warwick Rd. Rain 7G 67
Warwick Rd. Sidc 2F 112
Warwick Rd. S'hall 4K 69
Warwick Rd. Sutt 6A 122
Warwick Rd. Th Dit 9D 102
Warwick Rd. T Hth 7L 107
Warwick Rd. Twic 7C 86
Warwick Rd. Well 2G 97
Warwick Rd. W Dray 3J 143
Warwick Row. SW1 4F 74
Warwickshire Path. SE8 8K 77
Warwickshire Rd. N16 9C 44
Warwick Sq. EC4 9M 59
Warwick Sq. SW1 6G 75
Warwick Sq. M. SW1 5G 75
Warwick St. W1 1G 75
Warwick Ter. E10 3B 46
(off Lea Bri. Rd.)
Warwick Ter. SE18 7B 80
Warwick Way. SW1 6F 74
Warwick Way. Crox G 6A 8
Warwick Way. Dart 8J 99
Warwick Yd. EC1 7A 60
Washington Av. E12 9K 47
Washington Clo. E3 6M 61
Washington Ho. E17 9K 29
(off Priory Ct.)
Washington Rd. E6 3G 63
Washington Rd. E18 9D 30
Washington Rd. SW13 8E 72
Washington Rd. King T 6L 103
Washington Rd. Wor Pk 4F 120
Washpond La. Warl 9A 140
Wasps R.U.F.C.
(Queen's Pk. Rangers F.C.)
2F 72
Wastdale Rd. SE23 7H 93
Watchfield Ct. W4 6A 72
Watch, The. N12 4A 26
Watcombe Cotts. Rich 7L 71
Watcombe Pl. SE25 9F 108
Watcombe Rd. SE25 9F 108
Waterbank Rd. SE6 9M 93
Waterbeach Rd. Dag 2G 65
Water Brook La. NW4 3G 41
Watercress Pl. N1 3C 60
Waterdale. 3H 5
Waterdale (Junct.) 4H 5
Waterdale. Brick 3J 5
Waterdale Rd. SE2 7E 80
Waterden Cres. E15 1L 61
Waterden Rd. E15 1L 61
Waterer Gdns. Tad 9H 135
Waterer Ho. SE6 1A 110
Waterer Ri. Wall 8H 123
Waterfall Clo. N14 3G 27
Waterfall Cotts. SW19 3B 106
Waterfall Rd. N11 & N14 4F 26
Waterfall Rd. SW19 3B 106
Waterfall Ter. SW17 3C 106
Waterfall Wlk. N14 1F 26
Waterfield Clo. SE28 2F 80
Waterfield Clo. Belv 4L 81
Waterfield Gdns. SE25 8B 108
Waterfields Way. Wat 6H 9
Waterford Ho. W11 1K 73
(off Kensington Pk. Rd.)
Waterford Rd. SW6 8M 73
(in two parts)
Waterford Way. NW10 1F 56
Waterfront, The. Els 8F 10
Water Gdns. Stan 6F 22
Water Gdns., The. W2 9C 58
Watergardens, The.
King T 3A 104
Watergate. EC4 1M 75
Watergate St. SE8 7L 77
Watergate, The. Wat 2H 21
Watergate Wlk. WC2 2J 75
Waterhall Av. E4 4C 30
Waterhall Clo. E17 8H 29
Waterhead. NW1 6G 59
(off Varndell St.)
Waterhead Clo. Eri 8C 82
Waterhouse Clo. E16 8H 63
Waterhouse Clo. NW3 1B 58
Waterhouse Clo. W6 5H 73
Waterhouse Sq. EC1 8L 59
Wateridge Clo. E14 4L 77
Wateringbury Clo. Orp 7F 112
Water La. E15 2C 62
Water La. EC3 1C 76
Water La. N9 1F 28
Water La. NW1 3F 58
Water La. SE14 8G 77
Water La. Ilf 8C 48
Water La. K Lan 2A 4
Water La. King T 5H 103
Water La. Purf 5L 83
Water La. Rich 4H 87
Water La. Sidc 8K 97
(in two parts)
Water La. Twic 7E 86
Water La. Wat 6G 9
Water Lily Clo. S'hall 3A 70
Waterloo Bri. WC2 & SE1 1K 75
Waterloo Clo. E9 1G 61
Waterloo Clo. Felt 7D 84
Waterloo Gdns. E2 5G 61
Waterloo Gdns. Romf 4B 50
Waterloo Pas. NW6 3K 57
Waterloo Pl. SW1 2H 75
Waterloo Pl. Cars 5D 122
(off Wrythe La.)
Waterloo Pl. Kew 7L 71
Waterloo Pl. Rich 3J 87
Waterloo Rd. E6 3G 63
Waterloo Rd. E7 1D 62
Waterloo Rd. E10 5L 45
Waterloo Rd. NW2 6E 40
Waterloo Rd. SE1 2K 75
Waterloo Rd. Eps 4B 134
Waterloo Rd. Ilf 9A 32
Waterloo Rd. Romf 3C 50
Waterloo Rd. Sutt 7B 122
Waterloo Rd. Uxb 4A 142
Waterloo Ter. N1 3M 59
Waterlow Ct. NW11 5M 41
Waterlow Rd. N19 6G 43
Waterman Building. E14 3K 77
Waterman Clo. Wat 8F 8
Watermans. Romf 3D 50
Watermans Clo. King T 4J 103
Watermans Ct. Bren 7H 71
(off High St.)
Watermans M. W5 1J 71
Waterman St. SW15 2H 89
Waterman's Wlk. EC4 1B 76
(off Allhallows La.)
Watermans Wlk. SE16 3J 77
Waterman Way. E1 2F 76
Watermead. Felt 7C 84
Watermead Ho. E9 1J 61
Watermead La. Cars 2D 122
Watermeadow Clo. Eri 8F 82
Watermeadow La. SW6 1A 90
Watermead Rd. SE6 1A 110
Watermead Way. N17 1E 44
Watermen's Sq. SE20 4G 109
Water M. SE15 3G 93
Watermill Bus. Cen. Enf 4K 17
Watermill Clo. Rich 9G 87
Water Mill Ho. Felt 8L 85
Watermill La. N18 5C 28
Watermill Way. SW19 5B 106
Watermill Way. Felt 8K 85
Water Mill Way. S Dar 6M 115
Watermint Clo. Orp 8H 113
Watermint Quay. N16 5E 44
Water Rd. Wemb 4K 55
Waters Edge. SW6 9G 73
Watersedge. Eps 6A 120
Watersfield Way. Edgw 7H 23
Waters Gdns. Dag 1L 65
Waterside. E17 4G 45
Waterside. Beck 5K 109
Waterside. Dart 4C 98
Water Side. Uxb 8A 142
Waterside. W Dray 8G 143
Waterside Bus. Cen.
Iswth 3F 86
Waterside Clo. E3 4K 61
Waterside Clo. SE16 3E 76
Waterside Clo. Bark 9E 48
Waterside Clo. H Wood 7L 35
Waterside Clo. N'holt 6K 53
Waterside Clo. Surb 4J 119
Waterside Dri. W on T 9E 100
Waterside Ho. E14 3M 77
(off Admirals Way)
Waterside Pl. NW1 4E 58
Waterside Point. SW11 8C 74
Waterside Rd. S'hall 4L 69
Waterside Trad. Cen. W7 4C 70
Waterside Way. SW17 1A 106
Watersmeet Way. SE28 9G 65
Waterson St. E2 6C 60
Waters Pl. SW15 1G 89
Watersplash Clo. King T 7J 103
Watersplash La. Hay 5E 68
(in two parts)
Waters Rd. SE6 9C 94
Waters Rd. King T 6M 103
Waters Sq. King T 7M 103
Water St. WC2 1L 75
(off Maltravers St.)
Waterton. Swan 8B 114
Water Tower Clo. Uxb 1C 142
Water Tower Hill. Croy 6B 124
Water Tower Pl. N1 4L 59
Waterview Ho. E14 8J 61
(off Carr St.)
Waterways Bus. Cen. Enf 2K 17
Waterworks Corner (Junct.)
9C 30
Waterworks La. E5 7H 45
Waterworks Rd. SW2 5K 91
Waterworks Yd. Croy 5A 124
Watery La. SW20 6K 105
Watery La. Hay 6C 68
Watery La. N'holt 5G 53
Watery La. Sidc 3F 112
Wates Way. Mitc 1D 122
Wateville Rd. N17 8A 28
Watford. 6F 8
Watford Arches Retail Pk.
Wat 7H 9
Watford By-Pass. Edgw 4M 23
Watford By-Pass. Stan 9F 10
Watford Clo. SW11 9C 74
Watford Enterprise Cen.
Wat 8C 8
Watford F.C.
(Vicarage Rd. Stadium)
7F 8
Watford Fld. Rd. Wat 7G 9
Watford Heath. 1H 21
Watford Heath. Wat 9H 9
Watford Heath Farm. Wat 9J 9
Watford Ho. Romf 5K 35
(off Redruth Rd.)
Watford Metro Cen. Wat 9A 8
Watford Rd. E16 8E 62
Watford Rd. Crox G 8A 8
Watford Rd. Els 8F 10
Watford Rd. Harr 5E 38
Watford Rd. K Lan 5A 4
Watford Rd. N'wd 7D 20
Watford Rd. Rad 1C 10
Watford Sports & Leisure Cen.
6G 5
Watford Way. NW4 2E 40
Watford Way.
NW7 & NW4 4C 24
Watkin Rd. Wemb 8M 39
Watkins Ct. N'wd 8D 20
Watkins Ho. E14 3A 78
(off Manchester Rd.)
Watkinson Rd. N7 2K 59
Watling. 7B 24
Watling Av. Edgw 8A 24
Watling Ct. EC4 9A 60
(off Watling St.)
Watling Ct. Els 8H 11
Watling Farm Clo. Stan 1G 23
Watling Gdns. NW2 2J 57
Watling Ga. NW9 2C 40
Watlings Clo. Croy 1J 125
Watling St. EC4 9A 60
Watling St. SE15 7C 76
Watling St. Bexh 3M 97
Watling St. Dart & Bean 6L 99
Watling St. Els 4G 11
Watlington Gro. SE26 2J 109
Watney Cotts. SW14 2A 88
Watney Mkt. E1 9F 60
Watney Rd. SW14 2A 88
Watney's Rd. Mitc 9H 107
Watney St. E1 9F 60
Watson Av. E6 3L 63
Watson Av. Sutt 4J 121
Watson Clo. N16 1B 60
Watson Clo. SW19 3C 106
Watson Gdns. H Wood 9J 35
Watson's M. W1 8C 58
Watsons Rd. N22 8K 27
Watsons St. SE8 8L 77
Watson St. E13 5F 62
Watsons Yd. NW2 7E 40
Wattendon Rd. Kenl 8M 137
Wattisfield Rd. E5 8G 45
Watts Bri. Rd. Eri 7D 82
Watts Clo. N15 3C 44
Watts Gro. E3 8L 61
Watts La. Chst 5M 111
Watts La. Tedd 2E 102
Watts Point. E13 4E 62
(off Brooks Rd.)
Watts Rd. Th Dit 2E 118
Watts St. E1 2F 76
Watts St. SE15 9D 76
Wat Tyler Ho. N8 1J 43
(off Boyton Rd.)
Wat Tyler Rd.
SE10 & SE3 1A 94
Wauthier Clo. N13 5M 27
Wavel Ct. E1 2G 77
(off Garnet St.)
Wavel Ct. Croy 7B 124
(off Hurst Rd.)
Wavell Clo. Chesh 1E 6
Wavell Dri. Sidc 5C 96
Wavel M. N8 2H 43
Wavel M. NW6 3M 57
Wavel Pl. SE26 1D 108
Wavendon Av. W4 6B 72
Waveney Av. SE15 3F 92
Waveney Clo. E1 2E 76
Waveney Ho. SE15 3F 92
Waverley Av. E4 4K 29
Waverley Av. E17 1B 46
Waverley Av. Kenl 8C 138
Waverley Av. Surb 1M 119
Waverley Av. Sutt 4M 121
Waverley Av. Twic 7K 85
Waverley Av. Wemb 1K 55
Waverley Clo. E18 8G 31
Waverley Clo. Brom 9H 111
Waverley Clo. Hay 5B 68
Waverley Clo. W Mol 9L 101
Waverley Ct. NW3 2D 58
Waverley Ct. NW6 3J 57
Waverley Ct. SE26 2G 109
Waverley Ct. Enf 5A 16
Waverley Cres. SE18 6B 80
Waverley Cres. Romf 7G 35
Waverley Gdns. E6 8J 63
Waverley Gdns. NW10 5K 55
Waverley Gdns. Bark 5C 64
Waverley Gdns. Ilf 9A 32
Waverley Gdns. N'wd 8E 20
Waverley Gro. N3 1J 41
Waverley Ind. Est. Harr 1B 38
Waverley Pl. N4 7M 43
Waverley Pl. NW8 5B 58
Waverley Rd. E17 1A 46
Waverley Rd. E18 8G 31
Waverley Rd. N8 4J 43
Waverley Rd. N17 7F 28
Waverley Rd. SE18 6A 80

averley Rd. SE25 ....8F 108
averley Rd. Enf 5M 15
averley Rd. Eps 7F 120
averley Rd. Harr 7J 37
averley Rd. Rain 7F 66
averley Rd. S'hall 1L 69
averley Rd. Stoke D 6A 132
averley Vs. N17 ....9D 28
averley Way. Cars 8C 122
averton Ho. E3 ....4K 61
averton Rd. SW18 ....6A 90
averton St. W1 ....2E 74
avertree Ct. SW2 ....7J 91
avertree Rd. E18 ....9E 30
avertree Rd. SW2 ....7K 91
axlow Cres. S'hall 9L 53
axlow Ho. Hay 8H 53
axlow Rd. NW10 ....5A 56
axwell Clo. Pinn 9H 21
axwell Farm Ho. Pinn 9H 21
axwell La. Pinn 9H 21
ayborne Gro. Ruis 4A 36
aye Av. Houn 9E 68
Vayfarer Rd. N'holt 6H 53
Vayfield Link. SE9 ....5B 96
Vayford St. SW11 ....1C 90
Vayland Av. E8 ....1E 60
Vayland Clo. E8 ....1E 60
Vayland Ho. SW9 ....1L 91
(off Robsart St.)
Vaylands. Hay 8B 52
Vaylands. Swan 8D 114
Vaylands Mead. Beck 5M 109
Vaylett Ho. SE11 ....6K 75
(off Loughborough St.)
Vaylett Pl. SE27 ....9M 91
Vaylett Pl. Wemb 9H 39
Vayman Ct. E8 ....2F 60
Vayne Clo. Orp 5D 128
Vayneflete Tower Av.
Esh 5L 117
Vayne Kirkum Way. NW6 ...1K 57
Vaynflete Av. Croy 5M 123
Vaynflete Sq. W10 ....1H 73
Vaynflete St. SW18 ....8A 90
Vayside. NW11 ....6J 41
Vayside. SW14 ....4A 88
Vayside. New Ad 8M 125
Vayside Av. Bush 8B 10
Vayside Av. Horn 7H 51
Vayside Clo. N14 ....8G 15
Vayside Clo. Romf 1D 50
Vayside Ct. Brick W 3K 5
Vayside Ct. Twic 5G 87
Vayside Ct. Wemb 8L 39
Vayside Gdns. Dag 1L 65
Vayside Gro. SE9 ....1K 111
Vayside M. Ilf 3L 47
Vayville Rd. Dart 6M 99
Veald Clo. SE16 ....6F 76
Veald Clo. Brom 4J 127
Veald La. Harr 9B 22
Veald Ri. Harr 7D 22
Veald Rd. Brtwd 1K 35
Veald Rd. Uxb 5E 142
Veald Sq. E5 ....7E 44
Vealdstone. 1C 38
Vealdstone Rd. Sutt 4K 121
Veald, The. Chst 3K 111
Veald Way. Hay 6C 52
Veald Way. Romf 4M 49
Vealdwood Gdns. Pinn 6M 21
Veale Rd. E4 ....3B 30
Veall Clo. Purl 4K 137
Veall Ct. Pinn 2J 37
Veall Grn. Wat 5F 4
Veardale Gdns. Enf 3B 16
Weardale Rd. SE13 ....3B 94
Wearmouth Ho. E3 ....8K 61
(off Joseph St.)
Wear Pl. E2 ....6F 60
(in two parts)
Wearside Rd. SE13 ....3M 93
Weatherbury. W2 ....9L 57
(off Talbot Rd.)
Weatherbury Ho. N19 ......8H 43
(off Wedmore St.)
Weatherley Clo. E3 ....8K 61
Weaver Clo. E6 ....1M 79
Weaver Clo. Croy 6D 124
Weavers Clo. Iswth 3C 86
Weavers Ho. E11 ....4E 46
(off New Wanstead)
Weavers La. SE1 ....2C 76
Weavers Ter. SW6 ....7L 73
(off Micklethwaite Rd.)
Weaver St. E1 ....7E 60
Weavers Way. NW1 ....4H 59
Weaver Wlk. SE27 ....1A 108
Webb Clo. W10 ....7G 57
Webber Clo. Els 8H 11
Webber Clo. Eri 8F 82
Webber Row. SE1 ....3M 75
(in two parts)
Webber St. SE1 ....3L 75
Webb Est. E5 ....5E 44
Webb Gdns. E13 ....7E 62
Webb Ho. SW8 ....8H 75
Webb Ho. Dag 8L 49
(off Kershaw Rd.)
Webb Ho. Felt 9J 85
Webb Pl. NW10 ....6D 56
Webb Rd. SE3 ....7D 78
Webbscroft Rd. Dag 9M 49
Webb's Rd. SW11 ....3D 90
Webbs Rd. Hay 6F 52
Webb St. SE1 ....4C 76
Webheath. NW6 ....3K 57
Webster Clo. Horn 8H 51
Webster Clo. Oxs 6A 132
Webster Clo. Wal A 6M 7
Webster Gdns. W5 ....2H 71
Webster Rd. E11 ....8A 46
Webster Rd. SE16 ....4E 76
Weddell Ho. E1 ....7H 61
(off Duckett St.)
Wedderburn Rd. NW3 ......1B 58
Wedderburn Rd. Bark 4C 64
Wedgewood Clo. N'wd 7A 20
Wedgewood Ct. Bex 6K 97
Wedgewood Ct. Brom 7D 110
(off Cumberland Rd.)
Wedgewood Ho. SW1 ......6F 74
(off Churchill Gdns.)
Wedgewood M. W1 ....9H 59
Wedgwood Ho. E2 ....6H 61
(off Warley St.)
Wedgwood Ho. SE11 ......4L 75
(off Lambeth Wlk.)
Wedgwood Wlk. NW6 ......1M 57
(off Dresden Clo.)
Wedgwood Way. SE19 .....4A 108
Wedlake Clo. Horn 6J 51
Wedlake St. W10 ....7J 57
Wedmore Av. Ilf 8L 31
Wedmore Ct. N19 ....7H 43
Wedmore Gdns. N19 ......7H 43
Wedmore M. N19 ....8H 43
Wedmore Rd. Gnfd 6B 54
Wedmore St. N19 ....8H 43
Wednesbury Gdns. Romf 7K 35
Wednesbury Grn. Romf 7K 35
Wednesbury Rd. Romf 7K 35
Weech Rd. NW6 ....9L 41
Weedington Rd. NW5 ......1E 58
Weedon Ho. W12 ....9E 56
Weekley Sq. SW11 ....2B 90
Weigall Rd. SE12 ....4E 94
Weighhouse St. W1 ....9E 58
Weighton M. SE20 ....6F 108
Weighton Rd. SE20 ....6F 108
Weighton Rd. Harr 8B 22
Weihurst Ct. Sutt 7C 122
Weihurst Gdns. Sutt 7B 122
Weimar St. SW15 ....2J 89
Weirdale Av. N20 ....2D 26
Weir Hall Av. N18 ....6B 28
Weir Hall Gdns. N18 ......5B 28
Weir Hall Rd. N18 & N17 ....5B 28
Weir Rd. SW12 ....6G 91
Weir Rd. SW19 ....9M 89
Weir Rd. Bex 6M 97
Weir Rd. W on T 1E 116
Weirside Gdns. W Dray 2H 143
Weir's Pas. NW1 ....6H 59
Weiss Rd. SW15 ....2H 89
Welbeck Av. Brom 1E 110
Welbeck Av. Hay 7F 52
Welbeck Av. Sidc 7E 96
Welbeck Clo. N12 ....5B 26
Welbeck Clo. Borwd 5L 11
Welbeck Clo. Eps 9E 120
Welbeck Clo. N Mald 9D 104
Welbeck Ct. W14 ....5K 73
(off Addison Bri. Pl.)
Welbeck Ho. W1 ....9F 58
(off Welbeck St.)
Welbeck Rd. E6 ....6H 63
Welbeck Rd. Barn 8C 14
Welbeck Rd. Harr 6M 37
Welbeck Rd. Sutt 4B 122
Welbeck St. W1 ....8E 58
Welbeck Vs. N21 ....2A 28
Welbeck Wlk. Cars 3B 122
Welbeck Way. W1 ....9F 58
Welbourne Rd. N17 ....1D 44
Welby Ho. N19 ....5H 43
Welby St. SE5 ....9M 75
Welch Pl. Pinn 8G 21
Welcome Ct. E17 ....5L 45
(off Boundary Rd.)
Welcomes Rd. Kenl 9A 138
Welcome Ter. Whyt 8D 138
Welcote Dri. N'wd 6B 20
Weldon Clo. Ruis 5F 52
Weldon Ct. N21 ....7K 15
Weldon Dri. W Mol 8K 101
Weld Pl. N11 ....5F 26
(in two parts)
Welfare Rd. E15 ....3C 62
Welford Clo. E5 ....8H 45
Welford Ct. NW1 ....3F 58
(off Castlehaven Rd.)
Welford Ct. SW8 ....1G 91
Welford Ct. W9 ....8L 57
(off Elmfield Way)
Welford Pl. SW19 ....1J 105
Welham Rd.
SW17 & SW16 ......2E 106
Welhouse Rd. Cars 3C 122
Wellacre Rd. Harr 4F 38
Wellan Clo. Sidc 4F 96
Welland Ct. SE6 ....8K 93
(off Oakham Clo.)
Welland Gdns. Gnfd 5D 54
Welland Ho. SE15 ....3G 93
Welland M. E1 ....2E 76
Wellands Clo. Brom 6K 111
Welland St. SE10 ....7A 78
Well App. Barn 7G 13
Wellbrook Rd. Orp 6L 127
Wellby Ct. E13 ....4G 63
Well Clo. SW16 ....1K 107
Well Clo. Ruis 8J 37
Wellclose Sq. E1 ....1E 76
Wellclose St. E1 ....1E 76
Wellcome Av. Dart 3J 99
Wellcome Cen. for
Medical Science. 7H 59
(off Euston Rd.)
Well Cottage Clo. E11 ......4G 47
Well Ct. EC4 ....9A 60
(in two parts)
Welldon Ct. Harr 3C 38
Welldon Cres. Harr 3C 38
Well End. 2B 12
Well End Rd. Borwd 1A 12
Weller Ho. SE16 ....3E 76
(off George Row)
Weller Pl. Orp 3L 141
Wellers Ct. NW1 ....5J 59
Wellers Gro. Chesh 1A 6
Weller St. SE1 ....3A 76
Welles Ct. E14 ....1L 77
(off Premiere Pl.)
Wellesford Clo. Bans 9K 135
Wellesley Av. W6 ....4F 72
Wellesley Av. N'wd 5D 20
Wellesley Clo. SE7 ....6G 79
Wellesley Ct. NW2 ....7E 40
Wellesley Ct. W9 ....6A 58
(off Maida Va.)
Wellesley Ct. Sutt 3J 121
Wellesley Ct. Rd. Croy 4B 124
Wellesley Cres. Twic 8C 86
Wellesley Gro. Croy 4B 124
Wellesley Ho. NW1 ....6H 59
(off Wellesley Pl.)
Wellesley Ho. SW1 ....6F 74
(off Ebury Bri. Rd.)
Wellesley Lodge. Sutt 9L 121
(off Worcester Rd.)
Wellesley Mans. W14 ......6K 73
(off Edith Vs.)
Wellesley Pde. Twic 9C 86
Wellesley Pk. M. Enf 4M 15
Wellesley Pas. Croy 4A 124
Wellesley Pl. NW1 ....6H 59
Wellesley Pl. NW5 ....1E 58
Wellesley Rd. E11 ....3E 46
Wellesley Rd. E17 ....4L 45
Wellesley Rd. N22 ....9L 27
Wellesley Rd. NW5 ....1E 58
Wellesley Rd. W4 ....6L 71
Wellesley Rd. Croy 3A 124
Wellesley Rd. Harr 3C 38
Wellesley Rd. Ilf 7M 47
Wellesley Rd. Sutt 8A 122
Wellesley Rd. Twic 9B 86
Wellesley St. E1 ....8H 61
Wellesley Ter. N1 ....6A 60
Wellfield Av. N10 ....1F 42
Wellfield Gdns. Cars 1C 136
Wellfield Rd. SW16 ......1J 107
Wellfields. Lou 5L 19
Wellfield Wlk. SW16 ......2K 107
(in two parts)
Wellfit St. SE24 ....2M 91
Wellgarth. Gnfd 2F 54
Wellgarth Rd. NW11 ......6M 41
Well Gro. N20 ....1A 26
Well Hall Pde. SE9 ....3K 95
Well Hall Rd. SE9 ....2J 95
Well Hall Roundabout (Junct.)
........2J 95
Well Hill. 8M 129
Well Hill. Orp 8M 129
Well Hill La. Orp 8M 129
Wellhouse La. Barn 6G 13
Wellhouse Rd. Beck 8L 109
Welling. 2F 96
Wellingborough Ho.
Romf 5K 35
(off Redruth Rd.)
Welling High St. Well 2F 96
Wellington. N8 ....2J 43
(in two parts)
Wellington Arch. 3E 74
(off Duke of Wellington Pl.)
Wellington Av. E4 ....2L 29
Wellington Av. N9 ....3F 28
Wellington Av. N15 ....4D 44
Wellington Av. SE18 ......4M 79
Wellington Av. Houn 4L 85
Wellington Av. Pinn 8K 21
Wellington Av. Sidc 5E 96
Wellington Av. Wor Pk 5G 121
Wellington Bldgs. SW1 .....6E 74
Wellington Clo. SE14 ......9H 77
Wellington Clo. W11 ....9L 57
Wellington Clo. Dag 3A 66
Wellington Clo. W on T 3D 116
Wellington Clo. Wat 3K 21
Wellington Ct. NW8 ....5B 58
(off Wellington Rd.)
Wellington Ct. SW1 ....3D 74
(off Knightsbridge)
Wellington Ct. SW6 ....9M 73
(off Maltings Pl.)
Wellington Ct. Hamp 2B 102
Wellington Ct. Pinn 8K 21
(off Wellington Rd.)
Wellington Ct. Stanw 6C 144
Wellington Cres. N Mald ...7A 104
Wellington Dri. Dag 3A 66
Wellington Dri. Purl 2K 137
Wellington Est. E2 ....5G 61
Wellington Gdns. SE7 ......7G 79
Wellington Gdns. Twic 1B 102
Wellington Gro. SE10 ......8B 78
Wellington Hill. Lou 1E 18
Wellington Ho. E16 ....2E 78
(off Pepys Cres.)
Wellington Ho. NW3 ....2D 58
(off Eton Rd.)
Wellington Ho. W5 ....6J 55
Wellington Ho. N'holt 3L 53
(off Farmlands, The)
Wellington Ho. Wat 4G 9
(off Exeter Clo.)
Wellingtonia Av. Hav 4A 34
Wellington Mans. E10 ......6L 45
Wellington M. N7 ....2K 59
(off Roman Way)
Wellington M. SE7 ....7G 79
Wellington M. SE22 ....3E 92
Wellington M. SW16 ......9H 91
Wellington Monument. 3E 74
(off Hyde Pk. Corner)
Wellington Mus. 3E 74
Wellington Pde. Sidc 4E 96
Wellington Pk. Est. NW2 ....6E 40
Wellington Pas. E11 ....3E 46
(off Wellington Rd.)
Wellington Pl. E11 ....3E 46
Wellington Pl. N2 ....3C 42
Wellington Pl. NW8 ....6B 58
Wellington Rd. E6 ....4K 63
Wellington Rd. E7 ....9D 46
Wellington Rd. E10 ....6J 45
Wellington Rd. E11 ....3E 46
Wellington Rd. E17 ....2J 45
Wellington Rd. NW8 ....5B 58
Wellington Rd. NW10 ......6H 57
Wellington Rd. SW19 ......8L 89
Wellington Rd. W5 ....4G 71
Wellington Rd. Belv 6K 81
Wellington Rd. Bex 4H 97
Wellington Rd. Brom 8G 111
Wellington Rd. Croy 2M 123
Wellington Rd. Dart 5G 99
Wellington Rd. Enf 7C 16
Wellington Rd. Felt 4C 84
Wellington Rd. Hamp 2B 102
Wellington Rd. Harr 1C 38
Wellington Rd. Orp 1F 128
Wellington Rd. Pinn 8K 21
Wellington Rd. Uxb 4A 142
Wellington Rd. Wat 4F 8
Wellington Rd. N. Houn 2K 85
Wellington Rd. S. Houn 3K 85
Wellington Row. E2 ....6D 60
Wellington Sq. SW3 ....6D 74
Wellington St. SE18 ....5L 79
Wellington St. WC2 ....1K 75
Wellington St. Bark 4A 64
Wellington Ter. E1 ....2F 76
Wellington Ter. N8 ....1L 43
(off Turnpike La.)
Wellington Ter. W2 ....1L 73
Wellington Ter. Harr 6B 38
Wellington Way. E3 ....6L 61
Welling United F.C. 2G 97
Welling Way. SE9 & Well 2A 96
Well La. SW14 ....4A 88
Wellmeadow Rd.
SE13 & SE6 ....5C 94
(in two parts)
Wellmeadow Rd. W7 ....5E 70
Wellow Wlk. Cars 3B 122
Well Pl. NW3 ....8B 42
Well Rd. NW3 ....8B 42
Well Rd. Barn 7G 13
Wells Clo. N'holt 6G 53
Wells Clo. S Croy 7C 124
Wells Ct. NW6 ....5L 57
(off Cambridge Av.)
Wells Dri. NW9 ....6B 40
Wells Gdns. Dag 1M 65
Wells Gdns. Ilf 5J 47
Wells Gdns. Rain 2D 66
Wells Ho. EC1 ....6L 59
(off Spa Grn. Est.)
Wells Ho. SE16 ....4G 77
(off Howland Est.)
Wells Ho. W5 ....2H 71
(off Grove Rd.)
Wells Ho. Bark 3E 64
(off Margaret Bondfield Av.)
Wells Ho. Brom 2F 110
(off Pike Clo.)
Wells Ho. Eps 6L 133
Wells Ho. Rd. NW10 ....8C 56
Wellside Clo. Barn 6G 13
Wellside Gdns. SW14 ......3A 88
Wells M. W1 ....8G 59
Wellsmoor Gdns. Brom 7L 111
Wells Pk. Rd. SE26 ....9E 92
Wells Path. N'holt 6C 52
Wells Pl. SW18 ....6A 90
Wells Ri. NW8 ....4D 58
Wells Rd. W12 ....3G 73
Wells Rd. Brom 6K 111
Wells Rd. Eps 6L 133
Wells Sq. WC1 ....6K 59
Wells St. W1 ....8G 59
Wellstead Av. N9 ....9H 17
Wellstead Rd. E6 ....5L 63
Wells Ter. N4 ....7L 43
Wells, The. 6L 133
Wells, The. N14 ....9H 15
Wellstones. Wat 6F 8
Well St. E9 ....3G 61
Well St. E15 ....2C 62
Wells Way. SE5 ....7B 76
Wells Way. SW7 ....4B 74
Wells Yd. N7 ....1L 59
Wells Yd. Wat 5F 8
Well Wlk. NW3 ....9B 42
Well Way. Eps 7L 133
Wellwood Clo. Coul 6J 137
Wellwood Rd. Ilf 6E 48
Welsby Ct. W5 ....8G 55
Welsford St. SE1 ....5E 76
(in two parts)
Welsh Clo. E13 ....6E 62
Welsh Ho. E1 ....2F 76
(off Wapping La.)
Welshpool Ho. E8 ....4E 60
(off Welshpool St.)
Welshpool St. E8 ....4E 60
(in two parts)
Welshside. NW9 ....4C 40
(off Ruthin Clo.)
Welshside Wlk. NW9 ......4C 40
Welstead Ho. E1 ....9F 60
(off Cannon St. Rd.)
Welstead Way. W4 ....5D 72
Welsummer Way. Chesh 1D 6
Weltje Rd. W6 ....5E 72
Welton Ct. SE5 ....9C 76
Welton Ho. E1 ....8H 61
(off Stepney Way)
Welton Rd. SE18 ....8C 80
Welwyn Av. Felt 5D 84
Welwyn St. E2 ....6G 61
Welwyn Way. Hay 7C 52
Wembley. 1J 55
Wembley Arena. 9L 39
Wembley Commercial Cen.
Wemb 7H 39
Wembley Conference Cen.
........9L 39
Wembley Hill Rd. Wemb 8K 39
Wembley Park. 8L 39
Wembley Pk. Bus. Cen. Wemb
........9M 39
Wembley Pk. Dri. Wemb 9K 39
Wembley Retail Pk.
Wemb 9M 39
Wembley Rd. Hamp 5L 101
Wembley Stadium. 9L 39
Wembley Stadium Ind. Est.
Wemb 9M 39
Wembley Way. Wemb 2M 55
Wemborough Rd. Stan 8F 22
Wembury M. N6 ....5G 43
Wembury Rd. N6 ....5F 42
Wemyss Rd. SE3 ....1D 94
Wendela Ct. Harr 7C 38
Wendell Rd. W12 ....4D 72
Wenderholme. S Croy 7B 124
(off S. Park Hill Rd.)
Wendle Ct. SW8 ....7J 75
Wendling Rd. Sutt 3B 122
Wendon St. E3 ....4K 61
Wendover. SE17 ....6C 76
(in two parts)
Wendover Clo. Hay 7J 53
Wendover Ct. NW2 ....8L 41
Wendover Ct. NW10 ......7M 55
Wendover Ct. W1 ....8E 58
(off Chiltern St.)
Wendover Ct. Brom 7F 110
(off Wendover Rd.)
Wendover Dri. N Mald 1D 120
Wendover Ho. W1 ....8E 58
(off Chiltern St.)
Wendover Ho. Wat 9C 8
(off Chenies Way)
Wendover Rd. NW10 ....5D 56
Wendover Rd. SE9 ....2H 95
Wendover Rd. Brom 8F 110
Wendover Way. Bush 8A 10
Wendover Way. Horn 1G 67
Wendover Way. Orp 1E 128
Wendover Way. Well 4E 96
Wend, The. Coul 6H 137
Wendy Clo. Enf 8D 16
Wendy Way. Wemb 4J 55
Wenham Ho. SW8 ....8G 75
Wenlake Ho. EC1 ....7A 60
(off Old St.)
Wenlock Barn Est. N1 ......5B 60
(off Wenlock St.)

Wenlock Ct.—West La.

Wenlock Ct. N1 5B 60
Wenlock Gdns. NW4 2F 40
Wenlock Rd. N1 5A 60
Wenlock Rd. Edgw 7M 23
Wenlock St. N1 5A 60
Wennington. 1J 83
Wennington Rd. E3 5H 61
Wennington Rd. Rain 7E 66
Wensdale Ho. E5 7E 44
Wensley Av. Wfd G 7D 30
Wensley Clo. N11 6E 26
Wensley Clo. SE9 5K 95
Wensley Clo. Romf 5L 33
Wensleydale Av. Ilf 9J 31
Wensleydale Gdns. Hamp 4M 101
Wensleydale Pas. Hamp 5L 101
Wensleydale Rd. Hamp 3L 101
Wensley Rd. N18 6F 28
Wenta Bus. Cen. Wat 1H 9
Wentbridge Path. Borwd 2L 11
Wentland Clo. SE6 8B 94
Wentland Rd. SE6 8B 94
Wentway Ct. W13 7D 54 (off Ruislip Rd. E.)
Wentworth Av. N3 7L 25
Wentworth Av. Els 7K 11
Wentworth Clo. N3 7M 25
Wentworth Clo. SE28 9H 65
Wentworth Clo. Ashf 9F 144
Wentworth Clo. Hayes 4E 126
Wentworth Clo. Mord 2L 121
Wentworth Clo. Orp 7C 128
Wentworth Clo. Surb 4H 119
Wentworth Clo. Wat 2D 8
Wentworth Ct. W6 7J 73 (off Paynes Wlk.)
Wentworth Ct. Twic 9C 86
Wentworth Cres. SE15 8E 76
Wentworth Cres. Hay 4B 68
Wentworth Dene. Wey 7A 116
Wentworth Dri. Dart 5E 98
Wentworth Dri. Pinn 3E 36
Wentworth Dwellings. E1 9D 60 (off Wentworth St.)
Wentworth Fields. Hay 5B 52
Wentworth Gdns. N13 3M 27
Wentworth Hill. Wemb 6K 39
Wentworth M. E3 7J 61
Wentworth Pk. N3 7L 25
Wentworth Pl. Stan 6F 22
Wentworth Rd. E12 9H 47
Wentworth Rd. NW11 4K 41
Wentworth Rd. Barn 5H 13
Wentworth Rd. Croy 2L 123
Wentworth Rd. S'hall 5G 69
Wentworth St. E1 9D 60
Wentworth Way. Pinn 2J 37
Wentworth Way. Rain 6F 66
Wentworth Way. S Croy 6E 138
Wenvoe Av. Bexh 1M 97
Wepham Clo. Hay 8H 53
Wernbrook St. SE18 7A 80
Werndee Rd. SE25 8E 108
Werneth Hall Rd. Ilf 1L 47
Werrington St. NW1 5G 59
Werter Rd. SW15 3J 89
Wescott Way. Uxb 5A 142
Wesleyan Pl. NW5 9F 42
Wesley Av. E16 2E 78
Wesley Av. NW10 6B 56
Wesley Av. Houn 1J 85
Wesley Clo. N7 7K 43
Wesley Clo. SE17 5M 75
Wesley Clo. Harr 7A 38
Wesley Clo. Orp 7G 113
Wesley Ct. SE16 4F 76
Wesley Rd. E10 5A 46
Wesley Rd. N2 8C 26
Wesley Rd. NW10 4A 56
Wesley Rd. Hay 1E 68
Wesley's House Chapel & Mus. of Methodism. 7B 60
Wesley Sq. W11 9J 57
Wesley St. W1 8E 58
Wessex Av. SW19 7L 105
Wessex Clo. Ilf 4C 48
Wessex Clo. King T 5M 103
Wessex Clo. Th Dit 4D 118
Wessex Ct. Barn 6H 13
Wessex Ct. Beck 5J 109
Wessex Ct. Stanw 5C 144
Wessex Dri. Eri 1C 98
Wessex Dri. Pinn 7J 21
Wessex Gdns. NW11 6J 41
Wessex Ho. SE1 6D 76
Wessex La. Gnfd 6B 54
Wessex Rd. H'row A 1A 144
Wessex St. E2 6G 61
Wessex Wlk. Bex 8C 98
Wessex Way. NW11 6J 41
Westacott. Hay 8C 52
Westacott Clo. N19 6H 43
West Acres. Esh 9K 117
West Acton. 9L 55
Westall Rd. Lou 5M 19
West App. Orp 9A 112
W. Arbour St. E1 9H 61
West Av. E17 2M 45
West Av. N2 1M 41
West Av. N3 6L 25
West Av. NW4 3H 41
West Av. Hay 1D 68
West Av. Pinn 4K 37
West Av. S'hall 1K 69
West Av. Wall 7J 123
W. Avenue Rd. E17 2L 45
West Bank. N16 5C 44
West Bank. Bark 4M 63
West Bank. Enf 4A 16
Westbank Rd. Hamp H 3A 102
West Barnes. 8F 104
W. Barnes La. N Mald & SW20 9E 104 (in two parts)
West Beckton. 9H 63
West Bedfont. 5D 144
Westbeech Rd. N22 1L 43
Westbere Dri. Stan 5H 23
Westbere Rd. NW2 9J 41
West Block. SE1 3K 75 (off Addington St.)
Westbourne Av. W3 9B 56
Westbourne Av. Sutt 4J 121
Westbourne Bri. W2 8A 58
Westbourne Clo. Hay 7G 53
Westbourne Cres. W2 1B 74
Westbourne Cres. M. W2 1B 74 (off Westbourne Cres.)
Westbourne Dri. SE23 8H 93
Westbourne Gdns. W2 9M 57
Westbourne Green. 9K 57
Westbourne Gro. W11 & W2 1K 73
Westbourne Gro. M. W11 9L 57
Westbourne Gro. Ter. W2 9M 57
Westbourne Ho. SW1 6F 74 (off Ebury Bri. Rd.)
Westbourne Ho. Houn 7L 69
Westbourne Pde. Hil 7F 142
Westbourne Pk. Pas. W2 8L 57 (in two parts)
Westbourne Pk. Rd. W11 & W2 9J 57
Westbourne Pk. Vs. W2 8L 57
Westbourne Pl. N9 3F 28
Westbourne Rd. N7 2K 59
Westbourne Rd. SE26 3H 109
Westbourne Rd. Bexh 8H 81
Westbourne Rd. Croy 1D 124
Westbourne Rd. Felt 9D 84
Westbourne Rd. Uxb 7F 142
Westbourne St. W2 1B 74
Westbourne Ter. SE23 8H 93 (off Westbourne Dri.)
Westbourne Ter. W2 9A 58
Westbourne Ter. M. W2 9A 58
Westbourne Ter. Rd. W2 8M 57
Westbourne Ter. Rd. Bri. W2 8A 58 (off Westbourne Ter. Rd.)
Westbridge Clo. W12 3E 72
Westbridge Rd. SW11 9B 74
West Brompton. 7M 73
Westbrook Av. Hamp 4K 101
Westbrook Clo. Barn 5B 14
Westbrook Cres. Cockf 5B 14
Westbrook Dri. Orp 3H 129
Westbrooke Cres. Well 2G 97
Westbrooke Rd. Sidc 8B 96
Westbrooke Rd. Well 2F 96 (in two parts)
Westbrook Ho. E2 6G 61 (off Victoria Pk. Sq.)
Westbrook Rd. SE3 9F 78
Westbrook Rd. Houn 8K 69
Westbrook Rd. T Hth 5B 108
Westbrook Sq. Barn 5B 14
Westbury. Chesh 3D 6
Westbury Av. N22 1M 43
Westbury Av. Clay 8D 118
Westbury Av. S'hall 7L 53
Westbury Av. Wemb 3J 55
Westbury Clo. Ruis 5E 36
Westbury Clo. Shep 1A 116
Westbury Clo. Whyt 9D 138
Westbury Ct. Bark 4B 64 (off Westbury Rd.)
Westbury Gro. N12 6L 25
Westbury Ho. E17 2K 45
Westbury La. Buck H 2G 31
Westbury Lodge Clo. Pinn 1H 37
Westbury Pl. Bren 7H 71
Westbury Rd. E7 2F 62
Westbury Rd. E17 2K 45
Westbury Rd. N11 6J 27
Westbury Rd. N12 6L 25
Westbury Rd. SE20 5H 109
Westbury Rd. W5 9J 55
Westbury Rd. Bark 4B 64
Westbury Rd. Beck 7J 109
Westbury Rd. Brom 5H 111
Westbury Rd. Buck H 2G 31
Westbury Rd. Croy 1B 124
Westbury Rd. Felt 7H 85
Westbury Rd. Ilf 7L 47
Westbury Rd. N Mald 8B 104
Westbury Rd. N'wd 4C 20
Westbury Rd. Wat 7F 8
Westbury Rd. Wemb 3J 55
Westbury St. SW8 1G 91 (off Portslade Rd.)
Westbury Ter. E7 2F 62
Westcar La. W on T 8F 116
W. Carriage Dri. W2 1C 74 (in two parts)
W. Central St. WC1 9J 59
W. Centre Av. NW10 7F 56
West Chantry. Harr 8M 21
Westchester Dri. NW4 1H 41
West Clo. N9 3D 28
West Clo. Ashf 9C 144
West Clo. Barn 7F 12
West Clo. Cockf 6E 14
West Clo. Gnfd 5A 54
West Clo. Hamp 3J 101
West Clo. Rain 7F 66
West Clo. Wemb 6K 39
Westcombe Av. Croy 2J 123
Westcombe Ct. SE3 8D 78
Westcombe Dri. Barn 7L 13
Westcombe Hill. SE3 8E 78
Westcombe Lodge Dri. Hay 8C 52
Westcombe Pk. Rd. SE3 7C 78
West Comn. Rd. Brom & Kes 3E 126
West Comn. Rd. Uxb 1B 142
Westcoombe Av. SW20 5D 104
Westcote Ri. Ruis 5A 36
Westcote Rd. SW16 2G 107
West Cotts. NW6 1L 57
Westcott Clo. N15 4D 44
Westcott Clo. Brom 9K 111
Westcott Clo. New Ad 1M 139
Westcott Cres. W7 9C 54
Westcott Ho. E14 1L 77
Westcott Rd. SE17 7M 75
Westcott Way. Sutt 2G 135
West Ct. E17 2L 45
West Ct. Houn 8A 70
West Ct. Wemb 7G 39
Westcroft Clo. NW2 9J 41
Westcroft Clo. Enf 2G 17
Westcroft Gdns. Mord 7K 105
Westcroft Rd. Cars 6E 122
Westcroft Sq. W6 5E 72
Westcroft Way. NW2 9J 41
W. Cromwell Rd. W14 & SW5 6K 73
W. Cross Cen. Bren 7E 70
W. Cross Route. W10 & W12 1H 73
W. Cross Way. Bren 7F 70
Westdale Pas. SE18 7M 79
Westdale Rd. SE18 7M 79
Westdean Av. SE12 7F 94
W. Dean Clo. SW18 5M 89
West Dene. Sutt 8J 121
W. Dene Dri. H Hill 5H 35
W. Dene Way. Wey 5C 116
Westdown Rd. E15 9A 46
Westdown Rd. SE6 6L 93
West Drayton. 3J 143
W. Drayton Pk. Av. W Dray 4J 143
W. Drayton Rd. Uxb 9F 142
West Dri. SW16 1G 107
West Dri. Cars 2B 136
West Dri. Harr 6B 22
West Dri. Sutt 1H 135
West Dri. Tad 9H 135
West Dri. Wat 9F 4
West Dri. Gdns. Harr 6B 22
West Dulwich. 8B 92
West Ealing. 1F 70
W. Ealing Bus. Cen. W13 1E 70
W. Eaton Pl. SW1 5E 74
W. Eaton Pl. M. SW1 5E 74 (off W. Eaton Pl.)
Wested La. Swan 2E 130 (in two parts)
W. Ella Rd. NW10 3C 56
West End. 7K 117 (Esher)
West End. 5H 53 (Northolt)
W. End Av. E10 3B 46
W. End Av. Pinn 2H 37
Westend Clo. NW10 3A 56
W. End Ct. NW6 3M 57
W. End Ct. Pinn 2H 37
W. End Gdns. Esh 7K 117
W. End Gdns. N'holt 5G 53
W. End La. NW6 1L 57 (in two parts)
W. End La. Barn 6H 13
W. End La. Esh 9K 117
W. End La. Hay 8A 68
W. End La. Pinn 1H 37
W. End Rd. Ruis 7C 36
W. End Rd. S'hall 2J 69
Westerdale Rd. SE10 6E 78
Westerfield Rd. N15 3D 44
Westergate. W5 8J 55
Westergate Ho. King T 8H 103 (off Portsmouth Rd.)
Westergate Rd. SE2 7J 81
Westerham. NW1 4G 59 (off Bayham St.)
Westerham Av. N9 3B 28
Westerham Clo. Sutt 2L 135
Westerham Dri. Sidc 5F 96
Westerham Ho. SE1 4B 76 (off Law St.)
Westerham Lodge. Beck 4L 109 (off Park Rd.)
Westerham Rd. E10 5M 45
Westerham Rd. Kes 8H 127
Westerley Cres. SE26 2K 109
Western Av. NW11 4H 41
Western Av. W5 & W3 7K 55
Western Av. Dag 2A 66
Western Av. Den & Uxb 1A 142
Western Av. Gnfd & W5 5B 54
Western Av. Romf 9G 35
Western Av. Uxb & Ruis 2A 52
Western Av. Bus. Pk. W3 7M 55
Western Beach Apartments. E16 1E 78
Western Circus (Junct.) 1D 72
Western Ct. N3 6L 25
Western Ct. NW6 5K 57
Western Ct. W3 9B 56
Western Ct. Romf 3C 50 (off Chandlers Way)
Western Dri. Shep 1B 116
Western Gdns. W5 1L 71
Western International Mkt. S'hall 5F 68
Western La. SW12 6E 90
Western Mans. New Bar 7M 13 (off Gt. North Rd.)
Western M. W9 7K 57
Western Pde. New Bar 7L 13
Western Pathway. Rain 3F 66
Western Perimeter Rd. W Dray & H'row A 9G 143
Western Pl. SE16 3G 77
Western Rd. E13 5G 63
Western Rd. E17 3A 46
Western Rd. N2 2D 42
Western Rd. N22 9K 27
Western Rd. NW10 7A 56
Western Rd. SW9 2L 91
Western Rd. SW19 & Mitc 5B 106
Western Rd. W5 1H 71
Western Rd. Romf 3C 50
Western Rd. S'hall 5G 69
Western Rd. Sutt 7L 121
Western Ter. W6 6E 72 (off Chiswick Mall)
Western Vw. Hay 3D 68
Westernville Gdns. Ilf 5A 48
Western Way. SE28 4B 80
Western Way. Barn 8L 13
West Ewell. 9C 120
Westferry Cir. E14 2K 77
Westferry Rd. E14 1K 77
West Fld. Asht 9K 133
Westfield. Lou 7H 19
Westfield Av. S Croy 5B 138
Westfield Av. Wat 2H 9
Westfield Clo. NW9 1A 40
Westfield Clo. SW10 8A 74
Westfield Clo. Enf 5J 17
Westfield Clo. Sutt 6K 121
Westfield Clo. Wal X 4F 6
Westfield Ct. NW10 6H 57 (off Chamberlayne Rd.)
Westfield Ct. Surb 9H 103 (off Portsmouth Rd)
Westfield Dri. Harr 2H 39
Westfield Gdns. Harr 2H 39
Westfield Gdns. Romf 4G 49
Westfield Ho. SE16 5H 77 (off Rotherhithe New Rd.)
Westfield Ho. SW18 7M 89
Westfield La. Harr 3H 39 (in two parts)
Westfield Pk. Pinn 7K 21
Westfield Pk. Dri. Wfd G 6J 31
Westfield Rd. NW7 3B 24
Westfield Rd. W13 2E 70
Westfield Rd. Beck 6K 109
Westfield Rd. Bexh 2A 98
Westfield Rd. Croy 4M 123
Westfield Rd. Dag 9J 49
Westfield Rd. Mitc 6C 106
Westfield Rd. Surb 9H 103
Westfield Rd. Sutt 6K 121
Westfield Rd. W on T 2J 117
Westfields. SW13 2D 88
Westfields Av. SW13 2C 88
Westfields Rd. W3 8M 55
Westfield St. SE18 4H 79
Westfield Wlk. Wal X 4F 6
Westfield Way. E1 6J 61
Westfield Way. Ruis 8C 36
W. Garden Pl. W2 9C 58
West Gdns. E1 1F 76
West Gdns. SW17 3C 106
West Gdns. Eps 2C 134
Westgate. W5 6J 55
Westgate Cen., The. E8 4F 60 (off Bocking St.)
Westgate Clo. Eps 7B 134
Westgate Ct. SE12 7E 94 (off Burnt Ash Hill)
Westgate Ct. SW9 2L (off Canterbury Cre
Westgate Ct. Wal X 8D
Westgate M. W10 7J (off West Ro
Westgate Rd. SE25 8F 1
Westgate Rd. Beck 6M 1
Westgate Rd. Dart 5H (in two part
Westgate St. E8 4F
Westgate Ter. SW10 6M
Westglade Ct. Kent 3H
West Green. 2M
W. Green Pl. Gnfd 4B
W. Green Rd. N8 2M
West Gro. SE10 9A
West Gro. W on T 7F 1
West Gro. Wfd G 6G
Westgrove La. SE10 9A
W. Halkin St. SW1 4E
West Hallowes. SE9 7H
W. Hall Rd. Rich 9M
Westhall Rd. Warl 9E 138 & 9H 13
West Ham. 4E
W. Ham La. E15 3B
West Hampstead. 2M
W. Hampstead M. NW6 2M
West Ham United F.C. (Upton Pk.) 5H
W. Harding St. EC4 9L
Westharold. Swan 7B 1
West Harrow. 5A
W. Hatch Mnr. Ruis 6D
Westhay Gdns. SW14 4M
West Heath. 7H
W. Heath Av. NW11 6L
W. Heath Clo. NW3 8L
W. Heath Clo. Dart 5D
W. Heath Ct. NW11 6L
W. Heath Dri. NW11 6L
W. Heath Gdns. NW3 7L
W. Heath Rd. NW3 7L
W. Heath Rd. SE2 7G
W. Heath Rd. Dart 5D
West Hendon. 5E
West Hertfordshire Crematorium. Wat 4H
West Herts Golf Course. 4A
West Hill. 5K
West Hill. SW15 & SW18 6H
West Hill. Dart 5H
West Hill. Eps 5M 13
West Hill. Harr 7C 3
West Hill. Orp 4K 14
West Hill. S Croy 2C 13
West Hill. Wemb 6K 3
W. Hill Av. Eps 5M 13
W. Hill Ct. N6 8E 4
W. Hill Ct. Eps 5A 13 (off Court La.
W. Hill Dri. Dart 5G 9
Westhill Pk. N6 7D 42 (in two parts
W. Hill Ri. Dart 5H 99
W. Hill Rd. SW18 5K 89
W. Hill Way. N20 1M 25
Westholm. NW11 2M 41
West Holme. Eri 9A 82
Westholme. Orp 2C 128
Westholme Gdns. Ruis 6E 36
Westhope Ho. E2 7E 60 (off Derbyshire St.
Westhorne Av. SE12 & SE9 6E 94
Westhorpe Gdns. NW4 1G 41
Westhorpe Rd. SW15 2G 89
West Ho. Clo. SW19 7J 89
West Ho. Cotts. Pinn 2H 37
Westhurst Dri. Chst 2M 111
W. India Av. E14 2L 77
W. India Dock Rd. E14 1K 77 (in two parts)
W. India Ho. E14 1L 77 (off W. India Dock Rd.)
West Kensington. 5K 73
W. Kensington Ct. W14 6K 73 (off Edith Vs.)
W. Kensington Mans. W14 6K 73 (off Beaumont Cres.)
West Kilburn. 6K 57
Westlake. SE16 5G 77 (off Rotherhithe New Rd.)
Westlake Clo. N13 3L 27
Westlake Clo. Hay 7J 53
Westlake Rd. Wemb 7H 39
Westland Av. Horn 6J 51
Westland Clo. Leav 7D 4
Westland Clo. Stanw 5C 144
Westland Ct. N'holt 6H 53 (off Seasprite Clo.)
Westland Dri. Brom 4D 126
Westland Ho. E16 2L 79 (off Rymill St.)
Westland Pl. N1 6B 60
Westland Rd. Wat 4F 8
Westlands Clo. Hay 5E 68
Westlands Ct. Eps 7A 134
Westlands Ter. SW12 5G 91
West La. SE16 3F 76

Willett Ho.—Winch Ho.

Willett Ho. E13 . . . 5F 62
(off Queens Rd. W.)
Willett Pl. T Hth . . . 9L 107
Willett Rd. T Hth . . . 9L 107
Willett Way. Orp . . . 9B 112
William Allen Ho. Edgw . . . 7K 23
William Banfield Ho. SW6 . . . 1K 89
(off Munster Rd.)
William Barefoot Dri. SE9 . . . 1L 111
William Blake Ho. SW11 . . . 9C 74
William Bonney Est. SW4 . . . 3H 91
William Booth Rd. SE20 . . . 5E 108
William Carey Way. Harr . . . 4C 38
William Caslon Ho. E2 . . . 5F 60
(off Patriot Sq.)
William Channing Ho. E2 . . . 6F 60
(off Canrobert St.)
William Clo. N2 . . . 1B 42
William Clo. SE13 . . . 2A 94
William Clo. Romf . . . 8A 34
William Clo. S'hall . . . 3A 70
William Cobbett Ho. W8 . . . 4M 73
(off Scarsdale Pl.)
William Cory Promenade. Eri . . . 6C 82
William Ct. W5 . . . 8G 55
William Covell Clo. Enf . . . 2K 15
William Dromey Ct. NW6 . . . 3K 57
William Dunbar Ho. NW6 . . . 5K 57
(off Albert Rd.)
William Dyce M. SW16 . . . 1H 107
William Ellis Way. SE16 . . . 4E 76
(off St James's Rd.)
William Evans Ho. SE8 . . . 5H 77
(off Bush Rd.)
William Evans Rd. Eps . . . 3L 133
William Farm La. SW15 . . . 2F 88
William Fenn Ho. E2 . . . 6E 60
(off Shipton Rd.)
William IV St. WC2 . . . 1J 75
William Gdns. SW15 . . . 4F 88
William Gibbs Ct. SW1 . . . 4H 75
(off Old Pye St.)
William Gunn Ho. NW3 . . . 1C 58
William Guy Gdns. E3 . . . 6M 61
William Henry Wlk. SW8 . . . 7H 75
William Hunt Mans. SW13 . . . 7G 73
William Margrie Clo. SE15 . . . 1E 92
William M. SW1 . . . 3D 74
William Morley Clo. E6 . . . 4H 63
William Morris Clo. E17 . . . 1K 45
William Morris Gallery. . . . 1L 45
William Morris Ho. W6 . . . 7H 73
William Morris Way. SW6 . . . 2A 90
William Nash Ct. Orp . . . 7G 113
William Paton Ho. E16 . . . 9F 62
William Pike Ho. Romf . . . 4B 50
(off Waterloo Gdns.)
William Pl. E3 . . . 5K 61
William Pl. Orp . . . 8G 113
William Rathbone Ho. E2 . . . 6F 60
(off Florida St.)
William Rd. NW1 . . . 6G 59
William Rd. SW19 . . . 4J 105
William Rd. Sutt . . . 7A 122
William Rushbrooke Ho. SE16 . . . 5E 76
(off Rouel Rd.)
Williams Av. E17 . . . 8K 29
William Saville Ho. NW6 . . . 5K 57
(off Denmark Rd.)
William's Bldgs. E2 . . . 7G 61
Williams Clo. N8 . . . 4H 43
Williams Clo. SW6 . . . 8J 73
Williams Dri. Houn . . . 3L 85
Williams Gro. N22 . . . 8L 27
Williams Gro. Surb . . . 1G 119
Williams Ho. E9 . . . 4F 60
(off King Edward's Rd.)
Williams Ho. NW2 . . . 8G 41
(off Stoll Clo.)
William's La. SW14 . . . 2A 88
Williams La. Mord . . . 9A 106
William Smith Ho. Belv . . . 4L 81
(off Ambrook Rd.)
Williamson Clo. SE10 . . . 6D 78
Williamson Ct. SE17 . . . 6A 76
Williamson Rd. N4 . . . 4M 43
Williamson St. N7 . . . 9J 43
Williamson Way. NW7 . . . 6J 25
William Sq. SE16 . . . 1J 77
(off Sovereign Cres.)
Williams Rd. W13 . . . 2E 70
Williams Rd. S'hall . . . 5J 69
Williams Ter. Croy . . . 8L 123
William St. E10 . . . 4M 45
William St. N17 . . . 7D 28
William St. SW1 . . . 3D 74
William St. Bark . . . 3A 64
William St. Bush . . . 5H 9
William St. Cars . . . 5C 122
Williams Way. Bex . . . 8C 98
William White Ct. E13 . . . 4G 63
(off Green St.)
William Wood Ho. SE26 . . . 9G 93
(off Shrublands Clo.)
Willifield Way. NW11 . . . 2K 41
Willingale Clo. Wfd G . . . 6G 31
Willingale Rd. Lou . . . 3M 19
Willingdon Rd. N22 . . . 9M 27
Willinghall Clo. Wal A . . . 5K 7
Willingham Clo. NW5 . . . 1G 59
Willingham Ter. NW5 . . . 1G 59
Willingham Way. King T . . . 7L 103
Willington Ct. E5 . . . 8J 45
Willington Rd. SW9 . . . 2J 91
Willis Av. Sutt . . . 8C 122
Willis Clo. Eps . . . 6M 133
Willis Ct. T Hth . . . 1L 123
Willis Ho. E14 . . . 1M 77
(off Hale St.)
Willis Rd. E15 . . . 5D 62
Willis Rd. Croy . . . 2A 124
Willis Rd. Eri . . . 5A 82
Willis St. E14 . . . 9M 61
Will Miles Ct. SW19 . . . 4A 106
Willmore End. SW19 . . . 5M 105
Willoughby Av. Croy . . . 6K 123
Willoughby Dri. Rain . . . 3C 66
Willoughby Gro. N17 . . . 7F 28
Willoughby Highwalk. EC2 . . . 8B 60
(off Moor La.)
Willoughby Ho. E1 . . . 2F 76
(off Reardon Path)
Willoughby Ho. EC2 . . . 8B 60
(off Moor La.)
Willoughby La. N17 . . . 6F 28
Willoughby Pk. Rd. N17 . . . 7F 28
(in two parts)
Willoughby Pas. E14 . . . 2L 77
(off W. India Av.)
Willoughby Rd. N8 . . . 1L 43
Willoughby Rd. NW3 . . . 9B 42
Willoughby Rd. King T . . . 5K 103
Willoughby Rd. Twic . . . 4G 87
(in two parts)
Willoughbys, The. SW15 . . . 2C 88
Willoughby St. WC1 . . . 8J 59
(off Gt. Russell St.)
Willoughby Way. SE7 . . . 5F 78
Willow Av. SW13 . . . 1D 88
Willow Av. Den . . . 2A 142
Willow Av. Sidc . . . 5E 96
Willow Av. Swan . . . 7D 114
Willow Av. W Dray . . . 1K 143
Willowbank. . . . 1A 142
Willow Bank. SW6 . . . 2J 89
Willowbank. Coul . . . 6J 137
Willow Bank. Rich . . . 9F 86
Willowbank Pl. S Croy . . . 1M 137
Willow Bri. Rd. N1 . . . 2A 60
(in two parts)
Willowbrook. Hamp H . . . 2M 101
Willowbrook Est. SE15 . . . 8E 76
Willow Brook Rd. SE15 . . . 8D 76
Willowbrook Rd. S'hall . . . 4L 69
Willowbrook Rd. Stai . . . 8C 144
Willow Bus. Cen., The. Mitc . . . 1D 122
Willow Bus. Pk. SE26 . . . 9G 93
Willow Clo. SE6 . . . 7D 94
Willow Clo. Bex . . . 5K 97
Willow Clo. Bren . . . 7G 71
Willow Clo. Brom . . . 9K 111
Willow Clo. Buck H . . . 3H 31
Willow Clo. Horn . . . 8F 50
Willow Clo. Orp . . . 2F 128
Willow Cotts. Hanw . . . 9J 85
Willow Cotts. Rich . . . 7L 71
Willow Ct. E11 . . . 7C 46
(off Trinity Clo.)
Willow Ct. EC2 . . . 7C 60
(off Willow St.)
Willow Ct. NW6 . . . 3J 57
Willow Ct. W4 . . . 8C 72
(off Corney Reach Way)
Willow Ct. W9 . . . 8L 57
(off Admiral Wlk.)
Willow Ct. Edgw . . . 4J 23
Willow Ct. Harr . . . 8D 22
Willowcourt Av. Harr . . . 3F 38
Willow Cres. E. Den . . . 1A 142
Willow Cres. W. Den . . . 1A 142
Willowdene. N6 . . . 5D 42
Willowdene. SE15 . . . 8F 76
Willow Dene. Bus H . . . 9C 10
Willow Dene. Pinn . . . 9H 21
Willowdene Clo. Twic . . . 6A 86
Willowdene Ct. N20 . . . 9A 14
(off High Rd.)
Willow Dri. Barn . . . 6J 13
Willow End. N20 . . . 2L 25
Willow End. N'wd . . . 6E 20
Willow End. Surb . . . 3J 119
Willowfields Clo. SE18 . . . 6C 80
Willow Gdns. Houn . . . 9L 69
Willow Gdns. Ruis . . . 7D 36
Willow Grange. Sidc . . . 9F 96
Willow Grn. NW9 . . . 8C 24
Willow Grn. Borwd . . . 7B 12
Willow Gro. E13 . . . 5E 62
Willow Gro. Chst . . . 3L 111
Willow Gro. Ruis . . . 7D 36
Willowhayne Dri. W on T . . . 2F 116
Willowhayne Gdns. Wor Pk . . . 5G 121
Willowherb Wlk. Romf . . . 7G 35
Willow Ho. W10 . . . 7H 57
(off Maple Wlk.)
Willow Ho. Short . . . 6C 110
Willow La. SE18 . . . 5K 79
Willow La. Mitc . . . 9D 106
Willow La. Wat . . . 7E 8
Willow Lodge. SW6 . . . 9H 73
Willow Mead. Chig . . . 3E 32
Willowmead Clo. W5 . . . 8H 55
Willow Mere. Esh . . . 6A 118
Willow Mt. Croy . . . 5C 124
Willow Path. Wal A . . . 7L 7
Willow Pl. SW1 . . . 5G 75
Willow Rd. E12 . . . 8K 47
Willow Rd. NW3 . . . 9B 42
Willow Rd. W5 . . . 3J 71
Willow Rd. Dart . . . 7G 99
Willow Rd. Enf . . . 5C 16
Willow Rd. Eri . . . 9E 82
Willow Rd. N Mald . . . 8A 104
Willow Rd. Romf . . . 4J 49
Willow Rd. Wall . . . 9F 122
Willows Av. Mord . . . 9M 105
Willows Clo. Pinn . . . 9G 21
Willowside Ct. Enf . . . 5M 15
Willows Path. Eps . . . 6M 133
Willows Ter. NW10 . . . 5D 56
(off Rucklidge Av.)
Willows, The. E6 . . . 3K 63
Willows, The. Beck . . . 5L 109
Willows, The. Borwd . . . 3L 11
Willows, The. Clay . . . 8C 118
Willows, The. Lou . . . 8H 19
Willows, The. Wat . . . 9F 8
Willow St. E4 . . . 9B 18
Willow St. EC2 . . . 7C 60
Willow St. Romf . . . 2A 50
Willow Ter. Eyns . . . 4J 131
Willow Tree Clo. E3 . . . 4J 61
Willow Tree Clo. SW18 . . . 7M 89
Willow Tree Clo. Hay . . . 7G 53
Willowtree Clo. Uxb . . . 8A 36
Willow Tree Ct. Sidc . . . 2E 112
Willow Tree Ct. Wemb . . . 1H 55
Willow Tree La. Hay . . . 7G 53
Willow Tree Wlk. Brom . . . 5F 110
Willowtree Way. T Hth . . . 5L 107
Willow Va. W12 . . . 2E 72
Willow Va. Chst . . . 3M 111
Willow Vw. SW19 . . . 5B 106
Willow Wlk. E17 . . . 3K 45
Willow Wlk. N2 . . . 9B 26
Willow Wlk. N15 . . . 2M 43
Willow Wlk. N21 . . . 8K 15
Willow Wlk. SE1 . . . 4C 76
Willow Wlk. Dart . . . 4G 99
Willow Wlk. Ilf . . . 7M 47
Willow Wlk. Orp . . . 5M 127
Willow Wlk. Sutt . . . 5K 121
Willow Way. N3 . . . 7M 25
Willow Way. SE26 . . . 9G 93
Willow Way. W11 . . . 1H 73
Willow Way. Eps . . . 8B 120
Willow Way. Rad . . . 1D 10
Willow Way. Romf . . . 6M 35
Willow Way. Sun . . . 8E 100
Willow Way. Twic . . . 8M 85
Willow Way. Wemb . . . 8E 38
Willow Wood Cres. SE25 . . . 1C 124
Willow Wren Wharf. S'hall . . . 5F 68
Will Perrin Ct. Rain . . . 4E 66
Willrose Cres. SE2 . . . 6F 80
Willsbridge Ct. SE15 . . . 7C 76
Wills Cres. Houn . . . 5M 85
Wills Gro. NW7 . . . 5E 24
(in two parts)
Wilman Gro. E8 . . . 3E 60
Wilmar Clo. Hay . . . 7B 52
Wilmar Clo. Uxb . . . 3B 142
Wilmar Gdns. W Wick . . . 3M 125
Wilmcote Ho. W2 . . . 8M 57
(off Woodchester Sq.)
Wilment Ct. NW2 . . . 8G 41
Wilmer Clo. King T . . . 2K 103
Wilmer Cres. King T . . . 2K 103
Wilmer Gdns. N1 . . . 4C 60
(in two parts)
Wilmerhatch La. Eps . . . 9M 133
Wilmer Lea Clo. E15 . . . 3B 62
Wilmer Pl. N16 . . . 7D 44
Wilmers Ct. NW10 . . . 4B 56
(off Stracey Rd.)
Wilmer Way. N14 . . . 5H 27
Wilmington. . . . 9G 99
Wilmington Av. W4 . . . 8B 72
Wilmington Av. Orp . . . 4G 129
Wilmington Ct. SW16 . . . 4J 107
Wilmington Ct. Rd. Dart . . . 9E 98
Wilmington Gdns. Bark . . . 2B 64
Wilmington Sq. WC1 . . . 6L 59
(in two parts)
Wilmington St. WC1 . . . 6L 59
Wilmot Clo. N2 . . . 9A 26
Wilmot Clo. SE15 . . . 8E 76
Wilmot Cotts. Bans . . . 7M 135
Wilmot Pl. W7 . . . 2C 70
Wilmot Rd. E10 . . . 7M 45
Wilmot Rd. N17 . . . 1B 44
Wilmot Rd. Cars . . . 7D 122
Wilmot Rd. Dart . . . 4E 98
Wilmot Rd. Purl . . . 4L 137
Wilmot St. E2 . . . 7F 60
Wilmot St. NW1 . . . 3G 59
Wilmot Way. Bans . . . 6L 135
Wilmount St. SE18 . . . 5M 79
Wilmslow Ho. Romf . . . 5J 35
(off Chudleigh Rd.)
Wilna Rd. SW18 . . . 6A 90
Wilsham St. W11 . . . 2H 73
Wilshaw Ct. NW4 . . . 1E 40
Wilshaw Ho. SE8 . . . 8L 77
Wilshaw St. SE14 . . . 9L 77
Wilsmere Dri. Har W . . . 7C 22
Wilsmere Dri. N'holt . . . 1J 53
Wilson Av. Mitc . . . 5C 106
(in two parts)
Wilson Clo. S Croy . . . 7B 124
Wilson Clo. Wemb . . . 5K 39
Wilson Dri. Wemb . . . 5K 39
Wilson Gdns. Harr . . . 5A 38
Wilson Gro. SE16 . . . 3F 76
Wilson Rd. E6 . . . 6H 63
Wilson Rd. SE5 . . . 9C 76
Wilson Rd. Chess . . . 8K 119
Wilson Rd. Ilf . . . 5K 47
Wilson's Av. N17 . . . 9D 28
Wilson's Pl. E14 . . . 9K 61
Wilson's Rd. W6 . . . 6H 73
Wilson St. E17 . . . 3A 46
Wilson St. EC2 . . . 8B 60
Wilson St. N21 . . . 9L 15
Wilson Wlk. W6 . . . 5D 72
(off Prebend Gdns.)
Wilstone Clo. Hay . . . 7J 53
Wiltern Ct. NW2 . . . 2J 57
Wilthorne Gdns. Dag . . . 3M 65
Wilton Av. W4 . . . 6C 72
Wilton Clo. W Dray . . . 7H 143
Wilton Ct. E1 . . . 9F 60
(off Cavell St.)
Wilton Ct. Wat . . . 5G 9
(off Estcourt Rd.)
Wilton Cres. SW1 . . . 3E 74
Wilton Cres. SW19 . . . 4K 105
Wilton Dri. Romf . . . 7A 34
Wilton Est. E8 . . . 2E 60
Wilton Gdns. W on T . . . 3H 117
Wilton Gdns. W Mol . . . 7L 101
Wilton Gro. SW19 . . . 5K 105
Wilton Gro. N Mald . . . 1D 120
Wilton Ho. S Croy . . . 7A 124
(off Nottingham Rd.)
Wilton M. SW1 . . . 4E 74
Wilton Pde. Felt . . . 7F 84
Wilton Pl. SW1 . . . 3E 74
Wilton Pl. Harr . . . 4D 38
Wilton Rd. N10 . . . 9E 26
Wilton Rd. SE2 . . . 5G 81
Wilton Rd. SW1 . . . 4F 74
Wilton Rd. SW19 . . . 4C 106
Wilton Rd. Cockf . . . 6D 14
(in two parts)
Wilton Rd. Houn . . . 2H 85
Wilton Row. SW1 . . . 3E 74
Wilton Sq. N1 . . . 4B 60
Wilton St. SW1 . . . 4F 74
Wilton Ter. SW1 . . . 4E 74
Wilton Vs. N1 . . . 4B 60
(off Wilton Sq.)
Wilton Way. E8 . . . 2E 60
Wiltshire Av. Horn . . . 2K 51
Wiltshire Clo. NW7 . . . 5D 24
Wiltshire Clo. SW3 . . . 5D 74
Wiltshire Ct. N4 . . . 6K 43
(off Marquis Rd.)
Wiltshire Ct. Ilf . . . 2A 64
Wiltshire Ct. S Croy . . . 7A 124
Wiltshire Gdns. N4 . . . 4A 44
Wiltshire Gdns. Twic . . . 7A 86
Wiltshire La. Pinn . . . 1D 36
Wiltshire Rd. SW9 . . . 2L 91
Wiltshire Rd. Orp . . . 2E 128
Wiltshire Rd. T Hth . . . 7L 107
Wiltshire Row. N1 . . . 4B 60
Wilverley Cres. N Mald . . . 1C 120
Wimbart Rd. SW2 . . . 6K 91
Wimbledon. . . . 3K 105
Wimbledon (All England Lawn Tennis & Croquet Club) . . . 1J 105
Wimbledon Bri. SW19 . . . 3K 105
Wimbledon Clo. SW20 . . . 4H 105
Wimbledon Common. . . . 1E 104
Wimbledon Common Postmill & Mus. . . . 8F 88
Wimbledon F.C. (Selhurst Pk.) . . . 8C 108
Wimbledon Greyhound Stadium. . . . 1A 106
Wimbledon Hill Rd. SW19 . . . 3J 105
Wimbledon Lawn Tennis Mus. . . . 1J 105
(Centre Court, All England Lawn Tennis & Croquet Club)
Wimbledon Mus. of Local History. . . . 3J 105
Wimbledon Park. . . . 9L 89
Wimbledon Pk. Rd. SW19 & SW18 . . . 8J 89
Wimbledon Pk. Side. SW19 . . . 9H 89
Wimbledon Rd. SW17 . . . 1A 106
Wimbledon Stadium Bus. Cen. SW17 . . . 9M 89
Wimbolt St. E2 . . . 6E 60
Wimborne Av. Hay . . . 9F 52
Wimborne Av. Orp . . . 8D 112
Wimborne Av. S'hall . . . 5L 69
Wimborne Clo. SE12 . . . 4D 94
Wimborne Clo. Buck H . . . 2F 30
Wimborne Clo. Eps . . . 5C 134
Wimborne Clo. Wor Pk . . . 3G 121
Wimborne Ct. SW12 . . . 9G 91
Wimborne Ct. N'holt . . . 2L 53
Wimborne Dri. NW9 . . . 1L 39
Wimborne Dri. Pinn . . . 5H 37
Wimborne Gdns. W13 . . . 8F 54
Wimborne Gro. Wat . . . 1C 8
Wimborne Ho. E16 . . . 1D 78
(off Victoria Dock Rd.)
Wimborne Ho. NW1 . . . 7C 58
(off Harewood Av.)
Wimborne Ho. SW8 . . . 8K 75
(off Dorset Rd.)
Wimborne Rd. N9 . . . 2E 28
Wimborne Rd. N17 . . . 9C 28
Wimborne Way. Beck . . . 7H 109
Wimbourne Ct. N1 . . . 5B 60
(off Wimbourne St.)
Wimbourne St. N1 . . . 5B 60
Wimpole Clo. Brom . . . 8G 111
Wimpole Clo. King T . . . 6K 103
Wimpole M. W1 . . . 8F 58
Wimpole Rd. W Dray . . . 2H 143
Wimpole St. W1 . . . 8F 58
Wimshurst Clo. Croy . . . 3J 123
Winans Wlk. SW9 . . . 1L 91
Winant Ho. E14 . . . 1M 77
(off Simpson's Rd.)
Wincanton Ct. N11 . . . 6E 26
(off Martock Gdns.)
Wincanton Cres. N'holt . . . 1L 53
Wincanton Gdns. Ilf . . . 1M 47
Wincanton Rd. SW18 . . . 6K 89
Wincanton Rd. Romf . . . 3H 35
Winchcombe Bus. Cen. SE15 . . . 7C 76
Winchcombe Ct. SE15 . . . 7C 76
(off Longhope Clo.)
Winchcombe Rd. Cars . . . 2B 122
Winchcomb Gdns. SE9 . . . 2H 95
Winchelsea Av. Bexh . . . 8K 81
Winchelsea Clo. SW15 . . . 4H 89
Winchelsea Cres. W Mol . . . 6A 102
Winchelsea Ho. SE16 . . . 3G 77
(off Swan Rd.)
Winchelsea Rd. E7 . . . 8E 46
Winchelsea Rd. N15 . . . 1C 44
Winchelsea Rd. NW10 . . . 4B 56
Winchelsey Ri. S Croy . . . 8D 124
Winchendon Rd. SW6 . . . 9K 73
Winchendon Rd. Tedd . . . 1B 102
Winchester Av. NW6 . . . 4J 57
Winchester Av. NW9 . . . 1L 39
Winchester Av. Houn . . . 7K 69
Winchester Clo. E6 . . . 9K 63
Winchester Clo. SE17 . . . 5M 75
Winchester Clo. Brom . . . 7D 110
Winchester Clo. Enf . . . 7C 16
Winchester Clo. Esh . . . 6L 117
Winchester Clo. King T . . . 4M 103
Winchester Ct. W8 . . . 3L 73
(off Vicarage Ga.)
Winchester Dri. Pinn . . . 3H 37
Winchester Ho. SE18 . . . 8H 79
(off Portway Gdns.)
Winchester Ho. SW3 . . . 7B 74
(off Beaufort St.)
Winchester Ho. SW9 . . . 8L 75
Winchester Ho. W2 . . . 9A 58
(off Hallfield Est.)
Winchester Ho. Bark . . . 3E 64
(off Keir Hardie Way)
Winchester Pk. Brom . . . 7D 110
Winchester Pl. E8 . . . 1D 60
Winchester Pl. N6 . . . 6F 42
Winchester Rd. E4 . . . 7A 30
Winchester Rd. N6 . . . 5F 42
Winchester Rd. N9 . . . 1D 28
Winchester Rd. NW3 . . . 3B 58
Winchester Rd. Bexh . . . 1H 97
Winchester Rd. Brom . . . 7D 110
Winchester Rd. Felt . . . 9K 85
Winchester Rd. Harr . . . 2J 39
Winchester Rd. Hay . . . 8C 68
Winchester Rd. Ilf . . . 8B 48
Winchester Rd. N'wd . . . 9D 20
Winchester Rd. Orp . . . 6G 129
Winchester Rd. Twic . . . 5F 86
Winchester Rd. W on T . . . 3E 116
Winchester Sq. SE1 . . . 2B 76
(off Winchester Wlk.)
Winchester St. SW1 . . . 6F 74
Winchester St. W3 . . . 2A 72
Winchester Wlk. SE1 . . . 2B 76
Winchester Way. Crox G . . . 7A 8
Winchet Wlk. Croy . . . 1G 125
Winchfield Clo. Harr . . . 4G 39
Winchfield Ho. SW15 . . . 5D 88
Winchfield Rd. SE26 . . . 2J 109
Winch Ho. E14 . . . 4M 77
(off Tiller Rd.)

Winch Ho.—Wolseley Rd.

Winch Ho. SW10 . . . . .8A 74
(off King's Rd.)
Winchilsea Ho. NW8 . . . . . . .6B 58
(off St John's Wood Rd.)
Winchmore Hill. 9L 15
Winchmore Hill Rd.
N14 & N21 . . . . .1H 27
Winchmore Vs. N21 . . . . .9K 15
(off Winchmore Hill Rd.)
Winckley Clo. Harr 3K 39
Wincott St. SE11 . . . . .5L 75
Wincrofts Dri. SE9 . . . . .3B 96
Windall Clo. SE19 . . . . .5E 108
Windborough Rd. Cars 9E 122
Windermere. NW1 . . . . .6F 58
(off Albany St.)
Windermere Av. N3 . . . . .1L 41
Windermere Av. NW6 . . . . . . .4J 57
Windermere Av. SW19 . . . .7M 105
Windermere Av. Horn 1E 66
Windermere Av. Ruis 5G 37
Windermere Av. Wemb 5G 39
Windermere Clo. Dart 7F 98
Windermere Clo. Felt 7D 84
Windermere Clo. Orp 5M 127
Windermere Clo. Stai 7C 144
Windermere Ct. SW13 . . . . . .7D 72
Windermere Ct. Cars 5E 122
Windermere Ct. Kenl 7M 137
Windermere Ct. Wat 4E 8
Windermere Ct. Wemb 5G 39
Windermere Gdns. Ilf 3J 47
Windermere Gro. Wemb 6G 39
Windermere Hall. Edgw 5K 23
Windermere Ho. E3 . . . . .7K 61
Windermere Ho. New Bar . . .6M 13
Windermere Point. SE15 . . . .8G 77
(off Old Kent Rd.)
Windermere Rd. N10 . . . . . . .8F 26
Windermere Rd. N19 . . . . . . .7G 43
Windermere Rd. SW15 . . . .1C 104
Windermere Rd. SW16 . . . .5G 107
Windermere Rd. W5 . . . . .4G 71
Windermere Rd. Bexh 1A 98
Windermere Rd. Coul 7J 137
Windermere Rd. Croy 3D 124
Windermere Rd. S'hall 8K 53
Windermere Rd. W Wick . . .4C 126
Windermere Way.
W Dray 2J 143
Winders Rd. SW11 . . . . .1C 90
(in two parts)
Windfield Clo. SE26 . . . . . . .1H 109
Windham Av. New Ad 2B 140
Windham Rd. Rich 2K 87
Windings, The. S Croy 3D 138
Winding Way. Dag 8G 49
Winding Way. Harr 9C 38
Windlass Pl. SE8 . . . . .5J 77
Windlesham Gro. SW19 . . . .7H 89
Windley Clo. SE23 . . . . .8G 93
Windmill. WC1 . . . . .8K 59
(off New N. St.)
Windmill Av. Eps 3D 134
Windmill Av. S'hall 2A 70
Windmill Bridge Ho.
Croy 3C 124
(off Freemasons Rd.)
Windmill Bus. Cen. S'hall . . .2A 70
Windmill Bus. Village.
Sun 5C 100
Windmill Clo. SE1 . . . . .5E 76
(off Beatrice Rd.)
Windmill Clo. SE13 . . . . .1A 94
Windmill Clo. Eps 4D 134
Windmill Clo. Sun 4C 100
Windmill Clo. Surb 3G 119
Windmill Clo. Upm 7L 51
Windmill Clo. Wal A 7L 7
Windmill Ct. NW2 . . . . .2J 57
Windmill Ct. W5 . . . . .5G 71
(off Windmill Rd.)
Windmill Dri. NW2 . . . . .8J 41
Windmill Dri. SW4 . . . . .4F 90
Windmill Dri. Kes 6G 127
Windmill End. Eps 4D 134
Windmill Gdns. Enf 5L 15
Windmill Grn. Shep 2C 116
(off Walton La.)
Windmill Gro. Croy 1A 124
Windmill Hill. NW3 . . . . .8A 42
Windmill Hill. Enf 5M 15
Windmill Hill. Ruis 5D 36
Windmill La. E15 . . . . .2B 62
Windmill La. Barn 8D 12
Windmill La. Bus H 1C 22
Windmill La. Chesh 3E 6
Windmill La. Eps 4D 134
Windmill La. Gnfd 7A 54
Windmill La.
S'hall & Iswth 2A 70
Windmill La. Surb 1F 118
Windmill M. W4 . . . . .5C 72
Windmill Pas. W4 . . . . .5C 72
Windmill Ri. King T 4M 103
Windmill Rd. N18 . . . . .4B 28
Windmill Rd. SW18 . . . . .5B 90
Windmill Rd. SW19 . . . . . . .1F 104
Windmill Rd. W4 . . . . .5C 72
Windmill Rd. W5 & Bren 5G 71
Windmill Rd. Croy 2A 124
Windmill Rd. Hamp H 2M 101
Windmill Rd. Mitc 9G 107
Windmill Rd. Sun 5C 100
Windmill Rd. W. Sun 6C 100
Windmill Row. SE11 . . . . . . .6L 75
Windmill St. W1 . . . . .8H 59
(in two parts)
Windmill St. Bus H 1C 22
Windmill Ter. Shep 2C 116
Windmill Wlk. SE1 . . . . .2L 75
Windmill Way. Ruis 6D 36
Windmore Clo. Wemb 1E 54
Windover Av. NW9 . . . . .2B 40
Windrose Clo. SE16 . . . . .3H 77
Windrush. SE28 . . . . .2F 80
Windrush. N Mald 8M 103
Windrush Clo. N17 . . . . .8C 28
Windrush Clo. SW11 . . . . . . .3B 90
Windrush Clo. W4 . . . . .9A 72
Windrush La. SE23 . . . . .9H 93
Windrush Rd. NW10 . . . . . . .4B 56
Windsock Clo. SE16 . . . . . . .5K 77
Windsor Av. E17 . . . . .9J 29
Windsor Av. SW19 . . . . .5A 106
Windsor Av. Edgw 4M 23
Windsor Av. N Mald 9A 104
Windsor Av. Sutt 5J 121
Windsor Av. Uxb 4F 142
Windsor Av. W Mol 7L 101
Windsor Cen., The. N1 . . . . .4M 59
(off Windsor St.)
Windsor Clo. N3 . . . . .9J 25
Windsor Clo. SE27 . . . . .1A 108
Windsor Clo. Borwd 3L 11
Windsor Clo. Bren 7F 70
Windsor Clo. Chesh 3A 6
Windsor Clo. Chst 2M 111
Windsor Clo. Harr 8L 37
Windsor Clo. N'wd 9E 20
Windsor Cotts. SE14 . . . . . . .8K 77
(off Amersham Gro.)
Windsor Ct. N12 . . . . .5D 26
Windsor Ct. N14 . . . . .9G 15
Windsor Ct. NW2 . . . . .2J 57
(off Chatsworth Rd.)
Windsor Ct. NW3 . . . . .9L 41
Windsor Ct. NW11 . . . . .4J 41
(off Golders Grn. Rd.)
Windsor Ct. SE16 . . . . .1H 77
(off King & Queen Wharf)
Windsor Ct. SW3 . . . . .6C 74
(off Jubilee Pl.)
Windsor Ct. SW11 . . . . .1B 90
Windsor Ct. W2 . . . . .1M 73
(off Moscow Rd.)
Windsor Ct. King T 8H 103
(off Palace Rd.)
Windsor Ct. Pinn 1H 37
Windsor Ct. Sun 4E 100
Windsor Ct. Whyt 9D 138
Windsor Cres. Harr 8L 37
Windsor Cres. Wemb 8M 39
Windsor Dri. Ashf 9B 144
Windsor Dri. Barn 8D 14
Windsor Dri. Dart 5E 98
Windsor Dri. Orp 8E 128
Windsor Gdns. W9 . . . . .8L 57
Windsor Gdns. Croy 5J 123
Windsor Gdns. Hay 4B 68
Windsor Gro. SE27 . . . . .1A 108
Windsor Hall. E16 . . . . .2F 78
(off Wesley Av., in two parts)
Windsor Ho. E2 . . . . .6H 61
(off Knottisford St.)
Windsor Ho. N1 . . . . .5A 60
Windsor Ho. NW1 . . . . .6F 58
(off Cumberland Mkt.)
Windsor Ho. N'holt 2L 53
(off Farmlands, The)
Windsor M. SE6 . . . . .7A 94
Windsor M. SE23 . . . . .7J 93
Windsor M. SW18 . . . . .6A 90
(off Wilna Rd.)
Windsor Pk. Rd. Hay 8D 68
Windsor Pl. SW1 . . . . .4G 75
Windsor Rd. E4 . . . . .4M 29
Windsor Rd. E7 . . . . .1F 62
Windsor Rd. E10 . . . . .7M 45
Windsor Rd. E11 . . . . .6E 46
Windsor Rd. N3 . . . . .9J 25
Windsor Rd. N7 . . . . .8J 43
Windsor Rd. N13 . . . . .3L 27
Windsor Rd. N17 . . . . .9E 28
Windsor Rd. NW2 . . . . .2F 56
Windsor Rd. W5 . . . . .1J 71
(in two parts)
Windsor Rd. Barn 8H 13
Windsor Rd. Bexh 3J 97
Windsor Rd. Dag 8J 49
Windsor Rd. Enf 9D 6
Windsor Rd. Harr 8A 22
Windsor Rd. Horn 5G 51
Windsor Rd. Houn 1F 84
Windsor Rd. Ilf 9M 47
Windsor Rd. King T 4J 103
Windsor Rd. Rich 1K 87
Windsor Rd. S'hall 4K 69
Windsor Rd. Sun 3E 100
Windsor Rd. Tedd 2B 102
Windsor Rd. T Hth 6M 107
Windsor Rd. Wat 2G 9
Windsor Rd. Wor Pk 4E 120
Windsors, The. Buck H 2J 31
Windsor St. N1 . . . . .4M 59
Windsor St. Uxb 3A 142
Windsor Ter. N1 . . . . .6A 60
Windsor Wlk. SE5 . . . . .1B 92
Windsor Wlk. W on T 3H 117
Windsor Wlk. Wey 7A 116
Windsor Way. W14 . . . . .5H 73
Windsor Wharf. E9 . . . . .2L 61
Windsor Wood. Wal A 6L 7
Windspoint Dri. SE15 . . . . . .7F 76
Windus Rd. N16 . . . . .6D 44
Windus Wlk. N16 . . . . .6D 44
Windward Clo. Enf 8D 6
Windycroft Clo. Purl 5H 137
Windy Ridge. Brom 5J 111
Windy Ridge Clo. SW19 . . .2H 105
Wine Clo. E1 . . . . .1G 77
(in two parts)
Wine Office Ct. EC4 . . . . .9L 59
Winery La. King T 7K 103
Winfields Mobile Home Pk.
Wat 3M 9
Winford Ct. SE15 . . . . .9F 76
Winford Ho. E3 . . . . .3K 61
Winford Pde. S'hall 9M 53
(off Marconi Way)
Winforton St. SE10 . . . . .9A 78
Winfrith Rd. SW18 . . . . .6A 90
Wingate Cres. Croy 1J 123
Wingate Rd. W6 . . . . .4F 72
Wingate Rd. Ilf 1M 63
Wingate Rd. Sidc 3G 113
Wingate Trad. Est. N17 . . . . .7E 28
Wingfield Ct. Bans 7L 135
Wingfield Ct. Sidc 8D 96
Wingfield Ct. Wat 8A 8
Wingfield Ho. E2 . . . . .6D 60
(off Virginia Rd.)
Wingfield Ho. NW6 . . . . .5M 57
(off Tollgate Gdns.)
Wingfield M. SE15 . . . . .2E 92
Wingfield Rd. E15 . . . . .9C 46
Wingfield Rd. E17 . . . . .3M 45
Wingfield Rd. King T 3K 103
Wingfield St. SE15 . . . . .2E 92
Wingfield Way. Ruis 2F 52
Wingford Rd. SW2 . . . . .5J 91
Wingletye La. Horn 2K 51
Wingmore Rd. SE24 . . . . .2A 92
Wingrad Ho. E1 . . . . .8G 61
(off Jubilee St.)
Wingrave. SE17 . . . . .5B 76
(in three parts)
Wingrave Rd. W6 . . . . .7G 73
Wingreen. NW8 . . . . .4M 57
(off Abbey Rd.)
Wingrove. E4 . . . . .9L 17
Wingrove Ct. Romf 3A 50
Wingrove Dri. Purf 6M 83
Wingrove Rd. SE6 . . . . .8C 94
Wings Clo. Sutt 6L 121
Winicotte Ho. W2 . . . . .8B 58
(off Paddington Grn.)
Winifred Av. Horn 9H 51
Winifred Pl. N12 . . . . .5A 26
Winifred Rd. SW19 . . . . .5L 105
Winifred Rd. Coul 8E 136
Winifred Rd. Dag 7J 49
Winifred Rd. Dart 4F 98
Winifred Rd. Eri 6C 82
Winifred Rd. Hamp H 1L 101
Winifred St. E16 . . . . .2K 79
Winifred Ter. E13 . . . . .5E 62
(off Victoria Rd.)
Winifred Ter. Enf 9D 16
Winifred Whittington Ho.
Rain 8F 66
Winkfield Rd. E13 . . . . .5F 62
Winkfield Rd. N22 . . . . .8L 27
Winkley Ct. N10 . . . . .2F 42
(off St James's La.)
Winkley Ct. S Harr 8L 37
Winkley St. E2 . . . . .5F 60
Winkworth Cotts. E1 . . . . . . .7G 61
(off Cephas St.)
Winkworth Pl. Bans 6K 135
Winkworth Rd. Bans 6L 135
Winlaton Rd. Brom 1B 110
Winmill Rd. Dag 8K 49
Winnett St. W1 . . . . .1H 75
Winningales Ct. Ilf 9J 31
Winnings Wlk. N'holt 2J 53
Winnington Clo. N2 . . . . .4B 42
Winnington Ho. SE5 . . . . . . .8A 76
(off Wyndham Est.)
Winnington Rd. N2 . . . . .4B 42
Winnington Rd. Enf 2G 17
Winnipeg Dri. G Str 8D 128
Winnock Rd. W Dray 2H 143
Winn Rd. SE12 . . . . .7E 94
Winns Av. E17 . . . . .1K 45
Winns Comn. Rd. SE18 . . . . .7C 80
Winns M. N15 . . . . .2C 44
Winns Ter. E17 . . . . .1L 45
Winsbeach. E17 . . . . .9B 30
Winscombe Cres. W5 . . . . . .7H 55
Winscombe St. NW5 . . . . . . .8F 42
Winscombe Way. Stan 5E 22
Winsford Rd. SE6 . . . . .9K 93
Winsford Ter. N18 . . . . .5B 28
Winsham Gro. SW11 . . . . . . .4E 90
Winsham Ho. NW1 . . . . .6H 59
(off Churchway)
Winslade Rd. SW2 . . . . .4J 91
Winslade Way. SE6 . . . . . . .6M 93
Winsland M. W2 . . . . .9B 58
Winsland St. W2 . . . . .9B 58
Winsley St. W1 . . . . .9G 59
Winslow. SE17 . . . . .6C 76
Winslow Clo. NW10 . . . . .8C 40
Winslow Clo. Pinn 4F 36
Winslow Gro. E4 . . . . .2C 30
Winslow Rd. W6 . . . . .7G 73
Winslow Way. Felt 9H 85
Winslow Way. W on T 5G 117
Winsmoor Ct. Enf 5M 15
Winsor Park. 8M 63
Winsor Ter. E6 . . . . .8L 63
Winstanley Est. SW11 . . . . . .2B 90
Winstanley Rd. SW11 . . . . . .2B 90
Winstead Gdns. Dag 1A 66
Winston Av. NW9 . . . . .5C 40
Winston Churchill's Britain at
War Experience. 2C 76
(off Tooley St.)
Winston Churchill Way.
Wal X 6C 6
Winston Clo. Harr 6D 22
Winston Clo. Romf 2M 49
Winston Ct. Brom 5F 110
(off Widmore Rd.)
Winston Ct. Harr 7M 21
Winston Ho. N1 . . . . .5B 60
(off Cherbury St.)
Winston Ho. W13 . . . . .3E 70
(off Balfour Rd.)
Winston Ho. WC1 . . . . .7H 59
(off Endsleigh St.)
Winston Rd. N16 . . . . .9B 44
Winston Wlk. W4 . . . . .4B 72
Winston Way. Ilf 8M 47
Winstre Rd. Borwd 3L 11
Winter Av. E6 . . . . .4J 63
Winterborne Av. Orp 5B 128
Winterbourne Gro. Wey 8A 116
Winterbourne Ho. W11 . . . . .1J 73
(off Portland Rd.)
Winterbourne Rd. SE6 . . . . . .7K 93
Winterbourne Rd. Dag 7G 49
Winterbourne Rd. T Hth 8L 107
Winter Box Wlk. Rich 4K 87
Winterbrook Rd. SE24 . . . . . .5A 92
Winterburn Clo. N11 . . . . . . .6E 26
Winterdown Gdns. Esh 8K 117
Winterdown Rd. Esh 8K 117
Winterfold Clo. SW19 . . . . . .8J 89
Wintergreen Clo. E6 . . . . .8J 63
Winterleys. NW6 . . . . .5K 57
(off Albert Rd.)
Winter Lodge. SE16 . . . . .6E 76
(off Fern Wlk.)
Winter's Ct. E4 . . . . .3M 29
Winterslow Ho. SE5 . . . . .1A 92
(off Flaxman Rd.)
Winters Rd. Th Dit 2F 118
Winterstoke Gdns. NW7 . . . . .5E 24
Winterstoke Rd. SE6 . . . . . . .7K 93
Winters Way. Wal A 6M 7
Winterton Ct. SE20 . . . . . . .6E 108
Winterton Ct. King T 5H 103
(off Lwr. Teddington Rd.)
Winterton Ho. E1 . . . . .9G 61
(off Deancross St.)
Winterton Pl. SW10 . . . . .7A 74
Winterwell Rd. SW2 . . . . .4J 91
Winthorpe Rd. SW15 . . . . . . .3J 89
Winthrop Ho. W12 . . . . .1F 72
(off White City Est.)
Winthrop St. E1 . . . . .8F 60
Winthrop Wlk. Wemb 8J 39
Winton App. Crox G 7A 8
Winton Av. N11 . . . . .7G 27
Winton Clo. N9 . . . . .9H 17
Winton Ct. Swan 8C 114
Winton Cres. Crox G 7A 8
Winton Dri. Chesh 2E 6
Winton Dri. Crox G 8A 8
Winton Gdns. Edgw 7K 23
Winton Rd. Orp 6M 127
Winton Way. SW16 . . . . . . .2L 107
Wireless Rd. Big H 7H 141
Wirrall Ho. SE26 . . . . .9E 92
Wirral Wood Clo. Chst 3L 111
Wisbeach Rd. Croy 9B 108
Wisbech. N4 . . . . .6K 43
(off Lorne Rd.)
Wisborough Rd. S Croy 1D 138
Wisden Ho. SW8 . . . . .7K 75
Wisdom Ct. Iswth 2E 86
(off South St.)
Wisdons Clo. Dag 6M 49
Wise La. NW7 . . . . .5E 24
Wise La. W Dray 4H 143
Wiseman Rd. E10 . . . . .7L 45
Wise Rd. E15 . . . . .4B 62
Wiseton Rd. SW17 . . . . .7C 90
Wisham Wlk. N13 . . . . .6J 27
Wishart Rd. SE3 . . . . .1H 95
Wishford Ct. Asht 9K 133
Wisley Ct. S Croy 2B 138
Wisley Ho. SW1 . . . . .6H 75
(off Rampayne St.)
Wisley Rd. SW11 . . . . .4E 90
Wisley Rd. Orp 4E 112
Wistaria Clo. Orp 4M 127
Wisteria Clo. NW7 . . . . .6D 24
Wisteria Clo. Ilf 1M 63
Wisteria Gdns. Swan 6B 114
Wisteria Gdns. Wfd G 5E 30
Wisteria Rd. SE13 . . . . .3B 94
Witanhurst La. N6 . . . . .6E 42
Witan St. E2 . . . . .6F 60
Witham Clo. Lou 8J 19
Witham Ct. E10 . . . . .8M 45
Witham Ct. SW17 . . . . .9D 90
Witham Rd. SE20 . . . . .7G 109
Witham Rd. W13 . . . . .2E 70
Witham Rd. Dag 1L 65
Witham Rd. Iswth 9B 70
Witham Rd. Romf 3F 50
Withens Clo. Orp 8G 113
Witherby Clo. Croy 7C 124
Witherings, The. Horn 3J 51
Witherington Rd. N5 . . . . . . .1L 59
Withers Clo. Chess 8G 119
Withers Mead. NW9 . . . . .8D 24
Withers Pl. EC1 . . . . .7A 60
Witherston Way. SE9 . . . . . . .8L 95
Withycombe Rd. SW19 . . . . .6H 89
Withy Ho. E1 . . . . .7H 61
(off Globe Rd.)
Withy La. Ruis 3A 36
Withy Mead. E4 . . . . .3B 30
Withy Pl. Park 1M 5
Witley Ct. WC1 . . . . .7J 59
(off Coram St.)
Witley Cres. New Ad 8A 126
Witley Gdns. S'hall 5K 69
Witley Ho. SW2 . . . . .6J 91
Witley Ind. Est. S'hall 5K 69
Witley Rd. N19 . . . . .7G 43
Witney Clo. Pinn 6K 21
Witney Path. SE23 . . . . .9H 93
Wittenham Way. E4 . . . . .3B 30
Wittering Clo. King T 2H 103
Wittering Wlk. Horn 2G 67
Wittersham Rd. Brom 2D 110
Witts Ho. King T 7K 103
(off Winery La.)
Wivenhoe Clo. SE15 . . . . .2F 92
Wivenhoe Ct. Houn 3K 85
Wivenhoe Rd. Bark 5E 64
Wiverton Rd. SE26 . . . . . . .3G 109
Wixom Ho. SE3 . . . . .3G 95
Wix Rd. Dag 4H 65
Wix's La. SW4 . . . . .2F 90
Woburn. W13 . . . . .8F 54
(off Clivedon Ct.)
Woburn Av. Horn 9E 50
Woburn Av. Purl 3L 137
Woburn Clo. SE28 . . . . .9H 65
Woburn Clo. SW19 . . . . . . .3A 106
Woburn Clo. Bush 8A 10
Woburn Ct. E18 . . . . .9E 30
Woburn Ct. SE16 . . . . .6F 77
(off Masters Dri.)
Woburn Ct. Croy 3A 124
Woburn M. WC1 . . . . .7H 59
Woburn Pl. WC1 . . . . .7J 59
Woburn Rd. Cars 3C 122
Woburn Rd. Croy 3A 124
Woburn Sq. WC1 . . . . .7H 59
Woburn Tower. N'holt 6H 53
(off Broomcroft Av.)
Woburn Wlk. WC1 . . . . .6H 59
Wodehouse Av. SE5 . . . . .9D 76
Wodehouse Ct. W3 . . . . .4A 72
(off Vincent Rd.)
Wodehouse Rd. Dart 3L 99
Woffington Clo. King T 5G 103
Woking Clo. SW15 . . . . .3D 88
Wolcot Ho. NW1 . . . . .5G 59
(off Aldenham St.)
Woldham Pl. Brom 8G 111
Woldham Rd. Brom 8G 111
Wolds Dri. Orp 6L 127
Wolfe Clo. Brom 1E 126
Wolfe Clo. Hay 6F 52
Wolfe Cres. SE7 . . . . .6H 79
Wolfe Cres. SE16 . . . . .3H 77
Wolfe Ho. W12 . . . . .1F 72
(off White City Est.)
Wolferton Rd. E12 . . . . .9K 47
Wolffe Gdns. E15 . . . . .2D 62
Wolfington Rd. SE27 . . . . . .1M 107
Wolfram Clo. SE13 . . . . .4C 94
Wolftencroft Clo. SW11 . . . . .2C 90
Wollaston Clo. SE1 . . . . .5A 76
Wollett Ct. NW1 . . . . .3G 59
(off St Pancras Way)
Wolmer Clo. Edgw 4L 23
Wolmer Gdns. Edgw 3L 23
Wolseley Av. SW19 . . . . .8L 89
Wolseley Gdns. W4 . . . . .7M 71
Wolseley Rd. E7 . . . . .3F 63
Wolseley Rd. N8 . . . . .4H 43
Wolseley Rd. N22 . . . . .8K 27
Wolseley Rd. W4 . . . . .5A 72
Wolseley Rd. Harr 1C 38
Wolseley Rd. Mitc 2E 122
Wolseley Rd. Romf 5B 50

Wyldfield Gdns.—Zoffany St.

yldfield Gdns. N9 . . . 2D **28**
yld Way. Wemb . . . 2M **55**
yleu St. SE23 . . . 6J **93**
ylie Rd. S'hall . . . 4L **69**
yllen Clo. E1 . . . 7G **61**
ylo Dri. Barn . . . 8E **12**
ymans Way. E7 . . . 9G **47**
ymering Mans. W9 . . . 6L 57
(off Wymering Rd., in two parts)
ymering Rd. W9 . . . 6L **57**
ymond St. SW15 . . . 2G **89**
ynan Rd. E14 . . . 6M **77**
ynash Gdns. Cars . . . 7C **122**
ynaud Ct. N22 . . . 6K **27**
yncham Av. Sidc . . . 7C **96**
yncham Ho. Sidc . . . 8E 96
(off Longlands Rd.)
ynchgate. N14 & N21 . . . 1H **27**
ynchgate. Harr . . . 7C **22**
ynchgate. N'holt . . . 1K **53**
yncote Way. S Croy . . . 1H **139**
yncroft Clo. Brom . . . 7K **111**
yndale Av. NW9 . . . 4L **39**
yndcliff Rd. SE7 . . . 7F **78**
yndcroft Clo. Enf . . . 5M **15**
yndham Clo. Orp . . . 3A **128**
yndham Clo. Sutt . . . 9L **121**
yndham Ct. W7 . . . 5E **70**
yndham Cres. N19 . . . 8G **43**
yndham Cres. Houn . . . 5L **85**
yndham Deedes Ho. E2 . . . 5E 60
(off Hackney Rd.)
yndham Est. SE5 . . . 8A **76**
yndham Ho. E14 . . . 3M 77
(off Marsh Wall)
yndham M. W1 . . . 8D **58**
yndham Pl. W1 . . . 8D **58**
yndham Rd. E6 . . . 3H **63**
yndham Rd. SE5 . . . 8A **76**
yndham Rd. W13 . . . 4F **70**
yndham Rd. Barn . . . 1D **26**
yndham Rd. King T . . . 4K **103**
(in two parts)
yndhams Ct. E8 . . . 3D 60
(off Celandine Dri.)
yndhams Theatre. . . . 1J 75
(off St Martin's La.)
yndham St. W1 . . . 8D **58**
yndham Yd. W1 . . . 8D **58**
yneham Rd. SE24 . . . 4B **92**
ynell Rd. SE23 . . . 9H **93**
ynford Gro. Orp . . . 7F **112**
ynford Ho. N1 . . . 5K 59
(off Wynford Rd.)
ynford Pl. Belv . . . 7L **81**
ynford Rd. N1 . . . 5K **59**
ynford Way. SE9 . . . 9K **95**
ynlie Gdns. Pinn . . . 9F **20**
ynndale Rd. E18 . . . 8F **30**
ynne Ho. SE14 . . . 9H **77**
ynne Rd. SW9 . . . 1L **91**
ynnstay Gdns. W8 . . . 4L **73**
ynter St. SW11 . . . 3A **90**
ynton Gdns. SE25 . . . 9D **108**
ynton Gro. W on T . . . 5E **116**
ynton Pl. W3 . . . 9M **55**
ynyard Ho. SE11 . . . 6K 75
(off Newburn St.)
ynyard Ter. SE11 . . . 6K **75**
ynyatt St. EC1 . . . 6M **59**
yre Gro. Edgw . . . 3M **23**
yre Gro. Hay . . . 5E **68**
yresdale Cres. Gnfd . . . 6D **54**
yteleaf Clo. Ruis . . . 4A **36**
ythburn Ct. W1 . . . 9D 58
(off Wythburn Pl.)
ythburn Pl. W1 . . . 9D **58**
ythenshawe Rd. Dag . . . 8L **49**
ythens Wlk. SE9 . . . 5M **95**
ythes Clo. Brom . . . 6K **111**
Wythes Rd. E16 . . . 2J **79**
Wythfield Rd. SE9 . . . 5K **95**
Wyvenhoe Rd. Harr . . . 9A **38**
Wyvern Clo. Dart . . . 6G **99**
Wyvern Clo. Orp . . . 5F **128**
Wyvern Est. N Mald . . . 8E **104**
Wyvern Rd. Purl . . . 2M **137**
Wyvern Way. Uxb . . . 3A **142**
Wyvil Rd. SW8 . . . 8J **75**
Wyvis St. E14 . . . 8M **61**

X

Xylon Ho. Wor Pk . . . 4F **120**

Y

Yabsley St. E14 . . . 2A **78**
Yalding Gro. Orp . . . 8H **113**
Yalding Rd. SE16 . . . 4E **76**
Yale Clo. Houn . . . 4K **85**
Yale Ct. NW6 . . . 1M **57**
Yale Way. Horn . . . 9E **50**
Yaohan Plaza. NW9 . . . 1B **40**
Yarborough Rd. SW19 . . . 5B **106**
Yarbridge Clo. Sutt . . . 2M **135**
Yardley Clo. E4 . . . 7M **17**
Yardley Ct. Sutt . . . 6G **121**
Yardley La. E4 . . . 7M **17**
Yardley St. WC1 . . . 6L **59**
(in two parts)
Yarlington Ct. N11 . . . 5E 26
(off Sparkford Gdns.)
Yarmouth Cres. N17 . . . 3F **44**
Yarmouth Pl. W1 . . . 2F **74**
Yarmouth Rd. Wat . . . 2G **9**
Yarnfield Sq. SE15 . . . 9E **76**
Yarnton Way. SE2 . . . 3G **81**
Yarrow Cres. E6 . . . 8J **63**
Yarrow Ho. E14 . . . 4A 78
(off Stewart St.)
Yarrow Ho. W10 . . . 8G 57
(off Sutton Way)
Yateley Ct. Kenl . . . 6A **138**
Yateley St. SE18 . . . 4H **79**
Yates Ct. NW2 . . . 2H 57
(off Willesden La.)
Yates Ho. E2 . . . 6E 60
(off Roberta St.)
Yatton Ho. W10 . . . 8G 57
(off Sutton Way)
Yeading. . . . 7G 53
Yeading Av. Harr . . . 7J **37**
Yeading Ct. Hay . . . 7G **53**
Yeading Fork. Hay . . . 8G **53**
Yeading Gdns. Hay . . . 8F **52**
Yeading Ho. Hay . . . 8H **53**
Yeading La. Hay & N'holt . . . 9F **52**
Yeading Wlk. N Har . . . 3K **37**
Yeadon Ho. W10 . . . 8G 57
(off Sutton Way)
Yeames Clo. W13 . . . 9E **54**
Yearby Ho. W10 . . . 7G 57
(off Sutton Way)
Yeate St. N1 . . . 3B **60**
Yeatman Ho. Wat . . . 9E **4**
Yeatman Rd. N6 . . . 4D **42**
Yeats Clo. NW10 . . . 1C **56**
Yeats Clo. SE13 . . . 1B **94**
Ye Corner. Wat . . . 8H **9**
Yeend Clo. W Mol . . . 8L **101**
Yeldham Ho. W6 . . . 6H 73
(off Yeldham Rd.)
Yeldham Rd. W6 . . . 6H **73**
Yellowpine Way. Chig . . . 4F **32**
Yelverton Clo. Romf . . . 8H **35**
Yelverton Lodge. Twic . . . 6G 87
(off Richmond Rd.)
Yelverton Rd. SW11 . . . 1B **90**
Ye Market. S Croy . . . 7B 124
(off Selsdon Dri.)
Yenston Clo. Mord . . . 1L **121**
Yenstone Ct. Wat . . . 5E **8**
Yeoman Clo. E6 . . . 1M **79**
Yeoman Clo. SE27 . . . 9M **91**
Yeoman Ct. SE1 . . . 6D 76
(off Cooper's Rd.)
Yeoman Ct. Houn . . . 8K **69**
Yeoman Rd. N'holt . . . 3J **53**
Yeomanry Clo. Eps . . . 4D **134**
Yeomans Acre. Ruis . . . 4E **36**
Yeomans M. Iswth . . . 5B **86**
Yeoman's Row. SW3 . . . 4C **74**
Yeoman St. SE8 . . . 5J **77**
Yeomans Way. Enf . . . 4G **17**
Yeoman's Yd. E1 . . . 1D 76
(off Chamber St.)
Yeomen Way. Ilf . . . 6A **32**
Yeo St. E3 . . . 8M **61**
Yeovil Clo. Orp . . . 4C **128**
Yeovil Ho. W10 . . . 7G 57
(off Sutton Way)
Yeovilton Pl. King T . . . 2G **103**
Yerbury Rd. N19 . . . 8H **43**
(in two parts)
Yester Dri. Chst . . . 4J **111**
Yester Pk. Chst . . . 4K **111**
Yester Rd. Chst . . . 4J **111**
Yetev Lev Ct. E5 . . . 6E **44**
Yevele Way. Horn . . . 5J **51**
Yew Av. W Dray . . . 1J **143**
Yewbank Clo. Kenl . . . 7B **138**
Yew Clo. Buck H . . . 2H **31**
Yewdale Clo. Brom . . . 3C **110**
Yewfield Rd. NW10 . . . 2D **56**
Yew Gro. NW2 . . . 9H **41**
Yew Ho. SE16 . . . 3H 77
(off Woodland Cres.)
Yewlands Clo. Bans . . . 7A **136**
Yew Pl. Wey . . . 5D **116**
Yews Av. Enf . . . 9B **6**
Yews, The. Ashf . . . 9F **144**
Yew Tree Bottom Rd.
Eps . . . 8F **134**
Yew Tree Clo. N21 . . . 9L **15**
Yewtree Clo. N22 . . . 8G **27**
Yewtree Clo. N Har . . . 2M **37**
Yewtree Clo. Well . . . 9E **80**
Yew Tree Clo. Wor Pk . . . 3C **120**
Yew Tree Ct. NW11 . . . 3K 41
(off Bridge La.)
Yew Tree Ct. Els . . . 8H **11**
Yew Tree Ct. Sutt . . . 9A 122
(off Walnut M.)
Yew Tree Gdns. Chad H . . . 3J **49**
Yew Tree Gdns. Eps . . . 7A **134**
Yew Tree Gdns. Romf . . . 3B **50**
Yew Tree Lodge. SW16 . . . 1G **107**
Yew Tree Lodge. Romf . . . 3B 50
(off Yew Tree Gdns.)
Yew Tree Rd. W12 . . . 1D **72**
Yewtree Rd. Beck . . . 7K **109**
Yew Tree Rd. Uxb . . . 4D **142**
Yew Tree Wlk. Houn . . . 4K **85**
Yew Tree Wlk. Purl . . . 2A **138**
Yew Tree Way. Croy . . . 2J **139**
(in four parts)
Yew Wlk. Harr . . . 6C **38**
Yiewsley. . . . 2J 143
Yiewsley Ct. W Dray . . . 2J **143**
Yoakley Rd. N16 . . . 7C **44**
Yoke Clo. N7 . . . 2J **59**
Yolande Gdns. SE9 . . . 4J **95**
Yonge Pk. N4 . . . 8L **43**
York Av. SE17 . . . 6A **76**
York Av. SW14 . . . 4A **88**
York Av. W7 . . . 2C **70**
York Av. Hay . . . 8A **52**
York Av. Sidc . . . 8C **96**
York Av. Stan . . . 8F **22**
York Bri. NW1 . . . 7E **58**
York Bldgs. WC2 . . . 1J **75**
York Clo. E6 . . . 9K **63**
York Clo. SE5 . . . 1A 92
(off Lilford Rd.)
York Clo. W7 . . . 2C **70**
York Clo. Mord . . . 8M **105**
York Ct. N14 . . . 3J **27**
York Cres. Borwd . . . 4B **12**
York Cres. Lou . . . 5J **19**
Yorke Ga. Wat . . . 4E **8**
York Gdns. W on T . . . 4H **117**
York Ga. N14 . . . 9J **15**
York Ga. NW1 . . . 7E **58**
York Gro. SE15 . . . 9G **77**
York Hill. SE27 . . . 9M **91**
York Hill. Lou . . . 5J **19**
York Ho. E16 . . . 2E 78
(off De Quincey M.)
York Ho. SE1 . . . 4K **75**
York Ho. W1 . . . 8D 58
(off York St.)
York Ho. Borwd . . . 4L 11
(off Canterbury Rd.)
York Ho. Enf . . . 3B **16**
York Ho. King T . . . 4K 103
(off Elm Rd.)
York Ho. Wemb . . . 9L **39**
York Ho. Pl. W8 . . . 3M **73**
Yorkland Av. Well . . . 2D **96**
Yorkley House. W10 . . . 7G 57
(off Sutton Way)
York Mans. SW5 . . . 6M 73
(off Earls Ct. Rd.)
York Mans. SW11 . . . 9E 74
(off Prince Of Wales Dri.)
York Mans. W1 . . . 8E 58
(off Chiltern St.)
York M. NW5 . . . 1F **58**
York M. Ilf . . . 8L **47**
York Pde. Bren . . . 6H **71**
York Pl. SW11 . . . 2B **90**
York Pl. WC2 . . . 1J 75
(off Villiers St.)
York Pl. Dag . . . 2A **66**
York Pl. Ilf . . . 7L **47**
York Pl. Mans. W1 . . . 8D 58
(off Baker St.)
York Ri. NW5 . . . 8F **42**
York Ri. Orp . . . 4C **128**
York Rd. E4 . . . 4L **29**
(in two parts)
York Rd. E7 . . . 2E **62**
York Rd. E10 . . . 8A **46**
York Rd. E17 . . . 3H **45**
York Rd. N11 . . . 6H **27**
York Rd. N18 . . . 6F **28**
York Rd. N21 . . . 9B **16**
York Rd. SE1 . . . 3K **75**
York Rd. SW18 & SW11 . . . 3A **90**
York Rd. SW19 . . . 3A **106**
York Rd. W3 . . . 9A **56**
York Rd. W5 . . . 4G **71**
York Rd. Bren . . . 6H **71**
York Rd. Croy . . . 2L **123**
York Rd. Dart . . . 6K **99**
York Rd. Houn . . . 2M **85**
York Rd. Ilf . . . 8L **47**
York Rd. King T . . . 4K **103**
York Rd. New Bar . . . 7A **14**
York Rd. N'wd . . . 9E **20**
York Rd. Rain . . . 3B **66**
York Rd. Rich . . . 4K **87**
York Rd. S Croy . . . 2H **139**
York Rd. Sutt . . . 8L **121**
York Rd. Tedd . . . 1C **102**
York Rd. Uxb . . . 3B **142**
York Rd. Wal X . . . 6E **6**
York Rd. Wat . . . 7G **9**
York Rd. Wey . . . 7A **116**
Yorkshire Clo. N16 . . . 8C **44**
Yorkshire Gdns. N18 . . . 5F **28**
Yorkshire Grey (Eltham Hill)
(Junct.) . . . 5H 95
Yorkshire Grey Pl. NW3 . . . 9A **42**
Yorkshire Grey Yd. WC1 . . . 8K 59
(off Eagle St.)
Yorkshire Rd. E14 . . . 9J **61**
Yorkshire Rd. Mitc . . . 9J **107**
Yorkshire St. E14 . . . 9J **61**
York Sq. E14 . . . 9J **61**
York St. W1 . . . 8D **58**
York St. Bark . . . 4A **64**
York St. Mitc . . . 2E **122**
York St. Twic . . . 7E **86**
York St. Chambers. W1 . . . 8D 58
(off York St.)
York Ter. Enf . . . 2A **16**
York Ter. Eri . . . 9A **82**
York Ter. E. NW1 . . . 7E **58**
York Ter. W. NW1 . . . 7E **58**
Yorkton St. E2 . . . 5E **60**
York Way. N7 & N1 . . . 2H **59**
York Way. N20 . . . 3D **26**
York Way. Borwd . . . 4B **12**
York Way. Chess . . . 9J **119**
York Way. Felt . . . 9J **85**
(in two parts)
York Way. Wat . . . 9H **5**
York Way Ct. N1 . . . 4J **59**
York Way Est. N7 . . . 2J **59**
Young Ct. NW6 . . . 3J **57**
Youngmans Clo. Enf . . . 3A **16**
Young Rd. E16 . . . 9G **63**
Youngs Bldgs. EC1 . . . 7A 60
(off Old St.)
Youngs Ct. SW11 . . . 9E **74**
Youngs Rd. Ilf . . . 3B **48**
Young St. W8 . . . 3M **73**
Young Vic Theatre, The. . . . 3L 75
(off Cut, The)
Yoxall Ho. W10 . . . 7G 57
(off Sutton Way)
Yoxley App. Ilf . . . 4A **48**
Yoxley Dri. Ilf . . . 4A **48**
Yukon Rd. SW12 . . . 6F **90**
Yule Clo. Brick W . . . 3K **5**
Yunus Khan Clo. E17 . . . 3L **45**

Z

Zampa Rd. SE16 . . . 6G **77**
Zander Ct. E2 . . . 6E **60**
Zangwill Rd. SE3 . . . 9H **79**
Zealand Av. W Dray . . . 8H **143**
Zealand Ho. SE5 . . . 1A 92
(off Denmark Rd.)
Zealand Rd. E3 . . . 5J **61**
Zelah Rd. Orp . . . 2G **129**
Zenith Lodge. N3 . . . 7M **25**
Zennor Rd. SW12 . . . 7G **91**
Zennor Rd. Ind. Est.
SW12 . . . 7G **91**
Zenoria St. SE22 . . . 3D **92**
Zermatt Rd. T Hth . . . 8A **108**
Zetland Ho. W8 . . . 4M 73
(off Marloes Rd.)
Zetland St. E14 . . . 8M **61**
Zig Zag Rd. Kenl . . . 8A **138**
Zion Ho. E1 . . . 9G 61
(off Jubilee St.)
Zion Pl. T Hth . . . 8B **108**
Zion Rd. T Hth . . . 8B **108**
Zoar St. SE1 . . . 2A **76**
Zoffany St. N19 . . . 7H **43**

HOSPITALS and HOSPICES
covered by this atlas
with their map square reference

N.B. Where Hospitals and Hospices are not named on the map, the reference
given is for the road in which they are situated.

ACTON HOSPITAL 3L **71**
Gunnersbury La.
LONDON
W3 8EG
Tel: 020 83831133

ARCHERY HOUSE 5M **99**
Bow Arrow La.
DARTFORD
DA2 6PB
Tel: 01322 622222

ASHFORD HOSPITAL 8C **144**
London Rd.
ASHFORD
Middlesex
TW15 3AA
Tel: 01784 884488

ATHLONE HOUSE 6D **42**
Hampstead La.
LONDON
N6 4RX
Tel: 020 83485231

ATKINSON MORLEY'S HOSPITAL
........................4F **104**
31 Copse Hill
LONDON
SW20 0NE
Tel: 020 89467711

BARKING HOSPITAL 3D **64**
Upney La.
BARKING
Essex
IG11 9LX
Tel: 0208 9838000

BARNES HOSPITAL 2C **88**
S. Worple Way
LONDON
SW14 8SU
Tel: 020 88784981

BARNET HOSPITAL 6H **13**
Wellhouse La.
BARNET
Hertfordshire
EN5 3DJ
Tel: 020 82164000

BECKENHAM HOSPITAL 6K **109**
379 Croydon Rd.
BECKENHAM
Kent
BR3 3QL
Tel: 020 82896600

BECONTREE DAY HOSPITAL 7J **49**
508 Becontree Av.
DAGENHAM
Essex
RM8 3HR
Tel: 0208 9841234

BELVEDERE DAY HOSPITAL 4E **56**
341 Harlesden Rd.
LONDON
NW10 3RX
Tel: 020 84593562

BELVEDERE PRIVATE CLINIC 6G **81**
Knee Hill
LONDON
SE2 0AT
Tel: 020 83114464

BETHLEM ROYAL HOSPITAL, THE
........................2L **125**
Monks Orchard Rd.
BECKENHAM
Kent
BR3 3BX
Tel: 020 87776611

BLACKHEATH BMI HOSPITAL, THE
........................2D **94**
40-42 Lee Terrace
LONDON
SE3 9UD
Tel: 020 83187722

BOLINGBROKE HOSPITAL 4C **90**
Bolingbroke Gro.
LONDON
SW11 6HN
Tel: 020 72237411

BRACTON CENTRE, THE 8D **98**
Bracton La., Leyton Cross Rd.
BEXLEY
Kent
DA2 7AF
Tel: 01322 294300

BRITISH HOME & HOSPITAL FOR
INCURABLES 2M **107**
Crown La.
LONDON
SW16 3JB
Tel: 020 86708261

BROMLEY HOSPITAL 8F **110**
Cromwell Av.
BROMLEY
BR2 9AJ
Tel: 020 82897000

BUSHEY BUPA HOSPITAL 9D **10**
Heathbourne Rd., Bushey Heath
BUSHEY
Hertfordshire
WD23 1RD
Tel: 020 89509090

CAMDEN MEWS DAY HOSPITAL 2G **59**
1-5 Camden M.
LONDON
NW1 9DB
Tel: 020 75304780

CANE HILL FORENSIC MENTAL HEALTH
UNIT 9G **137**
Brighton Rd.
COULSDON
Surrey
CR5 3YL
Tel: 01737 556300

CARSHALTON WAR MEMORIAL HOSPITAL
........................8D **122**
The Park
CARSHALTON
Surrey
SM5 3DB
Tel: 020 86475534

CASSEL HOSPITAL, THE 1H **103**
1 Ham Comn.
RICHMOND
Surrey
TW10 7JF
Tel: 020 89408181

CENTRAL MIDDLESEX HOSPITAL 6A **56**
Acton La.
LONDON
NW10 7NS
Tel: 020 89655733

CHADWELL HEATH HOSPITAL 3F **48**
Grove Rd.
ROMFORD
RM6 4XH
Tel: 020 89838000

CHARING CROSS HOSPITAL 7H **73**
Fulham Pal. Rd.
LONDON
W6 8RF
Tel: 020 88461234

CHASE FARM HOSPITAL 2L **15**
127 The Ridgeway
ENFIELD
Middlesex
EN2 8JL
Tel: 020 83666600

CHELSEA & WESTMINSTER HOSPITAL
........................7A **74**
369 Fulham Rd., LONDON
SW10 9NH
Tel: 020 87468000

CHELSFIELD PARK HOSPITAL 7J **129**
Bucks Cross Rd.
ORPINGTON
Kent
BR6 7RG
Tel: 01689 877855

CHESHUNT COMMUNITY HOSPITAL
........................4E **6**
King Arthur Ct.
Cheshunt
WALTHAM CROSS
Hertfordshire
EN8 8XN
Tel: 01992 622157

CLAYPONDS HOSPITAL 5J **71**
Sterling Pl.
LONDON
W5 4RN
Tel: 020 85604011

CLEMENTINE CHURCHILL HOSPITAL, THE
........................8D **38**
Sudbury Hill
HARROW
Middlesex
HA1 3RX
Tel: 020 88723872

COLINDALE HOSPITAL 9C **24**
Colindale Av.
LONDON
NW9 5HG
Tel: 020 89522381

CROMWELL HOSPITAL, THE 5M **73**
162-174 Cromwell Rd.
LONDON
SW5 0TU
Tel: 020 74602000

DEVONSHIRE HOSPITAL, THE 8E **58**
29-31 Devonshire St.
LONDON
W1G 6PU
Tel: 020 74867131

EALING HOSPITAL 3B **70**
Uxbridge Rd.
SOUTHALL
Middlesex
UB1 3HW
Tel: 020 89675000

EAST HAM MEMORIAL HOSPITAL
........................3H **63**
Shrewsbury Rd.
LONDON
E7 8QR
Tel: 0208 5865000

EASTMAN DENTAL HOSPITAL & DENTAL
INSTITUTE, THE 7K **59**
256 Gray's Inn Rd.
LONDON
WC1X 8LD
Tel: 020 79151000

EDENHALL MARIE CURIE CENTRE
........................1B **58**
11 Lyndhurst Gdns.
LONDON
NW3 5NS
Tel: 020 77940066

EDGWARE COMMUNITY HOSPITAL
........................7M **23**
Burnt Oak B'way.
EDGWARE
Middlesex
HA8 0AD
Tel: 020 89522381

EPSOM DAY SURGERY UNIT
........................5D **134**
The Old Cottage Hospital
Alexandra Rd.
EPSOM
Surrey
KT17 4BL
Tel: 01372 739002

EPSOM GENERAL HOSPITAL 7A **13**
Dorking Rd.
EPSOM
Surrey
KT18 7EG
Tel: 01372 735735

ERITH & DISTRICT HOSPITAL 7B **8**
Park Cres.
ERITH
Kent
DA8 3EE
Tel: 020 83022678

FARNBOROUGH HOSPITAL 6L **12**
Farnborough Comn.
ORPINGTON
Kent
BR6 8ND
Tel: 01689 814000

FINCHLEY MEMORIAL HOSPITAL 7A **2**
Granville Rd.
LONDON
N12 0JE
Tel: 020 83493121

FLORENCE NIGHTINGALE DAY HOSPITAL
........................8C **5**
1B Harewood Row
LONDON
NW1 6SE
Tel: 020 7259940

FLORENCE NIGHTINGALE HOSPITAL
........................8C **5**
11-19 Lisson Gro.
LONDON
NW1 6SH
Tel: 020 72583828

GAINSBOROUGH CLINIC, THE 4L **7**
22 Barkham Ter.
LONDON
SE1 7PW
Tel: 020 79285633

GARDEN HOSPITAL, THE 1G **4**
46-50 Sunny Gdns. Rd.
LONDON
NW4 1RP
Tel: 020 84574500

GOODMAYES HOSPITAL 3E **4**
Barley La.
ILFORD
Essex
IG3 8XJ
Tel: 020 89838000

GORDON HOSPITAL 5H **7**
Bloomburg St.
LONDON
SW1V 2RH
Tel: 020 87468733

GREAT ORMOND STREET HOSPITAL FOR
CHILDREN 7J **5**
Gt. Ormond St.
LONDON
WC1N 3JH
Tel: 020 74059200

GREENWICH & BEXLEY COTTAGE HOSPIC
........................6G **8**
185 Bostall Hill
LONDON
SE2 0QX
Tel: 020 83122244

GROVELANDS PRIORY HOSPITAL
........................1J **2**
The Bourne
LONDON
N14 6RA
Tel: 020 88828191

GUY'S HOSPITAL 2B **7**
St Thomas St.
LONDON
SE1 9RT
Tel: 020 79555000

GUY'S NUFFIELD HOUSE 3B **76**
Newcomen St.
LONDON
SE1 1YR
Tel: 020 79554257

HAMMERSMITH & NEW QUEEN
CHARLOTTE'S HOSPITAL 9F **56**
Du Cane Rd.
LONDON
W12 0HS
Tel: 020 83831000

HARLEY STREET CLINIC, THE 8F **58**
35 Weymouth St.
LONDON
W1G 8BJ
Tel: 020 79357700

HAROLD WOOD HOSPITAL 8J **35**
Gubbins La.
ROMFORD
RM3 0BE
Tel: 01708 345533

HAYES GROVE PRIORY HOSPITAL
.........................4E **126**
Prestons Rd.
BROMLEY
BR2 7AS
Tel: 020 84627722

HEART HOSPITAL, THE 8E **58**
16-18 Westmoreland St.
LONDON
W1G 8PH
Tel: 020 75738888

HEATHVIEW DAY CENTRE 7G **81**
Lodge Hill
LONDON
SE2 0AY
Tel: 020 83197100

HENDERSON HOSPITAL 1M **135**
Homeland Dri.
SUTTON
Surrey
SM2 5LY
Tel: 020 86611611

HIGHGATE PRIVATE HOSPITAL 4D **42**
17 View Rd.
LONDON
N6 4DJ
Tel: 020 83414182

HILLINGDON HOSPITAL 8D **142**
Pield Heath Rd.
UXBRIDGE
Middlesex
UB8 3NN
Tel: 01895 238282

HOLLY HOUSE HOSPITAL 2F **30**
High Rd.
BUCKHURST HILL
Essex
IG9 5HX
Tel: 0208 5053311

HOMERTON HOSPITAL 1H **61**
Homerton Row
LONDON
E9 6SR
Tel: 020 85105555

HORNSEY CENTRAL HOSPITAL 3H **43**
Park Rd.
LONDON
N8 8JL
Tel: 020 82191700

HOSPITAL FOR TROPICAL DISEASES
.........................7G **59**
Mortimer Mkt.
Capper St.
LONDON
WC1E 6AU
Tel: 020 73879300

HOSPITAL OF ST JOHN & ST ELIZABETH
.........................5B **58**
60 Gro. End Rd.
LONDON
NW8 9NH
Tel: 020 72865126

KING EDWARD VII'S HOSPITAL
SISTER AGNES 8E **58**
5-10 Beaumont St.
LONDON
W1G 6AA
Tel: 020 74864411

KING GEORGE HOSPITAL 3E **48**
Barley La.
ILFORD
Essex
IG3 9YB
Tel: 020 89838000

KING'S COLLEGE HOSPITAL
.........................1B **92**
Denmark Hill
LONDON
SE5 9RS
Tel: 020 77374000

KING'S COLLEGE HOSPITAL, DULWICH
.........................3C **92**
E. Dulwich Gro.
LONDON
SE22 8PT
Tel: 020 77374000

KING'S OAK BMI HOSPITAL, THE
.........................2L **15**
The Ridgeway
ENFIELD
Middlesex
EN2 8SD
Tel: 020 83709500

KINGSBURY COMMUNITY HOSPITAL
.........................2L **39**
Honeypot La.
LONDON
NW9 9QY
Tel: 020 89031323

KINGSTON HOSPITAL 5M **103**
Galsworthy Rd.
KINGSTON UPON THAMES
Surrey
KT2 7QB
Tel: 020 85467711

LAMBETH HOSPITAL 2J **91**
108 Landor Rd.
LONDON
SW9 9NT
Tel: 020 74116100

LATIMER DAY HOSPITAL 8G **59**
40 Hanson St.
LONDON
W1W 6UL
Tel: 020 73809187

LEWISHAM UNIVERSITY HOSPITAL
.........................4M **93**
Lewisham High St.
LONDON
SE13 6LH
Tel: 020 83333000

LISTER HOSPITAL, THE 6F **74**
Chelsea Bri. Rd.
LONDON
SW1W 8RH
Tel: 020 77303417

LITTLE BROOK HOSPITAL 5M **99**
Bow Arrow La.
DARTFORD
DA2 6PH
Tel: 01322 622222

LIVINGSTONE HOSPITAL 6K **99**
East Hill
DARTFORD
DA1 1SA
Tel: 01322 622222

LONDON BRIDGE HOSPITAL
.........................2B **76**
27 Tooley St.
LONDON
SE1 2PR
Tel: 020 74073100

LONDON CHEST HOSPITAL 5G **61**
Bonner Rd.
LONDON
E2 9JX
Tel: 020 73777000

LONDON CLINIC, THE 7E **58**
20 Devonshire Pl.
LONDON
W1G 6BW
Tel: 020 79354444

LONDON FOOT HOSPITAL 7G **59**
33 & 40 Fitzroy Sq.
LONDON
W1P 6AY
Tel: 020 75304500

LONDON INDEPENDENT HOSPITAL
.........................8H **61**
1 Beaumont Sq.
LONDON
E1 4NL
Tel: 020 77900990

LONDON LIGHTHOUSE 9J **57**
111-117 Lancaster Rd.
LONDON
W11 1QT
Tel: 020 77921200

LONDON WELBECK HOSPITAL 8E **58**
27 Welbeck St.
LONDON
W1G 8EN
Tel: 020 72242242

MAITLAND DAY HOSPITAL 9G **45**
143-153 Lwr. Clapton Rd.
LONDON
E5 8EQ
Tel: 020 89195600

MAUDSLEY HOSPITAL, THE 1B **92**
Denmark Hill
LONDON
SE5 8AZ
Tel: 020 77036333

MAYDAY UNIVERSITY HOSPITAL ...1M **123**
Mayday Rd.
THORNTON HEATH
Surrey
CR7 7YE
Tel: 020 84013000

MEADOW HOUSE HOSPICE 3B **70**
Ealing Hospital, Uxbridge Rd.
SOUTHALL
Middlesex
UB1 3HW
Tel: 020 8967 5179

MEADOWS, THE, E.M.I UNIT 2K **11**
Castleford Clo.
BOREHAMWOOD
Hertfordshire
WD6 4AL
Tel: 020 89534954

MEMORIAL HOSPITAL 1L **95**
Shooters Hill
LONDON
SE18 3RZ
Tel: 020 88565511

MIDDLESEX HOSPITAL, THE 8G **59**
Mortimer St.
LONDON
W1N 8AA
Tel: 020 76368333

MILDMAY MISSION HOSPITAL 6D **60**
Hackney Rd.
LONDON
E2 7NA
Tel: 020 76136300

MOLESEY HOSPITAL 9L **101**
High St.
WEST MOLESEY
Surrey
KT8 2LU
Tel: 020 89414481

MOORFIELDS EYE HOSPITAL 6B **60**
162 City Rd.
LONDON
EC1V 2PD
Tel: 020 72533411

MORLAND ROAD DAY HOSPITAL 3L **65**
Morland Rd.
DAGENHAM
Essex
RM10 9HU
Tel: 0208 5932343

NATIONAL HOSPITAL FOR NEUROLOGY &
NEUROSURGERY (FINCHLEY), THE
.........................2C **42**
Gt. North Rd.
LONDON
N2 0NW
Tel: 020 78373611

NATIONAL HOSPITAL FOR NEUROLOGY &
NEUROSURGERY, THE 7J **59**
Queen Sq.
LONDON
WC1N 3BG
Tel: 020 78373611

NELSON HOSPITAL 6K **105**
Kingston Rd.
LONDON
SW20 8DB
Tel: 020 82962000

NEW EPSOM & EWELL COTTAGE
HOSPITAL, THE 3J **133**
W. Park Rd.
EPSOM
Surrey
KT19 8PH
Tel: 01372 734834

NEW VICTORIA HOSPITAL 5C **104**
184 Coombe La. W.
KINGSTON UPON THAMES
Surrey
KT2 7EG
Tel: 020 89499000

NEWHAM GENERAL HOSPITAL
.........................7G **63**
Glen Rd.
LONDON
E13 8SL
Tel: 020 74764000

NORTH LONDON HOSPICE 3A **26**
47 Woodside Av.
LONDON
N12 8TT
Tel: 020 83438841

NORTH LONDON NUFFIELD
HOSPITAL, THE 4L **15**
Cavell Dri.
ENFIELD
Middlesex
EN2 7PR
Tel: 020 83662122

NORTH MIDDLESEX HOSPITAL, THE
.........................5C **28**
Sterling Way
LONDON
N18 1QX
Tel: 020 88872000

NORTHWICK PARK HOSPITAL
.........................5E **38**
Watford Rd.
HARROW
Middlesex
HA1 3UJ
Tel: 020 88643232

NORTHWOOD & PINNER COMMUNITY
HOSPITAL 8E **20**
Pinner Rd.
NORTHWOOD
Middlesex
HA6 1DE
Tel: 01923 824182

OBSTETRIC HOSPITAL, THE 7G **59**
Huntley St.
LONDON
WC1E 6DH
Tel: 020 73879300

OLDCHURCH HOSPITAL 4C **50**
Oldchurch Rd.
ROMFORD
RM7 0BE
Tel: 01708 746090

ORPINGTON HOSPITAL 6D **128**
Sevenoaks Rd.
ORPINGTON
Kent
BR6 9JU
Tel: 01689 815000

PARKLANDS DAY HOSPITAL
.........................4J **133**
W. Park Hospital
Horton La.
EPSOM
Surrey
KT19 8PB
Tel: 01883 388300

PARKSIDE HOSPITAL 9H **89**
53 Parkside
LONDON
SW19 5NX
Tel: 020 89718000

PEACE HOSPICE, THE 5E **8**
Peace Dri.
WATFORD
WD1 3AD
Tel: 01923 330330

PENNY SANGHAM DAY HOSPITAL
. . . . .4K **69**
Osterley Pk. Rd.
SOUTHALL
Middlesex
UB2 4EU
Tel: 020 85719676

PLAISTOW HOSPITAL 5G **63**
Samson St.
LONDON
E13 9EH
Tel: 020 85866200

**PORTLAND HOSPITAL FOR WOMEN &
  CHILDREN, THE** 7F **58**
209 Gt. Portland St.
LONDON
W1N 6AH
Tel: 020 75804400

PRINCESS ALICE HOSPICE 7L **117**
W. End La.
ESHER
Surrey
KT10 8NA
Tel: 01372 468811

PRINCESS GRACE HOSPITAL 7E **58**
42-52 Nottingham Pl.
LONDON
W1U 5NY
Tel: 020 74861234

PRINCESS LOUISE HOSPITAL 8H **57**
St Quintin Av.
LONDON
W10 6DL
Tel: 020 89690133

PROSPECT HOUSE, E.M.I. UNIT
. . . . .5E **8**
Peace Dri.
off Cassiobury Dri.
WATFORD
WD1 3XE
Tel: 01923 693900

**PURLEY & DISTRICT WAR MEMORIAL
  HOSPITAL** 3L **137**
Brighton Rd.
PURLEY
Surrey
CR8 2YL
Tel: 020 84013000

QUEEN ELIZABETH HOSPITAL
. . . . .8J **79**
Stadium Rd.
LONDON
SE18 4QH
Tel: 020 88366000

QUEEN MARY'S HOSPITAL 2E **112**
Frognal Av.
SIDCUP
Kent
DA14 6LT
Tel: 020 83022678

QUEEN MARY'S HOSPITAL 8A **42**
23 E. Heath Rd.
LONDON
NW3 1DU
Tel: 020 74314111

QUEEN MARY'S HOSPITAL FOR CHILDREN
. . . . .3A **122**
Wrythe La.
CARSHALTON
Surrey
SM5 1AA
Tel: 020 82962000

QUEEN MARY'S UNIVERSITY HOSPITAL
. . . . .5E **88**
Roehampton La.
LONDON
SW15 5PN
Tel: 020 87896611

REDFORD LODGE PSYCHIATRIC HOSPITAL
. . . . .2E **28**
15 Church St.
LONDON
N9 9DY
Tel: 020 89561234

RICHARD HOUSE CHILDREN'S HOSPICE
. . . . .1H **79**
Richard Ho. Dri.
LONDON
E16 3RG
Tel: 020 75110222

RICHMOND HEALTHCARE HAMLET . . .2J **87**
Kew Foot Rd.
RICHMOND
Surrey
TW9 2TE
Tel: 020 89403331

RODING HOSPITAL (BUPA) 1H **47**
Roding La. S.
ILFORD
Essex
IG4 5PZ
Tel: 020 85511100

ROEHAMPTON PRIORY HOSPITAL
. . . . .3D **88**
Priory La.
LONDON
SW15 5JJ
Tel: 020 88768261

ROYAL BROMPTON HOSPITAL 6C **74**
Sydney St.
LONDON
SW3 6NP
Tel: 020 73528121

ROYAL BROMPTON HOSPITAL (ANNEXE)
. . . . .6B **74**
Fulham Rd.
LONDON
SW3 6HP
Tel: 020 73528121

ROYAL FREE HOSPITAL, THE 1C **58**
Pond St.
LONDON
NW3 2QG
Tel: 020 77940500

ROYAL HOSPITAL FOR NEURO-DISABILITY
. . . . .5J **89**
West Hill
LONDON
SW15 3SW
Tel: 020 87804500

**ROYAL LONDON HOMOEOPATHIC
  HOSPITAL, THE** 8J **59**
Gt. Ormond St.
LONDON
WC1N 3HR
Tel: 020 78378833

ROYAL LONDON HOSPITAL (MILE END)
. . . . .7H **61**
Bancroft Rd.
LONDON
E1 4DG
Tel: 020 73777920

**ROYAL LONDON HOSPITAL
  (WHITECHAPEL)** 8F **60**
Whitechapel Rd.
LONDON
E1 1BB
Tel: 020 73777000

**ROYAL MARSDEN HOSPITAL
  (FULHAM), THE** 6B **74**
Fulham Rd.
LONDON
SW3 6JJ
Tel: 020 73528171

**ROYAL MARSDEN HOSPITAL
  (SUTTON), THE** 2A **136**
Downs Rd.
SUTTON
Surrey
SM2 5PT
Tel: 020 86426011

**ROYAL NATIONAL ORTHOPAEDIC
  HOSPITAL** 2F **22**
Brockley Hill
STANMORE
Middlesex
HA7 4LP
Tel: 020 89542300

**ROYAL NATIONAL ORTHOPAEDIC
  HOSPITAL (OUTPATIENTS)** 7F **58**
45-51 Bolsover St.
LONDON
W1W 5AQ
Tel: 020 89542300

**ROYAL NATIONAL THROAT, NOSE &
  EAR HOSPITAL** 6K **59**
330 Gray's Inn Rd.
LONDON
WC1X 8DA
Tel: 020 79151300

**ROYAL NATIONAL THROAT, NOSE & EAR
  HOSPITAL - SPEECH & LANGUAGE UNIT**
. . . . .8G **55**
10 Castlebar Hill
LONDON
W5 1TD
Tei: 020 89978480

ST ANDREW'S AT HARROW
. . . . .7C **38**
Bowden Ho. Clinic
London Rd.
HARROW
Middlesex
HA1 3JL
Tel: 020 89667000

ST ANDREW'S HOSPITAL 7M **61**
Devas St.
LONDON
E3 3NT
Tel: 020 74764000

ST ANN'S HOSPITAL 3A **44**
St Ann's Rd.
LONDON
N15 3TH
Tel: 020 84426000

ST ANTHONY'S HOSPITAL 4H **121**
London Rd.
LONDON
SM3 9DW
Tel: 020 83376691

ST BARTHOLOMEW'S HOSPITAL
. . . . .8M **59**
West Smithfield
LONDON
EC1A 7BE
Tel: 020 73777000

ST BERNARD'S HOSPITAL 3B **70**
Uxbridge Rd.
SOUTHALL
Middlesex
UB1 3EU
Tel: 020 89675000

ST CHARLES HOSPITAL 8H **57**
Exmoor St.
LONDON
W10 6DZ
Tel: 020 89692488

ST CHRISTOPHER'S HOSPICE
. . . . .2G **109**
51-59 Lawrie Pk. Rd.
LONDON
SE26 6DZ
Tel: 020 87789252

ST CLEMENT'S HOSPITAL 6K **61**
2A Bow Rd.
LONDON
E3 4LL
Tel: 020 73777000

ST EBBA'S 1A **134**
Hook Rd.
EPSOM
Surrey
KT19 8QJ
Tel: 01883 388300

ST FRANCIS HOSPICE 3C **34**
The Hall
Broxhill Rd.
Havering-atte-Bower
ROMFORD
RM4 1QH
Tel: 01708 753319

ST GEORGE'S HOSPITAL (TOOTING)
. . . . .2B **106**
Blackshaw Rd.
LONDON
SW17 0QT
Tel: 020 86721255

ST GEORGES HOSPITAL (HORNCHURCH)
. . . . .1J **67**
117 Suttons La.
HORNCHURCH
Essex
RM12 6RS
Tel: 01708 465000

ST HELIER HOSPITAL 3A **122**
Wrythe La.
CARSHALTON
Surrey
SM5 1AA
Tel: 020 82962000

ST JOHN'S AND AMYAND HOUSE
. . . . .6E **8**
Strafford Rd.
TWICKENHAM
TW1 3AD
Tel: 020 87449943

ST JOHN'S HOSPICE 5B **5**
Hospital of St John & St Elizabeth
60 Gro. End Rd.
LONDON
NW8 9NH
Tel: 020 72865126

ST JOSEPH'S HOSPICE 4F **6**
Mare St.
LONDON
E8 4SA
Tel: 020 85256000

ST LUKE'S HOSPITAL FOR THE CLERGY
. . . . .7G **5**
14 Fitzroy Sq.
LONDON
W1T 6AH
Tel: 020 73884954

ST LUKE'S KENTON GRANGE HOSPICE
. . . . .3H **3**
Kenton Grange
Kenton Rd.
HARROW
Middlesex
HA3 0YG
Tel: 020 83828000

ST LUKE'S WOODSIDE HOSPITAL
. . . . .2E **42**
Woodside Av.
LONDON
N10 3HU
Tel: 020 82191800

ST MARY'S HOSPITAL 9B **5**
Praed St.
LONDON
W2 1NY
Tel: 020 77256666

ST PANCRAS HOSPITAL 4H **59**
4 St Pancras Way
LONDON
NW1 0PE
Tel: 020 75303500

ST RAPHAEL'S HOSPICE 3H **12**
St Anthony's Hospital
London Rd.
SUTTON
Surrey
SM3 9DW
Tel: 020 83354575

ST THOMAS' HOSPITAL 4K **75**
Lambeth Pal. Rd.
LONDON
SE1 7EH
Tel: 020 79289292

SHIRLEY OAKS HOSPITAL 2G **125**
Poppy La.
CROYDON
CR9 8AB
Tel: 020 86555500

SLOANE HOSPITAL, THE 5B **110**
125-133 Albemarle Rd.
BECKENHAM
Kent
BR3 5HS
Tel: 020 84666911

SOUTH BROMLEY HOSPICE CARE
. . . . .6D **126**
Orpington Hospital
109 Sevenoaks Rd.
ORPINGTON
Kent
BR6 9JX
Tel: 01689 605300

SOUTHWOOD HOSPITAL 5E **42**
70 Southwood La.
LONDON
N6 5SP
Tel: 020 83408778

SPRINGFIELD UNIVERSITY HOSPITAL
. . . . .9C **90**
61 Glenburnie Rd.
LONDON
SW17 7DJ
Tel: 020 86826000

STONE HOUSE HOSPITAL 5M **99**
Cotton La.
DARTFORD
DA2 6AU
Tel: 01322 622222

URBITON HOSPITAL 1J **119**
Ewell Rd.
SURBITON
Surrey
KT6 6EZ
Tel: 020 83997111

SUTTON GENERAL HOSPITAL 2M **135**
Cotswold Rd.
SUTTON
Surrey
SM2 5NF
Tel: 020 82962000

EDDINGTON MEMORIAL HOSPITAL
.......................3C **102**
Hampton Rd.
TEDDINGTON
Middlesex
TW11 0JL
Tel: 020 84088210

HORPE COOMBE HOSPITAL 1A **46**
714 Forest Rd.
LONDON
E17 3HP
Tel: 020 85208971

TOLWORTH HOSPITAL 4L **119**
Red Lion Rd.
SURBITON
Surrey
KT6 7QU
Tel: 020 83900102

TRINITY HOSPICE 3F **90**
30 Clapham Comn. N. Side
LONDON
SW4 0RN
Tel: 020 77871000

UNITED ELIZABETH GARRETT
ANDERSON & SOHO HOSPITALS
FOR WOMEN 6H **59**
144 Euston Rd.
LONDON
NW1 2AP
Tel: 020 73872501

UNIVERSITY COLLEGE HOSPITAL ...7G **59**
Gower St.
LONDON
WC1E 6AU
Tel: 020 73879300

UPTON DAY HOSPITAL 3J **97**
14 Upton Rd.
BEXLEYHEATH
Kent
DA6 8LQ
Tel: 020 83017900

WALTON COMMUNITY HOSPITAL ...4F **116**
Rodney Rd.
WALTON-ON-THAMES
Surrey
KT12 3LD
Tel: 01932 220060

WATFORD GENERAL HOSPITAL 7F **8**
60 Vicarage Rd.
WATFORD
WD18 0HB
Tel: 01923 244366

WELLINGTON HOSPITAL, THE 6B **58**
8a Wellington Pl.
LONDON
NW8 9LE
Tel: 0207 5865959

WEST MIDDLESEX UNIVERSITY HOSPITAL
......................1E **86**
Twickenham Rd.
ISLEWORTH
Middlesex
TW7 6AF
Tel: 020 85602121

WEST PARK HOSPITAL 4J **133**
Horton La.
EPSOM
Surrey
KT19 8PB
Tel: 01883 388300

WESTERN OPHTHALMIC HOSPITAL
......................8D **58**
153 Marylebone Rd.
LONDON
NW1 5QH
Tel: 020 78866666

WHIPPS CROSS HOSPITAL 4B **46**
Whipps Cross Rd.
LONDON
E11 1NR
Tel: 020 85395522

WHITTINGTON NHS TRUST 7G **43**
Highgate Hill
LONDON
N19 5NF
Tel: 020 72723070

WILLESDEN COMMUNITY HOSPITAL
......................3E **56**
Harlesden Rd.
LONDON
NW10 3RY
Tel: 020 84591292

RAIL, CROYDON TRAMLINK, DOCKLANDS LIGHT RAILWAY AND LONDON UNDERGROUND STATIONS

with their map square reference

A

Abbey Wood Station. Rail 4G **81**
Acton Central Station. Rail 2B **72**
Acton Main Line Station. Rail 9A **56**
Acton Town Station. Tube 3L **71**
Addington Village Stop. CT 8L **125**
Addiscombe Stop. CT 3E **124**
Albany Park Station. Rail 8H **97**
Aldgate Station. Tube 9D **60**
Aldgate East Station. Tube 9D **60**
Alexandra Palace Station. Rail 9J **27**
All Saints Station. DLR 1M **77**
Alperton Station. Tube 4H **55**
Ampere Way Stop. CT 3K **123**
Anerley Station. Rail 5F **108**
Angel Station. Tube 5L **59**
Angel Road Station. Rail 5G **29**
Archway Station. Tube 7G **43**
Arena Stop. CT 9G **109**
Arnos Grove Station. Tube 5G **27**
Arsenal Station. Tube 8L **43**
Ashford Station. Rail 9D **144**
Ashtead Station. Rail 9J **133**
Avenue Road Stop. CT 6H **109**

B

Baker Street Station. Tube 7D **58**
Balham Station. Rail & Tube 7F **90**
Bank Station. Tube & DLR 9B **60**
Banstead Station. Rail 6K **135**
Barbican Station. Rail & Tube 8A **60**
Barking Station. Rail & Tube 3A **64**
Barkingside Station. Tube 1B **48**
Barnehurst Station. Rail 1A **98**
Barnes Station. Rail 2E **88**
Barnes Bridge Station. Rail 1D **88**
Barons Court Station. Tube 6J **73**
Battersea Park Station. Rail 8F **74**
Bayswater Station. Tube 1M **73**
Beckenham Hill Station. Rail 2A **110**
Beckenham Junction Station. Rail & CT 5L **109**
Beckenham Road Stop. CT 5J **109**
Beckton Station. DLR 8L **63**
Beckton Park Station. DLR 1K **79**
Becontree Station. Tube 2H **65**
Beddington Lane Stop. CT 1G **123**
Belgrave Walk Stop. CT 8B **106**
Bellingham Station. Rail 9M **93**
Belmont Station. Rail 2M **135**
Belsize Park Station. Tube 1C **58**
Belvedere Station. Rail 4M **81**
Bermondsey Station. Tube 4E **76**
Berrylands Station. Rail 8M **103**
Bethnal Green Station. Rail 7F **60**
Bethnal Green Station. Tube 6G **61**
Bexley Station. Rail 7L **97**
Bexleyheath Station. Rail 1J **97**
Bickley Station. Rail 7J **111**
Bingham Road Stop. CT 3E **124**
Birkbeck Stop. CT 7G **109**
Blackfriars Station. Rail & Tube 1M **75**
Blackheath Station. Rail 2D **94**
Blackhorse Lane Stop. CT 2E **124**
Blackhorse Road Station. Rail & Tube 2H **45**
Blackwall Station. DLR 1A **78**
Bond Street Station. Tube 9F **58**
Borough Station. Tube 3A **76**
Boston Manor Station. Tube 5E **70**
Bounds Green Station. Tube 6H **27**
Bow Church Station. DLR 6L **61**
Bowes Park Station. Rail 7J **27**
Bow Road Station. Tube 6L **61**
Brent Cross Station. Tube 5H **41**
Brentford Station. Rail 7G **71**
Bricket Wood Station. Rail 3L **5**
Brimsdown Station. Rail 4J **17**
Brixton Station. Rail & Tube 3L **91**
Brockley Station. Rail 2J **93**
Bromley-by-Bow Station. Tube 6A **62**
Bromley North Station. Rail 5E **110**
Bromley South Station. Rail 7E **110**
Brondesbury Station. Rail 3K **57**
Brondesbury Park Station. Rail 4J **57**
Bruce Grove Station. Rail 9D **28**
Buckhurst Hill Station. Tube 2H **31**
Burnt Oak Station. Tube 8A **24**
Bushey Station. Rail 8H **9**
Bush Hill Park Station. Rail 8D **16**

C

Caledonian Road Station. Tube 2K **59**
Caledonian Road & Barnsbury Station. Rail 3K **59**
Cambridge Heath Station. Rail 5F **60**
Camden Road Station. Rail 3G **59**
Camden Town Station. Tube 4F **58**
Canada Water Station. Tube 3G **77**
Canary Wharf Station. DLR 2L **77**
Canary Wharf Station. Tube 2M **77**
Canning Town Station. Rail, DLR & Tube 9C **62**
Cannon Street Station. Rail & Tube 1B **76**
Canonbury Station. Rail 1A **60**
Canons Park Station. Tube 7J **23**
Carpenders Park Station. Rail 3H **21**
Carshalton Station. Rail 6D **122**
Carshalton Beeches Station. Rail 8D **122**
Castle Bar Park Station. Rail 8D **54**
Catford Station. Rail 6L **93**
Catford Bridge Station. Rail 6L **93**
Chadwell Heath Station. Rail 5H **49**
Chalk Farm Station. Tube 3E **58**
Chancery Lane Station. Tube 8L **59**
Charing Cross Station. Rail & Tube 2J **75**
Charlton Station. Rail 6G **79**
Cheam Station. Rail 9J **121**
Chelsfield Station. Rail 7F **128**
Cheshunt Station. Rail 3F **6**
Chessington North Station. Rail 7J **119**
Chessington South Station. Rail 9H **119**
Chigwell Station. Tube 3M **31**
Chingford Station. Rail 9C **18**
Chislehurst Station. Rail 6L **111**
Chiswick Station. Rail 8A **72**
Chiswick Park Station. Tube 5A **72**
Church Street Stop. CT 4A **124**
City Thameslink Station. Rail 9M **59**
Clapham Common Station. Tube 3G **91**
Clapham High Street Station. Rail 2H **91**
Clapham Junction Station. Rail 2C **90**
Clapham North Station. Tube 2J **91**
Clapham South Station. Tube 5F **90**
Clapton Station. Rail 7F **44**
Claygate Station. Rail 8C **118**
Clock House Station. Rail 5J **109**
Cockfosters Station. Tube 6E **14**
Colindale Station. Tube 1C **40**
Colliers Wood Station. Tube 4B **106**
Coombe Lane Stop. CT 7G **125**
Coulsdon South Station. Rail 8H **137**
Covent Garden Station. Tube 1J **75**
Crayford Station. Rail 5D **98**
Cricklewood Station. Rail 9H **41**
Crofton Park Station. Rail 4K **93**
Crossharbour & London Arena Station. DLR 4M **77**
Crouch Hill Station. Rail 5K **43**
Croxley Station. Tube 8A **8**
Croxley Green Station. Rail 7B **8**
Croydon Central Stop. CT 4A **124**
Crystal Palace Station. Rail 3E **108**
Custom House for ExCeL Station. Rail & DLR 1F **78**
Cutty Sark Station. DLR 7A **78**
Cyprus Station. DLR 1L **79**

D

Dagenham Dock Station. Rail 6K **65**
Dagenham East Station. Tube 1A **66**
Dagenham Heathway Station. Tube 2K **65**
Dalston Kingsland Station. Rail 1C **60**
Dartford Station. Rail 5J **99**
Debden Station. Tube 6M **19**
Denmark Hill Station. Rail 1B **92**
Deptford Station. Rail 8L **77**
Deptford Bridge Station. DLR 9L **77**
Devons Road Station. DLR 7M **61**
Dollis Hill Station. Tube 1E **56**
Drayton Green Station. Rail 9D **54**
Drayton Park Station. Rail 9L **43**
Dundonald Road Stop. CT 4K **105**

E

Ealing Broadway Station. Rail & Tube 1H **71**
Ealing Common Station. Tube 2K **71**
Earl's Court Station. Tube 5M **73**
Earlsfield Station. Rail 7A **90**
East Acton Station. Tube 9D **56**
Eastcote Station. Tube 5G **37**
East Croydon Station. Rail & CT 4B **124**
East Dulwich Station. Rail 3C **92**
East Finchley Station. Tube 2C **42**
East Ham Station. Tube 3J **63**
East India Station. DLR 1B **78**
East Putney Station. Tube 4J **89**
Eden Park Station. Rail 9L **109**
Edgware Station. Tube 6M **23**
Edgware Road Station. Tube 8C **58**
Edgware Road Station. Tube 8C **58**
Edmonton Green Station. Rail 2E **28**
Elephant & Castle Station. Rail & Tube 5A **7**
Elmers End Station. Rail & CT 8H **10**
Elm Park Station. Tube 9F **5**
Elmstead Woods Station. Rail 3J **11**
Elstree & Borehamwood Station. Rail 6L **1**
Eltham Station. Rail 4K **9**
Elverson Road Station. DLR 1M **9**
Embankment Station. Tube 2J **7**
Emerson Park Station. Rail 5J **5**
Enfield Chase Station. Rail 5A **1**
Enfield Lock Station. Rail 1J **1**
Enfield Town Station. Rail 5C **1**
Epsom Station. Rail 5B **13**
Epsom Downs Station. Rail 7F **13**
Erith Station. Rail 6C **8**
Esher Station. Rail 4B **11**
Essex Road Station. Rail 3A **6**
Euston Station. Rail & Tube 6H **5**
Euston Square Station. Tube 7G **5**
Ewell East Station. Rail 2F **13**
Ewell West Station. Rail 1C **13**
Eynsford Station. Rail 6H **13**

F

Fairlop Station. Tube 8B **3**
Falconwood Station. Rail 3B **9**
Farningham Road Station. Rail 6M **11**
Farringdon Station. Rail & Tube 8M **5**
Feltham Station. Rail 7F **8**
Fenchurch Street Station. Rail 1C **7**
Fieldway Stop. CT 9M **12**
Finchley Central Station. Tube 8L **2**
Finchley Road Station. Tube 2A **5**
Finchley Road & Frognal Station. Rail 1A **5**
Finsbury Park Station. Rail & Tube 7L **4**
Forest Gate Station. Rail 1E **6**
Forest Hill Station. Rail 8G **9**
Fulham Broadway Station. Tube 8L **7**
Fulwell Station. Rail 1B **10**

G

Gallions Reach Station. DLR 1M **7**
Gants Hill Station. Tube 4L **4**
Garston Station. Rail 8J
George Street Stop. CT 4A **12**
Gidea Park Station. Rail 2F **5**
Gipsy Hill Station. Rail 2C **10**
Gloucester Road Station. Tube 5A **7**
Golders Green Station. Tube 6L **4**
Goldhawk Road Station. Tube 3G **7**
Goodge Street Station. Tube 8H **5**
Goodmayes Station. Rail 6E **4**
Gordon Hill Station. Rail 3M **1**
Gospel Oak Station. Rail 9E **4**
Grange Hill Station. Tube 4B **3**
Grange Park Station. Rail 7M **1**
Gravel Hill Stop. CT 8J **12**
Great Portland Street Station. Tube 7F **5**
Greenford Station. Rail & Tube 4B **5**
Green Park Station. Tube 2G **7**
Greenwich Station. Rail & DLR 8M **7**
Grove Park Station. Rail 9F **9**
Gunnersbury Station. Rail & Tube 6M **7**

H

Hackbridge Station. Rail 4F **12**
Hackney Central Station. Rail 2F **6**
Hackney Downs Station. Rail 1F **6**
Hackney Wick Station. Rail 2L **6**
Hadley Wood Station. Rail 2A **1**
Hainault Station. Tube 7C **3**
Hammersmith Station. Tube 5G **7**
Hampstead Station. Tube 9A **4**
Hampstead Heath Station. Rail 9C **4**
Hampton Station. Rail 5L **10**
Hampton Court Station. Rail 8C **10**
Hampton Wick Station. Rail 5G **10**
Hanger Lane Station. Tube 6J **5**
Hanwell Station. Rail 1C **7**
Harlesden Station. Rail & Tube 5B **5**
Harold Wood Station. Rail 8K **3**
Harringay Station. Rail 4L **4**
Harringay Green Lanes Station. Rail 4M **4**
Harrington Road Stop. CT 7G **10**
Harrow & Wealdstone Station. Rail & Tube 2C **3**
Harrow-on-the-Hill Station. Rail & Tube 4C **3**
Hatch End Station. Rail 7L **2**
Hatton Cross Station. Tube 3D **8**
Haydons Road Station. Rail 2A **10**
Hayes Station. Rail 3E **12**
Hayes & Harlington Station. Rail 4D **6**
Headstone Lane Station. Rail 8M **2**